The Motion Picture Guide

★ ★ ★ ★ ★ ★ ★ ★ ★ ★ ★ ★ ★ ★

1993 Annual

The Motion Picture Guide

1993 Annual
(The Films of 1992)

Editorial Director : James Pallot
Editor : John Miller-Monzon
Design and Production : Peter Hajduk
Assistant Editor : David Straussman

BASELINE

New York • Beverly Hills • Paris • Toronto • Tokyo

Published by BASELINE II, Inc., 838 Broadway, New York, NY 10003

ISBN: 0-933997-00-0 THE MOTION PICTURE GUIDE (10 Vols.)
ISBN: 0-933997-11-6 THE MOTION PICTURE GUIDE INDEX (2 Vols.)
ISBN: 0-918432-95-2 THE MOTION PICTURE GUIDE 1993 ANNUAL (THE FILMS OF 1992)

Printed in the United States
First Edition

1 2 3 4 5 6 7 8 9 10

TABLE OF CONTENTS

FOREWORD

The 1993 *Motion Picture Guide Annual,* covering films released during 1992, is the eighth supplement to the original, ten-volume *Motion Picture Guide* and the third to appear under the imprint of BASELINE.

We have continued to build upon the improvements in last year's *Annual*, setting a new record for films covered (529 full-length entries) and introducing three new features.

The first of these is a breakdown of Academy Award nominees and winners, arranged by film. If a film won, or was nominated for, an Award, all the relevant information is now included in tabular form after the credit listings for that title. In addition to this new, at-a-glance format, we have preserved the listing of all the year's Oscars at the back of the volume.

You will also notice two new tables in the *Indices* section, grouping films by country of origin and by major releasing company. The first is particulary useful for keeping an eye on those countries most actively involved in co-productions; the second provides a handy guide to the combined offerings of the big studios.

The *Motion Picture Guide* and its annual supplements are maintained by BASELINE's staff and more than 25 contributors under the direction of editor John Miller-Monzon. I would like to extend my thanks to John; to Peter Hajduk, for the care he brings to the design and production of this volume; to David Straussman, for his invaluable support; and to Jane Klain, Kent Greene and David Lugowski for their contributions to the *Obituaries* section. I hope you enjoy the fruits of their labors and I welcome, as always, any comments you may have about the *Annual.*

The Year In Review

Some of us have been saying it for years, but 1992 spelled it out plainly for all to see. Increasingly, the major studios are churning out bland, mass-produced entertainment that is conceived and developed by committee and that relies on saturation marketing to capture the public's imagination. Meanwhile, audiences looking for fresh, original material are turning inevitably to the independent sector, where alternative voices face a continual financial struggle to make themselves heard.

Nothing made this schism more apparent than the 1992 Academy Award nominations, which saw independent films from Merchant/Ivory's *Howards End* through John Sayles's *Passion Fish* dominate the major categories. The one exception was Clint Eastwood's *Unforgiven* which, made through his Malpaso Productions company from a script written in the mid-1970s, hardly counts as a typical studio project.

The closest we've seen to a masterpiece for some time, *Unforgiven* is a complex tale that ironically undermines our ideas about the western, only to deliver a climax as legendary as the shootout at the O.K. Corral. Just as Eastwood's film revitalized an all-but-defunct genre, Neil Jordan's *The Crying Game* defied any kind of categorization, starting out as a political thriller but then collapsing all our expectations with potent, unsettling force. Like both these movies, Carl Franklin's *One False Move* centered around an inter-racial relationship; one of the few new black directors to emerge last year, Franklin did so in triumphant style, crafting a moody, intelligent thriller about three outlaws on a doomed cross-country road trip. Quentin Tarantino's *Reservoir Dogs*, another low-budget crime drama, got a lot more attention from the critics, few of whom could see past the gore; despite too many art-film touches, it's a brilliantly constructed reflection on loyalty and betrayal. Similar ground was covered, with less technical and narrative finesse, by Nick Gomez's *Laws of Gravity*. Abel

Ferrara's *Bad Lieutenant*, meanwhile, put Harvey Keitel through a sordid, post-Scorsesian wringer.

Not every independent film of 1992 explored the bloodier aspects of the American underworld. *Howards End* and *Enchanted April* were acclaimed—and imported—literary adaptations which, if both too resolutely *tasteful*, nonetheless offered a refreshing, quasi-feminist perspective. Allison Anders' *Gas Food Lodging* was a grittier and more poignant reflection on the feminine lot, while the major studio "women's picture" *A League of Their Own* proved a bland, calculating mix of *Fried Green Tomatoes* and baseball bats.

A dismayingly high number of experienced directors turned out material ranging from the disappointing to the disastrous. Francis Ford Coppola's *Bram Stoker's Dracula*, though a marvel of baroque production and costume design, was a muddled, overstuffed mess. Barry Levinson's *Toys* was unanimously decreed a flop, as was Ridley Scott's *1492: The Conquest of Paradise*. *Twin Peaks: Fire Walk With Me* was conclusive evidence that David Lynch had fallen victim to his own publicity, while Brian De Palma proved equally capable of producing a paranoid, hallucinatory self-parody with *Raising Cain*. In the year that Neil Jordan regained his pre-Hollywood form, fellow brit Stephen Frears slid the other way with the toothless, big-budget satire, *Hero*.

Robert Altman, meanwhile, enjoyed a spectacular career revival with "The Player," a barbed, multi-layered Hollywood satire peppered with celebrity cameos. "Player" star Tim Robbins, in turn, made his directorial debut with the Altmanesque "Bob Roberts," developed from a "Saturday Night Live" sketch about a right-wing folk singer turned politician. Music was also a key factor in "Singles," a gem of a romantic comedy from Cameron Crowe which used the sounds of the new Seattle bands as an appropriate backdrop to a deftly observed story about lovelorn twenty-somethings.

If you took "Singles" and turned it inside out you'd get something like "Husbands and Wives," one of Woody Allen's best films in years. Like Crowe's film, "Husbands and Wives" brings a documentary-style gaze to bear on two central, unstable couples. But while *Singles* is shot through with the optimism of youth, Allen's is a weary admission of defeat. (Allen's characters have it rosy, though, compared with the phony real-estate salesman who, in David Mamet's *Glengarry Glen Ross*, curse their way ever deeper into despair.)

At the box office, two "franchise" pictures, *Batman Returns* and *Lethal Weapon 3,* proved that brand-name recognition can compensate for shoddy product: the first played like a series of trailers for the spectacular action film it could have been, while the second turned the easygoing charm of its predecessors into a lumpen formula. *Alien3* looked as if it might take the saga in an interesting new direction, but ultimately lost its way in a maze of artfully dank tunnels.

Three stars proved their seemingly indestructible financial worth: Kevin Costner made a hit out of the critically despised *The Bodyguard*; Mel Gibson managed to sell even *Forever Young* to a sizeable audience; and Macauley Culkin powered *Home Alone 2* to a gross of over $170 million. Al Pacino scored a more artistic triumph, with his Oscar-winning performance as a blind ex-officer in *Scent of a Woman* helping turn a mediocre script into a fine film. Robert Redford made a creditable comeback as both director (*A River Runs Through It*) and actor (*Sneakers*).

Meanwhile, a pumped-up Tom Cruise apparently lacked the box-office muscle to make a hit out of *Far and Away*, though he fared better opposite Jack Nicholson in *A Few Good Men*. Eddie Murphy seemed unable to halt an inevitable decline, appearing in the progressively disappointing *Boomerang* and *The Distinguished Gentleman*. The failure of *Stop! Or My Mom Will Shoot* may at last have convinced Sylvester Stallone that comedy is not his *forte*.

Newcomers to the stellar ranks included Daniel Day-Lewis, who was afforded many, many profile shots against ravishing natural backgrounds in *The Last of the Mohicans*; Steven Seagal, who may even have betrayed a sense of humor in *Under Siege*; and Sharon Stone, who, on the strength of *Basic Instinct*, landed $2.5 million to star in 1993's disastrous *Sliver*, another Joe Eszterhas-scripted "erotic" thriller.

In a departure from the norm of recent years, Hollywood seemed to score more consistently with comedies than with action-adventure pictures: *My Cousin Vinny*, *White Men Can't Jump*, *Housesitter*, *Honeymoon in Vegas* and *Sister Act* all surpassed the expectations of both studio accountants and critics. A biopic mini-revival saw *Malcolm X* score a modest hit, while *Chaplin*, *Hoffa* and *The Babe* did little to either educate or entertain.

Honorable mentions: *Aladdin*, for the Genie's verbal and visual pyrotechnics; *A Midnight Clear*, Keith Gordon's story of soldiers behind the lines in WWII, for its lyricism and quiet absurdity; *Mississippi Masala*, Mira Nair's interracial love story, for its low-key realism and winning central performances; *Deep Cover*, for Bill Duke's edgy direction of Jeff Goldblum and Larry Fishburne; *Night on Earth*, for its superb European cast members; and *The Waterdance*, Neal Jimenez's drama set in a paraplegic ward, for its defiantly irreverent wit. (One wheelchair-bound patient to another, after narrowly avoiding a crash during a joyride in a hijacked hospital van: "Lucky we're already crippled!") Maybe it wasn't such a bad year after all.

James Pallot
New York City
May 1993

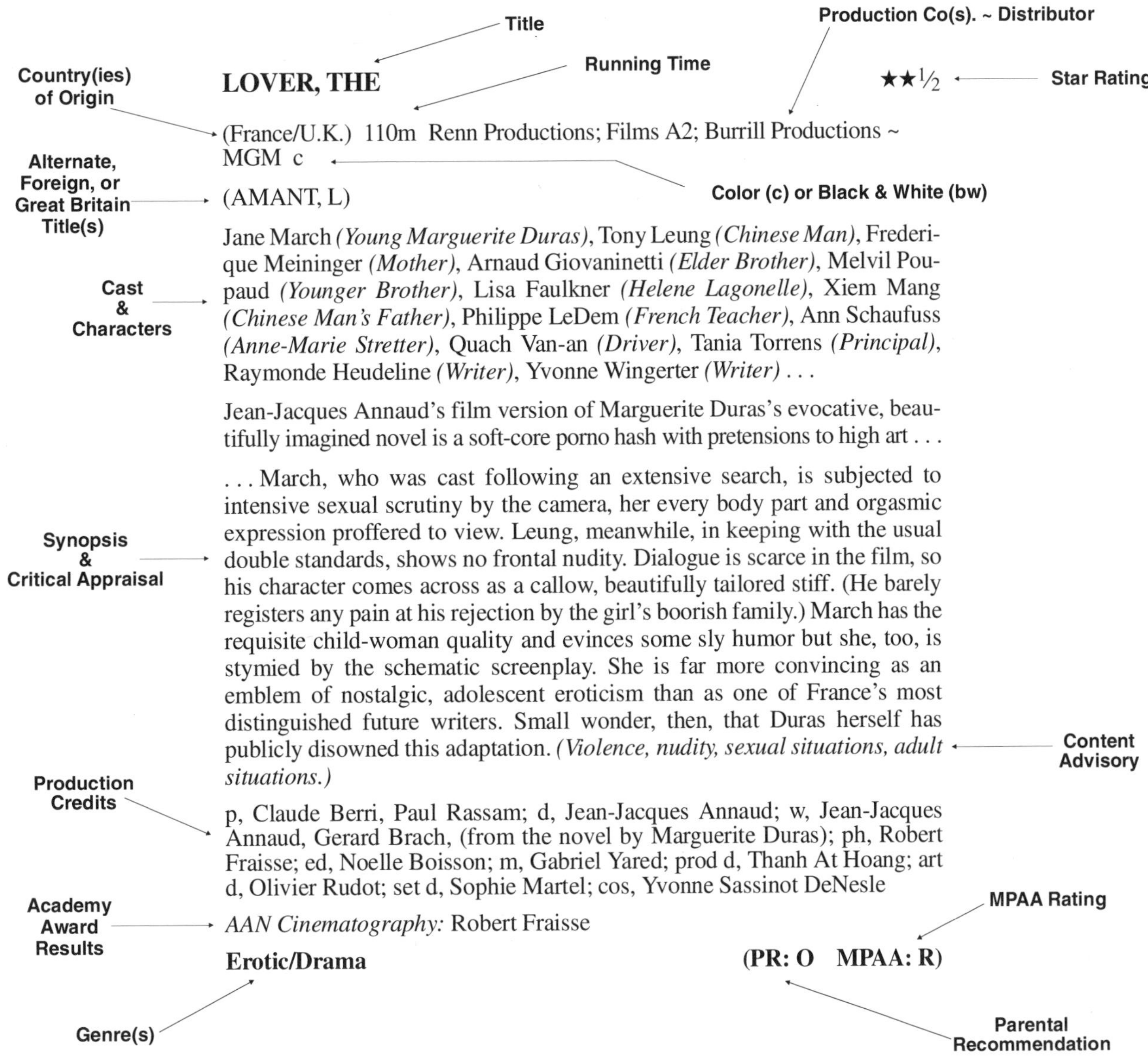

Title
Production Co(s). ~ Distributor
Country(ies) of Origin
Running Time
Star Rating
LOVER, THE
★★½
(France/U.K.) 110m Renn Productions; Films A2; Burrill Productions ~ MGM c
Alternate, Foreign, or Great Britain Title(s)
Color (c) or Black & White (bw)
(AMANT, L)
Cast & Characters
Jane March (Young Marguerite Duras), Tony Leung (Chinese Man), Frederique Meininger (Mother), Arnaud Giovaninetti (Elder Brother), Melvil Poupaud (Younger Brother), Lisa Faulkner (Helene Lagonelle), Xiem Mang (Chinese Man's Father), Philippe LeDem (French Teacher), Ann Schaufuss (Anne-Marie Stretter), Quach Van-an (Driver), Tania Torrens (Principal), Raymonde Heudeline (Writer), Yvonne Wingerter (Writer) . . .
Jean-Jacques Annaud's film version of Marguerite Duras's evocative, beautifully imagined novel is a soft-core porno hash with pretensions to high art . . .
Synopsis & Critical Appraisal
. . . March, who was cast following an extensive search, is subjected to intensive sexual scrutiny by the camera, her every body part and orgasmic expression proffered to view. Leung, meanwhile, in keeping with the usual double standards, shows no frontal nudity. Dialogue is scarce in the film, so his character comes across as a callow, beautifully tailored stiff. (He barely registers any pain at his rejection by the girl's boorish family.) March has the requisite child-woman quality and evinces some sly humor but she, too, is stymied by the schematic screenplay. She is far more convincing as an emblem of nostalgic, adolescent eroticism than as one of France's most distinguished future writers. Small wonder, then, that Duras herself has publicly disowned this adaptation. (Violence, nudity, sexual situations, adult situations.)
Content Advisory
Production Credits
p, Claude Berri, Paul Rassam; d, Jean-Jacques Annaud; w, Jean-Jacques Annaud, Gerard Brach, (from the novel by Marguerite Duras); ph, Robert Fraisse; ed, Noelle Boisson; m, Gabriel Yared; prod d, Thanh At Hoang; art d, Olivier Rudot; set d, Sophie Martel; cos, Yvonne Sassinot DeNesle
Academy Award Results
MPAA Rating
AAN Cinematography: Robert Fraisse
Erotic/Drama
(PR: O MPAA: R)
Genre(s)
Parental Recommendation

INFORMATION KEY

Titles
All entries are arranged alphabetically by title, with articles (A, AN, THE) appearing after the main title. Where appropriate, alternate titles (AKA), Great Britain titles (GB), and foreign-language titles are listed parenthetically.

International Productions
When a film has been produced by a country or countries other than the US, these are noted in parentheses on the first line following the title.

Production Companies/Distributor
The film's production company or companies are listed first, with a tilde separating them from the distributor.

Production Credits
The credits for the creative and technical personnel of a film include: p (producer); d (director); w (writer); ph (cinematographer); ed (editor); m (music composer); md (music director); prod d (production designer); art d (art director); set d (set decorator); cos (costumes); fx (special effects); anim (animation); ch (choreography); makeup; stunts; tech (technical adviser).

Academy Award Results
Academy Award information is preceded by *AA,* for a winner, or *AAN,* for a nominee, followed by the category and the name of the recipient, where appropriate.

Genres
Each film is classified by up to three genres drawn from the following list: Action, Adventure, Animated, Biography, Children's, Comedy, Crime, Dance, Disaster, Docudrama, Documentary, Drama, Erotic, Fantasy, Historical, Horror, Martial Arts, Musical, Mystery, Opera, Political, Prison, Religious, Romance, Science Fiction, Sports, Spy, Thriller, War, Western.

Parental Recommendations
The parental recommendation (PR) provides parents with an indication of the film's suitability for children. The recommendations are as follows: AA – good for children; A – acceptable for children; C – cautionary, some scenes my be objectionable for children; O – objectionable for children.

Film Reviews

ACES: IRON EAGLE III ★★½

98m Aces Eagles Productions; Ron Samuels Entertainment; Carolco Pictures ~ New Line Cinema c

Louis Gossett, Jr. *(Colonel Charles "Chappy" Sinclair)*, Rachel McLish *(Anna)*, Christopher Cazenove *(Palmer)*, Sonny Chiba *(Horikoshi)*, Horst Buchholz *(Leichman)*, Paul Freeman *(Kleiss)*, Ray Mancini *(Chico)*, Mitchell Ryan *(Simms)*, Robert Estes *(Doyle)*, Fred Dalton Thompson *(Stockman)*, Phill Lewis *(Tee Vee)*, Tom Bower *(Crawford)*, Juan Fernandez *(Escovez)*, J.E. Freeman *(Ames)*, Inez Perez *(Mrs. del Prado)*, Branscombe Richmond *(Rapist)*, Paul Weber *(Crewman)*, Rick Sky Garcia *(Crackhead)*, Bob Minor *(Bigman)*, Father Nacho *(Priest)*, Nick Sean Gomez *(Juan)*, Adrian A. Oviedo *(Javier)*, David Herrera *(Luis Morales)*, Estrella Reyes *(Little Girl)*, Majorie Shields *(Secretary)*, Fred Smith *(Security Chief)*

After two outings pounding Middle East dictators, indefatigable fighter pilot Chappy Sinclair takes on a WWII Nazi running cocaine out of South America in ACES: IRON EAGLE III, a fitfully entertaining, cartoonish action-adventure.

The fade-in finds Chappy (Louis Gossett Jr.) flying in an airshow of war-vintage fighters with aces from England (Christopher Cazanove), Germany (Horst Buchholz) and Japan (Sonny Chiba). After the show, Chappy gets word that an old friend has been killed in a crash while flying a shipment of coke in an Air Force jet. Going to his friend's apartment in search of answers, he discovers his friend's sister, Anna (Rachel McLish), who's been hiding out there after escaping from Nazi war criminal turned South American cocaine tycoon Kleiss (Paul Freeman, most famous for playing virtually the same character in RAIDERS OF THE LOST ARK). Kleiss has been holding Anna hostage to force her brother to fly the coke into the US. As soon as she can catch her breath, she intends to return and join rebel forces planning to attack Kleiss's compound.

Chappy promptly volunteers to help her, also enlisting his squadron of aging aces. The manager of the airshow (Fred Dalton Thompson) puts up token resistance to the use of his planes before outfitting them with superchargers, rocket launchers and laser tracking gear. To make the ethnic mix complete, a street-smart ghetto kid (Phill Lewis) stows away for the fight after helping Anna escape from some bad guys. Despite being grossly outgunned and outmanned, Chappy and his "boys" succeed in their mission and get away with only one casualty (Chiba, who goes down, kamakazi-style, taking a loaded cocaine transport plane with him) before adjourning to Chappy's backyard for a nice barbecue dinner.

ACES is one of those old-fashioned Saturday matinee movies they just don't make anymore, and it's all too easy to see why. For starters, the age of these aces would put WWII sometime between Korea and Vietnam, making it painfully obvious that ACES is someone's demented idea of an updated period film. It would be easy to believe a team of war heroes getting together shortly after the war to track down escaped Nazi war criminals in South America, but, evidently fearful of not making contact with today's jaded audiences, the producers opted for a modern mishmash that adds cocaine dealing to Nazi sins and throws in a ghetto kid for no particular reason except to sell tickets to other ghetto kids. And this all pales next to the glaring absurdity of WWII-era rust buckets getting into dogfights with state-of-the-art jets at the film's climax—and winning. The air of cinematic schizophrenia permeating the screenplay (by Kevin Elders, who also contributed to the two previous EAGLE outings) results in a film that is too silly to take seriously yet too solemn to enjoy as pure escapist froth.

Though hobbled by its script, however, ACES almost soars on the strength of its sterling cast and muscular direction. Gossett is as classy as ever, giving the old-fashioned virtues his character represents a simple dignity, conviction and purity. Veteran action star Buchholz brings vim and vigor to his role as a reformed Nazi sworn to redeem himself in battle with his unreformed foe. Cazanove brings back the cheerio spirit of the British Empire in the role they probably couldn't afford to get Roger Moore to play.

Martial arts veteran Chiba goes for Toshiro Mifune grandeur and humanity in his performance and is remarkably affecting. Freeman, of course, is dependably oily as the ultra-villain, though he has surprisingly little screen time for a criminal mastermind. Among the younger cast members, bodybuilder McLish is a true discovery, both sexy and likable enough on her own terms to escape being dubbed a female Schwarzenegger, though that is the obvious pigeonhole. In the thankless "ghetto kid" role, Lewis is relaxed, funny and capable.

Keeping the action cooking with undue fuss, director John Glen is also a veteran, having spent an unwholesome chunk of his career as a key player in the James Bond series, leading up to the director role on the last half-dozen or so outings. Needless to say, this is the kind of film he can do in his sleep. And if someone had thought to nudge him awake during the story sessions, ACES might have been aces all around. *(Violence, profanity.)*

p, Ron Samuels; d, John Glen; w, Kevin Elders, (from the characters created by Elders and Sidney J. Furie); ph, Alec Mills; ed, Bernard Gribble; m, Harry Manfredini; prod d, Robb Wilson King; set d, Daniel Boxer; cos, Lesley Nicholson

Action/Adventure (PR: C MPAA: R)

ADAM'S RIB ★★★

(U.S.S.R.) 75m Mosfilm ~ October Film c

(REBRO ADAMA)

Inna Churikova *(Nina)*, Svetlana Ryabova *(Lidia)*, Masha Goloubkina *(Nastya)*, Yelena Bogdanova *(Grandmother)*, Andrei Toloubeyev, Andrei Kasyanov

Soviet helmer Vyacheslav Krishtofovich's fourth feature offers an intimate view of contemporary Muscovite life as exemplified by three generations of one Russian family, cramped together in a small apartment.

The film opens with a static image, the painting of a bucolic river town hanging on the wall near the grandmother's (Yelena Bogdanova) sleeping niche. Paralyzed, she must rely on her daughter, Nina (Inna Churikova), and granddaughters, Lidia (Svetlana Ryabova) and Nastya (Masha Goloubkina), for her every need. Her only means of expression is a ship's bell above her bed, the legacy of the presumed grandfather, seen in what looks like a faded wartime photograph aboard a ship. Nina is a guide at a local museum; her two daughters, about ten years apart, are the products of two earlier marriages. Lidia works in an office where she is having an affair with her married supervisor, while fifteen-year-old Nastya is still at trade school. Despite her youth, Nastya displays a wily sense of the demands of daily life; she fakes a limp to avoid a long queue for the bus and defines communism as having the local butcher for a friend.

While Lidia must deal with her insecurity concerning her lover, Nina is being courted by a visitor from the provinces, a senior factory controller in town for a training course. Evgeny is clearly director Krishtofovich's idea of the average Russian: shy and laconic, he is contrasted favorably with Nina's earlier husbands, Victor, a government official; and Sasha, who works in the theater and is of Jewish origin. Grandmother apparently had something to do with the failed marriages, since Nina accuses her of this when the bell is rung at a key point in Evgeny's courtship.

The various strands in the plot reach a culmination at a dinner party, ostensibly in celebration of Grandmother's birthday, during which Nina's ex-husbands meet Evgeny, and Nastya drops an unexpected bombshell—she's pregnant. At first everyone laughs at her joke, but quickly realizes that she's dead serious. When Misha, her boyfriend, shows up drunk at their door, only the provincial Evgeny has both the common sense and the will to avoid a disgrace, in a scene displaying both peasant amiability and force. After the menfolk disperse, the three women begin to discuss the best way to deal with Nastya's decision to have the child. Part way through their talk they start to hear a voice singing. With too strong a pull at the bell's rope, the grandmother has been struck by the clapper and her paralysis cured. The film ends with a freeze frame of the now erect and vocal grandmother.

Despite a somewhat thin storyline, ADAM'S RIB provides a well-observed view of modern Russian life from a welcome feminine perspective. Krishtofovich, whose 1987 debut, SINGLE WOMAN SEEKS LIFE COMPANION, was also released in the US, has been quoted as saying that the effort to understand women is one of the worthiest occupations of a man, and except for the modest Evgeny, most of the men in ADAM'S RIB are lamentable. Lidia's lover is treacherous, while Misha is not sure whether to go to law school or become a criminal. Victor, the most successful, is a pompous name-dropper who can't wait to retell some story about officialdom, while Sasha is simply a sentimental drunk.

The women on the other hand are fairly strong, particularly Nina and Nastya, while Lidia is cast as the far-too-idealistic romantic; it's Lidia who is critical of Nastya's wily ways, yet she herself falls victim to the simplest betrayal. ADAM'S RIB confirms the Russian variant on an old joke: If two men and a woman were sent to a deserted island, and discovered two years later, what would be their status? In the Russian punch line, the two men are seen seated at a conference table discussing the working class—*i.e.* the woman laboring in the field behind them. *(Adult situations, profanity.)*

d, Vyacheslav Krishtofovich; w, Vladimir Kounine, Anatol Kourtchatkin, (from his novel *House of Young Women*); ph, Pavel Lebedev; ed, Inna Brozhovskaya; m, Vadim Khrapatchev

Drama **(PR: C MPAA: NR)**

ADJUSTER, THE ★★

(Canada) 102m Ego Film Arts; Family Viewing Pictures ~ Orion Classics c

Elias Koteas *(Noah Render)*, Arsinee Khanjian *(Hera)*, Maury Chaykin *(Bubba)*, Gabrielle Rose *(Mimi)*, Jennifer Dale *(Arianne)*, David Hemblen *(Bert–The Head Censor)*, Rose Sarkisyan *(Seta–Hera's Sister)*, Armen Kokorian *(Simon–Hera's Child)*, Jacqueline Samuda *(Louise–The Maid)*, Gerard Parkes *(Tim)*, Patricia Collins *(Lorraine)*, Don McKellar *(Tyler–The Young Censor)*, John Gilbert *(The Doctor)*, Stephen Ouimette *(Larry–The Butterfly Collector)*, Raoul Trujillo *(Matthew–His Lover)*, Tony Nardi *(The Motel Manager)*, Paul Bettis *(The Wild Man of the Billboards)*, Frank Jefferson *(Simon as a Baby)*

THE ADJUSTER is the sort of film that gives serious cinema a bad name. Elliptical, disconnected and apparently endlessly allusive, its narrative is simultaneously minimalist and impossibly convoluted.

Noah Render (Elias Koteas) is an insurance adjuster; his job requires him to sift through the minutiae of other people's ruined lives and assign a dollar value to their most intimate and invaluable possessions. He frequently engages in sexual liaisons with his clients, all of whom seem to be in a state of shock. Or so he tells them. Noah's wife Hera (Arsinee Khanjian) works for the Canadian censorship board, and spends her days deciding what sort of material is and is not appropriate for general viewing. She secretly films unsuitable material to show to her sister, Seta (Rose Sarkisyan), a recent immigrant who speaks no English and is fascinated by her younger sibling's life. Hera has nightmares, and Seta ritualistically burns photographs of her old neighborhood, destroyed by war. They all live in a sterile model home in a half-finished housing development in the middle of nowhere. The stasis of the Renders' lives is soon disrupted. Noah enters into a troubling relationship with a homosexual client, and Hera is caught in the act of illicit taping by a new censor, who thinks he's found a kindred spirit with whom to share a perverted interest in pornography. Bubba (Maury Chaykin) and Mimi (Gabrielle Rose), wealthy lovers who amuse themselves by orchestrating elaborate sexual games, further upset matters. Bubba convinces the Renders that he's making a movie and their house would be the perfect location, so they move out temporarily, taking up residence in the same motel where Noah regularly houses his clients. Noah's carefully compartmentalized life comes apart as his two worlds—the world of his family and that of his devastated client/lovers—are brought together.

This, his fourth feature, is probably the most accessible work by Canadian filmmaker Atom Egoyan (NEXT OF KIN, FAMILY VIEWING, SPEAKING PARTS), but that hardly means it's an exercise in mainstream moviemaking. THE ADJUSTER is all set-up with no payoff; the plot takes forever to describe because of the wealth of detail that makes up the back story, but once the stage is set, one is faced with the fact that nothing happens.

THE ADJUSTER is emphatically a film of ideas, a film about order and chaos, loss and accumulation, surface and interior. The characters are designed to embody and illustrate these issues, with the result that they're largely uninvolving. Once you get what they stand for, there's not much reason to watch them, except for the superficial fun of seeing them go through their paces. Noah Render is the most fleshed out characterization, and his determination to quantify the world, to attach arbitrary but consistent meaning to things, is both touching and absurd. When he asks the cost of a dog pictured in a snapshot or observes of some provocative photographs of a client in bed that they don't show much background, THE ADJUSTER verges on being genuinely, sharply funny. But all too often, Egoyan settles for being "provocative" in the worst possible sense of the word.

The film is relentlessly self-referential, awash in photographs and movies, dreams and memories and tableaux vivants; the viewer is adrift in a sea of symbolic signifiers, an ocean of images dense with meaning. Noah poised at the window of his model home, firing arrows into a billboard depicting a grimly happy family; Hera with her portable camera whirring at her hip in a darkened screening room; Mimi in cheerleader drag; Noah and a client making love as he continues a verbal inventory of her possessions; so clever, so meaningful, so very dull. It's provocative, but what it largely provokes is a feeling of irritated despair. *(Nudity, sexual situations.)*

p, Atom Egoyan; d, Atom Egoyan; w, Atom Egoyan; ph, Paul Sarossy; ed, Susan Shipton; m, Mychael Danna; prod d, Linda

Del Rosario, Richard Paris; set d, Linda Del Rosario, Richard Paris; cos, Maya Mani

Drama **(PR: C MPAA: R)**

ADVENTURES IN DINOSAUR CITY ★
88m Golden Ratio Films; Luigi Cingolani Productions ~ Republic Pictures Home Video c

Omri Katz *(Timmy)*, Shawn Hoffman *(Mick)*, Tiffanie Poston *(Jamie)*, Marc Martorana *(Tops)*, Tony Doyle *(Rex)*, Pete Koch, Megan Hughes, Mimi Maynard, Steven Anderson

In an attempt to cash in on the current popularity of anything reptilian, screenwriters Willie Baronet and Lisa Morton have come up with ADVENTURES IN DINOSAUR CITY, a feeble fantasy about three teens hurled back in time to the days when scaly monsters roamed the earth.

Timmy (Omri Katz), Mick (Shawn Hoffman) and Jamie (Tiffanie Poston) are three upper-middle-class teenagers who love to watch cartoons featuring a crime-fighting tyrannosaurus named Rex (Tony Doyle), his sidekick, Tops (Marc Martorana), and a cuddly lizard called Forey. Coincidentally, their scientist parents have developed a device with the power to transport plant and animal life-forms to past eras. Whether or not the device can also transport humans is unknown. Before leaving on business, the parents instruct Timmy, Mick and Jamie to turn off the TV, get their homework done and, above all, stay out of the laboratory. Within moments after their parents' departure, however, the siblings are exploring the lab and testing out all the gadgets they can lay their hands on. One such device, hooked up to a big-screen TV monitor, starts to sputter and act strangely, sucking the kids through the screen and back into the prehistoric era.

Here, to their delight, Timmy, Mick and Jamie meet Rex, Tops and Forey in the flesh. Together they embark on a series of adventures, culminating in the foiling of a plot by evil tyrannosaurus Mr. Big to destroy Dinosaur City and its inhabitants. Having overcome loin-cloth-clad Neanderthals as well as hostile reptiles, the children finally return to their own place and time.

Lackluster is the kindest word one can use to describe ADVENTURES IN DINOSAUR CITY, a badly acted, directed, photographed, edited and scored picture. Worst of all are the costumes and production design; the sets look like papier-mache mock-ups and the dinosaur outfits are too dreadful even to be considered corny. Released straight to video, ADVENTURES IN DINOSAUR CITY is, at best, a mindless diversion for undiscriminating young viewers. Adults will find it downright unbearable.

p, Luigi Cingolani; d, Brett Thompson; w, Willie Baronet, Lisa Morton, (from the story by Baronet); ph, Rick Fichter; ed, W. Peter Miller, Elizabeth Canney; m, Fredric Teetsel; prod d, Michael Stuart

Fantasy/Adventure **(PR: A MPAA: PG)**

ADVENTURES IN SPYING ★★
91m Moviestore Entertainment ~ New Line Home Video c

Bernie Coulson *(Brian McNichols)*, Jill Schoelen *(Julie Converse)*, Seymour Cassel *(Ray Rucker)*, Michael Emil *(Professor Hardwick)*, G. Gordon Liddy *(Al Dorn)*

While this very mild film has more to do with the fine points of an amateur stakeout than actual espionage, its given title—ADVENTURES IN SPYING—betrays the filmmakers' juvenile approach to their subject.

The story takes place in fictional Rockwater, where young, handsome Brian McNichols (Bernie Coulson) runs across a mysterious man (G. Gordon Liddy). Convinced he has just faced dangerous killer Al Dorn—presumed dead in a car explosion—and lured by a $50,000 reward for his capture, Brian stakes out the house where the man is being sheltered by an older person. Simultaneously, police detective Ray Rucker (Seymour Cassel) suspects Dorn is still alive and conducts his own zealous investigation. Invited by his new friend Julie Converse (Jill Schoelen) to a college reception, Brian realizes that Professor Hardwick (Michael Emil), a respected chemistry professor, is the person hiding Dorn.

Brian follows Hardwick after the reception and watches him transport what looks like cocaine to a nearby boat. Meanwhile, Dorn kidnaps Brian's kid brother when he steps too close to the house, just as detective Rucker's search brings him to Rockwater. Brian and Julie follow Dorn's car as he takes Brian's brother into the boat where Hardwick's powder is being shipped. Rucker answers their call for police help, quickly taking charge of the situation. It turns out that Rucker is a crooked detective, tracing Dorn for back bribes owed him. As Dorn lures Rucker into his own racket—ripping off the big drug cartels with fake cocaine—Bernie summons the Rockwater and federal police. The bad guys go to jail, Brian's brother is saved and Brian and Julie enjoy their just rewards.

Made for the pre-teen market, ADVENTURES IN SPYING is a light, predictable action comedy which is not meant to be taken seriously. Accordingly, more time is lavished on its photogenic teen heroes than on the plot's crime angle, forcing writer-director Hil Covington to resort to the tried-and-true stylistic trope of the "incredible coincidence." Brian just happens to run into America's most wanted killer, who has a deal with the town's revered chemistry professor, who's honored at the very same party Brian is invited to attend. While this lightness of tone is harmless enough, ADVENTURES IN SPYING's overall mediocrity of screenplay and direction—punctuated by an irritatingly tacky musical score—prevents even the mindless enjoyment of an unpretentious movie.

Appealing leads are crucial in the success of movies like this. Unfortunately, Bernie Coulson and Jill Schoelen are just pretty faces, too bland to hold any enduring interest. G. Gordon Liddy proves to be no actor, his only expression being a menacing glare in his best "Watergate" fashion, which wears thin after ten minutes. Only Seymour Cassel—an interesting actor too often wasted in silly roles—and Michael Emil perform with any sense of professionalism. ADVENTURES IN SPYING is recommended only to those in search of inconsequential, unoriginal entertainment.

p, Eugene Mazzola, Miles Mogulesco; d, Hil Covington; w, Hil Covington; ph, Peter Warrilow; ed, Dennis O'Connor; m, James Stemple

Comedy/Action/Crime **(PR: C MPAA: PG-13)**

AFFENGEIL ★★★
(Germany) 87m Rosa Von Praunheim Produktion ~ First Run Features c

Lotti Huber, Rosa Von Praunheim, Helga Sloop, Gertrud Mischwitzki, Thomas Woischnig, Hans Peter Schwade, Frank Schafer

"You can't just enter a universe in the middle!" admonished a young "Dungeons & Dragons" player to the protagonist of Steven Spielberg's E.T. THE EXTRA-TERRESTRIAL. This profound observation is relevant to the uninitiated viewer of

AFFENGEIL, a quirky experimental documentary from maverick German filmmaker Rosa Von Praunheim.

Born Holger Mischwitzki, Von Praunheim has remained a more marginal figure than several of his contemporaries in the New German Cinema movement. Whereas Fassbinder, Herzog, Schlondorff and Wenders have been intermittently fascinated by America and on occasion have toyed with the mainstream, Von Praunheim has remained a staple of museum and festival screenings. A prolific, openly gay filmmaker, he has made issues of politics and sexuality, particularly gay and lesbian sexuality and the politics of AIDS, the major focus of much of his work. AFFENGEIL is a different matter: it's a mostly lighthearted, sometimes poignant, and playfully experimental profile of a remarkable woman, actress/dancer/free-spirit Lotti Huber, and her ten-year or so relationship with the filmmaker.

Subtitled "A Trip through Lotti's Life", AFFENGEIL is not a traditional star profile or a standard documentary. It would make an excellent triple bill with Maximilian Schell's MARLENE, an unconventional portrait of Marlene Dietrich, and Orson Welles's F FOR FAKE, a witty meditation on the sometimes fictional nature of reality. AFFENGEIL investigates what constitutes the documentary approach to filmmaking. By filming obviously staged events, problematizing the veracity of interview subjects and acknowledging and analyzing the biases of the writer-director, this often fascinating film makes the audience wonder what is real and what is fiction.

The film begins with a little toy stage and whimsical background music that would not be out of place in a puppet show. The opening credits are drawn on a slate with brightly colored chalk. We first see Lotti Huber as a charming little old lady puttering around in a camera shop. She asks the salesperson if she can have a free catalogue. He gives her the booklet and walks away while Lotti totters over to a fancy video camcorder on display. There's a cut to a close-up of her eyes darting back and forth in an exaggerated manner. She then quickly places the camera in her valise, leaves the store, gets directions from a uniformed gentleman (a policeman? a soldier?) and he gallantly helps her across the street.

Lotti arrives at an apartment and presents the now gift-wrapped camera to a strapping, dark, bespectacled man whom we soon learn is Rosa Von Praunheim himself. He eyes the gift suspiciously and asks if it was stolen. "In the world of big business," she replies, "we call it a transaction." Lotti wants Rosa to make a documentary about her. "And you will film my life. As I am. How I laugh . . . how I cry . . . how I dance . . . how I live. Just as I am!" Rosa squeezes fresh orange juice and walks down a corridor where we see posters for his films—including some with Lotti—and shelves of books. He joins the older woman on the couch and pops a video into a VCR. We see Lotti on a stage against a black background. Dressed in black with a black cape decorated with sparkling golden designs, she seems at times to be floating across the stage surrounded by stars. In front of an unseen audience, she begins to tell her colorful life story.

The rest of the film consists of interviews, photographs, film clips, field trips and numerous arguments between the documentarian and his subject—some obviously staged, some convincingly real. We frequently return to the little old woman on stage playing to her appreciative audience. "Just as I am," instructed Lotti and just how is she? Perhaps Rosa puts it best when he describes his first impressions of her: "What a gaudy beast! So theatrical and affected and artificial!" Claiming to be seventy-five-years-old at the time of filming, Frau Huber has the kind of face, figure and personal style that would only appear in American films in the work of John Waters.

Short, chubby and overly made-up, Lotti is a genial grotesque and a consummate performer; she is always acting. Consequently she is a vastly entertaining interview subject as she recounts her many adventures. However, one begins to wonder after awhile if all her stories could possibly be true. Von Praunheim plants these suspicions by beginning some scenes as if depicting an interview or documenting a meeting and pulling back to reveal we are watching a video on a monitor while Lotti denounces it as untrue, inaccurate or cliched.

As a youth in Weimar Germany, Huber was encouraged by her independent mother to concentrate on her studies. "Forget kitchen, church and children. Study! Everything else comes later." With such encouragement from home, Lotti developed into an unconventional artistic personality. Dancer, restaurateur, teacher, model, movie extra and finally actress, Lotti had a rich and varied life. Although a German Jew, her family allegedly never took Nazism too seriously until Lotti was placed in a concentration camp in 1937. The love of her life was Hilbert, a tall blond German who was the son of the mayor. An old school friend reported her to the SS for breaking German race laws as a "Jewess" living with an Aryan man. Hilbert was thrown into prison where he was shot while she went to a camp in punishment for her forbidden love. This powerful sequence is abetted by documentary footage of the concentration camp and prison executions and then undermined somewhat by Lotti's vaguely ludicrous interpretive dance of the experience. Von Praunheim invites us to speculate as to which piece of "evidence" is most real.

Frau Huber tells her audience that the tale of her escape is "unbelievably fantastic" but neglects to tell the story! She skips to how she was invited to study music and dance at the Conservatory of Music in Jerusalem and went on to gain fame as a dancer of pantomimes and parodies. A delicious dramatization depicts Lotti dancing in a Cairo cabaret before an enthusiastic King Farouk with the irrepressible actress playing both parts. Clearly this is not a normal sober documentary.

Like an initially delightful guest who eventually overstays her welcome, AFFENGEIL goes on for much too long. It would have been a much stronger film at half its 90-minute length. Lotti's reflections on such important issues as the parallels between the rise of Nazism and the skinhead movement are well meaning but obvious. Perhaps the ideal viewer for this film is one who is intimately familiar with her work in previous Von Praunheim films. Nonetheless AFFENGEIL is a memorable experience that—like its subject—is often fabulous. *(Profanity, nudity, sexual situations.)*

p, Rosa Von Praunheim; d, Rosa Von Praunheim; w, Rosa Von Praunheim; ph, Klaus Janschewski, Mike Kuchar; ed, Mike Shephard; m, Maran Gosov, Thomas Marquard; set d, Volker Marz

Documentary **(PR: C MPAA: NR)**

AFRAID OF THE DARK ★★

(U.K./France) 92m Sovereign Pictures; Telescope Films; Les Films Ariane ~ Fine Line Features c

James Fox *(Frank)*, Fanny Ardant *(Miriam)*, Paul McGann *(Tony Dalton)*, Clare Holman *(Rose)*, Robert Stephens *(Dan Burns)*, Susan Woolridge *(Lucy Trent)*, Ben Keyworth *(Lucas)*, Star Acri *(1st Girl at Wedding/Cementary/Jane)*, Niven Body *(Ice Cream Man/Shop Owner)*, Sheila Burrell *(Meg)*, Frances Cuka *(Mrs. Dalton)*, Gerard DiMiglio *(Wedding Guest/Policeman with Walkie Talkie)*, Jeremy Flynn *(Jim Gilbert)*, Laurence Harrington *(Mr. Lewis/Man with Centerfold)*, Oona Howard *(Georgia/Girl on Embankment)*, Rosalind Knight *(Edith Simpkins)*, Hilary Mason *(Basement Woman)*, Catriona McColl *(Blind Woman at Reach Out House)*, Daniel Andre Pageon *(Wedding Guest/Po-*

liceman at Lucy Trent's), Colleen Passard *(Nurse with Knitting)*, Lola Peploe *(2nd Girl at Wedding/Cemetery)*, Struan Rodger *(Window Cleaner)*, Jean Serret *(Blind Man at Reach Out House/Bob)*, Ed Stobart *(Guest who Toasts/Police Driver)*, Gwynneth Strong *(Blind Mother with Baby)*, Cassie Stuart *(Red Head/Centerfold Woman)*, David Thewlis *(Tom Miller/Locksmith)*

Exploring the fantasy world of a stricken child, AFRAID OF THE DARK offers potent testimony that the greatest horrors lurk in the imagination.

Eleven-year-old Lucas (Ben Keyworth) lies in bed listening to his father, Frank (James Fox), and blind mother, Miriam (Fanny Ardant), whisper about a slasher who has been razoring the faces of blind women. The following day, he accompanies his mother to her knitting class at the local clinic for the blind where everyone is scared about the horrific incidents. Miriam asks him to escort her friend Rose (Clare Holman) to a photographer's (Paul McGann) studio where she is having her engagement portrait taken. After safely dropping her off, he catches sight of another blind woman having her face cut through his telescope. Running home, he passes the clinic's window cleaner, the photographer and the clinic locksmith—all of them seem threatening, like culprits. He wanders out on the railroad tracks just as the slasher attacks someone else on a deserted train platform. That night, Lucas, a compulsive explorer and sneak, slips out of his house. He passes the photo studio where the photographer is taking coerced pornographic shots of Rose. Suddenly the photographer pulls out a razor blade and lightly traces her face and body with it. Lucas dashes in and plunges the weapon into the photographer's eye.

Lucas suddenly comes to—he's wearing thick glasses that make his deep brown eyes seem grotesquely large. It's all been an awful nightmare and his parents are actually whispering about the eye operation he needs. His half-sister, Rose, is fussing with a wedding gown, for it's her wedding day. No one has any time for Lucas, especially as Miriam is very pregnant. During the wedding reception she goes into labor and she and Frank rush to the hospital leaving Lucas behind. The bride and groom depart as well, and in the confusion, someone steps on Lucas's glasses. Fortunately the optometrist nearby gives him a new pair. Lucas makes his way home and a beloved neighborhood dog, Toby, tries to follow him inside. Lucas removes his glasses and suddenly the beast appears to be rabid and on the attack. Lucas plunges one of his mother's knitting needles into the dog's eye and it falls, cracking its neck on the sidewalk.

Frank arrives home late to find the doors bolted and the house pitch dark. Lucas has put all the lightbulbs in the baby's crib. Miriam arrives with the newborn child, Tess, and admonishes Lucas to keep away, he's running a fever. Clutching a knitting needle, he snatches Tess and runs into the graveyard next door. A gang of blind people chase him—his mother and father, the photographer, the window cleaner and others. Just as he lifts the needle he wakes up in an operating room. He can see. His parents visit his hospital room and lay baby Tess in his arms. Lucas looks into their pale, tired faces and asks, "Did I kill Toby?"

AFRAID OF THE DARK is a taut, intelligent pyschodrama that pulls the audience into Lucas's deluded state of not being able to distinguish between nightmare and reality. Mark Peploe, the screenwriter best known for his collaborations with Antonioni and Bertolucci (THE PASSENGER and THE LAST EMPEROR, respectively), carefully measures his pace and shrewdly ignores American horror conventions, suggesting violence rather than covering the screen in gore and restricting the plot to the true realm of endless possibilities, the human mind, rather than resorting to absurd jaunts into the supernatural. He also cannily employs ubiquitous symbols of domesticity—knitting needles, toys, a newborn child—and common fears—blindness, abandonment, being watched—to create an unusually chilling film. Aside from James Fox's wooden performance all the other principals are intense and convincing—especially the luminous Fanny Ardant and Clare Holman in their deft switches between blind and sighted characters. Young Ben Keyworth is truly disturbing as Lucas. His deadpan performance is trimmed with a terrifying edge of repressed pyschosis.

Because AFRAID OF THE DARK is so engrossing, it's easy to ignore certain incongruities, first in a logic that does not succeed in linking its themes of voyeurism, oedipal complexes and fear of physical harm and then those in Lucas's overly mature imagination. The perversions he dreams up are far too sophisticated for a little boy. Nonetheless, AFRAID OF THE DARK does its job as a horror film and makes one consider some difficult and ugly issues as well. *(Violence, nudity, adult situations.)*

p, Simon Bosanquet; d, Mark Peploe; w, Mark Peploe, Frederick Seidel; ph, Bruno DeKeyzer; ed, Scott Thomas; m, Jason Osborn; prod d, Caroline Amies; art d, Stephen Scott; cos, Louise Stjernsward

Drama **(PR: C MPAA: R)**

ALADDIN ★★★½

90m Walt Disney Productions ~ BV c

VOICES OF: Scott Weinger *(Aladdin)*, Robin Williams *(Genie)*, Linda Larkin *(Jasmine)*, Jonathan Freeman *(Jafar)*, Frank Welker *(Abu/Narrator)*, Gilbert Gottfried *(Iago)*, Douglas Seale *(Sultan)*, Lea Salonga *(Singing Jasmine)*, Charlie Adler, Jack Angel, Corey Burton, Philip Clarke, Jim Cummings, Jennifer Darling, Debi Derryberry, Bruce Gooch, Jerry Houser, Vera Lockwood, Sherry Lynn, Mickie McGowan, Patrick Pinney, Phil Proctor *(Voices)*

Disney scored a cinematic hat trick with its three animated releases, THE LITTLE MERMAID, BEAUTY AND THE BEAST and ALADDIN. The last of these, however, gets by more on energy and flash than on the integration of score, story and character that elevated the first two.

Based on the tale from *1001 Arabian Nights*, ALADDIN follows the adventures of the title character (Scott Weinger), a poor Arabian boy who steals to live, and the Genie who helps him get his wishes. We first see Aladdin in the marketplace, stealing and conniving his way out of trouble with his monkey, Abu (Frank Welker). Meanwhile, in the Sultan's (Douglas Seale) palace, the evil vizier Jafar (Jonathan Freeman) has learned that Aladdin is the "chosen one" who will inherit a magical lamp, and orders his henchmen to kidnap the boy. Also on her way to the marketplace is Jasmine (Linda Larkin), the Sultan's daughter, in disguise as a commoner. The princess isn't allowed outside the palace walls, and has secretly escaped to sample life outside. Aladdin helps Jasmine out of trouble when she takes an apple from a merchant without paying for it, and in return, she has Jafar's men let Aladdin go when he's captured. The two develop an attraction for each other, which is thwarted by the Sultan's decree that Jasmine must marry a prince.

When Aladdin is again taken into custody he's thrown in jail, where he meets an old man (actually Jafar in disguise) who promises to help him escape if he leads him to the Cave of Wonders where the magic lamp is located. Aladdin does this and finds the lamp, which Jafar grabs from his hands as the boy is climbing out of the cave. Abu bites Jafar, and the lamp, Aladdin and Abu tumble back down, deep into the cave. Rubbing the lamp to clean away centuries of dust, he inadvertently conjures up its occupant, a wild, free-form genie (Robin Williams), who explains that Aladdin is now his master. To illustrate his super powers, the Genie whisks Aladdin and Abu out of the cave on a flying carpet, and tells Aladdin he can grant him three wishes. For the first wish, the better to woo Princess Jasmine, he turns Aladdin into a prince, which further infuriates Jafar, now determined more than ever to possess the lamp, marry the princess and become Sultan. With the help of his parrot Iago (Gilbert Gottfried), Jafar steals the lamp, leading to a climactic battle of magic between Aladdin and the now super-powerful wizard.

ALADDIN coasts along so breezily, and with such a surfeit of energy and good humor, that its weaknesses are not readily apparent. Robin Williams is the film's main selling point, but it's surprising how strong the rest of the film is; the Genie doesn't appear until thirty or forty minutes in, and things are pretty entertaining up to that point. Like most Disney classics, the real stars are the supporting characters: Abu and the flying carpet though voiceless (Abu does make some Donald Duck-like noises) are good comic relief, and Gottfried, as annoying as his screaming madman bit is in person, provides a marvelous smart-aleck counterpoint to the somber Jafar.

Williams's famous improvisational skills take the animation to a whole new level; it's obvious that directors John Musker and Ron Clements just let him loose with the script and then chose the best parts to animate. As a result, the Genie can become, in split-second succession, Ed Sullivan, Arnold Schwarzenegger, a French waiter and Groucho Marx. The pace and range of references in Williams's dialogue lends the proceedings a wild, irreverent tone never before seen in a Disney film (it's closer to old Warner Bros. cartoons, actually), and one with a winking, self-conscious knowledge of the mechanics of story-telling and movie-making. After his big number, "Friend Like Me," the Genie actually holds up an applause sign!

The Disney folks have even allowed some jokes at their own expense, including a brief sight gag on the DisneyWorld commercials. The film is full of dazzling action sequences, including the opener when Aladdin is chased through the marketplace, and a dizzying, fiery ride through the Cave of Wonders, which owes a large debt to the INDIANA JONES trilogy (and seems destined to become a new ride at DisneyWorld).

The score, much of it by the lyricist Howard Ashman and composer Alan Menken, the brilliant team responsible for THE LITTLE MERMAID and BEAUTY AND THE BEAST, is not that memorable, however, and in light of those films now sounds a bit formulaic. There's the aforementioned Big Production Number for the Genie, the love duet for the Aladdin and Jasmine, and so on, and while they're pleasant enough, none really have the freshness or wit of the previous two scores. In fairness, however, it must be noted that the lyrics contributed to "Arabian Nights," "Friend Like Me" and "Prince Ali" by the late Ashman are far superior to Tim Rice's efforts on "One Jump Ahead," "A Whole New World" and "Prince Ali Reprise." (Ashman died of complications from AIDS in 1991.)

Other slight letdowns are the somewhat bland Jasmine and Aladdin, who seem designed mainly to appeal to the nascent hormonal stirrings of the preteens in the audience. Aladdin, it has been noted by the animators, has been largely modeled on superstar Tom Cruise, while the Princess, in a slightly disturbing bit of backsliding following BEAUTY AND THE BEAST's independent Belle, is a cartoon pin-up, with a ridiculously thin waist and more cleavage than any previous Disney heroine. If only their personalities had been as developed as their physiques, ALADDIN could have been a classic adventure-comedy. It's a wild, exhilarating ride nonetheless.

p, John Musker, Ron Clements; d, John Musker, Ron Clements; w, Ron Clements, John Musker, Ted Elliot, Terry Rossio; ed, H. Lee Peterson; m, Alan Menken; art d, Bill Perkins; anim, Ed Gombert, Rasoul Azadani, Kathy Altieri, Vera Lanpher, Don Paul, Steve Goldberg

AA Best Score: Alan Menken; *AA Best Song:* Alan Menken (Music) and Tim Rice (Lyrics); *AAN Best Song:* Alan Menken (Music) and Howard Ashman (Lyrics); *AAN Sound:* Terry Porter, Mel Metcalfe, David J. Hudson, and Doc Kane; *AAN Sound Effects Editing:* Mark Mangini

Animated/Comedy/Musical (PR: AA MPAA: G)

ALAN & NAOMI ★★½

95m South Gate Entertainment; Leucadia Film Corporation; The Maltese Companies Inc ~ Triton Pictures c

Lukas Haas *(Alan Drucker Silverman)*, Vanessa Zaoui *(Naomi Kirschenbaum)*, Michael Gross *(Sol Silverman)*, Amy Aquino *(Ruth Silverman)*, Kevin Connolly *(Shaun Kelly)*, Zohra Lampert *(Mrs. Liebman)*, Victoria Christian *(Mrs. Kirschenbaum)*, Charlie Dow *(Joe Condello)*, Randy Williams *(Ken Newman)*, Mary McMillan *(Mrs. Landley)*, Richard K. Olsen *(Finch)*, Stacy Moseley *(Gloria)*, Mark Fincannon *(Mr. Kirschenbaum)*

A compassionate and determinedly modest debut from producer and Sundance cofounder Sterling VanWagenen, ALAN & NAOMI boasts fine central performances from juvenile star Lukas Haas and newcomer Vanessa Zaoui.

Alan Silverman (Haas), already in the dog house with some of his classmates for being a gangly sissy, is desperate to prove himself on the stickball team when his loving parents, Sol and Ruth (well played by Michael Gross of TV's "Family Ties" and Amy Aquino), deal their only son a devastating blow, virtually ordering him to sacrifice his afterschool playtime in order to serve as Good Samaritan to a new neighbor's young ward, a French girl named Naomi Kirschenbaum (Zaoui) who is suffering from catatonia as a result of witnessing the brutal death of her father, a member of the French Resistance, at the hands of the Nazis. When Alan, not understanding her tormented background or fully grasping the extent of her present plight, first meets Naomi, he's repulsed by her and resentful of having to spend his afternoons with an unresponsive girl who does nothing but stare into space while mechanically ripping newspapers to shreds. As these sessions continue, however, Alan begins to take a personal interest in his charge and begins working hard to reach her. The breakthrough comes when Alan, a passably good ventriloquist, uses his dummy to communicate with Naomi. She responds through her ragged doll and a friendship blossoms, first between dummy and doll, and eventually between the two youngsters themselves.

Initially embarrassed about his involvement with the troubled Naomi, Alan avoids telling the truth to his best friend Shaun (Kevin Connolly) and, as a result, he almost loses Shaun's friendship forever. Finally, Alan confesses all to Shaun and takes him to meet Naomi. At first, Shaun refuses to forgive Alan for his fibs, but all is forgiven after a local bully, shouting racial slurs, pounces on the smaller Alan and Shaun comes to his friend's defense. Near the conclusion, Naomi suffers a relapse, hides in a cellar and smears soot over her face. The touching finale finds Alan comforting Naomi on a bench outside the sanitorium where she has been taken by Mrs. Liebman (Zohra Lampert), her guardian. She's reverted to her previous catatonic state, but Alan's assured expression effectively conveys his hope for her future.

Set during the mid-1940s, some viewers will likely criticize ALAN & NAOMI for not offering a tougher, more realistic view of its subject matter, such as the unsparing portrait of Annie Sullivan and Helen Keller offered by Arthur Penn in THE MIRACLE WORKER. In truth, Jordan Horowitz's screenplay is decidedly sentimental, largely eschewing the more unpleasant aspects of Naomi's recovery, but the film remains a sweetly affecting coming-of-age story that younger audiences, and tender-hearted older viewers, will doubtlessly appreciate. The Brooklyn period settings have been faithfully recreated by production designer George Goodridge in Wilmington, North Carolina. *(Adult situations.)*

p, David Anderson, Mark Balsam; d, Sterling VanWagenen; w, Jordan Horowitz, (from the novel by Myron Levoy); ph, Paul Ryan; ed, Cari Coughlin; m, Dick Hyman; prod d, George Goodridge; art d, Barbara Kahn Kretschmer; cos, Alonzo V. Wilson

Drama **(PR: A MPAA: PG)**

ALBERTO EXPRESS ★★

(France) 98m Alliance Films et Communication; Cine Cinq ~ MK2 Productions USA c

Sergio Castellitto *(Alberto)*, Nino Manfredi *(Alberto's Father)*, Marie Trintignant *(Clara)*, Marco Messeri *(The Controller)*, Jeanne Moreau *(The Baroness)*, Eugenia Marruzzo *(Juliette)*, Dennis Goldson *(Diamond Tooth Man)*, Roland Amstutz *(Waiter)*, Dominique Pinon *(Train Conductor)*, Nanni Tamma *(Grandfather)*, Michel Aumont *(Man in Debt)*, Thomas Langmann *(Young Alberto)*

You may feel you owe your parents a great deal, but perhaps not as much as the hero of ALBERTO EXPRESS. Arthur Joffe's comedy adventure takes the concept of familial debt quite literally, but it's one that can't fuel this uneven movie.

The film opens with a teenage Alberto meeting with his father (Nino Manfredi), who explains the family tradition of sons repaying fathers, literally, for the costs of raising them. His father then takes out an adding machine and has his son add as he lists the costs of all his meals, clothes, furniture and assorted childhood expenses, finally arriving at a total of over thirty million lire. He then explains that Alberto cannot have a child without first repaying his debt, and implies grave consequences if he doesn't comply. Alberto, stunned, then leaves home, and we cut to fifteen years later, in Paris, where he and his French wife are awaiting the arrival of their first child. Alberto, realizing he is now in deep trouble since he hasn't paid back his father, impulsively boards a train to Rome.

Panicked and unsure of his plans, he wanders the train and meets people from his past, including an old school coach and a former flame (Marie Trintignant). After emptying her wallet, Alberto still doesn't have enough cash to pay his debt, and with the aid of a young-though-hardly-innocent boy, he goes through the entire train while its passengers are asleep, taking jewels, credit cards and whatever valuables he can lay his hands on. Alberto joyously realizes he now has enough loot, and in a half-crazed, illogical stunt, he climbs on top of the moving train to reach the conductor and tell him to speed up. Of course, the bag containing his loot opens while he's speaking to the conductor, and all the cash, jewels and valuables blow away.

More despondent than ever, Alberto again wanders the train where he enters a strange, darkened car that seems to be the tomb of a mysterious, oraculer-like woman (Jeanne Moreau, in a thankless cameo), who tells him what he's "searching for" is in the last car of the train. He goes there and finds his grandfather, great-grandfather and other white-haired ancestors poring over old receipts and ledgers, attempting to determine their "debts." While listening to them bicker over who owes what to whom, Alberto realizes that none of his ancestors have fully paid back their fathers, and the relieved son now arrives in Rome to find his father. Father and son initially clash, but Dad eventually comes to realize the travesty of the tradition.

ALBERTO EXPRESS ostensibly wants to make a statement regarding the debt one owes to parents, but it takes such a long, muddled route getting there that most viewers will lose interest before the film's conclusion. Given its initial premise, much could have been done with Alberto's predicament, but confining almost all the action to a train, and one populated with sketchy characters at that, doesn't help matters. The film's tone is as noncommittal as Alberto himself: indifferent, confused and not particularly likable, he comes off as a *shnook*, a terminal screw-up who at times seems quite unconcerned with his fate. Much of this can be attributed to Sergio Castellitto's vague, half-hearted performance.

If the whole train trip is a dream, or an attempt by Alberto to go back over his life, director and co-screenwriter Joffe has curiously given us little knowlege of it, so when Alberto's former girlfriend says, "I'm glad you robbed me," after discovering he's ripped her off, we're astonished. Is Alberto dreaming? Is Marie just an incredibly charitable person? Most importantly, we're given no background and no indication of Alberto's relationship with his father, so a story that could have carried some emotional weight (how to repay a person who gave you so much) or comedic possibilities (how to quickly raise a large amount of cash to pay back someone who's going to "do harm" to you) in the end, has neither. *(Profanity, nudity, adult situations.)*

p, Maurice Bernart; d, Arthur Joffe; w, Arthur Joffe, Jean-Louis Benoit, Christian Billette, (adapted from his story); ph, Philippe Welt; ed, Castro-Brechignac; m, Angelique, Jean-Claude Nachon

Comedy/Adventure **(PR: C MPAA: NR)**

ALIEN3 ★★½

135m Fox; Brandywine Productions ~ Fox c

Sigourney Weaver *(Ripley)*, Charles S. Dutton *(Dillon)*, Charles Dance *(Clemens)*, Paul McGann *(Golic)*, Brian Glover *(Andrews)*, Ralph Brown *(Aaron)*, Danny Webb *(Morse)*, Christopher John Fields *(Rains)*, Holt McCallany *(Junior)*, Lance Henriksen *(Bishop)*, Chris Fairbank *(Murphy)*, Carl Chase *(Frank)*, Leon Herbert *(Boggs)*, Vincenzo Nicoli *(Jude)*, Pete Postlethwaite *(David)*, Paul Brennen *(Troy)*, Clive Mantle *(William)*, Peter Guinness *(Gregor)*, Dhobi Oparei *(Arthur)*, Philip Davis *(Kevin)*, Niall Buggy *(Eric)*, Hi Ching *(Company Man)*, Danielle Edmond *(Newt)*

Perhaps no major film of 1992 suffered more negative advance word than ALIEN3. Rumors of script and production problems ran rampant prior to its oft-delayed release, and the project had been entrusted to a director, David Fincher, whose only previous experience was in glossy music videos. Yet the resulting film, though not nearly up to the level of its two predecessors, does contain several noteworthy elements, not the least of which is the heroic performance of returning star Sigourney Weaver.

The film opens with a renegade alien prowling the spacecraft Sulaco (the original film took place aboard the Nostromo, an enormous mineral tanker), in which the ALIENS survivors—Ripley (Weaver), Corporal Hicks and little Newt (Danielle Edmond)—are headed home in hypersleep. The alien causes an equipment malfunction that ejects an escape shuttle containing the passengers; the craft crash-lands on nearby Fiorina 161, a bleak prison planet. Only Ripley survives the crash, finding herself in the midst of a group of hardened criminals who haven't seen a woman in ages. The men have adopted a monastic religious doctrine, and superintendent Andrews (Brian Glover) doesn't like the idea of a female distraction in their presence.

Nonetheless, Ripley (who, like the others, is forced to have her head shaved due to the planet's lice problem) wins the grudging respect of Dillon (Charles Dutton), the group's spiritual leader, and the trust of the facility's doctor, Clemens (Charles Dance). Fearing that an alien might have accompanied her to Fiorina, Ripley persuades Clemens to perform an autopsy on Newt's corpse, even though she refuses to reveal details of the "contagion." The autopsy yields negative results, but Ripley's worries turn out to be well founded; an infected canine spawns a new alien, which quickly evolves and begins to prowl the facility and kill the helpless prisoners.

Realizing what's happening, Ripley reactivates the remains of the android Bishop, who confirms her fears and advises her that the all-powerful Company must certainly know of the alien's existence. Shortly thereafter, both Clemens and Andrews are brutally killed, prompting Ripley and the remaining men desperately to plot a way to dispatch the creature despite their lack of weapons. In a subsequent encounter with the alien, Ripley is at first puzzled when it passes up a chance to kill her; but then a terrible certainty grows in her mind and, using a bio-scanner on the downed shuttlecraft, she discovers that an alien queen is gestating inside her.

The dwindling survivors are ultimately able to trap the alien in a foundry and douse the beast with molten lead; when this still doesn't kill it, Ripley showers it with water, and the rapid cooling shatters the monster to fragments. Just then, a Company spacecraft arrives, and Bishop's human creator (Lance Henriksen) offers Ripley a promise that the alien inside her can be safely extracted and destroyed. But Ripley knows that the Company, as it always has, wants the creature for its Bioweapons Division, and jumps into the pit of molten metal, ending the alien threat once and for all.

ALIEN3 is certainly the most nihilistic of the trilogy, killing off all the second installment's sympathetic characters save Ripley, only to have her commit the ultimate act of sacrifice at the climax. Its *mise-en-scene* is also bleaker than that of its predecessors: a dank, run-down industrial complex that is noticeably free of the gleaming high-tech gadgets sprinkled liberally throughout the first two installments. The film also suffers from too many extended, confusing chase scenes, particularly during the last third of the film. Nevertheless, director Fincher is to be congratulated for infusing an expensive (reportedly $60 million) studio film with a distinctive personal style, and for maintaining that style consistently throughout; ALIEN3 could be described as the most expensive art film ever made. (Whereas the original was indebted to surrealist H.R. Giger and French illustrator Moebius, this third installment owes a debt to the work of 16th century Flemish master Brueghel.)

As in the previous ALIEN films, Weaver's performance anchors the story. With her striking new crew-cut appearance, she's a gutsy presence that an audience will follow even through questionable material—which, unfortunately, is what we get. As long as Fincher is setting up the situation and dealing with alien attacks, the film works fine, with a strong, scary opening and a couple of moments (particularly Clemens's death at the hands of the alien) that are blood-freezing. But as it goes on, the dialogue degenerates into a series of profane exchanges reminiscent of a Joel Silver actioner, and it becomes clear that, aside from Clemens and Dillon, the supporting characters are going to remain bald, barely intelligible ciphers. The screenplay, credited to producers David Giler and Walter Hill with Larry Ferguson (earlier drafts were contributed by cyperpunk novelist Wiliam Gibson and screenwriters Eric Red, David Twohy, John Fasano, and Greg Pruss), contains several logistical errors, not the least being the notion that one alien can infect *two* beings. Also confusing is Ripley's foolish refusal to explain her suspicions for nearly half the movie.

In the film and Fincher's defense, however, it should also be noted that ALIEN3 serves—quite astonishingly, considering its studio origins and astronomic budget—as a powerful AIDS metaphor, and was apparently intended as such; it seems no mere coincidence, for example, that most of the prisoners, as styled by Fincher, look like they just stepped out of an ACT UP meeting.

By turns compelling and annoying, ALIEN3 ultimately frustrates, but there's enough good stuff on view to make Fincher's next film something to look forward to. *(Violence, excessive profanity, adult situations.)*

p, Gordon Carroll, Walter Hill, David Giler; d, David Fincher; w, David Giler, Walter Hill, Larry Ferguson, (from a story by Vincent Ward, based on characters created by Dan O'Bannon and Ronald Shusett); ph, Alex Thomson; ed, Terry Rawlings; m, Elliot Goldenthal; prod d, Norman Reynolds; art d, James Morahan, Fred Hole; set d, Belinda Edwards; cos, Bob Ringwood, David Perry; fx, George Gibbs, Richard Edlund, Tom Woodruff, Jr., Alec Gillis

AAN Visual Effects: Richard Edlund, Alec Gillis, Tom Woodruff, Jr., and George Gibbs

Science Fiction/Action/Horror (PR: O MPAA: R)

ALL – AMERICAN MURDER ★★★

93m Enchantment Films; Greenwich Films ~ Prism Entertainment c

Christopher Walken *(P.J. Decker)*, Charlie Schlatter *(Artie Logan)*, Joanna Cassidy *(Erica Darby)*, Josie Bissett *(Tally Fuller)*, Amy Davis *(Wendy Stern)*, Richard Kind *(Lou Alonzo)*, Mitchell Anderson *(Wendy)*, J.C. Quinn, Craig Stout, Woody Watson, Angie Brown

For freshman Artie Logan, a college education means majoring in murder. Filled with overheated one-liners, ALL – AMERICAN MURDER infuses a complicated mystery plot about a young man wrongly accused of murder with incendiary suspense and a "Twin Peaks" style conclusion. Not since THE LAST OF SHEILA has there been such an entertaining blend of homicide and humor.

For anyone planning the perfect crime, the embittered, attitude-oozing Artie Logan (Charlie Schlatter) is the perfect patsy. With a family quick to believe the worst about him and a questionable personal history involving arson, this schlemiel is given one last chance by his pompous father to prove he's worthy of his privileged upbringing. Shunted off to a bible-thumping college in the midwest, Artie is bored senseless until he meets campus queen Tally Fuller (Josie Bisset). He sees her not only as a dream girl but as a symbol of the wholesome values his father wants him to espouse. No wonder Artie's shaken to the core when someone torches Tally following their first date—every available clue points to him.

Another big-city refugee, Detective Decker (Christopher Walken) investigates the allegedly open-and-shut case but doesn't share the quick rush to judgment of his compatriots on the force. Giving Artie the benefit of the doubt, he appeals to the student's renegade spirit and allows him to go out and find evidence that might clear him. Trying to solve the whodunit leads Artie to a dead end at first because Tally seems to have been such a squeaky-clean beacon of virtue. Once he realizes that Miss Pillar of College Society was just a role that Tally assumed to please her family and friends, however, the pieces start to fall into place.

The campus turns out to be a cross between PEYTON PLACE and WHO'S AFRAID OF VIRGINIA WOOLF? If Artie didn't light Tally's fire, who did? Was it Tally's jock boyfriend with whom she snorted coke and enjoyed kinky threesomes? Should Artie be afraid of that brain-damaged handyman who sniffs lacy underwear and stealthily snaps pornographic photos of the students? Could the killer be the dean's wife, Erica Darby (Joanna Cassidy), a boozehound who's already seduced Artie but may have been tiring of her husband's non-stop carousing? And what about Tally's dumpy pal Wendy Stern (Amy Davis) who had learned that her treacherous friend had secretly blackballed her at a sorority? Before the film's chilling conclusion, several of these duplicitous characters meet untimely ends. At the climax, Artie manages to vindicate Decker's belief in him and to unmask the real "killer."

ALL – AMERICAN MURDER is a cheeky thriller strewn with enough red herrings to baffle the most inveterate armchair detectives. Almost impossible to review without divulging information that will spoil the surprise ending, ALL – AMERICAN MURDER is fast-paced fun that is short on logic but abundant in thrills.

Surrounded by wonderful actors, Schlatter (HEARTBREAK HOTEL, 18 AGAIN!) walks a fine line between outright obnoxiousness and youthful exhuberance. Walken, appropriately saturnine, hits all the right notes as the dogged cop who has a hunch about Artie's innocence. Even better are Amy Davis as a sharp-tongued collegiate outcast who fails to remold herself in her school's white-bread image and the always reliable Joanna Cassidy (THE STEPFORD WIVES, WHO FRAMED ROGER RABBIT), memorable as an alcoholic who's a sexual den mother for fraternity row.

Riddled with a senseless barrage of one-liners (not all of which hit their intended target), ALL – AMERICAN MURDER manages to amuse without ever sacrificing suspense. What lends the movie distinction is the subtext that the outward appearance of goodness may mask all manner of insidious evildoing. What the film does is expose the worms lurking under the surface of this bedrock of the community—a Christian college. And what an intriguing group of worms they are—the cleancut jock who's a sex addict, and the holier-than-thou dean who believes retribution may come in the form of sexual flagellation in bed.

In Barry Sandler's clever screenplay, no one is exempt from blame, as the audience questions the mentality of both religious zealots who hide behind their claims of being "saved" and the facile cynicism of the local cops who are more interested in a quick arrest than in finding a killer. In penetrating the layers of hypocrisy beneath an institution and the surrounding community's feigned chasteness and rectitude, this thriller forges its mystery with a much more finely detailed foundation than is the case with run-of-the-mill policers. Like Tally, who is far more complex than she appears to be, ALL – AMERICAN MURDER is a social satire about conformity, camouflaged as a darkly comic thriller. *(Violence, substance abuse, profanity.)*

p, Bill Novodor, Anson Williams; d, Anson Williams; w, Barry Sandler; ph, Geoff Schaaf; ed, Jonas Thaler; m, Rod Slane; art d, Jim French

Crime/Thriller/Mystery **(PR: O MPAA: R)**

ALL THE VERMEERS IN NEW YORK ★★★½

87m Complex Corporation; American Playhouse Theatrical Films ~ Strand Releasing c

Emmanuelle Chaulet *(Anna)*, Katherine Bean *(Nicole)*, Grace Phillips *(Felicity)*, Laurel Lee Kiefer *(Ariel Ainsworth)*, Gracie Mansion *(Herself)*, Gordon Joseph Weiss *(Gordon)*, Stephen Lack *(Mark)*, Roger Ruffin *(Max)*

Largely improvised by maverick independent American filmmaker Jon Jost, and leavened by some social commentary and even a touch of fantasy, ALL THE VERMEERS IN NEW YORK is a melancholy romance about a couple who meet, do *not* fall in love and literally disappear.

Anna (Emmanuelle Chaulet) shares a nice apartment with Felicity (Grace Phillips) and Nicole (Katherine Bean). An expatriate Frenchwoman, Anna is studying for a part in a Chekov play and is experiencing some difficulty, while Felicity works in a tony art gallery and Nicole is an aspiring opera singer. The apartment seems to be paid for by investments made by Felicity's father in her name, about which she is beginning to have moral qualms. The question of investments also concerns Mark (Stephen Lack), who is employed on Wall Street as a financial broker; the extended sequences of him at work, studying his VDT and talking to his clients, are among the best parts of the film.

Mark relieves the pressure he faces at work by studying the Vermeers in New York City's museums, five at the Metropolitan and three at the Frick Collection, and at the former he spots Anna. She resembles one portrait, *Head of a Young Woman*, and he passes her a note to meet for coffee. They do later, though she brings along Felicity as a chaperone and pretends not to understand English. Mark sees through her ruse and they begin to date. He is beginning to hate his job and has some morbid preoccupations. When they visit the World Trade Center, he tells her it reminds him of the passage from life to hell; he later mentions reincarnation to a colleague.

Although it seems clear that Mark and Anna never become lovers, he still gives her $3,000 from the petty cash around his apartment when she claims to need it for rent. Actually, in one of the few scenes that reveals her motives, Anna says she misses France and her boyfriend there. Mark, meanwhile, has a day at work marked by huge losses; later, studying a Vermeer at the Metropolitan, he starts bleeding from his ear. Panicking, he goes to the phone to call Anna and tell her he loves her. About to leave for the airport, she gets his message on a machine and rushes to the museum to find his dead body in the phone booth. She, in turn, studies the Vermeer, which in turn, seems to absorb her literally.

Jon Jost has described ALL THE VERMEERS IN NEW YORK as "an elegy for a decade bathed in delusion and corruption." While Anna appears as nothing more than a self-obsessed young actress, Mark is besotted with her, or rather his image of what—based on her features—she *should* be. She is also corrupt enough to bamboozle him out of cash, in an atmosphere of easy money symbolized by Felicity's wealthy father and the neo-classic corridor of Wall Street wealth upon which Jost's camera lingers. Mark is, indeed, the only delineated character and perhaps the only sympathetic one.

Jost's film emphasizes interiors and furnishings, his camera lingering on scattered copies of *The Economist* in Felicity's room, the almost European view from the window of Mark's apartment, a photographic portrait of Anna reflected in a framed print on a nearby wall. Wonderfully lit and painstakingly constructed, ALL THE VERMEERS IN NEW YORK does have some of the merits of the artist it honors. *(Adult situations.)*

p, Henry S. Rosenthal; d, Jon Jost; w, Jon Jost, (from his idea); ph, Jon Jost; ed, Jon Jost; m, Jon A. English; art d, Jon Jost

Drama/Romance/Fantasy (PR: C MPAA: NR)

ALMOST PREGNANT ★½

96m ANA Productions ~ Columbia TriStar Home Video c

Tanya Roberts *(Linda)*, Joan Severance *(Maureen)*, Jeff Conaway *(Charlie Andeson)*, Dom DeLuise *(Doctor Beckhard)*, Christopher Michael Moore *(Ray Burns)*, John Calvin *(Gordon Mallory)*

Superficially similar to PROMISES, PROMISES, the notorious 1963 Jayne Mansfield skinflick, ALMOST PREGNANT contrives, via lightheaded performances and direction, to make impotence and explicit wife-swapping as cutesy as they're ever going to get.

"Spermwise, you're shooting blanks," opines Dr. Beckhard (Dom DeLuise) to Charlie Alderson (Jeff Conaway), whose marriage to kittenish, motherhood-obsessed Linda (Tanya Roberts) has produced no offspring. Linda refuses artificial insemination, but all the doctor's treatments fail to boost Charlie's sperm count. Undaunted, Linda convinces poor Charlie to hunt up a "surrogate father," an appropriate male to perform stud service. The top prospect is Gordon Mallory (John Calvin), a self-absorbed poet, complete with mini-goatee, who's sired numerous kids with his dutiful earth-mother wife Maureen (Joan Severance).

Gordon enthusiastically agrees to impregnate Linda as long as Maureen isn't told. Charlie becomes depressed over his wife's regular sessions with Gordon and starts a counter-affair with the neglected Maureen. Meanwhile, Linda has learned that the deceitful Gordon had a vasectomy to prevent swelling his family further. Stunned, she continues the sex with him to avoid hurting Charlie, while turning to Charlie's homely but unspayed cousin Ray Burns (Christopher Michael Moore) for further furtive intercouse. The whole thing resolves at a Christmas party that sees both women pregnant, back with their respective spouses, and everybody happy.

Viewers will just be happy that it's over, though ALMOST PREGNANT contrives to be less offensive than it might be, with only mild naughty language, bouncy music and cheerful turns from the actors. Roberts and Conaway play their comic parts in a fairly low-key fashion, leaving Calvin, Severance and DeLuise to do most of the mugging. Former model and *Playboy* centerfold Joan Severance has in the past stolen whole movies from the nominal superstars in BIRD ON A WIRE and SEE NO EVIL, HEAR NO EVIL. Her role here muffles her effervescent presence by turning it into a joke; even though Maureen looks like a million bucks, her moody husband treats her like a scullery maid, and she meekly accepts the abuse as the price to be paid for living with "genius."

ALMOST PREGNANT went to home video in a by-now-familiar dual format gimmick. Box art displayed a woman's underwear-clad torso; red lace meant it was the unrated version, with abundant nudity and graphic sex, while white lace signified the trimmed-down R-rated edition. The softcore stuff mostly occurs in the form of daydream sequences and time-filling montages, easily excisable, highly gratuitous, and wholly crass. While Tanya Roberts and Joan Severance are svelte and shapely specimens of femininity, one montage lingers on a melon-breasted body double who's obviously neither of them, a suggestion of the priorities here.

Apart from that lapse, director Michael DeLuise (son of Dom and an actor himself, mainly for TV) orchestrates the whole thing with a sure hand for someone in his early twenties. As if to comment on his precocity, DeLuise *fils* is depicted as an ovum in a director's chair in the opening computer-animated title sequence set in a uterine system. *(Nudity, sexual situations, adult situations, profanity.)*

p, Ray Haboush, Michael Kastenbaum; d, Michael DeLuise; w, Fred Stroppel; ph, Glen Kershaw; ed, Irit Raz; prod d, Damon Medlon; art d, Lou Trabbie; set d, Laura Sampson; cos, Terri King

Comedy (PR: O MPAA: R)

AMANT, L

(SEE: LOVER, THE)

AMANTES ★★★★

(Spain) 103m PCSA; Television Espanola ~ Aries Film Releasing c

Victoria Abril *(Luisa)*, Jorge Sanz *(Paco)*, Maribel Verdu *(Trini)*

With AMANTES, veteran Spanish director Vicente Aranda finally achieved wide international exposure and critical acclaim. Made in 1991, this tragic story of forbidden passions and betrayed innocence was one of the outstanding foreign films to reach US screens.

Madrid, 1955. Paco (Jorge Sanz), having completed his required military service, hopes to find work and marry his fiancee, Trini (Maribel Verdu), the housemaid to Paco's former commander. Paco lodges in a room rented by Luisa (Victoria Abril), a young widow and part-time grifter. Frustrated by his unfruitful job hunt and by Trini's refusal to sleep with him until they're married, Paco offers little resistance when Luisa seduces him, initiating an affair. Upon learning of his infidelity, Trini reluctantly gives herself to Paco, hoping to keep him away from Luisa. Though Paco promises to break up the affair, he succumbs to Luisa's sexual allures. Luisa declares her love for Paco, urging him to kill Trini and start a new life with her. Paco takes Trini to a town outside Madrid, under the pretense of marriage but with murder in his mind. Luisa follows them, unsure of Paco's resolve. Disarmed by Trini's trusting self, Paco confesses his true intentions. Unable to bear living without his love, Trini allows Paco to kill her. Luisa is about to leave town when Paco catches up with her on the railroad station. As they embrace, a title informs us that the police captured the pair three days after Trini's murder.

One of the founders of the "Barcelona School" during the 1960s, Aranda is fairly unknown outside Spain, in spite of a distinguished career. Unlike Carlos Saura, who often favors dense allegories, Aranda works with straightforward plots, often adapted from literary sources. In films like CAMBIO DE SEXO, LA MUCHACHA DE LAS BRAGAS DE ORO and AVENTIS/SI TE DICEN QUE CAI, the frailties of Spanish society are mirrored in stories of troubled man-woman relations, in which sex plays a key role.

Based on a real-life murder case, AMANTES follows Aranda's strategy of exposing the moral corruption of Franco's Spain through one specific incident. While not a strident political tract, the film subtly stresses the tragic effects of oppressive moral codes on its three characters. Trini firmly rejects Paco's sexual advances; she has been taught the ideal of the virginal bride, saving herself for her lawfully wedded husband. Crushed by Paco's infidelity, Trini seeks solace from her employer's wife, who teaches her the facts of life: men are promiscuous by nature, unable to control their sexual appetites. The only way to keep a man away from other women is through sex; what he can get at home, he won't seek elsewhere.

Society's moral double standard—condoning male promiscuity while enforcing female subservience—extends beyond the bedroom, oppressing women who seek fulfillment outside the home. Victim of this situation is Luisa, brutalized by her late husband and by the petty thieves with whom she collaborates in order to supplement her income from rent and from her clerical job in a pharmacy. Luisa sees in Paco's youth a glimmer of hope, a second chance at happiness, which is why she holds on to him so tightly. Paco is portrayed as a determined and well-intentioned, but ultimately weak man; powerless against his unemployment rut and Trini's moral conduct, he willingly gets involved in Luisa's sexual and criminal games.

Aranda presents this potentially salacious story with taste and intelligence. His characters are not cardboard villains/heroes but human beings caught in a no-win situation. The highly charged sex scenes are provocative without being vulgar. This sexual intensity helps audiences understand Paco's attraction to Luisa, who gives him the forbidden pleasures of the flesh in more ways than one. Aranda's handling of Trini's murder is understated, relying on the power of suggestion to create a stronger impact.

AMANTES benefits from a first-rate cast headed by Victoria Abril. A frequent collaborator of Aranda's (having worked in CAMBIO DE SEXO, LA MUCHACHA DE LAS BRAGAS DE ORO, TIEMPO DE SILENCIO and AVENTIS, among others), Abril reveals the humanity and sadness behind Luisa's calculating actions. Jorge Sanz and Maribel Verdu are equally outstanding as the weak-willed Paco and the innocent Trini.

AMANTES is a refreshing rarity in our quality-starved cinematic age: an intense, well-crafted drama for mature audiences. *(Nudity, sexual situations, adult situations.)*

p, Pedro Costa; d, Vicente Aranda; w, Vicente Aranda, Alvaro Del Amo, Carlos Perez Merinero; ph, Jose Luis Alcaine; ed, Teresa Font; m, Jose Nieto; art d, Josep Rosell; cos, Nereida Bonmati

Drama **(PR: O MPAA: R)**

AMERICAN DREAM ★★★½

100m Cabin Creek Films ~ Prestige Films/Miramax c

Lewie Anderson, Ray Rogers, Jesse Jackson

The human cost of a major American corporation's reorganization in the town of Austin, Minnesota, is chronicled in this ambitious, socially concerned documentary from filmmaker Barbara Kopple, her long-awaited follow-up to HARLAN COUNTY, U.S.A.

In 1984, the Hormel Company's management announced a cut in the hourly wage, from an average of $10.69 to $8.25, with similar reductions in benefits and an end to incentive payments that equalled a 50 percent cut for some categories of worker. The grandchildren and great-grandchildren of European immigrants, the predominantly white laborers were predictably angry, as can be seen in their testimony at union hearings. One female employee says she doesn't begrudge the firm's shareholders their profit of $29 million, but the workers should be allowed to live in their $32,000 homes.

Local union president Ray Guyette not only echoed their grievances, but also contracted the services of Ray Rogers whose consulting firm, Corporate Campaign, pioneered public relations techniques to win labor's demands. Rogers's novel tactics not only antagonized Hormel's leaders, but far worse, rankled the counselors of different methods at the parent union, the United Food and Commercial Workers. Although it can be a confusing thread to follow, this dispute between Guyette and Lewie Anderson, the UFCW representative, gives the film an added piquancy.

Anderson states that the industry wants to return workers to the days of *The Jungle*, Upton Sinclair's expose of the meatpacking conditions at the turn of the century, but is very critical of Corporate Campaign's efforts to pressure Hormel's investors. His rational discussion of the relative forces arrayed in the struggle is contrasted with Guyette's emotional appeal to his membership that "belief will carry you a long way." Later, Guyette describes his idea of union methods in terms of the lyrics of a Bruce Springsteen song. Hormel counters with a two-tier wage system, the old, high pay for experienced workers, and a lower one for new employees. This is rejected, setting the stage for the first strike at Hormel's Austin plant in over fifty years.

The local's inexperience now began to destroy it, according to Anderson who reiterates the classic dictum that a strike is the union's final weapon and should be used with discretion, in a situation and at a time that favors the workers. Austin was not such a situation and the local foolishly decided to rewrite their contract in the middle of negotiations. The strike coincided with difficult industry-wide talks, and Anderson is shown in the midst of feverish talks and debates. His pragmatic view is underlined by his willingness to meet with industry representatives away from the public eye.

Hormel's final offer is to pay $10 per hour, but to freeze this rate for three years, and to Anderson's evident frustration, the local rejects it. Since their strike had already lasted over four months, some of the workers were becoming disillusioned with Guyette, despite a certain buoyancy generated by picket lines and food distributions. The Bergstrom brothers are split by the decision to return to work, and we witness the heartbreaking choice made by some 75 members of the local union. In a frankly desperate move, the over 1400 remaining strikers attempt to spread the strike to Hormel's other plants; they only succeed in getting 600 additional workers fired. Finally, the UFCW revokes its support, ceasing strike benefit payments, and negotiates a pay rate of $10.25 for that small fraction of the local union members who have crossed the picket line. Vacant store fronts in downtown Austin are a result, as well as the relocation of the defeated workers, including the woman who had earlier referred to their right to live in their middle-class homes.

While the primary story of the Hormel strike is sadly routine, the secondary tale of rival strategies and competing views of unionism as personified by Anderson and Guyette is *almost* riveting. Almost, because of the background material that Barbara Kopple could not or would not limit. This film is a traditionally constructed modern documentary, with a number of expected sequences of picket lines, worker testimony, stock footage from Hormel past and present and "talking heads" interview material. Some of this footage gets in the way of understanding the subtle differences between the local's tactics and the UCFW's advice.

Part of the near-tragedy inherent in this conflict is the fact that Guyette and Rogers may have the better instincts and philosophy, but the sillier sense of political fighting, while Anderson has the canny feel of a seasoned professional, if the less romantic views of a union's role. It is this ambiguity which gives AMERICAN DREAM its sophisticated sensibility, aside from the gloom of a failed local strike on the eve of a national recession. *(Profanity.)*

p, Barbara Kopple, Arthur Cohn; d, Barbara Kopple; ph, Peter Gilbert, Kevin Keating, Hart Perry, Mark Petersson, Mathieu Roberts; ed, Cathy Caplan, Tom Haneke, Larry Silk; m, Michael Small

Documentary/Political **(PR: C MPAA: PG-13)**

AMERICAN FABULOUS ★★★

105m Dead Jesse Productions ~ First Run Features c

Jeffrey Strouth

Subtitled "an evening of country wit and wisdom," AMERICAN FABULOUS offers viewers a fascinating, uninhibited glimpse at the raucous life and times of Jeffrey Strouth, its unknown star, who makes a spectacular, albeit sadly belated, debut. Shot during 1990 on videotape but blown up to 16mm for theatrical release, this autobiographical monologue was filmed while driving through the back roads and side streets of Strouth's hometown in southern Ohio, land of white clapboard houses and even whiter Baptists, in a black 1957 Cadillac.

Supporting Wordsworth's claim that the child is father to the man, Strouth recalls his early fascination with nuns, *flying* nuns, that is. His own father, a sometime Elvis impersonator and fulltime lout, was prone to drunken displays of violence while his longsuffering wife and six children ran for cover. Mrs. Strouth's many attempts to kill her spouse inspired Jeffrey's own botched effort to asphyxiate his father with bleach fumes. At fourteen, the troublesome Jeffrey was shipped to Fort Lauderdale to live with his now divorced father, but after bringing him home from the airport and removing a stack of porn magazines from the coffee table, his father left to purchase groceries and returned two weeks later; during the interim, Jeffrey was forced to prostitute himself to survive, which Strouth claims to have rather enjoyed.

The friends—role models, really—Strouth made along the way form a wildly colorful gallery of eccentrics straight out of the Southern Gothic tradition. There's Miss Earl, a toothless transvestite and avid roller-derby fan, the first homosexual Jeffrey ever met; Bill, aka Angie Marie, an obese short-order cook who moonlighted as a female impersonator at Ruthie's Golden Garter, a local lesbian dive; and Marie, the elaborately coiffed sixty-nine-year-old roadside waitress and good-time gal who decorated her prized trailer home with gifts from her legion of trucker boyfriends.

In the film's most harrowing passage, Strouth makes a chilling escape from a knife-wielding psychopath. Found blind (his single contact lens having flown out), almost naked and bleeding, he's thrown into a cell by the police and abandoned for two days without food or fresh water. Relocated to a Salvation Army center in Colorado, he finds work as a dishwasher and starts to put his life together.

Determined to find his fortune, Strouth eventually relocates to New York City, the height of his show-biz career being a stint as the gossipy caterpillar from *Alice in Wonderland* at Area, the era's hottest dance club. Sadly true to form, however, he's forced to sleep in the back of a car, his caterpillar costume the only protection against the nighttime cold. Heroin addiction is the next, and almost final, frontier.

AMERICAN FABULOUS is too long, but what saves it from being a crudely edited vanity production is that Strouth, his slender fingers stained with nicotine from an omnipresent cigarette, emerges as a vastly amusing raconteur—the sort of flamboyant, wildly individualistic creature whose escapades are as likely to inspire revulsion as admiration. Most viewers, however, will find it difficult to remain unmoved by Strouth's humanity and fundamental goodness, as well as the knowledge that, under different circumstances, he might have accomplished a great deal. Strouth died of AIDS, aged thirty-three, in 1992. *(Profanity.)*

p, Reno Dakota; d, Reno Dakota; w, Jeffrey Strouth; ph, Reno Dakota, Travis Ruse; ed, Reno Dakota

Documentary **(PR: C MPAA: NR)**

AMERICAN ME ★★½

119m YOY Productions; Sean Daniel Company; Olmos Productions ~ Universal c

Edward James Olmos *(Santana Montoya)*, William Forsythe *(JD)*, Pepe Serna *(Mundo)*, Danny De La Paz *(Puppet)*, Evelina Fernandez *(Julie)*, Cary-Hiroyuki Tagawa *(El Jupo)*, Daniel Villarreal *(Little Puppet)*, Sal Lopez *(Pedro)*, Daniel A. Haro *(Huero)*, Vira Montes *(Esperanza)*, Panchito Gomez *(Young Santana)*, Steve Wilcox *(Young JD)*, Richard Coca *(Young Mundo)*, Roberto Martin Marquez *(Acha)*, Dyana Ortelli *(Yolanda)*, Joe Aubel *(Tattoo Artist)*, Rob Garrett *(Zoot Riot Bystander)*, Lance August *(Young Sailor)*, Cody Glenn *(Older Sailor)*, Don Pugsley *(Police Officer)*, Albert Joe Medina, Jr. *(Street Mechanic)*, Alex Solis *(Street Mechanic)*, Raymond Amezquita *(Abuelito)*, Javier Castellanos *(Hazard Kid)*, Richard Lee-Sung *(Restaurant Owner)*, Eric Close *(Juvie Hall Attacker)*, Christian Klemash *(Blonde Kid in Yard)*, Brian Joe Holechek *(Juvie Officer)*, Rigoberto Jiminez *(Big Happy)*, Domingo Ambriz *(Pie Face)*, Ron Thompson *(Junkie)*, Glenn Shelton *(Visiting Room Guard)*, Scott Johnstad *(Visiting Room Guard)*, Abraham Verduzco *(Paulito–Age 7)*, Grace Morley *(JD's Friend)*, Vic Trevino *(Cheetah)*, Robby Robinson *(Drug Thief)*, Paul Bollen *(Doc)*, Guillermo Perez *(Willie-Vato)*, Robert Chavez *(Sparky)*, Rafael H. Robledo *(El Chucko)*, Modesto M. Sanchez *(Mo)*, Dennis Ryan Sacco *(Paulito–Age 11)*, Michael A. Shaner *(Tony Scagnelli Jr.)*, Tom S. Ventimiglia *(Segregation Guard)*, William Fetzer *(Processing Guard)*, Thomas Richard Gorman, III *(Processing Guard)*, George Padilla *(Mundo's Attorney)*, Humberto Madrigal *(Veneno)*, Jaime Gomez *(Eddie)*, Jose Guardado *(Samson)*, Jacob Vargas *(Paulito–Age 15)*, Daniel Lujan *(Mico–Age 9)*, Rodney Rincon *(Shoe Salesman)*, John Rangel *(Neto–Age 15)*, Robert Pucci *(Bodyguard)*, Tony Giorgio *(Don Antonio Scagnelli)*, Sabino Villalobos *(Tin Man)*, Armando Briseno *(Chuy)*, Mauricio Ernesto Anzueto *(Bam Bam)*, Manny Perry *(Arthur J.)*, Bennie Moore *(Ronnie Little)*, Alex Brown *(Eddie Johnson)*, William Smith *(Deacon)*, Gerald L. Walker *(BGF Member)*, William T. Amos *(Tank)*, Irma Aurea Garcia *(Lourdes)*, Roberto Alvarez *(Ralphy)*, Ken Medlock *(Cop)*, Rolando Molina *(Cop)*, Anna Lizarraga *(Julie's Mother)*, Steven Cisneros

An ambitious drama about gang warfare and the culture of violence, AMERICAN ME is nothing if not earnest. Unfortunately, this doesn't mean it's a particularly successful film; for every bluntly powerful moment, there's another that's crude and obvious, sometimes excruciatingly so.

Raised in the East Los Angeles barrio, Santana Montoya (Edward James Olmos) ignores his parents' attempts to make him into a citizen of the mainstream United States, a culture from which they themselves have been excluded—a point that isn't lost on their angry son. Santana finds his identity in a gang, formed with his friends Mundo (Pepe Serna) and JD (William Forsythe), a white boy who's adopted the Latino street culture as his own and is ready to kill anyone who has a problem with it. They spend years together in juvenile hall and, later, in prison, completing their criminal educations and hatching an ambitious plan to form a large-scale operation that will command respect both within and outside prison walls. They are all too successful.

Members of the gang drift in and out of prison, dealing drugs, murdering anyone who opposes them and protecting one another from the police and other gangs. Santana becomes a near mythical figure until, during a brief sojourn out from behind bars, he falls in love with Julie (Evelina Fernandez), whom he meets at a neighborhood party—it's an awkward relationship that's bound to end badly. Julie despises what drugs and guns and gangs have done to the Latino community, and she's unable to ignore Santana's part in its destruction; Santana is too brutalized by a lifetime in prison to forge a conventional, non-exploitative connection with a woman. But Julie forces him to reconsider the life he's made for himself, and when he goes back to prison, they continue to correspond. Perceived as a sign of weakness, this relationship dooms Santana, who's stabbed to death outside his cell by members of a rival prison gang.

The directorial debut of actor Edward James Olmos, probably best known for his role as enigmatic Lieutenant Martin Castillo on TV's long-running "Miami Vice" series, AMERICAN ME is earnest, sprawling and awkward. But there's no denying the intensity of feeling that drives it, and though it can't be called an unqualified success, the film is forthright and sometimes surprisingly moving. It gets off to a bad start, with the imprisoned Santana reading what will be his last letter to Julie. Full of sing-song rhyming slang and painful platitudes, Santana's voice-over doesn't convince you that this is a character to whom you want to listen for the better part of two hours. Even worse, Julie's voice joins in, and her plaintive whine ("It's as though you were two people . . . ") is truly grating. Fortunately, the movie then begins to tell Santana's story, starting with the story of his parents, Pedro (Sal Lopez) and Esperanza (Vira Montes) and the 1943 zoot-suit riot. The period sets look like what they are—sets—but at least we're out of Santana's head and into a world of color and action. Fifty years of Hispanic-American history proceeds to unfold through the prism of Santana's life, and AMERICAN ME skips back and forth between the barrio, juvenile hall and various prisons as he comes of age in a culture that celebrates strength, machismo, respect and gang loyalty at the expense of other, more conventional virtues.

AMERICAN ME covers a lot of familiar ground, especially as it chronicles Santana's early years. But individual scenes transcend the cliches, hammering home the ruthlessness of prison life and the inevitable changes it produces in men who spend their lives there. There's no glamour to the film's prison sequences, no fetishization and no romantic notions that penitentiaries are crucibles that fire strong men's bodies and souls. They're ugly, cruel and brutalizing; it's clear that the men who survive inside cripple themselves to do so, even when the maiming doesn't show. Olmos and his collaborators sweat the details—the distinctive way gang members button their shirts, the mechanics of getting tattoos or smuggling contraband within the prison (a particularly disgusting sequence)—and the payoff is a fully realized universe, claustrophobic but complete. The outside world is hardly a factor; Santana spends precious little time there, and the viewer follows suit. When he's out of prison, his world seems limited to drug dens and a few square blocks of the old neighborhood; a visit to the palatial home of a mafioso whose turf Santana's gang plans to invade seems as exotic as a trip to China's Forbidden City.

While excelling in its depiction of the familial nature of gang relationships, AMERICAN ME is less successful in handling the dynamics within the Montoya clan. Though one could argue that this is a reflection of Santana's experience, which shapes the film's worldview, it's still a problem. Saintly Esperanza, distant and embittered Pedro, impressionable Paulito, Santana's younger brother: they're all cliches, and while AMERICAN ME seems to aim for the scope of THE GODFATHER, the preponderance of shallow characterizations severely undermines its strength. One wants so much to like AMERICAN ME for its passion and its deglamorization of criminal life that it's painful to have to dwell on its flaws. But ultimately the flaws overwhelm it, dragging it down to the level of heartfelt propaganda. *(Violence, substance abuse, profanity, nudity, sexual situations, adult situations.)*

p, Sean Daniel, Robert M. Young, Edward James Olmos; d, Edward James Olmos; w, Floyd Mutrux, Desmond Nakano, (from story by Mutrux and Nakano); ph, Reynaldo Villalobos; ed, Arthur R. Coburn, Richard Candib; m, Dennis Lambert, Claude Gaudette; prod d, Joe Aubel; cos, Sylvia Vega-Vasquez

Prison/Drama **(PR: C MPAA: R)**

AMITYVILLE 1992: IT'S ABOUT TIME ★★½

95m ~ Republic Pictures Home Video c

Stephen Macht *(Jacob Sterling)*, Shawn Weatherly *(Andrea)*, Megan Ward *(Lisa)*, Damon Martin *(Rusty)*, Jonathan Penner *(Leonard)*, Nita Talbot *(Mrs. Wheeler)*, Dean Cochran *(Andy)*

It's unlikely that anyone is still seriously taking the AMITYVILLE films for horrific true-life sagas, as they were once marketed. Clearly, the filmmakers behind this latest installment have simply used the franchise to take off on their own supernatural tangents. There is barely any connection to the previous films, with AMITYVILLE 1992 even being set all the way across the country in California.

The one linking device is a clock from the original Amityville house unwittingly bought by developer Jacob Sterling (Stephen Macht) during a business trip to New York. He brings it home to his family—teenagers Lisa (Megan Ward) and Rusty (Damon Martin), but no wife—and puts it on the mantel, where, unbeknownst to anyone, it ejects mechanical devices and bolts itself into place. Clearly there's something wrong with this timepiece, and the first to notice is a neighborhood dog, which growls at it one day and then, unprovoked, attacks Jacob the next.

While his father recuperates from the deep bites in his leg, Rusty is startled when the room in which the clock sits seems to transform into a satanic crypt; later, Lisa is mysteriously locked inside the room. Rusty comes to realize that something strange is going on, but can't convince Jacob's girlfriend Andrea (Shawn Weatherly) that supernatural forces are at work. Soon, however, she encounters a grisly apparition in her bed, but her own suspicions are debunked by her psychiatrist friend Leonard (Jonathan Penner). He also seems to think that Rusty's just going through a phase, and explains away Jacob's increasingly antisocial behavior in psychological terms.

The one person who believes Rusty is his occultist neighbor, Mrs. Wheeler (Nita Talbot), who realizes that the room he saw was the sacrificial chamber of a centuries-old satanist and ultimately figures out where the clock came from. Eventually, of course, she is killed in a freak truck accident. Meanwhile, Leonard has a vision in which a jealous Jacob shoots him; the evil force transforms Lisa into a teen sexpot who lures her boyfriend Andy (Dean Cochran) to a horrible death; and Andrea discovers that Jacob's scale model of his housing development has transformed into a landscape of Amityville-style homes.

Leonard is ultimately hanged outside the house, while Andrea and Rusty are trapped inside with the now murderous Jacob. Fending off his attacks, Andrea breaks through the wall behind the clock and discovers enormous springs and gears; as a gas main opens on its own, she lights a spark that blows the device to pieces. Suddenly, everything reverts back to the day Jacob first arrived home with the clock. But Andrea realizes what is happening and smashes the clock to pieces, stopping the evil cycle from beginning anew.

AMITYVILLE 1992 is based on one of a series of books by John G. Jones, in which the author relates how the original house's evil spread across the country when its furnishings were sold off. As one more attempt to wring some quick profits out of the lingering fascination with this story, the latest installment benefits from not claiming any basis in reality and, in fact, is one of the best of the six films (including a 1989 TV movie starring Patty Duke) derived from it. The screenplay doesn't do much that's new with the possessed-house basics, but some of the details have been imaginatively conceived and the film has been directed in a persuasive, comparatively low-key style by Tony Randel (HELLBOUND: HELLRAISER II). For the most part, Randel eschews cheap shock effects for the first hour, holding the interest through more mundane scare situations before the blood-and-thunder final reels.

The idea that the clock existed long before the Amityville house and has been working its evil through the centuries is never really explored, nor is the suggestion that Rusty's awareness of the supernatural presence around him might be connected to his apparent interest in heavy metal. But the acting and writing of the central characters is just empathetic enough to keep the material plausible in context, though the character of Leonard—the story's obligatory Doubting Thomas—is too overwrought to be convincing, and marks him from the start as eventual cannon fodder for the evil force.

AMITYVILLE 1992 is just scary enough to justify the continuation of the franchise, and just in case anyone had any doubts, a further installment, AMITYVILLE 1993, had already completed principal photography by the onset of its namesake year. *(Violence, profanity, sexual situations, nudity.)*

p, Christopher DeFaria; d, Tony Randel; w, Christopher DeFaria, Antonio Toro, (from the story by John G. Jones); ph, Christopher Taylor; ed, Rick Finney; m, Daniel Licht; prod d, Kim Hix

Horror **(PR: O MPAA: R)**

ANIMAL INSTINCTS ★★½

94m Wilshire Film Ventures ~ Academy Entertainment c

Maxwell Caulfield *(David Cole)*, Jan-Michael Vincent *(Fletcher Ross)*, Mitch Gaylord *(Rod Tennison)*, Shannon Whirry *(Joanne Cole)*, Delia Sheppard *(Ingrid)*, John Saxon *(Otto Van Horne)*, David Carradine *(Lamberti)*, Tom Reilly *(Ken)*, Josh Cruze *(Hernandez)*, Erika Nann *(Dianne)*

Ripped from last year's tabloid headlines, ANIMAL INSTINCTS is a dramatization of one of the sleaziest sex scandals of the decade. If this direct-to-video release never attains the fanciful heights of reality, it rips off enough aspects of the case to quicken viewers' heartbeats.

Primed by a powerful tranquilizer, housewife Joanne Cole (Shannon Whirry) tells her tawdry tale in flashbacks. Worn down by financial woes, Joanne's policeman husband, David (Maxwell Caulfield) can't get aroused even though his wife looks like the Playboy Playmate of the Year. While Joanne simmers at home, David becomes embroiled in a war of nerves between sleazy topless-bar czar Lamberti (David Carradine) and hypocritical mayoral candidate Fletcher Ross (Jan-Michael Vincent). One day, after David catches Joanne getting her reception fine-tuned by a cable repairman, he becomes a tiger in bed. Postponing any thoughts of calling Dr. Ruth, the couple indulges in America's Sexiest Home Videos. Not only can Joanne earn money at home, but she has the double satisfaction of knowing her hunk-husband is going to pounce on her after filming her with one of her clients.

Their marital bliss and financial picture couldn't be brighter until one of Lamberti's hoods shows up as a customer, puts two and two together and tattles to his boss. To discredit his enemy Fletcher Ross, Lamberti blackmails David into setting up Ross with Joanne in full view of the couple's video camera. Before the scam can be pulled off, a lesbian client of Joanne's, Ingrid (Delia Sheppard), shows up at the wrong time, calls the police, and the scandal hits the fan as David is arrested by none other than his partner Rod Tennison (Mitch Gaylord), also one of Joanne's clients. Now notorious, the imaginative couple are attacked in a media circus, but the Coles' attorney Otto Van Horne (John Saxon) proposes the ingenious defense that nymphomania and a diet of tranquilizers drove Joanne to a pitch of desire that no single man could satisfy.

As a hard-hitting docudrama, ANIMAL INSTINCTS displays the right stuff and makes some cogent points about the many different levels of corruption in city government. Competently acted by such B-movie stalwarts as David Carradine (DUNE WARRIORS, MARTIAL LAW), Jan-Michael Vincent (HAUNTING FEAR, RAW NERVE) and Maxwell Caulfield (PROJECT: ALIEN, SUNDOWN: THE VAMPIRE IN RETREAT), the film captures the essence of macho double-dealing and political backstabbing. And in newcomer Shannon Whirry (OUT FOR JUSTICE) it has an alluring focal point who could probably bring down several municipal power structures.

Oddly enough, where ANIMAL INSTINCTS falls short is in the eroticism department. We don't feel the sweat or hear the moans; for a film founded on voyeurism, viewers really should feel closer to the action. Due to complacent direction and a screenplay that sometimes seems strung together from reenactments of TV tabloid shows, ANIMAL INSTINCTS never really turns up the heat. *(Violence, profanity, sexual situations.)*

p, Andrew Garroni; d, A. Gregory Hippolyte; w, Georges Des Esseintes; ph, Wally Pfister; ed, Kent Smith; m, Joseph Smith; prod d, Blair Martin

Erotic/Drama **(PR: O MPAA: R)**

ARMED FOR ACTION ★½

88m AIP Studios ~ AIP Home Video c

Joe Estevez *(Detective West)*, David Harrod *(Phil Towers)*, Rocky Patterson *(David Montel)*, J. Scott Guy *(Alex)*, Shane Boldin *(Jake)*, Barri Murphy *(Sarah)*, Tracy Spaulding *(Lori)*, John Pask *(Robertson)*, Kirk McKinney *(Thompson)*, Dean Nolen *(Agent Carter)*, Jack Gould *(Sheriff)*

Starring AIP veteran Joe Estevez and newcomer David Harrod, ARMED FOR ACTION is a slow-moving, formulaic action yarn.

Beleaguered sergeant Phil Towers (Harrod) is transporting hitman turned government witness David Montel (Rockey Patterson) to Los Angeles. While driving across the country, Phil and Montel pull into a small Western town for lunch. Meanwhile, good ol' boys Alex (J. Scott Guy) and Jake (Shane Boldin) have gone hunting. En route, they get a flat tire and walk back toward town where they encounter two suspicious-looking men in business suits, who have stopped by the side of the road. One of the strangers, Robertson (John Pask), who is clearly disturbed, becomes annoyed at Alex and Jake's request for help, shoots at them and hits Jake in the shoulder. As Alex and Jake are running back to town like a couple of scared rabbits, detectives West (Estevez) and Carter (Dean Nolen) stroll into town looking for Montel. It is later revealed that West and Carter are not cops, but mobsters working with Robertson, Thompson (Kirk McKinney) and several other bad-guy types who want to kill Montel before he can testify at a trial.

When Alex and Jake return to town, they discover that the Sheriff (Jack Gould) and Jake's girlfriend Lori (Tracy Spaulding) have been murdered. Walking into the local bar, they meet up with Phil and Montel who explain what's happening. Soon the mobsters surround the bar, but Montel, Phil, Alex and Jake manage to escape. The four take refuge in Alex's trailer home, where he just happens to have his own private arsenal. And before you can say testosterone, the final shootout begins. After the smoke clears, the mandatory female hostage, Sarah (Barri Murphy), is freed; and old rivals West and Montel have a showdown wherein West is killed and Montel escapes.

Clearly, some care was taken where photography and special effects were concerned. However, the characters are one-dimensional, and much of the acting is over-the-top. Estevez (SOULTAKER, DARK RIDER) often substitutes eye bulging for acting. And Pask's portrayal of a trigger-happy psycho is really overdone. The only really likable person in the movie is Montel and he's a convicted killer. Also, it is never revealed where this town is and the female characters are, for the most part, used as decoration. *(Excessive violence, excessive profanity, partial nudity.)*

p, Max Raven; d, Bret McCormick; w, Ted Prior; ph, D.H. Blood; ed, Blue Thompson; m, Ron Dilulio; art d, Richard Perrin; cos, Jane Slaughter

Action/Crime **(PR: C MPAA: NR)**

ARTICLE 99 ★★

99m Article 99 Productions; Orion ~ Orion c

Ray Liotta *(Dr. Richard Sturgess)*, Kiefer Sutherland *(Dr. Peter Morgan)*, Forest Whitaker *(Dr. Sid Handleman)*, Lea Thompson *(Dr. Robin Van Dorn)*, John C. McGinley *(Dr. Rudy Bobrick)*, John Mahoney *(Dr. Henry Dreyfoos)*, Keith David *(Luther Jerome)*, Kathy Baker *(Dr. Diana Walton)*, Eli Wallach *(Sam Abrams)*, Noble Willingham *(Inspector General)*, Julie Bovasso *(Amelia Sturdeyvant)*, Troy Evans *(Pat Travis)*, Lynne Thigpen *(Nurse White)*, Jeffrey Tambor *(Dr. Leo Krutz)*, Leo Burmester *(Shooter Polaski)*, Ernest Abuba *(Ikiro Tenabe)*, Rutanya Alda *(Ann Travis)*, Michelle Little *(Nurse Pierce)*, Emily Houpt *(Dr. Norris)*, Mark Lowenthal *(Dr. Wolin)*, Cheryl Collins *(Nurse Stevens)*, Sherry Roulette-Mosely *(Nurse Jones)*, Donna Thomason *(Nurse Lyles)*, Brenda Varda *(Nurse Nichols)*, Barbara Houston *(Nurse)*, Karon Wright *(Secretary)*, Rick Reed *(Maintenance Man)*, Jeff Reiland *(Maintenance Man)*, T. Max Graham *(Captain)*, Douglas Dirkson *(Freaked Patient)*, Ed Autry *(Mumbling Man)*, Meyer L. Goldman *(Mr. Ponzini)*, Vince Melocchi *(Tense Patient)*, Ted Shonka *(McCarthy)*, Gwendolyn Shepherd *(Personnel Clerk)*, Bonita Hanson *(Clerk at Front Desk)*, Kathleen Bergman *(Clerk)*, Davenia McFadden *(Clerk)*, James Medina *(Puzzled Intern)*, Rodney McCay *(Orderly)*, C.L. Foster, Jr. *(Cigarette Vet)*, Joe Greve *(Lobby Vet)*, Tracy Sloat *(Gomer Ward Nurse)*, Erik Holland *(Gomer Ward Patient)*, Debra Bluford *(Men's Ward Nurse)*, Larry Kirchner *(Men's Ward Patient)*, John Lafayette *(Neurologist)*, C. Craig Satterlee *(Radiologist)*, Lynn King *(Pathology Lab Tech)*, Vivian Ecclefield *(Reporter)*, Joe Lerer *(Reporter)*, Kathy Quinn *(Nurse in Cafeteria)*, Ann Redow *(Nurse in Bathroom)*, Jophery Brown *(Admitting Guard)*, Kevin Brief *(Sleeping Security Guard)*, Granvile O'Neal *(Security Guard)*, Henry Levingston *(Security Guard)*, Cantor Ira S. Bigeleisen *(Rabbi)*, Kevin Davidson *(Inspector General's Aide)*, Donald Bishop *(New Director)*, Harold Hauss *(Helicopter Pilot)*

The thorny issue of veterans receiving substandard treatment in tight-budgeted, bureaucracy-plagued Veterans Administration hospitals receives little real insight in ARTICLE 99, a routine effort that borrows its freeswinging comic style from M*A*S*H but timidly pulls most of its punches.

Dr. Peter Morgan (Keifer Sutherland) is an up-and-coming heart surgeon who signs on at a VA hospital for his internship. There he encounters a nightmarish morass of red tape in trying to treat his patients and "creeping cutbacks" in budgets that have led to the title's fictitious catch-22 rule, promising treatment to all veterans but immediately withdrawing it in the absence of hard evidence directly connecting their maladies to military service. To get around this rule, doctors admit patients for authorized service-connected treatments they don't need and then attempt to give them the unauthorized treatment they do need on the sly. Morgan forms a friendship with one such patient (they're dubbed "gomers" by the hospital staff), a dying World War II veteran named Sam Abrams (Eli Wallach). Sam's dilemma moves Morgan to endanger his career by joining a group of renegade doctors, led by Dr. Richard Sturgess (Ray Liotta), who steal supplies and equipment at night from a well-funded research lab in the hospital's basement to perform their unauthorized operations.

Unfortunately, the naive Morgan is duped by the hospital's dogmatic administrator, Dr. Henry Dreyfoos (John Mahoney), into setting up Sturgess's group to be secretly videotaped during one of their midnight raids. Dreyfoos uses the tape to force Sturgess to take a voluntary suspension and face charges in return for not exposing his co-conspirators (Forest Whitaker and John C. McGinley). Morgan solves this problem by walking off with the tape and giving it to Sturgess, who returns to the hospital in triumph to perform a heart bypass on one of his own gomers, a Korean War vet (Troy Evans). Meanwhile a group of dissident veterans, led by a double amputee (Keith David) and a stress syndrome victim (Leo Burmester), blockade the hospital, forcing the exposure of Mahoney's villainy to the VA inspector general (Noble Willingham), who promises to oust Mahoney and institute reforms to end the blockade.

ARTICLE 99 gets off to a strong start, only to get weaker and more predictable as it goes along. Helmer Howard Deutch (PRETTY IN PINK, SOME KIND OF WONDERFUL) sets the right tone of grey despair outside and farcical life-and-death chaos inside the beleaguered hospital. From his apprenticeship with John Hughes he also evidently learned how to move an ensemble cast crisply through its paces. Sutherland is for once perfectly cast as a smarmy careerist at first interested in nothing more than putting in his time and keeping his pampered ass covered. Liotta is also typically strong as the hospital's chief renegade. The talented supporting cast contributes strongly, especially Whitaker, McGinley, David (all "veterans" of Oliver Stone's acclaimed PLATOON) and Mahoney. The largely peripheral females are led by the talented Kathy Baker, Julie Bovasso, Lea Thompson and Michelle Little.

But even the best performances are diluted by Ron Cutler's routine screenplay which begins veering away from complexity and originality early on. The chief antagonists are flat and uninteresting. Despite having a fling with Baker, Liotta is presented as a kind of Mother Teresa in hospital whites, while Mahoney is so doggedly devoted to ensuring that nobody ever gets treated in his hospital that one is left wondering how he attained his position in the first place. The only character who changes, Sutherland's, only gets more boring as the film goes on. From the moment he first locks eyes with Thompson, one of Liotta's devoted protectors, we know his days as a selfish yuppie won't last to the next reel change. The veterans' blockade of the hospital functions more to add a dash of spectacle to the climax than to serve any dramatic purpose. But most disappointing of all is how the film pulls back from its promised indictment of the VA system. Never examined is the source of the "creeping cutbacks" that lead Mahoney to his fanatical penny-pinching. As a result, never confronted is the inspector general, who appears instead as the film's improbable *deus ex machina*. Its overall failure of nerve makes ARTICLE 99 a typically lame Hollywood pseudo-political drama whose bark is worse than its bite. *(Profanity, adult situations.)*

p, Michael Gruskoff, Michael I. Levy; d, Howard Deutch; w, Ron Cutler; ph, Richard Bowen; ed, Richard Halsey; m, Danny Elfman; prod d, Virginia L. Randolph; cos, Rudy Dillon; makeup, Christa Reusch

Comedy/Drama **(PR: C MPAA: R)**

AUNTIE LEE'S MEAT PIES ★

100m Steiner Films ~ Columbia TriStar Home Video c

Karen Black *(Auntie Lee)*, Pat Morita *(Chief Koal)*, Kristine Anne Rose *(Fawn)*, Michael Berryman *(Larry)*, Pat Paulsen *(Minister)*, Huntz Hall *(Farmer)*, Ava Fabian *(Magnolia)*, Teri Weigel *(Coral)*, David Perry *(Harold Ivers)*, Steven Quadros *(Bob Evans)*, Phil Simms *(Mr. Pasquale)*, Leslie Simms *(Mrs. Pasquale)*, Louie Bonanno *(Doc)*, Walter Lang *(John)*, Pia Reyes *(Sky)*, Grant Cramer *(Phil)*, Cort McCown *(Craig)*, Petra Verkaik *(Baby)*

A moronic little trifle, AUNTIE LEE'S MEAT PIES is set in the California desert town of "Penance" and stars Karen Black as the title character, who's renowned in the area for her tasty meat pies which she prepares and bakes, aided by her retarded brother Larry (Michael Berryman), in the basement of their secluded adobe ranch house.

The pies' main ingredient is, of course, human flesh, mixed with a "special blend of herbs and spices," which is provided by male hitchhikers and tourists enticed to the slaughterhouse by Lee's four shapely, cleavage-heavy nieces, Fawn (Kristine Anne Rose), Magnolia (Ava Fabian), Coral (Teri Weigel) and Sky (Pia Reyes). Local police chief Koal (Pat Morita), a fan of both Auntie and her pies, has no idea what's going on until he discovers a garbage bag full of human bones in Coral's car trunk, but he arrives too late to save a dopey New York private investigator, Harold Ivers (David Perry), and a sleazy heavy-metal rock quartet led by Doc (Louie Bonanno), all waylaid and messily dispatched by the girls.

Stumbling along the cannibal-themed trail blazed by THE FOLKS AT RED WOLF INN, THE TEXAS CHAINSAW MASSACRE, WELCOME TO ARROW BEACH and, of course, *Sweeney Todd*, AUNTIE LEE'S MEAT PIES is feebly co-written by director Joseph F. Robertson and producer/editor Gerald M. Steiner (who last collaborated on 1990's campy DR. CALIGARI), with plenty of genre-required female nudity and gore effects.

Mostly ineptly acted and shot on a shoestring budget in Fullerton, California, the film is neither funny nor horrific. In fact, the only shock here is the spirited participation of mainstream actors Karen Black and Pat Morita. TV's Pat Paulsen has one brief scene (but no dialogue) early on as a minister/victim, while the veteran Bowery Boys comic Huntz Hall turns up as a farmer, the understandably irritated neighbor of Auntie and the girls. *(Violence, substance abuse, nudity, profanity.)*

p, Gerald M. Steiner; d, Joseph F. Robertson; w, Joseph F. Robertson, Gerald M. Steiner; ph, Arledge Armenaki; ed, Gerald M. Steiner; prod d, James R. Shumaker; cos, Tess DiGagni

Horror/Comedy **(PR: O MPAA: R)**

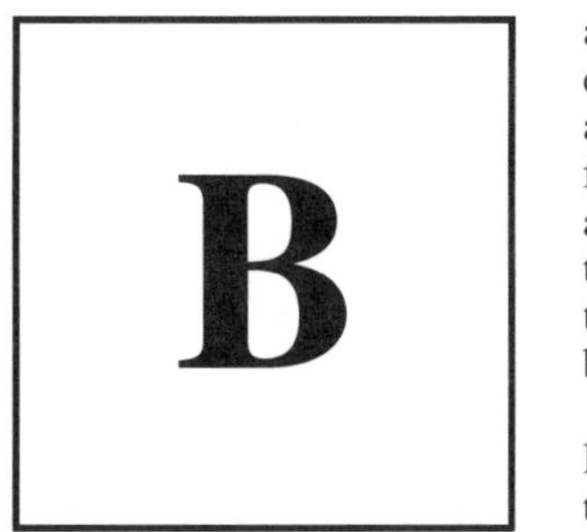

BABE, THE ★★½

115m Waterhorse Productions; Pipeline Productions; Finnegan-Pinchuk Productions ~ Universal c

John Goodman *(George Herman "Babe" Ruth)*, Kelly McGillis *(Claire Hodgeson-Ruth)*, Trini Alvarado *(Helen Woodford-Ruth)*, Bruce Boxleitner *(Jumpin' Joe Dugan)*, Peter Donat *(Harry Frazee)*, James Cromwell *(Brother Mathias)*, J.C. Quinn *(Jack Dunn)*, Joe Ragno *(Huggins)*, Richard Tyson *(Guy Bush)*, Ralph Marrero *(Francesco Stephano "Ping Bodie" Pezzolo)*, Bob Swan *(George Ruth, Sr.)*, Bernard Kates *(Colonel Jacob Ruppert)*, Michael McGrady *(Lou Gehrig)*, Stephen Caffrey *(Johnny Sylvester–Age 30)*, Gene Ross *(Brother Paul)*, Danny Goldring *(Carrigan)*, Andy Voils *(Young George Herman "Jidge" Ruth)*, Dylan Day *(Johnny Sylvester–Age 10)*, Laura Whyte *(Mrs. Ballister)*, James Andelin *(Asa)*, Guy Barile *(Torrio)*, Bernie Gigliotti *(Capone)*, Michael Nicolosi *(Jimmy Colosimmo)*, W. Earl Brown *(Herb Pennock)*, Barbara Faye Wallace *(Mrs. Pennock)*, Shannon Cochran *(Flapper)*, Michael Papajohn *(Heckler)*, Thom C. Simmons *(McKechnie)*, Gene Weygandt *(Mrs. Sylvester)*, Steve King *(Fuchs)*, Matt Doherty *(Boy in Car)*, Brendon DeMay *(Boy in Car)*, Brendan Hutt *(Boy at St. Mary's)*, Beep Iams *(Boy at St. Mary's)*, Jeffrey Wiseman *(Boy at St. Mary's)*, Rick Reardon *(Ernie Shore)*, Randy Steinmeyer *(Ty Cobb)*, Stevie Lee Richardson *(Eddie the Bat Boy)*, Elizabeth Greenberg *(Dorothy)*, Wayne Messmer *(Yankee Announcer)*, Larry Cedar *(Forbes Field Announcer)*, John Webb *(Eddie)*, Tanner King *(Joey)*, Erika Baltodano *(Shoeless Girl)*, Stavon Lovell Davis *(Boy with Radio)*, Tom Guarnieri *(Boy with Radio)*, Ken Gildin *(Hot Dog Vendor)*, Alan Johnson *(Orphanage Reporter)*, Michael Kendall *(Jack Warhop)*, Harry Hutchinson *(Tris Speaker)*, Michael Krawic *(Theatergoer)*, Sonny Mann *(Scoffer)*, Johanna McKay *(Yankee Wife)*, Cory Grant *(Inmate)*, Jim Ortlieb *(Scribe)*, Scott Haven *(Scribe)*, James Deuter *(Society Man)*, Ralph Foody *(Pittsburgh Man)*, Meg Thalken *(Johnny's Nurse)*, Ron West *(Spectator)*, Irma P. Hall *(Fanny Baily)*, Dana Lubotsky *(Julia)*, Patrick Clear *(Fedoras)*, William J. Norris *(Fedoras)*, Ron Dean *(Umpire Owens)*, Brett Hadley *(1st Umpire)*, Ken Kells *(2nd Umpire)*, Jeff Still *(3rd Umpire)*, Hank Robinson *(4th Umpire)*, Peter Siragusa *(Umpire Hildebrand)*, Vern Hazard *(1st Baseman)*, Harris Kal *(Pirates Catcher)*, Christopher Beacom *(2nd Baseman)*, Donald Bagley *(1st Barber Shop Quartet Member)*, Richard Kingdon *(2nd Barber Shop Quartet Member)*, Timothy McShane *(3rd Barber Shop Quartet Member)*, Chuck Sisson *(4th Barber Shop Quartet Member)*, Mark Ingram, Chuckie Anderson, Tyrone Blair, Thaddeus Expose, Roger Harris, Albert Smith *(Speakeasy Band Members)*, Marysue Redmann *(Mansrion Harpist)*, Ari Brown *(New Orleans Clarinetist)*, Joe Huppert *(Ansonia Pianist)*, Steve Jensen, Daniel Anderson, William Findlay, Michael Kocour, Brian Naylor, Russell Phillips, Paul Wertico *(Bistro Band Members)*, John S. Green *(Verbal Spectator)*, Melody Rae *(Verbal Spectator)*, Joan Elizabeth *(Verbal Spectator)*, Kara Zediker *(Redhead)*, Nicholas Rudall *(Brother Malcolm)*, John T Miltes *(Brother Lewis)*, Tricia Munford *(Jump's Wife (Ida))*, Alison Groh *(Dorothy–Age 2)*, Jade Rodell Tipton *(Baby Dorothy)*, Andrew Bendel *(Radio Announcer)*, Patrick Nugent *(Pittsburgh Announcer)*, James "Ike" Eichling *(Cigar Smoker)*, Shirley Spiegler-Jacobs *(Woman in Coffee Shop)*, Roy Hytower *(Elevator Operator)*, Amy Carlson *(Girl on Stairs)*, Michael Chesler *(Combs)*, Ron Marino *(Combs II)*, Brooke Linthicum *(Jump's Child)*, Randy Moll *(Meusal)*, Nicholas Satriano *(Lazzari)*, Ned Schmidtke *(Hospital Reporter)*

Thanks to Arthur Hiller's smoothly proficient direction, Haskell Wexler's evocative cinematography and an ingratiating performance by John Goodman, THE BABE goes down easy, like hot dogs and a beer at the ballpark on a summer afternoon. All these elements successfully obscure a lackluster script that plays fast and loose with the facts of Babe Ruth's life, transforming Ruth from the brilliant but emotionally troubled ball player that he was to a bacchanalian, redneck god.

The episodic scenario follows the life of George Herman Ruth (Goodman) for a period of thirty-three years, beginning with young Ruth's abandonment by his parents. His father deposits him at a Catholic school in Baltimore, where Ruth first picks up a bat and begins banging long balls over the school wall. He's eventually signed by the Boston Red Sox, where Ruth amazes teammates with his homerun abilities. He's then sold to the New York Yankees, where he becomes the heart of the Yankees team. Ruth brings his new wife Helen (Trini Alvarado) with him to the big city, but Helen prefers the quiet life on a farm to the New York high life, walking out on Ruth after one one-night stand too many. Ruth then marries Claire Hodgeson (Kelly McGillis), a worldly Ziegfeld showgirl who proves an equal companion for the fun-loving homerun king. But by this point, Ruth's home-run prowess has begun to fail him and he holds the hope that he will be hired as team manager by unsavory Yankees owner Colonel Jacob Ruppert (Bernard Kates). When this hope is dashed, Ruth quits and is hired by the Braves as a featured attraction, finding himself the laughingstock of fans and fellow players alike. Ruth musters up the remains of his talent and dignity and knocks three balls out of the ballpark in one game. As the fans respond with a frenzied ovation, Ruth drops his baseball hat in the dirt and walks out of the ballpark forever.

Even those unfamiliar with baseball lore have read or heard about Babe Ruth's famous called shot in the 1932 World Series, when he cryptically pointed over the scoreboard, then blasted the ball out of the ballpark—to the exact spot he'd indicated beforehand. When this moment is dramatized in THE BABE, one ballplayer turns to Lou Gehrig and exclaims, "He ain't human. He's an animal." "No. He's a God," Gehrig replies. In contrast, as Samuel Fuller recounts in *Cult Baseball Players*, "He was the King of Swat who could point to a spot in the bleachers and slam a homer to that exact spot. It wasn't ego. It was the highest form of his art: professionalism . . . . You could tell how much he loved the game. But more important, how much the game loved him." Fuller expresses awe for Ruth's talent, but it is grounded in a knowledge of Ruth's technical brilliance and his love of the game. Screenwriter John Fusco, however, portrays Ruth as a natural who can effortlessly pick up a bat for the first time and slam a ball over a fence. In THE BABE, Ruth is an alien being, a superman of baseball, a homerun powerhouse who is never shown to have any sense of the game but, who, through the money showered upon him by baseball, becomes a cornpone Bacchus, leaving mere mortals to chuckle and smirk in his wake. Unfortunately, Fusco's vulgar yet endearing Ruth is so much larger than life, so mythologized out of time or place, that his Babe is divorced from empathy or identity.

The Babe of THE BABE is a walking legend whose flaws are made lovable and whose only mortal desire is that good old fashioned bromide "the need for love." But his legendary status is never explored. THE BABE never shows the importance of baseball in turn-of-the-century American society, nor does the film explain Ruth's importance to the game. His celebrity, except for a few recreated newsreels, is never indicated. The Babe just is. Fans love him and cheer him. But why? How did he get that way? From "The House That Ruth Built" to Baby Ruth candy, Fusco never bothers to examine the meaning of celebrity and

Ruth's fame. With Fusco's comic-book script to overcome, John Goodman overrides it with a towering performance which doesn't stint on Ruth's churlishness, bitterness and rage, thereby giving his characterization a dimension the screenplay doesn't possess. Hiller and Wexler compliment Goodman's performance by visually conveying the underside of the baseball milieu, depicting the behind-the-scenes machinations with the dark-toned glow of the Inferno. These three demonstrate that sometimes the sheer force of artistry and professionalism can overcome mediocrity and indifference—a greater tribute to Babe Ruth than Fusco's formulaic, indifferent screenplay. *(Adult situations.)*

p, John Fusco; d, Arthur Hiller; w, John Fusco; ph, Haskell Wexler; ed, Robert C. Jones; m, Elmer Bernstein; prod d, James D. Vance; cos, April Ferry

Biography/Sports **(PR: A MPAA: PG)**

BACK IN THE U.S.S.R. ★★½

(U.S./U.S.S.R.) 89m Largo International; JVC Entertainment Inc.; Mosfilm ~ FoxVideo c

Frank Whaley *(Archer Sloan)*, Natalya Negoda *(Lena)*, Roman Polanski *(Kurilov)*, Andrew Divof *(Dimitri)*, Dey Young *(Claudia)*, Ravil Issyanov *(Georgi)*, Harry Ditson *(Whittier)*, Brian Blessed *(Chazov)*, Constantine Gregory *(Stanley)*, Alexei Yevdokimov *(Mikhail)*

History waits for no movie and recent transformative events in the former Soviet Union may have already dated this diverting romantic thriller. Touted as the first US film shot entirely on location in the Soviet Union, BACK IN THE U.S.S.R. provides an intriguing glimpse of "glasnost" in Moscow during the tumultuous Gorbachev era. This absorbing sociological backdrop is more interesting than the shopworn sub-Hitchcockian intrigues.

Plot machinations are set in motion with the excavation of a chest containing a precious Russian art treasure: a religious icon depicting the fabled Black Madonna. While transporting the treasure into town, a solemn, bearded monk is violently waylaid and the icon is stolen. Meanwhile, it's the last day in the U.S.S.R. for Archer Sloan (Frank Whaley), a vacationing American student. Curious about the nation's publicized changes, he had signed up for a group tour that covered all the official sights but still yearns to experience the "real Russia." As a citizen living that reality, the young and lovely Lena (Natalya Negoda) works as a reluctant neophyte hooker to survive these new uncertain times.

Unresponsive and unpaid, she gets booted out of the hotel suite of a boorish Englishman, Stanley (Constantine Gregory), who we learn is carrying the stolen icon in his valise. Cocky with his success, he attempts to renegotiate financial arrangements with his intended buyer in a tense telephone conversation. As Stanley showers, Lena creeps back and steals the valise. She runs into trouble in the lobby with the annoying hotel doorman but Archer gallantly comes to her aid and sees her to a taxi. He asks Lena to show him around town and they arrange to meet later at a local nightclub. The monk looks on ominously. The nervous Stanley goes to meet his buyer, Chazov (Brian Blessed), without the icon and gets murdered for his failure and greed.

Archer meets Lena at a rock club with her roommate, Georgi (Ravil Issyanov), who makes ends meet as a low-level black marketeer. The trio travels back to the cramped apartment the young Russians share with a senile doctor. Archer and Lena have a failed romantic interlude which propels the disquieted American back to his hotel where the monk awaits him, demanding the valise and threatening to call the police. Archer backtracks, grabs the bag and hops into a cab. The drunken cabbie abandons the lad in a deserted part of town where he gets robbed and beaten unconscious by thugs. Assuming that the "Russian Mafia" stole the icon, the young trio get deeply involed with the local criminal subculture. One gangster in particular, Kurilov (Roman Polanski), is especially threatening.

The plot thickens as Archer gets blamed for the murder of Stanley. He and Lena must avoid the police as they search for the icon and the monk who can clear his name. There follows a briskly paced series of episodes featuring sudden violence, shifting allegiances, surprising revelations and much local color before a climactic confrontation of most of the involved parties.

BACK IN THE U.S.S.R. invites viewers to identify with Archer as a sympathetic stranger in a strange land—a situation with many cinematic antecedents. The villain Chazov derides the debased modern character of Russian life in favor of the glorious past while the film itself evokes memories of similarly themed but far superior films: Carol Reed's THE THIRD MAN, Alfred Hitchcock's remake of his THE MAN WHO KNEW TOO MUCH and Polanski's FRANTIC leap to mind. These stories feature American innocents abroad, who learn—often with the help of an enigmatic native—the painful and humbling lesson that the world is a far darker and complex place than they had previously imagined.

By evoking these memories, BACK IN THE U.S.S.R. damns itself as second rate. While there are good performances, there are no great characters. The locations are authentic and attractive but they are not used imaginatively nor do we get a distinct sense of place. Moreover, the film lacks a great suspense set-piece—no one clings precariously to a national monument, there's no thrilling chase through the sewers, no showdowns in fabulous exotic locales. This may reflect a lack of budget as much as a lack of inspiration.

The participation of the great banished filmmaker Roman Polanski is both pleasurable and problematic. While in exile, Polanski directed the underrated FRANTIC wherein Harrison Ford has a harrowing adventure in Paris that puts BACK IN THE U.S.S.R. to shame. An efficient actor, Polanski starred in several of his films and made an indelible cameo appearance in CHINATOWN, a modern film noir classic that is also relevant; both films adopt a cynical conspiratorial view of crime, business and politics and Polanski's Kurilov echoes the earlier role in which he slits Jack Nicholson's nose. Kurilov, a larger part, commits comparable violence to the hero's body but this is a softer characterization. Tough but charismatic, he is more likable than the ostensible hero.

Frank Whaley's central performance suggests Joseph Cotton in THE THIRD MAN or Jimmy Stewart in THE MAN WHO KNEW TOO MUCH as reinterpeted by Michael J. Fox; the once-charming "aw shucks" idealism and middle American naivete has been curdled by pique and narcissism into a perhaps justified but certainly whiny self-pity. This offputting effect may be accidental or an intentional critique may be at work. In contrast Natalya Negoda (LITTLE VERA) is totally beguiling and displays genuine star potential. Her eyes convey depths that this little movie does not dare explore.

With its flaws and limitations, BACK IN THE U.S.S.R. is most worthwhile for its marginalia and subtexts. The end credits are followed by a silent image of a square crowded with smiling waving Russian children. The film provides a rare opportunity to see everyday Russian life in a mainstream Hollywood narrative. Just how much is accurate is hard to tell but there is a distinct impression of a curtain being pulled back to reveal a troubled society in transition.

In the film's most inspired conceit, Archer and Lena have their first kiss in the loud and gaudy nightclub in front of a movie screen. Projected on and around them are dramatic b&w scenes of WWII battles, hearkening back to an earlier era of international alliances. BACK IN THE U.S.S.R. may not be Hitchcock, but it isn't half bad. *(Violence, profanity, nudity, sexual situations.)*

p, Lindsay Smith, Ilmar Taska; d, Deran Sarafian; w, Lindsay Smith, (from the story by Smith and Ilmar Taska); ph, Yuri Neyman; ed, Ian Crafford; m, Les Hooper; prod d, Vladimir Philippov; set d, Yuri Osipenko, Nikolai Surovtsev; cos, Cynthia Bergstrom, Tatiana Lichmanova

Thriller/Romance **(PR: C MPAA: R)**

BACKTRACK ★½

98m Vestron Pictures; Precision Films; Mack-Taylor Productions; Dick Clark Productions; Backtrack Productions ~ Vestron Video c

Jodie Foster *(Anne Benton)*, Dennis Hopper *(Milo)*, Dean Stockwell *(John Luponi)*, Vincent Price *(Lino Avoca)*, John Turturro *(Pinella)*, Joe Pesci *(Leo Carelli)*, Fred Ward *(Pauling)*, Julie Adams *(Martha)*, G. Anthony Sirico *(Greek)*, Sy Richardson *(Captain Walker)*, Frank Gio *(Frankie)*, Helena Kalianiotes *(Grace Carelli)*, John Apicella *(Man at Refinery)*, Clifford Bartholomew *(Fed)*, Burke Byrnes *(Fed)*, Kevin Bourland *(Ad Agency Man)*, Carl David Burks *(Ad Agency Man)*, Grand Bush *(Bank Teller)*, Tod Davies *(Hit Woman)*, Satya De la Manitou *(Car Thug)*, Ayres Donno *(Girl in Restaurant)*, Bob Dylan *(Artist)*, Tomas Goros *(Golf Course Fed)*, Sarina Grant *(Hooker)*, Catherine Keener *(Trucker's Girl)*, Katherine La Nasa *(Waitress)*, Lauren Lloyd *(Margaret Mason)*, Anthony Pena *(Taos Sheriff)*, Robert Rothwell *(Ad Agency Executive)*, Charlie Sheen *(Bob)*, Gary Wills *(Police Sergeant)*, Michael Yama *(Technician)*, John Zenda *(Trucker)*

Though clearly intended to be something more than a routine thriller, BACKTRACK never transcends its generic limitations, and the surprisingly good cast ultimately founders.

Conceptual artist Anne Benton (Jodie Foster) creates electronic pieces (supplied by real-life artist Jenny Holzer) that flash glib but superficially significant statements, and her work has begun to attract major media attention. Driving home one night, she suffers a blowout on a deserted road and, while looking for help, witnesses a Mafia rubout. Killer Leo Carelli (Joe Pesci) spots her, but Anne escapes and goes to the police. They offer her a place in the federal witness protection program, but patrician mob boss Lino Avoca (Vincent Price) sends top-of-the-line but eccentric hitman Milo (Dennis Hopper) and his dopey partner Pinella (John Turturro) to silence her first. They kill her boyfriend, Bob (Charlie Sheen), but she escapes.

Months pass; Anne has severed all ties with her past and re-established herself in Seattle as an advertising copywriter. Milo, who never gives up, recognizes the text of a lipstick ad as one of Anne's catchphrases, and tracks her down. She flees again, to New Mexico; again he finds her. But this time he offers her a deal: he'll let her live, if she'll do anything and everything he asks. Milo's interest in Anne, it turns out, is more than professional, but not exactly what she thinks. He doesn't want her to be his sex slave, though sex is part of the equation. A man obsessed, Milo has fallen in love with Anne, and has no idea how to cope with the unfamiliar emotion. Astonishingly, after a rocky start, Anne realizes she has also fallen for him.

By failing to kill Anne, Milo has marked himself for death, and the two flee together to an isolated farm he owns. Avoca's men track them there, and they realize that in order to be free, they must return and confront their pursuers. The audacious plan they concoct works, and they escape together to a new life.

Directed by Hopper, BACKTRACK's credits carry the notorious "Alan Smithee" pseudonym, the sure sign of a helmer unhappy with the way his film has turned out. Shelved in 1989, when Vestron, the film's producer, went bankrupt, BACKTRACK was a troubled production that underwent extensive tinkering before being released theatrically in Europe as CATCHFIRE. Hopper was allowed to recut before the film was shown on cable television in the US in late 1991, but the result is still unsatisfying.

Shot after Hopper's COLORS and before THE HOT SPOT, the ambitious and attractively photographed BACKTRACK attempts to take genre conventions—the seemingly emotionless hitman falls for his intended victim thriller—and rework them. But, also like THE HOT SPOT, BACKTRACK amounts to considerably less than the sum of its parts, and nowhere is this more apparent than in the performances turned in by the hip but strangely disparate cast.

The resurgent Foster, who tackled this project between her Academy Award-winning performances in THE ACCUSED and THE SILENCE OF THE LAMBS, is outstanding as Anne, even saddled with a pretentiously named cat and a tacky seduction scene that misses no cliche, from bustier to garter belt. Hopper's performance, by contrast, is striking but miscalculated. Milo plays the saxophone, worships Charlie Parker and Hieronymous Bosch and tries to smash windows when he's frustrated, though he's comically unable to do so. He's the reincarnation of the insanely scary Frank Booth in David Lynch's BLUE VELVET, but with soul or something (so we can like him), and a ghastly accent that could only work if it were clearly a meta-accent, some sort of parody of the way New York lowlifes speak in the movies.

Meanwhile, John Turturro twitches, Charlie Sheen preens and Vincent Price is, yes, ghoulishly gracious as Don Lino Avoca, while Dean Stockwell is strangely recessive as mob lawyer John Luponi; perhaps it's his proximity to Hopper (with whom he appeared in BLUE VELVET) that makes one expect something more eccentric. Joe Pesci, whose name does not appear in the credits, falls back on manic mannerisms, and Bob Dylan's cameo (also uncredited) as an artist with a chainsaw is nothing more than an in-joke. None of them gives a really bad performance (except, perhaps, Hopper himself), but they all seem to be in different movies.

BACKTRACK is occasionally entertaining, but more often infuriating. It could have been far more interesting than it is, and the considerable talents of all involved are expended to little effect. *(Violence, sexual situations.)*

p, Dick Clark, Dan Paulson; d, Dennis Hopper; w, Rachel Kronstadt-Mann, Stephen L. Cotler, Lanny Cotler, (from the story by Kronstadt-Mann); ph, Edward Lachman; ed, David Rawlins; m, Curt Sobel; prod d, Ron Foreman; art d, Paul Marcotte; set d, Jeannie Laughlin; cos, Nancy Cone

Drama/Thriller **(PR: C MPAA: R)**

BAD CHANNELS ★

88m Full Moon Entertainment ~ Paramount Home Video c

Paul Hipp *(Dan O'Dare)*, Martha Quinn *(Lisa)*, Michael Huddleston *(Corky)*, Charlie Spradling *(Cookie)*, Daryl Strauss *(Bunny)*, Melissa Behr *(Ginger)*, Aaron Lustig *(Locknut)*, Victor Rogers *(Sheriff Hickman)*, Romel Reaux *(Flip Humble)*, Ian Patrick Williams

BAD CHANNELS is yet another slapdash direct-to-video release from Full Moon Entertainment, the Charles Band-headed company devoted to producing a steady flow of grade-B genre product.

Considering that the storyline involves terror at a radio station and the cast is headed by former MTV host Martha Quinn, the only surprise here is that she does not play the movie's DJ. That task falls to Paul Hipp as "Dangerous" Dan O'Dare, who likes to indulge in outrageous stunts like playing a 20-hour polka marathon until someone guesses the correct combination on the lock that keeps him chained to his chair. After a long introduction of such pointless hijinx, the film's real plot gets going, involving an alien being with a swollen head that drops to Earth with a robot sidekick and invades the station.

Pretty soon there's green slime everywhere, Dan and his engineer Corky (Michael Huddleston) are cringing in the control room and the alien is on the air, using a strange device to scope out cute women who are listening to the station. When it latches onto a likely subject, the creature sends a special transmission just to her, immersing her in a live music performance before zapping her out of her surroundings, shrinking her to a foot high and depositing her in a small glass case. In this manner, it procures a hot-to-trot waitress named Cookie (Charlie Spradling), airhead cheerleader Bunny (Daryl Strauss) and free-spirited nurse Ginger (Melissa Behr).

Meanwhile, a TV reporter named Lisa (Quinn) has been trying to get a story on Dan, and is right on the scene when the strange events begin to occur. The beleaguered DJ is reporting on the bizarre goings-on from inside the station, but nobody believes him, assuming it to be a "War of the Worlds"-style prank designed to pull in big ratings. Among the disbelievers are station owner Locknut (Aaron Lustig), local Sheriff Hickman (Victor Rogers) and Lisa's fellow TV personality Flip Humble (Romel Reaux)—that is, until the alien attempts to zap Lisa into its collection and instead captures a nerdy teenage fan.

The alien being reverses the process to empty the container for Lisa, and Dan sees the way to foil the alien's plan. Lisa soon becomes the creature's fourth captive, but Dan manages to revert her, Ginger and Cookie back to normal size, and they attack the being with the secret weapon Dan's discovered: household spray cleaner. The alien's head pops off, revealing a screeching plant monster beneath, but the group of humans manage to destroy it, the robot sidekick and the slime that's sealed over the doors. They emerge triumphant—not noticing at first that the miniaturized Bunny is still left behind.

BAD CHANNELS plays like a movie that was created around a couple of standing sets: the radio station and the hospital where Ginger works and a man contaminated by the slime is brought for observation. The negligible screenplay, credited to Jackson Barr, seems to have been created as the filmmakers went along, with little narrative drive and a general lack of motivation; it's never explained what the alien intends to do with the women it's shrunk once it takes them home. There's also no explanation of how the music-video fantasies that entrap its victims are created, or why they're necessary, but they do allow director Ted Nicolaou to pad the film's running time to over 80 minutes.

The musical sequences themselves are nothing to phone home about, with the exception of the warped and wild performance by Sykotik Sinfoney that entraps Ginger. Their piece not only captures the manic energy the rest of the film lacks, but serves as a commentary on it when the lead singer turns to the camera and screams, "It really sucks!" The cast all struggle against cartoon roles, with Hipp (recent star of Broadway's *Buddy*, based on the life of early rocker Buddy Holly) as the manic DJ coming off the best; Quinn, on the other hand, looks uncomfortable in a showcase that actually requires her to act.

The extraterrestrial being is not especially impressive, clad in black leather with a styrofoam head, and his robotic cohort looks like one of the makeshift contraptions from TV's "Mystery Science Theater 3000"—a venue where this movie would be entirely at home. *(Violence, profanity, adult situations.)*

p, Keith Payson, Ted Nicolaou; d, Ted Nicolaou; w, Jackson Barr, (from the idea by Charles Band); ph, Adolfo Bartoli; ed, Carol Oblath; m, Blue Oyster Cult; prod d, Everett Wilson

Science Fiction/Horror/Comedy (PR: C MPAA: R)

BAD LIEUTENANT ★★★½

96m Lt. Productions; Edward R. Pressman Film Corporation ~ Aries Film Releasing c

Harvey Keitel *(Lt.–The Lieutenant)*, Victor Argo *(Bet Cop)*, Paul Calderone *(Cop One)*, Leonard Thomas *(Cop Two)*, Robin Burrows *(Ariane)*, Frankie Thorn *(Nun)*, Victoria Bastel *(Bowtay)*, Paul Hipp *(Jesus)*, Brian McElroy *(Lt.'s Son)*, Frankie Acciario *(Lt.'s Son Number 2)*, Peggy Gormley *(Lt.'s Wife)*, Stella Keitel *(Lt.'s Daughter)*, John Steven Jones *(Black Kid Number 2)*, Anthony Ruggiero *(Lite)*, Vincent Laresca *(JC)*, G. Elvis Phillips *(Young Cop)*, Shawn McLean *(Black Kid Number 1)*, Stephen Chen *(Korean Store Owner)*, Fernando Velez *(Julio)*, Joseph Michael Cruz *(Paulo)*, Frank Adonis *(Large)*, Lambert Moss *(Veronica)*, Nicholas DeCegli *(Limelight Guide)*, Larry Mullane *(Detective Number 2)*, Zoe Tamarlaine Lund *(Zoe)*, Bo Dietl *(Detective Bo)*, Gene Canfield *(Irish Cop)*, Heather Bracken *(Nurse)*, Penny Allen *(Doctor)*, Eddie Daniels *(Jersey Girl)*, Bianca Bakiia *(Jersey Girl Number 2)*, Ed Kovens *(Monsignor)*, Jamie Sanchez *(Priest)*, Minnie Gentry *(Elderly Woman)*, Mike Fella *(Detective)*, Mike Ciravolo *(Detective Number 2)*, Iraida Polanco *(Momacita)*, John Cloghessy *(VO Announcer)*, Chris "Mad Dog" Russo *(VO Announcer Number 2)*, Warner Fusselle *(Play By Play Announcer)*

In a year when police corruption dominated the headlines from coast to coast, Abel Ferrara's blistering BAD LIEUTENANT couldn't have been more timely.

The Lieutenant (Harvey Keitel) is a New York City cop who's juggling two lives. At home, he's a family man who just wants the best for his wife and extended flock of relatives. On the job, he's a rogue cop heading for disaster. He drinks too much and has a wicked coke problem. He abuses suspects and extorts sexual favors from prostitutes and drug addicts, including his strung-out mistress (Zoe Tamarlaine Lund, who co-wrote the screenplay and starred in Ferrara's early cult hit, MS. 45). He's a compulsive gambler deep in hock to the Mafia. He's wired and getting more careless all the time; the walls are closing in and he doesn't have a clue how to fix things. All that changes when a young nun (Frankie Thorn) is raped during a robbery at a convent in Spanish Harlem. Rewards are offered by the Church and the Mafia—they're thugs, after all, but they're Catholic thugs who don't hold with sexually assaulting the good sisters.

The Lieutenant quickly launches his own investigation, figuring that he can use the reward money to pay off his debts. But much more importantly, his search takes on the aspect of a spiritual quest, even as he simultaneously indulges in a suicidal gambling spree that increases his indebtedness (to a dangerous and exasperated mob bookie) exponentially. A lapsed Catholic whose religious yearnings are resurfacing in a variety of disturbingly distorted forms, the Lieutenant believes that if he can avenge the nun's rape he'll be able to shake off the filth and degradation of his life and start all over. But things don't work out that way. She refuses to help him, insisting that she forgives her attackers and only wants to help them. He tracks them down anyway, but in a desperate bid for some fragment of the inner peace she enjoys, the Lieutenant lets the boys go. Shortly thereafter, he's shot to death by a mob flunkie.

Director of such stylish thrillers as CHINA GIRL and the extraordinary KING OF NEW YORK, Abel Ferrara has made his reputation by balancing lurid narratives and lush, seductive visuals. BAD LIEUTENANT is actually an aesthetic throwback to Ferrara's earliest work, 1979's DRILLER KILLER (in which he also starred as an artist driven to homicidal madness); it is harsh, gritty and utterly uncompromising. The photography has the bleak, documentary look of THE FRENCH CONNECTION, heavy on the hand-held camera; the editing is rough and jarring. One can empathize with the characters, but it's hard to imagine liking any of them—in fact, BAD LIEUTENANT is so overwhelmingly unpleasant that it's actually difficult to watch.

An actor whose recent performances have seldom lived up to the promise he showed in such films as MEAN STREETS, TAXI DRIVER and BLUE COLLAR, Harvey Keitel shone in two roles in 1992, both in low-budget films. Assured and impressive though he is in it, Keitel's part in Quentin Tarantino's RESERVOIR DOGS breaks no new ground. But in BAD LIEUTENANT, he's nothing short of extraordinary. Crude, corrupt, simultaneously revelling in self-loathing and desperate for some evidence of transcendence in a world whose sordidness is overwhelming, Keitel's Lieutenant is so far out of control he approaches some warped zen state: he's truly one with the vile universe in which he lives. Excellent supporting performances, including Lund's turn as a philosophizing junkie, round out the picture. Though hardly a film for all sensibilities, BAD LIEUTENANT has the courage of its own convictions, and follows them to the bitter end. *(Violence, substance abuse, profanity, nudity, sexual situations, adult situations.)*

p, Edward R. Pressman, Mary Kane; d, Abel Ferrara; w, Zoe Tamarlaine Lund, Abel Ferrara; ph, Ken Kelsch; ed, Anthony Redman; m, Joe Delia; prod d, Charles Lagola; set d, Stephanie Carroll; cos, David Sawaryn

Crime/Thriller **(PR: O MPAA: NC-17)**

BARBARIAN QUEEN II: THE EMPRESS STRIKES BACK ★

87m Concorde; Triana Films ~ Concorde c

Lana Clarkson *(Amathia–The Barbarian Queen)*, Greg Wrangler *(Aurion)*, Rebecca Wood *(Ziela)*, Elizabeth Jaeger *(Noki)*, Roger Cudney *(Hofrax)*, Alejandro Bracho *(Ankaris)*, Cecilia Tijerina *(Tamis)*, Orietta Aguilar *(Erigena)*, Carolina Valero *(Nabis)*, Monica Steuer *(Ethbek)*, Carlos Romano *(Peasant)*, Manuel Benitez *(Captain)*, Antonio Zubiaga *(King's Soldier)*, George Belanger *(1st Noble)*, John Sterlini *(2nd Noble)*, Patrick Welch *(Noble's Father)*, Auturo Ostos *(1st Soldier)*, Alejandro Landero *(2nd Soldier)*, Francisco Tostado *(3rd Soldier)*, Hector DeRubi *(4th Soldier)*, Memo Ayala *(Iron Man)*

Replete with gratuitous mud-wrestling, anachronistic attitudes and buxom actresses wearing fur-and-leather swimsuits at least three sizes too small, BARBARIAN QUEEN II: THE EMPRESS STRIKES BACK is a campy actioner for tired businessmen and oversexed amateur historians.

While evil usurper Ankaris (Alejandro Bracho) vies for the absent king's magical scepter, the monarch's daughter Amathia (Lana Clarkson) is in a quandary: if she wields the weapon prematurely, her father could die, but if she doesn't act soon her people will never slip out of those unattractive slave bracelets. Pressured by Ankaris's misogynist henchman Hofrax (Roger Cudney), Amathia foolhardily attempts escape only to be betrayed by Ankaris's ambitious daughter Tamis (Cecilia Tijerina), a teenage sorceress who's preoccupied with stealing Amathia's power and turning the beleaguered princess's suitor Aurion (Greg Wrangler) into her own boy toy.

En route to her execution, Amathia escapes the noose, befriends a forest Amazon named Ziela (Rebecca Wood), rescues a peddler's daughter and routs Hofrax's troops. Reigning over her newfound forest coterie, Amathia trains the good-hearted rabble, defeats a larger contingent of Ankaris's guards, pausing only to humiliate Hofrax and rekindle her affair with the wishy-washy Aurion. Lured into a trap when Ankaris starts executing the innocent en masse, Amathia endures treacherous torture, Hofrax's insults and a poisonous spider bite before being rescued by Aurion.

Attaining proof of her father's demise, Amathia seizes his scepter despite the machinations of Tamis who transforms herself into a witch. Ankaris mistakenly kills his own daughter and commits suicide, paving the way for Hofrax's downfall. Ultimately, Amathia decides that "the real magic is democracy" and wisely opts to forsake further bloodshed and rule with compassion and decency instead.

The cast of BARBARIAN QUEEN 2 seems to have assembled in between stints at a topless bar in the San Fernando Valley. Even on its own limited terms, the film suffers from action scenes that are as underdeveloped as the female cast is overdeveloped; from fanciful costuming that somehow spans the eons from Cave Man Couture to contemporary House of Suede and Leather; and from a needlessly complicated plot that relies too much on Amathia's flight-and-fight syndrome. As an excuse to stare at babes, it is altogether more successful.

Structurally magnificent, Lana Clarkson (BLIND DATE, THE HAUNTING OF MORELLA) could rank right up there with the Wonders of the Ancient World, positioned right after the Hanging Gardens of Babylon. As for bad movie lovers, they will no doubt be kept busy enjoying some ham from Tijerina as the delinquent teen and Cudney as mankind's first woman hater. The film, however, does boast one classic bad movie line. Tearing off Amathia's skimpy bikini top, Hofrax regards her proud breasts and sighs in disdain: "What an awesomely disgusting sight!"

Male chauvinists will doubtless be content with BARBARIAN QUEEN 2's mindless swordplay and constant parade of exposed female flesh; camp followers will enjoy the film's cheesy good-naturedness, dreadul art direction, and costumes by Genghis of Hollywood. *(Violence, nudity.)*

p, Alan Krone, Tony Norway; d, Joe Finley; ph, Francisco Bojorques; ed, Francisco Chiu; m, Chris Young; art d, Francisco Magallon; cos, Ignacia Aguilar

Action/Adventure **(PR: C MPAA: R)**

BASIC INSTINCT ★★½

122m Carolco Pictures; Le Studio Canal Plus; Basic Inst Inc ~ TriStar Pictures c

Michael Douglas *(Detective Nick Curran)*, Sharon Stone *(Catherine Tramell)*, George Dzundza *(Gus)*, Jeanne Tripplehorn *(Dr. Beth Gardner)*, Denis Arndt *(Lieutenant Walker)*, Leilani Sarelle *(Roxy)*, Bruce A. Young *(Andrews)*, Chelcie Ross *(Captain Talcott)*, Dorothy Malone *(Hazel Dobkins)*, Wayne Knight *(John Correli)*, Daniel Von Bargen *(Lieutenant Nilsen)*, Stephen Tobolowsky *(Dr. Lamott)*, Benjamin Mouton *(Harrigan)*, Jack McGee *(Sheriff)*, Bill Cable *(Johnny Boz)*, Stephen Rowe *(Internal Affairs Investigator)*, Mitch Pileggi *(Internal Affairs Investigator)*, Mary Pat Gleason *(Juvenile Officer)*, Freda Foh Shen *(Berkeley Registrar)*, William Duff-Griffin *(Dr. Myron)*, James Rebhorn *(Dr. McElwaine)*, David Wells *(Polygraph Examiner)*, Bradford English *(Campus Policeman)*, Mary Ann Rodgers *(Nurse)*, Adilah Barnes *(Nurse)*, Irene Olga Lopez *(Maid)*, Juanita Jennings *(Receptionist)*, Craig C. Lewis *(Bartender at Police Bar)*, Michael David Lally *(Detective)*, Peter Appel *(De-*

tective), Michael Halton *(Bartender at County Western Bar)*, Keith A. McDaniel *(Featured Dancer)*, Eric Poppick *(Coroner's Guy)*, Ron Cacas *(Policeman)*, Elsie Sniffen *(Roxy's Friend)*, Ken Liebenson, Lindy Rasmusson, Byron Berline, Eddie Dunbar, Tod McKibbin *(Doo Wah Riders Band Members)*, Julie Bond *(Hand Puppet Model)*

Some mysteries are compellingly ambiguous and deal with provocative themes. They effectively put their audiences through the ringer on many levels, leaving them satisfied though vaguely uneasy. Somewhere below that are mysteries that just leave you saying, "Huh?"

BASIC INSTINCT starts on the former level but descends to the latter before it's over. That's unfortunate. Nobody makes movies quite like Paul Verhoeven, the Dutchman who carved his place in international cinema with provocative and often sexually explicit films like SPETTERS, SOLDIER OF ORANGE and THE 4TH MAN before showing box-office muscle in America with ROBOCOP and TOTAL RECALL. But, though BASIC INSTINCT is certainly never boring, Verhoeven finally surrenders to a Joe Eszterhas screenplay that self-destructs in a ridiculous maze of red herrings and reversals that raise many more questions than they answer. By now, it must be acknowledged that Eszterhas utilizes the same basic premise for every screenplay he writes: someone whose livelihood depends on cool professional objectivity gets emotionally involved, to his or her extreme peril.

This time out, Michael Douglas is that someone—San Francisco homicide detective Nick Curran, whose past history includes accidentally killing innocent bystanders and losing a wife to suicide. As we meet him, he is undergoing mandatory therapy to keep his job and fighting a losing battle with his addictions to booze and cigarettes. It probably doesn't help much that he happens to be sexually involved with his therapist, Dr. Beth Gardner (Jeanne Tripplehorn). It doesn't help either that he later gets involved with the prime suspect in the gruesome icepick murder of a former rock star. Catherine Tramell (Sharon Stone) was the last person seen with the rocker. Being a writer, it also happens that she had previously authored a pulp thriller about a fading rock star who was murdered by his lover with an icepick.

In her new book, Tramell turns to the subject of a killer cop who gets involved with the wrong woman, using Curran as her model. Curran, obviously falling in love, turns back to the booze and the butts as his affair with Tramell reaches one steamy crescendo after another. Meanwhile, the bodies begin to pile up and suspicions come to be cast on everybody in shouting distance before settling mainly on Garner, who had a lesbian affair with Tramell while both were psychology students at UC Berkeley. Without giving it completely away, the ending involves a framing and someone getting away with multiple murders.

Actually, the ending won't come as much of a surprise to anyone familiar with the Eszterhas-scripted JAGGED EDGE. Like the earlier film, BASIC INSTINCT relies on an elaborate gimmick calculated to give the killer an airtight alibi that is shocking mainly because it defies all logic and credibility. Two crucial differences are that the killer in JAGGED EDGE didn't get away with it and, more important, JAGGED EDGE didn't rely on the convincing resolution of its central mystery to make it entertaining. In BASIC INSTINCT the mystery is pretty much the whole show. It has to be, since it's so complex and unwieldy that it consumes the final third of the film with enough "startling" revelations to make even the most avid mystery fan's teeth ache. Up until it loses its way, however, BASIC INSTINCT has the makings of a provocative take on sex, power and politics in contemporary American society.

Arriving aggressively panty-less for her first interrogation, Stone's Tramell threatens to expose the law as a reactionary male construct threatened by female sexuality—all merely by exposing herself to a roomfull of policemen. Before that, Verhoeven has introduced Tramell in otherworldly terms, like some more evolved being whose mercurial sexuality hints at a degree of enlightenment that has made conventional conceptions of law, ethics and morality intellectually irrelevant. Unfortunately, the screenplay's long-range intentions are much more banal than that, in the end turning downright anti-intellectual by making the most intelligent person in the film also the most vicious.

Along the way, Eszterhas also proves himself substantially guilty of the complaints lodged against him by gay activists who protested both the making and the release of BASIC INSTINCT. All the killers (yes, there are more than one) in the film are, indeed, bisexual or lesbian females. Verhoeven's attitude seems to sour along with the screenplay, though he tries to downplay the story's implicit equation of gay sexuality with murderous insanity. It could be a consequence of a European sensibility that he instinctively depicts sexuality as incidental to, rather than definitive of, his characters. However, it seems fully his intention to portray an American society that wallows in death, drawing its nourishment, vampire-like, from the blood of the innocent.

What seems to have drawn Verhoeven to BASIC INSTINCT is its grisly resolution, which leaves the corrupt, violent and evil escaping unscathed while the sympathetic characters are systematically slaughtered. It rings intellectually true but, as has been the case with all of Verhoeven's American films, there is no emotion to his indictment. In particular there is no sense of anger or outrage, as if Verhoeven himself were afraid of involving himself. As a result, for all of its bloodletting, BASIC INSTINCT remains a curiously bloodless film. *(Violence, profanity, nudity, sexual situations, adult situations.)*

p, Alan Marshall; d, Paul Verhoeven; w, Joe Eszterhas; ph, Jan De Bont; ed, Frank J. Urioste; m, Jerry Goldsmith; prod d, Terence Marsh; cos, Ellen Mirojnick

AAN Editing: Frank J. Urioste; *AAN Best Score:* Jerry Goldsmith

Erotic/Thriller **(PR: O MPAA: R)**

BASKET CASE 3: THE PROGENY ★★½

90m Shapiro/Glickenhaus Entertainment ~ MCA/Universal Home Video c

Kevin Van Hentenryck *(Duane Bradley)*, Annie Ross *(Granny Ruth)*, Dan Biggers *(Uncle Hal)*, Gil Roper *(Sheriff Griffith)*, James O'Doherty *(Little Hal)*, Tina Louise Hilbert *(Opal)*, Carla Morrell *(1st Twin)*, Carmen Morrell *(2nd Twin)*, Jackson Faw *(Bailey)*, Jim Grimshaw *(Baxter)*, Tim Ware *(Brennan)*, Jerry G White *(Banner)*, David Milford *(Brody)*, Jeff Winter *(Renaldo)*, Heather Place *(Ellice)*, Pierre Perea *(Simon)*, Bill Scully *(Leon)*, Denice Coop *(Eve)*, Rick Smailes *(Elmo)*, Donna Hall *(Arthur)*, James Scott *(Frederick)*, Larry Hurd *(Twister)*, Cedric Maurice *(Nuke)*, Fernando Perez-Lee *(Mooney)*, Charles Portney *(Platehead)*, Marty Polak *(Toothy)*, Dean Hines *(Mousey)*, Wendy Parham *(Brainiac)*, Bunny Phipps *(Mackerel)*, Diane Oxford *(Pearl)*, James Derrick *(Basil)*, Berl Boykins *(TV David)*

What's in the basket this year? As it happens, writer-director Frank Henenlotter has taken an interest in keeping his cult series from repeating itself, and BASKET CASE 3 feels more like an honest continuation of its predecessors' story than most low-budget sequels. Of course, familiarity has taken the edge off the horror by this point in the saga, but Henenlotter evidently realized this and has made the third installment the most overtly humorous of the three.

The story reunites the by-now-unbalanced Duane Bradley (Kevin Van Hentenryck) with his deformed, murderous twin Belial, yet it separates them too. After Duane tried to sew Belial back onto his side at the end of the last film, Belial has become angry with his brother and refuses to come out of his basket to see him, despite the entreaties of their keeper, Granny Ruth (Annie Ross). The new sequel continues the psychology of mutants theme from BASKET CASE 2, and also builds upon its most bizarre moment, the love scene between Belial and his lookalike girlfriend, Eve. As the new movie opens, Eve is expecting, and the brothers, Granny Ruth and the rest of her freakish charges head south to visit Uncle Hal (Dan Biggers), a doctor who can make this very unusual delivery.

BASKET CASE 3 hits a high point during their road trip as the freaks engage in a singalong, belting out the old tune "Personality" while Ross scat-sings an accompaniment. (As a founding member of Lambert, Hendricks and Ross, the seminal vocal jazz group, Ross wrote and recorded "Twisted," later popularized by Joni Mitchell, which in part explains her association with the BASKET CASE series.) Once they arrive at their destination, a small town in Georgia, Duane briefly meets an attractive girl named Opal (Tina Louise Hilbert) before the group arrives at Uncle Hal's mansion.

The freaks make themselves at home, and Uncle Hal, assisted by his enormous, multi-armed son Little Hal (James O'Doherty), helps Eve with her birth. The result is a dozen little baby Belials, and the assembled "family" is ecstatic, especially since Duane and Belial have been reconciled. But tragedy awaits; local sheriff Andrew Griffith (Gil Roper) has become suspicious of the goings-on at the mansion, and two of his deputies break into the house, where they suddenly happen upon the sleeping Eve and awaken her. Terrified by the sight, they shoot her dead with a shotgun, then steal the bassinet full of baby Belials as the freaks attempt to give chase.

The deputies bring the bassinet to the police station; Duane, meanwhile, is also arrested and thrown into one of the cells in the back. While he's imprisoned, Opal, who turns out to be the sheriff's daughter, arrives; proving to be a closet dominatrix, she attempts to seduce him. But then a suspicious-looking basket turns up on the front doorstep; inside, of course, is Belial, who attacks the deputies remaining in the station. In the ensuing melee, the lawmen and Opal are all killed and Duane escapes. Back at the mansion, Little Hal helps Belial assemble a mysterious device, which he uses to kill off the surviving deputies in their home. When the sheriff goes to confront Duane again, he finds out what this creation is: an enormous exo-skeleton piloted by Belial. A terrible fight ensues, ending with the sheriff falling face-first into the basket of baby Belials. When last seen, the freaks are overrunning a TV talk show . . . .

BASKET CASE 3 may be Henenlotter's (BRAIN DAMAGE, FRANKENHOOKER) slickest film yet, and those who enjoyed the gritty, grainy original may be put off by what appears to be an attempt to go mainstream. But the director's off-the-wall sensibilities are as evident here as ever, and the "Personality" singalong and Eve's birthing of the 12 lookalike infants are wonderfully weird highlights. Both of these sequences occur before the movie's midpoint, which helps, since the story isn't quite as strong as it was in BASKET CASE 2.

That film created some memorable antagonists in its tabloid reporter and sleazy detective; here, the Bradleys and company run up against a sheriff and his deputies, a more standardized movie threat. But if the plot isn't quite as compelling this time around, there are many memorable individual scenes, some of them effective straight horror (especially Eve's fate at the hands of the panicked deputies), more of them blackly comic.

It helps that Henenlotter has a cast that's right on the movie's twisted wavelength, including returning stars Van Hentenryck and Ross, who still seem completely at ease performing with a cast of made-up monsters; Roper, the stalwart sheriff who doesn't let the freaks faze him either; and Hilbert, who possesses the same cool beauty as BASKET CASE 2's Heather Rattray, as the surprisingly kinky sheriff's daughter.

The film, co-written by Robert Martin, looks great on a low budget, and although Gabe Bartalos and Dave Kindlon's special effects and makeup are more clever than convincing, they do a fine job on Belial himself, as well as the robotic creation he commandeers in the movie's later sequences. *(Excessive violence, profanity, sexual situations.)*

p, Edgar Ievins, Leonard Shapiro; d, Frank Henenlotter; w, Frank Henenlotter, Robert Martin; ph, Bob Paone; ed, Greg Sheldon; m, Joe Renzetti; prod d, William Barclay; art d, Caty Maxey; set d, Sharon Braunstein; cos, Carleen Rosado; fx, Gabe Bartalos; makeup, Dave Kindlon

Horror/Comedy **(PR: O MPAA: R)**

BATMAN RETURNS ★★½

126m Warner Bros.; Polygram Pictures ~ Warner Bros. c

Michael Keaton *(Batman/Bruce Wayne)*, Danny De Vito *(The Penguin/Oswald Cobblepot)*, Michelle Pfeiffer *(Catwoman/-Selina Kyle)*, Christopher Walken *(Max Shreck)*, Michael Gough *(Alfred–The Butler)*, Michael Murphy *(The Mayor of Gotham)*, Cristi Conaway *(The Ice Princess)*, Andrew Bryniarski *(Chip Shreck)*, Pat Hingle *(Police Commissioner Gordon)*, Vincent Schiavelli *(The Organ Grinder)*, Steve Witting *(Josh)*, Jan Hooks *(Jen)*, John Strong *(Sword Swallower)*, Rick Zumwalt *(Tattooed Strongman)*, Anna Katarina *(Poodle Lady)*, Gregory Scott Cummins *(Acrobat Thug One)*, Erika Andersch *(Knifethrower Dame)*, Travis McKenna *(Fat Clown)*, Doug Jones *(Thin Clown)*, Branscombe Richmond *(1st Terrifying Clown)*, Paul Reubens *(Penguin's Father)*, Diane Salinger *(Penguin's Mother)*, Stuart Lancaster *(Penguin's Doctor)*, Cal Hoffman *(Happy Man)*, Joan Jurige *(Happy Woman)*, Rosie O'Connor *(Adorable Little Girl)*, Sean M. Whalen *(Paperboy)*, Erik Onate *(Aggressive Reporter)*, Joey DePinto *(1st Shreck Security Guard)*, Steven Brill *(Gothamite 1)*, Neal Lerner *(Gothamite 2)*, Ashley Tillman *(Gothamite 3)*, Elizabeth Sanders *(Gothamite 4)*, Henri Kingi *(Mugger)*, Joan Giammarco *(Female Victim)*, Lisa Coles *(Volunteer Bimbo)*, Frank DiElsi *(Security 1)*, Biff Yeager *(Security 2)*, Robert Gossett *(TV Anchorman)*, Adam Drescher *(Crowd Member)*, Robert N. Bell, Niki Botelho, Susan Rossitto, Margarita Fernandez, Denise Killpack, Felix Silla, Debbie Lee Carrington *(Emperor Penguins)*

Director Tim Burton's storytelling skills have undergone no noticeable improvement since the original BATMAN in this bloated, murky, disjointed and meanspirited sequel that wastes the performances of its three leading villains.

In the promising prologue, an infant born deformed and with a bad attitude is dumped into a river by his horrified parents (Diane Salinger and Paul "Pee-Wee Herman" Reubens). Thirty-three years later, the infant reemerges as the villainous Penguin (Danny De Vito), who brings a circus-themed gang of killer tumblers, clowns and fire breathers to disrupt a Christmas tree lighting ceremony in Gotham City as cover for kidnapping tycoon Max Shreck (Christopher Walken). The Penguin has dirt on Shreck's secret history of social crimes and threatens to expose him unless he helps the Penguin reenter society to track down his parents. Forced to oblige, Shreck mounts a PR campaign that is so successful it catapults the Penguin into a race for mayor of Gotham against the earnest incumbent (Michael Murphy) who's run afoul of Shreck.

You-know-who (Michael Keaton) smells a rat in the Penguin. Digging into past news clippings, Batman discovers that, years earlier and for reasons never explained, the Penguin's gang kidnapped and murdered infants. The crime fighter suspects that Penguin may be planning another baby bloodbath and springs into action. He receives help from an unlikely quarter when Shreck's secretary, Selina Kyle (Michelle Pfeiffer), stumbles onto her boss's history of misdeeds and is summarily hurled from the top floor of his skyscraper. Miraculously resuscitated by a throng of feline vistors, Selina stitches a rubber raincoat into a tailored, tight-fitting costume and reemerges as Catwoman, sworn to vengeance against Shreck. Batman's alter-ego, fabulously wealthy Bruce Wayne, develops a yen for Catwoman's secretarial alter-ego, which further complicates the convoluted climax, involving Shreck locked in a cage in the Penguin's lair in the Arctic section of the Gotham Zoo and a flotilla of real penguins armed with tiny missiles to lay waste to the city. Batman, aided by faithful butler Alfred (Michael Gough), turns Penguin's penguins against him, destroying him and the zoo. Catwoman kills Shreck before apparently escaping for a future sequel.

The average Batman comic book (particularly the recent graphic novels by Frank Miller which reinvented Batman as a darker, tormented figure) is probably better plotted than this expensive mess. BATMAN RETURNS is crammed with enough incidents to fuel three movies, but never develops any pace, momentum or coherence. Things happen for no discernible reason and in no discernible order. Why the film even starts with the Penguin's origins is puzzling, since the major villain turns out to be Shreck, whose zany plan to hold Gotham's electricity for ransom might have been a better plot hook if it had been given more emphasis. For all his screen time, the Penguin remains an enigma from start to finish. Why he misspent his childhood killing other children is never explained; nor are his gang, who remain devoted despite not doing anything criminally or otherwise lucrative at any point during the film. And why anyone would want to live in the refrigerated bowels of a zoo with someone as ugly and relentlessly meanspirited as the Penguin is something that desperately needs explaining. Catwoman is nominally more compelling because she, at least, has a job. She also has strong motivation for getting even with Shreck.

Amid the otherwise undermotivated, dispiriting violence—attractive women being beaten and dropped off highrise buildings, machine guns being fired into crowds—Batman is virtually a guest star in his own movie, absent much of the time and not really dominating the action when he is around. Keaton's screen time is so scant that it's difficult to measure his performance. However, if the main criterion is being able to wear that suit without looking silly, he succeeds here as well as he did before. Pfeiffer gets the most mileage out of her sketchy character, making up in delicious attitude what Catwoman, as written, often lacks in dialogue.

The Penguin is thoroughly repulsive inside and out, but DeVito plays him with a demented, ravenous, randy glee that succeeds mainly in further highlighting the script's weaknesses. Though left out of the star billing, Walken deserves equal credit. As the only major character without an outrageous costume (true, his hairstyle would turn heads on Wall Street), he has to work harder to make an impression, and does, with just the right mixture of muted malevolence and tongue-in-cheek humor.

The major stale ingredient continues to be Burton, a visual genius who, by his own frequent admission, hasn't a clue about putting his creations together with movement, action and narrative. He could forge a career and a legacy out of overseeing future Batman films as a producer, but he really should be stopped before he directs again. *(Violence, profanity, adult situations.)*

p, Denise DiNovi, Tim Burton; d, Tim Burton; w, Daniel Waters, Sam Hamm, (from story by Waters and Hamm based on the characters by Bob Kane); ph, Stefan Czapsky; ed, Chris Lebenzon; m, Danny Elfman; prod d, Bo Welch; art d, Rick Heinrichs; set d, Cheryl Carasick; cos, Bob Rigwood, Mary Vogt; fx, Michael Fink, Dennis Skotak, John Bruno, Craig Barr; makeup, Ve Neill, Ronnie Specter, Stan Winston

AAN Visual Effects: Michael Fink, Craig Barron, John Bruno, and Dennis Skotak; *AAN Makeup:* Ve Neill, Ronnie Specter, and Stan Winston

Adventure/Crime/Fantasy (PR: C MPAA: PG-13)

BEASTMASTER 2: THROUGH THE PORTAL OF TIME ★★

107m Republic Pictures; Portal Productions; Films 21 ~ New Line Cinema c

Marc Singer *(Dar)*, Wings Hauser *(Arklon)*, Sarah Douglas *(Lyranna)*, Kari Wuhrer *(Jackie Trent)*, James Avery *(Captain Coberly)*, Robert Fieldsteel *(Bendowski)*, Robert Z'Dar *(Zavik)*, John Fifer *(Creature)*, Charles Hyman *(Inquisitor)*, Eric Waterhouse *(Exeter)*, Charles Young *(Lead)*, Arthur Malet, Michael Berryman, David Carrera, Carl Ciarfalio, Larry Dobkin, Steve Donmeyer, Richard Duran, Jim Eagle, Doug Franklin, Kyle Fredericks, Gordon Greene, Paul Goodman, Lawrence Mandley, Alva Megowan, Daniel O'Haco, Wayne Pere, Jeanne Pfleiger, Rex Pierson, Mark Roberts, David Sederholm, Vic Trevino, Dick Warlock, Dan Woren

When a genre wears itself out the next-to-last step is self-parody, and BEASTMASTER 2: THROUGH THE PORTAL OF TIME falls right in line. The foolish original came along in 1982, as part of a boomlet in CONAN-influenced sword-and-sorcery epics. But the theatrical market for wizards and warriors has since dried up, and this direct-to-video sequel drops the earnest attitude of its predecessor in favor of laughs.

The title hero is Dar (Marc Singer), a muscular barbarian who can communicate with and command a rather skimpy posse of animal friends—a tiger, an eagle and a pair of ferrets. In this adventure he's warned that his long lost brother Arklon (Wings Hauser), an evil monarch, has plans that could bring calamity to the universe. Sure enough, Arklon has linked up with Lyranna (Sarah Douglas), a shapely witch who wisecracks in modern slang—a trait she picked up from her travels in time and space via a "dimensional portal" to "a planet called LA."

As Arklon and Lianna putter with the portal an unforgivably perky Valley-girl teen named Jackie Trent (Kari Wuhrer) speeds through it in her red Porshe. "Way rad!" is her evaluation of Dar and his savage realm; she thinks he's with a circus. Arklon and Lyrrana go through the portal in search of the neutron detonator, a newfangled doomsday bomb hidden on a military base conveniently close to Los Angeles. Dar and Jackie pursue them, and lots of culture-shock gags ensue. The Beastmaster and his animal entourage get chased by the LAPD and stuck in the Griffith Park zoo, while Arklon and Lyranna shop for leather villainwear at a trendy Rodeo Drive-type boutique (staffed by a swish with the worst mock-French accent of the year). Eventually Arklon is destroyed, the neutron detonator is disarmed and Dar goes back to his homeworld. A neat punchline finds that red Porshe being worshipped there as a god.

Observant viewers will spot a credit stating that this whole rigmarole is "based" on a novel by fantasy and science-fiction author Andre Norton. Indeed, her 1959 work *The Beastmaster* was supposedly adapted for the first film, but when Norton read the screenplay she was so appalled that she dissociated her name from the project. On the advice of her agent, Norton got the credit restored for the sequel, even though she summed up both films as "atrocious." Neither storyline has anything to do with the literary precursor, a neat blend of space opera and Western involving a a spacegoing Navaho war hero who settles the Final Frontier with his fur-and-feathered allies.

No, the real *auteurs* behind BEASTMASTER 2 are two of the seven (!) credited screenwriters, specifically Jim Wynorski and R.J. Robertson, longtime Roger Corman cohorts with a nutty sense of humor and an appreciation of the B-Movie mentality. Wynorski in particular seems to specialize in camping up low-grade sequels. He's worked on DEATHSTALKER II, BIG BAD MAMA 2, THE RETURN OF SWAMP THING and others. So the satire in BEASTMASTER 2 hardly breaks new ground, but it's a tonic that makes the minutes pass more or less agreeably. The time-warp stuff isn't too original either; one gets the feeling it was an expediency that saved the producers the cost of building big, primordial sets in the Arizona desert.

The violence is mild, so bloodless that even Dar's pet eagle has a Tinkerbell-style recovery from a severe wound. If anything makes BEASTMASTER 2 questionable fare for impressionable kids (apart from swearing) it's MTV-personality Kari Wuhrer's hyper-sassy role as a rich senator's irresponsible daughter, first seen recklessly outracing the cops in her sportscar as she trills "I am *so* cool!" Parents may prefer Wings Hauser's Arklon as a role model. The bad news for mankind is that Jackie Trent stays on Earth at the end, but the filmmakers apparently forgot all about Lyranna, who just vanishes from the narrative. Too bad, because she's truly a fun vamp character played to the hilt by the sexy Douglas. Leading man Singer is appropriately deadpan and impressively pumped-up after ten years, even if his long blond hair in this outing is a stringy wig.

The film's highlight comes when the transplanted Dar does a double-take at an LA cinema marquee promoting a movie called . . . BEASTMASTER 2! There's more truth to that than one might think; LA was one of the few markets where this sequel received theatrical release before passing through the Portal of Home Video in 1992. *(Violence, profanity.)*

p, Sylvio Tabet; d, Sylvio Tabet; w, Jim Wynorski, R.J. Robertson, Sylvio Tabet, Ken Hauser, Doug Miles, (from the story by Wynorski and Robertson based on the characters created by Paul Pepperman and Don Coscarelli adapted from the novel *The Beastmaster* by Andre Norton); ph, Ronn Schmidt; ed, Adam Bernardi; m, Robert Folk; prod d, Allen Jones; art d, Patrick Tatopoulos; set d, Richard Kremer; cos, Betty Madden

Fantasy/Adventure **(PR: C MPAA: PG-13)**

BEATING HEART, A ★★★

(France) 100m Hachette Premiere; Union Generale Cinematographique; Avril SA; FR3 Films Production ~ MK2 Productions USA c

(COEUR QUI BAT, UN)

Dominique Faysse *(Mado)*, Thierry Fortineau *(Yves)*, Jean-Marie Winling *(Jean)*, Christophe Pichon *(Stephane)*, Steve Kalfa *(Luc)*, Coralie Seyrig *(Jeanne)*

It seems as if the French turn out intelligent love stories as briskly, effortlessly and competently as Hollywood turns out dopey, over-produced, impersonal action movies. A most charming case in point, A BEATING HEART hangs on the slight but tantalizing premise of what would happen if two strangers trading glances were to follow through on their initial interest.

The strangers make contact aboard an elevated train. Mado (Dominique Faysse) is an aging but attractive housewife and radio actress in a dreadful soap opera. The man, Yves (Thierry Fortineau), is hardly a dreamboat. Somewhat grungy, ill-kempt and emotionally volatile, he has an occupation, but once he meets Mado and immediately whisks her off to the nearest hotel room for an afternoon of passionate lovemaking, he has no other meaningful life. She doesn't want to see him again, but he insists on givinq her his phone number. She uses it at least in part, it seems, out of revenge when she suspects that her husband Jean (Jean-Marie Winling) is having an affair with a customer. Examining her life, she realizes that her marriage has become inert and empty since her teenage son moved out. She also becomes impatient with the tyrannical no-talent director of her radio show.

Yves, meanwhile, whom we see nothing of when he's not with Mado, becomes increasingly obsessed with her. Their affair becomes a succession of terse, anguished calls from public phones and meetings in out-of-the-way cafes leading to furtive couplings in anonymous hotel rooms and long walks afterwards, which often end in quarrels as Yves's infatuation intensifies his jealousy of Mado's married life. The bad news for Yves is that rather than breaking up her marriage, the affair seems to give Mado a new determination to make her life and marriage worthwhile. She keeps trying to break up with Yves, but he keeps pleading for one last chance, which she keeps giving him. Their final rendezvous is to be at one of their favorite hotels, but Mado arrives late after taking her son shopping. Yves has already left, but the clerk tells Mado that he has been staying in their room every day since the last time they made love there. Mado leaves a message for Yves that she will return the next day.

Helped by a capable cast, writer-director Francois Duperyon achieves an almost unnerving emotional intensity in A BEATING HEART, a small-scale love story that is at once utterly commonplace yet unfailingly engrossing and poignant. It also points to a possible reason that French love stories tend to make better films than their American counterparts. As evidenced herein, the French tend to view love as a part of life rather than as something separate, magical and exalted. Characters fall in love as a part of their daily existence, whereas in American films love is often seen as a form of escape or a secular means of transcendence.

What makes A BEATING HEART most "foreign" is that Duperyon finds Mado the realist more interesting than Yves the romantic. Their key scene comes unexpectedly, durinq one of their "final" meetings, when Yves has a street artist sketch Mado only to complain that the artist has failed to capture the confusion and frustration in her eyes. When the artist protests that he sees nothing there but happiness, Yves is outraged, but Mado suddenly realizes that she *is* basically happy with her life. She still loves Jean and begins paying more attention to him, as she does to her son and even to her acting job which, like everything else in her life, she begins pursuing with a new enthusiasm. Yves clearly doesn't fit into her life, but it is through him that Mado begins to feel better about herself. Hence, one suspects that long after the fadeout there will be many "final" meetings before it's finally over.

A BEATING HEART really is, as one character says, like a drum—familiar, even predictable, but nonetheless primal, compelling and, like so many French love stories, utterly unforgettable. *(Adult situations, sexual situations, nudity.)*

p, Rene Cleitman; d, Francois Dupeyron; w, Francois Dupeyron; ph, Yves Angelo, Francoise Collin, Florence Emir; ed, Francoise Collin; cos, Florence Emir

Drama/Romance **(PR: C MPAA: NR)**

BEAUTIFUL DREAMERS ★★★

(Canada) 107m Stairway Films; National Film Board of Canada ~ Hemdale Releasing c

Colm Feore *(Dr. Maurice Bucke)*, Rip Torn *(Walt Whitman)*, Wendel Meldrum *(Jessie Bucke)*, Sheila McCarthy *(Molly Jessop)*, Colin Fox *(Reverend Randolph Haines)*, David Gardner *(Dr. Lett)*, Tom McCamus *(Leonard Thorn)*, Barbara Gordon *(Agatha Haines)*, Marsha Moreau *(Birdie Bucke)*, Albert Schultz *(Dr. John Burgess)*, Angelo Rizacos *(Wallace)*, Gordon Masten *(John Carver)*, Gerry Quigley *(John Freeman)*, Roland Hewgill *(The Honorable Timothy Pardee)*, Roger Clown *(Kenneth)*, Peter Blais *(Delbert)*, R.D. Reid *(Karl Jessop)*, Martha Cronyn *(Lizzy)*, Jeff Braunstein *(Eddy)*, J. Winston Carroll *(Henderson)*, Bob Clout *(Dr. McAlpine)*, J.R. Zimmerman *(Chairman)*, Bernard Behrens *(Dr. Winslow)*, Doug Hughes *(Charles)*, Jefferson Mappin *(William)*, Tim MacMenamin *(Blacksmith)*, Chris Benson *(2nd Drunk)*, George Buza *(1st Drunk)*, Deborah Tennant *(Lady)*, Kory Taylor *(Loon Singer)*, Roy Wordsworth *(Player)*, Barrie Baldaro *(Umpire)*, Karen Kenedy *(1st Female Assistant)*, Damon Redfern *(Bowler)*

Veteran character actor Rip Torn stars as 19th-century poet Walt Whitman in BEAUTIFUL DREAMERS, a charming tale of sympathy, understanding and friendship.

Set in Canada circa 1880, the story revolves around Dr. Maurice Bucke (Colm Feore), a young psychiatrist who seeks to change some of the barbaric methods used to treat patients at his asylum. After meeting the radical and outspoken American writer Whitman at a medical conference in Philadelphia, Maurice decides Walt's philosophy of human compassion offers a new approach to treating the mentally ill.

As Maurice's consultant at the asylum in the town of London, Whitman is shocked to see patients strapped to beds, used as medical guinea pigs and so on. He convinces Maurice that the mentally ill need to be treated in a more humane way. Although Maurice's colleagues are extremely skeptical about his proposed changes, he goes ahead with them anyway. He abolishes the use of restraints or physical abuse, and instead starts exercise and dance programs for the asylum inmates. And slowly but surely, the hospital becomes a less dismal place and the patients become more receptive to therapy.

Meanwhile, back at the Bucke household, Maurice's wife Jessie (Wendel Meldrum) isn't sure she likes having a "free-thinker" like Whitman in her house. But after awhile, she gets used to the crusty but benign American. In the final scene, the town comes to see a cricket game between the asylum residents and the local team. Most of the patients aren't too coordinated, but just participating in an outdoor activity gives them a sense of accomplishment. A simple game of cricket has not only provided a good therapeutic outlet for them, but it helps the local residents realize that the mentally ill have the same kinds of needs as the rest of us.

Writer-director John Kent Harrison presents an important human interest story without being melodramatic or preachy. Also, the acting is very good indeed. Torn, in fact, is portraying Whitman for the second time; the first was in "Song of Myself," a 1976 TV presentation. Sheila McCarthy (I'VE HEARD THE MERMAIDS SINGING, STEPPING OUT), who plays a schizophrenic named Molly, delivers an especially moving and believable performance. And Francois Protat's photography gives viewers a real feel for the lush outdoor scenery. *(Violence, profanity, nudity, sexual situations.)*

p, Michael MacLear, Martin Walters; d, John Kent Harrison; w, John Kent Harrison; ph, Francois Protat; ed, Ron Wisman; prod d, Seamus Flannery; set d, Anthony Greco; cos, Ruth Secord

Drama/Historical **(PR: C MPAA: PG-13)**

BEBE'S KIDS ★★★

73m Hyperion Animation Company; Paramount ~ Paramount c

VOICES OF: Faizon Love *(Robin Harris)*, Vanessa Bell Calloway *(Jamika)*, Wayne Collins, Jr. *(Leon)*, Jonell Greene *(LaShawn)*, Marques Huston *(Kahlil)*, Tone-Loc *(Pee-Wee)*, Myra J. *(Dorothea)*, Nell Carter *(Vivian)*, John Witherspoon *(1st Card Player)*, Chino "Fats" Williams *(2nd Card Player)*, Rodney Winfield *(3rd Card Player)*, George Wallace *(4th Card Player)*, Brad Sanders *(Bartender)*, Reynaldo Rey *(Lush)*, Bebe Drake-Massey *(Barfly)*, Jack Lynch *(Richie)*, Phillip Glasser *(Opie)*, Louie Anderson *(Security Guard)*, Tom Everett *(2nd Security Guard)*, Kerrigan Mahan *(3rd Security Guard/Fun World Patrolman)*, Susan Silo *(Ticketlady/Saleswoman/Nuclear Mother/Rodney Rodent)*, Peter Renaday *(Announcer/President Lincoln/Impericon/Tommy Toad)*, Rich Little *(President Nixon)*, David Robert Cobb *(Titanic Captain)*, Barry Diamond *(Nuclear Father/Motorcycle Cop)*, Stanley B. Clay, Michelle Davison, Judi Durand, Greg Finley, Maui France, Jaquita Green, Jamie Gunderson, J.D. Hall, Doris Hess, Barbara Iley, Daamen Krall, John LaFayette, Tina Lifford, Josh Lindsay, Arvie Lowe, Jr., De'Vaughn Nixon, David Randolph, Noreen Reardon, Gary Schwartz, Cheryl Tyre Smith

The animated children's film BEBE'S KIDS is based on the popular nightclub act of the late Black comedian Robin Harris. Unusually for the genre, BEBE'S KIDS includes a healthy dose of realism, offering an alternately comic and poignant view of a group of mischievous latchkey children and their reluctant father-for-a-day.

A drunken Robin (voice of Faizon Love) tells the story of his relationship with girlfriend Jamika (Vanessa Bell Calloway) to a bartender. In a flashback, Robin tells how he met Jamika at a friend's funeral. He's immediately smitten by the beautiful secretary, his late friend's lover, but Jamika resists his advances. She agrees to give Robin a ride home, however, and makes a date with him when he befriends Leon (Wayne Collins, Jr.), her sweet son. Robin is ecstatic, but his joy quickly turns to exasperation when Jamika insists on bringing, in addition to Leon, several children she's babysitting—"Bebe's kid's." These tykes—LaShawn (Jonell Greene), Kahlil (Marques Huston) and Pee-Wee (Tone-Loc)—are quite a handful.

Robin drives the group to Fun World, a fascistic amusement park where uniformed security guards enforce strict rules and persecute Bebe's kids, who can never stay out of trouble. Just as Robin gets some time alone with Jamika, he runs into his ex-wife Dorothea (Myra J.) and her friend Vivian (Nell Carter), who decide to interfere in his date. As the women plot to make Jamika jealous, Bebe's kids pick on shy Leon. Then, however, the children unite to lead other kids in a rebellion against the amusement park's controllers. Kahlil is put on trial by a mechanized robot, but the kids escape and comandeer a pirate ship. Meanwhile, Robin proves his love to Jamika by confronting his ex-wife.

The group leaves Fun World and Robin takes Bebe's kids home to their run-down, dirty apartment, where their errant mother has left only a note. Although sympathetic to their plight, Robin orders the kids a pizza and leaves. Jamika quarrels with

Robin, who doesn't want to see the kids again. Back in the present, Jamika suddenly visits Robin at the bar, they reconcile and he walks toward her car—in which Leon, and Bebe's kids, are waiting. Resigned to his fate, Robin drives off with his extended family.

Reginald Hudlin's screenplay has a sophistication rarely seen in animated children's features, and includes some jokes that only adults will appreciate. The movie's slim narrative is sustained by Robin's snappy reactions to the kids' misbehavior. Like a Black animated W.C. Fields, Robin constantly deals with the kids' physical and verbal abuse. "I am pissed off to the highest level of pissivity!" he exclaims to Jamika as his day turns into a nightmare. Robin dubs Pee-Wee "test tube baby" and says the kids would "be better off in Ethiopia." He advises Leon to impress Bebe's awful offspring by showing self-confidence, then tells him to "knock the hell out of them kids!" Hudlin also makes several subtle points about the experience of African-Americans within a predominately white society. In a gift shop, Bebe's kids flip through racks of personalized items with names such as Joe, John and Peggy. "How come we can't ever find our names?" LaShawn wonders.

Director Bruce Smith is adroit in his use of animation. Robin's overweight, sluggish appearance and big round eyes make him instantly funny, while Jamika's sloe-eyed beauty lingers in the mind long after the movie ends. The drawing of Leon, however, should have had more depth; he appears as a generic good boy. Among Bebe's kids, Pee-Wee stands out as a baby whose facial expressions make him look older than his age.

The character of Pee-Wee also features the best voice work. The concept of a baby speaking like an adult is cliched, but rap star Tone-Loc's low, growly vocal style puts a wild spin on the idea. Pee-Wee is not cute—when he opens his mouth, he's downright menacing.

Other than a labored ending to the amusement park outing, and some unneeded musical interludes, BEBE'S KIDS is an excellent combination of witty entertainment and realistic social commentary.

p, Thomas L. Wilhite, Willard Carroll; d, Bruce Smith; w, Reginald Hudlin, (based on the characters created by Robin Harris); ed, Lynne Southerland; m, John Barnes; prod d, Fred Cline; anim, Lennie Graves, Chris Buck, Frans Vischer

Animated/Children's/Comedy (PR: C MPAA: PG-13)

BECOMING COLETTE ★★

(Germany/U.K./France) 97m Bibo Filmproduktions; BC Productions; Les Films Ariane; Wizan/Black Films; Peer Oppenheimer Productions; Becoming Colette Productions ~ Castle Hill c

Klaus-Maria Brandauer *(Henri Gauthier-Villars)*, Mathilda May *(Sidonie Gabrielle Colette)*, Virginia Madsen *(Polaire Sorel)*, Paul Rhys *(Chapo)*, John Van Dreelen *(Albert)*, Jean-Pierre Aumont *(Captain)*, Lucienne Hamon *(Sido)*, Georg Tryphon *(Creditor)*, Jockel Tschiersch, Frank Demules, Vincent Nadal, Maya Thebeault, Cecile Bois, Eva Probst, Patrick Fontana, Jean-Max Brua, Delphine Rich, Bertrand Treuil, Pierre Bayle, Valerie Abril, Peer Morkeborg, Valerie Ancel, Yvan Blanloeil, Cecile Aubague, Anne-Marie Rastel, Tracy Mueller, Kira Lingenberg, Costanze Moericke, Miriam Dreschler, Ines Goeritz, Miriam Wolff, Radestina Parvanova, Carola Schweiger, Anna Blank, Wendy Kamp, Nicola Futterer, Nicole Xavier-Zimmerman, Libby Farr, Sebastian Laas, Peter Mann, Wolfgang Fechner, Mladen Dean, Rainer Homann, Ared Hubert, Andrej Diamantstein, Karl Dick Schmidt, Connie Diem, Ralf Raeuker, Ulricke Sturzbecher, Alfred Hartung, Imad Tabsch, Thorsten Hiedel

Danny Huston's BECOMING COLETTE is a lushly photographed and erotically charged rendering of the life of legendary French authoress Gabrielle Colette.

Gabrielle (Mathilda May) is a beautiful country girl in her late teens. Well educated and independent, she is the daughter of an unsuccessful author, and she too has a fondness for writing. Gabrielle keeps a diary at her father's insistence. When a publisher from Paris, Henri Gauthier-Villars (Klaus-Maria Brandauer), visits her home, he is taken with the innocence and beauty of the young girl. Before long they are married and living in Henri's Paris apartment. The virginal Gabrielle gives herself fully to her new husband, unaware of his various mistresses and penchant for kinkiness. Soon after he arranges for a *menage a trois* with his favorite paramour, Polaire Sorel (Virginia Madsen), a seemingly wanton actress with the Folies Bergere. Gabrielle initially balks at the idea, but then willingly becomes lovers with her, bringing forth a newfound sexual liberation. Along with his carnal predilections, the manipulative Henri has a failing publishing house and growing debt due to his lavish spending. When he discovers Gabrielle's diary he realizes his problems are over. He convinces her to begin writing a novel based on her diary.

The result is a splendid tale of sexual awakening—the first of Colette's amazingly successful *Claudine* books. Henri insists, however, that the world would never accept such a novel from a female writer and therefore puts his name on the cover as the supposed author. Gabrielle reluctantly agrees and watches as her books become the rage of Europe. A virtual slave to her writing, and rarely able to leave her country house, she is living a very unfulfilled life. The occasional visits to Polaire, who has proven herself a true friend, and to a young Bohemian artist, Chapo (Paul Rhys), are all that keep her going. Henri's erratic behavior grows even more harsh—he spends all of their money on his lovers and rarely sees Gabrielle, and then only to pick up her most recent chapters.

The final blow occurs when Gabrielle learns that her mail has been intercepted by her husband. In fact, her father has fallen ill but Henri kept the news from her so that she would continue working. After visiting her papa she promises to turn her life around. Back in Paris she is ultimately betrayed anew when Henri promises to reveal Gabrielle as the true author of the books. At a meeting of France's literary elite, he once again claims the glory for himself. Chapo rises and identifies Gabrielle as the true scribe. She is finally liberated from the control of Henri who leaves in disgrace. Gabrielle takes her place at the top of the literary world.

The multifaceted relationship between Henri and Gabrielle, encompassing as it does the universal conflict between love and betrayal, is the catalyst for BECOMING COLETTE and it's on this intimate scale that Danny Huston's film works best. Even turning it into a triangular tale, upon Polaire's arrival, works because the focus remains on the human aspect. In capturing a large portion of someone's life, and certainly someone as complex as Colette, the narrative can get lost in the chronological pacing of the script. Thankfully that doesn't occur here. Instead, Ruth Graham's screenplay uses the author's early adulthood as the focal point of the story. Colette's formative years are made clear earlier through ample exposition and her success in later years, of course, is common knowledge.

Despite its heroine's relatively advanced age, BECOMING COLETTE is very much a coming of age story—both spiritually and sexually. Huston captures the story intelligently and truthfully, and with a nice dose of humor. The characterizations are wonderful. As Gabrielle, May (THE CRY OF THE OWL, NAKED TANGO) captures the change—from innocent schoolgirl to emancipated woman—with her expressive eyes and body language. She is that rare beauty whose performance could be overshadowed by her appearance. Her elocution and bearing are all that Colette's must have been, and a better casting choice is hard to imagine.

With his devilish performance as Henri, Brandauer continues to show why he's one of Europe's top stars. And Huston made a smart choice by not portraying Villars as a complete rogue. The poignant epilogue which suggests Henri's exoneration rings true and releases the character from a probable life of pain. As the sensual Polaire, Madsen (SLAM DANCE, THE HOT SPOT) shows surprising range. Nepotism works in this case, as Huston has cast his own wife in this pivotal role. They do their best to make her look merely attractive, but Madsen's beauty is hard to disguise.

Less successful are the larger scenes which begin to resemble badly staged costume epics. A backstage moment at the theater has a plethora of bumbling reporters crowded around the star Polaire—none of the actors seem to know what to do with themselves. When there are fewer than four characters onscreen, Huston is fine, but in the scenes requiring background action he loses control of the directorial reins. Also, there's a tendency when shooting period pieces to show off that era on an unnecessarily grand scale and unfortunately Huston follows suit. Berlin fills in admirably for the bustling streets of Paris, but the requisite shots of horse-drawn carriages, ornate costuming, big mustaches and extras extraordinaire are overly used. These all too familiar elements don't aid the story at all—but one would have to agree that an audience probably expects them.

With the previous MR. NORTH to his credit as well, Danny Huston is following in his famous father's footsteps by tackling films with substance and scale. BECOMING COLETTE may not seem like an obvious choice for a young American director, but he does a fine job with it, being backed up with a sturdy screenplay, solid cast and an engaging theme. *(Profanity, nudity, sexual situations, adult situations.)*

p, Peer Oppenheimer, Heinz Bibo; d, Danny Huston; w, Ruth Graham, Burt Weinshanker; ph, Wolfgang Treu; ed, Peter Taylor, Roberto Silvi; m, John Scott; prod d, Jan Schlubach, Berge Douy; cos, Barbara Baum

Biography/Drama **(PR: C MPAA: R)**

BED & BREAKFAST ★★★

97m Schwartzman Pictures ~ Hemdale Releasing c

Roger Moore *(Adam)*, Talia Shire *(Claire)*, Colleen Dewhurst *(Ruth)*, Nina Siemaszko *(Cassie)*, Ford Rainey *(Amos)*, Stephen Root *(Randolph)*, Jamie Walters *(Mitch)*, Cameron Arnett *(Hilton)*, Bryant Bradshaw *(Julius)*, Victor Slezak *(Alex Caxton)*, Jake Webber *(Bobby)*, Chevi Colton *(Hope Bowers)*, Frank Dolan *(Charlie Bowers)*, Harriet Rogers *(Elderly Shopper)*, Marceline Hugot *(Eloise)*, Bronia Stefan Wheeler *(Bessie)*, John Savoia *(Man at Church)*, Leila Carlin *(Mrs. Van Dyke)*, Samantha Belle *(Sam the Dog)*

Barely released in theaters, BED & BREAKFAST is nevertheless a low-key charmer from director Robert Ellis Miller recalling, though not quite as good as, his earlier REUBEN, REUBEN.

In a picturesque but rundown bed and breakfast hotel just outside one of those New England coastal towns populated entirely by crusty but lovable eccentrics, widowed Ruth (Colleen Dewhurst) lives with daughter Claire (Talia Shire) and granddaughter Cassie (Nina Siemaszko). Also a widow, Claire has been emotionally traumatized by revelations in an expose biography that her late husband, a famous 1960s activist, was a philanderer. But she still believes fervently in those ideals and tries to foster them in Siemaszko with a fundamentalist's zeal that has driven a wedge between them. Nevertheless, Cassie has put off pursuing her budding career as a musician and composer and Ruth avoids the romance she still fervently desires, both in order to care for Claire and help her through her troubles.

Their lives are shaken up by the arrival of Adam (Roger Moore), a charming con man who literally washes up on shore one day near their home, having been thrown off a boat by one of his wealthy victims. Concealing his past, he feigns amnesia to protect his "hostesses" from the possibility that the person who pitched him off the boat may come looking for him to finish the job. He also feigns skills as a handyman to earn his room and board. But he proves instead to be a skilled handyman of the heart in helping all three women get more out of life.

Adam encourages Cassie in her career ambitions, leading her to decide to move to New York City. Nudging Ruth leads her to finally bed the crusty but lovable lobster fisherman with whom she's had a long-running platonic relationship. He intervenes more directly with Claire, bedding and falling in love with her after a contentious courtship. But a run-in with the bad guys reminds Adam that his past could be a recurring problem. He steals away in the middle of the night. Showing her renewed zeal for life, Claire encourages her daughter to leave and her mother to move in with her lobster fisherman. She sells the bed and breakfast and joins Adam, who had earlier dropped hints about where he might head, to pursue her own ambitions to paint and run a coffee house.

Cindy Myers's screenplay could easily be criticized for being both fanciful and predictable. In its broad outlines, the plot for BED & BREAKFAST reads more like a pilot for a sitcom than a feature film, which could explain its quick route to home video. Details, however, are what count in a film like this. Miller's direction works well to minimize the screenplay's real weaknesses—a tendency towards melodrama in the plotting and preachiness in the dialogue—and play up its strengths—a respectfulness and genuine affection for its characters that prevents them from turning into stereotypes. Miller's particular strength is with actors. Has either Tom Conti or Kelly McGillis ever been as memorable as they were in REUBEN, REUBEN?

In one of her last performances, Dewhurst enlivens her familiar gritty authority with a sensuality usually denied women over 40 in Hollywood productions. Moore, meanwhile, though scarcely younger than Dewhurst and old enough to be Shire's father, is nevertheless nicely understated and plausible as the kind of worldly and world-weary man who might be just what the doctor ordered for Shire's grieving widow. He's more likably roguish than slick and even though his pairing with Shire is a given from the outset, it's not treated as a given in the screenplay, direction or Moore's performance. Hers is a love he has to earn. And it's one worth earning.

Shire's usual intensity works well here to define her character; combining a fiery passion and intelligence with a hard-headed integrity, she convinces that she would be a prize for any man. Siemaszko also well conveys her character's inherited passion, pride and intelligence despite an odd inconsistency in her character that has her neurotically embarrassed by her rapidly burgeoning physical womanhood while at the same time she's supposedly engaged in a no-sweat sexual relationship with her boyfriend.

While lacking the sharp wit brought to REUBEN, REUBEN by screenwriter Julius Epstein, BED & BREAKFAST has ample compensations in its performances, genuine good vibes and New England setting. *(Adult situations.)*

p, Jack Schwartzman; d, Robert Ellis Miller; w, Cindy Myers; ph, Peter Sova; ed, John F. Burnett; m, David Shire; prod d,

Suzanne Cavedon; art d, Ron Wilson; cos, Jennifer Von Mayerhauser

Romance/Comedy **(PR: C MPAA: R)**

BEETHOVEN ★★½
89m Ivan Reitman Productions ~ Universal c

Charles Grodin *(George Newton)*, Bonnie Hunt *(Alice Newton)*, Dean Jones *(Dr. Herman Varnick)*, Nicholle Tom *(Ryce Newton)*, Christopher Castile *(Ted Newton)*, Sara Rose Karr *(Emily Newton)*, Oliver Platt *(Harvey)*, Stanley Tucci *(Vernon)*, David Duchovny *(Brad)*, Patricia Heaton *(Brie)*, Laurel Cronin *(Devonia Peet)*, O-Lan Jones *(Biker Woman)*, Nancy Fish *(Miss Grundel)*, Craig Pinkard *(Homeless Man)*, Robi Davidson *(Mark)*, Sherri Paysinger *(Reporter)*, Patrick LaBrecque *(1st Bully)*, Jacob Kenner *(2nd Bully)*, Matthew Brooks *(3rd Bully)*, Chris Little *(Newsreader)*, Lisa Gerber *(Donna)*, Cory Danziger *(Mark's Friend)*, Colleen O'Hara *(Young Woman)*, Nicolas Mize *(Young Man)*, Maxine Elliot *(Old Woman)*, Stephanie Massman *(Young Woman)*, Cirroc Lofton *(1st Skateboarder)*, Chad Morton *(2nd Skateboarder)*, Melora Walters *(Pet Shop Owner)*, Holly Wortell *(2nd Nurse)*, Lorraine Marga *(Mother at Pet Store)*, Joseph Gordon-Levitt *(1st Student)*, Andres McKenzie *(2nd Student)*

As many a frustrated moviegoer will attest, most contemporary trailers endeavor to sell films with little regard to their actual content; creative editing makes heavy drama look like eroticism, satire seem to be slasher horror and absolutely *anything* appears to be an action adventure. In a refreshing departure from this maddening marketing strategy, the advance promo for BEETHOVEN promised audiences a predictable, dumb, family dog comedy—and that's exactly what this is.

The title character begins as a nameless St. Bernard pup in a pet store. A pair of comical burglars (whose resemblance to HOME ALONE's Joe Pesci and Daniel Stern will gain significance later on) raid the shop to seize dogs to sell for sadistic medical experiments. The puppy escapes from their van, however, and finds his way to the Newton household. Persnickety dad George Newton (Charles Grodin) cringes at the thought of a beast messing up his suburban castle, but his three children insist, so George promises to let the puppy stay for a brief time. That brief time runs to months, during which the St. Bernard swells to 185 pounds of enthusiastic fur, odor and drool.

Choosing his own name by howling when daughter Ryce (Nicholle Tom) pounds out the Fifth Symphony on the piano, Beethoven quickly proves his worth to the kids: its helps Ryce gain a boyfriend, backs up Ted (Christopher Castile) against school bullies, and rescues littlest daughter Emily (Sarah Rose Karr) from drowning. George still can't warm to the slobbering hound, and he's easily tricked into leaving the dog with malevolent veterinarian Dr. Varnick (Dean Jones). Varnick's the evil mastermind behind the dognappers from the start of the tale, and the huge Beethoven draws his greedy gaze because he needs a lab animal with a big, thick skull to test a new hollow-pointed bullet. Of course George has a change of heart, discovers Dr. Varnick's perfidy and liberates Beethoven (the old milquetoast "earns the respect of his loved ones through fighting" routine), adopting not only the St. Bernard but all the other captive canines.

BEETHOVEN is a safely banal concoction in the tradition of the bland live-action Disney features cranked out during the Magic Kingdom's dispirited years after Walt's death. That BEETHOVEN succeeded at the box office proved, in the year of BASIC INSTINCT, that a lucrative market still exists for family films—and not necessarily good ones.

At its heart BEETHOVEN is just a collection of Pavlovian kids-and-critters cliches that Hollywood has flogged to death since the days of D.W. Griffith: show the animal in peril, turn up the sad music; show the kid in peril, turn up the scary music; have the animal rescue the kid, then do a tension-relieving gag about the heroic animal soiling the living-room rug. One wonders what cosmic justice prevailed to make this film a smash while 1991's BINGO, which burlesqued the conventions of savior-pooch movies, bombed. Maybe St. Bernards mean big bucks, though (with the exception of Steven King's CUJO) when you've seen one trained St. Bernard you've pretty much seen them all, and Beethoven is played by a massive but uninspiring specimen named Chris.

The prizewinner among human performers here is Charles Grodin (THE HEARTBREAK KID, MIDNIGHT RUN), a sly, subdued comic actor who hits the right notes in George Newton's exasperated slow burns. The downright perverse casting of longtime Disney mainstay Dean Jones (THAT DARN CAT, THE SHAGGY D.A.) as the sadistic Varnick is fun at first, but the character's ham-handed exaggeration soon becomes grating.

Director Brian Levant made his movie debut helming the noxious PROBLEM CHILD 2. Executive producer Ivan Reitman became a comedy czar with titles like GHOSTBUSTERS and KINDERGARTEN COP. But one big name behind BEETHOVEN went unnoticed, concealed behind the literary pseudonym "Edmond Dantes" in the screenwriting credits. It was in fact John Hughes, of HOME ALONE fame (no wonder those two burglers looked familiar). Rumored to be as temperamental as he is successful, Hughes reportedly hid his authorship of BEETHOVEN partially because of a displeasure with Universal Pictures, and partially to avoid the brickbats of rabid anti-Hughes movie reviewers.

In the latter case, he was wise; critics have attacked his parade of middle-class middle-American comedies—FERRIS BUELLER'S DAY OFF, SOME KIND OF WONDERFUL, THE GREAT OUTDOORS, UNCLE BUCK, CAREER OPPORTUNITIES, CURLY SUE—as progressively cloying and repetitious, and BEETHOVEN indeed incorporates recognizable Hughes motifs like intermittent slapstick, canned familial warmth and situations stacked on the basic premise of kids—and in this case, a dog—who are a lot brighter and nicer than the uptight and/or malicious adults around them. Beethoven's not only a better parental unit than George Newton, he has more business sense; when a venal yuppie couple urge the oblivious George to sign a contract that would cost him his air-freshener factory, it's the dog that somehow figures that something's fishy and pulls a move with its leash that sends the fast-track nasties flying. Really, that's taking anthropomorphism a bit far, even for this picture. *(Violence, profanity.)*

p, Joe Medjuck, Michael C. Gross; d, Brian Levant; w, John Hughes, Amy Holden-Jones; ph, Victor J. Kemper; ed, Sheldon Kahn, William D. Gordean; prod d, Alex Tavoularis; art d, Charles Breen; set d, Gary Fettis

Comedy/Children's **(PR: A MPAA: PG)**

BEETHOVEN LIVES UPSTAIRS ★★★
(Canada) 52m Devine Videoworks; Eros Financial Investments Inc.; Classical Productions for Children Inc. ~ BMG Distribution c

Neil Munro *(Ludwig van Beethoven)*, Illya Woloshyn *(Christoph)*, Fiona Reid *(Mother)*, Paul Soles *(Schindler)*, Albert Schultz *(Uncle Kurt)*, Sheila McCarthy *(Sophie)*

A cursory but effective glimpse—and not much more than that—of musical genius Ludwig van Beethoven (1770-1827), BEETHOVEN

LIVES UPSTAIRS was derived from the "Classical Kids" recordings series.

Toronto teacher Susan Hammond hatched Classical Kids in 1988, as an entertaining way to introduce youngsters to the lives of the world's great composers. Each audio title is a historical docudrama depicting a Bach, Mozart or Vivaldi as seen through the wide eyes of a juvenile companion. David Devine, a director of children's videos starring the acclaimed entertainer Raffi, found out about Classical Kids and helped transfer its Beethoven installment to the small screen. The result is a modest little picture that should indeed enlighten schoolchildren but doesn't push the envelope far beyond that.

Beethoven's Boswell is Christophe (Illya Woloshyn), adolescent son of a Viennese widow who rents out a spare floor to the celebrated composer (Neil Munro). Christophe is far from starstruck; the legendary Beethoven, dogged by deafness and personal problems, dresses like a tramp and acts like a lunatic. With his stocky frame, unkempt hair and rude manner, Beethoven makes an embarrassing association for Christophe as he mutteringly stomps up the stairs, throws things at the maid and, half-naked, scrawls his music on walls and windowshades. Christophe's Uncle Kurt (Albert Schultz) explains Beethoven's private pain, rooted in a miserable childhood and, of course, the hearing disorder that prevents him from savoring the incomparable melodies filling his own mind.

Christophe becomes Beethoven's admirer, occasional helper and companion on daily walks with the composer, who is struggling to complete his epochal Ninth Symphony. Though Christophe never knows whether he's in the temperamental man's good graces or not, Beethoven ultimately gives the boy and his mother tickets to the symphony's debut performance on May 7, 1824—a momentous occasion during which Beethoven, unable to sense the audience ovation behind him, continued to conduct after the piece had finished. It was, in fact, Beethoven's final public appearance. He died three years later, and the film ends with a brief flash-forward to Beethoven's funeral.

BEETHOVEN LIVES UPSTAIRS follows the audio version's narrative closely, almost slavishly so, and one wishes that a little more time and trouble had gone into expanding the scope. Beethoven's music soars almost continually as background music, which was fine for the recording but a little strange in a visual drama with so much ado over the fact that Beethoven can't hear. Only a minor attempt is made to describe what made his compositions great, and purists may rightly complain that there's too much emphasis on the icon-busting portrait of the artist as dysfunctional egocentric, a sort of AMADEUS for kids. Plus the real Beethoven's last years included a bitter, antagonistic relationship with a teenage nephew over whom the composer fought a custody battle, a biographical snippet conveniently overlooked in this kid-friendly drama.

Be that as it may, this incomplete sketch of Beethoven is better than none, and for young viewers it serves as a nicely accessible entry to the topic without condescension, meaning that adults can also watch without pain. Illya Woloshyn is a bright and personable young narrator, while well-known Canadian character actress Sheila McCarthy (I'VE HEARD THE MERMAIDS SINGING, BEAUTIFUL DREAMERS) does an amusing turn as the household's long-suffering maid, repeatedly seen dodging the angry maestro's missiles. As Beethoven, Neil Munro glowers, laughs and composes with equal fervor and avoids the temptation to be just silly. Director Devine uses Prague (where AMADEUS was also lensed) as an effective substitute for old Vienna, though he has a distracting habit of employing tilted camera angles *a la* the old "Batman" TV show to reflect Beethoven's anguished mental state.

Once BEETHOVEN LIVES UPSTAIRS was completed there were plans to adapt other entries in the Classical Kids series, with Vivaldi nominated as the most likely followup.

p, Richard Mozer, David Devine; d, David Devine; w, Heather Conkie, (from the origional work by Barbara Nichol); ph, David Perrault; ed, Rick Morden; m, Ludwig van Beethoven; prod d, Cameron Porteous

Biography/Children's (PR: AA MPAA: NR)

BERNARD AND THE GENIE ★★½
70m BBC Enterprises; Attaboy-Talkback Productions ~ FoxVideo c

Alan Cumming *(Bernard Bottle)*, Lenny Henry *(Josephus–the Genie)*, Rowan Atkinson *(Charles Pinkworth)*, Dennis Lill *(Frank Kepple)*, Bob Geldof, Kevin Allen, Andre Bernard, Angie Clarke, David Forman, John Gabriel

Lenny Henry is a favorite in his native England, an actor and stand-up comedian sometimes compared to Eddie Murphy, not only for their common skin color but also in terms of his potential for international stardom. Unfortunately, Henry's highly touted American debut, the 1991 farce TRUE IDENTITY, fizzled at the box office.

He's somewhat better served by BERNARD AND THE GENIE, a droll British offering that casts him as Josephus, an ancient Mideastern chap imprisoned in a genie lamp by an angry wizard. Two thousand years later the lamp is accidentally rubbed by its present owner Bernard Bottle (Alan Cummings), a kindly fellow who's having a bad day; he's lost his art-collecting job for failing to defraud some old ladies; he's been framed for sexual harassment; his girlfriend has left him for his best mate; and the genie's explosive entrance lands him in the hospital. Things change once he and Josephus overcome their mutual shock, and Bernard takes the genie on a tour of London, where Josephus eagerly discovers fast food, ice cream, Barry White music and TERMINATOR 2. There's a minor plot with Bernard accused of stealing the "Mona Lisa" and killing a policeman, but Josephus's magical powers fix everything in an instant.

It happens to be Christmas, and Josephus knew Jesus personally: "He helped with the wine at my brother's wedding!" Upset at rampant commercialism of the Nativity, Bernard and Josephus take action, transforming a department-store Santa display into an enchanted grotto that makes wishes come true. Various children happily depart with a giant Paddington bear, a kid-sized sportscar and a real live Teenage Mutant Ninja Turtle (David Forman, the screen's original "Leonardo," cameos in full turtle gear). One could well argue that this also has nothing to do with the religious basis of Christmas, and neither do some revenge tricks the genie springs on Bernard's tormentors from earlier in the movie. The short feature ends when homesick Josephus beseeches Bernard to wish him back to his own era, and his friend and master complies.

Made for BBC-TV and released direct-to-video stateside, BERNARD AND THE GENIE is a cute confection so far as it goes. A limitation for Yank audiences is that many jokes revolve around Commonwealth celebrities; one had best be acquainted with Melvyn Bragg, Gary Lineker, Felicity Kendall, Kylie Minogue and Julian Lloyd-Webber (Andrew's brother). At least Bob Geldof should be no stranger. At one point Bernard wishes he could look like the Irish rock star, and the real Geldof plays him for the rest of the scene (the punchline is that onlookers mistake him for Mick Jagger).

Overall the humor is transitory, some of it off-color—a surprise to parents who may mistake this for children's fare—and highly dependent on the engaging actors. As the hapless Bernard, Alan Cumming is an appealingly downtrodden nice guy who makes the perfect foil for Josephus's expansive clowning. Henry certainly has charm, and between him, Robin Williams in ALADDIN and Ami Dolenz in MIRACLE BEACH, 1992 was a boom year for screen genies.

Prominently billed in the small role of Bernard's avaricious boss is Rowan Atkinson (THE TALL GUY, THE WITCHES), another comic performer considered one of Britain's best. Playing yet another supercilious prig (he fires employees with the line "Exit ye!"), does nothing here that we haven't seen many times before. (Screenwriter Richard Curtis has written extensively for Aktinson, including the British TV series "Black Adder", which has aired on PBS, and the movie "The Tall Guy".

Director Paul Weiland, meanwhile, suffered a transatlantic career catastrophe as the unfortunate behind the wheel of the costly Bill Cosby bomb LEONARD PART 6. Back on home soil for BERNARD AND THE GENIE, Weiland executes the gags with a quick pace, clever use of set design and small-scale special effects on what was obviously a modest budget. Go in peace, and sin no more. *(Violence, sexual situations.)*

p, Jacinta Peel; d, Paul Weiland; w, Richard Curtis; ph, Roger Pratt; ed, Ian Weil; m, Howard Goodall; prod d, John Beard, Rod McLean

Comedy/Fantasy (PR: A MPAA: NR)

BEST INTENTIONS, THE ★★★★

(Sweden) 182m Sveriges Television/SVT1 Drama Dept; Zweites Deutsches Fernsehen; Channel Four; RAI-TV Channel 2; La Sept; Danmarks Radio; YLE 2; Norsk Rikskringkasting; Rikisutvarpid-Sjonvarp ~ Samuel Goldwyn Company c

Samuel Froler *(Henrik Bergman)*, Pernilla August *(Anna Akerblom-Bergman)*, Max Von Sydow *(Johan Akerblom–Anna's Father)*, Ghita Norby *(Karin Akerblom–Anna's Mother)*, Bjorn Kjellman *(Ernst Akerblom–Anna's Brother)*, Borje Ahlstedt *(Carl Akerblom–Anna's Half-Brother)*, Bjorn Granath *(Oscar Akerblom–Anna's Half-Brother)*, Gunilla Nyroos *(Svea Akerblom–Oscar's Wife)*, Mikael Segerstrom *(Gustov Akerblom–Anna's Half-Brother)*, Eva Grondahl *(Martha Akerblom–Gustav's Wife)*, Mona Malm *(Alma Bergman–Henrik's Mother)*, Keve Hjelm *(Fredrik Bergman–Henrik's Paternal Grandfather)*, Margaretha Krook *(Blenda Bergman–Henrik's Aunt)*, Irma Christensson *(Ebba Bergman–Henrik's Aunt)*, Sif Ruud *(Beda Bergman–Henrik's Aunt)*, Lena Brogren *(Miss Lisen)*, Cecilia Lagerkvist *(Miss Siri)*, Lena Endre *(Frida Strandberg–Henrik's First Fiancee)*, Dan Johansson *(Justus Bark–Henrik's Fellow Student)*, Niklas Hald *(Baltzar Kugelman–Henrik's Fellow Student)*, Ernst-Hugo Jaregard *(Professor Sundelius)*, Hans Alfredson *(Reverend Gransjo)*, Lena T. Hansson *(Magda Sall)*, Lennart Hjulstrom *(Nordenson–Landowner and Owner of the Works)*, Marie Goranzon *(Elin Nordenson)*, Bjorn Gustavson *(Jesper Jakobsson)*, Roland Hedlund *(Herman Nagel–Works Manager)*, Elias Ringkvist *(Petrus Farg)*, Leif Forstenberg *(Mr. Johansson)*, Sara Arnia *(Mrs. Johansson)*, Boel Larsson *(Mia)*, Inga-Lill Ellung *(Mejan)*, Gun Jonsson *(Marta Lagerstam)*, Ernst Gunther *(Uncle Freddy)*, Marie Rickardson *(Marta Werkelin)*, Emy Storm *(Tekla Kronstrom)*, Barbro Kollberg *(Gertrud Tallroth)*, Inga Landgre *(Magna Flink)*, Inga Alenius *(Alva Nykvist)*, Tomas Bolme *(Jansson)*, Mikael Bengtsson *(Arvid Fredin)*, Pia Bergendahl *(Mrs. Fredin)*, Kare Santesson *(Mans Lagergren)*, Max Winderal *(Count Robert)*, Jan Blomberg *(Count Svante)*, Anita Bjork *(Queen Viktoria)*, Ake Lagergren *(Chamberlain Segersward)*, Bertil Norstrom *(Alopeus)*, Gaby Stenberg *(Matron Fanny)*, Gosta Pruzelius *(County Sheriff)*, Puck Ahlsell *(Clergyman Levander)*, Nils Eklund *(Churchwarden)*, Tord Peterson *(Coachman)*

There is nothing extraordinary about Henrik and Anna, the central couple of THE BEST INTENTIONS, except for the fact that they are the fictionalized parents of the great Swedish filmmaker Ingmar Bergman. Nevertheless, as remembered by the film's screenwriter, Bergman himself, and visualized by the director, fellow Scandinavian Bille August, they become profoundly moving examples of the power of human passion.

Henrik Bergman (Samuel Froler) is invited to dine with the grand, bourgeois Akerblom family by his seminary school-friend Ernst (Bjorn Kjellman). He falls in love instantly with Ernst's disarming, headstrong sister, Anna (Pernilla August). She soon visits the men at school and professes her attraction to Henrik. Disapproving Mrs. Akerblom (Ghita Norby) hears of their meeting and invites Henrik to the family summer house. While the others are out on a wagon ride, Mrs. Akerblom threatens to reveal to Anna that Henrik is already engaged to a devoted, voluptuous waitress, Frida (Lena Endre), if he doesn't dissociate himself from her daughter. Henrik leaves, and Mrs. Akerblom tells Anna about Frida.

The following winter, Frida finds Anna and begs her to take Henrik back, since he is losing his mind without her. Before she can contact him, however, Anna succumbs to tuberculosis and is sent to a sanatorium in Switzerland. She writes Henrik professing her continuing devotion, but her parents intercept the letter and Mrs. Akerblom burns it. After Anna recovers, her mother takes her on a trip to Italy to further postpone any contact with Henrik. While traveling they receive word that Mr. Akerblom has died. Stricken by grief and guilt, Mrs. Akerblom confesses to Anna what she did with the letter. Back in Sweden, Anna is reunited with Henrik and the two get engaged. They make a trip north to visit Henrik's mother and his new village parish. His mother, a simple woman, silently prays that God will stop their marriage.

Henrik and Anna arrive in the austere village of Forsboda during a factory workers' demonstration. They visit the small, sparse chapel and have a vicious fight about the upcoming wedding—they had planned a large celebration but now Henrik wants to be married in the village. Eventually the two are married in the sumptuous style Anna had wanted, but they skip their honeymoon and move directly to bleak Forsboda, where they are quickly accepted into village life; while Anna wins the appreciation of the village women and beautifies their home, Henrik's congregation grows. He allows the factory workers to hold a socialist meeting in the chapel, but is confronted by the sour industrialist, Nordenson (Lennart Hjulstrom). Anna gives birth to a little boy, Dag, and seems to bloom in motherhood. She and Henrik also take in an abused boy, Petrus (Elias Ringkvist).

Because of his good work in Forsboda, Henrik is asked by Queen Sophia to become the chaplain at a hospital in Stockholm. Dedicated to the village, Henrik refuses the offer, infuriating Anna. In the meantime, Nordenson has pulled his daughters out of confirmation class and turned the town against the Bergmans. They begin to discuss moving to Stockholm. Petrus overhears them, projects his terror onto little Dag, and tries to drown him. Anna, who has had all she can take, goes back to live with her family, leaving Henrik to a bitter, monk-like existence. After a harsh winter alone, Henrik makes his way to the Akerblom's home, and he and Anna decide to move to Stockholm.

A deeply satisfying film, THE BEST INTENTIONS, honored with the prestigious Palm d'Or at the 1992 Cannes Film Festival, uses its considerable length to examine the early relationship of Bergman's parents with uncompromising thoroughness. Nothing is rushed, not the initial delight of Henrik and Anna's union, nor their first agonizing separation, nor their explosive yet dependent marriage. The audience is pulled into their relationship by the pace as well as Bergman's perfect, translucent dialogue.

The relationship reflects the film's backdrop of class strife, but never does that become the film's central issue. It is a reality which coexists with the smaller world of their marriage. And Henrik's difficulties with the Akerbloms may be an example of class conflict, but they are not a parable for Marxist theory.

Similarly dedicated to truth is the development of characters: neither Anna nor Henrik is romanticized. With to-the-bone performances, Pernilla August and Samuel Froler expose Henrik and Anna as alternately violent, pathetic and heroically loving. Max Von Sydow is matchless as Anna's adoring father. Beautifully shot in shades of pearl and pale yellow and green, THE BEST INTENTIONS becomes a fully visceral film. One feels the chill of snow, first sunlight of spring, as well as the sweetness and awful vulnerability of Henrik and Anna's impossible love. *(Adult situations.)*

p, Lars Bjalkeskog; d, Bille August; w, Ingmar Bergman; ph, Jorgen Persson; ed, Janus Billeskov-Jansen; m, Stefan Nilsson; prod d, Anna Asp; cos, Ann Mari Anttila

Drama/Romance **(PR: C MPAA: NR)**

BEYOND DARKNESS ★½

(Italy) 94m Filmirage ~ Imperial Entertainment Corporation c

Gene Le Brock *(Peter)*, David Brandon *(Father George)*, Barbara Bingham *(Annie)*, Michael Stephenson *(Martin)*, Theresa F. Walker *(Carole)*, Stephen Brown *(Reverend Jonathan)*, Mary Coulson *(Bette)*

A few scary images fail to distinguish BEYOND DARKNESS, an Italian entry in the haunted house genre that's mostly content to pillage THE EXORCIST and POLTERGEIST—it even contains an angelic, blonde little girl named Carole.

Carole (Theresa F. Walker) moves with her father, a reverend named Peter (Gene Le Brock), her mother Annie (Barbara Bingham), and her brother Martin (Michael Stephenson) into a new house. The family is excited about their new dwelling, though it's a bit unnerving that the kids' room comes with a giant sculpture of a black swan. Carole discovers a brilliant light streaming from a hole in the wall, but when she calls Martin to see it, the light disappears. That night, however, Martin is startled to see the swan statue rocking by itself. Supernatural forces are clearly at work, and things come to a head one night while the family is having dinner. The radio suddenly turns on by itself and broadcasts strange, demonic chants, glasses and dishes fly off the shelves and a meat cleaver flies across the room and barely misses Peter. As if this isn't bad enough, the doors upstairs open to reveal horrible figures draped in black cloaks.

Peter goes to confront Rev. Jonathan (Stephen Brown), who sold him the house, and the elderly clergyman admits that he sent Jonathan and his family there on purpose: The place is haunted, having been built over the site of a mass witch-burning, and Jonathan figured that Peter, with the strength of his family behind him, would be able to exorcise the place. Jonathan also warns Peter to avoid Father George (David Brandon), another one of his pupils who has lost his faith after a frightening encounter with a child-murdering satanist, Bette (Mary Coulson), while serving his priestly duties at a nearby jail. Later, out on the street, Peter is accosted by George, who tries vainly to convince Peter to let him join him in combating the evil. That night, however, the spirits appear once again, terrorizing Peter's family and kidnapping Martin. George appears at the door as they are about to flee, and joins Peter in venturing into the spirits' realm to retrieve the boy. They appear to succeed, but soon discover that the child they have carried out is a supernatural impostor, and that the real boy is still being held by the ghosts.

The family decides to stay at the house another night, but when the bogus Martin tries to carry Carole into the spirit world, Peter insists that Annie take her to Jonathan's house. He and George then attempt an exorcism on the demonic child; they at first appear to be successful, but the boy is still possessed and leads George to his death. Peter goes back into the netherworld alone on a final attempt to reclaim his son, just as Annie arrives back at the house. Following Peter's trail into the beyond, she discovers him possessed as well, and about to deliver a fatal knife blow to their sleeping son, under the command of the witches' leader. But after a struggle, Peter regains control, and he and Annie stab the witch and flee with Martin. The house explodes as the couple and their son drive off—not noticing that Martin's eyes still bear the possessed gleam.

This attempt at a final scare is utterly predictable, and indeed it is BEYOND DARKNESS's utter familiarity that undoes it. Though the image of the large black swan is an eerie one, and the dark figures looming in doorways carry a chill or two in their early appearances, the frights in general are pedantic and the storyline proceeds with such predictability that the film loses its chance for true scariness. It also suffers from a problem plaguing many a haunted-house picture, that is, why don't the characters just leave? After the first outburst in the kitchen, the family foolishly decides to run upstairs instead of making a beeline for the front door, even though they have already been confronted by plenty of supernatural warnings.

Despite the filmmakers' best efforts, the characters are not especially compelling with their various religious crises, and it's a bit distracting that the leads all closely resemble more established Hollywood names. Le Brock is a dead ringer for Christopher Reeve, while Brandon bears more than a passing resemblance to "Twin Peaks" veteran Ray Wise and Bingham looks remarkably like Catherine Hicks. Their performances are okay, though they are frequently undone by their dialogue; the kids' lines are even worse, and Walker is an especially unconvincing young actress in any case.

BEYOND DARKNESS was originally known in Italy as LA CASA 5, marking it as part of a series that began with the retitled EVIL DEAD and EVIL DEAD II and continued with two unrelated films known as GHOSTHOUSE and WITCHERY in the US. Like TROLL 2, another 1992 direct-to-video release, BEYOND DARKNESS was written and directed by Claudio Fragasso under one of his pseudonyms, and like the former, his writing credit on the cassette box is a different *nom de film* from the one in the movie itself. Of interest to exploitation fans is that both movies feature costume design by Laura Gemser, better known for her appearances in numerous European softcore items, including a series of unofficial EMMANUELLE sequels. *(Violence, profanity, adult situations.)*

d, Claudio Fragasso; w, Claudio Fragasso, Sarah Asproon; ph, Larry J. Fraser; ed, Kathleen Stratton; m, Carlo Maria Cordio; art d, Thomas S. Lennox; cos, Laura M. Gemser

Horror **(PR: O MPAA: R)**

BEYOND JUSTICE ★★

(Italy) 113m Titanus Produzione ~ Vidmark Entertainment c

Rutger Hauer *(Tom Burton)*, Carol Alt *(Christine Sanders)*, Elliot Gould *(Lawyer)*, Omar Sharif *(Emir)*, Kabar Bedi *(Moulet)*, Brett Halsey *(Sal)*, Jan Bick Stewart, David Flosi, Larry Dolgen

Viewing BEYOND JUSTICE is like stepping into a Hollywood time machine and landing back in the heyday of John Wayne and Maureen O'Hara. Has the world really been waiting for another desert adventure featuring shieks, camels, heir-snatching and infidels filmed in a retro-style that matches the dated subject matter?

Millionairess Christine Sanders (former covergirl Carol Alt, doing a fair impression of Grace Kelly) should never have married Moulet (Kabar Bedi), an emir's black-sheep son, much less given birth to his child. Now Moulet's Koran-quoting father (Omar Sharif) claims his grandson Robert must take his rightful place ruling the family's desert empire. Who you gonna call when your rather brattish tyke is whisked off to North Africa? Why international soldier of fortune Tom Burton (Rutger Hauer), that's who. Despite sage counsel from an advisor, Sal (Brett Halsey), and an attorney (Elliot Gould), Christine insists on crashing the rescue party.

While the emir flaunts his kingdom before his young heir, Burton and company scheme to infiltrate his fortress by posing as arms dealers. Despite such glitches as a faulty radio, which forces Burton's partner to abandon him temporarily, and a sandstorm which gutsy Christine insists the rescue team endure, Burton is soon able to initiate his surprise attack from inside the fortress. With eventual assistance from the torn-between-two-worlds Moulet and a secret passageway, Robert is able to escape. When the emir pursues the heir-nappers, he's sidetracked by a vicious attack from an old enemy. Offered his choice of prep school or oasis, the boy who would be emir opts for a return ticket to America where he already lives like royalty.

The luminous photography captures the burnished gold of the desert sun; the lush musical score swells with epic abandon; the audience snoozes. Not one unpredictable moment mars the perfect undramatic arc of this suspenseless concoction. Somehow it's a comfort to realize that not even exploding tanks or loud inter-tribal warfare is going to shake you from your torpor. While the production values are superior and the cast is competent, the plot has been bounced over this particular camel hump once too often, and the actors have been hired to embody types rather than flesh-and-blood characters. Since the heroes are well-paid mercenaries, it's hard to root for them. Worse yet, the character of the coveted Robert is given such a spoiled personality and is portrayed by such a smug little trouper that you hope he will solve everyone's disagreements by getting killed in crossfire.

What BEYOND JUSTICE delivers is a tedious child-custody battle plunked down in the middle of a foreign legion fantasy. Mediocre from start to finish, the film is handsomely mounted but enervating. Poor Omar Sharif: he must be wondering how he got from David Lean's LAWRENCE OF ARABIA to this bargain basement corner of the Sahara. *(Violence.)*

d, Duccio Tessari; w, Adriano Bolzoni, Sergio Donati, Luigi Montefiori; ph, Giorgio Di Battista; ed, Mario Morra; m, Ennio Morricone; prod d, Luciano Sagoni

Action/Adventure **(PR: C MPAA: R)**

BIAN ZHOU BIAN CHANG
(SEE: LIFE ON A STRING)

BIG GIRLS DON'T CRY . . . THEY GET EVEN ★★
96m New Line; Perlman Productions; MG Entertainment; Katja Motion Pictures Inc. ~ New Line c

Hillary Wolf *(Laura Chartoff)*, David Strathairn *(Keith Powers)*, Margaret Whitton *(Melinda Powers)*, Griffin Dunne *(David Chartoff)*, Patricia Kalember *(Barbara Chartoff)*, Adrienne Shelly *(Stephanie Miller)*, Dan Futterman *(Josh Powers)*, Jenny Lewis *(Corrine)*, Ben Savage *(Sam)*, Trenton Teigen *(Kurt)*, Jessica Seely *(Emma)*, Jim Haynie *(Sheriff)*, Googy Gress *(Dad)*, Meagen Fay *(Mom)*, Leslie Engelberg *(Melissa)*, Ivory Ocean *(Teacher)*, Samir Kamoun *(Driver)*, Buck Kartalian *(Dog Owner)*, Keith E. MacKechnie *(Patrolman)*, Lori June Moore *(The Concerned Camper)*, Joseph D'Angerio *(Mr. Zordani)*, Cory Danziger *(Leonard)*, Sean Blackman *(1st Runaway Boy)*, Denis Heames *(2nd Runaway Boy)*, Joann Passantino *(Runaway Girl)*, Marc Grapey *(Employee)*, Angelina Estrada *(Rosario)*, Shaggy Murphy *(1st Kid)*, Reilly Murphy *(2nd Kid)*, Harmony Murphy *(3rd Kid)*, Michael Murphy *(4th Kid)*, Ethan Flinders *(5th Kid)*, Ashton Flinders *(6th Kid)*, Joey Sciacca *(Hunk)*, Jessica Seely *(Jessie)*, Bill Erickson *(1st Trooper)*, Salomon Marx *(2nd Trooper)*, Paul Short *(3rd Trooper)*

Rodney Dangerfield once joked about a kid who was so mean he'd glue worms to the sidewalk and watch the birds get hernias. Such is the hernial effort that director Joan Micklin Silver invests in BIG GIRLS DON'T CRY . . . THEY JUST GET EVEN, a tepid teenage angst sitcom, in a futile effort to wring some meaning and emotion from Frank Mugavero's shallow and rattleheaded screenplay.

Thirteen-year-old Laura Chartoff (Hillary Wolf), a lonely and unloved victim of multiple parental divorces and remarriages, introduces her "modern-day fairy tale . . . less simple and with lawyers." Laura lives with her current stepfather, Keith Powers (David Strathairn), an aloof and cold executive, and her frivolous, uncaring mother, Melinda (Margaret Whitton), while her biological father, David (Griffin Dunne), a reserved and unsuccessful artist, estranged from his second wife Barb (Patricia Kalember), is now cohabitating with his flighty young girlfriend Stephanie Miller (Adrienne Shelley), who is pregnant with twins. After a fight with Melinda and Keith, Laura runs away to a lakefront cabin being built by her older stepbrother Josh (Don Futterman). But when Laura spots Keith and Melinda driving up the cabin path, she takes off into the woods. Before long, she's reported missing and the remaining members of her extended family appear at the cabin to aid in the search.

In this rustic setting, the family members come to terms with each other, and Laura, realizing that there is no place like home, returns to the cabin and her family, taking Josh's advice that "You can't run away from these people." At one point in the film, when Laura is still on the run from her family, she is taken in by a terminally happy family that sings the "Brady Bunch" theme—and means it. After she regales the children with a tall tale about how her parents were secret agents killed by a foreign power, the Dad (Googy Gress), out of character, tells Laura that he doesn't appreciate being lied to, criticizing her glib attitude. And "glib" is the problem of the entire film.

By pitching BIG GIRLS DON'T CRY . . . THEY GET EVEN at a passionless sitcom level, writer Frank Mugavero trivializes Laura's problems and undercuts any emotional involvement with the characters. Laura addresses the camera like a pubescent Woody Allen ("My Mom worked all her life to get this shallow") and minimizes viewer empathy by spouting smart-alecky ripostes (confronting her Mom and Keith about a planned trip to Hawaii, she wails, "I hope you choke on poi . . . I hope the Don Ho Show really sucks") more appropriate to a thirtysomething character in a James L. Brooks movie than a teenage girl.

Mugavero further obscures character development by depicting Laura's step-siblings as television comedy brats (the stuck-up sister, the ten-year-old computer wiz, the cute toddler) with no substance beyond their cliched attributes. When Laura heads for the hills, the members of her extended family relate to one another in a thoroughly vacant, gag-like manner. This film's idea of a joke is everyone crowded around the cabin's bathroom mirror to brush their teeth.

The transparency of Mugavero's characters puts a heavy burden on Joan Micklin Silver to elicit energy and feeling out of thin air. And this she does, up to a point. The film is forever in motion, Micklin Silver adding an energetic pace to the film that compensates to some extent for the heavy-handed and obvious screenplay. Micklin Silver (HESTER STREET, CHILLY SCENES OF WINTER) has always been best at subtle relationships and quiet inflections between characters and, once again, she achieves more with a telling glance between David and Barb than any lame witticism ever could. Unfortunately, this forced extraction looks labored. Rather than conveying the whimsical effects of BETWEEN THE LINES and CROSSING DELANCEY, Silver too often descends to a John Hughes mode, recalling more often than not her disastrous LOVERBOY.

But without a well-developed screenplay, directorial nuance becomes divorced and empty. Milklin Silver strains and tries her mightiest, but she is striking a match in a vacuum of banality, and banality, in the film world of 1992, rages on like the Black Plague.

p, Laurie Perlman, Gerald T. Olson; d, Joan Micklin Silver; w, Frank Mugavero, (from the story by Mugavero, Mark Goddard and Melissa Goddard); ph, Theo Van De Sande; ed, Janice Hampton; m, Patrick Williams; prod d, Victoria Paul; art d, Brad Ricker; set d, Joyce Anne Gilstrap; cos, Jane Ruhm

Comedy/Drama **(PR: A MPAA: PG)**

BIKINI CARWASH COMPANY, THE
82m Krazy Karwash Kompany Inc. ~ New City c

Joe Dusic *(Jack McGowan)*, Kristie Ducati *(Melissa)*, Michael Wright *(Uncle Elmer)*, Neriah Napaul, Suzanne Browne

THE BIKINI CARWASH COMPANY is a film of such far-reaching stupidity and fatuousness that even the patience of its target audience—youthful, oversexed males—will be sorely tested.

A rube from Iowa, Jack McGowan (Joe Dusic), roams around a California beach teeming with buxom, nubile babes, in search of his Uncle Elmer's (Michael Wright) carwash, where he is to take over the management for the summer while his uncle leaves to tend to an allergic condition. Jack comes upon a group of top-heavy coeds who have just been bemoaning the depletion of their vacation funds. Melissa (Kristie Ducati) directs Jack to the carwash and plots with her friends to trick him into providing them with more vacation money. No sooner has Jack assumed his new duties than Melissa shows up and, after exposing her breasts to the impressed youth, persuades him to take her on as a business partner.

With the help of her bikini-clad friends, Melissa turns the carwash into a model of form and function—exposed female workers sudsing down spanking new cars. As a result, the carwash is a resounding success. A flasher and an irate district attorney appear at the carwash, but the rest of the film mostly concerns itself with the female carwashers performing their jobs in various states of undress. To round out the show, Jack and Melissa fall in love and Uncle Elmer returns to reveal his allergy as an aversion to underwear, compelling him to switch to the edible variety to help his sinuses. He also invites the kids back to work in his carwash next summer.

THE BIKINI CARWASH COMPANY will only appeal to immature males who are voyeuristic and horny. It's certainly not a film with any appeal for women—not readers of *Backlash* or *Revolution From Within*, at any rate. The women are all bimbos who hang around the beach with their dude boyfriends simply to hold court and wait for their breasts to pop out of their string bikini tops. It's almost a slap on the side of the head when one character reveals that she's a political science major (with this and THE DISTINGUISHED GENTLEMAN, American politics may never recover). The southern California landscape of THE BIKINI CARWASH is almost on par with Arthur Conan Doyle's *The Lost World*—pure fantasy. It's a whitebread WASP world with no blacks, Hispanics, Jews or even Eskimos to blot the racially pure landscape. These comely youths can also make love morning, noon and night in every position because, in this world, AIDS is nothing but a diet pill. It's a land where stupidity is way of life, where one character can say "I need something to cover my boobs" and another character can reply "I'll cover your boobs" and mean it.

The mentality of THE BIKINI CARWASH is like a smart virus. It creeps into your psyche and you either give in to moronic chortles or wince at the screen in stupefaction. The film's worldview can best be summed up by the fact that, halfway through its running time, the girls abandon cleaning cars in favor of soaping each other. As one character says to another, "Preposterous." As the other replies, "It's worse than that." *(Excessive nudity, sexual situations.)*

p, Buck Flower; d, Ed Hansen; w, Ed Hansen, Buck Flower; ph, Gary Orona; ed, Jose Ponce; m, Donald Mixon

Comedy **(PR: O MPAA: R)**

BIKINI SUMMER 2 ★
90m PM Entertainment ~ PM Home Video c

Jessica Hahn *(Marilyn Wetherspoon)*, Jeff Conaway *(Stu Stocker)*, Richard Arbolino *(Harry Wetherspoon)*, Avalon Anders *(Clarice)*, Melinda Armstrong *(Vanessa Wetherspoon)*, Maureen Flaherty *(Bridget Wetherspoon)*, Robert Miano *(Joshua)*, Brian Cassidy *(William)*

While one does not approach something called BIKINI SUMMER 2 with serious hopes of encountering the ghost of Ernst Lubitsch, this misbegotten "sequel" disappoints even the most modest expectations. Ironically, while it is totally inappropriate for young children, few mature adults will tolerate more than a few minutes of this cheerfully awful sex comedy.

"Yeah I'm ditching school and I'm heading out for the beach! Yeah there's something there my teachers just can't teach!" After a musical montage of bikini-clad beauties relaxing at the beach, Joshua (Robert Miano), a good-natured homeless person, spends $62 worth of change at a southern California liquor store. Joshua may be down and out in Malibu but he has many positive qualities; he's a sensitive, eloquent singer-songwriter. Moreover, he's devoted to Noreen, a former schoolteacher whom fate has made his companion on the road. They have their quarrels but they deeply care for each other. Their relationship is far healthier than that of Harry and Marilyn Wetherspoon (Richard Arbolino and Jessica Hahn), who live in a large luxurious home complete with pool, servants and a chauffeured limosine but lacking in love.

A successful real-estate developer, Harry claims to live only for work though he finds time to fool around with their buxom Latina maid. Furthermore, his work at the office consists primarily of sado-masochistic meetings with his mistress, Clarice (Avalon Anders). Frustrated by his lack of sexual attention, Marilyn contents herself with boxes of chocolate and frenzied telephone orders to a local home shopping network which is hosted by lusty TV personality Stu Stocker (Jeff Conaway). The unhappy couple has two fun-loving daughters, the sweet and generous 18-year-old Bridget (Maureen Flaherty), and her older dumber sister, Vanessa (Melinda Armstrong), who lives for the beach and her creature comforts. Other household members include William (Brian Cassidy), Harry's driver and Bridget's clandestine lover, and Mark, the vain, obsessive bodybuilder whose presence is never adequately explained.

The minimal plot is set in motion when William, rushing his boss to work, accidentally hits Joshua with the family limo. They carry the dazed homeless man inside, and Bridget befriends Joshua, cleans him up and takes him out in the limo to find Noreen. The girls persuade their cranky father—with the threat of a lawsuit—to allow the homeless couple to stay for a few weeks. Joshua utilizes this opportunity to sing a few songs and look for work while the girls take Noreen on a credit-card shopping spree. They decide to throw a poolside barbecue which is crashed by the local homeless community. Harry arrives, blows up and tosses everyone out. The girls also leave in solidarity with their new friends. They come up with a plot to regain their father's respect, help the homeless and become entrepreneurs in the process with an abandoned restaurant (owned by their father in simpler, happier times), local talent and a fortuitous financial windfall. All problems are resolved as the gang puts on a show.

Though neither funny nor sexy, BIKINI SUMMER 2 strains to suggest a raunchy cartoon come to life. However, it also bears a family resemblance to more innocent screen beach romps of the past such as the harmless series of "Beach Party" movies produced by American International Pictures in the early 1960s. Ineptly conceived and heavy-handed in execution, the modern variant is less funny, more cruel and more vulgar. Much of the film's alleged humor derives from watching the sexual humiliation and torture of the father at the hands of Mistress Clarice and a mysterious hooded woman called the Executioner. If one took these scenes seriously, they would be appalling. One assumes these are intended for those who find the mere notion of a dominatrix unspeakably amusing.

An unfortunate stab at displaying a social conscience contributes to this film's failure as even dumb entertainment. Yet, there is no sincere concern about any real-life issues expressed here. Joshua has simply opted out of the rat race, his homelessness being a moral choice, and he even has a substantial nest egg socked away. The message here is that the homeless are fine folk as long as they are actually lovable artistic eccentrics. To add insult to injury, Robert Miano and Michelle Conway are fairly touching as the homeless couple.

BIKINI SUMMER 2 reveals its true colors with its suspect representation of race, which begins subtly during the opening montage of exclusively white beach beauties cavorting. Most of the few males shown in this credit sequence are sleekly muscular Black men, engaged in such picturesque physical feats as stunt skateboarding, dancing and breakdancing on and off roller skates. The few white men we see are gawky and awkward—some even collapse with sexual excitement. What are we to make of this? As there are no Black male characters in the story proper, we can only assume that the intent is pure titillation of racial sexual fears and stereotypes. BIKINI SUMMER 2 features several broad ethnic caricatures including a promiscuous Latina maid, a grossly obese Black female cook and a homely asexual Japanese handyman. Harmless entertainment?

First time director (and original story contributor) Jeff Conaway is best known to TV viewers as Bobby Wheeler, the struggling actor/cabbie on the classic sitcom "Taxi." Still striving gamely, he approches the role of Stu Stocker with the zest of Joel Grey playing the Master of Ceremonies in CABARET. It is a sad spectacle to see a former member of the beloved "Taxi" ensemble so debased. At least his TV "infomercials" allow him to maintain some dignity.

Finally, BIKINI SUMMER 2 is touted as the feature acting debut of Jessica Hahn, a pseudo-celebrity by-product of some hazily remembered sex scandal with a public figure. Upon sober reflection, our advice to Miss Hahn: "Don't give up those late night infomercials, girl!" *(Violence, profanity, nudity, sexual situations.)*

p, Jean Levine; d, Jeff Conaway; w, Charles A. Kanganis, Joseph Merhi; ed, Melisa Sanchez; m, Jim Halfpenny; cos, Elizabeth Corbett

Comedy **(PR: O MPAA: R)**

BLACK ICE ★★

(U.S./Canada) 90m Saban Pictures; Entertainment Securities Ltd.; Fare Productions ~ Prism Entertainment c

Michael Nouri *(Ben Shorr)*, Joanna Pacula *(Vanessa)*, Michael Ironside *(Quinn)*, Mickey Jones *(Lloyd Carter)*

Cabbie and neophyte writer Michael Nouri is about to start up his meter for the fare of a lifetime in BLACK ICE. Before this cat-and-mouse game grows wearisome, it generates a fair amount of suspense.

After she botches a sexual blackmail scheme instigated by her corrupt superiors at the CIA, Vanessa (Joanna Pacula) runs for her life; hired to keep Congressman Eric Weaver (Arnie Olsen) in line, Vanessa is considered expendable when Weaver is accidentally killed after a post-coital argument. Instantly smitten with Vanessa, cabbie Ben Shorr (Nouri) drives her to the airport and then makes a deal to drive her to Seattle. Meanwhile agent Quinn (Michael Ironside) pursues his former top secret employee with the determination of Javert stalking Jean Valjean. After extracting their whereabouts from Ben's boss Lloyd Carter (Mickey Jones), Quinn cold-bloodedly murders the taxi company owner.

While feeding Ben fragments of her plight, Vanessa is betrayed by her contact in Minneapolis; she shoots the man. And although Quinn is temporarily waylaid for shooting at Ben and Vanessa, the local cops quickly release him. Wherever Vanessa flees, Quinn's agents have already paved the way for her capture, including the murder of her friend, a nurse in Billings, Montana. After Vanessa zaps a fake nurse with a heart fibrillator, she reveals her secret to Ben, tells him to disappear and heads for a train. Like all good cabbies, Ben is trained to see his customer to the door. Determined to cover up his own mistakes, Quinn pulls a gun on Vanessa in the train yard, but Ben intervenes. In the ensuing shootout, Vanessa is fatally shot, and a wounded Quinn stumbles into the path of an oncoming train.

Perfectly cast as a mystery woman, Pacula (GORKY PARK, THE KISS) is an enticing foil for Nouri's (FLASHDANCE, TOTAL EXPOSURE) guileless cabbie. And given one of his best showcases for abject villainy, Ironside (TOTALL RECALL, MCBAIN) gives spies everywhere a bad name. Too often, however, the film seems to fall in love with the admittedly gorgeous scenery, at the expense of dramatic tension. Also, the screenplay and direction falter in finding a balance between Nouri and Pacula's doomed romance and the basic run-for-your-life suspense mechanism; instead of complementing each other, these two angles get in each other's way. Nonetheless, even if the excitement is never allowed to grow to a fever pitch, BLACK ICE does have a few nerve-wracking moments, particularly the instant heart attack scene in the Montana clinic.

Crisper editing and a stronger focus on suspense rather than subtle human drama might have elevated BLACK ICE to a higher stratum. As it stands, it's an occasionally chilling thriller with a few too many stopovers. *(Extreme violence, profanity, nudity, sexual situations.)*

p, Robert Vince, Vonnie Von Helmolt; d, Neill Fearnley; w, Arne Olsen, John Alan Schwartz; ph, David Geddes; ed, Alan Lee; m, Amin Bahtia; prod d, Deanna Rhode; cos, Sharon Fedoruk

Thriller **(PR: O MPAA: R)**

BLACKBELT ★★½

Concorde ~ New Horizons Home Video c

Don "The Dragon" Wilson *(Jack Dillon)*, Richard Beymer *(Eddie DiAngelo)*, Deirdre Imershein *(Shanna)*, Alan Blumenfeld *(Will Sturges)*, "Bad" Brad Hefton *(Frank Ellis)*, Ernest Simmons *(Mercanary)*, Mitch Borrow *(Rene)*, Mathias Hues *(John Sweet)*, Jack Verell *(Bobby Machado)*, Barbara Graham *(Barbara)*, Lord Kimberly *(Mother Sweet)*, Tim Backer, Gerry Blank, Jim Graden, Ian Jacklin, John Graden

Make no mistake, BLACKBELT star Don "The Dragon" Wilson is the genuine chopsocky article. As an actor, he's merely adequate. But as a kickboxer, Wilson outclasses all the other martial arts heroes currently inflicting bodily harm.

Content with teaching self-defense, only reluctantly does Jack Dillon (Wilson) heed his former police partner's call to become a bodyguard. Can Dillon save popular songstress Shanna (Deirdre Imershein) from a self-destructive relationship with her manager Bobby Machado (Jack Verell)? (In this low-rent version of THE BODYGUARD, Wilson has a better haircut than Kevin Costner, but Imershein doesn't sing as well as Whitney Houston.) Machado is actually fronting for slimy music promoter Eddie DiAngelo (Richard Beymer) who plans to put out a hit on Shanna if she doesn't re-sign with him.

Matters are complicated by the appearance of John Sweet (Mathias Hues), a Vietnam vet, mercenary and serial killer who keeps his prostitute victims' ring fingers for trophies. Since Shanna has the misfortune of resembling Sweet's dead mother (Lord Kimberly), whom he seeks to kill over and over again, she's in double jeopardy from the psycho and DiAngelo. As the body count mounts (including Shanna's best friend and Dillon's ex-partner), Dillon and Shanna barely escape a mob hit. Although they survive the *de rigeur* car chase, Dillon has to defeat a kickboxing champ hired by DiAngelo and then go limb-to-limb against dozens of Sweet's bar buddies. In preparation for the kill, Sweet dresses Shanna up as his mom while Dillon is busy fighting a platoon of martial artists. When Dillon finally tangles with the massive Sweet, he conquers him with the help of Shanna who just happens to pick up a sword that Sweet impales himself upon.

Unfortunately, while BLACKBELT deserves credit for examining the seamier aspects of the glamorous record industry, writer-director Charles Philip Moore's screenplay raises some disturbing questions. Did the film really need to plumb the psychological depths in order to create credible motivations for both Shanna and Sweet? This may be the first martial arts movie to use incest as all-round psychological shorthand—Shanna was raped by her father; young Sweet was seduced into an affair with his mother—not that it develops these tragedies with any insight. The graphic scene of mother-son sex seems sorely out of place in an assembly-line action film. It's a shame that Sweet's sordid background seems intended to give the film a kinky undercurrent.

Overlooking that one major reservation, audiences will find that BLACKBELT goes about its high-kicking action business with the expected powerhouse fight sequences. *(Violence, sexual situations, adult situations.)*

p, Mike Elliott; d, Charles Philip Moore; w, Charles Philip Moore; ph, John Ulyanov; ed, Gabrielle Gilbert Reeves; m, David Wurst, Eric Wurst; prod d, Colin De Rouin; art d, Craig Muzio; set d, Anthony Stabley

Action/Crime/Martial Arts **(PR: O MPAA: R)**

BLAME IT ON THE BELLBOY ★★

(U.K./U.S.) 78m Hollywood; Bellboy Films Ltd. ~ BV c

Dudley Moore *(Melvyn Orton)*, Bryan Brown *(Charlton Black/Mike Lawton)*, Richard Griffiths *(Maurice Horton)*, Andreas Katsulas *(Scarpa)*, Patsy Kensit *(Caroline Wright)*, Alison Steadman *(Rosemary Horton)*, Penelope Wilton *(Patricia Fulford)*, Bronson Pinchot *(Bellboy)*, Jim Carter *(Rossi)*, Alex Norton *(Alfio)*, John Grillo *(Hotel Manager)*, Andrew Bailey *(Shady Character)*, Ronnie Stevens *(Man on Plane)*, Enzo Turrin *(Senior Policeman)*, Andy Bradford *(Italian Victim)*, Lindsay Anderson *(Mr. Marshall)*

Labored zaniness results when three men with similar names but very different missions check into the same Venice hotel at the same time in BLAME IT ON THE BELLBOY. In his feature debut, writer-director Mark Herman tries to revive the biting spirit of vintage British farce with tepid results.

Timid clerk Melvyn Orton (Dudley Moore) is in town to dispose of some of his mean boss's (director Lindsay Anderson, heard over the phone but never seen) money on a rundown villa as a tax shelter. Corpulent, married, small-town mayor Maurice Horton (Richard Griffiths), meanwhile, is in town to cheat on his wife with a computer-arranged travel date, Patricia Fulford (Penelope Wilton). Rounding out the trio, Mike Lawton (Bryan Brown) is a hitman in town to kill a local gangster, Scarpa (Andreas Katsulas). Thanks to a bellboy (Bronson Pinchot) whose English pronunciation leaves much to be desired, Horton winds up meeting a sexy real estate agent, Caroline Wright (Patsy Kensit), whom he believes to be his date, and Orton winds up trying to buy a villa from the gangster, while Lawton stalks Horton's date, believing her to be his "contract." It becomes easy to predict where the action goes from there. After much running around, Horton winds up buying the villa, blackmailed by the agent after Horton's wife, Rosemary (Alison Steadman), nearly walks in on them in bed. Orton winds up stealing the money he was supposed to have used to buy the villa, after inadvertently blowing up the gangster. Lawton collects the money earned by Orton and runs away with Horton's date, with whom he has fallen in love.

By naming one of his lead characters after late British playwright Joe Orton (whose own life story was the subject of Stephen Frears's film PRICK UP YOUR EARS), Herman invites comparison between his efforts here and the late master of British farce. But it's not a comparison that would have much point. Herman keeps his main characters separate for too long, necessitating extended frantic crosscutting that continues long after it has ceased to amuse. It was also a mistake to film on location in Venice. The best farces are staged in as small a space as possible—which is what makes the genre perfect for the stage and problematic for the screen—the more claustrophobic the better, to increase the comic tension. Here, the eerie, formidable beauty of Venice distracts from, rather than enhances, the action.

More importantly, BLAME IT ON THE BELLBOY comes to feel more and more coyly sanitized as it goes on, as if Herman were creating not a real British farce, but an incredible simulation, purposefully blunted and tamed for American consumption. It overemphasizes the punishment of the "bad" characters and the reward of the "good" characters—down to an end credit roll that seems almost as long as the film itself—precisely when a craftier writer (like Orton, whose writing was fueled by a truly corrosive wit) would be tightening the screws and making his audience squirm.

At least the performances are generally good. Even Moore is tolerable this time out, and most of the British veterans—Griffiths, Wilton and Steadman especially—give good, solid comedy performances. But it all comes down to the sum being much less than the individual parts. Despite sharing a producer (Steve Abbott) with the much funnier A FISH CALLED WANDA,

BLAME IT ON THE BELLBOY accomplishes little beyond making lust, greed and murder seem extraordinarily dull subjects for a comedy. *(Violence, profanity, adult situations.)*

p, Jennie Howarth, Steve Abbott; d, Mark Herman; w, Mark Herman; ph, Andrew Dunn; ed, Michael Ellis; m, Trevor Jones; prod d, Gemma Jackson; art d, Peter Roussell; set d, Peter Walpole; cos, Lindy Hemming

Comedy **(PR: C MPAA: PG-13)**

BLIND VISION ★★½

92m Saban Pictures; Vertigo Pictures ~ Worldvision Home Video c

Lenny Von Dohlen *(William Dalton)*, Deborah Shelton *(Leanne Dunaway)*, Stony Jackson *(Tony David)*, Robert Vaughn *(Mr. X)*, Ned Beatty *(Sergeant Dave Logan)*, Louise Fletcher *(Virginia Taylor)*, Catherine McGoohan *(Gloria Byers)*, T. Sean Foley *(Gregg Howard)*, Mary Jefferson *(Miss Sloan)*

Very nearly a hymn to voyeurism, BLIND VISION is an above-average thriller which stars Lenny Von Dohlen as William Dalton, a painfully shy man who from his menial position in the mailroom with buddy Tony David (Stony Jackson), is obsessed with unattainable co-worker Leanne Dunaway (Deborah Shelton).

Living across the street from her, William spies on Leanne through a camera equipped with a telephoto lens. She is also being watched by Mr. X (Robert Vaughn), who, also watched by William, visits her several times, at one point beating her up. William's landlady Miss Taylor (Louise Fletcher) in turn is always watching William with an amorous eye. One night, soon after leaving her, Leanne's lover Gregg Howard (T. Sean Foley) is killed with a razor, and Sgt. Logan (Ned Beatty) starts watching all of them.

The neatly convoluted plot by co-writers Winston Rickard and Shuki Levy (who also directed and co-edited) ultimately has William going over the edge into psycho territory and killing Mr. X (Leanne's estranged husband, who killed Gregg), but in a final showdown, Leanne, stirred by the purity of his love for her, steps in front of a bullet aimed at William and before dying confesses to Logan that *she* killed Mr. X, thus saving William.

If the characters who populate BLIND VISION are fairly standard, they're made fresh and interesting via the uniformly strong performances and the writing. The central relationship, or lack of one, is nicely delineated by the gently intent Von Dohlen, whose shyness is close to paralysis, and the sexy Shelton, late of De Palma's BODY DOUBLE and Levy's real-life spouse.

Levy, who directed last year's TWILIGHT BLUE, occasionally allows the pace to meander, which is lethal to a Hitchcockian ode like this, and surprisingly, for an unrated direct-to-video release, the violence and sex are fairly soft-pedaled. Despite the low budget, producer and co-editor Jonathon Braun has turned out a good-looking film, sharply photographed by Frank Byers. Shot in Norfolk, Virginia, in 1990. *(Violence, profanity, nudity, sexual Situations.)*

p, Jonathon Braun; d, Shuki Levy; w, Shuki Levy, Winston Rickard; ph, Frank Byers; ed, Shuki Levy, Jonathon Braun, Tony Lark, John Bryant; m, Shuki Levy; art d, Jayne Asman; set d, Mitchell Whitmore; cos, Candice Cain

Mystery/Thriller **(PR: O MPAA: NR)**

BLINK OF AN EYE ★★★

(Israel) 90m Chase Films Ltd. ~ Trimark Pictures c

Michael Pare *(Sam Browning)*, Janis Lee *(Katie Baker)*, Amos Lavie *(Mozzafar)*, Sasson Gabay *(Khalil)*, Uri Gavriel *(Izmir)*, Avi Keidar *(Captain in Jail)*, Jack Adalist *(Agent Tilson)*, Elkie Jacobs *(Noreen Baker)*, Jack Wieberker *(Alan Baker)*

Turning improbability into a cinematic virtue, BLINK OF AN EYE scores an escapist bullseye with one viscerally exciting action scene after another.

After allowing his headstrong daughter Katie (Janis Lee) to traipse off to war-torn Turkey and risk her life in the first place, no-nonsense CIA chief Alan Baker (Jack Wieberker) is so impressed by the troubled dreams of his wife Noreen (Elkie Jacobs) that he enlists the help of the CIA's experimental psychic warfare unit. Risking his career with what some might consider a misappropriation of government funds, Mr. Baker orders super jock Sam Browning (Michael Pare) to protect his darling daughter.

At first, Katie goes along with skeptical US military types like Tilson (Jack Adalist) who poke fun at our prescient hero. But when, as Sam predicted, the entire base is wiped out by terrorists trying to kidnap her, Katie changes her cynical tune. Because terrorist leader Mozzafar (Amos Lavie) wants to trade Katie for his imprisoned brother, Sam and Katie face a gauntlet manned by Mozzafar's crazed guerrillas. Even if they elude Mozzafar, they face capture by the military troops who are also seeking them at the instigation of Khalil (Sasson Gabay), a spineless prime minister.

Although Katie torches some rebels who've captured and tortured Sam, the terrorists are soon hot on their trail. With the sympathetic aid of Izmir (Uri Gavriel), a Kurd, Sam and Katie make it as far as an abandoned factory where they make a brave last stand. Even when blinded by an explosive blast, Sam is more than a match for the rebel-rabble. After the trio has systematically decimated the ranks of terrorists, Mr. Baker sends in a rescue helicopter (in violation of American foreign policy). Since Baker has forced the hand of the prime minister with a public relations statement to the world press, Khalil orders his troops to let the copter fly Sam and Katie to freedom.

Capitalizing on its mystic warrior scenario, THE BLINK OF AN EYE makes anything seem possible. Fortunately, Pare (EDDIE AND THE CRUISERS, THE LAST HOUR) has enough movie star magnetism not only to carry the outre storyline but also to offset the muffled performance of his pallid leading lady. As the pace accelerates, each new skirmish with the terrorists invigorates the film. Nothing, however, will prepare audiences for Pare's *coup de cinema*. Blinded, his psychic abilities grow razor-sharp and transform him into a sightless Jean-Claude Van Damme, able to kick in perfect opposition to each blow struck.

Far-out and ultra-patriotic, this celebration of all-American know-how may be fanciful, but as a hard-driving action film, it takes no prisoners. *(Violence, adult situations.)*

p, Jacob Kotzky; d, Bob Misiorowski; w, Edward Kovach; ph, David Gurfinkel; ed, Carmel Davies; m, Vladimir Horunzhy; prod d, Eytan Levy; set d, Amiram Lichter; cos, Rina Ziv

Action/Martial Arts **(PR: C MPAA: R)**

BLOOD ON THE BADGE

M.A.R.S. Productions ~ AIP Home Video c

Joe Estevez *(Captain Burton)*, David Harrod *(Detective Neil Farrow)*, Rocky Patterson *(Milo Truscott)*, Desiree LaFore *(Caroline/Alexandra)*, Melissa DeLeon *(Detective Jenny Webber)*, Todd A. Everett *(Bill Marshall)*, Dean Nolen, Monique Detraz

The title *Blood on the Badge* should be familiar to fans of the fondly remembered TV police comedy "Barney Miller"; it was the name of a Joseph Wambaugh-type novel penned with great pride by the dapper Detective Harris. The movie BLOOD ON THE BADGE, unfortunately, has nothing to do with sitcoms except that it provokes several laughs—all unintended.

The opening has Dallas lawman Neil Farrow (David Harrod) and partner Bill Marshall (Todd A. Everett) stumbling upon a warehouseful of weapons and "terrorists." A gunfight erupts and Marshall, a black man, is nailed. "I'm gonna get these guys who did this to him!" vows Detective Farrow at Marshall's hospital bedside. The avenging Anglo instantly traces the getaway van to Milo Truscott (Rocky Patterson), a politically powerful, millionaire backwoods pork farmer and raving racist apocalyptic Christian survivalist gun nut. Truscott and his henchman have been masquerading as Libyan death squads while murdering congressmen and diplomats, with the goal of triggering war in the Mideast and enabling neo-Confederates to seize the US government and ship all colored citizens back to Africa for mass genocide. He's also been selling bad sausage.

The movie could easily end right there, but before Farrow feeds Truscott to his own hogs the storyline stumbles through an hour of needless subplots, sex scenes and endless passages of expository dialogue. To add insult to injury, all this is given a ludicrous mystical bent; from time to time the comatose Bill's spirit materializes in ethereal light to provide clues or encouragement like "Hang in there, buddy. I'm watching your back." Our macho hero needs all the help he can get. At one point Farrow fails to recognize a strange symbol the villains paint on the wall. It's a cross—but the cop thinks it's a really skinny hand.

The token guest star is Martin Sheen's younger brother Joe Estevez (SOULTAKER, DARK RIDER), understandably angry as police Captain Burton. In a token stab at an in-joke, there's a minor character named Harkonnen, after the evil space dynasty in DUNE. Token women include Farrow's irritating new partner, Detective Jenny Weber (Melissa DeLeon). An Ivy League brat, Weber cautions Farrow that he shouldn't jump to conclusions over Truscott, because Texas teems with raving racist apocalyptic Christian survivalist gun nuts, and a good detective shouldn't just arrest the first one he finds.

Dallas-based schlockmeister Bret McCormick must know whereof he speaks, since BLOOD ON THE BADGE was made well before the 1993 conflict between federal troops and the heavily armed Branch Davidian survivalist cult in Waco. Lovers of the Lone Star State can take solace in this film's striking night views of Dallas, the movie's visual and emotional highlight. BLOOD ON THE BADGE was made entirely in Texas, and it escaped to the remaining planet via videocassette. *(Violence, profanity, nudity, sexual situations.)*

p, Bret McCormick; d, Bret McCormick; w, Bret McCormick, John Cianetti; ph, Adam Nunn; ed, Blue Thompson; m, Ron Dilulio; fx, Randy Moore

Crime/Thriller **(PR: O MPAA: NR)**

BLOODFIST IV: DIE TRYING ★★

Concorde ~ New Horizons Home Video c

Don "The Dragon" Wilson, Cat Sassoon, Amanda Wyss, Kale Browne, Liz Torres, Dan Martin, James Tolkan, Heather Lauren Olson

Rowdy but routine, BLOODFIST IV was part of a five-picture deal between Roger Corman's fertile Concorde Pictures and kickboxing star Don "The Dragon" Wilson. None of the last three BLOODFIST titles have had anything to do with each other apart from Wilson's involvement, and DIE TRYING goes through the motions as a kung-fu conspiracy thriller.

Wilson and his feet of fury portray Danny Holt, a repo man who gets the plot rolling by seizing the wrong BMW. (For some obscure reason the license plates have been switched.) While Danny's out to lunch evidoers raid the impound lot and massacre the whole staff in their desperate search for an innocent-looking box of chocolates left in the auto—the candy contains several Easter-bunniesful of nuclear detonators. The authorities naturally suspect Danny of being the psycho killer of his workmates and hunt him relentlessly. So do the evil weapons-smugglers, savvy FBI agents and CIA spooks who had originated the whole deal to funnel nukes into the Mideast.

The plot sustains attention through sheer momentum, with Danny's varied pursuers constantly outmaneuvering each other to get at the repo-man-who-knew-too-much. Wilson's self-choreographed martial-arts battles are lively but often absurd, even in context. BLOODFIST IV is one of those flicks that takes place in some alternate karate universe where every other person on the street has a black belt—even a pudgy Jackie Mason-lookalike who tangles with Wilson at the beginning—and each confrontation blooms into the action equivalent of a Broadway musical number, full of chopsocky mayhem and pseudo-oriental background muzak. One farfetched faceoff even occurs in a room filled with tear gas, where Wilson and his opponent are unable to breathe, but nevertheless can strip to the waist and kickbox like crazy.

Still, a climactic showdown with leather-clad villainess Cat Sassoon is disappointing; after being pummelled to a pulp, Danny rallies and demolishes the *dojo* dominatrix with some piddly pokes. Much blood spills to establish the deadliness of the heavies, but they degrade to low-level Disney dastards when they kidnap Danny's ever-so-cute daughter Molly (Heather Lauren Olson), tie her up, blow smoke in her face, and tease that her daddy doesn't love her anymore. The filmmakers seem to be on some crusade against tobacco, as the nicotine habit is shared by all Danny's antagonists. Love interest Amanda Wyss, in comparison, is a *reformed* smoker.

Another subtext attacks the much-abused LAPD, depicted here as malicious morons commanded by an overweight lady chief (Liz Torres) who gets fast food delivered to her at murder sites. And this isn't the hero's first brush with LA's finest; his wife was killed by a blue knight driving drunk, and the force covered it up and pinned the rap on Danny. In movies these days bright policemen are as rare as intelligent kung-fu scripts. Despite an overuse of slow-motion, director Paul Ziller keeps the narrative animated enough to render BLOODFIST IV: DIE TRYING passable for diehard action addicts. *(Violence, profanity.)*

p, Mike Elliott; d, Paul Ziller; w, Paul Ziller, (from the story by Robert Kerchner); ph, Christian Sebaldt; ed, David Beatty; m, David Wurst, Eric Wurst; prod d, Robin Nixson; art d, Dan Goldstein

Action/Thriller/Martial Arts **(PR: C MPAA: R)**

BLOODFIST III: FORCED TO FIGHT ★★★

88m Concorde ~ New Horizons Home Video c

Don "The Dragon" Wilson *(Jimmy Boland)*, Richard Roundtree *(Samuel Stark)*, Gregory McKinney *(Blue)*, Rick Dean *(Wheelhead)*, Richard Paul *(Bill Goddard)*, Charles Boswell *(Taylor)*, John Cardone *(Diddler)*, Brad Blaisdell *(Pisani)*, Stan Longinidus *(Leadbottom)*, Peter "Sugarfoot" Cunningham *(Champ)*, Tony DiBenedetto, Laura Stockman *(TV News Reporter)*, Maurice Smith, Joe Lewis

In 1992 several films stood out for the searing urgency with which they addressed American racism and redemption. One was MALCOLM X, maverick director Spike Lee's epic depiction of the slain leader's controversial life. And then there was . . . BLOODFIST III: FORCED TO FIGHT. No kidding. This sequel from the redoubtable Roger Corman's Concorde Pictures may not be scrutinized by pundits, civil rights leaders and social historians for years to come, but BLOODFIST III follows the best B-movie tradition of tackling larger issues and taboos within the framework of exploitation filler.

Actually, this movie has nothing to do with the previous BLOODFIST entries, except all-star World Kickboxing Association light heavyweight champ Don "The Dragon" Wilson. Wilson is, sadly, a bit of an anomaly in recent martial arts pictures: a hero who actually is of Asian (Japanese/Irish) descent. The Chinese, Japanese, Koreans and Thais may have developed the ancient martial arts, and Bruce Lee popularized the chopsocky genre, but you have to look hard for any leading Asian actors in American action films. Usually they're villains, wise mentors or doomed sidekicks. It's hardly coincidental that Wilson has condemned pernicious racism from time to time in his fistfests, and the penitentiary-bound BLOODFIST III has timely impact.

Wilson plays Jimmy Boland, a Japanese-American railroaded into the big house on a murder rap. When an acquaintance is sodomized and stabbed to death by the vicious jailhouse pusher, Boland retaliates by killing the drug lord in a martial-arts brawl. Both the victim and the pusher were black, but the bad guy was a partner of the prison's black gang commander Blue (Gregory McKinney), a self-styled militant whose walls are covered with Africa posters, and who wields power over the black inmate population through race baiting. He denounces Boland as a racist and orders revenge. Boland is offered protection by the Manson-like Wheelhead (Rick Dean), chieftain of the cellblock's white supremacists, but the hero refuses to be their homeboy. The calculating warden Taylor (Charles Boswell), seeing that Boland is a marked man, strategically places him in the same cell as Samuel Stark (Richard Roundtree), a self-taught lawyer (with Malcolm X and Elijah Muhammed portraits on *his* wall) who's made enemies of the administrators by handling the convicts' legal appeals.

"Knowledge is power," says Stark, indicating his law books. "This is my power," replies Boland, making a fist. Nonetheless, Stark recognizes that his new cellmate is a decent guy and finds him a job working with the non-hostile, ethnically mixed yard maintenance crew. Blue, meanwhile, despite his African-American rebel pose, is secretly an enforcer for Warden Taylor, and he now targets the meddling Stark for an attack. In the screenplay's sharpest irony, Blue allies himself with the avowed bigot Wheelhead; each rules through hatred and division, and both see Boland and Stark as threats to their standing in the prison community. The conspirators try to assassinate Stark during a Presidents' Day holiday, fomenting a full-scale prison riot in which Boland ultimately confronts his tormentors behind and outside the bars.

The climax, in which Boland actually resists killing Blue and Wheelhead, confirms that BLOODFIST III is operating several notches above the level of mere mayhem. True, there are enough brawls to satisfy such tastes, but none of them are extraneous to the plot. This is a rare action story in which action serves the story, not the other way around, and the plot, characters and implicit politics provide the reason to watch, even when the going gets brutal (actor-turned-director Oley Sassone is a long way from his earlier writing/producing chores on the Disney family tale WILD HEARTS CAN'T BE BROKEN).

As an actor the wiry Wilson has never been a terribly dynamic presence outside of the kickboxing arena, but here he stays within his range and gives a credible portrayal of a hardened tough. The screenplay is careful not to make him too much of a lamb, even when he sort-of-befriends a pathetic child molester Diddler (John Cardone), perenially tormented by the other prisoners. Richard Roundtree, best known for 1971's SHAFT, also lends a street-smart edge to Stark, a somewhat stock character who would usually be a prime candidate for plastic sainthood. Meanwhile villains Rick Dean and Gregory McKinney are given subtle shadings of humanity that balance their unchained malevolence. Richard Paul, commonly seen as stuffy Southern types on TV sitcoms, has a bit part as a Department of Corrections head whose double-dealings with the bowtied Warden Taylor inject a superfluous bit of cynicism.

Although there are no major female roles, the picture neatly meets its female nudity quota without violating the reality of the prison environment, via an inmate showing (Diddler works the projector) of the vintage kung-fu drive-in pic TNT JACKSON, starring the awesome Jeanne Bell. (That was another Corman release, of course.) As for BLOODFIST III: FORCED TO FIGHT, it had a brief showing in theaters with a video release quick to follow. A generic ad campaign (as well as the needless tie-in to the rest of the BLOODFIST titles) ensured that the picture would get overlooked as just another karate throwaway, but it's a superior specimen of both the martial-arts and prison genres. *(Violence, adult situations, substance abuse, sexual situations, profanity, nudity.)*

p, Roger Corman; d, Oley Sassone; w, Allison Burnett, Charles Mattera; ph, Rick Bota; ed, Eric L. Beason; m, Nigel Holton; prod d, James Shumaker

Action/Martial Arts **(PR: O MPAA: R)**

BOB MARLEY: TIME WILL TELL ★★

89m Initial Film & TV; Island Visual Arts; Polygram Video International ~ IRS Releasing c

Bob Marley

Bob Marley, the charismatic and controversial musician whose twenty-year career encompassed every style of Jamaican music from ska to reggae and whose songs expressed the sharp-edged emotionalism and political immediacy of revolutionary broadsides, is given exalted treatment in BOB MARLEY: TIME WILL TELL, a peripheral documentary on the late musician that spends most of its running time glorifying Marley the icon rather than celebrating his songs and his life.

The voice of Bob Marley is heard announcing "This is my story" and, after an impressive animated interlude that looks like flowing Bob Marley and the Wailers album covers, the film settles into a cursory examination of Marley's tragically short life, from his early recordings until his struggle against brain cancer, narrated by interviews with Marley, conducted at various points during his career. Marley's songs (including "Coming in from the Cold," "Trenchtown Rock," "Jammin," "No Woman No Cry," "Could You Be Loved," "Zimbabwe," "Lion of Judah," "Ambush in the Night," "Them Full Belly" and "Forever Loving Jah") serve as commentary upon his life and his political and religious beliefs. The film ends with extensive footage of Marley's state funeral in Jamaica of May 21, 1981, over the song "Get Up Stand Up."

Director Declan Lowney liberally peppers BOB MARLEY: TIME WILL TELL with Marley's songs, and the late musician's passion and fire is conveyed in the urgency of his lyrics and the fervor of his performance, particularly on "Curfew/Burnin and Lootin'," "I Shot the Sheriff," "War," "Exodus" and "Redemption Song." The power of these performances cuts through pretense and stridency like a pearl-edged hatchet felling a tree. As long as Lowney sticks to Marley's performances and his brilliantly lacerating songs, the film reveals the piercing genius of Bob Marley and the Wailers. But Lowney's stance on Marley is devotional, his legendary status taken for granted. Although Marley and his songs nominally narrate the film, Marley is frequently shown in slow-motion glory, his head tossed upwards to the sky, his poses joyous and redemptive, the deification complete.

Lowney feels no need to explain in any detail the story of Marley's life, his influences and the Kingston slums of ganja and poverty. Marley, to Lowney, was born almost full-blown into the Kingston music scene, a reggae Christ who was crucified at the cross of cancer for the sins of mankind. There are no markers or signposts for Bob Marley. BOB MARLEY: TIME WILL TELL glorifies Marley at the expense of the social milieu that formed reggae and the influences of other musicians upon the development of the music that Marley clearly and passionately loved. It would have been of great interest too if Lowney had spoken with Marley's friends, band members, family and associates and shown Marley to have had some contact with other members of the human race, simply in order to dispell the impression left by the film that he fell out of the sky.

Marley's performances in BOB MARLEY: TIME WILL TELL evoke such power that the songs overcome any obfuscation that is thrown in the way by the director. In "Curfew/Burnin' and Lootin'" and "Exodus," Lowney sticks with the performance and Marley burns through like a blinding sun. But Lowney, for most of the film, prefers to cut in news clippings of political events over Marley's songs, ruining the performance continuity and making the songs into psuedo-incendiary explosions that have reshaped history, akin to a pompous and over-bearing Michael Jackson MTV video clip. Wrapping these songs neatly in a politically correct bundle blunts their power and diminishes their potency, transforming songs of transcendence into out-of-date songs of protest. "Could You Be Loved" and "War," two of Marley's most moving songs, are sabotaged in this way. Lowney is so dewy-eyed in reverence that he can't leave well enough alone and allow Marley to speak for himself.

Since BOB MARLEY: TIME WILL TELL is basically preaching to the converted, new-comers to Marley's music will have to look elsewhere—to his albums—to appreciate his brilliance.

p, Rocky Oldham; d, Declan Lowney; ed, Peter Bensimon, Tim Thornton-Allen; m, Bob Marley and the Wailers; anim, Sue Young

Documentary/Biography/Musical (PR: C MPAA: NR)

BOB ROBERTS ★★½

(U.S./U.K.) 105m The Bob Roberts Co.; Working Title; Polygram Pictures ~ Paramount/Miramax c

Tim Robbins *(Bob Roberts)*, Giancarlo Esposito *(Bugs Raplin)*, Ray Wise *(Chet MacGregor)*, Rebecca Jenkins *(Delores Perrigrew)*, Harry J. Lennix *(Franklin Dockett)*, John Ottavino *(Clark Anderson)*, Robert Stanton *(Bart Macklerooney)*, Alan Rickman *(Lukas Hart III)*, Gore Vidal *(Senator Brickley Paiste)*, Brian Murray *(Terry Manchester)*, Jack Black *(Roger)*, Matthew Faber *(Calvin)*, Matt McGrath *(Burt)*, Shannon Holt *(Rita the Obsessive Fan)*, Brent Hinkley *(Bif the Patriot)*, James Spader *(News Anchor Chuck Marin)*, Pamela Reed *(News Anchor Carol Cruise)*, Helen Hunt *(Reporter Rose Pondell)*, Tom Atkins *(Dr. Caleb Menck)*, Merrilee Dale *(Polly Roberts)*, Eva Amurri *(Child in Hosptial)*, Jim West *(Bus Driver)*, Peter Gallagher *(News Anchor Dan Riley)*, Lynne Thigpen *(Kelly Noble)*, Bingo O'Malley *(Robert Roberts, Sr.)*, Kathleen Chalfant *(Constance Roberts)*, Ruth Lesko *(School Teacher)*, Kelly Willis *(Clarissa Flan)*, Anita Gillette *(The Mayor's Wife)*, Susan Sarandon *(News Anchor Tawna Titan)*, Fred Ward *(News Anchor Chip Daley)*, Charles Altman *(Debate Moderator)*, Staci Marcum *(Miss Philadelphia)*, Shira Piven *(Penn State Protester)*, Steve Pink *(Penn State Protester)*, Fisher Stevens *(Reporter Rock Bork)*, Gil Robbins *(Reverend Best)*, Angela Hall *(Choir Soloist)*, Lee Robbins *(Organ Player)*, John Cusack *(Host, "Cutting Edge Live")*, Bob Balaban *(Producer Michael Janes, "Cutting Edge Live")*, June Stein *(Carol, "Cutting Edge Live")*, Allan Nicholls *(Director, "Cutting Edge Live")*, Adam Simon *(Head Writer, "Cutting Edge Live")*, Ned Bellamy *(Uzi Kornhauser, "Cutting Edge Live")*, Natalie Strong *(Kala Kornhauser, "Cutting Edge Live")*, Robert Hegyes *(Reporter Ernesto Galleano)*, Larry John Meyers *(Police Spokesman)*, Pat Logan *(Policeman)*, Burnice Brourman *(Nurse)*, Tom Tully *(Reporter)*, Anthony DiLeo, Jr. *(Reporter)*, Jane Crawford *(Reporter)*, Gabrielle Robbins *(Singing Vigilante)*, Adele Robbins *(Vigilante)*, Brian Powell *(Vigilante)*, Paul Quinn *(Vigilante)*, Dean Robinson *(Vigilante)*, Jeffrey Foster *(Vigilante)*, Jeremy Piven *(Candle Seller)*, Lee Arenberg *(Religious Zealot)*, David Sinaiko *(Liberal)*, David Strathairn *(Bug's Attorney Mack Laflin)*, Ann Talman *(Reporter)*, Lamont Arnold *(Reporter)*, Hal O'Leary *(Senator Haydn)*, Don Brockett *(Chairman)*, Linda King *(DC Reporter)*, Nichole Bixler *(Dancer)*, Susan Shaw *(Dancer)*, Kristin Altfather, Jennifer Clippinger, Lori Doycich, Crystal Galipeau, Tracey Generalovich, Julie Harkness, Nadine Isenegger, Shari Jackson, Stephanie Lang, Erika Lingley, Cheryl Mann, Michelle Nagy, Keri Nowe, Elena Porco, Joy Short, Carolyn Sibray, Jennifer Stetor, Janine Willett *(Bob Roberts's Dancers)*

If good intentions could successfully make a film, then this one would be another CITIZEN KANE. Writer-director-star Tim Robbins is politically impeccable in terms of the issues he presents and the questions he raises, but it all brings to mind that famous mogul's quote about satire being the kind of thing that closes on Saturday night.

Bob Roberts (Robbins) is, as some pop biographer might describe him, "a young man in a hurry." A self-made millionaire, he's a folk-singing, right-wing senatorial candidate whose calculatedly repressive platform consists largely of a virulently anti-drug stance and an espousal of my-country-right-or-wrong, apple-pie values. Running against liberal incumbent Senator Brickley Paiste (Gore Vidal) of Pennsylvania, Roberts's campaign is fueled by a smug evasion of the issues and timely accusations of his opponent's sexual misconduct with a minor. He sings catchy ballads with titles like "Drugs Stink," "Complain, Complain, Complain," "My Land" and "Retake America." He's hounded by Bugs Raplin (Giancarlo Esposito), a liberal journalist who wants to ferret out the truth of his inside dealings with the very drug czars he rails so publicly against. Following his appearance on a "Saturday Night Live"-type TV show, there is a scuffle outside the studio and it appears that, in an assassination attempt in which Raplin is implicated, Roberts has been crippled from the waist down. Or has he?

The perils of neo-Fascistic, media-savvy politicos are indeed real, but this is all too calculated and bloodless to provide much in the way of truly provocative entertainment. It might have worked effectively as a TV sketch or short film, but the human element is in such short supply that most viewers' eyes will begin to glaze over when Robbins sings yet another "pointed" political song or presents one more view of Roberts's constituency, either sycophantic or sleazy. The songs are numbingly alike, and Robbins performs them with an unvarying, white-bread blandness. Robert Altman's classic NASHVILLE, which doubtlessly influenced Robbins, similarly used music in a political context, but those were real songs sung by performers like Henry Gibson, Barbara Harris and Ronee Blakley, whose love for them both transcended and drove home the moralizing.

BOB ROBERTS takes the form of a documentary being made about the candidate's campaign—a conceit which has a further distancing effect, as everyone is obviously acting for the camera, whether facing down the interviewer's questions or making the familiar "No paparazzi, please" gestures. The supposedly inadvertent moments of unstaged behavior likewise have a uniform predictability, the breath of life squeezed out of them by this tract-like approach. Robbins has rounded up a host of Hollywood's liberal elite: Susan Sarandon, Fred Ward, John Cusack, James Spader, Pamela Reed, Helen Hunt, Peter Gallagher, et al., to spice up the proceedings. But, as in THE PLAYER, these glorified cameos carry little weight. They're essentially a series of lightweight satirical takes on bubble-headed local news anchors—not exactly a hard target.

The writing is especially thin in the chaotic TV comedy show sequence, which gives no idea of the program's style or the reasons for its audience popularity. (As usual, Robbins favors the big, flamboyant gesture here, having a rebellious anti-Roberts employee literally pull the plug on the show.) Nor is the virtuosically roaming, one-take camerawork enough to convince us of the excitement of the events being recorded. Robbins ransacks some familiar media images—the faithful assembling beneath the stricken candidate's bedroom window (as if for John Lennon at the Dakota), Robbins sitting in a wheelchair *a la* George Wallace—but it's this type of simplistic expositional shorthand that does the film in.

Alan Rickman has perfected his brand of beady-eyed sleaze as Roberts's heinously corrupt financial backer, but as all the characters are conceived in the same cardboard vein, his viciousness has nothing to play against. About two-thirds into the film, the character of Roberts's wife pops up, appropriately blonde and wholesomely supportive, but that's all the information we're given about her. (She has no lines.) Likewise, there is no real delving into Brickley Paiste's persona, although Vidal, a born performer, has an elegant authority and magisterial comic verve with the material he has been given.

Robbins disastrously chooses to have the Raplin character deliver a climactic to-the-camera hysterical diatribe in which all the obviousness that has gone before is explained to us in excruciating detail. BOB ROBERTS dives headlong into the very kind of preachiness it seems to want to warn us against and, incidentally, gives Esposito a chance to twitch, sputter, bug his eyes and shriek in a manner already gruesomely, humorlessly familiar from his work with Spike Lee. *(Violence, profanity, adult situations.)*

p, Forrest Murray; d, Tim Robbins; w, Tim Robbins; ph, Jean Lepine; ed, Lisa Churgin; m, David Robbins; prod d, Richard Hoover; art d, Gary Kosko; set d, Brian Kasch; cos, Bridget Kelly

Comedy/Political **(PR: C MPAA: R)**

BODY WAVES ★

80m Concorde ~ New Horizons Home Video c

Bill Calvert *(Rick Matthews)*, Leah Lail *(Stacy Curtis)*, Jim Wise *(Donner)*, Dick Miller *(Father)*, John Crane *(Joe)*, Marc Grapey *(Larry)*, Michael James McDonald *(Squirrely)*, Larry Linville *(Himmel)*, Gloria LeRoy *(Mother)*, Roger Corman

Directed by newcomer P.J. Pesce, BODY WAVES is a predictable, slow-moving comedy which futilely resorts to tacky humor for laughs.

Rich Matthews (Bill Calvert) works for his father (Dick Miller) in an anal/rectal cream factory. Unhappy with his current career choice, Rick tells his father he wants to leave the company. Confounded by his son's decision, Rick's Dad challenges him to make $3,000 in three weeks. If Rick can do this, he has his freedom. Not wasting a minute, Rick goes into business with his enterprising friend Donner (Jim Wise) selling suntan lotion on the beach. But after awhile, the two can't give the stuff away. Although Rick is having difficulty selling the lotion he has no trouble attracting bikini-clad females. Rick's mastery of flirting with the opposite sex is witnessed by three local nerds—Joe (John Crane), Larry (Marc Grapey) and Squirrely (Michael James McDonald). Desperate to get laid, they offer Rick—surprise!—$3,000 to give them "cool lessons."

Meanwhile, evil politician Himmel (Larry Linville, of TV's "M*A*S*H" fame) is trying to shut down radio station KOOL where Rick's girlfriend Stacy Curtis (Leah Lail) works. After about a week of "cool lessons," Rick sends his students out on a trial run to pick up babes. Not surprisingly, none of them are successful. With the clock ticking, Rick makes up some special cologne and tells the nerds that it will drive the chicks crazy. This also fails to work. As a last resort, Larry, Joe and Squirrely ask their computer, "Clorisha," what to do. She tells them to become rappers. Calling themselves the Goo Boys, they somehow know how to rap, dance and gesticulate, and of course, become overnight successes. Rick gets his money, the nerds get laid and radio station KOOL is saved.

There are a few genuinely funny moments in BODY WAVES, but otherwise it fails as a comedy. The storyline (Pesce and Bo Zenga wrote the screenplay) is sophomoric, the physical humor doesn't work and the dialogue is often ridiculous. At one point Donner says: "We don't get the fundage unless those geeks get some pump action." This pretty much sums up the tone of the movie, dude. *(Profanity, partial nudity, sexual situations.)*

p, Mike Elliott; d, P.J. Pesce; w, Bo Zenga, P.J. Pesce; ph, Bob Paone; ed, John Shepphird; m, James Harry; prod d, Jane Hoffman, Kathleen Coates

Comedy **(PR: C MPAA: R)**

BODYGUARD, THE ★★

114m TIG Productions; Kasdan Pictures ~ Warner Bros c

Kevin Costner *(Frank Farmer)*, Whitney Houston *(Rachel Marron)*, Gary Kemp *(Sy Spector)*, Bill Cobbs *(Devaney)*, Ralph Waite *(Herb Farmer)*, Tomas Arana *(Portman)*, Michele Lamar Richards *(Nicki)*, Mike Starr *(Tony)*, Christopher Birt *(Henry)*, DeVaughn Nixon *(Fletcher)*, Gerry Bamman *(Ray Court)*, Joe Urla *(Minella)*, Tony Pierce *(Dan)*, Charles Keating *(Klingman)*, Robert Wuhl *(Oscar Host)*, Debbie Reynolds *(Herself)*, Daniel Tucker Kamin *(Thuringer)*, Ethel Ayler *(Emma)*, Sean Cheesman *(Rory)*, Richard Schiff *(Skip Thomas)*, Chris Connelly *(Oscar Arrivals MC)*, Nathaniel Parker *(Clive Healy)*, Bert Remsen *(Rotary President)*, Donald Hotton *(Reverend Hardy)*, Nita Whitaker *(Oscar Singer)*, Patricia Healy *(1st Sound Winner)*, Blumen Young *(2nd Sound Winner)*, Rob Sullivan *(Best Sound Presenter)*, Jennifer Lyon-Buchanan *(Best Song Winner)*, Stephen Shellen *(Tom Winston)*, Victoria Bass *(Woman in Green)*, Abbey Vine *(Ben Shiller)*, Phil Redrow *(Video Director)*, Joseph Hess *(Cuban Husband)*, Marta Velasco *(Cleaning Woman)*, Joe Unger *(Journalist)*, Gwen Seliger *(Rachel's Valet)*, Susan Traylor *(Dress Designer)*, Pat Van Patten *(Woman in Restaurant)*, Shelley A. Hill *(Mother at Restaurant)*, Amy Lou Dempsey *(Little Girl at Restaurant)*, Rosie Lee Hooks *(Thrift Shop Owner)*, Ken Myles *(1st Sound Technician)*, Robert L. Feist *(2nd Sound Technician)*, Charles Bazaldua *(TV Director)*, Tracye Logan *(Girl on Stairway)*, Art Spaan *(Billy Thomas)*, Douglas Price *(Pantages Assistant)*, Ellin LaVar *(Rachel's Hairstylist)*, Joseph Zabrosky *(Skip's Assistant)*, Rollin Jarrett *(Miami Reporter)*, David M. Morano *(Fontainebleau Barkeeper)*, Carla Lizzette Mejia *(Fontainebleau*

Maid), Linda Thompson *(Female Academy Member)*, David Foster *(Oscar Conductor)*, Towanna King *(Rachel's Assistant)*

In 1988, songstress Cyndi Lauper made her film debut in the ill-fated VIBES, for which Lauper, costar Jeff Goldblum and director Ken Kwapis were subjected to the most undeserved critical slings and arrows of recent memory. But more energy, chemistry and offbeat charm can be found in any extract from VIBES than in the entire running time of THE BODYGUARD, a dreary, turgid melodrama featuring the much ballyhooed debut of pop diva Whitney Houston.

Frank Farmer (Kevin Costner) is an ex-secret serviceman who, racked with guilt because he was off-duty the day Reagan was shot, is now a bodyguard for hire. And as is usually the case with movie star professionals, he is the best. When Rachel Marron (Whitney Houston), pop singer extraordinaire and Academy Award nominee, receives death threats and exploding dolls, she hires Farmer to beef up the security at home and serve as her bodyguard. Rachel takes an instant dislike to Farmer which means that before long they will become lovers. This comes to pass after Rachel asks Farmer out on a date and Farmer takes her to see YOJIMBO. But the next morning Farmer recovers his professional demeanor and informs Rachel that he wants no emotional involvement with his clients. After that, Rachel and Farmer spend most of their time scowling at each other, until another threat is made on Rachel's life.

Fearing for Rachel and her eight-year-old son, Farmer takes Rachel and her entourage to his father's mountain cabin for safety. But even in this secluded retreat, her life is again threatened. Her sister Nicki (Michele Lamar Richards), jealous of her success, reveals to Farmer that she hired an assassin to kill Rachel. Moments later, the assassin makes another attempt and kills Nicki by mistake. Rachel is despondent but still insists on attending the Academy Awards to see if she wins the Oscar for best actress. At the telecast, Farmer is on pins and needles but comes upon an old secret service buddy, Portman (Tomas Arana), whose unevenly set eyes immediately mark him as the killer. Before the evening is over, Rachel is named as Best Actress and she takes a long, long, long walk to the podium. Portman strikes, but Farmer leaps into the path of the bullets (which, we can only assume, he would have done if he'd been there on March 31, 1981) and saves Rachel. Time passes and Farmer, his arm in a sling, meets Rachel at an airport runway. Stopping the plane, she leaps into Farmer's arms and they kiss passionately.

Based on a decade-old screenplay by Lawrence Kasdan, THE BODYGUARD should have remained in Kasdan's drawer. It echoes the worst aspects of previous flops like THE FAN and THE OSCAR without any attempt at reworking the lame plot mechanizations and characterizations of those films. Instead, director Mick Jackson glosses over the shoddiness with a cheap-jack MTV burnish that ultimately serves to point up to a greater degree the botched narrative. Jackson lingers on Rachel's rich trappings, neglecting the screenplay and abandoning any efforts at suspense or character motivations. But Jackson isn't solely to blame, for Kasdan's screenplay is an abomination which never sufficiently explains the attraction between the two leads, let alone what kind of individuals they are.

Rachel is a cypher who lives in a big, luxurious house right out of "Lifestyles of the Rich and Famous." But the audience is never told why she's so popular, what makes her an Oscar-calibre actress, and why fans would be driven to a murderous frenzy because of her talent. The beautiful, albeit bland, Whitney Houston smiles and looks like a movie star but her eyes are dead. Frank Farmer, performed by Costner in a macho deadpan (and the worst haircut since Harrison Ford's in PRESUMED INNOCENT), is equally deadening, a man whose tormented past consists of pining regretfully for a replay of the day of Reagan's assassination. Farmer's a tinderbox of fulminating lethargy, whose constipated irritation at every other character in the film almost becomes a Brechtian audience distancing device but certainly offers no insight into the character. The burden of carrying the film falls squarely on the shoulders of these two stars but instead of fireworks, it becomes more a matter of Irresistible Force meeting Immovable Object with the laws of physics abandoned. Houston and Costner fume around each other like impotent bulls. They spend most of the running time avoiding eye contact, their star personas confining them within themselves.

THE BODYGUARD is another example of a failure that could have been aborted in the planning stages. But the concept must have made the movie executives salivate during their pre-production meetings. And when the writer and co-star are also the producers, who's around to disagree? *(Some violence, mild profanity, adult situations.)*

p, Lawrence Kasdan, Jim Wilson, Kevin Costner; d, Mick Jackson; w, Lawrence Kasdan, (from his story); ph, Andrew Dunn; ed, Richard A. Harris, Donn Cambern; m, Alan Silvestri; prod d, Jeffrey Beecroft; art d, William Ladd Skinner; set d, Lisa Dean; cos, Susan Nininger

AAN Best Song: David Foster (music) and Linda Thompson (lyrics); *AAN Best Song:* Jud Friedman (music) and Allan Rich (lyrics)

Romance/Thriller **(PR: C MPAA: R)**

BOOMERANG ★★½

118m Imagine Films Entertainment; Hudlin Bros; Paramount ~ Paramount c

Eddie Murphy *(Marcus Graham)*, Robin Givens *(Jacqueline)*, Halle Berry *(Angela)*, David Alan Grier *(Gerard)*, Martin Lawrence *(Tyler)*, Grace Jones *(Strange)*, Geoffrey Holder *(Nelson)*, Eartha Kitt *(Lady Eloise)*, Chris Rock *(Bony T)*, Tisha Campbell *(Yvonne)*, Lela Rochon *(Christie)*, John Witherspoon *(Mr. Jackson)*, Bebe Drake-Massey *(Mrs. Jackson)*, John Canada Terrell *(Todd)*, Leonard Jackson *(Chemist)*, Jonathan P Hicks *(Lady Eloise's Butler)*, Irv Dotten *(Box Office Clerk)*, Tom Mardirosian *(Salesman)*, Melvin Van Peebles *(Editor)*, Rhonda Jensen *(Waitress)*, Alyce Webb *(Noreen)*, Louise Vyent *(Woman From Holland)*, Frank Rivers *(Husband)*, Angela Logan *(Wife)*, Chuck Pfeifer *(French Businessman)*, Ray Dowell *(Pretty Receptionist)*, Reginald Hudlin *(Street Hustler)*, Warrington Hudlin *(Street Hustler)*, Andre Blake *(Waiter)*, Kenny Blank *(Kenny)*, Khanya Mkhize *(Khanya)*, Chris Rowland *(Kid)*, Erica Catherine Smith *(Kid)*, De'Von Young *(Kid)*, Daryl "Chill" Mitchell *(Street Photographer)*, Gene "Groove" Allen *(Street Photographer)*, Naydia Sanford *(Kissable Girl)*, Michelle Griffin *(Kissable Girl)*, Jewel Allsion Gittens *(Kissable Girl)*, Frank Tarsia *(Strange's Escort)*, Ronald Edward Ziegler *(Strange's Escort)*, Scott Baird *(Strange's Escort)*, Jeff McBride *(Strange's Escort)*, Herb Kerr *(Strange's Photographer)*, Al Cerullo *(Helicopter Pilot)*, Gary Frith *(Usher)*, Sandy Moore *(Usher)*, Olga Meredíz *(Guard)*, Tracy Douglas *(Attractive Woman)*

More interesting than entertaining and too long by far, BOOMERANG, which marks Eddie Murphy's return to the screen after a two-year hiatus, is a melancholy romantic comedy with a surprisingly bleak resolution for escapist summer fare.

Marcus Graham (Murphy) is a womanizing marketing director for a cosmetics firm who enjoys ample success in the bedroom as well as the boardroom before being demoted after his company is taken over by a European company founded by batty Lady Eloise (Eartha Kitt). Forced to report to new, sexy, hard-driving lady boss Jacqueline (Robin Givens), Marcus also finds himself losing the power position in the bedroom, when he is seduced first by Lady Eloise and then by Jacqueline, who promptly makes Marcus's sexual prowess the talk among the gals around the water cooler at work. Among those getting the word is outrageous supermodel Strange (Grace Jones), who tries to make Marcus's sexual cooperation a precondition for her cooperation on the company's new marketing campaign. Jacqueline reads the contractual riot act to Strange, salvaging the kind of situation that Marcus used to be able to finesse without breaking a sweat.

His self-esteem eroded to the point of disintegration, Marcus loses his confidence at work and risks catastrophe when he allows his avant-garde advertising director, Nelson (Geoffrey Holder), free rein over the first ad spots featuring Strange, with disastrous results. Taking pity on Marcus, creative assistant Angela (Halle Berry) steps in to help him save the ad campaign. Their relationship heats up outside the office as well, endangering Marcus's relationship with his best friend, Gerard (David Alan Grier), who had been dating Angela. Marcus then endangers his relationship with Angela, with whom he has fallen in love, by yielding to a one-night return engagement with Jacqueline. When the dust clears, Marcus patches things up with Angela, but the film actually ends with no peace in the battle of the sexes as Marcus and his two friends, Gerard and Tyler (Martin Lawrence), celebrate their male bond atop a Manhattan rooftop.

In their first outing following the critical and commercial success of the low-budget HOUSE PARTY, director Reginald Hudlin and producer Warrington Hudlin show themselves fully up to the demands of shepherding an all-star cast through an expensive production—maybe too much so. If anything, BOOMERANG is too controlled for its own good. The Hudlins' work here falls into the tradition of Lubitsch and Wilder, neither noted for wild spontaneity but both creators of sophisticated romantic romps with a darkness not too far beneath the surface gaiety. Here, the relationship between sex and power is handled with a frankness and directness rarely seen in American movies since Wilder's THE APARTMENT.

Marcus makes the mistake of believing that his power over women comes from his personal charm, when it actually stems from the same place it does for most men—their position in society. Once he loses that position, his egoism is such that he doesn't at first realize how much he's lost. When Lady Eloise and Jacqueline use him, he persists in believing that he is using them—until his run-in with Strange lets him know otherwise and forces him to realize how far he's fallen. Still, the lesson doesn't quite take when he later undervalues his relationship with Angela by going back to his old ways. Despite the nominally upbeat resolution of having Marcus reconcile with Angela, the Hudlins end the film with Marcus and his friends alone, still failing to comprehend the implications of women assuming socially powerful roles.

Unfortunately, BOOMERANG's provocative premise remains largely undeveloped in the screenplay by regular Murphy collaborators Barry W. Blaustein and David Sheffield, working from a story by Murphy himself. In his choice of material, Murphy seems to favor stories that have a fable-like quality to them. (How else to explain THE GOLDEN CHILD?) Sharing the same writers, BOOMERANG most resembles COMING TO AMERICA in attempting to make a statement on relations between the sexes within a fantasy framework. Directed with considerably more charm and grace than the earlier film, BOOMERANG suggests how such an approach could bring the romantic comedy into modern times, with its all-black casting being only the most visible of its innovations. But suggesting isn't the same thing as accomplishing. *(Adult situations.)*

p, Brian Grazer, Warrington Hudlin; d, Reginald Hudlin; w, Barry W. Blaustein, David Sheffield, (from story by Eddie Murphy); ph, Woody Omens; ed, Earl Watson; m, Marcus Miller; prod d, Jane Musky; art d, William Barclay; set d, Alan Hicks; cos, Francine Jamison-Tanchuck

Romance/Comedy **(PR: C MPAA: R)**

BRAIN DONORS

90m Lame Duck Productions; Zucker Brother Productions; Paramount ~ Paramount c

John Turturro *(Roland T. Flakfizer)*, Bob Nelson *(Jacques)*, Mel Smith *(Rocco Melonchek)*, Nancy Marchand *(Lillian Oglethorpe)*, John Savident *(Lazlo)*, George De La Pena *("The Great" Volare)*, Spike Alexander *(Alan)*, Juli Donald *(Lisa)*, Teri Copley *(Blonde)*

From its ugly claymation credits to its inexplicable title, BRAIN DONORS is a profoundly unsuccessful, uncredited and extremely loose remake of the 1935 Marx Brothers classic A NIGHT AT THE OPERA that brings no credit to anyone involved with its production.

Wealthy and foolish widow Lillian Oglethorpe (Nancy Marchand) decides to honor her late husband's memory by founding a ballet company. To the fury of her stuffy lawyer, Lazlo (John Savident), she appoints opportunistic ambulance chaser Roland T. Flakfizer (John Turturro) director. He rashly assures her he can sign up The Great Volare (George De La Pena), a temperamental, world famous dancer of indeterminate nationality. With moronic sidekicks Jacques (Bob Nelson) and Rocco Melonchek (Mel Smith), Flakfizer blunders through the world of ballet dancing, giving offense at every opportunity and helping a couple of sweet young dancers (Spike Alexander and Juli Donald) get their big break.

That BRAIN DONORS (originally titled "Lame Ducks," which at least had some faint connection with the subject matter) has no plot to speak of isn't really the problem. Neither, after all, does A NIGHT AT THE OPERA. The problem is that it's extraordinarily unfunny, despite the strenuous efforts of all involved. Surprisingly enough, those involved include the team of screenwriter Pat Proft and executive producers Jerry and David Zucker (fourth partner Jim Abrahams is missing), of AIRPLANE! fame. The world of classical ballet is certainly not without its absurdities; in fact, the ZAZ team poked malicious and on-the-money fun at some of them in TOP SECRET! You'd think that between them they'd have been able to come up with at least a couple of funny bits, if not a coherently entertaining film. But the deadly elements in BRAIN DONORS outweigh the promising ones by a substantial margin, and the results are excruciating.

John Turturro, best known for his accomplished work in such films as the Coen brothers' BARTON FINK and Spike Lee's DO THE RIGHT THING, is possessed of the sort of offbeat looks that often drive performers to comedy out of sheer self-defense. But looking funny isn't necessarily the same as *being* funny, and Turturro isn't. He certainly gives his all, but the endless mugging, eye-rolling and frantic rushing about is merely exhausting. Bob Nelson specializes in whimsical physical comedy (often more annoying than amusing), while Mel Smith is a crude foil; Nancy Marchand and John Savident are on hand to provide the sort of puffed up dignity that demands to be deflated in the crudest possible manner. As Volare, dancer George De La Pena rants and sputters through a dreary series of indignities (A NIGHT AT THE OPERA's famous stateroom sequence is re-staged in his dressing room); he's so colorless that it's shocking to recall that this was the star of Herbert Ross's overwrought NIJINSKY.

Director Dennis Dugan, of 1990's notorious PROBLEM CHILD (a purportedly comic twist on the BAD SEED scenario), shows no more flair for comic material than the cast. In all, BRAIN DONORS has little to recommend it.

p, James D. Brubaker, Gil Netter; d, Dennis Dugan; w, Pat Proft; ph, David M. Walsh; ed, Malcolm Campbell; m, Ira Newborn; prod d, William J. Cassidy; art d, Frank Richwood; set d, Jeannie Gunn; cos, Robert Turturice

Comedy **(PR: A MPAA: PG)**

BRAM STOKER'S DRACULA ★★★½

130m Columbia; American Zoetrope; Osiris Films ~ Columbia c

Gary Oldman *(Count Vlad Dracul/Dracula)*, Winona Ryder *(Mina Murray/Elisabeta)*, Anthony Hopkins *(Professor Abraham Van Helsing)*, Keanu Reeves *(Jonathan Harker)*, Richard E. Grant *(Dr. Jack Seward)*, Cary Elwes *(Lord Arthur Holmwood)*, Bill Campbell *(Quincey P. Morris)*, Sadie Frost *(Lucy Westenra)*, Tom Waits *(R.M. Renfield)*, Monica Bellucci *(Dracula's Bride)*, Michaela Bercu *(Dracula's Bride)*, Florina Kendrick *(Dracula's Bride)*, Jay Robinson *(Mr. Hawkins)*, I.M. Hobson *(Hobbs)*, Laurie Franks *(Lucy's Maid)*, Maud Winchester *(Downstairs Maid)*, Octavian Cadia *(Deacon)*, Robert Getz *(Priest)*, Dagmar Stanec *(Sister Agatha)*, Eniko Oss *(Sister Sylva)*, Nancy Linehan Charles *(Older Woman)*, Tatiana Von Furstenberg *(Younger Woman)*, Jules Sylvester *(Zoo Keeper)*, Hubert Wells *(Zoo Keeper)*, Daniel Newman *(News Hawker)*, Honey Lauren *(Peep Show Girl)*, Judi Diamond *(Peep Show Girl)*, Robert Buckingham *(Husband)*, Cully Fredricksen *(Van Helsing's Assistant)*, Don Lewis *(Shadow Puppeteer)*, Fred Spencer *(Shadow Puppeteer)*, Mitchel Evans, James Murray, Van Snowden, Mark Bryan Wilson *(Additional Puppeteers)*

Francis Ford Coppola reasserted his position as one of the most important mainstream filmmakers of his generation with BRAM STOKER'S DRACULA, an energetic and entertaining retelling of one of moviedom's most often told tales.

Coppola's reworking of the Dracula legend gives the Count more of a "backstory" than is customary. A Transylvanian Count sworn to defend the Catholic faith, Vlad Dracul (Gary Oldman) is known for his implacable viciousness towards his "heathen" enemies. After winning a battle during the Crusades of the 16th century, he impales his enemies on spears and is rumored to have eaten their flesh and swallowed their blood. Before his triumphant return home, however, his young bride Elisabeta (Winona Ryder) is given a false message that Dracul has been killed. Donning her wedding gown, she leaps to her death from Dracul's castle into the icy river hundreds of feet below. When Dracul is informed that Elisabeta's soul is damned as a result of her suicide, he renounces his faith and plunges his sword into a cross, causing it to gush forth blood, which the crazed nobleman catches in a sacred chalice and drinks. The sacrilege seals his fate for an eternity during which he must feed off the blood of the living.

Centuries later, young real estate agent Jonathan Harker (Keanu Reeves) visits the Count (now known as Dracula) at his castle in Transylvania to close a deal on some London properties. Dracula glimpses a photo of Harker's fiancee, Mina Murray (Ryder), and is immediately obsessed, believing her to be the reincarnation of his dead bride. Leaving Harker behind as a prisoner in his castle, the Count moves to London and befriends Mina, who finds herself inexorably attracted to this haunted Eastern European aristocrat. Under cover of night, though, this handsome, cultivated being takes on a variety of grotesque incarnations and commits a series of unspeakable acts. These make him the target of a hunt undertaken by blood disease specialist Abraham Van Helsing (Anthony Hopkins), the escaped-and-returned Harker and three suitors of Mina's sexy best friend Lucy Westenra (British actress Sadie Frost, in her American debut), an early victim of the Count. They hound Dracula from his nocturnal resting place in London, a ruined abbey, and pursue him back to Transylvania, where he is laid to rest by Mina herself, who puts Dracula out of his eternal misery by impaling his heart and then decapitating him.

BRAM STOKER'S DRACULA is as outrageous, fantastic and florid as THE GODFATHER is slow, stately and realistic. Both films demonstrate the flamboyant director's taste for the operatic, with their crashing visual and musical crescendos. It's hard to watch the extraordinary sequence in DRACULA during which Coppola crosscuts between the marriage of Mina and Jonathan and the ravishing of Lucy by Dracula (in the form of a wolf) without being reminded of the famed climax of THE GODFATHER, in which Michael Corleone's bloody rampage against his enemies is crosscut with the christening of his son. Overall, though, the style of DRACULA bears a greater resemblance to Coppola's more personal ONE FROM THE HEART in its utter, willful dissociation from any recognizable reality, plunging instead into the heady cinematic realms of fairy tales, dreams and myths.

DRACULA was shot almost entirely on a soundstage and its deliberate artificiality is underscored by special effects that subvert, rather than create, the illusion of, reality. The costumes and set designs have a baroque richness that makes the film seem at times more like a moving picture book than a moving picture. (The museum-quality costumes by acclaimed multi-media designer Eiko Ishioka are particularly stunning.) This impression is reinforced by James V. Hart's screenplay, which preserves Stoker's original epistolary device of telling the story through journal entries, diaries and letters written by the principal characters. Rather than trying to reinvent the saga radically, Coppola seems to embrace DRACULA's rich movie heritage with sly homages to everything from the Tod Browning-Bela Lugosi classic, to Herzog's NOSFERATU and even, with his breakneck pacing and breathless, cliffhanger climaxes, the horror films of England's Hammer studios.

What Coppola also adds, with considerable assistance from Ryder and Frost, is an eroticism that tilts the story away from Harker and Van Helsing towards Mina and Lucy. (One of the most sought-after actresses of her generation, Ryder originally brought Hart's screenplay to Coppola's attention. In gratitude, she is breathtakingly photographed by cinematographer Michael Ballhaus.) In common with other Coppola heroines, Mina is much wiser than the men around her and therefore capable of perceiving Dracula's essentially tragic nature; it is the strength of his passion that has turned him into a life-destroying creature. Mina defeats Dracula not by opposing him but embracing him, redefining his evil in human terms and defusing it with love. The message should not be lost on modern audiences who frequently respond with neo-Victorian terror to the venereal "blood sickness" of AIDS.

For all its violence and eroticism, DRACULA espouses a morality that encompasses rather than excludes, and brings understanding and sympathy rather than fear, hatred and terror. Beyond Coppola's unquestioned mastery of his medium and the rich, energetic performances of his attractive cast (with the exception of the embarassingly stiff Keanu Reeves), it is that sense of human affirmation that makes DRACULA more than a great horror film. *(Violence, nudity, sexual situations, adult situations.)*

p, Francis Ford Coppola, Fred Fuchs, Charles Mulvehill; d, Francis Ford Coppola; w, James V. Hart, (from the novel *Dracula* by Bram Stoker); ph, Michael Ballhaus; ed, Nicholas C. Smith, Glen Scantlebury, Anne Goursaud; m, Wojciech Kilar; prod d, Thomas Sanders; art d, Andrew Precht; set d, Garrett Lewis; cos, Eiko Ishioka; makeup, Tom C. McCarthy, David E. Stone

AAN Art Direction: Thomas Sanders (Art Direction) and Garrett Lewis (Set Decoration); *AA Costume Design:* Eiko Ishioka; *AA Makeup:* Greg Cannom, Michele Burke, and Matthew W. Mungle; *AA Sound Effects Editing:* Tom C. McCarthy and David E. Stone

Horror/Romance/Fantasy (PR: C MPAA: R)

BREAKING THE RULES ★

100m Management Company Entertainment Group ~ Miramax c

Jason Bateman *(Phil Stepler)*, C. Thomas Howell *(Gene Michaels)*, Jonathan Silverman *(Rob Konigsberg)*, Annie Potts *(Mary Klingsmith)*, Kent Bateman *(Mr. Stepler)*, Shawn Phelan *(Young Phil)*, Jackey Vinson *(Young Gene)*, Marty Belafsky *(Young Rob)*, Mark Rosenblatt *(Bartender)*, Krista Kesreau *(Rob's Date)*, Frank Wagner *(Justice of the Peace)*, Manual Pickett *(Minister AZ)*, Angelbreath Cobb *(Widow AZ)*, Eurlyne Epper *(Red Woman)*

A poor excuse for a teen road movie, BREAKING THE RULES manages to live up to its makers' reputations. Coming from director Neal Israel (POLICE ACADEMY, BACHELOR PARTY) and producers Jonathan D. Krane (MICKI AND MAUDE, BLIND DATE) and Kent Bateman (TEEN WOLF TOO), this is a dubious distinction at best.

Phil Stepler (Jason Bateman), a free-spirited college dropout, brings together his childhood best friends—Gene Michaels (C. Thomas Howell), a young Lothario past his prime, and Rob Konigsberg (Jonathan Silverman), an uptight med student with musical ambitions—to their hometown, Cleveland. Formerly songwriting partners, Gene and Rob have been estranged ever since Gene slept with Rob's girlfriend. Phil wants to reconcile his friends, which he manages by confessing his painful secret: he has contracted leukemia, which he hides behind his cheerful disposition. With barely a month left to live, Phil wants his friends to join him in a cross-country trek to Los Angeles, en route to a "Jeopardy!" audition.

In typical road movie fashion, the young men go through numerous small adventures on this trip of their lives. They run into a friendly bear; a beautiful blonde (Krista Kesreau) picks up shy Rob, only to baptize him into her born-again faith; they meet Mary Klingsmith (Annie Potts), a vivacious middle-aged waitress who joins them in their cruise; they witness a sad funeral, which prompts Phil to beg his friends not to mourn his imminent passing; Phil marries Mary in Reno, after which—as a gesture of friendship—he lets Rob sleep with her; finally in California, Phil dies in Mary's arms. Back in Cleveland, Mary takes Gene and Rob away from Phil's funeral, and they watch Phil's videotaped farewell, joining him in a nostalgic singalong.

BREAKING THE RULES aims to be a heart-warming road movie, a bittersweet comedy wherein true friendship triumphs over death. What we get instead is a rich kid's fantasy of "rebelliousness" that's all empty posturing. How revolutionary can you be with a new van and Daddy's American Express card? As for breaking rules, the only "transgressions" are Rob's dissatisfaction with his medical studies, imposed by his father, in favor of his real vocation as a musician (with no indication of his actually leaving medical school after Phil's funeral), Phil's own failed college career—a *fait accompli* before the whole adventure starts—and his impulsive marriage to an older woman. Rather than rule-breaking, what we have here is nothing more than all-American wish-fulfillment.

Tired cliches abound, from the inevitable reconciliation of strained friends and a doomed but brave terminally ill character to an utterly condescending view of womanhood. Rob's "date" is a zombified born-again Christian, portrayed as a calculating fanatic out to lure hot-blooded boys into her cult. Mary is inexplicably enchanted with these "wild and crazy" youths, readily agreeing to leave her town, marry the dying Phil and bed bashful Rob.

The cast of minor heartthrobs is energetic, but does very little acting. As the dour Gene, C. Thomas Howell (THE HITCHER, SOUL MAN) maintains a sour disposition throughout the movie, his smile resembling a grotesque mask. Jonathan Silverman (BRIGHTON BEACH MEMOIRS, WEEKEND AT BERNIES) portrays Rob as a big baby, giggling nervously in the presence of women and whining about his frustrated musical aspirations. Jason Bateman (TEEN WOLF TOO, TV's "The Hogan Family") shows just how superficial his acting talent is, overdoing Phil's happy facade and failing to make his agonies credible. Poor Annie Potts (GHOSTBUSTERS, TV's "Designing Women") has yet another wretched film role as Mary, the mature woman who plays second banana to three vapid young men.

BREAKING THE RULES could be seen as a metaphor, courtesy of producer Kent Bateman, for his son Jason's own dying career: just as Phil is racing against time to fulfill his aspirations, Bateman *fils* must've hoped to rescue his faltering career. With another bomb—it failed miserably at the box office—Bateman's career could be headed for Phil's fate. BREAKING THE RULES is a forgettable, clumsy movie, its appeal limited to the leading actors' fan clubs.

p, Jonathan D. Krane, Kent Bateman; d, Neal Israel; w, Paul Shapiro; ph, James Hayman; ed, Tom Walls; m, David Kitay; prod d, Donald Light-Harris; set d, Andy Bernard; cos, Giovanna Ottobe-Melton

Comedy/Drama (PR: C MPAA: PG-13)

BREATHING FIRE ★

Golden Pacific Productions ~ Imperial Entertainment Corporation c

Jonathan Ke Quan *(Charlie Moore)*, Jerry Trimble *(Michael Moore)*, Eddie Saavedra *(Tony Moore)*, Ed Neil *(David Moore)*, Laura Hamilton *(Annie)*, Wendell C. Whitaker *(Tank)*, Drake Diamond *(Peter Stern)*, Jaqueline Pulliam, Juan Ojeda, "Bolo" Yeung

There's bad and then there's enjoyably bad, which accounts for the lonely one-star rating accorded BREATHING FIRE, a decidedly unenjoyable martial arts saga.

Stuffed with action, empty of sense, the semi-coherent plot commences with a gold heist by a criminal quintet masterminded by hawk-faced businessman Michael Moore (Jerry Trimble), with the compliance of cringing bank exec Peter Stern (Drake Diamond). In a possible tribute to the Teenage Mutant Ninja Turtles, the robbers lock up the loot and make key impressions in a plastic pizza that they then divide among themselves to ensure honor among thieves. Stern wants out of the deal, however. Michael has the wimp and his wife both killed, but their busty teenage daughter Annie (Laura Hamilton) escapes with the precious pizza slice. She seeks sanctuary with her father's old Vietnam buddy, David Moore (Ed Neil), a grease-stained outcast who improbably snaps into form as an invincible kung fu fighting machine when the bad guys attack. He also happens to be Michael's brother, and unknowingly brings Annie to the archvillain's mansion for protection.

Here Annie encounters two kung fu kids who are the real stars of the story: Michael's biological son Tony (Eddie Saavedra) and his adopted son Charlie (Jonathan Ke Quan), a Vietnamese orphan. The latter tells anyone who'll listen that he's searching for his mysterious origins; it won't take viewers long to deduce that Charlie's peasant mom was mistaken for Viet Cong and gunned down by Michael back in the rice paddies. That bald fact takes Charlie the whole movie to uncover, as he and Eddie engage in fight after fight against Dad's evil cohorts.

With two official directors listed, and a third—Rick Mitchell—acknowledged in the closing credits for "additional scenes," BREATHING FIRE doesn't stay on a single tack for very long, alternating cold-blooded murder with comic slapstick, sometimes quite inexplicably as Charlie and Eddie tussle with a trio of chopsocky midgets and re-enact the famous fence-painting incident from Twain's *Adventures of Tom Sawyer*. The centerpiece of the picture has David Moore crippled by Michael in one brawl (Michael first pastes on a little mustache that effectively prevents his brother from recognizing him!). While David sulks, Charlie and Eddie beg that he tutor them in his brand of 'Nam-vet-fu, and soon David is putting the boys through the torturous training regimen that these movies love to chronicle.

There's an incredibly racist portrayal of gold-robber Tank (Wendell C. Whitaker), a big, blubbering Black goon who turns informer on the other criminals and, of course, gets killed as a reward—a typical fate for African-American characters in genre films like this. The karate tournament epilogue finds Eddie, upset that Charlie got Dad sent to jail, pummeling his half-brother nearly to death and then reconciling, a heartfelt message of Better Living Through Violence. The acting is often terrible, and hardly enhanced by badly post-synced dialogue, but otherwise production values are better than one would expect for such a jerry-built effort. Appropriately, the closing credits contain numerous spelling errors. *(Violence, profanity.)*

p, Raymond Mahoney; d, Lou Kennedy, Brandon DeWilde; w, Wayne John, Raymond Mohoney, (from the story by Delon Tanners); ph, Henry Chinon; ed, William Young; m, Paul Hertzog

Crime/Action/Martial Arts (PR: C MPAA: R)

BRENDA STARR ★

87m AM/PM Productions; Tribune Entertainment Company; Mystery Man Productions Inc.; Tomorrow Entertainment Inc. ~ Triumph Releasing c

Brooke Shields *(Brenda Starr)*, Timothy Dalton *(Basil St. John)*, Tony Peck *(Mike Randall)*, Diana Scarwid *(Libby "Lips" Lipscomb)*, Nestor Serrano *(Jose–Seaplane Pilot)*, Jeffrey Tambor *(Vladimir)*, June Gable *(Luba)*, Charles Durning *(Editor Francis I. Livright)*, Kathleen Wilhoite *(Reporter Hank O'Hare)*, John Short *(Cub Reporter Pesky Miller)*, Eddie Albert *(Police Chief Maloney)*, Mark Von Holstein *(Donovan O'Shea–Public Enemy Number 3)*, Henry Gibson *(Professor Gerhardt Von Kreutzer)*, Ed Nelson *(President Harry S. Truman)*, Tom Aldredge *(The Fake Captain Borg)*, Matthew Cowles *(The Real Captain Borg)*, Avner Eisenberg *(Carlos–Magnificent)*, Mary Lou Rosato *(Esperanza–Wife)*, Rex Pierson *(Boris–Bullyboy)*, Dave Efron *(Mischa–Bullyboy)*, Dario Carnevale *(Young Guide From India)*, Sergio Pereira *(Young Portugese Taxi Driver)*, Antoni Corone *(Karl–Burly Sailor)*, Joshua Sussman *(Carl–Burly Bartender)*, Bean Reathal *("Globe" Editor)*, Robert Weil *(Gus–"Flash" City Room)*, Pola Miller *(Gypsy Fortune Teller)*, Tod Booth *(1st Reporter)*, George Marshall Ruge *(2nd Reporter)*, Cyndi Vicino *(Nurse)*, Steve Tiger *(Chief of Agape Natives)*, Carmen Jovet *(San Juan Saleslady)*, Ramon Saldana *(Spanish Policeman)*, Carlos A. Martir *(Petshop Owner)*, William Agosto *(Street Vendor)*, Antonio Fabrizio *(Cargo Plane Pilot)*, Bob Noble *(Maitre d')*, Dean Morris *(Diego)*, Jeannine Falcon *(Jiva)*, Mitch Harwood *(Ras Poppa)*, Linda Dempsey *(Tinka)*, Lenny Baker *(Leonardo)*, Randall Thompson *(Zukini)*, Stephan Thompson *(Skypup)*, The Capoeira Dancers

Caught up in legal problems since its production in 1986, BRENDA STAR finally achieved negligible release in early 1992, and the only surprise about the fact that it had spent six years on the shelf is the fact that it didn't remain there.

The herky-jerky plot makes the fatal mistake of proceeding from the idea that its protagonist is fictional, hardly a good idea when attempting to convince an audience to believe in a comics-derived character. The movie is based on the popular strip by Dale Messick, who in this screenplay has left the daily drawing work to young artist Mike Randall (Tony Peck). He's getting sick of this job and says so out loud during one stint at his easel—but he then gets the startle of his life when Brenda (Brooke Shields) interrupts his work to chastise him for his bad attitude.

Viewers are then plunged into Brenda's world, where she always goes the extra mile to get a story, even if it involves being taken hostage by the crooks she's covering. This inspires the anger of Libby "Lips" Lipscomb (Diana Scarwid), her chief rival. Soon Brenda's onto the story of her career, that of a Nazi scientist who has developed an amazing new fuel and is hiding out in the Amazonian jungle. In the course of pursuing the doctor and her story, she runs afoul of the viciously competitive Libby, as well as a pair of inept Russian spies, Vladimir (Jeffrey Tambor) and Luba (June Gable). To complicate matters, Mike has willed himself into Brenda's world to try to lure her back to the strip she's abandoned, and begins to fall in love with her. Meanwhile, Brenda's fallen for a mysterious, handsome, eye-patched hero, Basil St. John (Timothy Dalton), who turns up to rescue her from tight situations.

Another facile attempt to bring a four-color character to the big screen, BRENDA STARR joins such recent flops as CAPTAIN AMERICA and THE PUNISHER in hammering another nail into the genre's crowded coffin. The screenplay is a total mess, trying to maintain a comic-strip feel while also poking fun at the conventions of the form, and Robert Ellis Miller's direction is strained in its attempts at comedy and simply inept in the action scenes. A sequence in which Brenda escapes from the Russians and precipitates a melee in a market square looks like it was assembled from outtakes left over after the good angles were used; in another priceless moment, Brenda and company are about to be thrown from a boat into a piranha-infested river, and escape by jumping off the other side! Technically the movie's okay, but all those years spent dormant haven't done much for the usually great Freddie Francis photography; some of the shots are as washed out and discolored as an old high-school science film.

The acting is pretty shabby as well. Shields (THE BLUE LAGOON, ENDLESS LOVE) is gorgeous but has a hard time displaying either dramatic or comic range, while Dalton (THE LIVING DAYLIGHTS, LICENCE TO KILL) looks like he's desperately waiting for that call from Cubby Broccoli. And poor Scarwid (INSIDE MOVES, SILKWOOD), who's done fine work in the past, is forced to play Libby as stiffly and abrasively as possible, perhaps explaining why she hasn't done any significant work since making this film. But at least she gets off easier than most of the other supporting female characters (including Kathleen Wilhoite as another reporter, Hank O'Hare), who are made to look unaccountably butch. In particular, Gable's Russian villainess looks startlingly like Monique Mercure in NAKED LUNCH—and she at least had the excuse of really being Roy Scheider. *(Violence, adult situations.)*

p, Myron A. Hyman; d, Robert Ellis Miller; w, Noreen Stone, James David Buchanan, Delia Ephron, (from the story by Buchanan and Stone based on the comic strip by Dale Messick); ph, Freddie Frances; ed, Mark Melnick; m, Johnny Mandel; prod d, John Lloyd; art d, Steven Schwartz; set d, Richard Villalobos; cos, Peggy Farrell

Adventure/Comedy/Fantasy (PR: A MPAA: PG)

BRIDE OF KILLER NERD

74m Riot Pictures ~ Tempe Video c

Toby Radloff *(Harold Kunkle)*, Heidi Lohr *(Thelma Crump)*, Kathleen Hogan *(Jackie)*, Louis DeJulius *(Jimbo)*, Lynette Ray *(Marzie)*, Tim Redmond *(Matt)*, Mimsel Dendak *(Rachael)*, Michael McClendon *(Tom)*, Karrie King *(Frankie)*, Joe Wack *(Johnny)*, Christopher Ashmun *(Hood)*, Tom Pettis *(Mr. Reynolds)*, Marc Andreyko *(Dave)*, Deena Stamm *(Connie)*, Virginia Scott *(Mother)*, Niko DePofi *(T.J.)*, Lori Scarlett *(Jenny)*, Amy Rupnik *(Young Girl)*, Laura Tsai *(1st Girl)*, Courtney Davison *(2nd Girl)*, Katie Polit *(3rd Girl)*, Tom Cullison *(TV Announcer)*

This dreadful follow-up to the 1991 direct-to-video gore film manages to make its negligible predecessor look good. Lacking even the minor surreal elements of the first KILLER NERD, this is homemade blood-and-guts at its worst.

Harold Kunkle (Toby Radloff), the titular gory geek, has moved on to a new job as a data processor, where he is looked down on by his fellow workers. But soon he finds true love in the person of Thelma Crump (Heidi Lohr), a high school senior who is regularly tormented by her nasty classmates. The pair meet in church while the priest is giving a sermon on loneliness, and soon are spending blissful days and nights together. Thelma's so happy that she doesn't think it unusual when Jackie (Kathleen Hogan) and Marzie (Lynette Ray), two of her tormentors, claim they've changed their ways and invite Thelma and Harold to a party at the house of Marzie's boyfriend Matt (Tim Redmond).

The couple attend despite Harold's reservations, and soon his worries prove founded; he is goaded into getting falling-down drunk by Matt and his pal Jimbo (Louis DeJulius), while Jackie and Marzie make up the oblivious Thelma to look like a freak. She and Harold flee the party in humiliation, but Thelma later hears Harold talking in his drunken sleep about his previous murders, inspiring her to lead Harold in another round of revenge. After dispatching Frankie (Karrie King) and Johnny (Joe Wack), who have been making out in a car, the pair invade the house.

The place is now deserted save the two couples and Rachael (Mimsel Dendak), whom Harold stabs in the shower, and Tom (Michael McClendon), who is lured upstairs and impaled. Harold and Thelma then drag Marzie downstairs, tie her to a chair, shave her head and plant an ax in her skull; looking for her, Jimbo is jumped by Harold while Thelma hacks up Matt upstairs. She then goes after Jackie, who manages to electrocute Thelma in the bathtub; Harold bursts in on the scene, strangles Jackie and spirits away the body of his beloved. Six months later, he's still living a happy life with her skeleton.

It's hard to say what is more unpleasant to watch in BRIDE OF KILLER NERD: the grotesquely unflattering close-ups of its actors; the sadistic humiliations visited upon Thelma; or the gross murders carried out by the Killer Nerds. One particularly sickening moment features Johnny being held in place by Harold while Thelma performs oral sex on him, followed by her biting off his penis. Little attempt is made to build up true sympathy for the protagonists—the film seems as disdainful of Thelma's nerdy qualities as the other characters—and nothing is made of the fact that Thelma is played by the same actress, Lohr, who portrayed the girl Harold had a crush on in the first KILLER NERD.

About the only praiseworthy element of this misbegotten sequel is the fact that the ending seems to preclude the possibility of a SON OF KILLER NERD. *(Excessive violence, profanity, substance abuse, nudity.)*

p, Mark Steven Bosko, Wayne A. Harold; d, Mark Steven Bosko, Wayne A. Harold; w, Mark Steven Bosko, Wayne A. Harold; ph, Alan Stevens; ed, Dick Myers; m, Sean Carlin; set d, Lance Kittel

Horror/Comedy (PR: O MPAA: NR)

BRIEF HISTORY OF TIME, A ★★★½

(U.S./U.K.) 80m Amblin Entertainment; Anglia Television; Gordon Freedman Productions ~ Triton Pictures c

Stephen Hawking, Jane Hawking, Isobel Hawking, Janet Humphrey, Mary Hawking, Basil King, Derek Powney, Norman Dix, Robert Berman, Gordon Berry, Roger Penrose, Dennis Sciama, John Wheeler, Brandon Carter, John Taylor, Kip Thorne, Don Page, Christopher Isham, Brian Whitt, Raymond LaFlamme

Director Errol Morris has taken a daunting subject—one man's lifelong obsession with the creation of the universe—and fashioned a uniquely thought-provoking entertainment highlighted by an unexpected dose of wit. While not as riveting as some of his earlier work, Morris's A BRIEF HISTORY OF TIME is nonetheless an outstanding documentary.

The film's magnificent opening shot, a stellar landscape, is something you'd expect to see in a planetarium, not a movie theater. It's followed by the eerily disembodied voice of the film's subject, Stephen Hawking, who is arguably the world's foremost astronomer. "What came first, the chicken or the egg?" queries Hawking. A chicken's head promptly pops into view, setting the atmosphere for the next ninety minutes—education through wry humor. Preferring to call himself a cosmologist, Hawking has, over the past three decades, taken the field and turned it upside down and inside out. Indeed, having rebutted Einstein's theory of general relativity well in advance of his scientific peers, Hawking has become a legend in his own time.

A BRIEF HISTORY OF TIME follows Stephen from his birth in England in 1942. Fascinated with the stars since childhood, he was accepted to Oxford on early admissions. Never really applying himself (because he didn't need to), he spent more time sipping beer with his college chums than hitting the books. Lazy by nature and all too easily bored with his studies, he always found plenty of time to play coxswain on the university rowing team. A fellow student recalls how Hawking finished ten questions on a mathematics exam in little over an hour, while his contemporaries managed to conquer only one and a half answers during a four-hour period. Still, Hawking himself admits that he was unfocused and not sure what to do with his gift. After completing his studies at Oxford in 1962, he went on to Cambridge for his Ph.d. This is where destiny finally caught up with him.

While at Cambridge, Hawking began to have trouble with his balance and often dropped things. Tests revealed that he was suffering from ALS, commonly known as Lou Gehrig's disease. Doctors also confirmed that he would progressively lose all motor functions and that only his heart, brain and lungs would remain unaffected. Worse still, they gave him only two or three years to live. After understandably succumbing to depression, Stephen soon met his future wife Jane, who gave him new hope to go on. He became determined to defeat ALS and for the first time in his life he became focused on his future and his work.

In the 1960s Hawking began to make significant scientific advances, becoming well known for his theories about black holes and the "Big Bang." Convinced—due to his disbelief in quantum mechanics—that Einstein's assumptions were incorrect, Hawking instead envisioned an ever-expanding universe that possibly had no beginning at all. Delving deeper into the nature of black holes, Hawking deduced that time and space were interchangeable. He also developed an explanation for the presence of what looked like radiation near the horizon of a black hole—anything sucked into the vortex was expelled in the form of radiation-like light. Though some of his findings were later revised by others (and many by himself), Hawking single-handedly answered questions which had puzzled the scientific mind for centuries. (Although not religious himself, Hawking made it clear that his theories did not necessarily exclude the presence of God, a declaration which softened an initial hostility on the part of the Church.)

By the 1980s Hawking had lost all use of his hands and was confined to a wheelchair. When his vocal chords failed him, a system was devised by which small finger movements could provoke his computer to punch up words on the screen. These words were then filtered through a speech synthesizer, enabling Hawking to "talk" again. Today, at his home in England, Hawking continues to unravel the mysteries of the universe, which he's now convinced will eventually collapse into nothingness.

The fact that Stephen Hawking's life is nearly as fascinating as his discoveries is what doubtless compelled Morris to document them both. Done in true documentary style, A BRIEF HISTORY OF TIME is dominated by talking heads, graphs and charts and just the right amount of scientific data to keep an audience interested without going over its head. The director keeps to his earlier format by never asking questions on camera, preferring to let various relatives (notably quirky themselves), scientists and friends piece together Hawking's compelling history. And while his extraordinary intellect is everywhere apparent, Hawking's self-effacing wit and charm make this a very accessible story for the general public. When he mentions that the world will destroy itself in two hundred billion years he wryly notes, "It doesn't bother me, because I don't expect to be around to see it."

A BRIEF HISTORY OF TIME is informative but accessible. When the numbers get too difficult for the layman to follow, Morris has a formidable solution—graphics that come alive on the screen. For instance, in one monologue, Hawking begins describing what happens to time and space at the entrance to a black hole—pretty deep stuff. By floating a giant Rolex watch into the picture as his prop, and showing the effects of time on the watch's face, the situation becomes utterly clear. He does this again later with a broken cup and saucer which put themselves back together again. The only real flaw in the film is that the findings of so many previous astronomers are alluded to so briefly—a better sense of the prevailing theories would have helped here.

Throughout, the one constant is the clicking of Hawking's computer keyboard as he searches for the next word to put into a sentence. Immobile in his wheelchair, yet with his mind racing through another dimension, this stationary protagonist is fascinating to watch and impossible not to admire. Ultimately, A BRIEF HISTORY OF TIME is as much about one person's triumph over adversity as it is about the mysteries of astronomy.

p, David Hickman; d, Errol Morris; w, Stephen Hawking, (from his book); ph, John Bailey, Stefan Czapsky; ed, Brad Fuller; m, Philip Glass; prod d, Ted Bafaloukos; art d, David Lee

Documentary **(PR: A MPAA: G)**

BROKEN NOSES ★★★

77m Kira Films ~ Kino Home Video bw/c

Andy Minsker, Mount Scott Boxing Club Members

Fashion photographer Bruce Weber, best known for his *GQ* spreads and provocative Calvin Klein ads, turned documentary filmmaker for this offbeat portrait of lightweight boxer Andy Minsker. While lacking any compelling story or structure, BROKEN NOSES combines stylized cinematography, an ironic jazz score and unconventional direction to create an intriguing personality profile.

The film begins with an explanation of its genesis: while photographing athletes at a 1983 sports festival Weber crossed paths with officials who objected to his suggestive, idiosyncratic studio shots of the US Olympic Boxing Team. After being forbidden to work with the controversial artist, Minsker came to pose. Rumors of how subjects would be shot with "weird haircuts" and "skimpy" swimsuits supposedly attracted the young pugilist. Weber chose to make the athlete the subject of his film. The resulting project was not a typical profile of a boxer (scenes of his bouts are minimal) but an experimental, elliptical portrait of an eccentric character.

Forsaking any neat narrative or genre structure, BROKEN NOSES interweaves a number of contrived interviews, photo sessions and home-movie-like scenes in an impressionistic mood-piece with Minsker as its photogenic center. Andy's minor fame as a boxer becomes incidental and is recalled only in scrapbook pictures, memories and stories told to the very young boys he trains in his hometown. The film opens with one of Weber's trademark black-and-white studio shoots, as Minsker and his stable are filmed posing—weird haircuts and all. Subsequent scenes alternate between lengthy monologues and dialogues in the Minsker home and quirky montages of Andy training with his pupils.

Both types of presentation deliberately undercut typical assumptions about the life of a macho fighter. Dreamy jazz ballads and love songs contrast with the images of prepubescent boys slugging it out. And for every scene of tough guy Andy teaching his students to "be a man" (by enduring the pain of "broken noses") another shows the boxer in a domestic setting (ironing, babysitting) where he talks through problematic relationships with his mother, father and stepparents. The revelation that he was physically abused as a child is one of the few psychological insights offered by the film. The rest of his story remains vague and is presented only superficially.

But the overall aesthetic generated by the film is one consistent with Weber's infamous commercial photography. While no overtly sexual material is seen, BROKEN NOSES lingers intimately and voyeuristically over the sight of athletic bodies, creating a wash of decidedly homoerotic imagery. Within the fashion industry Weber has been credited with redefining the ways in which men are photographed. This, his feature debut, extends that reputation, making the usually shirtless Minsker look like another ad for "Obsession," which in fact he became.

The visual fascination for Minsker, however, wears thin as the film winds on with little development of his character. In fact, Weber's fixation on what he calls at the end of the movie an "unforgettable" personality, may be too personal and idiosyncratic—not broadly appealing. He dedicates BROKEN NOSES to Chet Baker, the jazz trumpeter whose music scores much of the film and who became the subject of Weber's second feature documentary, the far more compelling LET'S GET LOST. The director tells us at the outset that Andy resembles a "young Chet Baker." While this is obviously true to those familiar with the musician, it scarcely seems grounds for devoting an entire film to a young man whose own story is only vaguely told and only partly interesting.

Weber's forte remains one of creating beautiful artifice and evocative black-and-white visuals, a talent that BROKEN NOSES shows to good effect. But a better developed sense of narrative and character might have enriched his debut film's thematic qualities. As presented, the beauty of Weber's work is only skin deep. *(Mild profanity, adult situations.)*

d, Bruce Weber; ph, Jeff Priess; ed, Phyllis Famiglietti, Howie Weisbrot; art d, Sam Shahid

Documentary/Sports (PR: C MPAA: NR)

BRONX WAR, THE ★

95m Filmworld International Productions ~ Academy Entertainment c

Joseph B. Vasquez *(Tito Sunshine)*, Frances Colon *(Maria)*, Charmaine Cruz *(Rachel)*, Andre Brown *(Caesar)*, Fabio Urena *(Tony)*, Miguel Sierra *(Crazy)*, Marlene Forte, Kim West, J.E. Gonzalez, Yvonne Fidias

Joseph B. Vasquez's insipid, ultra-violent drama, THE BRONX WAR, fails in nearly every aspect of filmmaking. A weak story, poor acting, substandard production values and laborious pacing all add to an abysmal conclusion.

Things in the Latino 'hood are nasty. Small time drug hustler Tito Sunshine (Joseph B. Vasquez) and his posse are feeling the pressure from the big, bad Black gang headed by Caesar (Andre Brown). At Tito's bar, he and his brother, Tony (Fabio Urena) have a heated sit down with the opposing leader. Caesar tells them he's looking for Tito's sister-in-law Rachel (Charmaine Cruz) who stole his cache of heroin. Tito plays dumb although he's hiding her in his Bronx apartment. Confronting Rachel, Tito buys her story that it was her dead boyfriend who stole the drugs. He vows to protect her from Caesar.

Things begin to turn grim on the streets as Caesar sends a hitman after the brothers. The gang members demand war but Tito refuses to let them go head to head in battle against Caesar's larger posse. Tito is then snatched off the streets by Caesar, who takes him to lunch to work out a payment plan for Rachel's arrears. The Latinos think he's been killed and take to the streets. Crazy (Miguel Sierra), an out of control madman, gets a gun and blows away Caesar's brother and girlfriend. This means war. Next to go are four crooked policemen who die in a torrent of shotgun blasts.

Tito arrives back at his club and is astonished to find out that his boys have started this street battle. He reluctantly agrees to end the warfare once and for all. Over the next two days, virtually all of his gang are killed, including his brother. Tito rips off his gold chains and falls into his wife Maria's (Frances Colon) arms, swearing off the life of a drug dealer for good.

As a student film, THE BRONX WAR would have been considered flawed. As a professional effort, it's nearly unwatchable, laughable when it's meant to be somber. Vasquez, who also wrote the screenplay, had great possibilities with this story. The world of Hispanic gangs has never been explored deeply, and that alone could have made for a good tale. Instead his characters become caricatures and the story falls flat. The pacing of the story is atrocious, with scenes three times as long as they require.

The violence is schlocky and will remind viewers of a cheap horror film. One guy takes a bullet to the chest but somehow ends up with eight wounds. Vasquez even has the absurd notion of creating a music video-like sequence where gang members are being gunned down while a stripper dances to the music. The film is underlit and the sound quality is at times uneven. Save for Vasquez's and Urena's passable performances as the brothers, the acting, or lack of it, can only be explained as par for the course.

Director Vasquez opens his picture with a written message telling the viewer some disturbing drug related statistics. This heavy-handed method is meant to give the film some sense of purpose—here's the problem, now let's show you the solution—instead it only trivializes the real issue.

THE BRONX WAR is about as exploitative as a film can get. If the filmmaker was expecting it to find an audience of inner-city youth, he may be vastly disappointed. Teen gang members will certainly find this amateurish offering unacceptable. *(Excessive violence, excessive profanity, nudity.)*

p, Elizabeth Frankel; d, Joseph B. Vasquez; w, Joseph B. Vasquez; ph, Gordon Maynard; ed, Michael Schweitzer; m, Tasso Zapanti, Wayne Gorbea

Crime/Drama (PR: O MPAA: NR)

BROTHER'S KEEPER ★★★½

120m Creative Thinking International; American Playhouse Theatrical Films; Hand-to-Mouth Production ~ American Playhouse Theatrical Films c

Delbert Ward, Roscoe Ward, Lyman Ward

In BROTHER'S KEEPER, the award-winning documentary from Joe Berlinger and Bruce Sinofski, an outcast's arrest on murder charges pits the members of a simple farming community against the local bureaucracy.

The four Ward brothers were well known in Munnsville, a rural town in upstate New York; they had been born and raised there over six decades earlier and lived on their dairy farm like poor laborers. Their water-stained wooden cabin had minimal electricity, no central heating and no running water or indoor plumbing. Even their friends, who blithely refer to them as the "boys," admit that they don't wash or change their clothes very often. The Wards present a sorry picture for filmmakers Berlinger and Sinofski as their camera takes in the piles of dirty clothes on yellowed mattresses, a refrigerator brown from accumulated grime and their shaggy, grizzled beards. Still, their milking equipment is spotless and the brothers do show a certain inventiveness in using a delapidated school bus as an animal shed and in keeping their old tractor in some kind of repair.

When the oldest brother, Bill, was found dead in the bed he shared for years with Delbert, most people felt it was a natural death, until a brief autopsy revealed some indecisive anomalies. Barely literate, the three surviving brothers were questioned by the police who succeeded in eliciting a confession from Delbert Ward that he smothered his brother. Later, Delbert consistently maintained that the police demonstrated how he may have strangled Bill in the course of a long, tiring interrogation. He agreed and found himself locked up for the first time in his life. Despite his eccentric shabbiness, Delbert Ward's neighbors quickly rallied to his defense, collecting the $10,000 in bail within a day.

Partly fueling this effort was the animosity between the region's farmers and the local officialdom. The young, smooth-faced police and court officers in dark suits, posed speaking in front of rows of law books, are in sharp contrast with the older Ward supporters usually dressed in t-shirts and feed caps. Noticeable also is the irony that the former are largely the descendants of what used to be called the "new" immigrants from southern and eastern Europe, while the latter are the offspring of distant "old" immigrants from northwestern Europe.

Despite these possible prejudices, some local farmers are forthright about the ambiguity surrounding Bill Ward's death. One man recalls a traditional bovine Heimlich maneuver that Delbert may have used to try to revive a dying Bill, while another feels it may simply have been a mercy killing. A further complication is earlier testimony by Lyman Ward that implicated his brother, though a visibly shaking Lyman later revokes it during Delbert's trial.

BROTHER'S KEEPER offers a rich tapestry of rural American life in both light and dark shades. Chief among the film's impressions is the good-natured acceptance of the Ward brothers as shabby recluses and the help and friendliness extended to them following Delbert's arrest. A strong sense of community is evoked as Thurston, a local, walks through the cemetery noticing how many of the dead were his friends. The chewing tobacco advertised on roadside signboards is actually consumed by the people onscreen and it is not only the Ward brothers who show the effects of negligible dental care or working with large animals and dangerous equipment.

Just as the Ward case received a great deal of media attention, so too has BROTHER'S KEEPER. Among its many honors, the film garnered the coveted Audience Award at the 1992 Sundance Film Festival and year-end accolades from the National Board of Review and the New York Film Critics Circle. *(Adult Situations.)*

p, Joe Berlinger, Bruce Sinofski; d, Joe Berlinger, Bruce Sinofski; w, Joe Berlinger, Bruce Sinofski; ph, Douglas Cooper; ed, Joe Berlinger, Bruce Sinofski; m, Jay Ungar, Molly Mason

Documentary/Crime **(PR: C MPAA: NR)**

BUFFY THE VAMPIRE SLAYER ★★

86m Buffy Films; Kuzui Enterprises; Sandollar Productions ~ Fox c

Kristy Swanson *(Buffy)*, Donald Sutherland *(Merrick)*, Paul Reubens *(Amilyn)*, Rutger Hauer *(Lothos)*, Luke Perry *(Pike)*, Michele Abrams *(Jennifer)*, Hilary Swank *(Kimberly)*, Paris Vaughan *(Nicole)*, David Arquette *(Benny)*, Randall Batinkoff *(Jeffrey)*, Andrew Lowery *(Andy)*, Sasha Jenson *(Grueller)*, Stephen Root *(Gary Murray)*, Candy Clark *(Buffy's Mom)*, Natasha Gregson Wagner *(Cassandra)*, Mark DeCarlo *(Coach)*, Tom Janes *(Zeph)*, James Paradise *(Buffy's Dad)*, David Sherrill *(Knight)*, Liz Smith *(Reporter)*, Paul M. Lane *(Robert Berman)*, Toby Holguin *(Vampire Fan)*, Eurlyne Epper-Woldman *(Graveyard Woman)*, Andre Warren *(Newscaster)*, Bob "Swanie" Swanson *(Referee)*, Erika Dittner *(Cheerleader)*, J.C. Cole *(Biker)*, Tony Maxwell *(Student)*, Tarra Greenhut *(Female Student)*, Michael S. Kopelow *(Timid Student)*, Jaime Seibert *(Deep Student)*, Ricky Dean Logan *(Bloody Student)*, Anthony Haynes *(Unidentified Schoolboy)*, Bobby Aldridge, Amanda Anka, Chino Binamo, Al Goto, Terry Jackson, Mike Johnson, Sarah Lee Jones, Kim Robert Kosci, Clint Lilley, Chi Muoi-lo, Jimmy N. Roberts, David Rowden, Kenny Sacha, Ben R. Scott, Kurtis Epper Sanders, Sharon Schaffer, Lincoln Simonds *(Vampires)*

If you've seen BUFFY THE VAMPIRE SLAYER's poster, you've seen the movie. Otherwise, this pallid crossbreeding of vampire horror with Valley Girl vamping has no surprises.

Tall, blond and very fit, Buffy (Kristy Swanson) is an average movie version of an LA high-school student (including the fact that Swanson, however comely, is a bit old for the part). Her averageness vanishes, however, the day she discovers—via dreams and a visitation from veteran vampire fighter Merrick (Donald Sutherland)—that she is the latest descendant of a race of vampire slayers dedicated to the extinction of the blood-sucking subspecies. This turns out to be a very convenient occurrence: Buffy's city of angels is currently under siege from vampires led by Lothos (Rutger Hauer) and Amilyn (Paul Reubens), who've wandered the Earth since sometime before the Crusades and have managed to vanquish Buffy and Merrick in their earlier incarnations through the generations.

After some token whining—she is a Val, after all—Buffy rises to the occasion, though not before Lothos and Amilyn have apparently decimated Buffy's high school and turned most of her classmates into bloodsuckers. Aided by handsome town outcast Pike (Luke Perry), Buffy has her showdown at the senior dance, creating an overnight run on wooden stakes by impaling her erstwhile classmates and, eventually, Lothos and Amilyn, making the world safe once again for mallrats from Burbank to Woodland Hills.

Mixing vapid t'n'a Valley Girl comedy with bloodthirsty vampire horror evidently seemed like a great idea to someone, somewhere at some time. In practice, however, the screenplay, by sitcom veteran Joss Whedon, doesn't have anything new to add to either genre. Neither does director Fran Rubel Kuzui (TOKYO POP), who betrays little flair for either genre, resulting in more a clumsy collision than a creative clash. The comedy consists of the same old pert-bottomed, perky-breasted teenagers scampering through malls, cooing over buff dudes and speaking in tongues. The horror is mostly vampire camp, despite BUFFY's having an apparently higher body count than most straightforward treatments of the theme.

On the acting side, Swanson is earnest, attractive and a bodacious athlete (she'd do well in a kung-fu Valley Gal comedy), while TV heartthrob Perry is pleasantly laidback and engagingly chivalrous to the point of trimming his trademark sideburns to win the heart of the Buff woman. The two villains, however, are a disappointment. Hauer tries for arch self-parody, a mistake since the Dutch actor accomplishes much the same in most of his straight roles. The effect here is overkill. Reubens, in his first substantial role since dropping his Pee-Wee Herman persona, is afforded little opportunity to display much comic inventiveness, cast as a retread "Renfield" to Hauer's "Count." Despite that, his death scene—a sort of vampire ballet of spasms, puking and twitching—is about the only real laugh in the film (something the filmmakers sensed, since the scene is replayed over the closing credits). On the whole, however, the mood is one of tired resignation. *(Violence.)*

p, Kaz Kuzui, Howard Rosenman; d, Fran Rubel Kuzui; w, Joss Whedon; ph, James Hayman; ed, Camilla Toniolo, Jill Savitt; m, Carter Burwell; prod d, Lawrence Miller; art d, Randy Moore, James Barrows; set d, Claire Bowin; cos, Marie France

Comedy/Horror **(PR: C MPAA: PG-13)**

CABEZA DE VACA ★★★½

(Mexico/Spain) 111m American Playhouse Theatrical Films ~ Concorde c

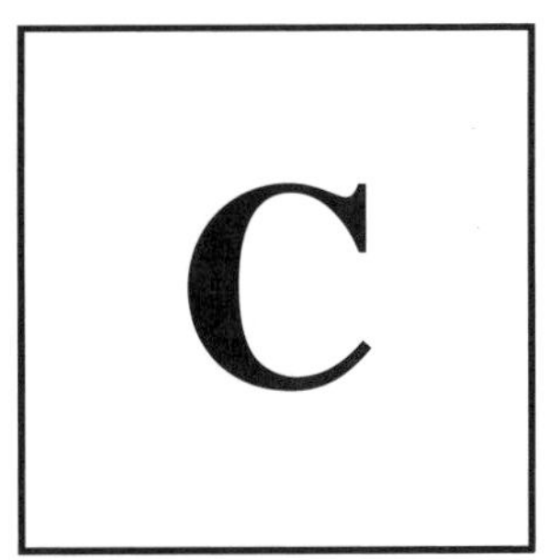

Juan Diego *(Alvar Nunez Cabeza de Vaca)*, Daniel Gimenez Cacho *(Dorantes)*, Roberto Sosa *(Cascabel/Araino)*, Carlos Castanon *(Castillo)*, Gerardo Villarreal *(Estebanico)*, Roberto Cobo *(Lozoya)*, Jose Flores *(Malacosa)*, Eli "Chupadera" Machuca *(Hechicero)*, Farnesio DeBernal *(Fray Suarez)*, Josefina Echanove *(Anciana Avavar)*, Max Kerlow *(Hombre de la Armadura)*, Oscar Yoldi *(Esquivel)*, Ramon Barragan *(Panfilo de Narvaez)*, Julio Solorzano Foppa *(Alcaraz)*, Javier Escobar Villarreal *(Young Iguase Indian)*, Victor Hugo Salcedo *(Iguese Chief)*, Jorge Santoyo *(Aide de Camp)*, Juan Sanchez Duarte *(Giant)*, Adyari Chazaro *(Dead Girl)*, Mayra Serbulo *(Iguase Lover)*, Jose Manuel Poncelis *(Wounded Indian)*, Hector Tellez *(Cart Driver)*, Victor Hugo Martin Del Campo *(Young Soldier)*, Adriana Guzman *(Woman in Giants Village)*, Yvonne Leyton *(Woman in Giants Village)*, Santiago Carrillo *(Indian Singer)*, Alejandro Carrillo *(Indian Singer)*, Santiago Lopez *(Indian Singer)*, Geraldo Martinez *(Avavar Guard)*, Abel Woolrich, Juan Carlos Martinez, Gerardo Duran, Alfredo Mejia Baron, Alejandro Tamayo *(Shipwrecked Men)*, Antero Chavez *(Spanish Drummer)*, Jose Salinas *(Witch Doctor)*, Jesus Vazquez *(Body in Spanish Chest)*, Gerardo Sanchez, Sara Iliana Sanchez, Gisela I. Sanders, Dulce Maria Villarreal *(Dwellers in Floating Village)*, Groupo de Danza Mexico Hue huecoyotl *(Avavar Indians)*, Armando Flores, Isreal Villa, Nayelli Zepeda, Juana Dorantes, Alicia Sanchez *(Avavar Dancers)*

Being the 500th anniversary of Columbus's "discovery" of the Americas, 1992 saw the release of several historical films related to the conquest of the continent. (1492: THE CONQUEST OF PARADISE and CHRISTOPHER COLUMBUS: THE DISCOVERY immediately come to mind.) Made in 1990, Nicolas Echevarria's CABEZA DE VACA stands out for its high production values and its well-drawn revisionist take on the Spanish colonizing enterprise.

The film recounts Alvar Nunez Cabeza de Vaca's eight-year trek across the hitherto unexplored regions of the Gulf of Mexico, one of the most astonishing feats in early American history. Treasurer to the 1528 Florida expedition headed by Panfilio de Narvaez, Cabeza de Vaca (Juan Diego) and a small group of soldiers survive the expedition's shipwreck and land on unknown territory. Captured in a bloody ambush, Cabeza de Vaca becomes the slave of a shaman and his armless dwarf assistant. After learning the witch doctor's trade and curing a tribal chief's blindness, Cabeza de Vaca is freed, equipped with magic stones and amulets. He comes across fellow survivors of the Narvaez expedition, who travel with him on foot across vast territories.

Cabeza de Vaca's curative powers gain him and his companions the trust of the native tribes they encounter, but as they approach Spanish presence, he is talked into abandoning his shaman practice; he could be imprisoned as a heretic madman. Spanish soldiers find Cabeza de Vaca and his three companions, taking them to their outpost. The soldiers are slave hunters, expecting Cabeza de Vaca's help in capturing natives. Appalled by his compatriots' rapacious cruelty toward a people he has learned to respect, Cabeza de Vaca vows to tell his story.

A noted Mexican ethnographic documentarian, Echevarria makes his feature-length debut with CABEZA DE VACA, adapted from Cabeza de Vaca's book *Naufragios* by Echaviarra and Guillermo Sheridan. And a stunning debut it is; through outstanding art direction, locations, costumes, sets and photography, the film effectively transports the audience back in time to the sweltering, dangerous jungles faced by the Spanish explorers of the 1500s. Echevarria draws from his ethnographic background in his detailed depiction of tribal life: celebrations, feasts, religious and curative ceremonies are presented in an involving, uncondescending way. By not translating the diverse indigenous languages, Echevarria makes audiences experience the way the Spaniards must have felt, perplexed at not comprehending the natives while fascinated by their customs.

When captured and enslaved, Cabeza de Vaca's immediate reaction is anger at his powerlessness against what he considers "godless creatures" who can't even speak his own language. As time passes, he learns to live among the natives—at first because he has no choice, but eventually seeing positive qualities in the tribes he meets. He finds a common thread in the shaman's rituals, which resemble Catholic ceremonies in the use of chants and sacred objects. In fact, Cabeza de Vaca's version of the shaman mixes Latin phrases with native amulets, harmonizing Christian and pagan rituals. America's inhabitants are no godless savages. The Spanish *conquistadores*, on the other hand, are portrayed as overtly cruel pillagers who crack under extreme pressure.

Captain Narvaez willingly abandons his battered group to their own fates after the shipwreck disaster: "Spain has ended here!" is his response to Cabeza de Vaca's demands for leadership. Astray with no food, we learn from one soldier, Narvaez's men descend to murder and cannibalism. Cabeza de Vaca faces the consequences of Spanish conquest in a mortally wounded native, struck by a musket bullet. "There's no reviving this one" is his remark as he removes the bullet. Nowhere in the tribes he has lived with has he found the inhuman propensity latent in his own race.

While most often compared to the revisionist Western DANCES WITH WOLVES, CABEZA DE VACA's strong visual style best recalls Werner Herzog's AGUIRRE, THE WRATH OF GOD. Striking sequences like the sight of a mad monk—seven lances stuck in his back—deliriously chanting Latin prayers as he displays a wooden cross, and the concluding scene, showing a monumental cross carried along a desert by native slaves—Echevarria's most eloquent visual metaphor—share Herzog's spectacular style, without overwhelming the film's message.

Notwithstanding its stately pace and the uneven acting (in the title role, Juan Diego could have used some subtlety and control), CABEZA DE VACA deserves to be watched for its necessary reinterpetation of history as well as its impressive cinematic merits. *(Violence, nudity.)*

p, Bertha Navarro, Rafael Cruz, Jorge Sanchez, Julio Solorzano Foppa; d, Nicolas Echevarria; w, Guillermo Sheridan, Nicolas Echevarria, (from the book *Naufragios* by Alvar Nunez Cabeza de Vaca); ph, Guillermo Navarro; ed, Rafael Castanedo; m, Mario Lavista; art d, Jose Luis Aguilar; set d, Angeles Martinez; cos, Totita Figueroa

Historical/Drama/Adventure (PR: C MPAA: R)

CAFE ROMEO ★★★

93m First Cafe Productions; Axelia Productions; Telefilm Canada ~ Republic Pictures Home Video c

Catherine Mary Stewart *(Lia)*, Jonathan Crombie *(Bennie)*, Michael Ironside *(Natino)*, John Cassini *(Tierno)*, Michael Tiernan *(Piero)*, Jay Brazeau *(Dean)*, Campbell Lane *(Enzo)*, Denalda

Williams *(Vera)*, Joseph Campanella *(Nino)*, Rae Scrivano *(Nick)*

Infused with authentic Italian-Americanisms rather than the usual cliches, this is a gentle *post*-coming-of-age story; everyone in it has already botched a first fling with love or suffered from a hasty career decision. Although a bit placid and predictable, CAFE ROMEO is a welcome relief after so many movies in which the participants behave like hand-waving refugees from La Scala.

Studying at a dental college, and investing money under the tutelage of go-getter Tierno (John Cassini), starry-eyed Bennie (Jonathan Crombie) wonders whether life has more to offer than safe career choices and smart investments. He pines for his long-time crush Lia (Catherine Mary Stewart) who regrettably married the wrong man, Bennie's cousin Piero (Michael Tiernan). Handcuffed by her husband's sexism, Lia is prevented from accepting a dream apprenticeship as a dress designer in New York City. Forced by his father into the local Mafia, Piero is consumed with self-doubt when he realizes he has no taste for violence.

When Bennie's uncle Nino (Joseph Campanella) dies and bequeaths his home and restaurant to his restless nephew, Bennie gravely disappoints his mother by moving out, pouring all his energy into making the bistro a popular neighborhood haunt and transforming Nino's house into a safe haven for Lia, who's left Piero, and Vera (Denalda Williams), who's dumped Bennie's womanizing brother Nick (Rae Scrivano). Buoyed up by this new extended family, Bennie and Lia are both able to follow their dreams and make space in their lives for each other. Although Piero is shipped off to the old country, Bennie has surmounted any conventions his parents placed in his path.

What shines through CAFE ROMEO is the film's genuine affection for its characters. What's most refreshing about Frank Procopio's screenplay is that not everyone achieves a happy ending. Although it never rises to any extraordinary dramatic heights, CAFE ROMEO does its modest job well and studies a coterie caught at the crossroads—friends since childhood, these small-towners must all go their separate ways.

In structural terms, none of the overlapping subplots ever seem extraneous; they dovetail satisfyingly with the central romance. With a good ear for the way people speak, Procopio also zeros in on the little antagonisms experienced even by people who care about each other. Since MOONSTRUCK first struck a popular chord, moviegoers have been plagued by loud-mouth imitators. Do we need to see more colorful eccentrics elbow each other off the screen while they scream out their ethnicity? Audiences would do well to soak up the more relaxed, humane atmsophere of CAFE ROMEO where not every character is larger than life.

Speaking in a whisper rather than shouting out its dramatic concerns in a thick accent, CAFE ROMEO spins its yarns with dignity and transparent honesty. Making its audience feel warm all over, it delves into the lives of ordinary people without patronizing them. *(Violence, profanity.)*

p, Richard Davis, Robert Vince; d, Rex Bromfield; w, Frank Procopio; ph, Philip Linzey; ed, Richard Benwick; m, Amin Bhalia, Cos Natola; prod d, Robert Logevall; cos, Carla Hetland

Drama/Romance **(PR: C MPAA: R)**

CAGED FEAR ★½

103m European American Entertainment ~ New Line Home Video c

David Keith *(Tommy Lang)*, Deborah May *(Deputy Warden Charles)*, Ray Sharkey *(Warden Hayes)*, Karen Black *(Blanche)*, Kristen Cloke *(Krissie Bell)*, Charlie Stradling *(Joy)*, Rick Dean *(Ray)*, Loretta Devine, Paddi Edwards

If the filmmakers had infused its you-won't-believe-a-minute-of-this storyline with a little more voltage, CAGED FEAR might have been a camp classic. As it stands, this direct-to-video embarrassment offers several attractions for purveyors of the intrinsically stupid.

Loyal small-town gal Krissie Bell (Kristen Cloke) takes the rap for her ne'er-do-well fiance Tommy Lang (David Keith), a recent parolee, when, too poor to purchase an engagement ring for his betrothed, he robs the jewelry store instead. Fed up with his reckless behavior, Krissie forces Tommy out of their getaway car, only to find herself quickly in the custody of the local authorities. The gruff men in blue know Tommy's responsible, but when Krissie refuses to implicate him in the botched heist, they throw *her* in the slammer instead. Fugitive-on-the-lam Tommy hides out from cracker cops while new arrival Krissie is accosted by prison guard Major Ray (Rick Dean), propositioned by an assortment of tough lesbians and attacked for integrating her friendships.

In a distinctly farfetched stroke of good fortune, Tommy manages to take advantage of a close encounter with a roving prison warden, Hayes (Ray Sharkey), who conveniently dies while chasing Tommy in his car. Determined to spring his girlfriend, Tommy disguises himself as Warden Hayes in order to infiltrate the prison—and not a moment too soon! Krissie has already broken a cardinal rule by resisting the advances of the sapphic Deputy Warden Charles (Deborah May) and angered the general prison populace by involving herself in a lesbian tug-of-war that ends in homicide.

Falling rather easily into the role of peace-keeping guardian, Tommy slips up when he lets a lascivious trustee spot his prison tattoo. By the time Deputy Warden Charles catches on to Tommy's harebrained hoax, Krissie has been sent to the penitentiary version of THE SNAKE PIT and the caged women are seething with revolt. After Tommy risks his life to free Krissie in sick bay, she rushes right back into the fray to be at his side. Tired of her non-stop insults impugning his abilities, Major Ray shoots down Deputy Warden Charles instead of Tommy the ersatz peacekeeper. Temporarily satisfied with Deputy Charles's blood, the inmates return to their cells. Free of bad meals, communal showering and racial discrimination, Krissie drives off with Tommy into the sunset of some scriptwriter's horizon in which the cops are going to forget all about the time Tommy and Krissie have left to serve on their prison sentences.

Viewers may be left with the surreal impression that the filmmakers simply took plot elements from classics like CAGED and CAGED HEAT, had them rewritten by comedy writers, and then rewritten *again* by disgruntled former employees of the State Correctional Board. No style dominates; the tone isn't tongue-in-cheek but the plotting cannot bear the weight of serious examination. If only the movie had stooped to more inspired depths like the scene in which Karen Black caps off her psycho-cameo by peeing on Krissie! Despite her innumerable recent appearances in similarly low-grade fare, this surely marks the nadir of Black's once shining career.

The few remaining stalwarts in Black's fan club must be crying out, "No, Karen, it *isn't* better to keep working!" Return to the stage, become a director through the AFI or guest star on TV's "Murder, She Wrote." No one should diminish their integrity by appearing in roles that force you to piss on another character as well as your fans. *(Extreme violence, profanity, nudity, sexual situations.)*

p, Gregory Vanger, Ed Elbert, Terry Kahn; d, Bobby Houston; w, Bobby Houston, Lisa Sutton, (from the story by Houston, Ed Elbert and Terry Kahn); ph, Alan Caso; ed, Erica Flaum; m, Toby Fitch; prod d, Clare Scarpulla; art d, Mike Costanza

Drama/Crime **(PR: O MPAA: R)**

CAN IT BE LOVE ★★
90m Hit Entertainment ~ Academy Entertainment c

Charles Klausmeyer *(Jim)*, Richard Beaumont *(David)*, Mary Ann Mixon *(Lisa)*, Jennifer Langdon *(Jesse)*, Blake Pickett *(Dyanne)*, Marcus "Wally the Wall" Mueller *(Pig Iron)*

Can it be another sun-baked excuse for sexual basking under the Florida skies? If you're the kind of viewer who perspires just thinking about tan lines and thong bikinis, CAN IT BE LOVE is your pail of beach sand.

Two geeks land in Fort Lauderdale with but one plan in mind: to score, score, score. While Jim (Charles Klausmeyer) pines for true love with a big-breasted smalltown girl, his buddy Dave (Richard Beaumont) dreams of dating a Delta sorority slut. After running afoul of a muscleman named Pig Iron (Wally "The Wall" Marcus Mueller), the boys get duped out of a room deposit by a sleazy hotelier and nearly miss a date with potential main squeezes Lisa (Mary Ann Mixon) and Jesse (Jennifer Langdon). Before all this, the college nerds have also found time to drool at a wet T-shirt contest and to witness a buxom babe being covered with whipped cream.

Romantic salvation for Dave and Jim arrives when ersatz sorority chick Dyanne Drake (Blake Pickett) reveals that she's really a private detective. By midnight, Dyanne must locate the missing heiress to a fortune; her only clue is that the girl is a Delta with a rose tatoo in a private place. Enlisting the boys' help, Dyanne transforms the two rubes into hot jocks so that they can finesse the entire sorority into disrobing. After a few more scrapes with Pig Iron who's been hired by a rival faction laying claim to the late millionaire's money, the fellows discover that Lisa is the rose-tatooed heiress just in the nick of time.

Inane, sexist and filled with enough contemporary music to fill a stack of CDs, CAN IT BE LOVE is surprisingly painless. As the two dweebs-in-the-woods, Klausmeyer and Beaumont exhibit expert comic timing and laid-back personalities that keep this thinly plotted comedy skipping along.

Since the women are gorgeous, and some of the gags (one Delta girl's favorite book is *Bambi's Pop-Up Christmas*) are occasionally funny, CAN IT BE LOVE is perfect party fare for horny teens and their leering college-age counterparts. However, women who do not gauge their own worth by the size of their brassieres and who wouldn't strip on the flimsiest of pretexts offered by a frat brat, may want to avoid this sun-drenched journey into the male libido. *(Profanity, nudity.)*

p, Bob Gallager, Brian Shuster; d, Peter Maris; w, William R. Milling, Hesh Rephun; ph, Jerry Wolfe; ed, Trebor Nirobk; m, Steve Weiss; art d, Jackie Pereira

Comedy **(PR: C MPAA: R)**

CANDYMAN ★★★½
101m Propaganda Films ~ TriStar c

Virginia Madsen *(Helen Lyle)*, Tony Todd *(Candyman)*, Xander Berkeley *(Trevor Lyle)*, Kasi Lemmons *(Bernadette Walsh)*, Vanessa Williams *(Anne-Marie McCoy)*, DeJuan Guy *(Jake)*, Marianna Eliott *(Clara)*, Ted Raimi *(Billy)*, Ria Pavia *(Monica)*, Mark Daniels *(Student)*, Lisa Ann Poggi *(Diane)*, Adam Philipson *(Danny)*, Eric Edwards *(Harold)*, Carolyn Lowery *(Stacey)*, Barbara Alston *(Henrietta Mosely)*, Sarina Grant *(Kitty Culver)*, Latesha Martin *(Baby Anthony)*, Lanesha Martin *(Baby Anthony)*, Michael Culkin *(Purcell)*, Bernard Rose *(Archie Walsh)*, Glenda Starr Kelly *(Crying Mother)*, Kenneth A. Brown *(Castrated Boy)*, Caesar Brown *(Tough Guy)*, Terrence Riggins *(Gang Leader)*, Gilbert Lewis *(Detective Frank Valento)*, Rusty Schwimmer *(Policewoman)*, Baxter Harris *(Detective)*, John Rensenhouse *(Attorney)*, Mika Quintard *(TV Reporter)*, Doug MacHugh *(1st Orderly)*, Carol Harris *(2nd Orderly)*, Stanley DeSantis *(Dr. Burke)*, Diane Peterson *(Nurse)*, Michael Wilheim *(Priest)*

Serious, straightforward cinematic terror is hard to come by in this age of wisecracking slashers and comic-horror sequels, but CANDYMAN is a riveting exception. This down-and-dirty yet literate shocker is the scariest film since THE SILENCE OF THE LAMBS and joins BRAM STOKER'S DRACULA as one of the best supernatural movies in years.

Derived from British author Clive Barker's short story "The Forbidden," CANDYMAN concerns a Chicago-based doctoral student named Helen Lyle (Virginia Madsen), who's working on a paper about urban legends with her friend Bernadette Walsh (Kasi Lemmons). One of the myths they're focusing on concerns a spirit called Candyman, who supposedly appears before anyone who says his name five times into a mirror—then slaughters them with a hook hand. When Helen learns that a murder in the nearby Cabrini Green housing projects has been attributed to Candyman, she and Bernadette investigate, and Helen discovers a shrine to the legendary phantom in a back room. The pair also encounter a young single mother, Anne-Marie McCoy (Vanessa Williams), who confirms the residents' belief that Candyman haunts their building and has committed several killings there.

Later, at a dinner with her professor husband Trevor (Xander Berkeley), Helen learns the legend of Candyman's origin: the son of a slave who had won fame as a portrait artist in the 1800s, he had an affair with a white female subject and was killed by a lynch mob, who sawed off his painting hand and had him stung to death by bees. Returning to Cabrini Green for further research, Helen is attacked by a local gang leader who has been using the Candyman legend to terrorize the residents into submission.

Surviving to testify against him, Helen sees him convicted of the murder and thinks she has put an end to the Candyman legend. But then Candyman himself (Tony Todd) appears before her, intoning that she has destroyed the belief that has kept him alive, and that he now must shed innocent blood to prove himself. Helen passes out, only to wake up in Anne-Marie's apartment, drenched in blood; Anne-Marie's dog has been slaughtered and her baby kidnapped. Arrested for the crimes, Helen protests her innocence and is eventually bailed out by her husband. Then Candyman reappears in her apartment and, after lulling Helen into a trancelike state, butchers Bernadette when the latter comes to visit.

Taken to a mental hospital, Helen has another encounter with the evil spirit; upon coming out of a month under heavy sedation, however, she is shown a videotape of the "confrontation"—she's the only one visible. It seems as if Helen may have been hallucinating, and committing the crimes herself, but then Candyman appears again and slaughters the psychiatrist interviewing her. The phantom wants to drive Helen to join him in death, and live forever with him in legend.

Escaping from the hospital, Helen returns to her apartment, only to find that Trevor has taken up with one of his female students. Realizing that she is alone in her plight, Helen goes to the housing projects to confront Candyman, who has been keeping Anne-Marie's baby alive in his lair and intends to sacrifice it. Resisting his further entreaties to join him (despite discovering that she is the reincarnation of his original love), Helen goes to rescue the baby from inside a pile of junk that the Cabrini Green residents have set up for a bonfire.

As they set the heap ablaze, Helen manages to impale Candyman with a blazing piece of wood and crawl out, her clothes and hair on fire, to deliver the child back to Anne-Marie before she dies. Later, after Helen's funeral (at which the Cabrini Green residents appeared in tribute), Trevor sits in his bathroom, disgusted by his abandonment of Helen and his relationship with the coed. Turning to the mirror, he repeats Helen's name five times . . . .

It's one of the many strengths of CANDYMAN that its story is actually about something, beyond a group of characters getting brutally hacked up. Writer-director Bernard Rose, who previously explored the shadowy world of dreams in 1988's PAPERHOUSE, here turns his gruesome material into a dark meditation on the nature of urban legends.

The notion of a legendary monster who kills to reassert himself in people's beliefs, and thus stay "alive," is intriguing, as is the way the Cabrini Green residents cling to the myth as a way to rationalize the violence of their daily lives. The film is notable for the way in which it manages to utilize ghetto realities without condescending to its black characters, or exploiting the more obvious shock possibilities of a black villain pursuing a white heroine. Instead, the well-observed characters and settings add an extra depth to the scary moments, which are indeed graphic and startling.

Rose builds excellent tension, playing for a while with the notion of whether Helen may in fact be guilty of the murders, before plunging into a heart-pounding third act and a wickedly funny coda. The glimpses of Candyman's victims are quite graphic—Rose is certainly not averse to ladling on the blood—but the actual onscreen violence is limited. The murders are more heard than seen, though they're certainly some of the most disgusting-*sounding* deaths in recent memory.

CANDYMAN's acting also shines, from Madsen's (SLAM DANCE, THE HOT SPOT) forceful work as the confused but resilient heroine and Tony Todd's imposing villain to Williams's excellent portrayal of the beleaguered but proud young mother. Genre fans will get a kick out of the presence of familiar faces Berkeley (the doomed foster father in TERMINATOR 2) and Lemmons (Jodie Foster's FBI-trainee roommate in SILENCE OF THE LAMBS). And special mention must be made of Philip Glass's superlative score, which combines synthesizers, piano and chorus to haunting and evocative effect. *(Violence, nudity, adult situations.)*

p, Alan Poul, Sigurjon Sighvatsson, Steve Golin; d, Bernard Rose; w, Bernard Rose, (from the short story "The Forbidden" by Clive Barker); ph, Anthony B. Richmond; ed, Dan Rae; m, Philip Glass; prod d, Jane Ann Stewart; art d, David Lazan; set d, Kathryn Peters; cos, Leonard Pollack; fx, Bob Keen

Horror **(PR: O MPAA: R)**

CANVAS ★½

(Canada/U.K.) 94m Optima Productions; Mark Forstater Productions ~ LIVE Home Video c

Gary Busey *(Ozzie Decker)*, John Rhys-Davies *(Nick)*, Vittorio Rossi *(Frank Dante)*, Cary Lawrence *(Nathalie)*, Nick Cavaiola *(Tony Dante)*, Jonathan Palis *(Alfie)*, Michael McGill *(Chris Williams)*, Alexandra Innes *(Anna Maxwell)*, Nicola LaMorgia

A dysfunctional pair of siblings work out their relationship against a backdrop of murder and art world scams in CANVAS, a handsomely shot but rather anemic art-of-crime thriller.

Bombastic Ozzie Decker (Gary Busey) not only runs the most prestigious art gallery in town but has a highly profitable sideline in theft; beware his return policy because disgruntled customers are likely to end up stuffed into a car trunk. Struggling artist Frank Dante (Vittorio Rossi) hooks up with wily Decker because he needs a quick $40,000 to help his ne'er-do-well brother Tony (Nick Cavaiola) out of a jam with a druglord. How many artists *manques* not only get to see their work represented in a tony art gallery but also are personally selected by the gallery owner to hijack truckloads of fine art? Still, the biggest question is why Frank continues to help his screwed up brother.

Accompanied by Decker's long-time associate Nick (John Rhys-Davies), Frank begins his life of crime smoothly. Unfortunately, he wrecks a stolen painting when he and Nick are shot at by a peeved millionaire during a bungled burglary. The enraged Decker doesn't care about their running for their lives; now he has to explain a damaged Klee to a customer. To ensure Frank's cooperation in heisting a Cezanne for bitchy Anna Maxwell (Alexandra Innes), who's already sore about the loss of the Klee, nasty Decker kidnaps Frank's girlfriend Nathalie (Cary Lawrence). After gunfire with a guard who wounds Nick, Frank hands over the pilfered Cezanne only to discover Decker intends to eliminate him and Nathalie.

Dreaming of a one-way ticket to Greece and fed up with the itchy trigger finger of his boss, Nick kills Decker. Picking up big bucks from Anna Maxwell at the airport, Frank turns over the Cezanne money to Nick, who gives him an heirloom which he can hock for enough loot to help brother Tony. Although Frank and Nathalie return to normalcy, old Nick dies while waiting for his flight. In an ironic touch, Nick's money is tossed into the trash by a small child.

What attracted backers and actors to this paint-by-numbers screenplay? Surely it wasn't the creaky script's ability to build suspense; instead of creating a crescendo of nail-biting scenes, CANVAS manufactures car chases and quick exits from burglaries.

Any chance the film might have had for commercial success as an action potboiler is wrecked by the inclusion of the saga of Frank and his whiny brother who already caused him one prison stretch. A mob hit is the very least this unappealing character deserves (particularly as enacted by Nick Cavaiola as a cross between Uriah Heep and Howie Mandel). Niggling questions about motivation slap down one's potential interest at every turn. How did Decker stay in business so long when he seems to kill off a quarter of his clientele? Thugs in the Yakuza can't match his impressive tally of victims. And what about that doormat Nathalie? How many women would forgive Frank for constantly placing his errant brother's welfare ahead of any concerns for their own safety? Most damaging of all, there's no sense of the twisted hold Decker has over Frank and how the latter might attempt to extricate himself.

As an action movie, CANVAS suffers from muddy motivations and a dull suspense palette. The colors of the subject matter are bold but the controlling strokes applying that color are carelessly blunt. *(Violence, profanity.)*

p, Jean Zaloum; d, Alain Zaloum; w, Alain Zaloum, Brenda Newman; ph, Stephen Reizes; ed, Patrick Moore; m, Mike Hewer; prod d, Michael Joy; set d, Paul Hotte, Ginette Robitaille; cos, Nicoletta Massone

Crime/Drama **(PR: C MPAA: R)**

CAPTAIN AMERICA ★★

(U.S./Yugoslavia) 97m 21st Century Productions; Jadran Film; Marvel Entertainment Group ~ Columbia TriStar Home Video c

Matt Salinger *(Steve Rogers/Captain America)*, Ronny Cox *(Tom Kimball)*, Ned Beatty *(Sam Kolawetz)*, Darren McGavin *(General Fleming)*, Michael Nouri *(Lieutenant Colonel Louis)*, Melinda Dillon *(Mrs. Rogers)*, Francesca Neri *(Valentina de Santis)*, Bill Mumy *(Young General Fleming)*, Kim Gillingham *(Bernice Stewart/Sharon)*, Scott Paulin *(The Red Skull)*, Carla Cassola *(Dr. Maria Vaselli)*, Massimilio Massimi *(Tadzio de Santis)*, Wayde Preston *(Jack)*, Norbert Weisser *(Alaskan Surveyor)*, Garette Ratliff *(Young Tom Kimball)*, Bernarda Oman *(Tadzio's Mother)*, Mustafa Nadarevic *(Tadzio's Father)*, Tonko Lonza *(Tadzio's Mentor)*, Edita Lipovsek *(Tadzio's Aunt)*, Ljubica Dujmovic *(Tadzio's Grandmother)*, Galliano Pahor *(Fascist General)*, Milan Kristofic *(Nazi General)*, Giulio Marini *(Nazi General)*, Aldo Galleazzi *(German Scientist)*, Ljubomir Strgacic *(German Scientist)*, Slvko Sestak *(German Scientist)*, Petar Tomac *(Italian Vendor)*, Bruno Grdadolnik *(Italian Vendor)*, Autun Nalis *(Old Repairman)*, Mario Kovac *(Repairman–as a Boy)*, Zoran Pollupec *(Implant Doctor)*, Adrianne Marcich Dumicic *(VA Nurse)*, Fay Finver *(Lab Technician)*, Frank Finver *(Lab Technician)*, Peter Mulrean *(Lab Technician)*, Catherine Farrell *(Roz)*, Mia Begovic *(Young Italian Woman)*, Matko Raguz *(Italian Woman's Husband)*, Donald Standen *(Red Skull's Bodyguard)*, Dragana Zigic, Judranka Katusa, Rafaelle Burunelli, Robert Egon, Igor Serdar *(Perfect Young Italians)*, Sven Medvesek *(Pietro)*, Gary Epper *(Mr. Erlich)*, Sonja Gregus *(Resistance Fighter)*, Rene Medvesek *(Resistance Fighter)*, Demeter Bitenc, Relja Basic, Velemir Chytil, Drago Klobucar, Gordon Piculjan *(Industrialists)*, Frank Papia *(Paramedic)*, Christopher Whitney *(Boy at Beach)*, Beth Ann Bowen *(Girl at Beach)*, Gerda Shepherd *(Jack's Nurse)*, Trek Potter *(Boy Scout)*, Sarah Wasson *(Little Girl)*, Thomas Beatty *(Young Sam Kolawetz)*, Jon Beatty *(War Veteran)*, Ann Bell *(Tom Kimball's Mother)*, Scott Del Amo *(Tom Kimball's Father)*, John M. Johnson *(Sharon Double)*, Robert Reitmeier *(Bandstand Musician)*, John S. Reynolds *(Bandstand Musician)*, Lee Westenhofer *(Bandstand Musician)*

Unlike DC Comics mainstays Batman and Superman, Marvel Comics characters have made distinctly unheroic leaps to the silver screen, with misfires like SWAMP THING, THE PUNISHER and, most notably, HOWARD THE DUCK. Having recently marked his 50th anniversary in print, Captain America is the latest Marvel icon to suffer a rattletrap cinematic treatment with this 1990 effort, belatedly released to home video.

The plot remains faithful to the WWII orgins of Captain America, which is a bit of a drawback in itself; classic though he is, Captain America is easily the squarest crime fighter in Marvel's stable, preceding editor Stan Lee's popular 1960s formula for "heroes with hang-ups," flawed titans with neuroses and troubled personal lives. CAPTAIN AMERICA tries to bridge the generations with a wildly convoluted storyline.

It opens in Italy circa 1936, where Mussolini's stormtroopers seize a boy genius and subject him to "Project Rebirth," fiendish experiments to create Axis super warriors. The child emerges, hideously scarred and inhumanly strong, as a bad guy dubbed the Red Skull (Scott Paulin). The scientist behind Project Rebirth, Dr. Maria Vasseli (Carla Cassola), rebels and defects to the US, where she perfects the process for the Allies. Amid low-tech sparking and crackling, polio-stricken volunteer Steve Rogers (Matt Salinger), is thus transformed into a mighty blond hunk. Directly afterwards a Nazi spy assassinates Dr Vasseli, leaving pumped-up Rogers, code-named Captain America, as our secret hope for victory over the Red Skull. "He'll be the living symbol of what this country stands for," says an official as Rogers, outfitted in his trademark red, white and blue tights (explained as a custom-made fireproof uniform), parachutes into enemy territory to tackle the superfoe.

But the Red Skull beats up Captain America, fastens him to a flying bomb and launches the early ICBM at Washington, DC. The warhead is about to strike the White House when Captain America at last thinks to kick its tailfin and send it offcourse. The rocket lands in Alaska, where Captain America remains frozen until 1993, when he's thawed out by surveyors. In the meantime the Red Skull has become a conspiracy theorist's dream, masterminding all kinds of wickedness for the highest bidder (his crimes include the murders of the Kennedy brothers and Martin Luther King). Now Mr. Skull is being consulted by the pollution industry, who want to eliminate the new environmental-activist US President Tom Kimball (Ronny Cox).

Kimball's best buddy, newspaperman Sam Kolawetz (Ned Beatty) has spent years piecing together the story of the Red Skull, and he recognizes the escaped iceman as Captain America. So does the Red Skull, who sends some bored-looking henchmen to terminate the hero. With Kolawetz's help Steve Rogers makes his way back to his boyhood home in California and reunites with his long-ago sweetheart, now old and married to someone else. She's conveniently killed by the Red Skull's agents, leaving daughter Sharon (Kim Gillingham plays both mother and offspring) to accompany Rogers to Italy for a final confrontation with the meanies who have kidnapped President Kimball and are preparing him for a mind control implant.

The wide-ranging story keeps Captain America sidelined most of the time, well away from the center of things until the climactic battle (when he finally dons his tights again). In fact, so much time is spent on the Red Skull that one wonders why they didn't name the picture after him instead. With his mutilated face clumsily masked by plastic surgery, the Red Skull looks like a gangster grotesque from DICK TRACY, and the screenplay tries hard to work up a touch of tragic pathos for him in the end.

Historically, Captain America has always been at something of a loss without a war to fight, and the tale's abrupt switch from anti-fascist heroics to ecological concern takes some force out of the character. As Rogers, stage and screen actor Matt Salinger (REVENGE OF THE NERDS, POWER) is valiant but stiff, and he gets into an annoying habit—shared by all the good guys here, as in comics—of letting his mouth hang open stupidly. His superpowers are never really defined, so it's hard to tell what Rogers could or could not survive (the same is true for the Red Skull, thus assuring his resurrection for any sequels). Physically, Salinger (the son of J.D. Salinger) is augmented by a padded muscle suit that emphasizes rippled abdominals, but leaves his arms relatively skinny; as a result, Captain America seems to sport a formidable beer gut—perhaps he moonlights as Bud Man.

The special effects rely heavily on stunts (when they try anything else, like the flying bomb, they look pretty threadbare), a logical choice for veteran martial arts director Albert Pyun (CYBORG), whose action sequences often verge on incoherency. Pyun's major achievement in CAPTAIN AMERICA is keeping the knotted plot understandable, but, along with screenwriters Stephen Tolkin and Laurence Block, he works in some cute touches in the quieter moments. Two kids (the young Tom Kimball and Sam Kolawetz, in fact) witness one of Cap's 1943 feats and debate who this costumed hero could be, name-dropping a roster of comic characters from the Human Torch to the Sub-Mariner. Then in 1993 a newly revived Captain America is alarmed by all the German and Japanese-made consumer goods he sees.

Pyun isn't above a gaffe, though. Look closely at an old-timey montage that chronicles Tom Kimball's political ascension via newspaper articles. Though the Kimball-oriented headlines keep changing, the text underneath doesn't—and it's readable as a divorce scandal involving one of the San Diego Padres. *(Violence, profanity.)*

p, Menahem Golan; d, Albert Pyun; w, Stephen Tolkin, (from the story by Tolkin and Lawrence J. Block based on the characters created by Joe Simon and Jack Kirby); ph, Philip Alan Waters; ed, John Poll; m, Barry Goldberg; prod d, Douglas Leonard; cos, Heidi Kaczenski

Action/Adventure/Fantasy (PR: C MPAA: PG-13)

CAPTAIN RON ★½

104m Hybrid Productions; Touchstone; Touchwood Pacific Parters I ~ BV c

Kurt Russell *(Captain Ron)*, Martin Short *(Martin Harvey)*, Mary Kay Place *(Katherine Harvey)*, Benjamin Salisbury *(Benjamin Harvey)*, Meadow Sisto *(Caroline Harvey)*, Emannuel Logrono *(General Armando)*, Jorge Luis Ramos *(General's Translator)*, J.A. Preston *(Magistrate)*, Tanya Soler *(Angeline)*, Raul Estela *(Roscoe)*, Jainardo Batista *(Mamba)*, Dan Butler *(Zachery)*, Tom McGowan *(Bill)*, Katherine Franco *(Sneezing Woman)*, Clement Talkington *(Bicycle Messenger)*, Craig Rondell *(Fiance)*, Paul Anka *(Donaldson)*, Shanti Kahn *(Patti)*, Marty Eli Schwartz *(Supervisor)*, John Scott Clough *(Garth)*, Katherine Calzada *(Barbara)*, Diego De La Texera *(Man with Rifle)*, Roselyn Sanchez *(Island Girl)*, Janine Okada *(Wong's Waitress)*, Eliseo Lopez *(Old Man)*, Gustavo Cerezo *(Handsome Guerrilla)*, Efrain "Chico" Rosario, Jose Ciro, Silvestre Ramos Gonzalez, Antonia Valdes Lazo, Jose Angel Ortiz, Gustavo Rodriguez, Victor Emilio Rodriguez *(Guerrillas)*, Ralph Arrieta *(Dutch Dude)*, James Dudley *(Dutch Dude)*, David Canal, Edwin Delgado, Carlos Miranda, Gil Baldiris *(Pirate)*

Former Disney juvenile star Kurt Russell looks right at home in CAPTAIN RON, a bland, seagoing, feature-length sitcom which recycles the displaced-dad theme from the studio's recent hit WHAT ABOUT BOB? to little effect.

Russell plays the title character, a dreadlocked, drydocked bum hired to pilot a boat, *The Wanderer*, which was once supposed to have belonged to Clark Gable and Carole Lombard. The boat has been inherited from a long-forgotten uncle by a yuppie family consisting of Martin Harvey (Martin Short), his wife Katherine (Mary Kay Place), their budding teenage daughter Caroline (Meadow Sisto) and pre-adolescent son Benjamin (Benjamin Salisbury). Though not shipwrecked, *The Wanderer*, docked in the Caribbean, does turn out to be more of a wreck than a ship, a point injudiciously relayed to boat broker Donaldson (Paul Anka), who plans to junk it as soon as it hits port in Miami. Rather than leaving the sailing to Ron, Martin hauls his family south to soak up some adventure that, of course, gets out of hand.

Though plagued by a sense of indirection that causes him to navigate past island stops on the trip, Ron otherwise proves an expert seaman. He also proves more popular with Martin's family than Martin himself. Under Ron's influence Caroline is soon out getting tattooed while Benjamin drinks beer and gambles at Monopoly with Ron's "friend," an island hooker, and Ron gets some hands-on experience of his own while teaching Katherine how to work the ship's wheel. Martin's family, all of whom were initially opposed to the trip, wind up having more fun than Martin, who means to put a stop to it by firing Ron forthwith. Unfortunately, it's a little too forthwith because Martin also throws Ron's paramour ashore before she can get paid for winning a game of strip Monopoly, leading her pimp to ambush the Martin vessel and steal it away to Cuba.

There Martin and family stage a daring rescue with some last-minute help from Ron, who even manipulates the rescue to make Martin look like the hero, restoring Martin's manhood and status as head of his clan and his boat. When the moment comes to turn over the boat, which has undergone an amazing transformation after just a little scrubbing and swabbing, Martin instead turns back to the sea leaving Donaldson sputtering on the dock.

Like virtually every Disney comedy released for the last several years, CAPTAIN RON starts well but gets soggier as it goes along. As usual, the cast can't really be faulted. Russell has just the right mix of saltiness and warmth as Ron. Place is also appealing as the mom of the piece, predictably keeping her wits while her husband loses his and still managing to fill a pair of cutoffs in eye-catching fashion. The kids are capable though standard-issue sitcom charmers. The glaring problem is Short's miscasting in a role that seems perversely calculated to display none of his comic talents.

To say the least, the thankless role as the slow-burning responsible member of the ensemble is ill-suited to someone who set a new standard for inspired lunacy on "SCTV," the landmark comedy series which showcased Short in roles ranging from hyperactive super-schnook Ed Grimley to "the kid from DELIVERANCE." Even if he'd intended to expand his range—an affliction that seems peculiar to comedy topliners—this is a less-than-ideal vehicle. The "displaced dad" angle seems arbitrarily grafted onto the screenplay for no better reason than that it worked in WHAT ABOUT BOB?, in which psychiatrist-dad Richard Dreyfuss found himself vying with lovable-lunatic patient Bill Murray for the affections of his family. In fact, there is no compelling reason whatsoever for Martin's dislike of Ron, but Thom Eberhardt and John Dwyer's screenplay is rarely logical, much less inspired.

After setting up a HOOK-style climax of a sea battle with real-life "pirates of the Caribbean," the actual action consists largely of Ron below deck on the ship's radio screaming for Coast Guard assistance. Despite the appealing window dressing, it all amounts to yet another ho-hum entry from a studio that now seems bent on "perfecting" a new genre in the fatally forgettable big-star comedy. *(Adult situations.)*

p, David Permut, Paige Simpson; d, Thom Eberhardt; w, Thom Eberhardt, John Dwyer, (from his story); ph, Daryn Okada; ed, Tina Hirsch; m, Nicholas Pike; prod d, William F. Matthews; art d, James Truesdale; set d, Jeff Haley, Irvin E. Jim Duffy Jr.; cos, Jennifer Von Mayrhauser

Comedy (PR: C MPAA: PG-13)

CENTER OF THE WEB ★½

91m One for the Money; Action International Pictures Inc.; Winters Group; Sovereign Investment Group ~ Pyramid Releasing Corporation c

Robert Davi *(Richard Morgan)*, Charlene Tilton *(Kathryn Lockwood)*, Ted Prior *(John Phillips)*, Bo Hopkins *(Frank Allesendro)*, William Zipp *(Tony)*, Tony Curtis *(Stephen Moore)*, Charles Napier

A convoluted political thriller with knee-jerk paranoid underpinnings, CENTER OF THE WEB lacks the edge it takes to distinguish itself from other examples of this popular genre.

John Phillips (Ted Prior) is an acting teacher, and his girlfriend Kathryn Lockwood (Charlene Tilton) an ambitious young prosecuting attorney. As he waits on the street one night for

Kathryn, Phillips's life takes an unexpected turn. A limousine pulls up and he's ordered inside by two men with guns. As they speed down the streets, another car pursues and opens fire. His abductors clearly think Phillips is someone else, but who? When the shootout is over, Phillips is arrested and thrown into jail; Kathryn bails him out. When Phillips returns home, he finds his possessions gone and a mysterious stranger from the Justice Department, Richard Morgan (Robert Davi), waiting for him.

Morgan explains that Phillips was mistaken for a murdered hit man named John Logan, and tells him that unless he impersonates Logan so the Justice Department can find out what Logan was up to, Phillips will go to jail. Phillips reluctantly agrees, and he and Kathryn are sworn to secrecy. She immediately breaks her vow, consulting an old family friend, Stephen Moore (Tony Curtis), with ties to the intelligence community; Moore has looked out for her ever since her father's suicide in the wake of a scandal that threatened to ruin his political career. Phillips, meanwhile, is drawn ever deeper into a conspiracy he can't figure out, no matter how hard he tries.

When he tries to stop the assassination of the Governor (the very man who ruined Kathryn's father years earlier), he instead finds himself framed as the killer. Phillips returns to Kathryn, arriving at almost the same time as her boss, District Attorney Frank Allesendro (Bo Hopkins) and two cops. They claim they're there to arrest Phillips, who forces Kathryn to escape with him and reveals that he's not an acting teacher at all, but a "deepcover" federal agent. He also convinces her that even Allesandro is part of the plot. Kathryn lures the unsuspecting Phillips to Moore, thinking he'll help her, only to discover that Moore is behind the entire complex scheme. It was he who murdered her father and made it look like a suicide, so that if the Governor ever needed to be killed, Kathryn could be framed, with vengeance for her father's death the motive. Morgan arrives and tries to kill Moore, who shoots him. Kathryn grabs Phillips's gun and kills Moore.

Though clearly produced on a limited budget, CENTER OF THE WEB is an acceptable paranoid political thriller that never transcends the form (as does, say, THE MANCHURIAN CANDIDATE), but does manage to avoid becoming hopelessly mired in its own complicated plot. The cast is a direct-to-video dream (though the film did receive a limited theatrical release, even playing New York's Times Square, it was clearly intended for the home market), a collection of marginal has-beens and never-quite-weres who rescue the material from the curse of out-and-out bad acting without ever being good enough to make viewers forget the film's low-budget origins.

Surprisingly, the film's worst performance comes from Curtis, who's simultaneously wooden and over-emphatic; it also hurts that the man at the center of the web—who's carefully shot from behind furniture and cloaked in shadows to hide his face—is revealed as Curtis far too early in the film, courtesy of his distinctive, grating accent. *(Violence.)*

p, Ruta K. Aras; d, David A. Prior; w, David A. Prior; ph, Andrew Parke; ed, Tony Malanowski; m, Greg Turner; art d, Linda Lewis; cos, Lenny Baron

Political/Thriller **(PR: C MPAA: R)**

CHAINS OF GOLD ★★

95m Management Company Entertainment Group ~ Academy Entertainment c

John Travolta *(Scott Barnes)*, Marilu Henner *(Jackie)*, Joey Lawrence *(Tommy Burke)*, Bernie Casey *(Sergeant Palco)*, Ramon Franco *(James)*, Hector Elizondo *(Lieutenant Ortega)*, Benjamin Bratt *(Carlos)*, Conchata Ferrell *(Martha)*, Tammy Lauren *(Rachel)*, Raphael Rey Gomez *(Bobby)*

To its minor credit, CHAINS OF GOLD maintains a sincere urgency about its subject matter that's a change from the often execrable kill-them-and-quip insouciance typical of buddy-cop romps that trawl this territory.

Set in drug-soaked Miami, this particular bit of vice centers on Scott Barnes (John Travolta), a recovering alcoholic whose boozing caused his small son's car-wreck death. Now a maverick social worker, Scott gets personally involved in his cases, especially that of Tommy Burke (Joey Lawrence), a plucky adolescent burdened with a disabled, drunken single mom. Scott's so cool he even joins Tommy on window-breaking expeditions to make sure the lad stays out of trouble, but it's already too late: Tommy's supplying his dysfunctional family with cash earned dealing drugs for the YIP—the Youth Incentive Program, a fiendishly well organized cocaine combine run by a murderous twenty-one-year-old multimillionaire named Carlos (Benjamin Bratt).

Carlos is the kind of celluloid gangster who spends so much time devising tortures for his own underlings that one wonders how he ever gets anything else done. Little Tommy thus gets forced into cruel narco-slavery, working day and night in the YIP's crack-packaging plant, suffering Dickensian degrees of duress with scores of other captive youngsters. On the outside Tommy's frantic family contacts Scott, who finds his cop co-workers either evasive or apathetic about the mighty drug ring. When Scott learns his ex-lover Jackie (Marilu Henner) is now Carlos's very own lawyer, he goes undercover, using Jackie's influence to pass himself off as an aspiring upscale pusher. Soon the hero learns that Tommy's to be executed for an escape attempt. While a secret police operation has infiltrated the YIP at the highest level, the authorities won't blow it just to save one boy, so Scott launches a one-man rescue.

It climaxes in a set of action scenes right out of James Bond, highlighted by Scott momentarily eluding the baddies by sliding down the sloped side of a modern apartment building. He also leaps across an upraised bridge gap and faces doom in Carlos's dreaded alligator pit. "This motion picture is based upon actual events," trumpets an opening title, but the major concession to reality onscreen is that Scott's various scrapes ruin his dinner jacket. Actually, the movie vividly shows how drug kingpins utilize children as sellers, lookouts or couriers; they're easy to control and expendable, and even if the juveniles get arrested the system will put them back on the streets in no time.

Most of the personnel involved have their roots in TV. John Travolta (credited as one of the film's three screenwriters) bounded from "Welcome Back Kotter" heartthrob to superstardom via SATURDAY NIGHT FEVER and GREASE before hitting a stretch of duds. He still holds center stage well, but Scott's do-gooder concern, mixed with his own fight to stay sober, gets a trite, melodramatic treatment. Vague hints about Scott's former lifestyle as a high-flyer spawn an in-joke about erstwhile disco king Travolta's own career: reunited with old friends, Scott gestures at a nearby dance floor and says, "This, you know—it's not *me*." The elegant Marilu Henner (JOHNNY DANGEROUSLY, NOISES OFF) has a thankless role as the doomed romantic interest. Young Joey Lawrence acts properly imperiled, but his character could have been a more streetwise Artful Dodger and less a naive Oliver Twist. The material might have gained an sharper edge had Tommy Burke been any race other than lily-white. Then again, maybe not.

Director Rod Holcomb is a longtime TV helmer, and this 1989 production was intended as his theatrical debut. But after sitting in limbo for a couple of years the $10 million CHAINS OF

GOLD finally made an inauspicious bow on the Showtime cable network in 1991. It was unchained on home video the following year. *(Violence, substance abuse, profanity, adult situations, sexual situations.)*

p, Jonathan D. Krane; d, Rod Holcomb; w, John Petz, Linda Favila, Anson Downes, John Travolta; ph, Dariusz Wolski, Bruce Surtees; ed, Chris Nelson; m, Trevor Jones; prod d, George Goodridge; art d, Barbara Peterson; cos, Nile Samples

Crime/Drama (PR: O MPAA: R)

CHAPLIN ★★

(U.K./U.S.) 144m Carolco Pictures; Le Studio Canal Plus; RCS Video; Lambeth Productions Ltd. ~ TriStar Pictures bw/c

Robert Downey, Jr. *(Charlie Chaplin)*, Geraldine Chaplin *(Hannah Chaplin)*, Paul Rhys *(Sydney Chaplin)*, John Thaw *(Fred Karno)*, Moira Kelly *(Hetty Kelly/Oona O'Neill)*, Anthony Hopkins *(George Hayden)*, Dan Aykroyd *(Mack Sennett)*, Marisa Tomei *(Mabel Normand)*, Penelope Ann Miller *(Edna Purviance)*, Kevin Kline *(Douglas Fairbanks)*, Milla Jovovich *(Mildred Harris)*, Kevin Dunn *(J. Edgar Hoover)*, Diane Lane *(Paulette Goddard)*, Nancy Travis *(Joan Barry)*, James Woods *(Lawyer Scott)*, Hugh Downer *(Charlie–Age 5)*, Tom Bradford *(Charlie–Age 14)*, Matthew Cottle *(Stan Laurel)*, David Duchovny *(Rollie Totheroh)*, Francesca Buller *(Minnie Chaplin)*, Peter Crook *(Frank Hooper)*, Donnie Kehr *(Sound Engineer)*, Michael Blevins *(David Raskin)*, Nicholas Gatt *(Sydney–Age 9)*, Bill Paterson *(Stage Manager)*, Anthony Bowles *(Conductor)*, Bryan Coleman *(Drunk)*, Howard "Lew" Lewis *(Workhouse Official)*, P.H. Moriarty *(Workhouse Official)*, Brian Lipson *(Warder)*, Alan Ford *(Warder)*, Liz Porter *(Matchgirl)*, Ultan Ely-O'Carroll *(Rummy Binks)*, Marcus Eyre *(Policeman)*, Anwar Adaoui, Ben Bilson, Matthew Cartwright, Ian Covington, Adam Goodwin, Milly Gregory, Sam Holland, Josh Maguire, Daniel Sherman, Luke Strain, Frankie Sullivan *(Lambeth Kids)*, Karen Salt *(Little Girl)*, Gerald Sim *(Doctor)*, Una Brandon-Jones *(Inmate)*, Audrey Leybourne *(Inmate)*, Graham Sinclair *(Master of Ceremonies)*, Karen Lewis, Andree Bernard, Carole Jahme, Jacqueline Leonard, Claire Perriam, Theresa Petts *(Yankee Doodle Dancers)*, David Gant *(London Maitre d')*, Mary Healey *(Mrs. Karno)*, Malcolm Terris *(Stallholder)*, Phil Brown *(Projectionist)*, Ena Baga *(Pianist)*, Mario Govoni *(Swiss Butler)*, David Mooney *(Wedding Photographer)*, C.J. Golden *(Bride's Mother)*, Raymond Lynch *(Bride's Father)*, Peter Georges *(Groom)*, Mike Randelman *(Groom's Mother)*, Mike Peluso *(Groom's Father)*, Caroline Cornell, Ann Fairlie, Paul Hayes, Dennis Vero *(Wedding Guests)*, Nick Corello *(Masseur)*, Richard Fast *(Bronco Billy Anderson)*, Maria Pitillo *(Mary Pickford)*, Brad Parker *(Party Photographer)*, Yoshio Be *(Chauffeur)*, David Totheroh *(Cameraman)*, Jack Totheroh *(Cameraman)*, Jack Ritschel *(William Randolph Hearst)*, Heather McNair *(Marion Davies)*, Laura Bastianelli, Joy Claussen, Paul Bruno Grenier, Marykate Harris, Charles Howerton, Jason Logan, Renata Scott, Mike Villani *(Dinner Guests)*, Jerry Jenson *(Hotel Porter)*, Larry Randolph *(Waiter)*, Alan Charoff *(Federal Marshal)*, Dana Craig *(Federal Marshal)*, Kennedy Grant *(Federal Marshal)*, Ken MaGee *(Federal Marshal)*, Ben Whitrow *(Station Master)*, Edward Crangle *(Young Autograph Hunter)*, Stuart Richman *(Barman)*, Mark Vegh *(Barman)*, Caroline Guthrie *(Courting Couple)*, Lawrence Lambert *(Courting Couple)*, Robert Stephens *(Ted The Drunk)*, Tim Chaplin, Nick Edmett, David Finch, Mark Long, Tommy Wright *(Working Men)*, Leonard Kirby *(Young Fan)*, Sean O'Bryan *(Lewis Seeley)*, Deborah Maria Moore *(Lita Grey)*, Donald Elson *(Prop Man)*, Sky Rumph *(Charles Chaplin, Jr.–Age 7)*, Bradley Pierce *(Sydney Chaplin, Jr.–Age 6)*, Richard James *(Pianist)*, William Dennis Hunt *(US Maitre d')*, Norbert Weisser *(German Diplomat)*, Vicki Frederick, Gene Wolande, Michael Adler, Iris Bath, Thomas K. Belgrey, Tom Preston, Mary Stark, Annie Waterman *(Party Guests)*, Noah Margetts *(Clapper Boy)*, Rhett Smith *(Tennis Party Guest)*, John Standing *(Butler)*, Michael Goorjian *(Adult Charles Chaplin, Jr.)*, Michael Cade *(Adult Sydney Chaplin, Jr.)*, Todd Mason Covert, Phil Forman, Charley J. Garrett, Jerry Giles, Howard Hughes, Jayson Kane, Michael Miller, John Otrin, J. Michael Patterson, Paul Sinclair, Terrence Stone, Ralph Votrian *(Reporters)*, Emma Lewis *(Production Assistant)*

With CHAPLIN, director Richard Attenborough (GANDHI) again attempted an earnest historic profile of epic proportions. Though this stodgy portrait of the great entertainer's life is never nearly as fascinating as its subject, it's worth seeing for the lead performance of Robert Downey, Jr. The actor ages almost fifty years through the course of the film and the resemblance to Chaplin, in mien and movement, is uncanny. Downey's virtuosity, thought, is stifled by the director's stultifying, encyclopedic approach to Chaplin's life.

This see-Europe-in-five-days trip through Chaplin's fifty-four-year career begins with his dirt-poor London boyhood as the son of failed vaudevillian mother, Hannah (played by Chaplin's real-life daughter, Geraldine) who has begun a slow descent into insanity. It tracks his early London vaudeville career; his arrival in the US in 1913 and phenomenal success in the early days of the American film industry; his formation, with Douglas Fairbanks (Kevin Kline), Mary Pickford (Maria Pitillo) and D.W. Griffith of the United Artists studio; his sometimes turbulent working relationship with his half-brother/manager Sydney (Paul Rhys); his scandalous liaisons with, and series of marriages to, young women; his loss of an unjust paternity suit brought against him by Joan Barry (Nancy Travis); the animosity borne him by J. Edgar Hoover (Kevin Dunn), resulting in his tainting as a "Communist" and forced exile from the US; his happy, thirty-five-year marriage to fourth wife Oona O'Neill (Moira Kelly), daughter of playwright Eugene (she bore him eight children and they lived together in Vevey, Switzerland, until his death in 1977 at the age of eighty-eight); and his triumphant return to the US in 1972 to recieve an honorary Oscar for his life's work.

CHAPLIN recreates the early days of silent moviemaking, sketching portraits of figures ranging from Mack Sennett (Dan Aykroyd) to Edna Purviance (Penelope Ann Miller) to wife #3 Paulette Goddard (Diane Lane). The speed with which these figures are paraded past our eyes, however, tends to reduce everything to a senseless blur.

Attenborough and his screenwriters fail to impose sufficient dramatic structure on the overabundance of material, and never get to grips with what it was that made Chaplin tick. The screenplay is structured as a series of flashbacks recounted by Chaplin to publisher George Hayden (Anthony Hopkins). Hayden, the film's only fictional character, is visiting the aged filmmaker at his Swiss home to discuss Chaplin's pending autobiography (on which this film is partly based). It's a thankless acting task, and the questions are baldly contrived. ("Lita [Grey] was your second wife, okay? She gave you two sons who you adored. This book is over 500 pages long. Yet you only devoted five lines to her. Why?") Cut to Lita (Deborah Maria Moore) . . . .

It's only in those rare moments when Downey imitates Chaplin in performance, mimicking his singular waddle with trademark bowler hat, undersized waistcoat, baggy pants and Hitleresque mustache, that the screen comes alive. Few of the other actors are anything more than ciphers. Moira Kelly, for example, plays both Hetty Kelly, Chaplin's first love, and wife

Oona, but is barely onscreen long enough to make an impression. The exceptions are Geraldine Chaplin, a standout playing her own pathetically crazed grandmother, and Kevin Kline as Douglas Fairbanks—a great friend of Chaplin's and the silent screen's most famous swashbuckler.

The last minutes of the film are devoted to an on-screen readout, a *whatever became of* appendix to the lives of the characters depicted: Fred Karno (John Thaw), the London impresario who gave Chaplin his first job in vaudeville, went bankrupt in 1926 and died penniless; Mack Sennet's reign as "King of Comedy" ended with the talkies—almost forgotten, he was awarded a special Oscar in 1937; Sennett's girlfriend Mabel Normand (Marisa Tomei) was involved in the scandal surrounding the murder of director William Desmond Taylor in 1922 and her career never fully recovered.

CHAPLIN boasts meticulous production values, particularly Stuart Craig's and Chris Butler's art and set direction. But sumptuous sets and costumes cannot make up for a fundamental lack of directorial vision. At some point, Chaplin tells his publisher: "If you want to understand me, watch my movies." It's the truest line in the film.

p, Richard Attenborough, Mario Kassar; d, Richard Attenborough; w, William Boyd, Bryan Forbes, William Goldman, (from the story by Diana Hawkins based on the biography *Chaplin: His Life and Art* by David Robinson and *My Autobiography* by Charles Chaplin); ph, Sven Nykvist; ed, Anne V. Coates; m, John Barry; prod d, Stuart Craig; art d, Mark Mansbridge, John King; set d, Chris A. Butler, Stephenie McMillan; cos, John Mollo, Ellen Mirojnick

AAN Best Actor: Robert Downey, Jr.; *AAN Best Score:* John Barry; *AAN Art Direction:* Stuart Craig (Art Direction) and Chris A. Butler (Set Decoration)

Biography/Drama (PR: C MPAA: PG-13)

CHILDREN OF THE NIGHT ★★★

91m Fangoria Films ~ Columbia TriStar Home Video c

Karen Black *(Karen Thompson)*, Peter DeLuise *(Mark Gardener)*, Ami Dolenz *(Lucy Barrett)*, Maya McLaughlin *(Cindy Thompson)*, Evan Mackenzie *(Frank Aldin)*, Garrett Morris *(Matty)*, David Sawyer *(Czakyr)*, Josette DiCarlo *(Officer Gates)*, Shirley Spengler-Jacobs *(Grandma)*

The second of three 1992 video releases from Fangoria Films, CHILDREN OF THE NIGHT is a straightforward vampire thriller that proceeds with style and a refreshing lack of gimmickry. Though not especially revisionist, the movie does introduce a few new ideas to the bloodsucker lore, such as creatures that can live underwater.

That's where the story's lead ghoul, Czakyr (David Sawyer), is lying dormant as the story opens—in the flooded crypt beneath a church in the small town of Allburg. And who should happen along but a pair of teenaged girls, Lucy Barrett (Ami Dolenz) and her visiting friend Cindy Thompson (Maya McLaughlin). Lucy's getting ready to leave town for college, and with Cindy is taking part in the local ritual of swimming the crypt, "to wash the dirt of this town off forever." In the process, Lucy loses her cross necklace during her swim, and the icon awakens Czakyr, who attacks Cindy as Lucy flees in terror.

Shortly thereafter, Frank Aldin (Evan MacKenzie), a priest in a nearby town who's friendly with Cindy's mother Karen (Karen Black), reveals to his teacher friend Mark Gardener (Peter DeLuise) that Cindy has become a vampire and infected Karen as well; Frank has barricaded them into an upstairs room and feeds them blood-engorged leeches. Responding to his friend's plea to find out what's going on, Mark travels to Allburg just in time to save Lucy from her grandmother, who, like just about everyone else in town, has now been transformed by the evil Czakyr. Investigating at the local lodge, Mark and Lucy are captured by the locals and confronted by the towering, deformed Czakyr, but manage to escape. Picked up by town drunk Matty (Garrett Morris), who has commandeered a religious van, they flee to a deserted lumber mill.

While the others are asleep, Lucy is visited by the vampirized Cindy, who has put her mother out of her misery and enlists Lucy's help in destroying Czakyr. Mark and Matty awaken, find Lucy gone, and rush to town to save her, dispatching numerous vampires along the way; down in the crypt, Czakyr kills Cindy but is overwhelmed by his former youthful followers, who rise from the water to attack him. He survives, though, and attacks Mark and Lucy in the church; just as he's about to put the fatal bite into Lucy, Matty drives the religious van through a wall, the huge crucifix on the front impaling Czakyr, destroying him and freeing the town from the vampire curse.

Although there's little in CHILDREN OF THE NIGHT that is truly surprising, it moves confidently, with pacing that really picks up in the second half; once it gets cooking, the film's action doesn't stop. Despite the modest budget, director Tony Randel (HELLBOUND: HELLRAISER II) and cinematographer Richard Michalak pack their contribution to the 1992 vampire film boom with moody atmosphere. As with his previous film, Randel goes less for quick jolts than for scenes that build a mounting sense of terror. The screenplay by Nicolas Falacci provides him ample opportunity, with the early "feeding" scene of Karen and Cindy providing one of the film's most chilling moments.

Earnest performances all around help, and "Saturday Night Live" alumn Morris's comic relief is funny without overwhelming the seriousness of the situation. Although the makeup work by KNB EFX is efficiently gruesome, the movie doesn't become the gorefest that HELLBOUND was. Even so, there are a few elements here that are recognizable from Randel's earlier work, such as a scene of two creatures thrashing carnally inside a cocoon, and the Christopher Young-ish score by Daniel Licht (who worked with Young on the music for the HELLRAISER films).

Unlike Kathryn Bigelow's brilliant NEAR DARK, CHILDREN OF THE NIGHT doesn't reinvent the subgenre it deals with, but nor does it try to; it's the kind of solid, scary, unpretentious low-budget horror film that's gotten scarce in this age of needless sequels and dumb comic terror. *(Violence, profanity.)*

p, Christopher Webster; d, Tony Randel; w, Nicolas Falacci, Tom Holliday, William Hopkins, (from the story by Falacci, Hopkins, Tony Randel, Christopher Webster); ph, Richard Michalak; ed, Rick Roberts; m, Daniel Licht; prod d, Kim Hix

Horror/Thriller (PR: O MPAA: R)

CHILDREN, THE ★★★

(U.K./West Germany) 115m Isolde Films; Film Four International; Arbo Films & Maram ~ Hemdale Home Video c

Ben Kingsley *(Martin Boyle)*, Kim Novak *(Rose Sellars)*, Geraldine Chaplin *(Joyce Wheater)*, Siri Neal *(Judith)*, Joe Don Baker *(Cliffe Wheater)*, Rosemary Leach *(Miss Scope)*, Donald Sinden *(Lord Wrench)*, Britt Ekland *(Lady Wrench)*, Karen Black *(Sybil Lullmer)*, Mark Asquith *(Terry)*, Marie Helvin *(Princess Buondelmonte)*, Terence Rigby *(Duke of Mendip)*, Rupert Graves *(Gerald Ormerod)*, Anouk Fontaine *(Blanca)*, Eileen Hawkes *(Beechy)*, Ian Hawkes *(Bun)*, Hermione Eyre *(Zinnie)*, Robert Stephens *(Dobree)*, Edward Michie *(Chippo)*, Magdalen Asquith, Edward Asquith

Ben Kingsley heads a talented cast in THE CHILDREN, a well-directed and visually stunning film adaptation of the Edith Wharton novel.

Set in 1920s Europe, the story revolves around a middle-aged engineer, Martin Boyne (Kingsley), whose life is turned upside down when he takes in a group of children. After five years of corresponding with the now-widowed Rose Sellars (Kim Novak), Martin finally journeys overseas to marry her. But enroute he stops in Venice to see old college chum Cliffe Wheater (Joe Don Baker), a loud American who's in shipping. Cliffe and his wife Joyce (Geraldine Chaplin) have a number of children—some hers, some his and some adopted. After spending several weeks with the children and their nanny Miss Scope (Rosemary Leach), Martin travels to the mountains to be with Rose. Trying to sort out trouble with her husband's will, Rose asks Martin to wait another year before marrying her.

In the meantime, Cliffe and Joyce's teenage daughter Judith (Siri Neal) shows up at Rose's door with her younger siblings in tow. Their parents are having marital problems and the children eventually convince Martin to become their legal guardian. It isn't long before Martin's commitments to the children interfere with his relationship with Rose. Worse, his eventual crush on fifteen-year-old Judith jeopardizes his social standing. Exasperated, Rose goes to France on vacation and she and Martin finally break up. Five years later, alone and ailing, Martin returns to Europe where he runs into the children. At the film's close, it is uncertain whether or not he will get involved with them again.

Director Tony Palmer (WAGNER, TESTIMONY) has done a skillful job of bringing THE CHILDREN to the screen. Kingsley, Novak, Chaplin, Baker and the rest of the cast all deliver solid performances. And newcomer Neal is especially believable as Judith, a spoiled but mature-beyond-her-years adolescent. Nic Knowland's photography and the production design by Chris Bradley and Paul Templeman are not to be overlooked either. Add authentic-looking costumes and it's as though Wharton's imagery has leapt from the pages of her book onto the screen.

p, Tony Palmer; d, Tony Palmer; w, Timberlake Wertenbaker, (from the novel by Edith Wharton); ph, Nic Knowland; ed, Tony Palmer; prod d, Chris Bradley, Paul Templeman; cos, John Hibbs

Drama/Romance **(PR: A MPAA: NR)**

CHINA O'BRIEN II ★

86m Golden Harvest Films Ltd. ~ Imperial Entertainment Corporation c

Cynthia Rothrock *(China O'Brien)*, Richard Norton *(Matt Conroy)*, Keith Cook *(Dakota)*, Frank Magner *(Frank Atkins)*, Harlow Marks *(Charlie Baskin)*, Tiffany Soter *(Jill Atkins)*, Tricia Quai *(Annie Atkins)*, Douglas Caputo *(Kurt)*, J.R. Glover *(Chester)*

The old saying about Chinese food holds equally true for the CHINA O'BRIEN movies: you see one, and right away you're hungry again. There's barely any susbstance to these clone vehicles for pixyish martial-arts ingenue Cynthia Rothrock.

Part one concluded with the petite O'Brien (Rothrock) succeeding her late father as sheriff of tiny Beaver Creek. Now, thanks to the lady's flying feet and fists of fury, it's been designated the safest community in the state—even though there's a streetfight every two minutes so Sheriff O'Brien and her karate posse can show off their skills. The stunts get more expensive when Beaver Creek is invaded by legions of heavily armed marauders, led by hirsute Vietnam vet cum narcotics lord Charlie Baskin (Harlow Marks). He escaped from prison and wants revenge on an ex-associate, Frank Atkins (Frank Magner), residing in Beaver Creek with a cache of embezzled drug money.

Wave after wave of villainous mercenaries attack and get cut down by China and her deputies. There's no real excitement because O'Brien never makes a wrong move, never gets injured, never breaks a sweat, never loses. Her elaborately choreographed battles are lively but rote, predictable as aerobics routines. The only good guys who catch a punch occasionally are supporting sparmates: China's platonic best pal, Special Forces commando Matt Conroy (Richard Norton, sporting an incongruous Australian accent) and one-handed faithful Indian sidekick Dakota (Keith Cooke, covering two minorities in one). But they always bounce back, and the defeat of sleazy Baskin is as dull as it is certain.

The movie shares this dreary disinterest with the original CHINA O'BRIEN. Both also have the same fuzzy photography, location shooting in Park City, Utah, and identical offscreen personnel, from longtime chopsocky director Robert Clouse (ENTER THE DRAGON) on down. The pictures were probably shot back-to-back, as further evidenced by the reappearance of distinctive evil-henchmen from one film to another.

Rothrock's impressive form is no mere act; she earned five black-belt titles before retiring from martial arts competition in 1985. She since has cranked out a number of action flicks in Hong Kong and the US, and the CHINA O'BRIEN bookends were indeed produced under the auspices of the Hong Kong-based Golden Harvest company. In her other efforts Rothrock displays genuine acting ability and a gamine charm that deserves a better showcase than these no-frills combat marathons. *(Violence, profanity, sexual situations.)*

p, Fred Weintraub, Sandra Weintraub; d, Robert Clouse; w, James Hennessy, Craig Clyde, (from the story by Sandra Weintraub); ph, Kent Wakeford; ed, Mark Harrah; m, David Wheatley, Paul F. Antonelli; art d, John Told

Action/Crime/Martial Arts **(PR: O MPAA: R)**

CHRISTOPHER COLUMBUS: THE DISCOVERY ★★

(U.S./Spain) 120m Christopher Columbus Productions Inc. ~ Warner Bros. c

Marlon Brando *(Tomas de Torquemada)*, Tom Selleck *(King Ferdinand)*, George Corraface *(Christopher Columbus)*, Rachel Ward *(Queen Isabella)*, Robert Davi *(Martin Pinzon)*, Catherine Zeta-Jones *(Beatriz)*, Oliver Cotton *(Harana)*, Benicio Del Toro *(Alvaro)*, Mathieu Carriere *(King John)*, Manuel De Blas *(Vicente Pinzon)*, Glyn Grain *(De La Cosa)*, Peter Guinness *(Fra Perez)*, Nigel Terry *(Roldan)*, Nitzan Sharron *(Benjamin)*, Steven Hartley *(Terreros)*, Hugo Blick *(De Torres)*, Nigel Harrison *(Gonzalo)*, Chris Hunter *(Morales)*, Simon Dormandy *(Bives)*, Christopher Chaplin *(Escobedo)*, Michael Gothard *(Inquisitor's Spy)*, Clive Arrindell *(Lord Guarco)*, Richard Cubison *(Isaac)*, Mark Long *(Joseph)*, Nicholas Selby *(Monsignor Camos)*, John Grillo *(Chios Mapmaker)*, Serge Malik *(Alcalde of Malaga)*, Joseph Long *(1st Alguazil)*, Branscombe Richmond *(Indian Chieftain)*, Tailinh Forest Flower *(Indian Girl)*, Anthony Sarda *(Indian Brave)*, Gerard Langlais *(Indian Guide)*, Michael Halphie *(Chios Vendor)*, Genevieve Allenbury *(Harana's Wife)*, Michael Gunn *(Prison Officer)*, Vincent Pickering *(Healthy Prisoner)*, Trevor Sellers *(First Mate of Pinta)*, Caleb Lloyd *(Diego–Age 8)*, Andrew Dicks *(Diego–Age 11)*, Georgi Fisher *(Fernando)*, Steven Fletcher *(Rodrigo de Triana)*, Ivan De Bono *(Sailor in Tavern)*

CHRISTOPHER COLUMBUS: THE DISCOVERY was mounted by the father-son producers of the SUPERMAN series in official celebration of the 500th anniversary of Columbus's first voyage to the New World. This daft biographical epic reveals that the Europeans came West in search of many things: a new trade route to India and China; new souls to be converted to Christianity; new sources of gold; and new girlfriends with larger breasts.

Columbus (George Corraface, who's dropped the "s" from the end of his first name since starring in Peter Brook's epic MAHABHARATA) is first seen mixing it up with some treacherous Turks who are trying to steal his valuable maps to the great ocean over which he hopes one day to sail. (These same Turks have been disrupting European trade with the Far East.) It is Columbus's plan to prove the world is round by sailing West in order to reach the East. Exclusive rights to this new trading route will go to whichever monarch backs Columbus's expedition, with the explorer's take being a percentage of the trading gross. His brother makes little headway with either the English or the French monarchs and Columbus himself is kept in Spain by King Ferdinand (Tom Selleck) and Queen Isabella (Rachel Ward). As these two indulge in lengthy deliberations over their decision, Isabella's Rasputin-like Grand Inquisitor and confessor, the feared Torquemada (Marlon Brando), asks Columbus inscrutable questions and flays heretics in the basement. Looking haggard from his work as a mapmaker and mercilessly mocked by street urchins, Columbus takes solace in the company of his voluptuous child bride.

Having failed in her efforts to convert Spain's Jews to Christianity, Isabella has Torquemada throw them out of the country and takes a new interest in Columbus's plan as a means of spreading her faith to the New World. Columbus mounts his famous expedition, overcoming all the standard complications—Portugese attempts to sabotage the mission, dissent among his officers, mutiny among his crew, bad weather, hallucinations, etc. The New World itself is a paradise, especially for Columbus, who takes a pop-eyed interest in a native chieftain's young daughter. (She bears an uncanny resemblance to his child-bride at home, except that she wears nothing at all to cover breasts at least twice the size of his wife's.)

Columbus heads home without having discovered his route to the East, but with plenty of gold and a sampling of converted souls. He's forced to leave a third of his officers and crew behind when his fascination with the chieftain's daughter—chaste though it remains—leads to the sinking of one of his ships. Paradise turns sour for those left behind when the natives, fed up with their guests' raping, fighting and proselytizing, slaughter the whole scurvy bunch. Columbus also goes a little crazy on the voyage home but pulls himself together in time to present his bounty to the king and queen and be officially awarded his piece of the trading action.

Under the direction of James Bond veteran John Glen, CHRISTOPHER COLUMBUS: THE DISCOVERY tries to deliver lusty adventure, pitched battles and cartoonish history. But its screenplay, whose credited coauthors include the writers of THE GODFATHER and GANDHI, also aims for depth and complexity as it tries to address the dubious gifts Columbus brought to the New World, like rats, syphilis and slavery. The result is an oddly conflicted film.

Columbus starts out, improbably, as a swashbuckling trader with a crazy dream. From there, he segues to ladies' man, then to Queegish captain obsessed with order and discipline. At no time, however, is he credible as someone capable of planning and carrying out his audacious mission. And he's the most clearly defined character in the film. His sergeant-at-arms is the most curious. He trades secret sexy winks with Columbus's wife in Spain, yet he had a liaison with her sister, only to denounce her as a whore when she became pregnant with his child. Along on the voyage, of course, is the bastard son, who swears that only one of them will return to Spain alive and, amazingly, is never tossed overboard.

These token attempts at depth consistently run aground with Glen at the helm, who seems to get quickly bored when his characters aren't trying to either kill or have sex with each other. The big-star cast, understandably, keeps looking as if they can't quite believe how they're dressed or what they're doing. Selleck looks like he's having trouble willing his way into the mindset of a Spanish monarch. Brando puts in the most expensive—and pointless—cameo since he last fleeced the Salkinds for SUPERMAN.

Rachel Ward (AFTER DARK, MY SWEET; AGAINST ALL ODDS) gives simultaneously the flashiest and most thoughtful performance. Her Isabella burns with the eery, unhealthy glow of latent religious mania. The classically trained Corraface, scheduled to star in Sir David Lean's adaptation of Joseph Conrad's *Nostromo* until the great filmmaker's death in 1991, handles Columbus's violent mood swings with remarkable aplomb. If anything, this film may one day occupy roughly the same position in Corraface's career that KING KONG does in Jessica Lange's. *(Violence, nudity, sexual situations, adult situations.)*

p, Ilya Salkind; d, John Glen; w, John Briley, Cary Bates, Mario Puzo, (from his story); ph, Alec Mills; ed, Matthew Glen; m, Cliff Eidelman; prod d, Gil Parrondo; art d, Terry Pritchard, Luis Koldo; cos, John Bloomfield

Historical/Biography/Adventure (PR: C MPAA: PG-13)

CITY OF JOY ★★

(France/U.K.) 134m Lightmotive; Pricel S.A. ~ TriStar c

Patrick Swayze *(Max Lowe)*, Pauline Collins *(Joan Bethal)*, Om Puri *(Hasari Pal)*, Shabana Azmi *(Kamla Pal)*, Art Malik *(Ashoka)*, Ayesha Dharker *(Amrita Pal)*, Santu Chowdhury *(Shambu Pal)*, Imran Badsah Khan *(Manooj Pal)*, Nabil Shaban *(Anouar)*, Debtosh Ghosh *(Ram Chander)*, Suneeta Sengupta *(Poomina)*, Mansi Upadhyay *(Meeta)*, Shyamanand Jalan *(Godfather/Ghatak)*, Shyamal Sengupta *(Gangooly)*, Rudraprasad Sengupta *(Chomotkar)*, Baroon Chakraborty *(Said)*, Masood Akhtar *(Rassoul)*, Loveleen Mishra *(Shanta)*, Pavan Malhotra *(Ashish)*, Anashua Mujumdar *(Selima)*, Dipti Dave *(Schoolgirl)*, Aloke Roychoudhury *(Aristotle John)*, Siv Sankar Banerjee *(Goonda)*, Aloknanda Datta *(Schoolgirl's Mother)*, Chakradhar Jena *(Mehboub)*, Sunil Mukherjee *(Hotel Porter)*, Chetna Jalan *(Court Judge)*, Ravi Jhankal *(Obstructing Policeman)*, Debraj Roy *(Binal)*, Charubala Chokshi *(Binal's Wife)*, Durba Datta *(Margareta)*, Tamal Raichowdhury *(Surya)*, Sanjay Pathak *(Shoba)*, Anjan Dutt *(Dr. Sunil)*, Debasish Banerjee *(Dr. Sunil's Assistant)*, Swatilekha Sengupta *(Hotel Manageress)*, Sami Ahmad *(Bartender)*, Chhotu Bhai *(Thug)*, Rana Mitra *(Thug)*, Siddharth Roy *(Thug)*, Manu Mukherjee *(Waiter at Hamburger Bar)*, John Nair *(Selima's Son)*, Subrata Sen Sharma *(Minister at Railway Station)*, Sujan Mukherjee *(Subash)*, Satya Banerjee *(Subash's Father)*, Paresh Ghosh *(Subash's Uncle)*, Saran Chatterjee *(Subash's Uncle)*, Gouri Sankar Panda *(Subash's Uncle)*, Sudip Banerjee *(Subash's Uncle)*, Kajal Chaudhury *(Hasari's Mother)*, Iftekhar *(Hasari's Father)*, Chitra Sen *(Angry Woman)*, Keira Jane Malik *(Young Patient)*, Arunodoy Theater Group *(Special Crowd in City of Joy)*

Renowned for both his social conscience and the epic scale of his films, British helmer Roland Joffe (THE KILLING FIELDS, THE MISSION) is on familiar dramatic terrain with CITY OF JOY, a burnished portrait of personal redemption and native empowerment in India, the Third World nation synonymous with overpopulation and grinding poverty.

In search of the most basic needs, the farming family of Hasari Pal (Om Puri), among countless others, migrates to Calcutta to escape a disastrous drought in Bihar, India's poorest state. Woefully unprepared and frightened, instead of work they find a foul, teeming metropolis of inhuman congestion. Meanwhile, in an unnamed American city, Dr. Max Lowe (Patrick Swayze) loses a child on the operating table. Abruptly fleeing his stressful but privileged position, he arrives in Calcutta seeking to find—or redeem—his soul. (Oddly enough, although he's chosen India rather than, say, Kenya or Brazil, Max has no idea that Indians do not kill, much less *eat* cows; understandably, hamburgers are nonexistent.) One night, Max naively but chastely gets drunk with a hooker, and is then assaulted and robbed by local thugs. The Pals are sleeping nearby on the street. Hasari nobly comes to the stranger's aid, though by logic he should have no desire to enter a brawl he cannot even see around the corner. Hasari takes Max to the clinic in the City of Joy, a poetically named slum of Indian untouchables, outcasts of society who exist in a wretched ward but where, in sharp contrast to the affluent communities of the world, people are generous and full of life.

CITY OF JOY is based on a fine book of the same name by Dominique Lapierre, which shapes real-life drama and the semi-fictional, the epic and the intimate, into a mosaic relevant to our times. Entirely absent from the film is the central, saintly Polish priest Stephan Kovalski, who made extraordinary physical and spiritual efforts to raise human dignity from the depths of squalor. He's transformed into Joan Bethal (Pauline Collins), the compassionate, dedicated but less devout head of the City of Joy clinic. When Joan saves Max from an angry policeman, he's drawn into the eddy that is the City of Joy. In a vivid scene, shot largely in available light, Max delivers the baby of a leprous mother. The grainy realism is more effective than greater production efforts made elsewhere. "If your heart is clean, nothing happens," Hasari's wife says to her spouse as she enters the lepers' hovel to assist Max. Later, this baby, underfed because his mother must sell part of the milk ration for rent money, subjects Max to a watery baptism, an impromptu moment that enriches the film with its innocence and humanity.

Max's confusion about his work at the clinic or in a life adrift clashes with Joan's insistence that he make a choice: his life, or real life, here in the City of Joy. She boils it down to three choices: Run; spectate; or commit. Max eventually commits, but his Western ways irk the local godfather, a fat, cynical creature who extorts from the poor in exchange for "protection." When the City of Joy builds a clinic for the lepers, at Max's urging the inhabitants refuse the requisite payment to the godfather. His goons pillage and kill until the graft is proffered to Ashoka (Art Malik), the godfather's lieutenant. Hasari works for the godfather as a rickshaw puller, a job which turns humans into beasts of burden who toil in deadly heat and air for a few daily rupees. His tuberculosis is typically fatal for the impoverished who cannot afford medicine. Worse, Ashoka takes away his rickshaw because, as a denizen of the City of Joy, he sided with his family and community, not his employer.

This loss of livelihood sparks a clash between Max and Hasari, whose only option now is to sell his blood for the few rupees that he, as the head of the house, must provide. The rituals of life—healing the endless waves of sick; celebrating the violent but cleansing monsoon; and the wedding of Hasari's daughter after much haggling over the dowry—are well observed. Justice is served upon Ashoka, Hasari defends his family and personal dignity, and the gold medallion which once hung around Max's neck serves a far more meaningful purpose. But the film is weakened by its flattened perspective, more inclined to self-centered peace of Western mind than the milieu of very complex Indian agony. Given its enormous production expenses, this film, ironically, could only be produced by a Hollywood studio and, as such, simplified. Still, CITY OF JOY is not so much to be criticized as admired for the virtue it so passionately displays. *(Violence, adult situations.)*

p, Jake Eberts, Roland Joffe; d, Roland Joffe; w, Mark Medoff, (from the novel by Dominique Lapierre); ph, Peter Biziou; ed, Gerry Hambling; m, Ennio Morricone; prod d, Roy Walker; art d, Asoke Bose; set d, Rosalind Shingleton; cos, Judy Moorcroft

Drama **(PR: C MPAA: PG-13)**

CLASS ACT ★½

98m Wizan/Black Films; Gordy/DePasse Productions; Warner Bros. ~ Warner Bros. c

Christopher Reid *(Duncan Pinderhughes)*, Christopher Martin *(Blade)*, Andre Rosey Brown *(Jail Guard)*, Meshach Taylor *(Duncan's Dad)*, Mariann Aalda *(Duncan's Mom)*, Loretta Devine *(Blade's Mom)*, Rick Ducommun *(Parole Officer Reichert)*, Tony Simotes *(Dr. Oppenheimer)*, Scott Jensen *(Prison Guard)*, Simply Marvalous *(Miss Jackson)*, Jack "The Rapper" Gibson *(Janitor)*, Raye Birk *(Principal Kratz)*, Rhea Perlman *(Miss Joanne Simpson)*, Graham Galloway *(Latin Student)*, Gabe Green *(Rashid)*, Philip Perlman *(Teacher)*, Doug E. Doug *(Popsicle)*, Alysia Rogers *(Damita)*, Lamont Johnson *(Wedge)*, Kwawe Holland *(Squirrley Kid)*, Karyn Parsons *(Ellen)*, Randy Jandt *(Dorky Kid)*, Reginald Ballard *(Fruity)*, David Basulto *(Go-Go)*, John Hostetter *(Football Coach)*, Ivory Ocean *(Wrestling Coach)*, Patricia Fraser *(Mrs. Ipswitch)*, Thomas Mikal Ford *(Mink)*, George Alvarez *(Tommy)*, Michael Whaley *(Tyrone)*, Guy Margo *(1st Damita's Neighbor)*, Darcell Crayton *(2nd Damita's Neighbor)*, Lance Crouther *(1st Bad Dude)*, Baldwin C. Sykes *(2nd Bad Dude)*, Skip O. Carwell *(3rd Bad Dude)*, Mark "DJ Wiz" Eastmond *(D.J.)*, Greg Collins *(Cop)*, Sam McMurray *(Skip Wankman)*, Jody Savin *(1st St Peter's Student)*, Lisa Lord *(2nd St Peter's Student)*, Pauly Shore

As the Fat Boys demonstrated in DISORDERLIES, the social stridency of rap music does not mix well with crude, antediluvian slapstick. And now Kid 'N' Play, the popular rap duo that scored high-energy hilarity in HOUSE PARTY, offer further proof with the intensely juvenile CLASS ACT.

CLASS ACT regurgitates the old mistaken identity comic formula that reaches back to *A Comedy of Errors* and *The Prince and the Pauper*, only updating it to a South Central Los Angeles high school, where, due to a contrived switching of student records, two newcomers to the high school, Duncan Pinderhughes (Christopher "Kid" Reid) and Blade (Christopher "Play" Martin), are mistaken for one another. Duncan and Blade are complete opposites—Duncan a shy, straight-A student and Blade a street tough on parole. When Duncan and Blade manage to meet two attractive female classmates, Damita and Ellen (Alysia Rogers and Karyn Parsons), they reluctantly agree to continue with the charade in order to continue seeing the girls. After a series of confused complications, Duncan and Blade are chased by the local drug gang into a cut-rate wax museum that features the likenesses of Jerry Lewis, Christopher Lloyd, Larry Fine and other notables. There they vanquish the bad guys and confess their real identities to the girls, who, being true-blue types, stick with the guys anyway. As a coda, Duncan and Blade appear on a local TV quiz show, where they get the right answers and win honor and fame for their high school.

At this rate, can a remake of THE THREE STOOGES MEET HERCULES with Kriss Kross be far behind? Despite an up-to-date hipness and a sexually aware subtext in which girlfriends readily dispense condoms to their rarin' to go boyfriends, CLASS ACT, with its low voltage slapstick and cartoonish characterizations, feels decidedly secondhand, nothing more than a retread of such 60s drive-in teen flicks as SKI PARTY, MUSCLE BEACH PARTY and IT'S A BIKINI WORLD, with Tommy Kirk and Dwayne Hickman transformed into Kid 'N' Play.

Randall Miller directs the film with a sledgehammer intensity that pounds John Semper and Cynthia Freidlob's screenplay into dust. Like William Asher's beach films of the 60s, the graceless crudity of the direction overwhelms the shallowness of the screenplay, allowing only the most obtuse viewer not to understand what is happening in the film at any given point. In a 60s world of drive-in movies and triple bills, this style permitted the viewer to relax his gaze upon the film for other pursuits, from getting a hot dog to concentrating on the companion seated next to him in his car, and still come back to the film at any point and know immediately what was going on. But CLASS ACT, showcased on its own in a 90s multiplex, only serves to expose its blandness and its thin and belabored comedy.

The film is also confused in its political priorities. CLASS ACT seems to want to be a role model film for inner-city teens, teaching the importance of responsibility and education. But the film holds Duncan's world up to ridicule, from his shallow parents to ineffectual school administrators and ignorant high school teachers. At the same time, Blade's street world is depicted as more honest than Duncan's world of phonies, from Blade's ability to wing a biology lecture, to his cool clothes and shiny red car. All of this renders the sudden, head-banging inclusion of an anti-drug rap song performed by Kid 'N' Play halfway through the film not only jarring and unconvincing, but hard-headed, insincere and cynical.

CLASS ACT is so misguided that even the filmmakers themselves have thrown in the towel. As a coda to the film, Kid 'N' Play appear as themselves to wrap up stray plotlines. When Play threatens to retell the story from Blade's point of view, in a rap HE SAID, SHE SAID mode, Kid grabs him and physically drags him off camera, exhorting him by saying, "They're not going to sit through this again!" No truer words have ever been spoken. *(Adult situations.)*

p, Todd Black, Maynell Thomas; d, Randall Miller; w, John Semper, Cynthia Freidlob, (from the story by Michael Swerdlick, Wayne Rice, and Richard Brenne); ph, Francis Kenny; ed, John F. Burnett; m, Vassal Benford; prod d, David L. Snyder; set d, Robin Peyton

Comedy **(PR: C MPAA: PG-13)**

CLEARCUT ★★★½

(Canada) 96m Cinexus; First Canadian Artists ~ Northern Arts Entertainment c

Ron Lea *(Peter Maguire)*, Graham Greene *(Arthur)*, Rebecca Jenkins *(Female Reporter)*, Michael Hogan *(Bud Rickets)*, Floyd Red Crow Westerman *(Wilf Redwing)*, Tia Smith *(Polly)*, Tom Jackson *(Tom Starblanket)*, Raoul Trujillo *(Eugene)*, Michael Millar *(1st News Cameraman)*, Kim Hansen *(2nd News Cameraman)*, Steve Mousseau *(Nasty Cop)*, Phil Harris *(Policeman on Bullhorn)*, John Boylan *(Bud's Lawyer)*, Dee McCafferty *(Guide)*, Michael J. Reynolds *(Hunter)*, Andrew Proctor *(1st Regional Police Officer)*, Jari Sarkka *(2nd Police Officer)*, David A. Sutton *(Pilot)*, Thierry Bannon *(Sweat Lodge Singer)*, Harvey Churchill *(Sweat Lodge Singer)*

Darkly compelling despite being eerily unresolved, CLEARCUT is a crossbreeding of DELIVERANCE-style suspense with social consciousness, and helped immeasurably by a barn burner of a performance from Graham Greene as a murderously vengeful Native American who may or may not be real.

Despite his best efforts, Peter Maguire (Ron Lea), a Toronto lawyer working for a Canadian Native American tribe to stop "clear cut" logging on their tribal lands, is no match for the logging corporation's fleet of top lawyers. Traveling to his clients' reservation to deliver the grim news of his latest loss, he finds that the corporation has already begun operations opposed by Indian protesters. Pouring out his anger and bitterness over his failure to tribal elder Wilf Redwing (Floyd Red Crow Westerman) during a hallucinogenic session in a religious sweat lodge, Peter is later confronted in his motel room by Arthur (Greene).

A stranger whom Peter first encountered at the demonstration, Arthur now proposes a policy of no retreat, no surrender against the lumber company, beginning with the kidnapping and murder of Bud Rickets (Michael Hogan), the local logging plant's foreman. To show he can back up his words, Arthur begins by terrorizing a TV news crew in the room next door whose loud partying has kept Peter awake. Only Peter's intervention prevents Arthur from bashing in the heads of the two men in the room and raping the woman they find. Instead, the tormentors-turned-victims are left tied up while Arthur, with Peter in tow, goes in search of Rickets.

Finding him at a gas station, they kidnap him and take him into the woods. There, Arthur begins torturing Rickets by slowly skinning him alive. He later pays two hunters to go away and leave them alone and kills two policemen. All along, he challenges Peter to stop his rampage by fighting him. When Peter finally is prodded into action, Arthur dives into the river, disappears beneath the surface and is never seen again. Back in civilization, however, Peter spots a distinctive piece of jewelry that belonged to Arthur now around the neck of a child on the reservation.

Under the skilled direction of Richard Bugajski (whose blistering 1982 feature THE INTERROGATION was banned by the Polish government, finally resurfacing to great acclaim at the 1989 Toronto Festival of Festivals), CLEARCUT is as enigmatic as its central character. At different points in the film, Arthur is variously perceived or described as a drifter with a strong sociopathic streak, a terrorist hired by the tribe to make the lumber company more "sympathetic" to their point of view, and not a man at all but a spirit, conjured up by the tribal spiritual leaders to stop the destruction of their forest. It's also possible that he's none of the above. Starting with the motel confrontation, it seems mostly as if Arthur may be a figment of Peter's imagination, a twisted, outsized embodiment of his own impotent rage at slights big and small to which he consistently turns the other cheek out of social conditioning. Only Wilf knows for sure, and he's not saying.

Neither is Bugajski, who presents the tale from Peter's point of view, a questionable point of view at best. In the role, Lea is not the most charismatic of actors, which seems to be the whole idea. He's playing a most uncharismatic character, whose alliance with the Indians has a vaguely patronizing quality to it. He seems angrier at his courtroom setbacks than his Indian clients do despite the fact that the outcome has little or no effect on his own life. His motivation for following Arthur seems therefore unclear. Throughout he seems to be in some sort of dreamlike state, insubstantial and ineffectual, like a man having a nightmare who is unable to wake up. By extension, modern life itself is seen as a waking nightmare in which nothing, from savage confrontational violence to sophisticated legal maneuvering, seems able to prevent the gradual destruction of the planet. The meek may inherit the earth, but they won't hold onto the logging rights.

As CLEARCUT shows, they'll be lucky to hold onto their sanity. If Bugajski has made an absorbing, enigmatic film, Greene (DANCES WITH WOLVES, THUNDERHEART) is clearly the main attraction. His work here is the kind of classic star turn that leaps from the screen and burns itself into the memory despite being anything but a typical star role. Most stars are almost pathologically image-conscious, but his character never explains himself and is never explained by anyone else while he's skinning, shooting and menacing those around him. Although Rob Forsyth's screenplay, based on M.T. Kelly's novel *A Dream Like Mine*, would have easily accommodated a portrayal of Arthur as a noble savage taking his last stand or a minority driven mad by oppression, Greene seems to have taken the far trickier approach of playing Arthur as Peter's dark side, which is, finally, the most dramatically logical approach to take.

The combined efforts make CLEARCUT a film that is frustrating both as art, for its lack of resolution, and as politics, for its lack of clear villains and heroes and little in the way of a clear message. But echoing Peter's dilemma, it has a dreamlike, or nightmarish, authority that makes it linger in the memory in a way a more forthcoming film may not have. *(Extreme violence, profanity, adult situations.)*

p, Stephen J. Roth, Ian McDougall; d, Richard Bugajski; w, Rob Forsyth, (from the novel *A Dream Like Mine* by M.T. Kelly); ph, Francois Protat; ed, Michael Rea; m, Shane Harvey; prod d, Perry Gorrara; art d, Kenneth Watkins; set d, Gareth Wilson; cos, Kathy Vieira

Thriller/Fantasy **(PR: C MPAA: R)**

CLOSE TO EDEN ★★★½

(U.S.S.R./France) 120m Camera One; Hachette Premiere; UGC; Studio Trite ~ Miramax c
(URGA)

Badema *(Pagma)*, Bayaertu *(Gombo)*, Vladimir Gostukhin *(Sergei)*, Babuskha *(Grandma)*, Larissa Kuznetsova *(Marina)*, Jon Bochinski *(Stanislas)*, Bao Yongyan *(Bourma)*, Wurinile *(Bouin)*, Wang Zhiyong *(Van Biao)*, Baoyinhexige *(Bayartou)*, Nikolai Vachtiline *(Nikolai)*

More than a few lifetimes since the glory days when Genghis Khan conquered Eurasia, Mongolia has languished on the periphery of the modern age, with scant international influence and few major industries to speak of. Still, it may come as a surprise to most Westerners that the bucolic existence led by some Mongols has undergone little change in hundreds of years. Until recently, that is. Stunningly photographed on the vast steppes of China's Inner Mongolia, Nikita Mikhalkov's CLOSE TO EDEN is a poetic and richly cinematic ode to a way of life which, after centuries of stasis, is finally vanishing.

In the opening scene, Gombo (Bayaertu), an expert horseman, ambushes his lovely young wife, Pagma (Badema, no slouch on a horse, either), with the aid of an *urga*, a long pole with a noose at the end which the landlocked Mongols use to corral their livestock; stuck vertically into the ground, it's also a signal to others that a couple is making love in the open fields nearby. Much to his chagrin, Gombo's amorous advances are met with fierce resistance from Pagma; by Chinese law, they are only allowed two children, and they've already got three, including a newborn who will likely be turned away from school.

Though isolated, Gombo and his family aren't entirely cut off from the outside world, which appears one day in the form of Sergei (Vladimir Gostukhin), a jovial Russian laborer who's helping to build a transcontinental road in Mongolia. After driving for twenty-four hours straight, he falls asleep at the wheel of his truck, goes off the road and almost crashes into a small lake. He jumps out to refresh himself, only to stumble across a decomposing corpse in the fields. Quickly sobered, he hastily retreats to his vehicle, but panics and drives his truck into the water after all. Sergei is promptly rescued by Gombo (the corpse, it turns out, was a beloved uncle), but there's nothing to be done until the following day, so he brings Sergei back to his *yurga*, or homestead.

Once there, Sergei watches with a combination of fascination and repulsion, but mostly the latter, as Gombo kills and skins a sheep with a few deft incisions, then expertly disembowels it. Sensing that he's insulted his hosts by refusing their offer of the delectable cooked meat, Sergei capitulates, and also partakes of some very potent home brew. (The actors, including the adorable Wurinile, who plays little Bouin, make a remarkably convincing family, such is their warmth and naturalness.) In one of the film's most charming moments, Bourma (Bao Yongyan), their oldest child, reveals herself to be a surprisingly accomplished accordionist, much to Sergei's drunken delight.

That night, a frustrated Gombo and resolute Pagma once again a reach a sexual stalemate. Pagma, who, unlike her husband, grew up in the city, shocks Gombo by suggesting that he travel into town to purchase condoms. She also asks him to buy a TV. The following day, Gombo helps Sergei pull his truck out of the lake. In return, he drives Gombo into town—the same town where Sergei, along with his unhappily displaced wife and their young son, now lives in a modern apartment. After promising to reunite with his new friend, Gombo enters the local pharmacy, but he's too embarrassed by the presence of female salesclerks to make a purchase.

That evening, while carousing with his new friend in a local nightclub, Sergei drunkenly lectures a fellow countryman on the sadly devalued Russian soul. Next, he staggers onstage and forces the band to play a mournful lament about the Russian soldiers who died defending their homeland; the musicians merely follow the notes tattooed on Sergei's back, a souvenir from his own youthful army career. Sergei is quickly arrested, but Gombo and Van Biao (Wang Zhiyong), the musician who taught Bourma how to play the accordian, come to his rescue.

The following day, Gombo returns to the homestead with the promised TV—but no condoms. En route, he has a dream in which he's confronted by Genghis Khan, who admonishes him for lacking the warrior spirit that made their people great. Pagma quickly sees through her husband's feeble excuse—the pharmacy was out of stock—but, touched by his tremendous desire to have another child (Genghis Khan, after all, was a fourth child, and Gombo himself was seventh), she steps outside and beckons him to join her in the fields. The film comes full circle, with Gombo once again giving chase after Pagma, only this time the *urga* stands proudly in the ground.

CLOSE TO EDEN brilliantly juxtaposes two melancholy spirits, Russian and Mongolian, both at odds with the 20th century. But then, as the film gently implies, what society—apart from our own grasping, relentlessly forward-thinking nation—isn't? While often downright anthropological in its keen observation of the rural Mongolian lifestyle, the film deftly underscores their commonality with all mankind. In the film's bittersweet, ironic coda, Gombo and Pagma's fourth child, Genghis, has grown up and become a gas station attendant, and the vast Mongolian steppes have become home to nuclear reactors.

This is a wise, deeply affecting film, marking a considerable departure for Mikhalkov (who, along with brother and fellow filmmaker Andrei Konchalovsky, are the scions of a Russian creative dynasty), best known for DARK EYES, and arguably his best to date. With its subtly and beautifully expressed themes, it's the work of not only a master filmmaker, but an artist of rare vision and deep humanity.

d, Nikita Mikhalkov; w, Nikita Mikhalkov, Roustam Ibraguimbekov, (from his story based on an idea by Mikhalov); ph, Villenn Kaluta; ed, Joelle Hache; prod d, Aleksei Levtchenko; cos, Irina Guinno

AAN Best Foreign Language Film:

Drama/Romance **(PR: A MPAA: NR)**

CODE NAME: CHAOS ★
96m Vestron Pictures; Corunna ~ LIVE Home Video c

Diane Ladd *(Alice)*, Brian Kerwin *(Jim)*, Robert Loggia *(Mac)*, David Warner *(Cleague)*, Alice Krige *(Isabelle)*, Freddie Jones *(Filator)*, William Allen Young *(Rob)*, Carlos Douglas *(Chu Chu)*, Angus MacInnes *(Vic)*

Facetiously dedicated to spies everywhere, CODE NAME: CHAOS deals with that most fun-loving bunch of cut-ups: CIA agents. It's this puerile comedy's contention that self-serving, renegade spies could set up shop in a storybook country and reap financial benefits by manufacturing fake global conflicts.

Unfortunately for these slick sell-outs in picturesque Moressa, the US government sends agent Jim (Brian Kerwin), who's more loyal to his country than to his bank account. Finding it necessary for business to smoke out a Russian defector, head spy Mac (Robert Loggia), trustworthy aide-de-camp Alice (Diane Ladd), demolition expert Rob (William Allen Young) and British ally Cleague (David Warner) all endeavor to make the Soviet Filator (Freddie Jones) come in from the cold. While squeaky clean Jim dodges bomb-bursts and quickly sizes up the deadly intentions of his fellow Americans, the CIA financial wizards sieze Filator and launch a bogus Russian threat to world security.

Aided by Isabelle (Alice Krige), a beautiful loyalist to the tiny principality of Patria, Jim escapes a freighter explosion and staunches the flow of damage at CIA headquarters in Moressa. While the CIA cutthroats gamble on a falling world economy, Jim and Isabelle risk their lives gathering info about a fabricated Russian star wars crisis. After Mac and Cleague crash their helicpoter in pursuit of the good guys, Alice shifts all their investments around. What she doesn't realize is that battered but unbowed Jim is tired of the spy games; rather than return to America with proof of the CIA plot, he's decided to remain in Patria with Isabelle. While Alice can content herself with romance with Filator, the others will be less pleased to know their biggest financial hoax yet has proven a big bust.

Witless and frenetic, CODE NAME: CHAOS doesn't have the directorial control, clever dialogue or visual grace to instill any of its mean-spirited assassination attempts and treacheries with a sense of humor. The actors screech at each other like children at a shouting match; the confusing plotline trips over itself; only the scenic photography delights. Was this screenplay shoved in a trunk and forgotten and then taken out after Glasnost? Why produce it now that its cold-war shenanigans have lost their satiric point? The plot contortions strangle the film's forward momentum and the high-decibel acting wears away at any residual affection viewers may have for the cast.

Combining murder plots with banal romantic vignettes is like crossing THE MANCHURIAN CANDIDATE with A MIDSUMMER NIGHT'S DREAM. While Krige and Kerwin emote as if they were in a serious romantic thriller, the other cast members are gesticulating and grimacing like marionettes struggling to come to life and form their own comedy club. Only Ladd (WILD AT HEART, RAMBLING ROSE) salvages her reputation by underplaying. But what is one to make of the usually reliable Warner and Loggia? Seeing the forceful Loggia mug his way through this dismal comedy is as upsetting as catching Brando doing a guest spot on "Hee Haw." Dated and ill-conceived, CODE NAME: CHAOS is a mind-numbing, caper comedy with a paucity of thrills and laughter approaching the level of our national debt.

p, John Levy, John Davis; d, Anthony Thomas; w, Anthony Thomas; ph, Mike Southon; ed, Jim Clark; m, Hans Zimmer, Fiachra Trench; prod d, Gemma Jackson; art d, Sophie Becher; cos, Imogen Mangus

Comedy **(PR: C MPAA: R)**

COEUR QUI BAT, UN
(SEE: BEATING HEART, A)

COLD HEAVEN ★
105m Hemdale Picture Corporation; Management Company Entertainment Group; Schwartzman Pictures ~ Hemdale Releasing Corporation c

Theresa Russell *(Marie Davenport)*, Mark Harmon *(Dr. Alex Davenport)*, James Russo *(Daniel Corvin)*, Talia Shire *(Sister Martha)*, Will Patton *(Father Niles)*, Richard Bradford *(Monsignor Cassidy)*, Julie Carmen *(Anna Corvin)*, Diana Douglas *(Mother St. Agnes)*, Seymour Cassel *(Tom Farrelly)*, Castulo Guerra *(Dr. DeMencos)*, Daniel Addes *(Dr. Mendes)*, Jim Ishida *(Dr. Tanaki)*, Jeanette Miller *(Sister Katarina)*, Martha Milliken *(Sister Anna)*, Margarita Cordova *(Registrar)*, Sal Lopez *(Young Doctor)*, Gary Pagett *(Doorman)*, Helen Boll *(Maid)*, Dennis Kelly *(1st Doctor)*, David Meyers *(2nd Doctor)*, Claudia Harrington *(1st Nurse)*, Valerie Hastings *(2nd Nurse)*, Susan Sells *(3rd Nurse)*, Carmela Rioseco *(Mexican Nurse)*, Sam Vlahos *(Alvarado)*, David Rodriguez *(Cab Driver)*, Alex Alexander *(Waitress)*

With COLD HEAVEN, an often incoherent adaptation of Brian Moore's novel, director Nicholas Roeg proves that even when he's boring he can still be interesting.

Marie Davenport (Theresa Russell), the pampered wife of a successful doctor, Alex (Mark Harmon), has chosen a Mexican vacation to tell her husband she's leaving him for one of his medical colleagues, Daniel Corvin (James Russo). Before she can break the news, Alex is hit by a boat while swimming, crushing his skull and apparently killing him. The next day, when Alex's body disappears from the local morgue, Marie suspects that he may not have been dead in the first place. But that doesn't stop her from continuing on to a rendezvous with Corvin at the resort where much of the action takes place.

There, while awaiting Corvin, Marie is surprised to find Alex staying at the same hotel—ashen, oozing from his head wound and raving about plots against his life. Taking a walk on the grounds of a nearby mission, Marie has a vision of a young girl rising from a creek at the bottom of a seaside cliff. She is driven to reveal this apparition to the local monsignor (Richard Bradford) and urges him to construct a shrine to the Virgin Mary at the creek. The monsignor dismisses Marie's claims, but the story catches the interest of a young priest (Will Patton) after a nun (Talia Shire) tells him that she had dreamed of Marie and her vision long before Marie's arrival at the mission.

The situation at the resort becomes exceedingly awkward with the arrival of Corvin, who has left his own wife (Julie Carmen) to be with Marie and finds himself examining Alex and checking him into a hospital. Though Marie never tells Alex of her affair with Corvin, Alex puts two and two together and, after being released from the hospital, decides to make a quiet exit from Marie's life. Returning with the nun to the site of her vision,

Marie has her own revelation about what she must do and races back to the hotel, into Alex's arms.

Nothing ever really clicks in COLD HEAVEN, a weird cross-mixture of genres that dips and whizzes from Hitchcockian suspense to religious inspirational to romantic melodrama to Edgar Allen Poe and beyond. It doesn't help that Roeg's approach to narrative remains as fuzzy as ever. For the longest time, it's never clear whether Marie actually planned with Corvin to kill Alex or just to leave him. Alex's reappearance is similarly treated in such a way that it's not clear, at first, whether he actually has reappeared or is just a figment of Marie's feverish imagination. The exact nature of Marie's vision and precisely why it makes such an impact on her is never quite clear either, although Marie does reveal that she was an extremely devout girl who renounced God following the untimely death of her beloved mother.

As COLD HEAVEN goes on Roeg seems uninterested in or unable to tie up his three major plots compellingly; instead he lets them run awkwardly on parallel tracks to the film's perfunctory end. Yet what Roeg has consistently managed with authority throughout his career—or at least since 1970's PERFORMANCE—is to give cinematic shape to the psychological disintegration, amid the violent chaos of modern life, of his protagonists. Here, if nothing else, he brings conviction and clarity to Maria's plight as a lapsed Catholic whose paralyzing guilt over her adultery seems to drive her to religious mania.

Russell's anxious vacuity as an actress, which has elsewhere garnered her a reputation as perhaps the world's greatest bad actress, becomes an asset in Roeg's films. She's like some sort of caged animal here, perpetually on the edge of panic while trapped in an infernal triangle between two inadequate men, one representing domesticity so dreary that he seems more lively as a "dead" man than he did when he was "alive," and the other representing destructive, self-absorbed lust. Completing the triangle is the power of the Divinity, who has chosen her, like a deranged Mary Magdalene, to deliver the Word to the doubting priests.

It never makes much sense. But, at its best, COLD HEAVEN is anything but run-of-the-mill. When it's working, it's bizarre, bewildering, infuriating and frequently inexplicable, but it's also a fascinating psycho-puzzle of a movie that is silly as often as it is sublime. Roeg and Russell may never appear on the Oscar stage together hoisting twin statuettes; however, it's all but impossible to imagine what modern cinema would be without them. *(Violence, adult situations, nudity, profanity.)*

p, Allan Scott, Jonathan D. Krane; d, Nicolas Roeg; w, Allan Scott, (from the novel by Brian Moore); ph, Francis Kenny; ed, Tony Lawson; m, Stanley Myers; prod d, Steve Legler; art d, Nina Ruscio; set d, Cliff Cunningham; cos, Del Adey-Jones

Thriller/Fantasy **(PR: O MPAA: R)**

COLD JUSTICE ★½

(U.K.) 102m Father Jim Productions; East End Films ~ Columbia TriStar Home Video c

Roger Daltrey *(Keith Gibson)*, Dennis Waterman *(Father Jim)*, Ralph Foody *(Ernie)*, Ron Dean *(Stan)*, Penelope Milford *(Eileen)*, Bert Rosario *(Pacito)*, Robert Carricart *(Paco)*, Joe Greco *(Mr. Swan)*, Larry Brandenburg *(Ray)*, Bridget O'Connell *(Debbie)*, Bonnie Sue Arp *(Sylvie)*, Matthew Wertz *(Nicko)*, John Moherlein *(Bronski)*, Diane Charles *(Tracey)*, Ernest Perry, Jr. *(Tucker)*

Apparently the screenwriters responsible for this saloon saga have been reading too much William Saroyan. Anecdotal yet besotted with its own plot, COLD JUSTICE requires a scorecard more than a review; all the philosophizing bums and neighborhood bar heroes get lost in the shuffle.

With the yuppies nipping at their heels, long-time bar patrons self-pityingly cry into their beer. Former fight pro Keith Gibson (Roger Daltrey) wants to renounce petty crime and box his way back to glory. Amateur singer Pacito (Bert Rosario) longs to be the Puerto Rican Robert Goulet, but is troubled by his senile father, Paco (Robert Carricart), who has lost his faith in the Church. Unwed, slightly retarded Debbie (Bridget O'Connell) frets about her pregnancy, catches the baby's fickle father making out with a barmaid and loses her job. Into all these inconsequential, drab lives comes Father Jim (Dennis Waterman), an unconventional British priest who meddles as often as he drinks—which is often. No one pays attention when pesky wino-cynic Ernie (Ralph Foody) points out that, despite Father Jim's claims, there were no English chaplains in the American armed services. Instead, they trust the priest with the proceeds of their benefit fundraiser.

But where is this trusted advisor when Debbie buys a gun and ends her life, or when Gibson loses his sight as a result of boxing in a rigged bout, or when barkeep Stan (Ron Dean) cowers because he thinks he's angered local mobster Mr. Swan (Joe Greco)? Clearly the charlatan priest is too busy dreaming up cons when the chips are down. Although Father Jim gets his greedy paws on Paco's secret lottery winnings, he makes the mistake of absconding with the charity loot which contains a generous gift from Mr. Swan. The mobster does not like being ripped off; it's a point of pride for him. Divine retribution strikes Father Jim when Mr. Swan and his henchman catch up with the fake priest. Fittingly, they crucify him.

Exactly what is the point of this peripatetic examination of faith in one's fellow man? That one should check the references of foreign clerics? That crotchety old alcoholics are better at spotting phonies than less accomplished drunks? That mentally impaired girls should wear condoms when dating hockey-loving romeos? Worn down by more intertwined storylines than you'll find in any three Robert Altman movies, the audience stuck with COLD JUSTICE can only wonder whether the film's losers are simply incredibly dense or perpetually inebriated.

It's distressing to see Daltrey and Penelope Milford wasted here, but it's downright perplexing to read star Dennis Waterman's name listed as one of the writers and producers. Did he really think that this watered-down pitcher of highballs was a juicy showcase for his talents? If so, he's as deluded as the lost souls Father Jim cons. Actually, the entire cast should fall down on its knees and pray for career guidance. *(Violence, profanity, adult situations.)*

p, Ross Cameron, Dennis Waterman, Robert Hudecek; d, Terry Green; w, Terry Green, Trevor Preston, Dennis Waterman; ph, Dusty Miller; ed, Tom Morrish, Crispin Green; prod d, Bill Arnold; art d, Pat Raney; set d, Joel Prihoda; cos, Jay Hurley

Drama/Crime **(PR: O MPAA: R)**

COLLISION COURSE ★★

96m Interscope Communications; DeLaurentiis Entertainment Group; Sign of the Ram Productions ~ HBO Video c

Pat Morita *(Investigator Fujitsuka Natsuo)*, Jay Leno *(Detective Tony Costas)*, Ernie Hudson *(Shortcut)*, Chris Sarandon *(Philip Madras)*, John Hancock *(Lieutenant Ryerson)*, Tom Noonan *(Scully)*, Al Waxman *(Dingman)*, Dennis Holahan *(Derek Jeryd)*, Soon-Teck Ho *(Kitao)*, Randall "Tex" Cobb *(Kosnic)*, Kevin Hagan

Amid much fanfare, beloved "Tonight Show" host Johnny Carson finally retired in 1992, after three decades as a late-night institution. As every devotee knows, Carson had a stunted career as a movie actor, and on TV he would occasionally joke about his less-than-memorable influence on the big screen. It seems only fitting that his chosen successor, convivial smart-aleck comedian Jay Leno, also have a celluloid skeleton rattling around his closet, and so it was that the 1989 Leno vehicle COLLISION COURSE was hauled out of storage and onto home video the same year Leno took Carson's parking space. It's a workaday buddy-cop comedy, though the storyline is almost interesting in spite of itself.

Detective Tony Costas (Leno) is a convivial smart-aleck cop in the car capital, Detroit. When an old pal from the force is mowed down by high-powered ammunition in a junkyard, Costas bucks the system and investigates the case personally. It turns out that maverick auto executive Derek Jerryd (Dennis Holahan) has kept his company afloat via a partnership with underworld boss Philip Madras (Chris Sarandon). To give Jerryd's new car a technical edge, Madras bribed a Japanese businessman to sneak the revolutionary new "Kodama Motors" engine prototype into the US, but the smuggler died at the hands of Madras's strong-arm henchmen. Madras is now searching the Motor City for the hidden engine prototype, and so is investigator Fujitsuka Natsuo (Pat Morita), an elfin Tokyo lawman with orders to bring back the valuable hardware—or else. Costas and Natsuo form the usual uneasy, bickering alliance as they chase down the bad guys, turning from rival cops into cross-cultural pals.

COLLISION COURSE's formulaic premise is bolstered by the clash between East and West, explored, however shallowly, by screenwriters Frank Darius Namei and Robert Resnikoff. The courteous little Natsuo is referred to disparagingly as "Tojo," "Honda," "the Kamikaze"—and that's just by the police. But if anything the tale implies criticism of the Yanks, who are racist, rude and boundlessly violent (one of the villains is a gun-happy survivalist who keeps a live grenade next to his plastic Jesus). There's one scene—meant to be funny but extremely uncomfortable to anyone familiar with Nippon-hating Detroit—in which Costas and Natsuo chase a baddie into a blue-collar bowling alley, then find themselves surrounded by angry working-class roughnecks who commence a beefy debate with Natsuo over global economics and protectionism. This moment concludes with the standard action-comedy setpiece of a slapstick fistfight, with lots of acrobatic camera sweeps as the soundtrack blares one of the film's many non-hit songs.

Leno, who had smaller roles in the earlier SILVER BEARS and AMERICAN HOT WAX, comes across as an immensely likeable guy, comfortable in front of the cameras and quick with his line readings, but he doesn't exactly set the frame on fire. Maybe it's the comedian's habit of letting his tongue hang out during the chase scenes, or a silly running gag making him a ladies' man when the plot has no romance, but he brings no extra juice to a screenplay that sorely needs a jump-start. The likeable Noriyuki "Pat" Morita has a pat role to play, the standard inscrutable-oriental type given to Confucian-style remarks like "Destiny bring us together." An amusing but too-rare insight into his character is that whenever the placid, polite Natsuo phones home to Tokyo his superior vigorously berates him as a worthless bumbler; Natsuo listens stoically on the line, playing it cool for the benefit of the American cops watching uncomprehendingly. Natsuo describes himself as one of the very few Japanese who knows no martial arts (a dig at Morita's KARATE KID movies), but in the ludicrous ending he foils the heavies with a superhuman kung-fu kick of a sort unseen since the days of Billy Jack.

The real star of COLLISION COURSE is Detroit itself, here a sparkling and funky urban setting. The climax manages to involve the famous Detroit Grand Prix, a motor race with a track that wound right through downtown (in the years since this was made it relocated to nearby Belle Isle). The rest was filmed at the DeLaurentiis Entertainment Group studios in Wilmington, North Carolina. There was trouble on the assembly line for this $13 million production, which went through no fewer than three directors—John Guillerman, Bob Clark and Lewis Teague—before completion. But COLLISION COURSE stalled when DEG declared bankruptcy, and was truly a day late and a dollar short by the time it made its debut on home video. *(Violence, substance abuse, profanity.)*

p, Howard W. Koch Jr., Ted Field, Robert W. Cort; d, Lewis Teague; w, Frank Darius Namei, Robert Resnikoff; ph, Donald E. Thorin; ed, Jerry Greenberg; m, Ira Newborn; prod d, Harry Pottle; art d, Bill Durrell; set d, Garrett Lewis; cos, Ron Talsky

Action/Comedy **(PR: A MPAA: PG)**

COLOR ADJUSTMENT ★★½

88m Signifyin' Works ~ California Newsreel c

Ruby Dee *(Narration)*, Esther Rolle, Henry Louis Gates, Jr., Norman Lear, Alvin Poussaint, Herman Gray, Diahann Carroll, David Wolper, Hal Kanter, Sheldon Leonard, Steve Bochco, Tim Reid, Daphne Reid

Acclaimed documentarian Marlon T. Riggs won an Emmy in 1987 for his public-TV program "Ethnic Notions," a survey of various stereotypes applied to African-Americans over the years. Its companion piece is COLOR ADJUSTMENT, which enjoyed both theatrical and broadcast exposure in 1992, and deals with the inadequate depiction of blacks on network TV.

From the 1950s TV incarnation of radio stereotypes Amos and Andy to "The Cosby Show" in the 1980's, Riggs (TONGUES UNTIED) sees a pattern of subverting racial identity and equality. Black characters were either harmlessly comical buffoons or sanitized into shallow, segregated reflections of their pallid white counterparts—happy, successful and, recently, yuppified. Even so-called breakthrough TV, like the Diahann Carroll sitcom "Julia" (1968-71) placed its idealized Black heroine into an impossibly color-blind society that interviewee Carroll admits was blandly one-dimensional. Riggs occasionally turns to an assortment of opinion-leaders, actors and TV producers for anecdotes and social commentary, all supporting the idea that prime-time Blacks are thoroughly whitewashed.

It's a sad but familiar refrain that a minority has been shortchanged in the media. Riggs does offer a few insights, like the admission from "Julia" producer Hal Kanter (with an Emmy Award looming over his shoulder) that his show was a form of penance for "Amos and Andy." A virtually forgotten, realistic drama of the early 60s, "East Side, West Side," (featuring young George C. Scott and James Earl Jones) looks stark and bracing even by modern standards. Couch potatoes may be shocked to realize that not until the 1970s sitcom "Good Times" was an *intact* Black family, with both mother and father, allowed to take center stage—and that was only because lead Esther Rolle demanded a husband (the role played by John Amos), instead of being the usual widowed "mammy" figure. And gentlemanly crooner Nat King Cole, host of an intermittant variety show in the 1950s, struck terror into the hearts of white station owners, much as angry "gangsta rappers" do today.

COLOR ADJUSTMENT is neither a comparative history lesson, nor really a critique of what constitutes entertainment. The filmmaker's concern is image, how the African-American is presented to countless viewers. "If TV alone can liberate us," intones narrator Ruby Dee, "it continues to mold how we are seen and defined." But there's something terribly facile about the thesis Riggs proposes. He contends that TV has always pandered to a sham vision of the American Dream: a superficial, consumer-crazed, affluent utopia with no relevance to the real world. Riggs makes his point by intercutting news footage of late-60s race riots and anti-war violence with clips of what was on the tube at the time—"Gilligan's Island," "Bewitched" and "Julia"—and he quotes producer Aaron Spelling: "Television is cotton candy for the eyes." So when Blacks reach ascendancy on the air via "The Cosby Show" (and to a lesser extent "The Jeffersons"), Riggs and his panel of smug academics claim that no worthwile goal has been achieved, and nothing has changed. The Huxtables are merely Ozzie and Harriet with dark skin, and the query "Is this positive?" is superimposed over the smiling visage of Bill Cosby.

In other words, COLOR ADJUSTMENT is, well, rigged. It presents a no-win situation, a set-up in which any Black who succeeds on the tube is demonized for selling out. As an alternative to Cosby, Riggs and his assembled scholars hail "Frank's Place," a short-lived 1988 comedy-drama that got the leper treatment from CBS, shuffled around to so many time slots that leading lady Daphne Maxwell Reid's own mother couldn't find it. One wonders, if the tables were turned and "Frank's Place" had been a smash while "The Cosby Show" languished, whether COLOR ADJUSTMENT would have adjusted its own opinion of the two programs.

Riggs informed a newspaper reporter that he pursued Bill Cosby for nine months for an onscreen interview to defend himself, but to no avail. When COLOR ADJUSTMENT premiered, with its sour take on the Huxtables, an upset Cosby phoned Riggs and explained his refusal. Riggs: "Essentially he said he did not want to engage in a public debate about dissension within the Black community. He felt it would harm our overall unity as a people. I find that very old-fashioned and quite regressive."

The point is well taken, but Riggs has his own blinders. By spotlighting prime time exclusively COLOR BLINDNESS skips the late-night stardom of Eddie Murphy and Arsenio Hall, daytime's Oprah Winfrey and Bryant Gumbel, and Bill Cosby's Saturday-morning kids' show "Fat Albert and the Cosby Kids," whose urban setting was far removed from the Huxtable's comfortable lifestyle. (Dare anyone mention "Soul Train?") The politically correct commentators slam the mini-series "Roots" for obliquely suggesting that the struggle of American Blacks ended with Reconstruction; nobody refers to its followup "Roots: The Next Generation." Riggs omits shows with integrated casts like "The Mod Squad," "Mission Impossible," "Laugh-In" and "Star Trek." Variety shows hosted by Sammy Davis Jr., Flip Wilson and Leslie Uggams are ignored. Finally COLOR ADJUSTMENT is hobbled by being current only to 1988, which excludes the taboo-nudging satire of Fox TV's "In Living Color," the video incarnation of "In the Heat of the Night," the widely acclaimed "I'll Fly Away" and others.

In the fall 1992 TV season alone there were six new shows starring Black performers or set within the Black community. Marlon Riggs is quite correct in questioning what such roles—typically on sitcoms rather than the more prestigious dramatic format—represent, and what relevance they contain for America still stricken by entrenched prejudice and inequities. Unfortunately, COLOR ADJUSTMENT, with its easy cynicism and built-in failure mode, makes little progress toward answers.

p, Marlon T. Riggs, Vivian Kleiman; d, Marlon T. Riggs; w, Marlon T. Riggs; ph, Rick Butler, Michael Anderson; ed, Deborah Hoffman; m, Mary Watkins

Documentary **(PR: A MPAA: NR)**

COMMON BONDS ★★½

(Canada) 108m R&R; The Movie Group; Chaindance Productions ~ Academy Entertainment c

(AKA: CHAINDANCE)

Michael Ironside *(J.T. Blake)*, Rae Dawn Chong *(Ilene)*, Brad Dourif *(Johnny Reynolds)*, Bruce Glover *(Casey)*, Ken Pogue, Sheila Moore, Leslie Carlson, Janne Mortil

The irreverent FBC series "In Living Color" once did a sketch called "My Left Foot of Fury," in which disabled Irish poet Christie Brown teamed up with Jean-Claude Van Damme to kickbox evildoers. There are times when COMMON BONDS is hardly less absurd. The biggest surprise is how much of it the actors manage to pull off.

Set in Canada, the opening finds troublemaker J.T. Blake (Michael Ironside) just released from prison. Straightaway he finds his favorite hookers hosting a hated police sergeant and raises a ruckus that puts him right back in the stir. This time Blake lands in Mountain Hill Federal Penitentiary, where he gets to participate in a truly bizarre experiment in corrections: due to Ottawa's budget cuts, a nearby nursing home for the severely handicapped lacks personnel, so pragmatic liberal social worker Eileen Curtis (Rae Dawn Chong) recruits work-released convicts as caregivers. No mere nurses, the prisoners are literally chained to the wheelchairs of their helpless charges—the idea is that the cellblock toughs will learn compassion from the patients, while the bewildered patients will gain survival skills by being cuffed to career criminals and maniacs.

Blake meets his match in his assignee, Johnny Reynolds (Brad Dourif), a hospital hellion crippled by cerebral palsy and self-pity. Johnny intentionally soils himself, throws food around and rages at Blake, "I didn't ask for you!" The convict feels equal loathing for Johnny, but after long hours of pushing the wheelchair and escorting him to the toilet, Blake develops sympathy and understanding for his companion. Johnny begins to behave and introduces Blake to the poetry of Dylan Thomas and e.e. cummings, proving there's more to life than punching out cops.

Though it sounds like sentimental slush, a welcome hard edge to the material makes COMMON BONDS work better than it sounds. Blake's conversion to model prisoner comes a little too rapidly, and so the filmmakers throw in a Van Damme-nable plot complication, a malevolent convict named Casey (Bruce Glover). This smirking meanie runs the jailhouse rackets with the complicity of corrupt guards, and he gleefully abuses his own wretched wheelchair-mate. Blake rebels and gets the creep carted off to a tougher prison. Casey escapes, and when Blake and Johnny go on a furlough visit to the city, he seizes the chance for revenge. The token menace overshadows a sensitive subplot about Blake persuading a squeamish prostitute to give Johnny his first dose of sexual healing. Instead the drama climaxes with violence and gunfire, the villain vanquished, and Johnny sustaining a melon-sized bullet wound and comforted by Blake in the ambulance. It's an ending right out of a typical mismatched-buddy-cop adventure.

Originally released in Canada as CHAINDANCE, COMMON BONDS was a personal project for star Michael Ironside, who receives credit as co-screenwriter and co-producer. The Canadian actor has long been a fixture in action pictures and thrillers, either as vicious bad guys or steely heroes. His COMMON BONDS performance does a nice job at broadening the actor's range within the boundaries of a restrictive screen persona, and this the first film in a long time in which Michael Ironside can smile and not look like a hungry wolf. Still, one wishes that Blake's path to redemption was a little rockier and didn't necessitate the formula external threat.

Long consigned to weirdo parts (like the voice of "Chucky" in the CHILD'S PLAY horror films), Brad Dourif faces the daunting comparison with Daniel Day-Lewis's Oscar-winning turn in MY LEFT FOOT. Dourif is equal to the physical challenge. His thin, contorted body makes Johnny's condition agonizingly real, and often his strangled voice is just barely intelligible. More than that, Dourif conveys the personality beneath all that pathology—and with it the fact that Johnny Reynolds is not a nice guy at the outset. He's needlessly churlish, sometimes absolutely disgusting and as much in need of an attitude adjustment as Blake.

There's rare sophistication in not depicting this CP victim as a saintly sufferer, which makes COMMON BONDS doubly disappointing when this farfetched but unique tale, directed by Allan Goldstein, segues into cliches. *(Violence, profanity, sexual situations, adult situations, nudity.)*

p, Richard Davis; d, Allan A. Goldstein; w, Michael Ironside, Alan Aylward; ph, Tobias Schliessler; ed, Allan Lee; m, Graeme Coleman; prod d, Phil Schmidt; art d, Clyde Klotz; set d, Barry Kemp; cos, David Lisle

Prison/Drama **(PR: O MPAA: NR)**

COMPLEX WORLD ★★★
81m Heartbreak Hits ~ Hemdale c

Stanley Matis *(Morris Brock)*, Margot Dionne *(Gilda)*, Allen Oliver *(Harpo)*, Daniel Von Bargen *(Malcolm)*, Joe Klimek *(Alex–The Janitor)*, Jay Charbonneau *(Klem)*, Dan Welch *(Jeff Burgess)*, Ernesto Luna *(Hotel Waiter)*, Bob Owczarek *(Robert Burgess)*, Dorothy Gallagher *(Miriam)*, David P.B. Stevens *(Larry Newman)*, Rich Lupo *(The Mayor)*, Captain Lou Albano *(Boris Lee)*, NRBQ *(1st Band in the Documentary)*, Roomful of Blues *(2nd Band in the Documentary)*, Tilman Gandy, Jr. *(Himself)*, Lucinda Dohanan *(Maggie the Bartender)*, Molly Fitch *(Jeff's Girlfriend)*, Bree *(The Wino)*, Norm Buerklin *(Richard Holden)*, Russ *(Biker Lieutenant)*, Sport Fisher, Rudy Cheeks, Jeff Shore, Thomas Enright, John Rufo, Tom Dequattro, Ed Vallee *(Young Adults Members)*, Frank Secundo *(Bill)*, Dan Gosch *(1st Horny Guy)*, Peter Gerety *(Biker)*, Becca Lish *(Biker)*, Ray Parker *(Heartbreak Hotel Doorman)*, John Burt *(Heartbreak Hotel Doorman)*, Zeek *(Bearded Man)*, Miriam Lupo *(Woman with Handbag)*, Keith Jochim *(Harvey–The Backup)*, Michael Cobb *(Phil–The Bartender)*, Martin Sarna *(College Boy)*, Laura Callella *(College Girl)*, Michael Balcanoff *(Freddy–The Biker)*, Charles Lynch *(Nice Guy)*, Chandler Travis *(Paul–The Bartender)*, Pitt Harding *(Sober Guy)*, Paul Buxton *(Drunk Guy)*, Hillary Chaplin *(Bonita–The Bartender)*, John Savoia *(Jack–The Promoter)*, Andrew Mutnick *(Jerry)*, Terry Adams *(Lenny)*, Tom Ardolino *(Randy)*, Tom Jones *(Cameraman)*, Chance Langton *(Man in the Girl's Room)*, Michael Poisson *(The Reporter)*, Dawn Davis *(Ruby)*, Christine Barker *(FBI Secretary)*, Nick Hasomeras *(Drunk Fighter)*, David Blue *(Drunk Fighter)*, Deb Davis *(Heimlich Dancer)*, William Damkobler *(Mayor's Voice)*, Steve Linder *(Guy in Law Suit)*, Max Alexander *(Drug Dealer)*, The Smithereens *(Bar Boys)*, Blaze *(Dog at Diner)*

During its aborted theatrical run one critic likened COMPLEX WORLD to a wild night on the town without a punishing hangover the next day. Made in Providence, Rhode Island, the film version is a thoroughly crazed, go-for-broke rock'n'roll cult comedy with no rules but enough order imposed by first-time feature filmmaker Jim Wolpaw that the whole melee pulls together and somehow works.

The opening sets the tone with a sick gag introducing the semi-pivotal character Morris Brock (Stanley Matis), a bespectacled loser whose life was warped by the world fame twin brother Ralph garnered for shooting himself while still in the incubator—history's youngest suicide. Overwhelmed by Ralph's "success," Morris has grown up an angry nerd who writes hostile folk songs denouncing women, the dead and New Jersey. Morris also belongs to a small terrorist cell, and for their next bourgeois bomb target the urban guerrillas fixate on the only place that allows Morris in to perform: a lively dive called the Heartbreak Hotel.

The Heartbreak Hotel is run by the supremely mellow Jeff Burgess (Dan Welch), the estranged son of monstrous right-wing presidential candidate Robert Burgess (a tired Strangelovian stereotype, played by Bob Owczarek). It's the elder Burgess who secretly controls the terrorists. Their humorless leader Malcolm (Daniel Von Bargen) is a CIA stooge whose mission is to wipe out the nightspot because of the potential embarrassment it poses to the politician. Meanwhile the city wants to raze the Heartbreak Hotel for the valuable downtown real estate, and the mayor pays a bestial motorcycle gang called the Scum of the Earth (their Civil War-buff chieftain portrayed by pro wrestling's Captain Lou Albano) to trash the place that very night.

With a beer keg full of explosives set to go off at 1 a.m., the narrative strands chronicle the apocalyptic soiree in a series of segments labeled with title-cards like "Death Makes You Smart" and "God Told Us to Laugh at You"—lines taken verbatim from the dialogue. In the thick of a packed house of party-hearty patrons, the laid-back Jeff Burgess simply ignores Malcolm's ransom demand, driving the ultra-serious terrorist into impotent rage. Meanwhile one of the marauders, an icy gunman named Harpo (Allen Oliver), waiting in the getaway van, overhears the strange sermons of a streetcorner preacher. Silently and lethally Harpo is Born Again and proceeds to stalk his own terrorist cohorts. Elsewhere, a "clone band," the worst Beatles lookalikes of all time, are doing drugs in the basement when they receive a phone call from Elvis Presley, dialing from the afterlife to warn the skeptical cretins of their imminent demise. Meanwhile . . .

It all builds to a satisfyingly insane finale that goes right over the edge, exactly where a conventional comedy would have backed away. Some of the bits and situations in COMPLEX WORLD fall flat—especially the tiresome anti-commie rants of Robert Burgess—and having Jeff alternate narration with Morris Brock creates a confusion of voiceovers. But the bulk of the picture is consistently, almost effortlessly amusing. It nearly looks too easy. After all, self-indulgent backyard endeavors like this are what give tyro auteurs a bad name. James Wolpaw is no rank amateur, however, but an Oscar-nominated documentarian (for the short KEATS AND HIS NIGHTINGALE: A BLIND DATE) and professed admirer of Robert Altman, who in M*A*S*H and NASHVILLE also handled interlocking plotlines and running characters. Wolpaw pulls off the same kind of nimble juggling act, though with no pretensions other than good, subversive fun.

COMPLEX WORLD derived from Wolpaw's own college-era adventures as a bartender at the selfsame Heartbreak Hotel shown onscreen (the club no longer exists, alas). Wolpaw's roommate Rich Lupo ran the hangout, and as Wolpaw delved deeper into his movie career the two of them envisioned a freewheeling feature about the club. Filmed in haphazard, documentary style, with a vague script and much improvisation, the 35mm production ballooned from a $275,000 effort into a $1 million one that took about five years to complete. When finally finished it ran for months in cinemas in Providence and Boston and earned enthusiastic reviews during a nearly unadvertised 1992 New York City run. But distributor Hemdale cancelled plans for an expanded release. Wolpaw subsequently slapped Hemdale with a lawsuit, which may be why Hemdale Home Video's COMPLEX WORLD isn't the most common tape in the rental stores.

For lovers of the offbeat it's worth a search. Stanley Matis is a bizarre club performer whose onscreen persona doesn't differ much from the demented Morris Brock. That fateful street evangelist is a genuine preacher, Tilman Gandy, Jr., who authored his own bizarre pavement homilies. Part traditional fire-and-brimstone, part stand-up schtick, the Gospels according to Gandy are hilarious and heartfelt, just the right revival for the last temptation of Harpo. Real-life bands make guest appearances on the Heartbreak Hotel's stage, including Roomful of Blues and NRBQ; members of the latter are also cast as the zonked-out "BeatLegends" in the basement, whose response to the ghostly Elvis contact is to mock the King with tasteless jokes about Jimi, Janis and Jesus.

But the spotlight belongs to the Young Adults, New England "mock-rockers" and former backup musicians for Bo Diddley who'd actually split years earlier but reunited for this film. Expressively exuberant, the Young Adults perform pieces like "I Married a Tree," "Why Not Kill Yourself" and "Let's Get Naked and Break Things" (plus the eponymous "Complex World") that are just as tastelessly deranged as the Stanley Matis set but good-natured and infectiously rambunctious—and you can dance to them, especially a raunchy physical routine based on the Heimlich maneuver. *(Violence, substance abuse, profanity, sexual situations.)*

p, Rich Lupo, Geoff Adams, Denis Maloney; d, James Wolpaw; w, James Wolpaw, (screenplay); ph, Denis Maloney; ed, Steven Gentile; m, Steven Snyder; set d, Deb Davis; makeup, James Bienkowsky

Musical/Comedy **(PR: O MPAA: R)**

COMRADES IN ARMS ★

88m Cinema Sciences Corporation ~ Republic Pictures Home Video c

Lance Henriksen *(Rob Reen)*, Lyle Alzado *(General Rada)*, John Weiner *(Khaleel)*, John Christian *(Frank White)*, Dierdre Coleman *(Natasha)*, Phillip Stimpson *(Sergeant Stomper)*, Lorna Courtney *(Anka)*, Rick Washburn

An insipid gung-ho actioner, COMRADES IN ARMS posits Lance Henriksen as CIA chieftain Rob Reen, who orders his crack, undercover military terrorist squad, led by loose-cannon warrior Captain Frank White (John Christian), to eradicate powerful Third World drug trafficker Khaleel (John Weiner).

After a nighttime raid fails, White learns Khaleel has set his sights on the "vast untapped marketplace" of the former Soviet Union and eastern Europe, where the "decentralizing governments are weak" and they can take advantage of the new class of "private capitalists" for street operations. Enter the Russians, led by General Rada (Lyle Alzado), who send *their* crack military unit, led by Colonel Kotchev (Steven Kaman) to participate in the maneuvers to get rid of Khaleel, whose drug cartels represent, to them, the "world's new third superpower." However, due to the bickering between the Americans and the Russians, the next raid on Khaleel, at his Colombia stronghold, also fails. The furious Reen indicates White will be the scapegoat, so he and his remaining men return to Moscow with Kotchev, who is similarly threatened by Rada, where the pair gain some grudging respect for each other and join forces for a final mission against Khaleel, set in a deserted cavernous Prague factory.

As dumb as its titular acronym, COMRADES IN ARMS strains to update its WWII-type formula (Kotchev blusters about the Americans' "pathetic imperialist war in Iraq"), and the scrambled plot makes little sense, falling back on hoary cliches like White's vodka-drinking bout and sexual fling with Russian soldier Natasha (Dierdre Coleman); White's veteran Viet Nam War buddy "Sergeant Stomper" (Phillip Stimpson), too wounded to evacuate, suicidally staying behind, propped against a tree with his M16, to delay Khaleel's pursuit of the fleeing good guys; and, of course, the dying Khaleel's final words to White and Kotchev: "I'll see you in hell!" To make matters worse, the screenplay also features just plain eye-opening weirdness, such as Khaleel's beautiful girlfriend Anka (Lorna Courtney) infiltrating the Washington, D.C., CIA headquarters by killing a single guard and spraying Reen's top-secret meeting with automatic fire.

Director J. Christian Ingvordsen, who also co-wrote and co-produced, fails to enliven any of this material. The expository scenes are static and the action scenes are confusing, often composed of men jumping into the frame to fire their state-of-the-art weaponry at the camera. The nighttime combat sequences, photographed by Steven Kaman (who also plays Kotchev and edited and co-wrote) do have an odd, ironic physical beauty all on their own which has nothing to do with the plot. The movie's low budget necessitated the use of stock footage to stand in for the picture's worldwide locales, which adds further chaos—most of the movie was shot in Canada.

The acting is barely adequate, although Weiner is fine as the insane, messianic sociopath Khaleel. Former pro football player and second-billed Alzado appears in only two scenes (one of them in long shot), for a combined total of about two minutes' screen time. The film screened at the 1991 Cannes Film Festival market and was released in the US direct-to-video. *(Violence, profanity.)*

p, J. Christian Ingvordsen, Steven Kaman, John Weiner; d, J. Christian Ingvordsen; w, J. Christian Ingvordsen, Steven Kaman, John Weiner; ph, Steven Kaman; ed, Steven Kaman; m, Paul Avgerinos

War/Action **(PR: O MPAA: R)**

CONFESSIONS OF A SERIAL KILLER ★★½

80m Concorde ~ New Horizons Home Video c

Robert A. Burns *(Daniel Ray Hawkins)*, Dennis Hill *(Moon Lawton)*, Berkley Garrett *(Sheriff Will Gaines)*, Sidney Brammer *(Molly)*, Dee Dee Norton *(Monica)*, Ollie Handley *(Doctor Earl Krivics)*, Demp Toney *(Doris)*, Eleese Lester *(Karen Grimes)*, Colom Keating *(Detective Barnes)*, John Browning *(Doctor Spivey)*

Considering that its video packaging is clearly intended to capitalize on the critical and commercial success of both THE SILENCE OF THE LAMBS and HENRY: PORTRAIT OF A SERIAL KILLER, CONFESSIONS OF A SERIAL KILLER turns out to be better than expected, a psycho chiller that becomes more effective as it goes along. Like HENRY, it's based on the true-life exploits of Henry Lee Lucas, who claimed to have killed hundreds of women in the course of his exploits.

Daniel Ray Hawkins (Robert A. Burns, who was also the film's production designer) has been captured and narrates his vicious deeds to Sheriff Will Gaines (Berkley Garrett). Hawkins, who grew up with a mother who had sex with numerous strange men as he and his little sister watched, killed his first victim at fifteen, and has evaded capture by sticking to the Texas highways. Sometimes his victims get away, including a hitchhiker whose escape we witness, but more often they would become one in his long string of victims. After a while, he hooks up with a brute named Moon Lawton (Dennis Hill), who at one point helps him rape and murder a young woman named Karen Grimes (Eleese Lester). Gaines and his men at first believe that Hawkins is simply claiming responsibility for this crime based on what he's read in the papers (an echo of the real Lucas case), but Hawkins leads them to her remains to prove his culpability. He also informs them of several boxes of Polaroids of his victims stashed in a bus station locker, further proof of his and Moon's murderous deeds.

The second half of the film is an extended flashback that begins when Moon's sister Molly (Sidney Brammer) joins the duo after fleeing her job in a "massage parlor." Hawkins is at first doubtful, but soon Molly is helping them lure unwary victims. One day, Hawkins and Molly attempt to procure a new car by posing as hitchhikers, and think they've found a victim when a middle-aged doctor, Earl Krivics (Ollie Handley), pulls over to change a flat tire. Prevented from killing Dr. Krivics by the presence of a nearby police car lying in wait for speeding vehicles, Hawkins and Molly help him with the tire, and are talked into accompanying him back to his house, where he also runs an appliance repair service and gives them and Moon jobs.

Dr. Krivics's assistant, Doris (Demp Toney), and his college-age daughter, Monica (Dee Dee Norton), are suspicious of the trio, who at first keep their continuing murders clandestine. Soon, however, Doris discovers evidence of the bloodshed in their living quarters; she is discovered and stabbed to death by Molly. Getting tired of their situation, Moon abandons Hawkins and Molly; he is soon picked up in Louisiana, and a Texas cop arrives to question Molly; she shoots him dead. At the same time, Hawkins tries to drag Monica off to defile her, but Molly protests and slashes him on the arm; in return, Hawkins murders her. After a lengthy chase, he also captures and kills Monica, and it is this last murder that ultimately leads to his capture.

Although bearing a 1987 copyright, CONFESSIONS OF A SERIAL KILLER appears to have been made even earlier than HENRY, and one can't help but make the comparison by which the former suffers. HENRY's director John McNaughton managed to achieve the difficult balancing act of telling the story through the title character's eyes and making him an intriguing character without encouraging identification with or sympathy for him. On the other hand, CONFESSIONS OF A SERIAL KILLER's writer-director Mark Blair doesn't have the same skill, and often literally shoots scenes from his villain's point-of-view, making some of the murder scenes and their buildup sleazy instead of scary. And by starting his movie with Hawkins in jail, Blair loses the unpredictability that made HENRY so good, in addition to negating the possibility of an equally chilling ending. CONFESSIONS OF A SERIAL KILLER doesn't so much conclude as fade out. There's also some second-hand psychology involved here that doesn't work, and was more effectively suggested in McNaughton's film.

Nonetheless, there's more texture to this movie than most regional slasher flicks, with a backroads verismilitude that effectively abets the subject matter. Burns has been a production designer on a slew of low-budget chillers (including THE HOWLING, RE-ANIMATOR and THE TEXAS CHAINSAW MASSACRE), and his work behind the scenes is at least as good as his performance as Hawkins, which convincingly suggests the banal nature of this killer even though it lacks added dimension. The other actors do good, naturalistic work, however, and once the film grounds itself in one continuous story instead of a series of flashbacks, it has the chance to build some solid tension.

CONFESSIONS OF A SERIAL KILLER is not as gratuitously bloody as it might have been, particularly given that its end credits include one for Kim Fusch as "Body Parts," and it creates some of its best chills through suggestion. But it is still decidedly adult material that might well have had the same ratings problems as HENRY had it been distributed theatrically. *(Violence, substance abuse, profanity, nudity, sexual situations, adult situations.)*

p, Cecyle Osgood Rexrode; d, Mark Blair; w, Mark Blair; ph, Layton Blaylock; ed, Sheri Galloway; m, William Penn; prod d, Robert A. Burns

Horror/Crime **(PR: O MPAA: NR)**

CONSENTING ADULTS ★★

95m Hollywood; Touchwood Pacific Partners I; Pakula Productions; C.A. Productions ~ BV c

Kevin Kline *(Richard Parker)*, Mary Elizabeth Mastrantonio *(Priscilla Parker)*, Kevin Spacey *(Eddy Otis)*, Rebecca Miller *(Kay Otis)*, Forest Whitaker *(David Duttonville)*, E.G. Marshall *(George Gordon)*, Kimberly McCullough *(Lori Parker)*, Billie Neal *(Annie Duttonville)*, Benjamin Hendrickson *(Jimmy Schwartz)*, Lonnie Smith *(Dr. Pettering)*, Joe Mulherin *(Bo)*, Rick Hinkle *(Singer in Mahoney's Band)*, Artis Edwards, Jr. *(Atlanta Police Officer)*, Jerry Campbell *(Prison Guard)*, Ginny Parker *(Martha)*, Judson Vaughn *(Max Roth)*, Ed Grady *(Mr. Watkins)*, Suzanne Stewart *(Mrs. Watkins)*, Bruce Evers *(Maxie)*, Nance Plachta *(Woman in Blues Connection)*, L. Warren Young *(Musician in Blues Connection)*, Edward Seamon *(Hotel Desk Clerk)*, Shelly Pinsky *(Woman in Dressing Room)*, Thomas Saccio *(Johnny Rocco)*, D.L. Anderson *(Phone Company Woman)*, Janette Lane Bradbury *(Dry Cleaner Lady)*, Tommy Cresswell *(Charleston Detective)*, Robert C. Treveiler *(Charleston Deputy)*, Michael L. Nesbitt *(Charleston Deputy)*, Michelle Moore *(Trudy Seaton)*, Deborah Lucas *(Birthday Party Girl)*, Jennifer Swago *(Birthday Party Girl)*, Suzi Selman *(Birthday Party Girl)*, Mark Wood, Meredith Brasher, Jeffrey Charlton, Michelle Smith, Dean Taylor, Nan McElroy *(Christmas Carolers)*, Mary K.E. Packer-Phillips, Jeannie E. Davis, Laura Griffin, Robb Harleston, Rachel C. MacRae, Susan T. Haidary *(Rehab Counselors)*

CONSENTING ADULTS shows that the urban thriller genre spawned by FATAL ATTRACTION has run out of gas. Viewers who have seen such films as THE HAND THAT ROCKS THE CRADLE, SINGLE WHITE FEMALE and UNLAWFUL ENTRY are unlikely to enjoy this derivative effort; it's the same paranoid mayhem—and not as much fun.

Commercial jingle composer Richard Parker (Kevin Kline) and his wife Priscilla (Mary Elizabeth Mastrantonio), bored with their work and humdrum marriage, are intrigued by their fast-living new neighbors Eddy (Kevin Spacey) and Kay Otis (Rebecca Miller, the daughter of playwright Arthur Miller). Richard becomes friends with financial advisor Eddy—a lover of money, motorcycles and sailing—and lusts after beautiful blonde Kay after hearing her amateur torch singing and catching glimpses of her naked through his study window. The neighbors become even closer when Eddy arranges a car insurance scam to get Richard out of debt. Later, Eddy suggests that he and Richard have sex with each other's spouses, trading beds in the middle of the night so their wives won't know. Richard rejects the idea, but finally buckles under Eddy's pressure. The men's plan succeeds, but the next morning Kay is found bludgeoned to death with a baseball bat, and the police arrest Richard.

Repelled by the wife-swapping trick and believing Richard guilty of murder, Priscilla divorces him. Insurance investigator David Duttonville (Forest Whitaker) tells Richard that Eddy had a $1.5 million insurance policy out on Kay. He also offers the shocking news that Priscilla and his daughter are living with Eddy. Richard thinks he hears Kay's singing voice on a radio show, and finds the neighbor who was believed to be dead. Kay explains that Eddy had another woman killed in her place. When Richard leaves Kay alone, Eddy kills her. The composer rushes to Eddy's house to rescue Priscilla. Eddy has set a deadly trap for Richard, but Priscilla saves her ex-husband by killing Eddy with a baseball bat. As the movie ends, the Parkers are moving into a new house, far away from any neighbors.

Everything about CONSENTING ADULTS seems half-hearted because we've seen it all before. As in the other recent thrillers, boring yuppies are terrorized by outwardly trustworthy but inwardly psychopathic people. The hero makes unbelievably stupid mistakes, leaving himself vulnerable to the villain. Then there's an obligatory duel to the death between good and evil. CONSENTING ADULTS follows the formula to the letter. Alan J. Pakula directs the film in an oddly languid manner that often dissipates what little suspense exists. Long, slow pans appear in scenes that demand quick cuts. Richard's discovery of Kay singing at a bar, for instance, should have been dispensed with more quickly. We *know* it's her.

The unbelievable screenplay by Matthew Chapman doesn't help Pakula, either. On two occasions, Richard improbably leaves women in peril. When Priscilla is living with Eddy, Richard confronts her with a tape of Kay singing. He demands she play it for Eddy—and when she does so, Eddy is immediately on the defensive. Later, Richard leaves the rediscovered Kay alone after spending days searching for her. Naturally, she ends up slaughtered the second Richard disappears. Another major plot question is why Priscilla runs off with Eddy after Richard is arrested—it all happens offscreen. The movie cries out for at least a brief scene depicting Priscilla's sexual and/or emotional attraction to Eddy.

Kevin Spacey (WORKING GIRL, GLENGARRY GLEN ROSS) makes the most of the showy part of Eddy, giving him the smooth, charming exterior of an Alfred Hitchcock villain. Spacey's funniest moment is when he sings Irving Berlin's "Cheek to Cheek" to Richard after their bed switching scheme has worked ("Heaven . . . I'm in Heaven"). Unfortunately, Spacey vanishes from the screen for long periods as the story follows wimpy Richard's attempts to investigate Eddy while out on bail. Kevin Kline (THE BIG CHILL, A FISH CALLED WANDA) tries hard but his character remains that of a one-dimensional victim. As for the actresses, Mastrantonio and Miller have little to do or say.

One good aspect of CONSENTING ADULTS is that it may finally put an end to this string of thrillers. Now that filmmakers have dealt with the killer mistress, nanny, cop, roommate, and neighbor, there may be only one subject left—the killer maid? *(Violence, adult situations.)*

p, David Permut, Alan J. Pakula; d, Alan J. Pakula; w, Matthew Chapman; ph, Stephen Goldblatt; ed, Sam O'Steen; m, Michael Small; prod d, Carol Spier; art d, Alicia Keywan; set d, Gretchen Rau; cos, Gary Jones, Ann Roth

Thriller **(PR: O MPAA: R)**

CONTE DE PRINTEMPS ★★★

(France) 107m Films du Losange; Compagnie Eric Rohmer ~ Orion Classics c

Anne Teyssedre *(Jeanne)*, Hugues Quester *(Igor)*, Florence Darel *(Natasha)*, Eloise Bennett *(Eve)*, Sophie Robin *(Gaelle)*, Marc Lelon, Francois Lamore

Along with Claude Chabrol, probably the most durable of the surviving French New Wavers, Eric Rohmer returns after a too-long absence from American screens with another of his gently wry tales of the eternal tug-of-war between the heart and the head that will typically enrapture his admirers and confound his detractors.

The typically Rohmer-esque wisp of a plot revolves around a Paris philosophy teacher, Jeanne (Anne Teyssedre), who finds herself at loose ends when her apartment is temporarily occupied by her cousin while Jeanne's boyfriend is out of town. It is Jeanne's quirk that she is unable to live in her boyfriend's apartment when he is not there because she detests his disorderliness. On a whim, she accepts an invitation to a party thrown by an old schoolfriend. There, she strikes up a conversation with Natasha (Florence Darel), a classical pianist. When Jeanne airs her apartment dilemma, Natasha immediately offers lodging in her own Paris home.

As roomies, the two women become fast friends, though Jeanne finds herself more involved in Natasha's family intrigues than she would like, primarily Natasha's plot to break up the relationship between her divorced father, Igor (Hugues Quester) and a brittle, blond academic, Eve (Eloise Bennett). Natasha's main grievance is her suspicion that Eve has stolen a family-heirloom necklace. It begins to seem as if Natasha is pushing Jeanne and Igor into a romance during a weekend at her family's country house. Igor, who is gradually breaking up with Eve, seems game. However, Jeanne's insistence on order asserts itself when Igor tries to seduce her. She grants Igor three requests. When one of them isn't to make love, Jeanne withdraws without any real regrets—Igor didn't much appeal to her anyway. Clearing out of Natasha's Paris home, Jeanne finds the necklace, which had long ago been dropped by Igor into an old shoe.

Eric Rohmer remains one of a fast-dwindling number of world-class directors whose works can restore one's faith in life and the cinema. They are a tonic in an age of diminishing consciousness and conscience, proof that, somewhere in the world, there are still people capable of translating lucid thought and emotion into works of narrative art that ennoble, rather than belittle, the human experience. As they typically consist of little more than characters talking, watching a Rohmer film can be, as a character in Arthur Penn's NIGHT MOVES once famously put it, "like watching paint dry." But there can be no more profound a canvas than the one Rohmer has chosen and few painters capable of bringing that canvas as alive as Rohmer does.

As if to add more fuel to the fire laid by his detractors, in a traditionally auteurist sense, Rohmer has been making essentially the same film over and over again. It is typically about love, usually lost in the distance between thought and action—thus the talk. Here, Jeanne's fixation on order leads to a fixation on protocol that borders on a kind of mania that would seem to exclude all spontaneity from her life. And the scenario would seem to endorse her point of view, as acting on a whim early on leads her deep into the heart of a contentious family and worse, when she's cast as a weapon wielded by a manipulative, neglected daughter against a feckless father's equally manipulative girlfriend.

It becomes increasingly difficult to side with Jeanne as her willed detachment and denial of experience begins to seem inhuman. Yet the vital constant in Rohmer's works is that the heart always has its own agenda and in this context the talk becomes as important for what it conceals as for what it reveals. As is true with all the characters in Rohmer's ensemble, we come to respect and understand Jeanne and see her reticence not as denial but as an expression of who she is. Through her, we are faced with the truth that sometimes discretion really is the better part of valor.

More often than not throughout his career, Rohmer's interest has been taken up with those like Jeanne who hesitate, for the very simple yet profound reason that it is in our moments of hesitation that we are most human. In those moments, everything we have thought, felt, learned, been taught and have inherited, all come to a point. And it is in these moments that most of Rohmer's films reside, including this delicious slice of life, one of a projected series inspired by the four seasons. (The second installment, A WINTER'S TALE, was glowingly reviewed at the 1992 New York Film Festival, but has yet to be released in the US.)

For those willing to meet them half-way, Rohmer's films are anything but boring. In fact, they are adventures of the most exquisite sort. Unpredictable yet predestined, passionate yet meticulously reasoned, crammed with dry talk yet achingly erotic in the pauses between the talk, they are finally as enigmatic as they are seemingly plain, offhanded and anti-cinematic. In fact, for more than three decades, Rohmer has lovingly taken his camera where few others have dared tread. And he has done it, by and large, without roaming very far from Paris and the rooms in his people's lives, which are, like the rooms in our souls, cluttered, dusty and comfortably familiar, yet always tantalizingly alive with the infinite possibilities for discovery, surprise and enchantment.

Eric Rohmer has been making the same film over and over again. And as long as he does, there's still hope. *(Adult situations.)*

p, Margaret Menegoz; d, Eric Rohmer; w, Eric Rohmer; ph, Luc Pages, Philippe Renaut; ed, Maria-Luisa Garcia; m, Ludwig Van Beethoven, Robert Schumann, Jean-Louis Valero

Romance/Comedy **(PR: C MPAA: PG)**

COOL WORLD ★

102m Paramount ~ Paramount c

Gabriel Byrne *(Jack Deebs)*, Kim Basinger *(Holli Would)*, Brad Pitt *(Frank Harris)*, Janni Brenn-Lowen *(Mom Harris)*, William Frankfather *(Cop)*, Greg Collins *(Cop)*, Michele Abrams *(Jennifer Malley)*, Carrie Hamilton *(Comic Bookstore Cashier)*, Stephen Worth *(Store Patron)*, Murray Podwal *(Store Patron)*, VOICE OF: Jenine Jennings *(Craps Bunny)*, Gregory Snegoff *(Bash)*, Candy Milo *(Bob/Lonette)*, Maurice LaMarche *(Interrogator/Doc Whiskers/Mash/Drunk Bar Patron/Super Jack)*, Joey Camen *(Interrogator/Slash/Holli's Door)*, Michael David Lally *(Sparks)*, Charles Adler *(Nails)*, Patrick Pinney *(Bouncer)*, Deirdre O'Connell *(Isabelle Malley)*, Lamont Jackson *(Lucky's Bouncer)*, Paul Benvictor *(Valet)*, Big Yank *(Plaza Bouncer)*, Frank Sinatra, Jr.

This highly touted 1992 release marks director Ralph Bakshi's return to films after almost a decade, and while his work has always been erratic, and many times ludicrously violent and nihilistic, it has nevertheless broken new ground in animation, with films like FRITZ THE CAT and HEAVY TRAFFIC. But COOL WORLD, a mix of animation and live action, is a near-total disaster.

The film opens in Las Vegas, right after WWII, as returning war hero Frank Harris (Brad Pitt) buys a motorcycle. When he and Mom (Janni Brenn-Lowen) ride off for a celebratory spin, they crash, possibly fatally. Frank, however, is sucked into Cool World, a sort of animated version of Hell, through the efforts of a scientist who's working on some sort of bridge between the "real world" and Cool World (one of many elements in the film that's never fully explained). Frank stays in this 'toon purgatory as a cop, on the lookout for any sort of criminal behavior, especially the ultimate Cool World taboo: sex between a "doodle" (a cartoon character) and a "noid" (a human). Oddly enough, he seems to be the only human there.

The film then flashes forward to the present where cartoonist Jack Deebs (Gabriel Byrne) is being released from jail after serving time for killing a man he found with his wife (this point, as well as the wife, are never mentioned again). Jack is the successful author of a series of "Cool World" comic books, and one night he too is pulled in, thanks to Holli Would (Kim Basinger), the ultimate blonde seductress. Holli's desperate to become "real" by having sex with a human, and she spends most of her time trying to bed Jack, in a scenario that appears to be scripted by a group of horny fourteen-year-old boys.

When they finally do consummate their relationship, Frank is understandably displeased, and he goes after the pair, at one point even following them into the real world. Meanwhile Holli keeps shifting back between her "doodle" and "noid" selves (her doodle self is now a clown, for some reason) and tells Jack the only way she can become truly "real" is to get to "the Spike," some sort of pointy object on top of a Vegas hotel. With Jack and Frank in pursuit, she reaches it, and all three characters are happily reincarnated as doodles. (At least that's how the film appears to wind up; the last few scenes go by so fast it's hard to tell what's happening.)

In summarizing the plot, it's clear that COOL WORLD suffers from one of the sloppiest, most unfocused screenplays in recent memory; there's]ittle logic, even of the absurd cartoon kind, to explain the action. For instance: if Holli wants so badly to be real, why is she a cartoon again at the end? And why isn't the scientist who brought Frank into Cool World not seen again until the end of the film? Most importantly, if Jack created Cool World, couldn't he just destroy it, or change the rules to suit his own purposes? The concept of an artist trapped in his own creation is loaded with possibilities, especially given the underground-comics angle of the film: that this idea is never exploited is the most glaring example of the missed opportunities in the screenplay.

Of course, plot holes and illogic could be forgiven if COOL WORLD had interesting characters or impressive visual effects. Given WHO FRAMED ROGER RABBIT?'s stunning integration of live action and animation, these effects are even more disappointing: whenever a noid puts an arm around a doodle, it looks like he's cradling thin air. And Bakshi's annoying predilection for the grotesque and violent reaches a new low here. Except for the embarrassingly juvenile Holli Would (two-dimensional in every sense of the word) and Frank's bumbling insect sidekick, the doodles are thoroughly repulsive and, worse, unfunny. (One is a baby-like character who smokes, suspiciously like Baby Herman in ROGER RABBIT.) "Cruel World" would be a better name for this place, for literally every time we see other doodles they're hitting each other with hammers and axes, having safes dropped on one another, and getting killed in various gory ways.

Ironically, the last ten minutes of the film, with Jack transformed into a Dudley Do-Right-ish superhero, are surprisingly funny, although they seemed tacked-on, as if from an earlier, more comprehensible version of the film. But they can't redeem COOL WORLD, which could have been a more thoughtful, hip answer to ROGER RABBIT, and is instead a loud, confused mess. *(Violence, profanity, sexual situations.)*

p, Frank Mancuso, Jr.; d, Ralph Bakshi; w, Mark Victor, Michael Grais, Larry Gross, (from the story by Ralph Bakshi and Frank Mancuso, Jr.); ph, John A. Alonzo; ed, Steve Mirkovich, Annamaria Szanto; m, Mark Isham; prod d, Michael Corenblith; art d, David James Bomba; set d, Merideth Boswell; cos, Malissa Daniel; anim, Bruce Woodside

Animated/Comedy/Fantasy (PR: C MPAA: PG-13)

COUSIN BOBBY ★★★

65m Tesauro SA; Clinica Estetico ~ Cinevista c

Robert Castle, Jonathan Demme

Hollywood hotshot and sometime—STOP MAKING SENSE, HAITI DREAMS OF DEMOCRACY— documentarian Jonathan Demme is finally unable to resist turning this profile of his activist reverend cousin into a B-movie rabble-rouser. But when it really focuses on his cousin, COUSIN BOBBY offers a fascinating and engrossing portrait of humanist activism.

Every family should have a Cousin Bobby, if not to keep them sane then to keep them honest and, mostly, to keep them together. It's therefore ironic that, as Demme mentions early on, he hadn't seen his cousin, the Reverend Robert Castle of St. Mary's Episcopal Church in Harlem, in some thirty years. When we first see Castle he's celebrating Mass in the middle of a Harlem intersection to demonstrate the need for a traffic light and to draw attention to a sinkhole that has gone unrepaired by the city. In his sermon, Castle uses the two seemingly minor complaints as an emblem of government neglect, a form of gradual genocide, against the area's ethnic groups—and he's utterly convincing. From that fiery opening, however, what's most remarkable about Castle is how humble and utterly human he is. He takes racism and bigotry as a personal affront against a civilized sensibility. And he takes a personal interest in his parishioners, from holding their mail for them to visiting them when they are ill or fallen on bad times and doing whatever he can to help them.

A man like this, one would think, should be held up as a paragon for all to aspire to. Instead, Castle was exiled from his chosen inner-city turf during the early 1960s for openly challenging authorities and generally being an activist before it was considered fashionable for clerics to be involved in the material, as well as spiritual, lives of their parishioners. More controversial was Castle's later involvement with and support of the Black Panthers. Yet, for all the screen time it receives, the film is exasperatingly hazy on this point. Never given is Castle's contrast of his experiences with the violent image of the group given in the press and elsewhere.

At one point, apparently thinking he was off camera and out of microphone range, Castle tells Demme that he doesn't want to romanticize the Panthers in any way. From that aside, it might be drawn that Castle was ambivalent about his involvement with the Panthers to the extent of supporting their social activities while deploring their violence. But no serious elaboration is forthcoming in the film itself. Instead, Demme cuts—in a film about a man for whom any kind of willful violence is apparently anathema—to a lame sequence of rap music over a montage of footage from famous urban race riots. One wonders if Castle had final-cut approval. One also wonders if Demme has ever actually been in the middle of an urban riot, in the same way one wonders about the wartime experiences, or lack thereof, of warmongering writers, politician and filmmakers.

Castle returns, however, to save Cousin Jonathan's film. Revisiting the now-repaired sinkhole from the film's beginning, he notes that he practically had to start his own civil rights movement just to get the job done. But the tone of this comment is more bleakly comic than genuinely bitter—it's just another day in the life, after all. In general, COUSIN BOBBY is at its best when conveying Castle's deep humanity, making not only the man but his example accessible, and in the process almost, though not quite, making Demme forget that he's a Hollywood filmmaker for whom excess equals success. It may not make everybody who sees it cast off their own self-centered lifestyles but, at the very least, it might make some of us track down that old friend, classmate or cousin who took the road less travelled.

p, Edward Saxon; d, Jonathan Demme; ph, Ernest Dickerson, Craig Haagensen, Tony Jannelli, Jacek Laskus, Declan Quinn; ed, David Greenwald; m, Anton Sanko

Documentary (PR: A MPAA: NR)

CRI DU HIBOU, LE

(SEE: CRY OF THE OWL, THE)

CRISSCROSS ★★½

101m Hawn/Sylbert Movie Company; MGM ~ MGM c

Goldie Hawn *(Tracy Cross)*, Arliss Howard *(Joe)*, James Gammon *(Emmett)*, David Arnott *(Chris Cross)*, Keith Carradine *(John Cross)*, J.C. Quinn *(Jetty)*, Steve Buscemi *(Louis)*, Paul Calderon *(Blacky)*, Cathryn DePrume *(Oakley)*, Nada Despotovich *(Kelly)*, David Anthony Marshall *(Blondie)*, Deirdre O'Connell *(Shelly)*, Anna Levine Thomson *(Monica)*, Neil Giuntoli *(Snyder)*, Christy Martin *(Termina)*, Damian Vantriglia *(Buggs)*, Derrick Velez *(Cruz)*, Frank Military *(Harvey)*, John Nesci *(Connie)*, Annie McEnroe *(Mrs. Sivil)*, Tim Settimi *(Mr. Sivil)*, Carol Hankamp *(Mrs. Smethurst)*, Brother Paul Johnson *(Brother Timothy)*, Ronald Cellilo *(Eggs Over Easy)*, Gregory Wolf *(Carrot Eater)*, Ray Bastenero *(Truck Driver)*, Rebel *(Himself)*

Comedienne Goldie Hawn gets gritty with mixed results in CRISSCROSS, a downbeat family drama set in Key West on the eve of the first lunar landing in 1969.

Hawn plays Tracy Cross, abandoned by her Navy-pilot husband who came back from Vietnam stressed-out and unable to cope with domestic life. After sinking into drink for an extended period, John Cross (Keith Carradine) went on a fast, took a vow of silence and eventually divorced Tracy to become a groundskeeper at a monastery. To keep herself and her space-buff son, Chris (David Arnott), afloat, Tracy has just taken a "promotion" to dancing at the go-go club where she's been working as a bartender. During the day, she also works as a waitress in exchange for room and board at the hotel where she lives with Chris, who delivers papers to contribute to the household income.

The folks at the hotel are not a savory bunch. Gruff owner Emmett (James Gammon) is salty but basically kind. Not so, though, his hard-bitten cook, who sends Chris on night runs for fish supposedly for the kitchen that are stuffed with cocaine. Chris gets wise to the scheme and begins stealing the cocaine to sell for extra money so his mom can quit dancing. What he doesn't know is that his buyers, as well as the nice guy, Joe (Arliss Howard), who's come into town and stolen Tracy's heart, are actually undercover drug cops who have targeted the drug ring—and Chris.

Under the direction of former cinematographer Chris Menges (A WORLD APART), CRISSCROSS is an effective mood piece much of the time. But it's all but done in by a pretentious, preachy, reactionary screenplay. You would expect a film directed by a cinematographer to look good (Menges won Oscars for his camerwork on THE KILLING FIELDS and THE MISSION), and CRISSCROSS doesn't let down on that count. Key

West has a burnished, hungover look and mood to match its story about people whose lives have gone quietly and sadly off track. And the performances are generally low-key and effective.

Narrating the story, newcomer Arnott is either onscreen or on the soundtrack virtually every moment of the film's running time. Though his thick South Florida drawl is hard to decipher at times, he does a surprisingly good job of carrying the film with an engaging mixture of precocious worldliness and baffled innocence. Gammon also stands out as the hotel owner. Goldie Hawn, however, is badly miscast.

Droopiness is not Hawn's style though it's one she's chosen for a performance that never feels completely real. Amid the plug-ugly character players and weather-beaten extras that provide realistic detailing, she just can't help looking, well, like a movie star. Nobody who grew up on Hawn as the giggly go-go dancer on TV's "Laugh-In" is likely to believe that she despises dancing. Those who didn't aren't likely to, either, since she's opted (and Hawn is an actress with enough clout to demur, if so inclined) to go through the film wearing a pair of cutoffs precisely trimmed to allow just the slightest hint of her perfectly-shaped derriere to peek through. The problem thus isn't that she dances half-naked for a living, but that she does it in such a toilet, as Hawn's is a bottom that deserves to strut in only the *best* of sleazy bars.

Howard (FULL METAL JACKET, MEN DON'T LEAVE) is relaxed and likable as always, but he has "nark" written all over him from the second he walks onscreen, and he doesn't have nearly enough to do otherwise. Carradine also gets short shrift in what amounts to a cameo as Hawn's husband. However, Hawn's miscasting notwithstanding, this is overall a highly watchable cast whose charm goes a long way towards making CRISSCROSS tolerable entertainment.

The real problem is Scott Sommer's screenplay, adapted from his own novella, which is filled with far more portentous themes, symbols and motifs than comfortably fit onscreen, none of them particularly illuminating or original. It doesn't help either that, at its heart, the substance of Sommer's screenplay is essentially neo-conservative self-flagellation over the 1960s — which would be fine if only the 70s and 80s hadn't come afterwards. CRISSCROSS is a schematic horror story about the so-called disintegration of the nuclear family that gives its characters just enough individuality and depth to make its politics transparent and intrusive. The incidental pleasures from the cast and Menges's direction provide some compensation, but not quite enough. As message movies go, CRISSCROSS could have used more movie and less message. *(Adult situations.)*

p, Anthea Sylbert; d, Chris Menges; w, Scott Sommer, (from his novella); ph, Ivan Strasburg; ed, Tony Lawson; m, Trevor Jones; prod d, Crispian Sallis; art d, Dayna Lee; set d, Leslie Morales; cos, Lisa Jensen

Drama **(PR: C MPAA: R)**

CRITTERS 4 ★½

94m Nicolas Entertainment; New Line ~ New Line Home Video c

Terrence Mann *(Ug)*, Paul Witthorne *(Ethan)*, Anders Hove *(Rick)*, Angela Bassett *(Fran)*, Don Keith Opper *(Charlie)*, Eric DaRe *(Bernie)*, Anne Elizabeth Ramsay *(Dr. McCormick)*, Brad Dourif *(Al Bert)*

Picking up immediately where the previous entry in the CRITTERS series left off, this sequel largely lacks, among other things, one very important element: the critters themselves.

Earthly critter hunter Charlie (Don Keith Opper) is mopping up after the tenement action of CRITTERS 3 when he comes upon some unhatched critter eggs in the basement. But he's prevented from destroying them by the appearance of the hologram form of Ug (Terrence Mann), which appears before him, instructing him that these are the last surviving form of the species, and intergalactic law prohibits their extinction. An unmanned space pod arrives to pick up the eggs, but Charlie also gets caught within it and is whisked into space.

Some 50 years later, a small spacecraft traversing the galaxy comes upon the pod, and it is brought inside. The small crew, which includes hot-tempered captain Rick (Anders Hove), level-headed pilot Fran (Angela Bassett), youthful Ethan (Paul Whitthorne), eccentric computer expert Al Bert (Brad Dourif) and Bernie (Eric DaRe), receive a transmission from the Terracor company instructing them not to tamper with the pod, but to bring it to a nearby space station. Although the crew is offered three times the usual salvage payment, Rick tries to force more money out of Terracor before Fran stops him. Once the group arrives at the station, however, they discover that the place has been abandoned, and that its nuclear reactor is on yellow alert.

Increasingly frustrated, Rick breaks into the pod; he's discovered by Ethan, whom he threatens and then knocks unconscious. The frightened Charlie then crawls out from inside the pod and is similarly attacked by Rick, whom he tries to warn about the danger that's arrived with him. But the critter eggs have already hatched, and the little monsters immediately set upon Rick, killing him before rolling off into the depths of the station. Charlie revives Ethan, and the two manage to make it back to the others; the rest of the crew have already discovered Rick's body, and Charlie, after getting over the shock of finding himself in the 21st century, convinces them of what's going on.

Using a computer card, Al discovers that the station contains a biological research lab that had been used to create warfare organisms. Bernie then swipes the card in order to break into the pharmaceutical storeroom to steal drugs, but is killed by the critters. As the survivors make ready to leave the station, another spaceship arrives, and Charlie is happy to see his old friend Ug among the landing party. However, the familiar face turns out to actually be Terracor Counselor Tetra (Mann), concerned only with safely retrieving the critters, and he shoots Al when the latter confronts him. Tetra then sends his stormtroopers out to find the eggs, but Ethan locks them in the genetics lab, where the critters have mutated themselves into even more grotesque killers.

With the nuclear core now on the verge of meltdown, Ethan confronts Tetra with what he claims are the last remaining eggs, and Charlie ultimately shoots the villain. After fighting off one of the mutated critters, Ethan joins Fran and Charlie on Tetra's ship, and the group takes off with Charlie at the helm just in time to escape the exploding station.

By the fourth film in a monster-movie series, it's hardly advisable to play coy with the creatures, but that's exactly what the makers of CRITTERS 4 have done. The screen time allotted the little monsters could hardly be more than ten minutes or so; the rest of the running time is taken up with pat conflicts, underheated character development and lots of techno-speak. As in the previous films, this entry attempts to appeal to young audiences by making its protagonist a teenager, yet misses the sense of anarchic humor and gleeful critter mischief that were really behind the original's success.

Director Rupert Harvey worked as a producer on the previous CRITTERS films, and his debut at the helm is good-looking but largely bereft of dramatic interest. There's more hardware on view than in the earlier installments, and the special effects are generally impressive for a low-budget project, but they're used in the service of a derivative plot that borrows liberally from the last two ALIEN films and even the original STAR WARS (as when Charlie and Ethan get trapped in a giant trash compartment).

The cast is decent in undemanding parts, with the prolific Dourif (SPONTANEOUS COMBUSTION, GRIM PRAIRIE TALES) barely given the chance to exercise his offbeat acting muscles and Bassett hardly overshadowing her earlier work in BOYZ N THE HOOD and CITY OF HOPE, or Spike Lee's epic MALCOLM X. Even the Critters seem to be going through the motions, which hopefully marks the end of this clearly exhausted series. *(Violence, profanity.)*

p, Barry Opper, Rupert Harvey; d, Rupert Harvey; w, Joseph Lyle, David J. Schow; ph, Tom Callaway; ed, Terry Stokes; m, Peter Manning Robinson; prod d, Philip Dean Foreman; art d, Jeff Wallace; fx, Frank Ceglia

Science Fiction/Horror (PR: C MPAA: PG-13)

CROSSING THE BRIDGE ★★

103m Outlaw Productions; War Wagon Productions Inc.; Columbia TriStar Home Video ~ BV c

Josh Charles *(Mort Golden)*, Jason Gedrick *(Tim Reese)*, Stephen Baldwin *(Danny Morgan)*, Cheryl Pollak *(Carol Brockton)*, Rita Taggart *(Kate Golden)*, Hy Anzell *(Manny Goldfarb)*, Richard Edson *(Mitchell)*, Ken Jenkins *(Lou Morgan)*, Abraham Benrubi *(Rinny)*, David Schwimmer *(John Henderson)*, Bob Nickman *(Baldy)*, James Krag *(Smiling Jack)*, Rana Haugen *(Monica)*, Jeffrey Tambor *(Uncle Alby)*, Todd Tidgewell *(Ricky Toller)*, Daniel Hawke *(1st High School Senior)*, Jerry Lynn *(2nd High School Senior)*, Sean Waltman *(3rd High School Senior)*, Thomas McCarthy *(Chris Adams)*, Kevin McLauglin *(1st Player)*, Jay Kopita *(Himself)*, Nelson C. Williams *(Ed Baker)*, Chris Forth *(Tracy)*, David Brinkley *(1st Border Guard)*, Brian Grandison *(2nd Border Guard)*, James Cada *(3rd Border Guard)*, Bill Schoppert *(Supervisor)*, Jaclyn Ross *(Faye Collins)*, Daniel Blinkoff *(Randy Silverman)*, Miriam Johnson *(Ellen)*, Steven Kissel *(Elan)*, Tammara Meloy *(Sue)*, Fawzy Simon *(Ollie)*, Isabell Monk *(Professor)*, Bruce Baum *(Guy Who Looks Like Bruce Baum)*, Benny S. Cannon *(Free)*, Steve Cochran *(Ant)*, T. Mychael Rambo *(Carlyle)*, Marvette Knight *(Woman Border Guard)*, Sharon Howard *(Woman at Desk)*, Mike Binder *(Narrator)*

Three young guys face a crossroads to maturity in CROSSING THE BRIDGE, an autobiographical drama that offers too little to distinguish itself from every other film about three young guys facing a crossroads to maturity.

The story, set during the late 1970s, is told from the point of view of Mort Golden (Josh Charles, standing in for writer-director Mike Binder, who wrote the screenplay for COUPE DEVILLE and has appeared in comedy specials on HBO), an aspiring writer and stand-up comic. Having graduated from high school in a grungy town on the outskirts of Detroit, Mort is facing the future with pals Tim Reese (Jason Gedrick), a victim of child abuse with a psycho-sized chip on his shoulder, and ex-high school football star Danny Morgan (Stephen Baldwin, brother of Alec, Daniel and William). Only Mort has anything resembling a plan. Tim single-handedly fights gangs of kids from his old school for money, while Danny, the trio's ostensible "leader," mostly looks cool and drives around in the trio's designated party wagon, an unregistered old blue sedan. The three drink endless beers and chain-smoke cigarettes to bide the time between outings to go-go bars across the bridge in Canada. These outings attract the attention of a local drug dealer who offers the trio a hefty fee to transport hashish across the border from Canada into the US.

While trying to decide whether or not to accept, Mort gets fired from his job in a typewriter repair shop by his uncle (Jeffrey Tambor), who believes Mort caused a friend's (Hy Anzell) fatal heart attack. Mort also tries to reignite an old relationship with an ex-girlfriend (Cheryl Pollak) who has gone to college in Canada. Danny's life is upturned when his single dad decides to sell the family house and move into an apartment with his girlfriend—and without Danny. Tim meanwhile continues to simmer in his domestic private hell. The three accept the deal, though Mort begins having second thoughts when he's awarded a full scholarship to a college writing program. Going across the bridge, they stop off long enough for Mort to bed down his old flame before going on to an isolated farm where they find that the cargo is to be heroin rather than hashish. After a violent run-in with head dope dealer Mitchell (Richard Edson) that leaves Tim beaten to a pulp, the three return only to realize what they're risking and abandon the sedan at the border.

Although coming-of-age stories have long been a literary staple, CROSSING THE BRIDGE attempts to revive the relentlessly pop-scored sagas that spread into theaters like fungus after the success of 1973's AMERICAN GRAFFITI and didn't peter out until the genre's inevitable debasement in the PORKY'S sex films and the FRIDAY THE 13TH slashers of the 80s. These days, the genre continues to limp along in small-screen variations ranging from quasi-pornographic videos to "star-studded" network telemovies. But for all intents and purposes, it's a dead horse, and it's quite beyond Binder's powers here to breathe any new life into it.

Virtually all coming-of-age dramas rely on the same stock characters as the ones on display here, from the sensitive guy perpetually on the quest to lose his virginity to the troubled teen perpetually in hot water with his "old man." They usually face a life-threatening, future-altering crisis, whether it's adulthood itself or its metaphoric embodiments, from Jason the hockey-masked slasher to the porcine pimp Porky himself. And they always do so to the tune of pop songs of the era that waft across the soundtrack telegraphing every stock emotion and theme. But CROSSING THE BRIDGE has even fewer surprises than usual, since only the dimmest of viewers could fail to grasp going in that a film distributed by a Walt Disney subsidiary is not likely to endorse drug smuggling as an acceptable middle-class career pursuit.

The acting throughout is fine and the period detail is solid and evocative, including an unbilled, speechless cameo as one of the drug dealers by rocker and ex-druggie Dave Crosby (or somebody looking astoundingly like him). (Since this is supposedly the 70s, however, where's the disco music?) But the same is true of countless other sensitive coming-of-age sagas. Binder may well go on to more interesting work in the future, but this time he's tackled one genre badly in need of at least a decade-long hiatus. *(Violence, substance abuse, profanity, adult situations.)*

p, Jeffrey Silver, Robert Newmyer; d, Mike Binder; w, Mike Binder; ph, Tomy Sigel; ed, Adam Weiss; m, Peter Himmelman; prod d, Craig Stearns; art d, Jack D.L. Ballance; set d, Ellen Totleben; cos, Carol Ramsey

Drama (PR: O MPAA: R)

CROSSING, THE ★★½

(Australia) 94m Beyond International Group ~ South Gate Entertainment c

Danielle Spencer *(Meg)*, Russell Crowe *(Johnny)*, Robert Mammone *(Sam)*, Daphne Gray *(Jean)*, George Whaley *(Sid)*, Jacqy

Phillips *(Marion)*, Patrick Ward *(Nev)*, May Lloyd *(Peg)*, Emily Lumbers *(Jenny)*, Rodney Bell *(Shorty)*, John Blair *(Bill)*, Les Foxcroft *(Granddad)*

George Ogilvie's THE CROSSING is a tense, small-town romantic drama set in the Australian outback.

Johnny (Russell Crowe of PROOF), the son of a smothering mother and dead war-hero father, has just proposed and made love for the first time to Meg (Danielle Spencer). The next day, Anzac Day, when the small town honors its war dead, sees the return of Sam (Robert Mammone), who had left for "the city" to study art. He and Meg had been lovers before he left without saying goodbye. Now, finding his life empty without her, he has returned to take her back. As the bored, provincial locals look on, Sam tries to win Meg back in the middle of the town's Anzac Day parade. Meg rejects him, but is suddenly uneasy with the idea of staying with Johnny. Meg's father had walked in on Johnny and Meg making love and, by lunch time, the entire town was excitedly anticipating their wedding date.

Goaded on by the locals, Johnny challenges Sam to a car race for honor and Meg's hand. When the race ends in a tie and almost costs both men their lives, Sam decides he's had enough and packs to leave. But at the last second he also decides to do what he didn't before by finding Meg at a local dance to say goodbye. As they dance, a drunk and angry Johnny shows up. Seeing Sam and Meg together, he stomps off to his car, pursued by Meg. As they speed off followed by Sam, he notices that they're about to get hit by a train at a crossing. Unable to stop Johnny, Sam runs him off the road and himself into the crossing. In the film's coda, Johnny is seen placing flowers at Sam's grave as Meg looks on.

With a plotline as simple and as melodramatic as a romantic pop ballad, THE CROSSING is nevertheless directed and played with an urgency and intelligence that sets a strong, tense mood without crossing over into kitsch or self-indulgent artiness. Ogilvie (who co-directed MAD MAX: BEYOND THUNDERDROME with George Miller) and screenwriter Ranald Allan make fate itself the major player. The plot is efficiently set in motion when Meg and Johnny's lovers' idyll is invaded by Meg's father. As Meg later fingers a charm bracelet, already doubting the decision she has made, Ogilvie cuts to an identical charm dangling from Sam's wrist as he drives toward the town. At the same time, the director intercuts dark, ominous images of the train being coupled to its engine and track junctions clicking into position to draw it precisely to its fatal and fateful destination.

The townspeople function as a multi-generational Greek chorus, both commenting and acting as a catalyst on the main action as their individual stories emerge in bits and pieces. A spiteful young man stirs things up between Sam and Johnny by phoning in a taunting dedication to a local radio station. By way of explaining his bitterness, we later see him loading his dead-drunk father into his car. Waitress Peg (May Lloyd), derided as the town's "loose woman," yearns to leave for the unnamed city from whence Sam came and urges Meg to come with her, leaving her posturing macho suitors behind. Thus Meg is torn in three directions at once: Johnny with his safe but stifling stability; Sam and his alluring but dangerous romanticism; and just leaving everything and everyone behind. She finally turns to her mother for guidance, who advises her that she would be lucky to find a man who will stand by her. "But how do you know you've made the right choice?" Meg asks. "You never do," is the reply.

And that is what THE CROSSING is really about. We can never know what fate holds, and yet fate is ignored or tempted only at a terrible price. It's a theme and a story that has the power and purity of a ballad, underscored by the story's lack of specificity; it's difficult to tell not only where the story takes place but when. The characters seem contemporary but the cars and songs on the soundtrack belong to the 1960s (albeit interpreted by contemporary artists like The Proclaimers and David Bowie's Tin Machine). At the same time THE CROSSING easily asserts the importance of this story happening in this town to these characters with an unpretentious lyricism and conviction, making it another on a growing list of recent outstanding direct-to-video finds. *(Profanity, adult situations, brief nudity.)*

p, Sue Seeary; d, George Ogilvie; w, Ranald Allan; ph, Jeff Darling; ed, Henry Dangar; m, Martin Armiger; prod d, Igor Nay; art d, Kim Darby; cos, Katie Pye

Romance/Drama **(PR: C MPAA: R)**

CRY OF THE OWL, THE ★★★½

(France/Italy) 102m Italfrance Films; CiViTeCaSa Films ~ R5/S8 c

(CRI DU HIBOU, LE)

Christophe Malavoy *(Robert)*, Mathilda May *(Juliette)*, Virginie Thevenet *(Veronique)*, Jacques Penot *(Patrick)*, Jean-Pierre Kalfon *(Commissioner)*, Patrice Kerbrat *(Marcello)*

With THE CRY OF THE OWL, adapted from a novel by Patricia Highsmith, Gallic director Claude Chabrol has fashioned yet another of his biting black comedies of murderously ill manners.

Robert (Christophe Malavoy, who also starred in Chabrol's recent adaptation of Flaubert's MADAME BOVARY) is a mechanical artist who also illustrates nature books, drawing birds of prey with huge, mad eyes. Recovering from a bout of depression and a divorce from his shrewish wife Veronique (Virginie Thevenet) in Paris, he has moved to the quiet town of Vichy and taken a job with a local firm. For relaxation, he spies on his neighbor, pretty Juliette (Mathilda May, yes, the naked space vampire from Tobe Hooper's LIFEFORCE). There's nothing salacious about it. In fact, Robert soon comes out in the open to introduce himself to Juliette and to explain that he merely admired her happy, orderly and satisfied life and enjoyed watching her live it.

Robert's description of her causes Juliette to question whether she really *is* that happy or satisfied and whether her life may be too ordered. She impulsively breaks off her engagement to her swinish fiance Patrick (Jacques Penot) and begins romantically pursuing Robert. Enraged, Patrick seeks revenge. With the help of a spiteful Veronique, he goes into hiding after fighting with Robert to make it appear as though Robert has murdered him. Ironically, Robert has no interest in Juliette beyond friendship. Realizing this, Juliette commits suicide—after knitting him a nice sweater.

After Juliette's death, Patrick's rage turns hotter, causing him to take potshots at Robert's house at night. However, instead of killing Robert, he injures a kindly doctor and is indicted on attempted-murder charges. Goaded by Veronique and feeling he has nothing to lose, Patrick goes to Robert's house to "take care of him once and for all." Instead, Patrick and Veronique kill each other with the knife intended for Robert. Feeling himself responsible, Robert is left frozen with indecision over whether he should put his own fingerprints on the knife.

In all of Claude Chabrol's films, scratch the bourgeoisie and you'll find raging monsters underneath. But if that were all there were to Chabrol, he would probably be George Romero. By his own admission, however, Chabrol is at heart middle class himself. And that is what makes his films so compelling and complex. It is impossible to pinpoint Chabrol's own ethos in his films because there is a little bit of him in everybody on the screen.

On one level, THE CRY OF THE OWL is a gruesome tale of middle-class horror in which an innocent young man is drawn into the twisted lives of a group of people who feed off of the innocence of others. And Veronique and Patrick are both the type of cold-blooded, predatory abusers who are recurring villain figures in Chabrol films. But Robert, interestingly enough, doesn't triumph over these antagonists through resourcefulness. He does so through utter passivity, accentuated by Chabrol's casting of the blandly handsome Malavoy in the role of Robert. And there's something a little gruesome about that as well. Robert keeps his distance from Juliette, telling her, "A dream image should remain in dreams." With Patrick and Veronique, he simply waits for them to come to him, as if knowing that within their rage and stupidity lie the seeds of their own destruction. In fact, virtually all of the bloodshed in THE CRY OF THE OWL would have been averted had Robert, like the other characters, remained closeted within his own obsessions.

Juliette was ready to marry and probably would have had a tolerable life with Patrick, had Robert not stepped from behind her trash fire like the angel of death about whom Juliette tells Robert she frequently dreams. Inspired by Robert's independence from Veronique, she breaks off with Patrick, but rather than standing on her own, she merely replaces him as an object of masochistic adoration with Robert. And Veronique was on the verge of granting Robert an uncontested divorce before Robert drove Patrick to her, breaking up her pending engagement to a rich suitor. There is a sense throughout that Robert, rather than being the victim is in fact the instigator, upsetting the realities of the other characters to control their fates in a way in which he feels he is unable to control his own.

Beneath the social concerns central to Chabrol's films is their poignant sense of the extreme fragility of our images of ourselves and our worlds and how just the slightest nudge at the right time and in the right place can cascade us into nightmarish chaos. In respect to Highsmith, whose novel *Strangers on a Train* was turned into an electrifying thriller by Alfred Hitchcock in 1951, it's clear that what appealed to both directors is her brilliantly rigorous worst-case scenarios of what can happen when a voyeur steps out of his role to confront his victim or when a man has a conversation with a stranger on a train.

THE CRY OF THE OWL is no STRANGERS ON A TRAIN; Chabrol seems just plain too jovially bourgeois to whip himself up to the state of moral implacability that characterizes Hitchcock's utter control of the medium. But, in its own way, THE CRY OF THE OWL is just as unforgettable. *(Violence, adult situations.)*

p, Antonio Passalia; d, Claude Chabrol; w, Claude Chabrol, Odile Barski, (from the novel by Patricia Highsmith); ph, Jean Rabier; ed, Monique Fardoulis; m, Mathieu Chabrol; art d, Jacques Leguillon

Drama **(PR: C MPAA: NR)**

CRYING GAME, THE ★★★★

(U.K.) 112m Palace Pictures ~ Miramax c

Stephen Rea *(Fergus)*, Miranda Richardson *(Jude)*, Forest Whitaker *(Jody)*, Jim Broadbent *(Col)*, Ralph Brown *(Dave)*, Adrian Dunbar *(Maguire)*, Jaye Davidson *(Dil)*, Breffini McKenna *(Tinker)*, Joe Savino *(Eddie)*, Birdie Sweeney *(Tommy)*, Andree Bernard *(Jane)*, Tony Slattery, Jack Carr, Brian Coleman

A perverse moral tale preaching the oldest of lessons—that love conquers all—THE CRYING GAME was helped by clever marketing to seduce an unexpectedly wide audience. The film presents a lushly romantic vision of a cruel, arbitrarily violent world in which the apparently safe harbor of love is actually filled with mysterious eddies and invisible rocks.

Fergus (Stephen Rea), a foot soldier in the IRA, is part of a small group led by ferocious idealogues Jude (Miranda Richardson) and Maguire (Adrian Dunbar). They kidnap a British soldier, Jody (Forest Whitaker), in Northern Ireland (the only place they'll still call you "nigger" to your face, he observes) and hold him in exchange for a group of imprisoned IRA members; if they're not released within three days, Jody will die.

As the tense and exhausted comrades take turns guarding Jody, a tentative friendship forms between Fergus and the frightened captive. This hothouse relationship is spawned, in part, by their proximity, but also because, as Jody shrewdly and somewhat desperately observes, it's in Fergus's nature to show kindness.

Aware of his ruthless colleagues' growing contempt for what they perceive to be his weakness, if not outright disloyalty, Fergus pointedly accepts the task of killing their captive when it becomes apparent that British officials are not going to comply with their demands. But things go terribly wrong. As Fergus marches Jody into the woods at gunpoint, the prisoner suddenly breaks into a run, imploring Fergus not to shoot and reminding him of his essential goodness. Fergus gives chase, but the surprisingly agile Jody quickly removes his restraints and gains additional speed, only to run into a road and collide fatally with an oncoming vehicle. It's a British armored car, and within moments the IRA fortress is under attack. Fergus escapes, leaving Maguire and Jude trapped in a hail of gunfire.

Fergus flees Ireland and melts into London's underground of undocumented Irish workers, assuming a new name, working at menial jobs and keeping a low profile. Haunted by the memory of Jody, he looks up the dead man's lover, Dil (Jaye Davidson), a photograph of whom Jody had earlier shown him. Alternately seductive and petulant, childish and grave, desperately needy and infuriatingly aloof, Dil soon has Fergus bewitched. But Fergus is tormented by his past, trapped by the lies (mostly of omission) he has told Dil and, as their relationship grows ever more intimate, tortured by the fact that he has an entire other life of which she is unaware. Still, it's Fergus who's in for the biggest shock, when he learns Dil has a secret as well: "she" is really a man. To his own amazement, Fergus is unable to repudiate Dil; when Jude and Maguire reappear unexpectedly, demanding that he help them with one last assassination, it's fear for Dil's safety that makes him comply. The killing—a suicide mission for Fergus—is a botch, resulting in Maguire's death instead. Hungry for revenge, Jude appears at Dil's apartment, only to be gunned down by Dil, who's been devastated by the news of Fergus's complicity in Jody's death. Fergus, true to his gentlemanly nature, takes the rap for Dil and goes to prison, where Dil visits him regularly, cheerfully counting down the many days until his release.

THE CRYING GAME's audacity is remarkable, and extends far beyond its "controversial" subject matter. In fact, its utter belief in the power of love to overcome all obstacles may be its boldest conceit; while a conventional Hollywood romance pretends to place roadblocks in the paths of its lovers, THE CRYING GAME presents Dill and Fergus with a real dilemma and refuses to opt for the easy ending. Who, after all, doubts that the Hollywood remake would make certain to have Dil die saving Fergus (from the police, Jude, whatever . . .), allowing him to love her safely in the abstract, rather than in the all-too-obstinate flesh? And while THE BODYGUARD reaped praise for the color-blind affair between its protagonists, played by Whitney Houston and Kevin Costner (who fall into bed without ever noticing they're different colors, gushed the critics), THE CRYING GAME tweaks the same question—beautiful, barely black woman/white man—with the telling details that lift it out of the realm of pre-fab fantasy: Fergus and Dil may not be daunted by race, but they notice.

Nevertheless, writer-director Neil Jordan, whose credits include THE COMPANY OF WOLVES and MONA LISA, trusts in the power of fantasy to make reality bearable. He just never forgets that deception is dangerous, particularly when it's ourselves we seek to deceive. Dil is a relatively conventional dreamer, like every girl with a much-broken heart who retreats by degrees into a dream world of storybook romance; her veil-draped apartment is a refuge that could easily become Miss Haversham's cobwebbed chamber. Fergus, by contrast, is an everyman tormented by the repressed implications of his brief relationship with Jody. Disturbed by its intensity, he goes for the classic dodge—transference onto the wife/girlfriend/sister of the unacceptable object of desire. The problem is that Dil—the *real* Dil, rather than Fergus's guilty fantasy, sparked by the haunting snapshot in Jody's wallet—isn't an acceptable object either. Jordan's conclusion seems to be that if men insist on turning women into fantasy objects, they'll just have to live with the results, a radical proposition indeed.

Thematic issues aside, THE CRYING GAME pulls off a tremendously difficult technical feat; its screenplay contains not one, but *two*, wrenching twists, each of which could easily derail the narrative in the hands of a lesser storyteller. But Jordan not only makes it work, he makes it seem inevitable. Viewers are introduced to the story of Fergus's growing friendship with the captive and doomed Jody (classic, but always good for a sharply observed retelling), then have the rug pulled out from under them when Jody dies barely a third of the way into the film—you have to go back to PSYCHO to find a top-billed star as heedlessly dispensed with as is Whitaker. Fergus's relationship with Dil seems to be proceeding along conventional lines until the moment of revelation, at which point the average film would consider it had done its job and bring things to a swift close. But THE CRYING GAME keeps on going, patiently playing its story out to its appointed, ironic end. *(Violence, nudity, sexual situations.)*

p, Stephen Woolley; d, Neil Jordan; w, Neil Jordan; ph, Ian Wilson; ed, Kant Pan; m, Anne Dudley; prod d, Jim Clay; art d, Chris Seagers; set d, Martin Childs; cos, Sandy Powell

AAN Best Picture: Stephen Woolley (Producer); *AAN Best Actor:* Stephen Rea; *AAN Best Supporting Actor:* Jaye Davidson; *AAN Director:* Neil Jordan; *AA Best Original Screenplay:* Neil Jordan; *AAN Editing:* Kant Pan

Drama/Romance/Thriller **(PR: C MPAA: R)**

CTHULHU MANSION ★½

92m Filmagic; Golden Pictures; Walrus Pictures ~ Republic Pictures Home Video c

Frank Finlay *(Chandu)*, Marcia Layton *(Lisa)*, Brad Fisher *(Hawk)*, Melanie Shatner *(Eva)*, Luis Fernandez Alves *(Chris)*, Kaethe Cherney *(Candy)*, Paul Birchard *(Billy)*, Frank Brana *(Felix)*, Ronald Feaval *(Fatman)*, Pascal Muzadi *(Larry)*, Emile Linder *(Eddie)*, Jack Jamison *(1st Guard)*, Angel Blanco *(2nd Guard)*, Jorge Bernal *(3rd Guard)*, Ivan Almagro *(1st Grip)*, Jeff Espinoza *(2nd Grip)*, Steve Jordan *(Policeman)*, Larry Ann Evans *(Hot Dog Lady)*

The writings of H.P. Lovecraft have inspired some memorable recent horror films, most notably those of Stuart Gordon (RE-ANIMATOR and FROM BEYOND). But that's certainly not the case with CTHULHU MANSION, which announces its dubious credentials right away by announcing that it's "based on the writings of H.P. Lovecraft." Writer-director Juan Piquer Simon's last straight horror film, SLUGS, was rather schlocky but at least appeared to hew fairly close to its literary source (the Shaun Hutson novel); this one doesn't even seem to be trying.

CTHULHU MANSION stars Frank Finlay as Chandu, a magician whose dabbling in the black arts once caused his assistant, who also happened to be his wife, to burst into flames during a levitation act. In the present day, he's using his daughter Lisa (Marcia Layton) in his shows, but soon tragedy of a non-supernatural type strikes. Seeking escape from a botched drug deal, a gang of punks kidnap Chandu, Lisa and his mute bodyguard Felix (Frank Brana). The gang's leader, Hawk (Brad Fisher), forces Chandu to help sneak the gang out of the amusement park, which is now crawling with cops, and take them to his mansion.

Once there, Hawk insists that Chandu dress a gunshot wound that his brother Chris (Luis Fernandez Alves) has suffered, but the young man's condition continues to deteriorate. An evil force has been unleashed in the house, heralded by a vision of Chandu's deceased wife that appears to the magician. As various manifestations of the hellish force pick off the punks one by one, Chandu struggles to find a way to stop it before it engulfs the entire house; he is unsuccessful, however, and ends up absorbing the malignance that has overtaken Chris into his own body. Chris and Lisa flee to safety as the house, with Chandu inside, is sucked down into the bowels of hell.

The questionable highlight of CTHULHU MANSION is a moment of unintentional hilarity early on, as Chandu's hijacked car approaches a police checkpoint with his own party of three and the five punks crammed into it. Hawk instructs his gang to hide, and when the vehicle reaches the gate, only our three heroes can be seen inside the vehicle. Then, once the car has pulled away, everyone's back in their original positions. Where did the five punks go? Why, they were hiding under blankets on the floor, of course!

The unintended amusement pops up again every so often once the group arrives at the titular mansion (its name and some stray "Cthulhu" literature lying around the house are the only real connections to Lovecraft's work), but not often enough to make this a camp classic on the order of Simon's earlier PIECES. Instead, there's a long, *long* series of arguments and fisticuffs, as well as a minor subplot in which the suffering Chris befriends Lisa, before the negligible terrors begin.

Slowly but surely and oh-so-predictably, the punks are done in by a shower stall that fills with blood, feisty vines and some leftover monster claws from Simon's ENDLESS DESCENT that pull a girl into a refrigerator. Of course, since—with the exception of Chris—the punks are all mean and obnoxious, there's no horror associated with their deaths; there is a bit of blather about how their evil natures helped unleash the wicked spirits residing beneath the mansion, but it's never really developed or explored. Nor are the punks' characters given any more than cursory personalities or performances; for his part, Finlay spends the early portions of the film looking like an aged Bela Lugosi and the rest looking like an aged British character actor who can't believe he got roped into this Euroschlock. *(Violence, profanity, substance abuse.)*

p, Jose G. Maesso, J.P. Simon; d, J.P. Simon; w, J.P. Simon, (from the stories by H.P. Lovecraft); ph, Julio Bragado; ed, Paul Aviles; m, Tim Souster; prod d, Pablo Alonso; art d, Eduardo Hidalgo; cos, Maria Caceres

Horror/Fantasy **(PR: O MPAA: R)**

CUP FINAL ★★★

(Israel) 110m Local Productions ~ First Run Features c

Moshe Ivgi *(Cohen)*, Muhamed Bakri *(Ziad)*, Suheil Haddad *(Omar)*, Salim Dau, Bassam Zuamut, Yussef Abu Warda, Gassan Abbass, Sharon Alexander, Johnny Arbid, Sami Samir

An effort to reconcile some of the differences between Israelis and Palestinians, Eran Riklis's CUP FINAL uses the cliche of a beleagured platoon with a POW whom they eventually come to accept as a fellow pawn in the larger political struggle. The catalyst for this realization is a shared love for soccer and a devotion to the Italian national team in the World Cup match.

Cohen (Moshe Ivgi) is far from a ferocious warrior; he has trouble buckling his helmet's chin strap and laments his army's Lebanese incursion as undue interference with his Plans to attend the match in Barcelona. Heightening the irony is a brief aside in which a fellow reservist admonishes him for voting Conservative. Soon, however, this Israeli Sad Sack has a lot more to worry about; Cohen and his far tougher commander are captured by a wildly heterogenous crew. While the Muslim leader Ziad (Muhamed Bakri), has all the earmarks of a born leader, tough and lean, laconic and sensible, and his second-in-command, Omar (Suheil Haddad) looks the typical politicized intellectual with long hair and mended glasses, the others range from a very devout and implausibly fat farmer to a brooding, belligerent fighter whom only Ziad seems able to control.

In their effort to get to Beirut, they have to dodge the road-bound Israeli patrols and occasional unknown and unseen snipers, as well. In one firefight they lose their higher-ranking prisoner and one of their own too. In the casual conversations between panicky situations, they learn that Cohen is a soccer fan and that he shares an enthusiasm for things Italian with Ziad and Omar who had been university students in Italy before joining the PLO. It also appears that one of the fighters, George, is a Christian-Marxist who uses his Crucifix to gain entry to an Israeli Army medical site to get needed supplies.

Trained at England's National Film and Television School, Riklis highlights some of the amusing sequences in Eyal Halfon's screenplay. Besides the Israeli Army doctor who thinks he remembers Omar from an Odessa medical school, there is the Lebanese torn between his devotion to the rules of hospitality and his fear at harboring armed guerillas. Later, at a party to celebrate a relative's marriage, one of the female guests naturally chooses Cohen as her dance partner, while an Israeli patrol, guns at the ready, scans the festivities.

As they near Beirut, tensions increase and their idle games at soccer or billiards take on a nasty tone. The lone zealot manages to capture Cohen alone and proposes to torture him, but is met by the genuine embarrassment of the others at this show of hatred. During the final approach to the city, Cohen is freed by his own side, while Ziad is wounded. The final scene shows Cohen weeping at the deaths of people he had learned are not so different from himself.

Director Riklis and screenwriter Halfon have refurbished an old format. THE LOST PATROL, the basic model, dates back to 1934, while the character study of POW and captors was a theme in both the Soviet THE FORTY-FIRST and Hollywood's own COUNTER-ATTACK. CUP FINAL's sole strength lies in its confrontation of an Israeli Everyman with a heroic Palestinian, proof of the director's sense of drama and fair play. *(Profanity.)*

p, Michael Sharfshtein; d, Eran Riklis; w, Eyal Halfon, (from the story by Eran Riklis); ph, Amnon Salomon; ed, Anat Lubarsky; m, Raviv Gazit

War/Drama/Sports **(PR: C MPAA: NR)**

CUTTING EDGE, THE ★★½

101m TCE Film Productions; Interscope Communications; MGM ~ MGM c

D.B. Sweeney *(Doug Dorsey)*, Moira Kelly *(Kate Moseley)*, Roy Dotrice *(Anton Pamchenko)*, Terry O'Quinn *(Jack Moseley)*, Dwier Brown *(Hale)*, Chris Benson *(Walter Dorsey)*, Kevin Peeks *(Brian)*, Barry Flatman *(Tuttle)*, Rachelle Ottley *(Lorie)*, Steve Sears *(Spindler)*, Nahanni Johnstone *(German Girl)*, Michael Hogan *(Doctor)*, R.D. Reid *(Calgary Cop)*, Dick Grant *(Olympic Commentator)*, Melanie Miller *(Olympic Commentator)*, Judy Blumberg *(Nationals Commentator)*, Robin Cousins *(Nationals Commentator)*, Chick Roberts *(Drunk)*, Edwin Stephenson *(Costumer)*, Arthur Rowsell *(Assistant Costumer)*, Jojo Starbuck *(Interviewer)*, France Gauthier *(French Official)*, Roger Perlard *(French Official)*, Graham Harley *(Official)*, Pierre Peloquin *(International Reporter)*, Peter Messaline *(International Reporter)*, Maya Toman *(International Reporter)*, Kirsten Kieferle *(Woman in Bar)*, Sam Aaron *(Man in Bar)*, Larry Armstrong, Frank Dooley, Linda Hanchar, Adrian Pellett *(People in Bar)*, Rhys M. Berthiaume *(Aerobics Instructor)*, Joanne Nisbett *(Ballet Instructor)*, Robert Buck *(Butler)*, Tiina Muir *(Nyman)*, Christine Hough *(Smilkov)*, Doug Ladret *(Brushkin)*, Krista Coady *(Dubois)*, Brian Geddeis *(Gercel)*, Penny Papaioannou *(Weiderman Twin)*, Raoul LeBlanc *(Weiderman Twin)*, Michelle Menzies *(Yumez)*, Kevin Wheeler *(Weaver)*, Patricia MacNeil *(1st Nationals Pair)*, Cory Watson *(1st Nationals Pair)*, Janice Yeck *(2nd Nationals Pair)*, Scott MacDonald *(2nd Nationals Pair)*, Allison Gaylor *(1st Olympic Pair)*, John Robinson *(1st Olympic Pair)*, Kim Esdaile *(2nd Olympic Pair)*, Sean Rice *(2nd Olympic Pair)*, Haley Williams *(3rd Olympic Pair)*, John Jenkins *(3rd Olympic Pair)*

A calculated throwback to old-fashioned romances, THE CUTTING EDGE could be used as a classroom example of correct, if not necessarily compelling, screenwriting technique. It sets up its situation, in which antagonistic characters are thrown together and fall in love, and plays it out to logical perfection.

Doug Dorsey (D.B. Sweeney) is a working-class kid with a gift for playing hockey; he looks as though he's headed for a major career until a minor but irreparable eye injury sidelines him. Kate Moseley (Moira Kelly) is a spoiled rich girl whose bid for Olympic figure skating fame is defeated by her nasty temperament. She's such a bitch no one can stand her, and all her daddy's (Terry O'Quinn) money can't change that. Crafty old Russian coach Anton Pamchenko (Roy Dotrice) pairs the two, and soon they're bickering by day and conspicuously ignoring one another by night. Doug has to relearn skating (he thinks figure skating is such a sissy business that he tells his friends back home that he's shipped out with the merchant marines), and Kate needs to accept that yes, she can learn something from somebody else. They form an inspired partnership (he gives her sex and she gives him class, to invert the old Astaire/Rogers formula) and progress to the Olympic tryouts. Along the way they fall in love, though at first they both do their best to deny it. In an improbable but perfectly predictable ending, they admit their mutual attraction moments before skating out to Olympic stardom, sealing their declaration not with a kiss, but with a novel and difficult stunt.

Perhaps the reason THE CUTTING EDGE seems so oddly old fashioned is that the romantic conventions by which it plays have in recent years been usurped by the buddy movie, exemplified by the wildly successful LETHAL WEAPON series. At least where American films are concerned, today's viewers seem to expect their opposites-attract couples to be of the same sex variety, and (in mainstream movies, anyway) expect them not to end up in bed together. They just learn tolerance, acceptance and understanding as chaste friendship blossoms. That's not to say you don't have mismatched couples falling for one another in contemporary movies, just that their affairs are seldom the focal point. It's as though today's moviemakers have lost faith in romance, pure and simple, as a subject. Even THE BIG EASY, a longstanding favorite of contemporary romantics, tries to insure that audiences won't get bored by surrounding its love affair with a murder mystery and lashings of New Orleans atmosphere, while PRETTY WOMAN—probably the closest thing to an old-fashioned romance movie in years—tricks up the fairy tale story line with class comedy and yuppie angst.

Directed by Paul Michael Glaser (formerly half of that Ur-buddy couple, TV's "Starsky and Hutch"), THE CUTTING EDGE also seems anachronistic in its PG-rated treatment of sex; there's scarcely more of it than you'd find in a similar film made in the 1940s, and what there is takes place discretely off screen. The movie's thrills are mostly of the athletic variety, and though diehard ice skating fans were no doubt disappointed by the rapid-fire editing required to conceal—quite effectively—the use of doubles for Kelly and Sweeny, the ice-skating scenes are in fact well photographed and competently used to delineate the developing relationship between the two skaters.

Clearly designed to be a family entertainment, THE CUTTING EDGE has a by-the-numbers quality that's only partly concealed by smooth production values and consistent—if uninspiring—performances.

p, Ted Field, Karen Murphy, Robert W. Cort; d, Paul M. Glaser; w, Tony Gilroy; ph, Elliot Davis; ed, Michael E. Polakow; m, Patrick Williams; prod d, David Gropman; art d, Dan Davis; set d, Steve Shewchuk; cos, William Ivey Long; ch, Robin Cousins

Romance/Sports **(PR: A MPAA: PG)**

DADDY AND THE MUSCLE ACADEMY ★★★

(Finland) 65m Filmitakomo; YLE TV2 Documentary ~ Zeitgeist Films c

Tom of Finland/Touko Laaksonen, Bob Mizer, Nayland Blake, Durk Dehner, Etienne, Isaac Julien

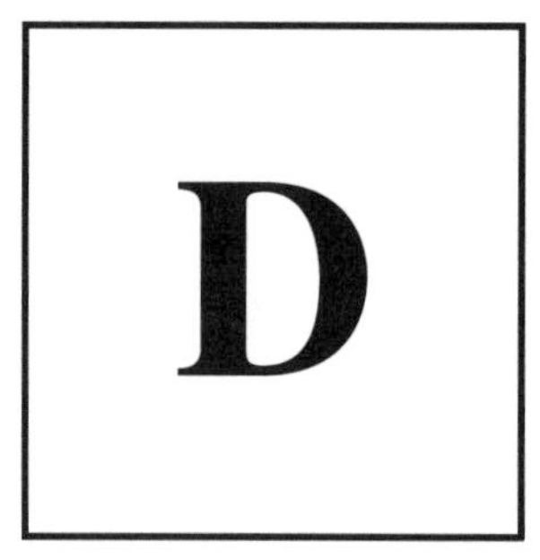

When, under the now legendary moniker "Tom of Finland," Touko Laaksonen's brazenly homoerotic artwork first began appearing on the pages of American "physique" magazines like *Athletic Model Guide* during the 1950s, his robust, handsome and refreshingly forthright male figures provided positive role models for confused adolescents and guilt-wracked adults alike. Now, following Laaksonen's death in November 1991 at seventy-one, Ilppo Pohjola's stylish DADDY AND THE MUSCLE ACADEMY examines his lasting contribution to gay culture.

Quite simply, Tom of Finland brought homoerotic imagery into the 20th century and, in the process, helped generations of gay men, previously banished to sissydom and derided as the "third" or "indeterminate" sex, redefine themselves. It's certainly no small innovation that his hyper-masculine bikers, laborers, servicemen and cowboys, among other macho archetypes, cruise each other openly and, rather than groping each other furtively in dark alleys or seedy hotel rooms, are invariably situated in open-air, scenic settings. More importantly, Tom's men don't appear to be even remotely conflicted by their "deviant" sexuality, coming across instead as supremely well adjusted individuals who thoroughly and shamelessly indulge their same-sex proclivities.

Perhaps wary of his growing renown (or, given his age and conservative background, reluctant to forsake his hard-earned status in mainstream society), Laaksonen waited until 1973 before finally abandoned his advertising career to concentrate exclusively on his homoerotica. With success, however, came problems. His work was widely pirated, leading to the creation of the Tom of Finland Foundation to promote, protect and preserve his efforts.

Largely funded by that Los Angeles-based organization, DADDY AND THE MUSCLE ACADEMY effectively charts the development of Tom's idealized male figures, from beautiful long-lashed and tender-hearted youths to, in keeping with his own evolving fantasies, more physically mature, but still seemingly tender-hearted, blue-collar icons. According to Laaksonen himself, his work stems from the school of photo-realism, characterized by extremely meticulous depiction of detail. Not surprisingly, his early illustrations were inspired by, and inspired in turn, the photographs he found on the pages of his beloved American "physique" magazines.

Interestingly, it wasn't until the 1960s, when photographic technology reached new heights of sophistication that, just to remain competitive, Tom began, in what became his trademark, to grossly exaggerate the male genitalia; the figures in his earlier work may be impossibly beautiful, but they *are* realistically proportioned.

Tom of Finland's major innovation was to subvert the macho image, something that has had a profound impact on American pop culture: today, in the worlds of fashion, advertising, rock music and beyond, everyone from Madonna to Helmut Newton to Gianni Versace has appropriated the Tom of Finland aesthetic.

DADDY AND THE MUSCLE ACADEMY is supremely stylish and, thanks to Laaksonen's own reflections and additional commentary by the likes of *AMG* founder Bob Mizer, fellow illustrator Etienne and British filmmaker Isaac Julien, often insightful. It's not without its drawbacks, however. For one thing, hearing grown men repeatedly utter "I'm a Tom's man" on the soundtrack grows more than a little tiresome. Worse, the leather netherworld that Pohjola depicts, a supposed recreation of Tom's milieu, is well executed but decidedly underwhelming—is there any significance to the fact that the purported "Tom's men" in this recurring footage are, almost without exception, decidedly average specimens of manhood? Well, as Laaksonen himself admits, the male figures who populate his illustrations are his personal archetypes, mere fantasies, and most poor fellows fall far short of the mark.

On a more disturbing level, Laaksonen, who was born circa 1920 and "discovered" his sexuality with German soldiers during WWII, freely admits to the influence Nazi propaganda had on his artwork—a provocative but understandably controversial factor which is largely unexplored by Illpo. (*Sexual situations, adult situations.*)

p, Kari Paljakka, Alvaro Pardo; d, Ilppo Pohjola; w, Ilppo Pohjola; ph, Kjell Lagerroos; ed, Jorma Hori; m, Elliot Sharp

Documentary/Biography (PR: O MPAA: NR)

DAHONG DENGLONG GAOGAO GUA

(SEE: RAISE THE RED LANTERN)

DAMAGE ★★★

(France/U.K.) 112m Nouvelles Editions de Film; Skreba Damage ~ New Line Cinema c

Jeremy Irons *(Dr. Stephen Fleming)*, Juliette Binoche *(Anna Barton)*, Miranda Richardson *(Ingrid)*, Rupert Graves *(Martyn)*, Ian Bannen *(Edward Lloyd)*, Leslie Caron *(Elizabeth Prideaux)*, Peter Stormare *(Peter Wetzler)*, Gemma Clark *(Sally)*, Julian Fellowes *(Donald Lyndsaymp)*, Tony Doyle *(Prime Minister)*, Raymond Gravell *(Raymond)*, Susan Engel *(Miss Snow)*, David Thewlis *(Detective)*, Benjamin Whitrow *(Civil Servant)*, Jeff Nuttall *(Trevor Leigh Davies MP)*, Roger Llewellyn *(Palmer)*, Jason Morell *(Young Man at Sothebys)*, Barry Stearn *(Prime Minister's Aide)*, Linda Delapena *(Beth)*, Francine Stock *(TV Interviewer)*, Henry Power *(Henry)*, Simon DeDeney *(Young Man at DTI)*, Luc Etienne *(Lutetia Receptionist)*

With DAMAGE, based on the novel by Josephine Hart, acclaimed French director Louis Malle has created one of the coldest movies about sex ever to hit the screen. Although Malle's austere style isn't immediately compelling, the film develops a power that builds to a devastating conclusion.

Married, successful English Parliament member Dr. Stephen Fleming (Jeremy Irons) has an intense first meeting with his son Martyn's (Rupert Graves) girlfriend, Anna Barton (Juliette Binoche), at a cocktail party. When Anna phones him at work, Stephen immediately arranges a sexual rendezvous. Martyn, a newspaper editor, later introduces Anna to his family, and she reveals over dinner, to the dismay of Stephen's wife, Ingrid (Miranda Richardson), that her brother committed suicide.

Stephen invites Anna to accompany him on a Brussels business trip, but she goes to Paris with Martyn instead. Besotted by Anna, Stephen finds her there and has sex with her in a church doorway. Later, he suggests leaving Ingrid for her, but Anna refuses his plea. Stephen meets Anna's ex-boyfriend Peter at her apartment. Anna tells him her late brother had been incestuously jealous of her relationship with Peter. He slit his wrists, and afterwards, Anna asked Peter to sleep with her.

At Ingrid's country estate, Martyn announces he's marrying Anna. When Stephen tries to dissuade his son, Martyn, ironically, accuses him of not understanding true passion. Sensing Anna's affair with Stephen, her mother, Elizabeth (Leslie Caron), begs him to let her go. Stephen calls Anna and tells her their relationship has to end. However, Anna sends him a key to a love nest, making it clear that she will marry Martyn and still maintain their affair. The two arrange a tryst, and Martyn walks in unexpectedly when they are making love. Shocked by catching them in bed, Martyn backs out the door and falls off the apartment balcony to his death.

Stephen reveals everything to the police, and Ingrid turns on him in a fury. Stephen resigns from Parliament in disgrace, and when he tries to see Anna, she won't speak to him. Years later, a broken Stephen shuffles into a dilapidated apartment somewhere on the continent, where he has a photo of himself, Martyn and Anna blown up on a wall. Sitting before the photo, Stephen reveals in a voiceover that he saw Anna just once more—with Peter and a child. "She was no different than anyone else," he sadly concludes.

DAMAGE's plot is pure soap opera melodrama, but Malle imbues the material with an almost morbid seriousness that matches David Hare's irony-free screenplay. Stephen arranges his first meeting with Anna in two terse sentences: "Give me your address. I'll be there in an hour." After that, there's no talking, as Stephen and Anna grapple on the floor of her ultramodern, tomb-like apartment. Strangely enough, the sex scenes are so mechanical that the recent NC-17 flap over this movie seems ridiculous: no one could possibly find this material erotic. In fact, Stephen and Anna's many couplings look cold, especially when Malle dresses them up with arty lighting through Venetian blinds.

As the movie hits its last third, however, we finally know the characters well enough that the sexual obsession theme becomes hypnotic. Although Stephen's fixation on Anna is never explained, watching him stalk to his doom becomes perversely entertaining. It helps that Malle never wavers from his highly stylized tone. His most successful scenes are silent, showing Stephen waiting for Anna like a lost puppy, or holding the key to their apartment up to his mouth as she smiles at him behind Martyn's back.

As the aristocratic yet emotionally vulnerable Stephen, Irons is perfectly cast, his grey, haggard appearance making a striking contrast with Binoche's ivory skin and "black helmet" haircut (an unmistakable nod to Louise Brooks's Lulu in PANDORA'S BOX). Although Binoche's couture wardrobe is distracting, her recurrent, inscrutable smile is memorable, as is the gaze that she and Irons exchange when they first meet. Miranda Richardson (DANCE WITH A STRANGER, THE CRYING GAME) turns in a ferocious performance as the scorned wife, with her sarcastic display of her naked body to Irons a dramatic highlight. Leslie Caron makes a satisfying, if brief, return to the screen in the film's only comic role. The ending is worth waiting for: a bizarre meditation on the folly of Stephen's and Anna's entire relationship. The last line—and the close-up of her photograph—sum up his tragedy. *(Nudity, sexual situations, profanity.)*

p, Louis Malle; d, Louis Malle; w, David Hare, (from the novel by Josephine Hart); ph, Peter Biziou; ed, John Bloom; m, Zbigniew Preisner; prod d, Brian Morris; art d, Richard Earl; set d, Jill Quertier; cos, Milena Canonero

AAN Best Supporting Actress: Miranda Richardson

Drama/Erotic **(PR: O MPAA: R)**

DAMNED IN THE USA ★★½

(U.K.) 68m Berwick Universal Pictures; Uptown Media Associates; Channel Four ~ DIUSA Releasing c

Reverend Donald Wildmon, Christie Hefner, Jesse Helms, Alphonse D'Amato, Jimmy Tingle, Andres Serrano, Dennis Barrie, Luther Campbell, Lou Reed, Judge David Albanese, Representative Thomas J. Downey, James Ford, Charles Freeman, Senator Gordon Humphrey, Harry Lunn, Norma Ramos, Peter Reed, Joe Reilly, Philip Yenawine

The reverend Donald Wildmon's failed attempt to block distribution of DAMNED IN THE USA certainly reaped its share of headlines, but he needn't have bothered. For a film addressing the censorship debate which has raged in this country during the past few years, Paul Yule's feature is surprisingly tepid.

Among the mediums under steady attack from the likes of Wildmon's American Family Association, a highly organized and vocal mainstay of the Christian Right, are films, TV, popular music, books, photography, performance art and stand-up comedy. (Appropriately, the film features extensive—if not particularly incisive—commentary by liberal comedian Jimmy Tingle.) Notables who've been taken to task by the "family values" platform include performance artist Karen Finley, who has been known to smear her nude body with chocolate sauce to make a point, to say nothing of her expertise with various tubers; Andres Serrano, whose notorious "Piss Christ" photograph incited the wrath of Alfonse D'Amato, who perceived it as an affront to Christians; rap impresario Luther Campbell, whose group 2 Live Crew was brought to court on obscenity charges for their "As Nasty As They Wanna Be" album; and Robert Mapplethorpe, whose formalist imagery, including a self-portrait featuring the handsome artist with a bullwhip intimately esconded, are denounced as "sickness masquerading as art." (Yule devotes a considerable amount of the film's running time to the closing of the Mapplethorpe exhibit at the Contemporary Arts Centre in Cinncinati, and the trial on obscenity charges which followed.)

The Far Right seems blind to the idea that the higher purpose of art is to challenge society's values, not uphold them; although the embattled NEA has not always been quick to make the point, free societies aren't supposed to censor art. It's ironic and disturbing that the artists consistently under attack by organizations like the AFA are the very ones whose work underscores the diversity and richness of contemporary American culture. Then again, cultural complexity is not a concept the AFA embraces. What Wildmon earnestly describes as the "heart and soul of civilization" looks, acts and sounds suspiciously like a bunch of racist, sexist, homophobic, white Christian heterosexuals. (One of the organization's uglier mandates is to limit the exposure of minorities on TV—if the black population is 12%, they shouldn't represent more than 12% of the characters on our screens!) As Christie Hefner, the articulate president of Playboy Enterprises (the AFA successfully lobbied the chain of 7-11 convenience stores to stop carrying *Playboy* magazine) points out, the AFA is just a fringe group—a highly organized fringe group perhaps, but a fringe group nonetheless.

Despite Wildmon's exhortations to the contrary, Yule's film is quite balanced. Wildmon gets plenty of opportunity to express exactly what he feels; if he comes across—even to himself, apparently—as a fool, it's not because the film has been edited with a bias toward the liberal left. But DAMNED IN THE USA is an unremarkable, if solid, effort, adding little fuel or insight to an important debate. *(Adult situations, sexual situations.)*

p, Paul Yule; d, Paul Yule; ph, Mark Benjamin, Robert Achs, Luke Sacher; ed, John Street

Documentary/Political **(PR: C MPAA: NR)**

DANCE MACABRE
21st Century Productions; Power Pictures; Lenfilm ~ Columbia TriStar Home Video c

Robert Englund *(Anthony Wager/The Madame)*, Michelle Zeitlin *(Jessica)*, Alexander Sergeyev *(Alex)*, Irena Davidoff *(Olga)*, Nina Goldman *(Claudine)*, Julene Renee *(Angela)*, Natasha Fesson *(Natasha)*, Marianna Moen *(Ingrid)*

Originally intended as a sequel to the Robert Englund version of THE PHANTOM OF THE OPERA, DANCE MACABRE is based on a cinematic ruse so transparent, obvious and cliched it boggles the mind. The result is a misbegotten mix of PSYCHO, SUSPIRIA and co-executive producer Harry Alan Towers's beloved TEN LITTLE INDIANS theme.

Anthony Wagner (Englund) runs a ballet academy in St. Petersburg, Russia, with a woman known as "The Madame" who's supposedly Wagner's old love Svetlana, confined to a wheelchair after a motorcycle accident. (Unfortunately for viewers, from the moment she first appears onscreen, it's glaringly clear that "The Madame" is actually Englund in pasty makeup and a wig, and all the scenes of Wagner having "conversations" with her in an upstairs room don't hide the dual-identity trick one bit.) Wagner takes a special interest in accepting a reluctant American student named Jessica (Michelle Zeitlin) when he sees that she bears a striking resemblance to the young Svetlana.

Once Jessica begins her dance training, the other girls start falling victim to a mysterious killer. First, Jessica's roommate Claudine (Nina Goldman) is drowned in the academy's hot tub; then Angela (Julene Renee) is hanged at the St. Petersburg Ballet, where the troupe has gone for a special class. The Madame explains the disappearances by telling the other girls that their friends have returned home suddenly, and lets them out for a night at a nearby club to relax (and allow for some gratuitous rock 'n' roll sequences). While Jessica continues a developing romance with a local photographer named Alex (Alexander Sergeyev), another student, Natasha (Natasha Fesson), is thrown in front of a moving subway train. When a fourth death occurs—Ingrid (Marianna Moen), who has recently kicked a drug habit, is tossed from a window to her death, which is explained to the girls as a suicide—the other students finally get the idea that sticking around may not be a good idea and withdraw from the academy.

Wagner convinces Jessica to stay for one-on-one training with him, and soon she discovers what the audience has figured out from the start: Wagner and The Madame are one and the same, and the real Svetlana is a corpse sitting in an upstairs room. After a confrontation that results in the deaths of both Alex and Wagner's assistant Olga (Irina Davidoff), Wagner, who killed the others to eliminate Jessica's competition, forces her to continue her sessions with him. But when she goes for her audition before the St. Petersburg Ballet, Jessica refuses to play "Svetlana" for Wagner, leading him to jump, in a fit of mania, off a balcony to his death.

It's hard to decide which aspect of DANCE MACABRE is more idiotic: the girls, who never cotton to the resemblance between Wagner and The Madame and take a while to find the string of disappearances and "accidents" strange, or the screenplay, which asks the audience to accept this foolishness at face value. Writer-director Greydon Clark tries to fudge the issue by having Wagner, Alex, The Madame and Olga make themselves scarce just before each murder, but anyone with any familiarity with the genre will see through all this right away.

It's almost a subsidiary point that none of the murders themselves are the least bit scary, and that Jessica is too utterly vapid to engender any sympathy at all. How can one be scared for a girl who, after all her friends have left due to the strange events, easily accepts Wagner's invitation to stick around when she never wanted to attend the school in the first place? The Russian settings are pretty but used only for travelogue value, and the movie throws in exploitation elements as if programmed by a computer: MTV club scene here, gratuitous sex scene there.

Considering that veteran director Clark (SATAN'S CHEERLEADERS, JOYSTICKS) and producer Menahem Golan were also responsible for 1990's THE FORBIDDEN DANCE, this film's only virtue is that, when Jessica proclaims she wants to abandon ballet for her "own style" of dancing, she isn't later seen doing the *lambada. (Violence, substance abuse, nudity, sexual situations.)*

p, Menahem Golan; d, Greydon Clark; w, Greydon Clark, Michael J. Murray; ed, Earl Watson; m, Dan Slider

Horror **(PR: O MPAA: R)**

DANCE WITH DEATH ★★½
90m Concorde ~ HBO Video c

Maxwell Caulfield *(Shaughnessy)*, Barbara Alyn Woods *(Kelly Preston/Dominique)*, Martin Mull *(Art)*, Elena Sahagen *(Jodie)*, Michael James McDonald *(Henry)*, Tracey Burch *(Whitney)*, Steven Lloyd Williams *(Dermot)*, Drew Snyder *(Hopper)*, Maria Ford, Catya Sassoon

Until the ending scene carries the expression "carrying a torch" to a far-fetched extreme, DANCE WITH DEATH is moderately entertaining sleaze for audiences with a yen for perfectly proportioned females, a predilection for red herrings and a taste for colorfully reprobate murder suspects.

On the surface, this sexploitation whodunit is about Kelly Preston (Barbara Alyn Woods) an ambitious reporter who goes undercover to crack the case of the topless-dancer killings. Yet it's equally fascinated by that reporter's growing interest in her new sideline as an exotic dancer. Also walking on the wild side of life are: Dermot (Steven Lloyd Williams), a horny bartender with no luck with the ladies; Art (Martin Mull), the even hornier proprietor of the seedy club and a part-time blackmailer; and Jodie (Elena Sahagen), a tough lesbian who has an eye for new girl Kelly and makes a quick recovery after her last girlfriend does the death-dance with the psycho killer. Kelly's own boss, editor Hopper (Drew Snyder), has a checkered past involving sexual assault charges and a proclivity for dating strippers, including one of the serial killer's victims.

When cop-in-charge Shaughnessy (Maxwell Caulfield) solicits Kelly's cooperation, she admits her suspicions about her sexist pig boss, but Shaughnessy collects damaging evidence against club patron Henry (Michael James McDonald), a leering customer who's handy with a blade. By the time a few more dancers fall prey to the killer, the oddly intense policeman beds Kelly and insists she renounce her sideline on the nude dance circuit. Then, once the cops shoot nutty Henry in self-defense, the case is officially closed. Although Kelly's creepy boss bumps off Art for blackmailing him, he's not the real culprit. Actually, the killer is the purity-obsessed cop, Shaughnessy. After Kelly realizes he's a sicko, he closes in for the kill. But never underestimate a reporter who can dance topless; Shaughnessy does his own final dance with death as Kelly literally sets him ablaze.

Some viewers may be offended by what might be considered soft-core titillation in which helpless exotic terpsichoreans are stalked to death and made to pay for the sick fantasies of male America. But since the arousal factor takes a back seat to the detective work and since just as many men die as women during the running time, feminists may not wish to be too critical. After all, a gutsy career woman cracks the case without sacrificing her independence on the job—or in the bedroom. Even after sleeping with the handsome killer, Kelly never wavers in trying to get her scoop.

Whatever deeper meanings about career integrity or male-female relationships you care to derive from this tassel-twirler, DANCE WITH DEATH is good escapism for heavy-breathers and crime buffs alike. It may not be socially redeeming, but it never commits the cardinal sin of being boring. *(Violence, profanity, sexual situations.)*

p, Mike Elliott; d, Charles Philip Moore; w, Daryl Haney; ph, Bill Molina; ed, Christopher Roth; prod d, James Schumaker; art d, Amy Ancona; set d, Kendal Schaefer; cos, Loretta Pickering

Erotic/Thriller **(PR: O MPAA: R)**

DANZON ★★★

(Mexico) 120m Instituto Mexicano de Cinematografia; Macondo Cine Video; Fondo de Fomento a la Calidad Cinematografica; Television Espanola; Tabasco Films; Gobierno del Estado de Veracruz ~ Sony Pictures Classics c

Maria Rojo *(Julia)*, Carmen Salinas *(Dona Ti)*, Blanca Guerra *(Chocolate)*, Tito Vasconcelos *(Susy)*, Victor Vasconcelos *(Ruben)*, Margarita Isabel *(Silvia)*, Chely Godinez *(Tere)*, Martha Navarro *(Bruja)*, Daniel Rergis *(Carmelo)*, Adjari Chazaro *(Perla)*, Cesar Sobrevals *(Chucho)*, Ines Jacome *(Victoria)*, Emiliano Guerra *(Hijo de la Colorado)*, Mikhail Kaminin *(Russian Sailor)*, Rodrigo Gomez *(Mulatto)*, Luis Gerardo *(Juan)*, Sergio Colmenares *(Karla)*, Angel Del Valle *(Yadira)*, Nicolas Castro *(Cook)*, Juan Hernandez *(1st Official)*, Ruben Benitez *(Officer Martinez)*, Chato Cejudo *(Guerito)*, Indio Mendoza *(Master of Ceremonies)*, Javier Molina *(Drunk)*, Rosario Gonzalez *(Viejita Parque Zamora)*, Chato Reyes *(Presumido)*, Miguelito *(Maletero)*, Norma Leyva *(Mujer en Fondo)*, Claudia Rodriguez *(Young Woman)*, Rocio Rodriguez *(1st Woman)*, Roberto Ortiz *(Locutor Xeu)*, Adolfo Aldana *(Lozano)*, Carlos Catalan *(Galan Salon Los Angeles)*, Micke Del Villar *(Galan Salon Los Angeles)*, Victor Carpintiero

A favorite on the international festival circuit—indeed, the first Mexican film in over a dozen years to be featured in the prestigious Director's Fortnight at Cannes—DANZON marks filmmaker Maria Novaro's return to the screen following LOLA, her acclaimed 1990 debut.

Julia (Maria Rojo), a middle-aged widow, leads a contented life: she works as a Mexico City telephone operator, taking every Wednesday evening off to enjoy her sole passion, dancing at the local club. When her longtime dance partner, Carmelo (Daniel Rergis), disappears without an explanation, Julia travels to Veracruz—his hometown—to look for him. With the help of Susy (Tito Vasconcelos), a transvestite performer she befriends, Julia inquires all over town, to no avail. Discouraged after missing a ship her partner supposedly was working on, Julia meets a young tugboat sailor (Victor Carpintiero), who's attracted to her. The attraction is mutual, but Julia is reluctant to go out with him because of his youth. Resigned to the failure of her search, she gives in to her feelings and has a brief affair with the sailor, after which she returns to Mexico City. Back in the dance hall, Julia allows herself to dance with another man. As she dances, someone cuts in: it's her missing partner, back as mysteriously as he vanished.

While LOLA chronicled the daily struggles of a single mother with hard-hitting realism, DANZON could be seen as Novaro's deliberate reaction to her previous project's style; the screenplay (written in collaboration with her sister Beatriz) is a fable-like story inspired by traditional modes of Latin American popular culture and their effect on people's lives.

Novaro's subject is the *danzon*, a Latin American musical genre that sings of lost loves and betrayals with a light—almost cheerful — resignation mirrored in its soft, graceful rhythym (very different from the fatalistic *bolero*). Like many middle-aged and older women, Julia takes the danzon very seriously; it is "the most important thing in her life" for her, and she vainly tries to pass her dancing tradition on to her daughter. When her partner disappears, she refuses to dance with anyone else. The dance has become a ritual for her, and in her mind she cannot deviate from her accepted routine.

Julia's trip to Veracruz begins as a quest, a search for her missing partner. As it develops, this quest turns into an inner voyage of self-examination; after initial desperation, the good people she meets, including Dona Ti (Carmen Salinas), the kindly owner of the hotel she stays in, make her realize that there is more to life than her dogmatic beliefs. Veracruz teaches her to look at her romantic notions in a different light: life is best enjoyed spontaneously, without rigid preconceptions. Julia repositions her cultural values in a new, life-affirming philosophy.

Novarro succeeds in giving her film the rhythyms of the music she loves; in essence, DANZON is literally a cinematic danzon, gracefully moving from contentment to sadness to desperation to resignation and happiness. The musical numbers performed by the featured bands give the film a warm, nostalgic mood. Maria Rojo shines above the good cast, giving a touching performance as the romantic Julia.

Its good points aside, DANZON has some serious flaws. The story is founded on the strong pull the missing partner has on Julia. Unfortunately, he's nothing but a cipher, appearing only fleetingly in the opening sequences—hardly enough time to establish a rapport with the audience. It's hard to identify with Julia's longing for someone we don't really know. Susy's character does not rise above the stereotype of the sentimental homosexual who gives moral support to the protagonist and suffers in silence for being rejected by society. DANZON purports to be a critique of old-fashioned cultural perceptions, but its gentle, grit-free approach replicates the old romantic genres of Mexico's "Golden Age" with little irony.

In the end, DANZON is a triumph of style over substance, a well-made film that will leave its audiences with a smile on their faces as it raises a point so subtle as to be easily missed among the gorgeous strains of the dance-hall bands. *(Adult situations.)*

p, Jorge Sanchez; d, Maria Novaro; w, Maria Novaro, Beatriz Novaro; ph, Rodrigo Garcia; ed, Nelson Rogriguez, Maria Novaro; art d, Marisa Pecanins, Norberto Sanchez

Romance/Drama/Dance **(PR: C MPAA: PG-13)**

DARK HORSE ★★½

89m D Horse Inc. ~ LIVE Home Video c

Mimi Rogers *(Dr. Susan Hadley)*, Ed Begley, Jr. *(Jack Mills)*, Ari Meyers *(Allison Mills)*, Samantha Eggar *(Mrs. Curtis)*, Tab Hunter *(Perkins)*, Chad Smith *(Clint)*, Bojesse Christopher *(Michael Aarons)*, Natasha Gregson Wagner *(Martha)*, Donovan Leitch *(J.B. Hadley)*, Brooke Cuskey *(Amy)*

"Kate & Allie" star Ari Meyers heads the cast in DARK HORSE, a moving story of a young girl's struggle with change and personal tragedies.

High school student Allison Mills (Meyers) is trying to cope with the death of her mother, relocating from LA to northern California and living with an over-protective father, Jack Mills (Ed Begley, Jr.). Eager to defy her father and do something wild, Allison sneaks out one night with her felony-bound boyfriend Clint (Chad Smith). After they get into town, Clint gets drunk, and picks up another girl, and Allison, in a fit of adolescent rage, drives off with Clint's truck and crashes it.

As punishment, Allison must do ten weeks of community service. She's assigned to Dr. Susan Hadley (Mimi Rogers) who raises horses and works with handicapped children on her ranch. Allison is not thrilled with doing chores or taking orders from Susan, but gets used to the routine and eventually gets to like life on the ranch. And she quickly becomes attached to Jet, an injured horse that money-hungry owner Perkins (Tab Hunter) wants to race.

After finally nursing Jet back to health, Susan and Allison transport him back to Perkins. But enroute they have an accident and Allison is seriously injured while trying to free Jet from his trailer. Allison and the horse both survive but are terribly crippled. Feeling defeated, Allison is resigned to spending her days sitting alone in a wheelchair. Attempts by family and friends to motivate Allison to try to walk again fail. In the final scene, a ranch hand accidentally leaves a tractor in gear which crashes into the barn. Jet falls down but eventually manages to stand up and even start running. Simultaneously, Allison finally stands up and begins slowly to walk again.

The obvious parallel in DARK HORSE is, needless to say, Jet the horse and Allison the troubled teen. However, J.E. MacLean's screenplay is geared toward children and the film does succeed in presenting a tale of overcoming adversity and growing up. The most affecting scene is between Brooke Cuskey and Meyers. Cuskey plays Amy, a young girl who's been on crutches her whole life. She gives Allison her crutches and very assertively tells her to stand up. Director David Hemmings has presented this exchange in a way that is straightforward and not sappy. The rest of the cast is equally competent, but Rogers (SOMEONE TO WATCH OVER ME, THE RAPTURE), who's a very powerful actress, doesn't have a very challenging role.

p, Allan Glaser; d, David Hemmings; w, J.E. MacLean, (from the story by Tab Hunter); ph, Steve Yaconelli; ed, Marjorie O'Connel; m, Roger Bellon; art d, Prudence Hemmings, Bernard Hyde; set d, Mary Hislop; cos, Dona Granata

Drama/Children's **(PR: A MPAA: PG)**

DAUGHTERS OF THE DUST ★★★★

113m Geechee Girls Productions; American Playhouse Theatrical Films ~ Kino International c

Adisa Anderson *(Eli Peazant)*, Barbara O *(Yellow Mary)*, Cheryl Lynn Bruce *(Viola)*, Cora Lee Day *(Nana Peazant)*, Geraldine Dunston *(Viola's Mother)*, Vertamae Grovensor *(Hairbraider)*, Tommy Hicks *(Mr. Snead)*, Kaycee Moore *(Haagar)*, Eartha D. Robinson *(Myown)*, Alva Rogers *(Eula Peazant)*, Cornell "Kofi" Royal *(Daddy Mac)*, Catherine Tarver *(Woman with Baby)*, Bahni Turpin *(Iona Peazant)*, Kai Lynn Warren *(The Unborn Child)*, Trula Hoosier *(Trula)*, Umar Ubdurrahman *(Bilal)*, Malik Farrakhan *(Newlywed Man)*, Sherry Jackson *(Older Cousin)*, Ervin Green *(Baptist Minister)*, Marcus Humphrey *(Boatman)*, Bernard Wilson *(Boatman)*, Althea Lang *(Newlywed Woman)*, Jasmine Lee *(Peazant Baby)*, Dalisia Robinson *(Peazant Baby)*, Willie Faulkner *(Peazant Man)*, Joe Taylor *(Peazant Man)*, Frank Brown *(Peazant Man)*, Rueben Fripp *(Peazant Man)*, Derrick Coaxum *(Peazant Boy)*, Neil Howard *(Peazant Boy)*, Jared Warren, Zenovia Green, Taira Miller, Tiffanye Hills *(Peazant Children)*, Jamer Freeman *(Pete)*, Detrell Freeman *(Re-Pete)*, Vivian Dawson *(Rice Husker)*, Inez Griffin *(Rice Husker)*, M. Cochise Anderson *(St. Julen Lastchild)*, Darrel Cook *(Moss Gatherer)*, Julius Cook *(Moss Gatherer)*, Benjamin Gillens *(Minister's Assistant)*, Ronald Daise *(Processional Man)*, Marie Smalls *(Woman Being Baptizied)*, Lonnie Moon, Dewitt Parker, Emma Robinson, Taylor Thompson, Virginia Green, Maceo Griffin, Archie Thomas, Raymond Paige, Ervena Falkner, J.R. Wilson, Wilhemina Wilson *(Baptismal Processional Members)*, Tarell Brown, Shanna Parker, Belle White, Stanley White, Maxine Royale, Georgia Wiggins, Carolyn Garris, Ella Powell, Bernice Jenkins, Lilian Johnson, Jackie Parker *(Indigo Plantation Workers)*, Sharria Johnson *(Young Nana Peazant)*, Leroy Simmons, Jr. *(Young Daddy Mac)*, Leroy Simmons *(Shad Peazant)*

The first feature-length film by a female African-American filmmaker to receive theatrical release in the US, Julie Dash's DAUGHTERS OF THE DUST explores one day on a Sea Island as three generations of women confront their common past, their futures and each other.

In 1902, two members of the Peazant family, straitlaced Viola (Cheryl Lynn Bruce) and worldly Yellow Mary (Barbara O) make the crossing to one of South Carolina's Sea Islands to pick up the rest of the family and escort them in a move to the North. Trula (Trula Hoosier), Mary's soulmate, accompanies her and the thoroughly modern Mr. Snead (Tommy Hicks) goes along to document the excursion. But they arrive to find the rest of the family conflicted over leaving. Eli (Adisa Anderson) is trying to convince the Peazant matriarch, stubborn, old Nana (Cora Lee Day) that leaving means progress for the whole family. Eli is also struggling with his young wife Eula (Alva Rodgers) because she's carrying another man's baby—the unborn narrator of the day's events.

Haagar (Kaycee Moore) and the other women of her generation are frustrated with Nana and her ties to the past and the Island, but Hagaar's daughter, Iona (Bahni Turpin) wants to remain behind with her Cherokee boyfriend, St. Julen Lastchild (M. Cochise Anderson). Citified Viola and Yellow Mary are at first put off by the backwater habits of their family, but they begin to enjoy reacquainting themselves. Mary and Trula stroll on the beach with Eula. Viola gives all the teenage girls an etiquette lesson. In the afternoon, the family gathers on the beach to indulge in a luscious picnic of gumbo, corn bread, rice, shrimp and crab.

After the meal, the Peazant women air their old grievances, attacking Yellow Mary for her questionable morals and Nana for her attachment to the ways of their African ancestors. A passionate outburst by Eula breaks them down and brings them together, and they all walk into the woods to receive a blessing from Nana. She stands in front of an arch formed by the curve in a great, fallen tree, and literally entwines animism and Christianity, asking her relatives to kiss a bible tied with a charm, to bide her family on their way North.

Yellow Mary and Eula decide to remain on the Island with Nana—they are her spiritual heirs. The rest of the family boards a rickety, wooden boat headed North, save Iona who pulls away at the last minute and rushes to St. Julen Lastchild.

In her poetic feature debut, independent filmmaker Julie Dash abandons traditional narrative forms in order to create a new way of looking at the lives of these African-American women. She presents their day as a collage of images: snippets of arguments and confessions; blued hands wringing cloth in vats of indigo dye; girls dancing on the beach; cabin walls decorated with flamboyant drawings; and always quilts, the symbol of the beauty and internal coherence underlying their varied experiences.

Through this impressionistic style Dash, who reportedly spent thirteen years getting DAUGHTERS OF THE DUST off the ground, is able to investigate the basic theme of generations struggling for and against progress and also to present a volume of information about each character individually, the gorgeous and isolated physical setting, the daily customs that reveal the link between African and Sea Island culture—all details that inform the severity of the family's conflict.

Grounding DAUGHTERS OF THE DUST are forceful performances from all of the Peazant women, especially Cora Lee Davis, Barbara O and Alva Rodgers. These three actresses are utterly unselfconscious emotionally. The direction of the other characters is at times inconsistent, moments of theatricality disrupting the more open, natural style of most of the film.

Releasing one's self to the new rhythm of this film can be difficult; the story is allusive, the Island history sketchy, and the precise relationships of the family members undefined. Yet, if her suggestive presentation escapes straightforward analysis, one cannot help but be mesmerized by Dash's unique vision. *(Adult situations.)*

p, Julie Dash, Arthur Jafa; d, Julie Dash; w, Julie Dash; ph, Arthur Jafa; ed, Amy Carey, Joseph Burton; m, John Barnes; prod d, Kerry Marshall; art d, Michael Kelly Williams; cos, Arline Burks

Drama/Historical **(PR: A MPAA: NR)**

DAY IN OCTOBER, A ★★½

97m Just Betzer Films; Kenneth Madsen Film Productions; Panorama Film International ~ Castle Hill Productions c

D.B. Sweeney *(Niels Jensen)*, Kelly Wolf *(Sara Kublitz)*, Tovah Feldshuh *(Emma Kublitz)*, Daniel Benzali *(Solomon Kublitz)*, Ole Lemmeke *(Larson)*, Kim Romer *(Arne)*, Anders Peter Bro *(Kurt)*, Lars Oluf Larsen *(Willy)*, Morten Suurballe *(Peter)*, Jens Arentzen *(Paul)*, Lily Weiding *(Secretary)*, Arne Hansen *(Hansen)*, Jorgen Teytaud *(Fisherman)*, Jorgen Bidstrup *(Moviegoer)*, Dale Lovett *(Policeman)*, Thomas Hogsbro *(Danish Nazi)*, Anina Ritterband Rosenbaum *(Little Girl)*, Daglan *(Rabbi)*, Benjamin Levy *(Cantor)*, Klaus Hjuler *(Young Dane)*

While its title refers to the successful evacuation of some 7,000 Jews from Denmark to neutral Sweden on the eve of their arrest and deportation by the occupying Nazis in 1943, A DAY IN OCTOBER focuses on the plight of one particular family as they face this historic event.

Denmark would seem to be an exceptional case in occupied Europe. First, it was ruled not by the German Army or the dreaded SS, but by the officials of the Foreign Ministry who ruled with kid gloves for some time. The country also did not have a deep tradition of extreme right-wing politics like France or of anti-Semitism like Poland. There is also a hint of links to high-ranking anti-Nazis in the complex realm of German officialdom. Most of this material is missing from A DAY IN OCTOBER, which rather suggests that the rescue operation was improvisational, though one would think that the arrival of several thousand refugees on Swedish shores practically overnight would involve some preparation.

The Kublitz family appear well-off Danish Jews: father Solomon (Daniel Benzali) works as a bookkeeper at the local radio-parts factory while his young daughter Sara (Kelly Wolf) works at a nearby cinema. That cinema becomes the site of the prankish act of a group of saboteurs when they jam a genuine Nazi newsreel and substitute a looped version of a sequence from TRIUMPH OF THE WILL that has Storm Troopers and SS men marchingn backwards and forwards doing the "Lambeth Walk." Headed by Niels Jensen (D.B. Sweeney), the saboteurs quickly advance to more ambitious projects.

They prepare a primitive bomb disguised in a box of beer bottles. Unfortunately a thirsty worker triggers the bomb prematurely and in the ensuing shootout with German troops, a number of the saboteurs are shot and wounded, but Niels gets away despite a bullet in his shoulder. Sara discovers his unconscious body and drags him into the family shed. Solomon, meanwhile, frets about the senselessness of the bombing and the possible retaliation by the Germans. Sara's mother, Emma (Tovah Feldshuh), discovers her with the wounded Niels and decides to use her nurse's skills to help him.

At the factory, Solomon witnesses the arrest of the two surviving saboteurs and sees them apparently kept locked in a wing of the plant. Later, in conversation with Sara, he admits that the factory is making weapon parts and agrees to try to contact the pair of prisoners. Feigning a need for supplies, he gains acccess to the factory wing and discovers that they are already dead and have been propped up as bait in a prepared trap for their comrades.

That realization and Sara's influence persuades Solomon to plant the new bomb Niels has made in a place where it will destroy the weapons production wing. This sabotage coincides with the report that the seizure of all Danish Jews is being planned, so that the Kublitzs' fate now lies in the hands of Niels Jensen's resistance group. Unfortunately, a local Danish Nazi, Larsen (Ole Lemmeke), whose anti-Semitism has fuelled his suspicion of Kublitz, has taken it upon himself to follow the bookkeeper. Larsen soon confronts Sara in the hiding place she shares with Niels.

Despite very good performances from Benzali and Lemmeke, as respectively the unwilling saboteur and the quiet racist, A DAY IN OCTOBER is a competent collection of cliches. The sly obstruction of German security troops and the occasional unwillingness of troops to insist on the arrest of the odd Jew was better depicted in George Seaton's THE COUNTERFEIT TRAITOR some thirty years ago. *(Violence, adult situations.)*

p, Just Betzer, Philippe Rivier; d, Kenneth Madsen; w, Damian F. Slattery; ph, Henning Kristiansen; ed, Nicolas Gaster; m, Jens Lysdal, Adam Gorgoni; prod d, Sven Wichmann; set d, Torben Baekmark Pedersen; cos, Lotte Dandanell

Historical/War/Romance **(PR: C MPAA: PG-13)**

DEAD CERTAIN ★½

(Canada/U.K./U.S.) 93m DB Films; IF-Films ~ Hemdale Home Video c

Francesco Quinn *(John Reed)*, Brad Dourif *(John Barnes)*, Joel Kaiser *(Frank Jones)*, Karen Russell, Jonathan Grinner

Moviedom's infatuation with serial killers continues in DEAD CERTAIN, a slick, sick slice of nastiness that film forensics should quickly identify as a takeoff on Jonathan Demme's THE SILENCE OF THE LAMBS.

Back in 1979 John Barnes was convicted of cutting the heart out of girlfriend Debbi Jones (the proof apparently being that he's portrayed by veteran screen nutcase Brad Dourif). Flash ahead to the present, when Barnes, a pathetic human wreck still protesting his innocence, is discharged, much to the fury of the investigating Detective John Reed (Francesco Quinn). Reed is a real piece of work, making BAD LIEUTENANT's Harvey Keitel look like Officer Friendly: Reed's a slovenly, unshaven, vicious, lapsed Catholic addicted to heroin and hookers, trailing behind him a shattered marriage and an unresolved obsession with the long-dead Debbi. During custodial visits with his small son he takes the tyke to a favorite nudie bar where they swap profane precinct shop talk about the Jones case.

Reed is "dead certain" that Barnes is guilty, and when a freshly gutted female corpse turns up the cringing ex-con immediately gets thrown back in the clink. But the bloody butcherings continue. Obviously Barnes isn't responsible, but he's had taunting calls and letters from the copycat killer, and Reed reluctantly cozies up to his former prime suspect for advice on nabbing the new slasher on the block. Barnes claims to know nothing, and the whole grim business drags on for a hellish 110 minutes before the murderer is fingered (literally—he amputates digits as part of his modus operandi): he's Frank Jones (Joel Kaiser), little-known brother of Debbi. It seems he too felt Barnes got off easy, and took up serial-killing to drive the accused over the edge.

In that he succeeds. An amoral conclusion finds Barnes committing suicide, while Reed cleans up his act and regains his kids. (Frank helpfully disembowelled the detective's ex-wife.) A final tableau shows the restored family in a happy domestic setting—but the miracle of flashbacks reveals that it was really jilted lover John Reed who slaughtered Debbi all those years ago and pinned the guilt on Barnes.

Writer-director Anders Palm renders this ugly yarn in fever-dream fashion, abetted by cinematographer John DeBorman's florid lensing techniques: infrared b&w film stock for the flashbacks, scanlined video for stalker stuff, flashing strobes for the antihero's druggy visions, and rainwashed nocturnal neon noir for everything else. Like an oil slick on stagnant water it's an interesting sight but unhealthy to ingest. The performances are equally crazed, and lines of dialogue are typically prefaced by "You sick bastard!" Freaky Frank introduces himself at one point as "the Candyman," though any resemblance to the similarly titled 1992 horror release flatters neither it nor DEAD CERTAIN, which arrived in most territories as a direct-to-video castoff. *(Violence, substance abuse, profanity, nudity, sexual situations, adult situations.)*

p, Anders Palm, Mark Cutforth; d, Anders Palm; w, Anders Palm; ph, John DeBorman; ed, Roy Burge; m, Charlie Mole, Richard Derbyshire; art d, Nick White

Thriller/Crime **(PR: O MPAA: R)**

DEADBOLT ★½

95m Image Organization; Allegro Films ~ New Line Home Video c

Justine Bateman, Adam Baldwin, Chris Mulkey, Michele Scarabelli, Cyndi Pass, Isabelle Truchon

To call it "Single White Male" would be an insult to SINGLE WHITE FEMALE, but DEADBOLT is virtually a sex-reversed carbon copy of that better-known hit, this time starring Justine Bateman as a remarkably dense med student who takes in a male roommate and gets, as they say, more than she bargains for.

Concerned about being alone and unprotected in the big city after breaking up with her lawyer husband (Chris Mulkey), med school student Bateman advertises for a male roommate (presumably, since no females apply) after her spacious, stylish apartment is broken into. Her first choice is pre-empted from moving in after his skull is crushed with a car jack handle, leaving the field clear for easygoing, attractive Adam Baldwin, whose first hints of weirdness are low-key enough. Like Michael Keaton in PACIFIC HEIGHTS, Baldwin appears to have no job, yet he pays for everything with big wads of cash. But he is a skilled carpenter and begins doing minor remodeling and repair jobs around the apartment, which endears him to Bateman immediately.

Much fussier Mulkey, who's trying to win Bateman back, finds that Baldwin has left no paper trail whatsoever during his life. In the face of such fact-checking, Baldwin is of course forced to murder Mulkey by getting him drunk and inducing him to commit suicide. Baldwin goes on to get Bateman fired from her research job, steals her loan application from the mail so she runs short of money and later kills her suspicious best friend, apparently the sole person at Bateman's med school who's at all curious about why she's stopped showing up for class.

While Bateman is away in the country for a few days to recover from Mulkey's "suicide," Baldwin radically redecorates the apartment, adding bars and soundproofing to Bateman's bedroom in which he imprisons her upon her return. Winning Baldwin's trust enough to let her out for a candlelight dinner, Bateman spikes his dessert with some botulism culture from her research lab she had apparently been stowing at home for just the right occasion. Escaping and finding shelter at the apartment of a friend (Michele Scarabelli), Bateman awaits the inevitable arrival of Baldwin and, after some minor skirmishing (the man is addled by botulism, after all), manages to dump him through a skylight to his death.

Though mounted with conviction by director Doug Jackson and acted with more skill than it deserves, DEADBOLT is one suspense thriller most likely to cause its chills from the ferocious winds blowing through the huge holes in its scenario.

Forget wondering why cagey city girl Bateman would suddenly turn over a set of her keys to a guy with no discernible personal history. Forget trying to figure out why Bateman, a responsible student and would-be research scientist, brings a bottle of botulism home from the lab and stores it in a kitchen cabinet within easy reach of a young child who often visits her. And definitely forget questioning why the police don't even begin to get suspicious until well after practically everybody Bateman has known since she was an infant dies violently in the space of a week while she herself seems to disappear from the face of the earth.

Why is this movie even called DEADBOLT? Granted, it's a nifty title, but deadbolts do not figure prominently either in the plot or the climax. A more logical title would have been "Botulism," but that undoubtedly would have been too perfect a preemptive review as well as a description of the plot. In fact, DEADBOLT isn't even bad enough to be sickening. It's just more of the same. *(Violence, adult situations.)*

p, Tom Berry, Franco Battista; d, Doug Jackson; w, Mara Trafficante, Frank Rehwaldt; ph, Rodney Gibbons; ed, Yves Langlois; m, Milan Kymlicka; prod d, Perri Gorrara; set d, Amy Burt; cos, Aline Gilmore

Thriller **(PR: C MPAA: R)**

DEADLY BET ★★½

93m Pepin/Merhi Productions ~ PM Home Video c

Charlene Tilton *(Isabella)*, Jeff Wincott *(Angelo Scala)*, Steven Vincent Leigh *(Rico Daraby)*, Ray Mancini *(Charlie)*, Jerry Tiffe *(Frank)*, Patty Toy *(Xmas)*, Mike Toney *(Johnny)*, Michael Delano *(Greek)*, Sherrie Rose *(Doris)*, Carl Butto

There's a lot of ROCKY and a bit of HONEYMOON IN VEGAS in DEADLY BET, a cut-above-average kickboxing opus starring Jeff Wincott (best known for TV's "Night Heat" series) as Las Vegas gambler Angelo Scala, who's just run out of luck.

Idyllic plans to move to Colorado with his fiancee Isabella (Charlene Tilton, the petite star of TV's "Dallas") are dashed as Angelo, in hopes of financial security for their fresh start, has stupidly put Isabella up as collateral on a bet, and then loses a kickboxing bout to Rico Daraby (Steven Vincent Leigh), who controls the Vegas underground fighting business. Fed up with Angelo's behavior, Isabella shacks up with the rich suave Rico, while Angelo, losing a basketball game bet to a loan shark called the Greek (Michael Delano), is forced to work for the Greek collecting bad debts, along with thug Johnny (Mike Toney). With

Isabella out of his life, Angelo boozily hits the skids but soon recovers, gives up alcohol and gambling, and trains for a half-million-dollar-stakes, winner-take-all, fifty-man kickboxing tournament. After besting Rico in the grueling penultimate bout, Angelo is reunited with Isabella and they head out to Colorado.

The most interesting aspect of Joseph Merhi and Robert Tiffe's screenplay is not Angelo's fairly cliched plight but the love-hate relationship between Isabella (who doesn't know Angelo has bet and lost her to Rico) and the slimy but charming Rico, who is excellently played by Leigh, a veteran of similar action fare (CHINA WHITE, RING OF FIRE). Richard W. Munchkin's direction is undistinguished but fully adequate, with the kickboxing sequences expertly choreographed (by Eric Lee) and performed by Leigh and Wincott, whose acting skills are more incisive as a fighter than as a lover. DEADLY BET is a well mounted production for the prolific LA team of Joseph Merhi and Richard Pepin, the latter also responsible for the sharp-looking cinematography.

Boxing fans will note former lightweight boxing champ Ray "Boom Boom" Mancini in a small role as the minor hoodlum Charlie. Released direct-to-video. *(Violence, sexual situations, profanity.)*

p, Joseph Merhi, Richard Pepin; d, Richard W. Munchkin; w, Joseph Merhi, Robert Tiffe; ph, Richard Pepin; ed, John Weidner, Geraint Bell; m, Louis Febre; prod d, Greg Martin; art d, Greg Martin; cos, Christine Boudreaux

Crime/Action/Martial Arts (PR: O MPAA: R)

DEADLY CURRENTS ★★★

(Canada) 115m Associated Producers ~ Spotlight Public Relations & Marketing c

Lieutenant Kobi Motiv, Juliano Mor, Amir Kolban, Hayan Yacoub, Shim Navon

Admirably balanced and superbly crafted, if a trifle slick, DEADLY CURRENTS is Simcha Jacobovici's documentary examination of an ancient but, sadly, ongoing conflict.

In 1980, the Israeli government decided to promote increased Jewish settlement in the West Bank, provoking protest from Palestinian Arab leaders who view the region as their birthright and spiritual homeland. In December 1987, Muslim residents of the West Bank and Gaza launched a series of violent demonstrations against Israeli authorities. This *intifada*, or uprising, has continued to the present day in a cycle of protest and police reaction that has led to the deaths of hundreds of demonstrators and a crisis of Israeli control in the occupied territories.

With its arresting visuals, DEADLY CURRENTS underscores the fact that, while the Israeli-Palestinian conflict stems from the expansion of Islam from Arabia during the 7th century, it is being played out on a modern stage; the Israeli soldiers are armed with sophisticated weaponry and the *shabab*, as the Palestinian youth activists are known, may fight with rocks and molotov cocktails, but their typical uniform consists of brand-name sweat suits and sneakers. They're also armed with spray cans, which they deftly wield to write political slogans. And, in their ongoing efforts to elicit international sympathy, the Palestinians have been cannily playing the *intifada* to the TV camera. The film also alleges that the more unscrupulous members of the foreign press, always on the make for a story, habitually provoke incidents.

The Israeli soldiers interviewed in the film, particularly Lieutenant Kobi Motiv, come across as resolute and unyielding. Defending themselves against frequent accusations of brutality, they claim that, except in extreme circumstances, only rubber bullets are fired; unfortunately, these can do considerable damage, particularly to a child's tender flesh—and children, the film makes clear, are an active part of the *intifada*. Of course, the Palestinian Arabs, who resent the increasingly oppressive methods employed by their adversaries, come across as equally determined. While some express the desire merely to live in freedom and dignity in their own land, and not to destroy the state of Israel, there are clearly other, less conciliatory factions with a disquieting habit of brutally murdering known—or suspected—collaborators.

Not surprisingly, it's the artists—choreographers, theater directors, musicians—from both sides of the conflict who address its human toll. Of particular interest is Juliano Mor, a provocative Tel Aviv street performer of both Palestinian and Israeli extraction. The entire situation, it is suggested by a Palestinian journalist, is exacerbated by the traditional middle-eastern character—volatile, emotional and quite difficult for Westerners to grasp.

One possible solution is the creation of two states, Jewish Israel and Arab Palestine; certainly, as one Israeli academic suggests, the future of Israel is endangered if the current occupation continues unabated—Israel will become a fascist state and international sympathy will reside with the Arabs. But is either side willing to share? The film's final, woeful impression is of two ancient, not dissimilar cultures—both after all, are preoccupied with ethnicity and affirmation—locked in a death dance. *(Violence, adult situations.)*

p, Simcha Jacobovici, Elliott Halpern, Ric Esther Bienstock; d, Simcha Jacobovici; ph, Mark MacKay; ed, Steve Weslak; m, Stephen Price

Documentary/Political (PR: C MPAA: NR)

DEATH BECOMES HER ★★½

105m Universal ~ Universal c

Meryl Streep *(Madeline Ashton)*, Bruce Willis *(Ernest Menville)*, Goldie Hawn *(Helen Sharp)*, Isabella Rosselini *(Lisle Von Rhumans)*, Sydney Pollack *(Doctor)*, Michael Caine, Ian Ogilvy *(Chagall)*, Adam Storke *(Dakota)*, Nancy Fish *(Rose)*, Alaina Reed Hall *(Psychologist)*, Michelle Johnson *(Anna)*, Mary Ellen Trainor *(Vivian Adams)*, William Frankfather *(Mr. Franklin)*, John Ingle *(Eulogist)*, Clement Von Franckenstein *(Opening Man)*, Petrea Burchard *(Opening Woman)*, Jim Jansen *(Second Man)*, Mimi Kennedy *(Second Woman)*, Paula Tocha *(Landlord)*, Mark Davenport *(Eviction Cop)*, Thomas Murphy *(Eviction Cop)*, Michael Mills *(Police Officer)*, Sonia Jackson, Jill C. Klein, Jean Pflieger, Debra Jo Rupp, Carol Ann Susi, Kay Yamamoto *(Psychiatric Patients)*, Jacquelyn K. Koch *(Messenger Girl)*, Anya Longwell *(Chagall Receptionist)*, Stuart Mabray *(Chagall Security)*, Louise Rapport *(Older Woman at Party)*, Colleen Morris *(Starlet)*, Jonathan Silverman *(Jay Norman)*, Meg Wittner *(Woman at Book Party)*, Carrie Yazel *(Girl at Dakota's)*, Michael A. Nickles, John Enos, Dan Clark, Fabio, Joel Beeson *(Lisle's Body Guards)*, Ron Stein *(Elvis)*, Bonnie Cahoon *(Greta Garbo)*, Stephanie Anderson *(Marilyn Monroe)*, Bob Swain *(Andy Warhol)*, Eric Clark *(James Dean)*, Dave Brock *(Jim Morrison)*, Lydia Peterkoch *(Blonde with Jim Morrison)*, Phillip Cooper *(Coroner)*, Ernest Harada *(Coroner)*, Susan Kellermann *(Second Doctor)*, Kevin Caldwell *(Medical Technician)*, Alex P. Hernandez *(Medical Technician)*, Donna Ekholdt *(Sobbing Nun)*, Tammy Gantz *(Sobbing Nun)*, Melissa Martin *(Sobbing Nun)*, Jeff Adkins, Cheryl Baxter, Cameron English, Ed Forsyth, Bob Gaynor, Don Hesser, Michael Higgins, Kenneth Hughes, Kenneth Knaff, Glean Lewis, Keith McDaniel, Charles McGowan, Regan Patno, Lacy Darryl Phillips, Matt Sergott, Paul Thorpe, Sergio Trujillo *(Dancers)*, Randy Crenshaw *(Singer)*, Jon Joyce *(Singer)*, Jerry Whitman *(Singer)*

This broad, heavy-handed black comedy from director Robert Zemeckis strives for both socially pointed satire and wacky escapism. Unsurprisingly, DEATH BECOMES HER winds up being neither.

Noted plastic surgeon Ernest Menville (Bruce Willis) finds himself caught in the middle of a lifelong feud between his fiancee, book editor and aspiring novelist Helen Sharp (Goldie Hawn), and aging Broadway star Madeline Ashton (Meryl Streep). As the film opens, Menville is already failing the "Madeline Ashton test," being administered by a wary Helen at a tacky musical version of *Sweet Bird of Youth* starring the conspicuously under-talented Ashton. As most of the audience dives for the exits, Menville sits transfixed, much to his girlfriend's chagrin, and he's later thunderstruck when he meets the actress, in a calculated state of *deshabille*, in her dressing room.

Losing Menville sends Helen over the edge into a deep, deep depression, marked by a disturbing weakness for canned vanilla frosting, that develops into an unquenchable thirst for revenge against her rival. (The sight of an obscenely overweight Hawn is truly astonishing, and beautifully underplayed; it's by far her best moment.) Meanwhile, Madeline has—thanks to her husband Ernest's expert ministrations—found a whole new career as a movie star. But she's beginning to sag again, and so, heeding the advice of her beautician, the desperate actress visits a mysterious Beverly Hills cult priestess, Lisle Von Rhumans (Isabella Rossellini), from whom she obtains a youth serum with the Faustian side-effect of also granting eternal life, whatever the condition of the user's body.

A newly svelte Helen then reappears on the scene and persuades Menville to do away with Madeline so the original couple can be reunited. Menville initially resists the plan, but ends up "assisting" Madeline in her spectacular fall down a flight of stairs. The immortal Madeline bounces back and gets her revenge by killing Helen who, having also partaken of Lisle's serum, proves equally un-killable. Deciding they both need Menville's cosmetic skills to keep their battered bodies in presentable condition, the women form an alliance and try to force Menville to drink the serum and join them in an eternal triangle. He refuses and escapes from a gathering of the undead at Lisle's gothic mansion. At his funeral some years later, the two women, alive but looking much the worse for wear, get into a fight and pull each other down the steps outside the church, both shattering into a pile of disembodied limbs. Their arguing heads, however, remain intact and alive.

DEATH BECOMES HER itself was evidently chopped up late into its post-production, almost invariably a sign of panic behind the scenes over a movie that isn't working with preview audiences. Trailers prominently featured a sequence involving Willis wrestling Streep's living-dead body out of their home freezer that was nowhere to be found in the released film. However, whether the film would have been any funnier with that or any other excised footage is debatable.

The film is more fundamentally flawed by Zemeckis's (BACK TO THE FUTURE, WHO FRAMED ROGER RABBIT) cartoonish approach to the delicate material. This works against any involvement with the characters, who remain one-dimensional grotesques throughout, or the narrative, which goes nowhere beyond its initial premise. The only real plot twist—the disclosure that Helen, as well as Madeline, has swallowed the youth serum—was also virtually given away in the film's trailers. The most telling weakness is that Zemeckis has chosen a genre—black comedy—that traditionally flattens its characters in order to make satirical points about life or society, without having much of interest or originality to say on either topic.

Lacking any real satirical bite, DEATH BECOMES HER makes a late attempt to fashion Menville into a "hero" when he rejects both women and goes on to live a worthwhile life. However, such a turnabout is implausible, to say the least, from a wife-murderer who is too easily let off the hook for his crime. And since the film demonstrates little genuine interest in its characters during the bulk of its running time, Menville's sudden redemption seems disingenuous at best and a desperate, last-ditch attempt to save the film at worst. In either case, the ploy doesn't work and only highlights the weaknesses in both the screenplay and the direction.

DEATH BECOMES HER lacks the conviction to get beyond the self-loathing vanity of its female protagonists and address the wider issue of society's attitudes toward women over forty. On the other hand, it lacks an appealing protagonist, depriving the mass audience of anyone to root for. The real culprit is an ongoing mentality in Hollywood filmmaking that mandates a false dichotomy between art and entertainment and is therefore unable to cope with films or filmmakers who try to combine the two in any challenging way.

The major victims in this case are the lead performers, most notably Streep, whose legendary precision and seemingly inexhaustible inventiveness continue to put her in a class by herself. Willis is more restrained, and therefore funnier, than usual and Hawn continues to mature into a potentially interesting actress. Rossellini, while no match for her costars, is nonetheless used to good advantage in a typically offbeat role. But a failure of nerve behind the camera and, presumably, in the editing room prevents DEATH BECOMES HER from being the kind of genuinely cutting comedy it could, and indeed *should* have been, given the talent involved. Far from the worst film of 1992, it nevertheless has to rank as one of the year's bigger disappointments. *(Adult situations, profanity.)*

p, Robert Zemeckis, Steve Starkey; d, Robert Zemeckis; w, Martin Donovan, David Koepp; ph, Dean Cundey; ed, Arthur Schmidt; m, Alan Silvestri; prod d, Rick Carter; art d, Jim Teegarden; set d, Jackie Carr; cos, Joanna Johnston; fx, Ken Ralston, Doug Chiang,, Tom Woodruff, Doug Smythe

AA Visual Effects: Ken Ralston, Doug Chiang, Doug Smythe, and Tom Woodruff

Comedy/Fantasy **(PR: C MPAA: PG-13)**

DEATH HOUSE

Double Helix Films; First International Pictures ~
AIP Home Video Inc. c

Dennis Cole *(Derek Keillor)*, John Saxon *(Colonel Burgess)*, Anthony Franciosa *(Vic Moretti)*, Michael Pataki *(Franco Moretti)*, Tane McLure *(Tanya Karrington)*, Howard George, Alex Courtney, William Selby, David S. Freeman, Ron O'Neal

Durable B-movie actor John Saxon marks his feature directorial debut—sort of—with DEATH HOUSE, an ugly mutt of a motion picture.

Rewrites and postproduction difficulties show clearly in a tangled plot that begins with down-and-out Vietnam vet Derek Keillor (Dennis Cole) hired as a chauffeur by patriotic crook Vic Moretti (Anthony Franciosa). In no time Derek beds the mobster's sexy blonde movie-actress moll, and an angry Moretti frames the hero for murder, getting him sent to a hellhole of a prison, where the sleazy story detours into an AIDS-inspired horror-conspiracy scenerio.

Fanatical Colonel Burgess (Saxon, doing a takeoff on Oliver North) has been covertly conducting grisly experiments on death-row residents with the lab-created HV8-B virus, initially a behavior-altering disease that will turn the average lifer into a drooling, kill-crazy lunatic ("Imagine an army like that!" beams

Burgess). But the HV8-B strain has some *bad* points: it's highly contagious—spread by body fluids—and victims transform into putrefying cannibal zombies. When a contaminated prison chaplain accidentally drips slime from his nose into a communion chalice, HV8-B spreads through the cellblock, causing a convict revolt led rather improbably by the colorless Derek. Though Burgess favors the idea of a man-made plague "toughening" America, he brings in troops and puts the penitentiary under armed quarantine.

It remains for the courageous 'Nam vet to fend off the zombies, his rebellious fellow inmates and Vic Moretti, while a sexy blonde biochemist-turned-investigative-TV-reporter named Tanya (Tane McClure) labors to find a cure, although Derek comes up with the vaccine first. He and selected survivors (the token heroic Black guy gets killed at the last minute, as usual) reach freedom through a secret tunnel, and Burgess is dismembered by zombies as bombs blow the Death House to bits. But the virus reaches the outside world via an infected Burgess henchman.

In an autobiographical chapter of his 1992 book *The New Poverty Row*, cheapie filmmaker Fred Olen Ray takes credit (sic) for much of DEATH HOUSE, claiming he was brought in to doctor up the fraught efforts of novice helmer Saxon. "There was no script per se. I was handed a piece of paper from which I created the entire climax of the picture." Yet three writers are listed onscreen, perhaps a noble gesture of sharing the blame. From its grotesque, paranoid politics to loving closeups of bloody wounds to gratuitous nudity (heroine McClure gets her grand unveiling in a dream sequence), this toxic sludge is lowbrow cinema on a high plane indeed, though one must admire the use of "Chemical Warfare" by the Dead Kennedys as a closing theme.

Perhaps the kindest interpretation of *un film de John Saxon* is that its commando hero balances Saxon's 1980 European-made opus CANNIBALS IN THE STREETS, in which returned Vietnam vets were themselves psychos with a lust for human flesh acquired during war duty. DEATH HOUSE was done in 1988, but escaped to the public on home video in 1992. *(Violence, profanity, sexual situations, adult situations.)*

p, Nick Marino; d, John Saxon; w, William Selby, Devin Frazer, Kate Wittcomb; ph, John Fante; ed, Gary Blair; prod d, Regina Argentina; set d, Todd Morrison; cos, Sheera Von Puttkamer

Horror/Thriller **(PR: O MPAA: NR)**

DEATHSTALKER IV: MATCH OF TITANS ★½
(U.S.) Concorde ~ Concorde c

Rick Hill *(Deathstalker)*, Maria Ford *(Dionara)*, Bret Baxter Clark *(Vanist)*, Michelle Moffett *(Kana)*, Jocko Rossitch *(Rakshia)*, Anya Pencheva *(Janeris)*, Rumen Dimitrov *(Eldron)*

At the climax of DEATHSTALKER IV: MATCH OF TITANS, an army of musclemen who'd earlier been turned to stone come back to life. Viewers will wait in vain for that same happy fate to transform the leaden cast of this tacky adventure yarn.

Deathstalker (Rick Hill) returns in search of Eldron (Rumen Dimitrov), a hale and hearty fellow who accidentally switched cutlasses with him. He instead encounters the Herculean Vaniat (Brett Baxter Clark), whose manager offers to make Deathstalker a fighter. Actually, Deathstalker needs all of his Nautilus-honed power to rescue two damsels in distress, one of whom, Dionara (Maria Ford), is a deposed warrior princess out to reclaim her throne. After these pectorally perfect good guys battle some creatures who look like pussycats on gland-enhancers, they meet Queen Kana (Michelle Moffett), who's planning a big tourney. Unbeknownst to them, this devious royal saps the strength of every weight-training hunk she seduces, chemically transforming them into park statues. When our titular hero stumbles upon the sequestered stone men, Kana and her minister revive them in order to capture Deathstalker, who soon finds his own beefcake is starting to marbleize. En route to the ring for her competitive bout, Dionara manages to slip Deathstalker the anti-stone elixir. Kana, meanwhile, tries to seduce the teasing Vaniat, but she's the one who ends up turned to stone. After some poorly choreographed fight sequences, Dionara retrieves her royal pendant, the erstwhile statuary go back to lifting free weights and Deathstalker gets his sword back and gallops off.

this is another sword-and-sandal epic with cheesy costumes that resemble the hand-me-downs of a dozen DeMille spectaculars, and canned muzak reminiscent of your local shopping mall.

True, different criteria apply when one is evaluating low-budget action flicks, particularly if they're set in ancient times. Yet even judging it against lowered standards, DEATHSTALKER IV is a 90-pound weakling among gladiator films. While one can overlook actors who think Stanislavsky was Lenin's successor and a screenplay that reduces ancient history to a series of "You started it" playground fights, one does expect some expert brawling and zippy editing. Still, its unpretentiousness, its ludicrous anachronisms and its tongue-and-cheek dialogue (however poorly delivered) give it some muscle in the action adventure arena.

DEATHSTALKER's many fans can pump themselves up with the rampant good-naturedness, liberal nudity, and comforting knowledge that a hard body was an essential tool for survival in barbarian epochs. *(Violence, nudity.)*

p, Steve Rabiner, Howard R. Cohen; d, Howard R. Cohen; w, Howard R. Cohen; ph, Emil Wagenstein; ed, Nadia Tsenova; m, Simo Lazarov; prod d, Joseph Munchin; art d, Ivan Andrev, Tsvetana Iankova

Action/Adventure **(PR: C MPAA: R)**

DEEP BLUES ★★★
91m Radio Active Films; Oil Factory Ltd ~ Tara Releasing c

"Big" Jack Johnson, Roosevelt "Booba" Barnes, Junior Kimbrough, Jessie Mae Hemphill, R.L. Burnside, Booker T. Laury, Lonnie Pitchford, Jack Owens, Bud Spires, David A. Stewart, Jessie Mae's Fife and Drum Band, Wade Walton, Robert Palmer *(Narration)*

Blues, specifically the gutsy delta variety, is the subject of DEEP BLUES, an illuminating and inspiring documentary put together by filmmaker Robert Mugge and writer-music critic Robert Palmer.

Palmer, who's covered popular music for *Rolling Stone* and the *New York Times* among others, is an effective guide for this trip into Mississippi: he grew up in neighboring Arkansas, and has both played the music and organized festivals devoted to it. He obviously has a great affection and respect for his subject, and although he's not the most professional-sounding narrator, he's an engaging and friendly host, never pedantic or windy. At the start of the film, he's joined by Eurythmics founder Dave Stewart, who wants Palmer's help in recording some of the legendary blues musicians who inspired him as a youth. Stewart, with his shades, carefully trimmed beard and omnipresent cigarette, resembles a Doonesbury cartoon of a wealthy Brit rock star, but apparently has a genuine interest in the music, although he drops out of the film about a third on to finish a tour.

The film takes us from Memphis, Tennessee, where Palmer and Stewart meet on famed Beale Street, into rural Mississippi, traveling from the northern part of the state into the delta, one of the many birthplaces of the blues. Along the way, we're treated to interviews and frequently lengthy performances by various blues artists, who, while obscure, have greatly influenced better-known names. Jesse Mae Hemphill illustrates where blues rhythms came from with her fife-and-drum group, a piece of musical antiquity that is still evident in that part of the country. Roosevelt "Booba" Barnes, a performer and juke joint owner, does a long, somewhat spooky number in which he plays guitar with his teeth.

Another highlight is "Big" Jack Johnson, known as the "Oil Man" for his deliveries of heating oil during the day and sizzling blues at night; he also does a soul-oriented original, "Daddy, When Is Mama Comin' Home?" Lonnie Pitchford gives a demonstration of a "diddly bow," a one-stringed instrument made of wire, and concludes the film, fittingly, with two songs by blues pioneer (and recently, best-selling recording artist) Robert Johnson. Although many of the performers do use such modern inventions as electric guitars, the music is more primitive than the blues many viewers may be familiar with: the chord changes are not always I-IV-V blues patterns, frequently staying on one, sometimes minor chord for long stretches, giving it a haunting, dark tone, like an electric version of some centuries-old occult chant.

The film provides some informative background material, from a visit to a voodoo shop where many will be interested to learn finally what a "mojo" is, to a barbershop that served as an informal meeting place for many notable blues performers. Palmer is mindful to show the conditions that contributed to the blues, explaining how it grew out of a way of life on plantations and rural farms. He also reminds us the blues was created by people so far down the socio-economic scale it was, and to some extent still is, "outlaw culture."

Director Robert Mugge's style complements Palmer's narrative, having performers do long (sometimes too long) pieces without the camera getting in the way. The scenes of shacks, long expanses of flat land and highway and a nighttime sky so blue it appears painted, all add to the film's rural, hopeful-yet-desolate atmosphere. For this is a world not often seen in documentaries, even musical ones. As cliched as it sounds, music for these performers is inextricably linked to their lives, their work and their attitudes.

DEEP BLUES not only shows the evolution of a musical style, but is a rare opportunity to see the practitioners of that style, many of whom have never been recorded or filmed.

p, Eileen Gregory, John Stewart; d, Robert Mugge; ph, Erich Roland; ed, Robert Mugge; md, Robert Palmer

Documentary/Musical **(PR: A MPAA: NR)**

DEEP COVER ★★★½

112m New Line; Image Organization ~ New Line c

Larry Fishburne *(Russell Stevens, Jr./John Q. Hull)*, Jeff Goldblum *(David Jason)*, Victoria Dillard *(Betty McCutcheon)*, Charles Martin Smith *(Jerry Carver)*, Clarence Williams, III *(Ken Taft)*, Gregory Sierra *(Felix Barbosa)*, Rene Asa *(Hector Guzman)*, Alex Colon *(Molto)*, Roger Guenveur Smith *(Eddie)*, Sydney Lassick *(Gopher)*, Kamala Lopez, Julio Oscar Mechosa, James T. Morris, Arthur Mendozo, Sandra Gould, Cory Curtis, Glynn Turman *(Russell Stevens, Sr.)*, Def Jef, Lionel Matthews

The best B-movies, by definition, do what A-movies can't. The lower the budget, the more pointedly political a film can be, although most B-movies today don't take that advantage and are content merely to ape bigger-budgeted hits. DEEP COVER is a welcome exception, a New Age noir tale that recasts the traditional crime thriller's hard-boiled cynicism within contemporary society's slippery new morality—with disturbing results.

Russell Stevens, Jr. (Larry Fishburne) is a man who becomes his own worst enemy. Having watched his junkie father die violently, shot to death while robbing a liquor store, he determines that he will make his life the opposite of his father's. He becomes a cop, but the rage of his youth and the criminal conditioning of his upbringing remain. That's why the DEA, in the form of Jerry Carver (Charles Martin Smith), recruits him to go so far undercover that the idea of a normal life has no meaning. As Carver points out, all the weaknesses that work against Stevens's ever becoming an outstanding cop suddenly become strengths. Stevens is made over into John Q. Hull, a street dealer who moves up quickly, thanks to buy money provided by the authorities. He is "adopted" by crooked drug-dealing lawyer David Jason (Jeff Goldblum), who makes him a partner in his venture to create a new designer drug, completely legal and with none of the messy hassles associated with importing cocaine.

Through Jason, Stevens meets his targets, South American kingpins who are the dealers behind the dealers. However, Stevens is left out in the cold when the DEA decides that the top dealer, an influential politician, may someday be useful to the State Department. They call off the investigation. But by that time, of course, Stevens is in too deep. He decides to go on, but his lone-wolf tactics lead to several underworld murders and cost the life of a sympathetic cop (Clarence Williams, III). The DEA decides to whitewash Stevens's vigilantism in Congressional hearings. But Stevens has plans of his own.

DEEP COVER is one of those rare genre films in which guns cause far more problems than they solve. Co-written by Michael Tolkin (THE PLAYER) and Henry Bean (INTERNAL AFFAIRS), DEEP COVER also does what neither THE PLAYER nor INTERNAL AFFAIRS could do. It names names and points fingers up the ladders of power, drawing parallels between its fictional South American aspiring despot and real-life figures, particularly Panama's Manuel Noriega, whom the US government supported as bulwarks against communism despite the violence and corruption they caused. It also shows how enforcing drug laws can turn cops into criminals in a more detailed, plausible and compelling way than the higher-profile RUSH.

More importantly, DEEP COVER examines issues like personal morality, ethics and even spirituality to a degree usually unheard of in a genre film, much less in generic studio features. In that, it most closely resembles Tolkin's own THE RAPTURE, an erratic but compelling inquiry into spirituality in a numbingly secular age. Specifically, both films, through RAPTURE's female protagonist and DEEP COVER's black protagonist, ask what is left to those who were left out of the "Reagan revolution" of the 1980s, when a lot of white boys with MBAs looted the economy and left the rest of the country working harder for less in the recession-plagued 90s. The answer in both cases is, not much. THE RAPTURE's heroine is left in jail, having killed her daughter because "God" told her to, and DEEP COVER's nominal "hero" is left with $11 million in drug money and moral paralysis as to what to do about it.

Actor-turned-filmmaker Bill Duke continues to impress. He is a former TV director who's flowered on the big screen rather than going the more familiar route of making big-screen movies that seem more like TV shows with dirty words and nudity. He brings a real stamp of originality to both this film and his earlier A RAGE IN HARLEM, but he also brings a real moral gravity and personal vision that is becoming increasingly rare in any kind of commercial filmmaking. Not surprisingly, he's been able to attract top talent to both films. In this case, Goldblum justly received attention for his scary, offbeat portrayal of the corrupt lawyer Jason. But Fishburne—not for the first time, nor for the last—gives the film its real weight. He shares with Goldblum the ability to project intelligence and feeling, in this case brought to a character who must rethink and recreate himself almost on a second-by-second basis. Smith is properly corrosive as the DEA agent, and Gregory Sierra, the nice-guy Hispanic cop Chano from the old "Barney Miller" sitcom, is a real surprise here as Goldblum's ruthlessly sadistic higher-up in the drug chain.

In its focus on a bleak new world of diminished expectations and the people who live there groping for meaning, DEEP COVER may well herald the real future of American cinema. It's an artful piece of filmmaking, but it feels depressingly real all the way through. *(Violence, substance abuse, profanity, adult situations.)*

p, Henry Bean, Pierre David; d, Bill Duke; w, Henry Bean, Michael Tolkin, (from his story); ph, Bojan Bazelli; ed, John Carter; m, Michel Colombier; prod d, Pam Warner; art d, Daniel W. Bickel; set d, Donald Elmblad; cos, Arlene Gant

Crime/Thriller **(PR: O MPAA: R)**

DELICATESSEN ★★★★

(France) 97m Constellation Production; Union Generale Cinematographique; Hachette Premiere ~ Miramax c

Marie-Laure Dougnac *(Julie Clapet)*, Dominique Pinon *(Louison)*, Karin Viard *(Miss Plusse)*, Jean-Claude Dreyfus *(The Butcher)*, Ticky Holgado *(Mr. Tapioca)*, Anne-Marie Pisani *(Mrs. Tapioca)*, Edith Ker *(The Grandmother)*, Mickael Todde *(Lucien)*, Boban Janevski *(Remi)*, Jacques Mathou *(Roger Kube)*, Jean-Francois Perrier *(Mr. Interligator)*, Sylvie Laguna *(Mrs. Interligator)*, Rufus *(Robert Kube)*, Howard Vernon *(Mr. Potin)*, Chick Ortega *(The Facteur)*, Patrick Paroux *(Rolls)*, Jean-Luc Caron *(Janvier)*, Eric Averlant *(Tourneur)*, Dominique Betenfield *(Paumeau)*, Maurice Lamy *(Pank)*, Marc Caro *(Fox)*, Raymond Forestier *(Milan)*, Dominique Defever *(Trappe)*, Bernard Flavien *(Brelan)*, Robert Baud *(Voltange)*, Dominique Zardi *(The Taxi Driver)*, Pascal Benezech *(Mr. Houy)*

Cannibalism serves as a potent metaphor for social oppression in DELICATESSEN, the darkly stylish feature debut by French animators Jean-Pierre Jeunet and Marc Caro.

This surreal, blackly comic fable is set in a run-down apartment building sometime in the dystopian near future. The landlord of the building also runs the butcher shop on the ground floor, and keeps his tenants supplied with meat by chopping up hapless applicants for the job of building superintendent. The problem is that the butcher's mousey, nearsighted daughter, Julie Clapet (Marie-Laure Dougnac), keeps falling in love with these sirloins-to-be. In the past, gastronomical necessity has overcome romantic yearning. However, she insists that the newest arrival, Louison (Dominique Pinon, who made such an indelible impression in Jean-Jacques Beineix's DIVA), is different. The butcher doesn't believe her, but something makes him hold off from doing in the newest superintendent until well after the neighbors begin complaining about the lack of meat in their diet.

The butcher's hesitation leaves Julie enough time to contact a group of radical vegetarians who live in the sewers below the city; they stage a daring rescue, only to come away with the butcher's voluptuous girlfriend Miss Plusse (Karin Viard) instead. Back at the building, the mob of angry tenants, led by the butcher, close in on the superintendent and his sweetheart. But true love—and rundown plumbing—prevail when the lovers arrange a watery deluge that vanquishes the would-be flesh eaters and demolishes most of the building's insides. The roof is left intact, and it is there that the lovers are seen placidly playing a duet at the fadeout, he on his saw and she on her cello.

DELICATESSEN is not as grisly as its premise might suggest. Much of the mayhem and violence takes place offscreen, and the main stylistic influences are Carne, Prevert, Dali and Bunuel, rather than Tobe Hooper. Carno and Jeunet construct a series of vignettes — some hilarious, some grotesque — of the tenants, often as seen through the eyes of two spying little boys. They include an old man who keeps his basement apartment flooded to raise escargots (one of the *slimiest* scenes in screen history); a prim matron who hears mysterious voices—actually a malicious upstairs neighbor speaking through the building vents—telling her to do away with herself (something she attempts, via a series of elaborate Rube Goldberg-style set-ups); and two brothers who support themselves by constructing moo-ing noisemakers. Into this bizarre, painstakingly rendered universe wanders the new superintendent, a former clown still mourning the death of his "partner," a chimpanzee who came to an ugly end when he was eaten by other members of their circus troupe.

For all its cartoonish artificiality, DELICATESSEN does hit home: we all pay the butcher to feed us, while not letting us know too much about where the food comes from. The film merely takes this familiar phenomenon to its logical conclusion. By placing cannibalism within a social context, it zeroes in on the extent to which we feed on each other and, in hard times, how the big fish readily feed on the small.

Ideas aside, DELICATESSEN is a funny film with a surprisingly sweet romance at its center. As a director's piece, it's a nonstop *tour de force* of ingenuity, inspiration and wit, performed by a cast of wonderfully talented unknowns. But it's also a reminder that most of the best comedies make us laugh as an alternative to crying. *(Violence, adult situations.)*

p, Claude Ossard; d, Jean-Pierre Jeunet, Marc Caro; w, Adrien Gilles; ph, Darius Khondji; ed, Herve Schneid; m, Carlos D'Alessi; prod d, Jean-Philippe Carp, Kreka Kjnakovic; set d, Aline Bonetto; cos, Valerie Pozzo DiBorgo

Comedy/Fantasy **(PR: C MPAA: R)**

DELTA HEAT ★★

91m Harham Group; Karen Films; Sawmill Entertainment ~ Academy Entertainment c

Anthony Edwards *(Mike Bishop)*, Lance Henriksen *(Jackson Rivers)*, Betsy Russell *(Vicky Forbes)*, Rod Masterson *(Crawford)*, John "Spud" McConnell *(LaSalle)*, Clyde Jones *(Clayborne)*, Linda Dona, Jack David Harris

The moviegoing year came to an unremarkable close with DELTA HEAT, a curdled mix of gunplay and gumbo — the umpteenth variation on the buddy-cop formula.

The LAPD traces a new designer drug to New Orleans, where one officer turns up murdered and mutilated Cajun-voodoo-style. The victim's partner, silly California pretty-boy Detective Mike Bishop (Anthony Edwards), arrives in Bayou Country with an earring, a disco-dance wardrobe and a vow of vengeance. The killer's style was the trademark of Antoine Forbes, a legendary crimelord who supposedly perished in a fiery shootout and explosion years ago. One of the last Louisiana lawmen to hunt Forbes was clean-cut New Orleans officer Crawford (Rod Masterson). Another was Jackson Rivers (Lance Henricksen), now an embittered, hook-handed, swamp-dwelling hermit.

The odd couple of gaunt, grumbly Rivers and natty, numbskull Bishop swap the expected wisecracks as they prowl the backstreets, docks and verandas of the Big Easy, following up unresolved strands of the Forbes case. Soon the informers they locate are turning up murdered, each with one of Rivers's favorite cigarettes by the body. Bishop decides Rivers is some sort of drug-smuggling psycho throwback to Antoine Forbes (who indeed survived, as a scarred, vegetative husk in a nursing home), but when he aids Rivers's swamp hovel the real evildoers reveal themselves—Crawford and his corrupt precinct cohorts.

The climax shows what happens when a screenwriter paints himself into a corner. The villains have Bishop and Rivers captive and helpless; there's no possible way the heroes can hope to escape. So the bad guys abruptly and pointlessly turn against each other, giving the partners the opportunity to triumph after all.

Released direct-to-video at the end of December, DELTA HEAT is at its best when the sublimely saturnine Lance Henricksen (ALIENS, NEAR DARK) is in full swing as the grizzled Cajun cop, a showy role he relishes with scenery-chewing delight. Even Edwards looks good playing off the character contrast. Otherwise Det. Bishop seems like he should be carrying a surfboard, not a badge. The rest of the cast have fun with Big Easy accents and attitudes, and the Southern-fried speech patterns flavor the dialogue (sexy heroine Betsy Russell, on Bishop's cologne: "What is that *pugnacious* aroma?"), but the overall self-consciousness of the effort doesn't so much preserve the on-location New Orleans atmosphere as stuff it and mount it for display.

An inordinate amount of humor derives from the homespun torture methods Rivers uses to make suspects confess; violence on balance isn't as severe as it could have been, but there's enough of it to please fans and put off those who are not naturally enamored of the cross-cultural clashes of buddy cops. The inevitable barroom brawl is accompanied by the music and onscreen appearance of Rockin' Dopsie and the Zydeco Twisters, who contribute the soundtrack tunes "Josephine Pas Se Ma Femme" and "LaFayette Two Step." *(Violence, profanity, sexual situations, nudity.)*

p, Richard L. Albert, Rudy Cohen; d, Michael Fischa; w, Sam A. Scribner, (from the characters created by Bruce Akiyama and Richard L. Albert); ph, Avi Karpick; ed, Rob Edwards, Robert Gordon; m, Christopher Tyng; prod d, Don Day; cos, Stacey Chance

Crime/Thriller **(PR: O MPAA: R)**

DEMON IN MY VIEW, A ★

(Germany) 99m First City Productions; Pro-ject Filmverlag ~ Vidmark Entertainment c

Anthony Perkins *(Arthur Johnson)*, Uwe Bohm *(Anthony Johnson)*, Sophie Ward *(Helen Schweizer)*, Deborah Lacey *(Linthea)*, Stratford Johns *(Stanley Caspian)*, Brian Bovell *(Winston Mervin)*, Charmain May *(Auntie Grace)*, James Aubrey *(Brian Kotowsky)*, Carole Hayman *(Vesta Kotowsky)*, Choy-Ling Man *(Li-Li Chan)*, Michael Simpkins *(Jonathan Dean)*, Hans Peta Hallwachs *(Roger Schweizer)*, Sam Smart *(Barry)*, Terence Hardiman *(Inspector)*, Tilly Blackwood *(Beryl)*, Sally Rogers *(Maureen Cowan)*, Justine Glenton *(Bridget)*, Steven O'Donell *(Young Stanley)*, Leon Black *(Leroy)*, Nick Dawney *(Arthur as a Child)*, Simon Bright *(Steve)*, Rocky Samrai *(David)*, David Willis *(Television Interviewer)*, Pete Lee Wilson *(Richard Harrison)*, Peter Barnes *(Potter)*

Struggling with a tony British accent, the late Anthony Perkins does his best to energize A DEMON IN MY VIEW, a boring psychodrama that utterly wrecks the gripping Ruth Rendell novel on which it's based.

For years, Arthur Johnson (Perkins) has kept his dirty, sadistic little secrets to himself. Going a little mad on occasion and killing a nurse or a hooker, Arthur usually gets his kicks making love in his cellar to a mannequin dressed up as his mother. Mentally taxed to the max with memories of his homicidal impulses, this depraved mama's boy is unhinged when a second Mr. Johnson named Anthony (Uwe Bohm) moves into his apartment building. Smitten with a married woman he left behind in Germany, Anthony has traveled to London to write about the elusive serial killer. When the emotionally stable Anthony unwittingly gives away Arthur's beloved dummy to kids planning a Guy Fawkes Day bonfire, Arthur steps up a campaign of intercepting his alter ego's mail, leading Anthony to believe that his married lover has dumped him.

Breathing a sigh of relief when a neighbor is accused of the unsolved crimes, Arthur makes the brash mistake of attacking a new, long-haired victim who turns out to be a man with a photographic memory of his assailant's face. A police sketch is soon displayed on TV. As the fates close in, the deranged Arthur's mail trickery ends when lady fair Helen Schweizer (Sophie Ward) arrives and redeclares her love for Anthony. However, when Helen's angry husband Roger (Hans Peta Hallwachs) turns up, he mistakes Arthur Johnson for his wife's sweetheart and blasts the wrong man away.

Skimming the storyline with its provocative elements of letter-crossed adulterers, sado-sexual flashback, and the juxtaposition of the two vastly disparate Mr. Johnsons, one might assume that this film would achieve some level of psychological penetration. Wrong assumption. Snail-paced and ineptly directed, A DEMON IN MY VIEW fails to plumb the psychological depths of either character and never develops any sort of symbiosis between the two men. It's as if the filmmakers reasoned that the novel's premise was intrinsically intriguing, then proceeded to concentrate solely on the exposition.

In terms of interconnectedness, the two Mr. Johnsons and the actors playing them might have been edited in from two different films. Where's the eerie *doppleganger* effect? Where's the sense of one man's identity being usurped by another's? What is sorely missing (even if one overlooks the invisibility of atmosphere and incredible lack of suspense) is the absence of pathos for Mr. Johnson. Even if he's a killer, we're meant to feel sympathy for him because of his dark childhood. Somehow there is no guiding intelligence behind this film: it's a cut-and-paste job produced and directed with little flair or depth.

Lastly, what an unfitting swan song this represents for actor Anthony Perkins, whose classic performance in PSYCHO overshadowed superb work (FEAR STRIKES OUT, FRIENDLY PERSUASION) that preceded it and underrated performances (PRETTY POISON, CRIMES OF PASSION) that followed it. *(Violence, sexual situations, adult situations.)*

p, David Kelly, Martin Bruce-Clayton; d, Petra Haffter; w, Petra Haffter, (from the novel by Ruth Rendell); ph, Frank Bruhne; ed, Moune Barius; prod d, Josef Sanktjohanser; art d, Andrew Rothschild; cos, Shuna Harwood

Thriller **(PR: O MPAA: R)**

DEMONIC TOYS ★

86m Full Moon Entertainment ~ Paramount Home Video c

Tracy Scoggins *(Judith)*, Bentley Mitchum *(Mark)*, Michael Russo *(Lincoln)*, Jeff Weston *(Matt)*, Daniel Cerney *(Little Boy)*, Barry Lynch *(Hesse)*, Ellen Dunning *(Anne)*, Pete Schrum *(Charnetski)*

With DEMONIC TOYS, Full Moon Entertainment attempts to recycle one of its own most popular ideas with little success. Essentially a rehash of the company's PUPPETMASTER series, this film suffers from a hackneyed story and unimaginative creatures.

The setting is an old toy warehouse where a motley group of innocents and not-so-innocents wind up being terrorized by playthings come to life. Serving as the key protagonist is Judith

(Tracy Scoggins), a policewoman whose undercover meeting with a couple of thugs goes awry. Her partner and lover, Matt (Jeff Weston), is shot to death, whereupon Judith pursues the creeps into the building. One of them, Hesse (Barry Lynch), has been wounded in the gunplay; stumbling into a white-lit circle in one of the rooms, he bleeds onto the floor, resurrecting a demon that brings a group of toys to life which promptly attack and kill him.

Meanwhile, Judith has caught up to the other punk, Lincoln (Michael Russo), and handcuffs him after a violent struggle. But as she makes ready to deliver Lincoln to justice, the doors slam shut and mysteriously lock, along with the windows. (Intelligence not being one of her key character traits, Judith fails to realize that she could easily shoot the locks off to escape.) Within moments, the toys in the warehouse begin to mass against everyone in sight. Among the potential victims are a hunky Chunky Chicken delivery man named Mark (Bentley Mitchum), security guard Charnetski (Pete Schrum) and homeless girl Anne (Ellen Dunning), who's been hiding in the building (and comes in handy for providing exposition).

Judith soon finds out that she faces a potentially worse fate than death at the toys' hands: the possessive spirit controlling the playthings, which manifests on occasion as a creepy little boy (Daniel Cerney), plans to be reborn through the child she's expecting. (Not explained, of course, is why a policewoman who knows she's pregnant would have taken on a dangerous undercover assignment in the first place.) However, there's also a good spirit on the premises that takes the physical form of a tin soldier to help Judith out. As the supporting players fall victim to the toys and Mark goes about fighting them off, Judith is abducted by the evil spirit, which takes the form of the deceased Matt and ties her down, preparing to be reborn through her. But the benevolent tin soldier spirit intervenes, takes the guise of another young boy and fights off the evil one.

Although it pours on its fair share of blood and gore, DEMONIC TOYS is rarely frightening, in part because the special effects by John Buechler are unconvincing and in part because the characters are so foolish. In a typical scene, a deadly toy advances on the fallen Hesse, who keeps his arm outstretched (ostensibly in horror) long enough for the creature to get a good bite into his hand. The toys themselves are a largely derivative lot; the wisecracking Baby Oopsy-Daisy comes off like an infant Chucky, the man-sized killer teddy bear is a straight lift from executive producer Charles Band's earlier—and far superior—DOLLS and the design of a vicious jack-in-the-box is a direct steal from the Chiodo Bros.' KILLER KLOWNS FROM OUTER SPACE.

Just how a jack-in-the-box (which one presumes would have to remain pretty stationary) could be a legitimate threat is one of the many questions never convincingly resolved by director Peter Manoogian and screenwriter David S. Goyer; they simply run through a bunch of stock horror situations which are neither scary nor campily entertaining. The actors fight a losing battle with their simplistic, largely obnoxious roles and dumb, carelessly obscene dialogue (sample exchange: "Is that a cigarette in your mouth?" "No, it's your dick!"); Scoggins (TIME BOMB, PLAY MURDER FOR ME) is especially unconvincing as the overglamorous policewoman who gives new meaning to the term "model officer." *(Violence, profanity.)*

p, Anne Kelly; d, Peter Manoogian; w, David S. Goyer, (from the idea by Charles Band); ph, Adolfo Bartoli; ed, Andy Horvitch; art d, Billy Jett; cos, Robin Lewis; fx, John Buechler

Horror/Fantasy **(PR: O MPAA: R)**

DESERT KICKBOXER ★

85m 21st Century Film Corporation; Wells Company Ltd. ~ HBO Video c

John Haymes Newton *(Joe Highhawk–Hawk)*, Judie Aronson *(Claudia Valente)*, Sam DeFrancisco *(Anthony Valente)*, Paul L. Smith *(Santos)*, Michael M. Foley *(Bruno)*, Robert O'Reilly, Barry Lynch, Biff Manard

A tepid action saga, DESERT KICKBOXER concerns a half-breed Arizona lawman named Joe Highhawk, or Hawk (John Haymes Newton), who is haunted by the memory of having killed a man in a San Francisco kickboxing match years earlier.

He runs across gorgeous accountant Claudia Valente (Judie Aronson) and her dimwitted brother Anthony (Sam DeFrancisco), who are fleeing from dangerous Mexican drug king Santos (Paul L. Smith), mainly because they've stolen $20 million of his loot. Hawk decides to help them, even though they are technically felons, since he's been after Santos for a long time. Obstacles in their path include a mean biker gang and Hawk's crooked sheriff (Robert O'Reilly), who leads Santos and his heavies to a final showdown at Hawk's isolated desert trailer. In the finale melee, Anthony is killed but Hawk, breaking his promise never to kill again, demolishes the villains.

Star Newton, who played the lead in the short-lived TV series "Superboy," is the year's most dismal new action hero, whose attempt at mythic taciturnity reads more as if he just can't find his surfboard on a really great beach day. However, there's nothing much in the film to help him out, with a cliched screenplay, stodgy direction by Isaac Florentine, rote acting, and clumsy action and martial arts sequences, the latter poorly choreographed, with last-gasp overuse of slow-motion, by Florentine.

As usual for the genre, the villain, played by veteran Paul L. Smith (POPEYE, HAUNTED HONEYMOON), comes off best. Originally titled DESERT HAWK, this film was released direct-to-video. *(Violence, profanity, nudity.)*

p, William G. Dunn, Jr.; d, Isaac Florentine; w, Isaac Florentine, Jim Lotfi, (from the story by Florentine); ph, David "Dudy" Namir; ed, Karen Horn; m, Roy J. Ravio; prod d, Heather Lynn Ross; cos, Sashanna Kaplan

Crime/Action/Martial Arts **(PR: O MPAA: R)**

DESIRE AND HELL AT SUNSET MOTEL ★

90m Sunset Productions; Planet Productions ~ FoxVideo c

Sherilyn Fenn *(Bridey DeSoto)*, Whip Hubley *(Chester DeSoto)*, David Hewlett *(Deadpan Winchester)*, David Johansen *(Auggie March)*, Paul Bartel *(Manager)*, Kenneth Tobey *(Captain Holiday)*, Parker Whitman *(Boss)*, Shannon Sturges *(Louella)*, Eric Welch *(Eddie)*, Larry Spinak *(Waiter)*, Chuck Swain *(Hula-Hoop Boy)*

A comedy noir of the ultra-cheap variety, shot at the deserted Flamingo Motel in Santa Monica, DESIRE AND HELL AT SUNSET MOTEL is a long-winded, stage-bound travesty with a belabored hipness so smug and depleting that the film becomes an exposition of sham and stupidity.

Chester DeSoto (Whip Hubley) checks into the Sunset Motel in 1950s Anaheim for a sales meeting of the Tiny Plastic Toy Company. Accompanying him is his sultry sexpot wife, Bridey (Sherilyn Fenn), a woman whose desires run the gamut from an obsession for seeing Disneyland to taking midnight swims in the motel swimming pool wearing alluring black negligees. Soon after signing the register, Bridey is making advances on loitering Lothario Auggie March (David Johansen), who also happens to be blackmailing Chester for past Communist associations. Chester is busily engaged in hiring a sleazy psychotic beatnik appropriately named Deadpan Winchester (David Hewlett) to get the goods on his wife.

Amongst all the sordid maneuverings, the pompous and effete motel manager (Paul Bartel) is fussily spying through his shuttered office window at this jumbled collection of screwballs. The narrative line collapses in torpid and ramshackled scenes involving amnesia, hoola-hoops and murder. Ultimately, Deadpan is arrested by the cops for having killed blackmailer Auggie, and the DeSotos, joyous at having manipulated Deadpan into eliminating their blackmailer, fall into bed together as Bridey breathlessly intones, "Take me to Disneyland."

At one point well into the jumble of DESIRE AND HELL AT SUNSET MOTEL, a supporting character, musing to himself, states with grim finality "There's a lot less to this than meets the eye" and there is a no truer line of dialogue spoken in the film. First time writer-director Alan Castle strives for a jokey, stylistically dense parody of 1950s potboilers, but fails completely. Castle, with clunky direction and a badly paced over-the-top screenplay containing dialogue dipped in a curious amalgam of Somerset Maugham and James Elroy ("They say radioactive things have a half life as they decay. I think I'm radioactive"), is seemingly unable to muster enough energy or inspiration to take advantage of Jamie Thompson's impressively evocative cinematography.

The film is further stunted by the flat line readings of the actors, who appear to be playing out an extended form of a particularly bad Second City TV sketch, the parodic elements further blunted by a self-conscious post-modernist smirk. Sherilyn Fenn (TV's "Twin Peaks," RUBY) lends a sultry presence to the proceedings, but her acting ability teeters wildly from parody to self-parody. David Hewlett joins her in performing in a thoroughly psychotic manner, while Whip Hubley in contrast is completely bland and forgettable. Paul Bartel, David Johansen and Kenneth Tobay all lend their moral support to the project but are all cast adrift and abandoned in the uncharted waters of a production without a rudder. *(Sexual situations.)*

p, Donald P. Borchers; d, Alan Castle; w, Alan Castle; ph, Jamie Thompson; ed, James Gavin Bedford; m, Doug Walter Castle; prod d, Michael Clausen; set d, Jacqueline Lemmon; cos, Betty Pache Madden

Comedy/Thriller **(PR: C MPAA: PG-13)**

DEVIL'S DAUGHTER, THE ★★½

(Italy) 112m Penta Film; ADC ~ Republic Pictures Home Video c
(SETTA, LA)

Kelly Leigh Curtis *(Miriam)*, Herbert Lom *(Gran Vecchio)*, Maria Angela Giordano *(Kathryn)*, Tomas Arana *(Damon)*, Erica Sinisi *(Sara)*, Donald O'Brien *(Jonathan)*, Michel Hans Adatte *(Franz)*, Roberto Corbiletto *(Martin)*, Niels Gullov *(Mr. Heins)*, Angelika Maria Boeck *(Mrs. Heins)*, Carla Cassola

Though it does not transcend its genre limitations, THE DEVIL'S DAUGHTER uses the genre's conventions intelligently, and the result is highly watchable.

Southern California, 1970: a band of hippies living in a desert commune is slaughtered by a Manson-esque drifter who swears allegiance to Satan and a mysterious figure in a limousine, who speaks ominously of others whose time will come. Cut to Frankfurt, Germany, 1991: a mild looking, middle-aged man leaves his family, saying he's going to buy some milk. Instead he follows a young girl home and murders her, cutting out her heart and fleeing into the subway. When he's caught, he commits suicide. A sick old man (Herbert Lom), carrying a parcel wrapped in brown paper, embarks on a long bus trip; a shy schoolteacher, Miriam (Kelly Curtis, sister of horror-movie veteran Jamie Lee Curtis) nearly runs him over on the road in the quiet suburb where she lives. She brings him to her home, where he dies mysteriously, and she's plunged into a nightmare of bizarre dreams and acts of horror.

The old man is part of a mysterious sect, dedicated to Satan, and Miriam has been chosen to bear his son. The warning signs of supernatural nastiness are all around her: strange blue glop pours from the taps; her pet rabbit behaves weirdly; there's a message from the dead man on her answering machine and the cloth that covered his face takes on an eerie life; her best friend is brutally murdered; a student draws a strange, extinct insect—the very one the old man carried with him and placed in Miriam's nose, causing her to have strange dreams—and the camera tracks restlessly, nervously, intensely through the halls and cellar of Miriam's house, as though propelled by, well yes—the devil himself. But she doesn't know what to make of it all until it's too late, and she has been forced to bear her unnatural child.

It's standard enough stuff until the end, when THE DEVIL'S DAUGHTER throws the viewer a surprising curve: given the option of raising her child or turning him over to the cult, Miriam opts to hurl herself and the baby into the flames of a blazing automobile wreck. But when the emergency crews arrive, she alone is pulled from the ashes, miraculously unscathed and astonished that her unearthly child loved her enough to protect her from the fire.

What distinguishes THE DEVIL'S DAUGHTER from a slew of other evil-cult movies is the breathtaking beauty of its images, nowhere better demonstrated than in a hallucinatory dream, initiated when the strange insect (it's referred to as a scarab, though it hardly looks like one) crawls up Miriam's nose and into her brain. Following her pet rabbit through a field bright with flowers, she finds herself beneath a tree glittering with metal charms that tinkle in the breeze; the dream becomes a nightmare with the appearance of a great black bird that envelopes her in its wings and tears at her flesh. The scene in which, beneath a moonlit sky, cultists delicately insert a set of silver hooks into a woman's face, then lovingly peel it away from her skull, runs a close second. Photographed by Raffaele Mertes, THE DEVIL'S DAUGHTER rejects the crude darkness of most horror films, and replaces it with a rich palette of densely colored shadows and strangely eerie daylight.

THE DEVIL'S DAUGHTER breaks no new ground on the narrative front: its story owes much to ROSEMARY'S BABY, doctored with touches of everything from THE WICKER MAN to ALICE IN WONDERLAND. Actor-turned-director Michele Soavi's third film, following BLOODY BIRD and THE CHURCH, THE DEVIL'S DAUGHTER (which was released in his native Italy as LA SETTA, "The Sect"), shows clearly the influence of his mentor, Dario Argento, whose glorious and horrific visual sense has found him a wide cult following among fans of European horror films. But it is supremely beautiful, and surprisingly haunting. Almost two hours long, the film twists and turns in ways that are wildly improbable, but compelling nonetheless, despite the hollow dubbing that mars Italian films with English-language soundtracks. *(Violence, nudity, sexual situations.)*

p, Dario Argento, Mario Cecchi Gori, Vittorio Cecchi Gori; d, Michele Soavi; w, Dario Argento, Giovanni Romoli, Michele Soavi, (from the story by Argento, Romoli and Soavi); ph, Raffaele Mertes; m, Pino Donaggio; cos, Vera Cozzolino

Horror **(PR: C MPAA: R)**

DIARY OF A HITMAN ★½

90m Continental Film Group; Vision pdg ~ Vision International c

Forest Whitaker *(Dekker)*, Sherilyn Fenn *(Jain)*, Sharon Stone *(Kiki)*, Seymour Cassel *(Koenig)*, James Belushi *(Shandy)*, Lewis Smith *(Zidzyk)*, Lois Chiles *(Sheila)*, John Bedford-Lloyd, Jake Dengel, Wayne Crawford

The basis for DIARY OF A HITMAN was a stage drama called *Insider's Price*, by Kenneth Pressman, and although the playwright adapted his own work for the screen the film's theatrical origins are painfully clear.

The introspective hit man is Dekker (Forest Whitaker), a veteran assassin-for-hire who's tried but largely failed to remain indifferent to his profession. Now his eyesight is failing and his weapon arm pains him. With one more hit he'll have enough cash to retire, but the latest contract is unusually gruesome. A dubiously reformed hood named Zidzyk (Lewis Smith) has accepted Jesus as his savior, and now wants his wife dead (because she knows too much) and their infant child slaughtered with a body part brought back as proof.

Debuting director Roy London, a prominent Hollywood acting coach, keeps the first act moving with restless energy and the anti-hero's neuroses-ridden daily routine, as he attempts to put off his deadly errand for as long as he can. But the picture takes a real nosedive in the long, single-set segment when Dekker finally faces his target, Jain (Sherilyn Fenn). She's a dipsy child-woman who reacts to her impending doom with a sitcom-ful of hysterical antics: she babbles, does a striptease and recreates a high-school cheerleading routine. Then Dekker's halfhearted attempt to shoot her is interrupted by a visit from Jain's floozy sister (Sharon Stone in a hideous cameo). One finds oneself wishing that Dekker would pull the trigger already and get the movie over with, but instead he becomes Jain's valiant defender against a second hit man sent by Zidzyk. The born-again creep himself gets blasted by Dekker in his "true church," a porno parlor, permitting a wholly gratuitous display of sleaze ("He is risen!" Zidzyk exults, masturbating).

For a story that purports to confront lofty moral issues, all DIARY OF A HIT MAN has to say is Murdering People Is Very Bad, a trite theme that hardly gains interest as it crumbles Dekker's already shaky resolve. To London's considerable discredit, the thespians *declaim* their lines to the farthest balcony, and the situations and dialogue follow the florid extremes of off-Broadway psychodrama. The redoubtable Forest Whitaker's (BIRD, THE CRYING GAME) strong presence props up this stuff only partway, though he has solid support from Seymour Cassel as the hit man's paternalistic manager, who buys Dekker an expensive silencer so the noise won't damage the killer's hearing. Fenn (OF MICE AND MEN, RUBY) isn't believable for a single frame, and Jim Belushi chews the scenery as a flamboyant cop.

DIARY OF A HIT MAN played mainly at film festivals before coming to home video, although its Los Angeles run expanded after the picture won the audience prize at the Seventh Annual Santa Barbara Film Festival. It was an independent production, set and shot in Pittsburgh with additional filming in Sharon, Pennsylvania, and Youngstown, Ohio, for a budget of $2.5 million. *(Violence, substance abuse, profanity, nudity, sexual situations, adult situations.)*

p, Amin Q. Chaudhri; d, Roy London; w, Kenneth Pressman, (from his play *Insider's Price*); ph, Yuri Sokol; ed, Brian Smedley-Aston; m, Michel Colombier; prod d, Stephen Hendrickson; art d, Rusty Smith; set d, Karin Wiesel; cos, Calista Hendrickson

Crime/Drama **(PR: O MPAA: R)**

DIGGSTOWN ★★

97m Schaffel/Eclectic Films Production; Diggstown Productions; Axis Productions; MGM ~ MGM c

(GB: MIDNIGHT STING)

James Woods *(Gabriel Caine)*, Louis Gossett, Jr. *("Honey" Roy Palmer)*, Bruce Dern *(John Gillon)*, Oliver Platt *(Fitz)*, Heather Graham *(Emily Forrester)*, Randall "Tex" Cobb *(Wolf Forrester)*, Thomas Wilson Brown *(Robby Gillon)*, Duane Davis *(Hambone Busby)*, Willie Green *(Hammerhead Hagan)*, Orestes Matacena *(Victor Corsini)*, Kim Robillard *(Sheriff Stennis)*, John Short *(Corney "Buster" Robbins)*, Michael McGrady *(Frank Mangrum)*, Roger Hewlett *(Sam Lester)*, Rocky Pepeli *(Buck Holland)*, Jeff Benson *(Tank Miller)*, James Caviezel *(Billy Hargrove)*, Frank Collison *(Prison Guard)*, Marshall Bell *(Warden Bates)*, Raymond Turner *(Slim Busby)*, Wilhelm Von Homburg *(Charles Macum Diggs)*, George D. Wallace *(Bob Ferris)*, John Walter Davis *(Chet Willis)*, Alex Garcia *(Minoso Torres)*, Cyndi James Gossett *(Mary Palmer)*, Kenneth White *(Ben Culver)*, David Fresco *(Fish)*, Benny Urquidez *(Referee)*, Jeremy Roberts *(Sonny)*, Michael DeLorenzo *(Paulo)*, Troy A. Smith *(Betting Guard)*, Larry Ham *(Betting Guard)*, David Candreva *(Coach)*, Jose Alcala *(Boxing Kid)*, Victor Koliacos *(Boxing Kid)*, Nelly Bly *(Emily's Friend)*, Laura Mae Tate *(Marcy)*

Michael Ritchie's DIGGSTOWN attempts to blend the boxing excitement of the ROCKY series with the comic con man shenanigans of THE STING. When the screenplay deals with matters outside the ring, however, the film can't compete with its models.

Con man Gabriel Caine (James Woods), convicted of peddling phony fine art, continues to do business from behind bars in a Georgia prison. Caine directs the prison's boxing matches and helps convicts escape. Caine sends his partner Fitz (Oliver Platt) to a small Southern community called Diggstown, where he promptly cheats locals by pretending to be a rube and then winning big at cards and pool. After Caine is released from jail, to the chagrin of his enemy, Warden Bates (Marshall Bell), he joins Fitz and tangles with John Gillon (Bruce Dern), a ruthless businessman who owns all of Diggstown's land.

Caine bets Gillon that his boxer "Honey" Roy Palmer (Louis Gossett, Jr.) can defeat any ten of Diggstown's top male fighters in a twenty-four-hour period. The major challenge for Caine, however, is convincing forty-eight-year-old, washed-up Palmer to step again into the ring. Although he mistrusts Caine, Palmer eventually agrees to the scheme. Caine gets financial backing from mobster Victor Corsini (Orestes Matacena) in his bet with Gillon. Meanwhile, he also romances Emily Forrester (Heather Graham), the beautiful sister of a boxer convict Caine befriended in jail.

As Palmer trains, he is inspired by Charles Macum Diggs (Wilhelm Von Homburg), the wheelchair-bound, mute former pugilist the town is named after. When the fights commence, however, Gillon has plenty of aces up his sleeve, including Hammerhead Hagan (Willie Green), the only opponent to have ever defeated Palmer in his pro career. The fighter valiantly beats Hagan and eight others, but then Gillon, with the help of Warden Bates, brings out an awesome fighter from Caine's former jail. Caine gives a signal, however, and the fighter lets Palmer win.

Boxing scenes in movies usually can't lose, and DIGGSTOWN delivers the goods in a loud, fast, frenetic style. Its director, Michael Ritchie, has shown skill with such sports movies as THE BAD NEWS BEARS and SEMI TOUGH. Since DIGGSTOWN's screenplay, by Steven McKay, is poor, Ritchie has the right idea: speed past the cliches as quickly as possible, getting to the more dynamic fight scenes. He seems to shoot from every kind of angle, flashing from the fight, to the bell, to the crowd, to Caine, to Palmer and to Gillon. It's dizzying, yet effective.

Unfortunately, Ritchie's technique can't hide the film's many flaws. Most importantly, Woods's jumpy acting makes it impossible for you to enjoy his character's cons. Dressed in "Miami Vice"-style blazers, loafers and shades, he can hardly stand still. And Woods can't be sympathetic, even when the screenplay forces him into gooey scenes with Heather Graham, who plays the most obvious of love interests (and who inexplicably disappears near the end of the movie). Gossett doesn't fare much better—he's obviously too old and out-of-shape for the part. You find yourself staring at his little paunch. Meanwhile, Dern is so oily he might as well be playing Woods's part.

The movie's most glaring problem, however, is the screenplay. One of its many idiocies shows Palmer's glimpses of Charles Diggs, who has become a vegetable due to Gillon's chicanery. Near the end, when it looks as though Palmer will lose, he spots Diggs in the stands. If you don't think Diggs's suddenly alive look will propel Palmer to victory, you've seen very few films. And whenever screenwriter McKay needs a cheap laugh, he gives Woods a dick joke. Woods is actually most funny when he stands quietly in a long-sleeved, droopy sweater, listening to Gossett rant and rave.

But McKay is intent on overwriting. Bursts of important plot material will suddenly appear as dialogue in an action scene. You can't concentrate on what's happening. Video watchers may want to fast-forward to the boxing scenes; otherwise, DIGGSTOWN is a bust. *(Violence, profanity, adult situations.)*

p, Robert Schaffel; d, Michael Ritchie; w, Steven McKay, (from the novel *The Diggstown Ringers* by Leonard Wise); ph, Gerry Fisher; ed, Don Zimmerman; m, James Newton Howard; prod d, Steve Hendrickson; art d, Okowita; set d, Barbara Drake; cos, Wayne A. Finkelman

Comedy/Sports **(PR: C MPAA: R)**

DISCRETE, LA ★★★★

(France) 94m Productions Lazennec; Sara Films; FR3 Films Production; Canal Plus; Centre National de la Cinematographie ~ MK2 Productions USA c

Fabrice Luchini *(Antoine)*, Judith Henry *(Catherine)*, Maurice Garrel *(Jean)*, Marje Bunel *(Solange)*, Francois Toumarkine *(Manu)*, Brice Beaugier *(Solange's Friend)*

A stark parable of love betrayed, LA DISCRETE boasts two strong lead performances and sharp direction by Christian Vincent, who also co-wrote the richly detailed screenplay with Jean-Pierre Ronssin.

Both young and prematurely jaded Parisians, Antoine (Fabrice Luchini) and Catherine (Judith Henry) would hardly be anyone's idealistic idea of romantic young lovers. A government clerk who freelances as a rewrite editor of upscale pornography, Antoine prides himself on being a love-'em-and-leave-'em type who has recently been dumped for the first time by his latest conquest, Solange (Marje Bunel), leaving him angry and eager for revenge. Egged on by his vaguely demonic editor Jean (Maurice Garrel)—whom Vincent frames in his office surrounded by manuscript boxes bearing the scrawled name of "Sade" on their spines—Antoine enters into a hellish agreement to seduce, humiliate and abandon a woman while recording the details in an erotic journal to be published by Jean for wealthy patrons.

Antoine's quarry turns out to be the gamine-like Catherine, whom he initially lures with the promise of freelance secretarial work. No innocent herself, Catherine has had to leave her London job as an *au pair* after an affair she was having with her employer's husband started to turn serious. Weary of men who just want her for sex, she has avoided involvements. She nevertheless finds herself attracted to Antoine despite his transparent attempts to manipulate her by alternating cruelty and indifference with charm and flowers. Instead, she becomes the manipulator, testing his devotion even as he maintains the fiction in his "journal" that he is in control. When something like a conscience begins asserting itself, Antoine tries quitting the project, but Jean angrily holds him to their agreement.

Once Antoine accomplishes his "goal" he finds he has fallen completely in love with Catherine and submits his resignation as she is about to leave for a weekend with her parents in the country. Seeking revenge of his own, Jean contacts Catherine with a new assignment—typing Antoine's "memoir." After reading the document, she writes to Antoine, breaking off their relationship without giving any reason. Antoine returns to his favorite haunt, a cafe where his relationship with Catherine had blossomed, to meet Solange.

Vincent recognizes an essential but ugly truth that lies at the core of this heart-wrenching tale—that we tend to try to make over our lovers to fit our own ideals and fantasies. Vincent gets rich comic mileage out of the disparity between Antoine's writings, which appear as voiceover narration, and the truth. While Catherine is indifferent, Antoine writes of how she is beginning to yield to his "diabolical" stratagems. To his editor, Antoine feigns indifference, claiming that Catherine is too homely and too plain to be a worthy conquest. Yet, as Antoine continues to scribble, Catherine captures his heart through the transformative power of his art, however degraded. As he recreates her as a fictional character, she takes on an irresistible attraction to him, and almost against her will, she becomes the woman he has created in his writing—bright, charming and overpoweringly sensual. Yet again, art also betrays when Jean betrays Antoine simply by revealing to Catherine the original motivation for his courtship of her.

As it does in life, art creates and art destroys. As it does to Antoine, art lays bare our basest instincts for actions, existing as a permanent record of the contemptible reasons we often have for doing what turn out to be good things. For all the spare, economical elegance and subtle power with which LA DISCRETE (the title refers to the code name Antoine gives Catherine in his manuscript) articulates its themes, it never appears to be manipulated or manipulative. Rather its themes grow from the material and the characters, acted with passion and realism by its players. Richly ironic, erotic, ephemeral, intellectually provocative and downright earthy, LA DISCRETE is one of those deceptively small films that rocks the soul with its almost offhanded insights into eternal human truths. It's as good as Rohmer's best, with a lot less talk and a much harder edge. *(Adult situations, nudity.)*

p, Alain Rocca; d, Christian Vincent; w, Jean-Pierre Ronssin, Christian Vincent; ph, Romain Winding; ed, Francois Ceppi; m, Jay Gottlieb; set d, Sylvie Olive; cos, Marie Malterre; makeup, Michele Constantinides

Romance/Comedy/Drama **(PR: O MPAA: NR)**

DISTINGUISHED GENTLEMAN, THE ★★

105m Hollywood; Touchwood Pacific Partners I ~ BV c

Eddie Murphy *(Thomas Jefferson Johnson)*, Lane Smith *(Dick Dodge)*, Sheryl Lee Ralph *(Miss Loretta)*, Joe Don Baker *(Olaf Anderson)*, Victoria Rowell *(Celia Kirby)*, Grant Shaud *(Arthur Reinhardt)*, Kevin McCarthy *(Terry Corrigan)*, Charles S. Dutton *(Elijah Hawkins)*, Victor Rivers *(Armando)*, Chi *(Homer)*, Sonny Jim Gaines *(Van Dyke)*, Noble Willingham *(Zeke Bridges)*,

Gary Frank *(Iowa)*, Daniel Benzali *("Skeeter" Warburton)*, Cynthia Harris *(Vera Johnson)*, Susan Forristal *(Ellen Juba)*, Autumn Winters *(Mickey Juba)*, James Garner *(Jeff Johnson)*, Doris Grau *(Hattie Rifkin)*, Frances Foster *(Grandma)*, Sarah Carson *(Kimberly)*, Mel Owens *(Bo Chandler)*, Brad Koepenick *(Rafe Simon)*, John Doolittle *(Ira Schecter)*, Rosanna Huffman *(Mrs. Bridges)*, Dianne Turley Travis *(Mrs. Dodge)*, Tom Dahlgren *(Chief of Police)*, Tom Finnegan *(Ethics Committee Chair)*, Marty Kaplan *(Ned Grable)*, Cliff Bemis *(Gun Lobbyist)*, Prudence Barry *(Teacher)*, Nina Totenberg *(Election Anchor)*, Julianna McCarthy *(Blue Haired Lady)*, Daniel Petrie, Jr. *(Asbestos Lobbyist)*, Dion Anderson *(Distilled Spirits Lobbyist)*, Stu Levin *(Tobacco Lobbyist)*, Richard Anders *(Poultry Lobbyist)*, Brian Gelatto *(Crabhouse Waiter)*, Roger Reid *(Florida Reporter)*, Angela Stribling *(DC Anchor)*, Patricia Ciaffa *(DC Correspondent)*, David A. Penhale *(Voting Husband)*, Cordis Heard *(Voting Wife)*, Gary Price *(Taxi Driver)*, Tommy Boggs *(Tommy Boggs)*, J.D. Williams

Late 1992 saw the release of two films featuring an American flag in their opening credits. Both dealt with an African-American whose intelligence, vision and determination enabled him to turn the American political world upside down. One of these was Spike Lee's epic MALCOLM X. The other is the flip side of that heroic vision, a piece of cotton candy called THE DISTINGUISHED GENTLEMAN.

Thomas Jefferson Johnson (Eddie Murphy) is a con man who one day realizes that the similarity of his name to that of recently departed Florida Congressman Jefferson Davis Johnson could just get him elected to the House of Representatives. Campaigning as "Jeff Johnson" (his near-namesake's informal moniker), he wins the election without having given a speech or even made a public appearance. Once installed in Washington, Johnson and his cohorts are completely baffled by their new surroundings until they enlist the services of the former congressman's administrative aide, Reinhardt (Grant Shaud).

Johnson is welcomed into Congress, and soon finds that his experience as a con artist makes him a natural player of the influence-peddling game. His biggest coup is to land a lucrative position on the all-important Power and Industry Committee, chaired by Dick Dodge (Lane Smith); it's not as easy for him to pull the wool over the eyes of beautiful *pro bono* lobbyist Celia Kirby (Victoria Rowell) and her righteous liberal uncle, the Reverend Elijah Hawkins (Charles S. Dutton). Johnson's mercenary impulses finally lose out to his nobler side when he decides to blow the whistle on a Dodge-engineered coverup involving cancer-causing powerlines placed near schools in his district.

Thanks to Jonathan Lynn's pedestrian direction and an uninspired script, THE DISTINGUISHED GENTLEMEN does little to pull Eddie Murphy's career out of what looks like a consistent, if gentle, decline. On occasion, the former box-office champ is very funny: Johnson's acceptance speech is a hilarious pastiche of boilerplate political cliches, and his ability to adopt different characters and accents on demand remains a delight to watch. There's just not enough good material, however, to sustain the comic pace. The supporting cast is terrific, with highest marks going to Smith as the unctuous power-monger. *(Profanity.)*

p, Leonard Goldberg, Michael Peyser; d, Jonathan Lynn; w, Marty Kaplan, (from the story by Kaplan and Reynolds); ph, Gabriel Beristain; ed, Barry B. Leirer, Tony Lombardo; m, Randy Edelman; prod d, Leslie Dilley; art d, Ed Verreaux; set d, Dorree Cooper; cos, Francine Jamison-Tanchuck

Comedy **(PR: C MPAA: R)**

DO OR DIE ★½

97m November Down Co. ~ Malibu Bay Films c

Pat Morita *(Kaneshiro)*, Erik Estrada *(Richard Estaban)*, Dona Speir *(Donna Hamilton)*, Roberta Vasquez *(Nicole Justin)*, Bruce Penhall *(Bruce Christian)*, Cynthia Brimhall *(Edy)*, Bill Bumiller *(Lucas)*, Michael Shayne *(Shane Abilene)*, Stephanie Schick *(Atlanta Lee)*, Carolyn Liu *(Silk)*, Ava Cadell, Richard Cansino, Chu Chu Malave, Skip Ward, James Lew, Eric Chen

They're called T & E movies — the "E" stands for "explosions"—and they've been cranked out for years now by the Hawaii-based husband-and-wife team of Andy and Arlene Sidaris. He's a former Emmy-winning director for ABC Sports, while she wrote and produced TV's "The Hardy Boys/Nancy Drew Mysteries"; together, they've been responsible for a series of distinctive action-sexploitation spectacles starring a recurring cast of delectable federal agents who enjoy hot sex and deadly danger in equal doses. Part *Playboy* video, part gun-lovers' wet dream, the typical Malibu Bay Films production plays a few theaters but more often reaches salivating fans via home cassette.

The 1992 entry DO OR DIE gets off to a strong start before settling down to the usual exhibit of blazing bullets, squealing tires and luscious bodies. Two of the latter, undercover-agent babes Donna Hamilton (Dona Speir) and Nicole Justin (Roberta Vasquez) are kidnapped and brought before Kaneshiro (Pat Morita), a shadowy crimelord the pair has crossed too often. He doesn't kill them, but coolly warns that he's dispatched six separate teams of assassins who will most assuredly send the curvaceous cops to that big hot tub in the sky.

Released to their certain fate, the imperiled ladies call on their cohorts for backup. There's Shane Abilene (Michael Shayne), virile adventurer who can't shoot accurately with anything smaller than a grenade launcher (can there be some subtle bedroom metaphor at work here?); hunky Colonel Richard Estaban—listed as "Estevez" in the closing credits, but in any case played by Erik Estrada; Edy (Cynthia Brimhall), who has huge breasts; Atlanta Lee (Stephanie Schick), who has *huger* breasts; CIA hardbody Bruce Christian (Bruce Penhall); and a stud named Lucas (Bill Bumiller) to make sure everyone has a partner for the abundant lovemaking that ensues in between the chase scenes. One would think that characters running for their lives would have more urgent plans than coitus, but this is a Sidaris film, so there.

It's quite possible to mix frisky sex and action—witness the James Bond series—but DO OR DIE disappoints when the assassins attack. The fearsome hit men (and women) are a dull bunch, defeated with tired regularity and little suspense. Even Kaneshiro loses his menace; the narrative periodically visits him in his supervillain pad where he wastes valuable scheme time luxuriating in sensual massages from Asian wench Silk (Carolyn Liu). His computer screen shows the successive hit teams vanquished, video-game fashion, and finally he himself is cornered with minimal fuss.

The role is an impressive change of pace for Noriyuki "Pat" Morita. Best known as Arnold Takahashi on TV's "Happy Days" sitcom and the kindly martial-arts master in the KARATE KID series, he makes an effective, all-powerful bad guy until the screenplay turns him into a campy hedonist. The other familiar face, Estrada, is no stranger to the Sidaris team; he was the heavy in the previous installment, GUNS, ultimately blown to bits by a rocket launcher. Resurrections and reversals are nothing new to the series, though, and heroine Roberta Vasquez portrayed a doomed temptress in perhaps the best of the whole lot, PICASSO TRIGGER.

To liven things up the plot turns travelogue, roving from Hawaii to Arizona to Louisiana to Dallas for different showdowns. The Arizona interlude, set during a radio-controlled-aircraft fly-in, provides some diverting sights (both gunfire and evildoer Ava Cadell, who has huge breasts *and* a Cinemascope derriere). But the Bayou locations look oppressively overcast and dreary, even if they do provide an excuse for a country-and-western musical number that gives the girls yet another chance to shake their formidable tambourines. *(Violence, nudity, sexual situations, profanity.)*

p, Arlene Sidaris; d, Andy Sidaris; w, Andy Sidaris; ph, Mark Morris; ed, Michael Haight; m, Richard Lyons; prod d, Cherie Day Ledwith

Action **(PR: O MPAA: NR)**

DR. GIGGLES ★

93m Largo Entertainment; Dark Horse Entertainment ~ Universal c

Larry Drake *(Dr. Evan Rendell)*, Holly Marie Combs *(Jennifer Campbell)*, Cliff DeYoung *(Tom Campbell)*, Glenn Quinn *(Max Anderson)*, Keith Diamond *(Officer Joe Reitz)*, Richard Bradford *(Officer Hank Magruder)*, Michelle Johnson *(Tamara)*, John Vickery *(Dr. Chamberlain)*, Nancy Fish *(Elaine Henderson)*, Sara Melson *(Coreen)*, Zoe Trilling *(Normi)*, Darin Heames *(Stu)*, Deborah Tucker *(Dianne)*, Doug E. Doug *(Trotter)*, Denise Barnes *(Leigh)*, Patrick Cronin *(Sheriff Harper)*, Joshua Nielsen *(Danny Atchley)*, William Dennis Hunt *(Evan's Father)*, Nicholas Mastrandea *(Young Evan)*, William Earl Ray *(Psychiatrist)*, Danny Perkin *(Specks)*, Pieter Dawson *(Doctor)*, Todd Tolces *(1st Security Guard)*, Mario DePriest *(1st Orderly)*, Jerry Counsil *(1st Surgeon)*, Mark C. Vincent *(2nd Surgeon)*, Britt Magnuson *(1st Nurse)*, Annie Wanberg *(2nd Nurse)*, Russ Fast *(Anesthesiologist)*, Troy Barron *(Young Magruder)*, Marianne Doherty *(OR Nurse)*

A cliched throwback to the early 1980s slasher genre, DR. GIGGLES transplants the heart of a NIGHTMARE ON ELM STREET sequel—wisecracking killer—into the body of HALLOWEEN — psycho killer returns to his hometown to slash anew—but lacks the wit of the former or the tension of the latter.

Evan Rendell (Larry Drake of TV's "LA Law"), who thinks he's a physician and is nicknamed "Dr. Giggles" for his tendency to titter in times of stress, escapes from an asylum after butchering a couple of workers. He then heads for his hometown of Moorehigh, where he sets up a makeshift office in the house where he grew up. The place is now the stuff of local legend—when Evan was a boy, his father murdered several people in an attempt to find a heart to replace that of his dying wife; the townsfolk killed Rendell and his son disappeared without a trace.

Today, teenager Jennifer Campbell (Holly Marie Combs) is having heart problems of her own, and is told by town doctor Chamberlain (John Vickery) that she may need an operation. This, compounded by memories of her mother dying in a hospital, is severely troubling Jennifer and straining her relationships with her father Tom (Cliff DeYoung), his new wife Tamara (Michelle Johnson), and her own boyfriend Max Anderson (Glenn Quinn). Meanwhile, four of Jennifer's friends go exploring the old Rendell place; two of them are locked in and dispatched by Dr. Giggles. The next to go is the nosy old lady (Nancy Fish) who lives next door; as with all his victims, Dr. Giggles dispatches her with a piece of outsized medical equipment drawn from a seemingly bottomless doctor's bag.

The bad doctor goes on to dispatch two more hapless teens, then invades Jennifer's house and kills Tamara before going up to Jennifer's room. There he finds evidence of the girl's heart condition and vows to "save" her. He pursues her to the carnival, where Jennifer has discovered Max in a clinch with fellow student Coreen (Sara Melson); following the three into a hall of mirrors, Dr. Giggles kills Coreen and takes off in pursuit of Jennifer as Max watches helplessly. The police manage to find Jennifer before Dr. Giggles does, and after hearing her and Max's story, young Officer Joe Reitz (Keith Diamond) begins to believe the Rendell legend is true. Sure enough, older Officer Magruder recounts to Reitz that he was a rookie when the earlier Rendell massacre took place, and that he alone witnessed young Evan cutting his way out of his mother's corpse—his father had sewn him inside—before the boy disappeared.

Still stalking Jennifer, Dr. Giggles wounds Tom in his house and kills Magruder when the latter stops by; but Magruder has managed to shoot and wound him, and he is forced to return to his old house and extract the bullet himself. He then abducts Jennifer from Dr. Chamberlain's office, killing Chamberlain in the process, and spirits her to his "operating room," where he will give her a new heart—one of many he's extracted from his victims. But the operation is interrupted by the arrival of Reitz, who dies trying to save Jennifer, and then Max, who rescues her after a chase and struggle in the house's basement offices. Dr. Giggles apparently dies in an ensuing explosion—but then turns up at the hospital where Jennifer is to undergo a real operation. She manages to fight back, however, and kill him with the grotesque surgical devices he was planning to use on her.

DR. GIGGLES has exactly two effective moments, neither of which occurs during the movie's main action: the opening credit sequence, which takes us on a computer-generated trip through the bloodstream before Giggles's scalpel slices in; and the unnerving flashback to when the young Evan climbs bloodily out of his mother's corpse. Everything about the film's basic story, on the other hand, proceeds with a disheartening lack of originality, logic or thrills.

The characters themselves are one-dimensional stereotypes, from the idiot teenagers who talk only in partyspeak to the knucklehead adults who don't bother to turn the lights on even after they've discovered a bloody body on the floor. Their actions occur not because they make dramatic sense, but solely to motivate the simplistic storyline. Thus, Jennifer, who's been told to wear a heart-monitoring device and avoid stressful situations, carelessly tosses the device away early on and, instead of escaping into the crowded carnival after the hall of mirrors pursuit, decides to lead a long chase through the nearby woods. She's one resilient girl, though; during the climax, she's able to walk barefoot on floors where glass has been shattered and spilled water has been electrified.

The film's original story was written by Graeme Whifler, also responsible for the bizarre cult mini-classic SONNY BOY, but what co-screenwriter and director Manny Coto (JACK IN THE BOX, COVER-UP) has turned out is groaningly conventional, from the teen-sex-begets-violence horror scenes to the ridiculous "shocker" ending to the medically themed, sub-Freddy Krueger one-liners that make up just about all of Dr. Giggles's dialogue. And although the look is fairly slick, the occasional directorial flourishes often get silly. In a scene apparently inspired by HUSBANDS AND WIVES, the handheld camera lurches from one character to another until it appears to lose track of what it's supposed to be focusing on.

Given the one-note level of Dr. Giggles, it's not surprising that Drake doesn't appear to be having much fun with the role, even when, at the climax, he turns and intones to the audience, "Is there a doctor in the house?" What this project really needed was a script doctor. *(Excessive violence, sexual situations.)*

p, Stuart M. Besser; d, Manny Coto; w, Manny Coto, Graeme Whifler; ph, Robert Draper; ed, Debra Neil; m, Brian May; prod d, Bill Malley; art d, Alan Locke; set d, C.C. Rodarte

Horror/Comedy **(PR: O MPAA: R)**

DOCTOR MORDRID ★★

74m Full Moon Entertainment ~ Paramount Home Video c

Jeffrey Combs *(Doctor Mordrid)*, Brian Thompson *(Kabal)*, Yvette Nipar *(Samantha)*, Jay Acovone *(Tony Gaudio)*, Keith Coulouris *(Adrian)*, Julie Michaels *(Irene)*

Clearly an attempt to establish a new fantasy-hero franchise, DOCTOR MORDRID appears to have been an ambitious idea severely tempered by budgetary restrictions. Clocking in at only 74 minutes, its storyline could probably fit within a single comic book, with a couple of pages left over for the letters column.

Jeffrey Combs, who won genre acclaim for his work in RE-ANIMATOR and BRIDE OF RE-ANIMATOR, stars as the titular sorcerer, a being from another dimension who maintains an Earthly facade as the landlord of a Manhattan apartment building. As the story opens, he receives word from the all-seeing Monitor that his nemesis, Kabal (Brian Thompson), has escaped from imprisonment in his home dimension and is plotting to use black magic to take over the world. The glowering villain has, in fact, been appearing at various points around the globe, staging robberies of alchemic materials (platinum, diamonds etc.) that he needs to further his plot. He's also taken up with a pair of amateur satanists, Adrian (Keith Coulouris) and Irene (Julie Michaels), the latter of whom he kills after seducing her, whereupon he drains every drop of blood from her body.

While planning his counterattack against Kabal, Dr. Mordrid has become friendly with Samantha (Yvette Nipar), who works as a consultant to the police on occult matters and just happens to live in Mordrid's building. A relationship begins to develop, and when Irene's body is discovered, she has her policeman friend Tony Gaudio (Jay Acovone) visit with Mordrid for help—but Gaudio recognizes a symbol on one of Mordrid's talismans as the same one found on Irene's body and has him arrested. At the same time, Kabal has granted Adrian the gift of immortality, whereupon the punk gets himself arrested so he can strike at Mordrid; Samantha helps Mordrid escape before this can happen, though. He reveals to her that he and Kabal are brothers, each devoted to one of the opposite extremes of the potential of magic.

Realizing that Kabal is about to put his plans into motion at a museum, and with no time to get there physically, Mordrid releases his spirit from his body, leaving Samantha to guard it, and confronts the villain. Kabal has already begun his preparations, and animates a tyrannosaurus skeleton to attack intruding security guards; but Mordrid brings a mammoth skeleton to life, and it fights off the dinosaur and skewers Kabal before he can complete his evil magic. Mordrid then returns to his body just as Samantha is fighting off another attack by Adrian; the thug boldly challenges some cops who arrive on the scene, but Kabal had lifted his protective spell before dying, and Adrian is shot in the leg and taken away. Mordrid bids Samantha goodbye; he must leave for his own dimension for a time, but promises to return again—which he does the following Christmas Eve.

Some observers in the comics world noted the similarities between the title character of DOCTOR MORDRID and the Marvel Comics hero Dr. Strange, a comparison that is partly explained by the film's genesis; it was originally conceived by producer Charles Band and Marvel writer Jack Kirby as "Dr. Mortalis," back when Band was still heading up Empire Pictures. After Empire collapsed and Band set up Full Moon, the project was revived under its current title. Given the results, though, this hero is not likely to see many more adventures.

Although the setup is promising and some of the settings look great for the low budget, DOCTOR MORDRID's storyline is underdeveloped and, even with the abbreviated running time, cluttered with superfluous elements. The material involving the police is tired, old-hat stuff, and the subplot involving Adrian being made invincible ultimately makes no sense, since Kabal robs him of his power before receiving any indication that Adrian has carried out his murderous mission. Clearly, grounding much of the story in the real world was motivated by budgetary concerns, but the time might have been better spent further developing the relationship between Mordrid and Samantha. Combs and Nipar make an attractive couple, and Combs in general makes a convincing Mordrid, but there's not enough for them to do. Once again, filmmakers attempting to launch a franchise have forgotten that the first film has to stand out enough to warrant one. *(Violence, profanity, nudity.)*

p, Charles Band; d, Charles Band, Albert Band; w, C. Courtney Joyner, (from the idea by Charles Band); ph, Adolfo Bartoli; ed, Lauren Schaffer; m, Richard Band; prod d, Milo

Fantasy/Action **(PR: O MPAA: R)**

DOES THIS MEAN WE'RE MARRIED? ★★

(France) 93m Chrysalide Films ~ New Line Home Video c

Stephane Freiss *(Nick)*, Patsy Kensit *(Deena)*, Mouss Diouf *(Booker)*, Anne-Marie Pisani *(Claire)*, Joseph Momo *(Malik)*, Roxiane *(Asa)*, Jean-Marc Truong *(Hong)*, Valerie Stephen *(Madeleine)*, An Luu *(May Lin)*, Mapi Galan *(Antonella)*, Fedele Papalia *(Valenti)*, Andre Chaumeau *(Fournier)*, Pierre Belot *(Charles)*, Laura Benson *(Helene)*, Loic Brabant *(Thierry)*, Hugues Profy *(Carlo)*, Maite Nahyr *(Anna Liebman)*, Michel Prud'homme *(Official)*, Dominique Hulin *(Tiny)*, Michel Pilorge *(Pinot)*, Jean-Michel Dagory *(Concierge's Husband)*, Liliane Rovere *(Colette Brialy)*

In the spirit of Peter Weir's GREEN CARD, DOES THIS MEAN WE'RE MARRIED? tells the story of an American trying to become a French citizen. Unfortunately, director Carole Wiseman's version lacks the comic panache and romantic chemistry of the 1990 Gerard Depardieu vehicle.

Deena (Patsy Kensit) is a beautiful stand-up comic who "marries" Nick (Stephane Freiss) in order to get her green card. Nick, a struggling musician, goes along with the charade in exchange for Fr12,000. Deena and Nick part ways thinking they've got it made—she's got her green card and he can pay off his equipment. But this is just the beginning of their troubles, and their involvement with each other. After leaving the court house ceremony, Nick and his collaborator Booker (Mouss Diouf) enter the subway and are mugged.

Meanwhile, a French immigration official comes to Deena's apartment to ask some questions. Thinking quickly, Deena's roommate Claire (Anne-Marie Pisani) tells the agent she's moved. Later, Deena goes to stay with Nick, so when the agent comes to his place, it'll look like they're really married. However, they are not able to convince the mistrusting official, and must come in for questioning. Deena and Nick pass the interview and actually start to like each other, but part ways once again.

Returning to her apartment that night, Deena discovers that she is being evicted. Apparently, her chubby, compulsive gambler roomie Claire hasn't paid the rent in three months. Unable to find her own place, Deena goes back to Nick's. He lets her stay in the spare room. Eventually, Deena gets an agent and a lot of work doing stand-up and finally her own place. But Nick's luck continues to be bad. A credit card company that Deena and ex-roommate Claire scammed for Fr12,000, has repossessed Nick's electronic equipment since he's Deena's "husband." Deena ends up borrowing the money from Claire, and the equipment is returned.

Things are going well until Deena goes to Nick's place after an audition and finds him fooling around with Claire. Being an infamous womanizer, Nick's attempts to explain that it was Claire's hormones working overtime and not his, fail to convince Deena. A few weeks later, Nick and Booker finally sell a song, and Deena and Nick start seeing each other. At the film's close, Deena's mother dies and the two return to the US as a real married couple.

DOES THIS MEAN WE'RE MARRIED? is technically well produced, but the often slow-paced action and screenwriter Grant Morris's silly dialogue prevent it from being an entertaining romantic comedy. However, the film does manage to present an accurate picture of artists' frustrations. The scene where Nick becomes angry after realizing that a record producer hasn't even listened to his demo tape, is well executed and believable. *(Profanity, partial nudity, sexual situations.)*

p, Monique Annaud; d, Carol Wiseman; w, Grant Morris, Nancy Heikin-Pepin; ph, Yves Dahan; ed, Suzanne Lang-Willar; set d, Brigitte Perreau

Romance/Comedy **(PR: C MPAA: PG-13)**

DOLLY DEAREST ★★

94m Patriot Pictures; Channeler Entertainment; Cineast Group ~ Trimark Entertainment c

Denise Crosby *(Marilyn Reed)*, Rip Torn *(Dr. Karl Resnick)*, Sam Bottoms *(Eliot Reed)*, Chris Demetral *(Jimmy Reed)*, Candy Hutson *(Jessica Reed)*, Lupe Ontirveros *(Camila)*, Will Gotay *(Luis)*, Alma Martinez *(Alva)*, Enrique Renaldo *(Estrella)*, Brass Adams *(Bob Larabe)*

A competent but redundant horror film, DOLLY DEAREST amounts to a gender switch on the CHILD'S PLAY films, only this time it's an ancient evil instead of Brad Dourif that possesses the titular plaything.

The spirit is released when archaeologist Bob Larabe (Brass Adams) digs into what appear to be some ancient Mayan ruins in Mexico; as he tries to pry open a heavy stone door, it suddenly flies off and crushes him to death. The evil force (represented by an animated red doodle) then invades a nearby abandoned toy factory. But it's not abandoned for long; the Reed family arrives in the area shortly thereafter, with father Eliot (Sam Bottoms) planning to take over the place to put out his new "Dolly Dearest" line. When the family checks out the factory, young daughter Jessica (Candy Hutson) is entranced by the finished dolls left by the previous owner, and takes one of them home.

Pretty soon, she's spending all her time with the doll, and her mother Marilyn (Denise Crosby) starts to notice she's acting funny. The girl is especially belligerent towards the family's maid, Camila (Lupe Ontirveros), who confides to Marilyn that she fears evil forces are at work. Marilyn scoffs at her superstitions, and Camilla announces that she plans to leave; but before she can, the doll electrocutes her in the house's basement while Eliot and Marilyn are out.

Meanwhile, archaeologist Karl Resnick (Rip Torn), an associate of Larabe's, has traveled to the area to continue his friend's work. When he reactivates the dig, he finds that the ruins are not Mayan, but relics of the ancient, devil-worshipping Sanzia cult. Jessica's older brother Jimmy (Chris Demetral) has become fascinated by the ruins, and sneaks out of the house one night to "assist" Resnick at the site. At the same time, Eliot's assistant Luis (Will Gotay) is attacked by the other possessed dolls at the factory, causing him to have a fatal heart attack.

Jimmy discovers the body and, when he is brought home, explains his interest in the Sanzia cult to his parents. This piques the interest of Marilyn, who is becoming distraught over Jessica's increasingly disturbed behavior, and the next day she goes to ask Resnick about the cult. He tells her of a legend that the cult tried to breed the offspring of the devil, a child with the body of a human and the head of a goat. The legend is confirmed when Marilyn goes to visit Camila's sister Alva (Alma Martinez), who lives in a nearby convent, but Resnick insists that the story has no basis in fact.

Marilyn soon discovers the truth, however, when she arrives home and is confronted by the living, talking doll, which is indeed possessed by the devil-child's spirit and intends to corrupt Jessica and any other children it can claim. Attempting to shoot the doll, Marilyn is attacked by Jessica and drops her shotgun, but Jimmy takes up the weapon and blows the doll away, freeing his sister from its hold. Meanwhile, at the factory, Eliot is attacked by the other possessed dolls, but is saved by the arrival of Resnick, who has discovered the devil-child's corpse in the crypt and realized the legend is true. Marilyn and the children arrive, and while Eliot and Resnick lay dynamite in the factory, Jimmy goes to set some at the dig. The explosives he places destroy the ruins, and despite vicious opposition from the dolls, Eliot and Resnick manage to set enough dynamite to blow the factory and the dolls to kingdom come.

DOLLY DEAREST might have gotten away with its derivative basic premise had the details been filled in with more imagination, but this is standardized, predictable stuff from beginning to end. From the opening scene, all the elements fall neatly into place: nuclear family to be terrorized; young child to be possessed; helpful scientist around to explain it all; and various supporting characters who are so obviously destined for nasty fates that it's hard to get worked up about them. This is especially true in the case of Camila, who knows supernatural evil when she senses it and is immediately earmarked to pay for her correct suppositions.

The dolls themselves (created by Michael Burnett) are spooky-looking enough, and director Maria A. Lease's best effects are created by having the living toys scurrying around in the background. There are some tense moments as the plot unfolds, but the movie is uneven in its horrors; after developing the personal story of Jessica's possession, the story shifts to the multiple threat at the factory and loses some of its personal horror. And Lease is not averse to falling back on cliches as ancient as the evil spirits, like a cat that jumps out of a corner for a fake scare.

The climax's suspense is muddled as well—the dolls are shown putting out the fuses on the dynamite laid by the heroes, but then the factory blows up anyway—and occasional dumb dialogue also gets in the way. The most groan-worthy line belongs to Crosby, once she learns the truth about what's happening to Jessica: "I'm not losing my daughter to some goddamn seven-hundred-year-old goat head!" *(Violence, profanity.)*

p, Daniel Cady; d, Maria A. Lease; w, Maria A. Lease, (from the story by Lease, Rod Nave and Peter Sutcliff); ph, Eric D. Anderson; ed, Geoffrey Rowland; m, Mark Snow; prod d, Brooke Wheeler; art d, Pepie Tuers; cos, Scott Tomlinson

Horror **(PR: O MPAA: R)**

DOUBLE EDGE ★★½

(Israel) 86m Castle Hill Productions Inc. ~ Castle Hill Productions c

Faye Dunaway *(Faye Milano)*, Amos Kollek *(David)*, Muhamad Bakri *(Mustafa Shafik)*, Makram Khouri *(Ahmed Shafik)*, Michael Schneider *(Max)*, Shmuel Shiloh *(Moshe)*, Anat Atzmon *(Censor)*, Ann Belkin *(Sarah)*, Teddy Kollek, Abba Eban, Meir Kahane, Hanan Ashrawi, Ziad Abu Za'Yad, Naomi Altarez

Despite its controversial topic and occasional documentary flavor, DOUBLE EDGE is a ploddingly predictable melodrama about Israeli-Palestinian issues.

Faye Milano (Faye Dunaway) is an American photojournalist with a minimal background for her first foreign assignment in Israel, since she can't speak any of the languages and is still carrying in her baggage a selection of the popular books on the relevant issues. To judge from an opening conversation with a graying Israeli reserve officer, David (Amos Kollek), to whom she gives a ride, Faye seems slightly pro-Palestinian. Later, she learns that David is a writer and nephew to Jerusalem's mayor and uses his romantic interest in her to get an interview with Mayor Kollek.

Here the fictional narrative combines with a documentary impulse, since Faye does a series of interviews with real political representatives on both sides of the issue. Despite these interviews, Faye displays an incredible ability to go off half-cocked with fragmentary leads that she does not bother to complete or confirm. She also likes to counterpoint her print stories with conflicting photographs, so her interview with Mayor Kollek is illustrated with a shot of an Israeli policeman clubbing a Palestinian schoolgirl, who incidentally spat at her for her intercession.

Upon her arrival in Jerusalem, Faye hears of an incident in which a Palestinian boy was shot after having smashed in the skull of an Israeli soldier with a hurled brick. In her effort to report the story, Faye is invited to the Shafik household and meets the dead boy's elder brother Mustafa (Mohammed Bakri). She is received with that traditional Arab hospitality that always seems at such odds with the thickening tensions. Her clandestine photograph of Mustafa's later arrest earns the revocation of her press credentials since it includes a clear close-up of an arresting officer who is found with his throat cut. The Israeli army censor tells Faye that had she submitted the photo they would have cropped the guard's face, perhaps saving his life. A trifle chastened, Faye still submits the story of an injured Palestinian boy, who, it turns out, was hurt in a household accident and flown by army helicopter to the hospital burn unit. In the final sequence, as the frame freezes, Faye finds herself uncomfortably in a situation similar to the one she had heard about on the radio during her first day in Jerusalem.

The device of using naive or prejudiced reporters in situations they can barely fathom is not new. Joseph L. Mankiewicz did it about the first Indo-Chinese war in THE QUIET AMERICAN, based on the novel by Graham Greene, and so did John Wayne and Ray Kellogg about the Vietnam war, in 1968's THE GREEN BERETS. In DOUBLE EDGE, Faye Milano emerges as foolish as the transposed settler from New York's upper west side who frantically waves his automatic because of a couple of burning car tires that earlier an Israeli Army patrol had sensibly ignored. She cannot fit the incidents of cold-blooded ruthlessness she eventually witnesses on both sides into a simple framework of good guys and bad guys. *(Adult situations.)*

p, Amos Kollek, Rafi Reibenbach; d, Amos Kollek; w, Amos Kollek; ph, Amnon Salomon; ed, David Tour, Vicki Hiatt; m, Mira J. Spektor; cos, Rakefet Levy, Bernardine Morgan

Political/Thriller **(PR: C MPAA: PG-13)**

DOUBLE TROUBLE ★★

87m Motion Picture Corporation of America ~ Motion Picture Corporation of America c

Peter Paul *(Peter Jade)*, David Paul *(David Jade)*, Roddy McDowall *(Philip Chamberlain)*, A.J. Johnson *(Danitra)*, Collin Bernsen *(Whitney Regan)*, David Carradine *(Mr. C)*, Bill Mumy *(Bob)*, James Doohan *(Chief O'Brien)*, Troy Donahue *(Leonard Stewart)*, Steve Kanaly *(Kent)*, Gregory McKinney *(Ellis)*, Willie C. Carpenter *(Michaelson)*, Bobbie Brown *(Helga)*, Darcy LaPier *(Julie)*, Philip H. Fravel *(Ed)*, Tim Stack *(Albers)*, John Paragon *(Krevoy)*, Tito Larriva *(Reg)*, Robert Evan Collins *(Rosehill)*, Bill Moynahan *(Guard)*, Lynne Marie Stewart *(Policewoman)*, Stefanos Miltsakakis *(Jeremy)*, Henry Polic II *(Stephen Tarlow)*, Charles Aaronberg *(Receptionist)*, Nancy Marlowe *(Andrea King)*

At least the acting lessons paid off for Peter and David Paul, massively muscled twin bodybuilders who've appeared in a fistful of B pictures under the moniker "The Barbarian Brothers." In the quirky but forgettable DOUBLE TROUBLE the pumped-up pair finally play slightly fresher characters than the expected big, dumb brutes.

David Paul essays David Jade, a big, not-so-dumb hardworking cop (with Schwarzenegger posters on his apartment walls). Peter thesps as Peter Jade, David's black-sheep twin, a show-off cat burglar who phones the police to brag about his robberies and clowns for the security cameras. During a jewel heist Peter comes across an odd object and pockets it. The thingamajig turns out to be a top secret key to a vast underground diamond repository. Evil businessman Philip Chamberlain (Roddy McDowell) plans to use it to grab an incalculable fortune for himself, in what he calls "the most brilliantly conceived and successful ripoff since the invention of junk bonds." To this end Chamberlain kills David's partner on the force and threatens the key-snatching Peter.

So the strapping siblings from opposite sides of the tracks team up to defeat the bad guy. It's not that difficult because the double-crossing Chamberlain rubs out his own co-conspirators with almost mundane regularity, boiling the whole thing down to a one-against-two faceoff with the Jade boys. Also in the heroes' favor is some rather desperate plotting that sees them inexplicably escaping from a sealed vault and somehow arriving at Chamberlain's getaway plane well ahead of the villian.

DOUBLE TROUBLE may stumble over its own storyline, but as no-brainer entertainment it does provide diversion. The real creativity went into casting. That typically gruff police chief who orders David and Peter to work together is none other than James Doohan, finally taking a belated respite from his long-running role as Chief Engineer Scott in the "Star Trek" universe. David Carradine has a Hannibal-Lecter-type bit as Peter's smooth criminal mentor, locked up in prison but still available to dispense underworldly wisdom. Former child star Bill Mumy makes a memorably baby-faced assassin. A.J. Johnson, as David's slain partner Danitra, impresses with her buoyant attitude and mile-high platform shoes. Unfortunately, she's Black—the mark of sure doom for partners in airhead cop adventures. The officer who succeeds Danitra turns out to be a milquetoast preppie, and actor Collin Bernsen wrings bona fide laughs from the trite stock character.

Then there are the Pauls, a couple of human tanks previously showcased in vehicles like THE BARBARIANS and THINK BIG. Their comic sense is well developed also, though this screenplay foolishly serves up pathos as the duo reminisce about their late Alzheimer's disease-afflicted father. Outlaw Peter is a dapper *bon vivant*, while lawman David is a straight-arrow slob; both, however, agree on a sanctimonious anti-steroids statement injected into the dialogue early on—even though wastrel Peter claims he exercises his monstrous muscles not through honest workouts but with rhythmic electric shocks. This dubious bit of phys ed accounts for the presence of a high-voltage contraption in Peter's pad that he employs to torture a Chamberlain henchman, in a scene that's more sadistic than funny.

The violence in DOUBLE TROUBLE is distatefully, needlessly extreme (guest star Troy Donahue gets murdered in particularly sickening fashion), ruling out the picture for children, who otherwise would be the ideal audience for the singular Brothers Paul. *(Excessive violence, profanity.)*

p, Brad Krevoy, Steven Stabler; d, John Paragon; w, Jeffrey Kerns, Kurt Wimmer, Chuck Osborne, (from the story by Wimmer and Osborne); ph, Richard Michalak; ed, Jonas Thaler; prod d, Johan LeTenoux; set d, Marisol Jimenez; cos, Greg LaVoi

Action/Comedy **(PR: O MPAA: R)**

DOUBLE VISION

(France/Canada) 92m Cameras Continentales; Telescene Film Group; Gemini Film ~ Republic Pictures Home Video c

Kim Cattrall *(Lisa/Caroline)*, Gale Hansen *(Michael)*, Christopher Lee *(Mr. Bernard)*, Macha Meril *(Jimmy)*

Twins, good and evil, biological and symbolic, must be one of the hoariest movie devices. Doubles and doppelgangers abound throughout countless interesting thrillers. Hitchcock practically made them a stylistic signature and Brian De Palma picked up the torch with SISTERS and RAISING CAIN. David Cronenberg did his part with DEAD RINGERS. SINGLE WHITE FEMALE mines the same territory and Bette Davis served double duty in several movies. When faced with this tired device in DOUBLE VISION, the greatest mystery in the mind of the viewer should not be "Whodunnit?" but "Why bother?" Caroline (Kim Cattrall) is troubled by bad dreams. She and her twin sister, Lisa, are little girls playing by a body of water. Suddenly they are in a small rowboat and Lisa stands up and begins rocking it back and forth while little Caroline screams. Their father comes running to help but before he can get there, the adult Lisa lies dead in the water near a small waterfall. Caroline wakes up screaming.

Concerned by her nightmare, she telephones Lisa overseas in London. Groggy and hungover, Lisa fails to get to the telephone before Caroline hangs up to greet her stolid fiance, Michael (Gale Hansen). Back in London, Lisa is picked up by her South Asian boyfriend, Jimmy (Macha Meril), an aspiring actor making a living as a cabbie. He playfully torments her by playing loud music as he drives her to an audition for *Othello*. Lisa blows the audition and declares that Desdemona was a wimp. From there she goes to her job as a waitress in an Italian restaurant before dashing to an appointment with her lover, an elegant older gentleman, Mr. Bernard (Christopher Lee). She truly loves her elderly beau but he refuses to leave his wife.

Caroline has a far quieter lifestyle. She works in a laboratory apparently in the same medical center where Michael works as a surgeon. Still troubled by her dreams, she decides that Lisa needs her help. Since they are set to be married that coming weekend, Michael suggests that they go to London for their honeymoon. After she has a vision of Lisa's face in the water of the laboratory sink, Caroline decides she must travel immediately. She flies to London and is promptly mistaken for Lisa wherever she goes. Her premonitions get stronger and more dire. Meanwhile Lisa has crashed the Bernards' party in the country where they are celebrating the christening of a grandchild. Madame Bernard attempts to stop Lisa while alluding to a mysterious "arrangement" they have but the young woman is determined to cause a scene. Mr. Bernard arranges to meet her later in the boathouse down by the river. Lisa goes to the boathouse and gets murdered by an offscreen assailant. Suffering sympathetically in Lisa's apartment, Caroline collapses. When she is summoned by the police to view Lisa's body the next day, Caroline hears her sister's voice saying, "Don't run away this time." Caroline promptly returns to London, dresses up in her twin's sultriest outfit, and proceeds to "become" Lisa as she searches for the killer. She must confront her own dark half as she walks on the wild side to discover how Lisa lived and died.

Based on a short story by Mary Higgins Clark, hyped in the trailer as the "Modern Mistress of Suspense," DOUBLE VISION feels like a very small idea stretched out over a feature-length movie. Still, some entertainment value could have been salvaged if the story were told with a modicum of style and intelligence. Vivid performances and a resonant subtext may have helped a bit as well. However this direct-to-video release lacks any of these positive qualities.

The personality differences between the twins are purely academic. Caroline is a cipher and Lisa is a cipher with attitude. There is no hint of what their relationship was like. Furthermore the pace of the film is inexplicably and excruciatingly slow and there are no surprises. Anyone who manages to stay awake for the first half hour should be able to deduce easily the identity of the killer. The film's most thrilling moment occurs when the the end credits finally start their crawl up the screen. *(Violence, sexual situations.)*

p, Steve Walsh; d, Robert Knights; w, Tony Grisoni, (from the short story by Mary Higgins Clark); ph, Bruno De Keyzer; ed, Chris Wimble; m, Graham Sacher; prod d, Caroline Amies; art d, Tom Brown; cos, Shuna Harwood

Thriller **(PR: C MPAA: PG-13)**

DRIVE ★★★

86m Megagiant Entertainment ~ MEI Releasing bw

David Warner *(The Driver)*, Steve Antin *(The Passenger)*, Dedee Pfeiffer *(The Girl)*

Actor David Warner tends to lose his head in his movies, usually figuratively, as in MORGAN and STRAW DOGS, though at least once literally, in THE OMEN II. So it's business as usual in Jefery Levy's DRIVE as Warner turns an endless morning commute into a hilarious ride into the madness of lucidity, taking his hapless passenger with him.

Ryan O'Neal and Walter Hill notwithstanding, Warner is The Driver, driving pasty, weary Passenger (Steve Antin) to distraction even before the film's first image appears. Warner and Antin are heard arguing over a noise Warner thinks he hears his engine making. From there, they set out on their commute, apparently to respective jobs at computer makers IBM and Apple, somewhere in the far-flung vicinity of Los Angeles. It's also an hour and a half, each way, of automotive torture for Antin, as Warner spends most of the time testing out his "bits," half-cracked semi-semiotic diatribe-analyses covering cultural phenomena from football to pornography. In the intervals, Warner harangues Antin about his worthless life, destined to wind up, like Warner's, trapped in a steel cell on wheels on an eternal commute with way too much time to contemplate a life spent "rushing from one mistake to another."

Internally, and later externally, Antin anguishes over the breakup of his relationship with The Girl (Dedee Pfeiffer, Michelle's younger sister, who herself tends to show up in some pretty odd movies, like this one, and commendably so). She's seen but never heard as Antin first trickles, then pours out, his heart to Warner, for whom the breakup is only confirmation that The Passenger is, like himself, just another loser, smart enough to know it but not smart enough to do anything about it. The only real plot incident has the two involved in a minor fender-bender resulting in The Driver's getting bawled out by the other commuter and getting his face pushed in.

Eventually, The Passenger proposes they make a film about their commute, and it begins to seem as if DRIVE is that film, complete with cutaways to a script and Warner blowing a take. Abruptly, however, with a tear in his eye, The Driver runs out of things to say, stopping in the middle of a busy freeway to turn the wheel over to The Passenger.

Director and co-writer Jefery Levy shows a great deal of promise, as do his collaborators, from co-writer Colin MacLeod to cinematographer Steven Wacks, in this ingenious film that gets a feature's worth of mileage from the most minimalist ingredients imaginable. Despite its almost constant digressions, the screenplay stays tightly focused because the digressions spring from, and therefore define, the characters. Indeed, since the characters are never shown actually arriving at work, it could be said that the entire film is a digression. At the same time, it draws its grain of truth from the fact that most people are defined by their digressions.

In terms of dramatic style, DRIVE lands somewhere between Samuel Beckett, in its wry comic bleakness, and monologists such as Spalding Gray and Joe Frank, in its intellectual explorations of the possibilities of the inner life. Cinematically, the film is distinguished by a similar stylistic precision, recalling the early comically absurdist films of Roman Polanski. But the real driving force behind DRIVE is David Warner's performance. Warner is both seen and heard for virtually the film's entire length. His ability to hold the screen is a wonder to behold in a *tour de force* performance remarkable for its range of expression as well as a restraint that is all the more crucial for a character who's clearly on mental overload.

Antin is an unusually amiable straight man under the circumstances, enduring Warner's onslaughts without ever noticeably wilting. Rounding out the trio, as fantasy girls go, Pfeiffer more than fills the bill. *(Adult situations, profanity.)*

p, Jefery Levy; d, Jefery Levy; w, Colin MacLeod, Jefery Levy; ph, Steven Wacks; ed, Lauren Zuckerman; m, Charles H. Bisharat, Dr. Lee; prod d, J. Levy; art d, Scott Miller

Comedy **(PR: C MPAA: NR)**

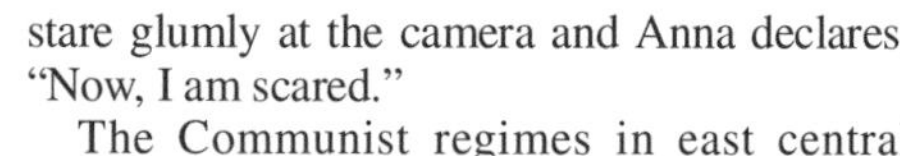

EAR, THE ★★★

(Czechoslovakia) 91m Barrandov Film Studios ~ International Film Exchange bw (UCHO)

Jirina Bohdalova *(Anna)*, Radoslav Brzobohaty *(Ludvik)*, Gustav Opocensky *(Conrade)*, Miloslav Holub *(General)*, Lubor Tokos *(Minister)*, Borivoj Navratil *(Cejnar)*, Jiri Cisler *(Secret Agent Standa)*

The plight of an opportunistic Communist bureaucrat torn between ambition and the changing tide of official loyalty provides the theme for THE EAR, a Czech film made over twenty years ago, stuck on the censors' shelf and released for exhibition by the changes in central Europe.

Scripted by director Karel Kachyna with Jan Prochazka, THE EAR also features a mordacious portrait of the unhappy marriage between Anna (Jirina Bohdalova), a tavern keeper's daughter, and Ludvik (Radoslav Brzobohaty), a smooth provincial functionary. Characteristically, when we first see them, Anna is drunk and he, preoccupied upon their early return from an official state reception. In a series of flashbacks, Ludvik recalls the whispered gossip and strong innuendo that the head of his ministry has been arrested along with several other officials. This fear of a purge is buttressed by the offhand remarks by some of the high-ranking and uniformed Soviet officers at the Party.

Of more immediate discomfort to the couple is the apparent loss of their house keys and a car that seems to be keeping watch on their street. Once at home, Ludvik notices a number of anomalies that heighten his fears: the electric power has been cut, the phone line is dead and strangers seem to have occupied the neighboring house where one of the arrested ministers lived. A frantic Ludvik even sets the toilet seat on fire in a maddened effort to destroy what he thinks may be incriminating papers. Suddenly the power is restored and the phone line reestablished, but now a team of men has assembled at their gate and demands entry.

This palpable threat effects a near reconciliation between the bickering couple, as she readies some warm clothes and he advises her how to protect their valuables. The visitors, recognizable as secret policemen from a flashback, appear genial and say they've come to return the house keys left behind at the party and to continue some late night drinking. Relieved at the apparent reprieve, the normally fastidious Ludvik joins them in their revels at the kitchen table. And with the threat diminished, Anna and Ludvik later resume their mutual abuse.

She reminds him of his crass opportunism in both marrying her and his political loyalty, catering to whoever is in power. Indeed in one of the flashbacks we've already seen how he was careful to remind people of the distance between himself and his dishonored superior, and how he joked with an old army pal, now a member of the secret police team. Anna even goes so far as to start doing the dishes, a task she normally avoids, and discovers a brand new "bug" or "ear" behind the sink. Together they search the house and discover three "ears" placed, he realizes, by the visiting drinkers. They now realize that the missing keys, like the power cut, were part of a procedure they had interrupted by their premature arrival from the banquet.

Now expecting an early morning arrest, the couple once again seem reconciled, especially after Ludvik's attempt at suicide is thwarted by police thoroughness in their earlier removal of his gun from its holster. So sure of arrest is he that Ludvik confuses the gate bell with the telephone's ringing. The call, however, is not a peremptory summons to prison, but rather a celebratory announcement of his promotion from Deputy to Minister. They stare glumly at the camera and Anna declares, "Now, I am scared."

The Communist regimes in east central Europe, like their model in Russia, had the unenviable reputation of being goverments that periodically destroyed their own, and particularly their most talented, supporters. In its droll blend of personal corruption and Stalinist practices, THE EAR does not focus on the idealistic victims, the Karl Radeks or Nikolai Bukharins destroyed by this system, but on an opportunistic survivor, the ballast aboard a tyrannical ship of state. For American audiences this, the nineteenth film from director Kachyna, could be seen as a mixture of WHO'S AFRAID OF VIRGINIA WOOLF? and THE CONVERSATION. In addition, the two leads bear a slight resemblance to Laurence Harvey and Simone Signoret.

Filmed in high-contrast b&w, the film features several satirical close-ups of Soviet and Czech officials, vodka glasses in hand, and the whole question of the pending political purge is compared openly to a primitive conga-line dance. THE EAR is also an exemplar of the art of the political film in eastern Europe with the fine hairline between the banned and the presentable at the censors' discretion. Ironically, the political changes that allowed the film to be finally seen have also destroyed the tension that called such art into being. THE EAR is now something of historic document on celluloid. *(Adult situations.)*

p, Karel Vejrik; d, Karel Kachyna; w, Karel Kachyna, Jan Prochazka, (from his story); ph, Josef Illik; ed, Miroslav Hanek; m, Svatopluk Havelka; prod d, Ester Krumbachova, Ladislav Winkelhofer; art d, Oldrich Okac; cos, Ester Krumbachova

Political/Thriller **(PR: C MPAA: NR)**

EDWARD II ★★

(U.K.) 91m Working Title; Uplink ~ Fine Line Features c

Steven Waddington *(Edward II)*, Andrew Tiernan *(Piers Gaveston)*, Tilda Swinton *(Queen Isabella)*, Nigel Terry *(Mortimer)*, John Lynch *(Spencer)*, Dudley Sutton *(Bishop of Winchester)*, Jerome Flynn *(Kent)*, Jody Graber *(Prince Edward)*, Kevin Collins *(Lightborn–the Jailor)*, Jill Balcon, Barbara New, Andrea Miller, Brian Mitchell, David Glover, John Quentin, Andrew Charleson *(Chorus of Nobility)*, Roger Hammond *(Bishop of York)*, Allan Corduner *(Poet)*, Annie Lennox *(Singer)*, Tony Forsyth *(Captive Policeman)*, Lloyd Newson *(Dancer)*, Nigel Charnock *(Dancer)*, Mark Davis *(Sailor)*, Andy Jeffrey *(Sailor)*, Barry John Clarke *(Man with Snake)*, John Henry Duncan *(Altar Boy)*, Thomas Duncan *(Altar Boy)*, Giles DeMontigny, Jonathan Stables, Michael Watkins, Robb Dennis *(Soldiers of the Guard)*, David Oliver, Chris McHallem, Chris Adamson, Danny Earl *(Thugs)*, Kim Dare *(Wild Girl)*, Kristina Overton *(Wild Girl)*, Trevor Skingle *(Gym Instructor)*, Christopher Hobbs *(Equery)*, Sandy Powell *(Seamstress)*, Kate Temple *(Seamstress)*, Andrew Lee Bolton *(Masseur)*, Liz Ranken *(Sexy Girl)*, Renee Eyre *(Sexy Girl)*, Sharon Munro *(Sexy Girl)*, Daniel Bevan, Ian Francis, James Norton, Tristam Cones *(Youth)*, Jocelyn Pook, Abigail Brown, Sonia Slany, Dinah Beamish *(Elektra Quartet Members)*

Derek Jarman's EDWARD II is calculated to offend, staging Christopher Marlowe's 16th-century tragedy in a timeless limbo and emphasizing the work's sexual themes if not to the exclusion, then very much to the diminution, of all others.

Edward II (Steven Waddington), King of England, is neglecting his marital duties for a robust affair with boyhood companion Piers Gaveston (Andrew Tiernan), son of a knight. Edward's wife, the icily beautiful and ferociously willful Queen Isabella (Tilda Swinton), is hurt, then enraged by his indifference. His nobles disapprove doubly, on the grounds that the relationship is homosexual and that it disturbs the social order. They attempt to force him to banish Gaveston, and though Edward realizes he is flouting custom with dangerous boldness, even for a king—or perhaps especially for a king—he fails to see the plot that is taking shape around him. Isabella conspires with Kent (Jerome Flynn) to overthrow her husband and install their young son, Prince Edward (Jody Graber), on the throne. Loyal to Gaveston to the end, the king is arrested and brutally murdered in custody.

Brief synopsis can scarcely do justice to the complexity of Edward II's story of love, betrayal, politics, ambition, greed and murder. In fact, Christopher Marlowe's play has long been criticized for its bewilderingly rapid shifts of alliance and enmity, though these same elements, along with its frank and sympathetic exploration of homosexual love, contribute to its startling freshness more than 300 years after it was written.

British filmmaker Derek Jarman, whose aesthetic orientation is intensely visual, is well known for his iconoclastic and eccentric (sometimes a bit too preciously so) approach to historical subjects; he's particularly drawn to material in which he can freely mix the sacred and the profane. Shot in Latin, SEBASTIAN, which marked the former production designer's feature directorial debut, was a homoerotic exploration of the life of martyr St. Sebastian, traditionally depicted as a comely youth pierced by numerous arrows (the image was a favorite of Japanese writer Yukio Mishima); it was followed by JUBILEE, THE TEMPEST, and THE LAST OF ENGLAND and CARAVAGGIO, both released in the US in 1988. An outspoken gay activist, Jarman's politics (he went public with his HIV-positive status shortly after being diagnosed in December 1986) are an integral part of his art. In EDWARD II, Jarman bluntly equates the sexual prejudices (and, by extension, intolerance of any form of difference) of 16th-century England with those of contemporary society. Shot on a set that resembles a vast, grey basement, the film hedges the issue of period and employs distancing devices to break the fictional illusion. Some cast members appear in Elizabethan costume, while others wear modern dress; a scene in which citizens riot is staged with contemporary policemen and gay activists bearing up-to-the-minute placards, and Edward and Gaveston dance to a mournful ballad sung by gender-bending Annie Lennox, who saunters around a corner and then melts back into the darkness. Though striking, this methodology seems pointless. The text itself makes clear that there's nothing dated about EDWARD II, and that its concerns are as vital today as when it was written. Jarman's lavish conceits verge on so much lily-gilding.

Though the issue of class is inextricably woven into the narrative, in Jarman's consideration it takes a back seat to homophobia, and the passion of his convictions makes him visually didactic. Star-crossed leads Waddington and Tiernan are costumed, groomed and shot with painstaking flattery; the scenes of Edward and Gaveston together—wrestling, bantering and making love—are composed with tender care, emphasizing the glistening beauty of their nearly identical pale skin and red hair. Among the other cast members, only Jarman regular Swinton is afforded equally striking treatment. But her Isabella is an *haute couture* gargoyle, a harpie with brilliantly lacquered fingernails; every increase in her bitterness and determination to strip Edward of his throne is mirrored in her ever higher hairdos, larger earrings and redder lipstick. It comes as no great surprise when she finally rips out a man's throat with her teeth—she's both beauty and the beast.

Tiernan and Swinton turn in the film's best performances. She delicately captures Isabella's initial hurt and confusion as Edward turns away from her, then skillfully delineates the way in which she transmutes her pain into cold fury and determination for revenge. Tiernan gives a less complex performance, but captures flawlessly Gaveston's common compulsion to flaunt before the aristocracy his privileged position as the King's consort; he knows better, but he can't help himself. Waddington is the weak side of the triangle. Though convincingly besotted, he's unconvincing as royalty; however much Edward may reject convention, he was born and raised to be king, and it's disconcerting to see no sign of it. Veteran actor Nigel Terry (THE LION IN WINTER, EXCALIBUR) brings to his less flashy but pivotal role as Mortimer, Isabella's lover and co-conspirator, the unflinching competence one expects from him.

Despite its faults, EDWARD II is both unusual and thought provoking. For all its fashionably post-modern production, it's far more compelling viewing than more conventional renditions of similar material, which often gives off the musty air of the museum. *(Violence, nudity, sexual situations.)*

p, Steve Clark-Hall, Antony Root; d, Derek Jarman; w, Derek Jarman, Stephen McBride, Ken Butler, (based on the play by Christopher Marlowe); ph, Ian Wilson; ed, George Akers; m, Simon Fisher Turner; prod d, Christopher Hobbs; art d, Rick Eyres; ch, Lloyd Newson, Nigel Charnock

Historical/Drama **(PR: O MPAA: R)**

EFFICIENCY EXPERT, THE ★★★

(Australia) 95m Meridian Films; Smiley Films ~ Miramax c (GB: SPOTSWOOD)

Anthony Hopkins *(Wallace)*, Ben Mendelsohn *(Carey)*, Alwyn Kurts *(Mr. Ball)*, Toni Collette *(Wendy)*, Bruno Lawrence *(Robert)*, Rebecca Rigg *(Cheryl)*, Russell Crowe *(Kim)*, John Walton *(Finn)*, John Flaus *(Gordon)*, Jeff Truman *(Ron)*, Gary Adams *(Kevin)*, Leslie Baker *(Gwen)*, Jacob Kino *(Marvin)*, Angela Punch McGregor *(Caroline)*, Dan Wyllie *(Frank Fletcher)*

An amusing, if sentimental, look at one small battlefield in the war for the global marketplace, THE EFFICIENCY EXPERT depicts Australia, or more specifically the town of Spotswood, Victoria, as a preserve of eccentricity and human kindness.

We first see Spotswood's workers through the unsympathetic, indeed shocked, eyes of Wallace (Anthony Hopkins), a three-piece-suited expert who seems to specialize, for a hefty commission, in preparing ailing businesses for sale to devouring super-national conglomerates. The Balls Moccasin Factory in Spotswood reminds Wallace of his grandfather's old house. The workers, most of whom seem to *wear* moccasins, he notices, are a jovial, cheery lot who chat amiably during work hours and converge en mass on the cafeteria for a lunch hour that resembles a cross between a knitting circle and a town hall meeting.

Presiding over this gentle anarchy is Mr. Ball (Alwyn Kurts), a paternal boss who thinks of expanding his firm and talks of steady profits to a bewildered Wallace, who stares in amazement at the thin, handwritten ledger books that comprise the firm's total business records. While most of the adult male employees spend a considerable part of their time preparing for a miniature car race, young Carey (Ben Mendelsohn) cannot help thinking and looking at Mr. Ball's daughter, Cheryl (Rebecca Rigg), whose tight dress is at a contrast with the relatively tomboyish Wendy (Toni Collette), an old friend and fellow worker who notes Carey's interest with growing dismay.

Wallace is friendly with the Balls employees, but distant—after all, he knows all too well what his recommendations often mean, and if he doesn't, he has the ugly labor unrest at nearby Durmack's factory to remind him. He is doubly shocked when he discovers that his colleague has multiplied the number of suggested firings in order to speed up the deal with an American firm from which they will profit. Wallace's shock deepens when his home and car are vandalized.

By contrast the lads at the Balls shipping room are all kindness and light, eagerly offering to repair Wallace's car and giving him a lift in the factory van. The changes he had suggested, including partitions and staggered lunch hours, are calmly ignored or neatly avoided. Unfortunately, an ambitious young salesman, Kim (Russell Crowe), Carey's tough rival for Cheryl's attentions, has stolen a set of books to show Wallace, accounts that paint a far more accurate and grimmer picture of the old firm's finances. Mr. Ball, it seems, has kept his plant in the fiscal black by selling off nearby properties.

Wallace must tell a tearful Mr. Ball that he will have to let go of half his employees, but requests a week's delay in the promulgation of the cuts. In the meantime, the shipping room lads ask if Wallace could help them in the forthcoming miniature car races, since one of the team has hurt his thumb in the repair of Wallace's Rover. Initially reluctant, Wallace agrees and, in the great filmic revelatory tradition, enjoys himself thoroughly as model cars are hurled through the air in imitation of some Hollywood chase film. That pleasure soon has effects as Wallace revises his suggestions to Mr. Ball.

Directed in the style of the post war British comedies from Ealing Studios, THE EFFICIENCY EXPERT has several throwaway scenes like Carey's young brother Kevin (Gary Adams), reading Orwell and Tolstoy late into the night. But director Mark Joffe, having previously worked on a documentary about the great Australian comic Barry Humphries, a/k/a Dame Edna Everage, does display a nice flair for comedy. Of special note, the film's primary location, an abandoned factory, was filled by production designer Chris Kennedy with the findings from old factories, rummage shops and garage sales to create a wondrous atmosphere of antiquated equipment and dated advertising posters.

p, Timothy White, Richard Brennan; d, Mark Joffe; w, Max Dann, Andrew Knight; ph, Ellery Ryan; ed, Nicholas Beauman; m, Ricky Fataar; prod d, Chris Kennedy; art d, Hugh Bateup; cos, Tess Schofield

Comedy **(PR: A MPAA: PG)**

ELEGANT CRIMINEL, L' ★★½

(France) 125m Partners Productions; Union Generale Cinematographique; Cine Cinq; Hachette Premiere ~ RKO Pictures Distribution c

Daniel Auteuil *(Pierre Lacenaire)*, Jean Poiret *(Allard)*, Marie-Armelle Deguy *(Princess Ida)*, Maiwenn LeBesco *(Hermine)*, Jacques Weber *(Arago)*, Patrick Pineau *(Avril)*, Samuel Labarthe *(Lusignan)*, Francois Perier *(Lacenaire's Father)*, Genevieve Casile *(Lacenaire's Mother)*

Daniel Auteuil gives a wonderfully deranged performance in L'ELEGANT CRIMINEL, the otherwise uneven biography of a notorious 19th-Century French thief and murderer.

Auteuil plays Pierre Lacenaire, who was also portrayed in the Marcel Carne classic, CHILDREN OF PARADISE. As this film begins, Lacenaire is about to face the guillotine together with his accomplice, Avril (Patrick Pineau). A flamboyant figure (imagine, if you can, equal parts Quentin Crisp and Charlie Manson), Lacenaire has turned aside the court's offer of mercy, describing his criminal career as a form of slow suicide he hopes will reach fruition with his beheading. He has also written an autobiography describing his gruesome exploits in detail that he has turned over to state security official Allard (Jean Poiret) to edit and have published after his death. As Allard works on the manuscript—his editing mostly consisting of censorship—the past life of Lacenaire unfolds.

The product of a smothering, sexually provocative mother and a distant, disdainful father, Lacenaire went on to a Jesuit education under a bullying, pedophilic cleric. He begins his career by stealing from his parents, first outright, then by deception when he cons his father out of a sizable sum to pay a gambling debt. He then enlists in the military to pass the time until his father dies and he can come into his inheritance. Upon leaving the military, however, he finds that his father has died bankrupt, causing Lacenaire to begin his criminal career in earnest. He teams up with a street urchin, Hermine, to commit street robberies. This same urchin reappears as a comely, amoral teen (Maiwenn LeBesco) after Lacenaire's death to seduce and move in with Allard, largely to have access to Lacenaire's memoir.

Moving on to bigger and better things, Lacenaire gets himself arrested and put into prison so he can make contact with the criminal underworld and recruit "professional accomplices," including Avril. Lacenaire is finally caught after one particularly bloody rampage in which he and a cohort with a fondness for ice-picks murder an old couple in their sleep to rob their silver shop. As a prisoner, Lacenaire becomes a major celebrity, which is also in keeping with his ambitions. At long last, Lacenaire goes to the guillotine, unrepentant and impeccably dressed.

To say the least, Lacenaire's story is hardly the stuff of a dry French costume drama. But that is precisely what L'ELEGANT CRIMINEL keeps threatening to become under co-writer Francis Girod's self-defeating direction. His method here, which backfires badly, is to have the movie jump freely, at times haphazardly, from the past to the present, revolving around Lacenaire's incarceration leading up to his execution in 1836, the editing of his manuscript by Allard and Arago (Jacques Weber), whom Lacenaire has asked to write an introduction, and Hermine, who herself jumps freely between Allard and Arago. The past, one must assume, is drawn from Lacenaire's actual memoir, which progresses in tone from colorful roguishness to dark, obsessive violence, along the way draining itself of any possible sympathy for its protagonist, as it should. Presumably, the idea is to distance the audience from either the allure of Lacenaire's outlaw life or the hypocritical bourgeois society that tracked him down and put him down. But it's finally difficult to deduce what Girod's intentions might have been.

There are a lot of strong ideas and powerful scenes floating around in L'ELEGANT CRIMINEL, perhaps too many. Girod can't stick with any single subplot or idea long enough for it to make its point. In fact, his pattern seems to be to cut away the moment a scene, character or theme threatens to engage either the intellect or emotions, which has the effect of upending the film and setting it back to square one every few minutes. The result is more irritating than enlightening and finally outright boring with a screenplay that is as overrun with dialogue as it is fragmented. If Lacenaire hadn't employed more conventional weapons, he almost certainly could have talked his victims to death.

Despite that, Auteuil's (best known to American audiences for JEAN DE FLORETTE and its sequel, MANON OF THE SPRING) audacious performance keeps the film from sinking irrevocably into some highbrow movie netherworld between anti-Chabrol and sub-Godard. In fact, the entire cast is generally strong, from the durable Poiret to the beguiling LeBesco. Girod's direction, in bits and pieces, suggests a major talent at work, which makes it all the more exasperating that L'ELEGANT CRIMINEL isn't a better film. *(Violence, adult situations.)*

p, Ariel Zeitoun; d, Francis Girod; w, Georges Conchon, Francis Girod; ph, Bruno DeKeyzer; ed, Genevieve Winding; m, Laurent Petitgirard; art d, Jacques Bufnoir; cos, Yvonne Sassinot DeNesle

Biography/Historical/Drama (PR: O MPAA: NR)

EMMANUELLE 6 ★

(France) 77m Everest Productions; Korda Films; Societe Generale de Gestion Cinematographique ~ New Horizons Home Video c

Natalie Uher *(Emmanuelle)*, Jean-Rene Gossart *(Professor Simon)*, Gustavo Rodriguez *(Tony Harrison)*, Tamira *(Uma)*, Thomass Ozermuller *(Benton)*, Hassan Guerrar *(Carlos)*, Luis Carlos Mendes *(Morales)*, Dagmar Berger, Rania Raja, Edda Kopke, Ilena D'Arcy

Poor Emmanuelle. The dazed young thing (Natalie Uher) arrives at the French country estate of loopy, bald-headed psychiatrist Professor Simon (Jean-Rene Gossart) with a romping case of amnesia, which has robbed her of her "instinctually sexual personality." It's now hidden behind the "curtain of her subconscious," a loss that EMMANUELLE 6 ranks as a major world disaster worthy of live CNN coverage.

Under Simon's care, Emmanuelle begins to relive her trauma. In flashbacks Emmanuelle and four other models set off on a fashion-jewelry-show cruise to Caracas, supervised by Benton (Thomass Ozermuller), the insurance agent for the valuable jewelry. The randy ship captain, Tony Harrison (Gustavo Rodrigues), arranges to steal the jewels for wealthy estate-owner Morales (Luis Carlos Mendes), who sends the girls, plus Indian stowaway Uma (Tamira), off to the local slavemarket, a fate from which they are saved by Uma's blowgun-armed tribe. Not unexpectedly, the stress of all this sends Emmanuelle wandering off into the jungle, from which she emerges weeks later with no memory of her ordeal. At film's end, wisely dumping Simon, Emmanuelle trots off into a barren field for a little masturbatory exercise, which apparently cures her.

Upon her debut in 1974, EMMANUELLE was touted as a model of the new, liberated, sexually empowered woman. The earlier entries were somewhat more interesting, unintentionally functioning as neo – colonialist revenge tales, as rich, jaded French or Italian intellectuals, male and female alike, invaded exotic locales to romp with the natives in a fashion forbidden them in Paris or Rome. But since taking over the EMMANUELLE "franchise" in 1984, producer Alain Siritzky has run the series right into the ground, catering to the commonest of male prurient fantasies.

EMMANUELLE 6 features yet another attractive but talentless one-shot star; a contrived and choppy storyline by screenwriter Jean Rollin (better known as a low budget horror-auteur), featuring, to cover the holes, a perfervid narration by shrink Gossart; inept direction by Bruno Zincone (with the "erotic" scenes shot by former fashion photographer Otto Weisser, for which he received co-director credit); and all of it atrociously dubbed into English. The sex scenes are surprisingly listless, tending to lesbian couplings. Clearly the worst of the series, EMMANUELLE 6 opened in French theaters in 1988 and has only now been released in the US direct-to-video.

For the record, the film shares only the character name with its predecessors: EMMANUELLE; EMMANUELLE, JOYS OF A WOMAN; GOODBYE EMMANUELLE (all with Sylvia Kristel); EMMANUELLE 4 (with Mia Nygren); and EMMANUELLE 5 (with Monique Gabrielle). Something to watch for: since 1985, producer Siritzky has been annually promising a TV series . . . . *(Nudity, sexual situations.)*

p, Alain Siritzky; d, Bruno Zincone, Otto Weisser; w, Jean Rollin, (from the story by Emmanuelle Arsan); ph, Max Montheillet, Serge Godet; ed, Michel Crivallero; m, Olivier Day

Erotic/Drama (PR: O MPAA: NR)

ENCHANTED APRIL ★★★

(U.K.) 101m Miramax ~ Miramax c

Josie Lawrence *(Lottie Wilkins)*, Miranda Richardson *(Rose Arbuthnot)*, Joan Plowright *(Mrs. Fisher)*, Polly Walker *(Lady Caroline Dester)*, Alfred Molina *(Mellersh Wilkins)*, Jim Broadbent *(Frederick Arbuthnot)*, Michael Kitchen *(George Briggs)*, Neville Phillips *(Vicar)*, Stephen Beckett *(Jonathan)*, Mathew Radford *(Patrick)*, Davide Manuli *(Beppo)*, Vittorio Duse *(Domenico)*, Adriana Fachetti *(Francesca)*, Anna Longhi *(Costanza)*

Light, airy and utterly charming, this is one romantic comedy that lives up to its title, a feat all the more surprising for having come from the director and brilliant star of the grim, nightmarish DANCE WITH A STRANGER.

Miranda Richardson, who played the doomed Ruth Ellis in director Mike Newell's celebrated 1985 drama, is Rose Arbuthnot, a deeply moral wife in an unlikely marriage with Frederick (Jim Broadbent), a worldly author of risque boudoir biographies (*The Sins of Madame Pompadour* is his latest). But it is her rather ditsy acquaintance, Lottie Wilkins (Josie Lawrence), who first spots the ad for a one-month rental of an Italian villa on a rainy afternoon in London. In an equally unlikely marriage, Wilkins is the tentatively freespirited wife of Mellersh (Alfred Molina), an officious accountant who treats her like a child. Convincing Rose that a month away from their husbands would do them a world of good, Lottie also brings in two other co-renters—the widowed Mrs. Fisher (Joan Plowright), who has withdrawn into her memories of now-dead poets she has known and is so snooty she initially demands references from Wilkins and Arbuthnot, and the rich and beautiful Lady Caroline Dester (Polly Walker), the heart's desire of every man in London (including, unbeknownst to Rose, her husband), who needs a month away from her usual social whirl.

Having finalized the arrangements with the villa owner, George Briggs (Michael Kitchen), Rose and Lottie hurry off to Italy to make the villa habitable for their co-renters only to find they've already arrived, chosen rooms and made meal arrangements with the serving staff. There is some initial friction, particularly between Mrs. Fisher and Lady Caroline. But, on the whole, the villa exerts a kind of magic over them that is threatened when Lottie, who had most wanted to get away from her husband, winds up writing him to come and join her. She convinces Rose to do the same, although she assumes her husband will be so busy promoting his book that he may not even read her telegram. In fact he doesn't, but he comes to the villa anyway—in pursuit of Lady Caroline. Meanwhile, Briggs drops by—in pursuit of Rose, whom he has mistakenly assumed to be a widow. Lottie's husband also arrives—bent on doing business with Lady Caroline. But instead of causing embarrassments and complications, both husbands also fall under the villa's charm and come to a new appreciation of their wives. Lady Caroline finds herself in the unaccustomed position of being a fifth wheel, while Mrs. Fisher is quietly rejuvenated.

If ENCHANTED APRIL, based on the fanciful 1923 novel by Elizabeth Von Arnim, seems like an unlikely follow-up for the director and star of DANCE WITH A STRANGER, think again. Newell is hardly a one-note director, nor is Richardson an actress of limited range. After their 1985 collaboration, Newell went on to make THE GOOD FATHER, eliciting one of Anthony Hopkins's best performances as a man consumed with revenging himself against his divorced wife. Richardson, meanwhile, has shown amazing range. In her furthest cry from Ruth Ellis, she more than held her own playing a hilariously harebrained Queen Elizabeth opposite Rowan Atkinson in his British TV series, "Blackadder." And her recent turns in Neil Jordan's THE CRYING GAME and Louis Malle's DAMAGE have shown her off to brilliant advantage.

In lesser hands, ENCHANTED APRIL could have been impossibly treacly, but Newell and screenwriter Peter Barnes imbue the material with a distinctively feminist bent; what all four women have in common is a need for relief from the oppression of men who have compartmentalized them each in his own way. The "magic" comes from the men in the story being compelled to reacquaint themselves with these women on their own terms and coming away richer for it. Beautifully acted by its ensemble and sumptuously photographed, ENCHANTED APRIL is indeed enchanting, but there is much more to it than meets the eye. *(Adult situations.)*

p, Ann Scott; d, Mike Newell; w, Peter Barnes, Elizabeth Von Arnim, (from her novel); ph, Rex Maidment; ed, Dick Allen; m, Richard Rodney Bennet; prod d, Malcolm Thornton; cos, Sheena Napier

AAN Best Supporting Actress: Joan Plowright; *AAN Best Adapted Screenplay:* Peter Barnes; *AAN Costume Design:* Sheena Napier

Romance/Comedy **(PR: C MPAA: PG)**

ENCINO MAN ★★

89m Hollywood ~ BV c

Sean Astin *(Dave Morgan)*, Brendan Fraser *(Link)*, Pauly Shore *(Stoney Brown)*, Megan Ward *(Robyn Sweeney)*, Robin Tunney *(Ella)*, Michael DeLuise *(Matt)*, Patrick Van Horn *(Phil)*, Dalton James *(Will)*, Rick Ducommun *(Mr. Brush)*, Jonathan Quan *(Kim)*, Mariette Hartley *(Mrs. Morgan)*, Richard Masur *(Mr. Morgan)*, Ellen Blain *(Teena Morgan)*, Esther Scott *(Mrs. Mackey)*, Steven Elkins *(Mr. Beady)*, Wanda Acuna *(Maria)*, Furley Lumpkin *(Science Teacher)*, Peter Allas *(Officer Sims)*, Michole Briana White *(Kathleen)*, Rose McGowan *(Nora)*, Jack Noseworthy *(Taylor)*, Christian Hoff *(Boog)*, Sicily Rossomando *(Senorita Vasquez)*, Erick Avari *(Raji)*, Gerry Bednob *(Kashmir)*, Douglas McCallie *(Police Officer)*, R.D. Carpenter *(Truck Driver)*, Kyle-Scott Jackson *(Intimidating Cop)*, Jeffrey Anderson-Gunter *(Bartender)*, Noel L. Walcott, III *(Rastadude)*, Mark Adair *(Peyton)*, Jose Luis Lozano *(Charlie)*, Sandra Hess *(Cave Nug)*, Deborah Johnson, Julianne Christie, Toni Herkert, Therese Kablan, Jerri Renee Griffin *(Fresh Nugs)*, Heather Bennett *(Mountain Nug)*, Melinda Armstrong *(Mountain Nug)*, Boris the Dog *(Buffie the Dog)*, Mike Muir, Stephen Perkins, Dean Pleasants, Adam Siegel, Robert Trujillo *(Infectious Grooves Band Members)*, Richard Montoya *(Enrique)*, Ric Salinas *(Loco)*, Herbert Siguenza *(Chuly)*

An amusing idea goes nowhere in ENCINO MAN, the Disney debut from the producers behind the acclaimed documentary HEARTS OF DARKNESS: A FILMMAKER'S APOCALYPSE.

Recycling the stone-aged teenage plot about the two dweebs who make good, Sean Astin and Pauly Shore co-star as Encino High seniors Dave Morgan and Stoney Brown, who are facing graduation as failures. Dave has lost his lifelong love, Robyn Sweeney (Megan Ward), to the school goon Matt (Michael DeLuise, son of Dom). Stoney, meanwhile, lives in a little Valley world of his own with its own language and "wacky" outlook on life. Dave's quest for popularity has reached the obsessive point where he is digging his own swimming pool in his family's backyard in order to host a righteous after-prom party. It is from there that one of Southern California's frequent earthquakes unearths the title caveman (Brendan Fraser) in a cake of ice.

After thawing, "Link" proves so "rad" that Dave sees him as a shortcut to high-school popularity, as well as a way to win back Robyn. At school, Link is palmed off as an exchange student from "Estonia" who causes high-spirited mayhem around Encino High while placing Dave and Stoney in the social spotlight. Dave's plan goes awry, however, when Robyn and Link become attracted to each other and Matt begins to suspect Link's true origins. Dave and Stoney have a brief falling-out over Dave's exploitation of Link after a fed-up Dave tries to abandon Link by the side of a road. But everybody gets back together in time to defeat Matt, who tries to expose Link's caveman-hood at the prom. The romantic impasse between Robyn and Dave is solved by the last-minute unearthing of Link's sexy cave-girlfriend (Sandra Hess). At the fadeout, Dave and Robyn are blissfully sucking face while Stoney addresses the camera and promises to be back.

Judging by the fadeout, Disney seems to think it has a new franchise in Shore, the rubber-faced son of comedian Sammy Shore and comedy club owner Mitzi Shore who stars on an allegedly popular MTV cable show. Not only is he featured here; according to ENCINO MAN's presskit, he has been signed to a three-picture deal with Disney subsidiary Hollywood Pictures to do—who knows what. Maybe he'll be teamed with Jim Varney to add teen appeal to upcoming "Ernest" movies. But all seriousness aside, ENCINO MAN is a less-than-stellar calling card for a subpar talent.

The film itself is a drab, lifeless farce that manages to make not only the "Bill and Ted" movies and WAYNE'S WORLD, but even STRANGE BREW, seem fresh and original by comparison. In what is fast becoming the signature of the Disney comedy style, its potentially intriguing premise gets systematically watered down in numbingly routine, derivative comedy situations and half-baked, warmhearted homilies. Awkwardly sidestepped is any serious or satirical exploration of the film's ticklish premise—unleashing an earthy half-animal in a school full of hormone-wired teenaged girls and their preening, blow-dried boyfriends. In the age of AIDS and clarion calls for a return to family values, the most relating to be done here is between Dave and Stoney, with Robyn functioning as a sort of brain-dead adornment who gravitates from Matt to Link to Dave for no discernible reason except that it's where the plot puts her.

For the most part, anything resembling a genuine plot is pushed back to give a showcase for Shore, a scenery chewer without conviction or noticeable talent, whose deficits as an actor and comedian have evidently remained safely hidden in the zap-happy MTV format until now. Fraser (SCHOOL TIES) seems to have some talent for physical comedy but, despite having the film named after his character, he seems over-edited and reined-in, as though the filmmakers saw him in constant danger of stealing the film from Shore. While he's in the spotlight, however, he resembles an amusing younger version of Christopher Lambert's Tarzan.

Astin also tries hard, but his character is an unappealing nonentity who really has no business getting the girl. Richard Masur and Mariette Hartley are funny but, despite being billed over the over-ubiquitous Shore, they have little more than cameo roles here as Dave's placidly baffled parents.

All told, ENCINO MAN is yet another "zany" Disney comedy that is little more than the sum total of its trailers. *(Adult situations, substance abuse.)*

p, George Zaloom, Les Mayfield; d, Les Mayfield; w, Shawn Schepps, (from the story by Schepps and George Zaloom); ph, Robert Brinkmann; ed, Eric Sears, Michael Kelly; m, J. Peter Robinson; prod d, James Allen; set d, Cheryal Kearney; cos, Marie France

Comedy/Fantasy **(PR: C MPAA: R)**

ENID IS SLEEPING
(SEE: OVER HER DEAD BODY)

ESCAPE FROM . . . SURVIVAL ZONE ★★★
85m Living Spirit Pictures ~ AIP Home Video c

Terence Ford *(Jack Slater)*, Paris Jefferson *(Kath Hanzaker)*, Raymond Johnson *(Benjamin Gibson, Jr.)*, Truce Mitchell *(Sean McBain)*, Ivan Rogers *(Lewis T. Holden)*

ESCAPE FROM . . . SURVIVAL ZONE is a surprisingly effective sci-fi psychodrama, composed of equal parts BLADE RUNNER, BATMAN and "The Twilight Zone." Long on atmosphere and angst, it's regrettably short on production values, which in many ways weakens the punch.

The year is 1998 and the US is on the brink of a nuclear war due to a white hot confrontation in the Persian Gulf. Broadcast news has become what NETWORK once satirized—a series of shock sound bites that devote as much time to reporting on the death of the President's dog as it does to the mounting tensions in the Persian Gulf. TV news cameraman Jack Slater (Terence Ford), recently returned from covering the conflict in the Persian Gulf, spends most of his time drowning his nightmarish recollections of the televised death of his soundman in a vat of alcohol. Kath Hanzaker (Paris Jefferson), the spunky reporter of the stricken unit, wants Slater to snap out of his stupor but she too is haunted by the soundman's death. Enter Benjamin Gibson, Jr. (Raymond Johnson), who, seeing what wrecks Slater and Kath are, suggests they join him on a four-week survival training course on the obscure Survival Island in order to be prepared for the next emergency the team may face covering the impending war. Kath agrees to go and, although skeptical, Slater goes along.

Once there, the trio is victimized by Lewis T. Holden (Ivan Rogers) and Sean McBain (Truce Mitchell), the paranoid ex-Marines who run Survival Island. Suspicious, Slater and Ben sneak into Holden and McBain's barracks and discover that the former was once on trial for murder and had written a rambling, psychotic treatise on post-nuclear war survival. As Ben reads the news clippings of Holden's murder trial, a hidden figure lobs a hand grenade at him, killing him. Slater and Kath determine that the camp is run by a bunch of lunatics and attempt an escape. The real madman turns out to be McBain, who kills Holden and tries to kill Slater so that he and Kath can survive the impending nuclear war together. Slater returns and kills the maniacal McBain, but not before Kath is killed. As Slater leans on the entrance to a rescue helicopter in a shocked stupor, a news team runs up to him and the reporter recognizes him. Looking at Slater's stunned countenance he asks him, "I thought you were in the Gulf covering the peace talks."

ESCAPE FROM . . . SURVIVAL ZONE manages to convey the mental terror of a world seized by apocalyptic terror. This is accomplished not by ornate special effects or a baroque musical score, but by concentrating on individual characters who must come to grips with the chaos surrounding them.

Kath and Slater register their hopelessness and desperation by going about their duties with helpless resignation. Slater drinks to blunt his pain and Kath spends nights awaking from nightmares. Director Chris Jones centers on these two tortured souls by beginning scenes with roving close-ups of their personal belongings, much in the way that Hitchcock gave audiences a sense of James Stewart's character at the beginning of REAR WINDOW. Jones intimates through small touches the sense of a world at a breaking point: signs that say "The end of the world is here" and "All firearms to be checked at bar before service"; Ben paging through *Guns Magazine* like someone flipping through the latest issue of *Vanity Fair*; and a desolate highrise Marriott Marquis headquarters for Callington Communications.

Mark Talbot-Butler and Jones's screenplay compliments the latter's direction in its sparse, barking dialogue (a mugger tells his partner, "When you're in this town, you gotta think violence"; a crazed gunman holding a hostage shrieks "Money puts this guy way above the law"). Together they almost compensate for the film's jarringly low production values. Given the budget of a BATMAN or a TOTAL RECALL, ESCAPE FROM . . . SURVIVAL ZONE could have been molded into a disturbing, bleak science fiction masterpiece. Although Jones is more often than not effective in creating a mood of malaise and moral bankrupcy, how much grander the film could have been with conceptual artist Syd Mead or production designer Lawrence G. Paull working with the director.

ESCAPE FROM . . . SURVIVAL ZONE is a film trapped in its own Survival Zone. Never theatrically released and relegated to the ongoing sludge of video releases, this is one film that deserves to be rescued from video limbo. Even given its limitations, it's still much better than most of the grade A releases unspooling in suburban multiplexes. *(Violence, profanity, adult situations.)*

p, Genevieve Jolliffe, Chris Jones; d, Chris Jones; w, Chris Jones, Mark Talbot Butler; ph, Jon Walker; ed, Mark Talbot Butler

Science Fiction/Action **(PR: O MPAA: NR)**

EUROPA
(SEE: ZENTROPA)

EVIL CLUTCH ★
88m Troma Inc.; Fomar Film ~ Rhino Home Video c

Coralina C. Tassoni *(Cindy)*, Diego Ribon *(Tony)*, Luciano Crovato *(Algernoon)*, Elena Cantarone *(Arva)*, Stefano Molinari *(Fango)*

EVIL CLUTCH is another Italian zombie gorefest, but, unlike such forebears as THE GATES OF HELL and NIGHT OF THE ZOMBIES, this one is less inspired by DAWN OF THE DEAD than by THE EVIL DEAD. It features a similarly small cast and heavy use of a roving camera, but like many other spaghetti shockers, it confuses gross-outs with honest chills.

Actually, the film's biggest flaw is that nothing happens for such long stretches of time. In a prologue, a mysterious woman named Arva (Elena Cantarone) seduces a young man named Fango (Stefano Molinari), before extruding a clawed hand from between her legs that savages him in the crotch. Meanwhile a vacationing couple, Cindy (Coralina C. Tassoni) and Tony (Diego Ribon), are driving through the Alps; near a small cemetery, they pick up the screaming Arva, who claims an evil force is chasing her. Tony ventures into the graveyard to check things out, and the camera starts swirling around him so much that even he notices it.

Continuing on to a small town, the couple next encounter Algernoon (Luciano Crovato, looking remarkably like Jim Varney's alter ego, Ernest P. Worrell), a strange man on a motorcycle who speaks with an electronic voice box which, he says, "makes me sound like a ro-boat." He informs them he's a writer of horror stories and that true evil exists in the region, but the couple are mostly annoyed by his presence, or as Cindy puts it, "That guy's got the power to put me in a bad mood." Later, he shows up again when Cindy and Tony set out to go camping in a nearby forest. They disregard his warnings, however, and after a *very* long series of hiking-through-the-forest scenes, the two wind up at the house where Arva had claimed her previous victim.

Needless to say, Arva's still hanging around and at first appears hospitable, but soon things turn nasty. Arva attempts to seduce Tony, splashing his face with a gross liquid in the process; he soon takes sick, much to Cindy's dismay. The couple are then set upon by a now zombified Fango, but succeed in chaining him up in a basement room; as they flee into the woods, however, Tony is overcome by the evil influence and attacks Cindy. She runs off, and Tony is met once again by Arva, who ravishes him before attempting to feed him to a living tree. He's saved by the arrival of Algernoon, who chops through the attacking roots and then hacks off Arva's clawed appendage when she unleashes it on him.

Ultimately, Arva kills Algernoon. Tony, now back to normal, is attacked by Fango, who severs his hands. He finds his way back to Cindy, who goes looking for help and finds only the dead Algernoon. Meanwhile, Fango reattacks and beheads Tony, and then joins the now undead Algernoon in assaulting Cindy once more. But she finds a handy chainsaw and fells Algernoon with it, then uses a mirror to reflect the rays of the rising sun onto Fango, who melts away as a result. Cindy survives to see the dawn—but so does Arva.

While the plot of EVIL CLUTCH is as thin on paper as that of THE EVIL DEAD, director Andreas Marfori lacks the sense of pacing and ever-building intensity that allowed Sam Raimi to convert his material into a classic horror story. The imitative camerawork apes Raimi's trademark swooping shots and long tracking scenes from the evil nemesis's point of view, but without the sense of purpose. Here, the camera races along the ground, around the characters and through buildings, and . . . nothing happens. In fact very little happens through much of the film, which sees fit to pad out its nothing storyline with endless shots of the couple's Jeep traversing scenic country roads and characters walking (or running, or searching) through the trees.

Early on, when Algernoon tells the couple one of his stories, Marfori even throws in excerpts from his short film GORY SAND to bolster the running time. These scenes, along with the opening attack on Fango by Arva, are the only instances of gore (the movie's only real purpose) for a long time; when the violence finally starts in the third act, it's much more disgusting than scary. Troma picked up this 1988 production with the apparent intent of a theatrical release, but not surprisingly, it wound up debuting on home video. *(Excessive violence, substance abuse, sexual situations, profanity.)*

p, Agnese Fontana; d, Andreas Marfori; w, Andreas Marfori; ph, Marco Isoli; ed, Fabrizio Polverari; m, Adriano M. Vitali; art d, Gianni Albertini

Horror **(PR: O MPAA: R)**

EXILED IN AMERICA ★½

84m Burnhill Productions ~ Prism Entertainment c

Edward Albert *(Filipe Soto)*, Wings Hauser *(Fred Jenkins)*, Kamala Lopez *(Marla Soto)*, Stella Stevens *(Sonny Moore)*, Maxwell Caulfield *(Joe Moore)*, Viveca Lindfors *(Dr. Helena Lindenheim)*, John Considine *(Dr. Tom Robinson)*, Gary Werntz *(Carl Mahler)*, Gina Gallego, Rodrigo Obregon, Bill Cobbs, Marilyn Hassett

An underwhelming, low-budget political drama, EXILED IN AMERICA concerns the real-life "Sanctuary" movement, an underground church-based network that welcomes refugees and rebels escaping murderous Latin American dictatorships. Sanctuary became an anathema to Washington in the Rambo-minded 1980s, when human rights took a back seat to Cold War arms shipments and Contra gunmen.

Writer-director Paul Leder (working from the play *Sanctuary*, by William Norton, Sr.) casts the conflict in hackneyed terms, with Filipe Soto (Edward Albert), heroic revolutionary from an unnamed banana republic, on the run in small-town California. Tortured—and brutally castrated—by thugs in his native land, Filipe languishes in a safehouse while his pretty wife Marla (Kamala Lopez), posing as a widow, takes a waitress job in a nearby diner. There she draws the unwanted affections of Joe Moore (Maxwell Caulfield), a young alcoholic in thrall to his insanely possessive mother Sonny (Stella Stevens), owner of the eatery. Ever since a car crash caused by drunken Joe, Sonny's pretended to be paralyzed just to keep her son under her thumb, and she sure doesn't enjoy his flirting with the new girl.

Meanwhile a death squad from the anonymous Latin country arrives on US soil and starts blowing away anyone in contact with Soto. The lead heavy is rogue CIA agent Carl Mahler (Gary Werntz), an expressionless Aryan who doesn't argue when one doomed activist compares him to Hitler's SS. The villains' path leads to Sunny's Diner, where a frantic Filipe has fled in delirium. He raises the assembled citizens' political consciousness by suffering torture flashbacks; he addresses the wheelchair-bound Sonny as though she were a fellow victim and mistakes Joe for a visiting yank reporter (but he speaks to them all in English, making this key scene even less convincing than it sounds). Fortunately local Sheriff Fred Jenkins (Wings Hauser) sympathizes with the refugees, and the government goons bite the dust in a lackluster shootout. Filipe perishes, but the tragedy permits Joe—his own manhood intact—to walk away with Marla after all, in what looks like one of those many "alternative" endings to CASABLANCA that cineastes keep talking about.

Like that Humphrey Bogart classic, EXILED IN AMERICA is based on an obscure stage play, and there the parallels end. This film's politics are simplistic, humdrum polemics in which the Reagan-esque Mahler and his crew slaughter every nun, doctor and innocent bystander they please. Soto's big soliloquy reveals the crime that turned him into a fugitive: a Catholic university instructor, he taught students that most un-American doctrine, Thou Shalt Not Kill. The performances are unedifying at best, with veteran glamour queen Stella Stevens (THE POSEIDON ADVENTURE, CHAINED HEAT) in a rare non-sexpot role, even though the incest-tinged relationship between Sonny and Joe is torrid enough on its own terms.

EXILED IN AMERICA might at least have had timeliness on its side had it come out during the thick of the Salvadoran crisis several years ago, but the 1990 production didn't debut on home video until 1992. *(Violence, substance abuse, profanity, adult situations.)*

p, Ralph Tornberg, Paul Leder; d, Paul Leder; w, Paul Leder, (from the play by William Norton, Sr.); ph, Francis Grumman; ed, Paul Leder; m, Jay Asher; cos, Ewa Zbroniec

Political/Drama **(PR: C MPAA: NR)**

EYE OF THE EAGLE 3 ★★½

91m Concorde ~ New Horizons Home Video c

Steve Kanaly *(Major Verdum)*, Ken Wright *(Jim McAdams)*, Peter Nelson *(Captain Wheeler)*, John Vargas *(Pvt. Wolfdreamer)*, Carl

Franklin *(Sgt. Devereux)*, Leo Martinez *(Tovar)*, Joe Zucchero *(General George Mayfield)*, Frederick Bailey *(M.P. Kowalski)*

Here's a rarity—a Vietnam War movie that actually transpires during the time of Uncle Sam's original involvement. You'll look in vain for contemporary soldiers of fortune restaging their old skirmishes. Nor will you find any intrepid Perot-inspired heroes looking for MIAs. The plot of EYE OF THE EAGLE 3 actually unfolds during the heat of combat in the 1960s.

In a manner recalling the legendary Gen. George S. Patton, Jr., the flamboyant Major Verdum (Steve Kanaly) plans all his strategies with as little interference from the Pentagon or his immediate superiors as possible. Verdum is so tough, the Vietnamese lie awake at night dreaming up ways to get rid of him. No wonder the Cong jump for joy when General George Mayfield (Joe Zucchero) incarcerates Verdun for vigilantism in the field. Having already sent his pride-and-joy unit to buttress a Marine contingent, Verdun has no intention of remaining in stir and abandoning them to the vagaries of fools like Mayfield. While he frets behind bars, his elite troops welcome an influx of mountain guerrillas but wonder where the hell their reinforcements are.

What they *don't* welcome is a fresh-from-West Point commander, Captain Wheeler (Peter Nelson) who berates the grungy troops about hygiene and lack of discipline. Having already sized up their desperate fix by sending in a spy posing as a UPI photographer, the enemy closes in. Wheeler refuses to request help but soon cracks under the mounting pressure. Taking charge, Corporal McAdams (Ken Wright) saves the day with some tricky manuevers. By appealing to M.P. Kowalski (Frederick Bailey), Verdun breaks out of the brig. While the good guys keep the Viet Cong busy with napalm explosions, Verdun flies into the fray with two borrowed helicopters. The rule-breaking Major rescues his men who have done a remarkable job of containing the enemy anyway. Although the Viet Commies don't wipe out the Verdum team, they can still gloat about the chances of his getting a court martial. But that consideration must be saved for "Eye of the Eagle 4."

Slam-bang action and a clear-cut delineation of the buddy system are the hallmarks of EYE OF THE EAGLE 3, which clearly sympathizes with the grunts in the combat zone. Since action aficionados love take-charge personalities and hate wimpy authority figures, this film cagily lets viewers root for the heroes in two ways: they get to cream the Viet Cong *and* demonstrate that only front-liners know how to win a war. With Major Verdum acting as coach and head cheerleader, EYE OF THE EAGLE 3 represents the War Film as Football Game.

Unfortunately, the filmmakers don't maximize suspense by cutting from the combat scenes to the imprisoned Major footage with any dexterity. In fact, the Major-in-jail scenes stop the film cold. Still, weekend warrior-types will enjoy the anti-Pentagon stance, the bomb blasts, bullet sprays, and the heady aroma of napalm. *(Violence, profanity.)*

d, Cirio H. Santiago; w, Carl Franklin, M.A. Solomon, Dan Cacliasso; ph, Joe Batac, Vic Anao; ed, Edgardo Vinarao; m, Justin Lord; art d, Ben Delira

War/Action/Adventure **(PR: C MPAA: R)**

EYE OF THE STORM ★★★

(Germany/U.S.) 98m Senator Films; EuroFilm Productions; Style Productions ~ New Line Home Video c

Craig Sheffer *(Ray)*, Bradley Gregg *(Steven)*, Lara Flynn Boyle *(Sandra Gladstone)*, Leon Rippy *(Sheriff)*, Dennis Hopper *(Marvin Gladstone)*

Released theatrically in Germany but direct-to-video stateside, EYE OF THE STORM, a German-US co-production, is an eerie and tragic story of two brothers haunted by their past.

In the opening scene, a young boy, Steven (Bradley Gregg), watches as his motel proprietor parents are murdered by thieves. Running away from the killers, Steven jumps out of a window and is blinded by the fall. Ten years later, Steven and his older brother Ray (Craig Sheffer) are running the motel, ironically named the Easy Rest Inn. One day, redneck drunk Marvin Gladstone (Dennis Hopper) and his gum-chewing floosie wife Sandra (Lara Flynn Boyle) check into the Easy Rest. Several fights later, Marvin walks out on Sandra but returns the next day. Ray tries to talk Marvin into leaving for good, but he refuses. The two get into a fight, and in a psychotic rage (he thinks Marvin's the thief who murdered his parents), Ray kills his guest.

Sandra, meanwhile, gets close to Steven and isn't aware that Marvin is dead. She finds Marvin's watch and confronts Ray with it. Ray convinces Sandra that Steven stole the watch. He further convinces her that Steven was in a mental institution for two years and warns her not to tell the authorities about the theft, or they'll take Steven away. But in a later conversation she has with Steven, he implies that Ray might have killed Marvin. Packing to leave, Sandra is stopped by Ray who tries to kill her. During the ensuing struggle, Sandra blasts Ray with the gun Marvin left in their room. Hearing all the commotion, Steven, who was in the shed, stumbles to the motel where Sandra tells him that his brother is dead. But, from the FATAL ATTRACTION school of dramatics, Ray suddenly jumps up and tries to kill Sandra again, only to be shot dead by Steven. At the film's close, Sandra and Steven drive off together.

Director Yuri Zeltser has put together an effective thriller, eliciting strong performances from his actors. Gregg (STAND BY ME, CLASS OF 1999), in particular, is very convincing as the blind and fearful younger brother. In addition, Karl Walter Lindenlaub's cinematography helps to punctuate this story which illustrates the devastating effects of holding onto a tragic past. *(Excessive violence, substance abuse, profanity.)*

p, Carsten H.W. Lorenz, Oliver Eberle; d, Yuri Zeltser; w, Yuri Zeltser, Michael Stewart; ph, Karl Walter Lindenlaub; ed, Michael J. Duthie; m, Christopher Franke; art d, Michael Manson; cos, Laurie Henriksen

Thriller/Crime **(PR: C MPAA: R)**

FALLING FROM GRACE ★★½

100m Columbia; Little b Pictures Corporation~ Columbia c

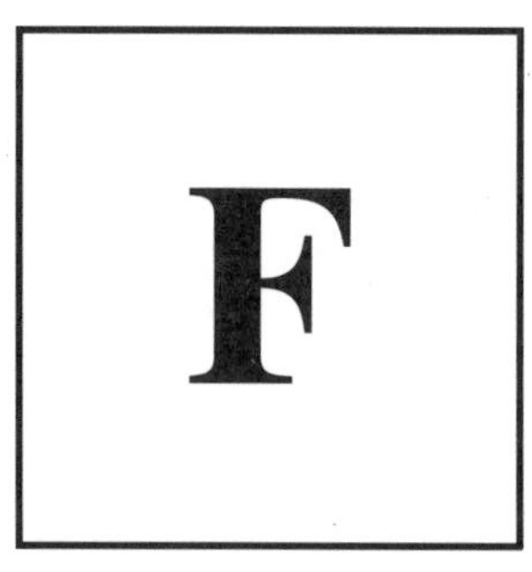

John Mellencamp *(Bud Parks)*, Mariel Hemingway *(Alice Parks)*, Claude Akins *(Speck Parks)*, Dub Taylor *(Grandpa Parks)*, Kay Lenz *(P.J. Parks)*, Larry Crane *(Ramey Parks)*, Kate Noonan *(Linda)*, Deirdre O'Connell *(Sally Cutler)*, John Prine *(Mitch Cutler)*, Brent Huff *(Parker Parks)*, Joanne Jacobson *(Marian Parks)*, Tracy Cowles *(Bobby Tucker)*, Melissa Ann Hackman *(Terri Jo Parks)*, Mary Tom Crain *(Grandma Parks)*, Sigmund Balaban *(Country Club Manager)*, Gary Boebinger *(Turdis)*, Toby Myers *(Luke)*, Margie Hopper *(Mrs. Pendergrass)*, Donna Cowles *(Mrs. Sacks)*, Elizabeth Anne Bowen *(Checker Girl)*, Hilda Marie Bolden *(Checker Girl)*, Edna Ryan Booker *(Mrs. Green)*, Matthew J. Correll *(Parking Attendant)*, Mary Cowles *(Waitress)*, Teddi Jo Mellencamp, Thomas Judd, Kasey Robinson, Eric White, Aaron White *(P.J.'s Children)*, Terra Cowles *(Sally's Child)*, Derek Davis *(Sally's Child)*, Joe Mellencamp *(Band Leader)*, Bentley Austin, Criag Austin, Eric Austin, Glenn Dalton *(Pure Jam Band Members)*

This acting and directing debut from rock star John Mellencamp had only a brief run in theaters early in the year, and it's easy to see why: FALLING FROM GRACE is an unusually downbeat story for the popular rocker to choose as his film debut.

Mellencamp plays singer Bud Parks, returning to his hometown of Oak City, Indiana, for his grandfather's eightieth birthday. Bud has brought his glamorous "California wife," Alice (Mariel Hemingway), and young daughter to meet the Parks clan, and what a dysfunctional brood it is: there's sister Sally (Deidre O'Connell), who's married to the hard-drinking, frequently absent Mitch Cutler (folksinger John Prine, in a fine, low-keyed performance); father Speck (Claude Akins), somewhat estranged from his famous son and known for his way with women; and Speck's illegitimate son Ramey (Larry Crane, Mellencamp's real-life bandmate). As if things weren't incendiary enough, Bud's brother Parker (Brent Huff) is married to P.J. (Kay Lenz), Bud's former high-school school sweetheart.

Bud's return to his hometown sets off all sorts of long-held hostilities and rivalries. Mitch resents Bud for his "handouts," Speck is both jealous of and cold towards Bud, and P.J. seems eager to rekindle their romance. She tells him, matter-of-factly, that she's having an affair with Speck, and seems just as eager to start something with Bud. Eventually Bud and P.J. do have a brief fling, and Bud begins to be drawn back into the smalltown world he left to become a star. His ambivalence about his fame leads him to consider giving it all up and staying in Oak City, and he extends his visit to two weeks there, from the originally scheduled three days. Bud's plans for a possible life with P.J. are derailed, however, when she tells him she would have married him if he'd asked her, but he's now "16 years too late," and she's content to stay married to Parker while having affairs on the side.

Speck, meanwhile, means to add another woman to his collection, and makes a pass at Alice, who bonks him on the head. She begins to suspect Bud's infidelity and soon returns to LA with their daughter. Bud confronts his father after Alice tells him about Speck. They have a fight in a diner, and Bud, now drowning in self-pity and smalltown nihilism, tries an old high-school stunt: "riding the cage," in which he's strapped into a metal cage in the back of a pick-up truck, and dumped onto the highway while the vehicle is speeding along the road. Bud is badly hurt, and while he's recuperating in the hospital, Alice comes to see him, hinting at a reconciliation.

FALLING FROM GRACE does a good job at capturing the stifling feeling of small town life; virtually every Oak City denizen is either resigned to spending the rest of his or her life there, or trying to blot out this inevitability through alcohol or sex. Thanks to the authenticity of Larry McMurtry's screenplay, and Mellencamp's surprisingly competent direction, the film is more compelling than it might seem from the above description. At the same time, it would have been more effective if Mellencamp's character had been fleshed out: we've seen this brooding rock star type a million times.

Mellencamp, as if to prove he doesn't need to perform to hold our attention, never sings in the film, so we're given no reasons for Bud's success; one scene, where he's sitting on a porch aimlessly strumming a guitar, is a tease. Bud might as well be a movie star or a famous author—the film never takes advantage of his musical background to illustrate the talent that enabled him to escape a future of chicken farming. Likewise, we never learn why Bud would even consider abandoning his hard-won fame (not to mention a genuinely loving family) to go back to Oak City, whether it be self-loathing, restlessness or the inexorable pull of his smalltown roots. (The closest the film gets to this is P.J.'s comment to Bud that "nobody ever controlled you and nothing ever stopped you.") FALLING FROM GRACE hints at some of this, but a little more depth and insight would have helped this promising first effort. *(Violence, profanity, brief nudity.)*

p, Harry Sandler; d, John Mellencamp; w, Larry McMurtry; ph, Victor Hammer; ed, Dennis Virkler; prod d, George Corsillo; art d, Todd Hatfield; set d, Sandi Cook

Drama **(PR: C MPAA: PG-13)**

FAR AND AWAY ★★

140m Imagine Films Entertainment ~ Universal c

Tom Cruise *(Joseph Donelly)*, Nicole Kidman *(Shannon Christie)*, Thomas Gibson *(Stephen)*, Robert Prosky *(Christie)*, Barbara Babcock *(Nora Christie)*, Colm Meaney *(Kelly)*, Eileen Pollock *(Molly Kay)*, Michelle Johnson *(Grace)*, Douglas Gillison *(Dermody)*, Wayne Grace *(Bourke)*, Barry McGovern *(McGuire)*, Niall Toibin *(Joe)*, Rance Howard *(Tomlin)*, Clint Howard *(Flynn)*, Cyril Cusack *(Danty Duff)*, Gary Lee Davis *(Gordon)*, Jared Harris *(Paddy)*, Steven O'Donnell *(Colm)*, Peadar Lamb *(Farmer)*, Mark Mulholland *(1st Peasant)*, P.J. Brady *(2nd Peasant)*, Wesley Murphy *(Landlord)*, Jimmy Keogh *(Priest)*, J.G. Devlin *(1st Villager)*, Gerry Walsh *(2nd Villager)*, Brendan Cauldwell *(Tavern Keeper)*, Derry Power *(Peter)*, Noel O'Donovan *(Matthew)*, MacDara O'Fatharta *(John)*, Eileen Colgan *(1st Lady)*, Kate Flynn *(2nd Lady)*, Joan O'Hara *(3rd Lady)*, Frankie McCafferty *(Map Vendor)*, Poll Moussilides *(Hat Vendor)*, Pat Kinevane *(Irish Vendor)*, Donncha Crowley *(Flag Vendor)*, Tim McDonnell *(Fruit Vendor)*, Todd Hallowell *(1st Thug)*, Kenneth McCluskey *(2nd Thug)*, Brendan Ellis *(Rebel Leader)*, Jeffrey Andrews *(Coniff)*, Judith McIntyre *(Glenna)*, Rynagh O'Grady *(Olive)*, Martin Ewen *(Lamplighter)*, Brendan Gleeson *(Social Club Policeman)*, Frank Coughlan *(Doctor)*, Hoke Howell *(Crew Boss)*, Arnold Kuenning *(Old Man)*, Rocco Sisto *(1st Immigrant)*, Michael Ruud *(2nd Immigrant)*, DonRe Sampson *(Railworker)*, Harry Webster *(Derelict)*, Mark Wheeler *(Officer)*, William Preston *(Blacksmith)*, Pauline McLynn, Joanne McAteer, Elizabeth Kemler, Cara Wilder, Aedin Moloney *(Prostitutes)*, Helen Montague *(Piano Player Prostitute)*, John-Clay Scott, Clay Lilley, Cole McKay, James Jude Courtney, Jeff

Ramsey, Anthony DeLongis *(Boxers)*, Carl N. Ciarfalio *(Italian Boxer)*, Tim Monich *(Bigoted Man)*, Alecia LaRue *(Boston Maid)*, Ian Elliot *(Turner)*, Bobby Huber *(Social Club Thug)*, Julie Donatt *(1st Social Club Woman)*, Louisa Marie *(2nd Social Club Woman)*, Brian Munn *(1st Henchman)*, Bob Dolman *(Honest Bob)*, Phillip V. Caruso *(I.M. Malone)*, Tom Lucy *(Immigration Policeman)*

Intermittently entertaining but extremely uneven, the Irish immigration epic FAR AND AWAY plays like a theme park attraction: viscerally exciting but detached, impersonal and dull.

Tom Cruise stars as Joseph Donelly, a tenant farmer in Ireland circa 1892 who starts off determined to settle a score with Stephen (Thomas Gibson), the ruthless landlord's agent who caused his father's death and torched the Donelly homestead over unpaid rent as Joseph was laying his paterfamilias to rest. Instead, he gets sidetracked by the landowner's lovely daughter, Shannon Christie (Nicole Kidman), who abruptly, and illogically, sweeps Joseph away to accompany her to America, where she intends to pick up land of her own in the Oklahoma Land Rush.

Unfortunately, Shannon is robbed by a con man on the ship, leaving her and Joseph penniless in Boston. Joseph makes contact with the local working-class Irish community and, passing Shannon off as his sister, scrounges lodging for them in a boisterous whorehouse and jobs in a food plant plucking chickens. Joseph becomes a bare-knuckle boxing champion and the apple of the eye of busty bar dancer Grace (Michelle Johnson). Matched up in a big fight with the Italian champion, however, he loses when he's distracted by a city councilman pawing Shannon.

After finding themselves once again penniless and back on the streets, Shannon is shot by the owner of a home which she and Joseph have broken into for temporary shelter. Unable to care for her, Joseph reluctantly returns her to her family. He then gets a job building the railroad west before finally hitching up with a wagon train headed to Oklahoma. There, he's reunited with Shannon, who has come west with her family. During the land rush itself, Joseph faces off with Shannon's beau, Stephen, before claiming a prized piece of land.

FAR AND AWAY may very well be the first dramatic film shot in 70mm wide-screen Panavision since David Lean's RYAN'S DAUGHTER, but Ron Howard has along way to go before he becomes a filmmaker in Lean's artistic league. His treatment of Ireland and its people is almost embarrassingly cartoonish, depicting a country overrun by rosy-nosed leprechauns who spend all their time digging up spuds, drinking, brawling and throwing rocks at rich people.

Cruise looks no more at home than any Hollywood star would be dropped into a gaggle of strenuously colorful Irish character actors, but his Irish brogue is at least convincing. As the rich, spoiled daughter of the landowner, Kidman looks more at home. But as an actress, she remains a cool beauty rather than a fiery lassie, which makes her fiery lassie continuously problematic.

From the Lean parody of the Irish section, Howard switches to something resembling half-baked Capra when he brings his lovers to America, mixing self-conscious populism with conservative cynicism in his depiction of the Boston Irish politicos as being even crueler and more exploitive than the Irish landowners Joseph left behind. Nonetheless, this is by far the most engaging part of the film if only because it's the only section that isn't utterly predictable. As the film moves west, however, Howard seems to lose his grip entirely.

Despite being, like everything else in the film, lavishly staged and photographed, Joseph's time on the railroad is little more than a time-killer for him to have loving flashbacks of Shannon that inspire him to Oklahoma. Yet, after taking the effort to set up an emotional reunion between these would-be lovers, the actual scene is dismayingly flat and obligatory, a mood extending to the climactic land rush, in which sensational staging and stunt work is overcome by yawning predictability.

Given the genuine promise he showed as a director of quirky comedies like NIGHT SHIFT and SPLASH, Howard has seemed to get overblown and boring in a hurry, starting with the flashy but empty COCOON and leading to the elephantine but undistinguished BACKDRAFT, which has already been adapted into a Universal theme park attraction. FAR AND AWAY could yield a bare-knuckle boxing stunt show and maybe an Oklahoma land rush thrill ride. What it will never yield, however, is the kind of connection to those deep wells of emotional crosscurrents that made Lean's films at times almost unbearably intimate despite their often massive scale.

The major difference is that, for Lean, complex, challenging characters were the whole point of the film while Howard seems to find complexity of any kind a nuisance. Hence, while nobody ever made a carnival ride out of LAWRENCE OF ARABIA, Ron Howard's films seem as though they would be incomplete without them. *(Violence, adult situations.)*

p, Brian Grazer, Ron Howard; d, Ron Howard; w, Bob Dolman, (from the story by Dolman and Ron Howard); ph, Mikael Salomon; ed, Daniel Hanley, Michael Hill; m, John Williams; prod d, Jack T. Collis, Allan Cameron; art d, Jack Senter; set d, Richard Goddard; cos, Joanna Johnston

Romance/Adventure **(PR: C MPAA: PG-13)**

FATAL INSTINCT ★

93m Baby Dica Productions; Nucleus Entertainment ~ New Line Home Video c

Michael Madsen *(Cliff Burden)*, Laura Johnson *(Catherine Merrims)*, Tony Hamilton *(Bill Hook)*, Tommy Redmond Hicks *(Captain Merrihew)*, Richard Foronjy *(Cy Tarr)*, Jody Bradley *(Alan)*, Jan Marlyn *(Rosie)*, Barry Laws *(Bartender)*, Robin Jameson *(Ally Barrett)*, Rick Johnson *(Tennis Instructor)*, Rick Bartz *(Detective Schutte)*, Paul Lyell *(MD Officer)*, Kim McKamy *(Frank Stegner's Girlfriend)*, Gene Armor *(Frank Stegner)*, Joanne Laura *(Receptionist)*, Scott Mitchell *(Beaumont Detective)*, Rick Zeller *(Beaumont Detective)*, Jerry Recter *(Detective Rickey Jones)*, Gary Lee Reed *(LA Detective)*, Cynthia Haffield *(Girl in Bar)*

For victims of amnesia who discover themselves inside a video store and can't quite recall the name of that actor who's the son of Spartacus and who have a fuzzy recall of the titles of recent hit movies, the numbingly dull and cheap FATAL INSTINCT should trigger a complete recovery.

Frank Stegner (Gene Armor) is murdered at a Southern California resort hotel and laid-back detective Cliff Burden (Michael Madsen) is sent to investigate. Burden finds out that the hotel is definitely in the off-season because, aside from Frank and his girlfriend (Kim McKamy), the only two people at the hotel the night of the murder were the hotel manager Cy Tarr (Richard Foronjy) and the beautiful hotel owner Catherine Merrims (Laura Johnson). Cliff immediately suspects Catherine of the murder and begins following her and ransacking her room at the hotel. But before long, he becomes sexually involved with her and the two engage in a torrid love affair.

But Burden is getting pressured from his boss, Captain Merihew (Tommy Redmond Hicks), to solve the case. He finds out that Catherine is a woman with a past, having moved to Southern California after shooting a burglar and rejecting her therapist, who promptly killed himself. As the case unfolds, Burden discovers that the dead therapist is actually alive, now under the moniker of Bill Hook (Tony Hamilton). And Hook has Catherine under his obsessive psychotherapeutic spell. Burden realizes that Hook is the killer of Frank Stegner after finding Frank's girlfriend murdered. He races back to the hotel and finds Catherine held at bay by Hook. After a shootout, Burden kills Hook, but not before Hook pumps some bullets into Catherine. At the film's fadeout, Burden sits by the hotel swimming pool and smokes a cigarette.

Obviously, these filmmakers had no compunction about exploiting the tremendous popularity of FATAL ATTRACTION and BASIC INSTINCT to create an artificial demand for their product, but all FATAL INSTINCT manages to achieve is to evoke a weak impression of the originals; there's no desire to expand or embellish on the popular "erotic thriller" genre currently dominating the direct-to-video marketplace and, increasingly, movie theaters. While not painful or difficult to sit through, FATAL INSTINCT's main problem is its shoddiness, which, in the fashion world equivalent, would be an Oscar de la Renta knock-off manufactured in Newark.

George D. Putnam's threadbare screenplay was clearly calculated to bask in the success of BASIC INSTINCT, containing not one moment of interest or suspense in itself. When Hook is discovered to be the murderer, the only surprise is why it took so long for Cliff to figure it out. Putnam's screenplay is a paint-by-numbers clone, only with some of the paints missing. The actors also seem to be in on the listlessness of the venture with Michael Madsen (THELMA & LOUISE, RESERVOIR DOGS) appearing bored and sounding like Danny Aiello in slow motion. Only Laura Johnson plays her part a peg above mediocrity. The perfunctory location shooting is limited to mostly two locations—the hotel and the police department office. This may have been interesting in the days of Edwin S. Porter, but in 1992 it's merely tiresome and flat.

With all the unused writing, acting and filmmaking talents waiting on tables, parking cars and writing film reviews, it is vastly depressing to know that films like FATAL INSTINCT will continue to get made while artists of originality and vision starve. *(Violence, excessive nudity, excessive profanity.)*

p, Stacy Codikow; d, John Dirlam; w, George D. Putnam; ph, John Dirlam; ed, Rachel Igel; m, Stephen Allen, Bobby Crew; prod d, Gary Lee Reed

Erotic/Thriller **(PR: O MPAA: R)**

FATE

114m Paul Entertainment ~ Academy Entertainment c

Stuart Paul *(Jake Blackburn)*, Cheryl M. Lynn *(Chelly)*, Kaye Ballard *(Judy)*, Yuda Barkan *(Sy)*, Patrick Wright *(Louie)*, Paul Bashkin *(Lenny)*, Delaney Lucas *(Sylvie)*, William F. Collard, Johnathon Woods, Billie Wallace, Susannah York, Bonnie Paul, Cindy Roberts

New Age mysticism runs rampant throughout FATE, an amorphous comedy-drama toplining writer-director Stuart Paul as Jake Blackburn, an easygoing LA writer who lives with his nutty-but-nurturing family in a shabby house wedged between looming skyscrapers.

The Blackburn homestead, of course, is meant to symbolize a homely alternative to stressful modern life. Get it? Jake meets and romances Chelly (Cheryl M. Lynn), a model whose California good looks hide a traumatic childhood of abuse and molestation by an alcoholic father. Jake and Chelly are a happy West Coast couple at first; he's into ESP and astrology, while she digs mermaids and "sea spirits." But Chelly starts drinking heavily, acts promiscuous, wakes up screaming and talks casually of drowning herself. Jake fears that Chelly's psychological scars are more than even psychics can handle, and when she goes into a schizoid frenzy he hits her. Chelly retaliates by moving in with a sleazy new boyfriend, while Jake howls to the night sky for a sign from God—or gods.

God obliges with a manifestation of Bohini, an ancient yogi who starts channelling through Jake's meddlesome mama, Judy (Kaye Ballard). Speaking with a vaudeville Hindu accent, Judy utters banalities like "Only through love can you get a love-energy connection," and performs some miraculous cures on family members. "Everything in this world is so hard—yet it's so easy!" exclaims Jake, grokking. (For more on grokking, read Robert A. Heinlein's *Stranger in a Strange Land*.) On Bohini's cue Jake saves Chelly from her latest suicide attempt and they marry.

Oh there's more, much more, including the screenplay that Jake is doing, an Indian picture that finally goes before the cameras with the blonde Chelly in a caveman suit as a most unconvincing Native American. There's also a crazed horoscope "scientist," who, after Jake's star chart crashes a computer, runs around shouting that the hero is blessed, fated, ordained, destined, the messiah—or something, never clearly delineated.

Whatever Bohini's therapeutic powers, he's a washout at healing ham performances, and the supporting cast generally mug like maniacs. Leading-man Paul tries hard to cultivate an amiable schnook persona, but the whole effort carries the distasteful odor of a vanity production. Only Cheryl M. Lynn hits some of the right notes as the troubled Chelly, but for the wrong reasons; her line readings are so wooden and monotone that when this mannequin suddenly goes into ungovernable hysterics the contrast in character is truly disturbing.

Like the fictitious Blackburns, the Paul clan make movies a family activity, mixing trendy metaphysics with naive gropings at social issues in a karmic kitsch of Capra, Casteneda and MacLaine—that's Shirley Maclaine. 1988's EMANON starred Stuart as a Christ figure dwelling among the homeless, while 1990's ETERNITY tackled reincarnation, media manipulation and toxic waste. FATE quickly followed them to the home-video afterlife. *(Substance abuse, adult situations, profanity.)*

p, Dorothy Koster-Paul, Hank Paul; d, Stuart Paul; w, Stuart Paul, Dorothy Koster-Paul; ph, John Lambert; ed, Jack Tucker; m, Michel Legrand; prod d, Robert Farthing

Comedy/Romance **(PR: C MPAA: PG-13)**

FATHER ★★★

(Australia) 106m Barron Films; Transcontinental Films ~ Northern Arts Entertainment c

Max Von Sydow *(Joseph Meuller)*, Carol Drinkwater *(Anne Winton)*, Julia Blake *(Leah Zetnick)*, Steven Jacobs *(Bobby Winton)*, Tim Robertson *(George Coleman)*, Simone Robertson, Kahli Sneddon, Nicholas Bell, Bruce Alexander, Denis Moore, Jon Concannon, Reg Evans, Eve Von Bibra, Nic Lathouris, Brenda Addie, Kate Langroek, Josephine Eberhard, Scott Lucey, Colin Vancao, Nancy Black, Anthony Evans, James Sugden, Jane Anthony, Ben Mitchell, Richard Cordner, George Zocopoulos, Colin Batrouney, Susan Arnold, Donna Woodhouse, Anthony Fletcher, Bianna Briam, Bob Bright, Terry Emery, John Braybrook, Les Toth, Robert Morgan, Tibor Gyapjas, Monica Jaeger, Glynis Jones, Bernadette Doyle, Ross Mogeridge, David Gray, John Bishop, Michael Joshua, Alan Lovett, Bill Tisdall, Bill Manderson, Tom Gutteridge, John Devlin, Scott Board

Shortly after FATHER begins, the happy domestic life of a grandfather in Melbourne ends when a TV news show reveals the charge that he was the commander of a dreaded SS execution squad in the Baltic. Although his family rallies to his successful defense at the inevitable court trial, there are lingering doubts that gain strength and result in a more personal condemnation.

Joseph Meuller (Max Von Sydow) seems the ideal grandfather, trading silly jokes with his two granddaughters on whom he dotes shamelessly. Meuller also advises his daughter Anne Winton (Carol Drinkwater) and son-in-law Bobby (Steven Jacobs) on how to manage the hotel he founded. As we watch him accompany his grandchildren to school, Meuller is being observed by a middle-aged woman and filmed by a clandestine camera crew. Later, that woman, Leah Zetnick (Julia Blake), calls Anne to advise her to watch a weekly news program. On that show, it is alleged that Joe Meuller is, in reality, Franz Kessler who commanded the murder squad that killed Leah Zetnick's parents during WWII. She has even unearthed a photograph of a man in SS uniform who resembles a young Meuller. While Anne and Bobby look on aghast, Mueller rushes to the bathroom to be sick.

Their dismay turns into real dread when they realise that they are now besieged by teams of cameramen, so they decide to leave for a vacation at the seashore. While there, they are visited by the TV producer who wants an exclusive interview and is willing to impart the news that the federal authorities are about to issue an indictment of Meuller. Anne takes her father to an isolated shack in the outback, while she prepares, with the family lawyer, George Coleman (Tim Robertson), to defend her father.

In the courtroom, Meuller argues that any proof of his identity was destroyed in the Dresden firestorm, while Anne goes to the TV producer to trade an exclusive interview for his help. Apparently, he supplies information about Leah Zetnick's past, including a ruined engagement in England, her false charges against another German emigre and her own brief spell of hospitalization. George reduces her to tears on the witness stand, and Meuller is exonerated. Despite the celebration of his victory at the hotel, Bobby warns Anne that there may have been something to the charges, reminding her of his own Vietnam War experiences.

Meanwhile, Leah Zetnick has decided to take matters into her own hands and goes to the hotel packing an automatic pistol. By hiding in the bathroom, she manages to sneak into the Wintons' apartment and, drawing a bead on Meuller, forces the adults into the bedroom, making a point of sparing the children any unrest. Talking to Anne, Leah tells her how she is going to trust her with the burden she has borne since the war and then proceeds to blow her own brains out.

To Anne's shock, her father seems unconcerned with the woman's suicide, and she starts to question him severely about his past. Was he just a simple Afrika Korps veteran, as he has long claimed? She demands to know what happened to the real Joseph Meuller and her father admits that he had assumed this identity in the POW camp after the real Meuller had killed himself. With a cold fury, Anne demands her father leave the house and have nothing more to do with her children. In the closing scenes we see the emotional toll Anne's decision takes on her, and the genuine pain it causes the real Franz Kessler.

Directed by John Power from a screenplay by Tony Cavanaugh and Grahame Hartley, FATHER's account of a highly dramatic, if unusual, domestic situation is seen from a nearly feminist viewpoint, since the principal movers are both women, Anne and Leah, while Meuller, at one point, contemplates running away to the northern coastal town of Darwin. Leah is also characterized as a devout daughter, intent on avenging her parents' murder, and her apartment is full of books, documents and wartime photographs. Leah appeals directly several times to Anne and finally succeeds in having her extract a confession from Meuller. Even the final punishment, the exclusion from the happy domestic circle, seems a particularly distaff judgment.

A minor, but haunting element in the film, is Leah's signature tune, a childish voice singing an odd march, "Ilya's Song" at key moments in the narrative. *(Adult situations.)*

p, Damien Parer; d, John Power; w, Tony Cavanaugh, Grahame Hartley; ph, Dan Burstall; ed, Kerry Regan; m, Peter Best; prod d, Phil Peters; art d, Bernadette Wynack; cos, Jeannie Cameron

Drama/War **(PR: C MPAA: NR)**

FATHERS AND SONS ★★½

99m Asbury Park Productions; Columbia TriStar Home Video; Addis/Wechsler ~ Pacific Pictures Distribution Company c

Jeff Goldblum *(Max Fish)*, Rory Cochrane *(Ed Fish)*, Mitchell Marchand *(Smiley)*, Famke Janssen *(Kyle)*, Rocky Carroll *(Flo)*, Natasha Gregson Wagner *(Lisa)*, Ellen Greene *(Judy)*, Samuel L. Jackson *(Marshall)*, Joie Lee *(Lois)*, Rosanna Arquette *(Miss Athena)*, Mitchell Disend *(Shore Killer)*

This modest film about family values as practiced by a refugee from LA's movie industry seems to have been a heartfelt desire of director Paul Mones for some time. Based on Mones's own screenplay, FATHERS AND SONS has some good elements but lacks the necessary detail to make it more than the sum of its parts.

Max Fish (Jeff Goldblum) once made movies, but now owns and manages a bookshop in the New Jersey shore town where he lives with his teenage son, Ed (Rory Cochrane). A widower, Max is troubled by his son's growing coolness toward him, though he does recognize it as one of his own traits. For his part, Ed seems to have a chameleon's gift for protective coloration; he hangs around with an older, delinquent crowd, yet ponders the fate of the dolphins whose diseased bodies wash up on the beach near the boardwalk that serves as the town's main street.

Ed and his high school pal, Smiley (Mitchell Marchand), seem to accept the drug dealing of Smiley's brother Flo (Rocky Carroll) as easily as the fears about a mad killer whose victims are occasionally glimpsed by the camera as they are discovered by the Asbury Park and Belmar police. Complicating life for Ed and Smiley is the emergence of a new psychedelic drug called "chew"; it's supposedly the substance chewed by South American shamans to achieve visions, hence the odd name.

The real catalysts in the film's narrative, however, are two women, Kyle (Famke Janssen) and Lisa (Natasha Gregson Wagner). Max meets Kyle wholesomely enough at a footrace in which they are contestants, while Ed discovers Lisa at a "chew" session. While Max's relationship with Kyle seems to prosper (she attends the opening night presentation of a modernized *Don Quixote* in which he naturally stars), Ed discovers that Lisa is too promiscuous for his taste. Ed forsakes the premiere of the local play and instead bites into some "chew" to commune with the dolphins and his dead mother, but meets the dreaded shore killer instead.

Filmed locally in the towns that dot the New Jersey shoreline, FATHERS AND SONS features an interracial friendship without fanfare and charming subplots involving a local fortune teller, Miss Athena (Rosanna Arquette), and Max's stage-bound romance with a fellow performer, Judy (Ellen Greene), but they tend to emphasize a central tepidity.

Despite the authentic locale, Max's bookshop is an amateur effort with a lot more bookshelf space than books, leaving him more than ample free time to indulge in jogging and local theatrics. Ed and Smiley's flirtation with street violence seems far too casual, though Smiley does suffer a broken arm and concussion for courting a far tougher guy's girl. Ed has harbored a resentment over his mother's death that he blames on Max since the couple had fought in LA and she died from cancer shortly after their move to the Jersey shore. Father and son's reconciliation serves as the film's ending.

The several good performances and the engaging modesty of FATHERS AND SONS are, however, not quite enough to ennoble it. *(Profanity, adult situations.)*

p, Jon Kilik; d, Paul Mones; w, Paul Mones; ph, Ron Fortunato; ed, Janice Keunelian; m, Mason Daring; prod d, Eve Cauley; art d, Pauly Weimer; set d, Roberta Holinko; cos, Lynn Pickwell

Drama/Romance **(PR: C MPAA: R)**

FAVOUR, THE WATCH, AND THE VERY BIG FISH, THE ★★

(U.K./France) 92m Films Ariane; Umbrella Films; Fildebroc~ Trimark Pictures c

Bob Hoskins *(Louis Aubinard)*, Jeff Goldblum *(Pianist)*, Natasha Richardson *(Sybil)*, Michel Blanc *(Norbert)*, Jacques Villeret *(Charles)*, Angela Pleasence *(Elizabeth)*, Jean-Pierre Cassel *(Zalman)*, Samuel Chaimovitch *(Grandfather)*, Sacha Vikouloff *(Violinist)*, Claudine Mavros *(Mother Superior)*, Carlos Kloster *(Bishop)*, Yvonne Constant *(The Prostitute)*, Martine Ferriere *(Charles's Mother)*, Gerald Morales *(1st Chauffeur)*, Yannick Evely *(2nd Chauffeur)*, Jacques Herlin *(Man with Hooked Nose)*, Eric Averlant *(Taxi Driver)*, Gerard Zalcberg *(Freed Prisoner)*, Daniel Lombart *(Theo)*, Jean-Michel Ribes *(Blind Man)*, Artus DePenguern *(Saint Francois)*, Beth McFadden *(Young Girl in Sugar Club)*, Louba Guertchikoff *(1st Old Woman)*, Janine Darcey *(2nd Old Woman)*, Mireille Franchino *(3rd Old Woman)*, Mado Maurin *(4th Old Woman)*, Gilette Barbier *(5th Old Woman)*, Nicolas DiGiacomo *(Small Boy in Lingerie Shop)*, Jean-Claude Deret *(Grandfather)*, Pamela Goldblum *(Large Woman)*, Maximilien Seide *(Small Boy in the Metro)*, Claire Magnin *(Mother in the Metro)*, Gisele Soban *(1st Passer-By)*, John Arnold *(2nd Passer-By)*, Philippe Dormoy *(Young Man in the Cinema)*, Maurice Herman *(1st Apostle)*, Pascal Beckar *(2nd Apostle)*, Edouard Hastings *(3rd Apostle)*, Michel Sebban *(4th Apostle)*, Jean-Francois Vlerick *(5th Apostle)*, Geoffrey Carey *(6th Apostle)*, Caroline Jacquin *(Receptionist at Sound Studio)*, Patrick Albenque *(Sound Engineer)*, Andre Chaumeau *(Ice Cream Vendor)*, Denys Fouqueray *(Waiter at Cafe Liberte)*, Caroline Loeb *(Waitress at the Shabby Cafe)*, Lylia Dalskaia *(Singer in the Restaurant)*, Fedle Papalia *(Barman at the Sordid Bar)*, Louis Navarre *(The Baker)*, Anne Levy *(The Baker's Wife)*, Jacques Potin *(1st Spectator)*, Hilton McConnico *(2nd Spectator)*, Sylvie Laporte *(Coat Seller)*, Julien Calderbank *(Blind Child)*, Dhan Olivier *(Jungle Man)*, Jenny Legros *(Jungle Woman)*, Jean-Claude Gillet *(Arab Fish Seller)*, Fazia Boussoffara *(Mustapha's Woman)*, Charles-Andre Eisler *(Tramp Neighbor)*, Oleg Ponomarenko *(Musician at Restaurant Tzigane)*, Pascal DeLoutchek *(Musician at Restaurant Tzigane)*

Take talents like Jeff Goldblum, Bob Hoskins and Natasha Richardson and put them together in a comedy and you should have a funny movie. Against all odds, however, THE FAVOUR, THE WATCH, AND THE VERY BIG FISH only succeeds intermittently in amusing, conveying more the waste of a good cast than movie magic.

Louis Aubinard (Hoskins) is a "devotional photographer" of religious themes in search of the perfect Christ model who succeeds, in a roundabout way, when the favor he does for an actor friend brings him together with Sybil (Richardson). A leg waxer in a beauty shop, Sybil does acting work on the side, primarily as a moaner for porno loops, which brings her together with Louis. She's also the one with the watch, given to her by a little girl at a dinner club, where Sybil also works as a waitress, as payment to make the house pianist (Jeff Goldblum) smile. Sybil decides to make him smile in the traditional way in which women often make men smile, but she must wait four days as it's her "time of the month."

In the meantime, a violinist sweeps Sybil off her feet, sending the smitten pianist into a rage during which he assaults the violinist and is put into prison. Sybil and Louis have a significant moment together as porno co-moaners, leading Sybil to con a large sum of money out of Louis to care for her sick grandfather and to buy a coat for the pianist, who's coming out of prison the following day.

Louis goes to the prison, where Sybil stands him up. But he eventually hooks up with the pianist, who's not only the perfect Christ model, but also has star quality enough to make him an overnight celebrity—along with a couple of "miracles." Thinking Louis to be yet another contender for Sybil's affections, the pianist goes bonkers yet again, bringing about the ending and bringing Louis and Sybil together for the final fadeout.

Unfortunately, THE FAVOUR, THE WATCH, AND THE VERY BIG FISH sounds a lot funnier than it really is. (The very big fish, by the way, has nothing to do with anything. It makes a cameo appearance before disappearing into a meat grinder.) While certainly not suffering from a shortage of incidents, the plot never picks up much momentum. Instead, it plays like one thing after another, piling on one outrageous gag after another without ever seeming to have much of a point. As a result, the film doesn't so much wind up as wind down, exhausting itself, and its audience, long before it's over.

As other recent casualties can attest, from Ted Kotcheff's FOLKS! to Peter Bogdanovich's strained mounting of Michael Frayn's NOISES OFF, pure farce is one of the trickiest movie forms to pull off successfully; even reigning master Blake Edwards hasn't really done it in years. But writer-director Ben Lewin, adapting a French short story, barely gets out of first gear. His ideas are rarely either fresh or imaginative and his sense of pacing is virtually nonexistent. Scene after scene lumbers along gracelessly when it should dance. What charm, and what few laughs there are, come from the cast's efforts to breathe life into Lewin's comedy corpse.

Hoskins does what he's been doing too often over the last few years, bringing wit and warmth to largely witless, unengaging material. He remains one of the best, most resourceful actors working in films today. But when is somebody going to get him a decent script? Much the same could be said for Richardson (PATTY HEARST, THE HANDMAID'S TALE), who has similarly been burning up her career, wasting her luscious, thinking-man's sex appeal in mediocre, unsexy movies. Rounding out the leading trio, Goldblum continues to amaze. Is there another actor on earth right now who could play a modern-day Christ as a slightly distracted, and more-than-a-little annoyed, unwilling celebrity and make it not only funny but utterly believable?

But the real surprise is Michel Blanc, who played the obsessed voyeur to a poignant perfection in MONSIEUR HIRE, who's so hilarious as Hoskins's oh-so-despicably-French boss that the two should think about making a movie series as a team. Unfortunately, as with the other actors, he is at his best when he's most able to make you forget how utterly uninspired a film this otherwise is. *(Adult situations, nudity, profanity.)*

p, Michelle DeBroca; d, Ben Lewin; w, Ben Lewin, (from the short story "Rue Staint-Sulpice" by Marcel Ayme); ph, Bernard

Zitzermann; ed, John Grover; m, Vladimir Cosma; art d, Juan Carlos Conti; set d, Frederic Pesquer; cos, Elisabeth Tavernier

Comedy **(PR: C MPAA: R)**

FEED ★★★
76m Video Democracy ~ Original Cinema c

George Bush, Bill Clinton, Pat Buchanan, Ross Perot, Paul Tsongas, Bob Kerrey, Tom Harkin, Jerry Brown, Jacques Barzaghi, Hillary Clinton, Gennifer Flowers, Arnold Schwarzenegger

Compiling the unused portions of news conferences and speeches transmitted via satellite during the 1992 New Hampshire primary campaign, filmmakers Kevin Rafferty and James Ridgeway, abetted by Brian Springer, have assembled an amusing series of vignettes, full of those little moments of silly vanity to which senators, governors and congressmen may be especially prone when faced by anything with a lens.

The electioneering style in New Hampshire was an especially rich vein of embarrassing moments since there were innumerable small groups before which the aspirants had to appear. So, we see Senator Bob Kerry standing in the snow in front of a handful of supporters, some of whom are clearly well below voting age, and fretting over the wires and electrical connections hanging out of his overcoat pockets, and with good reason, since he ends up unable to hear the distant newscaster's introduction or questions.

Former governor Jerry Brown continually primps in front of the camera and complains about the knot of his tie when it is clearly his oversized shirt collar that is the problem. Later, in an obvious cheap shot, we see Brown literally bend into the camera frame while using a nasal spray. Larded in between such segments, President Bush appears patiently waiting for the official signal to start smiling. Two things emerge clearly from Bush's appearance: one is how grim he can look and secondly that he has apparently nothing to occupy his valuable time while he sits there leaden and silent.

One amusing bipartisan failing is the reluctance to be seen actually wearing the eyeglasses needed by most of these middle-aged stumpers to check speeches and schedules printed in anything less than teleprompter-size lettering. The two strongest segments, however, do not involve the major candidates at all. On her way from a restaurant session of pressing the female flesh, Hillary Clinton is approached by a well-wisher who turns out to be homeless. Corporate lawyer Clinton quickly delegates his attentions to a campaign functionary with whom the poor man has a brief, sad chat. The other sequence involves a local newsman who is gossiping with a fellow anchor as they wait for their news "feed" to begin, and apparently refers to a reporter from a larger network as a "Shylock," just the kind of off-hand remark that would have gotten any of the politicos into big trouble.

Oddly enough, Paul Tsongas scores the biggest points and gets equally stumped. Tsongas succeeds rather sharply when he comments on Sam Donaldson who upstages him at a local press conference. At what might be the same locale, a New Hampshire resident baffles the candidate by asking him if he knows the price of a gallon of milk—Tsongas clearly does not.

Exploiting as it does the common ground of show business and politics, FEED is both amusing and a little cheap, since anyone having make-up applied in close-up would look foolish, particularly full-faced presidential candidates. Still, Rafferty and Ridgeway, who collaborated previously with Anne Bohlen on the gripping BLOOD IN THE FACE, do emphasize the scrutiny to which these men are subjected and the odd combination of sincerity and guile that underlie any modern political campaign. *(Adult situations.)*

p, Kevin Rafferty, James Ridgeway; d, Kevin Rafferty, James Ridgeway; ph, Kevin Rafferty, Jenny Darrow, Sarah Durham; ed, Sarah Durham, Kevin Rafferty

Documentary/Political/Comedy **(PR: C MPAA: NR)**

FERNGULLY: THE LAST RAINFOREST ★★½
(Australia/U.S.) 72m FAI Films; Youngheart Productions; Interscope Communications ~ Fox c

VOICES OF: Tim Curry *(Hexxus)*, Samantha Mathis *(Crysta)*, Christian Slater *(Pips)*, Jonathan Ward *(Zak)*, Robin Williams *(Batty Koda)*, Grace Zabriskie *(Magi Lune)*, Geoffrey Blake *(Ralph)*, Robert Pastorelli *(Tony)*, Richard "Cheech" Marin *(Stump)*, Tommy Chong *(Root)*, Tone-Loc *(The Goanna)*, Townsend Coleman *(Knotty)*, Brian Cummings *(Ock)*, Kathleen Freeman *(1st Elder)*, Janet Gilmore *(1st Fairy)*, Naomi Lewis *(2nd Elder)*, Danny Mann *(Ash)*, Neil Ross *(3rd Elder)*, Pamela Segall *(2nd Fairy)*, Anderson Wong *(Rock)*, Lauri Hendler, Rosanna Huffman, Harvey Jason, Dave Mallow, Paige Nan Pollack, Holly Ryan, Gary Schwartz *(Additional Voices)*

Widely noted as a "politically correct" animated feature, FERNGULLY is nonetheless a pleasing adventure that provides enough entertainment to make its occasionally overstated message go down easy.

The titular forest is a region that has thrived in the absence of humans; it was once threatened by an evil force called Hexxus (the voice of Tim Curry), who was imprisoned inside a great tree by the fairy Magi Lune. Now aging, Magi (Grace Zabriskie) is tutoring young fairy Crysta (Samantha Mathis) in the ways of magic and the wonders of nature. Crysta, whose friends include the amorous Pips (Christian Slater) and a fruit bat named Batty Koda (Robin Williams), who has escaped from an experimental lab, is curious about the world beyond the forest, and ventures out one day despite Magi's warnings.

On the edge of the woods, Crysta witnesses a logging machine tearing up the trees; when she sees it bearing down on a young lumberjack named Zak (Jonathan Ward), she shrinks him to her size to save him. At first angered by his predicament (Crysta is unable to restore him to normal height), Zak later comes to admire and respect the wonders of the forest as Crysta reveals them to him. The two also become attracted to each other, much to Pips's chagrin.

Meanwhile, the logging machine has torn up the tree containing Hexxus; the vile spirit takes over the machine and aims it toward Ferngully. Magi Lune creates a giant tree for the forest spirits to hide in—and expires as a result—but Crysta decides to confront the creature. While Batty (who has overcome his prejudice against humans) flies Zak into the machine to stop it, Crysta plants a seed within Hexxus, one that grows around and consumes him under the fairies' power. She is also able to return Zak to normal, and he leaves the fairy community, promising to help stop humans from continuing the destruction of the forests.

FERNGULLY was one of the first major-studio feature cartoons to follow in the wake of Disney's recent successes in the field, and the inspiration shows in more ways than one. Its heroine Crysta recalls Ariel from THE LITTLE MERMAID; not only does she share the latter's independence and yearning to learn about the mysterious world of humans, but she's similarly sexed-up: impossibly slender, Crysta flits about the forest barefoot and wearing the skimpiest costume the MPAA's G rating will allow. Like BEAUTY AND THE BEAST, FERNGULLY attempts to instruct as well as entertain, but where the earlier film taught a subtle lesson (about the skin-depth of physical beauty), this one wears its save-the-forest message on its sleeve.

Nonetheless, there are many pleasingly novel elements to FERNGULLY. Because it was produced by an Australian firm, the film's background animal cast is populated not by the usual bunnies, deer and squirrels but kangaroos, koalas and even a goanna—a monitor lizard—with the voice of Tone-Loc (who sings "If I'm Goanna Eat Somebody, It Might as Well Be You"). The song score is nicely varied, with the more up-to-date numbers, abetted by amusingly eccentric lyrics, outshining the more traditional ballads. Hexxus's "Toxic Love" (given a superbly creepy rendition by Curry) manages to rhyme "acid rain" with "chow mein," and Williams's Batty Koda sings what is probably the only rap number you'll ever hear about animal experimentation.

Though his performance plays as something of a warmup for his virtuoso turn in Disney's ALADDIN, Williams adds a good amount of high spirits to the ensemble; he and Curry (THE ROCKY HORROR PICTURE SHOW, Ridley Scott's LEGEND) are standouts among a generally effective voice cast. The animation, while not as complex as Disney's recent work, is fluid and colorful, with some striking backgrounds and a strong "natural" feel that's somewhat surprising, given director Bill Kroyer's background handling the computerized visuals of TRON.

Despite some moments that seem overly commercially calculated (as when the miniature Zak finds his lost Walkman in the forest and switches it on, and the fairies start boogieing to "Land of a Thousand Dances"), FERNGULLY makes for above-average family entertainment.

p, Wayne Young, Peter Faiman; d, Bill Kroyer; w, Jim Cox, (from the stories "FernGully" by Diana Young); ed, Gillian Hutshing; m, Alan Silvestri; art d, Susan Kroyer, Ralph Eggleston; anim, Charles Leland Richardson, Tony Fucile

Animated/Fantasy/Musical (PR: AA MPAA: PG)

FEW GOOD MEN, A ★★★

138m Manhattan Project; Castle Rock Entertainment ~ Columbia c

Tom Cruise *(Lieutenant J.G. Daniel Kaffe)*, Jack Nicholson *(Colonel Nathan R. Jessep)*, Demi Moore *(Lieutenant Commander JoAnne Galloway)*, Kevin Bacon *(Captain Jack Ross)*, Kiefer Sutherland *(Lieutenant Jonathan Kendrick)*, Kevin Pollak *(Lieutenant Sam Weinberg)*, James Marshall *(Private First Class Louden Downey)*, J.T. Walsh *(Lieutenant Colonel Matthew Markinson)*, Christopher Guest *(Dr. Stone)*, J.A. Preston *(Judge Randolph)*, Matt Craven *(Lieutenant Dave Sprading)*, Wolfgang Bodison *(Lance Corporal Harold W. Dawson)*, Xander Berkeley *(Captain Whitaker)*, John M. Jackson *(Captain West)*, Noah Wyle *(Corporal Jeffrey Barnes)*, Cuba Gooding, Jr. *(Corporal Carl Hammaker)*, Lawrence Lowe *(Bailiff)*, Josh Malina *(Orderly)*, Oscar Jordan *(Steward)*, John M. Mathews *(1st Guard)*, Aaron Sorkin *(Man in Bar)*, Al Wexo *(2nd Guard)*, Frank Cavestani *(1st Agent)*, Jan Munroe *(Jury Forman)*, Ron Ostrow *(MP)*, Matthew Saks *(David)*, Harry Caesar *(Luther)*, Michael DeLorenzo *(Private First Class William T. Santiago)*, Geoffrey Nauffts *(Lieutenant Sherby)*, Arthur Senzy *(Robert C. McGuire)*, Cameron Thor *(Commander Lawrence)*, David Bowe *(Commander Gibbs)*, Gene Whittington *(Mr. Dawson)*, Maud Winchester *(Aunt Ginny)*, The Association of Former Fish Drill Team Members of Cadets at Texas A & M University *(Drill Team)*

This courtroom drama has more ham than you'll find on any Christmas table. Despite the massive hype, A FEW GOOD MEN is little more than a star vehicle for famous names who exert themselves with less than stellar results.

When two Marines, Pfc. Louden Downey (James Marshall) and Lance Cpl. Harold W. Dawson (Wolfgang Bodison), are accused of murdering Pfc. William Santiago (Michael DeLorenzo) on the US Navy base at Guantanamo Bay in Cuba, hotshot Navy lawyer Lieut. J.G. Daniel Kaffe (Tom Cruise) is assigned to defend them. As is his custom, Kaffe wants to plea-bargain, but his co-counsel, Lieut. Comdr. JoAnne Galloway (Demi Moore), senses a Marine conspiracy, and the young lawyer comes to agree with his antagonistic partner.

The two stoic defendants are uncommunicative at first, but under interrogation reveal that they were ordered to perform a "Code Red"—a secret form of hazing—on Santiago after he threatened to reveal Dawson's illegal firing at a Cuban watchtower. (For those unfamiliar with US history, the American presence on Cuban soil is a legacy of the Spanish-American War.) The result was Santiago's accidental death, apparently poisoned by the rag stuffed down his throat before his mouth was taped shut. Dawson and Downey claim that they received the orders from their superior, Lieut. Jonathan Kendrick (Kiefer Sutherland). Tough career officer Col. Nathan R. Jessep (Jack Nicholson) of the US Marine Corps, however, denies any involvement by the leadership.

Kaffe, Galloway and their research partner, Lieut. Sam Weinberg (Kevin Pollak), have little hope of winning against prosecuting attorney Capt. Jack Ross (Kevin Bacon). Kaffe's worst fears are realized when Downey admits on the stand that Dawson, and not Kendrick, ordered him to perform the Code Red. Lieut. Col. Matthew Markinson (J.T. Walsh), however, confides to Kaffe that Jessep personally ordered the Code Red as a punishment for Santiago's defiance of the Marine Corps chain of command. (Santiago had gone over Jessep's head, writing letters to Washington offering to testify against Dawson and asking to be transferred off the base.) Markinson, however, commits suicide before he can testify.

Hoping finally to live up to the reputation of his late father, an illustrious attorney, Kaffe pins his last hope on goading Jessep into admitting that he ordered the hazing. Kaffe faces a court martial if he's wrong, but the attorney gets a damaging admission from Jessep and wins the case. Although the Marines are found innocent, they receive a dishonorable discharge.

The celebrated Jack Nicholson is A FEW GOOD MEN's biggest liability. He continues the trend of self-parody that he began in BATMAN, over-enunciating every line and failing to inject any subtlety into this portrait of a bully. At the not-so-tender age of thirty, fellow superstar Tom Cruise still appears too young for his part, failing to convince us that he has the intelligence or the courage to take on Jessep. Cruise looks like a hyperactive student involved in the big high-school debate, and throws in an embarassing drunk scene to boot.

Actress Demi Moore talks tough but barely registers onscreen. To show distress, she bites her lower lip. Cruise and Moore are required to play out the usual male/female antagonism: she hates him at first but then really grows to respect him (though the obligatory sex scene is thankfully missing here). Unfortunately, Cruise and Moore have similar blank green eyes and open-mouthed expressions that add up to zero in the chemistry department.

Sutherland's character is a future Jessep, and the young actor gives a similarly villainous performance. Pollak, meanwhile, is annoying as a stereotypically Jewish straight man to Cruise and Moore. Only Walsh, Bodison, and the resurgent Bacon (JFK, CRIMINAL LAW) turn in natural performances.

Aaron Sorkin's screenplay, based on his hit Broadway play, strikes an unsuccessful balance between drama and comedy.

Cruise gets jokey lines to make him look cute, but they all fall flat. "And the hits just keep on coming," he remarks after learning Moore will be co-counsel with him. "Well, Zippa Dee Doo Da!" he yells when he discovers an amazing bit of evidence that his defendants had not previously revealed. Cruise's dialogue, which makes him seem nerdy rather than hip, is blended with long expositionary monologues from the other characters.

In the film's defense, Rob Reiner directs at a fairly fast clip, avoiding the dull pitfalls of many other courtroom pictures. Bacon's expert interrogation of Marshall is particularly fine, showing how a case can unravel in an instant. A few good moments in the courtroom, however, are not enough to save A FEW GOOD MEN. *(Adult situations.)*

p, David Brown, Rob Reiner, Andrew Scheinman; d, Rob Reiner; w, Aaron Sorkin, (from his play); ph, Robert Richardson; ed, Robert Leighton; m, Marc Shaiman; prod d, J. Michael Riva; art d, David Klassen; set d, Michael Taylor; cos, Gloria Gresham

AAN Best Picture: David Brown (Producer), Rob Reiner (Producer), and Andrew Scheinman (Producer); *AAN Best Supporting Actor:* Jack Nicholson; *AAN Editing:* Robert Leighton; *AAN Sound:* Kevin O'Connell, Rick Kline, and Bob Eber

Drama **(PR: C MPAA: R)**

FIELD OF FIRE ★½

96m Concorde ~ HBO Video c

David Carradine *(General Corman)*, Eb Lottimer *(Sgt. Duncan)*, Scott Utley *(Senator)*, Don Barnes *(Jimmy T.)*, David Anthony Smith *(Lt. Reynolds)*, Jim Moss *(Wilson)*, Tonichi Fructouso *(Jeff)*, Ruben Ramos *(Major Ho)*, Henry Strzalkowski *(Hawk)*

When a valuable air ace, Major Wilson (Jim Moss), is shot down behind enemy lines in Vietnam, the American military headed by General Corman (David Carradine) initiates a desperate rescue mission: find Wilson before the Commies can torture information out of him. Simplistic and boringly brutal, FIELD OF FIRE traces the jungle slogging of Yankee saviors who escort Wilson through this hostile terrain.

Whether blowing up paddle boats containing the sequestered enemy or engaging "gooks" in hand-to-hand combat, Uncle Sam's boys, headed by Sgt. Duncan (Eb Lottimer), always manage to outsmart the Viet Reds. Although Wilson is soon plagued by jungle rot, he puts on a brave face as he and his rescuers climb what seems like every mountain in Vietnam. Unfortunately, their radio hook-up was tampered with back at headquarters, and the soldiers lose contact with General Corman. Ambushed and then surrounded after they run for cover, things look bleak. While one martyrdom-embracing hero holds the line, the others drag Wilson into an underground bunker and start praying. Locating a copter in Laos, General Corman proves he's a hands-on kind of guy and flies through a hail of bullets himself in order to save Wilson and his own men. Outsmarting the enemy, Corman saves his fighting men and Major Wilson—proving himself a hero and saving the US government from a major embarrassment.

During WWII, propaganda films served a specific function, successfully stirring audiences' patriotic feelings and thereby fueling the war effort. These days, all the retro-Vietnam War films glutting the direct-to-video market seem pointless. Why whip up hysteria over a lost cause? Certainly, during the actual course of that tragic conflict, audiences weren't beseiged by gung-ho salutes that made them want to go out and bayonet a Commie (and this despite the fact that, thanks to the glory of TV, Vietnam was the first such conflict to invade American living rooms). Attitudes were too complex. Today, it's disheartening to witness the Vietnam conflict recast as a good vs. evil action tableau. How can these tacky, warmongering movies view such a muddied, confusing conflict in such a clear-cut, arrogant manner?

Even as an athletic action movie, FIELD OF FIRE fails to ignite. Not one combat scene is staged well enough to shake this slow-moving film out of its lassitude. If you're going to grind out Vietnam replays as an excuse for jingoism then at least provide some technical razzle-dazzle and skill at staging action sequences. Falling asleep on the bayonet of its own lowly ambitions, FIELD OF FIRE reeks of deja vu. This film needs to go back to basic training. *(Violence, profanity.)*

p, Roger Corman; d, Cirio Santiago; w, David A. Thomas; ph, Joe Batac, Vic Anao; ed, Edgardo Vinaro; m, Justin Lord; prod d, Joe Mari Avellana; art d, Ronnie Cruz

War/Action/Adventure **(PR: C MPAA: R)**

FINAL ANALYSIS ★★

124m Witt-Thomas Productions; Roven/Cavallo Entertainment; Warner Bros. ~ Warner Bros. c

Richard Gere *(Isaac Barr)*, Kim Basinger *(Heather Evans)*, Uma Thurman *(Diana Baylor)*, Eric Roberts *(Jimmy Evans)*, Paul Guilfoyle *(Mike O'Brien)*, Keith David *(Detective Huggins)*, Robert Harper *(Alan Lowenthal)*, Agustin Rodriguez *(Pepe Carrero)*, Rita Zohar *(Dr. Grusin)*, George Murdock *(Judge Costello)*, Shirley Prestia *(District Attorney Kaufman)*, Tony Genaro *(Hector)*, Katherine Cortez *(Woman Speaker)*, Wood Moy *(Dr. Lee)*, Corey Fischer *(Forensic Doctor)*, Jack Shearer *(Insurance Consultant Doctor)*, Lee Anthony *(Judge)*, Derick Alexander *(Ambulance Driver)*, Abigail Van Alyn *(Night Nurse)*, Rober Bearde *(Orderly)*, Dennis Matthews *(Ambulance Attendant)*, Tessa Konig-Martinez *(Woman Witness)*, Ernie Davis *(Young Tough)*, Rico Alaniz *(Old Spanish Man)*, Charlie Holiday *(Jury Foreman)*, Jeff Tanner *(Dinner Companion)*, Jeff Smolek *(Hospital Security)*, John Roselius *(Sheriff's Deputy)*, Michael Sayles *(Deputy Guard)*, Anna Nicholas *(Ex-Girlfriend)*

Innumerable films are indebted to the great Alfred Hitchcock, perhaps the most emulated director in history. But these homages, while often technically adept, usually lack the psychological nuance and ambiguity that were Hitchcock's forte. With its dangerous ethics and sexual obsession, FINAL ANALYSIS attempts to repackage VERTIGO, the celebrated auteur's 1958 masterpiece, for the taboo-laden 9Os.

Psychiatrist Isaac Barr (Richard Gere) is treating Diana Baylor (Uma Thurman), an apparently neurotic, obsessive-compulsive young woman who harbors deeply guilty suppressed memories of childhood sexual abuse by her father, and the action she took to avenge it. Her older sister, she says, knows much more about the event. Heather Evans (Kim Bassinger) appears on Isaac's doorstep in classic rainy-night fashion, expressing great worry about Diane, who in her agitation has procured a gun and displays every sign of breakdown. Diane's plight, however, is soon secondary to the reluctant but mutual lust between Heather and Isaac; his libido negates his professional discretion and they quickly fall into bed. After their erotic gratification, Isaac listens to what he presumes to be a candid diagnosis of Diane.

After this brief encounter, Heather returns home to Jimmy (Eric Roberts), her vain, reptilian, domineering husband, whom she fears and perhaps even loathes. At Isaac's next session with Diane, he is more interested in Heather than her sister's psyche. Her Freudian fears exacerbated, Diane becomes addled and envious. Word association — "violet, violence, violates" — suggests a psychorama of confused, traumatized sexuality. But Heather, it seems, has demons of her own. Jimmy's priggery at an elite restaurant elicits her contempt, which she cools, or stokes, with a glass of wine, perhaps deliberately inducing a rare and mysterious "pathological intoxication." Heather is beautiful, but also fiercely self-destructive, a potentially lethal combination for all concerned.

Isaac, nonetheless, is further smitten and intrigued by the forbidden Heather. His state of mind is symbolized by their tryst at an abandoned, phallic seaside lighthouse somewhere near the Golden Gate Bridge. Isaac wades in further when he shadows Jimmy and Heather at a bar, his gaze a bit too lingering, and is admonished by the thuggish spouse. Arriving home, she liberally swigs some cold medicine, then snaps into a murderous rage from the alcohol it filters into her blood. The weapon is a functional Maguffin; her alibi of pathological intoxication is akin to SPELLBOUND's amnesia—innocence by reason of incapacity.

Isaac retains a lawyer friend on Heather's behalf. Much momentum is lost during the rather tepid trial. Diane lurks in the background; the link to her therapy is not yet clear. The case rests on the viability of Heather's defense, which is, in effect, temporary insanity. She is confined to an asylum, subject to periodic review. But Isaac deduces that Diane's "violet, violence, violates" is only verbatim Freud, and that he has been set up by the sisters in an elaborate scheme for them to acquire Jimmy's mobster fortune now that his Greek brother and sole heir is conveniently dead.

Isaac confronts Heather, who counters with threats to have him disbarred for malpractice and indicted for homicide. And she can substantiate her claims: Isaac's fingerprints are on the murder weapon she retains. Isaac, however, keenly counters her devious mind with wiles of his own. As Heather's scheme unravels, she escapes the asylum, nearly murders the fellow Isaac has assigned to tail "Diane," and almost puts the incriminating evidence into the hands of Detective Huggins (Keith David), who distrusts the liberal psychiatrist. The denouement occurs at a predictable venue, the irony all but washed away in the acrophobic setting. Clearly, the writer or director was the wrong man who knew too much Hitchcock.

Director Phil Joanou has crafted some impressive sequences with master cinematographer Jordan Cronenweth (who shot Joanou's earlier STATE OF GRACE). The tight story by Robert Berger and Wesley Strick provides sufficient red herrings. The love triangle of sorts supplies the physical appeal (though some viewers may balk at accepting Gere as cerebral doctor, hot lover *and* clever sleuth). But a gripping internal dynamic has not been conferred upon the proceedings so much as grafted, its concoction of handsome boilerplate filched from a worn but wizardly grab bag. FINAL ANALYSIS fails, beyond a shadow of a doubt, to captivate the way a new spin on Hitchcock should.

p, Charles Roven, Paul Junger Witt, Tony Thomas; d, Phil Joanou; w, Wesley Strick, (from the story by Strick and Robert Berger); ph, Jordan Cronenweth; ed, Thom Noble; m, George Fenton; prod d, Dean Tavoularis; art d, Angelo Graham; set d, Bob Nelson; cos, Aude Bronson-Howard

Crime/Drama **(PR: C MPAA: R)**

FINAL IMPACT ★½

102m Pepin/Merhi Productions ~ PM Home Video c

Lorenzo Lamas *(Nick Taylor)*, Kathleen Kinmont *(Maggie)*, Mike Worth *(Danny Davis)*, Jeff Langton *(Jake Gerard)*, Frank Reeves *(Stevie)*, Mike Toney *(Joe)*, Mimi Lesseos *(Roxy)*, Kathrin Lautner *(Kimber)*, Gary Daniels *(4th Fighter)*, Lance Harris *(3rd Fighter)*, Pete Cunningham *(1st Fighter)*, Ian Jacklin *(2nd Fighter)*, Azhakd Fariborz *(Fighter)*, Art Camacho *(Fighter)*, Michele Grassnick *(Foxy Boxer)*, Erika Nann *(Foxy Boxer)*

Since concluding his assignment as a prime-time hunk on the long-running TV soap opera "Falcon Crest," the genetically blessed Lorenzo Lamas (son of Fernando Lamas and Arlene Dahl) has reinvented himself as a martial arts star in a series of direct-to-video action potboilers.

His latest, FINAL IMPACT, cannily casts the veteran stud as over-the-hill kickboxer Nick Taylor, boozy proprietor of a sleazy sports bar. Once a winner, Nick hit the spiritual skids after meanie Jake Gerard (Jeff Langton) defeated him in the ring, taking Nick's title and wife. Now a newcomer named Danny Davis (Mike Worth), "light-heavyweight champ of the great state of Ohio," is bound for Las Vegas to compete against Gerard in the kung-fu finals, and the kid seeks out his hero Nick for advice. Nick puts the young contender through the usual strenuous personal training exercises that are always a priority in these fight flicks.

The cliched plot pushes the envelope slightly with Nick Taylor, who's not the expected ROCKY-esque underdog but a genuinely bitter, self-absorbed lush who cultivates little sympathy as he grooms Danny to be his instrument of revenge on Jake. Nick isn't even permitted to live to the fade-out; fatally injured by Jake in a street showdown, he repents on his hospital deathbed just before Danny's climactic bout.

The tag-team directors Stephen Smoke and Joseph Merhi know well how to photograph a brawl, and had they merely delivered on the promise of a knockout finale FINAL IMPACT would have succeeded on its own lowly terms. Instead it fouls out. After a pounding that puts him on the canvas for a nine count, Danny totters to his feet and KO's the deadly Jake Gerard with two or three lackluster blows. The onscreen spectators cheer Mike's victory upset, but home viewers are more likely to cry "Fix!"

The cast is serviceable, with Mike Worth looking like a skinny high school nerd until he sheds his sweatshirt and reveals a taut, muscular physique. The rather pudgy villain Jeff Langton bears a strong resemblance to the sand-kicking "Bully on the Beach" in those famous old ads for the Charles Atlas bodybuilding course. Romantic lead Kathleen Kinmont (married to Lorenzo Lamas in real life) contributes her own variety of body language, but the picture's sexy opening-credit montage of voluptuous lady wrestlers in peek-a-boo outfits oiling up for a performance gives a misleading impression of a high T&A component. *(Violence, substance abuse, profanity, sexual situations.)*

p, Joseph Merhi, Richard Pepin; d, Joseph Merhi, Stephen Smoke; w, Stephen Smoke; ph, Richard Pepin; ed, Geraint Bell, John Weidner; m, John Gonzalez, Louis Febre

Action/Martial Arts **(PR: O MPAA: R)**

FINE ROMANCE, A ★

(Italy) 83m CEP Produzione Cinematografica; Silvio Berlusconi Communications; ReteItalia ~ Castle Hill Productions c

Julie Andrews *(Pamela Picquet)*, Marcello Mastroianni *(Cesareo Gramaldi)*, Ian Fitzgibbon *(Bobby Picquet)*, Jean-Pierre Castaldi *(Marcel)*, Jean-Jacques Dulon *(Dr. Noiret)*, Maria Marchado *(Miss Knudson)*, Dennis Grey *(Madame Legris)*, Jean-Michel Cannone *(Dr. Picquet)*, Catherine Jarret *(Marguerite Gramaldi)*, Francoise Michaud *(Madeleine)*, Herve Hiolle *(Hospital Doctor)*, Yvette Petit *(1st Concierge)*, Michele Amiel *(2nd Concierge)*, Ronald Mills *(Maitre'd)*, Michele Buczynski *(Photo Shop)*, Isidro Arruti *("Hotel Patricular")*

Gene Saks's listless comedy, A FINE ROMANCE, is distinguishable for many reasons. It fails to evoke any laughs, wastes the talents of two fine performers and may be the first motion picture in history to make Paris look unattractive.

Cesareo Gramaldi (Marcello Mastroianni) arrives home to find out that his young wife has left him for another man. Across town, Pamela Piquet (Julie Andrews) discovers that her husband has also flown the coop and is bedding Cesareo's wife. The disgruntled duo meet in a restaurant to try and figure out a solution to their mutual predicament; they both confess to wanting their spouses back. Cesareo, while missing his wife dearly, is nevertheless attracted to the staid Englishwoman, Pamela. Pamela views him as she does every Italian man—a leech in a nice suit. He begs her to go out to dinner but she refuses.

A month later, she finds Cesareo sleeping in one of the beds at a hospice she helps run. He confesses to severe depression, his always legendary drinking having gotten even worse. Pamela is now determined to help him through this ordeal. They take a holiday together at a country spa hoping it will get them both in a better state of mind. Cesareo puts on a good front, but he's really keeping fit by chasing a voluptuous instructor and sneaking booze into his room. Pamela has just about had it with his animalistic behavior. Cesareo, however, is falling in love with her.

Back in Paris, Pamela finally decides he isn't so bad and agrees to sleep with him. Last-minute jitters cause her to end up doing just that—sleep. They have grown quite fond over the past weeks, but it's apparent each is still pining for their respective mates. Before long their wishes are granted. Pamela's husband returns home, as does Cesareo's wife. All seems back to normal, but the gods have intervened. Pamela and Cesareo exchange love letters and rendezvous at a nearby hotel to consummate their affair. They now have their spouses and their true loves.

A FINE ROMANCE is a fine disaster. Rarely has a film boasted so many glaring errors. The story, always headed for the predictable happy ending, is a jumble of unfunny, heavy-handed vignettes. Screenwriter Ronald Harwood, adapting from the play *Tchin-Tchin* by Francois Billetdoux, obviously felt it didn't matter why the protagonists' spouses walked out. By ignoring the reasons he only added more ambiguity to a film which cries out for some definition. The only source of conflict seems to be, will the spouses come back? One should hope for their own sake that they don't. Staying as far away from the screen as possible is the best advice here.

Flat scene follows flat scene, and it ultimately takes quite an imagination to figure out just what the two leads see in each other. There is also a subplot involving Pamela's yuppie son, which is too absurd to dissect. Technically the film is harshly overlit, washing out the actors' faces. The wretched dialogue grows worse as the movie progresses. Holding up two glasses of liquor, Mastroianni observes, "I order two of everything. It's faster." That zinger may be the funniest line of the film, and it comes after an excruciatingly long opening scene. Never has the City of Lights had such a bad rendering on celluloid.

The film's dearth of professionalism can only be attributed to director Gene Saks. Trying desperately to raise a laugh, and failing at every turn, Saks (a multiple Tony Award-winning director long associated with Neil Simon) betrays little flair for the filmic medium. He may have struck a deal with the owners of the Eiffel Tower, though: the monument appears in at least a dozen separate scenes. There also appears to be a peculiar proliferation of Americans in Paris, as evinced by several waiters and bit players with decidedly Yankee accents.

Andrews tries her best in this silly role, but she is undone by anemic dialogue and unfiltered lighting. Mastroianni only looks tired. The chemistry between them is non-existent, but this too can be traced back to the abysmal screenplay. To add insult to injury, the film's moral suggests that adultery is okay, even wonderful, between consenting partners. A perfect ending for such an egregious folly. *(Sexual situations.*

p, Arturo LaPegna, Massimiliano LaPegna; d, Gene Saks; w, Ronald Harwood, (from the play *Tchin-Tchin* by Francois Billetdoux); ph, Franco DiGiacomo; ed, Richard Nord, Anna Poscetti; m, Pino Donaggio; md, Natale Massara; art d, Jean Michel Hugon, Michel Albournac; cos, Gianni Versace

Comedy/Romance (PR: C MPAA: PG-13)

FINEST HOUR, THE ★

105m 21st Century Film Corporation ~ Columbia TriStar Home Video c

Rob Lowe *(Hammer)*, Gale Hansen *(Dean)*, Tracy Griffith *(Barbara)*, Eb Lottimer *(Bosco)*, Baruch Dror *(Greenspan)*, Daniel Dieker *(Albie)*, Michael Fountain *(Carter)*, Evyatar Lazar *(Moonjean)*, Henry Taejoon Lee *(T.J.)*, Ari Sorko-Ram *(Petersen)*, Erik Degn *(Thurston)*, Natan Sgan-Cohen *(Franklin)*, Jon J. Herson *(Dr. Cortese)*, Uri Gavriel *(Commander)*, John Phillips *(Simmons)*, Jack Widerker *(Taylor)*, Gilia Stern *(Diane)*, Ava Haddad *(Isabel)*, Gregory Tal *(Big Soldier)*, Tristan Ray Lawson *(Joshua)*

Former brat packer Rob Lowe strikes a blow for freedom and star slumming in THE FINEST HOUR, a daft but enjoyable actioner from veteran shlockmeister Menahem Golan revolving not around Desert Storm but — for budgetary reasons, no doubt — the less incendiary Desert Shield.

Lowe is known through the entire film by his last name, Hammer. He doesn't rap, but he is tough. How tough? When his commanding officer at Navy SEALS school in San Diego asks which recruits think they can whip his butt, Hammer immediately steps forward—and the commander doesn't challenge him. *Whooo!* Only one guy in the SEALS school is tough enough to be Hammer's buddy, and that's sensitive, introspective Dean (Gale Hanson) who says, in voiceover, that he came to the SEALS from Annapolis to conquer his fear of water. Before the viewer is allowed to mull over what a guy with a fear of water is doing in the Navy to begin with, we're plunged into stock footage aplenty featuring familiar Desert Storm faces from President Bush to Wolf Blitzer. And there's Hammer, right in the thick of it.

He's temporarily separated from Dean after marrying the gal of Dean's dreams, pretty marine biologist Barbara (Tracy Griffith) whose choice of the carousing, womanizing Hammer can only mean that she lost a bet. The two SEAL buddies are brought back together after emerging as the force's top mini-sub specialists and sent to check out Iraqi development of biological warfare weapons on an island in the Strait of Hormuz. Hammer gets blown up, not once, but twice for his trouble. The second time kills him but not before he and Dean knock out the bioweapon development center. Though Barbara was on the verge of leaving Hammer for Dean just before the fatal mission, Dean is alone at the fadeout, his ever-helpful voiceover explaining that "the death of Hammer was the death of us." Huh? Not only that, we never do learn the answer to the film's other burning question: Did Dean conquer his fear of water?

For an action film, there's not much action in THE FINEST HOUR. Nor is there much romance or drama. However, director Shimon Dotan manages to cover up most of the time by keeping what action there is fast and frenzied. SEALS training is a blur of guys flailing in the mud and being tied up and dropped into a water tank to teach them not to drown. Hammer marries Barbara while out on a pizza run. All the film's "war" scenes take place on a single, cheesy set that looks left over from a Jackie Chan action comedy on which, it seems, Hammer and Dean take out the entire Iraqi army without expending too much energy or too many bullets.

Lowe, who seems to have based his mustachioed character on TV's comically blustery "Major Dad," puts forth his best acting effort to keep a straight face during such scenes as the one in which he fondles a nurse's shapely calves to elicit her breathless and instantaneous cooperation in getting himself sprung from a military hospital. Griffith and Hansen are worth noting for keeping their dignity throughout, the former especially during not one, but two scenes in which she's dropped into water fully clothed All that and more doesn't make THE FINEST HOUR anything like a fine film, but it is curiously entertaining. *(Violence, brief nudity.)*

p, Menahem Golan; d, Shimon Dotan; w, Shimon Dotan, Stuart Schoffman; ph, Avi Karpik; ed, Netaya Anbar, Bob Ducsay; m, Walter Christian Rothe; prod d, Avi Avivi; cos, Rochelle Zaltzman

War/Action **(PR: C MPAA: R)**

FINISHING TOUCH, THE ★★★

82m Concorde ~ Columbia TriStar Home Video c

Michael Nader *(Sam Stone)*, Shelley Hack *(Hannah Stone)*, Arnold Vosloo *(Mikael Gant)*, Art Evans *(Lt. Mormon)*, Clark Johnson *(Det. Gilliam)*, Ted Raimi *(Det. Arnold)*, John Mariano *(Nick Sorvino)*, Howard Shangraw *(Marty)*

One wades through scores of obscure video releases just in the hopes of finding one visually arresting, intelligently written thriller. Stacked beside the steady stream of illogical murder mysteries and juvenile crime dramas, the stylish THE FINISHING TOUCH may seem even better than it is.

Someone with a depraved artistic bent is slicing up women in Los Angeles, and it's not a pretty picture. High-strung Detective Sam Stone (Michael Nader) is forced to reteam with his ex-wife Hannah (Shelley Hack) who agrees to work undercover to ensnare the murderer. The emotional baggage carried by this troubled pair forms an interesting subtext for this yarn about trust and lust, as Hannah becomes involved with prime suspect Mikael Gant (Arnold Vosloo). Ostensibly set up as a target for the killer's next homicidal expression, Hannah loses her objectivity when Gant displays a powerful brushstroke technique in the boudoir. Are Stone's instincts about Gant colored by jealousy, or should the coppers be tailing Nick Sorvino (John Mariano), a pornographer, rape suspect and former employee of Gant's with a grudge for being fired?

In a warehouse that ships out kiddie videos, Stone discovers a stash of snuff movies starring all of the serial killer's victims. Although Gant is arrested, he's released for lack of sufficient evidence; Hannah feels she's made a mess of her police work and any potential relationship with Gant. After Stone traces Sorvino to a kinky s & m rendezvous, he's forced to shoot the low-life; the police consider the snuff murder case closed. Storming off the force, Hannah returns to Gant to apologize, but instead discovers that he's not only the real psychopath but he also has an aversion to dates who kiss and tell. Arriving in the nick of time, Stone grapples with Gant. At the climax, Hannah gets knocked out but revives and shoots Gant in his crotch, thus ending a life of crime and art.

Unlike run-of-the-mill maniac movies, THE FINISHING TOUCH boasts carefully planned atmospheric touches and psychological insights. Its sole objective isn't merely to keep viewers awake in between the graphic slay sequences; instead it develops the characters' personalities to such a degree that we have an interest in them beyond their involvement in finding out whodunit.

Exploring the unresolved relationship of Stone and Hannah, THE FINISHING TOUCH juxtaposes their estranged sexuality with the fulfillment Hannah gets from Gant. Wildly possessive of his ex-wife, Stone cannot go on with his own life. Interestingly, the volatile Stone seems more off-balance than the murder suspect. Not only does the film maintain a high level of sexual tension, it also keeps viewers guessing about the true murderer's identity, not by dispensing the usual red herrings but by offering us several viable suspects.

Painting an ugly portrait of crime-solving in urban America, THE FINISHING TOUCH employs its art world background evocatively. Creepy and sometimes suprisingly erotic, this thriller presents a blood-spattered canvas where life is cheap but the profits from murder are high. At the same time, it takes no prisoners as it confronts a contemporary battle of the sexes. An unusually sophisticated crime thriller. *(Violence, profanity, sexual situations.)*

p, Steve Rabiner; d, Fred Gallo; w, Anthony L. Greene, (from the story by Green and Rodger S. Grossman); ph, Mark Parry; ed, Glenn Garland; m, Darryl Way; prod d, Hector Velez

Erotic/Thriller **(PR: O MPAA: R)**

FLIRTING ★★★½

(Australia) 96m Kennedy-Miller Productions ~ Samuel Goldwyn Company c

Noah Taylor *(Danny Embling)*, Thandie Newton *(Thandiwe Adjewa)*, Nicole Kidman *(Nicola Radcliffe)*, Bartholomew Rose *("Gilby" Fryer)*, Felix Nobis *(Jock Blair)*, Josh Picker *("Baka" Bourke)*, Kiri Paramore *("Slag" Green)*, Marc Gray *(Christopher Laidlaw)*, Greg Palmer *(Colin Proudfoot)*, Joshua Marshall *("Cheddar" Fedderson)*, David Wieland *("Possum" Piper)*, Craig Black *("Pup" Pierdon)*, Leslie Hill *(Greg Gilmore)*, Jeff Truman *(Mr. Morris Cutts)*, Marshall Napier *(Mr. Rupert Elliott)*, John Dicks *(Reverend Consti Nicholson)*, Kym Wilson *(Melissa Miles)*, Naomi Watts *(Janet Odgers)*, Lisa Spinadel *(Barbara Howe)*, Francesca Raft *(Fiona Spry)*, Danielle Lyttleton *(Jean Thomas)*, Jacqui Fifer *(Stacey Burt)*, Fiona Press *(Mrs. Archer)*, Maggie Blinco *(Miss Guinevere MacReady)*, Jane Harders *(Miss Sylvia Anderson)*, Malcolm Robertson *(Bruce Embling)*, Judi Farr *(Sheila Embling)*, Freddie Paris *(Solomon Adjewa)*, Femi Taylor *(Letitia Adjewa)*, Gillian Hyde *(Dr. Alison Pierce)*, Harry Lawrence *(Motel Manager)*, Michael Williams *(Sonny Liston)*, Kurt Frey *(Jean-Paul Sartre)*

This sequel to writer-director John Duigan's acclaimed THE YEAR MY VOICE BROKE is intelligently written and marvelously acted. Set during the turbulent 60s, in the not so turbulent Australian countryside, FLIRTING is both charming and poignant, a universal story of the innocence of youth and the emergence of emotional maturity.

Danny Embling (Noah Taylor) is a bright and sensitive teenager forced to make his way through a restrictive and very proper boarding school. His days are spent fending off school bullies and chatting about the absurdity of it all with his best chum, Gilby Fryer (Bartholomew Rose). Danny keeps his sense of humor even after some students make fun of his occasional stutter. While watching a school rugby match, he lays eyes on a beautiful young student, Thandiwe Adjewa (Thandie Newton), from the girl's boarding school which sits tantalizingly across the lake. He is immediately smitten with Thandiwe's exotic looks—the only black girl at an otherwise all white stronghold—and her obvious intellect. Shortly thereafter, at a debate, they win each other over with equally inspiring arguments and agree to meet at a social mixer the following week.

Though excited by the impending date, Thandiwe is also having trouble with some of her classmates, particularly Nicola Radcliffe (Nicole Kidman), a snobbish upperclassman. Meanwhile, the boys' school's tyrannical headmaster refuses to let Danny go to the dance because his hair is too long. Exhibiting a surprising bravado, he sneaks into the affair anyway and collects Thandiwe. They steal off to his dormitory where they share their first kiss, determined to see each other again soon.

Over the next few weeks they grow closer as Danny surreptitiously rows across the connecting lake to the female academy. They explore their sexuality and ultimately fall in love. Thandiwe sends him a love letter which is intercepted by one of the bullies. Infuriated, Gilby reports the theft to the headmaster. When the student is reprimanded he believes Danny ratted him out and challenges him to a boxing match. In front of a huge gathering, Danny is pulverized but gains the respect of many of the students. Thandiwe has also made headway and is now highly regarded amongst her peers, even winning the loyal friendship of Nicola.

When the two schools collaborate on a theatrical production, Thandiwe and Danny spend more and more time together, eventually introducing their parents on the night of the play. Thandiwe's father, Solomon (Freddie Paris), is a Ugandan dissident concerned with the growing strife in his country. Danny's parents, Sheila and Bruce (Judi Farr and Malcolm Robertson), are slightly taken back when they realize their son is dating a black girl. Weeks later Thandiwe receives notice that the violence in her home country has worsened and that her father is in dire trouble. She is forced to leave Australia and Danny.

The lovers plan their last night together and run off to a small motel for the event. When the schoolmaster and his counterpart at the girl's school find out, they track them down and break into the room where the couple are in bed. Thandiwe and Danny say goodbye with hopeful promises to see each other soon. Danny is expelled from the school and returns home to work at his father's pub. Through letters, he finds out that Thandiwe's father was killed and that she has since moved to Nairobi. Danny dreams of when they will be back in each other's arms.

While there are light moments throughout, FLIRTING is rather more serious than its name implies. True, Duigan focuses on the simple love story between two teenage outsiders, yet he makes it clear that the world around Danny and Thandiwe is changing rapidly, giving the film a broader dramatic context that is its strong point.

Aided by a literate screenplay and fine performances from his ensemble cast, Duigan depicts the awkward changes which all teenagers encounter with compassion and unblinking realism. In fact, this story could be set anywhere—anywhere where authority and rebellion can be found. At the same time, Duigan filters in a keen sense of time—it's 1965—and place with sparing use of news clips and expositional information, but the effect is never heavy handed. For instance, one finds out that America is sending her first troops into Vietnam through a passing shot of a television set. This works doubly in that it not only identifies the era, but it also captures universal themes which will unfold in the film. Duigan also manages to pinpoint the different mentality levels of the students by addressing world events. While Danny and Thandiwe are concerned with the troubled state of the planet, most of the other students are having trouble organizing their sock drawers.

FLIRTING's central love story works on many levels, not the least of which is that the issue of an interracial romance barely comes into play. Instead Duigan trains his camera on the confusing and exploratory aspects of first love, never belittling the emotions of the young protagonists. Taylor, as the fish out of water Danny, is flawless in his interpretation of character, displaying an uncanny depth seldom found in juvenile actors. He never appears to be acting—only living the experiences of a wise-beyond-his-years manchild. The exceptionally pretty Newton is graceful and charming as Thandiwe. From the first frame there is never a doubt she'll win over her schoolmates. Kidman (DEAD CALM, FAR AND AWAY) has a fine turn in the underwritten role of Nicola. The entire group of students are well cast and diverse in type and style.

While there are stylistic similarities between this and other coming-of-age tales, Duigan's screenplay has a depth of intelligence which makes FLIRTING stand out among films in this genre. In addition, the act of placing a likable character in a hostile environment, and giving him wonderful words to speak and a bright light at the end of the tunnel, has an appeal that never grows old. Both beautiful and at times painful to watch, FLIRTING leaves one wanting more, which is exactly what John Duigan has in mind. The final installment of this projected trilogy should be on the screen before too long. *(Sexual situations.)*

p, George Miller, Terry Hayes, Doug Mitchell; d, John Duigan; w, John Duigan; ph, Geoff Burton; ed, Robert Gibson; prod d, Roger Ford

Drama/Romance **(PR: A MPAA: NR)**

FOLKS! ★★

109m Penta Pictures; Victor Drai Productions ~ Fox c

Tom Selleck *(Jon Aldrich)*, Don Ameche *(Harry Aldrich)*, Anne Jackson *(Mildred Aldrich)*, Christine Ebersole *(Arlene Aldrich)*, Wendy Crewson *(Audrey Aldrich)*, Robert Pastorelli *(Fred)*, Michael Murphy *(Ed)*, Kevin Timothy Chevalia *(Kevin)*, Margaret Murphy *(Maggie)*, Joseph Miller *(Jerry)*, T.J. Parish *(Steve)*, John McCormack *(Howard)*, Peter Burns *(Another Trader)*, Jon Favreau *(Chicago Taxi Driver)*, Jackye Roberts *(Gail)*, Kevin Barry Howe *(FBI Agent)*, Christopher J. Campbell *(1st Taxi Driver)*, Omar Cabral *(Dr. Aviano)*, Marilyn Dodds Frank *(Mrs. Henney)*, Doris Carey Ferguson *(Nurse)*, Will Knickerbocker *(2nd Taxi Driver)*, George O. Petrie *(Sammy)*, Ilse Earl *(Lois Elliott)*, Mal Jones *(Retired Doctor)*, Sid Raymond *(Retired Attorney)*, George O *(Doorman)*, Bob Gordon *(William)*, Jerry Hotchkiss *(1st Neighbor)*, Dee Dee Deering *(1st Neighbor's Wife)*, Evelyn Brooks *(Retired Lawyer's wife)*, Robert Escobar *(Florida Cop)*, Wanda Christine *(County Nurse)*, Joseph R. Ryan *(Patient)*, Teri McEvoy *(1st Reporter)*, Ross Gottstein *(2nd Reporter)*, Thomas Richter *(Agent)*, Frankie DaVila *(Shoe Salesman)*, Toni Fleming *(Lady Shoe Buyer)*, Juan Ramirez *(Shoe Store Owner)*, Nydia Rodriguez Terracina *(Shoe Store Owner's Wife)*, Frank Dominelli *(1st Thug)*, Tom Milanovich *(2nd Thug)*, Mary Seibel *(Condo Manager)*, Richard Sullivan Lee *(Police Officer)*, Gerald Owens *(Dr. Bush)*, Angelo Anthony Buscaglia, Jr. *(Tow Truck Driver)*, Evan Lionel *(Gang Leader)*, Magic Slim *(Blues Singer)*, Tony Mockus, Jr. *(Chicago Cop)*, James Andelin *(Lenny)*, O. Boyd Clow *(Lenny's Partner)*, Mike Barger *(Paramedic)*, Mario Nieves *(2nd Cousin)*, Juan Olmedo *(1st Cousin)*, Connie Scurlock *(Mother)*

Can absurdist comedy have a heart? Should it? That question is posed by FOLKS!, a very black comedy from screenwriter Robert Klane, about a deranged senior citizen who turns his son's life into a living hell.

Jon Aldrich (Tom Selleck) is the laid-back Chicago Stock Exchange wheeler-dealer with a beautiful wife, Audry (Wendy Crewson), two cute kids, a dog and a nice apartment, whose life is about to go completely down the toilet. It all starts unassumingly enough when he gets a call that his mother, Mildred (Anne Jackson), needs a minor operation. It seems that his father, Harry (Don Ameche), can't be found, so Jon will need to sign the consent form. Arriving there, he finds his mother lucid and in good spirits. But he also finds that his father is in an advanced state of senile dementia. Despite Jon's best efforts, his father manages to destroy half the trailer park where he lives before burning down his own trailer.

Meanwhile, the FBI closes down Jon's company in Chicago as part of a sting investigation and freezes Jon's assets, leaving him penniless and unable to earn a living. Nevertheless, Jon brings his parents back to Chicago to live with his family, where the disasters escalate. Before it's over, Jon will lose his wife, kids and apartment, along with various parts of his body, from a piece of his ear to a testicle, before yielding to his father's one lucid suggestion—that Jon end his misery by getting rid of them in an "accident." Driven to desperation, Jon decides to comply. However, the last-minute discovery of a valuable stock certificate held by Jon's father prevents euthanasia and puts Jon's family and life back together.

Even if Tom Selleck has yet to break through to big-screen stardom, he can hardly be accused of picking bland, safe star vehicles to further his career. FOLKS! embodies more ugly truths about American life than most American movies are comfortable with. At the same time, it tries to soften its impact with big-scale comic destruction and a wish-fulfillment ending. But realism and fantasy make an uncomfortable mix, cancelling each other out and making FOLKS! neither fish nor fowl, neither dark gallows farce nor sunny feelgood froth.

For two-thirds of the film, it's hard to decide whether to laugh at or be appalled by some truly amazing stuntwork and big-scale buffoonery when each scene ends with Selleck's character in the hospital, with yet another body part removed and another piece of his sanity chipped away. At the end of the second act, Selleck sits, catatonic, in his empty apartment (his furniture removed by creditors). What brings him back to life is his decision to carry out his parents' wish to murder them.

For the final third, we don't know whether to laugh at or be appalled by Selleck's attempts to murder a couple of old people by such methods as pushing them onto the highway in a gas-drenched Ford Pinto. FOLKS! kicks into its standard comedy resolution when Selleck, finding he just hasn't the heart—or lack of it—to kill his parents, leaves it to his greedy sister, Arlene (Christine Ebersole), to do the deed, leading to a sensational, cliffhanger ending, in which the hapless parents are put into a plane rigged to crash with Selleck hanging onto the wing.

The points are sharply made that today's yuppies will have some hard decisions to make as increasingly sophisticated medical technology keeps their parents alive longer than ever and, the most basic American truth of all, that money changes everything. But, despite hitting close to home, FOLKS! finally has more moral baggage than it can comfortably carry. Its social truths deflate its comedy value while its comedy element prevents it from getting any kind of a grip on the serious issues it raises.

As he has in the past, Robert Klane (WHERE'S POPPA?) demonstrates that his reach exceeds his grasp when it comes to writing a mixture of sentiment and satire. And, despite the return of Ted Kotcheff, who directed Klane's recent hit, WEEKEND AT BERNIE'S, the results manage to feel simultaneously provocative, stale and predictable as it becomes apparent that FOLKS!, having bitten off more than it can chew, will revert to mediocrity by its fadeout.

Neither particularly funny nor particularly moving, FOLKS! tries hard, but it only winds up proving that being different doesn't necessarily mean being better. *(Violence, adult situations.)*

p, Victor Drai, Malcolm R. Harding; d, Ted Kotcheff; w, Robert Klane; ph, Larry Pizer; ed, Joan E. Chapman; m, Michel Colombier; prod d, William J. Creber; set d, Scott Jacobson, Jean Alan; cos, Jay Hurley

Comedy **(PR: C MPAA: PG-13)**

FOR THOSE ABOUT TO ROCK ★★

84m the Acme Company ~ Warner Home Video c

AC/DC, Metallica, The Black Crowes, Pantera, Electro Shock Therapy

Shot in the wake of the Soviet coup of 1991, FOR THOSE ABOUT TO ROCK intermixes glossed moments of political change with lots of standard, headbanging heavy metal music.

When Russian and American music promoters received permission to mount a huge outdoor rock concert in post-Soviet Moscow, film and video crews recorded the event from beginning to end. This MTV-styled rockumentary combines the conventions of the rock concert film (WOODSTOCK-influenced behind the scenes interviews, footage of the local reactions, etc.) with the kinetic, video-toasted look of the all-music channel.

The film begins with the inscription that in August 1991 "the young challenged the old" in the political battle that resulted in the overthrow of Gorbachev and the eventual installation of Boris Yeltsin. From there images of heavy rockers are supposed to represent the agents of political change who threw up barricades against the hard-liners and brought freedom to a repressive regime. Footage of Lenin and Brezhnev give way to shots of Yeltsin riding a tank and 500,000 screaming metalheads. Headbanging concert revelers clash with head-beating riot police trying to impose order on the unruly crowd.

Amid it all the "Monsters of Rock USSR" concert goes on. Those "cowboys from hell," Pantera, open the program with three numbers including "Primal Concrete Sledge" and "Psycho Holiday." The Moscow metal culture is shown turning out in force, looking much like their American counterparts, sporting tattered jeans, leather, tattoos, long hair and devil masks. Their raucous set is followed by a song from local Russian grunge-metal band E.S.T., who sing about bullying policeman—as the lyrics are illustrated by a montage of concert disorder and club-toting military forces. The supposed celebration of freedom and the "end to violence" threatens to end in chaos when the promoter appears on stage telling the metal-hungry fans to "settle down or we'll have to listen to Neil Diamond the rest of our lives."

Disorder seems to give way to drunken revelry as The Black Crowes play a short set that concludes with a cover of Bob Dylan's "Rainy Day Woman." The song's refrain "Everybody must get stoned," evokes images of multitudes of young Russian men hoisting bottles of vodka. Two somber interludes offset three songs by Metallica. One shows video footage from the evening of the violent August coup, the other a memorial service for those who died in the fighting. The Australian group AC/DC wrap up the event with a longer set, playing their hit "Highway to Hell" and concluding with the anthem that gives FOR THOSE ABOUT TO ROCK its name. The production concludes with impromptu scenes of the rock stars paying irreverent visits to the sights of Moscow.

Fans of heavy metal, and of the featured bands in particular, will obviously enjoy the performances showcased in FOR THOSE ABOUT TO ROCK. The links between Metallica and martyrdom for democracy, however, are troubling.

This huge event was obviously historic. The mere fact that such a show could be staged was a significant symbol of change in the liberated atmosphere of the new Russia. And the tension-releasing feelings of empowerment channeled through blaring rock guitars must have been tremendously cathartic for many. But the poignant scenes of memorials for those who died and scenes of pro-democracy heroes battling tyranny make the chaotic concert seem at odds with those constructive forces rather than in league with them; instead of peace signs, fans throughout the heavy metal mob flash only middle fingers and devil's horns.

No matter how much one might enjoy the music, the mood of the concert—even as documented by people trying to promote their efforts as good—leans more toward nihilistic anarchy than democratic liberation, more toward hooliganism than fandom. That being the case, it seems unfortunate that the chroniclers of this important cultural event should try simply to pass off their efforts as part of a victory for democracy. Rock on, but think about it sometimes. *(Profanity, violence.)*

p, Curt Marvis; d, Wayne Isham

Documentary/Musical **(PR: C MPAA: R)**

FOREVER YOUNG ★★½

102m Warner Bros.; Icon Productions ~ Warner Bros. c

Mel Gibson *(Daniel)*, Jamie Lee Curtis *(Claire)*, Elijah Wood *(Nat)*, Isabel Glasser *(Helen)*, George Wendt *(Harry)*, Joe Morton *(Cameron)*, Nicholas Surovy *(John)*, David Marshall Grant *(Wilcox)*, Robert Hy Gorman *(Felix)*, Millie Slavin *(Susan Finley)*, Michael Goorjian *(Steven)*, Veronica Lauren *(Alice)*, Art LaFleur *(Alice's Father)*, Eric Pierpont *(Fred)*, Walt Goggins *(Gate MP)*, Amanda Foreman *(Debbie)*, Karla Tamburrelli *(Blanche)*, Robert Munns *(Wrong Harry)*, J.D. Cullum *(Frank)*, Ava Lazar *(Waitress at Diner)*, Richard Ryder *(Pilot at Airshow)*, Michael Briggs *(Pilot at Airshow)*, Kenny Ransom *(Officer at Warehouse)*, Jared Chandler *(Officer at Warehouse)*, Jon Menick *(Doctor at Airfield)*, Paul Ganus *(Airbase Personnel)*, Jason Iorg *(Airbase Personnel)*, Mary Ellen Moore *(Ticket Woman)*, Miriam Beesley *(Woman at Picnic)*, Lisa Savage *(Woman at Picnic)*, Cody Burger *(Boy at Picnic)*, Dean Hallo *(Man at Picnic)*, Greg Allan Martin *(Man at Picnic)*, Joel McKinnon Miller *(Man at Picnic)*, William Marquez *(Doctor at Hospital)*, Steve Hinton, Jr. *(Boy with Ice Cream)*, John Bourg *(Daniel–Age 11)*, Ara Maxwell *(Helen–Age 11)*

Like 1991's LATE FOR DINNER, FOREVER YOUNG is a "deep-freeze" drama: a romance featuring a character who is cryogenically preserved and then revivified in a later era. In this case, a mildly intriguing idea has been insufficiently developed; the presence of Mel Gibson, however, still made a fairly respectable hit out of this unabashed tear-jerker.

Daniel (Mel Gibson) is a 1939 test pilot completely devoted to his girlfriend Helen (Isabel Glasser). Just after he has once again failed to get up the courage to propose marriage, she is hit by a truck and falls into a coma from which, according to the doctors, she may never recover. Crushed, Danny approaches his best friend Harry (George Wendt) and asks to be the subject in his next cryogenic experiment; unable to stand the pain of waiting for his beloved either to revive or die, he agrees to be deep-frozen for one year.

Cut to the present day, as two boys, Nat (Elijah Wood) and Felix (Robert Hy Gorman), find and accidentally open the "freezer" while playing in an old air force warehouse. Released from his frozen state, Danny sets about trying to discover what went wrong, and why he's been frozen for so long. In the process, he moves in with Nat and his single mother, Claire (Jamie Lee Curtis), to both of whom he gets very attached. Meanwhile, the Army is also very keen to find out what happened to their long-forgotten experiment. Things get progressively sniffly as the film moves toward a grand, emotional climax.

Relentlessly corny, FOREVER YOUNG gets off to a bad start in every department—screenplay, direction, editing and acting. There is an explanation for what went wrong with the experiment, but can we really believe that no one would notice a freezer big enough to hold Mel Gibson, sitting among plane parts? Or that his character would adjust to modern life so easily? Somehow, though, the film seems to come to life as it goes along, with some well-written, keenly observed scenes. (There's a very good one in which Danny teaches Nat how to fly an old plane, using trinkets in Nat's treehouse, with the camera behaving as though they're really in flight.) The last ten minutes of the film are absolutely irresistible.

Put together with a little more care and inspiration, FOREVER YOUNG could have been a massive hit. There's a huge potential audience for this sort of GHOST-ly romance, and many of Gibson's female fans prefer to see him without fast cars and guns (in a nice bit of self-referential humor, Gibson screams to Curtis, as she swings a car out of the road and over a drop, "You drive like I do!"). FOREVER YOUNG misses its shot at capturing that market. *(Mild profanity.)*

p, Bruce Davey; d, Steve Miner; w, Jeffrey Abrams; ph, Russell Boyd; ed, Jon Poll; m, Jerry Goldsmith; prod d, Gregg Fonseca; art d, Bruce A. Miller; set d, Jay R. Hart

Romance/Adventure **(PR: A MPAA: PG)**

1492: THE CONQUEST OF PARADISE ★

(U.S./Spain/France/U.K.) 140m Due West Productions; Pere Fajes; Legende; CYRK ~ Paramount c

Gerard Depardieu *(Christopher Columbus)*, Armand Assante *(Sanchez)*, Sigourney Weaver *(Queen Isabella)*, Loren Dean *(Older Fernando)*, Angela Molina *(Beatrix)*, Fernando Rey *(Friar Marchena)*, Michael Wincott *(De Moxica)*, Tcheky Karyo *(Pinzon)*, Kevin Dunn *(Captain Mendez)*, Frank Langella *(Luis de Santangel)*, Mark Margolis *(Bobadilla)*, Kario Salem *(Arojaz)*, Billy Sullivan *(Fernando Age–10)*, John Heffernan *(Brother Buyl)*, Arnold Vosloo *(Guevara)*, Steven Waddington *(Bartolome)*, Fernando G. Cuervo *(Giacomo)*, Jose Luis Ferrer *(Alonso)*, Bercelio Moya *(Utapan)*, Juan Diego Botto *(Diego)*, Achero Manas *(Ship's Boy)*, Fernando Garcia Rimada *(King Ferdinand)*, Albert Vidal *(Hernando de Talavera)*, Isabel Prinz *(Duenna)*, Angela Rosal *(Pinzon's Wife)*, Jack Taylor *(Vicuna)*

History has not been well served by Hollywood this year. Following Warner Bros.' ill-fated CHRISTOPHER COLUMBUS: THE DISCOVERY comes Paramount's 1492: THE CONQUEST OF PARADISE, a lumbering journey that conveys none of the joy or mystery of exploration. Star Gerard Depardieu's unintelligible line readings and director Ridley Scott's murky mise-en-scene make it a hard film to hear and see, let alone like.

Yearning to follow a Western route to Asia, explorer Christopher Columbus (Depardieu) presents his case to the Spanish royal council in 1492. Only the Queen's treasurer Sanchez (Armand Assante) supports the idea, and Columbus is refused. With a banker's help, however, he gets an audience with Queen Isabella (Sigourney Weaver), and convinces her to finance his voyage. The explorer is so obsessed by his quest that he neglects his mistress Beatrix (Angela Molina) and two sons. Columbus and his men set sail on the Nina, the Pinta and the Santa Maria. After weeks of navigating by the stars and not reaching land, Columbus faces the near-mutiny of his sailors. His inspiring speech about their mission, however, convinces the weary, hungry men to continue and they finally land in Haiti.

The Spaniards quickly befriend the local natives, learning their language and customs and believing the land a paradise. Columbus takes some Indians and their meagre gold jewelery back to Queen Isabella, who is delighted with the explorer's success. But when Columbus returns to the West Indies with Spanish noblemen, he finds that the sailors he left behind have been massacred. Instead of punishing the Indians, however, Columbus establishes a colonial government. A mass rebellion occurs after Spanish nobleman De Moxica (Michael Wincott) persecutes some natives. After hearing about Columbus's chaotic administration, Queen Isabella sends another man to supervise the colony and summons the explorer to return to Spain, where he is promptly thrown in prison. The Queen later releases him, however, and agrees to let him make one more voyage.

1492: THE CONQUEST OF PARADISE has managed the impossible: to make Columbus's story dull. It meanders along for two and a half hours without creating the slightest ripple of interest. Former TV commercials director Ridley Scott (ALIENS, BLADE RUNNER, THELMA & LOUISE) indulges his passion for shadows and darkness, an idea that just doesn't work in an epic historical film; the grim lighting makes all the actors look grey. And Scott lingers over every scene. When the director finally gets to the landing in Haiti, a dramatic highpoint, he overdoes it by using the big slow-mo approach. Meanwhile, Roselyne Bosch's screenplay includes some unintentionally funny dialogue. Columbus's meeting with the Queen turns into a flirtation as he asks her how old she is. Another scene has Friar Marchena (Fernando Rey) deck Columbus when the explorer goes berserk in his church.

Unfortunately, the most amusing part of the film is Depardieu's awkward performance. The actor, so marvelous in his native tongue, has trouble speaking English, and his thick accent makes even the simplest sentences difficult to comprehend. "De lund eez dere. De lund eez closh," he says to convince a sailor they will soon finish the voyage. Depardieu's hangdog expression and substantial girth also contribute to the laughable effect. As Isabella, Sigourney Weaver deports herself with a stiffness befitting a soap opera queen, not a true monarch; it's as though she doesn't quite know what to do with her body in the elaborate costumes. Assante looks like *he* should have played Columbus. Michael Wincott, who portrays the evil De Moxica, uses his strong features to good effect. On the other hand, his costume is distracting, reminding one of pop star Michael Jackson's outfits—a black leather jumpsuit with a low-slung, silver-studded belt.

Although Columbus's achievements and motives have been subjected to criticism in recent years, the legendary explorer deserves a better filmic treatment on the occasion of the 500th anniversary of his discovery of the new world. *(Violence, adult situations.)*

p, Alain Goldman, Ridley Scott; d, Ridley Scott; w, Roselyne Bosch; ph, Adrian Biddle; ed, Francoise Bonnot, William Anderson; m, Vangelis; prod d, Norris Spencer; art d, Benjamin Fernandez, Leslie Tomkins; set d, Ann Mollo; cos, Charles Knode, Barbara Rutter

Historical/Biography/Adventure (PR: C MPAA: PG-13)

FREDDIE AS F.R.O.7 ★½

90m Hollywood Road Film Productions ~ Miramax c

VOICES: Ben Kingsley *(Freddie the Frog)*, Jenny Agutter *(Daffers)*, John Sessions *(Scottie)*, Brian Blessed *(El Supremo)*, Nigel Hawthorne *(Brigadier G.)*, Sir Michael Horden *(The King)*, Phyllis Logan *(Nessie)*, Jonathan Pryce *(Trilby)*, Billie Whitelaw *(Messina)*, Prunella Scales, David Ashton

A British animated import, FREDDIE AS F.R.O.7 is a poorly plotted, badly executed parody of James Bond movies.

The story begins in the distant past, where a recently widowed magician-king (Sir Michael Horden) lives in a coastal castle with his preteen son and heir, Prince Freddie (Ben Kingsley). Determined that young Frederic shall never be King, Messina (Billie Whitelaw), his wicked aunt, does away with the lad's father and turns the Prince into a frog. Before being squashed by the ugly, venomous Messina, the Frog Prince escapes by plunging into the sea; Messina turns herself into a cobra and pursues him. With the aid of Nessie (Phyllis Logan), a Loch Ness monster-style creature, the Frog Prince successfully eludes Messina.

After a musical dance interlude, the story flashes forward several centuries to contemporary Paris, where Freddie the Frog is now a six-foot tall amphibian known as Secret Agent F.R.O.7—an eccentric blend of Inspector Clouseau and James Bond. Meanwhile, Messina has joined forces with El Supremo (Brian Blessed), a latter-day combination of Adolf Hitler and Napoleon Bonaparte whose singular motto is, "I will rule the world . . . ha ha ha ha!"

El Supremo has invented a device that shrinks tall buildings into seeming oblivion and, in conjunction with Messina, has caused such historic London landmarks as the Tower of London and Buckingham Palace to disappear. His other high-tech weaponry includes a sleep-ray which can effectively benumb every man, woman and child in the British Isles. In desperation, British intelligence dispatches an urgent message to Paris requesting the services of Freddie to help them out of their dilemma.

Freddie gets wind of El Supremo's next target, namely, Big Ben. In company with Daffers (Jenny Agutter), a pretty, karate-practicing, female British agent, and Scottie (John Sessions), Daffers's very Scottish fellow agent, Freddie ensconces himself and partners in Big Ben's interior, figuring that the only way to capture the villians is to hide inside the landmark just prior to its disappearance. He and his fellow agents are caught in the Big Ben snatch and wind up prisoners of Messina and El Supremo in an impenetrable fortress deep within the bowels of a mountain. Ultimately—and again with the help of Nessie, the gentle sea monster—Freddie and friends escape the clutches of Messina and El Supremo and become national heroes. Freddie is knighted by the Queen and settles down with Daffers.

FREDDIE AS F.R.O.7 is woefully lacking in the plot and pacing department; the film gets off to a less-than-action-packed start and never really picks up. The dialogue is listless and flat, and never achieves the witty, tongue-in-cheek effect for which it is clearly striving. The vocal performances are competent, if uninspired, with Brian Blessed going a little over the top and Billie Whitelaw achieving the desired level of menace. Most of the songs are unmemorable, though the "Evilmainya" number performed by Grace Jones is visually striking, with its hundreds of high-stepping, jack-booted soldiers.

The animation is generally competent, but hardly extraordinary. While this feature has some good moments sprinkled among its extended, dull stretches, it is light years behind Disney's BEAUTY AND THE BEAST or THE LITTLE MERMAID.

p, Jon Acevski, Norman Priggen; d, Jon Acevski; w, Jon Acevski, David Ashton; ph, Rex Neville; ed, Alex Rayment; m, David Dundas, Rick Wentworth; art d, Paul Shardlow; anim, Richard Fawdry, Tony Guy, Mike Stewart

Animated/Musical/Children's (PR: AA MPAA: PG)

FREEJACK ★★

108m Morgan Creek Productions; Freejack Productions ~ Warner Bros. c

Emilio Estevez *(Alex Furlong)*, Anthony Hopkins *(McCandless)*, Mick Jagger *(Vacendak)*, Rene Russo *(Julie Redlund)*, David Johansen *(Brad Hines)*, Jonathan Banks *(Michelette)*, Grand Bush *(Boone)*, Amanda Plummer *(Nun)*, John Shea *(Morgan)*, Esai Morales *(Ripper)*, *Vincent Schiavelli*

It's hard not to go in with some expectations when a film boasts the credentials this one does, from a screenplay co-written by Ronald Shusett (TOTAL RECALL, ALIEN), to villainous co-starring turns from Mick Jagger and Anthony Hopkins. Alas, even the lowest expectations go unmet by FREEJACK, which turns out to be an inexplicably lame, penny-pinched futuristic actioner.

Emilio Estevez adds to his groaning gallery of wooden portrayals as big-time race driver Alex Furlong, who's about to get creamed on the track. The event is being eagerly anticipated from the future by bounty hunter Vacendak (Jagger), who supplies strapping young bodies to the old and infirm. His client is big-shot corporate executive McCandless (Hopkins), who is already dead, but who appears to his underlings as a video hologram and whose spirit is being temporarily kept alive in a high-tech facility until a suitable body can be found.

A barrage of electronic gadgetry is used to spirit Furlong's body out of the past just seconds prior to his pulverization in the arranged accident. A radical lobotomy will then be performed to remove his own mind and replace it with McCandless's. Naturally, something goes wrong. Furlong regains consciousness in the future and escapes Vacendak's evil clutches before the scheduled brain transfer can take place, making him the outlaw "free-jack" of the title. The remainder of the movie is given over to a tedious array of chases, with Vacendak after Furlong and the latter determined to uncover the reason he's being pursued. Meanwhile, Vacendak also tries to ferret out the traitor in his midst who's passing on his moves and strategies to an unknown third party interested in bringing Furlong back dead, rather than alive.

FREEJACK insists that we care about Furlong's plight, but it never quite gets around to explaining why. Instead, it expects us to get so caught up in the schematic succession of double-crosses, triple-crosses, chases and pitched gun battles that we don't notice there isn't all that much going on. The "surprises" are fairly transparent from the outset, but what's imponderable is how the future got to be the way it's portrayed here—it's not even clear how many years hence the main action is set.

Furlong's pal from the present, his sleazy manager, Brad Hines (former New York Dolls singer David Johansen), and his girlfriend, Julie Redlund (Rene Russo), who's somehow become McCandless's girl Friday, seem barely to have aged more than a few days since Furlong left them in the present. Yet society has changed drastically, ruled by huge corporations (as in ROLLERBALL), with cities that have become uninhabitable battlegrounds of warring factions (as in ESCAPE FROM NEW YORK), all dark, damp and dirty (as in BLADE RUNNER). Unlike the movies it emulates, however, FREEJACK is all surfaces with no soul, and compounds its derivativeness by not making sense on any level except as a tired retread of better films. Even on its most basic level, as a head-banging action thriller, it's woefully lacking in craft.

The screenplay takes forever developing the uneasy alliance between Furlong and Vacendak against their common enemy, Michelette, a standard-issue corporate sleazoid intent on overthrowing McCandless (who is nonetheless given some snap and vigor as played by WISEGUY's Jonathan Banks). Vacendak, meanwhile, comes across as less a formidable foe than an incompetent nincompoop who takes forever figuring out who the traitor is while letting Furlong give him the slip too easily time after time. If Vacendak is the best bounty hunter the future has to offer, then we really are in trouble.

None of these other weaknesses is helped at all by Geoff Murphy's sluggish direction and the film's overall cheapjack production values, which sustain a mood of solemn silliness throughout, from futuristic "vehicles" that look suspiciously like painted-over city street sweepers, to Vacendak's ridiculous disco-maniac, hellbent-for-leather attire. Beyond Banks and Hopkins, the acting is also generally uninspired, with Jagger suffering from an extreme shortage of screen time—and Estevez suffering from a notable surplus. And who'd want to inhabit Emilio's body anyway?

One could go on and on, but it would have even less point than the film itself. Altogether, FREEJACK is forgettable sci-fi that is best forgotten by all involved. *(Violence, profanity.)*

p, Ronald Shusett, Stuart Oken; d, Geoff Murphy; w, Ronald Shusett, Steven Pressfield, (screenplay) Dan Gilroy, (from the novel *Immortality Inc.* by Robert Sheckley); ph, Amir Mokri; ed, Dennis Virkler; m, Trevor Jones; prod d, Joe Alves; art d, Jim Taylor; set d, Bruce Gibeson; cos, Lisa Jensen

Science Fiction/Action (PR: C MPAA: R)

FROZEN ASSETS ★½

96m Frozen Assets Productions ~ RKO Pictures Distribution c

Shelley Long *(Dr. Grace Murdock)*, Corbin Bernsen *(Zach Shepard)*, Larry Miller *(Newton Patterson)*, Dody Goodman *(Mrs. Patterson)*, Matt Clark *(J.F. Hughes)*, Jeanne Cooper *(Zach's Mother)*, Paul Sand *(McTaggert)*, Gloria Camden *(Gloria the Madam)*, Teri Copley *(Peaches)*, Gerrit Graham *(Lewis Crandall)*, John Mallory Asher *(Bobby Murdock)*, Jennifer Lewis *(Jomisha)*, John Bloom *(Ed Walker)*, Sara Ballentine *(Valentine)*, Gary Basey *(Clarence)*, Collin Bernsen *(Lomax)*, Vicky Vose *(Cindy Andrews)*, Duffy Epstein *(Bob Gould)*, Michele Lane *(Mommy in Classroom)*, Tara Brooks *(Tara)*, Lauren Brooks *(Lauren Walker)*, Karen Boettcher-Tate *(Mrs. Walker)*, Linda Altus *(Expectant Mother)*, Lee Imperial *(Expectant Father)*, Jerry Basham *(Hotel Clerk)*, Barbara Irvin *(Hotel Clerk's Wife)*, Colleen Mason *(Maddie)*, Lindsey Hutchison *(Cheerleader)*, Christie Blackmon *(Cheerleader)*, Sheryl Mary Lewis *(Picketing Housewife)*, Michelle Guthrie *(Sheila)*, Ivy Wharton *(Miss Armstrong)*, Jacqueline Desnet *(Receptionist)*, Michael Weisman *(NPI Guard)*, Don Scorby *(TGC Guard)*, Lee Carau *(Black-eyed Man)*, Sandi St. John *(Black-eyed Man's Wife)*, Charles Bernard *(Zach Shepard's Father)*, Brandon Wolff *(Youngest Walker Son)*, Lauren Moran *(Gladys)*, Walt Hoppert *(Donor)*, Dallas McKennon *(Stud of the Year/Octogenarian)*, Sandra Holt, Mimi Maynard, Kimberly Beck, Michael Hagerty, Holly Kane, Randy Kirby, Don Maxwell, Tony Pope, Udana Power, Thomas Lee Tully *(Voices)*

Curdled whimsy continues to be the hallmark of Shelley Long's post-"Cheers" career, as demonstrated in FROZEN ASSETS, the comedienne's latest film appearance since departing the long-running hit sitcom.

Zach Shepard ("L.A. Law" star Corbin Bernsen, previously paired with Long in HELLO AGAIN) is a mediocre middle-management executive in a mammoth Los Angeles holding company who's bucking for a VP spot after the former holder of the office has a mental meltdown. In order to earn the promotion, Shepard must revive a foundering smalltown bank in Hobart, Oregon, managed by Dr. Grace Murdock (Long). Actually, it's a sperm bank which has been run into the red by too many bum donations and her charitable tendencies towards women unable to conceive.

Along the way Bernsen picks up a hitchhiker, Newton Patterson (Larry Miller), who's actually a mental clinic escapee on his way back to his mom's home in Hobart. After finding that his company has put him up in the vermin-infested town brothel, Shepard takes up Patterson on his offer to bunk with him and his dotty mom (Dody Goodman) and even hires Patterson to help him out at the bank. The plan to save the clinic comes from a major sperm merchant offering a cash infusion only if Shepard can come up with a massive quantity of spilled seed within a tight deadline.

The enterprising Shepard concocts a contest to award part of the profits to the local man with the highest sperm count. He converts the clinic into something resembling a masturbation salon and shoehorns local hookers (including former sitcom star Teri Copley) into tight-fitting nurse uniforms to staff the facility and stimulate business. The clinic meets the deadline and Shepard delivers the goods. However, his boss reneges on the promised promotion, causing Shepard to abscond with the semen and hold it hostage. Cornered by cops, Shepard dumps the truckload of frozen "assets" into the town's river.

At the climactic town rally to give out the sperm award, Shepard is about to confess that there is no prize when Patterson reveals his true identity—he's the owner of Shepard's company. He steps forward with the prize money and gives Shepard his boss's job and first assignment—to get the truck out of the river before it creates a semen slick. Moved by Shepard's heroics, Grace, whose attraction to Shepard has been festering throughout the film, finally dumps her stuffy beau, Lewis Crandall (Gerrit Graham), and follows her new man.

Those finding jokes about masturbation and sperm banks endlessly amusing may enjoy FROZEN ASSETS. Others will most likely find it endlessly annoying. The screenplay suffers from the same kind of fuzzy underdevelopment that has also kept Long's past films, such as DON'T TELL HER IT'S ME and TROOP BEVERLY HILLS, from being anything special. Like the other two, FROZEN ASSETS, despite an original premise, abounds in stock situations predictably resolved by cardboard-thin characters with no real comic bite, creating that all-too-familiar *deja vu* feeling, and this long before the cutesy, sperm-infested credits have finished unfurling.

As might be drawn from the synopsis, Long really doesn't have all that much to do except struggle with her attraction to Bernsen while being appalled by his tacky tactics to return the bank to profitability. As a result, she's afforded little chance to showcase her gift for physical comedy, getting her only real laugh when she dives off a dais at the end to follow her man. Of the rest of the cast, Miller, a top stand-up comic, gets the film's best laughs by bringing imaginative shtick to his over-familiar character. Bernsen tries no less gamely than Miller, but he never makes much of an impression, and becomes the main casualty of the wan scripting.

Director George Miller (THE MAN FROM SNOWY RIVER, THE NEVERENDING STORY II) keeps the action moving smoothly and crisply, but FROZEN ASSETS never manages to amount to much more than moving wallpaper, inoffensive but relentlessly uninteresting. *(Profanity, adult situations.)*

p, Don Klein; d, George Miller; w, Don Klein, Thomas Kartozian; ph, Ron Latoure, Geza Sinkovics; ed, Larry Bock; m, Michael Tavera; prod d, Dorian Vernacchio, Deborah Raymond; set d, Caroline Perzan; cos, Ann Culotta

Comedy **(PR: C MPAA: PG-13)**

GAS FOOD LODGING ★★★★

100m Cineville Partners II; Seth Willenson Inc. ~ IRS Releasing c

Brooke Adams *(Nora)*, Ione Skye *(Trudi)*, Fairuza Balk *(Shade)*, James Brolin *(John Evans)*, Robert Knepper *(Dank)*, David Landsbury *(Hamlet)*, Jacob Vargas *(Javier)*, Donovan Leitch *(Darius)*, Chris Mulkey *(Raymond)*, Laurie O'Brien *(Thelma)*, Julie Condra *(Tanya)*, Adam Biesk *(Brett)*, Leigh Hamilton *(Kim)*, Diane Behrens *(Hostess)*, J. Mascis *(Cecil)*, Tiffany Anders *(Persi)*, Sissy Boyd *(Rocio)*, Jeffrey McDonald *(Langhaariger)*, Bill Kemp, Graci Lund

Bleak and beautiful, GAS FOOD LODGING is what people are asking for when they say they long for emotionally honest movies that examine the lives of real people.

Nora (Brooke Adams) is a divorced truck stop waitress in desolate Laramie, New Mexico, the kind of place people barely notice unless they need to fill up one way or the other. Her older daughter, beautiful Trudi (Ione Skye), is bored and rebellious, fast becoming the town tramp; Nora desperately wants to save her from the dead-end of teen pregnancy, but her screeching tirades only widen the gap between them. Her younger daughter, Shade (Fairuza Balk), by contrast, is immersed in the fantasy world of Mexican exploitation movies, living for the exploits of the noble and long-suffering Elvia Rivera. Shade dreams shyly of playing matchmaker for her mother, but her one attempt is a comic disaster: the handsome cowboy she selects is the same man with whom Nora has been having a secret affair for years, and their blind date is a study in awkward politeness.

Trudi meets the offbeat Dank (Robert Knepper), an English geologist who seems to hold out the promise of true love, while Shade pursues a doomed and embarrassing crush on Darius (Donovan Leitch), the town weird boy. But while Trudi is again disappointed—Dank leaves on a rock collecting expedition and fails to return—Shade finds first love with a Mexican neighbor, Javier (Jacob Vargas), and Nora falls for the guy who comes to install their satellite dish. Pregnant Trudi leaves to have her baby at a Laramie home for unwed mothers, and Shade stays behind; she learns that Dank was killed in an accident, and vows that someday—when Trudi is less bitter and angry—she'll tell her he hadn't abandoned her after all.

Some reviewers carelessly, though with the best intentions, compared GAS FOOD LODGING, director Allison Anders's first solo feature (she co-directed 1987's BORDER RADIO with fellow UCLA classmates Kurt Voss and Dean Lent) to Peter Bogdanovitch's THE LAST PICTURE SHOW, but the films share little beyond a desolate small-town setting. While THE LAST PICTURE SHOW chronicles a dying town, GAS FOOD LODGING is about a town that *won't* die, though everyone who lives there is dying by degrees. Based on Richard Peck's *Don't Look and It Won't Hurt*, it's a film about women—and, to a lesser degree, men—whose lives are so circumscribed that every dust mote and heat ripple over the blacktop is charged with significance.

Nora, Trudi, and Shade each react to the painful emptiness of their world differently, but are united by their single-minded determination to force meaning into their lives. Nora lives to be a good mother to her daughters, determined to set a good example at the expense of her own emotions and regardless of whether or not they care or even notice. Trudi seeks affirmation through sex, not because she needs the approval of men, but because she derives strength from her power to say yes; it's a painful strength, she divulges to Dank in a moment of poignant self-revelation: raped by a group of local boys, she decided it was better to pursue sex aggressively than refuse and risk having the illusion of control brutally stripped away. Shade, the dreamer her name suggests, takes conventional refuge in a rich fantasy life. She's destined (doomed, perhaps) to be a writer by her keen awareness of the intricate network of wheels and cogs spinning beneath the apparently placid surface of life.

Through these three women, Anders examines racism, economic oppression and the numbing effect of the infinite highway—America's favorite "boy" metaphor for existence—on the lives of those who wait by the endless road side. Anders has a fine eye for detail: a near-empty movie theater, cave walls turned by ultraviolet light into a shimmering fantasy of glowing colors, a box of buttons and other worthless treasures carefully hidden beneath a bed. Fine performances from Adams, Skye and, especially, Balk (RETURN TO OZ, VALMONT), who miraculously manages to delineate the prickly world of the awkwardly bright adolescent without ever becoming cloying, help make GAS FOOD LODGING a richly evocative look at lives in waiting. *(Adult situations.)*

p, Daniel Hassid, William Ewart, Seth M. Willenson; d, Allison Anders; w, Allison Anders, (from the novel *Don't Look and It Won't Hurt* by Richard Peck); ph, Dean Lent; ed, Tracy S. Granger; m, J. Mascis; prod d, Jane Ann Stewart; art d, Lisa Denker, Carla Weber; set d, Mary Meeks; cos, Susan Bertram

Drama **(PR: C MPAA: R)**

GATE II ★★

(Canada) 90m Epic Productions; Alliance Entertainment; Vision pdg ~ Triumph Releasing c

Louis Tripp *(Terry)*, Simon Reynolds *(Moe)*, James Villemaire *(John)*, Pamela Segall *(Liz)*, Neil Munro *(Art)*, James Kidnie *(Mr. Coleson)*, Irene Pauzer *(Teacher)*, Larry O'Brey *(1st Representative)*, Elva Mai Hoover *(Doctor)*, Gerry Mendicino *(Maitre d')*, Mark Saunders *(Waiter)*, Todd Waite *(Wine Steward)*, Edward Leefe *(Busboy)*, Andrea Ladanyi *(Minion)*, Carl Kraines *(Terry Transformed)*, Layne Coleman *(Priest)*

The videocassette market has spawned innumerable sequels to films of which no one has ever heard, and GATE II is one of them. That's not to say that Tibor Takacs's THE GATE is a bad movie; just that it's a very minor one that would hardly strike the average moviegoer as a likely candidate for a sequel. After all, that 1987 release's only real asset was some imaginative special effects work, particularly a walking corpse that dissolved into a hoard of tiny, chattering demons. Cool enough to rent, though hardly compelling enough to get most people to shell out $7.50 at a movie theater. Still, GATE II was made and received a limited theatrical release before joining its predecessor on video store shelves.

Young Terry (Louis Tripp) is going through a bad time. His alcoholic father has lost his job as a pilot, and Terry himself is a Grade A geek with few friends; as for the opposite sex, well, things are truly dismal in the teen romance department. But he has a plan. Everyone else dismisses the story that some local kids opened up the gate of Hell in their backyard as nonsense; Terry knows better. With the help of a computer and a book of spells, Terry plans to reopen the gate and make a deal with the powers of darkness to improve his lot. His ceremony is interrupted by local toughs John (James Villemaire) and Moe (Simon Reynolds), and John's not-so-tough girlfriend Liz (Pamela Segall). Like it or not, they're in it together when the incantation works and a tiny demon materializes.

At first, things go well. Terry wishes that his father would get his old job back, and it happens. Liz asks for a new car and the cash for a major shopping spree, and they're there. But soon it all goes terribly wrong. Terry's father is horribly injured in an on-the-job accident, the goods dissolve into excrement, and John and Moe become possessed by demonic forces. Liz and Terry must team up to reverse the spell and close the Gate a second time, before chaos reigns on the earth. Not only do they manage to do so, but all the damage they've done is reversed—even the hamster Terry sacrificed for the first ritual is brought back to life.

The virtues of THE GATE were modest, and those of GATE II are even more so. The little demon, a stop-motion creation that recalls the work of Ray Harryhausen (JASON AND THE ARGONAUTS, CLASH OF THE TITANS and many, many others), is foremost among them, and played for more charm than the throng of similar creatures in the first film. It's more a sprite than a monster, a mischievous imp that's forever being stuffed into bags and boxes and jars from which it invariably escapes and wreaks havoc. The demon is far and away the most interesting character in the film, utterly eclipsing the stereotypical kids—with the exception of Terry's father, adults scarcely seem to exist. John is a bully, Moe a hanger-on, Liz a misunderstood girl whose bad exterior hides a good heart and Terry a smart misfit traumatized by the tyranny of teen society. Nothing new in that department.

The story is just an extended, updated riff on the fairy tale about the couple who get a limited number of wishes and employ them badly, finally using the last one to undo all the others and restore things to normal. There's a nice set of morals there about being careful what you wish for and not getting anything for nothing, but who wants to be preached at by a low-budget horror movie? *(Violence.)*

p, Andras Hamori; d, Tibor Takacs; w, Michael Nankin; ph, Bryan England; ed, Ronald Sanders; m, George Blond Heim; prod d, William Beeton; cos, Beth Pasternak; fx, Frank Carere, Randall William Cook

Horror/Comedy **(PR: O MPAA: R)**

GETTING MARRIED IN BUFFALO JUMP ★★½
(Canada) 98m Canadian Broadcasting Corporation ~ Academy Entertainment c

Wendy Crewson *(Sophie Ware)*, Paul Gross *(Alex)*, Marion Gilsenan *(Vera)*, Victoria Snow *(Eleanor)*, Murray Crunchley *(Robert)*, Kyra Harper *(Annie)*, Ivan Horsley *(Alex's Father)*, Diane Gordon, Florence Paterson, Alexander Brown

An effective, unashamedly old-fashioned love story, BUFFALO JUMP follows the emotional trials and tribulations of Sophie Ware (Wendy Crewson), who has just inherited the family ranch in rural Alberta and moved back from Toronto, determined to run it, over the objections of her mother, Vera (Marion Gilsenan), who wants to sell the rundown place.

As Sophie knows nothing at all about the business, she hires her handsome old high-school friend Alex (Paul Gross), who has also just returned home, having abandoned fifteen years earlier his Indian lover Annie (Kyra Harper) and then-infant son Benny. He proposes marriage to Sophie as a business arrangement, and the course of the film takes up this off-and-on relationship as it turns into love and a "genuine" marriage. Adding to Sophie's predicaments are her current boyfriend Robert (Murray Crunchley), who teaches math at the local high school, and a visit from her citified, wisecracking friend Eleanor (Victoria Snow) from Toronto.

Written by John Frizzell from a novel by Susan Haley, and shot entirely from Sophie's point-of-view, BUFFALO JUMP touches all the familiar "women's film" bases but also surprisingly delves into more serious themes like racism against Indians (Annie) and Ukrainians (Alex's family are immigrants), before sentimentally tying up every loose end in sight: Alex and his now-teenaged son are reconciled, as is Alex with both his father and Annie (who has since remarried), while Sophie becomes best friends with the initially belligerent Annie and draws closer to her mother. The actors deliver uniformly fine performances, easily overcoming the fact that their characters are largely predictable.

Director Eric Till (whose earlier theatrical features like HOT MILLIONS and THE WALKING STICK led to a career in Canadian TV) has provided a detailed look at small-town life, with its homey, honky-tonk cafe and July 4th parade and rodeo, often offset by quietly pernicious rumor-mongering. Well produced on a small budget, the movie was shot admidst the gorgeous, sparsely populated scenery of Pincher Creek, Cowley and Lundbreck, Alberta, and features a neat country and western soundtrack with a couple of tunes by K.D. Lang. Originally telecast by the CBC in November 1990, the picture was released domestically direct-to-video.

p, Flora Macdonald; d, Eric Till; w, John Frizzell, (from the novel by Susan Haley); ph, Nikos Evdemon; ed, Bruce Lange; m, Eric N. Robertson, K.D. Lang; art d, Paul Ames; cos, Hilary Corbett

Romance/Drama **(PR: C MPAA: PG-13)**

GHOULIES III: GHOULIES GO TO COLLEGE
94m Porthos Foundations; Vestron Pictures ~ LIVE Home Video c

Kevin McCarthy *(Professor Ragnar)*, Evan MacKenzie *(Skip Carter)*, Patrick Labyorteaux *(Mookey)*, Marcia Wallace *(Miss Boggs)*, Griffin O'Neal, Thom Adcox, Sarah Lilly, Marcia Wallace, Eva LaRue, Hope Marie Carlton

Prolific B-movie producer Charles Band, who sired the original GHOULIES back in 1985, has declared that the reason his initial GREMLINS takeoff did any business at all was its attention-getting ad campaign: a bald, green mini-ogre emerging from a toilet bowl, with the tagline "They'll Get You in the End."

This sub-moronic comic sequel perpetuates the potty fixation. A supernatural bowl covered with gargoyle faces and known as the "Porcelain Vessel" has long served as a commode in the Beta Theta Zeta frat house at Glazier University. Diabolical dean, Professor Ragnar (Kevin McCarthy), wants to become all-powerful through black magic, and he uses a spell provided by a comic book to invoke a trio of dwarf demons who pop out of the Luciferian latrine. They are, of course, three of the "Ghoulies" from the previous films: the bald one, a rat-creature and a mutant pussycat. That's still not cretinous enough for the filmmakers, who endow the evil imps with Three Stooges mannerisms as they bop heads, gouge eyes and kick groins. Their path of death and destruction is blamed on overzealous fraternity jerks celebrating "Prank Week." Finally Greek lovers Skip Carter (Evan MacKenzie) and Erin (Eva Larue) wise up—so to speak—and permanently flush Ragnar, but not before he and his Ghoulies meld into one visually impressive composite monster.

This installment boasts the best special effects of any GHOULIES picture so far, which is no surprise considering that make-up ace John Carl Buechler is directing. But it is also the lowliest of the whole ugly lot, an ordeal for any viewer with brain cells. Gags, stereotypes and vulgarity are trawled from the septic discharge of NATIONAL LAMPOON'S ANIMAL HOUSE-inspired farces, with much time expended on the raunchy BTZ guys and their pursuit of girls, drugs and a paper-and-tinsel "Prank Crown" that looks like the thing Jughead used to wear. It's a Hollywood-burnout's-eye-view of college life as an orgiastic keg party and nonstop panty raid, although Brent Olson's screenplay drops the names of Magritte, Man Ray and Roy Lichtenstein in a futile try for academic ambiance.

And that's even before the Ghoulies show up. Chattering immortal lines like "Who cut the cheese?" and beating the Stooges schtick into the ground, they wear out their welcome at once, even though Buechler's puppet creations manage a wider range of facial expressions this time out. Their antics include an encounter with a monolith-like refrigerator stocked with 2001 (get it?) bottles of beer, and an ambush on familiar TV face Marcia Wallace, playing Ragnar's secretary. "She's famous," quoth a Ghoulie. "She's on 'Newhart!'" (Wallace actually acted on the older "Bob Newhart Show," but that's a lot of syllables.) If GHOULIES GO TO COLLEGE seems a bit out of step with the times, there's a good reason: distribution company Vestron went out of business (thanks in part to junk like this), leaving the movie on the shelf until its home video release a few years later. *(Violence, substance abuse, profanity, nudity, sexual situations.)*

p, Iain Paterson; d, John Carl Buechler; w, Brent Olson, (from the characters created by Luca Bercovici and Jeffery Levy); ph, Ronn Schmidt; ed, Adam Bernhardi; m, Michael Lloyd, Reg Powell; prod d, Stephen Greenberg; set d, Maggie Martin; cos, Beatrix Aruna Pasztor

Comedy/Horror **(PR: O MPAA: R)**

GIVING, THE ★½

100m Three Cats Inc.; Jeremiah Pollock Associates ~ Northern Arts Entertainment bw

Kevin Kildow *(Jeremiah Pollock)*, Lee Hampton *(Gregor)*, Satya Cyprian *(Tiffany)*, Kellie A. McKuen *(Ashley)*, Gail L. Green *(Ruth)*, Stephen Hornyak *(Gale)*, Oliver Patterson *(MacAdam)*, Paul Boesing *(The Boss)*, Russell Smith *(Carl Lepus)*, Michael McGee *(Yurgen)*, Southern Comfort *(Luthor)*, Eleanor Ruth Alpert *(Lola)*, Joel "Wolf" Parker *(Cortez)*, Lois D. Yaroshefsky *(Thelma)*, Lionel Stoneham *(Slam)*, Flo Hawkins *(Graffiti Painter)*, James Asher Salt *(Stefan)*, Larry Nicola *(Emcee)*, Rick Wolf *(Wayne)*, Gina Elten *(Phoenicia)*, Jake *(Asphalt)*, Brian Tucker *(Police Officer)*, Nick Erickson *(Anchorman)*, Scotty *(Horseman)*, Paul H. Rosas *(Dealer)*, Marilyn Stoneham *(Shana)*, James Arzagamartin *(Laramie)*, David Gilison *(Says Hey)*, Martha Kincare *(Sylvia)*, Mike McGlone *(Jogger)*, Howard Smith *(Security Guard)*, Cevin Cathell *(Carol)*, Russell Garner *(Graft)*, Jacklin Townson *(Daphne)*, Greg Wardell *(Killer)*, Jay Lewis *(Sushi Cashier)*, Tamara Eden *(Sushi Geisha)*, Jeff Matsushita *(Sushi Chef)*, Eric Lewy *(Yuppie)*, Tim Correa *(Store Clerk)*, Mark Morgan *(Fires Gun)*, Eames Demetrios *(Bank Guard)*, Gentile Culpepper *(Skull)*, Wojciech Fabjaniak *(Police)*, Dahlia Greer *(Police)*, L.C. Edwards *(Hotel CLerk)*, William A. Moody *(Moronsco)*, Quentin Johnson *(Farm Kid)*, Shakir Cherry *(Farm Kid)*

Stuck somewhere between social drama and flashy fantasy, THE GIVING is an allegorical tale revolving around the relationships between the guilty rich and the defiantly destitute which engages the eye without rousing either the head or the heart.

Jeremiah Pollock's (Kevin Kildow) skills as a Los Angeles computer programmer have netted him a cushy job with a salary somewhere in the low six figures along with corporate perks like a free BMW and Marina Del Ray condo from his bank employer, for whom he's designed and installed an ATM program in record time. Pollock's vanity plate, HACKER1, hints at an anarchic spirit that surfaces when he tries to do something worthwhile for the city's teeming homeless population. He thinks it's enough that he gives huge amounts at charity benefits until he's frozen into inaction when he encounters security guards harassing a homeless group. The group's irascible leader Gregor (Lee Hampton) challenges Pollock's sincerity and accuses him of being a charity junkie whose lavish contributions are meant only to assuage his guilt over earning so much for doing so little. To prove Gregor wrong, Pollock goes on a private hunger strike and rigs his own bank's ATM system to dispense money to anyone holding a code number which Pollock changes daily and distributes to the homeless. Gregor accumulates a nest egg towards his dream of buying land in LA for an urban farm that would be a refuge for the homeless. But at the same time he still sneers at Pollock for providing money to crack junkies who smoke themselves to death.

Eventually, Pollock's plot is discovered by his bosses who decline to prosecute but fire Pollock and mangle his personal and credit profiles to ensure that he becomes a capitalist outcast. Moving into a seedy Skid Row hotel after being ousted from his condo, Pollock is allowed to keep the BMW, which he inadvertently uses to lead the bank's private security forces to the homeless group, which they terrorize to recover what money they can. Pollock is bludgeoned by one of his own erstwhile co-workers and dies while Gregor's urban farm, bought with the stolen bank money, flourishes.

The grandson of designers Charles and Ray Eames, writer-producer-director Eames Demetrios has designed a film that looks at its best like advertising for men's cologne and at its worst like a freshman film school assignment suffering from budget bloat. Whether that helps or hurts THE GIVING's social message is difficult to determine since it's nearly impossible to pin down just what the social message is supposed to be. The screenplay is amateurish, self-indulgent and wincingly whimsical, depicting the homeless as cute, colorful urban pioneers and their yuppie nemeses as either wanton goons or simpering liberals who can't understand why the homeless spit on their money.

Why Pollock's talents are worth anything is never established—what's so great about an ATM that anyone can loot without a bank card? The program itself looks like incoherent gibberish that would doubtless daunt any typical bank customer. Why anyone should care about Pollock as a person is equally elusive. He keeps saying he wants to give till it hurts, and after a very short time it's hard not to wish he'll attain some amount of pain for the irritations he inflicts with his long, windy, pointless monologues. Pollock and Gregor deserve each other, since Gregor is little more than the obnoxious embodiment of Pollock's guilt, another overbearing blowhard whose own monologues deal with how much he hates people who give him money for the wrong reasons.

Mostly THE GIVING plays as if it should be congratulated for having been made at all rather than for having been made well, which it isn't. Its plot resembles Luis Bunuel's classic VIRIDIANA, and its penchant for slick but empty surrealist imagery raises the even more ominous possibility that Demetrios, along with executive producer Tim Disney (grand-nephew of Walt), thinks he really does have something in common with the grand old man of surrealism. In fact, they couldn't hold his martini. Bunuel made films about human vanity, whereas THE GIVING is a vanity film and no more genuinely subversive than an Obsession ad. *(Violence, profanity.)*

p, Tim Disney, Eames Demetrios, Cevin Cathell; d, Eames Demetrios; w, Eames Demetrios; ph, Antonio Soriano; ed, Bruce Barrow, Nancy Parker; prod d, Diane Romine Clark, Lee Shane

Drama **(PR: C MPAA: NR)**

GLADIATOR ★★

88m Columbia; Price Entertainment ~ Columbia c

Cuba Gooding, Jr. *(Lincoln)*, James Marshall *(Tommy)*, Robert Loggia *(Pappy Jack)*, Ossie Davis *(Noah)*, Brian Dennehy *(Horn)*, John Heard *(John Riley)*, Richar Lexsee *(Father in Park)*, T.E. Russell *(Spits)*, Tab Baker *(Storm Trooper)*, Dwain A. Perry *(Storm Trooper)*, Joan Schwenk *(Secretary)*, Raul Salinas *(Teen in Classroom)*, Marctwaine Nettles-Bey *(Teen in Classroom)*, Derek Anunciation *(Teen in Classroom)*, Cara Buono *(Dawn)*, Francesca P. Roberts *(Miss Higgins)*, Emily Marie Hooper *(Belinda)*, Jon Seda *(Romano)*, Lance Slaughter *(Shortcut)*, Vonte Sweet *(Tidbits)*, Antoine Roshell *(Scarface)*, John Louis Williams *(School Guard)*, Anthony Fitzpatrick *(Collector)*, Kevin Casey *(Collector)*, Thomas Charles Simmons *(Leo)*, Laura Whyte *(Millie)*, Mary Flynn *(Teen in Diner)*, Jill Kiblinger *(Teen in Diner)*, Mark Phillip Raff *(Teen in Diner)*, Harve Kolzow *(Timekeeper)*, Jeon-Paul Griffin *(Black Death)*, Mik Scriba *(1st Referee)*, Michael Glienna *(Black Death Corner Man)*, Mike A. Burgos *(Odds Board Man)*, Kenneth Scott Coopwood *(Bookie)*, Tony Gios *(Bookie)*, Johnny Lira *(Bookie)*, Desi Singh *(Bookie)*, David Burton *(Bettor)*, Chilton Shellito *(Bettor)*, James Ike Eichling *(Cop on Take)*, Debra Sandlund *(Charlene)*, Blake Dollard *(Heavyweight Fighter)*, Johnny Bellino *(Dawn's Father)*, Theorn "Touche" Lykes *(Bodyguard)*, Julian S. Campo *(Bodyguard)*, David Spence Perkins *(Fight Fan)*, Virgil Strauss *(2nd Referee)*, John W. Wilson *(3rd Referee)*, Franklin Jones *(Ring Manager)*, Anthony "Primo" LaCassa *(Romano's Cornerman)*, Brian O'Shea *(4th Referee)*, Patrick Outlaw *(Lincoln's Opponent)*, Hector Pena *(Tommy's Opponent)*, Mike Nussbaum *(Doctor)*, John M. Watson, Sr. *(Hospital Patient)*, Jena Wynn *(Laura Lee)*

From Rouben Mamoulian's GOLDEN BOY and Martin Ritt's THE GREAT WHITE HOPE to John Houston's FAT CITY and Martin Scorsese's RAGING BULL, in the movies a boxing match is never just a boxing match—it's a metaphor, a spectacle, a microcosmic embodiment of the struggles within the human soul.

Did audiences cheer Sylvester Stallone's Rocky Balboa through countless rounds and six films because they doubted the outcome, or because they loved watching him prance around a ring in decorative trunks? Of course not—Rocky and its sequels are all about the triumph of the underdog, the comeuppance of the smug and the wealthy, the unlikely victory of fairness in an unfair world. GLADIATOR trades on the same message in a slightly different package, packing a plea for racial tolerance between the punches and assuring viewers that everything will indeed be alright if we can just work together.

White-bread suburbanite Tommy Riley (James Marshall) is an anomaly in his new school in a tough, inner-city Chicago neighborhood. But he can box, and that's enough to earn him the respect of at least some of his classmates, the ones who see the sport as a way out of the grinding poverty of their lives. Recruited by an unscrupulous promoter, Riley enters the ring reluctantly (alcoholic father, gambling debts, etc.) and keeps swearing he won't fight again. But wealthy and brutal Horn (Brian Dennehy), the ghetto Mephistopheles who controls the boxing rackets, won't let him go. Riley is a rare commodity, a white fighter in a sea of black and Hispanic faces, and Horn smells money in the exploitation of racial tensions in the ring.

Riley becomes friendly with two of his fellow fighters, a cocky, sweet-natured Hispanic youth and the proud, ambitious Lincoln (Cuba Gooding, Jr.), who's black. It's no great surprise when the former winds up beaten to a brain-dead pulp by an unscrupulous opponent, and the latter finds himself facing off against Riley in the ring; not for nothing is the film called GLADIATOR. Lincoln and Riley refuse to fight, realizing they have a common enemy in Horn. Riley's taunting invitation to the older man to go one-on-one with him provides the film with its obvious but satisfying conclusion.

GLADIATOR is filmmaking by the numbers, if a particularly glossily executed package: director Rowdy Herrington (ROADHOUSE) mixes a top-ten soundtrack, handsome stars of all colors, little guy vs. the system conflict and an up-beat message swaddled in enough cynical layers to make it palatable to today's superficially tough audiences, and manages to keep it all moving surprisingly smoothly. The only place it's a little short is on the love interest front, and that's to be expected: boxing is the quintessential man's world, so it's only fitting that wives and girlfriends take a back seat to the sweaty joys of punching bags and jockstraps.

The cast is better than average, ranging from Ossie Davis as a wise coach to Robert Loggia as a smarmy recruiter; Brian Dennehy stands out as the truly loathsome bully boy Horn, a slumlord of the soul. Leads James Marshall and Cuba Gooding, Jr. (of "Twin Peaks" and BOYZ 'N' THE HOOD fame, respectively) are called upon to do little more than glower attractively, and do so. John Heard's role as Riley's father lends new meaning to the phrase "phone it in"; after a brief scene in which he resolves to make up for his past failures, he leaves town and occasionally calls to see how his son is faring.

Despite its fairy-tale narrative, GLADIATOR's boxing sequences are strikingly vivid and brutal. The bouts are nothing if not visceral and occasionally they're truly disturbing, reminding the viewer of the savagery that lies right below the brittle surface of the sweet science. GLADIATOR breaks no new ground, but it pays off scrupulously, fulfilling—in fact, catering to—audience expectations at every turn. This may not sound like much of an achievement, but when theaters are full of movies that don't deliver on their implicit promises, it's nice to see a movie that gives audiences exactly what they've paid for. *(Violence.)*

p, Frank Price, Steve Roth; d, Rowdy Herrington; w, Lyle Kessler, Robert Mark Kamen, (from the story by Kamen and Djordje Milicevic); ph, Tak Fujimoto; ed, Peter Zinner, Harry B. Miller, III; m, Brad Fiedel; prod d, Gregg Fonseca; art d, Bruce Miller; set d, Jay R. Hart; cos, Donfeld

Drama/Sports **(PR: C MPAA: R)**

GLENGARRY GLEN ROSS ★★★★

100m Zupnik Enterprises Inc. ~ New Line c

Al Pacino *(Ricky Roma)*, Jack Lemmon *(Shelley "The Machine" Levine)*, Alec Baldwin *(Blake)*, Ed Harris *(Dave Moss)*, Alan Arkin *(George Aaronow)*, Kevin Spacey *(John Williamson)*, Jonathan Pryce *(James Lingk)*, Bruce Altman *(Mr. Spaniel)*, Jude Ciccolella *(Detective)*, Paul Butler *(Policeman)*

Though underplotted and weakly motivated, GLENGARRY GLEN ROSS is a seamy slice of life from acclaimed playwright David Mamet, providing a searing showcase for one of the most remarkable all-star ensembles of the year.

Featuring no single protagonist, this foul-mouthed drama revolves around a real estate operation in which weary practitioners of the telephone investment scam ply their thievery. The currency of the trade is the "lead," an initial expression of interest from potential buyers who are usually lured by the promise of a "free gift" to sit through the salesman's pitch. The setting, Premiere Properties, gets a royal shaking up in the very first scene by consulting supersalesman Blake (Alec Baldwin), whose motivation strategy is brutally simple—sell or get out. The problem is that the leads the salesmen are being forced to use have been long since picked over for qualified buyers. New leads are available but only to those who can close deals on the old leads. Blake's ultimatum sets up a mad scramble in the office.

Veteran supersalesman Shelly "The Machine" Levine (Jack Lemmon) trained the office's current sales leader, Ricky Roma (Al Pacino). But the stale leads are thwarting his efforts as much as those of the others, his situation desperately complicated by a daughter in the hospital with a chronic illness. Moss (Ed Harris) is just plain fed up and draws fellow salesman Aaronow (Alan Arkin) into a plot to burglarize the office, steal the leads and sell them to a rival. Aaronow isn't too thrilled, but there's another conspirator who is already set up to take the fall for the burglary. What drama there is hinges on whether the third party is Levine or Roma, himself driven to desperation when his locked-in deal with a henpecked prospect (Jonathan Pryce) unravels.

Whereas most films would focus on the details of the theft itself, Mamet's screenplay doesn't reveal exactly what happened, and it's clear that he isn't particularly interested. Instead, GLENGARRY GLEN ROSS focuses on the various salesmen as they sustain themselves by reliving past glories in the desiccated present.

Adapted from Mamet's Pulitzer Prize-winning play, the film is an absurdist reduction of the Hobbesian all-male ethos of unchecked aggression tempered only by fierce bonding among members of the group who cover for each other against bigger and more fierce aggressors. They are like dinosaurs who don't realize they're extinct. They just go on plying their transparent cons on would-be victims who are generally either smarter or crazier than they are.

What's never clear is whether Mamet wants us to mourn their passing, as Arthur Miller did a generation earlier in *Death of a Salesman*, or celebrate it. In the film's most telling scene, Levine goes to see what he thinks to be a hot prospect, only to find the husband, not the wife he had spoken to. The man treats Levine with a weary condescension which, given the nonstop bluster of Mamet's dialogue, the audience could easily have shared were it not for the extremely high quality of the acting.

Lemmon, in particular, brings with him the resonance of one of filmdom's most durable careers. In GLENGARRY GLEN ROSS, he tackles the type of role he's justly renowned for, a downtrodden individual who, in previous incarnations, has always found some form of salvation by achieving self-knowledge. In this instance, however, salvation is not forthcoming; the screws continue to tighten on Levine until he is driven to the type of cravenly desperate act that was only an unspoken alternative in Lemmon's earlier films.

The rest of the cast is no less inspired. Pacino, never known for ensemble work, starts cocky and confident as Roma, only to shrink before our eyes as his miserable "prospect" flees to report him to the authorities. Arkin is wonderfully low-key and cagy. Harris, one of the most underutilized actors around, brings real acid to his all-American striver who proves the most coldly cynical of the group. In the key supporting role—aside from Baldwin's one-scene barn burner and Pryce's painfully indecisive victim of Roma's sales prowess—you can almost see the ulcers forming in the stomach of Kevin Spacey, as the beleaguered office manager who tries to maintain a tough facade but is just smart enough to know that, essentially, he's a world-class loser.

Not surprisingly, GLENGARRY GLEN ROSS's stage origins are its greatest liability. Movies crave movement and this one simply doesn't have much. But, in compensation, Foley turns the screenplay's staginess into an asset, creating a claustrophobic vision of hell as a place where we're all fighting for survival, clutching a sweat-stained, dog-eared pile of bad leads. *(Pervasive profanity.)*

p, Jerry Tokofsky, Stanley R. Zupnik; d, James Foley; w, David Mamet, (from his play); ph, Juan Ruiz-Anchia; ed, Howard Smith; m, James Newton Howard; prod d, Jane Musky; art d, Robert K. Shaw, Jr., Bill Barclay; set d, Robert J. Franco; cos, Jane Greenwood

AAN Best Supporting Actor: Al Pacino

Drama **(PR: O MPAA: R)**

GODZILLA VS. BIOLLANTE ★★½

(Japan) 104m Toho Company Ltd. ~ HBO Video c

Kunihiko Mitamura, Yoshiko Tanaka, Masanobu Takashima, Megumi Odaka, Toru Minegishi, Ryunosuke Kaneda, Koji Takahashi, Kazuma Matsubara, Yasuko Sawaguchi, Toshiyuki Nagashima, Yoshiko Kuga, Majot Beoi, Derrick Holmes, Soleiman Mehdizadeh, Abdallah Helal, Kurt Cramer, Brian Uhl, Aijdin Yamanlar, Beth Blatt, Robert Corner

After bringing their celebrated monster back to cinematic life in GODZILLA 1985, the Toho company launched a new series of battling-monster sequels with this 1988 production, a talky and slightly overlong opus that nonetheless delivers the goods for monster fans.

While mopping up after Godzilla's destructive rampage through Tokyo (the monster is now imprisoned inside the volcanic Mt. Mihara), a special army scientific unit retrieves some of the monster's oversized cells. A gunman from the Arab Republic of Saradia shoots down the soldiers and steals the cells, which wind up at the Saradia Institute of Biotechnology. There, Japanese scientist Dr. Sherigami, who left Japan after criticism of his radical work, and his daughter, Erica, plan to work with the cells to spawn plantlife hardy enough to grow in deserts. But a terrorist bomb destroys the lab and kills Erica.

Five years later, Dr. Sherigami has returned to Japan, where he secludes himself in a small botanical lab. He is occasionally assisted by a young woman named Asuko, whose psychic friend Miki seems to have the ability to "hear" what plants are "thinking." Asuko's boyfriend, young Dr. Kerishima, works for a corporation that hopes to use the Godzilla cells to create a bacterium that can consume radioactive material; Dr. Sherigami is approached to work on this project, but turns the offer down. He then changes his mind, however, provided he can have the cells for a week to do some research on his own.

Carrying on the experiments he and Erica had begun, Sherigami grafts one of Godzilla's cells to that of a rose; the result is a bizarre plantlike creature that grows at an incredible rate. After killing a pair of industrial spies that break into Sherigami's lab, it escapes into the nearby lake, where it grows to titanic size. Meanwhile, the American Biomajor Corporation faxes a threat to the company working on the antinuclear bacteria: hand over the Godzilla cells to them, or they'll explode a bomb that will cause Mt. Mihara to erupt and free Godzilla. But when Kerishima and an associate go to the rendezvous with Biomajor, the Saradian gunman intervenes to steal the cells, preventing the remote deactivation of the bomb in the process. The explosive goes off, Mt. Mihara erupts, and Godzilla is unleashed upon Japan once more.

Col. Karake is put in charge of the defensive forces, but neither battleships nor a revamped version of the Super-X aircraft that had previously battled Godzilla can stop the monster. He comes ashore and encounters Sherigami's plant monster, which the scientist has dubbed Biollante; an incredible battle ensues, with Biollante battling Godzilla with fanged tentacles, but it is no match for Godzilla and dies in flames, its spores drifting into the air.

Returning to the sea, Godzilla heads for Osaka. Meanwhile, Kerishima and a partner raid the Saradian Oil Company headquarters and retrieve the stolen cells. Miki is brought in to try to repel Godzilla with her psychic powers, but she only puts him off for a short time. It is enough, however, for the military and the scientists to come up with a plan. After the Super-X forces Godzilla into position, the monster is shot with the anti-nuclear bacteria. Since the monster lives off radioactivity, this will theoretically kill him. But the bacteria's effectiveness is blunted by Godzilla's cold-blooded nature, and a new plan must be set up. The monster is lured into the midst of a group of heat-generating climate-control devices that will raise his body temperature. But the plan has an unexpected side effect: the storm clouds it creates cause the Biollante spores to recombine, and the two monsters fight another terrible battle.

The now more reptilian Biollante is once again defeated, but the bacteria within Godzilla take effect and the monster collapses. But just then the vengeful Saradian gunman shoots down Sherigami. Kerishima chases after him, and their fight leads them into the midst of the heat-generating mines, one of which vaporizes the gunman. Then Godzilla awakens and, apparently tired of wreaking havoc for the time being, returns to the sea.

As one can easily infer from its synopsis, GODZILLA VS. BIOLLANTE is considerably more plot-heavy than previous entries, and in fact is so overstocked with supporting characters that it's 40 minutes or so before any serious monster action gets started. Even though all of the players have some impact on the central storyline, the screenplay seems needlessly complex, and some of the most entertaining characters are the peripheral ones. Chief among these is Col. Gondo of the National Land Bureau, which has been on alert since Godzilla's last rampage for signs of the monster's return. He's been so bored with his inactivity that, as another character points out, he almost seems to wish for the monster's return. When it finally transpires, he dies heroically after firing the lethal bacteria shot into the monster's mouth.

There are also some amusing details in the settings: two characters meet in the "Godzilla Memorial Lounge," which bears an enormous, monster-footprint-shaped skylight apparently left by Godzilla's last visit. As expected, the dubbing results in some unintentional humor as well, with lines like, "You think you're Romeo out of Shakespeare's tragedy; well, I'm not going to be Juliet, that's for certain," and, spoken by Dr. Sherigami about the towering Biollante, "What you're seeing is no ordinary plant." Of course, fans know that this is part and parcel of the Godzilla film experience. What they're there for is the monster sequences, which certainly deliver once they get started. They don't belie their man-in-a-suit-on-miniature-sets nature, and the destruction and battle scenes are vivid, exciting and, when the two monsters go at it in nighttime settings, fairly atmospheric as well.

The version of GODZILLA VS. BIOLLANTE released by HBO Video is the full-length original cut of the film and, in a bonus for fans, is letterboxed. Many editions that circulated on the US underground video market prior to this official release were cut by nearly 20 minutes, making an already overcomplicated plot completely incomprehensible. *(Monstrous violence, profanity.)*

p, Shogo Tomiyama; d, Kazuki Omori; w, Kazuki Omori, (from the story by Shinichiro Kobayashi); ph, Yudai Kato; ed, Michiko Ikeda; m, Koichi Sugiyama; prod d, Shigekazu Ikuno; cos, Kanji Kawasaki

Science Fiction/Fantasy **(PR: A MPAA: PG)**

GUILTY AS CHARGED ★★

95m IRS Media ~ IRS Releasing c

Rod Steiger *(Ben Kallin)*, Lauren Hutton *(Liz Stanford)*, Heather Graham *(Kimberly)*, Lymon Ward *(Mark Stanford)*, Isaac Hayes *(Aloysius)*, Zelda Rubenstein *(Edna)*, Erwin Keyes *(Deek)*, Michael Beach *(Hamilton)*

Rod Steiger stars as a high-voltage vigilante in GUILTY AS CHARGED, a dark, distasteful satire in the grisly tradition of Paul Bartel's EATING RAOUL.

Steiger plays meat mogul Ben Kallin, who went around the bend sometime after his family was ax-murdered by a recently paroled killer. Having built his own private death row in the basement of his high-volume butchering plant, he kidnaps ex-cons who got what he judges to be too-light sentences for their crimes. Kallin then invites the families of their victims to witness the ex-cons' executions in his custom-made, throne-like, home-brew electric chair, featuring a huge set of angel wings, from which, Kallin is convinced, the criminals will ascend to heaven once they have repented for their crimes to the families.

The film cuts awkwardly from Kallin's killings to the corrupt antics of gubernatorial hopeful Mark Stanford (Lymon Ward), who solicits campaign contributions from major-league polluters with the promise of a blind eye once he is elected. Standford's representatives approach Kallin, whose rectitude at first prevents him from participating in the shady under-the-table payoffs. Kallin changes his mind, however, when he learns, from pretty parole officer, Kimberly (Heather Graham) working on Stanford's campaign, that Stanford is an unabashed supporter of the death penalty. What he doesn't know is that Stanford has a personal reason for adding the capital punishment plank to his platform.

At the start of his campaign, Stanford murdered his secretary-mistress, who had threatened to expose his political improprieties, and framed a mugger for the crime. Frustrated by his inability to win himself an appeal, the mugger breaks out of prison only to fall into Kallin's hands. His freelance frying is to be witnessed by the governor-to-be at the climax, barring a last-minute reprieve from Stanford's embittered wife, Liz (Lauren Hutton), and maid, Edna (Poltergeist's tiny psychic Zelda Rubenstein), who have been accumulating incriminating evidence against Stanford.

Despite some moments of grim, dark humor, GUILTY AS CHARGED is one of those one-joke satires whose joke runs out long before the movie does. Charles Gale's screenplay starts with an intriguing premise, but the execution proves to be both predictable and uninspired. The dialogue and characters are also dull and uninvolving. Witty repartee throughout the film generally consists of one character insulting another and the other character screaming back, "Shut up!"

Other parts of GUILTY AS CHARGED are padded with long-winded monologues from Kallin, rendered in the overbearing, scenery–devouring style that has been the hallmark of Steiger's acting career. The supporting cast is generally competent if similarly uninspired, though Graham, an angelic beauty, is eminently watchable throughout. Coming closest to stealing the film is, of all people, veteran composer and musician Isaac Hayes, who has some truly funny moments as one of Kallin's crazed henchmen and musically contributes the film's funky, hummable closing theme.

A presentation of record company IRS Media's filmmaking arm, GUILTY AS CHARGED boasts a mood-setting score by, guitarist Steve Bartek of Oingo Boingo (of which BATMAN composer Danny Elfman is also an alumnus) and additional contributions from Animal Logic. Byrnadette DiSanto's expressionistic production design and Richard Michalack's shadowy cinematography are also first-rate. Unfortunately, however, none of that compensates for the mock-outrageous mediocrity of the film overall.

GUILTY AS CHARGED is yet another offbeat B–movie that's all dressed up with no place to go. *(Violence, profanity, adult situations.)*

p, Randolph Gale; d, Sam Irvin; w, Charles Gale; ph, Richard Michalak; ed, Kevin Tent; m, Steve Bartek; prod d, Byrnadette DiSanto; art d, Ian Hardy

Horror/Comedy **(PR: O MPAA: R)**

GUN IN BETTY LOU'S HANDBAG, THE ★★½

89m In the Bag Productions Inc.; Interscope Communications; Touchstone ~ BV c

Penelope Ann Miller *(Betty Lou Perkins)*, Eric Thal *(Alex Perkins)*, Alfre Woodard *(Ann)*, Julianne Moore *(Elinor)*, Andy Romano *(Herrick)*, Ray McKinnon *(Frank)*, William Forsythe *(Beaudeen)*, Xander Berkeley *(Marchat)*, Michael O'Neill *(Jergens)*, Christopher John Fields *(Brown)*, Cathy Moriarty *(Reba)*, Billie Neal *(Gail)*, Gale Mayron *(Pearl)*, Faye Grant *(Charleen)*, Reathel Bean *(Bob Barnes)*, Marian Seldes *(Margaret Armstrong)*, Ellen McElduff *(Joan)*, Marisa Miller *(April)*, Paul Bates *(Officer Finney)*, Bill Mullen *(Officer George)*, Meat Loaf *(Larry)*, Catherine Keener *(Suzanne)*, Cordell Jackson *(Bathroom Lady)*, Bernard Canepari *(Mayor)*, Deborah Spector *(Cashier)*, Barry Hannah *(Court Clerk)*, Red West *(Judge)*, Lida Burris Gibson *(Lydia Williams)*, Ralph Braseth *(Reporter)*, M.J. Etua *(Reporter)*, Christine Joyce *(Reporter)*, Mark Magill *(Glen)*, Merrill Healy *(Gary)*, Don Keith Opper *(Dell)*, Jane Smithwick *(Freckled Girl)*, Jeff O'Haco *(Bar Fighter)*, Ruddy L. Garner *(FBI Wiretapper)*, Adam Shankman *(Timid Man)*, Laura Boenheim *(Autograph Girl)*, Suzanne Kent *(Townsperson)*, Nash Germany *(Teenage Boy)*, Lesha Campbell *(Teenage Girl)*, Robert Jackson *(Irate Man)*, Ann Fisher-Wirth *(Young Matron)*, Kay McDuffie *(Perm)*, Margaret Graham *(Perm)*, Billy Holcomb *(Farmer)*, John McCauley *(Farmer)*, Charles Treas *(Old Man)*, Amanda Zenil *(Radical Girl)*, Dianna Miranda *(Chiropractor)*, Frank Welker *(Scarlet's Vocals)*, Barton Segal *(Barton)*

Penelope Ann Miller transcends her material in THE GUN IN BETTY LOU'S HANDBAG, a half-baked Disney comedy that also half-benefits (the first half, to be exact) from the sly, subversive direction of Allen Moyle.

Betty Lou Perkins (Miller), the prim assistant librarian in Tettley, Missouri ("played" by Oxford, Mississippi), is ready to explode. Her cop husband, Alex (Eric Thal, the Talmudic scholar who stoked Melanie Griffith's religious fervor in A STRANGER AMONG US), would rather stay around the station house to investigate the town's first murder case in a decade than come home to celebrate his wedding anniversary. Meanwhile, a modest fundraiser Betty Lou's supervising at her library threatens to balloon into the social nightmare of the decade as all the social climbers in the area try to put their useless two cents into the planning.

Outside her work and her home, Betty Lou is further plagued by the nonstop whining of her single sister, Elinor (Julianne Moore, very funny and a ringer for Miller), but she finally topples over the edge when she can't even get her husband on the phone to tell him she has stumbled upon the murder weapon while out walking her dog. So, instead of turning the gun in, she turns herself in as the notorious motel killer sought by Alex.

In jail she blossoms in a way she couldn't as a cop's wife, particularly under the fashion tutelage of her hooker-cellmate Reba (Cathy Moriarty). Alex is astounded, depressed and finally suspended from the force for interfering with the investigation of his own wife. Meanwhile, the real killer, vicious New Orleans mobster Beaudeen (William Forsythe), shows up in Tettley to retrieve an incriminating tape he believes to be in Betty Lou's possession and kidnaps her fresh-out-of-law-school attorney Ann (Alfre Woodard); this in turn brings about the climactic husband and wife reunion.

If the mantle of auteurism has passed from the hands of directors to the heads of studio, then there's currently no studio genre more reliably rubber-stamped than the Disney/Touchstone/Hollywood comedy. As if Disney were still making amends for the enjoyably nasty RUTHLESS PEOPLE, virtually all of them can be described thusly: "Bright start, boring end."

Such is the case with THE GUN IN BETTY LOU'S HANDBAG, yet another wacky, madcap caper comedy, despite Moyle's (TIMES SQUARE, PUMP UP THE VOLUME) hand. Yet, while it's on, the film is a honey—sparkling, enjoyable, fast-paced, well-acted and unpredictable. But it finally paints itself into a corner, with a premise quite beyond resolution within the context of the Disney vision of cinematic domestic tranquility shored up against a dangerous, chaotic world. That world is filled with everything from all-purpose vicious gangsters (SISTER ACT and V.I. WARSHAWSKI), to scandal-mongering journalists (STRAIGHT TALK), apparent adulteresses and uninvited gays (PASSED AWAY), and, most memorably of all, mad nannies (THE HAND THAT ROCKS THE CRADLE). Whoever's making the big production decisions at Disney must not get out much.

Moyle makes clear early on that the "gun" in Betty Lou's handbag is carried by all women who have ever compartmentalized themselves in the lives of their men and in their workplaces only to be betrayed, disappointed and otherwise dumped on. THE GUN IN BETTY LOU'S HANDBAG sets out to show us how lucky we are that most don't use it. By a single, simple and silly act of rebellion, Betty Lou upends not only her whole town but that very Disney vision of Pollyanna life, in which men are likable lunks (modelled after Goofy?) and women are neglected, though kept superficially busy in home and out.

THE GUN IN BETTY LOU'S HANDBAG dares to suggest that the Disney fantasy, attractive though it may be, would likely drive anyone actually forced to live it as nuts as it does Betty Lou, who plausibly begins to find prison a viable alternative to her Stepford life on the outside. With "family values" on everyone's lips, someone's bound to let the air out of these tires real quick. Betty Lou's gun has no bullets in it at the end, either literally or figuratively. The bad guys get safely put away and everybody hugs at the end (though curiously, Ann, the only nonwhite among the principals, is still tied up at the fadeout).

But who's Disney kidding, anyway? Most of their recent formulaic comedies haven't been blockbusters. This new thing called TV has the bland market cornered. If Disney really wants people to go out and spend seven bucks, they need to give them something worth going out for. THE GUN IN BETTY LOU'S HANDBAG isn't quite it. Bright start, boring end. *(Violence, profanity.)*

p, Scott Kroopf; d, Allan Moyle; w, Grace Cary Bickley; ph, Charles Minsky; ed, Janice Hampton, Erica Huggins; m, Richard

Gibbs; prod d, Michael Corenblith; art d, David James Bomba; set d, Merideth Boswell Charbonnet; cos, Lisa Jensen

Comedy **(PR: C MPAA: PG-13)**

GUYVER, THE ★★

92m Guyver Productions ~ New Line Home Video c

Mark Hamill *(Max)*, Vivian Wu *(Mizky)*, Jack Armstrong *(Sean)*, David Gale *(Balcus)*, Michael Berryman *(Lisker)*, Jimmie Walker *(Striker)*, Spice Williams *(Weber)*, Peter Spellos *(Ramsey)*, Willard Pugh *(Castle)*, Jeffrey Combs *(Dr. East)*, David Wells *(Gordon)*, Deborah Gorman *(Ms. Jensen)*, Greg Paik *(Toomer)*, Linnea Quigley *(Actress)*, Michael Deak *(Director)*, Johnnie Saiko *(Craig)*, Ted Smith *(Ronnie)*, Doug Simpson *(Quinton)*, Danny Gibson *(Instructor)*, Jay Kelley *(Lab Scientist)*

No, it's not "MacGyver," it's THE GUYVER, and one can only wish that the creativity that went into that erstwhile hit TV show had gone into this film. Based on a popular Japanese comic character created by Yoshiki Takaya, the story has a lot of potential that is frittered away with a shallow screenplay.

Fleeing through the Los Angeles night, scientist Dr. Tetsu Segawa (Greg Paik) is cornered in a storm drain by a bunch of goons led by Lisker (Michael Berryman). They demand that he hand over a mysterious object in a metal case he holds—little knowing that he has stashed the object nearby. The doctor suddenly transforms into a reptilian creature, but so does Lisker, who kills him and takes the case. The next day, CIA agent Max Reed (Mark Hamill)—with whom Dr. Segawa had arranged a meeting and who witnessed his death from afar—goes to notify the doctor's daughter Mizky (Vivian Wu) of his death. She's at a martial arts class being taken by her boyfriend Sean (Jack Armstrong).

Sean yearns to be a kung fu master but, in time-honored tradition, he lacks the concentration. He does notice Max's interest in Mizky, and later follows the two to the site of Dr. Segawa's murder. There he stumbles upon the device the doctor had hidden, a strange metal object the size of a hubcap called the Guyver. He can't figure out what it is, but later, when he gets in a fight with a street gang, the thing seems to come to life, encasing him in a suit of armor that allows him to vanquish his foes before retracting into his body. It is this object that Lisker was supposed to retrieve, but the metal case he presents to his boss, Fulton Balcus (David Gale), head of the Chronos Corporation, contains a toaster instead. Enraged, Balcus orders Lisker to track down Mizky.

Max, meanwhile, has explained to Mizky that he's been investigating the Chronos Corporation, and that Dr. Segawa was supposed to deliver the Guyver to him. As Sean is coming to visit her, and Max is staked out outside her apartment, Lisker and company attempt to kidnap Mizky. But Sean and Max get the better of them for a moment and flee, with Lisker and the other goons—one of whom, Striker (Jimmie Walker), has transformed into a monster—in hot pursuit. The chase leads to an abandoned warehouse, where Lisker and the rest also transform into creatures, and Sean calls on the power of the Guyver to protect him. The armor wraps itself around him and a lengthy fight ensues but, when Lisker pulls a controlling cell from Sean's forehead, his body disintegrates.

Max and Mizky are captured and taken to the Chronos labs, where Balcus reveals that he's been using an ancient alien power to transform humans into Zoanoids, his monstrous henchmen. The Guyver is another manifestation of this power, one that will allow him to rule the world, and it appears to be slowly regenerating itself from the controlling cell. Mizky attempts to steal the cell but, in the resulting melee, it is swallowed by one of Balcus's creatures. Soon Sean, who is now one with the Guyver, is reborn and tears his way out of the monster's body. He manages to fight off all the attacking beasts and free the captured Max from the transformation chamber, but the latter metamorphoses into a giant bug before dying. An enraged Balcus then transforms into a giant dragon and attempts to kill Sean, but the young man uses the Guyver's power to blow him to pieces. He then reverts back to normal and leaves with Mizky, not knowing that the monstrous Striker has survived.

THE GUYVER represents another welcome infusion of Asian fantasy into American genre production, but the result doesn't resemble the top-flight fantasy of films like A CHINESE GHOST STORY so much as it does an episode of the old "Ultraman" TV show. No doubt there was a wealth of Japanese material to work with, but screenwriter Jon Purdy has concocted situations that are a lot less imaginative than the science-fiction trappings and creature designs. One of the main problems is a rather uninteresting lead character. Sean is the traditional KARATE KID-style hero who must learn discipline. Even so, his persona disappears beneath the Guyver's armor in the second half of the movie. The rest of the characters are comic-strip level, from Wu's poorly acted damsel in distress to Hamill's CIA man, who's unusually forthcoming about his assignments.

Of course, this is essentially a comic-strip movie, so that shouldn't be too much of a problem. But there are no additional levels or interesting plot twists to attract viewers older than kids, and directors Screaming Mad George and Steve Wang throw in a lot of lame comic relief, from a clumsily telegraphed bit where the monstrous Striker stumbles onto a horror movie set—and confronts "Scream Queen" Linnea Quigley—to dumb rap dialogue delivered by the same character (Walker's character even gets a silly "Good Times" in-joke as the movie's punchline). On the other hand, both George and Wang are special effects artists who clearly viewed this as a showcase for their work, and their monster designs are varied and very well executed.

The creature effects are, in fact, the highlight of THE GUYVER, even if the climactic set pieces are a little too reminiscent of THE FLY and ALIENS. The fight scenes are fairly well staged, too, but they go on for too long, further pointing up the fact that they are all THE GUYVER has to offer. *(Violence, profanity.)*

p, Brian Yuzna; d, Screaming Mad George, Steve Wang; w, Jon Purdy, (from characters by Yoshiki Takaya); ph, Levie Isaacks; ed, Andy Horvitch; m, Matthew Morse; prod d, Matthew C. Jacobs; set d, Julie Brooke Beattie; cos, Linda "Lulu" Meltzer

Science Fiction/Action **(PR: C MPAA: PG-13)**

HAIRDRESSER'S HUSBAND, THE ★★★★
(France) 84m Lambart Productions; TF1 Films Production; PAC ~ Triton Pictures c
(MARI DE LA COIFFEUSE, LA)

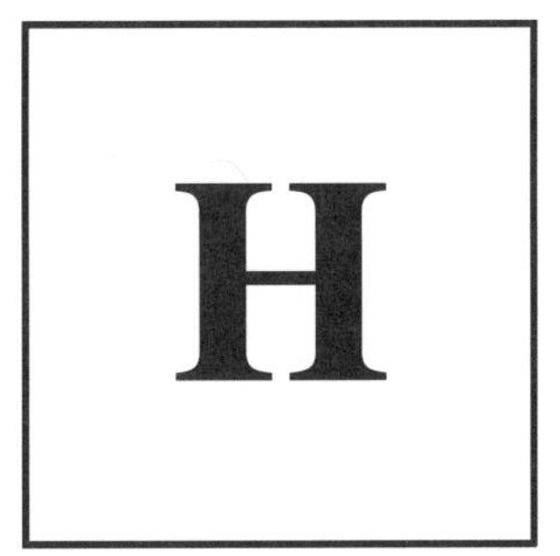

Jean Rochefort *(Antoine)*, Anna Galiena *(Mathilde)*, Roland Bertin *(Antoine's Father)*, Maurice Chevit *(Agopian)*, Philippe Clevenot *(Morvoisieux)*, Jacques Mathou *(Mr. Chardon)*, Claude Aufaure *(Gay Customer)*, Albert Delpy *(Donecker)*, Henry Hocking *(Antoine–Age 12)*, Ticky Holgado *(Morvoisieux Son-in-Law)*, Michele Laroque *(Adopted Child's Mother)*, Anne-Marie Pisani *(Madame Shaeffer)*, Pierre Meyrand *(Antoine's Brother)*, Yveline Ailhaud *(Antoine's Mother)*, Julien Bukowski *(Gloomy Man)*, Youssef Hamid *(Tunisian Customer)*, Laurence Ragon *(Madame Chardon)*, Arlette Tephany *(Antoine's Sister-in-Law)*, Christophe Pichon *(Antoine's Brother Age–12)*, Thomas Rochefort *(Little Edouard)*

Director Patrice Leconte follows up MONSIEUR HIRE, his recent art-house hit, with another exquisite tale of obsessive love. THE HAIRDRESSER'S HUSBAND is lighter than its predecessor but tinged with heartache nonetheless.

From an early age, after an erotic experience with his childhood barber, Antoine (Jean Rochefort) has had a single ambition in life: to marry a hairdresser. He finally meets the shampoo girl of his dreams, Mathilde (Anna Galiena), who has inherited a shop from its elderly owner, Agopian (Maurice Chevit), and has centered her life entirely around the shop ever since. Antoine comes into the shop and proposes immediately, drawing little more than an embarrassed blush from Mathilde. However, when he returns, three weeks later, she accepts his proposal before learning his name. They get married in the shop and have a rushed honeymoon before returning and making the shop their private island of bliss, frequently closing in the afternoon to make love in full view of the street.

However, cracks begin to appear in this barber shop of Eden as Mathilde becomes obsessively preoccupied that Antoine's love for her may fade as she grows older. She extracts from Antoine the promise that, should he ever stop loving her, he'll leave her rather than pretend otherwise. Meanwhile, Antoine is prompted to recall how he found his childhood hairdresser dead, a suicide. One stormy night, Mathilde bolts from the shop. Antoine seems to sense what is about to happen but is helpless to stop her. Mathilde throws herself off a levy, leaving Antoine a note telling him that she finds this fate preferable to losing Antoine by increments. Afterward, Antoine sits in the shop as he did before, unable to accept his loss, and patiently waits for her to return.

Based mainly on a series of light comedies he made before breaking through with MONSIEUR HIRE, Leconte was reportedly dubbed by one critic "the French John Landis." As hard as it is to imagine that the director of OSCAR and ANIMAL HOUSE could ever create something as delicate as MONSIEUR HIRE or THE HAIRDRESSER'S HUSBAND, the idea is not as outlandish as it sounds. Especially in the films of Blake Edwards, for a contemporary example, but going back to Charlie Chaplin and Buster Keaton, there has always been a deep streak of underlying bleakness in film comedies, mainly stemming from a deep dissatisfaction with the world as it is.

Leconte's style in THE HAIRDRESSER'S HUSBAND is realistic, yet his plot is the stuff of fables or fantasy, leading to a tension between style and content that only grows as Mathilde's romanticism begins to seem more like a phobia of the world and change and Antoine begins to seem more pathetic for not having a life of his own. Still, what is seen of the world indicates that it is not a happy place, either. One customer's wife leaves him to care for their children alone. Another woman drags in her adopted son, telling Antoine and Mathilde never to adopt. For a while, it is made to seem as if it's possible for Antoine and Mathilde to be in the world but not of it. But at some point the world must be faced, since to delay is to only increase the consequences, even in a small, idyllic French village where it is possible to make love in the front window of a shop in the middle of the afternoon and not have anyone see you. Still, until that point, Leconte makes the ride a sweet one.

Never has love-soaked indolence seemed so attractive in a movie as it is here as conveyed by Rochefort, whose Antoine is as avid a devourer of the minutiae of a life apparently truly minute as if it were a grand feast. Galiena's Mathilde, meanwhile, is like the answer to an indolent sensualist's prayer, a woman of dark, earthy beauty living only to be loved—and living in terror of the day when she might be loved no more. Love truly is a drug in THE HAIRDRESSER'S HUSBAND, but it is the one drug to which everyone strives to be addicted. Leconte understands this, but he also understands what happens when we wake up. And that is what makes a film as slight as this seem like a story for the ages, a rapturous epic of the heart that is gripping, intoxicating and unforgettable. *(Sexual situations, adult situations.)*

p, Thierry DeGanay; d, Patrice Leconte; w, Patrice Leconte, Claude Klotz, (from the story by Leconte); ph, Eduardo Serra; ed, Joelle Hache; m, Michael Nyman; prod d, Ivan Maussion; art d, Ivan Maussion

Romance/Drama **(PR: C MPAA: R)**

HAND THAT ROCKS THE CRADLE, THE ★★★½
110m Interscope Communications; Rockin' Cradle Productions; Hollywood ~ BV c

Annabella Sciorra *(Claire Bartel)*, Rebecca De Mornay *(Peyton Flanders)*, Matt McCoy *(Michael Bartel)*, Ernie Hudson *(Solomon)*, Julianne Moore *(Marlene)*, Madeline Zima *(Emma Bartel)*, John DeLancie *(Doctor Mott)*, Kevin Skousen *(Marty)*, Mitchell Laurance *(Lawyer)*, Justin Zaremby *(Schoolyard Bully)*, Eric Melander *(Baby Joe)*, Jennifer Melander *(Baby Joe)*, Ashley Melander *(Baby Joe)*, Cliff Lenz *("Seattle Today" Host)*, Penny LeGate *("Seattle Today" Host)*, Mary Anne Owen *(Dr. Mott's Nurse)*, Therese Xavier Tinling *(Receptionist)*, Todd Jamieson *(Surgeon)*, Laura Ferri *(Emergency Room Nurse)*, Dee Dee Van Zyl *(Emergency Room Nurse)*, Cristine McMurdo-Wallis *(Peyton's Nurse)*, Sara Jennifer Sharp *(Peyton's Nurse)*, Susan Chin *(Newscaster)*, Kimberly Hill *(Newscaster)*, Jane Jones *(Woman in Park)*, Ericka Matson, Robert James, Aimee Kanemori, Elaine Micklesen *(Children in Schoolyard)*, Brian Finney *(Botanical Gardens Worker)*, Stephen West *(Federal Express Clerk)*, David Scully *(Male Lab Worker)*, Julie Clemmons *(Female Lab Worker)*, Joseph Franklin *(Man at Cleaners)*, Tom Francis *(Marlene's Assistant)*, Jeff Conkel *(Paramedic)*, Patrick Ryals *(Policeman)*, Chip Lucia *(Realtor)*

This jovially sinister, middle-class morality-tale-cum-horror-show is predictable and implausible. It's also one of the most entertaining films of its type since John Schlesinger's similiar yuppies-in-peril thriller, PACIFIC HEIGHTS.

Newly arrived in Seattle, Claire and Michael Bartel (Annabella Sciorra and Matt McCoy) are a prosperous suburban couple with one young daughter, Emma (Madeline Zima), and a baby boy on the way. When mildly retarded Solomon (Ernie Hudson)

shows up from a local self-help charity to build them a fence, Claire tells him it's to keep people out, as well as in. The outside world intrudes, however, after Clair is sexually abused by her new gynecologist. When she files charges, other patients come forward with similiar charges and lawsuits. The doctor commits suicide, leaving his pregnant wife Peyton (Rebecca De Mornay) broke and homeless and contributing to her miscarriage. While recovering, Peyton sees Claire's picture and hears her name on the TV news and becomes obsessed with revenge.

After her release, Peyton charms her way into the Bartel household as a live-in nanny. She then systematically turns Emma, Michael and even the baby against Claire. She shares secrets with Emma; she shows up in the kitchen in a diaphanous nightgown at three in the morning for Michael's benefit; and she secretly breast-feeds the baby so he will refuse his own mother's milk. Despite being reminded by family friend Marlene (Julianne Moore) that "The hand that rocks the cradle/Is the hand that rules the world," Claire remains oblivious to Peyton's treachery. (Naturally, when Marlene discovers how right she is about Peyton, her life expectancy is drastically curtailed.) After reducing Claire to a nervous, helpless wreck, Peyton launches the final, deadly phase of her master plan to squeeze Claire entirely out of her own family.

At the climax, Peyton learns too late what villains of her ilk always learn too late: don't mess with the nuclear family! Up to that point, though, director Curtis Hanson and screenwriter Amanda Silver (the latter marking an auspicious debut) let viewers have an awful lot of unwholesome fun watching her try. Hanson, a skilled craftsman and Hitchcock imitator, allowed dull, complicated plots to addle his past films, THE BEDROOM WINDOW and BAD INFLUENCE. That's not a problem here.

The plot moves with finely crafted momentum, barrelling through its manifest implausibilities to underscore the tense psychological conflict between a deranged but sympathetic villainess and a likable but flawed heroine. Mistrust and prejudice are the main weapons Peyton brings to bear in her plot against Claire. She exploits Michael's tendency to mistrust Claire's competence as a wife and mother; Claire's doubts as to the nature of Michael's relationship with an old flame; and both Michael's and Claire's subconscious prejudice against the black, retarded Solomon.

THE HAND THAT ROCKS THE CRADLE's plot is as old as the medium itself, with Solomon, the wise and kindly retainer, pitted against Peyton, the devious, seductive vamp, for the soul of the good mother and her family. And it works as well here as it ever has, helped by clever plotting and careful casting. Consolidating her rise to stardom, Sciorra (TRUE LOVE, JUNGLE FEVER) excels at the harder and key job of maintaining audience interest in a character that at times verges on stupidity. The sadly underrated De Mornay (TRIP TO BOUNTIFUL, DEALERS), no less commanding here than she was as Tom Cruise's hardboiled hooker girlfriend in RISKY BUSINESS, is nothing short of astounding as Peyton.

In a villainous acting coup, De Mornay imbues her wholesome good looks with a controlled, terrifying blankness betrayed only by the slightest occasional facial ticks. She also carries herself with a nastily enticing eroticism, among other things recalling Woody Allen's joke about sex being bad only when it's done right. *(Violence, profanity, adult situations.)*

p, David Madden; d, Curtis Hanson; w, Amanda Silver; ph, Robert Elswit; ed, John F. Link; m, Graeme Revell; prod d, Edward Pisoni; art d, Mark Zuelzke; set d, Sandy Reynolds-Wasco; cos, Jennifer Von Mayrhauser

Thriller **(PR: C MPAA: R)**

HAPPY HELL NIGHT

Brisun Entertainment; Pavlina Ltd; Petersen Productions Inc.~ Quest Entertainment c

Nick Gregory *(Eric)*, Frank Hughes *(Sonny)*, Laura Garney *(Liz)*, Charles Cragin *(Father Malius)*, Ted Clark *(Ned Bara)*, Darren McGavin, Jesse Walken, Winston Mayes, Scott Tyler

HAPPY HELL NIGHT is the decrepit mule train of slasher films, taking up the rear and sweeping up the malignant droppings of the FRIDAY THE 13TH, HALLOWEEN and NIGHTMARE ON ELM STREET series, not to mention scores of other horror gore-fests of the 1980s.

Holed up in the dank cell of a madhouse for 25 years after he went on a killing spree, carving up college freshmen during Hell Night in 1965, the emaciated Father Malius (Charles Cragin) sits silently in his cell awaiting the call to murder again. He doesn't have much longer to wait, for local fraternity students are preparing for their traditional Hell Night hazing. At the instigation of sleazy college cable personality Ned Bara (Ted Clark), the Phi Delta fraternity decides to break into the madhouse to snap a picture of the lunatic.

To wreak vengeance on his younger brother, Sonny (Frank Hughes), for sleeping with his girlfriend, Liz (Laura Garney), Eric (Nick Gregory), a big man on campus, selects his brother Sonny, a new Phi Delta pledge, to go snap the photo of Malius. Arriving at the madhouse, Sonny's plans to photograph the lunatic go awry and the murderous priest escapes and heads for the fraternity house with a pickaxe and proceeds to carve up the college freshmen. As the corpses pile up, Eric and Sonny's father (Darren McGavin) arrives to help defeat Malius, only to become another victim.

Finally, performing an ancient ritual, Liz, Sonny and Eric destroy Malius. But, unbeknownst to them, Malius isn't corporeal—he's an evil spirit. When Liz reassures Eric in the back of an ambulance that "everything's gonna be alright now," Malius is seen driving the ambulance, stating sardonically, "No problem."

Representing the last gasp of an exhausted horror formula, HAPPY HELL NIGHT lacks a single moment of originality or inventiveness. Writer-director Brian Owens appears to be relying on the viewers' tacit acceptance of the horror conventions employed herein, as if their very familiarity will compensate for Owens's listless and confused presentation. The film recycles the supernatural slasher, the sexually promiscuous victims, the bloody killings and the ritualistic expulsion of evil with a liturgical monotone. It's all terribly predictable and boring.

Although cutting quite a swath with his pickaxe, Malius lacks even the marginal enigmatic allure of such horror luminaries as Jason and Freddy. Instead, he resembles a nightmare amalgam of John Qualen's Muley from THE GRAPES OF WRATH and Gandhi. Talking like a debauched Tex Avery cartoon dog, mouthing witticisms like "no kidding" when one of his victims shrieks that he can't stop the bleeding of his severed hand, Malius comes across like Droopy with a bloody pickaxe.

Although top-billed Darren McGavin has a mere four scenes in HAPPY HELL NIGHT, the erstwhile TV heartthrob does supply the biggest laugh. After McGavin is attacked by Malius, he's deposited on a bed where he dies. But when Sonny looks back on the bed, McGavin is gone. Searching for McGavin, he comes upon a prone body with a pickaxe tucked under his arm. Thinking it's Malius, Sonny grabs the pickaxe and gives the body a good jab, only to see the luckless McGavin bolt upright, the pickaxe embedded in his chest, screaming like a banshee. *(Excessive violence, profanity, nudity.)*

p, Leslie Sunshine, Pavlina Proevska; d, Brian Owens; w, Brian Owens, Ron Petersen, Michael Fitzpatrick; ph, Sol Negrin; ed, David Mitchell; m, Nenad Bach; prod d, Miljen Kljakovic

Horror **(PR: O MPAA: NR)**

HARD PROMISES ★★
95m Stone Group Pictures; High Horse Films ~ Columbia c

Sissy Spacek *(Chris Coalter)*, William Petersen *(Joey Coalter)*, Brian Kerwin *(Walter Humphrey)*, Mare Winningham *(Dawn)*, Jeff Perry *(Pinky)*, Olivia Burnette *(Beth Coalter)*, Peter MacNichol *(Stuart Coalter)*, Ann Wedgeworth *(Chris's Mom)*, Amy Wright *(Shelley)*, Lois Smith *(Mrs. Bell)*, Dorothy Deavers *(Mrs. Bentson)*, Ed Geldart *(Mr. Bentson)*, Niles Williamson *(Howard)*, Lucy Childs *(Edna)*, Margaret Bowman *(Walt's Mom)*, Jerry Haynes *(Walt's Dad)*, Josh Stoppelwerth *(Walt's Nephew)*, Turk Pipkin *(Tucker)*, James Prince *(Phillip)*, Albert G. "Zeke" Mills *(Grandpa)*, Gerry Becker *(Minister)*, Ann Hamilton *(Minister's Wife)*, Larry Brandenburg *(Garber)*, Brandon Smith *(Lyle)*, Blue Deckert *(Ray)*, Joe Berryman *(Stan)*, Mark Voges *(Judd)*, Woody Watson *(William)*, Margaret Wiley *(Trudy)*, James Black *(Gameshow Husband)*, Suzanne Savoy *(Gameshow Wife)*, Melodee Bowman *(Miss Bowman)*, Joey Coomer *(Peter Pan)*, Julius Tennon *(Football Coach)*, Schuyler Fisk *(Mary)*, Shannon Sedwick *(Neighbor)*, Alissa Alban, Angie Bolling, Coquina Dunn, Mona Lee Fultz, C.K. McFarland *(Bachlorette Party Guests)*, David Alex-Barton, Steev Riccardo, Kevin Cooney, David Breax, Jay W. Davis *(Wedding Band Members)*, Leslie Sachs *(Mail Woman)*, Jack Lilley *(Cowboy)*, Clay Lilley *(Cowboy)*, Keith McCaslim *(Cowboy)*

A pleasant cast brightens HARD PROMISES, an otherwise overly familiar small-town romantic comedy stronger on basic warmth and decency than sparkling wit.

Joey Coalter (William Petersen) has been married to Chris (Sissy Spacek) for 12-1/2 years. But it's a marriage that has been anything but conventional. Chris estimates that Joey has only actually been home one-quarter of the time they've been married. For the rest, Joey has indulged his insatiable wanderlust and unquenchable thirst for adventure, travelling around the world and working at odd jobs, while Chris has stayed at home, teaching at the local school and raising their daughter Beth (Olivia Burnette). The arrangement suits Joey fine, and to Beth he's a hero. But to Chris, he's strictly a heel.

That's why she has finally divorced him to marry stable-but-dull businessman Walter Humphry (Brian Kerwin). In a last bid to keep her parents together, Beth sends Joey an invitation to the wedding, which reaches him somewhere on the prairie, where he is regaling fellow cowhands with tall tales of tawny Tahitian beauties. Joey drops everything and heads home to stop the pending nuptials, but, as the cashier at the local bake shop warns him, it's going to take more than a box of Chris's favorite muffins to smooth things over this time. Well, not much more. In fact, the muffins work fine to lure Chris into a pre-wedding-night fling with Joey, even if they don't do much to patch up the rocky marriage.

But generally, HARD PROMISES is commendably sensible and sensitive about the affairs of the heart. It also updates some of the conventions of the screwball comedy besides letting Chris sow a few final wild oats before marrying Walt, who spends his own pre-wedding-night passed out in a bar. In most films of this type, the woman gets engaged to a decent dullard (Ralph Bellamy spent much of his early career playing this character) as a ploy to win back her straying, likable rogue of an ex-husband (often played by Cary Grant). Chris, however, has no such ulterior motive. She really does love Walt, who really is a likable guy. She also really loves Joey. She just doesn't want to be married to him anymore and be left home alone while he wanders around the world.

The complexities of these adult relationships take their toll mainly on Beth, who becomes sullen and withdrawn as it becomes apparent that her plot to keep her parents together isn't going to work. However, nobody emerges scarred for life. Instead, a staple of relationship films in recent years, everybody gets to learn something: Chris learns that Joey's still-potent charms aren't enough to sway her from her determination to have a stable homelife; Walt learns not to expect Chris to put Joey entirely out of her heart; Joey learns that he's just not the marrying kind; and Beth learns that she doesn't have to lose her father just because her mother has a new husband. It helps that director Martin Davidson (THE LORDS OF FLATBUSH) manages to make this play more like a breezy country-and-western ballad than the cinematic group therapy session suggested above. The cast helps even more.

William Petersen's High Horse Films produced HARD PROMISES and, despite Spacek's top billing, this is really his show. While he may never rate with the likes of Nicholson, Beatty and Pacino as screen-hunk superstars go, Petersen (TO LIVE AND DIE IN LA, MANHUNTER) is completely at home in modest films like this, where effort and easy likability count for more than charisma. Spacek, on the other hand, still has charisma to burn, but she's also enough of a team player to give an enjoyable ensemble performance here as the kind of strong-headed, big-hearted woman any man would be proud to vie for. Kerwin (MURPHY'S ROMANCE, TORCH SONG TRILOGY) is similarly solid as the man who loves her enough to let her go and Burnette is a natural charmer as the daughter. Strong support comes especially from the reliable Mare Winningham, as Spacek's salty best friend, Peter McNichol, as her comically nerdy lawyer, and Amy Wright, amusing in a too-small part as an eccentric member of the wedding party.

Together, they can't quite overcome the tedious telemovie thinness of Jule Selbo's screenplay, but they do make HARD PROMISES a reasonably entertaining diversion. *(Adult situations.)*

p, Cindy Chvatal, William Petersen; d, Martin Davidson; w, Jule Selbo; ph, Andrzej Bartkowiak; ed, Bonnie Koehler, Rick Shaine; m, George S. Clinton; prod d, Dan Leigh; set d, Leslie Rollins; cos, Susan Gammie

Romance/Comedy **(PR: A MPAA: PG)**

HARD-BOILED ★★★½
(Hong Kong) 126m Milestone Pictures ~ Rim Film Distributors c

Chow Yun-fat *(Inspector Yuen)*, Tony Leung *(Tony)*, Teresa Mo *(Teresa)*, Philip Chan *(Pang)*, Anthony Wong *(Johnny Wong)*, Bowie Lam *(Yuen's Partner)*, Kwan Hoi-shan *(Mr. Hoi)*, Cheung Jue-lin *(Mad Dog)*, Philip Kwok

Released in the US just as director John Woo was himself venturing to Hollywood, HARD-BOILED is the Hong Kong action specialist's biggest film yet. Taking the gunplay to even more hyperbolic extremes than before, Woo's new movie doesn't have quite the melodramatic kick of his classic THE KILLER, but the same themes of loyalty, honor and violence are explored to nearly the same impact.

Woo's perennial leading man Chow Yun-fat stars as police inspector Yuen, nicknamed "Tequila," who is first seen moonlighting as a jazz musician in a Hong Kong club. We're soon plunged into the more violent side of Tequila's world, as he and his partner (Bowie Lam) battle a gang of gunrunners in a restaurant. His partner is killed, and Tequila is subsequently browbeaten by his commander, Pang (Philip Chan), who has become increasingly frustrated with Tequila's overly violent tactics. Meanwhile, Tequila is trying to rekindle a relationship with coworker Teresa (Teresa Mo), who has been receiving frequent gifts of white roses. As it happens, the flowers come with coded messages from an undercover gangland source that Teresa passes on to Pang.

As Tequila will later discover, the notes are being sent by Tony (Tony Leung—not the actor from THE LOVER), a cop working undercover as a hitman for aging crime boss Mr. Hoi (Kwan Hoi-shan). After shooting a member of Hoi's gang who had gone over to work for Johnny Wong (Anthony Wong)—the gunrunner Tequila is pursuing—Tony is courted by Johnny to join his gang, as he's poised to take over Hoi's business. Tequila is alerted to the imminent takeover by his own informant, Little Ko, and sneaks into Hoi's warehouse just before Johnny's gang invades the building and kills most of Hoi's workers. In the ensuing shootout, Hoi is killed by Tony, who is then spared by Tequila, who recognizes him from a previous encounter. He's beginning to suspect Tony's true identity, but Pang won't give him a straight answer when he confronts him.

Tequila tracks Tony to the boat where he lives just in time to help protect him from a vengeful gang of Hoi's men. Then Johnny's men arrive and Tequila leaves. Johnny has discovered Little Ko's treachery, and Tony volunteers to kill him. But he leaves the informant alive long enough for him to deliver a message to Tequila: Johnny's armory is located in the heavily fortified basement of a local hospital. Little Ko is taken to the hospital, but Johnny's vicious henchman Mad Dog (Cheung Jue-lin) arrives there and kills him. Tequila is also there, however, as are Pang, Teresa and other cops posing as doctors and nurses; teaming with Tony, who has decided to help him bring Johnny down, Tequila invades Johnny's underground fortress. There they are confronted by Mad Dog, who beats them in a vicious fight and locks them inside the armory.

Meanwhile, Johnny orders his men to seal off the building, taking the patients hostage and killing any who try to escape. As more police arrive and the death toll grows, Tequila and Tony escape from the basement, blasting their way through Johnny's men and helping the other cops free the patients from the now-burning building. While the evacuation continues and a SWAT team outside picks off Johnny's men, Tony goes off to take down Johnny while Tequila helps Teresa rescue babies from the nursery. Outside, Tequila is confronted once again by Johnny, who has taken Tony hostage. The villain forces Tequila to humiliate himself in front of him, before Tony grabs Johnny's gun and fires through his own body and Johnny's. The crime boss is killed, but Tony appears to survive to abandon his life of violence.

In a sort of reverse on THE KILLER, this time it's Yun-fat who plays the cop while his costar is the hitman, but as before, the lines are not so easily defined. Tequila, like many American cop heroes, disdains the rules that keep him from doing his job effectively, while Tony is actually a policeman who finds himself increasingly unable to cope with the violent demands of his undercover work. (Reportedly, the cop angle of his character was not originally part of the film as planned, but was added in deference to actor Leung's pop-idol status in Hong Kong.) Although Yun-fat does forceful work as always, it is Leung's character that is more complex and intriguing, as he is constantly forced to switch loyalties and cope alone with his murderous deeds (he creates origami paper cranes as totems of each person he's killed). In particular, the confrontation between Tony and Mr. Hoi just prior to the latter's shooting is a riveting scene.

If these themes aren't enough to mark HARD-BOILED as Woo's work, the incredible action sequences leave no doubt that the master of the form is once again at work. The opening gunfight in the restaurant is worthy of the climax of any American actioner, and the entire last 40 minutes of the film is one long, breathtaking setpiece in the hospital, with one tense confrontation and shootout after another. Woo never lets the pace slacken or the action become repetitive, and his constantly moving camera keeps the audience consistently involved; there's one Steadicam shot, following Tequila and Tony from one floor of the hospital, into an elevator, onto another floor and into another gunfight, that's truly stunning. Even amidst all the bullets, bombs and blood, however, Woo always keeps the characters in focus, with affecting moments and surprises throughout, as when Mad Dog reveals a surprising moral dimension during the climax.

The cut of HARD-BOILED that played Chinese-language theaters in America is a slightly trimmed version of Woo's original director's cut (shown at the 1992 Toronto Festival of Festivals), shorn of several minutes for violence and running-time concerns. Either version, however, offers ample evidence of Woo's considerable talent, and given his burgeoning US career, it may well represent his last work on home soil for quite some time. *(Excessive violence, adult situations, profanity.)*

p, Linda Kuk, Terence Chang; d, John Woo; w, Barry Wong, (from the story by John Woo); ph, Wang Wing-heng; ed, David Wu, Kai Kit-wai; m, Michael Gibbs; prod d, James Leung; art d, Joel Chong; stunts, Cheung Jue-luh

Crime/Action/Drama (PR: O MPAA: NR)

HEAVEN IS A PLAYGROUND ★★½

111m Aurora Productions; Heaven Corporation ~ Columbia TriStar Home Video c

D.B. Sweeney *(Zack Telander)*, Michael Warren *(Byron Harper)*, Richard Jordan *(David Racine)*, Victor Love *(Truth)*, Bo Kimble *(Matthew Lockhart)*, Janet Julian *(Dalton)*, Nigel Miguel *(Casey)*, Kendall Gill, Cylk Cozart, Hakeen Olajuwon, Terry Bradley

In 1974 *Sports Illustrated* writer Rick Telander spent a season observing life on New York City's public basketball courts. The resulting memoir, *Heaven Is a Playground*, is a fascinating document that weaves sports into sociology with its depiction of disenfranchized young Blacks for whom the game of basketball is no mere diversion but a self-defining discipline, an extended family, and—if they're good enough—a ticket out of the ghetto via college athletic scholarships. It's an illuminating read for sports fans and non-fans alike. This movie version relocates the action to Chicago's Cabrini Green neighborhood and spreads a thick layer of fiction over the book's themes and personalities. Despite some dramatic fouls, the material retains enough interest and insight to score.

The author here is clumsily reinvented as Zack Telander (D.B. Sweeney), a whitebread type who, despite his unlikely background as a law school grad, has always wanted to participate in the street basketball leagues of the inner city playgrounds. He presents himself to local legend Byron Harper (Michael Warren), a ticket scalper by trade but freelance talent scout by avocation. With zeal bordering on obsession, Byron organizes trouble-prone kids into disciplined teams and sets up exhibition matches on the asphalt courts, with college recruiters present if any player shows promise.

Initially Byron and his boys don't trust the strange Caucasian dude loitering on their turf, until Zack demonstrates his knowledge of contract law. Byron's adopted son Truth (Victor Love) looks like he has the right stuff to turn pro, and Byron wants all the legal counsel he can get as he maneuvers to sign Truth with high-powered sports agent David Racine (Richard Jordan). Meanwhile the subplots proliferate. Zack discovers another basketball prodigy, Matthew Lockhart (Bo Kimble), a player of near-mythic prowess who's been practicing alone and unseen following a knee injury. Zack also finds himself reluctantly in charge of one of the playground teams, a seemingly hopeless collection of troublemakers who want so much to shoot hoops that they'll take coaching from a white outsider.

Eventually Zack and Byron clash over how to manage the unpredictable Truth. The boy has a drug habit fed by his inflated but fragile ego, and after Matthew bests him in an impromptu one-on-one Truth dies of a cocaine seizure behind the wheel of his luxury sportscar. In the wake of the tragedy Zack and Byron reconcile, forming a permanent partnership to cultivate and guide young champions out of the projects.

Despite lapses into melodrama, HEAVEN IS A PLAYGROUND succeeds in capturing the allure and urgency that basketball holds for these street partisans, especially when Zack's team of misfits finally pull together and hold their own against more seasoned players before rain stops the game. Theirs is a completely insignificant playground match, but one senses the pride they gain through the minor victory.

Admittedly, there's an element of racial condescension in the Zack character and the way he functions as sort of a guide for white viewers into the heart of darkest Afro-America. Voiceover narration attempts to flesh out the role, and that Zack ultimately elects to remain in Cabrini Green is an unexpected touch, but the whole thing would have seemed more sensible had it remained faithful to the source material and made Zack/Rick the reporter he was. (Rick Telander himself makes cameo appearance as a bartender.) D.B. Sweeney's (EIGHT MEN OUT, MEMPHIS BELLE) insistent good nature brings likability, if not believability, to the role.

Michael Warren's strong performance sharpens but doesn't resolve the ambiguities in Byron Harper, put forth as either a selfless humanitarian helping underprivileged kids to succeed, or a hustler basking in the reflected glory—and profit—of his homegrown champions. There's the lingering suspicion that Byron adopted and raised Truth more for his athletic potential than anything else, and the lack of parental feeling contributes to the boy's downfall. As Truth, Victor Love (NATIVE SON) was cast for his thespian talents rather than his fast break; despite Truth's ballyhooed feats on the court he's barely shown playing the game onscreen. But the penalty goes to Richard Jordan's hammy Racine, a Grinch-like corporate villain better suited to chasing Little Eva across the ice than exploiting Black sports talent.

Real-life basketball stars took part in HEAVEN IS A PLAYGROUND. At one point Chicago Bulls sensation Michael Jordan was cast as loner Matthew Lockheart, but when he backed out the filmmakers scouted Bo Kimble, who made all-American during his days at Loyola Marymount University and was later picked up by the New York Knicks. He turns in a fine performance, but devotees should know that Lockheart's superhuman hang time—he can snatch a dollar bill from atop a backboard and leave four quarters in change during the arc of a single jump—was staged with the help of a few apple crates stacked out of the frame. Hakeem Olajuwon of the Houston Rockets has a scene as an NBA professional used as a ringer to humble the playground leagues, and college luminaries Terry Bradley and Kendall Gill appear. Extras were recruited from the Chicago division of the Midnight Basketball League, an association of ex-gang members who channel their energies into sporting competition.

In a case of home video coming to the rescue, HEAVEN IS A PLAYGROUND—which saw theatrical exhibition only in Chicago during 1991—did strong business as a 1992 cassette release, and by early 1993 there was talk of developing the film into a network TV series. *(Violence, substance abuse, profanity.)*

p, Keith Bank, Bill Higgins; d, Randall Fried; w, Randall Fried, (from the book by Rick Telander); ph, Tom Richmond; ed, Lou Angelo; m, Patrick O'Hearn; prod d, Gregory William Bolton; set d, Karen Bruck; cos, Susan Kaufmann

Sports/Drama **(PR: C MPAA: R)**

HELL MASTER ★

92m Dolphin Productions Ltd. ~ AIP Home Video c

John Saxon *(Professor Saxon)*, David Emge *(The Reporter)*, Amy Raasch *(Shelley)*, Edward Stevens *(Drake)*, Sean Sweeney *(Joel)*, Jeff Rector *(Jesse)*, Lisa Sheldon Miller, Sarah Barkoff

A lurid, low-budget horror discard from the wild world of Michigan cinema, HELL MASTER opens in 1969, with a title crawl explaining that the Kant Institute was the site of the "Nietzsche Experiments" to create mental super-soldiers for Uncle Sam. In the process, nutty Professor Saxon (John Saxon) turned a disused chapel into a mad lab slaughterhouse before an outraged administrator shot him in the head.

Twenty years later the institute is still grooming a superior class of students, although in the film's lone crowd shot they're the usual collegiate jocks, nerds and bimbos, just getting their lectures over headphones, that's all. Soon the visible campus population drops to about a dozen and the murders resume. It seems that Professor Saxon didn't die all those years ago, but supercharged his brainwaves and projected a duplicate of himself to take the fatal bullet. Now having assembled an "army" of four zombified street people and a nun(!), Saxon has returned to obtain mass quantities of mutant-manufacturing narcotics hidden in the tunnels beneath the chapel.

Opposing the forces of evil are some pretty pallid heroes. There's a mischevious little girl (Sarah Barkoff), sole survivor of an earlier Saxon attack; Shelley (Amy Raasch), a psychic coed; and a crusading reporter (David Emge). After interminable dreams-vs-reality bits and much killing and stalking, Shelley decides to fight the mind-controlling Saxon on his own terms; she allows herself to be injected with the Nietzsche drug. The final faceoff between the two somehow turns into a theological debate over the existence of God, Saxon taking the atheist position while Shelley defends the notion of an ethical supreme being.

Let's hope God's got more going for Him than this film. Writer-producer-director-editor Douglas Schulze (who also receives credit for art direction and set design) knows a few neat camera tricks, which he simply uses over and over again, chiefly perspective shots of long halls with distant doorways sometimes bathed ominously in red light, sometimes bathed ominously in green light.

In a strictly visual sense, John Saxon's Professor Saxon is one of the more memorable horror villains of late, stylishly clad in a flowing black leather trenchcoat, his right arm fitted with a spring-loaded triple syringe array, his left arm installed with an extra-large catheter tube for shooting up his own veins. Otherwise this baddie is as exciting as his name. Obviously intended to combine the worst elements of Freddy Krueger and Timothy Leary, Professor Saxon has the usual goal of world-domination-thru-zombie-slaves, and his diatribes against God don't translate into depth.

Besides theology and the 60s drug culture, Schulze loads the narrative with political asides about social activism and conservatism, the latter ridiculously embodied in Jesse (Jeff Rector), a whip-wielding student fascist whom Shelley's psychic insight unmasks as . . . a bedwetter. (We couldn't make this up, folks.) More compelling is Joel (Sean Sweeney), a handicapped genius who strikes a Faustian bargain with Saxon because he's convinced that a dose of Nietzsche serum will let him cast away his crutches. It only turns him into another slimy ghoul, and his friends blow him away with barely a second thought.

Executive producer of the film was Nathan J. White, who mixed chills and religion more effectively a few years back when he wrote and directed a nightmarish oddity called THE CARRIER, also a Michigan product. As for HELL MASTER, it went directly to home video with a title and ad campaign designed to recall the better-known HELLRAISER series, even fashioning one of its zombies—a carved-up baldie dubbed "Bobby Razorface"—to resemble the Pinhead figure from the Clive Barker movies. *(Violence, profanity, substance abuse, adult situations.)*

p, Douglas Schulze; d, Douglas Schulze; w, Douglas Schulze; ph, Michael Goi; ed, Douglas Schulze; m, John Traynor; art d, Douglas Schulze; set d, Douglas Schulze

Horror **(PR: O MPAA: NR)**

HELLRAISER III: HELL ON EARTH ★★★

92m Fifth Avenue Entertainment; Nostradamus Pictures Inc.; Trans Atlantic Entertainment ~ Dimension Pictures c

Terry Farrell *(Joey Summerskill)*, Doug Bradley *(Pinhead/Elliott Spencer)*, Paula Marshall *(Terri)*, Kevin Bernhardt *(J.P. Monroe)*, Ken Carpenter *(Doc/Camerahead)*, Peter Boynton *(Joey's Father)*, Aimee Leigh *(Sandy)*, Lawrence Mortorff *(Bum)*, Brent Bolthouse *(Club D.J.)*

British horror master Clive Barker's best-known story gets another workout in HELLRAISER III: HELL ON EARTH, a film that's more conventional than its predecessors but still delivers the goods to genre fans.

The terror begins when J.P. Monroe (Kevin Bernhardt), the owner of a decadent New York nightclub called the Boiler Room, purchases the torture pillar last seen at the end of HELLBOUND: HELLRAISER II as a decorative item for the club. Soon thereafter, Joey Summerskill (Terry Farrell), a young TV newswoman frustrated in her attempts to be assigned major stories, is present at a hospital when a young man is brought in, chains seemingly operated by unseen forces pulling at his skin and eventually ripping him apart. Attempting to track down Terri (Paula Marshall), the girl who came in with the unfortunate young man, Joey learns that she is an ex-girlfriend of J.P.'s, and that the horrific death was somehow related to the pillar, which J.P. has installed in his apartment above the club. Terri also presents Joey with a puzzlebox, one that can unleash the demonic spirits known as Cenobites, which she removed from the pillar before leaving J.P.'s place.

J.P., meanwhile, has shed some of his blood on the pillar and awakened the spirit of Pinhead (Doug Bradley), the Cenobites' leader, who is trapped within it. Promising him gifts of pleasure and pain, Pinhead convinces J.P. to sacrifice a young girl named Sandy (Aimee Leigh) to him. When the insecure Terri returns to J.P., she nearly meets the same fate but manages to turn the tables, and Pinhead kills J.P. Now freed of the pillar, Pinhead seduces Terri, who has figuratively and literally lost her ability to dream, with the offer to join him in his world of ultimate physical sensation. She succumbs, and soon Pinhead has invaded the Boiler Room, his supernatural powers sending chains and other devices down to slaughter its guests.

Investigating the pillar, Joey has discovered that only the puzzlebox has the power to send its demons back to hell. She is also visited in a dream by the ghost of Elliott Spenser, the WWI army officer whom the puzzlebox transformed into Pinhead, who tells her that his demonic incarnation can only win complete freedom from hell by convincing Joey to hand over the box voluntarily. While investigating the carnage at the club, Joey is confronted by Pinhead and his Cenobite followers, who include the resuscitated J.P., Terri, Doc (Ken Carpenter), her cameraman whose camera has become part of his skull, and the club's D.J. (Brent Bolthouse), who now fires lethal CDs pulled from his head. Joey attempts to flee the creatures, but even hiding in a church can't deter Pinhead's demonic advance.

Finally confronting the demons at a construction site, Joey uses the box to send them back to hell—or so she thinks. Pinhead tricks her into handing over the box by disguising himself as the ghost of Joey's father, who died in Vietnam, and then prepares to turn her into a Cenobite herself. But Spenser's spirit reappears and recombines with Pinhead, and Joey manages to banish them both to hell once and for all. She then submerges the box in a wet cement foundation—but the building erected upon it winds up having boxlike designs as decor in its lobby.

At first, HELLRAISER III promised to abandon completely the Gothic sensibilities of its British-made predecessors and embrace the simplistic characteristics of mass-market American horror. Unlike the first two films, this one was shot in the US; original creator Clive Barker was nowhere to be found in the original credits; and HELLBOUND director Tony Randel was dropped in favor of Anthony Hickox, whose previous works (the WAXWORK films and SUNDOWN: THE VAMPIRE IN RETREAT) had little of the surrealism or depth that characterized the HELLRAISER movies. Fortunately, anchored by Peter Atkins's solid screenplay, Hickox does by far his best work with this film, and Miramax, which ultimately picked up the US distribution rights, lured Barker back to supervise reshoots and lend his name as executive producer. The result, while it still owes as much to the ELM STREET films as to its true antecedents, is an effective piece of rock 'n' roll horror.

The movie certainly benefits from expanding the role of its lead villain, Pinhead, without sanitizing him. Originally a shadowy figure lurking on the edges of the boundaries between earth and hell, the character is now allowed a larger part in the action, and Bradley's creepy delivery, either promising unearthly pleasures or horrible fates (best line: "Come to me and die, while you still have the option of doing so quickly!"), make him a most effective monster. The way in which he taps into his victims' fears, doubts and desires to further his own plans to spread hell on earth is creepily effective, particularly in his pivotal scenes with J.P. and Terri, and the character is given a black sense of wit without resorting to Freddy-style one-liners.

This, unfortunately, is not the case with the supporting Cenobites, whose overly literalized designs (combining them with key devices from their previous lives as humans) smacks of Americanized gimmick horror. And the rules of hell, which have been greatly expanded from the first two films, are not completely thought out, but rather called into play at the screenplay's convenience. Nonetheless, HELLRAISER III goes farther with its horror than many recent genre items, reaching its apex in a sequence in which Pinhead invades the church and enacts a grotesque travesty of both the communion (force-feeding a priest bits of his own flesh) and the crucifixion. *(Excessive violence, substance abuse, profanity, nudity, sexual situations, adult situations.)*

p, Lawrence Mortorff; d, Anthony Hickox; w, Peter Atkins, (from the characters created by Clive Barker); ph, Gerry Lively; ed, Christopher Cibelli; m, Randy Miller; prod d, Steve Hardie; art d, Tim Eckel; set d, David Koneff; cos, Leonard Pollack

Horror **(PR: O MPAA: R)**

HELLROLLER
Hollywood International Pictures; Off the Wall Productions ~ Black Diamond Video c

Ron Litman *(Eugene)*, Mary Woronov *(Eugene's Aunt)*, Michelle Bauer *(Michelle Novak)*, Elizabeth Kaitan *(Lizzy)*, Hyapatia Lee *(Dancer)*, David Sterry *(Dr. Kosloff/King of the Bums)*, Ruth Collins *(Eugene's Mother)*, Tammara Souza *(Bunny)*, G.J. Levinson *(Donald)*, Dink O'Neil *(Tony Sky)*, Wendy Spahr *(Lisa Dye)*, Johnny Legend *(Street Punk)*, Eric Caidin *(Street Punk)*, Lonn Wade *(Siamese Twin)*, Sean Wade *(Siamese Twin)*, Lucia Mortato *(Hooker)*, Lisa Shea *(Girl in Elevator)*, Jeff David *(Guy in Elevator)*, Rene Gonzalez *(Sheila)*, William Quigley *(Gym Bouncer)*, William Hoversten *(Mugging Victim)*, Katie Amstutz *(Baglady)*, Howard Hollis *(Preacher)*, Webb Garwood *(Detective)*, Douglas Dunning *(Englishman)*, Lee Forbes *(TV Interviewee)*, Michael Lacoy *(TV Interviewee)*, Mary Craig *(TV Interviewee)*, Kenneth Klinkowski *(Fire Juggler)*, Ed'Ge, Stuart Wall, Jason Goodwin, Joe Green, Bruce Mercury, Todd Roman, Jeff Wright *(Bums)*

The idea of a wheelchair-bound serial killer is not the most frightening in the world—particularly as handled in the thoroughly inept HELLROLLER, made by individuals who could charitably be described as creatively impaired.

The titular terror is Eugene (Ron Litman), who's been raised on the street by his aunt (Mary Woronov, wisely taking the pseudonym Penny Arcade) ever since his prostitute mother (Ruth Collins) was murdered in the attack that crippled him. When another pair of punks rape and murder his aunt, Eugene is driven round the bend and seeks revenge on society. Going into a gym to get in shape for his assault, Eugene and his wheelchair are promptly tossed out by the musclebound doorman, but he's rescued by a friendly bum named Donald (G.J. Levinson), who helps him get murderous revenge. The two then go to kill swimsuit model Michelle Novak (Michelle Bauer), but when Donald proves uncooperative, Eugene goads Michelle into helping him kill his partner before finishing off Michelle himself.

Eugene's murderous rampage continues, as he slaughters a dancer (Hyapatia Lee), a hooker (Lucia Mortato) and a pair of young criminals (Elizabeth Kaitan and Tammara Souza) he briefly befriends. Seeking the ultimate revenge on the wealthy, he engages the services of a mad scientist, Dr. Kosloff (David Sterry), who concocts a potion that, when introduced into water, will turn rich people into bums. The ploy works, but then the King of the Bums (Sterry), angered by Eugene's exploits, sends the other street people out to kill him. Eugene attacks and kills the King, but the other bums tear him apart.

The climactic shot of Eugene's head in a garbage can is a fitting epitaph for HELLROLLER, a pathetic, shot-on-video affair that's been cropped at the top and bottom with black bars (occasionally cutting off the actors' heads) in an attempt to make this look like a letterboxed movie. It's the only attempt at class in a film that otherwise dwells on seedy, unredeemable and uninteresting characters, copious but sloppy gore and grossly misogynistic exploitation of its actresses.

At least twice in HELLROLLER, the action stops for several minutes of leering at the women posing nude, bathing or showering before Eugene gets down to business; some of them don't even utter a word before they're slaughtered. The filmmakers probably thought they were being tactful by leaving the rapes of Eugene's mother and aunt offscreen at the beginning, but any goodwill they've earned in that department evaporates long before they present one of Eugene's nameless, half-naked female victims being burned to death with an iron.

The murders themselves are too ineptly presented (not to mention distasteful) to be scary, and the attempts at humor are largely on the level of the signature letters of a TV station—KRAP 69—whose news broadcasts periodically interrupt the action. It's probably taking HELLROLLER too seriously to protest its mindless exploitation of the homeless and the handicapped, or to expect any kind of depth in the performances. The saddest part of all is seeing Mary Woronov (ROCK 'N' ROLL HIGH SCHOOL, EATING RAOUL), a veteran of so many entertaining exploitation films, taking part in this bilge; judging by the movie's complete lack of production values, she couldn't possibly have done this for the money. *(Excessive violence, excessive nudity, profanity, sexual situations.)*

p, Stuart Wall, G.J. Levinson; d, G.J. Levinson; w, Stuart Wall, G.J. Levinson; ph, G.J. Levinson; ed, W.F. Heldmyer; m, Randy Greif, Static Effect; art d, Alan Brody

Horror/Comedy **(PR: O MPAA: NR)**

HERO ★★½
112m Columbia ~ Columbia c
(GB: ACCIDENTAL HERO)

Dustin Hoffman *(Bernie LaPlante)*, Geena Davis *(Gale Gayley)*, Andy Garcia *(John Bubber)*, Joan Cusack *(Evelyn)*, Kevin J. O'Connor *(Chucky)*, Maury Chaykin *(Winston)*, Stephen Tobolowsky *(Wallace)*, Christian Clemenson *(Conklin)*, Tom Arnold *(Chick)*, Warren Berlinger *(Judge Goines)*, Cady Huffman *(Flight Attendant Leslie)*, Susie Cusack *(Donna O'Day)*, James Madio *(Joey)*, Richard Riehle *(Robinson)*, Daniel Leroy Baldwin *(Fireman Denton)*, Don Yesso *(Elliott)*, Don Pugsley *(Jury Foreman)*, Lee Wilkof *(Prosecutor)*, Steven Elkins *(1st Bailiff)*, Leslie Jordan *(Court Official)*, Raymond Fitzpatrick *(2nd Bailiff)*, Bobby C. Collins *(Mendoza)*, Richard Montoya *(Vargas)*, Ricardo Salinas *(Mendoza's Friend)*, Herbert Siguenza *(Espinosa)*, Don S. Davis *(Probation Officer)*, Darrell Larson *(Flight Attendant Freddy)*, Harry Northup *(Mr. Fletcher)*, Jordan Bond *(Richie Fletcher)*, Eric Poppick *(Mr. Smith)*, Julia Barry *(Kelly)*, Marnie Mosiman *(Susan)*, William Duff Griffin *(Mr. Brown)*, Peggy Roeder *(Bag Lady on TV)*, Katrina Cerio *(Makeup Artist)*, Kevin Jackson *(Inspector Dayton)*, Don Gazzaniga *(Fire Captain)*, Lance Kinsey *(Paramedic)*, Michael Talbott *(State Police Officer)*, John Ackerman *(Bag Man)*, Paul Hewitt *(Parker)*, Marita Geraghty *(Joan)*, Shirley Pierce *(Anchorwoman-Channel 4)*, Sam Derence *(Reporter-Channel 8)*, Rick Plastina *(Reporter-Channel 13)*, Martin Schienle *(Allen in Coma)*, Jeff Garlin *(News Vendor)*, John M. Watson, Sr. *(African-American Wannabee)*, John Mohrlein *(Fighter Wannabee)*, Tony Fitzpatrick *(Fighter Wannabee)*, Vito D'Ambrosio *(Another Wannabee)*, Jay Leggett *(Mud Face Wannabee)*, Dev Kennedy *(Tall Wannabee)*, Darryl David *(Tough Prisoner)*, Terry Muller *(Tough Prisoner)*, James Alfred Whitaker *(Tough Prisoner)*, Collins Williams Daniels *(Rasta Prisoner)*, I.M. Hobson *(Waiter/Captain)*, William Newman *(Millionaire)*, Clea Lewis *(Sylvia)*, Jeff Kline *(Street Kid)*, John Merrill *(Street Kid)*, Lynn Oddo *(Buxom Woman)*, Milton L. Cobb *(Vietnam Vet)*, Robert Pabst *(Vietnam Vet)*, Tom Milanovich *(Guard at Jail)*, Cordis Heard *(Nurse Roberts)*, Mandy Duncan *(Teen in Hospital)*, Gerardo Murillo-Carr *(Teen in Hospital)*, Henry Brown *(Hospital Guard)*, Robert Munns *(Doctor)*, Tamar Teufenkjian, Jose Reyes, Michael Mullen, D'Angelo Ferreri, Kody Cullum *(Children in Hospital)*, Heidi McNeal *(Teenage Girl at Hospital)*, Michael O'Dwyer *(Cop at Hospital)*, Ed Scheibner *(Donna's Boyfriend)*, James Callahan *(Police Chief)*, D David Morin *(Fireman on Ledge)*, Dan Healy *(George Bush Look-A-Like)*, Margery Jane Ross *(Barbara Bush Look-A-Like)*, Chevy Chase

First-rate talent in front of and behind the camera fails to save HERO, an insistently Capra-esque social comedy, from being a lumbering bore.

Bernie LaPlante (Dustin Hoffman) has tried to live a low-profile life. In fact, it's his creed, which he tries to pass on to the young son, Joey (James Madio), of his ex-wife, Evelyn (Joan Cusack). But the only result is that Bernie has a low life to match his low profile. A small-time Chicago thief, he's about to be put into prison for trying to sell stolen house paint. Though his main business is stolen credit cards, he moves just about anything and everything from the dreary walk-up where he lives alone.

Fate intervenes when Bernie finds himself at the scene of a plane crash and, against his nature, helps the survivors—including hot-shot TV reporter Gale Gayley (Geena Davis)—escape. Bernie tries to fade back into anonymity, but Gayley's station offers a million-dollar reward for the first exclusive interview with the "Angel of Flight 104." Before Bernie can come forward, he's arrested yet again in a credit-card sting. Meanwhile, a homeless man who had given him a ride home from the crash, John Bubber (Andy Garcia), claims the reward.

Lionized by the media, Bubber sincerely enjoys being a popular inspirational figure and doing good works under his hero's mantle. But his good-heartedness comes back to torture him for living a lie. Bernie comes to Gayley's attention when her credit cards, which Bernie stole from her while rescuing her, surface after his arrest. But before she can put two and two together, Bubber is out on a high ledge threatening suicide. Bernie joins him there and brings him back in with a deal—Bubber can remain the "hero" and Bernie will stay in the background for a piece of the million. On the way in, Bernie slips and almost falls, saved only by Bubber's quick reactions. Bubber gets to be a hero after all.

It's beginning to seem as if Hollywood is systemically unable to get anything right. Most of the time, stories feel over-digested and too thought out, betraying a craven fear of giving offense to any group or individual among the two hundred million-plus potential audience. Directed by the usually incisive Stephen Frears (MY BEAUTIFUL LAUNDRETTE, DANGEROUS LIAISONS) and written by the usually elegant and eloquent David Webb Peoples (BLADE RUNNER, UNFORGIVEN), HERO seems fatally under-digested. It's difficult to quite know either what it's about or what it's "about," though the main target seems to be the press.

Gayley is a pneumatic airhead accurately described by her assignment editor (an uncredited and bald Chevy Chase) as a reporter pretending to be a real person. HERO revolves around her willingness to accept style over substance in taking Bubber at face value rather than investigating him. That he's a sensitive, photogenic hunk is enough for both her and her viewers, who will Bubber into the role with such conviction that he is soon charming chronically ill children at the hospital, even as Bernie is trying to call his bluff.

None of this is particularly amusing, let alone trenchant, meaningful or believable. Moreover, the film insults its audience by depicting them as a teeming mass of grubby idiots prone to mindless worship of any empty-headed sex symbol foisted upon them by a pandering press. As such—and this has been true of most Hollywood press satires of the past decade or so—HERO reveals less about the fourth estate than it does about a filmmaking establishment that feels itself arrogantly above the scrutiny of mere reporters and accountability to mere moviegoers.

Aside from a few moments of comedy between Davis and Chase (in a relationship lifted almost unaltered from THE FRONT PAGE), HERO is an embarrassment best forgotten by everyone involved.

p, Laura Ziskin; d, Stephen Frears; w, David Webb Peoples, (from the story by Peoples, Laura Ziskin and Alvin Sargent); ph, Oliver Stapleton; ed, Mick Audsley; m, George Fenton; prod d, Dennis Gassner; art d, Leslie McDonald; set d, Nancy Haigh; cos, Richard Hornung

Comedy/Drama **(PR: C MPAA: PG-13)**

HIGHWAY 61 ★★★

(Canada) 110m Shadow Shows Entertainment Corporation ~ Skouras Pictures c

Valerie Buhagiar *(Jackie Bangs)*, Don McKellar *(Pokey Jones)*, Earl Pastko *(Mr. Skin/"Satan")*, Peter Breck *(Mr. Watson)*, Art Bergmann *(Otto)*, Jello Biafra *(1st Customs Agent)*, Hadley Obodiac *(2nd Customs Agent)*, Tav Falco *(Motorcycle Gang Leader)*, Tracy Wright *(Margo)*, Johnny Askwith *(Claude)*, Namir Khan *(Funeral Director)*, Steve Fall *(Jeffrey–The Corpse)*, Larry Hudson *(Nathan–The Manservant)*, Elizabeth Pritchard *(Louise Watson)*, Chantal Ettles *(Missie Watson)*, Alithea Watters *(Minnie Watson)*, Ellen Carlisle *(Mother)*, Brooks Rapley *(Mother's Little Helper)*, Ann Shipman *(Pickerel Falls Reporter)*, Michael Vendruscolo *(Pickerel Falls Photographer)*, David McFarlane *(Satan's Neighbor)*, Peter Lynch *(Bingo Angry Man)*, Alma Doyle *(Bingo Angry Woman)*, Caroline Gillis *(Bingo Attendant)*, Ray Gabourie *(Bingo Caller)*, Jimmy Watson *(Highway Panhandler)*, Willie Selkirk *(Motel Clerk)*, Robert Theodore *(Rock Band Manager)*, Kevin Carlisle *(1st Rock Band Member)*, Charlie Azzopardi *(2nd Rock Band Member)*, Jimmy Lynch *(3rd Rock Band Member)*, Ken Sinclair *(4th Rock Band Member)*, Lad Shaga *(Gun Dealer)*, Clarence Haynes *(Motel Meat Eater)*, E.G. Daniels *(Motel Vegetarian)*, Jay Patterson *(Bus Driver)*, Sweety Dog *(Iggy Pup)*

An eventful, music-oriented road movie that defies easy classification, HIGHWAY 61 reconfirms that Canadians are quite leery of the US, that huge, loud neighbor from whence so many marvels and nightmares come.

The title refers to a stretch of highway that longitudinally spans the continent, linking New Orleans at one end with Thunder Bay, Ontario, at the other. It's in the little town of Pickerel Falls that Pokey Jones (Don McKellar), a humble barber and frustrated trumpet player, is thrust into the spotlight when an anonymous, drunken youth happens to die of exposure in his yard. Enter Jackie Bangs (Valerie Buhagiar), a rock 'n' roll roadie on the run with a fortune in cocaine. She claims the dead kid is her brother and pursuades Pokey to drive her and the body down to New Orleans for the family funeral. In reality she's stashed the coke down the throat of the corpse and has to smuggle it to her drug connection in the Big Easy. The pine coffin precariously perched atop his vintage Ford Galaxy, naive Pokey and hard-hearted Jackie set off down Highway 61 into America, "the Land of Kings" notes Pokey with deadpan sincerity in his postcards to a Guns 'n' Roses fan back home.

The characters they encounter on the US side of the border run the gamut from threatening to very, very, *very* threatening. There's Watson (Peter Breck) a gun-toting lug obsessed with "good family music" and ruthlessly grooming his motherless brood of children for wholesome showbiz stardom; a mansionful of Jackie's has-been rocker friends, wasting away in dissolute, twilight existence—an environment straight out of the Eagles' "Hotel California"; but most of all there's a certain Mr. Skin (Earl Pastko). He's gaunt, malevolent, and happy to purchase the immortal soul of anyone who crosses his path. It seems the deceased boy had sold out to Mr. Skin (the price? a free concert ticket), and now the devil wants his due, pursuing the protagonists all the way down to New Orleans to get his claws on that cadaver.

HIGHWAY 61 traverses the backroads of fame, fortune and tawdry ambition that compromise the American Dream, and while it takes a few strange detours, it's well the worth the trip. Handsomely mounted for $1.2 million, the film was inspired by the Bob Dylan song "Highway 61 Revisited" (the road passes through Dylan's hometown of Hibbing, Minnesota, and in one scene Pokey plays homage to the house where the music legend grew up). Director Bruce McDonald is one of the rising stars of Canadian cinema, having made his feature debut in 1989 with the well-received ROADKILL, and like that film HIGHWAY 61 boasts a screenplay by actor Don McKellar, who makes his characters quirky, ideal traveling companions.

A riff on New Orleans barber *cum* cornet player Buddy Bolden, Pokey Jones may be somewhat timid and slow to catch on but he's nobody's fool when it comes to standing down a rowdy biker gang (all it takes is a good haircut and a shave) or confronting Satan in his lair. Valerie Buhagiar looks and acts like a heavy metal Mona Lisa, whose smile may be genuine or just another deceit as she ends Pokey's virginity at gunpoint and leads the hapless Ontarian deeper into *terra incognita.* Punk rock star and monologist Jello Biafra, no stranger to legal hassles himself, has a juicy cameo as an uptight American border cop; the former Dead Kennedy's frontman barely contains the sarcasm in the finger-wagging antidrug warning he unloads at the two Canadians early on.

The real scene-stealer, though, is Earl Pastko's Mr. Skin, a big-as-folklore embodiment of diabolical evil. It's a bit of a letdown, in fact, when Pokey tracks him down (in New Orleans *everybody* can point out where Satan lives) and finds that this Lucifer's roots are less than supernatural. He's just an elaborate wacko who lost his mind after the death of Elvis Presley. Still, he's got several walls filled with polaroids of those from whom he agreed to purchase souls—some for as little as $20 or a pint of bourbon. Now that's scary.

Dedicated to a bluesman named Blind Boy Grunt, HIGHWAY 61 has a soundtrack with a peculiar skimming of rock, pop, jazz and gospel—everything from Tom Jones to the Ramones to Andre Crouch. The picture's exhibition covered less territory, unfortunately, receiving mainly film festival and art house exhibition in the US. *(Violence, substance abuse, profanity, nudity, sexual situations, adult situations.)*

p, Bruce McDonald, Colin Brunton; d, Bruce McDonald; w, Don McKellar, (from the story by McKellar, Bruce McDonald, Allan Magee); ph, Miroslaw Baszak; ed, Michael Pacek; m, Nash the Slash; art d, Ian Brock

Drama/Comedy **(PR: O MPAA: R)**

HIGHWAY TO HELL ★★½

92m Goodman-Rosen Production; Josa Productions; High Street Productions; Hemdale Picture Corporation; Sovereign Pictures ~ Hemdale Releasing Corporation c

Patrick Bergin *(Beelzebub)*, Chad Lowe *(Charlie Sykes)*, Kristy Swanson *(Rachel Clark)*, Adam Storke *(Royce)*, Pamela Gidley *(Clara)*, Richard Farnsworth *(Sam)*, Jarrett Lennon *(Adam)*, C.J. Graham *(Sergeant Bedlam/"Hellcop")*, Lita Ford *(Hitchhiker)*, Gilbert Gottfried *(Hitler)*, Kevin Peter Hall *(Charon)*, Anne Meara, Jerry Stiller, Amy Stiller, Ben Stiller

An unusual combination of the Orpheus myth, contemporary horror and pop-culture satire, HIGHWAY TO HELL is an engaging if not always successful genre entry.

Young Charlie Sykes (Chad Lowe) is eloping to Las Vegas with his girlfriend Rachel Clark (Kristy Swanson). Fearful that Rachel's disapproving parents might have sent the cops after them, Charlie decides to take a back road through the desert. He stops at the Last Chance gas station for a fill-up, and Sam (Richard Farnsworth), the elderly proprietor, warns him to stay awake on the road ahead. But Charlie falls asleep at the wheel and nearly crashes his car; the couple are then confronted by the Hellcop (C.J. Graham), a hulking scarred figure who kidnaps Rachel and spirits her away to the netherworld.

Racing back to Sam for help, Charlie learns that numerous young women—including Sam's own fiancee Clara—have disappeared on the road over the years, and that if he means to rescue Rachel, he must catch up with the Hellcop before he reaches Hell City. Sam lends Charlie his old car, a rifle and some shells, and after being chased by a real cop, Charlie manages to drive through a dimensional barrier and into hell itself.

Rachel, meanwhile, has attempted to escape the Hellcop when he stops at Pluto's Diner, but she is grabbed by a biker gang led by the hotheaded young Royce (Adam Storke), who hands her back over to the demonic officer. After his own run-in with Royce's gang, Charlie catches up to Hellcop, but is run off the road by him after a chase. His damaged car is picked up by Beezlebub (Patrick Bergin), an easygoing mechanic who claims to be able to fix anything and has a young boy named Adam (Jarrett Lennon) assisting him. Beezlebub tells Charlie that Rachel is safe from claiming by the devil when Charlie admits she's not a virgin; he then fixes Charlie's car and sees him off. But Adam stows away in the car, and reveals to Charlie that his entire family was killed by Hellcop. Charlie promises to take Adam back to earth with him once he rescues Rachel.

Arriving at Hoffa's casino, Charlie discovers Rachel trapped in a cage and attempts to free her, but Hellcop shows up and shoots him before spiriting Rachel away again. Beezlebub, who has been looking for Adam, "fixes" Charlie and revives him, then attempts to talk Charlie out of his attempted rescue. He fails, and Adam stays behind with Beezlebub as Charlie drives on. He eventually catches up to Hellcop's car, parked outside some caves; there he meets Royce's girlfriend, who turns out to be Clara (Pamela Gidley). She warns Charlie that he, like herself, will be forced to make a choice that might doom him if he presses on, but he does, and successfully resists the temptations of a demon disguised as Rachel.

Crossing the river Styx, Charlie finds Rachel in the devil's lair; the dark lord tries to tempt Rachel into staying, but Charlie talks him into letting them leave. Fending off more of hell's denizens and eluding the pursuing Hellcop, Charlie and Rachel once again encounter Beezlebub, who they realize is actually the devil himself. Charlie insists on taking Adam with him, and Beezlebub, who admires the young man's goodness of spirit, agrees to a contest: if Charlie can outrace the Hellcop, he can take Rachel and Adam back, but if not, he'll have to leave them both behind. Using a nitro booster hidden in Sam's car, Charlie wins the race and emerges back on earth—but the angry Hellcop follows them and attempts to kill Charlie before being blown away by Rachel with Sam's shotgun.

A surprisingly capable little horror comedy, HIGHWAY TO HELL could have become something of a cult item with the proper handling. Unfortunately, embattled distributor Hemdale kept it on the shelf for over a year and then dumped it out for a quickie release with a lousy ad campaign. The movie deserved better. Although its mixture of comedy and chills is somewhat uneven, Brian Helgeland's screenplay is consistently inventive, and director Ate De Jong (DROP DEAD FRED) offers a fast-paced and generally entertaining ride with some good action scenes and in-jokes.

One of the funniest sights in hell is the "Good Intentions Paving Company," which turns people who say things like "I only slept with my boss to advance my professional career" into road surfacing. There's also a throwaway shot of a table in the lounge at Hoffa's casino which has spaces reserved for the likes of Moammar Qaddafi, D.W. Botha and . . Jerry Lewis.

On the horror side, HIGHWAY TO HELL benefits from strong makeup effects by Steve Johnson (particularly Hellcop's inscription-carved face) and brief stop-motion sequences by Randall William Cook. The subplot involving Charlie's attempts to bring Adam back to the real world is not as maudlin as one might expect, and the action sequences are well-executed. The actors generally acquit themselves well, with Lowe a sympathetic hero and Swanson (BUFFY THE VAMPIRE SLAYER) bringing pluck and energy to what is largely a thankless role. Bergin (SLEEPING WITH THE ENEMY, LOVE CRIMES) has less to do than his star billing might suggest, but does a good job nonetheless as the well-spoken devil.

Although some of the sequences appear to suffer from lack of coverage, De Jong does provide the film with a strong visual look and an offbeat atmosphere; Robin Vidgeon's sun-baked photography gives the desert locations a forbidding feel; and the score by Hidden Faces is properly eccentric. HIGHWAY TO HELL is no masterpiece, but it *is* a genuine video find. *(Violence, profanity, sexual situations.)*

p, Mary Anne Page, John Byers; d, Ate De Jong; w, Brian Helgeland; ph, Robin Vidgeon; ed, Todd Ramsey, Randy Thornton; m, Hidden Faces; prod d, Philip Dean Foreman; set d, Lynda Burbank; cos, Florence Kemper

Horror/Comedy **(PR: O MPAA: R)**

HIRED TO KILL ★★

91m Allstar Pictures Ltd. ~ Paramount Home Video c

Brian Thompson *(Frank Ryan)*, Oliver Reed *(Michael Bartos)*, Jose Ferrer *(Rallis)*, George Kennedy *(Thomas)*, Michelle Moffet *(Ana)*, Barbara Lee Alexander *(Sheila)*, Jordanna Capra *(Joanna)*, Kendall Conrad *(Daphne)*, Kim Lonsdale *(Sivi)*, Jude Mussetter *(Dahlia)*, Penelope Reed *(Katrina)*, David Sawyer *(Louis)*

Despite its can't-win premise, HIRED TO KILL marshalls just enough flair to make one wish it were a lot better.

Beefy Brian Thompson plays Frank Ryan, a pugnacious globe-trotting soldier of fortune summoned by self-proclaimed "businessman" Thomas (George Kennedy), a shady manipulator with congressional ties and a taste for covert conspiracies. He pays Ryan to go to a tropical banana republic and kill Rallis (Jose Ferrer), a revolutionary who threatens American interests. Unfortunately, Rallis is housed in an impregnable fortress overseen by death-squad commander Michael Bartos (Oliver Reed)—and a computer has concluded that the only way Ryan can penetrate it is to masquerade as a swishy photographer on a fashion shoot with six sexy models.

Cranky Frank doesn't want any girls in tow: "From Eve to Margaret Thatcher, [women] have managed to screw up history!" These females aren't bimbo mannequins, though, but a handpicked bunch of fellow mercenaries, ex-terrorists and outlaw broads. Much screen time is devoted to these Magnificent Six and their transformation from hellcats to slinky fashion plates with crack combat skills, thanks to a training regimen rife with Frank's crude male-chauvinist remarks. At last the adventurers embark on their mission, but things aren't what they seem. The feared Rallis turns out to be a courageous captive dissident whom Thomas has marked for termination at the behest of evil Arabs. When Frank figures out he's been made an expendable patsy in an assassination doublecross, his team releases Rallis and turns the tables on Thomas.

While the betrayals and plot twists tie the tale's logic in loops, one is still grateful for the distraction from the main conflict between Frank and his distaff comrades. The avowedly amoral commando goes way beyond "cute" neanderthal sexism into genuine violence, raping freedom-fighter Ana (Michelle Moffett), who immediately becomes his willing love slave, just as accompanying ex-girlfriend Sheila (Barbara Lee Alexander) conveniently bites the dust in battle. That Ryan spares Rallis's life is supposed to represent some sort of dawning conscience in the hero, but he's still a one-dimensional misanthropic goon.

Brian Thompson (COBRA, LIONHEART) has previously played nemesis to such heavyweights as Sylvester Stallone and Jean-Claude Van Damme, displaying an easy attitude and humor that hinted of better things. Here he's got one extraordinary scene in which, keeping up the homosexual facade, he kisses bewildered villain Oliver Reed full on the lips, but otherwise this is no breakthrough role.

Its politically incorrect protagonist aside, HIRED TO KILL ultimately stands or falls by how it handles the central gimmick of an all-girl strike force, a situation tailor-made for crass exploitation T & A. Yes indeed, there's the inevitable music-video display of evening-gown and swimwear modelling, followed by a perfectly gratuitous poolside catfight. On balance, however, there's less cheesecake than there could have been. The women are capable actresses, believably unglamorous before their camouflage makeovers, and when the shooting starts they get as good as they give—although messy action sequences make it tough to tell who dies and who doesn't.

Despite exotic settings and generous stunts, production values lean to the shabby side. Street signs display fresh hand-lettering, and a subterranean cave has a soundstage-smooth floor. Codirector-writer-producer Nico Mastorakis is a vetern B-movie *auteur* whose films are a real mixed bag of good and sleazeball elements, and HIRED TO KILL makes no exception. *(Violence, profanity, nudity, sexual situations, adult situations.)*

p, Isabelle Mastorakis, Nico Mastorakis; d, Nico Mastorakis, Peter Rader; w, Nico Mastorakis, Kirk Ellis, Fred C. Perry, (from the story by Mastorakis); ph, Andreas Bellis, Michael Stringer; prod d, Michael Stringer

Action/Adventure **(PR: O MPAA: R)**

HOFFA ★★

140m Edward R. Pressman Film Corporation; Jersey Films; Fox; Isgro Productions ~ Fox c

Jack Nicholson *(James R. Hoffa)*, Danny De Vito *(Bobby Ciaro)*, Armand Assante *(Carol D'Allesandro)*, J.T. Walsh *(Fitzsimmons)*, John C. Reilly *(Pete Connelly)*, Frank Whaley *(Young Kid)*, Kevin Anderson *(Robert Kennedy)*, John P. Ryan *(Red Bennett)*, Robert Prosky *(Billy Flynn)*, Natalija Nogulich *(Jo Hoffa)*, Nicholas Pryor *(Hoffa's Attorney)*, Paul Guilfoyle *(Ted Harmon)*, Karen Young *(Young Woman at RTA)*, Cliff Gorman *(Solly Stein)*, Joanne Neer *(Soignee Woman)*, Joe V. Greco *(Loading Foreman)*, Jim Ochs *(Kreger Worker)*, Joe Quasarano *(Dock Worker)*, Don Brockett *(Police Captain)*, Nicholas Giordano *(Cop)*, Dale Young *(Father Doyle)*, Jennifer Nicholson *(Nurse Nun in White)*, Don Vargo *(Driver with Pistol)*, Anthony Cannata *(Organizer)*, Valentino Cimo *(Assailant #1)*, Willy Rizzo *(Scialla)*, Tom Finnegan *(Teamster President)*, Kirk Palmer Anderson *(Driver with Flat)*, Sam Nicotero *(Counterman at Laundry)*, John Malloy *(Counterman at Roadhouse)*, Louis Giambalvo *(RTA Representative)*, Robert Eurich *(Reporter #1)*, Robert Maffia *(Reporter #2)*, Gerry Becker *(Business Negotiator)*, Shirley Prestia *(Hoffa's Secretary)*, John

Hackett *(Bladesdale)*, Peter J. Reinemann *(Working Man)*, Joey Dal Santo *("Joey" Boy at RTA)*, Kevin Crowley *(Reporter)*, Tomasino Baratta *(D'Allesandro's Man)*, Angela Block *(Hoffa's Daughter)*, Anna Marie Knierim *(Teamster Widow)*, Staci Marie Marcum *(Woman in Cabin)*, Alton Bouchard *(Airplane Pilot)*, Dennis Tolkach *(Airplane Pilot)*, John Judd *(Senate Policeman)*, Jeffrey Howell *(Senate Reporter)*, Fred Scialla *(Castratore)*, Christopher Otto *(Young Reporter)*, Annette DePetris *(Newspaper Secretary)*, William Cameron *(State Trooper)*, Rudy E. Morrison *(Copa Thug)*, Joanne Deak *(Woman in Penthouse)*, Richard Schiff *(Government Attorney)*, Allison Robinson *(Ciaro's Attorney)*, Steve Witting *(Eliot Cookson)*, Kathy Hartsell *(Dancer with Cigarette)*, Philip Perlman *(Maitre d')*, Sean P. Bello *(Party Crasher)*, Robert Feist *(Bouncer)*, Peter Spellos *(Man in Crowd)*, Steven E. Goldsmith *(Bailiff)*, Marty Perlov *(Bartender)*, Tim Gamble *(Prosecutor)*, Thomas A. Van Tiem, Sr. *(Judge)*, Thomas D. Mahard *(Bartender)*, Gary Houston *(Government Agent in Bar)*, Dinah Lynch *(Barbara Hoffa)*, Jillian Alyse Cardillo *(Granddaughter)*, Jacqulyne Marie Cardillo *(Granddaughter)*, Chet Badalato *(Hoffa's Driver)*, David Regal *(Newsman)*, Paul M. White *(Young Driver)*, James "Ike" Eichling *(Prison Guard)*, Dean Wells *(1st Convict)*, Bill Dalzell, III *(2nd Convict)*, Samson Barkhordarian *(Official at Hall)*, Alex A. Kvassay *(Airplane Pilot)*, Larry John Meyers *(Newsman)*, Cha Cha Ciarcia *(D'ally's Financial Adviser)*, Sherri Mazie *(Reporter)*, Dave Shemo *(Young Reporter)*, David Calvin Berg *(Committee Chairman)*, David Sconduto *(Social Club Waiter)*

Despite Jack Nicholson's galvanizing portrayal, HOFFA is a cold, remote, neo-religious pageant featuring the controversial, belligerent labor leader as the working man's deity—a dangerous demagogue in a gray suit.

The story is told as an extended flashback while aging Hoffa flunky Bobby Ciaro (Danny De Vito) and recently pardoned Teamster leader James R. Hoffa (Nicholson) cool their heels at a run-down truckers' diner, awaiting the arrival of underworld figure Carol D'Allesandro (Armand Assante). The two plan to cut a deal with D'Allesandro to wrest control of the Teamsters' Union away from Hoffa's own chosen successor, Frank Fitzsimmons (J.T. Walsh). Hoffa's life is recalled and recreated from the viewpoint of the fictitious Ciaro: Hoffa sneaking from truck to truck in the wee hours of the morning to recruit truckers into the union; his shady dealings with the mob; a bitter strike organized by Hoffa that results in a riot and multiple deaths; Hoffa squaring off against Robert Kennedy (Kevin Anderson) in public hearings; Hoffa's incarceration and subsequent pardon by President Richard M. Nixon. While Ciaro waits inside the diner, he befriends a young trucker (Frank Whaley) who is apparently awed by him. To give the boy a kick, he permits him to deliver coffee to Hoffa, who's waiting outside the diner in his Lincoln Continental. But the kid turns out to be a plant and guns down both Hoffa and Ciaro. The two are dumped into the back of the Lincoln and the car is driven into the back of a truck that then disappears into the sunset.

HOFFA unravels through the skewed, glorifying gaze of Bobby Ciaro, casting the film in a sycophantic haze that no amount of David Mamet profanities or Jack Nicholson pyrotechnics can surmount. The film visualizes Hoffa in episodic tableaux that convey nothing about the labor leader's motivations, his emotions, his desires or his private life. According to the filmmakers, Hoffa is a walking myth playing out his destiny in front of newsmen, television cameras and Senate committees. While Bobby Ciaro should have been presented as a small, supportive Everyman—much like Karl Malden's Omar Bradley in PATTON—more screen time is spent on De Vito than his character warrants, further frustrating audience interest in Hoffa and propelling the labor leader into an untouchable historical realm.

This glacial attitude toward Hoffa carries over into De Vito's direction. Carried away by the possibilities of Panavision, De Vito creates perfectly composed images that, though frequently overflowing with human bustle, are far too studied. When a strikers' march turns into a brawl, De Vito removes himself from the scene, craning up into the sky, looking down on the heated confrontation like a giant sitting on his haunches observing the ants. De Vito's chilliness makes HOFFA into a posed museum piece, his scholarly cinematic technique so icy that he makes Stanley Kubrick look like Frank Borzage.

Nicholson's potentially great performance is sadly wasted here. The actor relies on James Cagney's earlier take on Huey Long in A LION IN THE STREETS, bringing a throat-cutting passion to Hoffa's fiery oratory and an attack dog's ferocity to his bitter feud with Robert Kennedy. But De Vito gives Nicholson a closer relationship with microphones than with any human characters, and his performance becomes correspondingly strident. An early, telling scene occurs as Hoffa and Ciaro ride to a strike site. Nicholson's trademark glint is replaced by a glassy stare as he waxes philosophical to Ciaro about the Teamsters' Union, saying that "the fucking local is a ship upon the sea."

In HOFFA, a storm is raging, the ship is sinking and all that remains above water is Nicholson's dead eyes.*(Violence, excessive profanity, nudity.)*

p, Edward R. Pressman, Caldecott Chubb, Danny DeVito; d, Danny De Vito; w, David Mamet; ph, Stephen H. Burum; ed, Lynzee Klingman, Ronald Roose; m, David Newman; prod d, Ida Random; art d, Gary Wissner; cos, Deborah L. Scott; makeup, Ve Neill, Greg Cannom, John Blake

AAN Cinematography: Stephen H. Burum; *AAN Makeup:* Ve Neill, Greg Cannom, and John Blake

Biography/Drama **(PR: C MPAA: R)**

HOME ALONE 2: LOST IN NEW YORK ★★½

113m Hughes Entertainment; Fox ~ Fox c

Macaulay Culkin *(Kevin McCallister)*, Joe Pesci *(Harry)*, Daniel Stern *(Marv)*, Catherine O'Hara *(Kate McCallister)*, John Heard *(Peter McCallister)*, Devin Ratray *(Buzz)*, Hillary Wolf *(Megan)*, Maureen Elisabeth Shay *(Linnie)*, Michael C. Maronna *(Jeff)*, Gerry Bamman *(Uncle Frank)*, Terrie Snell *(Aunt Leslie)*, Jedidiah Cohen *(Rod)*, Senta Moses *(Tracy)*, Daiana Campeanu *(Sondra)*, Kieran Culkin *(Fuller)*, Anna Slotky *(Brooke)*, Tim Curry *(Concierge)*, Brenda Fricker *(Pigeon Lady)*, Dana Ivey *(Desk Clerk)*, Rob Schneider *(Bellman)*, Leigh Zimmerman *(Fashion Model)*, Ralph Foody *(Gangster)*, Clare Hoak *(Gangster)*, Monica Devereux *(Hotel Operator)*, Bob Eubanks *(Ding-Dang-Dong Host)*, Rip Taylor *(1st Celeb)*, Jaye P. Morgan *(2nd Celeb)*, Jimmie Walker *(3rd Celeb)*, Patricia Devereux *(1st Contestant)*, Aimee Devereux *(2nd Contestant)*, A.M. Columbus *(1st Skycap O'Hare)*, Joe Liss *(2nd Skycap O'Hare)*, Teri McEvoy *(3rd Agent-New York Gate/O'Hare)*, Ally Sheedy *(Ticket Agent)*, Harry Hutchinson *(Ticket Taker)*, Clarke P. Devereux *(Ticket Taker)*, Sandra Macat *(Flight Attendant)*, Venessia Valentino *(Flight Attendant)*, Andre Lachaumette *(Man on Plane)*, Rick Shafer *(Peter Look Alike)*, Rod Sell *(Officer Bennett)*, Ron Canada *(Cop in Times Square)*, Cedric Young *(Cop in Central Park)*, William Dambra *(1st Arresting Cop in Central Park)*, Mark Morettini *(2nd Arresting Cop in Central Park)*, Fred Krause *(Cliff)*, James Cole *(Security Guard)*, Donald Trump *(Himself)*, Warren Rice *(Doorman)*, Thomas Civitano *(Plaza Marketing Director)*, Daniel Dassin *(Waiter)*, Donna Black *(Health Club Woman)*, Abdoulaye N'Gom

(Bead Vendor), Peter Pantaleo *(Airport Van Driver)*, Michael Hansen *(Airport Van Driver)*, Michael Goldfinger *(Limo Driver)*, Mario Todisco *(Cab Driver)*, Clarke Devereux *(Evidence Specialist)*, Anthony Cannata *(Sergeant in Toy Store)*, Eleanor Columbus *(Little Girl in Toy Store)*, Karen Giordano *(1st Streetwalker)*, Fran McGee *(2nd Streetwalker)*, Leonard Tepper *(Sleeping Man)*, Kevin Thomas *(Geeky Kid)*

Remember those violent films of the 1980s, in which a madman would torture and murder young women? Now that we're into the kinder, gentler 90s, HOME ALONE 2: LOST IN NEW YORK offers viewers a similar mentality, only sanitized for children: now a kid sets a man on fire next to a toilet full of kerosene, so that the man will humiliate himself as well as burn to a crisp. Welcome to the family movie of 1992.

In this blockbuster sequel to the hugely popular original, it's a year later, and Kevin McCallister (Macaulay Culkin) is still treated lousily by his Chicago family, making him once again wish they'd leave him alone. Sure enough, when the family heads to the airport for a vacation in Florida, they're in such a rush that they run too fast for Kevin, and he follows the wrong adult onto a plane bound for New York. Again, once he's realized his mistake, he happily adapts to the situation, touring the city and getting himself into a suite at the luxurious Plaza Hotel, despite the suspicions of an officious concierge (Tim Curry).

Meanwhile, Kevin's old nemeses, Harry and Marv (Joe Pesci and Daniel Stern), have escaped from jail and are roaming New York, looking to rob toy stores and get revenge on the resourceful tyke. As before, Kevin fends off the two with routines ranging from the aforementioned toilet attack on Marv to a staplegun in the face for Harry. He also develops a relationship with a homeless woman played by Brenda Fricker.

HOME ALONE 2 pales next to its predecessor. For all its demerits, the first film did an astounding job of encapsulating a child's rage toward the adult world, with Kevin's sadistic treatment of the crooks a seemingly fair return for the treatment he'd been getting from grown-ups in general. The second time around, everything seems forced. From the opening moments of the film we know Kevin will be left behind, so writer-producer John Hughes and director Chris Columbus play with us, making us think one thing will go wrong, and then letting it be another. But all the developments are weak: would airline attendants really let a child onto a plane without making sure of his destination?

After the clever way Kevin foiled the crooks before, using a video of a gangster film, he now does the same trick using a sequel to it. Even the parents' moment of realization (the most memorable scene of the first film, now probably the most famous jump-cut since BREATHLESS) disappoints. Most importantly, this time the film fails to make us believe that Kevin wants his family back the way he did in HOME ALONE. His life on the streets of New York seems almost idyllic, despite his problems with the two crooks.

It's morally that HOME ALONE 2 is the most disturbing. On the one hand, it's nice to see a movie that shows a kid on the streets of Manhattan, without having him instantly mugged or killed—the street people are weird but harmless. On the other hand, the kid turns around and wreaks violence beyond belief on his hapless attackers/victims. It will be fascinating to see how the generation of children that has made these films so successful matures. Will they be better adjusted, having vicariously expressed their aggression through Kevin's adventures? Or will they be the most sadistic generation ever, nostalgically heaving bricks at people's heads from the tops of buildings, humming "Somewhere in My Memory"? *(Violence.)*

p, John Hughes; d, Chris Columbus; w, John Hughes, (from his characters); ph, Julio Macat; ed, Raja Gosnell; m, John Williams; prod d, Sandy Veneziano; art d, Gary Lee; set d, Marvin March; cos, Jay Hurley

Comedy/Children's **(PR: C MPAA: PG)**

HOMEBOYS ★

91m JWP Production; DB Films ~ AIP Home Video c

David Garrison *(Murphy)*, Todd Bridges *(Johnny Davis)*, Ron Odriozola, Keo Michaels, Sigrid Salazar

True to the AIP studio tradition, the amateurish HOMEBOYS is an ultra-low-budget, teen-oriented genre film quickly produced to capitalize on contemporary trends.

Emilio and Hector Sanchez (Ron Odriozola and Keo Michaels) are brothers raised in an East LA barrio. Emilio becomes a college-educated cop, while homeboy Hector joins the neighborhood gang, the High Rollers. The "gang-bangers" become involved in a turf war with the rival Bloods and a drug-laced sting operation with an undercover cop. The older Emilio continually warns his brother about the dangers of gang life, but his moralistic lectures meet with angry rejection. Hector recruits their little brother Luis into the High Rollers. Meanwhile, Emilio falls in love with Vanessa (Sigrid Salazar), an anti-gang social crusader. He deepens his resolve to fight gang activity, despite being harangued by Officer Murphy (David Garrison), his racist partner.

Violence between the Black and Hispanic gangs escalates. After Bloods kill one of Hector's group in a drive-by shooting, the High Rollers retaliate, accidentally killing a young child. Emilio finds a black headband at the scene of the crime—evidence that Hector's gang was involved. Despite warnings from Murphy, the rookie cop chases down his brother and warns him that police are onto his crimes. Unrepentant, the other members of the gang, led by Ramon, murder the undercover policeman who had posed as their drug supplier. They then take Vanessa and Emilio hostage. But when Hector sees what they have done he turns against Ramon and helps the couple escape.

In a final act of revenge against the Sanchez brothers the remaining High Rollers abduct Luis. Police surround their house and a shootout takes place: Murphy is shot and wounded; Ramon shoots one gang member himself, cops kill another; Hector finally kills Ramon. Afterwards, just as Emilio convinces his brother to start his life over, gang turncoat Hector is killed in yet another vengeful drive-by shooting.

A weak imitation of films like John Singleton's BOYZ N THE HOOD, Dennis Hopper's COLORS and Joseph B. Vasquez's HANGIN' WITH THE HOMEBOYS, this AIP cheapie obviously seeks to capitalize on the success of the aforementioned fresh, gritty portayals of gang life, urban ghetto neighborhoods and racially charged conflicts with police. However, HOMEBOYS fails to convey any of the slice-of-life drama or sincere social engagement that its precursors created.

Not only does it fall short in terms of performance (clumsy acting, lifeless ersatz hip-hop music) and production values (home-movie sets, a cliche-ridden screenplay), this direct-to-video effort appropriates the look and talk of the "homeboy" genre in obviously exploitive ways. Stereotypical white racist cops, bloody drive-by shootings and gang "colors" are paraded for their own sake, in hopes that such hot-button issues might sell in the climate of the Rodney King beating. Pale moralizing about such acute social problems comes out of the character's mouths, but their insincerity only compounds the film's shamelessness. And, as if realizing this bad faith, violence and racial animus might not sell enough videos, plenty of gratuitous female nudity is thrown in to boot.

In a final act of schlockmeistery, HOMEBOYS promotes itself as starring Todd Bridges of "Different Strokes" fame. But Bridges appears in only one scene. His character, a kid from the projects who shunned crime for the straight life of an advertising executive, rings no truer than any other in this sham homeboy drama. *(Violence, profanity, nudity, sexual situations.)*

p, James A. Holt, Lindsay Norgard; d, Lindsay Norgard; w, Peter Foldy; ph, Kurt Brabbee; ed, Steve Rasch; m, John W. Scott; prod d, Mark Richardson

Drama/Action **(PR: O MPAA: NR)**

HOMICIDAL IMPULSE ★½
84m Concorde ~ LIVE Home Video c

Scott Valentine *(Tim Casey)*, Charles Napier *(Doogan)*, Vanessa Angel *(Deborah)*, Talia Balsam *(Emma)*, Mary Ellen Dunbar *(Paula)*, Michael Traeger *(Belcher)*, Brian Cousins *(Kent)*, Dominic Huffman *(Campbell)*

PRESUMED INNOCENT meets FATAL ATTRACTION with diminishing returns. Steamy crime melodramas can be entertaining trash when they boast well-rounded central characters who are flawed by their regrettable tendency to think with their genitals. In HOMICIDAL IMPULSE, stick figures scream at each other, while the director flubs his presentation of plot complications that come from left field and beyond.

Diligent Assistant DA Tim Casey (Scott Valentine) gets passed over for promotion because he has obviously failed Assertiveness 101. Somehow, his macho boss, DA Doogan (Charles Napier), can't see that Casey has a little killer instinct in his soul. Although claiming to be Doogan's niece, new kid in the office Deborah (Vanessa Angel) spots Tim's career potential and champions him, although she's really Doogan's mistress. Thanks to her machinations, Tim's stock rises along with his self-confidence, and he becomes a puppet for Deborah's hidden agenda—her own career advancement.

Although he drops his main squeeze Emma (Talia Balsam), Tim's not quite ready to murder Doogan to keep Vanessa happy. Lying about incest from "Uncle Doogan," Deborah gets Tim all riled up and drugs him into believing he's murdered Doogan (a homicide Debbie's already committed). Convincing Tim to dispose of Doogan for her, the unbalanced Deborah reveals her true colors and threatens to discredit him if he doesn't continue to play ball with her. She also manages to remove her competition for Tim's affections.

While Deborah tries to point the finger of suspicion, resourceful Tim has already planted body parts in her pad. Deftly pinning the murders of Doogan and Emma on Deborah before he blows her away, not only has Tim gotten off the hook from two crimes he didn't commit, but he is also the natural candidate to replace Doogan as DA.

That double-whammy surprise ending is a nifty tie-up for an exceedingly sloppy thriller. Since Deborah seems to have the words "femme fatale" stamped on her forehead, it's hard to feel sympathy for the easily duped assistant DA. Required to jump through large loopholes in David Tausik's screenplay, Deborah is poorly written and unpersuasively limned by Vanessa Angel. Although their sex scenes have some sizzle, Valentine (MY DEMON LOVER, WRITE TO KILL) really only shines as an actor when he finally turns the tables on his manipulative lover.

All the actors are abandoned by a meretricious screenplay that requires the audience to suspend disbelief until they must rebel at how insulting to their intelligence the film is. Shabby to begin with, HOMICIDAL IMPULSE needlessly crosses over to the realm of horror with gratuitous scenes of Valentine dismembering and melting down his late boss. At times, we seem to be watching a training film produced by John Wayne Gacy.

Part sex melodrama, part gore movie, and all rip-off, HOMICIDAL IMPULSE is only worthwhile as a cinematic primer on the qualities necessary to succeed in politics. *(Extreme violence, sexual situations.)*

p, Mike Elliott; d, David Tausik; w, David Tausik

Erotic/Thriller **(PR: O MPAA: R)**

HONEY, I BLEW UP THE KID ★★
89m Walt Disney Productions; Touchwood Pacific Parters I ~ BV c

Rick Moranis *(Wayne Szalinski)*, Marcia Strassman *(Diane Szalinski)*, Robert Oliveri *(Nick Szalinski)*, Daniel Shalikar *(Adam Szalinski)*, Joshua Shalikar *(Adam Szalinski)*, Lloyd Bridges *(Clifford Sterling)*, John Shea *(Hendrickson)*, Keri Russell *(Mandy)*, Ron Canada *(Marshall Brooks)*, Amy O'Neill *(Amy Szalinski)*, Michael Milhoan *(Captain Ed Myerson)*, Gregory Sierra *(Terence Wheeler)*, Leslie Neale *(Constance Winters)*, Julia Sweeney *(Nosey Neighbor)*, Linda Carlson *(Nosey Neighbor)*, Lisa Mende *(Lab Technician)*, John Paragon *(Lab Technician)*, Ken Tobey *(Smitty)*, Bill Moseley *(Federal Marshall)*, Ed Feldman *(Las Vegas Couple)*, Suzanne Kent *(Las Vegas Couple)*, Alex Daniels *(Uncle Yanosh)*, Robert Jaffe *(Motorcycle Officer)*, Ron Lawrence *(Motorcycle Officer)*, John Hora *(Helicopter Observer)*, Mary Ellen Moore *(Police Woman)*, Randy Swallow *(Vegas Reporter)*, Pamela Cederquist *(Vegas Reporter)*, James M. Lauten *(Vegas Reporter)*, Shannon M. Steger *(Nevada Militia)*, Minori Goto *(Japanese Tourist)*, Mamoru Kanai *(Japanese Tourist)*, Gregory McCurdy *(Police Officer)*, David Scates *(Rock Fan in Crowd)*, Marion Palmer *(Hard Rock Reporter)*, Kathy Pastor *(Hard Rock Hostess)*, Bill Loska *(Highway Patrol Officer)*, Sammy *(Quark–the Dog)*

The whole gang is back for HONEY, I BLEW UP THE KID, the expected sequel to Disney's surprise 1989 hit, but somehow the magic has fled—if there ever was any in the first place.

Rick Moranis returns as Wayne Szalinski, the crackpot inventor who shrunk his family in HONEY, I SHRUNK THE KIDS. Wayne is now installed in a comfortable Las Vegas suburb and is working for a conglomerate led by snooty superbrain Hendrickson (John Shea). The conglomerate has bought his size-alteration device and has a cadre of top scientists poring over it to try and figure out how it works. They can't get the machine to function, and won't listen when Wayne thinks he has an answer. Undeterred, Wayne sneaks into the lab over the weekend to test his theory, bringing along son Nick (Robert Oliveri) and baby Adam (Daniel and Joshua Shalikar). Wayne's attempt, of course, works all too well.

Adam gets in the way of the ray, which alters his body chemistry so that whenever he's near an electrical field he grows in size. Getting near a microwave oven causes him to sprout to seven feet in height. An attempt to calm him down in front of the television causes him to double that size. Then Hendrickson gets into the act by baby-napping Adam and attempting to transport him back to the lab in a truck past high-tension lines that cause him to shoot to 112 feet. Completely beyond anyone's control, Adam toddles off towards the bright lights of the Vegas strip.

Wayne chases Adam with his old prototype ray gun, hoping to get him to stand still long enough to zap him back to normal size. It's only at the end, however, that he hits on the idea of zapping Mom (Marcia Strassman) to the approximate size of the Statue of Liberty, allowing her to subdue the overgrown infant. Everyone gets zapped back to normal, except for Nick and his new girlfriend, Mandy (Keri Russell), who have been in Adam's pocket all along.

Despite the impressive special effects, HONEY, I BLEW UP THE KID offers few surprises. The visual gag of a giant-sized infant is the only real joke the film has and it wears thin in a hurry. The plot is perfunctory and simple, presumably to cater to the attention span of a pint-sized audience. The slapstick is labored and the film as a whole is surprisingly emotionless.

The cast is capable from the top down, including nice cameos by familiar faces like Lloyd Bridges, Gregory Sierra and "Creature Features" veteran Ken Tobey (THE THING). But there's little for them to do besides react to the special effects. There's little tension and few real laughs. What there *is* plenty of is shrewd product placement. Adam's clothes, which grow along with him, are dotted with familiar trademarks that are in your face through most of the film. Las Vegas is so big, bright and shiny, you'd barely believe that anyone actually gambles there.

Director Randal Kleiser (GREASE) does what he can to inject life and wit into the proceedings. While searching for his old ray gun in a corporate warehouse, Wayne is irritated to come across instead the "Rosebud" sled from CITIZEN KANE. But such moments are few and far between. Too much of the time, HONEY, I BLEW UP THE KID plays like a Joe Dante (GREMLINS) film without Dante's anarchic sensibility and, especially, without his sharp, playful comic intelligence.

p, Dawn Steel, Edward S. Feldman; d, Randal Kleiser; w, Thom Eberhardt, Peter Elbling, Garry Goodrow, (from his story based on the characters created by Stuart Gordon, Brian Yuzna and Ed Naha); ph, John Hora; ed, Michael A. Stevenson, Harry Hitner; m, Bruce Broughton; prod d, Leslie Dilley; art d, Ed Verreaux; set d, Dorree Cooper; cos, Tom Bronson

Comedy/Children's (PR: A MPAA: PG)

HONEYMOON IN VEGAS ★★★½

95m Castle Rock Entertainment; Lobell/Bergman Productions~ Columbia c

James Caan *(Tommy Korman)*, Nicolas Cage *(Detective Jack Singer)*, Sarah Jessica Parker *(Betsy/Donna)*, Pat Morita *(Mahi)*, Johnny Williams *(Johnny Sandwich)*, John Capodice *(Sally Molars)*, Robert Costanzo *(Sidney Tomashefsky)*, Anne Bancroft *(Bea Singer)*, Peter Boyle *(Chief Orman)*, Burton Gilliam *(Roy)*, Brent Hinkley *(Vern)*, Dean Hallo *(Lyle)*, Seymour Cassel *(Tony Cataracts)*, Jerry Tarkanian *(Sid Feder)*, Keone Young *(Eddie Wong)*, Danny Kamekona *(Niko)*, John McMahon *(Chris)*, Lisa Poggi *(Laura)*, Ben Stein *(Walter)*, Teddy Bergman *(David)*, Tiiu Leek *(Anchorwoman)*, Angela Pietropinto *(School Parent)*, Anna Lobell *(Airport Passenger)*, Joanna Lipari *(JFK Agent)*, Josh Nelson *(Guy in Little Italy)*, Johnny Cha Cha *(Cha Cha)*, Captain Haggerty *(Businessman)*, Lonnie Schuyler *(Pool Guy)*, Ernie Shavers *(Himself)*, Gwen Greenhalgh *(Cigarette Girl)*, Connie Kissinger *(Ticket Agent–Kauai)*, Jay Richardson *(Ticket Agent–San Jose)*, Tony Shalhoub *(Buddy Walker)*, Brad Blumenthal *(Waiter)*, J.J. Bostick *(Valet)*, David Buccella *(Bellhop)*, Cathy Celario *(Croupier)*, Esmond Chung *(Cop)*, Ray Favaro *(Clerk)*, Koko Kanealii *(2nd Cop)*, Sasha Semenoff *(2nd Waiter)*, Sly Smith *(Hotel Guard)*, John Patrick *(Poker Instructor)*, Jim Hamilton *(Minister)*, Bruno Hernandez *(Little Elvis)*, Clearance Giddens *(Black Elvis)*, Robert Kim *(Oriental Elvis)*, Eddie Bear, Gary Benson, George Chung, Elvis, Jr., David Jenner, E.P. King, Johnny Lawson, Roddy Ragsdale, Rick Marino *(Elvis Impersonators)*

Still working his way through the Coppola repertory company, writer-director Andrew Bergman follows up his Brando coup, THE FRESHMAN, with HONEYMOON IN VEGAS, an edgy romantic comedy featuring James Caan as a gambler without a heart of gold.

Private detective Jack Singer (Nicolas Cage, Coppola's nephew and star of RUMBLE FISH and PEGGY SUE GOT MARRIED) is trying hard to defy his mother's deathbed decree that he never marry. But still he finds he can't cross that final threshold, even though the lady in his life, Betsy (Sarah Jessica Parker), is beginning to lose patience with her longtime beau's reluctance. When she gives him an ultimatum, Jack proposes that they immediately fly to Las Vegas and tie the knot. What stops them once they get there is gambler Tommy Korman (Caan), who recognizes in the pneumatic Betsy the spitting image of his own late wife.

Determined to separate Jack and Betsy, Tommy invites the young man to a high-stakes "hotel courtesy" poker game. (One of the other players, Sid Feder, is played by no less than famed UNLV basketball coach Jerry Tarkanian, chewing on a cocktail napkin as the betting gets tense.) Still stalling on his marriage proposal, Jack accepts and soon finds himself indebted to the veteran gambler to the tune of $65,000. Jack is less than thrilled by the deal Korman then proposes—that the gambler be allowed to spend the weekend with Betsy, in exchange for cancelling out Jack's debt. Betsy is even less taken with the idea, but is so fed up with Jack by this point that she agrees, as much out of spite as anything else.

What neither has reckoned on is that Korman intends to spend his weekend with Betsy not in Vegas, where Jack can at least keep an eye on them, but in Hawaii. Jack follows the couple there, but has virtually no idea where to look for them. Meanwhile, Betsy is prodded into accepting Korman's marriage proposal, partly by the fact that she's unable to reach Jack back at their hotel. Korman and Betsy return to Vegas to tie the knot, but Betsy develops cold feet; this brings out the gambler's true colors, as he uses bribes, and finally threats, to try and force her compliance. Meanwhile, Jack makes a last-minute, THE GRADUATE-style intervention, hitching a plane ride to the city with a parachute group called "The Flying Elvises" and jumping from the sky to save the day.

Like his earlier THE FRESHMAN, Bergman's HONEYMOON IN VEGAS is a shaggy-dog tale about a neurotic, basically amiable guy who finds his mettle tested under strange circumstances. Bergman is less concerned with plot than with simply putting his characters into bizarre, almost surrealistic situations to see how they'll squirm their way out. The overall structure may be shaky but, scene-by-scene, HONEYMOON IN VEGAS is one of the most charmingly funny films of the year, full of hilarious throwaway moments and giddy visual conceits typified by the Flying Elvises.

Bergman elicits first-rate performances, from Caan's cool, canny star turn, to Cage's marvelously controlled rising hysteria, to Parker's sensible but confused would-be bride. As with THE FRESHMAN, the cameos alone are worth the price of admission; Peter Boyle, in particular, almost steals the movie as a native Hawaiian "king" with a passion for show tunes. HONEYMOON IN VEGAS adds up to a thoroughly enjoyable outing, as smart as it is funny, from one of the last of the true comic stylists. *(Profanity, adult situations.)*

p, Mike Lobell; d, Andrew Bergman; w, Andrew Bergman; ph, William A. Fraker; ed, Barry Malkin; m, David Newman; prod d, William A. Elliott; art d, John Warnke; set d, Linda DeScenna; cos, Julie Weiss

Romance/Comedy (PR: C MPAA: PG-13)

HOT CHOCOLATE ★★

(France) 93m Chrysalide Films; Canal Plus ~ LIVE Home Video c

Bo Derek *(B.J. Cassidy)*, Robert Hays *(Eric Ferrier)*, Francois Marthouret *(Hubert)*, Howard Hesseman *(Mr. Cassidy)*, Patricia Millardet *(Lucretia)*, Vincent Cassell *(Dede)*, Hella Petri *(La Marquise Pipo)*, David Martin *(Gaston)*, Jean-Yves Gauthier *(Jean-Pierre)*, Amidou *(Beauregard)*

Inevitably perhaps, most contemporary co-productions lack the distinctive flavor of one particular country of origin. When you view a film and start to wonder how much financing came from each nation involved, something's amiss. As a comedy, HOT CHOCOLATE is neither French champagne nor domestic beer, but somehow the cast enlivens the material often enough that the film doesn't seem like a joke made meaningless after having been retold by too many UN delegates.

Although his chocolate factory has been the family business for centuries, Hubert (Francois Marthouret) yearns for ready cash. Loyal chauffeur and business advisor Eric Ferrier (Robert Hays) begs him to reconsider liquidating, while Hubert's ex-wife, Lucretia (Patricia Millardet), threatens to monkey wrench any prospective deals by constantly endeavoring to revive their marriage. On the other side of the Atlantic, Texas heiress B.J. Cassidy (Bo Derek) cultivates her sweet tooth for acquisitions by offering to add the unprofitable chocolate business to her portfolio. Mistakenly expecting a refugee from TV's "Dallas," Eric doesn't realize that B.J. is the prospective buyer. The two rendezvous at several scenic locations, but B.J. also doesn't fathom the full extent of his ties to Hubert.

Meanwhile, Hubert is being vamped by Lucretia and the local workers have united in protest against what they fear is the imminent shutdown of the chocolate factory. Charming the suspicious rank and file, B.J. doesn't just propose a takeover, she offers a lucrative partnership with a million dollar bonus for Hubert. While Eric remains skeptical of B.J.'s intent and infatuated with her beauty, Hubert accepts the deal only to end up trapped in an elevator while two punks make off with the bonus. After B.J. lassos the desperadoes, Eric can no longer suppress his feelings for her. Serendipitously, the villagers retain their beloved place of employment, Eric captures B.J.'s heart, and Hubert gets lots of money and a second chance with the persistent Lucretia.

Thanks to the light touch of farceurs like Hays and Marthouret, HOT CHOCOLATE elicits more affection from its audience than its screenplay would ordinarily merit. Hampered by an all-purpose muzak score and a hoary mistaken-identity plot that only Fred and Ginger could have transcended, HOT CHOCOLATE still leaves a sweet aftertaste.

Perfectly cast for once, Derek (10, BOLERO) responds to Hays's comedic aplomb and, of course, looks radiant enough to make any man stumble all over himself. The fairy tale settings are seductive; the plot complications whiz by painlessly. If there is nothing distinctive about the film and if the mesh of international players never achieves a satisfying ensemble, several players stand out including the flamboyant Millardet. In addition, the scenes of rioting peasants are hilarious and reach a level of lunacy that this romantic farce usually finds outside its grasp.

Sweet but inconsequential, HOT CHOCOLATE proves that you can whip up a tasty confection even with some missing ingedients (like assured direction, captivating musical scoring). While this isn't the yummiest romantic comedy available for consumption, Hays and company make it much more than just another stale farce. *(Mild violence, some adult situations.)*

p, Monique Annaud; d, Josee Dayan; w, Ginny Cerrella, Maryedith Burrell; ph, Jean-Pierre Aliphat; ed, Michele Robert-Lauliac; prod d, Richard Cahours De Virgile; cos, Annie Quesnel-Boursaus

Romance/Comedy **(PR: C MPAA: PG-13)**

HOURS AND TIMES, THE ★★★

60m Antarctic Pictures ~ Good Machine bw

David Angus *(Brian Epstein)*, Ian Hart *(John Lennon)*, Stephanie Pack *(Marianne)*, Robin McDonald *(Quinones)*, Sergio Moreno *(Miguel)*, Unity Grimwood *(Mother)*

Its subject matter is limiting and its austere technique may leave most viewers cold; nonetheless THE HOURS AND TIMES ranks as one of the notables of 1992.

Armed with a paltry budget, b&w film stock, antiquated equipment, dedicated personnel and plane tickets for Spain, independent LA filmmaker Christopher Munch audaciously tackled one of the most sensational bits of gossip in rock 'n' roll history, that the great John Lennon had a homosexual love affair with Beatles manager Brian Epstein in the early 1960s. Such tabloid fodder often results in headline-grabbing quickies like "John and Yoko: A Love Story," 1985's widely scorned network TV movie. Munch's approach, however, represents the opposite extreme. THE HOURS AND TIMES is a compact speculative playlet that scales its legendary figures down to life-size via minute, almost mundane neorealism. Using not a moment more of screen time than necessary, this featurette covers a brief 1963 vacation in Barcelona that Lennon is known to have taken with Epstein.

It is the dawn of Beatlemania, just before success rockets the lads from Liverpool into pop-culture demigods. Brian Epstein (David Angus), elegant and cultured, recognizes a rough genius in the streetwise young Lennon—plus a powerful homoerotic allure. The manager wants to expose the musician to the ambiance and architecture of Spain, as well as define the terms of their relationship. John Lennon (Ian Hart) is married and newly a father, and clearly uncomfortable with both duties. He knows of Brian's attraction and mischieviously baits the other man by having a one-night fling with an obliging stewardess. Epstein tries to relieve his overwhelming loneliness with a Spanish nobleman and a bellboy, but he really wants John. The film's one onscreen love scene is unflinching but not exceptionally graphic: John allows Brian to join him in the hotel bathtub, but after some frantic kissing, the Beatle backs out. "So that which never was is now ended," concludes Brian, sadly but without rancor. The two finish up their holiday on an amicable but rather inconclusive note.

While producer-director-writer-cinematographer Christopher Munch is American, both main actors are British. David Angus is a classically trained thespian and longtime participant in London theater and television. Ian Hart had no need to fabricate a Liverpool accent; a native of that city, he has done much acting on stage and on TV. Both do fine jobs, though it's frankly difficult to get a sense of Lennon and Epstein from the thin slices of their lives shown here.

Likewise, THE HOURS AND TIMES as a whole seems overspecialized and a bit arcane, making no attempt to pull in the uninformed audience with spoonfed history or heavy-handed nostalgia. The viewers are expected to have done their homework: Brian makes John promise that they'll take another such trip together in ten years, and one must already know that it was not to be. As the Beatles rose up the charts Brian Epstein became estranged from them professionally and personally, dying of a drug overdose—a possible suicide—in 1967.

Cynics might propose that had THE HOURS AND TIMES enjoyed major studio backing, it might have been a slick piece of razzamatazz like the giddy but shallow Jerry Lee Lewis biopic GREAT BALLS OF FIRE. But the film shows more discipline than that, its tight scope and severity no mere accident. Munch, whose previous efforts include two unreleased features, modeled his monochrome photography after the Beatle's own A HARD DAY'S NIGHT, and probably wouldn't have included any Lennon/McCartney songs—even if the budget had permitted their use.

THE HOURS AND TIMES won a Special Jury Prize for Artistic Excellence at the 1992 Sundance Film Festival and the prestigious Wolfgang Staudte Prize at that year's Berlin Film Festival. The subsequent New York City opening took place with practically no advertising but gained enough publicity and positive critical comment to result in bookings nationwide at festivals and specialty houses. *(Nudity, adult situations, sexual situations, profanity.)*

p, Christopher Munch; d, Christopher Munch; w, Christopher Munch; ph, Christopher Munch; ed, Christopher Munch

Drama **(PR: C MPAA: NR)**

HOUSE IV ★★½

94m International Artists; Cunningham Productions ~ New Line Home Video c

Terri Treas *(Kelly Cobb)*, William Katt *(Roger Cobb)*, Scott Burkholder *(Burke)*, Melissa Clayton *(Laurel Cobb)*, Denny Dillon *(Verna Clump)*, Dabbs Greer *(Dad)*, Ned Romero *(Ezra)*, Ned Bellamy *(Lee)*, John Santucci *(Charles)*, Mark Gash *(Grosso)*, Kane Hodder *(Talking Pizza)*

The arrival of HOUSE IV no doubt caused confusion among genre fans who wondered what happened to HOUSE III. The former was retitled THE HORROR SHOW for domestic release, and to avoid confusion between the US and overseas markets, the latter was titled HOUSE IV. All clear?

In any case, this entry, unlike the two previous unrelated follow-ups, directly continues the story of the original HOUSE. William Katt returns as haunted-homeowner Roger Cobb, who has not aged appreciably even though he has a new wife, Kelly (Terri Treas), with whom he has a twelve-year-old daughter, Laurel (Melissa Clayton). He's not around for very long, as he and his family get into a bad car accident while visiting their summer house. Laurel winds up confined to a wheelchair after the crash, while Roger is so badly burned that Kelly forces herself to have his life-support turned off. She and Laurel then move back into the summer house, which she sets about renovating. Soon, however, Kelly is plagued by terrifying supernatural apparitions and visions of Roger's death in the hospital. She's also being hounded by Roger's ne'er-do-well brother Burke (Scott Burkholder), who seems uncommonly anxious to get his hands on the house; he's in cahoots with a grotesque little man called Mr. Grosso (Mark Gash), who wants the land the house sits on for his toxic waste-disposing needs.

After the ghostly visions (including one which almost causes Kelly to stab Laurel to death in her sleep) become too much for her to stand, Kelly visits a local Indian shaman, who reveals that the house is indeed built over sacred ground. Yet the land is the site of positive energy, a healing spring that's bubbled up through the floorboards in the basement. Soon Kelly is once again visited by spirits—but this time, they are the specters of two of Grosso's thugs, whom Kelly follows to the top of a nearby hill. There she witnesses a replay of the car accident that crippled Laurel and killed Roger, and which was actually caused by a rifle shot from one of the goons.

It's not long before the gunmen make a return visit to the house for real, but the spirit, which Kelly now realizes is that of Roger, trying to frighten her away from the house and out of danger, causes the thugs to shoot each other. As Burke arrives to claim the house himself, the spring in the basement roils over and finally bursts through the house like a geyser; as Kelly drags Laurel to safety, its healing waters fall upon the girl's legs and restore her ability to walk. Burke manages to escape as well, but the spirit has one final trick in store and leads him into the arms of the law.

Avoiding the lame silliness of HOUSE II and the gruesome literalness of THE HORROR SHOW/HOUSE III, this new installment manages to capture some of the balance between scares and humor that made the original HOUSE entertaining. It may not be quite believable that the combination of the ghostly attacks and Burke's increasingly threatening visits doesn't drive heroine Kelly away from the titular dwelling, but it is nice to see a genre film in which the heroine braves her terrors alone and doesn't depend on a male savior.

Director Lewis Abernathy and screenwriters Geof Miller (who penned DEEPSTAR SIX with Abernathy) and Deirdre Higgins build nicely on the mystery as to what's behind the hauntings: if it's Katt's ghost, why is he malevolent? The ultimate explanation, while not entirely plausible in context, pleasingly combines the supernatural with the psychological, and some of the hauntings are effectively scary (like the scene where Kelly almost stabs Laurel) and funny (Kane Hodder, famous among horror fans for playing Jason in the last two FRIDAY THE 13TH films, turns up as the face in a talking pizza).

There are a few logical loopholes allowed to slip through in the interest of the drama; the potential of the magic spring to heal the crippled Laurel quickly becomes apparent to the audience, but the movie saves it for the emotional climax. And although the balance of horror and comedy is pretty consistent inside the dwelling, HOUSE IV often becomes really loopy when it ventures outside. A particular case in point is the scenes involving Mr. Grosso and his goons, which look like they were lifted from a Warner Bros. cartoon. The thugs act like the ones who used to threaten Bugs Bunny, and the lead villain (who likes to listen to Mozart's "Concerto de Grosso") disguises his nefarious activities by having "NON-" painted onto barrels labeled "TOXIC WASTE." There's also a bit based on Grosso's health problems that's one of the most disgusting things seen in recent movies.

While sometimes fun, this material doesn't jibe at all with the rest of the film, and some of the screenplay's events strain credibility even given the supernatural elements. But HOUSE IV has enough good stuff in it to elevate it above many recent sequels and make it worth a look. *(Violence, adult situations, profanity.)*

p, Sean S. Cunningham; d, Lewis Abernathy; w, Geof Miller, Deirdre Higgins, (from the story by Miller, Higgins, Jim Wynorski and R.J. Robertson); ph, Jim Mathers; ed, Seth Gavin; m, Harry Manfredini; prod d, Milo Needles; set d, Ildiko Toth; cos, Mona May

Horror/Fantasy/Comedy **(PR: O MPAA: R)**

HOUSE OF USHER, THE ★

90m 21st Century Productions; Breton Film Productions ~ RCA/Columbia Pictures Home Video c

Oliver Reed *(Roderick Usher)*, Donald Pleasence *(Clive Usher)*, Romy Windsor *(Molly McNulty)*, Rufus Swart *(Ryan Usher)*, Norman Coombes *(Mr. Derrick)*, Anne Stradi *(Mrs. Derrick)*, Carole Farquhar *(Gwen)*, Philip Godewa *(Dr. Bailey)*

Edgar Allen Poe's tales of "mystery and imagination" inspired a memorable cycle of low-budget horror films in the 1960s, specifically the Roger Corman adaptations—including HOUSE OF USHER and MASQUE OF THE RED DEATH—that have come to be regarded as classics of the genre. The early 90s have seen another onslaught of Poe titles, with recent versions of THE PIT AND THE PENDULUM, MORELLA, THE PREMATURE BURIAL, THE BLACK CAT and even a second, less fortunate Corman run-in with MASQUE OF THE RED DEATH. In this field of undistinguished entries, the 1992 video release THE HOUSE OF USHER is especially disposable.

Set in the present day despite period costumes, it follows the perils of LA hairstylist Molly McNulty (Romy Windsor), when her fiancee, handsome young heir Ryan Usher (Rufus Swart), gets invited to visit the ancestral Usher estate in England. Some phantoms in the road cause Ryan to crash the car, and the helpless Molly is carried into the cardboard-and-papier mache Usher mansion as a prisoner in the clutches of obsessed aristocrat Roderick Usher (Oliver Reed). He tells her Ryan was killed in the accident and that he, Roderick, must now impregnate Molly to continue the accursed Usher bloodline. Later it transpires that Ryan was not killed, but purposely entombed alive in the family crypt.

Ryan's crazy father, Clive (Donald Pleasence), a frizzy-haired goof with a dinky hobbyist drill attached to one hand, subsequently escapes from his upstairs cell and goes on a psycho driller-killer rampage, as the "ancient" mansion crumbles around the terrified Molly. The sadistic butler, Mr. Derrick (Norman Coombes), carries a large fish around at odd moments and castrates the family doctor with a hungry rat. His wife (Anne Stradi), a gaunt Billie Whitelaw type, utters the movie's best line to Molly: "I know you've got a lot on your mind, but while you're here—could you do something with my hair." None of it makes very much sense, even less of it is scary, and the ending reveals it has all been a daydream. Quoth the viewer: "Nevermore!"

International Z-movie producer Harry Alan Towers previously purloined Poe's good name for a fistful of potboilers, including yet another MASQUE OF THE RED DEATH. Like its companions, THE HOUSE OF USHER was filmed cheaply in South Africa with a few big-name actors involved. Here it's imposing Oliver Reed, game for the role but totally miscast as the creepy Roderick Usher, a hypersensitive aesthete who can't tolerate strong scents, bright light or certain colors. Reed's just too robust for such a neurasthenic character, undercutting the concept of a mental and genetic defective bent on perpetuating his justly extinct clan in the name of aristocracy.

Pleasence is at least in his element as a twitchy lunatic, but the part slips into embarrassment as he literally dances through the corridors with his dimestore power tool buzzing for victims. Repeated, painful closeups of the little drill bit poking through the walls emphasize that this HOUSE OF USHER is only chintzy drywall and plaster, painted and stippled to resemble stone. Though some decor is eye-catching, carnival spookhouses have better production values. In fact, the most impressive acting is pert Romy Windsor's pretense that a styrofoam tomb lid is really heavy granite as she strains to rescue Ryan.

From such low-budget orgins did Roger Corman once weave respectable gothic horror, and sometimes diverting camp humor. But New Zealand-born director Alan Birkinshaw shows little flair either way, and has a habit of holding shots for a few seconds longer than necessary to milk the few gore scenes childishly for all they're worth. The sexual stuff is also very mild, despite a videocassete-box promise of eroticism. This THE HOUSE OF USHER isn't the worst thing that ever happened to Poe onscreen, but it's close enough. *(Violence, sexual situations, adult situations, profanity)*

p, Alan Harry Towers; d, Alan Birkinshaw; w, Michael J. Murray, (from the story *The Fall of the House of Usher* by Edgar Allen Poe); ph, Jossi Wein; ed, Michael J. Duthie; m, George A. Clinton, Gary Chang; prod d, Leonardo Coen Cagli; art d, Leith Ridney; cos, Dianna Cilliers

Horror **(PR: O MPAA: R)**

HOUSE ON TOMBSTONE HILL, THE

95m Troma Inc. ~ AIP Home Video c

Mark Zobian *(Ron)*, Victor Verhaeghe *(Bob)*, Sarah Newhouse *(Jamie)*, Doug Gibson *(Mark/Old Lady)*, John Cerna *(Steve)*, Naomi Kooker, Eugene Sautner

Even the tombstone turns in an unconvincing performance in THE HOUSE ON TOMBSTONE HILL, a wretched chiller that wastes little time on plot. No sooner does its coed cast of annoying young renovators set foot in the haunted Leatherby mansion than the slaughter begins.

Sealed in, they're stalked by a withered old lady (played pointlessly in drag by Doug Gibson, the actor who also plays her first victim, Mark), feeble in appearance but superhuman in strength. The kids she hacks to death rise again as cruel ghouls who try to kill their former buddies, and no real explanation for all this is offered apart from an old news item about an unsolved stabbing and suicide. The only way to stop the undead is to bash their skulls in, but sole survivor Ron (Mark Zobian) neglects one corpse and gets wasted in the grim "surprise" ending that will be no surprise to splatter-savvy viewers who will correctly see the whole thing as a poor rip-off of Sam Raimi's far superior THE EVIL DEAD.

Among THE HOUSE ON TOMBSTONE HILL's many failings is the unskilled cast's utter inability to register fear. Opportunities at humor, meanwhile, are seldom exploited ("I hate this house!" complains punk Bob [Victor Verhaeghe] as a jagged window chews him in half). Considering the dire quality of the acting, the fact that most of the picture is dialogue-free constitutes a small mercy. The real star is the makeup work (supervised by Ed French) emphasizing facial gashes that make most of the characters look like road maps, but the onscreen gore is accompanied by an overinsistent sucking noise that sounds like a straw at the bottom of a soda bottle. At least the transsexual crone getup is credible.

Made in New York State, this movie bears a copyright title of "The Dead Come Home" and date of 1988. It mouldered in obscurity until its 1992 videocassette release. *((Excessive violence, profanity.)*

p, Melisse Lewis, James Riffel; d, J. Riffel; w, J. Riffel; ed, Valerie Schwartz; m, Remote Control Music; art d, Janice Irwin

Horror **(PR: O MPAA: NR)**

HOUSESITTER ★★★

100m Imagine Films Entertainment ~ Universal c

Steve Martin *(Newton Davis)*, Goldie Hawn *(Gwen)*, Dana Delany *(Becky)*, Julie Harris *(Edna Davis)*, Donald Moffat *(George Davis)*, Peter MacNicol *(Marty)*, Richard B. Shull *(Ralph)*, Laurel Cronin *(Mary)*, Ray Cooper *(Moseby)*, Christopher Durang *(Reverend Lipton)*, Heywood Hale Broun *(Travis)*, Cherry Jones *(Patty)*, Vasek Simek *(Karol)*, Suzanne Whang *(Moseby's Secretary)*, Mary Klug *(Lorraine)*, Alice Duffy *(Hazel)*, Ken Cheeseman *(Harv)*, Tony V. *(Bus Driver)*, Ricardo Pitts-Wiley *(Bus*

Driver), Belle McDonald *(Aunt Betty)*, Bill McDonald *(Uncel Ray)*, Kevin O'Brien *(Caterer Truck Driver)*, Maggie Steig, Molly D. Gerard, David Hannegan, Edward Mason, Grenville Cuyler *(Party Guests)*, Rose-Ann San Martino *(Shopkeeper)*, Hazel Gardner *(Mother with Stroller)*, Phyllis Jubett Gould *(Dobb's Mill Pedestrian)*, George Michael Jones *(Restaurant Guest)*, Moira J. McCarthy *(Restaurant Guest)*, Michael Nurse *(Dedication Ceremony Speaker)*, Howe F. Perrigo *(Bus Person)*, Patricia Madden *(China Shop Proprietor)*

Steve Martin and Goldie Hawn make for a surprisingly agreeable pair in Universal's HOUSESITTER, an enjoyably warped romantic comedy about the importance of creative lying to a happy marriage.

Architect Newton Davis (Martin) is so madly in love with his childhood sweetheart, Becky (Dana Delaney), that he designs and builds a home for them in their hometown before he even pops the question. Shocked and depressed when she says no, he can't bring himself to sell the house. After seeking a night of solace in the arms of Gwen (Hawn), a waitress, Newton sneaks out on her in the middle of the night. Embarrassed by his inability to commit himself even for an entire night, he decides to sell the house as a way to free himself from his torch for Becky. Gwen meanwhile seems to be taking revenge on Newton for sneaking out when she goes to his hometown and moves into his house. She tells everyone that she's Newton's new bride and uses what he's told her about the house, the town and the people in it to bluff her way into the hearts of his friends and family, from Becky to Newton's mom, Edna (Julie Harris) and dad, George (Donald Moffat).

The plot thickens when Newton returns home to ready his house for sale. But after his initial panic dies down, Newton begins to see a way to win Becky as well as to extricate himself and Gwen from the mutual embarrassment of their one-night stand and her massive con job. He arranges with Gwen for them to have a "separation" over her "affair" with an old flame, figuring that he can win Becky's sympathy. Instead, the situation predictably continues to snowball to the film's climactic scene—a reception for the couple thrown mainly so that Newton can win a promotion at work. The real complication, however, is that Gwen has become less interested in leaving either him or the house, having fallen in love with both.

With this, his sixth film, director Frank Oz (DIRTY ROTTEN SCOUNDRELS, WHAT ABOUT BOB?) emerges as a masterful orchestrator of sophisticated comedy. At the heart of HOUSESITTER is a remarkably complex idea for a commercial comedy that takes the old saw about the webs we weave when we practice to deceive to its logical conclusion, the point at which the lie, repeated and elaborated, becomes more real than and infinitely preferable to the bleaker reality it supplants.

Lies also become the roundabout way by which truth is attained. Gwen thinks she has fallen in love with Newton's house when, in fact, she has fallen in love with the architect himself. Newton, meanwhile, believes that his stalking out of Gwen's apartment comes from his love for Becky when, in fact, he has fallen in love with Gwen, threatening his blissful self-flagellation over failing with Becky. Each believes that maintaining the masquerade of their "marriage" will help them attain separate ends when, in fact, the brilliance of their masquerade becomes the foundation upon which they build their own romance.

Thus, the lies and tales each tells to further the deception are something more than jokes. As the film goes on, they become their means of mutual seduction, eventually becoming unconscious love sonnets each sends to the other as the deception takes on its own weight and reality. Gwen actually has no more desire to continue her life as a con artist than Newton does to spend his life with Becky who, as beautifully played by Delaney (LIGHT SLEEPER and TV's acclaimed "China Beach"), is Gwen's equal as a resourceful manipulator but is, at heart, as cold as Gwen is hot. Though its ending is assured from the second Gwen and Newton first make contact, like any good romantic comedy, HOUSESITTER generates interest through the process by which Gwen and Newton finally come together rather than through the result itself. In short, on this trip, most of the fun is in getting there.

The performers and performances are uniformly first-rate. Martin continues to be one of the most engaging and inventive talents on the screen today while Hawn, for a change, is well cast in a role that puts her considerable talents to their best advantage. Delaney, meanwhile, is enigmatic and enticing as well as cold and manipulative, giving a real heat to the kind of "other woman" character usually played for broad parody. We may not want Newton to spend his life with her, but we can't help feeling sorry he never got past second base in the film's funny interrupted seduction scene between them.

Uncommonly classy support comes from both Harris and Moffat, in a nice change of pace from his usual casting as the epitome of WASP evil, along with Christopher Durang, Richard B. Shull, Peter MacNicol and many others, making HOUSESITTER an increasingly rare case of a movie that looks as good on paper as it does on the screen. *(Adult situations, profanity.)*

p, Brian Grazer; d, Frank Oz; w, Mark Stein, (from the story by Grazer and Stein); ph, John A. Alonzo; ed, John Jympson; m, Miles Goodman; prod d, Ida Random; art d, Jack Blackman, Jeff Sage; set d, Tracey A. Doyle; cos, Betsy Cox

Romance/Comedy **(PR: A MPAA: PG)**

HOWARDS END ★★★★

(U.K.) 140m Merchant-Ivory Productions; Nippon Herald Films; Channel Four ~ Sony Pictures Classics c

Anthony Hopkins *(Henry Wilcox)*, Vanessa Redgrave *(Ruth Wilcox)*, Helena Bonham Carter *(Helen Schlegel)*, Joseph Bennett *(Paul Wilcox)*, Emma Thompson *(Margaret Schlegel)*, Prunella Scales *(Aunt Juley)*, Adrian Ross-Magenty *(Tibby Schlegel)*, Jo Kendall *(Annie)*, James Wilby *(Charles Wilcox)*, Jemma Redgrave *(Evie Wilcox)*, Ian Latimer *(Station Master)*, Sam West *(Leonard Bast)*, Mary Nash *(Pianist)*, Siegbert Prawer *(Man Asking a Question)*, Susan Lindeman *(Dolly Wilcox)*, Nicola Duffett *(Jacky Bast)*, Mark Tandy, Andrew St. Clair, Anne Lambton, Emma Godfrey, Duncan Brown, Iain Kelly *(Luncheon Guests)*, Atlanta White *(Maid at Howards End)*, Gerald Paris *(Porphyrion Supervisor)*, Allie Byrne, Sally Geoghegan, Paula Stockbridge, Bridget Duvall, Lucy Freeman, Harriet Stewart, Tina Leslie *(Blue Stockings)*, Mark Payton *(Percy Cahill)*, David Delaney *(Simpson's Carver)*, Mary McWilliams *(Wilcox Baby)*, Barbara Hicks *(Miss Avery)*, Rodney Rymell *(Chauffeur)*, Luke Parry *(Tom–the Farmer's Boy)*, Antony Gilding *(Bank Supervisor)*, Crispin Bonham Carter *(Colonel Fussell)*, Patricia Lawrence *(Wedding Guest)*, Margery Mason *(Wedding Guest)*, Jim Bowden *(Marlett)*, Alan James *(Porphyrion Chief Clerk)*, Jocelyn Cobb *(Telegraph Operator)*, Peter Darling *(Doctor)*, Terence Sach *(Delivery Man)*, Brian Lipson *(Police Inspector)*, Barr Heckstall-Smith *(Helen's Child)*, Simon Callow *(Music Lecturer)*

In less skilled hands, this lush adaptation of E.M. Forster's celebrated novel could easily have turned into glossy melodrama. HOWARDS END, after all, has all the lurid elements of a Judith Krantz opus: a stolen inheritance; a rich merchant thoughtlessly wrecking the life of a lowly clerk; the same bigwig, a very proper widower, marrying the elder sister of his son's ex-lover—but not before his sordid love affair with the clerk's common-law wife is revealed at his gala engagement party; his sister-in-law's out-of-wedlock pregnancy; and, finally, a murder. Instead, HOWARDS END is a jewel in the crown of the Merchant/Ivory production team; a scintillating period piece put together with style, intelligence and taste.

Forster's 1910 study of bourgeois ethics and improprieties in Edwardian England tracks two middle-class families, the Wilcoxes and Schlegels, who represent two diametrically opposed sets of values. The prosperous, materialistic Wilcoxes are emotionally stunted snobs obsessed with class distinctions and status. The emancipated Schlegel sisters, on the other hand, are vital, vibrant and voluble; silence seems an anathema for these young women. Margaret (Emma Thompson), older and more responsible, is energized by intellectual diversity; Helen (Helena Bonham-Carter), impulsive and emotional, leads more with her heart than her head. Both share an innate sense of justice and a fervent belief—their father was a philosopher—that a person's dreams are the real coin of the realm.

As a houseguest at the Wilcoxes' country house, Howards End, Helen Schlegel falls in love with the younger Wilcox son, Paul, and writes home that she's engaged. It soon becomes clear, though, that the penniless Paul has no intention of marrying Helen, and relations between the families are broken off.

Several months later, the Wilcoxes inadvertently take a London flat across from the Schlegels, and Margaret pays a courtesy call on the kindly Ruth Wilcox (Vanessa Redgrave), now obviously quite ill. They immediately form a deep bond. Ruth admires Margaret's warmth and intellectual curiosity ("We never discuss anything at Howards End . . except sports"), and rightly feels they're kindred spirits. Margaret also seems to share something of Ruth's mystical bond to Howards End—not just a piece of real estate, but a symbol of all things spiritual, rural and non-materialistic. Just before Ruth dies, she impulsively wills Howards End to Margaret in a scribbled note. The Wilcoxes discover and destroy the note and Margaret remains ignorant of Ruth's gesture.

One day, after attending a lecture on Beethoven, Helen accidentally takes an umbrella belonging to Leonard Bast (Sam West), a timid clerk intent on self-improvement. He follows her home in a downpour to collect it, but is so intimidated by the Schlegels that he declines their invitation to come in and take tea with them and their brother Tibby (Adrian Ross-Magenty).

Bast does, however, take Margaret's card, which is then discovered by his blowsy, vulgar, live-in fiancee, Jacky (Nicola Duffet). When Bast doesn't come home one weekend (he's off on a mystical trek through the countryside), Jacky becomes convinced he's having an affair with Margaret and goes to the Schlegels' home to confront her. Bast then visits the Schlegels to apologize for Jacky's intrusion, and the sisters are charmed by his earnest intellectual and cultural aspirations. They take him under their wing, moved by his desire to create a more meaningful life for himself and Jacky, who he's promised to marry (more out of decency than love) when he turns twenty-one. Acting on the advice of Henry Wilcox (Anthony Hopkins), Ruth's widowed husband, they urge Bast to leave his current job, since his employers are apparently headed for bankruptcy. Bast takes the advice and leaves his employers (who turn out to have been in fact very solvent) for a new job with a company that soon folds.

Meanwhile, Margaret and Henry Wilcox have renewed their acquaintance and, over both families' objections, plan to marry at his magnificent new Shropshire estate. Prior to the wedding, Bast, nearly destitute, tells the sisters of his dire straits. Margaret implores Henry to hire him—after all, it was his bad advice that created the situation—but he couldn't care less. Helen is infuriated by Henry's callousness and shows up at her sister's engagement party with the near-starving young couple in tow. A very drunk Jacky recognizes Henry and reveals that she was formerly his mistress. An enraged Henry insists on breaking the engagement, but Margaret demurs, insisting that everything can be smoothed out. To preserve their relationship, she writes Helen a note saying that "there is no room in Henry's business for Mr. Bast."

Helen spends a night with Bast, who is now wed to Jacky, before leaving for an extended trip abroad. She also has Tibby send Bast a five-thousand-pound check (the bulk of her fortune), which is returned uncashed.

Eight months after Margaret and Henry are married (to the utter disapproval of his children), Helen sends her sister a message from Germany. She wishes to come back to England to retrieve her books, which are now in storage at Howards End, and then immediately return to Germany without seeing her sister or new brother-in-law. Margaret confronts her at the house and discovers that Helen is very pregnant—the result of her night with Bast, who remains unaware of her situation.

An outraged Henry wants Helen off his property, but the two sisters defy him and spend the night at Howards End. Henry despatches his pompous, self-righteous son Charles (James Wilby) to deal with the situation; coincidentally, Charles arrives the next morning, only minutes before a very needy Bast shows up to try and borrow some money from Margaret. Charles realizes that Bast is the man responsible for Helen's condition and starts a scuffle that ends with Bast dying, crushed under a falling bookcase.

Like the novel, the film ends on an ironic note. The following summer, while Helen and her baby romp in the garden of Howards End, a tired Henry gathers his family inside to read them his new will. All his money will go to his children, but he leaves Howards End to his wife and, after her death, to her nephew, Helen's illegitimate child. "It's curious," says his daughter-in-law. "Mrs. Wilcox wanted Margaret to have the house, and now she has it after all." When Margaret asks Henry what she'd meant, he answers off-handedly that it was nothing; just something his poor wife had scribbled on a piece of paper before she died.

Marking the 16th collaboration for producer Ismael Merchant, director James Ivory and screenwriter Ruth Prawer Jhabvala, HOWARDS END is filled with a myriad of meticulous details that have come to exemplify the Merchant/Ivory style, and set it apart from most imitators. (The recent adaptation of Forster's WHERE ANGELS FEAR TO TREAD, for example, hardly measures up.) Coupled with its extraordinarily apt casting, the film's sumptuous and yet understated production design, Richard Robbins's lush musical score and Tony Pierce-Roberts's camerawork exquisitely capture the flavor of the period.

Although Emma Thompson's marvelously subtle performance has received widespread acclaim, the film's secondary performances—notably by West, Wilby, Duffet, Scales and Lindeman (son Charles's whiny wife)—are entirely first class and should not go unnoticed.

p, Ismail Merchant; d, James Ivory; w, Ruth Prawer Jhabvala, (from the novel by E.M. Forster); ph, Tony Pierce-Roberts; ed, Andrew Marcus; m, Richard Robbins; prod d, Luciana Arrighi; art d, John Ralph; set d, Ian Whittaker; cos, Jenny Beavan, John Bright

AAN Best Picture: Ismail Merchant (Producer); *AA Best Actress:* Emma Thompson; *AAN Best Supporting Actress:* Vanessa Redgrave; *AAN Director:* James Ivory; *AA Best Adapted Screenplay:* Ruth Prawer Jhabvala; *AAN Cinematography:* Tony Pierce-Roberts; *AAN Best Score:* Richard Robbins; *AA Art Direction:* Luciana Arrighi (Art Direction) and Ian Whittaker (Set Decoration); *AAN Costume Design:* Jenny Beavan and John Bright

Drama/Historical (PR: A MPAA: PG)

HUGH HEFNER: ONCE UPON A TIME ★★★
91m Lynch/Frost Productions ~ IRS Releasing c

Hugh Hefner, James Coburn

Despite its release under the Lynch/Frost banner, this feature-length documentary on the founder of *Playboy* magazine, on its surface at least, is a surprisingly tame affair that seems to gloss over the controversies and turmoil surrounding its subject. A closer look, however, reveals that HUGH HEFNER: ONCE UPON A TIME works in mysterious ways.

Expanded from a segment of David Lynch and Mark Frost's failed documentary series for the Fox network, "American Chronicles," HUGH HEFNER: ONCE UPON A TIME maintains an almost obsessive focus on its subject whose story, for better or worse, has become part of American lore. A struggling copywriter and failed cartoonist, Hefner and a partner started *Playboy*—oddly enough while Hefner worked for a children's magazine publisher to make ends meet—on a wing and a prayer in 1953. He also had a little bit of luck by including a now-famous nude calendar photo of Marilyn Monroe just as she was becoming the nation's top box-office draw.

That first issue, which carried no date because Hefner wasn't sure he'd ever publish another, sold a respectable 50,000 copies. Not missing the lesson of the Monroe photo, Hefner developed the *Playboy* formula of hedonism in its lifestyle features and an adventurous liberal bent in its news and fiction editorial. But what propelled it into popularity and notoriety was its photo spreads featuring nude, nubile girls next door, the *Playboy* Playmates.

By 1971, *Playboy*'s circulation had reached seven million. Nine hundred thousand keyholders patronized the international string of night clubs and resorts spawned by the magazine's success and Hefner was poised to conquer Atlantic City with a $130 million casino. But a series of scandals, setbacks and changes in society eroded the empire in the next decade. Battered but unbeaten, *Playboy* survived into the 80s largely because Hefner turned over the reins to his daughter by his first marriage, Christie Hefner, a canny businesswoman who aggressively downsized the organization, shedding its clubs and other unrelated businesses, while at the same time overseeing its generally successful expansion into home video and pay TV.

After suffering a stroke in 1985, Hefner downsized his own life, dropping out of the day-to-day running of the corporation and marrying 1989 Playmate of the Year Kimberley Conrad. Made with the cooperation of its subject, HUGH HEFNER: ONCE UPON A TIME carries no startling new revelations either about the man or his empire. What it does have is a finely tuned sense of Hefner's story as a uniquely American tale about the infinite possibilities of remaking oneself.

The early parts of the film use Hefner's home movies to portray the archetypal nerd, a gawky kid who was the product of a repressed Methodist upbringing. What inspired his first "re-emergence" was, of all things, an early exposure to the FLASH GORDON serials featuring the dashing space hero pulling the lovely heroine (pointedly braless in the clips featured) out of one scrape after another at the hands of Ming the Merciless before escaping in Gordon's phallic spaceship. Hefner remade himself as a dashing big man on campus and took over the school magazine, where he instituted a photo feature spotlighting the "Coed of the Month."

At the helm of *Playboy*, he remade himself again, into a social philosopher and crusader for liberal causes. As the magazine became an empire, he remade himself yet again, though unsuccessfully, into a jet-setting capitalist, wheeling and dealing from aboard his jet-black DC-9. He was forced to sell his Atlantic City casino when the New Jersey Gaming Commission turned down his application for a license. The other clubs and resorts became a cash hemorrhage and the magazine came to appear stodgy and outdated with the popularity of X-rated videos and raunchier competition on the newsstands.

HUGH HEFNER: ONCE UPON A TIME touches on all this, as well as the suicide of his assistant, Bobbie Arnstein, while under the scrutiny of the DEA, which posthumously exonerated her of drug-dealing charges, and the more recent murder of Playmate Dorothy Stratten. As the pace picks up late in the film, figures ranging from Peter Bogdanovich to William F. Buckley, Jerry Falwell and Susan Brownmiller all check in with denunciations, with Falwell and Brownmiller agreeing from polar opposite ends of the political spectrum that *Playboy* ought to be banned.

Throughout, Hefner manages to remain something more than a soft-core pornographer and exploiter of women and something less than a great thinker but always undeniably a classic American enigma wrapped inside a mystery. Surprisingly enough, at least to the millions of heterosexual males who still admire him, Hefner never, for a moment, looks quite comfortable in his own skin. Even in the newly filmed interview footage, he looks as he always has: wrung out, his eyes darting like those of a caged animal, clutching his omnipresent pipe as if it were a lifeline to his sanity.

Woody Allen once quipped that the Constitution guarantees us the pursuit of happiness, but it doesn't guarantee that we'll catch it. It is that odd undercurrent of melancholy that raises HUGH HEFNER: ONCE UPON A TIME from a sophisticated puff piece into something resembling art. *(Adult situations, nudity.)*

p, Gary H. Grossman, Robert Heath; d, Robert Heath; w, Gary H. Grossman, Robert Heath, Michael Gross; ph, Van Carlson, Dustin Teel, Tony Zapata; ed, Michael Gross; m, Charlotte Lansberg

Documentary/Biography (PR: C MPAA: NR)

HUMAN SHIELD, THE ★★½
90m Global Pictures; GG Israel Studios ~ Cannon Pictures c

Michael Dudikoff *(Doug Matthews)*, Tommy Hinkley *(Ben Matthews)*, Hana Azoulay-Hasfari *(Lila Haddilh)*, Steve Inwood *(Ali Dallal)*, Uri Gavriel *(Tanzi)*, Avi Keidar *(Sager)*, Geula Levy *(Nanny)*, Gil Dagon *(Daud)*, Michael Shillo *(Joe Albalo)*, Roberto Pollak *(Bashir)*, Albert Illouz *(Dallal's Driver)*, Gilles Ben-David *(Dallal's Aide)*, Irving Kaplan *(Sid Cromwell)*, Nagy Tarabshi *(Ben's Guard)*, Eitan Londner *(Ben's Guard)*, Gilatt Ankori *(Laura Matthews)*, Mati Seri *(Taxi Driver)*, Isaac Saadi *(Taxi Driver)*, Gilya Stern *(Stewardess)*, Avi Cohen *(Blackmarketeer)*, Boni Sue Marcus *(US Reporter)*, Jack Adalist *(US Reporter)*, Linda Harris *(British Commentator)*, Shosha Goren *(Kurdish Grandma)*, Igal Adika *(Kurdish Host)*, Shmuel Matalon *(Checkpoint Guard)*, Michael Eleazar *(Iraqi Officer)*, Ofer Shikartsi *(Passport Clerk)*, Megan Lawson *(Laura's Baby)*, Eran Mengel *(Physical Therapist)*

Apparently usurping South American drug cartels as the B-movie villains of choice, the Iraqis get another low-budget bashing in THE HUMAN SHIELD, a routine but capable action thriller directed by genre veteran Ted Post.

A prologue recounts how American advisor Doug Matthews (Michael Dudikoff) helped train the Iraqi military in tactics during their war against Ayatollah Khomeini only to object when Iraqi commander Ali Dallal (Steve Inwood) turns those tactics against unarmed Iraqi civilians, presumably the Kurds, who oppose Iraqi leader Saddam Hussein. In preventing his summary execution of an elderly woman and a baby, Matthews dishonors Dallal by cutting his face. The action picks up with the evacuation of Americans from Iraq after the Iraqi invasion of Kuwait. At the airport, Dallal orders Doug's brother Ben (Tommy Hinkley) to be held as a hostage. After running into inaction from the US government Doug takes matters into his own hands, sneaking back into Iraq to free his brother.

He soon learns that the woman he had fallen in love with during his previous stay, Lila (Hana Azoulay-Hasfari), had married Dallal to secure Doug's freedom after his previous run-in with Dallal. Now, with the help of her sympathetic Iraqi guards, Lila does what she can to help Doug evade Dallal's wrath and free Ben. Eventually Dallal learns of Lila's collaboration, tries to imprison her in their home and schedules Ben's immediate execution where he's being held, in an Iraqi chemical weapons plant. Breaking free of his own captors, Doug frees Lila before going to the plant, where he frees Ben before killing Dallal and blowing up the plant.

Hampered by a ham-handed, hole-laden screenplay, THE HUMAN SHIELD nevertheless is remarkably sturdy action fare, with an attention to character rare in the B-movie arena. Dudikoff (AVENGING FORCE, AMERICAN NINJA 2), one of the more engagingly low-key B action stars, is appropriately cast in a film in which the real protagonists are the Iraqi characters who help him at great personal risk and in some cases at the cost of their lives. This is not the typical low-budget rip-off of the RAMBO movies in which big, tough Americans come in and save small, helpless natives from cartoonish monsters. Here, there's nothing idealistic about Doug's mission. He's there to save his brother and get out just as, in Post's earlier Vietnam drama GO TELL THE SPARTANS, the Americans came in to accomplish a seemingly simple mission and get out.

As with the earlier film, THE HUMAN SHIELD becomes more complex as it goes along rather than building to a simple climax. For one thing, Doug is an evident amateur at covert infiltration. He draws attention to himself repeatedly with his ineptitude and is rescued by Iraqis who are beaten, raped and slaughtered for their trouble. The villain, Dallal, is an oaf and a monster but one with beliefs and a code of honor that leads him to revenge. In terms of the screenplay, one might question, to no avail, why Dallal waits until Ben is about to leave before he begins tormenting him or why Lila didn't use her sympathetic guards to get away from Dallal once Doug was safely out of the country.

If nothing else, however, THE HUMAN SHIELD demonstrates, as do other truly memorable action films, that a little thoughtful attention to character and theme and the respect for the audience they imply can compensate for a multitude of lesser sins. *(Violence.)*

p, Christopher Pearce, Elie Cohn; d, Ted Post; w, Mann Rubin, (from the story by Rubin and Michael Werb); ph, Yossi Wein; ed, Daniel Cahn, Matthew Booth; m, Stephen Barber; prod d, Itzik Albalak; art d, Yehuda Ako

Action/War **(PR: C MPAA: R)**

HUNTING ★★

(Australia) 97m Boulevard Films ~ Paramount Home Video c

John Savage *(Michael Bergman)*, Guy Pearce *(Sharp)*, Kerry Armstrong *(Michelle Harris)*, Rebecca Rigg *(Debbie McCormack)*, Jeffrey Thomas *(Larry Harris)*, Rhys McConnochie *(Bill Stockton)*, Nicholas Bell *(Piggott)*, Ian Scott *(Holmes)*, Stephen Whittaker *(Roberts)*, Stacey Valkenburg

Failing to deliver on its arty symbolism, HUNTING can best be appreciated as a poison-pen letter to media moguls like Rupert Murdoch and Ted Turner. The film's often remarkable visual style can't disguise the fact that its central romance is a rather dull affair.

Bored with marriage to her earnest but chronically unemployed hubby Larry (Jeffrey Thomas), lowly secretary Michelle Harris (Kerry Armstrong) is swept off her feet when media czar Michael Bergman (John Savage) drops by to take a meeting with her boss. Dazzled by his wealth and impressed by his knowledge of erogenous zones, this mousy Cinderella blinds herself to her lover's more unsavory personality traits. When Larry makes muffled threats to his cuckolding rival, Bergman clears the field by having Larry killed in a manner suggesting suicide. Whether blackmailing public officials or gobbling up foreign corporations, the American tycoon indulges his passion for Michelle until she starts to see through his facade.

Worried about over-extending himself financially and angry at Michelle's failure to toe the traditional mistress line, Bergman attempts to buy off his plaything and even beds her best friend. Michelle, however, is too passionate to let go. When she goes too far and insults him at a business dinner, Bergman puts her in her place by raping her on the table in front of his constituents. Having tired of her lover's sanctimonius appearances on telethons and finally recognizing just how blackhearted Bergman is, Michelle rids the world of the power broker right on the eve of his greatest business triumph, thus proving that even a media mogul can be stopped with a bullet.

A lot of carefully thought-out cinematography has been lavished on a sex-and-power-as-aphrodisiac yarn that could have been better told at half the length. Instead of exploring the finer points of what makes a workaholic mover and shaker tick and how he deliberately snuffs out his sensitive side, HUNTING reiterates examples of his power lust and uncontrollable temper.

Although John Savage (INSIDE MOVES, SALVADOR) leaves his boyish image far behind by giving a scarily intense turn as the CEO from Hell, and Jeffrey Thomas is solid in what could be tagged the Liam Neeson role, Kerry Armstrong falls short as the object of everyone's affection. With Armstrong's pallid presence in the central role, the film falls apart as viewers lose patience with her character—her soul searching comes across as mere whining. You may even ask yourself what makes Michelle so judgmental when she is an adulteress who initially liked wearing cultured pearls and being screwed by a master manipulator. Staring into the camera but failing to capture viewers with her blank gaze, Amrstrong hardly seems likely to have a man-who's-had-everybody panting for her favors.

Still, not all blame for this film's disintegration rests with Armstrong. Bergman is a one-dimensional villain with not enough shadings to make this battle of the sexes absorbing. Making him such a transparent rotter turns Michelle into a bit of a dope; viewers need to see Bergman's seductive powers working overtime. Without the added tensions more fleshed-out characters might have provided, HUNTING becomes a cautionary tale about a beauty and a recalcitrant beast who can't be changed by the former's kiss. *(Violence, sexual situations, adult situations.)*

p, Frank Howson; d, Frank Howson; w, Frank Howson; ph, David Connell, Dan Burstall; ed, Philip Reid; m, John French,

David Herzog; prod d, John Dowding; art d, Bernadette Wynack; set d, Victoria Rowell; cos, Aphrodite Kondos

Drama **(PR: O MPAA: R)**

HURRICANE SMITH ★★½
(Australia) 96m Village Roadshow ~ Warner Home Video c

Carl Weathers *(Billy "Hurricane" Smith)*, Cassandra Delaney *(Julie)*, Tony Bonner *(Howard Fenton)*, Jurgen Prochnow *(Charlie Dowd)*, David Argue *(Shanks)*, John Ewart *(Julie's Grandfather)*

Depending on their susceptibility to muscular acting and fish-out-of-water adventure yarns, viewers may have a "G'day" at this CROCODILE DUNDEE in reverse. Although its plot has been handled so often it's liable to disintegrate from overuse, the Australian Gold Coast scenery, local color and snappy supporting cast combine to make HURRICANE SMITH look *almost* second-hand.

Mourning his mother's death, construction worker Billy "Hurricane" Smith (Carl Weathers) flies down under to locate his missing sister, a playgirl with a weakness for drugs. His search takes him to the swank pad of a pimp, Shanks (David Argue), and whore-with-a-heart-of-gold, Julie (Cassandra Delaney), who both knew his errant sibling. Unflappable even after being tortured by his sister's former employer, crimelord Charlie Dowd (Jurgen Prochnow), who's secretly waging a turf war against his partner Howard Fenton (Tony Bonner), Hurricane is not about to blow town without finding out what Charlie did to his sister. He soon wins the support of Julie, her pimp and her Yank-hating grandpa (John Ewart) who helps Hurricane locate Howard. For abetting this big lug, Julie is nearly captured and sent to feed the sharks, the preferred method of dismissal among Aussie criminals.

Not only does Shanks endure a savage beating to help Hurricane, he also stops a few bullets for him when they storm Charlie's mansion in search of the now-kidnapped Julie. Ever busy Charlie has already blown up Howard in an explosion which almost kills Hurricane, and has murdered his own girlfriend just to eliminate loose ends. With the SWAT team called in, Charlie uses Julie as a shield after his men are wiped out. Climbing onto the bottom of a chopper Charlie has comandeered, Hurricane battles the villain in a manner worthy of a 1940s cliffhanger, particularly since the wounded pilot lapses in and out of consciousness. Once Charlie has been dropped into the maws of some hungry sharks (the same grisly fate that befell the hero's sister), Hurricane is free to make plans to bring Julie stateside, presumably where they will not run into any of her former customers.

Short on logic and long on punch power, HURRICANE SMITH capitalizes on its Yank-down-under motif so successfully that one wouldn't be surprised to hear that a sequel is in the works. While he may not be able to act rings around Wesley Snipes or Larry Fishburne, Weathers is the premiere African-American action hero of our day. Improbably handsome and built like Schwarzenegger's trainer, Weathers saunters across the screen with classic movie-star assurance. Because of the low-key confidence he exudes, you have no difficulty believing he can strong-arm dozens of men and still have energy to maul a few dozen more without seriously damaging that magnificent physique.

Although Prochnow provides his by now standard rip-off of Conrad Veidt, the other supporting cast members pitch in with full-bodied, lively characterizations, particularly Argue who emerges as a sort of overage Artful Dodger expanding Fagin's domain to include prostitution, and Ewart as the feisty old innkeeper who damns all Yankees. With its stunning photography and equally colorful rogues' gallery of players, HURRICANE SMITH may not pack the punch of a hurricane but neither is it an ill wind blowing action fans no good. *(Violence, profanity, nudity.)*

p, Stanley O'Toole, Daniel O'Toole; d, Colin Budds; w, Peter A. Kinloch; ph, John Stokes; ed, Pippa Anderson; prod d, Martin Hitchcock

Action/Adventure **(PR: O MPAA: R)**

HUSBANDS AND LOVERS ★½
(Italy) 91m Metrofilm; PAC Srl ~ Columbia TriStar Home Video c
(VILLA DEL VENERDI, LA)

Julian Sands *(Stefan)*, Joanna Pacula *(Alina)*, Tcheky Karyo *(Paolo)*, Laura Wendel *(Louisa)*, Marco DiStefano *(Piero)*, Sonia Topazio *(Perla)*, Jean Valerie *(Luisa's Mother)*

Alternately torpid and unintentionally hilarious, HUSBANDS AND LOVERS utterly trivializes the Alberto Moravia novel upon which it is based. Judging from the shiny, healthy tresses of the leads and how self-consciously they toss their manes, you might think this glossy sexual rondelay were written by Alberto VO5.

Stricken by the chronic ennui that once afflicted the heroines of Antonioni and Resnais, Alina (Joanna Pacula) not only wants her screenwriter husband Stefan (Julian Sands) to condone her affair with pianist Paolo (Tcheky Karyo) but also to indulge her need for honesty by relishing the details of her vacation from marriage. Obsessed with his wife, Stefan gets no satisfaction from any of the other women he beds and can barely concentrate on his new screenplay about a teenage nymphet. Peeved with his wife's running commentary on her infidelity with kinky Paolo, Stefan keeps breaching the terms of their open marriage agreement. But ultimately Alina and Paolo cross the thin line between love and hate when he spanks, rapes, then beats her. Having failed to kill Alina during one of his voyeuristic forays, Stefan welcomes back the retired sexual pioneer when she tires of touching up her bruises. Truly made for each other, they can now indulge in boring conversations about love and pain, pausing only to have conventional sex.

If only the running time weren't so padded out with stunning scenery, HUSBANDS AND LOVERS might have been a bad movie classic. It's too slow for that, but it could still serve as a model for anyone wishing to parody foreign films of the 60s. Never in the history of cinema have there been two such supremely self-absorbed bores, intellectualizing all the vitality out of their passions. If only the pace were picked up and viewers could get to the unintentionally hilarious pronouncements sooner! The occasional pleasure of staring at beautiful bodies—male and female, for once—is far outweighed by the torture of witnessing their ludicrous emotional posturing and their zombie-like ramblings.

When Pacula utters lines like "He wanted to rip the sex out of me!" with Garbo-like detachment, what other response is there but snickers? Whenever the camera holds on Pacula or Sands, the sexual dynamics seem to shrivel before our eyes because neither actor commands our attention. Long before the fade-out, you'll give up caring whether Sand's sexual frustration symbolizes his writer's block or vice versa. As for Sands (increasingly a good indication that you're watching a bomb), he seems to be stuck in a rut doing his own version of Jeremy Irons sans talent. Never has seriousness seemed so funny or so prolonged. *(Violence, sexual situations, profanity.)*

p, Galliano Juso; d, Mauro Bolognini; w, Sergio Bazzini, (from the novel *The Friday Villa* by Alberto Moravia); ph, Giuseppe Lanci; ed, Sergio Montanari; m, Ennio Morricone; prod d, Claudio Cinini; cos, Alberto Spiazzi, Giorgio Armani

Drama **(PR: O MPAA: R)**

HUSBANDS AND WIVES ★★★★
107m TriStar Pictures ~ TriStar Pictures c

Woody Allen *(Gabe Roth)*, Mia Farrow *(Judy Roth)*, Judy Davis *(Sally)*, Juliette Lewis *(Rain)*, Liam Neeson *(Michael)*, Sydney Pollack *(Jack)*, Lysette Anthony *(Sam)*, Nick Metropolis *(TV Scientist)*, Cristi Conaway *(Shawn Grainger)*, Timothy Jerome *(Paul)*, Rebecca Glenn *(Gail)*, Galaxy Craze *(Harriet)*, John Doumanian *(Hampton's Party Guest)*, Gordon Rigsby *(Hampton's Party Guest)*, Ron Rifkin *(Rain's Analyst)*, Ilene Blackman *(Receptionist)*, Blythe Danner *(Rain's Mother)*, Brian McConnachie *(Rain's Father)*, Bruce Jay Friedman *(Peter Styles)*, Benno Schmidt *(Judy's Ex-Husband)*, Jeffrey Kurland *(Interviewer/Narrator)*, Ron August *(Rain's Ex-lover)*, John Bucher *(Rain's Ex-lover)*, Matthew Flint *(Rain's Boyfriend)*, Jerry Zaks, Caroline Aaron, Jack Richardson, Nora Ephron, Ira Wheeler *(Dinner Party Guests)*, Kenneth Edelson, Michelle Turley, Victor Truro, Kenny Vance, Lisa Gustin, Anthony Nocerino *(Gabe's Novel Montage)*, Philip Levy *(Taxi Dispatcher)*, Connie Picard *(Banducci Family Member)*, Steve Randazzo *(Banducci Family Member)*, Tony Turco *(Banducci Family Member)*, Adelaide Mestre *(Banducci Family Member)*, Jessica Frankston *(Birthday Party Guest)*, Merv Bloch *(Birthday Party Guest)*

It is unfortunate that HUSBANDS AND WIVES will be remembered as the film that mirrored, with unnerving accuracy, a real-life domestic struggle that was being reported in the popular media just as the movie first appeared in theaters. Inextricably linked in the public mind with the messy, painful dispute that erupted between its director-writer-star, Woody Allen, and his longtime partner and leading lady, Mia Farrow, HUSBANDS AND WIVES is nevertheless one of Allen's strongest films ever; a powerful, painful and occasionally funny reflection on the limitations of love and marriage. It's hard to imagine any people leaving this film with gossip on their mind.

Noted author Gabe Roth (Allen) teaches creative writing at Columbia University in New York City. His wife of ten years, Judy (Farrow), works as an editor for an art magazine. To Gabe and Judy's genuine shock, their best friends Jack (Sydney Pollack) and Sally (Judy Davis) announce that they are splitting up. Jack pursues a beautiful aerobics instructor, Sam (Lysette Anthony), while Judy fixes Sally up with an earnest coworker (Liam Neeson), whom she'd secretly like for herself. Meanwhile, Gabe becomes increasingly infatuated with Rain (Juliette Lewis), a bright young student in his class.

Based around a romantic hexagon that could have been conceived by Erich Rohmer, HUSBANDS AND WIVES is a far harsher film than Rohmer would have made. Many scenes are painful and even violent, particularly one in which Jack takes Sam to a party, gets drunk and starts an ugly fight with her.

Allen structures HUSBANDS AND WIVES as a pseudo-documentary. It's shot with an obviously hand-held camera, edited with jump cuts and, most effectively, employs an unseen, unexplained filmmaker (Jeffrey Kurland) who interviews each of the protagonists, giving the whole an unsettling intimacy.

The performances are superlative throughout, with top honors going to Judy Davis (BARTON FINK, NAKED LUNCH), who blazes through the picture with devastating urgency. The grand surprise, though, is director Sydney Pollack, who projects consummate ease and authenticity in his first major role. (Pollack had small but effective bit parts in TOOTSIE and DEATH BECOMES HER.)

HUSBANDS AND WIVES self-consciously refers to, and/or undercuts, several earlier Allen films: Gabe writes a passage about the personality of sperm that almost plagiarizes EVERYTHING YOU ALWAYS WANTED TO KNOW ABOUT SEX; the neo-documentary format is reminiscent of ZELIG; the ending recalls CRIMES AND MISDEMEANORS, etc. The most notable example of this, though, is what could be called the "Allen montage." Often, his films have ended with a series of relatively optimistic musings—memories in ANNIE HALL, reasons to stay alive in MANHATTAN, thoughts on the Marx Brothers in HANNAH AND HER SISTERS, things worth hanging on for in CRIMES AND MISDEMEANORS. Here, Gabe gives that montage as a speech, going through all the reasons he and Judy should stay together. When he finishes, she responds by saying, "Yeah, but it's all over and we know it." Allen has undercut all our expectations, and the result is devastating.

HUSBANDS AND WIVES takes a while to find its rhythm, and the jumpy camerawork is occasionally obtrusive—especially in the opening scene. But it's an extremely powerful and provocative work, the true follow-up to CRIMES AND MISDEMEANORS. At the end of the film, the interviewer asks Gabe about his next novel. Gabe responds that it will be "less confessional, more political. Can I go now, is this over?" It is clearly a heartfelt plea.

For the record, TriStar Pictures capitalized on the Allen/Farrow scandal by opening HUSBANDS AND WIVES on many more screens than usual for one of the reclusive director's pictures, hoping that mainstream audiences would feel compelled to see the film and scour it for clues about the real-life drama unfolding in the tabloids. Ultimately, though, the film grossed a mere $10 million—not much more than an average Allen film. *(Violence, extreme profanity, nudity, sexual situations.)*

p, Robert Greenhut; d, Woody Allen; w, Woody Allen; ph, Carlo DiPalma; ed, Susan E. Morse; prod d, Santo Loquasto; art d, Speed Hopkins; set d, Susan Bode; cos, Jeffrey Kurland

AAN Best Supporting Actress: Judy Davis; *AAN Best Original Screenplay:* Woody Allen

Comedy/Drama **(PR: C MPAA: R)**

I DON'T BUY KISSES ANYMORE ★★½
112m Web-Marc Pictures ~ Skouras Pictures c

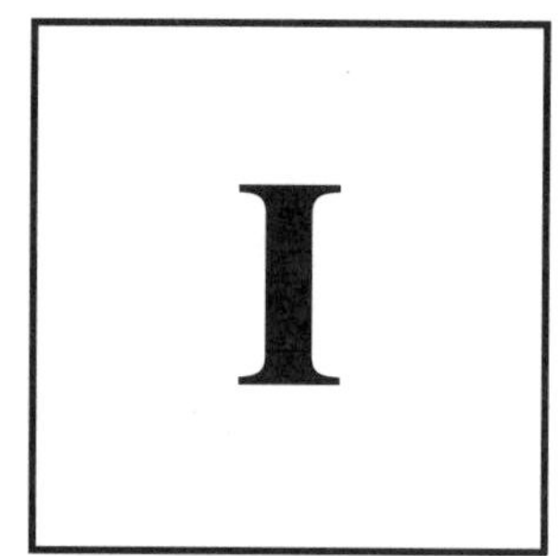

Jason Alexander *(Bernie Fishbine)*, Nia Peeples *(Theresa Garabaldi)*, Lainie Kazan *(Sarah Fishbine)*, Lou Jacobi *(Gramps)*, Eileen Brennan *(Frieda)*, David Bowe *(Norman Fishbine)*, Michele Scarabelli *(Connie Klinger)*, Hilary Shepard *(Ada Fishbine)*, Marlena Giovi *(Louise Garabaldi)*, Ralph Monaco *(Albert Garabaldi)*, Arleen Sorkin *(Monica)*, Cassie Yates *(Melinda)*, Al Ruscio *(Uncle Dominic)*, Lela Ivey *(Alice)*, Matthias Hues *(Eric)*, Larry Storch *(Giora)*, Michael Laskin *(Melvin Fishbine)*, Barbara Pilavin *(Grandma Garabaldi)*, Janna Levenstein *(Angela Garabaldi)*, Robert Do'Qui *(Fred)*, Candy Milo *(Mother in Candy Store)*, Rance Howard *(Elderly Man)*, Jean Speegle Howard *(Elderly Woman)*, David Dolph Benbow *(Mark Thurston)*, Jamie Donovan *(Larry)*, Jack Ong *(Bowling Alley Clerk)*, Benny Grant *(Lenny Fishbine)*, Deborah Grant *(Linda Fishbine)*, Spencer Klein *(Boy in Candy Store)*, Julianne Michelle *(Girl in Candy Store)*, Carolyn Henessey *(Bowling Alley Waitress)*, Ken Oberheu *(1st Waiter)*, Ross McKerras *(Mr. Dill)*, Suzan Hughes *(Waitress in Health Spa)*, Damien Klitou *(Young Bernie Fishbine)*

I DON'T BUY KISSES ANYMORE is a tissue-thin but sweet little romantic comedy.

Philadelphia shoe salesman Bernie Fishbine (Jason Alexander), a personable, lonely bachelor, still lives at home with his overbearing mother Sarah (Lainie Kazan) and grandfather (Lou Jacobi). Bernie's only real flaw is his obesity, which isn't helped by his daily visits to his friend Frieda's (Eileen Brennan) candy store, where he typically buys a half dozen chocolate kisses. One night on the bus he meets Theresa Garabaldi (Nia Peeples), a beautiful graduate student who moonlights as a singer at her uncle's Italian restaurant. Bernie is instantly smitten and tries to trim his waistline by dieting and working out at Theresa's gym, and while they become tentative friends, the romance is strictly one-sided; Theresa is secretly using Bernie as the subject of her graduate thesis "The Psychological Study of an Obese Male."

On the verge of proposing marriage, Bernie accidentally discovers the paper and broken-heartedly heads for a solo vacation in Mexico. Back home, Bernie mopingly resumes his old habits. Taking matters into their own hands, Sarah and Gramps meet at the restaurant with Theresa, who's finding she misses Bernie more than she thought she would and, in effect, propose marriage for Bernie, complete with the engagement ring. Theresa heads Bernie off at the candy store, and after he vents his anger, they seal their future together with a nonchocolate kiss.

The slender plot is well filled out by writer Jonnie Lindsell, but I DON'T BUY KISSES ANYMORE's chief drawback is the surprisingly uneven acting from its seasoned cast. Director Robert Marcarelli relies on too much unflattering, ethnically stereotypical hamming (also a flaw in Beeban Kidron's otherwise engaging USED PEOPLE) to pass for character development. Kazan and Jacobi are especially guilty here, although they do provide the film's biggest laughs. At the opposite end of this scale, the underplaying young leads Alexander (WHITE PALACE, TV's "Seinfeld" and a Tony Award winner for *Jerome Robbins' Broadway*) and Peeples (NORTH SHORE, TV's "Fame") do share a genial chemistry, but the latter's abrupt change of heart remains a bit unbelievable. Peeples also hasn't the voice to carry the old standards in her repertoire at the restaurant bandstand.

This modestly budgeted movie, well designed by Byrnadette DiSanto and photographed by Michael Ferris, uses its Philadelphia locales well. Oddly in keeping with the decidedly old-fashioned tale that unfolds, the city looks as if it were still reassuringly in the 1950s. *(Adult situations.)*

p, Mitchel Matovich; d, Robert Marcarelli; w, Jonnie Lindsell; ph, Michael Ferris; ed, Joanne D'Antonio; m, Cobb Bussinger; prod d, Byrnadette DiSanto; cos, Patte Dee

Romance/Comedy (PR: A MPAA: PG)

ILLUSIONS ★
95m Apricot Entertainment; Crystal Sky Communications ~ Prism Entertainment c

Heather Locklear *(Jan)*, Robert Carradine *(Greg)*, Emma Samms *(Laura)*, Ned Beatty *(George)*, Susannah York *(Dr. Sanders)*

In a damsel-in-distress thriller, when the heroine suffers a nervous breakdown and her shrink is reluctant to release her from psychiatric care, you know she's unlikely to celebrate another wedding anniversary with her husband. Therefore, it should come as no surprise to viewers of ILLUSIONS that archaeologist Greg (Robert Carradine) is going to drive his wife Jan (Heather Locklear) round the bend with that old MIDNIGHT LACE treatment. Yet, even after viewing this murky thriller, the why and how of his actions remain baffling—not because of clever twists in the screenplay but because the bogus plot points are so ineptly presented onscreen.

Why is Dr. Sanders (Susannah York) reluctant to release Jan from her institution? Who's that weird handyman Greg hired and why does he keep feeding nervous Jan all those ghost stories? And who's that sultry Laura (Emma Samms) who drops by unannounced and pretends to be Greg's sister? Judging from their hot smooches she's either an impostor, or this film is actually about incest. Since viewers will figure out what's going on in record time anyway, it will not spoil anyone's fun to know Greg plans to wig out his wife with drug-induced visions that will lead her to "shoot" Laura. Innocently using her own set of bullets, Jan actually does shoot Laura—and kills her.

In the interim, kooky George the handyman (Ned Beatty) demands more money for his part in the let's-get-Jan plot. Showing a remarkable lack of concern for his dead mistress, the cool-headed Greg next poisons George with a drug that makes the murder look like a heart attack. As this mystery builds to its incredible climax, the drugged and whacked-out Jan pulls herself together long enough for a quickie "shotgun" divorce from her tormentor.

Whether it's the film-to-video transfer or its own shoddy cinematography, ILLUSIONS is an appalling-looking thriller. For these sado-masochistic exercises to work, an aura of glamour must pervade. Think of SLEEPING WITH THE ENEMY and DECEIVED, two recent entries that weren't masterpieces but at least sported attractive sheens. Since these films are merely soap operas with the stakes raised, the scoring, art direction, cinematography and costuming are all essential elements. Without that glossy Hollywood patina, the lady-in-danger movie falls apart. Combine this grave tactical error with sloppy suspense plotting and mundane direction and you have a total failure.

Add Heather Locklear's (FIRESTARTER, THE RETURN OF THE SWAMP THING) stone-faced acting into the equation, and whatever minimal thrills the film musters quickly dissipate. Acting up a spritz instead of a storm, Locklear tries hard but always sounds like she's giving a dramatic reading for her talent spot at a local beauty pageant. Her co-stars are scarcely above this level themselves. Without production values and forceful performances, this GASLIGHT clone grows dim rather quickly. *(Violence, adult situations.)*

p, Steven Paul, Michael Canale, Gary Preisler; d, Victor Kulle; w, Peter Colley, (from his play *I'll Be Back Before Midnight*); ph, George Hosek; ed, Jack Tucker; prod d, Carlos Barbosa; art d, Richard Brunton; cos, Deborah Slate

Thriller **(PR: C MPAA: R)**

IMPORTANCE OF BEING EARNEST, THE ★
123m Eclectic Concepts Limited; Paco Global Inc. ~ Eclectic Concepts/Paco Global Inc. c

Brock Peters *(Doctor Chausible)*, C.C.H. Pounder *(Miss Prism)*, Obba Babatunde *(Lane)*, Wren T. Brown *(Algernon)*, Chris Calloway *(Gwendolyn)*, Lanei Chapman *(Cecily)*, Barbara Isaacs *(Merriman)*, Daryl Roach *(Jack)*, Ann Weldon *(Lady Bracknell)*, Sylvester Hayes *(Butler)*

The notion of reworking *The Importance of Being Earnest*, Oscar Wilde's classic if severely conventioned 1895 play, using a modern-dress African-American cast while retaining its London setting and most of Wilde's trademark epigrammatic dialogue is an idea whose time should never have come.

This ill-conceived and artificial updating concerns the comic misadventures of two young aristocrats, Algernon (Wren T. Brown) and Jack (Daryl Roach), who each take on the name Ernest in order to snare two comely ladies, Cecily (Lanei Chapman) and Gwendolyn (Chris Calloway), who will only marry men bearing that name. Standing in the way of both men is the impervious Lady Bracknell (Ann Weldon), Algernon's aunt, who takes an interest in the pedigree of any who dare to marry into the family. The action shifts midway from Algernon's London townhouse to his country estate, where the men's "Ernest" deceptions are revealed and straightened out, even to Lady Bracknell's demanding satisfaction, largely by a surprise revelation that Algernon and Jack, who was "misplaced" as an infant by governess Miss Prism (C.C.H. Pounder), are really brothers, thus paving the way for the union of the two couples, as well as that of Dr. Chausible (Brock Peters) and Miss Prism.

The language especially is a problem; it's modernized a bit (Lady Bracknell sneers at rap music and prefers jazz, for instance) in Kurt Baker and Peter Andrews's screenplay, but the late 19th-century rhythms and inflections become ludicrous given the film's modern setting and the fact that no one in the cast is even attempting a British accent. (Why not have switched locales to Los Angeles, where most of this film was shot?) Also ludicrous is the plot and its unwieldy contrivances, which, arguably, have little to do with the Black experience in any country at any time period.

First-time director Baker too often strands his actors in stagey tableaux, and the filmmakers' attempts to "open up" the play are mostly forced. Even a technically able production might have helped, but the sound is deficient, the production design crude and the cinematography mostly bleached out (perhaps due to being shot on videotape then transferred to film). Given all the flaws of this low-budget effort, which is nearly unwatchably long, only veterans Brock Peters (CARMEN JONES, STAR TREK IV) and Ann Weldon (SHAMPOO, BIRD) come off well; the other actors simply look uncomfortable.

Wilde's play has been filmed twice before, the most notable of the two being Anthony Asquith's 1952 version starring Michael Redgrave, Edith Evans, Margaret Rutherford and Joan Greenwood. This version premiered in October, 1991, at a Harvard University film symposium "Blacks in Black & White and Color."

p, Nancy Carter Crow; d, Kurt Baker; w, Peter Andrews, Kurt Baker, (from the play by Oscar Wilde); ph, Mark Angell; ed, Tracy Alexander; m, Roger Hamilton Spotts

Romance/Comedy **(PR: A MPAA: G)**

IN GOLD WE TRUST ★★
89m Little Bear Films ~ AIP Home Video c

Jan-Michael Vincent *(Oliver Moss)*, Sam J. Jones *(Jeff Slater)*, Sherrie Rose *(Debbie)*, James Phillips *(Greg)*, Michi McGee *(Sal-Kam)*, Robert Cespedes *(George)*, Nappon Gomarachun *(Colonel Lavia)*, Christoph Kluppel *(Christoph)*

This film features enough warring factions to keep UN delegates busy around the clock for the next decade. Set somewhere along the Thai-Cambodian border, IN GOLD WE TRUST requires a good memory to sort out who's on whose side. Once again Vietnam's ghost haunts an action flick as a Ross Perot-type heads a rescue mission to free MIAs with gold.

Embittered at being forgotten by their country for so long, the renegade POWs led by the deranged Jeff Slater (Sam J. Jones) intercept the ransom intended to free them. After obtaining the booty contained in an all-but-impenetrable container, they foolishly kill the man with the combination and spend much of the film's running time figuring out how to unlock or blow open the safe. While they search for a hiding place from rebel forces and the local military, the US government dispatches noble Oliver Moss (Jan-Michael Vincent) and his associates to retrieve the dough and carry out the mission—never realizing that their former comrades-in-arms, the Slater Bunch, have already nabbed their own ransom.

Encountering mountain guerrillas led by Moss's long-lost love Sal-Kam (Michi McGee), Moss enlists them in locating the missing treasure as well as Sal-Kam's sister who has been kidnapped by Slater and used as his love slave. Complicating matters is the participation of Sal-Kam's father in the botched transfer of money-for-MIAs, but he ends up dead. Foolhardily, Slater has hidden the ransom container in a cave populated by Japanese troops apparently living there since WWII. Before the Rising Sun can rise again, Slater's right-hand man, Greg (James Phillips), pretends to be a loyal Yankee and leads Moss's contingent and the rebels into a trap.

Temporarily forced to team up to retrieve the safe from the Japanese, Moss's fighters and Slater's renegade band attack their mutual enemy. In the climactic melee, Slater's Russian crony Christoph (Christoph Kluppel) cancels out the spirit of Glasnost with his machine gun; Sal-Kam's sister bites the dust; the Japanese MIAs are all eliminated; Slater and his goons don't live to spend any of Uncle Sam's money, which goes to help the rebel cause; Moss's buddies return home; and Moss stays behind to help Sal-Kam raise a lot of little guerrillas.

No one views an action film to demand logic, but one does expect an exercise in military machismo to be less confusing. How, for example, have those Japanese soldiers existed in hiding—and for how many years? They dance around as if they've been waiting for Mothra to save them. With so many brands of guerrillas, and Cambodian forces, and turncoat Americans, was it necessary to write the forgotten Japanese into the screenplay? Is the film saying that all nations abandon their fighting men when expedient? If so, they left out a few countries. Even without the Japanese, IN GOLD WE TRUST is already populated with too many double-crosses and betrayals. Maybe it doesn't matter how many brands of bad guy there are, since we can recognize Jan-Michael Vincent's crew as the heroes. Tellingly, the film offers a rare opportunity to hiss MIAs as villains.

Putting confusion aside, action fans can enjoy martial arts demonstrations in the cavernous cave, muscular *mano a mano* combat, colorful explosions, and the profane banter of traitorous Americans enterprising enough to cut out the middle man and steal their own ransom. Hobbled with a tortuous script, IN GOLD WE TRUST musters up some vigorous, hard-edged action for the non-discriminating. *(Violence, profanity, some nudity.)*

p, Chalong Pakdivijit; d, Chalong Pakdivijit; w, Tony S. Suvat, Buncherd Dhawee, (from the story by Norman Puemin); ph, Visidh Santhavee; ed, Peter Charles; m, Hummie Mann

Action/Martial Arts **(PR: O MPAA: NR)**

IN THE HEAT OF PASSION ★★
84m Concorde ~ Concorde c

Sally Kirkland *(Lee Adams)*, Jack Carter *(Stan)*, Nick Corri *(Charlie Bronson)*, Michael Greene *(Sanford Adams)*, Gloria LeRoy *(Betty)*, Carl Franklin *(Detective Rooker)*, Carlos Carrasco *(Perez)*, Jack Carter *("Crimebusters" Host)*, Charles Philip Moore

A fitfully clever film noir that exists mainly to exude sensual steam, IN THE HEAT OF PASSION garnishes a formulaic story with 1990s trimmings.

Charlie Bronson (Nick Corri) is a struggling young Hollywood actor who makes such an impact portraying the notorious Montclair Hills serial rapist on "Crimebusters," a sleazy reality TV show (and a neat takeoff on the hit FBC program "America's Most Wanted"), that he's publicly mistaken for the unidentified psychopath. Most of the time, though, Charlie pumps gas in the barrio where he lives. When ultra-sexy, rich psychiatrist Lee Adams (Sally Kirkland) drives in for service, Charlie's dipstick leads him into the danger zone. The stud thespian carries on a frenzied affair with the enticing Lee, literally under the nose of her middle-aged dullard spouse Sanford (Michael Greene). When Sanford finally finds out about the infidelity, he's killed in a violent struggle with the lovers. Lee gets the idea to tell police that the still-at-large Montclair Hills rapist committed the murder, and a nervous Charlie soon finds himself recalled by "Crimebusters" to reprise the role for a special broadcast about Sanford's death. Thus the hapless protagonist edgily reenacts for the cameras a homicide he himself committed.

If it sounds like a set-up, it is. "Don't you know that shrinks are the craziest people," wisecracks Lee's secretary; the only surprise delivered by the remainder of IN THE HEAT OF PASSION is the heroine's motive for sending Charlie to his ruin. It's an appropriate and cynical closer, but not quite enough to save the picture. Excessive footage is spent unrewardingly on the couplings between Charlie and Lee, with much nudity and double-entendre dialogue better suited to a low-grade sitcom. When Charlie, disguised as a friendly TV repairman, trysts with Lee while Sanford grumbles in another room, one can almost hear the laugh track. Corri can't do much with the underwritten, basically unsympathetic fall guy he plays. The exquisitely overripe Kirkland (ANNA, COLD FEET), often seen as a good-natured sexpot, is supposed to be somewhat sinister here, but she's far more femme than fatale.

IN THE HEAT OF PASSION was made under the stewardship of exploitation czar Roger Corman, so it's not unusual that it goes straight for the gonads. Producer-writer-director Rodman Flender came to Corman's Concorde-New Horizons group right out of Harvard, and after serving as director of advertising Flender became, at the tender age of 27, the B-movie factory's head of production. IN THE HEAT OF PASSION is clearly the work of no dummy (whether it was intended for dummies is another matter), and its tangential nudge at today's crime-based media is the highlight. Jack Carter has fun as the blustery host of "Crimebusters," and second-unit director Charles Philip Moore does a gonzo cameo early on as a street person who loudly claims to be a missing key witness in the JFK assassination conspiracy. *(Violence, substance abuse, profanity, nudity, sexual situations, adult situations.)*

p, Rodman Flender; d, Rodman Flender; w, Rodman Flender; ph, Wally Pfister; ed, Patrick Rand; m, Art Wood, Ken Rarick; prod d, Hector Velez; art d, Patrick Lees; set d, Aaron Osborne; cos, Meta Jardine

Romance/Thriller **(PR: O MPAA: R)**

IN THE SOUP ★★★½
93m Will Alliance Company; Pandora Film; Why Not Productions; Odessa Films; Alta Films; Mikado Film; Cacous Films ~ Triton Pictures bw/c

Steve Buscemi *(Adolpho Rollo)*, Seymour Cassel *(Joe)*, Jennifer Beals *(Angelica)*, Pat Moya *(Dang)*, Will Patton *(Skippy)*, Jim Jarmusch *(Monty)*, Carol Kane *(Barbara)*, Elizabeth Bracco *(Hooker)*, Sully Boyer *(Old Man)*, Steven Randazzo *(Louis Bafardi)*, Frank Messina *(Bafardi Brother)*, Stanley Tucci *(Gregoire)*, Rockets Redglare *(Guy)*, Debi Mazar, Ruth Malaczech

A semi-autobiographical black comedy from writer-director Alexandre Rockwell, IN THE SOUP is a wry and biting yarn highlighted by a cast of quirky characters and an outlandish and twisting plot line.

Adolpho Rollo (Steve Buscemi) is an unemployed man with a dream. He's determined to see his five-hundred-page mega-screenplay, "Unconditional Surrender," made into a film. Convinced that his life's work isn't like other films—it's art—Adolpho has never considered selling it for something as trivial as money. That is, until the singing Bafardi Brothers (Steven Randazzo and Frank Messina), his bullying landlords, threaten bodily harm to the aspiring filmmaker. "Can a blind man direct a movie?" one of them inquires ominously. Desperate for cash, Adolpho appears on a cable talk show in the buff. The producer, Monty (Jim Jarmusch), only gives him forty bucks for the gig—hardly enough to appease the brothers. Dejected, Adolpho is forced to place an advertisement in the paper for a financial backer. He waits out the dry period sitting in a local coffee shop and watching his neighbor, Angelica (Jennifer Beals), a beautiful Hispanic waitress, serve espresso to the regulars. He's convinced that she will star in his movie and maybe his life. She won't give him the time of day.

It isn't long before Adolpho receives a response to the ad. He arrives at a Grammercy Park apartment and is thrust into the mysterious world of Joe (Seymour Cassel), an aging yet virile shyster. Without seeing the screenplay, Joe quickly hands Adolpho a thousand dollars as a gesture of good will. Then he abruptly dismisses the filmmaker with a big kiss so that he can make love with his nymphomaniac girlfriend, Dang (Pat Moya). One thing is for sure, Joe believes that Adolpho has what it takes to make a great movie—even if he would prefer a simple love story instead of Adolpho's surreal epic of Nietzsche, Dostoyevsky and table-tennis balls. Soon after, Joe invites his new partner to dinner along with Joe's hemophiliac thug brother, Skippy (Will Patton), who sizes up Adolpho.

Later that night, Angelica's ex-husband, Gregoire (Stanley Tucci), an emotional Frenchman she mistakingly married for her green card, knocks on Adolpho's door and begs to sleep on his floor. The next morning he's gone but has left one of Angelica's shoes behind. On Christmas morning, Joe tells him it's time they raised money for their film. He coerces Adolpho to join him as he steals a new Porsche from a cop's driveway. Adolpho's suspicions are confirmed—he's involved with a crook. Joe justifies the larceny by adding another forty thousand to the film's kitty. His intoxicating lifestyle soon overtakes Adolpho who accompanies him on other heists, getting caught up in Joe's web of charm, power and money.

As the dollars roll in, Adolpho begins sending flowers to Angelica on a daily basis. She begins to warm up to him, and when Joe sees that his young charge is in love, he sets up a four-way New Year's Eve date. On the appointed night everything seems to be going well—Adolpho and Angelica are getting along splendidly, Joe has called Gregoire and scared him into paying up the three thousand dollars that he owes Angelica, and there's plenty of good champagne. Then Joe tries to slip his tongue down Angelica's throat, and the party comes to a crashing end.

Adolpho is in too deep now to quit, almost able to see his film being shot. Joe and Skippy have come up with a master plan to raise all of the needed funds in one fell swoop. It's a drug deal and Adolpho will be the pick-up man. When the scheme goes awry, Skippy is murdered and Adolpho runs off to find Joe who has taken Angelica to get her money from Gregoire. Joe already knows about Skippy's death and suggests they drive out to the beach to work things out. Once there, a fight breaks out between the trio. Angelica grabs Joe's gun and accidentally fires it. For a moment they think Joe is shot, but when he smiles and says, "I fooled ya," Angelica storms off leaving Joe and Adolpho to wander the beach. They sit in the sand and Joe convinces Adolpho to make his movie—whatever it takes. Adolpho agrees but now he tells Joe it will be a simple love story about him, Joe and Angelica. Then Joe dies—the bullet had struck him after all.

Alexandre Rockwell (HERO, SONS) has taken bits and pieces of his early filmmaking days, thrown in some outlandish fiction and ended up with a smart and original portrait of show business from the outside looking in. IN THE SOUP is sarcasm personified. Rockwell even gives his alter ego the pretentious name of Adolpho Rollo, an obvious homage to the likes of Godard and other European auteurs. Ranging from slapstick, to hip, to poignant, the film manages to encompass a full range of personalities while remaining true to its story.

Shooting in dramatically lit b&w, Rockwell accents the low-budget nature of the protagonist's own dream project. The film's narration, though virtually dismissed in the second act, is always entertaining—offering some of the film's best dialogue. One hilarious trick has Adolpho's narration voicing an opinion about Skippy who is seated next to him in the car. As if hearing the thought process, Skippy says, "What?" The tongue in cheek dream sequences are tremendously melodramatic and effectively funny. Oddly though, the most memorable scene isn't comedic at all, but deals with an elderly, confused man (Sully Boyer) who is lost in his thoughts.

There isn't enough one could say about the casting in this film—it's simply perfect. The story is elevated by the chemistry and sense of improvisation between Buscemi and Cassel. Rockwell was fortunate to match up these two talented performers. Busecmi, with his non-Hollywood looks and Everyman quality, is the perfect foil for Cassel's slick and manipulative aging gangster. Cassel charms the camera in every frame—effortlessly convincing the audience why Adolpho could so easily be sucked into his lifestyle. Beals (Rockwell's wife) plays Angelica shrewdly and with believable ethnicity. Patton continues to add to his list of bizarre madmen with an impressive turn as Skippy. Tucci, as the tormented Gregoire, is a standout, and cameos by Jarmusch and Carol Kane as the sleazy cable show producers are understated hilarity.

The film would have been better served by eliminating a few of the ideas which may have worked in the screenplay but don't in the final print. The sequence with the ape and the midget, while sardonic enough in tone and a slap at gangster films, seems silly and out of place. The dramatic ending also has been seen before in other shapes and forms and could have been strengthened. Overall though, IN THE SOUP is consistently winning and uniquely eccentric. *(Profanity.)*

p, Jim Stark, Hank Blumenthal; d, Alexandre Rockwell; w, Alexandre Rockwell, Tim Kissell; ph, Phil Parmet; ed, Dana Congdon; m, Mader; prod d, Mark Friedberg; art d, Ginger Tougas; set d, Rik Armour; cos, Elizabeth Bracco

Comedy/Crime **(PR: C MPAA: NR)**

INCIDENT AT OGLALA ★★★

93m Seven Arts; Spanish Fork Motion Picture Company; The Dakota Film Corporation; Carolco Pictures ~ Miramax c

Robert Redford *(Narration)*, Leonard Peltier, John Trudell

Robert Redford served as executive producer and narrator of INCIDENT AT OGLALA, Michael Apted's documentary companion piece to his fictional THUNDERHEART. The film addresses the mystery surrounding the deaths of two FBI agents on the Pine Ridge reservation on June 26, 1975.

By the mid-1970s, the Pine Ridge reservation had become the poorest in the nation, plagued by poverty, alcoholism and violence. The situation was exacerbated both by the corrupt Pine Ridge Tribal Council and its newly elected president Dick Wilson, and a US government intent on intimidating supporters of the newly organized American Indian Movement.

It was in this atmosphere that two FBI agents assigned to Pine Ridge were called in to investigate the whereabouts of one Jimmy Eagle, who was wanted by the authorities for stealing cowboy boots. The agents, thinking they were following Jimmy Eagle's red pickup truck, pulled the truck over in an area known as Jumping Bull, populated by radical members of the American Indian Movement. Shots were fired and some area residents, apparently thinking they were under fire themselves, proceeded to shoot back at the agents. When the hail of bullets subsided, the two agents and one Native American were left dead.

There was no investigation concerning the death of the Native American, but the FBI arrested three men in connection with the death of the agents. The first two, Dino Butler and Bob Robideau, were brought to trial but cleared of the charges. The third, Leonard Peltier, was extradicted from Canada and, in a separate trial, found guilty of the two murders. The FBI, however, had allegedly intimidated witnesses into giving false accounts and tampered with documents in order to obtain the arrest. Peltier, professing his innocence, now serves two consecutive life terms in prison.

An acknowledged master of the documentary format, Apted (28 UP, BRING ON THE NIGHT) utilizes some of the same techniques that were showcased in Erroll Morris's THE THIN BLUE LINE—minimalist dramatizations, eyewitness interviews, selected scanning of court documents and transcripts. Apted presents a scathing picture of Nixon-era paranoia in which the FBI and federal authorities, in a desperate attempt to avoid losing a second murder conviction, ran roughshod over Constitutional guarantees; the factual discrepancies, and the testimonies of coerced witnesses, consitute a chilling indictment of a federal power structure gone out of control.

INCIDENT AT OGLALA is even more effective in establishing the context for the Pine Ridge murders, showing how the American Indian Movement arose as a reaction to the venal US government and the power-hungry Dick Wilson. In the film's most harrowing sequence, various Pine Ridge residents dispassionately recount the most horrible acts of terror carried out by the Wilson-organized GOON squad (for Guardians of the Oglala Nation) in order to frighten families into leaving the reservation. Referring to the FBI killings, Madonna Thunder Hawk is recorded as saying, "There were shootouts going on all the time . . . before that and after that."

Apted's tight documentary structure begins to unwind after the Peltier conviction, leaving many questions unanswered. (What became of Dick Wilson? Was the death of a coerced witness in a car crash accidental? Why has the government refused to hear new evidence in the case?) The most glaring misstep is the introduction, during the last few minutes of the film, of a mysterious Mr. X, who claims to have killed the agents. The man's appearance so late in the film, without a sufficient examination of his assertions, ends INCIDENT AT OGLALA on a note of puzzlement and disbelief that detracts from the careful layering of evidence we have seen during the preceding 80 minutes.

Even given the questionable confessions of Mr. X, however, INCIDENT AT OGLALA presents sufficient evidence to warrant a re-examination of Leonard Peltier's case.

p, Arthur Chobanian; d, Michael Apted; ph, Maryse Alberti; ed, Susanne Rostock

Documentary/Political **(PR: A MPAA: PG)**

INDIO 2-THE REVOLT ★½

(Italy) 99m RPA International ~ LIVE Home Video c

Marvelous Marvin Hagler *(Sergeant Iron)*, Frank Cuervo *(Indian Guide)*, Dirk Galuba *(Vincent Van Eyck)*, Tetchie Agbayani *(Mrs. Morrell)*, Maurizio Fardo *(Father Leonard)*, Jacqueline Carol *(Mama Lou)*, Charles Napier *(IMC president)*

About ten years ago Italian exploitation filmmakers were cranking out sickening safari-splatter epics with titles like CANNIBAL HOLOCAUST and ULTIMO MONDO CANNIBALE, drenched with blood and gore and depicting the grisly atrocities of savage jungle primitives. What a difference a decade makes. Now those villainous headhunters are noble rain forest dwellers, heroically raising righteous spears to defend Mother Earth against evil industrial despoilers of the environment. There's still plenty of blood and gore, though, which is the point.

INDIO 2-THE REVOLT is suitably revolting, and its politically correct massacres should please hopeless action fans. It's a step down from the earlier INDIO, escapist stuff that starred Francesco Quinn as Daniel Morrell, a skilled US Marine commando and South American tribal prince who used Rambo tactics to drive off bulldozers of IMC Corporation, a malevolent multinational bent on devouring Morrell's verdant habitat. Obviously Quinn (the son of actor Anthony Quinn) couldn't or wouldn't come back for an encore, so here an anonymous extra portrays Morrell by keeping his back to the camera in a prologue that sees the hero easily betrayed and slain. Even post-mortem photos hide the face of Quinn's stand-in, but the remains are nonetheless recognized by Morrell's Marine Corps mentor, Sergeant Jake Iron (Marvelous Marvin Hagler). Iron gets time off from boot camp so he can go avenge his buddy, as though vendetta leave is perfectly routine in the Leathernecks.

Once in the wilderness Iron meets Morrell's people, hiding from the depredations of IMC, which uses Indian slaves to build a construction road. In charge of the infernal project is, naturally, a white South African named Vincent Van Eyck (Dirk Galuba); the beastly Boer is the same guy who murdered Morrell. Iron inspires the natives with the story of Spartacus, and leads the aboriginal avengers in an ultimately triumphant battle against IMC and its mercenaries. The road to victory is an arduous one for characters and viewers alike though, and subplots include a weapons-raid on a bordello/drughouse/arsenal run by the grotesque Mama Lou (Jaqueline Carol), a fat madame with lethal metal teeth. Later, Van Eyck strafes the natives with "White Cloud"—not the fabric softener, but a deadly chemical that creates cheap dry-ice bubbles on the river. Sergeant Iron, discouraged by this display of Mr. Wizard-level special effects, elects to quit. Yes, just quit. But while walking back home he's given a boost by the sight of legions of painted warriors materializing out of the underbrush (a truly impressive crowd shot), and rejoins them for the climactic attack.

Former world heavyweight boxer Marvelous Marvin Hagler fits the bill physically as a knockabout action star, and can expect more roles of this type even though his acting is as wooden as the trees he's trying to save. Even so, there's something very tentative about this Sergeant Iron guy, who, as a Black man, is expected to identify with persecuted Third World peoples and kick that Afrikaaner's white honky butt. But one never loses sight of the fact that Morrell's tribe would have fought just as fiercely even if Iron had never shown up, the suspicion compounded when the Marine throws in the towel at the first sign of real trouble. While it's nice to see natives who aren't the usual submissive victims helpless without Anglo guidance, the whole thing goes against the film's iconographic treatment of Hagler as hero. In keeping with Marvelous Marvin's athletic prowess, the Sergeant's got fists of, well, iron; cracks from those mighty mitts send baddies sailing twenty feet through the air, put out Mama Lou's lights for good, and stop Van Eyck's heart during Iron's final one-on-one grudge match with the archvillian (who, until that cardiac punch, is giving Hagler a worse thrashing than Sugar Ray Leonard ever did).

It's fifty times the workout that Hagler got in the first INDIO, in which his big movie debut turned out to be a passive cameo. But the original, done by the same filmmaking team, was a classier picture all the way through, with cleaner photography, a personable antagonist, played by Brian Dennehy, and—believe it or not—a low body count. Daniel Morrell mainly sabotaged equipment and work schedules, killing only a few IMC thugs and even leaving Dennehy alive, albeit unemployed, at the conclusion. INDIO 2-THE REVOLT revels in death and mutilation, with one of Hagler's blows squirting a splat of blood right onto the camera lens. The IMC marauders habitually cut off the heads and ears of their victims, and later a bullet is removed from a wounded child in closeup; all with the same slurpy sound effect. There's also a terrific explosion, followed by a landslide. Not surprisingly, any ecological profundities are generally ignored amidst all the mayhem. *(Violence, profanity, substance abuse, nudity.)*

p, Filiberto Bandini; d, Anthony M. Dawson; w, Gianfranco Bucceri, Filiberto Bandini, (from his story); ph, Roberto Benvenuti; ed, Angela Cipriani; m, Pino Donaggio

Action/Adventure **(PR: O MPAA: R)**

INDOCHINE ★★½

(France) 155m Paradis Films/General D'Images; BAC Films; Orly Films; Cine Cinq; Cinemanuel ~ Sony Pictures Classics c

Catherine Deneuve *(Eliane)*, Vincent Perez *(Jean-Baptiste)*, Linh Dan-pham *(Camille)*, Jean Yanne *(Guy)*, Dominique Blanc *(Yvette)*, Henri Marteau *(Emile)*, Carlo Brandt *(Castellani)*, Gerard Lartigau *(The Admiral)*, Hubert Saint-Macary *(Raymond)*, Andrzej Seweryn *(Hebrard)*, Mai Chau *(Shen)*, Alain Fromager *(Dominique)*, Chu Hung *(Mari De Sao)*, Jean-Baptiste Huynh *(Etienne Adult)*, Thibault DeMontalembert *(Charles-Henri)*, Eric Nguyen *(Tanh)*, Trinh Van-thinh *(Minh)*, Tien Tho *(Xuy)*, Thi Hoe Tranh Huu Trieu *(Madame Minh Tam)*, Nguyen Lan Trung *(Kim)*, Nhu Quynh *(Sao)*

Although thoroughly French, Regis Wargnier's INDOCHINE, starring Gallic icon Catherine Deneuve, is as calculated and pre-packaged as anything conceived in contemporary Hollywood.

This florid, would-be epic centers on Eliane (Deneuve), the doyenne of a rubber plantation in French colonial Indochina, and her greatest joy, her adopted Indochinese daughter Camille (Linh Dan-pham). Their rapport is so complete that they regularly wow the other planters at parties with a very piquant mom-and-daughter tango. Eliane's dignified existence is further enlivened by the appearance of Jean-Baptiste (Vincent Perez), a dashing French officer whose orders initially bring him into hostile contact with the plantation owner. The capable young soldier seduces first mother and then, more lastingly, daughter.

The enraged Eliane pulls strings to have Jean-Baptiste transferred to the remote regions of the Gulf of Tonkin, but lovestruck Camille doggedly pursues him. En route, she hooks up with a pack of Communist rebels, is taken prisoner by the French and becomes a legend of the resistance when she kills a sadistic officer. Camille is then reunited with Jean-Baptiste, and the star-crossed lovers have a son together before literally disappearing into the horizon, leaving the stoic, noble Eliane to pass their story onto their child.

The filmmakers responsible for INDOCHINE seem to have reasoned that, to make the kind of money a GONE WITH THE WIND or DR. ZHIVAGO rakes in, you have to spend it; at an estimated $21 million, this is one of the costliest productions in the history of the French cinema. They also tried to cover all the commercial bases by throwing in a "colorful" historical background; a host of age-encrusted racial and dramatic stereotypes; some artily torrid sex scenes; a dash of gore; and, most essentially, a star synonymous with Gallic charm and glamor.

Wargnier's direction has a miniseries-like impersonality. He shamelessly pumps things up from time to time with clarions of thundering muzak, prettily overripe photography and the odd, artfully composed set piece (opium dens and whorehouses galore; Eliane and Jean-Baptiste consummating their passion in the back seat of her car, while her chauffeur dutifully stands outside in the rain, etc.) Four individuals are credited with the screenplay, which is a rummage sale of bad ideas, operatic coincidence and tired cliches.

A charismatic, even eccentric, performance in the lead role, *a la* Laurence Olivier in THE BETSY, can on occasion redeem this kind of clunky melodrama. INDOCHINE, however, gives us a Deneuve who, in the grandest MGM tradition of Greer Garson, is too pallid and ladylike to provide any real juice. It should be remembered that her most memorable film appearances have been as a beautiful, passive *reactor* to the surreal promise of life as envisioned by such as Bunuel or Polanski. INDOCHINE's Eliane is, above all else, a feisty instigator of the events around her, and calls for more than elegant posing in diaphanous tea gowns and the occasional set of a chiseled jaw.

The men in the cast go too far in the other direction. Perez seems to think he's in a pirate swashbuckler, while Jean Yanne, as a longtime admirer of Eliane, is an obstreperous bore in the tradition of Jose Ferrer at his noisiest. Lin Dan Pham's Camille is predictably delicate, abject and touching; only Dominique Blanc, a kind of pocket-sized Gallic Bette Davis, breaks through the tedium with a flashy turn in the small part of a wayward Frenchwoman. *(Violence, substance abuse, nudity, sexual situations, adult situations.)*

p, Eric Heumann, Jean Labadie; d, Regis Wargnier; w, Erik Orsenna, Louis Gardel, Catherine Cohen, Regis Wargnier; ph, Francois Catonne; ed, Genevieve Winding; m, Patrick Doyle; cos, Gabriella Pescucci, Pierre-Yves Gayraud

AAN Best Actress: Catherine Deneuve; *AA Best Foreign Language Film:*

Drama/Romance/Historical (PR: C MPAA: PG-13)

INNOCENT BLOOD ★

115m Lee Rich Productions; Landis/Belzberg ~ Warner Bros. c

Anne Parillaud *(Marie)*, Anthony LaPaglia *(Joe Gennaro)*, Robert Loggia *(Sal "The Shark" Macelli)*, David Proval *(Lenny)*, Rocco Sisto *(Gilly)*, Don Rickles *(Emmanuel Bergman)*, Chazz Palminteri *(Tony)*, Tony Sirico *(Jacko)*, Tony Lip *(Frank)*, Kim Coates *(Ray)*, Marshall Bell *(Marsh)*, Leo Burmester *(Flinton)*, Rohn Thomas *(Coroner)*, Angela Bassett *(US Attorney Sinclair)*, Luis Guzman *(Morales)*, Tom Savini *(News Photographer)*, Christopher Lee *(Count Dracula)*, Peter Cushing *(Van Helsing)*, Dan Quayle *(Vice President of the United States)*, Ike *(German Shepherd)*, Gil Cates, Jr. *(Dog Boy)*, Charlie Gomorra *(Gorilla)*, Lamont Arnold *(Morgue Desk Man)*, Yancey Arias *(Coroner's Assistant)*, Frank Oz *(Pathologist)*, Pitty Jennings *(Reporter)*, David Early *(Reporter)*, Forrest J. Ackerman *(Stolen Car Man)*, Elaine Kagan *(Frannie Bergman)*, Bela Lugosi *(Count Dracula)*, Michael Ritchie *(Night Watchman)*, Bernard Hocke *(Motel Clerk)*, Sam Raimi *(Roma Meats Man)*, Dario Argento *(Paramedic)*, Alfred Hitchcock *(Man with Cello Case)*, Marina Durell *(Nurse)*, Harry Gions *(Orderly)*, Steve Johnson *(Orderly)*, Robert Walker *(Bruno)*, Linnea Quigley *(Nurse)*, Michael Wolk *(Surgeon)*, Russ Cochran *(Panhandler)*, Teri Weigel, Lisa Ann Baker, Christina Jimenez, Christina Bowers, Kim Currow, Christina Diaz, Kim Melton, Robin Place, Regina Poole, Tracy Rolen, Tammy Ulm, Katrina Witt, Maribe Zolli *(Melody Lounge Dancers)*, Ron Roth *(Gus)*, Vic Noto *(Tommy)*, Jerry Lyden *(Vinnie)*, Rick Avery *(Cab Driver)*, Bob Minor *(Bus Driver)*

Director John Landis returns to horror-comedy territory with INNOCENT BLOOD, a vampire yarn that shares the uneven quality of Landis's previous entry in the genre, AN AMERICAN WEREWOLF IN LONDON.

Marie (Anne Parillaud, making her American film debut after scoring in the lead of Luc Besson's LA FEMME NIKITA) is an ageless bloodsucker who only preys on evil people, taking care to shoot her victims in the head to prevent their own return from the dead. With a Pittsburgh mob war going on, she has a perfect cover for her activities, as Mafioso Sal "The Shark" Macelli (Robert Loggia) is attempting a bloody takeover. She encounters one of Macelli's underlings, Joe Gennaro (Anthony LaPaglia), but senses an inner goodness in him and spares him, electing instead to seduce, vampirize and kill Tony (Chazz Palminteri). Joe shows up the scene of Tony's death; he is in fact an undercover cop, but US Attorney Sinclair (Angela Bassett) thinks he's getting in too deep and intentionally blows his cover by planting his picture in the paper, revealing his true identity.

Macelli is enraged to find out about the ruse, but shortly thereafter he encounters Marie and, turned on by her defiant attitude toward his crude advances, takes her home to his mansion. He thinks he's about to get lucky, but soon she's tearing his throat out and drinking his blood. He manages to shoot her in the struggle, however, and the shot alerts Macelli's waiting driver, forcing Marie to flee before she can finish the crimelord off. Joe arrives at the scene and, after an angry confrontation with Macelli's lawyer, Emmanuel Bergman (Don Rickles), he spots Marie and tracks her to a shuttered store, where she threatens him before disappearing.

Meanwhile, the now vampiric Macelli has awakened in the morgue, stolen a car and crashed it attempting to get to Bergman's house. Overhearing a report of the crash, Marie commandeers Joe's car to get there. She reveals her true nature to Joe and explains that Macelli has become a vampire and must be stopped. Arriving at the crash site, Joe attempts to explain the situation to his fellow cops, but Marie feigns innocence and they ridicule Joe's story. He continues on to Bergman's mansion, where he's attacked by the undead Macelli, who instructs his goons to lock Joe in the trunk of his car. Macelli then attacks Bergman and drinks his blood before taking off with his goons and the captured Joe; but Marie follows them and saves Joe from being fed into a garbage masher.

With the sun about to rise, Macelli drives off to find shelter, and Marie and Joe lose him after a pursuit and are forced to take cover of their own in a motel room. The hospitalized Bergman, however, disintegrates before the horrified staff when the blinds in his room are opened. At first wary of Marie, Joe comes to trust her, and they make love.

As the sun sets, Macelli calls two of his associates to the meat locker where he's taken refuge and gives Lenny (David Proval) the bite before putting him in his trunk. Driving to his club, Macelli opens the trunk and reveals Lenny to be almost good as new, before announcing to the assembled thugs that he can make them immortal, and that in this state they'll be able to take over the city. Marie and Joe arrive at the club and after rescuing a pair of cops who have been grabbed by the vampires, dispatch Macelli's undead underlings. Macelli himself jumps from the roof and, despite being smashed between a colliding car and bus, continues to proclaim his plans for conquest. But Joe manages to set Macelli on fire, and then shoots him into burning pieces. Upset by the carnage she has caused, Marie sets out to walk into the rays of the rising sun, but Joe stops her, and she realizes that staying with him will allow her to feel more human.

Landis attempts to combine chuckles and chills, but he can't merge the two as successfully as contemporaries like Joe Dante and Sam Raimi. INNOCENT BLOOD's crime and horror trappings are all presented straight—the tough, foul-mouthed gangsters, the gory vampire attacks—but the movie is pitched with a jokey attitude that prevents them from resonating at a visceral level. This approach extends to the technical credits: Mac Ahlberg's slick photography is glossy rather than Gothic, and Ira Newborn's score sounds more appropriate to "Dragnet" than Dracula.

Looked at the other way, INNOCENT BLOOD can be seen as a comedy interrupted by periodic outbursts of gruesome violence, which are undeniably well executed by special makeup effects ace Steve Johnson; the vampiric Bergman's disintegration in the hospital room is a particular highlight. But the blood and guts are presented far too literally for them to sit easily alongside the comic elements. Landis also throws in a raft of horror in-jokes, with mixed results; his *de riguer* director's cameos are fun—Raimi appears as a meat locker worker and Dario Argento turns up as an ambulance attendant—but the incessant shots of old, and better, vampire movies on the various characters' TVs become distracting and annoying.

The actors, at least, get the tones right, with LaPaglia (BETSY'S WEDDING, 29TH STREET) as an effective straight man, Loggia (SCARFACE, PRIZZI'S HONOR) with the right combination of threatening malice and lethal humor and Rickles playing his comic role well without his usual abrasive persona. Parillaud makes for a sympathetic and convincing vampire protagonist, with her appealing accent lending Marie an exoticism she might have lacked with an American actress. Given the apparent intention to make this a strong woman's role, though, it's a shame that she becomes a sex object in a few key moments. *(Excessive violence, profanity, nudity, sexual situations.)*

p, Lee Rich, Leslie Belzberg; d, John Landis; w, Michael Wolk; ph, Mac Ahlberg; ed, Dale Beldin; m, Ira Newborn; prod d, Richard Sawyer; set d, Peg Cummings; cos, Deborah Nadoolman; makeup, Steve Johnson

Horror/Comedy **(PR: O MPAA: R)**

INSIDE EDGE ★★

84m Frank Cinelli Productions ~ Atlantic Home Video c

Michael Madsen *(Richard Montana)*, Richard Lynch *(Mario Gio)*, Rosie Vela *(Lisa Zamora)*, George Jenesky *(Hip-Hop)*, Tony Peck *(Dan Nealy)*, Branscombe Richmond *(Henderson)*, Clifford Dalton *(Chief Deming)*, D. Paul Thomas *(Matt Reeves)*, David Shark *(Randy)*, Harold MacPherson *(Precinct Guard)*, Bill Swann *(Billy Boy)*, Jorge Alberto *(Abeyla)*, Antonio Iarve *(Mr. Ortiz)*

A busy but inconsequential urban crime thriller, INSIDE EDGE toplines Michael Madsen as tough cop Richard Montana, who's been using decidedly unorthodox means to topple drug kingpin Mario Gio (Richard Lynch). Up until now, Gio has been largely amused by Montana's endeavors. His latest escapade, busting Gio cohort Hip-Hop (George Jenesky), results in a $150,000 civilian lawsuit against the department and angers police chief Deming (Clifford Dalton). In retaliation, Deming slights Montana by promoting a rival officer, Henderson (Branscombe Richmond), to lieutenant; Montana blames Henderson for the earlier death of his partner. Against the warnings of his current partner and friend, Dan Nealy (Tony Peck), Montana falls for Gio's girlfriend, Lisa Zamora (Rosie Vela), a sultry cafe singer, who soon realizes she can use him to get revenge on Gio, who hasn't delivered on his promise to help her career. She gets Gio and Montana together; strengthening his own crime position, Gio starts feeding him information on his drug rivals, and when Montana brings them down, he is lionized by the press and Deming reluctantly promotes him.

Now, however, Gio has the goods on Montana, so he blackmails him into making a $5 million drug buy, during which Hip-Hop is killed, in Miami from Mr. Ortiz (Antonio Iarve). With lists provided by Lisa, Montana sells the drugs directly to Gio's dealers. Gio catches on to the scam; in a final shootout, Gio, Nealy (who was on Gio's payroll all along) and his henchmen are killed by Montana and Lisa, leaving the latter pair facing an undetermined future, except that they now have a suitcase full of tax-free cash.

Given its complex storyline (it's actually fairly well laid out, except for the disappointingly inconclusive ending), INSIDE EDGE should have been more interesting than it is, particularly regarding the entwined love/hate relationships among Montana, Gio and Lisa. But Vincent Gutierrez and William Tannen's screenplay does little more than establish this theme; otherwise, director Warren Clark is content to lay out the standard genre violence.

Veteran heavy Lynch (SWORD AND SORCERERS, PUPPET MASTER III) is, as usual, excellent as the villainous slimeball. Rosie Velez (THE TWO JAKES) is competent as the femme fatale; in addition, she expertly belts out two bluesy songs, "Can't Walk Away from Your Love" and "Heavy Rain." Hero Michael Madsen (THELMA AND LOUISE, THE DOORS), on the other hand, is more problematical; with a strong director and good material, Madsen has contributed some memorable screen characters. Lacking that, however, he's simply twitchily laconic, a second-rate James Dean. Whether or not he's improvising some dialogue herein, Madsen's scenes are draggy and unfocused, and the crucial question of whether he's a good cop or a corrupt one is much less interesting—and it's ultimately ignored by the movie—than Lisa's playing both him and Gio against each other.

INSIDE EDGE is well done technically, although Russell Moore's production design has a few gaffes: Montana's neat and clean apartment, for instance, doesn't reflect his working-class-hero character as effectively as his scruffy clothes and car do. Released direct-to-video, this LA-set movie was shot entirely on location in Baja California. *(Violence, substance abuse, profanity, nudity.)*

p, William Tannen; d, Warren Clark; w, Vincent Gutierrez, William Tannen, (from the screenplay by Gutierrez); ph, Eric Van Haren Noman; ed, Michael Keusch; m, Scott Douglas Maclachlan, Clay Manska, Glenn Aulepp; prod d, Russell Moore; cos, Ted Giammona

Crime/Action/Thriller **(PR: O MPAA: R)**

INSPECTOR LAVARDIN ★★★½

(France) 100m Marin Karmitz Productions; Films A2; Television Suisse Romande; CAB Productions ~ MK2 Productions USA c

Jean Poiret *(Inspector Jean Lavardin)*, Bernadette Lafont *(Helene Mons)*, Jean-Claude Brialy *(Claude Alvarez)*, Jacques Dacqmine *(Raoul Mons)*, Hermine Claire *(Veronique Manguin)*, Jean-Luc Bideau *(Max Charnet)*, Pierre-Francois Dumeniaud *(Marcel Vigouroux)*, Florent Gibassier *(Francis Li Bihan)*, Guy Louret *(Buci)*, Jean Depusse *(Volga)*, Marc Adam *(Adam)*, Michel Dupuy *(Frogman)*, Serge Feuillet *(Priest)*, Michel Fontayne *(Bouncer)*, Philippe Froger *(Director)*, Chantal Gresset *(Eve)*, Claire Ifrane *(Tobacconist)*, Herve Lelardoux *(1st Right-Minded Man)*, Lisa Livane *(Right-Minded Woman)*, Guy Parigot *(2nd Right-Minded Man)*, Robert Mazet *(Leon)*, Maurice Regnaut *(Pierre Manguin)*, Odette Simonneau *(Denise)*

The recent success of Claude Chabrol's STORY OF WOMEN and MADAME BOVARY, both starring Isabelle Huppert, helped bring about the belated US release of two of the director's formerly overlooked efforts, 1987's THE CRY OF THE OWL and the previous year's INSPECTOR LAVARDIN. A deliciously entertaining sequel to the French hit POULET AU VINAIGRE, INSPECTOR LAVARDIN continues the adventures of a most unorthodox police detective, played by the late Jean Poiret.

Raoul Mons (Jacques Dacqmine) is a pious, portly writer of boring novels who, as the film begins, is seen throwing his considerable weight behind the banning of a sacreligious play in his provincial town. The next day he is found dead, face down and naked on some rocks by the sea, with the word "pig" scrawled across his back.

Inspector Lavardin begins his inquiry into the murder by interrogating the family, consisting of twice-widowed Helene (Bernadette Lafont), also an old flame of Lavardin's; Veronique (Hermine Claire), her teenage daughter by her equally tragic previous marriage; and her indolent gay brother Claude (Jean-Claude Brialy), a widower who spends his time creating meticulously painted sculptures of the eyes of the famous. None of these puts up even a pretense of grief for the late Mons, whom Helene married for money when the death of her first husband left her bankrupt, and who was despised by both Veronique and Claude. The group of possible suspects eventually extends to include a sleazy disco owner (Jean-Luc Bideau), from whom Mons rented a bachelor's pad equipped with a video camera mounted over the bed; and a stagehand with the banned theatrical troupe, who is apparently Claude's paid lover.

As he did in POULET AU VINAIGRE, Lavardin shows little regard for the presumption of innocence—much less basic civil rights—as he bullies and threatens his way to the truth. Once he has completed his recreation of the crime, he extends his role to judge and jury, framing the innocent and absolving the guilty according to his personal code of justice. All this is based on his finding that the real villain of the piece was none other than the late Mons himself.

Though not among his greatest works, INSPECTOR LAVARDIN is typically Chabrolian in its jovial skewering of middle-class pretensions. As usual, Chabrol's characters affect a moral rectitude quite at odds with their underlying swinishness. Ironically, Lavardin uses his detective's shield as a cover for his own abusive tactics, the only difference being that he is on the side of law and order.

INSPECTOR LAVARDIN lacks the sense of outrage that characterizes Chabrol's best work. On the other hand, it has an exquisitely unfussy, serene style that echoes the late films of Hitchcock and Bunuel. Chabrol shares with Hitchcock a delight in unfolding a devious, well-crafted suspense narrative, as well as an ambivalence about police and other figures of societal authority. With Bunuel he shares the wry amusement of an aging *enfant terrible* who finally recognizes that he has himself become a pillar of the bourgeoisie he so despises.

Poiret plays Lavardin with a no-nonsense earthiness that recalls the great Jean Gabin. Lafont worked with the director in his first film, LE BEAU SERGE, and Brialy in his second, LES COUSINS, contributing to the impression that INSPECTOR LAVARDIN is the work of a group of old friends and comfortably kindred spirits. *(Adult situations.)*

p, Marin Karmitz; d, Claude Chabrol; w, Claude Chabrol, Dominique Roulet; ph, Jean Rabier; ed, Monique Fardoulis, Angela Braga-Mermet; m, Mathieu Chabrol; art d, Benoit-Fresco; cos, Magali Fustier

Mystery/Thriller **(PR: C MPAA: NR)**

INTO THE SUN ★½

100m Into the Sun, Inc.; Vidmark Entertainment ~ Trimark Pictures International c

Anthony Michael Hall *(Tom Slade)*, Michael Pare *(Captain Paul Watkins)*, Deborah Maria Moore *(Major Goode)*, Terry Kiser *(Mitchell Burton)*, Brian Haley *(Lieutenant DeCarlo)*, Michael St. Gerard *(Lieutenant Wolf)*, Linden Ashby *(Dragon)*, Jack Heller *(Commandant)*, Ted Davis *(Yosef)*, Hunter Von Leer *(Lieutenant Colonel Reynolds)*, Casey Stengel *(Technican)*, Melissa Moore *(Female Sergeant)*, Chino Binamo *(1st Soldier)*, Richard Epper *(2nd Soldier)*, Raffe *(1st Enemy Guard)*, Tim Moran *(2nd Enemy Guard)*, Eddie Yansick *(Bedouin)*, Ahbaru Zetlina *(Executioner)*, Nayyer Bilal *(Bedouin with Knife)*

A handsome but preposterous action adventure, INTO THE SUN must have sprung from a desperate story conference. It's an unholy union of TOP GUN and THE HARD WAY. If originality won wars, then this screenplay would be classified 4-F.

The fun begins "somewhere over the Mediterranean Sea," where US fighter pilot Paul "Shotgun" Watkins (Michael Pare) and his macho flyboy friends have a close encounter of the opening-credits kind with some unfriendly Mirage warplanes of a never-to-be-named foreign power. Back at the base Watkins is given an unexpected ground assignment: callow Hollywood superstar Tom Slade (Anthony Michael Hall) has been cast in an armed forces picture and wants to tag along with a real Top Gunner to research his role. With the introduction of Slade, INTO THE SUN nearly takes off in a fresh, interesting direction.

Initially the actor isn't the spoiled stumblebum one expects, but a friendly, if self-absorbed, dude to whom everything comes too easily. Before Watkins's unbelieving eyes, Slade instantly masters the computer flight simulator, proves immune to oxygen-deprivation in a pressure chamber, and even starts to romance Major Goode (Deborah Maria Moore), a commanding officer with cover girl looks who happens to be Watkins's lover. The closest INTO THE SUN comes to honest emotion is when Watkins drops his stoic facade and laments, "You know what really gets me about Slade? He's good at everything . . . he doesn't even really have to try."

There's a legitimate concept lurking here, derivative or not. How does an outside tinseltown personality like, for example, Tom Cruise get along with the real-life naval aviators he's supposed to play? But, as with THE HARD WAY, the contrast has no edge whatsoever because "reality" in this film turns out to be as laughable as any celluloid fluff. Watkins takes Slade up in the air in an F-16 to humble the brat packer with aerial acrobatics. Suddenly that never-to-be-named foreign power attacks the American squadron, and Slade and Watkins get shot down in enemy territory. Slade instantly devolves into a silly stereotype of a California pretty boy threatening to sue Watkins and griping about the lack of tanning lotion as the odd couple wander the wastelands.

The film flubs its chance at an award from the Arab Anti-Defamation League, as treacherous Bedouins capture the pair and hand them over to the hostage-hungry warlord and Yassir Arafat lookalike, but then the greedy nomads kidnap Slade back again because he's a star. Slade and his Arab Merry Men rescue Watkins from execution, and the two Yanks blow up the nation-state's entire military infrastructure while escaping a nonstop, absolutely unbelievable fracas strongly reminiscent of 1991's parody HOT SHOTS. INTO THE SUN was in fact promoted as a comedy, but it's hard to tell at this level of exaggeration. Some of the better bits: the avaricious Arab tribesman drive pickups and listen to Country and Western ballads, and while in their sandy clutches a nervous Slade leans over to Watkins and whispers, "My real name's Greenbaum!"

The picture does look good: its relatively modest $6 million budget is betrayed only by the skimpy homebase of the desert despot. Flight sequences are more exciting than usual for this breed, and were achieved using basic modelwork mixed with stock footage of the Peruvian Air Force. But when the battles begin the quality of the material crashes to the ground. It's energetic but predictable as a flight plan, moviemaking on autopilot. The soundtrack in particular feels like car-chase music from every cop TV series ever made.

Anthony Michael Hall (THE BREAKFAST CLUB, EDWARD SCISSORHANDS), a young actor whose career has been on a roller coaster of hits, flops and the usual publicized-bouts-with-alcohol, contritely told the press that his temperamental antics made things miserable for director Fritz Kiersch during the shoot, but Hall can't catch all the flak for such monumental banality. As Mitchell Burton, Tom Slade's high-strung manager, Terry Kiser overacts enough to revive vaudeville. Linden Ashby borrows Bruce Dern mannerisms in his small, but showy part as an American mercenary flying for the villians. As the good-looking major with an arsenal of low-cut party dresses, Moore (she's Roger Moore's daughter, previously seen onscreen under the name Deborah Barrymore) is never more than decorative. Michael Pare (EDDIE AND THE CRUISERS, STREETS OF FIRE) comes off best; the B-movie action star essays "Shotgun" Watkins with a proper blend of cool professionalism and understated humor.

INTO THE SUN played theaters in Washington, D.C., Dallas and elsewhere before ejecting into home video later in the year. *(Violence, profanity, sexual situations.)*

p, Kevin M. Kallberg, Oliver G. Hess; d, Fritz Kiersch; w, John Brancato, Michael Ferris, (from the story by Ferris and Brancato); ph, Steve Grass; ed, Barry Zetlin; m, Randy Miller; prod d, Gary T. New; art d, Dana Torrey; set d, A. Rosaline Crew

Action/Adventure/Comedy (PR: O MPAA: R)

INVASION OF THE SPACE PREACHERS ★

100m Big Pictures ~ Rhino Home Video c

Jim Wolfe *(Walter Bennett)*, Guy Nelson *(Rick Lowery)*, Eliska Hahn *(Nova)*, Gary Brown *(Reverend Lash/Kritar)*, Jesse Johnson *(Vic20)*, Vince Edwards *(Theodore Daniels)*, Cameron Macarelli *(Steven)*, John Ricks, Jimmy Walker, Stacy Weddington, John Marshall

"It's sort of like 'Green Acres' meets BLADE RUNNER." That's producer-writer-director Daniel Boyd's unhelpful summation of INVASION OF THE SPACE PREACHERS, an obscure, boring comic mishmash, filmed entirely in West Virginia under the title *Strangest Dreams*.

Rick Lowery (Guy Nelson) and Walter Bennett (Jim Wolfe) are urbanites from Ohio who motor into the rural countryside for a much-needed vacation and less-welcome gags about urine and "The Dukes of Hazzard." The city slickers stop at a community that seems friendly enough, but every once in a while the folksy inhabitants complain about having the "strangest dreams" and go into a trance when they hear the hypnotic voice of the neighborhood's whip-wielding evangelist, Reverend Lash (Gary Brown). "My world is a better one," intones the unearthly preacher during his "Lash of God" radio show. He's an alien, of course, an extraterrestrial criminal called Kritar. Soon Rick and Walt witness the arrival of an interstellar bounty-hunter (in a canvas-and-chickenwire starship that looks like a gourd) hot on Kritar's trail.

These ETs take the form of bug-eyed monsters while traveling the cosmos, but otherwise they're perfectly humanoid, and the bounty-hunter transforms into a Daryl Hannah lookalike named Nova (Eliska Hahn). Walt falls for the sexually naive galactic cutie, but their romance has to wait; Kritar has bribed a politician to transmit the next mind-melting Reverend Lash sermon worldwide via satellite. Gloats the villain: "I will bestow upon me the most corrupt and powerful position on this planet—president of the United States!" The fate of mankind lies in the hands of Rick, Walt, Nova and the druggie members of a forest hippie commune headed by a Nicaraguan mercenary. It's a long hundred minutes before Kritar and his henchmen get shot up by the assembled townspeople, whose hail of bullets somehow manages to miss hostage Rick. One really doesn't care whether Rick survives or not, just as long as the picture finally ends.

The performances are uniformly grotesque, with one actor portraying a midget by standing on his knees. Except for the nifty insectoid-alien costumes, production values are threadbare, while the energy level is laggard and the spoofing light-years away from funny. There's no profound satire of religion, sci-fi, any particular church, or any particular *anything*, except a flash of cleverness when Walt gets out of a jam by quoting "Klaatu barada nikto," from the classic DAY THE EARTH STOOD STILL.

Slightly closer to the heart of filmmaker Boyd's *oeuvre* is a throwaway joke about a goonish local who poses as the banjo-strumming mute from DELIVERANCE to entertain gawking tourists, then speechifies, "It's cheap, exploitive tactics like this that contribute to a negative, unrealistic image of the contemporary Appalachian!" Boyd, a former West Virginia State University instructor, has labored mightily to create a movie industry in the Mountain State with native talent. His first picture, CHILLERS, was a fair terror anthology and his latest, PARADISE PARK, stars a gallery of country-and-western music stars as denizens of a trailer camp awaiting a visit from God. In between came INVASION OF THE SPACE PREACHERS (in which Boyd cameos as co-proprietor of a roadside exhibit, the Amazing House of Dung). It was filmed in venues like Cabin Creek, Sissonville, Garretts Bend and Tornado on a budget of about $100 thousand with a crew of unpaid volunteers from local colleges. Boyd transferred the celluloid footage to videotape for editing and final release, which might explain the film's flat, bleached-out look.

The film came out as a rather hard to find videocassette. Cult-movie fans attracted by odd cheapies with novelty titles may want to inspect INVASION OF THE SPACE PREACHERS if they can find it, but it's not worth an intensive search. *(Violence, substance abuse, profanity, nudity, sexual situations.)*

p, David Wohl, A.V. Gallagher, Daniel Boyd; d, Daniel Boyd; w, Daniel Boyd; ph, Bill Hogan; ed, Daniel Boyd; m, Michael Lipton; prod d, Steve Gilliland; art d, Bradford Boll, Brian Young

Science Fiction/Comedy (PR: O MPAA: NR)

JENNIFER EIGHT ★★½

127m Scott Rudin Productions ~ Paramount c

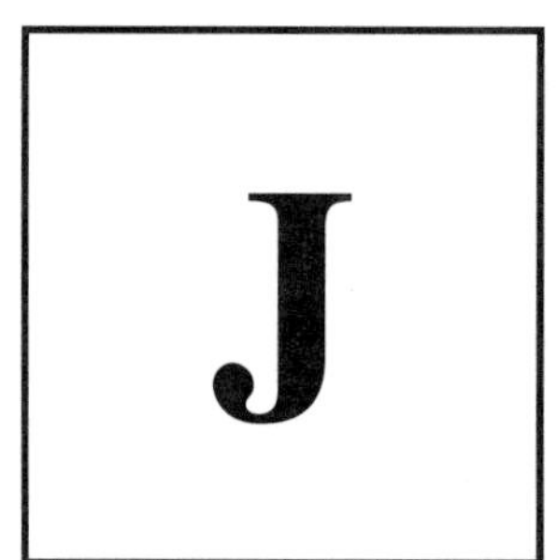

Andy Garcia *(John Berlin)*, Lance Henriksen *(Freddy Ross)*, Uma Thurman *(Helena Robertson)*, Graham Beckel *(John Taylor)*, Kathy Baker *(Margie Ross)*, Kevin Conway *(Citrine)*, John Malkovich *(St. Anne)*, Perry Lang *(Travis)*, Nicholas Love *(Bisley)*, Michael O'Neill *(Serato)*, Paul Bates *(Venables)*, Bob Gunton *(Goodridge)*, Lenny Von Dohlen *(Blattis)*, Bryan Larkin *(Bobby Rose)*, Debbon Ayer *(Amanda)*, Eddie Korbich *(Myopic Janitor)*, Stephen Piemonte, II *(Trimble)*, Ken Camroux *(Pathologist)*, Carol Jeanne Schneider *(Ann)*, Deborah Spector *(Emerson)*, Frank Birney *(Expert)*, Mike Winlaw *(Male Reporter)*, Jeffrey Josephson *(Popeye)*, T.J. Hageboeck *(Max)*, Jaylene Hamilton-Larose *(Woman Reporter)*, Joe Drago *(St. Anne's Assistant)*, Jonas Quastel *(Lab Technician)*, Charles "Mark" Eaton *(Airplane Pilot)*

Despite a gimmicky, underdeveloped plot, JENNIFER EIGHT is a moody, atmospheric thriller, featuring several fine performances and marking a promising major studio debut by writer-director Bruce Robinson.

John Berlin (Andy Garcia) is a cop teetering toward burnout from life on the streets of LA and the collapse of a bad marriage. At the invitation of an old friend, fellow cop Freddy Ross (Lance Henriksen), Berlin bolts from the LAPD for a supposedly quieter life in rural California with the Eureka police force. Instead, Berlin immediately prickles his new colleagues, including one who was passed over for promotion to make room for Berlin, by reopening the case of a serial killer of blind girls that went unsolved despite a full-time six-month effort by the department. The title of the film comes from the code name for the case, which has already cost the lives of seven.

Berlin becomes convinced that "Jennifer 8" will be blind student Helena Robertson (Uma Thurman), who was the roommate of the last victim. The case comes to obsess Berlin, despite an almost complete lack of hard evidence, and he becomes romantically involved with Robertson, who resembles his ex-wife. Concerned for his friend's physical and emotional welfare, Ross accompanies Berlin on a stakeout at Robertson's school after leaving Robertson at a party with Ross's wife Margie (Kathy Baker). When they see lights in the closed school, Berlin investigates and is knocked unconscious, awakening to find that Ross has been shot to death with his gun.

After a grueling interrogation by FBI agent, St. Anne (John Malkovich), Berlin is arrested for murder but bailed out by Margie, who wants him to avenge the death of her husband. Instead, she becomes the avenger herself when she masquerades as Helena and is cornered by the killer in Helena's school dorm. The killer reveals himself to be the passed-over cop—his killing spree prompted by a traumatic childhood spent attending a school for blind girls—before Margie shoots him dead.

In the unusual case of JENNIFER EIGHT it's meant as a compliment that the thriller plot is by far the least interesting aspect of this otherwise absorbing drama. It's also meant as a compliment that the film recalls Nicholas Ray's small-scale noir classic ON DANGEROUS GROUND, in which stressed-out city cop Robert Ryan is exiled north, to "Siberia," where he's sensitized by his involvement with blind girl Ida Lupino while investigating a local murder case. Like Ray, Robinson (WITHNAIL AND I, HOW TO GET AHEAD IN ADVERTISING) demonstrates a strong affinity for isolated, alienated individuals in a hostile environment.

For most of its running time, JENNIFER EIGHT is effectively and powerfully built around the echoing existences of Robertson, whose blindness makes her easy prey to the fear and panic of isolation, and Berlin, whose absorption in his gruesome work has left him similarly isolated and fearful. Where the film falls apart is in failing to follow through on Berlin's growing dependence on Helena as he finds himself blindsided after being framed for Ross's murder. Like ON DANGEROUS GROUND—indeed, almost all of Ray's films—JENNIFER EIGHT is finally about two "cripples" reaching out to each other on common, and dangerous, ground.

Ultimately, due either to studio interference, as was rumored, or bad judgment, Robinson damages his film by separating Helena and Berlin at the film's climax for the sake of the "surprise" ending. Then he resorts to the kind of nickel-and-dime aberrant child psychology more appropriate to low-budget slasher films to explain his killer. But along the way, besides creating some poignant movie moments, Robinson elicits fine performances from his excellent cast, especially Garcia and Thurman, neither of whom has been more compelling than they are here. Henriksen and Baker lend typically sterling support and Malkovich is suitably noirish.

Its flaws prevent JENNIFER EIGHT from being one of the year's best, but the film's virtues make it far better than most and ample enough reason to keep an eye out for Robinson's next effort. *(Violence, profanity, nudity, adult situations.)*

p, David Wimbury, Gary Lucchesi; d, Bruce Robinson; w, Bruce Robinson; ph, Conrad L. Hall; ed, Conrad Buff; m, Christopher Young; prod d, Richard MacDonald; art d, William Durrell, Jr., John Willett; set d, Casey C. Hallenbeck, Elizabeth Wilcox

Romance/Thriller (PR: C MPAA: R)

JOHNNY STECCHINO ★★★½

(Italy) 100m Penta Film; CG Group Tiger Cinematografica ~ New Line Cinema c

Roberto Benigni *(Dante/Johnny Stecchino)*, Nicoletta Braschi *(Maria)*, Paolo Bonacelli *(D'Agata)*, Franco Volpi *(Minister)*, Ivano Marescotti *(Randazzo)*, Alessandro DeSantis *(Lillo)*, Domenico Minutoli *(Chief of Police)*, Guilio Donnini *(Cardinal)*, Gaetano Sperandeo *(1st Picciotto)*, Gaetano Campisi *(2nd Picciotto)*, Loredana Romito *(Gianna)*, Ignazio Pappalardo *(Filippo Cozzamara)*, Salvatore Scallia *(Judge)*, Vito Zappala *(Marshal)*, Luciana Palombi *(Mrs. Festa)*, Giorgia O'Brien *(Minister's Wife)*, Giorgio Trestini *(Doorman)*, Angela Conti Imperioli *(1st Girl at the Party)*, Daniela Mango *(2nd Girl at the Party)*, Salvatore Borgese *(Iganzio)*, Carlo Amedeo Mangiu *(Barber)*, Giuseppe Viola *(Spectator)*

Best known to American audiences for his work with independent filmmaker Jim Jarmusch, Roberto Benigni is poised to become the next great European screen comedian. As director, writer and star of the tremendously funny JOHNNY STECCHINO, Benigni has placed himself in an enviable position—someone able to work in front of, behind and alongside the camera, all with equal panache.

The film begins as an impossibly beautiful woman pours out her heart to Dante (Benigni). The sappy faced Roman looks on stoically as she pleads for forgiveness and begs him to make love. As it turns out, the girl is merely telling him the story of an earlier encounter with her old boyfriend. Always the last guy to get the girl, Dante precariously suggests he take her home. Brushing him off like lint, she refuses. Leaving a party that night, Dante is nearly run over by a beautiful woman, Maria (Nicoletta Braschi), who is zipping her sports car through town. Maria apologizes to the hapless Dante, but when she gets a close look at his face, she can't believe it. She utters, "You're like a dream," before passing out in his arms. Flattered but confused, he runs off to find help for Maria. When he returns, she and her car are gone.

The next day, Dante is floating on air as he tells his pal Lillo (Alessandro DeSantis), a high school student with Downs Syndrome, about his magnificent episode from the previous evening. Dante, who drives Lillo's school bus, then proceeds to do his favorite magician's act by stealing two bananas from a local fruit vendor. He returns home from work that night to find the ravishing Maria waiting at his door. She only stays for a brief moment—long enough to eat some cake. If Dante was confused before, now he's dumbstruck. Things get stranger when an insurance man shows up and Dante begins flailing his right hand around—he's been claiming a false injury suit for years. Dante finally locates Maria's hotel and surprises her with a visit.

The couple spend a wonderful day together touring Rome, with Maria buying Dante a new suit and encouraging him to use a toothpick. Strangest of all, she begins to call him Johnny and draws a mole below his right eye. Dante doesn't mind—he's finally got his girl. The next day Maria promptly disappears again. Heartbroken, Dante mopes around the apartment with Lillo. Then Maria calls, inviting Johnny to her mansion in Palermo. He arrives the next day happy as a puppy and is greeted by a man claiming to be Maria's uncle, D'Agata (Paolo Bonacelli)—in reality a low-life gangster with a serious cocaine habit who works for the mysterious woman. He greets Dante with amazement and also calls him Johnny.

Dante is soon welcomed by a radiant Maria who shows him to his bedroom. The delighted houseguest believes it will only be a matter of time before they will consummate their relationship. Secretly watching the visitor from behind a closet door, however, is the real Johnny "Toothpick" Stecchino (Benigni again), Maria's husband and a notorious Mafioso who has recently earned the ire of his fellow mob leaders. The plan is that Maria will march the unwitting Dante, a dead ringer for Stecchino, around town until the bad guys knock him off, leaving Maria and the Toothpick to live happily ever after. The cold gangster who can't stand to be kissed by his wife isn't very impressed with Dante. "He don't look nothing like me. He's got the face of a wimp!"

The next day Dante rises early to seek out his daily breakfast of bananas. Just as he is about to pilfer one, a carload of hoodlums working for the infamous mobster, Filippo Cozzamara (Ignazio Pappalardo), spot him and open fire. He runs straight to the police and screams that the fruit shop owner has tried to murder him. Later that night, while attending the opera with Maria, he causes a mass exodus just by his presence. He believes it's just because he didn't pay for a banana at intermission. Maria, desperate to get him rubbed out, takes him to a very public party where he ends up offering a bag full of cocaine, which Uncle D'Agata told him was a cure for diabetes, to the town's Cardinal (Guilio Donnini).

The next day Maria has a clandestine meeting with the fearsome Cozzamara and tells him she'll deliver her husband. Shortly thereafter, Dante is paraded into a barbershop where he is surrounded by numerous ugly hoods. Meanwhile Maria and the real Johnny are on their way to South America. While they stop at a gas station, Johnny is surprised to find the bathroom stalls filled with hitmen. Maria has out-schemed her husband. Dante is still safe and entertaining the barbershop hoods. Maria, a wealthier widow, takes Dante back to Rome and his old life. Lillo is waiting for him at the door.

Benigni has written a screenplay that perfectly suits his acting and directing sensibilities. At moments poignant and other times just this side of a Marx Brothers film, JOHNNY STECCHINO is designed to showcase the hyphenate's strengths—physical comedy and sheer versatility. The rubber-faced comedian commands the screen from the first frame, playing Dante the lovable schlemiel. Benigni has one of those faces that elicits chuckles before a word is uttered, and his Dante evokes belly laughs as he is pursued by half of Sicily, in a role that might have been written for Peter Sellers or Jerry Lewis.

If Dante is the Everyman with a dream, then Johnny the gangster is the tough—or, at least, semi-tough—side of Benigni. As Johnny, Benigni slows his body movements and plays his devotion to mamma with a twisted edge. Though Johnny is more neurotic than Dante, Benigni plays both roles with abandon and makes the transitions work with a wide range of comic tricks. Some scenes seem written just to showcase his physical skills, but all the plot lines are nevertheless neatly resolved in the third act. Benigni has also surrounded himself with a uniformly strong cast, headed by Braschi as the scheming and eccentric Maria.

JOHNNY STECCHINO is that rare and welcome phenomenon, a film that provokes sustained waves of laughter throughout. It's also a surprisingly poignant take on unrequited love, set against a variety of extremely inviting Italian backdrops. Since JOHNNY STECCHINO has become the highest-grossing Italian picture of all time, it's safe to say that we'll be seeing a lot more of Benigni. In fact, he's already been snagged by Blake Edwards to star in the upcoming SON OF THE PINK PANTHER. *(Adult situations, substance abuse.)*

p, Mario Cecchi Gori, Vittorio Cecchi Gori; d, Roberto Benigni; w, Roberto Benigni, Vincenzo Cerami, (from the story by Benigni and Cerami); ph, Giuseppe Lanci; ed, Nino Baragli; m, Evan Lurie; art d, Paolo Biagetti; set d, Giancarlo Sensidoni; cos, Gianna Gissi

Comedy **(PR: C MPAA: R)**

JOHNNY SUEDE ★★

95m Vegas Films; Balthazar Pictures; Arena Films; Starr Pictures ~ Miramax c

Brad Pitt *(Johnny Suede)*, Richard Boes *(Man in Tuxedo)*, Cheryl Costa *(Woman in Alley)*, Michael Luciano *(Mr. Clepp)*, Calvin Levels *(Deke)*, Nick Cave *(Freak Storm)*, Ralph Marrero *(Bartender)*, Wilfredo Giovanni Clark *(Slick)*, Alison Moir *(Darlette)*, Peter McRobbie *(Flip Doubt)*, Ron Vawter *(Winston)*, Dennis Parlato *(Dalton)*, Tina Louise *(Mrs. Fontaine)*, Michael Mulheren *(Fred Business)*, Wayne Maugans *(Ned Business)*, Catherine Keener *(Yvonne)*, Joseph Barry *(The Cowboy)*, John David Barone *(Bernard)*, Tom Jarmusch *(Conan)*, Samuel L. Jackson *(B-Bop)*, Evelyn Solann *(Old Woman)*, Ashley Gardner *(Ellen)*, Ahmed Ben Larby *(Cab Driver)*

This surrealistic fable from cinematographer turned writer-director Tom DiCillo tries very hard to be hip. Sometimes it succeeds, but more often it simply collapses under the weight of its own absurdity.

Johnny Suede (Brad Pitt) is a young man who aspires to be a rock 'n' roll star in the mold of his 1960s idol, Ricky Nelson. Johnny has the right look, the right attitude and the largest pompadour in town, but a crucial element is still missing—he lacks a cool pair of shoes. Late one night, while he is leaving a downtown nightclub, a pair of black suede shoes literally drop from the heavens into his path. The newly complete and confident youth then meets the mysterious Darlette, a beautiful bohemian. They sleep together after she tells him about her boyfriend—a man with a penchant for hitting her. Johnny considers going after the cad until Darlette mentions her beau's gun. Instead, a deal is worked out; Johnny will see her every other day.

Hurting for rent money, Johnny pawns his guitar until his best friend, Deke (Calvin Levels), fronts him the cash to get it back and the two begin to form a band. Inexplicably, Darlette grows tired of Johnny and ends their relationship. Weathering a depression, Johnny eventually meets Yvonne (Catherine Keener). She's a few years older and certainly wiser than the budding idol. They begin a romance, but Johnny still dreams about Darlette. Yvonne teaches Johnny about life and love, but he remains cautious about getting too close to her.

When his band falls apart, Johnny appeals to aging punk rocker Freak Storm (Nick Cave) for guidance. Freak takes the young man's last twenty dollars and promises him some recording time, which never materializes. Johnny moves in with Yvonne, but she throws him out after he cheats on her with a stranger. After spending the night sitting in a diner, where he dreams about death and midgets, Johnny returns to Yvonne and apologizes for his behavior. What was really missing from his life was true love, not a pair of suede shoes.

JOHNNY SUEDE's stylish, dreamlike mood and abstract dialogue cannot compensate for its unsatisfying storyline and characters. Indeed, it's only Brad Pitt's (A RIVER RUNS THROUGH IT, THELMA & LOUISE) performance that makes the film watchable through to the end. Pitt certainly has screen-idol looks, but also demonstrates a vulnerability and confusion that round out his character. And DiCillo takes advantage of Pitt's comic abilities, allowing for some genuinely funny moments: Johnny rushing out the door to beat up Darlette's boyfriend, only to return swiftly when he is told the man carries a gun; Yvonne inducting the young man into the mysteries of the female anatomy. Moments like these, though, can't make up for a weak overall plot.

The main problem is that Johnny is almost entirely passive. He is pushed through the story, very rarely fighting back or generating any real conflict. As the only completely sane character, Keener (BACKTRACK, SWITCH) helps matters somewhat.

JOHNNY SUEDE remains intriguing on a visual level, thanks to the deliberately generic, anonymous urban setting, some Fellini-esque casting choices and, above all, Johnny's outrageous pompadour hairstyle. Ultimately, though, this is a derivative blend of surface elements from three far better films: Martin Scorsese's AFTER HOURS, Jonathan Demme's SOMETHING WILD and David Lynch's BLUE VELVET. *(Profanity, sexual situations.)*

p, Ruth Waldburger, Yoram Mandel; d, Tom DiCillo; w, Tom DiCillo; ph, Joe DeSalvo; ed, Geraldine Peroni; m, Jim Farmer; prod d, Patricia Woodbridge; art d, Laura Brock; cos, Jessica Haston

Comedy/Romance **(PR: C MPAA: R)**

JOURNEY OF HONOR ★★★

(Japan) 107m Sho Kosugi Corporation; Mayeda Productions~ MCA/Universal Home Video c

Sho Kosugi *(Mayeda)*, David Essex *(Don Pedro)*, Kane Kosugi *(Yorimune)*, Christopher Lee *(King Philip)*, Norman Lloyd *(Father Vasco)*, Ronald Pickup *(Captain Crawford)*, John Rhys-Davies *(El Zaidan)*, Polly Walker *(Cecilia)*, Dylan Kussman *(Smitty)*, Toshiro Mifune *(Lord Takugawa Ieyasu)*, Miwa Takada *(Yadogimi)*, Nijiko Kiyokawa *(Counselor)*, Yuki Sugimura *(Chiyo Mayeda)*, Ken Sekiguchi *(Ishikawa)*, Naoto Shigemizu *(Nakamura)*, Yuji Sawayama *(East Army General)*, Toni Sosic *(Dutch)*, Savic Milutin *(First Pistoleer)*, Miomir Radevic *(Second Pistoleer)*, Shinsuke Shirakura *(Daisuke Mayeda)*, Masashi Muta *(Daisuke Mayeda)*, Dusko Vujnovic *(Ibrahim)*, Stevan Minja *(Salim)*, Ljubomir Skiljevic *(Taskmaster)*, John Stewart *(1st Sailor)*, Dragomir Stanojevic-Kameni *(2nd Sailor)*, Bora Stojanovic *(Royal Chamberlin)*, Osamu Yayama *(Samurai in Edo Castle)*, Kenji Miura *(Interpreter for Ieyasu)*, Manami Mitani *(Interpreter for Yadogimi)*, Hidekazu Utsumi *(1st Page)*, Tadashi Ogasawara *(2nd Page)*, Akira Hoshino, Kenji Yasunaga, Shogo Ikegami, Junichiro Hayama, Yoshiaki Iguchi *(Retainers for Ieyasu)*, Toshimi Yamaguchi, Toshimi Ogiwara, Satoru Fukasaku, Yuki Nasaka, Kazuhiro Taketoshi, Takashi Odajima *(Samurai Guards for Ieyasu)*, Don Pedro Colley *(Voice-Over Narrator)*

Best-known to American audiences as the star of ENTER THE NINJA and its sequels, Japanese lead Sho Kosugi produces as well as stars in the rousing JOURNEY OF HONOR, an old-fashioned, lavishly produced swashbuckler.

Mayeda (Kosugi) is a samurai in 17th-century Japan whose clan, headed by Lord Ieyasu (Toshiro Mifune), is at war with another clan for control of the country. The rival clan has outfitted itself with punk-burning muskets which give them an advantage except when it rains and the water snuffs out the punks, making the rifles impossible to fire. Ieyasu dispatches Mayeda to Spain, accompanied by Ieyasu's young heir Yorimune (Kane Kosugi), to purchase five thousand flintlock rifles, which are immune to the rain.

Among Yorimune's entourage is, of course, a traitor, Yorimune's Catholic spiritual advisor Father Vasco (Norman Lloyd), who cuts a deal with the rival clan to assassinate Mayeda and Yorimune and see to it that the flintlocks never get delivered in return for wealth and power. The assassination attempt, aboard their ship piloted by the hard-drinking Captain Crawford (Ronald Pickup), is thwarted by Mayeda. However, in the process, the chest filled with gold to pay for the rifles falls overboard. Arriving in Spain penniless at the court of King Philip (Christopher Lee), Mayeda makes little progress in convincing the King to release the rifles on credit until he saves the King's life during a rebel attack. However, Mayeda also earns the enmity of the King's advisor, Don Pedro (David Essex), by winning the heart of his fiancee Cecilia (Polly Walker), who turns out to be Crawford's long-lost daughter, unwillingly bartered into marriage with Don Pedro.

Crawford eludes Don Pedro's attempts to capture his ship, only to run into Moroccan pirate El Zaidan (John Rhys-Davies), who has received information on their valuable cargo from Vasco. Now imprisoned in Morocco, Mayeda impresses El Zaidan with his samurai skills and wins a deal for his and Yorimune's freedom if he can defeat Don Pedro in mortal combat. Mayeda wins and, despite having to fight El Zaidan also, who tries to renege on his bargain, sails off into the sunset with Yorimune and Cecilia by his side.

JOURNEY OF HONOR bypassed an American theatrical release and went directly to home video, but that's no reason to shun it. What makes this film refreshingly different is precisely what might turn off action-movie junkies weaned on Indiana Jones, Rambo and even THE CRIMSON PIRATE.

Unlike the traditional American action hero, Kosugi's samurai hero is self-effacing to a fault. Though he's onscreen practically from the first moments, it's not even apparent he's to be the film's hero until Lord Ieyasu actually sends him on his mission. And this is after both his wife and young son, standing in for Yorimune, have given their lives to protect the young Lord. Yorimune is arrogant, disdainful and generally obnoxious until he matures during their adventure, but Mayeda casts him not so much as a sharp glance, so complete is his sense of duty. Mayeda doesn't even resist when, unaware of the priest's treachery, Yorimune countermands Mayeda's orders that Vasco be left in Spain. Mayeda's courtship of Cecilia is meanwhile courtly to the point of reticence.

There is a shortage of action sequences for a film of this type since Mayeda can't act, but only react to threats against his young charge. There is also a shortage of the usual swashbuckling romance, since Mayeda, whatever his feelings for Cecilia, can let nothing deter him from his duty. Yet, when the action sequences do come, they are exciting and imaginatively staged, which will come as no surprise to anyone familiar with Kosugi's past films. Perhaps compensating for the lack of romance, Mayeda walks in on Cecilia nude in her bath, although its motivation is a friendly rather than romantic gesture by Mayeda, since communal bathing is part of his culture.

Nelson Gidding's screenplay, based on a story co-written by Gidding and Kosugi, is a quirkily engaging mixture of historical drama and outrageous plot turns smoothly negotiated by veteran director Gordon Hessler, whose past outings with Kosugi include PRAY FOR DEATH. The star cameos, for another refreshing change, are all well cast, with Walker (ENCHANTED APRIL, PATRIOT GAMES) an appealing and feisty heroine and Mifune the obvious standout, bringing personality and charm to his brief part in an unusual action film that values chivalry and old-fashioned adventure over blood, gore and explosions. *(Violence, brief nudity.)*

p, Sho Kosugi; d, Gordon Hessler; w, Nelson Gidding, (from the story by Gidding and Sho Kosugi); ph, John Connor; ed, Bill Butler; m, John Scott; prod d, Adrian Gorton

Historical/Adventure/Action (PR: C MPAA: PG-13)

JUICE ★★½

94m IMPix Inc; Island World; Moritz/Heyman Productions ~ Paramount c

Omar Epps *(Quincy "Q")*, Tupac Shakur *(Bishop)*, Jermaine Hopkins *(Steel)*, Khalil Kain *(Raheem)*, Cindy Herron *(Yolanda)*, Vincent Laresca *(Radames)*, Samuel L. Jackson *(Trip)*, George O. Gore *(Brian)*, Grace Garland *(Quincy's Mother)*, Queen Latifah *(Ruffhouse M.C.)*, Idina Harris *(Keesha)*, Victor Campos *(Quiles)*, Eric Payne *(Frank)*, Sharon Cook *(Record Store Clerk)*, Darien Berry *(Blizzard)*, Maggie Rush *(Myra)*, Mark "Flex" Knox *(Contest Auditioner)*, Rony Clanton *(Detective Markham)*, Mike Badalucco *(Detective Kelly)*, Jacqui Dickerson *(Sweets)*, Pablo Guzman *(TV Reporter)*, Randy Frazier *(Steel's Father)*, Latanya Richardson *(Steel's Mother)*, Oran "Juice" Jones *(Snappy Nappy Dugout)*, Mitchell Marchand *(Kid at Trip's)*, Corwin Moore *(Sam)*, Lauren Jones *(Raheem's Mother)*, Birdie M. Hale *(Bishop's Grandma)*, L.B. Williams *(Bishop's Father)*, Donald Faison *(Student)*, Eddie Joe *(Bartender)*, John Patrick McLaughlin *(1st Cop)*, Norman Douglass *(2nd Cop)*, John DiBenedetto *(3rd Cop)*, Christopher Rubin *(Doctor)*, Juanita Troy-Keitt *(Homeless Woman)*, Ed Lover *(Contest Judge)*, Dr. Dre *(Contest Judge)*, Fab 5 Freddie *(Himself)*, Erik Sermon *(Bar Patron)*, Parrish Smith *(Bar Patron)*

"Juice" is street slang for respect and power, and the quest for it is at the heart of this directorial debut from Ernest Dickerson, Spike Lee's longtime cinematographer. Unlike the somewhat older milieu of Lee's films, JUICE, like many recent black-oriented features, is concerned with young people and their lives on and off the streets.

The lead characters are a quartet of teenaged friends: Quincy, known as "Q" (Omar Epps), Raheem (Khalil Kain), Bishop (Tupac Shakur) and Steel (Jermaine Hopkins). They spend little time in school, preferring to spend their days hanging in their Harlem neighborhood. While Raheem keeps up an argumentative relationship with his girlfriend (with whom he's already had a child) and the volatile Bishop looks for trouble with a rival gang, Q dreams of becoming a DJ; he plans to enter an upcoming contest, calling himself "Gee Q." After he and his friends shoplift some records in preparation for the contest, Q runs into an old friend in a bar who's just gotten out of jail. He turns out to be preparing to hold the place up; Bishop wants to join in, but Q holds him back. Later, watching TV at Steel's house, the friends see on the news that the friend was killed in the robbery attempt, yet Bishop still chides the others as cowards for not taking part.

Further seeking an outlet for his violent urges, Bishop convinces the others to help him hold up a store whose owner had once chased them out at gunpoint. Q is reluctant, in part because of conscience and in part because Bishop plans to stage the robbery the night of the DJ contest. He's persuaded to take part, however, and after winning the first round of the contest, joins the others for the stickup. The plan goes awry, however, and Bishop shoots the store owner, then Raheem when the latter turns on him. The three survivors return to the contest, where the cops question them but decide not to take them in.

Soon thereafter, Bishop begins to notice that Q and Steel are avoiding him, and after threatening Q, he tracks down Steel one night and shoots him. Bishop sets up Q to look like the culprit, but the latter realizes this and agrees to meet with his former friend. Buying a gun from Trip (Samuel L. Jackson), the older proprietor of a local hangout, Q heads for the meeting but decides to throw the weapon away; Bishop, however, has no such compunctions and tries to shoot him. Q escapes into a building where a party is being held, but Bishop follows him and confronts him on the roof. A struggle ensues, and Bishop falls over the side; Q tries to save him, but Bishop plunges to his death. An onlooker tells Q, "You got juice," but Q can only look at him and walk away.

The obvious comparison point for JUICE is the previous year's BOYZ N THE HOOD; like John Singleton's Oscar-nominated film, this one tells the story of a group of youths of varying levels of ambition whose lives are torn apart by violence. What prevents JUICE from achieving the same heights is its more conventional action-thriller approach; instead of illuminating or commenting on the social realities that surround the boys and influence their behavior, Dickerson is content to tell their story in more genre-movie terms.

This is not to say that JUICE doesn't succeed on those terms. Dickerson, who wrote the screenplay with Gerard Brown, invests the film with a gritty, evocative urban feel and sets it to a pulsating rap soundtrack, featuring over a dozen songs and a strong score by Hank Shocklee and the Bomb Squad. Music also proves to be important to the story in addition to backing it, and setting up the DJ contest as the story's centerpiece is an effective touch. Not only does it give Q a goal of celebrity to shoot for without lifting the film from its inner-city reality, but the ecstatic excitement of his "showdown" with another DJ contrasts nicely with the tension of the robbery scene that immediately follows it. A couple of rap artists contribute strong work in front of the cameras as well, with Shakur (of the group Digital Underground) a frighteningly menacing Bishop and Queen Latifah contributing a nice cameo turn as the contest's tough but friendly MC.

The other actors do equally good work, maintaining interest even after the story trajectory becomes clear and the film moves to the inevitable action climax. Omar Epps is fine as the film's moral center; unlike his friends, who have resigned themselves to various levels of dead-end futures, he fights the forces that would drag him down and tries to make something of himself. Not a new idea, certainly, but one that can still work with a strong and colorful approach, and that's what Dickerson brings to this film. With this very promising directorial debut, he proves himself worthy of "juice" in the filmmaking world. *(Violence, profanity, sexual situations.)*

p, David Heyman, Neal H. Moritz, Peter Frankfurt; d, Ernest Dickerson; w, Gerard Brown, Ernest Dickerson, (from his story);

ph, Larry Banks; ed, Sam Pollard, Brunilda Torres; m, The Bomb Squad; prod d, Lester Cohen; set d, Alyssa Winter; cos, Donna Berwick

Drama/Action **(PR: O MPAA: R)**

JUMPIN' AT THE BONEYARD ★★★½
107m Boneyard Productions; Kasdan Pictures ~ Fox c

Tim Roth *(Manny)*, Alex Arquette *(Danny)*, Danitra Vance *(Jeanette)*, Kathleen Chalfant *(Mom)*, Samuel L. Jackson *(Mr. Simpson)*, Luis Guzman *(Taxi Driver)*, Elizabeth Bracco *(Cathy)*, Jeffrey Wright *(Derek)*

Writer-director Jeff Stanzler has made a stunning feature debut with JUMPIN' AT THE BONEYARD. This moving and dark tale of the trickle-down effect of drug abuse rings true with a resonance not often seen in contemporary American cinema. Its haunting images remain with the viewer long after leaving the theater.

Manny (Tim Roth), an unemployed Irish-American, is awakened in his Bronx apartment early one morning when he hears two intruders rummaging around the kitchen. Armed with a baseball bat, he confronts them, only to discover his younger brother, Danny (Alex Arquette), a ravaged crack addict, and his junkie girlfriend, Jeanette (Danitra Vance). The duo were in search of goods to sell for drug money. In response to this betrayal, Manny administers a brutal beating, but he also recognizes that he has precious little time to help his brother before it's too late.

After confiscating their crack vials, Manny forces Danny and Jeanette into the car for a trip further north in the borough. There he coaxes Danny from the vehicle and takes him to a graveyard where their father is buried. As it grows dark, the volatile Manny continues to test Danny's limits by forcing him to play a familiar game from their childhood. "What would you do if the bogeyman reached up and grabbed your leg," he asks. The game spooks Danny, while Jeanette watches nervously from the car as she smokes some leftover cocaine.

The next morning, Manny convinces Danny to visit their mother (Kathleen Chalfont) who's been estranged from her wayward son for years. Unfortunately, Jeanette, with Danny's permission, fled with Manny's car during the long night. Without a car at their disposal, the duo must walk through their old stomping grounds which have become a dangerous ghetto wasteland. Danny needs to get cleaned up first, so they visit a community center where the compassionate director, Mr. Simpson (Samuel L. Jackson), allows him to use one of their showers. As Danny scrubs off months of dirt, Simpson and Manny concoct a plan to get him into an upstate drug rehab.

Cleaned up and wearing fresh clothes, supplied by Simpson, Danny looks presentable enough for the visit home. After a run-in with a local teenage pusher, they speed up their sobering exodus through the Bronx—encountering sheer devastation everywhere. Finally they find a cab and make an unscheduled stop at the school of Manny's young son Derek (Jeffrey Wright). Danny has never seen his nephew before. Before long, though, Manny's ex-wife, Cathy (Elizabeth Bracco), shows up and they have a huge argument in the playground. Cathy berates Manny for not supporting their son. The next stop is Manny's apartment where he finally convinces Danny to enter the rehab program. Manny tells him they will go together so that he'll have family there. Danny reluctantly agrees as long as he can talk to Jeanette first.

They go to their mother's house but she is too overcome to face Danny. They have an awkward reunion on two sides of a bedroom door. Danny confesses his sins through the wall and promises her he is going to get straightened out. Leaving the apartment, the brothers are confronted by an ill-tempered Jeanette. She and Danny argue when he tells her he's leaving town for a clinic. She goes off and pulls a gun, pumping a bullet into Manny who dies in his anguished brother's arms.

The power of JUMPIN' AT THE BONEYARD is in its simplistic storyline. Not weighed down with innumerable plot twists, it remains an intimate and often depressing chronicle of human and urban decay. Jeff Stanzler is a gifted filmmaker. With his grasp of technique and storytelling abilities, it is hard to imagine that this is his first feature. He captures perfectly the horrors and confusion of people who've lost control of their lives. The drugs which have nearly destroyed Danny are the most tangible evidence of this, but Manny, being overly violent and unfocused on his own future, has weaknesses every bit as revealing; it would have been easy for Stanzler to present Manny in a heroic mode, yet he made the character weak in ways that show there are no complete paragons. Manny's failure to maintain a relationship, or even pay child support, is in contrast to his linear goal of getting his brother well. It's also ironic that Danny, weak and addicted, is the one who has found some sort of love, albeit conditional, with Jeanette.

In the role of Manny, Roth is exceptional. His ability to convey his character's complexities makes this one of the strongest performances of the year. Roth will inevitably be compared to a young De Niro, and truth be told, there are similarities, but his depth as an actor is all his own. As Danny, Arquette captures the vacuous and pitiful strains of drug addiction with complete believability. Not flashy in any way, he then takes the role to a new level by showing the pain he feels at being a disappointment to his family and himself. As his tormented girlfriend, Vance is well cast, ably grasping the contradictory aspects of hustle and fear.

JUMPIN' AT THE BONEYARD is successful filmmaking for the simple reason that it rings completely true. It's bleak, scary and utterly real—refusing to allow one to be complacent about an issue which is everywhere. Its scant theatrical release was perhaps inevitable, but it should find a lasting audience in the video marketplace. It certainly deserves it. *(Violence, profanity, substance abuse.)*

p, Nina R. Sadowsky, Lloyd Goldfine; d, Jeff Stanzler; w, Jeff Stanzler; ph, Lloyd Goldfine; ed, Chris Tellefsen; m, Steve Postel; prod d, Caroline Wallner; cos, Natasha Landau

Drama **(PR: C MPAA: R)**

JUST LIKE IN THE MOVIES ★★½
90m Alon Kasha Productions ~ Cabriolet Films c

Jay O. Sanders *(Ryan Legrand)*, Katherine Borowitz *(Tura Erickson)*, Alan Ruck *(Dean Erickson)*, Michael Jeter *(Vernon Jackson)*, Mark Margolis *(John Zanasco)*, Alex Vincent *(Carter Legrand)*, Lauren Thompson *(Alice)*, Richard Council *(Robert)*, Margaret Devine *(Val)*, Martha Gehman *(Leda)*, Jon Sidel *(Jon Sidel)*, Joyce Reehling *(Sara Zaloom)*, Larry Pine *(Michael Stone)*, Fred Sanders *(Astronoment)*, Francis Conroy *(Simone Kassler)*, Kurt Peterson *(Robert Kassler)*, Helen Hanft *(Darcy Simons)*, Mark Lotito *(Man in Fatigues)*, Steve Rankin *(Mr. Magic)*, Michael Jefferson *(Punk)*, Tom Mandirosian *(Mr. Zang)*, Ilene Kristen *(Julia)*, Ralph Marrero *(Driver)*, Silvio Luciano *(Child)*, Paul Bates *(Don)*, Frances Guinan *(Olaf)*, Steven Marcus *(1st Man)*, Reg E. Cathey *(2nd Man)*, Sam Guncler *(3rd Man)*, Marcella Lowrey *(1st Woman)*, Judith Cohen *(2nd Woman)*, Dani Klein *(3rd Woman)*, Emma Terese *(4th Woman)*, Nealla Spano *(Emily)*, Joni Dee Bostwick *(Dance Instructor)*

Not particularly incisive, but refreshingly unpretentious, JUST LIKE IN THE MOVIES explores one man's premature midlife crisis.

Screenwriters and co-directors Bram Towbin and Mark Halliday wear their titles ironically as they follow the adventures of thirty-four-year-old Ryan Legrand (Jay O. Sanders), a private investigator who seems to specialize in recording marital infidelities for his divorce-bound clients. His partners in the none-too-successful business are equipment whiz Vernon Jackson (Michael Jeter, whose homeless drag queen was one of the highlights of THE FISHER KING) and cameraman Dean Erickson (Alan Ruck), a low-key bohemian-type whose constant razzing of Ryan's spartan love life adds to the latter's frustrations, which also include an ex-wife, Alice (Lauren Thompson), who feels herself well rid of him, and their seven-year-old son, Carter (Alex Vincent), who's the brightest spot of his life.

Through a computer-dating service, Ryan meets Tura Erickson (Katherine Borowitz), an earnest free spirit, ruled by her emotions just as Ryan is by thought and analysis, whom he falls in love with but is unable to commit to. Increasingly jealous when Tura breaks off the affair, Ryan begins to follow her and record her comings and goings from his surveillance van, leading to her further irritation and his further isolation and despair.

The filmmakers' designs here are nothing if not ambitious, as they blend Ryan's surveillance jobs, his dates with Tura and resulting stasis-producing indecision and fear, his weekend outings with Carter and unsuccessful dating, mostly doubling with his buddy Dean, who has an easy way with women. Despite their material's potential, Towbin and Halliday never come to terms with Ryan's character flaws, which include a quick temper and impatience, even with his son, and ultimately leaves him stranded in Antonioni-land. (The film ends with Tura's initial phone-message response to his dating-service tape.)

There are some good ideas here. For instance, the evidence Ryan painstakingly collects for his clients prompts them to break down in pain, further highlighting his own lack of strong emotional involvement with anyone. And there's a good deal of humor, including some strong social criticism, in a pair of scenes directed at sophisticated New York social life. The huge cast is full of quirky players, some very amusing, like comic Steve Rankin as Mr. Magic, an accountant who moonlights as a kids' party clown, and Margaret Devine as Val, an addled bubblehead stranded, ultimately in a batting cage, on a date with Ryan. But many of these characters also unfortunately fall flat.

Square-jawed Jay O. Sanders, the familiar veteran character actor (GLORY, JFK), is fine as the hero, but he can't overcome the movie's uneven tone, which veers inconclusively from linked comic to dramatic setpieces. Oddly dated by the use of 16mm film instead of video for Ryan's undercover sleuthing, the low-budget picture, largely shot in Manhattan and East Hampton, L.I., carries a 1989 copyright and received a brief theatrical run in May 1992 before release on video. *(Profanity, substance abuse, adult situations.)*

p, Alon Kasha; d, Bram Towbin, Mark Halliday; w, Bram Towbin; ph, Peter Fernberger; ed, Jay Keuper; m, John Hill; prod d, Marek Dobrowolski; art d, Kate Conklin; set d, John Marrett; cos, Linda Fisher

Comedy/Drama **(PR: C MPAA: R)**

K2 ★½

(U.K.) 111m Trans Pacific Films; Majestic Films International; K2 Film Productions NV~ Paramount c

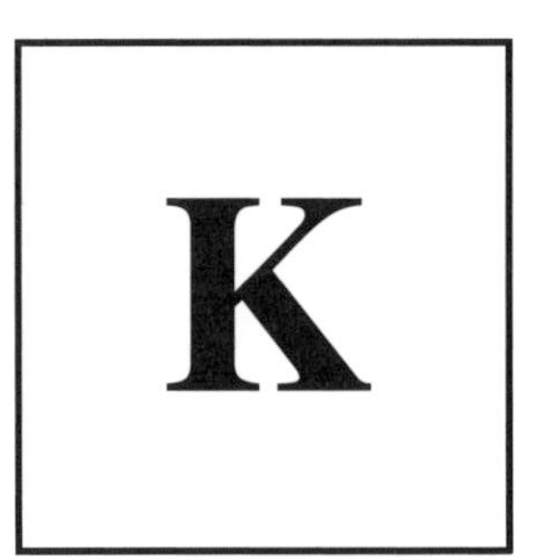

Michael Biehn *(Taylor Brooks)*, Matt Craven *(Harold Jamieson)*, Raymond J. Barry *(Claiborne)*, Hiroshi Fujioka *(Takane Shimuzu)*, Luca Bercovici *(Dallas Woolf)*, Patricia Charbonneau *(Jacki Metcalfe)*, Julia Nickson-Soul *(Cindy)*, Jamal Shah *(Malik)*, Annie Grindlay *(Lisa)*, Elena Stiteler *(Tracey)*, Blu Mankuma *(Man in Wheelchair)*, Charles Oberman *(Tony)*, Christopher M. Brown *(Carl)*, Leslie Carlson *(Dexter)*, David Cubitt *(Peter)*, Edward Spatt *(Mike)*, Andrew Spat *(Todd)*, Antony Holland *(Priest)*, Kehli O'Byrne *(Pam)*, Lillian Carlson *(Secretary)*, Laurie Briscoe *(Handsome Woman)*, Badi Uzzaman *(Ibrahim)*, Rajeb Shah, Ibrahim Zahid, Ali Ka, Ali Khan, Abdul Karim, Ghulam Abbas, Asghar Khan, Mr. Shaban *(Balti Porters)*, Nazir Sabir *(Balti Liaison Officer)*, Shah Jehan *(Balti Liaison Officer)*, Tim Van Rellim *(Steiner)*, Gabrielle Dellal *(Frenchwoman)*, Hadji Mejdi *(Lambardar)*

A molehill has been made of a mountain. Patrick Myers's stunning play about two characters in search of survival on K2, the world's second highest peak, fails to scale any cinematic heights at all.

The original theatrical piece, mounted on Broadway in 1983, has been effectively enlarged, and the two mountain-climbing protagonists given fleshed-out identities. Bachelor Taylor Brooks (Michael Biehn), owner of a silver metallic Porsche convertible, is a wiseguy and womanizing assistant DA, whose idea of a good time is picking up gals who are "wet, wild and willing." (He'll go to any lengths to impress them, including lithely scampering up the side of a building, like Spiderman, to reach their apartment.) Harold Jamieson (Matt Craven) is an introspective physicist, and happily married with a young child. They're old friends, ying and yang tempermentally, who share a mutual, obsessive passion for the challenge of the climb.

Philosophically, Harold (nicknamed "H") climbs because, when he stands on top of a mountain, for just a second he feels *the truth*; Taylor climbs because there are none. (H: "If there are no answers, why don't you look for one?" Taylor: "That's why I climb mountains.") On a recent vacation, a planned 10-day trip on Mount McKinley, they barely escaped with their lives after an overhead jet created an avalanche. Two in their party died. Understandably, Harold's beautiful Asian-American wife Cindy (Julia Nickson-Soul) isn't at all pleased when the pair decide to scale K2, "the toughest mountain in the world" because "half of the people who go there don't come back." (At 28,250 feet, it's a bit lower than Everest's 29,028, but is considered a more difficult ascent.)

In Pakistan, they join a team headed by billionare Philip Claiborne (Raymond J. Barry), with Dallas Woolf (Luca Bercovici), Taylor's "sworn enemy" since law school, veteran climber Takane Shimuzu (Hiroshi Fujioka) and Clairborne's girlfriend Jacki Metcalfe (Patricia Charbonneau), who's along for the ride. Mirroring "Murphy's Law" ("If anything can go wrong, it will"), almost all of the native porters abandon them just four hours from the base camp. There's tons of equipment yet to bring up, but Taylor delivers the mountain climber's equivalent of Henry V's impassioned speech at Agincourt ("We're a team!"), and a few Sherpas remain.

At 20,000 feet, Philip becomes ill, requires oxygen and can't continue. (Wonderful photography here, of the mountain at night, and the geodesic-domed tents lighted from the inside.) Philip gives orders that only two of the four men can go to the summit, Dallas and Takane, but the latter is killed and the former is missing. By this time, Philip is coughing blood and near death, and Jacki has radioed for a rescue helicopter. But Taylor and "H" are raring to try to reach the summit. Philip warns them that if they're not back in time, within twenty-four hours, they'll leave without them.

Scared, with no rope, tent or oxygen and just one can of chicken soup between them, the pair are successful and plant flags and take photos. On their way back to the camp, "H" falls on a sheet of ice and breaks his leg. They're both stranded on a ledge 1,250 feet below the summit. "H" becomes delirious and wants to die, and asks Taylor to look after his son. At first, Taylor doesn't want to leave him ("You're the only real friend I have. My work is with scum and lies and compromise. You have grace and nobility.") But Taylor is a born survivor and goes for help. En route, he finds Dallas's frozen body, takes his rope and drags "H" down the mountain where the chopper appears to save the day and, one assumes, the two of them. (In the play, the ending isn't as hopeful, and "H" likely perishes.)

Much of the filming took place on Mt. Waddington, in Canada, and at the base of the real K2 in the Karakoram range in northern Kashmir. The mountain-climbing sequences are visually scenic and well done. Not so the predictable screenplay and pedestrian acting, which reduces this high-minded attempt to deal with areas of friendship and personal nobility to a pseudo-sentimental buddy film. The original 95-minute play, a drama with no intermission, almost never got on the boards. Its single stage set, featuring a spectacular 55-foot ice-covered wood and styrofoam mountaintop, was condemned as a fire hazard by the NYPD. Fortunately, remedial measures were taken and the play opened in time to qualify for that year's Tony Awards—where Ming Cho Lee won one for best scenic design.

p, Jonathan Taplin, Marilyn Weiner, Tim Van Rellim; d, Franc Roddam; w, Scott Roberts, Patrick Meyers, (from his play); ph, Gabriel Beristain; ed, Sean Barton; m, Chaz Jankel; prod d, Andrew Sanders; art d, Richard Hudolin, Stephen Simmonds; set d, Ted Kuchera; cos, Keith Denny

Drama/Sports/Action **(PR: C MPAA: R)**

KICK OR DIE

87m Anglo Pacific Film ~ AIP Home Video c

Kevin Bernhardt *(Don Potter)*, Holaday Mason *(Eve Campo)*, Tim Wallace *(Craig)*, Joe Stewardson *(John Campo)*, Antonio Caprari *(Red)*, Terry Norton *(Jean)*

Much as a rose by any other name would still smell as sweet, the renamed NO HARD FEELINGS still reeks. KICK OR DIE, the new moniker slapped on this five-year-old South African actioner, does nothing to improve the film's idiocy and cut-rate fisticuffs.

After several female coeds are attacked by a mysterious rapist, Don Potter (Kevin Bernhardt), kickboxer *par excellence*, is hired to protect the beleaguered university's distaff population from further assaults. In the course of this assignment, Potter falls head over heels for attractive singer Eve Campo (Holaday Mason). Another rival for Eve's affections is Potter's old macho antagonist, Craig (Tim Wallace). As sure as a roll of the dice will never abolish chance, Craig happens to be the college rapist and has set his sights on Eve. During an addle-brained chase, Craig becomes the recipient of an officer's bullet as Potter utters the punchline, "No hard feelings, buddy."

As written and directed by Henro Mohr, KICK OR DIE's chief failing is that it wobbles uncontrollably and without warning from the glaringly obvious to the glaringly moronic. Mohr eschews any form of suspense by making Craig so malignant and lowbrow that the only one who seems shocked by his actions is Potter. Viewers are left stupefied at the obtuseness of the film's characters, who clearly inhabit a world of their own. Mohr also blunts any interest in his narrative by promoting dreary stereotypes. Granted, this is a South African production, but even so, its half-witted attempt to make the rapist appear to be a Black man is so shallow and retrograde that the device becomes cynically calculating and appallingly insensitive.

Another questionable maneuver Mohr pulls out of his ratty magician's hat is setting up the audience for an intense, kick-boxing finale that never occurs. It seems that one well-placed bullet can quickly allay just about any ancient Asian discipline. Unfortunately, this ploy leaves the audience waiting 85 minutes for a cathartic release that never happens, rendering viewers limp and slack-jawed.

The title KICK OR DIE, although much more belligerent in tone, should be replaced by NO HARD FEELINGS. At least with its original title, the filmmakers would be making their apologies to the audience in advance. *(Excessive violence.)*

p, Chris Davies, Lionel A. Ephraim; d, Henro Mohr; w, Henro Mohr; ed, Simon Grimley

Martial Arts/Action (PR: O MPAA: R)

KICKBOXER 3: THE ART OF WAR ★★½

92m Vision International; Kings Road Entertainment; MPC ~ Kings Road Entertainment c

Sasha Mitchell *(David Sloan)*, Dennis Chan *(Xian Chow)*, Richard Comar *(Lane)*, Noah Verduzco *(Marcos)*, Ian Jacklin *(Martine)*, Althea Miranda *(Isabella)*, Ricardo Petraglia *(Alberto)*, Gracindo Junior *(Pete)*, Miguel Orniga *(Marelo)*, Milton Goncalves *(Sergeant)*, Manitu Felipe *(Machado)*

Starting with Jean-Claude Van Damme in KICKBOXER and ending up with Sasha Mitchell in KICKBOXER 3: THE ART OF WAR is a little like working your way down from Steve Reeves to Richard Simmons. Still, if Mitchell is a lightweight entry in the action hero sweepstakes, he's quite adept at the manly art of kicking the crap out of people.

While sight-seeing in Rio de Janeiro prior to an international kickboxing championship, ace American athlete David Sloan (Mitchell) learns firsthand about the local mean streets. Accompanied by his sage companion Xian Chow (Dennis Chan), David is ripped off by a street urchin named Marcos (Noah Verduzco) whose beautiful sister Isabella (Althea Miranda) may be the next target of a child prostitution ring. Although our warm-hearted hero unofficially adopts the little beggar, he doesn't realize that Lane (Richard Comar), his friendly fight promoter, is actually the kiddie pimp. At an exhibition match to benefit homeless children (you can tell this film has a social conscience), local hero Machado (Manitu Felipe) is nearly killed by Lane's star attraction Martine (Ian Jacklin) before David steps into the ring and challenges the bully to a grudge match.

After Isabella is kidnapped David begins investigating the city's sleazy underworld. Meanwhile, Lane has propositioned him to take a fall in the kickboxing championship. Instead, David and Xian acquire illegal arms and invade a crimelord's house, only to discover that Lane is the chief child-trafficker. Unfortunately, Lane has virginal Isabella under wraps and intends to use her as a bargaining chip in persuading David to over-train and lose the upcoming bout. Foolishly, the slimeball bets a bundle he can't afford to lose against the exhausted David, who naturally recovers enough of his strength to win his match. He then retrieves Isabella, but not before inducing Lane's head honcho to betray and kill the louse.

As lithe and muscled as Sasha Mitchell is, that's how toneless and flabby this sequel's plotting is. How many failed rescue attempts can the filmmakers expect an audience to endure? Naturally, the plotline is dropped often enough for Mitchell to kick some life into the movie. Not only is the martial arts quota potently satisfied but the action movie mayhem scenes are also suspenseful and dynamic. In fact, as long as the plot remains in the background, KICKBOXER 3 delivers the wallop action fans expect. Saving street children is all well and good as long as it doesn't detract from all that heart-pounding violence.

A power kicker in the self-defense category, Mitchell is agreeable as an actor but somewhat hampered by a thin voice. On the other hand, Richard Comar oozes avarice from every pore and truly commands an audience's attention. He makes you believe he'd sell anyone of any age to turn a profit. Overall, the film has an abundance of hissable villains and also convincingly portrays the vice underbelly of Rio. It's not a knock-out, but KICKBOXER 3 contains enough crunch-and-punch to satisfy action devotees. *(Violence, sexual situations.)*

p, Michael D. Pariser; d, Rick King; w, Dennis A. Pratt; ph, Edgar Moura; ed, Daniel Loewenthal; m, Harry Manfredini; prod d, Clovis Bueno; cos, Isabela Braga

Action/Martial Arts (PR: C MPAA: R)

KILL CRUISE ★★★

(Germany) 99m Rialto Film; Rocket Pictures ~ MCA/Universal Home Video c

Jurgen Prochnow *(Skipper)*, Elizabeth Hurley *(Lou)*, Patsy Kensit *(Su)*, Franz Buchrieser *(Owner of the California)*, Grazyna Szapolowska *(Mona)*, Mario Stock *(Paul Pelikan)*

Expatriate German actor Jurgen Prochnow may have been wishing he were back on DAS BOOT. In KILL CRUISE, a queasily entertaining seagoing suspense thriller, he plays a character known only as "Skipper," but this ain't "Gilligan's Island."

What little viewers need to know about Skipper is etched in during a brief prologue. His sailing yacht, the "Bella Donna," is being tossed in a stormy sea off Gibraltar while his best friend—and the man who was about to take his wife away from him—is drowning overboard. Still on deck, Skipper clearly wishes he could help, but he cannot. Authorities clear him of responsibility, but his wife, Mona, doesn't and leaves him. Retiring to his favorite bar, the California Club, Skipper orders a drink and bitterly declares that he'll set sail the next day. "After all, why stay," he grumbles.

Six months later, he's still muttering the same thing; it's now an act, and Skipper has become a local joke. Two hookers with dubious musical ambitions enter the bar and sing a song. Afterward one of them, Lou (Elizabeth Hurley) performs a striptease while the other, Su (Patsy Kensit), takes a seat at a table. Lou beckons Skipper over to the stage and asks him to collect tips for her. He does, and later the three retire to his yacht for an evening of carnal delights.

The next day, the hungover Skipper discovers to his horror that he's promised Su and Lou a trip to Barbados. At first he demurs, but after being taunted by the owner of the California Club, he decides to do it on a whim. To many men, being on a yacht alone with two beautiful women of loose virtue would be a dream come true. But the Skipper is a seasoned sailor, wise enough to know that three strangers in a boat on the open sea for the four weeks it takes to reach Barbados can have unpredictable, perhaps even deadly, results. Before too long, his worst fears seem to be coming true.

To give away much more of the plot of KILL CRUISE would be to give away most of the reason for seeing it. Writer-director Peter Keglevic has pretensions to Polanski and Hitchcock in this KNIFE IN THE WATER with a PSYCHO windup. But the ending becomes obvious once one realizes that only two of the three characters reveal much of themselves as the film goes on. Despite that, however, Keglevic gets more than halfway to his goal, cleverly playing on our expectations and playing with what we know and, especially, what we think we know about who's doing what with whom and to whom.

The suspense hinges largely on Skipper's enigmatic character, nicely sustained by Prochnow's tight-lipped performance. Is his growing unease justified by his sea experience? Or have the wounds he still nurses over his broken marriage made him an embittered misogynist? Or is he, as one of the ladies declares, simply crazy? Whatever the reason, despite the carnal possibilities, he retires chastely to his quarters each night to record in his log his dark premonitions of trouble to come.

Keglevic orchestrates the moods of this elemental drama with devious precision from a slight unease, to a gnawing tension, to pure panic, to a quiet—too quiet, of course—resolution before he unleashes his final, decisive bit of Grand Guignol just when you thought it was safe to go back up on deck again. Even to comment on the lead performances would be to risk giving away too much. However, the three stars play Keglevic's exercise in cinematic sleight of hand for all it's worth.

Since coming to international prominence in DAS BOOT, Prochnow (DUNE, THE SEVENTH SIGN) has had problems finding his niche, but here he's marvelously assured; one of the film's best incidental pleasures is simply watching him perform the multitude of minute tasks it takes to make a yacht sail. Even so, KILL CRUISE will make you think long and hard the next time someone invites you for that seagoing vacation you've always dreamed of. *(Violence, profanity, adult situations.)*

p, Matthias Wendlandt; d, Peter Keglevic; w, Peter Keglevic; ph, Edward Klosinski; ed, Susanne Schett; m, Brynmor Jones; prod d, Mario Stock; cos, Ulrike Schutte

Suspense/Thriller **(PR: O MPAA: R)**

KILL LINE

93m Rocky Group Inc.; Clark Film Company Inc. ~ Hemdale Home Video c

Bobby Kim *(Joe Lee)*, Michael Parker *(Sheriff Mark)*, Marlene Zimmerman *(Oggie)*, Mark Williams *(Lou)*, C.R. Valdez, Ben Pfeifer, H. Wayne Lowery, Michael Ford, Paul Rohrer

This inert specimen of martial-artlessness stars a certain Bobby Kim, billed as the "Charles Bronson of Tae Kwondo," no doubt because his craggy, mustachioed visage vaguely resembles the veteran Occidental star. And possibly because Kim's appearance in this film consitutes a career Death Wish. The very least one should get out of even the lowliest kung-fu flick is action, but KILL LINE is as exciting as watching bones mend.

Kim glumly plays Joe Lee, a hard-luck Asian-American who was stuck in prison while his rural family got massacred by bad guys convinced that Joe had stashed a fortune on their prairie homestead. Once paroled, Joe trudges to the remote gravesite to pay his respects. But the evildoers, led by a corrupt yahoo sheriff and a razor-slashing priest (he kills people, then presides over the Mass at their funerals), are on the lookout. They beat Joe. They burn Joe. They throw Joe off a cliff. Joe gradually starts to realize that the bad guys have it in for him, and he wonders whether it has anything to do with the money he was falsely convicted of stealing back when he was a courier for some shady missionaries.

After that deadly dull setup, Joe belatedly trounces his tormentors with a little tae kwondo and lots of explosives and ammunition. Finally, hero and villain alike agree that Joe wasn't the thief at all—the loot was embezzled by a well-known TV evangelist. Joe invades the holy man's "Center for the Less Fortunate" in New York and rakes the set with gunfire during a live broadcast. Then he leaves, and the filmmakers try to tidy up the whole mess with a zany, rambling end title that explains and apologizes for the TV preacher's criminal activities and points out that he did perform a lot of good deeds in his ministry as well. It really must be seen to be believed, but viewers are best advised to do neither.

Released inauspiciously to home video, KILL LINE was filmed in, as the end credits awkwardly phrase it, "Number One City in the Nation 1988 City and County of Pueblo, Colorado." *(Violence, substance abuse, profanity, nudity, sexual situations, adult situations.)*

p, Robert W. Kim; d, Richard H. Kim; w, Richard H. Kim; ph, Maximo Munzi; ed, Randall C. McBride; m, Kelly Bryarly, Patrick Dowling

Action/Thriller/Martial Arts **(PR: O MPAA: R)**

KILLER IMAGE ★½

(Canada) 97m Groundstar Entertainment; Storia Films ~ Groundstar Entertainment c

M. Emmet Walsh *(Sam Kane)*, John Pyper-Ferguson *(Max Oliver)*, Krista Errikson *(Shelly)*, Michael Ironside *(Luther Kane)*, Barbra Gajewskia *(Stacey)*, Paul Austin *(Ric Oliver)*, Chantelle Jenkins *(Lori)*, Kristie Baker *(Carrie)*

Without strangling the audience's interest, a clever thriller must twist and turn its plot with finesse. Instead of being caught off-guard, viewers of KILLER IMAGE are likely to choke on the plot reversals, red herrings, and unmotivated surprises.

When Max Oliver (John Pyper-Ferguson) investigates the untimely demise of his brother Ric (Paul Austin), his partner in a photographic business, his own safety becomes a tenuous matter. Discovered snapping pictures of Luther Kane (Michael Ironside) murdering Stacey (Barbara Gajewskia), the bimbo girlfriend of Luther's brother Senator John Kane (M. Emmet Walsh), Ric was quickly dispatched by Luther. Looking for Ric's negatives, the unhinged Luther ransacks Max's apartment and begins harassing Max, who hasn't a clue about the incriminating photos.

Duping a prostitute named Lori (Chantelle Jenkins) into entertaining Max, Luther slays the trusting streetwalker, crazy-glues Max's hand to the murder weapon, and takes photos of guilty-looking Max in order to blackmail him into relinquishing Ric's negatives. After being forced to take a ride with Lori's corpse in a roller coaster, Max temporarily escapes Luther's clutches, but Ric's girlfriend Carrie (Kristie Baker) isn't so

lucky. The increasingly deranged Luther removes Stacey's corpse from a body bag long enough to photograph it, and then dumps the other dead women's bodies in Max's apartment to brand him a serial killer.

Meanwhile fugitive Max finally unearths the Luther-photos from a motor bike and lays a trap, a plan complicated when Luther kidnaps Max's friend Shelley (Krista Errikson) and kills his own brother, who was not delighted to learn Luther executed his mistress. Concealing dozens of cameras in the forest where he has agreed to rendezvous with Luther and Shelley, Max terrorizes camera-shy Luther. Before Luther can pick up all the incriminating photos or kill Max and Shelley, he does everyone a favor by falling off a cliff.

The above synopsis is a cursory detailing of all the ins and outs of a needlessly complicated mystery maze. This convoluted thriller grows nuttier and nuttier just like its psychotic villain. In a film not distinguished by a seductive visual style, it is hard to overlook the complete absence of logic. Trying but failing to enrich itself with multi-leveled subtexts, KILLER IMAGE doesn't draw satisfying parallels between the two sets of brothers nor does it develop the political cover-up involving Senator John Kane's scandalous affair with Stacey. Instead of tightening the screws as Max uses his talents to play Polaroid P.I., the movie veers off on too many tangents, and the body pile-up could be the envy of a teen slasher film.

Although Pyper-Ferguson draws the audience in with his animal magnetism, Ironside has become the Jack Palance of the 90s—one was enough. The thrills dissipate as the pacing slacks off every time Luther pulls a new dirty trick. Sneaky surprises enliven the film but don't build up the level of suspense. Rather than frightening or intriguing viewers, KILLER IMAGE only succeeds in making them more and more incredulous. *(Violence, nudity, sexual situations.)*

p, Rudy Barichello, David Winning, Bruce Harvey; d, David Winning; w, Jaron Summers, David Winning, Stan Edmonds, (from his idea); ph, Dean Bennett; ed, Alan Collins; m, Stephen Foster; art d, Bruce Sinski

Thriller **(PR: O MPAA: R)**

KILLER TOMATOES EAT FRANCE! ★★

Four Square Productions ~ FoxVideo c

John Astin *(Professor Gangrene)*, Steve Lundquist *(Igor/Louis)*, Angela Visser *(Marie)*, Marc Price *(Michael)*, J.R. Morley, Rick Rockwell

Made under the simple philosophy of milk-it-to-death, this sequel accurately proclaims itself "Part IV of the Tomatoes Trilogy" that commenced with the cheapo satire ATTACK OF THE KILLER TOMATOES and followed with RETURN OF THE KILLER TOMATOES and KILLER TOMATOES STRIKE BACK. Once again the original *artistes* John DeBello, J. Stephen Peace and Constantine Dillon haul out the premise of deadly vegetables on the warpath and load it with broad spoofs of everything they can think of.

The frustrating thing is that DeBello, Peace and Dillon really do know how to be funny, seeding their send-ups with some of the brightest movie parody this side of THE NAKED GUN. But they refuse to let go of the fifteen-year-old premise, and a killer-tomato movie is like a good stand-up comic endlessly doing variations of the same routine. This installment does indeed relocate to France, where the series's perennial villain, fright-wigged Prof. Gangrene (John Astin), inexplicably resurrected since his demise last time, has set up headquarters with his feral tomatoes in an ancient, tourist-filled castle.

Gangrene plans to control all France through his handsome bonehead sidekick Igor (Steve Lundquist), who resembles old engravings of a prophesied King Louis XVII who will regain the throne when the correct omens are fulfilled. This necessitates another killer tomato attack, so Gangrene kidnaps "F.T.," or Fuzzy Tomato, the cuddly lab-created mutant who's a friend to all humanity and currently tours in a "We Are the World"-type musical event promoting man-tomato brotherhood. The villain replaces F.T. with one of the wicked tomatoes, which performs an incendiary tomato gangstah rap that makes the audience riot, and tomato war four is on.

Opposing the menace is Michael (Marc Price), an actor first shown lamenting his role in a killer tomatoes film. Consequently he tells everybody that he's Michael J. Fox, especially a naive French beauty named—as absolutely all the Frenchwomen in this movie are named—Marie (Angela Visser), who thinks herself hideous because she's not fat and homely like the nudes in classical paintings. Their rocky romance compels a despairing Michael to join the tomato-fighting French army, where he finds that a comrade (also played by Steve Lundquist) is in fact the *real* destined-to-be Louis XVII.

The viewer should realize just how adept a team of satirists are on duty here when they cram in a parody of PLATOON within a parody of old WWII newsreels within a parody of Dumas's *The Man in the Iron Mask* within a killer-tomato spectacle. It's not an easy feat to sustain that level of intricate silliness for a feature running-time, and in the wake of AIRPLANE! many a merry prankster has tried with pathetic results. Among the highlights here are battle scenes filmed using toy soldiers and vehicles so obviously fake that when a tank blows up it drops a huge Duracell battery right next to Michael. The hero also braves Prof. Gangrene's "Basement of Death"—an ordinary, cluttered suburban cellar where forgotten mousetraps, leftover xmas lights, piles of board games and a vibrating washing machine pose nonstop peril in a well-timed slapstick setpiece.

But most of KILLER TOMATOES EAT FRANCE! isn't that fresh. The title creatures now feature grimacing animatronic faces and fangs, evidently inspired by the way the killer tomatoes looked in a TV kiddie cartoon version that aired in 1991. The tomatoes can talk but rarely have anything witty to say, and gone is the earlier films' ludicrous image of people running and screaming in mortal terror from inert garden produce. The rule for killer tomatoes seems to be the bigger the duller, although a giant specimen introduced as "The PhanTomato of the Opera" raises a smile. Taking the comedy franchise to France allows *beaucoup de* jokes based on Gallic stereotypes and culture, but they're out of step with the Hollywood genre gags that seasoned the preceding tomato flicks.

As for acting, get real. John Astin, the congenially mad Gomez from TV's "Addams Family," is a master of mordant, deadpan humor that finds little opportunity in this screenplay's frantic mugging. The hunky Lundquist, for the record, is in real life a 1984 Olympic gold medalist with a thriving second career as a tanning-products entrepreneur. His thespic turns in the killer tomato epics don't exactly take the bronze, but the oxenlike Igor is consistently amusing.

The best in the cycle to date was probably RETURN OF THE KILLER TOMATOES. "To date" must be added since this chapter ends with Gangrene foiled as always, but getting away and vowing another escapade. Naturally KILLER TOMATOES EAT FRANCE! premiered on home video, and a command to rewind the tape after watching is included in the mocking opening credits.

p, J. Stephen Peace, John DeBello; d, John DeBello; w, John DeBello, Constantine Dillon, J. Stephen Peace; ph, Kevin Morrisey; ed, Beth Accomando; m, Rick Patterson; prod d, Robert Brill; art d, Debbie DeVilla; set d, Christopher Vail; cos, Victoria Petrovich

Comedy **(PR: A MPAA: NR)**

KISS ME A KILLER ★★

74m Concorde ~ Califilm c

Julie Carmen *(Teresa)*, Robert Beltran *(Tony Montero)*, Guy Boyd *(Jake)*, Ramon Franco *(Ramon)*, Charles Boswell *(Dennehy)*, Sam Vlahos *(Father Dominguez)*, Brad Blaisdell *(Tom)*, A.C. Santos *(Pedro)*, Ray Victor *(Carlos)*, Tony Rael *(Ruben)*, Addison Cook *(Painter)*, Pancho Sanchez *(Pancho Sanchez)*,

Marita DeLeon *(Girl Entering Club)*, Monica Sanchez *(Girl Entering Club)*, Armando Morales *(Keyboardist)*, Eddie Resto *(Bassist)*, Willie Loya *(Conga Player)*, David Romero *(Timabli Player)*, Sal Cracchiolo *(1st Trumpeter)*, Marcos Loya *(2nd Trumpeter)*, R.T. Berrick, Pamela Duarte, Juanito Garcia, Shirley Leiva, Dalila Megia, Johny Trivino, Jairo Zabalelta *(Renee Victor Dancers)*

This quickie from Roger Corman tries to make the most of its weak novelty of taking place in the Latino community of Los Angeles. Ethnicity gets smeared over KISS ME A KILLER's hackneyed plot like hot sauce; here's an erotic thriller that intercuts its gratuitous nude scenes with gratuitous shots of rice and beans cooking on the stove. Call it "The *Caballero* Always Rings Twice."

The Circle Club is an East LA lounge owned by blustery, middle-aged Anglo Jake (Guy Boyd) whose lovely but stifled young wife Teresa (Julie Carmen) waits the tables. When the club's headlining salsa singer faints away drunk, a handsome patron named Tony Montero (Robert Beltran) suddenly takes the stage and croons *canciones* so well that Jake hires him at once. In no time Tony seduces Teresa, and the two copulate all over tables and kitchen counters. Tony asks his lover to run away with him, but Teresa doesn't want to abandon the bar biz. So they conspire to murder Jake in an alleyway outside. But the victim survives the shooting, and Tony throws off suspicion by claiming the gunman was Ramon (Ramon Franco), one of his old homeboys. After an oblivious Jake returns home from the hospital Tony and Teresa try again, and this time they succeed in killing the poor chump and making it look accidental. No sooner has Teresa taken over management of the Circle Club than Ramon visits and blows away her dear Tony as revenge for that earlier frame-up.

It's listless film noir from first-time director Marcus DeLeon, with suitably dark photography and good actors getting by in underwritten roles. Even though he's supposed to be overbearing, Guy Boyd's character comes across as the warmest and most likable of the bunch, leaving an unspoken and uncomfortable impression for the viewer that Jake's marked for death because he's older and/or white. Tony remains a cipher about whom nothing insightful is learned. Carmen is basically a symphony of sulks, though she's got a good gimmicky moment when, as a dutiful Catholic, Teresa confesses to her priest that she's going to rub out her husband. The *padre*, bound by the confidentiality of the confessional, spends the rest of the movie glaring at her in silence.

KISS ME A KILLER came and went rapidly in theaters in 1991, mainly playing in urban centers with large Hispanic or Latino populations. It surfaced in home video's cultural melting-pot the next year, but retained its barrio beat with a soundtrack full of original songs by Marcus Loya, performed by Robert Beltran. *(Violence, profanity, substance abuse, adult situations, sexual situations, nudity.)*

p, Catherine Cyran; d, Marcus DeLeon; w, Christopher Wooden, Marcus DeLeon; ph, Nancy Schreiber; ed, Glenn Garland; m, Nigel Holton; prod d, James R. Schumaker; art d, Amy B. Ancona; set d, Aaron Osborne; cos, Meta Jardine

Erotic/Thriller **(PR: O MPAA: R)**

KUFFS ★★½

101m Evansgideon Productions ~ Universal c

Christian Slater *(George Kuffs)*, Milla Jovovich *(Maya Carlton)*, Ric Waugh, Steve Holladay, Chad Randall, Clarke Coleman *(Hoods)*, Leon Rippy *(Kane)*, Craig Benton *(Paint Store Owner)*, Ashley Judd *(Wife of Paint Store Owner)*, Bruce Boxleitner *(Brad Kuffs)*, Joshua Cadman *(Bill Donnelly)*, Mary Ellen Trainor *(Nikki Allyn)*, Aki Aleong *(Mr. Chang)*, Henry G. Sanders *(Building Owner)*, Dom Magwili *(Restaurant Owner)*, Father Kevin Leidich *(Priest)*, E. Keith Polk *(Emergency Room Doctor)*, Susan Schelling *(Emergency Room Nurse)*, Troy Evans *(Captain Morino)*, Loren Blackwell *(Stuart Burkis)*, Kim Robillard *(Peter Coca)*, Gary Munch *(Detective)*, Don Schlossman *(Police Officer)*, George De La Pena *(Sam Jones)*, Janis Uhley *(Street Singer)*, Lu Leonard *(Harriet)*, Roger Rook *(Gun Salesman)*, Don S. Davis *(Gun Instructor)*, Tony Goldwyn *(Ted Bukovsky)*, Phil Mishkin *(Inspector Doug Sticks)*, Jon Greene *(Cop)*, Stephen Park *(Officer Favaro)*, Julie Strain *(Kane's Girl)*, Zona Jaguar *(Kane's Girl)*, Erik Rondell *(Counterman)*, Ross Partridge *(Robert)*, John Apicella *(Janitor)*, Tim Davison *(Jumper)*, Megan Derry *(Nurse)*, Ryan Cutrona *(Florist)*, Scott Williamson *(Alan Eddy)*, Dennis Holahan *(Dr. Carlton)*, Patricia J. Earnest *(Mrs. Carlton)*, Thunder *(Thunder)*, Joe Hart *(Gun Salesman)*, Allan Apone *(Taxi Driver)*, Kenny Endoso *(Japanese Businessman)*, Al Goto *(Japanese Hood)*, Willie Leong *(Japanese Hood)*, Karen D'Ettore *(Baby Sarah)*, Kelly D'Ettore *(Baby Sarah)*

In one of his best roles to date, KUFFS star Christian Slater turns in an ingratiating performance as a smart-alecky high school dropout with a secret passion for law and order.

As the film opens, twenty-one-year-old George Kuffs (Slater) has just written a letter to his pregnant girlfriend, Maya Carlton (Milla Jovovich), explaining that she'd be better off without him. Following this act of desertion, George heads for San Francisco to help his older brother Brad (Bruce Boxleitner) celebrate his birthday. Shortly after George arrives, however, Brad is gunned down in cold blood in front of him. Seeking revenge, George is determined to track down his brother's killer at all costs. He learns he has inherited Brad's Patrol Special franchise, a private police district that Brad operated with the cooperation of the SFPD. (Patrol Specials originated during San Francisco's Barbary Coast days when the city police were so desperate for help that they sold off districts to private enterprise, letting them do the policing.)

Sam Jones (George De La Pena), a rival Patrol Special cop, tries to convince George that he would be better off selling his inheritance; when that fails, Jones decides to have George eliminated in another way. In his own attempt to nail Bruce's killer, George doesn't hesitate to pull off a number of wildly outlandish capers to the chagrin of the local police. Ultimately, George corners the killer and has a happy reunion with his former live-in girlfriend, but not before the body count reaches tremendous proportions.

Crisply paced and directed with a genuine flair for action comedy by Bruce A. Evans, KUFFS is fun to watch, despite the fact that it goes too far in the ultra-violent murder-and-mayhem department. One clever stroke here is that Evans utilizes the gimmick of having Slater address the camera directly, as if explaining his actions to an unseen friend. This is a well worn theatrical device, but in KUFFS it works extremely well.

As entertaining as KUFFS is, however, it would be difficult to recommend to anyone but die-hard action fans. The problem is that Evans and Raynold Gideon's screenplay tries to inject too many elements—romantic comedy, slapstick, satire, revenge melodrama, ultra-violent action—into one film and the end result is an overabundance of frenetic mayhem that tends to detract heavily from the fascinating central character's emotional maturation. And the filmmakers' emphasis on knockabout action, spectacular shootouts and explosions also robs the movie of much of its underlying core of lighthearted fun. The cast plays off each other well. Particularly fine is Tony Goldwyn (GHOST, TRACES OF RED), seen here briefly as a muddled San

Francisco cop assigned to keep an eye on Slater who gets into trouble when he's caught with his pants down in the company of the chief's wife.

A film of profound credibility and stark realism KUFFS most assuredly is not, but, despite its faults, and on its own level, it's loads of fun. *(Excessive violence, profanity.)*

p, Raynold Gideon; d, Bruce A. Evans; w, Bruce A. Evans, Raynold Gideon; ph, Thomas Del Ruth; ed, Stephen Semel; m, Harold Faltermeyer; prod d, Victoria Paul, Armin Ganz; cos, Mary E. Vogt; ch, Karole Armitage

Action/Crime/Comedy **(PR: O MPAA: PG-13)**

LADY DRAGON ★★★

97m Rapi Films ~ Imperial Entertainment Corporation c

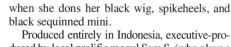

Cynthia Rothrock *(Kathy Gallager)*, Richard Norton *(Ludwig Hauptman)*, Robert Ginty *(Gibson)*, Bella Esperance *(Susan)*, Hengky Tornando *(Allan)*, Thomas Forcher *(John)*, Piet Burnama *(Grandfather)*, Advent Bangun *(Ringo)*, Diaz Tangkilisan *(Boy)*, H.I.M. Damsyik *(Chin)*, Henry Surentu *(Sonny)*, Syarief Friant *(Mario)*, Gino Makasutji *(Andre)*, Tanaka *(Hans)*

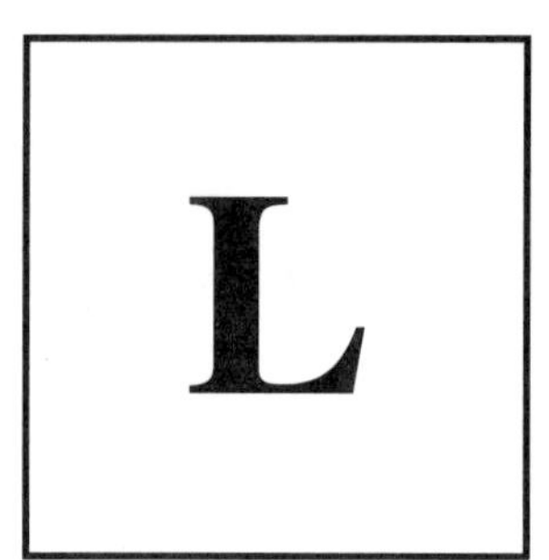

Distaff martial arts star Cynthia Rothrock has one of her better outings as LADY DRAGON, aka Kathy Gallager, an embittered young woman who's still mourning the year-old murder of her husband, on their wedding day, by local crime czar Richard Norton.

Stuck in Indonesia, Gallager makes a bare living in kickboxing matches run by Chin (H.I.M. Damsyik). Warned off revenge by her best friend Gibson (Robert Ginty), Gallager dons a disguise and visits Ludwig Hauptman (Norton), who rapes her, beats her up and dumps her body in the countryside. She's found by Grandfather (Piet Burnama), a mute martial arts sage, who with his young grandson (Diaz Tangkilisan) nurses her back to health and teaches her some new fighting techniques.

Months later, Gallager infiltrates Hauptman's company Imperial Export (he's shipping cocaine and heroin in barrels marked "powdered milk") by befriending his business partner Susan (Bella Esperance). She discovers undercover cop Allan (Hengky Tornando) also working there. Gallager's ruse is uncovered by the turncoat Gibson, who's on Hauptman's payroll. Gallager kills him, and Susan and Hauptman retaliate by burning down Grandfather's house and kidnapping him, forcing her into a big-stakes showdown kickboxing match, overseen by Chin, which Gallager gruellingly wins. Her revenge thus sated, Allan and the police haul off Susan and what's left of Hauptman, and Gallager drives off with her new "family," Grandfather and the boy, to rebuild his house.

Clifford Mohr's screenplay incorporates some specifics from other films (Gallager's murdered-groom predicament from THE BRIDE WORE BLACK; her slow physical recovery/martial arts tutelage from HARD TO KILL and BLIND FURY) and generally recycles genre cliches in decent fashion, although the usual plot implausibilities still nag, such as Hauptman's failing to recognize the thinly disguised Gallager not once but twice. The film is entertainingly directed by David Worth (WARRIORS OF THE LOST WORLD, KICKBOXER) who also photographed it, with good orchestration of the kickboxing melees and lively car and motorcycle chases and shootouts.

Although veteran Robert Ginty (THE EXTERMINATOR, HARLEY DAVIDSON AND THE MARLBORO MAN) is wasted in a surprisingly tiny and extraneous role, the acting is good, with the usually heroic Norton (this former Chuck Norris protege was Rothrock's bad-guy-smashing sidekick in CHINA O'BRIEN) excellent as the kind of slimy villain who enjoys rape and torture, setting his traitorous minions on fire, and watching local peasant women bloodily splashing after a ruby he tosses into his swimming pool.

Norton and Rothrock's climactic crunching chopfest is one of the best martial arts displays of the year. Rothrock gets a lavish star intro here, like Clark Gable in THE MISFITS: the camera tracks up behind her and she suddenly swings around into a close-up, cuing the pumping theme music by Jim West. She's also better photographed here than usual, with better makeup and wardrobe, even diving into some big-star drop-dead glamour when she dons her black wig, spikeheels, and black sequinned mini.

Produced entirely in Indonesia, executive-produced by local prolific mogul Sam S. (who plays a bit part as a diplomat), and with better than average production values, LADY DRAGON was released direct-to-video. *(Violence, profanity, nudity, sexual situations.)*

p, Gope T. Samtani; d, David Worth; w, Clifford Mohr, (from the story by David Worth); ph, David Worth; ed, Amin Kertarahardja, Maruli Ara; m, Jim West; prod d, Hendro Tangkilisan

Crime/Action/Martial Arts (PR: O MPAA: R)

LADYBUGS ★½

91m Ruddy/Morgan Productions ~ Paramount c

Rodney Dangerfield *(Chester Lee)*, Jonathan Brandis *(Matthew/Martha)*, Jackee *(Julie Benson)*, Ilene Graff *(Bess)*, Vinessa Shaw *(Kimberly Mullen)*, Tom Parks *(Dave Mullen)*, Jeannetta Arnette *(Glynnis Mullen)*, Nancy Parsons *(Coach Annie)*, Blake Clark *(Coach Bull)*, Tommy Lasorda *(Coach Cannoli)*

Rodney Dangerfield has always had the potential to be one of the funniest men in American movies, and when filmmakers have taken advantage of that potential, the results have often been hilarious. Unfortunately, LADYBUGS squanders his talents in a cheap and crude comedy.

Dangerfield stars as Chester Lee, a working joe who hopes to win a long-overdue promotion in order to have the money to marry his longtime sweetheart, Bess (Ilene Graff). In an attempt to get in good with his boss, Dave Mullen (Tom Parks), Chester agrees to take on the job of coach for the Ladybugs, the girls' soccer team sponsored by Mullen's company. He figures the job should be easy, since the team has won the last two championships, but he soon finds that all but one of the young players this year are newcomers, none of them particularly skilled at the game. Drafting his assistant, Julie Benson (Jackee), to help him, Chester leads the Ladybugs into their first game of the season—which, naturally, ends in a crushing defeat.

Desperate for a solution to the team's problems, Chester enlists the help of Bess's son Matthew (Jonathan Brandis), with the idea that the boy, who possesses considerable athletic skills, can improve the Ladybugs' fortunes by dressing as a girl and joining the team. At first, the young man is naturally opposed to the idea, but he is convinced when he discovers that Kimberly (Vinessa Shaw), Mullen's beautiful daughter whom he has a crush on, is part of the team.

The Ladybugs begin to score one victory after another, and things start to look bright for Chester. But the other girls start to become upset that "Martha," their new teammate, is the only one capturing any glory on the team, and Bess ultimately discovers Chester's ruse and angrily breaks their engagement. Chester sinks into despair, but with encouragement from Matthew, he restores his faith in himself. He reveals the true identity of "Martha" to the other girls and tells them they're all winners, and the girls go on to win the championship game. Chester gets his promotion and wins back Bess, and all ends happily.

Considering that LADYBUGS was Dangerfield's first film in the six years since the smash hit BACK TO SCHOOL, it's all the more dispiriting that he chose for his follow-up project this witless and obnoxious comedy. The plot is a heavy-handed slog through THE BAD NEWS BEARS territory, with screenwriter Curtis Burch (the press notes claim this is his first major screenplay, though he also cowrote the equally inane 1983 teen-sex comedy JOYSTICKS) faithfully trotting out every predictable plot turn during the second half.

His worst offense, however, is the rather grotesque subplot about young Matthew being talked into adopting transvestism in order to help his potential stepfather, complete with jokes about which rest room to use and a scene in which he must rapidly switch roles from boy to girl and back again when Kimberly stops by for a visit. The screenplay even sinks to the level of using the ruse as the setup for an offensive later scene in which Chester, bemoaning his troubles in a bar, is mistaken for a child molester.

The blame hardly begins or ends with the screenplay, however. Whoever decided that Sidney J. Furie—whose prior credits include the action-movie flops SUPERMAN IV and THE TAKING OF BEVERLY HILLS—was the right director for a Dangerfield comedy should have their heads examined. He displays no sense of wit or comic timing, allows everything to be played as broadly as possible and can't even muster up any enthusiasm for the soccer scenes. The actors are pretty much left to their own devices, with Dangerfield occasionally scoring a good laugh but ultimately left to fall back on his old one-liners at numerous points. Jackee tries hard in a fairly demeaning part, while Brandis looks understandably embarrassed as Matthew/Martha.

The rest of the cast do what they can with their stock roles, and that includes the Ladybugs themselves—a p.c. team if ever there was one, complete with one Black, one Asian, one fat girl and one beauty (Shaw) who looks a good deal older than the rest of her teammates. Of course, this was probably intentional, to keep Matthew's attraction to her in good taste, but it's just about the *only* concession to good taste to be found in LADYBUGS. *(Profanity, adult situations.)*

p, Albert S. Ruddy, Andre E. Morgan; d, Sidney J. Furie; w, Curtis Burch; ph, Dan Burstall; ed, John W. Wheeler, Timothy N. Board; m, Richard Gibbs; prod d, Robb Wilson King; set d, Penny Stames; cos, Isis Mussenden

Comedy **(PR: C MPAA: PG-13)**

LANDSLIDE ★

(U.K.) 95m Northern Screen UK ~ Republic Pictures Home Video c

Anthony Edwards *(Bob Boyd)*, Tom Burlinson *(Howard)*, Melody Anderson *(Clare)*, Ronald Lacey *(Donner)*, Lloyd Bochner *(Bull Matterson)*, Joanna Cassidy *(Lucy)*, Ken James, William Colgate

A painfully bad, melodramatic thriller, LANDSLIDE bears all the hallmarks of a direct-to-video quickie: a couple of minor Hollywood stars-for-hire sleepwalking through their parts, multinational financing and a shoddy screenplay.

Bob Boyd (Anthony Edwards) is an amnesiac from a near-fatal car wreck. A geologist, he is hired by the Matterson Timber & Mining Company to survey its land, which abuts an unstable dam and property owned by its enemy, the Trinivant family. Despite Bob's report that the dam sits on shaky ground, Howard (Tom Burlinson), the evil son of powerful local patriarch Bull Matterson, plans to continue with his project and flood the land belonging to Clair Trinivant (Melody Anderson). Bob becomes drawn into the power struggle and gradually realizes that the past he can not remember ties him to the feud.

Local journalist Mac informs Bob that Claire is the widow of Frank, the son of Matterson's deceased partner John Trinivant. Ten years earlier, both men were reportedly killed in a fiery car crash, along with a mysterious "third man" hitchhiker, Robert Grant. Bob begins to suspect that his crash and the Trinivants' were one and the same. Mac suggests foul play by the Mattersons. Bob decides to investigate in an attempt to discover his own identity, interfering with Howard's nefarious business plans along the way. Before long he's become romantically involved with both Claire and Howard's sister Lucy (Joanna Cassidy). The Mattersons try to convince him he is really Grant and a victim of Claire's sabotage. But Bob takes Claire's side, as he begins to think he may be her husband Frank.

Conflicts come to a head as the dam begins to collapse, setting off a giant landslide. Bull Matterson suffers a spontaneous heart attack upon realizing that it was Frank who survived the wreck. In revenge, Howard, Lucy and their gun thugs hunt down Mac, Claire and Bob/Frank. The amnesiac hero escapes the manhunt to hear a deathbed confession by Bull and his honest partner Fred Donner. As the town is engulfed by the landslide, Frank rescues Claire, while the evil Howard is killed by the disaster he created.

Although nominally an action-thriller, LANDSLIDE spends most of its time having its hopelessly confused and confusing characters sort out their identities and relationships to one another. The central plot device—amnesia—is straight out of the worst of soap operas, but its dialogue and character motivations never fulfill even that low level of artfulness. Anthony Edwards is absolutely wooden as the leading man who bumbles through a series of unmotivated, poorly explained confrontations with the warring families. Is he Bob Boyd? Richard Grant? Robert Boyd Grant? Or Frank Trinivant? He is never quite sure. Neither are any of the other characters. And neither were the screenwriter or director. Nor are we.

At times the poorly thought out twists and confusing turns in the storyline are ludicrous enough to be unintentionally comical, as when Bob confronts old man Matterson with the question, "What if I'm Frank Trinivant?" to which Bull unexpectedly responds by clutching his heart and falling to the ground with all the histrionics of a Gilded Age thespian. The dialogue and narrative exposition sometimes rise to this comical status: "Why weren't you in a car wreck with your husband?" a suspicious Bob asks Claire. "I wanted to go, but . . . I had a cold!" she explains. For the most part, however, LANDSLIDE merely offers an avalanche of unconvincing plot developments and undramatic, unbelievable dialogue.

Somewhere amid the identity reversals, family business power plays and lumber mills (set in the Canadian northwest, the film was also shot in the Yugoslavian republics of Croatia and Slovenia) there seems to be some attempt to exploit David Lynch's "Twin Peaks" TV series, but any similiar sense of style, humor or mystery is absent. Surprisingly, the Croatian crew's low-budget special effects and miniatures in the film's disaster climax are executed in a fairly convincing manner though this comes as small comfort after the disastrous attempts at drama that precede it. *(Violence, profanity, sexual situations.)*

p, Stein Monn-Iversen; d, Jean-Claude Lord; w, Peter Palliser, (from the novel by Desmond Bagley); ph, Tom Pinter; ed, Terje Haglund; m, Bob Mithoff

Mystery/Action/Thriller **(PR: C MPAA: PG-13)**

LASER MOON

90m Triangle Films Inc.; Fitzgerald Filmcorp ~ Hemdale Home Video c

Traci Lords *(Barbara Fleck)*, Crystal Shaw *(Jacelyn)*, Harrison LeDuke *(Zane Wolf)*, Gail Russell *(Maria)*, Michael Hidrogo *(Cruz)*, Eric Goche *(Andy)*, Bruce Carter

The title suggests a science fiction movie, or perhaps a comedic take on new hemorrhoid treatments. Considering alternative approaches like this is the only fun to be had with LASER

MOON, which is actually billed as an erotic thriller—but doesn't succeed at being that either.

Traci Lords is the nominal star, but she's only got a supporting role as a policewoman on the trail of a serial killer who's been murdering women with a surgical laser device. Most of the movie is concerned with a late-night talk-show DJ, Zane Wolf (Harrison LeDuke), who spends his nights fielding phone calls from various eccentrics, including the troubled Maria (Gail Russell) who calls him every night. Outside the studio, Zane's got problems of his own: he's in the middle of unpleasant divorce proceedings with his wife, Jacelyn (Crystal Shaw). Little does he know that she's already taken a lover, Cruz (Michael Hidrogo), and little does *she* know that, in a completely superfluous and unresolved subplot, he's got another mistress and is plotting to kill Jacelyn once her divorce is finalized so the two of them can take off with the money.

Meanwhile, detective Vincent Musso (Bruce Carter) is on the case of the laser murders, which have been occurring on and around nights with full moons. Young Barbara Fleck (Lords) becomes his partner in the investigation, and spends a lot of the time trying to convince Musso that she's really qualified, and didn't just get the job because she's the mayor's daughter. The killer begins to call Zane's radio show, and the police decide to put a trace on incoming calls; this leads them to arrest Andy (Eric Goche). But while subsequently staking out Zane's radio station, Barbara hears his voice coming over distorted. Realizing he's just playing a prerecorded tape, she rushes to Jacelyn's house, where the killer is in the process of terrorizing Jacelyn. Barbara shoots the intruder, and unmasks him—revealing the attacker to be Zane. Sometime later, Musso is out fishing when an associate arrives to tell him that another body's been discovered.

"This movie really sucks," Lords comments at one point, and that's pretty much the best way to sum up this utterly tedious attempt to combine a traditional sex thriller with an introspective look at the life of a radio talk-show host.

Actually, the radically uneven nature of LASER MOON suggests that writer-director Douglas K. Grimm was either ashamed of making an exploitation movie and decided to "legitimize" it through the insertion of all of Zane's soul searching, or was originally intending to create a more dramatic film and was convinced to spice it up with sex and violence to make it an easier sell. In any case, the violent scenes are either perfunctory or unpleasant (or both, in a couple of places), the sex is decidedly unerotic, with the usual languorous couplings and the same saxophone music heard in every film of this type, and the characters and their situations are resolutely uninteresting.

Zane may have a TALK RADIO poster hanging in his studio, but that only serves to remind viewers that any five minutes of that Oliver Stone film had more wit, energy and humanity than Zane's boring monologues and his pat outside conflicts. Anyone expecting any steamy scenes (or even a significant role) for former porn star Lords will be disappointed, and one can only sympathize with Musso when he exclaims halfway through, "I don't know what to say when I'm sitting around waiting for somebody to get murdered." *(Violence, profanity, nudity, sexual situations.)*

p, Mark Paglia; d, Douglas K. Grimm; w, Douglas K. Grimm; ph, Kenneth Carmack; ed, Roger Schroeder, Ken Koenig; m, John Standish

Thriller/Erotic/Crime **(PR: O MPAA: NR)**

LAST OF THE MOHICANS, THE ★★½

122m Forward Pass Productions; Fox ~ Fox c

Daniel Day-Lewis *(Nathaniel Poe/Hawkeye)*, Madeleine Stowe *(Cora Munro)*, Russell Means *(Chingachgook)*, Eric Schweig *(Uncas)*, Jodhi May *(Alice Munro)*, Steven Waddington *(Major Duncan Heyward)*, Wes Studi *(Magua)*, Maurice Roeves *(Colonel Munro)*, Patrice Chereau *(General Montcalm)*, Edward Blatchford *(Jack Winthrop)*, Terry Kinney *(John Cameron)*, Tracey Ellis *(Alexandra Cameron)*, Justin M. Rice *(James Cameron)*, Dennis J. Banks *(Ongewasgone)*, Pete Postelthwaite *(Captain Beams)*, Colm Meaney *(Major Ambrose)*, Mac Andrews *(General Webb)*, Malcolm Storry *(Phelps)*, David Schofield *(Sergeant Major)*, Eric D. Sandgren *(Coureuu de Bois)*, Mike Phillips *(Sachem)*, Mark A. Baker *(Colonial Man)*, Dylan Baker *(Bougainville)*, Tim Hopper *(Ian)*, Gregory Zaragoza *(Abenaki Chief)*, Scott Means *(Abenaki Warrior)*, William J. Bozic, Jr. *(French Artillery Officer)*, Patrick Fitzgerald *(Webb's Adjutant)*, Mark Joy *(Henri)*, Steve Keator *(Colonial Representative)*, Don Tilley *(1st Colonial)*, Thomas E. Cummings *(2nd Colonial)*, David Mark Farrow *(Guard)*, Ethan James Fugate *(French Sappeur)*, F. Curtis Gaston *(1st Soldier)*, Eric A. Hurley *(2nd Soldier)*, Jared Harris *(British Lieutenant)*, Michael McConnell *(Sentry)*, Thomas John McGowan *(Rich Merchant)*, Alice Papineau *(Huron Woman)*, Mark J. Maracle *(Sharitarish)*, Clark Heathcliffe *(Regimental Sergeant Major)*, Sebastian Roche *(Martin)*, Joe Finnegan *(2nd Redcoat)*, Sheila Adams Barnhill *(Humming Woman)*

Just as Montgomery Clift offered audiences a new kind of Western hero in Howard Hawks's classic RED RIVER, so Daniel Day-Lewis transforms Randolph Scott's frontier ruggedness into modernist intensity in THE LAST OF THE MOHICANS, Michael Mann's remake of the 1936 film version of James Fenimore Cooper's novel.

This frontier saga takes place in a wilderness America circa 1757, where British colonists in New York become pawns in a power struggle between England and France during the French and Indian War. Hawkeye (Day-Lewis) is a frontier woodsman more at home with his adopted Mohican father, Chingachgook (Native American activist Russell Means), and brother, Uncas (Eric Schweig), than the white British colonials.

En route to meet their father, Colonel Munro (Maurice Roeves), at the local British fort, comely sisters Cora (Madeleine Stowe) and Alice Munro (Jodhi May) are escorted through hostile territory by British soldiers led by the insufferable Major Duncan Heyward (Steven Waddington), who has his sights set on marrying Cora. The travelers are attacked by the hateful Huron brave Magua (Wes Studi) and his band of Indians. At the last moment, Hawkeye appears to rescue Cora, Alice and Heyward and see them safely to their destination. Cora, at first repelled by Hawkeye, begins to fall in love with him.

When the group arrive at the fort, they find it under seige by the French. Eventually, Colonel Munro surrenders and is allowed to evacuate his soldiers in peace. As the British troops march off into the wilderness, however, Magua—with the permission of the French commander—breaks the agreement and ambushes the group, intent on killing Colonel Munro and abducting his daughters. (Magua has sworn revenge on Munro for the Colonel's earlier anti-Indian exploits.) All the British are killed except for Cora, Alice and Heyward, who are once again rescued by Hawkeye. Magua pursues the group, finally capturing them under a waterfall after Hawkeye escapes.

Hawkeye then makes his way to the Huron encampment and offers his life in exchange for those of Alice and Cora, only for Heyward to preempt Hawkeye's offer and redeem himself by giving his own life. A tribal elder then decrees that all outstanding animosities be resolved by "giving" Alice to Magua. Magua accepts the chance thus to spoil Munro's bloodline, but would clearly prefer simply to kill all concerned. Magua leaves with Alice and his band, pursued by Hawkeye, Cora, Uncas and

Chingachgook. They catch up with the Huron on a high mountain pass where Alice has committed suicide rather than accept her fate; Uncas tries to avenge her death but is killed by Magua, who is then bludgeoned to death by an enraged Chingachgook. Hawkeye and Cora, we presume, live happily ever after.

Director Michael Mann (THIEF; MANHUNTER; TV's "Miami Vice") here eschews his customary hip, urban locales in favor of the breathtaking colonial wilderness. If nothing else, THE LAST OF THE MOHICANS offers some of the most spectular landscapes ever seen on screen, as well as some highly charged, no-expense-spared battle scenes.

Given the two-dimensionality of the characters, the performances are all first-rate. Daniel Day-Lewis handily succeeds in making the leap from art house favorite to a running, jumping, shooting movie hero. Russell Means lends an emotional solidity to his portrayal of Chingachgook. But top acting honors must go to Wes Studi's Magua, who invests this arch-villain with a depth of passion and pain that makes him the centerpiece of the film.

Thanks to a cardboard, hackneyed screenplay, these formulaic characters never stray too far from expectations, and indulge in dialogue that occasionally verges on self-parody ("What are you looking at, Sir?" "I'm looking at you, Miss"). The predictable nature of the whole generates little in the way of suspense—there is never any doubt that Cora and Hawkeye will become lovers, nor any sense that Hawkeye will be injured during the fighting (he flings tomahawks and shoots flintlocks with both hands and gets the bad guys every time). The screenplay wears its Randolph Scott pedigree on its sleeve like a ring of worn Indian beads.

Mann, however, successfully overcomes the weak script by dint of sheer directorial bravura, delivering James Fenimore Cooper into the 1990s with roaring cannons and whizzing tomahawks. The *real* Hawkeye of THE LAST OF THE MOHICANS is not the man on the screen, but the man in the director's chair. *(Extreme violence.)*

p, Michael Mann, Hunt Lowry; d, Michael Mann; w, Michael Mann, Christopher Crowe, Philip Dunne, (from his screenplay, based on the adaptations by John L. Balderston, Paul Perez and Daniel Moore of the novel by James Fenimore Cooper); ph, Dante Spinotti; ed, Dov Hoenig, Arthur Schmidt; m, Trevor Jones, Randy Edelman; prod d, Wolf Kroeger; art d, Richard Holland, Robert Guerra; set d, Jim Erickson, James V. Kent

AA Sound: Chris Jenkins, Doug Hemphill, Mark Smith, and Simon Kaye

Action/Adventure/Historical (PR: O MPAA: R)

LAWNMOWER MAN, THE ★½

(U.K./U.S.) 105m Ben Jade Productions; Lane/Pringle Productions; Allied Vision; Fuji Eight Company ~ New Line Cinema c

Jeff Fahey *(Jobe Smith)*, Pierce Brosnan *(Dr. Lawrence Angelo)*, Jenny Wright *(Marnie Burke)*, Mark Bringleson *(Sebastian Timms)*, Geoffrey Lewis *(Terry McKeen)*, Jeremy Slate *(Father McKeen)*, Dean Norris *(Director)*, Colleen Coffey *(Caroline Angelo)*, Troy Evans *(Lieutenant Goodwin)*, Rosalee Mayeux *(Carla Parkette)*, Austin O'Brien *(Peter Parkette)*, Michael Gregory *(Security Chief)*, Joe Hart *(Patrolman Cooley)*, John Laughlin *(Jake Simpson)*, Ray Lykins *(Harold Parkette)*, Jim Landis *(Ed Waits)*, Mike Valverde *(Day Gate Guard)*, Dale Raoul *(Dolly)*, Daniel Silver *(1st Boy)*, Joey Simrin *(2nd Boy)*, Frank Collison *(Night Gate Guard)*, Jonathan Smart *(Assistant)*, Steffan Gregory Foster *(Letchworth)*, Doug Hutchison *(Security Technician)*, Denney Pierce *(Skinhead Guard)*, Roger Rook *(Older Guard)*, Randall Fontana *(Hotel Waiter)*, Mara Duronslet *(Young Woman Clerk)*, Duane Byrne *(Letchworth Buddy)*, Craig Hosking *(Helicopter Pilot)*

From its dreary title to its tedious and interminable special effects, THE LAWNMOWER MAN is yet another bad example of a genre whose good ones can be counted on the fingers of one hand—the Stephen King Movie.

It may seem glib and lazy to call Stephen King Movies a genre, given that they range in subject matter from horror and science fiction to the occasional straightforward drama, and that his active participation in their production varies tremendously. But sheer numbers (some two dozen films to date and no end in sight) demand it, and the films are characterized by a crudity and brutal obviousness that almost invariably overwhelm the sensibilities of all other participants.

With the exceptions of CARRIE, STAND BY ME and possibly THE SHINING, movies adapted from King's novels and short stories, as well as those from his original screenplays, are a sorry bunch. Given that THE LAWNMOWER MAN takes little from King beyond the title (at the time of the film's release he went public with his complaints that distributor New Line Cinema was cashing in on his name, though the fuss seemed suspiciously like an excuse to hype STEPHEN KING'S SLEEPWALKERS, which was released soon after), it may seem unfair to include it in the King ouevre, but life isn't fair.

Good natured Jobe Smith (Jeff Fahey) is the simple minded ward of a small-town church. Abused by his guardian, a perverted priest, Father Mckeen (Jeremy Slate), and exploited and mocked by many of the townspeople, Jobe still manages to achieve some small measure of happiness reading comic books, playing innocently with local children and mowing lawns. He's that hoary movie cliche, the happy idiot, and as such is ripe for what happens next. Handsome, principled Dr. Lawrence Angelo (Pierce Brosnan) works for a secret government agency, and his latest experiment has gone very wrong. Using a mixture of drug therapy and computer instruction (this is where the movie's gimmick, virtual reality, comes in), Angelo has figured out a way to make chimpanzees smarter. But his latest success has gone on a violent rampage and has had to be destroyed. Angelo, already afraid that his work will be exploited for its military applications, agrees to take a leave of absence, but soon finds himself bored and restless. What could be more natural than for him to decide to continue his experiments at home on a human subject . . . say, the retarded guy who mows his lawn?

If the inevitable course of the action isn't already clear, it becomes so once one has said that THE LAWNMOWER MAN is CHARLY by way of TRON. Jobe becomes progressively more intelligent, a change that dismays some—like the priest who finds he can no longer beat and terrorize him with impunity—and delights others, notably hot-to-trot young widow Marnie Burke (Jenny Wright) who never noticed Jobe's rippling muscles until his new, improved intellect moved him to take off his shirt on hot summer days. Perhaps everything would have been alright if Dr. Angelo's old employers had been able to resist the temptation to tamper with the formula, but tamper they do, and Jobe becomes a psychopath with messianic fantasies of world domination. Like some humanoid computer virus, he intends to invade the world's computers and show humanity the way to better living through subordination to computer generated "reality." It's up to Dr. Angelo to stop him before mankind is reduced to a hoard of mindless video-addicted zombies.

THE LAWNMOWER MAN's selling point—aside from King's name—was its extensive use of simulated virtual reality, a movie first. Virtual reality technology allows users to don special goggles and gloves and explore computer generated environments without ever leaving their chairs. The implications are pretty obvious ("What's next, fucking?" asks Angelo's wife peevishly when she catches him hooked up to a program that fakes the alliterative sensations of flying, floating and falling), and much screen time is given over to the computer worlds Angelo has designed. How much one enjoys these sequences is directly related to how much one loves state-of-the-art video game graphics, all liquid metal edges and bright, clean colors. What THE LAWNMOWER MAN's effects don't—in fact, can't—do is give the viewer the sense of experiencing a false three-dimensional reality, and that's a real drawback: it robs the "virtual reality" sequences of the only thing that might make them seem fresh and novel.

Movies from THE LAST STARFIGHTER to TRON (so dated that it's painful to watch) have put video game images on screen, and it's pretty dull stuff. Virtual reality aside, THE LAWNMOWER MAN suffers all the usual problems: the cliched story is further undermined by wooden performances (Fahey, his naturally dark hair stripped to the consistancy of a Harpo Marx fright wig, is particularly excruciating) and the inevitable unhappy ending, in which a chorus of telephones ring in a scary new world. *(Sexual situations.)*

p, Gimel Everett; d, Brett Leonard; w, Brett Leonard, Gimel Everett, (adapted from the short story by Stephen King); ph, Russell Carpenter; ed, Alan Baumgarten; m, Dan Wyman; prod d, Alex McDowell; cos, Mary Jane Fort; fx, Frank Ceglia, Paul Haines, Tom Ceglia, Reel EFX Inc., Reel Time, Angel Studios, The Goosney Company, Homer & Associates Inc., Xaos Inc., Magical Media Industries, David Stipes Productions

Science Fiction **(PR: C MPAA: R)**

LAWS OF GRAVITY ★★★½
100m Meistrich Corporation ~ RKO Pictures Distribution c

Peter Greene *(Jimmy)*, Edie Falco *(Denise)*, Paul Schulzie *(Frankie)*, Tony Fernandez *(Tommy)*, James McCauley *(Kenny)*, Anibal Lierras *(Ray)*, Miguel Sierra *(Vasquez)*, Adam Trese *(Jon)*, Arabella Field *(Celia)*, Saul Stein *(Sal)*, Larry Meistrich *(Pete)*, Rick Greol *(Kevin)*, David Troup *(Sullivan)*, Patricia Sullivan *(Terry)*, John Gallagher, Eli Kabillio, William Sage, Dave Tuttle, Judith Boxley, Mark Chandler Bailey, Kim Gambino, Anthony Ingolglia, Dieidre Bodie-Henderson

Filmmaker Nick Gomez has fashioned an ultra-low-budget tale of urban losers that far surpasses any recent Hollywood product in terms of realistic characters and believable dialogue. An unblinking view of day-to-day life on the mean streets of Greenpoint, Brooklyn, LAWS OF GRAVITY captures this violent and gritty world without without being exploitative or sensationalist.

Jimmy (Peter Greene) and his lifelong friend Jon (Adam Trese) are two neighborhood punks who spend their days stealing, fighting and hanging out. Jimmy, at least, is in a stable domestic relationship with Denise (Edie Falco), and is beginning to question his lot in life; Jon, a few years younger, runs on a short fuse that seems to be getting even shorter. For these small-time thieves, a big haul consists of pilfering a box of sheets from the back of a van.

Jimmy, who is into the local loanshark, Tommy (Tony Fernandez), for a relatively sizeable amount, nevertheless turns down Tommy's offer to get him a real job at the Javits Center in Manhattan. "I ain't no garbageman," retorts Jimmy—though he's not above looting local department stores for chump change. Jon, moreover, is only one step ahead of the police, who have issued a summons for his arrest; this doesn't stop him from picking fights with virtually anyone who looks in the direction of his girlfriend Celia (Arabella Field). The endless cycle of stealing, brawling and drinking takes on new dimensions when another local, Frankie (Paul Schultzie), returns home from Florida.

A sociopath with boy-next-door looks, Frankie has brought with him a cache of stolen handguns which he convinces Jon and Jimmy to help him "move." Jon brazenly takes to carrying around a piece in his waistband, whipping it out at the slightest provocation. His erratic behavior finally causes Celia to leave him. Jimmy agrees to keep the guns hidden in his apartment until they find a taker. Denise, apparently the only person who holds a job, is less than delighted that Frankie is back in town and that her and Jimmy's apartment is being used to store weapons.

When the police finally catch up with Jon and arrest him, Jimmy decides to sell the guns to the local fence at a cut-price rate so he can raise bail money for his friend. Frankie finds out that his guns have been sold without his knowledge, leading to a nighttime confrontation that leaves Jon brutally murdered and Jimmy's fragile life shattered.

LAWS OF GRAVITY's shoestring budget (reputedly only $38 thousand) forced some interesting choices on writer-director Nick Gomez. The use of a hand-held camera (masterfully employed by Jean De Segonzac), and frequent lack of master shots, gives the film a compelling *cinema verite* feel. This is complemented by the improvisational quality of the dialogue and the realistically drawn characters.

Gomez's keen eye for casting is one of the film's strongest attributes, with an entire group of virtual unknowns turning in uniformly credible performances. Particularly strong is Greene as Jimmy, a man who knows he should be somewhere else in life but fails to make it happen. As the swaggering, volatile Jon and the cooly evil Frankie, Trese and Schulzie are completely believable. In the sympathetic role of Denise—the only character with a legitimate chance of getting out of the neighborhood—Falco is simply wonderful. (She later turned up, together with some other LAWS OF GRAVITY alumni, in a Gomez-directed episode of Barry Levinson's NBC cop series, "Homicide.")

Nick Gomez has made a stunning portrait of urban life that is unglamorous, unsettling and highly uncommercial. LAWS OF GRAVITY inevitably drew comparisons to a masterpiece of another era, Scorsese's MEAN STREETS, which also chronicles the lives of urban misfits. While there are stylistic similarities between the two, LAWS OF GRAVITY should be judged solely on its own merits—great storytelling, strong performances and gritty realism. *(Violence, profanity, adult situations.)*

p, Larry Meistrich, Bob Gosse; d, Nick Gomez; w, Nick Gomez; ph, Jean De Segonzac; ed, Nick Gomez, Tom McArdle; prod d, Monica Bretherton

Drama **(PR: O MPAA: R)**

LEAGUE OF THEIR OWN, A ★★½
128m Parkway Productions; Columbia ~ Columbia c

Tom Hanks *(Jimmy Dugan)*, Geena Davis *(Dottie Hinson)*, Lori Petty *(Kit Keller)*, Madonna *(Mae Mordabito)*, Rosie O'Donnell *(Doris Murphy)*, Megan Cavanagh *(Marla Hooch)*, Tracy Reiner *(Betty Horn)*, Bitty Schram *(Evelyn Gardner)*, Ann Cusack *(Shirley Baker)*, Anne Elizabeth Ramsay *(Helen Haley)*, Freddie Simpson *(Ellen Sue Gotlander)*, Renee Coleman *(Alice Gaspers)*, Robin Knight *("Beans" Babbitt)*, Patti Pelton *(Marbleann Wilkenson)*, Kelli Simpkins *(Beverly Dixon)*, Neezer Tarleton *(Neezer Dalton)*, Connie Pounds-Taylor *(Connie Calhoun)*, Kathleen Marshall *("Mumbles" Brockman)*, Sharon Szmidt *(Vivian Ernst)*, Pauline Brailsford *(Miss Cuthbert)*, David Strathairn *(Ira Lowenstein)*, Garry Marshall *(Walter Harvey)*, Jon Lovitz *(Ernie Capadino)*, Bill Pullman *(Bob Hinson)*, Justin Scheller *(Stilwell)*, Eddie Jones *(Dave Hooch)*, Alan Wilder *(Nelson)*, R.M. Haley *(Empathetic Umpire)*, Don Davis *(Racine Coach Charlie)*, Janet Jones *(Racine Pitcher)*, Brenda Ferrari *(Racine Pitcher)*, Tea

Leoni *(Racine 1B)*, Laurel Cronin *(Maida Gilespie)*, Robert Stanton *(Western Union Man)*, Wantland L. Sandel, Jr. *(Doctor)*, Joe Krowka *(Heckler)*, Harry Shearer *(Newsreel Announcer)*, Blaire Baron *(Margaret)*, Ryan Howell *(Jeffrey)*, Brian Boru Gleeson *(Bobby)*, David Franks *(Vacuum Salesman)*, Ryan Olsen *(Dollbody Kid)*, Ellie Weingardt *(Charm School Instructor)*, Larissa Collins *(Charm School Assistant)*, Douglas Blakeslee *(1st Doris Fan)*, Joseph Slotnick *(2nd Doris Fan)*, Brian Flannery *(1st Autograph Kid)*, Stephen Feagley *(2nd Autograph Kid)*, Rae Allen *(Ma Keller)*, Gregory Sporleder *(Mitch Swaley)*, Eddie Mekka *(Mae's Guy in Bar)*, Stephen Mailer *(Kit's Date in Bar)*, Ray Chapman *(Ticket Scalper)*, Joette Hodgen *(Opera Singer)*, Lynn Cartwright *(Older Dottie)*, Kathleen Butler *(Older Kit)*, Eunice Anderson *(Older Mae)*, Vera Johnson *(Older Doris)*, Patricia Wilson *(Older Marla)*, Mark Holton *(Older Stilwell)*, Barbara Erwin *(Older Shirley)*, Betty Miller *(Older Betty)*, Eugenia McLin *(Older Elle Sue)*, Barbara Pilavin *(Older Helen)*, Marvin Einhorn *(Older Ira)*, Shirley Burkovich *(Older Alice)*, Dolores "Pickles" Dries *(Lady in Bleachers)*, Lisa Hand *(Shelly Adlard)*, Cheryl Jones *(Vickie Buse)*, Shelly Niemeyer *(KC Carr)*, Sally Rutherford *(Julie Croteau)*, Lita Scmitt *(Tonya Gilles Koch)*, Amanda Walker *(Kirsten Gretick)*, Brenda Watson *(Stacey Gustaferro)*

A summertime smash for Columbia Pictures, A LEAGUE OF THEIR OWN is a female ensemble piece in the style of classics like THE WOMEN and STAGE DOOR.

As the film opens, elderly Dottie Hinson (Lynn Cartwright, dubbed by Geena Davis) is preparing to travel to Cooperstown's Baseball Hall of Fame for a celebration of her career in the 1940s Women's Professional Baseball League. In a flashback, it is recalled how candy-bar manufacturer Walter Harvey (Garry Marshall) created the league after most male players were sent off to fight in WWII. Dottie, a catcher (now played by Davis), and her younger sister Kit Keller (Lori Petty), a pitcher, are spotted by baseball scout Ernie Capadino (Jon Lovitz). Dottie rejects a tryout offer, but relents when Ernie will only accept Kit along with her prettier and more athletically talented sister.

While Dottie misses her soldier husband, and Kit resents Dottie for her superiority, both sisters make the league. Their fellow players on the Rockford Peaches include promiscuous Mae Mordabito (Madonna); Mae's funny pal Doris Murphy (Rosie O'Donnell); sensitive Evelyn Gardner (Bitty Schram), who dotes on her bratty son Stilwell (Justin Scheller); and athletically gifted but homely and shy Marla Hooch (Megan Cavanagh).

Harvey's choice to manage the club, former baseball great Jimmy Dugan (Tom Hanks), would rather drink than work at first, but finally takes control, developing respect for Davis and the concept of women's baseball. While the league initially falters, the ladies generate so much positive publicity that it becomes a sensation. Kit's ongoing sibling rivalry with Dottie, however, threatens to destroy the Peaches. When Kit is traded to a rival club, she finally has the chance to shine. Dottie leaves the Peaches when her husband returns from war, but rejoins them in time to face Kit in the World Series.

Most of the credit for A LEAGUE OF THEIR OWN belongs to director Penny Marshall, who lets her actresses have fun with the story. Marshall lapses into sentimentality during the beginning flashback and ending, but the bulk of the film is a joyous mix of comedy, sports and drama. Marshall works with the large cast beautifully, giving each supporting actress an important bit, whether it be Madonna's tearful refusal to abandon hope for the league or O'Donnell's bitter speech about her loutish boyfriend. Much of the movie's strength comes from moments with these likable characters.

As Dottie, Geena Davis proves herself once again to be one of our most important actresses. In the manner of a true star, Davis lets her oversized, goofy good looks and appealing personality speak for themselves. Seldom has an actress in a lead role so subtly melded herself into a film; it's a triumph of underplaying. Davis (in a role originally intended for Debra Winger) is utterly convincing as the voice of common sense, who tolerates her sister's angst until she can stand it no longer; gently nudges Hanks to give up drinking by offering him a coke; and manages the Peaches herself by simply assigning positions. Davis's generosity as a performer also allows the other actresses to shine.

Petty (POINT BREAK) perfectly portrays an intense tomboy who lets sibling rivalry define her life. Madonna's part was tailor-made for her and she doesn't disappoint, giving an energetic performance as a former dance-hall hostess who sees baseball as her ticket out of poverty. In the film's most delirious scene, Mae does a lively dance at the Suds Bucket, a club where the women sneak in finally to have some postgame fun. Madonna is also amusing when exiting a confessional with a shocked priest. The pop superstar works well with O'Donnell—their joking camaraderie is one of the film's early pleasures.

Also in the early scenes, Megan Cavanagh steals the show as Marla. Cavanagh's wide-eyed, scared look when anyone comes near her is hilarious. As for the actors, Jon Lovitz doesn't fare too well in his brief but flashy role; it's another one of his "Saturday Night Live" sketch characters. Tom Hanks, on the other hand, gives his best performance in years. The movie's funniest scene shows Hanks trying to suppress his anger when Schram again misses the cutoff man during a game. And his exasperated delivery of the line "There's no crying in baseball!" has made it an instant classic. Hanks and Davis are convincing in their movie relationship, too—it's a rare platonic one based on mutual respect. They're delightful talking quietly on the team bus or squabbling by flashing duelling signs to a player up at bat.

Based on the true story of the women's league, the screenplay by Lowell Ganz and Babaloo Mandel features many cute lines, most of which fly. More scenes should have focused on the actual mechanics of baseball, but Marshall's clever cutting does make the actresses look like they're really playing. And the final baseball confrontation between Dottie and Kit has a twist; it ends with a slide instead of the strikeout pitch you expect.

p, Elliot Abbott, Robert Greenhut; d, Penny Marshall; w, Lowell Ganz, Babaloo Mandel, (from the story by Kim Wilson and Kelly Candaele); ph, Miroslav Ondricek; ed, George Bowers; m, Hans Zimmer; prod d, Bill Groom; art d, Tim Galvin; set d, George DeTitta, Jr.; cos, Cynthia Flynt

Comedy/Sports **(PR: A MPAA: PG)**

LEAP OF FAITH ★★

110m Paramount ~ Paramount c

Steve Martin *(Jonas Nightengale)*, Debra Winger *(Jane)*, Lolita Davidovich *(Marva)*, Liam Neeson *(Will)*, Lukas Haas *(Boyd)*, Meat Loaf *(Hoover)*, Philip Seymour Hoffman *(Mart)*, M.C. Gainey *(Tiny)*, La Chanze *(Georgette)*, Delores Hall *(Ornella)*, John Toles-Bey *(Titus)*, Albertina Walker *(Lucille)*, Ricky Dillard *(Ricky)*, Vince Davis *(Roger)*, Troy Evans *(Dade)*, Phyllis Somerville *(Dolores)*, David L. Emmons *(Jerry Joe)*, Mark Walters *(Calvin)*, James N. Harrell *(Ramsey)*, Vernon Grote *(Rafe)*, Margaret Bowman *(Woman with Cherries Hat)*, Jennifer Snyder *(Glitter Jeans Girl)*, Deborah Hope *(Glitter Jeans Mother)*, Ed K. Geldart *(Brown Jacket)*, Marietta Marich *(Mrs. Hawkins)*, Grover Washington *(Old Black Man)*, Suzi Mclaughlin *(Weatherworn Woman)*, Salvador Hernandez *(Young Man)*, Casey Hammer *(Nineteen)*, Blue Deckert *(Jake)*, Jane Milburn *(Sadie)*, Norm Colvin *(1st Man)*, Maria Arita *(Female TV Anchor)*, Dave Hager *(Trucker)*, Jason McGuire *(Tough Kid)*, Melodee Bowman *(Calvin's Wife)*, Shirley Ash, Angela Blair, Cornelius Clark, Georgie Ellis, Tommy Ray Green, Felicia House, Tarsha Jackson, La Dale Kemp, Lizz Lee, Lawrence Matthews, Gheri LeGree-McDonald, Shun Pace-Rhodes, Stephanie Stephens, Cherrie Thompson, Leon P. Turner, Lulanger Washington, III, Gabrielle West, Leroy Williams, Eugene Young, IV *(Angels of Mercy)*

The main pleasure of this comedy is that it's completely forgettable. LEAP OF FAITH's lively spirit doesn't require any great thought, and star Steve Martin avoids much of the pretentious sentimentality that has plagued such recent work as L.A. STORY and FATHER OF THE BRIDE. Here, the wild and crazy guy is back, making you realize how much you missed him.

Phony traveling evangelist Jonas Nightengale (Martin) and his employees set up shop in a small Kansas town after their bus breaks down. With the aid of his savvy partner Jane (Debra Winger), who directs him through a hidden microphone, Jonas takes the locals' money and cons them into believing he can perform miracles, including helping a wheelchair-bound woman stand. Although honest town sheriff Will (Liam Neeson) falls for Jane, he mistrusts Jonas and tries to run him out of town. Meanwhile, Jonas pursues local waitress Marva (Lolita Davidovich), whose brother Boyd (Lukas Haas) lost the use of his legs in a car accident. Marva resists Jonas's advances because another preacher had once exploited her brother in a religious show.

When Jonas paints open eyes on a statue of Jesus, the townspeople declare it a miracle, and crowds jam the church to see the preacher. Will exposes Jonas's criminal past to the audience, but the preacher wins over the crowd with his oratory. In a genuinely miraculous turn of events that baffles and disturbs Jonas, Boyd regains the ability to walk during the show. When Boyd wants to leave town as part of Jonas's crooked caravan, however, Jonas can't live with his conscience. He hitches a ride out of town, leaving the boy with his sister and a happy Jane with Will. As Jonas leaves, the rain the drought-ridden townspeople have long prayed for begins to fall.

LEAP OF FAITH is a surprisingly gentle send-up of evangelism, not the hardest of targets. But Martin's character has more depth than most of his recent roles, making the movie an interesting character study of a man who can smoothly (and hilariously) rationalize cheating people out of their money. To Jonas, his brand of religion doesn't hurt anyone because it gives people entertainment. Martin is especially good with Winger, herself rebounding from a string of lackluster performances. (It's nice to see her good-humored, brassy personality used to good advantage.) Their relationship is a loving one that includes a lot of mutual jealousy, leading one to wonder why they aren't a romantic couple. Jonas gives Jane a puppy and a ruby ring during the movie, further confusing the issue.

Liam Neeson is so romance-novel-hunky that he manages to make you believe Winger could give up the excitement of the road for domesticity. The two of them don't even look ridiculous when they are surrounded by butterflies in the film's most corny romantic scene. The only trouble is, Neeson's thick Irish accent does seem distinctly out of place in Kansas. Meat Loaf, who plays bus driver and organist Hoover, has a natural presence; it would have been fun to see him as more of a comic foil for Martin.

Jonas's evangelist show reminds you of Martin's famous stand-up act—the "happy feet" come alive in the tent revival scenes. In these moments, director Richard Pearce wisely sets the camera back to show off Martin's graceful physical presence. Backed by the gospel choir "The Angels of Mercy," Jonas never stops moving around the stage. Jane's backstage microphone directions to Jonas are funny, as she pinpoints physical and emotional problems of audience members that the evangelist can exploit during the act.

Although the pace is consistently energetic, the melodramatic subplot involving Jonas and Boyd is cloying, mainly because the young boy's character is so saccharine-sweet. Our credibility is also strained by the ease with which Jonas manages to con an entire community. Overall, however, this is one of Martin's better, lighter vehicles. *(Sexual situations, adult situations.)*

p, Michael Manheim, David V. Picker; d, Richard Pearce; w, Janus Cercone; ph, Matthew F. Leonetti; ed, Don Zimmerman, Mark Warner, John F. Burnett; m, Cliff Eidelman; prod d, Patrizia Von Brandenstein; art d, Dennis Bradford; set d, Gretchen Rau; cos, Theadora Van Runkle

Comedy/Drama **(PR: C MPAA: PG-13)**

LEATHER JACKETS ★★½
90m Seven Inc.; Epic Productions ~ Epic Home Video c

D.B. Sweeney *(Mickey)*, Bridget Fonda *(Claudi)*, Cary Elwes *(Dobbs)*, Christopher Penn *(Big Steve)*, Jon Polito *(Fat Jack)*, Craig Ng *(Tron)*, Marshall Bell *(Stranger)*, James LeGros *(Carl)*, Neil Giuntoli *(Sammy)*, Ginger Lynn Allen *(Bree)*, Lisanne Falk *(Shanna)*, Viper *(Connie)*, Jon Pochran *(Anthony)*, Joseph H. Lewis *(Barfly)*, Dudi Trevor *(Mrs. Little)*, Phil Chong *(Vietnamese Bookie)*, Michael Champion *(Costello)*, Tony Cecere *(Pimp)*, Darryl Chan *(Su)*, Alicia Allain *(Jingles)*, Lee Drysdale *(Waiter)*

The presence of cult director Joseph H. Lewis in a brief bit as a semicoherent habitue of Fat Jack's bar is clearly prescient; at its best, LEATHER JACKETS, a crime melodrama about a group of young losers on the run, has all the merits of one of Lewis's energetic little B pictures of the 1940s and 1950s.

Small-time criminal Dobbs (Cary Elwes) and cohorts Carl (James LeGros), Big Steve (Christopher Penn), Sammy (Neil Giuntoli) and Anthony (Jon Pochran) rip off and kill a Vietnamese drug courier. Meanwhile, former gang member and Dobbs's longtime friend Mickey (D.B. Sweeney) quits his construction job and overcomes his shyness to propose to friend and neighbor Claudi (Bridget Fonda), who had earlier had an affair with Dobbs. The couple make plans to head for Los Angeles, where a job is waiting for Mickey. Dobbs and the gang refuse to flee the area, which would alert the police to their guilt, and hole up at Fat Jack's (Jon Polito), where they have planned a going-away party for Mickey.

The head of the Vietnamese cartel hires Tron (Craig Ng) to exact revenge, based on information passed to him by the corrupt cops. After drowning Anthony and using a deadly samurai blade to behead Sammy and Carl, and the latter's wife (Lisanne Falk) and child, Tron winds up at Fat Jack's as the cops arrive. In the ensuing shootout, the cops are killed, but Mickey, the wounded Dobbs and Big Steve escape, with Tron and his thugs in hot pursuit. They pick up Claudi and head for LA. Hours later, exhausted, they break into a motel room; Tron ambushes Big Steve, lops off his head and kills Dobbs, but, at the point of terrorizing Claudi, is dispatched by Mickey, using Dobbs's gun, although he is fatally skewered by Tron's blade. Soothed by the distraught Claudi, Mickey dies as the sun finally comes up, ending the long night of violence.

Produced by Cary's brother Cassian, LEATHER JACKETS is one of the truer exercises in modern film noir, with its existential storyline, relentlessly seedy production design and James Chressanthis's shadowy, color-drained cinematography. The picture unfolds almost in real time, most of it at night; as Claudi, cradling the dead Mickey's head, looks up into the rising, unseen-till-now sun, it's like a clear, fresh burst of salvation.

Debuting writer-director Lee Drysdale's film is much more explicitly violent than anything in Lewis's (GUN CRAZY, THE BIG COMBO) *oeuvre*, and oddly wordier, especially during its middle section, in which the trio Mickey, Dobbs and Claudi thrash out their past and present relationships. Even though this long sequence slows down the frenetic pace expertly established by Drysdale, it is well written and performed by his three attractive leads.

While she hasn't been given that neurotically feisty quality of many of Lewis's heroines, rising star Bridget Fonda (SINGLES, SINGLE WHITE FEMALE) quietly establishes her growing strength and clearheadedness as she describes her love affair—her first—with Elwes and her decision to end it. Likewise, actors D.B. Sweeney (MEMPHIS BELLE, THE CUTTING EDGE) and especially Cary Elwes (THE PRINCESS BRIDE, BRAM STOKER'S DRACULA), whose constant acerbic needling of Sweeney hides his jealousy that, unlike himself, the former has finally broken out of his losing rut of a life, fighting through the petty macho posturing holding them both back.

The story is fairly standard—again one thinks of Lewis, Don Siegel or the early Roger Corman—but Drysdale's brisk direction efficiently delineates the awful early bursts of violence which set his quartet on the run, then matches it with an equally suspenseful action finale. The plot still has its stumblers: the fourth member, played by Christopher Penn (FOOTLOOSE, RESERVOIR DOGS), is given very little to do, and the relative ease with which Sweeney wipes out three cold professional killers is a bit unbelievable.

The secondary performances are also good, particularly Craig Ng as the icily sleek, pony-tailed, black raincoated killer whose name signals his machine-like efficiency. Also memorable is Coen brothers' favorite Jon Polito (MILLER'S CROSSING, BARTON FINK) as the unfortunately oportunistic bar owner who tries to put the bite on Dobbs for the money and is knocked down a flight of stairs.

Unaccountably left on the shelf for several months, perhaps because of its downbeat ending, LEATHER JACKETS was released theatrically abroad during 1991, then went straight-to-video in the US the following year. *(Violence, substance abuse, profanity, nudity, sexual situations.)*

p, Cassian Elwes; d, Lee Drysdale; w, Lee Drysdale; ph, James Chressanthis; ed, Ned Humphreys; m, Shlomo Artzi; prod d, Phillip G. Thomas; set d, Helen Dersjant; cos, Shawna Leavell

Crime/Drama **(PR: O MPAA: R)**

LEAVING NORMAL ★★½

110m Mirage Enterprises; Universal ~ Universal c

Christine Lahti *(Darly Peters)*, Meg Tilly *(Marianne Johnson)*, Lenny Von Dohlen *(Harry Rainey)*, Maury Chaykin *(Leon "Crazy-As" Pendleton)*, Patrika Darbo *(66)*, Eve Gordon *(Emily Singer)*, James Eckhouse *(Rich Singer)*, Brett Cullen *(Kurt)*, James Gammon *(Walt)*, Lachlan Murdoch *(Marshall)*, Robyn Simons *(Sarah)*, Ken Angel *(Nuqaq)*, Darrell Dennis *(Clyde)*, Barbara Russell *(Izuzu Mother)*, Ahnee Boyce *(Izuzu Judy)*, Marc Levy *(Dave)*, Peter Anderson *(Spicy)*, Gordon Tootoosis *(Hank Amaruk)*, Rutanya Alda *(Palmer Hospital Nurse)*, Ray Godshall *(Mort)*, Tom Heaton *(Alec)*, Dierdre O'Connell *(Ellen)*, Gordon Tipple *(Danny)*, John Bear Curtis *(Michael)*, Paul Jarrett *(Charlie)*, Ed Solomon *(Jerk in Bar)*, Andrew Johnston *(Nearest Guy)*, Ben Ratner *(Next Nearest Guy)*, Timothy Webber *(Spicy's Friend)*, Sam Bob *(Delivery Guy)*, Marlane O'Brien *(Clara)*, Brenda McDonald *(Motel Clerk)*, Paul Stanley *(Man Customer)*, Rob Morton *(Bartender)*, Darryl Layne *(Topless Dancer)*, Julie Taggart *(Twelve-Year-Old Girl)*, Ruby Cox *(Woman)*, Desmond Smiley *(Minister)*, Dana Stevens *(Marianne's Mother)*, Ashlee Buhler *(Young Marianne)*, Jenny Drugan *(Young Emily)*, Colin James Munn, Dennis Marcenko, Richard Hopkins, John Ferreira, Darrell Mayes *(Colin James Band Members)*, Trisha Gagnon, Cathy-Anne Whitworth, Dave Schryver, Chris Stevens *(Tumbleweed Band Members)*

A few laughs, a few tears but also a few too many yawns are to be found in Edward Zwick's LEAVING NORMAL, a road movie that mainlines sugary whimsicality.

Marianne Johnson (Meg Tilly) yearns to settle down after a childhood spent moving around with her wandering parents and sister. But she can't stay put, even in adulthood. Married and living in Normal, Wyoming, she takes yet another powder after her husband takes a swing at her. On her way out of town—she's headed for Portland, Oregon, where her sister has settled down with a husband and two kids—Marianne meets up with hardbitten cocktail waitress Darly Peters (Christine Lahti), who's just found out that her former husband has died and left her a house and a small plot of land in Eternity Bluff, Alaska. Arriving in Portland, Marianne finds that her sister is *too* settled, a perfect suburban matron who can't keep from making Marianne feel inferior for her feckless ways. Impulsively, Marianne lights out again with Darly.

On the way they have adventures—hitchhiking after Darly's car breaks down and is stripped while the women go to get help; conning a randy truck driver (Maury Chaykin) and his sensitive partner (Lenny Von Dohlen) out of a ride and some money; travelling with a corpulent ex-waitress (Patrika Darbo) searching for true love who finds it in the unlikeliest place. In Alaska, Darly finds that there is no house—her husband never built it—and the daughter she abandoned 18 years earlier has disappeared. Her stock drops further when she loses her job—as a cocktail waitress in the only bar in town—after groin-kicking a guy (James Gammon) who gets ugly with her.

Darly is ready to leave town, but she finds Marianne reluctant. She's gotten a good job at the local hardware store and has befriended two homeless Eskimo teenagers whom she is teaching to read and write. Marianne and Darly have a falling out, leading Darly to turn a trick with the barroom masher, who's offered her money for dancing and sex, on her way out of town. Darly can't go through with it, but the masher is moved to give her two hundred dollars anyway. Darly returns "home" to Marianne, who has stayed on even after the sensitive truck driver has come to take her away. Together they build the house and have a happy, if offbeat, homelife with the two homeless kids.

THELMA AND LOUISE it ain't, but as far as it goes, LEAVING NORMAL is a pleasant ride. Tilly (AGNES OF GOD, VALMONT) has made a career out of playing sweetly ditzy flower-children like the character she essays here. But it wears remarkably well and Tilly remains one of the most watchable actresses around. Lahti also does well with a similarly one-note character she's also played to a fare-thee-well in films like HOUSEKEEPING and JUST BETWEEN FRIENDS. But it's an uphill battle throughout for the cast to overcome the uninspired, laboriously quirky characters overrunning Edward Solomon's screenplay, from Darbo's amusing turn as the unflaggingly optimistic fat girl to Gammon's masher with a soft spot for a sad story and Van Dohlen's lovestruck truck driver who writes bad poetry on the side.

Hindering their efforts, director Edward Zwick (GLORY, ABOUT LAST NIGHT) betrays too much of his "Thirtysomething" TV background in his tendency to fragment the action into annoying, elliptical 8-minute segments while deflating everything and everybody in sight into facile running jokes in need only of a laugh track. He tends to steer clear of anything that might have made LEAVING NORMAL distinctive, such as any exploration of Marianne's relationship with her sister, which at the beginning seems to be the film's subject only to become just another occasion for stale gags when Marianne arrives in Portland. Even the relationship between Darly and Marianne never gets far beyond its odd-couple premise. When all else fails, Zwick pulls back for one of those cosmic landscape shots that look pretty at first but only become redundant after a while.

Indeed, a spirit of redundancy pervades the entire film, considering how overworked quirkiness in the American Northwest has become via TV's "Northern Exposure" and "Twin Peaks." Despite its standout cast, LEAVING NORMAL is more whimsical weirdness where no more is needed. *(Adult situations, profanity.)*

p, Lindsay Doran; d, Edward Zwick; w, Edward Solomon; ph, Ralf D. Bode; ed, Victor DuBois; m, W.G. Snuffy Walden; prod d, Patricia Norris; art d, Sandy Cochrane; set d, Elizabeth Wilcox; cos, Patricia Norris

Comedy/Drama **(PR: C MPAA: R)**

LETHAL WEAPON 3 ★★½

118m Warner Bros.; Silver Pictures ~ Warner Bros. c

Mel Gibson *(Martin Riggs)*, Danny Glover *(Roger Murtaugh)*, Joe Pesci *(Leo Getz)*, Rene Russo *(Lorna Cole)*, Stuart Wilson *(Jack Travis)*, Steve Kahan *(Captain Murphy)*, Darlene Love *(Trish Murtaugh)*, Traci Wolfe *(Rianne Murtaugh)*, Damon Hines *(Nick Murtaugh)*, Ebonie Smith *(Carrie Murtaugh)*, Gregory Millar *(Tyrone)*, Nick Chinlund *(Hatchett)*, Jason Meshover-Iorg *(Young Cop)*, Alan Scarfe *(Herman Walters)*, Delores Hall *(Delores)*, Mary Ellen Trainor *(Dr. Stephanie Woods)*, Mark Pellegrino *(Billy Phelps)*, John Cenatiempo *(Smitty)*, Danny Wynands *(Hershel)*, Andrew Hill Newman *(Jaywalker)*, Kenneth Tigar *(Ernie/Detective)*, Pete Antico *(1st Henchman/Hubie)*, Sven-Ole Thorsen *(2nd Henchman)*, Paul Tuerpe *(3rd Henchman)*, Ronnie Alicino *(1st Squad Member)*, Henry Brown *(2nd Squad Member)*, Eric Briant Wells *(3rd Squad Member)*, Miguel Nunez *(4th Squad Member)*, Philip Moon *(5th Squad Member)*, Bobby Wynn *(Darryl)*, Sylvia Webb White *(Darryl's Mother)*, Danny Big Black *(Darryl's Father)*, Vincent Howard *(Preacher)*, Paul Hipp *(Doctor)*, Lauren Shuler-Donner *(Nurse)*, Stephen T. Kay *(Movie Director)*, Michael George Miller *(Movie Assistant Director)*, Henry Kingi *(Movie Gun Punk)*, Adam Klineberg *(Movie Cop)*, Michele Landry *(Young Woman)*, Scott M. Bryce *(Young Man)*, Del Emory *(Shower Cop)*, John Harms *(Cop)*, James Oliver *(Manager)*, Marian Collier *(Patron)*, Norman D. Wilson *(George)*, Thomas A. Geas *(Man at Hamburger Stand)*, Gene Williams *(Gangbanger)*, Selma Archerd *(Officer Selma)*, Harvey Fisher *(Murtaugh Neighbor)*, Edward Rosen *(1st Hockey Spectator)*, Jay Fiondella *(2nd Hockey Spectator)*, Steve Luport *(Welder)*, Anthony T. Pennelo *(Dead Guard)*, Jay Byron *(Guard)*, Germain Williams *(Conductor)*, David Lee Bynum *(Construction Worker)*, Steve Psaros *(1st Desk Cop)*, Paul Ganus *(2nd Desk Cop)*, Don Stanley *(1st Highway Patrolman)*, Maryellen Aviano *(2nd Highway Patrolman)*, Michael E. Klastorin *(CDR Worker)*, J. Mills Goodloe *(Harbormaster)*

While LETHAL WEAPON combined the drama of CIA corruption with the comedic, odd-couple pairing of psycho-Hamlet Martin Riggs (Mel Gibson) and straight-arrow Roger Murtaugh (Danny Glover), LETHAL WEAPON 2 attempted a more James Bond-ish combination of superhero action, romance and comedy. For the third installment, the filmmakers have opted to copy the formula of LETHAL WEAPON 2 to excess. Many of the gags are just reprises of jokes from the earlier film, and there is no attempt to flesh out existing characters.

The film opens with Riggs and Murtaugh engaged in a foolhardy attempt to defuse a huge car bomb, which goes off and destroys an entire building. As a result, the two are demoted to uniformed street cops, with Murtaugh having only one week left on the force before he is due to retire. The two then stumble onto, and foil, a bank robbery in which the criminals tote police guns equipped with armor-piercing "cop killer" bullets. Riggs and Murtaugh are brought into the investigation of the case, which centers around Jack Travis (Stuart Wilson), a vicious ex-cop who is apparently trading in stolen police weapons. The internal affairs department has been investigating Travis for some time, and the officer in charge, Lorna Cole (Rene Russo), has no desire to let our boys in on the case. The hostility between Cole and Riggs gradually gives way to mutual admiration (Riggs is suitably impressed by her kick-boxing skills), and the two eventually fall in love after a scene in which each exposes to the other a series of progressively more dramatic battle scars. Meanwhile, Murtaugh is guilt-stricken at having killed one of his son's best friends in a gun battle. Eventually waking up to the truth that the blame lies not with him, but with those crooks who sell guns "to babies," Murtaugh joins with Riggs and Cole in a climactic attack on Travis and his evil henchmen. Throughout, they are alternately helped and hindered by their sleazy aide-de-camp Leo Getz (Joe Pesci), who has been legitimized as a real-estate broker in this third installment of the series.

LETHAL WEAPON 3 appears to have been made on the fly, with the script being written, or improvised, on a week-by-week basis once production was already under way. The result is a disjointed pastiche of the earlier films, though with some undeniably effective action sequences, particularly the apocalyptic final shoot-out and the huge early explosion (for which the crew filmed a real-life demolition). The humor is patchy, and almost all derived from LW 1 or 2. Glover gets a chance to showcase his dramatic skills in the movie's best sequence, as he drunkenly reevaluates his life and nearly kills Gibson in a misunderstanding, and finally gets a love scene with Darlene Love, the singing great who's played his apparently chaste wife, Trish, throughout the series.

Undoubtedly the weakest installment to date, LETHAL WEAPON 3 nonetheless grossed nearly $150 million—very nearly as much as LW2 and more than double the take of the first film. It was released just weeks after Los Angeles was torn apart by riots in the wake of the Rodney King verdict, in which a group of white police officers was cleared of any wrongdoing in the vicious beating of an unarmed black motorist. Though this clearly didn't bother audiences, some critics found that LW3's cavalier, maverick cop attitude—including "gags" such as Riggs threatening to shoot someone for jaywalking—left a sour taste in the mouth. *(Violence, profanity, adult situations.)*

p, Richard Donner, Joel Silver; d, Richard Donner; w, Jeffrey Boam, Robert Mark Kamen, (from the story by Boam based on the characters created by Shane Black); ph, Jan De Bont; ed, Robert Brown, Battle Davis; m, Michael Kamen, Eric Clapton, David Sanborn; prod d, James Spencer; art d, Greg Papalia; set d, Richard Goddard

Action/Comedy/Crime **(PR: O MPAA: R)**

LIFE ON A STRING ★★★

(China/U.K./Germany) 110m Serene Productions; Pandora Film; Beijing Film Studio; China Film; Diva Film ~ Kino International c

(BIAN ZHOU BIAN CHANG)

Liu Zhongyuan *(The Saint)*, Huang Lei *(Shitou)*, Xu Qing *(Lanxiu)*, Ma Ling *(Noodleshop Owner's Wife)*, Zhang Zhenguan, Yao Jingou

Though its themes are obscure and its story ponderous, LIFE ON A STRING contains some of the most stupendous images of the year. Its events transpire against a backdrop of thundering waterfalls, sparkling mountain ranges, immense loessal plains, mist-fallen boulders and crags. These stunning vistas unfurl, bannerlike, in the widescreen format and leave lasting impressions on the eye—all in a film about blindness.

The setting is feudal China, where a sightless old musician, known simply as the Saint (Liu Zhongyuan), wanders purposefully with his young, also sightless apprentice Shitou (Huang Lei). As a youth the Saint was disciple to Grand Master, who told him that if he spent his days in ceaseless practice on the *sanxian* (a long necked banjo), his blindness would end. All the Saint had to do was break 1,000 strings in the course of playing. That task has consumed 60 years, and the count has reached the 990s. The Saint has no doubt that a cure is imminent; he only prays that he lives long enough to realize it. Meanwhile, to the scattered villagers and travelers who encounter him he is considered both a holy man and a lunatic.

The Saint preaches austerity and spiritual self-denial to the dutiful Shitou. But Shitou yearns for earthier pleasures, and a peasant girl named Lanxiu (Xu Qing) playfully flirts with the apprentice. The Saint disapproves, declaring, "We have our banjos. They are better than women." Even the Saint has doubts, however. He agonizes over temptations, banditry and civil wars that rage across the land, wondering if he really wants to see any of it after all. At last the moment arrives when the final string breaks. A concealed scroll then emerges from the Saint's instrument. The old man excitedly takes it to an apothecary—only to find that there is no cure after all. The Grand Master lied. The shattered Saint spends his few remaining days, still attended by Shitou, mournfully singing to crowds about the folly of blind faith.

LIFE ON A STRING represented China's entry at the 1992 Cannes Film Festival, a bitter irony, considering that its $1 million budget was financed by European interests, and the finished film remained banned from public exhibition in the People's Republic itself; a typical state of affairs in China's era of post-Tiananmen repression.

The Beijing government, free marketeer communists, viewed the project as a commercial product for export only; even so, their official approval came only after a three-month political scrutiny of the project. Foreign commentators nonetheless sifted through the film rather desperately for hidden anti-Beijing underpinnings, eventually concluding that it indicted charismatic leaders and their cults of personality. Filmmaker Chen Kaige himself claimed one scene, where jealous peasant boys pummel Shitou for his dalliance with Lanxiu, echoes the Tiananmen Square massacre. That seems a bit of a stretch. If anything LIFE ON A STRING resembles an epic fable whose precise moral has been lost to the ages, and a number of meanings can be read into its dense spectacle. That the regime could feel threatened by it speaks volumes.

The visuals are uncontestably awesome. LIFE ON A STRING was filmed in Shaanxi Province, and there's a story that during the darkest years of the Cultural Revolution merely looking upon such territory was forbidden, as the Red Guard feared its majesty would foster *bourgeois* emotions. Cinematographer Gu Changwei does justice to the scenery, and Chen Kaige composes each frame with an artisan's care. He restricts his camera movements to slow, formal pans and lengthy takes that tend to burden the storyline with frequent inertia, but impart a mythic poetry to the material. Most impressive is a lyrical series of long shots in which the Saint stops a war between two clans by hobbling into the midst of opposing armies and singing about peace and brotherhood. As the legendary minstrel's frail voice fills the soundtrack, the warriors unite around him to form a single, mighty procession.

The son of an established Beijing filmmaker, Chen Kaige rose to prominence in the more liberal climate of the the mid-1980s, coming to attention with pictures like YELLOW EARTH and THE BIG PARADE. At the 1988 Rotterdam Film Festival he was voted one of the top 20 directors of the future, and spent the ensuing years in America, where he studied and lectured at New York University, and earned a bit of notoriety for making his Western directorial debut with a Duran Duran music video. Along with fellow "Fifth Generation" filmmaker Zhang Yimou, he remains one of the most prominent international figures in the artistically strait-jacketed Chinese cinema. *(Violence, adult situations)*

p, Don Ranvaud; d, Chen Kaige; w, Chen Kaige, (from the short story by Shi Tiesheng); ph, Gu Changwei; ed, Pei Xiaonan; m, Qu Xiaosong; art d, Shao Ruigang

Drama **(PR: A MPAA: NR)**

LIFE ON THE EDGE ★★½
88m Movers & Shakers ~ Festival Film c

Jeff Perry *(Ray Nelson)*, Jennifer Holmes *(Karen Nelson)*, Ken Stoddard *(Tim)*, Michael Tulin *(Terry)*, Roger Callard *(Mike)*, Curtis Taylor *(Joey)*, Liz Sagal *(Mandy)*, Vaughn Armstrong *(Gary Hayes)*, Martine Beswike *(Linda James)*, Trish Doolan *(Guest)*, Kat Sawyer-Young *(Tovah Torrence)*, Greta Blackburn *(Joanie Hardy)*, Brent DeHart *(Guest)*, Thalmus Rasulala *(Truman Brown)*, Denny Dillon *(Shelli Summers)*, Tom Henschel *(Elliot Goldman)*, Susan Powell *(Dr. Carla Donahue)*, Tina Saddington *(Maid)*, Ralph Bruneau *(Walter Hughes)*, Jennifer Edwards *(Suzi Hughes)*, Jessie Scott *(Cathy Keats)*, Andrew Prine *(Roger Hardy)*, George C. Simms *(Calvin Shockley)*, Maria Melendez *(Pia Zumarragaray)*, Larry *(Punk Rocker)*, Doug Hale *(National Anchor)*, Jeff Kleiser, Suzanne DeGrandis, Eric Walczak, Dan Gorman, Joe Zimmerman, Diana Walczak, Karl Reichman, Linda Nelson, Levon Parian, Caleen Schons

LIFE ON THE EDGE finds a group of varied Los Angeles residents stranded at a party by a series of earthquakes and aftershocks, prompting them to review their lives or to pursue personal pleasures with comic results.

Ray Nelson (Jeff Perry) has good reason to examine his life, even before the seismograph needles start quivering. Nelson, a real estate promoter, is being threatened by two thugs for the repayment of a $100 thousand loan. Unfortunately for Nelson, his great hopes for profits from a development, Point Andreas, have failed, prompting him to attempt to forge his wife's signature on a legal document. For her part, Karen (Jennifer Holmes) doesn't seem too concerned over Ray's plight and rushes off to a neighbor's party just as the two loan collectors arrive to remind Ray of his debt.

That neighbor is Dr. Roger Hardy (Andrew Prine), a plastic surgeon whose voluptuous wife, Joanie (Greta Blackburn), is an example of his skills, enticing the stray males at the party into the pantry. Among the guests are Suzi (Jennifer Edwards), a mystic, and Walter (Ralph Bruneau), an engineer who uses his skills to design bungee equipment for her "skywalking" exercises. There are also two door-to-door missionaries, Tim and Terry (Ken Stoddard and Michael Tulin), who try to convert the guests at the party they have inadvertently crashed. Some of these folks have more important things on their minds: Tovah Torrance (Kat Sawyer-Young) angrily watches her rival on the local news in between screenings of a performance tape by Mandy (Liz Sagal) and the occasional feminist outbursts of a pregnant psychologist, Dr. Carla Donahue (Susan Powell); Shelli Summers (Denny Dillon) is torn between boasting of her years on diet plans and attacking the hors d'oeuvres, while Linda James (Martine Beswicke) retires to the bathroom to snort cocaine.

Galvanizing these characters and literally knocking out the television news reports about fighting in the Middle East is an 8.3 earthquake that only damages the Hardy residence but completely destroys Ray Nelson's home. He goes to tell his wife the bad news when she calmly announces her desire for a divorce and the fact that she has had a six-month affair with Roger Hardy. Bewildered, Ray groggily volunteers to accompany Truman Brown (Thalmus Rasulala) when the former actor and current earthquake insurance salesman goes for help. Along the way, Truman discloses that he and Roger are members of a survivalist group, part of whose holdings include $100 thousand in gold. Reconsidering the search for help, Ray returns on the sly to hunt through Roger's house for the cache of loot.

Sneaking from room to room, Ray discovers that the newscaster and performance artist are having an affair, while the dieter has camped out in front of the well-stocked refrigerator and one of the Bible thumpers has turned out to be a repressed homosexual. Ray is not alone in his quest; a suitably equipped Walter has discovered the bomb shelter in the basement but, fortunately for Ray, knocked himself unconscious when he triggered the opening mechanism. Ray easily spots the cigar box full of gold coins amid the canned foods, just as a sexually ravenous Joanie discovers *him.*

Unfortunately for Ray, a resourceful and rugged Roger has survived a car crash and, recognizing that the real estate promoter has violated both his wife and money, comes after him with a gun. An aftershock saves Ray, but he still has the pair of thugs to evade. Reconciled with Karen after his fight with Roger, Ray remembers the well-furnished bomb shelter just as the two hoods arrive looking for him. It serves not only as a good hiding place, but as the perfect sanctuary as the conflict in the Middle East spreads.

Amusing if predictable, Andrew Yates's LIFE ON THE EDGE does not expand beyond the limits of TV soap opera except for the use of explicit sex and suggestive language. While Jeff Perry is fine as the slightly bewildered, failed yuppie, the other performers seem too restricted, afraid to take their eccentric characters seriously. Yates and screenwriter Mark Edens would have better served their original premise if they had stretched the comic situation and performers to the limit. *(Sexual situations, adult situations, profanity.)*

p, Eric Lewald, Andrew Yates; d, Andrew Yates; w, Mark Edens; ph, Tom Fraser, Nick Von Sternberg; ed, Armen Minasian; m, Mike Garson; prod d, Amy Van Tries; art d, Greg P. Oehler, Gary McKinnon; set d, William J. Shaw

Comedy **(PR: C MPAA: NR)**

LIGHT IN THE JUNGLE, THE ★★½

100m Amritraj Entertainment; Toron International ~ LIVE Home Video c
(AKA: SCHWEITZER)

Malcolm McDowell *(Dr. Albert Schweitzer)*, Susan Strasberg *(Helene Schweitzer)*, Andrew Davis *(Lionel Curtis)*, Helen Jessop *(Amanda Hampton)*, John Carson *(Horton Herschel)*, Henry Cele *(Onganga)*, Patrick Shai *(Joseph)*, Barbara Nielsen, Michael Huff

Life magazine once described Dr. Albert Schweitzer (1875-1965) as, simply, the greatest man in the world. He was at once a missionary, physician, author, musician, philosopher, activist and winner of the Nobel Peace Prize. One of the brightest luminaries in Europe's intellectual firmament, Schweitzer chose to exile himself from society, ministering to disease-wracked natives deep in the African jungle, to set a living example for all Christianity. Dramatizing such a remarkable individual for the screen would tax many a filmmaker's talents, and the creators of THE LIGHT IN THE JUNGLE at best yield an intriguing but unsatisfactory sketch of the man and his deeds.

Except for a few brief flashbacks, the story eschews the epic sweep of typical biopics and concentrates on several days in the life of Dr. Schweitzer (Malcolm McDowell) at his volunteer-staffed hospital at Lambarene, Gabon, on Africa's west coast. The time is shortly after WWII, and Schweitzer is already renowned for his selfless dedication to the health and spiritual welfare of the natives, honored for his philosophy of reverence for all life—and, in political circles, reviled by some as an alleged anti-capitalist and by others for pro-colonial leanings.

A loose storyline finds Schweitzer at odds with two cultures: influential witch doctor Onganga (Henry Cele) declares that twins born to a native woman in the compound are a bad omen, and he demands ritual sacrifice of at least one of the infants. Meanwhile two arrogant Americans, a bombastic publisher and a stuffy socialite—personages right out of a Marx Brothers satire—arrive in Lambarene with a scheme to turn the humble settlement into a gleaming highrise clinic to draw planeloads of donations. While Schweitzer's hospital was indeed a magnet for skeptical journalists seeking to "expose" him, as well as the international jet set (the glamorous wife of director Otto Preminger was a favorite visitor), this subplot follows the trite showbiz conflict of the rogue-independent-pressured-to-sell-out-to-big-business, clunkily superimposed on humanitarianism.

Dr. Schweitzer opposes both threats with equal fervor. The antagonism with Onganga is like something out of an old "Daktari" episode. The parallel plot with the meddling high-society stiffs calls up some interesting questions about Schweitzer's administrative practices and attitudes, but few are answered. Schweitzer explains that the primitive, even squalid atmosphere of his hospital is essential; it evokes a welcoming African village, while a sterile, modern facility would repel potential patients. "Simple people need simple medicine," he declares. So a mentally disabled man is kept gibbering in a cage (the alternative, we're told, is that Onganga would drown him) and vital medicine spoils for lack of refrigeration. "Progress is the suicide of civilization," insists Schweitzer, shrugging off objections with insults and hymns.

Michel Potts and Patrick Lee's screenplay claims that Schweitzer ran his hospital like an autocrat, drove his volunteers relentlessly, and made little or no provisions for the future. When money runs low he promises to leave on a European concert tour, raising funds through his stirring organ renditions of Bach (whose music pervades the soundtrack). Another aside seems to challenge his reverence for all life. Schweitzer scorns a hunting expedition sent to kill a man-eating lioness, but later the beast mauls an acquaintence, and the doctor watches helplessly as the victim dies on the operating table. No conclusions are drawn from this tragedy, nor is there an epilogue to explain what happened to the Lambarene hospital after Schweitzer's passing (it still exists, but with the modern administration that the celluloid Schweitzer so disdains). A microscopic end credit states—inaccurately—that all the characters depicted in this film, save for Schweitzer and his wife (played adoringly by Susan Strasberg), are fictional.

Malcolm McDowell is best remembered as Alex, the sadistic future punk from A CLOCKWORK ORANGE. Consequently, his turn as the white-haired, gentle Schweitzer peaks in creative casting. Physically the transformation is believable, and though McDowell brings a Last-Angry-Man fire and intensity to *le grand docteur*, mere feistiness doesn't provide much insight into the historical figure and what made him what he was. Only a brief, cryptic reference is made to Schweitzer's "heresy" that estranged him from church hierarchy (in his scholarly writings the future missionary envisioned a Jesus more human and fallible than ecclesiasts could accept). The African setting maintains a sense of authenticity thanks to location shooting in Zimbabwe and the Ivory Coast. Indeed, it's often difficult to keep in mind that the drama takes place in the 20th century at all.

During his lifetime Dr. Schweitzer resisted attempts to turn him into Hollywood entertainment, reportedly threatening legal action to block a feature that was to be scripted by Irving Wallace (a choice quote from a Schweitzer biography: "I would rather burn in hell than have a film made of my life"). As much as THE LIGHT IN THE JUNGLE seems to bear out his concerns as a superficial work, it has an unusual, almost encouraging parentage. Producer Ashok Amritraj is an Indian-born former tennis pro who turned to moviemaking and has overseen various horror flicks, sex thrillers and kung-fu adventures, including the Jean-Claude Van Damme vehicle DOUBLE IMPACT, in addition to this uncharacteristically high-minded endeavor.

THE LIGHT IN THE JUNGLE was completed in 1990 and got shopped around for years at various international film markets, under different titles, including SCHWEITZER. It made a humble bow on American home video during 1992, an era in which, alas, anyone asked to name the greatest man in the world would more likely cite Schwarzenegger than Schweitzer. *(Violence, nudity.)*

p, Ashook Amritaj; d, Gray Hofmyer; w, Michel Potts, Patrick Lee; ph, Buster Reynolds; ed, Peter Grosett, Margaret-Anne Smith; m, Zane Cronje; prod d, Michael Philips; cos, Ruy Filipe

Biography/Historical **(PR: A MPAA: NR)**

LIGHT SLEEPER ★★★

103m Grain of Sand Productions ~ Fine Line Features c

Willem Dafoe *(John LeTour)*, Susan Sarandon *(Ann)*, Dana Delany *(Marianne)*, David Clennon *(Robert)*, Mary Beth Hurt *(Teresa)*, Victor Garber *(Tis)*, Jane Adams *(Randi)*, Paul Jabara *(Eddie)*, Robert Cicchini *(Guidone)*, Sam Rockell *(Jealous)*, Rene Rivera *(Manuel)*, David Spade *(Theological Cokehead)*, Steven Posen *(Hasid)*, Ken Ladd *(Carlos)*, Brian Judge *(Thomas)*, Vinny Capone *(Young Cuban)*, Christopher Todd Northrup *(Retro Yuppie)*, Paul Stocker *(Maitre d')*, Bernadette Jurkowski *(French Girl)*, Tatiana Von Furstenberg *(French Girl)*, Francesca Bonicoli *(1st Model)*, Elena Vannucci *(2nd Model)*, Jeff Telvi *(Male Model)*, Jennifer Fowler *(Woman at Bar)*, Gabrielle Stubbert *(Woman at Bar)*, James Saxenmeyer *(Bar Patron)*, Raymond Normandeau *(Chef)*, Arcoiris Medina *(Woman at Laundromat)*, Esteban Fernandez *(Concierge)*, Carolyn L.A. Walker *(Police Woman)*, Timothy Stickney *(Young Dominican)*, Joe Gironda *(Funeral Home Employee)*, Heather Rose Dominic *(Crackhead)*, Paul Stockman Smith *(Radio Announcer)*, Peter Macklin, Billy Joe Novinski, David Sukoff, Damien Corrente *(Baseball Card Fans)*, Ronald Sylvers *(Prison Guard)*

Former critic Paul Schrader is famous, perhaps infamous, for his stylish explorations of the dark side of the American psyche. While Schrader's early work, including his screenplay for TAXI DRIVER and his own films BLUE COLLAR and AMERICAN GIGOLO, drew critical praise and censure in equal parts, his more ambitious recent work—MISHIMA, LIGHT OF DAY, PATTY HEARST and THE COMFORT OF STRANGERS—has been largely dismissed. LIGHT SLEEPER, a study of a middle-aged drug dealer, is a return to his thematic roots.

Loner, insomniac and reformed junkie, John LeTour (Willem Dafoe) drifts through the Manhattan streets in a twilight cocoon. He delivers drugs for a living, coke and ecstasy and quaaludes ("white drugs for white people") for the upper-class clients of the glamorous Ann (Susan Sarandon), and writes in his diary during his sleepless off hours. Someone once told him that when a drug dealer starts keeping a diary it's time to retire, so he started writing and hasn't stopped, filling up notebook after notebook and throwing them away when he's done. At the age of forty, he's a little older than his clients, a little past his own using days and a little too damaged himself not to care when he sees habits out of control. Ann is talking about abandoning the business for herbal cosmetics, and LeTour can't quite envision a life without dealing.

He spots his old girlfriend, Marianne (Dana Delaney), one evening and gives her a lift, but she clearly wants nothing to do with him; she's clean and doesn't trust that he is. After another accidental meeting, this time at the hospital where her mother is dying, they briefly resume their troubled affair. His shock when she apparently jumps from the window of one of his clients drives LeTour to a near-fatal encounter with the man. LeTour survives by killing him and his bodyguards. Though sent to prison, LeTour realizes he has always loved Ann, and together they look forward to a new life after his release.

LIGHT SLEEPER may well be Schrader's best film, the melancholy continuation of a story that begins with TAXI DRIVER and the much-maligned AMERICAN GIGOLO. Superficially, maladjusted hack Travis Bickle, sleek hustler Julian Kay, and detached dealer John LeTour couldn't be more different, but they're brothers under the skin . . . brothers, or perhaps even the same man.

They're marginal characters, disposable men who only matter because of what they can do for people; they're just mechanisms. Bickle is raised from dreary anonymity to media stardom by a bloody quirk of fate; Kay, the most polished, sought-after hustler in Los Angeles is framed for a grisly murder because he's framable. LeTour just wants to get by, but even his modest ambitions are thwarted; with Ann abandoning the business, he'll either have to find himself a new boss or a new career, and he just isn't up to it.

Where TAXI DRIVER was all grit and fury and AMERICAN GIGOLO's glossy surface barely hid a core of hollow desperation, LIGHT SLEEPER has the texture of a dream. Not a nightmare, but a comfortable, familiar dream; while the movie purports to be about someone who can't sleep, it's actually about someone who won't wake up, and it's not hard to sympathize with his reluctance. Willem Dafoe's performance as LeTour is the glue that holds the film together, and it's a remarkable one. His white skin almost glows, and his haunted eyes never seem to connect; it's not that he's always looking over his shoulder, but that he seems never really to focus anywhere at all. Though his unusual features can often look disturbingly gargoyle-like, here Dafoe exudes a passive yearning that's as touching as it is unnerving.

Sarandon is also in fine form as Ann, whose brittle party girl shares the same skin with a shrewd entrepreneur and a genuinely kind woman. She may look flighty, but she's nobody's fool. LIGHT SLEEPER's ending sounds implausible on paper, a hybrid cross between the bloody rampage that ends TAXI DRIVER and the hint of redemption through love that concludes AMERICAN GIGOLO. But it's surprisingly effective on the screen, and the final close-up of Dafoe's face, eyes closed, is gently haunting.

p, Linda Reisman; d, Paul Schrader; w, Paul Schrader; ph, Edward Lachman; ed, Kristina Boden; m, Michael Been; prod d, Richard Hornung; art d, Jim Feng

Drama/Thriller **(PR: O MPAA: R)**

LILY WAS HERE ★★
(Netherlands) 115m Movies Film; BV Lenox Films Europe ~ SVS/Triumph Home Video c
(AKA: KASSIERE, DE)

Marion Van Thijn *(Lily)*, Thom Hoffman *(Arend)*, Monique Van De Ven *(Connyr)*, Coen Van Vrijburghe DeConingh *(Ted)*, Dennis Rudge *(Alan)*, Truus DeSelle *(Lily's Mother)*, Con Meyer *(Jake)*, Adrian Brine *(Inspector Doesburg)*, Yvonne Ristie *(Rita)*, Jeroen Planting *(Assistant Inspector)*, Gunar Gritters-Doublet *(Storenfried)*, Erik Beekes *(Juwelier)*, Hans Kesting *(Portier)*, Kees Hulst *(Emile)*, Jaloe Maat *(Helen)*, Beppie Melissen *(Bank Teller)*, Richard Messina *(American Officer)*

A desultory melodrama of troubled youth on the loose, LILY WAS HERE occurs in bleakly photographed urban Holland, where 17-year-old Lily (Marion Van Thijn) holds a dreary job at a checkout counter and barely tolerates her loveless home and lustful stepfather.

Her hopes center on her boyfriend Alan (Dennis Rudge), an American serviceman from a nearby Air Force base. He promised to bring her to the US but gets killed by thugs (he's Black of course; it's depressing that even foreign films mark minority characters as disposable lambs-to-the-slaughter). Lily is now pregnant and out of options. Determined to keep her baby, she runs away from home and comes under the sponsorship of Ted (Coen Van Vrijburghe DeConingh), a pimp who installs her in an apartment building as a specialty prostitute; she gives hand jobs to perverts turned on by pregnant, hostile nymphets.

A few months of this is all Lily can take. Moving to an expensive hotel, she pays the bills via armed robberies using an unloaded gun. She also starts a guarded love affair with Ted's good-hearted henchman Arend (Thom Hoffman). The police meanwhile, serious underachievers, take a long time tracking down the high-profile, distinctively tattooed, juvenile mom-to-be who's been a solo crime wave. Only after Lily gives birth do cops converge on the maternity ward. A sympathetic midwife, Connyr (Monique Van De Ven), has been looking after Lily's obstetric needs while shielding her from justice, and if you think that's liberalism run rampant, get a load of the climax when Lily, the newborn in her arms, strides confidently to freedom, right past an impassive chief inspector; Arend evidently had a heart-to-heart talk with the officer beforehand and got the girl instant amnesty.

Lily's walk on the wild side, neither sensationalized nor overly condemned, demonstrates how the heroine's headstrong determination enables her to have the child and survive the mean streets. But serious passion and sentiment rarely stir director Ben Verbong's screenplay. Lily's plight earns sympathy but only superficial interest, turning to mild annoyance late in the picture when she spouts a couple of lines that alternately glorify and bemoan her criminal acts. Arend properly gets fed up with the girl on more than one occasion, and at the heart of his inarticulate admonitions lie memories of another wayward hooker he loved, now deceased. But his character is hardly more than scenery; Lily is the focus of the picture, and while the sulkily attractive Van Thijn holds attention, her pouty defiance makes for a generally one-note performance. (Marion Van Thijn is in real life the daughter of Amsterdam's present mayor Eduard Van Thijn, which puts a whole different spin on why the law lets Lily off scot free.)

Whether it was the moody acoustic soundtrack by former Eurythmics member David Stewart or alienated-youth appeal, LILY WAS HERE became popular with underaged Dutch viewers. It even showed up on home video in the US in 1992, its box art suspiciously resembling that of the better-known Eurothriller LA FEMME NIKITA. *(Violence, profanity, sexual situations, adult situations, nudity.)*

p, Chris Brouwer, Haig Balian; d, Ben Verbong; w, Ben Verbong, Sytze Van Der Laan, (from the story by Verbong and Willem Jan Otten); ph, Lex Wertwijn; ed, Ton DeGraaff; m, David A. Stewart; prod d, Willem DeLeeuw; art d, Dorus Van Der Linden; cos, Yan Tax

Thriller/Drama **(PR: O MPAA: R)**

LINGUINI INCIDENT, THE ★★
98m GO Entertainment; Linguini Productions ~ Academy Pictures c

Rosanna Arquette *(Lucy)*, David Bowie *(Monte)*, Eszter Balint *(Vivian)*, Andre Gregory *(Dante)*, Buck Henry *(Cecil)*, Viveca Lindfors *(Miracle)*, Marlee Matlin *(Jeanette)*, Eloy Casados *(Tony Orlando)*, Michael Bonnabel *(Oliver)*, Maura Tierney, Lewis Arquette, Iman, Julian Lennon

Arty Manhattanites come under the less-than-razor sharp gaze of writer-director Richard Shepard in THE LINGUINI INCIDENT, a meek comedy of manners that revolves around the customers and employees of a frighteningly trendy restaurant.

Lucy (Rosanna Arquette) is an aspiring escape artist who makes ends meet waiting tables at Dali, a restaurant where the food is clearly secondary to decor and ambiance. Monte (David Bowie) is Dali's new bartender, an Englishman who quickly makes it clear that he's willing to marry anyone for a green card. Viv (Eszter Balint), Lucy's best friend, designs brassieres with knives concealed in the cups, the closest thing to an edge THE LINGUINI INCIDENT ever displays.

Quirky though things are, they're still not what they seem. Monte is a gambler, deeply in debt to Dali's supercilious owners Dante (Andre Gregory) and Cecil (Buck Henry). He draws Lucy and Viv into his convoluted schemes, and before you can say "plot device," they're all planning to rob the restaurant. At the same time, Monte and Lucy are falling—hesitantly and oh-so-reluctantly—in love. Things actually work out, though hardly as the conspirators had planned. The robbery, featuring Viv's "lethal cleavage," turns out to be good for business, Monte wins his last, desperate bet with Cecil and Dante, and Lucy decides to take a chance on romance.

This may be one of the eight million stories in the naked city, but at best it's a very slight one . . at worst it hardly seems to be a story at all. More than anything, THE LINGUINI INCIDENT plays as a series of quirky vignettes whose charm may elude the average viewer. Lucy's Houdini-esque ambitions provide endless opportunities for mild bondage gags, while Viv's aggressive foundation garments occasion in-the-know allusions to everything from performance art to feminist rage. Marlee Matlin's one-joke role as a bad-tempered, opportunistic and, of course, deaf cashier is funny once, but quickly wears thin. David Bowie is surprisingly charming in a hangdog sort of way, though his casting gives the role of Monte unexpected resonance not because of his rock star persona, but because he's obviously a bit old to be madcapping around the Lower East Side. Monte seems rather more pathetic than the filmmakers seem to have intended.

The film's best casting is Buck Henry and Andre Gregory as Dali's owners, guilty of every sin of self-ness one can imagine. They're impossibly self-centered, self-satisfied, self-indulgent, self-important and, of course, consummately selfish. They're also witty and self-aware, something to which the film as a whole aspires without success. The lion's share of THE LINGUINI INCIDENT's imagination seems to have been invested in set design, specifically, in the design of Dali. Though obvious, Dali is in fact a creditable parody of the monstrously overconceptualized restaurants in which New York specializes (the corkscrew bread is a particularly nice touch); it's a shame no other aspect of the movie rings as true. From Viv and Lucy's picturesque roof (where they sit and discuss men) to the occult shop staffed by a fright-wigged Viveca Lindfors, THE LINGUINI INCIDENT's locations are precious stereotypes, and the people who inhabit them are little better.

Unfavorable comparisons with Susan Seidelman's DESPERATELY SEEKING SUSAN, particularly in light of Arquette's casting, are inevitable, but they're also apt. DESPERATELY SEEKING SUSAN was genuinely quirky and offbeat, capturing the cheerful chaos of shiftless Downtown lives; THE LINGUINI INCIDENT is a pale pretender that tries too hard. *(Sexual situations.)*

p, Arnold Orgolini; d, Richard Shepard; w, Richard Shepard, Tamara Brott; ph, Robert Yeoman; ed, Sonya Polonsky; m, Thomas Newman; prod d, Marcia Hinds; art d, Bo Johnson; set d, Jerie Kelter; cos, Richard Von Ernst

Comedy/Drama **(PR: C MPAA: R)**

LITTLE NEMO: ADVENTURES IN SLUMBERLAND ★★

85m Tokyo Movie Shinsha Company Ltd.; TMS Entertainment Inc. ~ Hemdale Releasing c

VOICES OF: Gabriel Damon *(Nemo)*, Mickey Rooney *(Flip)*, Rene Auberjonois *(Professor Genius)*, Danny Mann *(Icarus)*, Laura Mooney *(Princess Camille)*, Bernard Erhard *(King Morpheus)*, William E. Martin *(Nightmare King)*, Alan Oppenheimer *(Oomp)*, Michael Bell *(Oompy)*, Sidney Miller *(Oompe)*, Neil Ross *(Oompa)*, John Stephenson *(Oompo/Dirigible Captain)*, Jennifer Darling *(Nemo's Mother)*, Greg Burson *(Nemo's Father/Voice of Flap)*, Sherry Lynn *(Bon Bon)*, Guy Christopher *(Courtier/Cop)*, Nancy Cartwright *(Page)*, Ellen Gerstell *(Page)*, Tress MacNeille *(Elevator Creature)*, Michael McConnohie *(Etiquette Master)*, Beau Weaver *(1st Teacher/ Cop)*, Michael Gough *(2nd Teacher)*, Kathleen Freeman *(Dance Teacher)*, Michael Sheehan *(Fencing Master)*, June Foray *(Librarian)*, Gregg Barger *(Equestrian Master)*, Bert Kramer *(Goblin)*, Bever-Leigh Banfield *(Woman)*

Over a decade ago, Ray Bradbury, the acclaimed sci-fi writer, conceived the idea of bringing to the screen a feature-length animated version of "Little Nemo," cartoonist Winsor McCay's turn-of-the-century comic strip about an imaginative boy and his many adventures in Slumberland. Despite all the effort, time and energy lavished on LITTLE NEMO: ADVENTURES IN SLUMBERLAND by the excellent talents involved, it is, finally, a disappointment.

The film opens with the perky title character in his bed, dreaming away the hours. Nemo (voice of Gabriel Damon) is an innocent, pure-minded child blessed with a vivid imagination that plays havoc during his dreams. One day the circus comes to town and that night Nemo dreams about four clowns wearing cone-shaped hats who, in the company of Professor Genius (Rene Auberjonois) fly in through his bedroom window. The professor tells Nemo that he is the lucky lad chosen by good King Morpheus (Bernard Erhard) to be the official playmate of Princess Camille (Laura Mooney), the king's beautiful and spunky daughter. In the company of Icarus (Danny Mann), his pet squirrel, Nemo travels, along with Professor Genius, aboard a turn-of-the-century showboat attached to a dirigible. En route to Slumberland, the realm of King Morpheus, the trio make a detour around Nightmareland, an evil place filled with demons who discharge thunder and lightning bolts.

Nemo finds Slumberland to be every child's dream of candy canes and circus clowns and just about any pleasure imaginable. Though at first cool toward Nemo, Princess Camille succumbs to his unassuming charms once the little commoner gets out of his pajamas and into something more befitting a royal playmate. When Nemo and Camille aren't making a tour of Slumberland or prancing about in the royal gardens, the boy is busy sharing his love of electric trains with King Morpheus. The King is so delighted with Nemo, he makes him his heir and presents the lad with the royal scepter and a golden key that opens all doors in Slumberland. However, there is one door that Nemo must promise the King never to open: the door to Nightmareland where all the demons are pent up.

Unfortunately, Nemo falls in with the likable Flip (Mickey Rooney), Slumberland's most notorious con artist. Although it is the cigar-chomping, brightly clad, black crow riding Flip who talks Nemo into taking a peek behind the door to Nightmareland, it is Nemo who chooses to take full blame and all responsibility for what happens next. Once the door is opened, all the demons escape Nightmareland and swirl and swarm into the palace to kidnap the King, taking him back to the very depths of Nightmareland. In the grand tradition of THE WIZARD OF OZ, the threesome remarkably overcome all obstacles and finally rescue King Morpheus. Suddenly realizing that there is no place like home, Nemo wakes up to find himself back in his warm bed . . . and to learn that a long-promised visit to the circus is now a sure thing.

Besides Bradbury (credited with the film's "concept"), LITTLE NEMO's contributors include co-directors William T. Hurtz and Masami Hata, screenwriters Chris Columbus and Richard Outten, the songwriting team of siblings Richard M. and Robert B. Sherman, and futuristic French illustrator Jean Moebius Giraud. Though often visually dazzling, the onscreen proceedings are too leisurely paced, unsophisticated and, ultimately, unoriginal to be of much interest to contemporary audiences. Only the youngest, most undiscriminating viewers with be satisfied.

Clearly, the filmmakers followed the path of least resistance when they elected to go with a predictable, tried-and-true formula, rather than attempt any genuine innovations of any kind. Sadly, LITTLE NEMO is an example of what can go wrong when creative forces from two diverse cultures unite. What should have been an ideal fusion of the more sophisticated Japanese style with the polished character work unique among American animators doesn't occur; the two styles more often clash and tend to undermine, rather than complement, one another.

While the various vocal performers are uniformly adequate, Flip is the only character given any interesting dialogue and veteran actor Mickey Rooney makes the most of it. Unfortunately, the rest of the dialogue is like LITTLE NEMO itself—predictable.

p, Yutaka Fujioka; d, William T. Hurtz, Masami Hata; w, Chris Columbus, Richard Outten, (from the story by Jean Moebius Giraud and Yutaka Fujioka from the comic strip *Little Nemo in Slumberland* by Winsor McKay); m, Thomas Chase, Steve Rucker; anim, Tokyo Movie Shinsha Company Ltd., Nobuo Tomizawa

Animated/Adventure/Children's **(PR: AA MPAA: G)**

LITTLE NOISES ★

110m Monument Pictures; Women's Film Company ~ Prism Entertainment c

Crispin Glover *(Joey Kremple)*, Tatum O'Neal *(Stella Winslow)*, John McGinley *(Stu Slovack)*, Rik Mayall *(Mathias Lichtenstein)*, Steven Schub *(Timmy Smith)*, Tate Donovan *(Elliott)*, Nina Siemaszko *(Dolores)*, Matthew Hutton *(Marty Slovack)*, Carole Shelley *(Aunt Shirley)*, Gianin Loffler *(Wayne Wacker)*, Caroline Farina, Barry Papick, Cathy Haase, Douglas D. Broe, Anthony Brito

Smug in attitude and decidedly pretentious in its approach, writer-director Jane Spencer's LITTLE NOISES is resoundingly defeated by its idiosyncratic leading man.

Failing even at the lowly job of perfume spritzer, the chronically unemployed Joey Kremple (Crispin Glover) angers his Aunt Shirley (Carole Shelley) with non-payment of rent and insults his equally untalented actor pal Timmy Smith (Steven Schub) whenever he isn't staring at the blank pages in his typewriter. What Joey wants is not to write but to be celebrated as a writer. When the woman he adores, Stella Winslow (Tatum O'Neal) enjoys a minor success in securing a production for one of her plays, Joey tires of dissembling about his prospects and stumbles onto a quick route to Yuppie-ville. If you can't be Bret Easton Ellis or Jay McInerney, then why not plagiarize the poetry of a talented friend, particularly if that poet is mute and a little slow on the uptake.

When pathetic Marty Slovack (Matthew Hutton) keeps shoving sheaths of poems at him, how can Joey resist, particularly when Marty's protective brother Stu (John McGinley) is killed while dealing drugs? Suddenly Joey's agent pal Mathias Lichtenstein (Rik Mayall) is keen on representing him, and the aftertaste of being evicted by his aunt is soon gone. Although Stella sees through Joey's ruse, he's already headed for minor celebrity status—and Marty winds up homeless in the gutter. Although Joey tries to assuage his conscience by tossing Marty a few bucks, it would seem his more immediate problem is where to locate another sucker. Salable primitive doggerel is hard to find.

Unappealingly photographed and directed with that we've-only-got-one-shot improvisatory air that plagues low-budget productions, LITTLE NOISES does offer reflections on the artistic process and selling out. Joey is a sort of contemporary Oblomov trapped by his own distaste for survival jobs and by the realization that as a writer he has precious little to offer a waiting world. Unfortunately, these and other promising themes (the conflict between artistic expression and the desire to have that expression garner approval from society; the plight of the struggling writer in an unsubsidized landscape; and the process by which some shed friends as they climb the ladder of success) are handled too blatantly in the film. Nor have the filmmakers chosen their leading man wisely.

To interpret this low-energy anti-hero, they should have chosen an actor with neurotic energy or at least one with some surface charm. Instead we have Crispin Glover (RIVER'S EDGE, WHERE THE HEART IS) calling attention to himself in the guise of a naturalistic performance. Stopping and starting sentences like a love child of Sandy Dennis and William Hickey, slurring words as if he were eating dialogue for sustenance, and staring with heavy-lidded torpor at each new dilemma, Clover distances us from his character instead of pulling us into his desperation.

Granted the film is poorly paced and the screenplay isn't well structured, and there are also mannered performances by Schub and Gianin Loffler, but the film's failure lies with Glover since this is primarily a one-man character study. Adrift in actor's anomie, Glover is so in tune with his own feelings, he's forgotten he's supposed to be performing for the film viewer's benefit, not merely his own. *(Violence, profanity.)*

p, Brad Gilbert, Michael Spielberg; d, Jane Spencer; w, Jane Spencer, Jon Zeiderman, (from the story by Spencer and Anthony Brito); ph, Makoto Watanabe; ed, Ernie Fritz; m, Kurt Hoffman, Fritz Van Orden; prod d, Charles Lagola; art d, Alison Cornyn; set d, Catie Dehaan; cos, Taylor Cheek

Drama **(PR: C MPAA: NR)**

LITTLE SISTER ★★½

94m Creative Edge Films ~ LIVE Home Video c

Jonathan Silverman *(Robert)*, Alyssa Milano *(Diana)*, George Newbern *(Mike)*, Jesse Dabson *(Chaz)*, Jerry Gideon *(Derry)*, Michelle Matheson *(Sybil)*, Moon Zappa *(Venus)*, Leilani Sarelle *(Catherine)*, Deborah Dillon *(Juliette)*, David Powladge *(Big Al)*, Jami Richards *(Zelda)*, Tia Carrere, Patrick Richwood, Jimmy Garfield, Christine Healy, Michael Berryman, Pamela Winslow, Twink Caplan, Mary Ann Mullerleile

Jonathan Silverman and Alyssa Milano star in LITTLE SISTER, an amusing story of cross-dressing and college life.

Freshman Robert (Silverman), anxious to follow in his alumnus father's footsteps, joins the college fraternity. But to become an official member, he must infiltrate the campus sorority house, Zeta Alpha Zeta, and steal an old painting of the sorority's founding sisters. Donning a wig, high heels, etc. and an English accent, Robert assumes the persona of "Roberta" and is let into Zeta Alpha Zeta. But as he's about to make off with the coveted painting, he decides to join the sorority for real in order to get close to coed Diana (Milano). And, of course, Diana becomes his "big sister."

During his stint as Roberta, Robert decides he likes being a sorority sister better than a frat brother. The Zeta girls seem to be very supportive of each other, whereas the frat boys take pleasure in silly rituals which humiliate the pledges. Also, Robert is able to hear firsthand how women feel about men, which enables him to expose Diana's boyfriend Darry (Jerry Gideon) for the jerk that he really is. At the film's close, Roberta, who has been nominated as the "Queen of Greek Week," reveals herself to be Robert during a speech. And, not surprisingly, Robert and Diana end up together.

Set in Washington state and directed by Jimmy Zeilinger from his own screenplay, LITTLE SISTER is a movie which effectively utilizes clever dialogue and subtle humor. As the romantic leads, Silverman (BRIGHTON BEACH MEMOIRS, CLASS ACTION) and Milano (TV's "Who's the Boss?") make an engaging pair. It's also particularly refreshing to see intelligent female characters in a college romp movie. Granted, Diana and her sorority sisters are socialites, but they're also confident women with minds of their own. *(Partial nudity, sexual situations.)*

p, Jeffrey Neuman; d, Jimmy Zellinger; w, Jimmy Zellinger; ph, Thomas Del Ruth; ed, Michael Ripps; m, Greg DeBelles; prod d, Jon Gary Steele; art d, Louisa Bonnie; set d, Nancy Arnold; cos, Terry Dresbach

Comedy/Romance **(PR: C MPAA: PG-13)**

LITTLE VEGAS ★★½

91m Sugar Entertainment; MacLang Productions ~ IRS Releasing c

Anthony John Denison *(Carmine DeCarlo)*, Catherine O'Hara *(Lexie)*, Anne Francis *(Martha Branstein)*, Michael Nouri *(Frank)*, Perry Lang *(Steve)*, Bruce McGill *(Harvey)*, Jerry Stiller *(Sam)*, P.J. Ochlan, John Sayles, Jay Thomas, Michael Talbot

"Vague" best describes LITTLE VEGAS, an inconsequential trifle that had the briefest acquaintance with theater screens before hitting cable TV and home video. Written and directed by performer Perry Lang, it's more like an actors' exercise than anything else, although those actors provide tidbits of transient pleasure.

The picture opens with Carmine DeCarlo (Anthony John Denison) stumbling in the desert, dishevelled and wearing a dress. Speaking to the viewer, he goes into a let-me-tell-you—how-I-got-this-way routine that intros a slack story about how Carmine and his kid reside in a tiny Nevada trailer-park community, on zero income. Once Carmine was a gigolo genuinely in love with wealthy matron Martha Branstein (Anne Francis), now deceased but seen in soft-edged flashbacks. Carmine still carries a torch for Martha's daughter, spacey and footloose Lexie (Catherine O'Hara), but she doesn't linger long in any one place or relationship.

Meanwhile Martha's son Harvey (Bruce McGill) is a brash go-getter trying to bankroll a local casino. He envisions turning the town into "Little Vegas," a small copy of the gambling mecca. "It's my dream," goes Harvey's mantra. Sam (Jerry Stiller), the aged trailer-park owner, is a melancholy relic of the original regime of mobsters who built up Las Vegas, and he wants nothing of the sort to spoil this tiny community. Carmine, meanwhile, is a recalcitrant exile from a New Jersey crime family who want him either back in the fold or dead. Occasionally his sharklike brother Frank (Michael Nouri) shows up to harass him, in scenes with an undertone of potential violence that quickly sober up the dreamy narrative.

Mostly, however, LITTLE VEGAS, just ambles amiably along, a smart and soft diversion that's enjoyable until one realizes that nothing much is happening here and nothing much is going to happen. The ensemble cast of notable but less-than-top-drawer names do very well, with the exception of its best-known player, Catherine O'Hara (BEETLEJUICE, HOME ALONE). She's supposed to be a footloose free spirit, but her underwritten role consists largely of smiling sweetly and vacantly. The remembered idyll between Carmine and Martha is a rare movie example of a warm older-woman/younger-man pairing, beschmaltzed by syrupy music.

Ultimately Harvey learns Sam's been concealing Martha's fortune from him, and he beats the old man, accidentally killing him. Sam's will leaves the money and trailer park in safe hands with Carmine, although where Lexie chooses to remain isn't at all clear. So why was Carmine stumbling in the desert, dishevelled and wearing a dress? To be absolutely honest . . . I forget. LITTLE VEGAS is *that* low-key. *(Violence, profanity, nudity, sexual situations, adult situations.)*

p, Peter MacGregor-Scott; d, Perry Lang; w, Perry Lang; ph, King Baggot; ed, John Tintori; m, Mason Darling; prod d, Michael Hartog; art d, Daniel Brewer; cos, Cynthia Flint

Comedy/Drama **(PR: O MPAA: R)**

LIVING END, THE ★★

92m Strand Releasing; Desperate Pictures Ltd. ~ October Films c

Mike Dytri *(Luke)*, Craig Gilmore *(Jon)*, Mark Finch *(Doctor)*, Mary Woronov *(Daisy)*, Johanna Went *(Fern)*, Darcy Marta *(Darcy)*, Scot Goetz *(Peter)*, Bretton Vail *(Ken)*, Nicole Dillenberg *(Barbie)*, Paul Bartel *(Twister Master)*, Stephen Holman *(7-11 Couple)*, Magie Song *(7-11 Couple)*, Peter Lanigan *(Three Stooges Member)*, Jon Gerrans *(Three Stooges Member)*, Jack Kofman *(Three Stooges Member)*, Christopher Mabli *(Neonazi)*, Michael Now *(Tarzan)*, Michael Haynes *(Jane)*, Peter Grame *(Gus)*, Craig Lee *(Arguing Couple at Ralphs)*, Torie Chickering *(Arguing Couple at Ralphs)*, J. Sidney Bestwick *(Buddhist)*

Reputedly made for a paltry $23,000 by underground LA filmmaker Gregg Araki, THE LIVING END is more admirable as a sheer technical feat of filmmaking than as a sustained dramatic narrative. It still makes worthwhile viewing, particularly for gay audiences starved of images.

No sooner has Jon (Craig Gilmore), a petulant, underemployed freelance film critic, learned that he's HIV-positive than he crosses paths with Luke (Mike Dytri), a handsome, aimless hustler who, Jon later discovers, is also afflicted with the deadly virus. Before long, and despite his better judgment, Jon finds himself accompanying Luke on an impromptu road trip to San Francisco where Luke promises to "figure something out." In fact, Luke is on the lam, having inadvertently killed a cop back in Los Angeles.

Liberated by their death sentences, these unlikely lovers embark on a freewheeling crime spree-cum-talkfest en route to northern California, but Jon eventually gets fed up with Luke's unrelenting self-destructiveness, leading to a cathartic resolution in the middle of nowhere.

This brazenly homoerotic hybrid of BONNIE AND CLYDE and THELMA & LOUISE gets off to a promising start but, once the protagonists hit the road together, THE LIVING END loses pace, finally stalling during an exceedingly boring middle section. The film's many sex scenes, while fairly graphic, lack credibility, partly because there seems to be an invisible sexual line that Dytri is unwilling to cross. (Whether the actor is gay or straight should be irrelevant; he's certainly handsome enough.)

The film's greatest weakness, however, is its cliche-ridden dialogue, something that only performances of tremendous authority can overcome. With the notable exception of Mary Woronov and Johanna Went as two psychotic lesbians who pick up Luke but botch their attempt to murder him, such performances are not forthcoming. A subplot involving Darcy Marta as a platonic friend of Jon's who loves him more than her own boyfriend is also uninvolving, largely because—like Winona Ryder in NIGHT ON EARTH—Darta appears to confuse chain-smoking with acting.

THE LIVING END is not without its pleasures, however. A graduate of USC and UCLA, Araki has a keen eye for composition, and the film's visuals are consistently engaging. Araki shot the film himself, with lighting assistance from fellow LA filmmaker Christopher Munch, employing a vivid color scheme that emphasizes blues, blacks and greens. THE LIVING END works most powerfully as an expression of rage over the ongoing catastrophe of AIDS; it's dedicated to "the hundreds of thousands who've died and the hundreds of thousands more who will die because of a big white house full of Republican f_ _ _heads."

Araki, whose previous "no-budget" features are THREE BEWILDERED PEOPLE IN THE NIGHT and THE LONG WEEKEND (O' DESPAIR), is a tremendously talented filmmaker who seems destined to hit his stride in the very near future. *(Violence, profanity, nudity, sexual situations, adult situations.)*

p, Marcus Hu, Jon Gerrans; d, Gregg Araki; w, Gregg Araki; ph, Gregg Araki; ed, Gregg Araki; m, Cole Coonce

Drama **(PR: O MPAA: NR)**

LOCKED-UP TIME ★★★

(Germany) 90m Alert Film; DEFA; Sender Fries Berlin bw (VERRIEGELTE ZEIT)

In a low-key example of high irony, LOCKED-UP TIME charts dogged filmmaker Sibylle Schonemann's quest to interview the officials who oversaw her detention, trial and imprisonment under the laws of the former German Democratic Republic.

The film opens at a nearly abandoned border control station that is being torn down by some of the same workers who originally put it up, and with the comment that a "job is a job," they express more happiness at their current work than their past achievement. Schonemann even catches a few sarcastic words from a former border guard who makes sure his face isn't caught by her camera. That border post, she informs viewers in a voiceover, was the one through which she passed in 1985, when with 40 other political prisoners, she was sent to West Germany as part of a quasi-official ransom deal.

Born and raised in Potsdam, it was Schonemann's and her husband's request to leave East Germany that caught the attention of the State Security Service or *Stasi*, from the German *Staatsicherheitsdienst*). Their emigration request evolved from the repeated rejection of their film projects at DEFA, the state-owned East German film studio, also located in Potsdam, where they worked.

Retracing her steps, Schonemann then takes us to the small town of Hohenleuben in the Gera region, the site of the most modern prison in the former republic. Staffed by a skeleton crew, the prison still stands as the town's outstanding feature and Schonemann revisits the facility's textile workshop and the resident warden or "educator" who has cast off her captain's uniform for the sake of a sympathetic interview. With a thin lipped smile, the warden can't remember any of the salient details in Schonemann's prison life, and when asked about the denial of a maternal visit or of her husband's letter, she refers to this or that obscure regulation.

Returning to Potsdam, Schonemann recalls the nighttime arrest that introduced her to a prison in the center of the town that she had never known existed where a moralistic aphorism from Lenin still adorns the wall. Her preliminary detention resulted in a very brief hearing at which her violation of Article 214 of the Criminal Code was confirmed and she was held for further questioning. Sitting in the same prison cell with her former cellmate, Brigitte or Punkt, they now laughingly recall how they discovered that each was a political prisoner. They also recall their interrogations, and the filmmaker even sights her former questioner in her view-finder.

Portly with narrow slit-like eyes, but a soft, almost insinuating, voice, the former interrogator is seen doing his laundry and calmly promises to speak with Schonemann at a later date, but then angrily waves her camera away. Her only really successful interview is with one of the three judges who found her guilty. That man admits his cowardice in the interpretation of law apparently drafted with just such cases as Schonemann's in mind. The courtroom in which she was condemned is now abandoned, a litter of chairs and a disconnected phone with the wreathed hammer-and-compass seal of the East German Republic still on the wall.

In an effort to discover the sources of the evidence at a trial, a thick folder of memos and depositions, Schonemann revisits DEFA where her former supervisors and colleagues seem to have helped incriminate her and her husband. The former director general of DEFA is very friendly, offering her his handshake and even waving cheerily at the camera, but then is unavailable for the interview he had promised to give. Moving further up the chain of bureaucratic command, Schonemann discovers a former *Stasi* lieutenant colonel, Peter Gericke. Now living in his summer house as a forester, Gericke talks willingly with the former political prisoner. He argues smoothly that accepting all the laws and regulations of the former government of necessity demanded the use of political police and their "partners," as he calls the many informers who made the work of the security service that much easier.

In closing, Schonemann visits the lawyer who had acted as an intermediary in her release and transit to the Federal Republic. The files in his office, he claims, concern some 35 thousand political prisoners. Despite the recent changes in Germany, the filmmaker and her family continue to live in Hamburg where they had relocated after their year in prison.

Sybille Schonemann's film is a study in subtleties. Since there was no physical torture or abuse and her term of imprisonment was relatively short, her story emphasizes the details of arrest and the ambiguity of the law and her status. The narrow exercise yard at the Hohenleuben prison and the specially designed vans with separate cells for each prisoner hint at the importance of political offenders to the state. Schonemann has told interviewers that she suspects she was arrested in order to discourage her fellow filmmakers at DEFA from emigrating and to stifle any dissident opinion at the studio.

LOCKED-UP TIME breaks the thin ground of the complex relationships among the citizenry of the former Communist republic where paternalism rivalled dictatorship as the major impulse. For some time this may be the dramatic theme of increasing numbers of films from East-Central Europe. *(Adult Situations.)*

p, Bernd Burkhardt, Alfred Hurmer; d, Sibylle Schonemann; ph, Thomas Plenert; ed, Gudrun Steinbruck; m, Thomas Kahane

Documentary/Political **(PR: C MPAA: NR)**

LONDON KILLS ME ★★★

(U.K.) 107m Working Title; Polygram Pictures ~ Fine Line Features c

Justin Chadwick *(Clint)*, Steven Mackintosh *(Muffdiver)*, Emer McCourt *(Sylvie)*, Roshan Seth *(Dr. Bubba)*, Fiona Shaw *(Headley)*, Brad Dourif *(Hemingway)*, Tony Haygarth *(Burns)*, Stevan Rimkus *(Tom Tom)*, Eleanor David *(Lily)*, Alun Armstrong *(Stone)*, Nick Dunning *(Faulkner)*, Naveen Andrews *(Bike)*, Garry Cooper *(Mr. G)*, Gordon Warnecke *(Mr. G's Assistant)*, Evelyn Doggart *(Mr. G's Girl)*, Chale Charles *(Mr. G's Girl)*, Joseph Alessi *(Plainclothes Policeman)*, David Hounslow *(Plainclothes Policeman)*, Ben Peel *(DJ at Party)*, Danny John-Jules *(Black Man at Party)*, Oliver Kester *(Black Thug at Party)*, Paudge Behan *(White Thug at Party)*, Yemi Ajibade *(Tramp)*, Anthony Cairns *(Busy Bee)*, Rowena King *(Melanie)*, Veronica Smart *(Woman Diner)*, Sandy McDade *(Woman Diner)*, Tracey MacLeod *(TV Interviewer)*, George Miller *(Mr. Runcipher)*, Philip Glenister *(Suited Man)*, Charlie Creed-Miles *(Kid in Loft)*, Delroy Nunes *(Kid in Loft)*, Karl Collins *(Barman)*, Sean Pertwee *(German Tourist)*, Pippa Hinchley *(German Tourist)*, Steven Lawrence *(Drug Dealer)*, Greg Saunders *(Rent Boy)*, Marianne Jean-Baptiste *(Nanny)*, Sally Whitman *(Mother)*, Leila Whitman *(Baby)*, James Caplan *(Boy in Country)*, Sarah Worth *(Girl in Country)*, Joe England *(Young Clint)*, Dave Atkins *(Heavy)*

The directorial debut for screenwriter Hanif Kureishi (SAMMY AND ROSIE GET LAID, MY BEAUTIFUL LAUNDERETTE), LONDON KILLS ME is a visceral, Dickensian tale of outcasts, drugs and upward mobility.

Clint (Justin Chadwick) is just turning twenty and has had enough of his lot as a small-time drug dealer and squatter, constantly scavenging for the next bag of hash to sell or a blanket to keep himself warm. One of a gang employed by his longtime chum and narcotics entrepreneur Muffdiver (Steven Mackintosh), Clint works alongside Burns (Tony Haygarth), Bike (Naveen Andrews) and Tom Tom (Stevan Rimkus). He sees a way out of his dead-end existence when a restaurant manager, Hemingway (Brad Dourif), offers him a waiting job on the condition that he can find a proper pair of shoes to wear to work. Clint decides to work one final week as a dealer so that he can raise enough cash to buy some appropriate footwear.

Clint bumps into his old friend Sylvie (Emer McCourt), a fallen beauty fresh from rehab. She's looking for a place to stay and a fix, and both her needs are met by Muffdiver when, implementing his latest plan, he and his gang break into a vacant second-floor apartment. With a good location on Whitehall Street, sleeping quarters for the staff, and a private bedroom for his new lover, Sylvie, Muffdiver is now able to indulge his business-tycoon fantasies—something about which the crew is less than thrilled.

Clint sells some hash to Headley (Fiona Shaw), a predatory older woman who fancies herself a protector of young bohemians. Then, still desperate for cash, he steals Muffdiver's bankroll and hides it on the roof of the building. Sent into a tailspin, the gang takes a trip to the countryside to get some fresh air, smoke hash and regroup. They end up at the house of Clint's mother, Lilly (Eleanor David), where her husband, Stone (Alun Armstrong), demonstrates his penchant for bad Elvis impersonations.

Back in London, the gang is forcefully evicted from the flat by the newly returned owners. Muffdiver is forced to leave town until the situation calms down, and Clint can't get to the stolen money. With only one day until his new job begins, he makes a last effort at procuring the needed footwear by pleading with Headley for a loan. She refuses his request unless sexual favors are built into the deal and he storms out of the apartment, after purloining a pair of boots which belong to someone who's using Headley's shower. Muffdiver and Sylvie try to convince Clint to join them on the lam, but he resists their entreaties. Clint arrives for work on time and with shoes that, it turns out, belong to Hemingway. Before long, it's obvious that he's a natural.

Kureishi brings both humor and pathos to his portrait of London's underworld, fashioning sympathetic, three-dimensional characters out of figures who are usually viewed as despicable villains. Kureishi's drug-dealers are confused, hopeful and desperate for love—not unlike the rest of humanity. Kureishi resists the temptation either to moralize about the story's more sober aspects or to let the jokes soften the drama's harder edges, treading a fine line between wit and despair with his trademark wry dialogue. Some occasional credibility-straining moments—as when no one seems to care that a group of squatters have broken into a posh flat, or when Muffdiver leaves his bankroll virtually sitting out in the open—are minor lapses in an otherwise well conceived plot.

Unusually, the fine cast are actually made to look like real drug users. As Clint, Chadwick is a standout, playing his character not as a vulture, but as a victim of society (and possibly, Kureishi hints, child abuse). If Clint is a grown version of Dickens's Oliver, then Mackintosh's Muffdiver is the modern-day Fagin. Muff's tough exterior is a means to an end, a thin veneer that is soon wiped away. What remains is a little boy caught between the fantasy of being a business tycoon and the sordid reality of his lifestyle. McCourt plays Sylvie with a delicateness which belies her tough surroundings. The rest of the gang is well cast, although they don't have much to do other than look stoned.

Kureishi's message is best summed up in the film's ironic epilogue. It's a few months later, and the cleaned-up, sharply dressed Clint has become the archetypal cool waiter. As we see him selling the restaurant's charm and hipness to a couple of tourists though, we realize that he's still a pusher. We're all selling something, Kureishi seems to be saying, whether it's drugs, food or our souls. How society views us is a result of the package we come in. *(Substance abuse, profanity, nudity.)*

p, Tim Bevan; d, Hanif Kureishi; w, Hanif Kureishi; ph, Edward Lachman; ed, Jon Gregory; m, Mark Springer, Sarah Sarhandi, Bruce Smith; prod d, Stuart Walker; art d, Diane Dancklefsen, Colin Blaymires; cos, Amy Roberts

Drama **(PR: C MPAA: R)**

LONELY HEARTS ★★★

106m Gibraltar Entertainment ~ LIVE Home Video c

Beverly D'Angelo *(Alma Bates)*, Eric Roberts *(Frank)*, Joanna Cassidy *(Erin)*, Herta Ware *(Annie)*, Sharon Farrell, Ellen Geer, Bibi Besch, Charles Napier

Film noir, almost by definition, implies seduction—usually a loner guy tempted by a dangerous dame, lured deeper and deeper by a siren's call to crime, deceit and doom. LONELY HEARTS is refreshing in its effective gender inversion: here a woman falls hard for the wrong man.

She's Alma Bates (Beverly D'Angelo), one of life's wallflowers. Pretty but overlooked, she lives with her grandmother Annie (Herta Ware), works at a Social Security office when not attending meetings of her self-help group for compulsive overeaters, and that's about it for night life. In desperation, Alma turns to the personals ads in the *LA Weekly* for companionship and links up with Frank (Eric Roberts), a handsome rake who completely charms her. But it's already been revealed to the viewer that Frank is a heartless con artist who targets middle-aged, single ladies. He earns their trust through romance, then siphons their fortunes and disappears.

Frank pulls his scam on Alma, but even after his betrayal she won't give up on him. Tracking the crook down through his vanity license plate, Alma gently blackmails Frank into letting her stay with him. She promises to help by posing as his adoring sister in the con game, giving support and counsel in the finer points of victimizing women. All goes smoothly at first, but Alma can't stomach the thought of Frank repeatedly wooing and bedding other partners right in front of her. Meanwhile the net is closing on the pair: one of Frank's ex-lovers has hired a no-nonsense private investigator, Erin (Joanna Cassidy), to track him down. When a failed scam results in murder the larcenous couple go on the run, ending when Frank takes Alma's grandmother as a hostage. Alma shoots him dead.

Producer, director and co-screenwriter Andrew Lane (MORTAL PASSIONS) knows this shadow territory well, and he upends the genre's conventions without violating them. Some thrillers portray dangerous females with venom bordering on misogyny, but LONELY HEARTS is more complex in its examination of women as both predator and prey.

Glib psychologists would doubtlessly explain Alma's infatuation with Frank as a natural extension of her latent eating disorder: "Compulsives tend to transfer their obsessions." But Frank's diagnosis is more to the point: "Nobody gets conned who doesn't want to be." On more than one occasion Alma tries to convince Frank to go straight, but he refuses, declaring that the life of a swindler is the only one he has ever known. Given a choice between leaving Frank—being alone again—and helping bury a corpse in the dead of night, Alma opts for the latter, until he turns on her own family.

Beverly D'Angelo, an underrated actress best known for comedy roles (NATIONAL LAMPOON'S VACATION, THE POPE MUST DIET), is excellent as the desperate heroine, neither pathetic nor unsympathetic as she's driven to extremes by her obsessive longing. As the *homme fatal* Eric Roberts (STAR 80, FINAL ANALYSIS) does equally well, conveying that even Frank is a victim of sorts as his schemes backfire on him. Cassidy's pithy suporting part as the distaff detective emphasizes the sexual role reversals.

Lane errs in staging one rather gratuitous death early on, making the plot's later, lethal bent feel anti-climactic. The second half moves at a languid pace and leans a bit heavily on the mood music, but overall LONELY HEARTS shows how a familiar screen setup can be energized by a healthy infusion of estrogen. *(Violence, sexual situations, adult situations, nudity, profanity.)*

p, Andrew Lane, Robert Kenner; d, Andrew Lane; w, Andrew Lane, R.E. Daniels, (from his story); ph, Paul Ryan; ed, Julian Semilian; m, David McHugh; prod d, Pam Woodbridge; art d, Carlos Barbosa; set d, Marty Huyette; cos, Libbie Aroff-Lane, Peggy Schnitzer

Crime/Thriller **(PR: O MPAA: R)**

LORENZO'S OIL ★★★½
135m Kennedy-Miller Productions ~ Universal c

Nick Nolte *(Augusto Odone)*, Susan Sarandon *(Michaela Odone)*, Peter Ustinov *(Professor Nikolais)*, Kathleen Wilhoite *(Deirdre Murphy)*, Gerry Bamman *(Doctor Judalon)*, Margo Martindale *(Wendy Gimble)*, James Rebhorn *(Ellard Muscatine)*, Ann Hearn *(Loretta Muscatine)*, Maduka Steady *(Omouri)*, Mary Wakio *(Comorian Teacher)*, Don Suddaby *(Don Suddaby)*, Colin Ward *(Jack Gimble)*, La Tanya Richardson *(Nurse Ruth)*, Jennifer Dundas *(Nurse Nancy Jo)*, William Cameon *(Pellerman)*, Becky Ann Baker *(Pellerman's Secretary)*, Mary Pat Gleason *(The Librarian)*, David Shiner *(Clown)*, Ann Dowd *(Pediatrician)*, Peter MacKenzie *(Immunosuppression Doctor)*, Paul Lazar *(Professor Duncan)*, Laura Linney *(Young Teacher)*, Helena Ruoti *(Judalon's Nurse)*, Luis Ruiz *(Judalon's Resident)*, Joyce Reehling *(Columnist)*, Barbara Poitier *(Nikolais Secretary)*, Mary Schmidt Campbell *(Principal)*, Michael O'Neill *(School Psycologist)*, William Thunhurst, Jr. *(Ear Specialist)*, Ann McDonough *(Dietician)*, Lianne Kressin *(Smiling Nurse)*, Nicolas Petrov *(World Bank Executive)*, Richard Cordery *(Suddaby's Senior Manager)*, Angus Barnett *(Suddaby's Junior Manager)*, Keiko McDonald *(Japanese Translator)*, Vladimir Padunov *(Russian Translator)*, David McFadden *(Father Killian)*, Carmen Piccini *(Cristina Odone)*, Aaron Jackson *(Francesco Odone)*, Neri Kyle Tannenbaum *(Female Lab Voice)*, Brad Einhorn *(Male Lab Voice)*, Noah Banks *(Lorenzo)*, Michael Haider *(Lorenzo)*, Cristin Woodworth *(Lorenzo)*, Billy Amman *(Lorenzo)*, E.G. Daily *(Lorenzo)*, Zack O'Malley Greenburg *(Lorenzo)*, Sandy Gore, Rocco Sisto, April Merscher, Nora Dunfee, Amelia Campbell, Keith Reddin *(Murphy Family)*, Eliot Brinton, Ayub Ommaya, Ryonosuke Shiono, James Merrill, Marie Nugent-Head, Zahra Ilkanipour *(Symposium Doctors)*, Nancy Chesney, John Mowod, Berta Van Zuiden, Susan Chapek, Shirley Tannenbaum, Charles R. Altman, Anthony Dileo, Nona Gerard, David Doepken, Kathryn Aronson, Lamont Arnold, Julie Marie Remele, Annie Loeffler, Lisa Montgomery *(Conference Parents)*, Raina Clifford, Todd Bella, Rachel Jones, Matthew Pyeritz, Daniel W. D'arcy, Justin Isfeld, Jeremy Beyer, Christine Merriman, Nicholas Wiese, Tia Delaney, Lamar Olivis, Ryan Thomas, Connie Cranden, C. Alex Roberts, Mack Hegyes, Eric Kunkle *(Special Children)*

LORENZO'S OIL marked a welcome return for acclaimed Australian filmmaker George Miller, who had not directed a feature since THE WITCHES OF EASTWICK in 1987.

This wrenching film tells the true tale of Augusto (Nick Nolte) and Michaela Odone (Susan Sarandon) and their fight to save the life of their son Lorenzo (Zack O'Malley Greenburg), after he is stricken with a rare and deadly disease. When Lorenzo is first diagnosed with Adrenolenkodystrophy (ALD), all that is known is that it affects only boys; it's brought on by a gene carried by the mother; and it destroys the fatty protective layer around nerves, resulting in extreme nervous disorders, blindness and certain death. A leading expert on ALD, Professor Nikolais (Peter Ustinov), is sympathetic, but his methodical cautiousness in searching for a cure frustrates the Odones. They decide to devote their lives to their own research, caring for the quickly deteriorating boy themselves as they race to develop their own unorthodox treatment. With the odds so drastically against them, and every hope just another chance to be hurt and disappointed, the couple find it hard to get support for their efforts even from the parents of other ALD boys. They nonetheless persevere and make a remarkable breakthrough.

Though LORENZO'S OIL may sound like a disease-of-the-week TV movie, it refuses to fit neatly into any genre, combining almost thriller-like suspense with a rigorously intelligent, neo-documentary approach to its subject.

Miller is a master of visceral violence. A licensed doctor, he drew his inspiration for MAD MAX from the grotesque sights he witnessed in hospital emergency rooms. With his latest film, he brings these horrors into the most frightening personal realm, using low-angle shots and ominous musical foreshadowing to dramatize Lorenzo's plight. The resulting work reveals the absolute horror of parenting a sick child, unleavened by sentimentality or nostalgia. Shockingly intense, it's reminiscent of THE EXORCIST, but with science instead of liturgy being the answer to the child's mysterious problem. (Actually, the Odones—he Italian, she Irish—are anything but faithless).

LORENZO'S OIL has other strengths beyond Miller's directorial pyrotechnics, its highest achievement being its uncompromising presentation of unconditional love. In the later stages of Lorenzo's disease, when he seems to have lost any grip on the world outside, Augusto hesitantly suggests that his son may no longer have a "soul"; his brain has deteriorated so far that he seems no longer capable of thought or emotion. Isn't there a point, we ask ourselves, when a person ceases to be a person, and we should stop feeling for that person as we once did? For Lorenzo's mother, the question does not even bear consideration. She condemns anyone who fails to share her zeal to some lower moral plane, banishing not only two capable nurses, but her own sister, from the house when they question the unqualified ardor of her crusade. Sarandon makes Mrs. Odone compelling, yet largely unsympathetic. We don't just applaud as she and her husband take on, and defeat, the bureaucracy of the medical establishment; we also recoil from her pious, pedantic self-righteousness. It's a brave, complex performance, and the centerpiece of a brave, complex film.

The eclectic mix of music in LORENZO'S OIL works brilliantly, and John Seale's harsh, uncompromising cinematography (quite different from his work with Peter Weir on WITNESS, THE MOSQUITO COAST and DEAD POETS SOCIETY) is excellent. The screenplay, by Miller and Nick Enright, does a fine job of balancing the various characters' points of view.

LORENZO'S OIL does have its weaknesses. Nolte's thick Italian accent sometimes makes it hard to understand what he's saying; the story of the Odones' quest is at least as draining as it is rewarding; and Miller's intense initial presentation of the disease leaves him with nowhere to build to in this inherently anti-climactic tale. This is, nevertheless, a one-of-a-kind drama that deserves to be seen; the story, not of a miracle cure, but—as a Swahili epigram at the opening of the film puts it—of "life as struggle." *(Violence.)*

p, George Miller, Doug Mitchell; d, George Miller; w, George Miller, Nick Enright; ph, John Seale; ed, Richard Francis-Bruce, Marcus D'Arcy, Lee Smith; prod d, Kristi Zea; art d, Dennis Bradford; set d, Karen A. O'Hara; cos, Colleen Atwood

AAN Best Actress: Susan Sarandon; *AAN Best Original Screenplay:* George Miller

Drama **(PR: C MPAA: PG-13)**

LOVE CRIMES ★
87m Miramax; Sovereign Pictures ~ Millimeter Films c

Sean Young *(Dana Greenway)*, Patrick Bergin *(David Hanover)*, Arnetia Walker *(Maria Johnson)*, James Read *(Stanton Gray)*, Ron Orbach *(Detective Eugene Tully)*, Fern Dorsey *(Colleen Dells)*, Tina Hightower *(Anne Winslow)*, Donna Biscoe *(Hannah)*, Danielle Shuman *(Dana—Age 6)*, David Shuman *(Lou Jay Greenway)*, Rebecca Wackler *(Cecillia)*, Jill Jane Clementis *(Lizbeth)*, Roe Sabordo *(Tamika)*, Sarah Bork *(Clarice Greenway)*, Diane Butler *(Kelly Andrews)*, Katheleen Rodgers *(Zenia)*, Linda D. Thompson *(Susan)*, Tasha Aver *(Linda)*, Dana L. Backwell *(Margie)*, Scott Kerr *(Mikey)*, Gary Bullock *(Joey)*, Yolanda Asher *(Kim)*, Peter Stanilias *(Patrick)*, Jim Harley *(Chief Ellis)*, Bob Banks *(Jamie)*, Sergeant Johnson Taylor *(Wilmer)*, Adrian Roberts *(Officer Riggs)*, Bob Hannah *(Detective Taylor)*, Hurley Daughtery *(1st Police Officer)*, Tom Rowan *(2nd Police Officer)*, Dennis Norton *(3rd Police Officer)*, Sonny Shroyer *(1st Plain Clothes Cop)*, Jimmy Meyers *(2nd Plain Clothes Cop)*, L. Warren Young *(3rd Plain Clothes Cop)*, Carl Bates *(4th Plain Clothes Cop)*, Charles Cheek *(5th Plain Clothes Cop)*, Joani Yarbrough *(Waitress)*, Jodi G. DuFresne *(Receptionist)*, Taylor Vickers *(Hooker)*, John Hambrick *(Man in Trailer)*, Scott Leftridge *(1st Bar Fight Man)*, Jonjo Mayo *(2nd Bar Fight Man)*, Lonnie R. Smith, Jr. *(Man in Hotel)*, James Mayberry *(Dennis)*, Leah Morgan *(Woman)*, Wayne Shorter *(Jazz Quartet Member)*, Ronnie Free *(Jazz Quartet Member)*, Joe Jones *(Jazz Quartet Member)*, Ben Tucker *(Jazz Quartet Member)*

Arguably a failure by conventional standards, LOVE CRIMES, a low-budget commercial foray by political filmmaker Lizzie Borden (BORN IN FLAMES, WORKING GIRLS), nevertheless effectively raises provocative questions about relations between the sexes within the context of a generic potboiler addled by underdeveloped characters and muddled plotting.

Inspired by real events, LOVE CRIMES revolves around a sex criminal (SLEEPING WITH THE ENEMY heavy Patrick Bergin) who represents himself as top fashion photographer "David Hanover" and uses the promise of a modelling career to lure victims from Atlanta-area shopping malls. He takes them back to their homes where he coerces them into being photographed in humiliating, sexually compromising poses. He then seduces and robs them, leaving the victims, typically lower-middle-class single career women, reluctant to press charges.

Herself a victim of childhood abuse, Atlanta assistant district attorney Dana Greenway (Sean Young) becomes obsessed with putting Hanover away, neglecting her active cases despite her inability to convince any of Hanover's victims to swear out a complaint. Her quest leads her to Savannah, where Hanover's activities show a pattern of escalating violence, including the severe beating of his latest victim. Lacking the support of either her own office or the local police, Greenway engages in a dangerous one-on-one game of cat-and-mouse with Hanover, putting herself in the position of a potential victim.

Though informed by a feminist sensibility, LOVE CRIMES is anything but a politically one-note movie. If anything, it suffers from an excess of ambiguity in its heroine and villain, well portrayed by unusually high-powered stars for a low-budget movie. Greenway is haunted by unresolved childhood traumas, presented in hazy flashbacks, in which, apparently, her abusive, womanizing father would lock her in a closet whenever he brought women home. He later accidentally kills one of his conquests who discovers the youngster cowering in the closet and tries to rescue her.

Presumably because of her childhood experiences, Greenway finds herself conflicted about Hanover, simultaneously repulsed by and attracted to him. Hanover is less developed. However, he is shown to be a tormented victim of his uncontrollable impulses to degrade women and horrified by his growing violent tendencies. His victims, many of them homely and lonely, are also conflicted about—and soiled by—Hanover's exploitation of their unfulfilled desires to be loved and lusted after.

At her best and most audacious, Borden uses a standard police thriller plot to paint a bleak though believable picture of a society in which both men and women are forced into roles that deny healthy sexuality and all but sanction coercion and self-loathing as normal parts of human sexual relations. It is thus a film, in Greenway's words, that probes the "grey area between seduction and rape" in which Hanover operates. The problem is that, in this case at least, an idea-driven film doesn't translate well into compelling drama.

Neither Greenway nor Hanover is developed much beyond the sum totals of their neuroses and the plotting suffers from an unengaging choppiness that suggests some tinkering in the editing room to make the film more generically conventional. (This, in fact, was precisely the case. Before the film's video release, however, Borden was given the opportunity to retool the film and reinsert several minutes of deleted footage; she seized the chance, of course.) The result, unfortunately, is only to draw undue attention to the kinds of character and plot implausibilities that, in a better-crafted film, would sail by in the wake of the dramatic momentum LOVE CRIMES never really develops.

Despite the film's shortcomings, Borden makes a strong enough case here that slickness isn't everything as she herself works to resolve her distinctively personal style of political filmmaking with the demands of a commercial marketplace that tends to shun both personality and politics. *(Adult situations, nudity, profanity.)*

p, Lizzie Borden, Randy Langlais; d, Lizzie Borden; w, Allan Moyle, Laurie Frank, (from story by Moyle); ph, Jack N. Green; ed, Nicholas C. Smith, Mike Jackson; m, Graeme Revell; prod d, Armin Ganz; art d, John E. "Jack" Marty, Tom Davick; set d, Joseph Litsch

Erotic/Thriller **(PR: O MPAA: R)**

LOVE FIELD ★★½

104m Sanford/Pillsbury Productions; Jacqueline Productions; Orion ~ Orion c

Michelle Pfeiffer *(Lurene Hallett)*, Dennis Haysbert *(Paul Cater)*, Stephanie McFadden *(Jonell Cater)*, Brian Kerwin *(Ray Hallett)*, Louise Latham *(Mrs. Enright)*, Peggy Rea *(Mrs. Heisenbuttal)*, Beth Grant *(Hazel)*, Johnny Ray McGhee *(Mechanic)*, Cooper Huckabee *(Deputy Swinson)*, Troy Evans *(Lieutenant Galvan)*, Mark Miller *(Trooper Exley)*, Pearl Jones *(Mrs. Baker)*, Janell McLeod *(Station Cashier)*, Bob Minor *(Barricade Policeman)*, Rhoda Griffis *(Jacqueline Kennedy)*, Bob Gill *(President Kennedy)*, Ron Shelly *(Secret Service Agent)*, Michael Milgrom *(TV Director)*, Chestley Price *(Porter)*, Nick Searcy *(FBI Man)*, Moses Gibson *(Driver)*, Dave Hager *(Station Master)*, Norm Heflin *(Phone Operator)*, Jon Maggard *(Redneck)*, Jonathan Wigan *(Redneck's Son)*, Brian Kay *(Friendly Man)*, Charles K. Bortell *(Cal Enright)*, Jack Canon *(Motel Manager)*, Resa Reagan *(Bathrobed Woman)*, Deborah Offner *(Police Dispatcher)*, Larry Butler *(Bullhorn Officer)*, Vickie Ross-Norris *(Vickie)*, Tiffany McHoney *(Foster Home Kid)*, Jesheka Winstead *(Foster Home Kid)*, Alma Woodard *(Woman at Counter)*, Ishmond Jones *(Mr. Baker)*, Bobbi Casto *(Bus Passenger)*, Bobbi Collins *(Bus Passenger)*, Caroline Goodwyn *(Bus Passenger)*, Bill Boyzett, William Shaw Urney, Rob Clotworthy, Burr DeBenning, Skay Kuter, Alan Oppenheimer, Joe Unger *(Announcers)*

Precisely the kind of oddball-hybrid for which Orion Pictures was once famous, LOVE FIELD was the studio's first release following its declaration of bankruptcy and subsequent restructuring in 1992.

Lurene Hallett (Michelle Pfeiffer) is a ditzy sixties Dallas housewife who married her high-school sweetheart, Ray (Brian Kerwin), and who worships Jackie Kennedy, down to making her own knockoffs of Jackie's designer wardrobe and emulating her bouffant hairdo. The film opens on the day of Kennedy's assassination, when Lurene just misses shaking the first lady's hand at Love Field because she's gone to retrieve a friend's (Peggy Rea) dropped purse. Subsequently determined to attend Kennedy's funeral—without knowing whether it will be in Washington or Massachusetts, and also without her husband's permission—she sneaks away in the middle of the night to catch a Greyhound east.

On the bus she befriends a black man, Paul Cater (Dennis Haysbert), and his young daughter Jonell (Stephanie McFadden), who are traveling to Philadelphia. What she doesn't know is that Cater, who identifies himself as "Johnson," is on the run after snatching his daughter from the abusive state home where she wound up after her mother died. Seeing bruises on Jonell, Lurene assumes the worst and calls the FBI from a bus station after their bus is involved in an accident. Almost as quickly realizing her mistake, she helps Cater and Jonell escape in a stolen car and travels with them.

En route to Virginia and the home of Mrs. Enright (Louise Latham), the mother of a friend of Lurene's, their car breaks down just outside of town. While Lurene goes for help, Cater runs afoul of some racists, who beat him up. After Lurene tends his wounds, the couple make love. The next day, they borrow Enright's car for the last leg of their trip. Lurene goes to meet her husband at a prearranged motel outside of Washington. When he beats her, she escapes with Cater's help, but they are finally captured at a police roadblock. After a year in prison, Cater is reunited with now-divorced Lurene and his now-thriving daughter.

A good rule of thumb for screenwriters might be to avoid using the Kennedy assassination in any way, shape or form for the next decade or so. In the case of LOVE FIELD, produced in 1990 from a screenplay by Don Roos (SINGLE WHITE FEMALE), the assassination functions as an unwieldy motivational device to bring about the transformation of Lurene's character. She abandons the comfortable liberalism of being a Kennedy supporter for a real activism sparked by her involvement with Cater, realizing that, Kennedy or no Kennedy, not much of substance has changed for Blacks in America. It's a nice idea, but it doesn't entirely work; despite Cater's assurances to the contrary, there *is* something more than passing strange about a woman who has made a life's obsession out of Jackie Kennedy. And it requires more range than Pfeiffer, or anyone else for that matter, can muster to effect a credible transition from a complete ditz in Kennedy drag to an intelligent individual.

On the upside, director Jonathan Kaplan (THE ACCUSED, HEART LIKE A WHEEL) displays an impressive talent for dramatically defining the ways in which institutions we have created to protect ourselves can come to oppress and degrade us. Thus, for Kaplan, Lurene doesn't need the Kennedy assassination to change her character, and he wisely downplays it whenever possible. It's enough for him and the film that she's a white woman traveling alone with a black man in 1963. The meat of the drama is thus the way in which two basically decent people become hunted outcasts for exercising perfectly reasonable rights—of a man to care for his daughter, and of a woman to travel with whomever she wants.

Purged of her character's ditziness, Pfeiffer is quite fine as an outlaw woman most men would want on their side. Though LOVE FIELD is a more serious film, Pfeiffer's performance demonstrates that she could just have easily played either Thelma or Louise, of which Lurene is a strange melding. Haysbert (who replaced actor Eriq LaSalle, who replaced Denzel Washington) is uncannily right for the character and for the time, bringing a real tenderness to his scenes with eight-year-old newcomer McFadden. He helps make LOVE FIELD a compelling drama, despite its umpteenth flogging of the Kennedy myth. *(Violence, profanity, adult situations.)*

p, Midge Sanford, Sarah Pillsbury; d, Jonathan Kaplan; w, Don Roos; ph, Ralf Bode; ed, Jane Kurson; m, Jerry Goldsmith; prod d, Mark Freeborn; art d, David Willson, Lance King; set d, Jim Erickson; cos, Peter Mitchell, Colleen Atwood

AAN Best Actress: Michelle Pfeiffer

Romance/Drama **(PR: C MPAA: PG-13)**

LOVE HURTS ★★½

106m Love Hurts Productions; Vestron Pictures ~ Vestron Video c

Jeff Daniels *(Paul Weaver)*, Cynthia Sykes *(Nancy Weaver)*, Judith Ivey *(Susan Volcheck)*, John Mahoney *(Boomer)*, Cloris Leachman *(Ruth Weaver)*, Amy Wright *(Karen Weaver)*, Mary Griffin *(Sarah Weaver)*, Thomas Allen *(David Weaver)*, Jo Livingston *(Harold Whipkey)*, Annabelle Weenick *(Miriam Whipkey)*, Matthew Carlton *(Doug Whipkey)*, Eve Smith *(Grandma Whipkey)*, Jack Willis *(Danny Volcheck)*, Brady Quaid *(Billy Volcheck)*, Peter Van Norden *(Frank)*, Adrian Ricard *(Roxy)*, Jodi Faith Cahn *(Jane)*, Daren Kelly *(Jane's Husband)*, Larry K. Collis *(Doorman)*, Sam Stoneburner *(Bob)*, Geraldine Court *(Laura)*, Frank Serrano *(New York Cabbie)*, Vernon Grote *(Pete)*, Burton Knight *(Flower Delivery Boy)*, Sean Galaise *(Billy's Friend)*, Emily Warfield *(Linda)*, Michelle DeMarco *(Marci)*, Tommie *(Puppy Girl)*, Jean Stephens *(Shelly)*, Harley McLane *(Bachelorette)*, Connie Speer *(Bachelorette)*, Lou Michaels *(Bachelorette)*, John Martin *(Sheriff)*, Chris Hauge *(Reverend Hopper)*, Deana Newcomb *(Wedding Photographer)*, Mona Lee Fultz *(Bridesmaid)*, Jan Dewitt *(Bridesmaid)*, Cynthia Dorn *(Bridesmaid)*, Floyd Dakil *(Tony)*, Doran Ingram *(Pool Shark)*, Mary Ann Smith *(Caterer)*, Helena Humann *(Lenabelle)*, Ken Paige *(Local Taxi Driver)*, Andrea Adams *(Night Cashier)*, Bob Girolami *(Lost New Yorker)*, Tim McCarver *(Mets Announcer)*

The latest from veteran helmer Bud Yorkin (COME BLOW YOUR HORN, TWICE IN A LIFETIME), LOVE HURTS bumps from quarrel to quarrel trying to find out whether there's anything funny about dysfunctional families.

Ex-baseball pro Paul Weaver (Jeff Daniels) is a sad, dishevelled Manhattanite pining for his estranged wife and kids in Pennsylvania but hooked on one-night stands. He is served divorce papers upon arriving home to his barren apartment after an anonymous encounter and decides he needs to visit his parents. At the same time, broken pipes force Paul's spouse, Nancy (Cynthia Skyes), and son and daughter to move into his parents' home. It also happens to be Paul's sister Karen's (Amy Wright) wedding weekend. After 10 hours on the highway, Paul dozes at the wheel and nearly smashes into an oncoming truck carrying small-town Susan Volchek (Judith Ivey) and her husband and son. Verging on a fight with the husband, Paul speeds off leaving Susan entranced.

Paul's long-suffering mother, Ruth (Cloris Leachman), is delighted to see him, but in a tizzy because she is about to serve lunch to her in-laws and her own alcoholic husband, Boomer (John Mahoney), hasn't yet arrived from his local bar. Paul's wife and nine-year-old daughter, Sarah (Mary Griffin), on the other hand, are not pleased to see him, and after an immediate confrontation, he storms out. He heads to the varsity ball field where he meets up with Susan again and nearly seduces her, but a wave of guilt forces him back to his parents' with a puppy for

Sarah. Once again, his arrival stimulates a screaming match and he ends up boozing with his dad. The cops bring both drunks home where his and Nancy's habitual row spins them into his old bedroom. They fall into bed and unknowingly on top of Sarah: "Is this a nightmare?" she screams. The reunion quickly explodes in a din of accusations and disappointment, and Paul spends the night in his car.

The next day is Karen's wedding. It's pouring. Boomer is drunk and ashamed and refuses to go into the church to give away the bride, and Karen refuses to exit her chamber to get married. Paul convinces her to go through with the wedding and escorts his sister down the aisle himself. In the hour preceding the reception, Paul runs into Susan and the two decide to sneak off to the "No-tell Motel." After feeding her the same lines he dished to his wife the night before and also to his last lover, Paul catches himself; he can't go through with it. Back at the reception, Boomer has sobered up and is dancing with an accepting Karen, but Sarah decides to run away upon sight of her own father. Paul catches her and asks her to move back to the city with him. She agrees as long as she can have the big room and paint it purple.

Marriage and pain are bound tightly in LOVE HURTS, and bound inextricably for those who have messed-up parents. The film's three generations keep replacing each other—Grandpa is a pathetic alcoholic, Paul a careening, irresponsible loser, and even David, the teenage son, is proving to be an emotionally distant ladies' man. The women are all forgiving but angrily turned inward. Outside of a couple of effervescently screwy scenes, such as when jabbering Grandma blithely wraps the bride Karen in Saran wrap before she braves the rain to reach the waiting limo, laughing at the family's mounting trials is like laughing at someone who has just slammed a finger in a door. With each scene, the characters' nerves tighten and Paul gets closer to the end of his rope. He seems to spoil everything he touches and to be lurching toward tragedy—Sarah having an accident perhaps, or Susan trying to commit suicide—which would turn LOVE HURTS into the straight drama it possibly should have been. A violent storm is necessary to burst the whole family's tension. But, instead, we are offered a queasy resolution—Karen goes through with her marriage and Sarah substitutes for her mom in Paul's house, which is more depressing than a tragedy as it offers no chance for change.

LOVE HURTS is a perfect companion to all those books characterizing dysfunctional families except without the solutions. The characters are well acted in their relentless pathos; thus they become increasingly repellant to watch. Only Sarah, probably the worst off of all, offers some variety and relief. She is miserable but savvy and ready to work her parents' divorce for everything she can get. Nowadays, maybe there isn't a way of halting the geometric disintegration of the nuclear family; however, comedy is a callous forum for this revelation. *(Adult situations.)*

p, Bud Yorkin; d, Bud Yorkin; w, Ron Nyswaner; ph, Adam Greenberg; ed, John C. Horger; prod d, Armin Ganz; set d, Leslie Rollins; cos, Elizabeth McBride

Comedy/Drama **(PR: C MPAA: R)**

LOVE POTION NO. 9 ★★½

104m Anarchy Productions; Fox ~ Fox c

Tate Donovan *(Paul Matthews)*, Sandra Bullock *(Diane Farrow)*, Mary Mara *(Marisa)*, Dale Midkiff *(Gary Logan)*, Hillary Bailey Smith *(Sally)*, Dylan Baker *(Prince Geoffrey)*, Anne Bancroft *(Madame Ruth)*, Blake Clark *(Motorcycle Cop)*, Bruce McCarty *(Jeff)*, Rebecca Staab *(Cheryl)*, Adrian Paul *(Enrico Pazzoli)*, Ric Reitz *(Dave)*, Steven Burnett *(Ron)*, Jordan Baker *(Joanne)*, Ken Strong *(Dick Webster)*, Gary Watkins *(Secret Service Agent)*, Scott Higgs *(Male Secretary)*, James Sbardellati *(Dino)*, Libby Whittemore *(R.T. Moreno)*, David Baer *(Marisa's Driver)*, Marc Gowan *(Priest)*, Esther Huston *(Mary)*, Lisa Coles *(Blonde at Bar)*, Timothy Martin *(Man at Bar)*, Susan Fassig *(Cheryl's Friend)*, Rob Cleveland *(Station Cop)*, Kathryn Firago *(Woman in Bridesroom)*, Jennifer Hale *(Catty Woman)*, Victoria Tabaka *(Catty Woman)*, David Dwyer *(Riot Cop)*, Virgil Beckham *(Riot Cop)*, Ann Taylor Boutwell *(Church Lady)*, Edith Ivey *(Church Lady)*, Andra Millian *(Matron)*

Writer-producer-director Dale Launer's breezy comedy LOVE POTION NO. 9 is the perfect date movie. It's light and fast-paced, with several funny moments and a predictably happy ending. Don't look for anything beyond that.

Paul Matthews (Tate Donovan) and Diane Farrow (Sandra Bullock) are two nerdy twentysomethings who have so much in common it almost hurts. They're both boring psychobiologists, specializing in the behavior patterns of primates. They also share adjoining apartments, listen to the same music, read the same books and have not been on a real date in years. Diane is resigned to sporadic middle-of-the-night visits from Gary Logan (Dale Midkiff), a user who can't find anybody else in the bars. Paul has such low self-esteem that he'll only talk to women when his friends give him money as a dare. When they set him up with a hooker, Marisa (Mary Mara), Paul spends two hours chatting. Desperate, Paul visits an enigmatic fortune teller, Madame Ruth (Anne Bancroft), who, after reading his palm and identifying his lack of female companionship, gives him some love potion number eight. It is guaranteed to make him irresistible to women.

Initially reluctant to try it, he throws the formula in the garbage. After seeing the effects of the potion on his cat and then on a chimpanzee at the lab, however, Paul and Diane agree to test the stuff on themselves. (The magic ingredient only works for four hours at a time, so they must constantly ingest more.) The pair agree not to see each other for three weeks, and then to report back and compare notes. Diane gets immediate results and is wooed, first by a dashing European car designer, Enrico Pazzoli (Adrian Paul), and then by Prince Geoffrey of England (Dylan Baker). Overnight, she is transformed from a frumpy wallflower to a siren surrounded by men—even the sleazy Gary begins showing her surprising respect. Paul, meanwhile, gets his revenge on a blonde who had previously made a fool of him, and then seduces an entire sorority house for good measure.

When the two get together to compare notes, they are both surprised to see the change in one another. They both are sporting cool haircuts, nice clothing and newfound confidence. They go out on a date of their own and get along so fabulously that, without the aid of the aphrodisiac, they end up in bed after a terrific night together.

Paul decides to propose marriage to Diane and shows up with a diamond ring and honeymoon tickets. Diane, though, has run off with Gary, who found out about the love potion and bought the remainder from Madame Ruth. After revisiting the fortune teller, Paul is given love potion number nine which, if swallowed, will identify true love. After various misadventures, Paul shows up just as Diane and Gary are about to be married. She sips the new potion and realizes that Paul is the real love of her life.

LOVE POTION NO. 9 achieves occasional moments of hipness or subtlety, but these are far outweighed by a preponderence of easy, tasteless gags. The material is helped by a charming cast. As the geeky monkey-doctor, Donovan (CLEAN AND SOBER, MEMPHIS BELLE) is a quirky presence, particularly hilarious in one extended monologue late in the film. Bullock makes a winning Cinderella figure and Mara (MR. SATURDAY NIGHT) gives an effectively over-the-top performance as the hooker.

LOVE POTION NO. 9 marks a disappointing directorial debut for Launer, whose screenplays include RUTHLESS PEOPLE, DIRTY ROTTEN SCOUNDRELS and MY COUSIN VINNY. *(Profanity.)*

p, Dale Launer; d, Dale Launer; w, Dale Launer; ph, William Wages; ed, Suzanne Pettit; m, Jed Leiber; prod d, Linda Pearl; art d, Thomas Minton; set d, Sally Nicolaou; cos, Timothy D'Arcy

Comedy/Romance **(PR: C MPAA: PG-13)**

LOVER, THE ★★½

(France/U.K.) 110m Renn Productions; Films A2; Burrill Productions ~ MGM c

(AMANT, L)

Jane March *(Young Marguerite Duras)*, Tony Leung *(Chinese Man)*, Frederique Meininger *(Mother)*, Arnaud Giovaninetti *(Elder Brother)*, Melvil Poupaud *(Younger Brother)*, Lisa Faulkner *(Helene Lagonelle)*, Xiem Mang *(Chinese Man's Father)*, Philippe LeDem *(French Teacher)*, Ann Schaufuss *(Anne-Marie Stretter)*, Quach Van-an *(Driver)*, Tania Torrens *(Principal)*, Raymonde Heudeline *(Writer)*, Yvonne Wingerter *(Writer)*, Do Minh-vien *(Young Boy)*, Helene Patarot *(Assistant Mistress)*, Jeanne Moreau *(Voice of Marguerite Duras)*

Jean-Jacques Annaud's film version of Marguerite Duras's evocative, beautifully imagined novel is a soft-core porno hash with pretensions to high art. Annaud focuses on *The Lover*'s most accessible aspects—"hot" sex scenes, the scenic pictorialism of 1930s Saigon, an overall ambiance of flushed exotica—and wholly misses the poetry, fatalism and brilliant economy which made Duras's prose as haunting as a recurring dream.

While on a ferry crossing the Mekong River, a fifteen-year-old French girl (Jane March) encounters a wealthy young Chinese man (Tony Leung) who will forever affect her life. They begin a torrid affair which provides her impoverished family with material gain, while simultaneously bringing on the disapprobation of a bigoted society. Her mother (Frederique Meininger) and brothers (Arnaud Giovaninetti and Melvil Poupaud) gladly accept the cash and fancy meals the Asian bestows, while treating him with the barely concealed contempt that is the unquestioned prerogative of their race and class. The girl, who is nothing if not enigmatic, finds herself rather the master in the relationship, for it is really the man who falls hard for her and suffers from outside pressures. The relationship ends when his family forces him to break with her and marry his designated-from-birth, aristocratic Chinese bride. However, the memory of him will obsess her through adulthood and greatly affect her as the writer she is to become.

Annaud (QUEST FOR FIRE, THE NAME OF THE ROSE) would have done well to study Frank Capra's most atypical, erotically astonishing film, THE BITTER TEA OF GENERAL YEN, which handled a similar story with real sensuality, romance and dramatic vigor. Although unseen, Jeanne Moreau is the most felicitously employed person in THE LOVER. Her magisterially jaded voice narrates the action and gives it some fitful flavor and a sense of something higher—like art—sorely lacking in the writing and direction.

Working on an obviously sizeable budget, Annaud offers some handsome visuals. The fabled first river crossing is given its full due, with the image of the girl, eccentrically clad in a man's fedora and gold high heels, leaning against a railing as the Asian's immense, gleaming limousine encroaches on her. In the film's single light-hearted moment, cleaning day at the girl's house is shown, with pails of water being sluiced across the floors, while her mother joyously pounds a piano and the kids go crazy. There's a tantalizing sequence, set in the girl's convent, in which she and a chum practice the tango in a hall shot through with late afternoon sun. And, of course, there are those sex scenes, which take place in a ramshackle room where only the thinnest, shuttered wall separates the writhing lovers from the teeming noise and smell of the streetmarket.

March, who was cast following an extensive search, is subjected to intensive sexual scrutiny by the camera, her every body part and orgasmic expression proffered to view. Leung, meanwhile, in keeping with the usual double standards, shows no frontal nudity. Dialogue is scarce in the film, so his character comes across as a callow, beautifully tailored stiff. (He barely registers any pain at his rejection by the girl's boorish family.) March has the requisite child-woman quality and evinces some sly humor but she, too, is stymied by the schematic screenplay. She is far more convincing as an emblem of nostalgic, adolescent eroticism than as one of France's most distinguished future writers. Small wonder, then, that Duras herself has publicly disowned this adaptation. *(Violence, nudity, sexual situations, adult situations.)*

p, Claude Berri, Paul Rassam; d, Jean-Jacques Annaud; w, Jean-Jacques Annaud, Gerard Brach, (from the novel by Marguerite Duras); ph, Robert Fraisse; ed, Noelle Boisson; m, Gabriel Yared; prod d, Thanh At Hoang; art d, Olivier Rudot; set d, Sophie Martel; cos, Yvonne Sassinot DeNesle

AAN Cinematography: Robert Fraisse

Erotic/Drama **(PR: O MPAA: R)**

LOWER LEVEL ★½

(U.S./Canada) 88m Neo Motion Pictures ~ Republic Pictures Home Video c

Elizabeth Gracen *(Hillary White)*, David Bradley *(Sam)*, Jeff Yagher *(Craig)*, Shari Shattuck, David H. Sterry

A glossy but base thriller that fuses FATAL ATTRACTION with DIE HARD, the lowbrow LOWER LEVEL sports a plot with more padding than the limbs of the stunt personnel.

Hillary White (Elizabeth Gracen) is a successful architect ensconced in a lonely executive suite atop the highrise office building she's just designed. She has a yuppie lover named Sam (David Bradley) who won't commit, and she vents her frustrations in torrid diary entries calling upon a handsome stranger to come and rescue her from this ivory tower (it sounds even dopier in voice-over). Unbeknownst to Hillary, a muscular meathead of a security guard named Craig (Jeff Yagher) is infatuated with her and surreptitiously reads her secret journal, taking her fantasies quite literally.

One day when the architect stays late, Craig locks up the building, trapping Hillary and Sam inside. Craig thus expects to force Hillary into a hot date with him; as the obsessed psycho later says, it seemed like a good idea at the time. When it fails, Craig tricks Sam into an open elevator shaft, then plays out lengthy cat-and-mouse scenes with the frantic heroine. "You really want to hurt me, huh?" posits Craig as Hillary bashes his skull with a fire extinguisher. The low blow of an ending has Craig abruptly choosing to dive off the roof, as if director Kristine Peterson just gave up when the stopwatch approached the ninety-minute mark.

Peterson knows how to create suspense using sounds and silences, but the dominant mood in LOWER LEVEL is frustration, with the minuscule cast behaving like idiots to prevent the tale from finishing early or logically. When Hillary and Sam find themselves sealed in the parking garage, what is their first impulse? To have sex, of course. The act gives Hillary a brainstorm, and she triggers the overhead sprinkler system; that doesn't save them, but it does offer viewers the sight of Gracen in a wet slip. Craig recovers instantly from violence and situations that would have killed anyone in reality, and the protagonists idiotically muff chance after chance to escape.

The sleek Gracen has been seen before in movie and TV roles, but she is most notorious as the 1982 Miss America winner, and the first wearer of the crown to pose later for *Playboy*. LOWER LEVEL had a low-profile release to home video. *(Violence, profanity, nudity, sexual situations.)*

p, Michael Leahy, W.K. Border; d, Kristine Peterson; w, Joel Soisson, (from the story by Michael Leahy, W.K. Border, Hilary Black); ph, Wally Pfister; ed, Nina Gilberti; m, Terry Plumeri; prod d, Dennis Brown; cos, Jami Burrows

Thriller **(PR: O MPAA: R)**

LUNATIC, THE ★★★

93m Paul Heller/John Pringle Productions; Island Pictures; Intrepid Productions; The Lunatic Company ~ Triton Pictures c

Julie T. Wallace *(Inga)*, Paul Campbell *(Aloysius)*, Reggie Carter *(Busha)*, Carl Bradshaw *(Service)*, Winston Stona *(Linstrom)*, Linda Gambrill *(Sarah)*, Rosemary Murray *(Widow Dawkins)*, Lloyd Reckord *(The Judge)*, Reggie Carter *(Voice of Strongheart Tree)*

Viewers who enjoyed THE GODS MUST BE CRAZY and BAGDAD CAFE will likely be delighted with Lol Creme's THE LUNATIC, an off-beat, droll saunter underneath the Jamaican Sun.

Improving upon the Lerner-Loewe song, Aloysius (Paul Campbell) doesn't just talk to the trees, he converses with all living creations—from cows to bushes. Picking up scraps of education by eavesdropping at the schoolhouse, this lunatic is a local eccentric, a fringe dweller who's barely tolerated. That outcast status changes when an Amazonian tourist enters his picturesque paradise. Part Eve, part serpent, Inga (Julie T. Wallace) tramples all over Mother Nature, introduces Aloysius to non-stop fornication, and dominates the simple-Simon peasant until he becomes her puppet. Snapping photographs like a shutter-fiend and grappling with the local customs and language like an explorer determined to conquer the New World, she seems to devour everyone and everything in her path.

Not content with one man, Inga also adopts Service Johnson (Carl Bradshaw), the local butcher, for fun and games. Before this *menage a trois* can settle into domestic bliss, however, Inga's papa cuts off her travel funds. Inga panics and insists her two pawns join her in burglarizing the home of civic leader Busha (Reggie Carter). Although Aloysius feels a loyalty to his community and even becomes a local hero at a cricket match, Inga is powerfully seductive. Unfortunately, the plot gets out of hand and Service nearly murders Busha who arrives home unexpectedly with his wife on church day.

During the ensuing trial Inga defends Aloysius for saving Busha's life before she herself is whisked back to Europe by her father. Forgiven by Busha and aquitted, Aloysius is adopted by a local widow who plans to take care of his spiritual and physical needs in the future. But despite her civilizing influence and the corrupting touch of a tourist, Aloysius can still communicate with plants and animals.

Depending on one's mood and taste for whimsy, THE LUNATIC could provide an exotic vacation from more mainstream fare. Without being condescending to Aloysius, its naive focal point, the film establishes its folksy tone from the outset and rarely falters. Since the lilt of the Jamaican language is so musical and the film's cinematography captures the drenching warmth of the West Indies sun, the viewer is comfortably lulled into accepting the far-fetched escapades.

Sweetly acted by the largely unfamiliar cast, THE LUNATIC gradually persuades viewers of the wisdom of the central character's world view. However, when the film introduces the trouble-making Inga, it often unwisely shifts its emphasis from folk humor to low comedy. As amusing as Julie T. Wallace is (she was indelible as the eponymous heroine of TV's "The Lives and Loves of a She-Devil"), she often threatens to pulverize this fable with overplaying in the broadest manner. Like Aloysius, the viewer is often in the position of being pleasantly but decidedly crushed by this statuesque dominatrix.

Directed by former 10CC member Lol Creme (who, along with partner Kevin Godley, became a pioneer in the music video field), THE LUNATIC triumphs over its shortcomings by always returning to form with a measure of gently breezy humor. *(Violence, profanity, sexual situations.)*

p, Paul Heller, John Pringle; d, Lol Creme; w, Anthony C. Winkler, (from his novel); ph, Richard Greatrex; ed, Michael Connell; m, Wally Badarou, Burning Flames; art d, Giorgio Ferrari; cos, Pat Griffiths

Comedy **(PR: O MPAA: R)**

LUNATICS: A LOVE STORY ★★½

87m Renaissance Pictures ~ Columbia TriStar Home Video c

Theodore Raimi *(Hank)*, Deborah Foreman *(Nancy)*, Bruce Campbell *(Ray)*, George Aguilar *(Comet)*, Brian McCree *(Presto)*

Despite its title, this offbeat, low-budget romantic comedy is *not* a spoof of Paul Mazursky's ENEMIES: A LOVE STORY. It is rather an original production of director Sam Raimi's (EVIL DEAD, DARKMAN) independent Renaissance Pictures, produced by and costarring Raimi regular Bruce Campbell. LUNATICS: A LOVE STORY's lineage is worth noting mainly due to its similarities to the EVIL DEAD movies, here played for laughs instead of shocks.

Theodore Raimi (Sam's brother; he played the thug who met a grisly end in DARKMAN by being thrust headfirst up through a manhole cover into heavy traffic by the terminally ticked-off title character) stars as nerdy Hank, a former mental patient and aspiring poet who hasn't left his downtown LA apartment since moving in six months earlier. Besides rampaging agoraphobia, he is also tortured by debilitating hallucinations of doctors trying to inject him with huge needles and perform lobotomies on him. Other hallucinations are less unpleasant, such as a lingerie model on a billboard across from his apartment who comes to life and pays him an afternoon visit.

Newly arrived from Iowa with boyfriend Ray (Campbell), Nancy (VALLEY GIRL's Deborah Foreman) meanwhile has come to think of herself as a jinx to everything she touches, including a cute puppy that immediately runs into the street and gets flattened by a truck only seconds after she pets it. After Ray abandons her, taking all her money with him, Nancy gets thrown out of her seedy hotel for getting behind on the rent and is left to wander the streets. She immediately gets in trouble with a menacing street gang after shooting off the toe of the gang leader with his own gun. Hiding out in a phone booth from the vengeful thugs, she gets a call from Hank, who has misdialed while trying to reach a 976 sex line. To get off the street, she offers to come and see Hank but, despite their shared love of poetry, she flees almost immediately when confronted by Hank's eccentric habits, like papering his entire apartment in tinfoil to keep the imaginary doctors from getting to him through his walls. Lovesmitten Hank conquers his fears, albeit not before wrapping most of his body in tinfoil, to follow and find Nancy in the nick of time, just as the gang leader, complete with his toe cast, is moving in for the kill.

Despite being credited to writer-director Josh Becker, LUNATICS: A LOVE STORY is easily at its best when it most resembles Raimi's own EVIL DEAD pictures, in which Campbell was plunged into a multi-sequel world of illusionary horrors after reading aloud from the Book of the Dead. Hank's hallucinations here are a running gag, made funnier by the filmmakers' making their obviously microscopic budget part of the gag. The results include some of the most unabashedly cheesy stop-motion effects since "Gumby," when Hank imagines tiny spiders popping out of his brain, and some of the most blatantly artificial rear-projection sequences since MARNIE, when Hank gets chased by a garbage truck he imagines to be a giant spider. At their best, also in common with the EVIL DEAD series, the hallucinations take on a riveting intensity that help to cover up a shaky screenplay. One scene, in which Hank imagines a city street splitting open under his feet, would look impressive in a film with many times the budget of LUNATICS. Next to scenes like these, however, the love story can't help but seem like pretty tepid stuff. And, in fact, there's barely enough to it to carry a feature-length film.

Still, LUNATICS, which is never less than intelligent throughout, is smart enough to end before it wears out its welcome entirely. And, along the way, Raimi keeps his hysteria likably low-key and Foreman, especially, brings a real sweetness to her character that gives the film a warmth it might otherwise have lacked. Though hardly a low-budget breakthrough, LUNATICS is nevertheless an agreeably imaginative change of pace from the usual B-movie exploitation fare, made more so by some of the most original genre filmmakers currently working. *(Violence, profanity, adult situations.)*

p, Bruce Campbell; d, Josh Becker; w, Josh Becker; ph, Jeff Dougherty; ed, Kaye Davis; m, Joseph Lo Duca; prod d, Peter Gurski

Comedy/Romance **(PR: C MPAA: PG-13)**

MAGICAL WORLD OF CHUCK JONES, THE ★★

100m Magical World Pictures; Industrial FX Productions ~ Warner Bros. c

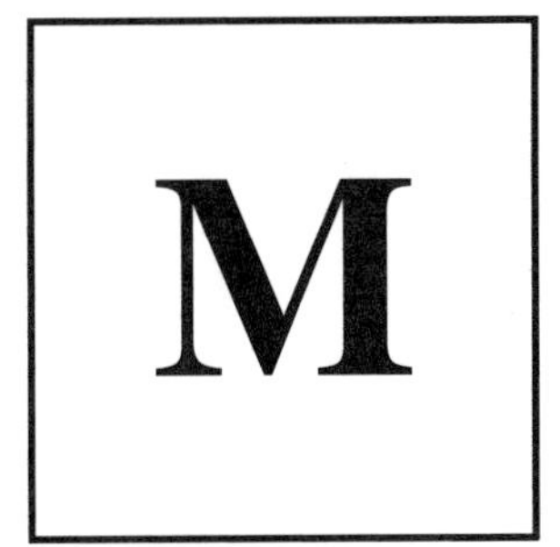

Steven Spielberg, Whoopi Goldberg, Ron Howard, Matt Groening, Leonard Maltin, Joe Dante, George Lucas, Steve Guttenberg, Chris Connelly, Danny Elfman, Gary Rydstrom, Fritz Freleng, Roddy McDowall, June Foray, Kathleen Helppie-Shipley, Maurice Noble, Roger Mayer, Linda Jones Claugh, Marian Jones, Valerie Kausen, Chuck Jones

Prepared in commemoration of animator Chuck Jones' eightieth birthday by George Daugherty, creator of the stage hit *Bugs Bunny on Broadway*, THE MAGICAL WORLD OF CHUCK JONES may be about the coolest birthday present anyone ever had, but average viewers may find themselves bored and baffled rather than enlightened or entertained.

Jones's accomplishments are certainly extensive and important and this "What's up Doc-umentary" contains snippets of numerous high points. While one of the top directors at Warner Bros. animation unit through the 1950s and early 60s, Jones steered Bugs Bunny, Daffy Duck, Elmer Fudd and Porky Pig through some of their most memorable adventures in THE RABBIT OF SEVILLE, noted for Elmer's timeless "Kill the Wabbit" aria set to Wagner's "Ride of the Valkyrie," DUCK AMUCK, in which animation's own "fourth wall" is broken down when an unseen artist torments Daffy during a labor dispute, and countless disasters visited upon Jones's creation Wile E. Coyote in his tireless pursuit of the Road Runner (Beep! Beep!).

During his later tenure with MGM, Jones turned to more abstract animation pieces such as THE DOT AND THE LINE and THE PHANTOM TOLLBOOTH while trying to breathe new life into that studio's hallmark "Tom and Jerry" cartoon series. But to most, Jones may actually be best-known for his collaboration with Dr. Seuss on a half-hour adaptation of the children's author's *How the Grinch Stole Christmas*, which has aired on network TV annually in the 25 years since it was first broadcast, to consistently high ratings.

Alas, THE MAGICAL WORLD OF CHUCK JONES is not the best introduction to either the man or his work. The bulk of the running time is devoted to testimonial tributes from the current Hollywood elite, starting with Steven Spielberg and ranging from Whoopi Goldberg to Ron Howard and Joe Dante—the director of GREMLINS who has probably the most compelling claim to being Jones's true creative heir—down to Steve Guttenberg, a tenuous choice who mainly seems interested in plugging his development deal at Paramount.

Clips from the cartoons are interspersed with these tributes. Sometimes they're grouped to illustrate a point made by the more informed toasters, such as Goldberg's explication of Jones's infallible sense of comic timing and film composer Danny Elfman's (BATMAN) notes on Jones' witty use of sound effects and Carl Stalling's usually underappreciated music. More often, unfortunately, the clips function as welcome, usually all-too-brief relief from the admittedly deserved but no less tiresome gush that largely dominates the film. What there is all too little of is any information on the history of Warner Bros. or Jones's place in it. The clips themselves aren't even completely identified until the end credits.

Given the type of film THE MAGICAL WORLD OF CHUCK JONES is—a testimonial by industry insiders *for* industry insiders—the sketchiness is not surprising. But for the general audience it's hard not to feel that a great opportunity was missed by not giving more time to Friz Freleng (Jones's mentor at Warner Bros.), Jones himself, who appears only briefly, and especially critic-historian Leonard Maltin. *(Cartoon violence.)*

p, David Ka Lik Wong, George Daugherty; d, George Daugherty; w, George Daugherty; ph, Peter Bonilla; ed, Peter E. Berger, Rick Trader; m, Cameron Patrick

Documentary (PR: A MPAA: PG)

MALCOLM X ★★★★

201m 40 Acres and a Mule Filmworks; Marvin Worth Productions ~ Warner Bros. c

Denzel Washington *(Malcolm X)*, Angela Bassett *(Betty Shabazz)*, Albert Hall *(Baines)*, Al Freeman, Jr. *(Elijah Muhammad)*, Delroy Lindo *(West Indian Archie)*, Spike Lee *(Shorty)*, Theresa Randle *(Laura)*, Kate Vernon *(Sophia)*, Lonette McKee *(Louise Little)*, Tommy Hollis *(Earl Little)*, James McDaniel *(Brother Earl)*, Ernest Thomas *(Sidney)*, Jean LaMarre *(Benjamin 2X)*, O.L. Duke *(Pete)*, Larry McCoy *(Sammy)*, Maurice Sneed *(Cadillac)*, Debi Mazar *(Peg)*, Phyllis Yvonne Stickney *(Honey)*, Scot Anthony Robinson *(Daniel)*, James E. Gaines *(Cholly)*, Joe Seneca *(Toomer)*, Latanya Richardson *(Lorraine)*, Wendell Pierce *(Ben Thomas)*, Michael Guess *(William X)*, Leland Gantt *(Wilbur Kinley)*, Giancarlo Esposito *(Thomas Hayer)*, Leonard Thomas *(Leon Davis)*, Roger Guenveur Smith *(Rudy)*, Craig Wasson *(TV Host)*, Graham Brown *(Dr. Payson)*, Gerica Cox *(Eva Marie)*, Kristan Rai Segure *(Saudi)*, Lauren Padick *(Lisha)*, Danielle Fletcher *(Attalah)*, Robinson Frank Adu *(Chuck)*, Aleta Mitchell *(Sister Robin)*, Curt Williams *(Mr. Cooper)*, John Ottavino *(Blades)*, John Reidy *(Simmons)*, Frances Foster *(Woman Outside Audubon Ballroom)*, Reggie Montgomery *(Dick Jones)*, David Patrick Kelly *(Mr. Ostrowski)*, Gary L. Catus *(Doctor)*, Sharon Washington *(Augusta)*, Shirley Stoler *(Mrs. Swerlin)*, Oran "Juice" Jones *(Hustler)*, Ricky Gordon *(Lionel Hampton)*, George Lee Miles *(Preacher)*, Raye Dowell *(Sister Evelyn Williams)*, Veronica Webb *(Sister Lucille Rosary)*, Abdul Salaam El Razaac *(Fox)*, Keith Smith *(Brother Gene)*, George Guidall *(Mr. Holway)*, James L. Swain *(Conductor)*, Pee Wee Love *(Speedy)*, Lawrence James *(Tully)*, Steve White *(Brother Johnson)*, K. Smith *(Roderick)*, Christopher Rubin *(Sophia's Husband)*, Matthew Harris *(Malcolm–Age 5)*, Zakee Howze *(Young Malcolm)*, Cytia Fontenette *(Hilda–Age 3)*, Marlaine Bass *(Hilda–Age 8)*, Benjamin Atwell *(Philbert–Age 1)*, Peter Dunn *(Philbert–Age 6)*, Dion Smack, Jr. *(Reginald–Age 2)*, Darnell Smith *(Elijah Muhammad's Grandson)*, TaiNesha Scott *(Elijah Muhammad's Granddaughter)*, Chelsea Counts *(Yvonne–Age 6 Months)*, Chela Counts *(Yvonne–Age 6 Months)*, Natalie Clanton *(Yvonne–Age 1)*, Jessica Givens *(Attalah)*, LaToyah Bigelow *(Quibillah–Age 3)*, Martaleah Jackson *(Ilyasah–Age 2 and 3)*, Tamaraleah Jackson *(Ilyasah–Age 2 and 3)*, Jasmine Smith *(Ilyasah–Age 2 and 3)*, Valentino Smith *(Wilfred–Age 4)*, David Thomas, Jr. *(Wilfred–Age 8)*, Simon Do-Ley *(Son of Elijah Muhammad and Secretary Evelyn Williams)*, Bill Goldberg *(The "John")*, Jonathan Peck *(Phone Voice)*, Leonard Parker *(Jason)*, Lennis Washington *(Mrs. Johnson)*, Dyan Humes *(Maid at Open Air Market)*, Lizabeth MacKay *(White Woman in Market)*, Terry Layman *(CIA Agent)*, Terry Sumter *(CIA Agent)*, Jasper McGruder *(Hotel Clerk)*, Mary Alice Smith *(School Teacher)*, Wyatt T. Walker *(Hospital Spokesperson)*, Hazel Medina *(Cashier Person)*, Wendy E. Taylor *(Numbers Woman)*, Ed Herlihy *(Joe Louis Announcer)*, Ralph Cooper, Sr. *(Radio Announcer)*, Christian J. Dacosta *(Passerby)*, Karen T. Duffy *(Sophia's Friend)*, Walter Jones *(Barber's Customer)*, Marc Phillips *(Photographer)*, Showman Uneke *(Hustler at Grand Central Station)*, Theara Ward *(Movie Goer)*, Larry Cherry *(Prison Barber)*, Clebert Ford, Grafton Trew, Rogers Simon, George T. Odom *(Barbers)*, Vincent Moscaritola *(Prison Guard)*, Larry Attile *(Guard Baines)*, Brendan Kelly *(Guard Cone)*, John Griesemer *(Guard Wilkins)*, Fia Porter *(Coed)*, Billy Mitchell *(1st Man)*, Kent Jackman *(2nd Man)*, Beatrice Winde *(Elderly Woman)*, Fracaswell Hyman *(Bartender)*, Rion Johnson *(Shoeshine Boy)*, Charles Weldon, Mike Hodge, Ira Little, Ilyasah Shabazz, Bahni Turpin *(Followers at Temple Number 7)*, Aaron Blackshear, Nilyne Fields, John David Washington, Rudi Bascomb, Muhammad Parks, Chinere Parry, Ian Quiles, Sharmeek Martinez *(Students in Harlem Classroom)*, Chuck Cooper, Damon Chandler, Shellye D. Broughton, Nicholas Barnwell, Sam Dixon, Barbara Smith *(Customers)*, Rome Neal, Earl Whitted, Michael C. Mahon, Addison Cook, Byron Utley, George Rafferty, Maxwell Sinovoi, Eric Swirsly *(Prisoners)*, Stewart J. Zully, Colleen Cowan, Armand Schultz, Reade Kelly, Janet Zarish, Annie Corley, Stephen James, Steven Randazzo, Christopher Skutch, William Swinton, Marcus Naylor, Anthony Nocerino *(TV Reporters)*, Gareth Williams, Stephen Hanan, Richard Schiff, David Berman *(JFK Reporters)*, Michael Imperioli *(Reporter at Fire Bombing)*, Steve Stapenhorst *(Reporter at Fire Bombing)*, Arthur French *(Pullman Porter)*, Lex Monson *(Pullman Porter)*, Judd Jones *(Pullman Porter)*, C.E. Smith *(Fountain Waiter)*, Erika Smith-Brown *(Waitress)*, Raymond Anthony Thomas *(Crowd Member)*, Delilah Picart *(Crowd Member)*, Michael Ralph *(Crowd Member)*, Monique Cintron, Jake-Ann Jones, Sharon Ferguson, Amelia "Mimi" Walker, Neisha Folkes-Le'Melle, Lenore Pemberton, Felicia Wilson, Yvette Brooks *(Hookers)*, Teresa Yvon Farley *(Young Hooker)*, Kiki Della Vecchia *(Teenage Whore)*, John Sayles *(FBI Agent)*, Martin Donovan *(FBI Agent)*, Jay Charbonneau *(Cop at Audobon)*, Joe Pentangelo, Mike Farley, Nick Muglia, David Reilly *(Mounted Police)*, Nick Turturro *(Boston Cop)*, James Murtaugh *(Cop at Harlem Station)*, William Fichtner *(Cop at Harlem Station)*, Tim Kelleher *(Cop at Harlem Station)*, Michael Cullen *(Desk Sergeant)*, James MacDonald *(Lieutenant)*, Steve Aronson, Bill Anagnos, Don Hewitt, Jery Hewitt *(Black Legion Members)*, Joe Fitos, Manny Siverio, Jack McLaughlin, Shaun O'Neil, Andy Duppin, Elmer Licciardello *(KKK Members)*, Matt Dillon *(DJ at the Harlem "Y" Dance)*, Renton Kirk *(DJ at the Harlem "Y" Dance)*, Tim Hutchinson, Andre Blair, Abdul Kakeem Hijrah, Rony Clanton *(Fruits of Islam)*, Scott Whitehurst, Eric Payne, Ali Abdul Wahbah, Terry Hodges, Kevan Gibbs, Dana Hubbard *(Malcolm's FOI)*, David Reivers, Robert Jason, Kevin Rock, Mansoor Najeeullah, Dion Graham, Zaahir Muhammad, Gregory Bargeman, Lee Summers, Rich Gordon, Larry Rushing *(Elijah Muhamad's FOI)*, Monty Ross *(MC–Roseland)*, Eddie Davis, Reggie Pittman, Patrick Rickman, Gerald Brazel *(Trumpet Players)*, Clark Gaton *(Trombone Player)*, Richard Owens *(Trombone Player)*, Douglas Purviance *(Trombone Player)*, Mark Gross *(Alto Saxophone Player)*, Cleave Guyton, Jr. *(Alto Saxophone Player)*, Javon Jackson *(Tenor Saxophone Player)*, Lance Bryant *(Tenor Saxophone Player)*, Danielle LeMelle *(Baritone Saxophone Player)*, David Fludd *(Piano Player)*, Marcus Lauper *(Bass Player)*, Dwayne "Cook" Broadnax *(Drummer)*, Preston Vismale *(Music Assistant)*, Miki Howard *(Billie Holiday)*, Terence Blanchard *(Trumpet Plyer)*, Bruce David Barth *(Piano Player)*, Rodney Whitaker *(Bass Player)*, William E. Kilson *(Drummer)*, Sonny Allen, Vanessa Benton, Cheryl Burr, Leslie Dockery, Cisco Drayton, Byron Easley, John Elejalde, Debra Elkins, Gina Ellis, Sharon Ferguson, John Festa, Robert H. Fowler, III, Ryan Francois, Phillip Gilmore, Jauquette Greene, Wendy King, Jerome Jamal Hardeman, Dawn Hampton, Monique Harcum, Raymond Harris, Delphine T. Mantz, Bernard Marsh, Greta Martin, Norma Miller, Frances Morgan, John Parks, Greg Poland, Judine Hawkins Richard, Eartha Robinson, Michelle Robinson, Traci Robinson, Ken Leigh Rogers, Eddie Sanabria, Eddie Shellman, Lynn Sterling, Keith Thomas, Debbie Williams, Charles F. Young, Anthony Dewitt *(Roseland Dancers)*, Cynthia Thomas *(Shorty's Dance Partner)*, Sharon Brooks, Laurie Ann Gibson, El Tahara Ibrahim, Keith Lewis, Dereque Whithurs *(Skeleton Crew Dancers)*, Steve Reed *(John F. Kennedy)*, Jodie Farber *(Jackie Kennedy)*, Randy Means *(Governor Connally)*, Columbia DuBose *(Nellie Connally)*, Vincent D'Onofrio *(Bill Newman)*, Cliff Cudney *(Limo Driver)*, George Marshall Ruge *(Secret Service Man)*, Bobby Seale *(1st Speaker)*, Al Sharpton *(2nd Speaker)*, Christopher Plummer *(Chaplain Gill)*, Karen Allen *(Miss Dunne)*, Peter Boyle *(Captain Green)*, William Kunstler *(The Judge)*, Ossie Davis *(Eulogy Performer)*

No film of 1992 generated more prerelease controversy than Spike Lee's epic retelling of the life of Malcolm X. Many doubted the outspoken director's ability or willingness to present an even-handed version of the slain civil rights leader's life—particularly given the personal nature of Lee's previous work. Yet MALCOLM X proves to be a surprisingly balanced portrayal of the man's life, taking him through many different stages without judgment or criticism.

The movie begins during WWII, when Malcolm Little (Denzel Washington) and his friend Shorty (Lee) are hustlers in Boston's Black Roxbury section. Malcolm's father was a Baptist minister hounded by the KKK, who killed him in a death crudely staged to look like a suicide; subsequently Malcolm's mother went slowly insane and lost her children to foster parents. Taking a job as a railroad porter, Malcolm winds up in Harlem, where he joins a numbers gang run by West Indian Archie (Delroy Lindo), using the name Detroit Red. But he's forced to flee back to Boston after scamming money from Archie. Malcolm, Shorty and Malcolm's former lover, Sophia (Kate Vernon), then begin to pull burglaries together. After the group is caught and arrested, Malcolm ends up in Charleston State Prison, where his fellow prisoner Baines (Albert Hall) introduces him to the Islamic religion.

Malcolm comes to embrace the teachings of Elijah Muhammad as a way of escaping the "mental prison" that white society has placed him in. He also adopts the name Malcolm X, rejecting the surname Little as bestowed on his family by a white slavemaster. He also educates himself by, among other things, reading the dictionary from cover to cover. Baines points out the common definitions of "white" and "black," the former of which is defined as positive and the latter as negative. While still in jail, Malcolm has a vision of Elijah Muhammad.

After he's released from jail, Malcolm actually meets Elijah Muhammad (Al Freeman, Jr.) and becomes a spokesman for the Nation of Islam; his gift for oratory leads him to become one of the Nation's key figures. Along the way, he meets Shorty and finds that his old gang has broken up; he also meets, and later marries, Betty Shabazz (Angela Bassett), a Muslim nurse. After Malcolm demonstrates his influence by leading hundreds on a march to a Harlem hospital where a fellow Muslim is recovering from a police beating, Elijah Muhammad makes him the Nation's national spokesman.

Malcolm continues to proclaim the evils of the white man, and rejects integration and non-violent resistance to racial oppression. Meanwhile, Baines and other members of the Nation have become threatened by his prominence and begin to plot against him. Malcolm later finds out that Elijah Muhammad, who is the subject of two paternity suits brought by Muslim women, is worried about Malcolm superseding him and is also scheming against him. After Malcolm gives an interview in which he seems to justify President Kennedy's assassination, Elijah Muhammad forbids him to speak on behalf of the Nation for 90 days.

Leaving the Nation after hearing of further plans to kill him, Malcolm makes a pilgrimage to Mecca where, surrounded by people of all colors and races worshipping the same teachings, he realizes that all men are brothers and renounces his separatist beliefs. This further angers the Nation, and Malcolm's house is later firebombed. Despite knowing of the danger, Malcolm goes ahead with a speaking engagement at the Audubon Ballroom, where he is assassinated, presumably by members of the Nation.

MALCOLM X opens with a pair of intercut images clearly designed to stir up strong feelings about the current state of race relations: the notorious video footage of unarmed black motorist Rodney King being beaten by white L.A. policemen; and an American flag burning down into the shape of an "X." Yet this is one of only a few times in MALCOLM X where director Lee, working from a screenplay he co-wrote with Arnold Perl (based on an earlier, uncredited screenplay by the late James Baldwin, which, in turn, was based on the "autobiography" by Alex Haley), wears his racial opinions on his sleeve. He's not presenting Malcolm X as a symbol, but has the respect to treat him as a man, one capable of great change as he navigates through a racially turbulent America. Some spectators initially feared that the movie would emphasize Malcolm the separatist, focusing on his campaign against whites; others felt it would lean too far in the direction of his later "one world" persona. The truth is that the film gives time to both these incarnations of Malcolm and more.

It's significant that Malcolm is first seen having his hair straightened—a symptom, it's suggested, of the desire to "be white"—and that Malcolm rejects a Black lover in the film's early section in favor of the white Sophia. It is the film's willingness to present all sides of Malcolm's character that makes it so persuasive as a biography. Only once or twice after that opening does Lee feel compelled to make a dramatic statement—as when Baines tells Malcolm to recall the evil done to him by whites in the past, and Lee presents a brief flashback montage to the previously seen white characters, all of whom are variously bigoted or insensitive. Paradoxically, this evenhandedness seems to blunt the film's power just a bit; the anger that drove DO THE RIGHT THING (still widely acknowledged as Lee's best film to date) is reduced here. This is not to say that the material isn't powerful; but in maintaining an equivocal point of view of the story's events, the movie occasionally lacks the emotional effect it might have had, had it "taken sides."

There is no denying, however, the passion in Denzel Washington's performance, a superlative job of acting that transcends impersonation and gets to the soul of the man. The audience never questions his feelings and motivations, and Washington impressively brings across Malcolm's power as an orator, whether he's making a fiery outdoor speech to Black followers or calmly, forcefully addressing a white collegiate audience. When footage of the real Malcolm is shown at the film's end, it's nearly impossible to tell the difference; it's enough to lead a viewer to measure the real thing against the performance, not the other way around.

The rest of the cast is equally fine, particularly Al Freeman, Jr., who does just as persuasive a job of portraying the aging Elijah Muhammad. Lee's technical command keeps the film moving at all times; its epic length was another topic of controversy, but although the movie feels long, it's never boring. One comes away from MALCOLM X with the feeling of having witnessed more than just a dramatized story, but having experienced a complex, meaningful and powerful life. *(Violence, profanity, adult situations.)*

p, Marvin Worth, Spike Lee; d, Spike Lee; w, Spike Lee, Arnold Perl, James Baldwin; ph, Ernest Dickerson; ed, Barry Alexander Brown; m, Terence Blanchard; prod d, Wynn Thomas; art d, Tom Warren; set d, Ted Glass; cos, Ruth E. Carter

AAN Best Actor: Denzel Washington; *AAN Costume Design:* Ruth E. Carter

Biography/Historical/Drama (PR: C MPAA: PG-13)

MAMBO KINGS, THE ★★½

(U.S./France) 101m King Mambo Inc.; Alcor Films; New Regency Films; Le Studio Canal Plus ~ Warner Bros. c

Armand Assante *(Cesar Castillo)*, Antonio Banderas *(Nestor Castillo)*, Cathy Moriarty *(Lanna Lake)*, Maruschka Detmers *(Delores Fuentes)*, Desi Arnaz, Jr. *(Desi Arnaz, Sr.)*, Celia Cruz *(Evalina Montoya)*, Roscoe Lee Browne *(Fernando Perez)*, Vondie Curtis-Hall *(Miguel Montoya)*, Tito Puente *(Himself)*, Talisa Soto *(Maria Rivera)*, Joe Petruzzi *(Carlo Ricci)*, Ahn Duong *(Ismelda Perez)*, Cordelia Gonzales *(Anna Maria)*, Theodora Castellanos *(Blanca)*, Lazaro Perez *(Pablo)*, Helena Carroll *(Mrs. Shannon)*, John Herrera *(Luis Fajardo)*, Colleen Fitzpatrick *(Redhead on Bus)*, Jose Duvall *(Nando)*, Joe Conzo *(Killer)*, Miller P. *(Killer's Girlfriend)*, Doug Barron *(Mike Wells)*, Jose Alberto *(Johnny Casanova)*, Frank Grillo *(Machito)*, Ron Thompson *(Empire MC)*, June Brown *(Portly Woman)*, Valerie McIntosh *(Tracy Blair)*, Jonathan Delarco *(Young Cesar)*, Salvador Miranda *(Young Nestor)*, Carlos Gomez *(Creep)*, Adrian Martinez *(Pablito)*, Rene Monteaqudo *(Robertico)*, Cecelia Neal Ortiz *(Leticia)*, Jessica Neal Ortiz *(Leticia)*, Thomas F. Duffy *(Mulligan)*, Martin Charles Warner *(Mac)*, Joycelyn O'Brien *(Gina)*, Jessica Diamond *(Secretary)*, Stephanie Blake *(Stripper)*, Ryan Howell *(Kid with Basketball)*, Anita Banderas *(Anita)*, Diana Manzo *(Amanda)*, Dawn McKinster *(Poolside Patron)*, Karen Assante *(Karen)*, Julie Pinson *(2nd Girlfriend)*, Cynthia Santos *(Mario's Girlfriend)*, Susie Stillwell *(Club Patron)*, Maiquel Saurez *(Cleaning Lady)*, Natalie Zimmerman *(3rd Girlfriend)*, Debra Scott *(Enchantment)*, Pablo Calogero *(Ramon)*, Scott Cohen *(Bernardito)*, Mario Grillo *(Mario)*, Ralph Irizarry *(Pito)*, Pete MacNamara *(Johnny Bing)*, Marcos Quintanilla *(Willie)*, J.T. Taylor *(Frankie Suarez)*, William Thomas, Jr. *(Xavier)*, Yul Vazquez *(Flaco)*

Art gallery entrepreneur-turned-film director Arne Glimcher has made a splashy, entertaining film of Oscar Hijuelos' Pulitzer Prize-winning novel, *The Mambo Kings Play Songs of Love*. Although a long way from art, THE MAMBO KINGS is actually an improvement on the book, which was a vastly overrated, rambling laundry list of evocative names and places of 1950s Manhattan.

In its attempt to tell the simplest of stories, Hijuelos's narrative bumped repetitively along in nostalgic fits and starts, vexingly interlaced with graphic sex scenes that always seemed to focus on the dimensions and prowess of Cuban male genitalia. Glimcher and screenwriter Cynthia Cidre have cannily chosen to film only the first half of the book, which cuts down on the redundancy and trowel-laden bathos of Hijuelos's conception.

THE MAMBO KINGS is the story of two brothers, Cesar (Armand Assante) and Nestor Castillo (Antonio Banderas), who leave their native Cuba to pursue their dream of making it big through their music in the Big Apple. Their natures are wildly contrasting: Cesar is a fiery, indefatigable womanizer and braggart, while Nestor, the more deeply talented of the two, is introspective, haunted by an overweening sadness at being deserted by a lover, Maria Rivera (Talisa Soto), back home. Onstage, however, their styles coalesce beautifully and their percolating, irresistible music makes them the rage of the nightclubs. Nestor pens what is to be their signature song, "Beautiful Maria of My Soul," which flies out of the record stores, and eventually captures the attention of that most famous of all Cubanos, Desi Arnaz.

The brothers are signed to a guest appearance on the "I Love Lucy" show and thereby attain the pinnacle of their careers. However, as these things always seem to go, success does not equal happiness. Nestor's marriage to the idealistic Delores (Maruschka Detmers) is blighted by his obsessive memory of Maria. Randy Cesar has an unholy desire for his sister-in-law, which he barely conceals, and he furthermore alienates music industry bigwigs with his arrogant bravado. Nestor dies in an auto crash on a snowy, drunken night, leaving all to mourn his untimely passing but remember him forever through his music.

The plot is right out of 40s programmers like CITY FOR CONQUEST, ORCHESTRA WIVES and BLUES IN THE NIGHT, full of steamy temptresses, hot-blooded musicians, shady promoters, sentimental family loyalties, jealousy and cigarette smoke. Glimcher does nothing to conceal its hoariness, smartly choosing instead to go for the gusto. He pours on the peacock-hued photography (Michael Ballhaus's lensing is on the money), gaudy editing, blindingly fast choreography, glamorous costumes and, most vitally, the score, a vibrant compendium of popular songs of the era and original compositions (by the *real* Mambo King, Tito Puente), with that itchy, celebratory beat dominating throughout. The high diva of Latin music, Celia Cruz, is triumphantly present in the small role of a nightclub owner. With her massive turbans and flounces, voodoo prescience and roof-raising pipes, she presides over the film like a benign, tiki-visaged goddess.

Assante (PRIVATE BENJAMIN, BELIZAIRE THE CAJUN) is the propulsive motor of the film, and he labors overtime, serving up flashing teeth, sexy sizzle and exploding tantrums in the venerable Gilbert Roland-Ricardo Montalban-Fernando Lamas tradition. His Cesar seems to operate on a gallon of coffee, a swig of rum and a handful of amphetamines—the hardest working Latino in show biz. While one may have preferred to see someone like Andy Garcia, an authentic Cubano, in the role, there is no denying Assante's electricity. His more-flash-than-depth performance is in perfect synch with the sketchy, hedonistic spirit of the film. Banderas's character is a thankless simp, but to it he brings his iconographic male-madonna looks, suffers prettily, and both speaks English and sings amazingly well.

The wittily Bronx-tongued Cathy Moriarty (RAGING BULL, SOAPDISH) is again wasted in the role of cigarette girl Lanna Lake (those names of Hijuelos's!). But decked out in an upswept do and glitteringly skintight fishtail dresses, she's a sight to behold and seems ready as always to give a ripe, funny performance, however stymied by Hijuelos's superficial characterization and the filmmakers' having added nothing to it. Detmers disappointingly displays none of her famous sexuality (so evident in Godard's CARMEN and Bellochio's DEVIL IN THE FLESH), which could have enlivened the part of Delores, one of those virginal domestic drudges dating back to Blasco-Ibanez. Desi Arnaz, Jr., with a padded nose, gives a respectful, slyly funny impersonation of his father. There's a charming moment when the Castillos' entire neighborhood assembles to greet their great home-grown television star, as he leaves their apartment.

The marriage of Nestor and Delores is the film's high point, with Cruz joyously cutting loose on a "Guantanamera" which has everyone onscreen, as well as in the audience, rocking. The entire era is visually embodied in the wordless presence of fashion model Ahn Duong, who appears as a nightclub denizen. Her starkly attenuated elegance, reminiscent of such period style emblems as Dovima and Lisa Fonssagrives, framed in a plush quilted booth, is marvelously evocative. There's a delightful "success" montage, with the cut-out figures of Duong and Roscoe Lee Browne (playing her music mogul inamorata), mamboing over ebullient big screen images of the Castillo brothers, revelling in the chips.

Glimcher's directorial hand is less sure when it comes to the many emotionally charged scenes between the brothers, and between Nestor and Delores. (Cidre's screenplay is barely serviceable.) When in doubt, he throws in visual fillips, like a determined Cesar posing with a disconsolate Nestor in a vintage photo booth, or a silent, lusciously desaturated flashback sequence between Nestor and Maria, which project feeling far more than any stilted dialogue. THE MAMBO KINGS may not be deep, but it's suffused with a sensuality that movie-lovers devour; Banderas and Soto on a Cuban beach easily rate as one of cinema's most gorgeous couplings. *(Substance abuse, profanity, nudity, sexual situations, adult situations.)*

p, Arnon Milchan, Arne Glimcher; d, Arne Glimcher; w, Cynthia Cidre, (from the novel *The Mambo Kings Play Songs of Love* by Oscar Hijuelos and the poem "Guantanamera" by Jose Marti); ph, Michael Ballhaus; ed, Claire Simpson; m, Robert Kraft, Carlos Franzetti; prod d, Stuart Wurtzel; art d, Steve Sarlad; set d, Kara Lindstrom; cos, Ann Roth, Gary Jones, Bridget Kelly; ch, Michael Peters

AAN Best Song: Robert Kraft (music) and Arne Glimcher (lyrics)

Drama/Musical **(PR: C MPAA: R)**

MAN TROUBLE ★½

108m Man Trouble Productions; Penta Pictures; American Filmworks; Budding Grove Productions; Touchwood Co Productions ~ Fox c

Jack Nicholson *(Harry Bliss)*, Ellen Barkin *(Joan Spruance)*, Harry Dean Stanton *(Redmond Layls)*, Beverly D'Angelo *(Andy Ellerman)*, Michael McKean *(Eddy Revere)*, Saul Rubinek *(Laurence Moncrief)*, Viveka Davis *(June Huff)*, Veronica Cartwright *(Helen Dextra)*, David Clennon *(Lewie Duart)*, John Kapelos *(Detective Melvenos)*, Lauren Tom *(Adele Bliss)*, Paul Mazursky *(Lee MacGreevy)*, Gary Graham *(Butch Gable)*, Betty Carvalho *(Socorro)*, Mark J. Goodman *(Talk Show Host)*, Robin Greer *(Actress)*, Sandy Ignon *(Director)*, Rustam Branaman *(Thug)*, Lenny Citrano *(Thug)*, Christopher Garr *(Thug)*, Rob LaBelle *(Barman)*, Raymond Cruz *(Balto)*, Ed Kerrigan *(Kenneth Dowler)*, Daniel J. Goojvin *(Vincent Gallardo)*, Thomas Griep *(Pianist)*, June Christopher *(Heidi Robles)*, Matt Ingersoll *(Fingerprinter)*, Rebecca Broussard *(Hospital Administrator)*, Mary Robin Redd *(Sonya)*, John D. Russo *(Old Man)*, Anthony Frederick *(1st Smoking Guy)*, Max Delgado *(2nd Smoking Guy)*, Jeff Record *(Male Nurse)*, Mary Pat Gleason *(Vita)*, Gordon Reinhart *(Therapist)*, David St. James *(Admissions Clerk)*, Susan Bugg *(Woman in Chorus)*, Virgil Frye *(Sturge)*, Ken Thorley *(Dr. Monroe Park)*, Gerrielani Miyazaki *(Japanese Hostess)*, Jennifer Yang *(Japanese Waitress)*, Suzanne Lodge *(On-Camera Reporter)*, Suzanne Q. Burdeau *(News Reporter)*, Ginger LaBrie *(News Reporter)*, Vilas *(Duke)*, Charles A. Tamburro *(Helicopter Pilot)*, Michael Tamburro *(Helicopter Co-Pilot)*, Jacqueline M. Allen, Stephen W. Anderson, Samela A. Beasom, Bernice Brightbill, Martha L. Cowen, Michelle A. Fournier, Linda Harmon, Ron Hicklin, Marie T. Hodgson, Laurel L. James, Darlene Koldenhoven, Cathy A. Larsen, Marti C. Pia, Gloria Grace Prosper, Ellen Rabineer, Paula Rasmussen-Novros, Mary Heller Rawcliffe, Sally Stevens, Susan Danielle Stevens, Diane O. Thomas, Maurita L. Thornburgh, Kerry E. Walsh, Kari Windingstad *(Chorus Members)*

Even his most fervent fans would have to concede that superstar Jack Nicholson will not go down in history as one of the great screen comedians. The dispiriting misfire MAN TROUBLE proves why.

Harry Bliss (Nicholson) is the owner of the "House of Bliss," a purveyor of attack dogs for personal protection. Harry's office is overrun with puppies, however, leaving him only one adult dog, Duke, with which to conduct business—which is no problem, since Harry has no clients. In fact, Harry has sold Duke to his ex-partner, Lee MacGreevy (Paul Mazursky), who is trying to track Harry down to take delivery. Now, though, Harry is avoiding MacGreevy because a call from distraught opera singer, Joan Spruance (Ellen Barkin) has brought him a new account—not to mention the chance of a new romantic conquest. Romantic conquests are actually Harry's true specialty—something that has put his marriage to Adele (Lauren Tom), a Japanese-American whom Harry refers to as "Iwo Jima," on the rocks.

Joan calls Harry after someone breaks into her apartment in search of a manuscript written by her sister, Andy Ellerman (Beverly D'Angelo). The manuscript contains information that could embarrass Andy's rich, powerful ex-lover, Red Layls (Harry Dean Stanton), but the search was fruitless because the manuscript, mailed by Andy to Joan, hasn't yet arrived. At the same time, Joan is being menaced by a would-be lover, Eddy Revere (Michael McKean), and bullied by her soon-to-be ex-husband, Lewis Duart (David Clennon), her conductor for an upcoming concert.

When Andy shows up, she's promptly kidnapped by Layls and his sleazy lawyer Laurence Moncrief (Saul Rubinek), who slips Harry a $15,000 check to steal the manuscript from Joan upon its arrival. Instead, Harry, who has fallen in love with Joan, helps her rescue her sister and later foils Eddy's attempt to force himself on Joan. After Adele throws Harry out, he and Joan live happily ever after with Duke, who has escaped from Harry's ex-partner.

On paper, MAN TROUBLE looks unbeatable. Besides the terrific accumulation of talent in front of the cameras, the film was directed by Bob Rafelson and written by co-producer Carole Eastman—a duo who last collaborated with Nicholson on FIVE EASY PIECES. Given the results, a criminal investigation more than a review might be in order.

MAN TROUBLE is abysmally amateurish from start to finish, never making any kind of sense on any level at any time during its running time. Its plot is incoherent, its characters idiotic and its stars are completely lacking in chemistry. Nicholson, in particular, fails to get any kind of take on his character, pushing Harry's slobbishness to unlikely extremes and coming across as genuinely mean-spirited, racially prejudiced and sexist in his scenes with Adele. Opposite Barkin, he seems lost somewhere between romance and farce. At still other times he descends to the kind of broad, graceless buffoonery that helped make GOIN' SOUTH unwatchable to all but his most diehard fans.

The always graceful Barkin comes closest to saving the film, much as she almost saved SWITCH, with sheer comic finesse. Her character makes even less sense than Nicholson's but, unlike him, Barkin has a true gift for physical comedy that makes her fun to watch—even in scenes where someone thought it would be a great idea to zoom in tight on her behind when she turned her back on the camera. D'Angelo, another gifted screen comedian, also helps matters during her few short scenes. But apart from its two female leads (and, of course, Duke, a German shepherd with personality to burn), MAN TROUBLE is mostly an irritating blur of mind-boggling vulgarity.

Eastman's screenplay seems to want to make salient points about female victimization and empowerment. It's awfully hard to take those ideas seriously, though, in a movie that goes for its biggest laughs from a Japanese-American woman with a speech impediment and a Mexican-American maid who spends most of the day fending off the amorous advances of a dog. *(Profanity, adult situations.)*

p, Bruce Gilbert, Carole Eastman; d, Bob Rafelson; w, Carole Eastman; ph, Stephen H. Burum; ed, William Steinkamp; m, Georges Delerue; prod d, Mel Bourne; set d, Samara Schaffer; cos, Judy Ruskin

Romance/Comedy **(PR: C MPAA: PG-13)**

MANIAC WARRIORS

(Canada) 91m North American Pictures ~ AIP Home Video c

Melanie Kilgour *(Danielle)*, William Smith *(Lucas)*, Scott Anderson *(Harris)*, Ken Farmer *(Chuck)*, Nancy Pataki *(Baalca)*, Tanya Orton *(Claudia)*, Joe Maffei *(Iodine)*, Andrew MacGregor *(Zak)*, Pauline Crawford *(Maria)*, Nick Amoroso *(Dax)*, Dave Gregg *(Rocket Man)*, Darlene DeVink *(April)*, Judy Reynolds *(June)*, Michael Metcalfe *(Ozzie)*, Paul Hogan *(Jack)*, Curt Bonn *(Arco)*, Richard Hendery *(1st Shepherd)*, Serge Houde *(2nd Shepherd)*, Andy Graffitti *(Grand Shepherd)*, Gordon Cook, Paul Dignard, Tom Felcan, John Haines, Lee Hatch, Bruce Hystad, Jeff Hystad, Bruce Huggett, Adam Longworth, David Napio, Helmut Peters, Ken Ralph, Gary Renfrey, Gary Taylor, Willis Taylor, Carmen Vacchiann, Rick Worthington, Bob Lessard, John Bassani, Rob Berridge, Merlin Bowe, Tim Chapman, Urbain Chartier, Wayne Confrey, Steve Cropper, Walter Langdon Davies, John Diablo, Cecil Drummond-Hay, Charlie Drummond-Hay, Jim Dyck, Steve Gumbert, Del Lambert, Ken Lester, Adam James Palmer, Ross Feltron, Scott McDonald, Pat McDonald, Pat McGarrigle, Alex Pankiw, Don Perrier, Taylor Prince, Dan Robinson, Micki Sacchari, Dave Stubbs, Don Wilson, Dave Wetson, John Woodcock, Art Yates, Ken Kryeger, Brian Philips, Fred Reber, Patrick Robinson, Harold Wyerch *(Raiders)*, Steve Franklin, Brett Jones, Nester Garandza, Bill Murray *(Shepherds)*, Andra Brown, Leslie Gmur, Lisa Larsen, Marny McKewan, Minna Setala, Laurie Martin, Susan Arnold, Lisa Clarke, Debra King, Patricia Maywood, Robin Rasberry, Larissa Mai, Lesley Wiebe, Susan Arnold *(Matrons)*, John Cowin, Carson Ferguson, Dale Loewen, Robert McNarland, Christine Peters, Derek Renfrey, Lesley Wiebe, Phaeder Williams, John Isaac, Andrew Long, Laura McNarland, Lauretta MacCarron, Brian Phillips, Debra Renfrey, Gwyneth Wiliams *(Wanderers)*, Robby Berner, Gerald Dyck, William Kelly, Rick Thompson, Ed Buquet, Don Demille, Brad Stewart, Art Watkins *(Cannibals)*, August Buquet *(Cannibal Girl)*, Camillia Mahal *(Cannibal Girl)*

And just who are the MANIAC WARRIORS? The year is 2050 and the world is a post-apocalyptic wasteland plagued by a deadly virus. The eponymous villains are a militaristic, government-sanctioned band of nomads who forcibly—they use needles—withdraw untainted blood from unwilling female victims to bolster their own immune systems. Locating these unwilling volunteers involves kidnapping, roadside executions and selective torture under such appalling conditions as execrable direction, exiguous acting and excretory camerawork.

Also along for the ride in this anemic action adventure inspired by the tragic AIDS epidemic are hooded figures already infected by the deadly virus, innocent hippie-like families who are constantly being massacred (even though we don't know their blood quality), and two sixties-style rebels, Zak (Andrew MacGregor) and Iodine (Joe Maffei), regarded as a subversive threat to the blood bank troops. Led by the butch Baalca (Nancy Pataki), the vampiric cruisers apparently are in collusion with bible-thumpers because the virginal, disease-free maidens they capture all have to have post-baptismal sex with Baalca's sidekick, a preacher referred to as the Grand Shepherd.

After her grandfather is slain and her sister abducted by the blood groupies, Danielle (Melanie Kilgour) forms a mutual protection society with taciturn loner Lucas (William Smith). When he's captured by the "hoods," she helps him escape; when she needs some firepower to free her sister, he pitches in. Although the underground rebels, Zak and Iodine, are seized by Baalca's clan and hanged upside down, a disgruntled guard gets high on their LSD and frees them. After assorted chases, scrapes, forays and flights, Danielle is reunited with her sister as the gonzo fighters join her and Lucas, by now her lover, in destroying Baalca's militia and silencing the hypocritical preacher.

In this slovenly photographed and sluggishly directed action adventure, even the special effects seem half asleep. Everything is monotonously violent; the repetitious persecution scenes are coated with an unpleasant veneer of sadistic glee. Lacking the sophistication for satire, MANIAC WARRIORS fails to draw blood when it attacks the warmongers and religious zealots who run the government in the not-so-distant future. Never rising to the level of competence, this future schlock plays out its running time with the shoddy feeling of a school assignment cribbed from an encyclopedia the night before it's due.

While the romantic leads are personable, their thesping won't displace Cronyn and Tandy, nor can they undo the damage done by the amatuerish playing of the remaining cast, which seems to suffer from recycled extras. Given the low humor and casual brutality inherent in the screenplay, the project was probably doomed. It's difficult for viewers to express enthusiasm for the film's dire glimpse at a disease-riddled future when the actors seem to be falling asleep while reciting the soporific dialogue.

Even low-low-budget action films have to drum up a little conviction, but this plasma-deprived expose of man's inhumanity to man is badly in need of a transfusion of talent. Sans energy or spirit, MANIAC WARRIOR is a DOA action adventure with no saving graces. *(Violence, profanity, sexual situations.)*

p, Lloyd Simandl, John A. Curtis; d, Lloyd Simandl, Michael Mazo; ph, Danny Nowak; ed, Fitzpatrick, Bert Bush; m, John Sereda; art d, Cecil Drummond-Hay

Action/Adventure/Science Fiction (PR: O MPAA: NR)

MARI DE LA COIFFEUSE, LA
(SEE: HAIRDRESSER'S HUSBAND, THE)

MARTIAL LAW 2: UNDERCOVER ★★½
92m M L Partnership ~ MCA/Universal Home Video c

Jeff Wincott *(Sean Thompson)*, Cynthia Rothrock *(Billie Blake)*, Billy Drago *(Captain Krantz)*, Paul Johansson *(Spencer Hamilton)*, Evan Lurie *(Tanner)*, L. Charles Taylor *(Danny Borelli)*, Sherrie Rose *(Tiffany)*, Deborah Driggs

This above average follow-up to 1991's action release MARTIAL LAW finds undercover partners Jeff Wincott and Cynthia Rothrock out for new adventures in the underworld as chief proponents of "Martial Law," the LAPD's elite, urban-warfare martial arts unit.

Sean Thompson (Wincott) is transferred to a new precinct, headed by Captain Krantz (Billy Drago), to teach "Martial Law" techniques to a new group of police, which includes his old police academy buddy Danny Birelli (L. Charles Taylor). When Birelli gets his neck broken in a drunk driving accident, Thompson is suspicious, but he's warned not to pursue the case by Krantz. In Birelli's demolished car Thompson finds a matchbook for the upscale Club Syntax, run by young crime mogul Spencer Hamilton (Paul Johansson), who had the upright Birelli eliminated for getting too close to Hamilton's crime organization. Thompson calls in Billie Blake (Rothrock) for help; she takes an undercover job as bartender in the club and befriends Hamilton's girlfriend Tiffany (Sherrie Rose), whom Hamilton has ordered to sleep with the crooked Krantz. Another corrupt on-the-payroll cop, Dobbs, is murdered just as he's about to inform on Hamilton and Krantz. Blake and Thompson kill Hamilton and his chief bodyguard Tanner (Evan Lurie) when they interrupt one of Hamilton's drug deals. And Krantz blows his own brains out just as Blake and Thompson arrive to arrest him.

This sequel was made by the same producing-directing-writing team that made MARTIAL LAW, and it's a better movie, chiefly in its deleting Chad McQueen (son of the late Steve McQueen), who embarrassingly had no screen presence or acting skills whatsoever. His character, Thompson, is ably filled by Jeff Wincott, who also starred in 1992's DEADLY BET. The equally cliched plot, as devised by Richard Brandes and Jiles Fitzgerald, is less unwieldy, as is the direction by Kurt Anderson. In an oddball, hey-it's-Hollywood switch, MARTIAL LAW's producer, Anderson, and director Steve Cohen have traded functions for the sequel; they've finally got it right.

The fist-and footicuffs are well choreographed by Jeff Pruitt; they are, after all, what makes these pictures succeed or fail. Former martial arts champ Rothrock, reprising her role from the first film, is still on the verge of genre stardom, although she has no other female competition as action heroine. Rothrock is all over the video store shelves (the CHINA O'BRIEN movies, FAST GETAWAY, the very good TIGER CLAWS), but her acting skills remain troublesomely less fluent than her martial arts expertise. Made in Canada, this film was released direct-to-video. *(Violence, profanity, nudity.)*

p, Steve Cohen; d, Kurt Anderson; w, Richard Brandes, Jiles Fitzgerald, (from the story by Pierre David); ph, Peter Fernberger; ed, Michael Thibault; m, Elliot Solomon; prod d, James R. Shumaker; set d, Sharo Reed; cos, Yana Syrkin

Crime/Action/Martial Arts (PR: O MPAA: R)

MATCH FACTORY GIRL, THE ★★★½
(Finland/Sweden) 70m Villealfa; Svenska Filminstitutet ~ Kino International c
(TULITIKKUTEHTAAN TYTTO)

Kati Outinen *(Iris)*, Elina Salo *(Iris's Mother)*, Esko Nikkari *(Iris's Stepfather)*, Vesa Vierikko *(Man in Dancehall)*, Reijo Taipale *(Singer)*, Silu Seppala *(Brother)*, Outi Maenpaa *(Workmate)*, Marja Packalen *(Doctor)*, Richard Reitinger *(Man in Bar)*, Helga Viljanen *(Office Employee)*, Kurt Siilas *(Policeman)*, Ismo Keinanen *(Policeman)*, Klaus Heydemann *(Worker)*

A darkly humorous fable, THE MATCH FACTORY GIRL chronicles, in extreme minimalist fashion, the transformation of an ugly duckling into a killer tigress. Utilizing perhaps only a half-dozen lines of dialogue, Finnish filmmaker Aki Kaurismaki relies instead on the lyrics of about a dozen songs to comment on the action.

Like some industrial documentary, the film opens with close-ups of the machinery used in making wooden matches, from the literal skinning of a section of tree trunk to the packaging and labeling of the bundles. Iris (Kati Outinen) has the deadeningly routine job of making sure the labels are properly stuck to the cartons. Her home life is as dreary as her job, since she lives in a shabby apartment with her mother (Elina Salo) and stepfather (Esko Nikkari), whom Iris supports with her meager earnings. On their part, they are international couch potatoes, watching the televised newscasts and sports broadcasts whether in English, French, Russian or Finnish. They eat the meals prepared by Iris in silence. Iris's few pleasures, to use the word loosely, include a half-liter glass of beer, the odd romance novel and a night at an alcohol-free dance where she sits uncourted on a bench tethered to the wall.

One pay day, she sees and buys a red floral print dress that her parents insist she return. Instead, she goes to a bar, wearing her new frock, where she meets a man (Vesa Vierikko) who takes her to his modern, middle-class apartment for the night. He leaves her in the morning with a thousand mark bill. On her part, Iris leaves a note asking him to call her; he never does. Iris shares the thousand marks with her brother (Silu Seppala), a cook who lives on his own, and the parents who believe she's returned the dress. When Iris learns she is pregnant, she sends her faithless lover a handwritten note full of cliched sentiments, only to receive a curt, typed reply and a money-order to pay for the abortion he demands. When her parents discover the facts, they demand she move out. She does, and into her brother's apartment (which features a jukebox and pool table as its principal furnishings). She also buys a box of rat poison. She prepares a bottled solution of the poison and pays visits to all those who have wronged her.

The final installment in Kaurismaki's acclaimed "proletarian trilogy" (the others being SHADOWS IN PARADISE and ARIEL), THE MATCH FACTORY GIRL is a wondrous antidote to the kind of sentimentality that figures so prominently in most mainstream films. It's almost as if Kaurismaki had deliberately decided to turn Charlie Chaplin on his head, particularly with the almost silent-film quality of this 70-minute feature. Although initially sympathetic, Iris becomes openly malevolent as she poisons both flowering plants and the odd barroom Lothario. Kaurismaki's presentation of Helsinki is characteristically grim and anonymous, either modern and bare or old and shabby.

The director, writer, producer and editor of the film, Kaurismaki has described it both as his "revenge on Robert Bresson" as well as a "piece of junk." He has also stated that he is not interested in middle-class family values, but rather in "losers." *(Adult situations.)*

p, Aki Kaurismaki; d, Aki Kaurismaki; w, Aki Kaurismaki; ph, Timo Salminen; ed, Aki Kaurismaki; cos, Tuula Hilkamo

Drama **(PR: C MPAA: NR)**

MAXIMUM BREAKOUT

93m Action International Pictures Inc. ~ AIP Home Video c

Bobby Johnston *(Travis)*, Eddie Hopper *(Reb)*, Carrie Murray *(Debbie)*, Sydney Coale Phillips *(Bobbi)*, Tom Blanton *(Loch)*, Steve Rally *(Suicide)*, Martin L. Keegan *(Professor)*, Stephen Bohrer *(Frank)*, Merl Waters *(Detective Wyatt)*, Tracy McReynolds *(Cowboy)*, Ron Litman *(Cowboy)*, Douglas Harter *(Kurt)*, Victor R. Wright *(Big Sam)*, Gerarde Imhoff *(Nigel Ryland)*, Larry Barsky *(Mr. O'Brien)*, Christine Kaye *(Mrs. O'Brien)*, Teddi Rae Prior *(Baby for Sale)*, Jenifer L. Blake *(Marian)*, Kristina Aras *(Police Woman)*

Obviously made on the cheap, MAXIMUM BREAKOUT teases with the promise of sleaze and sadism, but never delivers the goods.

Vacationing lovers Travis (Bobby Johnston) and Bobbi (Sydney Coale Phillips) encounter a nightmare on a lonely country road: two strangers lure them from their car, abduct Bobbi and beat Travis brutally. Six months pass; though Bobbi's family is wealthy, there's no ransom demand, and the police—even Travis's boss, Detective Wyatt (Merl Waters)—have all but given up. Only Travis, encouraged by Bobbi's best friend Debbie (Carrie Murray), continues to search.

Travis teams up with Debbie's brother Reb (Eddie Hopper), who assembles a posse to rescue Bobbi. The rest of the team consists of the Professor (Martin L. Keegan), a computer nerd who likes to blow things up; Loch (Tom Blanton), a gun-crazy nut case; and stuntman Sue (Steve Rally)—short for "suicide." Together they track Bobbi to an isolated ranch where blond, blue-eyed women are forced to bear children who are brokered to desperate couples by the sleazy Frank (Stephen Bohrer) and his boss, an icy bitch with a syrupy Southern accent.

With the help of a local cowboy, the team shoots its way into the baby ranch, killing the guards and rescuing the imprisoned women. To their horror, they discover that the woman behind this vicious racket is Debbie, who had Bobbi abducted so she could seduce Travis. Detective Wyatt appears fortuitously and kills her, then is in turn murdered by Frank. The wounded Loch shoots Frank and dies. Travis and Bobbi drive off together, leaving Reb with the body of his sister.

Though nominally an action adventure film, the generically titled MAXIMUM BREAKOUT contains little action, and punctuates what there is with long stretches of wooden dialogue meant to establish and explore the relationships between the barely differentiated characters. Photographed and edited in a flat, expedient style and lacking the verve, viciousness or sheer delight in luridness that might lift it above its limitations, MAXIMUM BREAKOUT is low budget filmmaking at its least interesting. *(Violence, nudity, sexual situations.)*

p, Ruta K. Aras; d, Tracy Lynch Britton; w, Michelle J. Carl; ph, Barry Wilson; ed, David Alan; m, Dennis Poore, Moshe Daaboul; art d, Jill Silvertone

Action/Crime/Drama **(PR: C MPAA: NR)**

MAXIMUM FORCE ★★

90m PM Productions ~ PM Home Video c

Sam J. Jones *(Michael Crew)*, Sherrie Rose *(Cody Randel)*, Jason Lively *(Rick Carver)*, Jeff Langton *(Iron)*, Victoria Hawley *(Julie)*, John Saxon *(Captain Fuller)*, Sonny Landham *(Pimp)*, Pam Dixon *(Sheila Stone)*, Mickey Rooney *(Chief of Police)*, Richard Lynch *(Max Tanebe)*

If lots of carnage, casual police brutality and macho posturing in the furtherance of justice is your idea of fun, you could do worse than MAXIMUM FORCE, an inconsequential yet diverting direct-to-video crime story. There is scant distracting social commentary or vexing moral ambiguity—just solid disposable entertainment.

The fun begins as Detective Rick Carver (Jason Lively) observes an illicit firearms transaction in a remote locale. Discovered, the bearded long-haired cop races to secure his precious surveillance equipment as the gun-toting bad guys approach in their helicopter. Carver loads some fancy weapon and runs off with the chopper in hot pursuit. Eluding the machine-gun fire, Carver takes aim and blows away the offending craft both in self-defense and to avenge the wanton destruction of his high-tech hardware. ("I was having a good day until you blew up my stuff! Goodbye," he whines as he fires his weapon.)

The criminal mastermind of this unnamed metropolis is Mr. Max Tanebe (Richard Lynch), an old fashioned gangster who speaks adoringly of the freedom and the business opportunities that America provided him when he was just a poor immigrant. Dealing in drugs, weapons, stolen goods and prostitutes has earned him an office atop a spectacular skyscraper. He even has the mayor and chief of police (Mickey Rooney) in his big pockets. Nonetheless several obsessed cops have repeatedly risked life and career to strike blows against Tanebe's evil empire. Captain Fuller (John Saxon) summons Carver, Detective Michael Crew (Sam J. Jones) and Detective Cody Randel (Sherrie

Rose) to a rundown loft and offers to supervise them in a special force exclusively devoted to battling Tanebe.

Each cop has a personal score to settle so they agree to eat, sleep, live and train together so as to function as one well-oiled machine—a Maximum Force. After a musical training interlude, they proceed to impede Tanebe's criminal operations. Infuriated, the gangster strikes back and the newly formed team incurs some heavy losses before confronting Tanebe in his lair.

With generous helpings of cartoon violence, quick personality sletches that pass for characterization and an essential silliness at its core, MAXIMUM FORCE feels like an extended episode of some lost minor Stephen J. Cannell cop show. Lacking the goofy charm of "The A-Team" or the moral gravity of "Wiseguy," this is a briskly paced succession of crime-film cliches edited in a slickly competent manner designed to deliver maximum impact for minimal budget. Ironically, topbilled star Sam J. Jones (best remembered as Dino De Laurentiis's FLASH GORDON) made a much stronger impression on TV last year as the seemingly invincible villain, Victory Smith, in the premiere episode of "The Hat Squad." As Crew, Jones, usually a clean-shaven blond, is brown-haired, unshaven, gravelly voiced and dull—a poor man's Don Johnson circa "Miami Vice."

Cheapie veteran John Saxon fares better than most of the undistinguished cast with his small role as the courageous Captain Fuller (a bow to "B-plus" auteur Samuel Fuller?). Cool and dignified, he deftly sketches in backgrounds for each of the characters during their first meeting. Motivations aside, capability is character for this crimefighting trio: Crews is the gruff hunky cop, as skilled in hand-to-hand combat as he is with his hefty hand gun; Carver is an oddball weapons specialist with a penchant for remote-controlled devices; and Cody, the female member (that is, love interest), is just one tough cookie who excels at undercover assignments. Personalities, interesting or otherwise, are not this film's main appeal with the notable exception of Mickey Rooney in a memorable cameo as the corrupt chief of police. Prowling the streets in his shadowy limo (the production probably couldn't afford an office set), Rooney delivers an overwrought lament about lost innocence that is unintentionally hilarious. This film is a long way from the ANDY HARDY series but the diminutive star remains a trooper.

MAXIMUM FORCE clearly aspires to be a stylish comic-book version of film noir. It's a dark, dark movie in which daylight is relegated to the pre-credit action scenes and, much later, a brief nightmare sequence. This is certainly for the best; the absurd old-age makeup on Richard Lynch looks terrible in bright light. The modest interior settings include a dimly lit nightclub, an oddly lit loft (a blue key light competes with a yellow and the shadows win), and a yellow-tinted conference room. The exteriors are mostly rather attractive shots of urban streets illuminated with lots of colorful neon. At times, all the smoke and tinted lights almost suggest a low-rent Ridley Scott.

There is nary an original idea to be found in MAXIMUM FORCE. In addition to the undeniable influence of TV cop shows, gimmicks and imagery are culled from THE DEAD POOL, Sam Fuller's UNDERWORLD USA and countless crime melodramas. Still, it is satisfying for exactly what it is: a modest, colorful action movie that delivers its unremarkable thrills with aplomb. *(Violence, profanity, sexual situations.)*

p, Richard Pepin, Joseph Merhi; d, Joseph Merhi; w, John Weidner, Ken Lamplugh; ph, Ken Blakey; ed, John Weidner; m, Louis Febre; prod d, Greg Martin

Action/Crime **(PR: O MPAA: R)**

MEATBALLS 4 ★★

91m Moviestore Entertainment ~ Moviestore Entertainment c

Corey Feldman *(Ricky Wade)*, Jack Nance *(Neil Peterson)*, Sarah Douglas *(Monica)*, Bojesse Christopher *(Wes)*, Johnny Cocktails *(Victor)*, J. Trevor Edmond *(Howie)*, Paige French *(Jennifer)*, John Mendoza *(Dick)*, Bentley Mitchum *(Kyle)*, Christy Thom *(Hillary)*, Deborah Tucker *(Kelly)*

Haven't audiences who've suffered through ROUND TRIP TO HEAVEN and ROCK 'N' ROLL HIGH SCHOOL FOREVER earned a rest from the singing-dancing-comedic talents of Corey Feldman? His presence notwithstanding, MEATBALLS 4 offers some mildly entertaining "how I spent my summer vacation getting laid and becoming a better teenager" escapism.

Strapped by a $200,000 mortgage on his Lakeside Resort and faced with dwindling enrollment, Neil Peterson (Jack Nance) may be forced to sell out to his state-of-the-art competitor, Monica (Sarah Douglas), who owns the popular Twin Oaks Camp. Determined to keep his coveted property, Neil calls back Ricky Wade (Corey Feldman), the best darned recreation director who ever lived. Since Ricky once went steady with Neil's granddaughter, Kelly (Deborah Tucker), who now dates Kyle (Bentley Mitchum), who's been passed over for the rec director's job in favor of Ricky, all is not smooth sailing at Lakeside. Under Ricky's tutelage all the campers, even the obese Victor (Johnny Cocktails), learn life lessons as they improve their ski-and-surf skills.

When underdog Lakeside bests Twin Oaks in a competition, Monica and her entourage resort to sabotage. As Lakeside faces bankruptcy, Ricky challenges the oppostion to a second mini-Olympics in which all the honest Lakesiders are defeated until Victor undercovers the Twin Oaks trickery. With clean competition restored, Neil hangs onto Lakeside, Kelly hangs all over Ricky and all the nubile and tumescent summer campers return home with memories of one helluva summer.

Inane and high-spirited, MEATBALLS 4 is no better or worse than dozens of other clones of MEATBALLS, SPRING BREAK or PORKY'S. In some ways it's actually more palatable. Sweeter-natured than its predecessors and less aggressively sexist, MEATBALLS 4 is a sort of stag-party fantasy for adolescents in which suntanned babes and stunt water-skiing demonstrations occupy equal amounts of screen time.

As the token authority figure, David Lynch regular Jack Nance (ERASERHEAD, BLUE VELVET) calls upon his distinctive comic persona to generate appealing laughter; at least he's not the kind of cruelly caricatured adult one finds in the *ouevre* of John Hughes. Writer-director Bob Logan's screenplay also has enough heart to score some points for the misfits of this world for whom summer camp may seem like a stretch in the Big House—although the fat jokes at Victor's expense go on for a little too long. Still, the sexism isn't too offensive and there's no homophobia, so why complain too vociferously? In fact, if triple-threat Corey Feldman doesn't rub you the wrong way, you might enjoy yourself. *(Profanity, nudity.)*

p, Donald P. Borchers; d, Bob Logan; w, Bob Logan; ph, Vance Burberry; ed, Peter H. Varity; m, Steve Hunter; prod d, Dorian Vernacchio, Deborah Raymond; cos, Angela Calin

Comedy **(PR: C MPAA: R)**

MEDICINE MAN ★★

104m Cinergi Productions; Hollywood ~ BV c

Sean Connery *(Dr. Robert Campbell)*, Lorraine Bracco *(Dr. Rae Crane)*, Jose Wilker *(Dr. Miguel Ornega)*, Rodolfo DeAlexandre *(Tanaki)*, Francisco Tsirene Tsere Rereme *(Jahausa)*, Elias Monteiro DaSilva *(Palala)*, Edinei Maria Serrio Dos Santos *(Kalana)*, Bec-Kana-Re Dos Santos Kaiapo *(Imana)*, Angelo Barra Moreira *(Medicine Man)*, Jose Lavat *(Government Man)*

Politically correct to a fault, MEDICINE MAN pleads for the preservation of the rain forest; were it a more compelling film, its message would doubtless do more good.

Dr. Robert Campbell (Sean Connery) is a bad-tempered loner whose biochemical research deep in the South American jungle is financed by a major US pharmaceutical company. Embittered by the death of his wife years earlier, Campbell drowns his sorrows in work and local liquor. Having lived among them for so long, he's accepted by the native tribal people as a kind of benevolent witch doctor—a medicine man. Exasperated by his refusal to file reports, his employers send Dr. Rae Crane (Lorraine Bracco) to his remote camp to find out what he's doing.

Even though his funding is at stake, Campbell is less than hospitable. He refuses to tell Crane what he's doing and treats her with barely concealed contempt. This state of affairs gradually improves as she comes around to his view of Amerindians as an enlightened culture living in harmony with the rain forest. Crane is also astonished when she learns the nature of Campbell's research: quite by accident he's discovered a cure for cancer. The problem is that he's lost the formula, and is desperately racing to reproduce it before a multinational logging company destroys the jungle. A fire destroys Campbell's lab, but he stays to rebuild, and Crane stays with him.

MEDICINE MAN's heart is in the right place, but its body is so uninteresting that few viewers ever discover it. It's two films in one, but this isn't a bonus: neither is compelling. The romantic comedy in the rain forest suffers from casting that, had it worked, would have been called bizarrely inspired. Since it doesn't, it's simply bizarre. The middle-aged Connery's much vaunted charm is little in evidence here; he's lumpen, disagreeable and not even particularly attractive. As Dr. Crane, Bracco is abrasive to an almost unbelievable degree; her name may be meant to foreshadow the empathy with nature she eventually achieves, but it leads one to think of the more appropriate birds after which she could have been named—starling, jay or crow, for example.

Crane is meant to be a no-nonsense careerist, a company woman and a scientist with a clear sense of purpose. But she's a shrew, shrill and obstinate; one keeps hoping she'll drown in a lake or be eaten by a jaguar. As a couple, Connery and Bracco generate no romantic sparks, and the screenplay doesn't help. It's possible that screenwriters Tom Schulman and Sally Robinson intended to subvert convention cleverly by not having Crane and Campbell sleep with one another, but since it's clear that we're meant to believe they've fallen deeply in love by the film's end it would be nice to sense that sex is a possibility.

The second film is an impassioned eco-adventure, one of several films with green themes announced by the movie industry recently, and one of the biggest actually to make it to the screen. Though dwarfed in scale by Hector Babenco's monumental AT PLAY IN THE FIELDS OF THE LORD, it seemed to have the greater commercial potential, and MEDICINE MAN did in fact open big, followed by a quick fadeout.

The film's sentiments are laudable, and it contains a few truly moving scenes of awesome trees falling before the bulldozers and devoured by flames. But the cliched story overshadows the film's political concerns, making them seem equally trite and awkward. Director John McTiernan, responsible for such action hits as PREDATOR and THE HUNT FOR RED OCTOBER, seems to have no feel for less blunt material, and his presentation of the jungle dwellers is particularly unsubtle. They're the same old noble savages, gentle, childlike and in touch with nature, ripe for ruination by "civilized" men and women, a stereotype as pervasive as it is simplistic. MEDICINE MAN tries hard to be a film for all tastes, but it ends up appealing to none. *(Adult Situations, profanity.)*

p, Andrew G. Vajna, Donna Dubrow; d, John McTiernan; w, Tom Schulman, Sally Robinson, (from the story by Schulman); ph, Donald McAlpine; ed, Michael R. Miller; m, Jerry Goldsmith; prod d, John Krenz Reinhart, Jr.; art d, Don Diers, Jesus Buenrostro; set d, Enrique Etevez; cos, Marilyn Vance-Straker

Drama/Romance **(PR: C MPAA: PG-13)**

MEDITERRANEO ★★

(Italy) 105m Penta Film; AMA Film ~ Prestige Films c
(AKA: Mediterranean)

Diego Abatantuono *(Sergeant Lo Russo)*, Claudio Bigagli *(Lieutenant Montini)*, Giuseppe Cederna *(Farina)*, Claudio Bisio *(Noventa)*, Gigio Alberti *(Strazzabosco)*, Ugo Conti *(Colasanti)*, Memo Dini *(Felice Munaron)*, Vasco Mirandola *(Libero Munaron)*, Vanna Barba *(Vasilissa)*, Luigi Montini *(Pope)*, Irene Grazioli *(Pastorella)*, Antonio Catalina *(Italian Pilot)*

Similar in theme to KING OF HEARTS, Philippe de Broca's charming antiwar fable, MEDITERRANEO tries to convince viewers that paradise is waiting just around the corner.

While investigating an apparently deserted island in the Aegean Sea during WWII, a brigade of misfit Italian soldiers led by Lt. Montini (Claudio Bigagli) is stranded, their ship sunk by a British attack. Cut off from any means of contact with the outside world, the soldiers soon discover that the island is far from deserted. Montini's assistant Farina (Giuseppe Cederna) discovers that the villagers have simply gone into hiding, believing their island under attack by the Germans. The soldiers notice that there are no young men in the village, and are informed by the local priest that they were taken prisoner by the Germans.

Lt. Montini and his men are welcomed into village life: Montini is invited to repaint the church's faded frescoes; Sgt. Lo Russo (Diego Abatantuono) organizes a soccer team; the Munaron brothers, Felice and Libero (Memo Dini and Vasco Mirandola), find a carnal playmate in the lovely shepherdess (Irene Grazioli); others share the favors of the town prostitute, Vasilissa (Vanna Barba). Farina is a virgin; he can't bring himself to sleep with Vasilissa and falls in love with her instead.

This sweet life passes undisturbed until one day an Italian pilot (Antonio Catalina) lands on the island because of engine trouble, and informs everyone of all the changes that have occurred since 1941. He leaves, promising to send a rescue mission. Spurred by his imminent departure, Farina finally makes love to Vasilissa, and they decide to marry. Soon after the wedding, a British navy boat comes to take the soldiers away. They also bring with them all the lost village men, disturbing various new relationships. Farina refuses to leave and hides in a barrel of olives, but the rest depart, the Munaron brothers waving furiously to the pregnant shepherdess as they are taken out to sea.

Forty years later, an elderly Lt. Montini returns to the island on a tourist boat. He sees Vasilissa's grave, but finds his trusty assistant Farina at their little blue house. Farina brings him to meet Sgt. Lo Russo, who returned years before, and the three old men settle in to spend the rest of their years on the island.

This pleasant fairy tale is the cinematic equivalent of a Club Med vacation. The rag-tag soldiers tumble through a predictable yarn of paradise found, tripping on worn but funny gags that make them all the more lovable. Their island is an Aegean jewel where the golden women are placid and friendly, the old men dance in the streets, and the priest invites them to reside in the mayor's house. It all comes too easily.

Director Gabriele Salvatores and screenwriter Vincenzo Monteleone forget—or overlook—the fact that these men are Mussolini's warriors, painting them instead as a jolly sporting team. They allow the innocent Farina blithely to marry the prostitute whom five of his friends frequent every day, and assume that isolated Greek peasants would instantly take these Italians to their bosom. Without any conflict, or real indication that these cheerful, seemingly well-adjusted fellows are running away from anything particularly unpleasant, the perfection of their surroundings has little impact.

One of the few moments of meaning in MEDITERRANEO is when Farina tearfully explains that he's deserting the army because he has no one, no home, in Italy. Diego Abatantuono is amusing as the bullish sergeant, and the other actors are appealing as well, tan and loose, easing into comradely jocularity. The two female characters are little more than walking dolls with coy expressions. They are pretty but vacuous, much like the film itself. *(Adult situations.)*

p, Gianni Minervini, Mario Cecchi Gori, Vittorio Cecchi Gori; d, Gabriele Salvatores; w, Vincenzo Monteleone; ph, Italo Petriccione; ed, Nino Baragali; m, Giancarlo Bigazzi, Marco Falagiani, Riccardo Cocciante; cos, Francesco Panni

Comedy/Romance **(PR: A MPAA: NR)**

MEGAVILLE ★★★

95m White Noise Productions; Heritage Entertainment ~ LIVE Home Video c

Billy Zane *(Raymond Palinov/Jensen)*, Kristen Cloke *(Christine)*, Grace Zabriskie *(Mrs. Panilov)*, Daniel J. Travanti *(Duprell)*, J.C. Quinn *(Newman)*, John Lantz *(Heller)*, Stefan Gierasch *(Dr. Vogel)*, Hamilton Camp, Leslie Morris, Raymond O'Connor, Vincent Guastaferro

Largely overlooked, this cynical, cyberpunk film noir is worth seeking out. With minimal special effects, lots of dark humor and a potent screenplay from writer-director Peter Lehner, MEGAVILLE demonstrates what can be done with a sharp idea and razor-edged attitude.

The plot carries faint echoes of the elephantine TOTAL RECALL. Deliberately vague in setting up its dystopic universe, MEGAVILLE takes place in some unspecified future when a chunk of the former US is now the Hemisphere, a bleak dictatorship combining chillier aspects of the Soviet Union and the Moral Majority. All forms of entertainment media are forbidden because they supposedly degrade societal values with their pervasive images of violence, sex and mockery (examples of the offending media are briefly shown; they're innocent old Keystone Kop comedies!), and to enforce the ban a squad of paramilitary Media Police raid the Hemisphere's dens of iniquity, smashing TV sets airing ancient Westerns.

Raymond Palinov (Billy Zane) is a young Media Policeman, troubled by sudden headaches and anomalous memory flashbacks. Despite his failing job performance he's recruited by Hemisphere's dreaded internal security agency, the CKS. They say he closely resembles a notorious outlaw and media-smuggler named Jensen. Palinov gets a remote-control transmitter implanted in his brain and, disguised as Jensen, he's sent to infiltrate Megaville, a neighboring nation-state that's an undisguised version of Los Angeles and a major source of media.

To his horror, Palinov/Jensen learns his mission is to set up a secret conduit to the Hemisphere for Megaville's latest and most addictive media, a headphone-shaped device called Dream-A-Life (DAL) that plunges the wearer's mind into a preselected artificial reality. The hero further discovers that he's not just portraying the fearsome Jensen, he *is* Jensen, his identity scrambled by a modified form of DAL lodged in his skull. The CKS want to distribute DAL themselves and keep the dissident elements of the Hemisphere drugged and docile. Jensen/Palinov finds himself at odds with both the CKS, who crudely discipline him with zaps from his neural implant, and Megaville hoods, who figured him as an infiltrator from the start. After numerous double-crosses and deceits the doomed Jensen forces rough justice to prevail in a desert climax derived from Von Stronheim's GREED.

The tale's acid metaphor for the War on Drugs seems superficial at best, but MEGAVILLE's main achievement is ambiance. Apart from Dream-A-Life ("Take a Vacation from Yourself") and the distorted visions from the brain implant, MEGAVILLE eschews visual f/x kitsch and expensive futuristic sets. Filmmaker Peter Lehner neatly places the whole Megaville segment in present-day LA (reminiscent of Jean-Luc Godard's use of contemporary Paris for another planet in ALPHAVILLE), while the Hemisphere's brooding, Byzantine architecture belongs with George Orwell's totalitarian Oceania in *1984*. Lehner obviously knows his movies, and MEGAVILLE opens with hardboiled voiceover narration straight out of a 1940s crime melodrama courtesy of a philosphical but amoral Megavillian named Newman—"new man"—who would assassinate his own president or son to protect DAL sales and sums up the first law of Megaville: "Never trust anybody but that ugly guy in the mirror."

None of the characters are remotely likable, with the exception of the bewildered hero played by Billy Zane (DEAD CALM, MEMPHIS BELLE). He's a short-lived composite personality—Jensen's ruthlessness married to Palinov's sheeplike submission, resulting in the only individual onscreen with a conscience and sense of decency. Durable character actor J.C. Quinn (SILKWOOD, BARFLY, THE ABYSS) steps out of relative anonymity to portray Newman, and cult actress Grace Zabriskie (DRUGSTORE COWBOY, WILD AT HEART) plays Palinov's pathetically doting mom, whose naked ambition makes her a convenient hostage for the CKS. Perhaps the most recognizable face onscreen is Daniel J. Travanti (Captain Frank Furillo on TV's "Hill Street Blues"), scene-stealingly sinister as Duprell, the gravel-throated CKS chief. Throughout the course of the picture his health decays, taking him from cane to wheelchair to sickbed to respirator; but his iron grip on power stays firm as he monitors all from his Hemisphere lair.

The typical film noir never had a simple plot, and MEGAVILLE makes no exception. Viewers accustomed to spoon-fed narratives may have as much difficulty as Billy Zane in figuring out what Jensen's supposed to be doing. The presidential assassination seems too tangential to the main story, almost as if a few scenes were missing. Also, the trick Jensen pulls to decapitate the CKS is cool but rather illogical and may demand a repeat viewing to get straight. This is easily accomplished, as MEGAVILLE circulated primarily as a low-profile B-movie home video release. That's a pity; a lot of thought and talent went into this small, deadly delicacy, and it deserves a wider audience. *(Violence, profanity, adult situations.)*

p, Christina Schmidlin, Andres Pfaeffli; d, Peter Lehner; w, Peter Lehner, Gordon Chavis; ph, Zoltan David; ed, Pietro Scalia; m, Stacy Widelitz; prod d, Milo Needles; art d, Troy Myers; cos, Shawna Leavell

Science Fiction/Action/Thriller **(PR: O MPAA: R)**

MEMOIRS OF AN INVISIBLE MAN ★★

102m Le Studio Canal Plus; Regency Enterprises; Alcor Films; Cornelius Production ~ Warner Bros. c

Chevy Chase *(Nick Halloway)*, Daryl Hannah *(Alice Monroe)*, Sam Neill *(David Jenkins)*, Michael McKean *(George Talbot)*, Stephen Tobolowsky *(Warren Singleton)*, Jim Norton *(Dr. Bernard Wachs)*, Pat Skipper *(Morrissey)*, Paul Perri *(Gomez)*, Richard Epcar *(Tyler)*, Steven Barr *(Clellan)*, Gregory Paul Martin

(Richard), Patricia Heaton *(Ellen)*, Barry Kivel *(Drunk Businessman)*, Donald Li *(Cab Driver)*, Rosalind Chao *(Cathy DiTolla)*, Jay Gerber *(Roger Whitman)*, Shay Duffin *(Patrick the Bartender)*, Edmund L. Shaff *(Edward Schneiderman)*, Sam Anderson *(Chairman of the House Committee)*, Elaine Corral *(News Anchor)*, Ellen Albertini Dow *(Mrs. Coulson)*, Jonathan Wigan *(Delivery Boy)*, I.M. Hobson *(Maitre d')*, Rip Haight *(Helicopter Pilot)*, Chip Heller *(Man Who Hails Taxi)*, Aaron Lustig *(Technician)*

As a crooked renegade CIA agent trying to recruit invisible yuppie Chevy Chase, Sam Neill implores him to "think of the adventures we'll have!" Unfortunately, it is the spirit of adventure that is distinctly lacking in MEMOIRS OF AN INVISIBLE MAN, a dismayingly flat and predictable, special-effects-laden action thriller.

The title dilemma of investment banker Nick Halloway (Chase) begins when he attends a presentation at a high-tech research company the morning after being instantly besotted by Boston lawyer-turned-social documentary filmmaker Alice Monroe (Hannah). Roaming the corridors of the high-tech firm in search of the men's room, Nick accidentally causes a helpful technician to spill a cup of coffee on a computer console, resulting in a massive short circuit that spreads throughout the building and somehow renders Nick invisible. His nemesis, David Jenkins (Neill), shows up at the scene of the catastrophe and, seeing the possibilities in an agent who can't be seen, spends the rest of the film trying to corral Nick. After Nick is reunited with Alice at a mutual friend's vacation home, they plot together to throw Jenkins off their trail once and for all and leave for some faraway place, where Nick plans to become a reclusive tycoon by wheeling and dealing over the phone. Jenkins's late kidnapping of Alice throws a wrench in the machinery, but only long enough for Nick to kill Jenkins as Jenkins has killed others, by throwing him off a roof.

MEMOIRS OF AN INVISIBLE MAN wants to be two types of films currently fashionable in Hollywood. The hook of a yuppie learning sensitivity in the wake of an outlandish catastrophe puts it in league with REGARDING HENRY and GHOST. Meanwhile, Nick's idealistic refusal to join Jenkins resembles the bogus pacifism of Schwarzenegger in TERMINATOR 2. It also means to establish Chase as a non-comic leading man. And Chase does keep the pratfalls to a minimum. However, the screenplay doesn't give him much of a non-comic character to play, leaving the star teetering uncomfortably between comedy and drama.

As it was in H.F. Saint's novel (which, oddly, has some moments of Chase-style humor that were left out of the film), Nick's invisibility is meant to be a physical correlative for his emotional detachment from the lives of those around him. Yet he's shown to be surrounded by people who like him, not the least of them being Hannah. It's also a little hard to buy Nick's moral superiority to Jenkins, since his only real goal is to give Jenkins the slip in order to withdraw from the mainstream of humanity and become a rich recluse. Jenkins is even less well defined than Nick. We never even know for sure whether he really intends to recruit Nick or kill him. Mostly he just seems to be chasing Chase because that's what bad guys do.

Similarly, it seems an oversight to establish Alice's brainy credibility as a documentary filmmaker without finding some meaningful way to integrate her background into the action. As the plot picks up speed, Alice instead becomes a standard heroine to match Chase's standard hero and Neill's standard villain. This is all the more dismaying considering that the screenplay is co-credited to William Goldman (MISERY, BUTCH CASSIDY AND THE SUNDANCE KID and many more). John Carpenter directs with what can only be described as slack disengagement when compared to the poignant urgency he injected into the similar STARMAN and the pure, bravura moviemaking joy he brought to his underrated action-comedy BIG TROUBLE IN LITTLE CHINA. Here, working with a far inferior screenplay, Carpenter is only occasionally able to evoke the suspense and excitement of his best past work. *(Violence, mild adult situations.)*

p, Bruce Bodner, Dan Kolsrud; d, John Carpenter; w, Robert Collector, Dana Olsen, William Goldman, (from the novel by H.F. Saint); ph, William A. Fraker; ed, Marion Rothman; m, Shirley Walker; prod d, Lawrence G. Paull; art d, Bruce Crone; set d, Rick Simpson

Science Fiction/Romance (PR: C MPAA: PG-13)

MIDNIGHT CLEAR, A ★★½

107m A&M Films; Tamrose Productions; Beacon Communications ~ InterStar Releasing c

Peter Berg *(Bud Miller)*, Kevin Dillon *(Mel Avakian)*, Arye Gross *(Stan Shutzer)*, Ethan Hawke *(Will Knott)*, Gary Sinise *("Mother" Wilkins)*, Frank Whaley *("Father" Mundy)*, John C. McGinley *(Major Griffin)*, Larry Joshua *(Lieutenant Ware)*, Curt Lowens *(German Soldier)*, Rachel Griffin *(Janice)*, Tim Shoemaker *(Morrie)*, Kelly Gately *(Young Hero German)*, Bill Osborn *(Sargeant)*, Andre Lamal *(German)*

An overabundance of sensitivity and a dearth of common sense dampen A MIDNIGHT CLEAR, a mawkish anti-war drama adapted from William Wharton's novel by actor-turned-director Keith Gordon (DRESSED TO KILL, CHRISTINE). This is Gordon's second outing behind the camera following his debut with THE CHOCOLATE WAR.

In the snowbound Ardennes in the late stages of WWII, the most intelligent soldiers the US Army could find are assembled into an elite reconnaissance squad. Their glory days, if they ever had any, are over. A third of the squad has already died in action, and those remaining are in poor shape. The senior officer, "Mother" Wilkins (Gary Sinise, director of OF MICE AND MEN and co-founder of Chicago's Steppenwolf Theatre), has suffered a nervous breakdown following news from home that his wife has suffered a miscarriage. Word of Wilkins's breakdown is kept from the rest of the squad by the story's narrator, Will Knott (Ethan Hawke), as they move out from base camp with orders to commandeer an abandoned house and use it to report on German troop movements. Instead of enemy resistance, they find a squad of ragtag Germans who shout goodnight messages, attack them with snowballs rather than bullets, and end up exchanging gifts with them around a makeshift Christmas tree. These soldiers, it turns out, want nothing more than to surrender. However, they fear retribution against families still in Germany if it looks as though they gave up without a fight.

The equally disillusioned American soldiers oblige by staging a phony skirmish. Knott lets his fellow soldiers know of Wilkins's conditions, and they leave Wilkins behind, with one of the other soldiers impersonating the senior officer to negotiate the Germans' surrender. However, Wilkins comes to the rescue when he hears shots being fired and the phony battle turns terribly real. The Germans are all killed, along with two of the Americans. When the dust clears, the squad concocts a phony story to cover up the atrocity, making Wilkins the hero so he can be discreetly decorated and sent home.

In interviews, Keith Gordon has cited Stanley Kubrick as a major influence, and that's apparent in the bleak yet lyrical style of A MIDNIGHT CLEAR. But Gordon lacks Kubrick's relentlessly sharp-eyed narrative focus and precision of craft. His screenplay keeps telling us things that it should be showing us, and shows us too much that has no real bearing on the story. His characters are flat and lack individuality. We're told that Knott's fellow squad members are exceptionally intelligent, but see little evidence of this, nor hear it in the dialogue that wavers between the mundane and the self-consciously poetic. One fleeting but typical example is Knott's observation that his full name, Will Knott, has been shortened by his fellow soldiers to "Won't." Throughout the film, nobody calls him anything but Knott, making the information either false or irrelevant.

Knott's narration is loaded with stale observations: war is a horrible waste, his commanders are stupid and callous, soldiers seem to swear a lot, etc. It becomes too easy to tune him out altogether, despite the rich expressiveness of the language adapted from Wharton's book. What never emerges is how these men live together and with themselves on a day-to-day basis. They exist as symbols of wasted youth, but never come alive as people. And if they never seem real, it's hard to care about who they are or what happens to them—the greatest irony of all in a movie attempting to place war in a human perspective.

A MIDNIGHT CLEAR looks good and is very well acted by its ensemble cast. But it belongs with countless other earnest, dull, well-meaning message films betrayed by good intentions. Gordon would do well to sit down with the films of his mentor for a closer look. *(Violence, profanity, adult situations.)*

p, Bill Borden, Dale Pollock; d, Keith Gordon; w, Keith Gordon, (from the novel by William Wharton); ph, Tom Richmond; ed, Donald Brochu; m, Mark Isham; prod d, David Nichols; art d, David Lubin; set d, Janis Lubin; cos, Barbara Tfank

War/Drama **(PR: C MPAA: R)**

MIDNIGHT FEAR ★½

90m Danyves Enterprises Ltd.; Crain Company ~ Rhino Home Video c

Craig Wasson *(Paul Prexton)*, David Carradine *(Sheriff Steve Hanley)*, August West *(Jenny)*, Page Fletcher *(John)*, Evan Richards *(David)*

File this one under the "nice try" category. MIDNIGHT FEAR is an underpopulated thriller that tries to keep the audience guessing. Trouble is, most of the time they'll guess right.

The locale is a logging town rocked by a bloody dismemberment and portentious mood music. As washed-up, boozing Sheriff Steve Hanley (David Carradine) tries to pull himself together and solve the slaying, the scene switches to a remote farm, where Jenny (August West), an attractive coed, has chosen to spend spring break house-sitting, horse-riding and fighting off unwanted sexual advances from fellow student David (Evan Richards), a self-described nerd who's obsessed with the heroine and, significantly, likes to quote the looney Jack Nicholson character from THE SHINING. Suddenly appearing on the scene are two menacing fugitives, scruffy Paul Prexton (Craig Wasson) and his deaf-mute brother, John (Page Fletcher), whom Paul has just liberated from a mental institution.

The setup is just too obvious, as a knife disappears from the kitchen and a horse turns up slaughtered. One is supposed to think that wild-eyed John or lustful Paul did it, but the pair couldn't be more of a red herring if they had fins and scales. Young David is the mad slasher, driven to kill because necrophilia is the only way he can succeed with girls, even on spring break. The pathetic John is also smitten with the terrified Jenny and tries to defend her, Quasimodo-fashion. But Sheriff Hanley deduces something suspicious is going down at the farm, and the stage is set for a downbeat ending that's only a shade less predictable than what's gone before.

The filmmakers certainly possess an interesting resume: Los Angeles-based Crain Productions make well-known educational videos in the series I AM JOE'S LUNG, I AM JOE'S HAND, I AM JOE'S HEART, etc. Lovers of movie gore may find that a splendid qualification, but MIDNIGHT FEAR is a classier production than it sounds. Director Bill Crain both avoids crass nudity and averts his camera from serious bloodletting, and cinematographer Michael Crain lends a dreamy, quality gloss to the nocturnal imagery. No, the problems are banal, transparent plotting (like most celluloid psychos, David is able to die and come back to life an indefinite number of times) and a skimpy storyline padded with long, dull interludes of skulking and lurking to push the running time to the 90-minute mark.

Lost in the stuffing is a fine turn by Carradine, whose frequent casting as stonefaced tough guys has lately left his acting talents sadly underrated. As Hanley, Carradine does a credible portrait of an alcoholic lawman fighting to stay focused and wrap up the case. Unfortunately he fades in and out of the tale, and one never even gets a hint of what drove Hanley to the bottle in the first place. The younger characters gain points for actually looking like they could be college-age, and damsel-in-distress West has a winsome vulnerability, even if Jenny's never quite as smart as she's supposed to be.

This production was originally called "Moonlight Sonata," after the piano piece that Jenny performs from time to time, and it was filmed in 1990 in Coeur d'Alene and Hayden, Idaho, for the home video and cable-TV markets. *(Violence, substance abuse, profanity, adult situations.)*

p, Pat Tagliaferro; d, Bill Crain; w, Bill Crain, Craig Hughes, Craig Wasson; ph, Michael Crain; ed, Brian Crain; m, Steve Edwards; art d, Rick Galbraith; cos, Karen Patch

Thriller **(PR: O MPAA: NR)**

MIDNIGHT STING

(SEE: DIGGSTOWN)

MIGHTY DUCKS, THE ★★½

100m Bombay Films; The Avnet/Kerner Company; Walt Disney Productions; Touchwood Pacific Partners I ~ BV c

Emilio Estevez *(Gordon Bombay)*, Joss Ackland *(Hans)*, Lane Smith *(Coach Reilly)*, Heidi Kling *(Casey)*, Josef Sommer *(Gerald Ducksworth)*, Joshua Jackson *(Charlie Conroy)*, Elden Ratliff *(Fulton Reed)*, Shaun Weiss *(Goldberg)*, M.C. Gainey *(Lewis)*, Matt Doherty *(Les Averman)*, Brandon Adams *(Jesse Hall)*, J.D. Daniels *(Peter)*, Aaron Schwartz *(Dave Karp)*, Garette Ratliff Henson *(Guy Germaine)*, Marguerite Moreau *(Connie)*, Jane Plank *(Tammy)*, Jussie Smollett *(Terry Hall)*, Vincent A. LaRusso *(Adam Banks)*, Daniel Tamberelli *(Tommy)*, Michael Ooms *(McGill)*, Casey Garven *(Larson)*, Hal Fort Atkinson, III *(Philip Banks)*, Basil McRae *(1st Northstar Playerr)*, Michael Modano *(2nd Northstar Playerr)*, John Beasley *(Mr. Hall)*, Stephen Dowling *(Referee)*, Brock Pierce *(Gordon–Age 10)*, Robert Pall *(Gordon's Father)*, John Paul Gamoke *(Mr. Tolbert)*, Steven Brill *(Frank Huddy)*, George Coe *(Judge Weathers)*, Dale Dunham *(Jury Foreman)*, Barbara Davidson *(Jeannie)*, Brad Peterson *(Cardinals Coach)*, John Oliver *(Cardinals Gaol)*, Jacqueline Kim *(Jane)*, Schumacher Garth *(Arresting Cop)*, Joe Howard *(Court Clerk)*, Scott Bryan *(1st Cardinal)*, Peter L. Mullin *(Referee)*, Mark Bradley *(Science Teacher)*, Bill Schoppert *(Official)*, Claudia Wilkens *(Principal)*, Jack White *(Utitity Ref)*, Peter Syvertsen *(Paramedic)*, Bob Miller *(Announcer)*

As sure as the next car payment is due or a new Michael Caine movie will be opening soon, Hollywood regularly mines the motherlode of hackneyed sports fantasies and produces vehicles like THE MIGHTY DUCKS, a streamlined, cliche-ridden underdog story that filled corporate coffers and wowed pre-schoolers who were too young to recognize hackwork.

Emilio Estevez stars as Gordon Bombay a brash, hotshot lawyer who, following his arrest on a drunk-driving charge, is given a leave of absence from his law firm by his boss Gerald Ducksworth (Josef Sommer) and sentenced to serve five hundred hours of community service coaching a hockey team consisting of a "pc" collection of pre-pubescent delinquents. At first Gordon, haunted by childhood memories of missing the final shot in a championship peewee hockey game, is less than enthusiastic about coaching the team ("I hate hockey and I hate kids," he declaims). But soon Gordon is redeemed, gaining the respect of the team, making them a hockey team to be reckoned with, and even succeeding is winning the peewee play-offs against his old team, the Hawks, and their cruelly badgering coach Reilly (Lane Smith). THE MIGHTY DUCKS ends with the team seeing Emilio Estevez off on a bus as he forsakes his career as a lawyer to try out for a position with a professional hockey team, his new love Casey (Heidi Kling) beaming as she sizes him up for the future.

THE MIGHTY DUCKS is the MacDonald's of popular movies. From the first scene (a flashback of Gordon losing the big game, shot in slow motion and a dream-like haze), the viewer knows exactly what he's getting, the only surprise being how utterly predictable it all is. The characters in the film might just as well not have proper names and instead opt for the D.W. Griffith brand of archetypal characters—Misunderstood Hero (Estevez), The Supportive Friend (Ackland), the Mean-Tempered Trainer (Smith), and, of course, The Dear One (Kling).

But it is not enough for THE MIGHTY DUCKS to celebrate its simplicity in concentrating on the underdog Ducks and their preordained success. Instead, the focus shifts to Gordon, jettisoning any attempt at creating distinctive members of the team, making the children faceless pawns in their coach's redemption. Unfortunately, Gordon's redemption is also by-the-book, this particular book being the textbook for Ganz and Mandell 101, in which an uninteresting and unappealing character is given intimations of a troubled past in lieu of any attempt at in-depth character development or emotional undertones. Steven Brill and Brian Hohlfield's flimsy screenplay puts a greater burden on the actors to carry the film. Unfortunately, the actors in THE MIGHTY DUCKS are as nondescript and interchangeable as their characters. Veterans Joss Ackland and Josef Sommer are left chewing whitebread with nothing to do and Emilio Estevez plays his role as if the actor himself was undergoing community service by appearing in the film.

Where the film does succeed is in director Stephen Herek's fast pace and upbeat tone, which manages to ride over most of the schmaltz and bathos. And Herek pumps up the peewee hockey games into a montage of cheers and slapshots that keeps the audience primed and charged (even taking a cue from Martin Scorcese in THE COLOR OF MONEY and Kevin Reynolds in ROBIN HOOD: PRINCE OF THIEVES with a point-of-view shot of a spinning hockey puck slamming through the net backing of a goal).

THE MIGHTY DUCKS is harmless enough, but its schematic retread of a screenplay and its lethargic acting detracts from the unassuming, passable entertainment it might have been.

p, Jon Avnet, Jordan Kerner; d, Stephen Herek; w, Steven Brill, Brian Hohlfield; ph, Thomas Del Ruth; ed, Larry Bock, John F. Link; m, David Newman; prod d, Randy Ser; art d, Tony Fanning; set d, Julie Kaye Fanton

Sports/Comedy **(PR: A MPAA: PG)**

MIKEY ★

Tapestry Films ~ Imperial Entertainment Corporation c

Josie Bissett *(Jessie)*, Lyman Ward *(Mr. Jenkins)*, John Diehl *(Neil)*, Ashley Laurence *(Gilder)*, Mimi Craven *(Rachel)*, Brian Bonsall *(Mikey)*, Whitby Hertford *(Ben)*, David Rogge *(Boyfriend)*

Directed with negligible flair by Dennis Dimster-Denk, MIKEY is the horrifying but implausible story of an angelic looking ten-year-old orphan who is anything but saintly.

The film opens with Mikey (Brian Bonsall) drowning his half-sister in the swimming pool and electrocuting his stepmother in the bathtub. When Daddy comes home, Mikey beats him to death with a baseball bat. The police assume an outsider killed Mikey's family, and the murderous tyke is soon adopted by the next set of parental units—Neil (John Diehl) and Rachel (Mimi Craven). After moving into his new home, Mikey befriends the little boy next door, Ben (Whitby Hertford), and develops a crush on Ben's teenage sister Jessie (Josie Bissett). But Mikey is unhappy to learn that Jessie has a boyfriend (David Rogge).

Meanwhile, at school, Mikey busies himself by drawing morbid pictures of dismembered people. Mikey's teacher, Miss Gilder (Ashley Laurence), shows one to the school shrink who thinks she's an alarmist. (We later discover that Mikey was abused by his real parents, but this is never discussed at any length.) After Mikey cuts up his own arm, Miss Gilder tries to get Neil and Rachel to take him to a psychologist, but they are not convinced Mikey has a problem. As Mikey's parents are conveniently hesitant, Mikey manages to bump off Jessie's boyfriend and the neighbor's cat.

It isn't until Rachel catches the rosy-cheeked maniac watching videotapes of his own misdeeds, that she decides Mikey is disturbed. By the end of the film, Mikey has murdered Rachel, Neil, Miss Gilder and the school shrink. And in the film's most gruesome scene, Mikey props up all the dead bodies in chairs around the dining room table. Mikey then leaves the house and walks along the highway where police pick him up. Once again he isn't checked out by the authorities and is adopted by family number three.

Dimster-Denk uses graphic violence to try and cover up holes in MIKEY's plot that you could drive a Mac truck through. How is it that a small child has such strength? Is he Pippi Longstocking's cousin? At least in movies like THE OMEN, we know the child has demonic powers. But in MIKEY, this kid's super strength is never explained. The scene where Mikey has arranged the dead bodies around the table is horrifying, to be sure. But how is it that a ten-year-old has not only dragged these bodies to the table, but propped them up in chairs as well? In fact, not one adult is able to defend himself or herself from this midget-sized Schwarzenegger. *(Excessive violence, profanity, sexual situations.)*

p, Peter Abrams, Robert Levy, Natan Zahavi; d, Dennis Dimster-Denk; w, Jonathan Glassner; ph, Tom Jewett; ed, Natan Zahavi, Omer Tal; m, Tim Truman; prod d, Nigel Clinker, Marcia Calosio

Horror **(PR: O MPAA: R)**

MIND, BODY & SOUL ★

93m AIP Studios; Rick Sloane Productions ~
AIP Home Video c

Wings Hauser *(John Stockton)*, Ginger Lynn Allen *(Brenda Carter)*, Jay Richardson *(Detective McKenzie)*, Tami Bakke *(Rachael)*, Michael McMillen *(Prison Guard)*, Jesse Kaye *(Carl)*, Ken Hill *(Shawn)*, Veronica Carothers *(Sacrifice Girl)*, Mark Richardson *(Demonic Spirit)*, Ken Merck *(Police Officer)*, Jeff Record *(Po-*

lice Officer), Robert Weston *(Police Officer)*, Toni Alessandrini *(Priestess Tura)*, Jo Brewer *(Joan Lake)*

Written and directed by Rick Sloane, MIND, BODY & SOUL is a slow-moving and badly produced film about an innocent young woman who gets caught up in a satanic cult.

In the opening scene, Brenda Carter's (porn superstar turned legit actress Ginger Lynn Allen) boyfriend, Carl (Jesse Kaye), takes her to a satanic meeting just for the hell of it; it's about time she knew what some of his hobbies are—devil worship, human sacrifice and so on. Brenda quickly becomes uncomfortable at the bizarre ceremony. And just as a woman is about to be murdered in a sadistic ritual, the cops raid the establishment. But somehow, all of the cult members manage to escape.

Brenda takes the police to Carl's apartment, but it has mysteriously burned down. Not believing her story about her boyfriend or her claim that she's not a cult member, the cops throw Brenda in jail. While incarcerated, attorney John Stockton (Wings Hauser) posts bail for Brenda and invites her to stay at his place. With nowhere else to go, she warily takes him up on his generous offer. A few days later, Brenda's cellmate, Rachael (Tami Bakke), shows up at John's house—she's got no place to stay either.

After a mutilated female body turns up with a satanic symbol carved into its chest, Brenda feels it's her civic duty to discuss her brush with the Devil on the "Joan Lake Show," a local TV talk program. When the taping's finished, a stagehand, Shawn (Ken Hill), drives Brenda home. But en route to John's house, one of the guards from the prison, who's also a cult member, tries to run them off the road. Fortunately, Brenda has Carl's satanic medallion with her. She stares at it, and before you can say "black magic," the guard's car runs off the road and he dies.

In the final scene, Brenda is nearly sacrificed during a satanic ritual, and it is revealed that John is the cult's leader. Shawn comes to her rescue, carrying with him Carl's magic medallion, which Brenda, once again summoning up her unexplained powers, uses to get free. As Shawn and Brenda make their implausible escape, they watch the meeting house burn down.

Although it contains some graphic violence, MIND, BODY & SOUL fails to terrify because of the abrupt editing and one too many plot holes. Why, for instance, doesn't Brenda become suspicious when John tells her not to call the police? And why don't the cops put the meeting place under surveillance once they've discovered where the cult gathers? But the film's most important flaw is scenes of violence against women which often incorporate sexual overtones. *(Violence, partial nudity, sexual situations.)*

p, Rick Sloane, Steve Flick; d, Rick Sloane; w, Rick Sloane; ph, Robert Hayes; ed, Rick Mitchell; m, Alan Dermarderosian; art d, Mark Richardson

Horror **(PR: O MPAA: R)**

MINDWARP ★★★

96m Fangoria Films ~ Columbia TriStar Home Video c

Bruce Campbell *(Stover)*, Marta Alicia *(Judy)*, Elizabeth Kent *(Cornelia)*, Angus Scrimm *(Seer)*, Wendy Sandow *(Claude)*, Mary Becker

There hasn't been a future as bleak as the one displayed in MINDWARP in some time. The movie, produced by Fangoria Films (an offshoot of the popular horror magazine) takes the audience through three different futuristic locations, each one more forbidding than the last. Fortunately, as the settings get worse, the movie gets progressively better, and MINDWARP ends up as an involving horror adventure.

The story opens in a white, sterile household where the young protagonist, Judy (Marta Alicia, whose performance starts out shaky but also improves with time), spends her life plugged into Infinisynth, a computer network that allows the population to live in a world of preprogrammed fantasy. But Judy's getting tired of living out these packaged dreams and longs for some real action in her life, and before you can say "Be careful what you wish for," she's deposited in the harsh, frightening wasteland that exists beyond "Inworld." After being menaced by deformed, humanoid creatures called Crawlers, Judy is rescued and befriended by Stover (Bruce Campbell of the EVIL DEAD films), a rugged hunter who takes Judy to his ramshackle house. The two share observations about their respective worlds, and eventually make love, but their solace is short-lived, as a group of Crawlers invade the house and drag the pair down into their subterranean domain.

Down below, Judy is subjected to the sadistic ministrations of Cornelia (Elizabeth Kent), while Stover is put in chains and forced into slave labor. The Crawlers' lair is filled with the scrap of previous civilizations and lorded over by a self-proclaimed mystic called the Seer (Angus Scrimm). Stover attempts an escape as Judy is brought before the ruler, but is caught; Judy witnesses the Seer sacrificing Cornelia's young handmaiden Claude (Wendy Sandow) in a giant chipper before being brought before him herself. There, he removes his headdress and reveals that he is in fact Judy's long-lost father, whom she has been yearning to know. He invites her to rule the underworld with him, but she rejects the idea; meanwhile, Stover, who has been imprisoned in a submerged cage and tortured with leeches, breaks free and once again intercedes to save Judy.

The Seer winds up being sent down into the chipper while Stover and Judy escape to the surface; once there, however, Stover succumbs to the leeches breeding inside him. At that point, Judy suddenly finds herself facing the Sysop, who runs Infinisynth; what she has just gone through was only a fantasy, and now she is being offered the chance to run the Infinisynth program. She accepts and takes the Sysop's position—and then wakes up from that fantasy, back in her room, just as she began.

One of the most impressive things about MINDWARP is its setting up of three very convincing futuristic environments on what was evidently a low budget; director Steve Barnett's previous work with Roger Corman (he headed up post-production at Corman's Concorde Pictures and directed HOLLYWOOD BOULEVARD II) no doubt helped out in this area. After a slow-paced start, the movie picks up once Judy hits the wasteland, with some impressive location photography in a landscape where white ice floes run up against black sand beaches. These scenes also benefit from introducing Campbell, whose rough-and-ready energy gives the film a boost. Once things get underground, PHANTASM veteran Scrimm brings a lot to his own role, playing his occasionally stilted lines with a sense of dignity and grandeur that makes the Seer a commanding presence, and his quiet imperiousness plays well off Campbell's brash action.

Given the current trend toward "fun" horror, Barnett keeps the mood surprisingly downbeat, and he and screenwriter Henry Dominick are startlingly merciless when it comes to the fates of their characters. This is especially true in the case of Claude, played with sympathetic expressiveness by newcomer Sandow; what happens to her threatens to send the movie over the line into distastefulness. However, Barnett has done well with material that might have been just gross in lesser hands, and admirably keeps the tone consistent all the way through to the end, even when the closing scenes try to be a little too tricky for their own good. *(Excessive violence, adult situations, sexual situations.)*

p, Christopher Webster; d, Steve Barnett; w, Henry Dominick; ph, Peter Fernberger; ed, Adam Wolfe; m, Mark Governor; prod d, Kim Hix

Science Fiction/Horror **(PR: O MPAA: R)**

MIRACLE BEACH ★½

Motion Picture Corporation of America ~ Columbia TriStar Home Video c

Pat Morita *(Gus)*, Martin Mull *(Donald Burbank)*, Dean Cameron *(Scotty McKay)*, Ami Dolenz *(Jeanie)*, Alexis Arquette *(Lars)*, Brian Perry *(Soup)*, Felicity Waterman *(Dana)*, Vincent Schiavelli, Allen Garfield, Hiroko, Gary Grant, Monique Gabrielle, Sydney Lassick

If you can tell a good joke you can get away with a lot, as any party drunk knows. But there are limits. Just ask whoever has to clean up after that drunk—or anybody who watches MIRACLE BEACH, sunny sexploitation salved, but not saved, by playful humor.

Up in the clouds is a cheapjack version of Mount Olympus or something, where magical figures like Santa Claus, the Easter Bunny and the Tooth Fairy wander around in dimestore costumes. A presiding leprechaun judges that Earth's been good lately ("Nuclear arms are out, democracy is in and they're starting to work very hard on that recycling thing"), so he sends a pretty genie named—what else?—Jeanie (Ami Dolenz) down to obey the commands of some lucky human. Jeanie's bottle ends up with Scotty McKay (Dean Cameron), a recently evicted young California beach bum. Scotty and his garage-dwelling cohorts Lars (Alexis Arquette) and Soup (Brian Perry) are delighted to meet Jeanie, who makes their wishes instantly come true. It's actually amusing for a while to see them get any absurd thing they want, granted happily—though with minimal special effects—by the genie.

Now housed in a luxury beach estate with live rock musicians in place of stereo and the Miss International swimsuit pageant staged on the grounds, Soup and Lars are sated. But Scotty's smitten with an unapproachable leggy supermodel, Dana (Felicity Waterman), who happens to live in the neighborhood. The only limit to Jeanie's power is she can't force lovers together, so she endows Scotty with money, moxie and multiple talents meant to attract Dana. The strategy works, and delectable Dana starts enticing Scotty toward her bed. But Jeanie realizes that Dana's a promiscuous tramp. "So what's the problem?" this film's target audience might well argue. Well, Jeanie's in love with Scotty herself and doesn't want to see him used. She does a few tricks to split Dana and the dupe, upsetting the leprechaun, but Scotty finally sees the light and pairs off with a now-mortal Jeanie for the finale.

Directed by Skott Snider, a former helmer of *Playboy* videocassettes, this male wish-fulfillment fantasy avoids a quick drowning in its own raunch through occasional clever gags (a Hollywood executive charges his expenses to the budget of "Hudson Hawk II") and a watchable cast. Ami Dolenz (daughter of erstwhile Monkee Mickey Dolenz) and Felicity Waterman each have a winning way with the camera that transcends their thankless roles, and they fill their bikinis fetchingly—though nude scenes are apportioned instead to the hordes of female extras.

Leading man Dean Cameron looks enough like Nicholas Cage to threaten havoc at the Francis Ford Coppola family reunion. Cameos include LA Clippers basketball star Gary Grant and pointless excerpts from past Brad Krevoy/Brian Stabler productions like THINK BIG and PURPLE PEOPLE EATER. The supporting cast contains some fine comic character performers, but Pat Morita plays it straight as Gus, a homeless guy who scorns a $10,000 handout from Scotty; this street person wants an honest job, not charity. Nice sentiment, but consider the message at the end when Gus turns out to be just another magical illusion. *(Nudity, sexual situations.)*

p, Brad Krevoy, Steve Stabler; d, Skott Snider; w, Scott Bindley; ph, Bernard Salzmann; ed, Emma Hickox; m, Eric Allaman; prod d, Gary Randall; art d, Paul Miller; set d, Amy Ancona; cos, Julia Schklair

Comedy/Fantasy/Romance **(PR: O MPAA: R)**

MIRROR IMAGES

94m Axis Films International ~ Academy Entertainment c

Deila Sheppard *(Kaitlin/Shauna)*, Jeff Conaway *(Jeff Blair)*, Julie Strain *(Gina Kaye)*, Nels Van Patten *(Joey Zoom)*, Korey Mall *(Gil)*, Ricard Arbolino *(Carter Sayles)*, Lee Anne Beaman, John O'Hurley, Buck Flower

Here's another one of those direct-to-video "thrillers" that are to pornography what "near beer" is to liquor. Strip MIRROR IMAGES of its feeble murder gimmick and superficial political cynicism and you're left with a soft-focus *Playboy* tape—or more accurately, *Penthouse*, the publication in which the charms of lead actress Delia Sheppard have previously been unveiled.

Ample quantities of Sheppard star in dual roles: she's Kaitlin, a voluptuous, redheaded California housewife neglected by yuppie husband Jeff (Jeff Conaway) who claims to be too busy with Republican electioneering to pay her any sexual attention. Meanwhile Kaitlin's twin sister, Shauna (Sheppard again),a voluptuous, wanton blonde, counts Jeff among her numerous lovers. Lonely Kaitlin visits Shauna's apartment but finds her sibling mysteriously absent. Impulsively she dons Shauna's trendy harlot wardrobe of Spandex, crucifixes and underwear too skimpy to serve any utilitarian purpose. Thus attired, Kaitlin begins a double life as a good-time girl, and Shauna's "gentlemen callers" can't tell the difference.

The plot thickens when one of Shauna's regulars turns out to be Jeff's GOP cohort, millionaire presidential candidate Carter Sayles (Richard Arbolino), in truth a corrupt, Halloween-masked serial-rapist-killer who uses his bankrupt airline business to smuggle heroin—whew! Kaitlin is rescued from the fiend by the timely arrival of Shauna, dressed in the cop uniform that she normally uses for s&m routines.

The filmmakers take every opportunity to pose the bad guys next to beaming portraits of Ronald Reagan and George Bush, but that's hardly the point. The main attractions are frequent skin shots of Sheppard, disporting herself in gauzy dream sequences and erotic interludes set to awful rock 'n' roll tunes. Some of the folks in the credits are hiding behind pseudonyms, and viewers may be feel similarly inclined. MIRROR IMAGES came out on cassettes offering the familiar choice of R-rated and more explicit unrated versions. *(Violence, substance abuse, profanity, excessive nudity, sexual situations, adult situations.)*

p, Andrew Garroni; d, Alexander Gregory Hippolyte; w, Rick Marx; ph, Paul Desatoff; ed, Kent Smith; m, Joseph Smith; prod d, Blair Martin; art d, Mike Shaw; cos, Ricardo Delgado, Lothar Delgado

Erotic/Thriller **(PR: O MPAA: R)**

MISSION OF JUSTICE ★★

95m Image Organization; Westwind Productions ~ Republic Pictures Home Video c

Jeff Wincott *(Kurt Harris)*, Brigitte Nielsen *(Dr. Rachel Olsen)*, Tony Burton *(Cedric Williams)*, Karen Shepard *(Lynn Steele)*, Matthias Hues *(Titus)*, Luca Bercovici, Billy Sly Williams, Cyndi Pass, Tom Wood

As slam-bang, kickboxing action films and vigilante revenge movies go, MISSION OF JUSTICE is only slightly above average.

Kurt Harris (Jeff Wincott) is a tough cop with a habit of using his martial arts expertise to trounce criminals who have it coming. He and his partner, Lynn Steele (Karen Shepard), rescue a woman from her violent boyfriend. When Sergeant Duncan lets the lout walk, and he subsequently commits murder, Harris punches out his boss and resigns from the force. The rogue cop soon finds a villain to direct his vigilante venom against when his friend Cedric Williams (Tony Burton), a former boxing champ, is murdered. As Harris soon learns, the killing was done by Dr. Rachel Olsen (Brigitte Nielsen), a cold-blooded, crypto-fascist psychologist trying to get elected mayor by posing as an anti-crime organizer. Her "Mission of Justice" cult uses martial arts and self-help philosophy to recruit ex-cons and wealthy patrons into her supposed crime watch group. With her thug brother Titus (Matthias Hues) and Machiavellian political consultant Roger, Dr. Olsen is poised to take over the city.

To expose the villains and avenge his friend's murder, Harris goes undercover, pretending to join the Olsen "family." His impressive martial arts abilities earn Harris a place within the organization's inner circle, but a suspicious Roger has his assistant Erin keep an eye on him. Harris wins Olsen's trust by busting up a drug deal, letting her crime-fighting "peacemakers" upstage the police. Meanwhile, Harris and an off-duty Steele uncover videotaped evidence that Olsen tortured as well as killed Cedric. When she discovers the video missing, Olsen has Sgt. Duncan assassinated and leads the police to suspect Harris.

With Steele's help, Harris eludes the police and teams up with Jimmy, a cult member who witnessed Cedric's murder and whose rich grandmother was bilked and murdered by the Mission. Titus captures Jimmy so that Olsen can torture him to get information. Steele and Harris videotape Olsen's crime. After winning a brutal fight against Erin and Titus, Harris interrupts a Olsen press conference by showing the torture session to reporters. The exposed villainess attacks the hero but is subdued. The vindicated Harris returns to the police force.

Compared to most films that feature a karate-chopping hero single-handedly defeating a gauntlet of goons, MISSION OF JUSTICE is competently acted. The real-life martial artists who play several of the parts, in fact, perform more convincingly than the statuesque but decidedly wooden Nielsen (ROCKY IV, BEVERLY HILLS COP II), the film's sole marquee name. While the storyline and action threaten to become overly complicated with subplots, director Steve Barnett, a Roger Corman protege, keeps things moving.

There is little redeeming value in the shallow moralizing of the vigilante hero, who will put his boot upside the head of any number of crooks and cops to prove that violence is wrong. But Barnett knows that unrelenting action is the martial arts genre's prime directive. He allows just enough generic narrative development to create the thin layer of outrage that motivates the violent combat scenes. Fans of the genre may be satified, but not overwhelmed by Jeff Wincott's two-fisted, one-emotion showcase of brutality. *(Excessive violence, profanity.)*

p, Pierre David, Kurt Anderson; d, Steve Barnett; w, George Saunders, John Bryant Hedberg, (from the story by David Pierre); ph, Peter Fernberger; ed, Brent Schoenfeld; art d, Gary Randall; set d, Sharon Reed; cos, Yana Syrkin

Action/Crime/Martial Arts (PR: O MPAA: R)

MISSISSIPPI MASALA ★★★½

(U.S./U.K.) 118m Mira Nair Films; SCS Films; Palace Pictures; Film Four International ~ Samuel Goldwyn Company c

Denzel Washington *(Demetrius)*, Sarita Choudhury *(Mina)*, Roshan Seth *(Jay)*, Sharmila Tagore *(Kinnu)*, Charles S. Dutton *(Tyrone)*, Joe Seneca *(Williben)*, Ranjit Chowdhry *(Anil)*, Mohan Gokhale *(Pontiac)*, Mohan Agashe *(Kanti Napkin)*, Tico Wells *(Dexter)*, Yvette Hawkins *(Aunt Rose)*, Anjan Srivastava *(Jammubhai)*, Dipti Suthar *(Chanda)*, Varsha Thaker *(Kusumben)*, Ashok Lath *(Harry Patel)*, Natalie Oliver *(Alicia LeShay)*, Karen Pinkston *(Mrs. Morgan)*, Willy Cobbs *(Skillet)*, Mira Nair *(1st Gossip)*, Rajika Puri *(2nd Gossip)*, Sharon Williams *(Tadice)*, Cyreio Hughes *(D.J.)*, Stacy Swinford *(Bubba)*, Rick Senn *(Piggly Wiggly Checker)*, Jim Haffey *(White Truck Driver)*, Dillon Rozell Gross *(Police Officer)*, Larry Haggard *(Joe)*, E.W. Colvin *(Grandcraw)*, Joyce Murrah *(Lady at Lusco's)*, Kevin McNeil *(Clarence)*, Reverend Fred Matthews *(Grandaddy)*, Mahlon Bouldin *(Student)*, Buddy St Amant *(Biloxi Cop)*, James Dale *(Businessman)*, Ben Burford *(Bank Manager)*, Sam Sherrill *(Phinias T. Turnbull)*, Alix Henry Sanders *(Barber)*, Jerone Wiggins *(James)*, Sadie Carr *(Mildre)*, Richard Crick *(White Customer)*, Alix W. Sanders *(postman)*, Shung Moo-joo *(Chinese Customer)*, Jaimini Thaker *(Kanti Bhai)*, Hollis Pippin *(Sylvester Artiste III)*, Dewey Buffington *(Evangelist)*, Tony McGhee *(1st Rapper)*, J.D. Barrett *(2nd Rapper)*, Tre'demont Spearman *(3rd Rapper)*, Argentina Moore *(4th Rapper)*, Nora Boland *(1st Shop-at-Home Anchor Person)*, Patsy Garrett *(2nd Shop-at-Home Anchor Person)*, Konga Mbandu *(Okelo)*, Sahira Nair *(Young Mina)*, Michael Wawuyo *(Soldier on Bus)*, Phavin Parbario *(Young Jay)*, Emanuel Mudara *(Young Okelo)*, Immaculate Byakatonda *(Okelo's Mother)*, Amrit Panesar *(Mrs. Bedi)*, Jimmy Din *(Bharat)*, Bonnie M. Lubega *(Teacher)*, Sammy E.D. Senkumba *(Taxi Driver)*, Mayambala Ssekasi *(Prison Captain)*, Joseph Olita *(Idi Amin)*, Muteta Wilberforce *(Soldier at Roadblock)*

"Masala" refers to a mix of varied spices, and one of the strengths of MISSISSIPPI MASALA is its own collection of colorful characters. While its ostensible focus is on an interracial romance, the film's dramatic scope is wide enough to encompass not only those around the couple, and their reactions to the affair, but the events and forces that led to their coming together in the first place.

The lovers are Demetrius (Denzel Washington), a young black man who runs a carpet-cleaning business in Mississippi, and Mina (Sarita Choudhury), whose parents Jay (Roshan Seth) and Kinnu (Sharmila Tagore) run a local liquor store. Like many of their friends, Mina and her family are Indians who were expelled from Uganda in 1972 by Idi Amin, and Jay has been tirelessly seeking restoration for his confiscated property by the Uganda government ever since. Mina, working for her parents' boss Anil (Ranjit Chowdhry), accidentally runs his car into Demetrius's truck; after his initial upset, Demetrius becomes attracted to her. The feeling is mutual, and the pair begin a romance. Jay frowns upon the relationship, but Mina wins approval from Demetrius's family when she joins him at his father's birthday party.

The pair sneak off for a weekend at Biloxi Beach without her parents' knowing, but Anil and a friend are also there; they recognize Demetrius's truck and break into the couple's motel room. The couple are arrested, and Mina is bailed out by Jay, who demands that she stop seeing Demetrius. Demetrius's business gets boycotted by the many local Asian motel owners, but despite the pressure to separate them, the lovers cannot forsake each other. Meanwhile, Jay has begun to feel that he should return his family to Africa, and goes there himself when invited to a court hearing over his compensation by the government. But he arrives to find his old house in ruins and his best African friend now dead, and realizes that he and his family belong in the US. At the same time, Demetrius and Mina decide to leave Mississippi and make their way together elsewhere.

MISSISSIPPI MASALA was certainly not the only miscegenation-themed film to reach US screens in recent years, but Indian director Mira Nair, a Harvard graduate and former documentarian (INDIA CABARET) whose first narrative feature, SALAAM BOMBAY!, received widespread acclaim, gives the story an additional spin by focusing on two minority characters and exploring the specific conflicts between their two races, as opposed to the usual black vs. white histrionics.

The screenplay by Sooni Taraporevala avoids easy polemics about race relations, and while the point of view is decisively on the Indian side, they are, if anything, frequently shown as less tolerant than the black characters. Yet the film also sets up a convincing and understandable source of this disapproval, particularly that of Jay, in the expulsion of Asians from Uganda that sent thousands of families into forced relocations in America. In this way, MISSISSIPPI MASALA becomes as much a story about the outside forces and past events that influence the central love affair as it is about the affair itself. Jay's attempts to win compensation for what he lost in Africa form an affecting subplot, and the minor characters are fleshed out in such a way that the film comes to explore a whole pair of cultures, not just a story of two people.

Nonetheless, Demetrius and Mina's deepening relationship remains empathetic and moving, not least because of the strong performances in the central roles. Washington, in one of his first true romantic leads, does solid work as a man who is resistant but not blind to the social pressures working against the affair, and newcomer Choudhury is excellent as the rebellious Mina, effectively playing the non-conformist side of her character without ever losing sympathy. There's real romantic chemistry between the two as well, and their love scene in the Biloxi motel room generates real heat without indulging in the sultry silliness of so many recent erotic dramas. *(Sexual situations, profanity, nudity.)*

p, Michael Nozik, Mira Nair; d, Mira Nair; w, Sooni Taraporevala; ph, Edward Lachman; ed, Roberto Silvi; m, L. Subramaniam; prod d, Mitch Epstein; art d, Jefferson Sage; set d, Jeanette Scott; cos, Hope Hanafin

Drama/Romance (PR: C MPAA: R)

MISTRESS ★★★

108m Mistress Productions; Meir Teper Productions; Tribeca Productions ~ Rainbow Releasing/Tribeca Productions c

Robert Wuhl *(Marvin Landisman)*, Martin Landau *(Jack Roth)*, Jace Alexander *(Stuart Stratland, Jr.)*, Robert De Niro *(Evan M. Wright)*, Laurie Metcalf *(Rachel Landisman)*, Eli Wallach *(George Lieberhoff)*, Danny Aiello *(Carmine Rasso)*, Sheryl Lee Ralph *(Beverly Dumont)*, Jean Smart *(Patricia Riley)*, Tuesday Knight *(Peggy Pauline)*, Christopher Walken *(Warren Zell)*, Ernest Borgnine *(Himself)*, Vasek C. Simek *(Hans)*, Tomas R. Voth *(Stagehand)*, Mary Mercier *(Shelby's Waitress)*, Bill Rotko *(Valet)*, Dimitri Dimitrov *(Maitre d')*, Chuck Lowe *(Bernie)*, Frida S. Aradottir *(Mrs. Evan Wright)*, Raphaela Rose Primus *(Raphaela Wright)*, Stefan Gierasch *(Stratland, Sr.)*, Michael Kelley *(Guard at Gate)*, Jerome Dempsey *(Mitch)*, Roberta Wallach *(Nancy)*, Kathleen Johnson *(Party Guest)*, Leata Galloway, Nina Small, Tim Bagley, Byron Simpson, Debbie L. James, Dawn Hopper *(Mitch's Singing Students)*, Deirdre Hade *(Party Goer)*, Peter Kalos *(Party Goer)*, Gretchen Becker *(Hamburger Girl)*, Eileen Wilkinson *(Astrologer)*

Actor Barry Primus made his directorial debut with MISTRESS, a kind of low-rent parallel to Robert Altman's THE PLAYER. While Altman's far superior film skewers Hollywood's power elite, Primus brings his gently satirical gaze to bear on the rather less glamorous fringes of the filmmaking world.

Marvin Landisman (Robert Wuhl), a once promising young director whose film career was cut short by the on-camera suicide of actor Warren Zell (Christopher Walken), is now in his early forties, an embittered director of instructional cassettes for the home video market. While watching a print of GRAND ILLUSION in his shabby Los Angeles apartment, he receives a call from down-at-heel, ex-studio producer Jack Roth (Martin Landau). Roth has unearthed Marvin's long dormant, completely uncommercial screenplay about an artist who commits suicide and believes he has a shot at producing the film. Marvin agrees to cooperate, only on condition that not a word of his precious screenplay be changed and that he be allowed to direct.

Marvin, Roth and aspiring young writer Stuart Stratland, Jr. (Jace Alexander), son of a famous screenwriter, meet with three potential investors. George Lieberhoff (Eli Wallach), whose biggest claim to fame is that film industry people used to buy clocks in his store, will put up money if there's a role for his girlfriend, Peggy Pauline (Tuesday Knight), a talent-free Madonna lookalike. Carmine Rasso (Danny Aiello), a shady businessman with a repertoire of gruesome Vietnam stories, will put up money if . . there's a role for *his* girlfriend, Patricia Riley (Jean Smart), an airline stewardess and recovering alcoholic. Evan M. Wright (Robert De Niro), a slick, sleazy mini-mogul, will put up money if . . there's a role for his mistress, Beverly Dumont (Sheryl Lee Ralph), *and* the script is changed beyond recognition. (One of many complications is that Beverly, a genuinely talented black actress, is *also* sleeping with Carmine—something she's only too happy to use as leverage in order to guarantee getting the best part.)

After a crisis of conscience triggered by a split with his wife (Marvin had made her life unbearable for several years as a result of his obsession with the suicide screenplay), he realizes it's time to let go of that obsession and compromise his screenplay simply in order to get something made. He doesn't even bother to read Stratland's new script—which accommodates not only the wishes of the producers but the young writer's infatuation with Peggy—before attending the climactic party at which the investors are to sign their contracts. The party, however, turns into a disastrous series of amorous and professional mix-ups, and the deal falls apart. Disillusioned, Marvin resumes his day job.

One night, with Marvin once again watching GRAND ILLUSION in his apartment, he receives another phone call from Roth, who's found another investor interested in discussing the project. After categorically stating that he's not interested, Marvin relents and asks, "What time?"

Produced (along with Meir Teper) by De Niro through his Tribeca Productions, MISTRESS is a benign satire of life on the seedier edges of Tinseltown. But although the screenplay, by Primus and J.F. Lawton, has plenty of comic moments, it is poorly structured and develops little momentum, shifting from one loosely connected sketch to another. The occasional attempts to switch from comic to tragic mode are also misguided, quickly sliding from the serious to the maudlin.

MISTRESS, however, is saved by its witty, well-observed sense of place and some snappy dialogue, delivered to perfection by a talented cast with whom the director clearly has an affinity.

Although Robert Wuhl delivers a largely one-note performance as Marvin, Primus elicits bright performances from the other cast members, including Landau as Roth—a clinging, fawning figure whose sad desperation saves him from being a caricature. De Niro's turn as the ruthless investor is a hilariously comic send-up of his diabolic businessman from ANGEL HEART.

Given a better structured screenplay, MISTRESS might have given THE PLAYER a run for its money. Instead, it merely offers glimmers of what might have been, and settles for being a cinematic footnote. *(Profanity, adult situations.)*

p, Meir Teper, Robert De Niro; d, Barry Primus; w, Barry Primus, J.F. Lawton, (from the story by Primus); ph, Sven Kirsten; ed, Steven Weisberg; m, Galt MacDermot; prod d, Phil Peters; art d, Randy Grickson; set d, K.O. Fox; cos, Susan Nininger

Drama/Comedy **(PR: C MPAA: R)**

MO' MONEY ★★½

98m Wife and Kids Productions; Columbia ~ Columbia c

Damon Wayans *(Johnny Stewart)*, Stacey Dash *(Amber Evans)*, Joe Santos *(Lieutenant Raymond Walsh)*, John Diehl *(Keith Heading)*, Harry J. Lennix *(Tom Dilton)*, Marlon Wayans *(Seymour Stewart)*, Mark Beltzman *(Chris Fields)*, Quincy Wong *(Eddie)*, Kevin Casey *(Lloyd)*, Larry Brandenburg *(Businessman)*, Garfield *(Rock)*, Almayvonne *(Charlotte)*, Dick Butler *(Ted Forrest)*, Matt Doherty *(Kid)*, Evan Lionel Smith *(Detective Mills)*, James Deuter *(Mr. Shift)*, Rondi Reed *(District Attorney)*, Gordon McClure *(Reverend Pimp Daddy)*, Richard Hamilton *(Judge Harold Lake)*, Ken Earl *(Bailiff)*, John Allen *(Jewelry Store Clerk)*, David Razowsky *(Jewelry Store Clerk)*, Salli Richardson *(Pretty Customer)*, Pete Zahradnick *(Officer Deebs)*, Lorenzo Clemons *(Officer Royce)*, Bill Harris *(Joel)*, Greg Bermont *(Waiter)*, Will Zahrn *(Bum/Cop)*, Ike Eichling *(Taxi Driver)*, Renee A Lacour *(Rock's Mother)*, Robert Swan *(Detective Lawrence)*, Victor Cole *(Sargeant Tan)*, Eddie "Bo" Smith *(Large Man)*, Ted Topolski *(1st Inmate)*, A.C. Tony Smith *(Guy on Toilet)*, Michael Bacarella *(Habib)*, Jo Be Cerny *(Patrolman)*, Allison Gordy *(Prostitute)*, Jackie Hoffman *(Jill)*, Mollie Grabemann *(Receptionist)*, Bernie Mac *(Club Doorman)*, Mik Scriba *(Transit Cop)*, William King *(Correction Officer)*, Irma P. Hall *(Lady on Phone)*, James Spinks *(Tracy Stewart)*, Kahil El Zabor *(Congo Player)*, Ben Lin *(Chinese Cook)*, Sean A. Tate *(Kid)*, Pat "Soul" Scaggs *(Token Booth Clerk)*, Lauro Lopez *(Dentist)*, Jimmy Woodard *(Man on Street)*, Edward Cushing *(Repairman)*

In MO' MONEY, a street fable for the 90s, "Living Color's" Damon Wayans and his little brother Marlon savor and suffer the sin of greed.

Johnny and Seymour Stewart (Damon and Marlon, respectively) are streetwise young men from Brooklyn always looking to scam another buck. Just as they are flubbing a con, a Dynasty Credit Card executive dies in a car crash set-up. Transit police nab Johnny during his getaway, but he is sprung by his dead father's ex-partner, Lt. Mills (Evan Lionel Smith) who is also investigating the businessman's murder. Ignoring his little brother's disgust, Johnny decides to go straight. While selling books in a midtown square he meets gorgeous Amber Evans (Stacey Dash), an employee at Dynasty. He immediately wangles a job in the mailroom to be near her. Determined to win Amber from her rich boyfriend, a whitebread Black man, Johnny breaks down and steals a credit card. He and Seymour step out on a wild shopping spree. Johnny shows up at Amber's in a sharp new suit, and she falls into his arms—she was over her boyfriend anyway.

Unfortunately, Dynasty security head, Keith Heading (John Diehl), caught Johnny's theft on video and blackmails him into joining his vicious credit-card crime ring—he was the murderer. Amber begins to get suspicious about Johnny's new wealth, and so he decides he wants out of the ring. Seymour is sent to Keith, wire tapped, in an attempt to elicit evidence against him, but Keith catches on and abducts him. With the help of Amber and Lt. Mills, Johnny sets out to rescue his kid brother. He enters a bloody race to the death with Keith and wins Seymour, the girl and his pride.

In writing MO' MONEY Damon Wayans has created an accessible comedy that introduces his charms to a wide audience. Both he and his brother are fatally charismatic as Johnny and Seymour, and the sparky dynamic of their banter is one of the delights of the film. Unfortunately, Wayans watered down his audacious sense of humor for Hollywood, resorting occasionally to non-punchlines like "oh shit!" As the mature, thoughtful brother he can also be a bit wet, especially playing drama or romance, and his guilt-free, buzzing little brother threatens to upstage him. The rest of the major characters are what you would expect—the police are cops, and Keith is an appropriately crazed psychotic. Stacey Dash employs a two-note range as Amber, sexy and pouty. Watch for two uproarious minor characters in their irreverent "Living Color" mode, the sleazy singer/lawyer Reverend Pimp Daddy (Gordon McClure) and the perennially grinning, sex-starved Charlotte (Almayvonne).

There's plenty of action in MO' MONEY and a fair dosage of gratuitous violence too. The film ends with an absurd five minute car-chase scene which makes Johnny some sort of bullet-dodging, car-roof-riding superman in silly contrast to the morally confused and indecisive guy he seemed for most of the film. MO' MONEY is entertaining enough and funny enough, and cannily includes all the elements that entice popularity. But, perhaps after reaping the rewards for this film, Wayans will put his obvious talents toward a project that isn't about making more money. *(Violence, profanity, adult situations.)*

p, Michael Rachmil; d, Peter Macdonald; w, Damon Wayans; ph, Don Burgess; ed, Hubert C. De La Bouillerie; m, Jay Gruska; prod d, William Arnold; set d, Michael Claypool; cos, Michelle Cole

Comedy/Action **(PR: C MPAA: R)**

MOM AND DAD SAVE THE WORLD ★½

87m Michael Phillips Production; Mercury Entertainment; HBO; Cinema Plus; Douglas Films ~ Warner Bros. c

Teri Garr *(Marge Nelson)*, Jeffrey Jones *(Dick Nelson)*, Jon Lovitz *(Tod Spengo)*, Dwier Brown *(Sirk)*, Kathy Ireland *(Semage)*, Thalmus Rasulala *(General Afir)*, Wallace Shawn *(Sibor)*, Eric Idle *(Raff)*, Debbie Lee Carrington, Tony Cox, Ed Gale, Suzanne Ventulett, Michael Stoyanov, Danny Cooksey

Striving for the antic shoddiness of such cheapo cult films as SANTA CLAUS CONQUERS THE MARTIANS and FLESH GORDON, MOM AND DAD SAVE THE WORLD succumbs instead to its dim-witted screenplay and cloddish direction.

On a distant planet populated exclusively by imbeciles, good King Raff (Eric Idle) is overthrown and imprisoned by the dense Emperor Tod Spengo (Jon Lovitz). Peering through a telescope at a Southern California landscape, Spengo spies air-headed mom, Marge Nelson (Teri Garr). Obsessed with this average housewife, Spengo teleports Marge and her couch-potato husband, Dick (Jeffrey Jones), to his planet. Before long, Marge and Dick become embroiled in planetary revolution and Dick asserts himself as the leader of a misfit band of nutty revolutionaries set on restoring King Raff to the throne.

Co-written by Chris Matheson and Ed Solomon, MOM AND DAD SAVE THE WORLD is too calculating and self-serving by far, striving with a manic intensity for its own cult status. Lost on the filmmakers, unfortunately, is the fact that cult movies always possess a dark, disturbing subtext. MOM AND DAD SAVE THE WORLD, on the other hand, is all surface blather. The screenplay wades into a cesspool of dumb jokes of the "Bazooka Joe" variety and, in the absence of any comic variations, becomes very annoying *very* quickly. The actors (particularly Jon Lovitz) stomp around, pop their eyes and maul the scenery in a comic expressionism that can only be explained as a desperate attempt to convey the intended spirit of the film. Greg Beeman's oafish direction makes Jules White look like Ernst Lubitsch.

In it's terminally hip idiocy, MOM AND DAD SAVE THE WORLD recalls such aborted 1960s comedies as JOHN GOLDFARB PLEASE COME HOME and THE PHYNX, but its retrograde modernism places it squarely in a below-par Mel Brooks late-80s atmosphere. As such, tots with their brains addled by too much Super Nintendo may find the film enjoyable, but their parents will be squirming in their seats.

p, Michael S. Phillips; d, Greg Beeman; w, Ed Solomon, Chris Matheson; ph, Jacques Haitkin; ed, Okuwah Garrett; m, Jerry Goldsmith; prod d, Craig Stearns; art d, Randy Moore; set d, Dorree Cooper; cos, Robyn Reichek

Comedy/Science Fiction **(PR: A MPAA: PG)**

MONKEY BOY ★★½

104m Zenith Productions ~ Prism Entertainment c

John Lynch *(Peter Carson)*, Christine Kavanagh *(Alison)*, Kenneth Cranham *(Hennessey)*, Emer Gillespie *(Tracy Pickford)*, George Costigan *(Schaffer)*, David Calder *(Dr. Jenner)*, Sebastian Shaw *(Dr. Liawski)*, Pip Torrens *(Windeler)*, Gary Mavers *(Forester)*, Peter Armitage *(Sergeant Crichton)*, Douglas Mann *(Chad)*

MONKEY BOY is the American video-release title for a condensation of "Chimera," a British TV production originally broadcast as a four-part, three-hour-plus miniseries. One would imagine that this 105-minute version would have been cut to emphasize the title creature, but surprisingly, the beast has rather little to do even in this edition.

The cutting appears to have been most drastic in the early sections of the film; a massacre sequence that came at the very end of the first episode in the original version takes place barely five minutes into this one. The setting of the bloodshed is the Jenner Clinic, an apparent fertility clinic set out in the hills of Britain. One of the workers there is a nurse named Tracy Pickford (Emer Gillespie), who is the last victim in the rampage of a mysterious creature that has apparently been created within the facility. Her boyfriend, Peter Carson (John Lynch of HARDWARE) drives up to visit her the next day, only to be informed of the tragedy and given the brushoff by police and other investigating officials; he soon meets Forester (Gary Mavers), a man whose wife was a patient at the clinic and also fell victim.

Getting nowhere in trying to find out what happened, Peter teams with Alison (Christine Kavanagh), a doctor at the clinic who was away from the site the night of the massacre. He's unaware, however, that she's working with Hennessey (Kenneth Cranham), a government official in charge of cleaning up after the tragedy and covering up its particulars. Meanwhile, the creature responsible, an apelike humanoid (Douglas Mann) nicknamed Chad by its creators, has escaped into the countryside and evaded the search parties sent after it. The beast hides out at a nearby farm, where it kills the owners but then befriends their children.

Seeking information on the clinic, Peter enlists the investigative help of a journalist friend, who is ultimately killed by Hennessey's men, but not before feeding him information about Dr. Jenner (David Calder), the head of the facility. The trail leads Peter and Alison to Jenner's old partner, Dr. Liawski (Sebastian Shaw), who now resides in an old-age home, and a tape he provides them reveals the truth: the clinic was devoted to the creation of human/lower primate hybrids, which could be used as slave labor or for the harvesting of organs for transplant. Soon, Alison makes her own confession to Peter: she had been working with Chad at the lab, and, knowing that the increasingly intelligent creature would soon be killed, left its cage open to allow it to escape; she never expected the bloody aftermath and has been plagued with guilt since.

Peter and Alison eventually track Chad to the farm, where they talk it out of killing one of the children and spirit it to safety in Peter's car. But as police and Hennessey's men surround them, the distraught Forester appears and shoots the creature dead with a shotgun. Some time later, Hennessey goes to visit a new lab—a much larger facility, one that is breeding hundreds of the humanoid creatures.

Although distributor Prism Entertainment is selling MONKEY BOY as a monster revenge story, the movie is actually much more concerned with intrigue and thrills of a more prosaic kind. The opening massacre is vivid and scarily presented, with the death of Tracy (who seems to be set up as a key character) coming as a real shock, and there are a couple more murders and some teasing shots from Chad's point of view. But for the most part, the screenplay is taken up with investigations, confrontations and characters worrying variously over What They Have Wrought and What They've Gotten Themselves Into.

On this level, MONKEY BOY maintains a decent amount of interest, although, as a result of the tampering for American release, the story development appears rushed and certain subplots either don't pay off or go unexplored completely after being set up. There are more than a few tense sequences, though horror fans may well become restless waiting for Chad to do its thing. In the end, of course, the filmmakers intend for us to sympathize with the creature, which is only just reacting to the hostile world around it; perhaps this intention is responsible for the lack of blood-and-guts attack scenes.

In any case, it's best for prospective viewers to ignore the hard sell of MONKEY BOY's American campaign and be prepared for a more understated kind of monster story. *(Violence, adult situations.)*

p, Nick Gillott; d, Lawrence Gordon-Clark; w, Stephen Gallagher, (from his novel *Chimera*); ph, Ken Westbury; ed, Alan Pattillo; m, Nigel Hess; prod d, Chris Edwards

Horror/Thriller **(PR: O MPAA: NR)**

MONSTER IN A BOX ★★★

(U.K./U.S.) 90m The Jon Blair Film Company ~ Fine Line Features c

Spalding Gray

The third of acclaimed monologist Spalding Gray's performance works to be filmed (after SWIMMING TO CAMBODIA and "SPALDING GRAY: TERRORS OF PLEASURE," shown as an HBO comedy special), MONSTER IN A BOX shows Gray reaching a point of diminishing returns as an artist, though he's lost nothing as an entertainer.

The monster of the title is a 1900-page manuscript of a novel by Gray that is two years overdue at the publisher. The monologue relates what happened during those two years and becomes a study in creative procrastination. Gray recounts how, after obtaining the book contract, he sequestered himself at a writer's colony to get down to work, only to find himself soon going stir crazy. Salvation comes in the form of a call from Los Angeles to be artist-in-residence at a theater and produce a work of performance art consisting of onstage interviews with LA citizens who have no connection with the film business.

Along the way he has other memorable experiences: taking meetings with high-powered Hollywood agents eager to represent him following the success of SWIMMING TO CAMBODIA; living through his first West Coast earthquake; coping with a bout of AIDS paranoia; undergoing Freudian therapy; touring Russia with an odd cadre of stars including Daryl Hannah, Richard Gere and Carrie Fisher; going on a research mission to Nicaragua on behalf of Columbia Pictures for a proposed screenplay; and then going back to New York for a disastrous acting outing in a revival of *Our Town*. It ends with Gray's decision to take a vacation, connecting with his long-gestating novel about a man who is unable to take a vacation.

There was a time when well-turned talk was a major attraction at the movies, when screenplays by the likes of Ben Hecht, Billy Wilder and Preston Sturges occasionally made films more enjoyable to listen to than to watch. Now, it seems, talk movies have become a genre unto themselves, as witness diverse offerings from MY DINNER WITH ANDRE, to Oliver Stone's and Eric Bogosian's TALK RADIO, to Robert Altman's SECRET HONOR, to Richard Pryor's performance films, to Errol Morris's talking-head documentaries and Gray's own filmed monologues. While it's still possible, though increasingly improbable, that Hollywood will rediscover how to put smart talk and smart moviemaking back together, in the meantime worse things could happen than to have Gray on the scene every couple of years with his slightly bent reports on life in the rich-and-famous lane.

While a first-rank raconteur, however, Gray is not a great artist. Though he tries, he is unable to find any compelling parallels between the progress of his novel and the progress of his life. Writing the novel seems to be about Gray's attempts to resolve his relationship with his mother. However, Gray proves to be the least interesting character in his own life, a routinely neurotic New York gadfly and self-described "Freudianexistentialist" who seems most alive only when he is observing others. Though the determined emptiness of pop culture forms the common thread of Gray's anecdotes here (as well as in SWIMMING TO CAMBODIA), he all but admits to being hard pressed to find anything to say about it that hasn't been said before, if not better.

Still, Gray's ability to acknowledge his own limitations may be what is most engaging about him. SWIMMING TO CAMBODIA was elevated by the scope of its subject. Lacking a similarly weighty subject, MONSTER IN A BOX would have been a far more tedious film if Gray had forced scope upon it. By comparison, MONSTER IN A BOX is a chat where SWIMMING TO CAMBODIA was an ode. But even a good chat is hard to find in today's increasingly arid cultural environment. Films like MONSTER IN A BOX function almost as a form of intellectual titillation, teasing their audiences with the lost art of simple, intelligent, articulate conversation.

One can only wish Gray the best on his vacation—and hope he takes the trouble to find us and tell us all about it when he gets back. *(Adult themes.)*

p, Jon Blair; d, Nick Broomfield; w, Spalding Gray, (from his performance piece); ph, Michael Coulter; ed, Graham Hutchings; m, Laurie Anderson; art d, Ray Oxley

Documentary/Comedy **(PR: C MPAA: PG-13)**

MONTANA RUN, THE ★★

97m Paul-Thompson Films ~ Greycat Films c

Ron Reid *(Doug Atkin)*, Dan Lishner *(Brock Mason)*, Randy Thompson *(Andy Miller)*, Mayme Paul-Thompson *(Charlie McKnight)*

The hard lives and times of standup comedians is the subject of THE MONTANA RUN, a rambling, largely misguided road movie.

Working out of a condemned house in Tacoma, smalltime promoter Doug Atkin (Ron Reid) puts together standup comedy shows for one-week tours on the title's "Montana run" of seedy lounges, roughneck bars and college campuses. For his latest effort, he's conned Andy Miller (played by writer-producer-director Randy Thompson), a stuffy headliner from San Francisco, and Charlie McKnight (Thompson's wife, Mayme Paul-Thompson), a divorced-mom lady comic, to join him and his loutish MC Brock Mason (Dan Lishner) for a trip through what turns out to be comedy hell. At the first stop the accommodations consist of cots in the club owner's basement, which Andy forgoes for a motel room out of his own pocket and which Charlie avoids by running into an old friend in the club.

From there, motel rooms are provided, more or less, but the gigs get steadily worse. A show gets cancelled at one club, and that's the good news. At a college campus, Brock's sexist Andrew Dice Clay style goes over like porno loops in a convent. The last stop is a disaster all-around with Charlie getting hooted off the stage and Andy nearly getting into a fistfight after being heckled off the stage by a Nazi in the audience. Luckily, it's Brock's kind of crowd. He saves Andy and Charlie from being torn apart, but, since Brock was the only one of the three to go over with the audience, the club owner refuses to pay the full fee.

Between shows, Andy and Charlie seek mutual solace in each other's bed, only to wind up not speaking to each other the next day. There is a dazzling array of bad food, tacky roadside stops and travelers' tedium that leads to the fussy pro Andy's falling out with Doug over the atrocious conditions and nearly getting into a fight with Brock, a heavy drinker with a girl at each stop, who's nevertheless painfully jealous of Andy's success. Everybody arrives back in Tacoma in one piece, worse for the wear and tear but, in the case of Andy and Charlie, with a new, tentative relationship getting underway and doubtless new material for future monologues or cable comedy specials.

THE MONTANA RUN certainly has the details down, presenting a starkly realistic, worm's-eye view of comedy and comedians that was woefully lacking in the higher-profile PUNCHLINE. Its situations and characters are both plausible and believable in their day-to-day dreariness. And while that is the film's strength, it is also its weakness. PUNCHLINE may not have had much realism, but it at least tried to be entertaining. Going too far in the opposite direction, THE MONTANA RUN is a dreary film about dreary people living dreary lives. That they happen to be comedians, the implicit message seems to be, is only incidental.

As a result, THE MONTANA RUN is something of a cheat, a film about stand-up comedians that is never very funny. Its screenplay is clumsy and artless, not quite amateurish, but pretty close. The same goes for the direction, which aims for a rough, offhanded documentary style. This *auteurist* approach would have been fine if THE MONTANA RUN had attempted something beyond compiling every comedian's horror story about every nightmare gig and every sleazy road trip into a single film. As it is, the film's main question remains unanswered, mainly, given what a comedian has to do to survive and succeed, why would anyone become a comedian in the first place?

Inexplicably, the film makes no connection between the artist, the art and the environment from which the comedian's art arises. Or, to put it more simply, why aren't these people funnier than they are? What snippets we see of their stage shows are uninspired. Offstage, they never test or work on their material with any particular conviction. Early in the film, Andy is seen driving along and talking into a tape recorder, making observational notes for possible inclusion in his act. The device is dropped as quickly as it appears, but the film needed it, or something like it, to show the creative process which, presumably, is what should make a film about comedians on the road more inherently interesting than the same film about truck drivers or traveling salespeople.

In the parlance of the comedy profession, THE MONTANA RUN has a good setup, but no follow-through. And it certainly has no punchline. Nicely observed and generally well acted, THE MONTANA RUN is not without its modest virtues. But it could have benefitted by taking itself just a tad less seriously. *(Profanity, adult situations.)*

p, Randy Thompson; d, Randy Thompson; w, Randy Thompson, Ron Reid, Dan Lishner; ph, William Brooks Baum; m, Randy Thompson

Comedy/Drama **(PR: C MPAA: NR)**

MORTUARY ACADEMY ★

85m Landmark Films; Priority Films ~ RCA/Columbia Pictures Home Video c

Paul Bartel *(Dr. Paul Truscott)*, Mary Woronov *(Mary Purcell)*, Perry Lang *(Sam Grimm)*, Tracey Walter *(Dickson)*, Christopher Atkins *(Max Grimm)*, Lynn Danielson *(Valerie)*, Stoney Jackson *(James Dandridge)*, Anthony James *(Abbott Smith)*, Wolfman Jack *(Bernie Berkowitz)*, Cesar Romero *(Captain)*, Cheryl Starbuck *(Corpse)*, Charles Gherardi, Nedra Volz, Dona Speir

Cult movie personalities Paul Bartel and Mary Woronov scored a hit with EATING RAOUL, their coyly tasteless 1982 comedy of ill-manners. MORTUARY ACADEMY represents a gamey attempt to recapture some of that earlier movie's satirical bite. This one just bites.

With the humorous topics running the gamut from necrophilia to necrophilia, the plot concerns young med-school rejects Max (Christopher Atkins) and Sam Grimm (Perry Lang). The brothers Grimm stand to inherit a $2 million family business, a mortician school, but only if they enroll as students and pass an exhaustive regimen of sicko jokes about embalming and such, most of them presided over by instructor Mary Purcell (Woronov). "Is this going to be gory, Miss Purcell?" asks a pupil before a session with a cadaver. "I can't promise anything, but we can all hope," comes the typically sparkling reply.

The venal Dr. Paul Truscott (Bartel) not only molests female stiffs, but has embezzled a fortune from the business. When Dr. Truscott meets the dead girl of his dreams he elopes with the corpse for a sea cruise, leaving Miss Purcell and her pupils in the lurch. The mortuary academy is saved when they're commissioned by Bernie Berkowitz (Wolfman Jack) to work on a deceased superstar rock group killed by automobile air bags (beware, that's probably the best joke in the screenplay). One of the students formerly built amusement-park robots; using his animatronics skills the Grimms resurrect the band sufficiently to perform a final booking at a million-dollar bar mitzvah.

The movie peaks with the opening-credit sequence, which takes gruesome Victorian-era engravings of gross anatomy clinics and brings them to uproarious cartoon life to the tune of "Be True to Your School." After that it's all downhill. The photography is muddy, the lighting amateurish, and the performers' feigned enthusiasm for the project not enough to prevent overall putrefaction.

The filmmakers exhume moments from better movies to their own detriment: Dr. Truscott is shown reading *The Loved One*, Evelyn Waugh's classic satire of the funeral business, a reminder of Tony Richardson's 1965 film adaptation that's a thousand times sharper and funnier than anything on display here. The closing shipboard gag of Truscott and his rotted sweetheart quotes the finale of SOME LIKE IT HOT, possibly the best screen punchline of all time. This coda also trots out special guest star Cesar Romero for a few fruitless seconds.

Director Michael Schroeder made his debut with MORTUARY ACADEMY, but this 1988-copyrighted effort waited unseen and uncelebrated until late 1991 to crawl out on home video. By that time Schroeder had fattened his resume with slightly more upscale productions, chiefly crime thrillers like OUT OF THE DARK and RELENTLESS 2: DEAD ON. *(Excessive profanity, nudity, sexual situations.)*

p, Dennis Winfrey, Chip Miller; d, Michael Schroeder; w, William Kelman; ph, Roy H. Wagner; ed, Ellen Keneshea; m, David Spear; prod d, Jon Rothschild; art d, Gary New

Comedy **(PR: O MPAA: R)**

MR. BASEBALL ★★½

109m Sogo Produce; Outlaw Productions; Universal ~ Universal c

Tom Selleck *(Jack Elliot)*, Ken Takakura *(Uchiyama)*, Aya Takanashi *(Hiroko Uchiyama)*, Dennis Haysbert *(Max "Hammer" Dubois)*, Toshi Shioya *(Yoji Nishimura)*, Kohsuke Toyohara *(Toshi Yamashita)*, Toshizo Fujiwara *(Ryoh Mukai)*, Mak Takano *(Shinji Igarashi)*, Kenji Morinaga *(Hiroshi Kurosawa)*, Joh Nishimura *(Tomohiko Ohmae)*, Norihide Goto *(Issei Itoi)*, Kensuke Toita *(Akito Yagi)*, Naoki Fujii *(Takuya Nishikawa)*, Takanobu Hozumi *(Hiroshi Nakamura)*, Leon Lee *(Lyle Massey)*, Bradley Jay "Animal" Lesley *(Niven)*, Jun Hamamura *(Hiroko's Grandfather)*, Mineko Yorozuyo *(Hiroko's Grandmother)*, Shoji Ohoki *(Coach Hori)*, Tomoko Fujita *(Hiroko's Assistant)*, Kinzoh Sakura *(1st Umpire)*, Ikuko Saitoh *(Morita San)*, Hikari Takano *(Commercial Director)*, Tim McCarver, Sean McDonough, Art LaFleur *(Skip)*, Greg Goossen *(Trey)*, Nicholas Cascone *(Doc)*, Larry Pennell *(Howie Gold)*, Scott Plank *(Ryan Ward)*, Charles Joseph Fick *(Billy Stevens)*, Michael McGrady *(Duane)*, Frank Thomas *(Rookie)*, Michael Papajohn *(Rick)*, Rolando Rodriquez *(Manuel)*, Todd A. Provence *(Young Ball Player)*, Frank Mendoza *(Player-New York)*, Ken Medlock *(Umpire)*, Carrie Yazel *(Coed in Bed)*, Mary Kohnert *(Player's Wife)*, Makoto Kuno *(Japanese Sportscaster)*, Michiyo Washizukan *(Japanese Sportscaster)*, Shinsuke Aoki *(Nikawa)*, Rinzoh Suzuki *(Sato)*, Shintaro Mizushima *(Uchida)*, Nobuyuki Kariya *(Uemoto)*, Satoshi Jinbo *(Tsuboi)*, Masanao Matsuzaki *(Sugita)*, Shotaro Kusumi *(Takahashi)*, Katsushi Yamaguchi *(Kobayashi)*, Hiro Nagae *(Mutsui)*, Yoshimi Imai *(Ishimaru)*, Cin Chi Cheng *(Itami)*, Makoto Kaketa *(2nd Umpire)*, Shogo Nakajima *(3rd Umpire)*, Yoshiya Morita *(Yashiro/Coach)*, Takao Ito *(Katsura/Coach)*, Hidetaka Hoshino *(Adachi/Coach)*, Kazuhiko Migita *(Namiki/Dragons)*, Tsukumo Torisaka *(Anzai/Dragons)*, Kazukuni Mutoh *(Catcher/Giants)*, Hiroshi Masumoto *(Pitcher/Giants)*, Tomohisa Shoji *(2nd Base/Giants)*, Fumio Kubo *(Pitcher/Whales)*, Yasunori Itoh *(Catcher/Whales)*, Nobuhiko Matsunami *(Giants Manager)*, Masahiro Nakane *(Pitcher/Carp)*, Toshikatsu Ida *(Catcher)*, Shinichiro Miura *(Umpire)*, Yoshio Fukazawa, Kenji Anzai, Masato Ohsumi, Youichi Monda, Shinya Kagimoto, Hirokazu Nagano, Kazuo Asahi, Yuji Inoue *(Players)*

As high-profile Hollywood releases go, probably the most earthshaking thing about MR. BASEBALL is that there's nothing much earthshaking about it. Well suited to star Tom Selleck, it is laid-back, amiable and unpretentious while touching on serious themes lightly but intelligently.

Jack Elliot (Selleck) is a power hitter on the wane whose team trades him to a fate worse than Cleveland, a Japanese team that expects him to power them to a pennant. He's immediately taken in hand by his new team's no-nonsense coach, Uchiyama (Ken Takakura). He's also taken in hand by the more attractive but equally no-nonsense team promotions manager, Hiroko (Aya Takanashi), with whom Elliot becomes romantically involved before discovering that she's Uchiyama's daughter. No love is lost between Elliot and Uchiyama, the quintessential Japanese organization man who puts up with Elliot's initial prima-donna boorishness for the sake of a pennant, despite what he perceives to be the "hole" in Elliot's swing. Though Elliot is hot for awhile—the title comes from the nickname he is given by the initially adoring Japanese sports press—opposing pitchers eventually find his "hole," and Elliot slips into a slump.

The team's backers use Elliot's slump as an excuse to put him on indefinite suspension and inform Uchiyama that he shouldn't expect his own contract to be renewed unless he wins the pennant. Putting aside their running clubhouse skirmishes, Uchiyama and Elliot team up to put the slugger back into shape and earn him a second chance. Elliot's redemption is a mixed blessing for Hiroko, who fears that he'll eventually win his way back to an American team and leave her behind. All is resolved happily, however. Elliot and Uchiyama win the pennant, but it is Hammer, Elliot's fellow American on the team (Dennis Haysbert), who gets called back to America. When Elliot himself is called back later, in the film's epilogue, Hiroko is seen joining the other players' wives in the bleachers during practice with her cellular phone and portable fax working overtime.

There can be no argument that the plot of MR. BASEBALL is predictable to a fault. But it's anything but a lazy film. The game scenes in particular have a genuine excitement and realism usually lacking in sports movies. But the attention to detail in the big scenes filters down to the smaller scenes as well. The Japanese way of baseball is examined humorously but without caricature as an illustration of the Japanese cultural mania for perfection mixed with an openness to outside cultures or, as Hiroko tries to explain to Elliot, Japan's taking the best the world has to offer—and making it better. Though Elliot discovers one result is the best-tasting steak he's ever eaten, he is less comfortable with the pursuit of perfection when it's applied to his own physique. Though Elliot helps his team loosen up and enjoy the game more for its own sake, director Fred Schepisi, using a screenplay that itself could be a tribute to Japanese teamwork for the battalion of credited writers, makes it clear that it is Elliot, and presumably America itself, who has more to learn from Japan than vice versa.

Along with his taste for exercise, Elliot has also lost his taste for egalitarianism. Inherent in the Japanese approach to baseball is the idea that anyone who works hard and pitches in for the common goal can succeed. As the pampered superstar, Elliot seems more imperialistic than anyone he meets in Japan—a country supposedly steeped in imperialist culture. Tuning in to the Japanese way of doing things, more than a little ironically, puts Elliot back in touch with core American ideals of teamwork and equality. That is why the ending, Elliot's return to America, is oddly satisfying. On one level, Schepisi has too much respect for both cultures to opt for the more standard resolution of having Elliot be fully accepted by, or fully accepting, Japanese culture. But we're also left with the sense that Elliot will return a better American. *(Adult situations, profanity.)*

p, Fred Schepisi, Doug Claybourne, Robert Newmyer; d, Fred Schepisi; w, Gary Ross, Kevin Wade, Monte Merrick, (from story by Theo Pelletier and John Junkerman); ph, Ian Baker; ed, Peter Honess; m, Jerry Goldsmith; prod d, Ted Haworth; cos, Bruce Finlayson

Comedy/Sports **(PR: C MPAA: PG-13)**

MR. SATURDAY NIGHT ★★½

119m Face Productions; Castle Rock Entertainment ~ Columbia c

Billy Crystal *(Buddy Young, Jr.)*, David Paymer *(Stan Yankelman)*, Julie Warner *(Elaine)*, Helen Hunt *(Annie)*, Mary Mara *(Susan)*, Jerry Orbach *(Phil Gussman)*, Ron Silver *(Larry Meyerson)*, Sage Allen *(Mom)*, Jason Marsden *(Abie–Age 15)*, Michael Weiner *(Stan–Age 15)*, Larry Gelman *(Mr. Gimbel)*, Kay Freeman *(Mrs. Gimbel)*, Howard Mann *(Stage Manager)*, Julius Branca *(Stage Manager)*, Liz Georges *(Script Girl)*, William Wendell *(Announcer)*, Hartley Haverty *(Susan–Age 6)*, Will Jordan *(Ed Sullivan)*, Josh Byrne *(Abie–Age 6)*, Ben Diskin *(Stan–Age 6)*, Irving Wasserman *(Uncle Moe)*, Phil Forman *(Uncle Julius)*, Joe Shea *(MC)*, Michael Ben-Edward *(Fat Guy in Audience)*, Jackie Gayle *(Gene)*, Carl Ballantine *(Freddie)*, Slappy White *(Joey)*, Richard Mehana *(Sidney)*, Mark Lonow *(Producer)*, Conrad Janis *(Director)*, Tim Russ *(A.D.)*, Marc Shaiman *(Lucky Zinberg)*, Cantor Chayim Frenkel *(Cantor at Funeral)*, Jan Lucas *(Karen)*, Daniel Tisman *(Reece)*, Peter Kim *(1st Korean)*, Greg Paik *(2nd Korean)*, Eugene Kaufmann *(Old Man)*, Miranda Garrison *(Apacke Dancer)*, Alberto Toledano *(Apacke Dancer)*, Richard Kind *(Reporter)*, Jerry Lewis *(Himself)*, Edith Fields *(Woman in Commercial)*, Adam Goldberg *(Eugene Gimbel)*, Maria A. Ferrari Olivo *(Fat Guy's Wife)*, Talbot Perry Simons *(Man at Catskills)*, Lonnie Burr, Randy Doney, Joe A. Giamalva, Birl Johns *(TV Show Dancers)*, Shadoe Stevens *(Fred)*, Bert Copello *(Sullivan A.D.)*, Lindsay Crystal *(Screaming Girl)*, Jerry Gadette *(Stage Hand)*, William Yamadera *(Japanese Client)*, Lowell Ganz *(1st Writer)*, Babaloo Mandel *(2nd Writer)*, Gary Grossman *(Backstage Man)*, Bob Yerkes, Marinela Cimpoeru, Costin Cszimas, Voinea Dumitru, Adrian Smertcov *(Acrobats)*, Steven Kravitz *(Young Comic)*, Randy Crenshaw, Geoff Koch, Steve Lively, Rick Logan *("Buddy Buddy" Singers)*

The life of a stand-up comic, one would think, is inherently dramatic: the lowly beginnings, the need for acceptance, the ability to turn personal insecurities and fears into material—all provide great fodder for a film. So why do filmmakers keep blowing it? Two recent movies, 1988's PUNCHLINE and last year's THIS IS MY LIFE, attempted to deal with the subject but succumbed to cheap sentimentality and unfocused screenplays. Unfortunately, the same can be said for MR. SATURDAY NIGHT, comedian Billy Crystal's directorial debut.

The film is more ambitious, tracing the rise, fall and partial comeback of the fictional Buddy Young, Jr. (Crystal), who, though achieving some degree of fame, never quite reaches the top rung of the business. As adolescents, Buddy (real name Abie) and his brother Stan (David Paymer) entertain the usual stock collection of Jewish relatives in their Brooklyn home, then grab the opportunity to audition at a local theater. When Stan chickens out at the last minute, Buddy, determined to make it outside his living room, does their act alone, and it isn't long before he's headlining in the Catskills, and starring in his TV variety hour in the 1950s. When we see him in the present day, he's been reduced to playing old-age homes and retirement condos. Further hampering his career is the decision by his brother who's now become his agent, assistant and all-around gofer, to retire.

The film then jumps around between Buddy's successful days in the 50s and his attempts, in the present, to resurrect his career. He meets with a powerful agent who sets him up with a new, young colleague, Annie (Helen Hunt), who tries to find Buddy work: in commercials, warming up the audience at a game show and finally a nice-sized part in famous director Larry Meyerson's (Ron Silver) film. But the crochety, disagreeable comedian usually blows his chances: he deems the commercial unworthy of his talent, and refuses to accept a lesser part in the film when his original role falls through. Buddy not only alienates Annie and Stan, he's estranged from his daughter, Susan (Mary Mara), whom he ridicules in his act, and refers to in one scene as a "twice-divorced drug addict." But wouldn't you know, by the film's conclusion, everyone has tentatively made up, Buddy is working and he's learned to be a little bit nicer.

Given how much is missing from MR. SATURDAY NIGHT, it's surprising how entertaining it often manages to be. Buddy's act, which is a mix of Alan King, Don Rickles, generic Catskills shtick and Crystal himself (his trademark "Don't get me started" line is the title of Crystal's 1986 HBO comedy special), is amusing enough, although the scenes of him being "on" offstage, like an encounter with Jerry Lewis at the Friar's Club, are better. The film has a feel for period details and does, to its credit, explore one facet of Young's life in depth: his relationship with his long-suffering brother, who never developed the drive and aggressiveness that propelled Buddy to the top—well, the middle at least. He's the film's most developed character, and Paymer's dignified, understated performance helps immeasurably.

But the main problem with the film is the problem with Buddy: both would rather go for a quick punchline than the truth. Somewhere during his TV-show period, Buddy becomes an insensitive lout, and we're never clued into as to why. He's charming enough when romancing future wife Elaine (Julie Warner) in the Catskills, but not long after he's making fun of his daughter on national TV, offending his sponsors and getting cancelled, and blowing whatever chances he might have at a comeback through his boorishness. Indicative of the screenplay's split personality (co-written by Crystal) is a scene where Annie begins to chastise Buddy for his behavior and his brother appears unexpectedly to tell him their mother has died. What starts out as a probing, crucial scene then cuts to a funeral, where Buddy, in his eulogy, typically resorts to cheap jokes about his mother's huge, flabby arms, only to conclude by saying how protected he felt when they held him.

The film's treatment of Buddy's family is maddeningly sketchy: his mother is a fat, howling caricature; his wife is a cipher; and his daughter, who's in for some type of verbal abuse virtually every time she's onscreen, is given the film's most ludicrous scene, where she and Buddy try to reconcile. (Viewers are led to believe that years of neglect and pain can be alleviated by a single visit by the aged, flower-bearing dad). Annie, the only woman in the film with a personality, is somewhat more believable (Helen Hunt does the most she can with the part), but we're a bit surprised she'd spend so much time helping this belligerent old man, especially after their first hostile meeting.

MR. SATURDAY NIGHT works best if one watches for its jokes, and the brothers' relationship. It's fairly long on laughs, but short on insight. Maybe one day, someone *will* make that funny, dramatic film about the life of a comedian, but this isn't it. *(Profanity, adult situations.)*

p, Billy Crystal; d, Billy Crystal; w, Billy Crystal, Lowell Ganz, Babaloo Mandell; ph, Donald Peterman; ed, Kent Beyda; m, Marc Shaiman; prod d, Albert Brenner; art d, Carol Winstead Wood; set d, Kathe Klopp; cos, Ruth Myers

Comedy/Drama **(PR: C MPAA: R)**

MUNCHIE ★½

80m Concorde ~ Concorde c

Loni Anderson *(Cathy)*, Dom DeLuise *(Voice of Munchie)*, Andrew Stevens *(Elliott)*, Jaime McEnnan *(Gage Dobson)*, Arte Johnson *(Professor Cruikshank)*, Mike Simmrin *(Leon)*, Scott Ferguson *(Ashton)*, Love Hewitt *(Andrea)*, Toni Naples *(Mrs Blaylok)*, Monique Gabrielle *(Miss Laurel)*, Ace Mask *(Principal Thornton)*, Jay Richardson *(Mr. Kurtz)*, Angus Scrimm, George "Buck" Flower, Fred Olen Ray, Becky LeBeau, Brinke Stevens, Linda Shayne, Paul Herzberg, Chuck Cirino, R.J. Robertson

Roger Corman's MUNCHIES wasn't the worst GREMLINS knockoff (not while a tape called HOBGOBLINS is still around), but close enough. It featured a horde of Aztec puppet demons who all talked like Cheech Marin as they ate up a town. But enough bad memories. The 1992 followup MUNCHIE chooses to be a kiddie pic, a sort of Disney *manque* that's inoffensive as far as it goes, but hardly worth the talent involved.

Ignoring the origin and persona of the beasts in the earlier movie, this features just one Munchie, a stiff, pointy-earred animatronic troll with the voice of Dom DeLuise. In a flashback intro, the Munchie is crated up by its tormented owner and thrown off a cliff (the road sign reads: "Danger: Bottomless Pit"). Flash ahead to the present day, where young Gage Dobson (Jaime McEnnan) finds the crate in an abandoned mine. Bravely ignoring this continuity lapse, Gage releases the wisecracking beastie, who offers, genie-style, to grant the lad's every wish.

The boy asks for relief from school bullies, his failing grades, and the pompous Dr. Elliott Carlyle (Andrew Stevens) who's angling to marry Gage's gorgeous single mother Cathy (Loni Anderson). The mischievous Munchie accomplishes all these tasks using sorcery and slapstick. Then, with nothing else to do, the story shifts gears into a cheesy ripoff of ET, with Gage and Munchie on the run from the dissection-crazed Dr. Carlyle. At the climax Munchie levitates the rickety jeep they're driving and flies it across the face of the full moon, a Spielbergian image the Corman crew sniggeringly swipe.

Director Jim Wynorski and co-writer R.J. Robertson are prolific B-movie crafters who often season their celluloid junk food with warped humor. Initially they give Gage some funny daydream fantasies, but those abruptly cease. Also insufficiently exploited is the idea (propounded by Arte Johnson, playing an eccentric professor with an indefinable accent) that Munchie has guided human progress for eons, instructing Buddha, authoring all Shakespeare's works and inventing the automobile. The filmmakers trip over another plot point: Gage wants to win the love of a pretty classmate, and while fulfilling that wish Munchie gets the girl's widowed father romantically paired off with mom Cathy. Wouldn't that end up making Gage's desire sort of . . . illegal?

Jaime McEnnan and all the other child actors are wonderfully expressive; one sincerely hopes they get superior material. Stevens, frequently seen as ingratiating heroes, shows good comic timing in his change-of-pace role as a bad guy. As he did in the AN AMERICAN TAIL animated features, Dom DeLuise proves himself an excellent vocal artist; his energetic patter far outshines the dopey-looking mechanical doll from which it emanates. Looking like a pop-eyed cross between Bilbo Baggins and the Big Boy Restaurant logo, the Munchie prop goes through its paces with limited gestures and a frozen what-me-worry smirk on its face.

Lots of schlock-cinema vets make small cameos, including PHANTASM's Angus Scrimm, sexy young things Monique Gabrielle and Becky LeBeau, and the one and only Fred Olen Ray. A real surpise is the whimsical score by Chuck Cirino, a composer who's contributed chalk-against-blackboard synthesizer chords to too many horror pics. His MUNCHIE musical theme, however, is a pleasant little tune that's the nearest to magic this production ever gets. *(Substance abuse.)*

p, Mike Elliott; d, Jim Wynorski; w, Jim Wynorski, R.J. Robertson; ph, Don E. Fauntleroy; ed, Rich Gentner; m, Chuck Cirino; prod d, Stuart Blatt; art d, Carey Meyer; cos, Lisa Cacavas

Fantasy/Children's **(PR: A MPAA: PG)**

MUPPET CHRISTMAS CAROL, THE ★★½

85m Jim Henson Productions ~ BV c

Michael Caine *(Scrooge)*, Dave Goelz *(The Great Gonzo/Robert Marley/Bunsen Honeydew/Betina Cratchit)*, Steve Whitmire *(Rizzo the Rat/Bean Bunny/Kermit the Frog/Beaker/Belinda Cratchit)*, Jerry Nelson *(Tiny Tim Cratchit/Jacob Marley/Ma Bear/Ghost of Christmas Present)*, Frank Oz *(Miss Piggy/Fozzie Bear/Sam Eagle/Animal)*, David Rudman *(Peter Cratchit/Old Joe/Swedish Chef)*, Donald Austen *(Ghost of Christmas Present/Ghost of Christmas Yet to Come)*, Rob Tygner *(Ghost of Christmas Past/Ghost of Christmas Yet to Come)*, Karen Prell *(Ghost of Christmas Past)*, William Todd Jones *(Ghost of Christmas Past)*, Jessica Fox *(Ghost of Christmas Past)*, Steven MacKintosh *(Fred)*, Meredith Braun *(Belle)*, Robin Weaver *(Clara)*, Raymond Coulthard *(Young Scrooge)*, Russell Martin *(Young Scrooge)*, Theo Sanders *(Young Scrooge)*, Kristopher Milnes *(Young Scrooge)*, Edward Sanders *(Young Scrooge)*, Anthony Hamblin *(1st Boy)*, Fergus Brazier *(2nd Boy)*, David Shaw Parker *(Voice of Old Joe)*, Ian Allen, James Barton, Simon Buckley, Craig Crane, John Ecclestone, Ken Haines, Christopher Leith, Angie Passmore, Judy Preece, Gillie Robic, Dave Showler, Mark Alexander Todd, Victoria Willing, David Barclay, Joan Barton, Dave Bulbeck, Sue Dacre, Geoff Felix, Anthony Lymboura, Peter Passmore, Sally Preisig, Tim Rose, John Thirtle, Ian Tregonning, Robbie Barnett, Mike Bayliss, Marcus Clarke, Taylor David, Kate Frost, Ronnie LeDrew, Rebecca Nagan, Nigel Plaskitt, Peter Robbins, Kaefan Shaw, Ian Thom, Simon Williamson, Phil Woodfine *(Additional Muppet Performers)*

The first full-length Muppet feature since the tragic death of Jim Henson in 1990, THE MUPPET CHRISTMAS CAROL is a mixed bag of mixed moods. The somberness of Dickens's oft-filmed seasonal cautionary fable works at cross purposes with the Muppets, keeping their usual gentle anarchy at bay.

Despite the participation of Kermit the Frog as Bob Crachit, this retelling does not significantly deviate from the outlines of the well-known and well-worn Charles Dickens original. In Dickens's 19th-century London, miserly financier Ebenezer Scrooge (Michael Caine) prepares to spend Christmas alone—having given his long-suffering but loyal head clerk Crachit a rare day off to spend with his wife and family, including his crippled son Tiny Tim (Jerry Nelson)—despite an invitation from his equally long-suffering and loyal nephew Fred (Steven Mackintosh) to spend the holiday with him and his wife Clara (Robin Weaver). Preparing for bed on Christmas Eve, Scrooge is visited by the ghost of his late partner Jacob Marley (also Jerry Nelson), who is in death bound by chains he forged during his own selfish life that now prevent him from rising into heaven.

Affording Scrooge a second chance denied to him, Marley informs his ex-partner that he will be visited by three other spirits, those of Christmases past, present and future. The three spirits take Scrooge through his life, showing how he turned his back on his fellow man while he was still young to arrive old, alone and embittered in his present to face a bleak future and die alone. Seeing the error of his ways come Christmas morning, Scrooge buys the biggest goose in town as a gift for the Crachits, with whom he spends the holiday capped by a raise for Crachit and an offer to help with Tiny Tim's medical care without which, the ghost of Christmas future reveals, the youngster will die.

Besides Caine and a few others, most notably Meredith Braun in a poignant performance as Belle, Scrooge's lost love, the remainder of THE MUPPET CHRISTMAS CAROL's cast is filled by either the Muppets or creations of Jim Henson's Creature Shop, now under the supervision of the film's director, Henson's son Brian. Kermit (now voiced by Steve Whitmire) headlines the non-human cast as Crachit, with Kermit's longtime amour, Miss Piggy (Frank Oz), of course cast as Crachit's wife Emily. The Great Gonzo (Dave Goelz) frames the story as Dickens with sidekick Rizzo the Rat (Whitmire). Of the non-Muppet characters, the Ghost of Christmas Past, an ethereal, angel-like spirit, is the film's most memorable creation.

On the upside, the Muppets have survived the loss of Jim Henson in fine fettle. In the film's lighter moments they are as funny and feisty as ever and Michael Caine gives a surprisingly touching and thoughtful performance as Scrooge. However, instead of either a send-up or a straightforward rendition of the tale (which worked for Mr. Magoo), Brian Henson opts for a bit of both. The most telling result is a happy ending that feels forced, rushed and unearned along with a decided uncertainty in the Muppets' dramatic performances. It's easy to imagine Caine as Scrooge, who's so good here it's easy to hope that he will one day star in a "straight" version of *The Christmas Carol*. However, Miss Piggy winds up looking more than a little uncomfortable as the righteously vindictive Mrs. Crachit.

Still, parents understandably wishing to pass on the cartoonish ultra-violence of other such seasonal favorites as HOME ALONE 2 could do far worse than this kinder and gentler alternative.

p, Brian Henson, Martin G. Baker; d, Brian Henson; w, Jerry Juhl; ph, John Fenner; ed, Michael Jablow; m, Miles Goodman; prod d, Val Strazovec; art d, Alan Cassie, Dennis Bosher; set d, Michael Ford; cos, Polly Smith; ch, Pat Garrett

Children's **(PR: AA MPAA: G)**

MY COUSIN VINNY ★★★

119m Palo Vista Productions; Peter V. Miller Investment Corporation ~ Fox c

Joe Pesci *(Vincent La Guardia Gambino)*, Ralph Macchio *(Bill Gambini)*, Marisa Tomei *(Mona Lisa Vito)*, Mitchell Whitfield *(Stan Rothenstein)*, Fred Gwynne *(Judge Chamberlain Haller)*, Lane Smith *(Jim Trotter, III)*, Austin Pendleton *(John Gibbons)*, Bruce McGill *(Sheriff Farley)*, Maury Chaykin *(Sam Tipton)*, Pauline Meyers *(Constance Riley)*, Raynor Scheine *(Ernie Crane)*, James Rebhorn *(George Wilbur)*, Chris Ellis *(J.T.)*, Michael Simpson *(Neckbrace)*, Lou Walker *(Grits Cook)*, Kenny Jones *(Jimmy Willis)*, Thomas Merdis *(Man in Town Square)*, J. Don Ferguson *(1st Guard)*, Michael Genevie *(2nd Guard)*, Jeff Lewis *(1st Deputy)*, Ron Leggett *(2nd Deputy)*, Aubrey J. Osteen *(3rd Deputy)*, Larry Shuler *(Hotel Clerk)*, Suzi Bass *(Woman)*, Michael Burgess *(Prison Van Driver)*, Bill Coates *(Bailiff)*, Jill Lane Clements *(Courtroom Clerk)*, Muriel Moore *(1st Juror)*, Bob Penny *(2nd Juror)*

Clocking in at just under two hours, MY COUSIN VINNY moves at an extremely leisurely pace for a hyped-up Hollywood farce. But that's just one indication of what makes this appealingly quirky comedy stand apart from more run-of-the-mill fare.

Two college kids, Bill Gambini and Stan Rothenstein (Ralph Macchio and Mitchell Whitfield), make the common movie blunder of taking the southern route by auto across the country from New York to attend school in California. A stop at an Alabama roadside convenience store sets events in motion when

Bill inadvertently pockets a can of tuna fish without paying for it. Some distance up the road they are pulled over and arrested by local Sheriff Farley (Bruce McGill), who seems to be treating the shoplifting with uncommon zealousness, taking the two into custody and proceeding to sweat confessions out of them. A weary Bill offers to admit to everything, figuring it will mean signing a statement, paying a fine and being on his way. What he doesn't know is that he and Stan have been arrested for the murder of the convenience store clerk by two men fitting their description and driving a car similar to theirs who committed the crime just after Bill and Stan left.

This all lays the groundwork for the entrance of Bill's cousin, Vincent La Guardia Gambino (Joe Pesci), a lawyer who graduated from law school six years earlier but who only passed the bar exam six weeks ago and has never been in a courtroom. Negotiating his way through the Alabaman judicial system, Vinny is held in daily contempt by the curmudgeonly judge, Chamberlain Haller (Fred Gwynne), and faces being outfoxed by the wily district attorney, Jim Trotter, III (Lane Smith). However, he rises to the occasion by virtue of his inquisitive intelligence and with the unexpected help of his leggy girlfriend Mona Lisa Vito (Marisa Tomei), who's also a self-taught automotive expert.

Joe Pesci may never be an actor who can do it all, but on his own turf in MY COUSIN VINNY he projects a surprising depth, shrewdly bringing down his usual cartoonish Brooklyn bravado a few notches. The film also benefits from a sturdy, imaginative plot, constructed by screenwriter and co-producer Dale Launer (RUTHLESS PEOPLE, DIRTY ROTTEN SCOUNDRELS), that keeps finding new angles on its stock situations. But more importantly, it takes an uncommonly generous approach to its characters.

MY COUSIN VINNY starts with the stock stereotypes of redneck farce and gives them a depth over the course of the film that belies their appearances. The curmudgeonly judge turns out to be an Ivy League graduate who gives respect, once it's been earned. The sheriff is zealous, but he's also fair. The district attorney is wily, but he's also hospitable and accommodating. Vinny and Mona Lisa dress atrociously in the latest Brooklyn-Queens bowling-alley fashions and drive an elderly smoke-belching Cadillac. But they're both smarter than they look, combining Vinny's unnerving tendency to ask the right question at the right time with Mona Lisa's encyclopedic knowledge of the fabulous General Motors cars of the 1960s, for what turns out to be a one-two killer punch in the courtroom.

The film's cast is a comfortable ensemble of reliable veterans like Gwynne and McGill, underrated performers like Macchio and at least one hot newcomer in Tomei, an accomplished comedienne with intelligence and talent to match her knockout looks. But it's Pesci who really commands the leading credit with a smart, sensitive, lived-in portrayal as Vinny. One measure of a good performance is the extent to which it becomes impossible to imagine any other actor in the role. Pesci fills the measure to the point where the movie would have no point without him. A great part of the film's freshness undoubtedly has to be credited to British director Jonathan Lynn (NUNS ON THE RUN), whose outsider's eye keeps planting unexpected grace notes along the way.

MY COUSIN VINNY could have used some tightening up, but it's nevertheless a rare comedy that never quite gets around to wearing out its welcome. *(Profanity.)*

p, Dale Launer, Paul Schiff; d, Jonathan Lynn; w, Dale Launer; ph, Peter Deming; ed, Tony Lombardo; m, Randy Edelman; prod d, Victoria Paul; art d, Randall Schmook, Michael Rizzo; set d, Michael Seirton; cos, Carol Wood

AA Best Supporting Actress: Marisa Tomei

Comedy **(PR: C MPAA: R)**

MY FATHER IS COMING ★★

(U.S./Germany) 82m Hyena Filmproduktion; Norddeutscher Rundfunk; Bluehorse Films ~ Tara Releasing c

Shelley Kastner *(Vicky)*, Alfred Edel *(Hans)*, Mary-Lou Graulau *(Lisa)*, Dominique Gaspar *(Christa)*, Flora Gaspar *(Dora)*, David Bronstein *(Ben)*, Dominique D'Anthony *(Doris)*, Fakir Musafar *(Fakir)*, Annie Sprinkle *(Annie)*, Michael Masses *(Joe)*, Mario DeColumbia, Lynne Tillman, Ursule Molinaro

No, it probably won't play in Peoria, which can't be much of a loss to Peoria. MY FATHER IS COMING is a low-budget, cross-cultural smorgasbord of fleshly delights. It's set in New York City's fabled East Village, where German-emigre heroine Vicky (Shelley Kastner) lives in squalor and works as a waitress when she's not busy failing one acting audition after another. In her letters to Germany, however, Vicky has informed her bourgeois father Hans that she's a successful actress with a loving husband and stable home life. When Hans sends word that he's going to pay his daughter a visit, Vicky tries to maintain the ruse. She enlists her leather-clad, very gay roommate Ben (David Bronstein) to pose as her straight spouse, and—well, that's about it.

The filmmakers appear to lose interest in the sitcom premise, and after father shows up the action fragments into casually related subplots and vignettes. Vicky, as unsure of her gender preference as she is of her future, falls for a tantalizing stranger named Joe (Michael Masses) who turns out to be a transsexual, a woman surgically transformed into the ultimate sensitive guy. The revelation knocks Vicky off base and into the arms of her lesbian coworker Lisa (Mary Lou Graulau), where she deigns to stay.

Hans, stunned by his daughter's leap out of the closet, wanders through the Village where he encounters various nurturing oddballs, including a cheery, New Age sexologist (porn-star cum "performance artist" Annie Sprinkle) and an ardent body piercer (a fellow named Fakir Musafar who was featured in the documentary DANCES SACRED AND PROFANE and is definitely *not* aided by makeup prosthetics) who suspends himself from the ceiling by blades speared through his gaunt torso as he patiently explains the pursuit of spiritual pleasure through physical pain and mutilation. It looks as good as it sounds.

The film thus paints a weirdly idealized portrait of the Lower East Side as kind of Emerald City of the flesh, where one can randomly stroll into a seedy storefront or decaying warehouse and find a wonderful wizard of eros ready to minister to the confused and uptight. These sexual shamans take turns declaring how the body is just the envelope for the soul, do what makes you happy, don't dream it, *be* it, and so on, but the tone of the movie is more playful than doctrinaire. The informal narrative verges on amateurish as it roams about, skipping over transitional scenes and key moments.

One subplot has Hans unintentionally getting cast for a TV commercial, much to the despair of Vicky who's long hungered for such a gig herself. But the resulting commercial is never shown, and later father's evasive behavior hints that something pretty sordid might have occurred when he went to shoot the ad. Or did it? Hard to tell; Alfred Edel, a big, friendly bear of a man, plays Hans with the bemused distraction of a curious non-actor who happened to visit the set during filming and was never told to leave. Shelley Kastner, making her movie debut, is winsome and appealingly vulnerable. But the only real emotional impact is registered by Michael Massee, as Joe-who-used-to-be-Joan, when he sees that he's lost Vicky to another woman. His pain seems poignantly real, but the movie papers over it. *C'est la vie boheme.* Based in New York and Hamburg, scholar and film-maker Monika Treut's earlier efforts include the cult features SEDUCTION: THE CRUEL WOMAN and VIRGIN MACHINE. Treut is also the author of a book on de Sade and Sacher-Masoch, and her films confront and champion a multiplicity of sexual taboos and practices seldom addressed outside of abnormal-psychology texts. While a sense of humor makes MY FATHER IS COMING somewhat easier to take, this unrated film is only for the most adventuresome of tastes and forgiving of sloppy narrative techniques. *(Adult situations, sexual situations, nudity, profanity.)*

p, Monika Treut, Nicole Ma, Ulla Zwicker-Ritz, E. Scharfenberg; d, Monika Treut; w, Bruce Benderson, Monika Treut; ph, Elfi Mikesch; ed, Steve Brown; m, David Van Tieghem; art d, Robin Ford

Comedy **(PR: O MPAA: NR)**

MY GRANDPA IS A VAMPIRE ★

(New Zealand) 90m Tucker Productions; New Zealand Film Commission ~ Republic Pictures Home Video c

Al Lewis *(Vernon T. Cooger)*, Justin Gocke *(Lonny)*, Milan Borich *(Kanziora)*, Pat Evison *(Leah)*, Noel Appleby *(Ernie)*, David Weatherley *(Sergeant Dicky Ticker)*, Sean Duffy *(Derek)*, Sylvia Rands *(Cheryl)*, Phoebe Falconer *(Tammy)*, Chris McNair *(Ben)*, Ian Watkin *(Father Vincent)*, Beryl TeWiata *(District Nurse)*, Alistair Douglas *(Ghost Train Owner)*, Max Cryer *(Compere)*, Louise Perry *(Serene)*, Rebekah Davies *(Brigit)*, Lyn Waldegrave *(Polka Dot Woman)*, Ann Morris *(Betty Gutsell)*, Tina Grenville *(Winona Ticker)*, Robert Bruce *(Truckie)*, Joel Tobeck *(McDonald's Cashier)*, Mark Sadgrove *(Hamish McWhirter)*, Karl Burnett *(Joe)*, Penelope Collins *(Woman at Carnival)*, Jim Scorrar *(Cooger Double)*

An Australian import directed by David Blyth from a screenplay by Michael Heath, MY GRANDPA IS A VAMPIRE features Al Lewis, a veteran American TV actor, in the title role. Lewis aquits himself well in an otherwise unfunny farcical fantasy aimed at children.

Elderly Vernon T. Cooger (Lewis) lives with his homely, childless middle-aged daughter, Leah (Pat Evison), and his churlish son-in-law Ernie (Noel Appleby). During the summer holidays, Lonny, Leah's young nephew (Justin Gocke), is sent by his parents to visit Aunt Leah and Uncle Ernie. Lonny is an energetic boy who quickly makes friends with a neighbor, Kanziora (Milan Borich), and the two boys soon become intrigued with Lonny's eccentric Grandpa Vernon. The ailing Vernon, who spends most of his time in his bedroom with the blinds down—especially on sunny days—entertains the youths with magic tricks and stories. Grandpa Vernon tells the kids how much he appreciates and loves them for being his friends and for caring to spend so much time with an old man, so that he can drink in their youthful energy and, thereby, keep himself in finer fettle.

Grandpa's affection for the children is in sharp contrast to most of the other adults around them, who spend their time ordering the boys to do—or not to do—something, or shouting at them either to stay in the house or go outside and play—whatever best suits the adults for the moment. Lonny's life hits its lowest ebb when Grandpa Vernon, climaxing a particularly cheerful evening of entertaining the boys with magic tricks backlighted by a full moon outside his bedroom window, suddenly collapses. Grandpa dies and Lonny is devasted. Within a few hours of his own funeral, however, Grandpa turns up alive—or, more precisely, as a member of the living dead.

Initially, Lonny is scared out of his wits, but with Grandpa's reassurance that all is well, the problem becomes one of what does a boy do with a dead grandfather who's a genuine living, breathing vampire? He and Kanziora can't very well show Grandpa Vernon off to Lonny's aunt and uncle. A temporary solution is to hide Grandpa in the nursery shed behind Kanziora's folk's house. This works until picnic day at the beach, when the boys decide to smuggle Grandpa into the back of Uncle Ernie's station wagon. Once at the beach, the sun proves to be too hard on Grandpa, so the boys must quickly slip him out of the station wagon and into the shade of a nearby cave. They get to the cave, but not before they've encountered a trio of smart-aleck village girls, one of whom informs Lonny's aunt later that night about having seen Lonny and his friend in the company of a "weird old guy who looked like a mummy." Aunt Leah instructs Uncle Ernie to go fetch Grandpa Vernon from the cave and bring him home, but Ernie will have none of that. He is not about to live under the same roof with an active vampire despite Leah's protests that, "after all, he is my father."

Ernie eventually confronts Grandpa and the boys in the cave and is about to shove a stake into Grandpa's heart when the boys distract him and help Grandpa escape. Eventually, Grandpa shows up on stage at a local theatrical event and inadvertently steals the show with his good natured antics. All hell breaks lose when the village priest, Father Vincent (Ian Watkin), recognizes Grandpa as the man he'd recently buried. After the pandemonium subsides, Grandpa is again reunited with Lonny, Kanziora and Aunt Leah. Leah orders Ernie to cease and desist where her father is concerned. Finally, to keep peace in the family, Grandpa Vernon agrees to live forever, joining the other creatures of the night in their search for love and understanding. Lonny waves a tearful goodbye to Grandpa, but is consoled by the fact that Grandpa will go on existing as a gracious member of the living dead.

Originally released in Australia as GRAMPIRE, MY GRANDPA IS A VAMPIRE is one of those pictures that must have looked absolutely hilarious on paper. Unhappily, most of the potential humor and fun gets lost somewhere between the page and the screen.

The story continuity is often muddled, due in part to the film's haphazard direction, quirky editing and sluggish pacing. There is an ambiguity about the whole movie that becomes a source of constant frustration for the viewer. For one thing, the sound quality is poor and that problem, coupled with the thick Australian accents of many of the actors, makes it difficult, if not impossible, to make out stretches of dialogue. Also, there is an unneccessarily extended, anti-climactic epilogue sequence involving Lonny and Kanziora that seems tacked on at that point, since the main characters' fate has already been determined. What is the point of prolonging the story with this very talky scene during which the boys discuss life and death and their future existence?

Lewis is effective in the title role, but there is little he can do to breathe life into the uninspired, unfocused and repetitious screenplay. Justin Gocke as Lonny and, to a lesser extent, Milan Borich as Kanziora, infuse the film with much of the little verve it has and both youngsters are far better than the material they have to work with. The remaining players are merely adequate, as are the various production values, including the direction and cinematography.

Beyond the touching performances of Gocke and Borich and the few good moments Lewis has as Grandpa Vernon, MY GRANDPA IS A VAMPIRE has very little to recommend it.

p, Murray Newey; d, David Blyth; w, Michael Heath; ph, Kevin Hayward; ed, David Huggett; m, Jim Manzie; prod d, Kim Sinclair; art d, Kirsten Shouler; cos, Ngila Dickson

Children's/Fantasy/Comedy (PR: A MPAA: PG)

MY NEW GUN ★★½

99m New Gun Inc.; IRS Media ~ IRS Releasing c

Diane Lane *(Debbie Bender)*, James LeGros *(Skippy)*, Stephen Collins *(Gerald Bender)*, Tess Harper *(Kimmy)*, Bill Raymond *(Andrew)*, Bruce Altman *(Irwin)*, Maddie Corman *(Myra)*, Suzzy Roche *(Checkout Girl)*, Phillip Seymour *(Chris Hoffman)*, Patti Chambers *(Janice Phee)*, Stephen Pearlman *(Al Schlyen)*, Leslie Brett Daniels *(Waitress)*, Paul J.Q. Lee *(Desk Manager)*, Angela Marie Baker *(Maid at Ramada)*, Kent Gash *(Bell Hop)*, Gene Canfield *(Detective)*, Gussie Levy *(Grandma Mo)*, La Chanze *(Kelly Jane)*, Harry Blackman *(Bartender)*, Franke Hughes *(Cop Number 1)*, Kane Picoy *(Cop Number 2)*, Loni Ackerman *(Woman in Charge)*, Nancy Friedman *(Woman at Wedding)*, Matt Malloy *(Ray Benson)*

An impressive but uneven debut feature, Stacy Cochran's MY NEW GUN boasts high production values and a briskly paced narrative. It also suffers from an identity crisis and, despite the help of a uniformly strong cast, fails to fulfill its potential.

On the surface, Debbie (Diane Lane) and Gerald Bender (Stephen Collins) are the photogenic embodiment of the American dream. Gerald has a glowing reputation as a New Jersey radiologist and Debbie is his beautiful, somewhat passive wife. There doesn't seem to be much genuine warmth in their marriage, but there *is* plenty of boredom. When their newly engaged friends, Irwin (Bruce Altman) and Myra (Maddie Corman), come by for dinner, they bring along Myra's new surprise—a handgun they have purchased for their own protection. The next day, Gerald follows suit and buys a .38 revolver for his household. Debbie is very uncomfortable with the whole thing, especially when Gerald unsuccessfully tries to teach her how to use it.

Skippy (James LeGros), a mysterious neighbor from across the street who seems to hold a certain power over Debbie, pleads with her to borrow the gun. She refuses but Skippy helps himself to the piece anyway. When Gerald finds out, he retrieves the gun but accidentally shoots himself in the foot. While he recuperates in the hospital, Debbie and Skippy grow closer, though she's convinced he's up to no good. Skippy finally convinces her that he needs the gun to protect his mother, Kimmy (Tess Harper), a former country music star who has developed a taste for depressant drugs, from Andrew (Bill Raymond), a deranged faith healer. Skippy and Debbie fall into bed, and she seems to come alive for the first time in his arms. Skippy borrows the gun again, this time with Debbie's permission.

When Gerald comes home from the hospital he promptly asks Debbie for a divorce. Meanwhile, Skippy begins shifting his mother from hotel to hotel in order to stay one step ahead of Andrew. After Andrew visits Debbie and interrogates her about Kimmy's whereabouts, she realizes the seriousness of the situation. Debbie and Skippy tell their story to the police, who agree to shadow them until Andrew shows up. At Myra and Irwin's wedding, Andrew appears with an Uzi, but Debbie pulls out her gun and distracts him while the cops make their move and arrest him. The wedding goes on as Debbie and Skippy ride off into the distance.

While writer-director Stacy Cochran is to be commended for getting her first feature made barely a year after graduating from Columbia University's graduate film program, MY NEW GUN feels like two disparate films spliced together. The darkly comic first half satirizes suburban domesticity, while the second half degenerates into contrived melodrama topped by an unbelievable denouement.

MY NEW GUN's visuals are rich and effective. Cochran's sparing use of only a few locations is one way to keep a budget from going overboard, and her resourcefulness is to be commended; the film looks as though it cost five times the actual $2 million budget. The male-female relationships are well handled, if weakened by the film's stylistic shift. It's also a welcome change to see a film in which, despite the fact that a violent weapon functions as a key thematic element, there is virtually no violence. What little there is takes place off camera—a wise decision.

Cochran's keen eye for casting is apparent from the leads down to the bit parts. Lane (CHAPLIN, TV's "Lonesome Dove") is wonderful as the blossoming, liberated Debbie. Somewhat underused in recent years, she perfectly captures her character's transformation from suburban slave to independent achiever. LeGros (GUNCRAZY, DRUGSTORE COWBOY) is just spooky enough to pull off Skippy. As the quintessential yuppie, Collins is self-centeredness personified.

MY NEW GUN introduces a filmmaker who certainly has the ability to pique an audience's curiosity. If her story had maintained a more constant focus, it would have been more powerful and more entertaining. *(Profanity, adult situations.)*

p, Michael Flynn; d, Stacy Cochran; w, Stacy Cochran; ph, Edward Lachman; ed, Camilla Toniolo; m, Pat Irwin; prod d, Toby Corbett; set d, Catherine Davis; cos, Eugenie Bafaloukos

Thriller/Comedy (PR: C MPAA: R)

NAKED OBSESSION ★★

80m Concorde ~ Vestron Video c

William Katt *(Franklyn Carlyle)*, Rick Dean *(Sam Silver)*, Maria Ford *(Lynne Hauser)*, Wendy MacDonald *(Saundra Carlyle)*, Elena Sahagan *(Becky)*, Tommy Hinkley *(Mitch)*, Roger Craig *(Detective Ludlow)*, Ria Coyne *(Cynthia)*, Fred Olen Ray *(Announcer)*, Mac Ward *(Man)*, Harriet Harris *(Elderly Lady)*, Madison Stone *(Jezebel)*, Suzy Evans *(Table Dancer)*, Sherri Graham *(Waitress)*, Melinda Wesley *(Waitress)*

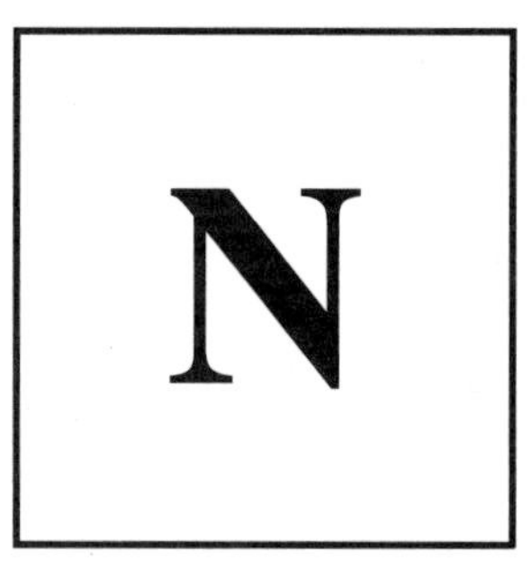

Proceeding from the assertion that NAKED OBSESSION is unabashedly exploitive swill, one must admit that it's *ambitious* swill. There seems to be more going on in the wild minds behind this noirish skinflick than can be found in a dozen "respectable" Hollywood films.

Franklyn Carlyle (William Katt) is an upright city councilman running for mayor on a law-and-order ticket, though he's clearly uncomfortable over slippery election-year pandering to "family values." Franklyn's campaign states that he'll tear down Dante's Square, the poetically dubbed red-light district, and one night Franklyn feels impelled to drive through the shabby 'hood he's pledged to demolish. There an unseen assailant knocks him on the head and takes his car and wallet. After an unconscious vision of a wickedly grinning Christ, Franklyn wakes to find himself in the company of shaggy, robed vagabond Sam Silver (Rick Dean), a dead ringer for that sleazy Jesus. Tootling on a panpipe and swigging blood-red wine, Sam calls himself a "missionary of enlightenment" as he ushers Franklyn into the Ying Yang Club, an area nudie bar.

Once inside, Franklyn is smitten with dancer Lynne Hauser (Maria Ford), a sweet-faced stripper who eventually entices the politician into a one-night stand. The angelic Lynne turns out to harbor a devilish hunger for sexual bondage, and a day later she's found dead in bed, Franklyn's discarded tie tight around her throat. Uninterested police rule the case an accidental suicide via autoeroticism, but soon Franklyn gets an anonymous blackmail note. Someone set him up, but who and why? Franklyn seeks the mysterious Sam for help, and a ridiculous climax takes place back at the Ying Yang Club, with Franklyn a captive audience for the masked murderess, whose facial covering is the last thing she removes while performing the ultimate striptease dance routine.

Trying to look surprised at the phantom's identity taxes William Katt's acting abilities to the utmost; viewers will have guessed the fatal femme long before she drops her, uh, pretenses, as Franklyn's obsessive secretary Becky (Elena Sahagun). Her guilt and garb are transparent because of a lack of remaining suspects, and because her early persona as an office busybody can't efface a busty body that, in this schlock milieu, demands unveiling. Franklyn's savior Sam has the last word before vanishing into thin air at the conclusion.

It's got no class, fizzles as a whodunit, and gets off on a meatmarket view of women that calls for all the female players to disrobe at one point or another—even if it takes a dream sequence to do it. But NAKED OBSESSION offers discriminating trash-hounds a fetid feast of religious and literary allusions, plus a sincerely proffered gutter-Taoist philosophy of life, the universe and all things sexy. "Cities are like people," states slum messiah Sam. "They got a light side and a dark side. It can't just be one or the other. You got to have that essential balance or things get all fucked up."

Franklyn at first seems the ultimate victim of the Dante's Square inferno (we never do find out who mugged him, and Sam remains suspect), but later he uncovers plots against him by his own bourgeois wife and best friend, and the maniacal murderer comes straight from his own careerist work environment. Katt is never more than functional as the bewildered hero; this picture belongs to Rick Dean's smugly dissolute urban mystic Sam Silver, a great character who lends more than a touch of the supernatural—he's the movie's pagan-funky attitude and fresh point of view. NFL running back Roger Craig has a guest role as a violent policeman who cuffs Sam to a drainpipe, crucifixion-style. Unlike his Nazarene forebear, Sam doesn't forgive this new centurion and stops the cop's heart with a glare.

Another cameo goes to notorious cheapie filmmaker Fred Olen Ray, making his acting debut as emcee at the Ying Yang Club. Debuting director Dan Golden was Ray's unit photographer who had Greatness Thrust Upon Him when he was pressed into service as a screenwriter to complete Fred's WIZARDS OF THE DEMON SWORD. Helming here for Roger Corman, Golden may be a helmer to watch, though the NAKED OBSESSION screenplay is mainly credited to Roger Dodson. Either way, the film lives up *and* down to its enthusiastic endorsement by drive-in movie maven Joe Bob Briggs: "The greatest topless bar flick ever made." Briggs granted Maria Ford his patented Hubbie Award—a hubcap—in the "Breast Actress" category.

For cult-movie connossieurs, NAKED OBSESSION stands comparison with Andy and Katt Shea Ruben's mid-1980s flesh-pot terror trilogy, STRIPPED TO KILL, STRIPPED TO KILL II and DANCE OF THE DAMNED. *(Violence, substance abuse, profanity, nudity, sexual situations, adult situations.)*

p, Ron Zwang; d, Dan Golden; w, Robert Dodson, (from the story by Dodson and Dan Golden); ph, Dick Buckley; ed, Gabrielle Gilbert-Reeves; m, Scott Singer; prod d, Johan LeTenoux; art d, Mark Walters, Hayden De M. Yates; cos, Paris Libby

Erotic/Thriller/Crime **(PR: O MPAA: R)**

NEAR MISSES ★½

(U.S./France) 93m Chrysalide Films; Canal Plus; The Movie Group ~ Media Home Entertainment c

Judge Reinhold *(Claude Jobert)*, Casey Siemaszko *(Colin Phipps)*, Rebecca Pauly *(Maggie)*, Cecile Paoli *(Molly)*, Kashia Figura *(Sasha)*, Muriel Combeau *(Toni)*, Bruce McGuire, Dominic Gould, Stuart Seide, Patrick Floersheim, Andrzej Jagora, Vernon Dobtcheff

The latest direct-to-video offering from the Gallic producers of THE MAID, MAY WINE and STROKE OF MIDNIGHT, NEAR MISSES is a desperate screwball farce which mistakes mix-ups and slamming doors for true wit.

Rather incongruously, it begins with a violent break-in at defense contractor Techtronics Industries, with legions of cops shot to death by the intruder. Claude Jobert (Judge Reinhold), a Techtronics employee instrumental to a top-secret satellite project, is thus summoned from the Phoenix home he shares with his spacey vegetarian wife Molly (Cecile Paoli) to the LA sprawl where he lives with glamorous blonde Maggie (Rebecca Pauly)—his other wife. Yes, Claude is a world-class bigamist, and with a mistress, Toni (Muriel Combeau), on the side. To make time for her, Claude pulls the ruse that fuels the plot: a Marine Reservist, he signs on for his annual two-week hitch at the US Embassy in Paris. Once there he commands lowly American trooper Colin Phipps (Casey Siemaszko) to assume his identity and rank.

While Claude enjoys a tropical idyll with Toni, Colin takes his place in Paris, only to be kidnapped by the Boris-Badenov-level stereotypes from the Soviet Embassy, who think he's the VIP

Jobert. By the time the commies realize their mistake, the real Claude has returned to Paris in a panic; both his wives, each having heard of her beloved husband's seizure, are in the city trying to secure his release. The Russians, afraid of drawing Kremlin wrath over snatching the wrong guy, urge Colin Phipps to continue masquerading as Jobert as they force him to "escape." Meanwhile the US diplomats come to suspect the real Claude of being some kind of double agent, due to his strange behaviour. Worse, the two Mrs. Joberts keep crossing each other's path, as Claude desperately tries to make sure they don't learn the truth about him.

And that's just the beginning. NEAR MISSES pumps out a torrent of misunderstandings and evasions, with all the participants, plus KGB, CIA, an assassin and a blustering blowhard of a Marine sergeant scrambling like NOISES OFF at 78 RPM, waving guns and punctuating their entrances and exits with expletives when the screenplay comes up with nothing remotely clever to say. The style's as tired as all the gags about Mikhail Gorbachev's birthmark, and characters run the gamut from annoying to irksome to pestiferous. Judge Reinhold mixes his off-center charm with a cloying smarminess fitting for a protagonist one is never sure whether to like or despise, but Siemaszko brings very little to his runty military role; he's Sad Sack without being particularly sad or sacked. The ladies are all pretty and dumb, holding up their low end of comedy with multiple catfights and repeated groin kicks.

Shot in France, NEAR MISSES is the latest in Chrysalide Films' series of trite, low-budget romantic romps toplining second-tier Yank actors. *(Profanity, adult situations, sexual situations, violence)*

p, Monique Annaud; d, Baz Taylor; w, Peter I. Baloff, David W. Wollert; ph, Yves Dahan; ed, Michele Robert-Lauliac; m, Didier Vasseur; art d, Nicolas Prier; cos, Annie Ducoulombier

Romance/Comedy (PR: C MPAA: PG-13)

NEON CITY ★★

(Canada) 107m Little Bear Films; Kodiak Films ~ Vidmark Entertainment c

Michael Ironside *(Harry Stark)*, Vanity *(Reno)*, Lyle Alzado *(Bulk)*, Nick Klar *(Tom)*, Richard Sanders *(Dickie Devine)*, Valerie Wildman *(Sandy)*, Juliet Landau *(Twink)*, Arsenio "Sonny" Trinidad *(Wing)*, Monte Markham *(Captain Raymond)*

Although Canada has turned out its share of cinematic wobblers over the years, they've been low on those post-nuke MAD MAX ripoffs that perpetually glut the direct-to-video market. Maybe Bob and Doug McKenzie's uproarious "Mutants of 2051 A.D." spoof from STRANGE BREW shamed the Canadian film industry for years. In any case, the moratorium has ended with NEON CITY, a film which also confirms a long-held suspicion that these apocalyptic actioners are a revival of the oft-pronounced-dead Western genre.

Instead of a horse-drawn wagon, this STAGECOACH retread features a turbocharged truck that conveys diverse misfits across the environmentally ravaged wastelands of 2053, where nomadic bandits, toxic mist, lethal sunbursts and those ever-popular mutants pose constant peril. The characters have to go from the frontier helltown of Jericho Station to glittering Neon City, one of the few strongholds of civilized society. The passengers are cynical bounty-hunter Harry Stark (Michael Ironside); his prisoner, a lovely escaped murderess named Reno (Vanity); Stark's bitter ex-wife Sandy (Valerie Wildman), now a mail-order bride for some lucky Neonian; a spoiled rich girl called Twink (Juliet Landau); vaudeville comic Dickie Devine (Richard Sanders); and a killer junkie disguised as a doctor, Tom (Nick Klar). There's also the hulking driver Bulk (Lyle Alzado) and a Mysterious Oriental (Arsenio Trinidad).

A formula plot wouldn't be a formula plot if it didn't work reliably time and again, and NEON CITY maintains some interest, even if there aren't many surprises. No sooner does Bulk mention he's got a dear sister in an outlying settlement than she's butchered in a bandit attack. Haughty Twink learns to be friends with her motley fellow travelers. The Mysterious Oriental turns out to be the missing scientist whose fiddling with the ozone layer brought on the whole ecological mess in the first place, but he redeems himself by rigging a raygun that blasts the marauding meanies. Stark hears the real story behind Reno's alleged crime, and falls in love with her for a drive-into-the-sunset close. That's not unexpected either given that Vanity looks every bit the sultry Prince protegee that she was, and not even gratuitous nose-picking will convince viewers that she's a hardbitten outlaw.

The rest of the cast is watchable, with Ironside (SCANNERS, TOTAL RECALL) again demonstrating why he's the premiere screen tough guy north of Eastwood—even if he lacks Clint's wise choice of screenplays. Richard Sanders's Red-Buttons-like turn as an itinerant clown gains a needed edge when it's revealed that his briefcase of props and magic gags includes a stock of deadly narcotics—the funnyman provides euthanasia service for the maimed and mutated as a sideline. A real-life casualty in 1992 was massive Lyle Alzado (CLUB FED, COMRADES IN ARMS), who succumbed to brain cancer he attributed to his longtime intake of steroids.

Director and supporting player Monte Markham uses the majestic Utah scenery well and manages the tricky feat of shooting the cramped truck interior with an energetic and fluid lens; paradoxically, action scenes feel wobbly and ill-prepared. There's also a ludicrous bit in which the voyagers discover and enjoy the world's last surviving hot tub.

At least Markham and his co-screenwriters put some thought into the 21st-century setting and its rich glossary of futurespeak slang. That's untypical for this variety of low-budget sci-fi action genre, in which the monosyllabic scripts seem to write themselves. NEON CITY is far from the worst ROAD WARRIOR rerun ever, although that's truly faint praise. *(Violence, substance abuse, profanity, sexual situations.)*

p, Schmidt Wolf, Jeff Begun, John Schouweiler; d, Monte Markham; w, Buck Finch, Jeff Begun, Monte Markham; ph, Timothy Galfas; ed, David Hagar; prod d, Fu Ding Cheng; set d, Steven Lee; cos, Debbie Shine

Action/Adventure/Science Fiction (PR: C MPAA: R)

NETHERWORLD ★★

91m Full Moon Entertainment ~ Paramount c

Michael Bendetti *(Corey Thornton)*, Holly Floria *(Dianne)*, Denise Gentile *(Delores)*, Anjanette Comer *(Mrs. Palmer)*, Robert Burr *(Mr. Yates)*, Robert Sampson *(Noah)*, Mark Kemble *(Barbu-Soir)*, Holly Butler *(Marilyn)*, Alex Datcher *(Mary Magdalene)*, Darlene Molero *(Hoyden-Harridan)*, Michael Lowry *(Stemsy)*, Candice Williams *(Afro-American Child)*, George Kelly *(Bijou)*, David Schmoeller *(Billy C.)*, Robert Labrosse *(Macho Man)*, Barret O'Brien *(Teen Boy)*, Kelsie Chance *(Nude Man)*, James T. Locascio *(Gun Man)*, Linda Ljoka *(Nona)*, A.C. Santa Cruz *(Masked Figure/Featured Female Dancer)*, Andrew Just *(Muscular Man)*, Patricia Heard *(Match Woman/Horrific Visage)*, Nicole Krummel *(Nude Woman)*, Edgar Winters *(Musician)*, Carol Brady *(Featured Female Dancer)*, Adolfo "Fito" Garcia *(Featured Male Dancer)*, Jessica Carvin *(Caucasian Child)*

Attractively mounted by Full Moon Entertainment, NETHERWORLD is a film of modest ambitions, but successful within its own limited parameters.

Corey Thornton (Michael Bendetti) receives a surprising legacy from his late, estranged father: a mansion in the Louisiana swamps, luxurious, beautiful and immensely valuable. But there are mysteries to be solved, foremost among them why Thornton senior left such riches to the son he abandoned. Corey is also haunted by dreams and hallucinatory visions of the gravely beautiful Delores (Denise Gentile), who worked at the raucous brothel that operates just down the river from the Thornton plantation and who seems to have had something to do with his father's death.

Corey promptly falls in love with Dianne Palmer (Holly Floria), whose mother (Anjanette Comer) oversees the Thornton property. Dianne warns him to have nothing to do with the brothel, but he's inexorably drawn there. Its basement holds secrets, strange creatures and succubi, and Corey slowly realizes that his father was deeply involved with black magic and hopes to return from the dead. Almost too late, Corey learns that his father's plan is to inhabit *his* body, and consign his soul to the netherworld. In a dream, Corey meets his father and the two fight it out. Corey triumphs, and returns to the land of the living; his father's soul is trapped in the body of a parrot, like those of many other unfortunates who came under Delores's spell.

Released direct-to-video, NETHERWORLD gets off to a surprisingly good start in the brothel of the damned: a belligerent, drunken client goes wandering where he shouldn't and comes upon an underground passageway whose inhabitants promise sensual pleasures tinged with danger. Needless to say, things go badly for him: as he has his way with the beckoning Delores, a disembodied hand detaches itself from some far-off wall and claws his face off. If the rest of the film kept up with the opening, it would be a small gem, but it quickly settles into long-winded exposition and the machinations of a conventional suspense story—what is the secret of the Thornton plantation, how did Thornton senior die, what does Mrs. Palmer know and why isn't she telling? It's all more than a little dull.

The film's high production values are a plus, and director David Schmoeller (CRAWLSPACE) keeps the action moving as quickly as the attenuated story allows. Though it would certainly have been a disappointment in theaters, NETHERWORLD plays fairly well on the small screen. For an audience whose expectations aren't too high, it's a diverting hour-and-a-half of supernatural entertainment. *(Violence, sexual situations.)*

p, Thomas Bradford; d, David Schmoeller; w, Billy Chicago, (from the idea by Charles Band); ph, Adolfo Bartoli; ed, Carol Oblath; m, David Bryan; art d, Billy Jett, James Fraser; set d, Elizabeth Shannon; cos, Lois Simbach

Fantasy/Horror **(PR: C MPAA: R)**

NEWSIES ★★

125m Walt Disney Productions ~ BV c

Christian Bale *(Jack Kelly/Frances Sullivan)*, David Moscow *(David Jacobs)*, Luke Edwards *(Les Jacobs)*, Max Casella *(Racetrack)*, Marty Belafsky *(Crutchy)*, Arvie Lowe, Jr. *(Boots)*, Aaron Lohr *(Mush)*, Trey Parker *(Kid Blink)*, Gabriel Damon *(Spot Conlon)*, Dee Caspary *(Snitch)*, Joseph Conrad *(Jake)*, Dominic Maldonado *(Itey)*, Matthew Fields *(Snipeshooter)*, Mark David *(Specs)*, Ivan Dudynsky *(Dutchy)*, Robert Feeney *(Snoddy)*, Michael A. Goorjian *(Skittery)*, Dominic Lucero *(Bumlets)*, David Sidoni *(Pie Eater)*, Kevin Stea *(Swifty)*, Bill Pullman *(Bryan Denton)*, Ann-Margret *(Medda Larkson)*, Ele Keats *(Sarah Jacobs)*, Jeffrey DeMunn *(Mayer Jacobs)*, Deborra-Lee Furness *(Esther Jacobs)*, Marc Lawrence *(Kloppman)*, Kevin Michaels *(Ten-Pin)*, Sylvia Short *(Nun)*, Melody Santangelo *(Nun)*, Lois Young *(Nun)*, JoAnn Harris *(Patrick's Mother)*, Gregg Kent-Smith *(Toby the Candy Butcher)*, David James Alexander *(Teddy Roosevelt)*, Robert Duvall *(Joseph Pulitzer)*, Michael Lerner *(Weasel)*, Kevin Tighe *(Snyder)*, Charles Cioffi *(Seitz)*, Shon Greenblatt *(Oscar Delancey)*, David Sheinkopf *(Morris Delancey)*, Mark Lowenthal *(Jonathan)*, William Boyett *(Judge Movealong Monahan)*, Ryan MacDonald *(Mayor Van Wyck)*, Frank Girardeau *(Chief of Police Devery)*, Shay Duffin *(Captain McSwain)*, Terry Kohl *(Bailiff)*, Tom Finnegan *(Bunsen)*, I.M. Hobson *(Gammon)*, Frank Novak *(Policeman)*, Ogie Banks, III, Daxon Calloway, Scott Caudill, D.J. Dellos, Chris Dupre, Dak Eubanks, Brian Friedman, Todd Jenkins, Terry Lindholm, Alan Luzietti, Kevin McCasland, Dean McFliker, James Earl Miller, David Evans, Craig Raclawski, Michael Rohrbacher, Gregg Russell, Joshua Wiener, Jesus Fuentes, Tony Gonzales, Robert Jaquez, Larry Jones, Kevin Kruger, David Larson, Patrick Lars Olsen, Travis Payne, Jim Raposa, Damon Butler, Christopher Bonomo, Bret Dieball, Rob Grayson, Michael Irvin, Eric Pesqueira, Scott Thysell, Jeff Thysell, Wes Veldink, Michael Warwick, Jason Yribar *(Newsies Dancers)*

Sumptuous production values and fitfully impressive choreography notwithstanding, NEWSIES was a major misfire for Disney Studios. That's a shame, because this intensely pro-labor musical drama, dealing with the late 1890s Gotham newsboys' strike against magnates Joseph Pulitzer and William Randolph Hearst, is a picture one really wants to like.

The time is 1899—one year after Teddy Roosevelt's famous charge up San Juan Hill—and the hard-working, impoverished newsies (boys who hawk "all the news that's fit to print" on the streets) are having a tough time making ends meet. Then Joseph Pulitzer (Robert Duvall) arbitrarily raises the wholesale cost of the newspapers, further cutting into the newsies' already slim profit margin. Led by rough-and-tumble Jack Kelly (Christian Bale) and the more intellectual David Jacobs (David Moscow), these street urchins form an all-singing, all-dancing picket line, determined not to give in to Pulitzer's cost-hikes. On the boys' side is an enthusiastic newspaper reporter, Bryan Denton (Bill Pullman), from a rival newspaper, who sticks his professional neck out for the newsies. Also sympathetic to their plight is a vaudeville showgirl, Medda Larkson (Ann-Margret), and finally, when all looks lost, New York Governor Teddy Roosevelt (David James Alexander) himself.

Opposing the heroes are an array of bullies, scabs and thugs, along with crooked politicians and, last but not least, two men audiences are supposed to love to hate: a Faginish newspaper distributor, Weasel (Michael Lerner), and a mean-as-they-come reform school warden Snyde (Kevin Tighe), who conspires with Pulitzer and others to arrest Jack and return him to the reform school from which he escaped years earlier. There are rescues, chases and street brawls galore, not to mention an overabundance of hoofing in the streets, before the story is neatly wrapped up in a typically upbeat—and extremely artificial—Disney ending.

Making his directorial bow, choreographer Kenny Ortega strains valiantly to breathe life into this misguided musical. On the one hand, NEWSIES aspires to be a throwback to the golden heyday of the Hollywood musical. On the other hand, it attempts to pay homage to the bleak, gritty, labor unrest movies of the Depression era. As for the cast, with the exception of Bale (EMPIRE OF THE SUN, HENRY V) who has more screen time and is given most of the best numbers to sing and dance, no one is allowed to stand out above the rest. Judged as an ensemble effort, every thespian acquits himself competently.

While a few of the dance numbers, especially the opening routine featuring dozens of high-stepping, leaping, spinning and prancing newsboys, are dazzling, too often they are lackluster and monotonous. The film cries out for at least one good love-song duet between Bale and his rather subdued love interest, Sarah Jacobs (played blandly by newcomer Ele Keats). Also, Ann-Margret's tremendous talent is virtually wasted. Even the two opportunities she has to perform potentially rousing rag-time-style tunes during her vaudeville act are painfully abbreviated, cut short by the demands of the plot.

While some of composer Alan Menken's (BEAUTY AND THE BEAST, ALADDIN) melodies are effective (though too contemporary to be genuinely compatible with the musical sounds of the 1890s), Jack Feldman, substituting for the late Howard Ashman, has penned lyrics that are, at best, mediocre. *(Mild violence, adult situations.)*

p, Michael Finnell; d, Kenny Ortega; w, Bob Tzudiker, Noni White; ph, Andrew Laszlo; ed, William Reynolds; m, Alan Menken, Danny Troob, J.A.C. Redford; art d, Nancy Patton; set d, Robert Gould; cos, May Routh; ch, Kenny Ortega, Peggy Holmes

Musical/Historical/Drama **(PR: A MPAA: PG)**

NICKEL & DIME ★★½

96m Hometown Pictures; Five and Ten Productions; Danielson/Moses Productions ~ Columbia TriStar Home Video c

C. Thomas Howell *(Jack Stone)*, Wallace Shawn *(Everett Willis)*, Lise Cutter *(Cathleen Markson)*, Roy Brocksmith *(Sammy Thornton)*, Lynn Danielson *(Destiny Charm)*, Kathleen Freeman *(Judge Lechter)*, Matthew Edison, Allan Rich, Mark Ralston, Eric Christmas, Carl Ballantine

The odd-couple pairing of C. Thomas Howell and Wallace Shawn is the brightest element of NICKEL & DIME, an otherwise mediocre comic action tale.

The story begins when flashy, free-spirited conman/lawyer Jack Stone (Howell), an "heir chaser," or specialist in probate cases, teams with straight-arrow accountant Everett Willis (Shawn), a forty-one-year-old man determinedly stuck in the fifties, whose idols are Hopalong Cassidy and Peggy Lee ("There's been no good music since 1955," he opines, mourning the advent of Elvis) to find the missing heir to the estate of a slain multimillionaire businessman.

Desperately broke, Stone has returned home to take over the impoverished legal business of his ill father, whom he's put into an old-age home, and hires Everett to straighten out his back taxes when the IRS sues him. With a frenetic but weak-kneed and almost totally implausible screenplay by Ben Moses (who also directed), Eddy Pollon and Seth Front, Stone and Everett initially loathe but grow to respect and learn from each other in the course of their adventure, as they are beset by villainous rival heir-sleuth Sammy Thorton (Roy Brocksmith) and a mobster (Matthew Edison) and his inept gunsels out to recover a cache of gems the dead businessman smuggled into the country (he replaced the pimientos with rubies in a shipment of olives).

Woefully coincidentally, Stone discovers that the missing heir is none other than the girlfriend, Cathleen Markson (Lise Cutter), now an assistant DA, he jilted seven years earlier at the altar, with whom he is soon reconciled, while Everett falls for wacky sweet-hearted hooker Destiny Charm (Lynn Danielson, who also produced this picture), which awkwardly completes the buddy-movie formula in which each man must have some female romantic interest, thus eliminating any possibility in viewers' minds of homosexual attraction.

The byplay between Howell (ET, SOUL MAN) and Shawn (the rotund, acclaimed playwright and sometime actor whose father, William, was the founder and publisher of the *New Yorker*) is often hilarious, although the filmmakers rely on too many post-dubbed jokes and wisecracks to help bolster the weak screenplay. While Moses's direction is strictly routine, with the action scenes especially flat, the movie is aided immensely by the presence of some delightful screen veterans, including Eric Christmas and Carl Ballantine as a pair of Howell's father's bickering cronies and Kathleen Freeman as a no-nonsence probate court judge.

Shot in late 1990 and released briefly in Los Angeles before heading to the video marketplace, NICKEL & DIME looks and feels like a busted TV pilot. And, for what it matters, the title is never explained. *(Sexual situations.)*

p, Lynn Danielson, Ben Moses; d, Ben Moses; w, Eddy Pollon, Seth Front; ph, Henry M. Lebo; ed, Joan E. Chapman; m, Stephen Cohn; prod d, George Costello; set d, Damon Medlen, Susan Benjamin; cos, Ann Lambert

Action/Comedy **(PR: A MPAA: PG)**

NIGHT AND DAY ★★★½

(France/Belgium/Switzerland) 90m Pierre Grise Productions; Paradise Films; George Reinhart Productions ~ Metropolis Film c
(NUIT ET JOUR)

Guilaine Londez *(Julie)*, Thomas Langmann *(Jack)*, Francois Negret *(Joseph)*

Inspired by Jean-Luc Godard, Chantal Akerman's career began with the short film BLOW UP MY CITY in 1968 and includes the groundbreaking JEANNE DIELMAN. The Belgian film-maker has frequently examined idealized notions of romance, something she does again in her latest work, the utterly charming NIGHT AND DAY.

Jack (Thomas Langmann) and Julie (Guilaine Londez) are young lovers recently arrived in Paris from the provinces. They have no phone, no friends and no ambitions—all that can wait until next year. By night Jack drives a cab, while Julie wanders the streets of Paris; by day they make love constantly. As for sleep . . . well, that can wait until next year too.

Late one afternoon, as Jack begins his shift, Julie meets Joseph (Francois Negret), who drives the cab during the day and is also a newcomer to the city. Julie spends an evening in his company, and then another, and before long they sleep together. Soon Julie's nights are as full as her days.

One Sunday, Jack's staid parents arrive unexpectedly from the provinces, but the young lovers' sexual greediness—they can't keep their hands off each other—quickly scares them off. Later, one dawn, after falling asleep beside Joseph in an air-conditioned hotel room, Julie awakens with a start and races to get home before Jack does—in her mind, her affair is only a betrayal if she's not there to greet her lover. She arrives in the nick of time but, from that moment on, worry and doubt begin to creep into the relationship; the idyll is over.

Joseph is hopelessly lovesick. When Jack asks Julie to accompany him one evening as he makes his rounds in the cab, Joseph cannot bear the separation, and tries to extract the promise—unforthcoming—that she'll never abandon him again. Finally, Julie decides to end the affair simply because, as she informs the devastated Joseph, Jack was there first. Later, after impulsively tearing down a wall in the apartment and repainting the rooms, she casually mentions her affair to Jack, prompting the film's bittersweet but true-to-life ending.

Widely considered one of the most important art-house filmmakers of the 1970s and 80s, Akerman later expressed a desire to make more commercially viable films, largely to escape the constant financial constraints of independent filmmaking. Although NIGHT AND DAY is by far her most commercial effort, it's nonetheless vintage Akerman.

The cinematography is lush, almost overripe, like a piece of technicolor candy. And the three young leads are shot in close-ups befitting Montgomery Clift, Elizabeth Taylor and James Dean. But Akerman's trademark minimalism and structuralism—suggesting Jarmusch and Ozu, respectively—is very much in evidence.

As Julie, Londez is radiant, with an expressive rather than pretty face and a firm, sturdy body. She has a more "masculine" physique than either of her male lovers (they're both wispy and delicately pretty), something that befits the story's gender reversal; rather than the traditional menage, wherein two women vie for the affection of a male, here it's the woman who undertakes dual affairs. And whereas the two men grow increasingly distraught by her refusal to commit—though Jack cannot pinpoint the cause of his malaise—Julie feels perfectly up to the challenge. She's also strong enough to walk away from them both when the time comes.

The youthful *joie de vivre* that fuels NIGHT AND DAY in its opening scenes starts to pall as the film progresses—these characters talk and talk and talk with an earnestness and self-importance that betrays their immaturity and which jaded viewers may find wearisome. On the whole, however, this is an engaging, welcome addition to the work of a consistently interesting and original filmmaker. *(Nudity, sexual situations, adult situations.)*

p, Martine Marignac, Maurice Tinchant; d, Chantal Akerman; w, Chantal Akerman, Pascal Bonitzer, (from the idea by Michel Vandestien); ph, Jean-Claude Neckelbrouck, Pierre Gordower, Bernard Delville, Olivier Dessalles; ed, Francine Sandberg, Camille Bordes Resnais; m, Marc Herouet; art d, Dominique Douret; cos, Brigitte Nierhaus, Michele Blondeel

Romance/Drama **(PR: C MPAA: NR)**

NIGHT AND THE CITY ★★★

98m Fox; TriBeCa Productions; PentAmerica Pictures ~ Fox c

Robert De Niro *(Harry Fabian)*, Jessica Lange *(Helen Nasseros)*, Cliff Gorman *(Phil)*, Alan King *("Boom-Boom" Grossman)*, Jack Warden *(Al Grossman)*, Eli Wallach *(Peck)*, Barry Primus *(Tommy Tessler)*, Gene Kirkwood *(Resnick)*, Pedro Sanchez *(Cuda Sanchez)*, Gerry Murphy *(1st Steel Jaw)*, Clem Caserta *(2nd Steel Jaw)*, Anthony Canarozzi *(Emmet Gorgon)*, David W. Butler *(Bonney)*, Byron Utley *(Frisker)*, Margo Winkler *(Judge)*, Maurice Shrog *(Gym Manager)*, Regis Philbin *(Himself)*, Joy Philbin *(Herself)*, Richard Price *(Doctor)*, Frank Jones *(Dugan)*, Tommy A. Ford *(Herman)*, Peter Bucossi *(Attacker)*, Bert Randolph Sugar *(Guy at Bar)*, Nathaniel E. Johnson *(Kid Client)*, Brenda Denmark *(Kid's Mom)*, Barry Squitieri *(Marty Kaufman)*, Lisa Vidal *(Carmen)*, Carol Woods *(Secretary)*, Joseph D'Onofrio *(Mike)*, Michael Badalucco *(Elaine's Bartender)*, Deborah Watkins *(Nun)*, Nandan Sage *(Gupta)*, Harsh Nayyar *(Faruz)*, Ben Lin *(Duk Soo Kim)*, John Polce *(Bouncer)*, Rosalind Malloff *(Frieda)*, Kennan Scott *(Kid on Phone)*, Henry Milligan *(Cotton)*, Victor Machado *(Santiago)*, Chuck Low *(Freddy DiMario)*, Lou Polo *(Jap Epstein)*, Louis Cantarini *(Boxing Official)*, John Quinn *(Bartender)*, Philip Carlo *(Peck's Guy)*, Cameron Lane *(1st Mugger)*, Sharrieff Pugh *(2nd Mugger)*, Mitchell Tex Low *(Delivery Man)*, Mitch Cunningham *(Kid at Disco)*, Dave Reilly *(2nd Cop)*, Leslie Bart *(Boom Boom's Secretary)*, Ann Devaney *(Gorgon's Girl)*, Lorenzo Palminteri *(Tommy Carver)*, Catherine Russell *(Singer)*

Flawed but engaging, this remake of Jules Dassin's 1950 film noir is updated in attitude and acting styles by Irwin Winkler and his superb cast, providing a rich slice of New York life.

Harry Fabian (Robert De Niro, stepping into one of Richard Widmark's best roles) is an ambulance-chasing injury lawyer who dreams of having the clout of boxing promoter "Boom Boom" Grossman (Alan King, at his vilest). While pursuing a typically flimsy lawsuit against one of Boom Boom's fighters, Cuda Sanchez (Pedro Sanchez), Fabian's eyes are opened when he visits a midtown gym teeming with pugilistic talent. Boom Boom has the lock on big promotions, but the less lucrative club fighting scene has languished, done in mostly by cable TV. Fabian dreams up a plan to recruit fighters and take over a disco for an evening of old-fashioned neighborhood boxing action. But he steps on far too many toes along the way.

Fabian is already sleeping with Helen Nasseros (Jessica Lange), the slightly blowsy, tough-as-nails wife of Phil (Cliff Gorman), the owner of his neighborhood bar, from whom he hopes to borrow most of the front money he needs. Having already irritated Boom Boom with his lawsuit, Fabian needles him even further by recruiting his brother, Al Grossman (Jack Warden), a former fighter whose career was ruined by Boom Boom, to be his talent scout. Boom Boom assigns two of his thugs to keep an eye on Al, who has a bad heart. They uncover Fabian's affair with Helen, which Boom Boom duly reports back to Phil. Phil beats up Helen and reports her forged liquor license, which was obtained for her by Fabian so she could open up her own bar after leaving Phil. He then welches on his deal to loan money to Fabian, beating him up as well.

Fabian finally gets the money from a moralizing loan shark, Peck (Eli Wallach). But when Al drops dead during a tussle on the day of the fight, Fabian and Helen find themselves on the run for their lives from Boom Boom's thugs. The thugs find Harry and shoot him, but fail to kill him. As Harry is carried off in an ambulance, Helen is at his side, ready to nurse him back to health so they can leave New York behind and open a bar somewhere else, as far away as possible from Boom Boom and Phil.

Comparisons between the directorial work of Winkler and Martin Scorsese are inevitable: Winkler co-produced some of Scorsese's best films, including RAGING BULL and GOODFELLAS; NIGHT AND THE CITY, like MEAN STREETS and TAXI DRIVER, sets Robert De Niro against a gritty New York City background; and Richard Price, by his own account, wrote the typically crisp and flavorful screenplay for Scorsese, who helped him develop it but finally passed on directing it. These comparisons, however, are not only unfair but irrelevant. Winkler has picked up some of Scorsese's distinctive directorial flourishes; but he tellingly dedicates his film to Dassin rather than Scorsese, and his version of NIGHT AND THE CITY is distinguished by a warmer, more benign approach to character and narrative.

Harry Fabian is neither bad enough nor mean enough to swim truly with the sharks he appears to envy. (In this, he's a character closer to KING OF COMEDY's Rupert Pupkin than to GOODFELLAS' Jimmy Conway, but he lacks even Pupkin's malignant edge.) He is genuinely awestruck at spotting a minor celebrity like Regis Philbin in a restaurant, and is attracted to being a fight promoter more by glamour than by money and power. It's these qualities that endear him to Helen (who's probably tough enough for both of them) and to us, but they also make him a loser within the framework of the movie. Inarticulate, neurotic and blindly driven by momentary needs and appetites, Harry and Helen may not be the most romantic of couples, but they ring true.

If NIGHT AND THE CITY has a problem, it's in a disjointed sense of period. At times, Winkler's film feels as though it's set, like Dassin's original, in the 50s, a time when boxers had the glamor we now associate with pop stars, and when fighters, writers and shady promoters would rub shoulders in Greenwich Village bars. The modernist sensibilities of the characters sometimes appear incongruous in this context, making the film seem like a brash, vibrant homage to a New York that no longer exists. What NIGHT AND THE CITY lacks in realism and subtlety, though, it makes up for in energy and vitality, with a punchy soundtrack helping maintain the pace. Like Harry Fabian, it desperately wants to be loved, and it pulls no punches trying to make sure that happens. *(Violence, profanity, adult situations.)*

p, Jane Rosenthal, Irwin Winkler; d, Irwin Winkler; w, Richard Price, Jo Eisinger, (from his screenplay based on the origional screenplay by Jules Dassin, based on the novel by Gerald Kersh); ph, Tak Fujimoto; ed, David Brenner; m, James Newton Howard; prod d, Peter Larkin; art d, Charley Beal; set d, Robert J. Franco; cos, Richard Bruno

Drama/Romance **(PR: C MPAA: R)**

NIGHT EYES 2 ★½

97m Two Eyes Productions; Amritraj Entertainment ~ Prism Entertainment c

Andrew Stevens *(Will Griffith)*, Shannon Tweed *(Marilyn)*, Richard Chaves *(Hector Mejenes)*, Tim Russ *(Jesse)*, Geno Silva *(Luis)*, John O'Hurley *(Turner)*, Dan Cashman *(Talbot)*, Tessa Taylor *(Vivian)*, Julian Stone *(Safecracker)*, Venus Baron *(Buxom Girl)*, Sarah Peery *(Beautiful girl)*, Shannon Retigan *(Bookstore Customer)*

The original NIGHT EYES blazed a trail in the direct-to-video market for lots of low-budget but glossy, erotic noir films that exploited fevered sex and nudity, with a murder tossed in now and then to keep the whole enterprise "respectably" anchored in the thriller realm. At least NIGHT EYES had a lambent touch of class, solid characterizations and an intriguing plot. This sequel is a shallow rerun with none of the above.

The new storyline follows the first so closely that one can't say if it's a sequel or a prequel or a remake. Once more Andrew Stevens is Will Griffith, handsome, straight-shooting security expert. Here he's hired to rig a high-tech alarm system for Hector Mejenes (Richard Chaves), a presidential candidate-in-exile from some unspecified banana republic. The suave would-be dictator has had attacks on his mansion by mystery gunmen, so Griffith sets up remote cameras and he monitors all that goes on—including the exercise workouts of Mejenes's sensuous, blonde American-born spouse Marilyn (Shannon Tweed).

Sure enough, Griffith falls in love with the healthy but neglected wife (and the frisky pair expose either square yards or feet of flesh, depending on whether one is watching the steamy unrated cassette or the scissored "R" version). As he did in the last movie, though, Will foolishly forgets his own cameras, which record the affair. While Mejenes is out of town his thug bodyguard Luis (Geno Silva) snatches the incriminating tape. Will figures out that Luis is behind the terrorist attacks and kills the villain, but Mejenes is the real mastermind, scheming to eliminate both the security man and Marilyn to win a sympathy vote in the upcoming election.

Andrew Stevens's affable charm has a hard time competing with the hero's stupidity. Delectable *Playboy* pinup Tweed (TWISTED JUSTICE, LAST CALL) is no stranger to sexpot roles, but at least she usually plays strong, no-nonsense females. Here she's the basic bimbo-in-jeopardy who can be counted on to kick the gun accidentally out of reach during every life or death struggle. Tim Russ portrays Will's partner Jesse; he's hip and friendly—and Black, so the savvy viewer knows right away he's dead meat. Sure enough, Jesse gets iced by Luis in a particularly sadistic sequence.

The original NIGHT EYES featured Tanya Roberts as the femme fatale who led Will Griffith astray, but in this retread it's Will's own *cojones* that nearly prove his undoing. The sequel operates in a moral void where the affair is sanctioned because Marilyn's husband doesn't pay her sufficient bedroom attention (he's only running for president, after all). The unrated sex scenes demonstrate the aphrodisiac potential of berries and gym equipment, while a gag romance scene in a bookstore (with a nerd carrying a paperback called—surprise!—"Night Eyes") provides low, low comedy. A much better joke is Will Griffith's nonreactive hound: the security expert owns the worst watchdog of all time. *(Violence, profanity, nudity, sexual situations, adult situations.)*

p, Ashok Amritraj; d, Rodney McDonald; w, Simon Louis Ward, (from the story by Andrew Stevens); ph, Kent Wakeford; ed, David H. Lloyd; prod d, Milo Needles; set d, Nicki Roberts; cos, Greg LaVoi

Erotic/Thriller **(PR: O MPAA: R)**

NIGHT ON EARTH ★★★

130m Locus Solus; Black Snake Productions ~ Fine Line Features c

Gena Rowlands *(Victoria Snelling)*, Winona Ryder *(Corky)*, Lisanne Falk *(Rock Manager)*, Alan Randolph Scott, I *(1st Rock Musician)*, Anthony Portillo *(2nd Rock Musician)*, Armin Mueller-Stahl *(Helmut Grokenberger)*, Giancarlo Esposito *(YoYo)*, Rosie Perez *(Angela)*, Richard Boes *(1st Cab Driver)*, Isaach De Bankole *(Driver)*, Beatrice Dalle *(Blind Woman)*, Pascal Nzonzi *(1st Passenger)*, Emile Abossolo-M'Bo *(2nd Passenger)*, Stephane Boucher *(Man in Accident)*, Noel Kaufmann *(Man on Motorcycle)*, Roberto Benigni *(Gino)*, Paolo Bonacelli *(Priest)*, Gianni Schettino *(1st Transvestite)*, Antonino Ragusa *(2nd Transvestite)*, Nicola Facondo *(Lover)*, Camilla Begnoni *(Lover)*, Romolo DiBiasi *(Angry Driver)*, Donatella Servadio *(Voice of Dispatcher)*, Matti Pellonpaa *(Mika)*, Kari Vaananen *(1st Man)*, Sakari Kuosmanen *(2nd Man)*, Tomi Salmela *(3rd Man)*, Eija Vilpas *(Voice of Dispatcher)*, Jaakko Talaskivi *(1st Factory Worker)*, Klaus Heydemann *(2nd Factory Worker)*

Akron-born Jim Jarmusch is one of America's least conventional filmmakers. Since his breakthrough STRANGER THAN PARADISE won the coveted camera d'or at the 1984 Cannes Film Festival he has gained a following for his odd, deceptively trivial narratives that unfold at their own pace and rely heavily on offbeat characters, unlikely settings and absurdist deadpan humor.

For the average moviegoer Jarmusch remains an aquired taste, but NIGHT ON EARTH, physically his most ambitious film, is also his most accessible. It's a compilation of five highly individual vignettes sharing a sublimely simple gimmick: they occur simultaneously, but span different time zones, continents and languages. The tentative relationships—or lack of same—between a taxi driver and his/her passenger(s) lie at the heart of each anecdote. The first, set at dusk in Los Angeles, is easily the weakest, focusing on a high-powered talent agent, Victoria (Gena Rowlands), getting a ride from the LA airport courtesy of a ragamuffin hack named Corky (Winona Ryder). Along the way

Victoria gets the idea that she can make the cabbie a superstar, but Corky politely declines; fame would ruin her career goal of becoming a mechanic. The dialogue in this one-joke playlet feels artificial and forced, and Ryder's tomboy persona comes across as a pure screen invention. She looks like a refugee from NEWSIES, complete with strategic smudge of soot on her cheek.

After that things only get better. The second part is a classic New York situation: streetwise YoYo (Giancarlo Esposito) learns that his friendly East German immigrant cabbie Helmut Grokenberger (Armin Mueller-Stahl) can barely drive or speak English, let alone find his way back to Brooklyn. Soon YoYo takes the wheel himself and tries to teach Helmut how to do his job, stopping on the way to pick up his motor-mouthed relative, Angela (Rosie Perez). It's a funny but hard-edged sketch about friendship growing out of the rockiest circumstances. Then on to Paris for something completely different: a much-abused driver (Isaach De Bankole) thinks he won't get any trouble from his latest fare, a hauntingly beautiful blind woman (Beatrice Dalle). But she's stronger, savvier and more abrasive than he could have imagined, and leaves him figuratively and literally a wreck. These two are the most successfully realized portions of NIGHT ON EARTH and either can stand on its own as a short subject.

The fourth story takes place in Rome and is a thin but rollicking bit of verbal slapstick for Tuscan comedian Roberto Benigni as Gino, a voluble oddball ferrying a weary old priest across town. On the way Gino confesses his many sexual sins to the unwilling clergyman—and the cabbie's bizarre adventures with sheep, vegetables and a sister-in-law prove too much for the holy father's ailing heart. Benigni, who previously appeared in Jarmusch's DOWN BY LAW, is a comedy superstar in Italy in both movie roles and stand-up performance. Off-color monologues like the one here are his specialty, and skillfull English subtitling preserves the hilarity of Gino's rant.

The somber, final portion of NIGHT ON EARTH occurs at dawn in frosty Helsinki, Finland, and suffers mainly from being an abrupt change in mood from what has gone before. Taxi driver Mika (Aki and Mika Kaurismaki regular Matti Pellonpaa) picks up two intoxicated workmen with a sleeping comrade. The revellers explain that their friend lost his job and drank himself into a stupor. Mika responds with a wrenching hard-luck story of his own that makes the conscious passengers grateful for their lot in life after all.

Jarmusch alters his style or intent to suit each segment, and more literal-minded viewers might complain of an absence of any overt unifying theme. Anthology films tend to play out unevenly, and NIGHT ON EARTH overall hangs together better than most. It's also on the longish side at more than two hours, but for entertainment content, this globe-trotting smorgasboard scores at least a solid three out of five.

Craggy-voiced singer-songwriter Tom Waits, a longtime Jarmusch associate, endowed NIGHT ON EARTH with a singular style of music, best described as caveman gypsy world-beat blues. *(Profanity, substance abuse, adult situations, sexual situations.)*

p, Jim Jarmusch; d, Jim Jarmusch; w, Jim Jarmusch; ph, Frederick Elmes; ed, Jay Rabinowitz; m, Tom Waits; set d, Johan LeTenoux; cos, Magda Bava, Claire Fraisse, Alexandra Welker, Gordon Barbara

Drama/Comedy **(PR: C MPAA: R)**

NIGHT RHYTHMS ★★

100m Wilshire Film Ventures; Axis Films International ~ Imperial Entertainment Corporation c

Martin Hewitt *(Nick West)*, Sam Jones *(Detective Jackson)*, David Carradine *(Vincent Machelli)*, Deborah Driggs *(Cinnamon)*, Delia Sheppard *(Bridget Masters)*, Tracy Tweed *(Honey)*, Jamie Stafford *(Kit)*, Patrice Leal *(Lila)*, Julie Strain *(Linda)*, Vincent Curto *(Joseph)*, Timothy C. Burns *(Edgar)*, Juliet James *(Sandra)*, Stephen Fiachi *(Cop)*, Theresa Ring *(Roxanne)*, Kristine Rose *(Marilyn)*, Carrie Bittner *(Elaine)*, Erika Nann *(Alex)*

Glossily produced by Andrew Garroni, NIGHT RHYTHMS is a lousy murder mystery, but—in the "unrated" video version—as X-rated voyeur fodder it's ok, especially for those too timid or self-deluding to rent the cheesily boxed but honest hardcore cassettes.

This ludicrously sexed-up production features Martin Hewitt as Nick West, a throaty, late-night KHPY radio talk-show host who caters, sometimes off the air as well, to his callers, all beautiful but lonely or frustrated women, to the bemusement of his program helper and call screener Bridget Masters (Delia Sheppard). When troubled, habitual caller Honey (Tracy Tweed) shows up in person, Nick dismisses Bridget and the pair have sex in the booth, the sounds of which are sent out over the air (an added turn-on for Honey). Approaching orgasm, Honey's moans turn to screams, and Nick, knocked unconscious, wakes up to find her dead beside him.

Nick flees to his local hangout, a bar run by Cinnamon (Deborah Driggs), who puts him up at her apartment as the cops, led by Detective Jackson (Sam Jones), search for him. Since, in her calls to Nick, Honey's main concern was breaking up with her jealous boyfriend, for whom she also worked as an exotic dancer at the plush Nirvana Club, Nick and Cinnamon, who are soon soulfully in love, go after him as the chief suspect: Vincent Machelli (David Carradine), who also dabbles in drugs, along with his henchman Joseph (Vincent Curto). But Machelli is soon accidentally killed by Nick, so he works through the list of suspects with the help of friends and fans, all the females of which, including Kit (Jamie Stafford), Lila (Patrice Leal) and Linda (Julie Strain), he winds up in bed with, before settling on Bridget, who's taken over his radio spot—and was a jealous lover of Honey, who dumped her. With Cinnamon prodding her by telephone, Nick traps Bridget into confessing to Honey's murder on-air.

Cued by its skin magazine-ish femme character names (Honey, Cinnamon et al.), NIGHT RHYTHMS sets off immediately into male fantasy-land, as Nick's nightly blatantly X-rated spiel—he in essence knowingly provides masturbatory images for his women callers—is more 900-number graphic than is allowable on KHYP's 108.9 FM bandwidth. Alan Gries and Robyn Sullivent's screenplay is hard put to provide a coherent plot, which, however deficient, is quickly lost amid the lushly filmed sex scenes; it's actually fairly extraneous in such fare, anyway. The dialogue is mostly risible, as is Nick's somewhat quaint soul-searching after he's found his ideal mate.

Director Alexander Gregory Hippolyte specializes in these sexathons (SECRET GAMES and CARNAL CRIMES, both starring Hewitt), and he's clearly out of his element whenever the two or three characters in any given scene aren't in the sack together. Fashionably stubbled, the handsome Hewitt (ENDLESS LOVE) has also been specializing in sexy videos lately, and he has his sensitive-eyed, God's-gift-to-women role down pat. The interchangeable women all look cut from the same cloth: serious haired, pneumatically bounteous, Frederick's-attired lookers (Sheppard and Strain are former Penthouse pets; Driggs, the heroine of last year's TOTAL EXPOSURE, was a Playboy centerfold). David Carradine, who should know better (along with Sam Jones), seems to be having fun as the flinty-eyed villainous strip-joint owner. *(Violence, profanity, excessive nudity, sexual situations.)*

p, Andrew Garroni; d, A. Gregory Hippolyte; w, Alan Gries, Robyn Sullivent; ph, Wally Pfister; ed, Kent Smith; m, Ashley Irwin; prod d, Blair Martin; cos, Ricardo Delgado, Lothar Delgado

Mystery/Crime (PR: O MPAA: NR)

976-EVIL II ★
93m CineTel Films ~ LIVE Home Video c

Patrick O'Bryan *(Spike)*, Rene Assa *(Professor Grubeck)*, Debbie James *(Robin)*, Brigitte Nielsen, Leslie Ryan *(Paula)*

There must have been *someone* looking forward to a sequel to 976-EVIL, but even those who were turned on by the Robert Englund-directed tale of telephone terror will likely find this a wrong number. Englund wisely sat out this needless follow-up, which strives mightily to make a connection with the original.

That nasty phone line to hell returns, as does hero Spike (Patrick O'Bryan), who traces the evil calls to a college town where one Professor Grubeck (Rene Assa) has been using the nasty number's powers to murderous ends. Once upon a time he was just your garden-variety serial killer; the movie's opening sequence features one of his murders, complete with a shower scene, dumb homages to Roger Corman and Joe Bob Briggs, and a screaming female victim who lies patiently waiting for Grubeck to drop a lethal spike into her body. Arrested for his crimes, Grubeck puts to use the powers of astral projection he's gained from the beyond, his spirit detaching from his body to wreak more havoc.

The first to go is the janitor who witnessed Grubeck's most recent murder, leading to his arrest; the villain's spirit appears in the motel where the old man's been sequestered and drags him onto the highway, where he's spectacularly splattered by an 18-wheeler. Though the punchline is an admittedly startling moment, the scene as a whole serves to point up the fact early on that director Jim Wynorski and screenwriter Eric Anjou never set up any plausible rules for Grubeck to follow. He simply turns up wherever he wants and does whatever he wants, sometimes an intangible spirit and sometimes a solid body, usually spewing out sub-Freddy one-liners.

The major subplot concerns Robin (Debbie James), a college coed with whom Grubeck was obsessed and who is now pursued by his projected spirit. The possibilities for him to *really* get inside her are ignored, however, in favor of a lot of scenes in which Grubeck kills her friends and others to try to get her attention. Meanwhile, Spike attempts to put a stop to Grubeck's reign of terror before Robin can fall victim to his murderous advances. At one point, he breaks into Grubeck's old office, whereupon a malevolent—and unexplained—force causes its inanimate objects to fly to life. Later, he goes to an occult bookstore, where the strange proprietor (Brigitte Nielsen, in a brief but much-touted cameo) helps clue him in as to what is going on. It all ends up with a confrontation between our heroes and Grubeck, with an annoying twist ending topping the package off.

Like most of director Jim Wynorski's (TRANSYLVANIA TWIST, THE HAUNTING OF MORELLA) work, 976-EVIL II attempts to blend horror and comedy elements, and only comes close to succeeding in a few instances. One of these is an amusing but protracted sequence in which Robin's friend Paula (Leslie Ryan) is sucked into a TV set showing IT'S A WONDERFUL LIFE, whose characters then turn into zombies from NIGHT OF THE LIVING DEAD and attack her. Unfortunately, the scene makes no sense in context; it's only in there because the filmmakers thought it would be a neat idea. 976-EVIL II never builds any real scares or tension; the actors are generally mediocre, and Zoran Hochstatter's photography has the floodlit, unatmospherically slick look of a quickie production.

The only really creditable element of the film is some fine car-crash material by the gifted low-budget stunt specialist Spiro Razatos, whose fine work, ironically, only serves to underscore how lacking the rest of 976-EVIL II is. *(Excessive violence, profanity, nudity.)*

p, Paul Hertzberg; d, Jim Wynorski; w, Erik Anjou; ph, Zoran Hochstatter; ed, Nina Gilberti; prod d, Gary D. Randall; set d, Amy Ancona; cos, Greg LaVoi; stunts, Spiro Razatos

Horror/Comedy (PR: O MPAA: R)

1991: THE YEAR PUNK BROKE ★★½
99m Geffen/DGC; Sonic Life/We Got Power ~ Tara Releasing bw/c

Sonic Youth, Nirvana, Dinosaur, Jr., Babes in Toyland, Gumball, The Ramones

We've already witnessed the birth and assimilation into the mainstream of punk rock, beginning in the late 1970s and early 80s, and now comes what could be called a punk documentary. 1991: THE YEAR PUNK BROKE is the visual equivalent of a punk album: raw, fast, loud, sometimes incoherent and defiantly uncommercial.

This film documents a tour of Europe in the summer of 1991 by New York music pioneers Sonic Youth, an increasingly popular outfit that combines avant-garde sound with the fury and attitude of punk. They perform about half of the film's songs, along with soon-to-be-huge Seattle grunge kings Nirvana, female thrashers Babes in Toyland and the somewhat more traditional critical favorites Dinosaur, Jr. The film features live performances intercut with backstage goofiness and "home movie"-type footage, much of it "narrated" or conducted by Sonic Youth guitarist Thurston Moore.

The movie is unlikely to win any new converts for Sonic Youth or the other bands. While the frenetic and disjointed camerawork suits much of this freeform, out-of-control music (the final audio/video blow-out that accompanies Sonic Youth's "Expressway to Your Skull" is a fitting climax), a whole movie's worth of it may make viewers feel like they've been force-fed hallucinogens and strapped into a rollercoaster; no doubt the film works better on video, seen in small doses. Ironically, the one relatively staid scene is an interview excerpt from MTV, the music video monolith largely responsible for mainstreaming quick-cut editing. The rest looks like it was shot by a hyperactive child and then edited with a buzzsaw. Obviously, director Dave Markey thinks his anti-film style complements his subject, but one wonders if any thought was given to how such a jagged, anarchic movie would play to an audience.

Sonic Youth's music is miles away from the "punk" pioneered by bands like the Sex Pistols and the Clash back in the 70s; as jarring as those bands appeared at first, they did utilize traditional song structures and chords. Sonic Youth uses "open tunings" to produce droning, feedback-laden pieces that can be structured into pounding, riff-based songs ("Kool Thing" and "Teenage Riot" are two of the film's more effective pieces) or out-and-out noise. They're not always easy to listen to, but they deserve credit for creating something genuinely new, even if it tends to degenerate into feedback and noise for noise's sake.

Dinsosaur, Jr. also uses punk and leader J. Mascis's impressive, frenzied guitar to put a spin on their songs; compared to the other bands in the movie, they're almost melodic. Nirvana, except for an unusually delicate rendition of "Polly," doesn't come off well at all; almost every "song" ends with them thrashing their instruments (leader Kurt Cobain actually jumps onto the drummer at one point), and one number has such awful sound it seems to have been recorded underwater. (Of course, this is in keeping with the anti-commercial aesthetic of the film; who needs good sound if you've got energy, right?) Babes in Toyland is like 70s band The Runaways on speed; so loud and fast they're like a parody of punk. Gumball plays a bunch of feedback called "Pre," although it's enlivened with some psychedelia-inspired computer graphics. Punk veterans the Ramones, on the other hand, should sue Markey; you'd never know what a witty band they are from the atrocious live sound of "Commando" (which also totally misses the tune's tongue-in-cheek lyrics).

Too much of 1991: THE YEAR PUNK BROKE is devoted to Youth guitarist Thurston Moore; he does some interviews with fans and musicians along the way, occasionally managing to make a good point in spite of himself (such as the observation on the media co-opting youth culture), but more often he rambles on like a spoiled kid who's been given his own tape recorder and can't think of anything to say, other than make as many scatalogical references as possible. Bassist-singer Kim Gordon gets to parody some scenes in Madonna's TRUTH OR DARE, but drummer Steve Shelley and guitarist Lee Ranaldo don't get much screen time, being either too camera-shy or too cool to care about giving a coherent picture of the band or themselves.

1991: THE YEAR PUNK BROKE is clearly a fan's film; those wanting to know more about Sonic Youth and the punk scene will find it entertaining part of the time; irritating and incredibly self-indulgent the rest. *(Profanity, substance abuse, adult situations.)*

d, Dave Markey; ph, Dave Markey; ed, Dave Markey

Documentary/Musical **(PR: C MPAA: NR)**

NOISES OFF ★★½

104m Amblin Entertainment; Touchstone ~ BV c

Carol Burnett *(Dotty Otley/Mrs. Clackett)*, Michael Caine *(Lloyd Fellowes)*, Denholm Elliott *(Selsdon Mowbray/The Burglar)*, Julie Hagerty *(Poppy Taylor)*, Marilu Henner *(Belinda Blair/Flavia Brent)*, Mark Linn-Baker *(Tim Allgood)*, Christopher Reeve *(Frederick Dallas/Philip Brent)*, John Ritter *(Garry Lejeune/Roger Tramplemain)*, Nicollette Sheridan *(Brooke Ashton/Vicki)*, Kate Rich *(Des Moines Stagehand)*, Zoe R. Cassavetes *(Miami Stagehand)*, Kim Sebastian *(Cleveland Stagehand)*, L.B. Straten *(Broadway Stagehand)*, J. Christopher Sullivan *(Miami Backstage Guard)*, Kimberly Neville *(Miami Usher)*, Cleveland O'Neal *(Miami Electrician)*, Roger Michelson *(Company Lighting Technician)*, Joe Hanna *(Company Soundman)*, Rosie DeSanctis *(Backstage Visitor)*, Jack McCall *(Broadway Usher)*, Keith Crowningshield *(Broadway Usher)*, Andrew Mapp *(Broadway Usher)*, Dianna Agostini *(Broadway Theatergoer)*, Bronson Dudley *(Bum at Curb)*, Drummond Erskine *(Backstage Doorman)*, Robert Armstrong, Dick Corman, Wendy Wilson, Matthew Robert Gottlieb, Dana Marley *(Additional Stagehands)*

By all accounts hilarious onstage, Michael Frayn's backstage farce receives a less-than-brilliant screen translation in NOISES OFF, a Touchstone production which boasts three terrific comic set-pieces with nothing to support them.

What plot there is roughly revolves around the production of a door-slamming bedroom stage farce whose chief attraction seems to be Nicollette Sheridan (TV's "Knots Landing") as a sexy blonde ingenue who spends most of the play scampering around in her brief, frilly underwear. With six months on the road to iron out the bugs before the show is scheduled to reach Broadway, director Lloyd Fellowes (Michael Caine) instead is horrified to find the show actually getting worse as time goes on. The three set-pieces consist of the final dress rehearsal before the play opens in Des Moines; a disastrous opening night in Miami; and a dismal collapse onstage in Cleveland. What causes the downward spiral is the increasingly knotty relationships developing behind the scenes.

Fellowes has recently switched his romantic attentions from stage manager Poppy Taylor (Julie Hagerty) to his sexy leading lady, Brooke Ashton (Sheridan), without knowing that Poppy is pregnant. Meanwhile, leading man Garry Lejeune (John Ritter) is wearing horns because the object of his affections, middle-aged character actress Dotty Otley (Carol Burnett), seems to have defected to dashing second lead Frederick Dallas (Christopher Reeve). To compound his problems, Fellowes is required to leave the company for long stretches to nurse a production of *Hamlet* in New York. Also, he, along with the rest of the cast, including female second lead Belinda Blair (Marilu Henner, who seems to fade into the scenery completely), has to keep a close eye on aging character actor Selsdon Mowbray (Denholm Elliott), who likes his liquor and has a tendency to forget his cues.

The film actually opens with Caine in a voiceover prologue on the play's Broadway opening night, explaining what the film is all about. It helps, but it doesn't really fill in the gaps. It's probably a sign of trouble early on in the dress rehearsal, the film's actual first scene, that the play within the play, as artfully terrible as it is, is actually more entertaining and engaging than the main plot and subplots involving the actors and director. And that's no mean feat, considering the calibre of talent that has been assembled for this film. Nevertheless, even in the dress rehearsal, the interruptions that are supposed to introduce the characters and relationships and get the film underway wind up being as much a source of annoyance and exasperation to viewers as they are to Fellowes. It thus becomes dispiriting to see the play's performance deteriorate as the film goes on, especially since neither the offstage characters nor their relationships get more interesting as time passes.

Somebody at some point in the production must have sensed the problem. NOISES OFF's credits include "additional editing," usually a dead giveaway of postproduction tinkering, and the film does seem to have been ruthlessly trimmed of any sense of the characters' lives backstage and reduced to the three play stagings, with just enough connecting material to make it seem like a movie. What's left, at least, plays to director Peter Bogdanovich's strengths as a director of physical comedy. He was, after all, the man who tried, and almost succeeded, in single-handedly restoring a Hawksian crispness and physical gracefulness to screen comedy in films like WHAT'S UP DOC? and PAPER MOON.

Here the "Bogdanovich touch" surfaces in dribs and drabs. The dress rehearsal is staged with a marvelous grace and exhilarating sense of joy in its feeling for the professionalism of the players. The second staging, in Des Moines, focuses on backstage antics that, at odd moments, reach a giddy surrealism, especially when Elliott (A PRIVATE FUNCTION, A ROOM WITH A VIEW), who's never had much of a reputation before as an accomplished *farceur*, comes to the fore. But precision and energy are not enough. As it becomes increasingly obvious that NOISES OFF never is going to come to life, the physical humor becomes less involving. By the Cleveland staging, when the show completely falls apart, it becomes downright nasty and painful to watch. Then there's the tacked-on, completely implausible, "upbeat" ending, which only further highlights the film's flaws.

Like any good farce, NOISES OFF is essentially dark in its view of human nature and is therefore wildly at odds with the fluffy, feelgood trend prevalent in the current crop of mainstream Hollywood comedies. As a result, the only truly amazing aspect about NOISES OFF is that anyone thought it would make a viable commercial film in the first place—especially from the studio that, since 1984, has dominated the marketplace with lightweight vehicles like THREE MEN AND A BABY, PRETTY WOMAN and SISTER ACT. *(Adult situations.)*

p, Frank Marshall; d, Peter Bogdanovich; w, Marty Kaplan, (from the play by Michael Frayn); ph, Tim Suhrstedt; ed, Lisa Day; m, Phil Marshall; prod d, Norman Newberry; art d, Daniel E. Maltese; set d, Jim Duffy

Comedy **(PR: C MPAA: PG-13)**

NUIT ET JOUR

(SEE: NIGHT AND DAY)

O

ODDBALL HALL ★★

87m Ravenhill Productions ~ Cannon Video c

Don Ameche, Burgess Meredith, Bill Maynard, Tullio Moneta, Tiny Skefile

Screen veteran Don Ameche leads a small cast of international irregulars through ODDBALL HALL, a slow but sweet caper comedy.

Four career criminals try to get out of the remote African village where they have been living undercover, masquerading as members of "Oddball Hall," an eccentric, secret fraternal order of fez-wearing samaritans. Having eluded capture for ten years, they hope to fence their stolen jewels and retire in Rio de Janeiro. But an unlikely string of events prevents their escape. The train which is to carry them out of town is perpetually delayed. And the real "Grand Noble Master" of the Oddball order comes to visit, eventually tipping the local constable off about the crooks.

More directly, the foursome must play out their role of benevolent "wizards" when the son of a local chieftan seeks their help in repairing his tribe's water pump. Mistaking the gentle youth for the Grand Noble Master, the Oddballs humor him until they can make their getaway. Although he plays along with their error, the group becomes fond of him and begin to soften in their criminal ways. Meanwhile, two ex-members of their gang who served time in prison, arrive looking for their share of the jewels. They give away the Oddballs' true identity, creating a chaotic, slapstick chase as the Master, town constable and two ex-cons pursue the gang and its adopted friend. The Oddballs manage to escape, but are unable to cash in their jewels. They do, however, repair their friend's water pump and decide to take up a happy life with the tribe.

Billed as "in the tradition of THE GODS MUST BE CRAZY," ODDBALL HALL plays on a similar premise—a bushman naif's misadventures in a town of bumbling white men—but fails to achieve much comic zip. Don Ameche (COCOON, FOLKS!) tries to pep up the slow story, but even his customary panache can't overcome the screenplay's lack of punch. Fellow veteran Burgess Meredith (THE DAY OF THE LOCUST, ROCKY), who receives equal billing, has few lines and seems to have merely lent his name to this minor project. Other supporting players never get the chance to develop recognizable characters. A general lack of chemistry among the ensemble cast and a hollowness to the humor both derive from the film's reliance on superficial racial and ethnic stereotyping. While Don Ameche's protagonist is so undeveloped that we don't even know his name, the characters with names are tagged by cheap-shot monikers: the Italian sidekick is "Goose" Linguini, the "native" (supposedly a member of the "Whimmoway" tribe) is Meetoo-U.

Fortunately the overall tone of the movie is not so patronizing. Instead the story, while often muddled, makes a turn toward sweetness. The attempt at all-out, screwball, chase comedy that accelerates at the climax lacks the requisite timing and wit. But the redeeming feelings of friendship that develop between the rehabilitated white adventurers and the African villagers come across as at least sincere. ODDBALL HALL might have had something more to recommend it if those relationships had been better developed narratively—and if its comedy had been significantly more lively. *(Mild profanity, nudity.)*

p, Alan Munro; d, Jackson Hunsicker; w, Jackson Hunsicker; ph, Avi Karpick; m, William T. Stromberg

Comedy **(PR: A MPAA: PG)**

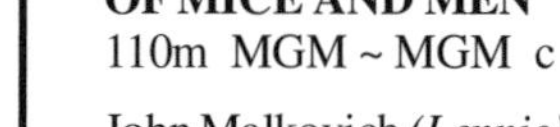

OF MICE AND MEN ★★½

110m MGM ~ MGM c

John Malkovich *(Lennie)*, Gary Sinise *(George)*, Ray Walston *(Candy)*, Casey Siemaszko *(Curley)*, Sherilyn Fenn *(Curley's Wife)*, John Terry *(Slim)*, Richard Riehle *(Carlson)*, Alexis Arquette *(Whitt)*, Joe Morton *(Crooks)*, Noble Willingham *(The Boss)*, Joe D'Angerio *(Jack)*, Tuck Milligan *(Mike)*, David Steen *(Tom)*, Moira Harris *(Girl in Red Dress)*, Mark Boone Junior *(Bus Driver)*

Actor-director Gary Sinise's respectful new version of John Steinbeck's Depression-era masterpiece is cautiously revisionistic, but with little effect. The look of the film offers an easy respite from the grimness of the story, but at a definite cost to its dramatic impact.

Wily, pragmatic George (Gary Sinise) and his infantile brute of a comrade, Lennie (John Malkovich), are bound, despite their wide differences, by a mutual need for companionship. They dream of having their own little ranch where they can be their own masters and Lennie can tend the small, furry creatures that he loves but is constantly destroying, so unaware is he of his own strength. On the run from the law, they find work on a migrant farm in California's San Joaquin Valley and, for a while, it seems as if their dream may eventually become a reality.

Their hopes are shattered, however, by the boss's bullying son Curley (Casey Siemaszko), who torments Lennie relentlessly, and by Curley's sexually frustrated wife (Sherilyn Fenn), whose need for companionship leads to her destruction at Lennie's unwitting, bewildered hands. Fearing George's wrath, Lennie escapes to the nearby woods. Realizing once and for all that there's no future with his simple-minded friend, George catches up to Lennie before the posse does and kills his friend in an act of euthenasia.

Of Mice and Men was first published in 1937 and was adapted for the screen two years later in a classic version directed by Lewis Milestone. Sinise, a co-founder of Chicago's acclaimed Steppenwolf Theater, seems to bring little to this new version other than an overriding concern with picturesque images: crystalline blue skies smile over shimmering fields of golden wheat, while the actors' tanned faces and worn denim clothes seem fresh out of a Ralph Lauren ad. Reading the book, one is constantly reminded of the poverty and desperation of the characters. In Sinise's cinematic retelling, there's not enough degrading dust or blistering heat; though the bunkhouse may be ramshackle, the gorgeous vistas which surround it make it seem a bucolic paradise.

As George, Sinise gives a performance almost identical to the one he did on stage as another Steinbeck hero, Tom Joad, in the Steppenwolf production of *The Grapes of Wrath*. He's a peculiarly withdrawn actor, more of an observer than an active participant, redolent of a Method cool which is inappropriate to the period. You never sense the conflicts and frustrations underpinning both his loyalty to Lennie and his desire to escape.

Malkovich, who is beginning to rival Charles Laughton for sheer take-no-prisoners hamminess, has a field day as Lennie. He emphasizes his bulging, wall-eyed look, makes his mouth an "o" of perpetual astonishment, furrows his substantial forehead and relishes Lennie's halting, childlike speech. (The deathless line, "Tell me about the rabbits, George!" only gains in camp value here.) The viewer may share much of George's exasperation with him, but it's difficult to judge whether it's the character or the portrayal which is the more irritating. The scene wherein Lennie crushes the hand of Curley (played with fine, snarling cockiness by Siemaszko, who gives the best performance in the film) has a frightening intensity—the Big Scary Malkovich Moment you've come to expect—but, for the most part, his performance is an egocentric stunt.

The director falters, too, with the nubile Sherilyn Fenn (RUBY, WILD AT HEART), who seemed ideally cast as Curley's wife. She is apparently under-directed, her natural sensuality buried beneath the heavy period makeup. (Fenn displays nothing like the teasing suggestiveness she radiated on TV's "Twin Peaks.") Ray Walston gives the kind of performance that is often nominated for Academy Awards—irascible, sympathetic and accompanied by a piteous, doomed dog. Black actor Joe Morton has a big scene as an embittered hunchback, which one assumes is Sinise's revisionist bow to political correctness, but the sequence, though powerful, fails to work.

As previously noted, all the farm hands are too generically well groomed—especially John Terry, who makes a very glamorous Slim, a hay-baling paragon of taciturn wisdom to rival Gary Cooper in his salad days. *(Violence, sexual situations, adult situations.)*

p, Russ Smith, Gary Sinise; d, Gary Sinise; w, Horton Foote, (from the novel by John Steinbeck); ph, Kenneth MacMillan; ed, Robert L. Sinise; m, Mark Isham; prod d, David Gropman; art d, Dan Davis; set d, Karen Schulz, Joyce Anne Gilstrap; cos, Shay Cunliffe

Drama **(PR: C MPAA: PG-13)**

OH, WHAT A NIGHT ★★½

(Canada) 93m Norstar Entertainment; Comfort Creek Productions Inc. ~ New Line Home Video c

Corey Haim *(Eric)*, Robbie Coltrane *(Todd)*, Barbara Williams *(Vera)*, Keir Dullea *(Thorvald)*, Genevieve Bujold *(Eva)*, Andrew Miller *(Donald)*

Teen star Corey Haim treks to the Great White North for OH, WHAT A NIGHT, a pleasant but undistinguished coming-of-age tale set in rural Ontario during the 1950s.

Haim plays Eric who lives out in the country with his widowed father, Thorvald (Keir Dullea), and stepmother, Eva (Genevieve Bujold). Still coming to terms with the death of his mother, Eric keeps a diary addressed to her in which he mainly chronicles his growing interest in girls. When not horsing around with his best pal Donald (Andrew Miller), himself coming to terms with his mother's imminent death from cancer, Eric gets "worldly" advice from friendly gas station owner Mr. Todd (Robbie Coltrane), mainly from his collection of pornographic novels—available for sale or leisurely perusal. More and more, however, Eric's time has been spent keeping vigil by a stream near his father's farm where the sexy, common-law farm wife next door, Vera (Barbara Williams), indulges in a daily nude swim accompanied by her young daughters.

Having struck up a friendly, playfully flirtatious relationship with Eric, Vera is at first shocked when she discovers his voyeuristic outpost, a trench he has dug lined with pinups and littered with cigarette butts. But instead of "exposing" him, she instead arrives at the stream the next day, sans daughters, and puts on a show for his benefit. When she later steps up the flirtation by sensually feeding him raspberries in a field while her abusive, hard-drinking husband dozes close by, Eric screws up his courage to pay her a visit one evening while her husband is out. Their moment of bliss in Vera's hayloft is cut short by the unexpected return of her husband, who abandons Vera the next day, leading her to move on as well.

On the plus side, OH, WHAT A NIGHT benefits from the able performances of its extremely likable cast under Eric Till's easygoing, unfussy direction accented by Brian Hebb's lush cinematography. Haim (LUCAS, LICENSE TO DRIVE) effectively counterpoints youthful rambunctiousness with a courtly politeness opposite Williams's sweet earthiness. The spirit of laid-back likability extends through the cast, even to the normally scene-chewing Coltrane (MONA LISA, THE POPE MUST DIET!). But the unceasing mellowness also results in a lack of substance that prevents the film from being anything special.

Richard Nielsen's screenplay seems to bend over backwards to avoid anything resembling dramatic conflict, especially between Eric and his stepmother. By Eric's account, Eva keeps him on an exceedingly short leash. What's odd about this is that Bujold (CHOOSE ME, DEAD RINGER), surprisingly, is barely in the film and when she is she barely has any dialogue. While Till seems generally surefooted in his treatment of Canadian rural life, OH, WHAT A NIGHT could generally have benefitted from a stronger sense of day-to-day life beyond the few asides and truncated scenes that create curiosity without quenching it.

Instead, the film's focus sharpens as it goes on to the "main event," Eric's deflowering, which, albeit sweetly and tastefully handled, most viewers will find predictable, even those unfamiliar with similar films from SUMMER OF '42 to THE GRADUATE. OH, WHAT A NIGHT is far from the worst of its kind, but it could have used a little less mellow and a little more meat. *(Adult situations.)*

p, Peter R. Simpson; d, Eric Till; w, Richard Nielsen; ph, Brian Hebb; ed, Susan Shipton; m, Ian Thomas; art d, David Moe; cos, Ruth Secord

Romance/Comedy **(PR: C MPAA: PG-13)**

ONCE UPON A CRIME ★½

100m Troublemakers Productions; Dino DeLaurentiis Communications ~ MGM c

John Candy *(Augie Morosco)*, James Belushi *(Neil Schwary)*, Cybill Shepherd *(Marilyn Schwary)*, Sean Young *(Phoebe)*, Richard Lewis *(Julian Peters)*, Ornella Muti *(Elena Morosco)*, Giancarlo Giannini *(Inspector Bonnard)*, George Hamilton *(Alfonso de la Pena)*, Roberto Sbaratto *(Detective Toussaint)*, Joss Ackland *(Hercules Popodopoulos)*, Ann Way *(Housekeeper)*, Geoffrey Andrews *(Butler)*, Caterina Boratto *(Madame de Senneville)*, Elsa Martinelli *(Carla the Agent)*, Riccardo Parisio Perrotti *(Customs Officer)*, Nino Richelmy *(Customs Officer)*, Mario DeCandia *(Witness)*, Giuseppe Perruccio *(Policeman)*, Alessandro Amen *(Porter)*, Francesco Angrisano *(Train Passenger)*, Georges Carlo *(Hotel de Paris Concierge)*, Benedetto Fanna *(Hotel de Paris Room Waiter)*, Christian Bianchi *(Casino Waiter)*, Marco Martinozzi *(Casino Waiter)*, Charles Dubourgeot *(Casino Employee)*

Michael Caine once revealed that he accepts film offers based on the shooting locations, making one wonder why he wasn't included in the cast of ONCE UPON A CRIME, a film where producer cum travel agent Dino DeLaurentiis provided what can be assumed were lovely accommodations in Monte Carlo. For filmgoers stuck viewing the result, their own vacation begins during the walk up the aisle and out of the theater.

In Rome, two bickering Americans, Phoebe and Julian Peters (Sean Young and Richard Lewis), find a missing dachshund and travel from Rome to Monte Carlo to collect a $5,000 reward offered for the dog's return. When they arrive in Monte Carlo, they discover the dog's murdered owner. Through a series of confused circumstances, they find themselves accused of murdering the owner, and a few other crackpot Americans—a compulsive gambler, Augie Morosco (John Candy), and a gauche husband and wife from Newark, Neil and Marilyn Schwary (James Belushi and Cybill Shepherd)—also find themselves implicated in the crime. Bringing this group together is Inspector

Bonnard (Giancarlo Giannini), who disconcertingly announces that the killers are the maid and the butler. Bonnard frees the group, lecturing them that "all your troubles came from distrust and fear." As a coda, it is revealed that the dachshund has inherited the owner's millions and the final shot shows gigolo Alfonso de la Pena (George Hamilton, who pops up throughout the film) romancing the dog.

Eugene Levy, late of "Second City TV" fame, makes his feature directorial debut with ONCE UPON A CRIME and clearly the golden days of "SCTV" are over. Levy directs with a club, keeping the actors screaming and hopping as if in the throes of a caffeine overdose. Of particular embarrassment is a scene where Belushi and Candy, overcome with gambling fever, go berserk inside a Monte Carlo casino and one in which Belushi and Shepherd have to hide carry-on luggage containing a chopped up corpse from a train conductor. Levy can't seem to tell if something is funny or not and keeps up the sledgehammer intensity throughout every scene, comic subtlety and timing abandoned in a desperate attempt for laughs—even pained ones.

The screenplay, astonishingly credited to seven screenwriters (two of whom, Charles Shyer and Nancy Meyers, were responsible for BABY BOOM and the 1991 remake of FATHER OF THE BRIDE), is so unstructured and pointless that it takes almost an hour before the four main characters even get to meet each other—and CRIMES AND MISDEMEANORS this isn't. Storylines are discarded like bon-bon wrappers. First ONCE UPON A CRIME is a caper movie. Then a comedy murder-mystery. Then nothing. Bonnard's solution to the murder is so abrupt and from so far afield that it seems more likely that the film had to end because Levy was running out of film stock.

The casting is like the pick of the Holywood unemployment line. Young and Lewis play their parts as if on a unpleasant blind date. Trying to act like a third-string Diane Keaton and Woody Allen, they are more reminiscent of Alan Carney and Wally Brown of ZOMBIES ON BROADWAY. In other roles, John Candy and James Belushi have never been more grating and repellent. The only survivor of the carnage is Giancarlo Giannini, whose bored and weary glances of contempt at the collection of third bananas mirror the feelings of the movie audience.

p, Dino DeLaurentiis; d, Eugene Levy; w, Charles Shyer, Nancy Meyers, Steve Kluger, Rodolfo Sonego, Giorgio Arlorio, Stefano Strucchi, Luciano Vincenzoni, (from the story by Sonego); ph, Giuseppe Rotunno; ed, Patrick Kennedy; m, Richard Gibbs; prod d, Pier Luigi Basile; set d, Gianfranco Fumagalli; cos, Molly Maginnis

Comedy/Mystery **(PR: A MPAA: PG)**

ONCE UPON A TIME IN CHINA ★★★★
(Hong Kong) 112m Film Workshop ~ Golden Harvest Films Ltd. c
(WONG FEI-HUNG)

Jet Li *(Wong Fei-hung)*, Yuen Biao *(Leung Foon)*, Jacky Cheung *(Buck Teeth Sol)*, Rosamund Kwan *(Aunt Yee)*, Kent Cheng *(Porky Lang)*

Tsui Hark's ONCE UPON A TIME IN CHINA is a truly dazzling achievement, even measured against Tsui's own considerable accomplishments and the hyperbolic standards of Hong Kong filmmaking, where riotous visual excess and surreal cross-cultural appropriations are the norm.

The year is 1875. Master Wong Fei-hung (Jet Li), a Confucian bone setter and righteous martial artist, establishes a clinic in Canton province and takes on several apprentices, including the comic Porky Lang (Kent Cheng) and Buck Teeth Sol (Jacky Cheung), who was raised in the West and scarcely even speaks his native language. Wong's associates also include the beautiful Aunt Yee (Rosamund Kwan), who has returned to China after many years abroad, bringing with her some strange and modern ideas. Their chaste romance is characterized by many subtle clashes of cultural and personal expectations. Though Wong aspires to a quiet life, dedicated to helping the weak and disenfranchised, circumstance forces him to rely frequently on his martial arts expertise in order to see justice done.

When Wong's clinic is burned down, he and his companions set out to right the many wrongs they see around them. A rival kung-fu master, amorally divorced from the spiritual component of his training, forces Wong to engage in a series of spectacular showdowns, but the real villain is creeping Westernization, embodied in the American soldiers who encourage opium addiction and coerce poor peasants to sail for America, where they'll wind up virtual slaves to the railroad barons. Wong and his compatriots win many battles (each more elaborately staged than the one before), but realize sadly that they are losing the war. China has been exposed to too many foreign influences for it to remain the same, and the modern world is encroaching relentlessly.

For fans of Hong Kong films, Tsui Hark is a superstar on the level of a Steven Spielberg or George Lucas. Born in Vietnam and trained at the University of Texas, he has written, directed and produced dozens of the most striking Hong Kong movies never seen in US theaters.

In fact, Tsui may be best known to mainstream American viewers for having fostered the career of John Woo, whose delirious THE KILLER received a limited release last year. It's a shame Tsui's own films aren't more familiar. Perhaps as a result of his American training, his pictures are far more accessible to Western audiences than the average Hong Kong fare. In particular, he demonstrates a consistent commitment to linear narrative (even in the face of outrageous story developments) that's very comforting, particularly when supported by careful production values.

The adventures of Master Wong are a longtime staple of Hong Kong genre cinema, so for Chinese viewers ONCE UPON A TIME IN CHINA is a revisionist exercise in the vein of YOUNG GUNS: the characters, settings and situations are familiar, but they're all delivered with a distinctly contemporary twist. The title, with its knowing nod to Sergio Leone's remaking of American national fables, ONCE UPON A TIME IN THE WEST, is the tip-off that Tsui's aim is to dust off old genre conventions and present them refreshed and revitalized and to a new generation of movie buffs. For US audiences, the material has very different implications.

While literally hundreds of Westerns have mapped out the history (or rather, the shifting cultural mythology) of America's frontier in the 1870s, China in the same period is a mystery, even though its growth was inextricably tied to developments in this country and in Europe. To the Western eye, ONCE UPON A TIME IN CHINA's mythmaking is manifestly alien in its particulars, but weirdly familiar in its dynamics. This juxtaposition of the conventional and the alien is riveting, and that's even before Tsui lets loose with the pyrotechnics.

ONCE UPON A TIME IN CHINA is a virtual non-stop festival of kung-fu display. Battles are staged in spectacular locales: at the opera, where the bad guys hide behind beneath brilliant traditional costumes and make-up; in a bizarrely out-of-place European-style restaurant; and in an enemy fortress full of ladders, which are deployed to astonishing effect. The action is lightning fast (though it shows few signs of the overcranking that Hong Kong pictures often use to up the ante) and balletically staged, living up to the choreographic potential often claimed—

but seldom truly realized—for martial arts pictures by their highbrow admirers.

What's unusual is that ONCE UPON A TIME IN CHINA, for all the opaqueness of the performances and awkwardness of the subtitles, is genuinely touching, suffused with a subtle sorrow at the passing of an era and the cruel awakening of an ancient culture to the brutal power of a new and aggressive one. *(Violence.)*

p, Raymond Chow; d, Tsui Hark; w, Tsui Hark, Yuen Kai-chi, Leung Yiu-ming, Tang Pik-yin; ph, David Chung, Bill Wong, Arthur Wong, Lam Kwok-wah, Chan Tung-chuen, Chan Pui-kai; ed, Mak Chi-sin; m, James Wong; prod d, Lau Man-hung; art d, Yee Chung-man; cos, Yu Ka-on

Action/Historical/Martial Arts (PR: C MPAA: NR)

ONE FALSE MOVE ★★★½
105m IRS Media ~ IRS Releasing c

Cynda Williams *(Fantasia/Lila)*, Bill Paxton *(Dale "Hurricane" Dixon)*, Billy Bob Thornton *(Ray Malcolm)*, Jim Metzler *(Dud Cole)*, Michael Beach *(Pluto)*, Earl Billings *(McFeely)*, Natalie Canerday *(Cherylann)*

Despite a strong start and good performances, this low-budget crime drama from director Carl Franklin is an ultimately disappointing exercise in "New Age noir." ONE FALSE MOVE is certainly edgier and less pretentious than most other films of its ilk, but it still suffers from an excess of attitude and a shortage of plot.

The film opens in suburban Los Angeles with the brutal murder of several family members and friends as part of a cash and cocaine robbery. The culprits are a nightmarish trio made up of a sadistic white-trash sociopath, Ray Malcolm (Billy Bob Thornton, who also co-wrote the screenplay); a Black, would-be criminal genius who has a mean way with a knife, Pluto (Michael Beach); and Fantasia (Cynda Williams), the femme fatale who set up the slaughter. Fantasia loses her nerve when it comes to turning over the murdered family's young son to the tender mercies of her colleagues, leaving him concealed in his hiding place and claiming he's nowhere in the house.

Piecing together accounts provided by neighbors with voices recorded on a videocam that was running during the slaughter, LA cops Cole and McFeely (Jim Metzler and Earl Billings) identify Pluto and Ray, both ex-cons, and discover that they're on their way to Star City, Arkansas, where Ray has an uncle. (In fact, the trio's plan is to go to Houston, convert the coke into cash, and then pass through Star City so that Fantasia can see her own baby boy.)

As Ray, Pluto and Fantasia wind their way through the Southwest on a road trip that becomes increasingly fraught and futile, Dud and McFeely go to Star City, where they team up with local sheriff "Hurricane" Dixon (Bill Paxton) to set a trap for the killers. Dixon, an overachiever of the "aw shucks" school, amuses the city cops with his puppyish small-town enthusiasm and aspirations to join the LA force. However, at the climax, it is he who faces the deadly gang alone.

After kicking off in gripping, grisly fashion, ONE FALSE MOVE veers somewhat off course. Narrative tension flags as the film turns into a character study of the sheriff who, despite Paxton's superb efforts to make him otherwise, is of insufficient interest to single-handedly hold our attention. (It turns out that Hurricane is more deeply implicated in the drama than just as a policeman. When Fantasia's real name, Lila, is discovered midway through the drama, it transpires that he once had an affair with the woman, and is the father of the child she is coming home to see.) Meanwhile, the energy and intensity of the opening is dissipated by dramatic lulls and credibility-straining lapses in logic. It's never explained why two major-league cops forego the pursuit of three cold-blooded killers in order to hole up in a backwater Arkansas town, where they spend most of the film eating, drinking and passively awaiting their quarry.

Director Franklin, an AFI graduate and veteran of low-budget Roger Corman epics like NOWHERE TO RUN and FULL FATHOM 5, gives a low-key, realistic feel to the criminals' travels, throwing in docudrama-styled titles to show which towns they're driving through. But it soon becomes apparent that his dangerous criminals are going to spend most of the film just driving around. Along the way, Pluto-as-criminal-mastermind loses credibility since he, Ray and Fantasia decide to do pretty much exactly what Dud, McFeely and Hurricane assume they will. Most of the film is spent crosscutting between the LA cops' vacation-like stay in Star City and the killer trio's road experiences, which do include some tensely effective scenes of violence: Fantasia shooting a highway patrolman, the drugs-for-cash exchange going bloodily awry.

ONE FALSE MOVE's imperfections are more those of genuine filmmakers honing their craft than of hacks lacking energy and vision; there is a terrific plot rattling around in here that just needs to be put together a little better. The cast is uniformly first rate, with Metzler, between his work here and in last year's equally noirish DELUSION, beginning to resemble a youthful Gig Young—wiry and hard-bitten but also graceful and charming when the situation calls for it. Also outstanding are Beach, Thornton and Williams, the first two as determinedly evil a duo as has been seen in a long time.

Franklin, aided by James L. Carter's excellent cinematography, injects a plentiful helping of moody tension. But ONE FALSE MOVE remains another case of less than meets the eye from a director and writers who surely have better films ahead of them. *(Violence, profanity, substance abuse, adult situations.)*

p, Jesse Beaton, Ben Myron; d, Carl Franklin; w, Billy Bob Thornton, Tom Epperson; ph, James L. Carter; ed, Carole Kravitz; m, Peter Haycock, Derek Holt; prod d, Gary T. New; art d, Dana Torrey; set d, Troy Myers; cos, Ron Leamon

Crime/Drama (PR: O MPAA: R)

ONE LAST RUN ★½
82m Blue Ice ~ Prism Entertainment c

Tracy Scoggins *(Cindy)*, Nels Van Patten *(Charlie)*, Ashley Laurence *(Jane)*, Craig Branham *(Tom)*, Jimmy Aleck *(Joe)*, Franz Weber *(Franz)*, Chuck Conners *(Buddy)*, Scot Schmidt, Russell Todd

Old hands at sports documentaries tried to enter the dramatic arena in ONE LAST RUN, and it looks it. The film has no story to speak of, just amazing skiing sequences piled on the lightest dusting of story.

Joe (Jimmy Aleck) woodenly narrates how he and buddies Nick (Russell Todd) and Tom (Craig Branham) have met annually for wild ski expeditions, but they're all feeling a bit jaded and have reluctantly decided that this year's run will be their last. At Lake Tahoe the trio find themselves snowed in overnight at a cozy chalet bar filled with other winter-sports enthusiasts, including Nick's old flame Jane (Ashley Laurence). After much drinking, introspection and ski-related product placement, Nick reunites with Jane, and the three men decide to continue meeting year after year.

That's it for the narrative, filler that marks time between skiing interludes. When characters are introduced extended flashbacks follow showing their prowess on the slopes. "I always thought Nick fell in love with [Jane] because she's a better skier than he is, especially in deep powder," comments Joe, cueing lengthy, striking shots of the lady whizzing across the majestic landscape.

A clownish hot-dogger named Charlie (Nels Van Patten) pops up; cut to him skiing while set on fire, then skiing into water. Also thrown in, for no other reason than visual interest, are scenes of "skeezers"—surfboards used in snow—and the crazy dudes who hang ten on them. The impressive ski stunts come courtesy of second-unit work by Warren Miller Entertainment. Miller, a legendary chronicler of the ski set, has made a career of turning out feature-length sports documentaries since 1947, perfectly plotless spectacles like WHITE MAGIC and EXTREME WINTER that consist of skiiers, surfers and sailors doing what they do best. ONE LAST RUN clumsily tries to integrate the Miller footage into a fiction scenario, and while the snowy stuff is as breathtaking as ever, the single-set scripted segments are just a flimsy distraction, even with supporting roles from sexy Tracy Scoggins, world speed champ Franz Weber, and a paternal Chuck Connors as the bar's proprietor. The picture is hardly painful to behold but still not recommended for anyone but true ski fiends devoted to the Warren Miller canon.

The credits state the skiing was filmed all over the world, literally: Colorado, Chile, Japan, British Columbia and elsewhere. The movie itself took a less circuitous direct-to-video route for its own tour. *(Substance abuse.)*

p, Peter Winograd, Glenn Gebhard; d, Peter Winograd, Glenn Gebhard; w, Glenn Gebhard, Peter Winograd; ph, Thomasy Callaway; ed, Tim Huntley; prod d, Virginia Lee

Sports/Drama **(PR: A MPAA: NR)**

ONLY YOU ★★

85m PRO FilmWorks; Day Job Films ~ LIVE Home Video c
(AKA: Love Stinks)

Andrew McCarthy, Kelly Preston, Helen Hunt

No filmmaker can spin a gossamer romantic comedy without a skein of star chemistry and charm. The two leads of ONLY YOU, Andrew McCarthy and Kelly Preston, don't possess that mystery ingredient that allows some performers to coast over pedestrian direction and bankrupt material.

A craftsman of doll houses with a childish attitude toward women, Clifford Codfrey (McCarthy) nearly has a nervous breakdown when his dream girl dumps him on the eve of their pre-nuptial trip to Mexico. Unable to retrieve his fare from Claire (Helen Hunt), a lovely and extremely patient travel agent, he storms off to a bar where he picks up Amanda (Kelly Preston) a beautiful but inebriated bimbo. Upon waking up south of the border with a hangover, Amanda agrees to stay with nerdish Cliff—with some liberal stipulations about space and freedom.

While this shallow siren leads Cliff around by the nose, he bumps into Claire, who's really a fledgling photographer staying at his hotel to shoot a travel brochure. While Amanda gambols with college jocks, Cliff serves as a model for Claire's photo shoot. Whenever he exhibits signs of good judgment, the tawny Amanda reels the sucker back in. Cliff finally abandons the scheming sexpot on a plane and tries to track down Claire, the true-blue love of his life. At a K-Mart-type department store he professes his love over the loudspeaker. For no discernible reason, Claire forgives him, providing the film with an unearned happy ending.

In defense of McCarthy and Preston, ONLY YOU would probably have taxed the allure of Cary Crant and Irene Dunne. Is the arrested romantic development of an insensitive clod really a fitting starting point for a light comedy? And how are viewers supposed to respond to the dream babe—although she emerges as the villain of the piece, isn't her self-absorption the perfect match for Cliff?

Watching this inane love triangle, one can only shake one's head and say real people do not behave this way. Cliff, Amanda and Claire are just stick figures poorly updated from the lovestruck fools and moony romantics of 1930s screwball comedies. In a contemporary context, their behavior is unpleasant or implausible at best. And since these swinging singles are interpreted by the charisma-less Preston and the color-less McCarthy, the viewer grows increasingly irritated by their sexual maneuverings and cutesy overplaying.

Because the reliable girlfriend-as-savior figure is played by the luminous Helen Hunt (THE WATERDANCE, MR. SATURDAY NIGHT), too much of our sympathy goes to her. The world does not need another comedy about a woman's ability to forgive almost anything in order not to end up alone on New Year's Eve. *(Nudity, sexual situations.)*

p, Morrie Eisenman, Wayne Allan Rice; d, Betty Thomas; w, Wayne Allan Rice; ph, Brian England; ed, Peter Teschner; prod d, A. Rosalind Crew; art d, Arlan Jay Vetter; cos, Deborah Waknin

Romance/Comedy **(PR: C MPAA: PG-13)**

ORIGINAL INTENT ★

97m Mission of Hope Productions; Marcarelli Productions ~ Paramount Home Video c

Jay Richardson *(Matthew Cameron)*, Candy Clark *(Jessica Cameron)*, Kris Kristofferson *(Jack Saunders)*, Martin Sheen *(Joe)*, Joseph Campanella *(Judge May)*, Cindy Pickett *(Marguerite)*, Bruce Jenner *(Dan Logan)*, Robert Do'Qui *(Ben)*, Virginia Capers *(Lily)*, Kurt Fuller *(Alex)*, Patrick Malone *(Bobby)*, Don Galloway *(Newsman)*, John Boyle, Caroline Gibbs, Jason Adams, Rick Johnson, Dominic Hoffman, Leslie Do'Qui, Linda Thompson

An overly sentimental social drama, ORIGINAL INTENT has its heart right out on its sleeve, wet and dripping.

Treacly and often amateurish, the homily-cum-story centers on Matthew Cameron (Jay Richardson), a prosperous lawyer with a happy family and affluent yuppie friends, all obsessed with food, fitness and finance. One day Matthew's old college buddy Alex (Kurt Fuller) asks him to aid a central LA homeless shelter, the Mission of Hope, in danger of demolition from dastardly developer Theodore Daniels (Vince Edwards), a one-note Simon LeGree who utters lines like "I don't want one brick of that building standing by this time next week!" Matthew gets his consciousness raised by visiting the sanctuary and meeting its noble operator Ben Reid (Robert Do'Qui) and a beaming assembly of poor folks, battered women, vagrant vets and perky ghetto kids. But the film's also a spiritual soap opera, as Matthew's fight for the Mission of Hope precipitates soul-testing crises at work and at home.

Matthew's wife Jessica (Candy Clark) loses her job and son Steven (Cameron Macarelli) lies comatose all because of dad's preoccupation with the homeless. "This is so unbelievable!" laments Jessica, bringing a richly unintentional laugh. The maddening thing about ORIGINAL INTENT is that it threatens to get interesting, only to backslide into ham-handed melodrama and simplistic politics. For instance, Matthew goes overboard in expunging his white-liberal guilt, forcing Jessica to volunteer for the soup kitchen and taking a personable black street kid Bobby (Patrick Malone) under his own roof when there's no room at the shelter. But Bobby disappears with the Camerons' luxury electronics, and Matthew throws a childish fit over the stolen video games, right in the midst of Ben's revival meeting. Then the hero mopes around haunted by flashback voices and the pic's gotta-hear-it-to-believe-it theme song. ". . . My dreams were stashed into some legal file/until I saw the eyes of a homeless child." One may rest assured that there's a happy ending thanks to the negative publicity the Scrooge-like capitalist villain gets in the media—it's revealed that when not occupied in crushing the weak he controls an eminently boycottable chain of toy stores.

Writer-director-producer Rob Marcarelli (I DON'T BUY KISSES ANYMORE) has little evident use for subtlety. He does, however, have a lot of charitably inclined celebrity associates in guest cameos, notably longtime homeless campaigner Martin Sheen, here staring into space as a basket case dubbed "Homeless Joe." Kris Kristofferson and Cindy Pickett make their contribution as indigents, Bruce and Linda Thompson Jenner as rich types. Leading-man Jay Richardson, a stalwart in B-and Z-grade movies, copes admirably with the script deficiencies, but the most potentially intriguing role in the whole thing goes to Kurt Fuller as Alex, the avatar of social activism who gets the plot rolling. Instead of the holy do-gooder one expects, he's pitched as a comic-relief buffoon, more class clown than Mother Theresa. He's cloying, obnoxious and frankly dislikeable, but it's an energetic and challenging creation compared to the cardboard saintliness of Ben and the other shelter helpers. Of course, Alex drops out of the narrative after his initial appearance.

Marcarelli, a prominent member of the Malibu Presbyterian Church, had a devil of a time finding a domestic theatrical distributor for ORIGINAL INTENT. The preachy production was finished in 1990, but never got to the big screen, loitering until 1992 before going straight to home video. *(Profanity.)*

p, Rob Marcarelli; d, Rob Marcarelli; w, Rob Marcarelli, Joyce Marcarelli; ph, John V. Fante; ed, Susan R. Crutcher; m, Ernie Rettino, Debby Kerner Rettino, C. Barny Robertson; prod d, Steven Michael Casey; set d, Jennifer Murphy; cos, Susan F. Camusi

Religious/Drama **(PR: A MPAA: PG)**

OTHER WOMAN, THE ★½

99m Axis Films International ~ Imperial Entertainment Corporation c

Adrian Zmed *(Greg Mathews)*, Lee Anne Beaman *(Jessica Mathews)*, Jenna Persaud *(Tracy Collins)*, Daniel Moriarity *(Carl)*, Craig Stepp *(Paul)*, Melissa Moore *(Elysse)*, Allison Berron *(Young Jessica)*, Sam Jones *(Mike Florian)*, Timothy C. Burns *(Pete Douglas)*, Beth Richard *(Cathy)*, Bill Bradshaw *(Scott)*, Stephen Fiachi *(Bob)*, Martine Anuszek *(Sheila)*, Victoria Deuschle *(Jessica's Mother)*, Regina Geisler *(Neighbor)*, Alan Gelfant *(Man at Bar)*, Sergio Lanza *(Delivery Man)*

Billed as an "erotic thriller," THE OTHER WOMAN is high in the titillation department, but the thriller element plays more like a Zalman King version of DESPERATELY SEEKING SUSAN without laughs.

Jessica Matthews (Lee Anne Beaman), a reporter for a Los Angeles newspaper, is consumed with being a successful reporter, much to the detriment of her marriage to Greg Matthews (Adrian Zmed), a bestselling self-help book author. When Greg announces that he must embark on a tour to promote his new book *Letting Go*, Jessica hardly notices. Instead, she becomes deeply immersed in researching an expose on influential businessman Mike Florian (Sam Jones). But her priorities begin to shift when, shortly after Greg's departure, she discovers suggestive photos of an attractive woman returned with Greg's laundry.

Making some calls, Jessica finds the woman in the photos to be one Traci Collins (Jenna Persaud), a sultry, sexy free spirit who lives in a walk-up apartment with an open door and makes her living as a prositute, escort and nude model. Following Traci around LA, Jessica becomes obsessed with her and finds herself envying her lifestyle. Agreeing to meet with her for lunch, Jessica befriends her in order to teach her a lesson about fooling around with her husband. But when Jessica confronts her about Greg's involvement, Traci denies having slept with him. Jessica follows her back to her apartment to apologize but finds Traci in the midst of a beating by her pimp, Carl (Daniel Moriarity). After Jessica chases Carl away, Traci snuggles up to her and they make love.

In the morning, Jessica steps into the shower and Traci's friend Paul (Craig Stepp) appears and they too make love. Unfortunately for Jessica, the whole night at Traci's has been a set-up and she has been videotaped with Traci and photographed with Paul. When this incriminating evidence is sent to her newspaper, she promptly loses her job. Arriving back home, she finds Florian there, revealing that he was the person responsible for her downfall. Right after Florian announces that he plans to kill her, Traci, having a change of heart, arrives in the nick of time to help Jessica fight off Florian, who is arrested.

When Greg returns, Jessica greets him in a sexy nightgown and they go to bed. As they make love, her ex-boss calls her and leaves a message on her phone machine that she now has a new and better job at the newspaper. Jessica, in voice-over, announces, "I found the other woman and she was me."

THE OTHER WOMAN attempts to be something more than a kinky, softcore porn skin-fest and for that it must be commended. Unfortunately, except for the nude scenes, it fails on almost all counts—as a thriller, as a romance, as a sexual manifesto and certainly as a feminist tract. In fact, Jessica's sexual "awakening" betrays a hideously conservative ideal—that is, the only "real" woman is the one who will forsake her career and submit herself fully to her man. It's true that Traci helps Jessica shed her sexual inhibitions, but only so that the neglectful wife can better serve her husband.

As much as the film fails in its "liberated" message, it also fails in its thriller aspect. Attempting to evoke films as disparate as VERTIGO, LAURA and SHARKEY'S MACHINE, THE OTHER WOMAN reveals neither character depth nor suspense. Jessica does not convince the viewer that she is so intrigued by Traci that she will squirm around with her at the first opportunity, in spite of a tacky flashback sequence of a younger Jessica catching her mother in bed with another woman. Nor does Traci deliver a convincing turnaround in coming to Jessica's aid from being in cahoots with Florian. And the climactic scene between Florian and Jessica is so ineptly staged that it delivers yocks instead of shocks.

THE OTHER WOMAN's chief fault is its dishonesty. To claim so much and deliver so little makes a viewer long for the simpler pleasures of TWO MOON JUNCTION. *(Profanity, excessive nudity.)*

p, Andrew Garroni, Alexander Gregory Hippolyte; d, Jag Mundhra; w, Georges Des Esseintes; ph, James Michaels; ed, Ron Resnick; m, Joseph Smith; prod d, Blair Martin; cos, Ricardo Delgado, Lothar Delgado

Erotic/Thriller **(PR: O MPAA: R)**

OUT FOR BLOOD ★★½

89m PM Entertainment ~ PM Home Video c

Don "The Dragon" Wilson *(John Decker)*, Shari Shattuck *(Joanna Montague)*, Michael DeLano *(Lieutenant Croft)*, Ron Steelman *(Doctor McConnell)*, Ken McLeod *(Blade)*, Todd Curtis *(Rick)*, Aki Aleong *(Hiroshi)*, Beau Billingslea *(Detective Hubbel)*, Roberta Vasquez *(Detective Price)*, Robert Miano *(Geisler)*, Addison Randall *(Bo)*, Pam Dixon *(Margaret)*, Art Comacho *(Street Dealer)*, Deron McBee *(1st Bodyguard)*, Dino Homsey *(2nd Bodyguard)*, Bob Schott *(Mad Biker)*, Joey Sagal *(Bubba)*

A lively if routine actioner, OUT FOR BLOOD stars Don "The Dragon" Wilson as John Decker, a savvy LA lawyer who is plagued by incomplete memories of the slaughter, fifteen months earlier, of his wife and son when they innocently stumbled into the middle of a boat-basin drug deal.

LAPD Lieutenant Croft (Michael DeLano) is annoyed at Decker's inability to identify the killers. Decker's "selective amnesia" is being treated by his friend Dr. McConnell (Ron Steelman). One night, while employing his martial arts skills to break up a street drug sale, Decker finds himself beginning to remember the painful events more clearly. He continues this violence-as-therapy against other drug dealers, and the media soon dubs this unknown vigilante as "Karateman." Croft's superiors are upset, since Karateman is doing their work for them to great popular approval.

Also upset is local drug king, Rick (Todd Curtis). Decker falls in love with art gallery owner Joanna Montague (Shari Shattuck), which angers Joanna's previous jilted boyfriend, mysterious businessman Geisler (Robert Miano). Decker also befriends Joanna's principal artist, the philosophizing Hiroshi (Aki Aleong). Decker's nightly violent forays eventually lead to Rick, who kidnaps Joanna and whom Decker now recognizes as his wife's murderer. In a dawn air-strip standoff, Decker rescues Joanna, McConnell is revealed as Rick's crime boss (he dies as his escape-route plane explodes, arranged by Geisler, who slyly thanks Decker for eliminating *his* drug-business competition) and Rick is gunned down by the suddenly appearing Croft, who announces (shades of the Dirty Harry opus MAGNUM FORCE) that he's now leading a cop vigilante gang "reporting directly to the mayor."

Despite its complicated, downright hallucinatory ending (the year's best bet for hitting the rewind button: did Croft really say that?), OUT FOR BLOOD is strictly formula genre fare, with the audience always one step ahead of Decker and the plot.

David S. Green's screenplay leans heavily on DEATH WISH and its myriad sequels and clones. Its most risible elements are Decker's solemn meetings with the all-seeing, all-knowing Hiroshi, who spouts orientalist nonsense with a straight face ("Violence could become a servant to peace, but beware when the servant becomes master"). Director Richard W. Munchkin (RING OF FIRE, DEADLY BET) keeps things moving sufficiently, with well-executed car chases, gun battles and martial arts displays (choreographed by Wilson and Eric Lee). As with other PM Entertainment direct-to-video releases (producers Richard Pepin and Joseph Mehri provide the initials), OUT FOR BLOOD is technically assured and features Pepin's usual excellent cinematography.

Star Don Wilson (DRAGONFLIGHT, the BLOODFIST series), a former World Kickboxing Association light heavyweight world kickboxing champion, seems determined to become a martial arts-driven action hero in the mold of Jean-Claude Van Damme and Steven Seagal. He's not much of an actor, but he has a certain boyish charm unusual in this macho movie world. *(Violence, substance abuse, profanity.)*

p, Richard Pepin, Joseph Mehri; d, Richard W. Munchkin; w, David S. Green; ph, Richard Pepin; ed, Paul G. Volk, John Weidner, Ron Cabreros; m, Louis Febre; prod d, William Martin

Action/Crime/Martial Arts **(PR: O MPAA: R)**

OUT ON A LIMB ★½

82m Interscope Communications; Universal ~ Universal c

Matthew Broderick *(Bill Campbell)*, Jeffrey Jones *(Matt Skearns/Mayor Peter Van Der Haven)*, Heidi Kling *(Sally)*, John C. Reilly *(Jim Jr.)*, Marian Mercer *(Ann Van Der Haven)*, Larry Hankin *(Darren)*, David Margulies *(Mr. Buchenwald)*, Courtney Peldon *(Marci Van Der Haven)*, Michael Monks *(Jim, Sr.)*, Andy Kossin *(Larry)*, Mickey Jones *(Virgil)*, Nancy Lenehan *(Miss Clayton)*, Noah Craig Andrews *(Julius)*, Ben Diskin *(Henry)*, Adam Wylie *(Bob)*, John Christian Graas *(Elliott)*, Bethany Richards *(Priscilla)*, Richard Allison *(1st Twin)*, Paul Allison *(2nd Twin)*, Rob Neukirch *(Steve)*, Lou DiMaggio *(Analyst)*, John Posey *(1st Analyst)*, Darrell Kunitomi *(2nd Analyst)*, Julie Araskog *(Julie)*, Robert Burr *(Travis)*, Christopher Grove *(Waiter)*, Danny Kovacs *(Mechanic)*, Shawn Schepps *(Cindy)*, Blaine Souza *(Jed)*, Mollie Stickney *(Teller)*, Marsha Mercant *(Woman in 1st Bank)*, Susan Brill *(Woman in 2nd Bank)*, Eve Child *(Woman in 3rd Bank)*, Tom McGraw *(Man in Bank)*, Michael Halton *(Utility Truck Driver)*, Deborah Goodrich *(Jenny)*, William Dean O'Neil *(Driver)*, Vivian Steindal *(1st Girl)*, Paul Hogue *(Little Boy)*, Elisebeth Hogue *(Little Girl)*, Carolyn DeLucia *(Woman on Street)*, Johnny Vega *(Highway Patrolman)*

Relentlessly unfunny and frantically directed to disguise its basic lack of inventiveness, OUT ON A LIMB, written by Daniel and Joshua Goldin and helmed by Francis Veber, fails to graft the style of a French farce onto an American action comedy.

Coyly narrated by Marci Van Der Haven (Courtney Peldon) in the form of a "How I Spent My Summer Vacation" tell-all to her grade-school class, the film begins with Marci begging her brother Bill Campbell (Matthew Broderick) to come home and investigate her suspicions about her stepfather, Mayor Van Der Haven (Jeffrey Jones). Although this trip could jeopardize the deal of his career, the boyish finance whiz journeys home to calm Marci's fears that her stepfather has an evil twin, Matt Skearns (Jones again), who took the rap for the Mayor years ago but has come back to collect $150,000 and exact some revenge.

Before Bill makes it to his frightened sister's side, he becomes entangled in the flight of Sally (Heidi Kling), a wigged-out fugitive who steals his car, clothing and wallet containing a vital telephone number in a business deal worth $140 million. Unfortunately, Sally tosses it into the messy hovel of the Jim Brothers (Michael Monks and John C. Reilly) and the search is on. While Bill chases after high-strung Sally, Skearns murders his brother, loses his spectacles, nearly buries one of the Jim Brothers alive, assumes the Mayor's identity and pursues Sally who just happened to witness Matt's fratricide.

Before Skearns can put a sizable dent in his late brother's bank account, he shows his true colors. With the bungling local cops in pursuit, Skearns nearly kills Bill and Sally, before he loses his glasses once more and drives his car off a road where the bridge is out. Despite the fact that the lost telephone number turns out to be a blessing that saves his company millions, Bill has had enough of the rat race. He decides to settle down with feisty Sally and even try to become the next mayor of Buzzsaw.

Not only is the idiotic plot run into the ground, the filmmakers compound their sins with the device of Marci's narration which injects a tone of moppety sweetness into the proceedings. If the audience isn't done in by the cuteness of the classroom scenes, then it's bound to be worn to a frazzle watching the cast do everything but froth at the mouth to make this material playable. And has there ever been a comic foil so obviously shoe-horned into the plot of a chase comedy (for no other reason than to provide romantic interest) than Sally? The telegraphed slapstick squelches any potential laughs; the direction exhibits little finesse; the writing doesn't juggle the subplots with any sense of building to a climax; the dialogue doesn't sparkle; the acting, in most cases, seems forced—as if right in the middle of filming the players realized how unfunny the scene was and visibly gave up hope.

Broderick's lop-sided grin and boyish appeal remain intact but he can't be expected to work miracles with this cloddish raw material. Connoisseurs of wonderful comediennes will appreciate the efforts of the under-utilized Marian Mercer (JOHN AND MARY, 9 TO 5). They may be less happy with the dueling performances of Jeffrey Jones, who plays his twin roles as though he's paying homage to John Lithgow in RAISING CAIN. *(Violence, some profanity.)*

p, Michael Hertzberg; d, Francis Veber; w, Daniel Goldin, Joshua Goldin; ph, Donald E. Thorin; ed, Glenn Farr; m, Van Dyke Parks; prod d, Stephen Marsh; set d, Peg Cummings

Comedy/Action **(PR: A MPAA: PG)**

OVER HER DEAD BODY ★★

100m Enid Productions; Davis Entertainment ~ Vestron Video c

(AKA: ENID IS SLEEPING)

Elizabeth Perkins *(June)*, Judge Reinhold *(Harry)*, Jeffrey Jones *(Floyd)*, Maureen Mueller *(Enid)*, Rhea Perlman *(Mavis)*, Brion James *(Trucker)*, Charles Tyner *(Man at Indian Burial Site)*, Henry Jones *(Old Man)*, Michael J. Pollard *(Hotel Manager)*, James Lashly *(Gas Station Attendant)*, Nicholas Love *(Robber)*, Alex Chapman *(Robber)*, Steven Schwartz-Hartley *(Fireman)*, Deenie Dakota *(Mary Lou)*, Maurice Phillips *(Cop at Indian Road Sign)*, Sean Pratt *(Joe Bob)*, Susan Cash *(Nether)*, Paula Johnson *(Mrs. Hopper)*, Carlton Beener *(Little Harry)*, Jami Lyn Greenham *(Little Enid)*, Casey Friel *(Little June)*, Phil Mead *(Sheriff)*, Ann Harris Thornhill *(Babs)*, Chris Yarnell *(Kid at Jakes)*, Owen Lorian *(Reporter)*, Carol Renee *(Cleaning Lady)*, John David Garfield *(Cop)*

A slapstick comedy of corpse abuse, OVER HER DEAD BODY was overshadowed by the the superficially similar dead-guy farce WEEKEND AT BERNIE'S, made around the same time. But this is far darker fare, opening with a baby-in-the-oven joke and heading south from there.

The film opens in a dreary little New Mexican town circa 1959, where hateful toddler Enid tries to roast her infant sister June alive. It then flashes ahead thirty years to the present. Enid (Maureen Mueller) is now a white-trash bitch with tacky Vegas clothing, a beehive hairdo and kookie sunglasses. To the strains of Tammy Wynette's "Stand By Your Man" Enid arrives unexpectedly at her puke-pink desert house and catches cop-husband Harry (the ever-askew Judge Reinhold) in bed with the adult June (Elizabeth Perkins). "D'ya mean to tell me you've been dinkin' my own stinkin' sister?!" Enid shrieks at her man, in a typical sample of the film's verbal wit. Her homicidal rage ends only when mousy June smashes a ceramic clown over her head, evidently killing her. The adulterous lovers pull themselves together and conspire to make Enid's death look like a traffic accident, a torturous exercise that takes the rest of the running time.

As a distracted Harry puts in a token appearance at work, the increasingly hysterical June drives all over the county with the corpse rigged with fishing line like a macabre puppet so onlookers will think Enid's still alive. But efforts to dispose neatly of the body go disasterously wrong time and time again. Foiling their scheme are a set of backwater grotesques straight from Gagwriting 101: there's Floyd (Jeffrey Jones), Harry's patrol partner, obsessed with urban violence and always chattering about the latest sicko mayhem; a senile garage mechanic (Henry Jones); a fey motel manager (Michael J. Pollard); some mutant desert cretins listening to a crazed radio evangelist; and a couple of murderous holdup men. "I'm gonna ride you like a Harley on a bad road," gurgles a lustful cowboy drunk (Brion James) to the spread-eagled Enid. He immediately passes out face-down in the cadaver's crotch, whereupon June comes upon the scene and scolds Enid: "I can't leave you alone for one second, can I?" All this and post-mortem flatulence too; one soon feels that the only cheap laugh left out is that Enid isn't dead after all. Guess what?

The ceramic clown used to whack Enid is an apt metaphor for the bludgeon-like quality of OVER HER DEAD BODY's humor, with its stereotyped yahoos, needless swearing, and single-situation plot. A comedy of frustration is always tough to pull off, but when a film's entire running time is expended on a couple of goofs failing repeatedly at the same task, it can become an equally frustrating ordeal for the audience unless some evolving element is introduced and developed in an interesting way.

In OVER HER DEAD BODY that's supposed to be the downtrodden June, played with a wounded expression by bleached-blonde Elizabeth Perkins. While she chauffeurs her late sister around in a yellow convertible June begins a one-way dialogue with the body, recapping their whole relationship, their dead-end lives in the podunk town, and their tawdry rivalry over Harry; it's the first meaningful conversation she's ever had with Enid, get it? June sustains not only an emotional pounding but a physical one, getting muddied, bloodied and charred (again) before the show ends. Perkins is the last actress one would expect to do a Wile E. Coyote act, but she performs the schtick with aplomb. June's breakdown is the funniest thing about the film .

The movie was filmed in and around Santa Fe in 1989 under the auspices of Vestron Pictures, the ill-fated motion picture division of Vestron Video. Vestron declared bankruptcy on the final week of shooting, and although the completed OVER HER DEAD BODY enjoyed some success on the domestic festival circuit, no US distributor took a chance on broad theatrical exhibition. Originally titled ENID IS SLEEPING, the comedy was released theatrically overseas, but was dubiously enshrined in the US as a 1992 B-grade video release.

Director and co-screenwriter Maurice Phillips (ANOTHER YOU) disapproved of the new title, but it turned out to be ironically apt; a lawsuit reportedly germinated from the OVER HER DEAD BODY video-box art because it used the faces of Elizabeth Perkins and Judge Reinhold without authorization, photographically transplanted atop the posed bodies of others. *(Violence, substance abuse, excessive profanity, sexual situations, adult situations.)*

p, John A. Davis, Howard Malin; d, Maurice Phillips; w, Maurice Phillips, James Whaley, A. J. Tipping; ph, Affonso Beato; ed, Malcolm Campbell; m, Craig Safan; prod d, Paul Peters; art d, Gershon Ginsburg; cos, Lisa Jensen

Comedy **(PR: O MPAA: R)**

OX, THE ★★★

(Sweden) 91m Sandrews Film & Teater; Sweetland Films AB; Nordisk Films Kompagni ~ First Run Features/Castle Hill Productions c

Stellan Skarsgard *(Helge)*, Ewa Froling *(Elfrida)*, Lennart Hjulstrom *(Svenning)*, Max Von Sydow *(The Vicar)*, Liv Ullmann *(Maria)*, Bjorn Granath *(Flyckt)*, Erland Josephson *(Silver)*, Rikard Wofff *(Johannes)*, Helge Jordal *(Navvy)*, Agneta Prytz *(Old Woman)*, Bjorn Gustafson *(Officer in Command)*, Jaqui Safra *(Shop Owner)*

Directed and co-written by Sven Nykvist, longtime cinematographer for Ingmar Bergman, THE OX boasts a superb cast of Bergman regulars and flawless cinematography. But the best efforts of Liv Ullmann, Erland Josephson and Max Von Sydow do little to relieve the film's mood of unmitigated gloom. This grim 19th-century period piece feels at least twice as long as its 91-minute running time. The true story on which THE OX is based is one of devastating hardship during the great Swedish drought of the late 1860s, when droves emigrated to the US. In Smaland, a small village hard hit by the famine, Helge (Stellan Skarsgard), a young tenant farmer, secretly kills one of the estate owner's remaining pair of oxen to feed his family through the long winter.

Justifiable as it might seem, it is a deceit which preys on his conscience. (A neighbor's casual remark about his appearance prompts him to tell his wife, "We can't eat anything today. We look too healthy.") Ultimately, the local vicar (Von Sydow) finds out, implores the conscience-stricken Helge to admit the crime, and assures him any censure would probably be mild. It isn't. The sentence "for unlawfully killing and eating an ox" is 40 strokes and a life of hard labor at one of Sweden's most notorious state prisons.

While Helge sweats out six merciless years until he's freed, his young wife Elfrida (Ewa Froling) has her own problems coping. With both her and their young daughter starving, Elfrida succumbs to the advances of an itinerant laborer in exchange for food. The brief encounter results in the birth of a son which Helge discovers, to his fury, upon his return home. Eventually, he forgives her, and the film ends with a superimposed legend: "Helge & Elfrida had 8 children. They all behaved very well."

Nykvist endows THE OX with an exquisitely photographed sense of melancholia. The wretchedness is suspended only once, in a scene that is all the more memorable for its rarity: on his way home from prison, Helge encounters a vivacious country woman who persuades him to dance at a local gathering. They're attracted to each other. She wants to kiss him—it would be his first bit of emotional, physical warmth in years. Instead, he tenderly caresses her with his eyes and gently touches her cheek before moving on. Not a word is spoken. The scene is brilliant—a rare, precious cinematic moment.

Nykvist's cast, including Ullmann, Josephson and Von Sydow in secondary roles, is exceptional. Skarsgard, considered the most successful Swedish actor of his generation, is brilliant in the lead role. Though generally unknown in America (he played Capt. Tupolev, Sean Connery's ill-fated adversary in HUNT FOR RED OCTOBER), he has received best actor awards at the Berlin Film Festival and twice at Stockholm's Guldabagge ceremony.

The film's origins are worth noting. Nykvist had always been intrigued by the story, first related to him by relatives from Smaland. His screenplay (co-written with editor Lass Summanen) was, in turn, based on a synopsis of the incident he had written in the mid-70s. Years later, through Woody Allen, he met American TV producer Jean Doumanian ("Saturday Night Live") at a dinner party and told her the tale. According to the first-time director, she was immediately interested in producing it, even after he "explained it would have to be filmed in Swedish."

Nykvist fares poorly with his pacing, story development and use of music. The tale is fascinating and poignant, but the unrelenting gloom ultimately becomes wearisome. A little humor would have been most welcome.

p, Jean Doumanian; d, Sven Nykvist; w, Sven Nykvist, Lasse Summanen, (screenplay); ph, Dan Myhrman; ed, Lasse Summanen; art d, Peter Hoimark; set d, Magnus Magnussön; cos, Inger Pehrsson

Drama/Historical **(PR: A MPAA: NR)**

PAINTING THE TOWN ★★★

78m Padded Cell ~ Zeitgeist Films c

Richard Osterweil

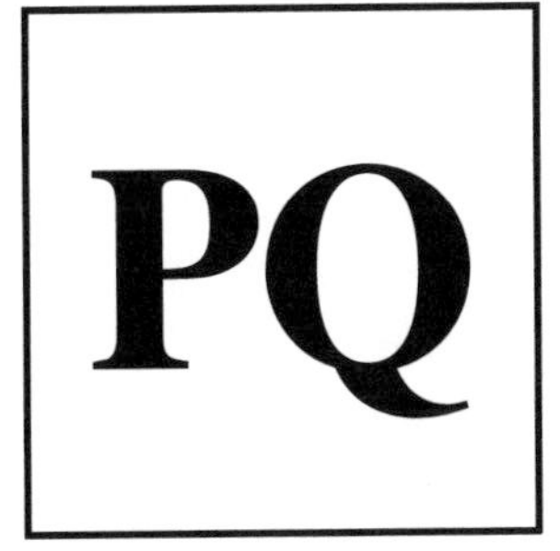

According to Richard Osterweil, the star of PAINTING THE TOWN and its sole *raison d'etre*, he moved to New York City in 1974 for the same reason everyone does: to spot celebrities. Osterweil is a painter, a rather unsuccessful calling he supports by driving cabs and checking coats at fancy restaurants. (He's prolific and, if somewhat derivative, surprisingly good, but his insistence on retaining visiting rights to his paintings has scared off most buyers.) His true metier, however, is crashing the parties, marriages and funerals of the rich and famous.

Osterweil's "social" conquests are many and varied. He's appeared at Gloria Steinem's fiftieth birthday fete; Leona Helmsley's celebrated trial for tax fraud; Imelda Marcos' trial, where the embattled former First Lady of the Philippines complimented him on his sneakers; and Phyllis George's wedding reception at Tavern on the Green. After being evicted from socialite Barbara de Portago's wedding, he put a curse on the marriage and vowed to attend her *next* one; true to his word, he did. The enterprising Osterweil forges invitations and, to crash particularly tight soirees, enlists friends who pose as paparazzi and shower him with attention as he sweeps into the lobby. (The heady whirl of power and prestige isn't the only attracttion for Osterweil—he's also there for the food.)

On a more somber note, Osterweil also crashed Richard Rodgers's funeral at Temple Emanu-El, where he escorted the elderly Helen Hayes and Lillian Gish out of the building; Warhol's funeral, where he and the Warhola clan were the only non-celebrities in attendance; and a shiva call for Leonard Bernstein at the fabled Dakota. He even crashed Roy Cohn's funeral—just to make sure he was dead. Osterweil doesn't view this practice as morbid, instead viewing himself as a witness to history. He's heard the great eulogized. Also, as Osterweil points out, "So I didn't know you in life. In death it's a different story."

The pixie-faced Osterweil is an unabashed elitist, but he's a refreshingly down-to-earth one who's nicknamed himself, *a la* DANCES WITH WOLVES, "Stands with Celebrities." He's also charmingly forthright about his obsession with various luminaries, including Katherine Hepburn (he once stole Hepburn's garbage, but was disappointed to find it quite commonplace), Princess Grace (after an accomplice managed to procure Grace's unlisted Manhattan number, Osterweil, posing as her son's school chum, called her the next time she was in town, and they chatted at length), and ballerina Suzanne Farrell. (For several years, the utterly devoted Osterweil scheduled his entire *life* around Farrell's performance schedule.) By his own admission, however, he identifies most strongly with that legendary gamine, Audrey Hepburn.

Osterweil has also been particularly obsessed with Mrs. Samuel Peabody, the glamorous, supremely regal socialite and fellow balletomane he admired from afar for several months before approaching her in front of the Public Theater. Unbeknownst to Peabody, he'd already begun a series of portraits of her and she's since become something of a muse. (Another recurrent theme in his artwork is the Romanov dynasty.) The upshot of Osterweil's obsessions? He's now good friends with Judy Peabody and actually receives invitations to the kind of events he used to crash, such as dinner with Brooke Astor and the Film Society of Lincoln Center's gala tribute to Audrey Hepburn.

Technically, PAINTING THE TOWN is barely adequate, displaying none of the structural or visual inventiveness that has refueled the documentary format in recent years. Instead, filmmakers Andrew Behar and Sara Sackner rely on the inherent allure of their previously unheralded subject to hold their audience—something Richard Osterweil is more than capable of doing.

p, Sara Sackner; d, Andrew Behar; w, Richard Osterweil; ph, Hamid Shams; ed, Sara Sackner, Andrew Behar; m, Peter Fish; prod d, Sara Sackner

Documentary **(PR: A MPAA: NR)**

PALE BLOOD ★

94m Noble Entertainment Group; Alpine Releasing Group ~ SVS/Triumph Home Video c

George Chakiris *(Michael Fury)*, Wings Hauser *(Van Vandemere)*, Pamela Ludwig *(Lori)*, Diana Frank *(Jenny)*, Darcy DeMoss *(Cherry)*, Earl Garnes *(Harker)*, Frazer Smith *(Frazer Kelly)*, Michael Palm *(Lead Singer)*, Steven Bramble *(Lori's Date)*, Randy Almazon, Frank Barajas, Sheryl Bence, Wanda Blunt, Den Daniel, Jr., Marc Leighton, Michaele Leighton, Mike Leighton, Michael Rosen, Rita Saiz, Tom Sidell *(People of the Night)*

Vampires have proven to be eerie and dramatically potent figures in the realm of dark fantasy, and PALE BLOOD positively aches to do something original with the lore of the undead. But the film never overcomes a serious anemia of good ideas and ways to handle them.

As the story opens, the body of a young Los Angeles woman has been found drained of blood, third in a series of killings by an unknown fiend dubbed the "Vampire Killer." Enter Michael Fury (George Chakiris), a mystery man of European origin who has an interest in the Vampire Killer. Through an agency he hires a *Nosferatu*-obsessed researcher, Lori (Pamela Ludwig), to help him; it's not clear whether the oft-mentioned "agency" denotes detective or modeling, as the slinky Lori makes bedroom eyes at the grim-faced Fury and passionately drapes herself all over the furnishings.

The viewer gets tipped off early that Mr. Fury is a real live undead, although he's a humane specimen who believes in drinking just the minimum amount of blood he needs without endangering his victim. And it's no great surprise that the Vampire Killer turns out to be Van Vandermere (Wings Hauser), a crazy "video artist" whose goal is to document a vampire on film. He's been faking the gory work of a bloodsucker so that a real one would eventually get curious and show up. Vandermere manages to trap Fury in a garlic-and-crucifix-lined vault and get the precious footage, but the tables turn when the lunatic lenser seizes Lori as a snack for the captive; she's secretly a vampire too, which explains her attitude but leaves the tale's logic as twisted as a hawthorne bush. The finale finds Vandermere confined, Renfield-like, to an insane asylum. No one believes his rantings about vampires, and the final shot suggests the whole movie has been a delusion. Or maybe that's wishful thinking.

The picture's best touch is a contractible portable coffin that accompanies Fury in his travels, and that's about it. Plotwise, PALE BLOOD just oozes along. Michael Fury's "investigation" into the murders consists of standing at his window looking moody or suffering repetitive and tiresome psychic visions. (Despite some prominent makeup artists involved, special effects are amazingly skimpy, consisting mainly of blood, blood and more blood.) Chakaris's (WEST SIDE STORY, IS PARIS BURNING?) stoic performance conveys little of the vampire mythos—except a hint of centuries-long boredom. At least Pamela Ludwig's (UNDER THE CHERRY MOON, IMMEDIATE FAMILY) over-the-top acting adds energy. Wings Hauser's muttering madman conveys more annoyance than menace.

Director V. Dachin Hsu (producer Michael W. Leighton also gets a closing co-direction credit) tries to give PALE BLOOD a neo-MTV look, with lots of shadows and German Expressionist sets, plus an unsuccessful attempt to capture an LA ambiance through lengthy shots of traffic jams over an audio montage of morning radio announcers—one of whom is a movie critic singing the praises of a new vampire flick called, of course, PALE BLOOD. Dream on, guys, although the movie reportedly took home a Golden Scroll Award from the broad-minded mavens of the Academy of Science-Fiction, Fantasy & Horror Films.

PALE BLOOD also indulges itself in the musical interludes, with too many visits to a Bram Stoker-themed nightspot called Drac's, where the band Agent Orange is headlining and lead vocalist Michael Palm mugs mercilessly for the camera as he performs songs like "So Strange" and "Bite the Hand that Feeds." *(Violence, profanity, nudity, sexual situations.)*

p, Omar Kaczmarczyk, Michael W. Leighton; d, V. Dachin Hsu, Michael W. Leighton; w, Takashi Matsuokoa, V. Dachin Hsu; ph, Gerry Lively; ed, Michael W. Leighton, Stewart Schill; m, Jan A.P. Kaczmarek; prod d, Shane Nelsen; art d, Dave Robinson; set d, Archie D'Amico

Horror **(PR: O MPAA: R)**

PAMELA PRINCIPLE, THE ★★

Axis Films International ~ Imperial Entertainment Corporation c

J.K. Dumont *(Carl Breeding)*, Veronica Cash *(Pamela)*, Troy Donahue *(Eddie)*, Shelby Lane, Frank Pesce

Basically an old-fashioned love triangle tricked up with a lot of nudity and sex, THE PAMELA PRINCIPLE somewhat remarkably but easily converts the torturously familiar 1940s "women's picture" into 90s sexploitation fare.

In the throes of a midlife crisis, Los Angeles dress-boutique owner Carl Breeding (J.K. Dumont) falls hard for Pamela (Veronica Cash), a knockout twenty-year-old model who sashays into his shop one slow afternoon. On the advice of his best friend, Eddie (Troy Donahue), Carl starts a steamy affair and cuts loose his wife (Shelby Lane) but eventually returns to hearth and home when he finds that he can't keep pace with his much younger lover, the deciding factor being when his own son (Frank Pesce) shows up for one of her wild, all-night bacchanals.

Like the earlier direct-to-video releases from the Garroni/Hippolyte/Gernert stable (MIRROR IMAGES, SECRET GAMES, THE OTHER WOMAN, NIGHT RHYTHMS), THE PAMELA PRINCIPLE boasts a high, nearly Lutheran morality (despite all the naughty shenanigans, Carl does go back to his wife), excellent production values, glossy no-blemishes cinematography, swank clothes and hairstyles and decent performances, with an added bonus of 60s heartthrob Troy Donahue, as well as Frank Pesce, whose true-life rags-to-riches story inspired last year's 29TH STREET. *(Profanity, nudity, sexual situations.)*

p, Andrew Garroni, Alexander Gregory Hippolyte; d, Toby Phillips; w, Toby Phillips, Alan Gries, Robyn Sullivent; ph, Dan Smith; ed, Kent Smith; m, Joseph Smith; prod d, Ed O'Reilly; cos, Ricardo Delgado, Lothar Delgado

Erotic/Drama **(PR: O MPAA: R)**

PANAMA DECEPTION, THE ★★★½

94m Empowerment Project ~ Empowerment Project c

Elizabeth Montgomery *(Narration)*, Abraham Alvarez, Carlos Cantu, Alma Martinez, Lou Diamond Phillips, Tony Plana, Rose Portillo, Lucy Rodriguez, Martha Velez, Carmen Zapata *(English-language Voiceovers)*

THE PANAMA DECEPTION, filmmaker Barbara Trent's follow-up to the equally controversial COVERUP: BEHIND THE IRAN-CONTRA AFFAIR, is a shocking expose of the dark side of American democracy.

US intervention in the affairs of Panama dates back to 1902, when the Colombian government rejected a US offer for construction of a transisthmian passageway in Panama. As a result, Panama, with US military backing, revolted against the Colombian government, resulting in Panama's separation from Colombia in 1903. Within a month Panamanian officials accepted an agreement that created a canal zone under the sovereign control of the US government "in perpetuity," and the Panama Canal was opened in 1914. In 1977, during the Carter administration, the Panamanian government and the US concluded a new canal treaty, the key provisions of which included integration of the Canal Zone with the rest of Panamanian territory and full Panamanian control of the canal in the year 2000.

The film alleges that General Manuel Noriega, for years the CIA's primary contact in Panama, was known to be involved in drug and arms trafficking, yet George Bush, first as director of the CIA (appointed by President Gerald R. Ford in 1976), then as Vice President during the Reagan administration, kept Noriega on the CIA payroll. Not surprisingly, given his US connections, Noriega became commander of the Panamanian Defense Forces, or PDF, in August 1983. Once in power, however, he cannily called for the cessation of US intervention in the affairs of Panama. In 1988, Noriega, by then the *de facto* ruler of the country, was indicted in the US on narcotics charges, but he refused to submit to US demands for his resignation and instead introduced a new wave of brutal oppression.

In May 1989, Noriega annulled election results that showed him losing to Guillermo Endara, seizing ballot boxes and employing goons to beat the opposition candidates, themselves illegally financed by the US government, and assumed the role of dictator. After an unsuccessful coup attempt in October 1989, the United States secretly mobilized 26,000 troops for an attack, known as operation "Just Cause," and invaded Panama on December 20. During the next several days, Noriega was captured and later brought to Miami to stand trial on narcotics charges.

The film argues convincingly that, despite President Bush's excuse of wanting to protect American lives and restore democracy, the *real* motive was the US government's determination to retain a military presence in Panama—and the canal itself. To do so, it was necessary to crush the PDF, for how can Panama ensure the future independence of the canal without it? Having invaded a heavily populated urban area, the US militia, by most civilian accounts, shot indiscriminately—though men between the ages of 15-55 were specific targets—and systematically burned buildings to flush out the PDF. Clearly, "peripheral damage" was not a concern. The film also alleges that the Panama invasion was a testing ground for the Persian Gulf invasion—and new technological weaponry; many civilians claim to have seen victims literally melt before their eyes or spontaneously bleed from every orifice.

The US military took elaborate efforts to conceal the number of dead, going so far as to seize control of local hospitals and morgues. The US government claims that there were 250 civilian casualties; by most other accounts, that figure is closer to 4,000—an enormous human toll. The videotape footage of mass graves being uncovered by stunned civilians months after the invasion is particularly damning evidence. Not surprisingly, Panama's white, English-speaking middle-class was largely unharmed.

Though widely condemned by the international community, the US action in Panama was barely criticized at home. But how much of the real picture did the American public receive? Trent argues that the American media were more than complicit; it's not just that the media act in the interests of the corporations, the media are *integral* to corporate America. Not surprisingly, access by American journalists and photographers was tightly controlled; they were only taken to see what the US government wanted them to see. The American public, consequently, didn't know what had happened until it was over. In addition, the Panamanian media were similarly suppressed, and any organization opposed to the US presence in Panama was destroyed.

The denouement? In 1991, US Congress passed a resolution to renegotiate the Panama Canal Treaty on the grounds that the Panamanian government could not adequately defend the canal, thus ensuring a continued US military presence into the 21st century. *(Some violence, adult situations.)*

p, Barbara Trent, David Kasper, Nico Panigutti, Joanne Doroshow; d, Barbara Trent; w, David Kasper; ph, Michael Dobo, Manuel Becker; ed, David Kasper; m, Chuck Wild, Ricky Barnes, Ismael Rivera, Jackson Browne, Jorge Strunz, Sting

AA Best Documentary Feature: Barbara Trent (Producer) and David Kasper (Producer)

Documentary/Political (PR: C MPAA: NR)

PASSED AWAY ★★½

96m Rank and File Productions Inc.; Hollywood ~ BV c

Bob Hoskins *(Johnny Scanlan)*, Blair Brown *(Amy Scanlan)*, Tim Curry *(Boyd Pinter)*, Frances McDormand *(Nora Scanlan)*, William Petersen *(Frank Scanlan)*, Pamela Reed *(Terry Scanlan)*, Peter Riegert *(Peter Syracusa)*, Maureen Stapleton *(Mary Scanlan)*, Nancy Travis *(Cassie Slocombe)*, Jack Warden *(Jack Scanlan)*, Diana Bellamy *(BJ)*, Don Brockett *(Froggie)*, Helen Lloyd Breed *(Aunt Maureen)*, Patricia O'Connell *(Mrs. Finch)*, Sally Gracie *(Mrs. Cassidy)*, Ruth Jarslow *(Mrs. Richfield)*, Alice Eisner *(Aunt Sissy)*, Louis Mustillo *(Carmine Syracusa)*, Ann Shea *(Louise)*, Tristan Tait *(Sam Scanlan)*, Sara Rue *(Megan Scanlan)*, Debra Rush *(Denise Scanlan)*, Patrick Breen *(Father Hallahan)*, Teri Polo *(Rachel Scanlan)*, Jayce Bartok *(Tony Scanlan)*, Antone DiLeo *(Enrique)*, Helena Ruoti *(Sheila Pajoli)*, Dylan Baker *(Unsworth)*, Jim Corr *(Daniel)*, Dan Futterman *(Tom)*, Andrida McCall *(Secretary)*, Jessie Keosian *(Mrs. Wysocki)*, Kathryn Aronson *(Claire Wysocki)*, Tommy LaFitte *(George Talbot)*, William Thunhurst, Jr. *(Father Ryan)*, Ruth Lesko *(Deirdre Floss)*, K.J. Roberts *(Liquor Delivery Man)*, Frank Seals, Jr. *(Flower Delivery Man)*, David L. Early *(Councilman Chaney)*, Kristin Minter *(Cousin Karen)*, Maggie Stewart *(Betty)*, Larry John Meyers *(1st Insurance Agent)*, Glenn Kubota *(2nd Insurance Agent)*, Katie Karlovitz *(Saleslady)*, Rick Applegate *(Unsworth's Guy)*, Harold O'Leary *(Bishop)*, Helen Lloyd-Breed *(Maureen)*, Richard Rauh *(Leering Man)*, Tom Tully *(Dr. G)*, Paul Mochnik *(Drunk Man)*, Jean Pierre Nutini *(Joe–Night Watchman)*, Steve Aronson *(Husband)*, Shirley Tannenbaum *(Wife)*

Bob Hoskins shepherds his zany family through the funeral of his father in PASSED AWAY, a Disney farce that replaces Dean Jones and hammy animals with peppery verbal humor and select "adult situations" before settling into an orgy of sitcom cliches.

Undergoing a midlife crisis, Johnny Scanlan (Hoskins) is thinking of trading in his tree-trimming business for a fishing boat and a life on the seas when his father Jack (Jack Warden) suddenly drops dead after "recovering" from open-heart surgery. Planning the funeral and burial, Johnny quickly finds himself overwhelmed, not only with organizing the old-fashioned Irish wake insisted upon by his mother, Mary (Maureen Stapleton), but also with the abundant life crises of the rest of his idiosyncratic family.

His handsome but dumb-as-dirt brother Frank (William Petersen), an aspiring union leader trying to follow in his father's footsteps, is being forced from his post by a vaguely Mafia-ish rival. Adding to Frank's woes are a shrewish, social-climbing wife (Debra Rush), a son who wears earrings and a very pregnant, unmarried daughter (Teri Polo). Rebellious sister Terry (Pamela Reed) ran away from home to marry star dancer-choreographer Boyd Pinter (Tim Curry) without knowing he was gay. Having long since divorced him, Terry still can't bring herself to arrive at the funeral without her ex in tow, which creates problems when Terry becomes attracted to funeral-home embalmer Peter Syracusa (Peter Riegert).

Sister Nora (Frances McDormand), a "liberation theologian" nun who's been working with the poor in El Salvador, shows up with her own man in tow, an illegal immigrant who's being hotly pursued by INS agents. Meanwhile, Johnny also finds himself considering leaving his wife Amy (Blair Brown), who opposes Johnny's fishy career change, to pursue the sexy, mysterious lady, Cassie Slocombe (Nancy Travis), who appears at the funeral without explanation and whom everybody assumes was Jack's mistress.

Like BLAME IT ON RIO (an earlier screenplay co-written with Larry Gelbart by Charlie Peters, who debuts here as a writer-director), PASSED AWAY promises more in risque outrageousness than it actually delivers. Like a number of recent Disney comedies, it also tries to drop in something for everyone while bending over backwards not to offend anyone, which prevents it from ever developing much of a personality.

After establishing the Scanlans as a clan of blustery, hard-drinking Irish Catholics, the film gradually downplays both their Irishness and their drinking as it goes on. The only drunkenness seen in the film is from the priest presiding over the funeral (who hilariously horrifies mourners with a screeching rendition of Cole Porter's "You're the Tops" during the wake). PASSED AWAY takes a slam at liberal politics by having family members refer to the brainless Frank as "the Kennedy of the family" (in part an inside joke: Petersen's most prominent TV role to date has been as family patriarch Joe in "The Kennedys of Massachusetts). The film also alludes to labor-union corruption in Frank's sketchy subplot. On the other hand, it generally endorses Nora's leftist activities on behalf of Salvadoran dissidents.

Terry's mid-wake liaison with Syracusa is one of the film's funniest comic set-pieces. However, Johnny never gets too far with Slocombe, whose relationship with Jack is revealed to have been not only absolutely pure, but something straight out of a 1930s' melodrama. Jack's own lifelong reputation as a womanizer is finally revealed to have been largely mythical, growing out of a single one-night stand many years earlier. Boyd's homosexuality is more talked-about than seen and dispensed with entirely when the character leaves the action long before the film is over. Johnny reconciles with Amy and even Rachel reunites with her boyfriend in time for the delivery of their baby—in the middle of Jack's funeral. Surveying the scene, Johnny decides, like THE WIZARD OF OZ's Dorothy, that there's more than enough adventure in his own backyard, leading him to abandon his plans for his new career.

Despite its studied inoffensiveness PASSED AWAY doesn't feel as hollow and strained as many recent Disney comedies. Though often overwritten, Peters's dialogue is also often howlingly funny and given sharp, smart readings by one of the strongest casts assembled for a studio comedy in recent memory. Virtually everybody here has been seen to better advantage in much better films, but there's not a throwaway performance in the bunch, with Petersen and McDormand (BLOOD SIMPLE, DARKMAN) especially showing a revelatory flair for poker-faced comedy.

Altogether, PASSED AWAY bodes well for the updated Disney formula of bringing fringe talent into the mainstream at bargain prices and is evidence that it may lead to good films in the future. As a viewer at a preview screening quipped, "It's not RULES OF THE GAME." True, but it ain't OSCAR, either. *(Adult situations, profanity.)*

p, Larry Brezner, Timothy Marx; d, Charlie Peters; w, Charlie Peters; ph, Arthur Albert; ed, Harry Keramidas; m, Richard Gibbs; prod d, Catherine Hardwicke; art d, Gilbert Mercier; set d, Gene Serdena; cos, Jennifer Von Mayrhauser

Comedy **(PR: C MPAA: PG-13)**

PASSENGER 57 ★½

90m Lee Rich Productions; Warner Bros. ~ Warner Bros. c

Wesley Snipes *(John Cutter)*, Bruce Payne *(Charles Rane)*, Tom Sizemore *(Sly Delvecchio)*, Alex Datcher *(Marti Slayton)*, Bruce Greenwood *(Stuart Ramsey)*, Robert Hooks *(Dwight Henderson)*, Elizabeth Hurley *(Sabrina Ritchie)*, Michael Horse *(Forget)*, Marc Macauley *(Vincent)*, Ernie Lively *(Chief Biggs)*, Duchess Tomasello *(Mrs. Edwards)*, Cameron Roberts *(Matthew)*, James Short *(Allen)*, Joel Fogel *(Doctor Bauman)*, Jane McPherson *(Nurse)*, Winston Bedford *(Doctor)*, Lori Bedford *(Surgical Receptionist)*, Kent Lindsey *(Agent Claflin)*, Rand MacPherson *(Swat Commander)*, Lou Bedford *(Attorney Phillips)*, Elena Ayala *(Lisa Cutter)*, Mike Speller *(Headwaiter)*, Kareen Germain *(Security Attendant)*, Michael Moss *(Agent Manning)*, Jim McDonald *(Agent Duncan)*, Zachary McLemore *(Norman)*, Lesa Thurman *(Norman's Mother)*, Janet Elder *(Screaming Woman)*, Alicia Allred *(Flight Attendant)*, Frank Causey *(Captain Whitehurst)*, Marty Connell *(First Officer)*, Frank Hart *(Flight Engineer)*, Tom Nowicki *(Sly's Assistant)*, Linda Vick *(Receptionist)*, Robert Midden *(Pistol-Whipped Passenger)*, Dennis Letts *(Frank Allen)*, Janis Benson *(Nora Allen)*, Gary Rorman *(Douglas)*, Lindsey Diamond *(Hostage Woman)*, Dean Carlberg *(Helicopter Pilot)*, James Brett Rice *(Cop 1)*, James Stone *(Cop 2)*, Henry J. McGauley *(Store Hold-Up Man)*, Michael D. Conner *(FBI Agent)*, Carl Cole *(Sharpshooter)*, Jack Gibson *(Reporter 1)*, Lisa Capriani *(Reporter 2)*

An action thriller from the Joel Silver school of Big Bang filmmaking, PASSENGER 57 smashes on the runway, an inflated cartoon of excess without a modicum of charm, wit or sense.

John Cutter (Wesley Snipes) is a snippy and imperious airline security expert (a friend tells him "You'd make a hell of a Republican") who finds himself aboard a flight to Los Angeles with the sneering and equally imperious Charles Rane (Bruce Payne), the latter being escorted by FBI agents to face terrorist bombing charges. Quite understandably, Rane wants to get off the plane before it lands in California and, while Cutter is in the bathroom, Rane's camouflaged cohorts take their cue and commandeer the aircraft. It is then up to Cutter and attractive airline attendant Marti Slayton (Alex Datcher) to sneak into the aircraft's underbelly and release the plane's fuel supply, forcing the plane to land on a small airstrip in Louisiana. Before landing, however, Cutter is kicked out of the plane onto the runway by one of Rane's henchmen, where two bonehead Southern deputies mistake him for one of the bad guys and arrest him.

As prisoners are released after the plane's landing, Rane ducks out the back way with two of his fellow terrorists. He strolls around a county fair, located conveniently nearby, where Cutter, having straightened out the comedy of errors with the local sheriff, stalks him, prompting an old-fashioned shoot-em-up. Rane's henchmen are killed and he's recaptured but he negotiates himself back onto the plane and it soon taxies down the runway with the remaining passengers. Confounding Rane, Cutter hops aboard and, after a hostage-taking stand-off and the obligatory killing of innocent bystanders, Cutter smacks Rane out of the airplane, GOLDFINGER-style. After the plane lands again, Marti and Cutter walk away from the bedlam to visit the fair.

PASSENGER 57 plays like a film Bruce Willis turned down. Incorporating elements of the DIE HARD blockbusters and the LETHAL WEAPON trilogy, the film has a battle-scarred familiarity, the deaths and explosions creating an unpleasant sense of *deja vu* in the viewer. Director Kevin Hooks knows how to press the action buttons, achieving the rhythm and look of the major 1980s action thrillers without the grit and panache that made those films exciting. Hooks invokes terrorists, plane crashes, gunfire and an ever-increasing body count like an old Nintendo game—the elements are all there, but viewers have played it one time too many.

The plot contrivances of PASSENGER 57 make the Zucker brothers' AIRPLANE look like a beacon of narrative economy—every plot point in David Loughery and Dan Gordon's derivative screenplay is set up like a sketch on "Saturday Night Live." Among the numerous unanswerable questions: why does a SWAT team decide to surprise Rane at his plastic surgeon's and how does he know they'll be bursting through the operating room door at exactly 6 p.m.? What is the chance in the real world of an airline security officer finding himself on an airplane teeming with unidentified terrorists? Why does Rane, instead of sneaking away after landing the airplane, decide to stroll to the local county fair, thereby allowing Cutter to hunt him down?

PASSENGER 57 offers the rare opportunity in American films for a mainstream audience to cheer for a black action hero, but this novel concept is immediately subverted by an inherent racism. Despite having Snipes mouth some hip catch-phrases ("Do you ever play roulette? Always bet on black"), most of the film reflects stereotypical perceptions of African-Americans: Snipes proudly tells his friend that he was patted down by an airport security woman because he is more physically endowed; he screams in pop-eyed mock terror as a hijacker tries to force him back to his seat; the sheriff's deputies arrest him at the airport because they cannot conceive of Snipes being a high-level security officer. The racism may be implicit, but it is certainly simmering below the surface.

This carries over into Wesley Snipes's performance, as if he knew what was happening but had to carry out his contract. Snipes, who looks like he sucked on a lemon before each take, doesn't play John Cutter as a character with an attitude—he's an *actor* with an attitude. The sarcastic, defensive and strident Cutter's favorite catchphrase is "I'm the best," and this without a hint of irony or humor. This guy means it.

PASSENGER 57 is a lazy, late entry in the action thriller sweepstakes that lacks excitement or interesting characters and has an undertone of sleaze. The nasty, cynical attitude of the film might best be summed up in a speech made by Rane to the frightened hostages on the hijacked airplane: "We will now continue with the remainder of the flight. If you don't want to wear your seat belts you don't have to." It's just a shame that movie theaters can't sell flight insurance for the rocky ride of PASSENGER 57. *(Excessive violence, profanity.)*

p, Dan Paulson, Lee Rich, Dylan Sellers; d, Kevin Hooks; w, David Loughery, Dan Gordon, (from story by Gordon and Stewart Raffill); ph, Mark Irwin; ed, Richard Nord; m, Stanley Clarke; prod d, Jaymes Hinkle; art d, Alan Muraoka; set d, Don K. Ivey

Action/Thriller **(PR: O MPAA: R)**

PASSION FISH ★★★½

136m Atchafalaya Films Inc.; Esperanza Productions ~ Miramax c

Mary McDonnell *(Mary-Alice Culhane)*, Alfre Woodard *(Chantelle)*, David Strathairn *(Rennie)*, Vondie Curtis-Hall *(Sugar LeDoux)*, Angela Bassett *(Dawn/Rhonda)*, Lenore Banks *(Nurse Quick)*, William Mahoney *(Max)*, Nelle Stokes *(1st Therapist)*, Brett Ardoin *(2nd Therapist)*, Michael Mantell *(Dr. Kline)*, Daniel Dupont *(Therapist)*, Chuck Cain *(Attendant)*, ShanaLedet Qualls *(1st Fan)*, Paula Lafleur *(2nd Fan)*, Maggie Renzi *(Louise)*, Marianne Muellerleile *(Drushka)*, Victoria Edwards *(Jessica)*, Amanda Carlin *(Perky)*, Elaine West *(Phoebe)*, Linda Castle *(Lawanda)*, Leigh Harris *(Kit)*, Leo Burmester *(Reeves)*, Mary Portser *(Precious)*, Nora Dunn *(Ti-Marie)*, Tom Wright *(Luther)*, Jennifer Gardner *(Albertine)*, Sheila Kelley *(Kim)*, Nancy Mette *(Nina)*, Shauntisa Willis *(Denita)*, John Henry *(Dr. Blades)*, Michael Laskin *(Redwood Vance)*

After forays into historical dramas and multi-character urban sagas, director John Sayles has returned to the kind of small, intimate film with which he first established his reputation. Tackling a subject that could easily have been turned into a sappy TV movie-of-the-week, PASSION FISH is instead a realistic, unsentimental "grown-up" movie.

It opens on a typically vivid Sayles image: soap opera actress Mary-Alice Culhane (Mary McDonnell) lying immobile in a hospital bed, watching herself walking and talking on TV. The nurse tells her she's been paralyzed from the waist down in a traffic accident (she was on her way to have her legs waxed), but her fear and anger have immobilized her as well: she refuses to participate in her physical therapy, and drowns her sorrows in endless TV watching and drinking. Moving back to her Louisiana Bayou hometown, Mary-Alice goes through a succession of caretakers (shown in a funny series of vignettes), ranging from Russian authoritarians to biker chicks.

The last hope for this self-proclaimed "bitch on wheels" is the quiet Chantelle (Alfre Woodard), who needs the job badly enough that she can't quit but refuses to put up with Mary-Alice's tantrums or stubbornness. At one point, tired of her refusal to go outdoors or do her exercises, she pushes the actress and her wheelchair out of the house and leaves her there, forcing her to wheel herself back in. "But it's all uphill," Mary-Alice complains, as Chantelle leaves. "So's life," the nurse shoots back.

The pair are visited by several friends and family members, including Mary-Alice's hard-drinking uncle, Reeves (Leo Burmester), who she obviously takes after; two schoolmates of the actress who were less than kind to her before she left to become famous; and Rennie (David Strathairn), the local handyman and childhood friend who's enlisted to make the house more handicapped-accessible. Although he's married with children, he begins to endear himself to Mary-Alice, while Chantelle captures the fancy of Sugar LeDoux (Vondie Curtis-Hall), a too-charming Black cowboy she's initially quite leery of.

Ironically, as Mary-Alice becomes more self-sufficient, she finds out that Chantelle is recovering too, from a drug-addicted past (thus explaining her disgust at Mary-Alice's constant drinking). Chantelle has also left behind a daughter, now living with her grandfather. Both women are trying to start over, grappling with new identities and responsibilities, and their isolated situation, as well as the subtle magic of the bayou, begins to change them, even more so after Rennie takes them on a boat ride through the swamp. There he shows them "passion fish"—the local superstition being that if you hold one of the small fish tight, and think of someone you love, that person will fall in love with you.

Never maudlin, and never opting for big dramatic climaxes, PASSION FISH succeeds most of the time, thanks to a typically deft Sayles screenplay and two fine, understated performances from McDonnell and Woodard. Sayles has created two wonderfully complex characters and given them a leisurely paced film more concerned with character development than with plot. The film's first half is so strong that it's hard to see how Sayles can sustain it, and, as it turns out, he can't.

The second half contains some unconnected scenes that, while not detracting from the film, seem a little out of place. A visit from three fellow soap-opera actresses has one of them go into a long monologue about a particularly humiliating audition for a low-budget UFO film. It's unclear whether the speech is intended to illustrate the somewhat ludicrous nature of their profession, or is simply a showpiece for a favorite actress. The revelation of Chantelle's daughter and drug-addicted past also feels a bit tacked-on; it comes too late in the film to be properly developed. Some more scenes between Rennie and Mary-Alice, or Chantelle and Sugar, would have worked better here.

Sayles's films are generally so true to life and feature such authentic dialogue that at times they're like documentaries, which makes his occasional lapses all the more jarring. There may actually be people as affected as Mary-Alice's two school friends (one played by "Saturday Night Live" thesp Nora Dunn); here they come off as cartoons. But for viewers willing to accomodate themselves to its rhythms, which are as unhurried as its bayou setting, Sayles has cooked up an affecting story, one that takes the audience on a slow ride into the swampland with two of its denizens, trying to re-define themselves in the "second act" of their lives. *(Substance abuse, profanity, adult situations.)*

p, Sarah Green, Maggie Renzi; d, John Sayles; w, John Sayles; ph, Roger Deakins; ed, John Sayles; m, Mason Daring; prod d, Dan Bishop, Dianna Freas; cos, Cynthia Flynt

AAN Best Actress: Mary McDonnell; *AAN Best Original Screenplay:* John Sayles

Drama/Romance **(PR: C MPAA: R)**

PATRIOT GAMES ★★½

113m Neufeld/Rehme Productions; Paramount ~ Paramount c

Harrison Ford *(Jack Ryan)*, Anne Archer *(Dr. Cathy Ryan)*, Patrick Bergin *(Kevin O'Donnell)*, Sean Bean *(Sean Miller)*, Thora Birch *(Sally Ryan)*, James Fox *(Lord Holmes)*, Samuel L. Jackson *(Robby Jackson)*, Polly Walker *(Annette)*, James Earl Jones *(Admiral James Greer)*, Richard Harris *(Paddy O'Neil)*, J.E. Freeman *(Marty Cantor)*, Alex Norton *(Dennis Cooley)*, Hugh Fraser *(Watkins)*, David Threlfall *(Inspector Highland)*, Alun Armstrong *(Owens)*, Berlinda Tolbert *(Sissy)*, Hugh Ross *(Barrister Atkinson)*, Gerald Sim *(Lord Justice)*, Pip Torrens *(First Aide)*, Thomas Russell *(Ashley)*, Jonathan Ryan *(Jimmy O'Reardon)*, Andrew Connolly *(Charlie Dugan)*, Karl Hayden *(Paddy Boy)*, Claire Oberman *(Lady Holmes)*, Oliver Stone *(Young Holmes)*, Tom Watt *(The Electrician)*, P.H. Moriarty *(Court Guard)*, Rebecca Mayhook *(School Girl)*, Roger Blake *(Constable)*, Martin Cochrane *(Constable)*, Tim Dutton *(Constable)*, Ellen Geer *(Rose)*, John Lafayette *(Winter)*, Duke Moosekian *(Ferro)*, Fritz Sperberg *(Spiva)*, Brenda Klemme *(Secretary)*, Allison Barron *(CIA Analyst)*, Theodore Raimi *(CIA Technician)*, Gregory Paul

Jackson *(Taxi Driver)*, Philip Levien *(Dr. Shapiro)*, Jesse Goins *(FBI Agent Shaw)*, John Shepard *(FBI Helicopter Pilot)*, Stephen Held *(FBI Rifleman)*, Debora Weston *(CNN Reporter)*, Bob Gunton *(Interviewer)*, Ivan Kane *(TV Reporter)*, Kim Delgado *(TV Reporter)*, Keith Campbell *(Ned Clark)*, Jeff Mandon *(Marine Guard)*, Eric Paul *(Marine Guard)*, Jeff Gardner *(Midshipman)*, Lester T. Tillery, Franklin Dam, Frankie Maldonatti, Bonnie Webster, Pamela Saxon, Leah Tabassi *(Midshipmen)*, Michael Ryan Way *(Avery)*, Fred Toma *(Arab Soldier)*, Ruben Garfias *(Anesthesiologist)*, Michael Francis Kelly *(O'Neil's Bodyguard)*

Ponderous and slow, PATRIOT GAMES is a thriller with few thrills, weighted down by obvious performances and an excess of family values.

Former CIA analyst Jack Ryan (Harrison Ford) is in London with his doctor wife, Cathy (Anne Archer) and small daughter, Sally (Thora Birch), when he happens upon an attack on Lord Holmes (James Fox), a member of the royal family, by a rogue IRA splinter group. Unable to stand simply by and watch, Ryan leaps into the fray, killing one of the terrorists and wounding another, the psychotic Sean Miller (Sean Bean). Miller is tried and convicted, swearing vengeance on Ryan all along. His co-conspirators, Kevin O'Donnell and Annette (Patrick Bergin and Polly Walker), spring him from police custody, and the games begin.

Ryan uses his CIA contacts to track the terrorists, but can't stop them from nearly killing Cathy and Sally on a highway near their home. They launch their final assault as Jack and Cathy are celebrating Sally's birthday (Lord Holmes is a guest), killing their bodyguards, cutting the phone lines and coming in with hightech weapons blazing. It all comes down to the inevitable one-to-one battle between Ryan and Miller; the latter is gorily dispatched with an anchor and the Ryans can again breath freely.

The sequel to the ponderous but highly profitable HUNT FOR RED OCTOBER, adapted from Tom Clancy's best-selling techno-thriller, PATRIOT GAMES is evidence of the painful dilemma into which the dissolution of the Soviet Union has placed the writers of spy thrillers. It's all very well to dredge up a few Nazis every now and again, but the fact of the matter is, communists were the best villains going. And now they're gone. Apparently sensing that the IRA isn't good enough on its own (pains are taken to point out that this group has broken off from the IRA proper; one wonders if the sensibilities of Irish-Americans were a consideration), the Irish terrorists are teamed for a while with Middle Eastern terrorists, who on their own don't really seem to scare Americans much but will do in a pinch to shore up a weak line-up.

Paramount's ad campaign for PATRIOT GAMES made much of the fact that there's never been a terrorist attack on American soil, but that's not really what the film is about. Terrorism is political, and the terrifying thing about it is that it can strike anywhere, at any time. Innocent people die horribly just because they were in the wrong restaurant or subway station at the wrong time. PATRIOT GAMES, on the other hand, is personal, just like dozens, if not hundreds, of less ballyhooed thrillers in which lone men (and occasionally women) must protect themselves and their families from vicious, implacable killers who will stop at nothing. So in the end, all this talk about the IRA is a smoke screen; Jack Ryan is just one more stand-up guy taking on the bogeyman.

As Ryan, Harrison Ford—replacing the much younger Alec Baldwin, who backed out of the sequel—seems ossified. As an actor he's at his best when he's thinking, not when he's doing; even though he's in fine shape, his blunt features and solid torso give the impression of heaviness. That's a plus when you consider that Ryan is an analyst, not a field man, but he then spends the film in the field, lumbering from clue to clue with determination unmatched by grace. He never seems more inert than in his scenes with Richard Harris.

A show-off and a frequent scenery chewer, Harris, who plays a smooth IRA spokesman, nevertheless seems to skate effortlessly around Ford whenever they share the screen. As the ruthless but highly photogenic trio of terrorists, Bergin, Walker and especially Bean opt for one-note characterizations. Their lips twitch, their eyes blaze, they hurl themselves around rooms with a theatrical excess of pent-up fury. The tone of a phone call from Miller to Ryan approximates "I'll get you and your little dog, too," and indicates the general level of performance.

Philip Noyce, director of the little-seen but much admired DEAD CALM and currently touted by Hollywood as heir apparent to the coveted thriller mantle, does a competent job with the material, but one expects more from both him and the estimated $45 million budget. *(Violence.)*

p, Mace Neufeld, Robert Rehme; d, Phillip Noyce; w, W. Peter Iliff, Donald Stewart, (from the novel by Tom Clancy); ph, Donald M. McAlpine; ed, Neil Travis, William Hoy; m, James Horner; prod d, Joseph Nemec, III; art d, Joseph P. Lucky; set d, John M. Dwyer; cos, Norma Moriceau

Thriller/Action **(PR: C MPAA: R)**

PEPI, LUCI, BOM AND OTHER GIRLS ON THE HEAP ★★★½

(Spain) 80m Figaro Films; Pepon Corominas Productions ~ Cinevista c

(PEPI, LUCI, BOM Y OTRAS CHICAS DEL MONTON)

Carmen Maura *(Pepi)*, Felix Rotaeta *(Policeman)*, Olvido "Alaska" Gara *(Bom)*, Eva Siva *(Luci)*, Diego Alvarez *(Little Boy)*, Concha Gregori, Kiti Manver, Cecilia Roth, Julieta Serrano, Christina S. Pascual, Jose Luis Aguirre, Carlos Tristancho, Eusebio Lazaro, Fabio DeMiguel, Assumpta Serna, Blanca Sanchez, Pastora Delgado, Carlos Lapuente, Richardo Franco, Jim Contreras, Ceesepe, Angela Fifa, Pedro Miralles, Agustin Almodvar, Ernique Naya, Juan Carrero, Tote Trenas, Los Pegamoides, Concha

Pedro Almodovar ingeniously makes the bizarre seem normal in PEPI, LUCI, BOM AND OTHER GIRLS ON THE HEAP, his subversive second feature.

A fascistic cop (Felix Rotaeta) busts into Pepi's (Carmen Maura) kitschy flat to hassle her over marijuana plants she grows in her window. She offers him sexual favors beneath a lifesize Wonder Woman poster—anything but the stealing of her virginity which she is saving to sell for a good price. He takes it anyway and Pepi plots her revenge. She enlists a streetwise teenage friend Bom (Olvido "Alaska" Gara), the band leader of "Bomitoni," and her musicians to rough up the cop. Pepi is delighted when they bump into him on a deserted street. The band pulls the wool over his eyes by aping a wandering opera troop and then jumps him. It turns out, though, that they ambushed the cop's twin brother.

Undaunted, Pepi inveigles a meeting with his spouse, a mousey housefrau named Luci (Eva Siva) and tries to get at him through her. She approaches Luci and convinces her to give her knitting lessons. Pepi lets Luci know she is after her husband at the first lesson. Luci doesn't seem to mind, she is willing to be bossed around by anyone—she likes it even, as displayed by her impassioned gasp when Pepi pokes her with a knitting needle. Bom comes to visit and it is immediately obvious that Luci and Bom are an S&M match made in heaven. Luci is introduced to the girls' rollicking scene of music, drugs and parties peopled with friends predisposed to any and every sexual flavor, and she loves it and leaves the vicious cop.

Pepi's father, meanwhile, is fed up with his daughter's lifestyle and and threatens to cut off her allowance. Imaginative woman that she is, Pepi finds a job at a quirky ad agency and quickly becomes queen bee. One night, the cop stalks Luci out with the girls at a disco. When she goes outside to get Bom cigarettes, he brutally attacks her, landing her bruised and broken in the hospital. It's the happiest she's ever been. After a few days Pepi and Bom discover what's happened and rush to save her. But Luci is blissful now that her husband has finally abused her and tells them to scat. Luci and Bom wander off disappointed but looking forward to the possibilities this turn in life might inspire.

Shot on 16mm after making several shorts like TWO WHORES and THE FALL OF SODOM, culminating in the Super-8 feature FUCK, FUCK, FUCK ME TIM, Almodovar's PEPI, LUCI, BOM AND OTHER GIRLS ON THE HEAP approaches a John Waters's aesthetic—one-take, bouncy camerawork and crackling sound, frantic almost improvised performances, and a color scheme suitable for a drinks menu at a Polynesian restaurant. Almodovar circles Waters's themes as well, including perversion, gender-role questions, social deviance and wickedness. What distinguishes Almodovar from Waters and other directors of their ilk is his unleashed optimism and delight in life. In some scenes he turns the project into a mad party for his friends, a collection of drag queens and rockers and other night creatures on the fringe, celebrating the end of the Franco years. He reigns over their hell-raising while also presenting an incisive examination of the macho police state this new freedom burst from.

As Pepi, Admodovar regular Carmen Maura strides though the center of this joyous anti-establishment mess on her long bandy legs. She's poodle-haired, ebullient and powerful, the childlike mother of the whole gang and the embodiment of Almodovar's impish, quicksilver vision. As her companions, Gara and Siva sparkle less but are also convincing in their quirky roles of cringing frump and misanthropic punk. Almodovar's trump is how homey these three feel. Through a few quiet moments when they are softly chatting or cooking, he brings the whole film down to earth and expresses how beautifully human, and therefore sympathetic, all the characters in his universe are. *(Violence, profanity, adult situations.)*

p, Pepon Coròminas; d, Pedro Almodovar; w, Pedro Almodovar; ph, Paco Fermenia; ed, Pepe Salcedo; cos, Manuela Camacho

Comedy **(PR: C MPAA: NR)**

PEPI, LUCI, BOM Y OTRAS CHICAS DEL MONTON
(SEE: PEPI, LUCI, BOM AND OTHER GIRLS ON THE HEAP)

PET SEMATARY II ★½

100m Pet II Productions ~ Paramount c

Anthony Edwards *(Chase Matthews)*, Edward Furlong *(Geoff Matthews)*, Clancy Brown *(Gus)*, Jason McGuire *(Drew)*, Jared Rushton *(Clyde)*, Jim Peck *(Dr. Yolander)*, Lisa Waltz *(Amanda)*, Darlanne Fluegel *(Renee Matthews)*, David Ratajczak, Reid Binion, Robert Easton

With just about every one of Stephen King's novels now covered by a movie or TV version, it was only a matter of time before unauthorized sequels started hitting the screen. PET SEMATARY II—which was not only unendorsed, but actually trashed in advance by King himself—establishes an instant nadir for unofficial adaptations of the modern horror master.

The protagonist is young Geoff Matthews (Edward Furlong) who in the film's opening moments watches in horror as his divorced actress mother Renee (Darlanne Fluegel) is electrocuted in a freak movie-set mishap. Instead of suing for big bucks, Jeff's father Chase (Anthony Edwards) takes the boy up to his hometown of Ludlow, Maine, to bury his ex-wife and open a veterinary practice while trying to rebuild his relationship with his son. At his new school, Jeff gets on the bad side of the bullying Clyde (Jared Rushton), but makes friends with the overweight Drew (Jason McGuire), who himself has problems at home with his bullying sheriff father Gus (Clancy Brown). As it turns out, Gus was Chase's old rival for Renee's affections, so there's plenty of tension to go around, even before the titular locale starts to figure into the picture.

Pretty soon, Jeff has been told of the pet cemetery and the ancient Indian burial grounds behind the site, which apparently can revive dead bodies planted there. He and Drew soon get a chance to test its powers, when Gus shoots Drew's dog Zowie in a fit of anger. The two boys bury the dog in the Indian cemetery, and soon he's returned to life, almost good as new. But when the animal is brought into Chase's office for a checkup, and Chase sends some of its blood to a lab for testing, the doctor is startled when he's informed that the samples seem to have come from a dead animal.

Soon, Zowie escapes from Chase's office and attacks Gus as the latter is about to beat Drew. The sheriff is soon lying dead from a torn-out throat, Drew and Jeff look at each other, and . . . . Gus is soon revived too, though he comes back with a moldy appearance, a taste for rough sex with wife Amanda (Lisa Waltz) and lousy table manners. Despite all this, Jeff, who is still grieving over his dead mother, starts to have the inevitable ideas, which haunt him in nightmares. Gus's actions soon take a turn for the horrific: he contrives the deaths of Amanda and Drew in a traffic accident, kills Clyde and buries him in the Indian grounds, and unearths Renee's body, presenting it to Jeff for the obvious purpose.

Meanwhile, Chase, unnerved by the strange recent events, has gone to see Ludlow's former vet, Dr. Yolander (Jim Peck), who warns him that horrible forces are at work in the town. But Chase doesn't heed the warnings in time; soon he is being threatened by a power-drill-wielding Gus, and discovering that his ex-wife has been brought back from the dead by a smiling Jeff. At the same time, a similarly undead, ax-wielding Clyde is waiting in the wings, and the climax finds father and son fending off his murderous attack in the attic, as Renee looks on and the house starts to burn down around them.

For all its many flaws, the original PET SEMATARY at least maintained a fidelity to its source novel; this one not only ignores the rules set up by the first movie but manages to contradict its own internal and dramatic logic as well. Although it's repeatedly stated that you must "bury your own" in order for the burial ground's powers to work, Gus manages to inter and revive Clyde, a character he shares no relation to; and despite a story setup that seems to demand that Furlong's character be the one to dig up his mother for resuscitation, it is Gus who hands over the corpse to him (in a scene that's shot in the style of a dream sequence, but is presented as a literal event). And the growing, personal sense of horror that powered King's book gets completely lost in Richard Outten's muddled screenplay. It's nearly forty minutes before the first character (actually, the dog) is reanimated, at which point the film rushes to compensate, winding up with an everybody-into-the-cemetery free-for-all in which just about everybody gets killed and/or brought back to life, as if director Mary Lambert felt the more the scarier.

Actually, it's just disgusting, especially when it comes to the numerous grotesque scenes of animal mutilation. For a film ostensibly concerned with the revivification of animals, this one dotes unpleasantly on shot dogs, slaughtered and skinned rabbits and, in the movie's sickest scene, a bunch of massacred kittens discovered by two little girls. The cast looks better on paper than that of the first PET SEMATARY, but Furlong walks through the proceedings with one-note sullenness, Edwards is restricted to a lot of disbelieving looks and dialogue and the female characters are ciphers. Only Brown manages to stand above the material; even as a zombie, he displays more life than the supposedly living characters. Pray tell, where can we bury this so that it *won't* come back for a third installment? *(Excessive violence, profanity, adult situations, sexual situations.)*

p, Ralph S. Singleton; d, Mary Lambert; w, Richard Outten; ph, Russell Carpenter; ed, Tom Finan; prod d, Michelle Minch; art d, Karen Steward; set d, Susan Benjamin; cos, Carleen Rosado

Horror **(PR: O MPAA: R)**

PETER'S FRIENDS ★★

(U.K./U.S.) 100m Renaissance Films; Samuel Goldwyn Company ~ Samuel Goldwyn Company c

Hugh Laurie *(Roger)*, Imelda Staunton *(Mary)*, Stephen Fry *(Peter)*, Emma Thompson *(Maggie)*, Kenneth Branagh *(Andrew)*, Alphonsia Emmanuel *(Sarah)*, Rita Rudner *(Carol)*, Phyllida Law *(Vera)*, Alex Lowe *(Paul)*, Tony Slattery *(Brian)*, Richard Briers *(Peter's Father)*, Alex Scott *(Paul)*, Edward Jewesbury *(Peter's Solicitor)*, Hetta Charnley *(Woman at Airport)*, Annie Davies *(Brenda–Babysitter)*, Magdelena Buznea *(Catsitter)*, Chris Pickles *(Chauffer)*, Nicki Wright *(Miranda–Brian's Wife)*, Bill Parfitt *(Ben–Age 1)*

Directed by English theatrical *wunderkind* Kenneth Branagh (HENRY V, DEAD AGAIN), PETER'S FRIENDS is a kind of English version of Lawrence Kasdan's 1983 reunion drama, THE BIG CHILL. Though not as affecting as the Kasdan film, it's infinitely zanier.

A pseudo-somber voiceover sets the tone: "There are some friends you are wedded to because of love, trust . . . or simple embarrassment." Over the opening credits, we see Peter (Stephen Fry) and his motley crew of friends staging a ridiculous (and unappreciated) musical revue at a formal New Year's party. It's 1982, their last time together before graduating.

After ten years pass (shown via fleeting newsreel footage documenting the era), Peter impulsively decides to throw a New Year's reunion at his recently inherited country house. Everyone's excited at the prospect, though a few experience severe separation anxiety before making the trip. The gentle Maggie (Emma Thompson), a delightfully neurotic publisher of self-help books who can't help herself enough to find a husband, leaves photos of herself around the apartment so her cat won't get lonely. Roger (Hugh Laurie) has a hard time getting his wife Mary (Imelda Staunton) to leave at all; she's practically traumatized at the thought of leaving behind their infant son, despite the presence of a perfectly competent babysitter.

Carol (Rita Rudner), the only American in the group, is the glitzy star of a successful American TV sitcom written by her husband Andrew (Branagh), a once-promising playwright who has found fame and fortune in Hollywood. A health nut and a snob, Carol comes dressed for a weekend at the Waldorf and literally runs for the "best" room (Peter's). Her renown fails to awe her companions, some of whom haven't even heard of her show. There's no TV in the house, and housekeeper Vera (Phyllida Law, mother of Emma Thompson) refuses a bribe to cook special weight-watching meals for her. Wondering aloud, Carol asks, "Did you ever see 'Upstairs, Downstairs'?"

Andrew, a recovering alcoholic, feels he owes Carol everything for "saving his life" (they met at an AA meeting in LA), but is in fact far from happy with the relationship. He briefly falls off the wagon before facing up to his dilemma, and the couple separate before the weekend is over, with Carol leaving early after a movie offer from California.

Roger and Mary are accomplished jingle writers whose normally blissful marriage has been threatened by a family tragedy. Months before, one of their twins died accidentally. Mary realizes she's unjustly blamed Roger for their infant's death, and the two eventually turn the reunion into a second honeymoon.

Gorgeous single swinger Sarah (Alphonsia Emmanuel), who had slept with all the guys years back, brings along low-brow married lover Brian (Tony Slattery), her latest cheating heart. He loses his charm for Sarah when he offers to leave his wife for her, and the group makes her understand the no-win basis of her serial relationships with married men.

Sweet, frumpy Maggie has also arrived with a secret agenda: to seduce Peter into marriage. (Carol gives her a cosmetic makeover after telling her she "makes Mother Theresa look like a hooker.") Maggie appears clad only in a robe at Peter's door late at night, imploring him to "fill me with your little babies." The stunned bachelor admits he's bisexual, kindly adding that if he weren't, "you'd be at the top of my list, along with Michele Pfeiffer and River Phoenix." Peter's condition turns into the film's one sour note. The revelation that he has taken a blood test and been found HIV-positive gives the film a tacked-on, exploitative ending.

PETER'S FRIENDS, while relaxed and blithely spirited, never quite achieves what it sets out to. The problem isn't the acting or direction, but the screenplay, written by US comedienne Rudner and her husband Martin Bergman, who was a classmate of Thompson's at Cambridge in the early 80s. The script is little more than a collection of gags that favors throwaway one-liners over character development. Peter and his friends come very close to being caricatures, with Rudner's showbiz celeb the most egregious—a cartoonish victim of her own excess. Rudner is a clever, funny performer, but there's just too much of her at the expense of everyone else. (One advantage of writing your own dialogue is that you can give yourself the most, and the best, lines.)

PETER'S FRIENDS tries to be a blend of Ealing comedy, Sturges and Capra, spiked with wisecracks trendy enough to satisfy the short attention span of a nightclub audience. Despite an enormously gifted cast, the result is closer to an extended segment of "Saturday Night Live" than to THE BIG CHILL or John Sayles's THE RETURN OF THE SECAUCUS SEVEN.

Director Branagh shows a flair for comedy and, except when Rudner is overdoing her thing, PETER'S FRIENDS has a light-hearted touch. The lively pace is helped by several rock and pop tunes from the time of Peter's and his friends' college days. Above all else, the film allows some of Britain's best young dramatic actors the chance to flex their funnybones. *(Profanity, nudity.)*

p, Kenneth Branagh; d, Kenneth Branagh; w, Rita Rudner, Martin Bergman; ph, Roger Lanser; ed, Andrew Marcus; m, Jacques Offenbach; prod d, Tim Harvey; cos, Susan Coates, Stephanie Collie

Comedy **(PR: C MPAA: NR)**

PHANTOM OF THE RITZ ★½

89m Hancock Park Productions Inc. ~ Prism Entertainment c

Peter Bergman *(Ed Blake)*, Deborah Van Valkenburg *(Nancy)*, Cindy Vincino *(Sally)*, Joshua Sussman *(The Phantom)*, Russell

Curry *(Marcus)*, Steve Geng *(Detective Lassarde)*, Frank Tranchina *(Dutch)*, The Coasters *(Themselves)*

Billed as a horror film but more of a backstage comedy, PHANTOM OF THE RITZ proves slightly more successful at the latter than at the former. In any case, it needed a little more ritz and a *lot* more Phantom.

The story opens in 1958, when a drag-racing accident causes the teenaged brother of one of the participants to be horribly burned. He ends up haunting the local Ritz movie theater, remaining even after the place has closed down. In the present day, the building, now fallen into grave disrepair, is bought by Ed Blake (Peter Bergman of the Firesign Theater), who hopes to renovate it and turn it into a 1950s rock 'n' roll club as therapy for his midlife crisis. With the help of his girlfriend, Nancy (Deborah Van Valkenburg), he sets about getting the place in shape, taking on the caustic Sally (Cindy Vincino) as his secretary and eloquent Black muscleman Marcus (Russell Curry) as his head of security. Meanwhile, detective Lassarde (Steve Geng) has been investigating the dismemberment deaths of bums in the area, little knowing that the Ritz's unseen inhabitant (Joshua Sussman) is behind them. He's upset at the new invaders on his turf, and soon the violence is spreading inside: first Dutch (Frank Tranchina), one of the workers, is murdered, and then Sally is kidnapped by the hulking fiend.

Ed is so caught up in his work on the Ritz that he begins to neglect Nancy, who responds by hanging out with an Elvis impersonator, one of many awful acts that Ed has been auditioning for the theater's opening night. They are later reconciled, however, and the opening is a smash, though Ed is later notified by Lassarde that two teenagers vanished from the vicinity of the theater (they were, in fact, killed by the Phantom). The following night marks an appearance by the Coasters (who sing their old hit "Yakkity Yak"), but in the midst of the festivities, Nancy is kidnapped by the Phantom, who spirits her to his underground lair. There, he reveals that he is also holding Sally, and that steroids he took while recovering from his burns have resulted in his monstrous state. Ed, Lassarde, Marcus and the security cops manage to find the secret room, and after a violent struggle, Nancy and Sally are saved, the place catches fire and the Phantom is left to die in the flames.

PHANTOM OF THE RITZ is a disappointment both in general and given the fact that its premise could have been worked into a scary and lively film. Brian De Palma, in fact, proved in PHANTOM OF THE PARADISE that Gaston Leroux's Phantom of the Opera could be transplanted into the world of rock 'n' roll with memorable results. But far too much of this film has nothing to do with either the horror of its particular Phantom or the 50s rock that its protagonist wants to provide a venue for. Instead, the increasingly tiresome screenplay focuses on all the problems and petty personal disputes surrounding the refurbishing of the Ritz, with intermittent laughs but no real comic momentum. By the time the Phantom makes his presence known in the climactic scenes, he almost seems to have wandered in from another movie.

The cast seems capable, but they're given little to do, with the exception of Russell Curry as the bodybuilder who also possesses an Ivy League vocabulary. He has the movie's best line, as he explains to Ed that he's gotten so educated just to startle people who think there's nothing to him but muscles: "How many people do you know who can benchpress 410 and know 30 English words beginning with 'x'?" There's an early suggestion that the filmmakers are savvy about B flicks when Ed notes that Nancy's video library contains "Klaus Kinski bloopers," but when her collection of awful movies also turns out to include director Allen Plone's previous film NIGHT SCREAMS, it should be taken as a warning. *(Violence, profanity.)*

p, Carol Marcus-Plone; d, Allen Plone; w, Allen Plone, Tom Dempsey, (from the novel *The Phantom of the Opera* by Gaston Leroux); ph, Ron Diamond; m, John Madara, Dave White, Wendy Frazier; set d, Anthony Ricardi; cos, Hope Hanafin

Horror/Comedy **(PR: O MPAA: R)**

PICTURES FROM A REVOLUTION ★★½

93m GMR Films ~ Kino Home Video c

Susan Meiselas, a photographer whose haunting pictures from Nicaragua during the struggle against Somoza's dictatorship received wide publication, returns to that beleaguered Central American country to retrace her steps and to interview some of the people she photographed ten years ago.

As she drives through the sun-drenched dusty villages of rural Nicaragua, Meiselas contrasts this intersection or that building site with a more dramatic moment when it served as the background to Sandinista battles with Somoza's National Guard. (Anastasio Somoza Garcia, head of the Nicaraguan National Guard, had Augusto Cesar Sandino—an insurgent fighting the continued presence of US occupation forces in Nicaragua—assassinated in 1934 and took over the presidency in 1937. Somoza and his sons Luis and Anastasio Somoza Debayle controlled the country until 1979.) Several veterans of those battles talk to Meiselas of their great hopes and current sadness, of living in an exhausted country with very little hope for a better life. One man talks of all the foreign economic pressures as an obstacle to the better living conditions he had fought for, while several women simply see the "time of the triumph" over Somoza as a flitting particle of hope in lives of grinding poverty.

One local hero of that time, however, asserts that the revolution had one overwhelming achievement—that they no longer have to fear the National Guard whose atrocities provoked the Sandinista revolution and whose victims were often literally dumped into the "valley of death" Meiselas had documented, replete with limp, tortured torsos. Now there's a small stone crucifix as a memorial to those nameless martyrs. Meiselas also photographed the National Guard troops, sometimes as the broken casualties of a street fight with the guerrillas, or as their marshaled prisoners. She interviews two former members of the National Guard, one who continued fighting as part of the Contras and lost his right hand. (Between 1981 and 1990 the US actively, if covertly, supported Contra rebels fighting the Sandinista regime.) Both recall their dead comrades and the maimed former lieutenant regrets having been simply a pawn of US interests as he assumes the Sandinistas must regret having played their small part in Soviet world politics.

Intellectually, the weakest part of Meiselas's film is the timidity with which she approaches the question of whether the Sandinista leadership betrayed their revolution, or made serious mistakes, or were simply unable to cope with external pressures and internal stresses. The surviving brother of three who supported the Ortega regime claims he had to leave for Canada, where he now works in an auto plant, but is not specific about details. The two officials interviewed are equally hazy about the successes of their revolution, talking instead about the imagery of Central America in foreign eyes. That discussion leads Meiselas to discover that many of the revolutionary wall murals have been painted over since Chamorro's electoral victory over Ortega. One of these popular images, an armed guerrilla preparing to hurl a Molotov cocktail, was drawn from one of Meiselas's photographs, and she muses on the transformation of her real picture into a less distinct and simpler image and symbol. Honestly, she does note how the revolution in Nicaragua was for her "the luxury of a dream" while for thousands of others it had a harder, concrete form.

The minor French novelist, Jules Valles, referred to the legacy of the Paris Commune as a "great confederation of sadness." PICTURES FROM A REVOLUTION, co-directed by Richard P. Rogers and Alfred Guzzetti, tries to captures this sense of pathos, whether in the frustrated ambition of the Toronto auto worker who had dreamed of becoming an engineer, or the unknown fate of a seven-year-old boy whose mother recalls his pride at being chosen for a scholarship in Cuba prior to training in the former Soviet Union. Unfortunately, the juxtaposition of her old photographs and current interviews seems pedestrian and predictable. Perhaps the use of a professional narrator and more imaginative scoring would have added the needed dimension. *(Violence, nudity.)*

p, Susan Meiselas, Richard P. Rogers, Alfred Guzzetti; d, Susan Meiselas, Richard P. Rogers, Alfred Guzzetti; ph, Richard P. Rogers; m, William Eldridge

Documentary/Political/War (PR: C MPAA: NR)

PLAY MURDER FOR ME ★★

80m Concorde ~ New Horizons Home Video c

Jack Wagner *(Paul Slater)*, Tracy Scoggins *(Tricia Merritt)*, William Burns *(Fred Merritt)*, Rodolfo Ranni *(Gregorius)*, Gerardo Romano *(Molina)*, Ivory Ocean *(Lou Venable)*

Many erotic thrillers these days rely on saxophones on the soundtrack to suggest primal, orgasmic feelings. Too often, the sultry sounds serve up a climax more convincing than the groping and spasmodic breathing of the lovers onscreen. Although tawdry shockers like PLAY MURDER FOR ME may herald a new sub-genre of "Unsafe Sex" melodramas, what transpires onscreen barely sizzles.

Of all the gin joints in the world, why did Tricia Merritt (Tracy Scoggins) have to walk into the blues bar featuring her down-on-his-luck old flame Paul Slater (Jack Wagner)? Having been burned by the smoldering vixen before, Paul is wary about accepting her husband Fred's (William Burns) invitation to play at an upcoming soiree. When Fred is paralyzed by gunshots inflicted by a business rival, Tricia soon tires of his self-pity and his sporadically successful attempts to rape her. As she cunningly vamps Paul back into an affair, it becomes apparent that the assault on Tricia's husband wasn't strictly a result of crime-lord turf wars.

As she models bruises given her by her unhinged mate, Tricia plays on her new lover's sympathies. Although she drives Paul wild enough to murder her spouse, Fred hands Paul the address of her latest love nest before he expires. Wrapped in the embrace of Fred's former business partner Molina (Gerardo Romano), Tricia is temporarily nonplussed when a hit man, Krieger (Francisco Cocuzza), remains loyal to her husband and kills Molina. While she manages to remove the Krieger obstacle, Tricia has less luck with Paul who's finally seen the light and who knifes Tricia during a final embrace before she can figure out a way to kill him first.

Ideally, as in the classics of the post-WWII film noir heyday, the melodrama of betrayal offers a complex network of self-destructive characters who succumb to their own delusions. In this lackluster effort, all the crimeworld characters seem to be visiting from another film; characters aren't satisfactorily intertwined. Fall guy Paul doesn't really connect with Tricia's husband—they don't fence with each other; there's no subtext. All we have is a femme fatale, a chump and an expendable husband stuck in a predictable suspense plot which offers no sharp reflections on human behavior and no dark sense of cynicism.

As for the actors, Jack Wagner represents a case of sending a boy to do a man's job; he only succeeds in playing one note—the musician's burned out demeanor. While marginally better, Scoggins has the curvature but not the subtle sexuality to dupe a man into risking his life. On the smoulder scale, the Scoggins-Wagner love scenes barely register. Without the erotic underpinning (despite the efforts of the saxophonist on the soundtrack) and without the sense that the characters can escape neither each other nor their harsh fates, PLAY MURDER FOR ME founders on the rocks of all those gangland double-crosses from out of left field. *(Violence, sexual situations, adult situations.)*

p, Roger Corman; d, Hector Olivera; w, J.P. Feinman

Erotic/Thriller (PR: O MPAA: R)

PLAY NICE ★★½

89m Smart Egg Pictures ~ Vidmark Entertainment c

Robey *(Jill/Rapunzel)*, Ed O'Ross *(Jack "Mouth" Penucci)*, Michael Zand *(Dennis Crichnore)*, Bruce McGill *(Capt Foxx)*, Ann Dusenberry *(Pam Crichnore)*, Scott Burkholder *(Harold Wiesen)*, Amy Steel *(Nancy)*, Sandy Faison *(Mrs. Holland)*, Mimi Maynard *(Mrs. Kessler)*, Hector Mercado *(Jay)*, Angel Ashley *(Susan Wright)*, Ron Canada *(Coroner)*

Pump up your average TV cop show with foul language and sardonic wit and some not-ready-for-prime-time sleaze, and you approximate the experience of viewing PLAY NICE. Although the storyline is stuffed with enough red herrings to stock a cannery for years, and the acting is sometimes on a level with "Star Search," this direct-to-video release boasts a no-nonsense precinct mentality and flashes of caustic black humor.

The tabloids have a field day as Rapunzel, a blonde-wigged babe, goes on a murder spree that gives coitus interruptus a whole new meaning. Burnt out by a recent divorce and separation from his daughter, and bugged by constant inquiries from internal affairs, Jack "Mouth" Penucci (Ed O'Ross) is the kind of shoot-from-the-hip lawman whose partners always request transfers. Saddled with a rookie, Dennis Crichnore (Michael Zand), Penucci pieces together a crime profile while staying one step ahead of a sleazy reporter, Harold Wiesen (Scott Burkholder), who is being fed official information from someone on the inside. During his investigation, Penucci springs back to life when he falls for obsequious Jill (Robey) who works for the Bureau of Social Services.

As the killings continue, two facts stand out: the murdered men are fathers with a history of sexually abusing their daughters and mousy Jill is turning into a tigress. By the time reporter Wiesen is silenced, Penucci realizes that Jill has assumed someone else's identity in order to have access to closed files and to facilitate her vigilante tactics. Abused as a child, this Rapunzel relives her traumas with an unhappy ending for her "daddy" of the evening. Arriving at the scene of her latest fatal incest tableau, Penucci and Crichmore tail her to a hotel basement where she knocks Jack unconscious and blasts Crichmore several times before Penucci awakens and stops Rapunzel's one-woman incest clean-up campaign.

If only PLAY NICE offered a few more viable murderess candidates and hadn't padded out its running time with reiterative exposition, this might have been a small-scale police classic. Unfortunately, the filmmakers' ambitions aren't matched by their abilities.

While the Jack-and-Jill psycho-sexual battle is meant to reflect somehow upon the killer's crime of passion, the sense of dangerous passion and out-of-control emotions is more theoretical than palpable in this film. Too much energy goes into teasing the audience with Jill's probable guilt; it is too obvious and too early when the viewer catches on to her little brown wren charade. The screenwriters' sleight-of-hand is clumsy on this key point. And in the film's early scenes, awkward staging is quite evident. Director Teri Treas seems to gain confidence as the film goes along. In fact, the crescendo of violence in the hotel basement at the film's climax is a real nail-biter.

As Rapunzel, the actress Robey lets her hair down nicely but doesn't shade her Plain Jane characterization effectively; she makes her character's hidden agenda apparent from the outset. A character actor in the Leo Rossi mold, Ed O'Ross is persuasive as the cop who's a little unhinged by passion himself.

Given the screenplay's dexterity in working in the incest motivation, one wishes it had a firmer grasp on the mechanics of suspense. For all its limitations, PLAY NICE offers a good supply of jolts and surprises. Compelling throughout, it will satisfy armchair detectives even if they work out the killer's identity rather quickly. In this instance the unraveling of the motives is as fascinating as whodunit. *(Violence, sexual situations.)*

p, Luigi Cingolani, Don Daniel; d, Teri Treas; w, Michael Zand, Chuck McCollum, (from the story by Zand, McCollum and Teri Treas)

Thriller/Crime **(PR: O MPAA: R)**

PLAYBOYS, THE ★★½

(U.S./Ireland) 110m Green Umbrella Films; Samuel Goldwyn Company ~ Samuel Goldwyn Company c

Albert Finney *(Constable Hegarty)*, Aidan Quinn *(Tom Casey)*, Robin Wright *(Tara Maguire)*, Milo O'Shea *(Freddie)*, Alan Devlin *(Malone)*, Niamh Cusack *(Brigid)*, Ian McElhinney *(Cassidy)*, Stella McCusker *(Rachel)*, Niall Buggy *(Denzil)*, Anna Livia Ryan *(Vonnie)*, Adrian Dunbar *(Mick)*, Lorcan Cranitch *(Ryan/John Joe)*, Aine NiMhuiri *(Mrs. Smith)*, Doreen Hepburn *(Nualla Ryan)*, Kilian McKenna *(Sean)*, Michele Forbes *(Maggie Rudden)*, P.J. Brady *(McMahon)*, Tony Rohr *(Kelly)*, Niall O'Brien *(Police Superintendent)*, Pat Laffan *(Duffy)*, Brian O'Leary *(Timmy)*, Stephen Holland *(Richie)*, Jimmy Keogh *(Liam)*, Shane Connaughton *(Customs Officer)*, Peter Morris *(Tara's Baby)*, James Morris *(Tara's Baby)*

Everybody has a story, which is the main problem with THE PLAYBOYS, an overstuffed if engaging drama set and shot in Ireland.

The closest the film comes to a central character, Tara Maguire (Robin Wright) gives birth as the movie begins. She's unmarried, which would be no big deal today. However, since this is a small town just south of the Northern Irish border during the 1950s, and she won't name the baby's father, it is a *very* big deal at the time. The town pastor has more influence over the people than even the mayor or the constable. And the pastor wants Tara to be married. The pastor notwithstanding, there are few who would cross Hegarty (Albert Finney), the town's big, gruff cop with a sullen, violent streak, who also happens to be in love with Tara and wants to marry her. Tara wants nothing to do with him and wants none of the pastor's scolding her from the pulpit, which he does, leading her to become an outcast of the town's polite society.

Tara also wants nothing to do with Tom Casey (Aidan Quinn), the handsome, genial lead player of a roving theatrical group, the Playboys. He wants plenty to do with her, however, which puts him at odds with Hegarty. It also puts him at odds with fate: Tara's last serious suitor committed suicide. And Hegarty's not looking too well himself. A recovering alcoholic, he's feeling pressure from his superiors for not cracking down on smuggling to and from Northern Ireland. It's not a task he warms to, since Tara happens to be one of the smugglers, whose latest shipment contains a very special package for an IRA partisan travelling incognito with the Playboys. The truth about Tara's baby almost sends Tom packing while the truth about Tom almost gets Tara to send him packing. Meanwhile Hegarty, realizing he has no hope with Tara, begins drinking again while mulling over some less-than-legal ways to get Tom out of the way.

Along with co-screenwriter Kerry Crabbe, Shane Connaughton (MY LEFT FOOT) wrote THE PLAYBOYS as a loving tribute to his own childhood in a similar town, where his father was indeed the constable. Not surprisingly, it aspires to be a rich, sweeping epic of yearning and fulfillment, hope and despair. The story, however, never quite finds a footing or focus, involving itself with too many crosscurrents and sub-plots within the town and within the troupe itself, lorded over by seasoned thespian and irrepressible schemer Freddie (Milo O'Shea). Though the writing is rich, sharp and detailed, there's nothing really tying it all together.

Some of the performances are terrific, though the leads are questionable. As demonstrated elsewhere, Quinn is engaging enough, but he still lacks star presence, as does Wright, who is radiantly beautiful but never quite convincing as a woman of such intense sexual allure that she drives men, literally, to drink and suicide. The real joys here are the supporting cast, particularly Finney, who has star presence to burn, and O'Shea, with whose theatrical troupe anyone would want to run away in a minute. They, along with Connaughton and Crabbe's sheer virtuosity as writers, make THE PLAYBOYS more watchable than most of what passes for screen entertainment. *(Adult situations.)*

p, William P. Cartlidge, Simon Perry; d, Gillies MacKinnon; w, Shane Connaughton, Kerry Crabbe; ph, Jack Conroy; ed, Humphrey Dixon; m, Jean-Claude Petit; prod d, Andy Harris; art d, Arden Gantly; cos, Consolata Boyle

Romance/Drama **(PR: C MPAA: PG-13)**

PLAYER, THE ★★★★

123m Avenue Entertainment; Spelling Entertainment ~ Fine Line Features c

Tim Robbins *(Griffin Mill)*, Greta Scacchi *(June Gudmundsdottir)*, Fred Ward *(Walter Stuckel)*, Whoopi Goldberg *(Detective Avery)*, Peter Gallagher *(Larry Levy)*, Brion James *(Joel Levison)*, Cynthia Stevenson *(Bonnie Sherow)*, Vincent D'Onofrio *(David Kahane)*, Dean Stockwell *(Andy Civella)*, Richard E. Grant *(Tom Oakley)*, Sydney Pollack *(Dick Mellen)*, Lyle Lovett *(Detective DeLongpre)*, Dina Merrill *(Celia)*, Angela Hall *(Jan)*, Leah Ayres *(Sandy)*, Paul Hewitt *(Jimmy Chase)*, Randall Batinkoff *(Reg Goldman)*, Jeremy Piven *(Steve Reeves)*, Gina Gershon *(Whitney Gersh)*, Frank Barhydt *(Frank Murphy)*, Mike E. Kaplan *(Marty Grossman)*, Kevin Scannell *(Gar Girard)*, Margery Bond *(Witness)*, Susan Emshwiller *(Detective Broom)*, Brian Brophy *(Phil)*, Michael Tolkin *(Eric Schecter)*, Stephen Tolkin *(Carl Schecter)*, Natalie Strong *(Natalie)*, Pete Koch *(Walter)*, Pamela Bowen *(Trixie)*, Jeff Weston *(Rocco)*, Steve Allen, Richard Anderson, Rene Auberjonois, Harry Belafonte, Shari Belafonte, Karen Black, Michael Bowen, Gary Busey, Robert Carradine, Charles Champlin, Cher, James Coburn, Cathy Lee Crosby, John Cusack, Brad Davis, Paul Dooley, Thereza Ellis, Peter Falk, Felicia Farr, Kasia Figura, Louise Fletcher, Dennis Franz, Teri Garr, Leeza Gibbons, Scott Glenn, Jeff Goldblum, Elliott Gould, Joel Grey, David Alan Grier, Buck Henry, Anjelica Huston, Kathy Ireland, Steve James, Maxine John-James, Sally Kellerman, Sally Kirkland, Jack Lemmon, Marlee Matlin, Andie MacDowell,

Malcolm McDowell, Jayne Meadows, Martin Mull, Jennifer Nash, Nicky Nolte, Alexandra Powers, Bert Remsen, Guy Remsen, Patricia Resnick, Burt Reynolds, Jack Riley, Julia Roberts, Mimi Rogers, Annie Ross, Alan Rudolph, Jill St. John, Susan Sarandon, Adam Simon, Rod Steiger, Joan Tewkesbury, Brian Tochi, Lily Tomlin, Robert Wagner, Ray Walston, Bruce Willis, Marvin Young

After the scathingly satirical eye he trained on NASHVILLE, and the righteous rage he expressed on behalf of an artist wronged in VINCENT AND THEO, Robert Altman brings a surprisingly benign gaze to bear on the world he knows and loves/hates best in THE PLAYER. A funny, fast-moving adaptation of Michael Tolkin's satirical novel about a Hollywood executive, THE PLAYER underscores its lethally accurate observations with more regret and sadness than genuine scorn.

Griffin Mill (Tim Robbins) is under attack on two fronts. In danger of being run out of his job by aggressive, up-and-coming rival Larry Levy (Peter Gallagher), he has also begun to receive a series of threatening postcards at the studio where he works. (We never learn the name of the studio, only its idiotic motto: "Movies . . . now more than ever.") Tending to the more potentially lethal problem first, Mill settles on spurned screenwriter David Kahane (Vincent D'Onofrio) as the prime suspect behind the postcards. One evening, after learning Kahane's whereabouts from the writer's beautiful live-in girlfriend, painter June Gudmundsdottir (Greta Scacchi), Mill travels out to a Pasadena movie theater to confront him. Mill plans to placate Kahane by purchasing his screenplay. Kahane, however, taunts Mill about the executive's professional problems, and Mill impulsively kills him in a parking lot.

Despite the dogged efforts of laid-back Pasadena detectives Avery and DeLongpre (Whoopi Goldberg and Lyle Lovett), Mill gets off scot-free. (The sole witness picks DeLongpre, rather than Mill, from a police lineup.) Piling irony upon irony, the postcards continue to arrive—Kahane was not the culprit.

Meanwhile, Mill gets a major professional boost thanks to a series of ironic reversals. He had schemed to oust Levy by persuading him to take on a must-fail project devoid of star talent. But the project eventually metamorphoses into a smash Bruce Willis-Julia Roberts vehicle, earning kudos for Levy *and* boosting Mill to head of the studio. The only loser here is Mill's former assistant-girlfriend, Bonnie Sherow (Cynthia Stevenson), who loses Mill to Gudmundsdottir and is fired by Levy for protesting his crass commercialism. The conclusion finds Mill taking a car-phone call from the presumed author of the postcards, now pitching a screenplay idea for a film which sounds a lot like THE PLAYER . . . .

Altman begins his film with a stylistic homage to the glory days of Hollywood—a bravura single-shot sequence that systematically introduces all the major characters and plot elements, recalling Orson Welles's celebrated opening to TOUCH OF EVIL. In case we miss the point, Altman includes a character in the sequence mourning the loss of filmmakers of Welles's calibre. The twist—which is about as bitter as THE PLAYER ever gets—is that these lines are spoken, not by a "creative executive," but by the head of studio security, Walter Stuckel (Fred Ward).

Altman wants the audience to know what it has lost, not only with his opening sequence but with repeated references to classic films via posters hung on office walls. These serve both to point up the mediocrity and inanity of the films currently being made, and as a wry commentary on various plot developments. Again, Altman is poking gentle fun rather than venting genuine ire.

The cast is uniformly wonderful. Robbins gives the most frighteningly bolted-down performance by a leading man since Harrison Ford's hideously repressed district attorney in PRESUMED INNOCENT. Scacchi (WHITE MISCHIEF, PRESUMED INNOCENT) has never been better cast than as the "ice queen" painter, and Goldberg has never been funnier. Ward proves he is becoming one of Hollywood's top character actors with a great turn in the style of the A STAR IS BORN-era Jack Carson. Dean Stockwell and Richard E. Grant are hilarious as the creative powers behind the dreadful project Mill foists onto Levy.

The list goes on, to Roberts and Willis, along with Lily Tomlin and Scott Glenn, as the stars of the films within the film; Buck Henry, writer of the original GRADUATE, seen here pitching a hilariously ludicrous sequel; Burt Reynolds bitching about producers over lunch; and 50 or so other celebrities seen in cameos that dot a film Altman reportedly brought in on an amazing $8 million budget. The film can justly be described as an embarrassment of riches, making it only too playeresque that it was initially rejected by every major studio in town. *(Violence, profanity, adult situations.)*

p, David Brown, Michael Tolkin, Nick Wechsler; d, Robert Altman; w, Michael Tolkin, (from his novel); ph, Jean Lepine; ed, Geraldine Peroni, Maysie Hoy; m, Thomas Newman; prod d, Stephen Altman; art d, Jerry Fleming; set d, Susan Emshwiller; cos, Alexander Julian

AAN Director: Robert Altman; *AAN Best Adapted Screenplay:* Michael Tolkin; *AAN Editing:* Geraldine Peroni

Comedy/Mystery **(PR: C MPAA: R)**

POISON IVY ★★½

100m MG Entertainment; New Line ~ New Line Cinema c

Sara Gilbert *(Sylvie Cooper)*, Drew Barrymore *(Ivy)*, Tom Skerritt *(Darryl Cooper)*, Cheryl Ladd *(Georgie Cooper)*, Alan Stock *(Bob)*, Jeanne Sakata *(Isabelle)*, E.J. Moore *(Kid)*, J.B. Quon *(Another Kid)*, Leonardo Dicaprio *(1st Guy)*, Michael Goldner *(Man in Car)*, Charley Hayward *(Tiny)*, Tim Winters *(Old Man)*, Billy Charles Kane *(James)*, Tony Ervolina *(Man on Screen)*, Mary Gordon Murray *(M.D.)*, Julie Jay *(Nurse Behind Desk)*, Charla Sampsel *(Orderly)*, Angel Broadhurst *(Death Rocker)*, Randall Caldwell *(Truck Driver)*, Tom Ruben *(Roofer)*, Lisa Passero *(Lisa)*, Lawrence Levy *(Jeff)*, Sandy Roth Ruben *(Estelle)*, Warren Burton *(Max)*

POISON IVY marks the entry of yet another pair of Roger Corman graduates—writer/director Katt Shea Ruben and her co-writer/producer/former husband Andy—into the mainstream. Ruben's work, which includes STRIPPED TO KILL, DANCE OF THE DAMNED and STREETS, has always emphasized mood and characterization over cheap thrills, and her new film is no exception.

The ad campaign, suggesting that Ivy (Drew Barrymore) covets her best friend's perfect life, is rather misleading; indeed, it is the fact that young Sylvie Cooper (Sara Gilbert) covets Ivy's freedom that leads them to connect. Sylvie's father Darryl (Tom Skerritt) is distant and neglectful, both of Sylvie and his wife Georgie (Cheryl Ladd), who is bedridden with emphysema. So rebellious Sylvie takes up with free spirit Ivy, who at first appears to be the only person she can trust. Soon, Ivy has insinuated herself into the Cooper family, spending all her time with Sylvie and also attracting the attention of Darryl. When Ivy contrives to take Sylvie's place helping Darryl host a cocktail party at his house, he ultimately succumbs to her charms, unable to resist the seduction even when Georgie discovers them in a clinch.

The unbalanced Ivy has been scheming to take Georgie's place—figuratively in Sylvie's life, literally in Darryl's—and completes her goal by causing Georgie to fall to her death from an upstairs window. When Ivy later takes Sylvie for a drive in Georgie's prized old Corvette, Sylvie begins to realize Ivy's responsibility in the death, and Ivy then crashes the car, leaving an unconscious Sylvie to appear responsible. After Darryl comes to visit her in the hospital and refuses to accept her claims about Ivy's true nature, Sylvie sneaks home to discover Ivy and her father making love. But Darryl is ultimately convinced of the truth, and after confronting Sylvie in Georgie's room, Ivy suffers the same fatal plunge from the window.

Although it's not as viscerally explicit as the subject matter promises, POISON IVY succeeds by creating psychologically compelling characters and situations that are more unnerving than out-and-out shocking. Not the least of its achievements was providing a perfect role to allow Drew Barrymore to make her transition into mature, adult roles; even though her title character is a teenager, she's more self-aware and cunning than anyone else in the film. Although she never has an outright nude scene, she manages to project a seductive, erotic aura that works to the story's advantage.

The potential for the film to lapse into a cliched teenage version of HAND THAT ROCKS THE CRADLE is skillfully avoided by the Rubens, who give all of their characters identifiable flaws and needs that Ivy can exploit. When it becomes clear that Ivy's up to no good, Ruben doesn't overplay her villainy, preferring to make her exploits more disturbing than jump-out-and-scare-you frightening. As a result, POISON IVY doesn't exactly keep one at the edge of one's seat throughout, but it certainly holds the interest.

Barrymore's effectively played combination of convincing pathology and precocious sexuality helps carry the film, and Gilbert is equally fine as the confused, conflicted Sylvie. Skerritt and Ladd do well enough in the secondary adult roles, but the most valuable support is provided by cinematographer Phedon Papamichael. A holdover from Ruben's Corman days, Papamichael drenches POISON IVY with atmosphere without resorting to conventional thriller lighting schemes. His work is striking but never obvious, a quality shared by most of the rest of the film.

Right down to Sylvie's final voiceover, which seems to be referring to one character but may actually be talking about another, POISON IVY strikes a pleasing balance between emotion and ambiguity. *(Violence, sexual situations, nudity.)*

p, Katt Shea Ruben, Andy Ruben; d, Katt Shea Ruben; w, Katt Shea Ruben, Andy Ruben, (from the story by Melissa Goddard and Peter Morgan); ph, Phedon Papamichael; ed, Gina Mittleman; m, Aaron Davies; prod d, Virginia Lee; art d, Hayden Yates; set d, Muchele Munoz; cos, Ellen Gross

Thriller/Drama **(PR: O MPAA: R)**

POPE MUST DIE!, THE
(SEE: POPE MUST DIET!, THE)

POPE MUST DIET!, THE ★½
(U.K.) 97m Palace Pictures; Miramax; Michael White Productions ~ Miramax c
(GB: POPE MUST DIE!, THE)

Robbie Coltrane *(Pope)*, Beverly D'Angelo *(Veronica Dante)*, Herbert Lom *(Vittorio Corelli)*, Alex Rocco *(Cardinal Rocco)*, Paul Bartel *(Monsignor Vitchie)*, Balthazar Getty *(Joe Don Dante)*, William Hootkins *(Cardinal Verucci)*, Robert Stephens *(Carmelengo)*, Annette Crosbie *(Mother Superior)*, Steve O'Donnell *(Rico)*, John Sessions *(Dino)*, Salvatore Cascio *(Paulo)*, Peter Richardson *(Bish)*, Khedija Sassi *(Luccia)*, Adrian Edmonson *(Rookie)*

Originally titled THE POPE MUST DIE! but re-titled before release due to protests from religious groups, THE POPE MUST DIET! is a crackpot amalgam of KING RALPH and THE GODFATHER PART III.

Following the death of the Pope, the corrupt Monsignor Vitchie (Paul Bartel) and Cardinal Rocco (Alex Rocco) attempt to install as his successor a shill for mob boss and international arms dealer Vittorio Corelli (Herbert Lom). But, due to a clerical error, country priest Guiseppe Albinizi (Robbie Coltrane)—a reluctant man of god who's more at home playing rock 'n' roll or fixing cars—is named as pope instead. Corelli is livid, but Cardinal Rocco assures him that he will be able to control Albinizi. Before long, however, the new pope uncovers financial chicanery at the Vatican Bank and cashiers Rocco. Conspiring with Vitchie to find a way of discrediting Albinizi, Rocco bugs the pope's bedroom and discovers that before he became a priest, Albinizi was involved with an American woman, Veronica Dante (Beverly D'Angelo). They had a son who is now a rock star and the lover of Corelli's young daughter.

Albinizi has been unaware of his son's existence until Veronica appears in the papal bedroom to inform him that the youth is now dying in a hospital—a victim of the wrath of Corelli, who, angered at the boy's relationship with his daughter, had killers plant a bomb under the rock star's trailer. During the explosion, his daughter was killed, further intensifying Corelli's wrath.

When the truth about Albinizi's past life is revealed, he is forced to resign as pope. When his son dies, however, a furious Albinizi interrupts the ceremony at which the new pope—Corelli—is being installed, and exposes him to the crowd as a gangster and arms dealer. Corelli snaps, shouting and wildly shooting his gun. A piece of the Sistine Chapel ceiling on which the head of God is painted is dislodged and falls on Corelli, killing him. Albinizi marries Veronica and his beautiful young papal attendant is crowned as the first female Pope.

THE POPE MUST DIET! begins at a feverish satirical pitch that soon degenerates into stupidity. It would have played much better as a parody of THE GODFATHER PART III—at least the assorted shootings, bombings and murders would have seemed a little more in context. As a genial comic hero, Robbie Coltrane's Father Albinizi is at odds with the tone of the rest of the film. Neither can he muster the joyful comic innocence of John Goodman in KING RALPH. Only veteran screen actor Herbert Lom, playing the film's most unsavory character, rises to the heights of operatic buffonery. In his moment of epiphany, shooting recklessly into the Sistine Chapel ceiling and roaring, "No more Mr. Nice Pope—back to the good old days," Lom achieves a comic apocalypse in an entirely different class from this dim-witted, mean-spirited film. *(Violence, profanity, nudity.)*

p, Stephen Woolley; d, Peter Richardson; w, Peter Richardson, Pete Richens; ph, Frank Gell; ed, Katherine Wenning; m, Jeff Beck, Anne Dudley; prod d, John Ebden; cos, Sandy Powell

Comedy **(PR: O MPAA: R)**

POUR SACHA ★★
(France) 114m Alexandre Films ~ MK2 Productions USA c

Sophie Marceau *(Laura)*, Richard Berry *(Sacha)*, Fabien Orcier *(Paul)*, Niels Dubost *(Simon)*, Frederic Quiring *(Michel)*, Gerard Darmon *(David Malka)*, Emmanuelle Riva *(Madame Malka)*, Shlomit Cohen *(Myriam)*, Jean-Claude DeGoros *(Dan Chemtov)*, Yael Abecassis *(Judith)*, Amit Goret *(Steve)*, Nissam Dau *(The*

Maskir), Ayelet Zorer *(Shoshana)*, Erza Kafri *(The Colonel)*, Amit Doron *(Salamon)*, Tali Atzmon *(Teacher)*

Co-produced by his protege, acclaimed director Diane Kurys (PEPPERMINT SODA, ENTRE NOUS, C'EST LA VIE), Alexandre Arcady's semi-autobiographical POUR SACHA is a bland if intermittently interesting drama.

Sacha (Richard Berry) has left his career as a Parisian philosophy professor to come to the Yardena Kibbutz, which lies just below the Golan Heights in Israel, to discover his Jewish roots. One of his students, Laura (Sophie Marceau), who is non-Jewish, has followed, desperately in love with him. (She's even put her budding career as a violinist on hold.) They have lived together passionately on the kibbutz for two years. Now, in June 1967, three more of Sacha's former students join them: Michel (Frederic Quiring), Simon (Niels Dubost) and Paul (Fabien Orcier), partly to help celebrate the 20th birthday of Laura, with whom they are also in varying degrees in love.

Sacha, however, has been inducted into the Army, although the tensions that will soon lead to the Six Days' War little effect the bucolic kibbutz life, to which the three newcomers begin to assimilate. Paul is deeply troubled, and at Laura's birthday party he shows home movies of them all back in Paris, including another member of the coterie, Myriam (Shlomit Cohen), who later committed suicide, for which Sacha feels responsible—he broke off their love affair—and which prompted his move to Israel.

With all this unresolved, the war breaks out, and Sacha is part of the Army unit that frees Jerusalem. Near to both the Syrian and Jordanian borders, the kibbutz is under constant threat, and the now bunker-living kibbutzniks finally learn that Sacha has been killed. After the war ends and Sacha is buried, Laura gets a letter addressed to Sacha from Myriam, delivered by her brother (Gerald Darmon), absolving Sacha of any connection with her death.

Veteran French filmmaker Alexandre Arcady has previously merged very personal themes with genre formulae in such films as his first, SIROCCO, about North African emigres in 1960s Paris; LE GRAND CARNAVAL, a WWII epic about the American army landing in Algeria; and BROTHERS IN ARMS, in which a Jewish cop and an Arab secret serviceman join forces to fight terrorism. (Arcady was born in Algeria, the North African country which, after years of guerrilla warfare, received its independence from French rule in 1962.) None of these films were released in the US. (His only "impersonal" film, the Belmondo romp HOLD UP was inventively remade by Bill Murray and Howard Franklin as QUICK CHANGE.) POUR SACHA is probably his most personal project; Arcady himself left Paris at age eighteen upon the suicide of a friend to stay on an Israeli kibbutz. Unfortunately, perhaps because he is so close to this material, POUR SACHA, cowritten, as are all of his films, with Daniel Saint-Hamont, is the weakest of his movies.

The central love story is remarkably, considering its attractive leads, uninvolving. And although it's 1967, permitting Sacha to tumble literally in the hay with a shapely Italian visitor, only to be dismissed by Laura as part of her lover's torment, reveals a blind spot common to many intellectual French male directors. (Laura knows Sacha loves only her, and he's only trying to protect her from too much intimacy, etc.) Arcady is also less tough-minded here than in his earlier films in dealing with the themes involved. While he does soft-pedal somewhat the usual filmic portrayal of kibbutz life as utopia (sun, work, sex, eating, drinking, sex, etc.), he never tackles, as we might expect him to (especially considering his background), the issues of the war, Arab and Israeli territorialism or the racism involved. Genre requirements are also more baldly utilized (the awkward if stylistically interesting manner the Myriam subject is inserted—Paul packed 16mm film cans in his luggage?!—and Sacha dying immediately after touching the Wailing Wall), so that the last reel (Laura's grief, Sacha's funeral, etc.) becomes lugubrious.

The production is a fine-looking one and boasts an excellent score by veteran Philippe Sarde. Secondary performers far outshine the leads, including a brief bit by Emmanuelle Riva, the luminous star of Resnais's HIROSHIMA, MON AMOUR, as Myriam's mother. The $8 million film was shot on location in Israel in late 1989 and early 1990, just as Iraq invaded Kuwait, which reportedly made the filming risky. *(Sexual situations, brief nudity.)*

p, Alexandre Arcady, Diane Kurys; d, Alexandre Arcady; w, Alexandre Arcady, Daniel Saint-Hamont, Antoine Lacomblez; ph, Robert Alazraki; ed, Martine Barraque; m, Philippe Sarde; prod d, Tony Egry; cos, Mimi Lempicka

Drama/War **(PR: C MPAA: NR)**

POWER OF ONE, THE ★★★

(U.S./Germany/France) 111m Regency Enterprises; Le Studio Canal Plus; Alcor Films; Village Roadshow ~ Warner Bros. c

Stephen Dorff *(PK–Age 18)*, Armin Mueller-Stahl *(Doc)*, Morgan Freeman *(Geel Piet)*, John Gielgud *(Headmaster St. John)*, Fay Masterson *(Maria Marais)*, Simon Fenton *(PK–Age 12)*, Guy Witcher *(PK–Age 7)*, Daniel Craig *(Sergeant Jaapie Botha)*, Alois Moyo *(Gideon Duma)*, Ian Roberts *(Hoppie Gruenwald)*, Marius Weyers *(Professor Daniel Marais)*, Nomadlozi Kubheka *(Nanny)*, Agatha Hurle *(Midwife)*, Nigel Ivy *(PK–As a Newborn)*, Tracy Brooks Swope *(Mother)*, Brendan Deary *(PK–Infant)*, Winston Mangwarara *(Tonderai Infant)*, Tonderai Masenda *(Tonderai)*, Cecil Zilla Mamanzi *(Ranch Foreman)*, John Turner *(Afrikaner Minister)*, Robbie Bulloch *(Jaapie Botha)*, Gordon Arnell *(Minister at Mother's Funeral)*, Jeremiah Mnisi *(Dabula Manzi)*, Paul Tingay *(Grandfather)*, Hywel Williams *(Captain)*, Michael Brunner *(Kommandant Van Zyl)*, Clive Russell *(Sergeant Bormann)*, Gart Van Niekerk *(Lieutenant Smit)*, Winston Ntshona *(Mlungisi)*, Ed Beeten *(Prison Commissioner)*, Dominic Walker *(Morrie Guilbert)*, Robert Thomas Reed *(School Fight Opponent)*, Roy Francis *(Referee)*, Clare Cobbold *(1st Maria's Friend)*, Natalie Morse *(2nd Maria's Friend)*, John Osborne *(Guard)*, Simon Shumba *(Man Without Pass)*, Stan Leih *(1st Van Cop)*, Rod Campbell *(2nd Van Cop)*, Adam Fogerty *(Andreas Malan)*, Tony Denham *(Boxing Partner)*, Eric Nobbs *(1st City Cop)*, Edward Jordan *(2nd City Cop)*, Brian O'Shaughnessy *(Colonel Bretyn)*, Faith Edwards *(Miriam Sisulu)*, Raymond Barreto *(Indian Referee)*, Liz Ngwenya *(Nganga Ancient Woman)*, Andrew Whaley *(Ticket Taker)*, Dominic Makuwachuma *(Joshua)*, Lungani Sibanda, Akim Mwale, Pesedena Dinah, Rosemary Chikobwe Sibanda, Joel Phiri, Peggy Moyo, David Khabo, David Guwaza *(Students)*, Robin Annison *(Anita)*, Christien Anholt *(Date at Dinner)*, Nigel Pegram *(1st Man Guest)*, Jon Cartwright *(Jacob)*, Reverend Peter Van Vuuren *(Minister at Maria's Funeral)*, Marcia Coleman *(Woman Guest)*, Banele Dala Moyo *(Boy Who Reads)*

Largely unheralded and unseen, THE POWER OF ONE is a rousing historical epic from director John G. Avildsen that provides a rare look at South African culture, history and politics. The story concerns an orphaned British youngster who becomes an unlikely hero by uniting the Black tribes of South Africa against their repressive Afrikaner rulers.

British South African PK (played at age seven by Guy Witcher, age twelve by Simon Fenton, and age eighteen by Stephen Dorff) gets an ugly taste of intolerance early in life on the eve of WWII.

Sent by his widowed mother to an Afrikaner boarding school, he becomes the object of abuse by older Afrikaner boys led by Jaapie Botha (Robbie Bulloch). PK is a victim of the old enmity between the British and the Afrikaners—an enmity heightened by Adolf Hitler's promise to drive the British from South Africa. When his mother dies, PK returns home for the funeral and confesses his problems at school to his Black nanny (Nomadlozi Kubheka), who calls in a witch doctor to help the boy find the confidence to overcome his fears of returning to school.

PK's only remaining relative, a grandfather he barely knows, later takes PK from the school and puts him under the tutelage of family friend Doc (Armin Mueller-Stahl), a renowned German pianist prevented from returning home by the war. Doc is imprisoned by the British under an alien-control act, but PK is allowed unlimited visits to him and winds up spending most of his time in the prison. There he also befriends Black prisoner Geel Piet (Morgan Freeman), who teaches PK how to box well enough to compete on an inter-prison boxing team. PK also becomes admired by the prison's multi-tribal Black population for resisting the racism of the British and Afrikaners and treating the members of the various tribes as equals.

Attempting to promote inter-tribal harmony, PK and Doc stage a concert at which the tribes sing together. Doc writes the music and Geel Piet the words, which criticize the white oppressors. Even though the songs are sung in the prisoners' native language, a sadistic prison guard recognizes the intent of the lyrics and murders Geel Piet.

At secondary school, PK earns the admiration of headmaster St. John (Sir John Gielgud), who promotes PK and his best friend Hoppie Gruenwald (Ian Roberts) for admission to Oxford. At a boxing match, PK spots and is smitten by Maria (Fay Masterson). He pursues her, despite the opposition of her philosopher father, Professor Daniel Marais (Marius Weyers), whose ideas form the basis of apartheid. PK also runs afoul of Botha, now a member of the state's brutal internal security forces, when he and Maria organize an underground school to teach South African Blacks to read and write with the help of Black boxing champion Gideon Duma (Alois Moyo). Maria is murdered by Botha's security forces during a raid on the school, but Botha is later killed by Duma while trying to kill PK. After some pursuading by Duma, PK turns down Oxford to help his fellow boxer establish more schools throughout the Black community in South Africa.

Director John G. Avildsen (ROCKY, THE KARATE KID) has been criticized for this latest of many attempts to tell the South African story from the point of view of a white character. Nonetheless, THE POWER OF ONE is a compelling historical fiction that uses the story of its protagonist to make its complex historical framework come grippingly alive.

As a British boy, PK is able to see both sides of the South African experience. He experiences prejudice firsthand, yet enjoys far more social mobility than a Black protagonist could have. His earliest education comes from his Black nanny, who instills in him a respect for Black South African culture that later motivates his resistance to aparthied. At his Afrikaner school, he sees how racist ideology is promulgated by religious teachings that argue the inferiority of the Blacks in Biblical terms. Through his friendship with Doc, he experiences the imperialism of his own people—more benign, but no less repugnant than the racism of the Afrikaners. Through his friendship with Geel Piet, he gains understanding of how inter-tribal conflicts can hinder the Black community's organized resistance to the white government. Through his conflict with Botha and romance with Maria, he sees the human faces behind apartheid: Botha is conditioned to hatred by a brutal upbringing, while the innocent Maria can see the truth of racial justice despite her own background.

All these diverse narrative strands find a strong focus in PK, a sensitive, intelligent and articulate narrator. He's also a bona fide hero. Directing Robert Mark Kamen's flawless adaptation of Bryce Courtenay's novel, Avildsen gives PK an interior life of grief, loss and loneliness that gives his heroism a moving poignancy.

The cast is as good as it looks on paper, with shining lead performances from Dorff and Masterson. The rousing soundtrack combines adaptations of African music, original music by Hans Zimmer and songs by South African star Johnny Clegg. Dean Semler's cinematography is rich, evocative and full of epic sweep. By necessity, the story is almost unremittingly downbeat, but THE POWER OF ONE is nonetheless a powerful, engrossing and enlightening tale that should not be missed. *(Violence, profanity.)*

p, Arnon Milchan; d, John G. Avildsen; w, Robert Mark Kamen, (from the novel by Bryce Courtenay); ph, Dean Semler; ed, John G. Avildsen; m, Hans Zimmer; prod d, Roger Hall; art d, Martin Hitchcock, Kevin Phipps; set d, Karen Brookes; cos, Tom Rand

Historical/Drama **(PR: C MPAA: PG-13)**

PRAYER OF THE ROLLERBOYS ★★½

(U.S./Japan) 94m Academy Home Entertainment; Fox/Lorber Associates; TV Tokyo Entertainment; Gaga Communications; Victor Company of Japan Inc. ~ Academy Entertainment c

Corey Haim *(Chris Griffin)*, Patricia Arquette *(Casey)*, Christopher Collet *(Gary Lee)*, J.C. Quinn *(Jaworski)*, Julius Harris *(Speedbagger)*, Devin Clark *(Miltie)*, Mark Pellegrino *(Bingo)*, Morgan Weisser *(Bullwinkle)*, G. Smokey Campbell *(Watt)*, Jake Dengel *(Tyler)*, John P. Connolly *(Pinky)*, Stanley Yale *(Grizzled Man)*, Loren Lester *(Anchorman)*, Tim Eyster *(Little Boy)*, James Patrick *(Rollerboy Guard)*, Cynthia Gatees *(Prostitute)*, Dal Trader *(Sargeant)*, Aron Eisenberg *(Teen Boy)*, Chad Taylor *(Partygoer)*, Bob Wills, Jr. *(Old Fisherman)*, Rodney Kagemaya *(Mr. Naboru)*

The world has ended so often in fantasy films that it's become a bad joke: my civilization collapsed and all I got was this lousy B movie. George Miller's MAD MAX and its countless imitators set the cliches in stone—desolate post-nuke music-video landscapes, barbaric mutants, loner/mercenary/samurai/cowboy/gunslinger heroes all waging the eternal fight for good against evil with armored motor vehicles and automatic weapons. At least PRAYER OF THE ROLLERBOYS comes up with a clever premise for its *apres*-apocalypse setting, but the saga that unravels therein goes out not with a bang but a whimper.

During a dynamic opening credit sequence a youthful narrator reveals that the bomb dropped here was not atomic but economic. Deficit spending and industrial disasters have plunged America into bottomless recession and "alien races foreclosed on our nation while we were locked in homeless camps," all leaving the once-proud US a disgraced, polluted third-world ghetto where the Dow Jones average falls 150 points daily, Harvard University has been relocated brick-by-brick to an acquisitive Japan, and thousands of American refugees try to slip over the border to look for jobs—in Mexico.

Though a weak central government tries to keep order, a rising force in the LA wastelands (played by a rubble-strewn Venice, California) is the Rollerboys, an elite street gang of young Aryan thugs who cruise the pavement in wedge formation atop in-line rollerskates, trademark white longcoats flapping artfully in sync. These dancing droogs gain power through protection rackets and drug-dealing, while their charismatic, crucifix-wearing leader Gary Lee (Christopher Collet) peddles white supremacy to kids via Rollerboy comic books and biblical injunctions about an upcoming "Day of the Rope" in which Caucasian America will triumph over ethnic parasites and foreign creditors.

The hero of the piece is Chris Griffin (Corey Haim), ex-pal of Gary Lee, now holding a chintzy delivery job and looking after trouble-prone little brother Milton (Devin Clark). Chris gets approached by cop Jaworski (J.C. Quinn) to go undercover as a Rollerboy and help get the goods on their chief. Chris accepts when he sees Milton seduced by the gang's propaganda—and their new drug, an addictive narcotic called "mist." So Chris passes a deadly initiation and starts hangin' with the R-boys. It turns out Gary Lee has vast investments in utilities, real estate and lawyers, and intends to turn the Rollerboys into a true neofascist political organization. They manufacture mist (ingredients provided by the Chinese), and once its use has spread through all "undesirable" levels of society Gary Lee plans to release a poisoned batch to get rid of all users in one swipe—the promised Day of the Rope—ushering in a Rollerboy Reich.

Having erected their neat little dystopia the filmmakers plod through it in predictable fashion, touching all the undercover-agent-in-jeopardy checkpoints still warm from genre reruns like STONE COLD and POINT BREAK. After some close scrapes and loopholes in logic, Chris leads the forces of relative law and order to raid the secret Rollerboy mist factory, but the showdown is routine. A sequel-pregnant open ending finds nothing really changed, all the pieces in place for another round; vengeful Gary Lee still runs his criminal empire from prison through a phalanx of lawyers, while Chris and his friends hit the road in an ex-Rollerboy relocation program. One gets the impression that screenwriter W. Peter Iliff had a lot more fun mischievously constructing the worst of all possible worlds (when a Rollerboy boasts that he's buying up America, an Asian businessman snorts, "Who would want it?") than in outfitting a satisfactory story.

Corey Haim (THE LOST BOYS, DREAM A LITTLE DREAM), the face that launched a thousand teen magazine covers, does okay in the roughneck action role, but despite all the death and mayhem a persistent sense of juvenilia hangs over PRAYER OF THE ROLLERBOYS. In fairness, the movie's major sin is guilt by association. So many awful ROAD WARRIOR retreads have chugged their way across screens big and small that to stand out from the convoy a new arrival has to be not merely good but very good, and realized in a ferociously fresh manner. While some viewers may think sci-fi skanks on skates an original concept, it's been done before, notably in the quasi-satirical ROLLER BLADE and SHREDDER ORPHEUS.

With its flip cynicism, thrash-punk futuristics and underaged, paper-thin characters, PRAYER OF THE ROLLERBOYS owes much to violent Japanese "manga" comics and their most resplendent transliteration to the cinema, the cartoon epic AKIRA. The relationship didn't stop at style; despite all the plot potshots at international corporate imperialists and avaricious Orientals, Japanese companies like Gaga Communications and TV Tokyo helped finance this film, which was a fledgling effort from the production end of Academy Entertainment, a prominent home-video distributor. *(Violence, substance abuse, profanity, adult situations, nudity, sexual situations.)*

p, Robert Mickelson; d, Rick King; w, W. Peter Iliff; ph, Phedon Papamichael; ed, Daniel Lowenthal; m, Stacy Widelitz; prod d, Thomas A. Walsh; art d, Jay Klein; set d, Natalie K. Pope; cos, Merrily Murray-Walsh

Science Fiction/Action/Crime (PR: O MPAA: R)

PRELUDE TO A KISS ★★

110m East 22nd Company Productions; Gruskoff/Levy Company; Fox ~ Fox c

Alec Baldwin *(Peter Hoskins)*, Meg Ryan *(Rita Boyle)*, Kathy Bates *(Leah Blier)*, Ned Beatty *(Dr. Boyle)*, Patty Duke *(Mrs. Boyle)*, Richard Riehle *(Jerry Blier)*, Stanley Tucci *(Taylor)*, Sydney Walker *(Julius–The Old Man)*, Rocky Carroll *(Tom)*, Debra Monk *(Aunt Dorothy)*, Ray Gill *(Uncle Fred)*, Ward Ohrman *(Minister)*, Annie Goldman *(Tin Market Musician)*, Frank Carillo *(Tin Market Musician)*, Sally Murphy *(1st Bridesmaid)*, Salli Richardson *(2nd Bridesmaid)*, Victoria Haas *(3rd Bridesmaid)*, Fern Persons *(Elderly Woman)*, Jobe Cerny *(Clerk)*, Josette DiCarlo *(Mother in Train Station)*, Peter Lloyd *(Jamaican Waiter)*, Richard C.W. Schulz *(Party Goer)*, Lucina Paquet *(Dancing Woman)*, Glendon Gabbard *(Dancing Man)*, Rob Riley *(Mr. Sokol)*, Jane Alderman *(Mrs. Sokol)*, The Upbeaters *("Pool" Band)*, Peter Hudson *(Hotel Band-Sax)*, Paul Hussey *(Hotel Band-Flute)*, Ozzie Wilkins *(Hotel Band-Trumpet)*, Robert Lindo *(Hotel Band-Trombone)*, Eric Miller *(Hotel Band-Piano)*, Andrew Fatta *(Hotel Band-Drums)*, Brian Jobson *(Hotel Band-Electric Guitar)*, Harold Williams *(Hotel Band-Bass)*, Peter Couch *(Piano Player)*

Alec Baldwin's redeeming love for insomniac barmaid Meg Ryan is sorely tested in the screen adaptation of *Prelude to a Kiss*, a talky, didactic fantasy-romance from the creators of LONGTIME COMPANION.

With few friends and no family, Peter Hoskins (Baldwin, reprising his role from the hit Broadway play), an editor of scientific journals on microfiche, is the quintessential urban lonely guy. One night at a party, however, all that changes when he meets Rita Boyle (Ryan), a lively, lovely insomniac, would-be graphic artist and full-time bartender in Chicago. Peter finds he can't get Rita out of his mind and, when he goes to see her at the bar where she works, he's relieved and overjoyed to find the feelings to be mutual. After a whirlwind courtship, the two get married at the home of Rita's parents (Ned Beatty and Patty Duke). Despite the fact that nobody at the wedding seems to know the elderly man (Sydney Walker) lingering at the fringes of the reception and nibbling on chicken wings, the good spirits of the day lead Rita to consent when he asks to kiss the bride.

Immediately afterwards, Rita begins acting extremely odd, not unlike the way she might act if she had switched souls with an elderly man. The elderly man, Julius, meanwhile, now begins lingering around Peter's house. As Peter begins to feel more and more alienated from Rita, he becomes more and more desperate. Out wandering one night in the rain, he winds up in the bar where Rita used to work, where he finds Julius. The two of them piece together what has happened and begin plotting how they might bring Julius back together with Rita to remedy the soul-switch. Once they do, they find that Julius has grown as bored with living in Rita's body as Rita has become desperate to get out of Julius's body, which, suffering from cancer, has less than a year to live.

It's hard to argue with PRELUDE TO A KISS's sentiments. But as a movie it's stilted, talky and dramatically inert, betraying its stage origins in its emphasis on character over action. Unfortunately, these characters aren't all that interesting. Baldwin's Hoskins is an overfamiliar type, the hapless romantic schlemiel whose life is transformed by love, as is Ryan's Rita, the urban gamine, descended from BREAKFAST AT TIFFANY's Holly Golightly, who is as charmingly whimsical in fiction as she would probably be unbearably whimsical in real life. Both suffer from that over-insistent brightness and over-articulate archness that is characteristic of many contemporary urban stage works. In short, they are both overwritten. They talk constantly and incessantly in clever aphorisms that make you wish they'd shut up a while and let their brains cool off. The problem is that they can't, since the plot, past its premise, is scant to nonexistent.

Perhaps there's been nothing quite like it on stage. However, as a movie, PRELUDE TO A KISS bears a distinct resemblance to the spate of body-switching comedies of recent years, 1988's BIG the most notable among them, that quickly wore out their welcomes with tired repetitions of the same sophomoric jokes and situations. Adapted by Craig Lucas from his own play, PRELUDE TO A KISS steers clear of comparisons to its hackneyed predecessors without ever finding anything of interest to replace the cliches. The chief innovation is in focusing on Hoskins, the man in the middle and, almost by definition, the least interesting of the trio; given the choice, most people would probably be more curious about what it would be like to be in somebody else's body than what it would be like to find all the interior qualities that attracted them to someone transferred into the least appealing package imaginable.

As too many current American movies that are awash neither in sex nor violence try to do, PRELUDE TO A KISS focuses its main energy on teaching its characters obvious, uplifting lessons. By finding himself more attracted to an elderly gentleman with the interior qualities of the woman he loves rather than a young, sexy woman with the soul of an elderly man, Hoskins learns of love that, in the words of Warren Zevon, "You can't start it like a car, and you can't stop it with a gun." Julius learns, despite having a youthful body, that life can be duller the second time around while Rita, who is portrayed as something of a cynic, learns the even more obvious lesson that youth can be wasted on the young. The problem is that the audience learns the lessons long before the characters do.

In fact, there's a good chance that many have learned them before they even walked into the theater, all of which, despite good performances all around (especially from the increasingly accomplished Ryan, who's so good at the "soul switch" she's eerie), make PRELUDE TO A KISS play more like a dirge. *(Adult situations.)*

p, Michael Gruskoff, Michael I. Levy; d, Norman Rene; w, Craig Lucas, (from his play *Prelude to a Kiss*); ph, Stefan Czapsky; ed, Stephen A. Rotter; m, Howard Shore; prod d, Andrew Jackness; art d, W. Steven Graham; set d, Cindy Carr; cos, Walker Hicklin

Romance/Fantasy **(PR: C MPAA: PG-13)**

PRIMARY MOTIVE ★★★

93m Ascension Films ~ FoxVideo c

Judd Nelson *(Andrew Blumenthal)*, John Savage *(Wallace Roberts)*, Sally Kirkland *(Helen Poulas)*, Justine Bateman *(Darcy Link)*, Frank Converse *(John Eastham)*, Joe Grifasi *(Paul Melton)*, Jennifer Youngs *(Stephanie Poulas)*, Malachi Throne *(Ken Blumenthal)*, Richard Jordan *(Chris Poulas)*, Larry "Ratso" Sloman

Patching together bits of real life ripped from the tabloids, the low-budget PRIMARY MOTIVE is a sharply written political melodrama which provides an entertaining trash wallow with a sort-of-famous all-star cast.

The son of a retired behind-the-scenes political powerplayer, Andy Blumenthal (Judd Nelson) wants to follow in his father's footsteps. His dad Ken (Malachi Throne) trades an endorsement to get Andy the second-in-command press job with a Republican hopeful for governor of Massachusetts during the primary campaign. Stately John Eastham's (Frank Converse) main liability as a candidate is his stubborn commitment to truth and integrity down to ordering a change in a campaign bumper sticker that omits the "for" in the "Eastham for Governor" slogan. This "quirk" drives dyspeptic press secretary Paul Melton (Joe Grifasi) to sputtering fits of impotent rage—out of Eastham's earshot of course. It also prevents Melton from running the kind of down-and-dirty campaign that he's sure he could win. His mood brightens, however, when Andy takes the sleaze initiative.

After inducing his girlfriend Darcy Link (Justine Bateman) to get a job on the opposing campaign of blue-collar, second-generation immigrant Chris Poulas (Richard Jordan), Andy gets a tip from her that Poulas has fabricated key parts of his background that have become the centerpiece of his candidacy. After confirming the allegations, Andy passes the information to reporter Wallace Roberts (John Savage). Cornered, Poulas decides to go the full denial route and turn the attack back on Roberts and his pro-Democrat paper. Impressed by Poulas's hubris, Darcy switches beds from Andy's to that of the married candidate and finds a way to exploit both her relationship with Andy and the suicide of Poulas's emotionally disturbed daughter by slipping a false story to Andy regarding the daughter for the sole purpose of exposing it at a press conference in order to discredit Roberts once and for all. This final, diabolically cynical press coup wins Poulas both the primary and the general election, with Darcy riding along not only as his mistress but also as his press secretary-designate.

PRIMARY MOTIVE has a fair share of plot holes. However, writer-director Daniel Adams, abetted by co-scripter William Snowden, manages to convey so plausibly the atmosphere and the personalities of a pressure-cooker election that even the holes seem to work in the film's favor.

For example, it wouldn't take a rocket scientist to expose the lies of Poulas's campaign since they are such whoppers. He falsely claims a degree from Yale and military service in Vietnam and overstates the income of his stock-brokering business fourfold. Of all the rocket scientists involved, however, only Andy thinks to verify Poulas's claims and even then it's only at the prodding of Darcy who, after walking off the street as a campaign volunteer, is immediately given enough up-close-and-personal access to Poulas to spot both the chinks in his armor and the weakness in his fly. None of this would be believable for a second were it not for the circus-like atmosphere that permeates real-life American politics from Bush dumping lunch in the Japanese premier's lap to Gennifer Flowers to Ross Perot on national TV exposing government plots to disrupt a family wedding with faked-up dirty pictures of his daughter-bride.

Clearly the fiction could never outstrip the reality, but what PRIMARY MOTIVE has that even BOB ROBERTS lacked as political satires go is an unmistakable feeling of behavioral realism. The seduction of power is almost palpable here in a way that makes the people going after it go a little crazy. The filmmakers are careful not to caricature Eastham, for example. His decency and integrity are made to seem genuine, but shouldn't he have more important things to worry about than bumper stickers? Poulas is portrayed with a similar humanity distorted by politics. And anyone who doubts either the plausibility or effectiveness of his own strategy should take a closer look at President Clinton's campaign that earned him a Teflon reputation in the face of almost nonstop allegations—some well-documented—against his own career and personality.

Conviction also helps, and Adams has drawn it in spades from his cast. Nelson is as bug-eyed and overwrought as ever and, for once, it fits his character. Bateman, meanwhile, imbues her character with a sexual delight in her manipulations. The supporting cast underplays effectively, particularly the reliable Jordan and, most surprisingly, Sally Kirkland as Poulas's run-ragged spouse. As the press secretary for whom no blow is too low, however, Grifasi virtually steals the film with the help of the screenplay's sharpest, funniest lines. Altogether they make PRIMARY MOTIVE fast-moving, mean-spirited fun. *(Profanity, adult situations.)*

p, Tom Gruenberg; d, Daniel Adams; w, Daniel Adams, William Snowden; ph, John Drake; ed, Jacqeline Carmody; prod d, Daniel Yarhi; art d, Axel Werner; set d, Jacques Bradette; cos, Julie Englesman

Political/Drama (PR: C MPAA: R)

PRIMO BABY ★★

(Canada) 110m Producers Group International; Victory Films Ltd. ~ Worldvision Home Video c

Duncan Regehr *(Charles Armstrong)*, Janet-Laine Green *(Ann Williams)*, Esther Purvis-Smith *(Paschal Draney)*, Tim Battle *(Clancy)*, Jackson Cole

After a respectable start out of the gate, this family drama of the horsey set eventually falls behind. Unlike the eponymous stallion hero, PRIMO BABY doesn't regain its footing by the finish line.

Esther Purvis-Smith, a young actress of Runyonesque looks and mannerisms, plays Paschal Draney, a tomboy delinquent who works as a runner for bookies at Canadian race tracks. Her uncaring father in jail, Paschal is assigned a foster home with Charles Armstrong (Duncan Regehr), a prestigious Alberta horse breeder. But Charles isn't so much interested in the girl's welfare as in finding a friend for teenage son Clancy (Tim Battle). In a wheelchair since the car accident that killed Mrs. Armstrong, Clancy's a self-pitying snob obsessed with the computerized champion-breeding program he's devised, and he wants no part of scruffy Paschal.

She's equally scornful of Clancy and the whole high-class household, but strikes a deal to stay if she can care for Primo Baby, a thoroughbred of illustrious lineage but otherwise doomed to the slaughterhouse because of a congenital eye defect that's made it almost blind. This horse was the first product of Clancy's breeding program, but unable to bear the disability the younger Armstrong lavishes his attention on his second creation, a filly named Saygold. Paschal knows that Primo's got the equine right stuff, and determines to train the unwanted animal to be a winner.

Actually, the first half of PRIMO BABY focuses almost exclusively on the humans, setting up Paschal's longing for her absent dad, Clancy's secret gambling habit, Charles's unresolved guilt over his wife's death and so on. Obviously everybody's going to end up healing everybody else in melodramatic sessions of cliche therapy, and the horses seem almost incidental, largely relegated to the sidelines despite portentious gab about Primo's gallantry and Saygold's promise. The movie probably would have been better had the beasts remained secondary, for things get silly when Paschal secretly enters Primo in the Calgary Cup race.

Officials refuse to admit a blind horse onto the track, whereupon Paschal raises a stink in the media that allegedly causes a firestorm of handicapped-animal-rights protests (we see one measly picket sign). Primo is granted an eye test, and while that conjures up hilarious images of the horse in an ophthalmologist's office reading letters off a wall chart it's really just an obstacle course that the beast passes in cliffhanger fashion. Primo gets to run in the event, all right, with Saygold nearby to act as a seeing-eye horse. At last comes the moment of truth, and Primo falls hopelessly behind. Of course he then rallies and comes in alongside Saygold, the tag team taking the trophy for the Armstrong Ranch.

The closing should live forever as a shining example of how *not* to end a film: the image area shrinks to a tiny box in which micro-thespians play out the final scenes, while the rest of the frame fills with a credit scroll and a booming pop tune (one of several on the soundtrack) vies with the dialogue for attention. Maybe it's decipherable on a wide cinema screen, but this Canadian production reached the US market on video. Those in search of elusive family entertainment will find it harmless, and nothing can dwarf that majestic Calgary scenery.

p, Eda Lever Lishman; d, Eda Lever Lishman; w, A.A. Lever, (from the story by Karen Jensen); ph, David Herrington; ed, Rick Benwick; m, Amin Bhatia, Luciano Giachetta; prod d, Rick Roberts

Children's/Sports/Drama (PR: A MPAA: NR)

PROFESSIONAL, THE ★★½

(Japan) 95m TMS Production ~ Streamline Pictures c

VOICES OF: Greg Snegoff *(Golgo 13)*, Michael McConnohie *(Leonard Dawson)*, Mike Reynolds *(Bragan)*, Edie Mirman *(Laura)*, Joyce Kurtz *(Cindy)*, Diane Michelle *(Rita)*, Kerrigan Mahan *(Pablo)*, David Povall *(Garvin)*, Ed Mannix *(Jefferson)*

This animated feature is definitely *not* for the LITTLE MERMAID crowd. Directed by Osamu Dezaki and Carl Macek, THE PROFESSIONAL is a dark and extremely violent story of murder for hire. Excessive violence, gratuitous bloodshed and a large dose of sex tend to overshadow the film's interesting art design and storyline.

Golgo 13 (Greg Snegoff) is an Asian assassin who works for anyone willing to pay his high price. A seemingly perfect male specimen, Golgo has never failed on a mission or with the ladies. The story opens as Golgo kills the son of a prominent Texas oil baron in California. Then he's off to Sicily to track down a reclusive Mafia leader. After bedding the mobster's supposed daughter, he finds out that she is actually the target. He blows her and her phalanx of bodyguards away. Before long though the unflappable killer begins to lose his cool—someone, he discovers, is trying to kill *him*. Through underground contacts Golgo learns that a coalition of Machiavellian proportions has been formed to do him in.

The CIA, FBI and other forces try to destroy him on various occasions but to no avail. Under the leadership of Leonard Dawson (Michael McConnohie), the oil tycoon whose son was a recent victim, these shadow groups are no match for the macho hit man. A master plan is concocted which will parlay the talent of three of the world's most notorious killers, Snake, Silver and Gold, to end Golgo's life at last. As he awaits his attackers, Golgo manages to knock off an aging former Nazi and luxuriate in his penthouse apartment with several nude playmates. Dawson is so desperate to see Golgo dead that he sacrifices his own daughter-in-law to the reptilian clutches of Snake.

The final confrontation takes place in Manhattan's Dawson Towers where Golgo fights the battle of a lifetime, finally prevailing over the three super killers—and he actually breaks a sweat. He confronts Dawson who discovers what Golgo knew all along: his son had felt he could never be the man his father wished. Instead of attempting suicide, however, he arranged for his own murder. Learning the overpowering truth, Dawson leaps out of an office window to his death.

THE PROFESSIONAL is one animated feature parents won't want to bring the kids to. There is more violence and sex on display than in most live-action films. Stylistically, however, there has never been anything quite like it before, and that makes for a unique film experience.

The elaborate animation techniques and dark color palette give the project a look unto itself. The numerous animators working on this film offer a cornucopia of effects from two to three dimensional and then to seemingly simplistic comic-book flatness. It will be regarded as a breakthrough in graphic technology, yet much of the innovativeness gets lost in the exploitative nature of gross violence and superfluous sex. The bloodshed is everywhere. Dezaki chooses to pay homage to the graphic novels of Takao Saito and fills the screen with gore. Heads explode, bullets slowly penetrate craniums and streamers of blood float from wounds with abandon.

The sexual encounters, while initially interesting and gorgeously drawn, are much too graphic to be effective. It begins to resemble soft porn. The film's strength, though, lies in its aforementioned technical achievement and in its humor. The Golgo character is an obvious take on the omnipotence and sexual power of James Bond. This man cannot be hurt. Even when his car blows up in a torrent of gunfire, Golgo walks away unscathed so that he may conquer another damsel in some exotic locale. It's surprising that this screenplay wasn't made into a live-action thriller instead of an animated one. It has plenty of action and a satisfying conclusion.

There is room for a wide array of genres within animation, as this thriller clearly demonstrates. However, it need not be as overly violent as seen here. Ultimately it only weakens the uniqueness of the project. THE PROFESSIONAL is to be praised for its technical virtuosity and clarity, but the decision where to draw the line was not nearly as well thought out. *(Excessive violence, excessive nudity, sexual situations.)*

p, Yutaka Fujioka, Mataichiro Yamamoto, Nobuo Inada, Carl Macek; d, Osamu Dezaki, Carl Macek; ph, Hirokata Takahashi; ed, Mitsuo Tsurubuchi; m, Toshiyuki Omori

Animated/Crime/Action (PR: O MPAA: NR)

PROJECT: SHADOWCHASER ★½

(U.K./Canada) 97m Prism Entertainment; Shadowchaser Ltd.; EGM Film International ~ Prism Entertainment c

Martin Kove *(Michael DaSilva)*, Meg Foster *(Sarah)*, Frank Zagarino *(Romulus)*, Paul Koslo *(Trevanian)*, Joss Ackland *("Kinderman")*, Ricco Ross *(Jackson)*, Robert Freeman *(Blackwood)*, Angie Hill Richmond *(Jonah)*, Brian Jackson *(President Evan Richards)*, Kymberley Huffman, John Pasternak, Eric Ray Livans, Andrew Lamond, Robert Jezek, John Chancer, David Oliver, Liza Ross, Steve Elm, Michael Morris

Here's another MixMaster picture that tosses two, maybe two-and-a-half familiar plots into the blender and comes out with a flavorless sludge of a movie. The recipe: take a big chunk of DIE HARD, toss in THE TERMINATOR and a bit of William Shatner's "Tek" novels, add a spritz of BIRD ON A WIRE or maybe TERROR IN BEVERLY HILLS, crown with a completely meaningless title and soundtrack music cribbed from BATMAN, and you have PROJECT: SHADOWCHASER.

The time: either the present or the cybernetic future, depending on what's being ripped off at the moment. The place: a big-city highrise hospital. An annoying young medico has the hots for an unwilling nurse, but this obnoxious subplot comes to a merciful end when mercenaries, disguised as paramedics, whip out their automatic weapons and commandeer the top floors. Their prize hostage is the President's daughter, Sarah (Meg Foster), brought in after a food-poisoning incident. In exchange for her life the bad guys demand $50 million, to be handed over by the chief executive in person.

For some reason the law, personified by a hard case named Trevanian (Paul Koslo), decides that the only man capable of leading a daring raid against the terrorists is the architect who designed the building. He's nearby but serving a suspended-animation life-sentence in a cryogenic prison. The cops go to thaw him out, but by mistake they instead revive Michael DeSilva (Martin Kove), an ex-football star doing time for killing a yahoo in self-defense. The jock, glad to be out of jail, goes along with the unintended masquerade as the emergency strike force assembles around him. But the commandos die in a freak elevator accident, leaving the imposter the lone good guy atop the captive skyscraper.

But that's *not* the main gimmick. This is: the muscular leader of the marauders is really Romulus (Frank Zagarino), a manlike warrior robot who slaughtered and escaped his government handlers during the opening credits. Soon his sinister creator, Dr. Kinderman (Joss Ackland), is at the hospital demanding that the billion-dollar android not be harmed during the rescue.

There's one, perhaps one-and-a-half, neat plot twists near the end concerning the terrorists' true motives, which are political, not financial. But for the most part PROJECT: SHADOWCHASER plays a shell game with three stock situations, and one gets to guess where the plot is hidden this time. There are the cat-and-mouse games with DeSilva and the terrorists; these don't evoke many thrills because half the time the heavies hardly care that the athlete's at large, their efforts at elimating him almost half-hearted. There's the Frankenstein factor of Romulus, boiling down to a one-on-one grudge match between the humanoid and the hero; it's predictable in the extreme, and viewers expecting a cool cyborg meltdown *a la* THE TERMINATOR will be disappointed as the robot comes back time and time again after being "killed," with a minimum of makeup f/x.

Lastly, there's the quarrelsome antics between DeSilva and the hellcat first daughter, which inevitably develops into an opposites-attact romance. The lady is played by turquoise-eyed Meg Foster (A DIFFERENT STORY, BLIND FURY), a unique presence who's the last actress in the world one would cast as a bimbo. Yet here she is in the sort of role Goldie Hawn now tries to escape—a spoiled princess shoehorned in a tight party dress, fussin', flirtin' and a-fightin' with her reluctant rescuer. Kove, a recurring villain in the KARATE KID series, goes through his leading-man part with good-natured zeal, while the massive Zagarino, veteran of B movies and his own exercise video, makes less of an impression. All the ancillary stuff going on tends to diminish Romulus's menace, and of course Schwarzenegger did it so much better. Ackland, an accomplished scene-stealer, oozes malevolence. Notable just for her looks is Angie Hill Richmond as a gun-toting androgyne named Jonah.

Director John E. Eyres musters comic-book flash and dazzle, and the fiery climax is a visual quotation of all that befell Bruce Willis in the DIE HARD adventures. It's physically impressive but marred by miniatures that aren't at all convincing even though end credits state some of the production was filmed at London's sprawling soundstages at Pinewood Studios. *(Violence, profanity.)*

p, John E. Eyres, Geoff Griffiths; d, John E. Eyres; w, Steven Lister; ph, Alan M. Trow; ed, Delhak Wreen; m, Gary Pinder; prod d, Mark Harris; art d, Simon Lamont; cos, Philip Crichton

Science Fiction/Action (PR: C MPAA: R)

PROM NIGHT IV-DELIVER US FROM EVIL ★★

95m ~ LIVE Home Video c

Nikki De Boer *(Megan)*, Alden Kane *(Mark)*, Joy Tanner *(Laura)*, Alle Ghadban *(Jeff)*, James Carver *(Father Jonas)*, Ken McGregor *(Father Jaeger)*, Brock Simpson *(Father Colin)*, Fab Filippo *(Jonathan)*

After chronicling the exploits of a prom queen from hell in the previous two installments, the PROM NIGHT series returns to the slasher formula of the first film. PROM NIGHT IV: DELIVER US FROM EVIL is stylishly shot and contains a few real scares, but it's not enough to elevate what has become a very tired plotline.

Like its predecessors, this one is set around Hamilton High School, opening with yet another tragedy that occurred there decades ago. Back in 1957, a randy prom-going couple were murdered in their car by Father Jonas (James Carver), a priest possessed by a demonic spirit. Discovered flagellating himself and sporting stigmata in the basement of the St. Basil Seminary, Father Jonas was taken to a nearby church, where an unsuccessful exorcism was performed. He has been imprisoned ever since in the bowels of the building, strapped down and kept under constant sedation. In the present, young novice priest Father Colin (Brock Simpson) is informed by the aging Father Jaeger (Ken McGregor) that it is his duty to take over the tending of Father Jonas, and never to let him go a day without being sedated. But shortly after Jaeger passes on, Colin neglects the injection through a combination of inquisitiveness and carelessness, and Jonas wakes up and escapes, murdering Colin before vanishing.

Meanwhile, a pair of Catholic school girls, inexperienced Megan (Nikki De Boer) and trampy Laura (Joy Tanner) are preparing for prom night. But they're not going to the actual event; along with their respective boyfriends, Mark (Alden Kane) and Jeff (Alle Ghadban), they're headed for the summer house of Mark's parents. Said house just happens to be—wouldn't you know it—the former St. Basil's Seminary, and Jonas is on his way there as well. The two couples arrive to find the place stripped of its electrical appliances, but decide there's still plenty they can do to keep occupied that only requires the upstairs beds.

While Jeff and Laura engage in violent coupling and Megan prepares to go all the way for the first time with Mark, a heavy breather lurks outside, peering through the windows. At least some of the breathing turns out to be coming from Mark's younger brother Jonathan (Fab Filippo), who has sneaked up to the house with a video camera and is busy taping all the risque activity; but he's attacked and killed by Jonas, who has also butchered a foul-mouthed motorist he's hitched a ride with. The mad priest then dispatches Laura, and crushes Jeff's head in his bare hands when the young man comes looking for her.

Searching for their friends, Megan and Mark are horrified when they discover their bodies tied to flaming crosses. With no way to escape the isolated building (they were delivered in a since-departed limo), Mark rushes to find the house's gun while Megan calls the police. They are then attacked by Jonas, who chases Mark to the roof; attempting to shoot him, Mark is stabbed by the madman and ultimately falls to his death. Taking up the gun, Megan ineffectively shoots Jonas before causing his immolation in a barn explosion. The police arrive, and both Jonas's body and Megan are taken away—but in his ambulance, Jonas's eyes snap open; so do Megan's, and now she bears the possessed look as well.

The best part of PROM NIGHT IV is its opening, which effectively sets up its premise and contains most of its creepiest material. The scenes in the catacombs beneath the church are dripping with atmosphere, and indeed, director Clay Borris demonstrates a creative way with a camera throughout, with plenty of sinuous tracking shots and unusual angles. The problem is that this kind of visual imagination can only go so far in the service of a tired plot, particularly one with such a limited number of victims that, as a result, they're made to spend an awful lot of time wandering around darkened hallways.

It doesn't help that the characters, despite showing occasional flashes of personality, are restricted to playing types—the good couple and the horny couple—with little in the way of meaningful dialogue. The screenplay attempts to give them more intelligence than the usual slasher film teens, but once Mark gets ahold of the gun, he doesn't stand his ground but instead runs to the snowy roof, where he is easy pickings for his attacker. And although Megan does think to call the police, and actually gets through, she never thinks to put shoes on, and thus steps barefoot onto broken glass not once but twice, the latter time resulting in a set of bloody footprints that lead the killer straight to her hiding place.

There are some chills in the latter section of the movie, but its general predictability and ridiculously cliched concluding scene keep PROM NIGHT IV stranded in mediocrity. *(Violence, profanity, nudity, sexual situations.)*

p, Ray Sager; d, Clay Borris; w, Richard Beattie; ph, Rick Wincenty; ed, Stan Cole; m, Paul Zaza; prod d, Ian Brock

Horror **(PR: O MPAA: R)**

PROOF ★★★½

(Australia) 86m House & Moorhouse Films ~ Fine Line Features c

Hugo Weaving *(Martin)*, Genevieve Picot *(Celia)*, Russell Crowe *(Andy)*, Heather Mitchell *(Martin's Mother)*, Jeffrey Walker *(Young Martin)*, Daniel Pollock *(Gary–the Punk)*, Frank Gallacher *(Vet)*, Frankie J. Holden *(Brian–Policeman)*, Saskia Post *(Waitress)*, Belinda Davey *(Doctor)*, Cliff Ellen *(Cemetery Caretaker)*, Tania Uren *(Customer)*, Robert James O'Neill *(Hoon)*, Anthony Rawling *(Hoon)*, Darko Tuscan *(Hoon)*, Adele Daniele *(Hoon)*, Roy Edmunds *(2nd Policeman)*, Lisa Chambers *(Nurse)*, Suzanne Chapman *(Chemist Girl)*, Angela Campbell *(High-heeled Woman)*, Oswaldo Malone *(Waiter)*, Carole Patullo *(Kiosk Girl)*, Covey *(Bill the Dog)*

Australian filmmaker Jocelyn Moorhouse makes a most auspicious debut with PROOF, a dry, dark comedy about a blind photographer and his efforts to find someone to trust in a world of lies and half-truths.

The disabled individual in question, Martin (Hugo Weaving), is apparently rich enough to do little else but walk his dog in the park and take pictures, a habit he picked up as a child when his mother gave him a camera he asked for as a gift. He now uses a modern auto-focus camera and aims at sounds and objects he feels with his hands. But, since he can never see what he photographs, he needs someone to describe what he has photographed, to provide "proof" of his existence. That used to be his mother's job until she passed away while Martin was still young. In the present, Martin has his housekeeper, Celia (Genevieve Picot), a dour, attractive but aging spinster who has become obsessed with her employer.

Celia constantly tries to seduce Martin, at one point even blackmailing him into spending an evening with her. But Martin harbors a deep distrust of women in general, since the death of his mother, and Celia in particular. Failing to entice Martin, Celia torments him in infinite, petty ways like moving the furniture, sneaking into the park to hold his dog so it cannot come when he calls him and, especially, taking furtive photographs of him, with which she has lined the walls of her apartment. Withholding himself is the main way in which Martin gets even. A new factor enters this sick little equation when Martin befriends Andy (Russell Crowe), a likable restaurant dishwasher, who at first proves a perfectly trustworthy "describer" for Martin's photographs. Together they also have fun, a concept foreign to Martin, such as getting into a brawl at a drive-in movie and then using Martin's blindness to dodge the police. The problem is that Celia is not a very sharing person.

PROOF unfolds with the clarity and purity of a fable, which makes it all the more disquieting. Moorhouse's subject is the lack of clarity in life, the inherent impurity of existence, in short, the impossibility of having proof of anything. As a result, the simplest situation in drama, the romantic triangle, here becomes a labyrinth of pure emotions finding their voice in impure ways, with the emotions themselves subject to myriad interpretations. Celia is obsessed with Martin, but does that mean she doesn't love him? Martin's attraction to Andy is more than a little homoerotic. But his most stable relationship so far has been with Celia and, despite his contempt for her, he finds himself, albeit to his horror, physically responding to her when she finally throws all caution to the wind and forces herself on him. Andy seems a real straightforward "bloke." But when he finds himself lusting after Celia, he proves to be easily her match when it comes to deceiving Martin.

Martin seems to have finally freed himself from the influence of his mother, who kept him sheltered and under her control throughout his youth, when he finds the courage to fire Celia. But has he? Or has he simply found another partner in torment in Andy? Moorhouse gives no clue, right up until the ending, when Andy apparently wins back Martin's trust by describing to him a photograph, the first he ever took, which the audience never gets to see. But by then Moorhouse has convinced us that it really doesn't matter. Even if we could see the photograph, it would still be open to interpretation. The metaphor of the blind photographer is daring at the outset, and Moorhouse sustains it brilliantly, bringing the film away from its initial pity for someone so dependent on others for his experience of the world. By the end, she has convinced us that we are all, after all, really blind, and utterly dependent on those around us for how we perceive the world. Our senses can be intact, but we can still be deceived, by ourselves as often as by others; even so, there can be worse things in life than being deceived.

For all its cerebral thematic crosscurrents, however, what is most remarkable about PROOF is how firmly and easily it stays on a human level. This is certainly an "art" film, but there is nothing "arty" about it. Moorhouse has written three full, rich characters who come vividly alive as acted by the excellent cast. Having laid a groundwork in her characters, the plot seems to unfold naturally from who they are, all of which leads to the richest irony of PROOF. Though unabashedly artificial and unrealistic from the outset, it never for a moment feels contrived. It deals with real issues of life, morality and existence in a vital, provocative way. But, in the end, PROOF is pure movie magic. *(Adult situations, Nudity.)*

p, Lynda House; d, Jocelyn Moorhouse; w, Jocelyn Moorhouse; ph, Martin McGrath; ed, Ken Sallows; m, Not Drowning Waving; prod d, Patrick Reardon; cos, Ccerri Barnett

Drama **(PR: C MPAA: R)**

PSYCHIC ★½

(Canada) 92m Allegro Films; Westwind Productions ~ Vidmark Entertainment c

Zach Galligan *(Patrick Costello)*, Catherine Mary Stewart *(Laurel Young)*, Michael Nouri *(Dr. Theodore Steering)*, Albert Schultz, Ken James, Clark Johnson, Lisa LaCroix, Andrea Roth

As basic and trite as its title, PSYCHIC presents Zach Galligan as Patrick Costello, a clairvoyant college student who uses his gift of second sight primarily to score with the chicks.

All this poor man's Edgar Cayce has to do is fondle an item belonging to a girl and he psychically knows all about her—interests, activities, turn-ons etc. Patrick tries to use his touchy-feelie ESP to cozy up to sexy scholar Laurel Young (Catherine Mary Stewart), but instead he gets visions of a local serial sex-killer in action. The otherworldly finger of guilt points to Laurel's steady boyfriend, Dr. Theodore Steering (Michael Nouri, in creepy low voice and dark glasses), an upstanding but unmistakably sinister psychologist. When Patrick presents his phantom "evidence" to the police they instead seize him as a suspect in the murders. Can Dr. Steering's rampage be stopped? Will true love triumph over evil and adversity? Does the high-school letter jacket Galligan wears hide the fact that he's too old for this role?

You don't need a crystal ball or tarot deck to foresee what will happen next in PSYCHIC, but a VCR or cable hook-up might help; the lacklustre occult thriller raced to reach both media, and while it showed up first on tape some might mistake it for a made-for-TV quickie, such is the predominant small-screen banality. The psychic visions of murder, which fulfill the R-rating's quotient of violence and nudity, indulge in hallucinatory f/x—distorted sound and color, plus interrupted motion thanks to removal of intermittant film frames.

Director George Mihalka used the same visual techniques for his earlier astral-projection chiller THE BLUE MAN (a.k.a. ETERNAL EVIL). *(Violence, profanity, nudity, sexual situations, adult situations.)*

p, Tom Berry, William Webb; d, George Mihalka; w, Miguel Tejada-Flores, Mark McQuade Crawford, William Crawford, Paul Koval; ph, Ludek Bogner; ed, Paul Ziller; prod d, Perri Gorrara; art d, Jasna Stefanovic; set d, Carolyn Gee; cos, Aline Gilmore

Horror/Thriller **(PR: O MPAA: R)**

PUBLIC EYE, THE ★★½

98m Public Eye Productions ~ Universal bw/c

Joe Pesci *(Leonard "The Great Bernzini" Bernstein)*, Barbara Hershey *(Kay Levitz)*, Richard Riehle *(Officer O'Brien)*, David Gianopoulos *(Portofino)*, Bryan Travis Smith *(Young Cop)*, Max Brooks *(Teen at Thompson Street)*, Richard Schiff *(Photographer–Thompson Street)*, Laura Ceron *(Puerto Rican Woman)*, Chuck Gillespie *(Cop–Puerto Rican Tenement)*, Christian Stolti *(Ambulance Attendant)*, Jack Denbo *(Photo Editor)*, Ellen McElduff *(Lonely Woman at Drugstore)*, Marge Kotlisky *(Rineman's Receptionist)*, Timothy Hendrickson *(Richard Rineman)*, Del Close *(H.R. Rineman)*, Henry Bolzon *(Photographer at Cafe)*, Jared Harris *(Danny the Doorman)*, Kevin Dorsey *(Singer)*, Gian-Carlo Scanduzzi *(Maitre d')*, Steve Forleo *(Hood)*, Mick McGovern *(Cop with Hood)*, Maurice Bravo *(1st Photographer)*, Tom Lauricella *(2nd Photographer)*, George Lugg *(3rd Photographer)*, Vinny Argiro *(Sergeant at Police Station)*, Gerry Becker *(Conklin)*, Tim Gamble *(Agent Chadwick)*, David Hull *(Thatcher White)*, Kyle Moore *(Young Agent)*, Bob Gunton *(Older Agent)*, Richard Foronjy *(Farinelli)*, Louie Lanciloti *(Mikey)*, Stanley Tucci *(Sal)*, Jerry Adler *(Arthur Nabler)*, Patricia Healy *(Vera)*, Peter Maloney *(Federal Watchman)*, Randall Stanton *(Federal Guard)*, Jason Wells *(Garage Attendant)*, Dominic Chianese *(Spoleto)*, Joe Guzaldo *(Spoleto's Lieutenant)*, Al Mancini *(Camera Shop Clerk)*, Joe Greco *(Villa Guard–Hitman)*, Ian Abercrombie *(Mr. Brown)*, Nick Tate *(Henry Haddock Jr.)*, Jean Zarzour *(Sal's Wife)*, Toni Fleming *(Sal's Mother)*, John M. Watson, Sr. *(Sculllion)*, Guido DiMarco *(Mr. D'Angelo)*, Teresa DiMarco *(Mrs. D'Angelo)*, Phil Locker *(Arresting Cop)*, Shay Duffin *(Chief of Police)*, John Farris *(Albert Gerard)*

The story of a 1940s tabloid photographer, THE PUBLIC EYE splendidly harkens back to old movies of the era. Writer-director Howard Franklin creates a film noir world only slightly weakened by confusing plot twists.

Tabloid photographer Leon "The Great Bernzini" Bernstein (Joe Pesci) takes gritty, slice-of-life photos of New York during WWII. Through his aggressiveness and friendly relations with cops and mobsters alike, Bernzy always gets the "money shot."

(The fact that his car comes equipped with a portable darkroom in the trunk doesn't hurt, either.) Bernzy's dream is to publish a collection of his work, but a top book publisher says his topics are too unsavory.

Cafe owner Kay Levitz (Barbara Hershey), the widow of a wealthy society figure, unexpectedly summons Bernzy to help her: a mysterious man named Portofino (David Gianopoulos) has claimed a stake in her business. Since Kay's husband trusted Bernzy, she hopes he can use his knowledge of low-life New York to investigate Portofino. Bernzy, infatuated with the beautiful Kay, agrees. Portofino's murdered body appears at Bernzy's apartment, however, and the photographer is questioned by the cops, FBI and Mafia. Bernzy realizes the murder involves two duelling mob families—Farinelli and Spoleto.

He photographs Sal (Stanley Tucci) snitching on his Farinelli family to Spoleto's (Dominic Chianese) organization. Bernzy confronts Sal and the double-dealing hood says Kay's husband was involved with the mob in the wartime black market. Bernzy gets Sal to promise advance information on where Spoleto's massacre of Farinelli's group will take place. Bernzy plans to photograph the bloody event, but Sal is killed before he can reveal the site. Eluding a Mafia hit man, Bernzy makes it to the right restaurant. Bernzy takes the pictures of a lifetime at the massacre and becomes a public hero for exposing the Mafia. Although Bernzy finally has the acclaim he always sought, he is devastated by Kay's betrayal: she admits to telling Spoleto his plans.

From the credit sequence of pictures developing in a darkroom to the final shot of a melancholy Bernzy riding through a cheering mob, THE PUBLIC EYE is a pleasure. Franklin, marking his solo directorial debut following 1990's QUICK CHANGE (co-directed with Bill Murray), deserves credit for bringing back the spirit, if not the substance, of the 1940s film noir genre. The early scenes are the most fascinating, as Franklin eschews plot considerations and simply shows Bernzy at work. The determined shutterbug—based, of course, on Weegee, the great tabloid photographer—doesn't hesitate to alter the scene for the perfect shot, throwing a dead man's hat next to his body. Later, he impersonates a priest in order to snatch pictures of a dying man in an ambulance.

But this is a movie, after all, and Franklin must abandon his perfectly plotless opening for a less interesting gangster story. Kay Levitz's explanation of her late husband's feelings towards Bernzy is puzzling. She's a contrived character. It gets even worse later as the convoluted story about black market gas coupons and mobsters overshadows Bernzy's professionalism.

Still, Franklin's shots, especially the gangster massacre as seen through Bernzy's lens, are stunning. One might have expected problems to arise from combining color footage with black-and-white photographs and montage sequences, but Franklin has no trouble; it's a well-planned blend. Franklin's screenplay includes many lines memorable for their simplicity. "Do you think a man like him can protect you from a man like me?" Spoleto asks Kay about Bernzy. The screenwriter also stays true to the 1940s period. "Kiss off!" a Mafia man tells Bernzy when he's pestered for a photograph.

As Bernzy, Joe Pesci avoids the scenery-chewing that has marred some of his other work. Despite his assertiveness on the job, Pesci shows Bernzy to be a gentle man easily swayed by a woman's attention. You immediately believe in his interest in Kay. Pesci is funny as well as sympathetic, however. He tells a cop about a fresh corpse: "I killed him to get the picture." Physically, Pesci's short stature is perfect for the part, and he's well decked out in the requisite grungy trench coat, hat and cigar.

Barbara Hershey (A WORLD APART, DEFENSELESS) plays the Mary Astor part from THE MALTESE FALCON with no irony. As soon as she starts her "I'm so helpless" speech to Pesci, you know she'll let him down somewhere along the way. It's too bad more couldn't have been done to make her character realistic. (Intriguingly enough, Hershey has stated that she based her performance on the late Cary Grant, who transformed himself from the lowborn Archibald Leach into the perfect, debonair Hollywood star.) Hershey's makeup is so thick, for example, she looks phony. Jerry Adler, who plays columnist-turned-Broadway-producer Arthur Nabler, has more chemistry with Pesci than Hershey does. *(Violence, adult situations.)*

p, Sue Baden-Powell; d, Howard Franklin; w, Howard Franklin; ph, Peter Suschitzky; ed, Evan Lottman; m, Mark Isham; prod d, Marcia Hinds-Johnson; art d, Bo Johnson, Dina Lipton; set d, Jan K. Berstrom; cos, Jane Robinson

Thriller/Romance **(PR: O MPAA: R)**

PUERTO RICAN MAMBO (NOT A MUSICAL), THE ★★

90m Pinata Films ~ Cabriolet Films c

Luis Caballero *(Himself)*, Howard Arnesson *(Boss)*, John Fulweiler *(Psychiatrist)*, John Leguizamo *(Paco)*, Ben Model *(Friend)*, Carolyn McDermott *(Store Clerk)*, Mike Robles *(Spanish Teacher)*, David Healy, Lucia Mendoza, Jeff Eyres, Susan Gaspar, Sandy McFadden, Carole M. Eckman, Mary Perez

A filmed performance by writer-comedian Luis Caballero, interspersed with sketches, THE PUERTO RICAN MAMBO (NOT A MUSICAL) focuses on the stand-up comic's plight as a "little dark guy with an accent." Amusing and often incisive, Caballero, with another improvisational comedy veteran, Ben Model, has created a funny film on a half-a-shoestring budget.

Filmed against a scrim, Caballero's performance posits the dilemma of the Puerto Rican as a vaguely defined ethnic group easily lost amid a welter of Hispanic groups including Mexicans, Dominicans, Panamanians and Hondurans. One of Caballero's running gags concerns the Western European appearance of the performers and newscasters on Spanish-language TV—not surprising, since they are often from Argentina. He also sends up the stereotypes cherished by white New Yorkers, as in a sketch in which a department store manager announces over the PA system that, despite the presence of a Puerto Rican browsing in the aisles, shoppers shouldn't panic. Another sketch spoofs the apparently widespread tendency to ask Puerto Ricans about drugs and how to get them. When he insists he doesn't sell drugs, claims Caballero, people ask him "What kind of Puerto Rican are you?"

Lamenting the failure of Puerto Ricans in the US to gain a significant footing in society (they don't even, for example, have their own Mafia), Caballero does boast of one exceptional national trait—the ability to go to the beach in style and to picnic anywhere. To illustrate these points, one of the performers, Mike Robles, portrays a family head preparing for the beach with a U-Haul truck and a manifest list running into several pages. To prove his argument about picnicking, Caballero includes a documentary segment filmed in what looks like Brooklyn's Prospect Park of family groups congregating around various makeshift barbecues.

The most ambitious and longest sequence is of a party attended by Caballero and his pal, Model, who make ridiculous small talk, punctuated by some hilarious set-pieces. Model, bespectacled with thinning hair, laments that women only talk to him to find out about their stereo sets, since he looks like a dull, technically competent sort. In one conversation Model says he spent the day at the nearby Jewish Museum—in a display case. Later, he is shown literally boring a girl to the point where she collapses. Luis, on his part, makes tactless remarks about "big blonde women with beautiful breasts" and angers one guest by telling him he could pass for Puerto Rican. Another guest, Paco (rising star John Leguizamo, credited as Johnny Leggs), boasts of his chameleon ability to blend in with any ethnic group, at which point he can then triumphantly announce that he *is* Puerto Rican.

Caballero and director Model have fashioned an amusing film, with the consistently gentle satire nicely handled by the ensemble company. Despite the limitations of both the budget and the performance styles, THE PUERTO RICAN MAMBO (NOT A MUSICAL) is a funny, honestly conceived and enacted portrayal of one man's view of his ethnic group. *(Profanity.)*

p, Ben Model; d, Ben Model; w, Ben Model, (from the comedy material by Luis Caballero); ph, Rosemary Tomosky-Franco, Vincent Manes, Paul A. Koestner; ed, Ben Model; m, Eddie Palmieri

Comedy **(PR: C MPAA: NR)**

PURE COUNTRY ★★

108m Warner Bros.; Jerry Weintraub Productions ~ Warner Bros. c

George Strait *(Dusty Wyatt Chandler)*, Lesley Ann Warren *(Lula Rogers)*, Isabel Glasser *(Harley Tucker)*, Kyle Chandler *(Buddy Jackson)*, John Doe *(Earl Blackstock)*, Rory Calhoun *(Ernest Tucker)*, Molly McClure *(Grandma Ivy Chandler)*, James Terry McIlvain *(Tim Tucker)*, Toby Metcalf *(J.W. Tucker)*, Mark Walters *(Al)*, Tom Christopher *(Dave-Dusty's Bodyguard)*, Jeffrey R. Fontana *(Eddie-Dusty's Bodyguard)*, Jeff Pettyman *(Bobby Louis)*, David Anthony, Mike D. Daily, Gene Elders, Terry Hale, Rondel Huckaby, Mike A. Kennedy, Benny McArthur, Rick McRae *(Dusty's Band)*, Sharon Thomas *(Monique James)*, Gil Glasgow *(Bartender)*, Julie Johnson *(Waitress)*, Fred Ellis *(Private Detective)*, Fred Fontana *(Courier)*, Kristen Michaels *(Hostess)*, Evelyn Purtak *(Assistant)*, Eric Randall *(Reporter)*, Loretta Holloway *(Reporter)*, Roy Kieffer *(Reporter)*, Bob Tallman *(Rodeo Announcer)*

Country superstar George Strait is so laid-back he barely registers onscreen in PURE COUNTRY, an unabashedly corny by-the-numbers drama.

Strait certainly doesn't have to stretch much to play singing star Dusty Wyatt Chandler who drops out of his big-star life to rediscover his roots. Under the influence of his longtime manager Lula Rodgers (Lesley Ann Warren), Dusty has watched his downhome country show gradually swell into a bloated spectacular of smoke, sparks and explosions. When he simply stops singing in the middle of his big finale and the audience doesn't seem to notice, Dusty decides enough is enough. Telling his drummer and best pal Earl Blackstock (erstwhile musician John Doe, one of the founding members of X, the seminal LA punk band) that he's "taking a walk," he winds up "walking" all the way back to his home town, where he touches base with his spry, slightly daft grandmother (Molly McClure) and falls in love with spunky tomboy Harley Tucker (Isabel Glasser), who's grittily determined to save the family ranch by winning a big barrel-race rodeo competition in Las Vegas.

Stuck without her star at the next gig, Lula puts her no-account gigolo boyfriend into Dusty's clothes and has him lip-synch his way through the show, causing an irritated Earl to turn in his resignation. Earl tracks down Dusty, closely followed by Lula, who hopes to round up Dusty in time for his next big show—in Las Vegas, of course. To further her ends, and create some very minor plot complications, Lula puts a crimp into Dusty's budding romance by telling Harley that she and Dusty are already married. Dusty returns, for the sake of the guys in the band and on the condition that Lula drop the special effects from the show, reschedule the missed gigs and patch things up with Harley. Harley wins her barrel race and is whisked, via limo, to Dusty's gig for a romantic reconciliation.

Everything that happens in PURE COUNTRY is preordained from its first few frames, so much so that director Christopher Cain tends to skip through many of the obligatory scenes, employing a sort of directorial shorthand that sometimes seems more like sleight-of-hand to plug the glaring holes in Rex McGee's screenplay. Granted, Strait's audience would not likely turn out to see the star battle terrorists or have a dangerous R-rated love affair with Sharon Stone. But it seems like something more than an oversight to bring Dusty back to his old honky-tonk, "where it all started," without having him jump up onstage and play a few numbers. In fact, this missed opportunity only serves to underscore the film's most unlikely notion, that Dusty could return to his home town and old honky tonk without being recognized by anyone, which would be something like Bruce Springsteen stopping off at the Stone Pony for a quick beer without turning a head.

If anything, PURE COUNTRY could have used more music and less scenario, given the shaky screenplay and Strait's somnambulent screen presence when he's doing anything *but* singing. To compensate, Cain turns up the volume—way up—on Warren, introducing her as a steamy vision in shrink-wrapped red leather that makes the most of her magnificent legs and cleavage. Glasser's strident spunkiness is no match for someone who could set a rock's hormones ablaze by just showing up and who here makes selling out seem the only reasonable alternative.

Unfortunately, Warren's (VICTOR/VICTORIA, CHOOSE ME) performance is not among her best due to a character so sketchy it's not even clear whether she works for Dusty or vice versa. Instead, they just seem to have some deep and unspoken bond that reduces Dusty to cantankerousness and Lula to facial-twitching lunacy, the latter thanks to monstrous, merciless closeups that make Warren look as though her head were going to explode at any second. More likely, she's holding back the urge to scream, "Wake up!" at her co-star. Even with Warren's presence, PURE COUNTRY is still a pretty dull row to hoe. Without her, it would have been a cinematic sedative, tickets available only by prescription. *(Mild adult situations and violence.)*

p, Jerry Weintraub; d, Christopher Cain; w, Rex McGee; ph, Richard Bowen; ed, Jack Hofstra; m, Steve Dorff; prod d, Jeffrey Howard; set d, Derek R. Hill

Romance/Drama/Musical **(PR: A MPAA: PG)**

PUSHED TO THE LIMIT

Mimi Productions; Stepping Out Inc. ~ Imperial Entertainment Corporation c

Mimi Lesseos *(Mimi)*, Verrel Lester Reed, Jr. *(Vern)*, Henry Hayshi *(Harry Lee)*, Greg Ostrin *(John Cordon)*, Michael Foley *(Nick)*, Phong Atwood *(Nick)*, James Bashaw *(Bodyguard)*, Barbara Braverman *(Mom)*, Christ Calven *(Inga)*, Darryl Cotton *(Priest)*, Terrance Curtis *(Tony)*, Alex Demir *(Mike)*, Pete Esposito *(1st Man)*, Alfons Giodano *(Fernel)*, Chad Hamilton *(Nephew)*, Lorraine Hawkin *(Terri)*, Jim Hooker *(FBI Agent)*, Terry Mack *(FBI Agent)*, Paul Wyanabi *(Kim)*, Louie Lesseos *(Louie)*, Eva Lesseos-Lypher *(Eva)*, Anna Maria *(Cousin)*, Arturo Mendoza *(2nd Pal)*, Jackie Merino *(Niece)*, Jonathan Mittleman *(Leonard Worthstein)*, Robert Morgenroth *(Doctor)*, Johnny Nungray *(2nd Man)*, Tino Orsini *(Byron)*, William Robinson *(Limo Driver)*, Rick Shaw *(Fred)*, Frank Trejo *(Frank)*, Edward Paul Zubia *(Dale)*, Amy Bancroft *(Sheeba)*, Ronda Kolodjl *(Bertha)*, Cynthia Prouder *(Quatro)*, Ulf Ranger *(Jack Stud)*, Mouchette Van Helsdingen *(Starella)*, Vivian Wickliffe *(Chata)*

Champion professional wrestler and kickboxer Mimi Lesseos strives for action stardom in the relentlessly inept PUSHED TO THE LIMIT and comes up empty.

The nominal story begins as Mimi (Lesseos) has just defeated Sheeba (Amy Bancroft) for the women's world wrestling title. To celebrate, she goes home to visit her family, catching her brother, Johnny (Gregg Ostrin) snorting cocaine in the bathroom. Mimi pleases her Mom (Barbara Braverman), who looks askance at her wrestling celebrity, by announcing that she is going to fill in for a Las Vegas dancer in a revue who has broken her leg. As she dances in the revue, Johnny is killed by rich Chinese drug dealer and kickboxing enthusiast Harry Lee (Henry Hayashi). Vowing revenge for her brother's murder, she challenges Lee's number one kickboxing bodyguard, Inga (Christi Calven), to a kickboxing match.

With the spiritual guidance of Vern (Verrel Lester Reed, Jr.), Mimi rises in the ranks of kickboxers to fight Inga. During Mimi's and Inga's fight to the death, the FBI, finding out about Lee's illicit drug operations, raids the kickboxing arena, causing a hysterical melee as the audience races for exits. Mimi's high-kicking renders Inga groggy and, in her stupor, thinking that Henry Lee is Mimi, Inga kickboxes him to death by cracking his spine and breaking his neck. Mimi wins the match and Inga is hauled away by the cops.

Susan Sontag in her seminal essay "Against Interpretation" refers to film as the most exciting and the most important of all art forms because of the "latitude it gives for making mistakes in it and still be good." But a film of the calibre of PUSHED TO THE LIMIT defies criticism by its multitude of mistakes, from Lesseos's self-aggrandizing screenplay to Michael Mileham's bungled direction—rendering it not good, not bad, but gleefully awful.

Lesseos, as screenwriter, graces her character with such a self-imposed layer of godlike goodness and saccharine self-importance, that she seems to be angling for the Nobel Peace Prize. At one point in the film, a family member tells Mimi that she is "a woman on the move and women admire that. You know, like a role model. You're a woman of the 90s." To which Mimi responds diffidently, "I don't know. I guess I am a role model." At another juncture in the film, arch villain Harry Lee tells her, "You not only have class and brains, but compassion as well." But this compassionate woman of the 90s is also a kickboxing wrestler of the most cold-hearted sort who dispassionately rises in the kickboxing ranks by snapping and breaking countless spines and necks. Mimi's cheery outlook (she responds to her mother's concern over Johnny's drug dealing by saying, "Nobody's perfect") hides a not too hidden bloodlust (she tells Vern after first seeing Harry Lee, "Let's kill him now"), which makes her deification very disturbing.

Thankfully, Michael Mileham's incompetent direction blunts any glorification of Lesseos. Mileham directs with his eyes closed—scenes are jumbled and the point of scenes obscured by characters who block the camera lens. The sound is garbled and indistinct and the editing is clumsy and unstructured (disregarding any editing principles, the film repeatedly cuts from Johnny's murder to Mimi's Las Vegas dance number, which looks like THE RITE OF SPRING meets TARZAN). Technically the film works like a bad porno movie without the sex scenes.

It is unclear to whom PUSHED TO THE LIMIT will appeal. As a kickboxing demonstration, it is defeated by the atrociously directed fight scenes. As a film featuring a strong role model for women, it is defeated by the abject egoism of the star. As campy trash, it is defeated by its neo-fascist conservatism. But as a truly bad film, you can't get any better—or worse—than this shoddy and cheapjack ego trip.

p, Mimi Lesseos; d, Michael Mileham; w, Mimi Lesseos; ph, Bodo Holst; ed, Peter Cohen; m, Miriam Cutler

Action/Martial Arts **(PR: C MPAA: R)**

QUARREL, THE ★★½

(Canada) 88m Atlantis Films; Apple & Honey Productions; Comweb Productions ~ American Playhouse Theatrical Films c

Saul Rubinek *(Hersh Rasseyner)*, R.H. Thomson *(Chaim Kovler)*

A gently ironic, but essentially Hasidic, debate between two middle-aged Jews who are reunited after more than a decade forms the dramatic core of THE QUARREL, a modest film about man's relationship to his God.

A large part of the film's ironic mood stems from its setting in postwar Montreal. It's 1948, and a huge cross dominates the city's Mont Royal Park where, by pure chance, Chaim Kovler (R.H. Thomson) meets old childhood rival and now Rabbi Hersh Rasseyner (Saul Rubinek). They had been fellow students at a religious school, until Chaim left to pursue a career as a writer and the war separated them further by sending Chaim to Siberia and Hersh to Auschwitz. Their wartime experiences and the fate of their old lives and friends in Bialystok, Poland, start them on their views of religion, although Chaim still defers to his old training and hesitates to light up a cigarette during a day that is sacred to practicing Jews.

Since Chaim writes for the Yiddish press, there is no question of assimilation and the film seems to counterpoint this theme by its setting. As in prewar Poland, the two Jews are almost surrounded by an alien culture. French is heard as they wander by the people in the park. They are alone except for an ingratiating female who accosts Chaim. He'd met and slept with her the night before; she's apparently a very young Auschwitz survivor and, as it turns out, one of Hersh's most passionate students.

In their debate Hersh makes the persuasive argument for a religiously based morality since reason alone could be seen as a support for the crimes committed by either Stalin's Communism or Hitler's Nazism. Chaim, however, counters that if he knew God, he'd put him on trial. Though they never reconcile their differences on this issue, the two do come together on more personal questions. Chaim had left his wife and children behind when he left for Russia since he mistakenly thought only men were being seized for forced labor, while Hersh never got along with a severe father who tended to favor his brightest student, Chaim. On this theme they can absolve each other of guilt and renew their ruptured friendship.

Despite its occasional charms (Chaim always nervously notes how Hersh brushes away the dirt on any surface they sit on) and its evocative representation of postwar Montreal, THE QUARREL is only for selected tastes. The whole film, called "a sort of Jewish MY DINNER WITH ANDRE" by one Canadian critic, may be just too self-involved and philosophical. Besides the Jewish reaction to wartime genocide, screenwriter David Brandes and director Eli Cohen have taken on one of the grandest themes possible, God and man, and such topics do not make for easy entertainment.

p, Kim Todd, David Brandes; d, Eli Cohen; w, David Brandes, (based on the play by Joseph Telushkin and the story "My Quarrel with Hersh Rasseyner" by Chaim Grade); ph, John Berrie; ed, Havelock Gradidge; m, William Goldstein; prod d, Michael Joy; art d, Michael Joy

Drama **(PR: A MPAA: NR)**

RADIO FLYER ★½

120m Stonebridge Entertainment; Donner/Shuler-Donner Productions ~ Columbia c

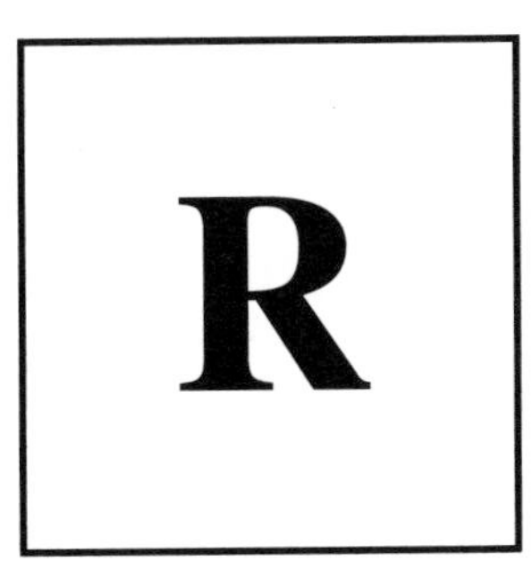

Lorraine Bracco *(Mary)*, John Heard *(Daugherty)*, Adam Baldwin *(The King)*, Elijah Wood *(Mike)*, Joseph Mazzello *(Bobby)*, Ben Johnson *(Geronimo Bill)*, Sean Baca *(Fisher)*, Robert Munic *(Older Fisher)*, Garette Ratliff *(Chad)*, Thomas Ian Nicholas *(Ferdie)*, Noah Verduzco *(Victor Hernandez)*, Isaac Ocampo *(Jorge Hernandez)*, Kaylan Romero *(Jesus Hernandez)*, Abraham Verduzco *(Carlos Hernandez)*, T.J. Evans *(Big Raymond)*, Victor DiMattia *(Little Raymond)*, Adam Hendershott *(1st Boy)*, Daniel Bieber *(2nd Boy)*, Coleby Lombardo *(1st Fisher Friend)*, Mike Simmrin *(2nd Fisher Friend)*, Elden Ratliff *(3rd Fisher Friend)*, Lennard Camarillo *(4th Fisher Friend)*, Lois Foraker *(Aunt)*, William J. Bonnel *(Uncle)*, Henry LaPlante *(Priest)*, Stephen Kahan *(Coffee Shop Manager)*, Steven Anthony Jones *(Postman)*, Paul Tuerpe *(Market Cashier)*, Scott Lloyd Nimerfro *(Golfer)*, Reye Reed *(Restaurant Patron)*, Susan Gale Linn *(Waitress at Coffee Shop)*, Dawan Scott *(Bigfoot)*, James Oliver *(Gas Station Attendant)*, Michael Maiello *(Gas Station Patron)*, Hattie Schwartzberg *(1st Ticket Taker)*, Joan Hyman *(2nd Ticket Taker)*, John Mazzello *(School Boy)*, Hannah Wood *(School Girl)*, James W. Gavin *(Pilot)*, Tom Hanks *(Narration)*

The production woes of RADIO FLYER could themselves form the basis for a movie, what with the firing of writer-director David Mickey Evans, the replacement of Rosanna Arquette with Lorraine Bracco, the rewriting of the screenplay, the twice-delayed opening and the deposing of Columbia studio head Frank Price after production was completed. The resulting film is like a travesty of a Spielberg paean to childhood innocence—an uplifting fantasy about child abuse and suicide.

Two young boys are arguing over a toy airplane when their father (Tom Hanks) puts a stop to the fight by intoning, "History is all in the mind of the teller. Truth is in the telling." He then relates a tall tale from his childhood, beginning with a cross-country drive as Mary (Lorraine Bracco) and her two children, Mike (Elijah Wood) and Bobby (Joseph Mazzello), head to northern California to start a new life after being abandoned by the childrens' father. In California, Mary meets and marries a mechanic to whom the children refer as "The King" (Adam Baldwin) and the family moves into a lower-middle-class suburb. Ostracized by the neighborhood kids, Mike and Bobby take refuge in their own fantasy world.

When the King begins to abuse Bobby physically, the two children conceal the fact from their mother. They begin to fantasize about turning their Radio Flyer wagon into a makeshift aircraft so that Bobby can fly away from his miserable home life. When their dog, Shane, is injured by the King, Bobby decides to try and escape in the Radio Flyer that night. Mike leaves a note for their mother and the children prepare for Bobby's nocturnal journey. The King sees the note and chases them but the children elude him and, after a tearful farewell, Bobby takes off in his Radio Flyer, apparently successfully.

Bobby, we are told, later went on to be a successful pilot who traveled all over the world. As we cut back to the framing narrative, however, we see that the story-teller—Mike as an adult—is in tears, implying that Bobby died the night of his "flight" away from suburbia.

RADIO FLYER attempts to conjure childhood in magical, ethereal terms, but a film that addresses child abuse and suicide requires a sensitive directorial hand—a Richard Mulligan or a Francois Truffaut. Instead, RADIO FLYER is helmed by Richard Donner, director of SUPERMAN and the LETHAL WEAPON series. Donner's efforts at balancing grim reality with fantasy only succeed in clouding the issues at hand, with tricksy camerawork replacing directorial vision. The King is shot in disjointed close-ups (hand opening a can of beer, feet getting out of a pickup truck, fast cuts of a face) that make him a cipher rather than a character. When Bobby is beaten, it always happens off-camera, distancing the audience from the horror of what happens and thus making it harder to understand Bobby's motivation. The fantasy element involving the Radio Flyer wagon is handled in an overblown Spielbergian style of almost religious intensity. But where Spielberg at his best conveys a sense of genuine awe and wonder, Donner gives us a secondhand mysticism ("Bobby could see the true potential of the wagon"). To add insult to injury, the images of RADIO FLYER cannot themselves convey what is happening, forcing Donner to rely upon Hanks's narration to explain the story. This preempts any possible emotional involvement in the film by baldly describing feelings that are not evident on the screen (after a particularly ludicrous dream sequence involving a giant buffalo, Hanks explains the scene by saying, "The dream had given me strength, a sudden sense of purpose"). *(Profanity, violence.)*

p, Lauren Shuler-Donner; d, Richard Donner; w, David Mickey Evans; ph, Laszlo Kovacs; ed, Stuart Baird, Dallas Puett; m, Hans Zimmer; prod d, J. Michael Riva; art d, David Frederick Klassen; set d, Michael Taylor; cos, April Ferry

Fantasy/Drama (PR: C MPAA: PG-13)

RAISE THE RED LANTERN ★★★½

(China/Hong Kong) 125m Era International; Salon Productions; China Film Co-Production Corporation ~ Orion Classics c

(DAHONG DENGLONG GAOGAO GUA)

Gong Li *(Songlian)*, Ma Jingwu *(Chen Zuoqian)*, He Caifei *(Meishan)*, Cao Cuifeng *(Zhuoyun)*, Jin Shuyuan *(Yuru)*, Kong Lin *(Yan'er)*, Ding Weimin *(Mother Song)*, Cui Zhihgang *(Doctor Gao)*, Chu Xiao *(Feipu)*, Cao Zhengyin *(Old Servant)*, Zhao Qi *(Chen Baishun–Housekeeper)*

While the People's Republic of China bids to become an international economic superpower, one of its most successful exports has also been the most embarrassing for the Beijing regime. He is Zhang Yimou, a master "Fifth Generation" filmmaker who emerged from the reopened Beijing Film Academy during the liberal climate of the early 1980s, and his historical dramas resonate with subtexts of repression, resistance and retribution.

Though they take place in the thematically "safe" era of pre-Mao feudalism, Zhang's films have rankled communist officialdom; his acclaimed JU DOU was banned on the mainland in 1991, just as it made history as the first Chinese picture to receive an Academy Award nomination for best foreign language film. And even though Zhang's screenplay for RAISE THE RED LANTERN (based on the 1989 novel *Wives and Concubines* by Su Tong) got a stamp of approval from the cultural watchdogs, the finished production met the same fate, censored at home while playing to great praise abroad.

Set in a wealthy 1920s Chinese household, the tale has the timeless quality of a fable, as a lovely nineteen-year-old named Songlian (Gong Li), forced to set aside her academic ambitions, resignedly sells herself to a rich man who already has three wives. "Let me be a concubine," she declares. "Isn't that a woman's fate?" Songlian arrives at the ancient, sprawling palace of Master Chen (Ma Jingwu), where she is welcomed as "Fourth Sister" in the aristocrat's harem. But beneath the polite surface boils a cauldron of intrigue and hatred, as rival wives scheme to win the Master's favor from day to day.

As the freshest arrival, Songlian gets the most of Chen's sexual attentions, until he's dragged away by the complaints of wife number three, Meishan (He Caifei), a onetime opera star who now craves the spotlight at home. Songlian is comforted by Second Sister, Zhuoyun (Cao Cuifeng), a kind-looking matron who is later accurately described by Meishan as having the face of the Buddah and the heart of a scorpion. By playing Songlian against Meishan and Yan'er (Kong Lin), a servant girl with whom Chen is dallying on the side, Zhuoyun eventually becomes the Master's favorite. A first wife, elderly and withdrawn, remains in the background.

Zhuoyun and Meishan have an edge in that each has given the Master a child; Songlian counters by faking pregnancy, but the ruse fails and the disgraced Fourth Sister permanently loses her status in the household. The abused Yan'er dies of heartbreak, and when Zhuoyun reveals Meishan's affair with the family doctor, Chen's lackeys brutally execute the diva. The film ends exactly one year after it began, with Songlian now hopelessly insane—and a new wife arriving apprehensively at the palace.

Almost all of this superbly rendered tragedy takes place within the confines of the Master's vast estate, and Zhang Yimou uses a mostly stationary camera to frame the characters within careful compositions of doorways, portals, canopies and courtyards. The severe, rigid style effectively turns the sumptuous residence into a metaphorical prison compound, the irony being that these women are their own jailers. Their strategems to gain dominance in this microcosmic society only reinforce their captivity and subservience to the likes of Chen. Zhang cannily avoids showing the Master clearly. His features are always obscured or averted, so even his age cannot be determined. He is the archetypal patriarchal oppressor—faceless, distant but ever-present in mind even when not in sight.

The translated title refers to a nightly ritual: each wife has her own house, and the one in which the Master chooses to sleep is festooned with huge red lanterns. In addition the chosen wife receives an elaborate foot massage (loud enough for the other wives to hear) and influence over the menu at meals. Such are the privileges over which these women destroy each other. As bleak as the material sounds, there is a certain sardonic humor, mostly from the spirited Meishan and even the Master himself, who's absolutely baffled as to why his spouses seem so discontented.

The sex and violence are left offscreen; nonetheless, the more prosaic commentators have stated that Zhang's use of sensuality in his films (not at all explicit by Western standards) is what really incurs the wrath of Beijing bureaucrats, rather than political content. Still, in one scene Songlian confronts the men who murdered Meishan and is told that nothing has happened—echoing Chinese denials of the Tienamen Square massacre of student protestors in June, 1989. A Hong Kong critic stated that Asian viewers would not miss the reference.

This handsome-looking $1 million production was financed by Taiwanese interests through a Hong Kong intermediary, and it was Hong Kong that submitted RAISE THE RED LANTERN as its official candidate for the 1992 Academy Award for best foreign language film, a move disapproved by Beijing. (The film eventually received a nomination, but lost to MEDITERRANEO.) Zhang Yimou endeared himself even less to the straight-laced Communist Party when he caused a scandal by leaving his wife for actress Gong Li, recurring star of his films. Nonethless, midway through 1992, after RAISE THE RED LANTERN reaffirmed Zhang as a rising star of world cinema, the party relented and approved a September release of the picture in China. The same decision freed up Zhang's latest, THE STORY OF QIU JU, also starring Gong Li, for mainland distribution. JU DOU, however, remains forbidden. *(Adult situations.)*

p, Chiu Fu-Sheng; d, Zhang Yimou; w, Ni Zhen, (from the novel *Wives and Concubines* by Su Tong); ph, Zhao Fei; ed, Du Yuan; m, Zhao Jiping; art d, Cao Jiuping, Dong Huamiao; cos, Huang Lihua

Drama **(PR: C MPAA: PG)**

RAISING CAIN ★½

95m Steller Jay Inc.; Universal; Pacific Western Productions ~ Universal c

John Lithgow *(Dr. Carter Nix/Cain/Josh/Margo)*, Lolita Davidovich *(Jenny)*, Steven Bauer *(Jack Dante)*, Frances Sternhagen *(Dr. Waldheim)*, Gregg Henry *(Lieutanent Terri)*, Tom Bower *(Sergeant Cally)*, Mel Harris *(Sarah)*, Teri Austin *(Karen)*, Gabrielle Carteris *(Nan)*, Barton Heyman *(Mack)*, Amanda Pombo *(Amy)*, Kathleen Callan *(Emma)*, Ed Hooks *(Coroner)*, Jim Johnson *(Night Clerk)*, Karen Kahn *(Saleslady)*, Noe Montoya *(Gardener)*, Riq Boogie Espinoza *(Gardener)*, Carolyn Morrell *(Newscaster)*, W. Allen Taylor *(Peters)*, Scott Townley *(Little Boy Josh)*, Mary Uhland *(Receptionist)*, Steve Schill *(Weatherman)*, James Van Harper *(Young Detective)*

Director Brian De Palma's eagerly awaited return to the psycho thriller genre that helped make him famous perfectly underscores the difference between plot and story in a film. "Story" refers to the events that occur, or are merely referred to, in a movie; "plot" refers to how these events are arranged in the screenplay. De Palma also wrote RAISING CAIN, and its story, upon synopsizing, seems fairly straightforward.

Carter Nix (John Lithgow) is a child psychologist who's become obsessed with the rearing of his little daughter. To this end, he's adopted a stay-at-home lifestyle and even installed a video camera in the girl's room, the better to be able to check on her. But his obsession has grown into dementia, and he embarks on a campaign to kill women he knows and steal their children. His intention is to deliver them to his father and his brother Cain (both of whom are also played by Lithgow), who plan to conduct psychological experiments on the kids, and who may also in fact exist only in Carter's mind.

Carter's wife Jenny (Lolita Davidovich) is slated to be Carter's last victim and their daughter the last subject. When Jenny, distressed by Carter's strange behavior of late, falls back into the arms of old lover Jack Dante (Steven Bauer), the daffy doc realizes that Jack is the perfect scapegoat for his crimes. After depositing the body of one of his victims in the trunk of Jack's car, Carter then goes after Jenny, imprisoning her in her own car and submerging her in a marsh (De Palma does his obligatory PSYCHO homage/pillage here). Jenny survives, however, leading to Carter's capture and Jack's exoneration.

As elderly Dr. Waldheim (Frances Sternhagen) reveals, Carter was the subject of bizarre psychological experiments himself as a child, and is now a schizophrenic who labors under the delusion that he must help his father continue his work. During a session with Dr. Waldheim, Carter overpowers her and escapes wearing her clothing and wig, intending to deliver his daughter to his father (who is, in fact, alive) and escape the country with him. Jenny follows him to the motel where Carter's father is staying, confronts the two men and struggles to take back her child. Jack arrives with the police, who shoot Carter's father dead as Jack saves the baby. Some time later, Jenny and Jack are back together and she takes her child to the park—where Carter, still in drag, is lurking.

As stated, that's the story of RAISING CAIN. The *plot*, however, is an utterly incoherent mishmash of flashbacks, dream sequences and voiceovers. Evidently, De Palma wanted to present different points of view and hallucinations, leaving the audience slowly to grasp how they all tie together, but all he succeeds in doing is thoroughly confusing the audience as to what's supposed to be going on, and even how it falls into place chronologically.

To make matters worse, all this cinematic bait-and-switching allows De Palma no time to explain anyone's motivation or backstory in a visual manner. Subsequently, the audience is subjected to big, unwieldy chunks of expository dialogue that even gimmicks like a five-minute tracking shot (during Sternhagen's explanation about Carter's background) can't make palatable. De Palma certainly lets all his visual stylistics hang out, but the result is ludicrously overdirected, leading to the completely berserk climax at the motel, complete with a raging storm, a man in a dress, slow-motion, beer-guzzlin' rowdies cheering from the sidelines and dialogue like, "Watch it! You're going to kill someone with that sundial!"

Better acting might have helped make RAISING CAIN more palatable, if not plausible, but only Lithgow seems to be having fun with his multiple role. Davidovich and Bauer play their parts with glum seriousness, with Bauer (SCARFACE, RUNNING SCARED) in particular seeming misdirected; in a police station scene where Jack and Jenny are questioned about the horrible events they've just undergone, all Jack seems interested in is jumping Jenny's bones. Davidovich (BLAZE, THE INNER CIRCLE), on the other hand, is just plain awful, and her stony performance clashes badly with the absurd melodramatics of De Palma's approach.

Every so often, a neat little moment will appear and RAISING CAIN will appear to be getting back on track, but like his schizophrenic villain, De Palma always winds up letting his worst instincts get the better of him. *(Violence, profanity, adult situations.)*

p, Gale Anne Hurd; d, Brian De Palma; w, Brian De Palma; ph, Stephen H. Burum; ed, Paul Hirsch, Bonnie Koehler, Robert Dalva; m, Pino Donaggio; prod d, Doug Kraner; art d, Mark Billerman; set d, Barbara Munch; cos, Bobbie Read

Thriller **(PR: O MPAA: R)**

RAMPAGE ★★½

97m DeLaurentiis Entertainment Group; Rampage Productions ~ Vestron Video c

Michael Biehn *(Anthony Fraser)*, Alex McArthur *(Charles Reece)*, Nicholas Campbell *(Albert Morse)*, Deborah Van Valkenburgh *(Kate Fraser)*, John Harkins *(Dr. Keddie)*, Art Lafleur *(Mel Sanderson)*, Billy Greenbush *(Judge McKinsey)*, Royce D. Applegate *(Gene Tippetts)*, Grace Zabriskie *(Naomi Reece)*, Carlos Palomino *(Nestade)*, Roy London *(Dr. Paul Rudin)*, Donald Hotton *(Dr. Leon Gables)*, Andy Romano *(Spencer Whalen)*, Patrick Cronin *(Harry Ballenger)*, Roger Nolan *(Dr. Ray Blair)*, Rosalyn Marshall *(Sally Ann)*, Whitby Hertford *(Andrew Tippetts)*, David A. Kimball *(Doctor in Flashbacks)*, Brenda Lilly *(Eileen Tippetts)*, Joseph Whipp *(Dr. George Mahon)*, Chip Heller *(Guard #1)*, Rodney Cornelius *(Guard #2)*, Dave Alan Johnson *(Del Cameron)*, Robert Broyles *(Joe Kautman)*, Edith Fields *(Rose Gurgan)*, Neal Hahn *(Mr. Hendriksen)*, Gale Beeman *(Mrs. Hendriksen)*, Marni Webb *(Mrs. Ellis)*, Paul Gaddoni *(Aaron Tippetts)*, Bernard Zanck *(Priest)*, Noreen Farley *(Waitress)*, Charlie Holliday *(Narc #1)*, Ken Jackson *(Narc #2)*, Miguel Najera *(Cardenas)*, John Petievich *(Jury Foreman)*, Miriam Gray, Tara O'Leary, Dorothy D. Johnson, George John, Edward Ivory *(Jurors)*, Violet Yip *(Court Clerk)*, Juliette Deinum *(Wendy)*, Robert Gonzales *(1st Guard)*, Steven A. Jones *(2nd Guard)*, Dr. Javad Jamshidi *(Dr. Jamshidi)*, Robert Knudsen *(ID Technician)*, Marina Valtierra *(ID Technician)*, Gaetano Comporato *(ID Technician)*, Clifford Milton *(Evidence Technician)*, Pamela Tarver *(Woman in Car)*, Chelsea Crank *(Molly Fraser)*, Margaret Rose Ott *(Mrs. Cardenas)*, S. Richard Goldman, Robert Wright, Colleen Casey-Rohde, Susan Thomas, Laura Moreno-Orrison, Leonard Neuman *(Emergency Room Technicians)*, Richard J. Baskin *(Attorney)*, Tino R. Enebrad, Jr. *(Officer)*, Robert Louis Raballo *(Patient)*, Angelo M. Vitale *(Assistant DA)*, Richard Markel *(Bailiff)*, Mack Haywood Flanders *(Sheriff)*, Erin Hazlett-Oakes *(Technologist)*, Nancy L. Sicotte *(Technologist)*, Elizabeth J. Prager *(Technologist)*, Michael Tamburro *(Helicopter Pilot)*, Peter McKernan, Jr. *(Co-Pilot)*

A courtroom drama focusing on both the horror of an apparently mad crime and the question of legal insanity, RAMPAGE is based on the real case of Richard Chase and the novel about it by California district attorney William Wood. Despite some ambiguity about the culprit's sanity, the emphasis in William Friedkin's screenplay is on the grief of the victims' relatives and the plight of the deputy district attorney, normally against the death penalty, who is asking for it in this case.

We first spot Charles Reece (Alex McArthur) wandering through a neat, typical suburban neighborhood and taking note of one particular house. A few days later, having purchased a Luger, he enters that house and shoots a man and two women whom he later mutilates to obtain body parts. While the police launch their investigation of this crime and the young deputy district attorney, Anthony Fraser (Michael Biehn), reevaluates his opinion of the death penalty in the light of this hideous murder, Reece attacks some neighbors whose dog he had poisoned earlier. Once again he kills and mutilates a woman and kidnaps one of her young sons, whose body is later discovered. Reece, however, has been identified and is soon arrested.

At the preliminary investigation, a weak-willed state psychiatrist, Paul Rudin (Roy London), assures Fraser that they do not have to worry about an insanity plea. Indeed, the good-looking, well-spoken Reece appears perfectly normal, as he did at the gun store, despite his household cellar with its collection of body parts, Nazi regalia, religious icons and pornography. The prosecutor, Fraser, is haunted by the death of his young daughter from pneumonia. Fraser's memories or fantasies about her are contrasted with Reece's own bloody imagery. In the course of his transit between courtroom and jail, Reece manages to kill his guards and escapes briefly. He is captured in a church into which he has broken in search of the sacred "blood" and apparently butchered the priest, a crime which Fraser is prohibited from mentioning at the trial.

The district attorney is not the only one with bad memories. The widower in the second series of murders, Gene Tippetts (Royce D. Applegate), leaves behind the house where his wife was killed and violated, and tells his surviving young son that they will leave the state and spend some time travelling. When Fraser implores him to be a witness, the man cites the crime as some sort of judgment with a fatalistic acceptance.

Although the question of Reece's sanity is the subject of the trial's second part, the subject emerges in open debate between Fraser and the defense psychiatrist, Keddie (John Harkins). Although Keddie testifies that he wants to understand the nature of Reece's madness, he had been seen earlier rather smoothly manipulating Rudin's fear of legal liability for having released Reece earlier from a stay in the local mental ward. The defense team eventually asks for a series of novel brain tests that reveal chemical imbalances, and the new findings indicate schizophrenia. The film ends with a chilling inter-title about Reece's chances for release from a mental hospital pending a possible cure.

No stranger to controversy, William Friedkin (THE EXORCIST, THE FRENCH CONNECTION) has tackled a far more serious topic than he can possibly handle. From the film's first quarter-hour, it seems to tip its hand and indicate that Reece is a cunning, if delusional, mass murderer, and the actual subject of the Nazis' extermination plans is raised in Fraser's debate with Keddie. Even Reece's apparently crazy foray into the church could be interpereted as a simple, if vicious, feint to confuse the issue.

For much of his youth, Reece seems to have led a fairly normal life, even enjoying a normal love affair with a high school girlfriend and working at a gas station. It seems clear that he could control some of his impulses to kill; that may be the fine legal point that Friedkin wants to highlight, but he doesn't quite do it. There is no apparent tension in Reece's personality, no internal struggle or debate at all, so that his calm, polite appearance seems a deception, not a thin and fragile veneer. By stressing that deceit, Friedkin has weakened his film. *(Excessive violence.)*

p, David Salven; d, William Friedkin; w, William Friedkin, (from the novel by William P. Wood); ph, Robert D. Yeoman; ed, Jere Huggins; m, Ennio Morricone; prod d, Buddyy Cone; art d, Carol Clements; set d, Nancy Nye

Crime/Thriller **(PR: C MPAA: R)**

RAPID FIRE ★★

96m Robert Lawrence Productions; Fox ~ Fox c

Brandon Lee *(Jake Lo)*, Powers Boothe *(Mace Ryan)*, Nick Mancuso *(Antonio Serrano)*, Raymond J. Barry *(Agent Stuart)*, Kate Hodge *(Karla Withers)*, Tzi Ma *(Kinman Tau)*, Tony Longo *(Brunner Gazzi)*, Michael Paul Chan *(Carl Chang)*, Dustin Nguyen *(Paul Yang)*, Brigitta Stenberg *(Rosalyn)*, Basil Wallace *(Agent Wesley)*, Al Leong *(Minh)*, Francois Chau *(Farris)*, Quentin O'Brien *(Agent Daniels)*, D.J. Howard *(Sharpy)*, Maurice Chasse *(Sharpy)*, Walter Addison *(Detective)*, John Vickery *(Detective)*, C'Esca Lawrence *(Lisa Stuart)*, Donald Li *(Tall Guard)*, Michael Chong *(John Lo)*, Jeff McCarthy *(Agent Anderson)*, Marvin Elkins *(Fireman)*, Steve Pickering *(Cop in Van)*, Ronald William Laurence *(Jail Guard)*, Will Kepper *(Jail Guard)*, Al Foster *(Jail Guard)*, Richard Schiff *(Art Teacher)*, Roy Abramsohn *(Agent Klein)*, Diana Castle *(Cop Gallery Ally)*, Chen Baoer Paul *(Laundry Worker)*, Cedric Young *(Chicago Uniform)*, Peter Russell *(Ambulance Driver)*

Despite a good supporting cast and pretensions to something more than standard martial-arts mayhem, RAPID FIRE demonstrates little more than the late Brandon Lee's ability to carry an action film.

The son of martial arts superstar Bruce Lee makes his major studio debut as Los Angeles art student Jake Lo, who gets caught up in a bloody three-way vendetta involving a grizzled Chicago cop, Mace Ryan (Powers Boothe), and a competing pair of drug kingpins, Antonio Serrano and Kinman Tau (Nick Mancuso and Tzi Ma). The mayhem is set in motion by Serrano, a Mafia drug distributor who wants a bigger piece of Far Eastern supplier Tau's business. Turned off from politics after witnessing the death of his father at Tiananmen Square, Lo is lured to a party of Chinese pro-democracy activists by a sexy figure model from one of his art classes. While there he witnesses the killing of the party sponsor, one of Tau's associates, by Serrano.

Placed under protective custody by federal agents, Lo is brought to Chicago to testify against Serrano where he barely escapes an attempt on his life by crooked agents. With nowhere else to turn, he teams up with Ryan and becomes romantically involved with Ryan's right-hand woman, Karla Withers (Kate Hodge), a tough but sexy Chicago cop. Ryan uses Lo as bait to lure Serrano into giving details of his next big drug shipment. But the arrest of Serrano turns into a pitched battle of bullets, fists and feet. When the smoke clears, Serrano has indeed been apprehended, but he's killed in custody by Tau's henchmen, forcing Ryan to use Lo once again as a pigeon.

Posing as a worker, Lo is sent into the heart of Tau's industrial laundry operation to find out how Tau manages to process his imported opium without soiling any shirts. Lo succeeds, but again things go haywire, forcing Lo to kill his way out to his final confrontation with Tau on the tracks of the Chicago El.

RAPID FIRE is little more than a classy resume film, hobbled by an overcomplicated, undermotivated screenplay. In a perhaps commendable effort to put a new twist into the usual action formula, the filmmakers create a layer of character development in Jake's problematic relationship with his father, which is echoed in his relationship with Ryan. However, the only real effect is to draw attention to the plot's more generic implausibilities, starting with what Lo is even *doing* in the middle of the film's two big battles. The father-son subplot never makes much sense even on its own terms anyway, with Lo attempting to obtain his father's files from the government for some reason or other that has no bearing on the main action. The simple fact is that martial-arts action movies work best when their plots maintain an elemental, almost boneheaded simplicity, hopefully leavened with humor—either intentional or unintentional.

In this case, an opportunity was missed with a talented cast. Mancuso (TIGER WARSAW, UNDER SIEGE) vamps shamelessly and entertainingly through his role as an overripe Mafioso. Boothe (SOUTHERN COMFORT, THE EMERALD FOREST), who can be funny, here mostly plays it straight with a cop who's as inept as he is tough, being unable to make simple arrests without shooting up half of Chicago. Ma (THE MONEY PIT, ROBOCOP 2), an accomplished stage veteran, takes top acting honors with a taut, businesslike performance as an entrepreneur whose chief enterprise happens to be death in a variety of forms—from bullets to white powders. Unfortunately, director Dwight Little can never seem to get his ensemble into anything resembling high gear.

Instead, the action feels bulky and slow-moving, belying the film's title. RAPID FIRE could have used more speed and fury and much less soul-searching static. Lee is the only real reason to watch this film, which gained a certain additional cachet after his death on the set of his next feature, THE CROW. RAPID FIRE proves him to have been an engaging, easygoing screen presence who handled action sequences with some of his father's style and grace. Lee had signed a multi-picture deal with Carolco, the high-profile production company responsible for films including TOTAL RECALL and BASIC INSTINCT, and was clearly on his way to bigger and better things. *(Violence, profanity, adult situations, nudity.)*

p, Robert Lawrence; d, Dwight H. Little; w, Alan B. McElroy, Cindy Cirile, Paul Attanasio, (based on the story by McElroy and Cirile); ph, Ric Waite; ed, Gib Jaffe; m, Christopher Young; prod d, Ron Foreman; art d, Charles Butcher; set d, Leslie Frankenheimer; cos, Erica Edell Phillips

Martial Arts/Action **(PR: C MPAA: R)**

RASPAD ★★★½

(U.S./U.S.S.R.) 105m Dovzheno Film Studios; Lavra Studio Productions ~ MK2 Productions USA bw/c

Sergei Shakurov *(Alexander Zhuralev)*, Tatiana Kochesmasova *(Ludmilla Zhuralev)*, Stanislas Stankevich *(Father Zhuralev)*,

Georgi Drozd *(Anatoli Stepanovich)*, Alexii Cerebriakov *(Valerii)*, Marina Mogilevskaya *(Lyuba)*, Alexii Gorbunov *(Shurik)*, Anatoli Groshevoi *(Ignatii)*, Nikita Buldovskii *(Kolka)*, Natalia Plohotniuk *(Maria)*, Nikilai Docenko *(Valentin Ivanovich)*; Valerii Sheptekita *(Dimitri Stepanovich)*, Valentina Masenko *(Nurse Lida)*, Taracik Mikitenko *(Dimka)*, Vladimir Olekceenko *(Ocip Lukich)*, Olga Kuznetcova *(Ludmilla's Friend)*, Victor Kondratiuk *(Priest)*, Russlan Ivanov *(Religious Man)*, Leonid Ynovskii *(Deputy of City Soviet)*, Alexei Koncovskii *(Fast Old Man)*, Sergei Gavriliuk *(Band Leader)*, Anatolii Vishnevskii *(Party Worker)*, Mikhail Kostiukovskii *(Scientist)*, Anatolii Skorohod *(Director of the Reactor)*

RASPAD is a hard-hitting Ukrainian film that details the horrors and aftermath of the Russian Chernobyl nuclear-reactor incident.

In April 1986, Soviet journalist Alexander Zhuralev (Sergei Shakurov) returns from assignment in Greece to his home in Kiev, only to discover, via an anonymous note, that his wife Ludmilla (Tatiana Kochesmasova) has been having an affair with his bureaucrat friend Shurik (Alexii Gorbunov). To consol himself, Alexander plans a visit with his friend Anatoli Stepanovich (Georgi Drozd), but before they can meet, a fiery explosion rips through one of the Chernobyl reactors, where Anatoli works, and he is one of the first victims. However, no announcements are made by the government, and life continues normally.

Newlyweds Valerii (Alexii Cerebriakov) and Lyuba (Marina Mogilevskaya) mount their motorcycle and set off on a camping honeymoon in the forests near Chernobyl. Soon towns near the site are being evacuated, and in Kiev (about 70 miles south of Chernobyl), Shurik tells Ludmilla about the accident and advises her to leave at once. Alexander, however, is able to find out nothing from his sources in the government. At the train station he discovers mass panic—all tickets are reserved for government officials and their friends. On their trip Valerii and Lyuba see dead animals and are startled by men in white radiation suits examining the area with their instruments; they flee to a church where an Easter mass is in progress. Still, no news from the government is forthcoming.

After a vodka-soaked Easter party, Alexander agrees to allow his wife and their son, Dimko (Taracik Mikitenko), to leave with Shurik only if he arranges access for Alexander to Chernobyl. He joins a small band of reporters on a helicopter that flies over the abandoned area, especially the town of Pripyat, where most of the Chernobyl workers lived. Stunned but feeling heroic for having been able to report on the disaster to his newspaper, Alexander returns home and finds that Ludmilla and Dimko have returned—they will face whatever future they have together as a family.

Translated into English as "collapse," RASPAD is much more than a chronicle of the Chernobyl accident. In it, producer-director-coscreenwriter Mikhail Belikov aims to document a country's entire moral, social, political, and economic disintegration. There are scores of concise and telling details here, from the small (Alexander has forgotten to bring a requested packet of soil from Greece, the homeland of his father, and so he fools the old man with some backyard dirt), to the medium (Ludmilla lies to Alexander about her affair; Valerii and Lyuba have bribed an official to send a relative to an old-age home so that they can take over their small, shared apartment), to the large (government officials tell Alexander there is no danger, then head their limos to the airport for the next flight out). Belikov reserves his greatest scorn for his own profession: the media—in the aftermath of the explosion, the TV channels (seen throughout the film) continue to carry only a marathon bicycle race.

Mostly documentary-like in style, RASPAD is savage and unsubtle in its catalogue of ills, yet it's beautifully controlled, avoiding both cliche and sentimentality, by Belikov, a former director of photography helming his third feature following 1981's THE SHORT NIGHT and 1985's HOW YOUNG WE WERE. The character Alexander is an obvious stand-in for Belikov, who was living in Kiev during the incident and has based his film on stories he heard from friends, relatives and colleagues.

In addition to Kiev, Belikov was allowed to shoot on actual locations, including the contaminated town of Pripyat (row after row of abandoned, deathly still apartment buildings and streets) and, most horrifyingly, the reactor areas of Chenobyl itself (for which scenes Belikov and his crew, three years after the fact, risked contamination themselves). Yet there are also touches of poetry here and some near surreal scenes (the sudden appearances of the white-suited figures at public outdoor events, which the government had allowed to go on after the explosion).

Beginning production with a $600,000 budget on the third anniversary of Chernobyl, and with the Soviet film industry in a collapse of its own, Belikov was technically aided (film stock, etc.) by American producer Peter Almond and the Pacific Film Fund, which brought the movie and Belikov to San Francisco for post-production. The film premiered at the 1990 Cannes Festival and reached US screens on the sixth anniversary of the disaster, the only other filmic treatment of which was a shamefully formulaic disaster movie the 1991 TV film called CHERNOBYL: THE FINAL WARNING. *(Profanity, adult situations.)*

d, Mikhail Belikov; w, Mikhail Belikov, Oleg Pridhodko; ph, Alexander Shagayev, Vassili Truschkovski; ed, Tatiana Magalis; m, Igor Senchuk; prod d, Inna Sichenkova, Vasilli Zaruva; cos, Valentia Gorlan

Drama **(PR: C MPAA: NR)**

REBRO ADAMA

(SEE: ADAM'S RIB)

REFRIGERATOR, THE ★★

86m Avenue D Films Ltd. ~ Avenue D Films Ltd. c

Julia Mueller *(Eileen Bateman)*, David Simonds *(Steve Bateman)*, Angel Caban *(Juan the Plumber)*, Phyllis Sanz *(Tanya)*, Nena Segal *(Eileen's Mother)*, Jaime Rojo *(Paolo–The Plumber's Assistant)*, Michelle DeCosta *(Young Eileen)*

THE REFRIGERATOR is billed as a supernatural horror comedy which ultimately is its downfall—too many chickens in the pot. First-time director Nicholas Jacobs's juxtaposition of genres is compelling in thought, but unfortunately on film the results just don't measure up.

Eileen (Julia Mueller) and Steve Bateman (David Simonds) are freshly married, carefree and faced with a bright future as they leave Ohio for their new life together in New York City. Steve has landed a new job, Eileen has her career as an actress to anticipate, and they've been told of a great apartment which is available. The only problem with this particular apartment is that it comes replete with a haunted refrigerator. The prospective renters aren't spooked off when a mysterious woman (Phyllis Sanz) appears out of nowhere offering the prophetic words, "Get out!"

After moving into the place, for a song, courtesy of a desperate landlord who has had trouble keeping tenants alive, the happy couple are suprised to find Steve's favorite cheese waiting in the fridge. It isn't long though before the fridge stops giving and starts taking. It begins emitting strange yellow light, oozes sludge and growls at all hours of the night. Steve's behavior grows stranger too as he becomes compelled to stand in front of the icebox in a trancelike state. This creates a growing chasm between the newlyweds; Eileen, who's begun having frightening flashbacks from her childhood, seems to be getting more attention from the building's plumber, Juan (Angel Caban), a sympathetic type who once dreamt of being a dancer in his native Bolivia.

Before long the refrigerator turns vicious and kills a maintenance man, then it swallows Eileen's mother in a gulp. Eileen begs Steve to throw it out, but even after Juan yells, "It is the gateway to Hell, the very devil himself," her hubby can't justify spending money for a new one. The final horrible night arrives and Steve is killed by Eileen as he tries to drag her off to Hell. This is followed by an orgy of kitchen appliances gone mad. Eileen and Juan barely escape with their lives, but go on to success as a flamenco team.

While the basic premise of THE REFRIGERATOR—take a couple of dream yuppies and plop them into a world of madness and horror—is satirical and wry, the final results aren't very satisfying. The main failure of the film is that none of the separate entities work on their own—the funny scenes generally aren't funny and the scary parts, while original in idea, aren't scary, only overly gory. On top of this, Jacobs throws in a couple of ultraserious segments involving the mother-daughter relationship that are completely out of place.

Mueller and Simonds as the jinxed couple offer up the right amount of exuberance and angst. Caban, though, as the plumber who looks more like an urban commando, best fits his role. Jacobs's eclectic use of music, from campy to melodramatic, is one of the highlights of the film. If he had put a little more punch in his screenplay, been more daring with his satire and put some real scares in the film, the end result would have made a lot more sense. Maybe his intentions weren't to make us laugh or get chills down our spine—it's a parody, after all. Perhaps he just wanted to make a statement about the inherent evil of domesticity. If so, it could have been done many other ways. *(Violence, profanity.)*

p, Christopher Oldcorn; d, Nicholas A.E. Jacobs; w, Nicholas A.E. Jacobs; ph, Paul Gibson; ed, P.J. Pesce, Nicholas Jacobs, Suzanne Pillsbury, Christopher Oldcorn; m, Don Peterkofsky, Chris Burke, Adam Roth; art d, Therese Deprez

Comedy/Horror **(PR: C MPAA: NR)**

RESERVOIR DOGS ★★★★

99m Dog Eat Dog Productions ~ Miramax c

Harvey Keitel *(Mr. White/Larry)*, Tim Roth *(Mr. Orange/Freddy)*, Michael Madsen *(Mr. Blonde/Vic)*, Christopher Penn *(Nice Guy/Eddie)*, Steve Buscemi *(Mr. Pink)*, Lawrence Tierney *(Joe Cabot)*, Randy Brooks *(Holdaway)*, Kirk Baltz *(Marvin Nash)*, Eddie Bunker *(Mr. Blue)*, Quentin Tarantino *(Mr. Brown)*, Rich Turner *(1st Sheriff)*, David Steen *(2nd Sheriff)*, Tony Cosmo *(3rd Sheriff)*, Stevo Poliy *(4th Sheriff)*, Michael Sottile *(Teddy)*, Robert Ruth *(Shot Cop)*, Lawrence Bender *(Young Cop/Voice for Background Radio Play)*, Linda Kaye *(Shocked Woman)*, Suzanne Celeste *(Shot Woman)*, Steven Wright *(Voice of K-Billy DJ)*, Laurie Latham, Maria Strova, Burr Steers, Craig Hamann *(Voices for Backround Radio Play)*

RESERVOIR DOGS boasts an extraordinary new talent leading a first-rate cast in one of the year's most original films.

The film starts with several men dressed in black suits sitting around a table in a diner, debating topics including the real meaning of the Madonna song, "Like a Virgin." After the opening credit sequence, we cut to the aftermath of a jewelry heist gone awry. The protagonists, whom we previously met in the diner, are strangers who address each other using false names assigned by the heist's organizer, Joe Cabot (Lawrence Tierney). Wounded Mr. Orange (Tim Roth) is screaming and flailing but mostly bleeding in the back seat of a car driven by Mr. White (Harvey Keitel), who's trying to comfort and reassure him. They return to the gang rendezvous, an abandoned warehouse somewhere in Los Angeles, where they meet Mr. Pink (Steve Buscemi), who has escaped with the stolen diamonds. Convinced there is a traitor in their gang, Pink proposes to White that they simply leave Orange to die and split the jewels. Their deliberations are interrupted by Mr. Blonde (Michael Madsen), who has brought along a cop, Marvin Nash (Kirk Baltz), he took as a hostage.

Later, "Nice Guy" Eddie (Christopher Penn) arrives, sent by his father, Cabot, to try and straighten out the mess. He takes White and Pink with him to get rid of the cars they used, while Blonde stays behind and tortures the cop. After slashing the cop's face and cutting off one of his ears, Blonde pours kerosene on him. Before he can set him on fire though, Orange, who had been unconscious, wakes up and kills Blonde. He then reveals to the cop that he's an undercover detective who has infiltrated the gang—something already discovered by Cabot, who arrives furious and prepares to shoot Orange. Orange protests his innocence, claiming he shot Blonde because *he* had revealed himself to be the cop. The now-returned White believes Orange and, to protect him, pulls a gun on Cabot, leading Eddie to pull a gun on White. The stand-off ends with the three men shooting each other and Eddie and Cabot dying. Pink is killed when he tries to escape alone with the diamonds, not knowing that the warehouse has been surrounded by police waiting for Orange's signal to move in. Orange reveals his identity to White, who is killed by the police as he's killing Orange.

As in GLENGARRY GLEN ROSS, the actual heist in RESERVOIR DOGS is never seen. What was supposed to happen is disclosed via flashbacks that etch in the backgrounds of key players White, Orange, Blonde, Eddie and Joe. We also see bits and pieces of the bloody aftermath and find out that, rather than being a victim of police gunfire or his colleagues' bad aim, Orange was shot by a woman whose car he was stealing while accompanied by White. Orange returns fire, killing the woman, and writer-director Quentin Tarantino pauses for just the briefest moment to allow the realization to sink in that Orange, a cop, has just murdered an innocent bystander.

Tarantino has listed both Howard Hawks and Jean-Luc Godard as being among his favorite filmmakers, and RESERVOIR DOGS is indebted to both. The Godard influence is apparent in the fragmentation of the narrative, which deconstructs the criminal subculture as a parody of "legitimate" capitalism. But the tone is more absurdly comic, looking back to certain Hawks films in which bloodshed becomes a kind of gruesome farce. (The cop endures having his face slashed, his ear cut off and being doused with kerosene, only to come out of it concerned that his good looks have been ruined.)

The film's look and themes also recall those of Hawks. Avoiding artful, fussy compositions, Tarantino constructs much of RESERVOIR DOGS from simple medium-shot long takes. The torture sequence is staged in real time—endless minutes of it, with the newly ominous 70s pop classic "Stuck in the Middle with You" playing on the soundtrack. Other real-time scenes include the opening diner session and another bloodless but harrowing sequence in which Orange "proves" his authenticity to Eddie by recounting a long, fictional reminiscence about a bad drug deal.

RESERVOIR DOGS also puts a post-modernist spin on the classic Hawksian theme of professionalism. The gangsters keep defining and redefining the meaning of the term, while their actions undercut their words by proving these addled sociopaths to be anything but "professional." In Tarantino's vision, the age of heroic competence is as dead as his characters are at the fadeout. Or it could be that his gang just had bad role models. They share a passion for the pop music of the Nixon era (heard on a fictional radio station, with comedian Steven Wright providing the voice of the deejay), a time when the nation's most powerful professionals proved more than capable of bungling things.

Thus RESERVOIR DOGS is a hard film to watch, but for more than the obvious reasons. Beyond the sting of its violence, there is also the sting of recognition. If Tarantino manages not to get neutered either by critic-sycophants or studio politics, he'll undoubtedly be one of the top filmmaking talents of the 90s. *(Extreme violence, pervasive profanity.)*

p, Lawrence Bender; d, Quentin Tarantino; w, Quentin Tarantino; ph, Andrzej Sekula; ed, Sally Menke; m, Karyn Rachtman; prod d, David Wasco; cos, Betsy Heimann

Crime/Drama **(PR: O MPAA: R)**

RESURRECTED, THE ★★½

106m Eurobrothers, N.V.; Scotti Brothers Pictures Distribution ~ Live Home Video c

John Terry *(John March)*, Jane Sibbett *(Claire Ward)*, Chris Sarandon *(Charles Dexter Ward/Joseph Curwin)*, Richard Romanus *(Lonnie Peck)*, Laurie Briscoe *(Holly Tender)*, Ken Cameroux *(Captain Ben Szandor)*, Patrick Pon *(Raymond)*, Bernard Cuffling *(Doctor Waite)*, Charles Kristian *(Ezra Ward)*, Megan Leitch *(Eliza)*, Deep Roy *(Main Monster)*

An ambitious but not entirely successful attempt to bring another H.P. Lovecraft tale to the screen, THE RESURRECTED is a slick adaptation of *The Case of Charles Dexter Ward*, the author's only novel-length work.

The book is written as a series of recollections-within-recollections, a device that is retained for the film and which proves one of its biggest problems.

The film's opening scene finds P.I. John March (John Terry) ruminating about his current, horrifying case; we then, via flashback, see how that case began. John is approached by Claire Ward (Jane Sibbett), who's become worried about her husband Charles (Chris Sarandon). It seems that he's been performing strange experiments in the basement, and has been fixated on duplicating the results of his ancestor, Joseph Curwin (also played by Sarandon), who had been working to reanimate the dead. Curwen apparently did not come to a good end, and neither did his experiments: he wound up creating misshapen monsters formed from human remains. This has not deterred Charles, however, who has ended up creating the same type of horrific creatures as his predecessor. But as John probes deeper and deeper into the case, he finds that these beasts are not as shocking as the ultimate result of Charles's bizarre work. Descending into the catacombs beneath his house, the protagonists discover that Charles has not only revived Curwen's experiments, but Curwen himself.

THE RESURRECTED has quite a few good things going for it: vivid monster effects by Todd Masters; a screenplay by Brent V. Friedman that takes a respectful approach to the Lovecraft original; and strong direction by Dan O'Bannon. After scoring a cult classic with the comic chiller RETURN OF THE LIVING DEAD, one might expect that O'Bannon would follow the lead of RE-ANIMATOR director Stuart Gordon and milk Lovecraft's material for gruesome black humor, but he plays the horrors refreshingly straight.

But fidelity to its source also results in the movie's biggest flaw. Although the multiple-flashback format lends the film a more literary feel than many of its ilk, it also stunts the story's dramatic development. The gambit just doesn't work on film, a medium which generally requires a more streamlined form of storytelling, particularly in this genre. Nonetheless, O'Bannon does a good job of maintaining viewer interest; he allows the film to unfold at a deliberate pace, never stretching for cheap shocks or gratuitous use of the supernatural as a catch-all explanation for weird events. Masters's monster creations are outrageously grotesque but pulled off convincingly, and there's an especially nice handling of the revelation of Charles's final deed (keep your eyes on the teeth).

For his part, Sarandon (DOG DAY AFTERNOON, THE PRINCESS BRIDE) performs his dual role quite well, with decent if unspectacular support from the rest of the cast. It's just a shame that all the time-hopping makes it hard to appreciate fully all of their efforts. With some patience, however, there are rewards to be found in THE RESURRECTED, and if retaining the structure is problematic, at least this is one filmization of a book that's clearly working to approximate the tone of its source. *(Violence, adult situations, profanity.)*

p, Mark Borde, Kenneth M. Raich; d, Dan O'Bannon; w, Brent V. Friedman, (from the novel *The Case of Charles Dexter Ward* by H.P. Lovecraft); ph, Irvin Goodnoff; ed, Russell Livingstone; m, Richard Band; prod d, Brent Thomas; art d, Doug Byggdin; set d, Christine MacLean; cos, Marcella Robertson

Horror **(PR: O MPAA: R)**

RIVER RUNS THROUGH IT, A ★★½

123m The Big Sky Motion Picture Co.; North Fork Motion Picture Company ~ Columbia c

Craig Sheffer *(Norman MacLean)*, Brad Pitt *(Paul MacLean)*, Tom Skerritt *(Reverend MacLean)*, Brenda Blethyn *(Mrs. MacLean)*, Emily Lloyd *(Jesse Burns)*, Edie McClurg *(Mrs. Burns)*, Stephen Shellen *(Neal Burns)*, Joseph Gordon-Levitt *(Young Norman)*, Vann Gravage *(Young Paul)*, Nicole Burdette *(Mabel)*, Susan Traylor *(Rawhide)*, Michael Cudlitz *(Chub)*, Rob Cox *(Conroy)*, Buck Simmonds *(Humph)*, Fred Oakland *(Mr. Burns)*, David Creamer *(Ken Burns)*, Madonna Reubens *(Aunt Sally)*, Arnold Richardson *(Old Norman)*, MacIntyre Dixon *(Police Sergeant)*, William Hootkins *(Mr. Murchison)*, Jess Schwidde *(Mr. Sweeney)*, Chuck Adamson *(Harry the Editor)*, Rex Kendall *(Reporter)*, Jack Kroll *(Reporter)*, Martina Kreidl *(Secretary at Newspaper)*, Noah Snyder *(Copy Boy at Newspaper)*, Margot Kiser *(Sal)*, Philip A. Braun *(Dealer at Lolo)*, Tracy Mayfield *(Bouncer at Lolo)*, Anne Merrem *(Hooker at Lolo)*, Chuck Tweed *(Drunk in Jail)*, Prudence Johnson *(Pavilion Singer)*, D. Gorton *(Pavilion Announcer)*, Lincoln Quesenberry *(Drunk in Alley)*, Hawk Forssell *(Bouncer at Speakeasy)*, Jim Dunkin *(Speakeasy Bartender)*, Jacob Snyder *(Piano Player)*, Kathy Scharler *(Waitress at Speakeasy)*, Don Jeffery *(Black Jack)*, Byron Dingman *(Speakeasy Patron)*, Cecily Johnson *(Speakeasy Patron)*, Caleb Shiff *(Young John)*, Robert Redford *(Narration)*

Directed by Robert Redford, A RIVER RUNS THROUGH IT employs picture-postcard Montana scenery as a backdrop for a vapid family melodrama.

Norman (Craig Sheffer) and Paul MacLean (Brad Pitt) grow up in a Montana town under the stern but loving guidance of their Presbyterian minister father, Reverend MacLean (Tom Skerritt), and soft-spoken mother (Brenda Blethyn). After school lessons, the Reverend lets the boys share his greatest passion—fly fishing. To the elder MacLean, the sport is almost a religion.

Young Paul is continually rebelling against the Reverend, while Norman is the responsible son. When they grow up, Norman goes away to college and Paul stays in Montana, becoming a newspaper reporter. When Norman returns from college, he is disturbed by Paul's gambling, drinking and skirt-chasing, but can do little to stop his brother's downward spiral. The Reverend is also unable to control his youngest son, but puts pressure on Norman to choose a career. Meanwhile, Norman falls in love with Jesse Burns (Emily Lloyd), a flapper he meets at a party.

Their romance is complicated by Jesse's eccentric Methodist family and a visit from her Hollywood brother Neal (Stephen Shellen), who looks down on Norman. The MacLean brothers take Neal fly fishing, but he ends up making love to the town prostitute and getting sunburned in the grass. When Paul takes Norman to a gambling den, Norman gets disgusted and leaves him there. To Norman's surprise, Paul makes it out of the speakeasy alive.

The men and their father go on a nostalgic fishing trip, during which Paul makes the catch of a lifetime. Later, however, what the family most dreaded happens—Paul is murdered, and Norman must inform his devastated parents. At the end, Norman becomes a professor and settles down with Jesse.

Some 12 years after making his directorial debut with ORDINARY PEOPLE, Robert Redford once again turns his attention to the story of a family. His directorial style, however, involves little more than a tendency to use huge close-ups of every performer—particularly Sheffer and Pitt, who are continually shown looking at each other, even when they have nothing to say. Redford's close-ups of Skerritt are equally bizarre—light is always reflecting off his glasses.

While Redford centers on the actors, the screenplay wallows in cliches. Richard Friedenberg, who adapted Norman MacLean's autobiographical novella, does little to make this depiction of 1920s Montana fresh, and Norman's narration is chock-full of platitudes about nature and life: "Life is not a work of art," etc. Compounding the situation is the fact that fly fishing isn't the most visually dynamic of sports. Even set against the Sierra Club beauty of Redford's Montana, it's hard to get excited by fisherman casting their lines into the water.

Sheffer (SOME KIND OF WONDERFUL, NIGHTBREED) proves himself too stiff to carry a lead role. The more attractive Pitt (JOHNNY SUEDE, THELMA & LOUISE) has star presence to burn, but Redford doesn't get an especially distinctive performance from him—he mugs his way through the movie. Most disappointing is the use of Lloyd, who has struggled through many clunky supporting roles since her sparkling debut in WISH YOU WERE HERE. The part of Jesse is another one. Her function is to play "the girl"—period. The underrated Skerritt (ALIEN, TOP GUN) has no real meaty scenes as the father, though his spirit hangs over the picture. *(Adult situations, sexual situations.)*

p, Patrick Markey, Robert Redford; d, Robert Redford; w, Richard Friedenberg, (from the novella by Norman MacLean); ph, Philippe Rousselot; ed, Lynzee Klingman, Robert Estrin; m, Mark Isham; prod d, Jon Hutman; art d, Walter Martishius; set d, Gretchen Rau; cos, Bernie Pollack

AAN Best Adapted Screenplay: Richard Friedenberg; *AA Cinematography:* Philippe Rousselot; *AAN Best Score:* Mark Isham

Drama **(PR: A MPAA: PG)**

ROAD TO RUIN ★★½

94m Chrysalide Films; Canal Plus ~ LIVE Home Video c

Peter Weller *(Jack Sloan)*, Carey Lowell *(Jessie Taylor)*, Michel Duchaussoy *(Julien Boulet)*, Rebecca Pauly *(Arabella)*, Sylvie Laguna *(Sarah)*, Takashi Kawahara *(Toshi)*, Edith Vernes *(1st Assistant)*, Frederique Feder *(2nd Assistant)*, Emmanuel Fouquet *(3rd Assistant)*, Nathalie Presles *(Jacqueline)*, Pierre Belot *(Jason)*, Eleonore Klarwein *(Woman)*, Nathalie Auffret *(Woman–Art Gallery)*, William Doherty *(Producer)*

The real star of ROAD TO RUIN, an innocuous but often winsome romantic comedy topping Peter Weller and Carey Lowell, is Paris itself, as lovingly photographed by Jean-Yves LeMener.

Jack Sloan (Weller) is a rich, high-powered American businessman who has lived in Paris for the past 20 years. But for all his wealth Jack is unhappy, with no family or close friends, except for his business partner Julien Boulet (Michel Duchaussoy). His girlfriends seem all the same, a parade of identically beautiful but frivilous women who are mainly interested in his money. Then he meets Jessie Taylor (Lowell), a successful model. Although she is unimpressed by his savoir faire and limos, he pursues her all over Paris; she finally relents, and they become lovers.

However, Jack soon worries that Jessie played hard to get only as a ploy to snare him ultimately for his money. So he concocts a scheme with Julien to strip himself of his $25 million assets, to be safely temporarily transferred into dummy accounts and corporations, and tells Jessie that he has lost everything in the stockmarket, to see if she sticks by him. He rents a scummy apartment and starts training as an assistant manager at a fast-food joint called Le Quick Hamburger. The perceptive Jessie suspects something is afoot, so she fakes her own kidnapping, and when Jack attempts to reclaim his loot to pay the $2 million "ransom" he finds that the cheating Julien has handled the paperwork too well and now owns all of Jack's wealth.

Now truly penniless, Jack confesses his plot to Jessie, who is offended by his attitude and leaves him. Ultimately they reunite and, with Jessie playing a prostitute, trap Julien into a confession. At fadeout Jessie and Jack walk off in connubial bliss, as the sun sets over the Eiffel Tower.

While even Tracy and Hepburn couldn't have pulled this one off, stars Peter Weller (ROBOCOP, NAKED LUNCH) and Carey Lowell (LICENSE TO KILL, THE GUARDIAN) are personable and perform well enough, but there is little chemistry sparking between them, and Erick Anjou's blandly transparent, often harebrained screenplay doesn't help them much. Faring best among the actors is the veteran Duchaussoy who has worked with many of the great European directors and is best known for his four films with Claude Chabrol. They are, in chronological order, LA FEMME INFIDELE, QUE LA BETE MEURE, LA RUPTURE and NADA.

Charlotte Brandstrom's direction is strictly routine, with its farcical comic moments especially flat, but the production, shot in English by a French crew, is quite glossy and stylish, just like Jack's expensive Armani suits. *(Profanity, brief nudity, sexual situations.)*

p, Monique Annaud; d, Charlotte Brandstrom; w, Erick Anjou, (from the story by Richard Gitelson and Eric Freiser); ph, Jean-Yves LeMener; ed, Michel Robert-Lauliac; m, John Goldstein; prod d, Bertrand Seitz; cos, Valerie L'Annee

Romance/Comedy **(PR: C MPAA: R)**

ROADSIDE PROPHETS ★★

96m New Line; Swinson/Stankey Productions ~ Fine Line Features c

John Doe *(Joe Mosely)*, Adam Horovitz *(Sam)*, Timothy Leary *(Salvadore)*, Arlo Guthrie *(Harvey)*, David Carradine *(Othello Jones)*, John Cusack *(Caspar)*, David Anthony Marshall *(Dave Coleman)*, Judith Thurman *(Stripper)*, Biff Yeager *(Bartender)*, Sonna Chavez *(Angie Abbott)*, Erica Rogers *(Housekeeper)*, J.D. Cullum *(Mr. Andres)*, Ebbe Roe Smith *(Journalist)*, David Swinson *(Fred Neiman)*, Aaron Lustig *(Morning Desk Clerk)*, Pam Lambert *(Mini-Mart Cashier)*, Beth DePatie *(Daisy)*, Barton Heyman *(Sheriff Durango)*, Don Cheadle *(Happy Days Manager)*, Jeanne McCarthy *(1st Happy Days Waitress)*, Viva Vinson *(2nd Waitress)*, Lee Arenberg *(Happy Days Cook)*, Nancy Lenehan *(Vegas Motel 9 Desk Clerk)*, Manny Chevrolet, Dick Rude, Tony Ruglio, Billy Ferrick, Flea, Pete Weiss *(Too Free Stooges Band Members)*, Jennifer Balgobin *(Ms. Labia Mirage)*, Lena Madjerac *(Kitty)*, Stephen Tobolowsky *(Ranger Bob)*, John Snyder *(Hank)*, Bill Cobbs *(Oscar)*, Lin Shaye *(Celeste)*, Harry Caesar *(Jesse)*, Ed Pansullo *(Hiram)*, Onice Bodozian *(Four Jack Bartender)*, Greg "Spoonie" Sporledder *(Deputy)*, Patti Tippo *(Casino Cashier)*, Nic Ratner *(Casino Casualty)*, Harty Grinner *(Jackpot Motel 9 Employee)*, Ellie Raab *(Gloria)*, Hector *(Ramblin Dog)*

Abbe Wool's ROADSIDE PROPHETS wants to be some sort of post-modern 90's EASY RIDER, but for the most part it's as aimless and uninspired as its two main characters.

Joe Mosely (John Doe of the LA punk band X) is a factory worker more interested in his vintage cycle than anything else. When Joe meets fellow employee Dave, they trade bike talk and go to a local bar where Dave (in one of the film's too-infrequent attempts at warped humor) is electrocuted playing a video game. Dave had talked glowingly about the Nevada town of Eldorado, so Joe has him cremated, puts his ashes in an old motorcycle gas tank, and sets off to deposit his friend there.

Two people are soon interfering with his plans, however: Angie, (whom we hear on the phone, but never see) from his personnel office keeps calling him, offering to provide more sick days to continue his trip, in exchange for a romantic rendezvous on his return. Then there's Sam (Adam Horovitz of rap/punk trio the Beastie Boys), a crazy kid who's been following Joe, and buys a bike to accompany him to Eldorado. The pair meet up with an assortment of supposedly colorful characters along the way, including truck driver Salvadore (Timothy Leary); bartender Harvey (Arlo Guthrie), who tells tales of "prehistoric" fish he's caught; a guitar-playing hermit named Othello Jones (David Carradine), who gets the boys high and tells them about Roman gladiators; and Caspar (John Cusack), an anarchist.

Like all mismatched cinematic couples, Joe and Sam get on each other's nerves, and split up when Sam refuses to stay in anything but a Motel 9, a chain he appears to have an unnatural attachment to. They do hook up again in Las Vegas, where they gamble away their money and their bikes, finally making it to Eldorado where they scatter Dave's ashes. Broke and unsure of what to do, they meet a teenage runaway on the highway. Sam, who up until that point has been critical of every one of the "prophets" they've met, decides to go with the kid to look after her, while Joe stays behind, hinting at a possible reunion down the road.

Doe (SLAM DANCE, BORDER RADIO), who's been fine in other films (and whose rugged good looks could garner him a role as Harrison Ford's brother), is fairly believable as the world-weary Joe, but Horovitz (the son of playwright Israel Horowitz), with his whining and goofy grin, seems as if he's about to break into a Jerry Lewis impression; he's more annoying than funny.

The lack of plot could be overlooked if the folks Sam and Joe met on their journey were remotely memorable, but almost every encounter is the same: they run into some eccentric for four or five minutes (sometimes shorter—don't blink or you'll miss Leary and Guthrie), Sam proclaims that they're insane and drives off. Writer-director Wool obviously wants to make some sort of statement about life in Reagan/Bush America, having characters spout off about nuclear power, the media and the dichotomy of rich and poor, but the "prophets" are onscreen for such a short time nothing registers. (One wonders whether this is a fault of the actors as well. Perhaps Wool rounded up a bunch of friends and then had them improvise their parts; Leary and Guthrie, especially, appear to have written their own lines.)

Towards the second half of the film, things do pick up slightly: Sam and Joe meet a couple who are both dying (she from AIDS, he from cancer), which naturally brings up some important issues, and Joe talks with a motel proprietor who regrets the passive role he played in his own life, emphasizing the importance of friends and love. This is a turning point in the film, since it leads to Joe's reunion with Sam, and Sam confessing the reason for his Motel 9 obsession: his parents left and checked into one when he was a child, and were never heard from again. But by then we're too uninterested by what's gone on before to be affected by these two fairly passive characters.

What could have been a fun, or at least uniquely weird journey is defeated by a lackadaisical screenplay and a lack of imagination. If only the film had been as lively as its soundtrack, which features performances by Doe and his X-mates, Bug Lamp, the Pogues and others. *(Brief violence, substance abuse, profanity, nudity.)*

p, Peter McCarthy, David Swinson; d, Abbe Wool; w, Abbe Wool, (from the idea by David Swinson); ph, Tom Richmond; ed, Nancy Richardson; m, Pray For Rain; prod d, J. Rae Fox; cos, Prudence Moriaty

Comedy/Drama/Adventure **(PR: C MPAA: R)**

ROCK-A-DOODLE ★★½

74m Sullivan-Bluth Studios; Goldcrest ~ Samuel Goldwyn Company c

VOICES OF: Glen Campbell *(Chanticleer)*, Eddie Deezen *(Snipes)*, Sandy Duncan *(Peepers)*, Charles Nelson Reilly *(Hunch)*, Ellen Greene *(Goldie)*, Phil Harris *(Patou)*, Christopher Plummer *(The Duke)*, Toby Scott Ganger *(Edmond)*, Kathryn Holcolmb *(Mother)*, Jason Marin *(Mark)*, Stan Ivar *(Dad)*, Christian Hoff *(Scott)*, Will Ryan *(Stuey)*, Sorrell Booke *(Pinky)*

Since striking out on his own, former Disney animator Don Bluth has created a number of lushly animated films (THE SECRET OF NIMH, AN AMERICAN TAIL, THE LAND BEFORE TIME, ALL DOGS GO TO HEAVEN) whose superior imagery is undercut by weak narratives. With this latest release, Bluth does a better job of telling a concise, coherent story, but the quality of the animation doesn't quite match the high standard of his earlier work.

The filmmakers have given a new, contemporary, rock 'n' roll twist to the old story of Chanticleer, the fabled rooster who caused the sun to rise each morning with his robust crowing. Borrowing liberally from THE WIZARD OF OZ, the brief live-action opening introduces the film's hero, Edmond (Tony Scott Granger), a little farm boy who's going through the trauma of a ferocious thunderstorm which has caused heavy flooding, endangering the family homestead. Knocked unconscious, Edmond reawakens in the animated world—much like his own—of Chanticleer (Glen Campbell). One morning Chanticleer fails to crow, and is shocked when the sun nevertheless rises of its own accord. Humiliated, Chanticleer departs for the big city to seek his fortune.

Shortly thereafter a devastating rainstorm strikes the barnyard and flood waters threaten to overwhelm the family farm. Convinced that only Chanticleer's crowing can bring back the sun and save them, Edmond is preparing to set off in search of the rooster when Duke (Christopher Plummer), a wicked owl, enters the boy's bedroom. To thwart the youngster, the Duke utilizes his magic powers and turns Edmond into a fluffy white kitten. But

Duke underestimates his tiny foe's determination. The kitten recruits Patou (Phil Harris), a trusty old farm dog; Peepers (Sandy Duncan), a very bright mouse; and Snipes (Eddie Deezen), a wise-cracking magpie, to journey with him in search of Chanticleer.

After several perilous adventures, the group track down Chanticleer at a nightclub where they discover their favorite rooster is now a rock 'n' roll superstar known as "The King." Unhappily, they can't get close to Chanticleer because he's too well guarded by bouncers hired by his manager, Pinky (Sorrell Booke), to keep enthusiastic fans at bay. Edmond and his pals finally gain the ear of Goldie (Ellen Greene), Chanticleer's glamorous pheasant showgirl girlfriend. Even Goldie is, at first, reluctant to cooperate, but she finally relents and the group's urgent message reaches the singing rooster at last. As might be expected, Chanticleer returns to the barnyard in the nick of time and saves the day. By the time Edmond the kitten has been restored to his animated human form, and then the real Edmond awakens from his dream, the little boy has learned, just as Dorothy Gale did in Kansas, that there's no place like home.

While ROCK-A-DOODLE has precious little to offer adults (other than the *very* young at heart), it should delight all children under the age of twelve. The artists lending their vocal talents to this production are uniformly adept, although there are no standouts. Charles Nelson-Reilly is featured as Hunch, the evil owl Duke's inept nephew. Robert Folk's musical score and original songs are, for the most part, quite good. Folk's lyrics are fresh and his music lively, and two of his songs provide the picture with its major highlights.

p, Don Bluth, Gary Goldman, John Pomeroy; d, Don Bluth; w, David N. Weiss, (from the story by Weiss, Don Bluth, John Pomeroy, T.J. Kuenster, David Steinberg and Gary Goldman); ed, Bernie Caputo, Fiona Trayler, Lisa Dorney; m, Robert Folks; prod d, Dave Goetz; art d, Don Moore; anim, Tom Higgins, Tamara Anderson, Paul Kelly, Jan Haylor

Animated/Musical/Children's (PR: AA MPAA: G)

ROCK & ROLL COWBOYS

(Australia) Cinefunds Limited; Somerset Films ~ Hemdale Home Video c

Peter Phelps *(Eddie)*, David Franklin *(Mickey)*, Dee Krainz *(Karla)*, John Doyle *(Damien Shard)*, Nikki Coghill *(Teena Tungsten)*, Ben Franklin *(Harvey Glutzman)*, Greg Parke *(Stevie Van Blitz)*, Ron Blanchard *(Uncle Sam)*, Robin Copp *(James)*

Lost: one coherent plot. Please return to ROCK & ROLL COWBOYS, an Australian sci-fi pop-music satire, copyrighted 1987, that became 1992 home-video esoterica in the US. What happens makes THE ROCKY HORROR PICTURE SHOW, a genre relation, look like a model of straightforward narrative.

Mickey (David Franklin) is a harried sound engineer for a glam-rock band fronted by conceited Stevie Van Blitz (Greg Parke) and pretty Teena Tungsten (Nikki Coghill). Mickey wants to write love songs and play keyboard with the ensemble, but Stevie won't have it, even though Teena's secretly sweet on the kid. One night Mickey follows a moving, mesmerizing, spiked sphere next door to Damien Shard (John Doyle), a Mephistopheles type armed with the "Psychotronic Alpha Sampler." This infernal device edits and remixes brain waves like a synclavier manipulates sound, with the effect of making dreams come true—but the band's interested because it means they can play music without their instruments, or something like that.

Much goes on that makes no obvious sense. One musician tries to steal the Psychotronic Alpha Sampler and ends up thinking he's a monkey. Mickey dreams of wrestling a skeleton underwater (special cinematography credit to the illustrious marine documentarians Ron and Valerie Taylor, of all people) and is summoned to a seedy church where an ominous figure offers him a strange potion. A robotic "Sample Squad" in gas masks and yellow jumpsuits jog through the cramped, futuristic urban scenery zapping band members and bystanders with more spiked spheres. The culprit is Damien Shard's boss, a kiddie-show TV evangelist called Uncle Sam (Ron Blanchard) who hosts the twerpy Sunday-morning "Cowboys for God" program on which he rails against the evils of rock 'n' roll. His master plan is unclear: to destroy all music except country-and-western gospel; steal the souls of the characters; turn everyone into mindless zombies; or popularize romantic ballads through Mickey. The ending leaves more questions, as a deaf roadie, immune to the Psychotronic Alpha Sampler, seemingly saves Mickey and Teena—or are they only in his mind?

The performances are generally grotesque, none more so than Ben Franklin as the band's manager Harvey Glutzman, a middle-aged, Nazi-obsessed, greed-driven pervert who enacts weirdo S&M fantasies and Egyptian pagan rituals while the camera dwells on his droopy belly. The dialogue doesn't often go beyond yelling and screaming. It says a lot for the vibrant, late-blooming Aussie film industry that even Down Under duds tend to be more stylish than antipodal counterparts, and director Rob Stewart invests this material with enough low-budget visual flash to make this worth a glance—a very brief glance—from the incautiously curious.

The musical numbers have energy to spare, and the songs by David Skinner are worthy of life beyond turkeydom. Notable for their appearance is a hard-rock group called the Escape Band, whose wardrobe of woolly animal hides, horns, tusks, chains and shoulder pads rivals the primordial garb of those American speed-metal barbarians, Gwar. *(Substance abuse, profanity, sexual situations.)*

p, James Michael Vernon, Jan Tyrell; d, Rob Stewart; w, David R. Young; ph, Joseph Pickering; ed, Amanda Robson; m, David Skinner; prod d, Michael Ralph; art d, Ian Gracie; cos, Helen Hooper

Musical/Comedy/Science Fiction (PR: C MPAA: NR)

ROCK SOUP ★★★

81m Rock Soup Productions Inc. ~ First Run Features bw

Kalif Beacon

A soup kitchen for the homeless, set up, staffed and run by the homeless themselves, is the subject of Lech Kowalski's ROCK SOUP, an engaging documentary filmed in the vicinity of Tompkins Square Park on New York City's Lower East Side.

On a rainy late afternoon, a series of tight, panning shots introduces us to the muddy lot with lean-tos and tents on East 9th Street called the "Plaza Culturelle" where the Rainbow Kitchen is located. Negotiating the wooden boards set up on the ground, Kowalski's camera focuses on the steaming vat of food that serves the poor, a recurring image in the film. Most, but by no means all, of the homeless are male Blacks and Hispanics to whom we are introduced only after the establishing scenes of anarchic poverty.

As the film continues there is an emerging pattern to life at the "Plaza." The same wood-fed fires that prepare the meals also serve to heat water for washing, and with the next day's dawn we see some of the regulars washing and preparing for their 500 or 1,000 daily customers. Though some of the food is donated, to judge from negotiations between the cook, an unnamed woman with kepi and boots and a local well-wisher, most of it is literally found among restaurant and grocery store discards. The wood is simply pried away from shipping pallets and fed into a simple fire over which rests a grillwork.

The Rainbow Kitchen owes its existence to Halif Beacon, a bearded fellow with a tall chimney sweeper's hat adorned with the stars and bars of a folded confederate flag. With squinting, amused eyes, Beacon tells the story of "rock soup," depicting the communal process by which each individual adds a needed element to prepare a meal. And, indeed, the "Plaza Culturelle" would appear an anarchist success story bound by the limits of the burned out tenement and the patrolling pairs of police glimpsed through the chain-link fence that surrounds the lot. New York's city planners, however, seem to have had other plans for the lot occupied by Beacon and his friends.

The proposal to build a housing project for the elderly on the same grounds stimulates Beacon and some of his allies to voice their protest at a community board meeting. With a droll deftness, Beacon unrolls official maps and charts to prove that the ground is unsuited to large construction, while others mix a cogent political analysis with religious imagery and apocalyptic visions. Sadly, there are also those who need the housing, so the community discussion degenerates into screaming matches between the elderly poor and the homeless, young poor, while the handsomely attired politicos and housing planners look on in discomfort.

The film ends almost as it had begun with a camera panning literally at the ground underfoot where the litter is marked with graffiti of the people who support the Rainbow Kitchen.

Lech Kowalski has had a long interest in the lives of people on the Lower East Side. In 1983, Kowalski filmed some incidents in the life of a drug addict in GRINGO, with sympathy alarming to some critics. Filmed in 1988, ROCK SOUP is also very sympathetic towards its subject and skirts the serious question of any addiction among its players. The degradation of the public shelters is discussed, ironically by a friendly food deliverer, while one of the kitchen regulars recalls the brutal hazing to which Beacon was subjected when he first appeared. While several of the regulars speak fluently and movingly of their plight, some of the conversations among the habituees of the kitchen are almost incoherent and garbled.

Despite its charms, as an example of self-help and cooperation, the kitchen is a limited boon. The muddy walkways and scrounged food are no solution to a serious dilemma, a position voiced in ROCK SOUP by a local city council member, despite the romantic appeal of Beacon and his eccentric friends. *(Profanity.)*

p, Lech Kowalski; d, Lech Kowalski; ph, Doron Schlair; ed, Lech Kowalski; m, Chico Freeman

Documentary **(PR: C MPAA: NR)**

ROOTS OF EVIL ★★

95m Grand Am Ltd; Global Pictures ~ Cannon Video c

Alex Cord *(Jake Osbourne)*, Delia Sheppard *(Marisa)*, Charles Dierkop *(Collins)*, Jillian Kesner *(Brenda Murphy)*, Jewell Sheppard *(Wanda)*, Brinke Stevens *(Candy)*, Randall Brady *(Johnny Malone)*, Deanna Lund, Gregg Cummings, Kate Murtagh

A pretentiously titled police caper, ROOTS OF EVIL is a routine blood-and-sex story of little consequence save for a key plot device.

A serial killer is on the loose, going after prostitutes *a la* Jack the Ripper. Detective Jake Osbourne (Alex Cord) and his partner and lover, Sergeant Brenda Murphy (Jillian Kesner), take on the case with the help of their contacts in the Los Angeles underworld. Matters get complicated with the murder of powerful drug lord Tony Fontana in his mansion, which they are also assigned to investigate. All clues point to sleazy pimp Johnny Malone (Randall Brady) as Fontana's killer, since he was seen leaving the mansion after the shooting. Osbourne and Murphy interrogate the drug lord's widow, Marisa (Delia Sheppard), and Candy (Brinke Stevens), an exploitation movie actress who was Malone's ex-lover, about Malone's whereabouts.

Meanwhile, the serial killer is identified by Wanda (Jewel Sheppard)—one of Murphy's prostitute contacts—as Detective Collins (Charles Dierkop). A trap is set for Collins, who quickly bites the bait and is killed in a shootout. After surviving an attempt on his life, Osbourne discovers the culprits in the Fontana case: none other than Marisa, who plotted with Candy to frame Malone and escape together to lesbian bliss. The film ends as violently as it began, with an assualt by a new serial killer.

Overall, ROOTS OF EVIL is quite ordinary as a crime story, with desperate murders, dedicated officers and enough violence to satisfy the average action-film aficionado. The sleazy underground locale makes for very lurid scenes, including a three-minute S&M dance followed by an unusually graphic and long sex scene, meant as local color and atmosphere but needlessly stalling the narrative. The characters are strictly cardboard, from the tough-talking detective to the tough-but-sexy female partner, from the psycho serial killer (infatuated with his heartless mother, with whom he has two senseless conversations) to hard-as-nails-but-vulnerable prostitutes. Typically, the female characters are presented as pathetic victims in need of male help; even Sgt. Murphy has to be rescued from the punk she battles with when we first see her by gallant Detective Osbourne.

Which leads to ROOTS OF EVIL's most intriguing point: the use of prostitutes as underworld contacts by the police department. When hooker Wanda is brought into police headquarters for booking, Brenda informs the arresting officer that Wanda is "very valuable to me. I need her on the street. Wanda is one of the best snitches I have," and Brenda sees to it that she goes back on the street to perform her trade. One would think that the police force would rehabilitate those criminals who help them in their work. But instead of steering her to a better life, Brenda lets Wanda loose into the prostitution ring, regardless of the obvious risks. The fact that it is a female officer who voices this policy makes for an interesting figure, woman as exploiter of woman. A serious filmmaker could have made a shattering comment on this unsavory aspect of crime fighting; in ROOTS OF EVIL, it is an accepted fact, not criticized in the least.

Nothing highlights the third-rate quality of ROOTS OF EVIL like its cast, comprised of veteran third-rate actors who perform in a tired, lackadaisical way. As Detective Jake Osbourne, Alex Cord speaks in an affected "tough guy" voice which, matched with his frozen face, makes for a ludicrous character. Jillian Kesner's only talent as Brenda Murphy is her amazing resemblance to Valerie Perrine. Charles Dierkopf overacts wildly as serial killer Collins. The rest of the cast goes through the motions, save for one very good actor who goes unbilled; his character, Detective Fred, appears nowhere on the final credits, an unprofessional oversight on the filmmaker's part.

A little social conscience could have made ROOTS OF EVIL a flawed yet interesting film. Alas, we are given a predictable, unexceptional film, one among hundreds of cheaply made action movies for the video market. *(Violence, nudity, adult situations.)*

p, Sidney Niekerk; d, Gary Graver; w, Adam Berg; ph, Gary Graver; ed, William Schaeffer; m, Duane Sciacqua; set d, Ted Tunney

Action/Crime **(PR: O MPAA: R)**

ROUND TRIP TO HEAVEN ★½

97m Vertigo Pictures; Saban Pictures ~ Prism Entertainment c

Corey Feldman *(Larry)*, Ray Sharkey *(Stoneface)*, Zach Galligan *(Steve)*, Julie McCullough *(Lucille)*, Rowanne Brewer *(April)*, Lloyd Battista *(Mike)*, John Stewart *(1st Man)*, Sandy Doll *(Melanie)*, Brent Corman *(Brandon)*, Michael Fosberg *(1st Policeman)*, Al Ruscio *(Uncle Roy)*, Kristine Rose *(Tina)*, Joey Travolta *(Ed)*, Michael Milhoan *(Melvin)*, Miguel Nunez, Jr. *(Leon)*, Pat Harrington, Jr. *(George)*, Buddy Daniels *(Valet)*, Mimi Eisman *(Stella)*, Cyndi Pass *(Cindy)*, Robyn Killian *(Carol)*, Stephen Dimon *(Blonde Hunk)*, Billy Hufsey *(Announcer)*, Scott Brandon *(1st Bellman)*, Noam Kaniel *(Piano Player)*, Musetta Vander *(Miss Moscow)*, Lilyan Chauvin *(Chaperone)*, Amber *(Desk Clerk)*, Shuki Levy *(2nd Man)*, Mark Burton *(3rd Policeman)*, Joe George *(Detective Hoot)*

An imbecilic college-age caper film, ROUND TRIP TO HEAVEN melds the standard young-adult sex farce onto an innocents-on-the-lam adventure. As with others in this jock fantasy sub-genre, a luxury car figures as prominently in the plot as the requisite dream girl.

Shaking the coppers, a felon named Stoneface (Ray Sharkey) stashes his purloined loot in the trunk of a car that just happens to be maintenanced by Larry's (Corey Feldman) uncle's dealership. Tired of life as party animal Boingo the Clown, who entertains tots and dallies with their suburban mothers, Larry decides to fix and borrow one of his uncle's Rolls-Royces. Persuading his cousin Steve (Zach Galligan) to join him on a wild weekend in Palm Springs, Larry is unaware that the Rolls contains a fortune in cash. While Larry dreams of super model April Summers (Rowanna Brewer), he learns that his pal Lucille (Julie McCullough) has been selected for a modeling seminar hosted by Ms. Summers.

As the coincidences pile up in place of laughs, the cops tail Stoneface, who pursues the boys in a hijacked cab while the boys blissfully drive to Palm Springs in the borrowed Rolls. Having smooth-talked their way into jobs at a hotel, Steve discovers the moolah while Larry resumes his Boingo character to perform at a surprise party for April. Although two bumbling cops try to entrap Stoneface by leading him to the boys' room, he eludes capture. With Stoneface closing in, Larry poses as a movie producer while Steve romances a Russian model. By the Keystone cops-style finale, the ineffectual cops finally catch up to Stoneface as Steve discovers the joys of puppy love with the Russian, and Larry finally realizes that Lucille is the only babe for him.

Intent on titillating its youthful audience, ROUND TRIP TO HEAVEN only veers from the business of inducing leers long enough to dispense stale jokes and keep viewers awake with some cops-and-robbers car chases. While goosing the plot along artificially, it celebrates female pulchritude. When even that grows tiresome, some forgettable song is tossed in. When that doesn't work, the idiot cops return to diminishing laughter. Yet all that camouflage can't disguise the fact that this is an adolescent wet dream. Gorgeous half-naked women interrupt enough of ROUND TRIP TO HEAVEN to satisfy its target audience of horny college jocks.

Fortunately, Galligan and McCullough have natural charm, and a few supporting players rise above the general tedium. If, however, you find star Corey Feldman resistible to the degree that you would rather face atomic radiation than share a bomb shelter with him, avoid taking this direct-to-video release. The sorry spectacle of watching this actor more suited to character roles once again preening as a handsome leading man makes one realize that egos in Hollywood have grown to frightening proportions. He has the irritating energy of the teenaged Mickey Rooney but without the saving grace of any of Rooney's talent. *(Some violence, profanity, nudity.)*

p, Ronnie Hadar; d, Alan Roberts; w, Shuki Levy, Winston Richards; ph, Jim Mathers; ed, Greg Sanders; m, Noam Kaniel, Shuki Levy; prod d, Robert Benedict; art d, Heather Ross; set d, Heather Ross

Comedy **(PR: C MPAA: R)**

ROVER DANGERFIELD ★★

74m Rover Dangerfield Productions; Warner Bros.; Hyperion Pictures ~ Warner Home Video c

VOICES OF: Rodney Dangerfield *(Rover)*, Susan Boyd *(Daisy)*, Dana Hill *(Danny)*, Sal Landi *(Rocky)*, Ned Luke *(Raffles)*, Ronnie Schell *(Eddie)*, Shawn Southwic *(Connie)*

The creators of the charming and imaginative THE BRAVE LITTLE TOASTER have joined forces with comedian Rodney Dangerfield on ROVER DANGERFIELD, an animated vanity production that seeks to transplant Dangerfield's ribald nightclub persona into a tubby cartoon dog. The result is a confused hybrid creation, suspended in a twilight zone between Don Bluth's benign but dull children's fare and Ralph Bakshi's gratingly hip work.

Rover Dangerfield (voice of Rodney Dangerfield) is a street-smart mutt whose owner, Connie (Shawn Southwic), is a blonde and beautiful Las Vegas showgirl. But her sleazy, Chester Gould-esque boyfriend, Rocky (Sal Landi), takes a disliking to Rover and when Connie leaves to go on the road, he shoves Rover in a sack and chucks him off the Hoover Dam. Rescued by two fishermen, Rover finds himself in the country, where he is taken in by a farmer and his little boy Danny (Dana Hill). Out in the country, Rover's urban style is seemingly useless, although he does manage to fall in love with the girl dog next door, Daisy (Susan Boyd).

Gradually, Rover manages to adapt to farm life but this idyll is shattered when the farmer mistakenly thinks that Rover has killed his prize turkey. Taking Rover into the woods to shoot him, the farmer is attacked by a pack of wolves. Rover comes to the rescue to save the farmer and becomes a local celebrity. When Connie sees his picture in a Las Vegas newspaper, she arranges to pick up Rover and take him back to the city. But back in Las Vegas, Rover is depressed. Connie drives back to the farm and Rover is reunited with Daisy, who surprises him with a tiny brood of puppies.

Dangerfield's brilliantly honed comic persona is that of a crude, loudmouthed loser who defends himself against an uncaring world with harsh insults. ("Rodney, what do you do for a living?" "What do I do for a living? I get guys for your sister.") In his film work, Dangerfield has tapped into this persona, toned down the undercurrent of anger, and in his most successful efforts, CADDYSHACK and BACK TO SCHOOL, turned him into an ultra-rich, no-nonsense lout. When he's tried to make himself endearing, as in EASY MONEY, the result has been too cloying by far.

Much to the detriment of ROVER DANGERFIELD, it is the kinder, gentler Rodney that finds his way into the film and this attempt to turn the Dangerfield persona into a lovable and cute cartoon character short-circuits the entire movie. If Dangerfield had extended his original persona into the cartoon and stuck to life in Las Vegas, ROVER DANGERFIELD might have worked as a sassy, irreverent LADY AND THE TRAMP. As it is, however, when Rover gets to the farm and must bounce his cracks off of cute but harmless barnyard animals, the promising hard edge is encrusted with treacle—it's quite a jump from "I love your pom-poms" to "I'd give up a bone for you."

But ROVER DANGERFIELD could still have been saved if the animation was creative and unique. Alas, it's extremely variable—from the undistinguished farm animals, to the menacing Rocky, to the comic Rover. The film begins with a promising parody of the computer-animated opening tracking shot from Disney's THE RESCUERS DOWN UNDER but rapidly descends to a cut above Saturday morning cartoon fare; the contrast between the computer-enhanced images and the shoddy cel work is jolting. Without a careful transition between the two elements, the film looks hurried and cheap, as if made by committees in different countries.

At the end of the film, Rover talks to himself under a tree and, like Woody Allen in HUSBANDS AND WIVES, bemoans his fate by sighing "I blew it." Since Rodney Dangerfield wrote and produced ROVER DANGERFIELD, along with supplying the title voice and writing the songs, it is not Rover who blew it, but Rodney himself.

p, Thomas L. Wilhite, Willard Carroll; d, James George, Robert Seeley; w, Rodney Dangerfield, (from the story by Dangerfield and Harold Ramis); ed, Tony Mizgalski; m, David Newman; prod d, Fred Cline

Comedy/Children's **(PR: AA MPAA: G)**

RUBIN & ED ★★★

(U.K.) 82m Rubin & Ed Inc.; Working Title ~ IRS Releasing c

Crispin Glover *(Rubin Farr)*, Howard Hesseman *(Ed Tuttle)*, Karen Black *(Rula)*, Michael Greene *(Mr. Busta)*, Brittnew Lewis *(Poster Girl)*

Many low-budget films strive to be genuinely offbeat with stories, characters and situations that just aren't ready for big-studio treatment. Perhaps because it doesn't strive, RUBIN & ED, a shaggy dog buddy-buddy comedy, singularly succeeds in being genuinely quirky fun.

Rubin Farr (Crispin Glover) lives in a motel managed by his mother, where he mostly stays in his room listening to music, dreaming of a love affair with a bikini poster pinup girl (Brittnew Lewis) and mourning the death of his cat, whose corpse he is keeping in the freezer until he can find the right spot to bury it. Ed Tuttle (Howard Hesseman), meanwhile, is a would-be yuppie without style, smarts or slickness who works for real estate guru Mr. Busta (Michael Greene) as a recruiter for Busta's $3,000 "seminars." They are brought together when Rubin's mom orders him out of his room to face the world and make a friend he can bring home for dinner.

However, the world may never be ready to face Rubin, who, in his undersized polyester disco-nerd outfit, accented by platform shoes that become handy defensive weapons in tight spots, inspires fear, loathing and, mostly, ridicule. Ed, of course, sees raw material for real-estate success in Rubin while the latter sees in the former the dinner guest he needs to placate his mom. When Rubin's mom is late for dinner, Rubin decides that it would be a good time to bury his cat in the Utah desert, where he and Ed head after Rubin commandeers Ed's car, which is actually on loan from Mr. Busta.

In the desert, Busta's car breaks down and Rubin and Ed separate over a disagreement on where the nearest town is. Ed is attacked by ants and returns to the car, which he repairs and decides to drive back after learning that Busta has reported the car stolen. Rubin, meanwhile, knocks himself unconscious while exploring a cave and dreams of being the King of the Echo People. As king, he owns the world's biggest platform shoes and enjoys an inner-tube float on a placid lake while his cat goes water-skiing behind a boat piloted by Rubin's dream girl. His reverie is disrupted by Ed, who has returned to find him after an attack of conscience.

They return to Busta's headquarters just long enough for Rubin to disrupt the seminar by announcing his new regal status. Busta gives chase only to collide, literally, with police intent on arresting him for stealing his own car, leaving Rubin and Ed to wander down a dark alley and argue, as they have throughout the film, over which of them is the bigger failure.

RUBIN & ED is a warm, funny and well-crafted celebration of eccentricity with terrific performances from Glover and Hesseman, who could easily be the perfect comedy duo for the post-modern age.

While not sacrificing an iota of Rubin's weirdness, Glover plays him with a dead-shot comic sureness, demonstrating admirable restraint and discipline. Hesseman similarly scores comic points with Ed by keying in on the character's humanity while letting his own buttoned-down weirdness speak for itself. The odd moments when he parrots the inspirational ravings of his guru, in particular, are blissful moments of comic inspiration, and the rapport he establishes with Glover goes a long way toward making the film enjoyable. Both are extremely well served by writer-director Trent Harris who maintains an easy mood of lunacy throughout. Harris's ability to get the best from his actors is readily apparent in the lead performances, but the real bonus comes with Karen Black, as Ed's shrewish, materialistic ex-wife, who is funnier and much more attractively photographed here than she has been in a while.

Throw in the remaining perks like Frederic Myrow's wryly funny electronic music score and Bryan Duggan's unpretentiously expressive cinematography on locations in Salt Lake City and surrounding environs and the sum total is one of those increasingly rare cases that make wandering through the wilderness of alternative cinema worthwhile. *(Mild profanity.)*

p, Paul Webster; d, Trent Harris; w, Trent Harris; ph, Bryan Duggan; ed, Brent Schoenfeld; m, Fredric Myrow; prod d, Clark Hunter; set d, Michelle Spaddro; cos, Lawane Cole

Comedy **(PR: C MPAA: PG-13)**

RUBY ★★

110m Polygram Pictures; Propaganda Films ~
Triumph Releasing c

Danny Aiello *(Jack Ruby)*, Sherilyn Fenn *(Candy Cane)*, Frank Orsatti *(Action Jackson)*, Jeffrey Nordling *(Hank)*, Jane Hamilton *(Telephone Trixie)*, Maurice Benard *(Diego)*, Joe Viterelli *(Joseph Valachi)*, Robert S. Telford *(Senator)*, John Roselius *(Detective Smalls)*, Lou Eppolito *(Detective Taylor)*, J. Marvin Campbell *(Bus Counter Tender)*, David Duchovny *(Officer Tippit)*, Richard Sarafian *(Proby)*, Joe Cortese *(Louie Vitali)*, Marc Lawrence *(Santos Alicante)*, Arliss Howard *(Maxwell)*, Tobin Bell *(David Ferrie)*, Tony Conforti *(Mickey the Shoe)*, Joseph Pecoraro *(Jinx)*, Joey DePinto *(Carmine)*, Carmine Caridi *(Sam Giancana)*, Leonard Termo *(Tony Ana)*, Steven Elkins *(Hotel Clerk)*, Richard Emanuel *(Bellhop)*, Gerard David *(JFK – Las Vegas)*, Patrick Jude *(Tony Montana)*, Willie Garson *(Lee Harvey Oswald)*, John Solari *(Lenny Doyle)*, Scott Lawrence *(Dillon)*, Cody Glenn *(Guard)*, Mike Lundy *(Dallas Television Announcer)*, Jim Ryan *(Dallas Television Announcer)*, Bill Seward *(Dallas Television Announcer)*, Kevin Wiggins *(JFK – Dallas)*, Mary Chris Wall *(Jackie Kennedy)*, Sean McGraw *(Governor Connally)*, Terri Zagrodnick *(Mrs. Connally)*, David Steen *(Sheriff's Deputy)*, Ron DeRoxtra *(Pressman)*, Alan Ackles *(Pressman)*, Bob Hess *(Pressman)*, Jay Dowd *(Pressman)*, Tina Rucker *(Pressman)*, Rodger Boyce *(Police Chief)*, James Healy *(Uniformed Policeman)*, Brad Leland *(Patrolman)*, Jim Brewer *(Detective)*,

Wirt Cain *(Detective)*, Ritch Brinkley *(Attorney Howard)*, Tim Green *(Judge)*, Norman Bennett *(Driver)*

Though RUBY is bound to suffer in comparison to Oliver Stone's JFK in terms of sheer cinematic pizzazz, this largely fictionalized historical drama is nevertheless a quietly engrossing contribution to the Kennedy assassination myth. In its dreamy, elegiac mixing of history and fiction, RUBY is closer in tone to E.L. Doctorow's works than to the muckraking tabloid antics of Stone's epic.

The film centers on Jack Ruby (Danny Aiello), the shadowy Dallas strip-club owner who emerged from obscurity just long enough to murder alleged Kennedy assassin Lee Harvey Oswald (Willie Garson)—an image captured on nationwide television and indelibly stamped in our collective memories.

In the wake of his ascension to power, Fidel Castro has imprisoned Santos Alicante (Marc Lawrence), who had been in charge of the mob's casinos in Cuba. In fact, Castro's swift expulsion of the forces of gambling and corruption from Cuba has left the mob obsessed with killing him. Ruby, a peripheral figure in the Mafia crime organization, is drawn closer to the nexus of power when another minor mob soldier fails—influenced by rogue elements within the CIA—to deliver exploding cigars for killing Castro. Taking on the assignment, Ruby goes to Cuba accompanied by his newest discovery, Sheryl Ann Dujean (Sherilyn Fenn), renamed "Candy Cane," whom he stumbled upon in a Dallas bus terminal and now hopes to use to curry favor with Santos.

Upon his arrival, however, Ruby finds that the assignment is not to kill Castro but Santos. Ruby instead kills his handler and returns to the US. He's a hero to the Mob, but in deep disfavor with the CIA, particularly in the form of agent Maxwell (Arliss Howard), who offers Ruby the chance to redeem himself by finishing his original assignment to kill Castro. It appears that Ruby has become a victim of yet another ruse, however, when it turns out that the real interest of the Mob and the CIA is in Candy, who becomes one of Kennedy's mistresses. The Mob wants Candy to deliver a message to the President to call his brother, the Attorney General, off the Mafia so that they, with the CIA, can continue in their plot to kill Castro. When Candy refuses, she's sent back to Ruby, as events move toward the inevitable assassination of Kennedy and Ruby's killing of Oswald in hopes of exposing the alliance between the mob and the CIA.

Less docudrama than melodrama, RUBY attempts to be a meditation on the loss of innocence symbolized by Kennedy's assassination. In the world according to British writer Stephen Davis (whose credits include the HBO production "Yuri Nosenko, KGB," and who is here adapting his play *Love Field*), America's fall actually began long before the assassination. By 1963, the government has become a shadow body, accountable to no one and capable of unholy alliances with common criminals.

As portrayed by Aiello and Fenn, Ruby and Cane are two sides of the same coin. Both are tough, big-hearted outsiders who embody what is left of the American pioneering spirit. The difference is that Ruby clings to the old-fashioned values of loyalty and honor that prove to be his downfall, while Cane is more modern, capable of making deals to fulfill her ambitions—though only up to a point.

Much of the thematic ground covered here by Davis has been covered better elsewhere. In fact, RUBY might have been better had it played even faster and looser with history. As it is, it comes most alive during its wildest flights of fancy, particularly in the scenes involving Howard's disturbingly deranged CIA agent or Tobin Bell's quietly weird David Ferrie (making a nice contrast with Joe Pesci's hysterical Ferrie in JFK). Along the way, Fenn manages to bring real erotic heat to her modest striptease sequences, suggesting that RUBY might have benefitted from the broader, burlesque approach of the similarly intentioned INSIGNIFICANCE.

Nevertheless, Davis, as he did in "Yuri Nosenko, KGB," manages to give the gray banality of government some eerie overtones, while director John Mackenzie (no stranger either to crime, in THE LONG GOOD FRIDAY, or espionage, in THE FOURTH PROTOCOL) makes the most of a talented cast. At its best, RUBY is as surreal and haunting as JFK is viscerally wrenching, adding a minor yet respectable chapter to "the story that won't go away." *(Violence, profanity, adult situations.)*

p, Sigurjon Sighvatsson, Steve Golin; d, John MacKenzie; w, Stephen Davis, (from his play *Love Field*); ph, Phil Meheux; ed, Richard Trevor; m, John Scott; prod d, David Brisbin; art d, Kenneth A. Hardy; set d, Lauri Gaffin; cos, Susie DeSanto

Drama/Crime/Historical **(PR: C MPAA: R)**

RUNESTONE, THE ★★★

107m Runestone Corporation; Hyperion Entertainment; Signature Communications ~ LIVE Home Video c

Alexander Godunov *(The Clockmaker)*, Peter Riegert *(Fanducol)*, Joan Severance *(Marla Stewart)*, William Hickey *(Lars Hagstron)*, Tim Ryan *(Sam Stewart)*, Mitchell Laurance *(Martin Almquist)*, Lawrence Tierney *(Chief Richardson)*, Dawan Scott *(Fenrir)*, Chris Young *(Jacob)*, Donald Hotton *(Ask Franag)*, Erika Schickel *(Angela)*, Bill Kalmenson *(Lester)*, Arthur Malet *(Stoddard)*, John Hobson *(Marotta)*, Anthony Cistaro *(Detective)*, Merilyn Carney *(Tawny)*, Greg Wrangler *(Bob)*, Ed Corbett *(Janitor)*, William Utay *(Truckdriver)*, Carl Parker *(Elevator Operator)*, Josef Rainer *(1st Boardmember)*, Christopher Holder *(2nd Boardmember)*, Susan Lentini *(1st Wife)*, Kelly Miller *(2nd Wife)*, Sam Menning *(Wino)*, Gil Perez *(Alberto)*, Gary Lahti *(Sanders)*, Ralph Monaco *(Cabbie)*, Peter Bigler *(Harris)*, Richard Molinare *(Pulsski)*, Rick Marzan *(Strange)*, Kim Delgado *(Reynolds)*, David Newman *(Graves)*, Joshua Cox *(Crossley)*, Vanessa Easton *(Nurse)*, Carol Hickey *(1st Bespectacled)*, Lisa Dinkins *(2nd Bespectacled)*, Eben Ham *(1st Policeman)*, Layne Beamer *(2nd Policeman)*, Matthew Boyett *(Village Boy)*

Proof of what a talented group of people can do with standardized material if they treat it with intelligence, THE RUNESTONE is quite a pleasant surprise, a deft and intriguing low-budget horror item that deserved much better handling than it received.

The title refers to a Norse relic discovered in a Pennsylvania mine that is covered with inscrutable lettering and features a horrific carving of a monster in its center. Brought back to New York City, the runestone begins to have a profound effect on Martin Almquist (Mitchell Laurance), the archaeologist who is keeping the discovery in his loft. Pretty soon he vanishes, and soon thereafter, a series of mutilation murders befalls the city. Marla Stewart (Joan Severance), Martin's ex-lover who just happens to have married another archaeologist, Sam (Tim Ryan), thinks there's a connection, but can't convince wise-guy detective Fanducol (the usually taciturn Peter Riegert, in a refreshing change-of-pace performance).

Only an old expert in Norse mythology, Lars Hagstron (William Hickey), thinks the unearthing of the runestone might have led to Martin's transformation into something large, furry and nasty, but he falls prey to the beast shortly after explaining things to Marla, who is then pursued through Central Park by the beast. Also getting involved in the mayhem is a mysterious clockmaker (Alexander Godunov), who's waiting in the wings with a method of combating the monster; Fanducol's gruff chief Richardson (Lawrence Tierney), who thinks the culprit is "maybe a guy in a bullet-proof vest and a dog suit"; and a young man named Jacob

(Chris Young) who will ultimately deliver the *coup de grace* to the monster.

Despite strong reviews and exposure at a couple of film festivals, THE RUNESTONE managed to land only one theatrical playdate in LA, where it was foolishly marketed as one of the multitude of "sexy thrillers" currently cluttering up the marketplace. The movie is adult, to be sure, but only in its gratifyingly mature approach to its characters and their reactions to the situations, even if what we've basically got here is a big hairy monster running amok. THE RUNESTONE piles on almost too many subplots and characters, and plods occasionally trying to keep them all sorted out, but the characters are developed and, more importantly, acted well enough that the movie never founders for long. It's nice to see a film where the characters appear to have lives beyond the boundaries of the film's story, and react to the terrors that confront them not with cliches but in the way real people might.

That's not to say that the movie is all character development; writer-director Willard Carroll, working from a novella by Mark E. Rogers, keeps things jumping with vicious monster attacks and, as the story goes on, increasingly spectacular sequences in which squads of cops try to no avail to shoot the monster down. The creature itself, designed by Lance Anderson, doesn't reinvent the man-in-a-suit approach, but it remains convincing because the characters all react to it believably. Carroll's scare sequences sometimes fall prey to convention—when the beast chases Marla through Central Park, you just know she'll be accosted by some thugs, whose assault of her will soon be rudely interrupted—but his directorial confidence makes the scenes work just the same.

Further benefiting from strong technical contributions, especially Misha Suslov's evocative photography and David Newman's strong score, THE RUNESTONE is an invigorating change from the usual camp approach to low-budget horror. *(Violence, profanity, sexual situations.)*

p, Thomas L. Wilhite, Harry E. Gould, Jr.; d, Willard Carroll; w, Willard Carroll, (from the novella by Mark E. Rogers); ph, Misha Suslov; ed, Lynne Southerland; m, David Newman; prod d, Jon Gary Steele; art d, Stella Wang; set d, Nancy Arnold; cos, Terry Dresbach

Horror **(PR: O MPAA: R)**

SARAFINA! ★★½

(U.S./U.K./France/South Africa) 96m Distant Horizon; Ideal Films; BBC Enterprises; Vanguard Films; Les Films Ariane; Videovision Enterprises; Hollywood; Miramax ~ BV c

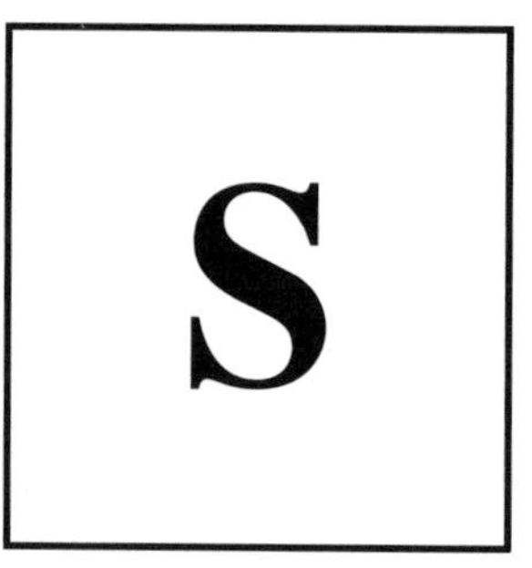

Leleti Khumalo *(Sarafina)*, Whoopi Goldberg *(Mary Masembuko)*, Miriam Makeba *(Angelina)*, John Kani *(School Principal)*, Dumisani Dlamini *(Crocodile)*, Mbongeni Ngema *(Sabela)*, Sipho Kunene *(Guitar)*, Tertius Meintjes *(Lieutenant Bloem)*, Robert Whithead *(Interrogator)*, Somizi "Whacko" Mhlongo *(Fire)*, Nhlanhla Ngema *(Stimela)*, Faca Kulu *(Eddie)*, Wendy Mseleku *(China)*, Mary Twala *(Sarafina's Grandmother)*, James Mthoba *(Sarafina's Uncle)*, Greg Latter *(1st Policeman)*, Gideon DeWet *(2nd Policeman)*, Nicky Rebelo *(1st Soldier)*, James Whyle *(2nd Soldier)*, Bheki Mqadi *(Moses)*, Michele Bestbier *(Mrs. Hendriks)*, Patrick Ndlovu *(Victor Gumede)*, David Manqele *(Preacher)*, Sibusiso Ngema *(Funeral Leader)*, Zanele Sangweni *(Lindiwe)*, Ayanda Nhlangothi *(Thuleni)*, Bafana Hendriks *(Jabu)*, Pheto Wildeman *(Nhlanhla)*, Xolani Dlamini *(Sarafina's Brother)*, Siya Ngcobe *(Sarafina's Brother)*, Louis Seboko *(Joe Masembuko)*, Sam Ngakane *(Guitar's Father)*, Doris Sehula *(Woman Shopper)*, Dominic Skosana *(1st Prison Guard)*, Ishamel Boikanyo *(2nd Prison Guard)*, Siphamandla Ngcamu *(1st Testimony/Crocodile Gang Member)*, Khanyo Maphumulo *(2nd Testimony)*, Vukani Dlamini *(3rd Testimony)*, Dipuo Lehlongwa *(4th Testimony/Sarafina's Friend)*, Mfana "Jones" Hlope *(5th Testimony/Crocodile Gang Member)*, Congo Radebe *(Silence)*, Thulani Didi *(Crocodile Gang Member)*, Vincent Ngobese *(Crocodile Gang Member)*, Vukani "Marko" Dlamini *(Crocodile Gang Member)*, Gugwana Dlamini *(Sarafina's Friend)*, Khululiwe Sithole *(Sarafina's Friend)*, Batho Mhlongo *(Sarafina's Friend)*, Billy Mashigo *(Shebeen Drinker)*, Dixon Malele *(Shebeen Drinker)*, Eric Seema *(Shebeen Drinker)*, Velaphi Msini *(Teacher)*, Mate Bashe *(Teacher)*, Princess Msala *(Teacher)*, Sbongile Dingatha *(Woman Shopper)*, Olga Mvicane *(Woman Shopper)*, Prince *(Jaeger)*, Sindiswa Dlathu, Mabusi Gumede, Khanyo Maphumulo, Mmabatho Ramoupi, Sonto Khumalo, Nonhlanhla Sithole, Seipati Sothoane, Sindisiwe Sokhela, Velile Mchunu, Brian "Jazz" Mazibuko, John Lata, Mazwe Shabalala, Phakiso Motloung, Sduduzo Mtethwa, Thulani Mofokeng, Dipuo Lehlongwa, Vukani Dlamini, Khululiwe Sithole, Gugwana Dlamini, Thapi "Joko" Khambule, Gugu Mkhize, Lerato Wildeman, Nokuzola Dhlathu, Futhi Mhlongo, Rayhana Myles, Sibonakaliso Sothoane, Zanele Radebe, Alfred Ndlovu, Cyprian Shandu, Mabonga Khumalo, Nkosana Mzolo, Sduduzo Mbili, Skhumbuzo Kubheka, Sindane Mbatha, Siphamandla Ngcamu, Mfana "Jones" Hlope, Batho Mhlongo, Thulani Didi, Vincent Ngobese *(Dancers)*

Movie musicals have traditionally had lightweight storylines, though exceptions like WEST SIDE STORY and ALL THAT JAZZ successfully dealt with darker, more serious subjects. Set against a backdrop of political struggle in South Africa, SARAFINA! fails to join that select group.

Adapted from the hit Broadway show, SARAFINA! tells the story of an idealistic Black schoolgirl in 1970s South Africa, Sarafina (Leleti Khumalo), who has imaginary conversations with Nelson Mandela and dreams of being a great superstar. The story traces her painful journey from innocent teenager to revolutionary, against the backdrop of the 1976 student uprisings.

At Sarafina's school there is only one teacher, Mary Masembuko (Whoopi Goldberg), who offers an alternative to the Eurocentric worldview propounded by her colleagues. As Mary is warned by the white authorities that she should change her style, Sarafina becomes more aware of the quasi-revolutionary activities practiced by some of the boys in her school, and of the evil doings of Police Constable Sabela (Mbongeni Ngema), a Black who gleefully helps the white authorities torture and suppress his people.

When Mary is finally arrested and taken away during a class, her students refuse to accept her replacement, and rebel. The police are called in and shoot at the students, killing many; rebellion ignites all over the township, with Sarafina joining the others in pouring gasoline on Sabela and burning him to death. She is arrested, learns of Mary's unkind fate, but lives to incorporate Mary's noble views and dream of Mandela's release.

As pure drama, SARAFINA! works pretty well. But the musical chorus numbers interspersed throughout the narrative lack the qualities that could have made them integral to the story (the balletic symbolism of the fighting in WEST SIDE STORY, the ironic juxtaposition of CABARET or the presentation of happy simplicity, ripe for destruction, in FIDDLER ON THE ROOF). The songs seem accidental; even Goldberg's marvelous leading of the children in the Lord's Prayer seems incongruous and unreal in this film.

If the songs were catchy or memorable enough, most viewers wouldn't care that they didn't make sense. Sadly, that's not the case here, partly because the South African accents make the words hard to understand. To add insult to injury, the stagey performances of the songs, similiar to those in NEWSIES, generally offer the viewer the emotional involvement of watching an aerobics class.

The biggest problem, though, is the narrative. While it makes sense to concentrate on an "average" schoolkid in the telling of this story, we cannot but wonder—especially during the opening musical number in which Sarafina's fantasy of superstardom is shown—why we're concentrating on this particular girl. Khumalo is a charming screen presence but, in the end, there are other kids in the class we are more concerned about.

Although anti-apartheid films have not made for good box-office in the US (CRY FREEDOM and A DRY WHITE SEASON preceded SARAFINA! in their mediocre audience turnouts), the film was a hit in South Africa. *(Violence.)*

p, Anant Singh, David M. Thompson; d, Darrell James Roodt; w, William Nicholson, Mbongeni Ngema, (from his play); ph, Mark Vicente; ed, Peter Hollywood, Sarah Thomas, David Hietner; m, Stanley Myers; prod d, David Barkham; ch, Michael Peters

Musical/Drama **(PR: C MPAA: PG-13)**

SAVAGE INSTINCT ★

82m New Gold Productions ~ AIP Home Video c

Debra Sweaney *(Susan Morris)*, Sean P. Donahue *(Terk)*, Brian Oldfield *(Mongo)*, Jerry Johnson *(Georgie)*, Paul Aenri *(Apples)*, Rodger Arilsen *(Buck)*, Mike Donahue *(Frankie)*, J. Brown *(Mr. Wilson)*, Michael Terranova *(Joey)*, Bob Frazier *(Jake)*, Sean McCarty *(Billy)*, Eversley Forte *(Benny)*, Steve Lee *(Chang)*, Rick Slater *(Big J.)*, Satch Williams *(Gasser)*, Monique Mullen *(Star)*, Paul Gomez *(Philip)*, Paul Roder *(Geno)*, Lor-Michael Ringuette *(Cecil)*, Douglas Huttleston *(Jamie)*

Distributed by the Tiffany's of cheapjack sleaze, Troma Inc., SAVAGE INSTINCT wears its shoddiness on its sleeve, with results so absurd it borders on camp.

Young, attractive and recently widowed Susan Morris (Debra Sweaney) decides upon a day trip into the countryside in order to check out homes suitable to a widow's pension. While house-hunting, Susan witnesses an unsavory drug transaction, conducted by a nasty gang of reprobates, headed by Mongo (Olympic medalist Brian Oldfield), who immediately tags her as an uncooperative witness. Mongo and the gang pursue her, capture her and attempt to torture her, but Susan, like Harry Houdini, is always good for a last minute escape. After one particularly harrowing confrontation, Susan zips to a backyard toolshed and after minimal gnashing of teeth suddenly becomes a martial arts expert and begins to practice her newfound craft upon recalcitrant gang members.

Writer-director Patrick G. Donahue grandly holds up the distinguished auteurist tradition of Edward D. Woods, Jr. and Hugo Haas. Donahue creates a senseless idiot world in SAVAGE INSTINCT—a world in which cause and effect do not matter. Oblivious to character development and narrative meaning, Donahue blithely leaves unexplained how a trip to the woodpile can transform a former merry widow into, not only a martial arts expert, but, also, a killing machine. Donahue also errs in portraying Mongo's gang as vile and reprehensible cutthroats in order to maneuver Susan into dangerous and exploitative positions, only to become suddenly an inept bunch of lunkheads so that she can find a way out of their clutches at the last possible second.

Donahue's world in SAVAGE INSTINCT is a world of cartoon terror. Men are depicted as slobbering beasts with only one thing on their minds—a hat. Women inhabit this world on the assumption that they will almost surely be attacked, raped or killed. When Susan is picked up by a group of guys out for a joy ride, it is an even bet that before the car makes a stop at the next red light, she'll be fighting off their slobbering and leering mugs. And even though this world of sexual horror may not be too far from the truth, Donahue uses his exaggeration of reality for the purposes of quick exploitation, so that when Susan discovers her thunderball fists, the solution is so far-fetched that it becomes no solution at all. But in Donahue's ridiculously dangerous world, it is little wonder that Susan subliminally knows the secrets of martial arts. Women have to have this knowledge encoded in their DNA in order to survive.

Unfortunately, Donahue lacks the *joie de vivre* that would permit SAVAGE INSTINCT to cross the fine line between campiness and dreadfulness—bargain basement production values and subterranean acting do not a camp movie make. Donahue's unmitigated incompetence lends the film a funereal air that cannot be overcome. Instead, SAVAGE INSTINCT holds the viewer's attention solely by its sheer, gape-jawed amateurishness. It was originally produced in 1989 and has more aliases—"Edge of Fear," "They Call Me Macho Woman"—than a thug on the run. *(Excessive violence, profanity.)*

p, Patrick G. Donahue; d, Patrick G. Donahue; w, Patrick G. Donahue; ph, Mike Pierce; art d, Lee Mason

Action/Martial Arts **(PR: O MPAA: NR)**

SCANNERS III: THE TAKEOVER ★★★

(U.S./Canada) 101m Malofilm Group; Lance Entertainment ~ Republic Pictures Home Video c

Liliana Komorowska *(Helena Monet)*, Valerie Valois *(Joyce Stone)*, Steve Parrish *(Alexa Monet)*, Collin Fox *(Dr. Elton Monet)*, Daniel Pilon *(Michael–the Lawyer)*, Michel Perron *(Charlie)*, Harry Hill *(Doctor Baumann)*, Christopher Macabe *(George)*, Michael Copeman *(Mitch)*, Claire Cellucci *(Suzy)*, Peter Wright *(Mark Dragon)*, Charles Landry *(Sam)*, Chip Chuipka *(Thomas Drake)*, Jean Frenette *(Max)*, Sith Sekae *(Monk)*

An improvement on the previous SCANNERS II: THE NEW ORDER, this second sequel to David Cronenberg's original combines the usual head-busting action with some effective humor and a heavy dose of style.

Alexa Monet (Steve Parrish) is one of the "scanners" born with telepathic powers as the result of an experimental drug taken by their mothers in the 1950s. While showing off his powers at a party, he accidentally causes the death of a friend, and goes into hiding at a Thai monastery. Two years later, his adopted sister Helena (Liliana Komorowska) is suffering from migraines. As a result of her own telepathic capabilities, she cannot stop the thoughts of others from entering her mind. Her adoptive father, Dr. Elton Monet (Collin Fox), is working on a treatment, and shows her a sample of an electronic patch that might be able to quell the "voices" for a 24-hour period.

Despite his warnings that the patch is still in the experimental phase, the anguished Helena tries one on, and soon the "voices" have gone. But she also starts to display a malevolent attitude, and uses her powers to humiliate her sexist boss, Mark Dragon (Peter Wright), in a restaurant. She then steals Dr. Monet's case of patches and goes to the clinic of Dr. Baumann (Harry Hill), with whom her father had been working and who had once subjected her to sadistic experiments in the interest of "curing" her. She telekinetically blows his head off, then tells the other Scanner patients—who have been largely reduced to a group of mental defectives—that the patches are their ticket to domination over the "normals" who have oppressed them.

As the patches start to run out, Helena goes to Dr. Monet's place; when he refuses to create more for her, she drowns him in his hot tub and tells his attorney, Michael (Daniel Pilon), that the death was accidental. Concerned about Helena's behavior, and knowing that she stands to inherit control of Monet Pharmaceuticals, Michael seeks out Alex in Thailand. But one of Helena's scanner thugs follows him there and telepathically sets a group of street fighters on Michael; they kill him, but Alexa realizes what's going on and uses his powers to kill the thugs and the scanner. As he heads for home, Helena has taken over Monet Pharmaceuticals and plans a ruthless corporate strategy, while assigning Joyce Stone (Valerie Valois), a chemist who was Alexa's girlfriend, to use Dr. Monet's material to figure out how to make more patches.

While seducing a handsome underling at her apartment with the TV on, Helena is startled to find out that she can use a televised signal to control people's minds and realizes she can use this ability to effect her goal of world domination. Upon arriving home, Alexa discovers a tape she's made and, after nearly falling victim to its influence, realizes what she's up to. He confronts her at her office, but she puts off his suspicions and tells him that Joyce is working at the Baumann Clinic. Going to see her there, Alexa is instead set upon by Helena's scanner thugs, whom he escapes after a lengthy fight and chase.

Alex goes to Joyce's place, where she confirms his fears that Helena has become megalomaniacal. Alexa is later set upon again by Helena's scanner corps and winds up hospitalized; meanwhile Helena catches Joyce going through her files, and tells her that she's discovered how to manufacture more patches before putting Joyce under her telepathic control. Alexa escapes from the hospital just as Helena, whose company has taken over a major TV network, plans to broadcast a lethal psychic signal during a football game. Fending off attacks by Helena's thugs and freeing Joyce from her spell, Alexa fights a terrible psychic duel with his sister. Her patch falls off during the battle and, realizing what has happened and what she's done, Helena electrocutes herself. Alexa and Joyce leave the studio, not noticing that Helena's spirit has entered the TV equipment.

Rather than attempting to improve on Cronenberg's original formula, the makers of SCANNERS III have wisely gone for the approach of having fun with it, creating a fairly outlandish scenario and finding plenty of humorous possibilities in their telepathic characters. The major subplot of Helena transmitting her psychic vibes over the airwaves is introduced in a very funny scene in which, while in the throes of passion, she influences the host and guest of a TV talk show to start pawing each other. Helena's humiliation of Mark, in which she makes him start disco dancing and ultimately hurls him into a piano, is also fun, and Komorowska makes Helena a wickedly entertaining villainess without losing the touch of humanity that makes her, ultimately, a sympathetic victim as well.

Director Christian Duguay, who also helmed SCANNERS II, keeps the action fast and furious, from the kickboxing fight in Thailand—a scene clearly influenced by Asian action films—to the lengthy chase between Alexa and the scanner killers, which ends with a spectacular motorcycle stunt and a well-filmed punchline in which Alexa causes the film series's first underwater exploding head. Duguay and the screenwriters move the story along at a good clip, with clever setups—the first sign of Helena's altered personality is her casual psychic destruction of a bird—and satisfying payoffs, and a good deal more creativity than one might expect from a film like this. SCANNERS III is still a schlock film at heart, but it's a most entertaining and engaging one. *(Violence, profanity, nudity, sexual situations.)*

p, Rene Malo; d, Christian Duguay; w, B.J. Nelson, Rene Malo, David Preston, Julie Richard, (based on the characters created by David Cronenberg); ph, Hughes DeHaeck; ed, Yves Langlois; m, Marty Simon; prod d, Michael Joy; art d, Lynn Trout; set d, Andre Chamberland; cos, Laurie Drew

Science Fiction/Horror/Action (PR: O MPAA: R)

SCENT OF A WOMAN ★★★½

157m City Light Films; Universal ~ Universal c

Al Pacino *(Lt. Col. Frank Slade)*, Chris O'Donnell *(Charlie Simms)*, James Rebhorn *(Mr. Trask)*, Gabrielle Anwar *(Donna)*, Philip S. Hoffman *(George Willis Jr.)*, Richard Venture *(W.R. Slade)*, Bradley Whitford *(Randy)*, Rochelle Oliver *(Gretchen)*, Margaret Eginton *(Gail)*, Tom Riis Farrell *(Garry)*, Nicholas Sadler *(Harry Havemeyer)*, Todd Louiso *(Trent Potter)*, Matt Smith *(Jimmy Jameson)*, Gene Canfield *(Manny)*, Frances Conroy *(Christine Downes)*, June Squibb *(Mrs. Hunsaker)*, Ron Eldard *(Officer Gore)*, Sally Murphy *(Karen Rossi)*, Michael Santoro *(Donny Rossi)*, Alyson Feldman *(Francine Rossi)*, Erika Feldman *(Francine Rossi)*, Julian Stein *(Willie Rossi)*, Max Stein *(Willie Rossi)*, Anh Duong *(Sofia)*, Leonard Gaines *(Freddie Bisco)*, David Lansbury *(Michael)*, Joseph Palmas *(Bellhop)*, Baxter Harris *(George Willis Sr.)*, Francie Swift *(Flight Attendant)*, Michel Simon *(Oak Room Waiter)*, William Beckwith *(Oak Room Maitre d')*, Mansoor Najeeullah *(Skycap)*, J.T. Cromwell *(Ballroom Waiter)*, Peter Carew *(Bootblack)*, Paul Stocker *(Doorman)*, Michael Lisenco *(Cab Driver)*, Divina Cook *(Night Maid)*

Based on 1975's PROFUMO DI DONNA, a popular Italian import starring Vittorio Gassman, SCENT OF A WOMAN offers the familiar tale of two disparate people learning about life, and each other, during a long, eventful journey. That one of them is disabled may remind some of RAIN MAN, but this film is substantially different, thanks to a wonderfully fiery main character, and a tour-de-force performance by Al Pacino.

We first see Pacino's companion, Charlie Simms (Chris O'Donnell), at a typical East Coast prep school, surrounded by lots of privileged, obnoxious classmates who patronize him as they socialize with him. Charlie, like countless other cinematic prep schoolers, doesn't fit in; he's a poor scholarship boy from Oregon. One night he sees his "friends" set up an elaborate practical joke at the expense of the Dean. He knows who the culprits are but refuses to squeal, despite both the Dean's carrot (a guaranteed place at Harvard) and his stick (expulsion). Charlie is given until the resumption of classes after Thanksgiving to reconsider his decision.

Over the Thanksgiving break, Charlie, lacking the funds to fly home, takes a weekend job as a "caretaker and companion" for Frank Slade (Pacino), a blind, retired Army Colonel who lives nearby. At their first meeting Frank is arrogant and bullying, but the family practically runs off on vacation before Charlie has a chance to back out. He gets an additional shock when Frank orders him to pack for a trip to New York. Charlie weakly protests and wants to know the purpose of the trip, but is told on the plane that information will be given to him on a strictly "need to know basis." On the flight, Frank—a highly decorated officer and former aide to Lyndon Johnson—expounds on his deep appreciation of women, flirting with the stewardess and showing off his amazing ability to recognize colognes and scents.

It is not until they sit down to dinner in an elegant Manhattan restaurant that Frank, after quite a few shots of Jack Daniels, reveals his plan: to see his family, have a few great meals, make love to a beautiful woman, and then "blow [his] brains out." Charlie is stunned but there's little he can do; he's stuck with Frank for the weekend. The pair's adventures include a visit to a high-class hooker (Charlie waits dutifully downstairs in the limo); an evening at a bar where Frank dances a memorable tango with the beautiful young Donna (Gabrielle Anwar); and a test-drive joyride in a Ferrari, with a petrified Charlie yelling navigational instructions to a gleeful Frank. Charlie and Frank also pop in unexpectedly for a tension-filled Thanksgiving dinner at Frank's brother's home. Here Charlie learns, from Frank's bitter nephew, about the act of drunken stupidity that led to the Colonel's handicap: showing off during a demonstration by juggling hand grenades, he was blinded when one of them went off.

Gradually, Frank begins to take a liking to Charlie, giving him advice about life and forcing him to re-examine where his loyalties should lie at school. When Frank finally attempts suicide, Charlie wrestles the gun away from him and tearfully convinces him that his life, however reduced from what it formerly was, is still worth living. The eventful weekend over, Charlie returns to school to face a disciplinary hearing in front of the entire school. Frank unexpectedly appears and, acting as Charlie's surrogate parent, pleads his case, effectively sparing him from expulsion.

Although parts of SCENT OF A WOMAN are formulaic and sentimental, it is a generally satisfying film, thanks largely to Pacino's riveting performance. This part is a gift for an actor, and Pacino has a great time with it, adopting a hoarse, slightly Southern-inflected accent. He convinces us that this gruff, hard-drinking man is still capable of great tenderness and charm, as illustrated by the celebrated tango scene. (In one of the film's best lines, Slade tries to pick up the lovely young woman by telling her she needs protection from all the womanizers there.) O'Donnell takes a somewhat bland part and plays it naively and innocently enough to be believable, without overdoing it.

Unfortunately, SCENT OF A WOMAN opts for a big showdown in order to conclude things on a feel-good, triumphant note; a film about Frank and Charlie getting to know each other doesn't seem to be enough for director Martin Brest and screenwriter Bo Goldman. The climactic hearing is played like a prize fight, and its logic is muddled. Charlie must either side with the Dean, a pompous figure who had no qualms about exploiting Charlie's insecurity; or his "friends," who are such condescending creeps that informing on them doesn't seem so awfully unthinkable. Frank's self-consciously rousing speech attacks both sides, and doesn't seem to know what point to make except for a very vague one about standing up for what you believe in—not much help if there's no option that you *can* believe in. It's clear that Frank, who seems to have lost faith in all institutions, views the school as yet another factory turning out unquestioning conformists, and sees in it the same system that sent promising young men like himself off to war to be killed or damaged for life. He's a complex character, full of passion, regret, and a certain amount of self-loathing, and some more reflective scenes between him and Charlie would have been more illuminating.

SCENT OF A WOMAN does hook us in, largely thanks to Pacino's landmark performance, but a little trimming could have turned this from a good film into a great one. *(Violence, profanity, sexual situations, adult situations.)*

p, Martin Brest; d, Martin Brest; w, Bo Goldman, (from the characters created by Ruggero Maccari and Dino Risi, from the novel *Il Buio e il Miele* by Giovanni Arpino); ph, Donald E. Thorin; ed, William Steinkamp, Michael Tronick, Harvey Rosenstock; m, Thomas Newman; prod d, Angelo Graham; art d, W. Steven Graham; set d, George DeTitta, Jr.; cos, Aude Bronson-Howard; ch, Jerry Mitchell, Paul Pellicoro

AAN Best Picture: Martin Brest (Producer); *AA Best Actor:* Al Pacino; *AAN Director:* Martin Brest; *AAN Best Adapted Screenplay:* Bo Goldman

Drama **(PR: C MPAA: R)**

SCHOOL TIES ★★

107m Jaffe-Lansing Productions; Paramount ~ Paramount c

Brendan Fraser *(David Greene)*, Matt Damon *(Charlie Dillon)*, Chris O'Donnell *(Chris Reece)*, Randall Batinkoff *(Rip Van Kelt)*, Andrew Lowery *(McGivern)*, Cole Hauser *(Jack Connors)*, Ben Affleck *(Chesty Smith)*, Anthony Rapp *(McGoo)*, Amy Locane *(Sally Wheeler)*, Peter Donat *(Headmaster Dr. Bartram)*, Zeljko Ivanek *(Cleary)*, Kevin Tighe *(Coach McDevitt)*, Michael Higgins *(Mr. Gierasch)*, Ed Lauter *(Allan Greene)*, Peter McRobbie *(Chaplain)*, John Cunningham *(Grayson Dillon)*, Elizabeth Franz *(Jane Dillon)*, Matt Hofherr *(Gray Dillon)*, Jeff Hochendoner *(Bear)*, Rick Rodgers *(Nick)*, John Sprerdakos *(Kocus)*, Edward Seamon *(Weezer)*, Dan Desmond *(Mr. Wheeler)*, Claudia Everest *(Mrs. Wheeler)*, Leon B. Stevens *(Tom Keating)*, Cody Conklin *(Sarah)*, Benari Poulten *(Petey)*, Stanton Denman *(Miller)*, Sean Kent *(Keller)*, Luke Jorgensen *(Rick)*, Kent Osborne *(Emile)*, Jayce Bartok *(Jack)*, Jeff Nichols *(Donald)*, James Quinn *(1st Boy)*, Ryan Anderson *(2nd Boy)*, Will Lyman *(Swanson)*, William Meisle *(Winchester Headmaster)*, Susan Johnston *(Mary Ellen)*, Sandra Landers *(Joyce)*, Ken Garito *(Don)*, Karen Shallo *(Edie)*, Gregory Chase *(Cal Reynolds)*, Alice Duffy *(Chaperone)*, Thomas Rhett Kee *(Boy in Shower)*, Jane Nichols *(Swimming Coach)*, Colin F. Lydon *(Boy in Dining Room)*, David Caldwell Allen *(Annoucer)*

The stolid social prejudice drama of the 1950s gets an ineffective updating in SCHOOL TIES, the story of an ultra-WASP boys' prep school that brings a Jewish student in as a scholarship ringer to quarterback their football team.

David Greene (Brendan Fraser) is a local football star from blue-collar Scranton who's plucked from almost-certain obscurity at the start of his senior year of high school to quarterback the team at exclusive St. Matthew's Prep, an Ivy League "feed school." Familiar with anti-Semitic prejudice in his home town, Greene elects to keep his religion secret at the school, even though it means biting his tongue against ethnic jokes and shirking his religious obligations by playing football on Rosh Hashanah.

After weathering some initial resentment from Charlie Dillon (Matt Damon), the boy he replaces, the two wind up friends as Dillon becomes Greene's chief blocker on the field. However, losing his position on the team is just the first stop on Dillon's downward spiral, seemingly at David's hands. He also loses his girlfriend Sally Wheeler (Amy Locane) to the hunky Greene.

Overhearing some loose talk at an alumni party, Dillon learns of Greene's religion and begins mobilizing the other students to make his life miserable. Greene hangs tough, although he loses Sally. But Dillon steps up the harassment, framing Greene for cheating on a final exam and exploiting the anti-Semitism of the school's honor system enforcement committee. When it looks certain that Greene will get expelled, a third student steps forward who knows the truth and it is Dillon who winds up leaving.

As these films go, SCHOOL TIES is more simplistic and has its dice more loaded than usual. To begin with, David doesn't seem particularly religious. He doesn't eat kosher, and he goes along to get along. And the film constantly underscores his "averageness" to make his acceptance by his classmates more plausible. His classmates, meanwhile, are the kind of uptight, overprivileged quasi-Nazis that somehow wind up all in one place in films like this. At any rate, they'd hardly fit anyone's idea of future leaders of commerce and society.

In the real world, it's more likely that Greene's working-class background would work harder against his acceptance at a snooty prep school than his religious beliefs, but SCHOOL TIES largely ignores this angle. Instead, it takes an odd side trip into the tremendous pressure on the student scions of powerful families to follow tradition and get into top schools. Besides Dillon's cheating, another student has a nervous breakdown after flunking a French exam.

Movies set in a school environment have their own tradition of showing the protagonist finally rejecting the destructive competitive pressures, from IF, which ends with an armed insurrection no less, to the famous ending of THE PAPER CHASE, in which the hero throws away his law school grade report without looking at it. In SCHOOL TIES, the "system" barely comes under question. Greene fully comprehends that he's being kept in school not because of some outburst of altruism from St. Matthew's administrators, but because having a star quarterback is more important to them than maintaining their ethnic purity. Greene ends up by informing the headmaster that he will use them to get into a first-rate school just as they are using him to win at football.

In this "pragmatic" resolution, SCHOOL TIES seems to accept educational elitism as earnestly as it rejects religious elitism. It's as if some forms of elitism are more elite than others when, in fact, elitism itself is the root of the social evil the film denounces. Its integrity thus compromised, and having little else going for it, SCHOOL TIES can't help but be an inferior film. *(Profanity.)*

p, Sherry Lansing, Stanley R. Jaffe; d, Robert Mandel; w, Dick Wolf, Darryl Ponicsan, (from the story by Wolf); ph, Freddie Francis; ed, Jerry Greenberg, Jacqueline Cambas; m, Maurice Jarre; art d, Steven Wolff; set d, Rosemary Brandenburg; cos, Ann Roth

Drama **(PR: C MPAA: PG-13)**

SCORCHERS ★½

(U.K./U.S.) 88m Goldcrest; Scorchers Productions; Nova Films; PRO FilmWorks ~ FoxVideo c

Emily Lloyd *(Splendid)*, Jennifer Tilly *(Talbot)*, Leland Crooke *(Jumper)*, Faye Dunaway *(Thais)*, James Earl Jones *(Bear)*,

Denholm Elliott *(Howler)*, James Wilder *(Dolan)*, Anthony Geary, Luke Perry

Adapting a play to the screen is often a tricky business. Dialogue that crackles across the stage may sound artificial and forced in a film, while rich characters somehow transform into unconvincing stereotypes. Playwright-turned-writer-director David Beaird struggles mightily to turn his theatrical trilogy into a compelling movie, but the results are fairly risible.

SCORCHERS offers many traveling shots of the Louisiana bayou accompanied by flavorful zydeco music. One such sequence opens the film, as the camera comes upon a riverside shack where Thais (Faye Dunaway), the town whore, is locked in a carnal embrace with the Preacher (Anthony Geary, Luke of "General Hospital" fame). The Preachers's absence at church delays the wedding of Splendid (Emily Lloyd) to Dolan (James Wilder) and the anxious father of the bride, Jumper (Leland Crooke), fumes about the delay.

Splendid frets about losing her virginity to Dolan, whom her father refers to as the "Human Hard-On," while Talbot (Jennifer Tilly) laments that her husband of six months never wants to have sex.

The missing minister finally shows up and marries the young couple. Everyone then gathers for a lavish reception, exept Talbot, who goes home in search of her aloof husband, growing increasingly agitated when she cannot find him. Shrieking, she grabs a pistol from a drawer, loads it and heads out into the night.

Splendid, meanwhile, leads Dolan on a mad chase around the house, crying to her father for help. We next meet Howler (Denholm Elliot) dancing alone to classical music in a bar presided over by Bear (James Earl Jones). The gentle Englishman was once hailed as a great actor but, for reasons never adequately explained, he has become the town drunk. Bear is short-tempered and chronically insecure but oddly devoted to Howler, for whom he stocks the jukebox with classical music.

Meanwhile neither Jumper nor "Moby Dick" is able to persuade Splendid to perform her wifely duties: the transition from virgin to wife is too sudden for her. In contrast, Talbot has become more aggressive: she deduces that her husband is with the town whore and goes lookin for Thais, who has dropped by Bear's place to chat.

Splendid finally reveals the true source of her fears: her mother died giving birth to her and she fears a similar fate if she has sex. Meanwhile Talbot shoots out the windows at Bear's place, then stomps in and confronts her nemesis, who admits that her husband pays $100 for each visit. Thais proceeds to vent her spleen about how no one cares about her own needs while she treats her customers lovingly, prompting Howler to praise her acting ability. Talbot then learns that her father—the Preacher—is another satisfied customer!

Jumper gets Splendid to engage in a psychodramatic exercise, which ends in tears of joy for all involved. At Bear's place, Talbot is advised not to act like a preacher's daughter between the sheets, and she trudges off home, where her husband lies sprawled across the bed. He awakens as Talbot undresses and makes passionate love to her, despite her initial resistance. Splendid and Dolan are similarly entwined in the presumably happy conclusion. Meanwhile, at Bear's, Thais has left for the evening. The grumpy barkeep makes a selection on the jukebox and a piece by Mahler fills the air. Having seen the light, he and Howler dance about slowly and happily.

In a desperate attempt to add some action to this tepid talkfest, Beaird has the camera careen about in a lunatic fashion. Talbot's first trip home is rendered with a shaky handheld camera accompanied by a thumping heartbeat on the soundtrack, inadvertently suggesting the ominous point-of-view shot of a stalker in a slasher movie. Later, when Talbot appears at the wedding party with murder on her mind, everything shifts to portentous slow motion *a la* Brian De Palma. The incessant crosscutting between the various characters' storylines is inelegant at best—perhaps these three stories were originally separate acts.

While one may forgive a neophyte filmmaker for lapses in craft and taste, Beaird bungles the direction of actors as well. The scenes of Splendid evading her husband are depicted in a vulgar slapstick manner. Nearly every scene is played far too broadly for the frail material. Good performers are wasted or made to look silly, with James Earl Jones a particular embarrassment. Faye Dunaway looks terrific in a glamorous star turn but her Thais is an abstraction. Denholm Elliot seems to be on hand merely to provide a touch of class but his character's function is a mystery. Only Leland Crooke, who originated the role of Jumper on stage, begins to suggest a believable character; even he, though, is undermined by his underwritten part. The emotional core of the film is the scene in which Splendid has an imaginary meeting with her dead mother. While the scene is affecting, the sentiments are obvious and the ideas simple-minded.

One approaches this kind of film expecting to find the qualities of a good play: well-staged scenes, strong performances, literate writing and sharp observations about the human condition. Here however, the only rational female is the town whore, the threat of domestic violence is played for laughs and part of the happy ending could be interpreted as a rape.

Seeing the names of the impressive cast listed on the box may warm the hearts of many unsuspecting video store browsers but viewers should avoid SCORCHERS unless they want to get burned. *(Profanity, sexual situations, adult situations.)*

p, Morrie Eisenman, Richard Hellman; d, David Beaird; w, David Beaird, (from his play); ph, Peter Deming; ed, David Garfield; m, Heidi Kaczenski; prod d, Bill Eigenbrodt; art d, Rosalind Crew; set d, Rosalind Crew; cos, Heidi Kaczenski

Comedy/Drama **(PR: C MPAA: R)**

SECRET FRIENDS ★½

97m Whistling Gypsy Productions Ltd.; Channel Four; Film Four International; Briar Patch Film Corporation ~ Briar Patch Film Corporation c

Alan Bates *(John)*, Gina Bellman *(Helen)*, Frances Barber *(Angela)*, Tony Doyle *(Martin)*, Joanna David *(Kate)*, Colin Jeavons *(Vicar)*, Rowena Cooper *(Vicar's Wife)*, Ian McNeice *(1st Businessman)*, Davyd Harries *(2nd Businessman)*, Niven Boyd *(British Rail Steward/Patient)*, Martin Whiting *(Young John)*, Roy Hamilton *(Singer)*, Nicholas Russell-Pavier *(Musician)*, Colin Ryan *(Musician)*, David Swift *(Musician)*

Madness is in the eye of the audience. And in the world according to Dennis Potter, there exist a myriad of "realities" that one can inhabit. You simply have to accept the idea that one perception may be just as valid as another. That's the *modus operandi* of SECRET FRIENDS, a schizophrenic think-piece concocted and directed by Potter, who does not serve his original novel *Ticket to Ride* very well. Lovers of deliberate obfuscation will, however, probably enjoy Potter's fling with confusion.

Welcome to the world of John (Alan Bates) who's haunted by a *doppelgaenger* who encourages him to kill his wife, Helen (Gina Bellman), because he's fixated on the notion that she's a whore who can't escape her sordid past. (Was his wife once a call girl or is she just another victim of John's misogyny?) In frenetic fragments suggesting John's tortured psyche, snippets of the character's past, present and possible future collide. Often we glimpse his troubled childhood in which a stern, disciplinarian father (Colin Jeavons) and a mute mother (Rowena Cooper) cripple him psychologically.

On occasion, we spy upon Pinteresque domestic scenes including one in which the unraveling John has an affair with a family friend, Angela (Frances Barber in the film's only noteworthy performance). Sometimes, we simply sit beside John on a train to London as he journies between breakdown and sanity while dreaming of uxoricide. By the climax, John is literally a prisoner of his fantasies; it becomes apparent that we have been witnessing the twisted imaginings of the protagonist throughout. Our view of reality has been distorted through his unique perspective.

Who is the secret friend of the title? It is the childlike essence of John—the brave, spontaneous spirit that's been oppressed by life. By the time John's troubled mind splinters into a hundred pieces, however, viewers may not care about his brutalized childhood or his career as a botanical artist or his warped alter-ego visions. As the narrative glides by in lightning bursts of memories followed by drawn-out present-day delusions, the stream of consciousness doesn't illuminate John's condition. He remains a cipher. Instead of being drawn inside the man's pathetic madness, most viewers will become frustrated by the flashy cinematic techniques and bored by the realization that John is less a character than the filmmaker's own secret friend, an excuse to show off his cleverness.

Shucking off the conventions of traditional narrative filmmaking is a tricky proposition unless the storyline is complex enough to challenge viewers' emotions as well as their intellects. Having a multi-faceted character or two for the audience to hold onto is a wise precaution to take; SECRET FRIENDS does not carry the weight of THE MANCHURIAN CANDIDATE or DREAMSCAPE or even the 1940s thriller THE LOCKET because the filmmaker has focused all his attention on the technique and not enough on delineating in depth the protagonist's skewed perception of reality.

Unlike "Pennies from Heaven" or "The Singing Detective," two Potter masterworks, the paranoid fantasy on tap is a nightmare that neither frightens nor involves. Potter's carefully thought out, worked-over descent into bedlam is a monument to cryptic philosophizing. That unsatisfying attempt to get inside John's head only takes us as far as Potter's brain, which no doubt clicked away with excitement as he threw film conventions and caution to the wind. It is an excitement not likely to be shared by those trying to make sense of SECRET FRIENDS. *(Violence, adult situations.)*

p, Rosemarie Whitman; d, Dennis Potter; w, Dennis Potter, (from his novel *Ticket to Ride*); ph, Sue Gibson; ed, Clare Douglas; m, Nicholas Russell-Pavier; prod d, Gary Williamson

Drama/Fantasy **(PR: O MPAA: NR)**

SECRET GAMES

Wilshire Film Ventures ~ Imperial Entertainment Corporation c

Martin Hewitt *(Eric)*, Michelle Brin *(Julianne)*, Billy Drago *(Mark Langford)*, Delia Sheppard, Catya Sassoon, Sabrina Mesko, Kimberly Williams

The tribulations of the rich, beautiful and naked in Beverly Hills are the focus of this inane soft-porn warming over of Bunuel's classic BELLE DU JOUR.

Michelle Brin, admittedly a ringer for Catherine Deneuve in looks if not in talent, plays Julianne who, neglected by her architect husband Mark Langford (Billy Drago), and bored with shopping, joins a ritzy daytime brothel in search of afternoon orgasms. Shy at first, she warms up with some mild lesbianism, topless sunbathing and parading around in frilly undergarments before taking on her first male client, the mysterious Eric (Martin Hewitt). Not only does Eric bring her to earthshaking orgasms, but he also chats with her afterwards. Julianne is, of course, smitten by this hunk who not only torques her body but is interested in her mind. She is, however, tormented by nightmares about her Catholic school upbringing in which she's mauled by a gay-porn magazine cover model in front of a miniskirted nun with great legs.

What these nightmares might mean is never explored before Eric's dark wacko side emerges. He wants to own Julianne and will stop at nothing. During one session, he "discreetly" snaps photographs of Julianne frolicking with a fellow lady of the day. He mails samples of the photos to Mark along with an offer to turn over the negatives for $10,000, but his real intention is to murder Mark in order to take possession of Julianne. Having escaped her bedroom-cell in Eric's apartment, Julianne arrives at the scene in the nick of time to kill Eric as he's about to kill Mark.

Not likely to erase memories of V: THE HOT ONE, porn legend Annette Haven's hard-core reworking of BELLE DU JOUR, much less Bunuel's classic itself, SECRET GAMES is the kind of movie for which pay cable was invented. The plot is minimal and nonsensical, the gals are gorgeous, and the action, in the unrated version at least, is about as salacious as it gets outside the "Adults Only" section of the video store.

The plot, when it gets going, resembles "Charlie's Angels" on an off week when the other prostitutes team up with Julianne to put Eric out of commission, sneaking around Beverly Hills in limousines and skittering in and out of mansions in the dead of night in tight miniskirts and nosebleed-inducing heels. Another highlight is the male bouncer of the brothel, who keeps an industrial key copier handy at his workplace, allowing him to copy all of Eric's keys to facilitate Julianne's later escape from Eric's luxuriously appointed holding cell. The handiest of handymen, he also services the madam of the house whenever she gets too heated up from watching her employees at work through the clever closed-circuit cameras she's scattered throughout the house.

But for the most part, SECRET GAMES is geared to lovers of lingerie and the ladies who wear it; in one long sequence, having little to do with anything else in the film, the daytime prostitutes demonstrate their skills at striptease for one another. In this kind of context, acting seems superfluous. But, for the record, Drago (THE UNTOUCHABLES, DIPLOMATIC IMMUNITY) is terrible as ever, while Hewitt (ENDLESS LOVE, CARNAL CRIMES) actually does act, and it's very distracting. Brin has the right idea. As Jack Nicholson advised in interviews while he was playing the Joker in BATMAN, she let the costumes do the acting. *(Sexual situations, nudity.)*

p, Andrew Garroni; d, A. Gregory Hippolyte; w, Georges Des Esseintes; ph, Thomas F. DeNove, Walter Pfister; ed, Kent Smith; prod d, Blair Martin; cos, Richardo Delgado

Erotic/Drama **(PR: O MPAA: R)**

SEEDPEOPLE ★

87m Full Moon Entertainment ~ Paramount Home Video c

Sam Hennings *(Tom Baines)*, Andrea Roth *(Heidi Tucker)*, Dane Witherspoon *(Brad Yates)*, David Dunard *(Ed)*, Holly Fields *(Kim Tucker)*, Bernard Kates *(Doc Roller)*, Anne Betancourt *(Mrs. Santiago)*, John Mooney, Charles Bouvier, Sonny Carl Davis

Executive producer Charles Band should be ashamed of the "Based on an original idea" credit he's given himself; SEEDPEOPLE is a blatant ripoff of INVASION OF THE BODY

SNATCHERS, quite possibly designed to beat Abel Ferrara's upcoming major studio remake into the marketplace.

Even the wraparound device is derivative, as our hero, Tom Baines (Sam Hennings) recounts his story of invasion and possession from a hospital bed. The story proper takes place in Tom's hometown of Comet Valley, where he arrives after a long absence just as the only bridge leading in or out is being closed down for repairs. There he gets a room at a bed-and-breakfast run by his old flame, Heidi Tucker (Andrea Roth), and encounters local sheriff, Brad Tates (Dane Witherspoon), the new man in Heidi's life. The expected conflicts ensue, but Tom soon has more to worry about: alien spores have recently landed nearby on a fallen meteorite, spawning bizarre plantlife that has begun to possess the populace. Some of the townsfolk are already exhibiting the blank, emotionless symptoms; one of them is Heidi's housekeeper Mrs. Santiago (Anne Betancourt), of whom Heidi's young daughter Kim (Holly Fields) is suspicious. The girl has also glimpsed Mrs. Santiago's alter ego—a rolling plant monster—but no one except Tom will believe her.

The only other person in town who is convinced of the invasion is crazy old Doc Roller (Bernard Kates), who has taken to outfitting himself with fluorescent lights (which can repel the alien creatures). Eventually, thanks to a videotape made by Kim, Tom convinces Heidi of the danger and the two set out to stop the aliens. This they manage to do, curing the locals of the possessing force with a barrage of fluorescents and blowing up a truckload of outgoing pods, which have been harvested by the enslaved humans. Back at the hospital, Tom wraps up his frightening story, only to find inevitably that the nightmare is just beginning . . . .

Boasting cheaper production values than usual for a Full Moon production, SEEDPEOPLE never looks chintzier than when its monsters are onscreen. These creations by John Buechler, who usually does better on his low budgets, are among the most laughable movie monsters in recent years, rendering the film more reminiscent of FROM HELL IT CAME than the intended inspiration. In true Full Moon tradition, the monsters were even given cute nicknames ("Sailor," "Tumbler" and "Shooter") in the event of a merchandising possibility that understandably never came to pass.

The rest of the movie is just as lacking, with Peter Manoogian's uninspired direction on a par with Jackson Barr's feeble screenplay. (Barr's been writing an awful lot of low-budget vehicles these days, and really should take a break to recharge his creative batteries.) The actors are competent at best, though to be fair, they weren't given much to work with. The most thankless role belongs to Fields, a twenty-one-year-old actress attempting vainly to pass as a thirteen-year-old. In the final analysis, though, she comes off as no less—or more—believable than anything else in this science fiction shambles. *(Violence, profanity.)*

p, Anne Kelly; d, Peter Manoogian; w, Jackson Barr, (from the origional idea by Charles Band); ph, Adolfo Bartoli; ed, Bert Glatstein, Tom Barrett; m, Boby Mithoff; prod d, R. Clifford Searcy; art d, Everett D. Wilson; cos, Lois Simbach

Science Fiction/Horror **(PR: O MPAA: R)**

SETTA, LA

(SEE: DEVIL'S DAUGHTER, THE)

SEVERED TIES ★

96m Fangoria Films ~ Columbia TriStar Home Video c

Oliver Reed *(Dr. Hans Vaughan)*, Elke Sommer *(Helena Harrison)*, Garrett Morris *(Stripes)*, Billy Morrisette *(Harrison Harrison)*, Johnny Legend *(Preacher)*, Denise Wallace *(Eve)*, Roger Perkovich *(Lorenz)*, Bekki Vallin *(Uta)*, Gerald Shidell *(Doctor Harrison)*

"Severed concept" is more like it. As a gross-out for teen viewers, SEVERED TIES passes muster, but as a horror film laced with black comedy, it's a messy hybrid of THE RE-ANIMATOR and THE BEAST WITH FIVE FINGERS with a little CREEPING UNKNOWN for good measure.

Haunted by flashbacks of his father's murder (a killing actually committed by his mother), juvenile genius Harrison Harrison (Billy Morrisette) poutily demands a better grade of cadavers for his experiments in genetics. Surreptiously working for NordKem, his mother, Helena (Elke Sommer), and her paramour, Dr. Hans Vaughan (Oliver Reed), want him to finish up his father's uncompleted research in gene-splicing and organ regrowth. During a rebellious snit, suspicious Harrison escapes with a top secret vial but loses his arm in a metal security door in his lab. Going out on a limb, Harrison injects the fluid into his severed limb and the arm reattaches but has a mind of its own; no one's ever accused Harrison of being disarming, but his limb can detach and re-attach itself at will.

Befriended by a peg-legged derelict, Stripes (Garrett Morris), Harrison encounters a subterranean band of homeless sewer-dwelling amputees. After arming himself against Preacher (Johnny Legend), their cruel leader, Harrison kills this revivalist, then sends his opinionated appendage and new-found sewer-gal pal, Eve (Denise Wallace) over to his old lab to retrieve ingredients. While Harrison perfects his research, Eve is captured by Helena and Dr. Vaughan who plan to use her as an all-purposes genetic guinea pig. Injecting fluids into all the outcast defectives, Harrison creates a veritable army, but he and Stripes have difficulty controlling the unruly troops. Although these newly empowered misfits defeat the NordKem plot by destroying Dr. Vaughan, Helena joins Eve in a splicing chamber (an idea lifted from David Cronenberg's THE FLY); although restored to life, Eve is possessed by the spirit of Helena.

If the sight of dismemberment chills you to the marrow then SEVERED TIES may engross you as it grosses you out. Then again, you might have just as much fun watching surgical training films.

Serious sci-fi buffs will be turned off by the screenplay's inconsistencies about "arms" control, its off-putting jokey tone, its poorly integrated flashback sequences, its repellent undercurrent of sadism and the dismaying presence of veteran actors who deserve better than playing fall guys in this adolescent house of horrors. Nothing is developed with any degree of intelligence or consistency in John Nystrom and Henry Dominic's screenplay; nothing in Damon Santostefano's direction rises above the level of hackwork. Though credit can go to the special effects for being gruesome if not particularly frightening and a one-armed salute to Morrisette's enthusiastic performance, one is left with little else to recommend.

Apt to make the impressionable gag and the discerning shake their heads in disgust, SEVERED TIES may find itself rejuvenated some day on TV's "Mystery Science Theater," the cemetery of all bad movies. There, this loathsome film may get the comic dissection it deserves. *(Extreme violence.)*

p, Christopher Webster; d, Damon Santostefano, Richard Roberts; w, John Nystrom, Henry Dominic, (from the story by Damon Santostefano and David A. Casci); ph, Geza Sinkovics; ed,

Richard Roberts; m, Daniel Licht; prod d, Don Day; cos, Susan Bertram

Science Fiction/Horror/Comedy **(PR: O MPAA: R)**

SEX CRIMES ★

90m Life Entertainment ~ Atlantic Home Video c

Jeffrey Osterhage *(Rick Massey)*, Maria Richwine *(Rosanna)*, Fernando Garzon *(Victor)*, Craig Alan *(Max)*, Grace Morley *(Cynthia)*, Danny Trejo *(Palmer)*, James Distefano *(Tony)*, Joan Moran *(Prosecutor)*, Norm Coupe *(Judge)*, Richard Haje *(Jack)*, Derek Mitchell *(Lawrence)*, Ron Howard George *(1st Bartender)*, Nicholas Hill *(Punk)*, David Eisenstein *(Edward)*, Carlos Cestero *(Forensic Man)*, Agustin Mendez *(Mendez)*, Raymond D. Turner *(Nolton)*, Danelle Gregorio *(Public Defender)*

Produced, directed and co-written by David Garcia, SEX CRIMES starts out as a promising portrait of cryptofeminist rage, but quickly collapses into substandard action fare.

Rosanna (Maria Richwine) is a rising Los Angeles prosecutor who is brutally raped but keeps quiet about it. She's upset at the number of cases that are thrown out of court on technicalities, but when she is appointed to a judgeship, "the first Hispanic woman on the bench," as her associate Edward (David Eisenstein) proclaims, she's even more tied to the letter of the law. Donning various disguises, Rosanna begins hunting down and executing these released hardened criminals, all of whom escaped charges of violence against women.

Detective Rick Massey (Jeffrey Osterhage) and his partners, Victor (Fernando Garzon) and Cynthia (Grace Morley), all tough undercover cops working in the LAPD's "unit of last resort with hardcore criminals," are on the trail of serial rapist/killer Palmer (Danny Trejo), who tape records his torturing of his victims and leaves the tapes with the bodies as calling cards. They are a little distracted by the new skein of murders, since the victims are all two-time-losing scum. Rick and Rosanna strike up a friendship and soon become lovers. Rosanna steals Palmer's latest tape from Rick and recognizes him by voice as her rapist. While she's out nailing Palmer, Rick searches her apartment and finds the tape and her disguises. Later when she confesses to him, Rick announces that her spree is over and destroys the tape, and they begin making love.

Joan Moran and David Garcia's screenplay is particularly incompetent in stitching together a coherent plot, even in its technical details (both Palmer and Rosanna leave enough fingerprints at their crime scenes to sink them both). And under Garcia's lumbering direction (even the gore effects are clumsy), it takes laughingly and anticlimactically forever to reach its last-reel thesis. Rick exonerates Rosanna's killings with this mouthful: "We are stuck with courts that are prisoners of laws created by a political system that doesn't work." What he doesn't mention is the incompetant police work on display in this film, resulting in cases being thrown out of court.

The distaff DEATH WISH vigilante received its first and still best outing in Abel Ferrara's no-nonsense thriller MS. 45. Here, Rosanna's clearly psychopathic behavior (she first shoots her victims in the genitals then moves on to slashed wrists, the injections of battery acid, etc.) remains totally unexplored, and she's apparently left, at film's end, with Rick's collaboration, as a still functioning trial judge! The performances are uniformally meagre, with Osterhage at least turning in a semblance of a character.

This low-budget production looks cheap throughout; perhaps significantly, no production designer or art director is credited. *(Violence, substance abuse, profanity, nudity, sexual situations.)*

p, David Garcia; d, David Garcia; w, Joan Moran, David Garcia, (from the story by Frank Cinelli); ph, Keith Holland; ed, Peter Cohen; m, Scott Douglas MacLachlan, Clay Manska, Glen Aulepp

Crime/Action **(PR: O MPAA: R)**

SEXUAL RESPONSE ★★

87m Response Productions ~ Columbia TriStar Home Video c

Shannon Tweed *(Eve)*, Catherine Oxenberg *(Kate)*, Vernon Wells *(Philip)*, Emile Levisetti *(Edge)*, David Kriegel *(Peter)*

The overly ambitious SEXUAL RESPONSE yearns to be an erotic psycho-thriller rife with meaningful commentary about romantic attraction as well as media ethics. Although the thrills are impacted negatively by the sex scenes, and although deeper thematics fade from view, this movie does get the down-and-dirty sexuality right.

Radio talk show hostess Eve (Shannon Tweed) handles her call-in guests' questions about relationships with tact and patience, but her own seemingly perfect marriage leaves her curiously unfulfilled. Since dominating husband Philip (Vernon Wells) treats her more as property than as a valued domestic partner, the pampered wife is ripe for the barstool blandishments of Edge (Emile Levisetti). Trotting after him to his cool artist pad, she quickly becomes an adultery statistic. Although Eve literally goes over the Edge, she's confused when he deposits a life-sized nude sculpture of her on her front lawn. As the requisite saxophone blares on the soundtrack, passion flares until Edge steals her husband's gun.

Fearing discovery by Philip, Eve involves her friends Kate (Catherine Oxenberg) and Peter (David Kriegel) in rifling through Edge's studio while she keeps him busy elsewhere. But why does Philip drug Eve? Could he be hiding a history he shares with Edge? As the body count of innocent bystanders mounts (Kate and Peter find out too much about Philip's former life), Eve, Edge and Philip engage in mortal combat. Conveniently clearing the way for the lovers, Philip gets impaled on one of Edge's more phallic sculptures. Since Philip was a fugitive from justice for many years after killing Edge's mother, Eve can consider herself lucky as she contemplates a full sex life with her late husband's son from a previous marriage.

When Tweed and Levisetti tear off their clothes, you can almost hear the buttons pop. On that count alone SEXUAL RESPONSE merits applause. The film also offers sterling support from Oxenberg as the true blue pal who goes where angels fear to tread and gets murdered. Unfortunately, the film isn't entirely successful at mating its erotic content with its unusual thriller subplot.

Had the filmmakers stuck to the basic FATAL ATTRACTION scenario, it would have made for a more ordinary film with the compensation of compact suspense. In throwing in that plot thread cribbed from THE STEPFATHER, it becomes diffuse and less effective. Although the near-misses and murders are suprising, the plentiful sex scenes detract from the primary driving force of the revenge plot involving Edge versus Phillip. Somehow, the sexual core of the film never seems integrated with the submerged storyline concerning Edge's family feud; the pseudo-Oedipal revelations hit viewers too late for maximum shock value.

Still, SEXUAL RESPONSE generates some spontaneous combustion between its central characters. And, in what marks a rarity for puritanical American cinema, it can claim the distinction of giving its adulterers a happy ending. *(Violence, nudity, sexual situations.)*

p, Ashok Amritraj; d, Yaky Yosha; w, Brent Morris, Eric Diamond; ph, Ilan Rosenberg; ed, David H. Lloyd; m, Richard

Berger; prod d, Arlan Jay Vetter; art d, Yudo Ako; cos, Alexis Scott

Erotic/Thriller **(PR: O MPAA: R)**

SHADOWS AND FOG ★★
83m Orion ~ Orion c

Woody Allen *(Kleinman)*, Kathy Bates *(Prostitute)*, John Cusack *(Student Jack)*, Mia Farrow *(Irmy)*, Jodie Foster *(Prostitute)*, Fred Gwynne *(Hacker's Follower)*, Julie Kavner *(Alma)*, Madonna *(Marie)*, John Malkovich *(Clown)*, Kenneth Mars *(Magician)*, Kate Nelligan *(Eve)*, Donald Pleasence *(Doctor)*, Lily Tomlin *(Prostitute)*, Philip Bosco *(Mr. Paulsen)*, Robert Joy *(Spiro's Assistant)*, Wallace Shawn *(Simon Carr)*, Kurtwood Smith *(Vogel's Follower)*, Josef Sommer *(Priest)*, David Ogden Stiers *(Hacker)*, Eszter Balint *(Woman with Baby)*, Michael Kirby *(Killer)*, James Rebhorn *(Vigilante)*, Victor Argo *(Vigilante)*, Daniel Von Bargen *(Vigilante)*, Camille Saviola *(Landlady)*, Tim Loomis *(Dwarf)*, Katy Dierlam *(Fat Lady)*, Dennis Vestunis *(Strongman)*, Anne Lange *(Prostitute)*, Andrew Mark Berman *(Student)*, Paul Anthony Stewart *(Student)*, Thomas Bolster *(Student)*, Fred Melamed *(Undesirables Onlooker)*, Greg Stebner *(Police Chief)*, Peter Appel, John C. Reilly, Brian Smiar, Michael P. Troy, Remak Ramsey, Ron Turek *(Cops at Police Station)*, Peter McRobbie *(Bartender)*, Ira Wheeler *(Cop with Priest)*, Rebecca Gibson *(Baby)*, Robert Silver *(Hacker's Follower)*, Charles Cragin *(Spiro)*, W.H. Macy *(Cop with Spiro)*, Tom Riis Farrell *(Vigilante with Spiro)*, Ron Weyand *(Vigilante with Spiro)*, Richard Riehle *(Roustabout)*, Max Robinson *(Roustabout)*

In the 15 years since he cemented his reputation with the Oscar-winning ANNIE HALL, Woody Allen has made films ranging from the sublime to the downright embarassing. He has also shown a regrettable predilection for stylistic perfection over emotional intensity (THE PURPLE ROSE OF CAIRO, Allen's self-avowed personal favorite, is a prime example). Though generally perceived as a failure, SHADOWS AND FOG was still one of the more interesting releases of 1992.

Allen's 21st feature (not including WHAT'S UP TIGER LILY?) is set in an unnamed Eastern European town and shot in an expressionist style, apparently in homage to the great German films of the 1920s, with Kurt Weill music behind the whole film. Kleinman (Allen), a timid clerk who hopes for nothing more in life than a promotion, is visited by a group of vigilantes who want his help in tracking down a serial killer. Kleinman doesn't understand how he can help, or what they want him to do, but they still expect him to do it.

At a nearby circus, sword swallower Irmy (Mia Farrow) leaves her noncommittal lover, the clown (John Malkovich), after finding him in bed with acrobat Marie (Madonna). She comes to the town and is rescued from the dangerous streets by a prostitute (Lily Tomlin) who takes her to a brothel; there, Irmy shyly befriends the other prostitutes (including Kathy Bates and Jodie Foster). Some customers come in, including the student Jack (John Cusack), who demands to take Irmy to bed. She refuses, but he keeps bidding higher until she finally agrees—and finds to her surprise that she is capable of enjoying sex.

Meanwhile, Kleinman visits the doctor (Donald Pleasence) who is examining the bodies of the murderer's victims. After he leaves, the doctor is murdered by the killer. The police investigate, find a glass that Kleinman had used, and take it away for fingerprinting. When an innocent friend of Kleinman's is arrested for the murders, Kleinman goes to the police station to lend him support, and sees the glass. At the same time, Irmy is brought in for whoring without a license and, in the confusion, Kleinman steals the glass. He and Irmy leave and confront someone who they think is the killer, but who turns out to be Kleinman's boss, a Peeping Tom. Feeling guilty at having accepted money for sex, Irmy gives some of her earnings to a poor woman on the street with a baby.

The vigilantes come across Kleinman, find the glass on his person, and accuse him of the murders; he flees. The clown, who has been looking for Irmy—and has learned from Jack of her infidelity—catches up with her. As they argue, they find the body of the poor woman, and rescue her baby. The clown doesn't want it at first, but soon becomes enamored of it and wants another. Kleinman flees to the brothel but, when it's searched by the police, speeds off to the circus. There, Irmy is stalked by the real killer but saved by Kleinman, who in turn is saved by a magician who uses magic tricks to trap the murderer. Kleinman, seeing the power of illusion over reality, decides to join the circus as an apprentice to the magician.

Allen fans will notice several familiar elements in SHADOWS AND FOG, including the influence of Bergman (particularly THE MAGICIAN and SAWDUST AND TINSEL); the philosophical exchanges between unlikely individuals; and the casting of Mia Farrow as a woman who befriends the Allen character after being abused by her partner. Allen has assembled a celebrity-studded cast, though not all his choices work: Madonna seems out of place, and her seduction of Malkovich is unerotic and unbelievable. There are some stylistic lapses, too, notably the insistent, distracting panning of the camera during the conversation between Farrow and the prostitutes.

While Allen's desire to tackle Big Moral Issues has resulted in some interesting work, SHADOWS AND FOG works on an almost exclusively cerebral level. It's hard not to wish he would return to the more emotionally involving—and funnier—territory of ANNIE HALL and MANHATTAN. Allen has stated in an interview with the *Los Angeles Times* that he believes he's never made a truly great film. SHADOWS AND FOG takes him no closer to that goal. *(Violence, adult situations.)*

p, Robert Greenhut; d, Woody Allen; w, Woody Allen; ph, Carlo DiPalma; ed, Susan E. Morse; m, Kurt Weill; prod d, Santo Loquasto; art d, Speed Hopkins; set d, George DeTitta, Jr., Amy Marshall; cos, Jeffrey Kurland

Comedy/Mystery **(PR: C MPAA: PG-13)**

SHAKES THE CLOWN ★
86m IRS Media ~ IRS Releasing c

Bobcat Goldthwait *(Shakes the Clown)*, Julie Brown *(Judy)*, Bruce Baum *(Ty the Rodeo Clown)*, Steve Bean *(Beaten Mime in Park)*, Blake Clark *(Stenchy the Clown)*, Eliza Coyle *(Enthusiastic Mime)*, Paul Dooley *(Owen Cheese)*, Gerald F. Edelstein *(2nd Party Dad)*, Robin Williams *(Mime Jerry)*, Jack Gallagher *(Officer Crony)*, Aige Gosney *(Billy)*, Kathy Griffin *(Lucy)*, Florence Henderson *(The Unknown Woman)*, Scott Herriott *(Floor Director)*, Melissa Hurley *(Producer at Bigtime Cartoon Circus)*, Tim Kazurinsky *(1st Party Dad)*, Tom Kenny *(Binky the Clown)*, Paul Kozlowski *(Hoho the Clown)*, Jeremy S. Kramer *(Detective Boar)*, Sydney Lassick *(Peppy the Clown)*, Joel Murray *(Milkman)*, Bob Nickman *(Gas Station Owner)*, LaWanda Page *(Female Clown Barfly)*, Shane Ricci *(Obnoxious Kid at Party)*, Adam Sandler *(Dink the Clown)*, Johnny Silver *(Clown Tailor)*, Cary Smith *(Mom at Party)*, Dan Spencer *(Boots the Clown)*, Greg Travis *(Randi the Rodeo Clown)*, Tony V. *(Broken Saddle Bouncer)*, Tom Villard *(Dirthead in Car)*, Martin Charles Warner *(Male Clown Barfly)*

"The CITIZEN KANE of Alcoholic Clown movies" was the critical comment used as a tagline for SHAKES THE CLOWN, a bizarre comedy that stretches its central gimmick thinner than watered-down carnival taffy.

Set in a mythical "Palukaville," no-class metropolis and lard capital of the US, the film proposes that professional clowns, despite their cheery exteriors, have a darker side in the form of a boozing, brawling subculture—like truckers, cowboys or sailors. Here clowns pal around with their own kind, drinking to excess in clown bars, swapping profane clown shop talk and beating up mimes, every clown's natural enemies. It's a cute idea, definitely worth a short subject or series of TV sketches, but here bloated into a feature-length vehicle for writer-director-star Bob "Bobcat" Goldthwait, whose distinctive grungy persona previously graced a couple of POLICE ACADEMY sequels and bombs like BURGLAR and HOT TO TROT.

At least here Goldthwait has a role suited to his dissipated manner with Shakes, a besotted slob of a clown who staggers from one kiddie-birthday-party engagement to another. His speech-impeded bowling-champ girlfriend Judy (Julie Brown) can't make him face the fact that he's an "awcohowic," and Shakes soon wrecks a house on a drunken binge. Fired from the clown booking agency, he drinks himself into a stupor, and is framed for homicide by a successful but untalented TV clown named Binky (Tom Kenny), a cocaine-crazed psycho who's just bludgeoned Shakes's ex-boss to death with a juggling pin. What passes for a plot deals with Shakes's attempt to clear his name and save Judy, kidnapped by the sinister Binky after the murderer simply blurts out his guilt to her in a scene that proves Goldthwait should have enlisted a good co-writer to help him over the rough spots.

The better parts of SHAKES THE CLOWN are the ambience moments in Shake's favorite tavern, the Twisted Balloon, where Palukaville's clown community gathers to get plastered, their circled eyes bleary and sullen, cigarettes drooping from grease-paint smiles on their lips as they snarl insults and four-letter words back and forth. There's novelty in hostile clown rummies who swear and perform unwholesome bodily functions, but in the course of the uneventful storyline, the joke gets very old, very fast.

Shakes isn't a very likable hero at all; he's drunk all the time, cheats on his girlfriend (debauching TV sitcom mom Florence Henderson for openers), and even Judy admits that he's no good in bed. Shakes's one reedeeming feature is that, when halfway sober he's a skilled party clown (and here Goldthwait goes through superhuman feats of gymnastics with the help of pathetically obvious stunt doubles). Shakes ultimately joins Alcoholics Anonymous, attending their meeting in full circus regalia. But nobody will see SHAKES THE CLOWN as a powerful plea for sobriety.

Shakes comes equipped with a couple of sidekicks (Adam Sandler and Blake Clark in the thankless supporting parts of Dink and Stenchy) who drink just as much as he does but "can hold their liquor," and guzzle beer as the trio speeds through Palukaville and outmaneuvers a pair of bonehead comedy cops (Jeremy S. Kramer and Jack Gallagher in the *really* thankless supporting parts of Boar and Crony). Tom Kenny scores a minor thespian coup as the deranged, Vegas-style Binky, doing an amusing job with the concept of a neurotic joker who's incapable of being intentionally funny. The same cannot be said of comic-turned-superstar Robin Williams (he's listed in the credits as Marty Fromage), who doesn't generate a single laugh from his cameo as a mime instructor. Way down in the cast among the veteran stand-ups one finds Bruce Baum as a villainous rodeo clown. Baum has made numerous hysterical short films for TV, and he probably could have done well with his subject matter in a fraction of the running time.

Forced to come up with a *raison d'etre* for SHAKES THE CLOWN, Goldthwaite told the *Los Angeles Times* that it was an allegory of the dog-eat-dog world of stand-up comedy, and that the mime-bashing parodied homophobia. After some experience writing, producing and directing short films, he penned the film's screenplay—expanding from a stage comedy skit—and shopped it around for years, encountered rejection and revulsion at every studio until he took it to I.R.S. Media, an outfit with a record of financing outre material. With his wife Ann Luly credited as producer, Goldthwait said the budget "cost about eight minutes of WAYNE'S WORLD."

Despite a certain cult notoriety that sprang up immediately around its subversive premise, SHAKES THE CLOWN did poor business, and only played major cities before going to home video later in the year. *(Excessive profanity, excessive substance abuse, sexual situations, adult situations.)*

p, Paul Colichman, Ann Luly-Goldthwait; d, Bobcat Goldthwait; w, Bobcat Goldthwait; ph, Elliot Davis, Bobby Bukowski; ed, J. Kathleen Gibson; m, Tom Scott; prod d, Pamela Woodbridge; cos, Stephen M. Chudej

Comedy **(PR: O MPAA: R)**

SHAKING THE TREE ★★½

98m Reality Productions; Magnificent Mile Productions; Castle Hill Productions ~ Castle Hill Productions c

Arye Gross *(Barry)*, Gale Hansen *(John "Sully" Sullivan)*, Doug Savant *(Michael)*, Steven Wilde *(Terry "Duke" Keegan)*, Courteney Cox *(Kathleen)*, Christina Haag *(Michelle)*, Michael Arabian *(Nickel)*, Dennis Cockrum *(Mr. Bannelli)*, Nathan Davis *(Grandpa Sullivan)*, Ron Dean *(Duke's Father)*, Kristin Messner *(Bridgette)*, Terry "Turk" Muller *(Ape)*, Ned Schmidtke *(Mr. Jack)*, Maurice Chasse *(Cashier at Stubby's)*, Dick Sasso *(New Yorker in Van)*, John Malloy *(Christmas Tree Lot Owner)*, Eva Quiroz *(Brunette at Bar)*, Dennis Kelly *(Sully's Father)*, Louie Lanceloti *(Cab Driver)*, Terry Moloney *(Barry's Work Buddy)*, Mick Scriba *(Tony Villanova)*, Barbara Robertson *(Nurse)*, Joey Tomaska *(Richie)*, Kirk Thatcher *(Craps Player)*

If it wasn't for the above-average ensemble performances, Duane Clark's SHAKING THE TREE would be bland fare indeed. That the viewer actually cares for the characters is a tribute to the talented young cast.

John "Sully" Sullivan (Gale Hansen), Terry "Duke" Keegan (Steven Wilde), Barry (Arye Gross) and Michael (Doug Savant), though from different backgrounds and with decidedly different interests, have stuck together through thick and thin ever since their high school days in the late 1970s. Now, a decade later (it's the holiday week between Christmas and New Year's Eve, 1989), they are forced to come to grips with the drastic changes that are about to take place in their lives.

Sully is a foolish, compulsive gambler who has gotten in over his head and now must pay the piper with money he does not have or face life-threatening consequences. Duke, a pugilist-turned-bartender, is on the verge of quitting the only job he's ever had. Barry is a real-estate wiz-kid who's just broken up with his fiancee, Michelle (Christina Haag), and is, at best, at loose ends. The philandering Michael is a professor of literature and struggling novelist whose wife, Kathleen (Couretney Cox), is about to give birth to their first child.

Michael's visions of impending fatherhood and the ball-and-chain existence that will follow in its wake cause him to panic, and he promptly seduces one of his female students. Fortunately for him, he backs off in the nick of time. Duke eventually pulls himself together while the friends rally around Sully in his time of greatest need. Barry finally overcomes his nervousness about getting married and it is to be assumed that he will have a happy reunion with his fiancee. In short, all four friends do a lot of growing up during that final week of 1989.

Unfortunately, this story of male bonding has been done many times before, often better. Also, the picture runs out of steam midway through. For example, there is a long, dull baseball game played out in Chicago's Comiskey Park that contributes virtually nothing to the plot other than to help pad the film's running time. Co-written by co-star Steven Wilde and director Duane Clark (the son of TV personality Dick Clark), SHAKING THE TREE, while sensibly structured and coherent, is filled with genre cliches and never less than 100 percent predictable.

That Clark's movie isn't livelier, spunkier and more original is truly a shame because the players are all so enjoyable. One wants to root for them to overcome their difficulties and make real men of themselves, but the desire to participate actively in this story is greatly hindered by the monotone patness of the plot. *(Profanity, adult situations)*

p, Robert J. Wilson; d, Duane Clark; w, Duane Clark, Steven Wilde; ph, Ronn Schmidt; ed, Martin L. Bernstein; m, David E. Russo; prod d, Sean Mannion; cos, Susan Michel Kaufman

Comedy/Drama **(PR: C MPAA: R)**

SHINING THROUGH ★★

127m Sandollar Productions; Fox ~ Fox c

Michael Douglas *(Ed Leland)*, Melanie Griffith *(Linda Voss)*, Liam Neeson *(Franze-Otto Dietrich)*, Joely Richardson *(Margrete Von Eberstien)*, John Gielgud *(Sunflower)*, Francis Guinan *(Andrew Berringer)*, Patrick Winczewski *(Fishmonger)*, Anthony Walters *(Dietrich's Son)*, Victoria Shalet *(Dietrich's Daughter)*, Sheila Allen *(Olga Leiner)*, Stanley Beard *(Linda's Father)*, Sylvia Syms *(Linda's Mother)*, Ronald Nitschke *(Horst Drescher)*, Hansi Jochmann *(Hedda Drescher)*, Peter Flechtner *(S.S. Officer at Fishmonger)*, Alexander Hauff *(S.S. Officer at Fishmonger)*, Claus Plankers *(S.S. Officer at Fishmonger)*, Renate Cyll *(Woman in Fish Market)*, Dana Gladstone *(Street Agitator)*, Lorinne Vozoff *(Personnel Director)*, Mathieu Carriere *(Von Haefler)*, Deirdre Harrison *(USO Singer)*, Wolf Kahler *(Border Commandant)*, Wolfe Morris *(Male Translator)*, William Hope *(Kernohan)*, Nigel Whitmey *(1st GI in Canteen)*, Rob Freeman *(2nd GI in Canteen)*, Lisa Orgolini *(Girl in Canteen)*, Jay Benedict *(Wisecracker in War Room)*, Thomas Kretschmann *(Man at Zurich Station)*, Klaus Munster *(Cab Driver)*, Markus Napier *(S.S. Officer)*, Constanze Engelbrecht *(Stayson Von Neest)*, Martin Hoppe *(German Soldier)*, Fritz Eggert *(German Soldier)*, Ludwig Haas *(Hitler)*, Clement Von Franckenstein *(BBC Interviewer)*, Lorelei King *(Leland's New Secretary)*, Hans Martin Stier *(Truck Driver)*, Wolfgang Heger *(Bus Conductor Kinderstrasse)*, Michael Gempart *(Man at Kinderstrasse)*, Hana Maria Pravda *(Babysitter)*, Lutz Weillich *(Train Station Guard)*, Wolfgang W. Muller *(Bus Conductor)*, Markus Kissling *(Swiss Border Guard)*, Anna Tzelniker *(Cleaning Woman)*, Andrzej Borkowdki *(German Refugee)*, Simon DeDeney *(S.S. Man)*, Tusse Silberg *(Woman Dinner Guest at Drescher's)*, Suzanne Roquette *(Woman Dinner Guest at Drescher's)*, Janis Martin *(Opera Singer)*

Despite its occasionally excessive derring-do and cliched romanticism, SHINING THROUGH is the kind of rousing entertainment that was a Hollywood staple back in the 1940s.

Linda Voss (Melanie Griffith) is a half-Jewish, half-Irish working girl from Queens, New York. The year is 1940 and Hitler is sweeping across Europe. Linda takes dictation for a living, but she dreams of being swept up in the kind of excitement that, thus far, only the colorful characters she sees onscreen, in the spy thrillers she has a passion for, seem to experience. Born with enough guts, passion and intelligence to arm a battery of spies—male or female—Linda is driven by two fantasies: to go behind enemy lines in Berlin to rescue her Jewish relatives and to convince her boss, lawyer Ed Leland (Michael Douglas), that she is both his intellectual and romantic equal.

Behind Linda's breathy, little-girl voice and outward vulnerability lies a tough, determined woman, and it doesn't take her long to realize that Ed is much more than a successful lawyer. The unusual letters he dictates (which she figures out are in code) and his habit of disappearing abruptly for extended periods of time, convinces Linda that Ed is, indeed, a spy. What is Ed really up to? And how can she convince him to take her seriously as a volunteer spy for the US? While Linda is doing her best to win Ed to her way of thinking, the pair become involved in a love affair.

Once the US officially enters the war—thanks to Pearl Harbor—Ed is finally revealed as a high-ranking colonel in the Office of Strategic Services. The war also brings to a halt their love affair since Ed feels that, now that his duty will lead him into perilous situations, it wouldn't be fair to Linda to tie her down to a relationship which might end in tragedy. Linda drowns her woes in work at the information center of the War Department. However, she has never lost sight of her goal to get into action . . . and one day her chance for glory comes.

Fluent in German and thoroughly versed in German customs and manners, Linda sees herself as the ideal candidate to replace one of Ed's key operatives in Germany when that spy is killed. Ed tries to dissuade her, but Linda persists and finally wins him over. Her assignment is to infiltrate the home of a high-ranking Nazi official. What happens to Linda once she arrives in Berlin is the stuff edge-of-your-seat cliffhangers are made of.

Admittedly, SHINING THROUGH is loaded with romance, sentimentality and passionate emotionalism, and many will consider this Melanie Griffith vehicle hopelessly cliched. But aren't these the very ingredients that made scores of the movies of the 1930s, 40s and early 50s so much fun to watch?

David Seltzer's screenplay, if not always plausible, is otherwise acceptable. While some of the dialogue may seem corny and dated to younger viewers, one should remember that people actually talked this way 50 years ago—Seltzer has done a respectable job of pinning down the idioms, speech patterns and rhythms of the early 40s. His direction is also appropriately paced and he's gleaned very effective performances from costars Griffith and Douglas, along with the supporting cast which includes John Gielgud as Sunflower, one of Douglas's operatives behind enemy lines; Liam Neeson as Franze-Otto Dietrich, the high-ranking Nazi official in whose home Griffith works as a nanny to his children; and Joely Richardson as Margrete Von Eberstien, a talented young German woman who apparently works with Gielgud and who befriends Griffith.

Production-wise, SHINING THROUGH is highly polished, with exquisite camerawork from cinematographer Jan de Bont and superior contributions from production designer Anthony Pratt and costume designer Marit Allen. Plaudits must also go to Michael Kamen's sweepingly potent musical score which more than accomplishes its essential task of helping to carry the audience through the action-packed events taking place onscreen. *(Adult situations.)*

p, Howard Rosenman, Carol Baum; d, David Seltzer; w, David Seltzer, (from the novel by Susan Isaacs); ph, Jan De Bont; ed, Craig McKay; m, Michael Kamen; prod d, Anthony Pratt; art d, Desmond Crowe, Kevin Phipps; set d, Peter Howitt; cos, Marit Allen

Romance/Thriller/War **(PR: C MPAA: R)**

SHOOTING ELIZABETH ★½

(France) Mate Productions ~ LIVE Home Video c

Jeff Goldblum *(Harold Pigeon)*, Mimi Rogers *(Elizabeth Pigeon)*, Burt Kwouk, Simon Andrell, Cristina Higueras, Juan Echanove

The spectre of the Italian film classic DIVORCE, ITALIAN STYLE haunts this bloodless farce. Clumsy and contrived, SHOOTING ELIZABETH suffers from plodding direction and star Jeff Goldblum's inability to turn a sow's ear screenplay into a silken black comedy.

Shrinking under the scrutiny of his increasingly shrewish wife Elizabeth (Mimi Rogers), Harold Pigeon (Jeff Goldblum) hatches a fool-proof scheme to rid himself of his ball-and-chain. Even when threatened at gunpoint, Elizabeth is so controlling, she refuses to surrender her jewelry to a burglar. Or are viewers only privy to her husband's jaundiced viewpoint? Promising Elizabeth a second honeymoon as a last resort to save their marriage, Harold lays plans for her demise. Point by point, the plot unravels. For example, Harold booked their old honeymoon suite because he needed a room that overlooked the ocean—now its balcony juts over a garden. Worse yet, Elizabeth undermines her mate's murderous intent by behaving like the loving woman he married many years ago.

Driven to exasperation by her husband's erratic behavior, Elizabeth vanishes without a word. However, Harold doesn't have long to enjoy his unexpected crime-free freedom because the police suspect him of actually murdering his wife. One by one, details of his homicidal bumbling return to haunt him—a bullet shot through a pillow, a note he'd forced Elizabeth to write and testimony from the punks who sold him a gun. Arrested at work and condemned by public opinion, Harold must desperately seek Elizabeth in order to clear his name. Abetted by a priestly mountain guide, he locates his wife, tells her the truth and reclaims her love. Although their marriage had been rocked by a miscarriage, the newly reunited couple decide to try marriage and parenthood again.

Remarkably witty in THE TALL GUY, Goldblum doesn't seem naturally funny when saddled with poor material. Not only does the screenplay's underlying nastiness vitiate the comedy, but the cast members' lack of conviction also dilutes the promised hilarity.

If you portray Rogers's character as a shrike in order to kick the murder plot into high gear, you can't shift gears and suggest some of her abrasiveness may be in the eye of the beholder. Moreover, she's not bitchy in a high comedic way, therefore the opportunity for a sophisticated commentary on the male-female connubial battleground is forsaken. And if Elizabeth is really a misunderstood sweetheart, then Harold becomes even more unlikable for trying to dispose of her.

No one, from screenwriter to director to cast members, demonstrates the slightest skill at making black comedy palatable. One ends up mired in questions about the two leads' motives. Was Elizabeth making Harold squirm by deliberately disappearing? Isn't Harold more interested in finding Elizabeth to save his own skin than he is in rekindling their marriage? When this many motivational clouds are on the comedy horizon, a film is in trouble.

If Elizabeth forgives her hubby for his comical flirtation with killing her, she is remarkably understanding, much more tolerant than audiences are likely to be toward this shot-to-pieces, sour comedy. *(Profanity, adult situations.)*

p, Monique Annaud, Mate Cantero; d, Baz Taylor; w, Robbie Fox; ph, Javier G. Salmones; art d, Ferran Sanchez

Comedy **(PR: C MPAA: PG-13)**

SILK ROAD, THE ★★

(Japan/China) 126m Daiei Company Ltd.; Dentsu Inc.; Marubeni ~ Trimark Pictures c

Koichi Sato *(Zhao Xingde)*, Toshiyuki Nishida *(Zhu Wangli)*, Tsunehiko Watase *(Li Yuanhao)*, Daijiro Harada *(Weichi Kuang)*, Takahiro Tamura *(Tsao Yanhui)*, Anna Nakagawa *(Tsurpia)*, Yoshiko Mita *(Woman of Xixia)*

Junya Sato's THE SILK ROAD, a large-scale Chinese-Japanese co-production, is watered-down Kurosawa, a comic book spectacle without subtext or emotional involvement.

In the year 1026, royal prince Li Yuanhao (Tsunehiko Watase) forms an army to raid merchants who travel the 5000-mile expanse of the silk road in China. On the road, traveling with a group of merchants, is Zhao Xingde (Koichi Sato), a student tagging along with a caravan en route to the city of Xixia, where Zhao hopes to learn to read and write the Xixian dialect. But Li's troops, led by Zhu Wangli (Toshiyuki Nishida), attack the caravan and Zhao is taken prisoner. Zhu becomes impressed with Zhao after witnessing his bravery during a ferocious battle and becomes further impressed when he discovers that Zhao can write.

Li's army is ordered to capture a fortress on the silk road, the Ganzhou Fortress, and Zhao rescues the daughter of the ruler of Ganzhou, Tsurpia (Anna Nakagawa), and hides her from Li's army. They fall in love and sneak away, but they are caught by Zhu, who promises that he will watch after Tsurpia if Zhao will go to Xixia to learn the language and translate for Prince Li. Zhao leaves for Xixia but is ordered to compile a dictionary and is gone for two years. He returns to find that Tsurpia is to be married to Li. On the day of the wedding, Tsurpia tries to kill Li and, when she fails, jumps to her death. Zhu reveals that he too has fallen in love with Tsurpia and vows revenge on Li.

In the city of Dun-huauang, a center of learning, Zhu plots to surprise Li during his visit to the city. But the plan fails and Li attacks the city. Zhu charges to his death with the remnants of his army, but not before he manages to hold off the destruction so that Zhao can rescue priceless parchments in the Dun-huauang library. Zhao takes the parchments and hides them in a secluded cave, where they remained preserved for 800 years.

THE SILK ROAD starts out as a mindless adventure saga and ends up as a paean to librarians and archivists (". . . about the people who helped to save the sutras, history tells us nothing and everything," lectures the narrator). But this genuflection to learning is about as vital to this film as immense, second-unit battle scenes would be to 84 CHARING CROSS ROAD. The sole interest in THE SILK ROAD lies in its battle scenes and mindless adventure rules the day.

Unfortunately, this mindlessness is of the unfocused variety, thanks to THE SILK ROAD's rambling narrative structure. The least that should be expected in films of this type is that the audience should care what happens to the hero, but Koichi Sato is completely bland as the hero and his character drifts along from battle to battle, unimportant and unnoticed. Why, viewers will wonder, is Zhu so impressed by him and why is Tsurpia so attracted to him? Sato's lackluster screen presence leaves the film without a center, putting greater emphasis on the film's battle scenes. But the battles never rise above the cartoon level. Though mounted impressively enough, they lack the psychological and metaphysical undercurrents evident in Kurosawa's THE HIDDEN FORTRESS, the film THE SILK ROAD most aspires to.

Director Sato, in apparent desperation, tries to make more of the film than it is by inserting time-lapse shots with macro-close-ups of flora and fauna, making the film at odd times look like a cross between WOMAN IN THE DUNES and KOYAAN-

ISQATSI. No matter how Sato shakes it, THE SILK ROAD can only be what it is—a hokey, overblown, cardboard epic. *(Violence.)*

p, Atsushi Takeda, Kazuo Haruna; d, Junya Sato; w, Tsuyoshi Yoshida, Junya Sato, (from the story by Yasushi Inoue); ph, Akira Shizuka; ed, Akira Suzuki; m, Masaru Sato; art d, Hiroshi Tokuda, Kou Honglie

Historical/Adventure **(PR: C MPAA: PG-13)**

SIMPLE MEN ★★★

(U.S./U.K.) 105m Zenith Productions; Fine Line Features; American Playhouse Theatrical Films; True Fiction Pictures; Simple Productions ~ Fine Line Features c

Robert Burke *(Bill McCabe)*, William Sage *(Dennis McCabe)*, Karen Sillas *(Kate)*, Elina Lowensohn *(Elina)*, Martin Donovan *(Martin)*, Chris Cooke *(Vic)*, Jeffrey Howard *(Ned Rifle)*, Holly Marie Combs *(Kim)*, Joe Stevens *(Jack)*, Damian Young *(Sheriff)*, Marietta Marich *(Mom–Meg)*, John Alexander MacKay *(Dad–William McCabe Sr)*, Bethany Wright *(Mary)*, Richard Reyes *(Security Guard)*, James Hansen Prince *(Frank)*, Ed Geldart *(Cop at Desk)*, Vivian Lanko *(Nun)*, Alissa Alban *(Waitress)*, Margaret A. Bowman *(Nurse Louise)*, Jo Perkins *(Nurse Otto)*, Mary McKenzie *(Vera)*, Matt Malloy *(Boyish Cop)*

In this, his third feature, Hal Hartley covers familiar territory, a quietly anarchic world where articulate, lovelorn, aimless characters come together more by chance than anything else. Nonetheless, SIMPLE MEN represents a substantial leap forward for this prolific filmmaker. It's also graced with the refreshingly adult, if occasionally indulgent, dialogue which has become Hartley's trademark.

After masterminding a computer heist, Bill McCabe (Robert Burke) is double-crossed by his girlfriend Vera (Mary McKenzie) and partner Frank (James Hansen Prince). Suddenly solo and on the lam, he inadvertently hooks up with his younger brother, Dennis (William Sage), an erstwhile philosophy student who's determined to track down their absentee father, William McCabe (John Alexander MacKay), the notorious "shortstop anarchist." A former major-league ball player, McCabe has recently been apprehended, twenty-three years after hurling a bomb on the steps of the Pentagon—an action which resulted in several innocent deaths.

Together, Bill and Dennis head for the hospital where their father's been taken following a heart seizure, only to discover that he's staged a masterful escape. They next approach their long-suffering mother for possible leads; all she can offer them is a faded snapshot of a bathing beauty named Tara, with a Long Island telephone number scrawled on the back. Unfortunately, it's disconnected. Undaunted, the brothers pool their meager resources and get as far as Lindenhurst (Hartley's hometown and favorite locale), where they stay just long enough to become embroiled with a cigarette-smoking nun, an alluring Catholic schoolgirl, a frustrated biker and the local authorities. The film reaches its first comic peak when Dennis and Bill make their getaway on a motorcyle while the nun and an overly officious cop tussle over a pendant of the Blessed Virgin Mary.

Brokenhearted and bitter over Vera's betrayal, Bill has declared that instead of falling for the next beautiful blond he meets, as is his custom, he's going to make her fall for *him*, then torment her with his studied indifference. As luck would have it, their motorcycle soon breaks down on a seemingly deserted byway where they happen upon Kate (Karen Sillas), a blond beauty whose companion, Elina (Elina Lowensohn), is having an epileptic fit in a nearby field. Fearing the imminent return of her ex-husband Jack (Joe Stevens), a recently released con, Kate invites the brothers to stay on for a few days, which incites the jealousy of Jack's best friend Martin (Martin Donovan), who's hopelessly in love with Kate. By now, of course, so is Bill.

The McCabe siblings finally trace the number to a local house, but it's been burned to the ground. Meanwhile, Dennis begins to suspect that the mysterious, mercurial Elina is somehow involved with his father. No sooner has he discovered that she's his old man's girlfriend, however, than she vanishes. And Tara, it turns out, is no lady—it's Martin's fishing vessel, also visible in the snapshot. Dennis drives off to confront his father while Bill, having won Kate's heart, deals with the surprisingly meek Jack. But the law finally catches up with Bill, who sacrifices his own freedom to ensure his father's safety.

Hartley is one of the few contemporary American filmmakers who's managed to create his own cinematic universe, even if it is overwhelmingly white, heterosexual and curiously underpopulated. SIMPLE MEN is also a little too self-conciously quirky at times, the biggest blunder being the admittedly beautiful Elina—there is no intrinsic reason for her character to be a Romanian expatriate subject to epileptic fits.

His chiseled good looks notwithstanding, Robert Burke is a curious choice for leading man, considering his limited range as an actor. While equally handsome, William Sage fares somewhat better as Burke's befuddled younger brother, but neither performance overrides the fact that the McCabe boys locate their father a little too easily. After all, he's eluded the FBI for over two decades, yet Bill and Dennis more or less stumble into him. Also, for never having seen his father, Dennis is decidedly underwhelmed when they finally come face to face. Rounding out the cast, Martin Donovan is typically engaging and newcomer Damian Young scores as a sheriff with marital woes, but it's a sweetly woebegone Karen Sillas who's the real standout.

On the whole, SIMPLE MEN is beautifully structured, less piecemeal than either THE UNBELIEVABLE TRUTH or TRUST, with seemingly random or throwaway bits of business dovetailing effortlessly as the story unfolds. The gorgeous acoustic score is credited to one Ned Rifle, a pseudonym for the multi-talented Hartley.

d, Hal Hartley; w, Hal Hartley; ph, Michael Spiller; ed, Steve Hamilton, Hal Hartley; m, Hal Hartley; prod d, Daniel Ouellette; art d, Therese DePrez; set d, Jeff Hartmann; cos, Alexandra Welker

Drama/Comedy **(PR: C MPAA: R)**

SINGLE WHITE FEMALE ★★½

107m SWF Productions; Guber-Peters Entertainment Company ~ Columbia c

Bridget Fonda *(Allison Jones)*, Jennifer Jason Leigh *(Hedra Carlson)*, Steven Weber *(Sam Rawson)*, Peter Friedman *(Graham Knox)*, Stephen Tobolowsky *(Mitchell Meyerson)*, Frances Bay *(Elderly Neighbor)*, Michele Farr *(Myerson's Assistant)*, Tara Karsian *(Mannish Applicant)*, Christiana Capetillo *(Exotic Applicant)*, Jessica Lundy *(Talkative Applicant)*, Rene Estevez *(Perfect Applicant)*, Tiffany Mataras *(Twin)*, Krystle Mataras *(Twin)*, Amelia Campbell *(Check Cashier)*, Ken Tobey *(Desk Clerk)*, Eric Poppick *(Nosy Neighbor)*, Kim Sykes *(TV Reporter)*, Michael James Collins *(Cashier Manager)*, George Gerdes *(Super)*, Jerry Mayer *(News Vendor)*, Robert Martin Steinberg *(Hedy's Date)*, Leslie A. Sank *(Woman in Club)*, Ron Athey *(Bartender)*, Kaaren Boothroyd *(Bookstore Customer)*, Jack Wilson *(Man in Cage)*

Though it may look like just another entry in the booming "lover/nanny/secretary from hell" genre, SINGLE WHITE FE-

MALE is a darkly realistic thriller with some eerily original moments. Directed by Barbet Schroeder (REVERSAL OF FORTUNE, BARFLY), it easily rises above its competitors while remaining faithful to the conventions of edge-of-your-seat filmmaking.

Allison Jones (Bridget Fonda) is an attractive, ambitious young woman who has lived in Manhattan for less than a year. While her professional star is on the rise—she has created a computer software package that will revolutionize the fashion world—her personal life is a mess. Ally has just broken off her engagement to her fiance, Sam Rawson (Steven Weber), after discovering that he has been sleeping with his ex-wife.

Allie finds platonic comfort in her gay male neighbor, Graham Knox (Peter Friedman), an actor with a sensitive shoulder to lean on. Realizing that the only way to hold onto her spacious rent-controlled apartment on the Upper West Side is to find a roommate, she places an ad and interviews a succession of unsuitable candidates before settling on the shy, frumpy Hedra Carlson (Jennifer Jason Leigh).

Aimless and underemployed, Hedy quickly fills the void left in her new roommate's life by Sam's abrupt departure. The rather self-centered Allie, meanwhile, is only too happy to allow her new roommate to cook and clean for her. Their friendship deepens when Hedy brings home an adorable and—unbeknownst to Allie—very expensive puppy; she later discovers the receipt and confronts Hedy, but can't bring herself to part with the creature. In another, more disturbing sign of her growing attachment to Allie, Hedy erases Sam's phone messages when he calls to plead for a reconciliation. Before long, she's even begun emulating the more sophisticated Allie in dress and manner. Allie passes off this strange behavior as that of an insecure but well-intentioned woman. When she and Sam patch things up, though, Hedy's more aggressive personality begins to emerge.

One afternoon, while Allie and Sam are out of the apartment, the puppy, which Allie has grown to love, plunges mysteriously to its death. Before long, Hedy's closet contains the exact same clothes as Allie's and the increasingly unstable young woman has even had her hair cut and dyed to match her roommate's chic look, revealing a startling resemblance between the two women. More than a little unnerved, Allie begins to investigate her roommate's background and discovers that she is not who she claims to be. Meanwhile, Hedy makes a transition from oddball roommate to psycho killer.

No sooner has Allie confided her mounting suspicions to Graham than he receives a brutal beating from Hedy. Then, posing as Allie, Hedy lets herself into Sam's hotel room, performs fellatio on him, then ends his life with a blow from one of her high heels. Next to go is Mitchell Meyerson (Stephen Tobolowsky), a lecherous client of Allie's who had earlier nearly raped her. Hedy's twisted logic assures her that Allie will thank her for this protective care, but when Allie responds by trying to escape, the violence is turned toward her. The two women engage in an extended battle deep in the basement of the building, where Allie's instincts for survival finally prevail.

Don Roos's screenplay and Schroeder's patient direction make SINGLE WHITE FEMALE an atypical thriller, complete with well-crafted scenes which actually let viewers get to know the characters who inhabit the story. The suspense is heightened by deliberately languid pacing, as in the long, mysterious opening shot of the apartment building which makes the edifice—not unlike the Dakota in Roman Polanski's classic ROSEMARY'S BABY—an an eerie partner in the upcoming sequence of events. (For the record, the Beaux-Arts beauty on display here is the fabled Ansonia at Broadway and 73rd.) The small cast also heightens the sense of isolation that suffuses the narrative.

Fonda (SINGLES, SCANDAL) continues to show her growing range as an actress. Her Allie is full of contradictions—a confident businesswoman one moment and a scared child the next. She's also willful, spoiled and—as she demonstrates by spying on Hedy while she masturbates in bed—hardly above reproach. (There is, in fact, a subtle but pronounced homoerotic subtext to Allie and Hedy's relationship. It becomes rather more obvious when, believing that she's just strangled Allie, Hedy kisses her full on the mouth.) As the dangerous Hedy, Jason Leigh (RUSH, LAST EXIT TO BROOKLYN) doesn't resort to any of the standard tricks of the trade in her chilling portrayal of a psychopath—she does it all with her eyes. The rest of the cast is uniformly strong, particularly Tobolowsky as an obnoxious businessman.

SINGLE WHITE FEMALE is a small film that enjoyed a major studio release. It has the production values of a Hollywood blockbuster (Academy Award-winning costume designer Milena Canonero makes her debut as a production designer), but is more satisfying for being more limited in scope. *(Violence, profanity, nudity, sexual situations.)*

p, Barbet Schroeder; d, Barbet Schroeder; w, Don Roos, (from the novel *SWF Seeks Same* by Jon Lutz); ph, Luciano Tovoli; ed, Lee Percy; m, Howard Shore; prod d, Milena Canonero; art d, P. Michael Johnston; set d, Anne H. Ahrens; cos, Milena Canonero

Thriller **(PR: O MPAA: R)**

SINGLES ★★★½

99m Warner Bros. ~ Warner Bros. c

Bridget Fonda *(Janet Livermore)*, Campbell Scott *(Steve Dunne)*, Kyra Sedgwick *(Linda Powell)*, Sheila Kelley *(Debbie Hunt)*, Jim True *(David Bailey)*, Matt Dillon *(Cliff Poncier)*, Bill Pullman *(Dr. Jamison)*, James LeGros *(Andy)*, Devon Raymond *(Ruth)*, Camilo Gallardo *(Luiz)*, Ally Walker *(Pam)*, Eric Stoltz *(Mime)*, Jeremy Piven *(Doug Hughley)*, Tom Skerritt *(Mayor Weber)*, Peter Horton *(Jamie)*, Bill Smillie *(Boston Doctor)*, Chuck McQuary *(Garage Opener Clerk)*, Christopher Kennedy Masterson *(Steve–Age 10)*, Matt Magnano *(1st Kid)*, Jaffar Smith *(2nd Kid)*, Dana Eskelson *(Club Girl)*, Mykol Hazsen *(Club Bouncer)*, Art Cahn *(Magazine Stand Clerk)*, Michael Su *(Ted)*, Jane Jones *(Denise)*, Johnny "Sugarbear" Willis *(Rick)*, Randy Thompson *(Stu)*, Paul Giamatti *(Kissing Man)*, Alicia Roper *(Kissing Woman)*, Xavier McDaniel *(Himself)*, Wayne Cody *(Himself)*, Eddie Vedder *(Eddie)*, Stone Gossard *(Stone)*, Cameron Crowe *(Club Interviewer)*, Jeff Ament *(Jeff)*, Pat DiNizio *(Sid)*, Chris Cornell *(Chris)*, Thomas A. Doyle *(Wrong Phone Number)*, Alice Marie Crowe *(Dr. Jamison's Nurse)*, Joan Giammarco *(Receptionist)*, Jim Hechim *(Rich)*, Heather Hughes *(Lauren)*, Tim Burton *(Brian)*, "Crazy Steve" Olsen *(Rob)*, Bernard Bentley *(Spiro)*, Stephen Rutledge *(Charles)*, Daniel Johnson *(Sean)*, Bruce Pavitt *(Bruce)*, Michael Gardner *(Mike)*, Sandra Grant *(Waitress)*, Karen Denice LaVoie *(Hostess)*, Tom Francis *(Deputy Mayor)*, Jerry Ziesmer *(Councilman Jordan Fisher)*, Nina Escudero *(Airline Clerk)*, Dan Wartman *(Single Kid on Plane)*, Amy Hill *(Hospital Nurse)*, Mike Parker *(Mover)*

Rolling Stone contributor turned writer-director Cameron Crowe pulled off a near-impossible feat with his first film, SAY ANYTHING: he made an intelligent, endearing, non-sappy teen romance. With his follow-up, SINGLES, Crowe ambitiously tackles the romantic lives of a group of twentysomething characters, as played out against Seattle's burgeoning music scene.

SINGLES is more a series of interlocking vignettes than a straightforward narrative; the film is divided into "chapters" and characters occasionally talk directly to the screen, to introduce themselves or comment on the action (a device that could have been used more often).

We first meet Linda Powell (Kyra Sedgwick), who works for an environmental agency and, like most of her colleagues, is both longing for and wary of love; the opening scenes show her falling for and ultimately getting taken in by a seemingly innocent "foreign exchange student." At one of Seattle's many dance clubs she meets Steve Dunne (Campbell Scott), an urban planner, and they make tentative, hesitant moves toward a relationship. When Linda accidentally becomes pregnant, the two decide to marry, and seem headed for happiness until a car accident in which Linda loses the baby. Shaken up and even more cautious than before, they split, although each obviously harbors strong feelings for the other.

Steve's U-shaped singles apartment complex also houses Janet Livermore (Bridget Fonda), Cliff Poncier (Matt Dillon) and the cute but rather vacuous Debbie Hunt (Sheila Kelly). Janet, Steve's trusted advisor on matters of the heart, is currently hung up on Cliff, the spacey lead singer of grunge-metal band Citizen Dick (played by members of Seattle sensation Pearl Jam). Cliff is more devoted to the band than to his quasi-girlfriend, and Janet makes several attempts to win him over before she finally breaks off the relationship. Debbie, meanwhile, is trying to make the perfect "film" of herself for a video dating service. (In an in-joke cameo, she enlists the services of an up-and-coming director, played by BATMAN mastermind Tim Burton.)

That SINGLES works is thanks to Crowe's deft, incisive writing, although one's age and relationship experiences will undoubtedly affect one's critical opinion. The film's success is largely due to its finely observed details: the discussions of how long you should wait after a date before calling someone back, or the games you play to try to convince yourself someone is attracted to you. In a small scene sure to raise some chuckles of recognition, Janet throws wadded-up balls of paper at her wastebasket, telling herself she'll call Cliff back if she gets one in.

If our own wounded and confused souls aren't enough to complicate things, Crowe says, advanced technology is no help: in SINGLES, someone will give a partner the automatic garage-door opener to signify commitment, only to rush out and get a new one when the affair abruptly breaks up. In another instance, an attempted reconciliation is quashed when an over-the-phone apology is eaten by an uncooperative answering machine.

Mercifully, Crowe hasn't added a syrupy orchestral score to cue the audience during emotional scenes. Instead, there's plenty of music from former Replacements front man Paul Westerberg and some of the Seattle bands who rose to national prominence in 1992: Alice in Chains, Soundgarden and many others. (The only notable omission is Nirvana, whose popularity peaked during the film's post-production, making Kurt Cobain and crew too expensive to include on the soundtrack). The angry, angst-ridden music acts as an effective counterpoint to the characters' seemingly cool, collected psyches. Crowe has winningly captured the dilemma of many urban singles in the 90s, giving dramatic examples of how supposedly rational people blow their big chances at love through fear, bad judgment or over-analysis.

Some scenes could have been trimmed a bit, and the characters sometimes seem too downright nice, but SINGLES is funny and accurate and, most notably, plays to its audience's intelligence rather than its libido. *(Profanity, sexual situations.)*

p, Richard Hashimoto, Cameron Crowe; d, Cameron Crowe; w, Cameron Crowe; ph, Ueli Steiger; ed, Richard Chew; m, Paul Westerberg; prod d, Stephen J. Lineweaver; art d, Mark Haack; set d, Clay Griffith

Romance/Comedy **(PR: C MPAA: PG-13)**

SISTER ACT ★★½

96m Touchstone ~ BV c

Whoopi Goldberg *(Deloris)*, Maggie Smith *(Mother Superior)*, Kathy Najimy *(Mary Patrick)*, Wendy Makkena *(Mary Robert)*, Mary Wickes *(Mary Lazarus)*, Harvey Keitel *(Vince LaRocca)*, Bill Nunn *(Eddie Souther)*, Robert Miranda *(Joey)*, Richard Portnow *(Willy)*, Ellen Albertini Dow, Carmen Zapata, Pat Crawford Brown, Prudence Wright Holmes, Georgia Creighton, Susan Johnson, Ruth Kobart, Susan Browning, Darlene Koldenhoven, Sheri Izzard, Edith Diaz, Beth Fowler *(Choir Nuns)*, Rose Parenti *(Sister Alma)*, Joseph Maher *(Bishop O'Hara)*, Jim Beaver *(Clarkson)*, Jenifer Lewis *(Michelle)*, Charlotte Crossley *(Tina)*, A.J. Johnson *(Lewanda)*, Desreta Jackson *(1st Teenage Girl)*, Zatella Beatty *(2nd Teenage Girl)*, Skye Bassett *(3rd Teenage Girl)*, Lois DeBanzie *(Immaculata)*, Isis Carmen Jones *(Little Deloris)*, Max Grodenchik *(Ernie)*, Joseph G. Medalis *(Henry Parker)*, Michael Durrell *(Larry Merrick)*, Robert Jimenez *(News Reporter)*, Toni Kalem *(Connie LaRocca)*, Kevin Bourland *(Pilot)*, David Boyce *(Croupier)*, Timothy J. Pedegana *(Gambler)*, Terry Wills *(Salesman)*, David M. Parker *(Bartender)*, Nicky Katt *(Waiter)*, Mike Jolly *(1st Biker)*, Jeremy Roberts *(2nd Biker)*, Eugene Greytak *(The Pope)*

Despite its tremendous commercial success, Touchstone's SISTER ACT is yet another Disney comedy that keeps threatening to get genuinely interesting, only to veer back into by-the-numbers banality.

The main plot is triggered when Reno lounge singer Deloris (Whoopi Goldberg) walks in on her lover, thug Vince LaRocca (Harvey Keitel), killing an informer. Deciding her life expectancy would be severely limited otherwise, Deloris takes an offer from a cop, Eddie Souther (Bill Nunn), to go temporarily undercover until she can testify against LaRocca. Her new identity? A nun in a San Francisco convent presided over by a stern Mother Superior (Maggie Smith), the only person in the place who knows Deloris's true identity. Since Deloris makes an unconvincing holy sister, the Mother Superior strikes a bargain with her: she will confine herself to her room and come out only to coach the convent choir, an ensemble of jaw-dropping ineptness.

Though it means ousting incumbent director Sister Mary Lazarus (Mary Wickes), Deloris soon turns the choir around into a hymn-singing girl group whose repertoire includes pop classics like "My Guy" and "I Will Follow Him," reworked into religious anthems. Soon, the church is packed for every service, attracting the attention of the Pope himself, who drops in for a "show." Their new fame gets the nuns more involved in the neighborhood, and also puts Deloris at loggerheads with the Mother Superior, under whose leadership the convent has become more isolated over the years. Deloris's notoriety also breaks her cover, leading LaRocca to make one last attempt to stop her from testifying.

Though it was SISTER ACT's major selling point, the idea of hip, singing nuns bringing down the house wears thin quickly. But the lines of tension that arise as a result suggest some intriguing directions the filmmakers chose not to take. The primary subplot, revolving around Deloris's efforts to get the convent members more involved in their depressed neighborhood, leads to some well-written and excellently acted scenes between Deloris and the Mother Superior. The latter, it turns out, originally came to her assignment with the same aspirations that Deloris now harbors, but ended up cutting almost all contact between the convent and its surroundings. What caused this change in heart, though, is never explored. Instead, the filmmakers opt for a cutesy montage of nuns running around the neighborhood, skipping rope and hip-hop dancing with their neighbors.

There is also a more ticklish subplot that half-develops between Deloris and attractive young novice Mary Robert (Wendy Makkena). The early scenes between them have the quality of a nervous flirtation—especially one in which the novice peers anxiously up and down the hall of the convent before closing the door to Deloris's room behind her and presenting her with a gift of an alarm clock in the shape of a flower. Needless to say, any nascent sexual tensions remain both unexplored and unresolved; like the scenes between Deloris and the Mother Superior, they belong in a different film from one in which nuns flee through the streets of Reno with a bunch of goofy gangsters in hot pursuit.

Director Emile Ardolino (THREE MEN AND A LITTLE LADY, DIRTY DANCING) deserves some credit for using the subplots to give SISTER ACT at least a suggestion of depth. Even more deserving of credit is the cast itself. Goldberg's work here never loses its texture, edge or originality, allowing her to shine opposite Smith, who is so good that she barely seems to be acting. The supporting cast is consistently funny, from those already mentioned, like Wickes—a smoothly assured comedy veteran who also starred in both THE TROUBLE WITH ANGELS and its sequel, WHERE ANGELS GO, TROUBLE FOLLOWS—to Kathy Najimy, whose maniacally sunny-spirited Sister Mary Patrick keeps threatening to steal the picture. *(Adult situations.)*

p, Teri Schwartz; d, Emile Ardolino; w, Paul Rudnick, Eleanor Bergstein, Jim Cash, Jack Epps, Jr., Carrie Fisher, Robert Harling, Nancy Meyers; ph, Adam Greenberg; ed, Richard Halsey; m, Marc Shaiman; prod d, Jackson DeGovia; cos, Molly Maginnis

Comedy/Musical **(PR: A MPAA: PG)**

SLUMBER PARTY MASSACRE 3

77m Concorde ~ New Horizons Home Video c

Keely Christian *(Jackie)*, Brittain Frye *(Ken)*, M.K. Harris *(Morgan)*, David Greenlee *(Duncan)*, Lulu Wilson *(Juliette)*, Maria Ford *(Maria)*, Brandi Burkett *(Diane)*, Hope Marie Carlton *(Janine)*, Maria Claire *(Sonia)*, Garon Grigsby, David Kriegel, David Lawrence, Wayne Grace, Marta Kober, Devon Jenkin

The major novelty of the SLUMBER PARTY MASSACRE series is that all this sleazy exploitation fodder has been written and directed by women. Yes, the fairer sex is responsible for the spectacle of lingerie-clad lovelies being menaced and mutilated by madmen wielding enormous phallic power drills.

At least SLUMBER PARTY MASSACRE II flirted with satire. The latest installment is grim, no-frills splatter dreck which sets its intellectual watermark by opening on a bikinied volleyball match. The participating beach bunnies hold a slumber party that night while their parents are absent. The girls engage in scintillating dialogue ("Your hair looks real good pulled back like that"), play truth-or-dare and practice striptease routines, while their horny boyfriends outside pull various pranks to gain entry.

Meanwhile someone is butchering the kids one by one. The murderer is unmasked halfway through; he's all-American college boy Ken (Brittain Frye), an impotent psycho-driller-killer due to abuse by his late cop uncle—police are depicted throughout the film as moronic cretins. Ken messily whittles down the movie's squealing bimbo population (Victim: "If I said something that made you angry I take it all back!"), getting quite bloodied himself in the process. Whenever a lamp is smashed over his head he drops the drill, but only heroine Jackie (Keely Christian) has the climactic enlightenment to pick up the tool and turn it against its owner.

On a purely technical level SLUMBER PARTY MASSACRE 3 is first-rate, which is no asset as gore flows by the hoseful. The young thespians emote with demo-reel sincerity, and talented character actor M.K. Harris goes to waste as a twitchy neighbor. Director Sally Mattison also wrote and performed the soundtrack songs "Pale Imitation" and "Hold Your Fire," while other musical credit goes to the aptly named band High Class Trash. *(Excessive violence, substance abuse, excessive profanity, nudity, sexual situations, adult situations.)*

p, Catherine Cyran; d, Sally Mattison; w, Catherine Cyran; ph, Jurgen Baum; ed, Tim Amyx; m, Jamie Sheriff; prod d, Stephanie Lytar, Gary Randall; cos, Sandra Araya Jensen

Horror **(PR: O MPAA: R)**

SMOOTH TALKER ★

89m Reivaj Films ~ Academy Entertainment c

Joe Guzaldo *(Carl Waters)*, Peter Crombie *(Jack Perdue)*, Stuart Whitman *(Lt. Gallagher)*, Burt Ward *(Lab Technician)*, Sydney Lassick *(Mr. Nathan)*, Blair Weickgenant *(Lisa Charles)*, Suzanne Ager *(Candy)*, Neil Bronco *(Neighbor)*, Paul Raci *(Perry)*

If telephone-sex services have set Alexander Graham Bell spinning in his grave, then the proliferation of phone-sex-slasher movies should do the same for film pioneers like Edison and the Brothers Lumiere. Since the mid-1980s there have been a handful of lowly potboilers about murderous perverts stalking the teleporn girls, and SMOOTH TALKER adds nothing but deadweight to the microgenre.

Surly cop Carl Waters (Joe Guzaldo) is having no luck nabbing the mysterious "976 Killer," who has so far left three female sex-chat employees permanently disconnected. Carl also carries a torch for his imperiously gorgeous ex-wife Lisa (Blair Weickgenant), an assistant district attorney. She can't stand him, but lets herself get hit on by all the other horny males in City Hall, especially clean-cut defense lawyer Jack Purdue (Peter Crombie). Guess who the serial murderer turns out to be? Carl gets to rescue Lisa from Jack in the nick of time, but not after a lengthy and distressing subplot about police efforts to pin the crimes on an innocent man. At one point Carl and cohorts scheme to frame the suspect for drug possession so they can lock him up in the absence of any other proof. If that implies criticism of law-enforcement zealots, it doesn't come through very well in this portrait of the boys in blue at work.

It's all awfully predictable, with Jack signifying his guilt from the get-go when he jokes about having just poisoned his spouse. Though nudity and gore isn't as excessive as others of its ilk, SMOOTH TALKER looks generally grungy and cheap, the only real class supplied by a Humphrey Bogart poster that Carl keeps on his wall. Weickgenant is a looker, though; one marvels that this regal beauty and the obscenity-snarling flatfoot ever got hitched in the first place. Some veteran character actors fill out the supporting cast, and Batmaniacs will hearken to the sight of TV's Robin, Burt Ward, as an audio technician. Evidently movie police now have entire labs devoted to the burgeoning science of phone-sex-homicide. *(Violence, excessive profanity, nudity, sexual situations, adult situations.)*

p, Eduardo Montes, Craig Shapiro; d, Tom E. Milo; w, Darrah Whitaker, (from the story by Eduardo Montes); ph, Stan Lazan; ed, Sandra Adair; m, Tony Roman; prod d, Brian Densmore; cos, Debrae Little

Thriller **(PR: O MPAA: NR)**

SNAKEEATER III . . . HIS LAW ★
109m Cinepix ~ Paramount Home Video c

Lorenzo Lamas *(Jack Kelly–SnakeEater)*, Minor Mustain *(Cowboy)*, Tracy Cook *(Hildy)*, Holly Chester *(Fran)*, Scott "Bam Bam" Bigelow *(Goose)*, Chip Chuipka *(Turk)*, Tracy Hway *(Vivian)*, Una Kay *(Marge Molison)*, Gordon Atkinson *(George Molison)*, Walker Boone *(Lieutenant Durkey)*, Chris Benson

The law of diminishing returns is clearly in evidence in this third installment of the Canadian-made SNAKEEATER series, which began in 1990 as a showcase for former TV heartthrob Lorenzo Lamas.

Adapted by John Dunning (who co-wrote and produced the first two entries as well) from a novel by Glenn Ducan, SNAKEEATER III has virtually no plot. Cop Jack Kelly (Lamas), who confusingly only goes by the name Soldier (as the robust title tune proclaims), is suspended from the police force for his Dirty Harry-like antics in breaking up a diner robbery. He is hired by the distraught parents of Vivian (Tracy Hway), who ten months earlier was abducted by a gang of bikers she infiltrated, gathering sociological data for a college thesis, and used as a sexual toy, then stumbled back into civilization reduced to a nymphomaniacal, nearly vegetative state. Now she's back with the bikers again, and Jack sets off to rescue her, aided by private investigator cohort Cowboy (Minor Mustain), ex-biker gal now topless dancer Fran (Holly Chester), and Jack's girlfriend Hildy (Tracy Cook).

The film, like the first two, directed by George Erschbamer, has so little plot that it has Vivian running away twice, forcing Jack and his pals through a repetative skein of fist, gun and kung-fu fights with evil hoodlums led by Goose (Scott "Bam Bam" Bigelow) and Turk (Chip Chuipka). This is weak-kneed by-the-numbers action stuff, with stunts choreographed by Jim Dunn, and it's mostly cartoonishly staged. The best action setpiece, in which our heroes are surrounded in a cheap motel room and escape by blasting through the flimsy walls of the units next to theirs, is embarrassingly lifted almost intact from the superb 1987 vampire chiller NEAR DARK. Erstwhile "Falcon Crest" star Lorenzo Lamas has the proper macho swagger but is almost totally unconvincing as an action hero. Then again, he gets little help from his artistic surroundings here, which include loopy dialogue like "These bikers stand out like a Great Dane's balls."

The SNAKEEATER series (named from the hero's "elite Marine fighting unit" in Vietnam) is produced by the veteran Canadian B-movie team of Dunning and Andre Link, who were responsible for much better movies through the 1970s and 80s, including the MEATBALLS pictures and a pair of David Cronenberg chillers, THEY CAME FROM WITHIN and RABID. For what it's worth, SNAKEEATER III does boast a first for the genre: the grungy bikers are outfitted with cellular phones on their Harleys. *(Violence, profanity, nudity, sexual situations.)*

p, Irene Litinsky, John Dunning; d, George Erschbamer; w, John Dunning, (from the novel *Rafferty's Rules* by Glenn Ducan); ph, Jacques Fortier; ed, Jacques Jean; m, John Massari; prod d, Richard Tasse

Action/Martial Arts **(PR: C MPAA: R)**

SNEAKERS ★★★
125m Universal; Lasker/Parkes Productions ~ Universal c

Robert Redford *(Martin Bishop)*, Sidney Poitier *(Crease)*, Dan Aykroyd *(Mother)*, David Strathairn *(Whistler)*, River Phoenix *(Carl Arbogast)*, Mary McDonnell *(Liz)*, Timothy Busfield *(Dick Gordon)*, Ben Kingsley *(Cosmo)*, Stephen Tobolowsky *(Dr. Werner Brandes)*, Eddie Jones *(Buddy Wallace)*, Donal Logue *(Dr. Gunter Janek)*, Lee Garlington *(Dr. Elena Rhyzkov)*, George Hearn *(Gregor)*, Bodhi Elfman *(Centurion S&L Night Guard)*, Jo Jo Marr *(College-Aged Cosmo)*, Gary Hershberger *(College-Aged Martin Bishop)*, Denise Dowse *(Bank Teller)*, Hanyee *(Bank Secretary)*, Time Winters *(Homeless Man)*, Jun Asai *(Piano Prodigy)*, John Shepherd *(Collidge Institute Guard)*, Ellaraino *(Mrs. Crease)*, Shayna Hollinquist *(Melissa Crease)*, Dayna Hollinquist *(Melissa Crease)*, Jacqueline Brand, Julie Gigante, Victoria Miskolczy, David Speltz *(Kiev String Quartet Members)*, Leslie Hardy *(Gregor's Date)*, John Moio *(Gregor's Chauffeur)*, James Craven *(FBI Agent)*, R.C. Everbeck *(2nd FBI Agent)*, Ernie Tetrault *(TV Anchorman)*, Lori Hall *(NSA Phone Operator)*, George Kee Cheung *(Chinese Restuarant Singer)*, Hayward Soo Hoo *(Chinese Restaurant Waiter)*, Michael Kinney *(Playtronics Desk Guard-Day)*, Rudy Francis Nementz *(Playtronics Desk Guard-Day)*, Ralph Monaco *(Playtronics Lobby Guard-Day)*, Paul Jenkins *(Playtronics Lobby Guard-Night)*, Al Foster *(Playtronics Desk Guard-Night)*, George Hartmann *(Playtronics Stairwell Guard)*, Jeffrey Daniel Phillips *(Playtronics Perimeter Guard)*, Michael Boston *(Playtronics Perimeter Guard)*, Anthony Winters *(Male NSA Agent)*, Jeff Joy *(Male NSA Agent)*, Amy Benedict *(Female NSA Agent)*, James Earl Jones *(Mr. Bernard Abbott)*

Robert Redford returns to his 1970s roots with SNEAKERS, an enjoyable caper comedy that recalls his string of socially conscious comedies with director Michael Ritchie.

For years, former 60s radical and computer hacker Martin Brice (Redford) has lived an undercover existence, wanted for electronically transferring funds from the bank accounts of Richard Nixon and his ilk to those of Greenpeace and other liberal organizations. Brice's partner, Cosmo (Ben Kingsley), apparently got caught and subsequently died in prison. Now Brice has a new last name, Bishop, and a career. He heads a group of computer and security specialist misfits who breach corporate security systems as a way of analyzing their weaknesses and recommending improvements. Bishop has a policy of never working for the government, but two representatives claiming to be from the National Security Agency, Dick Gordon and Buddy Wallace (Timothy Busfield and Eddie Jones), approach him with an offer he can't refuse. They have uncovered his past and threaten to turn him in unless he steals a computer code-breaking "black box" being developed by top mathematician Dr. Gunter Janek (Donal Logue), the agents believe, for the Russian government.

The theft goes easily enough, but when the mathematician is murdered the next day, Bishop and his crew smell a rat. Bishop turns over the box—which can break into any national computer network from the Federal Reserve to air traffic control systems—but barely escapes with his life when the agents try to kill him and his ex-CIA sidekick Crease (Sidney Poitier). Believing the Russians to be behind the skullduggery, Bishop confronts Gregor (George Hearn), a Russian diplomat friend. But the phony agents pull over Gregor's limousine and kill the diplomat and his driver with Bishop's gun. They then kidnap Bishop and take him to meet with Cosmo, whose death was a sham engineered by American organized-crime figures.

Using a toy-manufacturing company as a front, Cosmo now works for the mob and tries to blackmail Bishop into joining him by threatening to enter his current alias into the national crime computer system. Instead, Bishop rallies his forces, including his ex-girlfriend, Liz (Mary McDonnell), to steal the box back from Cosmo. Finally confronted by a real federal agent, Bernard Abbott (James Earl Jones), Bishop turns over the box, but without the computer chip required to make it work.

Though a little overlong, SNEAKERS is a generally engaging ensemble comedy. While the toplined Redford was written off in some quarters following the dismal commercial failure of his last starring vehicle, Sidney Pollack's HAVANA, the American moviegoing public has clearly welcomed him back.

Writer-director Phil Alden Robinson (FIELD OF DREAMS) and co-screenwriters Walter F. Parkes and Lawrence Lasker (who last turned computers into box-office bucks with WARGAMES) wisely soft-pedal the story's social commentary and keep the focus on the plot and characters, rather than forcing the high-tech bells and whistles to carry the film. Computers are inherently boring from a cinematic perspective, but what they do can be the makings of high drama.

The characters in SNEAKERS are well crafted to suit the actors playing them. Redford's specialty has always been to put a complex, modernist spin onto his ultra-handsome leading man persona. But Bishop is the first character he's had in some time that allows him to play—and look—his age. Poitier is similarly well served by his ex-CIA man with a shadowy past, though it's never made clear what led him from one end of the political spectrum to the other. Dan Aykroyd effectively underplays his role as a conspiracy-obsessed cryptographer, while the chameleon-like Kingsley effortlessly becomes a character that couldn't be further removed from his best-known performance, as GANDHI.

Elsewhere, McDonnell (PASSION FISH, DANCES WITH WOLVES) and River Phoenix (MY OWN PRIVATE IDAHO, RUNNING ON EMPTY), as the youngster of Redford's group, do a lot to widen the film's appeal. David Strathairn, as Redford's idealistic blind associate, and Stephen Tobolowsky, as the weak link in Kingsley's organization, also do fine work, helping make SNEAKERS one of the more entertaining films of the year. *(Violence, adult situations.)*

p, Walter F. Parkes, Lawrence Lasker; d, Phil Alden Robinson; w, Phil Alden Robinson, Lawrence Lasker, Walter F. Parkes; ph, John Lindley; ed, Tom Rolf; m, James Horner, Branford Marsalis; prod d, Patrizia Von Brandenstein; art d, Diane Wager; set d, Samara Schaffer; cos, Bernie Pollack

Comedy/Thriller/Action (PR: C MPAA: PG-13)

SOCIETY ★★½

99m Wild Street Pictures ~ Zecca Corporation c

Billy Warlock *(Bill Whitney)*, Connie Danese *(Nan)*, Ben Slack *(Dr. Cleveland)*, Evan Richards *(Milo)*, Patrice Jennings *(Jenny)*, Tim Bartell *(Blanchard)*, Charles Lucia *(Jim)*, Heidi Kozak *(Shauna)*, Brian Bremer *(Petrie)*, Ben Meyerson *(Ferguson)*, Devin Devasquez *(Clarissa)*, Maria Claire *(Sally)*, Conan Yuzna *(Jason)*, Jason Williams *(Jason's Friend)*, Pamela Matheson *(Mrs. Carlyn)*, Rohni Lee, Michael Schipper, Chris Claridge, Amy Obrand *(Ferguson's Gang Members)*, David Wiley *(Judge Carter)*, David Wells *(Sergeant Burt)*, Mike Diamant *(Cop in Woods)*, Raffaella Commitante *(Nurse at Hospital)*, Seely Abraham, Chris Anne, Laura Tulaska, Mike Colletta, Robb Willough, Tom Druzay, Allen Eisenhart, Michael Tony Merten, Donamari Tia, Thomas Lewis, Blanche Bimstein, Tom Rainone, Kristine Kauffman, Lisa Bal, Nicolle Durant, Daniel Heren, Caroline Lomas, C. John Merrill, Steven Morgan, Rick Widman, Chanel Ryan, Mark David, Don Storey, Robin Agee

More ambitious than the usual low-budget horror item, SOCIETY doesn't develop its provocative idea—when the rich feed off the lower classes, they do so literally—to the fullest, but has its share of intriguing and chilly moments along the way.

Teenager Bill Whitney (Billy Warlock) is a member of an upper-class family in Beverly Hills, but is starting to have doubts about his privileged life. As he tells his psychiatrist, Dr. Cleveland (Ben Slack), he's come to distrust his parents, who seem to lavish more attention on his sister, Jenny (Patrice Jennings). Bill's friend, Blanchard (Tim Bartell), who once dated Jenny, thinks something's wrong too, and one day, while getting something in the bathroom, Bill is startled when he sees Jenny taking a shower—through the glass door, the top half of her body appears to be on backwards. That day at the beach, Bill's status-obsessed girlfriend, Shauna (Heidi Kozak), implores him to get them invited to a party at the home of his snotty rival, Ferguson (Ben Meyerson), but his attempts are a failure and Shauna takes off. Then Blanchard appears, takes Bill aside and plays a tape he's secretly recorded of Jenny's recent coming-out party. From the sounds on the tape, the event apparently became an incestuous orgy at which an innocent victim was tortured and murdered.

A distraught Bill brings the tape to Dr. Cleveland; but when he returns the next day, the doctor plays it back, and the language and sounds appear completely innocent. The doctor lectures him about fitting in and obeying the rules of society before the confused Bill leaves. He arranges to meet with Blanchard to get another copy of the tape, but when he goes to the meeting place, he sees that Blanchard has had a fatal auto accident. Returning home, Bill is startled to find he's been invited to Ferguson's party; but when he goes and attempts to force information about the unnerving recent events from Ferguson, he's roughed up and thrown into the swimming pool. Later, however, he is seduced by Clarisa, a seemingly rebellious member of Ferguson's clique. Another of Ferguson's cronies, Petrie (Brian Bremer) contacts Bill, offering answers, but when Bill goes to meet him, Petrie turns up dead as well. Later, however, the "death" turns out to have been a hoax designed to embarrass Bill.

Bill starts to think he's going crazy—and so does Dr. Cleveland, who has him sedated and taken to a local hospital. There he finds that he has been pronounced dead even though he's still alive, and manages to escape to Clarisa's house. She warns him against investigating further, but Bill nonetheless returns home, where a reception for visiting Judge Carter (David Wiley) is to be held. But the guests, as well as his family, restrain Bill, and reveal that he was right all along: he is an outsider from society, brought up within it and raised to be their victim in a bizarre ritual called "shunting."

But the first to fall prey is the still-living Blanchard, who is brought out and restrained as the assembled guests sprout grotesque deformities and literally suck the life from him, melding into a huge, oozing mass as they do so. Despite the presence of Clarisa and Bill's best friend Milo (Evan Richards), who has infiltrated the party, Bill is set to be next in line, and although he briefly escapes—and discovers his family having a sickening, metamorphosing orgy in a back room—he too is prepared for "shunting." But in a last stand, Bill challenges Ferguson to a fight for his freedom, and manages to win, literally pulling his protean foe inside out. Bill, Milo and Clarisa escape into the night.

The directorial debut of prolific genre producer Brian Yuzna, SOCIETY sat on the shelf for a couple of years prior to a quickie release in Los Angeles, followed by its debut on home video. How one reacts to the film will have a lot to do with how accepting one is of a film that proceeds for most of its running time as a paranoid mystery with horrific overtones, only to become a graphic special effects festival in the final reels. The "shunting" orgy is an admittedly startling, lengthy sequence, with the party guests sprouting extended mouths and extremities and burrowing into their helpless victim, oozing slime all the while and eventually transforming into an enormous mass of quivering protoplasm. (On this evidence, both effects creator Screaming Mad George and his credit for "surrealistic makeup effects and design" seem quite well-named.) The intent appears to be the creation of the ultimate horror to pay off on Bill's seemingly paranoid suspicions, and although it's a properly shocking spectacle, its potency is depleted somewhat through the drawing out of the climactic action and injections of sick humor (his father's transformation makes literal Bill's earlier shouted insult, "Butthead!").

The film as a whole remains an entertaining and relatively intriguing thriller, though it might have benefited from a more complex development of its theme of outsiders in society, as opposed to the traditional suspense gambits it largely utilizes. Director Yuzna and screenwriters Woody Keith and Rick Fry also unnecessarily repeat themselves at times, as when the unsettling, obscured vision of Jenny's backwards body is repeated in full view with Clarisa and in the sequences involving Martin's "death," which is played too similarly to Blanchard's—not to mention Bill's curious lack of suspicion of rival Martin's intentions.

Nonetheless, SOCIETY has a level of originality and social satire not often seen in low-budget shockers. It's interesting to note that this film, with its out-in-the-open treatment of class differences, was a bigger critical and commercial success in England than its native America. *(Violence, profanity, nudity, sexual situations.)*

p, Keith Walley; d, Brian Yuzna; w, Woody Keith, Rick Fry; ph, Rick Fichter; ed, Peter Teschner; m, Mark Ryder, Phil Davies; prod d, Matthew C. Jacobs; art d, Kelle DeForrest

Horror/Mystery **(PR: O MPAA: R)**

SOLDIER'S TALE, A ★★½

(New Zealand) 99m Mirage Entertainment; Atlantic Entertainment; Vision Pictures ~ Atlantic Releasing Corporation c

Gabriel Byrne *(Saul Scourby)*, Marianne Basler *(Belle)*, Paul Wyett *(Charlie)*, Judge Reinhold *(The Yank)*

An oddly romantic WWII drama set amid the French countryside, with a darkly brooding lover and a compromised heroine, A SOLDIER'S TALE explores the uncomfortable kinship between war and rape.

Sergeant Saul Scourby (Gabriel Byrne) is adept at knifing enemy sentries and tells a flustered young recruit whom he has saved, Charlie (Paul Wyett), that feelings have no place in war; it is simply a job to get done. A few scenes later, when he spots Isabella (Marianne Basler), Scourby's intended sexual escapade is complicated by a trio of Resistance members who've arrived to take her to trial for treason. Cradling his sten-gun, the sergeant sends them packing and resolves to spend the weekend protecting her from the three, who retreat to the edge of her property.

After a joyless night of sex, Scourby learns that "Belle" had taken a German lover, a pilot later lost in the skies over England. In flashback, we see the dismay her liaison caused her widower father and the anger of her nosier neighbors. With the airman's presumed death, she soon took up with a young Frenchman whose Resistance activities precluded an affair with a Frenchwoman known to have had a Luftwaffe lover. As the weekend draws to a close, Scourby learns that she later had a relationship with a far less attractive German, a high-ranking officer in the SS security service, or SD.

The ambiguity surrounding Belle's life with the SD leader (it remains unclear whether he beat information out of her or was simply jealous of her former French lover) is mirrored by her complex attitude to her savior, the taciturn Scourby. Though he does try to rape her, later he's seen fixing things around the house in the manner of a middle-aged husband. He does make a misguided effort to find sanctuary for her at the local church, where the priest spouts Resistance platitudes yet is unwilling to make use of a young GI (Judge Reinhold) who comes by with gifts. He even muses about taking her away with him to Australia or New Zealand when the war is over. On her part, it is unclear whether Belle really is beginning to like Scourby; he is not overly charming or amusing or very educated, just a toughened "Tommy." Still, she knows he is the only thing standing between her and a Resistance firing squad, and had presumably thought little of becoming the consort the most sinister kind of German.

When Scourby is finally warned by his crass young lieutenant that he had better show up at their campsite or be considered AWOL, and that no help can be expected with the local Resistance, the sergeant must make a decision fast. He does, and one that combines his military skills and darker passions.

An interesting but slight character study, A SOLDIER'S TALE highlights the corrupt morality of wartime. Scourby thinks nothing of taking advantage of a lone woman; she has been exceedingly foolish in her choice of lovers; and the Resistance members cannot bother to think through the evidence that points to her possible innocence. *(Profanity, nudity, adult situations.)*

p, Larry Parr; d, Larry Parr; w, Grant Hinden Miller, Larry Parr, (from the novel by M.K. Joseph); ph, Alun Bollinger; ed, Michael Horton; m, John Charles; prod d, Ivan Maussion; art d, Reston Griffiths

War/Drama **(PR: C MPAA: R)**

SOLDIER'S FORTUNE ★★½

96m Soldier's Fortune Company; Box Office Partners ~ Republic Pictures Home Video c

Gil Gerard *(Robert E. Lee Jones)*, Dan Haggerty *(Hollis Bodine)*, Charles Napier *(Colonel Blair)*, P.J. Soles *(Debra)*, Barbara Bingham *(Susan Alexander)*, Grainger Hines *(Link)*, Janus Blythe *(Alex Prichard)*, Cynthia Guyer *(Jennifer Alexander)*, Wild Bill Mock *(Fresno Bob Bodine)*, George "Buck" Flower *(T. Max)*, Randy Harris *(Big Sam)*, Juan Garcia *(Low Eddie)*

In the action film arena, the Vietnam War has been relived *ad infinitum.*

Somehow unable to concede defeat, the film industry has inflicted on the American public an array of movies dealing with either rescuing MIAs and POWs, the bonding of mercenaries who were platoon buddies in 'Nam, an influx of crime into America by former Viet Cong and American traitors, or a combination thereof. While falling neatly into this cinematic scheme, SOLDIER'S FORTUNE at least conceals its hand for awhile.

When a rich teen, Jennifer Alexander (Cynthia Guyer), is abducted and her best friend slain, Jennifer's mother Susan (Barbara Bingham) contacts her not-so-beloved ex-husband, begs him to leave a military ruckus in Central America and asks his help in retrieving her child. After informing her ex, Robert E. Lee Jones (Gil Gerard), that the kidnapped teen is actually his daughter, the dumbstruck career soldier embraces instant fatherhood and complies. Rounding up a motley crew of former Vietnam comrades, Jones agrees to follow the abductors' orders. What no one realizes is that Susan's trustworthy assistant Debra (P.J. Soles) had led both teenage girls into a trap, which is part of a larger ambush set for Jones and company.

While Debra's motive is cash, her accomplice Colonel Blair (Charles Napier) hopes to wipe out the good guys who gave him so much grief over in South East Asia. Aided by the dead adolescent's vengeful sister Alex Prichard (Janus Blythe), an Air Force officer, the male crew thwarts an attempt by their nemeses to snatch the ransom without releasing Jennifer. In the shrapnel-spraying showdown, the bad guys trot out Debra, dressed in Jennifer's cheerleading outfit, and blow her away. Not fooled by this masquerade, Jones tricks Colonel Blair with a rigged bag of ransom money before finishing him off. Choking to death Blair's main henchman, Rojas (Orestes Matacena), who tortured him and Jones back in 'Nam, the mountainous T. Max (George "Buck" Flower) achieves a catharsis at last. Not only do the original Vietnam buddies survive but Jennifer is happily reunited with her parents who decide to give their relationship one more chance.

The tricky revenge manuevers manufactured by Blair and company in SOLDIER'S FORTUNE are divertingly complicated, and the action sequences are competently directed. These virtues, coupled with some tangy acting from the villains, allow this actioner to rise above the level of an average TV action series. In some ways, SOLDIER'S FORTUNE is "Combat" with more graphic violence or "Tour of Duty" with less philosophizing. Perhaps it is closest in spirit to "The A-Team" only without that show's cohesive ensemble.

In its favor, SOLDIER'S FORTUNE hoodwinks its audience into thinking it's witnessing a tangled kidnapping plot when it is actually on the sidelines of another replay of the Vietnam War. Further distracting us from the Battle of the Mercenaries is the clever way the film casts doubts on Susan's guilty-looking second husband and by its springing of the double-cross engineered by Susan's two-faced secretary. Better yet, the film dares to plop a feminist heroine right in the middle of the male-dominated adventure. Not only does Alex hold her own but also she's the one to rescue her counterparts on occasion.

Punched up with numerous demolitions and nifty special forces equipment gadgetry, this macho action film brings the Vietnam War to the streets of America where Yankee bravado and caginess naturally result in victory. Reassuringly, the film informs audiences that we lost the real war due to jungle foliage and the treachery of turncoats like Colonel Blair. *(Extreme violence, profanity.)*

p, Jeffrey C. Hogue, Michael J. Biber; d, Arthur N. Mele; w, Charles Douglas Lemay, Jeffrey C. Hogue, (from the story by Fred Olen Ray); ph, William Hayes; ed, Chris Roth; m, Chuck Cirino; prod d, Ted Tunney; art d, Edward T.E. Tunney

Action/War **(PR: C MPAA: R)**

SORORITY HOUSE MASSACRE 2

80m Concorde ~ New Horizons Home Video c

Melissa Moore, Robyn Harris, Stacia Zhivago, Dana Bentley, Michelle Verran, Orville Ketchum

Was the original SORORITY HOUSE MASSACRE really that successful? Well, like it or not, here's SORORITY HOUSE MASSACRE 2. Originally filmed as "Nighty Nightmare," this direct-to-video release is so bad director Jim Wynorski originally took his name off it, calling himself "Arch Stanton" instead. But now, here it is, with the director bravely putting his monicker back on and an instant-sequel title attached.

A bunch of babes move in to renovate a big old house (one that will look quite familiar to those who have seen a lot of Fred Olen Ray movies) and have a seance in which they attempt to call up the spirit of a man who killed a bunch of people in the manse years earlier. The ouija board they're using flies into the fireplace, but the girls get over their initial fright and prepare for bed (each one providing a topless shot before they get into their nighties). Meanwhile, a fat, drooling guy named Orville Ketchum has been lurking around, and appears to murder the girls one by one. But actually, one of the girls has been possessed by the old killer's spirit, and after a bit more misogynist mayhem, the ghost is put to rest. Or is it?

The five girls are played by Robyn Harris, Melissa Moore, Stacia Zhivago, Michelle Verran and Dana Bentley; their names and those of their characters are all that exist to differentiate them, unless one counts the fact that Harris has a British accent and Zhivago looks a lot like Laura Dern. It's bad enough that their only real purpose is to hang around in various states of undress and be terrorized—while saying things like, "Let's get changed for bed and have a seance!"—but they are presented as utter idiots with no personality, and the camera leers at them almost as enthusiastically as the inevitable maniac.

The acting, writing and direction in SORORITY HOUSE MASSACRE 2 is not so much bad as non-existent; there is something of a subplot attempted, in which a cop who was on the original murder scene continues to investigate it, to help pad out the running time to feature length. Of course, he does most of his investigative work at the local strip joint, just to allow a few *more* women to be shown topless. There's more padding when scenes of that first massacre are presented, and a further air of cheapness in the fact that they are taken from the original SLUMBER PARTY MASSACRE. (One of the survivors of that misogynist bloodshed, by the way, supposedly grew up to be one of this film's stripper characters; wonder what the feminist creators of SLUMBER would think of that!) One would assume that since the killer is set up as Orville Ketchum (supposedly playing "Himself"), the finale would at least allow some pro-female catharsis when the last girl defeats him, but the increasingly predictable "twist" ending even subverts that possibility.

Of course, there are those (and the filmmakers would probably be the first) who would argue that serious criticism is beside the point, that SORORITY HOUSE MASSACRE 2 is meant simply as a jokey, brainless good time. But movies like this are a blight on the video horror scene, taking up space that could be filled by a better, wittier, more ambitious low-budgeter that might not have the required naked women or bloodshed (though the effects in this one are of the cheapest, blood-splattering-on-the-walls type). The movie's real attitude towards its audience and its performers is inadvertently conveyed by an attempt at a funny end title that reads, "No actresses were hurt or mistreated while making this film." *(Violence, excessive nudity.)*

p, Shelly Stoker; d, Jim Wynorski; w, James B. Rogers, Bob Sheridan

Horror **(PR: O MPAA: NR)**

SOUTH CENTRAL ★★★

99m Ixtlan Productions; Monument Pictures; Enchantment Films ~ Warner Bros. c

Glenn Plummer *(Bobby Johnson)*, Carl Lumbly *(Ali)*, Byron Keith Minns *(Ray Ray)*, Lexie D. Bigham *(Bear)*, Vincent Craig Dupree *(Loco)*, LaRita Shelby *(Carole)*, Kevin Best *(Genie Lamp)*, "Big Daddy" Wayne *(Henchman)*, Allan Hatcher *(Baby Jimmie)*, Alvin Hatcher *(Baby Jimmie)*, Baldwin C. Sykes *(Ken Dog)*, Rana Mack *(Girl in Club)*, Diane Manzo *(Undercover Cop)*, Sal Landi *(Detective)*, Christian Coleman *(Jimmie–Age 10)*, Leonard Boyles *(Termite)*, Terrence Williams *(Boody)*, Reginald T. Dorsey *(Bastille)*, Tim DeZarn *(Buddha)*, Allen Michael Lerner *(Broken Nose)*, Julius LeFlore *(1st Prison Guard)*, Ivory Ocean *(Willie Manchester)*, Vickilyn Reynolds *(Willie's Wife)*, Linda Fontanette *(Neighbor Lady)*, Richard G. Camphuis *(1st Policeman)*, Starletta Dupois *(Nurse Shelly)*, George Mulholland *(2nd Prison Guard)*, Darren Leong *(Kim)*, Lanier Edwards *(Muslim)*, Clynell Jackson, III *(Intern)*, Donald Bakeer *(Dr. King)*, Bonnie Oda Homsey *(Patty Chin)*, Mark E. Anderson *(Sakett)*, Ron Chovance *(Parole Officer)*, Michael McNab *(2nd Policeman)*, Eugene Williams *(Local Tough)*, Musa Bakeer *(Young Boy)*

Director-writer Steve Anderson conjures up a realistic portrayal of Black ghetto life in SOUTH CENTRAL. More intimate than the recent rash of inner-city gang-themed films, this debut film focuses on relationships as much as the violence which is commonly associated with the genre. Although inconsistent in tone, it is an emotionally wrenching account of life on the mean streets of Los Angeles.

It's 1982 and Bobby Johnson (Glenn Plummer) has just been released from prison for armed robbery. Obviously unchanged from his stay in stir, Bobby rejoins his gang, the "Deuces," which he had formed with his friend Ray Ray (Byron Keith Minns). Ray Ray has gang expansion on the mind—envisioning the Deuces as the coming power in LA's criminal world. Bobby is anxious to rekindle his relationship with his wife, Carole (LaRita Shelby), and his infant son, Jimmie. Before long, he runs into trouble with a neighboring drug dealer who has been moving in on the Deuces' turf *and* Bobby's wife during his absence.

Bobby and the Deuces concoct a plan to kill the rival dealer. After ramming a car into the dealer's nightclub, Ray Ray hands Bobby a gun and watches as he pumps two bullets into his chest. Later that night, a somber Bobby has the Deuces' killer mark burned onto his face. After hiding out for a few months, Bobby agrees to take a ride with some gang members. When one of them, Loco (Vincent Craig Dupree), propositions a hooker who is an undercover cop, they are arrested. The police finger Bobby in the drug dealer's killing and he is convicted of murder. He holds his baby one last time before leaving for prison.

Ten years later, Bobby appears older and more pumped up from constantly lifting weights in the slammer. Having been turned down for parole a half dozen times, he is resigned to a long stay behind bars. He hears from outside that Ray Ray is building up the Deuces into the thousands—and that his former partner is using Bobby's son, Jimmie (Christian Coleman), now a ten-year-old, to steal car radios. Bobby breaks with the other Deuces inside and becomes open game. When some white inmates target him for an attack, Bobby is saved from the near beating by a fellow prisoner, Ali (Carl Lumbly).

Ali is a lifer and takes the bitter Bobby as his cell mate—extolling to him the virtues of the Muslim religion and redemption through love and education. Bobby initially is resistant to Ali's words, but after his boy is shot while stealing a radio, Bobby is desperate for some focus in his life. Ali breaks down and tells Bobby he lost his own son to the streets and was put in prison for killing his son's murderer. In time Bobby loses his anger and gains his self-worth back. He begins to understand the cycle of hate which has permeated his life. With Ali's help, Bobby is finally granted parole and given a chance for a fresh start. "Go save your son," are Ali's last words to Bobby before he leaves prison.

Back in the 'hood, things have changed. Carole is a full-blown PCP addict and Jimmie has been taken as a ward of the state and placed in a boys' home. When Bobby manages to get in to see his son, Jimmie is skeptical of this stranger, especially when Bobby tells him that violence and gang life are not the answer. He promises Jimmie he will get him out of the home but the boy is disappointed—this isn't the ruthless killer he has heard about for years. Jimmie is more interested in seeking revenge on the man who shot him, Willie Manchester (Ivory Ocean).

The next day, Bobby hears that his son has gone back to Ray Ray. Bobby arrives at the Deuces' warehouse where he confronts Ray Ray and Jimmie. Ray Ray treats Bobby like an outsider and refuses to give up the boy, as Bobby pleads with his son to stay away from the gang life. Then Ray Ray hands a gun to Jimmie and produces Willie Manchester for him to shoot. Bobby wrestles a gun away from Ray Ray's bodyguard, Bear (Lexie D. Bigham), and forces a standoff with Ray Ray. He begs him to release his son, who has now had his fill of gang violance. Ray Ray knows he owes Bobby ten years, so he allows father and son to leave—facing an uncertain future.

SOUTH CENTRAL is honorable in its intentions. Anderson refuses to glamorize the story, and that remains the true strength of the film. Instead, he offers a raw, moving portrait of a man who is forced to come face to face with himself and his chosen lifestyle. Drugs, violence and the gangs are the big picture, but the emotional impact of the father-son relationship is what viewers will remember. Loyalty and family play a large part of the film's underlying theme. The protagonist has always been loyal to the only family he had—the gang. But now he has his own family and that loyalty heavily outweighs the former. This family appeal is the reason gangs have proliferated in the ghetto, and Anderson never belittles that fact. Unfortunately, along with that family comes violent crime.

The storyline is successfully carried through to Bobby's redemption, and Anderson seems to be saying that there is still hope if the family unit can stay intact. Thankfully, the director keeps the violence at a tolerable level. He also has a keen ear for the nuances of South Central LA. The constant woosh of jets overhead adds a sense of realism to the neighborhood, which actually lies at the foot of the airport. Most directors would avoid such extraneous noise at all costs—it works here. Less successful is the film's tendency to be somewhat heavy-handed in its message. In one particular scene, the Deuces walk into a nightclub and the music stops as the entire crowd gawks at their presence. Cartoonish characters, especially noticeable in the prison sequences, also tend to weaken the film. The white prisoners, supposedly of the Aryan Nation, and some of the overacting junkies, are nothing more than cardboard cutouts.

Generally though, the story retains believability and is compelling to watch. The cast is uneven, but there are a few standouts. Plummer plays Bobby with a quiet intensity which works especially well against the backdrop of loudness. His naturalistic style is refreshing to watch, and the changes which occur in him, after he accepts his mistakes and later when he meets his son, are beautifully played. As the inspirational Ali, Lumbly is brilliant. He does more with his limited screen time than all of the larger roles. When he explains to Bobby about the hatred they both carry around inside, it is easily the strongest moment in the film. Coleman is a fine young actor. He plays both sides of Jimmy, child and tough hood, with convincing depth.

SOUTH CENTRAL is the type of film which gives people—regardless of race or nationality—hope. True, its message sometimes is laid on a little thick, but it would be hard to dislike a picture with so much genuine caring and good ambitions. It answers a very complex question rather simply. How do we stop the proliferation of gangs and crime? It starts in the home. *(Violence, profanity, substance abuse.)*

p, Janet Yang, William B. Steakley; d, Steve Anderson; w, Steve Anderson, (from the novel *Crips* by Donald Bakeer); ph, Charlie Lieberman; ed, Steve Nevius; m, Tim Truman; prod d, David Brian Miller, Marina Kieser; art d, Andrew D. Brothers; set d, Caroline Stover; cos, Mary Law Weir

Drama **(PR: C MPAA: R)**

SPIRITS ★

88m Cinema Group Productions; American Independent Productions ~ Vidmark Entertainment c

Erik Estrada *(Father Anthony Vicci)*, Carol Lynley *(Sister Jillian)*, Robert Quarry *(Dr. Richard Wicks)*, Brinke Stevens *(Amy Goldwyn)*, Kathrin Lautner *(Beth)*, Oliver Darrow *(Harry)*, Kaitlin Hopkins, Sandra Margot

Apart from a shapely nun who strips naked to reveal prominent bikini tan lines, SPIRITS has little new or interesting to offer.

It's an admitted rehash of THE LEGEND OF HELL HOUSE, with avuncular Dr. Richard Wicks (Robert Quarry) engaged in the study of "post-life energy forms." He gathers some pals together for a jaunt to the nearby haunted Heron mansion. Expedition members include Amy Goldwyn (Brinke Stevens), a no-nonsense psychic; Beth (Kathrin Lautner), a skeptic and self-proclaimed bitch; and lusty young Harry (Oliver Darrow), whose field may as well be occult gynecology, as he's bedded by a succubus the first night out.

Amy gets possessed and pulls the whole EXORCIST routine (an end credit gives special thanks to Father Merrin), pounding a nail into her hand and growling gutteral threats at the rest. The supernatural villain is the late Henri Picard, a fallen-priest-turned-serial-killer whose mummy abides in the cellar. Picard declares he will destroy each researcher through his or her own hidden evil. Beth's "evil" turns out to be that she's a closet lesbian, a telling example of how old-style morality creeps into even the sleaziest of exploitation chillers.

So where does the nude nun fit in? She's one of the demons tormenting Father Anthony Vicci (Erik Estrada), a handsome clergyman who was seduced by the malevolence of Heron House years ago. Finally the padre summons the courage to go and rescue the researchers. Father Anthony confronts Picard's reanimated skeleton with a psalmful of heavenly entreaties ("Go forth Christian soul! . . . Be at peace!"), though it takes a lethal splash of holy water to stop the bony fiend. The melting ghoul makes the only really impressive special effect in the picture.

Estrada, best-known for TV's "CHiPs," bravely faces B-moviehood. Robert Quarry has become a real chairman-of-the-board in this genre and looks comfortable. Scream queen Brinke Stevens gives a welcome hard edge to the stock character of the medium to whom nobody listens until it's too late. But SPIRITS is overall a horror hodgepodge of little import except that it's one of the more polished-looking productions of cheapie specialist Fred Olen Ray. This baron of low-budgetry has cranked out one potboiler after another over the past decade, and his filmmaking sense certainly has improved with mileage, if this $130,000 effort is any indication. Now if Ray could only come up with a screenplay.

Ray's most significant contribution to cinema last year was actually a book *The New Poverty Row: Independent Filmmakers as Distributors*, a shapeless but readable broth of movie business history, behind-the-scenes trivia, filmography and opinion. Ray outlines the travails of several exploitation mini-moguls, including Roger Corman, Jerry Warren, Al Adamson—and Fred Olen Ray himself. His autobiographical closing chapter runs down his own fraught Hollywood career, offers a spirited defense of his *oeuvre* and promises that he will never subject the world to his unreleased first feature, THE BRAIN LEECHES. One wishes him well. *(Violence, profanity, nudity, sexual situations, adult situations.)*

p, T.L. Lankford; d, Fred Olen Ray; w, Jeff Falls, R.U. King; ph, Gary Graver; ed, Chris Ross; m, Tim Landers; art d, Ted Tunny

Horror **(PR: O MPAA: R)**

SPLIT SECOND ★★

(U.K.) 90m Muse Productions; Split Second Productions; Challenge Films ~ InterStar Releasing c

Rutger Hauer *(Harley Stone)*, Kim Cattrall *(Michelle)*, Neil Duncan *(Dick Durkin)*, Michael J. Pollard *(The Rat Catcher)*, Pete Postlethwaite *(Paulsen)*, Ian Dury *(Jay Jay)*, Roberta Eaton *(Robin)*, Tony Steedman *(O'Donnell)*, Alun Armstrong *(Thrasher)*, Steven Hartley *(Foster)*, Sarah Stockbridge *(Tiffany)*, Colin Skeaping *(Drunk)*, Ken Bones *(Forensic Expert)*, Dave Duffy *(Nick "The Batman")*, Stewart Harvey-Wilson *(The Killer Player)*, Paul Grayson *(The Killer Player)*, Chris Chappel *(Rat Catcher's Assistant)*, Charlotte Hick *(Little Girl)*, Tina Smith *(Mutilated Woman)*, John Bennett *(Dr. Schulman)*, Martin Ronan *(1st Ambulance Attendant)*, Phil Smeeton *(2nd Ambulance Attendant)*, Morris Paton *(Jogger)*, Tony Sibbald *(Bald Man in Suit)*, Jason Wakins *(Coroner's Assistant)*, Tina Shaw *(Nighclub Stripper)*, Papillion Soo Lam *(Waitress)*, Rikki Howard *(Cage Security Policeman)*, Rob Edmonds *(Policeman)*, Alan Stocks *(Policeman)*, Padraig Casey *(Policeman)*, The Shend *(Precinct Policeman)*, Susan Aderin, Shelia Hyde, Jan Van Hool, Cathy Walker *(Precinct Policewomen)*, Angie Hill-Richmond *(Nurse)*, Havoc *(Dog)*, Vanessa Victor, Jadene Doran, Lorraine Pascal Woodward, Lisa Roudette, Bibi Bohorquez, Mayumi Cabrera *(Girls in Nightclub)*

In the grimly polluted future of SPLIT SECOND, an ill-matched pair of police detectives play a game of cat-and-mouse with a nonhuman killer. Besides portraying London as a cross between Calcutta and the south Bronx, writer Gary Scott Thompson adds a dollop of humor by teaming a tough cop with a stuffy Oxonian.

Clad in non-regulation black leather, Harley Stone (Rutger Hauer) seems perennially on the verge of dismissal from the metropolitan police. Obsessed with the peculiar murder of his partner years ago, he carries not only the physical, but the psychic scars of an encounter with the killer; Stone can sense when the miscreant is near. Following his hunch to a striptease bar, Stone is a few seconds too late to save a young blonde from having her chest cavity exposed and her heart actually torn out. There is also a note to Stone from the butcher smeared in blood on the bathroom mirror. At the frantically crowded police headquarters, Stone is introduced to his new partner, Dick Durkin (Neil Duncan) by an angry chief. As if in answer to the latter's complaint about Stone's habit of packing too many weapons, a refrigerator box arrives containing the victim's heart, with a nasty-looking bite taken out of it.

Durkin, in jacket with school tie and glasses, contrasts wildy with the violent Stone, who seems to thrive on a diet of sweet coffee and donuts. (Oddly, no one seems to question Stone's half-American accent or what he does as a detective between searches for the mysterious serial killer.) Barely tolerated by Stone, who teases him, Durkin begins to earn the more experienced man's respect when he recognizes the occult nature of the bloody graffiti smeared on the ceiling of victim number two, a male with the missing tell-tale organ. Stone then reveals that their prey may be something more than a human psychotic, since the plaster cast from the bite reveals teeth as long as most people's fingers.

Besides its dental talent, the creature soon reveals a few other skills as well. It steals a shotgun from a police car and manages to keep Stone and Durkin at bay despite their fusillade. The beast also leaves its bite on the shoulder of Michelle (Kim Cattrall), an old girlfriend and apparently another Yank in England. Although they are too slow to save victim number three, Durkin and Stone eventually realize that they prevented the removal of her heart, so they race to the police morgue just in time to catch a glimpse of their eight-foot tall opponent, who escapes by literally crashing through a steel door.

In a frankly amusing scene, the two detectives requisition enough guns to knock out a tank from the police armory while the stuffy quartermaster stares in shock. Now cursing as freely as Stone, Durkin the public-school boy copies his taste for sweets and coffee. There is also some discussion of the bloody graffiti and whether the heart-ripper is simply evil or "The Evil One" incarnate.

Whatever the beast may be, it is not stupid and rather easily separates Durkin from Stone and Stone from Michelle. She is soon abducted, but our toothsome beast has left a hint in the form of occult symbols carved onto an unconscious Durkin's chest. The two humans decipher the marks and return to the flooded London underground station where Stone had lost his earlier partner (as seen in flashback). They find Michelle, and the imposing antagonist finds them. In the battle that follows we finally get a good look at the demon and guage the amount of firepower it takes for Stone to finish it off.

Very fast-paced, SPLIT SECOND is an example of the men-versus-monster genre, with a British setting providing a fresh twist. The film's speed drowns any questions an audience may have about the presence of so many Americans in London, or the apparent lack of interest by the whole police force in a creature that can crash through its mortuary's steel door. Revealed as amphibious, the eight-foot monster seems to move around as quickly and quietly as a mouse. The scaly creature shares a dental scheme with the nemesis in Ridley Scott's ALIEN, but its origins are never explained, except for a generalized concern over global warming and pollution. *(Violence, profanity, nudity.)*

p, Laura Gregory; d, Tony Maylam; w, Gary Scott Thompson; ph, Clive Tickner; ed, Dan Rae; m, Francis Haines, Stephen Parsons; prod d, Chris Edwards; art d, Humphrey Bangham, Ian Baille; cos, Antoinette Gregory

Science Fiction/Horror/Thriller (PR: O MPAA: R)

SPOTSWOOD

(SEE: EFFICIENCY EXPERT, THE)

STATION, THE ★★½

(Italy) 91m Fandango srl ~ Aries Film Releasing c
(STAZIONE, LA)

Sergio Rubini *(Domenico)*, Margherita Buy *(Flavia)*, Ennio Fantastichini *(Danilo)*

American films are criticized, often rightly so, for the casual use of violence to get a cheap rise out of the audience. Even worthwhile plots descend to trite chases or fight sequences for the sake of a big action climax. A case in point was the 1990 blockbuster HOME ALONE, whose saccharine storyline was capped by a slapstick siege that many commentators felt bordered on sadism.

But slouching toward bedlam is by no means exclusive to Hollywood. The Italian production THE STATION starts off as a compact and poignant comedy-drama of human nature, then takes a dismaying 180-degree turn into a skull-cracking thriller to reach its resolution. Call it "Train Station Alone," although the plot predates the Macaulay Culkin hit by some time, being based on an Italian play that enjoyed a solid three-year run. THE STATION came to the screen with its stage cast intact, a screenplay by original playwright Umberto Marino and lead actor Sergio Rubini making his feature directorial debut.

Domenico (Rubini) is the birdlike, mother-dominated young night-attendant at a little country train station that's four kilometers from anywhere. One dark and stormy eve his lonely vigil gets an unexpected interruption—a passenger. She's Flavia (Margherita Buy), a wealthy, strikingly beautiful blonde desperate to catch a connecting train to Rome. The next one won't arrive until early morning, and in the interim Domenico does his awkward best to entertaining this once-in-a-lifetime visitor. There's a melancholy tone to the friendly, often funny interplay between the mismatched couple, fond of each other but worlds apart socially and otherwise. Then enter the token menace: Flavia's estranged boyfriend Danilo (Ennio Fantastichini), a burly creep who tried to use her rich family name to close a business deal. Flavia walked out on him at a party, and now the drunken thug wants to drag her back.

When Domenico timidly defends Flavia, Danilo fells him with one blow, and the bittersweet pathos of the earlier scenes rapidly evaporates. Domenico and Flavia barricade themselves inside the station, while Danilo rages murderously outside, tormenting the terrified but resourceful captives. Earlier Domenico proudly demonstrated how he's timed everything in the station, not only train departures but the way a loose, heavy cabinet door falls open every 20 minutes. Nobody will be surprised at where Danilo's head happens to be at the end of the next interval.

Before it takes a detour into STRAW DOGS territory, THE STATION makes a tender tableau, not too constricted by its limited settings and small cast. Scarecrow-thin, pinched-faced and sad-eyed, Rubini effectively holds center stage as the chatty but hopelessly provincial Domenico, trapped in the same dull job his father held, engaged to a local girl (off on a pilgrimage to Lourdes) but more enthusiastic about a long-planned vacation to Germany. Margherita Buy is sleek but sweet, although the hackneyed stalk-and-smash stuff barely gives her and Ennio Fantastichini a chance to develop their characters. At the end of the picture Domenico and Flavia, having shared the ready-mix adventure, regrettably but inevitably go their separate ways; not so Rubini and Buy, a married couple in real life. *(Violence, profanity, adult situations.)*

p, Domenico Procacci; d, Sergio Rubini; w, Sergio Rubini, Gianfilippo Ascione, Umberto Marino, (from his play); ph, Alessio Gelsini; ed, Angelo Nicoloni; m, Antonio DiPafi; prod d, Carolina Ferrara, Luca Gobbi

Comedy/Drama (PR: C MPAA: NR)

STAY TUNED ★★

89m ST Productions; Morgan Creek Productions ~
Warner Bros. c

John Ritter *(Roy Knable)*, Pam Dawber *(Helen Knable)*, Jeffrey Jones *(Spike)*, Eugene Levy *(Crowley)*, David Tom *(Darryl Knable)*, Heather McComb *(Diane Knable)*, Salt-N-Pepa *(Rap Artists)*, Cheryl James *(Salt)*, Sandy Denton *(Pepa)*, George Gray *(Mr. Grogan)*, Michael Hogan *(Duane)*, Jimi DeFlippis *(Garth)*

Two unoffending mice with the voices of John Ritter and Pam Dawber are relentlessly pursued through an appliance-gutted suburban tract house by a heartlessly mechanical Robocat, who performs his mission with such cold-blooded purpose that the automaton ends up destroying both itself and the suburban home as the two mice escape into another dimension. This wonderful, six-minute animated reprieve by the great Chuck Jones is the nearest Peter Hyams's spineless and dull comedy STAY TUNED ever gets to any sense of true satire, invention, or style.

Seattle couple Roy (John Ritter) and Helen (Pam Dawber) Knable get sucked into a satanic cable-TV dimension after Roy agrees to try out a satellite dish promoted by the devil's own right-hand man, Spike (Jeffrey Jones). Trapped into a heinous 666 channel, ricochetting from one nightmarish program to another, they must find their way back to the reality of suburban Seattle within 24 hours or their souls become the property of Beelzebub. With help from their electronics whiz son Darryl (David Tom), the Knables defeat Spike and rejoin their family in "reality."

Director Peter Hyams (OUTLAND, 2010, NARROW MARGIN) proves himself capable of displaying low voltage special effects but distinctly incapable of providing a context or a point of view. Hyams and screenwriters Tom S. Parker and Jim Jennewein seem to be angling for a more light-humored RUNNING MAN tinged with the existential thrust of a SHERLOCK JR. But the satiric point is ground down to a nub by the film's pointless "Saturday Night Live"-type sketch parodies ("Meet the Mansons," "Wayne's Underworld") whose weakly humorous premises become nothing more than that, flashing into view with labored joke and then vanishing like the thin wispy gags they are. Hyams's dim-witted blandness belies the toothless comedy, so that rather than exposing the dangerously homogenous pablum of current cable-TV programming, STAY TUNED has the look of the cable-TV gristle itself.

In its strange and convoluted way, STAY TUNED caves in to the same bilge that it wants to criticize. This deadening negation is further intensified by the casting of John Ritter ("Three's Company," "Hearts Afire") and Pam Dawber ("Mork and Mindy," "My Sister Sam"). Battle-scarred veterans of Sitcom Hell themselves, they play the Knables' Seattle reality as if already sucked into Spike's satellite dish. False and zombielike at the outset, it is with little surprise that they are less than horrified when confronted by the devil's own programming. Ritter and Dawber play their parts with a TV performer's even-tempered and empty-headed placidity, depriving the film of any depth or subtext.

With Hyams's direction, Parker and Jennewein's screenplay and Ritter and Dawber's performances, STAY TUNED is nothing more than the bland leading the bland, collapsing upon itself and disappearing into the TV screen like an electronic blip among the 625 scan lines.

d, Peter Hyams; w, Tom S. Parker, Jim Jennewein, (from the story by Parker, Jennewein and Richard Siegel); ph, Peter Hyams; ed, Peter E. Berger; m, Bruce Broughton; prod d, Philip Harrison; art d, Richard Hudolin; set d, Rose Marie McSherry; cos, Joe Tompkins; anim, Chuck Jones

Comedy/Science Fiction **(PR: C MPAA: PG)**

STAZIONE, LA
(SEE: STATION, THE)

STEAL AMERICA ★★½
94m Seamless Pictures; Pacific Film Fund ~ Tara Releasing bw

Clara Bellino *(Stella)*, Diviana Ingravallo *(Maria Maddelena)*, Kevin Haley *(Jack)*, Charlie Homo *(Christophe)*, Liza Monjauze *(Mickey)*, Christopher Fisher *(Ace)*, Cintra Wilson *(Carletta)*, Sean Parke *(Joey)*, Gina Ravarra *(Jeena)*

Lucy Phillips's STEAL AMERICA, more a chronological series of vignettes than a plot-driven narrative, gives us the intertwined stories of three twentysomething Europeans living in San Francisco.

Christophe (Charlie Homo), an indolent and diffident young Frenchman, who claims to want to see the American West of cowboy movies, procures a job as a valet parker because he likes the uniform—a white lab coat—and likes being on the street. Stella (Clara Bellino), a Swiss woman he met on the Greyhound bus en route to San Francisco, works in a postcard store where everything costs $2.99. Maria Maddelena (Diviana Ingravallo), an Italian expatriate, works in the kitchen of the restaurant where Christophe parks cars.

Their lives proceed in fits and starts. Stella is teaching herself Japanese with self-learning tapes. Maria and Christophe go to Coit Tower and talk about his desire to visit the desert and to own a big American car. Jack (Kevin Haley), a flirtatious American painter, comes into the postcard shop several times until Stella agrees to go out with him. Christophe flimflams $10 from a rich guy by telling him his tire is flat. Jack and Stella visit Jack's favorite park, with a stunning fog-bound view of the Bay Bridge. Maria and another women do a performance piece in the park where they frolic on a small patch of fake snow.

One morning, Christophe is fired. While he is standing outside the restaurant complaining to his friends a man demands that he park his car. Christophe gets in the car and just keeps going. He picks Stella up at the postcard store and arranges to meet Maria. They stop at a hotel, gorge themselves on room service, have the hotel bring around someone else's car and drive off. A series of postcards flashes on the screen: Silver City, NM; Van Horn, TX; Tulsa; New Orleans; San Francisco.

One year later, Maria is the MC at the Chi Chi Club where Stella is performing as Stella Bellino and the Flying Monkeys. Christophe has been enchanted by a "voodoo queen," been deported and followed her to Haiti. Two Japanese men scouting San Francisco for jazz singers offer Stella a series of gigs in Japan. Stella is working at a video store where everything costs $2.99. Jack is trying to move to New York, but his car only goes in reverse and he wants to consummate his relationship with Stella, which they finally do, staying in bed for three days.

Jack's car is irreparable so he arranges to get a drive-away car. There is a big going-away party. Maria is flying to New York; Jack is driving to New York; Stella is driving with Jack to Las Vegas and then flying to Tokyo. Jack and Stella drive off into the desert. They make it to Las Vegas, but he decides he's had enough. He abandons the car at the Las Vegas airport and says he is flying to Tokyo with Stella, though they walk off in opposite directions.

Expanded to feature length from a 45-minute short, STEAL AMERICA is shot in uninspired b&w and the plot and the characters are seamless; they are both aimless, at best only vaguely directional. This is not necessarily bad. The film stands in welcome contrast to most American movies where everything must be subsumed in and subservient to an overriding roller coaster of a plot. The characters do have quirky and interesting personalities, despite being directionless and irresponsible.

The performances are relaxed and appealing, though Diviana Ingravallo's earthy sexiness stands out. There is an interesting ambivalence about sex in the movie that is a great relief compared to the urgent heterosexuality of most films. Maria first arrives on a motorcycle with another women and is clearly coded as a lesbian, though she also goes on a date with Christophe. Stella seems to be living with Christophe, but still dates Jack, though she doesn't sleep with him for a year. When they do, it is shot in unprovocative motionless extreme close-ups of skin. There is mention of someone dying of AIDS, but no mention of condom use.

It's a relief to see a movie that does not use gratuitous violence and obsessive sex to hide its utter vacuousness, though one wishes the filmmaker were not as ambivalent as her characters.

p, Liz Gazzano, Lucy Phillips; d, Lucy Phillips; w, Lucy Phillips, Glen Scantlebury; ph, Jim Barrett, Glen Scantlebury; ed, Glen Scantlebury; m, Gregory Jones

Drama **(PR: C MPAA: NR)**

STEELE'S LAW
Po' Boy Productions ~ Academy Entertainment c

Fred Williamson *(John Steele)*, Bo Svenson *(Sheriff Barnes)*, Doran Inghram *(Joe Keno)*, Phyllis Cicero *(Rose Holly)*, Robin McGee, Paul Tepper

In his book *Blacks in American Films and Television* Donald Bogle regretfully writes off longtime action fixture Fred "The Hammer" Williamson as "a decent actor fighting to get out" who squanders his latent talent on unworthy schlock. That sounds like the cue for STEELE'S LAW, a direct-to-video leftover starring, produced and directed by Williamson, the once-feared AFL defensive back.

Detective John Steele (Williamson) is a maverick cop assigned to thwart certainly one of the more memorable assassination plots of the year: a cabal of racist Dallas businessman who dress like singing cowboys have hired Joe Keno (Doran Inghram), dreaded international hit man *and* serial killer of men, women, children and farm animals, to terminate the Iraqi ambassador, currently conducting a smashingly successful goodwill tour of the US. Against a pseudo-funk musical score that sounds like rusty playground swings, Steele chases Keno through the mean streets—or more precisely, the cheap streets; the budget of this shoddily-shot opus was evidently too low to permit an onscreen car explosion.

Things get very dull very fast, as Steele repeatedly walks into stupid traps set by the stupid villains, who are too stupid to kill him, so he stupidly escapes. In the end one of the bigoted bad guys gets impaled on the Iraqi flag, but the tale's anti-prejudice pretentions ring hollow when a limp-wristed homosexual stereotype sashays onscreen for some unwanted comic relief, or when filmmaker Williamson indulges in some gratuitous Japan-bashing.

STEELE'S LAW manages the tricky feat of being so bad that even the wealth of unintentional laughs can't make it fun on a camp level. *(Violence, profanity, nudity, sexual situations, adult situations.)*

p, Fred Williamson; d, Fred Williamson; w, Charles Johnson; ph, David Blood; ed, Doug Bryan; m, Mike Logan

Action **(PR: O MPAA: R)**

STEPHEN KING'S SLEEPWALKERS ★½
91m Ion Pictures; Victor & Grais Productions ~ Columbia c

Brian Krause *(Charles Brady)*, Madchen Amick *(Tanya Robertson)*, Alice Krige *(Mary Brady)*, Jim Haynie *(Ira)*, Cindy Pickett *(Mrs. Robertson)*, Ron Perlman *(Captain Soames)*, Lyman Ward *(Mr. Robertson)*, Dan Martin *(Andy Simpson)*, Glenn Shadix *(Mr. Fallows)*, Cynthia Garris *(Laurie)*, Monty Bane *(Horace)*, John Landis *(Lab Technician)*, Joe Dante *(Lab Assistant)*, Stephen King *(Cemetery Caretaker)*, Clive Barker *(Forensic Tech)*, Tobe Hooper *(Forensic Tech)*, Frank Novak *(Deputy Sheriff)*, Rusty Schwimmer *(Housewife)*, O. Nicholas Brown *(Officer Wilbur)*, Ernie Lively *(Animal Control Officer)*, Bojesse Christopher *(Crawford)*, Lucy Boryer *(Jeanette)*, Judette Warren *(Carrie)*, Stuart Charno *(Police Photographer)*, Karl Bakke *(Police)*, Diane Delano *(Police)*, Roger Nolan *(Stenta)*, Joey Aresco *(Victor)*, Donald Petersen *(Boy with Ear Ache)*, Hayden Victor *(Little Girl at School Bus)*, Michael Reid Mackay *("Charles" Sleepwalker)*, Karyn Sercelj *("Mary" Sleepwalker)*

Jacques Tourneur's CAT PEOPLE was a sexy, stylish and evocative horror movie about . . . well, people who metamorphose into cats. No doubt bestselling horror writer Stephen King admires the film and, whether conciously or not, chose to pay homage when he wrote SLEEPWALKERS. But like Paul Schrader, who remade CAT PEOPLE in 1982, King is defeated by the silliness of the metaphor: monstrous transformation as an analog of lust. It takes a sure and light touch to navigate such treacherous thematic waters, and King's approach is all sledgehammer vulgarity.

Mary Brady (Alice Krige) and her son Charles (Brian Krause) seem like ideal neighbors. Attractive, intelligent and charming, they're an exotic addition to the population of tiny Travis, Indiana—just how exotic, they'd prefer no one ever know. The Bradys are "sleepwalkers," shape-shifting cat creatures who feed on the life-force of virgins, and they may be the last of their race. The bizarre biology of sleepwalkers makes their survival a complicated matter: Charles must drain his victims and feed his mother in an incestuous ritual. The business is complicated and dangerous; they must move constantly to escape detection. In addition, common house cats recognize them for the monsters they are. Wherever the sleepwalkers go, cats torment them, hissing and plotting feline wickedness.

Charles selects perky and virtuous Travis native Tanya Robertson (Madchen Amick) as his next quarry, and their first date—on which they go to a cemetery to take photographs, at her suggestion—takes a nightmarish turn. Stunned and horrified by Charles's transformation into a vicious creature, Tanya fights back, mortally wounding him and escaping into the arms of the confused police. Bent on vengeance, Mary kidnaps Tanya, but the girl manages to destroy her.

STEPHEN KING'S SLEEPWALKERS is an unusually stupid and tedious film that seems aimed at viewers who have never seen a horror movie and will therefore be shocked and surprised by the idea that such apparently nice people as Mary and Charles Brady could be murderous, shape-shifting energy vampires. That's not to say that shopworn ideas can't be made fresh and interesting, only that SLEEPWALKERS doesn't manage to do so. In fact, it hardly seems to try. The plot fairly oozes contemptuous disdain for the audience, trotting out hoary cliches tricked up with high-tech special effects as though viewers will be so dazzled by the surface that they won't care there's nothing underneath.

Among many absurdities, one is asked to accept that though Charles and Mary are ancient, cunning hunters, the former would impulsively kill his English teacher (a bloated lecher with perverted intentions, to be sure) and taunt a local cop (even changing form in front of him) despite their need not to draw attention to themselves, at least not until after they've fed successfully. Viewers are also asked to swallow the idea that cats can see through the sleepwalkers' human disguise, and that the sleepwalkers live in mortal terror of them. Yes, of cats. The sight of hundreds of kitties staked out on the Brady lawn, blinking and swishing their tails, is meant to be ominous. Instead, it's ludicrous, funny enough that one might be tempted to think SLEEPWALKERS is a particularly deadpan horror parody. But it's not. In fact, the film's tone is annoyingly inconsistant. While most of the film is played absolutely straight, the scene in which Charles tries to kill Tanya is played for an incongruous, sub-Freddy Kreuger humor that actually verges on the distasteful.

Released within weeks of THE LAWNMOWER MAN, which also prominently featured King's name in its advertising (in lieu of any other virtues that could be extolled), SLEEPWALKERS is yet another addition to the panoply of dreadful films to issue in one form or another from King's prolific pen. SLEEPWALKERS has the distinction of being his first original screenplay, but this amounts to very little.

King and a number of other notable figures in the world of horror—including writer-director Clive Barker (HELLRAISER) and directors Tobe Hooper (THE TEXAS CHAINSAW MASSACRE), Joe Dante (THE HOWLING) and John Landis (AN AMERICAN WEREWOLF IN LONDON)—make brief, gratuitous appearances in the film. They're all clumped together, so one can't even rationalize watching it all the way through in order to spot the cameos. *(Violence, sexual situations.)*

p, Mark Victor, Michael Grais, Nabeel Zahid; d, Mick Garris; w, Stephen King; ph, Rodney Charters; ed, O. Nicholas Brown; m, Nicholas Pike; prod d, John DeCuir, Jr.; art d, Sig Tinglof; set d, Bruce A. Gibeson

Horror **(PR: C MPAA: R)**

STOP! OR MY MOM WILL SHOOT ★★
81m Northern Lights Media Corporation; Wizan/Black Films; Ivan Reitman Productions; Universal ~ Universal c

Sylvester Stallone *(Sergeant Joe Bomowski)*, Estelle Getty *(Tutti Bomowski)*, JoBeth Williams *(Lieutenant Gwen Harper)*, Roger Rees *(Parnell)*, Martin Ferrero *(Paulie)*, Gailard Sartain *(Munroe)*, John Wesley *(Tony)*, Al Fann *(Lou)*, Ella Joyce *(McCabe)*, J. Kenneth Campbell *(Ross)*, Nicholas Sadler *(Suicide)*, Dennis Burkley *(Mitchell)*, Jana Arnold *(Mitchell's Girl)*, Christopher Collins *(Gang Member)*, Mark Mikesell *(Uniformed Cop)*, Matthew Powers *(Taxi Driver)*, Richard Schiff *(Gun Clerk)*, Brigitta Stenberg *(Stewardess)*, Vanessa Angel *(Stewardess)*, Marjean Holden *(Stewardess)*, Joey DePinto *(Sergeant Ray Ban)*, Larry Campbell, Shari Ballard, Kimberley LaMarque, Amy Kirkpatrick, J. David Krassner *(Detectives)*, Patti Yasutake *(TV Newscaster)*, Norm Compton *(Thug)*, Matt Johnston *(Thug)*, A Michael Lerner *(Thug)*, J.W. "Corkey" Fornof *(Pilot)*, Charles Renneisen *(Pilot)*, John Sarviss *(Helicopter Pilot)*, Roydon E. Clark, Manuel Perry, Ving Rhames, Justin Derosa *(Bad Guys)*, Ernie Lively *(Man at Airport)*, Richard Suggett *(Truck Driver)*, Art T. Yago *(Skycap)*, Julia Montgomery *(Secretary)*, Shelley Hill *(Secretary)*

This lightheaded, generally painless fluff earned some of the most hostile reviews of the year, as critics' cups ran over with venom, spewed primarily at star Sylvester Stallone. Lately Stallone's been trying to hack a pathway out of the RAMBO jungle and into more diverse roles, and STOP! OR MY MOM WILL SHOOT is a rather too-calculated career move.

LAPD Sergeant Joe Bomowski (Stallone) is one of filmdom's typical shoot-em-up maverick officers of the law. Bullets and car chases don't phase Joe, but he's shaken when his diminutive, widowed mother Tutti (Estelle Getty) pops into town for a surprise visit. Just as Joe feared, Tutti undermines his macho image by displaying baby portraits to anyone within reach and telling embarrassing stories about his childhood. She also nags Joe about his clothes, kvetches over his messy apartment and interferes in his on-again-off-again romance with his department superior, Lt. Gwen Harper (the usually reliable JoBeth Williams, setting the women's movement back a millenium with a dithery performance).

Tutti washes her son's monstrous revolver in detergent, rendering it clean and shiny and unusable. To replace it she innocently visits a dealer in illegal arms, just in time to witness the hood's murder by persons unknown. Naturally Tutti refuses to help the police unless her son is assigned to the investigation, so Joe has to cope with his mom tagging along through a non-taxing plot involving an evil financeer dabbling in weapons-smuggling and S&L fraud. A major clue turns out to be that one of his henchmen has a persistent sneeze—that's the level of the material. The villain is played by acclaimed thespian Roger Rees, a long way from his stage role as Dickens' Nicholas Nickleby. Rees joins a number of British actors imported to play suave bad guys in Yank actioners; lately one must look no further than the first suspect with proper manners and diction to identify the criminal mastermind.

Even he's left alive at the end of this one, making STOP! OR MY MOM WILL SHOOT fairly mild in the violence department. Apart from a great dual on the tarmac between a getaway plane and a truck, the sequences are nothing spectacular, just done well enough to keep buffs amused; ditto the comedy. Stallone has long exercised humor both in the ROCKY series and his previous OSCAR, so there's really no novelty here, except for a nightmare bit showing the emasculated hero finding himself in a diaper again. That's a sight. Estelle Getty, popular on TV's geriatric sitcom "The Golden Girls," is okay as the busybody parent, stopping a hair short of Mr. Magoo style caricature. The doting-mother jokes are all familiar, but rendered with an earnest quality, as though a parent-offspring mediation group is to convene after the film ends.

This is Stallone striving to duplicate Arnold Schwarzenegger's KINDERGARTEN COP feat, cross-breeding a violent screen persona with cutesy sitcom farce. In both movies the brawny stars have it both ways, brandishing their big guns in outbursts of bloody mayhem, then counterpointing with warm, cuddly family fun. In Arnold's case the latter was a romp with a mob of unruly toddlers; Sylvester gets his yocks by sharing scenes with a meddlesome little old lady.

Both vehicles were produced by Ivan Reitman (GHOSTBUSTERS, LEGAL EAGLES), whose blockbuster comedies sometimes stretch themselves thin to appeal to the broadest possible audience. Although STOP! OR MY MOM WILL SHOOT took a pounding from critics, it did moderate business in theaters. *(Violence, profanity.)*

p, Ivan Reitman, Joe Medjuck, Michael C. Gross; d, Roger Spottiswoode; w, Blake Snyder, William Osborne, William Davies; ph, Frank Tidy; ed, Mark Conte, Lois Freeman-Fox; m, Alan Silvestri; prod d, Charles Rosen; art d, Diane Yates; set d, Don Remacle; cos, Marie France

Comedy/Action **(PR: C MPAA: PG-13)**

STORYVILLE ★½
110m Storyville Inc.; Davis Entertainment; Smart Egg-Cinema Enterprises Ltd; Grand Bay Films ~ Fox c

James Spader *(Cray Fowler)*, Joanne Whalley-Kilmer *(Natalie Tate)*, Jason Robards *(Clifford Fowler)*, Charlotte Lewis *(Lee Tran)*, Michael Warren *(Nathan LeFleur)*, Michael Parks *(Michael Trevallian)*, Chuck McCann *(Pudge Herman)*, Charles Haid *(Abe Choate)*, Chino Fats Williams *(Theotis Washington)*, Woody Strode *(Charlie Sumpter)*, Jeff Perry *(Peter Dandridge)*, Galyn Gorg *(Spice)*, Justine Arlin *(Melanie Fowler)*, Piper Laurie *(Constance Fowler)*, George Kee Cheung *(Xang Tran)*, Philip Carter *(Avner Hollister)*, Ron Gural *(Librarian)*, Fred Lewis *(Bennett Jones)*, Graham Timbes *(Sam Honess)*, Steve Forrest *(Judge Quentin Murdoch)*, Lionel Ferbos *(St. Alban's Pastor)*, Bernard Zette *(Tom Plunkett)*, Sally Ann Roberts *(Commentator)*, Jim Gleeson *(Lawyer)*

On the evidence of STORYVILLE, director and coscreenwriter Mark Frost seems to have learned all the wrong lessons from David Lynch, his partner on TV's "Twin Peaks." Frost's debut feature is a dippy, slow-moving exercise in Southern Fried tedium.

The scion of a powerful Louisiana political family, Cray Fowler (James Spader) is running his first election campaign. About to be divorced from his wife after she was caught in some compromising positions by a detective's still camera, Fowler is tempted by the advances of an exotic waitress, Lee Tran (Charlotte Lewis), at a fundraiser. At a later assignation in the French Quarter of New Orleans, he wrestles with her aikido-style before they slip into the hot tub, as a strategically placed video camera records everything. When Fowler wakes up, the waitress's father lies dead at the foot of the bed. Lee, who is nowhere to be seen, is charged in the killing, despite the fact that Fowler's fingerprints are all over the murder weapon and that his antics have been recorded on video.

In an attempt to save Lee and prevent the public airing of his dirty laundry, Fowler, a lawyer by training, steps forward to defend her, pitting himself against yet another object of his desire, sexy District Attorney Natalie Tate (Joanne Whalley-Kilmer). Fowler wins the case rather too easily, by producing a surprise witness in the middle of Natalie's cross-examination of

Lee. But his real agenda is to get to those who set him up in the first place. These include all the usual suspects, ranging from his political opponent to family patriarch Clifford Fowler (Jason Robards), who hatched the video scheme to keep Cray under his thumb. (Years earlier, it turns out, Clifford murdered Cray's father to prevent the airing of an earlier generation of family dirt involving bogus real-estate deeds.)

Getting through STORYVILLE's byzantine plot becomes a struggle to stay awake, as endless boring conversations and stifling set pieces are topped off by one of the dopiest courtroom climaxes in cinema history.

Frost tries to make everything moody and atmospheric but the results are strictly soporific; as a result, it's easier to isolate what's right about the film than to count the many ways in which it goes wrong. Ron Garcia's cinematography and Carter Burwell's score establish a convincing initial mood of menace. From an acting viewpoint, the film's only genuine heat comes from Whalley-Kilmer (SHATTERED, CROSSING THE LINE). Shoehorned into a succession of tight-fitting outfits, she contributes the jolt of lustful naughtiness that STORYVILLE otherwise lacks but is so desperately trying to achieve.

Otherwise, the actors seem hobbled by a flat, amateurish screenplay that is endlessly telling what it should be showing and relentlessly predictable in its unfolding. Seasoned veterans like Piper Laurie, Robards and Woody Strode put in listless one-or two-scene guest spots. Lewis—for some reason made up to look like the mysterious Asian character played by Joan Chen in "Twin Peaks"—is less enigmatic than alarmingly thin. Spader, meanwhile, sleepwalks through his role, offering us what seems like the umpteenth version of his wounded yuppie character. To be fair, he may just be caught in the general vortex of boredom that is STORYVILLE. *(Violence, profanity, nudity, adult situations.)*

p, David Roe, Edward R. Pressman; d, Mark Frost; w, Mark Frost, Lee Reynolds, (from the book *Juryman* by Frank Galbally and Robert Macklin); ph, Ron Garcia; ed, B.J. Sears; m, Carter Burwell; prod d, Richard Hoover; art d, Kathleen M. McKernin; set d, Brian Kasch; cos, Louise Frogley

Drama/Mystery **(PR: O MPAA: R)**

STRAIGHT TALK ★★

90m Robert Chartoff Productions; Hollywood; Sandollar Productions ~ BV c

Dolly Parton *(Shirlee Kenyon)*, James Woods *(Jack Russell)*, Griffin Dunne *(Alan)*, Michael Madsen *(Steve)*, Deirdre O'Connell *(Lily)*, John Sayles *(Guy Girardi)*, Teri Hatcher *(Janice)*, Spalding Gray *(Dr. Erdman)*, Jerry Orbach *(Milo Jacoby)*, Philip Bosco *(Gene Perlman)*, Charles Fleischer *(Tony)*, Keith MacKechnie *(Gordon)*, Jay Thomas *(Zim Zimmerman)*, Amy Morton *(Ann)*, Paula Newsome *(Ellen)*, Ralph Foody *(Desk Clerk)*, Robin Eurich *(Bill)*, Jeff Garlin *(Bob)*, Paul Dinello *(Casey)*, Barnet Kellman *(Director)*, Robert Kurcz *(Phil)*, Ray Toler *(Man at Strip Joint)*, Michael Oppenheimer *(Maitre d')*, Michael Jeffrey Woods *(Photographer)*, Tom Amandes *(1st Waiter)*, John Gegenhuber *(2nd Waiter)*, James Spinks *(1st Bartender)*, Greg Sobieski *(2nd Bartender)*, Scott Benjaminson *(Valet)*, Tom Webb *(Newscaster)*, Peter Sova *(Cabbie)*, Roger S. Christiansen *(Technical Director)*, Mary Ann Thebus *(Waitress)*, Alan Wilder *(Snake Man)*, Domenica Cameron-Scorsese *(1st Girl)*, Dana Lubotsky *(2nd Girl)*, Becky Wahlstrom *(3rd Girl)*, Tony Judge *(Officer)*, Susan Philpot *(Librarian)*, Dionne Lynn Nosek *(P.A.)*, Kate Buddeke *(Tina)*, Tracy Letts *(Sean)*, Jane Lynch *(Gladys)*, Anthony Cannata *(Bud)*, Joyce Hiller Piven *(Joan)*, Lorenzo Clemons *(Mr. Isaacs)*, Ron Livingston *(Soldier)*, Ray Friedeck *(Mr. Polonsky)*, Etel Billig *(Thelma)*, Irma P. Hall *(Ethel)*, Gilmary Doyle *(1st Fan)*, Jack Walsh *(Guard)*, Susan Messing *(Makeup Girl)*

Dolly Parton sweeps the windy city off its feet as a radio "psychologist" dispensing down-home wisdom in STRAIGHT TALK, a pleasant but lackluster romantic comedy from Hollywood Pictures.

Shirlee Kenyon (Parton) gets fired from her smalltown dance hall and fed up with her oafish boyfriend, Steve (Michael Madsen), on the same day. She moves to Chicago and, in response to a want ad for a radio station receptionist, stumbles into a studio where a newly hired shrink has failed to show up for air time. Shirlee gets mistaken for the missing psychologist and takes over the show, charming callers and listeners alike with her commonsense advice. The problem is that the station owner, Gene Perlman (Philip Bosco), has insisted on a bona fide Ph.D. to fill the slot, so the groveling station manager, Alan (Griffin Dunne), makes Shirlee over into "Dr." Shirlee.

Shirlee's ascendance attracts the attention of reporter Jack Russell (James Woods), who had bumped into her soon after she arrived in Chicago and knows the truth about her "credentials." Getting close to her in preparation for an expose, Russell instead falls for Shirlee and quits his paper rather than write his story. Shirlee, meanwhile, has had enough of living a lie, especially when it seems that some of her pat advice has caused a family breakup. On her premiere show for a nationwide radio network, she confesses the truth and flees the studio. Overwhelming popular demand, however, leads Shirlee back to her job and back into Russell's arms.

A half-baked attempt at Frank Capra-style sentimentality, STRAIGHT TALK is a populist comedy without any people in it. Despite being continually reminded of Shirlee's runaway popularity, the most we ever see of her fans is in one half-hearted street-crowd scene. Though filmed on location in Chicago, the film feels cramped and setbound. The performances are competent all around, but never inspired. The usually intense Woods makes little impact and even the ever-ebullient Parton seems barely interested. Dunne is funny, perhaps because he's the only character in the film with any personality.

In short, STRAIGHT TALK plays like a TV pilot (which should come as no surprise, since director Barnet Kellman also guided MURPHY BROWN through its first three seasons). In typical pilot fashion, the film introduces its key characters, concocts some mild complications to be unwound by the last reel and sends everyone home smiling. But it also seems to be holding back, as if it were getting ready for a long run. It has no real lows, but no real highs either; it has some cornpone humor, for Parton's core audience, but never turns into "Hee Haw"; Parton's songs can be heard over the soundtrack, but she never actually sings; STRAIGHT TALK has conversations sprinkled with effective one-liners, but it stops short of wit. And it is never, ever, pointed. In this context, the idea that Shirlee is single, sexually active and unapologetic about it seems downright subversive.

STRAIGHT TALK is yet another Hollywood attempt to recapture the feel of a vintage studio film, in this case a Capra comedy. But the result is so bland and toothless that it makes even mediocre Capra feel fiery by comparison. *(Adult situations.)*

p, Robert Chartoff, Fred Berner; d, Barnet Kellman; w, Craig Bolotin, Patricia Resnick, (from the story by Bolotin); ph, Peter Sova; ed, Michael Tronick; m, Brad Fiedel; prod d, Jeffrey Townsend; art d, Michael T. Perry; cos, Jodie Tillen

Comedy/Romance **(PR: A MPAA: PG)**

STRANGER AMONG US, A ★★

111m Sandollar/Isis Productions; Touchwood Pacific Partners I; Propaganda Films; Hollywood ~ BV c

Melanie Griffith *(Emily Eden)*, Eric Thal *(Ariel)*, John Pankow *(Levine)*, Tracy Pollan *(Mara)*, Lee Richardson *(Rebbe)*, Mia Sara *(Leah)*, Jamey Sheridan *(Nick Kemp)*, Jake Weber *(Yaakov)*, Ro'ee Levi *(Mendel)*, David Rosenbaum *(Mr. Klausman)*, Ruth Vool *(Mrs. Klausman)*, David Margulies *(Lieutenant Oliver)*, Ed Rogers, III *(Detective Tedford)*, Maurice Schell *(Detective Marden)*, James Gandolfini *(Tony Baldessari)*, Chris Collins *(Chris Baldessari)*, Burtt Harris *(Emily's Father)*, Ira Rubin *(French Rebbe)*, Francoise Granville *(French Rebbitzen)*, Rena Sofer *(Shayna)*, Shifra Lerer *(1st Yiddish Woman)*, Eleanor Reissa *(2nd Yiddish Woman)*, James Lovelett *(File Room Clerk)*, Jack Gill *(Zap Goon)*, Steve Hamilton *(Paramedic)*, Paul Zim *(Cantor)*, Drew Eliot *(Inspector)*, Alexander Pasmur, Jr. *(Klausman Son)*, John Louis Fischer *(Yussell)*, Jack Beers *(Rebbe's Assistant)*

Melanie Griffith stars as a tough New York police detective who gets religion when she goes undercover in the Brooklyn Hasidic community in Sidney Lumet's A STRANGER AMONG US. An unlikely crossbreeding of WITNESS and SISTER ACT, the film initially lives up to its ridiculous premise but actually gets better as it goes along.

Emily Eden (Griffith) is a maverick policewoman who likes to live on the edge but tends to get other people hurt; her partner, Nick Kemp (Jamey Sheridan), with whom she is "in deep lust," takes a knife in the stomach during a bust in which Eden decided not to call for back-up. Deciding that Eden may be strung a little too tightly, her sergeant assigns her to an apparently less troublesome case. She is sent to investigate the disappearance of a young Hasidic diamond cutter, who has vanished with diamonds worth three-quarters of a million dollars. Eden at first sees an open-and-shut case, but the plot thickens with the discovery of the diamond cutter's body stuffed behind the ceiling panels in his shop.

Eden decides to go undercover in the religious community to ferret out the killer, who may be among them. In the process, she develops a strong attraction for Ariel (Eric Thal), a Talmudic scholar who is already betrothed and who has his future carved out for him as a religious leader. Although dating, much less marriage, is completely out of the question, the attraction is mutual. Ariel begins breaking what Eden calls his "big rule" by visiting her without a chaperone, though their relationship remains platonic. Unexpectedly, Eden finds herself getting in touch with her spirituality through her contact with the Hasidim. Nevertheless, her initial suspicions prove to be true; the killer truly is among them, in the person of Mara (Tracy Pollan), a recent "convert" to conservative Judaism who had been engaged to the dead man.

Long before its release, A STRANGER AMONG US was dubbed "Vitness" by industry wags; one early review described it as a film about Hasidic Jews menaced by a vicious killer and too much Rembrandt lighting. At first, director Lumet and star Griffith seem determined to confirm the worst. The lighting, indeed, is so pretentiously Old Master-like in the scenes involving the Hassidim that one keeps expecting the camera to pull back and show an art class working feverishly at their canvasses. Griffith's initial credibility as a New York cop is also sorely lacking, especially given her tendency to show up at work dressed more for lunch at the Plaza than busting bad guys.

Fortunately, though, A STRANGER AMONG US gets better as it goes along. The characters take on depth as they approach the finish line, and the action becomes more engrossing—if also more implausable—as the plot develops. What starts as the search for a killer eventually becomes a surprisingly moving quest for spiritual wholeness. At the end of the film, nobody gets what they want, though most get what they either need or deserve.

After portraying some memorably corrupt cops in Q&A, Lumet presents Eden as the equivalent of a religious leader—someone whose experience with evil has both hardened her soul and opened her eyes. After a rocky start, Griffith pulls off the part beautifully, showing the character's awakening in small increments. Writer and co-producer Robert J. Avrech, whose last screenplay for Griffith was Brian DePalma's BODY DOUBLE, here does a fine job of delineating the tension between the worlds of the flesh and the spirit. Despite the high-concept kitchiness of its premise, A STRANGER AMONG US is a satisfying drama with genuine star quality at its core. *(Violence, profanity.)*

p, Steve Golin, Sigurjon Sighvatsson, Howard Rosenman; d, Sidney Lumet; w, Robert J. Avrech; ph, Andrzej Bartkowiak; ed, Andrew Mondshein; m, Jerry Bock; prod d, Philip Rosenberg; art d, Steven Graham; set d, Gary Brink; cos, Gary Jones, Ann Roth

Crime/Drama **(PR: C MPAA: PG-13)**

STREET CRIMES ★★½

94m PM Entertainment ~ PM Home Video c

Dennis Farina *(Brian O'Neal)*, Max Gail *(Flannigan)*, Mike Worth *(Tony Carter)*, Patricia Zehentmayr *(Susan O'Neal)*, James T. Morris *(Gerardo)*

Entertaining but nondescript and predictable, STREET CRIMES attempts to combine kick-boxing, urban gang violence and other elements of more hardcore action films with the tale of a young cop coming of age in troubled downtown Los Angeles.

Rookie policeman Tony Carter (Mike Worth) is taken under the wing of his partner, the seasoned veteran Brian O'Neal (Dennis Farina) as they combat prostitution, street crime and particularly a drug ring run by a Black gang led by Gerardo (James T. Morris). In attempting to quell Hispanic gang warfare, Tony is challenged to a kickboxing match by Jimmy (Ron Winston Yuan), which Tony wins, although the two eventually become friends. The bouts soon become regular events, with more cops joining in, becoming a positive force on the violence-splattered neighborhood. O'Neal helps fix up a community center, and the residents, seeing their neighborhood becoming less violent, pitch in, too.

Gerardo, however, sees this bonding as a threat to his drug business and begins harassing Tony, with whom he grew up, eventually killing Jimmy and kidnapping Susan (Patricia Zehentmayr), O'Neal's blind daughter, with whom Tony, fulfilling O'Neal's worst fears, has fallen in love. Tony and O'Neal rescue Susan, and Tony bests Gerardo in a brutal kickboxing showdown. As everyone files into the gym to celebrate, Tony ponders the beaten Gerardo's final words, that however strong the cops-neighborhood relationship is now, it eventually will "not make a difference."

Written by Stephen Smoke, who also directed, STREET CRIMES is strictly formula fare, but it downplays the usual genre violence and nudity in welcome favor of socially redeeming themes, which is also unusual in the tough action films of the seasoned low-budget production team of Charla Driver, Joseph Mehri and Richard Pepin (THE ART OF DYING, RING OF FIRE, A TIME TO DIE). Smoke's direction is adequate but routine, although the kickboxing bouts, both in and out of the ring, are well choreographed by Art Camacho. The acting is above average, especially by Farina (a former Chicago cop best known from TV's "Crime Stories") as a tough-tender cop still grieving for his wife and now in danger of "losing" his daughter to however worthy a suitor. *(Violence, profanity.)*

p, Charla Driver, Joseph Mehri, Richard Pepin; d, Stephen Smoke; w, Stephen Smoke; ph, Richard Pepin; ed, Ron Cabreros, Geraint Bell; m, John Gonzalez; prod d, Scott Maginnis; cos, Diana Phipps

Action/Crime/Martial Arts **(PR: C MPAA: R)**

SUNSET STRIP ★★

95m Contact Films ~ PM Home Video c

Michelle Foreman *(Heather)*, Jeff Conaway *(Tony)*, Shelley Michelle *(Veronica)*, Cameron *(Crystal)*, Gino Dentie *(Jack)*, Jerry Winsett *(Ted)*, Paul Bond *(David)*, Michelle Clunie *(Jonsey)*, Lori Jo Hendrix *(Tammy)*, Trisha Giallela *(Burn)*, Tim Abell *(Jerry)*, Brigitte Butler *(Candice)*, Helen Costa *(Eva)*, Jeff Miller *(Jimmy)*, Robert Leol *(Michael)*, Allison Cuffe *(Lori)*

Directed by Paul G. Volk, SUNSET STRIP is a formulaic, bargain-basement version of FLASHDANCE.

Heather (Michelle Foreman) lands a job at an LA striptease club in order to hone her dancing skills while she prepares for a dance contest. Nervous at first, Heather eventually gets used to performing in the rowdy, smoke-filled joint. She quickly befriends Crystal (Cameron), Jonsey (Michelle Clunie) and the other dancers. From here on, the movie basically jumps back and forth from Heather in dance class to Heather at the club—with literally half the film resembling a how-to video on striptease dancing. In between all of this, Heather gets involved with the suave club owner Tony (Jeff Conaway). And when the day of the big competition comes around, Heather wins the dance scholarship.

The characters in SUNSET STRIP are undeveloped, and consequently not sympathetic. But the actors manage to do a competent job with the material they've been given. (Nick Stone wrote the screenplay.) However, the film has several scenes which are photographed well by Ken Blakey. Particularly impressive is the b&w, slow-motion, flashback sequence wherein Heather, stripping for the first time, freezes up and then runs out of the club humiliated.

But in the final analysis, SUNSET STRIP is predictable and shamelessly structured after FLASHDANCE. Everything from the talk Heather has with the retired burlesque dancer, to the final scene at the dance competition, is modeled after the 1983 Jennifer Beals smash. *(Violence, partial nudity, sexual situations.)*

p, Nancee Borgnine; d, Paul G. Volk; w, Nick Stone; ph, Ken Blakey; ed, Paul G. Volk, John Gilbert; m, John Gonzalez; prod d, Richard Dearborn; cos, Christine Boudreaux

Drama **(PR: C MPAA: R)**

SUPERCOP: POLICE STORY III ★★★

(Hong Kong) 96m Golden Way ~ Golden Harvest Films Ltd. c

Jackie Chan *(Chen Chia-chu)*, Michelle Yeaoh *(Director Yang)*, Maggie Cheung *(May)*, Tsang Kong *(Big Brother Wei)*, Yuen Wah *(Panther)*, Lo Lieh *(The General)*, Tung Biao, Koo Kei-wah

With this second sequel to his enormously popular POLICE STORY, Jackie Chan edges ever closer to matching American action films in scope, even if his budgets are lower. This one cost $10 million, paltry by US standards but megabucks for a Hong Kong film, and one can only wish that the care lavished on the stunt sequences had been applied to the screenplay as well.

Chan reprises his role as Chan Chia-chu, who is drafted by his Hong Kong superiors to be the "supercop" requested by the police force in mainland China. They need someone to help them bring down an international drug ring run by Big Brother Wei (Tsang Kong), and Chan seems to fit the bill. But first, he must prove himself to Chinese police director Yang (Michelle Yeaoh), and does so in a martial arts duel with the best fighter on her squad. He then goes undercover in a prison camp, where he helps Wei's younger brother, known as "The Panther" (Yuen Wah) "escape" from the place. After some initial doubt, Wei's gang accepts Chan into their midst, but soon it looks like his cover might be blown. Chan has claimed to have family in a nearby town, and it just so happens that the gang will be shortly be passing by that very village. When he is forced to introduce the villains to his "family," Chan is surprised and relieved to find Yang and others on the force already there, posing as his fictitious relatives.

After a blazing firefight between the police and the gang at the villain's jungle fortress on the Thailand-Malaysia border, the action moves to a Malaysian resort hotel—where Chan's girlfriend May (Maggie Cheung) just happens to be vacationing in his absence. Spotting Chan at the hotel, and unable to get a straight answer about why he's there, May assumes that he is cheating on her. But then she winds up blowing his cover, and the gang, who plan to assassinate a prominent official in the city, take her hostage. Chan manages to rescue May, and then takes off after the escaping villains. The result is a chase by car, helicopter and finally atop a moving train, onto which Yang jumps by motorcycle to assist Chan in bringing down the bad guys.

SUPERCOP: POLICE STORY III shares many of the strengths and weaknesses of many of Chan's latter-day films. After he moved away from the big-budget, pure martial arts films that made his name (including the amazing PROJECT A, which remains one of the best kung-fu films ever made), his movies became more dependent on plot and big-scale stunts than his incredible hand-to-hand combat choreography. Like ARMOR OF GOD (another Chan title to get US exposure recently), POLICE STORY III is overly dependent on plot for the first two-thirds, and the action doesn't come as enjoyably thick and fast as in his all-martial-arts fests. But, as in most Asian genre films, the final half-hour makes it all worthwhile, and what makes Chan's work continually astonishing is that the actor does all his own stunts.

The movie also benefits from Chan's considerable comic skills—he's always incorporated humor into his films, and isn't afraid to be the butt of the jokes—and from costar Yeaoh, who proves to be every bit the martial artist he is. In fact, she may be the best of all the female sidekicks that have populated recent action films, treated with neither overt sensitivity nor sentimentality; she gets knocked down and jumps up again as much as Chan, and rarely gets into situations where she's dependent on him to save her. The scene in which Chan takes on Yang's best fighter, surprisingly and disappointingly, is done with sped-up visuals, but the action gets better as it goes along, culminating in the astonishing, extended final sequence that ends atop the speeding train. It's incredible stuff that takes the breath away. And, as usual, the film ends with outtakes of Chan and Yang getting into alternately funny and painful-looking accidents in the course of doing the action scenes. *(Violence.)*

p, Willie Chan, Tang King-sung; d, Stanley Tong; w, Tang King-sung, Ma Mei-ping, Lee Wei-yee; ph, Lam Kwok-wah; ed, Cheunng Yaeo-chung, Cheung Kai-fei; m, Lee Chun shing; art d, Oliver Wong; cos, Hung Wei-Chuk; stunts, Stanley Tong

Action/Crime/Martial Arts **(PR: C MPAA: NR)**

SWOON ★★½

90m Intolerance Productions; American Playhouse Theatrical Films ~ Fine Line Features bw

Daniel Schlachet *(Richard Loeb)*, Craig Chester *(Nathan Leopold, Jr.)*, Ron Vawter *(State's Attorney Crowe)*, Michael Kirby *(Detective Savage)*, Michael Stumm *(Doctor Bowman)*, Valda Z. Drabla *(Germaine Reinhardt)*, Natalie Stanford *(Susan Lurie)*, Isabela Araujo, Jill Buchanan, Mona Foot, Trash, Trasharama, Nashom Wooden *(Venus in Furs Divas)*, Peter Bowen *(Industrial Area Workman)*, Ryan Landry *(Ivory)*, Christopher Hoover *(Elektra Luxe)*, Paul Connor *(Bobby Franks)*, Brent Charleton *(Irving Hartman)*, Christopher Cangelosi *(Little Boy in Park)*, Dick Callaghan *(Country Workman)*, Craig Paull *(Country Workman)*, Carlos Rodriguez *(Country Workman)*, Emmitt Thrower *(Country Workman)*, Eric J. Wiggins, III *(Country Workman)*, Ken Howarth *(Sven Englund)*, Barry Liebowitz *(Mr. Franks)*, Judith Boxley *(Mrs. Franks)*, Julian Marynczak *(Workman in Marsh)*, Daniel Haughey *(Ornithologist)*, John Rowan *(Man With Newspaper)*, Stanley Taub *(Mr. Loeb)*, Robert Austin *(Allan Loeb)*, Barbara Bleier *(Mrs. Loeb)*, Ed Altman *(Mike Leopold)*, John A. Mudd *(Detective Sbarbaro)*, Robert Sullivan *(Night Desk Officer)*, Verne F. Hoyt *(Night Cop)*, James Cummings *(Interrogation Cop)*, Pepe Vives *(Night Detective)*, Malcolm A. Beers, Jr. *(Nathan Leopold, Jr.)*, Adina Porter *(Stenographer)*, Robert Read *(Clarence Darrow)*, Paul Schmidt *(Judge Caverly)*, Richard Elovich *(Doctor Hulbert)*, Christie MacFadyen *(Reporter)*, Robert McKanna *(Reporter)*, Bobby Reed *(Reporter)*, Mark Simpson *(Bailiff)*, Ray Wasik *(Mean Prison Guard)*, Jim Crawford *(Prison Barber)*, Jean Claude Monfort, Michael Nesline, Richard R. Upton, William Walters *(Clinic Doctors)*, Richard Schechner *(Radio Announcer)*, Burt Wright *(Warden)*, Glenn Backes *(James Day)*, Paul Rubin *(Father Weir)*, Philip Stanton *(Gene Lovitz)*, Dean C. Blanco, Catarina Borelli, Barry Cassidy, David Cheever, James Crafford, Steven Flum, Lou Galiardo, Carl M. George, Debra Goodman, Joseph Harding, Anna Kohler, Heidi Kriz, Scott K. Macarthur, John McGee, Dana Nasrallah, Jerome F. Richards, Hobson Sturtevant, Elizabeth Towson *(Courtroom Extras)*, Oscar Aleman, Emanuel Baetich, Robert Beck, Mike Diaz, Maddy Lederman, Tanya Taylor *(Press Conference Extras)*, Gary Lamadore *(Interrogation Cop)*, Michael Becker, Zoe Bissell, Gregg Bordowitz, Patricia Fabricant, Todd Haynes, Andrea Kislan, Pamela Koffler, Craig Paull, Nina Port, Emily Sherman, Lauren Zalaznick *(Phrenology Heads)*, Robert Funes, Timothy McCoy, Owen H. Ranft, Elion Sacker, Robert Vazquez, Alex Vean *(Prisoners)*, Addison Cook *(Prison Guard)*, Douglas Leland *(Prison Guard)*, John Ventimiglia *(Prison Guard)*, Douglas Crimp *(Prison Mugshot)*, Phelim Dolan *(Prison Mugshot)*, Jim Lyons *(Prison Mugshot)*

Hip to the nth degree and so self-conscious it verges on the suffocating, SWOON takes its inspiration in equal parts from 1924's sensational Leopold and Loeb case and Harlem drag balls by way of Madonna.

Wealthy Chicago teenagers Nathan Leopold, Jr. (Craig Chester) and Richard Loeb (Daniel Schlachet) are smart, spoiled and bored. They're embroiled in an intense, secret affair, whose fervor places them on a collision course with the straightlaced mores of middle America. They're outsiders on every level: homosexual in a family dominated culture, Jews in the Protestant midwest and sensualists in a bourgeois America that values puritan conformity above all else.

These two precocious teens intellectualize their outlaw sexuality into philosophical alienation, and begin to commit petty criminal acts—arson, vandalism—of escalating seriousness; eventually they kill fourteen-year-old Bobby Franks. Though they've planned a "perfect murder," the badly concealed body is quickly found and Loeb's glasses, uncovered nearby, lead the police to them. The two are arrested; under questioning, Loeb confesses and they're tried amidst vicious public opprobrium. State's Attorney Crowe (Ron Vawter) helps turn the trial into a prurient spectacle, hinting darkly about sexual sadism; Leopold and Loeb's smirking, superior attitudes both titillate and outrage the public and the media. Though they escape the death penalty, both go to prison, where Loeb is murdered. As a middle-aged man, Leopold is eventually released, marries and dies in obscurity.

The Leopold and Loeb case contained all the elements necessary to shock America in the 20s, the same elements that would make it into a true-crime bestseller today. The victim was an innocent child, the suspects educated and not connected to the criminal element. But more importantly, Leopold and Loeb lent (and lend) themselves to treatment as outsiders: wealthy Jewish homosexuals who may *look* like us, but are somehow safely, irrevocably different. That difference is at the heart of SWOON.

The case has inspired two movies before SWOON: Alfred Hitchcock's ROPE and Richard Fleischer's COMPULSION. As examinations of the case both were hampered by an inability to speak frankly about the conceptions of homosexuality that informed both the behavior of the two young men and the public reaction to their crime. But SWOON's writer and director, Tom Kalin, intends far more than a more factually correct recreation of a sordid murder case; though treated at the time as the crime of the century, by contemporary standards it's all (sadly) tame stuff and hardly merits another once over from the atrocity standpoint. Kalin instead weaves a dense and often beautiful net of allusions to ideas about homosexuality—social, scientific, philosophical and aesthetic—and traps Leopold and Loeb (or Babe and Dickie, as they call one another) within its meshes. Informed by radical gay politics and suffused with a strangled romanticism, SWOON is simultaneously provocative and infuriating, too intelligent to dismiss, but too enthralled by its own cleverness to escape being precious.

Shot in crisp, sparkling b&w, SWOON has the look of a too-cool-for-its-own-good jeans commercial, all avant-garde angles and compositional devices at the service of venal commerce. Kalin's sparse evocation of Chicago 70 years ago is a triumph of invention over budget. With little more than a period car and some strangely timeless clothing (the cloche hats reflect the appropriate period, but the suits wouldn't look out of place on today's streets), he suggests a stiffer, more proper America, one in which the words "sexual" and "politics" could never have been used in the same sentence and social rebellion had yet to acquire a marketable cachet. SWOON argues that with no models for living their lives as gay men, Leopold and Loeb were doomed; their sexual orientation isolated them from society, while their coddled upbringings prevented them from forging independent identities outside the mainstream. Craig Chester and Daniel Schlachet's performances as Leopold and Loeb are a particular asset, suggesting the mutable form of desire, and the power it wields in all its manifestations.

Kalin's use of anachronism (a touch-tone phone, a walkman, a newspaper with no date), which recalls the work of Derek Jarman (CARAVAGGIO, EDWARD II), seems designed to suggest the continuing relevance of SWOON's preoccupations—the ways in which sexuality determines social integration, the conflict between the public and the private self, the transformation of thwarted lust into anti-social behavior—but isn't used consistently enough. Its isolated manifestations just look wrong, and break the movie's often hypnotic spell. The same is true of the appearances by the "Venus in Furs Divas," an assortment of campily outfitted men in drag and women who *look* like men in drag reciting sado-masochistic verse. The device screams "formalism," but to what end?

SWOON is an intelligent, thoughtful piece of filmmaking, and its flaws do not diminish its achievement. The Leopold and Loeb case has been popularly thought of as an example of what can happen when bright but morally underdeveloped young men fall under the sway of Nietzchean philosophy, and SWOON returns philosophy to the bedroom, arguing persuasively that sexuality—in its social implications, as well as its private manifestations—is at the root of all behavior. *(Sexual situations, adult situations.)*

p, Christine Vachon; d, Tom Kalin; w, Tom Kalin, Hilton Als; ph, Ellen Kuras; ed, Tom Kalin; m, James Bennett; prod d, Therese Deprez; set d, Stacey Jones; cos, Jessica Haston

Drama/Crime/Historical (PR: C MPAA: NR)

TALONS OF THE EAGLE ★★

(Canada) 96m Film One Productions ~ MCA/Universal Home Video c

Billy Blanks *(Tyler Wilson)*, Jalal Merhi *(Michael Reed)*, James Hong *(Mr. Li)*, Priscilla Barnes *(Cassandra)*, Pan Qing Fu *(Himself)*, Eric Lee *(Bodyguard)*, Harry Mok *(Niko)*, Matthias Hues *(Khan)*, Kelly Gallant *(Tara)*

This subpar action film boasts a deficient screenplay and downright clumsy direction, although the martial arts sequences, choreographed by TALONS OF THE EAGLE's two stars and Pan Qing Fu are decent.

New York City DEA agent Tyler Wilson (Billy Blanks) is transferred to Toronto to help local cop Michael Reed (Jalal Mehri) bust up the powerful drug ring of Mr. Li (James Hong). The boys first undergo rigorous training to master the lethal "Eagle Claw" martial arts technique as practiced by Master Pan (Pan Qing Fu). Posing as entrants in Mr. Li's kickboxing tournament, a hobby partly devised to keep his brutal top bodyguard Khan (Matthias Hues) in shape and amused, Wilson and Reed impress Li enough (they save his life from an assassin) to gain $5,000-per-week jobs in Li's glitzy nightclub, an "adult playground" catering to Toronto's elite judges, politicians, businessman and the social set with prostitution and gambling.

The club is run by Li's girlfriend Cassandra (Priscilla Barnes), who is an undercover agent and quickly falls for Reed. The final-reel parade of battles features Wilson, Reed and Cassandra, aided by Master Pan's army of students, taking on and demolishing Khan, secondary Li bodyguards (Eric Lee, Henry Mok) and Li's cutthroat army, while the drug king himself is subdued by Reed, arrested and carted off to jail.

Kennedy's biggest failing, unfortunately a crucial one, is the final melee, which goes on far too long and is absolutely unsuspenseful, despite its staging in the candy-colored nightclub which is rigged to explode in five minutes. The pairing of Blanks (one of the few Black actors in the genre, who usually plays villains in more mainstream films like THE LAST BOY SCOUT) and Merhi (who also produced) is disastrous; both have done better previous work. Their combination herein seems to emphasize each other's already meager acting talents, and their attempt at LETHAL WEAPON-style wisecracking repartee falls pitifully flat.

The veteran Hong and the monstrously hulking blond Hues make fine villains. After a hiatus in her career, Barnes (THE LAST MARRIED COUPLE IN AMERICA, LICENCE TO KILL), who looks great, has resurfaced in B pictures like this; she seems a tad helpless for a wily undercover cop (Reed has to save her from a potential rapist); then again, she *is* able to pick a variety of locks with her earrings.

Like all of Mehri's Canadian-shot productions, TALONS OF THE EAGLE at least looks good. Although the boys surprisingly do not use their new, laboriously learned "Eagle Claw" technique (they do rip open a couple of trees with it during training), the film does feature one clever new wrinkle for the genre: Li effectively sports a deadly razor-blade-studded fan as a weapon. *(Violence, profanity, nudity, sexual situations.)*

p, Jalal Mehri; d, Michael Kennedy; w, J. Stephen Maunder; ph, Curtis Petersen; ed, Reid Dennison; m, VaRouje; art d, Jasna Stefanovich; set d, Rob Hepburn; cos, Erika Larner-Corbett

Action/Crime/Martial Arts (PR: O MPAA: R)

T

TERMINAL BLISS ★½

91m Terminal Bliss Productions Inc; Distant Horizon ~ Cannon Pictures c

Luke Perry *(John Hunter)*, Timothy Owen *(Alex Golden)*, Estee Chandler *(Stevie Bradley)*, Sonia Curtis *(Kirsten Davis)*, Micah Grant *(Bucky O'Connell)*, Alexis Arquette *(Craig Murphy)*, Heather Jones Challenge *(Tanya Bradley)*, Susan Nichols *(Judy Golden)*, Bruce Taylor *(Jack Hunter)*, Susan Satoris *(Lynn Hunter)*, Ann Pierce *(Mrs. Highton)*, George Grey *(Guidance Counselor)*, Roy Lind *(Andrew Hillier)*, Scott Kerr *(Republican)*, Peter Syrett *(Maitre d')*, Tara Heffner *(Daphne Miller)*, Jordan Alan *(Drug Buyer)*, Brian Cox *(Dream Surgeon)*, Brian Reily *(John Hunter–Age 10)*, Alex Harmon *(Alex Golden–Age 10)*

TERMINAL BLISS is an upper-class adolescent-angst melodrama that, although well-intentioned and heartfelt, mines the same ground as ORDINARY PEOPLE, PERMANENT RECORD, LESS THAN ZERO, HEATHERS and THE GRADUATE with less than enriching results.

Alex Golden (Timothy Owen) and John Hunter (Luke Perry) are two childhood friends from upper-class surroundings who have seen better days. Now in high school, these two prematurely dissolute youths spend their time driving around, going to parties, and getting high with their chums—Grateful Dead freak Craig Murphy (Alexis Arquette), drug dealer Bucky O'Connell (Micah Grant) and Bucky's hopped up girlfriend Kirsten Davis (Sonia Curtis). But the arrival of Alex's new girlfriend Stevie Bradley (Estee Chandler) sends Alex's friendship with John into a tailspin and it's not long before he finds John and Stevie snorting cocaine and having sex together, driving Alex into drug rehab and compelling Stevie to have an abortion.

In the meantime, John becomes more and more obnoxious. In spite of that, Stevie and Alex still socialize with him. At a birthday bash for Stevie's little sister, Tanya (Heather Jones Challenge), John convinces Alex and Stevie to come with him to his parents' lakehouse retreat. Alex and Stevie reluctantly agree to go and, as they wait for John, John rapes Tanya. Tanya says nothing about the incident to Stevie and off they go to the lakehouse, where John acts even more overbearing than usual. Stevie, disgusted by John, asks Alex if she can sleep in his room. In the morning, John and Alex go out on the lake to secure the lines on John's boat. When John submerges to tie down the anchor line, his foot gets caught in the rope and he drowns as Alex sits nonplussed in the rowboat. After John drowns, Alex goes back to the lakehouse and lies down with Stevie and they both silently cry.

The emotional problems of spoiled, rich teens with money to burn is not a subject that elicits much sympathy from movie audiences. This is not to say that the emotional turmoil of the upper classes cannot make for an interesting, thought-provoking film. (Woody Allen, after all, has been doing it for years.) But the world of TERMINAL BLISS, as envisioned by writer-director Jordan Alan, is a hermetically sealed and uninvolving world of cars, parties, sex and drugs. Reality does not intrude for a minute and the audience is shown no perspective beyond the stunted psyches of Alex and John—only fleeting hints of a larger world of parents, school and nascent responsibility.

Unfortunately, the psyches of Alex and John are empty shells. Alex begins the film as a cynical manic-depressive and ends the film as a cynical manic-depressive. The audience is given no clue as to why he feels such a deep attachment to John or why John's stealing Alex's girlfriend would land him in a drug clinic. John enters the film as a white-bread Staggerlee and simply becomes more intense as the film progresses—so much so that, by the time John gets to the lakehouse with Alex and Stevie, he enters the scene over a clap of thunder. John comes across as an other-worldly reprobate, the reasons for his actions obscure and unexplained. The other characters may be attracted to him for his boorishness, but when he drowns at the film's end, the audience is left untouched and unmoved.

It doesn't help matters any that Alan strives for unoriginality. Practically every scene in the film can be traced to another film of the same genre—the wild parties from LESS THAN ZERO, the graduation present for John from THE GRADUATE, the morose hero from ORDINARY PEOPLE. The cliches come thick and fast, riding roughshod over any attempt to create an original dramatic piece. This wholesale borrowing from other films creates a moviegoing *deja vu* that causes one to reflect wistfully upon coke-snorting Robert Downey, Jr. and anguished Timothy Hutton.

The performances, too, are stilted and overly familiar; these actors play their roles like they're in a sexed up ABC Afterschool Special. Timothy Owen whines and moans his way through his part like a cranky Steve Wright, and Estee Chandler can merely smile gamely through her unbelievable role as Stevie. Luke Perry attempts a star turn *a la* James Dean, but the character of John is so reprehensible that Perry's efforts at charm fall extremely flat, making the character that much more distasteful. TERMINAL BLISS is, itself, terminal. *(Substance abuse, sexual situations, profanity.)*

p, Brian Cox; d, Jordan Alan; w, Jordan Alan; ph, Gregory Smith; ed, Bruce Sinofsky; m, Frank W. Becker; prod d, Catherine Tirr; art d, David Poses; cos, Juliet Polcsa

Drama **(PR: O MPAA: R)**

TETSUO: THE IRON MAN ★★★

(Japan) 67m Kaiju Theatre ~ Original Cinema bw

Tomoroh Taguchi *(The Salaryman)*, Kei Fujiwara *(The Salaryman's Girlfriend)*, Nobu Kanaoka *(Woman in Glasses)*, Shinya Tsukamoto *(Young Metals Fetishist)*, Naomasa Musaka *(Doctor)*, Renji Ishibashi *(Tramp)*

Shinya Tsukamoto has infused TETSUO: THE IRON MAN with a graphic violence and sexuality that makes his featurette a wildly original departure from any standard sci-fi film, despite its lack of expensive, special effects.

In a disturbingly realistic scene prior to the opening credits, viewers see a young man (Tsukamoto) wandering through an abandoned factory. In between close-ups of discarded machinery and cables, the youth, a metals fetishist, carves open his upper thigh and starts to implant a piece of metal tubing. The next character viewers encounter is a bespectacled young man in a business suit, a typical "salaryman" (Tomoroh Taguchi), against a background of steel mill processes. While shaving, he notices a small metal "thorn" growing out of his face, and he seems to have flashbacks of a hit-and-run accident involving the metals fetishist.

While commuting to work, the salaryman has to fight off a young woman (Nobu Kanaoka) who is suddenly controlled by a mutant substance that converts her arm into a fungoid claw. Even the salaryman's dreams seem contaminated, since he has a nightmare in which a mutated woman sodomizes him with an enormous metallic phallus. Later, while making love to his girlfriend (Kei Fujiwara), the salaryman finds that he is changing into a collection of machinery and runs to hide. Undaunted, the woman tries to console him, until she realizes the extent of his mutation—his penis now boasts a power-driven screw head.

Throughout these sequences, presented at a very fast, almost dizzying pace, flashbacks occur to the metals fetishist and the car accident, sometimes on the salaryman's TV set. Eventually the salaryman and the telekinetic metals fetishist fight it out, in great monster movie tradition, at the abandoned factory in a dazzling display of stop-action effects. At the film's end, the two mutants are literally melded into a new entity that threatens to turn the world into metal, presumably in a recently made sequel, TETSUO 2: THE BODY HAMMER.

The frankly erotic element in TETSUO: THE IRON MAN would distinguish this production alone, but it also features a fractured continuity that demands attention, if only to figure out what is going on. The contortion of the narrative line, like the graphic emphasis on sex and blood, emphasizes the alien nature of mutation; Tsukamoto's creatures are not just plain folks with odd body parts, but original monsters. Although not for the priggish or squeamish, Tsukamoto's film does return genuine shock and horror to the science-fiction screen. *(Excessive violence, profanity, sexual situations.)*

p, Shinya Tsukamoto; d, Shinya Tsukamoto; w, Shinya Tsukamoto; ph, Kei Fujiwara, Shinya Tsukamoto; ed, Shinya Tsukamoto; m, Chu Ishikawa; art d, Shinya Tsukamoto; cos, Kei Fujiwara; fx, Shinya Tsukamoto

Science Fiction/Horror **(PR: O MPAA: NR)**

TEXAS TENOR: THE ILLINOIS JACQUET STORY ★★★

81m Arthur Elgort Ltd. ~ Rhapsody Films c

Illinois Jacquet, Walter Blanding, Jr., Arnett Cobb, "Wild" Bill Davis, Ron Della Chiesa, Dorothy Donegan, Dan Frank, Harry "Sweets" Edison, Dizzy Gillespie, John Grimes, Lionel Hampton, Al Hibbler, Milt Hinton, Mona Hinton, Matthew Hong, Javon Jackson, Jonah Jones, Emilio Lyons, Dan Morgenstern, Cecil Payne, Bob Porter, Sonny Rollins, John Simon, Buddy Tate, Clark Terry, Kenneth Bolds, Hugh Brodie, Bob Cunningham, Arthur Daniels, Randy Eckert, David Glasser, Frank Gordon, John Gordon, Larry Ham, Matt Haviland, Dick Griffin, Jim Leff, Tom Olin, Pat O'Leary, Edward Preston, Bernard Purdie, Joshua Roseman, Rudy Rutherford, Gary Sargent, Irwin Stokes, Aubrey Tucker, Gary Vosbein, Richard Wyands

TEXAS TENOR: THE ILLINOIS JACQUET STORY, Arthur Elgort's captivating documentary on tenor sax wizard Illinois Jacquet, gives just dues to one of the world's finest musicians. Considering the subject is virtually worshipped by many musical superstars, it's hard to imagine that his name is barely recognizable to the general public.

Illinois Jacquet has had a distinguished career that's spanned some fifty years. TEXAS TENOR follows the musician from 1988 through 1991 as the jazz saxophonist and conductor does what he does best—make beautiful music. Jacquet, like other great Southern Black musicians, came north just as soon as he was old enough to buy a train ticket. In his seventies now, he hasn't stopped moving since. In 1988 Jacquet and his newly formed big band are in the midst of a national tour of jazz clubs and larger venues. Jacquet is known as a "Texas Tenor," a term which relates not to where he lives—Jacquet was born in Louisiana—but to the sound which came to be identified by saxophonists in the past who played for big sound. Rooms were rarely miked in the heyday of jazz, and Jacquet liked to play to the back row.

Rising to fame in the forties, first as a star player in Lionel Hampton's orchestra, he then cemented his stature as a world class horn player when he joined Count Basie. He achieved his biggest success with the recording of "Flying Home," and many jazz musicians today credit his solo work on that song as the greatest saxophone instrumental ever recorded. His ability to articulate a musical phrase is simply awe-inspiring to fans and fellow performers alike. For the next few decades, Jacquet recorded countless albums and, like many other road veterans, toured continuously.

After being named artist in residence at Harvard, he was motivated to form his latest incarnation—"Illinois Jacquet's Big Band." The film follows Jacquet from a cramped backstage at the famous Blue Note jazz club in Manhattan, all the way through Europe on the band's debut tour. Along the way he plays at a variety of music festivals, visits a saxophone production factory, takes a sidewalk stroll around Paris while still finding time to rehearse and perform with a preternaturally talented group of musicians.

Arthur Elgort's tribute to a man who can make metal talk is tremendously satisfying to view. Through the clever use of archival footage and interviews with scores of world-class musicians—Dizzy Gillespie, Sonny Rollins and Les Paul, to name a few—one is exposed to a superstar in his field, yet barely known outside of the jazz world. TEXAS TENOR: THE ILLINOIS JACQUET STORY should change that.

Elgort finds piquant moments in a variety of locales. When Jacquet reminisces with some fellow jazz musicians, aboard a floating junket, the scene is amusingly touching. Shooting in grainy b&w, Elgort also eavesdrops backstage as Jacquet has his hair styled, chronicles an impromptu performance in an instrument repair shop and follows the protagonist as he gives a car tour of his well-manicured neighborhood.

Each musical sequence plays one-upmanship on the others, and Elgort captures the melodious sounds with aplomb. While fans stare at Jacquet's riffs with wide-eyed amazement, he merely views himself as a messenger of a music form. Some of the non-musical sequences are entertaining as well. When he and a fellow player shop for hats in an upscale Parisian boutique, they are no longer two accomplished musicians but a couple of kids in an expensive candy store. In a particularly poignant moment, Jacquet confesses to a radio disc jockey that the song "You Left Me All Alone," which he recorded decades earlier, now has new significance since all his fellow jazz musicians are passing away. Dizzy Gillespie is shown shortly before he died.

Elgort captures the surrounding characters with brief vignettes. Musicians, fans and friends filter in and out effectively, offering tidbits of information about Jacquet. Gillespie happily notes how Jacquet used to make more money gambling in the tour bus than he did from playing the horn. Jacquet's manager, Carol Scherick, is a constant presence whom Elgort addresses but astutely doesn't over emphasize, although her attendance is an important part of the "on the road" realism. The film is loaded with fine musicians, mostly unfamiliar to mainstream audiences, who give clarity to the history of this musical form and to Jacquet's pivotal position in the business.

The man himself, Illinois Jacquet, is low-key off stage, but he comes to life when he picks up the tenor sax. His contemporaries tell of a man who at one time was loud and possibly wild, now he is a classy well-worn giant, and he fits the role well. Jacquet is aware of his elevated stature, yet is humble enough to offer this on his bearing—"I only want to be part of something that will last."

The cinematography is superb, making the most of single-camera restrictions. In a stylish prologue, the use of eclectic close-ups and stark lighting set the mood for what is to follow. Sound, which is the hallmark of Jacquet's appeal, is uup to equally high levels. When he plays the solo from his most famous recording, "Flying Home," the technical achievements of light, sound and shot composition are in near perfect harmony.

TEXAS TENOR is a treat for music fans or anyone who appreciates true documentary biographies. The camera never gets in the way of the story, and one comes away with a better sense of history as told through wonderful music. Jacquet is representative of many great artists who might not be instantly recognizable, but his genius will now be indelibly etched on celluloid for future generations to admire.

p, Ronit Avneri; d, Arthur Elgort; ph, Morten Sandtroen; ed, Paula Heredia

Documentary/Musical **(PR: A MPAA: NR)**

THANK YOU AND GOOD NIGHT! ★★★
85m American Playhouse Theatrical Films; Red Wagon Films ~ Aries Film Releasing c

Mae Joffe, Jan Oxenberg

Jan Oxenberg's quest for knowledge about her dead maternal grandmother utilizes a number of styles and formats: home movies, life-size cut-outs, parodied quiz shows, fabricated interviews and outright fantasy sequences. Often funny, THANK YOU AND GOOD NIGHT! also explores the uneven relationship between Oxenberg's mother and grandmother, hinting at unspoken tensions and unnamed tragedies.

Oxenberg's persona at times is a cutout of herself as a scowling five-year-old, and one of the mysteries in the film is the reference to an older sister killed in a neighborhood car accident at the age of seven. One of the filmmaker's earliest memories of her grandmother is a visit to an old, ornate movie palace where they saw THE PAJAMA GAME. The "granny" cutout is of a stout, bespectacled, hearty woman which contrasts with the thin, acerbic, chain-smoking woman captured by Oxenberg's documentary sequences.

That grandmother, Mae Joffe, was to die of cancer and had already been stricken with diabetes. Born in Troy, New York, Jaffe reveals little of her life there or the reasons underlying the move downstate. Similarly, although native-born, Mae's fear about the Nazis and her sense of Jewish identity are never explored, though cited by Oxenberg as narrator.

What is investigated is the curious relationship between mother and Mae which seems to approach the love-hate level with nasty asides and frequent lapses in the filmed interviews and conversations. This tension changes as the grandmother's health declines precipitously; initially seen smoking and playing solitaire, she is soon confined to bed and cannot even stir a meal and is subsequently seen in a hospital. Oxenberg's film crew follows her into a radiation therapy session and provides the source for a fantasy sequence in which the Oxenberg cutout is shown with a miracle-cure machine.

The fantasy scenes often serve as a comment on the filmed commentary by family members as they discuss Mae's declining health and impending death. The five-year-old cutout also serves this function, so we see the scowling Jan on a psychiatric couch or riding the tractor that digs the graves at the family cemetery. All the while we hear her bemused voice asking questions about the nature of life and death in a mild satire of her more earnest brother. Even the most philosophically sophisticated discussion could not compete with the imagery of a ravished frail grandmother staring at the camera lens from what is to be her deathbed.

That death gives rise to an involved conversation as the family mourns in the prescribed religious fashion and Oxenberg plays with two fantasies: one a trip with a motley crew of the recently deceased, including a beer-toting carful of people dressed in bearsuits, through the Holland Tunnel toward the light of so-called "near-death experience"; the other a trip into space where the living meet the dead and their souvenirs.

After the grandmother's death, Oxenberg turns her camera on the disposition of the furnishings, including the salt and pepper shaker sets and the 21-inch color TV. It is during this part of the film that Oxenberg examines the death of her older sister about whom she remembers very little. The grandmother's death is partially an excuse to explore the issue of death and the various attitudes toward it on the part of surviving relatives.

Twelve years in the making, THANK YOU AND GOOD NIGHT! is a collage of the mundane and the imaginative exploring the by-ways of love and remorse. An experienced TV writer, Jan Oxenberg has made several short films and this production was made for American Playhouse Theatrical Films. Stylistically the film is similar to Syberberg's OUR HITLER, a debt Oxenberg has acknowledged along with Woody Allen's ANNIE HALL and Carlos Saura's CRIA. With its mixture of humor and pathos, the film has been compared to those of Allen and, like his films, THANK YOU AND GOOD NIGHT! wavers between the very amusing and the sentimental, though the actual death of a real person does tend to excuse the latter.

In a way, Oxenberg has squared the circle, since it would be tactless to criticize this film too harshly, especially for those documentary sequences that provide such a wonderful base from which to expand into the fantasy sections. Oddly droll, THANK YOU AND GOOD NIGHT! certainly expands the genre of documentary film, while providing an accessible variant of personal cinema for a wide audience. *(Adult situations.)*

p, Jan Oxenberg; d, Jan Oxenberg; w, Jan Oxenberg; ph, John Hazard, Sandi Sissel, Alicia Weber; ed, Lucy Winer; m, Mark Suozzo; prod d, Pamela Woodbridge; cos, Ellen Lutter

Documentary/Drama/Comedy (PR: A MPAA: NR)

THERE'S NOTHING OUT THERE ★
90m Grandmaster; Valkhn Films ~ Valkhn Films c

Craig Peck *(Mike)*, Wendy Bednarz *(Doreen)*, Mark Collver *(Jim)*, Bonnie Bowers *(Stacy)*, John Carhart, III *(Nick)*, Claudia Flores *(Janet)*, Jeff Dachis *(David)*, Lisa Grant *(Sally)*

A parody of monster movies, THERE'S NOTHING OUT THERE is not as clever as it imagines, and risks boring all but the most tolerant viewers.

It opens as pretty Sally (Lisa Grant), a videostore clerk, is stalked by an unseen monster. She escapes in her car, only to be captured in the woods by the creature. Cut to seven friends—three cute couples and Mike (Craig Peck), a goony loner who's seen every horror movie ever made—deciding to spend the weekend in a deserted house in the country. Are they perturbed when they pass Sally's abandoned car in the forest? Not on your life. Mike's endless warnings about monsters and madmen, delivered in a jokey but half-serious manner, quickly begin to wear on the nerves of his friends. But there is, in fact, reason for concern. A green monster is lurking outside the house, waiting to kill the boys and mate with the girls.

Its first victims are intellectual nerd David (Jeff Dachis) and Brazilian beauty Janet (Claudia Flores), who make the mistake of going for a romantic walk after dinner. Beautiful but stupid Jim (Mark Collver) and Stacy (Bonnie Bowers) are next. By the next morning, only Mike, Nick (John Carhart, III) and Doreen (Wendy Bednarz)—who's thoughtfully changed into her little striped bikini—are left. Nick goes off to town, so only Mike and Wendy are at home when the monster strikes again. They elude it by constructing clever traps with mirrors and shaving cream, and when Nick returns they manage to destroy the creature once and for all. They pick up a hitchhiker—the dazed Sally—as they drive off, but when they realize she may be under the monster's control, they abandon her by the roadside.

Horror parodies operate on the assumption that there's something inherently funny in exposing the shabby structural conventions of the vast majority of horror movies, no matter how many times it's demonstrated that that's just not so. Stripped of their thematic allusiveness and visual complexity, oneiric imagery and mythopoetic underpinnings, good horror movies aren't funny; they're just bad horror movies. THERE'S NOTHING OUT THERE is a bad horror movie hiding unsuccessfully behind the excuse "But it's supposed to be a *joke*."

First-time director Rolfe Kanefsky is clearly intimately familiar with the horror genre, and THERE'S NOTHING OUT THERE is a serviceable pastiche of that most cost-effective horror movie narrative: limited cast is terrorized in a deserted location. It's even occasionally funny. Mike's rant about those cats who seem to appear from nowhere to make people jump (" . . . what do they do, hang from the ceiling by their little claws?"), for example, is sure to get a chuckle from habitual horror moviegoers who have always wondered that very thing. But on the whole, THERE'S NOTHING OUT THERE is crude and obvious; the low budget ensures that it's ugly as well. In addition, there's a faint air of contempt about the whole business, and it's off putting. "Look how stupid horror movies are," it seems to be saying. But since the only people who will get the joke are people who watch horror pictures, how stupid does that make the movie's viewers?

There's a difference between movies that poke intelligent fun at generic conventions and movies that use them for a cheap laugh. John Landis's AN AMERICAN WEREWOLF IN LONDON, Joe Dante's THE HOWLING and even Kathryn Bigelow's NEAR DARK are excellent examples of the former approach, while THERE'S NOTHING OUT THERE is a textbook illustration of the latter. *(Violence, nudity, sexual situations.)*

p, Victor Kanefsky; d, Rolfe Kanefsky; w, Rolfe Kanefsky; ph, Ed Hershberger; ed, Victor Kanefsky; m, Christopher Thomas

Comedy/Horror (PR: C MPAA: NR)

35 UP ★★★
128m Granada Television Ltd.; Michael Apted Films ~ Samuel Goldwyn Company bw/c

Jackie, Bruce, Tony, Neil, John, Suzy, Charles, Andrew, Peter, Paul, Symon, Lynn, Susan, Nicholas

Michael Apted's celebrated documentary series, which has examined the effects of social, economic and cultural forces upon a group of English schoolchildren, chosen from varying economic backgrounds, as they age at seven-year intervals, has reached a curiously dispiriting plateau in 35 UP.

While previous installments of the series reflected on the physical and mental growth of the subjects—at seven, fourteen, twenty-one and twenty-eight—and how they managed to find a niche in the British social structure, now, at the age of thirty-five, the subjects are full fledged adults and have become reflective, bitter, and paunchy. For example, as Tony's life flashes onscreen, he is seen as a knockabout lower-class scrapper who becomes, briefly, a jockey, a pub owner, a movie extra and now, at thirty-five, a cab driver, stuck in his job and arguing with his wife and kids over dinner. Similarly, the lower-class triumvirate of Jackie, Lynn and Sue are now single parents who are forced into dead-end jobs in order to provide for their children. Even the upper-class subjects find themselves in lives of dull routine. The well-off Suzy, raising her children amidst the splendor of the English countryside, muses defensively that she can't change what she was born into.

The only dimly hopeful one of the bunch is Neil, the most unsettled member of the group, who, when asked if he feels that his life has been a failure, replies "Well, my life isn't over yet."

This stoic response reflects the underlying structure of Apted's fascinating project. No matter how many ruts the subjects find themselves in, there is no closure—either in the film or in their lives. The hints of future possibilities make 35 UP sad, bleak, hopeless yet, at the same moment, life-affirming, yearningly moving and refreshingly hopeful.

Beyond the class barriers that rule their lives, the other disturbing undercurrent of 35 UP is the subjects' ongoing celebrity based on their exposure in the films. By 35 UP, Apted's camera has become not merely a mirror of reality but reality itself. Jackie, Lynn and Sue reveal to Apted that they only reflect on their dead-end lives when Apted arrives with his camera to ask them. At another point in the film, Tony says, "I'm as good as other people, especially in this film." Although several of the original subjects declined to appear in 35 UP, citing invasion of privacy (Nick's wife; the upper-class Charles; and Symon, the only black participant, who decided to expose his family life no longer to public scrutiny), the others live their lives in a heightened super-reality, a life that is documented in distinct seven-year intervals with a visit from Apted and his film crew. By 35 UP, the subjects refer to their own previous film incarnations and react to the filmmaking process as a primary aspect of their existence.

35 UP is a God-like glimpse of the uninterrupted trajectory of lives that is vastly disturbing, cooly scientific and intensely emotional. As it unfolds, Apted reveals lives at the crossroads of capitulation or enervation. Despite the bleak outlook, Apted's film gives hope for a better life at 42.

p, Michael Apted; d, Michael Apted; w, Michael Apted; ph, George Jesse Turner; ed, Claire Lewis, Kim Horton

Documentary **(PR: A MPAA: NR)**

THIS IS MY LIFE ★★½

105m Frostback Productions; Fox ~ Fox c

Julie Kavner *(Dottie Ingels)*, Samantha Mathis *(Erica Ingels)*, Gaby Hoffman *(Opal Ingels)*, Carrie Fisher *(Claudia Curtis)*, Dan Aykroyd *(Arnold Moss)*, Bob Nelson *(Ed)*, Marita Geraghty *(Mia Jablon)*, Welker White *(Lynn)*, Caroline Aaron *(Martha Ingels)*, Kathy Ann Najimy *(Angela)*, Danny Zorn *(Jordan)*, Renee Lippin *(Arlene)*, Joy Behar *(Ruby)*, Estelle Harris *(Aunt Harriet)*, Sidney Armus *(Morris Chesler)*, David Eisner *(Oliver)*, Annie Golden *(Marianne)*, Tim Blake Nelson *(Dennis)*, Harvey Miller *(Lester)*, Patrick Rose *(Gary Garry)*, Kate McGregor-Stewart *(Jordan's Mom)*, Ellen Cleghorne *(TV Talk Show Host)*, Valerie Bromfield *(Dawna)*, Diane Sokolow *(Charlene)*, Tom Wood *(Billy)*, Louis DiBianco *(Norm Ingels)*, Barbara Stewart *(Joanne)*, Sylvia Kauders *(Evelyn)*, Faye Cohen *(Evelyn's Daughter)*, Theresa Tova *(Rochelle)*, Marcia DeBonis *(Linda)*, Heather Brown *(Jessica)*, Billy Van *(Agent)*, Bob Zidel *(Mr. Kaminski)*, Rabbi Dr. Joel Y. Zion *(Rabbi)*, John E. Johnson *(Martin)*, Joseph Mastrodominico *(Moving Man)*, Max Bernstein *(1st Tree Boy)*, Oly Obst *(2nd Tree Boy)*, Jacob Bernstein *(3rd Tree Boy)*, Zoe Hayes *(Girl in Mouse Costume)*, Renessa Blitz *(Lisa)*, Lisa Boynton *(Shawn)*, Audrey Webb *(Mrs. Fabricant)*, Katherine Greenwood *(Young Matron)*, Eric R. Mendelsohn *(Ice Cream Parlor Waiter)*, Bo Dietl *(Detective Wheedle)*

Marking the directorial debut of popular writer Nora Ephron, THIS IS MY LIFE is a low-key, likable story of mother-daughter conflict.

Dottie Ingels (Julie Kavner) is a single mother living in Queens who dreams of being a stand-up comedienne and tries out routines on customers at the Macy's makeup counter where she works. She gets her chance when her Aunt Harriet (Estelle Harris) suddenly passes away, leaving Dottie the house where she's been living with her daughters, sixteen-year-old Erica (Samantha Mathis) and ten-year-old Opal (Gaby Hoffman). Dottie decides to sell the place, move with her daughters to a Manhattan apartment, and use the rest of the money Harriet's left her to live on while she attempts to make it on the stand-up circuit. She manages to land an agent, Claudia Curtis (Carrie Fisher), who sends her out on tour while the girls are tended to by Dottie's aspiring comic friends.

The girls, particularly Erica, become incensed that their mother seems to be putting her ascending career before their needs. Erica seeks solace with her new boyfriend Jordan, (Danny Zorn), but still can't hide her anger when Dottie comes home to attend Opal's school play. Attempting to placate her kids, Dottie invites them to join her in Las Vegas, where she has a major club date. But Erica blows up at Dottie when the latter uses occasions from her daughter's life as material during a talk-show appearance, and both girls are startled when it appears their mother has taken a lover. At first, they believe the new man is a young stage technician that Opal's gotten a crush on, but they're even more mortified when they discover that he is in fact Arnold Moss (Dan Aykroyd), Claudia's boss and a major player on the comedy circuit.

When Dottie and the girls return to New York, Erica convinces Opal to run away with her to find their father, whom she's tracked down through a private detective. Taking a train to upstate New York, they find their father, Norm (Louis DiBianco), now remarried and, after an awkward visit, realize they can no longer be part of his life. Upon returning to Manhattan, they are greeted by Dottie, who was lterribly worried about them and was alerted to their return by Norm's new wife. The girls agree to try to adapt to their mother's new life and impending marriage to Moss, and she in turn agrees to give them more attention.

Nora Ephron is an acclaimed essayist (*Wallflower at the Orgy* and *Crazy Salad*), novelist (the roman-a-clef *Heartburn*) and screenwriter (SILKWOOD, WHEN HARRY MET SALLY . . .), who cowrote THIS IS MY LIFE with her humorist sister Delia. There's little doubt why she responded to Meg Wolitzer's novel *This Is Your Life*. The Ephron sisters themselves grew up living in the shadow of celebrity parents (the play and screenwriting team of Henry and Phoebe Ephron), and this movie, unlike the recent PUNCHLINE, deals less with the milieu of the stand-up comedy scene than the tensions created in the family of one aspiring performer.

Kavner (AWAKENINGS, SHADOWS AND FOG) is just right as Dottie, who ties in a gimmick (polka-dot dresses) with her name and strives to further her career to the point where she loses sight of her family responsibilities. That the character never loses the audience's sympathy is a tribute to Kavner's skill, and she also displays sharp comic timing both in her club scenes and in many moments off the stage as well. But the movie is only half her story; it's told as much from the daughters' point of view, particularly that of Erica, and Mathis shines in her role. A 180-degree turn from the punkish Nora she played so well in PUMP UP THE VOLUME, Erica is a more morose, insecure character, and Mathis portrays her with a great deal of sympathy and assurance. But she has her comic side too, and the scene in which she and her boyfriend embark on fumbling first sex together is played skillfully enough (by both Mathis and the very funny Zorn) to keep it from becoming embarrassing.

If the movie has a major flaw, it's that Dottie's climb to the top happens too fast to be completely convincing. She seems to hit the big time in an awful hurry, and although her routines are funny, they're not the kind of groundbreaking material that would seem likely to rocket someone from the cosmetic counter to "The Tonight Show" in a matter of months. There seems to be very little struggle involved, and the lousy material of Dottie's fellow aspiring comics is an obvious ploy to make her own "talent" stand out even more. It's a shame that this facet of the film isn't played with the realism of the dramatic scenes between Dottie and her daughters; if it were, THIS IS MY LIFE might have gone beyond the diverting but modest entertainment it is and wound up a true gem. *(Profanity, sexual situations, adult situations.)*

p, Lynda Obst; d, Nora Ephron; w, Nora Ephron, Delia Ephron, (from the novel *This Is Your Life* by Meg Wolitzer); ph, Bobby Byrne; ed, Robert Reitano; m, Carly Simon; prod d, David Chapman; art d, Barbra Matis; set d, Hilton Rosemarin, Jaro Dick; cos, Jeffrey Kurland

Comedy/Drama (PR: C MPAA: PG-13)

3 NINJAS ★★★

(U.S./South Korea) 87m Global Venture Hollywood Inc.; Sheen Productions ~ BV c

Victor Wong *(Grandpa)*, Michael Treanor *(Rocky)*, Max Elliott Slade *(Colt)*, Chad Power *(Tum Tum)*, Rand Kingsley *(Snyder)*, Alan McRae *(Sam Douglas)*, Margarita Franco *(Jessica Douglas)*, Kate Sargeant *(Emily)*, Joel Swetow *(Brown)*, Toru Tanaka *(Rushmore)*, Patrick Labyorteaux *(Fester)*, Race Nelson *(Marcus)*, D.J. Harder *(Hammer)*, Baha Jackson *(Bully)*, Scott Caudill *(Bully)*, Fritzi Burr *(Babysitter)*, Tasen Chou *(Store Owner)*, Clifton Powell *(FBI Agent Kurl)*, Al Septien *(FBI Agent Green)*

Mix in equal amounts of KARATE KID and HOME ALONE, stir in a couple doses of TEENAGE MUTANT NINJA TURTLES, add a dash of "chopsocky" action comedy, and you have 3 NINJAS, an entertaining, though hardly original, action comedy for youngsters ages six to twelve.

Ever since Rocky (Michael Treanor), Colt (Max Elliott Slade) and Tum Tum (Chad Power) can remember, the three brothers, ranging in age from seven to twelve, have been the grateful pupils of their maternal grandfather, ninja master Mori (Victor Wong). Mori shares his home and gardens with his three athletic grandsons where he also trains them in the technique of martial arts, much to the chagrin of their father, FBI Agent Sam Douglas (Alan McRae). He's on the trail of Hugo Snyder (Rand Kingsley), a notorious arms dealer and a ninja master in his own right, since he was once the pupil of Grandpa Mori himself.

When Sam gets too close to closing in on Synder, the ruthless arch criminal, who will stop at nothing to maintain the power structure of his despicable organization, orders Sam's three sons kidnapped and held hostage until Sam agrees to abandon his efforts to crush Snyder's operations once and for all. The crime boss sends a trio of not very bright punks to apprehend the boys. Fortunately, twelve-year-old Rocky, eleven-year-old Colt and seven-year-old Tum Tum spot trouble before the goons can execute their plans and this enables the boys to practice their karate skills on the bumbling would-be kidnappers.

Though they've clearly won the first round, the boys have not won the war, for Synder next dispatches a troop of ninja soldiers to accomplish what the dumbbell punks failed to do. Fortunately, the boys, well aware of the plot to capture them, visit Grandpa Mori for more intensive training. In their favor is the fact that the evil Synder was once Mori's pupil and since Grandpa taught Snyder everything he knows about kung fu, he is able to give his grandsons crucial pointers on how to defend themselves better against any future kidnapping attempts by Synder and his henchmen. Eventually, the boys are caught by the ninjas, but they refuse to lose their cool and a David-and-Goliath-like opportunity arises shortly after the boys are made prisoners in the hold of a ship docked off the Southern California coast.

Sam, who had previously disapproved of Mori's training his sons in the martial arts, is now extremely grateful to him and Sam and Mori join forces to rescue the youngsters. Meanwhile, the boys make their own plans to escape and bide their time, awaiting just the right moment to make a move. Ultimately, Mori is forced to meet Synder face to face and is challenged by Synder to best his former pupil in a vicious martial arts confrontation. What finally saves the boys, however, is the force of their own absolute faith in themselves and their own strong personalities: Rocky musters all the maturity of his young years and proves beyond doubt that he is in control of his own life; Colt, the wildest of the brothers, can now make his natural rambunctiousness pay off for him; and little Tum Tum, a boy used to being loved in a home where familial devotion is mutually shared, can now put his tremendous faith that everything will turn out alright to the test.

Since this is a Disney family film, it doesn't require a doctorate to guess the outcome. But 3 NINJAS offers much that youngsters, particularly boys, can identify with and, for its target audience at least, the film offers near perfect entertainment.

While adults may get a few chuckles from the proceedings, they will undoubtedly take note of some major flaws in the plot's plausibility. For example, early in the film the villain witnesses the martial arts prowess of the three youngsters he later orders kidnapped. Yet, despite his awareness of the boys' athletic abilities, and despite the fact that he already has in his employ a master martial arts henchman, Rushmore (Toru Tanaka), he nevertheless inexplicably hires three incompetent goons to carry out the initial kidnapping attempt. Of course, without the scenes where the boys outwit the goons in true HOME ALONE fashion, young audiences would be cheated out of the highlight slapstick comedy moments, so the filmmakers, obviously, felt justified in not concerning themselves too much over plot inconsistencies.

The three young actors portraying the title characters, Treaner, Slade and Power, are all scene stealers and Power is especially adorable. As their Grandpa Mori, Victor Wong, a veteran of such art films as DIM SUM and EAT A BOWL OF TEA, and mainstream pictures like THE LAST EMPEROR and THE GOLDEN CHILD, is splendid. Rand Kingsley and Toru Tanaka make convincingly menacing villains, while Alan McRae and Margarita Franco round out the cast as the boys' parents.

Director Jon Turteltaub is to be congratulated on keeping the proceedings exciting without resorting to unnecessary violence, and he directs with a sure hand from a competent screenplay that proves quite workable despite its plot discrepancies. In fact, everything about 3 NINJAS bespeaks a high degree of competence. While one could wish the film offered something more original than its strictly formula heroics, it benefits from a generous portion of charm. And most kids attending 3 NINJAS are likely to stand up and cheer the rousing, action-packed finale.

p, Martha Chang; d, Jon Turteltaub; w, Edward Emanuel, (from the story by Kenny Kim); ph, Richard Michalak; ed, David Rennie; m, Rick Marvin; prod d, Kirk Petruccelli; art d, Ken Kirchener, Greg Grande; set d, Carol Pressman; cos, Mona May

Children's/Action/Martial Arts (PR: A MPAA: PG)

THUNDERHEART ★★½

118m TriBeCa Productions; Waterhorse Productions; TriStar Pictures ~ TriStar c

Val Kilmer *(Ray Levoi)*, Sam Shepard *(Frank Coutelle)*, Graham Greene *(Walter Crow Horse)*, Fred Dalton Thompson *(William Dawes)*, Fred Ward *(Jack Milton)*, Sheila Tousey *(Maggie Eagle Bear)*, Chief Ted Thin Elk *(Grandpa Sam Reaches)*, John Trudell *(Jimmy Looks Twice)*, Julius Drum *(Richard Yellow Hawk)*, Sarah

Brave *(Maisy Blue Legs)*, Allan R.J. Joseph *(Leo Fast Elk)*, Sylvan Pumpkin Seed *(Hobart)*, Patrick Massett *(Agent Mackey)*, Rex Linn *(FBI Agent)*, Brian A. O'Meara *(FBI Agent)*, Duane Brewer *(Ranger)*, Lewis C Bradshaw *(Ranger)*, Dennis Banks *(Himself)*, Candy Hamilton *(School Teacher)*, Jerome Mack *(Maggie's Kid)*, Tom M. LeBeau *(Ray's Father)*, Bridgit P. Schock *(Ray's Mother)*, Terry Graber *(Doctor)*, David Crosby *(Bartender)*, Jerry Allan Hietala *(Drunken Brawler)*, Gordon Patterson *(Helicopter Pilot)*, Robin J. Saderup *(Helicopter Pilot)*, Buddy Red Bow *(Man at Powwow)*, Sam Adams, Robin Black Bird, Floyd Charging Crow, Elroy Cross, Charles Davis, Ernest Red Elk, Kenneth J. Richards, Severt Young Bear, Sr. *(Lakota Singers)*, Carlin Orville Morrison, Verland Theodore Phelps, Calvin Timothy Red Elk, Sr., Tim Owen Taggart, Melvin David Young Bear *(Powwow Singers)*

THUNDERHEART is an atmospheric thriller that tries to cover too many socially conscious bases for it to succeed completely as drama. Set on a North Dakota Native American reservation in the 1970s and directed by Michael Apted, it is loosely based on the real-life events that Apted investigated in his documentary, INCIDENT AT OGLALA.

Ray Levoi (Val Kilmer) is a cocky, buttoned-down young FBI agent who has done his best to suppress his Indian heritage (he's one-quarter Sioux). Precisely because he's a token Indian, he's sent to aid in the investigation of a possibly political murder on a reservation by his cynical supervisor, William Dawes (Fred Dalton Thompson), who's looking for public relations mileage from Levoi's mixed blood. Tough local agent Frank "Cooch" Coutelle (Sam Shepard) seems to have the case wrapped up before Levoi even arrives, with only the apprehension of the suspect, American Indian Movement radical Jimmy Looks Twice (John Trudell), left to be done.

While helping Coutelle track down the suspect, Levoi gradually becomes sensitized to Indian issues, partially from his attraction to Maggie Eagle Bear (Sheila Tousey), an earthy, politically active schoolteacher. Mockingly referred to by some—including gruff, savvy local cop Walter Crow Horse (Graham Greene)—as the "Washington Redskin," Levoi finds that he has an unaccountable standing with some of the tribal elders; according to one of the film's more mystical subplots, they "recognize" Levoi as Thunderheart, an Indian hero slain at the Wounded Knee massacre and now reincarnated to deliver them from their current troubles. As more killings take place, and as Walter provides him with some telling leads, Levoi comes to suspect—much to Coutelle's anger—that the case is not as cut and dried as the veteran agent would have him believe.

Eventually, Levoi discovers that a government-sponsored plan to mine uranium on the reservation is at the root of the killings. The mining is polluting the water supply and fueling a bloody conflict between the American Indian activists and the reservation's pro-government ruling council who, led by Jack Milton (Fred Ward), are not above using vigilante violence to further their aims. Coutelle, it turns out, is part of the problem rather than the solution, and the film ends with a climactic show-down between the pro-and anti-Government forces.

Apted is nearly as celebrated for his documentaries (7 UP, 14 UP etc.) as for features including GORILLAS IN THE MIST and COAL MINER'S DAUGHTER, and he has brought a cool, objective eye to his subject matter. Apted avoids sentimentalizing the Indians *a la* DANCES WITH WOLVES, celebrating the richness of their culture without turning a blind eye to their internal rivalries and degraded living conditions.

Despite its complexity, the plot is cleanly delineated and never becomes overly confusing. Roger Deakins's cinematography is rich and expressive, finding new, intriguing ways to look at settings that have graced hundreds of Hollywood Westerns.

The performances are uniformly thoughtful and well-detailed. Val Kilmer's transition from conservative bullheadedness to caring sensitivity comes a little too easily to be quite believable, but the character is never less than engaging. Shepard does his usual ornery routine and Greene is superb as the laconic Native American cop. Newcomer Tousey strikes just the right chords, neither too strident nor too soft, as the schoolteacher, and Indian activist Dennis Banks plays himself. As the film's clearest-cut villain, Ward makes so strong an impression that we wish he had more screen time.

The biggest problem with THUNDERHEART is its screenplay, by the prolific writer John Fusco (YOUNG GUNS, THE BABE), which attempts to touch on so many Indian-related issues that all of them end up getting short shrift. They also add so much exposition to the film's slow-moving second act that Kilmer begins to seem downright dense in failing to grasp Shepard's yawningly obvious duplicity. *(Violence, profanity.)*

p, Robert De Niro, Jane Rosenthal, John Fusco; d, Michael Apted; w, John Fusco; ph, Roger Deakins; ed, Ian Crafford; m, James Horner; prod d, Dan Bishop; art d, Bill Ballou; set d, Dianna Freas; cos, Susan Lyall

Thriller **(PR: C MPAA: R)**

TIGER CLAWS ★½

(Canada) 93m Tiger Claws Inc.; Film One Productions; Shapiro/Glickenhaus Entertainment ~ MCA/Universal Home Video c

Jalal Merhi *(Tarek Richards)*, Cynthia Rothrock *(Detective Linda Masterson)*, Bolo Yeung *(Chong)*, Robert Nolan *(Roberts)*, Kedar Brown *(Vince)*, John Webster *(Reeves)*, Ho Chow *(James)*, David Stevenson *(Harris)*, Gary Wong *(Ming)*, Mo Chow *(Chow)*, Bill Pickells

Despite an admittedly ambitious plot, TIGER CLAWS suffers from being grounded in a bonehead cops-and-ninjas formula.

Detective Linda Masterson (Cynthia Rothrock) is a policewoman who sees her chance to move from the robbery division into homicide when New York City is terrorized by the "Death Dealer," a murderer who targets martial arts masters. However proficient these *senseis* and *sifus* are supposed to be at defending themselves, they're carted to the morgue with clawlike gashes in their flesh.

Investigating officer Masterson, a martial arts expert, is given the case, but she's unwillingly paired with the force's other chopsocky ace, rogue cop Tarek Richards (Jalal Merhi). He recognizes on the bodies the mark of the ancient "tiger claw" school of martial arts, which emphasizes deadly gouging swipes with the hands. He himself trained in tiger until he felt its lethal power driving him crazy.

Linda and Tarek locate a tiger cult in Chinatown, and the latter manages to enroll as a disciple. But while the fighting flatfoots try to figure out which of the pupils is the Death Dealer, all ignore a strange, grinning hulk in the corner painting a giant tiger mural. He's Chong (Bolo Yeung), revealed early on to the audience as the serial clawer. Alone, he practices his fatal technique in front of a tiger altar, monster muscles crackling outrageously as he flexes.

The pumped-up Yeung has been in karate pictures from ENTER THE DRAGON to DOUBLE IMPACT, and he sure is the last opponent anyone would want to encounter in a darkened *shaolin*. But when his big showdown with Tarek finally rolls around, it's just too clear whose side the filmmakers are on. The cop can defeat this giant with his hands cuffed—and he does,

Chong's hokey dubbed-in tiger growls notwithstanding. It's just too lopsided a contest for fans expecting a terrific tussle, and the treatment brings little allure to the vaunted tiger style.

There's certainly room for an action film that treats martial arts as a philosophical discipline, not just another weapon in the War on Drugs, and TIGER CLAWS would have gained immeasurably had its story been set entirly in the world of competition and mystic secret societies. Instead it's framed by familiar crime buster cliches, and inept ones at that.

Except for the two stars, police here are monumentally stupid (and badly acted) as they suspect Tarek in the slayings, spurred by electioneering politicians howling for a quick arrest. But the heroes' undercover work wouldn't win any commendations anyway; it takes them the whole running time to discover Chong's guilt by some opaque deduction, and at that very instant the big guy coincidentally goes nuts and rampages throughout the city. In other words, Chong would have given himself away on schedule anyhow.

The maniac's motive is never spelled out, unless one happens to have a copy of the production notes, which claim that Chong is a fanatical tiger practitioner out to exterminate non-traditionalists and hot-dogging champs whom he sees as degrading the ancient forms. A crazed kung-fu fundamentalist is a great concept—it would certainly be fun to let such a character loose upon the movie industry.

Jalal Mehri, a holder of multiple black belts and operator of his own martial arts studio, was born in Brazil and raised in Beirut, confirming that these lone-wolf lawmen have a limitless range of accents to match their combat skills. Cynthia Rothrock, known as the female Bruce Lee, bids fair to become a major action star. She's certainly prolific, and makes a personal appearance on the videocassette of TIGER CLAWS to plug another one of her vehicles, MARTIAL LAW 2.

Despite this movie's pitiless villain, never let it be said that kung-fu masters lack a sense of humor; Bill Pickells portrays himself as one of Chong's early victims, an abusive, egocentric host of a self-defense program who gets thrashed into oblivion while his taped image on TV brags about his own invincibility. *(Violence, profanity.)*

p, Jalal Mehri; d, Kelly Makin; w, J. Stephen Maunder; ph, Curtis Petersen, Mark Willis; ed, Reid Dennison; m, VaRouje; art d, Michael Close; cos, Kate Healey

Action/Thriller/Martial Arts (PR: C MPAA: R)

TILL THERE WAS YOU ★★½
(Australia) 94m Sovereign Pictures; Ayer Productions; McElroy & McElroy ~ MCA/Universal Home Video c

Mark Harmon *(Frank Flynn)*, Jeroen Krabbe *(Robert "Viv" Vivaldi)*, Deborah Unger *(Anna)*, Shane Briant *(Rex)*, Ritchie Singer *(Robbo)*, Ivan Kesa *(Snowy)*, Lech Mackiewicz *(Muzza)*, Jeff Truman *(Nobby)*, Helen O'Connor *(Margot)*, Chief Telkon Watas *(Chief)*, Martin Garner *(Mr. Jimmy)*

Lushly photographed, sprinkled with jazzy interludes and smartly played by the attractive cast, the most negative remark one could make about TILL THERE WAS YOU is that it's all been seen before.

Jazz musician Frank Flynn (Mark Harmon) strikes a few sour notes when he goes searching for his missing brother Charlie in the South Pacific. He's given a cool reception by the constabulary, particularly after he's caught breaking curfew with a cooly beautiful blonde hitchhiker named Anna (Deborah Unger). After learning that his absent sibling has been clubbed to death, allegedly by natives, Flynn continues investigating the case at his own peril. With his suave Paul Henreid manner and competitive streak that extends to cheating at foot races, Robert "Viv" Vivaldi (Jeroen Krabbe), Charlie's former business associate, immediately leads the suspect parade.

Reencountering Anna (who turns out to be Viv's wife), Frank upsets the police with his Yankee inquisitiveness and irritates Viv with his amateur sleuthing. Having pushed all Viv's buttons and then beaten him at cards, Frank and Anna are forced to flee into the jungle. But what do those gold bars that Frank keeps stumbling upon have to do with the plot? Subscribing to their father's theory about a downed American bomber full of Japanese gold, Charlie explored the jungle before becoming a victim of Viv's jealousy regarding Anna.

Although Anna is recaptured, Frank is adopted by the quaint natives who teach him advanced bungee jumping, show him where the legendary plane went down, and then assist him in laying siege to Viv's house and vanquishing the villains. Investing his new-found wealth in a jazz club, Frank waits in New York until Anna deals with her own psychological baggage and widowhood before finally joining her beloved in that other jungle—New York City.

As adventure films go, TILL THERE WAS YOU deserves credit for throwing in everything but the kitchen sink: forbidden love in the tropics; a control-freak villain; sunken treasure; an oppressive military regime; adorable natives; death-defying escapes *a la* Indiana Jones. This flight of fancy is chock full of smooth professionalism but precious little inspiration.

Although Harmon and Unger are definitely lovely to look at, they pack the combined sex appeal of two pudding parfaits sitting on a diner refrigerator shelf. The beautiful title tune insinuates its way into the soundtrack at every appropriate turn, but it can't provide passion when the leading players don't create any sparks. As the deranged husband, Krabbe hams it up as if he were playing the title role in THE VILLAIN STILL PURSUED HER.

With all these not inconsiderable drawbacks, TILL THERE WAS YOU cannot be faulted for its handsome-looking romantic escapism. No matter how far-fetched the plot becomes, the mood music is inviting, the South Seas locale is alluring, and the stars are easy on the eyes. The film's exotic aura manages to carry you away even when the emotional drama is scarcely more exciting than a list of romantic stop-overs promised on a travel brochure. *(Violence, profanity, nudity.)*

p, Jim McElroy, Hal McElroy; d, John Seale; w, Michael Thomas; ph, Geoffrey Simpson; ed, Jill Bilcock; m, Graeme Revell; prod d, George Liddle; art d, Ian Allen; cos, Miv Brewer

Adventure/Mystery (PR: C MPAA: PG-13)

TO PROTECT AND SERVE ★★½
(Switzerland) 93m Apsicon Productions; Capital Entertainment ~ LIVE Home Video c

C. Thomas Howell *(Will Egan)*, Lezlie Deane *(Harriet)*, Richard Romanus *(Capt. Maloul)*, Joe Cortese *(Kazinsky)*, Zoe Trilling *(Beverly)*, Steve Ganon *(Lt. Burton)*, Rudy Ramos *(Aguilar)*, Tim Colgert *(Franklin)*, James Andronicus *(Garner)*, Jeffrey Anderson Gunter *(Teddy B.)*, Freemon King *(Ridley)*

Sporting top-of-the-line production values and confident direction, TO PROTECT AND SERVE is a gritty, above average crime thriller that plays like TV's erstwhile "Hill Street Blues" on testosterone.

Will Egan (C. Thomas Howell) is a burned-out cop whose life is changed after witnessing fellow officers execute a Rodney King-type beating on a perpetrator. Apparently, this nightbreed of crooked policemen have been in operation since Howell's own dad was killed in the line of duty years before. Although his former girlfriend Harriet (Lezlie Deane), a super cop, reluctantly partners Egan, she doesn't realize that he's working undercover for the internal affairs office. It seems they're after bigger game than the rogue cops, a group that includes Kazinski (Joe Cortese) and Aguilar (Rudy Ramos).

As the investigation heats up, the grafting cops start meeting their maker one by one, starting with Franklin (Tim Colgert) who's slain during a kinky sex scene with a prostitute; she may be the only one who can identify the cop killer. When Egan won't play ball by killing Teddy B. (Jeffrey Anderson Gunter), a drug-dealing informant, two of the choirboys do it for him but end up becoming homicide statistics themselves. By the time Egan acquires a shakedown diary from one of the surviving cops, Harriet suspects that he is the vigilante snuffing out crooked cops.

Lured by the whore who witnessed Franklin's killer running from the crime scene, Egan travels to a seedy section of town where he encounters the doubting Harriet disguised as the hooker. He is only slightly more surprised when their very own Captain Maloul (Richard Romanus), the chief of police, steps out of the shadows and demands the incriminating diary. In the ensuing Wambaugh-ian turn of events, Egan saves Harriet, executes the scummy captain (who also killed Howell's father), and prepares to turn the diary over to internal affairs.

Where TO PROTECT AND SERVE falters is in juggling the who's-really-doing-it suspense aspects of the screenplay. Also, once the internal affairs element is added, our suspicions shift immediately to the captain no matter how hard the screenplay keeps spotlighting Howell's possible guilt. Although amateur detectives may not be as easily led as the screenwriter hopes, the film's rogues gallery of rotten boys-in-blue is intriguing enough to hold one's interest.

Still feeling his way out of boyish roles, Howell (THE HITCHER, SOUL MAN) captures his character's angst without quite shaking off the aura of a juvenile lead trying to act more mature than he is. He lacks the heft for the role but it's a game try, and he's supported by a sterling contingent of some of today's finest character actors.

Reservations aside, TO PROTECT AND SERVE is an engrossing urban nightmare that raises some disturbing issues about loyalty and violence among professionals sworn to serve the public. It is persuasively grim enough to make police recruitment boards shudder. *(Violence, extreme profanity, adult situations.)*

p, Angela Schapiro; d, Eric Weston; w, Eric Weston, Freeman King, Kent Perkins, Darren Dalton; ph, Irv Goodnoff

Crime/Thriller **(PR: O MPAA: R)**

TO RENDER A LIFE ★★★

88m James Agee Film Project ~ James Agee Film Project c

The Glass Family, Robert Coles, Frederick Wiseman, Howard Raines, Jonathan Yardley

A contemporary tribute to *Let Us Now Praise Famous Men*, the 50-year-old book about Depression-era tenant farmers, Ross Spears's TO RENDER A LIFE not only mimics the style of James Agee's and Walker Evans's classic work, but also includes relevant comments from other writers and filmmakers who use the documentary method.

Spears's film opens with a panoramic view of a luxurious country estate, but then the camera draws back at increasing speed past a golf course, lake and shooting-range, winding up fifteen miles down a rural road before a simple shanty where Obea and Alice Glass live with their adopted daughter, Anita. Since they own the land on which they live in a house they built themselves, the Glasses are ineligible for any kind of aid from local, state or federal agencies; Obea and Alice are both missing teeth and look older than their years.

Copying the style of Walker Evans's photographs, TO RENDER A LIFE focuses on both human portraiture and the small details of daily life—no matter how common. For several long takes, the frame is filled with close-ups of discarded toys, rusting tools and an abandoned vehicle. The film also includes occasional readings from Agee's text, which one critic calls excessive, while another notes that it has passages of genius despite its flowery style.

Obea Glass supplements his meager income from restoring furniture by participating in shooting matches at which he earns boxes of foodstuffs. And we watch how Alice tends their wood-burning stove to make a starchy hot meal despite the 100-degree summer heat. Not only do they each chop wood, but they have to lug plastic bottles and pails of water from a nearby stream for their daily needs. A hard-working couple, the Glasses built their own house from timber and tarpaper; the close-ups of bent, rusty nails are proof of their handiwork. Poor but generous, the Glasses adopted Anita when her ailing health triggered Alice's maternal instincts.

Made over a period of three years, TO RENDER A LIFE notes a deterioration in Alice's health to which both an accident that wrecked their car, and the demise of the family's refrigerator, contribute. Woven into these observations is an editorial gloss concerning the responsibility of documentarians to their subjects, with input from Robert Coles, Frederick Wiseman, Tom Rosengarten, Howell Raines and others.

Despite the obvious affection that developed between the filmmakers and the Glasses (at one point Alice, energetically washing the floor, knocks out the camera), there is one detail that highlights the immense gap between film crew and subjects. Anita is given a still camera to take a parting shot of the director and his team; the camera is a very modern, very expensive Leica. After having seen the old-fashioned washing machine with attached wringer that Alice used (it died, like the fridge), the contrast is jolting. Still, TO RENDER A LIFE represents a plea for social justice that is needed now as much as ever.

d, Ross Spears; w, Silvia Kersusan; ph, Ross Spears

Documentary **(PR: A MPAA: NR)**

TOGETHER ALONE ★★★

87m P J Party Productions ~ Frameline bw

Todd Stites *(Bryan)*, Terry Curry *(Brian)*

Reputedly completed for a paltry $7,000 and already a sizable hit on the lesbian and gay festival circuit, TOGETHER ALONE works surprisingly well, given the obvious cinematic limitations of filming a straightforward if expansive conversation—one which takes place in a single setting, no less.

As the film opens, two attractive strangers are seen leaving an LA nightclub after picking each other up. They arrive at Bryan's (Todd Stites) modest studio apartment and, after some unseen sex, drift to sleep. Suddenly Bryan awakens with a jolt—he's had a disturbing dream involving Bill (Terry Curry). When Bill awakens, however, Bryan discovers that his new bedmate has lied; his *real* name is Brian. Bryan, who's HIV-negative and hasn't had anal intercourse in several years—if ever—is very upset; if Brian lied about his name, what *else* is he lying about? After all, in a rare moment of abandon for Bryan, they've just had unprotected sex.

Brian is disturbingly cavalier about practicing safe sex, admitting that he's never been tested because, as a perennial top man, he's never had to. As their conversation shifts from AIDS to sexual identity in general, Brian lashes out at the militant drag queens intent on outing the world. He hates labels like straight, gay, bisexual—at least during the 1960s and 70s you could explore your sexuality without being pigeonholed. Brian, not surprisingly, soon reveals that he enjoys sleeping with both sexes.

Bryan describes himself as yin, the feminine, passive principal in nature, to Brian's yang, or masculine, active principal; in Chinese cosmology, the two combine to produce all that comes to be. Underscoring this notion of oneness, Bryan and Brian discover that they've each had the same disturbing dream: they're on a big wooden raft on a river, navigating from islet to islet; Bryan leaps into the water, followed by Brian, who has difficulty swimming; suddenly the water has turned into air, and it's Brian who's at ease, whereas Bryan has difficulty flying; after watching the moon catch fire and feathers swirl around them, they both drift down to a tropical paradise.

Their mildly combative conversation continues. After Brian accuses Bryan of being incapable of making an emotional commitment, the latter recounts his one great love, Michael, a college roommate. Unfortunately, Bryan was closeted at the time—he had to flee to Europe to be liberated—and failed to act on his feelings. Brian, it turns out, also harbored a great love during college, for a strong, independent woman who combined the masculine and feminine traits he admires. Unfortunately, she angrily dumped Brian when, before proposing to her, he confessed his attraction to men.

When Bryan—who has, not surprisingly, pinned his romantic hopes on Brian—teasingly offers to have sex with Brian, the latter demurs. When pressed on the subject, he drops a bombshell: he's married, with one child and another on the way. Suddenly, the spectre of AIDS reappears; Brian, Bryan exclaims, has a cut on his penis. Fueling Bryan's fear is the fact that his own brother recently died of AIDS, contracted during an unprotected sexual encounter with a prostitute. Tired of defending himself, Brian decides it's time to leave, and the two part on ambivalent terms.

The shared dream may be a ridiculous conceit, but giving Brian a bisexual rather than gay orientation is a shrewd one; it allows filmmaker Castellaneta, in his feature debut, to touch upon topics—abortion, marriage—otherwise at some remove from the gay experience (though, obviously, the queer experience is not as hermetic as that comment might suggest). It's also a wee bit calculated, and the film treads a very thin line between public service announcement and drama. Also, while both characters emerge as reasonably complex, contradictory figures, they share certain traits—white, educated, emotionally stunted—that hardly mark them as alternative gay role models, mirroring, instead, the film's target audience. TOGETHER ALONE also suffers from a notable lack of passion, a trait which, along with films like THE LIVING END and SWOON, is a disturbing hallmark of the much heralded "New Queer Wave."

These considerations aside, TOGETHER ALONE is well worth seeing. The film is beautifully photographed and seamlessly edited—at no moment do the visuals succumb to the static nature of the material. True, Wayne Alabardo's score *is* intrusive, but there's a genuine dramatic arc to the material. Unlike the majority of contemporary American films, both independent and mainstream, which start off strong and quickly wane, this one grows more interesting as it goes along. *(Adult situations.)*

p, P.J. Castellaneta; d, P.J. Castellaneta; w, P.J. Castellaneta; ph, David Dechant; ed, P.J. Castellaneta, Maria Lee; m, Wayne Alabardo

Drama **(PR: C MPAA: NR)**

TOTO LE HEROS ★★★★

(Belgium/France/Germany) 90m Iblis Films; Les Productions Philippe Dussart; Metropolis Filmproduktion; RTBF Telefilms; FR3 Films Production; Zweites Deutsches Fernsehen; Jacqueline Pierreux ~ Triton Pictures c

Michel Bouquet *(Thomas–As an Old Man/Voice of Adult Thomas)*, Mireille Perrier *(Voice of Evelyne As an Old Woman/ Adult Evelyne)*, Jo De Backer *(Thomas–As an Adult)*, Thomas Godet *(Thomas–As a Child)*, Sandrine Blancke *(Alice)*, Fabienne Loriaux *(Thomas's Mother)*, Klaus Schindler *(Thomas's Father)*, Patrick Waleffe *(Voice of Thomas's Father)*, Didier DeNeck *(Mr. Kant)*, Peter Bohlke *(Alfred–As an Old Man)*, Michel Robin *(Voice of Alfred As an Old Man)*, Gisela Uhlen *(Evelyne–As an Old Woman)*, Christine Smeysters *(Mrs. Kant)*, Didier Ferney *(Alfred–As an Adult)*, Hugo Harold Harrisson *(Alfred–As a Child)*, Karim Moussati *(Celestin–As a Child)*, Pascal Duquenne *(Celestin–As an Adult)*, Francois Toumarkine *(Voice of Adult Celestin)*, Harry Cleven *(Gangster)*, Joose DePauw *(Pilot)*

A onetime professional clown named Jaco Van Dormael has made a remarkable feature filmmaking debut with TOTO LE HEROS, an enchanted plaything of a movie that takes full advantage of the narrative and reaffirms one's faith in cinema as a visual storytelling medium.

The plot pendulums back and forth through time, unraveling the obsessed thoughts of Thomas Van Hosebroeck (Michel Bouquet), a bitter old man in a retirement home, muttering darkly about conspiracies and vengeance as he packs his meager possessions and moves and sneaks out. His mind goes back to childhood, to his infancy in fact, when he firmly believes he was switched for another baby during a maternity ward fire. Thomas is convinced that the interloper grew to become Alfred Kant, the next-door neighbor, an overbearing rich kid who luxuriates in the stolen life that should have gone to Thomas.

Thomas's nominal parents, meanwhile, are a happy working-class couple. Father is a devil-may-care courier pilot who's flying for Alfred's family business when the plane crashes and kills him. Mother loses her sanity, leaving young Thomas and his headstrong adolescent sister Alice in charge of the household. Thomas falls in love with the indominatable girl (in his eyes they aren't really related). At the boy's urging, Alice sets a retaliatory fire on Alfred's property. In the inferno Alice is killed.

Adulthood finds Thomas a dispirited clerk in a bleak office. By chance he glimpses Evelyne, a grown-up incarnation of the lost Alice. They begin an affair, but the hated Alfred re-enters the picture. Now he is a prosperous businessman—and Evelyne's husband. Evelyne agrees to run away with Thomas, but she's late for their train station rendezvous. Certain he's been abandoned again, Thomas leaves the station, never seeing Evelyne arrive an instant later.

Now at sixty, Thomas at last perceives an opportunity to strike decisively against his lifelong secret nemesis. Alfred, a prominent industrialist, is the most hated man in the country for laying off countless factory workers. Thomas knows where Alfred hides out and plans to confront him and somehow take back his rightful existence. But while exploring Alfred's town residence, Thomas overhears political terrorists also scoping out the place; they plan to assassinate Alfred the next time he shows up. Thomas heads for Alfred's country house and warmly greets his former neighbor as an old pal. Alfred, nothing but a sad, lonely senior citizen, senses nothing amiss until Thomas locks him in the cellar and takes his car and clothing. Disguised as the industrialist, Thomas goes to the townhouse at the appointed hour and allows himself to be gunned down by the terrorists. Having regained his life after all, Thomas shouts with joy as as his ashes are scattered by plane over a cheery countryside.

TOTO LE HEROS centers on an abstract but resonant notion. After all, who, at one point or another, has not accused fate of having dealt him a bad hand from from the start? Thomas *knows* his destiny has been displaced, his many disappointments but confirmations of a cosmic fluke. The maternity-ward mixup, whether real or dreamed, colors his entire attitude, so that at the beginning of the film, as an old man ruminating over his strange, twisted life, he grumbles, "I haven't lived. Nothing ever happened to me. Nothing ever happened in this guy's story. Nothing." The sentiment cues the phantasmagoria of memories showing just how "uneventful" Thomas's years have been.

Other films have toyed with time, illusion and reality, to jazz up a straightforward story (the Oscar-winning ANNIE HALL is one of the best realized of these). And many a first-time auteur has tried every camera trick in the book and then some (CITIZEN KANE is a monumental example). In TOTO LE HEROS, however, the freeform follows function. One can hardly imagine any other way for the intricate, metaphysical premise to unfold than this controlled explosion of impressions. The multi-flashback structure evokes recurrent motifs and coincident images, notable family, fire and flight, making a comprehensible mosaic of it all.

Only a few characters get lost in the shuffle, notably Thomas's autistic younger brother Celestin, who just disappears after a while. The title personage may also be less than accessible for non-European viewers. Toto (a generic male nickname in Gallic argot, roughly equivalent to "Bud" or "Mack"), is an archetypal fantasy figure who pervades Thomas's daydreams. Looking like a stockier version of Inspector Clouseau, he is a fearless secret agent in Belgian comic-strip tradition, perpetually in battle against the forces of evil (gangster stand-ins for Alfred). Thomas repeatedly turns to Toto as an alter ego—himself on a different plane, where his thwarted existence is a great, hidden adventure. In the end Thomas and Toto become one as the hero wins the ultimate victory over Alfred by dying in his place.

Van Dormael originally envisioned TOTO LE HEROS as a film about children. The adult segments of the story evolved later, but the whole picture vividly evokes all the wonders and horrors of childhood, when new siblings arrive via odder means than the stork, and father's singing a popular song makes even the flowers dance. The six-decade chronology supposedly reaches to the year 2027, but the filmmakers decided they didn't want the distraction of a sci-fi production design, and they gave the entire tale an unspecific mid-20th-century look.

The actors are all perfectly cast. Michel Bouquet is one of France's most enduring stage and screen performers, while Jo De Backer (the mature Thomas) was an unknown in his first movie role. Writer-director Jaco Van Dormael himself had a stint as a clown with Belgium's "Big Flying Circus" (his wife Laurette was also a member of the troupe) before turning to motion picture work in the 1970s. He formed a close relationship with producer Pierre Drout, one of the administrators at a Brussels film institute where Van Dormael started an acclaimed series of shorts and documentaries.

In 1986 Van Dormael submitted the first draft of TOTO LE HEROS to Drouot, who spent two years gathering financing from numerous sources in Belgium, France and Germany (conveniently qualifying for a special grant available to any cinematic project made jointly by three European countries). The finished film cost $3.5 million—extravagant by Belgian standards—and met with both critical and commercial success on its home turf; among the awards it won was the prestigious Camera d'Or at Cannes in 1991.

This unusual picture proved to have a broad appeal, and Van Dormael thus summed up worldwide reaction: "In the United States and England there was more laughing. In Japan and Germany they were serious. In France I think they laughed and then cried." TOTO LES HEROS even garnered what history has proven to be a most doubtful tribute; it was announced that Hollywood's cultural imperialists planned to crank out a carefully Americanized remake. *(Violence, nudity, adult situations, sexual situations.)*

p, Pierre Drouot, Dany Geys; d, Jaco Van Dormael; w, Jaco Van Dormael; ph, Walther Vanden Ende; ed, Susana Rossberg; m, Pierre Van Dormael; art d, Hubert Pouille; cos, Suzanne Van Well

Drama/Comedy/Fantasy (PR: C MPAA: PG-13)

TOUCH AND DIE ★½

(U.K./France/Italy/Germany) 108m ITC Productions; TF1 Films Production; RAI-TV Channel 2; Taurus Film ~ Vestron Video c

Martin Sheen *(Frank Magentz)*, Renee Estevez *(Emma)*, David Birney *(Senator John Scanzano)*, Franco Nero *(Aquan)*, Veronique Jannot *(Catherine)*, Luca Venantini *(Carlo)*, Paolo Bonacelli *(Morelli)*, Horst Bucholz *(Limey)*, Kent Broadhurst *(Davis)*, Bazil Otoin *(The Major)*, Jacques Perrin *(Steuben)*

Imagine that Costa-Gavras, who has become expert in politically correct rabble-rousing, had become temporarily unhinged from exposure to radiation and had decided to expose the pro-Nuke movement. TOUCH AND DIE might be the end product of his delirium.

Hotshot American news bureau chief Frank Magentz (Martin Sheen) sniffs out a scoop when handless corpses start turning up all over Europe. Aided by his new assistant Carlo (Luca Venantini) and his visiting daughter, Emma (Renee Estevez), Magentz tracks down an African sailor who handled stolen plutonium on the vessel Black Mamba. While trying to implicate shipping magnate Steuben (Jacques Perrin) in international, wholesale nuclear theft, Frank falls for a pro-Nuke physicist, Catherine (Veronique Jannot), of the European Atomic Commission. Busy Frank also agrees to help an Italian secret police chief, Aquan (Franco Nero), in proving crooked cop Morelli (Paolo Bonacelli) has a "hand" in the conspiracy.

Traveling to Lutesh, Africa, Frank trades barbs with corrupt officials but manages to disrupt a nuclear flea market with the help of Limey (Horst Bucholz), a friend of a friend. Threading through this narrative that might have taxed Dickens's memory are the following events: Morelli pushes Carlo in front of a subway train but the kid escapes harm; Davis (Kent Broadhurst), the nuclear sales mastermind, threatens to kill everyone and formulates plans to kidnap Emma; Steuben commits suicide after telling Frank where the money trail leads; and Catherine takes an unplanned trip out of her hotel window after returning from Lutesh.

Why were the nuclear materials stolen and sold to the highest bidder? So that Davis and the atomic advocates could funnel money into the campaign fund of the candidate most likely to favor nuclear power when he becomes president. Incredibly, the duped politician is John Scanzano (David Birney), who just happens to be a close personal friend of Frank Magentz. After Scanzano fires his campaign manager, the nuclear lobby conspiracy is squelched, and Magentz writes the prize-winning expose of his career.

Perhaps if the vertiginous plotting that characterizes director Piernico Solinas and John Howlett's screenplay for TOUCH AND DIE were matched by a hallucinogenic directorial style, the film's paranoia might have had some impact. Hampered by perfunctory direction and bland cinematography and a ludicrously inappropriate musical score, the film emerges as even more preposterous.

The film's rabid anti-nuclear power stance is so poorly presented, most viewers will begin to feel sympathy for plutonium pushers everywhere. For one thing, actor Sheen needs to take a vacation from earnestness. For another thing, the film stockpiles so many storylines that even when they're tied together at the climax we feel oppressed by the over-plotting. Do we need the subplot of Franco Nero ferreting out a crooked cop? And isn't the news chief's daughter in the film only to provide a possible roadblock to his bringing the conspirators to justice quickly; if so, why is this subplot never developed? Have there ever been so many villains in one thriller?

Instead of concentrating on intertwining a few plot threads, the *modus operandi* of TOUCH AND DIE is to keep adding more principals and more conspiracy theories. Not only will this thriller fail to win over any converts, it will probably alienate those dedicated to blocking atomic power. A bad movie doesn't promote anyone's cause. *(Violence.)*

p, Evelyne Madec; d, Piernico Solinas; w, John Howlett, Piernico Solinas

Thriller/Crime **(PR: C MPAA: R)**

TOUS LES MATINS DU MONDE ★★★½

(France) 114m Film par film; Divali Films; DD Productions; Sedif; FR3 Films Production; Paravision International ~ October Films c

Jean-Pierre Marielle *(Monsieur de Saint Colombe)*, Gerard Depardieu *(Marin Marias)*, Anne Brochet *(Madeleine)*, Guillaume Depardieu *(Young Marin Marais)*, Caroline Sihol *(Madame de Sainte Colombe)*, Carole Richert *(Toinette)*, Violaine Lacroix *(Young Madeleine)*, Nadege Teron *(Young Toinette)*, Myriam Boyer *(Guignotte)*, Jean-Claude Dreyfus *(Abbe Mathieu)*, Yves Lambrecht *(Chabonnieres)*, Michel Bouquet *(Baugin)*, Jean-Marie Poirer *(Monsieur de Bures)*, Philippe Duclos *(Voice of Brunet)*, Yves Gourvil *(Voice of Lequieu)*

TOUS LES MATINS DU MONDE recounts the real-life story of master 17th-century French musician M. de Saint Colombe (Jean-Pierre Marielle) and his brilliant protege, Marin Marais. A grandly sentimental, eccentric romance, the film also tackles some hefty philosophical questions about the meaning and purpose of music. It's a heady, intoxicating mix.

The film's framing narrative introduces us to the mature Marais (a periwigged Gerard Depardieu at his bloated, foppish best), surrounded by his adoring students in the royal musical chambers. Despite having found fame and fortune as musical director at the court of Louis XIV, Marais is unfulfilled. Compared to his former mentor, the legendary Saint Colombe (Jean-Pierre Marielle)—a musical genius who created the *viol da gamba* by adding a seventh string to the viol—Marais feels like an impostor. He ruefully recalls his salad days as a student of Saint Colombe and lover of his mentor's elder daughter, Madeleine (Anne Brochet).

Stricken with grief after the death of his wife and left with two young daughters to raise, the legendary Saint Colombe had become a virtual recluse, refusing even a summons to play for the King. Apart from occasional performances with his gifted daughters, he spent his time obsessively practicing and composing melancholy pieces to keep alive the memory of his wife, who would often appear to him in a vision when he played.

Enter the teenage Marais (Guillaume Depardieu, son of Gerard), an aspiring musician with all the hubris and sex appeal of a modern rock star. Initially, Saint Colombe rejects Marais for his dazzling virtuosity ("You are a great acrobat but you're no musician"). But his sheltered daughters like the appealing stranger, so Marais is told to return in a month, when the maestro will reconsider. With Madeleine's covert help, Marais trains to meet her father's exacting standards. (For that month, they sneak under Saint Colombe's hideaway cabin to eavesdrop on his technique.) At the second audition, Saint Colombe tells Marais that he's "fit to play for the stage but [he] won't be a musician." Nevertheless, Marais is accepted as the reluctant maitre's sole pupil and moves into the household—and into Madeleine's bed.

Soon, however, the upwardly mobile Marais (he's the son of a poor shoemaker) is secretly moonlighting as a court violist. He's offered a permanent position and, bored with both Saint Colombe's stringent aesthetic and his daughter, he sells out for the baroque frippery of Versailles.

As a result of his departure, both Marais and Madeleine wither: he from loss of musical integrity, she from unrequited love. Unknown to Marais, Madeleine gives birth to his stillborn child, and never recovers from her heartbreak. Years later, when she has been taken seriously ill, Marais (now again played by Depardieu *pere*) is rushed to her bedside for a last meeting. He gives her a pair of shoes and plays "The Dreaming Girl," a song he had written for her when they were young. After he leaves she removes the satin ties from the shoes and hangs herself with them.

After the death of his daughter, Saint Colombe doesn't touch his viol for six months, and considers destroying the manuscript of a suite he has written called "Tomb of Sorrows." When Marais learns of this, he's horrified at the potential loss and becomes obsessed with hearing the piece. Every night for three years he rides to the cabin, hides outside the door, and listens to the master play. Finally, one cold night in January 1689, Saint Colombe hears him, and allows him to enter the cabin. After a disquisition on the nature of musical art, Saint Colombe opens his manuscript book and the two play a duet of "Tears." Marais, with tears in his eyes and using Madeleine's viol, creates the most beautiful sounds he has ever produced.

Cut to the present, years later. A phlegmatic Marais, still on his gilded seat in the royal concert chamber, sees a vision of Sainte Colombe, now smiling, in the doorway, who tells him, "I'm proud to have been your teacher. Please play me the air my daughter loved." As the picture fades to black, the sound of "Tears" fills the empty screen.

Though he's not on screen for very long, Gerard Depardieu gives a marvelously fussy performance as the older Marais. In an impressive film debut, his twenty-one-year-old son Guillaume portrays the aspiring artist as a young man with real charm and conviction. Anne Brochet and Carole Richert exude a winning blend of naivete and sophistication as the dutiful, talented daughters of a brilliant, eccentric father. Jean-Pierre Marielle's deadpan portrayal of Saint Colombe is wonderfully offbeat, filled with either long silences or aphorisms. ("Urinating is a chromatic descent; music exists to say things words cannot say.")

The relatively few words in TOUS LES MATINS DU MONDE were scripted by Pascal Quignard and director Alain Corneau, based on Quignard's novella of the same title (literally translated, *All the mornings of the world*, but closer in spirit to *Each day dawns but once*).

Despite the virtuoso performances, the driving force of TOUS LES MATINS DU MONDE is its music—original compositions of Saint Colombe and Marais, with additional works by Lully, Couperin and Savall, conducted and performed by Jordi Savall and the Concert of Nations. The sonorous tones of the viol fill the screen throughout its almost two-hour running time, making this a truly sublime experience for music lovers.

p, Jean-Louis Livi, French Ministry of Culture, Canal Plus; d, Alain Corneau; w, Alain Corneau, Pascal Quignard, (from his novel); ph, Yves Angelo; ed, Marie-Josephe Berroyer; m, Jordi Savall; prod d, Yves Angelo; cos, Corrine Jorry

Drama/Biography/Musical (PR: A MPAA: NR)

TOYS ★½

110m Baltimore Pictures; Fox ~ Fox c

Robin Williams *(Leslie Zevo)*, Michael Gambon *(The General)*, Joan Cusack *(Alsatia Zevo)*, Robin Wright *(Gwen)*, L.L. Cool J. *(Patrick)*, Donald O'Connor *(Kenneth Zevo)*, Arthur Malet *(Owens Owens)*, Jack Warden *(Zevo, Sr.)*, Debi Mazar *(Nurse Debbie)*, Wendy Melvoin *(Choir Soloist)*, Julio Oscar Mechoso *(Cortez)*, Jamie Foxx *(Baker)*, Shelly Desai *(Shimera)*, Blake Clark *(Hogenstern)*, Clinton Allmon *(Magraw)*, Art Metrano *(Guard at Desk)*, Tommy Townsend *(Tegnell)*, Kate Benton, Steve Park, Julie Hayden, Yeardley Smith *(Researchers)*, Ralph Tabakin *(Fred)*, Martha Faulkner *(Mary–Housekeeper)*, Alex Bookston *(Minister)*, Manny Portel *(Joe)*, Brooks Mondae *(Guard in General's Office)*, Sam Levinson *(War Room Player)*, Kevin West *(Technician)*, Jonathan McGarry *(Stupid Egghead)*, Jacque Lynn Colton *(Woman in Supermarket)*, Felton Anderson, III, Jenny Canales, Amy Arwen Gibbins, Michaela Herbon, Nicholas Herbon, Benjamin Hernandez, Sarah M. LeFever, Eric W. Miller, Jeffrey R. Miller, Kristy E. Miller, Tashequa J. Peterson, Heather Rogers, Denise J. Saucedo, Lisette Yvonne Saucedo, Summer Simaan, Jimmy Spooner, Sarah Yee *(Children of the World Choir)*, Lisel Brunson, Delores Finch, Lisa Fink, Jerry Goldman, Gerald McKinnie, Dolores E. Sebrasky, John Stevens, Roldan Nill Williams *(Factory Workers)*

In a disastrous throwback to his roots as a TV sketch writer, Barry Levinson created one of 1992's most notable flops in TOYS, a schmaltzy variety-show routine inflated into a rudderless mess of a fantasy.

Dying of a heart ailment, toymaker Kenneth Zevo (Donald O'Connor) entrusts the running of his factory after his death to his brother, an army general (Michael Gambon) with no more wars to fight. Zevo has a son, Leslie (Robin Williams), and a daughter, Alsatia (Joan Cusack), but he feels his children are too naive and innocent to run the factory. Upon the death of his brother, the General turns the once-happy factory into an oppressive assembly line, bringing in *his* son, Patrick (L.L. Cool J.), to run the security force. Leslie is left to supervise the manufacture of the simple, harmless toys that had made Zevo famous, while the General insidiously converts the plant into a manufacturing center for toys of war and destruction, training little boys to operate them through the use of video games.

When Leslie infiltrates the General's security system and discovers his nefarious plans, he determines to stop him. Pursued by killer toy tanks, Leslie makes his way through a human-size video maze into an abandoned warehouse, populated by rejected wind-up toys. With the aid of Patrick, Alsatia and his copy-room girlfriend, Gwen (Robin Wright), he fends off the General's army of destructive toys and ultimately vanquishes him. The factory resumes normal production, and Leslie's father's elephant-shaped mausoleum flies into the sky, blowing bubbles out of its alabaster trunk.

Trying for a post-modernist melding of THE 5,000 FINGERS OF DR. T and METROPOLIS, the best TOYS can achieve is a cross between a Rankin-Bass Christmas special and THE PAJAMA GAME. Levinson, whose best films (DINER, RAINMAN, AVALON) have been quiet character studies, eliminates character entirely from TOYS, preferring instead to allow the eye-popping production design by Ferdinando Scarfiotti and art direction by Edward Richardson to dwarf the actors into insignificance. Seemingly, Levinson wants to deliver an important statement via set design, but he has no idea what that important statement might be.

Glimmers of a satirical assault on the toy industry and American consumerism emerge during board meetings, at which topics such as the distinctions among various plastic vomit prototypes are discussed. But TOYS is striving (and failing) far too hard to be a fable for it to work as anything else. The factory, which stands alone in the middle of a huge Midwestern wheatfield, is a kind of utopian workers' community/theme park, where the happy drones joyfully slap together Zevo toys while singing, "It's the perfect job."

Given the addleheaded material, the actors have only themselves to depend on, and an air of doom suffuses their every inflection and movement. Robin Williams behaves like a dim-witted second cousin of a Kafka character. Too smart for the role, he attempts a muted version of his stream-of-consciousness schtick that is grating and un-funny. Joan Cusack opts for a metallic, performance-artist version of Dustin Hoffman's idiot-savant routine from RAINMAN, and comes across like Cher in slow motion. Michael Gambon tries to give a serious performance and achieves a hysterical amalgam of Adolf Hitler and Doctor Doom.

Originally developed at 20th Century-Fox in 1980 and by all accounts a dream project of Levinson's, TOYS is a failure of epic proportions and of the saddest sort—one in which innocence is victimized and vapidity reigns supreme.

p, Barry Levinson, Mark Johnson; d, Barry Levinson; w, Barry Levinson, Valerie Curtin; ph, Adam Greenberg; ed, Stu Linder; m, Hans Zimmer, Trevor Horn; prod d, Ferdinando Scarfiotti; art d, Edward Richardson; set d, Linda DeScenna; cos, Albert Wolsky; ch, Anthony Thomas

AAN Art Direction: Ferdinando Scarfiotti (Art Direction) and Linda DeScenna (Set Decoration); *AAN Costume Design:* Albert Wolsky

Fantasy/Comedy (PR: C MPAA: PG-13)

TRACES OF RED ★½

105m Nightlife Films; Samuel Goldwyn Company ~ Samuel Goldwyn Company c

James Belushi *(Jack Dobson)*, Lorraine Bracco *(Ellen Schofield)*, Tony Goldwyn *(Steve Frayn)*, William Russ *(Michael Dobson)*, Faye Grant *(Beth Frayn)*, Michelle Joyner *(Morgan Cassidy)*, Joe Lisi *(Lieutenant J.C. Hooks)*, Victoria Bass *(Susan Dobson)*, Melanie Tomlin *(Amanda)*, Jim Piddock *(Mr. Martyn)*, Ed Amatrudo *(Emilio)*, Daniel Tucker Kamin *(Prosecutor Dan Ayaroff)*, Harriet Grinnell *(Louis Dobson)*, Lindsey Jayde Sapp *(Nancy Frayn)*, Mario Ernesto Sanchez *(Tony Garidi)*, Joseph C. Hess *(Minnesota)*, Will Knickerbocker *(Tommy Hawkins)*, Edgar Allen Poe, IV *(Ian Wicks)*, Julian Byrd *(Squeeze Club Bartender)*, Billy Garrigues *(Phillip Norris)*, Lori Creevay *(Ellen's Receptionist)*, Michael George Owens *(Key West Priest)*, Tom Amick *(Wurtz's Friend)*, Rex Benson *(Hotel Manager)*, John T. Howe *(Funeral Priest)*, Gerald Beebe *(Angry Diner)*, Robert Farrell *(Detective)*, Artie Malesci *(Stevie B's Patron)*, Junior Biggs *(Snakepit Bartender)*, Katheryn Culliver Pierce *(Kimberly Davis)*, Gregory L. Richter *(Honor Guard Leader)*, Renate Schlesinger *(Ingrid)*

Despite having an interesting cast in a seamy mix of kinky sex, violence, dirty politics and dark family secrets, TRACES OF RED loses its bite in a messy pile of subplots.

Palm Beach homicide detective Jack Dobson (James Belushi) is investigating a series of grisly serial killings with partner Steve Frayn (Tony Goldwyn). Before the first killing, of a call girl, Dobson had witnessed the woman's pimp going up to her hotel room only minutes before the body was discovered. During the pimp's trial for the murder, at which Dobson testifies, he receives a threatening note printed by a computer printer with distinctive lettering flaws and sealed with a "kiss" made by a popular lipstick.

After a casual liaison with a restaurant waitress, Morgan Cassidy (Michelle Joyner), Dobson receives yet another note, warning that an unnamed woman will be garotted. When the waitress turns up dead, strangled with a phone cord, Dobson's suspicions turn to his other current lover, rich Palm Beach widow Ellen Schofield (Lorraine Bracco), who has a pronounced jealous streak. She uses the right lipstick, but none of her computer printers produce the tell-tale flaws. Then a third note appears, alluding to revenge on Dobson for childhood testimony he had given against his first-grade teacher in a child-molesting case.

Frayn takes off in solo pursuit of the teacher's surviving son, only to find that he had died a year earlier of AIDS. Complicating matters is the unexpected arrival of Ellen, who seduces Frayn in his hotel room. When Frayn returns home, he finds incriminating evidence has been planted in his garage. Ellen has also left an incriminating phone message at his home that was intercepted by his irritated wife, Beth (Faye Grant). Frayn sends his wife with Dobson to get away from their house and out of possible danger while he goes to meet with Ellen. Finding Ellen dead at her mansion, Frayn pursues a car he sees leaving to the campaign office of Dobson's brother Michael (William Russ), a politician running for local office.

Michael reveals to Frayn that Jack was actually molested by their own mother and not the teacher, who was used as a scapegoat to keep their family together. Ever since, Michael says, Jack's been unbalanced and tortured with guilt. Going to Jack's house, Michael and Frayn find the computer printer and further evidence linking Jack to the murders. Rushing to Jack's country cabin, Frayn shoots Jack, as it seems he is about to harm his wife. The story is covered up and Jack is buried with full honors for dying in the line of duty. Later, Michael has a date with one of his campaign workers. After getting her to confess that she, too, has slept with Jack, he begins strangling her with a phone cord, only to be interrupted by Frayn and Jack, whose death had been staged to draw Michael out into the open.

TRACES OF RED runs in so many directions at once that it winds up going nowhere. If it had been directed as a campy potboiler rather than an attempt at serious noir, it could have been trashy fun—especially given its first-rate cast.

Bracco seems to be having the most fun as the wanton widow of Palm Beach, who treats life as a banquet and sex as the main course. In the key role, however, Belushi is out of his depth and never able to suggest his problematic past with any conviction. To be fair, he's also let down by a screenplay that uses his childhood trauma more as a plot device than a character element. On the other hand, Russ does a lot more with a lot less to suggest his own family demons, handling his brief part with enough vivid, villainous energy to suggest that TRACES OF RED may be about the wrong character.

Despite his co-star billing, Goldwyn mostly lends support; a subplot involving some alleged hanky-panky between his character's wife and Dobson is never developed or explained. Like the rest of the characters, he spends most of the film chasing after endless plot developments.

Even including its daft twist of an ending, TRACES OF RED is moderately watchable, its byzantine plot recalling Mark Frost's STORYVILLE without also recalling that film's sleep-inducing torpor. *(Violence, profanity, nudity, sexual situations.)*

p, David V. Picker, Mark Gordon; d, Andy Wolk; w, Jim Piddock; ph, Timothy Suhrstedt; ed, Trudy Ship; m, Graeme Revell; prod d, Dan Bishop, Dianna Freas; cos, Hilary Rosenfeld

Mystery/Crime/Drama (PR: O MPAA: R)

TRAINED TO FIGHT ★½

Starlight Film ~ Imperial Entertainment Corporation c

Ken McLeod *(James Couffield)*, Matthew Ray Cohen *(Craig Tanner)*, Mark Williams *(Mark)*, Tang Tak Wing *(Wing Chan)*, Kendra Tucker *(Kimberly)*

Wise men say there are only about seven or eight basic plot concepts that underly all fiction. Now cut that figure in half. And again. You now have all the basic plot concepts available in kung fu movies, of which the direct-to-video release TRAINED TO FIGHT is a strenuous but workaday example.

It's KARATE KID PART 4 time as husky blond James Couffield shows up new in town to start college (he must have flunked several grades, because lead actor Ken McLeod looks amazingly mature for a freshman). James is a regional martial arts champ, and he finds his new roomate Mark (Mark Williams) not only holds numerous chopsocky trophies but also runs a self-defense school for inner-city kids. Mark plans to enter an upcoming tournament and win the $25 thousand prize to keep his dojo going—and beat rival Craig Tanner (Matthew Ray Cohen), racist psycho leader of a street gang called the White Tigers, who harass our heroes with their own blend of martial arts and bad acting.

James gets a job as a waiter at a Chinese restaurant, and during a White Tiger ambush he's saved by the cook Wing Chan (Tang Tak Wing), who turns out to be an invincible kung fu fighter. James begs Wing Chan to be his *sifu*, a revered instructor in martial arts tactics and thought. Finally Chan agrees, and viewers are subjected to the cliched setpiece of the main character going through all kinds of exotic training exercises which seem absurdly impossible at first, but which Chan can do with ease. They train barefoot on an ice rink; in holes on the beach; in an empty park at night. They train and train. This is one action pic that lives up to its title.

More so than many kung fu tales with this selfsame plot, TRAINED TO FIGHT emphasizes that the martial arts aren't all about bashing in somebody's head, but concern discipline, virtue and "being true to one's self." Like his Pat Morita counterpart in the KARATE KID series, Wing Chan is a engaging character to watch and seemingly sincere in his respect for the sport, exemplified by a transcendent moment when he practices alone in the woods, his ballet-like movements ultimately tracing a perfect Yin-Yang mandala in the dirt. But there's a dichotomy 99.9 percent of these karate kitsch pics never escape: no matter how eloquently the celluloid masters speak of harmony, balance, Tao, Te, Zen or whatever, the storyline's agenda is to kick ass. Period.

After all, this one wasn't called TRAINED TO BE TRUE TO ONE'S SELF, and James passes on combat techniques he learns to Mark in anticipation of the big grudge match with Craig Tanner. Before the tournament, however, the pals get into a street brawl with the White Tigers that leaves both Mark and Tanner injured. Against Wing Chan's wishes James enters the contest in Mark's place and defeats the White Tiger entrant, winning the prize money. The school is saved, and Chan judges that his disciple did the right thing.

It also says something about the simple mindset of these movies that arena opponents always have to be hateful monsters instead of honest competitors. James claims to have undergone a spiritual evolution under Wing Chan's tutelage, but all we see is that he successfully seduces sexy coed Kimberly (Kendra

Tucker) via acupuncture-derived oriental massage. She's not exactly a prizewinner either, starting out as a strident environmentalist fanatic who eventually sheds her innate pacifism and attends the tournament to see the White Tigers whipped. "I hope they get their heads bashed in!" declares the reformed peacenik.

Conscious viewers will note that top-billed actor Ken McLeod has in the end credits undergone a miraculous name change, listed there as "Ken Rendall Johnson" instead. As Wing Chan says, "With kung fu nothing is impossible." *(Violence, nudity, sexual situations.)*

p, William Yuen, Theresa Woo; d, Eric Sherman; w, Roxanne Reaver, Teresa Woo; ph, Jurg Walther; ed, Brian Varaday; m, David Bergeaud

Martial Arts/Action (PR: O MPAA: NR)

TRANCERS III: DETH LIVES ★★½
83m Full Moon Entertainment ~ Paramount Home Video c

Tim Thomerson *(Jack Deth)*, Melanie Smith *(R.J.)*, Andrew Robinson *(Colonel Daddy Muther)*, Tony Pierce *(Jason)*, Helen Hunt *(Lena)*, Megan Ward *(Alice)*, Hunter Von Leer *(Senator McCoy)*, R.A. Mihailoff *(Shark)*, Ed Beechner *(Lt. Ryan)*, Stephen Macht *(Harris)*, Telma Hopkins *(Commander Raines)*, Dawn Ann Billings

A distinct improvement on the previous entry in the TRANCERS series, this third installment is a small-scale but entertaining genre entry.

It's Christmas 1992 in Los Angeles, and former Trancer hunter Jack Deth (Tim Thomerson) is now making a living as a private detective. He's in the midst of divorce proceedings with his wife, Lena (Helen Hunt), but in an attempt at reconcilation, he makes arrangements to meet with her for dinner. Those plans are scuttled, however, by the arrival of Shark (R.A. Mihailoff), a scary-looking android emissary from the future who wisks Deth back "down the line" to the year 2352. There he encounters a wartorn Los Angeles in which the zombielike Trancers have slaughtered most of the "normals," and meets up with his former wife Alice (Megan Ward), now a colonel in the dwindling resistance against the Trancers. She sends him on yet another time jaunt—to 2005—when, she says, Lena will have found out who created the Trancers in the first place. Deth's mission is to track the responsible party and end the menace at its source.

Escaping another attack, Deth arrives at his destination year, where Colonel Daddy Muther (Andrew Robinson) has begun the trancing program as part of an elite underground military corps. After one of his "10th level" soldiers (Don Dowe) goes murderously berserk in a club, a lower-level female Trancer-to-be named R.J. (Melanie Smith) goes AWOL from the program. She winds up feeding information about Muther's program to Lena, now a newspaper reporter. Tracking her down after reading one of her stories, Deth finds that she has remarried and had a daughter since he mysteriously disappeared on her eight years before. She turns out to be hiding R.J., who agrees to help Deth bring Muther down and later proves herself by detecting that a cop who stops to question them is actually one of Muther's subjects. Before long, the pair are captured by Jason (Tony Pierce), a non-Trancer goon working for Muther, and brought to Muther's underground complex.

There the sadistic colonel forcibly reinstates R.J. back into the Trancer program, straps Deth down and gives him the first injection designed to turn him into a Trancer, but R.J. frees him just as influential Senator McCoy (Hunter Von Leer) is visiting Muther's facility. The pair shoot Jason, and Muther puts his soldiers on alert; Deth and R.J. take several of them down, but R.J. soon begins to feel the trancing drugs take hold and begs Deth to shoot her before she can turn on him, which he reluctantly does. He is then confronted by Lt. Ryan (Ed Beechner), one of Muther's best fighters, and is in danger of losing when Shark shows up again and saves him.

The android is incapacitated in a subsequent confrontation, however, and Muther confronts Deth, attempting to use his drug-accentuated influence over him to make Deth shoot himself. Deth resists, however, and kills Muther instead; Shark reactivates, and the pair return to 2352. There, Alice and her associates are now in charge of a glittering city, and, impressed by Deth's handling of his assignment, appoint him Peacekeeping Emissary of Time and Space. Deth, not especially thrilled with the appointment, nonetheless heads off with Shark for more adventures.

While TRANCERS III will probably appeal most to those who have already seen the first two installments, it can be enjoyed by the uninitiated who are able to extrapolate a bit from the dialogue and situations presented here. In any case, writer-director C. Courtney Joyner (who also wrote PUPPETMASTER III, the best entry in that Full Moon series) has kept his screenplay packed with incident. While not exactly complex, the film is certainly busy enough to sustain interest through the movie's brief running time. It's also clever in the way it manages to work almost all of the series' previously established characters into the story, provides a reasonable explanation for where the Trancers came from and includes an effective subplot about Lt. Ryan's younger brother Matt (Randal Keith), who wants to join the Trancer corps, only to fall victim to his own older brother in one of Muther's brutal staged combats.

Tim Thomerson continues to be this film series's greatest asset, delivering his tough-guy dialogue with assurance and finding humor in his character without playing against the material. Hunt, who was game enough to return to this low-budget franchise even as she was appearing in major films like MR. SATURDAY NIGHT and THE WATERDANCE, does well with her brief screen time, and Robinson is an effectively slimy villain.

Joyner stretches his limited resources pretty well and comes up with a couple of good action scenes, but regrettably lets an uncomfortable misogyny creep into his work; with the exception of Lena and the briefly seen future officials, every female character in the film dies a nasty and sometimes protracted death. It's an unfortunate indicator that TRANCERS III never really transcends its exploitation film status, even though it's in many ways an above-average example of the genre. *(Violence, profanity, sexual situations.)*

p, Albert Band; d, C. Courtney Joyner; w, C. Courtney Joyner; ph, Adolfo Bartoli; ed, Margaret Anne Smith, Lauren Schaffer; m, Mark Ryder, Phil Davies, Richard Band; prod d, Milo

Science Fiction/Action/Adventure (PR: O MPAA: R)

TRESPASS ★★½
101m Universal ~ Universal c

Bill Paxton *(Vince)*, Ice-T *(King James)*, William Sadler *(Don)*, Ice Cube *(Savon)*, Art Evans *(Bradlee)*, De'Voreaux White *(Lucky)*, Bruce A. Young *(Raymond)*, Glenn Plummer *(Luther)*, Stoney Jackson *(Wickey)*, T.E. Russell *(Video)*, Tiny Lister *(Cletus)*, John Toles-Bey *(Goose)*, Byron Minns *(Moon)*, Tico Wells *(Davis)*, Hal Landon, Jr. *(Eugene DeLong)*, James Pickens, Jr. *(Police Officer Reese)*, L. Warren Young *(Police Officer Foley)*

Originally entitled "The Looters" and scheduled for a summer 1992 release, TRESPASS was postponed to the Christmas season in order to distance it from the Los Angeles race riots triggered by the LAPD beating of Rodney King. Ironically, while flawed as a genre piece, the film implicitly pleads for racial understanding in its allegorical tale of a violent standoff between blacks and whites in a ruined factory.

Don and Vince (William Sadler and Bill Paxton) are two Arkansas firemen who think they've struck a mother lode when they're handed a "treasure map" leading to a million or more dollars' worth of gold stolen 50 years earlier from a Catholic church. The gold is concealed in a ceiling somewhere in a vast, abandoned factory in an East St. Louis ghetto. Sheer action-movie coincidence brings drug dealer King James (Ice-T) and his lieutenants to the factory on the same day as Don and Vince to carry out a revenge execution for the murder of one of their couriers.

Vince inadvertently witnesses the execution but escapes with Don's help before James can execute him. The pair also manage to take James's crippled junkie brother Lucky (De'Voreaux White) as a hostage. In the ensuing standoff, Vince and Don plot their escape with the gold helped by Bradlee (Art Evans), an old derelict living in the factory, before James can muster and mount an offensive on the single room in which they have taken refuge. As plans and negotiations are tried and fail, James must deal with growing dissension within his heavily armed ranks.

Raymond (Bruce A. Young), after finding Vince and Don's truck, also discovers their true reason for being in the factory. He enlists James's right-hand man Savon (Ice Cube) in his own plot to steal the gold while burning down the factory as a diversion. Meanwhile, after being promised a full share of the gold, Bradlee reveals a potential escape route. In the final fiery confrontation, Vince escapes with his life after Don is killed by Lucky, while Bradlee escapes with the gold.

Considered by some the successor to the late Sam Peckinpah, Walter Hill (48 HRS., JOHNNY HANDSOME), not unlike his mentor, makes action films that are conflicted almost to the point of paralysis. While Hill's instinctive intelligence has made him a critical favorite, the dark moral complexities of his scenarios haven't always been to the taste of the action movie audience, which has been spotty in supporting Hill's films.

Don is hard-bitten, greedy and cynical, but his bitterness seems earned in the wake of a bad marriage and messy divorce. Vince, meanwhile, is more traditionally heroic: good-natured, good-hearted and about to be married. But he also has the kind of stupidity that only belongs to the truly innocent, causing him to trigger the film's central crisis. The scenario eventually comes to center on James, the film's most intelligent character who refuses to consider the nature of his violent trade. Placing his brother in jeopardy causes James to reflect on his own situation, which leads to his doom.

The ideas, themes and symbols of TRESPASS never quite gel; the film, like other Hill efforts, fails to become more than the sum of its parts. The main problem is the razor-thin plot, which never overcomes the implausibility of its premise and fails to sustain much suspense. The action lumbers to an all too predictable climax. Yet, as has also typically been the case with Hill's films, the performances are solidly above average for the genre. Ice-T's James, in particular, conveys an uncommon poignancy in his inability to overcome a distrust of whites in general, and Don in particular; he's torn between trying to win the release of his brother without bloodshed, and risking losing the respect of his posse for appearing "soft."

While TRESPASS could have been a lot more compelling, it still displays far more style and intelligence than your average contemporary action thriller. *(Violence, profanity.)*

p, Neil Canton; d, Walter Hill; w, Robert Zemeckis, Bob Gale; ph, Lloyd Ahern; ed, Freeman Davies; m, Ry Cooder; prod d, Jon Hutman; art d, Charles Breen; set d, Beth Rubino; cos, Dan Moore

Action/Drama/Crime (PR: C MPAA: R)

TROLL 2

95m Epic Productions; Filmirage ~ Epic Home Video c

Michael Stephenson *(Joshua)*, Connie McFarland *(Holly)*, George Hardy *(Michael)*, Margo Prey *(Diana)*, Robert Ormsby *(Seth)*, Deborah Reed *(Creedence)*, Jason Wright *(Elliott)*, Darren Ewing *(Arnold)*, Jason Steadman *(Drew)*, David McConnell *(Brent)*, Gary Carison *(Sheriff Freak)*, Mike Hamill *(Bells)*

Italian ripoffs of successful American films are a constant factor on the exploitation movie scene, but rarely is the result as idiotic as TROLL 2, a film that makes the moderately entertaining original look like a Spielberg blockbuster.

The plot (which, of course, has nothing to do with that of its inspiration) centers on young Joshua Waits (Michael Stephenson), who's been having visions of his grandpa, Seth (Robert Ormsby), even though the old gentleman passed away six months before. Grandpa likes to tell Joshua scary stories about evil goblins who live in the forest, and soon begins to warn the boy that he'll be facing similar terrors in the real world.

As it happens, he and his parents, Michael and Diana (George Hardy and Margo Prey), and sister Holly (Connie McFarland) are about to take a vacation, on a strange kind of exchange program in which they'll be switching houses with a family from the small town of Nilbog. (Get it? It takes the characters about half the film to figure it out.) Both during the trip and once they arrive, Joshua continues to have visions of Seth, who warns him that the goblins are lurking about, and will conspire to have him and his family eat tainted food that will turn them into half-flesh, half-plants, the creatures' favorite food. One such warning occurs just as they're about to sit down to a lunch left for them by the locals, but Joshua thinks quickly and stops them from eating by urinating (offscreen, thankfully) all over the table.

Meanwhile, Holly's obnoxious boyfriend, Elliott (Jason Wright), has followed the Waitses to Nilbog in a motor home with three friends. One of the young men, following a pretty girl he sees running through the woods, winds up at a church that actually serves as the domain of Creedence (Deborah Reed), a witch who acts as high priestess for the goblins. The girl foolishly drinks a potion proffered by Creedence, and turns into a human guacamole salad that is devoured by a group of the creatures; her would-be rescuer winds up being turned into a human potted plant with branches growing out of his limbs. While Joshua is busy stumbling onto a meeting of goblins in human guise (whose leader rails against the evils of eating hamburgers and hot dogs) and his family continue to wonder why he's acting so strange, Creedence and the trolls plot to ensnare the family with a dinner reception at the house.

After Creedence seduces one of Elliott's friends (an encounter that begins with mutual nibbling on a corn on the cob and ends with barrels of popcorn falling all over the couple), the party takes place, and the Waitses are about to eat some tainted food when Seth's spirit intervenes, zapping one of the townspeople to a troll-shaped skeleton and giving away the village's terrible secret. Soon our heroes are on the run from a legion of the stunted monsters, but Seth's ghost appears once more, whisking Joshua to Creedence's lair, where the Stonehenge rock that gives the beasts their power rests. Seth then gives Joshua a secret weapon in a backpack, warning him not to use it until absolutely necessary. Needless to say, that time comes very quickly, and as the trolls are advancing on the helpless family, Joshua reaches into the pack and produces—a bologna sandwich! Gobbling down the sandwich, and protected from the vegetarian monsters by the meat in his system, Joshua is able to lead his family to concentrate, and the force of their wills destroys the goblins. The exhausted Waitses return home—but forget about the Nilbog family still living in their house, and Joshua soon witnesses his vegetized mother being devoured by the trolls.

That synopsis pretty much says it all, but suffice it to say that TROLL 2's moronic story is not the least bit made palatable by the dialogue; this must be the first fantasy film where the evil witch admonishes the young hero not to employ the secret weapon by saying, "Think of the cholesterol!" There are hints on occasion that the whole thing might have been intended as a spoof, but the horror scenes are played too straight (and with too much emphasis on gloppy makeup effects) for a tone of intentional amusement to hold for long. In any case, the laughter turns sour during the several sequences in which poor Joshua is subjected to grotesque horrors, particularly in the unforgivable final scene.

The actors are all terrible, but can hardly have been expected to do sterling work given the unspeakable lines and tone-deaf direction, both the responsibility of Claudio Fragasso. He's billed in the film as "Drago Floyd," though someone at Epic Home Video got the pseudonyms crossed and—among many other errors—ascribed the script to Fragasso's other *nom de film*, "Clyde Anderson," on the cassette boxes and ads.

Of course, any attempt to obscure the names of those involved in the making of this fiasco can only be construed as an act of mercy. TROLL 2 is really as bad as they come. *(Violence, profanity, adult situations.)*

d, Drago Floyd; w, Clyde Anderson, (from his story); ph, Federiko Slonisko; ed, Vania Strigenoff

Fantasy/Horror **(PR: O MPAA: PG-13)**

TULITIKKUTEHTAAN TYTTO
(SEE: MATCH FACTORY GIRL, THE)

TUNE, THE ★★★½
69m ~ October Films c

VOICES OF: Daniel Nieden *(Del)*, Maureen McElheron *(Didi)*, Marty Nelson *(Mayor/Mr. Mega/Mrs. Mega)*, Emily Bindiger *(Dot)*, Chris Hoffman *(Wiseone/Surfer/Tango Dancer/Note)*, Jimmy Ceribello *(Cabbie)*, Ned Reynolds *(Houndog)*, Jeff Knight *(Bellhop)*, Jennifer Senko *(Surfer/Note)*

Bill Plympton, whose imaginative and outrageous short cartoons, including 25 WAYS TO QUIT SMOKING, ONE OF THOSE DAYS and the Oscar-nominated YOUR FACE, have highlighted many an animation festival, makes his feature debut with this delightful musical comedy. While it maintains the wicked wit and singular personality of Plympton's earlier work, THE TUNE also serves as a showcase for some fine song work by his longtime collaborator Maureen McElheron.

THE TUNE's story, in fact, serves merely as a skeleton on which to hang a number of McElheron's memorable tunes, which in turn serve as a springboard for Plympton's wild creativity. The lead character is Del (voice of Daniel Nieden), a young songwriter who is given an ultimatum by his boss, Mr. Mega (Marty Nelson) of Mega Music: come up with a surefire hit in 47 minutes, or he's fired. Compounding Del's plight is the fact that losing his job will also mean the loss of his sweetheart, Didi (McElheron), who is Mega's secretary and has been yearning to return to her small hometown.

Going on a drive to seek inspiration, Del winds up in the bucolic village of Flooby Nooby, where the mayor greets him and explains that he has to write songs that come from the heart, not simply string together words that rhyme. For further guidance, the mayor takes Del to see the Wiseone (Chris Hoffman), who speaks in riddles and whose head transforms into animals and objects. The duo then stop at a diner, where the waitress, Dot (Emily Bindiger), sings a song that inspires the food to amorous activity. Another of the diner's inhabitants, a dog (Ned Reynolds) that impersonates Elvis, belts out an ode to his hairdo. Suddenly realizing that he's late for his meeting with Mr. Mega and in danger of losing Didi, Del imagines himself at the "Lovesick Hotel," where every suite offers a different manner for the lovelorn to end it all.

Help is on the way, however, in the form of a cabdriver (Jimmy Ceribello), who picks Del up and sings a blues song about the nose he loved and lost. But Del winds up deposited on a desert island, where a couple of surfers demonstrate the unique dances they've come up with to combat boredom. They then show Del the way to Mega Music, where he encounters Didi and heads into his meeting with Mr. Mega. He offers up the songs he's heard on his travels, as well as one he has just completed himself, but Mr. Mega hates them all and fires Del. Heartbroken, and realizing they are soon to be separated forever, Del and Didi sing a heartfelt love ballad—and Mr. Mega overhears it. Driven to tears by the song, Mega proclaims it a surefire smash, and Del and Didi face a future of happily ever after.

While the animated features from Disney forever strive for realistic—or at least naturalistic—effects, Plympton's pencil-and-watercolor visuals take the opposite approach. He delights in exploiting the possibilities of animation to manipulate and change familiar forms, and THE TUNE is rife with anthropomorphism and the distortion of the human anatomy.

The former is most delightfully on display during Dot's "Isn't It Good Again" number, which features romantic tableaux involving such comestible couples as ham and eggs and apple pie and ice cream. In the latter area, the highlight is a hilarious scene in which Del witnesses two men abusing each other's heads in ever more bizarre ways; this sequence, bearing the title PUSH COMES TO SHOVE, was released as a separate short by Plympton during THE TUNE's production to help raise completion funds.

Though some of THE TUNE's humor has a black streak, it contains nothing unpleasant or really unsuitable for children. The exaggeration and stylization take the edge off the few moments of violence, and Plympton's wonderful eye for detail makes this a treat for audiences of any age. He always looks for the extra laugh in a scene; when the cabdriver sings the "No Nose Blues" and sees proboscises popping up everywhere he looks, one tree sprouts an eye before being nudged to its correct shape by the nose next to it. There are also plenty of in-jokes for animation buffs; one of the dances performed by the surfers is "The Pencil-Rough," and a suite in the Lovesick Hotel contains Lupo the Butcher, the title star of Danny Antonucci's cult gore cartoon.

On a budget that was probably a hundredth of ALADDIN or BEAUTY AND THE BEAST, Plympton has created an animated feature of equal entertainment value. *(Mildly adult situations.)*

p, Bill Plympton; d, Bill Plympton; w, Bill Plympton, Maureen McElheron, P.C. Vey; ph, John Donnelly; ed, Merril Stern; m, Maureen McElheron

Animated/Musical/Comedy **(PR: A MPAA: NR)**

24 HOURS TO MIDNIGHT ★★
91m ~ AIP Home Video c

Cynthia Rothrock *(Devon Grady)*, Stack Pierce *("White Powder" Chan)*, Bernie Pock *(Lester McQueen)*, Myra *(Lee Ann Jackson)*, Leo T. Fong *(Mr. Big)*

This actioner could easily sink into the compost heap of cheesy, martial arts fist-fests glutting the video market, but in its open lack of pretension and no-holds-barred looniness, 24 HOURS TO MIDNIGHT rises to the top of the heap.

The festivities begin when local gangster "White Powder" Chan (Stack Pierce), in an effort to deter two government witnesses from testifying against him and exposing his organized crime operation, has his gang members mow them down. Unfortunately for Chan, the wife of one of the deceased witnesses happens to be Devon Grady (Cynthia Rothrock), a martial arts expert, who vows vengeance upon Chan's gang for the murder of her husband. Donning black ninja garb, Devon skulks around in the wee hours, enlisting her ninja paraphernalia to off Chan's gang members.

As Devon wreaks her revenge, two very busy cops, Lee Ann Jackson (Myra) and Lester McQueen (Bernie Pock), who are apparently the only two cops in town, attempt to track down the mysterious killer while juggling sundry robberies and teenage gang wars that constantly intrude to sidetrack their investigation. Finally, Chan meets with Mr. Big (Leo T. Fong) in an abandoned warehouse to cement a drug deal, but Devon was there first, planting a bomb that blows all the bad guys to smithereens. She escapes scot free to cool it down Mexico way and Jackson and McQueen are reassigned by the police department to crowd control duty.

24 HOURS TO MIDNIGHT unreels like a bargain-basement THE BRIDE WORE BLACK grafted onto a live-action "Streetfighter." Its low budget smacks you in the face like a karate chop. All the exterior action appears to have been shot on a pre-dawn stretch of Wilshire Boulevard; the dialogue is post-synced CHIMES AT MIDNIGHT-style; the performances are glaringly amateurish; and the narrative construction is repetitive and cliche-ridden. But the film's mantra-like revenge plot and dreary production values are more than compensated for by Leo T. Fong's relentlessly screwy dialogue, which makes the ears bleed in an Edward Wood, Jr. bleat. (Where else can you hear cops say lines like "You know what they say . . . kill them all and let God sort them out" or "Are you the guy they call . . . Spunky?")

Fong's crackpot dialogue is supplemented by his teasing disregard of his own hoary plot. Fong assumes that the audience is hip to the plot and could care less about whether the narrative makes sense or not. He also has no compunction about tweaking the nose of the audience and the genre. (For example, when Jackson bemoans the latest unsolved murder and tells McQueen that she longs for a good, old-fashioned robbery, no sooner does she mouth her wish than a police dispatcher tells the two hapless cops to proceed to a robbery at a convenience store.) For a genre so often overwhelmed by "serious artist" pretensions and raging egos, Fong's take is like a blast of cold air during a heat wave.

Although it suffers from a few gratuitous skin shots and flash-point exploitation, 24 HOURS TO MIDNIGHT has enough engagingly off-kilter moments to give the undiscriminating viewer a mental rest cure from the latest Oliver Stone or Spike Lee extravaganza and refuel his critical faculties for another whack at David Lynch. *(Excessive violence, nudity.)*

d, Leo T. Fong; w, Leo T. Fong

Action/Martial Arts/Crime (PR: C MPAA: NR)

TWIN PEAKS: FIRE WALK WITH ME ★
135m Twin Peaks Productions Inc.; Lynch/Frost Productions; CiBy 2000 ~ New Line Cinema c

Sheryl Lee *(Laura Palmer)*, Ray Wise *(Leland Palmer)*, Moira Kelly *(Donna Hayward)*, Kyle MacLachlan *(Special Agent Dale Cooper)*, David Bowie *(Phillip Jeffries)*, Chris Isaak *(Special Agent Chester Desmond)*, Harry Dean Stanton *(Carl Rodd)*, Dana Ashbrook *(Bobby Briggs)*, Kiefer Sutherland *(Sam Stanley)*, Phoebe Augustine *(Ronette Pulaski)*, Peggy Lipton *(Norma Jennings)*, James Marshall *(James Hurley)*, Grace Zabriskie *(Sarah Palmer)*, Pamela Gidley *(Teresa Banks)*, David Lynch *(Gordon Cole)*, Madchen Amick *(Shelly Johnson)*, Miguel Ferrer *(Albert Rosenfield)*, Heather Graham *(Annie Blackburn)*, Jurgen Prochnow *(Woodman)*, Gary Bullock *(Sheriff Cable)*, Frank Silva *(Bob)*, Al Strobel *(Phillip Michael Gerard)*, Frances Bay *(Mrs. Tremond)*, Eric DaRe *(Leo Johnson)*, Rick Aiello *(Cliff Howard)*, Catherine E. Coulson *(Log Lady)*, Chris Pedersen *(Tommy)*, Victor Rivers *(Buck)*, Jon Huck *(FBI Agent)*, Mike Malone *(FBI Agent)*, Joe Berman *(Bus Driver)*, Yvonne Roberts *(1st Prostitute)*, Audra L. Cooper *(2nd Prostitute)*, John Hoobler *(Pilot)*, Kimberly Ann Cole *(Lit the Dancer)*, Elizabeth Ann McCarthy *(Giggling Secretary)*, C.H. Evans *(Jack at Hap's)*, Paige Bennett *(French Girl at Hap's)*, G. Kenneth Davidson *(Old Guy at Hap's)*, Ingrid Brucato *(Curious Women)*, Chuck McQuarry *(Medic)*, Margaret Adams *(Fat Trout Neighbor)*, Carlton L. Russell *(Jumping Man)*, Calvin Lockhart *(The Electrician)*, Jonathan J. Leppell *(Mrs. Tremond's Grandson)*, David Brisbin *(Second Woodman)*, Andrea Hays *(Heidi)*, Steven Hodges, William Ungerman, Joseph "Simon" Szeibert, Gregory "Smokey" Hormel, Joseph L. Altruda *(Band at Roadhouse)*, James Parks *(Service Station Mechanic)*, Jane Jones *(School Teacher)*, Karin Robison *(Angel in Train Car)*, Lorna MacMillan *(Angel in Red Room)*, Julee Cruise *(Roadhouse Singer)*, Gary Hershberger *(Mike Nelson)*, Sandra Kinder *(Irene at Hap's)*, Lenny Van Dohlen *(Harold Smith)*, Michael J. Anderson *(Man from Another Place)*, Walter Olkewicz *(Jacques Renault)*

Casting alone saves TWIN PEAKS: FIRE WALK WITH ME, a "prequel" to David Lynch's cult TV series that finds the celebrated filmmaker at an uncharacteristically low ebb.

The ghost who haunted the series, Laura Palmer (Sheryl Lee), holds the spotlight here as a troubled teen leading a double life in the eponymous town. By day she's a top student hanging out with her innocent best friend Donna Hayward (Moira Kelly) and nice-guy boyfriend Bobby Briggs (Dana Ashbrook). By night, she's an overheated coke fiend carrying on a sleazy liaison with dope dealer James Hurley (James Marshall). After dark, she trades in her pleated skirts and bobby sox for high heels and garter belts, presumably paying for her habit by being an attraction at an underground sex club run by the loathsome Jacques Renault (Walter Olkewicz), where she gets pawed over by drunken loggers.

The source of Laura's self-destructiveness is traced to long-term sexual abuse by her father, Leland (Ray Wise), who, while possessed by evil spirit Bob (Frank Silva), has regularly raped her since she was twelve. When Laura realizes that she is leading Donna down a similar path of doom, she has an attack of conscience leading her to face up to the truth about herself and her father. Leland, meanwhile, stumbles upon Laura's secret life when his mistress inadvertently sets him up on a "date" with Laura during an out-of-town business trip.

Driven mad by jealousy, he follows Laura and friend Ronette Pulaski (Phoebe Augustine) to a sex party with Renault and Leo Johnson (Eric DaRe) in an abandoned railroad car. It is there that he knocks Leo unconscious and scares off Renault before beating Ronette into a coma and murdering his daughter, dumping her body into the river, where it surfaces for the first scene of the series.

It's getting to be an old story, but TWIN PEAKS: FIRE WALK WITH ME apparently underwent some drastic trimming before reaching American screens, somehow losing 20 minutes of its original running time after it was nearly booed off screens during its world premiere at the 1992 Cannes Film Festival. What's left isn't *that* bad, but it's far from Lynch's best work.

The feverish conviction that made Lynch's earlier films as controversial as they were gripping has given way to a cheap-looking, cheesy campiness here. Besides rehashing the series—also provided are back stories on characters such as town poet Harold Smith (Lenny Van Dohlen), filling in how he wound up with Laura's diary, and the source of Bobby's enmity with Leo (he killed one of Leo's drug couriers)—TWIN PEAKS also rehashes Lynch's obsession with the dark underbelly of small-town life that he had already treated more compellingly in BLUE VELVET.

Here, he doesn't have much to add, except possible consumer deception. Despite prominent listings among the cast, such series regulars as Peggy Lipton, Madchen Amick, Miguel Ferrer and Kyle MacLachlan have little more than one-or-two-scene cameo roles, as do guest stars such as David Bowie and Kiefer Sutherland. Further down the cast list, we must have blinked and missed appearances by other listed series stars like Jack Nance, Wendy Robie, Joan Chen and Michael Horse—or maybe they were among the casualties in the cutting room.

What redeems TWIN PEAKS, if anything, is Lee's performance, a fearsomely commanding star turn following token appearances in the series (as Laura's look-alike cousin, also murdered by Leland) and in WILD AT HEART. While Lynch ladles on the random weirdness around the edges, it is Lee who keeps the film centered, with a harrowing but poignantly sympathetic portrait of a woman's descent into horror and madness. *(Violence, substance abuse, profanity, nudity, sexual situations.)*

p, Francis Bouygues, Gregg Fienberg; d, David Lynch; w, David Lynch, Robert Engels; ph, Ron Garcia; ed, Mary Sweeney; m, Angelo Badalamenti; prod d, Patricia Norris; set d, Leslie Morales; cos, Patricia Norris

Drama/Fantasy **(PR: O MPAA: R)**

TWIN SISTERS ★½

(Canada) 92m Image Organization; Allegro Films; Eurogroup Films ~ Vidmark Entertainment c

Frederic Forrest *(Steve Delvaux)*, Stepfanie Kramer *(Carol Mallory/Lynn Cameron)*, James Brolin *(Michael)*, Susan Almgren *(Sophie)*, Robert Morelli, Lawrence Dane, Richard Zeman, Vlasta Vrana

A flaccid and flat-footed suspense yarn, TWIN SISTERS showcases glamorous Stepfanie Kramer, erstwhile star of the TV police show "Hunter," in a dual role as, logically, twin sisters.

Lynn Cameron (Kramer) is a high-priced prostitute and denizen of the Montreal underworld, and the opening credits are barely over when she witnesses a murder engineered by the usual Evil Businessman and flees for her life, only to disappear in a gas explosion. Carol Mallory (Kramer again), Lynn's estranged sibling, is an upstanding and proper Beverly Hills housewife, who heads north to determine what really happened to her twin.

Naturally Lynn's old clients leeringly mistake the newcomer for the lost call girl. This gives Carol the idea to masquerade as luscious Lynn and see what happens. Of course this draws the attention of the Evil Businessman, who thinks that Lynn's still alive and tries to terminate the lady again and again via a hulking hit man. The latter's repeated failures to nail Carol are strongly reminiscent of the Road Runner cartoons, and hardly scarier.

The heroine finally outwits that crazy coyote of a hit man, but there's one more twist to the tale, and sharp viewers should have little trouble guessing what it is. After all, one doesn't hawk two Stepfanie Kramers in a movie called TWIN SISTERS and then get rid of one right away. But it would have taken a filmmaker with the panache of Hitchcock or Brian De Palma (who did the evil-twin benchmark SISTERS in 1973) to uplift this mundane scenario. Instead director Tom Berry lets the plot unroll with a minimum of flair until that final, feeble trick. It would all be at the level of a stale TV movie-of-the-week but for an erotic nude interlude with Susan Almgren, as a fellow hooker.

Kramer is merely watchable as she goes through peril in a succession of tight dresses. James Brolin (GABLE AND LOMBARD, GAS FOOD LODGING) has little to do as Carol's neglectful husband, leaving Frederic Forrest to steal the picture (admittedly not too difficult) as a believably rumpled Canadian cop with a guilty conscience, who at one point declines an offer of easy sex with a lonely, lovely Carol. Now that's a surprise. *(Violence, nudity, sexual situations, adult situations.)*

p, Tom Berry, Jean Mark Paland, Franco Battista; d, Tom Berry; w, David Preston, Tom Berry, (from the story by Pierre David, Jean-Marc Paland and Julie Richard based on the idea by Andre Koob); ph, Rodney Gibbons; ed, Yves Langlois; m, Lou Forestieri; prod d, Richard Tasse; set d, Frank Sanna; cos, Francoise Lecours

Thriller **(PR: O MPAA: NR)**

UCHO
(SEE: EAR, THE)

ULTIMATE DESIRES
(Canada) 93m North American Pictures ~ North American Releasing c

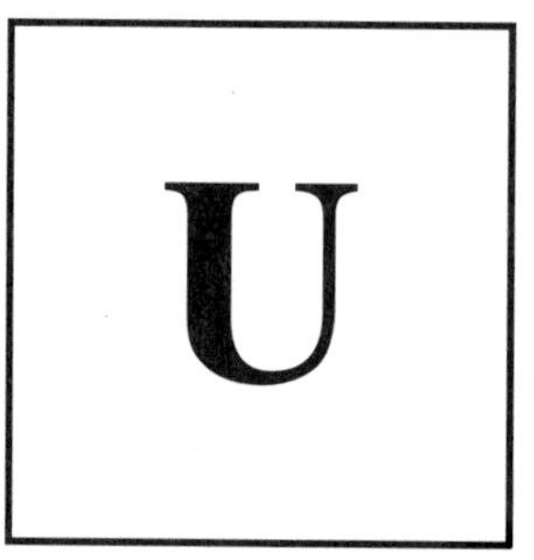

Tracy Scoggins *(Samantha Stewart)*, Marc Singer *(Jonathan)*, Brion James *(Wolf)*, Robert Morrison *(Arthur Kettner)*, Marc Bennet *(Pierce)*, Suzy Joachim *(Vicky)*, Marc Bauer *(David)*

Direct from Vancouver music-video hell comes this tarted-up mongrel of an erotic/political thriller that's so overwrought it rises to tabloid-level surrealism. Released on video under the title ULTIMATE DESIRES, it just may lure movie trash aficionados who'd thought they'd seen it all.

Amidst much smoke, shadows and fog, portentious voice-overs, dream sequences and incoherent Steadicam sweeps, the film relates the ultralurid tale of Samantha Stewart (Tracy Scoggins), a prim, bespectacled public defender in a neon-lit American metropolis. Her sheltered life changes when she gives a lift to Vicky (Suzy Joachim), a sexy prostitute on the run from assassins of "za Brotherhood," an underworld tribunal of silhouetted guys with funny facial hair, crazy post-synced voices and lines like "We cannot rest until we have the broach!" Vicky the hooker is soon murdered, but not before passing on the broach to Samantha, who decides from their brief meeting that the late B-girl was her best friend in the whole world. Logically, the heroine concludes it's fun to be a whore, and she adopts Vicky's attitude, wardrobe and street corner.

Samantha "discovers the darkest aspects of her own sexuality," as the publicity notes put it. On screen this translates into the succulent Scoggins donning a fetishistic assortment of lingerie and lace and preening in front of her window at night, as disco melodies on the soundtrack reach saturation. This, plus her repeated inquiries into Vicky's death, draw the attention of the broach-hungry Brotherhood. "The blame for a new Cold War must fall in Soviet hands, not in ours!" declares a Mr. Big with a voice uncannily like that of Oscar the Grouch from "Sesame Street."

A handsome agent named Jonathan (Marc Singer), supposedly employed by the Brotherhood, seduces and saves Samantha, blowing up the whole cabal of baddies in their purple lair. In what passes for an explanation Jonathan tells Samantha that he's part of a joint conspiracy-within-the-conspiracy between the CIA and the KGB to kill the peaceful US and Russian presidents and plunge the world back into the immensely profitable two-superpower arms race. He departs to do his bit, leaving Samantha back to dressing like a librarian again, sadder and wiser.

So what do we learn from ULTIMATE DESIRES? First and foremost that the direct-to-video filler market has a bottomless (more often topless) appetite for erotic psychosexual cheap-thrillers, like NIGHT EYES, BODY CHEMISTRY, MIRROR IMAGES etc. Some of these debased relatives of BODY HEAT and BASIC INSTINCT venture into softcore territory, but ULTIMATE DESIRES doesn't get quite so explicit, confining itself mainly to Scoggins acting out the whole Frederick's of Hollywood catalogue. Not until late in the film does Samantha actually have sex with Jonathan, superhuman self-control for the genre. When the bedroom scenes roll around the voyeurs will get what they want.

Second, producer-director Lloyd A. Simandl has little faith in Washington's New World Order, as further evidenced in his later PROJECT: SHADOWCHASER, an equally garish action/science fiction melange with a government coup and an ill-fated president involved. ULTIMATE DESIRES certainly doesn't lack ambition as the filmmakers expand from T & A noir into global intrigue, but the sleaze negates any nihilistic intent.

Third lesson: on the soundtrack someone named Cathy St. Germain belts out a cover version of "What About Love" that's as torrid as Heart's original hit single. ULTIMATE DESIRES, meanwhile, remains a poor imitation of a movie. *(Violence, substance abuse, profanity, nudity, sexual situations, adult situations.)*

p, Lloyd Simandl, John Curtis; d, Lloyd Simandl; w, Ted Hubert; ph, Danny Knovak; ed, Derek Whelan; m, Braun Farnon, Robert Smart; art d, Scott Richardson

Erotic/Thriller/Political **(PR: O MPAA: R)**

ULTRAVIOLET ★★½
Concorde ~ Concorde c

Esai Morales *(Nick)*, Patricia Healy *(Kristen)*, Stephen Meadows *(Sam)*

Despite Esai Morales's florid acting, ULTRAVIOLET emerges as an above-average trapped-like-desert-rats thriller.

Determined to give their marriage a second chance, ranger Sam (Stephen Meadows) and his visiting estranged wife, Kristen (Patricia Healy), forget about trips to a counsellor when they are attacked by loony Nick (Morales), who introduces himself by cold-bloodedly killing his traveling companion in front of them. After knocking Sam temporarily out of commission with a bullet, Nick forces Kristen to chauffeur him in her motor home. Despite such wily ploys as draining off gas and leaving clues behind her, Kristen is constantly counter-checked by Nick, an embittered artist who's decided to "mold" her into his ideal woman.

When Sam recovers sufficiently to attempt a rescue, Nick slows him down with a rattlesnake bite. Forced to submit to his advances, Kristen botches a chance to knife Nick and then starts playing along with his megalomania. Pleading to be taken to a local watering hole, Kristen is not saved by any of the tavern types, but they do humiliate the citified Nick enough for him to lure one good ol' boy away and kill him. Dragging his perfect mate on the road again, Nick is furious when Sam trails after them with a state trooper. After pumping lead into the cop, Nick goes a few rounds with Sam and winds up chained to a jeep. During the ensuing climax, the vehicle starts sinking inexorably into a hole; the desert sands suck up the jeep with madman attached.

Hostage melodramas such as DEPERATE HOURS and WHEN YOU COMIN' BACK, RED RYDER? offer audiences a chance to applaud upright Americans faced with deranged criminals who threaten the social fabric of their lives. While most viewers spend some time questioning their identities and paying lip service to good citizenship, they're really interested in watching the scummy hostage-takers "get theirs." What gives ULTRAVIOLET a distinctive edge is that in dissecting its villain's brain viewers realize why a criminal type so easy to overlook or dismiss is so dangerous. Handsome and extroverted, Nick could probably fool a lot of people as long as they didn't make the mistake of disparaging his work. For nutty Nick, the desert becomes a Garden of Eden where his very life will be a work of art not subject to critics or financees and where he can begin again with a neo-Eve. Viewers will be equally intrigued by the resourcefulness of the feminist heroine who outsmarts her tormentor on several occasions and never sits back awaiting a last-minute rescue by the cavalry.

Grippingly directed by Mark Griffiths, ULTRAVIOLET knows where to angle its camera for maximum effect whenever a rattler's about to strike or a psycho's about to snap. Only in the country-western bar scene does the film lose momentum because this primal drama is best left played out in the burning desert; introducing other characters at a late point in the story only dilutes the suspense.

Except for those moments when Morales calls too much attention to himself, ULTRAVIOLET remains an engrossing cat-and-mouse game with a desert-sun intensity and has a denoument with an undeniably rousing impact. *(Violence, sexual situations.)*

p, Catherine Cyran; d, Mark Griffiths; w, Gordon Cassidy; ph, Gregg Heschong; ed, Kevin Tent; m, Ed Tomney; prod d, Carlos Barbosa; art d, Richard Brunton; set d, Tamara Murphy; cos, Leesa Evans

Erotic/Thriller **(PR: O MPAA: R)**

UNDER SIEGE ★★½

100m Le Studio Canal Plus; Alcor Films; Regency Enterprises ~ Warner Bros. c

Steven Seagal *(Casey Ryback)*, Damian Chapa *(Tackman)*, Troy Evans *(Granger)*, David McKnight *(Flicker)*, Lee Hinton *(Cue Ball)*, Patrick O'Neal *(Captain Adams)*, Gary Busey *(Commander Krill)*, Glenn Morshower *(Ensign Taylor)*, Leo Alexzander *(Lieutenant Smart)*, John Rottger *(Commander Green)*, Brad Rea *(Marine Guard)*, Michael Weldon *(Lieutenant Ballard)*, Bernie Casey *(Commander Harris)*, Rickey Pierre *(Kitchen Helper)*, Raymond Cruz *(Ramirez)*, Duane Davis *(Johnson)*, Tommy Lee Jones *(William Strannix)*, Erika Eleniak *(Jordan Tate)*, Colm Meaney *(Daumer)*, Eddie Bo Smith, Jr. *(Shadow)*, Richard Jones *(Pitt)*, Tom Reynolds *(Wave)*, Tom Muzila *(Cates)*, Kirk Burroughs, Frank Ferrara, George Kee Cheung, Adam James, Jim Chimento, Michael Gaylord James, Craig Dunn, Miguel Nino, Daniel Dupont, David Webster *(Commandos)*, Gene Barge, Richard Davis, Anthony G. Brown, Tad Robinson, Hiram Bullock, Wendell Wayne Stewart, Christopher Alan Cameron *("The Bail Jumpers")*, Tom Wood *(Private Nash)*, Jerone Wiggins *(Sammy Lee)*, Joseph F. Kosala *(Engine Room Watch Officer)*, Ousuan Elam *(Marine)*, Richard Piemonte *(Marine)*, Daniel H. Friedman *(Spoon)*, Gregory G. Stump *(Bridge Officer)*, David U. Hodges *(Bridge Watchman)*, Bruce Bozzi *(F-18 Pilot)*, Craig A. Pinkard *(Submariner)*, Sandy Ward *(Calaway)*, Conrad E. Palmisano *(Strike Team Leader)*, Luis J. Silva *(Luigi)*, Michael Des Barres *(Damiani)*, Nate Robinson *(Ship's Doctor)*, Gary Gardner *(Marine)*, Nick Mancuso *(Tom Breaker)*, Andy Romano *(Admiral Batesy)*, Drucilla A. Carlson *(Captain Spellman)*, Ralph Wesley Carey *(Naval Aide)*, Joseph R. John *(Chief of Staff)*, Dennis Lipscomb *(Trenton)*, Dale A. Dye *(Captain Garza)*, Robert Nichols *(Colonel Sarnac)*, E. Daniel Corte, Jr. *(CIA Aide)*

Steven Seagal has carved his own profitable niche as an action hero who largely fights, not international terrorists and other fanciful enemies from without, but renegade elements within our own government and law-enforcement agencies. Despite its dashes of originality, UNDER SIEGE, Seagal's latest, is yet another B movie with bloated production values.

Former Navy SEAL Casey Ryback (Seagal), a top undercover operative in his day, has since been demoted to the post of personal cook to the Captain of the Missouri (Patrick O'Neal). Busted for his insubordinate conduct against the US invasion of Panama, Ryback now even refuses to wear his dress whites when President Bush visits the ship. Ryback becomes suspicious when the ship's second-in-command, Commander Krill (Gary Busey), abruptly cancels a long-planned dinner in honor of the Captain's birthday in favor of a "surprise" party featuring a rock band, outside catering and topless dancing by a Playboy bunny (Erika Eleniak).

To keep Ryback from double-checking with the Captain, Krill provokes the brawny cook into taking a swing at him and then has Ryback imprisoned in the galley meat locker. Ryback's worst fears are realized when the singer with the rock band, Strannix (Tommy Lee Jones), turns out to be a renegade CIA agent who, with his "caterers," takes over the ship. Strannix's plan is to hold the crew hostage until he can rendezvous with a submarine and off-load the MISSOURI's weaponry to be sold on the international market. After teaming up with the bunny—who was given knock-out pills to make her sleep through the takeover—and a few of the ship's remaining officers, Ryback deploys his finely honed killing skills to retake the destroyer and bring down a missile Strannix has launched towards Honolulu.

Reteaming with Seagal (ABOVE THE LAW) and Jones (who also played a crazy super-villain in THE PACKAGE), Andrew Davis directs with more punch than personality, leaning on special effects and stuntwork rather than his solid cast. During its opening scenes, however, UNDER SIEGE promises to be the best of its kind since John McTiernan's DIE HARD, which balanced its spectacle with wit, ingenuity and attention to details.

Jones and Busey, two underrated actors, are creepy-funny in an anarchic, postmodern manner; they've both been credited, in an issue of the *LA Weekly*, by screenwriter J.F. Lawton for their contributions to the storyline. It was Jones's idea to masquerade as the rock singer, leading him to spend most of the film dressed in his leathers, bandana and sunglasses. Busey, meanwhile, elected to assassinate the ship's Captain while in female drag, donned for a comedy routine that was part of the "party." This leads to the film's scariest funny moment in which, still in drag, Krill wonders aloud if he really needs the psychiatric evaluation the now-dead Captain had planned for him.

Unfortunately, once the stolid Seagal takes over, the action quickly settles into a predictable high-tech groove of explosions, gunplay and gore. Though as capable at staging explosions as anybody, Davis still has no more real feeling for character or suspense than he did with either THE PACKAGE or ABOVE THE LAW. Lawton has also said that the "bunny" subplot was Seagal's own idea, though little is made of the relationship. After putting up some initial token resistance, Eleniak essentially becomes Seagal's spear carrier then, inexplicably, his girlfriend. Giving Seagal a pneumatic main squeeze, Lawton said, necessitated the jettisoning of his own subplot, involving a female officer on a Coast Guard ship who tracks the MISSOURI during the struggle. Also probably jettisoned was a more interesting film.

Despite being Seagal's biggest hit to date, UNDER SIEGE remains another specimen of the big-budget action film in dull decline. *(Violence, profanity, brief nudity.)*

p, Steven Reuther, Arnon Milchan, Steven Seagal; d, Andrew Davis; w, J.F. Lawton, John Mason, Michael Rae; ph, Frank Tidy; ed, Robert A. Ferretti, Dennis Virkler, Don Brochu, Dov Hoenig; m, Gary Chang; prod d, Bill Kenney; art d, Bill Hiney; set d, Rick Gentz; cos, Richard Bruno

AAN Sound: Don Mitchell, Frank A. Montano, Rick Hart, and Scott Smith; *AAN Sound Effects Editing:* John Leveque and Bruce Stambler

Action/Thriller **(PR: C MPAA: R)**

UNDER SUSPICION ★★
(U.K./U.S.) 99m Carnival Films & Theater Ltd. ~ Columbia c

Liam Neeson *(Tony Aaron)*, Kenneth Cranham *(Frank)*, Maggie O'Neill *(Hazel)*, Alan Talbot *(Powers)*, Malcolm Storry *(Waterston)*, Martin Grace *(Colin)*, Kevin Moore *(Barrister)*, Stephen Oxley *(Hotel Deskman)*, Colin Dudley *(Hotel Waiter)*, Richard Graham *(Denny)*, Alison Ruffelle *(1st Chambermaid)*, Michael Almaz *(Simon Stasio)*, Victoria Alcock *(2nd Chambermaid)*, Tony Hughes *(Undertaker)*, Alphonsia Emmanuel *(Selina)*, Laura San Giacomo *(Angeline)*, Pamela Sholto *(Housekeeper)*, Stephen Moore *(Roscoe)*, Alan Stocks *(Paul)*, Nicolette McKenzie *(Mrs. Roscoe)*, Tommy Wright *(Hotel Janitor)*, Lee Whitlock *(Ben)*, Alex Norton *(Prosecuting Lawyer)*, Noel Coleman *(Judge)*, Kenneth Hadley *(Forensic Scientist)*, Danny Schiller *(Defence Lawyer)*, Joanna Brookes *(Travel Agent)*, Andrew Dunford *(Clerk of the Court)*, Roy Sampson *(Foreman of the Jury)*, P.J. Davidson *(Executioner)*, Steve Murray *(Executioner's Assistant)*, Christopher Whittingham *(Prison Warder)*, Terry John *(Switchboard Operator)*, Max Cane *(Switchboard Operator)*, Gordon Salkilld *(Prison Governor)*

A morose thriller set during the 1950s in the gloomy British seaside town of Brighton, UNDER SUSPICION is so suffused with tawdry bitterness that it's unpleasant to watch, which is perhaps why it failed to find many fans among critics and moviegoers.

Tony Aaron (Liam Neeson) is a cop who can't keep his pants zipped, and the inevitable trouble ensues. While staking out a gangster's house with his partner, Aaron slips in for a bit of fun with the gangster's blowsy moll, Hazel (Maggie O'Neil). The gangster comes home unexpectedly and all hell breaks loose; when the dust settles, Aaron is bounced off the force and barely avoids prosecution. He becomes a private detective and makes a scant living doing divorce work.

The punitive divorce laws of the period require proof of infidelity as grounds; Aaron's specialty is arranging compromising photographs, with Hazel, now his wife, as the other woman. It's a sleazy but predictable living, so imagine Aaron's surprise when he bursts into a hotel room, camera in hand, only to find Hazel and his client, a wealthy American painter, slaughtered. The painter's body has been mutilated as well: his thumb, with which he had signed his paintings, is gone.

Aaron's old police pal Frank (Kenneth Cranham) is placed in charge of the investigation, which at first revolves around two women: the painter's cool widow, Selina (Alphonsia Emmanuel), and his alluring student-turned-mistress, Angeline (Laura San Giacomo). Each owns many of the dead man's valuable artworks (more valuable than ever since his death) and Aaron suspects a plot to forge more, using the amputated thumb to make them appear indisputably real. The glamorous Angeline seems the more likely murder suspect, which is no doubt why Aaron takes up with her. To his surprise, he finds himself falling in love.

Suspicion soon falls on Aaron himself; the victims were killed with his gun, which is recovered near the scene, and though he has no good motive, he also has a flawed alibi. The circumstantial evidence seems increasingly damning, particularly after a local man (a married homosexual tormented by a blackmailer) commits suicide and leaves a note naming Aaron as the killer. Aaron is arrested and tried, found guilty and sentenced to die. Shortly before the execution, Frank makes a shocking discovery: the missing thumb, preserved in alcohol, hidden amidst Angeline's paints. Frank's new evidence saves Aaron and condemns Angeline, who goes to jail protesting her innocence.

In a brief epilogue, viewers learn that Aaron and Selina were co-conspirators in the painter's murder. She masterminded the plan to forge her husband's paintings, and he both committed the murder and framed Angeline. The two escape justice in sunny Florida, far from the dreary beaches of Brighton.

Although not an altogether successful film, UNDER SUSPICION does convey a palpable sense of time and place. In its delineation of the sexual repression and hypocrisy of the late 50s, the depressing architecture of decaying seaside towns, the sense that buried secrets and unspoken truths are poisoning the very soil and blighting everyone who walks on it, this 1992 release recalls such often underestimated films as Basil Dearden's SAPPHIRE and VICTIM.

Writer-director Simon Moore manages both to keep the complicated plot moving and to give his characters plenty of room in which to assert themselves. Disappointingly, the film's weakest performance comes from Laura San Giacomo; though certainly beautiful, she fails to convey the sense of mystery Angeline requires. Rather than a femme fatale, San Giacomo seems too much like the girl next door in borrowed soignee clothes; her performance comes together in only one brief—though extemely good—scene, following Angeline's conviction for murder. Walking in the prison yard, dressed in shapeless grey, she asks Aaron to tell her the truth, to whisper it in her ear. Though we don't hear what he says, the looks that wash over her face are painfully evocative.

The craggily handsome Neeson, on the other hand, is phenomenally good. He dares to allow Tony Aaron to be unlikable—vain, self-centered and crass—and creates a far more interesting character than the usual down-at-the-heels-but-good-at-heart rogue of a private eye American audiences have come to expect. Aaron is a weak and unprincipled man, and his sordid job has magnified his faults, turning him into the worst possible version of himself.

On balance, UNDER SUSPICION is an underrated thriller, well worth the effort required to shake the depression it induces. *(Violence, nudity, sexual situations.)*

p, Brian Eastman; d, Simon Moore; w, Simon Moore; ph, Vernon Layton; ed, Tariq Anwar; m, Christopher Gunning; prod d, Tim Hutchinson; art d, Tony Reading; set d, Stephenie McMillan; cos, Penny Rose

Thriller **(PR: C MPAA: R)**

UNFORGIVEN ★★★★½
130m Malpaso Productions; Warner Bros. ~ Warner Bros. c

Clint Eastwood *(William Munny)*, Gene Hackman *(Sheriff "Little Bill" Daggett)*, Morgan Freeman *(Ned Logan)*, Richard Harris *(English Bob)*, Jaimz Woolvett *(The "Schofield Kid")*, Saul Rubinek *(W.W. Beauchamp)*, Frances Fisher *(Strawberry Alice)*, Anna Thomson *(Delilah Fitzgerald)*, David Mucci *(Quick Mike)*, Rob Campbell *(Davey Bunting)*, Anthony James *(Skinny Dubois)*, Tara Dawn Frederick *(Little Sue)*, Beverley Elliott *(Silky)*, Liisa Repo-Martell *(Faith)*, Josie Smith *(Crow Creek Kate)*, Shane Meier *(Will Munny)*, Aline Levasseur *(Penny Munny)*

While most of Hollywood appeared to have forgotten how to make watchable, let alone good, movies in 1992, veteran Clint Eastwood reminded his peers how it's done with UNFORGIVEN, his most purely entertaining and thematically ambitious film as a director-star to date.

Wyoming, the 1880s. William Munny (Clint Eastwood) is a former murderer who, transformed by the love of a good woman, gave up a life of indiscriminate killing to raise a family and try his hand at pig farming. With his wife now dead and his farm a failure, Munny is lured back into the killing game by the "Schofield Kid" (Jaimz Woolvett), an aspiring young gunfighter who brings the older man word of a bounty being offered in the frontier town of Big Whiskey. (After a cowboy slashed the face of a prostitute there, the woman's co-workers have offered a reward for the death of the attacker and his accomplice.) Munny refuses the young man's offer of partnership but later reconsiders, leaves his two children in charge of the property and, together with his old sidekick Ned Logan (Morgan Freeman), sets off to join Schofield.

The autocratic sheriff of Big Whiskey, "Little Bill" Daggett (Gene Hackman), has treated the slashing incident with the gravity of a traffic violation, ordering the culprits to pay a fine in the form of horses. (In keeping with the film's critique of sexual politics the fine is due, not to the disfigured woman, but to the brothel-keeper who paid good money for her and is now out of pocket.) Daggett is furious when he finds out the prostitutes have put a price on the men's heads, making his town a magnet for professional gunslingers. He outlaws firearms in Big Whiskey and brutally beats and humiliates the first bounty hunter to defy the ban, English Bob (Richard Harris). A notorious shootist who has crossed paths with Daggett before, Bob is accompanied by a "biographer," W.W. Beauchamp (Saul Rubinek), who has chronicled Bob's (heavily embellished) exploits in several cheap novels but soon transfers his allegiance to the more down-to-earth sheriff.

Munny, Ned and Schofield arrive in Big Whisky during a torrential downpour. Munny, who has a fever, is left in the bar on the first floor of the brothel while his cohorts go upstairs to "negotiate" with the prostitutes—i.e., take advances on the reward money in the form of "free ones." Alerted to the arrival of more armed men, Daggett and his deputies viciously beat Munny and throw him into the street, where he is rescued by his escaping partners and taken into the hills.

After Munny's recovery, the three ambush one of the two cowboys. Munny, however, is forced to be the rifleman, since Ned finds he no longer has the stomach for killing. (En route to Big Whiskey, the two have discovered that Schofield is short-sighted, incapable of shooting anything more than 20 yards away.) Ned decides to return home, foregoing his share of the reward and leaving his companions to tackle the second slasher alone. On the way he is captured by Daggett's men, tortured to death and left on display outside the bar/bordello.

Munny and Schofield track the second cowboy to a heavily guarded ranchhouse, where the man eventually makes a rashly unaccompanied trip to the privy and is shot at point-blank range by Schofield. While waiting for a rendezvous with the woman who will bring their reward, Schofield confesses that, contrary to his earlier boastings, he had never killed a man before, and is horrified at what he has done. The woman arrives with the money and with news of Ned's death, prompting Munny to go back into Big Whiskey alone to exact his murderous revenge.

UNFORGIVEN was written by David Webb Peoples (BLADE RUNNER) in the late 70s. The screenplay was originally optioned by Francis Ford Coppola, but production was stymied after Coppola's pet project, ONE FROM THE HEART, pushed his Zoetrope Studios into bankruptcy. Eastwood bought the script after Coppola's option lapsed in the early 80s and sat on it until he felt he would be old enough to play the aging gunfighter.

It's easy to see why Eastwood was drawn by Peoples's screenplay. Munny is descended in a direct line from Eastwood's two most famous characters: the Man with No Name, from his 60s Westerns with Sergio Leone, and Dirty Harry, the anti-hero of Don Siegel's urban Westerns. Leone's presence is most strongly felt in the revisionist content of UNFORGIVEN, while Siegel's influence is in the film's lean, moody, no-nonsense style. Both of Eastwood's directorial mentors are acknowledged in the film's on-screen dedication, "to Sergio and Don."

The West of UNFORGIVEN is a place of few illusions, despite a mythology of heroism symbolized by the pulp biographer Beauchamp. Sheriff Daggett ruptures this mythology by telling the writer the inglorious real story behind one of the scenes described in his books. The pattern is reprised throughout the film, as awe-struck tales of earlier heroes and exploits are undercut by cynical, down-to-earth dismissals—until the climax, when Munny pulls off a gunslinging feat of genuinely mythic proportions. At that point, Beauchamp gets one more lesson in the mythology of the West when Munny, boasting neither Bob's elegant bravado nor Daggett's phony moral code, sums up the secret of his success with the simple declaration that "I've always been lucky at killing."

As with Leone's masterworks, UNFORGIVEN depicts a West driven solely by forces of commerce—not ideals of freedom or manifest destiny—with killing being Munny's sole marketable skill. Like Don Siegel's San Francisco, scabrously evoked in DIRTY HARRY, UNFORGIVEN's frontier is one where civilization is constantly threatened by savagery. Its skewered values typified by the lopsided "punishment" initially doled out to the slashers, Big Whiskey needs Munny and his "luck" at killing to restore some kind of absolute moral standard. Yet, just as Eastwood's occasional efforts to abandon his nihilist screen persona have been inconclusive, so is Munny haunted by his inability to escape the role society has decreed for him. Though he's the only protagonist left standing when the smoke clears, his story is the only one with the status of tragedy, his flaw being his very invincibility.

At the time of UNFORGIVEN's release, Eastwood told interviewers that he planned to drop out of acting altogether and concentrate on directing. If so, UNFORGIVEN bodes well for his future. Of Eastwood's directorial efforts, it's the first to establish its mood early on and sustain it without the lapses, lumpiness and *longeurs* that have addled some of his past films. His inspiration evidently comes from Peoples's screenplay, which is formally flawless, yet consistently suprising in the twists and spins it puts on traditional Western themes and characters.

The cast—for once in an Eastwood-helmed film—is universally strong. Hackman, Freeman and Harris don't do anything they haven't done before, but the roles suit their personae to a degree where they approach archetypal status. The same applies to Eastwood, who casts himself as part of an ensemble rather than as the conscious star.

And that's as it should be. With UNFORGIVEN, Eastwood achieves a new level of authority as a filmmaker and actor who has nothing to prove.*(Violence, profanity, adult situations.)*

p, Clint Eastwood; d, Clint Eastwood; w, David Webb Peoples; ph, Jack N. Green; ed, Joel Cox; m, Lennie Niehaus; prod d, Henry Bumstead; art d, Rick Roberts, Adrian Gorton; set d, Janice Blackie-Goodine

AA Best Picture: Clint Eastwood (Producer); *AAN Best Actor:* Clint Eastwood; *AA Best Supporting Actor:* Gene Hackman; *AA Director:* Clint Eastwood; *AAN Best Original Screenplay:* David Webb Peoples; *AAN Cinematography:* Jack N. Green; *AA Editing:* Joel Cox; *AAN Art Direction:* Henry Bumstead (Art Direction) and Janice Blackie-Goodine (Set Decoration); *AAN Sound:* Les Fresholtz, Vern Poore, Dick Alexander, and Rob Young

Western **(PR: C MPAA: R)**

UNIVERSAL SOLDIER ★★

98m Universal Soldier Inc.; IndieProd Company; Adelson/Baumgarten Productions; Centropolis Film Productions ~ TriStar c

Jean-Claude Van Damme *(Luc Devreux)*, Dolph Lundgren *(Andrew Scott)*, Ally Walker *(Veronica Roberts)*, Ed O'Ross *(Colonel Perry)*, Jerry Orbach *(Dr. Gregor)*, Leon Rippy *(Woodward)*,

Tico Wells *(Garth)*, Ralph Moeller *(GR76)*, Robert Trebor *(Motel Owner)*, Gene Davis *(Lieutenant)*, Drew Snyder *(Charles)*, Tom "Tiny" Lister, Jr. *(GR55)*, Simon Rhee *(GR61)*, Eric Norris *(GR86)*, Michael Winther *(Technician)*, Joseph Malone *(Huey)*, Rance Howard *(Mr. Devreux)*, Lilyan Chauvin *(Mrs. Devreux)*, Monty Laird *(Attendant)*, Joanne Baron *(Waitress)*, Lupe Ontiveros *(Maid)*, Jack Moore *(Witzy)*, John Storey *(Clark)*, Bradford Bancroft *(Powell)*, Thomas Rosales *(Wagner)*, Trini Tran *(Vietnamese Girl)*, Tai Thai *(Vietnamese Boy)*, Rachel Wagner *(Girl in Motel)*, Brandon Lambdin *(Boy in Motel)*, Ned Bellamy *(FBI Agent)*, Paul Raczkowski *(Briefing Officer)*, Daniel Demorest *(Radio Operator)*, Tanner Gill *(Masked Gunman)*, Eddie Braun *(Sniper)*, Walter R Robles *(Sniper)*, Jophery Brown *(Thug)*, Dona Hardy *(Old Woman)*, Leon Delaney *(Patrolman)*, George Fisher *(Patrolman)*, Dave Efron, Myron L. Lapka, David DiGregorio, Rhino Michaels *(Truckers)*, R.D. Carpenter, Duane Davis, Shane Dixon, Joel Kramer, Rodd Wolff *(Policemen)*, Leilani Jones *(Reporter at Hoover Dam)*, Mike Rauseo *(Reporter at Hoover Dam)*, Stephen Wolfe Smith *(Reporter at Hoover Dam)*, Tom Taglang *(Soldier)*, Michael Jai White *(Soldier)*, John Anthony D'Angelo, Roger B. Ellsworth, Matt Thomas, Mirron E. Willis *(Sharpshooters)*, Allan Wyatt, Jr. *(Local)*, Allan Graf *(Cook)*, Kamel Krifa *(HT)*, John DeMita *(Television News Crew Member)*, Jill Jaress *(Television News Crew Member)*

Action-movie ennui sets in early in UNIVERSAL SOLDIER, a lugubrious thriller featuring two of the biggest, beefiest boys of the B cinema.

Luc Devreux (Jean-Claude Van Damme) and Andrew Scott (Dolph Lundgren) are US soldiers who kill each other in Vietnam when the former interferes with the latter's My Lai-style slaughter of a friendly village. Listed as MIA, they are actually flash-frozen and shipped to a top-secret facility where a team of mad scientists led by Colonel Perry (Ed O'Ross) turn the two, with other select specimens, into bionic supersoldiers known as "Unisols." While helping foil a terrorist takeover of the giant "McKinley Dam" (played in stoic style by the real-life Hoover Dam), Devreux starts having flashbacks to his former life, and makes a break from his robotic pals. The increasingly human Devreux teams up with a spunky TV reporter, Veronica Roberts (Ally Walker), with whom he trades wisecracks while they are chased across much of the Midwest by Scott (who's also regaining his former, sadistic identity), and also by Colonel Perry and the police—who capture the duo long enough for Scott to catch up with them. Thinking they have destroyed Scott in a truck crash, Veronica takes Devreux home to his Cajun parents in Louisiana, only to have Scott catch up with them one last time for a final confrontation that ends with Scott being put through a giant wood mulcher.

The biggest—possibly only—real surprise to UNIVERSAL SOLDIER is that the cast acquits itself quite well. Walker takes top honors as a "Murphy Brown"-style heroine who—as usual for the genre—doesn't have much to do except act scared, run like hell and trade quips with the hero. But she does so with grit, humor and grace. And while no one familiar with his B work will ever mistake Van Damme for Cary Grant, he does possess a basic amiability that makes the two a surprisingly engaging pairing.

Lundgren, meanwhile, has genuine, cocky, big-star charisma that he marshals to good effect here, slyly underplaying his outsized, paranoid villain, whose hobbies include making stylish necklaces from the ears of his victims. UNIVERSAL SOLDIER's real problem is a screenplay that's all premise and no story, laboriously setting in place its sole idea—a tortured and obvious reworking of Schwarzenegger's TERMINATOR epics—and taking it nowhere. With no real plot tying them together, the impressively staged big scenes become empty exercises in logistics, while the smaller scenes never develop any momentum. *(Extreme violence, profanity.)*

p, Craig Baumgarten, Allen Shapiro, Joel B. Michaels; d, Roland Emmerich; w, Richard Rothstein, Christopher Leitch, Dean Devlin; ph, Karl Walter Lindenlaub; ed, Michael J. Duthie; m, Christopher Franke; prod d, Holger Gross; art d, Nelson Coates; set d, Alexander Carle

Action/Thriller **(PR: C MPAA: R)**

UNLAWFUL ENTRY ★★★

111m Daybreak Productions; Largo Entertainment ~ Fox c

Kurt Russell *(Michael Carr)*, Ray Liotta *(Officer Pete Davis)*, Madeleine Stowe *(Karen Carr)*, Roger E. Mosley *(Officer Roy Cole)*, Ken Lerner *(Penny)*, Deborah Offner *(Jerome Lurie)*, Carmen Argenziano *(Jerome Lurie)*, Andy Romano *(Captain Hayes)*, Johnny Ray McGhee *(Ernie Pike)*, Dino Anello *(Leon)*, Sonny Davis *(Neighbor Jack)*, Harry E. Northup *(Sergeant McMurtry)*, Sherrie Rose *(Girl in Jeep)*, Alicia Ramirez *(Taco Stand Worker)*, Ruby Salazar *(Rosa)*, Spider Madison *(Goatee)*, Myim Rose *(Layla)*, T.J. McInturff *(Layla's Kid)*, Tony Longo *(Big Anglo)*, Oscar Abadia *(Radio Announcer)*, Lynn Eastman *(Candace Lurie)*, David Taylor Moran *(Party Guest)*, Leslie James *(Party Guest)*, Chris Coombs *(Valet)*, Matthew Levy, Dorian Daneau, Marisa Durboraw, Royce Minor *(Kids in Classroom)*, Judy Hoy *(Waitress)*, Dick Miller *(Impound Clerk)*, Bob Minor *(Detective Murray)*, Curt Boulware *(Tall Detective)*, Craig Mizutari *(Narcotics Detective)*, Paul Bollen *(Plainclothes Cop)*, Ed DeFusco *(Plainclothes Cop)*, Djimon *(Prisoner on Beach)*, Jeffrey Beale *(Prisoner on Beach)*, Richard Narita *(Detective Nobu)*, Eduardo Migre *(Transfer Guard)*, Peter Dupont *(Deputy)*, Nora Heflin *(Woman Lawyer)*, Charles David Richards *(Bailiff)*, Chuck Bennett *(Judge Darabont)*, Robet M. Steinberg *(Deputy District Attorney)*, Victor Brandt *(Attorney Gershon)*, Michael Milgrom *(Prisoner)*, Jim Selzer *(Prison Guard)*, Bill Rogers *(Prison Guard)*, Bobby Costanzo *(Bail Bondsman)*, Skip Carwell *(Prisoner on Phone)*, Catherine Paolone *(Operator)*, Ed Beechner *(Motorcycle Cop)*

In the wake of the 1992 Rodney King beating, it was temporarily difficult to portray the LAPD in too dark a light to be credible. But UNLAWFUL ENTRY pushes the envelope about as far as it can go. With a no-exit scenario daring for a commercial film, this thriller gives audiences a chilling taste of what life might be like in a police state when the men in blue turn against those they are sworn to protect.

Michael and Karen Carr (Kurt Russell and Madeleine Stowe) are a yuppie couple living in an upscale part of town whose peace of mind is upset by an intruder coming in through their skylight one night. The intruder doesn't take anything except Karen, briefly, as a hostage, before dumping her in the swimming pool and making his escape. The Carrs call in the police, one of whom, Pete Davis (Ray Liotta), takes an interest in the couple's case. He cuts through department red tape and expedites speedy installation of a security system in the Carrs' house.

When Michael expresses an interest in getting revenge on the intruder, Pete invites him on a "ridealong" with his partner, Officer Roy Cole (Roger E. Mosley). After dropping Cole off, Pete takes Michael out to arrest the man who broke into the Carr's house, offering Michael a chance to take some revenge using Pete's nightstick. Michael declines, but Pete happily administers a vicious beating, leaving Michael deeply suspicious of Pete's mental stability. He suggests that Pete should get some professional help and, especially, stay far away from him and his wife in the future. But Pete takes neither suggestion, instead beginning to prey on the couple, and in particular on Karen.

When Michael files a complaint against Pete's unwanted attentions (he appears in the couple's bedroom one night when they are making love, just to "check that everything's O.K."), Pete uses his police connections to destroy Michael's business reputation. Encountering bemused apathy from Pete's superiors in the LAPD, Michael then turns to Cole—whom Pete then murders. As his crowning infamy, Pete has Michael framed on drug charges, leaving the way clear for him to move in on Karen. Michael takes matters into his own hands after making bail.

Director Jonathan Kaplan and screenwriter Lewis Colick's apparent target is society's acceptance of more—and more vicious—cops as an all-purpose panacea for social problems, extending Kaplan's (OVER THE EDGE, THE ACCUSED) preoccupation with the consequences of repression in a different social arena. Thankfully, however, UNLAWFUL ENTRY's disquieting storyline is not entirely plausible.

Audiences are asked to believe that a psychopathic rogue cop not only escapes detection, but flourishes, with decorations and the unquestioning support of his peers and superiors. When his partner is killed under extremely suspicious circumstances, the investigation consists of a few routine questions at the scene, instead of the formal inquiry that is the real routine in the LAPD, as well as most other police departments in the civilized world. Also, Pete's powers at times verge on the supernatural. Just how did he get keys to the Carr house, allowing him to come and go at will? (And why didn't the Carrs get their locks changed after Pete walked in on them having sex?) Just how does Pete manage such feats as having all of Michael's credit cards cancelled and fabricating enough parking tickets to get his car impounded? These and other questions go unanswered in what is nonetheless an uncommonly effective movie that hits disturbingly close to home.

Liotta (GOODFELLAS, SOMETHING WILD) gives a definitively creepy performance, his clear blue eyes and crinkly smile making him simultaneously charming and disgusting. The most genuinely chilling aspect of UNLAWFUL ENTRY is his ability to draw us inside his head, sharing—despite ourselves—the insidious seduction of his seemingly unlimited power. *(Violence, profanity, nudity, adult situations)*

p, Charles Gordon; d, Jonathan Kaplan; w, Lewis Colick, (from the story by Colick, John Katchmer and George D. Putnam); ph, Jamie Anderson; ed, Curtiss Clayton; m, James Horner; prod d, Lawrence G. Paull; art d, Bruce Crone; set d, Rick Simpson; cos, April Ferry

Thriller/Action **(PR: O MPAA: R)**

URGA
(SEE: CLOSE TO EDEN)

USED PEOPLE ★★½
120m Largo Entertainment ~ Fox c

Shirley MacLaine *(Pearl)*, Marcello Mastroianni *(Joe)*, Kathy Bates *(Bibby)*, Marcia Gay Harden *(Norma)*, Jessica Tandy *(Frieda)*, Sylvia Sidney *(Becky)*, Bob Dishy *(Jack)*, Emma Tammi *(Young Bibby)*, Asia Vieira *(Young Norma)*, Lee Wallace *(Uncle Harry)*, Louis Guss *(Uncle Normy)*, Gil Filar *(Mark)*, Maia Filar *(Rhonda)*, Irving Metzman *(Uncle Al)*, Matthew Branton *(Swee'Pea)*, David Gow *(Bill the Jeweler)*, Doris Roberts *(Aunt Lonnie)*, Helen Hanft *(Aunt Ruthie)*, Jeremy Trancz *(Cousin Matthew)*, Stuart Stone *(Cousin Stevie)*, Rosario Russo *(Theresa)*, Charles Cioffi *(Paolo)*, Diane D'Aquila *(Rose)*, Joe Pantoliano *(Frank)*, Sam Hutchinson *(Crying Baby)*, Ida Bernardini *(Aunt Louisa)*, Jane Richardson *(Joy)*, Janet Richardson *(Carla)*, Philip Williams *(Vic)*, Michael Ricupero *(Eddie)*, Genevieve Langlois *(French Teacher)*, Luba Goy *(Nursing Home Staff Member)*, Dominic Cuzzocrea *(Rabbi)*, Jim Millan *(Priest)*, Stephanie Voves *(Girl at Wedding)*

While it was advertised as a warm, feel-good family comedy *a la* MOONSTRUCK, this film is actually a bit more. It may remind viewers of other "crazy family" films, but USED PEOPLE is somewhat darker, harsher and more rewarding than first impressions would indicate.

The film is set in Queens, New York, in 1969, just as two miracles are about to occur: man's landing on the moon, and the Met's world series victory. Pearl Berman (Shirley MacLaine) and her family are returning from her husband's funeral, back to an apartment crammed with food, bickering relatives and nosy neighbors. One visitor is Joe (Marcello Mastroianni) whom no one seems to know; he claims to have known the deceased, and barges into the bedroom where Pearl has sequestered herself to ask if she'd like to have coffee sometime. Pearl's family and friends are aghast at his brazenness, including Pearl's mother, Frieda (Jessica Tandy), and daughters, Bibby (Kathy Bates) and Norma (Marcia Gay Harden).

Pearl, upset as she is, begins to consider Joe's offer, and they do meet "for coffee" in a bar, where Joe tells her how he came to know her late husband, and her. He recounts that Mr. Berman came into the bar one night ready to leave Pearl, but Joe convinced him to go home, take his wife wordlessly in his arms, and dance with her. (This last incident is shown in flashback at the opening of the film.) Joe confesses he watched the whole incident from the street below, and for the last 23 years has been in love with Pearl. Pearl runs out of the bar, more out of guilt for feeling something for this stranger, than out of shock, as she later explains.

Bibby and Norma, both divorced, have their own troubles: Bibby has a weight problem, two kids and a dead-end job, and is forced to live with Pearl; Norma, still coping with losing a child three years before, dresses up as various movie stars to distract herself. Her son, who is always referred to as Swee'pea although he's about ten, now considers himself "invincible," thanks to his late grandfather "protecting" him, and tempts fate several times, convinced nothing bad will happen to him. Frieda and her friend Becky (Sylvia Sidney), when they're not one-upping each other over who has worse physical ailments, are trying to decide where to spend their remaining years: a retirement home in Queens vs. Florida.

To make up for their first uncomfortable meeting, Joe prepares an elaborate Italian dinner for Pearl and both their families, which once again ends in chaos: Bibby and Norma have a fight; Joe's psychiatrist son-in-law flirts with Norma; and Swee'pea attempts to convince the doctor to take him as a client, convinced he's going insane. Nevertheless, Joe continues his courtship of Pearl: he delivers an air conditioner to her apartment; writes her a song; and becomes a surrogate grandfather for Swee'pea, rescuing him from several of his attempts at immortality. While rearranging her apartment after Bibby leaves for California, Pearl comes across the note and the money that her husband was going to leave her the night Joe met him. Pearl sees that Joe was telling the truth, her attitude begins to change and eventually they do wind up together.

Although the score is occasionally heavy-handed, USED PEOPLE is not as saccharine as it might have been, thanks to actor-turned-screenwriter Todd Graff and rising British director Beeban Kidron (ANTONIA & JANE), making her Hollywood film debut. When we first meet them, many of the characters are not particularly likable, and the various plots don't always resolve themselves with tears and hugs. The Berman women are all coping with unfulfilled and disappointing lives, and it shows in their actions and their dialogue; these are people who find it easier to pick each other apart than to show affection. Bates and MacLaine have a scene where each lets out years of repressed feelings and hurt; it's fairly jolting, and rare to see a mother-daughter conflict expressed so bluntly.

The film does have some lapses, most notably Norma, who comes off more as a nutty "character" than a fully developed one. (The scene where she tries to seduce the psychiatrist in order to stop him from seeing her son is especially ludicrous.) Joe, also, seems too good to be true, his kindness and understanding in sharp contrast to the people around him. Mastroianni's accent is sometimes impenetrable as well.

The film does have a feel for Jewish family life that some may find all-too-authentic (right down to details like the running gag of the relatives arguing over which highway is the quickest), as well as subtle ways of illustrating the persistance of behavior patterns from generation to generation, with Norma's son's embarrassing moniker being a descendant of "Bibby," the diminutive of Barbara that is *still* how Pearl addresses her daughter. But just when things get too cranky or too painfully true for comfort, Kidron inserts a lovely scene of people all over the neighborhood watching the moon landing, from apartments, fire escapes and rooftops; played simply, but adding a slightly magical touch to the film. It seems to say that even in the most ordinary of lives, some magic is still possible. *(Profanity, sexual situations.)*

p, Peggy Rajski; d, Beeban Kidron; w, Todd Graff, (from his play *The Grandmother Plays*); ph, David Watkin; ed, John Tintori; m, Rachel Portman; prod d, Stuart Wurtzel; art d, Gregory Paul Keen; set d, Hilton Rosemarin; cos, Marilyn Vance-Straker

Romance/Comedy/Drama **(PR: C MPAA: PG-13)**

VAGRANT, THE ★★

91m Brooksfilms; Vagrant Productions Inc.; Le Studio Canal Plus ~ MGM/UA Home Video c

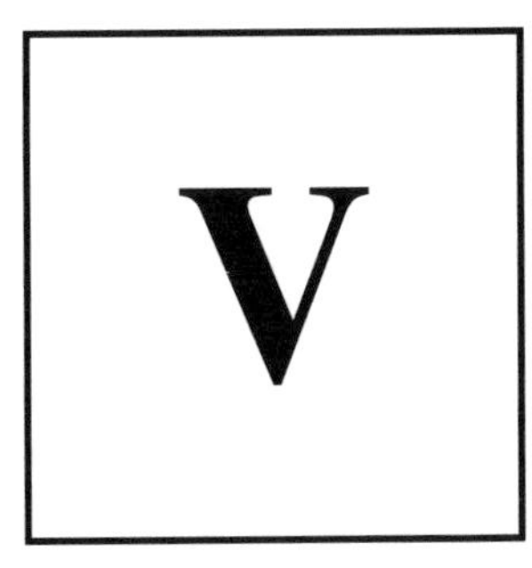

Bill Paxton *(Graham Krakowski)*, Michael Ironside *(Lieutenant Ralf Barfuss)*, Marshall Bell *(The Vagrant)*, Mitzi Kapture *(Edie Roberts)*, Colleen Camp *(Judy Dansig)*, Patrika Darbo *(Doatti)*, Mark McClure *(Chuck)*, Stuart Pankin *(Mr. Feemster)*, Derek Mark Lochran *(Detective Lackson)*, Mildred Brion *(Mrs. Howler)*

Yet another yuppie nightmare thriller, THE VAGRANT posits a Bum from Hell making life miserable for an uptight young professional. Unfortunately, unlike its more realistically played counterparts, this movie's approach is an awkward marriage of cheap laughs and queasy shocks.

The yuppie in question is Graham Krakowski (Bill Paxton), a young financial analyst who's working toward a promotion at his office and buys a new house across from a vacant lot. The lot is home to a gnarled, rangy vagrant (Marshall Bell), who's apparently not satisfied with outdoor living and enters the house on a regular basis. The intrusion doesn't stop after Graham moves in, and the homeowner, unnerved by the vagrant's gruesome appearance and unwanted presence, has the bum arrested. But the vagrant is soon harassing him anew, and Graham responds by installing eight-foot walls and a ring of spotlights around his house.

But even this doesn't work when Graham's girlfriend Edie Roberts (Mitzi Kapture) comes to visit; while he's at work, Edie takes pity on the bum and invites him in for some food. Graham is close to the breaking point, and Edie soon leaves him; shortly thereafter, both his neighbor, Mrs. Howler (Mildred Brion), and a real estate agent, Judy Dansig (Colleen Camp), with whom Graham had a fling, are brutally murdered. Investigating Lt. Ralf Barfuss (Michael Ironside) discovers parts of the victims' bodies in Graham's home, and the hapless yuppie soon finds himself on trial for murder.

During the trial, however, Graham's mother dies of a heart attack while acting as a character witness for her son, and Graham is let off. He takes to the road, eventually landing a job at a trailer park. But the vagrant has followed him there, and after killing the elderly owner's dog (inspiring a heart attack in the owner himself), he attacks Graham as he's fleeing in his car. After finding the vagrant's belongings in the back seat, Graham discovers that the bum is actually a disgraced professor who's using him as a guinea pig in a psychological experiment, attempting to prove that a stable professional man will revert to the animal inside under enough pressure. Graham goes after the vagrant in a dilapidated amusement park, where he also runs into Barfuss and another policeman; Barfuss is killed by the vagrant, but the other cop manages to blow the tramp away. Graham has retained his humanity, but can't shake the memories of the vagrant.

THE VAGRANT's premise—a downtrodden homeless man exacting symbolic vengeance against an uptight member of the wealthy class—could have produced a dark and disturbing tale with resonant undertones, a perfect expression of Robin Wood's "return of the repressed" theory of horror. Instead, director Chris Walas (the makeup effects artist who also helmed THE FLY II) and screenwriter Richard Jeffries camp up the material and only go for the most obvious shocks, resulting in a wildly uneven and frustrating movie with a few good individual moments.

Most of these are derived from the sight of the horrific vagrant invading the sanctity of house and home; but since the character is not fleshed out in any significant way, the potential for more meaningful shocks is lost. And the explanation behind the vagrant's terrorization of Graham is ridiculously over-literal and a cheat, as is the previously silent villain suddenly uttering psychobabble during the final confrontation. Similarly, the film negates the possibility of a claustrophobic, housebound climax by moving Graham to the trailer park for the final reels, yet never explores the ironic potential of having him wind up a vagrant himself.

Equally disappointing is the way the film wastes a strong genre cast: ALIENS' Paxton is given a practically unplayable character, and of TOTAL RECALL's Bell and Ironside, the latter chews the scenery. As if to guard against being seen as exploiting a very real social problem, the filmmakers play a good deal of the material as a big joke, with clunky comedy out of a bad Mel Brooks movie. (Brooks's company, in fact, produced the film.) This includes a burlesque dialogue sequence about the vagrant's urinating in the bushes, multiple pratfalls by Paxton as he encounters the bum, the glaringly out-of-place scene of Graham's mother's death and even silly character names (in addition to those mentioned above, Graham's boss is named "Mr. Feemster").

THE VAGRANT should have been as single-minded and relentless as its villain, but it ends up as confused as its protagonist. *(Violence, profanity, sexual situations.)*

p, Gillian Richardson; d, Chris Walas; w, Richard Jeffries; ph, John J. Connor, Jack Wallner; ed, Jay Ignaszewski; m, Christopher Young; prod d, Michael Bolton; art d, Eric Fraser; set d, Andrew Bernard; cos, Katherine D. Dover

Horror/Comedy (PR: O MPAA: R)

VAMPIRE HUNTER D ★

(Japan) 80m Ashi ~ Streamline Pictures c

Michael McConnohie, Barbara Goodson, Jeff Winkless, Edie Mirman, Kerrigan Mahan, Steve Kramer, Steve Bulen, Joyce Kurtz, Lara Cody, Tom Syner, Kirk Thornton

A Japanese-produced feature, VAMPIRE HUNTER D employs overly simplistic "Speed Racer"-style animation to illustrate an extremely convoluted narrative that tries to combine elements of samurai action films, American Westerns, horror films and futuristic sci-fi.

12,090 A.D. In this future Dark Age, powerful vampires have imposed a feudal state of terror on human beings. The formidable Count Magnus Lee, a descendant of Dracula, rules over a small village. When he puts his bite on an intrepid young woman, Doris, she vows to overthrow him. Doris teams up with a mysterious stranger, Vampire Hunter D, who agrees to use his considerable abilities to help her. As she later learns, he too is from the house of Dracula. But, being half human, D has given himself over to good.

The duo's quest is complicated, however, by the machinations of selfish townspeople and jealous members of Count Lee's court. The mayor's oily son, Greco, exposes Doris's vampire bite to the town when she rebuffs his sexual advances. Lee's daughter L'Amica wants the commoner Doris killed so she will not become the Count's new bride. And Lee's treacherous assistant Ray seeks D's death to curry favor with his master. Battling hordes of mutants, ghouls and demonic creatures along the way, D reaches the Count's castle, only to be ensnared by three snake-girls. The Count has Doris kidnapped and brought to the castle for their forced wedding. D uses his regenerative powers and escapes with Doris, back to the village.

Ray hunts them, using a special vampire-paralyzing lamp given him by Lee. Greco steals the lamp, allowing D to win an encounter with Ray. Meanwhile, L'Amica captures Doris, despite competition from Greco. In a second attack by Ray, D is gravely wounded. Thinking he has won the court's favor Ray asks Count Lee for promotion. Denied, he tries to assassinate the Count, but is himself killed by Lee. As the vampire wedding is about to transpire, a recovered D enters and kills his fellow Draculan. The evil empire vanquished, D quietly rides out of the village.

The animators try to liven up the crudeness of the characters' robotic motions and unsynched lips by giving VAMPIRE HUNTER D a dark, comic-book Gothic look. But any interest this might create is negated by several confusing action sequences, in which combatants jump and jerk about in illogical ways that are difficult to follow. More bothersome is the way in which every scene introduces unexplained plot twists and unmotivated character actions.

Perhaps because VAMPIRE HUNTER D tries to smash together so many different genres, the narration remains embattled throughout. At times the story takes turns that are simply bizarre and opaque: why, for example, do we learn well into the film that the hero has another creature of some sort embedded in the palm of his hand? Why does this hand with a face taunt the person in the body to which it is attached? And why does it eat dirt when it wants to revive the wounded hero? Such confusion might be funny if the entire narrative weren't so hard to follow. In its more lucid moments it is overly cliched—at least in this English language version of the original 1985 Japanese release.

VAMPIRE HUNTER D also plays its cartoon violence to an adult rather than a children's audience. The gruesomeness and gore are not excessive, but there are trite uses of profanity. Moreover, the heroine Doris is undressed several times and twice offers her body to the noble, repressed D ("You're a vampire hunter, aren't you? I need you. I'll give you three meals a day and you can sleep with me if you want.") While such "adult" comics and cartoons are common in Japan, US audiences usually associate animation with children and horror/sci fi with teens. This mishmash of genres offers little to any of these audiences. *(Violence, profanity, nudity.)*

p, Hiroshi Kato, Mitsuhisa Koeda, Yukio Nagasaki, Carl Macek; d, Toyoo Ashida, Carl Macek; w, Yasuhi Hirano; md, Noriyoshi Matsuura; art d, Toyoo Ashida

Animated/Horror/Science Fiction (PR: C MPAA: NR)

VAN GOGH ★★★½

(France) 175m Erato Films; Antenne 2; Le Studio Canal Plus; Les Films du Livradois ~ Sony Pictures Classics c

Jacques Dutronc *(Vincent Van Gogh)*, Alexandra London *(Marguerite Gachet)*, Gerard Sety *(Doctor Gachet)*, Bernard LeCoq *(Theo Van Gogh)*, Corinne Bourdon *(Jo)*, Elsa Zylberstein *(Cathy)*, Leslie Azzoulai *(Adeline Ravoux)*, Jacques Vidal *(M. Ravoux)*, Lisa Lametrie *(Madame Ravoux)*, Chantal Barbarit *(Madame Chevalier)*, Claudine Ducret *(Piano teacher)*

Covering much the same biographical ground as Robert Altman's acclaimed VINCENT & THEO, French director Maurice Pialat tackles the last two months of the artist's life in a mood of bemused contemplation.

The film begins with the arrival of Vincent (Jacques Dutronc) in Auvers, France, to be cared for by Dr. Gachet (Gerard Sety) for supposed epileptic fits and headaches. Gachet finds nothing physically wrong with him, but Vincent stays on in the town anyway to do some painting, first at the local hotel then, after his money runs out, moving in with Gachet and his precocious teenage daughter Marguerite (Alexandra London). Each morning Vincent rises with the farm workers and goes out to paint, returning at dusk. To help pay for his stay at the Gachet's, he paints both Marguerite and her father. Marguerite develops a crush on Vincent that quickens when she spies him cavorting with a prostitute who comes to visit him from Paris.

When Vincent's brother, Theo (Bernard LeCoq), comes to visit with his wife, Jo (Corinne Bourdon), and their new son—whom Theo has named after Vincent—Jo confesses to Vincent that Theo is becoming impossible to live with, due to increasing insanity brought on by the syphilis that will eventually kill him. Later, Vincent finds himself increasingly distracted by Marguerite's attentions and the fawning of Gachet, an art buff and collector. He moves back into the hotel, working as a waiter and bartender to pay his keep, and eventually goes back to Paris, where his increasing frustration over his stalled career leads him to fight with his brother, an art dealer who refuses to promote his work. When Vincent misses his train back to Auvers, a frantic Marguerite comes searching for him and is taken by Theo to the brothers' favorite brothel, where they find Vincent along with a drunken Toulouse-Lautrec and a bevy of prostitutes, one of whom tries to seduce Marguerite.

On the train back to Auvers, Vincent and Marguerite make love but then quarrel, upsetting Gachet, who has come to the station to meet them. Soon after, Vincent is discovered with an unexplained gunshot wound. Gachet lacks the expertise to operate on him to remove the bullet, but vetoes any move to a hospital. Vincent dies from the wound, but the film ends with Marguerite, dressed in mourning clothes, telling a young painter of her "friendship" with Vincent Van Gogh.

Early in his career Pialat was described, in Richard Roud's *Cinema: A Critical Dictionary*, as "discreet" and "restrained," even in his treatment of the most pathological areas of human behavior. Here, the two most "celebrated" events in Van Gogh's life—his severing of his own ear and his supposed suicide—both occur offscreen, the former alluded to by his prostitute companion as having taken place before the film begins, and the latter seen only in its aftermath.

In marked contrast to the ferocity of Altman's treatment, Pialat's approach remains low-key throughout. Where Altman's Vincent seemed to be a man in uninterrupted turmoil, Pialat's contention here is that Vincent could not have possibly been the anguished artist who is usually portrayed; he produced 70 works, including some of his most celebrated, in the last 67 days of his life. Pialat works through a slow accumulation of details in Vincent's life that come to make his death seem, not only unsurprising, but virtually Aristotelian in its inevitability.

For someone who apparently sought only to pursue his work in peace, Van Gogh's life is one of constant distractions: nubile teenaged girls throwing themselves at him (moving out of Gachet's house, Vincent becomes the apple of the eye of his innkeeper's young daughter); a beautiful whore he can't escape, even far from the streets of Paris; and, the real passion of his life, the baby nephew who bears his name. Even trying to stop drinking proves impossible; he's unable to resist a daily tipple with a vintner who befriends him after he indulges the vinter's retarded son with a rough portrait. Given his additional problems with his brother, it becomes difficult to see how Vincent accomplished so much in so little time. In context, his accomplishments become all the more miraculous. *(Nudity, adult situations.)*

p, Daniel Toscan DuPlantier, Sylvie Danton; d, Maurice Pialat; w, Maurice Pialat; ph, Emmanuel Machuel, Gilles Henri, Jacques Loiseleux; ed, Yann Dedet, Nathalie Hubert; m, Edith Vesperini; prod d, Philippe Pallut, Katia Vischkof

Historical/Biography/Drama (PR: C MPAA: R)

VENICE/VENICE ★½

108m Jagfilm ~ International Rainbow Pictures c

Nelly Alard *(Jeanne)*, Henry Jaglom *(Dean)*, Suzanne Bertish *(Carlotta)*, Daphna Kastner *(Eve)*, David Duchovny *(Dylan)*, Suzanne Lanza *(Dylan's Girlfriend)*, Vernon Dobtcheff *(Alexander)*, Klaus Helwig *(Dean's Sales Agent)*, John Landis *(Himself)*, Edna Fainaru *(Fan)*, Guido Colella *(Fan)*, Simonetta DeSantis *(Fan)*, Bracuitti Luca *(Waiter)*, Sarah Gristwood, Silvia Bizio, Dan Fainaru, Claudio Lazzaro, Phyllis Curott *(Journalists)*, Helmuth Bielendt, Dieter Achtel, Rafael Mueller, Klaus Fink, Doje-Kadoke Edgar, Miorelli Bruna, Prospero Bozzo, Roberto Rossi *(Interviewers)*, Melissa Leo *(Peggy)*, Diane Salinger *(Stephanie)*, Zack Norman *(Dennis)*, Christoph Henkel *(Hanno)*, Aimee Shoenberg *(Dean's Secretary)*, Marshall Barer *(Mark)*, David Colin Ross *(Mark's Piano Player)*, Mace Cahme, Marcus Chong, Pierre Cottrell, Mario Gonzalez, Leslie Oliver, Todd M Cahme, Helen Costa, Marlena Giovi, Michelle McIntosh, Lisa Richards, Robert Thomas *(Other Guests at Party)*, Barbara Bercu, Alpha Blair, Sue Cameron, Stacy Solon Foster, Cindy Friedl, Barbara Berque, Anna Bogdanovich, Deborah Carlisle, Victoria Foyt, Nancy Gold, Annette Goliti, Gayle Harbor, Marcia Jacobs, Elizabeth Kemp, Gina Lamond, Kyla MacTaggart, Robyn Rosenfeld, Charisse Savarin, Brenda Smith, Magie Song, Mary Gray, Andrea Harmon, Tracy James, Gaye Kruger, Carolyn McLuskie, Kathleen Matson, Ora Rubinstein, Deborah Skelly, Lisa-Marie Soble, Claudia Stedelin, Abidah Viera *(Interviewees)*

Indefatigable independent filmmaker Henry Jaglom offers another feature full of pseudo-insights and psycho-babble in VENICE/VENICE, a slicker, though only marginally less tedious, package than usual.

Starring as usual, Jaglom this time plays a character named Dean, a director with an affinity for really silly hats whose films, described but never shown, sound an awful lot like those made by one Henry Jaglom. A resolutely independent figure who makes small films about relationships, Dean gives interviews about how shocked he is to have been selected as the American representative to the jury of the Venice Film Festival, since his work has so little in common with the usual Hollywood output.

He is approached by Jeanne (Nelly Alard), a pretty, tongue-tied French journalist and admirer of his films, with whom he strikes up a tentative festival romance. After some hand-holding and rides in a gondola, however, they have a falling out over Dean devoting too much time to his festival business and not enough to her. However, that doesn't stop Jeanne from hopping on a plane and following Dean back to Venice, California, where he lives and works after the festival is over.

There she finds Dean deep into pre-production on his next film and looking for an actress to play his wife. She also finds near him one discarded lover, Carlotta (Suzanne Bertish), who was also with him in Italy, and a live-in, about-to-be-discarded lover, Peggy (Melissa Leo), whom Dean has also helped through some undefined emotional trauma. Jeanne sensibly decides to go back to the airport and hop on the next plane back to Paris, but is prevailed upon to stay by Peggy. Dean promises to spend the next day with Jeanne, but he has forgotten about the big audition for the spouse part in his film and confronts an office filled with ticked-off waiting actresses. Jeanne becomes bored and restive while waiting for Dean and impulsively decides to audition for the part, which she easily wins. The film ends with Jeanne and Dean in the editing room, looking over footage from the "Italy" section of VENICE/VENICE.

As always with a Jaglom opus, the main problem here is figuring out just where the director is in his own film.

The main gimmick in VENICE/VENICE is the ending, when what has seemed to be a straightforward romantic drama played out against the Venice backdrop turns out to be Dean's unfinished film. By duping his audience, Jaglom is apparently trying to make a statement about the relationship between movie illusion and hard reality. This is reinforced by the interviews, dotted throughout the film, in which strikingly beautiful women complain about the way their lives have not lived up to the movie illusions on which they were raised. It's a cheap statement that has been made often and with more wit elsewhere—almost any elsewhere, in fact.

Beyond that, there's not much more than the usual Jaglom blather. To deflect scrutiny from himself, Jaglom usually, as he does here, gives himself a different name; this way no one can accuse his work of being autobiographical. Yet the characters he plays are so undeveloped and uninteresting that the issue is moot.

In earlier films, Jaglom's character simply subjected audiences to endless monologues insisting on his sensitivity and stature. Now, it seems, he can hire actresses, like Allard, Leo and Bertish, to do that for him. He can also afford classier cinematography and better music than he has in the past. But take it all away and VENICE/VENICE is the same old ongoing, hellish cocktail party, filled with annoying, self-absorbed people no one wants to know, and from which most viewers will desperately want to flee after a very short time. *(Adult situations.)*

p, Judith Wolinsky; d, Henry Jaglom; w, Henry Jaglom; ph, Hanania Baer

Drama/Romance **(PR: C MPAA: R)**

VERRIEGELTE ZEIT

(SEE: LOCKED-UP TIME)

VILLA DEL VENERDI, LA

(SEE: HUSBANDS AND LOVERS)

VOICES FROM THE FRONT ★★★

92m Testing the Limits ~ Frameline c

Produced by Testing the Limits, VOICES FROM THE FRONT provides a primer on AIDS activism, relying on interviews with People with AIDS and other AIDS activists, documentary footage of demonstrations, and footage from TV broadcasts to tell the story of AIDS activism in America 1988-1991 systematically and effectively, always allowing AIDS activists and PWAs to speak for themselves.

The film starts with the beginning of AIDS activism—the decision not to be a victim, an AIDS sufferer—and explodes the myth of PWAs as helpless victims, as emaciated corpses lying near death in a hospital, by showing viewers forceful PWAs telling their own stories, juxtaposed with Ronald Reagan asserting his interest in AIDS and footage belying his statements.

AIDS activism emerged when PWAs demanded control of their own bodies. Their first reaction is "I'm going to die." The second reaction is to get involved. VOICES FROM THE FRONT then introduces the various AIDS activist organizations: the PWA Coalition, the first organization run solely by PWAs for PWAs; the AIDS Coalition to Unleash Power (ACT-UP), a "diverse non-partisan group of individuals united in anger and committed to direct action to end the AIDS crisis"; the Community Research Initiative, a grassroots drug testing organization; and the PWA Health Group which sells drugs that are otherwise unavailable.

VOICES FROM THE FRONT is punctuated with footage of demonstrations. In the first, activists take over the 5th International AIDS conference in Montreal and effectively reorient the conference from the insular concerns of scientists to the concerns of the people with the disease. The next one is called "Seize Control of the FDA" and was intended to force the Food and Drug Administration to speed up the nearly ten-year drug approval process. However, the FDA can't approve drugs that aren't being developed, so the next step is to "Storm the NIH (National Institutes of Health)," which weren't developing the drugs to cure opportunistic infections, but obsessively researching AZT, the one drug already approved. Another issue is that those drug trials that do exist systematically exclude women and people of color. This demonstration is wonderfully visual, with 20-foot poles spewing a rainbow of smoke, as well as numerous caustic signs.

The activists assert that the purpose of these demonstrations is to open dialogue with those in control. In addition, the activists prepare by learning the biology of the disease, the chemistry of the drugs and the economics of the healthcare system better than the so-called experts. The next problem is that the drugs that do exist, particularly AZT, are so expensive that the marketplace, rather than people's needs, controls healthcare. The AIDS activists attack this by demonstrating on Wall Street and even on the floor of the New York Stock Exchange, directing their protests at Burroughs-Wellcome, the manufacturer of AZT. Three days later the price is lowered 20 percent.

Next, the filmmakers detail the problems of the whole healthcare delivery system. Viewers hear a heart-wrenching plea on behalf of a doctor with AIDS who has been left for nine days in a hospital corridor, soiled by his own feces, surrounded by garbage, subject to drafts while desperately ill. The next expansion is to prevention. A demonstration at Shea Stadium during a Mets game targets safe sex using huge signs that declare: Men Wear Condoms, Women Get AIDS, No Glove, No Love. The activists also go to Chicago to demonstrate at the AMA and some insurance companies' headquarters. They target needle exchange programs so that intravenous drug users will no longer pass the virus to each other. They demonstrate in San Francisco, targeting the Immigration and Naturalization Service which keeps even tourists with HIV out of the US and at the 6th International Conference drown out Louis Sullivan, Secretary of Health and Human Services, the representative of the Reagan administration. The film ends with the Day of Desperation, a series of demonstrations during the height of the Gulf War, in Harlem for better housing, at Grand Central Station disrupting business as usual, interrupting commuters' lives as AIDS has disrupted activists' lives.

The film's poignant coda presents viewers with the pictures of 12 activists prominent in the film who have died since filming began. The power of VOICES FROM THE FRONT derives from the directness of its message. The fact that this was shot on video and transferred to film adds to the urgency.

The impassioned pleas of PWAs are never mediated by scientific experts. In fact, in an analysis of one particular Nightline episode, the filmmakers show how mainstream media favors the platitudes of government apologists over the activists. The government spokesmen are allowed to go on and on while the activists microphone is turned off.

There is so much information in VOICES FROM THE FRONT that it does begin to wear on the viewers. Generally, the filmmakers use music well to enhance the emotionality of the film, but their only real misstep is the over-use of a simplistic, annoying rap song about ACT-UP. Life is not a music video and the filmmakers have captured a great deal of real life. This is not the sort of film to sway ardent homophobes, but open-minded people who have no real connection to the AIDS movement will learn a great deal from it.

p, David Meiesan, Robyn Hutt, Sandra Elgear; d, David Meiesan, Robyn Hutt, Sandra Elgear; ed, David Meiesan, Robyn Hutt, Sandra Elgear

Political/Documentary (PR: A MPAA: NR)

VOYAGER ★★

(France/West Germany) 117m Bioskop Film; Action Films ~ Castle Hill Productions c

Sam Shepard *(Walter Faber)*, Julie Delpy *(Sabeth)*, Barbara Sukowa *(Hannah)*, Dieter Kirchlechner *(Herbert Henke)*, Traci Lind *(Charlene)*, Deborra-Lee Furness *(Ivy)*, August Zirner *(Joachim Henke)*, Thomas Heinze *(Kurt)*, Bill Dunn *(Lewin)*, Peter Berling *(Baptist)*, Lorna Farrar *(Arlene)*, Kathleen Matiezen *(Lady Stenographer)*, Lou Cuttell *(New York Doorman)*, Charles Hayward *(Joe)*, Irwin Wynn *(Dick)*, James Mathews *(Pilot)*, Perla Walter *(Restroom Attendant)*, Roland DeChandenay *(UNESCO Delegate)*, Jacques Martial *(African UNESCO)*, Brigitte Catillou *(Marianne)*, Philippe Morier Genoud *(Guillaume)*, Erica Lawson *(Judith)*

Dreamily paced and easy on the eyes, VOYAGER spans the globe from the 1930s to the 50s with muted soul-searching.

Racing from engineering assignment to assignment, Max Faber (Sam Shepard) runs away from emotional commitment and fervently practices his religion—Technology. By chance, Faber becomes plane-mates with Herbert Henke (Dieter Kirchlechner), the brother of a long-lost school-chum from Germany, Joachim Henke (August Zirner). After a plane crash forces them to land in the desert, the rigid Max decides to join Herbert on a fraternal visit, only to discover that Joachim has hanged himself. In flashbacks, viewers discover that Max impregnated Hannah (Barbara Sukowa), who grew so weary of his insensitivity that she married Joachim on the rebound.

Before long, tactless Max has brushed off another woman in New York, and the globe-trotter boards an ocean liner for France. On the waves, the insular Max comes to passionate life under the tutelage of a teenager, Sabeth (Julie Delpy). She represents pure feeling, you see, and even persuades Mr. No-nonsense to waste his time at the Louvre. Unable to break away from her, Max even proposes marriage while on an auto trip to Greece. While their love rages, Max learns a shocking secret just before Sabeth gets bitten by a snake and injures her head on a rock. Stunned, as his head swims with deja vu, Max realizes he has been sleeping with his own daughter. By the time ex-love Hannah enters the scene, this dysfunctional family is hit with Sabeth's death. Doomed to loneliness, Max wanders the globe once more.

While powerful metaphors for the search for existential identity and the bittersweet curse of sexual longing may leap off the pages of Max Frisch's *Homo Faber*, VOYAGER's source material, these themes scream at viewers in over-elaboration onscreen. After his versions of SWANN'S WAY and THE HANDMAID'S TALE, Schlondorff can be considered a major embalmer of difficult-to-transfer novels. Nor is the literal-minded director aided by stoic star Sam Shepard who's best at playing on-the-edge action types but who seems mighty befuddled by having to suggest interior states. When he reads the book's soul-searching lines as narration, his thin voice turns eloquence to mush.

But not all blame can be placed on the unpersuasive direction and static acting. One grows weary of the sexist notion that some middle-aged closet-romantic can only be saved by the sexual ministrations of a wise-beyond-her-years nymphet. This young blend of beauty and brains is a pin-up girl for the Camus calendar, the Existentialist's wet dream. Watching Shepard and Delpy failing to strike sparks while they bare their souls, one is less likely to be shocked by the incest gambit because their love-making seems so essentially chaste and austere anyway.

All the passion seems to have gone into the lush, memorable cinematography (including striking sepia tones for flashbacks). Maybe the novel's profundities are shallow anyway—using incest to symbolize a chracter's stunted spiritual growth may carry symbol-mindedness too far. Over-long and half-baked, this odyssey of a repressive sputters to a foregone conclusion. Moral: do you know where your chlldren are? *(Sexual situations.)*

p, Eberhard Junkersdorf; d, Volker Schlondorff; w, Rudy Wurlitzer, Volker Schlondorff, (from the novel *Homo Faber* by Max Frisch); ph, Pierre Lhomme, Yorgos Arvantis; ed, Dagmar Hirtz; m, Stanley Myers; prod d, Nicos Perakis; art d, Thierry Francois, Cherie Baker; set d, Frederque Lauzier, Doxi Nikolaidou, Pepeta Arvaniti, Itala Scandariato, Robin Schneider; cos, Barbara Baum

Drama/Romance **(PR: C MPAA: PG-13)**

WATERDANCE, THE ★★★½

106m No Frills Films; JBW ~ Samuel Goldwyn Company c

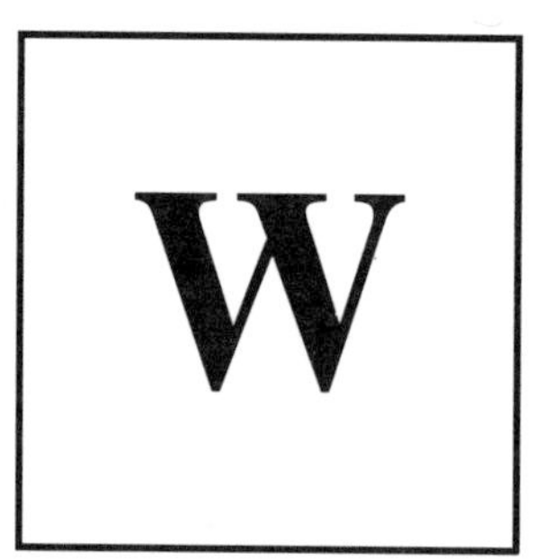

Eric Stoltz *(Joel Garcia)*, Wesley Snipes *(Raymond Hill)*, William Forsythe *(Bloss)*, Helen Hunt *(Anna)*, Elizabeth Pena *(Rosa)*, William Allen Young *(Les)*, James Roach *(Guy in the Electronic Wheelchair)*, Henry Harris *(Mr. Gibson)*, Tony Genaro *(Victor)*, Eva Rodriguez *(Victor's Wife)*, Erick Vigil *(Victor's Son)*, Edgar Rodriguez *(Victor's Son)*, Angelica Castell *(Victor's Daughter)*, Kimberly Scott *(Alice)*, Casey Stengal *(Vernon)*, Susan Gibney *(Cheryl Lynn)*, Elizabeth Dennehy *(Candy)*, Starletta DuPois *(Florence)*, Mirron E. Willis *(Doctor)*, Badja Djola *(Decton)*, Marco Ramos *(Tomas)*, David Aguilar *(Carlos)*, Thomas F. Duffy *(Harrison)*, Joey Ciccone *(2nd Biker)*, Chelsea Madison-Ciu *(Lucille)*, Fay Hauser *(Rachel Hill)*, Andrea Young *(Starletta Hill)*, Tai Thai *(Sang)*, Rick Lieberman *(David Albini)*, Ed Barkas *(Western Man)*, Lyla Chang, Sandra Lee, Kyu Na, Sanghyuk Shin *(Korean Singers)*, Joe Goddbiff *(Derelict Man)*, Pola Churchill *(Vernon's Wife)*, Barbara Alyn Woods *(Annabelle Lee)*, Joe Nipote *(Emcee)*, Jennifer Ryan *(Stripper)*, Adriana Barbor *(Stripper)*, Tony Simotes *(Phone Operator)*, Rebeca Ruth *(Shelia)*, William Forward *(Cop)*, Lara Cody, Ann Blessing, Thomas White, Reni Satoni, Andy Goldberg, Dean Wein, Jeffrey Scott Yesko *(Waila Group)*

Screenwriter and first-time director Neal Jimenez drew on personal experience for THE WATERDANCE, a tough-minded comedy-drama about three paraplegics coping with life in a wheelchair.

Joel Garcia (Eric Stolz) is a promising young novelist who broke his neck in a hiking accident. Garcia was having an affair with his married editor, Anna (Helen Hunt), who was about to leave her husband for him when Garcia's accident occurred. With his world turned upside down, Garcia begins having second thoughts about their relationship and questions whether Anna will stay with him in his new, physically dependent condition.

He has little regard or use for his wardmates at first, but gradually he gets to know them. A member of a biker gang, Bloss (William Forsythe) was broadsided by a car while riding drunk. Though an unapologetic redneck bigot, Bloss strikes up a bickering friendship with Black wardmate Raymond Hill (Wesley Snipes). Hill brags about his sexual prowess nonstop, in particular his past exploits with a stripper named Annabelle Lee. His only visible partner, though, is his wife, who is divorcing him and taking their daughter with her. Bloss bets Raymond that Annabelle Lee doesn't exist.

Despondent about his divorce, Raymond finally admits that his talk about Annabelle Lee was exactly that—just talk. However, when Bloss and Garcia "borrow" the hospital van for an illicit late-night outing to a local go-go bar, they discover the surprising truth.

Garcia eventually breaks off his affair with Anna, who leaves her husband nonetheless and, in a friendly capacity, helps Garcia find a wheelchair-accessible apartment. Bloss goes home, unsure of whether he'll ever see any injury money from the lawyer his mother has hired from a TV commercial. Raymond returns to the ward after attempting suicide.

As with his screenplay for RIVER'S EDGE, Jimenez refuses to yield to the temptation of squeezing a moral from a tragic situation. Jimenez's characters don't learn much of anything from their experiences. They're more like crazy stoics, just trying to keep their heads above water in a world where the water is rising faster than they can tread. Rather than making speeches, they make some noise and move on, often worse for the wear and tear. Their experiences do change them, but not necessarily for the better.

Jimenez, who codirected THE WATERDANCE with former UCLA classmate Michael Steinberg, recognizes what few admit in formulaic, feelgood Hollywood filmmaking: suffering doesn't always ennoble. More often, it diminishes us and makes it that much harder for us to hang onto our humanity. Sometimes Jimenez's characters don't succeed. When they do, the victories are usually temporary, lasting just until the next challenge.

THE WATERDANCE favors an episodic style, with few big dramatic moments. "Saddled" with a gorgeous girlfriend, Garcia spends most of the film intent on hurting her before she can hurt him by leaving him for a man who, as Bloss puts it, "can tune her engine." In a story thread that loosely parodies ONE FLEW OVER THE CUCKOO'S NEST, Bloss and Garcia take revenge on the hospital phone operator who cut off Raymond's desperate call before his suicide attempt. Jimenez undercuts the sentimental potential of his story with some effectively barbed humor (one wheelchair-bound patient to another, after narrowly avoiding a crash in the "hijacked" hospital bus: "Lucky we're already crippled!").

Jimenez's characters are believable rather than heroic, sympathetic if not always likable. The cast is generally good, with Hunt (MR. SATURDAY NIGHT, PEGGY SUE GOT MARRIED) taking top honors for giving substance to a relatively sketchy part. Stolz and Forsythe are solid and Snipes is extraordinary. He disappears so thoroughly into Raymond that it's hard to imagine the same actor as the slick, successful architect in Spike Lee's JUNGLE FEVER. Elizabeth Pena (JACOB'S LADDER) contributes an effective turn as the ward's head nurse.

The real star here, though, is Jimenez, a talented filmmaker who clearly has a lot more still to offer. *(Profanity, nudity, adult situations.)*

p, Gale Anne Hurd, Marie Cantin; d, Neal Jimenez, Michael Steinberg; w, Neal Jimenez; ph, Mark Plummer; ed, Jeff Freeman; m, Michael Convertino; prod d, Bob Ziembicki; cos, Isis Mussenden

Comedy/Drama **(PR: C MPAA: R)**

WATERLAND ★★½

(U.K./U.S.) 95m Palace Pictures; Fine Line Features; Pandora Cinema ~ Fine Line Features c

Jeremy Irons *(Tom Crick)*, Ethan Hawke *(Mathew Price)*, Sinead Cusack *(Mary Crick)*, John Heard *(Lewis Scott)*, Grant Warnock *(Young Tom)*, Lena Headey *(Young Mary)*, David Morrissey *(Dick Crick)*, Peter Postlethwaite *(Henry Crick)*, Cara Buono *(Judy Dobson)*, Callum Dixon *(Freddie Parr)*, Sean McGuire *(Peter)*, Ross McCall *(Terry)*, Camilla Hebditch *(Shirley)*, Maggie Gyllenhaal *(Maggie Ruth)*, Stewart Richman *(Ernest Atkinson)*, Siri Neal *(Helen Atkinson)*, Gareth Thomas *(Publican)*, Susannah Fellows *(Rebecca Scott)*, Colin Bruce, Kate Harper, Bradley Lavelle, Jana Sheldon, Scott Children, Alesh Hlozek, Kimberley Lakey, Tessa Wilkins *(Guests at Dinner Party)*, Tony Vogel *(Stan Booth)*, Paul Haigh *(RAF Man 1)*, Giles Thomas *(RAF Man 2)*, Larry John Meyers *(Senior Police Officer)*, Tina Benko *(Baby's Mother)*, Rohn Thomas *(Barman)*, Matyelok Gibbs *(Martha Clay)*, Jolyon Stephenson *(Joe)*, Nicholas Boyce *(Leroy)*, Miguel Montalvo *(Stephen Bates)*, Alison Everns *(Alison)*, Latoya Heard *(Julie)*, Kalvin Palmer *(Marshall)*, Jennifer Meyer *(Sara)*, Christine Christie *(Angie)*, Vanessa Pfulger *(Vanessa)*,

Monique Idelbird *(Girl)*, Joe Collis, Paul Hardy, Eric Dumbaugh, Hasmin Stremikis *(Boys)*, Stephanie Anderson, Fernando Cassas, Jeff Hoffman, Michael Hunter, Anne Kilpack, Sara Ittmann, Nadia Siraj, Josh Wheaton *(Other Pupils)*

Set in Pittsburgh and England's Fens—the low, flat marshlands where East Anglia meets the North Sea—WATERLAND sadly but perhaps inevitably fails to measure up to the acclaimed novel upon which it's based.

Tom Crick (Jeremy Irons) is a Pittsburgh high-school history teacher haunted by a tragic past. Mary (Sinead Cusack), his childhood sweetheart and wife of many years, is an increasingly unstable woman on the brink of madness. When she blithely announces at a dinner party that she's pregnant, Tom is duly stunned—this, he well knows, is impossible. As a result of the crisis in his marriage, painful memories from Tom's childhood begin to resurface, further disrupting the delicate balance of his life. When one of his students, Mathew Price (Ethan Hawke), questions the relevance of history to their lives, Tom, in an effort to bring history alive for his students, begins to recount his own traumatic childhood during WWII.

In a flashback, we are introduced to young Tom (Grant Warnock) and Mary (newcomer Lena Heady, who bears a remarkable resemblance to Cusack), and Tom's elder brother, Dick (David Morrissey), a simpleton. Both brothers are infatuated with Mary, but it's Tom with whom the girl has been spending secret, passionate afternoons in an abandoned windmill.

Then, in a fantasy flashback-within-a-flashback, the adult Tom enables his students to travel literally back in time to the Fens of 1911, a time when his maternal grandfather, Ernest Atkinson (Stewart Richman), owned and operated a famous brewery. When Atkinson lost a bid for Parliament, he took revenge by concocting a special batch of highly potent beer and dispersing it to the locals; in the resulting chaos, the brewery was burned to the ground, although Atkinson did manage to save one crate of his beer from the flames.

By 1922, the Atkinson mansion has become an asylum for war veterans. Atkinson, a broken man on the verge of madness, has retreated from the world. He is cared for by his faithful daughter Helen (Siri Neal), spawning rumors of incest. It's here that Helen meets Tom's father, a vet named Henry Crick (Peter Postlethwaite). They marry but, after giving birth to her second son, Tom, Helen succumbs to influenza. Before she dies, she gives Dick a key to a trunk in the attic, to be opened on his eighteenth birthday.

Back to the original flashback, where young Tom realizes that his elder brother has been courting Mary. When Mary announces that she is pregnant, Tom suspects that Dick is the father, though Mary protests that they never consummated their relationship; nonetheless, she is scared of the older boy and his reaction to the news. Shortly thereafter, Freddie Parr (Callum Dixon), a schoolmate of Tom's, is found floating in the river. Mary confesses that, afraid of implicating Tom, she had lied to Dick, telling him that Freddie was the father. The death is deemed a suicide by local authorities, but Tom, who's already spotted the marks on Freddie's neck and a suspicious beer bottle floating in the water, knows better.

When Tom confronts Dick with the truth, the latter goes haywire and forces Tom to read the letter in the trunk; it's from Atkinson, who, it turns out, is not Dick's grandfather but his father. (The trunk also contained twelve bottles of the infamous beer.) Now even more distraught, Dick speeds away on his motorbike, climbs a barge and dives into the water, swimming out to sea; presumably, he's never seen again (a point the film fails to clarify). Mary, wracked with guilt, visits a local midwife and undergoes a botched abortion, rendering her infertile. The old hag hands Tom a slop bucket, warning him not to look at the aborted fetus when he throws it into the river—it's bad luck. Tom looks.

Back in present-day Pittsburgh, Tom returns home and discovers that Mary has stolen a baby. She claims to have received him from God, who, it turns out, left him at the local Shop and Save. Acting quickly, Tom manages to return the infant to its hysterical mother without getting his wife arrested in the process. Shortly thereafter he's forced into early retirement for having deviated from the proscribed curriculum. As Price, who's warmed to Tom, points out, he's been "telling stories" for himself, not for the benefit of his students. Mary leaves Tom, who soon returns to the Fens, where he sees her strolling in the distance.

Gorgeously photographed, particularly the flashback sequences, WATERLAND strives to be an evocative mood piece. Occasionally it succeeds, but more often it's enervating and uninvolving. This is particularly disappointing considering director Stephen Gyllenhaal's impressive work on two recent TV movies, "A Killing in a Small Town" and "Paris Trout," the latter adapted from the acclaimed book by Pete Dexter.

In Graham Swift's highly idiosyncratic 1983 novel, Tom and Mary are in their mid-fifties; given the fact that they were adolescents during WWII, this screen adaptation would have to be set in the early 70s to account for the fortysomething Irons and Cusack—a point the film never clarifies. But that's a minor quibble. The film's most glaring fault is the fantasy element. Even though we're not supposed to take it at face value, the sight of Tom's contemporary students cavorting with the locals in a small English town circa 1911 is ludicrous. Worse still, these teens are utterly charmless. Ethan Hawke (DEAD POETS SOCIETY, WHITE FANG), in particular, substitutes bad-boy posturing for acting.

Credit is nevertheless due to screenwriter Peter Prince for his ambitious attempt to adapt Swift's novel. And Sinead Cusack, the daughter of famed actor Cyril Cusack and wife of Jeremy Irons, is superb as the adult Mary, easily overshadowing her husband's bland central performance.

p, Katy McGuinness, Patrick Cassavetti; d, Stephen Gyllenhaal; w, Peter Prince, (from the novel by Grahm Swift); ph, Robert Elswit; ed, Lesley Walker; m, Carter Burwell; prod d, Hugo Luczyc-Wyhowski; art d, Helen Rayner; cos, Lindy Hemming

Drama/Fantasy **(PR: C MPAA: R)**

WAXWORK II: LOST IN TIME ★★

104m Lost in Time Productions; Electric Pictures ~ LIVE Home Video c

Zach Galligan *(Mark Loftmore)*, Sophie Ward *(Eleanore Pratt)*, Patrick Macnee *(Sir Wilfred)*, Alexander Godunov *(Scarabus)*, Martin Kemp *(Baron Frankenstein)*, Monika Schnarre *(Sarah)*, Bruce Campbell *(John Wright)*, David Carradine *(Beggar)*, Mirina Sirtis *(Gloria)*, Michael DeBarres, John Ireland *(King Arthur)*, Maxwell Caulfield, Marina Sirtis, Jim Metzler, Billy Kane, Joe Baker, Ivan Markota

A slight improvement on the badly structured original, WAXWORK II briefly suggests how the two films' basic idea might really have worked. Unfortunately, it only proves that the best use of the format would be as a brief series of sketches, not a full-length film.

The movie opens with heroes Mark Loftmore (Zach Galligan) and Sarah (Monika Schnarre, replacing Deborah Foreman) escaping the burning wax museum where several of their friends had been sucked into the horrific displays and killed. They don't notice a living, crawling hand following them out, and it soon turns up at Sarah's home and bludgeons her father to death with a hammer. She manages to dispose of the murderous appendage bloodily in the garbage disposal, but that leaves her with nothing to back up her story when she's arrested for the murder.

The beleagured couple go looking for helpful evidence at the home of Sir Wilfred (Patrick Macnee), the occult expert who died in the previous adventure, where a home-movie message instructs them to use a time portal to stop the evil that still threatens Earth.

Using a sort of compass that guides them to time holes, Mark and Sarah first wind up as players in a Frankenstein story, where Mark grabs the doctor's book on life restoration that he believes can help exonerate Sarah. "Think about it," he explains in a typical line of dialogue. "If we can reanimate dead flesh, then the prosecution's case is out the window!"

Pretty soon the pair are separated; Mark winds up in a haunted-house homage to THE HAUNTING, complete with b&w photography and another masochistic role for EVIL DEAD star Bruce Campbell, while Sarah is thrust into the Sigourney Weaver role in an ALIENS takeoff. Mark appears in time to rescue her from the space beast, and the couple are then transported into a medieval setting, where Sarah is kidnapped by knights under the command of the sorcerer Scarabus (Alexander Godunov). He's got an evil plan to use black magic to impersonate King Arthur (John Ireland) and seize command of his kingdom, but after much drawn-out intrigue, Mark manages to expose his evil intentions.

He gets into a duel to the death with the evil magician, and the two wind up jumping quickly through several successive scenarios: Jekyll and Hyde's laboratory; a shopping mall inhabited by DAWN OF THE DEAD-style zombies (where Mark slices off and retrieves an undead hand); Victorian London, where Jack the Ripper is claiming another victim; a bedroom terrorized by Nosferatu (in which the Ripper winds up trapped); and finally Japan under attack by Godzilla.

Returning to Arthur's castle, Mark finally manages to defeat Scarabus, but when he and Sarah go to use the one time door that can take them home, only one of them will fit. Giving Sarah the zombie hand for evidence, Mark forces her to leave him and return home to exonerate herself. That she does, and as she leaves the courthouse an innocent woman, she is approached by a delivery man, who has a package that's been waiting for her for a very long time. It turns out to be another time compass, complete with a note from Mark to "Join Me"—which she does.

The late-coming sequence in which Mark and Scarabus's duel takes them through the montage of brief spoofs—complete with jumpy b&w photography in the NOSFERATU scene and bad dubbing in the Godzilla homage—is the best thing about WAXWORK II, since it allows each parody to make its simple point quickly before the transition to the next. The rest of the film, unfortunately, is fatally drawn out, with a wildly uneven mixture of tones.

Although, for the most part, the longer segments are played straight (complete with graphic gore, torture and sleazy attempted rape scenes), encoring writer-director Anthony Hickox peppers the film with dumb, sitcom-level humor and gags. The spoofy touches even extend to the music; when Sarah fights off the crawling hand that has murdered her father (an ostensibly serious battle), and the thing throws hot dog buns at her, strains of "Take Me Out to the Ball Game" are heard on the soundtrack.

The movie also relies way too much on coincidence and the characters' stupidity to keep the story moving. Mark is forever picking up and losing artifacts that could help his and Sarah's situation, and the rules of time-jumping are haphazardly presented; when Hickox finds himself in an expository corner, he simply has Sir Wilfred, in the guise of a raven, turn up to help Mark out. (In one of the screenplay's many awkward lines, he refers to the time-hopping scenario as "God's Nintendo game.") And the movie never explains how, if the the characters are supposed to be traveling through different historical eras, they wind up consorting with so many fictional characters.

Unfortunately, WAXWORK II: LOST IN TIME ends up little more than a good idea that needed a steadier hand at the helm. *(Excessive violence, profanity, sexual situations.)*

p, Nancy Paloian; d, Anthony Hickox; w, Anthony Hickox; ph, Gerry Lively; ed, Christopher Cibelli; m, Steve Schiff; prod d, Steve Hardie; art d, John Chichester; set d, David A. Koneff; cos, Mark Bridges

Fantasy/Horror/Comedy **(PR: O MPAA: R)**

WAYNE'S WORLD ★★½

95m Paramount ~ Paramount c

Mike Myers *(Wayne Campbell)*, Dana Carvey *(Garth Algar)*, Rob Lowe *(Benjamin Oliver)*, Tia Carrere *(Cassandra)*, Brian Doyle-Murray *(Noah Vanderhoff)*, Lara Flynn Boyle *(Stacy)*, Michael DeLuise *(Alan)*, Dan Bell *(Neil)*, Lee Tergesen *(Terry)*, Kurt Fuller *(Russell)*, Sean Gregory Sullivan *(Phil)*, Colleen Camp *(Mrs. Vanderhoff)*, Donna Dixon *(Dreamwoman)*, Frederick Coffin *(Officer Koharski)*, Michael G. Hagerty *(Davy)*, Chris Farley *(Security Guard)*, Meat Loaf *(Tiny)*, Charles Noland *(Ron Paxton)*, Robert Patrick *(Bad Cop)*, Ione Skye *(Elyse)*, Frank DiLeo *(Frankie Sharp–Mr. Big)*, Eric Crabb *(Guitar Store Clerk)*, Mark St. James *(Fellow Drummer)*, Harris Shore *(Detective)*, Peder Melhuse *(Detective)*, Don Amendolia *(Announcer)*, Carmen Filpi *(Old Man Withers)*, Anna Schoeller *(Girl Driver)*, Robin Ruzan *(Waitress)*, Alice Cooper *(Alice Cooper)*, Stan Mikita *(Stan Mikita)*, Ed O'Neill *(Mikita's Manager)*, George Foster *(Guitarist–Crucial Taunt Band Member)*, Anthony Focx *(Drummer–Crucial Taunt Band Member)*, Marc Ferrari *(Guitarist–Crucial Taunt Band Member)*, Stef Burns *(Guitarist–Alice Cooper's Band Member)*, Pete Freezin' *(Guitarist–Alice Cooper's Band Member)*, Greg Smith *(Bassist–Alice Cooper's Band Member)*, Derek Sherinian *(Keyboards–Alice Cooper's Band Member)*, Jimmy DeGrassio *(Drummer–Alice Cooper's Band Member)*

One of the surprise box-office smashes of 1992, WAYNE'S WORLD is a moderately successful translation of the popular "Saturday Night Live" sketch to the big screen. As its origins would suggest, the movie works better in small pieces than it does as a whole.

"Wayne's World" is the name of an underground public-access cable show broadcast from the Aurora, Illinois basement of teenager Wayne Campbell (Mike Myers). The program, on which he and best friend Garth (Dana Carvey) riff on their lives, music and favorite "babes," catches the attention of sleazy TV executive Benjamin Oliver (Rob Lowe), who sees in it a vehicle for video-arcade magnate and potential sponsor Noah Vanderhoff (Brian Doyle-Murray). Benjamin meets with Wayne and Garth and offers them a sizable advance for the rights to their show, and the startled boys agree.

Meanwhile, Wayne has become attracted to beautiful Asian rock singer Cassandra (Tia Carrere), while fending off the ferocious advances of his ex-girlfriend, Stacy (Lara Flynn Boyle). Benjamin, however, also has his eye on Cassandra. After sending the boys to Milwaukee with free tickets and backstage passes for an Alice Cooper concert, he seduces her with a music-video deal.

The first episode of the professionally produced, Vanderhoff-sponsored "Wayne's World" is broadcast, but Wayne has misgivings about the slicker, commercialized format and pokes fun at Vanderhoff on the air. After an argument with Benjamin, Wayne walks off the show, and also has fallings-out with Garth and Cassandra. But he's soon reconciled with his best friend and, acting on information passed on by a roadie at the Alice Cooper show, the pair arrange for footage of Cassandra performing to be transmitted to the limousine of record industry hotshot Frankie Sharp (Frank DiLeo). After presenting, and then disposing of, two alternate endings (one of which spoofs the "Scooby Doo" cartoons), Wayne reveals the story's true, happy conclusion: the three friends achieve their goals and Benjamin sees the error of his ways.

With their laid-back attitude, partying disposition and cheeky slang, Wayne and Garth are clearly cut from the same cloth as Bill and Ted, and their first big-screen vehicle is certainly entertaining. Myers and Carvey, having honed their act over years of TV sketches, carry off their dude personas effortlessly, and it's fun to watch these guys having a good time, particularly in the car singalong that put Queen's "Bohemian Rhapsody" back on the charts. Director Penelope Spheeris (THE BOYS NEXT DOOR, THE DECLINE OF WESTERN CIVILIZATION PART II), who has explored the serious side of both dead-end teens and the heavy-metal industry, gets the cheesy suburban milieu just right.

Unfortunately, Spheeris's comedy skills are not as finely honed, and the screenplay by Myers (with Bonnie and Terry Turner) provides her with distinctly limited material to work from. Unlike Bill and Ted, whose film vehicles sent them on jaunts through time, space and hell, Wayne and Garth remain planted in the familiar world of modern pop culture, and much of the humor is derived from sketch-style routines that trade on familiar sounds and images. (A cop tailing Wayne turns out to be the bad cyborg from TERMINATOR 2; arriving in Milwaukee, the guys appear in a pastiche of the title sequence from TV's "Laverne and Shirley"; when Wayne tries out an electric guitar in a store by playing some Led Zeppelin riffs, the manager points to a sign on the wall that reads: "No Stairway to Heaven!") Though some of these gags are undeniably funny, the humor is never developed beyond the initial idea.

WAYNE'S WORLD also has some unpleasant moments, particularly those involving Stacy, the ex-girlfriend who is loathed by Wayne and subjected to some violent slapstick pratfalls. It's the most offensive women's role in a movie since—well, since the same actress's role in THE DARK BACKWARD.

Nonetheless, it is refreshing to see a modern teen comedy with a minority actress (Carrere, quite fetching as the object of Wayne's desire) in the romantic lead, and Lowe does better by his slimy character here than he did in a similar role in the aforementioned THE DARK BACKWARD. A mixed bag, WAYNE'S WORLD may work better on the small screen—the concept's original home—than it did in theaters. *(Violence, profanity, mild sexual situations.)*

p, Lorne Michaels; d, Penelope Spheeris; w, Mike Myers, Bonnie Turner, Terry Turner, (from the characters created by Mike Myers); ph, Theo Van De Sande; ed, Malcolm Campbell; m, J. Peter Robinson; prod d, Gregg Fonseca; art d, Bruce Miller; set d, Jay Hart

Comedy **(PR: C MPAA: PG-13)**

WELCOME TO OBLIVION ★

80m Concorde; Iguana Films ~ Concorde c

Dack Rambo *(Kenner)*, Clare Beresford *(Grace)*, Meshach Taylor *(Elijah)*, Mark Bringelson *(Big)*, Charles Dougherty *(Zig)*, Ramsay Ross *(Lazarus)*, Diana Quijano *(Radio)*, Orlando Sacha *(Bishop)*, Emily Kreimer *(Shiela)*, Ramon Garcia *(Bad Guy)*, Tony Vasques *(Yorrick)*, David Killerby *(Buddy)*, Ian Igberg *(Horst)*

A poverty-stricken MAD MAX retread from Roger Corman's Concorde Pictures, WELCOME TO OBLIVION is set in 2058, after a nuclear war has reduced the Atlantic seaboard to a radioactive wasteland called Oblivion.

The requisite greedy Company sends tough "normal" (that is, radiation free) Kenner (Dack Rambo) there, reluctantly accompanied by the boss's son, Lazarus (Ramsay Ross), and his latest girlfriend, Sheila (Emily Kreimer), to secure zirconium mining rights, the mineral needed for bombs to repel an enemy alien threat. The trio is ambushed by Oblivion's cruel dictator, the Bishop (Orlando Sacha), and forced into slavery along with genetic mutant nomads called "Mutties," one of whom, a spunky fighter named Grace (Clare Beresford) Kenner soon falls in love with. Kenner wins a gladitorial contest (reminiscent of the one in MAD MAX BEYOND THUNDERDOME) and organizes the Mutties into an armed mutiny, along the way dispatching Elijah (Meshach Taylor), a turncoat Muttie who's been reporting to the Bishop. His army defeated in the last-reel battle, the Bishop reveals his true identity as an alien before self-destructing.

Legendary B-man Corman's 1980s-spawned Concorde Pictures specializes in extremely low budget movies released to video and cable TV, completely bypassing theatrical exhibition. Although he serves as executive producer on all of them, Corman seldom takes a screen credit, with good reason: these pictures are technically ragtag, derivative of other, better known films and just plain awful. (Most of his efforts, for Filmgroup and New World, from the 1950s through the 1970s were similarly technically threadbare, but they were also fun and often stylish.) If ULTRAWARRIOR is not the bottom of the barrel, it's certainly scraping wood, its badness turning it into unintentional parody.

For starters, Len Jenkin and Dan Kleinman's screenplay is a tired amalgam of Mad Max cliches, and its nearly nonstop action drags along boringly under director Augusto Tamayo. The special effects, with lots of stock footage from previous Corman films, are poor, as is the make-up. The acting is uniformly comatose; stars Dack Rambo (HIT LADY, RIVER OF DIAMONDS), Clare Beresford and Meshach Taylor (the MANNEQUIN films, TV's "Designing Women") barely register their characters.

Producer Luis Llosa (HOUR OF THE ASSASSIN, FULL FATHOM FIVE and others, all for Concorde) shot this movie in Peru, of all places, and, with its 1990 copyright, it came out briefly in 1991 on video as WELCOME TO OBLIVION. Someone named Kevin Tent then appeared, apparently rearranged some things and cut some fifteen minutes (he receives a co-director credit for his efforts), with the result now entitled ULTRAWARRIOR. *(Violence, profanity, nudity.)*

p, Luis Llosa; d, Augusto Tamayo, Kevin Tent; w, Len Jenkin, Dan Kleinman; ph, Cusi Barrio; ed, Augusto Tamayo, Dan Schalk; m, Kevin Klingler

Science Fiction/Action **(PR: O MPAA: R)**

WE'RE TALKIN' SERIOUS MONEY ★★½

104m CineTel Films ~ Columbia TriStar Home Video c

Leo Rossi *(Charlie)*, Dennis Farina *(Sal)*, Fran Drescher *(Valerie)*, John LaMotta *(Gino the Grocer)*, Peter Iacangelo *(Frankie the Beast)*, Catherine Paolone *(Rosemarie)*, Robert Costanzo *(Michael)*, John Kapelos *(Marty the Greek)*, Denis Arndt *(Jacubick)*, Jeanie Moore *(Amelia)*, Anthony Powers *(Joey Eggs)*, Len Pera *(Goon Behind Counter)*, John Spencer *(Rosemarie's Son)*, Maria Cavaiani *(Rosemarie's Daughter)*, Dona Hardy *(Old Lady)*, Dale Swan *(Guard)*, Peter Marc *(1st Jacubick Goon)*, Johnny Timko *(Tad)*, Richard Gilbert-Hall *(Rent-A-Car Guy)*, Blas Lorenzo *(1st Chicano)*, Joe George *(Uncle John)*, Elizabeth Austin *(Airline Agent)*, Kerry Dakota Dunne *(Bartender)*, Ed Blatchford *(1st*

Biker), Lou Bonacki *(Cop)*, James Jude Courtney *(2nd Biker)*, Cynthia Frost *(Connie)*, Barbara Alyn Woods *(Baggage Claim Clerk)*, Robert Harvey *(FBI Agent)*, Jennifer Gatti *(Sophia)*, Dennis Woodruff *(FBI Man)*, Monty McKee *(FBI Man)*

A congenial, slice-of-pizza comedy, WE'RE TALKING SERIOUS MONEY features two small-time crooks who can barely keep afloat in a sea of crime populated by bigger, nastier fish.

Forever dreaming of the get-rich-quick path to early retirement, Sal (Dennis Farina) resists the sensible career guidance of his girlfriend Valerie (Fran Drescher). Although such can't-miss schemes as St. Christopher medals with talking mouths did miss, enterprising Sal nonetheless talks buddy Charlie (Leo Rossi) into a bearer-bond theft for which they have to ante up ten thousand bucks for Sal's cousin, the inside man. When the snake of a relative skips town, the unwise guys are liable for this loan from Mafioso Gino the Grocer (John LaMotta). While Gino considers a bone-breaking repayment plan, Sal and Charlie take it on the lam to LA, where they crash with Sal's sister and hook up with Marty the Greek (John Kapelos). He inveigles the small-timers into an envelope theft from Marty's office where Sal and Charlie discover the dead body of Marty's partner.

After greedy Marty joins his associate in the hereafter, the bungling crooks adopt his shakedown scheme involving videos of grafting politicians accepting bribes from businessmen. During a dangerous extortion exchange with the suited sharks headed by Jacubick (Dennis Arndt), the white-collar rats take Sal hostage but Charlie manages to hang onto some of the incriminating tapes for insurance. Although Gino and a bodyguard arrive with palms outstretched, Charlie shakes them off long enough to rendezvous with the corporate criminals, free Sal and help capture the ring of corrupt businessmen with the aid of the FBI, who've been summoned by Valerie. Proving ingenious enough to play in the big crime leagues, Sal pays off Gino many times over, returns a substantial portion of the blackmail money to the FBI but splits the remaining $500,000 with Sal, who winds up hitched to Valerie over the closing credits.

Question for a proposed sequel: how long will it take Sal and Charlie to squander their newly acquired nest eggs—or have they learned their lessons? Although WE'RE TALKING SERIOUS MONEY puts viewers in the uncomfortable position of rooting for low-rung blackmailers over high-level CEO murderers, this caper comedy is best approached without too much scrutiny. The film does succeed in making us want Sal and Charlie to outwit the badder guys. Appealingly played by a veteran cast who can limn Italian-American traits without stereotyping them, this farce is so engagingly performed that the characters redeem predictable material. Although this type of hapless hood comedy has been done to death, this variant is vastly superior to fare like WISE GUYS and THE GANG THAT COULDN'T SHOOT STRAIGHT.

Displaying an abundance of heart, the filmmakers enhance even the minor characters (save for the villains) with warmth and loving detail. Deftly, the screenplay milks laughs from the characters rather than outlandish situations in themselves, and the direction never falls into the trap of frenetic pacing or overemphasis. Pleasantly surprising, WE'RE TALKIN' SERIOUS MONEY involves viewers in the friendship of two losers who finally make their big score. To the film's credit, Sal and Charlie are so beautifully etched and freshly played that audiences would likely have been just as interested in them if this comedy had been about their comical misadventures in failure rather than this one pipe dream that came true. *(Violence, profanity.)*

p, Paul Hertzberg; d, James Lemmo; w, James Lemmo, Leo Rossi; ph, Jacques Haitkin; ed, Steve Nevius; m, Scott Grusin; prod d, Dins Danielson; art d, Susan Benjamin; set d, Mary Buri; cos, Tom McKinley

Comedy **(PR: C MPAA: PG-13)**

WHERE ANGELS FEAR TO TREAD ★★

(U.K.) 112m Where Angels Fear to Tread Ltd.; Stagescreen Productions; Sovereign Pictures ~ Fine Line Features c

Helena Bonham Carter *(Caroline Abbott)*, Judy Davis *(Harriet Herriton)*, Rupert Graves *(Philip Herriton)*, Giovanni Guidelli *(Gino Carella)*, Barbara Jefford *(Mrs. Herriton)*, Helen Mirren *(Lilia Herriton)*, Thomas Wheatley *(Mr. Kingcroft)*, Sophie Kullman *(Irma)*, Vass Anderson *(Mr. Abbott)*, Sylvia Barter *(Mrs. Theobald)*, Eileen Davies *(Ethel)*, Siria Betti *(Hotel-keeper)*, Anna Lelio *(Perfetta)*, Luca Lazzareschi *(Spiridione)*, Sergio Falasca *(Carriage Driver)*, Giuseppe Vivenzio *(Carriage Driver)*, Evelina Meghangi *(Opera Singer)*, Gaetano Piro *(Hooded Man)*, Tullio Baccellini *(Postman)*, Lea Burroni *(Hotel Maid)*, Clementina Sguerri *(Hotel Maid)*, Charlie Pinsent *(Girl in Cafe)*, Alessandro Casini *(Gino's Baby)*

In the wake of A PASSAGE TO INDIA (1984), A ROOM WITH A VIEW (1985) and MAURICE (1987), two more screen adaptations of novels by E.M. Forster were released in 1992. The Merchant-Ivory production of HOWARDS END was a tremendous critical and commercial success, earning nine Oscar nominations and taking in over $25 million at the box-office. WHERE ANGELS FEAR TO TREAD, unfortunately, ran a very distant second. Though it closely follows the novel—written after Forster's first trip to Italy with his mother, when he was just twenty-six—much has been lost in the translation.

The rich and recently widowed Lilia Herriton (Helen Mirren) goes on a three-month Italian holiday to recover from her loss. Her late husband's family is only too glad to see her off, since they find her rather too provincial for their upper-class tastes. Lilia leaves her nine-year-old child in their care and is chaperoned by vicar's daughter Caroline Abbott (Helena Bonham Carter, a Merchant-Ivory regular also seen in HOWARDS END).

Lilia's in-laws are horrified and outraged when they receive a letter informing them that she is engaged to "someone she met at a hotel." Mrs. Herriton (Barbara Jefford) and spinster daughter Harriet (Judy Davis) dispatch lawyer and family member Philip Herriton (Rupert Graves) to Tuscany to rescue Lilia, but he's too late. She's already married to the very handsome, very charming and entirely unsuitable Gino Carella (Giovanni Guidelli). He is a poor local dentist's son—at age twenty-one, a little over half her age—and an opportunist who keeps his soon unhappy (and soon pregnant) wife confined at home while he gallivants, as is his custom, with the neighborhood lovelies.

The Herritons conclude that Lilia has been seduced by the country and write, telling her that any further communication should be via solicitor. But when Lilia dies in childbirth, Harriet and Philip return to Italy, intending to ransom the child from his father so that he can be "properly" raised in England. Much to their surprise, Gino refuses. Unable to understand, much less appreciate, the fact that Gino actually loves his son, the Herritons kidnap the baby, with dire results.

WHERE ANGELS FEAR TO TREAD may have elements of both tragedy and comedy, but the pedigree cast (most of them alumni from other Forster films) aren't particularly convincing at either. With the exception of the always wonderful Mirren (who dies off early on) and Guidelli (impressive here in his first English-language film), the actors bellow or fret their way through one-note characterizations. The film is mired by heavy-handed direction, which includes some attempts at humor that quickly descend into slapstick—as in a scene where Harriet attempts to enforce decorum on a raucously enthusiastic Italian opera audience at a performance of *Lucia di Lammermoor*.

WHERE ANGELS FEAR TO TREAD has structural problems, too. The most potentially interesting characters, Philip and Caroline, are largely peripheral to the story. Caroline, a poor maiden aunt in a family of rich relations, has the gumption to engage the Herritons in battle for the child. (She wants to raise the baby herself, and have him go to English schools at her expense.) Philip is a more or less neutral figure who comes out with a remarkable final admission. After the pair have returned to England, Caroline confides to Philip that she loves Gino. He responds: "If he had asked me, I would have given myself to him body and soul. I love him."

Other elements of the story are morally disquieting. From the time she goes to Italy until her death at least a year later, Lilia—of whom we've grown quite fond—is almost entirely negligent of her daughter back in England. And those responsible for causing the fatal accident of the finale show barely a trace of remorse at their actions.

Overall, this is an unsatisfactory experience—surprisingly, since the production stems from the same team that was behind TV's award-winning "Brideshead Revisited" (director Charles Sturridge and producer Derek Granger, who both co-wrote the screenplay with Tim Sullivan).

p, Derek Granger; d, Charles Sturridge; w, Tim Sullivan, Derek Granger, Charles Sturridge, (from the novel by E.M. Forster); ph, Michael Coulter; ed, Peter Coulson; m, Rachel Portman; prod d, Simon Holland; art d, Luigi Marchione, Marianne Ford; cos, Monica Howe

Drama/Romance **(PR: A MPAA: PG)**

WHERE THE DAY TAKES YOU ★★★
92m CineTel Films ~ New Line Cinema c

Dermot Mulroney *(King)*, Lara Flynn Boyle *(Heather)*, Balthazar Getty *(Little J.)*, Sean Astin *(Greg)*, James LeGros *(Crasher)*, Ricki Lake *(Brenda)*, Kyle MacLachlan *(Ted)*, Robert Knepper *(Rock Singer)*, Peter Dobson *(Tommy Ray)*, Stephen Tobolowsky *(Charles)*, Will Smith *(Manny)*, Adam Baldwin *(Officer Black)*, Laura San Giacomo *(Interviewer)*, Christian Slater *(Rocky)*, Nancy McKeon *(Vikki)*, Alyssa Milano *(Kimmy)*, David Arquette *(Rob)*, Debbie James *(Mrs. Burtis)*, Leo Rossi *(Mr. Burtis)*, Rachel Ticotin *(Officer Landers)*, Ken Kerman *(Older Cop)*, Cynthia Szigeti *(Counselor)*, Joey Dedio *(Teen)*, Dennis Phun *(Korean Man)*, Michael Maguire *(2nd Cop)*

This gritty portrait of teen runaways living, hustling and not always surviving on the streets of Los Angeles is a powerfully acted and disturbing vision of existence on the fringe. Writer-director Marc Rocco and fellow screenwriters Michael Hitchcock and Kurt Voss have clearly done their research for WHERE THE DAY TAKES YOU, allowing the story to ring true even if it sometimes barks a little loudly in the process.

King (Dermot Mulroney) has just been released from jail after a three month stay. As part of his parole, and with the enticement of ten dollars cash for each session, he agrees to let a non-threatening interviewer (Laura San Giacomo) videotape him being questioned about his experiences as a young homeless person. Back on the streets, King reunites with his ersatz family of juvenile delinquents, Little J. (Balthazar Getty), a hottempered youth, Crasher (James LeGros), a street philosopher and good soul, and Greg (Sean Astin), a junkie who is losing control of his methamphetamine habit. They are happy to see King back as he is their father figure on the mean streets and the only one who can keep them all together.

The eldest of the group, at all of twenty-one, King accepts the role of leader with both fierce protectiveness of his clan and self-doubts about his ability to take care of them. Things have changed a lot since King was in jail not the least of which is that his girlfriend is missing after having been a prostitute for a pimp squatter, Tommy Ray (Peter Dobson). The gang pay a visit to Tommy Ray and a near rumble ensues. A few days later, Brenda (Ricki Lake), Crasher's girlfriend, brings her friend Heather (Lara Flynn Boyle) around. A fresh arrival from Chicago, Heather is yet another product of a dysfunctional family. King takes to her quickly and she returns his admiration—eventually moving in with King under the freeway entrance, a popular spot for the homeless.

The gang spend their days wandering the asphalt jungle of Hollywood begging for change and passing the time. After they beat up Tommy Ray the stakes rise and everyone begins looking over their shoulders more often. Little J. steals a gun, which he keeps hidden in his jacket away from King, and Greg has graduated to heroine thanks to his sleazy pusher, Ted (Kyle MacLachlan). Late one night, Tommy Ray sneaks into the gang's encampment and attacks a sleeping King. When Tommy pulls his knife, Little J. shoots him in the back. Everyone scatters before the police arrive to find the body. King and Heather end up at the beach where they find a hotel room for the night and finally manage to consummate their relationship. She confesses to him that she left home after being sexually abused by her brother. King tells her about his father's penchant for needles, one reason why he left home.

While Greg and Little J. hide out from the police, King hatches a plan which will get them all out of town but first he has to find everyone. He soon finds a sick and stoned Greg at Ted's apartment and tells him where the group will rendezvous. Little J. finds King and goes with him. Waiting at the bus station they are unaware that Greg has been picked up by the cops and has told them of King's plan. Greg then overdoses on heroin and dies. The cops arrive at the bus station where they confront King and Little J. as Heather watches from the bus. Cornered, Little J. pulls out his pistol and the officers train their weapons on him. King jumps in front of Little J. as shots ring out. King is killed in a torrent of bullets. Nine months later, Heather watches the videotape of King in the interviewer's office. She has come to take Little J., the new "King," home—a home of concrete and violence.

Homelessness is not an attractive subject for a filmmaker, and Rocco is to be commended for even getting WHERE THE DAY TAKES YOU made. He accomplished this with a potent combination of a serious, almost documentary-style screenplay and a cast comprised of many of Hollywood's young actors on the rise.

The most affecting aspect Rocco captures is the sense of family which one wouldn't expect to find in this harsh environment. King is the personification of love and authority to his younger followers, giving them all the support and guidance one would expect from a caring parent. The irony is that nearly all of the characters left home because of family abuse. Rocco also knew that in order to keep an audience interested his film needed to have forward momentum, and he supplies it with the intrigue of Tommy Ray's death and the subsequent breakdown of King's family. In addition, the director shows the realistically monotonous side to living on the asphalt, panhandling and simply hanging out. The solemnness of the story is sometimes filled in with gallows humor which works splendidly and authenticates the message.

Casting choices couldn't have been better. Mulroney captures the essence of King, the leader, with complete accuracy. He offers up just the right amount of bravado, intelligence and compassion to have made it to the level of street icon he portrays.

Boyle accurately portrays a victim who has nowhere else to turn but the streets. She has a mysterious aura about her that works well for the role of Heather. Her sheer joy when she is finally able to take a shower is played with total childlike abandon which is the opposite of her normal reserved and cautious street persona. Getty is a standout as the youngest member, unable to fight off his personal demons as well as the others seem to do. Astin plays Greg with the frenetic energy that a speed freak plays. MacLachlin is genuinely scary as the dealer. The remaining cast, comprised of many young TV stars, rise to the occasion with believable portrayals.

The film falters in only a few spots, most notably during an extended musical sequence in the prologue which heavy-handedly tries to match up each lyric with a visual image. Also confusing is the plot line involving King's missing girlfriend. After King falls in love with Heather, the screenplay never mentions the other girl again. Some of the characters seem incompletely drawn. The police officers are never really defined, leaving one to ponder their compassion or lack thereof. Also unclear is the character of the interviewer. Is she a psychologist or some other professional working for a governmental agency? Rocco could have also shown more of the people who try to help the unfortunate teens who live on the street, but aside from a fleeting visit to a shelter, and the rehab center, there are no friendly faces in sight.

Regardless of these small miscalculations, WHERE THE DAY TAKES YOU has a consistently engaging narrative all the while resonating with accuracy and honesty. This film speaks the language of the young but there is a message for everyone. *(Violence, substance abuse, profanity.)*

p, Paul Hertzberg; d, Marc Rocco; w, Michael Hitchcock, Kurt Voss, Marc Rocco; ph, King Baggot; ed, Russell Livingstone; m, Mark Morgan; prod d, Kirk Petrucelli

Drama **(PR: C MPAA: R)**

WHISPERS IN THE DARK ★½

107m Paramount; Martin Bregman Productions ~ Paramount c

Annabella Sciorra *(Ann Hecker)*, Jamey Sheridan *(Doug McDowell)*, Anthony LaPaglia *(Detective Morgenstern)*, Jill Clayburgh *(Sarah Green)*, John Leguizamo *(Fast Johnny C.)*, Deborah Unger *(Eve Abergray)*, Anthony Heald *(Paul)*, Alan Alda *(Leo Green)*, Jacqueline Brookes *(Mrs. McDowell)*, Gene Canfield *(Billy O'Meara)*, Joseph Badalucco, Jr. *(Undercover Cop)*, Albert Pisarenkov *(Cab Driver)*, Malik *(Earring Vendor)*, Bo Dietl *(Detective Ditali)*, Allison Field, David H. Kramer, Dominic Marcus, Nicholas J. Giangiulio, Philip Levy, William Timoney, Sondra James, Karen Longwell, Lisa Vidal *(Voice Overs)*

Fresh from her performance as the world's dopiest mom in THE HAND THAT ROCKS THE CRADLE, Annabella Sciorra tackled the world's stupidest psychiatrist in WHISPERS IN THE DARK, a well-cast but insanely inept thriller.

Upscale Manhattan psychiatrist Anne Hecker (Sciorra) is suffering from bad dreams about one of her patients, a self-destructive blonde beauty named Eve Abergray (Deborah Unger) who's heavily into bondage, masochism and exhibitionism. These kinky motifs are deftly combined in the lurid tales Eve tells Anne, which then resurface in Anne's dreams. In these stories, Eve's rough, unnamed lover has been getting out of hand, to the point where he is threatening her life as well as her sanity.

Outside the office, Anne is drifting apart from her drunken and verbally abusive live-in boyfriend Paul (Anthony Heald) and seeking professional counsel from old friends, married psychiatrists Sarah and Leo Green (Alan Alda and Jill Clayburgh). She also begins an affair with dashing pilot Doug McDowell (Jamey Sheridan) that unexpectedly intrudes on her professional life when he's revealed to be Eve's brute lover.

Another of Anne's clients is "Fast" Johnny C. (John Leguizamo), an aspiring Hispanic artist and ex-con rapist. With Anne's help he is trying, with only limited success, to exorcise his misogyny through his art. He may not have much luck getting an NEA grant to paint his graphic pictures of tied-up and disemboweled blondes, but he somehow connects with Eve, a gallery owner and the ideal saleslady for his works among the chic downtown elite. There is thus no shortage of suspects for Detective Morgenstern (Anthony LaPaglia), an NYPD detective with neurotic baggage of his own, when Eve later shows up murdered.

Writer-director Christopher Crowe, whose last significant credit was the similarly lurid Vietnam thriller OFF LIMITS, seems set on saying something about the issue of trust: Anne trusts and mistrusts the wrong people. But WHISPERS IN THE DARK is too unbelievable at the narrative level for its story to carry any kind of thematic weight: Anne gets personally involved with her patients to the point of spying on Eve during a lunch meeting with her lover; later, when Eve reveals to Anne that said lover is dumping her, Anne chooses that moment to dump Eve as a patient, subsequently leaving Eve alone in her office when she goes to make a phone call in the middle of the session. Who can blame Eve for stealing some of Anne's files during the analyst's rude and unprofessional absence? And who can later blame her when she threatens to use those files for dastardly purposes after catching Anne and Doug together?

WHISPERS IN THE DARK gets sillier and less involving as it goes along, with most of the (unintentional) laughs coming from Anne's tendency to stumble on the major plot points about 20 minutes after they have become baldly obvious to every viewer. It becomes apparent, too, that Crowe centered his film on the wrong character. Eve is the only person in this sodden mess who engenders any real sympathy, while the two primary perpetrators who use and abuse her are made to seem the heroes.

The cast, from Sciorra to Alda to Unger and, especially, Clayburgh, lend the proceedings much more class than they deserve—though the poignant vulnerability that Sciorra deployed to good effect in THE HAND THAT ROCKS THE CRADLE is largely wasted here. Unger shows grace under pressure in a role that requires her, among other things, to disrobe and masturbate in Anne's office. *(Violence, profanity, nudity, adult situations.)*

p, Martin Bregman, Michael S. Bregman; d, Christopher Crowe; w, Christopher Crowe; ph, Michael Chapman; ed, Bill Pankow; m, Thomas Newman; prod d, John Jay Moore; set d, Justin Scoppa, Jr.; cos, John A. Dunn

Erotic/Thriller **(PR: O MPAA: R)**

WHITE MEN CAN'T JUMP ★★½

115m Finger Roll Inc; Fox ~ Fox c

Wesley Snipes *(Sidney Deane)*, Woody Harrelson *(Billy Hoyle)*, Rosie Perez *(Gloria Clemente)*, Tyra Ferrell *(Rhonda Deane)*, Cylk Cozart *(Robert)*, Kadeem Hardison *(Junior)*, Ernest Harden, Jr. *(George)*, John Marshall Jones *(Walter)*, Marques Johnson *(Raymond)*, David Roberson *(T.J.)*, Kevin Benton *(Zeke)*, Nigel Miguel *(Dwight "The Flight" McGhee)*, Duane Martin *(Willie Lewis)*, Bill Henderson *(The Venice Beach Boys Member)*, Sonny Craver *(The Venice Beach Boys Member)*, Jon Hendricks *(The Venice Beach Boys Member)*, Eloy Casados *(Tony Stucci)*, Frank Rossi *(Frank Stucci)*, Freeman Williams *(Duck Johnson)*, Louis Price *(Eddie "The King" Faroo)*, Alex Trebek *(Himself)*, Reggie Leon *(Reggie)*, Sarah Stavrou *(Etiwanda)*, Reynaldo Rey *(Tad)*, Lanei Chapman *(Lanei)*, Irene Nettles *(Real Estate Agent)*, Torri

Whitehead *(Tanya)*, Lisa McDowell *(Alisa)*, David Maxwell *(Malcolm)*, Dion B. Vines *(The Bank)*, Bill Caplan *(Tournament Announcer)*, Richard James Baker *(Tournament Referee)*, Amy Golden *(Big Guy's Girlfriend)*, Jeanette Srubar *(Little Guy's Girlfriend)*, Zandra Hill *(Sponsor)*, Fred P. Gregory *(Sponsor)*, Carl E. Hodge *(Pickup Truck Driver)*, Ruben Martinez *(Ruben)*, Gary Lazar *(Oki-Dog Businessman)*, Donna Howell *(Yolanda)*, Don Fullilove *(Jake)*, Johnny Gilbert *("JEOPARDY!" Announcer)*, Leonard A. Oakland *(Doctor Leonard Allen)*, Allan Malamud *(Rocket Scientist)*, Jeanne McCarthy *(Dressing Room Staffer)*, John Charles Sheehan *(Cop)*, Carl A. McGee *(Gambler)*, Chick Hearn *(NBA Announcer)*, Stu Lantz *(NBA Announcer)*, Ronald Beals, Joe Metcalf, Mahcoe Moore, Mark Hill, Eric Kizziee, Chalmer Maddox, Leroy Michaux, Joseph Duffy, Pete Duffy, Gary Moeller, Daniel Porto, Jake Roberts, Lester Hawkins, Jeffrey Todd *(Ballplayers)*

Ron Shelton's second outing since his breakout success with BULL DURHAM is a wheezy, exasperating disappointment. WHITE MEN CAN'T JUMP starts out wanting to be a high-energy remake of THE HUSTLER in a street-basketball setting, only to lose steam gradually along the way.

Literally coming out of nowhere, playground hoops phenomenon Billy Hoyle (Woody Harrelson) walks onto a tough Venice court and smokes the competition, including reigning champ Sidney Deane (Wesley Snipes), who is duly impressed. Or so it seems, until Deane conspires with some friends to con Hoyle out of the nest egg he's saved while living with his sexy, volatile girlfriend Gloria Clemente (Rosie Perez). Gloria knocks heads with Sidney's wife Rhonda (Tyra Ferrell), and together they come up with a plan for Sidney and Billy to compete in a sponsored two-on-two playground competition for a $5000 first prize. Sidney and Billy win easily, but Billy loses his half to Sidney on a foolish slamdunking bet on the way home (thus the film's title).

A disgusted Gloria walks out on Billy, but he wins her back by helping her achieve her lifetime ambition to compete on the game show "Jeopardy," which she wins easily. With her winnings, Gloria wants Billy to buy some decent clothes and get a straight job. Instead, Billy wants to take the money and bet it on one last playground match, teaming again with Sidney. At the match, Billy gets to prove that he is now one white man who can jump, slamming home the winning basket. But he returns to find Gloria gone, for good this time. Billy and Sidney go off into the sunset with Billy vowing to win Gloria back, if he can find her.

WHITE MEN CAN'T JUMP can never seem to decide whether it wants to be a comedy, a drama, a comedy-drama or a drama-comedy. In the long haul it succeeds at none of the above, although it still manages to feel generic. The film's choppiness and inconsistency seem to indicate some editing-room tampering, perhaps to dilute its drama and make it more mindlessly upbeat. But the film is such a complete mess it's truly hard to tell what Shelton might have had in mind. Billy is supposedly on the run from bookies from Louisiana after reneging on a deal to throw a crucial game as a college player. But the bookies are more goofy than menacing, providing stretches of seriocomic relief rather than advancing or motivating the plot. Billy is also supposedly a compulsive gambler and insanely possessive of Gloria. But Harrelson plays him most of the time more as a high-spirited overgrown kid than someone with serious problems.

Snipes's character makes even less sense. At least we know that Gloria doesn't approve of Billy's throwing his life and money away on basketball (which seems a paradoxical spasm of maturity from someone whose whole life is built around "Jeopardy"). But we never get any sense at all of Sidney's life with his wife. We're not even quite sure where they live. At one point, Sidney seems to be signing a lease on a house. Yet, late in the film, they're burglarized in the same seedy apartment complex they were in when the film began. As a straight job, Sidney seems to work out of a taco stand as a freelance tiling contractor. But we never actually see him laying tile, which may mean that it's just another hustle.

If Billy and Sidney don't make sense as individuals, it should come as no surprise that they don't make much sense as a team. After Sidney cons Billy, it makes some sense for them to team up for the two-on-two competition, since both would stand to make a profit. However, it's hard to see why Billy would then leave the woman he says he loves, and has just spent so much effort winning back, to go off with Sidney at the end. Sidney was able to pull strings to help get Gloria on "Jeopardy," which to Sidney means that Billy owes him a favor. But, considering that Sidney started the film by fleecing Billy of all he was worth, it would seem more like they were about even.

With little in the way of plot or characters, WHITE MEN CAN'T JUMP might be justified by its displays of basketball prowess, but even here the film falls flat. Harrelson and Snipes both look in shape and at the top of their game. Even so, Bird and Magic they're not. Shelton seems to have forgotten—or ignored—the qualities that made BULL DURHAM an unassuming, off-the-cuff success. Believable, engaging characters and a plot that was about something would have been a start. Instead, WHITE MEN CAN'T JUMP tries to be about so many things that it winds up being about nothing much at all. *(Profanity, adult situations.)*

p, Don Miller, David Lester; d, Ron Shelton; w, Ron Shelton; ph, Russell Boyd; ed, Paul Seydor, Kimberly Ray; m, Bennie Wallace; prod d, Dennis Washington; art d, Roger Fortune; set d, Robert R. Benton

Sports/Comedy **(PR: O MPAA: R)**

WHITE SANDS ★★

101m Morgan Creek Productions ~ Warner Bros. c

Willem Dafoe *(Ray Dolezal)*, Mary Elizabeth Mastrantonio *(Lane Bodine)*, Mickey Rourke *(Gorman Lennox)*, Samuel L. Jackson *(Greg Meeker)*, Mimi Rogers *(Molly)*, M. Emmet Walsh *(Bert Gibson)*, James Rebhorn *(Flynn)*, Maura Tierney *(Noreen)*, Beth Grant *(Roz)*, Alexander Nicksay *(Ben)*, Fredrick Lopez *(Delmar Blackwater)*, Miguel Sandoval *(Ruiz)*, John Lafayette *(Demott)*, Ken Thorley *(Kleinman)*, Jack Kehler *(Casanov)*, Royce D. Applegate *(Peterson)*, Megan Butler *(Goodman)*, Lisa Cloud *(Redhead)*, Steve Cormier *(Artie O'Brien)*, Steven Tyler *(Blonde FBI Agent)*, John David Garfield *(2nd FBI Agent)*, William P. Bennet *(Rodeo Clown)*, Tom Conner *(La Fonda Desk Clerk)*, Joy Bouton *(Sue)*, Meredith Marshall *(Rodeo Singer)*, Doc Phillips *(Rodeo Announcer)*, Ben Zeller *(Drifter)*, Karen Breeding *(Cowgirl)*

A kind of pop-art remake of Antonioni's THE PASSENGER, Roger Donaldson's enigmatic WHITE SANDS is ultimately undone by its labyrinthine, cumbersome plot.

The rough equivalent to Jack Nicholson's TV reporter in Antonioni's film, Willem Dafoe plays small-town New Mexico sheriff Ray Dolezal, who gets more than he bargained for when he investigates an apparent suicide in a remote part of his territory. The victim turns out to be an FBI agent who has with him a suitcase with half a million dollars in used bills. For reasons that are never entirely clear, Dolezal deduces that the "suicide" was actually a murder; from evidence in the man's motel room, the sheriff reasons that he was on his way to a meeting with somebody to buy something with the money. Dolezal decides to assume the dead man's identity, arranging the meeting and taking off with the money to see where it leads.

He quickly finds himself embroiled in an arms-dealing scheme. The dead man's partners were to be Gorman Lennox (Mickey Rourke), a shady entrepreneur, and Lane Bodine (Mary Elizabeth Mastrantonio), his rich, thrill-junkie girlfriend. Dolezal also quickly finds himself in hot water with the FBI, whose money was in the suitcase, which Dolezal turns over to Lennox to make the deal. The problem is that none of this gets Dolezal any closer to the agent's killer—at first. Meanwhile, Dolezal is put under pressure by the FBI, particularly anxious agent Greg Meeker (Samuel L. Jackson), either to recover or to repay the money. Dolezal's problems are compounded by demands from the arms suppliers for an additional quarter-million to close the deal.

Ironically, WHITE SANDS is at its best when it's least explicable. Not unlike the gripping DEEP COVER, which was released during the same month, WHITE SANDS tells the story of a decent cop who becomes a criminal in order to bring high-level wrongdoers to justice. Compared to Larry Fishburne's undercover cop in DEEP COVER, however, Dolezal has much hazier motivations, which is what edges WHITE SANDS—at least theoretically—into Antonioni territory.

Dolezal's life has been peaceful if humdrum (though it's hard to imagine any man having a humdrum life when his wife is played by Mimi Rogers, making an all-too-brief appearance). Then, out of the blue, he's confronted with a mystery that seems, well, right out of a movie—complete with cash, corpses, a reckless femme fatale and, of course, Mickey Rourke. All this proves a heady temptation for Dolezal, especially when Lane steps into the shower with him. But he remains a straight arrow, even down to fending off the exquisite temptress.

Arguably, THE PASSENGER reaches a point of diminishing returns at about the time it becomes apparent that there isn't going to be much of a plot. WHITE SANDS tries to remedy this, however, by backloading itself with far too much plot. When the real villains come forth in feverish profusion late in the film, they're forced to explain themselves in long, tiresome speeches that indict everything from the lack of accountability among elite law-enforcement organizations to the misconduct of American foreign policymakers. Thus, instead of leading to a crafty, emotionally cathartic payoff, WHITE SANDS gets more tiresome and banal as it goes along and all its threads are tied up with neat, if outlandish, explanations. WHITE SANDS would have been a better film if it had remained more dreamlike and less tied to plot mechanics. *(Violence, profanity, nudity.)*

p, William Sackheim, Scott Rudin; d, Roger Donaldson; w, Daniel Pyne; ph, Peter Menzies, Jr.; ed, Nicholas Beauman; m, Patrick O'Hearn; prod d, John Graysmark; art d, Michael Rizzo; set d, Michael Seirton; cos, Deborah Everton

Thriller **(PR: C MPAA: R)**

WHITE TRASH

85m Fred Baker Film & Video Company ~ Fred Baker Film & Video Company c

John Hartman *(Casino)*, Sean Christiansen *(John "Rio")*, Periel Marr *("Rotten" Rita)*, Wheaton James *(Percy)*, Jack Betts *(Father)*, Winnie Thexton *(Sister)*, Brian Patrick *(CC Charles)*, Robert Scarbro *(Boy Pickup)*, Janice Hightower *(1st Dyke)*, Niva Ruschell *(2nd Dyke)*, David Worcester *(Santa Claus)*, Rikki Roberts *(Woman in Wheelchair)*, Giovanni Lemm *(Houseboy)*, Niko Robinson *(Percy's Lady Friend)*, Jeffrey Thomas *(Percy's Friend)*, Stefan Bell *(Roller Skater)*, Mark Greenfield *(Street Hustler)*, Timothy Ball *(Limo Driver)*, Norman Lefebvre *(Toughguy at Burgerjoint)*, Elliot Taikeff *(Priest)*, Robbie Quine *(Street Hustler/Friend at Funeral)*, Helen Marsland *(Girl at Funeral)*, Greg Panos *(Pizzaman)*, Keith Camren, Traci Grabarncik, Kevin James, David Krieger, John Miler, Howard Thornton

Talky and amateurish, WHITE TRASH aspires to wring art from the miserable lives of street hustlers, but fails dismally.

Casino (John Hartman) and Rio (Sean Christiansen) are young Los Angeles street hustlers with few ambitions. Their roommate, seventeen-year-old Rita (Periel Marr)—also a prostitute—has recently found a focus for her life: she's pregnant by her boyfriend CC (Brian Patrick), and wants to have the baby, though she continues to hustle and use drugs. CC's death from AIDS precipitates a crisis in their lives. First, they must get wasted enough to make it through his funeral, a task made difficult by the fact that they're all broke. Rita sleeps with kinky dealer Percy (Wheaton James) in exchange for drugs. Then, after the funeral, CC's father (Jack Betts) and sister (Winnie Thexton) come by to visit. They offer to take Rita back to New Jersey with them, so she can have CC's baby. Rio and Casino taunt them, but CC's family eventually depart with Rita, leaving the two hustlers to return to the streets.

WHITE TRASH seems intended to be a gritty, razor-edged look at the hopeless lives of three Hollywood hustlers, laced with trenchant observations about race, class and sexual oppression in contemporary Los Angeles. The lurid title and funky rap score might fool exploitation fans into thinking it's a sleazy, no-holds-barred wallow in the neon slime *a la* VICE SQUAD or any of the numerous slice-of-lowlife pictures designed to serve up vicarious thrills with a dash of legitimizing social censure, but WHITE TRASH doesn't deliver those goods.

Written by Mel Clay (THE SPOOK WHO SAT BY THE DOOR) and directed by Fred Baker (whose long career in motion pictures has taken him from acting to distribution), WHITE TRASH is righteously ambitious, determined not to paint prostitution in the fairy tale strokes of PRETTY WOMAN. It fails, however, to forge those high-minded aspirations into compelling drama. Some of the film's faults can be laid at the door of budget: the film is painfully set-bound, with most of the action (if relentless talk can be properly termed "action") taking place in the nondescript apartment Rio, Casino and Rita share, and the photography and lighting are at best competent. But its inadequacies run deeper.

The screenplay is shapeless, and while this may be intended as the structural reflection of the aimless lives of young hustlers, it makes it difficult to stick with the film—it's boring and pointless. Even worse, the individual scenes flop and flounder, feeling at best like improvised acting exercises and at worst like amateur self-indulgence. It's all talk, crafted to shock but without weight or impact; the result is off-putting, like hearing children mouth dirty words they clearly don't understand. Though the performers all seem to be trying their best, they're undermined at every turn by the film's technical inadequacies; it's possible none of them is up to making the material work, but they don't even get the chance to try.

In the end, WHITE TRASH succeeds neither as sexploitation nor as serious social commentary, failing at both because it's too dull to hold the attention of either highbrow or lowbrow audiences. *(Substance abuse, profanity, sexual situations, adult situations.)*

p, Fred Baker; d, Fred Baker; w, Mel Clay, (from his play); ph, Fred Baker; ed, Robert Simpson; m, Fred Baker; prod d, Mary Jane Bell; art d, Steven Nelson; cos, Rikki Roberts

Drama **(PR: O MPAA: NR)**

WHO SHOT PATAKANGO? ★★
104m Patakango Ltd. ~ Castle Hill Productions c

David Knight *(Bic Bickham)*, Sandra Bullock *(Devlin Moran)*, Kevin Otto *(Mark Bickham)*, Aaron Ingram *(Cougar)*, Brad Randall *(Patakango)*, Chris Cardona *(Freddie)*, Michael Puzzo *(Goldie)*, Christopher Crean *(Tony)*, Greg Marc Miller *(Vinnie)*, Damon Chandler *(Mr. Donnelly)*, Bridget Fogle *(Mitsy)*, Phil Rosenthal *(Principal)*, Cline Jordan *(Ricky–Dick)*, Ella Arolovi *(Marianna)*, Nicholas Reiner *(Carmen)*, Ben Digregorio *(Detective Levy)*, Marc Davenport *(Detective Driskill)*, Jim Flanagan *(Mr. Bickham)*, Joyce Ellen Hill *(Mrs. Bickham)*, Allison Eikeren *(Paula)*

WHO SHOT PATAKANGO? is an unceasingly cheery backward glance at life in a racially mixed 1950s high school. Bittersweet and episodic, the film's loose-knit narrative structure seems appropriate since this is the dreamchild of a husband and wife team of documentarians. Unfortunately, the filmmakers never piece together all their teen trials into a cohesive entity.

The title derives from an incident in which the shooting of a teenager suggests racial tensions to the media and neighborhood cops. (In reality, the nitwit shot himself while making a zip gun.) It is this film's interesting premise that Black and white students at Alexander Hamilton High School got along when left to their own devices, but that trouble arose in the form of outside gangs invading the school territory. Although poverty and violence encourage dropping out, the students portrayed onscreen remain in school without really taking advantage of the opportunity to learn.

Of all the mischievous students in his care, Mr. Donnelly (Damon Chandler) has highest hopes for Bic Bickham (David Knight). Troubled by his homelife with his embittered blind father (Jim Flanagan) and forever having to explain the facts of inner city life to his younger brother Mark (Kevin Otto), Bic flirts with juvenile deliquency. Along with his African-American counterpart Cougar (Aaron Ingram), Bic is brutally questioned by the cops about gang warfare. Although innocent of that charge, he's nearly caught stealing from parking meters to finance a date with dream girl Devlin Moran (Sandra Bullock).

A college coed from Sarah Lawrence, Devlin is the vision of a better life to which Bic decides to cling. After a chance meeting in Greenwich Village, the two fall madly in love despite the disparity of their backgrounds. As Bic and his buddies drift toward graduation, he worries about the future and frets that Devlin won't forgive him after he decks her former boyfriend with a pitcher of beer. Pooling energies with Cougar to produce the school talent show, Bic resolves to rise above his circumstances.

Highly personal and tripping over its own nostalgia, WHO SHOT PATAKANGO? is a glance backward that has the texture of a mosaic of fond memories insufficiently dramatized to involve anyone who wasn't there. Featuring the oldest-looking teenagers this side of WEST SIDE STORY, the film has its heart in the right place but its technique falters. Not only do all the little vignettes about Bic's friends fail to connect with the viewer but also the central romance is a tired, conventional Romeo and Juliet scenario.

Sometimes the gang attacks from local toughs are played for laughs, and the entire memory play seems superficial. Could life back then possibly have seemed so rosy? It's not the events themselves but the way the filmmakers portray them. The attitude is "Sure we had zip guns and chains, and we never paid attention in class but, man, wasn't that a time?" While the early rainbow coalition message is a heartwarming one, the film seems to be coloring THE BLACKBOARD JUNGLE with hues more appropriate to TV's "Happy Days." Imagine a high school where everyone is either the Fonz or one of the Jackson Five.

If you're in the mood for fifties rock 'n' roll and enjoy sappy romances, then you may enjoy WHO SHOT PATAKANGO? Others may not find much delectation in a film that puts vandalism and petty crime in the same fifties time capsule as "American Bandstand." Ah, the happy memories of hooliganism. *(Violence, profanity, nudity.)*

p, Halle Brooks; d, Robert Brooks; w, Robert Brooks, Halle Brooks; ph, Robert Brooks; ed, Robert Brooks, Halle Brooks; art d, Lionel Driskill

Drama **(PR: C MPAA: R)**

WILD ORCHID 2: TWO SHADES OF BLUE ★½
107m Blue Movie Blue Inc.; Vision pdg ~
Triumph Releasing c

Nina Siemaszko *(Blue)*, Tom Skerritt *(Ham)*, Robert Davi *(Sully)*, Brent Fraser *(Josh)*, Christopher McDonald *(Senator Dixon)*, Wendy Hughes *(Elle)*, Liane Curtis *(Mona)*, Joe Dallesandro *(Jules)*, Stafford Morgan *(Colonel Winslow)*, Don Bloomfield *(J.J. Clark)*, Captain Edwards *(Casey Sander)*, Bridgit Ryan *(Ruth)*, Lydie Denier *(Dominique)*, Gloria Rueben *(Celeste)*, Victoria Mahoney *(Mary)*, Kathy Hartsell *(Cathy)*, Lynn Gendron *(Del)*, Monica Anne Ekblad *(Ida)*, Julia Wakefield *(Judy)*, Deanne Jeffries *(Isadora)*, Merry Clayton *(Gospel Singer)*, Pat Crawford Brown *(Ms. Earlane)*, Frank Cavestani *(Business Man)*, Michael Villella *(Man With Mona)*, Jeanne R. Bates *(Mrs. Felt)*, Ben Hartigan *(Elderly Gentleman)*, Douglas Stark *(Usinger)*, Robert Keith *(Peter)*, Cary Lowenstein *(John)*, Bonnie Snyder *(School Secretary)*, Roger LaPage *(Referee)*, Clifford Goler *(Defenseman)*, Lance Reed *(Football Player)*, Sekou Bunch *(Bass Player)*, Greg Leisz *(Guitar Player)*, Cindy Lair *(Girl in Brothel)*, Sigal Diamant *(Girl in Brothel)*, Jeff Alan Young *(Man in Oriental Suite)*

From softcore sex king Zalman King comes WILD ORCHID 2: TWO SHADES OF BLUE, a sequel in name only that either thankfully or regrettably has nothing to do with its predecessor.

Instead of the original's sex-crazed lady lawyer playing kinky games in Rio, this outing turns to a kinky morality tale of a hapless teenager forced into prostitution in steamy, sultry Southern California of the 1950s. Blue (Nina Siemaszko) dreams of nothing more than having a normal teenaged life with a nice boyfriend, a normal suburban mom and dad and all the other accessories. She meets the prospective boyfriend early in the film, Josh (Brent Fraser), a strapping, upstanding youth she meets outside a church, no less. But the two go their separate ways before anything can happen. And unfortunately (though fortunate for King's purposes), Blue's mother was a whore who's long since flown the coop and her dad, Ham (Tom Skeritt), is an itinerant jazz trumpeter with a nasty heroin habit.

When Ham misses a gig because he's too strung-out to blow, Blue yields her virginity to Ham's "old pal", clubowner Jules (Joe Dallesandro), in return for a fix for dear old dad. Ham gets happy, but the shock of how his fix was earned kills him. Dissatisfied with Blue's listless performance both as lover and waitress at his club, Jules sells her to Elle (Wendy Hughes), a high-class madam who specializes in catering to the kinky whims of senators and generals and such. Blue brings even less enthusiasm to their beds than she brought to Jules's. When a senator tries to break her icy reserve by hiring her for an evening of filmed gang rape, her chauffeur Sully (Robert Davi), who has fallen platonically in love with Blue, saves her.

They run away to the town of Blue's dreams, where Josh just happens to be the star of the high-school football team. Elle tracks Blue down and stages a special private screening of her film debut for Josh. But Josh remains steadfast in his love for Blue, leading to a clinch for the fadeout, while Elle slinks away, presumably setting the stage for yet another WILD ORCHID bouquet.

Resembling something like a dirty-minded John Hughes movie, WILD ORCHID 2's screenplay, also written by King, contains more than its share of howlers in its dialogue as well as in its plotting. Ham's description of his marriage to Blue's mom as a "piggyback ride to hell" sounds kinkier than anything that happens onscreen. King later takes a slap at the decline of American standards by having Elle coo that Blue would do well to study another whore's stripping technique because "she was trained in Paris." (Yes, but everyone knows the Japanese do it more efficiently.) Blue doesn't seem to do anything particularly erotically or efficiently. When she's not moping, whining or pouting, she has a bad habit of heaping contempt on her clients, at one point humiliating the guest of honor at a stag party in front of his well-heeled friends.

In light of such behavior, Elle's dedication to making Blue a whore for all seasons becomes downright baffling. But for all its loony plot contrivances and loopy dialogue, what WILD ORCHID 2 lacks, and badly needs, is a sense of humor. King (9½ WEEKS and cable TV's popular "Red Shoes Diaries") goes about his business here with a deadly earnestness, as though he were trying to make a Philip Kaufman (HENRY AND JUNE) film from a Russ Meyer (VIXEN) script. His sex scenes look erotic, conveying the impression of a man who has studied his *Penthouse* layouts very carefully. But there is little joy, forget about passion, to the sex itself, most of it grimly coerced by ugly men in tuxedos from women with the emotional range and heat of department store mannequins. The film's overall dourness and smarmy pseudo-decadence only contributes to a sex film that seems calculated to make its audiences swear off sex.

Despite her kewpie-doll face and curvaceous body, Siemaszko (BED & BREAKFAST, LITTLE NOISES) comes off more like a petulant girlfriend from hell than an obscure object of desire. She's not likely to make anyone forget WILD ORCHID's Carre Otis, as the lady lawyer who sweats on cue, not to mention Kim Basinger's refrigerator raid in 9-1/2 WEEKS. On the other hand, one good thing can certainly be said about WILD ORCHID 2: Mickey Rourke is nowhere in sight. *(substance abuse, nudity, sexual situations, profanity.)*

p, David Saunders, Rafael Eisenman; d, Zalman King; w, Zalman King, Patricia Louisiana Knop; ph, Mark Reshovsky; ed, Marc Grossman, James Gavin; m, George Clinton; prod d, Richard Amend; art d, Randy Eriksen; set d, Chance Rearden

Erotic/Drama **(PR: O MPAA: R)**

WILD WHEELS ★★★

64m ~ Tara Releasing c

Harrod Blank, Lisa Law, W.C. Rice, H.L. Gandy, Ron Snow, Gene Pool, Albert Guibarra, Larry Fuente, Bob Corbett, Renee Sherrer, Eric Staller, Jon Barnes, Dalton Stevens

Filmmaker Harrod Blank's WILD WHEELS is an amusing, sometimes surreal documentary on America's "art car" craze, in which, to put it in simplest terms, people decorate their cars and trucks.

That's where the simplicity ends, however; producer-director-cinematographer-editor Blank (the son of famed documentary filmmaker Les Blank, who contributed some cinematography here) has scoured a half dozen states across the US and found some eye-opening vehicles—about 45 appear in the film—along with their owners. Along with the expected religious fanatics, like the guy who has attached dozens of plumbing faucets to his car because God told him to, and UFO freaks, Blank has discovered some interesting, comparatively normal people, although none of them are at all what one could call introverted.

These include folks who have covered their cars with children's toys; a detailed, three-dimensional cityscape; mirrors; psychedelically blinking lights; horse figurines; copper sheeting molded into the shape of a hippopotamus; and just plain junk, but junk which has meaning to the "artist." The Rhinestone Cowboy has them not just all over his car but in his clothes and teeth; ditto the Button King, including his mailbox and coffin. One man so misses his dead wife that he has glued all her possessions, from jewelry to kitchen appliances, on his car. Jon Barnes's New York "Ultimate Taxi"—the only car that is plain on the outside—has a minidisco inside, replete with light show, sound system, and dry-ice fumes. Gene Pool's "portable environment" car is covered with real grass—we see him gluing on the seeds, nurturing the sprouts then tending and trimming his "lawn"—his car looks like a gently sloping hill with windows.

None of these people can say exactly why they do this, and there's little one can say about them as a class, except that they all seem to be rabid fans of swap meets. Filmmaker Blank traces this phenomenon to 1960s psychedelic buses (and Ken Kesey's famous one makes an appearance here). Blank is also revealed, at the end, as an enthusiast himself—his car is topped by a TV set with things coming out of it. The film's first sequence follows him (unidentified at this point) into court to fight a parking ticket, apparently one of an endless string, which Blank interprets as harassment because of the way his car looks. Surprisingly, there's little practical information detailed in the film, like how to do it, what glues to use or what you do if you get a flat or it starts raining while you're out on the road.

Backed by a soundtrack of pop, blues and folk music from Hendrix to Woody Guthrie to Charley Musselwhite, WILD WHEELS is a witty, deadpan, often fascinating look at a bit of arcane, peculiarly American culture. The film was released on video after Blank self-distributed it, mostly in California, often appearing with his weird VW beetle. *(Profanity.)*

p, Harrod Blank; d, Harrod Blank; ph, Paul Cope, Harrod Blank, Les Blank; ed, Harrod Blank

Documentary **(PR: A MPAA: NR)**

WILDFIRE ★★★

98m Zupnik Enterprises Inc.; Jerry Tokofsky Productions ~ MCA/Universal Home Video c

Steven Bauer *(Frank)*, Linda Fiorentino *(Kay)*, Will Patton *(Mike)*, Marshall Bell *(Lewis)*, Sandra Seacat *(Sissy)*, Richard Bradford *(Gene)*, Jonah Ellers-Isaacs *(Frank–age 5)*, Michelle Mayberry *(Kay–age 5)*, William Hall *(Bank Cop)*, Jack Spratt *(Fatman)*, Tony Amendola *(Lieutenant)*, O-Lan Jones *(Mrs. Johnson)*, Nancy Fish *(Roberta)*, Sarah Luck Pearson, Marc Siegler

Linda Fiorentino and Steven Bauer star in Zalman King's WILDFIRE, an involving film about passionate, obsessive love.

Kay (Fiorentino) and Frank (Bauer) grow up together in an orphanage. By the time they're teenagers, they get married, drop out of school and start their new life on the road. With a wife, and a baby on the way, Frank is desperate for money, and decides to hold up a bank with a toy gun. But as he's running away with the loot, he's shot by a cop and Kay, who becomes hysterical, runs over to Frank, falls down and seriously injures herself. After Frank is sent to prison and Kay loses her baby, she gives up on their future altogether and settles in with a foster family. Eight years later, Kay is happily married, to another man, Mike (Will Patton), and has two children.

Meanwhile, Frank, who's thought about nothing except Kay during his incarceration, comes looking for her as soon as he's released from prison. After several awkward encounters at the grocery store, the airport and even at her home, Kay begs Frank to leave town. But when Frank reveals he has learned that her birth mother is living in Stockton, Kay agrees to drive to California with him. Once in Stockton, Kay has a traumatic and heartbreaking encounter with her real mother—a tacky, foul-mouthed woman by the name of Roberta. By the movie's end, Frank and Kay end up in Mexico together, where Frank makes one last-ditch effort to convince Kay to stay with him. Kay still loves Frank, but being committed to a new husband and two small children, she turns him down. In the film's dramatic finale, Frank, who feels alone, abandoned and destined never to have a family of his own, commits suicide.

Shot in 1986 and released direct-to-video in 1992, WILDFIRE is a well-written film with strong performances by Fiorentino and Bauer. Fiorentino (AFTER HOURS, THE MODERNS) is convincing as a young woman who is torn between her past and her present. And Bauer (SCARFACE, RAISING CAIN) is adept at portraying the desperate but sympathetic Frank. The direction by Zalman King (TWO MOON JUNCTION, WILD ORCHID) is not to be overlooked either. The scene where Kay encounters her real mother is especially powerful. It effectively captures Kay's curiosity, apprehension and quiet revulsion. *(Profanity, sexual situations.)*

p, Jerry Tokofsky; d, Zalman King; w, Zalman King, Matthew Bright, (from his story); ph, Bill Butler; ed, Danford B. Greene, William Gordean; m, Maurice Jarre; prod d, Geoffrey Kirkland; art d, Geoffrey Kirkland; cos, Theadora Van Runkle

Romance/Drama **(PR: C MPAA: PG)**

WIND ★★

123m American Zoetrope; Filmlink International ~ TriStar c

Matthew Modine *(Will Parker)*, Jennifer Grey *(Kate Bass)*, Cliff Robertson *(Morgan Weld)*, Jack Thompson *(Jack Neville)*, Stellan Skarsgard *(Joe Heiser)*, Rebecca Miller *(Abigail Weld)*, Ned Vaughn *(Charley Moore)*, Peter Montgomery *(TV Commentator)*, Elmer Ahlwardt *(Sarge)*, Saylor Creswell *(Butler)*, James Rebhorn *(George)*, Michael Higgins *(Artemus)*, Ron Colbin *(Tad)*, Ken Kensei *(Swami)*, Bill Buell *(Danny)*, Tom Fervoy *(Jeff)*, Ron Palillo *(Tony)*, Matt Malloy *(Lyle)*, Mark Walsh *(Spider)*, Kim Sheridan *(Rubsey)*, Bruce Epke *(Sheik)*, Sean Leonard *(Mooney)*, Tom Darling *(Otis)*, John Sangmeister *(Skye)*, Stewart Silvestri *(Tuck)*, Jay Brown *(Hook)*, Mark McTeigue *(Mac)*, Mark Richards *(Bruno)*, Billy Bates *(Cat)*

Although director Carroll Ballard energetically conveys the visceral excitement of high-speed sailing in WIND, his film is scuttled by flat characterizations and a hackneyed screenplay.

In Newport, Rhode Island, Morgan Weld (Cliff Robertson) organizes a racing crew to defend the America's Cup. Among the crew is Will Parker (Matthew Modine), whose fear of success causes Weld to lose the race to an Australian ship. Desolate after the loss and abandoned by both the crew and his girlfriend Kate (Jennifer Grey), Will ambles around rudderless until he turns up in Nevada, where Kate and her new boyfriend, Joe Heiser (Stellan Skarsgard), are designing airplanes. Inspired by their work, Will convinces them to design a new type of boat to compete in the next America's Cup race. Armed with the innovative boat, the crew face the Australian defender Jack Neville (Jack Thompson) in a ROCKY-style conclusion.

As with his previous feature films, Ballard here attempts to dramatize the struggle between a human being and an essentially uncaring, irrational natural force. In THE BLACK STALLION and NEVER CRY WOLF, however, the drama succeeded because the environment functioned as a kind of character. That's not the case with WIND.

Despite Ballard's unique talent for capturing the power and energy of natural forces (the sailing scenes are truly exhilarating), he cannot overcome a derivative screenplay and bland performances. The script, in particular, shows tell-tale signs of having been tampered with by a committee. The work of iconoclastic screenwriter Rudy Wurlitzer (PAT GARRETT AND BILLY THE KID, WALKER) has apparently been watered down in the shuffle, although the raw-edged Nevada sequence and the unusual reading of the Joe Heiser character reflect the kind of film WIND might have been if Wurlitzer's contributions had been left untouched.

p, Mata Yamamoto, Tom Luddy; d, Carroll Ballard; w, Rudy Wurlitzer, Mac Gudgeon, Larry Gross, (from the story by Jeff Benjamin, Howard Chelsey, Kimball Livingston and Roger Vaughan); ph, John Toll; ed, Michael Chandler; m, Basil Poledouris; prod d, Laurence Eastwood; cos, Marit Allen

Drama/Sports **(PR: C MPAA: PG-13)**

WINTER IN LISBON, THE ★★

(Spain/France/Portugal) 100m Impala; Jet Films; Igeldo Zine; Sara Films; MGN Filmes e Espectaculos ~ Castle Hill Productions c

Dizzy Gillespie *(Bill Swann)*, Christian Vadim *(Jim)*, Helene De St. Pere *(Lucrecia)*, Fernando Guillen *(Malcolm)*, Michel Duperial *(Morton)*, Carlos Wallenstein *(Ramires)*, Isidoro Fernandez *(Oscar)*, Victor Norte *(Silveira)*, Mikel Garmendia *(Rigoletto)*, Aitzpea Goenaga *(Daphne)*, Klara Badiola *(Nurse)*, Ester Esparza *(Monja)*

Writer-director Jose Antonio Zorrilla's THE WINTER IN LISBON never really gets off the ground. The filmmaker ends up with an atmospheric assemblage of long, drawn out scenes made worse with feeble dialogue and unnecessary characters.

Jim (Christian Vadim) is a jazz pianist who plays in a well-known summer resort club called "Lady Bird." This particular summer a legendary horn player, Bill Swann (Dizzy Gillespie), is headlining the club, and Jim is his talented pianist. It isn't long before Lucrecia (Helene De St. Pere) walks into Jim's life. She is a beautiful yet mysterious blonde—the unhappy wife of a ruthless gangster. When their eyes meet, they know they must have each other, and she returns to the club late that night to begin the affair. As the summer progresses, Jim falls in love with her all the while knowing that some sinister plot is going on.

Lucrecia's husband, Malcolm (Fernando Guillen), and his cohorts, Ramires (Carlos Wallenstein) and Morton (Michel Duperial), are trafficking in arms for their master plan to overthrow the democratic government of Portugal. The summer romance ends quickly when Ramires's bodyguard is killed, and the criminal crew flee San Sebastian. Lucrecia says goodbye to Jim and is gone. Jim finds out what happened and is determined to find her again. He travels to Lisbon and finds himself in the middle of strange events. The arms deal is discovered, various shady characters end up dead and Bill Swann reunites with his favorite piano player and then dies in his arms. After a shoot-out with the last remaining bad guy, Jim and Lucrecia board a boat and sail away into the sunset.

When a director commits to making a movie, particularly a thriller, he must be aware of pacing. Fifteen minutes into THE WINTER IN LISBON the viewer is already fatigued, and only two or three scenes have played up to this point. The film has a wacky plot involving international intrigue and jazz music that is hard to fathom. Zorrilla tries valiantly to put all of these absurd parts together but is himself worn down in the process. The last half hour seems to go on forever.

As a writer, Zorrilla had an interesting idea about the affair between a loner pianist and a mysterious woman, but this too gets washed out by the big picture. The dialogue wavers between passable and silly, as in this remark from Lucrecia to Jim: "You'll always be a musician. I'm only a subtext." In the end, the story leaves too many unanswered questions, but even if the questions had been answered the film probably wouldn't be much better. The cast, particularly Vadim, try their best in a wasted effort. Gillespie plays beautiful music, but the scenes which really require him to act are a bit much for this fine musician. He does have one telling scene about the pain of racism, but it doesn't really have anything to do with the movie. A handful of secondary characters are in the way and only confuse the plot further.

THE WINTER IN LISBON probably would have made a better film if the screenplay had been pared down to focus on the love triangle aspect. Turning the tale into a story of espionage was a remarkably bad idea. *(Violence, nudity.)*

p, Angel Amigo; d, Jose Antonio Zorrilla; w, Jose Antonio Zorrilla, Mason Funk, (from the original screenplay by Funk based on the novel by Antonio Munoz Molina); ph, Jean Francis Gondre; ed, Pablo G. Del Amo, Ivan Aleso; m, Dizzy Gillespie; art d, Mario Alberto; set d, Augusto Mayer; cos, Javier Artinano

Thriller/Drama (PR: C MPAA: NR)

WISECRACKS ★★★

(Canada) 91m Zinger Films; National Film Board of Canada ~ Alliance Releasing c

Phyllis Diller, Whoopi Goldberg, The Clichettes, Faking It Three, Geri Jewell, Jenny Jones, Ellen DeGeneres, The Alexander Sisters, JoAnne Astrow, Joy Behar, Maria Callous, Dreenagh Darrell, Dorothy Hart, Maxine Lapiduss, Jenny Lecoat, Emily Levine, Paula Poundstone, Sandra Shamas, Carrie Snow, Pam Stone, Deborah Theaker, Robin Tyler, Kem Wayans, Lotus Weinstock, Gracie Allen, Eve Arden, Lucille Ball, Fanny Brice, Carol Burnett, George Burns, Carol Channing, Constance Collier, Cass Daley, Joan Davis, Marie Dressler, Duncan Sisters, Louise Fazenda, Gracie Fields, Molly Goldberg, Betty Hutton, Beatrice Lillie, Hattie McDaniel, Martha Raye, Ronald Reagan, Sophie Tucker, Mae West, Marie Wilson

Canadian filmmaker Gail Singer provides some answers to the question of what constitutes feminist humor with WISECRACKS, a combination of filmed performances by various stand-up comics, archival footage of comediennes from the early days of film and TV, and interviews.

Singer includes an extended interview with Phyllis Diller, who not only defines the various categories of funny female performers, but also deals with very practical questions of stage design. In archival footage, Diller demonstrates a performance style similar to Bob Hope's while tackling breast fixation, a risque topic at the time. The central question of whether to use sexual matters as the prime focus of humor runs throughout the film.

Some of the performers avoid the topic of sex and just comment about the absurdity of life in general; Paula Poundstone speaks hilariously about her neurotic cats while Joy Behar does a routine on people who insist on pressing elevator buttons even though someone else has already clearly done so. Jenny Jones lampoons the behavior of cheap men on dates and Emily Levine admits that one of her sexual fantasies is the sudden post coital death of the male. Lotus Weinstock spoofs simplistic advice for the lovelorn, while Deborah Theaker takes on the persona of a beleagured Emily Dickinson look-alike.

Many of the comics stress the importance of good audiences, and we see how they handle the occasional male heckler with a mixture of wit and nerve—though one of the performers does cite the difficulty of dealing with "likker'd-up" spectators in mixed groups.

There are also some highly unusual performances. The Alexander Sisters parody male rock groups, donning naked muscleman suits with removable genitalia; the Clichettes parody the egotism of the male torch singers featured on second-rate variety shows; and Faking It Three portray the ways in which three women from very different class backgrounds (with accents to match) might react to a range of pointed questions. Dorothy Hart uses her experiences at senior citizens' centers to highlight the humor in male memory loss, while Geri Jewell chronicles the misadventures of a cerebral palsy victim—which she is.

Whoopi Goldberg comes across as a little smug in an interview, claiming that she never auditions for parts and doesn't exploit Black themes—though her performance includes a sketch featuring a heavy "street" accent.

With more than 24 female performers from America, Canada and Britain, WISECRACKS offers a general overview of feminist humor, from the subtle to the absurd. Singer attempts to make the interviews serve as commentary on the performances, but the disparate nature of the material—from Marie Dressler's silent film antics to Mae West's off-hand comments at a gala reception—does not make for a neat match. *(Profanity.)*

p, Gail Singer, Signe Johannson; d, Gail Singer; ph, Zoe Dirse, Bob Fresco; ed, Gordon McClellan; m, Maribeth Solomon

Documentary/Comedy (PR: C MPAA: NR)

WITCHCRAFT IV: VIRGIN HEART

92m Vista Street Entertainment; Feifer/Miller Productions ~ Academy Entertainment c

Charles Solomon *(William Spanner)*, Julie Strain *(Belladonna)*, Clive Pearson *(Santara)*, Orien Richman *(Pete Wild)*, Diane Fowler *(Nora)*, Jason O'Gulihur *(Hal)*, Lisa Jay Harrington *(Lily Wild)*, Erol Munuz *(Lt. Hovis)*, Isaac Baruch *(Art)*, Barbara Dow

Billed as an erotic horror film, WITCHCRAFT IV is neither sexy nor scary, and for much of its running time doesn't seem to be attempting to be either. For the most part, it's a pedestrian mystery that's badly scripted even by low-budget standards.

While out in the woods for a romantic tryst, teenager Pete Wild (Orien Richman) falls out of a tree and is knocked unconscious; going for help, his girlfriend Nora (Diane Fowler) attempts to call the police, only to be abducted by a sinister man named Hal (Jason O'Gulihur). Pete is arrested for Nora's disappearance and apparent murder (she has, in fact, been killed in a satanic ritual), and his older sister Lily (Lisa Jay Harrington) goes to attorney William Spanner (Charles Solomon) for help. Will (a warlock who has suppressed his powers and the hero of the last two WITCHCRAFT films) has given up public defending, but is moved to help Lily clear Pete. Meeting with Lt. Hovis (Erol Munuz), who's in charge of the case, Will learns that the young man is being held as a suspect in a whole string of recent killings. While doing their own investigating, Will and Lily discover a matchbook from the Coven nightclub at the phone booth where Nora made her call; inside is written "BD-2:00."

That night, Will goes to check out the Coven, where he briefly runs into Hal and watches as the gorgeous dancer Belladonna (Julie Strain) performs a strip act. Figuring that she's the "BD" referred to on the matchbook, he follows her when she's taken home that night, but then sees her sneak out again and loses her when he attempts to find out where she's going. The next night, however, he successfully tracks her to the 2:00 Club, where she sings with a blues band. Meeting her afterwards, he shows her the matchbook and voices his suspicions; she professes not to know anything about the murder, and invites him back to her place.

There, she's in the midst of seducing him when someone knocks on the door, and has him hide in a closet before opening up. The visitor turns out to be Robert Santara (Clive Pearson), a popular local British DJ, who threatens and assaults Belladonna, telling her to stick to stripping and stop singing. When he leaves, Belladonna tells Will that Santara's her manager and that she owes him everything before becoming upset and throwing Will out.

Still getting nowhere with Lt. Hovis, who tells Will to stop his investigation, and entering into a passionate relationship with Belladonna, Will discovers that Santara broadcasts his show from somewhere other than his station's offices. He goes to talk to Art (Isaac Baruch), Belladonna's guitarist at the 2:00 Club, who says that the singer's plight is related to "the legend of the blues." Will discovers that the legend has to do with the Devil helping bluesmen with their music, and that a manager who looked very much like Santara aided numerous performers in the 1920s. Hal and another of Santara's thugs kill Art and then kidnap Will while he's with Belladonna, taking him out into the woods.

There, Santara's spirit instructs the goons to leave Will to him, then tells Will to meet with him at his studio beneath the Coven. There, Will discovers Lily tied down and confronts Santara and his henchmen; Santara turns out to be a satanic entity who attempts to convince Will to join him and use his powers to serve the dark side. But Will refuses, kills the henchmen and tears out Santara's heart after a struggle. He then frees Lily—who turns on him as well before being stabbed by Belladonna. She and Lt. Hovis, who is waiting upstairs, reveal that Lily was a disciple of Santara's who attempted to lure her unwilling brother into the fold; Hovis knew Pete was innocent, but held him in custody to help set Will up to lead him to the real killers. Will and Belladonna then leave through a back door while Lt. Hovis and his men mop up after the fight downstairs.

While there's a lot to criticize in WITCHCRAFT IV, its very worst element is its frequently idiotic dialogue. None of the characters are exempt, from Will (whose opening voiceover includes the line "I've given up looking for the perfect life; it just doesn't come naturally when you're a warlock") to Lily (who asks, upon their discovery of the matchbook, "Do you think it's a clue?") to the villainous Santara (when Will spits at him, he responds, "I'll take your saliva; we are the same!") to his irascible henchman Hal (when someone asks him the time, he snaps, "Do I look like Big Ben? Am I Swiss? Am I ticking?") to the teenagers in the opening scene, who talk entirely too much. It's a particular detriment for a film that's *mostly* talk, with a few attempted scary and sexy moments thrown in until it finally wraps up with some negligible supernatural histrionics.

Director-coscreenwriter James Merendino fails to give this film the style that would offset its low-budget look, favoring long, static two-shots for most of the dialogue scenes. Horror fans will be disappointed by the lack of creative scares and special effects, while those who might be attracted by the mystery element will find it pretty half-baked. The only conceivable audience for WITCHCRAFT IV are "erotic thriller" fans for whom a few flashes of skin are enough to justify a movie. *(Violence, profanity, nudity, sexual situations.)*

p, Holly MacConkey, Stephen Lieb; d, James Merendino; w, Michael Paul Gerard, James Merendino; ph, Kevin Morrisey; ed, Tony Miller; m, Miriam Cutler; prod d, Todd Warfield; art d, Java Delauria; cos, Caroline Leone

Horror/Mystery **(PR: O MPAA: R)**

WOMAN, HER MEN AND HER FUTON, A ★★

90m Interpersonal Films; First Look Pictures ~ Republic Pictures c

Jennifer Rubin *(Helen)*, Lance Edwards *(Donald)*, Grant Show *(Randy)*, Michael Cerveris *(Paul)*, Delaune Michel *(Gail)*, Robert Lipton *(Max)*, Richard Gordon *(Gay Man)*, Jennifer Zuniga *(Waitress)*, Kathryn Atwood *(Waitress)*, Kirsten Hall *(Sales Woman)*, Gary Cusano

Rising star Jennifer Rubin (THE DOORS, DELUSION) heads the cast in A WOMAN, HER MEN AND HER FUTON, a slow-moving drama about a would-be screenwriter who ends up using her casual affairs with men as material for a script.

Set in Los Angeles, the film opens with Helen (Rubin), an attractive twentysomething office worker, breaking up with her possessive boyfriend Paul (Michael Cerveris). Living beyond her means, Helen soon loses her car and her apartment, and eventually moves in with her friend Donald (Lance Edwards), an aspiring writer. Helen helps Donald with his screenplay, while secretly writing her own. In the meantime, Donald introduces Helen to Max (Robert Lipton), a producer who takes an interest in Helen and her screenplay.

Feeling cornered by Paul, Max and Donald, who also wants a relationship with her, Helen has a series of casual affairs. These flings and her past relationships end up in her screenplay. And before you can say "Masters & Johnson," she sells her script. By the end of the film, Helen moves out of Donald's place and drives off with futon in tow.

Written and directed by Mussef Sibay, A WOMAN, HER MEN AND HER FUTON drags in spots, but it's well acted and has good production values. It also intelligently addresses the issues of manipulation, frustration and false hope that take place within relationships. This is brought to bear in a key scene toward the end of the film, where Donald and Helen finally lay their cards on the table. After Helen says she doesn't want to get involved, Donald accuses her of leading him on and using him. Yet Donald has been deceitful too—pretending to be rich and initially claiming that he only wants to be her friend. *(Profanity, sexual situations, nudity.)*

p, Dale Rosenbloom, Mussef Sibay; d, Mussef Sibay; w, Mussef Sibay; ph, Michael Davis; ed, Howard Heard; m, Joel Goldsmith; prod d, Peter Paul Raubertas; art d, Florina Roberts; set d, Richard Way; cos, Lothar Delgado

Drama/Romance **(PR: C MPAA: R)**

WONG FEI-HUNG

(SEE: ONE UPON A TIME IN CHINA)

YEAR OF THE COMET ★★

89m Castle Rock Entertainment ~ Columbia c

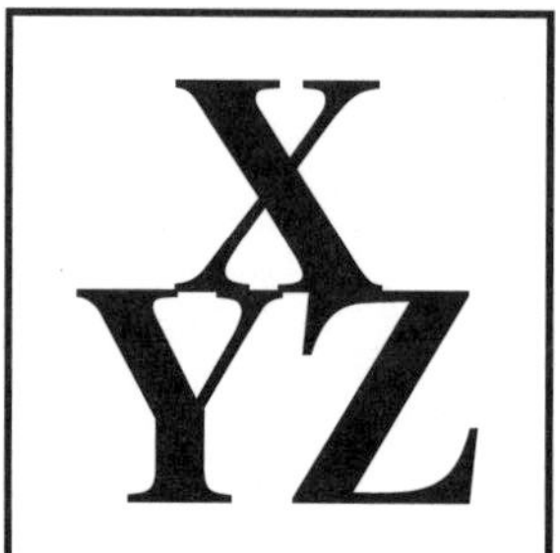

Penelope Ann Miller *(Maggie Harwood)*, Timothy Daly *(Oliver Plexico)*, Louis Jourdan *(Philippe)*, Art Malik *(Nico)*, Ian Richardson *(Sir Mason Harwood)*, Ian McNeice *(Ian)*, Timothy Bentinck *(Richard Harwood)*, Julia McCarthy *(Landlady)*, Jacques Mathou *(Doctor Roget)*, Arturo Venegas *(Luis)*, Chapman Roberts *(John)*, Nick Brimble *(Jaimie)*, Andrew Robertson *(Scottish Farmer)*, Shane Rimmer *(T.T. Kelleher)*, David Bamber *(Albert)*, Nicholas Ward Jackson *(Snobbish Wine Taster)*, Wilfred Bowman *(Spiros Nivanlos)*, Robert Hardy, Olivier Pierre, Martin Benson, Oliver Cotton

A dream project for writer William Goldman (BUTCH CASSIDY AND THE SUNDANCE KID) since he wrote it in the 1970s, this labored attempt to inject some modern irreverence into an old genre falls flat from having languished too long on the shelf and by being entrusted to the wrong director.

Maggie Harwood (Penelope Ann Miller) is the Americanized daughter of the owner of a very old, very conservative and very British wine-auctioning concern. Yearning to play a more important part in the male-dominated business, she gets her chance when her father assigns her to catalogue a wine cellar in an old Scottish estate. There, she discovers a huge bottle of wine bearing Napoleon's seal and dated 1811, the "year of the comet" and a legendary vintage. It's so legendary, in fact, that Margaret's father offers the bottle sight-unseen to a collector for $1 million, who snaps it up immediately. The collector sends his assistant, swaggering beer-swilling Oliver Plexico (Timothy Daly, of TV's "WINGS"), to collect his prize. Plexico and Margaret had met, and scrapped, earlier, at a winetasting. But there were supposedly sparks there and, before too long, they are wrestling between the sheets in Scotland while wrestling the wine away from mad scientist Philippe (Louis Jourdan), a tenant who had been renting the estate from its now-deceased owner and is now after a secret formula for an eternal-youth drug hidden under the bottle's label.

Goldman has had an uncanny affinity with directors throughout his career, especially those with a flair for comedy. BUTCH CASSIDY AND THE SUNDANCE KID was mounted to great popular and critical acclaim under George Roy Hill's direction and THE PRINCESS BRIDE, with Rob Reiner at the helm, has become a romantic cult favorite. Though Goldman, whose other successes include THE STEPFORD WIVES, ALL THE PRESIDENT'S MEN, MARATHON MAN and MAGIC (the latter two adapted from his own novels), has more than proved himself in a wide variety of genres, several of the same ingredients in SUNDANCE and BRIDE are present in this attempt to revive and rib the romantic comedy-adventure. But the results here are flatter than old champagne with Peter Yates at the helm. Yates, whose best films remain the dark and gritty underworld dramas BULLITT and THE FRIENDS OF EDDIE COYLE, has generally shown in his other films that bubbly is quite beyond him.

In this instance, YEAR OF THE COMET seems to lumber when it should soar. Despite the beautiful countryside and the abundant stuntwork, it always feels drab, strained and slow-moving. More than a little fault lies with the screenplay, however. Setting a cliffhanger in the "cutthroat" world of wine-tasting, while an amusing concept, presents limited cinematic possibilities, to say the least. And what's there hasn't improved with age. If Michael Douglas and Kathleen Turner didn't already own this turf with ROMANCING THE STONE and JEWEL OF THE NILE, YEAR OF THE COMET might have had possibilities. As it is, it limps along aimlessly, like THE PINK PANTHER with a hangover.

There is evidence that Goldman had some good thematic ideas. Harwood is a young lady in love with old wines. Plexico, meanwhile, is an old whiner, a once-dashing hero with back problems that make him put the plot on hold so he can get to a chiropractor. And Philippe is an old man obsessed with recapturing his youth. But these potentially intriguing characters are not fleshed out, and the plotting is listless and routine. The final nail in the coffin, as if it were needed, is that Daly and Miller have no chemistry together. Though Daly is amiable enough, Miller fails to inhabit the emotional core of her character, and therefore never seems quite to believe what she's being made to say. (Though, with some of Goldman's dialogue, it's hard to blame her.) She seems relieved during the romantic scenes because at least they connect to something comprehensible in human nature. Otherwise, there's nothing stellar about YEAR OF THE COMET. *(Adult situations.)*

p, Peter Yates, Nigel Wooll; d, Peter Yates; w, William Goldman; ph, Roger Pratt; ed, Ray Lovejoy; m, Hummie Mann; prod d, Anthony Pratt; art d, Desmond Crowe, Chris Seagers; set d, Stephen McMillan; cos, Marilyn Vance-Straker

Romance/Comedy/Adventure (PR: C MPAA: PG-13)

ZEBRAHEAD ★★★

100m Oliver Stone Productions; Ixtlan Productions; Columbia TriStar Home Video ~ Triumph Releasing c

Michael Rapaport *(Zack Glass)*, Kevin Corrigan *(Dominic)*, Lois Bendler *(Dominic's Mother)*, Dan Ziskie *(Mr. Cimino)*, DeShonn Castle *(Dee Wimms)*, N'Bushe Wright *(Nikki)*, Marsha Florence *(Mrs. Wilson)*, Shula Van Buren *(Michelle)*, Ron Johnson *(Nut)*, Ray Sharkey *(Richard Glass)*, Glenn Dossin *(Waiter)*, Martin Priest *(Saul)*, Shirley Benyas *(Helen)*, Jason Willinger *(Bobby)*, Jon Seda *(Vinnie)*, Jade Marisa Thomas *(Kathy)*, Bobby Joe Travis *(Angel)*, Liana Pai *(Connie)*, Idina Harris *(Nadine)*, Taunesha Butler *(Brenda)*, Tycie Person *(Sophie)*, Abdul Hassan Sharif *(Al)*, Lz Granderson *(Larry)*, Londie Jermain Fuller *(Jasmine)*, Paul Butler *(Otis Wimms)*, Yvette Hawkins *(Margaret)*, Candy Ann Brown *(Marlene)*, Luke Reilly *(Mr. Modell)*, Diane Jones *(Mrs. Jones)*, Harold Hogan *(Marlene's Boyfriend)*, Alberta Watson *(Phyliss)*, Lara Kramer *(Robin)*, Andrew Berlin *(Jake)*, William Ozier *(Reverend)*, Helen Shaver *(Diane)*

Writer-director Anthony Drazan's exploration of an interracial relationship, and its polarizing effects, is noticeably effective for its mature, uncompromising stance on the subject. ZEBRAHEAD manages to capture the bravado and streetwise essence of urban American youth without resorting to glossy tactics.

Zack Glass (Michael Rapaport) is hip-hop all the way. He walks the walk, talks the talk and spins rap at his high school's dances. The only thing that doesn't jibe is that Zack is white and Jewish. Nevertheless he is well acclimated in the predominantly Black Detroit high school. His best friend, Dee Wimms (DeShonn Castle), gets a kick out of Zack's pseudo-Black street image. Dee, himself an African-American, realizes this is Zack's way of fitting in.

At home Zack is used to his father Richard's (Ray Sharkey) ever present parade of female guests. Since Zack's mother died 12 years earlier he and his father have been on their own. Richard owns a downtown vintage record shop that is about to close since there are few folks left in the city. Dee's cousin, Nikki (N'Bushe

Wright), arrives from New York City and transfers into their school. Zack is immediately smitten with her, and broaches the subject with Dee of asking her out. Dee offers his blessing to Zack, unaware that this interracial pairing will start a chain effect of bad events.

Nut (Ron Johnson), a short fuse waiting to go off, is the first to hassle Zack. He has his own sights on Nikki, although she declines his persistant advances. However, she is thrilled when Zack asks her out for their first date. Nikki is cautious when she tells her mother, Marlene (Candy Ann Brown), about the impending night out. "He's different," is all she offers. They start the romance off slowly, neither one ever having dated outside their own race.

At a party, Zack's white friends embarrass Nikki and she runs off when his response isn't what she'd counted on. Meanwhile, Nut begins threatening Zack at every turn. They survive the inevitable hardships of their fledgling romance and start to forge a serious relationship, until Zack shows up at a local skating rink and finds Nikki being badgered by Nut. He confronts Nut who pulls out a handgun and begins shooting wildly. Dee ends up in the line of fire and is killed. After Dee's funeral, Zack returns to school only to find it a hotbed of racial tension waiting to explode. There will seemingly never be an end to this conflict.

This is not an action-packed picture. Instead, Drazan pulls the viewer in through consistently original dialogue and carefully drawn characters; the director also relies on the audience's familiarity with racial disharmony. Drazan doesn't try to offer solutions to the conflicts, choosing instead to put the issues on the table and let viewers figure out the answers for themselves. If a sense of helplessness pervades here, that was probably Drazen's intent. The brutal ending, while foreshadowed heavily, still arrives with a shock. In fact, it is clearly designed to increase the racial tension which hangs in the air from the first frame.

While Zack and Nikki may look at their romance as just two teenagers trying to find their own way in the world, many others harbor a much less enlightened view of miscegenation. It was daring for the helmsman to depic Zack as a white youth enamored of Black street culture, but this too works despite its possible exploitative aspects. The character can even be seen as non-racial, embodying qualities good and bad of all races.

Rapaport is a primary reason for the film's appeal. His performance as Zack is unerringly natural, never slipping into caricature. Wright is also well cast as Nikki. She is particularly strong in the scenes with Brown as her mother. Sharkey, while only in a few scenes, is fully plugged into his role. The supporting ensemble are generally up to the material. The musical score is superb, offering not only the expected rap tunes but also a wide variety of styles from classical to country and western.

When ZEBRAHEAD falters it is generally due to unfinished bits of business. The strained relationship between Zack and his father is the most glaringly evident example of this fate. Drazan allows for a buildup in tension to occur in the first reel, but pulls back causing their final confrontation to be forcefully but not credibly resolved. Some of the peripheral characters, while included to play devil's advocate for elements of the unfolding events, are needlessly in the way. The young demagogue who appears from time to time to spew forth racist rhetoric, while offering some comic relief, is unnecessary and only editorializes a story which can communicate its message without such obvious steering. The recurring motif of burning fires is just too surreal to be appreciated.

While ZEBRAHEAD may trip itself up on occasion, it is notable for its honest angle on the subject of race relations. Anthony Drazan is able to portray one small example of racial injustice and yet encompass feelings and emotions that go well beyond the story's locale. *(Violence, profanity.)*

p, Charles Mitchell, Jeff Dowd, William F. Willett; d, Anthony Drazan; w, Anthony Drazan; ph, Maryse Alberti; ed, Elizabeth Kling; m, Taj Mahal; prod d, Naomi Shohan; art d, Dan Whifler; set d, Penny Barrett; cos, Carol Oditz

Drama/Romance **(PR: C MPAA: R)**

ZENTROPA ★★½

(Denmark/France/Sweden/Germany) 114m Nordisk Film & TV A/S; Gunnar Obel Film; Gerard Mital Productions; Promotion Cinema Communications Productions; Telefilm ~ Prestige Films bw/c
(EUROPA)

Jean-Marc Barr *(Leopold Kessler)*, Barbara Sukowa *(Katharina Hartmann)*, Udo Kier *(Lawrence Hartmann)*, Ernst-Hugo Jaregard *(Uncle Kessler)*, Erik Mork *(Father Jaregard)*, Jorgen Reenberg *(Max Hartmann)*, Henning Jensen *(Siggy)*, Eddie Constantine *(Colonel Harris)*, Max Von Sydow *(Narrator)*, Lars Von Trier *(The Jew)*

The highly stylized ZENTROPA returns to what was once a classic setting for intrigue—a first-class sleeping compartment on a train crossing postwar occupied Germany. Using rear projection, superimposition and scenes that mix color with b&w, director and co-screenwriter Lars Von Trier has fashioned an atmospheric if convoluted drama peopled with devious schemers, robotic officials and anonymous grey masses.

A narrator (Max Von Sydow) introduces us to Leopold Kessler (Jean-Marc Barr), an American of sufficient Germanic background to speak the language. Leopold's uncle (Ernst-Hugo Jaregard) gets him a job as a sleeper-coach attendant with the Zentropa railway. A pacifist, Leopold claims he wants to help in German reconstruction; Leopold's uncle is a pompous prig who boasts about his position and disdains the shabby masses the company serves.

On his first night of work, Leopold meets one of the passengers, Katharina Hartmann (Barbara Sukowa), daughter of the railway's owner, Max Hartmann (Jorgen Reenberg). She has already familiarized herself with the young American and invites him to dinner at the family's villa—an offer Leopold's uncle exploits in order to get himself a free meal as his nephew's official chaperone. During the dinner, Leopold learns of the disaffection of the Hartmann son, Lawrence (Udo Kier), and becomes aware of Katharina's romantic interest in him. Another dinner guest, Father Jaregard (Erik Mork), condemns neither the Nazis nor the Allies, but rather those who—like Leopold—didn't take sides in the conflict. That wartime passions have not cooled is proven by bodies hanging from lampposts, glimpsed by Leopold from the train. They each bear a placard identifying them as Nazi guerrillas, or "Werewolves."

Shortly after the dinner, Leopold witnesses a "Werewolf" action. Two young boys, apparently friends of the Hartmanns, assassinate the newly appointed mayor of Ravenstein. During another evening at the Hartmanns, Leopold learns that Max Hartmann worked willingly with the former German government to transport victims to the extermination camps; moreover, Max persuades US Army Colonel Harris (Eddie Constantine) to clear his name of wrongdoing by blackmailing a Jew (Von Trier) into testifying that Max had hidden him from the Nazis. Hartmann, however, is remorseful enough to slash his wrists in his bathtub, at about the same time that Leopold and Katharina make love amid the model train setup in the villa's attic. Katharina admits that she was once a member of the "Werewolf" organization.

Several months later, Leopold is approached by Father Jaregard to help transport Hartmann's coffin for a funeral ceremony.

He must pass through the poorer sections of the train, which were formerly used as concentration camp transports, and whose emaciated passengers still resemble prisoners. The ceremony which he attends at times suggests a Nazi rally, as the drab onlookers stretch out their arms in the familiar salute towards the coffin. Leopold is also approached by the "Werewolf" leader, Siggy (Henning Jensen), who had orchestrated the Ravenstein assassination and suggests that the young American will be called upon in the near future. More imminent, however, are Leopold's marriage to Katharina (poverty-stricken since the death of her father), and an impending examination by railway officials to determine if he can keep his job.

The wedding, in a church without a roof, offers Siggy the opportunity he has been waiting for. After kidnapping Katharina, he forces Leopold to plant two bombs, one on a strategic bridge and one in the first-class cabin of the train. Leopold complies but, on the point of abandoning the train, is stricken with remorse and returns to defuse the device left in his cabin.

Having saved the lives of the passengers, Leopold is confronted by Colonel Harris, who leads him to Katharina: she is safe and sound—and under arrest, since, as she admits to Leopold, she never completely abandoned the "Werewolves." Visibly disturbed, Leopold retreats to his cabin, just as the re-routed train goes over the bridge, which explodes. His section of train falls into the river below and begins to sink. Trapped in his cabin, Leopold drowns aboard the first-class sleeper of the Zentropa line.

ZENTROPA is as muddled as it is stylized; set in Germany six months after the end of WWII, the word "Nazi" is never uttered on the soundtrack. There was a Nazi guerrilla organization called "Werewolf," but its activities were much more limited than the film suggests. Even Kessler's acceptance of such a menial job is somewhat credibility-straining. And the bodies hanging from lampposts seems more typical of Nazi practices than of the western Allies' efforts at denazification, which favored detailed questionnaires like the one back-projected during Max Hartmann's fraudulent trial. Still, the use of such cinematic devices is often striking, as is that of an overhead camera that peers through a gutted roof or captures an internal snowfall in the town's cathedral. *(Profanity, sexual situations, adult situations.)*

p, Peter Aalbaek Jensen; d, Lars Von Trier; w, Lars Von Trier, Niels Vorsel; ph, Henning Bendtsen, Jean-Paul Meurisse, Edward Klosinsky; ed, Herve Schneid; m, Joakim Holbek; prod d, Henning Bahs; cos, Manon Rasmussen

Thriller/Drama/Historical **(PR: C MPAA: R)**

Academy Awards

ACADEMY AWARDS

65th AWARDS OF THE ACADEMY OF MOTION PICTURE ARTS AND SCIENCES
(Listings in italics indicate winners)

Best Picture
Clint Eastwood, UNFORGIVEN
Stephen Woolley, THE CRYING GAME
David Brown, Rob Reiner, Andrew Scheinman, A FEW GOOD MEN
Ismail Merchant, HOWARDS END
Martin Brest, SCENT OF A WOMAN

Best Actor
Al Pacino, SCENT OF A WOMAN
Robert Downey, Jr., CHAPLIN
Stephen Rea, THE CRYING GAME
Denzel Washington, MALCOLM X
Clint Eastwood, UNFORGIVEN

Best Actress
Emma Thompson, HOWARDS END
Catherine Deneuve, INDOCHINE
Susan Sarandon, LORENZO'S OIL
Michelle Pfeiffer, LOVE FIELD
Mary McDonnell, PASSION FISH

Best Supporting Actor
Gene Hackman, UNFORGIVEN
Jaye Davidson, THE CRYING GAME
Jack Nicholson, A FEW GOOD MEN
Al Pacino, GLENGARRY GLEN ROSS
David Paymer, MR SATURDAY NIGHT

Best Supporting Actress
Marisa Tomei, MY COUSIN VINNY
Miranda Richardson, DAMAGE
Joan Plowright, ENCHANTED APRIL
Vanessa Redgrave, HOWARDS END
Judy Davis, HUSBANDS AND WIVES

Best Director
Clint Eastwood, UNFORGIVEN
Neil Jordan, THE CRYING GAME
James Ivory, HOWARDS END
Robert Altman, THE PLAYER
Martin Brest, SCENT OF A WOMAN

Best Original Screenplay
Neil Jordan, THE CRYING GAME
Woody Allen, HUSBANDS AND WIVES
George Miller, Nick Enright, LORENZO'S OIL
John Sayles, PASSION FISH
David Webb Peoples, UNFORGIVEN

Best Adapted Screenplay
Ruth Prawer Jhabvala, HOWARDS END
Peter Barnes, ENCHANTED APRIL
Michael Tolkin, THE PLAYER
Richard Friedenberg, A RIVER RUNS THROUGH IT
Bo Goldman, SCENT OF A WOMAN

Best Foreign Language Film
INDOCHINE (France)
CLOSE TO EDEN (Russia)
DAENS (Belgium)
SCHTONK (Germany)

Best Art Direction
Luciana Arrighi (Art Direction), Ian Whittaker (Set Decoration), HOWARDS END
Thomas Sanders (Art Direction), Garrett Lewis (Set Decoration), BRAM STOKER'S DRACULA
Stuart Craig (Art Direction), Chris A. Butler (Set Decoration), CHAPLIN
Ferdinando Scarfiotti (Art Direction), Linda DeScenna (Set Decoration), TOYS
Henry Bumstead (Art Direction), Janice Blackie-Goodine (Set Decoration), UNFORGIVEN

Best Cinematography
Philippe Rousselot, A RIVER RUNS THROUGH IT
Stephen H. Burum, HOFFA
Tony Pierce-Roberts, HOWARDS END
Robert Fraisse, THE LOVER
Jack N. Green, UNFORGIVEN

Best Costumes
Eiko Ishioka, BRAM STOKER'S DRACULA
Sheena Napier, ENCHANTED APRIL
Jenny Beavan, John Bright, HOWARDS END
Ruth Carter, MALCOLM X
Albert Wolsky, TOYS

Best Documentary Feature
Barbara Trent (Producer), David Kasper (Producer), THE PANAMA DECEPTION
David Haugland (Producer), CHANGING OUR MINDS: THE STORY OF DR. EVELYN HOOKER
Sally Dundas (Producer), FIRES OF KUWAIT
William Miles (Producer), Nina Rosenblum (Producer), LIBERATORS: FIGHTING ON TWO FRONTS IN WORLD WAR II
Margaret Smilov (Producer), Roma Baran (Producer), MUSIC FOR THE MOVIES: BERNARD HERRMANN

Best Documentary Short Subject
Thomas C. Goodwin (Producer), Gerardine Wurzburg (Producer), EDUCATING PETER
Geoffrey O'Connor (Producer), AT THE EDGE OF CONQUEST: THE JOURNEY OF CHIEF WAI-WAI
Wendy L. Weinberg (Producer), BEYOND IMAGINING: MARGARET ANDERSON AND THE "LITTLE REVIEW"
Richard Elson (Producer), Sally Bochner (Producer), THE COLOURS OF MY FATHER: A PORTRAIT OF SAM BORENSTEIN
Dorothy Fadiman (Producer), WHEN ABORTION WAS ILLEGAL: UNTOLD STORIES

Best Film Editing
Joel Cox, UNFORGIVEN
Frank J. Urioste, BASIC INSTINCT
Kant Pan, THE CRYING GAME
Robert Leighton, A FEW GOOD MEN
Geraldine Peroni, THE PLAYER

Best Makeup
Greg Cannom, Michele Burke, Matthew W. Mungle, BRAM STOKER'S DRACULA
Ve Neill, Ronnie Specter, Stan Winston, BATMAN RETURNS
Ve Neill, Greg Cannom, John Blake, HOFFA

Best Original Score
Alan Menken, ALADDIN
Jerry Goldsmith, BASIC INSTINCT
John Barry, CHAPLIN
Richard Robbins, HOWARDS END
Mark Isham, A RIVER RUNS THROUGH IT

Best Song
Alan Menken (music), Tim Rice (lyrics), ALADDIN
Alan Menken (music), Howard Ashman (lyrics), ALADDIN
David Foster (music), Linda Thompson (lyrics), THE BODYGUARD
Jud Friedman (music), Allan Rich (lyrics), THE BODYGUARD
Robert Kraft (music), Arne Glimcher (lyrics), THE MAMBO KINGS

Best Animated Short Film
Joan C. Gratz, MONA LISA DESCENDING A STAIRCASE
Peter Lord, ADAM
Michaela Pavlatova, RECI, RECI, RECI . . .
Paul Berry, THE SANDMAN
Barry J. C. Purves, SCREEN PLAY

Best Live Action Short Film
Sam Karmann, OMNIBUS
Jonathan Darby, Jana Sue Memel, CONTACT
Matt Palmieri, CRUISE CONTROL
Christian M. Taylor, THE LADY IN WAITING
Kenneth Branagh, SWAN SONG

Best Sound
Chris Jenkins, Doug Hemphill, Mark Smith, Simon Kaye, THE LAST OF THE MOHICANS
Terry Porter, Mel Metcalfe, David J. Hudson, Doc Kane, ALADDIN
Kevin O'Connell, Rick Kline, Bob Eber, A FEW GOOD MEN
Don Mitchell, Frank A. Montano, Rick Hart, Scott Smith, UNDER SIEGE
Les Fresholtz, Vern Poore, Dick Alexander, Rob Young, UNFORGIVEN

Best Sound Effects Editing
Tom C. McCarthy, David E. Stone, BRAM STOKER'S DRACULA
Mark Mangini, ALADDIN
John Leveque, Bruce Stambler, UNDER SIEGE

Best Visual Effects
Ken Ralston, Doug Chiang, Doug Smythe, Tom Woodruff, DEATH BECOMES HER
Richard Edlund, Alec Gillis, Tom Woodruff, Jr., George Gibbs, ALIEN3
Michael Fink, Craig Barron, John Bruno, Dennis Skotak, BATMAN RETURNS

Honorary Award
Federico Fellini

Gordon E. Sawyer Award
Erich Kaestner

Jean Hersholt Humanitarian Award
Audrey Hepburn
Elizabeth Taylor

Obituaries

OBITUARIES

(January 1 to December 31, 1992)

Adler, Stella
acting teacher, actress; also stage director
aka: Ardler, Stella
born: 1902, New York, NY
died: December 21, 1992, Los Angeles CA, age 91
educ: NYU; American Laboratory Theatre

One of America's most influential acting teachers, and one of few Americans to have studied the "method" with its originator, Constantin Stanislavsky; Adler's former students include Marlon Brando, Robert De Niro, Warren Beatty and Harvey Keitel. Adler began her career with the theater company of her father, the legendary Yiddish actor Jacob Adler, before appearing on Broadway and later joining the Group Theater at its inception in 1931. Her most famous performance was in The Group Theater's production of Clifford Odets's "Awake and Sing" in the 1930s. By the mid-1940s, after a schism with Lee Strasberg over his interpretation of the Stanislavsky "method", she turned to teaching, first at the Dramatic Workshop of the New School for Social Research in New York and, in 1949, full-time at her own school.

Alcoriza, Luis
director; also screenwriter, actor
born: 1920, Badajoz, Spain
died: December 3, 1992, Cuernvaca, Mexico, age 71

Co-wrote many of Luis Bunuel's Mexican classics. Alcoriza's own films as a director are little known outside Mexico.

Alison, Dorothy
actress
born: 1925, Australia
died: January 17, 1992, London, age 66

Australian-born supporting actress who spent much of her career in Great Britain, playing warm, approachable characters in films from "Reach for the Sky" (1956) to "The Nun's Story" (1959) to "Georgy Girl" (1966) to "Doctor Jekyll and Sister Hyde" (1971). Alison's most fondly remembered film performance may be her first, as the sympathetic teacher of the hearing-impaired who finally gets a young girl to utter sounds in Alexander Mackendrick's "Mandy" (1952). The renaissance in Australian filmmaking during the 1970s and 80s enabled Alison to act more in her native land, where she appeared in "A Cry in the Dark" (1988) and "Malpractice" (1989) and the TV miniseries "A Town Like Alice" (1981).

Almendros, Nestor
director of photography; also director
aka: Nestor, John
born: October 30, 1930, Barcelona, Spain
died: March 4, 1992, Manhattan NY, age 61
educ: Havana University (philosophy, literature); Centro Sperimentale di Cinematografia, Rome (cinematography); CCNY (film)

Award-winning international cinematographer who rose to prominence in the 1960s and 70s. Almendros's crisp black-and-white style recalled the early silent masters and he also did brilliant color work for Francois Truffaut (eight features, from 1969's "The Wild Child" to 1982's "Confidentially Yours") and Eric Rohmer (the black-and-white "My Night at Maud's" in 1969 and the sun-dappled "Claire's Knee" in 1970). During this period, Almendros collaborated with producer-director Barbet Schroeder on "More" (1969), "Maitresse" (1975) and the documentaries "General Idi Amin Dada" (1974) and "Koko, the Talking Gorilla" (1978). By the mid-70s Almendros was alternating between major American films and projects for European directors. With his Oscar-winning work on Terrence Malick's "Days of Heaven" (1978), Almendros introduced a completely natural look to his films, eschewing traditional studio lighting, filters and trickery for use of existing natural light in such features as "The Blue Lagoon" (1980) and "Sophie's Choice" (1982). In the 80s, while continuing to create luminous images for the likes of Robert Benton and Martin Scorsese, Almendros also directed two piercing interview-documentaries about political repression and human rights violations in Cuba: "Improper Conduct" (1983, with Orlando Jimenez-Leal) and "Nobody Listened" (1988, with Jorge Ulla). He authored an acclaimed book on cinematography, "A Man With A Camera" (1980).

Alzado, Lyle
professional athlete; also actor, spokesperson
born: April 3, 1949, Brooklyn NY
died: May 14, 1992, Portland OR, age 42

Burly professional football player noted for his aggressive, hard-hitting style as a defensive lineman on the field, and for an equally tough line of talk ("I don't think there's a man in America who can take me") off the field. Alzado leavened his growling with an occasional touch of humor in his modest film appearances and TV guest spots, but always boldly proclaimed his "hit hard, hit first" approach to sports and showbiz alike. Alzado was diagnosed with brain cancer in the early 1990s and became convinced that his use of steroids and growth hormones for nearly 20 years had caused his illness. He spent his last days, looking tired, drawn, and 120 pounds lighter than his 300-pound peak, warning body-conscious teenagers about the evils of "dream" drugs.

Anderson, John
actor
born: 1923, Clayton IL
died: August 7, 1992, Sherman Oaks CA, age 69
educ: University of Iowa

Prolific, versatile, light-haired charactor actor. Anderson's feature credits include "Psycho" (as the smarmy car salesman), Ossie Davis' "Cotton Comes to Harlem" (1970) and John Sayles' "Eight Men Out" (1988). His TV credits include over 500 roles, most recently among them a recurring role on "Dallas"; the short lived spin-off "Baby Boom"; and, as the title character's father, "MacGyver".

Anderson, Judith
actress
aka: Anderson, Dame Judith; Anderson, Frances
born: Anderson-Anderson, Frances Margaret, February 10, 1898, Adelaide, Australia
died: January 3, 1992, Santa Barbara CA, age 93

Leading Broadway star from the 1920s through the 50s, perhaps most famous for her savage, award-winning performance in 1947 as "Medea"; as a formidable Lady Macbeth (opposite Laurence Olivier in London in 1937 and Maurice Evans on Broadway in 1941); and as an interpreter of the neurotic heroines of Eugene

O'Neill (Nina in "Strange Interlude" in 1928 and Lavinia in "Mourning Becomes Electra" in 1932). Anderson made her film debut in 1933 and played the sinister housekeeper Mrs. Danvers in Hitchcock's "Rebecca" seven years later. It was the first, and most memorable, in a series of malevolent characer roles that exploited her severe features and commanding presence. Cast against type, Anderson made an effective Big Mama in Richard Brooks's film adaptation of "Cat on a Hot Tin Roof" (1958). Late in her career she gained a new following as campy grande dame Minx Lockridge on the TV soap opera, "Santa Barbara".

Andrews, Dana
actor
born: Andrews, Carver Dana, January 1, 1912, Collins MS
died: December 17, 1992, Orange County CA, age 83
educ: Pasadena Playhouse; Sam Houston State Teacher's College
Solid (sometimes to the point of being wooden), average-Joe leading man of the 1940s who specialized in earnest, embittered and/or disillusioned characters. Having worked as an accountant and a singer, Andrews entered films in the early 40s as a supporting player in Westerns. After portraying the victim of a lynch mob in "The Ox-Bow Incident" (1943), his career took off and he starred in a succession of strong vehicles, often as flawed heroes. Most memorable in urban settings, Andrews successfully teamed up with director Otto Preminger and co-star Gene Tierney for "Laura" (1944) and "Where the Sidewalk Ends" (1950); he was equally superb as the re-adjusting bombadier in "The Best Years of Our Lives" (1946) and as the unflinchingly honest prosecuting attorney in Elia Kazan's "Boomerang!" (1947). With his big-screen career on the wane, Andrews starred in prestige TV showcases in the 50s and headlined a daytime soap opera, "Bright Promise", in the late 60s. Andrews's second wife, Mary Todd, was an actress and his brother, Steve Forrest, an actor.

Arletty
actress
born: Bathiat, Arlette-Leonie, May 15, 1898, Courbevoie, France
died: July 24, 1992, Paris, France, age 94
Elegant, husky-voiced French star of the 1930s and 40s, remembered for her roles in four classics of poetic realism: "Hotel du Nord" (1938), "Daybreak" (1939), "The Devil's Envoys" (1942) and "Children of Paradise" (1945). With her striking features and aloof, mysterious air, Arletty was a kind of French Marlene Dietrich. In the 50s she divided her career between the stage and film until an accident in 1957 left her temporarily blind. Arletty returned to film in the war epic "The Longest Day" (1962) but recurring blindness sent her into retirement again soon after. Briefly jailed as a collaborator after WWII because of an affair with a German officer, she never married and had no children.

Arnold, Jack
director; also producer, actor
born: October 14, 1916, New Haven CT
died: March 17, 1992, Woodland Hills CA, age 75
educ: Ohio State University; AADA, New York NY
Former stage and movie actor who filmed numerous documentaries for the US State Department, the Army and private industry in the late 1940s and began making low-budget features in the early 50s. Arnold concocted some of that era's classic science fiction-horror films, notably the pioneering 3-D efforts "It Came from Outer Space" (1952) and "The Creature From the Black Lagoon" (1954) as well as "The Incredible Shrinking Man" (1957). A prolific director, mostly for Universal, Arnold worked in many genres, turning out 3-D mystery thrillers ("The Glass Web" 1953), teen exploitation flicks ("High School Confidential" 1958), blaxploitation actioners ("Boss Nigger" 1975), the wry Peter Sellers satire "The Mouse That Roared" (1959), and Bob Hope comedies including "Bachelor in Paradise" (1961) and "A Global Affair" (1964). By the mid-60s Arnold had turned his attention increasingly to TV, as a director on "Rawhide", "Perry Mason" "Buck Rogers in the 25th Century", "Wonder Woman" and "The Bionic Woman", and as producer-director of "Mr. Lucky" (1959-60) "Gilligan's Island" (1964-67) and "It Takes a Thief" (1968-70).

Atterbury, Malcolm
actor; also theater owner, theater operator, theater seminar instructor, TV host
born: February 20, 1907, Philadelphia PA
died: August 23, 1992, Beverly Hills CA, age 85
A veteran of the stage, TV and film, Atterbury was one of the most respected character actors in Hollywood from the early 1950s through the 80s. His height and gaunt features made him a natural for Westerns in his younger days, but he served just as well in thrillers, film noirs, horror quickies and cop movies. In his later years, his feisty yet friendly manner made Atterbury a favorite choice for colorful grandfather roles. He appeared in more than 75 features and 300 TV episodes in the course of his career. One of Atterbury's best-remembered appearances was in "North by Northwest", where he plays the weathered-looking, taciturn man who drily observes to Cary Grant that "That plane's dusting crops where there ain't no crops," setting the stage for one of Hitchcock's most celebrated set pieces. Prior to going to Hollywood in 1953, Atterbury's major contribution to the entertainment field was as a theater owner and operator. He and his wife Ellen ran two professional theaters: the Tamarack Playhouse, a summer stock theater in Lake Pleasant NY; and the Playhouse in Albany NY. The latter was the only Equity winter stock company in the country. In Albany, the Atterburys provided opportunities for the young talents of Grace Kelly, Kirk Douglas, Karl Malden, Cliff Robertson, Barbara Cook and Tom Bosley.

Audley, Maxine
actress
born: April 29, 1923, London
died: July 23, 1992, London, age 69
Incisive character actress trained in New York and London. Audley began appearing on the London stage in 1940 and in films and TV shows from the mid-1950s. Her screen credits include Sidney Franklin's "The Barretts of Wimpole Street" (1956), Laurence Olivier's "The Prince and the Showgirl" (1957), Charles Chaplin's "A King in New York" (1957), Carol Reed's "Our Man in Havana" (1960), John Huston's "Sinful Davey" (1969), and Terrence Fisher's "Frankenstein Must Be Destroyed" (1969). Audley was particularly memorable as the heroine's blind mother in Michael Powell's unnerving cult classic, "Peeping Tom" (1960). She also worked extensively on British radio and was popular on the British stage for over 50 years.

Aurenche, Jean
screenwriter
born: September 11, 1904, Pierrelatte, France
died: October 1992, age 88
Entered films in the early 1930s, wrote his first feature in 1936 and began a fruitful, lasting collaboration with co-writer Pierre Bost on "Douce" (1943). The team wrote numerous scripts for directors Claude Autant-Lara ("The Devil in the Flesh" 1946, "The Red Inn" 1951), Rene Clement ("The Walls of Malpaga" 1949, "Forbidden Games" 1951, "Gervaise" 1956) and Jean Delannoy ("God Needs Men" 1950). Though the work of Bost

and Aurenche came to typify the "quality" films so despised by the New Wave directors, their earlier screenplays had often been iconoclastic, dealing with controversial subjects and espousing progressive politics. After a series of generally undistinguished films in the 1960s, the team re-established its critical reputation with two fine, intricate dramas for Bertrand Tavernier, "The Watchmaker" (1973) and "The Judge and the Assassin" (1976).

Babbitt, Art

animator; also director of commercial department of Hanna-Barbera, animation instructor
born: Babitsky, Arthur, c. 1907, Omaha NE
died: March 4, 1992, Los Angeles CA, age 85

A master of character animation, Art Babbitt's career spanned the early days of sound animation at Terrytoons and Disney; the glory days of the lavish pre-war Disney features; the 1950s innovations of UPA; the limited commercial animation of Hanna-Barbera in the 60s; and the big-budget animated features of the late 80s and 90s. He was significant both for his extraordinary artistic achievements and for his central role in the fateful Disney animators' strike of 1941. As a leader in the cartoonists' union which clashed with management over wages and working conditions, Babbitt gained the lasting enmity of the paternalistic Walt Disney, with whom he nearly came to blows on the picket line during the height of the strike. Legend has it that Walt's bitterness over the strike motivated the waning of his interest in animated features in the 1940s and forever changed his attitude toward his staff. As an animator, Babbitt is best known for developing the personality of Goofy, one of the most beloved Disney characters. He also animated the Big Bad Wolf for the classic 1933 short, "The Three Little Pigs" and worked on such landmark Disney features as "Snow White", "Pinocchio", and "Dumbo". Perhaps his most celebrated work at Disney was his animation of the dancing mushrooms in the "Nutcracker Suite" sequence of "Fantasia". Babbitt also did memorable work for Warner Brothers, UPA, and Hanna-Barbera. He won more than 80 awards for independent TV commercials in the 1950s and 60s, including spots for the Ajax Cleanser elves and a popular ad involving a man who could not pronounce "Worcestershire Sauce". Babbitt headed the commercial department of Hanna-Barbera from 1966 to 1975 and taught master classes in animation at Richard Williams' London studio beginning in 1973. Babbitt's last work was on "The Thief and the Cobbler", a major animated feature not yet released.

Barber, Red

sportscaster, radio personality
born: Barber, Walter Lanier, c. 1908, Columbus MS
died: October 22, 1992, Tallahassee FL, age 84

A pioneer baseball sportscaster, "The Old Redhead" is generally acknowledged as being one of the very best practitioners of his craft. Over the course of his long career, Barber called play-by-play on the first night baseball game, the first televised game (during which he also announced the first TV commercials), the first televised World Series, and the first televised football games. The first man to be hired by Edward R. Murrow when the legendary newsman returned from World War II to run CBS News, he served as the network's director of sports. Barber garnered praise from some and criticism from others for his scrupulous impartiality during his broadcasts; one never had a sense that he was rooting for one team over another—a trait that sometimes irritated partisans (such as his employers). Barber became familiar to a new generation of fans through his Friday morning appearances on National Public Radio's "Morning Edition" for the last 11 years of his life. One did not need to be a sports fan to delight in hearing this great broadcaster's wonderfully tangy voice—so warmly evocative of leisurely summer afternoons—comment on the current sports scene in a crisp no-nonsense manner.

Bartholomew, Freddie

actor; also TV director
aka: Bartholomew, Fred C.
born: Bartholomew, Frederick Llewellyn, March 28, 1924, London
died: January 23, 1992, Sarasota FL, age 67

Curly-haired Hollywood child star whose earnest presence, refined British diction and angelic looks established him as a boxoffice favorite in the 1930s and 40s. After a few minor roles in British films, the ten-year-old was signed by MGM to star as Dickens's hero in David O. Selznick's production of "David Copperfield" (1935). He went on to play Greta Garbo's son in "Anna Karenina" (1935) and followed up with his two most popular roles: as the American boy who learns he is the heir to a dukedom in "Little Lord Fauntleroy" (1936) and as a pampered rich brat who is rescued and educated by rough fishermen in Rudyard Kipling's adventure yarn, "Captains Courageous" (1937). With a salary eclipsed only by that of child superstar Shirley Temple, Bartholomew was earning $2,500 a week by the late 30s, though his career began to wane after numerous court battles between his guardian-aunt and his parents over his earnings. After service in WWII he made a stab at a career in vaudeville and nightclubs before turning to TV, where he hosted a daytime program in the 1950s and then became associate director of a New York TV station. In the mid-1950s he again switched careers, this time joining New York's Benton and Bowles agency as an advertising executive.

Beatty, Robert

actor
born: October 19, 1909, Hamilton, Ontario, Canada
died: March 2, 1992, London, age 82
educ: University of Toronto; RADA, London

Craggy-faced, Canadian-born actor whose rugged appearance made him a natural for tough guy roles, especially in British crime films of the 1950s. Beatty's voice became familiar to North American listeners as he described the WWII bombings of London for the BBC's Overseas News Service and, after the war, as detective Philip O'Dell on radio. Beatty was a prolific performer on TV as well as in film through the 80s and portrayed President Ronald Reagan in the 1987 PBS dramatization "Breakthrough at Reykjavik".

Beck, Reginald

film editor
born: c. 1902, England
died: July 12, 1992, England, age 90

British film editor whose career spanned over 40 years. Beck helped to shape films as diverse as Laurence Olivier's "Henry V" (1944) and Rainer Werner Fassbinder's "Despair" (1978). He worked with American expatriate director Joseph Losey on 12 of his British films, including "Accident" (1967) and "The Go-Between" (1971).

Beloin, Edmund

screenwriter
born: April 1, 1910, Bristol CT
died: May 26, 1992, Pompano Beach FL, age 82
educ: NYU (medicine); Columbia University (medicine)

Hollywood screenwriter of the 1940s, 50s and 60s who started writing short stories and book reviews while a medical student. After writing jokes for Jack Benny's highly popular radio series,

Beloin got his start in Hollywood crafting the screenplays for two Benny vehicles, "Buck Benny Rides Again" (1940) and "Love Thy Neighbor" (1941). He would specialize in comedy throughout his career, penning such enjoyable films as "Lady on a Train" (1945) and "All in a Night's Work" (1961). Beloin collaborated on a number of films with Bob Hope ("My Favorite Brunette" 1947, "Road to Rio" 1947, "The Great Lover" 1949) and Jerry Lewis ("The Sad Sack" 1957, "Don't Give Up the Ship" 1959, "Visit to a Small Planet" 1960). In the 60s he also wrote for the TV comedies "Family Affair", "The Lucy Show" and "My Three Sons".

Benedek, Laslo
director; also producer
born: Benedek, Laszlo, March 5, 1907, Budapest, Hungary
died: March 11, 1992, Bronx NY, age 85
educ: University of Vienna (psychiatry)

Began his career at UFA and, after brief stints in France and England, arrived in the US in 1937. Benedek made his directorial debut a decade later with the Frank Sinatra vehicle "The Kissing Bandit" (1948) and teamed up with producer Stanley Kramer twice, for a faithful, if pedestrian adaptation of Arthur Miller's "Death of a Salesman" (1951) and "The Wild One" (1954), which remains a signature film of the 1950s, largely thanks to the charismatic presence of Marlon Brando as the silent, rebel biker. From the mid-1950s Benedek worked primarily in TV.

Berkeley, George
actor; also stage director
born: c. 1922
died: February 1, 1992, Glendale CA, age 70

Character actor who scored a slew of bit parts in TV and films, including Mel Brooks' "Life Stinks" (1991) and Samuel Fuller's "Pickup On South Street" (1953). For the most part Berkley stomped the boards or directed legit shows.

Blackwood, Christian
documentarian; also director photography, director
born: c. 1942, Berlin
died: July 22, 1992, New York NY, age 50

Child actor turned documentarian and director of photography whose career spanned 40 films over a 25-year period. Among his work as a cinematographer is Charlotte Zwerin's haunting "Thelonius Monk: Straight, No Chaser". As a documentarian, Blackwood generally focused on artists and filmmakers. His films include "Observations Under The Volcano" (1988), a behind-the-scenes look at director John Huston's adaptation of Malcolm Lowry's novel; "Roger Corman: Hollywood's Wild Angel" (1978); and "Signed, Lino Brocka" (1987), a portrait of the eminent Filipino director. His "Private Conversations: On the Set of 'Death of a Salesman'" (1985), a documentary about the filming of German director Volker Schlondorff's interpretation of the Arthur Miller play, won the grand prize at the Sundance Film Festival.

Bletcher, Arline
actress
born: c. 1893
died: July 3, 1992, Los Angeles CA, age 99

Former vaudevillian and Ziegfeld Girl who moved with her husband Billy Bletcher to Los Angeles, where she performed as a Bathing Beauty and he as a stock comic in Mack Sennett's repertory company. Bletcher never gained the prominence of her husband but worked with him in a series of silent comic two-reelers and features before he was teamed with Billy Gilbert by producer Hal Roach. Later Bletcher acted on the TV series "Wagon Train" (1957-65) for five years and played small film roles in "Thoroughly Modern Millie" (1967), "Pete's Dragon" (1977) and "Heaven Can Wait" (1978).

Booth, Shirley
actress, comedienne
born: Ford, Thelma Booth, August 30, 1898, New York NY
died: October 16, 1992, North Chatham MA, age 94

Celebrated Broadway star of long standing who graced two TV series and a handful of films with her warm, if often acerbic, presence. Leaving high school to pursue acting, Booth trod the boards in over 600 plays in stock before her career really got off the ground. Her Broadway debut came in the 1925 "Hell's Bells" (which also featured newcomer Humphrey Bogart) but it wasn't until a decade later that she enjoyed her first major success in George Abbott's Runyonesque comedy, "Three Men on a Horse". Booth's fortunes improved considerably after she originated the role of intrepid news photographer Liz Imbrie in the Broadway smash "The Philadelphia Story", starring Katharine Hepburn. Other notable Broadway roles followed: a wisecracking writer in "My Sister Eileen" (1940); an anti-fascist teacher in "Tomorrow the World" (1943); a vivacious gossip columnist in "Hollywood Pinafore" (1945); and, in a Tony-winning performance, the sophisticated secretary to a U.S. congresswoman in "Goodbye, My Fancy". The most important role of Booth's career came in 1950 with the Broadway production of William Inge's "Come Back, Little Sheba", in which she played a slovenly, gabby housewife wistfully hanging onto her illusions (embodied in her runaway dog, Sheba) and inadvertently driving her husband to drink. She recreated the role in Daniel Mann's film version and acted in several other features, notably "The Matchmaker" (1958), based on the Thornton Wilder play which later became "Hello, Dolly". For many TV viewers Booth is best remembered as "Hazel" (1961-66), the housekeeper extraordinaire forever warning "Mr. B" (Don DeFore) about the dangers of domestic life and undercutting his authority at every opportunity.

Brand, Neville
actor
born: August 13, 1921, Kewanee IL
died: April 16, 1992, Sacramento CA, age 70

Highly decorated WWII soldier who carved a niche as a tough-guy character actor, beginning with a role as a hood in the film noir, "D.O.A." (1950). Brand's rough-hewn features helped him project an air of menace in hard-boiled dramas, war films and westerns, most notably as the convict representative in "Riot in Cell Block 11" (1954). He portrayed gangster Al Capone three times: in "The George Raft Story" (1961), "The Scarface Mob" (1962) and TV's "The Untouchables". Brand also starred as a rowdy, occasionally bumbling Texas Ranger in the 1960s western series, "Laredo".

Brodie, Steve
actor
born: Stevens, John, November 25, 1919, Eldorado, KS
died: January 9, 1992, West Hills, CA, age 72

Rugged leading man of B Westerns and supporting player in numerous films who worked with some of Hollywood's most celebrated genre directors—Anthony Mann, Samuel Fuller, Mark Robson, and Jacques Tourneur. Brodie also appeared in several social problem pictures such as "Crossfire" (1947) and "Home of the Brave" (1949).

Brooks, Richard
director; also screenwriter, producer, novelist
born: May 18, 1912, Philadelphia PA
died: March 11, 1992, Beverly Hills CA, age 79
educ: Temple University, Philadelphia
Former radio journalist and Marine who co-wrote several hard-boiled, realistic dramas including Jules Dassin's "Brute Force" (1947), John Huston's "Key Largo" (1948) and Stuart Heisler's "Storm Warning" (1951). Brooks made his directorial debut in 1950 with the political thriller "Crisis" and turned out a number of taut, male-oriented features before landing in the spotlight with "The Blackboard Jungle" (1955). The violent, gritty schoolroom drama dealt with juvenile deliquency and racial tensions, catapulted Sidney Poitier to fame, and virtually introduced rock 'n' roll to the screen as Bill Haley's "Rock Around the Clock" blasted over the credits. Brooks consolidated his position in the front rank of Hollywood directors with several fine literary adaptations. "Elmer Gantry" (1960) was an explosive, award-winning version of Sinclair Lewis's expose of evangelists; "Cat on a Hot Tin Roof" (1958) and "Sweet Bird of Youth" (1962) were superb, if relatively tame, adaptations of the Tennessee Williams plays; and "In Cold Blood" (1967) was a suitably noirish treatment of Truman Capote's reality-based novel. Beginning with "The Professionals" (1966) and continuing through "Bite the Bullet" (1977), Brooks developed an interesting take on the western genre, using the frontier experience as a context to explore the relationship between tradition and change. His career tailed off in the 70s, though "Looking for Mr. Goodbar" (1977) featured a bravura central performance by Diane Keaton. In 1960 Brooks married actress Jean Simmons, who starred in his "Elmer Gantry" (1960) and "The Happy Ending" (1969).

Brown, Georgia
actress, singer
born: Klot, Lillian, October 21, 1933, London, England
died: July 5, 1992, London, England, age 58
First attracted attention on the nightclub and cabaret scene for her bluesy jazz intonations and later enjoyed considerable success on the Broadway and London stages. Brown made her breakthrough with a London staging of "The Threepenny Opera" in 1956 and is perhaps best remembered for originating the role of Nancy in the smash London and Broadway hit, "Oliver!". (She lost out to Shani Wallis when Carol Reed adapted the musical to film in 1968.) Although Brown began acting in films in 1957, the 1970s marked her busiest period. Typically cast in blowsy, bawdy roles, she enlivened such features as "The Fixer" (1968), "Tales That Witness Madness" (1973) and "The Seven Per-Cent Solution" (1976) and also appeared in the PBS miniseries "Shoulder to Shoulder" (1975) and "The Rebel" (1976). Late in life Brown returned to the London stage to perform in "42nd Street" and "Greek", and to Broadway for the revival of "Threepenny" starring Sting. She also lent her distinctively husky voice to the animated TV programs "Rick Moranis in Gravedale High" and the short-lived "Fish Police" before her sudden death at age 58.

Brown, James
actor
aka: Brown, Jim
born: March 22, 1920, Desdemona TX
died: April 11, 1992, Woodland Hills CA, age 72
After a brief stint as a teenage tennis player, Brown turned to acting in the early 1940s, mostly in B action films. He starred as the young romantic lead in "Our Hearts Were Young and Gay" (1944) and its sequel, "Our Hearts Were Growing Up" (1946), but is best known as Lt. Rip Masters, father figure to a young boy at an Old West outpost in the children's TV series "The Adventures of Rin Tin Tin". (The show ran from 1954 to 1959 and was later syndicated, with new introductions featuring Brown, in the 1970s.) Brown retired from film in the 1960s to become a manufacturer of body-building equipment but returned to the screen with a part in the spoof "Whiffs" (1975). Brown acted under the names James and Jim Brown and is not to be confused with black athlete-turned-film star Jim Brown or soul recording star James Brown.

Brown, Lucille
actress; also singer, dancer
aka: Brown, Lucille E.
born: c. 1918
died: August 21, 1992, Buffalo NY, age 74
Black American actress, singer and dancer who began her career at age 5 when Hal Roach took her out of an orphanage to play Farina for about a year in his "Our Gang" comedies. Brown's career in film was rather brief, though she did small roles in the later all-Black features "The Green Pastures" (1936) and "Stormy Weather" (1943). Brown also sang and danced for many years as the headliner of Babe Barlow and the Sugar Drops. Not to be confused with white American actress Lucille Brown, leading lady of a handful of modest films in the 1930s.

Carnovsky, Morris
actor; also stage director
born: September 5, 1897, St. Louis MO
died: September 1, 1992, Easton CT, age 94
Distinguished American stage actor with a background in Yiddish-language theater. Carnovsky worked with the Theater Guild on Broadway in the 1920s before becoming involved with New York's Group Theater, for whom he originated the roles of Dr. Levine in "Men in White", Jacob in "Awake and Sing!" and Mr. Bonaparte in "Golden Boy". In the late 1930s Carnovsky gravitated to Hollywood, where he began with a memorable turn as author Anatole France in the Oscar-winning "The Life of Emile Zola" (1937) and expounded his anti-fascist views in Lewis Milestone's "Edge of Darkness" (1943) and Herbert Biberman's "The Master Race" (1944). Compact and dignified whether playing heroes or villains, Carnovsky appeared in several fine films of the 40s and 50s including "Cornered" (1945), "Dead Reckoning" (1947), "Thieves Highway" (1949), "Gun Crazy" (1950) and the touching drama, "Our Vines Have Tender Grapes" (1945). Shortly after completing a role in Stanley Kramer's "Cyrano de Bergerac" (1950), Carnovsky was called upon to testify before the House Un-American Activities Committee. Refusing to compromise his rights or to vilify colleagues, Carnovsky was blacklisted but, partly thanks to the help of John Houseman, was able to revive his career in live theater. Portraying characters from Shylock to Lear (at the American Shakespeare Festival) and enjoying many of the plums of the classical and contemporary repertory during the next three decades, Carnovsky enjoyed his career peak late in life, though American films of that period were denied a singular talent.

Carrol, Regina
actress, entertainer; also TV host, columnist
born: Gelfan, Regina, c. 1943, Boston MA
died: November 4, 1992, St. George UT, age 49
Stage, TV and film actress of the 1960s and 70s best remembered by cultists for her work on the fringes of the industry. Carrol made her feature acting debut in "The Beat Generation" (1959), under her birth name, Regina Gelfan. During the 60s, she adopted the last name Carrol and appeared in several mainstream Hollywood films: John Ford's "Two Rode Together" (1961), "Viva Las Vegas" (1964) with Elvis Presley, and Sydney Pollack's directo-

rial debut, "The Slender Thread" (1965). She made TV guest appearances throughout the 60s on "Route 66", "Ozzie and Harriet" and "The Dinah Shore Show". In 1969 Carrol met her future husband, exploitation auteur Al Adamson, and subsequently worked on many of his films. Their collaborations included "Satan's Sadists" (1969), "Dracula vs. Frankenstein" (1971),"The Female Bunch" (1971), and "Blazing Stewardesses" (1975). Carrol made her final film appearance in Adamson's "Carnival Magic" (1982). Her later entertainment career primarily consisted of work on stage and in cabaret.

Carter, Beverly
actress; also TV writer
born: c. 1941
died: June 8, 1992, Athens, Greece, age 51
Actress who appeared in a host of TV series, including "Mannix" and "Bonanza", and films including "Herbie Rides Again" (1974). Carter later became a writer for TV's "Fantasy Island".

Cattani, Rico
producer, executive; also actor, manager
born: c. 1928, Italy
died: November 12, 1992, Los Angeles CA, age 64
A show business veteran for 50 years as an actor, producer and manager, Cattani formed his own production company, Cattani Films, after serving in various capacities for a number of other producers. Born in Italy, Cattani emigrated to America in 1957 and worked as a character actor in film and TV. He had a recurring role on "Combat", a top-rated ABC World War II drama of the 1960s. Cattani's feature credits include John Boorman's "Point Blank", Roger Corman's "The St. Valentine's Day Massacre" (both 1967) and "The Bamboo Saucer" (1968). He also appeared in the TV movies "The Smugglers" (1968) and "Advice to the Lovelorn" (1981).

Chaliapin Jr, Feodor
actor
aka: Chaliapin, Feodor
born: c. 1905, Moscow, Russia
died: September 17, 1992, Rome, Italy, age 87
Son and namesake of the internationally renowned operatic bass, Chaliapin moved to Hollywood from Paris to get out from under his father's shadow and began playing bit parts in silent films. He carved a niche for himself as a reliable character actor, one of his finest moments being his death in the arms of Gary Cooper at the start of "For Whom the Bell Tolls" (1943). After WWII Chaliapin moved to Italy, where he continued his film acting career. It was not until late in life, though, that he really made his mark, when an ill John Huston had to back out of playing the blind, murderous monk Jorge of Burgos in "The Name of the Rose" (1986). His career enjoyed a brief resurgence after that, and in "Stanley and Iris" he enjoyed a fine part as Robert De Niro's father. Chaliapin's best known role was his delightful turn as the dog-walking grandfather in "Moonstruck" (1987), forever greeting the moon with cries of "La luna! La luna!".

Clarke, Mae
actress
born: Klotz, Mary, August 16, 1910, Philadelphia PA
died: April 29, 1992, Woodland Hills CA, age 81
Blonde leading lady of the 1930s, a former cabaret dancer and Broadway actress. With attractive but unremarkable looks, Clarke kept very busy during her first decade in films, most notably as the woman on the receiving end of James Cagney's quicksilver temper. In "The Public Enemy" (1931), the film which made Cagney a star, Clarke received the famous grapefruit-in-the-face, and in "Lady Killer" (1933), Cagney dragged Clarke around by the hair. Clarke also suffered memorably at the hands of Frankenstein's monster; Boris Karloff carried her off on her wedding day in James Whale's marvelous 1931 film. Whale also gave Clarke a much more challenging role in "Waterloo Bridge" the same year. In the first screen version (twice remade with Vivien Leigh and Leslie Caron) of Robert Sherwood's play, Clarke was superb as the young woman forced into prostitution during WWI. Clarke appeared mainly in supporting roles from the 40s onward.

Clatworthy, Robert
art director; also production designer
born: Clatworthy, William Robert, c. 1911
died: March 2, 1992, age 80
Veteran Hollywood art director whose outstanding work includes Orson Welles' "Touch of Evil" (1958), Jack Clayton's "The Incredible Shrinking Man" (1957) and Alfred Hitchcock's "Psycho" (1960). Clatworthy won an Academy Award for his work on Stanley Kramer's all-star "Ship of Fools" in 1965.

Clore, Leon
producer
born: c. 1919, Brighton, England
died: February 9, 1992, London, England, age 73
Producer of commercials, documentaries and feature films who was instrumental in the careers of directors Lindsay Anderson and Karel Reisz.

Combs, Frederick
actor, acting teacher; also playwright, director
born: c. 1935
died: September 19, 1992, Los Angeles, age 57
Actor, playwright, director and acting teacher originated the role of Donald in the original Off-Broadway production of Mart Crowley's landmark gay-themed play, "The Boys in the Band" (1968). Combs went on to recreate the role in London and in William Friedkin's 1970 feature film. He appeared on TV in the soap "The Young and the Restless" and in various made-for-TV movies and miniseries including "The Users" (1978), "Roots: The Next Generations" (1979), and three titles directed by John Erman: "Moviola: The Silent Lovers" (1980), "Another Woman's Child" (1983), and "David" (1988). Combs also wrote several plays including "The Children's Mass", which he directed at the Cast Theater in Hollywood.

Connors, Chuck
actor
born: Connors, Kevin Joseph, April 10, 1921, Bay Ridge, Brooklyn NY
died: November 10, 1992, Los Angeles CA, age 71
educ: Seton Hall College, South Orange NJ
Imposing, lantern-jawed leading man of TV, most famous as Lucas McCain, the righteous, chain-smoking protagonist of ABC-TV's immensely popular "The Rifleman" (1958-63). Connors' six-foot-five frame helped him gain a position as a pro basketball player on the Boston Celtics after a stint in the military during WWII. He soon switched to baseball, playing for the Brooklyn Dodgers and the Chicago Cubs, but he was more distinguished for his comical sideline antics than his baseball prowess. Demoted to the Cubs' minor league farm, the old Los Angeles Angels of the Pacific Coast League, Connors took advantage of his new location to begin an acting career, appearing in at least a dozen features before his star-making TV role. "The Rifleman" featured the athlete-turned-actor as New Mexico homesteader

Lucas McCain, a diligent single father whose child-rearing duties were enlivened by gun battles with ornery varmints whom he dispatched with his trusty modified Winchester rifle. Several notable directors of genre features—Sam Peckinpah, Budd Boetticher, Joseph H. Lewis, Ida Lupino—toiled on this landmark TV Western. Connors's subsequent series included the cop/attorney drama "Arrest and Trial" (1963-64), opposite Ben Gazzara; the Westerns "Branded" (1965-66) and "Cowboy in Africa" (1967-68); the syndicated documentary "The Thrill Seekers" (1973), which he hosted and narrated; "The Yellow Rose" (1983-84); and the short-lived "Werewolf" (1987). TV movies include "The Police Story" (the 1973 pilot movie for the popular TV series), "The Horror at 37,000 Feet" (1973), "Banjo Hackett: Roamin' Free" (1976) and "Roots" (1977). Connors contemplated entering politics, but found politicians even more ornery than his old sagebrush adversaries. In 1973, at a party at President Nixon's vacation home, he met an unlikely fan—Soviet leader Leonid Brezhnev, who greeted his favorite actor with a big Russian bear hug. Connors presented Brezhnev with two six-guns. He was also on hand to honor his actor-turned-President friend on a 1985 CBS special entitled "An All-Star Party For 'Dutch' Reagan".

Cooper, Ralph

master of ceremonies; also actor, screenwriter
born: c. 1910s, New York NY
died: August 4, 1992, New York NY, age 80s

Best known for founding (in 1934) and emceeing the Amateur Night at the historic Apollo Theater, where talents such as Sarah Vaughan, Ella Fitzgerald and Billie Holiday received early exposure. Cooper also played supporting roles in Hollywood features such as Josef von Sternberg's "Blonde Venus" (1932), Henry King's "Lloyd's of London" (1936) and Irving Cummings' "White Hunter" (1936), and choreographed Cummings' Shirley Temple vehicle, "Poor Little Rich Girl" (1936). The star of several films produced for segregated Black audiences in the 1930s, Cooper appropriately served as special consultant to "The Cotton Club" (1984), Francis Ford Coppola's ode to 1930s Harlem night life.

Corday, Rita

actress
aka: Corday, Paula; Croset, Paule; Croset, Rita
born: Teipotemarga, Jeanne Paule, 1924, Switzerland
died: November 23, 1992, Century City CA, age 68

B-film lead who decorated five of RKO's "Falcon" detective films before signing with Universal to perform similar duties in Max Ophuls' "The Exile" (1947). Briefly using the professional names Paule and Rita Croset, Rita Corday eventually became Paula Corday when she played second leads in such light fare as "Because You're Mine" and "You for Me" (both 1952). Corday decorated two Boris Karloff chillers: she played the romantic lead in "The Black Castle" (1952) and a young mother desperately trying to arrange surgery for her crippled daughter in producer Val Lewton's "The Body Snatcher" (1945). After marrying producer Harold Nebenzal in 1954, Corday retired from the screen, making only occasional TV appearances thereafter.

Cristaldi, Franco

producer
born: October 3, 1924, Turin, Italy
died: July 1, 1992, Monte Carlo, Monaco, age 68
educ: Turin University (law)

Respected European producer who has backed films by most of the neo-realists and other major post-war Italian directors, including Luchino Visconti ("White Nights" 1957), Mario Monicelli ("Big Deal on Madonna Street" 1958), Marco Bellocchio, Francesco Rosi and Federico Fellini ("Amarcord" 1974 and "The Ship Sails On" 1983). Formerly married to Claudia Cardinale.

Cronin, Laurel

actress; also singer, dancer
born: c. 1939
died: October 26, 1992, Chicago, age 53

Actress, singer and dancer who was a fixture on the Chicago stage for 30 years. Cronin's feature credits include Steven Spielberg's "Hook" (1991), "Beethoven" (1992), Frank Oz's "Housesitter" (1992) and Penny Marshall's "A League of Their Own" (1992). She was a regular on the short-lived Blake Edwards-produced TV sitcom, "Julie", and her other TV credits include "Murphy Brown", "Brooklyn Bridge" and "Baby Talk", as well as the small-screen crime movies "Lady Blue", "Dillinger" and "Crime Story", the Abel Ferrara-directed pilot for the Michael Mann-produced TV series.

Daney, Serge

critic
born: c. 1944
died: June 11, 1992, Paris, age 48

French film critic whose career began during the heyday of the New Wave and who, like many of his peers, was particularly enamoured of Hollywood films. In 1964, Daney visited the dream factory itself, where he met some of the stars he admired the most—including Jerry Lewis. Daney's interview with Lewis was published in "Cahiers du Cinema", the influential journal which published the likes of Truffaut, Godard and Chabrol. This began a fruitful association with the publication which culminated in his taking over the editorial reins of "Cahiers" in the eventful year of 1968, when the magazine became highly politicized. Daney joined the daily newspaper "Liberation" as a critic and editorialist in 1982 while remaining editor of "Cahiers", and began a new film quarterly called "Trafic" in 1991.

Danova, Cesare

actor
born: March 1, 1926, Rome, Italy
died: March 19, 1992, Los Angeles CA, age 66

Suavely handsome leading man in Italian films of the late 1940s and 50s who signed with MGM in 1956. A prolific actor who was featured in more than 350 films and TV productions, Danova appeared in supporting roles in such Hollywood productions as "Tender is the Night" (1962), "Gidget Goes to Rome" (1963) and "Viva Las Vegas" (1964). He brought a smooth sophistication to the role of Harvey Keitel's mob-connected uncle Giovanni in Martin Scorsese's "Mean Streets" (1973). A frequent TV performer, Danova starred on his own series "Garrison's Gorillas" (1967) and was a guest on "The Rifleman", "Mission: Impossible" and "Murder, She Wrote", among others.

Danton, Ray

actor; also director
born: Danton, Raymond, September 19, 1931, New York NY
died: February 11, 1992, Los Angeles CA, age 60
educ: Carnegie Institute of Technology

Handsome lead with dark good looks and sleek black hair who began his career as a child actor on radio and appeared in early live TV dramas in New York. After making his film debut in "Chief Crazy Horse" (1954), Danton gained notice for his portrayal of Lillian Roth's first love in the soapy biopic "I'll Cry Tomorrow" (1955). Danton is best remembered for his portrayal of ruthless mobster "Legs" Diamond in both Budd Boetticher's gangster melodrama, "The Rise and Fall of Legs Diamond"

(1960), and the 1961 biopic of gangster Dutch Schultz, "Portrait of a Mobster". That same year he also starred in the title role of "The George Raft Story". In 1964 Danton moved to Italy, where he starred in numerous low-budget films and turned to directing with "Deathmaster" (1972). He formed his own production company in Barcelona before returning in 1975 to the US, where he become a TV director for Universal. Danton helmed episodes of "Cagney and Lacey", "Quincy", "Fame" and "Dallas" and served as supervising producer on "The New Mike Hammer" TV series (1986-87). Danton was at one time married to actress Julie Adams.

Darby, Ken

musical director, conductor, composer
born: c. 1909
died: January 24, 1992, Sherman Oaks CA, age 82

Three-time Oscar winner for his lush musical adaptations of Broadway musicals to film: "The King and I" (1956) and "Camelot" (1967), both in collaboration with Alfred Newman; and "Porgy and Bess" (1959), with Andre Previn. A leading musical scorer, conductor and songwriter in films from the late 1940s through the 60s, Darby wrote songs for "River of No Return", "Garden of Evil" (both 1954), "The Lieutenant Wore Skirts" (1955) and "Villa" (1958). He served as musical associate on the 1962 remake of Rodgers and Hammerstein's "State Fair" and, teamed with Alfred Newman, was Oscar-nominated for scoring Rodgers and Hammerstein's "South Pacific" (1958) and "Flower Drum Song" (1961) as well as "How the West Was Won" (1963).

Darrid, William

executive; also actor, novelist, scriptwriter, drama coach
born: c. 1923
died: July 11, 1992, Santa Monica CA, age 69

Actor, writer and studio executive who achieved moderate success in all three fields. A Neighborhood Playhouse alumnus, Darrid the actor worked almost exclusively on stage ("Inherit the Wind", "Reclining Figure") and TV. After moderate success stomping the boards he taught for a time at Bennington College and then started producing plays on Broadway, where his credits include "The Disenchanted", "The Andersonville Trial", and "A Cook for Mr. General". Shifting career gears yet again, the versatile Darrid later became a vice president at MCA/Universal, heading the East Coast literary and theater division in New York. In the 1970s, Darrid and his wife, Diana Douglas, moved to L.A. to focus on novel and script writing. His script based on the life of poet Hart Crane is being posthumously produced by stepson Michael Douglas's production company.

Dehner, John

actor; also animator
born: Forkum, John, November 23, 1915, Staten Island NY
died: February 4, 1992, Santa Barbara CA, age 76

Tall, distinguished-looking character player usually cast as villains or humorless authority figures. Dehner began his career as an animation assistant at Walt Disney Studios, worked as an Army publicist during WWII and, as a Los Angeles radio news reporter, editor and announcer, netted his station a Peabody Award for his coverage of the first UN conference in San Francisco in the late 1940s. Dehner started acting in films in the mid-1940s, eventually appearing in over 100 features, mostly westerns or action films. As sheriff Pat Garrett, he proved a notable foil to Paul Newman's Billy the Kid in Arthur Penn's "The Left-Handed Gun" (1958). Once voted "best radio voice" by "Radio Life Magazine", Dehner was a prolific radio performer during the 1950s, starring as J.B. Kendall, a Brit in the American West, on "Frontier Gentleman" and as Paladin on "Have Gun Will Travel". Throughout the 60s and 70s he made regular appearances on TV series including "The Westerner" (1960), "The Roaring Twenties" (1960-62), "The Don Knotts Show" (1970-71) "The Doris Day Show" (1971-73) and "Big Hawaii" (1977). Later roles included Secretary of State Dean Acheson in the miniseries "The Missiles of October" (1974); Admiral Ernest King in the miniseries "The Winds of War" (1983); Henry Luce in "The Right Stuff" (1983); and the judge in "Jagged Edge" (1985).

Delerue, Georges

composer; also conductor
born: March 12, 1925, Roubaix, France
died: March 20, 1992, Los Angeles CA, age 67
educ: Paris Conservatoire

Acclaimed international composer who first gained prominence with the emergence of the French New Wave. Delerue's prolific output includes ballets, operas, chamber pieces, orchestral works, a series of vocal melodies for the poems of Paul Eluard, and music for TV and plays. In the 1950s Delerue scored over 20 short films, including some documentaries directed by Alain Resnais. He moved into features with Pierre Kast's "Le Bel Age" (1959) and contributed memorable, evocative scores to New Wave features like Agnes Varda's "Opera-Mouffe" (1958), Resnais's "Hiroshima Mon Amour" (1959, the waltz theme on the jukebox), Truffaut's "Jules et Jim" (1961) and Godard's "Le Mepris/Contempt" (1963). Delerue's first US film was John Huston's "A Walk with Love and Death" (1969) and highlights of his prolific international career include "A Man for All Seasons" (1966), "Women in Love" (1969), "Julia" (1977) and "Platoon" (1986). His score for "A Little Romance" won the 1979 Oscar. Delerue's most frequent collaborators were Truffaut and Philippe De Broca, for whom he scored 16 films.

Dennis, Sandy

actress
born: Dennis, Sandra Dale, April 27, 1937, Hastings NE
died: March 2, 1992, Westport CT, age 54
educ: Wesleyan College, Nebraska; University of Nebraska; Actors Studio

Method-trained critics' darling of the 1960s who first made her name on Broadway with Tony Award-winning performances in "A Thousand Clowns" (1962) and "Any Wednesday" (1964). Dennis's high-pitched, neurotic style lent itself to quirky, eccentric roles in films such as "Splendor in the Grass" (1961, her debut). Her memorable performance as the irritating yet vulnerable young faculty wife in "Who's Afraid of Virginia Woolf" (1967) earned her an Oscar for best supporting actress, and her portrayal of an idealistic teacher in an inner-city school in "Up the Down Staircase" (1967) won her a best actress accolade from the Moscow Film Festival. Dennis turned in some fine performances in later films, notably "Come Back to the Five and Dime, Jimmy Dean, Jimmy Dean" (1982) and, in a hilarious cameo, Bob Balaban's overlooked "Parents" (1989). She made her final onscreen cameo as the wife of Charles Bronson in Sean Penn's directorial debut, "The Indian Runner" (1991), before her death the following year from ovarian cancer at age 54.

Deutsch, Helen

screenwriter; also lyricist
born: c. 1906, New York NY
died: March 14, 1992, Manhattan NY, age 85
educ: Barnard College

Award-winning screenwriter of the 1940s, 50s and 60s, primarily with MGM. A prolific writer who never learned to type but dictated her stories into a Dictaphone, Deutsch turned out more than 20 short stories for magazines and hundreds of newspaper articles as well as several plays and teleplays. She began her career in the theater, first managing the Provincetown Players and working as a publicist, later covering the theater beat for the "New York Herald-Tribune" and the "New York Times" and working for the Theater Guild. Deutsch entered films in 1944, collaborating on the adaptation of Enid Bagnold's novel "National Velvet" which catapulted the young Elizabeth Taylor to stardom. In the same year she scripted "The Seventh Cross", which starred Spencer Tracy as a refugee from a Nazi death camp. Deutsch's work ranged from espionage fluff ("Golden Earrings" 1947) to epic adventures ("King Solomon's Mines" 1950), psychological melodrama ("I'll Cry Tomorrow" 1955) and musicals ("The Unsinkable Molly Brown" 1964). Her best-loved film is "Lili" (1953), the charming classic about a childlike waif (Leslie Caron) smitten with a womanizing magician and loved by a crippled puppeteer (Mel Ferrer). Deutsch not only wrote the lyrics for the movie's hit song "Hi-Lili, Hi-Lo" but later wrote the libretto for "Carnival", the 1961 Bob Merrill Broadway musical based on the film.

Dietrich, Marlene

actress; also singer
aka: Von Losch, Maria Magdalena
born: Dietrich, Maria Magdalene, December 27, 1901, Berlin, West Germany
died: May 6, 1992, Paris, France
educ: Hochschule fur Musik, Berlin (violin); Max Reinhardt's Deutsche Theaterschule

There are only a handful of actors in the history of film whose personalities far extend the film frame, and Marlene Dietrich is one of these. More than just an actress, Dietrich has become one of the most recognizable figures of the 20th century—a Hollywood star who never imagined her profession to be more important than it was. After studying acting under the renowned Max Reinhardt, Dietrich began her film career in 1923 with "The Little Napoleon". She made over a dozen German films, including "Tragodie der Liebe" (1923), Alexander Korda's "A Modern Du Barry" and "Madame Wants No Children" (both 1926), and Maurice Tourneur's "The Ship of Lost Men" (1929), before being discovered by American director Josef von Sternberg, who was in Germany to cast the female lead in "The Blue Angel" (1930). The character of Lola Lola, a dance-hall girl who could drive a professor to the most extreme humiliations in the name of love, was perfect for Dietrich. With her sultry version of "Falling in Love Again," the entire world fell in love, for the first time, with Marlene Dietrich. Over the next five years at Paramount Pictures, Dietrich and von Sternberg sustained one of film's greatest creative collaborations through six films ("Morocco" 1930, "Dishonored" 1931, "Shanghai Express" 1932, "Blonde Venus" 1932, "The Scarlet Empress" 1934 and "The Devil is a Woman" 1935), each one considerably more abstract and several less commercially successful than "The Blue Angel". After the financial if not artistic failure of "The Devil Is a Woman", Dietrich and von Sternberg parted ways. In the ensuing decades Dietrich would act for some of the greatest directors—Ernst Lubitsch, Rene Clair, Raoul Walsh, Billy Wilder, Alfred Hitchcock, Fritz Lang and Orson Welles—and co-star with some of the greatest actors—Charles Boyer, James Stewart, John Wayne, Edward G. Robinson, Jean Gabin, Spencer Tracy and Burt Lancaster. During the early 1940s, her on-screen accomplishments were often overshadowed by her contributions to the war effort. After turning down a lucrative offer from Hitler to make films for her Nazi homeland, the anti-Fascist Dietrich retaliated by raising the spirits of American servicemen in numerous USO appearances. In the early 1960s Dietrich decided to bid farewell to the screen, deciding that her advancing years would be less obvious as a concert singer than as an actress. Her last film appearance, in "Just a Gigolo" (1979) opposite David Bowie, was only a brief one. She later became increasingly reclusive, refusing to be photographed. Though she was the subject of the 1984 documentary "Marlene", which she commissioned Maximillian Schell to direct, Dietrich refused to appear on camera.

Dixon, Joan

actress
born: c. 1930
died: February 20, 1992, Los Angeles CA, age 61

B movie actress of the 1950s whose work includes the films "Gun Play" and "Pistol Harvest" (both 1951).

Drake, Alfred

actor, singer
born: Capurro, Alfred, October 7, 1914, New York NY
died: July 25, 1992, New York NY, age 77
educ: Brooklyn College (English)

Actor and baritone who played leading roles in landmark Broadway shows including "Oklahoma!" and "Kiss Me Kate". Drake's good-humored performance as Hajj, a street poet made Emir of Bagdad for a day, in the hit musical "Kismet" won him a well-deserved Tony in 1954. A commanding presence, Drake also performed well in straight drama, including several Shakesperean roles. He made regular TV appearances in the 1950s, sometimes in broadcast versions of his stage successes; the most notable of his few film roles was Claudius opposite Richard Burton's "Hamlet" (1964).

Dunne, Philip

director, screenwriter; also producer
born: February 11, 1908, New York NY
died: June 4, 1992, Malibu California, age 84
educ: Harvard

Began his Hollywood career as a scenarist in the mid-1930s and scripted a number of first-rate productions incuding "How Green Was My Valley" (1941), "The Ghost and Mrs. Muir" (1947) and "The Robe" (1953). Directing from 1954, Dunne turned out a series of smoothly crafted, finely acted dramas, notably "Hilda Crane" (1956), "Blue Denim" (1959) and the suspense-filled "Lisa" (1962). He also served as a speech writer on the presidential campaigns of Adlai Stevenson and John F. Kennedy.

Eagle, Arnold

cinematographer, editor; also documentary still photographer, documentarian
born: c. 1910, Hungary
died: October 25, 1992, New York NY, age 82

A still photographer, cinematographer, editor and documentarian, Eagle emigrated to the US from Hungary with his family in 1929. He joined the Film and Photo League, an organization concerned with documentary photographs and newsreels, in 1932 and began photographing Orthodox Jews on Manhattan's Lower East Side two years later. (The photographs were posthumously published in a volume entitled "At Home Only With God".) Eagle worked for the WPA, as a freelance photographer for "The Saturday Evening Post" and as a cinematographer for both avant-garde filmmaker Hans Richter ("Dreams that Money Can Buy" 1946) and documentarian Robert Flaherty ("Louisiana Story" 1948). He also made several documentaries of his own, taught filmmaking at New York's New School for Social Research and contributed to books about modern art and the Actors Studio.

Elliott, Denholm
actor
born: May 31, 1922, London
died: October 6, 1992, Ibiza, Spain, age 70
educ: Malvern College, England; RADA
Consummate character player who began his screen career playing earnest, dependable young Englishmen in films like "The Cruel Sea" (1953). Over the next four decades, Elliott perfected the image of the slightly disreputable, often boozy ex-public school type, expertly playing a succession of rumpled conmen, journalists and professors. He won three British Film Awards for his roles in "Trading Places" (1983), "A Private Function" (1984) and "Defence of the Realm" (1985), and earned an Oscar nomination for his portrayal of Julian Sands's slightly shabby academic father in "A Room With a View" (1986). Modern American audiences know Elliott best as Marcus Brody, Harrison Ford's mentor and colleague in "Raiders of the Lost Ark" (1981) and "Indiana Jones and the Last Crusade" (1989). Elliott was married to first wife actress Virginia McKenna from 1954-56.

Enright, Dan
producer
born: c. 1918
died: May 22, 1992, Los Angeles California, age 74
Prolific TV producer responsible for several 1950s quiz shows. Enright was executive producer of the Emmy Award-winning TV-movie "Caroline" (1990) as well as a handful of feature films, most notably "Making Mr. Right" (1987).

Ephron, Henry
screenwriter; also producer, playwright, director
born: May 26, 1912, Bronx NY
died: September 6, 1992, Los Angeles CA, age 81
educ: Cornell
Playwright turned screenwriter and producer, known for his teaming with wife Phoebe Wolkind. Among his credits as a screenwriter are Henry King's "Carousel" (1956), which also marked the start of his producing career, and the Walter Lang films "There's No Business Like Show Business" (1954) and the Tracy/Hepburn classic "Desk Set" (1957). Ephron's final screenplay "Captain Newman, M.D." (1963) received an Oscar nomination for best screenplay adaptation. He was the father of screenwriter/director Nora Ephron.

Ferrer, Jose
actor; also director, stage producer, writer
born: Ferrer De Otero y Cintron, Jose Vicente, January 8, 1912, Santurce, Puerto Rico
died: January 26, 1992, Coral Gables FL, age 80
educ: Princeton (architecture, music composition)
Protean Broadway actor-director-producer whose noteworthy stage performances include Iago to Paul Robeson's "Othello" (1942), a Tony-winning "Cyrano de Bergerac" (1946) and the prince in the Noel Coward musical, "The Girl Who Came to Supper" (1964). Ferrer made his Hollywood debut in "Joan of Arc" (1948) and, thanks to his sonorous voice and urbane manner, excelled at playing pedants and snobs, like the pompous Nazi professor in Mel Brooks's 1983 remake of "To Be or Not to Be". He proved his versatility, though, as the murderous hypnotist in "Whirlpool" (1949), the defending officer in "The Caine Mutiny" (1954), the sadistic Turkish bey in "Lawrence of Arabia" (1962) and the ham actor in "Enter Laughing" (1966). Ferrer's work as a film director has been generally undistinguished, one exception being his scathing look at the TV industry, "The Great Man" (1956). He was married to actress Uta Hagen (1938-48) and singer Rosemary Clooney (1953-66), and his son is character actor Miguel Ferrer.

Ffrangcon-Davies, Gwen
actress; also singer
born: January 25, 1891, London
died: January 27, 1992, Essex, England, age 101
Legendary figure of the English stage and, in the words of the "New York Times", "a last link with the world of Victorian theater". Ffrangcon-Davies's career spanned 80 years, from a walk-on part in a 1911 performance of "A Midsummer Night's Dream" to an appearance in the 1992 Sherlock Holmes TV movie "The Master Blackmailer". She was hailed as the finest Juliet of her generation for her 1924 portrayal opposite the 19-year-old John Gielgud. Ffrangcon-Davies retired from the stage in 1970 but continued to work in radio and TV until the end of her life. She was made a Dame of the British Empire in 1991 after much campaigning by senior theatrical figures. At age 100, she was the oldest person to be so honored.

Field, Virginia
actress
born: Field, Margaret Cynthia, November 4, 1917, London
died: January 2, 1992, Palm Springs CA, age 74
British-born blonde second lead of the 1930s and 40s who, after a brief stage career and appearances in a few British features, moved to Hollywood in 1935; after an impressive American debut as a frisky barmaid in "Lloyds of London" (1936) she was soon typecast as the "other woman" in numerous films. Field was featured in "Captain Fury" (1939), "Waterloo Bridge" (1940) and "A Connecticut Yankee in King Arthur's Court" (1949) and also appeared in the "Mr. Moto" series of detective films as well as "Charlie Chan at Monte Carlo" (1937). Her first husband was actor Paul Douglas and her third was actor Willard Parker.

Fielding, Sol Baer
producer
born: c. 1909, New York, NY
died: September 2, 1992, Reseda, CA, age 83
Graphic artist turned Hollywood producer who made only four features: "Bright Road" (1953), starring Dorothy Dandridge and a debuting Harry Belafonte; "Jeopardy" (1953), starring Barbara Stanwyk and directed by John Sturges; "Tennessee Champ" (1954), with Shelly Winters; and "Trooper Hook" (1957), a western starring Barbara Stanwyck and Joel McCrea. Fielding retired from the film business in 1957 to work as a newspaper cartoonist.

Foreman, John C.
producer; also executive
born: c. 1925, Idaho Falls ID
died: November 20, 1992, Beverly Hills CA, age 67
Prolific producer whose first film, "Butch Cassidy and the Sundance Kid" (1969), was made through Newman-Foreman Productions, a company he formed with Paul Newman. The film brought Foreman his first Oscar nomination; he earned a second for "Prizzi's Honor" (1985), the last of four John Huston films that he produced.

Frankovich, Mike J.
executive, producer; also screenwriter, radio producer, radio commentator
aka: Frankovich, M. J.
born: Frankovich, Mitchell John, September 29, 1910, Bisbee AZ
died: January 1, 1992, Los Angeles CA, age 82
educ: UCLA
Began his career as a radio producer and commentator and entered films in 1938 as a screenwriter. In the early 1950s, Frankovich became an independent producer based in Europe. He joined Columbia Pictures' international division in England in 1955 and was involved in the David Lean-Sam Spiegel epics "The Bridge on the River Kwai" (1957) and "Lawrence of Arabia" (1962) as well as "Dr. Strangelove" (1964). After returning to the US as Columbia's vice president in charge of production in 1964, Frankovich was responsible for such films as "Cat Ballou" (1965), "A Man For All Seasons" (1966), "Guess Who's Coming to Dinner", "In Cold Blood" (both 1967) and "Oliver!" (1968). In 1968 he resigned to produce his own films, often comedies and frequently starring Goldie Hawn; one notable exception was John Wayne's swan song, "The Shootist" (1976).

Gardenia, Vincent
actor
born: Scognamiglio, Vincente, January 7, 1922, Naples, Italy
died: December 9, 1992, Philadelphia PA, age 70
Short, stocky character player whose furrowed brow, hawk nose and hearty manner made him an instantly recognizable figure on stage, screen and TV from the late 1950s. Starting as a professional actor in his mid-30s, Gardenia played supporting roles on Broadway in "Volpone" (1957), "Only in America" (1959) and "Seidman and Son" (1962) and in films including "The Hustler" (1961, playing a bartender) and "Mad Dog Coll" (1961, playing Dutch Schultz). He won a Tony for his performance in Neil Simon's "The Prisoner of Second Avenue" in 1972 and earned a New York Film Critics Award and his first Oscar nomination as the baseball team manager in "Bang the Drum Slowly" (1973). Gardenia appeared in many other Simon plays including "God's Favorite", in a role written specially for him by the playwright. He is perhaps best known as Archie Bunker's loquacious, ever-singing, culinary buff neighbor Frank Lorenzo on the CBS perennial, "All in the Family". Gardenia spent a considerable portion of his career playing huffy but good-hearted police officers, detectives, and station captains in TV movies including "Cops" (1973), "Muggable Mary: Street Cop" (1982), "The Dark Mirror" (1984) and "Brass" (1985), and films such as "Heaven Can Wait" (1978). His final film appearance was as the father of Joe Pesci in "The Super" (1991).

Gonzalez Sinde, Jose
screenwriter, director, producer; also executive
born: Gonzalez Sinde, Jose Maria, c. 1941, Madrid, Spain
died: December 20, 1992, Madrid, Spain, age 51
educ: Official School of Cinematography, Madrid (production and screenwriting)
A significant figure in the Spanish film industry of the 1970s, 80s and 90s, Gonzalez Sinde enjoyed a long collaboration as a writer and producer with Oscar-winning director Jose Luis Garci. The pair co-wrote "Pending Exam," "Green Pastures" (1979), and "Alone In the Early Hours." Gonzalez Sinde produced more than 50 features including "El Love Feroz", "Cantico" and "The Executioners." His work as a director included "Long Live the Middle Class" (1980) and "By the Pale Light of the Moon" (1986). Gonzalez Sinde also co-founded the Spanish Academy of Motion Picture Arts and Sciences and served as the director of regional TV network Tele-Madrid.

Goodwin Jr., Thomas
producer
born: Goodwin Jr., Thomas Campbell, c. 1941, Baltimore MD
died: December 11, 1992, Washington, D.C., age 51
educ: Harvard, Cambridge MA
Washington, D.C.-based producer who specialized in educational programming and began his career with Andy Warhol at The Factory. Goodwin worked on the controversial documentary series, "An American Family" (1973) and co-founded State of the Art, Inc., an award-winning production company. Goodwin's production credits include "Ellington Live!", a program showcasing students at Duke Ellington's School of the Arts, and "We Dig Coal", a tribute to women coal miners. His final project was the Oscar-winning short documentary "Educating Peter", about a Down's syndrome child.

Gosha, Hideo
director
born: c. 1931, Tokyo, Japan
died: August 30, 1992, Japan, age 63
educ: Meiji University
Successful Japanese director best known for his work in the samurai genre. Gosha's feature credits include "Onimasa" (1982), "The Gates of Flesh" (1988) and "Four Days of Snow and Blood" (1989).

Greenbaum, Brian
executive producer; also line producer, production manager, location manager, location scout
born: c. 1962
died: February 27, 1992, New York City, age 30
educ: Brown University, Rhode Island; University of Bamberg, Germany; University of Paris
Location scout turned production manager on several German-financed films, including Waltraud Ehrhardt's "Katzenjammer Kids" (1988), which he also executive produced. Greenbaum served as line producer for "Metropolitan" (1990), Whit Stillman's acclaimed directorial debut, and was executive producer on "Poison" (1991), the controversial independent feature directed by Todd Haynes. He also produced several music videos and commercials.

Hanalis, Blanche
TV writer
aka: Wodin, Blanche Hanalis
born: c. 1919
died: July 27, 1992, Los Angeles CA, age 73
Veteran TV writer known for warm-hearted family fare, biopics of great women and tales of remarkable little girls. Hanalis's greatest success was in developing the long-running TV series "Little House on the Prairie", which made former "Bonanza" star Michael Landon into a TV writer/director of renown. Her first major job in the industry was as staff writer on the fondly remembered 1960s fantasy spoof, "My Favorite Martian", starring Ray Walston and Bill Bixby. Much of Hanalis's subsequent work involved literary adaptations, usually in period settings. Other TV movie credits include "Christmas Eve" (1986), "Big Bend Country" (1981), "Portrait of a Rebel: Margaret Sanger" (1980), "Little Lord Fauntleroy" (1980), "My Africa" (1988), "Love Affair: The Eleanor and Lou Gehrig Story" (1978) and "Young Pioneers" (1976).

Hancock, John
actor
born: c. 1941, Hazen AK
died: October 12, 1992, Los Angeles, age 51
Thickset, affable African-American character player. Hancock got his first break appearing in the TV movie "The Monk" (1969), after which he began landing supporting roles in such films as "The In-Laws" (1979), "All the Marbles" (1981), Norman Jewison's faithful adaptation of Charles Fuller's "A Soldier's Story" (1984), and—as a figure loosely modeled on Al Sharpton—Brian De-Palma's disastrous "Bonfire of the Vanities" (1990). Hancock's recurring TV roles included "Family Ties", "Houston Knights", "L.A. Law", "Cop Rock" and "Love and War". While fully believable as a gentle, paternal character on "Family Ties", he is probably best remembered for his portrayals of no-nonsense authority figures like judges, police commissioners and religious leaders.

Henreid, Paul
actor; also director, producer
aka: von Henreid, Paul; von Wasel-Waldingau, Paul
born: von Hernreid Ritter, Paul George Julius, January 10, 1908, Trieste, Austria-Hungary (now Italy)
died: March 29, 1992, Santa Monica CA, age 84
educ: Institute of Graphic Arts, Vienna; Konservatorium Dramatic Arts, Vienna
Suave, romantic leading man who, in the 1940s and 50s, represented the epitome of continental charm. Henreid is best remembered as Ingrid Bergman's husband, the stoic Resistance leader Victor Laszlo, in "Casablanca" and for his classic bit of romantic business in "Now Voyager" (both 1942) in which he lit two cigarettes at the same time and handed one to Bette Davis. The scion of an aristocratic Austrian family, Henreid first worked as a designer and translator at a Vienna publishing firm until he was discovered in an acting school performance by Otto Preminger, who was then Max Reinhardt's managing director. Henreid became a leading man with Reinhardt's theater company and appeared in two Austrian films in the early 1930s before he moved to England because of his anti-Nazi sentiments. There he starred on the London stage and in films, ironically being cast as a Nazi officer in "Madman of Europe" and as a Gestapo agent in Carol Reed's "Night Train" (both 1940). Moving to the US in 1940, he was again cast as a German in the Broadway production "Flight to the West". Signing with RKO Radio Pictures in 1941, Henreid played his first heroic role as a Free French R.A.F. pilot in his Hollywood debut, "Joan of Paris" (1941). It was the first of many films in which he would dramatize the wartime plight of sympathetic Europeans. In the 50s Henreid starred in mediocre swashbucklers such as "Last of the Buccaneers" (1950) and "Thief of Damascus" (1952), and melodramas like "So Young, So Bad" (1950) and "Stolen Face" (1952). With his career as a romantic lead petering out he switched to producing and directing, especially on TV, where he directed numerous episodes of "Alfred Hitchcock Presents", "The Schlitz Playhouse", "G.E. Theater", "Maverick" and "Bracken's World". In 1964 Henreid reteamed with his "Now, Voyager" and "Deception" (1946) co-star Bette Davis, directing her in the dual roles of homicidal twin sisters in the campy suspense melodrama "Dead Ringers".

Hibben, Eleanor
nature cinematographer, documentarian; also TV host
born: c. 1899
died: August 31, 1992, Albuquerque NM, age 93
Wildlife cinematographer and filmmaker celebrated for her work with the Walt Disney Studio. With her husband Frank, Hibben shot many hours of nature footage in numerous farflung settings. Walt Disney saw their work in the 1940s and decided to initiate a popular series of nature short subjects and features utilizing their footage. While the final products can be justly criticized for their corny narration, goofy music, and shameless anthropomorphism, these films were a vivid introduction to the wonders of nature for generations of young people. The Hibbens had a yearlong network TV series in the 1950s. Their expeditions took them to seven continents and included 26 African safaris. Mrs. Hibben also devoted much of her time to nature and animal organizations.

Hill, Benny
comedian; also writer
born: Hill, Alfred Hawthorn, January 21, 1925, Southampton, England
died: April 20, 1992, Teddington, Southwest London, England, age 67
Chubby, round-faced British comedian, noted for his bawdy double entendres and outlandish comic sketches in which he either dressed in drag or was pursued by buxom women in scanty outfits. Described as "comedy of sexual regret" by novelist Anthony Burgess, Hill's cornball humor—a combination of expert mimicry and saucy music-hall sight gags—won him an international cult following during the 1970s and 80s as star of the popular syndicated Thames export, "The Benny Hill Show"; it also won him accusations of sexism which were partially responsible for the cancellation of his show in England in 1989.

Holloway, Sterling
actor; also comedian, singer
born: January 14, 1905, Cedartown GA
died: November 22, 1992, Los Angeles, age 87
educ: American Academy of Dramatic Arts
Tall, gangly, fair-haired character actor best known for his distinctive voice work with the Walt Disney Studio. Holloway began his career as an actor in the silent film "Casey at the Bat" (1927). He continued to work steadily, usually in local yokel roles, appearing in 12 films in 1933 alone. Among his feature credits are Frank Capra's "Meet John Doe" (1941), Preston Sturges' "The Beautiful Blonde From Bashful Bend" (1949) and Stanley Kramer's "It's a Mad, Mad, Mad, Mad World" (1963). Holloway's final film appearance was in 1977's "Thunder and Lightning". In 1941 Holloway began a long and fruitful collaboration with Disney when he lent his voice to the animated classic "Dumbo". It is his voice for which Holloway is chiefly remembered, a gravelly tenor that evoked whimsy and wonder, innocence and mischief. Among the Disney characters he brought to life are the Cheshire Cat in "Alice in Wonderland" (1951), Kaa the Snake in "The Jungle Book" (1967) and, best of all, Winnie the Pooh, the lovable bear from Christopher Robin's forest.

Howerd, Frankie
actor; also comic
born: Howard, Francis, March 6, 1921, York, England
died: April 19, 1992, London, England, age 70
Master of high camp, primarily remembered for his wrist-flicking, eye-rolling performance as a bawdy Roman slave in the double-entendre-crammed British TV series, "Up Pompeii". Howerd began his career in radio on a show called "Variety Band Box" and his films always remained secondary to his variety performances. His feature credits include "The Ladykillers" (1955), as a barrow-boy put upon by an old lady; "The Great St. Trinian's Train Robbery" (1966); "Carry On Doctor" (1967); "Up Pompeii" (1971), a movie version of his TV show; and "Sergeant Pepper's Lonely Hearts Club Band" (1978).

Hurrell, George
photographer
born: c. 1904
died: May 17, 1992, age 87
A key figure in the creation of Hollywood glamor, Hurrell was arguably the most important still photographer in the history of American commercial film. Hurrell's first important client was Ramon Novarro; his shot of the dashing star in courtly armor beside a white horse immediately marked the photographer as one who understood the fantasy that defined Hollywood. His real break, though, came when Novarro recommended him to Norma Shearer, then at the peak of her popularity. Shearer was trying to find a photographer to take some steamy snaps of her to convince her producer husband, Irving Thalberg, that with the coming of sound her sweet image could use a little sexy sophistication. Hurrell's flair for atmosphere, figure placement and artful lighting created a series of shots at once mythic and sensual, and Hurrell was suddenly in great demand by all of MGM's top female glamour stars. Hurrell worked primarily in black-and-white during Hollywood's golden years, creating halos around the subjects he sculpted with light while surrounding them with posh, quietly Art Deco settings. Flashy mirror effects and surprising intimacy amid the artifice mark a number of his finest works. Better than anyone else, Hurrell knew how to highlight Veronica Lake's silken hair and sulky hauteur, Jane Russell's earth-mother sensuality (for "The Outlaw") and Clark Gable's tongue-in-cheek masculinity. He even knew how to highlight the seemingly unattractive to stunning effect. His famous 1932 shot of a freckled Joan Crawford, for instance, tempers her gloriously tony chic with a touching vulnerability. The master craftsman also conquered color, both in the garish 1940s Technicolor musical mode and (more typically) in a subtle blend of pastels and half-tones. The durable Hurrell continued well into his eighties, shooting Arnold Schwarznegger and other current stars, and lending more than a dash of the style so essential to the cult of stardom.

Ireland, John
actor
born: Ireland, John Benjamin, January 30, 1914, Vancouver, British Columbia, Canada
died: March 21, 1992, Santa Barbara CA, age 78
Tall, lean former professional swimmer who appeared on Broadway and toured in Shakespeare in the late 1930s and early 40s before entering film in the mid-40s. A leading man in several notable westerns including "My Darling Clementine" (1946) and "Red River" (1948), Ireland was nominated for an Oscar for his forceful performance as the newspaper reporter who evolves from devotee to cynical denouncer of demagogue Willie Stark (Broderick Crawford) in "All the King's Men" (1949). A prolific performer in films and early TV, Ireland had made the transition to supporting roles by the mid-50s, playing cynical villains in films like "Gunfight at the O.K. Corral" (1956), "Spartacus" (1960) and "55 Days at Peking" (1962). By the late 60s he was turning up as the star of B-films and second-rate Italian productions like "The House of the Seven Corpses" (1974), "Salon Kitty" (1976) and "Satan's Cheerleaders" (1977), as well as appearing in big-budget fare such as "The Adventurers" (1970). Ireland regularly returned to the stage throughout his career and co-directed two features in the 1950s: "Outlaw Territory/Hannah Lee" (1953) and "The Fast and the Furious" (1954). He was married to actresses Elaine Sheldon (1940-49), Joanne Dru (1949-56) and Daphne Myrick Cameron (from 1962).

Ising, Rudolf
animator
aka: Ising, Rudy
born: Ising, Rudolf C., c. 1904
died: July 18, 1992, Newport Beach CA, age 88
One half of the Harman-Ising (reads "harmonizing") company, a partnership that ranked among the most important forces in American animated cartoon history. Harman-Ising established the great tradition of Warner Bros. animation which would eventually produce Bugs Bunny, Daffy Duck, Porky Pig et al. and offer the most significant challenge to Disney's domination of cartoon style and subject matter. The pair also played a major part in advancing the careers of major animators such as Friz Freleng, Bob Clampett and William Hanna (later of Hanna-Barbera). Ising's career began in 1922 as an inker and painter for Walt Disney's Kansas City, Missouri-based cartoon studio. The tiny studio produced "Newman Laugh-O-Grams", short animated commercials for local merchants that were shown in the Newman Theater. Ising's future partner, Hugh Harman, soon joined the company. After Disney headed west to fortune and glory, Harman-Ising formed their own studio which began producing Loony Tunes in 1930 for Warner Bros. The first major Loony Tunes star was Bosko, a young black boy who was the first cartoon character to speak actual dialogue; beginning with "Bosko the Talk-Ink Kid" in 1929, these cartoons synchronized dialogue on the soundtrack with action on the screen. (Disney's earlier "Steamboat Willie" had music and sound effects, but no dialogue.) The Bosko shorts were also notable for their sign-off, "That's all folks!," which would later become Porky Pig's stammering trademark. In 1931, the studio commissioned a second series of monthly sound cartoons. Harman-Ising named this series Merrie Melodies. Ising became the supervisor/director of this series while Harman concentrated on Bosko and other Looney Tunes. Though the cartoons were signed by both men they worked separately from this point on. Ising gravitated toward cute, cuddly Disney-esque characters, while Harman preferred more stylized creations. Ising's Merrie Melodies were music-oriented cartoons which generally featured one-shot characters, often in surprisingly accurate Depression-era settings. Harman-Ising parted ways with Warner Bros. over budget disputes and were contracted by MGM to produce color cartoons at double their previous budgets. These were beautiful if undistinguished. Ising's most notable creation was Barney Bear, the ancestor of Hanna-Barbera's Yogi Bear, whose personality was based on Ising's own lethargic nature. He also received the sole animation credit (though the animation was done primarily by the fledgling team of William Hanna and Joseph Barbera) on "Puss Gets the Boot", the 1940 cartoon debut for the immensely popular cat-and-mouse duo, Tom and Jerry.

Jaffe, Henry
producer; also lawyer
born: January 19, 1907, New York NY
died: September 11, 1992, Beverly Hills CA, age 85
educ: Columbia University; Columbia Law School
Veteran independent TV producer began his career as a guild lawyer. As a producer, Jaffe was involved in several of the more prestigious dramatic and musical variety shows of the 1950s: "Producers Showcase", "The Bell Telephone Hour", "Shirley Temple's Storybook", "Goodyear Playhouse", and "The Dinah Shore Chevy Show". He produced several popular specials such as "Peter Pan" starring Mary Martin, "Cyrano de Bergerac" starring Jose Ferrer, the Old Vic's "Romeo and Juliet" with Claire Bloom, and "Festival of Music" with Arthur Rubinstein and Marian Anderson. Jaffe also executive produced specials starring Dinah Shore, Wayne Newton, Stan Laurel, and Cheryl Ladd. His

production company, "Henry Jaffe Productions", produced the acclaimed 1968 NBC-TV special "Teacher, Teacher" starring David McCallum and Ossie Davis for the "Hallmark Hall of Fame". He also had critical success in the 1970s as the executive producer of "Dinah's Place" and "Dinah!" both showcasing the talents of Dinah Shore. His other credits include the TV-movies "Emily, Emily", "A Woman Called Moses", and "Aunt Mary".

Jaffee, James
executive
aka: Jaffee, Jamie
born: Jaffee, James M., c. 1952
died: June 5, 1992, Los Angeles CA, age 39
TV production executive who got his start as a production associate working for the team of Tom Patchett and Jay Tarses on the sitcoms "Open All Night" and "Buffalo Bill". Jaffee made it to executive status with a later and more successful sitcom created by Patchett, "Alf". In 1989 he helped Patchett and new partner Ken Kaufman form Patchett-Kaufman Entertainment (PKE) and served as executive in charge of production on such series as "Working Girl" and "Bagdad Cafe" and such TV movies as "Don't Touch My Daughter" (1991) and "Woman Scorned: The Betty Broderick Story" (1992).

Johnstone, Anna
costume designer
aka: Johnstone, Anna Hill
born: Robinson, Anna Johnstone, c. 1913
died: October 16, 1992, Lenox MA, age 79
Prolific Oscar-nominated costume designer was a frequent collaborator with directors Elia Kazan and Sidney Lumet. Johnstone's costume stylings graced such Kazan films as "On the Waterfront" (1954), "East of Eden" (1955), "Baby Doll" (1956), "A Face in the Crowd" (1957), "Wild River" (1960), "Splendor in the Grass" (1961), "America, America" (1963), and "The Last Tycoon" (1976). She also provided appropriate garb for many of Lumet's distinctive films: "Fail Safe" (1964), "The Pawnbroker" (1965), "Serpico" (1973), "Dog Day Afternoon" (1975), "Prince of the City" (1981), "The Verdict" (1982), "Daniel" (1983), "Garbo Talks" (1984), "Power" (1986), and "Running on Empty" (1988). Johnstone received Academy Award nominations for Francis Ford Coppola's "The Godfather" (1972) and Milos Forman's "Ragtime" (1981).

Jones, Allan
singer, actor
born: October 14, 1908, Old Forge PA
died: June 27, 1992, New York NY, age 85
educ: University of Syracuse (music)
Stalwart, curly-haired American leading man and singer, perhaps best remembered for handling the obligatory romantic role in two Marx Brothers comedies, "A Night at the Opera" (1935) and "A Day at the Races" (1937). Jones also played riverboat gambler Gaylord Ravenal opposite Irene Dunne in James Whale's marvelous 1936 adaptation of the stage classic "Show Boat". Possessing a genial personality and a fine baritone, Jones enjoyed modest success in Hollywood for several years without ever attaining the star status of which he seemed capable. He was played up as a second-string Nelson Eddy, and consequently never developed a distinctive persona of his own. After his film career waned, Jones kept busy with singing tours and stage work, including touring companies of shows from "Guys and Dolls" in the 1950s to "Man of La Mancha" in the 1970s. At one time married to actress and singer Irene Hervey, Jones was the father (by Hervey) of singer Jack Jones.

Katz, Ephraim
historian, author; also filmmaker
born: March 11, 1932, Tel Aviv
died: August 2, 1992, New York NY, age 60
educ: Hebrew University, Jerusalem (law, economics); Hunter College, New York (political science); NYU (cinema studies)
Sole author of the monumental critical-historical study of world cinema, "The Film Encyclopedia" (1979). The one-volume work accounts for major and minor figures of US, European and Third World cinema and includes entries on technical terms, national film industries and important cinematic schools and movements. It remains a landmark in American film scholarship. Katz also made numerous documentaries and educational and industrial films. His 1960 book "Minister of Death", co-written with Quintin Reynolds, was an account of the hunt and capture of Nazi war criminal Adolf Eichmann.

Keene, William Joseph
actor
born: c.1916
died: May 23, 1992, Los Angeles, CA, age 76
Veteran charactor actor from the days of live TV, best remembered as the minister on TV's "The Andy Griffith Show" and in the same role on the short lived spin-off "Mayberry, RFD".

Kelly, Jack
actor; also game show host
born: September 16, 1927, Astoria NY
died: November 7, 1992, Huntington Beach CA, age 65
Veteran TV and film actor who began his career as a child performer. Kelly was best known as the co-star of the popular Western series "Maverick", which ran on ABC-TV from 1957-62. As Bart Maverick he played the brother of James Garner's Bret Maverick; both were dapper gamblers and card-sharks who wandered throughout the West and got involved in all kinds of tongue-in-cheek mischief. Kelly's official film debut was "The Story of Alexander Graham Bell" (1939) starring Don Ameche, though he also appeared in the previous year's "Swing Your Lady", a minor Humphrey Bogart entry. Kelly's feature credits include Douglas Sirk's "No Room for the Groom" (1952), Bud Boetticher's "Red Ball Express" (1952) and the MGM science-fiction classic "Forbidden Planet" (1956). Kelly's other TV roles include Andrew Duggan, Andy's pal on "The Saga of Andy Burnett" segments of "Walt Disney Presents" (1957-58); a four-year stint as a gameshow host on "Sale of the Century" (1969-73); and Captain Arthur P. Ryan, Teresa Graves's hard-nosed superior officer on "Get Christie Love!" (1975). Kelly was also a regular on the Hardy Boys segments of "The Hardy Boys/Nancy Drew Mysteries" (1974-75), appeared in the pilot for "Vega$!" (1978), and played Lloyd Bridges in the ABC-TV biopic "Grace Kelly" (1983).

Kinney, Jack
animation director; also producer, animator
born: c. 1910
died: February 9, 1992, Glendale, CA, age 82
One of the few animation directors whose careers spanned the history of the field. Jack Kinney began in 1931 with Walt Disney, where he was directing cartoon shorts a decade later. When Disney began regular production of feature-length cartoons in the late 1930s and early 1940s, Kinney contributed to "Pinocchio"(1940), "Dumbo"(1941), "The Reluctant Dragon"(1941), "Saludos Amigos"(1943), "The Three Caballeros"(1945), and "Melody Time"(1948), while continuing to direct shorts. When

Disney diversified into TV in the mid 1950s, Kinney co-supervised the production of the new animation that linked together the old cartoons. He later produced cartoons for Saturday morning TV. Kinney's most enduring and celebrated contributions to the field were his Goofy "How To..." shorts in the 40s. While Disney was the undisputed leader in cartoon features during this period, their shorts were becoming staid compared to the anarchic offerings from Warner Brothers (Bugs Bunny & Co.) and MGM (Tom & Jerry). Jack Kinney and his brother, cartoon writer Dick Kinney, helped close the gap with their funny, fast-paced and often violent efforts.

Klein, Marty
talent agent, talent agency president; also road manager, standup comic
born: c. 1941, Montreal, Canada
died: October 25, 1992, Los Angeles CA, age 51
Major talent agent and president of the Agency for the Performing Arts (1977-92) who nurtured the careers of many prominent comedy performers. Klein's illustrious list of clients included Steve Martin, Martin Mull, David Letterman, John Candy, Rodney Dangerfield, Sam Kinison, Rowan & Martin and country & western legend Johnny Cash.

Koenekamp, Hans F.
camera operator, special effects cinematographer
born: December 3, 1891, Denison IA
died: September 12, 1992, Northridge CA, age 100
Pioneer in the field of special effects photography. Koenekamp began his career as a camera operator for Mack Sennett's Keystone studio, where he filmed such notables as Charlie Chaplin, Gloria Swanson and the famed Keystone Kops. He then went on to Vitagraph Studios, where he had a long working relationship with silent screen comedian Larry Semon. Among those films done with Semon are the original film version of "The Wizard of Oz" (1925) and "Spuds" (1927). In 1927 Koenekamp moved to the Warner Bros. special effects department, where he remained for 30 years. There he often lensed and directed second unit and special effects segments, with aviation effects his specialty. Among his credits were Max Reinhardt's Hollywood vision of the Bard's "A Midsummer Night's Dream" (1935), Howard Hawks' stirring "Air Force" (1943), Alfred Hitchcock's "Strangers on a Train" (1951)—which featured a memorable whirlwind runaway carousel sequence—and and John Huston's "The Treasure of the Sierra Madre" (1948). Aside from his work on features, Koenekamp was responsible for several technological innovations, including a synchronized motor connection between a background projector and a camera. Koenekamp was the father of Oscar-winning cinematographer Fred J. Koenekamp.

Krugman, Lou
actor
born: c. 1914, Passaic NJ
died: August 8, 1992, Burbank CA, age 78
Prolific radio, stage and TV actor who reportedly appeared on over 10,000 radio programs and performed over 700 commercial voiceovers. Krugman also appeared in a handful of feature films, among them Robert Wise's "I Want to Live!" (1958) and Billy Wilder's "Irma la Douce" (1963). His extensive TV credits include "I Love Lucy", "The Untouchables" and "Love, American Style".

Leclerc, Ginette
actress
born: Menut, Genevieve, February 9, 1912, Paris
died: January 1, 1992, Paris, age 79
Striking, voluptuous, brunette actress who appeared in over 100 French films from the early 1930s through the late 70s. Too often cast in vamp or "other woman" roles in mostly lightweight fare, Leclerc occasionally landed stronger roles or was effectively cast against type. 1938 was a banner year for the actress, with good roles in the women's prison drama "Prison Without Bars" and, as the errant spouse, in Marcel Pagnol's rural tale, "The Baker's Wife". The war years brought Leclerc perhaps her most memorable role, as the crippled Denise in the suspense classic "Le Corbeau" (1943), though she also distinguished herself in postwar years as one of the prostitutes in the "House of Madame Tellier" episode of the masterful Max Ophuls trilogy, "Le Plaisir" (1951). One of her rare English-speaking appearances was in Joseph Strick's adaptation of Henry Miller's "Tropic of Cancer" (1970).

Lee, Charles
comedy writer; also TV writer
born: c. 1914
died: October 18, 1992, Burbank CA, age 78
Veteran comedy writer who worked with comedian Bob Hope for 32 years. Lee's association with Hope began in the mid-1940s and continued through the mid-70s. Lee specialized in comic monologues and worked on Hope's films, TV specials, public appearances, and newspaper columns. Lee also traveled with Hope as he entertained the troops in Vietnam, Thailand, Germany, and Greenland.

Levitt, Ruby R.
art director, set designer
aka: Levitt, Ruby
born: c. 1907, New York NY
died: January 18, 1992, Woodland Hills CA, age 83
educ: Pratt Art Institute
Veteran art director and set designer who entered the film industry in the mid-1940s and worked consistently through the 70s, designing the sets for a wide range of films—from the film noir melodrama "Kiss the Blood Off My Hands" (1948) and the lush Douglas Sirk "women's picture" "Magnificent Obsession" (1954) to the low-budget sci-fi classic, "The Incredible Shrinking Man" (1957). Levitt earned Oscar nominations for her work on the picture-pretty "Pillow Talk" (1959), the popular classic "The Sound of Music" (1965) and Roman Polanski's retro film noir "Chinatown" (1974). She was also responsible for the deliciously creepy look of the TV series, "The Addams Family", in the mid-1960s.

Lewis, Juliet
producer, talent agent
died: July 21, 1992, New York NY
American TV producer who, together with her husband Lester Lewis, was responsible for several early TV series, game and talk shows from the late 1940s through the mid 50s. The game shows included "Movieland Quiz", "Who's the Boss?" and "Who's Whose?", while the talk shows included "Meet Betty Furness" and "Penthouse Party" (also hosted by Furness). The Lewises later became talent agents for the likes of Furness, Marlene Dietrich, Eva Gabor and Alfred Drake, with Ms. Lewis running the firm for several years after her husband's death in 1988.

Liss, Ted
actor; also director, acting coach
born: Liss, Theodore, c. 1919
died: March 3, 1992, Chicago IL, age 72

Character actor known primarily as an acting coach. Liss started off as a child actor working on radio serials and later with Orson Welles's Mercury Theatre. He was seen in films like "Call Northside 777" (1948) with James Stewart and Lee J. Cobb, as well as "Mahogany" (1975) with Diana Ross and Billy Dee Williams. Liss formed the Ted Liss Studio Acting Workshop and coached actors Tom Bosley, Geraldine Page and Virginia Madsen.

Little, Cleavon
actor; also singer
born: June 1, 1939, Chickasaw OK
died: October 22, 1992, Los Angeles CA, age 53
Stage-trained African-American comic actor who garnered international acclaim for his portrayal of Black Bart, the unlikely sheriff, in Mel Brooks' Western spoof "Blazing Saddles" (1974). Little's big break came with a turn in Peter Yates' "John and Mary" (1969), alongside Dustin Hoffman and Mia Farrow. In 1970 he starred on stage in Ossie Davis' musical "Purlie", for which he won a Tony and a Drama Desk award, and appeared in Davis' landmark Black independent film, "Cotton Comes to Harlem". Throughout his career, Little displayed a manic, livewire comic energy and a flamboyant, streetwise style of line delivery.

Lorentz, Pare
filmmaker; also screenwriter
born: December 11, 1905, Clarksburg WV
died: March 5, 1992, Armonk NY, age 92
educ: West Virginia Wesleyan College; University of West Virginia
Journalist and film critic who made two landmark documentaries while serving as film advisor to Franklin D. Roosevelt's US Resettlement Administration: "The Plow That Broke the Plains" (1936), about soil erosion in the West, and "The River" (1937), about flooding on the Mississippi. Despite Hollywood's resistance to Lorentz's subsidized films (the studios claimed unfair competition), his socially progressive work received widespread critical and popular support. In 1938 Lorentz was appointed head of the newly-formed US Film Service, a unit responsible for producing some noteworthy documentaries—including his dramatized study of infant and maternal mortality in America, "The Fight for Life" (1940)—before Congress withdrew its support in 1940. After a brief, unfruitful stint as a producer and director at RKO in Hollywood, Lorentz made over 200 short training films for the armed forces during WWII and oversaw the production of film, music and theater for re-education programs in the occupied countries after the war. He held two more government posts before setting up shop as a New York-based producer of commercial and industrial films in 1947, and lecturing on documentary filmmaking on the college circuit.

Luciano, Michael A.
editor; also editing supervisor
aka: Luciano, Michael
born: c. 1910
died: September 15, 1992, Los Angeles CA, age 82
Veteran Hollywood editor and longtime associate of director Robert Aldrich. Luciano was nominated for editing Oscars on four occasions for four Aldrich films: "Hush...Hush, Sweet Charlotte" (1964), "The Flight of the Phoenix" (1965), "The Dirty Dozen" (1967) and "The Longest Yard" (1974). His other collaborations with the cult director include "Kiss Me Deadly" (1955), "The Big Knife" (1955), "Whatever Happened to Baby Jane?" (1962), "The Killing of Sister George" (1968) and "Ulzana's Raid" (1972). Luciano also worked on several TV movies and received two Eddy awards for TV editing.

Lund, John
actor; also writer
born: February 6, 1913, Rochester NY
died: May 10, 1992, Coldwater Canyon CA, age 79
Strapping, stolid leading man of the postwar years. Lund enjoyed several good opportunities opposite Marlene Dietrich ("A Foreign Affair" 1948), Betty Hutton ("The Perils of Pauline" 1947) and Barbara Stanwyck ("The File on Thelma Jordan" 1949), but never displayed the magnetism needed to either catch the public's eye or match his more fiery costars. Before long he was playing the stooge fiance who loses Grace Kelly, first to Frank Sinatra and later to Bing Crosby, in the mediocre remake of "The Philadelphia Story", "High Society" (1956). Lund retired from acting in the early 1960s.

Maddow, Ben
screenwriter; also documentarian, director, author
aka: Wolff, David
born: c. 1909
died: October 9, 1992, Los Angeles CA, age 83
educ: Columbia University
Prolific screenwriter and documentarian from the 1930s through the 70s. Maddow began his career working within the American documentary movement in the 30s. In 1936 he co-founded the short-lived left-wing newsreel "The World Today". Under the pseudonym of David Wolff, Maddow co-wrote the screenplay to the Paul Strand-Leo Hurwitz documentary landmark, "Native Land" (1942). He earned his first feature screenplay credit with "Framed" (1947), and other screenplays include Clarence Brown's "Intruder in the Dust" (1949, an adaptation of the Faulkner novel), John Huston's "The Asphalt Jungle" (1950) and "The Unforgiven" (1960). As a documentarian he directed and wrote such films as "Storm of Strangers" and "The Stairs". Maddow made his solo directorial debut with the striking, offbeat feature "An Affair of the Skin" (1963), a well-acted story of several loves and friendships gone sour and marked by the rich characterizations which had distinguished his best screenplays. His final screenplay was for the horror melodrama "The Mephisto Waltz" (1970).

Markopoulos, Gregory
filmmaker; also teacher, critic
born: c. 1928, Toledo OH
died: November 13, 1992, Freiburg, Germany, age 64
educ: USC
A major but somewhat mysterious figure in the history of American avant-garde cinema, Markopoulos was part of the post-WWII re-emergence of experimental film which also included Kenneth Anger and Stan Brakhage. Like the similarly precocious Anger, the teenaged Markopoulos made his first film in 1947, the ambitious trilogy, "Du Sang, de la Volupte et de la Mort/Of Blood, of Desire and of Death", a 70-minute feature based partly on a novel by Pierre Louys. Not a prolific filmmaker, Markopoulos wrote his own screenplays and also photographed and edited his own works. His best-known and most influential films are "Twice a Man" (1963) and "The Iliac Passion" (1966). Distinguished by subtle but sensuous homoeroticism and a haunting use of loop printing and double exposure, these films explore cinema's capacity to represent time, subjectivity and myth. As with many avant-garde filmmakers, Markopoulos moved increasingly toward structural film as the decade waned (as in "Gammelion" 1968), focusing on the formal parameters of film to enable "new ways of seeing". He also made several collage-style film portraits of prominent cultural figures, among them "Political Portraits" (1969) and "Galaxie" (1966), which featured 30 three-minute portraits of figures including W.H. Auden, Jasper Johns, Jonas Mekas and Susan Sontag. Markopoulos was an

active and visible presence in American "underground" film of the 1960s. He wrote occasionally for the journal "Film Culture", taught at the Art Institute of Chicago, and featured figures from Andy Warhol to Taylor Mead in his films. After moving to Switzerland late in the decade, however, Markopoulos began to sever ties with colleagues and audiences alike. He asked critic P. Adams Sitney to remove the chapter of the landmark "Visionary Film: The American Avant-Garde" devoted to his films from the book's second edition because he felt it misquoted his writings; he even discouraged screenings of his films. Markopoulos continued working on films which, as yet, have been little seen, but several of his greatest efforts are part of the permanent collections of the Art Institute, the Museum of Modern Art, Anthology Film Archives and the Cinematheque Francaise.

Marton, Andrew
director; also 2nd unit director
born: Marton, Endre, January 26, 1904, Budapest, Hungary
died: January 7, 1992, Santa Monica CA, age 87
Hungarian-born director and second-unit director, best known for his action and adventure films, most memorably the thrilling chariot race sequence in the 1959 remake of "Ben Hur". Marton began his career as an editor at Vita Films in Vienna before going to Hollywood as Ernst Lubitsch's editor in 1923. He made his directorial debut there with "Two-O'Clock in the Morning" (1929) before returning to Germany as chief editor at the Tobin studios. In 1933 Marton left Germany and commuted between Switzerland, Hungary and England, where he directed "Wolf's Clothing" "Secret of Stamboul" (both 1936), and "School for Husbands" (1937). Marton returned to Hollywood in the early 1940s to film the ski sequences for "Two-Faced Woman" (1942), Greta Garbo's last feature. He replaced Compton Bennett as director of the African epic "King Solomon's Mines" (1950) after Bennett became ill. As a second-unit director Marton also shot sequences for such big-budget epics as "The Red Badge of Courage" (1951), "A Farewell to Arms" (1957) and "Cleopatra" (1963), as well as "Mrs. Miniver" (1942), "Cabin in the Sky" (1943), "Million Dollar Mermaid" (1952) and "Day of the Jackal" (1973).

Marx, Samuel
producer, screenwriter; also story editor, author
born: January 26, 1902, New York NY
died: March 2, 1992, Los Angeles CA, age 90
educ: Columbia School of Journalism
Marx moved from newspaper and trade journalism in New York to Hollywood in its 1930s heyday where, as story editor for MGM, he oversaw a stable of literary talents that included William Faulkner, F. Scott Fitzgerald, Ben Hecht, Charles MacArthur, Dorothy Parker and Moss Hart. Marx was involved in the acquisition of such classic film properties as "Grand Hotel" (1932), "The Thin Man" (1934), "Mutiny on the Bounty" (1935) and "Goodbye, Mr. Chips" (1939), as well as writing several original screenplays including "A Night at the Opera" and "Only Eight Hours/Society Doctor" (both 1935). After the death of Irving Thalberg in 1936, Marx shifted his focus to producing and was responsible for such MGM films as "The Longest Night" (1936); the first Andy Hardy film, "A Family Affair" (1937); and "Lassie Come Home" (1943). In the 1950s he began working in TV, serving as executive producer on several Desilu productions including "December Bride" as well as producing "General Electric Hour" and "Broken Arrow". In the 70s Marx became a full-time chronicler of Hollywood with his insider profiles of the industry: "Mayer and Thalberg: The Make-Believe Saints" (1975); "Rodgers and Hart: Bewitched, Bothered and Bedeviled" (1977, with Jan Clayton); "A Gaudy Spree: The Literary Life of Hollywood in the 1930s" (1987); and "Deadly Illusions: Jean Harlow and the Murder of Paul Bern" (1990). Marx frequently assisted researchers of the golden age of Hollywood, appearing in the 1979 Kevin Brownlow-David Gill "Hollywood" series as well as the TNT special series "MGM: When the Lion Roars", broadcast the month of his death in 1992.

Merritt, Michael
set designer
born: c. 1945
died: August 3, 1992, Chicago IL, age 47
Award-winning set designer who frequently worked with David Mamet. Merritt designed the original set for Mamet's play "American Buffalo" and served as production designer on the writer-director's three films: "House of Games" (1987), "Things Change" (1988) and "Homicide" (1991). Merritt also designed the sets for Arthur Hiller's Babe Ruth biopic, "The Babe" (1992), which was released in the same year that he died of cancer.

Miller, Harry
sound editor; also dialogue editor
born: 1904, Hampstead, England
died: October 23, 1992, London, age 88
Pioneer sound editor of the British film industry. Miller originated the concept of instant post-synchronized sound for Alfred Hitchcock's "Blackmail" (1929) when he arranged for British actress Joan Barry to speak the dialogue synchronously from the side of the soundstage for the film's leading lady, Czech actress Anny Ondra, who spoke heavily accented English. The credit title "dubbing editor" was created for Miller and first appeared in the credits for "Goodbye, Mr. Chips" (1939). His other credits include "The Four Feathers" (1939), "The Thief of Baghdad" (1940), David Lean's "Brief Encounter" (1945), and Laurence Olivier's "Henry V" (1945). Miller later became dialogue editor on several James Bond films including "From Russia With Love" (1963), "Goldfinger" (1964), "You Only Live Twice" (1967) and "On Her Majesty's Secret Service" (1969). Miller's later credits include "Chitty Chitty Bang Bang" (1968) and Fred Zinnemann's "A Man For All Seasons" (1966).

Miller, Hope
actress
aka: Lessman, Hope Miller
born: c. 1929
died: July 25, 1992, New York NY, age 63
Minor supporting player of 1940s and 50s stage, screen, and TV. In film, Miller appeared in such escapist fare as "Cry Murder" (1950) and Arch Oboler's "Bwana Devil" (1952), the first 3-D theatrical feature. On Broadway, she appeared opposite Fredric March in "Now I Lay Me Down to Sleep."

Mitchell, Chuck
actor
aka: Mitchell, Chuck "Porky"
born: c. 1928
died: June 22, 1992, Hollywood CA, age 64
Portly actor who was cast as the title character in the teen sex comedies "Porky's" (1981) and the final segment of the trilogy, "Porky's Revenge" (1985).

Mitchell, Robert
TV writer; also radio writer
born: c. 1918, Casper WY
died: October 13, 1992, Northridge CA, age 74

Veteran TV writer who began his career on radio. Mitchell's TV credits include "The Steve Allen Show", "Highway Patrol", "Maverick", "M Squad", "Adventures in Paradise", "Perry Mason", "Combat", "The High Chaparral", "Land of the Giants", "Cannon", "Charlie's Angels", "Hawaii Five-O", "Chips" and "Buck Rogers in the 25th Century".

Morley, Robert
actor; also novelist, playwright
born: May 25, 1908, Semley, Wiltshire, England
died: June 3, 1992, Reading, England, age 84
educ: Wellington College; RADA, London

Portly English character actor who first gained acclaim on the London stage for his title role in "Oscar Wilde". Morley successfully reprised the part on Broadway in 1938, leading to an invitation to Hollywood and an Oscar-nominated film debut as Louis XVI in "Marie Antoinette" (1938). A jovial comic figure who could equally convincingly erupt into rage, Morley portrayed several more royal or aristocratic types, including King George III, in "Beau Brummel" (1954); Louis XI, in "Quentin Durward" (1955); and the Earl of Manchester, in "Cromwell" (1970). Other real-life figures he played were Charles James Fox, in "The Young Mr. Pitt" (1942); Oscar Hammerstein, in "Melba" (1953); and W.S. Gilbert, in "Gilbert and Sullivan" (1953). A cultivated, erudite presence, Morley imposed a distinctive stamp both on his more serious films and on campy vehicles like "Theatre of Blood" (1973). In this cult classic, he played a pompous theater critic gruesomely dispatched by a Shakespearean actor (Vincent Price) whom he had panned.

Munro, Nan
actress
born: c. 1905, South Africa
died: June 16, 1992, London, England, age 87

South African-born actress who worked mostly on the English stage for more than 50 years. She made her film debut in "End of the Affair" (1955) opposite Van Johnson. Munro was most recently seen in the English comedy "Getting it Right" (1989) with Helena Bonham-Carter.

Murphy, George
actor; also dancer, singer, executive
born: July 4, 1902, New Haven CT
died: May 3, 1992, Palm Beach FL, age 89
educ: Yale

Genial American leading actor and singer-dancer who enjoyed 15 years of second-string stardom in Hollywood and, prefiguring Ronald Reagan (whom he rather resembled), later enjoyed success in California politics.

Naismith, Laurence
actor
born: Johnson, Lawrence, December 14, 1908, Surrey, England
died: June 5, 1992, Southport, Australia, age 83

Affable, gentlemanly British character actor of long stage experience who began making regular appearances in British and American films beginning in the late 1940s. Among his more than 50 credits are "The Happiest Days of Your Life" (1950), "Mogambo" (1953), "Lust for Life" (1956), "The Singer Not the Song" (1960), "The Trials of Oscar Wilde" (1960), "Cleopatra" (1963) and "Deadlier Than the Male" (1967). In the 60s, Naismith concentrated on theater, doing "Here's Love" and "A Time for Singing" on Broadway, and "The Apple Cart" and the 1970 revival of "The Winslow Boy". He is probably best remembered by contemporary audiences for his whimsical Merlin in Joshua Logan's film of "Camelot" (1967) and for encouraging Roger Moore and Tony Curtis to accept dangerous assignments each week in the tongue-in-cheek TV adventure series "The Persuaders".

Nelson, George R.
set designer, set decorator
aka: Nelson, George; Nelson, George 'Bob'
born: c. 1927
died: August 25, 1992, Hollywood CA, age 65

Veteran Hollywood set designer and decorator who worked steadily in the industry for nearly three decades. Nelson's feature credits include "All Fall Down" and "The Manchurian Candidate", both directed by John Frankenheimer and released in 1962; "The Graduate" (1967), "Carnal Knowledge" (1971) and "The Day of the Dolphin" (1973), all directed by Mike Nichols; and Coppola's "The Godfather, Part II" (1974) and "Apocolypse Now" (1979).

Nelson, Ruth
actress
born: c. 1905, Saginaw MI
died: September 12, 1992, New York NY, age 87

Distinguished stage actress who was a member of the innovative, politically committed Group Theater in the 1930s and played character roles in Hollywood films of the 40s. Nelson joined the Group Theater at its inception and shared in its popular and critical triumph with Clifford Odets' short play, "Waiting for Lefty" (1935). Portraying the wife of a cab driver moving toward union activism, Nelson established a style that would endure through the next decade: she brought a similar plaintive persona and subdued, understated performance style to her Hollywood films of the 40s, mostly playing supportive, working-class women in films like "A Tree Grows in Brooklyn" (1945), "Humoresque" (1946), "Till the End of Time" (1946) and "Mother Wore Tights" (1947). When her second husband, director John Cromwell, was blacklisted in the early 50s on suspicion of being a member of the Communist party, Nelson turned down a role in "Death of a Salesman" that would have required her to leave him in Los Angeles to return to the New York stage. Later years saw her primarily onstage, notably in the successful 1966 revival of "The Skin of Our Teeth", but she did return to screen work occasionally, most recently as the mother of Robert De Niro in "Awakenings" (1990).

O'Donnell, Gene
actor; also radio announcer
born: c. 1911
died: November 22, 1992, Woodland Hills CA, age 81

Character actor of the 1940s, 50s and 60s. O'Donnell began as a radio announcer working in Boston and New York before moving to LA where he signed a contract with Republic Studios. There he appeared in "The Ape" (1940) with Boris Karloff, "I'm Nobody's Sweetheart Now" (1940) and "The Devil Bat" (1941) with Bela Lugosi. After serving in the Army, O'Donnell moved back to LA, where he played the title character in "Barney Blake, Police Reporter" (1948) and Judy's (Patricia Crowley) brother in the comedy "A Date With Judy" (1951). O'Donnell's subsequent TV credits include guest stints on "Peyton Place", "The Big Valley" and "I Love Lucy". His later film work included "Pretty Boy Floyd" (1960), "Planet of the Apes" (1968) and "The Lawyer" (1970).

O'Neal, Frederick
actor, union president; also professor, author
born: August 27, 1905, Brooksville MS
died: August 25, 1992, New York NY, age 86
educ: New Theater School, American Theater Wing, NY
Veteran black American stage actor who also worked in film and TV. O'Neal's greatest impact on the industry was as a union leader: he was president emeritus of Actors' Equity Association and Associated Actors and Artistes of America. O'Neal was also a major figure in the black theater in New York City and London, where he founded and organized several theater companies and cultural organizations. The American Negro Theater, which O'Neal co-founded, gave a start to the careers of Harry Belafonte and Sidney Poitier. O'Neal's feature credits include Elia Kazan's "Pinky" (1949), Richard Brooks' "Something of Value" (1958), "Anna Lucasta" (1958), and Ossie Davis' "Cotton Comes to Harlem" (1970). O'Neal was also a regular on the 1960s cop sitcom, "Car 54, Where Are You?".

Oliver, David
actor
born: c. 1962
died: November 12, 1992, Los Angeles CA, age 30
Young stage, film and TV actor who played Sam Gardner, the twentysomething son of Richard Kiley, in the Emmy Award-winning NBC miniseries "A Year in the Life" (1986) and the subsequent TV series (1987-88). Previously Oliver had been a regular on the soap "Another World". After the end of "A Year in the Life" he did TV guest spots and a busted pilot ("Protect and Surf" 1989) and appeared in several TV movies and miniseries ("If It's Tuesday, It Still Must Be Belgium" 1987, "Miracle in the Wilderness" 1991). Oliver's film career included a starring role in "Defense Play" (1988) and small roles in Derek Jarman's "Edward the II" and Jim Abrahams' "Hot Shots" (both 1991). He also appeared on the San Diego stage. Oliver's final stage work was in "Elegies: An AIDS Anthology".

Pallero, Edgardo
producer
born: c. 1936
died: July 6, 1992, Buenos Aires, Argentina, age 56
Producer of several landmark Argentine films. Pallero started his career in the late 1950s as the producer of "Tiredie" and "Los Unidados", both directed by Fernando Birri. He later produced "Los Hijos de Fierro/The Sons of Fierro", directed by Fernando Solanas, and co-produced Jorge Sanjinee's "El Coraje del Pueblo/The Courage of the People". Pallero's last film was Tristan Bauer's "Despues de la Tormenta/After the Storm". This feature won the new director's prize for Bauer, primarily a documentarian, at the San Sebastian Film Festival.

Parks, Bert
TV host; also actor, singer
born: Jacobson, Bert, December 30, 1914, Atlanta GA
died: February 2, 1992, La Jolla CA, age 77
educ: Marist College, Atlanta
Best known as a popular TV game show host in the 1950s and the ever-smiling master of ceremonies for the Miss America beauty pageant. At age 19 Parks moved to New York, working first as a singer/straight man on "The Eddie Cantor Show" and then as a staff announcer for CBS radio before finding his niche as the enthusiastic host of the popular radio quiz programs "Break the Bank" and "Stop the Music" in the late 1940s. Parks's eager, affable style translated well to TV and by the early 1950s he was the ubiquitous host of both daytime and primetime game shows and variety series. Parks virtually became an American institution as the host of the annual Miss America pageant from its second telecast in 1955 until he was fired by producers seeking a younger image for the show (in the shape of Ron Ely) in 1980. A letter-writing campaign organized by Johnny Carson resulted in his return to his ceremonial post in 1990, and he once again serenaded the newly crowned Miss America with his signature song "There She Is, Miss America" at the pageant's finale. Although he received a standing ovation, the program was marred by gaffes and he was not asked to return. Parks's career was centered almost entirely on radio and TV, although in the 1960s he replaced Robert Preston as the title character in the Broadway hit, "The Music Man" and performed in road companies of musicals; he made his feature debut in "That's the Way of the World" (1975) and made a quirky cameo appearance as himself in "The Freshman" (1990).

Parsons Sr, Lindsley
producer, executive; also screenwriter
aka: Parsons, Lindsley
born: September 12, 1905, Tacoma WA
died: October 9, 1992, Burbank CA, age 87
educ: UCLA
Veteran film executive, producer and screenwriter. Parsons produced more than 150 theatrical features and three TV series in addition to supervising vast numbers of genre pictures as the production head of Monogram Studios and Allied Artists. He began as a newspaperman and moved into the entertainment industry as the publicity director of Monogram Pictures. Before long Parsons was churning out screenplays for B Westerns—nearly 20 in a five-year period—many starring a bright young talent named John Wayne. He went on to personally produce over 40 films, including some titles in the popular Charlie Chan and Bowery Boys series. Parsons' credits as a producer include films by such notable tough-guy B filmmakers as Bud Boetticher ("Black Midnight" 1949, "The Wolf Hunters" 1949, "The Killer Shark" 1950) and Phil Karlson. A sampling of his voluminous credits yields such colorful titles as "King of the Zombies" (1941), "Law of the Jungle" (1942), "Rhythm Inn" (1951), "Cry Vengeance" (1954), "Desert Pursuit" (1952), "Trail of the Yukon" (1949), "The Adventures of Kitty O'Day" (1944) and "Leave It to the Irish" (1944).

Peck, Ed
actor
born: c. 1917
died: September 12, 1992, Los Angeles CA, age 75
Granite-faced, raspy-voiced character player who often portrayed policemen or military types and convincingly wielded authority—and firearms—well into his sixties. Peck's first major TV credit was the title role in "Major Dell Conway of the Flying Tigers" (1951-52), a Sunday afternoon adventure series on the defunct DuMont network. (He succeeded Eric Fleming, who had played the action hero in the prime-time version of the series.) Peck is probably best remembered as Police Officer Kirk on "Happy Days", with other TV credits including "G.E. Theater", "The Super", "Semi-Tough", and the TV movie pilots for "Jigsaw" (1972) and "The Incredible Hulk" (1977).

Peixoto, Mario
director; also screenwriter
born: c. 1909, Brussels, Belgium
died: February 3, 1992, Rio de Janeiro, Brazil, age 83
educ: educated in London
Enigmatic, reclusive filmmaker whose one feature, "Limite/The Limit" (1929), is regarded as a classic of Brazilian cinema. Made

when the director was 19, "Limite" is a visually beautiful display of surrealistic cinema techniques depicting the visions of two men and a woman lost at sea in a lifeboat. The great Soviet filmmaker Sergei Eisenstein reportedly described it as "an extremely beautiful film" and an example of the "pure language of cinema". The film was virtually lost for 20 years. Restored in 1979 and relaunched on the art-house circuit, it was triumphantly screened in 1984 at the opening of the Berlin Film Festival and at the 1991 London Film Festival. Peixoto also wrote several screenplays, including "Onde a Terra Acaba/Where the Land Ends" and "A Alma Segundo Salustre/The Soul According to Salustre". He began shooting the first screenplay but the film was never finished.

Perkins, Anthony

actor; also director
born: April 4, 1932, New York NY
died: September 12, 1992, Los Angeles, age 60
educ: Columbia University; Rollins College

Began his career as a juvenile lead in the early 1950s and distinguished himself in films including "Tin Star" (1957) and, as baseball star Jim Piersall, "Fear Strikes Out" (1957). Perkins's gripping recreation of Piersall's mental problems made him a suitable choice for what would become his signature role, the mother-fixated Norman Bates in Hitchcock's classic thriller, "Psycho" (1960). He went on to appear in a number of interesting works, including Orson Welles's adaptation of Kafka's "The Trial" (1962), but could never quite shake the "Psycho" mantle. In the mid-1980s Perkins returned to the scene of his early triumph, reprising the Bates role in three progressively campy sequels, the second of which also marked his directorial debut. He was the son of actor Osgood Perkins (Johnny Lovo in "Scarface" 1932) and husband of Berry Berenson, who appeared opposite him in two films, "Remember My Name" (1978) and "Winter Kills" (1979).

Pettyjohn, Angelique

actress; also nightclub entertainer
aka: St. John, Heaven; Angelique
born: c. 1943
died: February 14, 1992, Las Vegas NV, age 48

Voluptuous, usually blonde, actress who began her career with decorative roles in such films as the Elvis Presley vehicle, "Clambake" (1967), and attracted some attention for her role as Agent Charlie, a male colleague of CONTROL agent Maxwell Smart (Don Adams), on TV's "Get Smart". During this period Pettyjohn also played the role for which she is best remembered, a silver lame bikini-clad "thrall" assigned to train Captain James T. Kirk (William Shatner) for battle in the "Star Trek" episode "The Gamesters of Triskelion". One of few performers to switch from mainstream films to porn, Pettyjohn made several hardcore flicks in the early 80s (billed as either "Angelique" or "Heaven St. John"), as well as the softcore comedy about strippers, "Takin' It Off" (1984).

Picon, Molly

actress
born: Pyekoon, Molly, June 1, 1898, New York NY
died: April 5, 1992, Lancaster PA, age 93

Celebrated musical comedy entertainer who began her career with Philadelphia's Arch Street Theater in 1912, later becoming a beloved star of New York's Second Avenue Yiddish stage and a cross-over Broadway performer. Petite and energetic, Picon worked prolifically in plays and vaudeville, making her Yiddish film debut in "Mazel Tov" (1924). In 1936 she traveled to Poland with Polish-born American director Joseph Green to star in the charming semi-musical "Yiddle With His Fiddle". Picone played an itinerant musician posing as a boy in order to travel the Polish countryside without sexual harassment. (The actress often used her slight stature and unglamourous looks to portray girls masquerading as boys.) While in Poland she also starred in Green's "Mamale" (1938) and, upon her return to the US, made a belated English-language starring debut in the Broadway play, "Morning Star". Picon spent much of the 1950s on tour with the USO and in various international fundraising efforts. The 1960s saw her career boosted by her spirited featured role in Jerry Herman's first Broadway musical, "Milk and Honey", which she soon followed with her English-language film debut as the mother of two playboy sons in Neil Simon's "Come Blow Your Horn" (1964). Picon played the definitive Jewish matchmaker, Yente, in "Fiddler on the Roof" (1971), and a bossy madam trying to recruit Barbra Streisand to prostitution in the comedy "For Pete's Sake" (1974). An indefatigable trouper, she continued to appear on stage in her one-woman show into her eighties.

Preston, Wayde

actor
born: c. 1929, Laramie WY
died: 1992, age 63

TV actor who starred as undercover government agent Christopher Colt on the Western series "Colt .45" from 1957-59. Like other Warner Bros. TV "walkout stars" Clint Walker, James Garner and Edd Byrnes, Preston walked off the show to protest his low salary during the 1958-59 season, but was replaced by Donald May. In the 60s he moved to Rome and followed actors Clint Eastwood and Lee Van Cleef in seeking a career in Italian "spaghetti" westerns, appearing in films including "Anzio", "Today It's Me—Tomorrow You" (both 1968), "A Long Ride From Hell" and "A Man Called Sledge" (both 1970). Preston returned to the US in the early 80s and made his final film appearance in "Captain America" (1990).

Ray, Satyajit

director; also screenwriter, composer
born: May 2, 1921, Calcutta, India
died: April 23, 1992, Calcutta, India, age 70
educ: Presidency College, University of Calcutta (science, economics); Santiniketan University (art history)

Satyajit Ray, India's only internationally renowned filmmaker, was born into a family prominent in Bengali arts and letters for fifteen generations. In 1940, after receiving his degree in science and economics, he attended Rabindranath Tagore's "world university" in rural Santiniketan. Tangore, the dominant figure in India's cultural renaissance, had a strong influence on Ray, whose humanist films reaffirm his Bengali heritage within a modern context. In 1942, Ray returned to Calcutta, where he spent the next ten years as layout artist and art director for a British-run advertising agency. In his spare time he wrote film scenarios, among them an adaptation of Tagore's novel, "Ghare Baire," which producers rejected when Ray refused to make changes. With India's independence in 1947, Ray co-founded Calcutta's first film society with Chidananda Das Gupta and wrote articles calling for a new cinema. His reputation as a graphic artist brought offers to illustrate books, including an abridged edition of Bibhuti Bhusan Banerjee's classic novel, "Pather Panchali," in 1946. After an influential encounter with Jean Renoir in Calcutta in 1949 and a business trip to London in 1950, where he saw Vittorio De Sica's "The Bicycle Thief "(1948), Ray set out to script and direct "Pather Panchali." The film, shot on location on weekends, failed to attract backers and could not be completed until a request from the Museum of Modern Art in New York to include it in their Indian art exhibit led the West

Bengal government—in an unprecendented move—to provide funds. "Pather Panchali" (1956) won several international awards and established Ray as a world-class director, as well as being a box-office hit at home. Artistic and financial success gave Ray total control over his subsequent films; in his numerous functions—writer, director, casting director, composer (since 1961) and cinematographer (since 1963)—he was able to continue Tagore's example in theater of welding the arts into a unified entity. Two sequels also based on the novel ("Aparajito" 1957, "The World of Apu" 1959) completed the acclaimed "Apu" trilogy, whose slow-paced realism broke with the song-and-dance melodramas of Indian cinema. Using long takes and reaction shots, slow camera movements, and—in "Kanchanjangha" (1962)—real-time narrative, Ray allows the meticulous accumulation of details to reveal the inner lives and humanity of diverse Bengali characters. In 1961, Ray revived "Sandesh," a children's magazine founded by his grandfather, to which he continued to contribute illustrations, verses and stories throughout his life. Beginning in 1969, he also made four popular children's films which contain an unobtrusive yet distinct political awareness. Earlier in his career, Ray was criticized by Indian critics for failing to deal with Calcutta's immediate social problems. And although he defended his humanist (versus ideological) approach, "Pratidwandi" (1971) signaled a shift toward political themes. In the 1970s, Ray's films acquired a bitter tone and deviated from his usual classical style, with the abrupt use of montage, jump cuts and flashbacks. Ray's "Ghaire Baire/The Home and the World" (1984) was a return to his first screen adaptation. While shooting, he suffered two heart attacks and his son, Sandip, completed the project from his father's detailed instructions. Ray continued to write prolifically, completing 13 half-hour TV screenplays to be directed by Sandip, and returned to directing in 1989 with an adaptation of Ibsen's "Enemy of the People". In 1992, the year of his death, Ray was awarded an honorary Oscar for "his rare mastery of the art of motion pictures, and for his profound humanitarian outlook, which has had an indelible influence on filmmakers and audiences throughout the world."

Reed, Robert

actor
born: Rietz, Jr., John Robert, c. 1933, Highland Park IL
died: May 12, 1992, Pasadena CA, age 59
educ: Northwestern University, Evanston IL; University of London

Tall, curly-haired actor, often cast as business-suited paternal types. Reed worked on mainly forgettable TV series from the 1960s, first gaining widespread notice as a crusading lawyer in "The Defenders". He is best remembered as "a man named Brady, with three boys of his own" on that corny 70s ode to the suburban family, "The Brady Bunch". Reed subsequently had major supporting roles on the miniseries "Rich Man, Poor Man" (1976) and "Roots" (1977).

Renie

costume designer
born: Brouillet, Irene, c. 1902
died: June 23, 1992, Pacific Palisades CA, age 90

A leading Hollywood costume designer from the mid-1930s through the 60s, associated with RKO during its peak years of the 30s and 40s. A former theatrical set designer and sketch artist for Paramount, Renie moved to RKO in 1937 and soon became responsible for garbing such stars as Ginger Rogers, Simone Simon and Laraine Day in films including "Tom, Dick, and Harry" (1941), "Cat People" (1942) and "Mr. Lucky" (1943). Throughout her career, Renie managed to evoke an understated elegance in her work. Her integration of glamour and working-girl motifs into Rogers' clothing as the proletariat "Kitty Foyle" (1940), for example, is highly typical of her style and remains probably her best-known work from this period. Freelancing during the 50s and 60s, Renie worked on such TV series as "Haywire" and "Space" and films including "A Man Called Peter" (1955), "The Three Faces of Eve" (1957) and "The Killing of Sister George" (1968). She also served as a designer for Shipstead & Johnson's during the height of their success with the Ice Follies. After three previous nominations, Renie won an Oscar for her hand in the creation of the lavish costumes for the infamous flop "Cleopatra" (1963).

Roach, Hal

producer; also screenwriter, director
born: January 14, 1892, Elmira NY
died: November 2, 1992, Los Angeles, age 100

Former mule skinner and gold prospector who stumbled into film in 1912, serving as stuntman and bit player in a number of Universal action films and westerns. With backing from Pathe, Roach and former Universal cohort Harold Lloyd formed the Rolin company in 1914 and commenced production on a series of comic shorts starring Lloyd. Such was the success of the "Lonesome Luke" films that Roach was able to take over a large, fully equipped studio in Culver City in 1919. There he continued to turn out successful comedies, distinguished from the Keystone company's product by an emphasis on narrative structure as opposed to sight gags. In 1921 Roach inaugurated the "Our Gang" series, which remained popular over the next two decades. Other notable productions included "Safety Last" (1923), starring Lloyd; "From Soup to Nuts" (1928), starring Laurel and Hardy (whom Roach had first teamed the previous year); and "Of Mice and Men" (1939), directed by Lewis Milestone. Although Roach became increasingly involved with the administration of his organization, he continued to enjoy occasional stints as a director. Actors who developed their careers under Roach's guidance included Mickey Rooney, Charlie Chase and ZaSu Pitts; directors included George Stevens, Norman Z. McLeod and Leo McCarey. Adept at staying abreast of developments within the industry, Roach moved into sound films in the early 1930s, switched to feature production (in partnership with his son, Hal Roach, Jr.) later in the decade, and turned his attention to TV in the late 1940s. The Hal Roach Television Corporation, formed in 1948, enjoyed intermittent success until its eventual demise in the late 1950s. Living until the age of 100, Roach was recognized late in life as one of the "grand old men" of the American cinema, and was honored with an honorary Oscar in 1983 "in recognition of his unparalleled record of distinguished contributions to the motion picture art form."

Robbins, Fred

TV personality; also interviewer
born: c. 1919
died: June 23, 1992, New York NY, age 73

Former radio and TV personality of the 1950s who emceed "The Eddie Fisher Coke Time Hour" and the NBC game show "Haggis Baggis". Robbins later became an interviewer and writer, co-writing a biography on Richard Pryor entitled "This Cat's Got Nine Lives". Robbins was most recently seen as an interviewer on CNN's "Showbiz Today".

Roberts, Meade

screenwriter; also playwright
born: Mednick, Robert, c. 1931
died: February 10, 1992, New York NY, age 61
educ: NYU

A playwright and screenwriter associated with Tennessee Williams, Roberts co-wrote the film adaptations of two of Williams's plays, "The Fugitive Kind" (1960) and "Summer and Smoke" (1961). He also appeared in two John Cassavetes films, "The Killing of a Chinese Bookie" (1976) and "Opening Night" (1977).

Robinson, Cardew
actor; also comedian, vaudevillian, writer
born: Robinson, Douglas, c. 1917, England
died: December 27, 1992, Rochampton, England, age 75
Veteran performer of the English stage, screen and radio, best known for portraying Cardew the Cad, an overgrown schoolboy character he created in the 1940s. This character became so popular that he was featured in a comic strip and resurfaced in the 1956 film "Fun at St. Fanny's". Robinson also worked on the London stage, most notably as King Pellinore in "Camelot" in the 1960s. During this period, he also pursued a career as a comedy writer, producing comic material for Peter Sellers and Dick Emery. Robinson also created the long-running radio show, "You've Got to Be Joking", and performed character roles in features including Roy Boulting's "Happy Is the Bride" (1958), "Where's Jack" (1969), Roman Polanski's "Pirates" (1986) and "Shirley Valentine" (1989).

Rose, David E.
producer, executive; also manager
born: c. 1895, Kansas City MO
died: August 21, 1992, Phoenix AZ, age 96
Former studio executive turned producer who began his career as the manager of Douglas Fairbanks. Rose produced a number of undistinguished British genre films in the 1950s and 1960s including "Island of Desire" (1952) with Linda Darnell and Tab Hunter; "Sea Devils" (1953) with Yvonne De Carlo and Rock Hudson; "Doctor Blood's Coffin" (1960); and Ray Milland's "Hostile Witness" (1968).

Rosenberg, Mark
producer
born: 1948, Passaic NJ
died: November 6, 1992, Stanton TX, age 44
educ: Bard College, NY; University of Wisconsin
At one time a literary agent who represented such writers and directors as John Badham, Paul Brickman, Alvin Sargent and David Seltzer, Rosenberg joined Warner Bros. as a vice president in the studio's production division in 1978. Five years later he became president of production worldwide, developing and overseeing "The World According to Garp", "Never Say Never Again (both 1983), "The Killing Fields" and "Greystoke: The Legend of Tarzan, Lord of the Apes" (both 1984). Rosenberg left Warners after seven years and soon thereafter partnered with Sydney Pollack at Mirage Enterprises, a company the director-producer had formed to help manage such films as "Absence of Malice" (1981), "Tootsie" (1982) and "Out of Africa" (1985). With Rosenberg's help, Pollack expanded Mirage's slate to producing "The Fabulous Baker Boys", "Major League" (both 1989), "Presumed Innocent" (1990) and "King Ralph" (1991). By the time the last of these films had reached audiences, however, Rosenberg and Pollack had parted company, with Rosenberg forming Spring Creek Productions with his wife, producer Paula Weinstein. In 1990 the duo signed a production agreement with Rosenberg's alma mater, Warners, on the studio's lot at Burbank. Rosenberg and Weinstein successfully helmed the HBO telefilm "Citizen Cohn" (1992), based on the life of shark attorney Ray Cohn, who began his career as assistant to Wisconsin senator Joe McCarthy during the 1950s. Spring Creek was filming "Flesh and Bone" and "Fearless" for Warners when Rosenberg was stricken by a heart attack at age 44.

Ross, Steve
executive
born: Ross, Steven J, September 19, 1927, Brooklyn NY
died: December 20, 1992, age 64
educ: Paul Smith's College
Entered the film industry when his father-in-law's limousine rental service expanded to include Kinney Systems parking lots, which then bought Ashley Famous Talent Agency and Warner Bros.-7 Arts in 1969. By 1972 Ross held the titles of chairman of the board and president and CEO of Warner Communications and was named co-chairman and co-CEO of the newly formed Time Warner Inc. in 1989.

Rowe, Bill
sound rerecorder
died: September 29, 1992, London, England
Prolific sound re-recordist who began working for Elstree Studios in the 1950s in their sound department. Rowe eventually became director of post-production at the studio and remained in that position until his death. In 1966 he received his first sound mixer credit, for "One Million Years B.C." (1966). Among the directors with whom Rowe worked are: Ken Russell, on "Tommy" (1975), "Valentino" (1977), and "The Lair of the White Worm" (1988); Roland Joffe, on "The Killing Fields" (1984), "The Mission" (1986) and "City of Joy" (1992); Stanley Kubrick, on "Barry Lyndon" (1975) and "The Shining" (1980); and Jim Henson, on "The Great Muppet Caper" (1981), "The Dark Crystal" (1982) and "Labyrinth" (1986). Other credits include "Batman" (1989), "Local Hero" (1983), "Chariots of Fire" (1981) and "Yentl" (1983). Rowe's final film work was on Roman Polanski's "Bitter Moon" (1992).

Russell, Robert W.
screenwriter, playwright
born: 1912
died: February 11, 1992, New York NY, age 79
educ: USC
After winning a Bronze Star for his WWII work photographing Merchant Marine ships in the Pacific Theater and his documentary propaganda film "Ring of Steel", Russell turned to screenwriting, scripting the comedies "The More the Merrier" (1943, with Frank Ross) which was Oscar nominated for best screenplay; "The Well-Groomed Bride" (1946); and "The Lady Says No" (1951). He also wrote more than 30 documentary, business and educational films and wrote the librettos for the Broadway musicals "Take Me Along" (1959), a musical version of Eugene O'Neill's "Ah, Wilderness" starring Jackie Gleason, and "Flora the Red Menace" (1965), starring Liza Minnelli.

Sanderson, Joan
actress
born: c. 1913, England
died: May 24, 1992, Norwich, England, age 79
English comic player known for her bossy roles in British TV series including "Please Sir!", "Me and My Girl" and "After Henry". Sanderson worked mostly on TV and on the British stage, with occasional small film roles in "The Great Muppet Caper" (1981) and Stephen Frears' "Prick Up Your Ears" (1987).

Sandlin, Edward L.
sound editor
born: c. 1922
died: November 13, 1992, Woodland Hills CA, age 70

Veteran sound editor who was honored with eight Emmy nominations—winning twice for the early miniseries "QBVII-Parts 1 & 2" (1974) and the acclaimed TV movie, "Raid on Entebbe" (1977)—over the course of his long career in TV and film. Sandlin also won numerous Golden Reel Awards for excellence in sound editing. His TV series credits include "Mannix", "Police Story", "Knightrider" and "Wiseguy"; his TV movies/miniseries work includes "The Winds of War" (1983) and the Bette Davis vehicle, "The Dark Secret of Harvest Home" (1978). Among Sandlin's feature credits are "Hair", "1941" (both 1979), "First Blood" (1982), "Wall Street" (1987), "Die Hard 2: Die Harder", "Jacob's Ladder" (both 1990) and "Alien 3" (1992).

Serpe, Ralph B.
producer; also distributor
aka: Serpe, Ralph
born: December 23, 1911, Portland, ME
died: October 24, 1992, Tarzana CA, age 81
educ: Columbia University

Serpe started his entertainment career as an independent theatrical agent and moved into the Italian film industry as vice president of the Scalera film Studios in Rome. A few years later he established a business relationship with Italian movie mogul Dino De Laurentiis that would serve him for most of his professional career. Working for Ponti-De Laurentiis Corp., Serpe negotiated production and distribution deals for a few classics of art cinema and several sprawling international co-productions. His credits include Federico Fellini's "La Strada" (1954) and "Nights of Cabiria" (1957) as well as "Ulysses" (1955), King Vidor's "War and Peace" (1956), John Huston's "The Bible" (1966) and "Barabbas" (1962). In the 1970s Serpe produced a number of American films that were borderline exploitation fare, including "Across 110th Street" (1972), "Mandingo" (1975) and "Drum" (1976), as well as classier material like William Friedkin's "The Brink's Job" (1978).

Shayne, Robert
actor
born: Dawe, Robert Shaen, October 4, 1900, Yonkers NY
died: November 29, 1992, Woodland Hills CA, age 92
educ: Boston University; Chicago University

Prolific supporting player of the Broadway stage, screen and TV, whose career lasted for over 60 years. Best known as Inspector Henderson on the popular syndicated series "The Adventures of Superman" (1952-57), Shayne's last role was the recurring part of Reggie, the blind news vendor, on another superhero series, "The Flash" (1990-91). On Broadway, he worked with Katherine Hepburn and Ethel Barrymore. Shayne appeared in nearly 100 films, sometimes as a lead, but usually a supporting player, often in B movies. His feature credits include "Hollywood Canteen" (1944), "Mr. Skeffington", "Rhapsody in Blue" (both 1945), "Smash-Up: The Story of a Woman" (1947), "Let's Live a Little" (1948) and "Tora! Tora! Tora!" (1970).

Shorr, Lester
director of photography; also camera operator, assistant cameraman
born: c. 1907, Brooklyn NY
died: July 28, 1992, Los Angeles CA, age 85

Shorr began his entertainment career during the silent film era but gained acclaim for his TV work, winning the first Emmy for cinematography in 1954. Shorr worked as director of photography for such TV series as "Bonanza", "Alfred Hitchcock Presents", "General Electric Theater", "Ford Star Jubilee", "Union Pacific", "The Rosemary Clooney Show", "Pete and Gladys", "The Beverly Hillbillies", "The Odd Couple" and "Eight is Enough." He also lensed the final gasps of "The Brady Bunch" TV franchise on "The Brady Girls Get Married" and "The Brady Brides". More importantly, Shorr helped pioneer the multiple-camera techniques that are now standard in TV cinematography. Shorr's feature films were generally low budget genre programmers with titles like "Three Bad Sisters" (1955), "Running Target" (1956), "The Peacemaker" (1956), "Hot Rod Rumble" (1957), "The Quick Gun" (1964), "Ride Beyond Vengeance" (1966) and "The McMasters" (1970). His more illustrious feature credits include the live-action sequences of Chuck Jones and Abe Levitow's "The Phantom Tollbooth" and Woody Allen's feature directorial debut, "Take the Money and Run" (1969).

Simon, Robert F
actor
aka: Simon, Robert
born: c. 1909
died: November 29, 1992, Tarzana CA, age 83

Veteran film and TV character actor of the 1950s through 80s who often played strong-minded, fatherly professional types. Simon moved to Hollywood in 1954 after a busy career on the Broadway stage. He worked steadily in supporting roles until his retirement in the early 80s, with feature credits including "The Last Angry Man", "Compulsion" (both 1959), John Ford's "The Man Who Shot Liberty Valence" (1962) and "Captain Newman M.D." (1963). Simon's small screen work encompassed made-for-TV movies, pilots, and recurring roles on "Bewitched", "M*A*S*H", and "The Amazing Spider-Man".

Sinclair, Ronald
film editor; also actor
born: January 21, 1924, Dunedin, New Zealand
died: 1992, Woodland Hills CA, age 68

Juvenile player turned film editor who retained his celebrity in his native New Zealand long after the end of his Hollywood acting career. Sinclair's feature credits include William Wellman's "The Light That Failed", "Tower of London" (both 1939), Alexander Korda's "That Hamilton Woman" (1941) and Raoul Walsh's "Desperate Journey" (1942). He also appeared in a series of children's adventure films featuring the Five Little Peppers (1939-40) In 1955 Sinclair began a long and fruitful collaboration with producer-director Roger Corman which led to a busy career in low-budget independent filmmaking. Sinclair edited Corman's directorial debut, "Five Guns West" (1955), and went on to work on at least a dozen of his films including "Machine Gun Kelly" (1958), "The Intruder" (1962), "The Premature Burial" (1962), "The Raven" (1963) and "The Trip" (1967). He also edited a number of films by another low-rent auteur with big ideas, Bert I. Gordon: "The Amazing Colossal Man", "Invasion of the Saucer Men" (both 1957), "War of the Colossal Beast", "Attack of the Puppet People", and "The Spider" (all 1958). This was guerrilla filmmaking for the drive-in teen market. The product was high concept, low-budget, and usually shot in a couple of weeks. A substantial portion of the footage shot for these economical marvels was doubtlessly saved through Sinclair's adept editing. He made a brief return to acting in "The Big Catch" (1969), a British children's film.

Steel, Pippa
actress
born: c. 1948, England
died: May 29, 1992, London, England, age 44
English character player who scored with a few film roles as well as in British TV and stage work. Steel is best remembered as the comic foil to Kelly Monteith in the English TV series "The Kelly Monteith Show". Her most prominent film role was that of Clementine Hozier in Richard Attenborough's "Young Winston" (1972).

Stoessel, Jessica
costume designer; also assistant costume designer
aka: Haston, Jessica; Haston Stoessel, Jessica
born: c. 1965
died: July 21, 1992, New York NY, age 27
educ: Fashion Institute of Technology
Up-and-coming costume designer whose career was cut tragically short by cancer. Stoessel (some of her recent credits list her as "Jessica Haston") entered the industry as an assistant costume designer and soon moved up to designing costumes for independent features such as "Poison" (1990) and "Swoon" (1992). Other feature credits include "Johnny Suede" (1992), "Wind" (where she assisted Marit Allen), "Agent Breaker/Cool Jerk" and "Sublet". For TV, she worked on "ABC Afterschool Specials" and CBS "Schoolbreaks" and the miniseries "Summer Stories". Stoessel also worked as a commercial stylist for various advertising agencies.

Sturges, John
director
born: Sturges, John Eliot, January 3, 1910, Oak Park IL
died: August 18, 1992, San Luis Obispo CA, age 82
educ: Marin Junior College, San Rafael CA
Reliable Hollywood craftsman who established his reputation in the mid-1950s with a series of intense, morally charged features such as "Bad Day at Black Rock" (1954) and "Gunfight at the OK Corral" (1957), before moving on to bigger—though not especially better—productions. Sturges began his career as an editor, co-directed the war documentary, "Thunderbolt" (1945), with William Wyler, and subsequently specialized in action and western features. Other notable films include "The Magnificent Seven" (1960), "The Great Escape" (1963) and—Howard Hughes's favorite movie—"Ice Station Zebra" (1968).

Summerfield, Marvin
art director; also set designer
born: c. 1913
died: September 13, 1992, Santa Monica CA, age 79
educ: USC, Los Angeles
Veteran art director and set designer who worked primarily on TV in the 1970s and 80s. Summerfield started his long entertainment career at MGM in 1936. He moved to TV in the 1960s and worked on "The Courtship of Eddie's Father" and "Please Don't Eat the Daisies". Summerfield served as art director for two long-running TV medical shows, "Medical Center" and "Trapper John M.D." He also worked on the TV version of "The Long Hot Summer" (1985). Summerfield's feature credits include "Honeymoon Hotel" (1964) and "Day of the Evil Gun" (1968).

Swarthout, Glendon
playwright, novelist; also screenwriter
born: Michigan
died: September 23, 1992, Scottsdale AZ
A Michigan native who moved to Arizona in 1959, Swarthout wrote more than 20 novels and many short stories, plays and film scripts. Films adapted from his work include Stanley Kramer's "Bless the Beasts & Children" (1971), "Where the Boys Are" (1960), Robert Rossen's "They Came to Cordura" (1959) and Don Siegel's "The Shootist" (1976), an affecting swan song for the Western starring John Wayne in his final film role. Swarthout's novel, "The Melodeon" was adapted by Stewart Stern for "A Christmas to Remember" (1978), a sentimental TV movie set during the Depression starring Jason Robards, Eva Marie Saint and Joanne Woodward.

Sweeney, Bob
actor, director; also producer
born: c. 1919
died: June 1, 1992, Westlake Village CA, age 73
Veteran TV, film and radio actor turned successful TV director and producer. Sweeney's entertainment career began in the waning days of the golden age of radio, first as an announcer and then as half of a popular comedy team. He moved on to the infant medium of TV where he made a niche for himself as a supporting player on several early sitcoms. Sweeney co-starred with Gale Gordon (later of "The Lucy Show") in a short-lived sitcom before landing what must have seemed like a plum role at the time: Fibber McGee on the NBC TV version of "Fibber McGee and Molly", the immensely popular radio sitcom. However the show failed and Sweeney shifted most of his attention to TV directing. As an actor, Sweeney is best known to film audiences as the smugly earnest undertaker in John Ford's "The Last Hurrah" (1958) and as Cousin Bob in Alfred Hitchcock's "Marnie" (1964). Sweeney directed most of the episodes in the first three years of the longrunning sitcom "The Andy Griffith Show". He next shifted generic gears as he went on to produce (with Bill Finnegan) the first six seasons of the immensely popular cop show, "Hawaii Five-O". Sweeney directed some episodes of that series as well as episodes of "That Girl", "Scarecrow and Mrs. King", "Matlock", and "Dynasty". He also helmed the popular "Andy Griffith Show" reunion TV movie, "Return to Mayberry" (1986).

Tavares, Albert
casting director, stage director; also acting teacher
born: c. 1953
died: July 28, 1992, Taunton MA, age 39
Experienced stage and casting director best known in film for handling the casting for Disney's acclaimed animated features "The Little Mermaid" (1989) and "Beauty and the Beast" (1991). Tavares's stage credits include casting and directorial work on the Broadway, off-Broadway, regional and international productions of such plays as "Smile", "Little Shop of Horrors", "A Little Night Music", "On the Town" and "I Think I'm in Here Somewhere". At the time of his death, Tavares had just completed casting Disney's animated follow-up to "Beauty and the Beast", "Aladdin" (1992).

Thompson, Marshall
actor; also director, screenwriter
born: Thompson, James Marshall, November 27, 1925, Peoria IL
died: May 18, 1992, Royal Oak, MI, age 66
educ: Occidental College, Los Angeles
A descendant of Supreme Court Justice John Marshall, this veteran of over 40 films is best remembered as the star of "Daktari", a popular family TV series set in Africa that ran on CBS from January 1966 to January 1969. The inspiration for the show was the feature film "Clarence the Cross-Eyed Lion" (1964) which Thompson starred in and co-wrote. Cast in naive

juvenile roles in MGM films of the 1940s, Thompson began playing a wide variety of roles as a mature lead or second lead. He appeared in Vincente Minnelli's "The Clock" (1945), John Ford's "They Were Expendable" (1945), William Wellman's "Battleground" (1949), Anthony Mann's "Devil's Doorway" (1950) and "The Tall Target" (1951), Herbert Ross's "The Turning Point" (1977) and Sam Fuller's "White Dog" (1982). He also faced down the uncanny in the likes of "Fiend Without a Face", "It! The Terror From Beyond Space" and "First Man in Space". Thompson spent much of his time in Africa in his later years, where he produced, directed, and acted in the documentary series "Orphans of the Wild".

Timberg, Sammy
composer, musical director for the Fleischer Studios;
also songwriter, vaudevillian
born: c. 1903
died: August 26, 1992, Scranton CT, age 89
A Hollywood composer, bandleader and vaudevillian, Timberg is fondly remembered for his musical contributions to the classic cartoons of the Fleischer brothers in the 1930s and 40s.

Trevey, Ken
TV scriptwriter; also TV producer
born: c. 1930
died: July 8, 1992, Los Angeles CA, age 62
Veteran TV writer who kept busy during the 1960s working on such series as "Wagon Train", "Branded" and "The Naked City". While continuing to write episodes for "Lou Grant", "Cannon" and "Matt Houston" during the 70s and 80s, Trevey also penned such made-for-TV movies as "The Weekend Nun" (1972), "Banjo Hackett: Roamin' Free" (1976), "Memories Never Die" (1982) and "LBJ: The Early Years" (1987).

Turner, Lloyd
TV writer; also cartoon writer
born: c. 1924
died: November 11, 1992, Shady Grove OR, age 68
Veteran TV writer who began his career in the Warner Bros. animation department, collaborating with Bill Scott on a series of frantically funny shorts directed by Arthur Davis. Turner/Scott collaborations included "Doggone Cats" (1947), "What Makes Daffy Duck?", "The Stupor Salesman" and "A Hick, a Slick, and a Chick" (all 1948). Shifting to TV, Turner collaborated with producer-animator Jay Ward in 1949 to create "Crusader Rabbit", the first TV cartoon series. He moved on to write and direct "Time for Beany" (1950), a puppet show about a boy and his sea serpent that formed the basis for the subsequent "Beany and Cecil" cartoon series. Turner rejoined Jay Ward and Bill Scott in 1959 to write for the seminal cartoon series "Rocky and His Friends" and its follow-up, "The Bullwinkle Show". Though the animation was limited, the scripting was clever, multi-layered (suitable for kids and parents alike) and satirical, earning enduring cult status for the show. Turner segued to live-action writing with the popular James Bond spoof "Get Smart" and worked on some of the most fondly remembered shows of the 70s: "The Partridge Family", "All in the Family", "Maude", "The Jeffersons", "The Mary Tyler Moore Show" and "Alice". He served as a producer on the "Maude" spinoff, "Good Times", and aided in the creation of "Mork and Mindy". In addition to writing for the series, Turner guided the cartoonish antics of the youthful Robin Williams as the executive creative consultant for the first two seasons.

Vallish Foote, Lillian
film producer; also theater producer
aka: Foote, Lillian V
born: c. 1923, Mt. Carmel PA
died: August 5, 1992, Princeton NJ, age 69
educ: Radcliffe College, Cambridge MA
Stage and screen producer who dealt exclusively with the work of her husband, Horton Foote. Feature producing credits include "1918" (1985) and "On Valentine's Day" (1986).

Von Zerneck, Peter
actor
born: c. 1908
died: June 10, 1992, Burbank CA, age 84
Character actor who worked mostly on TV and the stage. Von Zerneck landed the occasional plumb role, as in Alfred Hitchcock's "Notorious" (1946) and Billy Wilder's "A Foreign Affair" (1948), with Marlene Dietrich and Jean Arthur.

Wachsberger, Nathan
producer; also distributor, screenwriter
born: c. 1916
died: February 1, 1992, Beverly Hills, CA, age 75
Specialized in distributing European films in the US and vice versa. While European trade was curtailed during WWII, Wachsberger worked with George Jessel to set up a production company headquartered at 20th Century-Fox. After the war, he returned to distributing American films in Europe, and oversaw the production of numerous international co-productions in the 1950s, 60s and 70s. Wachsberger was the husband of actress Yvette Lebon.

Walker, Nancy
actress, comedian, singer; also director
aka: Swoyer, Myrtle
born: Swoyer, Anna Myrtle, May 10, 1922, Philadelphia PA
died: March 25, 1992, Studio City CA, age 69
Pint-sized comedienne-singer who electrified Broadway at age 19 with her debut as a wisecracking ugly-duckling blind date in the Hugh Martin-Ralph Blaine musical "Best Foot Forward" (1941). In 1943, Walker reprised the role in MGM's sassy film version and played a similar part in the remake of the Gershwins' "Girl Crazy." A child of vaudevillians, Walker parlayed her wickedly sarcastic deadpan delivery and unconventional looks into a unique comic persona. Perhaps her greatest showcase was "On the Town" (1944), as an aggressively man-chasing taxi driver who tries to persuade a sailor on leave to forego the tourist sites and "Come Up to My Place". Established as a Broadway favorite, Walker next starred as a Marxist coed in the George Abbott-directed musical "Barefoot Boy with Cheek" (1947) and as an heiress-turned-ballerina in the musical "Look Ma, I'm Dancing" (1948). She played Gladys in the acclaimed 1952 revival of "Pal Joey", starred in "Phoenix '55" (1953) and played opposite Phil Silvers in "Do-Re-Mi" (1960), a Comden-Green-Styne musical about jukebox rackets. On TV, Walker parlayed a high-profile paper towel commercial into a role as Rock Hudson's housekeeper on "McMillan and Wife" (1971-76). She later delighted viewers as Valerie Harper's overbearing Jewish mother, first on "The Mary Tyler Moore Show" and then on the spinoff series "Rhoda" (1974-78). In 1976 she played a wisecracking Hollywood talent agent in her own short-lived series and, when that failed, starred as a wisecracking Las Vegas landlady in "Blansky's Beauties!" (1977). Walker turned to directing with the Broadway production of James Kirkwood's "UTBU" in 1965 and subsequently became one of TV's busiest women directors, helming episodes of "The Mary Tyler Moore Show", "Rhoda"

and "Alice". She made her feature directing debut with the misbegotten Village People disco musical "Can't Stop the Music" (1980) and had returned to sitcoms, playing a mother with a black son-in-law in "True Colors", at the time of her death.

Welk, Lawrence
bandleader; also TV host, accordionist
born: March 11, 1903, Strasburg ND
died: May 17, 1992, Santa Monica CA, age 89
Genial American bandleader whose brand of "Champagne Music" lilted weekly across American TV airwaves for nearly three decades. Welk left home at age 21 to begin his career as an itinerant musician. He eventually formed his own "Biggest Little Band in America" and achieved success on the radio in the late 1930s with his band's bright, danceable renditions of popular songs. The label "Champagne Music" reportedly stuck after call-in listeners likened his music to the sipping of champagne. In the early 50s Welk and his band began performing on a local LA TV station, and viewer response was such that his program—considered hopelessly schmaltzy even in its prime—eventually went nationwide courtesy of ABC. Welk's Germanic accent (his parents were from Alsace-Lorraine) became a favorite of impersonators everywhere, his "Wunnerful, wunnerful" and "Ah-one an' ah-two" all but entering the American idiom. By the early 70s, Welk's unchanging format, replete with black tap dancer, middle-aged "Champagne Lady" vocalist and maidenly female singing trios, seemed even more out of touch, and ABC cancelled the show in 1971. Welk, however, had the last laugh, earning more money during the next 11 years of syndication than he ever did during his first 16 with ABC. If anything, a rapidly graying working-class America eager for nostalgic escapism embraced their keeper of the flame more warmly than ever before. The affable merrymaker continued waving his baton on TV and later on tour well into his eighties.

Westmoreland, Mary
studio hairstylist
born: c. 1911
died: April 6, 1992, Kailua-Kona HI, age 81
Studio hairstylist who worked in Hollywood from 1945 to 1975, at Columbia and 20th Century-Fox. Westmoreland's film credits include "The Manchurian Candidate" (1962), for which she styled Angela Lansbury, "Ship of Fools" (1965), "Born Yesterday" (1950) and "Devil at Four O'Clock" (1961). On TV, she handled hair for "The Flying Nun".

Whaley, Jim
TV host
born: c. 1948
died: August 2, 1992, Atlanta GA, age 44
Producer and host of "Cinema Showcase", a syndicated TV show which was created for Atlanta public TV station WPBA. The series was syndicated nationally and stayed on the air for 20 years, with Whaley interviewing such stellar figures as Lillian Gish, John Wayne, Henry Fonda, Kevin Costner, Meryl Streep and Eddie Murphy. He also conversed with major filmmakers including Alfred Hitchcock, Otto Preminger and Steven Spielberg.

Williams, Bill
actor
aka: Katt, William H.
born: Katt, Herman, c. 1916, Greenpoint (Brooklyn) NY
died: September 21, 1992, Burbank CA, age 76
educ: Pratt Institute, Brooklyn, NY
Blond stalwart of film and TV. Williams' all-American good looks usually led to him being cast in good-guy leads or second leads, sometimes opposite wife Barbara Hale. RKO groomed the boyish actor for stardom in the immediate postwar period, but despite the popular and critical success of "Till the End of Time" (1946), a story of returning WWII veterans, Williams was soon playing in modestly budgeted action pictures and crime dramas. He was best known for the title role of the syndicated 1950s TV series, "The Adventures of Kit Carson", in which the frontier scout was teamed up with Mexican sidekick El Toro (Don Diamond). Williams also had leading roles in another syndicated adventure series, "Assignment Underwater", and the sitcom "Date with the Angels", in which he played the husband of Betty White. He made guest appearances on a wide variety of TV series including "M Squad", "The Millionaire", "The Lawman", "77 Sunset Strip", "The Wild, Wild West", "Lassie", "Dragnet", "Marcus Welby, M.D.", and "Adam-12". Williams' many feature credits include "Thirty Seconds Over Tokyo" (1944), "Deadline at Dawn" (1946), "The Stratton Story" (1949), Frank Tashlin's "Son of Paleface" (1952) and Howard Hawks's "Rio Lobo" (1970).

Willis, Ted
writer
aka: Willis, Theodore
born: c. 1918
died: December 22, 1992, Chislehurst, England, age 74
Cited in "The Guiness Book of World Records" as the world's most prolific TV writer, Willis created 41 TV serials, wrote 37 stage plays, penned scripts for 39 feature films, churned out radio scripts and generated a dozen novels. He was also one of the pioneers of British "kitchen sink" drama in the late 1950s, producing gritty, realistic stories set in a working-class milieu.

Wolfe, Ian
actor; also pantomimist, singer, dancer
born: 1896, Canton IL
died: January 23, 1992, Los Angeles CA, age 95
Gaunt, wiry, prolific supporting player with a piercing stare, familiar from the hundreds of films in which he played mean or menacing characters in the course of a seven-decade career. After appearing on the Broadway stage, Wolfe made his film debut in his late 30s and, already balding, quickly won notice as Captain Bligh's cruel storekeeper and stool pigeon Maggs in "Mutiny in the Bounty" (1935). Wolfe went on to make more than 150 film appearances, often playing English or clerical characters, in films including the horror comedy "Homebodies" (1974, a starring role); Mike Nichols's "The Fortune" (1975, as the dithery old justice of the peace); "Creator" (1985); "Checking Out" (1988); and "Dick Tracy" (1990). Wolfe also played Wizard Tranquil on the 1983 TV series, "Wizards and Warriors".

Worden, Hank
acting
born: c. 1901
died: December 6, 1992, Los Angeles CA, age 91
Rodeo worker chosen, along with roommate Tex Ritter, to play a cowhand in Broadway's "Green Grow the Lilacs" in 1930. Worden later broke into films in Cecil B. DeMille's "The Plainsman" (1937) and appeared in over 100 movies during the next half-century. Typically cast in westerns, Worden ambled his way through a host of colorful supporting roles, including four for director John Ford. Although Worden played a memorable recurring cameo in David Lynch's "Twin Peaks" series shortly before his death, buffs are more likely to cherish his unforgettably

addled Old Mose ("Thank you kindly") in Ford's "The Searchers" (1956).

Wyatt Sr., Allan
stunt coordinator; also stunt double, stuntman, second unit director
aka: Wyatt, Allan
born: c. 1920
died: August 12, 1992, Burbank CA, age 72

Veteran stuntman, stunt coordinator and second unit director whose Hollywood career spanned four decades. Wyatt started out as a stunt double for Jon Hall in "The Last of the Redmen" (a 1946 adaptation of James Fenimore Cooper's "The Last of the Mohicans") and went on to stand in for such performers as Randolph Scott, Joel McCrea, Errol Flynn, Buddy Ebsen and George Montgomery. As a stunt coordinator, Wyatt worked primarily on Western and action movies such as Blake Edwards' "The Wild Rovers" (1971), "Dirty Mary Crazy Larry" (1974), "Duel at Diablo" (1966), "Valdez is Coming" (1971), "The Long Ride Home/A Time for Killing" (1967) and "Heaven With a Gun" (1969). His TV credits include "The Streets of San Francisco", "Barnaby Jones" and "The Quest". Wyatt's last feature credits include Amy Heckerling's "Fast Times at Ridgemont High" (1982) and Steven Spielberg's "E.T. The Extra-Terrestrial" (1982). His son, Allan, Jr., is also a stunt coordinator.

Wyler, Jorie
acting teacher; also director, actress
born: c. 1931
died: October 27, 1992, New York, NY, age 61
educ: AADA, New York (acting)

Stage director and veteran acting teacher who was a senior member of the Academy of Dramatic Arts in New York. Wyler's students included Danny DeVito, Peter Weller, Julia Duffy, John Savage, Michael Countryman and the late Cleavon Little. As an actress, she worked in theater, radio, films and TV, appearing on the series "The Rifleman".

York, Dick
actor
born: York, Richard, September 4, 1928, Fort Wayne IN
died: February 20, 1992, Grand Rapids MI, age 63

Best known as Darren Stephens, the befuddled husband of nose-twitching witch Samantha (Elizabeth Montgomery) on the long-running TV comedy, "Bewitched". York began his career as a child actor on radio in Chicago, most notably as Jack Armstrong, "the All-American boy". By the mid-1950s he had appeared on Broadway in "Tea and Sympathy" and "Bus Stop" and became a frequent guest performer on TV dramas and series such as "The Twilight Zone", "Wagon Train" and "Alfred Hitchcock Presents". York also entered films in the mid-50s: he was featured as former footballer Wreck in "My Sister Eileen" (1955) and played the schoolteacher tried for teaching evolution in "Inherit the Wind" (1960). York's first TV series was "Going My Way" (1962-63), based on the 1944 Bing Crosby film, but it is his co-starring role on "Bewitched" for which he remains best known. York remained with the show from its debut in 1964 to 1969, when problems stemming from an old back injury forced him to leave; he was replaced by Dick Sargent, who continued in the role until 1972. In the years after his retirement from acting York was active with his private fund-raising effort called Acting for Life, soliciting money for the homeless by telephone while confined to his home by emphysema and a degenerative spinal condition.

Indices

MASTER INDEX FOR MPG ANNUALS

Listed below are the titles of all films reviewed since 1984, with their year of release. This date will enable you to locate the *Motion Picture Guide* volume in which the film appears. All films released in 1984 can be found in volume IX of the original *Motion Picture Guide*. Films released during or after 1985 can be found in the *Motion Picture Guide Annual* for the year *following* the film's year of release (i.e. films of 1986 are reviewed in the 1987 *Annual*, films of 1987 in the 1988 *Annual*, etc.).

If a film has been reviewed, but is absent from the list below, the title in question was released prior to 1984 and may be found in the original, ten-volume set, which is arranged alphabetically by title.

B

C

D

E

I

LA DOUBLE VIE DE VERONIQUE (SEE: DOUBLE LIFE OF VERONIQUE, THE)(1991)
LA DUEDA INTERNA (SEE: VERONICO CRUZ)(1990)
LA FAMIGLIA (SEE: FAMILY, THE)(1987)
LA FEMME NIKITA (1991)
LA FLUTE A SIX SCHTROUMPFS (SEE: SMURFS AND THE MAGIC FLUTE, THE)(1984)
LA FRACTURE DU MYOCARDE (SEE: CROSS MY HEART)(1991)
LA GLOIRE DE MON PERE (SEE: MY FATHER'S GLORY)(1991)
LA GRIETA (SEE: ENDLESS DESCENT)(1991)
L.A. HEAT (1989)
LA HISTORIA OFICIAL (SEE: OFFICIAL STORY, THE)(1985)
LA LECTRICE (1989)
LA LEGENDA DEL RUDIO MALESE (SEE: JUNGLE RAIDERS)(1986)
LA LEI DEL DESEO (SEE: LAW OF DESIRE, THE)(1987)
LA MESSA E FINITA (SEE: MASS IS ENDED, THE)(1988)
LA MORT DE MARIO RICCI (SEE: DEATH OF MARIO RICCI, THE)(1985)
LA PASSION BEATRICE (SEE: BEATRICE)(1988)
LA PELICULA DEL REY (SEE: KING AND HIS MOVIE, A)(1986)
LA PETIT SIRENE (1984)
LA SEGUA (1985)
L.A. STORY (1991)
LA VIE EST RIEN D'AUTRE (SEE: LIFE AND NOTHING BUT)(1990)
LA VIE EST UN ROMAN (SEE: LIFE IS A BED OF ROSES)(1984)
LABYRINTH (1986)
LABYRINTH OF PASSION (1990)
L'ADDITION (1984)
LADIES CLUB, THE (1986)
LADIES OF THE LOTUS (1987)
LADIES ON THE ROCKS (1985)
LADRI DI SAPONETTE (SEE: ICICLE THIEF, THE)(1990)
LADY DRAGON (1992)
LADY IN WHITE (1988)
LADY JANE (1986)
LADY OF THE CAMELIAS (1987)
LADYBUGS (1992)
LADYHAWKE (1985)
LAIR OF THE WHITE WORM, THE (1988)
LAMBADA (1990)
L'AMI DE MON AMIE (SEE: BOYFRIENDS AND GIRLFRIENDS)(1988)
L'AMOUR PAR TERRE (SEE: LOVE ON THE GROUND)(1984)
LAMP, THE (SEE: OUTING, THE)(1987)
LAND BEFORE TIME, THE (1988)
LAND OF DOOM (1986)
LANDSCAPE IN THE MIST (1990)
LANDSCAPE SUICIDE (1986)
LANDSLIDE (1992)
L'ANNEE DES MEDUSES (1984)
L'ARGENT (1984)
LAS VEGAS WEEKEND (1985)
LASER MAN, THE (1988)
LASER MOON (1992)
LASSITER (1984)
LAST BOY SCOUT, THE (1991)
LAST CALL (1991)
LAST DRAGON, THE (1985)
LAST EMPEROR, THE (1987)
LAST EXIT TO BROOKLYN (1989)
LAST FLIGHT TO HELL (1991)
LAST HORROR FILM, THE (1984)
LAST HOUR, THE (1991)
LAST HUNTER, THE (1984)
LAST NIGHT AT THE ALAMO (1984)
LAST OF THE FINEST, THE (1990)
LAST OF THE MOHICANS, THE (1992)
LAST RESORT (1986)
LAST RIDE, THE (1991)
LAST RITES (1988)
LAST STARFIGHTER, THE (1984)
LAST STRAW, THE (1987)
LAST TEMPTATION OF CHRIST, THE (1988)
LAST WARRIOR, THE (1989)
LATE FOR DINNER (1991)
LATE SUMMER BLUES (1988)
LATENT IMAGE (1988)
LATINO (1985)
LAUGHTERHOUSE (1984)
LAW OF DESIRE, THE (1987)
LAWNMOWER MAN, THE (1992)
LAWS OF GRAVITY (1992)
LE BON PLAISIR (1984)
LE CHATEAU DE MA MERE (SEE: MY MOTHER'S CASTLE)(1991)
LE COMPLOT (SEE: TO KILL A PRIEST)(1989)
LE DECLIN DE L'EMPIRE AMERICAIN (SEE: DECLINE OF THE AMERICAN EMPIRE, THE)(1986)
LE DUE VITE DI MATTIA PASCAL (SEE: TWO LIVES OF MATTIA PASCAL, THE)(1985)
LE GRAND BLEU (SEE: BIG BLUE, THE)(1988)
LE GRAND CHEMIN (SEE: GRAND HIGHWAY, THE)(1988)
LE JUPON ROUGE (SEE: MANUELA'S LOVES)(1987)
LE LEOPARD (1984)
LE LIEU DU CRIME (SEE: SCENE OF THE CRIME)(1986)
LE PETIT AMOUR (SEE: KUNG FU MASTER)(1989)
LE POUVOIR DU MAL (SEE: POWER OF EVIL, THE)(1985)
LE THE AU HAREM D'ARCHIMEDE (SEE: TEA IN THE HAREM OF ARCHIMEDE)(1985)
LEAGUE OF THEIR OWN, A (1992)
LEAN ON ME (1989)
LEAP OF FAITH (1992)
LEATHER JACKETS (1992)
LEATHERFACE: THE TEXAS CHAINSAW MASSACRE III (1990)
LEAVING NORMAL (1992)
LEGAL EAGLES (1986)
LEGAL TENDER (1991)
LEGEND (1985)
LEGEND OF BILLIE JEAN, THE (1985)
LEGEND OF SURAM FORTRESS (1985)
LEGEND OF THE WHITE HORSE (1991)
LEMON SISTERS, THE (1990)
LENA'S HOLIDAY (1991)
LEONARD PART 6 (1987)
LES FAVORIS DE LA LUNE (SEE: FAVORITES OF THE MOON)(1985)
LES GUERISSEURS (SEE: ADUEFUE)(1988)
LES INNOCENTS (SEE: INNOCENT, THE)(1988)
LES NOCES DE PAPIER (SEE: PAPER WEDDING)(1991)
LES NUITS DE LA PLEINE LUNE (SEE: FULL MOON IN PARIS)(1984)
LES PLOUFFE (1985)
LES PORTES TOURNANTES (SEE: REVOLVING DOORS, THE)(1988)
LES RIPOUX (SEE: MY NEW PARTNER)(1984)
LES TROIS COURONNES DU MATELOT (SEE: THREE CROWNS OF THE SAILOR)(1984)
LESS THAN ZERO (1987)
LET HIM HAVE IT (1991)
LET IT RIDE (1989)
L'ETAT SAUVAGE (1990)
LETHAL OBSESSION (1988)
LETHAL WEAPON (1987)
LETHAL WEAPON 2 (1989)
LETHAL WEAPON 3 (1992)
LET'S GET HARRY (1987)
LETTER TO BREZHNEV (1986)
LEVIATHAN (1989)
L'HOMME BLESSE (1985)
LICENCE TO KILL (1989)
LICENSE TO DRIVE (1988)
LIEBESTRAUM (1991)
LIES (1984)
LIFE AND NOTHING BUT (1990)
LIFE IS A BED OF ROSES (1984)
LIFE IS A LONG QUIET RIVER (1990)
LIFE IS CHEAP . . . BUT TOILET PAPER IS EXPENSIVE (1990)
LIFE IS SWEET (1991)
LIFE ON A STRING (1992)
LIFE ON THE EDGE (1992)
LIFE STINKS (1991)
LIFEFORCE (1985)
LIGHT IN THE JUNGLE, THE (1992)
LIGHT OF DAY (1987)
LIGHT SLEEPER (1992)
LIGHT YEARS (1988)
LIGHTHORSEMEN, THE (1988)
LIGHTNING—THE WHITE STALLION (1986)
LIGHTSHIP, THE (1986)
LIKE FATHER, LIKE SON (1987)
LILY IN LOVE (1985)
LILY WAS HERE (1992)
LIMIT UP (1989)
LINGUINI INCIDENT, THE (1992)
LINK (1986)
LIONHEART (1990)
LIONHEART (1991)
LISA (1990)
LISTEN TO ME (1989)
LISTEN TO THE CITY (1984)

M

P

Q

R

T

U

UN DIMANCHE A LA CAMPAGNE (SEE: SUNDAY IN THE COUNTRY, A)(1984)
UN HOMBRE DE EXITO (SEE: SUCCESSFUL MAN, A)(1987)
UN HOMBRE VIOLENTE (1986)
UN HOMME AMOUREUX (SEE: MAN IN LOVE, A)(1987)
UN HOMME ET UNE FEMME: VINGT ANS DEJA (SEE: MAN AND A WOMAN: 20 YEARS LATER, A)(1986)
UN MONDE SANS PITIE (SEE: LOVE WITHOUT PITY)(1991)
UN PASAJE DE IDA (SEE: ONE-WAY TICKET, A)(1988)
UN WEEK-END SUR DEUX (SEE: EVERY OTHER WEEKEND)(1991)
UN ZOO LA NUIT (SEE: NIGHT ZOO)(1987)
UNBEARABLE LIGHTNESS OF BEING, THE (1988)
UNBELIEVABLE TRUTH, THE (1990)
UNBORN, THE (1991)
UNCLE BUCK (1989)
UNCONSCIOUS (SEE: FEAR)(1986)
UNDER COVER (1987)
UNDER SATAN'S SUN (1988)
UNDER SIEGE (1992)
UNDER SUSPICION (1992)
UNDER THE BOARDWALK (1990)
UNDER THE CHERRY MOON (1986)
UNDER THE GUN (1989)
UNDER THE VOLCANO (1984)
UNDYING LOVE (1991)
UNE FLAME DANS MON COEUR (SEE: FLAME IN MY HEART, A)(1990)
UNFAITHFULLY YOURS (1984)
UNFINISHED BUSINESS (1985)
UNFINISHED BUSINESS . . . (1987)
UNFORGIVEN (1992)
UNHOLY, THE (1988)
UNINVITED, THE (1988)
UNIVERSAL SOLDIER (1992)
UNLAWFUL ENTRY (1992)
UNREMARKABLE LIFE, AN (1989)
UNTERGANGENS ARKITEKTUR (SEE: ARCHITECTURE OF DOOM)(1991)
UNTIL SEPTEMBER (1984)
UNTIL THE END OF THE WORLD (1991)
UNTOUCHABLES, THE (1987)
UP THE CREEK (1984)
UPHILL ALL THE WAY (1986)
URAMISTEN (SEE: PHILADELPHIA ATTRACTION, THE)(1985)
URANUS (1991)
URGA (SEE: CLOSE TO EDEN)(1992)
USED PEOPLE (1992)
UTU (1984)

V

VAGABOND (1985)
VAGRANT, THE (1992)
VALENTINO RETURNS (1989)
VALET GIRLS (1987)
VALHALLA (1986)
VALMONT (1989)
VALS, THE (1985)
VAMP (1986)
VAMPING (1984)
VAMPIRE HUNTER D (1992)
VAMPIRES IN HAVANA (1985)
VAMPIRE'S KISS (1989)
VAN GOGH (1992)
VANISHING, THE (1991)
VARIETY (1984)
VASECTOMY: A DELICATE MATTER (1986)
VENDETTA (1986)
VENICE/VENICE (1992)
VERA (1987)
VERNE MILLER (1988)
VERONICO CRUZ (1990)
VERRIEGELTE ZEIT (SEE: LOCKED-UP TIME)(1992)
VERY CLOSE QUARTERS (1986)
VESNICKO MA STREDISKOVA (SEE: MY SWEET LITTLE VILLAGE)(1985)
V.I. WARSHAWSKI (1991)
VIA APPIA (1991)
VICE ACADEMY (1989)
VICE ACADEMY III (1991)
VICE VERSA (1988)
VICOLI E DELITTI (SEE: CAMORRA)(1986)
VIDEO DEAD (1987)
VIEW TO A KILL, A (1985)
VIGIL (1984)
VILLA DEL VENERDI, LA (SEE: HUSBANDS AND LOVERS)(1992)
VILLE ETRANGERE (SEE: FOREIGN CITY, A)(1988)
VINCENT AND THEO (1990)
VINDICATOR (SEE: DESERT WARRIOR)(1985)
VIOLATED (1986)
VIOLENT BREED, THE (1986)
VIOLETS ARE BLUE (1986)
VIRGIN HIGH (1991)
VIRGIN QUEEN OF ST. FRANCIS HIGH, THE (1987)
VIRUS KNOWS NO MORALS, A (1986)
VISA U.S.A. (1987)
VISION QUEST (1985)
VISSZASZAMLALAS (SEE: COUNTDOWN)(1985)
VITAL SIGNS (1990)
VLCI BOUDA (SEE: WOLF'S HOLE)(1987)
VOICES FROM THE FRONT (1992)
VOLUNTEERS (1985)
VOODOO DAWN (1991)
VOYAGER (1992)
VROEGER IS DOOD (SEE: BYGONES)(1988)

W

WAIT FOR ME IN HEAVEN (1988)
WAIT UNTIL SPRING, BANDINI (1991)
WAITING FOR THE MOON (1987)
WALK LIKE A MAN (1987)
WALK ON THE MOON, A (1987)
WALKER (1987)
WALKING ON WATER (SEE: STAND AND DELIVER)(1988)
WALKING THE EDGE (1985)
WALL STREET (1987)
WALTZING REGITZE (1991)
WANNSEE CONFERENCE, THE (1987)
WANTED: DEAD OR ALIVE (1987)
WAR AND LOVE (1985)
WAR BIRDS (1989)
WAR OF THE ROSES, THE (1989)
WAR PARTY (1989)
WAR ZONE (SEE: DEADLINE)(1987)
WARDOGS (1987)
WARLOCK (1991)
WARM NIGHTS ON A SLOW MOVING TRAIN (1987)
WARNING SIGN (1985)
WARRIOR AND THE SORCERESS, THE (1984)
WARRIOR QUEEN (1987)
WARRIORS OF THE WASTELAND (1984)
WARRIORS OF THE WIND (1984)
WATCHERS (1988)
WATER (1985)
WATER AND SOAP (SEE: ACQUA E SAPONE)(1985)
WATERDANCE, THE (1992)
WATERLAND (1992)
WAXWORK (1988)
WAXWORK II: LOST IN TIME (1992)
WAYNE'S WORLD (1992)
WE THINK THE WORLD OF YOU (1989)
WE THREE (1985)
WEDDING BAND (1990)
WEDDING IN GALILEE (1988)
WEEDS (1987)
WEEKEND AT BERNIE'S (1989)
WEEKEND PASS (1984)
WEEKEND WARRIORS (1986)
WEININGER'S LAST NIGHT (1991)
WEININGERS NACHT (SEE: WEININGER'S LAST NIGHT)(1991)
WEIRD SCIENCE (1985)
WELCOME HOME (1989)
WELCOME HOME, ROXY CARMICHAEL (1990)
WELCOME IN VIENNA (1988)
WELCOME TO 18 (1986)
WELCOME TO GERMANY (1988)
WELCOME TO OBLIVION (1992)
WENDY CRACKED A WALNUT (SEE: ALMOST)(1991)
WE'RE NO ANGELS (1989)
WE'RE TALKIN' SERIOUS MONEY (1992)
WESTLER (SEE: EAST OF THE WALL)(1986)
WETHERBY (1985)
WHALES OF AUGUST, THE (1987)
WHAT ABOUT BOB? (1991)
WHAT COMES AROUND (1986)
WHAT WAITS BELOW (1986)
WHAT YOU TAKE FOR GRANTED (1984)
WHATEVER IT TAKES (1986)
WHAT'S THE TIME, MR. CLOCK? (1985)
WHEELS OF FIRE (SEE: DESERT WARRIOR)(1985)
WHEELS OF TERROR (SEE: MISFIT BRIGADE, THE)(1988)
WHEN FATHER WAS AWAY ON BUSINESS (1985)
WHEN HARRY MET SALLY . . . (1989)
WHEN NATURE CALLS (1985)

X

Y

Z

FILMS BY COUNTRY OF ORIGIN

A bullet before the title indicates a film co-produced by more than one country

Australia
CROSSING, THE
EFFICIENCY EXPERT, THE
FATHER
• FERNGULLY: THE LAST RAINFOREST
FLIRTING
HUNTING
HURRICANE SMITH
PROOF
ROCK & ROLL COWBOYS
TILL THERE WAS YOU

Belgium
• NIGHT AND DAY
• TOTO LE HEROS

Canada
ADJUSTER, THE
BEAUTIFUL DREAMERS
BEETHOVEN LIVES UPSTAIRS
• BLACK ICE
• CANVAS
CLEARCUT
COMMON BONDS
• DEAD CERTAIN
DEADLY CURRENTS
• DOUBLE VISION
GATE II
GETTING MARRIED IN BUFFALO JUMP
HIGHWAY 61
KILLER IMAGE
• LOWER LEVEL
MANIAC WARRIORS
NEON CITY
OH, WHAT A NIGHT
PRIMO BABY
• PROJECT: SHADOWCHASER
PSYCHIC
QUARREL, THE
• SCANNERS III: THE TAKEOVER
TALONS OF THE EAGLE
TIGER CLAWS
TWIN SISTERS
ULTIMATE DESIRES
WISECRACKS

China
• LIFE ON A STRING
• RAISE THE RED LANTERN
• SILK ROAD, THE

Czechoslovakia
EAR, THE

Denmark
• ZENTROPA

Finland
DADDY AND THE MUSCLE ACADEMY
• MATCH FACTORY GIRL, THE

France
• 1492: THE CONQUEST OF PARADISE
• AFRAID OF THE DARK
ALBERTO EXPRESS
BEATING HEART, A
• BECOMING COLETTE
• CITY OF JOY
• CLOSE TO EDEN
CONTE DE PRINTEMPS
• CRY OF THE OWL, THE
• DAMAGE
DELICATESSEN
DISCRETE, LA
DOES THIS MEAN WE'RE MARRIED?
• DOUBLE VISION
ELEGANT CRIMINEL, L'
EMMANUELLE 6
• FAVOUR, THE WATCH, AND THE VERY BIG FISH, THE
HAIRDRESSER'S HUSBAND, THE
HOT CHOCOLATE
INDOCHINE
INSPECTOR LAVARDIN
• LOVER, THE
• MAMBO KINGS, THE
• NEAR MISSES
• NIGHT AND DAY
POUR SACHA
• POWER OF ONE, THE
• SARAFINA!
SHOOTING ELIZABETH
• TOTO LE HEROS
• TOUCH AND DIE
TOUS LES MATINS DU MONDE
VAN GOGH
• VOYAGER
• WINTER IN LISBON, THE
• ZENTROPA

Germany
AFFENGEIL
• BECOMING COLETTE
DEMON IN MY VIEW, A
• EYE OF THE STORM
KILL CRUISE
• LIFE ON A STRING
LOCKED-UP TIME
• MY FATHER IS COMING
• POWER OF ONE, THE
• TOTO LE HEROS
• TOUCH AND DIE
• ZENTROPA

Hong Kong
HARD-BOILED
ONCE UPON A TIME IN CHINA
• RAISE THE RED LANTERN
SUPERCOP: POLICE STORY III

Ireland
• PLAYBOYS, THE

Israel
BLINK OF AN EYE
CUP FINAL
DOUBLE EDGE

Italy
BEYOND DARKNESS
BEYOND JUSTICE
• CRY OF THE OWL, THE
DEVIL'S DAUGHTER, THE
FINE ROMANCE, A
HUSBANDS AND LOVERS
INDIO 2 - THE REVOLT
JOHNNY STECCHINO
MEDITERRANEO
STATION, THE
• TOUCH AND DIE

Japan
GODZILLA VS. BIOLLANTE
JOURNEY OF HONOR
• PRAYER OF THE ROLLERBOYS
PROFESSIONAL, THE
• SILK ROAD, THE
TETSUO: THE IRON MAN
VAMPIRE HUNTER D

Mexico
• CABEZA DE VACA
DANZON

Netherlands
LILY WAS HERE

New Zealand
MY GRANDPA IS A VAMPIRE
SOLDIER'S TALE, A

Portugal
• WINTER IN LISBON, THE

South Africa
• SARAFINA!

South Korea
• 3 NINJAS

Spain
• 1492: THE CONQUEST OF PARADISE
AMANTES
• CABEZA DE VACA
• CHRISTOPHER COLUMBUS: THE DISCOVERY

PEPI, LUCI, BOM AND OTHER GIRLS ON THE HEAP
• WINTER IN LISBON, THE

Sweden

BEST INTENTIONS, THE
• MATCH FACTORY GIRL, THE
OX, THE
• ZENTROPA

Switzerland

• NIGHT AND DAY
TO PROTECT AND SERVE

U.K.

• 1492: THE CONQUEST OF PARADISE
• AFRAID OF THE DARK
• BECOMING COLETTE
• BLAME IT ON THE BELLBOY
• BOB ROBERTS
• BRIEF HISTORY OF TIME, A
• CANVAS
• CHAPLIN
• CHILDREN, THE
• CITY OF JOY
COLD JUSTICE
CRYING GAME, THE
• DAMAGE
DAMNED IN THE USA
• DEAD CERTAIN
EDWARD II
ENCHANTED APRIL
• FAVOUR, THE WATCH, AND THE VERY BIG FISH, THE
HOWARDS END
K2
LANDSLIDE
• LAWNMOWER MAN, THE
• LIFE ON A STRING
LONDON KILLS ME
• LOVER, THE
• MISSISSIPPI MASALA
• MONSTER IN A BOX
• PETER'S FRIENDS
POPE MUST DIET!, THE
• PROJECT: SHADOWCHASER
RUBIN & ED
• SARAFINA!
• SCORCHERS
• SIMPLE MEN
SPLIT SECOND
• TOUCH AND DIE
• UNDER SUSPICION
• WATERLAND
WHERE ANGELS FEAR TO TREAD

U.S.

ACES: IRON EAGLE III
ADVENTURES IN DINOSAUR CITY
ADVENTURES IN SPYING
ALADDIN
ALAN & NAOMI
ALIEN3
ALL THE VERMEERS IN NEW YORK
ALL-AMERICAN MURDER
ALMOST PREGNANT
AMERICAN DREAM
AMERICAN FABULOUS
AMERICAN ME
AMITYVILLE 1992: IT'S ABOUT TIME
ANIMAL INSTINCTS
ARMED FOR ACTION
ARTICLE 99
AUNTIE LEE'S MEAT PIES
BABE, THE
• BACK IN THE U.S.S.R.
BACKTRACK
BAD CHANNELS
BAD LIEUTENANT
BARBARIAN QUEEN II: THE EMPRESS STRIKES BACK
BASIC INSTINCT
BASKET CASE 3: THE PROGENY
BATMAN RETURNS
BEASTMASTER 2: THROUGH THE PORTAL OF TIME
BEBE'S KIDS
BED & BREAKFAST
BEETHOVEN
BERNARD AND THE GENIE
BIG GIRLS DON'T CRY . . . THEY GET EVEN
BIKINI CARWASH COMPANY, THE
BIKINI SUMMER 2
• BLACK ICE
BLACKBELT
• BLAME IT ON THE BELLBOY
BLIND VISION
BLOOD ON THE BADGE
BLOODFIST III: FORCED TO FIGHT
BLOODFIST IV: DIE TRYING
BOB MARLEY: TIME WILL TELL
• BOB ROBERTS
BODY WAVES
BODYGUARD, THE
BOOMERANG
BRAIN DONORS
BRAM STOKER'S DRACULA
BREAKING THE RULES
BREATHING FIRE
BRENDA STARR
BRIDE OF KILLER NERD
• BRIEF HISTORY OF TIME, A
BROKEN NOSES
BRONX WAR, THE
BROTHER'S KEEPER
BUFFY THE VAMPIRE SLAYER
CAFE ROMEO
CAGED FEAR
CAN IT BE LOVE
CANDYMAN
• CAPTAIN AMERICA
CAPTAIN RON
CENTER OF THE WEB
CHAINS OF GOLD
• CHAPLIN
CHILDREN OF THE NIGHT
CHINA O'BRIEN II
• CHRISTOPHER COLUMBUS: THE DISCOVERY
CLASS ACT
CODE NAME: CHAOS
COLD HEAVEN
COLLISION COURSE
COLOR ADJUSTMENT
COMPLEX WORLD
COMRADES IN ARMS
CONFESSIONS OF A SERIAL KILLER
CONSENTING ADULTS
COOL WORLD
COUSIN BOBBY
CRISSCROSS
CRITTERS 4
CROSSING THE BRIDGE
CTHULHU MANSION
CUTTING EDGE, THE
DANCE MACABRE
DANCE WITH DEATH
DARK HORSE
DAUGHTERS OF THE DUST
DAY IN OCTOBER, A
• DEAD CERTAIN
DEADBOLT
DEADLY BET
DEATH BECOMES HER
DEATH HOUSE
• DEATHSTALKER IV: MATCH OF TITANS
DEEP BLUES
DEEP COVER
DELTA HEAT
DEMONIC TOYS
DESERT KICKBOXER
DESIRE AND HELL AT SUNSET MOTEL
DIARY OF A HITMAN
DIGGSTOWN
DISTINGUISHED GENTLEMAN, THE
DO OR DIE
DOCTOR MORDRID
DOLLY DEAREST
DOUBLE TROUBLE
DR. GIGGLES
DRIVE
ENCINO MAN
ESCAPE FROM . . . SURVIVAL ZONE
EVIL CLUTCH
EXILED IN AMERICA
EYE OF THE EAGLE 3
• EYE OF THE STORM
FALLING FROM GRACE
FAR AND AWAY
FATAL INSTINCT
FATE
FATHERS AND SONS
FEED
• FERNGULLY: THE LAST RAINFOREST
FEW GOOD MEN, A
FIELD OF FIRE
FINAL ANALYSIS
FINAL IMPACT
FINEST HOUR, THE
FINISHING TOUCH, THE
• FOLKS
FOR THOSE ABOUT TO ROCK
FOREVER YOUNG
• 1492: THE CONQUEST OF PARADISE
FREDDIE AS F.R.O.7
FREEJACK
FROZEN ASSETS

GAS FOOD LODGING
GHOULIES III: GHOULIES GO TO COLLEGE
GIVING, THE
GLADIATOR
GLENGARRY GLEN ROSS
GUILTY AS CHARGED
GUN IN BETTY LOU'S HANDBAG, THE
GUYVER, THE
HAND THAT ROCKS THE CRADLE, THE
HAPPY HELL NIGHT
HARD PROMISES
HEAVEN IS A PLAYGROUND
HELL MASTER
HELLRAISER III: HELL ON EARTH
HELLROLLER
HERO
HIGHWAY TO HELL
HIRED TO KILL
HOFFA
HOME ALONE 2: LOST IN NEW YORK
HOMEBOYS
HOMICIDAL IMPULSE
HONEY, I BLEW UP THE KID
HONEYMOON IN VEGAS
HOURS AND TIMES, THE
HOUSE IV
HOUSE OF USHER, THE
HOUSE ON TOMBSTONE HILL, THE
HOUSESITTER
HUGH HEFNER: ONCE UPON A TIME
HUMAN SHIELD, THE
HUSBANDS AND WIVES
I DON'T BUY KISSES ANYMORE
ILLUSIONS
IMPORTANCE OF BEING EARNEST, THE
IN GOLD WE TRUST
IN THE HEAT OF PASSION
IN THE SOUP
INCIDENT AT OGLALA
INNOCENT BLOOD
INSIDE EDGE
INTO THE SUN
INVASION OF THE SPACE PREACHERS
JENNIFER EIGHT
JOHNNY SUEDE
JUICE
JUMPIN' AT THE BONEYARD
JUST LIKE IN THE MOVIES
KICK OR DIE
KICKBOXER 3: THE ART OF WAR
KILL LINE
• KILLER TOMATOES EAT FRANCE
KISS ME A KILLER
KUFFS
LADY DRAGON
LADYBUGS
LASER MOON
LAST OF THE MOHICANS, THE
• LAWNMOWER MAN, THE
LAWS OF GRAVITY
LEAGUE OF THEIR OWN, A
LEAP OF FAITH
LEATHER JACKETS
LEAVING NORMAL
LETHAL WEAPON 3
LIFE ON THE EDGE
LIGHT IN THE JUNGLE, THE
LIGHT SLEEPER
LINGUINI INCIDENT, THE
LITTLE NEMO: ADVENTURES IN SLUMBERLAND
LITTLE NOISES
LITTLE SISTER
LITTLE VEGAS
LIVING END, THE
LONELY HEARTS
LORENZO'S OIL
LOVE CRIMES
LOVE FIELD
LOVE HURTS
LOVE POTION NO. 9
• LOWER LEVEL
LUNATIC, THE
LUNATICS: A LOVE STORY
MAGICAL WORLD OF CHUCK JONES, THE
MALCOLM X
• MAMBO KINGS, THE
MAN TROUBLE
MARTIAL LAW 2: UNDERCOVER
MAXIMUM BREAKOUT
MAXIMUM FORCE
MEATBALLS 4
MEDICINE MAN
MEGAVILLE
MEMOIRS OF AN INVISIBLE MAN
MIDNIGHT CLEAR, A
MIDNIGHT FEAR
MIGHTY DUCKS, THE
MIKEY
MIND, BODY & SOUL
MINDWARP
MIRACLE BEACH
MIRROR IMAGES
MISSION OF JUSTICE
• MISSISSIPPI MASALA
MISTRESS
MO' MONEY
MOM AND DAD SAVE THE WORLD
MONKEY BOY
• MONSTER IN A BOX
MONTANA RUN, THE
MORTUARY ACADEMY
MR. BASEBALL
MR. SATURDAY NIGHT
MUNCHIE
MUPPET CHRISTMAS CAROL, THE
MY COUSIN VINNY
• MY FATHER IS COMING
MY NEW GUN
NAKED OBSESSION
• NEAR MISSES
NETHERWORLD
NEWSIES
NICKEL & DIME
NIGHT AND THE CITY
NIGHT EYES 2
NIGHT ON EARTH
NIGHT RHYTHMS
976-EVIL II
1991: THE YEAR PUNK BROKE
NOISES OFF
ODDBALL HALL
OF MICE AND MEN
ONCE UPON A CRIME
ONE FALSE MOVE
ONE LAST RUN
ONLY YOU
ORIGINAL INTENT
OTHER WOMAN, THE
OUT FOR BLOOD
OUT ON A LIMB
OVER HER DEAD BODY
PAINTING THE TOWN
PALE BLOOD
PAMELA PRINCIPLE, THE
PANAMA DECEPTION, THE
PASSED AWAY
PASSENGER 57
PASSION FISH
PATRIOT GAMES
PET SEMATARY II
• PETER'S FRIENDS
PHANTOM OF THE RITZ
PICTURES FROM A REVOLUTION
PLAY MURDER FOR ME
PLAY NICE
• PLAYBOYS, THE
PLAYER, THE
POISON IVY
• POWER OF ONE, THE
• PRAYER OF THE ROLLERBOYS
PRELUDE TO A KISS
PRIMARY MOTIVE
PROM NIGHT IV - DELIVER US FROM EVIL
PUBLIC EYE, THE
PUERTO RICAN MAMBO (NOT A MUSICAL), THE
PURE COUNTRY
PUSHED TO THE LIMIT
RADIO FLYER
RAISING CAIN
RAMPAGE
RAPID FIRE
• RASPAD
REFRIGERATOR, THE
RESERVOIR DOGS
RESURRECTED, THE
RIVER RUNS THROUGH IT, A
ROAD TO RUIN
ROADSIDE PROPHETS
ROCK SOUP
ROCK-A-DOODLE
ROOTS OF EVIL
ROUND TRIP TO HEAVEN
ROVER DANGERFIELD
RUBY
RUNESTONE, THE
• SARAFINA!
SAVAGE INSTINCT
• SCANNERS III: THE TAKEOVER
SCENT OF A WOMAN

SCHOOL TIES
• SCORCHERS
SECRET FRIENDS
SECRET GAMES
SEEDPEOPLE
SEVERED TIES
SEX CRIMES
SEXUAL RESPONSE
SHADOWS AND FOG
SHAKES THE CLOWN
SHAKING THE TREE
SHINING THROUGH
• SIMPLE MEN
SINGLE WHITE FEMALE
SINGLES
SISTER ACT
SLUMBER PARTY MASSACRE 3
SMOOTH TALKER
SNAKEEATER III . . . HIS LAW
SNEAKERS
SOCIETY
SOLDIER'S FORTUNE
SORORITY HOUSE MASSACRE 2
SOUTH CENTRAL
SPIRITS
STAY TUNED
STEAL AMERICA
STEELE'S LAW
STEPHEN KING'S SLEEPWALKERS
STOP! OR MY MOM WILL SHOOT
STORYVILLE
STRAIGHT TALK
STRANGER AMONG US, A
STREET CRIMES
SUNSET STRIP
SWOON
TERMINAL BLISS
TEXAS TENOR: THE ILLINOIS JACQUET STORY
• THANK YOU AND GOOD NIGHT
THERE'S NOTHING OUT THERE
THIS IS MY LIFE
35 UP
• 3 NINJAS
THUNDERHEART
TO RENDER A LIFE
TOGETHER ALONE
TOYS
TRACES OF RED
TRAINED TO FIGHT
TRANCERS III: DETH LIVES
TRESPASS
TROLL 2
TUNE, THE
24 HOURS TO MIDNIGHT
TWIN PEAKS: FIRE WALK WITH ME
ULTRAVIOLET
UNDER SIEGE
• UNDER SUSPICION
UNFORGIVEN
UNIVERSAL SOLDIER
UNLAWFUL ENTRY
USED PEOPLE
VAGRANT, THE
VENICE/VENICE
VOICES FROM THE FRONT
WATERDANCE, THE
• WATERLAND
WAXWORK II: LOST IN TIME
WAYNE'S WORLD
WE'RE TALKIN' SERIOUS MONEY
WELCOME TO OBLIVION
WHERE THE DAY TAKES YOU
WHISPERS IN THE DARK
WHITE MEN CAN'T JUMP
WHITE SANDS
WHITE TRASH
WHO SHOT PATAKANGO?
WILD ORCHID 2: TWO SHADES OF BLUE
WILD WHEELS
WILDFIRE
WIND
WITCHCRAFT IV: VIRGIN HEART
WOMAN, HER MEN AND HER FUTON, A
YEAR OF THE COMET
ZEBRAHEAD

U.S.S.R.

ADAM'S RIB
• BACK IN THE U.S.S.R.
• CLOSE TO EDEN
• RASPAD

West Germany

• CHILDREN, THE
• VOYAGER

Yugoslavia

• CAPTAIN AMERICA

FILMS RELEASED BY MAJOR STUDIOS

BUENA VISTA

Walt Disney Productions
Hollywood Pictures
Touchstone Pictures

3 NINJAS
ALADDIN
BLAME IT ON THE BELLBOY
CAPTAIN RON
CONSENTING ADULTS
CROSSING THE BRIDGE
DISTINGUISHED GENTLEMAN, THE
ENCINO MAN
GUN IN BETTY LOU'S HANDBAG, THE
HAND THAT ROCKS THE CRADLE, THE
HONEY, I BLEW UP THE KID
MEDICINE MAN
MIGHTY DUCKS, THE
MUPPET CHRISTMAS CAROL, THE
NEWSIES
NOISES OFF
PASSED AWAY
SARAFINA!
SISTER ACT
STRAIGHT TALK
STRANGER AMONG US, A

COLUMBIA

BRAM STOKER'S DRACULA
FALLING FROM GRACE
FEW GOOD MEN, A
GLADIATOR
HARD PROMISES
HERO
HONEYMOON IN VEGAS
LEAGUE OF THEIR OWN, A
MO' MONEY
MR. SATURDAY NIGHT
RADIO FLYER
RIVER RUNS THROUGH IT, A
SINGLE WHITE FEMALE
STEPHEN KING'S SLEEPWALKERS
UNDER SUSPICION
YEAR OF THE COMET

MGM

CRISSCROSS
CUTTING EDGE, THE
DIGGSTOWN
LOVER, THE
OF MICE AND MEN
ONCE UPON A CRIME

PARAMOUNT

1492: THE CONQUEST OF PARADISE
BEBE'S KIDS
BOOMERANG
BRAIN DONORS
COOL WORLD
JENNIFER EIGHT
JUICE
K2
LADYBUGS
LEAP OF FAITH
NETHERWORLD
PATRIOT GAMES
PET SEMATARY II
SCHOOL TIES
WAYNE'S WORLD
WHISPERS IN THE DARK

TRISTAR

BASIC INSTINCT
CANDYMAN
CHAPLIN
CITY OF JOY
HUSBANDS AND WIVES
THUNDERHEART
UNIVERSAL SOLDIER
WIND

TWENTIETH CENTURY FOX

ALIEN3
BUFFY THE VAMPIRE SLAYER
FERNGULLY: THE LAST RAINFOREST
FOLKS!
HOFFA
HOME ALONE 2: LOST IN NEW YORK
JUMPIN' AT THE BONEYARD
LAST OF THE MOHICANS, THE
LOVE POTION NO. 9
MAN TROUBLE
MY COUSIN VINNY
NIGHT AND THE CITY
PRELUDE TO A KISS
RAPID FIRE
SHINING THROUGH
STORYVILLE
THIS IS MY LIFE
TOYS
UNLAWFUL ENTRY
USED PEOPLE
WHITE MEN CAN'T JUMP

UNIVERSAL

AMERICAN ME
BABE, THE
BEETHOVEN
DEATH BECOMES HER
DR. GIGGLES
FAR AND AWAY
HOUSESITTER
KUFFS
LEAVING NORMAL
LORENZO'S OIL
MR. BASEBALL
OUT ON A LIMB
PUBLIC EYE, THE
RAISING CAIN
SCENT OF A WOMAN
SNEAKERS
STOP! OR MY MOM WILL SHOOT
TRESPASS

WARNER BROS.

BATMAN RETURNS
BODYGUARD, THE
CHRISTOPHER COLUMBUS: THE DISCOVERY
CLASS ACT
FINAL ANALYSIS
FOREVER YOUNG
FREEJACK
INNOCENT BLOOD
LETHAL WEAPON 3
MAGICAL WORLD OF CHUCK JONES, THE
MALCOLM X
MAMBO KINGS, THE
MEMOIRS OF AN INVISIBLE MAN
MOM AND DAD SAVE THE WORLD
PASSENGER 57
POWER OF ONE, THE
PURE COUNTRY
SINGLES
SOUTH CENTRAL
STAY TUNED
UNDER SIEGE
UNFORGIVEN
WHITE SANDS

FILMS BY STAR RATING

All films in this volume are listed below by their star ratings. The ratings are:

★★★★★ = Masterpiece; ★★★★ = Excellent; ★★★ = Good; ★★ = Fair; ★ = Poor; No Star Rating = Without Merit

★★★★½

UNFORGIVEN

★★★★

AMANTES
BEST INTENTIONS, THE
CRYING GAME, THE
DAUGHTERS OF THE DUST
DELICATESSEN
DISCRETE, LA
GAS FOOD LODGING
GLENGARRY GLEN ROSS
HAIRDRESSER'S HUSBAND, THE
HOWARDS END
HUSBANDS AND WIVES
MALCOLM X
ONCE UPON A TIME IN CHINA
PLAYER, THE
RESERVOIR DOGS
TOTO LE HEROS

★★★½

ALADDIN
ALL THE VERMEERS IN NEW YORK
AMERICAN DREAM
BAD LIEUTENANT
BRAM STOKER'S DRACULA
BRIEF HISTORY OF TIME, A
BROTHER'S KEEPER
CABEZA DE VACA
CANDYMAN
CLEARCUT
CLOSE TO EDEN
CRY OF THE OWL, THE
DEEP COVER
FLIRTING
HAND THAT ROCKS THE CRADLE, THE
HARD-BOILED
HONEYMOON IN VEGAS
IN THE SOUP
INSPECTOR LAVARDIN
JOHNNY STECCHINO
JUMPIN' AT THE BONEYARD
LAWS OF GRAVITY
LORENZO'S OIL
MATCH FACTORY GIRL, THE
MISSISSIPPI MASALA
NIGHT AND DAY
ONE FALSE MOVE
PANAMA DECEPTION, THE
PASSION FISH
PEPI, LUCI, BOM AND OTHER GIRLS
  ON THE HEAP
PROOF
RAISE THE RED LANTERN
RASPAD
SCENT OF A WOMAN
SINGLES
TOUS LES MATINS DU MONDE
TUNE, THE
VAN GOGH
WATERDANCE, THE

★★★

ADAM'S RIB
AFFENGEIL
ALL-AMERICAN MURDER
AMERICAN FABULOUS
BEATING HEART, A
BEAUTIFUL DREAMERS
BEBE'S KIDS
BED & BREAKFAST
BEETHOVEN LIVES UPSTAIRS
BLINK OF AN EYE
BLOODFIST III: FORCED TO FIGHT
BROKEN NOSES
CAFE ROMEO
CHILDREN OF THE NIGHT
CHILDREN, THE
COMPLEX WORLD
CONTE DE PRINTEMPS
COUSIN BOBBY
CUP FINAL
DADDY AND THE MUSCLE ACADEMY
DAMAGE
DANZON
DEADLY CURRENTS
DEEP BLUES
DRIVE
EAR, THE
EFFICIENCY EXPERT, THE
ENCHANTED APRIL
ESCAPE FROM . . . SURVIVAL ZONE
EYE OF THE STORM
FATHER
FEED
FEW GOOD MEN, A
FINISHING TOUCH, THE
HELLRAISER III: HELL ON EARTH
HIGHWAY 61
HOURS AND TIMES, THE
HOUSESITTER
HUGH HEFNER: ONCE UPON A TIME
INCIDENT AT OGLALA
JOURNEY OF HONOR
KILL CRUISE
LADY DRAGON
LIFE ON A STRING
LIGHT SLEEPER
LOCKED-UP TIME
LONDON KILLS ME
LONELY HEARTS
LUNATIC, THE
MEGAVILLE
MINDWARP
MISTRESS
MONSTER IN A BOX
MY COUSIN VINNY
NIGHT AND THE CITY
NIGHT ON EARTH
OX, THE
PAINTING THE TOWN
POWER OF ONE, THE
PRIMARY MOTIVE
ROCK SOUP
RUBIN & ED
RUNESTONE, THE
SCANNERS III: THE TAKEOVER
SIMPLE MEN
SNEAKERS
SOUTH CENTRAL
SUPERCOP: POLICE STORY III
TETSUO: THE IRON MAN
TEXAS TENOR:
  THE ILLINOIS JACQUET STORY
THANK YOU AND GOOD NIGHT!
35 UP
3 NINJAS
TO RENDER A LIFE
TOGETHER ALONE
UNLAWFUL ENTRY
VOICES FROM THE FRONT
WHERE THE DAY TAKES YOU
WILD WHEELS
WILDFIRE
WISECRACKS
ZEBRAHEAD

★★½

ACES: IRON EAGLE III
ALAN & NAOMI
ALIEN3
AMERICAN ME
AMITYVILLE 1992: IT'S ABOUT TIME
ANIMAL INSTINCTS
BABE, THE
BACK IN THE U.S.S.R.
BASIC INSTINCT
BASKET CASE 3: THE PROGENY
BATMAN RETURNS
BEETHOVEN
BERNARD AND THE GENIE
BLACKBELT
BLIND VISION
BOB ROBERTS
BOOMERANG
COLOR ADJUSTMENT

COMMON BONDS
CONFESSIONS OF A SERIAL KILLER
CRISSCROSS
CROSSING, THE
CUTTING EDGE, THE
DAMNED IN THE USA
DANCE WITH DEATH
DARK HORSE
DAY IN OCTOBER, A
DEADLY BET
DEATH BECOMES HER
DEVIL'S DAUGHTER, THE
DOUBLE EDGE
ELEGANT CRIMINEL, L'
EYE OF THE EAGLE 3
FALLING FROM GRACE
FATHERS AND SONS
FERNGULLY: THE LAST RAINFOREST
FOREVER YOUNG
GETTING MARRIED IN BUFFALO JUMP
GODZILLA VS. BIOLLANTE
GUN IN BETTY LOU'S HANDBAG, THE
HEAVEN IS A PLAYGROUND
HERO
HIGHWAY TO HELL
HOME ALONE 2: LOST IN NEW YORK
HOUSE IV
HUMAN SHIELD, THE
HURRICANE SMITH
I DON'T BUY KISSES ANYMORE
INDOCHINE
JENNIFER EIGHT
JUICE
JUST LIKE IN THE MOVIES
KICKBOXER 3: THE ART OF WAR
KUFFS
LAST OF THE MOHICANS, THE
LEAGUE OF THEIR OWN, A
LEATHER JACKETS
LEAVING NORMAL
LETHAL WEAPON 3
LIFE ON THE EDGE
LIGHT IN THE JUNGLE, THE
LITTLE SISTER
LITTLE VEGAS
LOVE FIELD
LOVE HURTS
LOVE POTION NO. 9
LOVER, THE
LUNATICS: A LOVE STORY
MAMBO KINGS, THE
MARTIAL LAW 2: UNDERCOVER
MIDNIGHT CLEAR, A
MIGHTY DUCKS, THE
MO' MONEY
MONKEY BOY
MR. BASEBALL
MR. SATURDAY NIGHT
MUPPET CHRISTMAS CAROL, THE
MY NEW GUN
NICKEL & DIME
1991: THE YEAR PUNK BROKE
NOISES OFF
OF MICE AND MEN
OH, WHAT A NIGHT
OUT FOR BLOOD
PASSED AWAY
PATRIOT GAMES
PICTURES FROM A REVOLUTION
PLAY NICE
PLAYBOYS, THE
POISON IVY
PRAYER OF THE ROLLERBOYS
PROFESSIONAL, THE
PUBLIC EYE, THE
QUARREL, THE
RAMPAGE
RESURRECTED, THE
RIVER RUNS THROUGH IT, A
ROAD TO RUIN
ROCK-A-DOODLE
SARAFINA!
SHAKING THE TREE
SINGLE WHITE FEMALE
SISTER ACT
SOCIETY
SOLDIER'S TALE, A
SOLDIER'S FORTUNE
STATION, THE
STEAL AMERICA
STREET CRIMES
SWOON
THIS IS MY LIFE
THUNDERHEART
TILL THERE WAS YOU
TO PROTECT AND SERVE
TRANCERS III: DETH LIVES
TRESPASS
ULTRAVIOLET
UNDER SIEGE
USED PEOPLE
WATERLAND
WAYNE'S WORLD
WE'RE TALKIN' SERIOUS MONEY
WHITE MEN CAN'T JUMP
ZENTROPA

★★

ADJUSTER, THE
ADVENTURES IN SPYING
AFRAID OF THE DARK
ALBERTO EXPRESS
ARTICLE 99
BEASTMASTER 2: THROUGH THE PORTAL OF TIME
BECOMING COLETTE
BEYOND JUSTICE
BIG GIRLS DON'T CRY . . . THEY GET EVEN
BLACK ICE
BLAME IT ON THE BELLBOY
BLOODFIST IV: DIE TRYING
BOB MARLEY: TIME WILL TELL
BODYGUARD, THE
BUFFY THE VAMPIRE SLAYER
CAN IT BE LOVE
CAPTAIN AMERICA
CHAINS OF GOLD
CHAPLIN
CHRISTOPHER COLUMBUS: THE DISCOVERY
CITY OF JOY
COLLISION COURSE
CONSENTING ADULTS
CROSSING THE BRIDGE
DELTA HEAT
DIGGSTOWN
DISTINGUISHED GENTLEMAN, THE
DOCTOR MORDRID
DOES THIS MEAN WE'RE MARRIED?
DOLLY DEAREST
DOUBLE TROUBLE
EDWARD II
ENCINO MAN
FAR AND AWAY
FAVOUR, THE WATCH, AND THE VERY BIG FISH, THE
FINAL ANALYSIS
FOLKS!
FOR THOSE ABOUT TO ROCK
FREEJACK
GATE II
GLADIATOR
GUILTY AS CHARGED
GUYVER, THE
HARD PROMISES
HIRED TO KILL
HOFFA
HONEY, I BLEW UP THE KID
HOT CHOCOLATE
HUNTING
IN GOLD WE TRUST
IN THE HEAT OF PASSION
INNOCENT BLOOD
INSIDE EDGE
JOHNNY SUEDE
KILLER TOMATOES EAT FRANCE!
KISS ME A KILLER
LEAP OF FAITH
LILY WAS HERE
LINGUINI INCIDENT, THE
LITTLE NEMO: ADVENTURES IN SLUMBERLAND
LIVING END, THE
MAGICAL WORLD OF CHUCK JONES, THE
MAXIMUM FORCE
MEATBALLS 4
MEDICINE MAN
MEDITERRANEO
MEMOIRS OF AN INVISIBLE MAN
MISSION OF JUSTICE
MONTANA RUN, THE
MY FATHER IS COMING
NAKED OBSESSION
NEON CITY
NETHERWORLD
NEWSIES
NIGHT RHYTHMS
ODDBALL HALL
ONLY YOU
OVER HER DEAD BODY
PAMELA PRINCIPLE, THE
PETER'S FRIENDS
PLAY MURDER FOR ME
POUR SACHA
PRELUDE TO A KISS
PRIMO BABY

PROM NIGHT IV – DELIVER US FROM EVIL
PUERTO RICAN MAMBO (NOT A MUSICAL), THE
PURE COUNTRY
RAPID FIRE
REFRIGERATOR, THE
ROADSIDE PROPHETS
ROOTS OF EVIL
ROVER DANGERFIELD
RUBY
SCHOOL TIES
SEXUAL RESPONSE
SHADOWS AND FOG
SHINING THROUGH
SILK ROAD, THE
SPLIT SECOND
STAY TUNED
STOP! OR MY MOM WILL SHOOT
STRAIGHT TALK
STRANGER AMONG US, A
SUNSET STRIP
TALONS OF THE EAGLE
24 HOURS TO MIDNIGHT
UNDER SUSPICION
UNIVERSAL SOLDIER
VAGRANT, THE
VOYAGER
WAXWORK II: LOST IN TIME
WHERE ANGELS FEAR TO TREAD
WHITE SANDS
WHO SHOT PATAKANGO?
WIND
WINTER IN LISBON, THE
WOMAN, HER MEN AND HER FUTON, A
YEAR OF THE COMET

★½

ALMOST PREGNANT
ARMED FOR ACTION
BACKTRACK
BEYOND DARKNESS
CAGED FEAR
CANVAS
CAPTAIN RON
CENTER OF THE WEB
CLASS ACT
COLD JUSTICE
CRITTERS 4
CTHULHU MANSION
DEAD CERTAIN
DEADBOLT
DEATHSTALKER IV: MATCH OF TITANS
DIARY OF A HITMAN
DO OR DIE
EXILED IN AMERICA
FIELD OF FIRE
FINAL IMPACT
FREDDIE AS F.R.O.7
FROZEN ASSETS
GIVING, THE
HOMICIDAL IMPULSE
HUSBANDS AND LOVERS
INDIO 2 – THE REVOLT
INTO THE SUN
K2
KILLER IMAGE
LADYBUGS
LAWNMOWER MAN, THE
LOWER LEVEL
MAN TROUBLE
MIDNIGHT FEAR
MIRACLE BEACH
MOM AND DAD SAVE THE WORLD
MUNCHIE
NEAR MISSES
NIGHT EYES 2
ONCE UPON A CRIME
ONE LAST RUN
OTHER WOMAN, THE
OUT ON A LIMB
PASSENGER 57
PET SEMATARY II
PHANTOM OF THE RITZ
POPE MUST DIET!, THE
PROJECT: SHADOWCHASER
PSYCHIC
RADIO FLYER
RAISING CAIN
ROUND TRIP TO HEAVEN
SECRET FRIENDS
SHOOTING ELIZABETH
STEPHEN KING'S SLEEPWALKERS
STORYVILLE
TERMINAL BLISS
TIGER CLAWS
TOUCH AND DIE
TOYS
TRACES OF RED
TRAINED TO FIGHT
TWIN SISTERS
VENICE/VENICE
WHISPERS IN THE DARK
WILD ORCHID 2: TWO SHADES OF BLUE

★

ADVENTURES IN DINOSAUR CITY
AUNTIE LEE'S MEAT PIES
BAD CHANNELS
BARBARIAN QUEEN II: THE EMPRESS STRIKES BACK
BIKINI SUMMER 2
BODY WAVES
BREAKING THE RULES
BREATHING FIRE
BRENDA STARR
BRONX WAR, THE
CHINA O'BRIEN II
CODE NAME: CHAOS
COLD HEAVEN
COMRADES IN ARMS
COOL WORLD
DEMON IN MY VIEW, A
DEMONIC TOYS
DESERT KICKBOXER
DESIRE AND HELL AT SUNSET MOTEL
DR. GIGGLES
EMMANUELLE 6
EVIL CLUTCH
FATAL INSTINCT
FINE ROMANCE, A
FINEST HOUR, THE
1492: THE CONQUEST OF PARADISE
HELL MASTER
HOMEBOYS
HOUSE OF USHER, THE
ILLUSIONS
IMPORTANCE OF BEING EARNEST, THE
INVASION OF THE SPACE PREACHERS
LANDSLIDE
LITTLE NOISES
LOVE CRIMES
MIKEY
MIND, BODY & SOUL
MORTUARY ACADEMY
MY GRANDPA IS A VAMPIRE
976–EVIL II
ORIGINAL INTENT
PALE BLOOD
SAVAGE INSTINCT
SCORCHERS
SEEDPEOPLE
SEVERED TIES
SEX CRIMES
SHAKES THE CLOWN
SMOOTH TALKER
SNAKEEATER III . . . HIS LAW
SPIRITS
THERE'S NOTHING OUT THERE
TWIN PEAKS: FIRE WALK WITH ME
VAMPIRE HUNTER D
WELCOME TO OBLIVION

NO STAR RATING

BIKINI CARWASH COMPANY, THE
BLOOD ON THE BADGE
BRAIN DONORS
BRIDE OF KILLER NERD
DANCE MACABRE
DEATH HOUSE
DOUBLE VISION
FATE
GHOULIES III: GHOULIES GO TO COLLEGE
HAPPY HELL NIGHT
HELLROLLER
HOUSE ON TOMBSTONE HILL, THE
KICK OR DIE
KILL LINE
LASER MOON
MANIAC WARRIORS
MAXIMUM BREAKOUT
MIRROR IMAGES
PUSHED TO THE LIMIT
ROCK & ROLL COWBOYS
SECRET GAMES
SLUMBER PARTY MASSACRE 3
SORORITY HOUSE MASSACRE 2
STEELE'S LAW
TROLL 2
ULTIMATE DESIRES
WHITE TRASH
WITCHCRAFT IV: VIRGIN HEART

FILMS BY GENRE

Films belonging to more than one genre are listed under each appropriate category

Action

ACES: IRON EAGLE III
ADVENTURES IN SPYING
ALIEN3
ARMED FOR ACTION
BARBARIAN QUEEN II: THE EMPRESS STRIKES BACK
BEYOND JUSTICE
BLACKBELT
BLINK OF AN EYE
BLOODFIST IV: DIE TRYING
BLOODFIST III: FORCED TO FIGHT
BREATHING FIRE
CAPTAIN AMERICA
CHINA O'BRIEN II
COLLISION COURSE
COMRADES IN ARMS
DEADLY BET
DEATHSTALKER IV: MATCH OF TITANS
DESERT KICKBOXER
DO OR DIE
DOCTOR MORDRID
DOUBLE TROUBLE
ESCAPE FROM . . . SURVIVAL ZONE
EYE OF THE EAGLE 3
FIELD OF FIRE
FINAL IMPACT
FINEST HOUR, THE
FREEJACK
GUYVER, THE
HARD-BOILED
HIRED TO KILL
HOMEBOYS
HUMAN SHIELD, THE
HURRICANE SMITH
IN GOLD WE TRUST
INDIO 2 - THE REVOLT
INSIDE EDGE
INTO THE SUN
JOURNEY OF HONOR
JUICE
K2
KICK OR DIE
KICKBOXER 3: THE ART OF WAR
KILL LINE
KUFFS
LADY DRAGON
LANDSLIDE
LAST OF THE MOHICANS, THE
LETHAL WEAPON 3
MANIAC WARRIORS
MARTIAL LAW 2: UNDERCOVER
MAXIMUM BREAKOUT
MAXIMUM FORCE
MEGAVILLE
MISSION OF JUSTICE
MO' MONEY
NEON CITY
NICKEL & DIME
ONCE UPON A TIME IN CHINA
OUT FOR BLOOD
OUT ON A LIMB
PASSENGER 57
PATRIOT GAMES
PRAYER OF THE ROLLERBOYS
PROFESSIONAL, THE
PROJECT: SHADOWCHASER
PUSHED TO THE LIMIT
RAPID FIRE
ROOTS OF EVIL
SAVAGE INSTINCT
SCANNERS III: THE TAKEOVER
SEX CRIMES
SNAKEEATER III . . . HIS LAW
SNEAKERS
SOLDIER'S FORTUNE
STEELE'S LAW
STOP! OR MY MOM WILL SHOOT
STREET CRIMES
SUPERCOP: POLICE STORY III
TALONS OF THE EAGLE
3 NINJAS
TIGER CLAWS
TRAINED TO FIGHT
TRANCERS III: DETH LIVES
TRESPASS
24 HOURS TO MIDNIGHT
UNDER SIEGE
UNIVERSAL SOLDIER
UNLAWFUL ENTRY
WELCOME TO OBLIVION

Adventure

ACES: IRON EAGLE III
ADVENTURES IN DINOSAUR CITY
ALBERTO EXPRESS
BARBARIAN QUEEN II: THE EMPRESS STRIKES BACK
BATMAN RETURNS
BEASTMASTER 2: THROUGH THE PORTAL OF TIME
BEYOND JUSTICE
BRENDA STARR
CABEZA DE VACA
CAPTAIN AMERICA
CHRISTOPHER COLUMBUS: THE DISCOVERY
DEATHSTALKER IV: MATCH OF TITANS
EYE OF THE EAGLE 3
FAR AND AWAY
FIELD OF FIRE
FOREVER YOUNG
1492: THE CONQUEST OF PARADISE
HIRED TO KILL
HURRICANE SMITH
INDIO 2 – THE REVOLT
INTO THE SUN
JOURNEY OF HONOR
LAST OF THE MOHICANS, THE
LITTLE NEMO: ADVENTURES IN SLUMBERLAND
MANIAC WARRIORS
NEON CITY
ROADSIDE PROPHETS
SILK ROAD, THE
TILL THERE WAS YOU
TRANCERS III: DETH LIVES
YEAR OF THE COMET

Animated

ALADDIN
BEBE'S KIDS
COOL WORLD
FERNGULLY: THE LAST RAINFOREST
FREDDIE AS F.R.O.7
LITTLE NEMO: ADVENTURES IN SLUMBERLAND
PROFESSIONAL, THE
ROCK-A-DOODLE
TUNE, THE
VAMPIRE HUNTER D

Biography

BABE, THE
BECOMING COLETTE
BEETHOVEN LIVES UPSTAIRS
BOB MARLEY: TIME WILL TELL
CHAPLIN
CHRISTOPHER COLUMBUS: THE DISCOVERY
DADDY AND THE MUSCLE ACADEMY
ELEGANT CRIMINEL, L'
1492: THE CONQUEST OF PARADISE
HOFFA
HUGH HEFNER: ONCE UPON A TIME
LIGHT IN THE JUNGLE, THE
MALCOLM X
TOUS LES MATINS DU MONDE
VAN GOGH

Children's

BEBE'S KIDS
BEETHOVEN
BEETHOVEN LIVES UPSTAIRS
DARK HORSE
FREDDIE AS F.R.O.7
HOME ALONE 2: LOST IN NEW YORK
HONEY, I BLEW UP THE KID
LITTLE NEMO: ADVENTURES IN SLUMBERLAND
MUNCHIE
MUPPET CHRISTMAS CAROL, THE
MY GRANDPA IS A VAMPIRE
PRIMO BABY
ROCK-A-DOODLE

ROVER DANGERFIELD
3 NINJAS

Comedy

ADVENTURES IN SPYING
ALADDIN
ALBERTO EXPRESS
ALMOST PREGNANT
ARTICLE 99
AUNTIE LEE'S MEAT PIES
BAD CHANNELS
BASKET CASE 3: THE PROGENY
BEBE'S KIDS
BED & BREAKFAST
BEETHOVEN
BERNARD AND THE GENIE
BIG GIRLS DON'T CRY . . . THEY GET EVEN
BIKINI CARWASH COMPANY, THE
BIKINI SUMMER 2
BLAME IT ON THE BELLBOY
BOB ROBERTS
BODY WAVES
BOOMERANG
BRAIN DONORS
BREAKING THE RULES
BRENDA STARR
BRIDE OF KILLER NERD
BUFFY THE VAMPIRE SLAYER
CAN IT BE LOVE
CAPTAIN RON
CLASS ACT
CODE NAME: CHAOS
COLLISION COURSE
COMPLEX WORLD
CONTE DE PRINTEMPS
COOL WORLD
DEATH BECOMES HER
DELICATESSEN
DESIRE AND HELL AT SUNSET MOTEL
DIGGSTOWN
DISCRETE, LA
DISTINGUISHED GENTLEMAN, THE
DR. GIGGLES
DOES THIS MEAN WE'RE MARRIED?
DOUBLE TROUBLE
DRIVE
EFFICIENCY EXPERT, THE
ENCHANTED APRIL
ENCINO MAN
FATE
FAVOUR, THE WATCH, AND THE VERY BIG FISH, THE
FEED
FINE ROMANCE, A
FOLKS!
FROZEN ASSETS
GATE II
GHOULIES III: GHOULIES GO TO COLLEGE
GUILTY AS CHARGED
GUN IN BETTY LOU'S HANDBAG, THE
HARD PROMISES
HELLROLLER
HERO
HIGHWAY 61
HIGHWAY TO HELL
HOME ALONE 2: LOST IN NEW YORK
HONEY, I BLEW UP THE KID
HONEYMOON IN VEGAS
HOT CHOCOLATE
HOUSE IV
HOUSESITTER
HUSBANDS AND WIVES
I DON'T BUY KISSES ANYMORE
IMPORTANCE OF BEING EARNEST, THE
IN THE SOUP
INNOCENT BLOOD
INTO THE SUN
INVASION OF THE SPACE PREACHERS
JOHNNY STECCHINO
JOHNNY SUEDE
JUST LIKE IN THE MOVIES
KILLER TOMATOES EAT FRANCE!
KUFFS
LADYBUGS
LEAGUE OF THEIR OWN, A
LEAP OF FAITH
LEAVING NORMAL
LETHAL WEAPON 3
LIFE ON THE EDGE
LINGUINI INCIDENT, THE
LITTLE SISTER
LITTLE VEGAS
LOVE HURTS
LOVE POTION NO. 9
LUNATIC, THE
LUNATICS: A LOVE STORY
MAN TROUBLE
MEATBALLS 4
MEDITERRANEO
MIGHTY DUCKS, THE
MIRACLE BEACH
MISTRESS
MO' MONEY
MOM AND DAD SAVE THE WORLD
MONSTER IN A BOX
MONTANA RUN, THE
MORTUARY ACADEMY
MR. BASEBALL
MR. SATURDAY NIGHT
MY COUSIN VINNY
MY FATHER IS COMING
MY GRANDPA IS A VAMPIRE
MY NEW GUN
NEAR MISSES
NICKEL & DIME
NIGHT ON EARTH
976 – EVIL II
NOISES OFF
ODDBALL HALL
OH, WHAT A NIGHT
ONCE UPON A CRIME
ONLY YOU
OUT ON A LIMB
OVER HER DEAD BODY
PASSED AWAY
PEPI, LUCI, BOM AND OTHER GIRLS ON THE HEAP
PETER'S FRIENDS
PHANTOM OF THE RITZ
PLAYER, THE
POPE MUST DIET!, THE
PUERTO RICAN MAMBO (NOT A MUSICAL), THE
REFRIGERATOR, THE
ROAD TO RUIN
ROADSIDE PROPHETS
ROCK & ROLL COWBOYS
ROUND TRIP TO HEAVEN
ROVER DANGERFIELD
RUBIN & ED
SCORCHERS
SEVERED TIES
SHADOWS AND FOG
SHAKES THE CLOWN
SHAKING THE TREE
SHOOTING ELIZABETH
SIMPLE MEN
SINGLES
SISTER ACT
SNEAKERS
STATION, THE
STAY TUNED
STOP! OR MY MOM WILL SHOOT
STRAIGHT TALK
THANK YOU AND GOOD NIGHT!
THERE'S NOTHING OUT THERE
THIS IS MY LIFE
TOTO LE HEROS
TOYS
TUNE, THE
USED PEOPLE
VAGRANT, THE
WATERDANCE, THE
WAXWORK II: LOST IN TIME
WAYNE'S WORLD
WE'RE TALKIN' SERIOUS MONEY
WHITE MEN CAN'T JUMP
WISECRACKS
YEAR OF THE COMET

Crime

ADVENTURES IN SPYING
ALL – AMERICAN MURDER
ARMED FOR ACTION
BAD LIEUTENANT
BATMAN RETURNS
BLACKBELT
BLOOD ON THE BADGE
BREATHING FIRE
BRONX WAR, THE
BROTHER'S KEEPER
CAGED FEAR
CANVAS
CHAINS OF GOLD
CHINA O'BRIEN II
COLD JUSTICE
CONFESSIONS OF A SERIAL KILLER
DEAD CERTAIN
DEADLY BET
DEEP COVER
DELTA HEAT
DESERT KICKBOXER
DIARY OF A HITMAN
EYE OF THE STORM
FINAL ANALYSIS
HARD-BOILED
IN THE SOUP
INSIDE EDGE

KUFFS
LADY DRAGON
LASER MOON
LEATHER JACKETS
LETHAL WEAPON 3
LONELY HEARTS
MARTIAL LAW 2: UNDERCOVER
MAXIMUM BREAKOUT
MAXIMUM FORCE
MISSION OF JUSTICE
NAKED OBSESSION
NIGHT RHYTHMS
ONE FALSE MOVE
OUT FOR BLOOD
PLAY NICE
PRAYER OF THE ROLLERBOYS
PROFESSIONAL, THE
RAMPAGE
RESERVOIR DOGS
ROOTS OF EVIL
RUBY
SEX CRIMES
STRANGER AMONG US, A
STREET CRIMES
SUPERCOP: POLICE STORY III
SWOON
TALONS OF THE EAGLE
TO PROTECT AND SERVE
TOUCH AND DIE
TRACES OF RED
TRESPASS
24 HOURS TO MIDNIGHT

Dance

DANZON

Documentary

AFFENGEIL
AMERICAN DREAM
AMERICAN FABULOUS
BOB MARLEY: TIME WILL TELL
BRIEF HISTORY OF TIME, A
BROKEN NOSES
BROTHER'S KEEPER
COLOR ADJUSTMENT
COUSIN BOBBY
DADDY AND THE MUSCLE ACADEMY
DAMNED IN THE USA
DEADLY CURRENTS
DEEP BLUES
FEED
FOR THOSE ABOUT TO ROCK
HUGH HEFNER: ONCE UPON A TIME
INCIDENT AT OGLALA
LOCKED-UP TIME
MAGICAL WORLD OF CHUCK JONES, THE
MONSTER IN A BOX
1991: THE YEAR PUNK BROKE
PAINTING THE TOWN
PANAMA DECEPTION, THE
PICTURES FROM A REVOLUTION
ROCK SOUP
TEXAS TENOR: THE ILLINOIS JACQUET STORY
THANK YOU AND GOOD NIGHT!
35 UP
TO RENDER A LIFE
VOICES FROM THE FRONT
WILD WHEELS
WISECRACKS

Drama

ADAM'S RIB
ADJUSTER, THE
AFRAID OF THE DARK
ALAN & NAOMI
ALL THE VERMEERS IN NEW YORK
AMANTES
AMERICAN ME
ANIMAL INSTINCTS
ARTICLE 99
BACKTRACK
BEATING HEART, A
BEAUTIFUL DREAMERS
BECOMING COLETTE
BEST INTENTIONS, THE
BIG GIRLS DON'T CRY . . . THEY GET EVEN
BREAKING THE RULES
BRONX WAR, THE
CABEZA DE VACA
CAFE ROMEO
CAGED FEAR
CANVAS
CHAINS OF GOLD
CHAPLIN
CHILDREN, THE
CITY OF JOY
CLOSE TO EDEN
COLD JUSTICE
COMMON BONDS
CRISSCROSS
CROSSING THE BRIDGE
CROSSING, THE
CRY OF THE OWL, THE
CRYING GAME, THE
CUP FINAL
DAMAGE
DANZON
DARK HORSE
DAUGHTERS OF THE DUST
DIARY OF A HITMAN
DISCRETE, LA
EDWARD II
ELEGANT CRIMINEL, L'
EMMANUELLE 6
EXILED IN AMERICA
FALLING FROM GRACE
FATHER
FATHERS AND SONS
FEW GOOD MEN, A
FINAL ANALYSIS
FLIRTING
GAS FOOD LODGING
GETTING MARRIED IN BUFFALO JUMP
GIVING, THE
GLADIATOR
GLENGARRY GLEN ROSS
HAIRDRESSER'S HUSBAND, THE
HARD – BOILED
HEAVEN IS A PLAYGROUND
HERO
HIGHWAY 61
HOFFA
HOMEBOYS
HOURS AND TIMES, THE
HOWARDS END
HUNTING
HUSBANDS AND LOVERS
HUSBANDS AND WIVES
INDOCHINE
JUICE
JUMPIN' AT THE BONEYARD
JUST LIKE IN THE MOVIES
K2
LAWS OF GRAVITY
LEAP OF FAITH
LEATHER JACKETS
LEAVING NORMAL
LIFE ON A STRING
LIGHT SLEEPER
LILY WAS HERE
LINGUINI INCIDENT, THE
LITTLE NOISES
LITTLE VEGAS
LIVING END, THE
LONDON KILLS ME
LORENZO'S OIL
LOVE FIELD
LOVE HURTS
LOVER, THE
MALCOLM X
MAMBO KINGS, THE
MATCH FACTORY GIRL, THE
MAXIMUM BREAKOUT
MEDICINE MAN
MIDNIGHT CLEAR, A
MISSISSIPPI MASALA
MISTRESS
MONTANA RUN, THE
MR. SATURDAY NIGHT
NEWSIES
NIGHT AND DAY
NIGHT AND THE CITY
NIGHT ON EARTH
OF MICE AND MEN
ONE FALSE MOVE
ONE LAST RUN
ORIGINAL INTENT
OX, THE
PAMELA PRINCIPLE, THE
PASSION FISH
PLAYBOYS, THE
POISON IVY
POUR SACHA
POWER OF ONE, THE
PRIMARY MOTIVE
PRIMO BABY
PROOF
PURE COUNTRY
QUARREL, THE
RADIO FLYER
RAISE THE RED LANTERN
RASPAD
RESERVOIR DOGS
RIVER RUNS THROUGH IT, A
ROADSIDE PROPHETS
RUBY
SARAFINA!
SCENT OF A WOMAN

SCHOOL TIES
SCORCHERS
SECRET FRIENDS
SECRET GAMES
SHAKING THE TREE
SIMPLE MEN
SOLDIER'S TALE, A
SOUTH CENTRAL
STATION, THE
STEAL AMERICA
STORYVILLE
STRANGER AMONG US, A
SUNSET STRIP
SWOON
TERMINAL BLISS
THANK YOU AND GOOD NIGHT!
THIS IS MY LIFE
TOGETHER ALONE
TOTO LE HEROS
TOUS LES MATINS DU MONDE
TRACES OF RED
TRESPASS
TWIN PEAKS: FIRE WALK WITH ME
USED PEOPLE
VAN GOGH
VENICE/VENICE
VOYAGER
WATERDANCE, THE
WATERLAND
WHERE ANGELS FEAR TO TREAD
WHERE THE DAY TAKES YOU
WHITE TRASH
WHO SHOT PATAKANGO?
WILD ORCHID 2: TWO SHADES OF BLUE
WILDFIRE
WIND
WINTER IN LISBON, THE
WOMAN, HER MEN AND HER FUTON, A
ZEBRAHEAD
ZENTROPA

Erotic

ANIMAL INSTINCTS
BASIC INSTINCT
DAMAGE
DANCE WITH DEATH
EMMANUELLE 6
FATAL INSTINCT
FINISHING TOUCH, THE
HOMICIDAL IMPULSE
KISS ME A KILLER
LASER MOON
LOVE CRIMES
LOVER, THE
MIRROR IMAGES
NAKED OBSESSION
NIGHT EYES 2
OTHER WOMAN, THE
PAMELA PRINCIPLE, THE
PLAY MURDER FOR ME
SECRET GAMES
SEXUAL RESPONSE
ULTIMATE DESIRES
ULTRAVIOLET
WHISPERS IN THE DARK
WILD ORCHID 2: TWO SHADES OF BLUE

Fantasy

ADVENTURES IN DINOSAUR CITY
ALL THE VERMEERS IN NEW YORK
BATMAN RETURNS
BEASTMASTER 2: THROUGH THE PORTAL OF TIME
BERNARD AND THE GENIE
BRAM STOKER'S DRACULA
BRENDA STARR
CAPTAIN AMERICA
CLEARCUT
COLD HEAVEN
COOL WORLD
CTHULHU MANSION
DEATH BECOMES HER
DELICATESSEN
DEMONIC TOYS
DOCTOR MORDRID
ENCINO MAN
FERNGULLY: THE LAST RAINFOREST
GODZILLA VS. BIOLLANTE
HOUSE IV
MIRACLE BEACH
MUNCHIE
MY GRANDPA IS A VAMPIRE
NETHERWORLD
PRELUDE TO A KISS
RADIO FLYER
SECRET FRIENDS
TOTO LE HEROS
TOYS
TROLL 2
TWIN PEAKS: FIRE WALK WITH ME
WATERLAND
WAXWORK II: LOST IN TIME

Historical

BEAUTIFUL DREAMERS
CABEZA DE VACA
CHRISTOPHER COLUMBUS: THE DISCOVERY
DAUGHTERS OF THE DUST
DAY IN OCTOBER, A
EDWARD II
ELEGANT CRIMINEL, L'
1492: THE CONQUEST OF PARADISE
HOWARDS END
INDOCHINE
JOURNEY OF HONOR
LAST OF THE MOHICANS, THE
LIGHT IN THE JUNGLE, THE
MALCOLM X
NEWSIES
ONCE UPON A TIME IN CHINA
OX, THE
POWER OF ONE, THE
RUBY
SILK ROAD, THE
SWOON
VAN GOGH
ZENTROPA

Horror

ALIEN3
AMITYVILLE 1992: IT'S ABOUT TIME
AUNTIE LEE'S MEAT PIES
BAD CHANNELS
BASKET CASE 3: THE PROGENY
BEYOND DARKNESS
BRAM STOKER'S DRACULA
BRIDE OF KILLER NERD
BUFFY THE VAMPIRE SLAYER
CANDYMAN
CHILDREN OF THE NIGHT
CONFESSIONS OF A SERIAL KILLER
CRITTERS 4
CTHULHU MANSION
DANCE MACABRE
DEATH HOUSE
DEMONIC TOYS
DEVIL'S DAUGHTER, THE
DR. GIGGLES
DOLLY DEAREST
EVIL CLUTCH
GATE II
GHOULIES III: GHOULIES GO TO COLLEGE
GUILTY AS CHARGED
HAPPY HELL NIGHT
HELL MASTER
HELLRAISER III: HELL ON EARTH
HELLROLLER
HIGHWAY TO HELL
HOUSE IV
HOUSE OF USHER, THE
HOUSE ON TOMBSTONE HILL, THE
INNOCENT BLOOD
MIKEY
MIND, BODY & SOUL
MINDWARP
MONKEY BOY
NETHERWORLD
976 – EVIL II
PALE BLOOD
PET SEMATARY II
PHANTOM OF THE RITZ
PROM NIGHT IV – DELIVER US FROM EVIL
PSYCHIC
REFRIGERATOR, THE
RESURRECTED, THE
RUNESTONE, THE
SCANNERS III: THE TAKEOVER
SEEDPEOPLE
SEVERED TIES
SLUMBER PARTY MASSACRE 3
SOCIETY
SORORITY HOUSE MASSACRE 2
SPIRITS
SPLIT SECOND
STEPHEN KING'S SLEEPWALKERS
TETSUO: THE IRON MAN
THERE'S NOTHING OUT THERE
TROLL 2
VAGRANT, THE
VAMPIRE HUNTER D
WAXWORK II: LOST IN TIME
WITCHCRAFT IV: VIRGIN HEART

Martial Arts

BLACKBELT
BLINK OF AN EYE
BLOODFIST IV: DIE TRYING
BLOODFIST III: FORCED TO FIGHT
BREATHING FIRE
CHINA O'BRIEN II
DEADLY BET
DESERT KICKBOXER
FINAL IMPACT
IN GOLD WE TRUST
KICK OR DIE
KICKBOXER 3: THE ART OF WAR
KILL LINE
LADY DRAGON
MARTIAL LAW 2: UNDERCOVER
MISSION OF JUSTICE
ONCE UPON A TIME IN CHINA
OUT FOR BLOOD
PUSHED TO THE LIMIT
RAPID FIRE
SAVAGE INSTINCT
SNAKEEATER III . . . HIS LAW
STREET CRIMES
SUPERCOP: POLICE STORY III
TALONS OF THE EAGLE
3 NINJAS
TIGER CLAWS
TRAINED TO FIGHT
24 HOURS TO MIDNIGHT

Musical

ALADDIN
BOB MARLEY: TIME WILL TELL
COMPLEX WORLD
DEEP BLUES
FERNGULLY: THE LAST RAINFOREST
FOR THOSE ABOUT TO ROCK
FREDDIE AS F.R.O.7
MAMBO KINGS, THE
NEWSIES
1991: THE YEAR PUNK BROKE
PURE COUNTRY
ROCK-A-DOODLE
ROCK & ROLL COWBOYS
SARAFINA!
SISTER ACT
TEXAS TENOR:
THE ILLINOIS JACQUET STORY
TOUS LES MATINS DU MONDE
TUNE, THE

Mystery

ALL – AMERICAN MURDER
BLIND VISION
INSPECTOR LAVARDIN
LANDSLIDE
NIGHT RHYTHMS
ONCE UPON A CRIME
PLAYER, THE
SHADOWS AND FOG
SOCIETY
STORYVILLE
TILL THERE WAS YOU
TRACES OF RED
WITCHCRAFT IV: VIRGIN HEART

Political

AMERICAN DREAM
BOB ROBERTS
CENTER OF THE WEB
DAMNED IN THE USA
DEADLY CURRENTS
DOUBLE EDGE
EAR, THE
EXILED IN AMERICA
FEED
INCIDENT AT OGLALA
LOCKED – UP TIME
PANAMA DECEPTION, THE
PICTURES FROM A REVOLUTION
PRIMARY MOTIVE
ULTIMATE DESIRES
VOICES FROM THE FRONT

Prison

AMERICAN ME
COMMON BONDS

Religious

ORIGINAL INTENT

Romance

ALL THE VERMEERS IN NEW YORK
BACK IN THE U.S.S.R.
BEATING HEART, A
BED & BREAKFAST
BEST INTENTIONS, THE
BODYGUARD, THE
BOOMERANG
BRAM STOKER'S DRACULA
CAFE ROMEO
CHILDREN, THE
CLOSE TO EDEN
CONTE DE PRINTEMPS
CROSSING, THE
CRYING GAME, THE
CUTTING EDGE, THE
DANZON
DAY IN OCTOBER, A
DISCRETE, LA
DOES THIS MEAN WE'RE MARRIED?
ENCHANTED APRIL
FAR AND AWAY
FATE
FATHERS AND SONS
FINE ROMANCE, A
FLIRTING
FOREVER YOUNG
GETTING MARRIED IN BUFFALO JUMP
HAIRDRESSER'S HUSBAND, THE
HARD PROMISES
HONEYMOON IN VEGAS
HOT CHOCOLATE
HOUSESITTER
I DON'T BUY KISSES ANYMORE
IMPORTANCE OF BEING EARNEST, THE
IN THE HEAT OF PASSION
INDOCHINE
JENNIFER EIGHT
JOHNNY SUEDE
LITTLE SISTER
LOVE FIELD
LOVE POTION NO. 9
LUNATICS: A LOVE STORY
MAN TROUBLE
MEDICINE MAN
MEDITERRANEO
MEMOIRS OF AN INVISIBLE MAN
MIRACLE BEACH
MISSISSIPPI MASALA
NEAR MISSES
NIGHT AND DAY
NIGHT AND THE CITY
OH, WHAT A NIGHT
ONLY YOU
PASSION FISH
PLAYBOYS, THE
PRELUDE TO A KISS
PUBLIC EYE, THE
PURE COUNTRY
ROAD TO RUIN
SHINING THROUGH
SINGLES
STRAIGHT TALK
USED PEOPLE
VENICE/VENICE
VOYAGER
WHERE ANGELS FEAR TO TREAD
WILDFIRE
WOMAN, HER MEN AND HER
FUTON, A
YEAR OF THE COMET
ZEBRAHEAD

Science Fiction

ALIEN3
BAD CHANNELS
CRITTERS 4
ESCAPE FROM . . . SURVIVAL ZONE
FREEJACK
GODZILLA VS. BIOLLANTE
GUYVER, THE
INVASION OF THE SPACE PREACHERS
LAWNMOWER MAN, THE
MANIAC WARRIORS
MEGAVILLE
MEMOIRS OF AN INVISIBLE MAN
MINDWARP
MOM AND DAD SAVE THE WORLD
NEON CITY
PRAYER OF THE ROLLERBOYS
PROJECT: SHADOWCHASER
ROCK & ROLL COWBOYS
SCANNERS III: THE TAKEOVER
SEEDPEOPLE
SEVERED TIES
SPLIT SECOND
STAY TUNED
TETSUO: THE IRON MAN
TRANCERS III: DETH LIVES
VAMPIRE HUNTER D
WELCOME TO OBLIVION

Sports

BABE, THE
BROKEN NOSES
CUP FINAL
CUTTING EDGE, THE

DIGGSTOWN
GLADIATOR
HEAVEN IS A PLAYGROUND
K2
LEAGUE OF THEIR OWN, A
MIGHTY DUCKS, THE
MR. BASEBALL
ONE LAST RUN
PRIMO BABY
WHITE MEN CAN'T JUMP
WIND

Suspense

KILL CRUISE

Thriller

ALL – AMERICAN MURDER
BACK IN THE U.S.S.R.
BACKTRACK
BAD LIEUTENANT
BASIC INSTINCT
BLACK ICE
BLIND VISION
BLOOD ON THE BADGE
BLOODFIST IV: DIE TRYING
BODYGUARD, THE
CENTER OF THE WEB
CHILDREN OF THE NIGHT
CLEARCUT
COLD HEAVEN
CONSENTING ADULTS
CRYING GAME, THE
DANCE WITH DEATH
DEAD CERTAIN
DEADBOLT
DEATH HOUSE
DEEP COVER
DELTA HEAT
DEMON IN MY VIEW, A
DESIRE AND HELL AT SUNSET MOTEL
DOUBLE EDGE
DOUBLE VISION
EAR, THE
EYE OF THE STORM
FATAL INSTINCT
FINISHING TOUCH, THE
HAND THAT ROCKS THE CRADLE, THE
HOMICIDAL IMPULSE
ILLUSIONS
IN THE HEAT OF PASSION
INSIDE EDGE
INSPECTOR LAVARDIN
JENNIFER EIGHT
KILL CRUISE
KILL LINE
KILLER IMAGE
KISS ME A KILLER
LANDSLIDE
LASER MOON
LIGHT SLEEPER
LILY WAS HERE
LONELY HEARTS
LOVE CRIMES
LOWER LEVEL
MEGAVILLE
MIDNIGHT FEAR
MIRROR IMAGES
MONKEY BOY
MY NEW GUN
NAKED OBSESSION
NIGHT EYES 2
OTHER WOMAN, THE
PASSENGER 57
PATRIOT GAMES
PLAY MURDER FOR ME
PLAY NICE
POISON IVY
PSYCHIC
PUBLIC EYE, THE
RAISING CAIN
RAMPAGE
SEXUAL RESPONSE
SHINING THROUGH
SINGLE WHITE FEMALE
SMOOTH TALKER
SNEAKERS
SPLIT SECOND
THUNDERHEART
TIGER CLAWS
TO PROTECT AND SERVE
TOUCH AND DIE
TWIN SISTERS
ULTIMATE DESIRES
ULTRAVIOLET
UNDER SIEGE
UNDER SUSPICION
UNIVERSAL SOLDIER
UNLAWFUL ENTRY
WHISPERS IN THE DARK
WHITE SANDS
WINTER IN LISBON, THE
ZENTROPA

War

COMRADES IN ARMS
CUP FINAL
DAY IN OCTOBER, A
EYE OF THE EAGLE 3
FATHER
FIELD OF FIRE
FINEST HOUR, THE
HUMAN SHIELD, THE
MIDNIGHT CLEAR, A
PICTURES FROM A REVOLUTION
POUR SACHA
SHINING THROUGH
SOLDIER'S TALE, A
SOLDIER'S FORTUNE

Western

UNFORGIVEN

FILMS BY MPAA RATING

The Motion Picture Association of America (MPAA) currently grades films according to the following codes:

G GENERAL AUDIENCES (All ages admitted)
PG PARENTAL GUIDANCE SUGGESTED (Some material may not be suitable for children)
PG-13 PARENTS STRONGLY CAUTIONED (Some material may be inappropriate for children under 13)
R RESTRICTED (Under 17 requires accompanying parent or adult guardian)
NC-17 NO CHILDREN UNDER 17 ADMITTED
NR NOT RATED

G

ALADDIN
BRIEF HISTORY OF TIME, A
IMPORTANCE OF BEING EARNEST, THE
LITTLE NEMO: ADVENTURES IN SLUMBERLAND
MUPPET CHRISTMAS CAROL, THE
ROCK-A-DOODLE
ROVER DANGERFIELD

PG

ADVENTURES IN DINOSAUR CITY
ALAN & NAOMI
BABE, THE
BEETHOVEN
BIG GIRLS DON'T CRY . . . THEY GET EVEN
BRAIN DONORS
BRENDA STARR
COLLISION COURSE
CONTE DE PRINTEMPS
CUTTING EDGE, THE
DARK HORSE
EFFICIENCY EXPERT, THE
ENCHANTED APRIL
FERNGULLY: THE LAST RAINFOREST
FOREVER YOUNG
FREDDIE AS F.R.O.7
GODZILLA VS. BIOLLANTE
HARD PROMISES
HOME ALONE 2: LOST IN NEW YORK
HONEY, I BLEW UP THE KID
HOUSESITTER
HOWARDS END
I DON'T BUY KISSES ANYMORE
INCIDENT AT OGLALA
LEAGUE OF THEIR OWN, A
MAGICAL WORLD OF CHUCK JONES, THE
MIGHTY DUCKS, THE
MOM AND DAD SAVE THE WORLD
MUNCHIE
MY GRANDPA IS A VAMPIRE
NEWSIES
NICKEL & DIME
ODDBALL HALL
ONCE UPON A CRIME
ORIGINAL INTENT
OUT ON A LIMB
PURE COUNTRY
RAISE THE RED LANTERN
RIVER RUNS THROUGH IT, A
SISTER ACT
STAY TUNED
STRAIGHT TALK
3 NINJAS
WHERE ANGELS FEAR TO TREAD
WILDFIRE

PG-13

ADVENTURES IN SPYING
AMERICAN DREAM
BATMAN RETURNS
BEASTMASTER 2: THROUGH THE PORTAL OF TIME
BEAUTIFUL DREAMERS
BEBE'S KIDS
BLAME IT ON THE BELLBOY
BREAKING THE RULES
BUFFY THE VAMPIRE SLAYER
CAPTAIN AMERICA
CAPTAIN RON
CHAPLIN
CHRISTOPHER COLUMBUS: THE DISCOVERY
CITY OF JOY
CLASS ACT
COOL WORLD
CRITTERS 4
DANZON
DAY IN OCTOBER, A
DEATH BECOMES HER
DESIRE AND HELL AT SUNSET MOTEL
DOES THIS MEAN WE'RE MARRIED?
DOUBLE EDGE
DOUBLE VISION
FALLING FROM GRACE
FAR AND AWAY
FATE
FINE ROMANCE, A
FOLKS!
1492: THE CONQUEST OF PARADISE
FROZEN ASSETS
GETTING MARRIED IN BUFFALO JUMP
GUN IN BETTY LOU'S HANDBAG, THE
GUYVER, THE
HERO
HONEYMOON IN VEGAS
HOT CHOCOLATE
INDOCHINE
JOURNEY OF HONOR
KUFFS
LADYBUGS
LANDSLIDE
LEAP OF FAITH
LITTLE SISTER
LORENZO'S OIL
LOVE FIELD
LOVE POTION NO. 9
LUNATICS: A LOVE STORY
MALCOLM X
MAN TROUBLE
MEDICINE MAN
MEMOIRS OF AN INVISIBLE MAN
MONSTER IN A BOX
MR. BASEBALL
NEAR MISSES
NOISES OFF
OF MICE AND MEN
OH, WHAT A NIGHT
ONLY YOU
PASSED AWAY
PLAYBOYS, THE
POWER OF ONE, THE
PRELUDE TO A KISS
RADIO FLYER
RUBIN & ED
SARAFINA!
SCHOOL TIES
SHADOWS AND FOG
SHOOTING ELIZABETH
SILK ROAD, THE
SINGLES
SNEAKERS
STOP! OR MY MOM WILL SHOOT
STRANGER AMONG US, A
THIS IS MY LIFE
TILL THERE WAS YOU
TOTO LE HEROS
TOYS
TROLL 2
USED PEOPLE
VOYAGER
WAYNE'S WORLD
WE'RE TALKIN' SERIOUS MONEY
WIND
YEAR OF THE COMET

R

ACES: IRON EAGLE III
ADJUSTER, THE
AFRAID OF THE DARK
ALIEN3
ALL – AMERICAN MURDER
ALMOST PREGNANT
AMANTES
AMERICAN ME
AMITYVILLE 1992: IT'S ABOUT TIME
ANIMAL INSTINCTS
ARTICLE 99
AUNTIE LEE'S MEAT PIES
BACK IN THE U.S.S.R.
BACKTRACK
BAD CHANNELS
BARBARIAN QUEEN II: THE EMPRESS STRIKES BACK
BASIC INSTINCT
BASKET CASE 3: THE PROGENY
BECOMING COLETTE
BED & BREAKFAST
BEYOND DARKNESS
BEYOND JUSTICE
BIKINI CARWASH COMPANY, THE
BIKINI SUMMER 2
BLACK ICE
BLACKBELT
BLINK OF AN EYE
BLOODFIST IV: DIE TRYING
BLOODFIST III: FORCED TO FIGHT
BOB ROBERTS
BODY WAVES
BODYGUARD, THE
BOOMERANG
BRAM STOKER'S DRACULA
BREATHING FIRE
CABEZA DE VACA
CAFE ROMEO
CAGED FEAR
CAN IT BE LOVE
CANDYMAN
CANVAS
CENTER OF THE WEB
CHAINS OF GOLD
CHILDREN OF THE NIGHT
CHINA O'BRIEN II
CLEARCUT
CODE NAME: CHAOS
COLD HEAVEN
COLD JUSTICE
COMPLEX WORLD
COMRADES IN ARMS
CONSENTING ADULTS
CRISSCROSS
CROSSING THE BRIDGE
CROSSING, THE
CRYING GAME, THE
CTHULHU MANSION
DAMAGE
DANCE MACABRE
DANCE WITH DEATH
DEAD CERTAIN
DEADBOLT
DEADLY BET
DEATHSTALKER IV: MATCH OF TITANS
DEEP COVER
DELICATESSEN
DELTA HEAT
DEMON IN MY VIEW, A
DEMONIC TOYS
DESERT KICKBOXER
DEVIL'S DAUGHTER, THE
DIARY OF A HITMAN
DIGGSTOWN
DISTINGUISHED GENTLEMAN, THE
DR. GIGGLES
DOCTOR MORDRID
DOLLY DEAREST
DOUBLE TROUBLE
EDWARD II
ENCINO MAN
EVIL CLUTCH
EYE OF THE EAGLE 3
EYE OF THE STORM
FATAL INSTINCT
FATHERS AND SONS
FAVOUR, THE WATCH, AND THE VERY BIG FISH, THE
FEW GOOD MEN, A
FIELD OF FIRE
FINAL ANALYSIS
FINAL IMPACT
FINEST HOUR, THE
FINISHING TOUCH, THE
FOR THOSE ABOUT TO ROCK
FREEJACK
GAS FOOD LODGING
GATE II
GHOULIES III: GHOULIES GO TO COLLEGE
GLADIATOR
GLENGARRY GLEN ROSS
GUILTY AS CHARGED
HAIRDRESSER'S HUSBAND, THE
HAND THAT ROCKS THE CRADLE, THE
HEAVEN IS A PLAYGROUND
HELLRAISER III: HELL ON EARTH
HIGHWAY 61
HIGHWAY TO HELL
HIRED TO KILL
HOFFA
HOMICIDAL IMPULSE
HOUSE IV
HOUSE OF USHER, THE
HUMAN SHIELD, THE
HUNTING
HURRICANE SMITH
HUSBANDS AND LOVERS
HUSBANDS AND WIVES
ILLUSIONS
IN THE HEAT OF PASSION
INDIO 2 – THE REVOLT
INNOCENT BLOOD
INSIDE EDGE
INTO THE SUN
JENNIFER EIGHT
JOHNNY STECCHINO
JOHNNY SUEDE
JUICE
JUMPIN' AT THE BONEYARD
JUST LIKE IN THE MOVIES
K2
KICK OR DIE
KICKBOXER 3: THE ART OF WAR
KILL CRUISE
KILL LINE
KILLER IMAGE
KISS ME A KILLER
LADY DRAGON
LAST OF THE MOHICANS, THE
LAWNMOWER MAN, THE
LAWS OF GRAVITY
LEATHER JACKETS
LEAVING NORMAL
LETHAL WEAPON 3
LIGHT SLEEPER
LILY WAS HERE
LINGUINI INCIDENT, THE
LITTLE VEGAS
LONDON KILLS ME
LONELY HEARTS
LOVE CRIMES
LOVE HURTS
LOVER, THE
LOWER LEVEL
LUNATIC, THE
MAMBO KINGS, THE
MARTIAL LAW 2: UNDERCOVER
MAXIMUM FORCE
MEATBALLS 4
MEGAVILLE
MIDNIGHT CLEAR, A
MIKEY
MIND, BODY & SOUL
MINDWARP
MIRACLE BEACH
MIRROR IMAGES
MISSION OF JUSTICE
MISSISSIPPI MASALA
MISTRESS
MO' MONEY
MORTUARY ACADEMY
MR. SATURDAY NIGHT
MY COUSIN VINNY
MY NEW GUN
NAKED OBSESSION
NEON CITY
NETHERWORLD
NIGHT AND THE CITY
NIGHT EYES 2
NIGHT ON EARTH
976 – EVIL II
ONE FALSE MOVE
OTHER WOMAN, THE
OUT FOR BLOOD
OVER HER DEAD BODY
PALE BLOOD
PAMELA PRINCIPLE, THE
PASSENGER 57
PASSION FISH
PATRIOT GAMES
PET SEMATARY II
PHANTOM OF THE RITZ
PLAY MURDER FOR ME
PLAY NICE
PLAYER, THE

POISON IVY
POPE MUST DIET!, THE
PRAYER OF THE ROLLERBOYS
PRIMARY MOTIVE
PROJECT: SHADOWCHASER
PROM NIGHT IV – DELIVER US FROM EVIL
PROOF
PSYCHIC
PUBLIC EYE, THE
PUSHED TO THE LIMIT
RAISING CAIN
RAMPAGE
RAPID FIRE
RESERVOIR DOGS
RESURRECTED, THE
ROAD TO RUIN
ROADSIDE PROPHETS
ROOTS OF EVIL
ROUND TRIP TO HEAVEN
RUBY
RUNESTONE, THE
SCANNERS III: THE TAKEOVER
SCENT OF A WOMAN
SCORCHERS
SECRET GAMES
SEEDPEOPLE
SEVERED TIES
SEX CRIMES
SEXUAL RESPONSE
SHAKES THE CLOWN
SHAKING THE TREE
SHINING THROUGH
SIMPLE MEN
SINGLE WHITE FEMALE
SLUMBER PARTY MASSACRE 3
SNAKEEATER III . . . HIS LAW
SOCIETY
SOLDIER'S TALE, A
SOLDIER'S FORTUNE
SOUTH CENTRAL
SPIRITS
SPLIT SECOND
STEELE'S LAW
STEPHEN KING'S SLEEPWALKERS
STORYVILLE
STREET CRIMES
SUNSET STRIP
TALONS OF THE EAGLE
TERMINAL BLISS
THUNDERHEART
TIGER CLAWS
TO PROTECT AND SERVE
TOUCH AND DIE
TRACES OF RED
TRANCERS III: DETH LIVES
TRESPASS
TWIN PEAKS: FIRE WALK WITH ME
ULTIMATE DESIRES
ULTRAVIOLET
UNDER SIEGE
UNDER SUSPICION
UNFORGIVEN
UNIVERSAL SOLDIER
UNLAWFUL ENTRY
VAGRANT, THE
VAN GOGH
VENICE/VENICE
WATERDANCE, THE
WATERLAND
WAXWORK II: LOST IN TIME
WELCOME TO OBLIVION
WHERE THE DAY TAKES YOU
WHISPERS IN THE DARK
WHITE MEN CAN'T JUMP
WHITE SANDS
WHO SHOT PATAKANGO?
WILD ORCHID 2: TWO SHADES OF BLUE
WITCHCRAFT IV: VIRGIN HEART
WOMAN, HER MEN AND HER FUTON, A
ZEBRAHEAD
ZENTROPA

NC-17

BAD LIEUTENANT

NR

ADAM'S RIB
AFFENGEIL
ALBERTO EXPRESS
ALL THE VERMEERS IN NEW YORK
AMERICAN FABULOUS
ARMED FOR ACTION
BEATING HEART, A
BEETHOVEN LIVES UPSTAIRS
BERNARD AND THE GENIE
BEST INTENTIONS, THE
BLIND VISION
BLOOD ON THE BADGE
BOB MARLEY: TIME WILL TELL
BRIDE OF KILLER NERD
BROKEN NOSES
BRONX WAR, THE
BROTHER'S KEEPER
CHILDREN, THE
CLOSE TO EDEN
COLOR ADJUSTMENT
COMMON BONDS
CONFESSIONS OF A SERIAL KILLER
COUSIN BOBBY
CRY OF THE OWL, THE
CUP FINAL
DADDY AND THE MUSCLE ACADEMY
DAMNED IN THE USA
DAUGHTERS OF THE DUST
DEADLY CURRENTS
DEATH HOUSE
DEEP BLUES
DISCRETE, LA
DO OR DIE
DRIVE
EAR, THE
ELEGANT CRIMINEL, L'
EMMANUELLE 6
ESCAPE FROM . . . SURVIVAL ZONE
EXILED IN AMERICA
FATHER
FEED
FLIRTING
GIVING, THE
HAPPY HELL NIGHT
HARD – BOILED
HELL MASTER
HELLROLLER
HOMEBOYS
HOURS AND TIMES, THE
HOUSE ON TOMBSTONE HILL, THE
HUGH HEFNER: ONCE UPON A TIME
IN GOLD WE TRUST
IN THE SOUP
INSPECTOR LAVARDIN
INVASION OF THE SPACE PREACHERS
KILLER TOMATOES EAT FRANCE!
LASER MOON
LIFE ON A STRING
LIFE ON THE EDGE
LIGHT IN THE JUNGLE, THE
LITTLE NOISES
LIVING END, THE
LOCKED – UP TIME
MANIAC WARRIORS
MATCH FACTORY GIRL, THE
MAXIMUM BREAKOUT
MEDITERRANEO
MIDNIGHT FEAR
MONKEY BOY
MONTANA RUN, THE
MY FATHER IS COMING
NIGHT AND DAY
NIGHT RHYTHMS
1991: THE YEAR PUNK BROKE
ONCE UPON A TIME IN CHINA
ONE LAST RUN
OX, THE
PAINTING THE TOWN
PANAMA DECEPTION, THE
PEPI, LUCI, BOM AND OTHER GIRLS ON THE HEAP
PETER'S FRIENDS
PICTURES FROM A REVOLUTION
POUR SACHA
PRIMO BABY
PROFESSIONAL, THE
PUERTO RICAN MAMBO (NOT A MUSICAL), THE
QUARREL, THE
RASPAD
REFRIGERATOR, THE
ROCK & ROLL COWBOYS
ROCK SOUP
SAVAGE INSTINCT
SECRET FRIENDS
SMOOTH TALKER
SORORITY HOUSE MASSACRE 2
STATION, THE
STEAL AMERICA
SUPERCOP: POLICE STORY III
SWOON
TETSUO: THE IRON MAN
TEXAS TENOR: THE ILLINOIS JACQUET STORY
THANK YOU AND GOOD NIGHT!
THERE'S NOTHING OUT THERE
35 UP
TO RENDER A LIFE
TOGETHER ALONE
TOUS LES MATINS DU MONDE

TRAINED TO FIGHT
TUNE, THE
24 HOURS TO MIDNIGHT
TWIN SISTERS

VAMPIRE HUNTER D
VOICES FROM THE FRONT

WHITE TRASH
WILD WHEELS
WINTER IN LISBON, THE
WISECRACKS

FILMS BY PARENTAL RECOMMENDATION (PR)

AA – good for children; A – acceptable for children;
C – cautionary, some scenes may be objectionable for children; O – objectionable for children

AA

ALADDIN
BEETHOVEN LIVES UPSTAIRS
FERNGULLY: THE LAST RAINFOREST
FREDDIE AS F.R.O.7
LITTLE NEMO: ADVENTURES IN SLUMBERLAND
MUPPET CHRISTMAS CAROL, THE
ROCK-A-DOODLE
ROVER DANGERFIELD

A

ADVENTURES IN DINOSAUR CITY
ALAN & NAOMI
BABE, THE
BEETHOVEN
BERNARD AND THE GENIE
BIG GIRLS DON'T CRY . . . THEY GET EVEN
BRAIN DONORS
BRENDA STARR
BRIEF HISTORY OF TIME, A
CHILDREN, THE
CLOSE TO EDEN
COLLISION COURSE
COLOR ADJUSTMENT
COUSIN BOBBY
CUTTING EDGE, THE
DARK HORSE
DAUGHTERS OF THE DUST
DEEP BLUES
EFFICIENCY EXPERT, THE
FLIRTING
FOREVER YOUNG
GODZILLA VS. BIOLLANTE
HARD PROMISES
HONEY, I BLEW UP THE KID
HOUSESITTER
HOWARDS END
I DON'T BUY KISSES ANYMORE
IMPORTANCE OF BEING EARNEST, THE
INCIDENT AT OGLALA
KILLER TOMATOES EAT FRANCE!
LEAGUE OF THEIR OWN, A
LIFE ON A STRING
LIGHT IN THE JUNGLE, THE
MAGICAL WORLD OF CHUCK JONES, THE
MEDITERRANEO
MIGHTY DUCKS, THE
MOM AND DAD SAVE THE WORLD
MUNCHIE
MY GRANDPA IS A VAMPIRE
NEWSIES
NICKEL & DIME
ODDBALL HALL
ONCE UPON A CRIME
ONE LAST RUN
ORIGINAL INTENT
OUT ON A LIMB
OX, THE
PAINTING THE TOWN
PRIMO BABY
PURE COUNTRY
QUARREL, THE
RIVER RUNS THROUGH IT, A
SISTER ACT
STRAIGHT TALK
TEXAS TENOR: THE ILLINOIS JACQUET STORY
THANK YOU AND GOOD NIGHT!
35 UP
3 NINJAS
TO RENDER A LIFE
TOUS LES MATINS DU MONDE
TUNE, THE
VOICES FROM THE FRONT
WHERE ANGELS FEAR TO TREAD
WILD WHEELS

C

ACES: IRON EAGLE III
ADAM'S RIB
ADJUSTER, THE
ADVENTURES IN SPYING
AFFENGEIL
AFRAID OF THE DARK
ALBERTO EXPRESS
ALL THE VERMEERS IN NEW YORK
AMERICAN DREAM
AMERICAN FABULOUS
AMERICAN ME
ARMED FOR ACTION
ARTICLE 99
BACK IN THE U.S.S.R.
BACKTRACK
BAD CHANNELS
BARBARIAN QUEEN II: THE EMPRESS STRIKES BACK
BATMAN RETURNS
BEASTMASTER 2: THROUGH THE PORTAL OF TIME
BEATING HEART, A
BEAUTIFUL DREAMERS
BEBE'S KIDS
BECOMING COLETTE
BED & BREAKFAST
BEST INTENTIONS, THE
BEYOND JUSTICE
BLAME IT ON THE BELLBOY
BLINK OF AN EYE
BLOODFIST IV: DIE TRYING
BOB MARLEY: TIME WILL TELL
BOB ROBERTS
BODY WAVES
BODYGUARD, THE
BOOMERANG
BRAM STOKER'S DRACULA
BREAKING THE RULES
BREATHING FIRE
BROKEN NOSES
BROTHER'S KEEPER
BUFFY THE VAMPIRE SLAYER
CABEZA DE VACA
CAFE ROMEO
CAN IT BE LOVE
CANVAS
CAPTAIN AMERICA
CAPTAIN RON
CENTER OF THE WEB
CHAPLIN
CHRISTOPHER COLUMBUS: THE DISCOVERY
CITY OF JOY
CLASS ACT
CLEARCUT
CODE NAME: CHAOS
CONTE DE PRINTEMPS
COOL WORLD
CRISSCROSS
CRITTERS 4
CROSSING, THE
CRY OF THE OWL, THE
CRYING GAME, THE
CUP FINAL
DAMNED IN THE USA
DANZON
DAY IN OCTOBER, A
DEADBOLT
DEADLY CURRENTS
DEATH BECOMES HER
DEATHSTALKER IV: MATCH OF TITANS
DELICATESSEN
DESIRE AND HELL AT SUNSET MOTEL
DEVIL'S DAUGHTER, THE
DIGGSTOWN
DISTINGUISHED GENTLEMAN, THE
DOES THIS MEAN WE'RE MARRIED?
DOUBLE EDGE
DOUBLE VISION
DRIVE
EAR, THE
ENCHANTED APRIL

ENCINO MAN
EXILED IN AMERICA
EYE OF THE EAGLE 3
EYE OF THE STORM
FALLING FROM GRACE
FAR AND AWAY
FATE
FATHER
FATHERS AND SONS
FAVOUR, THE WATCH, AND THE VERY BIG FISH, THE
FEED
FEW GOOD MEN, A
FIELD OF FIRE
FINAL ANALYSIS
FINE ROMANCE, A
FINEST HOUR, THE
FOLKS!
FOR THOSE ABOUT TO ROCK
1492: THE CONQUEST OF PARADISE
FREEJACK
FROZEN ASSETS
GAS FOOD LODGING
GETTING MARRIED IN BUFFALO JUMP
GIVING, THE
GLADIATOR
GUN IN BETTY LOU'S HANDBAG, THE
GUYVER, THE
HAIRDRESSER'S HUSBAND, THE
HAND THAT ROCKS THE CRADLE, THE
HEAVEN IS A PLAYGROUND
HERO
HOFFA
HOME ALONE 2: LOST IN NEW YORK
HONEYMOON IN VEGAS
HOT CHOCOLATE
HOURS AND TIMES, THE
HUGH HEFNER: ONCE UPON A TIME
HUMAN SHIELD, THE
HUSBANDS AND WIVES
ILLUSIONS
IN THE SOUP
INDOCHINE
INSPECTOR LAVARDIN
JENNIFER EIGHT
JOHNNY STECCHINO
JOHNNY SUEDE
JOURNEY OF HONOR
JUMPIN' AT THE BONEYARD
JUST LIKE IN THE MOVIES
K2
KICKBOXER 3: THE ART OF WAR
LADYBUGS
LANDSLIDE
LAWNMOWER MAN, THE
LEAP OF FAITH
LEAVING NORMAL
LIFE ON THE EDGE
LINGUINI INCIDENT, THE
LITTLE NOISES
LITTLE SISTER
LOCKED–UP TIME
LONDON KILLS ME
LORENZO'S OIL
LOVE FIELD
LOVE HURTS
LOVE POTION NO. 9
LUNATICS: A LOVE STORY
MALCOLM X
MAMBO KINGS, THE
MAN TROUBLE
MATCH FACTORY GIRL, THE
MAXIMUM BREAKOUT
MEATBALLS 4
MEDICINE MAN
MEMOIRS OF AN INVISIBLE MAN
MIDNIGHT CLEAR, A
MISSISSIPPI MASALA
MISTRESS
MO' MONEY
MONSTER IN A BOX
MONTANA RUN, THE
MR. BASEBALL
MR. SATURDAY NIGHT
MY COUSIN VINNY
MY NEW GUN
NEAR MISSES
NEON CITY
NETHERWORLD
NIGHT AND DAY
NIGHT AND THE CITY
NIGHT ON EARTH
1991: THE YEAR PUNK BROKE
NOISES OFF
OF MICE AND MEN
OH, WHAT A NIGHT
ONCE UPON A TIME IN CHINA
ONLY YOU
PANAMA DECEPTION, THE
PASSED AWAY
PASSION FISH
PATRIOT GAMES
PEPI, LUCI, BOM AND OTHER GIRLS ON THE HEAP
PETER'S FRIENDS
PICTURES FROM A REVOLUTION
PLAYBOYS, THE
PLAYER, THE
POUR SACHA
POWER OF ONE, THE
PRELUDE TO A KISS
PRIMARY MOTIVE
PROJECT: SHADOWCHASER
PROOF
PUERTO RICAN MAMBO (NOT A MUSICAL), THE
PUSHED TO THE LIMIT
RADIO FLYER
RAISE THE RED LANTERN
RAMPAGE
RAPID FIRE
RASPAD
REFRIGERATOR, THE
ROAD TO RUIN
ROADSIDE PROPHETS
ROCK & ROLL COWBOYS
ROCK SOUP
ROUND TRIP TO HEAVEN
RUBIN & ED
RUBY
SARAFINA!
SCENT OF A WOMAN
SCHOOL TIES
SCORCHERS
SHADOWS AND FOG
SHAKING THE TREE
SHINING THROUGH
SHOOTING ELIZABETH
SILK ROAD, THE
SIMPLE MEN
SINGLES
SNAKEEATER III . . . HIS LAW
SNEAKERS
SOLDIER'S TALE, A
SOLDIER'S FORTUNE
SOUTH CENTRAL
STATION, THE
STAY TUNED
STEAL AMERICA
STEPHEN KING'S SLEEPWALKERS
STOP! OR MY MOM WILL SHOOT
STRANGER AMONG US, A
STREET CRIMES
SUNSET STRIP
SUPERCOP: POLICE STORY III
SWOON
THERE'S NOTHING OUT THERE
THIS IS MY LIFE
THUNDERHEART
TIGER CLAWS
TILL THERE WAS YOU
TOGETHER ALONE
TOTO LE HEROS
TOUCH AND DIE
TOYS
TRESPASS
24 HOURS TO MIDNIGHT
UNDER SIEGE
UNDER SUSPICION
UNFORGIVEN
UNIVERSAL SOLDIER
USED PEOPLE
VAMPIRE HUNTER D
VAN GOGH
VENICE/VENICE
VOYAGER
WATERDANCE, THE
WATERLAND
WAYNE'S WORLD
WE'RE TALKIN' SERIOUS MONEY
WHERE THE DAY TAKES YOU
WHITE SANDS
WHO SHOT PATAKANGO?
WILDFIRE
WIND
WINTER IN LISBON, THE
WISECRACKS
WOMAN, HER MEN AND HER FUTON, A
YEAR OF THE COMET
ZEBRAHEAD
ZENTROPA

O

ALIEN3
ALL–AMERICAN MURDER
ALMOST PREGNANT

AMANTES
AMITYVILLE 1992: IT'S ABOUT TIME
ANIMAL INSTINCTS
AUNTIE LEE'S MEAT PIES
BAD LIEUTENANT
BASIC INSTINCT
BASKET CASE 3: THE PROGENY
BEYOND DARKNESS
BIKINI CARWASH COMPANY, THE
BIKINI SUMMER 2
BLACK ICE
BLACKBELT
BLIND VISION
BLOOD ON THE BADGE
BLOODFIST III: FORCED TO FIGHT
BRIDE OF KILLER NERD
BRONX WAR, THE
CAGED FEAR
CANDYMAN
CHAINS OF GOLD
CHILDREN OF THE NIGHT
CHINA O'BRIEN II
COLD HEAVEN
COLD JUSTICE
COMMON BONDS
COMPLEX WORLD
COMRADES IN ARMS
CONFESSIONS OF A SERIAL KILLER
CONSENTING ADULTS
CROSSING THE BRIDGE
CTHULHU MANSION
DADDY AND THE MUSCLE ACADEMY
DAMAGE
DANCE MACABRE
DANCE WITH DEATH
DEAD CERTAIN
DEADLY BET
DEATH HOUSE
DEEP COVER
DELTA HEAT
DEMON IN MY VIEW, A
DEMONIC TOYS
DESERT KICKBOXER
DIARY OF A HITMAN
DISCRETE, LA
DO OR DIE
DR. GIGGLES
DOCTOR MORDRID
DOLLY DEAREST
DOUBLE TROUBLE
EDWARD II
ELEGANT CRIMINEL, L'
EMMANUELLE 6
ESCAPE FROM . . . SURVIVAL ZONE
EVIL CLUTCH
FATAL INSTINCT
FINAL IMPACT
FINISHING TOUCH, THE
GATE II
GHOULIES III:
GHOULIES GO TO COLLEGE
GLENGARRY GLEN ROSS
GUILTY AS CHARGED
HAPPY HELL NIGHT
HARD–BOILED
HELL MASTER
HELLRAISER III: HELL ON EARTH
HELLROLLER
HIGHWAY 61
HIGHWAY TO HELL
HIRED TO KILL
HOMEBOYS
HOMICIDAL IMPULSE
HOUSE IV
HOUSE OF USHER, THE
HOUSE ON TOMBSTONE HILL, THE
HUNTING
HURRICANE SMITH
HUSBANDS AND LOVERS
IN GOLD WE TRUST
IN THE HEAT OF PASSION
INDIO 2 – THE REVOLT
INNOCENT BLOOD
INSIDE EDGE
INTO THE SUN
INVASION OF THE SPACE PREACHERS
JUICE
KICK OR DIE
KILL CRUISE
KILL LINE
KILLER IMAGE
KISS ME A KILLER
KUFFS
LADY DRAGON
LASER MOON
LAST OF THE MOHICANS, THE
LAWS OF GRAVITY
LEATHER JACKETS
LETHAL WEAPON 3
LIGHT SLEEPER
LILY WAS HERE
LITTLE VEGAS
LIVING END, THE
LONELY HEARTS
LOVE CRIMES
LOVER, THE
LOWER LEVEL
LUNATIC, THE
MANIAC WARRIORS
MARTIAL LAW 2: UNDERCOVER
MAXIMUM FORCE
MEGAVILLE
MIDNIGHT FEAR
MIKEY
MIND, BODY & SOUL
MINDWARP
MIRACLE BEACH
MIRROR IMAGES
MISSION OF JUSTICE
MONKEY BOY
MORTUARY ACADEMY
MY FATHER IS COMING
NAKED OBSESSION
NIGHT EYES 2
NIGHT RHYTHMS
976–EVIL II
ONE FALSE MOVE
OTHER WOMAN, THE
OUT FOR BLOOD
OVER HER DEAD BODY
PALE BLOOD
PAMELA PRINCIPLE, THE
PASSENGER 57
PET SEMATARY II
PHANTOM OF THE RITZ
PLAY MURDER FOR ME
PLAY NICE
POISON IVY
POPE MUST DIET!, THE
PRAYER OF THE ROLLERBOYS
PROFESSIONAL, THE
PROM NIGHT IV – DELIVER US
FROM EVIL
PSYCHIC
PUBLIC EYE, THE
RAISING CAIN
RESERVOIR DOGS
RESURRECTED, THE
ROOTS OF EVIL
RUNESTONE, THE
SAVAGE INSTINCT
SCANNERS III: THE TAKEOVER
SECRET FRIENDS
SECRET GAMES
SEEDPEOPLE
SEVERED TIES
SEX CRIMES
SEXUAL RESPONSE
SHAKES THE CLOWN
SINGLE WHITE FEMALE
SLUMBER PARTY MASSACRE 3
SMOOTH TALKER
SOCIETY
SORORITY HOUSE MASSACRE 2
SPIRITS
SPLIT SECOND
STEELE'S LAW
STORYVILLE
TALONS OF THE EAGLE
TERMINAL BLISS
TETSUO: THE IRON MAN
TO PROTECT AND SERVE
TRACES OF RED
TRAINED TO FIGHT
TRANCERS III: DETH LIVES
TROLL 2
TWIN PEAKS: FIRE WALK WITH ME
TWIN SISTERS
ULTIMATE DESIRES
ULTRAVIOLET
UNLAWFUL ENTRY
VAGRANT, THE
WAXWORK II: LOST IN TIME
WELCOME TO OBLIVION
WHISPERS IN THE DARK
WHITE MEN CAN'T JUMP
WHITE TRASH
WILD ORCHID 2:
TWO SHADES OF BLUE
WITCHCRAFT IV: VIRGIN HEART

NAME INDEX

Individuals included in the cast or credit sections of the film reviews in this volume are listed below. Names are arranged alphabetically by function as follows:

Actors
Animators
Art Directors
Choreographers
Cinematographers
Costumes
Directors
Editors
Makeup
Music Composers
Music Directors
Producers
Production Designers
Screenwriters
Set Decorators
Source Authors
Special Effects
Stunts

ACTORS

Aguilar, Orietta
BARBARIAN QUEEN II: THE EMPRESS STRIKES BACK
Aguirre, Jose Luis
PEPI, LUCI, BOM AND OTHER GIRLS ON THE HEAP
Agutter, Jenny
FREDDIE AS F.R.O.7
Ahlsell, Puck
BEST INTENTIONS, THE
Ahlstedt, Borje
BEST INTENTIONS, THE
Ahlwardt, Elmer
WIND
Ahmad, Sami
CITY OF JOY
Aiello, Danny
MISTRESS
RUBY
Aiello, Rick
TWIN PEAKS: FIRE WALK WITH ME
Ailhaud, Yveline
HAIRDRESSER'S HUSBAND, THE
Ajibade, Yemi
LONDON KILLS ME
Akhtar, Masood
CITY OF JOY
Akins, Claude
FALLING FROM GRACE
Alan, Craig
SEX CRIMES
Alan, Jordan
TERMINAL BLISS
Alaniz, Rico
FINAL ANALYSIS
Alard, Nelly
VENICE/VENICE
Alban, Alissa
HARD PROMISES
SIMPLE MEN
Albanese, Judge David
DAMNED IN THE USA
Albano, Captain Lou
COMPLEX WORLD
Albenque, Patrick
FAVOUR, THE WATCH, AND THE VERY BIG FISH, THE
Albert, Eddie
BRENDA STARR
Albert, Edward
EXILED IN AMERICA
Alberti, Gigio
MEDITERRANEO
Alberto, Jorge
INSIDE EDGE
Alberto, Jose
MAMBO KINGS, THE
Alcala, Jose
DIGGSTOWN
Alcock, Victoria
UNDER SUSPICION
Alda, Alan
WHISPERS IN THE DARK
Alda, Rutanya
ARTICLE 99
LEAVING NORMAL

Aldana, Adolfo
DANZON
Alderman, Jane
PRELUDE TO A KISS
Aldredge, Tom
BRENDA STARR
Aldridge, Bobby
BUFFY THE VAMPIRE SLAYER
Aleck, Jimmy
ONE LAST RUN
Aleman, Oscar
SWOON
Alenius, Inga
BEST INTENTIONS, THE
Aleong, Aki
KUFFS
OUT FOR BLOOD
Alessandrini, Toni
MIND, BODY & SOUL
Alessi, Joseph
LONDON KILLS ME
Alex-Barton, David
HARD PROMISES
Alexander, Alex
COLD HEAVEN
Alexander, Barbara Lee
HIRED TO KILL
Alexander, Bruce
FATHER
Alexander, David James
NEWSIES
Alexander, Derick
FINAL ANALYSIS
Alexander, Jace
MISTRESS
Alexander, Jason
I DON'T BUY KISSES ANYMORE
Alexander, Max
COMPLEX WORLD
Alexander, Sharon
CUP FINAL
Alexander, Spike
BRAIN DONORS
Alexzander, Leo
UNDER SIEGE
Alfredson, Hans
BEST INTENTIONS, THE
Alicia, Marta
MINDWARP
Alicino, Ronnie
LETHAL WEAPON 3
Allain, Alicia
LEATHER JACKETS
Allas, Peter
ENCINO MAN
Allen, David Caldwell
SCHOOL TIES
Allen, Gene "Groove"
BOOMERANG
Allen, Ginger Lynn
LEATHER JACKETS
MIND, BODY & SOUL
Allen, Gracie
WISECRACKS
Allen, Ian
MUPPET CHRISTMAS CAROL, THE

Allen, Jacqueline M.
MAN TROUBLE
Allen, John
MO' MONEY
Allen, Karen
MALCOLM X
Allen, Kevin
BERNARD AND THE GENIE
Allen, Penny
BAD LIEUTENANT
Allen, Rae
LEAGUE OF THEIR OWN, A
Allen, Sage
MR. SATURDAY NIGHT
Allen, Sheila
SHINING THROUGH
Allen, Sonny
MALCOLM X
Allen, Steve
PLAYER, THE
Allen, Thomas
LOVE HURTS
Allen, Woody
HUSBANDS AND WIVES
SHADOWS AND FOG
Allenbury, Genevieve
CHRISTOPHER COLUMBUS: THE DISCOVERY
Allison, Paul
OUT ON A LIMB
Allison, Richard
OUT ON A LIMB
Allmon, Clinton
TOYS
Allred, Alicia
PASSENGER 57
Almagro, Ivan
CTHULHU MANSION
Almayvonne
MO' MONEY
Almaz, Michael
UNDER SUSPICION
Almazon, Randy
PALE BLOOD
Almgren, Susan
TWIN SISTERS
Almodvar, Agustin
PEPI, LUCI, BOM AND OTHER GIRLS ON THE HEAP
Alpert, Eleanor Ruth
GIVING, THE
Alston, Barbara
CANDYMAN
Alt, Carol
BEYOND JUSTICE
Altarez, Naomi
DOUBLE EDGE
Altfather, Kristin
BOB ROBERTS
Altman, Bruce
GLENGARRY GLEN ROSS
MY NEW GUN
Altman, Charles R.
BOB ROBERTS
LORENZO'S OIL
Altman, Ed
SWOON

Altruda, Joseph L.
TWIN PEAKS: FIRE WALK WITH ME
Altus, Linda
FROZEN ASSETS
Alvarado, Trini
BABE, THE
Alvarez, Abraham
PANAMA DECEPTION, THE
Alvarez, Diego
PEPI, LUCI, BOM AND OTHER GIRLS ON THE HEAP
Alvarez, George
CLASS ACT
Alvarez, Roberto
AMERICAN ME
Alves, Luis Fernandez
CTHULHU MANSION
Alzado, Lyle
COMRADES IN ARMS
NEON CITY
Amandes, Tom
STRAIGHT TALK
Amatrudo, Ed
TRACES OF RED
Amber
ROUND TRIP TO HEAVEN
Ambriz, Domingo
AMERICAN ME
Ameche, Don
FOLKS!
ODDBALL HALL
Amen, Alessandro
ONCE UPON A CRIME
Amendola, Tony
WILDFIRE
Amendolia, Don
WAYNE'S WORLD
Ament, Jeff
SINGLES
Amezquita, Raymond
AMERICAN ME
Amick, Madchen
STEPHEN KING'S SLEEPWALKERS
TWIN PEAKS: FIRE WALK WITH ME
Amick, Tom
TRACES OF RED
Amidou
HOT CHOCOLATE
Amiel, Michele
FINE ROMANCE, A
Amman, Billy
LORENZO'S OIL
Amoroso, Nick
MANIAC WARRIORS
Amos, William T.
AMERICAN ME
Amstutz, Katie
HELLROLLER
Amstutz, Roland
ALBERTO EXPRESS
Amurri, Eva
BOB ROBERTS
Anagnos, Bill
MALCOLM X
Ancel, Valerie
BECOMING COLETTE

Andelin, James
BABE, THE
FOLKS!
Anders, Avalon
BIKINI SUMMER 2
Anders, Richard
DISTINGUISHED GENTLEMAN, THE
Anders, Tiffany
GAS FOOD LODGING
Andersch, Erika
BATMAN RETURNS
Anderson, Adisa
DAUGHTERS OF THE DUST
Anderson, Chuckie
BABE, THE
Anderson, D.L.
CONSENTING ADULTS
Anderson, Daniel
BABE, THE
Anderson, Dion
DISTINGUISHED GENTLEMAN, THE
Anderson, Eunice
LEAGUE OF THEIR OWN, A
Anderson, III, Felton
TOYS
Anderson, Kevin
HOFFA
Anderson, Kirk Palmer
HOFFA
Anderson, Lewie
AMERICAN DREAM
Anderson, Lindsay
BLAME IT ON THE BELLBOY
Anderson, Loni
MUNCHIE
Anderson, Louie
BEBE'S KIDS
Anderson, M. Cochise
DAUGHTERS OF THE DUST
Anderson, Mark E.
SOUTH CENTRAL
Anderson, Melody
LANDSLIDE
Anderson, Michael J.
TWIN PEAKS: FIRE WALK WITH ME
Anderson, Mitchell
ALL-AMERICAN MURDER
Anderson, Peter
LEAVING NORMAL
Anderson, Richard
PLAYER, THE
Anderson, Ryan
SCHOOL TIES
Anderson, Sam
MEMOIRS OF AN INVISIBLE MAN
Anderson, Scott
MANIAC WARRIORS
Anderson, Stephanie
DEATH BECOMES HER
WATERLAND
Anderson, Stephen W.
MAN TROUBLE
Anderson, Steven
ADVENTURES IN DINOSAUR CITY
Anderson, Vass
WHERE ANGELS FEAR TO TREAD

Anderson-Gunter, Jeffrey
ENCINO MAN
Andrell, Simon
SHOOTING ELIZABETH
Andrew
35 UP
Andrews, Geoffrey
ONCE UPON A CRIME
Andrews, Jeffrey
FAR AND AWAY
Andrews, Julie
FINE ROMANCE, A
Andrews, Mac
LAST OF THE MOHICANS, THE
Andrews, Naveen
LONDON KILLS ME
Andrews, Noah Craig
OUT ON A LIMB
Andreyko, Marc
BRIDE OF KILLER NERD
Andronicus, James
TO PROTECT AND SERVE
Anello, Dino
UNLAWFUL ENTRY
Angel, Jack
ALADDIN
Angel, Ken
LEAVING NORMAL
Angel, Vanessa
HOMICIDAL IMPULSE
STOP! OR MY MOM WILL SHOOT
Angrisano, Francesco
ONCE UPON A CRIME
Angus, David
HOURS AND TIMES, THE
Anholt, Christien
POWER OF ONE, THE
Anka, Amanda
BUFFY THE VAMPIRE SLAYER
Anka, Paul
CAPTAIN RON
Ankori, Gilatt
HUMAN SHIELD, THE
Ann-Margret
NEWSIES
Anne, Chris
SOCIETY
Annison, Robin
POWER OF ONE, THE
Anthony, David
PURE COUNTRY
Anthony, Jane
FATHER
Anthony, Lee
FINAL ANALYSIS
Anthony, Lysette
HUSBANDS AND WIVES
Antico, Pete
LETHAL WEAPON 3
Antin, Steve
DRIVE
Anunciation, Derek
GLADIATOR
Anuszek, Martine
OTHER WOMAN, THE

Anwar, Gabrielle
SCENT OF A WOMAN

Anzai, Kenji
MR. BASEBALL

Anzell, Hy
CROSSING THE BRIDGE

Anzueto, Mauricio Ernesto
AMERICAN ME

Aoki, Shinsuke
MR. BASEBALL

Apicella, John
BACKTRACK
KUFFS

Apone, Allan
KUFFS

Appel, Peter
BASIC INSTINCT
SHADOWS AND FOG

Appleby, Noel
MY GRANDPA IS A VAMPIRE

Applegate, Rick
PASSED AWAY

Applegate, Royce D.
RAMPAGE
WHITE SANDS

Aquino, Amy
ALAN & NAOMI

Arabian, Michael
SHAKING THE TREE

Aradottir, Frida S.
MISTRESS

Arana, Tomas
BODYGUARD, THE
DEVIL'S DAUGHTER, THE

Aras, Kristina
MAXIMUM BREAKOUT

Araskog, Julie
OUT ON A LIMB

Araujo, Isabela
SWOON

Arbid, Johnny
CUP FINAL

Arbolino, Richard
BIKINI SUMMER 2
MIRROR IMAGES

Archer, Anne
PATRIOT GAMES

Archerd, Selma
LETHAL WEAPON 3

Ardant, Fanny
AFRAID OF THE DARK

Arden, Eve
WISECRACKS

Ardoin, Brett
PASSION FISH

Ardolino, Tom
COMPLEX WORLD

Arenberg, Lee
BOB ROBERTS
ROADSIDE PROPHETS

Arentzen, Jens
DAY IN OCTOBER, A

Aresco, Joey
STEPHEN KING'S SLEEPWALKERS

Argento, Dario
INNOCENT BLOOD

Argenziano, Carmen
UNLAWFUL ENTRY

Argiro, Vinny
PUBLIC EYE, THE

Argo, Victor
BAD LIEUTENANT
SHADOWS AND FOG

Argue, David
HURRICANE SMITH

Arias, Yancey
INNOCENT BLOOD

Arilsen, Rodger
SAVAGE INSTINCT

Arita, Maria
LEAP OF FAITH

Arkin, Alan
GLENGARRY GLEN ROSS

Arlin, Justine
STORYVILLE

Armitage, Peter
MONKEY BOY

Armor, Gene
FATAL INSTINCT

Armstrong, Alun
LONDON KILLS ME
PATRIOT GAMES
SPLIT SECOND

Armstrong, Jack
GUYVER, THE

Armstrong, Kerry
HUNTING

Armstrong, Larry
CUTTING EDGE, THE

Armstrong, Melinda
BIKINI SUMMER 2
ENCINO MAN

Armstrong, Robert
NOISES OFF

Armstrong, Vaughn
LIFE ON THE EDGE

Armus, Sidney
THIS IS MY LIFE

Arnaz, Jr., Desi
MAMBO KINGS, THE

Arndt, Denis
BASIC INSTINCT
WE'RE TALKIN' SERIOUS MONEY

Arnell, Gordon
POWER OF ONE, THE

Arnesson, Howard
PUERTO RICAN MAMBO (NOT A MUSICAL), THE

Arnett, Cameron
BED & BREAKFAST

Arnette, Jeannetta
LADYBUGS

Arnia, Sara
BEST INTENTIONS, THE

Arnold, Jana
STOP! OR MY MOM WILL SHOOT

Arnold, John
FAVOUR, THE WATCH, AND THE VERY BIG FISH, THE

Arnold, Lamont
BOB ROBERTS
INNOCENT BLOOD
LORENZO'S OIL

Arnold, Susan
FATHER
MANIAC WARRIORS

Arnold, Tom
HERO

Arnott, David
CRISSCROSS

Arolovi, Ella
WHO SHOT PATAKANGO?

Aronson, Judie
DESERT KICKBOXER

Aronson, Kathryn
LORENZO'S OIL
PASSED AWAY

Aronson, Steve
MALCOLM X
PASSED AWAY

Arp, Bonnie Sue
COLD JUSTICE

Arquette, Alexis
JUMPIN' AT THE BONEYARD
MIRACLE BEACH
OF MICE AND MEN
TERMINAL BLISS

Arquette, David
BUFFY THE VAMPIRE SLAYER
WHERE THE DAY TAKES YOU

Arquette, Lewis
LINGUINI INCIDENT, THE

Arquette, Patricia
PRAYER OF THE ROLLERBOYS

Arquette, Rosanna
FATHERS AND SONS
LINGUINI INCIDENT, THE

Arrieta, Ralph
CAPTAIN RON

Arrindell, Clive
CHRISTOPHER COLUMBUS: THE DISCOVERY

Arruti, Isidro
FINE ROMANCE, A

Arunodoy Theater Group
CITY OF JOY

Arzagamartin, James
GIVING, THE

Asa, Rene
DEEP COVER

Asahi, Kazuo
MR. BASEBALL

Asai, Jun
SNEAKERS

Ash, Shirley
LEAP OF FAITH

Ashbrook, Dana
TWIN PEAKS: FIRE WALK WITH ME

Ashby, Linden
INTO THE SUN

Asher, John Mallory
FROZEN ASSETS

Asher, Yolanda
LOVE CRIMES

Ashley, Angel
PLAY NICE

Ashmun, Christopher
BRIDE OF KILLER NERD

Ashrawi, Hanan
DOUBLE EDGE

Ashton, David
FREDDIE AS F.R.O.7

Askwith, Johnny
HIGHWAY 61

Asquith, Edward
CHILDREN, THE

Asquith, Magdalen
CHILDREN, THE

Asquith, Mark
CHILDREN, THE

Assa, Rene
976-EVIL II

Assante, Armand
1492: THE CONQUEST OF PARADISE
HOFFA
MAMBO KINGS, THE

Assante, Karen
MAMBO KINGS, THE

Astin, John
KILLER TOMATOES EAT FRANCE!

Astin, Sean
ENCINO MAN
WHERE THE DAY TAKES YOU

Astrow, JoAnne
WISECRACKS

Athey, Ron
SINGLE WHITE FEMALE

Atkins, Christopher
MORTUARY ACADEMY

Atkins, Dave
LONDON KILLS ME

Atkins, Tom
BOB ROBERTS

Atkinson, Gordon
SNAKEEATER III . . . HIS LAW

Atkinson, III, Hal Fort
MIGHTY DUCKS, THE

Atkinson, Rowan
BERNARD AND THE GENIE

Attile, Larry
MALCOLM X

Atwell, Benjamin
MALCOLM X

Atwood, Kathryn
WOMAN, HER MEN AND HER FUTON, A

Atwood, Phong
PUSHED TO THE LIMIT

Atzmon, Anat
DOUBLE EDGE

Atzmon, Tali
POUR SACHA

Aubague, Cecile
BECOMING COLETTE

Aubel, Joe
AMERICAN ME

Auberjonois, Rene
LITTLE NEMO: ADVENTURES IN SLUMBERLAND
PLAYER, THE

Aubrey, James
DEMON IN MY VIEW, A

Aufaure, Claude
HAIRDRESSER'S HUSBAND, THE

Auffret, Nathalie
ROAD TO RUIN

August, Lance
AMERICAN ME

August, Pernilla
BEST INTENTIONS, THE

August, Ron
HUSBANDS AND WIVES

Augustine, Phoebe
TWIN PEAKS: FIRE WALK WITH ME

Aumont, Jean-Pierre
BECOMING COLETTE

Aumont, Michel
ALBERTO EXPRESS

Austen, Donald
MUPPET CHRISTMAS CAROL, THE

Austin, Bentley
FALLING FROM GRACE

Austin, Criag
FALLING FROM GRACE

Austin, Elizabeth
WE'RE TALKIN' SERIOUS MONEY

Austin, Eric
FALLING FROM GRACE

Austin, Paul
KILLER IMAGE

Austin, Robert
SWOON

Austin, Teri
RAISING CAIN

Auteuil, Daniel
ELEGANT CRIMINEL, L'

Autry, Ed
ARTICLE 99

Avari, Erick
ENCINO MAN

Aver, Tasha
LOVE CRIMES

Averlant, Eric
DELICATESSEN
FAVOUR, THE WATCH, AND THE VERY BIG FISH, THE

Avery, James
BEASTMASTER 2: THROUGH THE PORTAL OF TIME

Avery, Rick
INNOCENT BLOOD

Aviano, Maryellen
LETHAL WEAPON 3

Ayala, Elena
PASSENGER 57

Ayala, Memo
BARBARIAN QUEEN II: THE EMPRESS STRIKES BACK

Ayer, Debbon
JENNIFER EIGHT

Aykroyd, Dan
CHAPLIN
SNEAKERS
THIS IS MY LIFE

Ayler, Ethel
BODYGUARD, THE

Ayres, Leah
PLAYER, THE

Azmi, Shabana
CITY OF JOY

Azoulay-Hasfari, Hana
HUMAN SHIELD, THE

Azzopardi, Charlie
HIGHWAY 61

Azzoulai, Leslie
VAN GOGH

Babatunde, Obba
IMPORTANCE OF BEING EARNEST, THE

Babcock, Barbara
FAR AND AWAY

Babes in Toyland
1991: THE YEAR PUNK BROKE

Babuskha
CLOSE TO EDEN

Baca, Sean
RADIO FLYER

Bacarella, Michael
MO' MONEY

Baccellini, Tullio
WHERE ANGELS FEAR TO TREAD

Backer, Tim
BLACKBELT

Backes, Glenn
SWOON

Backwell, Dana L.
LOVE CRIMES

Bacon, Kevin
FEW GOOD MEN, A

Badalato, Chet
HOFFA

Badalucco, Jr., Joseph
WHISPERS IN THE DARK

Badalucco, Michael
JUICE
NIGHT AND THE CITY

Badema
CLOSE TO EDEN

Badiola, Klara
WINTER IN LISBON, THE

Baer, David
LOVE POTION NO. 9

Baetich, Emanuel
SWOON

Baga, Ena
CHAPLIN

Bagley, Donald
BABE, THE

Bagley, Tim
MISTRESS

Bailey, Andrew
BLAME IT ON THE BELLBOY

Bailey, Frederick
EYE OF THE EAGLE 3

Bailey, Mark Chandler
LAWS OF GRAVITY

Baird, Scott
BOOMERANG

Bakeer, Donald
SOUTH CENTRAL

Bakeer, Musa
SOUTH CENTRAL

Baker, Angela Marie
MY NEW GUN

Baker, Becky Ann
LORENZO'S OIL

Baker, Dylan
LAST OF THE MOHICANS, THE
LOVE POTION NO. 9
PASSED AWAY

Baker, Joe
WAXWORK II: LOST IN TIME

Baker, Joe Don
CHILDREN, THE
DISTINGUISHED GENTLEMAN, THE

Baker, Jordan
LOVE POTION NO. 9

Baker, Kathy
ARTICLE 99
JENNIFER EIGHT

Baker, Kristie
KILLER IMAGE

Baker, Lenny
BRENDA STARR

Baker, Leslie
EFFICIENCY EXPERT, THE

Baker, Lisa Ann
INNOCENT BLOOD

Baker, Mark A.
LAST OF THE MOHICANS, THE

Baker, Richard James
WHITE MEN CAN'T JUMP

Baker, Tab
GLADIATOR

Bakiia, Bianca
BAD LIEUTENANT

Bakke, Karl
STEPHEN KING'S SLEEPWALKERS

Bakke, Tami
MIND, BODY & SOUL

Bakri, Muhamed
CUP FINAL
DOUBLE EDGE

Bal, Lisa
SOCIETY

Balaban, Bob
BOB ROBERTS

Balaban, Sigmund
FALLING FROM GRACE

Balcanoff, Michael
COMPLEX WORLD

Balcon, Jill
EDWARD II

Baldaro, Barrie
BEAUTIFUL DREAMERS

Baldiris, Gil
CAPTAIN RON

Baldwin, Adam
DEADBOLT
RADIO FLYER
WHERE THE DAY TAKES YOU

Baldwin, Alec
GLENGARRY GLEN ROSS
PRELUDE TO A KISS

Baldwin, Daniel Leroy
HERO

Baldwin, Stephen
CROSSING THE BRIDGE

Bale, Christian
NEWSIES

Balgobin, Jennifer
ROADSIDE PROPHETS

Balint, Eszter
LINGUINI INCIDENT, THE
SHADOWS AND FOG

Balk, Fairuza
GAS FOOD LODGING

Ball, Lucille
WISECRACKS

Ball, Timothy
WHITE TRASH

Ballantine, Carl
MR. SATURDAY NIGHT
NICKEL & DIME

Ballard, Kaye
FATE

Ballard, Reginald
CLASS ACT

Ballard, Shari
STOP! OR MY MOM WILL SHOOT

Ballentine, Sara
FROZEN ASSETS

Balsam, Talia
HOMICIDAL IMPULSE

Baltodano, Erika
BABE, THE

Baltz, Kirk
RESERVOIR DOGS

Bamber, David
YEAR OF THE COMET

Bamman, Gerry
BODYGUARD, THE
HOME ALONE 2:
LOST IN NEW YORK
LORENZO'S OIL

Bancroft, Amy
PUSHED TO THE LIMIT

Bancroft, Anne
HONEYMOON IN VEGAS
LOVE POTION NO. 9

Bancroft, Bradford
UNIVERSAL SOLDIER

Banderas, Anita
MAMBO KINGS, THE

Banderas, Antonio
MAMBO KINGS, THE

Bane, Monty
STEPHEN KING'S SLEEPWALKERS

Banerjee, Debasish
CITY OF JOY

Banerjee, Satya
CITY OF JOY

Banerjee, Siv Sankar
CITY OF JOY

Banerjee, Sudip
CITY OF JOY

Banfield, Bever-Leigh
LITTLE NEMO: ADVENTURES IN
SLUMBERLAND

Bangun, Advent
LADY DRAGON

Banks, Bob
LOVE CRIMES

Banks, Dennis
THUNDERHEART

Banks, Dennis J.
LAST OF THE MOHICANS, THE

Banks, III, Ogie
NEWSIES

Banks, Jonathan
FREEJACK

Banks, Lenore
PASSION FISH

Banks, Noah
LORENZO'S OIL

Bannen, Ian
DAMAGE

Bannon, Thierry
CLEARCUT

Bao Yongyan
CLOSE TO EDEN

Baoyinhexige
CLOSE TO EDEN

Barajas, Frank
PALE BLOOD

Baratta, Tomasino
HOFFA

Barba, Vanna
MEDITERRANEO

Barbarit, Chantal
VAN GOGH

Barber, Frances
SECRET FRIENDS

Barbier, Gilette
FAVOUR, THE WATCH, AND THE
VERY BIG FISH, THE

Barbor, Adriana
WATERDANCE, THE

Barclay, David
MUPPET CHRISTMAS CAROL, THE

Barer, Marshall
VENICE/VENICE

Barge, Gene
UNDER SIEGE

Bargeman, Gregory
MALCOLM X

Barger, Gregg
LITTLE NEMO: ADVENTURES IN
SLUMBERLAND

Barger, Mike
FOLKS!

Barhydt, Frank
PLAYER, THE

Barile, Guy
BABE, THE

Barkan, Yuda
FATE

Barkas, Ed
WATERDANCE, THE

Barker, Christine
COMPLEX WORLD

Barker, Clive
STEPHEN KING'S SLEEPWALKERS

Barkhordarian, Samson
HOFFA

Barkin, Ellen
MAN TROUBLE

Barkoff, Sarah
HELL MASTER

Barnes, Adilah
BASIC INSTINCT

Barnes, Denise
DR. GIGGLES

Barnes, Don
FIELD OF FIRE

Barnes, Jon
WILD WHEELS
Barnes, Peter
DEMON IN MY VIEW, A
Barnes, Priscilla
TALONS OF THE EAGLE
Barnes, Roosevelt "Booba"
DEEP BLUES
Barnett, Angus
LORENZO'S OIL
Barnett, Robbie
MUPPET CHRISTMAS CAROL, THE
Barnhill, Sheila Adams
LAST OF THE MOHICANS, THE
Barnwell, Nicholas
MALCOLM X
Baron, Alfredo Mejia
CABEZA DE VACA
Baron, Blaire
LEAGUE OF THEIR OWN, A
Baron, Joanne
UNIVERSAL SOLDIER
Baron, Venus
NIGHT EYES 2
Barone, John David
JOHNNY SUEDE
Barr, Jean-Marc
ZENTROPA
Barr, Steven
MEMOIRS OF AN INVISIBLE MAN
Barragan, Ramon
CABEZA DE VACA
Barreto, Raymond
POWER OF ONE, THE
Barrett, J.D.
MISSISSIPPI MASALA
Barrie, Dennis
DAMNED IN THE USA
Barron, Allison
PATRIOT GAMES
Barron, Doug
MAMBO KINGS, THE
Barron, Troy
DR. GIGGLES
Barry, Joseph
JOHNNY SUEDE
Barry, Julia
HERO
Barry, Prudence
DISTINGUISHED GENTLEMAN, THE
Barry, Raymond J.
K2
RAPID FIRE
Barrymore, Drew
POISON IVY
Barsky, Larry
MAXIMUM BREAKOUT
Bart, Leslie
NIGHT AND THE CITY
Bartel, Paul
DESIRE AND HELL AT SUNSET MOTEL
LIVING END, THE
MORTUARY ACADEMY
POPE MUST DIET!, THE
Bartell, Tim
SOCIETY
Barter, Sylvia
WHERE ANGELS FEAR TO TREAD
Barth, Bruce David
MALCOLM X
Bartholomew, Clifford
BACKTRACK
Bartok, Jayce
PASSED AWAY
SCHOOL TIES
Barton, James
MUPPET CHRISTMAS CAROL, THE
Barton, Joan
MUPPET CHRISTMAS CAROL, THE
Bartz, Rick
FATAL INSTINCT
Baruch, Isaac
WITCHCRAFT IV: VIRGIN HEART
Barzaghi, Jacques
FEED
Bascomb, Rudi
MALCOLM X
Basey, Gary
FROZEN ASSETS
Basham, Jerry
FROZEN ASSETS
Bashaw, James
PUSHED TO THE LIMIT
Bashe, Mate
SARAFINA!
Bashkin, Paul
FATE
Basic, Relja
CAPTAIN AMERICA
Basinger, Kim
COOL WORLD
FINAL ANALYSIS
Baskin, Richard J.
RAMPAGE
Basler, Marianne
SOLDIER'S TALE, A
Bass, Marlaine
MALCOLM X
Bass, Suzi
MY COUSIN VINNY
Bass, Victoria
BODYGUARD, THE
TRACES OF RED
Bassani, John
MANIAC WARRIORS
Bassett, Angela
CRITTERS 4
INNOCENT BLOOD
MALCOLM X
PASSION FISH
Bassett, Skye
SISTER ACT
Bastel, Victoria
BAD LIEUTENANT
Bastenero, Ray
CRISSCROSS
Bastianelli, Laura
CHAPLIN
Basulto, David
CLASS ACT
Bateman, Jason
BREAKING THE RULES
Bateman, Justine
DEADBOLT
PRIMARY MOTIVE
Bateman, Kent
BREAKING THE RULES
Bates, Alan
SECRET FRIENDS
Bates, Billy
WIND
Bates, Carl
LOVE CRIMES
Bates, Jeanne R.
WILD ORCHID 2: TWO SHADES OF BLUE
Bates, Kathy
PRELUDE TO A KISS
SHADOWS AND FOG
USED PEOPLE
Bates, Paul
GUN IN BETTY LOU'S HANDBAG, THE
JENNIFER EIGHT
JUST LIKE IN THE MOVIES
Bath, Iris
CHAPLIN
Batinkoff, Randall
BUFFY THE VAMPIRE SLAYER
PLAYER, THE
SCHOOL TIES
Batista, Jainardo
CAPTAIN RON
Batrouney, Colin
FATHER
Battista, Lloyd
ROUND TRIP TO HEAVEN
Battle, Tim
PRIMO BABY
Baud, Robert
DELICATESSEN
Bauer, Marc
ULTIMATE DESIRES
Bauer, Michelle
HELLROLLER
Bauer, Steven
RAISING CAIN
WILDFIRE
Baum, Bruce
CROSSING THE BRIDGE
SHAKES THE CLOWN
Baxter, Cheryl
DEATH BECOMES HER
Bay, Frances
SINGLE WHITE FEMALE
TWIN PEAKS: FIRE WALK WITH ME
Bayaertu
CLOSE TO EDEN
Bayle, Pierre
BECOMING COLETTE
Bayliss, Mike
MUPPET CHRISTMAS CAROL, THE
Bazaldua, Charles
BODYGUARD, THE
Be, Yoshio
CHAPLIN
Beach, Michael
GUILTY AS CHARGED
ONE FALSE MOVE

Beacom, Christopher
BABE, THE
Beacon, Kalif
ROCK SOUP
Beale, Jeffrey
UNLAWFUL ENTRY
Beals, Jennifer
IN THE SOUP
Beals, Ronald
WHITE MEN CAN'T JUMP
Beaman, Lee Anne
MIRROR IMAGES
OTHER WOMAN, THE
Beamer, Layne
RUNESTONE, THE
Beamish, Dinah
EDWARD II
Bean, Katherine
ALL THE VERMEERS IN NEW YORK
Bean, Reathel
GUN IN BETTY LOU'S HANDBAG, THE
Bean, Sean
PATRIOT GAMES
Bean, Steve
SHAKES THE CLOWN
Bear, Eddie
HONEYMOON IN VEGAS
Beard, Stanley
SHINING THROUGH
Bearde, Rober
FINAL ANALYSIS
Beasley, John
MIGHTY DUCKS, THE
Beasom, Samela A.
MAN TROUBLE
Beatty, Jon
CAPTAIN AMERICA
Beatty, Ned
BLIND VISION
CAPTAIN AMERICA
ILLUSIONS
PRELUDE TO A KISS
Beatty, Thomas
CAPTAIN AMERICA
Beatty, Zatella
SISTER ACT
Beaugier, Brice
DISCRETE, LA
Beaumont, Richard
CAN IT BE LOVE
Beaver, Jim
SISTER ACT
Beck, Kimberly
FROZEN ASSETS
Beck, Robert
SWOON
Beckar, Pascal
FAVOUR, THE WATCH, AND THE VERY BIG FISH, THE
Beckel, Graham
JENNIFER EIGHT
Becker, Gerry
HARD PROMISES
HOFFA
PUBLIC EYE, THE
Becker, Gretchen
MISTRESS
Becker, Mary
MINDWARP
Becker, Michael
SWOON
Beckett, Stephen
ENCHANTED APRIL
Beckham, Virgil
LOVE POTION NO. 9
Beckwith, William
SCENT OF A WOMAN
Bedford, Lori
PASSENGER 57
Bedford, Lou
PASSENGER 57
Bedford, Winston
PASSENGER 57
Bedford-Lloyd, John
DIARY OF A HITMAN
Bedi, Kabar
BEYOND JUSTICE
Bednarz, Wendy
THERE'S NOTHING OUT THERE
Bednob, Gerry
ENCINO MAN
Beebe, Gerald
TRACES OF RED
Beechner, Ed
TRANCERS III: DETH LIVES
UNLAWFUL ENTRY
Beekes, Erik
LILY WAS HERE
Beeman, Gale
RAMPAGE
Beener, Carlton
OVER HER DEAD BODY
Beers, Jack
STRANGER AMONG US, A
Beers, Jr., Malcolm A.
SWOON
Beesley, Miriam
FOREVER YOUNG
Beeson, Joel
DEATH BECOMES HER
Beeten, Ed
POWER OF ONE, THE
Begley, Jr., Ed
DARK HORSE
Begnoni, Camilla
NIGHT ON EARTH
Begovic, Mia
CAPTAIN AMERICA
Behan, Paudge
LONDON KILLS ME
Behar, Joy
THIS IS MY LIFE
WISECRACKS
Behr, Melissa
BAD CHANNELS
Behrens, Bernard
BEAUTIFUL DREAMERS
Behrens, Diane
GAS FOOD LODGING
Belafonte, Harry
PLAYER, THE
Belafonte, Shari
PLAYER, THE
Belafsky, Marty
BREAKING THE RULES
NEWSIES
Belanger, George
BARBARIAN QUEEN II: THE EMPRESS STRIKES BACK
Belgrey, Thomas K.
CHAPLIN
Belkin, Ann
DOUBLE EDGE
Bell, Ann
CAPTAIN AMERICA
Bell, Dan
WAYNE'S WORLD
Bell, Marshall
DIGGSTOWN
INNOCENT BLOOD
LEATHER JACKETS
VAGRANT, THE
WILDFIRE
Bell, Michael
LITTLE NEMO: ADVENTURES IN SLUMBERLAND
Bell, Nicholas
FATHER
HUNTING
Bell, Robert N.
BATMAN RETURNS
Bell, Rodney
CROSSING, THE
Bell, Stefan
WHITE TRASH
Bell, Tobin
RUBY
Bella, Todd
LORENZO'S OIL
Bellamy, Diana
PASSED AWAY
Bellamy, Ned
BOB ROBERTS
HOUSE IV
UNIVERSAL SOLDIER
Belle, Samantha
BED & BREAKFAST
Bellino, Clara
STEAL AMERICA
Bellino, Johnny
GLADIATOR
Bellman, Gina
SECRET FRIENDS
Bello, Sean P.
HOFFA
Bellucci, Monica
BRAM STOKER'S DRACULA
Belot, Pierre
DOES THIS MEAN WE'RE MARRIED?
ROAD TO RUIN
Beltran, Robert
KISS ME A KILLER
Beltzman, Mark
MO' MONEY
Belushi, James
DIARY OF A HITMAN
ONCE UPON A CRIME
TRACES OF RED

Bemis, Cliff
DISTINGUISHED GENTLEMAN, THE
Ben-David, Gilles
HUMAN SHIELD, THE
Ben-Edward, Michael
MR. SATURDAY NIGHT
Benard, Maurice
RUBY
Benbow, David Dolph
I DON'T BUY KISSES ANYMORE
Bence, Sheryl
PALE BLOOD
Bendel, Andrew
BABE, THE
Bender, Lawrence
RESERVOIR DOGS
Bendetti, Michael
NETHERWORLD
Bendler, Lois
ZEBRAHEAD
Benedict, Amy
SNEAKERS
Benedict, Jay
SHINING THROUGH
Benezech, Pascal
DELICATESSEN
Bengtsson, Mikael
BEST INTENTIONS, THE
Benigni, Roberto
JOHNNY STECCHINO
NIGHT ON EARTH
Benitez, Manuel
BARBARIAN QUEEN II: THE EMPRESS STRIKES BACK
Benitez, Ruben
DANZON
Benjaminson, Scott
STRAIGHT TALK
Benko, Tina
WATERLAND
Bennet, Marc
ULTIMATE DESIRES
Bennet, William P.
WHITE SANDS
Bennett, Chuck
UNLAWFUL ENTRY
Bennett, Eloise
CONTE DE PRINTEMPS
Bennett, Heather
ENCINO MAN
Bennett, John
SPLIT SECOND
Bennett, Joseph
HOWARDS END
Bennett, Norman
RUBY
Bennett, Paige
TWIN PEAKS: FIRE WALK WITH ME
Benrubi, Abraham
CROSSING THE BRIDGE
Benson, Chris
BEAUTIFUL DREAMERS
CUTTING EDGE, THE
SNAKEEATER III . . . HIS LAW
Benson, Gary
HONEYMOON IN VEGAS
Benson, Janis
PASSENGER 57
Benson, Jeff
DIGGSTOWN
Benson, Laura
DOES THIS MEAN WE'RE MARRIED?
Benson, Martin
YEAR OF THE COMET
Benson, Rex
TRACES OF RED
Bentinck, Timothy
YEAR OF THE COMET
Bentley, Bernard
SINGLES
Bentley, Dana
SORORITY HOUSE MASSACRE 2
Benton, Craig
KUFFS
Benton, Kate
TOYS
Benton, Kevin
WHITE MEN CAN'T JUMP
Benton, Vanessa
MALCOLM X
Benvictor, Paul
COOL WORLD
Benyas, Shirley
ZEBRAHEAD
Benzali, Daniel
DAY IN OCTOBER, A
DISTINGUISHED GENTLEMAN, THE
Beoi, Majot
GODZILLA VS. BIOLLANTE
Bercovici, Luca
K2
MISSION OF JUSTICE
Bercu, Barbara
VENICE/VENICE
Bercu, Michaela
BRAM STOKER'S DRACULA
Beresford, Clare
WELCOME TO OBLIVION
Berg, David Calvin
HOFFA
Berg, Peter
MIDNIGHT CLEAR, A
Bergendahl, Pia
BEST INTENTIONS, THE
Berger, Dagmar
EMMANUELLE 6
Bergin, Patrick
HIGHWAY TO HELL
LOVE CRIMES
PATRIOT GAMES
Bergman, Kathleen
ARTICLE 99
Bergman, Peter
PHANTOM OF THE RITZ
Bergman, Teddy
HONEYMOON IN VEGAS
Bergmann, Art
HIGHWAY 61
Berkeley, Xander
CANDYMAN
FEW GOOD MEN, A
GUN IN BETTY LOU'S HANDBAG, THE
Berlin, Andrew
ZEBRAHEAD
Berline, Byron
BASIC INSTINCT
Berling, Peter
VOYAGER
Berlinger, Warren
HERO
Berman, Andrew Mark
SHADOWS AND FOG
Berman, David
MALCOLM X
Berman, Joe
TWIN PEAKS: FIRE WALK WITH ME
Berman, Robert
BRIEF HISTORY OF TIME, A
Bermont, Greg
MO' MONEY
Bernal, Jorge
CTHULHU MANSION
Bernard, Andre
BERNARD AND THE GENIE
Bernard, Andree
CHAPLIN
CRYING GAME, THE
Bernard, Charles
FROZEN ASSETS
Bernardini, Ida
USED PEOPLE
Berner, Robby
MANIAC WARRIORS
Bernhardt, Kevin
HELLRAISER III: HELL ON EARTH
KICK OR DIE
Bernsen, Collin
DOUBLE TROUBLE
FROZEN ASSETS
Bernsen, Corbin
FROZEN ASSETS
Bernstein, Jacob
THIS IS MY LIFE
Bernstein, Max
THIS IS MY LIFE
Berque, Barbara
VENICE/VENICE
Berrick, R.T.
KISS ME A KILLER
Berridge, Rob
MANIAC WARRIORS
Berron, Allison
OTHER WOMAN, THE
Berry, Darien
JUICE
Berry, Gordon
BRIEF HISTORY OF TIME, A
Berry, Halle
BOOMERANG
Berry, Richard
POUR SACHA
Berryman, Joe
HARD PROMISES

Berryman, Michael
AUNTIE LEE'S MEAT PIES
BEASTMASTER 2: THROUGH THE PORTAL OF TIME
GUYVER, THE
LITTLE SISTER
Berthiaume, Rhys M.
CUTTING EDGE, THE
Bertin, Roland
HAIRDRESSER'S HUSBAND, THE
Bertish, Suzanne
VENICE/VENICE
Besch, Bibi
LONELY HEARTS
Best, Kevin
SOUTH CENTRAL
Bestbier, Michele
SARAFINA!
Bestwick, J. Sidney
LIVING END, THE
Beswike, Martine
LIFE ON THE EDGE
Betancourt, Anne
SEEDPEOPLE
Betenfield, Dominique
DELICATESSEN
Betti, Siria
WHERE ANGELS FEAR TO TREAD
Bettis, Paul
ADJUSTER, THE
Betts, Jack
WHITE TRASH
Bevan, Daniel
EDWARD II
Beyer, Jeremy
LORENZO'S OIL
Beymer, Richard
BLACKBELT
Bhai, Chhotu
CITY OF JOY
Biafra, Jello
HIGHWAY 61
Bianchi, Christian
ONCE UPON A CRIME
Bideau, Jean-Luc
INSPECTOR LAVARDIN
Bidstrup, Jorgen
DAY IN OCTOBER, A
Bieber, Daniel
RADIO FLYER
Biehn, Michael
K2
RAMPAGE
Bielendt, Helmuth
VENICE/VENICE
Biesk, Adam
GAS FOOD LODGING
Big Yank
COOL WORLD
Bigagli, Claudio
MEDITERRANEO
Bigeleisen, Cantor Ira S.
ARTICLE 99
Bigelow, LaToyah
MALCOLM X
Bigelow, Scott "Bam Bam"
SNAKEEATER III . . . HIS LAW

Biggers, Dan
BASKET CASE 3: THE PROGENY
Biggs, Junior
TRACES OF RED
Bigham, Lexie D.
SOUTH CENTRAL
Bigler, Peter
RUNESTONE, THE
Bilal, Nayyer
INTO THE SUN
Billig, Etel
STRAIGHT TALK
Billings, Dawn Ann
TRANCERS III: DETH LIVES
Billings, Earl
ONE FALSE MOVE
Billingslea, Beau
OUT FOR BLOOD
Bilson, Ben
CHAPLIN
Bimstein, Blanche
SOCIETY
Binamo, Chino
BUFFY THE VAMPIRE SLAYER
INTO THE SUN
Binder, Mike
CROSSING THE BRIDGE
Bindiger, Emily
TUNE, THE
Bingham, Barbara
BEYOND DARKNESS
SOLDIER'S FORTUNE
Binion, Reid
PET SEMATARY II
Binoche, Juliette
DAMAGE
Birch, Thora
PATRIOT GAMES
Birchard, Paul
CTHULHU MANSION
Bird, Robin Black
THUNDERHEART
Birk, Raye
CLASS ACT
Birney, David
TOUCH AND DIE
Birney, Frank
JENNIFER EIGHT
Birt, Christopher
BODYGUARD, THE
Biscoe, Donna
LOVE CRIMES
Bishop, Donald
ARTICLE 99
Bishop, John
FATHER
Bisio, Claudio
MEDITERRANEO
Bissell, Zoe
SWOON
Bissett, Josie
ALL-AMERICAN MURDER
MIKEY
Bitenc, Demeter
CAPTAIN AMERICA

Bittner, Carrie
NIGHT RHYTHMS
Bixler, Nichole
BOB ROBERTS
Bizio, Silvia
VENICE/VENICE
Bjork, Anita
BEST INTENTIONS, THE
Black, Craig
FLIRTING
Black, Danny Big
LETHAL WEAPON 3
Black, Donna
HOME ALONE 2: LOST IN NEW YORK
Black, Jack
BOB ROBERTS
Black, James
HARD PROMISES
Black, Karen
AUNTIE LEE'S MEAT PIES
CAGED FEAR
CHILDREN OF THE NIGHT
CHILDREN, THE
PLAYER, THE
RUBIN & ED
Black, Leon
DEMON IN MY VIEW, A
Black, Nancy
FATHER
Blackburn, Greta
LIFE ON THE EDGE
Blackman, Harry
MY NEW GUN
Blackman, Ilene
HUSBANDS AND WIVES
Blackman, Sean
BIG GIRLS DON'T CRY . . . THEY GET EVEN
Blackmon, Christie
FROZEN ASSETS
Blackshear, Aaron
MALCOLM X
Blackwell, Loren
KUFFS
Blackwood, Tilly
DEMON IN MY VIEW, A
Blain, Ellen
ENCINO MAN
Blair, Alpha
VENICE/VENICE
Blair, Andre
MALCOLM X
Blair, Angela
LEAP OF FAITH
Blair, John
CROSSING, THE
Blair, Tyrone
BABE, THE
Blais, Peter
BEAUTIFUL DREAMERS
Blaisdell, Brad
BLOODFIST III: FORCED TO FIGHT
KISS ME A KILLER
Blake, Andre
BOOMERANG

Blake, Geoffrey
FERNGULLY: THE LAST RAINFOREST
Blake, Jenifer L.
MAXIMUM BREAKOUT
Blake, Julia
FATHER
Blake, Nayland
DADDY AND THE MUSCLE ACADEMY
Blake, Roger
PATRIOT GAMES
Blake, Stephanie
MAMBO KINGS, THE
Blakeslee, Douglas
LEAGUE OF THEIR OWN, A
Blanc, Dominique
INDOCHINE
Blanc, Michel
FAVOUR, THE WATCH, AND THE VERY BIG FISH, THE
Blanchard, Ron
ROCK & ROLL COWBOYS
Blanchard, Terence
MALCOLM X
Blancke, Sandrine
TOTO LE HEROS
Blanco, Angel
CTHULHU MANSION
Blanco, Dean C.
SWOON
Blanding, Jr., Walter
TEXAS TENOR: THE ILLINOIS JACQUET STORY
Blank, Anna
BECOMING COLETTE
Blank, Gerry
BLACKBELT
Blank, Harrod
WILD WHEELS
Blank, Kenny
BOOMERANG
Blanks, Billy
TALONS OF THE EAGLE
Blanloeil, Yvan
BECOMING COLETTE
Blanton, Tom
MAXIMUM BREAKOUT
Blatchford, Edward
LAST OF THE MOHICANS, THE
WE'RE TALKIN' SERIOUS MONEY
Blatt, Beth
GODZILLA VS. BIOLLANTE
Blaze
COMPLEX WORLD
Bleier, Barbara
SWOON
Blessed, Brian
BACK IN THE U.S.S.R.
FREDDIE AS F.R.O.7
Blessing, Ann
WATERDANCE, THE
Blethyn, Brenda
RIVER RUNS THROUGH IT, A
Blevins, Michael
CHAPLIN
Blick, Hugo
CHRISTOPHER COLUMBUS: THE DISCOVERY
Blinco, Maggie
FLIRTING
Blinkoff, Daniel
CROSSING THE BRIDGE
Blitz, Renessa
THIS IS MY LIFE
Bloch, Merv
HUSBANDS AND WIVES
Block, Angela
HOFFA
Blomberg, Jan
BEST INTENTIONS, THE
Bloom, John
FROZEN ASSETS
Bloomfield, Don
WILD ORCHID 2: TWO SHADES OF BLUE
Blue, David
COMPLEX WORLD
Bluford, Debra
ARTICLE 99
Blumberg, Judy
CUTTING EDGE, THE
Blumenfeld, Alan
BLACKBELT
Blumenthal, Brad
HONEYMOON IN VEGAS
Blunt, Wanda
PALE BLOOD
Bly, Nelly
DIGGSTOWN
Blythe, Janus
SOLDIER'S FORTUNE
Board, Scott
FATHER
Bob, Sam
LEAVING NORMAL
Bochco, Steve
COLOR ADJUSTMENT
Bochinski, Jon
CLOSE TO EDEN
Bochner, Lloyd
LANDSLIDE
Bodie-Henderson, Dieidre
LAWS OF GRAVITY
Bodison, Wolfgang
FEW GOOD MEN, A
Bodozian, Onice
ROADSIDE PROPHETS
Body, Niven
AFRAID OF THE DARK
Boebinger, Gary
FALLING FROM GRACE
Boeck, Angelika Maria
DEVIL'S DAUGHTER, THE
Boenheim, Laura
GUN IN BETTY LOU'S HANDBAG, THE
Boes, Richard
JOHNNY SUEDE
NIGHT ON EARTH
Boesing, Paul
GIVING, THE
Boettcher-Tate, Karen
FROZEN ASSETS
Bogdanova, Yelena
ADAM'S RIB
Bogdanovich, Anna
VENICE/VENICE
Boggs, Tommy
DISTINGUISHED GENTLEMAN, THE
Bohdalova, Jirina
EAR, THE
Bohlke, Peter
TOTO LE HEROS
Bohm, Uwe
DEMON IN MY VIEW, A
Bohorquez, Bibi
SPLIT SECOND
Bohrer, Stephen
MAXIMUM BREAKOUT
Boikanyo, Ishamel
SARAFINA!
Bois, Cecile
BECOMING COLETTE
Boland, Nora
MISSISSIPPI MASALA
Bolden, Hilda Marie
FALLING FROM GRACE
Boldin, Shane
ARMED FOR ACTION
Bolds, Kenneth
TEXAS TENOR: THE ILLINOIS JACQUET STORY
Boll, Helen
COLD HEAVEN
Bollen, Paul
AMERICAN ME
UNLAWFUL ENTRY
Bolling, Angie
HARD PROMISES
Bolme, Tomas
BEST INTENTIONS, THE
Bolster, Thomas
SHADOWS AND FOG
Bolthouse, Brent
HELLRAISER III: HELL ON EARTH
Bolton, Andrew Lee
EDWARD II
Bolzon, Henry
PUBLIC EYE, THE
Bonacelli, Paolo
JOHNNY STECCHINO
NIGHT ON EARTH
TOUCH AND DIE
Bonacki, Lou
WE'RE TALKIN' SERIOUS MONEY
Bonanno, Louie
AUNTIE LEE'S MEAT PIES
Bond, Jordan
HERO
Bond, Julie
BASIC INSTINCT
Bond, Margery
PLAYER, THE
Bond, Paul
SUNSET STRIP
Bones, Ken
SPLIT SECOND

Bonham Carter, Crispin
HOWARDS END
Bonham Carter, Helena
HOWARDS END
WHERE ANGELS FEAR TO TREAD
Bonicoli, Francesca
LIGHT SLEEPER
Bonn, Curt
MANIAC WARRIORS
Bonnabel, Michael
LINGUINI INCIDENT, THE
Bonnel, William J.
RADIO FLYER
Bonner, Tony
HURRICANE SMITH
Bonomo, Christopher
NEWSIES
Bonsall, Brian
MIKEY
Booke, Sorrell
ROCK-A-DOODLE
Booker, Edna Ryan
FALLING FROM GRACE
Bookston, Alex
TOYS
Boone Junior, Mark
OF MICE AND MEN
Boone, Walker
SNAKEEATER III . . . HIS LAW
Booth, Tod
BRENDA STARR
Boothe, Powers
RAPID FIRE
Boothroyd, Kaaren
SINGLE WHITE FEMALE
Boratto, Caterina
ONCE UPON A CRIME
Bordowitz, Gregg
SWOON
Borelli, Catarina
SWOON
Borgese, Salvatore
JOHNNY STECCHINO
Borgnine, Ernest
MISTRESS
Borich, Milan
MY GRANDPA IS A VAMPIRE
Boris the Dog
ENCINO MAN
Bork, Sarah
LOVE CRIMES
Borkowdki, Andrzej
SHINING THROUGH
Borowitz, Katherine
JUST LIKE IN THE MOVIES
Borrow, Mitch
BLACKBELT
Bortell, Charles K.
LOVE FIELD
Boryer, Lucy
STEPHEN KING'S SLEEPWALKERS
Bosco, Philip
SHADOWS AND FOG
STRAIGHT TALK
Bostick, J.J.
HONEYMOON IN VEGAS
Boston, Michael
SNEAKERS
Bostwick, Joni Dee
JUST LIKE IN THE MOVIES
Boswell, Charles
BLOODFIST III: FORCED TO FIGHT
KISS ME A KILLER
Botelho, Niki
BATMAN RETURNS
Botto, Juan Diego
1492: THE CONQUEST OF PARADISE
Bottoms, Sam
DOLLY DEAREST
Bouchard, Alton
HOFFA
Boucher, Stephane
NIGHT ON EARTH
Bouldin, Mahlon
MISSISSIPPI MASALA
Boulware, Curt
UNLAWFUL ENTRY
Bouquet, Michel
TOTO LE HEROS
TOUS LES MATINS DU MONDE
Bourdon, Corinne
VAN GOGH
Bourg, John
FOREVER YOUNG
Bourland, Kevin
BACKTRACK
SISTER ACT
Boussoffara, Fazia
FAVOUR, THE WATCH, AND THE VERY BIG FISH, THE
Bouton, Joy
WHITE SANDS
Boutwell, Ann Taylor
LOVE POTION NO. 9
Bouvier, Charles
SEEDPEOPLE
Bovasso, Julie
ARTICLE 99
Bovell, Brian
DEMON IN MY VIEW, A
Bowden, Jim
HOWARDS END
Bowe, David
FEW GOOD MEN, A
I DON'T BUY KISSES ANYMORE
Bowe, Merlin
MANIAC WARRIORS
Bowen, Beth Ann
CAPTAIN AMERICA
Bowen, Elizabeth Anne
FALLING FROM GRACE
Bowen, Michael
PLAYER, THE
Bowen, Pamela
PLAYER, THE
Bowen, Peter
SWOON
Bower, Tom
ACES: IRON EAGLE III
RAISING CAIN
Bowers, Bonnie
THERE'S NOTHING OUT THERE
Bowers, Christina
INNOCENT BLOOD
Bowie, David
LINGUINI INCIDENT, THE
TWIN PEAKS: FIRE WALK WITH ME
Bowles, Anthony
CHAPLIN
Bowman, Margaret
HARD PROMISES
LEAP OF FAITH
SIMPLE MEN
Bowman, Melodee
HARD PROMISES
LEAP OF FAITH
Bowman, Wilfred
YEAR OF THE COMET
Boxleitner, Bruce
BABE, THE
KUFFS
Boxley, Judith
LAWS OF GRAVITY
SWOON
Boyce, Ahnee
LEAVING NORMAL
Boyce, David
SISTER ACT
Boyce, Nicholas
WATERLAND
Boyce, Rodger
RUBY
Boyd, Guy
KISS ME A KILLER
Boyd, Niven
SECRET FRIENDS
Boyd, Sissy
GAS FOOD LODGING
Boyd, Susan
ROVER DANGERFIELD
Boyer, Myriam
TOUS LES MATINS DU MONDE
Boyer, Sully
IN THE SOUP
Boyett, Matthew
RUNESTONE, THE
Boyett, William
NEWSIES
Boykins, Berl
BASKET CASE 3: THE PROGENY
Boylan, John
CLEARCUT
Boyle, John
ORIGINAL INTENT
Boyle, Lara Flynn
EYE OF THE STORM
WAYNE'S WORLD
WHERE THE DAY TAKES YOU
Boyle, Peter
HONEYMOON IN VEGAS
MALCOLM X
Boyles, Leonard
SOUTH CENTRAL
Boynton, Lisa
THIS IS MY LIFE
Boynton, Peter
HELLRAISER III: HELL ON EARTH
Boyzett, Bill
LOVE FIELD

Bozic, Jr., William J.
LAST OF THE MOHICANS, THE
Bozzi, Bruce
UNDER SIEGE
Bozzo, Prospero
VENICE/VENICE
Brabant, Loic
DOES THIS MEAN WE'RE MARRIED?
Bracco, Elizabeth
IN THE SOUP
JUMPIN' AT THE BONEYARD
Bracco, Lorraine
MEDICINE MAN
RADIO FLYER
TRACES OF RED
Bracho, Alejandro
BARBARIAN QUEEN II: THE EMPRESS STRIKES BACK
Bracken, Heather
BAD LIEUTENANT
Bradbury, Janette Lane
CONSENTING ADULTS
Bradford, Andy
BLAME IT ON THE BELLBOY
Bradford, Richard
COLD HEAVEN
DR. GIGGLES
WILDFIRE
Bradford, Tom
CHAPLIN
Bradley, David
LOWER LEVEL
Bradley, Doug
HELLRAISER III: HELL ON EARTH
Bradley, Jody
FATAL INSTINCT
Bradley, Mark
MIGHTY DUCKS, THE
Bradley, Terry
HEAVEN IS A PLAYGROUND
Bradshaw, Bill
OTHER WOMAN, THE
Bradshaw, Bryant
BED & BREAKFAST
Bradshaw, Carl
LUNATIC, THE
Bradshaw, Lewis C.
THUNDERHEART
Brady, Carol
NETHERWORLD
Brady, P.J.
FAR AND AWAY
PLAYBOYS, THE
Brady, Randall
ROOTS OF EVIL
Brailsford, Pauline
LEAGUE OF THEIR OWN, A
Bramble, Steven
PALE BLOOD
Brammer, Sidney
CONFESSIONS OF A SERIAL KILLER
Brana, Frank
CTHULHU MANSION
Branagh, Kenneth
PETER'S FRIENDS
Branaman, Rustam
MAN TROUBLE
Branca, Julius
MR. SATURDAY NIGHT
Brand, Jacqueline
SNEAKERS
Brandauer, Klaus-Maria
BECOMING COLETTE
Brandenburg, Larry
COLD JUSTICE
HARD PROMISES
MO' MONEY
Brandis, Jonathan
LADYBUGS
Brando, Marlon
CHRISTOPHER COLUMBUS: THE DISCOVERY
Brandon, David
BEYOND DARKNESS
Brandon, Scott
ROUND TRIP TO HEAVEN
Brandon-Jones, Una
CHAPLIN
Brandt, Carlo
INDOCHINE
Brandt, Victor
UNLAWFUL ENTRY
Branham, Craig
ONE LAST RUN
Branton, Matthew
USED PEOPLE
Braschi, Nicoletta
JOHNNY STECCHINO
Braseth, Ralph
GUN IN BETTY LOU'S HANDBAG, THE
Brasher, Meredith
CONSENTING ADULTS
Bratt, Benjamin
CHAINS OF GOLD
Braun, Eddie
UNIVERSAL SOLDIER
Braun, Meredith
MUPPET CHRISTMAS CAROL, THE
Braun, Philip A.
RIVER RUNS THROUGH IT, A
Braunstein, Jeff
BEAUTIFUL DREAMERS
Brave, Sarah
THUNDERHEART
Braverman, Barbara
PUSHED TO THE LIMIT
Bravo, Maurice
PUBLIC EYE, THE
Braybrook, John
FATHER
Brazeau, Jay
CAFE ROMEO
Brazel, Gerald
MALCOLM X
Brazier, Fergus
MUPPET CHRISTMAS CAROL, THE
Breax, David
HARD PROMISES
Breck, Peter
HIGHWAY 61
Bree
COMPLEX WORLD
Breed, Helen Lloyd
PASSED AWAY
Breeding, Karen
WHITE SANDS
Breen, Patrick
PASSED AWAY
Bremer, Brian
SOCIETY
Brenn-Lowen, Janni
COOL WORLD
Brennan, Eileen
I DON'T BUY KISSES ANYMORE
Brennen, Paul
ALIEN3
Brewer, Duane
THUNDERHEART
Brewer, Jim
RUBY
Brewer, Jo
MIND, BODY & SOUL
Brewer, Rowanne
ROUND TRIP TO HEAVEN
Brialy, Jean-Claude
INSPECTOR LAVARDIN
Briam, Bianna
FATHER
Briant, Shane
TILL THERE WAS YOU
Brice, Fanny
WISECRACKS
Bridges, Lloyd
HONEY, I BLEW UP THE KID
Bridges, Todd
HOMEBOYS
Brief, Kevin
ARTICLE 99
Briers, Richard
PETER'S FRIENDS
Briggs, Michael
FOREVER YOUNG
Bright, Bob
FATHER
Bright, Simon
DEMON IN MY VIEW, A
Brightbill, Bernice
MAN TROUBLE
Brill, Steven
BATMAN RETURNS
MIGHTY DUCKS, THE
Brill, Susan
OUT ON A LIMB
Brimble, Nick
YEAR OF THE COMET
Brimhall, Cynthia
DO OR DIE
Brin, Michelle
SECRET GAMES
Brine, Adrian
LILY WAS HERE
Bringelson, Mark
WELCOME TO OBLIVION
Bringleson, Mark
LAWNMOWER MAN, THE

Brinkley, David
CROSSING THE BRIDGE
Brinkley, Ritch
RUBY
Brinton, Eliot
LORENZO'S OIL
Brion, Mildred
VAGRANT, THE
Brisbin, David
TWIN PEAKS: FIRE WALK WITH ME
Briscoe, Laurie
K2
RESURRECTED, THE
Briseno, Armando
AMERICAN ME
Brito, Anthony
LITTLE NOISES
Bro, Anders Peter
DAY IN OCTOBER, A
Broadbent, Jim
CRYING GAME, THE
ENCHANTED APRIL
Broadhurst, Angel
POISON IVY
Broadhurst, Kent
TOUCH AND DIE
Broadnax, Dwayne "Cook"
MALCOLM X
Brochet, Anne
TOUS LES MATINS DU MONDE
Brock, Dave
DEATH BECOMES HER
Brockett, Don
BOB ROBERTS
HOFFA
PASSED AWAY
Brocksmith, Roy
NICKEL & DIME
Broderick, Matthew
OUT ON A LIMB
Brodie, Hugh
TEXAS TENOR:
THE ILLINOIS JACQUET STORY
Broe, Douglas D.
LITTLE NOISES
Brogren, Lena
BEST INTENTIONS, THE
Brolin, James
GAS FOOD LODGING
TWIN SISTERS
Bromfield, Valerie
THIS IS MY LIFE
Bronco, Neil
SMOOTH TALKER
Bronstein, David
MY FATHER IS COMING
Brookes, Jacqueline
WHISPERS IN THE DARK
Brookes, Joanna
UNDER SUSPICION
Brooks, Evelyn
FOLKS!
Brooks, Lauren
FROZEN ASSETS
Brooks, Matthew
BEETHOVEN

Brooks, Max
PUBLIC EYE, THE
Brooks, Randy
RESERVOIR DOGS
Brooks, Sharon
MALCOLM X
Brooks, Tara
FROZEN ASSETS
Brooks, Yvette
MALCOLM X
Brophy, Brian
PLAYER, THE
Brosnan, Pierce
LAWNMOWER MAN, THE
Broughton, Shellye D.
MALCOLM X
Broun, Heywood Hale
HOUSESITTER
Brourman, Burnice
BOB ROBERTS
Broussard, Rebecca
MAN TROUBLE
Brown, Abigail
EDWARD II
Brown, Alex
AMERICAN ME
Brown, Alexander
GETTING MARRIED IN BUFFALO JUMP
Brown, Andra
MANIAC WARRIORS
Brown, Andre Rosey
BRONX WAR, THE
CLASS ACT
Brown, Angie
ALL-AMERICAN MURDER
Brown, Anthony G.
UNDER SIEGE
Brown, Ari
BABE, THE
Brown, Blair
PASSED AWAY
Brown, Bobbie
DOUBLE TROUBLE
Brown, Bryan
BLAME IT ON THE BELLBOY
Brown, Caesar
CANDYMAN
Brown, Candy Ann
ZEBRAHEAD
Brown, Christopher M.
K2
Brown, Clancy
PET SEMATARY II
Brown, Duncan
HOWARDS END
Brown, Dwier
CUTTING EDGE, THE
MOM AND DAD SAVE THE WORLD
Brown, Frank
DAUGHTERS OF THE DUST
Brown, Gary
INVASION OF THE SPACE PREACHERS
Brown, Graham
MALCOLM X

Brown, Heather
THIS IS MY LIFE
Brown, Henry
HERO
LETHAL WEAPON 3
Brown, J.
SAVAGE INSTINCT
Brown, Jay
WIND
Brown, Jerry
FEED
Brown, Jophery
ARTICLE 99
UNIVERSAL SOLDIER
Brown, Julie
SHAKES THE CLOWN
Brown, June
MAMBO KINGS, THE
Brown, Kedar
TIGER CLAWS
Brown, Kenneth A.
CANDYMAN
Brown, O. Nicholas
STEPHEN KING'S SLEEPWALKERS
Brown, Pat Crawford
SISTER ACT
WILD ORCHID 2:
TWO SHADES OF BLUE
Brown, Phil
CHAPLIN
Brown, Ralph
ALIEN3
CRYING GAME, THE
Brown, Stephen
BEYOND DARKNESS
Brown, Tarell
DAUGHTERS OF THE DUST
Brown, Thomas Wilson
DIGGSTOWN
Brown, W. Earl
BABE, THE
Brown, Wren T.
IMPORTANCE OF BEING EARNEST, THE
Browne, Kale
BLOODFIST IV: DIE TRYING
Browne, Roscoe Lee
MAMBO KINGS, THE
Browne, Suzanne
BIKINI CARWASH COMPANY, THE
Browning, John
CONFESSIONS OF A SERIAL KILLER
Browning, Susan
SISTER ACT
Broyles, Robert
RAMPAGE
Brua, Jean-Max
BECOMING COLETTE
Brucato, Ingrid
TWIN PEAKS: FIRE WALK WITH ME
Bruce
35 UP
Bruce, Cheryl Lynn
DAUGHTERS OF THE DUST
Bruce, Colin
WATERLAND

Bruce, Robert
MY GRANDPA IS A VAMPIRE
Bruna, Miorelli
VENICE/VENICE
Bruneau, Ralph
LIFE ON THE EDGE
Brunner, Michael
POWER OF ONE, THE
Brunson, Lisel
TOYS
Bryan, Scott
MIGHTY DUCKS, THE
Bryant, Lance
MALCOLM X
Bryce, Scott M.
LETHAL WEAPON 3
Bryniarski, Andrew
BATMAN RETURNS
Brzobohaty, Radoslav
EAR, THE
Buccella, David
HONEYMOON IN VEGAS
Buchanan, Jill
SWOON
Buchanan, Pat
FEED
Bucher, John
HUSBANDS AND WIVES
Buchholz, Horst
ACES: IRON EAGLE III
TOUCH AND DIE
Buchrieser, Franz
KILL CRUISE
Buck, Robert
CUTTING EDGE, THE
Buckingham, Robert
BRAM STOKER'S DRACULA
Buckley, Simon
MUPPET CHRISTMAS CAROL, THE
Bucossi, Peter
NIGHT AND THE CITY
Buczynski, Michele
FINE ROMANCE, A
Buddeke, Kate
STRAIGHT TALK
Buell, Bill
WIND
Buerklin, Norm
COMPLEX WORLD
Buffington, Dewey
MISSISSIPPI MASALA
Bugg, Susan
MAN TROUBLE
Buggy, Niall
ALIEN3
PLAYBOYS, THE
Buhagiar, Valerie
HIGHWAY 61
Buhler, Ashlee
LEAVING NORMAL
Bujold, Genevieve
OH, WHAT A NIGHT
Bukowski, Julien
HAIRDRESSER'S HUSBAND, THE
Bulbeck, Dave
MUPPET CHRISTMAS CAROL, THE
Buldovskii, Nikita
RASPAD
Bulen, Steve
VAMPIRE HUNTER D
Buller, Francesca
CHAPLIN
Bulloch, Robbie
POWER OF ONE, THE
Bullock, Gary
LOVE CRIMES
TWIN PEAKS: FIRE WALK WITH ME
Bullock, Hiram
UNDER SIEGE
Bullock, Sandra
LOVE POTION NO. 9
WHO SHOT PATAKANGO?
Bumiller, Bill
DO OR DIE
Bunch, Sekou
WILD ORCHID 2:
TWO SHADES OF BLUE
Bunel, Marje
DISCRETE, LA
Bunker, Eddie
RESERVOIR DOGS
Buono, Cara
GLADIATOR
WATERLAND
Buquet, August
MANIAC WARRIORS
Buquet, Ed
MANIAC WARRIORS
Burch, Tracey
DANCE WITH DEATH
Burchard, Petrea
DEATH BECOMES HER
Burdeau, Suzanne Q.
MAN TROUBLE
Burdette, Nicole
RIVER RUNS THROUGH IT, A
Burford, Ben
MISSISSIPPI MASALA
Burger, Cody
FOREVER YOUNG
Burgess, Michael
MY COUSIN VINNY
Burgos, Mike A.
GLADIATOR
Burke, Robert
SIMPLE MEN
Burkett, Brandi
SLUMBER PARTY MASSACRE 3
Burkholder, Scott
HOUSE IV
PLAY NICE
Burkley, Dennis
STOP! OR MY MOM WILL SHOOT
Burkovich, Shirley
LEAGUE OF THEIR OWN, A
Burks, Carl David
BACKTRACK
Burlinson, Tom
LANDSLIDE
Burmester, Leo
ARTICLE 99
INNOCENT BLOOD
PASSION FISH
Burnama, Piet
LADY DRAGON
Burnett, Carol
NOISES OFF
WISECRACKS
Burnett, Karl
MY GRANDPA IS A VAMPIRE
Burnett, Steven
LOVE POTION NO. 9
Burnette, Olivia
HARD PROMISES
Burns, George
WISECRACKS
Burns, Peter
FOLKS!
Burns, Robert A.
CONFESSIONS OF A SERIAL KILLER
Burns, Stef
WAYNE'S WORLD
Burns, Timothy C.
NIGHT RHYTHMS
OTHER WOMAN, THE
Burns, William
PLAY MURDER FOR ME
Burnside, R.L.
DEEP BLUES
Burr, Cheryl
MALCOLM X
Burr, Fritzi
3 NINJAS
Burr, Lonnie
MR. SATURDAY NIGHT
Burr, Robert
NETHERWORLD
OUT ON A LIMB
Burrell, Sheila
AFRAID OF THE DARK
Burroni, Lea
WHERE ANGELS FEAR TO TREAD
Burroughs, Kirk
UNDER SIEGE
Burrows, Robin
BAD LIEUTENANT
Burson, Greg
LITTLE NEMO: ADVENTURES IN
SLUMBERLAND
Burt, John
COMPLEX WORLD
Burton, Corey
ALADDIN
Burton, David
GLADIATOR
Burton, Mark
ROUND TRIP TO HEAVEN
Burton, Tim
SINGLES
Burton, Tony
MISSION OF JUSTICE
Burton, Warren
POISON IVY
Burunelli, Rafaelle
CAPTAIN AMERICA
Buscaglia, Jr., Angelo Anthony
FOLKS!

Buscemi, Steve
CRISSCROSS
IN THE SOUP
RESERVOIR DOGS
Busey, Gary
CANVAS
PLAYER, THE
UNDER SIEGE
Busfield, Timothy
SNEAKERS
Bush, George
FEED
Bush, Grand
BACKTRACK
FREEJACK
Butler, Brigitte
SUNSET STRIP
Butler, Damon
NEWSIES
Butler, Dan
CAPTAIN RON
Butler, David W.
NIGHT AND THE CITY
Butler, Diane
LOVE CRIMES
Butler, Dick
MO' MONEY
Butler, Holly
NETHERWORLD
Butler, Kathleen
LEAGUE OF THEIR OWN, A
Butler, Larry
LOVE FIELD
Butler, Megan
WHITE SANDS
Butler, Paul
GLENGARRY GLEN ROSS
ZEBRAHEAD
Butler, Taunesha
ZEBRAHEAD
Butto, Carl
DEADLY BET
Buxton, Paul
COMPLEX WORLD
Buy, Margherita
STATION, THE
Buza, George
BEAUTIFUL DREAMERS
Buznea, Magdelena
PETER'S FRIENDS
Byakatonda, Immaculate
MISSISSIPPI MASALA
Bynum, David Lee
LETHAL WEAPON 3
Byrd, Julian
TRACES OF RED
Byrne, Allie
HOWARDS END
Byrne, Duane
LAWNMOWER MAN, THE
Byrne, Gabriel
COOL WORLD
SOLDIER'S TALE, A
Byrne, Josh
MR. SATURDAY NIGHT
Byrnes, Burke
BACKTRACK
Byron, Jay
LETHAL WEAPON 3
Caan, James
HONEYMOON IN VEGAS
Caballero, Luiș
PUERTO RICAN MAMBO (NOT A MUSICAL), THE
Caban, Angel
REFRIGERATOR, THE
Cable, Bill
BASIC INSTINCT
Cabral, Omar
FOLKS!
Cabrera, Mayumi
SPLIT SECOND
Cacas, Ron
BASIC INSTINCT
Cacho, Daniel Gimenez
CABEZA DE VACA
Cada, James
CROSSING THE BRIDGE
Cade, Michael
CHAPLIN
Cadell, Ava
DO OR DIE
Cadia, Octavian
BRAM STOKER'S DRACULA
Cadman, Joshua
KUFFS
Caesar, Harry
FEW GOOD MEN, A
ROADSIDE PROPHETS
Caffrey, Stephen
BABE, THE
Cage, Nicolas
HONEYMOON IN VEGAS
Cahme, Mace
VENICE/VENICE
Cahme, Todd M.
VENICE/VENICE
Cahn, Art
SINGLES
Cahn, Jodi Faith
LOVE HURTS
Cahoon, Bonnie
DEATH BECOMES HER
Caidin, Eric
HELLROLLER
Cain, Chuck
PASSION FISH
Cain, Wirt
RUBY
Caine, Michael
DEATH BECOMES HER
MUPPET CHRISTMAS CAROL, THE
NOISES OFF
Cairns, Anthony
LONDON KILLS ME
Calder, David
MONKEY BOY
Calderbank, Julien
FAVOUR, THE WATCH, AND THE VERY BIG FISH, THE
Calderon, Paul
CRISSCROSS
BAD LIEUTENANT
Caldwell, Kevin
DEATH BECOMES HER
Caldwell, Randall
POISON IVY
Calhoun, Rory
PURE COUNTRY
Callaghan, Dick
SWOON
Callahan, James
HERO
Callan, Kathleen
RAISING CAIN
Callard, Roger
LIFE ON THE EDGE
Callella, Laura
COMPLEX WORLD
Callous, Maria
WISECRACKS
Callow, Simon
HOWARDS END
Calloway, Chris
IMPORTANCE OF BEING EARNEST, THE
Calloway, Daxon
NEWSIES
Calloway, Vanessa Bell
BEBE'S KIDS
Calogero, Pablo
MAMBO KINGS, THE
Calven, Christ
PUSHED TO THE LIMIT
Calvert, Bill
BODY WAVES
Calvin, John
ALMOST PREGNANT
Calzada, Katherine
CAPTAIN RON
Camacho, Art
FINAL IMPACT
Camarillo, Lennard
RADIO FLYER
Camden, Gloria
FROZEN ASSETS
Camen, Joey
COOL WORLD
Cameon, William
LORENZO'S OIL
Cameron
SUNSET STRIP
Cameron, Christopher Alan
UNDER SIEGE
Cameron, Dean
MIRACLE BEACH
Cameron, Sue
VENICE/VENICE
Cameron, William
HOFFA
Cameron-Scorsese, Domenica
STRAIGHT TALK
Cameroux, Ken
RESURRECTED, THE
Camp, Colleen
VAGRANT, THE
WAYNE'S WORLD
Camp, Hamilton
MEGAVILLE

Campanella, Joseph
CAFE ROMEO
ORIGINAL INTENT
Campbell, Amelia
LORENZO'S OIL
SINGLE WHITE FEMALE
Campbell, Angela
PROOF
Campbell, Bill
BRAM STOKER'S DRACULA
Campbell, Bruce
LUNATICS: A LOVE STORY
MINDWARP
WAXWORK II: LOST IN TIME
Campbell, Christopher J.
FOLKS!
Campbell, G. Smokey
PRAYER OF THE ROLLERBOYS
Campbell, Glen
ROCK-A-DOODLE
Campbell, J. Kenneth
STOP! OR MY MOM WILL SHOOT
Campbell, J. Marvin
RUBY
Campbell, Jerry
CONSENTING ADULTS
Campbell, Keith
PATRIOT GAMES
Campbell, Larry
STOP! OR MY MOM WILL SHOOT
Campbell, Lesha
GUN IN BETTY LOU'S
HANDBAG, THE
Campbell, Luther
DAMNED IN THE USA
Campbell, Mary Schmidt
LORENZO'S OIL
Campbell, Nicholas
RAMPAGE
Campbell, Paul
LUNATIC, THE
Campbell, Rob
UNFORGIVEN
Campbell, Rod
POWER OF ONE, THE
Campbell, Tisha
BOOMERANG
Campeanu, Daiana
HOME ALONE 2:
LOST IN NEW YORK
Camphuis, Richard G.
SOUTH CENTRAL
Campisi, Gaetano
JOHNNY STECCHINO
Campo, Julian S.
GLADIATOR
Campos, Victor
JUICE
Camren, Keith
WHITE TRASH
Camroux, Ken
JENNIFER EIGHT
Canada, Ron
HOME ALONE 2:
LOST IN NEW YORK
HONEY, I BLEW UP THE KID
PLAY NICE

Canal, David
CAPTAIN RON
Canales, Jenny
TOYS
Canarozzi, Anthony
NIGHT AND THE CITY
Candreva, David
DIGGSTOWN
Candy, John
ONCE UPON A CRIME
Cane, Max
UNDER SUSPICION
Canepari, Bernard
GUN IN BETTY LOU'S
HANDBAG, THE
Canerday, Natalie
ONE FALSE MOVE
Canfield, Gene
BAD LIEUTENANT
MY NEW GUN
SCENT OF A WOMAN
WHISPERS IN THE DARK
Cangelosi, Christopher
SWOON
Cannata, Anthony
HOFFA
HOME ALONE 2:
LOST IN NEW YORK
STRAIGHT TALK
Cannon, Benny S.
CROSSING THE BRIDGE
Cannone, Jean-Michel
FINE ROMANCE, A
Canon, Jack
LOVE FIELD
Cansino, Richard
DO OR DIE
Cantarini, Louis
NIGHT AND THE CITY
Cantarone, Elena
EVIL CLUTCH
Cantu, Carlos
PANAMA DECEPTION, THE
Cao Cuifeng
RAISE THE RED LANTERN
Cao Zhengyin
RAISE THE RED LANTERN
Capers, Virginia
ORIGINAL INTENT
Capetillo, Christiana
SINGLE WHITE FEMALE
Caplan, Bill
WHITE MEN CAN'T JUMP
Caplan, James
LONDON KILLS ME
Caplan, Twink
LITTLE SISTER
Capodice, John
HONEYMOON IN VEGAS
Capone, Vinny
LIGHT SLEEPER
Capra, Jordanna
HIRED TO KILL
Caprari, Antonio
KICK OR DIE
Capriani, Lisa
PASSENGER 57

Caputo, Douglas
CHINA O'BRIEN II
Carau, Lee
FROZEN ASSETS
Cardillo, Jacqulyne Marie
HOFFA
Cardillo, Jillian Alyse
HOFFA
Cardona, Chris
WHO SHOT PATAKANGO?
Cardone, John
BLOODFIST III: FORCED TO FIGHT
Carew, Peter
SCENT OF A WOMAN
Carey Ferguson, Doris
FOLKS!
Carey, Geoffrey
FAVOUR, THE WATCH, AND THE
VERY BIG FISH, THE
Carey, Ralph Wesley
UNDER SIEGE
Carhart, III, John
THERE'S NOTHING OUT THERE
Caridi, Carmine
RUBY
Carillo, Frank
PRELUDE TO A KISS
Carison, Gary
TROLL 2
Carlberg, Dean
PASSENGER 57
Carlin, Amanda
PASSION FISH
Carlin, Leila
BED & BREAKFAST
Carlisle, Deborah
VENICE/VENICE
Carlisle, Ellen
HIGHWAY 61
Carlisle, Kevin
HIGHWAY 61
Carlo, Georges
ONCE UPON A CRIME
Carlo, Philip
NIGHT AND THE CITY
Carlson, Amy
BABE, THE
Carlson, Drucilla A.
UNDER SIEGE
Carlson, Leslie
COMMON BONDS
K2
Carlson, Lillian
K2
Carlson, Linda
HONEY, I BLEW UP THE KID
Carlton, Hope Marie
GHOULIES III:
GHOULIES GO TO COLLEGE
SLUMBER PARTY MASSACRE 3
Carlton, Matthew
LOVE HURTS
Carmen, Julie
COLD HEAVEN
KISS ME A KILLER
Carnevale, Dario
BRENDA STARR

Carney, Merilyn
RUNESTONE, THE
Caro, Marc
DELICATESSEN
Carol, Jacqueline
INDIO 2 - THE REVOLT
Caron, Jean-Luc
DELICATESSEN
Caron, Leslie
DAMAGE
Carothers, Veronica
MIND, BODY & SOUL
Carpenter, Ken
HELLRAISER III: HELL ON EARTH
Carpenter, R.D.
ENCINO MAN
UNIVERSAL SOLDIER
Carpenter, Willie C.
DOUBLE TROUBLE
Carpintiero, Victor
DANZON
Carr, Jack
CRYING GAME, THE
Carr, Sadie
MISSISSIPPI MASALA
Carradine, David
ANIMAL INSTINCTS
DOUBLE TROUBLE
FIELD OF FIRE
MIDNIGHT FEAR
NIGHT RHYTHMS
ROADSIDE PROPHETS
WAXWORK II: LOST IN TIME
Carradine, Keith
CRISSCROSS
Carradine, Robert
ILLUSIONS
PLAYER, THE
Carrasco, Carlos
IN THE HEAT OF PASSION
Carrera, David
BEASTMASTER 2: THROUGH THE PORTAL OF TIME
Carrere, Tia
LITTLE SISTER
WAYNE'S WORLD
Carrero, Juan
PEPI, LUCI, BOM AND OTHER GIRLS ON THE HEAP
Carricart, Robert
COLD JUSTICE
Carriere, Mathieu
CHRISTOPHER COLUMBUS: THE DISCOVERY
SHINING THROUGH
Carrillo, Alejandro
CABEZA DE VACA
Carrillo, Santiago
CABEZA DE VACA
Carrington, Debbie Lee
BATMAN RETURNS
MOM AND DAD SAVE THE WORLD
Carroll, Diahann
COLOR ADJUSTMENT
Carroll, Helena
MAMBO KINGS, THE
Carroll, J. Winston
BEAUTIFUL DREAMERS
Carroll, Rocky
FATHERS AND SONS
PRELUDE TO A KISS
Carson, John
LIGHT IN THE JUNGLE, THE
Carson, Sarah
DISTINGUISHED GENTLEMAN, THE
Carter, Brandon
BRIEF HISTORY OF TIME, A
Carter, Bruce
LASER MOON
Carter, Jack
IN THE HEAT OF PASSION
Carter, Jim
BLAME IT ON THE BELLBOY
Carter, Nell
BEBE'S KIDS
Carter, Philip
STORYVILLE
Carter, Reggie
LUNATIC, THE
LUNATIC, THE
Carteris, Gabrielle
RAISING CAIN
Cartwright, Jon
POWER OF ONE, THE
Cartwright, Lynn
LEAGUE OF THEIR OWN, A
Cartwright, Matthew
CHAPLIN
Cartwright, Nancy
LITTLE NEMO: ADVENTURES IN SLUMBERLAND
Cartwright, Veronica
MAN TROUBLE
Caruso, Phillip V.
FAR AND AWAY
Carvalho, Betty
MAN TROUBLE
Carver, James
PROM NIGHT IV - DELIVER US FROM EVIL
Carvey, Dana
WAYNE'S WORLD
Carvin, Jessica
NETHERWORLD
Carwell, Skip
UNLAWFUL ENTRY
Carwell, Skip O.
CLASS ACT
Casados, Eloy
LINGUINI INCIDENT, THE
WHITE MEN CAN'T JUMP
Cascio, Salvatore
POPE MUST DIET!, THE
Cascone, Nicholas
MR. BASEBALL
Casella, Max
NEWSIES
Caserta, Clem
NIGHT AND THE CITY
Casey, Bernie
CHAINS OF GOLD
UNDER SIEGE
Casey, Kevin
GLADIATOR
MO' MONEY
Casey, Padraig
SPLIT SECOND
Casey-Rohde, Colleen
RAMPAGE
Cash, Susan
OVER HER DEAD BODY
Cash, Veronica
PAMELA PRINCIPLE, THE
Cashman, Dan
NIGHT EYES 2
Casile, Genevieve
ELEGANT CRIMINEL, L'
Casini, Alessandro
WHERE ANGELS FEAR TO TREAD
Caspary, Dee
NEWSIES
Cassas, Fernando
WATERLAND
Cassavetes, Zoe R.
NOISES OFF
Cassel, Jean-Pierre
FAVOUR, THE WATCH, AND THE VERY BIG FISH, THE
Cassel, Seymour
ADVENTURES IN SPYING
COLD HEAVEN
DIARY OF A HITMAN
HONEYMOON IN VEGAS
IN THE SOUP
Cassell, Vincent
HOT CHOCOLATE
Cassidy, Barry
SWOON
Cassidy, Brian
BIKINI SUMMER 2
Cassidy, Joanna
ALL-AMERICAN MURDER
LANDSLIDE
LONELY HEARTS
Cassini, John
CAFE ROMEO
Cassola, Carla
CAPTAIN AMERICA
DEVIL'S DAUGHTER, THE
Castaldi, Jean-Pierre
FINE ROMANCE, A
Castanon, Carlos
CABEZA DE VACA
Castell, Angelica
WATERDANCE, THE
Castellanos, Javier
AMERICAN ME
Castellanos, Theodora
MAMBO KINGS, THE
Castellitto, Sergio
ALBERTO EXPRESS
Castile, Christopher
BEETHOVEN
Castle, DeShonn
ZEBRAHEAD
Castle, Diana
RAPID FIRE
Castle, Linda
PASSION FISH
Castle, Robert
COUSIN BOBBY

Casto, Bobbi
LOVE FIELD
Castro, Nicolas
DANZON
Catalan, Carlos
DANZON
Catalina, Antonio
MEDITERRANEO
Cates, Jr., Gil
INNOCENT BLOOD
Cathell, Cevin
GIVING, THE
Cathey, Reg E.
JUST LIKE IN THE MOVIES
Catillou, Brigitte
VOYAGER
Cattrall, Kim
DOUBLE VISION
SPLIT SECOND
Catus, Gary L.
MALCOLM X
Caudill, Scott
NEWSIES
3 NINJAS
Cauldwell, Brendan
FAR AND AWAY
Caulfield, Maxwell
ANIMAL INSTINCTS
DANCE WITH DEATH
EXILED IN AMERICA
WAXWORK II: LOST IN TIME
Causey, Frank
PASSENGER 57
Cavaiani, Maria
WE'RE TALKIN' SERIOUS MONEY
Cavaiola, Nick
CANVAS
Cavanagh, Megan
LEAGUE OF THEIR OWN, A
Cave, Nick
JOHNNY SUEDE
Cavestani, Frank
FEW GOOD MEN, A
WILD ORCHID 2: TWO SHADES OF BLUE
Caviezel, James
DIGGSTOWN
Cazenove, Christopher
ACES: IRON EAGLE III
Cecere, Tony
LEATHER JACKETS
Cedar, Larry
BABE, THE
Cederna, Giuseppe
MEDITERRANEO
Cederquist, Pamela
HONEY, I BLEW UP THE KID
Ceesepe
PEPI, LUCI, BOM AND OTHER GIRLS ON THE HEAP
Cejudo, Chato
DANZON
Celario, Cathy
HONEYMOON IN VEGAS
Cele, Henry
LIGHT IN THE JUNGLE, THE

Celeste, Suzanne
RESERVOIR DOGS
Cellilo, Ronald
CRISSCROSS
Cellucci, Claire
SCANNERS III: THE TAKEOVER
Cenatiempo, John
LETHAL WEAPON 3
Cerebriakov, Alexii
RASPAD
Cerezo, Gustavo
CAPTAIN RON
Ceribello, Jimmy
TUNE, THE
Cerio, Katrina
HERO
Cerna, John
HOUSE ON TOMBSTONE HILL, THE
Cerney, Daniel
DEMONIC TOYS
Cerny, Jobe
MO' MONEY
PRELUDE TO A KISS
Ceron, Laura
PUBLIC EYE, THE
Cerullo, Al
BOOMERANG
Cerveris, Michael
WOMAN, HER MEN AND HER FUTON, A
Cespedes, Robert
IN GOLD WE TRUST
Cestero, Carlos
SEX CRIMES
Cha Cha, Johnny
HONEYMOON IN VEGAS
Chadwick, Justin
LONDON KILLS ME
Chaimovitch, Samuel
FAVOUR, THE WATCH, AND THE VERY BIG FISH, THE
Chakiris, George
PALE BLOOD
Chakraborty, Baroon
CITY OF JOY
Chalfant, Kathleen
BOB ROBERTS
JUMPIN' AT THE BONEYARD
Challenge, Heather Jones
TERMINAL BLISS
Chambers, Lisa
PROOF
Chambers, Patti
MY NEW GUN
Champion, Michael
LEATHER JACKETS
Champlin, Charles
PLAYER, THE
Chan, Darryl
LEATHER JACKETS
Chan, Dennis
KICKBOXER 3: THE ART OF WAR
Chan, Jackie
SUPERCOP: POLICE STORY III
Chan, Michael Paul
RAPID FIRE

Chan, Philip
HARD-BOILED
Chance, Kelsie
NETHERWORLD
Chancer, John
PROJECT: SHADOWCHASER
Chandler, Damon
MALCOLM X
WHO SHOT PATAKANGO?
Chandler, Estee
TERMINAL BLISS
Chandler, Jared
FOREVER YOUNG
Chandler, Kyle
PURE COUNTRY
Chang, Lyla
WATERDANCE, THE
Channing, Carol
WISECRACKS
Chanze, La
LEAP OF FAITH
MY NEW GUN
Chao, Rosalind
MEMOIRS OF AN INVISIBLE MAN
Chapa, Damian
UNDER SIEGE
Chapek, Susan
LORENZO'S OIL
Chaplin, Christopher
CHRISTOPHER COLUMBUS: THE DISCOVERY
Chaplin, Geraldine
CHAPLIN
CHILDREN, THE
Chaplin, Hillary
COMPLEX WORLD
Chaplin, Tim
CHAPLIN
Chapman, Alex
OVER HER DEAD BODY
Chapman, Lanei
IMPORTANCE OF BEING EARNEST, THE
WHITE MEN CAN'T JUMP
Chapman, Ray
LEAGUE OF THEIR OWN, A
Chapman, Suzanne
PROOF
Chapman, Tim
MANIAC WARRIORS
Chappel, Chris
SPLIT SECOND
Charbonneau, Jay
COMPLEX WORLD
MALCOLM X
Charbonneau, Patricia
K2
Charles
35 UP
Charles, Chale
LONDON KILLS ME
Charles, Diane
COLD JUSTICE
Charles, Josh
CROSSING THE BRIDGE
Charles, Nancy Linehan
BRAM STOKER'S DRACULA

Charleson, Andrew
EDWARD II
Charleton, Brent
SWOON
Charlton, Jeffrey
CONSENTING ADULTS
Charnley, Hetta
PETER'S FRIENDS
Charno, Stuart
STEPHEN KING'S SLEEPWALKERS
Charnock, Nigel
EDWARD II
Charoff, Alan
CHAPLIN
Chartier, Urbain
MANIAC WARRIORS
Chase, Carl
ALIEN3
Chase, Chevy
HERO
MEMOIRS OF AN INVISIBLE MAN
Chase, Gregory
SCHOOL TIES
Chasse, Maurice
RAPID FIRE
SHAKING THE TREE
Chatterjee, Saran
CITY OF JOY
Chau, Francois
RAPID FIRE
Chaudhury, Kajal
CITY OF JOY
Chaulet, Emmanuelle
ALL THE VERMEERS IN NEW YORK
Chaumeau, Andre
DOES THIS MEAN WE'RE MARRIED?
FAVOUR, THE WATCH, AND THE VERY BIG FISH, THE
Chauvin, Lilyan
ROUND TRIP TO HEAVEN
UNIVERSAL SOLDIER
Chaves, Richard
NIGHT EYES 2
Chavez, Antero
CABEZA DE VACA
Chavez, Robert
AMERICAN ME
Chavez, Sonna
ROADSIDE PROPHETS
Chaykin, Maury
ADJUSTER, THE
HERO
LEAVING NORMAL
MY COUSIN VINNY
Chazaro, Adjari
DANZON
Chazaro, Adyari
CABEZA DE VACA
Cheadle, Don
ROADSIDE PROPHETS
Cheek, Charles
LOVE CRIMES
Cheeks, Rudy
COMPLEX WORLD
Cheeseman, Ken
HOUSESITTER
Cheesman, Sean
BODYGUARD, THE
Cheever, David
SWOON
Chen, Eric
DO OR DIE
Chen, Stephen
BAD LIEUTENANT
Cheng, Kent
ONCE UPON A TIME IN CHINA
Cher
PLAYER, THE
Chereau, Patrice
LAST OF THE MOHICANS, THE
Cherney, Kaethe
CTHULHU MANSION
Cherry, Larry
MALCOLM X
Cherry, Shakir
GIVING, THE
Chesler, Michael
BABE, THE
Chesney, Nancy
LORENZO'S OIL
Chester, Craig
SWOON
Chester, Holly
SNAKEEATER III . . . HIS LAW
Cheung, George Kee
SNEAKERS
STORYVILLE
UNDER SIEGE
Cheung, Jacky
ONCE UPON A TIME IN CHINA
Cheung Jue-lin
HARD-BOILED
Cheung, Maggie
SUPERCOP: POLICE STORY III
Chevalia, Kevin Timothy
FOLKS!
Chevit, Maurice
HAIRDRESSER'S HUSBAND, THE
Chevrolet, Manny
ROADSIDE PROPHETS
Chi
DISTINGUISHED GENTLEMAN, THE
Chi-Muoi Lo
BUFFY THE VAMPIRE SLAYER
Chianese, Dominic
PUBLIC EYE, THE
Chiba, Sonny
ACES: IRON EAGLE III
Chickering, Torie
LIVING END, THE
Child, Eve
OUT ON A LIMB
Children, Scott
WATERLAND
Childs, Lucy
HARD PROMISES
Chiles, Lois
DIARY OF A HITMAN
Chimento, Jim
UNDER SIEGE
Chin, Susan
HAND THAT ROCKS THE CRADLE, THE
Chinlund, Nick
LETHAL WEAPON 3
Chokshi, Charubala
CITY OF JOY
Chong, Marcus
VENICE/VENICE
Chong, Michael
RAPID FIRE
Chong, Phil
LEATHER JACKETS
Chong, Rae Dawn
COMMON BONDS
Chong, Tommy
FERNGULLY: THE LAST RAINFOREST
Chou, Tasen
3 NINJAS
Choudhury, Sarita
MISSISSIPPI MASALA
Chovance, Ron
SOUTH CENTRAL
Chow Yun-fat
HARD-BOILED
Chowdhry, Ranjit
MISSISSIPPI MASALA
Chowdhury, Santu
CITY OF JOY
Choy-Ling Man
DEMON IN MY VIEW, A
Christensson, Irma
BEST INTENTIONS, THE
Christian, John
COMRADES IN ARMS
Christian, Keely
SLUMBER PARTY MASSACRE 3
Christian, Victoria
ALAN & NAOMI
Christiansen, Roger S.
STRAIGHT TALK
Christiansen, Sean
WHITE TRASH
Christie, Christine
WATERLAND
Christie, Julianne
ENCINO MAN
Christine, Wanda
FOLKS!
Christmas, Eric
NICKEL & DIME
Christopher, Bojesse
DARK HORSE
MEATBALLS 4
STEPHEN KING'S SLEEPWALKERS
Christopher, Guy
LITTLE NEMO: ADVENTURES IN SLUMBERLAND
Christopher, June
MAN TROUBLE
Christopher, Tom
PURE COUNTRY
Chu Hung
INDOCHINE
Chu Xiao
RAISE THE RED LANTERN

Chuipka, Chip
SCANNERS III: THE TAKEOVER
SNAKEEATER III . . . HIS LAW

Chung, Esmond
HONEYMOON IN VEGAS

Chung, George
HONEYMOON IN VEGAS

Churchill, Harvey
CLEARCUT

Churchill, Pola
WATERDANCE, THE

Churikova, Inna
ADAM'S RIB

Chytil, Velemir
CAPTAIN AMERICA

Ciaffa, Patricia
DISTINGUISHED GENTLEMAN, THE

Ciarcia, Cha Cha
HOFFA

Ciarfalio, Carl
BEASTMASTER 2:
THROUGH THE PORTAL OF TIME

Ciarfalio, Carl N.
FAR AND AWAY

Cicchini, Robert
LIGHT SLEEPER

Ciccolella, Jude
GLENGARRY GLEN ROSS

Ciccone, Joey
WATERDANCE, THE

Cicero, Phyllis
STEELE'S LAW

Cimo, Valentino
HOFFA

Cimpoeru, Marinela
MR. SATURDAY NIGHT

Cin Chi Cheng
MR. BASEBALL

Cintron, Monique
MALCOLM X

Cioffi, Charles
NEWSIES
USED PEOPLE

Ciravolo, Mike
BAD LIEUTENANT

Cirino, Chuck
MUNCHIE

Ciro, Jose
CAPTAIN RON

Cisler, Jiri
EAR, THE

Cisneros, Steven
AMERICAN ME

Cistaro, Anthony
RUNESTONE, THE

Citrano, Lenny
MAN TROUBLE

Civitano, Thomas
HOME ALONE 2:
LOST IN NEW YORK

Claire, Hermine
INSPECTOR LAVARDIN

Claire, Maria
SLUMBER PARTY MASSACRE 3
SOCIETY

Clanton, Natalie
MALCOLM X

Clanton, Rony
JUICE
MALCOLM X

Claridge, Chris
SOCIETY

Clark, Blake
LADYBUGS
LOVE POTION NO. 9
SHAKES THE CLOWN
TOYS

Clark, Bret Baxter
DEATHSTALKER IV:
MATCH OF TITANS

Clark, Candy
BUFFY THE VAMPIRE SLAYER
ORIGINAL INTENT

Clark, Cornelius
LEAP OF FAITH

Clark, Dan
DEATH BECOMES HER

Clark, Devin
PRAYER OF THE ROLLERBOYS

Clark, Eric
DEATH BECOMES HER

Clark, Gemma
DAMAGE

Clark, Matt
FROZEN ASSETS

Clark, Roydon E.
STOP! OR MY MOM WILL SHOOT

Clark, Ted
HAPPY HELL NIGHT

Clark, Wilfredo Giovanni
JOHNNY SUEDE

Clarke, Angie
BERNARD AND THE GENIE

Clarke, Barry John
EDWARD II

Clarke, Lisa
MANIAC WARRIORS

Clarke, Marcus
MUPPET CHRISTMAS CAROL, THE

Clarke, Philip
ALADDIN

Clarkson, Lana
BARBARIAN QUEEN II:
THE EMPRESS STRIKES BACK

Claugh, Linda Jones
MAGICAL WORLD OF CHUCK
JONES, THE

Claussen, Joy
CHAPLIN

Clay, Stanley B.
BEBE'S KIDS

Clayburgh, Jill
WHISPERS IN THE DARK

Clayton, Melissa
HOUSE IV

Clayton, Merry
WILD ORCHID 2:
TWO SHADES OF BLUE

Clear, Patrick
BABE, THE

Cleghorne, Ellen
THIS IS MY LIFE

Clemenson, Christian
HERO

Clementis, Jill Jane
LOVE CRIMES

Clements, Jill Lane
MY COUSIN VINNY

Clemmons, Julie
HAND THAT ROCKS THE
CRADLE, THE

Clemons, Lorenzo
MO' MONEY
STRAIGHT TALK

Clennon, David
LIGHT SLEEPER
MAN TROUBLE

Cleveland, Rob
LOVE POTION NO. 9

Cleven, Harry
TOTO LE HEROS

Clevenot, Philippe
HAIRDRESSER'S HUSBAND, THE

Clifford, Raina
LORENZO'S OIL

Clinton, Bill
FEED

Clinton, Hillary
FEED

Clippinger, Jennifer
BOB ROBERTS

Cloghessy, John
BAD LIEUTENANT

Cloke, Kristen
CAGED FEAR
MEGAVILLE

Close, Del
PUBLIC EYE, THE

Close, Eric
AMERICAN ME

Clotworthy, Rob
LOVE FIELD

Cloud, Lisa
WHITE SANDS

Clough, John Scott
CAPTAIN RON

Clout, Bob
BEAUTIFUL DREAMERS

Clow, O. Boyd
FOLKS!

Clown, Roger
BEAUTIFUL DREAMERS

Clunie, Michelle
SUNSET STRIP

Coady, Krista
CUTTING EDGE, THE

Coates, Bill
MY COUSIN VINNY

Coates, Kim
INNOCENT BLOOD

Coaxum, Derrick
DAUGHTERS OF THE DUST

Cobb, Angelbreath
BREAKING THE RULES

Cobb, Arnett
TEXAS TENOR:
THE ILLINOIS JACQUET STORY

Cobb, David Robert
BEBE'S KIDS

Cobb, Jocelyn
HOWARDS END

Cobb, Michael
COMPLEX WORLD
Cobb, Milton L.
HERO
Cobb, Randall "Tex"
COLLISION COURSE
DIGGSTOWN
Cobbold, Clare
POWER OF ONE, THE
Cobbs, Bill
BODYGUARD, THE
EXILED IN AMERICA
ROADSIDE PROPHETS
Cobbs, Willy
MISSISSIPPI MASALA
Cobo, Roberto
CABEZA DE VACA
Coburn, James
HUGH HEFNER: ONCE UPON A TIME
PLAYER, THE
Coca, Richard
AMERICAN ME
Cochran, Dean
AMITYVILLE 1992:
IT'S ABOUT TIME
Cochran, Russ
INNOCENT BLOOD
Cochran, Shannon
BABE, THE
Cochran, Steve
CROSSING THE BRIDGE
Cochrane, Martin
PATRIOT GAMES
Cochrane, Rory
FATHERS AND SONS
Cockrum, Dennis
SHAKING THE TREE
Cocktails, Johnny
MEATBALLS 4
Cody, Lara
VAMPIRE HUNTER D
WATERDANCE, THE
Cody, Wayne
SINGLES
Coe, George
MIGHTY DUCKS, THE
Coffey, Colleen
LAWNMOWER MAN, THE
Coffin, Frederick
WAYNE'S WORLD
Coghill, Nikki
ROCK & ROLL COWBOYS
Cohen, Avi
HUMAN SHIELD, THE
Cohen, Faye
THIS IS MY LIFE
Cohen, Jedidiah
HOME ALONE 2:
LOST IN NEW YORK
Cohen, Judith
JUST LIKE IN THE MOVIES
Cohen, Matthew Ray
TRAINED TO FIGHT
Cohen, Scott
MAMBO KINGS, THE
Cohen, Shlomit
POUR SACHA

Colbin, Ron
WIND
Cole, Carl
PASSENGER 57
Cole, Dennis
DEATH HOUSE
Cole, J.C.
BUFFY THE VAMPIRE SLAYER
Cole, Jackson
PRIMO BABY
Cole, James
HOME ALONE 2:
LOST IN NEW YORK
Cole, Kimberly Ann
TWIN PEAKS: FIRE WALK WITH ME
Cole, Victor
MO' MONEY
Colella, Guido
VENICE/VENICE
Coleman, Brian
CRYING GAME, THE
Coleman, Bryan
CHAPLIN
Coleman, Christian
SOUTH CENTRAL
Coleman, Clarke
KUFFS
Coleman, Dierdre
COMRADES IN ARMS
Coleman, Layne
GATE II
Coleman, Marcia
POWER OF ONE, THE
Coleman, Noel
UNDER SUSPICION
Coleman, Renee
LEAGUE OF THEIR OWN, A
Coleman, Townsend
FERNGULLY:
THE LAST RAINFOREST
Coles, Lisa
BATMAN RETURNS
LOVE POTION NO. 9
Coles, Robert
TO RENDER A LIFE
Colgan, Eileen
FAR AND AWAY
Colgate, William
LANDSLIDE
Colgert, Tim
TO PROTECT AND SERVE
Collard, William F.
FATE
Collet, Christopher
PRAYER OF THE ROLLERBOYS
Colletta, Mike
SOCIETY
Collette, Toni
EFFICIENCY EXPERT, THE
Colley, Don Pedro
JOURNEY OF HONOR
Collier, Constance
WISECRACKS
Collier, Marian
LETHAL WEAPON 3

Collins, Bobbi
LOVE FIELD
Collins, Bobby C.
HERO
Collins, Cheryl
ARTICLE 99
Collins, Christopher
STOP! OR MY MOM WILL SHOOT
STRANGER AMONG US, A
Collins, Greg
CLASS ACT
COOL WORLD
Collins, Jr., Wayne
BEBE'S KIDS
Collins, Karl
LONDON KILLS ME
Collins, Kevin
EDWARD II
Collins, Larissa
LEAGUE OF THEIR OWN, A
Collins, Michael James
SINGLE WHITE FEMALE
Collins, Patricia
ADJUSTER, THE
Collins, Pauline
CITY OF JOY
Collins, Penelope
MY GRANDPA IS A VAMPIRE
Collins, Robert Evan
DOUBLE TROUBLE
Collins, Ruth
HELLROLLER
Collins, Stephen
MY NEW GUN
Collis, Joe
WATERLAND
Collis, Larry K.
LOVE HURTS
Collison, Frank
DIGGSTOWN
LAWNMOWER MAN, THE
Collver, Mark
THERE'S NOTHING OUT THERE
Colmenares, Sergio
DANZON
Colon, Alex
DEEP COVER
Colon, Frances
BRONX WAR, THE
Colton, Chevi
BED & BREAKFAST
Colton, Jacque Lynn
TOYS
Coltrane, Robbie
OH, WHAT A NIGHT
POPE MUST DIET!, THE
Columbus, A.M.
HOME ALONE 2:
LOST IN NEW YORK
Columbus, Eleanor
HOME ALONE 2:
LOST IN NEW YORK
Colvin, E.W.
MISSISSIPPI MASALA
Colvin, Norm
LEAP OF FAITH

Comacho, Art
OUT FOR BLOOD

Comar, Richard
KICKBOXER 3: THE ART OF WAR

Combeau, Muriel
NEAR MISSES

Combs, Holly Marie
DR. GIGGLES
SIMPLE MEN

Combs, Jeffrey
DOCTOR MORDRID
GUYVER, THE

Comer, Anjanette
NETHERWORLD

Commitante, Raffaella
SOCIETY

Comporato, Gaetano
RAMPAGE

Compton, Norm
STOP! OR MY MOM WILL SHOOT

Conaway, Cristi
BATMAN RETURNS
HUSBANDS AND WIVES

Conaway, Jeff
ALMOST PREGNANT
BIKINI SUMMER 2
MIRROR IMAGES
SUNSET STRIP

Concannon, Jon
FATHER

Concha
PEPI, LUCI, BOM AND OTHER GIRLS ON THE HEAP

Condra, Julie
GAS FOOD LODGING

Cones, Tristam
EDWARD II

Conforti, Tony
RUBY

Confrey, Wayne
MANIAC WARRIORS

Conkel, Jeff
HAND THAT ROCKS THE CRADLE, THE

Conklin, Cody
SCHOOL TIES

Connaughton, Shane
PLAYBOYS, THE

Connell, Marty
PASSENGER 57

Connelly, Chris
BODYGUARD, THE
MAGICAL WORLD OF CHUCK JONES, THE

Conner, Michael D.
PASSENGER 57

Conner, Tom
WHITE SANDS

Conners, Chuck
ONE LAST RUN

Connery, Sean
MEDICINE MAN

Connolly, Andrew
PATRIOT GAMES

Connolly, John P.
PRAYER OF THE ROLLERBOYS

Connolly, Kevin
ALAN & NAOMI

Connor, Paul
SWOON

Conrad, Joseph
NEWSIES

Conrad, Kendall
HIRED TO KILL

Conroy, Frances
SCENT OF A WOMAN

Conroy, Francis
JUST LIKE IN THE MOVIES

Considine, John
EXILED IN AMERICA

Constant, Yvonne
FAVOUR, THE WATCH, AND THE VERY BIG FISH, THE

Constantine, Eddie
ZENTROPA

Conti, Ugo
MEDITERRANEO

Contreras, Jim
PEPI, LUCI, BOM AND OTHER GIRLS ON THE HEAP

Converse, Frank
PRIMARY MOTIVE

Conway, Kevin
JENNIFER EIGHT

Conzo, Joe
MAMBO KINGS, THE

Cook, Addison
KISS ME A KILLER
MALCOLM X
SWOON

Cook, Darrel
DAUGHTERS OF THE DUST

Cook, Divina
SCENT OF A WOMAN

Cook, Gordon
MANIAC WARRIORS

Cook, Julius
DAUGHTERS OF THE DUST

Cook, Keith
CHINA O'BRIEN II

Cook, Sharon
JUICE

Cook, Tracy
SNAKEEATER III . . . HIS LAW

Cooke, Chris
SIMPLE MEN

Cooksey, Danny
MOM AND DAD SAVE THE WORLD

Coombes, Norman
HOUSE OF USHER, THE

Coombs, Chris
UNLAWFUL ENTRY

Coomer, Joey
HARD PROMISES

Cooney, Kevin
HARD PROMISES

Coop, Denice
BASKET CASE 3: THE PROGENY

Cooper, Alice
WAYNE'S WORLD

Cooper, Audra L.
TWIN PEAKS: FIRE WALK WITH ME

Cooper, Chuck
MALCOLM X

Cooper, Garry
LONDON KILLS ME

Cooper, Jeanne
FROZEN ASSETS

Cooper, Phillip
DEATH BECOMES HER

Cooper, Ray
HOUSESITTER

Cooper, Rowena
SECRET FRIENDS

Cooper, Sr., Ralph
MALCOLM X

Coopwood, Kenneth Scott
GLADIATOR

Copello, Bert
MR. SATURDAY NIGHT

Copeman, Michael
SCANNERS III: THE TAKEOVER

Copley, Teri
BRAIN DONORS
FROZEN ASSETS

Copp, Robin
ROCK & ROLL COWBOYS

Corbett, Bob
WILD WHEELS

Corbett, Ed
RUNESTONE, THE

Corbiletto, Roberto
DEVIL'S DAUGHTER, THE

Cord, Alex
ROOTS OF EVIL

Cordery, Richard
LORENZO'S OIL

Cordner, Richard
FATHER

Cordova, Margarita
COLD HEAVEN

Corduner, Allan
EDWARD II

Corello, Nick
CHAPLIN

Corley, Annie
MALCOLM X

Corman, Brent
ROUND TRIP TO HEAVEN

Corman, Dick
NOISES OFF

Corman, Maddie
MY NEW GUN

Corman, Roger
BODY WAVES

Cormier, Steve
WHITE SANDS

Cornelius, Rodney
RAMPAGE

Cornell, Caroline
CHAPLIN

Cornell, Chris
SINGLES

Corner, Robert
GODZILLA VS. BIOLLANTE

Corone, Antoni
BRENDA STARR

Corr, Jim
PASSED AWAY

Corraface, George
CHRISTOPHER COLUMBUS: THE DISCOVERY

Corral, Elaine
MEMOIRS OF AN INVISIBLE MAN

Correa, Tim
GIVING, THE

Correll, Matthew J.
FALLING FROM GRACE

Corrente, Damien
LIGHT SLEEPER

Corri, Nick
IN THE HEAT OF PASSION

Corrigan, Kevin
ZEBRAHEAD

Corte, Jr., E. Daniel
UNDER SIEGE

Cortese, Joe
RUBY
TO PROTECT AND SERVE

Cortez, Katherine
FINAL ANALYSIS

Cosmo, Tony
RESERVOIR DOGS

Costa, Cheryl
JOHNNY SUEDE

Costa, Helen
SUNSET STRIP
VENICE/VENICE

Costanzo, Robert
HONEYMOON IN VEGAS
WE'RE TALKIN' SERIOUS MONEY
UNLAWFUL ENTRY

Costigan, George
MONKEY BOY

Costner, Kevin
BODYGUARD, THE

Cottle, Matthew
CHAPLIN

Cotton, Darryl
PUSHED TO THE LIMIT

Cotton, Oliver
CHRISTOPHER COLUMBUS: THE DISCOVERY
YEAR OF THE COMET

Cottrell, Pierre
VENICE/VENICE

Couch, Peter
PRELUDE TO A KISS

Coughlan, Frank
FAR AND AWAY

Coulouris, Keith
DOCTOR MORDRID

Coulson, Bernie
ADVENTURES IN SPYING

Coulson, Catherine E.
TWIN PEAKS: FIRE WALK WITH ME

Coulson, Mary
BEYOND DARKNESS

Coulthard, Raymond
MUPPET CHRISTMAS CAROL, THE

Council, Richard
JUST LIKE IN THE MOVIES

Counsil, Jerry
DR. GIGGLES

Counts, Chela
MALCOLM X

Counts, Chelsea
MALCOLM X

Coupe, Norm
SEX CRIMES

Court, Geraldine
LOVE HURTS

Courtney, Alex
DEATH HOUSE

Courtney, James Jude
FAR AND AWAY
WE'RE TALKIN' SERIOUS MONEY

Courtney, Lorna
COMRADES IN ARMS

Cousins, Brian
HOMICIDAL IMPULSE

Cousins, Robin
CUTTING EDGE, THE

Covert, Todd Mason
CHAPLIN

Covey
PROOF

Covington, Ian
CHAPLIN

Cowan, Colleen
MALCOLM X

Cowen, Martha L.
MAN TROUBLE

Cowin, John
MANIAC WARRIORS

Cowles, Donna
FALLING FROM GRACE

Cowles, Mary
FALLING FROM GRACE

Cowles, Matthew
BRENDA STARR

Cowles, Terra
FALLING FROM GRACE

Cowles, Tracy
FALLING FROM GRACE

Cox, Brian
TERMINAL BLISS

Cox, Courteney
SHAKING THE TREE

Cox, Gerica
MALCOLM X

Cox, Joshua
RUNESTONE, THE

Cox, Rob
RIVER RUNS THROUGH IT, A

Cox, Ronny
CAPTAIN AMERICA

Cox, Ruby
LEAVING NORMAL

Cox, Tony
MOM AND DAD SAVE THE WORLD

Coyle, Eliza
SHAKES THE CLOWN

Coyne, Ria
NAKED OBSESSION

Cozart, Cylk
HEAVEN IS A PLAYGROUND
WHITE MEN CAN'T JUMP

Crabb, Eric
WAYNE'S WORLD

Cracchiolo, Sal
KISS ME A KILLER

Crafford, James
SWOON

Cragin, Charles
HAPPY HELL NIGHT
SHADOWS AND FOG

Craig, Dana
CHAPLIN

Craig, Daniel
POWER OF ONE, THE

Craig, Mary
HELLROLLER

Craig, Roger
NAKED OBSESSION

Crain, Mary Tom
FALLING FROM GRACE

Cramer, Grant
AUNTIE LEE'S MEAT PIES

Cramer, Kurt
GODZILLA VS. BIOLLANTE

Cranden, Connie
LORENZO'S OIL

Crane, Craig
MUPPET CHRISTMAS CAROL, THE

Crane, John
BODY WAVES

Crane, Larry
FALLING FROM GRACE

Crangle, Edward
CHAPLIN

Cranham, Kenneth
MONKEY BOY
UNDER SUSPICION

Cranitch, Lorcan
PLAYBOYS, THE

Crank, Chelsea
RAMPAGE

Craven, James
SNEAKERS

Craven, Matt
FEW GOOD MEN, A
K2

Craven, Mimi
MIKEY

Craver, Sonny
WHITE MEN CAN'T JUMP

Crawford, Jane
BOB ROBERTS

Crawford, Jim
SWOON

Crawford, Pauline
MANIAC WARRIORS

Crawford, Wayne
DIARY OF A HITMAN

Crayton, Darcell
CLASS ACT

Craze, Galaxy
HUSBANDS AND WIVES

Creamer, David
RIVER RUNS THROUGH IT, A

Crean, Christopher
WHO SHOT PATAKANGO?

Creed-Miles, Charlie
LONDON KILLS ME

Creevay, Lori
TRACES OF RED

Creighton, Georgia
SISTER ACT

Crenshaw, Randy
DEATH BECOMES HER
MR. SATURDAY NIGHT

Cresswell, Tommy
CONSENTING ADULTS

Creswell, Saylor
WIND

Crewson, Wendy
FOLKS!
GETTING MARRIED IN BUFFALO JUMP

Crick, Richard
MISSISSIPPI MASALA

Crimp, Douglas
SWOON

Crombie, Jonathan
CAFE ROMEO

Crombie, Peter
SMOOTH TALKER

Cromwell, J.T.
SCENT OF A WOMAN

Cromwell, James
BABE, THE

Cronin, Laurel
BEETHOVEN
HOUSESITTER
LEAGUE OF THEIR OWN, A

Cronin, Patrick
DR. GIGGLES
RAMPAGE

Cronyn, Martha
BEAUTIFUL DREAMERS

Crook, Peter
CHAPLIN

Crooke, Leland
SCORCHERS

Cropper, Steve
MANIAC WARRIORS

Crosbie, Annette
POPE MUST DIET!, THE

Crosby, Cathy Lee
PLAYER, THE

Crosby, David
THUNDERHEART

Crosby, Denise
DOLLY DEAREST

Cross, Elroy
THUNDERHEART

Crossley, Charlotte
SISTER ACT

Crouther, Lance
CLASS ACT

Crovato, Luciano
EVIL CLUTCH

Crow, Floyd Charging
THUNDERHEART

Crowe, Alice Marie
SINGLES

Crowe, Cameron
SINGLES

Crowe, Russell
CROSSING, THE
EFFICIENCY EXPERT, THE
PROOF

Crowley, Donncha
FAR AND AWAY

Crowley, Kevin
HOFFA

Crowningshield, Keith
NOISES OFF

Cruise, Julee
TWIN PEAKS: FIRE WALK WITH ME

Cruise, Tom
FAR AND AWAY
FEW GOOD MEN, A

Crunchley, Murray
GETTING MARRIED IN BUFFALO JUMP

Cruz, Celia
MAMBO KINGS, THE

Cruz, Charmaine
BRONX WAR, THE

Cruz, Joseph Michael
BAD LIEUTENANT

Cruz, Raymond
MAN TROUBLE
UNDER SIEGE

Cruze, Josh
ANIMAL INSTINCTS

Cryer, Max
MY GRANDPA IS A VAMPIRE

Crystal, Billy
MR. SATURDAY NIGHT

Crystal, Lindsay
MR. SATURDAY NIGHT

Cszimas, Costin
MR. SATURDAY NIGHT

Cubison, Richard
CHRISTOPHER COLUMBUS: THE DISCOVERY

Cubitt, David
K2

Cudlitz, Michael
RIVER RUNS THROUGH IT, A

Cudney, Cliff
MALCOLM X

Cudney, Roger
BARBARIAN QUEEN II: THE EMPRESS STRIKES BACK

Cuervo, Fernando G.
1492: THE CONQUEST OF PARADISE

Cuervo, Frank
INDIO 2 - THE REVOLT

Cuffe, Allison
SUNSET STRIP

Cuffling, Bernard
RESURRECTED, THE

Cui Zhihgang
RAISE THE RED LANTERN

Cuka, Frances
AFRAID OF THE DARK

Culkin, Kieran
HOME ALONE 2: LOST IN NEW YORK

Culkin, Macaulay
HOME ALONE 2: LOST IN NEW YORK

Culkin, Michael
CANDYMAN

Cullen, Brett
LEAVING NORMAL

Cullen, Michael
MALCOLM X

Cullison, Tom
BRIDE OF KILLER NERD

Cullum, J.D.
FOREVER YOUNG
ROADSIDE PROPHETS

Cullum, Kody
HERO

Culpepper, Gentile
GIVING, THE

Cumming, Alan
BERNARD AND THE GENIE

Cummings, Brian
FERNGULLY: THE LAST RAINFOREST

Cummings, Gregg
ROOTS OF EVIL

Cummings, James
SWOON

Cummings, Jim
ALADDIN

Cummings, Thomas E.
LAST OF THE MOHICANS, THE

Cummins, Gregory Scott
BATMAN RETURNS

Cunningham, Bob
TEXAS TENOR: THE ILLINOIS JACQUET STORY

Cunningham, John
SCHOOL TIES

Cunningham, Mitch
NIGHT AND THE CITY

Cunningham, Peter "Sugarfoot"
BLOODFIST III: FORCED TO FIGHT
FINAL IMPACT

Curott, Phyllis
VENICE/VENICE

Currow, Kim
INNOCENT BLOOD

Curry, Russell
PHANTOM OF THE RITZ

Curry, Terry
TOGETHER ALONE

Curry, Tim
FERNGULLY: THE LAST RAINFOREST
HOME ALONE 2: LOST IN NEW YORK
PASSED AWAY

Curtis, Cory
DEEP COVER

Curtis, Jamie Lee
FOREVER YOUNG

Curtis, John Bear
LEAVING NORMAL

Curtis, Kelly Leigh
DEVIL'S DAUGHTER, THE

Curtis, Liane
WILD ORCHID 2: TWO SHADES OF BLUE

Curtis, Sonia
TERMINAL BLISS

Curtis, Terrance
PUSHED TO THE LIMIT
Curtis, Todd
OUT FOR BLOOD
Curtis, Tony
CENTER OF THE WEB
Curtis-Hall, Vondie
MAMBO KINGS, THE
PASSION FISH
Curto, Vincent
NIGHT RHYTHMS
Cusack, Ann
LEAGUE OF THEIR OWN, A
Cusack, Cyril
FAR AND AWAY
Cusack, Joan
HERO
TOYS
Cusack, John
BOB ROBERTS
PLAYER, THE
ROADSIDE PROPHETS
SHADOWS AND FOG
Cusack, Niamh
PLAYBOYS, THE
Cusack, Sinead
WATERLAND
Cusack, Susie
HERO
Cusano, Gary
WOMAN, HER MEN AND HER FUTON, A
Cushing, Edward
MO' MONEY
Cushing, Peter
INNOCENT BLOOD
Cuskey, Brooke
DARK HORSE
Cutrona, Ryan
KUFFS
Cuttell, Lou
VOYAGER
Cutter, Lise
NICKEL & DIME
Cuyler, Grenville
HOUSESITTER
Cuzzocrea, Dominic
USED PEOPLE
Cyll, Renate
SHINING THROUGH
Cyprian, Satya
GIVING, THE
D'Amato, Alphonse
DAMNED IN THE USA
D'Ambrosio, Vito
HERO
D'Angelo, Beverly
LONELY HEARTS
MAN TROUBLE
POPE MUST DIET!, THE
D'Angelo, John Anthony
UNIVERSAL SOLDIER
D'Angerio, Joe
OF MICE AND MEN
D'Angerio, Joseph
BIG GIRLS DON'T CRY . . . THEY GET EVEN

D'Anthony, Dominique
MY FATHER IS COMING
D'Aquila, Diane
USED PEOPLE
D'arcy, Daniel W.
LORENZO'S OIL
D'Arcy, Ilena
EMMANUELLE 6
D'Ettore, Karen
KUFFS
D'Ettore, Kelly
KUFFS
D'Onofrio, Joseph
NIGHT AND THE CITY
D'Onofrio, Vincent
MALCOLM X
PLAYER, THE
Dabson, Jesse
LITTLE SISTER
Dachis, Jeff
THERE'S NOTHING OUT THERE
Dacosta, Christian J.
MALCOLM X
Dacqmine, Jacques
INSPECTOR LAVARDIN
Dacre, Sue
MUPPET CHRISTMAS CAROL, THE
Dafoe, Willem
LIGHT SLEEPER
WHITE SANDS
Daglan
DAY IN OCTOBER, A
Dagon, Gil
HUMAN SHIELD, THE
Dagory, Jean-Michel
DOES THIS MEAN WE'RE MARRIED?
Dahlgren, Tom
DISTINGUISHED GENTLEMAN, THE
Daily, E.G.
LORENZO'S OIL
Daily, Mike D.
PURE COUNTRY
Daise, Ronald
DAUGHTERS OF THE DUST
Dakil, Floyd
LOVE HURTS
Dakota, Deenie
OVER HER DEAD BODY
Dal Santo, Joey
HOFFA
Dale, James
MISSISSIPPI MASALA
Dale, Jennifer
ADJUSTER, THE
Dale, Merrilee
BOB ROBERTS
Daley, Cass
WISECRACKS
Dalle, Beatrice
NIGHT ON EARTH
Dallesandro, Joe
WILD ORCHID 2: TWO SHADES OF BLUE
Dalskaia, Lylia
FAVOUR, THE WATCH, AND THE VERY BIG FISH, THE

Dalton, Clifford
INSIDE EDGE
Dalton, Glenn
FALLING FROM GRACE
Dalton, Timothy
BRENDA STARR
Daltrey, Roger
COLD JUSTICE
Daly, Timothy
YEAR OF THE COMET
Dalzell, III, Bill
HOFFA
Dam, Franklin
PATRIOT GAMES
Dambra, William
HOME ALONE 2: LOST IN NEW YORK
Damkobler, William
COMPLEX WORLD
Damon, Gabriel
LITTLE NEMO: ADVENTURES IN SLUMBERLAND
NEWSIES
Damon, Matt
SCHOOL TIES
Damsyik, H.I.M.
LADY DRAGON
Dance, Charles
ALIEN3
Dane, Lawrence
TWIN SISTERS
Daneau, Dorian
UNLAWFUL ENTRY
Danese, Connie
SOCIETY
Dangerfield, Rodney
LADYBUGS
ROVER DANGERFIELD
Daniel, Jr., Den
PALE BLOOD
Daniele, Adele
PROOF
Daniels, Alex
HONEY, I BLEW UP THE KID
Daniels, Arthur
TEXAS TENOR: THE ILLINOIS JACQUET STORY
Daniels, Buddy
ROUND TRIP TO HEAVEN
Daniels, Collins Williams
HERO
Daniels, E.G.
HIGHWAY 61
Daniels, Eddie
BAD LIEUTENANT
Daniels, Gary
FINAL IMPACT
Daniels, J.D.
MIGHTY DUCKS, THE
Daniels, Jeff
LOVE HURTS
Daniels, Leslie Brett
MY NEW GUN
Daniels, Mark
CANDYMAN
Danielson, Lynn
MORTUARY ACADEMY
NICKEL & DIME

Danner, Blythe
HUSBANDS AND WIVES

Dante, Joe
MAGICAL WORLD OF CHUCK JONES, THE
STEPHEN KING'S SLEEPWALKERS

Danziger, Cory
BEETHOVEN
BIG GIRLS DON'T CRY . . . THEY GET EVEN

Darbo, Patrika
LEAVING NORMAL
VAGRANT, THE

Darcey, Janine
FAVOUR, THE WATCH, AND THE VERY BIG FISH, THE

DaRe, Eric
CRITTERS 4
TWIN PEAKS: FIRE WALK WITH ME

Dare, Kim
EDWARD II

Darel, Florence
CONTE DE PRINTEMPS

Darling, Jennifer
ALADDIN
LITTLE NEMO: ADVENTURES IN SLUMBERLAND

Darling, Peter
HOWARDS END

Darling, Tom
WIND

Darmon, Gerard
POUR SACHA

Darrell, Dreenagh
WISECRACKS

Darrow, Oliver
SPIRITS

Dash, Stacey
MO' MONEY

DaSilva, Elias Monteiro
MEDICINE MAN

Dassin, Daniel
HOME ALONE 2: LOST IN NEW YORK

Datcher, Alex
NETHERWORLD
PASSENGER 57

Datta, Aloknanda
CITY OF JOY

Datta, Durba
CITY OF JOY

Dau, Nissam
POUR SACHA

Dau, Salim
CUP FINAL

Daughtery, Hurley
LOVE CRIMES

Dave, Dipti
CITY OF JOY

Davenport, Marc
WHO SHOT PATAKANGO?

Davenport, Mark
DEATH BECOMES HER

Davey, Belinda
PROOF

Davi, Robert
CENTER OF THE WEB
CHRISTOPHER COLUMBUS: THE DISCOVERY
WILD ORCHID 2: TWO SHADES OF BLUE

David, Darryl
HERO

David, Eleanor
LONDON KILLS ME

David, Gerard
RUBY

David, Jeff
HELLROLLER

David, Joanna
SECRET FRIENDS

David, Keith
ARTICLE 99
FINAL ANALYSIS

David, Mark
NEWSIES
SOCIETY

David, Taylor
MUPPET CHRISTMAS CAROL, THE

Davidoff, Irena
DANCE MACABRE

Davidovich, Lolita
LEAP OF FAITH
RAISING CAIN

Davidson, Barbara
MIGHTY DUCKS, THE

Davidson, G. Kenneth
TWIN PEAKS: FIRE WALK WITH ME

Davidson, Jaye
CRYING GAME, THE

Davidson, Kevin
ARTICLE 99

Davidson, P.J.
UNDER SUSPICION

Davidson, Robi
BEETHOVEN

Davies, Annie
PETER'S FRIENDS

Davies, Eileen
WHERE ANGELS FEAR TO TREAD

Davies, Rebekah
MY GRANDPA IS A VAMPIRE

Davies, Tod
BACKTRACK

Davies, Walter Langdon
MANIAC WARRIORS

DaVila, Frankie
FOLKS!

Davis, "Wild" Bill
TEXAS TENOR: THE ILLINOIS JACQUET STORY

Davis, Amy
ALL-AMERICAN MURDER

Davis, Andrew
LIGHT IN THE JUNGLE, THE

Davis, Brad
PLAYER, THE

Davis, Charles
THUNDERHEART

Davis, Dawn
COMPLEX WORLD

Davis, Deb
COMPLEX WORLD

Davis, Derek
FALLING FROM GRACE

Davis, Don
LEAGUE OF THEIR OWN, A

Davis, Don S.
HERO
KUFFS

Davis, Duane
DIGGSTOWN
UNDER SIEGE
UNIVERSAL SOLDIER

Davis, Eddie
MALCOLM X

Davis, Ernie
FINAL ANALYSIS

Davis, Gary Lee
FAR AND AWAY

Davis, Geena
HERO
LEAGUE OF THEIR OWN, A

Davis, Gene
UNIVERSAL SOLDIER

Davis, Jay W
HARD PROMISES

Davis, Jeannie E.
CONSENTING ADULTS

Davis, Joan
WISECRACKS

Davis, John Walter
DIGGSTOWN

Davis, Judy
HUSBANDS AND WIVES
WHERE ANGELS FEAR TO TREAD

Davis, Mark
EDWARD II

Davis, Nathan
SHAKING THE TREE

Davis, Ossie
GLADIATOR
MALCOLM X

Davis, Philip
ALIEN3

Davis, Richard
UNDER SIEGE

Davis, Sonny
SEEDPEOPLE
UNLAWFUL ENTRY

Davis, Stavon Lovell
BABE, THE

Davis, Ted
INTO THE SUN

Davis, Vince
LEAP OF FAITH

Davis, Viveka
MAN TROUBLE

Davison, Courtney
BRIDE OF KILLER NERD

Davison, Michelle
BEBE'S KIDS

Davison, Tim
KUFFS

Dawber, Pam
STAY TUNED

Dawney, Nick
DEMON IN MY VIEW, A

Dawson, Pieter
DR. GIGGLES
Dawson, Vivian
DAUGHTERS OF THE DUST
Day, Cora Lee
DAUGHTERS OF THE DUST
Day, Dylan
BABE, THE
Day-Lewis, Daniel
LAST OF THE MOHICANS, THE
De Backer, Jo
TOTO LE HEROS
De Bankole, Isaach
NIGHT ON EARTH
De Blas, Manuel
CHRISTOPHER COLUMBUS: THE DISCOVERY
De Boer, Nikki
PROM NIGHT IV - DELIVER US FROM EVIL
De Bono, Ivan
CHRISTOPHER COLUMBUS: THE DISCOVERY
De la Manitou, Satya
BACKTRACK
De La Paz, Danny
AMERICAN ME
De La Pena, George
BRAIN DONORS
KUFFS
De La Texera, Diego
CAPTAIN RON
De Mornay, Rebecca
HAND THAT ROCKS THE CRADLE, THE
De Niro, Robert
MISTRESS
NIGHT AND THE CITY
De St. Pere, Helene
WINTER IN LISBON, THE
De Vito, Danny
BATMAN RETURNS
HOFFA
Deak, Joanne
HOFFA
Deak, Michael
GUYVER, THE
DeAlexandre, Rodolfo
MEDICINE MAN
Dean, Loren
1492: THE CONQUEST OF PARADISE
Dean, Mladen
BECOMING COLETTE
Dean, Rick
BLOODFIST III: FORCED TO FIGHT
CAGED FEAR
NAKED OBSESSION
Dean, Ron
BABE, THE
COLD JUSTICE
SHAKING THE TREE
Deane, Lezlie
TO PROTECT AND SERVE
Deary, Brendan
POWER OF ONE, THE
Deavers, Dorothy
HARD PROMISES

DeBanzie, Lois
SISTER ACT
DeBarres, Michael
WAXWORK II: LOST IN TIME
DeBenning, Burr
LOVE FIELD
DeBernal, Farnesio
CABEZA DE VACA
DeBonis, Marcia
THIS IS MY LIFE
DeCandia, Mario
ONCE UPON A CRIME
DeCarlo, Mark
BUFFY THE VAMPIRE SLAYER
DeCegli, Nicholas
BAD LIEUTENANT
DeChandenay, Roland
VOYAGER
Deckert, Blue
HARD PROMISES
LEAP OF FAITH
DeColumbia, Mario
MY FATHER IS COMING
DeCosta, Michelle
REFRIGERATOR, THE
DeDeney, Simon
DAMAGE
SHINING THROUGH
Dedio, Joey
WHERE THE DAY TAKES YOU
Dee, Ruby
COLOR ADJUSTMENT
Deering, Dee Dee
FOLKS!
Deezen, Eddie
ROCK-A-DOODLE
Def Jef
DEEP COVER
Defever, Dominique
DELICATESSEN
DeFlippis, Jimi
STAY TUNED
DeFrancisco, Sam
DESERT KICKBOXER
DeFusco, Ed
UNLAWFUL ENTRY
DeGeneres, Ellen
WISECRACKS
Degn, Erik
FINEST HOUR, THE
DeGoros, Jean-Claude
POUR SACHA
DeGrandis, Suzanne
LIFE ON THE EDGE
DeGrassio, Jimmy
WAYNE'S WORLD
Deguy, Marie-Armelle
ELEGANT CRIMINEL, L'
DeHart, Brent
LIFE ON THE EDGE
Dehner, Durk
DADDY AND THE MUSCLE ACADEMY
Deinum, Juliette
RAMPAGE

DeJulius, Louis
BRIDE OF KILLER NERD
Del Amo, Scott
CAPTAIN AMERICA
Del Campo, Victor Hugo Martin
CABEZA DE VACA
Del Toro, Benicio
CHRISTOPHER COLUMBUS: THE DISCOVERY
Del Valle, Angel
DANZON
Del Villar, Micke
DANZON
DeLancie, John
HAND THAT ROCKS THE CRADLE, THE
Delaney, Cassandra
HURRICANE SMITH
Delaney, David
HOWARDS END
Delaney, Leon
UNIVERSAL SOLDIER
Delaney, Tia
LORENZO'S OIL
Delano, Diane
STEPHEN KING'S SLEEPWALKERS
Delano, Michael
DEADLY BET
DeLano, Michael
OUT FOR BLOOD
Delany, Dana
HOUSESITTER
LIGHT SLEEPER
Delapena, Linda
DAMAGE
Delarco, Jonathan
MAMBO KINGS, THE
DeLeon, Marita
KISS ME A KILLER
DeLeon, Melissa
BLOOD ON THE BADGE
Delgado, Edwin
CAPTAIN RON
Delgado, Kim
PATRIOT GAMES
RUNESTONE, THE
Delgado, Max
MAN TROUBLE
Delgado, Pastora
PEPI, LUCI, BOM AND OTHER GIRLS ON THE HEAP
Della Chiesa, Ron
TEXAS TENOR: THE ILLINOIS JACQUET STORY
Dellal, Gabrielle
K2
Dellos, D.J.
NEWSIES
DeLongis, Anthony
FAR AND AWAY
DeLorenzo, Michael
DIGGSTOWN
FEW GOOD MEN, A
DeLoutchek, Pascal
FAVOUR, THE WATCH, AND THE VERY BIG FISH, THE

Delpy, Albert
HAIRDRESSER'S HUSBAND, THE

Delpy, Julie
VOYAGER

DeLucia, Carolyn
OUT ON A LIMB

DeLuise, Dom
ALMOST PREGNANT
MUNCHIE

DeLuise, Michael
ENCINO MAN
WAYNE'S WORLD

DeLuise, Peter
CHILDREN OF THE NIGHT

DeMarco, Michelle
LOVE HURTS

DeMay, Brendon
BABE, THE

Demetral, Chris
DOLLY DEAREST

Demetrios, Eames
GIVING, THE

DeMiguel, Fabio
PEPI, LUCI, BOM AND OTHER GIRLS ON THE HEAP

Demille, Don
MANIAC WARRIORS

Demir, Alex
PUSHED TO THE LIMIT

DeMita, John
UNIVERSAL SOLDIER

Demme, Jonathan
COUSIN BOBBY

DeMontalembert, Thibault
INDOCHINE

DeMontigny, Giles
EDWARD II

Demorest, Daniel
UNIVERSAL SOLDIER

DeMoss, Darcy
PALE BLOOD

Dempsey, Amy Lou
BODYGUARD, THE

Dempsey, Jerome
MISTRESS

Dempsey, Linda
BRENDA STARR

Demules, Frank
BECOMING COLETTE

DeMunn, Jeffrey
NEWSIES

Denbo, Jack
PUBLIC EYE, THE

Dendak, Mimsel
BRIDE OF KILLER NERD

DeNeck, Didier
TOTO LE HEROS

Deneuve, Catherine
INDOCHINE

Dengel, Jake
DIARY OF A HITMAN
PRAYER OF THE ROLLERBOYS

Denham, Tony
POWER OF ONE, THE

Denier, Lydie
WILD ORCHID 2: TWO SHADES OF BLUE

Denison, Anthony John
LITTLE VEGAS

Denman, Stanton
SCHOOL TIES

Denmark, Brenda
NIGHT AND THE CITY

Dennehy, Brian
GLADIATOR

Dennehy, Elizabeth
WATERDANCE, THE

Dennis, Darrell
LEAVING NORMAL

Dennis, Robb
EDWARD II

Dentie, Gino
SUNSET STRIP

Denton, Sandy
STAY TUNED

Depardieu, Gerard
1492: THE CONQUEST OF PARADISE
TOUS LES MATINS DU MONDE

Depardieu, Guillaume
TOUS LES MATINS DU MONDE

DePatie, Beth
ROADSIDE PROPHETS

DePauw, Joose
TOTO LE HEROS

DePenguern, Artus
FAVOUR, THE WATCH, AND THE VERY BIG FISH, THE

DePetris, Annette
HOFFA

DePinto, Joey
BATMAN RETURNS
RUBY
STOP! OR MY MOM WILL SHOOT

DePofi, Niko
BRIDE OF KILLER NERD

DePriest, Mario
DR. GIGGLES

DePrume, Cathryn
CRISSCROSS

Depusse, Jean
INSPECTOR LAVARDIN

Dequattro, Tom
COMPLEX WORLD

Derek, Bo
HOT CHOCOLATE

Derence, Sam
HERO

Deret, Jean-Claude
FAVOUR, THE WATCH, AND THE VERY BIG FISH, THE

Dern, Bruce
DIGGSTOWN

Derosa, Justin
STOP! OR MY MOM WILL SHOOT

DeRoxtra, Ron
RUBY

Derrick, James
BASKET CASE 3: THE PROGENY

Derry, Megan
KUFFS

Derryberry, Debi
ALADDIN

DeRubi, Hector
BARBARIAN QUEEN II: THE EMPRESS STRIKES BACK

Des Barres, Michael
UNDER SIEGE

Desai, Shelly
TOYS

DeSanctis, Rosie
NOISES OFF

DeSantis, Alessandro
JOHNNY STECCHINO

DeSantis, Simonetta
VENICE/VENICE

DeSantis, Stanley
CANDYMAN

DeSelle, Truus
LILY WAS HERE

Desmond, Dan
SCHOOL TIES

Desnet, Jacqueline
FROZEN ASSETS

Despotovich, Nada
CRISSCROSS

Detmers, Maruschka
MAMBO KINGS, THE

Detraz, Monique
BLOOD ON THE BADGE

Deuschle, Victoria
OTHER WOMAN, THE

Deuter, James
BABE, THE
MO' MONEY

Devaney, Ann
NIGHT AND THE CITY

Devasquez, Devin
SOCIETY

Devereux, Aimee
HOME ALONE 2: LOST IN NEW YORK

Devereux, Clarke P.
HOME ALONE 2: LOST IN NEW YORK

Devereux, Monica
HOME ALONE 2: LOST IN NEW YORK

Devereux, Patricia
HOME ALONE 2: LOST IN NEW YORK

Devine, Loretta
CAGED FEAR
CLASS ACT

Devine, Margaret
JUST LIKE IN THE MOVIES

DeVink, Darlene
MANIAC WARRIORS

Devlin, Alan
PLAYBOYS, THE

Devlin, J.G.
FAR AND AWAY

Devlin, John
FATHER

DeWet, Gideon
SARAFINA!

Dewhurst, Colleen
BED & BREAKFAST

Dewitt, Anthony
MALCOLM X

Dewitt, Jan
LOVE HURTS
DeYoung, Cliff
DR. GIGGLES
DeZarn, Tim
SOUTH CENTRAL
Dharker, Ayesha
CITY OF JOY
Dhlathu, Nokuzola
SARAFINA!
Diablo, John
MANIAC WARRIORS
Diamant, Mike
SOCIETY
Diamant, Sigal
WILD ORCHID 2: TWO SHADES OF BLUE
Diamantstein, Andrej
BECOMING COLETTE
Diamond, Barry
BEBE'S KIDS
Diamond, Drake
BREATHING FIRE
Diamond, Jessica
MAMBO KINGS, THE
Diamond, Judi
BRAM STOKER'S DRACULA
Diamond, Keith
DR. GIGGLES
Diamond, Lindsey
PASSENGER 57
Diaz, Christina
INNOCENT BLOOD
Diaz, Edith
SISTER ACT
Diaz, Mike
SWOON
DiBenedetto, John
JUICE
DiBenedetto, Tony
BLOODFIST III: FORCED TO FIGHT
DiBianco, Louis
THIS IS MY LIFE
DiBiasi, Romolo
NIGHT ON EARTH
Dicaprio, Leonardo
POISON IVY
DiCarlo, Josette
CHILDREN OF THE NIGHT
PRELUDE TO A KISS
Dickerson, Jacqui
JUICE
Dicks, Andrew
CHRISTOPHER COLUMBUS: THE DISCOVERY
Dicks, John
FLIRTING
Didi, Thulani
SARAFINA!
Dieball, Bret
NEWSIES
Diego, Juan
CABEZA DE VACA
Diehl, John
MIKEY
MO' MONEY
Dieker, Daniel
FINEST HOUR, THE
DiElsi, Frank
BATMAN RETURNS
Diem, Connie
BECOMING COLETTE
Dierkop, Charles
ROOTS OF EVIL
Dierlam, Katy
SHADOWS AND FOG
Dietl, Bo
BAD LIEUTENANT
THIS IS MY LIFE
WHISPERS IN THE DARK
DiGiacomo, Nicolas
FAVOUR, THE WATCH, AND THE VERY BIG FISH, THE
Dignard, Paul
MANIAC WARRIORS
Digregorio, Ben
WHO SHOT PATAKANGO?
DiGregorio, David
UNIVERSAL SOLDIER
Dileo, Anthony
LORENZO'S OIL
DiLeo, Antone
PASSED AWAY
DiLeo, Frank
WAYNE'S WORLD
DiLeo, Jr., Anthony
BOB ROBERTS
Dillard, Ricky
LEAP OF FAITH
Dillard, Victoria
DEEP COVER
Dillenberg, Nicole
LIVING END, THE
Diller, Phyllis
WISECRACKS
Dillon, Deborah
LITTLE SISTER
Dillon, Denny
HOUSE IV
LIFE ON THE EDGE
Dillon, Kevin
MIDNIGHT CLEAR, A
Dillon, Matt
MALCOLM X
SINGLES
Dillon, Melinda
CAPTAIN AMERICA
DiMaggio, Lou
OUT ON A LIMB
DiMarco, Guido
PUBLIC EYE, THE
DiMarco, Teresa
PUBLIC EYE, THE
DiMattia, Victor
RADIO FLYER
DiMiglio, Gerard
AFRAID OF THE DARK
Dimitrov, Dimitri
MISTRESS
Dimitrov, Rumen
DEATHSTALKER IV: MATCH OF TITANS
Dimon, Stephen
ROUND TRIP TO HEAVEN
Din, Jimmy
MISSISSIPPI MASALA
Dinah, Pesedena
POWER OF ONE, THE
Dinello, Paul
STRAIGHT TALK
Ding Weimin
RAISE THE RED LANTERN
Dingatha, Sbongile
SARAFINA!
Dingman, Byron
RIVER RUNS THROUGH IT, A
Dini, Memo
MEDITERRANEO
DiNizio, Pat
SINGLES
Dinkins, Lisa
RUNESTONE, THE
Dinosaur, Jr.
1991: THE YEAR PUNK BROKE
Dionne, Margot
COMPLEX WORLD
Diouf, Mouss
DOES THIS MEAN WE'RE MARRIED?
Dirkson, Douglas
ARTICLE 99
Disend, Mitchell
FATHERS AND SONS
Dishy, Bob
USED PEOPLE
Diskin, Ben
MR. SATURDAY NIGHT
OUT ON A LIMB
Distefano, James
SEX CRIMES
DiStefano, Marco
HUSBANDS AND LOVERS
Ditson, Harry
BACK IN THE U.S.S.R.
Dittner, Erika
BUFFY THE VAMPIRE SLAYER
Divof, Andrew
BACK IN THE U.S.S.R.
Dix, Norman
BRIEF HISTORY OF TIME, A
Dixon, Callum
WATERLAND
Dixon, Donna
WAYNE'S WORLD
Dixon, MacIntyre
RIVER RUNS THROUGH IT, A
Dixon, Pam
MAXIMUM FORCE
OUT FOR BLOOD
Dixon, Sam
MALCOLM X
Dixon, Shane
UNIVERSAL SOLDIER
Djimon
UNLAWFUL ENTRY
Djola, Badja
WATERDANCE, THE

Dlamini, Dumisani
SARAFINA!
Dlamini, Gugwana
SARAFINA!
Dlamini, Vukani
SARAFINA!
Dlamini, Xolani
SARAFINA!
Dlathu, Sindiswa
SARAFINA!
Do Minh-vien
LOVER, THE
Do'Qui, Leslie
ORIGINAL INTENT
Do'Qui, Robert
I DON'T BUY KISSES ANYMORE
ORIGINAL INTENT
Do-Ley, Simon
MALCOLM X
Dobkin, Larry
BEASTMASTER 2:
THROUGH THE PORTAL OF TIME
Dobson, Peter
WHERE THE DAY TAKES YOU
Dobtcheff, Vernon
NEAR MISSES
VENICE/VENICE
Docenko, Nikilai
RASPAD
Dockery, Leslie
MALCOLM X
Dodds Frank, Marilyn
FOLKS!
Doe, John
PURE COUNTRY
ROADSIDE PROPHETS
Doepken, David
LORENZO'S OIL
Doggart, Evelyn
LONDON KILLS ME
Dohanan, Lucinda
COMPLEX WORLD
Doherty, Marianne
DR. GIGGLES
Doherty, Matt
BABE, THE
MIGHTY DUCKS, THE
MO' MONEY
Doherty, William
ROAD TO RUIN
Dolan, Frank
BED & BREAKFAST
Dolan, Phelim
SWOON
Dolenz, Ami
CHILDREN OF THE NIGHT
MIRACLE BEACH
Dolgen, Larry
BEYOND JUSTICE
Doll, Sandy
ROUND TRIP TO HEAVEN
Dollard, Blake
GLADIATOR
Dolman, Bob
FAR AND AWAY
Dominelli, Frank
FOLKS!
Dominic, Heather Rose
LIGHT SLEEPER
Dona, Linda
DELTA HEAT
Donahue, Mike
SAVAGE INSTINCT
Donahue, Sean P.
SAVAGE INSTINCT
Donahue, Troy
DOUBLE TROUBLE
PAMELA PRINCIPLE, THE
Donald, Juli
BRAIN DONORS
Donat, Peter
BABE, THE
SCHOOL TIES
Donatt, Julie
FAR AND AWAY
Donegan, Dorothy
TEXAS TENOR:
THE ILLINOIS JACQUET STORY
Doney, Randy
MR. SATURDAY NIGHT
Donmeyer, Steve
BEASTMASTER 2:
THROUGH THE PORTAL OF TIME
Donnini, Guilio
JOHNNY STECCHINO
Donno, Ayres
BACKTRACK
Donovan, Jamie
I DON'T BUY KISSES ANYMORE
Donovan, Martin
MALCOLM X
SIMPLE MEN
Donovan, Tate
LITTLE NOISES
LOVE POTION NO. 9
Doohan, James
DOUBLE TROUBLE
Doolan, Trish
LIFE ON THE EDGE
Dooley, Frank
CUTTING EDGE, THE
Dooley, Paul
PLAYER, THE
SHAKES THE CLOWN
Doolittle, John
DISTINGUISHED GENTLEMAN, THE
Doran, Jadene
SPLIT SECOND
Dorantes, Juana
CABEZA DE VACA
Dorff, Stephen
POWER OF ONE, THE
Dormandy, Simon
CHRISTOPHER COLUMBUS:
THE DISCOVERY
Dormoy, Philippe
FAVOUR, THE WATCH, AND THE
VERY BIG FISH, THE
Dorn, Cynthia
LOVE HURTS
Doron, Amit
POUR SACHA
Dorsey, Fern
LOVE CRIMES
Dorsey, Kevin
PUBLIC EYE, THE
Dorsey, Reginald T.
SOUTH CENTRAL
Dos Santos Kaiapo, Bec-Kana-Re
MEDICINE MAN
Dossin, Glenn
ZEBRAHEAD
Dotrice, Roy
CUTTING EDGE, THE
Dotten, Irv
BOOMERANG
Doug, Doug E.
CLASS ACT
DR. GIGGLES
Dougherty, Charles
WELCOME TO OBLIVION
Douglas, Alistair
MY GRANDPA IS A VAMPIRE
Douglas, Carlos
CODE NAME: CHAOS
Douglas, Diana
COLD HEAVEN
Douglas, Michael
BASIC INSTINCT
SHINING THROUGH
Douglas, Sarah
BEASTMASTER 2:
THROUGH THE PORTAL OF TIME
MEATBALLS 4
Douglas, Tracy
BOOMERANG
Douglass, Norman
JUICE
Dougnac, Marie-Laure
DELICATESSEN
Doumanian, John
HUSBANDS AND WIVES
Dourif, Brad
COMMON BONDS
CRITTERS 4
DEAD CERTAIN
LONDON KILLS ME
Dow, Barbara
WITCHCRAFT IV: VIRGIN HEART
Dow, Charlie
ALAN & NAOMI
Dow, Ellen Albertini
MEMOIRS OF AN INVISIBLE MAN
SISTER ACT
Dowd, Ann
LORENZO'S OIL
Dowd, Jay
RUBY
Dowell, Raye
BOOMERANG
MALCOLM X
Dowling, Stephen
MIGHTY DUCKS, THE
Downer, Hugh
CHAPLIN
Downey, Jr., Robert
CHAPLIN
Downey, Representative Thomas J.
DAMNED IN THE USA
Dowse, Denise
SNEAKERS

Doycich, Lori
BOB ROBERTS
Doyle, Alma
HIGHWAY 61
Doyle, Bernadette
FATHER
Doyle, Gilmary
STRAIGHT TALK
Doyle, John
ROCK & ROLL COWBOYS
Doyle, Thomas A.
SINGLES
Doyle, Tony
ADVENTURES IN DINOSAUR CITY
DAMAGE
SECRET FRIENDS
Doyle-Murray, Brian
WAYNE'S WORLD
Dr. Dre
JUICE
Drabla, Valda Z.
SWOON
Drago, Billy
MARTIAL LAW 2: UNDERCOVER
SECRET GAMES
Drago, Joe
JENNIFER EIGHT
Drake, Larry
DR. GIGGLES
Drake-Massey, Bebe
BEBE'S KIDS
BOOMERANG
Drayton, Cisco
MALCOLM X
Drescher, Adam
BATMAN RETURNS
Drescher, Fran
WE'RE TALKIN' SERIOUS MONEY
Dreschler, Miriam
BECOMING COLETTE
Dressler, Marie
WISECRACKS
Dreyfus, Jean-Claude
DELICATESSEN
TOUS LES MATINS DU MONDE
Dries, Dolores "Pickles"
LEAGUE OF THEIR OWN, A
Driggs, Deborah
MARTIAL LAW 2: UNDERCOVER
NIGHT RHYTHMS
Drinkwater, Carol
FATHER
Dror, Baruch
FINEST HOUR, THE
Drozd, Georgi
RASPAD
Drugan, Jenny
LEAVING NORMAL
Drum, Julius
THUNDERHEART
Drummond-Hay, Cecil
MANIAC WARRIORS
Drummond-Hay, Charlie
MANIAC WARRIORS
Druzay, Tom
SOCIETY
Drysdale, Lee
LEATHER JACKETS
Duarte, Juan Sanchez
CABEZA DE VACA
Duarte, Pamela
KISS ME A KILLER
DuBose, Columbia
MALCOLM X
Dubost, Niels
POUR SACHA
Dubourgeot, Charles
ONCE UPON A CRIME
Ducati, Kristie
BIKINI CARWASH COMPANY, THE
Duchaussoy, Michel
ROAD TO RUIN
Duchovny, David
BEETHOVEN
CHAPLIN
RUBY
VENICE/VENICE
Duclos, Philippe
TOUS LES MATINS DU MONDE
Ducommun, Rick
CLASS ACT
ENCINO MAN
Ducret, Claudine
VAN GOGH
Dudikoff, Michael
HUMAN SHIELD, THE
Dudley, Bronson
NOISES OFF
Dudley, Colin
UNDER SUSPICION
Dudley, James
CAPTAIN RON
Dudynsky, Ivan
NEWSIES
Duff-Griffin, William
BASIC INSTINCT
Duffett, Nicola
HOWARDS END
Duffin, Shay
MEMOIRS OF AN INVISIBLE MAN
NEWSIES
PUBLIC EYE, THE
Duffy, Alice
HOUSESITTER
SCHOOL TIES
Duffy, Dave
SPLIT SECOND
Duffy, Joseph
WHITE MEN CAN'T JUMP
Duffy, Karen T.
MALCOLM X
Duffy, Pete
WHITE MEN CAN'T JUMP
Duffy, Sean
MY GRANDPA IS A VAMPIRE
Duffy, Thomas F.
MAMBO KINGS, THE
WATERDANCE, THE
DuFresne, Jodi G.
LOVE CRIMES
Dujmovic, Ljubica
CAPTAIN AMERICA
Duke, O.L.
MALCOLM X
Duke, Patty
PRELUDE TO A KISS
Dullea, Keir
OH, WHAT A NIGHT
Dulon, Jean-Jacques
FINE ROMANCE, A
Dumbaugh, Eric
WATERLAND
Dumeniaud, Pierre-Francois
INSPECTOR LAVARDIN
Dumicic, Adrianne Marcich
CAPTAIN AMERICA
Dumitru, Voinea
MR. SATURDAY NIGHT
Dumont, J.K.
PAMELA PRINCIPLE, THE
Dunard, David
SEEDPEOPLE
Dunaway, Faye
DOUBLE EDGE
SCORCHERS
Dunbar, Adrian
CRYING GAME, THE
PLAYBOYS, THE
Dunbar, Eddie
BASIC INSTINCT
Dunbar, Mary Ellen
HOMICIDAL IMPULSE
Duncan, John Henry
EDWARD II
Duncan, Mandy
HERO
Duncan, Neil
SPLIT SECOND
Duncan, Sandy
ROCK-A-DOODLE
Duncan Sisters
WISECRACKS
Duncan, Thomas
EDWARD II
Dundas, Jennifer
LORENZO'S OIL
Dunfee, Nora
LORENZO'S OIL
Dunford, Andrew
UNDER SUSPICION
Dunham, Dale
MIGHTY DUCKS, THE
Dunkin, Jim
RIVER RUNS THROUGH IT, A
Dunn, Bill
VOYAGER
Dunn, Coquina
HARD PROMISES
Dunn, Craig
UNDER SIEGE
Dunn, Kevin
CHAPLIN
1492: THE CONQUEST OF PARADISE
Dunn, Nora
PASSION FISH
Dunn, Peter
MALCOLM X

Dunne, Griffin
BIG GIRLS DON'T CRY . . . THEY GET EVEN
STRAIGHT TALK

Dunne, Kerry Dakota
WE'RE TALKIN' SERIOUS MONEY

Dunning, Douglas
HELLROLLER

Dunning, Ellen
DEMONIC TOYS

Dunning, Nick
LONDON KILLS ME

Dunston, Geraldine
DAUGHTERS OF THE DUST

Duong, Ahn
MAMBO KINGS, THE
SCENT OF A WOMAN

Duperial, Michel
WINTER IN LISBON, THE

DuPois, Starletta
SOUTH CENTRAL
WATERDANCE, THE

Dupont, Daniel
PASSION FISH
UNDER SIEGE

Dupont, Peter
UNLAWFUL ENTRY

Duppin, Andy
MALCOLM X

Dupre, Chris
NEWSIES

Dupree, Vincent Craig
SOUTH CENTRAL

Dupuy, Michel
INSPECTOR LAVARDIN

Duquenne, Pascal
TOTO LE HEROS

Duran, Gerardo
CABEZA DE VACA

Duran, Richard
BEASTMASTER 2: THROUGH THE PORTAL OF TIME

Durand, Judi
BEBE'S KIDS

Durang, Christopher
HOUSESITTER

Durant, Nicolle
SOCIETY

Durboraw, Marisa
UNLAWFUL ENTRY

Durell, Marina
INNOCENT BLOOD

Durning, Charles
BRENDA STARR

Duronslet, Mara
LAWNMOWER MAN, THE

Durrell, Michael
SISTER ACT

Dury, Ian
SPLIT SECOND

Duse, Vittorio
ENCHANTED APRIL

Dusenberry, Ann
PLAY NICE

Dusic, Joe
BIKINI CARWASH COMPANY, THE

Dutronc, Jacques
VAN GOGH

Dutt, Anjan
CITY OF JOY

Dutton, Charles S.
ALIEN3
DISTINGUISHED GENTLEMAN, THE
MISSISSIPPI MASALA

Dutton, Tim
PATRIOT GAMES

Duvall, Bridget
HOWARDS END

Duvall, Jose
MAMBO KINGS, THE

Duvall, Robert
NEWSIES

Dwyer, David
LOVE POTION NO. 9

Dyck, Gerald
MANIAC WARRIORS

Dyck, Jim
MANIAC WARRIORS

Dye, Dale A.
UNDER SIEGE

Dylan, Bob
BACKTRACK

Dytri, Mike
LIVING END, THE

Dzundza, George
BASIC INSTINCT

Eagle, Jim
BEASTMASTER 2: THROUGH THE PORTAL OF TIME

Earl, Danny
EDWARD II

Earl, Ilse
FOLKS!

Earl, Ken
MO' MONEY

Early, David
INNOCENT BLOOD
PASSED AWAY

Earnest, Patricia J.
KUFFS

Easley, Byron
MALCOLM X

Eastman, Lynn
UNLAWFUL ENTRY

Eastmond, Mark "DJ Wiz"
CLASS ACT

Easton, Robert
PET SEMATARY II

Easton, Vanessa
RUNESTONE, THE

Eastwood, Clint
UNFORGIVEN

Eaton, Charles "Mark"
JENNIFER EIGHT

Eaton, Roberta
SPLIT SECOND

Eban, Abba
DOUBLE EDGE

Eberhard, Josephine
FATHER

Ebersole, Christine
FOLKS!

Ecclefield, Vivian
ARTICLE 99

Ecclestone, John
MUPPET CHRISTMAS CAROL, THE

Echanove, Josefina
CABEZA DE VACA

Echanove, Juan
SHOOTING ELIZABETH

Eckert, Randy
TEXAS TENOR: THE ILLINOIS JACQUET STORY

Eckhouse, James
LEAVING NORMAL

Eckman, Carole M.
PUERTO RICAN MAMBO (NOT A MUSICAL), THE

Ed'Ge
HELLROLLER

Edel, Alfred
MY FATHER IS COMING

Edelson, Kenneth
HUSBANDS AND WIVES

Edelstein, Gerald F.
SHAKES THE CLOWN

Eden, Tamara
GIVING, THE

Edgar, Doje-Kadoke
VENICE/VENICE

Edison, Harry "Sweets"
TEXAS TENOR: THE ILLINOIS JACQUET STORY

Edison, Matthew
NICKEL & DIME

Edmett, Nick
CHAPLIN

Edmond, Danielle
ALIEN3

Edmond, J. Trevor
MEATBALLS 4

Edmonds, Rob
SPLIT SECOND

Edmonson, Adrian
POPE MUST DIET!, THE

Edmunds, Roy
PROOF

Edson, Richard
CROSSING THE BRIDGE

Edwards, Anthony
DELTA HEAT
LANDSLIDE
PET SEMATARY II

Edwards, Captain
WILD ORCHID 2: TWO SHADES OF BLUE

Edwards, Eric
CANDYMAN

Edwards, Faith
POWER OF ONE, THE

Edwards, Jennifer
LIFE ON THE EDGE

Edwards, Jr., Artis
CONSENTING ADULTS

Edwards, L.C.
GIVING, THE

Edwards, Lance
WOMAN, HER MEN AND HER FUTON, A

Edwards, Lanier
SOUTH CENTRAL
Edwards, Luke
NEWSIES
Edwards, Paddi
CAGED FEAR
Edwards, Victoria
PASSION FISH
Edwards, Vince
INVASION OF THE SPACE PREACHERS
Efron, Dave
BRENDA STARR
UNIVERSAL SOLDIER
Eggar, Samantha
DARK HORSE
Eggert, Fritz
SHINING THROUGH
Eginton, Margaret
SCENT OF A WOMAN
Egon, Robert
CAPTAIN AMERICA
Eichling, Ike
MO' MONEY
Eichling, James "Ike"
BABE, THE
HOFFA
Eichling, James Ike
GLADIATOR
Eikeren, Allison
WHO SHOT PATAKANGO?
Einhorn, Brad
LORENZO'S OIL
Einhorn, Marvin
LEAGUE OF THEIR OWN, A
Eisenberg, Aron
PRAYER OF THE ROLLERBOYS
Eisenberg, Avner
BRENDA STARR
Eisenhart, Allen
SOCIETY
Eisenstein, David
SEX CRIMES
Eisler, Charles-Andre
FAVOUR, THE WATCH, AND THE VERY BIG FISH, THE
Eisman, Mimi
ROUND TRIP TO HEAVEN
Eisner, Alice
PASSED AWAY
Eisner, David
THIS IS MY LIFE
Ekblad, Monica Anne
WILD ORCHID 2: TWO SHADES OF BLUE
Ekholdt, Donna
DEATH BECOMES HER
Ekland, Britt
CHILDREN, THE
Eklund, Nils
BEST INTENTIONS, THE
El Razaac, Abdul Salaam
MALCOLM X
El Zabor, Kahil
MO' MONEY
Elam, Ousuan
UNDER SIEGE

Eldard, Ron
SCENT OF A WOMAN
Elder, Janet
PASSENGER 57
Elders, Gene
PURE COUNTRY
Eleazar, Michael
HUMAN SHIELD, THE
Electro Shock Therapy
FOR THOSE ABOUT TO ROCK
Elejalde, John
MALCOLM X
Eleniak, Erika
UNDER SIEGE
Elfman, Bodhi
SNEAKERS
Elfman, Danny
MAGICAL WORLD OF CHUCK JONES, THE
Eliot, Drew
STRANGER AMONG US, A
Eliott, Marianna
CANDYMAN
Elizabeth, Joan
BABE, THE
Elizondo, Hector
CHAINS OF GOLD
Elkins, Debra
MALCOLM X
Elkins, Marvin
RAPID FIRE
Elkins, Steven
ENCINO MAN
HERO
RUBY
Ellaraino
SNEAKERS
Ellen, Cliff
PROOF
Ellers-Isaacs, Jonah
WILDFIRE
Elliot, Ian
FAR AND AWAY
Elliot, Maxine
BEETHOVEN
Elliott, Beverley
UNFORGIVEN
Elliott, Denholm
NOISES OFF
SCORCHERS
Ellis, Brendan
FAR AND AWAY
Ellis, Chris
MY COUSIN VINNY
Ellis, Fred
PURE COUNTRY
Ellis, Georgie
LEAP OF FAITH
Ellis, Gina
MALCOLM X
Ellis, Thereza
PLAYER, THE
Ellis, Tracey
LAST OF THE MOHICANS, THE
Ellsworth, Roger B.
UNIVERSAL SOLDIER

Ellung, Inga-Lill
BEST INTENTIONS, THE
Elm, Steve
PROJECT: SHADOWCHASER
Elovich, Richard
SWOON
Elson, Donald
CHAPLIN
Elten, Gina
GIVING, THE
Elvis, Jr.
HONEYMOON IN VEGAS
Elwes, Cary
BRAM STOKER'S DRACULA
LEATHER JACKETS
Ely-O'Carroll, Ultan
CHAPLIN
Emanuel, Richard
RUBY
Emery, Terry
FATHER
Emge, David
HELL MASTER
Emil, Michael
ADVENTURES IN SPYING
Emmanuel, Alphonsia
PETER'S FRIENDS
UNDER SUSPICION
Emmons, David L.
LEAP OF FAITH
Emory, Del
LETHAL WEAPON 3
Emshwiller, Susan
PLAYER, THE
Endoso, Kenny
KUFFS
Endre, Lena
BEST INTENTIONS, THE
Enebrad, Jr., Tino R.
RAMPAGE
Engel, Susan
DAMAGE
Engelberg, Leslie
BIG GIRLS DON'T CRY . . . THEY GET EVEN
Engelbrecht, Constanze
SHINING THROUGH
England, Joe
LONDON KILLS ME
English, Bradford
BASIC INSTINCT
English, Cameron
DEATH BECOMES HER
Englund, Robert
DANCE MACABRE
Enos, John
DEATH BECOMES HER
Enright, Thomas
COMPLEX WORLD
Epcar, Richard
MEMOIRS OF AN INVISIBLE MAN
Ephron, Nora
HUSBANDS AND WIVES
Epke, Bruce
WIND

Epper, Eurlyne
BREAKING THE RULES
Epper, Gary
CAPTAIN AMERICA
Epper, Richard
INTO THE SUN
Epper-Woldman, Eurlyne
BUFFY THE VAMPIRE SLAYER
Eppolito, Lou
RUBY
Epps, Omar
JUICE
Epstein, Duffy
FROZEN ASSETS
Erhard, Bernard
LITTLE NEMO: ADVENTURES IN SLUMBERLAND
Erickson, Bill
BIG GIRLS DON'T CRY . . . THEY GET EVEN
Erickson, Nick
GIVING, THE
Errikson, Krista
KILLER IMAGE
Erskine, Drummond
NOISES OFF
Ervolina, Tony
POISON IVY
Erwin, Barbara
LEAGUE OF THEIR OWN, A
Escobar, Robert
FOLKS!
Escudero, Nina
SINGLES
Esdaile, Kim
CUTTING EDGE, THE
Eskelson, Dana
SINGLES
Esparza, Ester
WINTER IN LISBON, THE
Esperance, Bella
LADY DRAGON
Espinoza, Jeff
CTHULHU MANSION
Espinoza, Riq Boogie
RAISING CAIN
Esposito, Giancarlo
BOB ROBERTS
MALCOLM X
NIGHT ON EARTH
Esposito, Pete
PUSHED TO THE LIMIT
Essex, David
JOURNEY OF HONOR
Estela, Raul
CAPTAIN RON
Estes, Robert
ACES: IRON EAGLE III
Estevez, Emilio
FREEJACK
MIGHTY DUCKS, THE
Estevez, Joe
ARMED FOR ACTION
BLOOD ON THE BADGE
Estevez, Renee
SINGLE WHITE FEMALE
TOUCH AND DIE

Estrada, Angelina
BIG GIRLS DON'T CRY . . . THEY GET EVEN
Estrada, Erik
DO OR DIE
SPIRITS
Etienne
DADDY AND THE MUSCLE ACADEMY
Etienne, Luc
DAMAGE
Ettles, Chantal
HIGHWAY 61
Etua, M.J.
GUN IN BETTY LOU'S HANDBAG, THE
Eubanks, Bob
HOME ALONE 2: LOST IN NEW YORK
Eubanks, Dak
NEWSIES
Eurich, Robert
HOFFA
Eurich, Robin
STRAIGHT TALK
Evans, Anthony
FATHER
Evans, Art
FINISHING TOUCH, THE
TRESPASS
Evans, C.H.
TWIN PEAKS: FIRE WALK WITH ME
Evans, David
NEWSIES
Evans, Larry Ann
CTHULHU MANSION
Evans, Mitchel
BRAM STOKER'S DRACULA
Evans, Reg
FATHER
Evans, Suzy
NAKED OBSESSION
Evans, T.J.
RADIO FLYER
Evans, Troy
ARTICLE 99
KUFFS
LAWNMOWER MAN, THE
LEAP OF FAITH
LOVE FIELD
UNDER SIEGE
Evely, Yannick
FAVOUR, THE WATCH, AND THE VERY BIG FISH, THE
Everbeck, R.C.
SNEAKERS
Everest, Claudia
SCHOOL TIES
Everett, Todd A.
BLOOD ON THE BADGE
Everett, Tom
BEBE'S KIDS
Everns, Alison
WATERLAND
Evers, Bruce
CONSENTING ADULTS
Evison, Pat
MY GRANDPA IS A VAMPIRE

Ewart, John
HURRICANE SMITH
Ewen, Martin
FAR AND AWAY
Ewing, Darren
TROLL 2
Expose, Thaddeus
BABE, THE
Eyre, Hermione
CHILDREN, THE
Eyre, Marcus
CHAPLIN
Eyre, Renee
EDWARD II
Eyres, Jeff
PUERTO RICAN MAMBO (NOT A MUSICAL), THE
Eyster, Tim
PRAYER OF THE ROLLERBOYS
Fab 5 Freddie
JUICE
Faber, Matthew
BOB ROBERTS
Fabian, Ava
AUNTIE LEE'S MEAT PIES
Fabio
DEATH BECOMES HER
Fabjaniak, Wojciech
GIVING, THE
Fabricant, Patricia
SWOON
Fabrizio, Antonio
BRENDA STARR
Fachetti, Adriana
ENCHANTED APRIL
Facondo, Nicola
NIGHT ON EARTH
Fahey, Jeff
LAWNMOWER MAN, THE
Fainaru, Dan
VENICE/VENICE
Fainaru, Edna
VENICE/VENICE
Fairbank, Chris
ALIEN3
Fairlie, Ann
CHAPLIN
Faison, Donald
JUICE
Faison, Sandy
PLAY NICE
Faking It Three
WISECRACKS
Falasca, Sergio
WHERE ANGELS FEAR TO TREAD
Falco, Edie
LAWS OF GRAVITY
Falco, Tav
HIGHWAY 61
Falcon, Jeannine
BRENDA STARR
Falconer, Phoebe
MY GRANDPA IS A VAMPIRE
Falk, Lisanne
LEATHER JACKETS
NIGHT ON EARTH

Falk, Peter
PLAYER, THE
Falkner, Ervena
DAUGHTERS OF THE DUST
Fall, Steve
HIGHWAY 61
Fann, Al
STOP! OR MY MOM WILL SHOOT
Fanna, Benedetto
ONCE UPON A CRIME
Fantastichini, Ennio
STATION, THE
Farber, Jodie
MALCOLM X
Fardo, Maurizio
INDIO 2 - THE REVOLT
Fariborz, Azhakd
FINAL IMPACT
Farina, Caroline
LITTLE NOISES
Farina, Dennis
STREET CRIMES
WE'RE TALKIN' SERIOUS MONEY
Farley, Chris
WAYNE'S WORLD
Farley, Mike
MALCOLM X
Farley, Noreen
RAMPAGE
Farley, Teresa Yvon
MALCOLM X
Farmer, Ken
MANIAC WARRIORS
Farnsworth, Richard
HIGHWAY TO HELL
Farquhar, Carole
HOUSE OF USHER, THE
Farr, Felicia
PLAYER, THE
Farr, Judi
FLIRTING
Farr, Libby
BECOMING COLETTE
Farr, Michele
SINGLE WHITE FEMALE
Farrakhan, Malik
DAUGHTERS OF THE DUST
Farrar, Lorna
VOYAGER
Farrell, Catherine
CAPTAIN AMERICA
Farrell, Robert
TRACES OF RED
Farrell, Sharon
LONELY HEARTS
Farrell, Terry
HELLRAISER III: HELL ON EARTH
Farrell, Tom Riis
SCENT OF A WOMAN
SHADOWS AND FOG
Farris, John
PUBLIC EYE, THE
Farrow, David Mark
LAST OF THE MOHICANS, THE

Farrow, Mia
HUSBANDS AND WIVES
SHADOWS AND FOG
Fassig, Susan
LOVE POTION NO. 9
Fast, Richard
CHAPLIN
Fast, Russ
DR. GIGGLES
Fatta, Andrew
PRELUDE TO A KISS
Faulkner, Lisa
LOVER, THE
Faulkner, Martha
TOYS
Faulkner, Willie
DAUGHTERS OF THE DUST
Favaro, Ray
HONEYMOON IN VEGAS
Favreau, Jon
FOLKS!
Faw, Jackson
BASKET CASE 3: THE PROGENY
Fay, Meagen
BIG GIRLS DON'T CRY . . . THEY GET EVEN
Faysse, Dominique
BEATING HEART, A
Fazenda, Louise
WISECRACKS
Feagley, Stephen
LEAGUE OF THEIR OWN, A
Feaval, Ronald
CTHULHU MANSION
Fechner, Wolfgang
BECOMING COLETTE
Feder, Frederique
ROAD TO RUIN
Feeney, Robert
NEWSIES
Feist, Robert
HOFFA
Feist, Robert L.
BODYGUARD, THE
Felcan, Tom
MANIAC WARRIORS
Feldman, Alyson
SCENT OF A WOMAN
Feldman, Corey
MEATBALLS 4
ROUND TRIP TO HEAVEN
Feldman, Ed
HONEY, I BLEW UP THE KID
Feldman, Erika
SCENT OF A WOMAN
Feldshuh, Tovah
DAY IN OCTOBER, A
Felipe, Manitu
KICKBOXER 3: THE ART OF WAR
Felix, Geoff
MUPPET CHRISTMAS CAROL, THE
Fella, Mike
BAD LIEUTENANT
Fellowes, Julian
DAMAGE

Fellows, Susannah
WATERLAND
Feltron, Ross
MANIAC WARRIORS
Fenn, Sherilyn
DESIRE AND HELL AT SUNSET MOTEL
DIARY OF A HITMAN
OF MICE AND MEN
RUBY
Fenton, Simon
POWER OF ONE, THE
Feore, Colm
BEAUTIFUL DREAMERS
Ferbos, Lionel
STORYVILLE
Ferguson, Carson
MANIAC WARRIORS
Ferguson, J. Don
MY COUSIN VINNY
Ferguson, Scott
MUNCHIE
Ferguson, Sharon
MALCOLM X
Fernandez, Esteban
LIGHT SLEEPER
Fernandez, Evelina
AMERICAN ME
Fernandez, Isidoro
WINTER IN LISBON, THE
Fernandez, Juan
ACES: IRON EAGLE III
Fernandez, Margarita
BATMAN RETURNS
Fernandez, Tony
LAWS OF GRAVITY
Ferney, Didier
TOTO LE HEROS
Ferrara, Frank
UNDER SIEGE
Ferrari, Brenda
LEAGUE OF THEIR OWN, A
Ferrari, Marc
WAYNE'S WORLD
Ferreira, John
LEAVING NORMAL
Ferrell, Conchata
CHAINS OF GOLD
Ferrell, Tyra
WHITE MEN CAN'T JUMP
Ferrer, Jose
HIRED TO KILL
Ferrer, Jose Luis
1492: THE CONQUEST OF PARADISE
Ferrer, Miguel
TWIN PEAKS: FIRE WALK WITH ME
Ferreri, D'Angelo
HERO
Ferrero, Martin
STOP! OR MY MOM WILL SHOOT
Ferri, Laura
HAND THAT ROCKS THE CRADLE, THE
Ferrick, Billy
ROADSIDE PROPHETS

Ferriere, Martine
FAVOUR, THE WATCH, AND THE VERY BIG FISH, THE
Fervoy, Tom
WIND
Fesson, Natasha
DANCE MACABRE
Festa, John
MALCOLM X
Fetzer, William
AMERICAN ME
Feuillet, Serge
INSPECTOR LAVARDIN
Fiachi, Stephen
NIGHT RHYTHMS
OTHER WOMAN, THE
Fichtner, William
MALCOLM X
Fick, Charles Joseph
MR. BASEBALL
Fidias, Yvonne
BRONX WAR, THE
Field, Allison
WHISPERS IN THE DARK
Field, Arabella
LAWS OF GRAVITY
Fields, Christopher John
ALIEN3
GUN IN BETTY LOU'S HANDBAG, THE
Fields, Edith
MR. SATURDAY NIGHT
RAMPAGE
Fields, Gracie
WISECRACKS
Fields, Holly
SEEDPEOPLE
Fields, Matthew
NEWSIES
Fields, Nilyne
MALCOLM X
Fieldsteel, Robert
BEASTMASTER 2: THROUGH THE PORTAL OF TIME
Fifa, Angela
PEPI, LUCI, BOM AND OTHER GIRLS ON THE HEAP
Fifer, Jacqui
FLIRTING
Fifer, John
BEASTMASTER 2: THROUGH THE PORTAL OF TIME
Figura, Kasia
NEAR MISSES
PLAYER, THE
Filar, Gil
USED PEOPLE
Filar, Maia
USED PEOPLE
Filippo, Fab
PROM NIGHT IV - DELIVER US FROM EVIL
Filpi, Carmen
WAYNE'S WORLD
Fincannon, Mark
ALAN & NAOMI
Finch, David
CHAPLIN
Finch, Delores
TOYS
Finch, Mark
LIVING END, THE
Findlay, William
BABE, THE
Fink, Klaus
VENICE/VENICE
Fink, Lisa
TOYS
Finlay, Frank
CTHULHU MANSION
Finley, Greg
BEBE'S KIDS
Finnegan, Joe
LAST OF THE MOHICANS, THE
Finnegan, Tom
DISTINGUISHED GENTLEMAN, THE
HOFFA
NEWSIES
Finney, Albert
PLAYBOYS, THE
Finney, Brian
HAND THAT ROCKS THE CRADLE, THE
Finver, Fay
CAPTAIN AMERICA
Finver, Frank
CAPTAIN AMERICA
Fiondella, Jay
LETHAL WEAPON 3
Fiorentino, Linda
WILDFIRE
Firago, Kathryn
LOVE POTION NO. 9
Fischer, Corey
FINAL ANALYSIS
Fischer, John Louis
STRANGER AMONG US, A
Fish, Nancy
BEETHOVEN
DEATH BECOMES HER
DR. GIGGLES
WILDFIRE
Fishburne, Larry
DEEP COVER
Fisher, Brad
CTHULHU MANSION
Fisher, Carrie
THIS IS MY LIFE
Fisher, Christopher
STEAL AMERICA
Fisher, Frances
UNFORGIVEN
Fisher, George
UNIVERSAL SOLDIER
Fisher, Georgi
CHRISTOPHER COLUMBUS: THE DISCOVERY
Fisher, Harvey
LETHAL WEAPON 3
Fisher, Sport
COMPLEX WORLD
Fisher-Wirth, Ann
GUN IN BETTY LOU'S HANDBAG, THE
Fisk, Schuyler
HARD PROMISES
Fitch, Molly
COMPLEX WORLD
Fitos, Joe
MALCOLM X
Fitzgerald, Patrick
LAST OF THE MOHICANS, THE
Fitzgibbon, Ian
FINE ROMANCE, A
Fitzpatrick, Anthony
GLADIATOR
Fitzpatrick, Colleen
MAMBO KINGS, THE
Fitzpatrick, Raymond
HERO
Fitzpatrick, Tony
HERO
Flaherty, Maureen
BIKINI SUMMER 2
Flanagan, Jim
WHO SHOT PATAKANGO?
Flanders, Mack Haywood
RAMPAGE
Flannery, Brian
LEAGUE OF THEIR OWN, A
Flatman, Barry
CUTTING EDGE, THE
Flaus, John
EFFICIENCY EXPERT, THE
Flavien, Bernard
DELICATESSEN
Flea
ROADSIDE PROPHETS
Flechtner, Peter
SHINING THROUGH
Fleischer, Charles
STRAIGHT TALK
Fleming, Toni
FOLKS!
PUBLIC EYE, THE
Fletcher, Anthony
FATHER
Fletcher, Danielle
MALCOLM X
Fletcher, Louise
BLIND VISION
PLAYER, THE
Fletcher, Page
MIDNIGHT FEAR
Fletcher, Steven
CHRISTOPHER COLUMBUS: THE DISCOVERY
Flinders, Ashton
BIG GIRLS DON'T CRY . . . THEY GET EVEN
Flinders, Ethan
BIG GIRLS DON'T CRY . . . THEY GET EVEN
Flint, Matthew
HUSBANDS AND WIVES
Floersheim, Patrick
NEAR MISSES
Florence, Marsha
ZEBRAHEAD
Flores, Armando
CABEZA DE VACA

Flores, Claudia
THERE'S NOTHING OUT THERE
Flores, Jose
CABEZA DE VACA
Floria, Holly
NETHERWORLD
Flosi, David
BEYOND JUSTICE
Flower, Buck
MIRROR IMAGES
Flower, George "Buck"
MUNCHIE
SOLDIER'S FORTUNE
Flower, Tailinh Forest
CHRISTOPHER COLUMBUS: THE DISCOVERY
Flowers, Gennifer
FEED
Fludd, David
MALCOLM X
Fluegel, Darlanne
PET SEMATARY II
Flum, Steven
SWOON
Flynn, Jeremy
AFRAID OF THE DARK
Flynn, Jerome
EDWARD II
Flynn, Kate
FAR AND AWAY
Flynn, Mary
GLADIATOR
Focx, Anthony
WAYNE'S WORLD
Fogel, Joel
PASSENGER 57
Fogerty, Adam
POWER OF ONE, THE
Fogle, Bridget
WHO SHOT PATAKANGO?
Foley, Michael
DESERT KICKBOXER
PUSHED TO THE LIMIT
Foley, T. Sean
BLIND VISION
Folkes-Le'Melle, Neisha
MALCOLM X
Fonda, Bridget
LEATHER JACKETS
SINGLE WHITE FEMALE
SINGLES
Fong, Leo T.
24 HOURS TO MIDNIGHT
Fontaine, Anouk
CHILDREN, THE
Fontana, Fred
PURE COUNTRY
Fontana, Jeffrey R.
PURE COUNTRY
Fontana, Patrick
BECOMING COLETTE
Fontana, Randall
LAWNMOWER MAN, THE
Fontanette, Linda
SOUTH CENTRAL
Fontayne, Michel
INSPECTOR LAVARDIN
Fontenette, Cytia
MALCOLM X
Foody, Ralph
BABE, THE
COLD JUSTICE
HOME ALONE 2: LOST IN NEW YORK
STRAIGHT TALK
Foot, Mona
SWOON
Foppa, Julio Solorzano
CABEZA DE VACA
Foraker, Lois
RADIO FLYER
Foray, June
LITTLE NEMO: ADVENTURES IN SLUMBERLAND
MAGICAL WORLD OF CHUCK JONES, THE
Forbes, Lee
HELLROLLER
Forbes, Michele
PLAYBOYS, THE
Forcher, Thomas
LADY DRAGON
Ford, Alan
CHAPLIN
Ford, Clebert
MALCOLM X
Ford, Harrison
PATRIOT GAMES
Ford, James
DAMNED IN THE USA
Ford, Lita
HIGHWAY TO HELL
Ford, Maria
DANCE WITH DEATH
DEATHSTALKER IV: MATCH OF TITANS
NAKED OBSESSION
SLUMBER PARTY MASSACRE 3
Ford, Michael
KILL LINE
Ford, Terence
ESCAPE FROM . . . SURVIVAL ZONE
Ford, Thomas Mikal
CLASS ACT
Ford, Tommy A.
NIGHT AND THE CITY
Foreman, Amanda
FOREVER YOUNG
Foreman, Deborah
LUNATICS: A LOVE STORY
Foreman, Michelle
SUNSET STRIP
Forestier, Raymond
DELICATESSEN
Forleo, Steve
PUBLIC EYE, THE
Forman, David
BERNARD AND THE GENIE
Forman, Phil
CHAPLIN
MR. SATURDAY NIGHT
Fornof, J.W. "Corkey"
STOP! OR MY MOM WILL SHOOT
Foronjy, Richard
FATAL INSTINCT
PUBLIC EYE, THE
Forrest, Frederic
TWIN SISTERS
Forrest, Steve
STORYVILLE
Forristal, Susan
DISTINGUISHED GENTLEMAN, THE
Forssell, Hawk
RIVER RUNS THROUGH IT, A
Forstenberg, Leif
BEST INTENTIONS, THE
Forsyth, Ed
DEATH BECOMES HER
Forsyth, Tony
EDWARD II
Forsythe, William
AMERICAN ME
GUN IN BETTY LOU'S HANDBAG, THE
WATERDANCE, THE
Forte, Eversley
SAVAGE INSTINCT
Forte, Marlene
BRONX WAR, THE
Forth, Chris
CROSSING THE BRIDGE
Fortineau, Thierry
BEATING HEART, A
Forward, William
WATERDANCE, THE
Fosberg, Michael
ROUND TRIP TO HEAVEN
Foster, Al
RAPID FIRE
SNEAKERS
Foster, David
BODYGUARD, THE
Foster, Frances
DISTINGUISHED GENTLEMAN, THE
MALCOLM X
Foster, George
WAYNE'S WORLD
Foster, Jeffrey
BOB ROBERTS
Foster, Jodie
BACKTRACK
SHADOWS AND FOG
Foster, Jr., C.L.
ARTICLE 99
Foster, Meg
PROJECT: SHADOWCHASER
Foster, Stacy Solon
VENICE/VENICE
Foster, Steffan Gregory
LAWNMOWER MAN, THE
Fountain, Michael
FINEST HOUR, THE
Fouqueray, Denys
FAVOUR, THE WATCH, AND THE VERY BIG FISH, THE
Fouquet, Emmanuel
ROAD TO RUIN
Fournier, Michelle A.
MAN TROUBLE

Fowler, Beth
SISTER ACT
Fowler, Diane
WITCHCRAFT IV: VIRGIN HEART
Fowler, III, Robert H.
MALCOLM X
Fowler, Jennifer
LIGHT SLEEPER
Fox, Colin
BEAUTIFUL DREAMERS
SCANNERS III: THE TAKEOVER
Fox, James
AFRAID OF THE DARK
PATRIOT GAMES
Fox, Jessica
MUPPET CHRISTMAS CAROL, THE
Foxcroft, Les
CROSSING, THE
Foxx, Jamie
TOYS
Foyt, Victoria
VENICE/VENICE
France, Maui
BEBE'S KIDS
Franchino, Mireille
FAVOUR, THE WATCH, AND THE VERY BIG FISH, THE
Franciosa, Anthony
DEATH HOUSE
Francis, Anne
LITTLE VEGAS
Francis, Ian
EDWARD II
Francis, Roy
POWER OF ONE, THE
Francis, Tom
HAND THAT ROCKS THE CRADLE, THE
SINGLES
Franco, Katherine
CAPTAIN RON
Franco, Margarita
3 NINJAS
Franco, Ramon
CHAINS OF GOLD
KISS ME A KILLER
Franco, Richardo
PEPI, LUCI, BOM AND OTHER GIRLS ON THE HEAP
Francois, Ryan
MALCOLM X
Frank, Dan
TEXAS TENOR: THE ILLINOIS JACQUET STORY
Frank, Diana
PALE BLOOD
Frank, Gary
DISTINGUISHED GENTLEMAN, THE
Frankfather, William
COOL WORLD
DEATH BECOMES HER
Franklin, Ben
ROCK & ROLL COWBOYS
Franklin, Carl
EYE OF THE EAGLE 3
IN THE HEAT OF PASSION
Franklin, David
ROCK & ROLL COWBOYS
Franklin, Doug
BEASTMASTER 2: THROUGH THE PORTAL OF TIME
Franklin, Joseph
HAND THAT ROCKS THE CRADLE, THE
Franklin, Steve
MANIAC WARRIORS
Franks, David
LEAGUE OF THEIR OWN, A
Franks, Laurie
BRAM STOKER'S DRACULA
Frankston, Jessica
HUSBANDS AND WIVES
Franz, Dennis
PLAYER, THE
Franz, Elizabeth
SCHOOL TIES
Fraser, Brendan
ENCINO MAN
SCHOOL TIES
Fraser, Brent
WILD ORCHID 2: TWO SHADES OF BLUE
Fraser, Hugh
PATRIOT GAMES
Fraser, Patricia
CLASS ACT
Fravel, Philip H.
DOUBLE TROUBLE
Frazier, Bob
SAVAGE INSTINCT
Frazier, Randy
JUICE
Frederick, Anthony
MAN TROUBLE
Frederick, Tara Dawn
UNFORGIVEN
Frederick, Vicki
CHAPLIN
Fredericks, Kyle
BEASTMASTER 2: THROUGH THE PORTAL OF TIME
Fredricksen, Cully
BRAM STOKER'S DRACULA
Free, Ronnie
LOVE CRIMES
Freeman, Charles
DAMNED IN THE USA
Freeman, David S.
DEATH HOUSE
Freeman, Detrell
DAUGHTERS OF THE DUST
Freeman, J.E.
ACES: IRON EAGLE III
PATRIOT GAMES
Freeman, Jamer
DAUGHTERS OF THE DUST
Freeman, Jonathan
ALADDIN
Freeman, Jr., Al
MALCOLM X
Freeman, Kathleen
FERNGULLY: THE LAST RAINFOREST
LITTLE NEMO: ADVENTURES IN SLUMBERLAND
NICKEL & DIME
Freeman, Kay
MR. SATURDAY NIGHT
Freeman, Lucy
HOWARDS END
Freeman, Morgan
POWER OF ONE, THE
UNFORGIVEN
Freeman, Paul
ACES: IRON EAGLE III
Freeman, Rob
SHINING THROUGH
Freeman, Robert
PROJECT: SHADOWCHASER
Freezin', Pete
WAYNE'S WORLD
Freiss, Stephane
DOES THIS MEAN WE'RE MARRIED?
Freleng, Fritz
MAGICAL WORLD OF CHUCK JONES, THE
French, Arthur
MALCOLM X
French, Paige
MEATBALLS 4
Frenette, Jean
SCANNERS III: THE TAKEOVER
Frenkel, Cantor Chayim
MR. SATURDAY NIGHT
Fresco, David
DIGGSTOWN
Frey, Kurt
FLIRTING
Friant, Syarief
LADY DRAGON
Fricker, Brenda
HOME ALONE 2: LOST IN NEW YORK
Friedeck, Ray
STRAIGHT TALK
Friedl, Cindy
VENICE/VENICE
Friedman, Brian
NEWSIES
Friedman, Bruce Jay
HUSBANDS AND WIVES
Friedman, Daniel H.
UNDER SIEGE
Friedman, Nancy
MY NEW GUN
Friedman, Peter
SINGLE WHITE FEMALE
Friel, Casey
OVER HER DEAD BODY
Fripp, Rueben
DAUGHTERS OF THE DUST
Frith, Gary
BOOMERANG
Froger, Philippe
INSPECTOR LAVARDIN

Froler, Samuel
BEST INTENTIONS, THE
Froling, Ewa
OX, THE
Fromager, Alain
INDOCHINE
Frost, Cynthia
WE'RE TALKIN' SERIOUS MONEY
Frost, Kate
MUPPET CHRISTMAS CAROL, THE
Frost, Sadie
BRAM STOKER'S DRACULA
Fructouso, Tonichi
FIELD OF FIRE
Fry, Stephen
PETER'S FRIENDS
Frye, Brittain
SLUMBER PARTY MASSACRE 3
Frye, Virgil
MAN TROUBLE
Fuente, Larry
WILD WHEELS
Fuentes, Jesus
NEWSIES
Fugate, Ethan James
LAST OF THE MOHICANS, THE
Fujii, Naoki
MR. BASEBALL
Fujioka, Hiroshi
K2
Fujita, Tomoko
MR. BASEBALL
Fujiwara, Kei
TETSUO: THE IRON MAN
Fujiwara, Toshizo
MR. BASEBALL
Fukasaku, Satoru
JOURNEY OF HONOR
Fukazawa, Yoshio
MR. BASEBALL
Fuller, Kurt
ORIGINAL INTENT
WAYNE'S WORLD
Fuller, Londie Jermain
ZEBRAHEAD
Fullilove, Don
WHITE MEN CAN'T JUMP
Fultz, Mona Lee
HARD PROMISES
LOVE HURTS
Fulweiler, John
PUERTO RICAN MAMBO (NOT A MUSICAL), THE
Funes, Robert
SWOON
Furlong, Edward
PET SEMATARY II
Furness, Deborra-Lee
NEWSIES
VOYAGER
Fusselle, Warner
BAD LIEUTENANT
Futterer, Nicola
BECOMING COLETTE

Futterman, Dan
BIG GIRLS DON'T CRY . . . THEY GET EVEN
PASSED AWAY
Gabay, Sasson
BLINK OF AN EYE
Gabbard, Glendon
PRELUDE TO A KISS
Gable, June
BRENDA STARR
Gabourie, Ray
HIGHWAY 61
Gabriel, John
BERNARD AND THE GENIE
Gabrielle, Monique
MIRACLE BEACH
MUNCHIE
Gaddoni, Paul
RAMPAGE
Gadette, Jerry
MR. SATURDAY NIGHT
Gagnon, Trisha
LEAVING NORMAL
Gail, Max
STREET CRIMES
Gaines, James E.
MALCOLM X
Gaines, Leonard
SCENT OF A WOMAN
Gaines, Sonny Jim
DISTINGUISHED GENTLEMAN, THE
Gainey, M.C.
LEAP OF FAITH
MIGHTY DUCKS, THE
Gajewskia, Barbra
KILLER IMAGE
Galaise, Sean
LOVE HURTS
Galan, Mapi
DOES THIS MEAN WE'RE MARRIED?
Gale, David
GUYVER, THE
Gale, Ed
MOM AND DAD SAVE THE WORLD
Galiardo, Lou
SWOON
Galiena, Anna
HAIRDRESSER'S HUSBAND, THE
Galipeau, Crystal
BOB ROBERTS
Gallacher, Frank
PROOF
Gallagher, Dorothy
COMPLEX WORLD
Gallagher, Jack
SHAKES THE CLOWN
Gallagher, John
LAWS OF GRAVITY
Gallagher, Peter
BOB ROBERTS
PLAYER, THE
Gallant, Kelly
TALONS OF THE EAGLE
Gallardo, Camilo
SINGLES

Galleazzi, Aldo
CAPTAIN AMERICA
Gallego, Gina
EXILED IN AMERICA
Galligan, Zach
PSYCHIC
ROUND TRIP TO HEAVEN
WAXWORK II: LOST IN TIME
Galloway, Don
ORIGINAL INTENT
Galloway, Graham
CLASS ACT
Galloway, Leata
MISTRESS
Galuba, Dirk
INDIO 2 - THE REVOLT
Gambino, Kim
LAWS OF GRAVITY
Gamble, Tim
HOFFA
PUBLIC EYE, THE
Gambon, Michael
TOYS
Gambrill, Linda
LUNATIC, THE
Gammon, James
CRISSCROSS
LEAVING NORMAL
Gamoke, John Paul
MIGHTY DUCKS, THE
Gandolfini, James
STRANGER AMONG US, A
Gandy, H.L.
WILD WHEELS
Gandy, Jr., Tilman
COMPLEX WORLD
Ganger, Toby Scott
ROCK-A-DOODLE
Ganon, Steve
TO PROTECT AND SERVE
Gant, David
CHAPLIN
Gantt, Leland
MALCOLM X
Gantz, Tammy
DEATH BECOMES HER
Ganus, Paul
FOREVER YOUNG
LETHAL WEAPON 3
Ganz, Lowell
MR. SATURDAY NIGHT
Gara, Olvido "Alaska"
PEPI, LUCI, BOM AND OTHER GIRLS ON THE HEAP
Garandza, Nester
MANIAC WARRIORS
Garber, Victor
LIGHT SLEEPER
Garcia, Adolfo "Fito"
NETHERWORLD
Garcia, Alex
DIGGSTOWN
Garcia, Andy
HERO
JENNIFER EIGHT
Garcia, Irma Aurea
AMERICAN ME

Garcia, Juan
SOLDIER'S FORTUNE
Garcia, Juanito
KISS ME A KILLER
Garcia, Ramon
WELCOME TO OBLIVION
Garcia, Rick Sky
ACES: IRON EAGLE III
Gardner, Ashley
JOHNNY SUEDE
Gardner, David
BEAUTIFUL DREAMERS
Gardner, Gary
UNDER SIEGE
Gardner, Hazel
HOUSESITTER
Gardner, Jeff
PATRIOT GAMES
Gardner, Jennifer
PASSION FISH
Gardner, Michael
SINGLES
Garfias, Ruben
PATRIOT GAMES
Garfield
MO' MONEY
Garfield, Allen
MIRACLE BEACH
Garfield, Jimmy
LITTLE SISTER
Garfield, John David
OVER HER DEAD BODY
WHITE SANDS
Garito, Ken
SCHOOL TIES
Garland, Grace
JUICE
Garlin, Jeff
HERO
STRAIGHT TALK
Garlington, Lee
SNEAKERS
Garmendia, Mikel
WINTER IN LISBON, THE
Garner, James
DISTINGUISHED GENTLEMAN, THE
Garner, Martin
TILL THERE WAS YOU
Garner, Ruddy L.
GUN IN BETTY LOU'S HANDBAG, THE
Garner, Russell
GIVING, THE
Garnes, Earl
PALE BLOOD
Garney, Laura
HAPPY HELL NIGHT
Garr, Christopher
MAN TROUBLE
Garr, Teri
MOM AND DAD SAVE THE WORLD
PLAYER, THE
Garrel, Maurice
DISCRETE, LA
Garrett, Berkley
CONFESSIONS OF A SERIAL KILLER
Garrett, Charley J.
CHAPLIN
Garrett, Patsy
MISSISSIPPI MASALA
Garrett, Rob
AMERICAN ME
Garrigues, Billy
TRACES OF RED
Garris, Carolyn
DAUGHTERS OF THE DUST
Garris, Cynthia
STEPHEN KING'S SLEEPWALKERS
Garrison, David
HOMEBOYS
Garrison, Miranda
MR. SATURDAY NIGHT
Garson, Willie
RUBY
Garven, Casey
MIGHTY DUCKS, THE
Garwood, Webb
HELLROLLER
Garzon, Fernando
SEX CRIMES
Gash, Kent
MY NEW GUN
Gash, Mark
HOUSE IV
Gaspar, Dominique
MY FATHER IS COMING
Gaspar, Flora
MY FATHER IS COMING
Gaspar, Susan
PUERTO RICAN MAMBO (NOT A MUSICAL), THE
Gaston, F. Curtis
LAST OF THE MOHICANS, THE
Gatees, Cynthia
PRAYER OF THE ROLLERBOYS
Gately, Kelly
MIDNIGHT CLEAR, A
Gates, Jr., Henry Louis
COLOR ADJUSTMENT
Gaton, Clark
MALCOLM X
Gatt, Nicholas
CHAPLIN
Gatti, Jennifer
WE'RE TALKIN' SERIOUS MONEY
Gauthier, France
CUTTING EDGE, THE
Gauthier, Jean-Yves
HOT CHOCOLATE
Gavin, James W.
RADIO FLYER
Gavriel, Uri
BLINK OF AN EYE
FINEST HOUR, THE
HUMAN SHIELD, THE
Gavriliuk, Sergei
RASPAD
Gayle, Jackie
MR. SATURDAY NIGHT
Gaylor, Allison
CUTTING EDGE, THE
Gaylord, Mitch
ANIMAL INSTINCTS
Gaynor, Bob
DEATH BECOMES HER
Gazzaniga, Don
HERO
Geary, Anthony
SCORCHERS
Geas, Thomas A.
LETHAL WEAPON 3
Geddeis, Brian
CUTTING EDGE, THE
Gedrick, Jason
CROSSING THE BRIDGE
Geer, Ellen
LONELY HEARTS
PATRIOT GAMES
Gegenhuber, John
STRAIGHT TALK
Gehman, Martha
JUST LIKE IN THE MOVIES
Geisler, Regina
OTHER WOMAN, THE
Gelatto, Brian
DISTINGUISHED GENTLEMAN, THE
Geldart, Ed
HARD PROMISES
LEAP OF FAITH
SIMPLE MEN
Geldof, Bob
BERNARD AND THE GENIE
Gelfant, Alan
OTHER WOMAN, THE
Gelman, Larry
MR. SATURDAY NIGHT
Gempart, Michael
SHINING THROUGH
Genaro, Tony
FINAL ANALYSIS
WATERDANCE, THE
Gendron, Lynn
WILD ORCHID 2: TWO SHADES OF BLUE
Generalovich, Tracey
BOB ROBERTS
Genevie, Michael
MY COUSIN VINNY
Geng, Steve
PHANTOM OF THE RITZ
Genoud, Philippe Morier
VOYAGER
Gentile, Denise
NETHERWORLD
Gentry, Minnie
BAD LIEUTENANT
Geoghegan, Sally
HOWARDS END
George, Carl M.
SWOON
George, Howard
DEATH HOUSE
George, Joe
ROUND TRIP TO HEAVEN
WE'RE TALKIN' SERIOUS MONEY
George, Ron Howard
SEX CRIMES

Georges, Liz
MR. SATURDAY NIGHT
Georges, Peter
CHAPLIN
Geraghty, Marita
HERO
THIS IS MY LIFE
Gerard, Gil
SOLDIER'S FORTUNE
Gerard, Molly D.
HOUSESITTER
Gerard, Nona
LORENZO'S OIL
Gerardo, Luis
DANZON
Gerber, Jay
MEMOIRS OF AN INVISIBLE MAN
Gerber, Lisa
BEETHOVEN
Gerdes, George
SINGLE WHITE FEMALE
Gere, Richard
FINAL ANALYSIS
Gerety, Peter
COMPLEX WORLD
Germain, Kareen
PASSENGER 57
Germany, Nash
GUN IN BETTY LOU'S HANDBAG, THE
Gerrans, Jon
LIVING END, THE
Gershon, Gina
PLAYER, THE
Gerstell, Ellen
LITTLE NEMO: ADVENTURES IN SLUMBERLAND
Getty, Balthazar
POPE MUST DIET!, THE
WHERE THE DAY TAKES YOU
Getty, Estelle
STOP! OR MY MOM WILL SHOOT
Getz, Robert
BRAM STOKER'S DRACULA
Ghadban, Alle
PROM NIGHT IV - DELIVER US FROM EVIL
Gherardi, Charles
MORTUARY ACADEMY
Ghosh, Debtosh
CITY OF JOY
Ghosh, Paresh
CITY OF JOY
Giallela, Trisha
SUNSET STRIP
Giamalva, Joe A.
MR. SATURDAY NIGHT
Giamatti, Paul
SINGLES
Giambalvo, Louis
HOFFA
Giammarco, Joan
BATMAN RETURNS
SINGLES
Giangiulio, Nicholas J.
WHISPERS IN THE DARK

Giannini, Giancarlo
ONCE UPON A CRIME
Gianopoulos, David
PUBLIC EYE, THE
Gibassier, Florent
INSPECTOR LAVARDIN
Gibbins, Amy Arwen
TOYS
Gibbons, Leeza
PLAYER, THE
Gibbs, Caroline
ORIGINAL INTENT
Gibbs, Kevan
MALCOLM X
Gibbs, Matyelok
WATERLAND
Gibney, Susan
WATERDANCE, THE
Gibson, Danny
GUYVER, THE
Gibson, Doug
HOUSE ON TOMBSTONE HILL, THE
Gibson, Henry
BRENDA STARR
Gibson, Jack
CLASS ACT
PASSENGER 57
Gibson, Laurie Ann
MALCOLM X
Gibson, Lida Burris
GUN IN BETTY LOU'S HANDBAG, THE
Gibson, Mel
FOREVER YOUNG
LETHAL WEAPON 3
Gibson, Moses
LOVE FIELD
Gibson, Rebecca
SHADOWS AND FOG
Gibson, Thomas
FAR AND AWAY
Giddens, Clearance
HONEYMOON IN VEGAS
Gideon, Jerry
LITTLE SISTER
Gidley, Pamela
HIGHWAY TO HELL
TWIN PEAKS: FIRE WALK WITH ME
Gielgud, John
POWER OF ONE, THE
SHINING THROUGH
Gierasch, Stefan
MEGAVILLE
MISTRESS
Gigante, Julie
SNEAKERS
Gigliotti, Bernie
BABE, THE
Gilbert, John
ADJUSTER, THE
Gilbert, Johnny
WHITE MEN CAN'T JUMP
Gilbert, Sara
POISON IVY
Gilbert-Hall, Richard
WE'RE TALKIN' SERIOUS MONEY

Gildin, Ken
BABE, THE
Gilding, Antony
HOWARDS END
Giles, Jerry
CHAPLIN
Gilison, David
GIVING, THE
Gill, Bob
LOVE FIELD
Gill, Jack
STRANGER AMONG US, A
Gill, Kendall
HEAVEN IS A PLAYGROUND
Gill, Ray
PRELUDE TO A KISS
Gill, Tanner
UNIVERSAL SOLDIER
Gillens, Benjamin
DAUGHTERS OF THE DUST
Gillespie, Chuck
PUBLIC EYE, THE
Gillespie, Dizzy
TEXAS TENOR: THE ILLINOIS JACQUET STORY
WINTER IN LISBON, THE
Gillespie, Emer
MONKEY BOY
Gillet, Jean-Claude
FAVOUR, THE WATCH, AND THE VERY BIG FISH, THE
Gillette, Anita
BOB ROBERTS
Gilliam, Burton
HONEYMOON IN VEGAS
Gillingham, Kim
CAPTAIN AMERICA
Gillis, Caroline
HIGHWAY 61
Gillison, Douglas
FAR AND AWAY
Gilmore, Craig
LIVING END, THE
Gilmore, Janet
FERNGULLY: THE LAST RAINFOREST
Gilmore, Phillip
MALCOLM X
Gilsenan, Marion
GETTING MARRIED IN BUFFALO JUMP
Ginty, Robert
LADY DRAGON
Gio, Frank
BACKTRACK
Giodano, Alfons
PUSHED TO THE LIMIT
Gions, Harry
INNOCENT BLOOD
Giordano, Karen
HOME ALONE 2: LOST IN NEW YORK
Giordano, Maria Angela
DEVIL'S DAUGHTER, THE
Giordano, Nicholas
HOFFA

Giorgio, Tony
AMERICAN ME
Gios, Tony
GLADIATOR
Giovaninetti, Arnaud
LOVER, THE
Giovi, Marlena
I DON'T BUY KISSES ANYMORE
VENICE/VENICE
Girardeau, Frank
NEWSIES
Girolami, Bob
LOVE HURTS
Gironda, Joe
LIGHT SLEEPER
Gittens, Jewel Allsion
BOOMERANG
Giuntoli, Neil
CRISSCROSS
LEATHER JACKETS
Givens, Jessica
MALCOLM X
Givens, Robin
BOOMERANG
Gladstone, Dana
SHINING THROUGH
Glasgow, Gil
PURE COUNTRY
Glasser, David
TEXAS TENOR:
THE ILLINOIS JACQUET STORY
Glasser, Isabel
FOREVER YOUNG
PURE COUNTRY
Glasser, Phillip
BEBE'S KIDS
Gleason, Mary Pat
BASIC INSTINCT
LORENZO'S OIL
MAN TROUBLE
Gleeson, Brendan
FAR AND AWAY
Gleeson, Brian Boru
LEAGUE OF THEIR OWN, A
Gleeson, Jim
STORYVILLE
Glenister, Philip
LONDON KILLS ME
Glenn, Cody
AMERICAN ME
RUBY
Glenn, Rebecca
HUSBANDS AND WIVES
Glenn, Scott
PLAYER, THE
Glenton, Justine
DEMON IN MY VIEW, A
Glienna, Michael
GLADIATOR
Glover, Brian
ALIEN3
Glover, Bruce
COMMON BONDS
Glover, Crispin
LITTLE NOISES
RUBIN & ED
Glover, Danny
LETHAL WEAPON 3
Glover, David
EDWARD II
Glover, J.R.
CHINA O'BRIEN II
Gmur, Leslie
MANIAC WARRIORS
Goche, Eric
LASER MOON
Gocke, Justin
MY GRANDPA IS A VAMPIRE
Goddbiff, Joe
WATERDANCE, THE
Godet, Thomas
TOTO LE HEROS
Godewa, Philip
HOUSE OF USHER, THE
Godfrey, Emma
HOWARDS END
Godinez, Chely
DANZON
Godshall, Ray
LEAVING NORMAL
Godunov, Alexander
RUNESTONE, THE
WAXWORK II: LOST IN TIME
Goelz, Dave
MUPPET CHRISTMAS CAROL, THE
Goenaga, Aitzpea
WINTER IN LISBON, THE
Goeritz, Ines
BECOMING COLETTE
Goetz, Scot
LIVING END, THE
Goggins, Walt
FOREVER YOUNG
Goins, Jesse
PATRIOT GAMES
Gokhale, Mohan
MISSISSIPPI MASALA
Gold, Nancy
VENICE/VENICE
Goldberg, Adam
MR. SATURDAY NIGHT
Goldberg, Andy
WATERDANCE, THE
Goldberg, Bill
MALCOLM X
Goldberg, Molly
WISECRACKS
Goldberg, Whoopi
MAGICAL WORLD OF CHUCK
JONES, THE
PLAYER, THE
SARAFINA!
SISTER ACT
WISECRACKS
Goldblum, Jeff
DEEP COVER
FATHERS AND SONS
FAVOUR, THE WATCH, AND THE
VERY BIG FISH, THE
PLAYER, THE
SHOOTING ELIZABETH
Goldblum, Pamela
FAVOUR, THE WATCH, AND THE
VERY BIG FISH, THE
Golden, Amy
WHITE MEN CAN'T JUMP
Golden, Annie
THIS IS MY LIFE
Golden, C.J.
CHAPLIN
Goldfinger, Michael
HOME ALONE 2:
LOST IN NEW YORK
Goldman, Annie
PRELUDE TO A KISS
Goldman, Jerry
TOYS
Goldman, Meyer L.
ARTICLE 99
Goldman, Nina
DANCE MACABRE
Goldman, S. Richard
RAMPAGE
Goldner, Michael
POISON IVY
Goldring, Danny
BABE, THE
Goldsmith, Steven E.
HOFFA
Goldson, Dennis
ALBERTO EXPRESS
Goldthwait, Bobcat
SHAKES THE CLOWN
Goldwyn, Tony
KUFFS
TRACES OF RED
Goler, Clifford
WILD ORCHID 2:
TWO SHADES OF BLUE
Goliti, Annette
VENICE/VENICE
Goloubkina, Masha
ADAM'S RIB
Gomarachun, Nappon
IN GOLD WE TRUST
Gomez, Carlos
MAMBO KINGS, THE
Gomez, Jaime
AMERICAN ME
Gomez, Nick Sean
ACES: IRON EAGLE III
Gomez, Panchito
AMERICAN ME
Gomez, Paul
SAVAGE INSTINCT
Gomez, Raphael Rey
CHAINS OF GOLD
Gomez, Rodrigo
DANZON
Gomorra, Charlie
INNOCENT BLOOD
Goncalves, Milton
KICKBOXER 3: THE ART OF WAR
Gong Li
RAISE THE RED LANTERN
Gonzales, Cordelia
MAMBO KINGS, THE

Gonzales, Robert
RAMPAGE
Gonzales, Tony
NEWSIES
Gonzalez, J.E.
BRONX WAR, THE
Gonzalez, Mario
VENICE/VENICE
Gonzalez, Rene
HELLROLLER
Gonzalez, Rosario
DANZON
Gonzalez, Silvestre Ramos
CAPTAIN RON
Gooch, Bruce
ALADDIN
Gooding, Jr., Cuba
FEW GOOD MEN, A
GLADIATOR
Goodloe, J. Mills
LETHAL WEAPON 3
Goodman, Debra
SWOON
Goodman, Dody
FROZEN ASSETS
Goodman, John
BABE, THE
Goodman, Mark J.
MAN TROUBLE
Goodman, Paul
BEASTMASTER 2: THROUGH THE PORTAL OF TIME
Goodrich, Deborah
OUT ON A LIMB
Goodson, Barbara
VAMPIRE HUNTER D
Goodwin, Adam
CHAPLIN
Goodwin, Jason
HELLROLLER
Goodwyn, Caroline
LOVE FIELD
Goojvin, Daniel J.
MAN TROUBLE
Goorjian, Michael
CHAPLIN
FOREVER YOUNG
NEWSIES
Goossen, Greg
MR. BASEBALL
Goranzon, Marie
BEST INTENTIONS, THE
Gorbunov, Alexii
RASPAD
Gordon, Barbara
BEAUTIFUL DREAMERS
Gordon, Bob
FOLKS!
Gordon, Diane
GETTING MARRIED IN BUFFALO JUMP
Gordon, Eve
LEAVING NORMAL
Gordon, Frank
TEXAS TENOR: THE ILLINOIS JACQUET STORY
Gordon, John
TEXAS TENOR: THE ILLINOIS JACQUET STORY
Gordon, Rich
MALCOLM X
Gordon, Richard
WOMAN, HER MEN AND HER FUTON, A
Gordon, Ricky
MALCOLM X
Gordon-Levitt, Joseph
BEETHOVEN
RIVER RUNS THROUGH IT, A
Gordy, Allison
MO' MONEY
Gore, George O.
JUICE
Gore, Sandy
LORENZO'S OIL
Goren, Shosha
HUMAN SHIELD, THE
Goret, Amit
POUR SACHA
Gorg, Galyn
STORYVILLE
Gorman, Cliff
HOFFA
NIGHT AND THE CITY
Gorman, Dan
LIFE ON THE EDGE
Gorman, Deborah
GUYVER, THE
Gorman, III, Thomas Richard
AMERICAN ME
Gorman, Robert Hy
FOREVER YOUNG
Gormley, Peggy
BAD LIEUTENANT
Goros, Tomas
BACKTRACK
Gorton, D.
RIVER RUNS THROUGH IT, A
Gosch, Dan
COMPLEX WORLD
Gosney, Aige
SHAKES THE CLOWN
Gossard, Stone
SINGLES
Gossart, Jean-Rene
EMMANUELLE 6
Gossett, Cyndi James
DIGGSTOWN
Gossett, Jr., Louis
ACES: IRON EAGLE III
DIGGSTOWN
Gossett, Robert
BATMAN RETURNS
Gostukhin, Vladimir
CLOSE TO EDEN
Gotay, Will
DOLLY DEAREST
Gothard, Michael
CHRISTOPHER COLUMBUS: THE DISCOVERY
Goto, Al
BUFFY THE VAMPIRE SLAYER
KUFFS
Goto, Minori
HONEY, I BLEW UP THE KID
Goto, Norihide
MR. BASEBALL
Gottfried, Gilbert
ALADDIN
HIGHWAY TO HELL
Gottlieb, Matthew Robert
NOISES OFF
Gottstein, Ross
FOLKS!
Gough, Michael
BATMAN RETURNS
LITTLE NEMO: ADVENTURES IN SLUMBERLAND
Gould, Dominic
NEAR MISSES
Gould, Elliott
BEYOND JUSTICE
PLAYER, THE
Gould, Jack
ARMED FOR ACTION
Gould, Phyllis Jubett
HOUSESITTER
Gould, Sandra
DEEP COVER
Gourvil, Yves
TOUS LES MATINS DU MONDE
Govoni, Mario
CHAPLIN
Gow, David
USED PEOPLE
Gowan, Marc
LOVE POTION NO. 9
Goy, Luba
USED PEOPLE
Graas, John Christian
OUT ON A LIMB
Grabarncik, Traci
WHITE TRASH
Grabemann, Mollie
MO' MONEY
Graber, Jody
EDWARD II
Graber, Terry
THUNDERHEART
Grace, Martin
UNDER SUSPICION
Grace, Wayne
FAR AND AWAY
SLUMBER PARTY MASSACRE 3
Gracen, Elizabeth
LOWER LEVEL
Gracie, Sally
PASSED AWAY
Graden, Jim
BLACKBELT
Graden, John
BLACKBELT
Grady, Ed
CONSENTING ADULTS
Graf, Allan
UNIVERSAL SOLDIER
Graff, Ilene
LADYBUGS
Graffitti, Andy
MANIAC WARRIORS

Graham, Barbara
BLACKBELT
Graham, C.J.
HIGHWAY TO HELL
Graham, Dion
MALCOLM X
Graham, Gary
MAN TROUBLE
Graham, Gerrit
FROZEN ASSETS
Graham, Heather
DIGGSTOWN
GUILTY AS CHARGED
TWIN PEAKS: FIRE WALK WITH ME
Graham, Margaret
GUN IN BETTY LOU'S HANDBAG, THE
Graham, Richard
UNDER SUSPICION
Graham, Sherri
NAKED OBSESSION
Graham, T. Max
ARTICLE 99
Grain, Glyn
CHRISTOPHER COLUMBUS: THE DISCOVERY
Grame, Peter
LIVING END, THE
Granath, Bjorn
BEST INTENTIONS, THE
OX, THE
Granderson, Lz
ZEBRAHEAD
Grandison, Brian
CROSSING THE BRIDGE
Grant, Benny
I DON'T BUY KISSES ANYMORE
Grant, Beth
LOVE FIELD
WHITE SANDS
Grant, Cory
BABE, THE
Grant, David Marshall
FOREVER YOUNG
Grant, Deborah
I DON'T BUY KISSES ANYMORE
Grant, Dick
CUTTING EDGE, THE
Grant, Faye
GUN IN BETTY LOU'S HANDBAG, THE
TRACES OF RED
Grant, Gary
MIRACLE BEACH
Grant, Kennedy
CHAPLIN
Grant, Lisa
THERE'S NOTHING OUT THERE
Grant, Micah
TERMINAL BLISS
Grant, Richard E.
BRAM STOKER'S DRACULA
PLAYER, THE
Grant, Sandra
SINGLES
Grant, Sarina
BACKTRACK
CANDYMAN
Granville, Francoise
STRANGER AMONG US, A
Grapey, Marc
BIG GIRLS DON'T CRY . . . THEY GET EVEN
BODY WAVES
Grassnick, Michele
FINAL IMPACT
Grau, Doris
DISTINGUISHED GENTLEMAN, THE
Graulau, Mary-Lou
MY FATHER IS COMING
Gravage, Vann
RIVER RUNS THROUGH IT, A
Gravell, Raymond
DAMAGE
Graves, Rupert
CHILDREN, THE
DAMAGE
WHERE ANGELS FEAR TO TREAD
Gray, Daphne
CROSSING, THE
Gray, David
FATHER
Gray, George
STAY TUNED
Gray, Herman
COLOR ADJUSTMENT
Gray, Marc
FLIRTING
Gray, Mary
VENICE/VENICE
Gray, Miriam
RAMPAGE
Gray, Spalding
MONSTER IN A BOX
STRAIGHT TALK
Grayson, Paul
SPLIT SECOND
Grayson, Rob
NEWSIES
Grazioli, Irene
MEDITERRANEO
Grdadolnik, Bruno
CAPTAIN AMERICA
Greco, Joe
COLD JUSTICE
PUBLIC EYE, THE
Greco, Joe V.
HOFFA
Green, Ervin
DAUGHTERS OF THE DUST
Green, Gabe
CLASS ACT
Green, Gail L.
GIVING, THE
Green, Janet-Laine
PRIMO BABY
Green, Jaquita
BEBE'S KIDS
Green, Joe
HELLROLLER
Green, John S.
BABE, THE
Green, Tim
RUBY
Green, Tommy Ray
LEAP OF FAITH
Green, Virginia
DAUGHTERS OF THE DUST
Green, Willie
DIGGSTOWN
Green, Zenovia
DAUGHTERS OF THE DUST
Greenberg, Elizabeth
BABE, THE
Greenblatt, Shon
NEWSIES
Greenburg, Zack O'Malley
LORENZO'S OIL
Greenbush, Billy
RAMPAGE
Greene, Ellen
FATHERS AND SONS
ROCK-A-DOODLE
Greene, Gordon
BEASTMASTER 2: THROUGH THE PORTAL OF TIME
Greene, Graham
CLEARCUT
THUNDERHEART
Greene, Jauquette
MALCOLM X
Greene, Jon
KUFFS
Greene, Jonell
BEBE'S KIDS
Greene, Michael
IN THE HEAT OF PASSION
RUBIN & ED
Greene, Peter
LAWS OF GRAVITY
Greenfield, Mark
WHITE TRASH
Greenhalgh, Gwen
HONEYMOON IN VEGAS
Greenham, Jami Lyn
OVER HER DEAD BODY
Greenhut, Tarra
BUFFY THE VAMPIRE SLAYER
Greenlee, David
SLUMBER PARTY MASSACRE 3
Greenwood, Bruce
PASSENGER 57
Greenwood, Katherine
THIS IS MY LIFE
Greer, Dabbs
HOUSE IV
Greer, Dahlia
GIVING, THE
Greer, Robin
MAN TROUBLE
Gregg, Bradley
EYE OF THE STORM
Gregg, Dave
MANIAC WARRIORS
Gregori, Concha
PEPI, LUCI, BOM AND OTHER GIRLS ON THE HEAP
Gregorio, Danelle
SEX CRIMES

Gregory, Andre
LINGUINI INCIDENT, THE
Gregory, Constantine
BACK IN THE U.S.S.R.
Gregory, Fred P.
WHITE MEN CAN'T JUMP
Gregory, Michael
LAWNMOWER MAN, THE
Gregory, Milly
CHAPLIN
Gregory, Nick
HAPPY HELL NIGHT
Gregus, Sonja
CAPTAIN AMERICA
Grenier, Paul Bruno
CHAPLIN
Grenville, Tina
MY GRANDPA IS A VAMPIRE
Greol, Rick
LAWS OF GRAVITY
Gress, Googy
BIG GIRLS DON'T CRY . . . THEY GET EVEN
Gresset, Chantal
INSPECTOR LAVARDIN
Greve, Joe
ARTICLE 99
Grey, Dennis
FINE ROMANCE, A
Grey, George
TERMINAL BLISS
Grey, Jennifer
WIND
Grey, Joel
PLAYER, THE
Greytak, Eugene
SISTER ACT
Griep, Thomas
MAN TROUBLE
Grier, David Alan
BOOMERANG
PLAYER, THE
Griesemer, John
MALCOLM X
Grifasi, Joe
PRIMARY MOTIVE
Griffin, Dick
TEXAS TENOR: THE ILLINOIS JACQUET STORY
Griffin, Inez
DAUGHTERS OF THE DUST
Griffin, Jeon-Paul
GLADIATOR
Griffin, Jerri Renee
ENCINO MAN
Griffin, Kathy
SHAKES THE CLOWN
Griffin, Laura
CONSENTING ADULTS
Griffin, Maceo
DAUGHTERS OF THE DUST
Griffin, Mary
LOVE HURTS
Griffin, Michelle
BOOMERANG

Griffin, Rachel
MIDNIGHT CLEAR, A
Griffin, William Duff
HERO
Griffis, Rhoda
LOVE FIELD
Griffith, Melanie
SHINING THROUGH
STRANGER AMONG US, A
Griffith, Tracy
FINEST HOUR, THE
Griffiths, Richard
BLAME IT ON THE BELLBOY
Grigsby, Garon
SLUMBER PARTY MASSACRE 3
Grillo, Frank
MAMBO KINGS, THE
Grillo, John
BLAME IT ON THE BELLBOY
CHRISTOPHER COLUMBUS: THE DISCOVERY
Grillo, Mario
MAMBO KINGS, THE
Grimes, John
TEXAS TENOR: THE ILLINOIS JACQUET STORY
Grimshaw, Jim
BASKET CASE 3: THE PROGENY
Grimwood, Unity
HOURS AND TIMES, THE
Grindlay, Annie
K2
Grinnell, Harriet
TRACES OF RED
Grinner, Harty
ROADSIDE PROPHETS
Grinner, Jonathan
DEAD CERTAIN
Gristwood, Sarah
VENICE/VENICE
Gritters-Doublet, Gunar
LILY WAS HERE
Grodenchik, Max
SISTER ACT
Grodin, Charles
BEETHOVEN
Groening, Matt
MAGICAL WORLD OF CHUCK JONES, THE
Groh, Alison
BABE, THE
Grondahl, Eva
BEST INTENTIONS, THE
Groshevoi, Anatoli
RASPAD
Gross, Arye
MIDNIGHT CLEAR, A
SHAKING THE TREE
Gross, Dillon Rozell
MISSISSIPPI MASALA
Gross, Mark
MALCOLM X
Gross, Michael
ALAN & NAOMI
Gross, Paul
GETTING MARRIED IN BUFFALO JUMP

Grossman, Gary
MR. SATURDAY NIGHT
Grote, Vernon
LEAP OF FAITH
LOVE HURTS
Groupo de Danza Mexico Huehuecoyotl
CABEZA DE VACA
Grove, Christopher
OUT ON A LIMB
Grovensor, Vertamae
DAUGHTERS OF THE DUST
Guardado, Jose
AMERICAN ME
Guarnieri, Tom
BABE, THE
Guastaferro, Vincent
MEGAVILLE
Guerra, Blanca
DANZON
Guerra, Castulo
COLD HEAVEN
Guerra, Emiliano
DANZON
Guerrar, Hassan
EMMANUELLE 6
Guertchikoff, Louba
FAVOUR, THE WATCH, AND THE VERY BIG FISH, THE
Guess, Michael
MALCOLM X
Guest, Christopher
FEW GOOD MEN, A
Guibarra, Albert
WILD WHEELS
Guidall, George
MALCOLM X
Guidelli, Giovanni
WHERE ANGELS FEAR TO TREAD
Guilfoyle, Paul
FINAL ANALYSIS
HOFFA
Guillen, Fernando
WINTER IN LISBON, THE
Guinan, Francis
JUST LIKE IN THE MOVIES
SHINING THROUGH
Guinness, Peter
ALIEN3
CHRISTOPHER COLUMBUS: THE DISCOVERY
Gullov, Niels
DEVIL'S DAUGHTER, THE
Gumball
1991: THE YEAR PUNK BROKE
Gumbert, Steve
MANIAC WARRIORS
Gumede, Mabusi
SARAFINA!
Guncler, Sam
JUST LIKE IN THE MOVIES
Gunderson, Jamie
BEBE'S KIDS
Gunn, Michael
CHRISTOPHER COLUMBUS: THE DISCOVERY

Gunter, Jeffrey Anderson
TO PROTECT AND SERVE
Gunther, Ernst
BEST INTENTIONS, THE
Gunton, Bob
JENNIFER EIGHT
PATRIOT GAMES
PUBLIC EYE, THE
Gural, Ron
STORYVILLE
Guss, Louis
USED PEOPLE
Gustafson, Bjorn
BEST INTENTIONS, THE
OX, THE
Gustin, Lisa
HUSBANDS AND WIVES
Guthrie, Arlo
ROADSIDE PROPHETS
Guthrie, Caroline
CHAPLIN
Guthrie, Michelle
FROZEN ASSETS
Guttenberg, Steve
MAGICAL WORLD OF CHUCK JONES, THE
Gutteridge, Tom
FATHER
Guwaza, David
POWER OF ONE, THE
Guy, DeJuan
CANDYMAN
Guy, J. Scott
ARMED FOR ACTION
Guyer, Cynthia
SOLDIER'S FORTUNE
Guyton, Jr., Cleave
MALCOLM X
Guzaldo, Joe
PUBLIC EYE, THE
SMOOTH TALKER
Guzman, Adriana
CABEZA DE VACA
Guzman, Luis
INNOCENT BLOOD
JUMPIN' AT THE BONEYARD
Guzman, Pablo
JUICE
Gwynne, Fred
MY COUSIN VINNY
SHADOWS AND FOG
Gyapjas, Tibor
FATHER
Gyllenhaal, Maggie
WATERLAND
Haag, Christina
SHAKING THE TREE
Haas, Ludwig
SHINING THROUGH
Haas, Lukas
ALAN & NAOMI
LEAP OF FAITH
Haas, Victoria
PRELUDE TO A KISS
Haase, Cathy
LITTLE NOISES

Hack, Shelley
FINISHING TOUCH, THE
Hackett, John
HOFFA
Hackman, Gene
UNFORGIVEN
Hackman, Melissa Ann
FALLING FROM GRACE
Haddad, Ava
FINEST HOUR, THE
Haddad, Suheil
CUP FINAL
Hade, Deirdre
MISTRESS
Hadley, Brett
BABE, THE
Hadley, Kenneth
UNDER SUSPICION
Haffey, Jim
MISSISSIPPI MASALA
Haffield, Cynthia
FATAL INSTINCT
Hagan, Kevin
COLLISION COURSE
Hageboeck, T.J.
JENNIFER EIGHT
Hager, Dave
LEAP OF FAITH
LOVE FIELD
Hagerty, Julie
NOISES OFF
Hagerty, Michael G.
FROZEN ASSETS
WAYNE'S WORLD
Haggard, Larry
MISSISSIPPI MASALA
Haggerty, Captain
HONEYMOON IN VEGAS
Haggerty, Dan
SOLDIER'S FORTUNE
Hagler, Marvelous Marvin
INDIO 2 - THE REVOLT
Hahn, Eliska
INVASION OF THE SPACE PREACHERS
Hahn, Jessica
BIKINI SUMMER 2
Hahn, Neal
RAMPAGE
Haid, Charles
STORYVILLE
Haidary, Susan T.
CONSENTING ADULTS
Haider, Michael
LORENZO'S OIL
Haigh, Paul
WATERLAND
Haight, Rip
MEMOIRS OF AN INVISIBLE MAN
Haim, Corey
OH, WHAT A NIGHT
PRAYER OF THE ROLLERBOYS
Haines, John
MANIAC WARRIORS
Haines, Ken
MUPPET CHRISTMAS CAROL, THE

Haje, Richard
SEX CRIMES
Hald, Niklas
BEST INTENTIONS, THE
Hale, Birdie M.
JUICE
Hale, Doug
LIFE ON THE EDGE
Hale, Jennifer
LOVE POTION NO. 9
Hale, Terry
PURE COUNTRY
Haley, Brian
INTO THE SUN
Haley, Kevin
STEAL AMERICA
Haley, R.M.
LEAGUE OF THEIR OWN, A
Hall, Alaina Reed
DEATH BECOMES HER
Hall, Albert
MALCOLM X
Hall, Angela
BOB ROBERTS
PLAYER, THE
Hall, Anthony Michael
INTO THE SUN
Hall, Delores
LEAP OF FAITH
LETHAL WEAPON 3
Hall, Donna
BASKET CASE 3: THE PROGENY
Hall, Huntz
AUNTIE LEE'S MEAT PIES
Hall, Irma P.
BABE, THE
MO' MONEY
STRAIGHT TALK
Hall, J.D.
BEBE'S KIDS
Hall, Kevin Peter
HIGHWAY TO HELL
Hall, Kirsten
WOMAN, HER MEN AND HER FUTON, A
Hall, Lori
SNEAKERS
Hall, William
WILDFIRE
Hallo, Dean
FOREVER YOUNG
HONEYMOON IN VEGAS
Hallowell, Todd
FAR AND AWAY
Hallwachs, Hans Peta
DEMON IN MY VIEW, A
Halphie, Michael
CHRISTOPHER COLUMBUS: THE DISCOVERY
Halsey, Brett
BEYOND JUSTICE
Halton, Michael
BASIC INSTINCT
OUT ON A LIMB
Ham, Eben
RUNESTONE, THE

Ham, Larry
DIGGSTOWN
TEXAS TENOR: THE ILLINOIS JACQUET STORY

Hamamura, Jun
MR. BASEBALL

Hamann, Craig
RESERVOIR DOGS

Hamblin, Anthony
MUPPET CHRISTMAS CAROL, THE

Hambrick, John
LOVE CRIMES

Hamid, Youssef
HAIRDRESSER'S HUSBAND, THE

Hamill, Mark
GUYVER, THE

Hamill, Mike
TROLL 2

Hamilton, Ann
HARD PROMISES

Hamilton, Candy
THUNDERHEART

Hamilton, Carrie
COOL WORLD

Hamilton, Chad
PUSHED TO THE LIMIT

Hamilton, George
ONCE UPON A CRIME

Hamilton, Jane
RUBY

Hamilton, Jim
HONEYMOON IN VEGAS

Hamilton, Laura
BREATHING FIRE

Hamilton, Leigh
GAS FOOD LODGING

Hamilton, Richard
MO' MONEY

Hamilton, Roy
SECRET FRIENDS

Hamilton, Steve
STRANGER AMONG US, A

Hamilton, Tony
FATAL INSTINCT

Hamilton-Larose, Jaylene
JENNIFER EIGHT

Hammer, Casey
LEAP OF FAITH

Hammond, Roger
EDWARD II

Hamon, Lucienne
BECOMING COLETTE

Hampton, Dawn
MALCOLM X

Hampton, Lee
GIVING, THE

Hampton, Lionel
TEXAS TENOR: THE ILLINOIS JACQUET STORY

Hanan, Stephen
MALCOLM X

Hanchar, Linda
CUTTING EDGE, THE

Hancock, John
COLLISION COURSE

Hand, Lisa
LEAGUE OF THEIR OWN, A

Handley, Ollie
CONFESSIONS OF A SERIAL KILLER

Hanft, Helen
JUST LIKE IN THE MOVIES
USED PEOPLE

Hankamp, Carol
CRISSCROSS

Hankin, Larry
OUT ON A LIMB

Hanks, Tom
LEAGUE OF THEIR OWN, A
RADIO FLYER

Hanna, Joe
NOISES OFF

Hannah, Barry
GUN IN BETTY LOU'S HANDBAG, THE

Hannah, Bob
LOVE CRIMES

Hannah, Daryl
MEMOIRS OF AN INVISIBLE MAN

Hannegan, David
HOUSESITTER

Hansen, Arne
DAY IN OCTOBER, A

Hansen, Gale
DOUBLE VISION
FINEST HOUR, THE
SHAKING THE TREE

Hansen, Kim
CLEARCUT

Hansen, Michael
HOME ALONE 2: LOST IN NEW YORK

Hanson, Bonita
ARTICLE 99

Hansson, Lena T.
BEST INTENTIONS, THE

Hanyee
SNEAKERS

Harada, Daijiro
SILK ROAD, THE

Harada, Ernest
DEATH BECOMES HER

Harbor, Gayle
VENICE/VENICE

Harcum, Monique
MALCOLM X

Hardeman, Jerome Jamal
MALCOLM X

Harden, Jr., Ernest
WHITE MEN CAN'T JUMP

Harden, Marcia Gay
USED PEOPLE

Harder, D.J.
3 NINJAS

Harders, Jane
FLIRTING

Hardiman, Terence
DEMON IN MY VIEW, A

Harding, Joseph
SWOON

Harding, Pitt
COMPLEX WORLD

Hardison, Kadeem
WHITE MEN CAN'T JUMP

Hardy, Dona
UNIVERSAL SOLDIER
WE'RE TALKIN' SERIOUS MONEY

Hardy, George
TROLL 2

Hardy, Leslie
SNEAKERS

Hardy, Paul
WATERLAND

Hardy, Robert
YEAR OF THE COMET

Harkin, Tom
FEED

Harkins, John
RAMPAGE

Harkness, Julie
BOB ROBERTS

Harleston, Robb
CONSENTING ADULTS

Harley, Graham
CUTTING EDGE, THE

Harley, Jim
LOVE CRIMES

Harmon, Alex
TERMINAL BLISS

Harmon, Andrea
VENICE/VENICE

Harmon, Linda
MAN TROUBLE

Harmon, Mark
COLD HEAVEN
TILL THERE WAS YOU

Harms, John
LETHAL WEAPON 3

Haro, Daniel A.
AMERICAN ME

Harper, Kate
WATERLAND

Harper, Kyra
GETTING MARRIED IN BUFFALO JUMP

Harper, Robert
FINAL ANALYSIS

Harper, Tess
MY NEW GUN

Harrell, James N.
LEAP OF FAITH

Harrelson, Woody
WHITE MEN CAN'T JUMP

Harries, Davyd
SECRET FRIENDS

Harrington, Claudia
COLD HEAVEN

Harrington, Jr., Pat
ROUND TRIP TO HEAVEN

Harrington, Laurence
AFRAID OF THE DARK

Harrington, Lisa Jay
WITCHCRAFT IV: VIRGIN HEART

Harris, Baxter
CANDYMAN
SCENT OF A WOMAN

Harris, Bill
MO' MONEY

Harris, Burtt
STRANGER AMONG US, A

Harris, Carol
CANDYMAN

Harris, Cynthia
DISTINGUISHED GENTLEMAN, THE

Harris, Ed
GLENGARRY GLEN ROSS

Harris, Estelle
THIS IS MY LIFE

Harris, Harriet
NAKED OBSESSION

Harris, Henry
WATERDANCE, THE

Harris, Idina
JUICE
ZEBRAHEAD

Harris, Jack David
DELTA HEAT

Harris, Jared
FAR AND AWAY
LAST OF THE MOHICANS, THE
PUBLIC EYE, THE

Harris, JoAnn
NEWSIES

Harris, Julie
HOUSESITTER

Harris, Julius
PRAYER OF THE ROLLERBOYS

Harris, Lance
FINAL IMPACT

Harris, Leigh
PASSION FISH

Harris, Linda
HUMAN SHIELD, THE

Harris, M.K.
SLUMBER PARTY MASSACRE 3

Harris, Marykate
CHAPLIN

Harris, Matthew
MALCOLM X

Harris, Mel
RAISING CAIN

Harris, Moira
OF MICE AND MEN

Harris, Phil
CLEARCUT
ROCK-A-DOODLE

Harris, Randy
SOLDIER'S FORTUNE

Harris, Raymond
MALCOLM X

Harris, Richard
PATRIOT GAMES
UNFORGIVEN

Harris, Robyn
SORORITY HOUSE MASSACRE 2

Harris, Roger
BABE, THE

Harrison, Deirdre
SHINING THROUGH

Harrison, Nigel
CHRISTOPHER COLUMBUS:
THE DISCOVERY

Harrisson, Hugo Harold
TOTO LE HEROS

Harrod, David
ARMED FOR ACTION
BLOOD ON THE BADGE

Hart, Dorothy
WISECRACKS

Hart, Frank
PASSENGER 57

Hart, Ian
HOURS AND TIMES, THE

Hart, Joe
KUFFS
LAWNMOWER MAN, THE

Harter, Douglas
MAXIMUM BREAKOUT

Hartigan, Ben
WILD ORCHID 2:
TWO SHADES OF BLUE

Hartley, Mariette
ENCINO MAN

Hartley, Steven
CHRISTOPHER COLUMBUS:
THE DISCOVERY
SPLIT SECOND

Hartman, John
WHITE TRASH

Hartmann, George
SNEAKERS

Hartsell, Kathy
HOFFA
WILD ORCHID 2:
TWO SHADES OF BLUE

Hartung, Alfred
BECOMING COLETTE

Harvey, Robert
WE'RE TALKIN' SERIOUS MONEY

Harvey-Wilson, Stewart
SPLIT SECOND

Harwood, Mitch
BRENDA STARR

Hasomeras, Nick
COMPLEX WORLD

Hassett, Marilyn
EXILED IN AMERICA

Hastings, Edouard
FAVOUR, THE WATCH, AND THE
VERY BIG FISH, THE

Hastings, Valerie
COLD HEAVEN

Hatch, Lee
MANIAC WARRIORS

Hatcher, Allan
SOUTH CENTRAL

Hatcher, Alvin
SOUTH CENTRAL

Hatcher, Teri
STRAIGHT TALK

Hauer, Rutger
BEYOND JUSTICE
BUFFY THE VAMPIRE SLAYER
SPLIT SECOND

Hauff, Alexander
SHINING THROUGH

Hauge, Chris
LOVE HURTS

Haugen, Rana
CROSSING THE BRIDGE

Haughey, Daniel
SWOON

Hauser, Cole
SCHOOL TIES

Hauser, Fay
WATERDANCE, THE

Hauser, Wings
BEASTMASTER 2:
THROUGH THE PORTAL OF TIME
EXILED IN AMERICA
MIND, BODY & SOUL
PALE BLOOD

Hauss, Harold
ARTICLE 99

Haven, Scott
BABE, THE

Haverty, Hartley
MR. SATURDAY NIGHT

Haviland, Matt
TEXAS TENOR:
THE ILLINOIS JACQUET STORY

Havoc
SPLIT SECOND

Hawke, Daniel
CROSSING THE BRIDGE

Hawke, Ethan
MIDNIGHT CLEAR, A
WATERLAND

Hawkes, Eileen
CHILDREN, THE

Hawkes, Ian
CHILDREN, THE

Hawkin, Lorraine
PUSHED TO THE LIMIT

Hawking, Isobel
BRIEF HISTORY OF TIME, A

Hawking, Jane
BRIEF HISTORY OF TIME, A

Hawking, Mary
BRIEF HISTORY OF TIME, A

Hawking, Stephen
BRIEF HISTORY OF TIME, A

Hawkins, Flo
GIVING, THE

Hawkins, Lester
WHITE MEN CAN'T JUMP

Hawkins, Yvette
MISSISSIPPI MASALA
ZEBRAHEAD

Hawley, Victoria
MAXIMUM FORCE

Hawn, Goldie
CRISSCROSS
DEATH BECOMES HER
HOUSESITTER

Hawthorne, Nigel
FREDDIE AS F.R.O.7

Hayama, Junichiro
JOURNEY OF HONOR

Hayden, Julie
TOYS

Hayden, Karl
PATRIOT GAMES

Hayes, Isaac
GUILTY AS CHARGED

Hayes, Paul
CHAPLIN

Hayes, Sylvester
IMPORTANCE OF BEING EARNEST, THE

Hayes, Zoe
THIS IS MY LIFE

Haygarth, Tony
LONDON KILLS ME

Hayman, Carole
DEMON IN MY VIEW, A

Haynes, Anthony
BUFFY THE VAMPIRE SLAYER

Haynes, Clarence
HIGHWAY 61

Haynes, Jerry
HARD PROMISES

Haynes, Michael
LIVING END, THE

Haynes, Todd
SWOON

Haynie, Jim
BIG GIRLS DON'T CRY . . . THEY GET EVEN
STEPHEN KING'S SLEEPWALKERS

Hays, Andrea
TWIN PEAKS: FIRE WALK WITH ME

Hays, Robert
HOT CHOCOLATE

Haysbert, Dennis
LOVE FIELD
MR. BASEBALL

Hayshi, Henry
PUSHED TO THE LIMIT

Hayward, Charles
VOYAGER
POISON IVY

Hazard, Vern
BABE, THE

Hazlett-Oakes, Erin
RAMPAGE

Hazsen, Mykol
SINGLES

He Caifei
RAISE THE RED LANTERN

Headey, Lena
WATERLAND

Heald, Anthony
WHISPERS IN THE DARK

Healey, Mary
CHAPLIN

Healy, Christine
LITTLE SISTER

Healy, Dan
HERO

Healy, David
PUERTO RICAN MAMBO (NOT A MUSICAL), THE

Healy, James
RUBY

Healy, Merrill
GUN IN BETTY LOU'S HANDBAG, THE

Healy, Patricia
BODYGUARD, THE
PUBLIC EYE, THE
ULTRAVIOLET

Heames, Darin
DR. GIGGLES

Heames, Denis
BIG GIRLS DON'T CRY . . . THEY GET EVEN

Heard, Cordis
DISTINGUISHED GENTLEMAN, THE
HERO

Heard, John
GLADIATOR
HOME ALONE 2: LOST IN NEW YORK
RADIO FLYER
WATERLAND

Heard, Latoya
WATERLAND

Heard, Patricia
NETHERWORLD

Hearn, Ann
LORENZO'S OIL

Hearn, Chick
WHITE MEN CAN'T JUMP

Hearn, George
SNEAKERS

Heathcliffe, Clark
LAST OF THE MOHICANS, THE

Heaton, Patricia
BEETHOVEN
MEMOIRS OF AN INVISIBLE MAN

Heaton, Tom
LEAVING NORMAL

Hebditch, Camilla
WATERLAND

Hechim, Jim
SINGLES

Heckstall-Smith, Barr
HOWARDS END

Hector
ROADSIDE PROPHETS

Hedlund, Roland
BEST INTENTIONS, THE

Heffernan, John
1492: THE CONQUEST OF PARADISE

Heffner, Tara
TERMINAL BLISS

Heflin, Nora
UNLAWFUL ENTRY

Heflin, Norm
LOVE FIELD

Hefner, Christie
DAMNED IN THE USA

Hefner, Hugh
HUGH HEFNER: ONCE UPON A TIME

Hefton, "Bad" Brad
BLACKBELT

Heger, Wolfgang
SHINING THROUGH

Hegyes, Mack
LORENZO'S OIL

Hegyes, Robert
BOB ROBERTS

Heinze, Thomas
VOYAGER

Helal, Abdallah
GODZILLA VS. BIOLLANTE

Held, Stephen
PATRIOT GAMES

Heller, Chip
MEMOIRS OF AN INVISIBLE MAN
RAMPAGE

Heller, Jack
INTO THE SUN

Helms, Jesse
DAMNED IN THE USA

Helppie-Shipley, Kathleen
MAGICAL WORLD OF CHUCK JONES, THE

Helvin, Marie
CHILDREN, THE

Helwig, Klaus
VENICE/VENICE

Hemblen, David
ADJUSTER, THE

Hemingway, Mariel
FALLING FROM GRACE

Hemphill, Jessie Mae
DEEP BLUES

Hendershott, Adam
RADIO FLYER

Henderson, Bill
WHITE MEN CAN'T JUMP

Henderson, Florence
SHAKES THE CLOWN

Hendery, Richard
MANIAC WARRIORS

Hendler, Lauri
FERNGULLY: THE LAST RAINFOREST

Hendricks, Jon
WHITE MEN CAN'T JUMP

Hendrickson, Benjamin
CONSENTING ADULTS

Hendrickson, Timothy
PUBLIC EYE, THE

Hendriks, Bafana
SARAFINA!

Hendrix, Lori Jo
SUNSET STRIP

Henessey, Carolyn
I DON'T BUY KISSES ANYMORE

Henkel, Christoph
VENICE/VENICE

Henner, Marilu
CHAINS OF GOLD
NOISES OFF

Hennings, Sam
SEEDPEOPLE

Henriksen, Lance
ALIEN3
COMRADES IN ARMS
DELTA HEAT
JENNIFER EIGHT

Henry, Buck
LINGUINI INCIDENT, THE
PLAYER, THE

Henry, Gregg
RAISING CAIN

Henry, John
PASSION FISH

Henry, Judith
DISCRETE, LA

Henry, Lenny
BERNARD AND THE GENIE

Henschel, Tom
LIFE ON THE EDGE
Henson, Garette Ratliff
MIGHTY DUCKS, THE
Hepburn, Doreen
PLAYBOYS, THE
Herbert, Leon
ALIEN3
Herbon, Michaela
TOYS
Herbon, Nicholas
TOYS
Heren, Daniel
SOCIETY
Herkert, Toni
ENCINO MAN
Herlihy, Ed
MALCOLM X
Herlin, Jacques
FAVOUR, THE WATCH, AND THE VERY BIG FISH, THE
Herman, Maurice
FAVOUR, THE WATCH, AND THE VERY BIG FISH, THE
Hernandez, Alex P.
DEATH BECOMES HER
Hernandez, Benjamin
TOYS
Hernandez, Bruno
HONEYMOON IN VEGAS
Hernandez, Juan
DANZON
Hernandez, Salvador
LEAP OF FAITH
Herrera, David
ACES: IRON EAGLE III
Herrera, John
MAMBO KINGS, THE
Herriott, Scott
SHAKES THE CLOWN
Herron, Cindy
JUICE
Hershberger, Gary
SNEAKERS
TWIN PEAKS: FIRE WALK WITH ME
Hershey, Barbara
PUBLIC EYE, THE
Herson, Jon J.
FINEST HOUR, THE
Hertford, Whitby
MIKEY
RAMPAGE
Herzberg, Paul
MUNCHIE
Hess, Bob
RUBY
Hess, Doris
BEBE'S KIDS
Hess, Joseph
BODYGUARD, THE
TRACES OF RED
Hess, Sandra
ENCINO MAN
Hesseman, Howard
HOT CHOCOLATE
RUBIN & ED
Hesser, Don
DEATH BECOMES HER
Heudeline, Raymonde
LOVER, THE
Hewgill, Roland
BEAUTIFUL DREAMERS
Hewitt, Don
MALCOLM X
Hewitt, Jery
MALCOLM X
Hewitt, Love
MUNCHIE
Hewitt, Martin
NIGHT RHYTHMS
SECRET GAMES
Hewitt, Paul
HERO
PLAYER, THE
Hewlett, David
DESIRE AND HELL AT SUNSET MOTEL
Hewlett, Roger
DIGGSTOWN
Heydemann, Klaus
MATCH FACTORY GIRL, THE
NIGHT ON EARTH
Heyman, Barton
RAISING CAIN
ROADSIDE PROPHETS
Hi Ching
ALIEN3
Hibbler, Al
TEXAS TENOR: THE ILLINOIS JACQUET STORY
Hick, Charlotte
SPLIT SECOND
Hickey, Carol
RUNESTONE, THE
Hickey, William
RUNESTONE, THE
Hicklin, Ron
MAN TROUBLE
Hicks, Barbara
HOWARDS END
Hicks, Jonathan P.
BOOMERANG
Hicks, Tommy
DAUGHTERS OF THE DUST
FATAL INSTINCT
Hidrogo, Michael
LASER MOON
Hiedel, Thorsten
BECOMING COLETTE
Hietala, Jerry Allan
THUNDERHEART
Higgins, Michael
DEATH BECOMES HER
SCHOOL TIES
WIND
Higgs, Scott
LOVE POTION NO. 9
Hightower, Janice
WHITE TRASH
Hightower, Tina
LOVE CRIMES
Higueras, Cristina
SHOOTING ELIZABETH
Hijrah, Abdul Kakeem
MALCOLM X
Hilbert, Tina Louise
BASKET CASE 3: THE PROGENY
Hill, Amy
SINGLES
Hill, Dana
ROVER DANGERFIELD
Hill, Dennis
CONFESSIONS OF A SERIAL KILLER
Hill, Harry
SCANNERS III: THE TAKEOVER
Hill, Joyce Ellen
WHO SHOT PATAKANGO?
Hill, Ken
MIND, BODY & SOUL
Hill, Kimberly
HAND THAT ROCKS THE CRADLE, THE
Hill, Leslie
FLIRTING
Hill, Mark
WHITE MEN CAN'T JUMP
Hill, Nicholas
SEX CRIMES
Hill, Rick
DEATHSTALKER IV: MATCH OF TITANS
Hill, Shelley
BODYGUARD, THE
STOP! OR MY MOM WILL SHOOT
Hill, Zandra
WHITE MEN CAN'T JUMP
Hill-Richmond, Angie
SPLIT SECOND
Hills, Tiffanye
DAUGHTERS OF THE DUST
Hinchley, Pippa
LONDON KILLS ME
Hines, Damon
LETHAL WEAPON 3
Hines, Dean
BASKET CASE 3: THE PROGENY
Hines, Grainger
SOLDIER'S FORTUNE
Hingle, Pat
BATMAN RETURNS
Hinkle, Rick
CONSENTING ADULTS
Hinkley, Brent
BOB ROBERTS
HONEYMOON IN VEGAS
Hinkley, Tommy
HUMAN SHIELD, THE
NAKED OBSESSION
Hinton, Lee
UNDER SIEGE
Hinton, Milt
TEXAS TENOR: THE ILLINOIS JACQUET STORY
Hinton, Mona
TEXAS TENOR: THE ILLINOIS JACQUET STORY
Hinton, Jr., Steve
FOREVER YOUNG
Hiolle, Herve
FINE ROMANCE, A

Hipp, Paul
BAD CHANNELS
BAD LIEUTENANT
LETHAL WEAPON 3
Hiroko
MIRACLE BEACH
Hjelm, Keve
BEST INTENTIONS, THE
Hjuler, Klaus
DAY IN OCTOBER, A
Hjulstrom, Lennart
BEST INTENTIONS, THE
OX, THE
Hlope, Mfana "Jones"
SARAFINA!
Hlozek, Alesh
WATERLAND
Ho Chow
TIGER CLAWS
Hoak, Clare
HOME ALONE 2: LOST IN NEW YORK
Hobbs, Christopher
EDWARD II
Hobson, I.M.
BRAM STOKER'S DRACULA
HERO
MEMOIRS OF AN INVISIBLE MAN
NEWSIES
Hobson, John
RUNESTONE, THE
Hochendoner, Jeff
SCHOOL TIES
Hocke, Bernard
INNOCENT BLOOD
Hocking, Henry
HAIRDRESSER'S HUSBAND, THE
Hodder, Kane
HOUSE IV
Hodge, Carl E.
WHITE MEN CAN'T JUMP
Hodge, Kate
RAPID FIRE
Hodge, Mike
MALCOLM X
Hodgen, Joette
LEAGUE OF THEIR OWN, A
Hodges, David U.
UNDER SIEGE
Hodges, Steven
TWIN PEAKS: FIRE WALK WITH ME
Hodges, Terry
MALCOLM X
Hodgson, Marie T.
MAN TROUBLE
Hoff, Christian
ENCINO MAN
ROCK-A-DOODLE
Hoffman, Cal
BATMAN RETURNS
Hoffman, Chris
TUNE, THE
Hoffman, Dominic
ORIGINAL INTENT
Hoffman, Dustin
HERO
Hoffman, Gaby
THIS IS MY LIFE
Hoffman, Jackie
MO' MONEY
Hoffman, Jeff
WATERLAND
Hoffman, Philip S.
LEAP OF FAITH
SCENT OF A WOMAN
Hoffman, Shawn
ADVENTURES IN DINOSAUR CITY
Hoffman, Thom
LILY WAS HERE
Hofherr, Matt
SCHOOL TIES
Hogan, Harold
ZEBRAHEAD
Hogan, Kathleen
BRIDE OF KILLER NERD
Hogan, Michael
CLEARCUT
CUTTING EDGE, THE
STAY TUNED
Hogan, Paul
MANIAC WARRIORS
Hogsbro, Thomas
DAY IN OCTOBER, A
Hogue, Elisebeth
OUT ON A LIMB
Hogue, Paul
OUT ON A LIMB
Holahan, Dennis
COLLISION COURSE
KUFFS
Holcolmb, Kathryn
ROCK-A-DOODLE
Holcomb, Billy
GUN IN BETTY LOU'S HANDBAG, THE
Holden, Frankie J.
PROOF
Holden, Marjean
STOP! OR MY MOM WILL SHOOT
Holder, Christopher
RUNESTONE, THE
Holder, Geoffrey
BOOMERANG
Holechek, Brian Joe
AMERICAN ME
Holgado, Ticky
DELICATESSEN
HAIRDRESSER'S HUSBAND, THE
Holguin, Toby
BUFFY THE VAMPIRE SLAYER
Holiday, Charlie
FINAL ANALYSIS
Holladay, Steve
KUFFS
Holland, Antony
K2
Holland, Erik
ARTICLE 99
Holland, Kwawe
CLASS ACT
Holland, Sam
CHAPLIN
Holland, Stephen
PLAYBOYS, THE
Holliday, Charlie
RAMPAGE
Hollinquist, Dayna
SNEAKERS
Hollinquist, Shayna
SNEAKERS
Hollis, Howard
HELLROLLER
Hollis, Tommy
MALCOLM X
Holloway, Loretta
PURE COUNTRY
Holman, Clare
AFRAID OF THE DARK
Holman, Stephen
LIVING END, THE
Holmes, Derrick
GODZILLA VS. BIOLLANTE
Holmes, Jennifer
LIFE ON THE EDGE
Holmes, Prudence Wright
SISTER ACT
Holt, Sandra
FROZEN ASSETS
Holt, Shannon
BOB ROBERTS
Holton, Mark
LEAGUE OF THEIR OWN, A
Holub, Miloslav
EAR, THE
Homann, Rainer
BECOMING COLETTE
Homo, Charlie
STEAL AMERICA
Homsey, Bonnie Oda
SOUTH CENTRAL
Homsey, Dino
OUT FOR BLOOD
Hong, James
TALONS OF THE EAGLE
Hong, Matthew
TEXAS TENOR: THE ILLINOIS JACQUET STORY
Hoobler, John
TWIN PEAKS: FIRE WALK WITH ME
Hooker, Jim
PUSHED TO THE LIMIT
Hooks, Ed
RAISING CAIN
Hooks, Jan
BATMAN RETURNS
Hooks, Robert
PASSENGER 57
Hooks, Rosie Lee
BODYGUARD, THE
Hooper, Emily Marie
GLADIATOR
Hooper, Tobe
STEPHEN KING'S SLEEPWALKERS
Hoosier, Trula
DAUGHTERS OF THE DUST
Hootkins, William
POPE MUST DIET!, THE
RIVER RUNS THROUGH IT, A

Hoover, Christopher
SWOON
Hoover, Elva Mai
GATE II
Hope, Deborah
LEAP OF FAITH
Hope, William
SHINING THROUGH
Hopkins, Anthony
BRAM STOKER'S DRACULA
CHAPLIN
EFFICIENCY EXPERT, THE
FREEJACK
HOWARDS END
Hopkins, Bo
CENTER OF THE WEB
Hopkins, Jermaine
JUICE
Hopkins, Kaitlin
SPIRITS
Hopkins, Richard
LEAVING NORMAL
Hopkins, Telma
TRANCERS III: DETH LIVES
Hoppe, Martin
SHINING THROUGH
Hopper, Dawn
MISTRESS
Hopper, Dennis
BACKTRACK
EYE OF THE STORM
Hopper, Eddie
MAXIMUM BREAKOUT
Hopper, Margie
FALLING FROM GRACE
Hopper, Tim
LAST OF THE MOHICANS, THE
Hoppert, Walt
FROZEN ASSETS
Hora, John
HONEY, I BLEW UP THE KID
Horden, Sir Michael
FREDDIE AS F.R.O.7
Hormel, Gregory "Smokey"
TWIN PEAKS: FIRE WALK WITH ME
Hornyak, Stephen
GIVING, THE
Horovitz, Adam
ROADSIDE PROPHETS
Horse, Michael
PASSENGER 57
Horsley, Ivan
GETTING MARRIED IN BUFFALO JUMP
Horton, Peter
SINGLES
Hoshino, Akira
JOURNEY OF HONOR
Hoshino, Hidetaka
MR. BASEBALL
Hosking, Craig
LAWNMOWER MAN, THE
Hoskins, Bob
FAVOUR, THE WATCH, AND THE VERY BIG FISH, THE
PASSED AWAY

Hostetter, John
CLASS ACT
Hotchkiss, Jerry
FOLKS!
Hotton, Donald
BODYGUARD, THE
RAMPAGE
RUNESTONE, THE
Houde, Serge
MANIAC WARRIORS
Hough, Christine
CUTTING EDGE, THE
Hounslow, David
LONDON KILLS ME
Houpt, Emily
ARTICLE 99
House, Felicia
LEAP OF FAITH
Houser, Jerry
ALADDIN
Houston, Barbara
ARTICLE 99
Houston, Gary
HOFFA
Houston, Whitney
BODYGUARD, THE
Hove, Anders
CRITTERS 4
Hoversten, William
HELLROLLER
Howard, Arliss
CRISSCROSS
RUBY
Howard, Clint
FAR AND AWAY
Howard, D.J.
RAPID FIRE
Howard, Jean Speegle
I DON'T BUY KISSES ANYMORE
Howard, Jeffrey
SIMPLE MEN
Howard, Joe
MIGHTY DUCKS, THE
Howard, Miki
MALCOLM X
Howard, Neil
DAUGHTERS OF THE DUST
Howard, Oona
AFRAID OF THE DARK
Howard, Rance
FAR AND AWAY
I DON'T BUY KISSES ANYMORE
UNIVERSAL SOLDIER
Howard, Rikki
SPLIT SECOND
Howard, Ron
MAGICAL WORLD OF CHUCK JONES, THE
Howard, Sharon
CROSSING THE BRIDGE
Howard, Vincent
LETHAL WEAPON 3
Howarth, Ken
SWOON
Howe, John T.
TRACES OF RED

Howe, Kevin Barry
FOLKS!
Howell, C. Thomas
BREAKING THE RULES
NICKEL & DIME
TO PROTECT AND SERVE
Howell, Donna
WHITE MEN CAN'T JUMP
Howell, Hoke
FAR AND AWAY
Howell, Jeffrey
HOFFA
Howell, Ryan
LEAGUE OF THEIR OWN, A
MAMBO KINGS, THE
Howerton, Charles
CHAPLIN
Howze, Zakee
MALCOLM X
Hoy, Judy
UNLAWFUL ENTRY
Hoyt, Verne F.
SWOON
Hozumi, Takanobu
MR. BASEBALL
Huang Lei
LIFE ON A STRING
Hubbard, Dana
MALCOLM X
Huber, Bobby
FAR AND AWAY
Huber, Lotti
AFFENGEIL
Hubert, Ared
BECOMING COLETTE
Hubley, Whip
DESIRE AND HELL AT SUNSET MOTEL
Huck, Jon
TWIN PEAKS: FIRE WALK WITH ME
Huckabee, Cooper
LOVE FIELD
Huckaby, Rondel
PURE COUNTRY
Huddleston, Michael
BAD CHANNELS
Hudlin, Reginald
BOOMERANG
Hudlin, Warrington
BOOMERANG
Hudson, Ernie
COLLISION COURSE
HAND THAT ROCKS THE CRADLE, THE
Hudson, Larry
HIGHWAY 61
Hudson, Peter
PRELUDE TO A KISS
Hues, Matthias
BLACKBELT
I DON'T BUY KISSES ANYMORE
MISSION OF JUSTICE
TALONS OF THE EAGLE
Huff, Brent
FALLING FROM GRACE
Huff, Michael
LIGHT IN THE JUNGLE, THE

Huffman, Cady
HERO

Huffman, Dominic
HOMICIDAL IMPULSE

Huffman, Kymberley
PROJECT: SHADOWCHASER

Huffman, Rosanna
DISTINGUISHED GENTLEMAN, THE
FERNGULLY: THE LAST RAINFOREST

Hufsey, Billy
ROUND TRIP TO HEAVEN

Huggett, Bruce
MANIAC WARRIORS

Hughes, Cyreio
MISSISSIPPI MASALA

Hughes, Doug
BEAUTIFUL DREAMERS

Hughes, Frank
HAPPY HELL NIGHT

Hughes, Franke
MY NEW GUN

Hughes, Heather
SINGLES

Hughes, Howard
CHAPLIN

Hughes, Kenneth
DEATH BECOMES HER

Hughes, Megan
ADVENTURES IN DINOSAUR CITY

Hughes, Suzan
I DON'T BUY KISSES ANYMORE

Hughes, Tony
UNDER SUSPICION

Hughes, Wendy
WILD ORCHID 2: TWO SHADES OF BLUE

Hugot, Marceline
BED & BREAKFAST

Hulin, Dominique
DOES THIS MEAN WE'RE MARRIED?

Hull, David
PUBLIC EYE, THE

Hulst, Kees
LILY WAS HERE

Humann, Helena
LOVE HURTS

Humes, Dyan
MALCOLM X

Humphrey, Janet
BRIEF HISTORY OF TIME, A

Humphrey, Marcus
DAUGHTERS OF THE DUST

Humphrey, Senator Gordon
DAMNED IN THE USA

Hunt, Bonnie
BEETHOVEN

Hunt, Helen
BOB ROBERTS
MR. SATURDAY NIGHT
ONLY YOU
TRANCERS III: DETH LIVES
WATERDANCE, THE

Hunt, William Dennis
CHAPLIN
DR. GIGGLES

Hunter, Chris
CHRISTOPHER COLUMBUS: THE DISCOVERY

Hunter, Michael
WATERLAND

Hunter, Tab
DARK HORSE

Huppert, Joe
BABE, THE

Hurd, Larry
BASKET CASE 3: THE PROGENY

Hurle, Agatha
POWER OF ONE, THE

Hurley, Elizabeth
KILL CRUISE
PASSENGER 57

Hurley, Eric A.
LAST OF THE MOHICANS, THE

Hurley, Melissa
SHAKES THE CLOWN

Hurt, Mary Beth
LIGHT SLEEPER

Hussey, Paul
PRELUDE TO A KISS

Huston, Anjelica
PLAYER, THE

Huston, Esther
LOVE POTION NO. 9

Huston, Marques
BEBE'S KIDS

Hutchinson, Harry
BABE, THE
HOME ALONE 2: LOST IN NEW YORK

Hutchinson, Sam
USED PEOPLE

Hutchinson, Tim
MALCOLM X

Hutchison, Doug
LAWNMOWER MAN, THE

Hutchison, Lindsey
FROZEN ASSETS

Hutson, Candy
DOLLY DEAREST

Hutt, Brendan
BABE, THE

Huttleston, Douglas
SAVAGE INSTINCT

Hutton, Betty
WISECRACKS

Hutton, Lauren
GUILTY AS CHARGED

Hutton, Matthew
LITTLE NOISES

Huynh, Jean-Baptiste
INDOCHINE

Hway, Tracy
SNAKEEATER III . . . HIS LAW

Hyde, Gillian
FLIRTING

Hyde, Shelia
SPLIT SECOND

Hyman, Charles
BEASTMASTER 2: THROUGH THE PORTAL OF TIME

Hyman, Fracaswell
MALCOLM X

Hyman, Joan
RADIO FLYER

Hystad, Bruce
MANIAC WARRIORS

Hystad, Jeff
MANIAC WARRIORS

Hytower, Roy
BABE, THE

Iacangelo, Peter
WE'RE TALKIN' SERIOUS MONEY

Iams, Beep
BABE, THE

Iarve, Antonio
INSIDE EDGE

Ibrahim, El Tahara
MALCOLM X

Ice Cube
TRESPASS

Ice-T
TRESPASS

Ida, Toshikatsu
MR. BASEBALL

Idelbird, Monique
WATERLAND

Idle, Eric
MOM AND DAD SAVE THE WORLD

Ifrane, Claire
INSPECTOR LAVARDIN

Iftekhar
CITY OF JOY

Igberg, Ian
WELCOME TO OBLIVION

Ignon, Sandy
MAN TROUBLE

Iguchi, Yoshiaki
JOURNEY OF HONOR

Ike
INNOCENT BLOOD

Ikegami, Shogo
JOURNEY OF HONOR

Iley, Barbara
BEBE'S KIDS

Ilkanipour, Zahra
LORENZO'S OIL

Illouz, Albert
HUMAN SHIELD, THE

Imai, Yoshimi
MR. BASEBALL

Iman
LINGUINI INCIDENT, THE

Imershein, Deirdre
BLACKBELT

Imhoff, Gerarde
MAXIMUM BREAKOUT

Imperial, Lee
FROZEN ASSETS

Imperioli, Angela Conti
JOHNNY STECCHINO

Imperioli, Michael
MALCOLM X

Ingersoll, Matt
MAN TROUBLE

Inghram, Doran
STEELE'S LAW

Ingle, John
DEATH BECOMES HER

Ingolglia, Anthony
LAWS OF GRAVITY

Ingram, Aaron
WHO SHOT PATAKANGO?

Ingram, Doran
LOVE HURTS

Ingram, Mark
BABE, THE

Ingravallo, Diviana
STEAL AMERICA

Innes, Alexandra
CANVAS

Inoue, Yuji
MR. BASEBALL

Inwood, Steve
HUMAN SHIELD, THE

Iorg, Jason
FOREVER YOUNG

Ireland, John
WAXWORK II: LOST IN TIME

Ireland, Kathy
MOM AND DAD SAVE THE WORLD
PLAYER, THE

Irizarry, Ralph
MAMBO KINGS, THE

Irons, Jeremy
DAMAGE
WATERLAND

Ironside, Michael
BLACK ICE
CAFE ROMEO
COMMON BONDS
KILLER IMAGE
NEON CITY
VAGRANT, THE

Irvin, Barbara
FROZEN ASSETS

Irvin, Michael
NEWSIES

Isaac, John
MANIAC WARRIORS

Isaacs, Barbara
IMPORTANCE OF BEING EARNEST, THE

Isaak, Chris
TWIN PEAKS: FIRE WALK WITH ME

Isabel, Margarita
DANZON

Isenegger, Nadine
BOB ROBERTS

Isfeld, Justin
LORENZO'S OIL

Isham, Christopher
BRIEF HISTORY OF TIME, A

Ishibashi, Renji
TETSUO: THE IRON MAN

Ishida, Jim
COLD HEAVEN

Issyanov, Ravil
BACK IN THE U.S.S.R.

Ito, Takao
MR. BASEBALL

Itoh, Yasunori
MR. BASEBALL

Ittmann, Sara
WATERLAND

Ivanek, Zeljko
SCHOOL TIES

Ivanov, Russlan
RASPAD

Ivar, Stan
ROCK-A-DOODLE

Ivey, Dana
HOME ALONE 2: LOST IN NEW YORK

Ivey, Edith
LOVE POTION NO. 9

Ivey, Judith
LOVE HURTS

Ivey, Lela
I DON'T BUY KISSES ANYMORE

Ivgi, Moshe
CUP FINAL

Ivory, Edward
RAMPAGE

Ivy, Nigel
POWER OF ONE, THE

Izzard, Sheri
SISTER ACT

J., L.L. Cool
TOYS

Jabara, Paul
LIGHT SLEEPER

Jackee
LADYBUGS

Jackie
35 UP

Jacklin, Ian
BLACKBELT
FINAL IMPACT
KICKBOXER 3: THE ART OF WAR

Jackman, Kent
MALCOLM X

Jackson, Aaron
LORENZO'S OIL

Jackson, Anne
FOLKS!

Jackson, Baha
3 NINJAS

Jackson, Brian
PROJECT: SHADOWCHASER

Jackson, Cordell
GUN IN BETTY LOU'S HANDBAG, THE

Jackson, Desreta
SISTER ACT

Jackson, Gregory Paul
PATRIOT GAMES

Jackson, III, Clynell
SOUTH CENTRAL

Jackson, Javon
MALCOLM X
TEXAS TENOR: THE ILLINOIS JACQUET STORY

Jackson, Jesse
AMERICAN DREAM

Jackson, John M.
FEW GOOD MEN, A

Jackson, Joshua
MIGHTY DUCKS, THE

Jackson, Ken
RAMPAGE

Jackson, Kevin
HERO

Jackson, Kyle-Scott
ENCINO MAN

Jackson, Lamont
COOL WORLD

Jackson, Leonard
BOOMERANG

Jackson, Martaleah
MALCOLM X

Jackson, Nicholas Ward
YEAR OF THE COMET

Jackson, Robert
GUN IN BETTY LOU'S HANDBAG, THE

Jackson, Samuel L.
FATHERS AND SONS
JOHNNY SUEDE
JUICE
JUMPIN' AT THE BONEYARD
PATRIOT GAMES
WHITE SANDS

Jackson, Shari
BOB ROBERTS

Jackson, Sherry
DAUGHTERS OF THE DUST

Jackson, Sonia
DEATH BECOMES HER

Jackson, Stoney
BLIND VISION
MORTUARY ACADEMY
TRESPASS

Jackson, Tamaraleah
MALCOLM X

Jackson, Tarsha
LEAP OF FAITH

Jackson, Terry
BUFFY THE VAMPIRE SLAYER

Jackson, Tom
CLEARCUT

Jacobi, Lou
I DON'T BUY KISSES ANYMORE

Jacobs, Elkie
BLINK OF AN EYE

Jacobs, Marcia
VENICE/VENICE

Jacobs, Steven
FATHER

Jacobson, Joanne
FALLING FROM GRACE

Jacome, Ines
DANZON

Jacquet, Illinois
TEXAS TENOR: THE ILLINOIS JACQUET STORY

Jacquin, Caroline
FAVOUR, THE WATCH, AND THE VERY BIG FISH, THE

Jaeger, Elizabeth
BARBARIAN QUEEN II: THE EMPRESS STRIKES BACK

Jaeger, Monica
FATHER

Jaffe, Robert
HONEY, I BLEW UP THE KID

Jagger, Mick
FREEJACK

Jaglom, Henry
VENICE/VENICE
Jagora, Andrzej
NEAR MISSES
Jaguar, Zona
KUFFS
Jahme, Carole
CHAPLIN
Jake
GIVING, THE
Jalan, Chetna
CITY OF JOY
Jalan, Shyamanand
CITY OF JOY
James, Adam
UNDER SIEGE
James, Alan
HOWARDS END
James, Anthony
MORTUARY ACADEMY
UNFORGIVEN
James, Brion
OVER HER DEAD BODY
PLAYER, THE
ULTIMATE DESIRES
James, Cheryl
STAY TUNED
James, Dalton
ENCINO MAN
James, Debbie
MISTRESS
976-EVIL II
WHERE THE DAY TAKES YOU
James, Juliet
NIGHT RHYTHMS
James, Ken
LANDSLIDE
PSYCHIC
James, Kevin
WHITE TRASH
James, Laurel L.
MAN TROUBLE
James, Lawrence
MALCOLM X
James, Leslie
UNLAWFUL ENTRY
James, Michael Gaylord
UNDER SIEGE
James, Richard
CHAPLIN
James, Robert
HAND THAT ROCKS THE CRADLE, THE
James, Sondra
WHISPERS IN THE DARK
James, Stephen
MALCOLM X
PLAYER, THE
James, Tracy
VENICE/VENICE
James, Wheaton
WHITE TRASH
Jameson, Robin
FATAL INSTINCT
Jamieson, Todd
HAND THAT ROCKS THE CRADLE, THE
Jamison, Jack
CTHULHU MANSION
Jamshidi, Dr. Javad
RAMPAGE
Jandt, Randy
CLASS ACT
Janes, Tom
BUFFY THE VAMPIRE SLAYER
Janevski, Boban
DELICATESSEN
Janis, Conrad
MR. SATURDAY NIGHT
Jannot, Veronique
TOUCH AND DIE
Jansen, Jim
DEATH BECOMES HER
Janssen, Famke
FATHERS AND SONS
Jaquez, Robert
NEWSIES
Jaregard, Ernst-Hugo
BEST INTENTIONS, THE
ZENTROPA
Jaress, Jill
UNIVERSAL SOLDIER
Jarmusch, Jim
IN THE SOUP
Jarmusch, Tom
JOHNNY SUEDE
Jarret, Catherine
FINE ROMANCE, A
Jarrett, Paul
LEAVING NORMAL
Jarrett, Rollin
BODYGUARD, THE
Jarslow, Ruth
PASSED AWAY
Jason, Harvey
FERNGULLY: THE LAST RAINFOREST
Jason, Robert
MALCOLM X
Jay, Julie
POISON IVY
Jean-Baptiste, Marianne
LONDON KILLS ME
Jeavons, Colin
SECRET FRIENDS
Jefferson, Frank
ADJUSTER, THE
Jefferson, Mary
BLIND VISION
Jefferson, Michael
JUST LIKE IN THE MOVIES
Jefferson, Paris
ESCAPE FROM . . . SURVIVAL ZONE
Jeffery, Don
RIVER RUNS THROUGH IT, A
Jefford, Barbara
WHERE ANGELS FEAR TO TREAD
Jeffrey, Andy
EDWARD II
Jeffries, Deanne
WILD ORCHID 2: TWO SHADES OF BLUE
Jehan, Shah
K2
Jena, Chakradhar
CITY OF JOY
Jenesky, George
INSIDE EDGE
Jenkin, Devon
SLUMBER PARTY MASSACRE 3
Jenkins, Bernice
DAUGHTERS OF THE DUST
Jenkins, Chantelle
KILLER IMAGE
Jenkins, John
CUTTING EDGE, THE
Jenkins, Ken
CROSSING THE BRIDGE
Jenkins, Paul
SNEAKERS
Jenkins, Rebecca
BOB ROBERTS
CLEARCUT
Jenkins, Todd
NEWSIES
Jenner, Bruce
ORIGINAL INTENT
Jenner, David
HONEYMOON IN VEGAS
Jennings, Jenine
COOL WORLD
Jennings, Juanita
BASIC INSTINCT
Jennings, Patrice
SOCIETY
Jennings, Pitty
INNOCENT BLOOD
Jensen, Henning
ZENTROPA
Jensen, Rhonda
BOOMERANG
Jensen, Scott
CLASS ACT
Jensen, Steve
BABE, THE
Jenson, Jerry
CHAPLIN
Jenson, Sasha
BUFFY THE VAMPIRE SLAYER
Jerome, Timothy
HUSBANDS AND WIVES
Jessie Mae's Fife and Drum Band
DEEP BLUES
Jessop, Helen
LIGHT IN THE JUNGLE, THE
Jet Li
ONCE UPON A TIME IN CHINA
Jeter, Michael
JUST LIKE IN THE MOVIES
Jewell, Geri
WISECRACKS
Jewesbury, Edward
PETER'S FRIENDS
Jezek, Robert
PROJECT: SHADOWCHASER
Jhankal, Ravi
CITY OF JOY

Jimenez, Christina
INNOCENT BLOOD

Jimenez, Robert
SISTER ACT

Jiminez, Rigoberto
AMERICAN ME

Jin Shuyuan
RAISE THE RED LANTERN

Jinbo, Satoshi
MR. BASEBALL

Jo Rupp, Debra
DEATH BECOMES HER

Joachim, Suzy
ULTIMATE DESIRES

Jobson, Brian
PRELUDE TO A KISS

Jochim, Keith
COMPLEX WORLD

Jochmann, Hansi
SHINING THROUGH

Joe, Eddie
JUICE

Joffe, Mae
THANK YOU AND GOOD NIGHT!

Johansen, David
DESIRE AND HELL AT SUNSET MOTEL
FREEJACK

Johansson, Dan
BEST INTENTIONS, THE

Johansson, Paul
MARTIAL LAW 2: UNDERCOVER

John
35 UP

John, George
RAMPAGE

John, Joseph R.
UNDER SIEGE

John, Terry
UNDER SUSPICION

John-James, Maxine
PLAYER, THE

John-Jules, Danny
LONDON KILLS ME

Johns, Birl
MR. SATURDAY NIGHT

Johns, Stratford
DEMON IN MY VIEW, A

Johnson, "Big" Jack
DEEP BLUES

Johnson, A.J.
DOUBLE TROUBLE
SISTER ACT

Johnson, Alan
BABE, THE

Johnson, Arte
MUNCHIE

Johnson, Ben
RADIO FLYER

Johnson, Brother Paul
CRISSCROSS

Johnson, Cecily
RIVER RUNS THROUGH IT, A

Johnson, Clark
FINISHING TOUCH, THE
PSYCHIC

Johnson, Daniel
SINGLES

Johnson, Dave Alan
RAMPAGE

Johnson, Deborah
ENCINO MAN

Johnson, Dorothy D.
RAMPAGE

Johnson, Jerry
SAVAGE INSTINCT

Johnson, Jesse
INVASION OF THE SPACE PREACHERS

Johnson, Jim
RAISING CAIN

Johnson, John E.
THIS IS MY LIFE

Johnson, John M.
CAPTAIN AMERICA

Johnson, Julie
PURE COUNTRY

Johnson, Kathleen
MISTRESS

Johnson, Lamont
CLASS ACT

Johnson, Laura
FATAL INSTINCT

Johnson, Lilian
DAUGHTERS OF THE DUST

Johnson, Marques
WHITE MEN CAN'T JUMP

Johnson, Michelle
DEATH BECOMES HER
DR. GIGGLES
FAR AND AWAY

Johnson, Mike
BUFFY THE VAMPIRE SLAYER

Johnson, Miriam
CROSSING THE BRIDGE

Johnson, Nathaniel E.
NIGHT AND THE CITY

Johnson, Paula
OVER HER DEAD BODY

Johnson, Prudence
RIVER RUNS THROUGH IT, A

Johnson, Quentin
GIVING, THE

Johnson, Raymond
ESCAPE FROM . . . SURVIVAL ZONE

Johnson, Rick
FATAL INSTINCT
ORIGINAL INTENT

Johnson, Rion
MALCOLM X

Johnson, Ron
ZEBRAHEAD

Johnson, Sharria
DAUGHTERS OF THE DUST

Johnson, Steve
INNOCENT BLOOD

Johnson, Susan
SISTER ACT

Johnson, Vera
LEAGUE OF THEIR OWN, A

Johnstad, Scott
AMERICAN ME

Johnston, Andrew
LEAVING NORMAL

Johnston, Bobby
MAXIMUM BREAKOUT

Johnston, Matt
STOP! OR MY MOM WILL SHOOT

Johnston, Susan
SCHOOL TIES

Johnstone, Nahanni
CUTTING EDGE, THE

Jolly, Mike
SISTER ACT

Jones, Brett
MANIAC WARRIORS

Jones, Cherry
HOUSESITTER

Jones, Cheryl
LEAGUE OF THEIR OWN, A

Jones, Chuck
MAGICAL WORLD OF CHUCK JONES, THE

Jones, Clyde
DELTA HEAT

Jones, Dean
BEETHOVEN

Jones, Diane
ZEBRAHEAD

Jones, Doug
BATMAN RETURNS

Jones, Eddie
LEAGUE OF THEIR OWN, A
SNEAKERS

Jones, Frank
NIGHT AND THE CITY

Jones, Franklin
GLADIATOR

Jones, Freddie
CODE NAME: CHAOS

Jones, George Michael
HOUSESITTER

Jones, Glynis
FATHER

Jones, Grace
BOOMERANG

Jones, Henry
OVER HER DEAD BODY

Jones, Ishmond
LOVE FIELD

Jones, Isis Carmen
SISTER ACT

Jones, Jake-Ann
MALCOLM X

Jones, James Earl
PATRIOT GAMES
SCORCHERS
SNEAKERS

Jones, Jane
HAND THAT ROCKS THE CRADLE, THE
SINGLES
TWIN PEAKS: FIRE WALK WITH ME

Jones, Janet
LEAGUE OF THEIR OWN, A

Jones, Jeffrey
MOM AND DAD SAVE THE WORLD
OUT ON A LIMB
OVER HER DEAD BODY
STAY TUNED

Jones, Jenny
WISECRACKS

Jones, Joe
LOVE CRIMES

Jones, John Marshall
WHITE MEN CAN'T JUMP

Jones, John Steven
BAD LIEUTENANT

Jones, Jonah
TEXAS TENOR: THE ILLINOIS JACQUET STORY

Jones, Judd
MALCOLM X

Jones, Kenny
MY COUSIN VINNY

Jones, Larry
NEWSIES

Jones, Lauren
JUICE

Jones, Leilani
UNIVERSAL SOLDIER

Jones, Mal
FOLKS!

Jones, Marian
MAGICAL WORLD OF CHUCK JONES, THE

Jones, Mickey
BLACK ICE
OUT ON A LIMB

Jones, O-Lan
BEETHOVEN
WILDFIRE

Jones, Oran "Juice"
JUICE
MALCOLM X

Jones, Pearl
LOVE FIELD

Jones, Rachel
LORENZO'S OIL

Jones, Richard
UNDER SIEGE

Jones, Sam
NIGHT RHYTHMS
OTHER WOMAN, THE

Jones, Sam J.
IN GOLD WE TRUST
MAXIMUM FORCE

Jones, Sarah Lee
BUFFY THE VAMPIRE SLAYER

Jones, Steven A.
RADIO FLYER
RAMPAGE

Jones, Tom
COMPLEX WORLD

Jones, Tommy Lee
UNDER SIEGE

Jones, Walter
MALCOLM X

Jones, William Todd
MUPPET CHRISTMAS CAROL, THE

Jonsson, Gun
BEST INTENTIONS, THE

Jordal, Helge
OX, THE

Jordan, Cline
WHO SHOT PATAKANGO?

Jordan, Edward
POWER OF ONE, THE

Jordan, Leslie
HERO

Jordan, Oscar
FEW GOOD MEN, A

Jordan, Richard
HEAVEN IS A PLAYGROUND
PRIMARY MOTIVE

Jordan, Steve
CTHULHU MANSION

Jordan, Will
MR. SATURDAY NIGHT

Jorgensen, Luke
SCHOOL TIES

Joseph, Allan R.J.
THUNDERHEART

Josephson, Erland
OX, THE

Josephson, Jeffrey
JENNIFER EIGHT

Joshua, Larry
MIDNIGHT CLEAR, A

Joshua, Michael
FATHER

Jourdan, Louis
YEAR OF THE COMET

Jovet, Carmen
BRENDA STARR

Jovovich, Milla
CHAPLIN
KUFFS

Joy, Jeff
SNEAKERS

Joy, Mark
LAST OF THE MOHICANS, THE

Joy, Robert
SHADOWS AND FOG

Joyce, Christine
GUN IN BETTY LOU'S HANDBAG, THE

Joyce, Ella
STOP! OR MY MOM WILL SHOOT

Joyce, Jon
DEATH BECOMES HER

Joyner, Michelle
TRACES OF RED

Judd, Ashley
KUFFS

Judd, John
HOFFA

Judd, Thomas
FALLING FROM GRACE

Jude, Patrick
RUBY

Judge, Brian
LIGHT SLEEPER

Judge, Tony
STRAIGHT TALK

Julian, Janet
HEAVEN IS A PLAYGROUND

Julien, Isaac
DADDY AND THE MUSCLE ACADEMY

Junior, Gracindo
KICKBOXER 3: THE ART OF WAR

Jurige, Joan
BATMAN RETURNS

Jurkowski, Bernadette
LIGHT SLEEPER

Just, Andrew
NETHERWORLD

Ka, Ali
K2

Kabillio, Eli
LAWS OF GRAVITY

Kablan, Therese
ENCINO MAN

Kafri, Erza
POUR SACHA

Kagan, Elaine
INNOCENT BLOOD

Kagemaya, Rodney
PRAYER OF THE ROLLERBOYS

Kagimoto, Shinya
MR. BASEBALL

Kahan, Stephen
LETHAL WEAPON 3
RADIO FLYER

Kahane, Meir
DOUBLE EDGE

Kahler, Wolf
SHINING THROUGH

Kahn, Karen
RAISING CAIN

Kahn, Shanti
CAPTAIN RON

Kain, Khalil
JUICE

Kaiser, Joel
DEAD CERTAIN

Kaitan, Elizabeth
HELLROLLER

Kaketa, Makoto
MR. BASEBALL

Kal, Harris
BABE, THE

Kalem, Toni
SISTER ACT

Kalember, Patricia
BIG GIRLS DON'T CRY . . . THEY GET EVEN

Kalfa, Steve
BEATING HEART, A

Kalfon, Jean-Pierre
CRY OF THE OWL, THE

Kalianiotes, Helena
BACKTRACK

Kalmenson, Bill
RUNESTONE, THE

Kalos, Peter
MISTRESS

Kamekona, Danny
HONEYMOON IN VEGAS

Kamin, Daniel Tucker
BODYGUARD, THE
TRACES OF RED

Kaminin, Mikhail
DANZON

Kamoun, Samir
BIG GIRLS DON'T CRY . . . THEY GET EVEN

Kamp, Wendy
BECOMING COLETTE

Kanai, Mamoru
HONEY, I BLEW UP THE KID

Kanaly, Steve
DOUBLE TROUBLE
EYE OF THE EAGLE 3

Kanaoka, Nobu
TETSUO: THE IRON MAN

Kane, Alden
PROM NIGHT IV - DELIVER US FROM EVIL

Kane, Billy
WAXWORK II: LOST IN TIME

Kane, Billy Charles
POISON IVY

Kane, Carol
IN THE SOUP

Kane, Holly
FROZEN ASSETS

Kane, Ivan
PATRIOT GAMES

Kane, Jayson
CHAPLIN

Kanealii, Koko
HONEYMOON IN VEGAS

Kaneda, Ryunosuke
GODZILLA VS. BIOLLANTE

Kanemori, Aimee
HAND THAT ROCKS THE CRADLE, THE

Kani, John
SARAFINA!

Kaniel, Noam
ROUND TRIP TO HEAVEN

Kanter, Hal
COLOR ADJUSTMENT

Kapelos, John
MAN TROUBLE
WE'RE TALKIN' SERIOUS MONEY

Kaplan, Irving
HUMAN SHIELD, THE

Kaplan, Marty
DISTINGUISHED GENTLEMAN, THE

Kaplan, Mike E.
PLAYER, THE

Kapture, Mitzi
VAGRANT, THE

Karim, Abdul
K2

Kariya, Nobuyuki
MR. BASEBALL

Karlovitz, Katie
PASSED AWAY

Karr, Sara Rose
BEETHOVEN

Karsian, Tara
SINGLE WHITE FEMALE

Kartalian, Buck
BIG GIRLS DON'T CRY . . . THEY GET EVEN

Karyo, Tcheky
1492: THE CONQUEST OF PARADISE
HUSBANDS AND LOVERS

Kastner, Daphna
VENICE/VENICE

Kastner, Shelley
MY FATHER IS COMING

Kasyanov, Andrei
ADAM'S RIB

Katarina, Anna
BATMAN RETURNS

Kates, Bernard
BABE, THE
SEEDPEOPLE

Katsulas, Andreas
BLAME IT ON THE BELLBOY

Katt, Nicky
SISTER ACT

Katt, William
HOUSE IV
NAKED OBSESSION

Katusa, Judranka
CAPTAIN AMERICA

Katz, Omri
ADVENTURES IN DINOSAUR CITY

Kauders, Sylvia
THIS IS MY LIFE

Kauffman, Kristine
SOCIETY

Kaufmann, Eugene
MR. SATURDAY NIGHT

Kaufmann, Noel
NIGHT ON EARTH

Kausen, Valerie
MAGICAL WORLD OF CHUCK JONES, THE

Kavanagh, Christine
MONKEY BOY

Kavner, Julie
SHADOWS AND FOG
THIS IS MY LIFE

Kawahara, Takashi
ROAD TO RUIN

Kay, Brian
LOVE FIELD

Kay, Stephen T.
LETHAL WEAPON 3

Kay, Una
SNAKEEATER III . . . HIS LAW

Kaye, Christine
MAXIMUM BREAKOUT

Kaye, Jesse
MIND, BODY & SOUL

Kaye, Linda
RESERVOIR DOGS

Kazan, Lainie
I DON'T BUY KISSES ANYMORE

Kazurinsky, Tim
SHAKES THE CLOWN

Ke Quan, Jonathan
BREATHING FIRE

Keating, Charles
BODYGUARD, THE

Keating, Colom
CONFESSIONS OF A SERIAL KILLER

Keaton, Michael
BATMAN RETURNS

Keator, Steve
LAST OF THE MOHICANS, THE

Keats, Ele
NEWSIES

Kee, Thomas Rhett
SCHOOL TIES

Keegan, Martin L.
MAXIMUM BREAKOUT

Keener, Catherine
BACKTRACK
GUN IN BETTY LOU'S HANDBAG, THE
JOHNNY SUEDE

Kehler, Jack
WHITE SANDS

Kehr, Donnie
CHAPLIN

Keidar, Avi
BLINK OF AN EYE
HUMAN SHIELD, THE

Keinanen, Ismo
MATCH FACTORY GIRL, THE

Keitel, Harvey
BAD LIEUTENANT
RESERVOIR DOGS
SISTER ACT

Keitel, Stella
BAD LIEUTENANT

Keith, David
CAGED FEAR

Keith, Robert
WILD ORCHID 2: TWO SHADES OF BLUE

Kelleher, Tim
MALCOLM X

Kellerman, Sally
PLAYER, THE

Kellermann, Susan
DEATH BECOMES HER

Kelley, Jay
GUYVER, THE

Kelley, Michael
MISTRESS

Kelley, Sheila
PASSION FISH
SINGLES

Kellman, Barnet
STRAIGHT TALK

Kells, Ken
BABE, THE

Kelly, Brendan
MALCOLM X

Kelly, Daren
LOVE HURTS

Kelly, David Patrick
MALCOLM X

Kelly, Dennis
COLD HEAVEN
SHAKING THE TREE

Kelly, George
NETHERWORLD

Kelly, Glenda Starr
CANDYMAN

Kelly, Iain
HOWARDS END

Kelly, Michael Francis
PATRIOT GAMES

Kelly, Moira
CHAPLIN
CUTTING EDGE, THE
TWIN PEAKS: FIRE WALK WITH ME
Kelly, Reade
MALCOLM X
Kelly, William
MANIAC WARRIORS
Kemble, Mark
NETHERWORLD
Kemler, Elizabeth
FAR AND AWAY
Kemp, Bill
GAS FOOD LODGING
Kemp, Elizabeth
VENICE/VENICE
Kemp, Gary
BODYGUARD, THE
Kemp, La Dale
LEAP OF FAITH
Kemp, Martin
WAXWORK II: LOST IN TIME
Kendall, Jo
HOWARDS END
Kendall, Michael
BABE, THE
Kendall, Rex
RIVER RUNS THROUGH IT, A
Kendrick, Florina
BRAM STOKER'S DRACULA
Kenedy, Karen
BEAUTIFUL DREAMERS
Kennedy, Dev
HERO
Kennedy, George
HIRED TO KILL
Kennedy, Mike A.
PURE COUNTRY
Kennedy, Mimi
DEATH BECOMES HER
Kenner, Jacob
BEETHOVEN
Kenny, Tom
SHAKES THE CLOWN
Kensei, Ken
WIND
Kensit, Patsy
BLAME IT ON THE BELLBOY
DOES THIS MEAN WE'RE MARRIED?
KILL CRUISE
Kent, Elizabeth
MINDWARP
Kent, Sean
SCHOOL TIES
Kent, Suzanne
GUN IN BETTY LOU'S HANDBAG, THE
HONEY, I BLEW UP THE KID
Kent-Smith, Gregg
NEWSIES
Keogh, Jimmy
FAR AND AWAY
PLAYBOYS, THE
Keosian, Jessie
PASSED AWAY
Kepper, Will
RAPID FIRE
Ker, Edith
DELICATESSEN
Kerbrat, Patrice
CRY OF THE OWL, THE
Kerlow, Max
CABEZA DE VACA
Kerman, Ken
WHERE THE DAY TAKES YOU
Kerr, Herb
BOOMERANG
Kerr, Scott
LOVE CRIMES
TERMINAL BLISS
Kerrey, Bob
FEED
Kerrigan, Ed
MAN TROUBLE
Kerwin, Brian
CODE NAME: CHAOS
HARD PROMISES
LOVE FIELD
Kesa, Ivan
TILL THERE WAS YOU
Kesner, Jillian
ROOTS OF EVIL
Kesreau, Krista
BREAKING THE RULES
Kester, Oliver
LONDON KILLS ME
Kesting, Hans
LILY WAS HERE
Ketchum, Orville
SORORITY HOUSE MASSACRE 2
Keyes, Erwin
GUILTY AS CHARGED
Keyworth, Ben
AFRAID OF THE DARK
Khabo, David
POWER OF ONE, THE
Khambule, Thapi "Joko"
SARAFINA!
Khan, Ali
K2
Khan, Asghar
K2
Khan, Imran Badsah
CITY OF JOY
Khan, Namir
HIGHWAY 61
Khanjian, Arsinee
ADJUSTER, THE
Khouri, Makram
DOUBLE EDGE
Khumalo, Leleti
SARAFINA!
Khumalo, Mabonga
SARAFINA!
Khumalo, Sonto
SARAFINA!
Kiblinger, Jill
GLADIATOR
Kidman, Nicole
FAR AND AWAY
FLIRTING
Kidnie, James
GATE II
Kiefer, Laurel Lee
ALL THE VERMEERS IN NEW YORK
Kieferle, Kirsten
CUTTING EDGE, THE
Kieffer, Roy
PURE COUNTRY
Kier, Udo
ZENTROPA
Kildow, Kevin
GIVING, THE
Kilgour, Melanie
MANIAC WARRIORS
Killerby, David
WELCOME TO OBLIVION
Killian, Robyn
ROUND TRIP TO HEAVEN
Killpack, Denise
BATMAN RETURNS
Kilmer, Val
THUNDERHEART
Kilpack, Anne
WATERLAND
Kilson, William E.
MALCOLM X
Kim, Bobby
KILL LINE
Kim, Jacqueline
MIGHTY DUCKS, THE
Kim, Peter
MR. SATURDAY NIGHT
Kim, Robert
HONEYMOON IN VEGAS
Kimball, David A.
RAMPAGE
Kimberly, Lord
BLACKBELT
Kimble, Bo
HEAVEN IS A PLAYGROUND
Kimbrough, Junior
DEEP BLUES
Kincare, Martha
GIVING, THE
Kind, Richard
ALL-AMERICAN MURDER
MR. SATURDAY NIGHT
Kinder, Sandra
TWIN PEAKS: FIRE WALK WITH ME
Kinevane, Pat
FAR AND AWAY
King, Alan
NIGHT AND THE CITY
King, Basil
BRIEF HISTORY OF TIME, A
King, Debra
MANIAC WARRIORS
King, E.P.
HONEYMOON IN VEGAS
King, Freemon
TO PROTECT AND SERVE
King, Karrie
BRIDE OF KILLER NERD
King, Linda
BOB ROBERTS

King, Lorelei
SHINING THROUGH
King, Lynn
ARTICLE 99
King, Rowena
LONDON KILLS ME
King, Stephen
STEPHEN KING'S SLEEPWALKERS
King, Steve
BABE, THE
King, Tanner
BABE, THE
King, Towanna
BODYGUARD, THE
King, Wendy
MALCOLM X
King, William
MO' MONEY
Kingdon, Richard
BABE, THE
Kingi, Henri
BATMAN RETURNS
Kingi, Henry
LETHAL WEAPON 3
Kingsley, Ben
CHILDREN, THE
FREDDIE AS F.R.O.7
SNEAKERS
Kingsley, Rand
3 NINJAS
Kinmont, Kathleen
FINAL IMPACT
Kinney, Michael
SNEAKERS
Kinney, Terry
LAST OF THE MOHICANS, THE
Kino, Jacob
EFFICIENCY EXPERT, THE
Kinsey, Lance
HERO
Kirby, Leonard
CHAPLIN
Kirby, Michael
SHADOWS AND FOG
SWOON
Kirby, Randy
FROZEN ASSETS
Kirchlechner, Dieter
VOYAGER
Kirchner, Larry
ARTICLE 99
Kirk, Renton
MALCOLM X
Kirkland, Sally
IN THE HEAT OF PASSION
PLAYER, THE
PRIMARY MOTIVE
Kirkpatrick, Amy
STOP! OR MY MOM WILL SHOOT
Kirkwood, Gene
NIGHT AND THE CITY
Kiser, Margot
RIVER RUNS THROUGH IT, A
Kiser, Terry
INTO THE SUN

Kislan, Andrea
SWOON
Kissel, Steven
CROSSING THE BRIDGE
Kissinger, Connie
HONEYMOON IN VEGAS
Kissling, Markus
SHINING THROUGH
Kitchen, Michael
ENCHANTED APRIL
Kitt, Eartha
BOOMERANG
Kivel, Barry
MEMOIRS OF AN INVISIBLE MAN
Kiyokawa, Nijiko
JOURNEY OF HONOR
Kizziee, Eric
WHITE MEN CAN'T JUMP
Kjellman, Bjorn
BEST INTENTIONS, THE
Klar, Nick
NEON CITY
Klarwein, Eleonore
ROAD TO RUIN
Klastorin, Michael E.
LETHAL WEAPON 3
Klausmeyer, Charles
CAN IT BE LOVE
Klein, Dani
JUST LIKE IN THE MOVIES
Klein, Jill C.
DEATH BECOMES HER
Klein, Spencer
I DON'T BUY KISSES ANYMORE
Kleiser, Jeff
LIFE ON THE EDGE
Klemash, Christian
AMERICAN ME
Klemme, Brenda
PATRIOT GAMES
Klimek, Joe
COMPLEX WORLD
Kline, Jeff
HERO
Kline, Kevin
CHAPLIN
CONSENTING ADULTS
Klineberg, Adam
LETHAL WEAPON 3
Kling, Heidi
MIGHTY DUCKS, THE
OUT ON A LIMB
Klinkowski, Kenneth
HELLROLLER
Klitou, Damien
I DON'T BUY KISSES ANYMORE
Klobucar, Drago
CAPTAIN AMERICA
Kloster, Carlos
FAVOUR, THE WATCH, AND THE VERY BIG FISH, THE
Klug, Mary
HOUSESITTER
Kluppel, Christoph
IN GOLD WE TRUST

Knaff, Kenneth
DEATH BECOMES HER
Knepper, Robert
GAS FOOD LODGING
WHERE THE DAY TAKES YOU
Knickerbocker, Will
FOLKS!
TRACES OF RED
Knierim, Anna Marie
HOFFA
Knight, Burton
LOVE HURTS
Knight, David
WHO SHOT PATAKANGO?
Knight, Jeff
TUNE, THE
Knight, Marvette
CROSSING THE BRIDGE
Knight, Robin
LEAGUE OF THEIR OWN, A
Knight, Rosalind
AFRAID OF THE DARK
Knight, Tuesday
MISTRESS
Knight, Wayne
BASIC INSTINCT
Knox, Mark "Flex"
JUICE
Knudsen, Robert
RAMPAGE
Kobart, Ruth
SISTER ACT
Kober, Marta
SLUMBER PARTY MASSACRE 3
Koch, Geoff
MR. SATURDAY NIGHT
Koch, Jacquelyn K.
DEATH BECOMES HER
Koch, Pete
ADVENTURES IN DINOSAUR CITY
PLAYER, THE
Kochesmasova, Tatiana
RASPAD
Kocour, Michael
BABE, THE
Koepenick, Brad
DISTINGUISHED GENTLEMAN, THE
Koffler, Pamela
SWOON
Kofman, Jack
LIVING END, THE
Kohl, Terry
NEWSIES
Kohler, Anna
SWOON
Kohnert, Mary
MR. BASEBALL
Kokorian, Armen
ADJUSTER, THE
Kolban, Amir
DEADLY CURRENTS
Koldenhoven, Darlene
MAN TROUBLE
SISTER ACT
Koliacos, Victor
DIGGSTOWN

Kollberg, Barbro
BEST INTENTIONS, THE
Kollek, Amos
DOUBLE EDGE
Kollek, Teddy
DOUBLE EDGE
Kolodjl, Ronda
PUSHED TO THE LIMIT
Kolzow, Harve
GLADIATOR
Komorowska, Liliana
SCANNERS III: THE TAKEOVER
Koncovskii, Alexei
RASPAD
Kondratiuk, Victor
RASPAD
Kong Lin
RAISE THE RED LANTERN
Konig-Martinez, Tessa
FINAL ANALYSIS
Koo Kei-wah
SUPERCOP: POLICE STORY III
Kooker, Naomi
HOUSE ON TOMBSTONE HILL, THE
Kopelow, Michael S.
BUFFY THE VAMPIRE SLAYER
Kopita, Jay
CROSSING THE BRIDGE
Kopke, Edda
EMMANUELLE 6
Korbich, Eddie
JENNIFER EIGHT
Kosala, Joseph F.
UNDER SIEGE
Kosci, Kim Robert
BUFFY THE VAMPIRE SLAYER
Koslo, Paul
PROJECT: SHADOWCHASER
Kossin, Andy
OUT ON A LIMB
Kostiukovskii, Mikhail
RASPAD
Kosugi, Kane
JOURNEY OF HONOR
Kosugi, Sho
JOURNEY OF HONOR
Koteas, Elias
ADJUSTER, THE
Kotlisky, Marge
PUBLIC EYE, THE
Kovac, Mario
CAPTAIN AMERICA
Kovacs, Danny
OUT ON A LIMB
Kove, Martin
PROJECT: SHADOWCHASER
Kovens, Ed
BAD LIEUTENANT
Kozak, Heidi
SOCIETY
Kozlowski, Paul
SHAKES THE CLOWN
Krabbe, Jeroen
TILL THERE WAS YOU
Krag, James
CROSSING THE BRIDGE
Kraines, Carl
GATE II
Krainz, Dee
ROCK & ROLL COWBOYS
Krall, Daamen
BEBE'S KIDS
Kramer, Bert
LITTLE NEMO: ADVENTURES IN SLUMBERLAND
Kramer, David H.
WHISPERS IN THE DARK
Kramer, Jeremy S.
SHAKES THE CLOWN
Kramer, Joel
UNIVERSAL SOLDIER
Kramer, Lara
ZEBRAHEAD
Kramer, Stepfanie
TWIN SISTERS
Kramer, Steve
VAMPIRE HUNTER D
Krassner, J. David
STOP! OR MY MOM WILL SHOOT
Krause, Brian
STEPHEN KING'S SLEEPWALKERS
Krause, Fred
HOME ALONE 2: LOST IN NEW YORK
Kravitz, Steven
MR. SATURDAY NIGHT
Krawic, Michael
BABE, THE
Kreidl, Martina
RIVER RUNS THROUGH IT, A
Kreimer, Emily
WELCOME TO OBLIVION
Kressin, Lianne
LORENZO'S OIL
Kretschmann, Thomas
SHINING THROUGH
Kriegel, David
SEXUAL RESPONSE
SLUMBER PARTY MASSACRE 3
Krieger, David
WHITE TRASH
Krifa, Kamel
UNIVERSAL SOLDIER
Krige, Alice
CODE NAME: CHAOS
STEPHEN KING'S SLEEPWALKERS
Kristen, Ilene
JUST LIKE IN THE MOVIES
Kristian, Charles
RESURRECTED, THE
Kristofferson, Kris
ORIGINAL INTENT
Kristofic, Milan
CAPTAIN AMERICA
Kriz, Heidi
SWOON
Kroll, Jack
RIVER RUNS THROUGH IT, A
Krook, Margaretha
BEST INTENTIONS, THE
Krowka, Joe
LEAGUE OF THEIR OWN, A
Kruger, Gaye
VENICE/VENICE
Kruger, Kevin
NEWSIES
Krummel, Nicole
NETHERWORLD
Kryeger, Ken
MANIAC WARRIORS
Kubheka, Nomadlozi
POWER OF ONE, THE
Kubheka, Skhumbuzo
SARAFINA!
Kubo, Fumio
MR. BASEBALL
Kubota, Glenn
PASSED AWAY
Kuenning, Arnold
FAR AND AWAY
Kuga, Yoshiko
GODZILLA VS. BIOLLANTE
Kullman, Sophie
WHERE ANGELS FEAR TO TREAD
Kulu, Faca
SARAFINA!
Kunene, Sipho
SARAFINA!
Kunitomi, Darrell
OUT ON A LIMB
Kunkle, Eric
LORENZO'S OIL
Kuno, Makoto
MR. BASEBALL
Kunstler, William
MALCOLM X
Kuosmanen, Sakari
NIGHT ON EARTH
Kurcz, Robert
STRAIGHT TALK
Kurland, Jeffrey
HUSBANDS AND WIVES
Kurts, Alwyn
EFFICIENCY EXPERT, THE
Kurtz, Joyce
PROFESSIONAL, THE
VAMPIRE HUNTER D
Kussman, Dylan
JOURNEY OF HONOR
Kusumi, Shotaro
MR. BASEBALL
Kuter, Skay
LOVE FIELD
Kuznetcova, Olga
RASPAD
Kuznetsova, Larissa
CLOSE TO EDEN
Kvassay, Alex A.
HOFFA
Kwan Hoi-shan
HARD-BOILED
Kwan, Rosamund
ONCE UPON A TIME IN CHINA
Kwok, Philip
HARD-BOILED
Kwouk, Burt
SHOOTING ELIZABETH

Kyu Na
WATERDANCE, THE

La Nasa, Katherine
BACKTRACK

Laas, Sebastian
BECOMING COLETTE

Labarthe, Samuel
ELEGANT CRIMINEL, L'

LaBelle, Rob
MAN TROUBLE

LaBrecque, Patrick
BEETHOVEN

LaBrie, Ginger
MAN TROUBLE

Labrosse, Robert
NETHERWORLD

Labyorteaux, Patrick
GHOULIES III:
GHOULIES GO TO COLLEGE
3 NINJAS

LaCassa, Anthony "Primo"
GLADIATOR

Lacey, Deborah
DEMON IN MY VIEW, A

Lacey, Ronald
LANDSLIDE

Lachaumette, Andre
HOME ALONE 2:
LOST IN NEW YORK

Lack, Stephen
ALL THE VERMEERS IN NEW YORK

Lacour, Renee A
MO' MONEY

Lacoy, Michael
HELLROLLER

LaCroix, Lisa
PSYCHIC

Lacroix, Violaine
TOUS LES MATINS DU MONDE

Ladanyi, Andrea
GATE II

Ladd, Cheryl
POISON IVY

Ladd, Diane
CODE NAME: CHAOS

Ladd, Ken
LIGHT SLEEPER

Ladret, Doug
CUTTING EDGE, THE

Lafayette, John
ARTICLE 99
BEBE'S KIDS
PATRIOT GAMES
WHITE SANDS

Laffan, Pat
PLAYBOYS, THE

LaFitte, Tommy
PASSED AWAY

LaFlamme, Raymond
BRIEF HISTORY OF TIME, A

LaFleur, Art
FOREVER YOUNG
MR. BASEBALL
RAMPAGE

Lafleur, Paula
PASSION FISH

Lafont, Bernadette
INSPECTOR LAVARDIN

LaFore, Desiree
BLOOD ON THE BADGE

Lagergren, Ake
BEST INTENTIONS, THE

Lagerkvist, Cecilia
BEST INTENTIONS, THE

Laguna, Sylvie
DELICATESSEN
ROAD TO RUIN

Lahti, Christine
LEAVING NORMAL

Lahti, Gary
RUNESTONE, THE

Lail, Leah
BODY WAVES

Lair, Cindy
WILD ORCHID 2:
TWO SHADES OF BLUE

Laird, Monty
UNIVERSAL SOLDIER

Lake, Ricki
WHERE THE DAY TAKES YOU

Lakey, Kimberley
WATERLAND

Lally, Michael David
BASIC INSTINCT
COOL WORLD

Lam, Bowie
HARD-BOILED

Lamadore, Gary
SWOON

Lamal, Andre
MIDNIGHT CLEAR, A

LaMarche, Maurice
COOL WORLD

LaMarque, Kimberley
STOP! OR MY MOM WILL SHOOT

LaMarre, Jean
MALCOLM X

Lamas, Lorenzo
FINAL IMPACT
SNAKEEATER III . . . HIS LAW

Lamb, Peadar
FAR AND AWAY

Lambdin, Brandon
UNIVERSAL SOLDIER

Lambert, Del
MANIAC WARRIORS

Lambert, Lawrence
CHAPLIN

Lambert, Pam
ROADSIDE PROPHETS

Lambrecht, Yves
TOUS LES MATINS DU MONDE

Lambton, Anne
HOWARDS END

Lametrie, Lisa
VAN GOGH

Lamond, Andrew
PROJECT: SHADOWCHASER

Lamond, Gina
VENICE/VENICE

Lamore, Francois
CONTE DE PRINTEMPS

LaMorgia, Nicola
CANVAS

LaMotta, John
WE'RE TALKIN' SERIOUS MONEY

Lampert, Zohra
ALAN & NAOMI

Lamy, Maurice
DELICATESSEN

Lancaster, Stuart
BATMAN RETURNS

Lanceloti, Louie
SHAKING THE TREE

Lanciloti, Louie
PUBLIC EYE, THE

Landau, Juliet
NEON CITY

Landau, Martin
MISTRESS

Landero, Alejandro
BARBARIAN QUEEN II:
THE EMPRESS STRIKES BACK

Landers, Sandra
SCHOOL TIES

Landgre, Inga
BEST INTENTIONS, THE

Landham, Sonny
MAXIMUM FORCE

Landi, Sal
ROVER DANGERFIELD
SOUTH CENTRAL

Landis, Jim
LAWNMOWER MAN, THE

Landis, John
STEPHEN KING'S SLEEPWALKERS
VENICE/VENICE

Landon, Jr., Hal
TRESPASS

Landry, Charles
SCANNERS III: THE TAKEOVER

Landry, Michele
LETHAL WEAPON 3

Landry, Ryan
SWOON

Landsbury, David
GAS FOOD LODGING

Lane, Cameron
NIGHT AND THE CITY

Lane, Campbell
CAFE ROMEO

Lane, Diane
CHAPLIN
MY NEW GUN

Lane, Michele
FROZEN ASSETS

Lane, Paul M.
BUFFY THE VAMPIRE SLAYER

Lane, Shelby
PAMELA PRINCIPLE, THE

Lang, Althea
DAUGHTERS OF THE DUST

Lang, Perry
JENNIFER EIGHT
LITTLE VEGAS
MORTUARY ACADEMY

Lang, Stephanie
BOB ROBERTS

Lang, Walter
AUNTIE LEE'S MEAT PIES
Langdon, Jennifer
CAN IT BE LOVE
Lange, Anne
SHADOWS AND FOG
Lange, Jessica
NIGHT AND THE CITY
Langella, Frank
1492: THE CONQUEST OF PARADISE
Langlais, Gerard
CHRISTOPHER COLUMBUS: THE DISCOVERY
Langlois, Genevieve
USED PEOPLE
Langmann, Thomas
ALBERTO EXPRESS
NIGHT AND DAY
Langroek, Kate
FATHER
Langton, Chance
COMPLEX WORLD
Langton, Jeff
FINAL IMPACT
MAXIMUM FORCE
Lanigan, Peter
LIVING END, THE
Lanko, Vivian
SIMPLE MEN
Lansbury, David
SCENT OF A WOMAN
Lantz, John
MEGAVILLE
Lantz, Stu
WHITE MEN CAN'T JUMP
Lanza, Sergio
OTHER WOMAN, THE
Lanza, Suzanne
VENICE/VENICE
LaPage, Roger
WILD ORCHID 2: TWO SHADES OF BLUE
LaPaglia, Anthony
INNOCENT BLOOD
WHISPERS IN THE DARK
Lapiduss, Maxine
WISECRACKS
LaPier, Darcy
DOUBLE TROUBLE
Lapka, Myron L.
UNIVERSAL SOLDIER
LaPlante, Henry
RADIO FLYER
Laporte, Sylvie
FAVOUR, THE WATCH, AND THE VERY BIG FISH, THE
Lapuente, Carlos
PEPI, LUCI, BOM AND OTHER GIRLS ON THE HEAP
Larby, Ahmed Ben
JOHNNY SUEDE
Laresca, Vincent
BAD LIEUTENANT
JUICE
Larkin, Bryan
JENNIFER EIGHT
Larkin, Linda
ALADDIN
Laroque, Michele
HAIRDRESSER'S HUSBAND, THE
Larriva, Tito
DOUBLE TROUBLE
Larry
LIFE ON THE EDGE
Larsen, Cathy A.
MAN TROUBLE
Larsen, Lars Oluf
DAY IN OCTOBER, A
Larsen, Lisa
MANIAC WARRIORS
Larson, Darrell
HERO
Larson, David
NEWSIES
Larsson, Boel
BEST INTENTIONS, THE
Lartigau, Gerard
INDOCHINE
LaRue, Alecia
FAR AND AWAY
LaRue, Eva
GHOULIES III: GHOULIES GO TO COLLEGE
LaRusso, Vincent A.
MIGHTY DUCKS, THE
Lashly, James
OVER HER DEAD BODY
Laskin, Michael
I DON'T BUY KISSES ANYMORE
PASSION FISH
Lasorda, Tommy
LADYBUGS
Lassick, Sydney
DEEP COVER
MIRACLE BEACH
SHAKES THE CLOWN
SMOOTH TALKER
Lata, John
SARAFINA!
Lath, Ashok
MISSISSIPPI MASALA
Latham, Laurie
RESERVOIR DOGS
Latham, Louise
LOVE FIELD
Lathouris, Nic
FATHER
Latimer, Ian
HOWARDS END
Latter, Greg
SARAFINA!
Laughlin, John
LAWNMOWER MAN, THE
Lauper, Marcus
MALCOLM X
Laura, Joanne
FATAL INSTINCT
Laurance, Mitchell
HAND THAT ROCKS THE CRADLE, THE
RUNESTONE, THE
Lauren, Honey
BRAM STOKER'S DRACULA
Lauren, Tammy
CHAINS OF GOLD
Lauren, Veronica
FOREVER YOUNG
Laurence, Ashley
MIKEY
ONE LAST RUN
Laurence, Ronald William
RAPID FIRE
Lauricella, Tom
PUBLIC EYE, THE
Laurie, Hugh
PETER'S FRIENDS
Laurie, Piper
STORYVILLE
Laury, Booker T.
DEEP BLUES
Lauten, James M.
HONEY, I BLEW UP THE KID
Lauter, Ed
SCHOOL TIES
Lautner, Kathrin
FINAL IMPACT
SPIRITS
LaVar, Ellin
BODYGUARD, THE
Lavat, Jose
MEDICINE MAN
Lavelle, Bradley
WATERLAND
Lavie, Amos
BLINK OF AN EYE
LaVoie, Karen Denice
SINGLES
Law, Lisa
WILD WHEELS
Law, Phyllida
PETER'S FRIENDS
Lawrence, Bruno
EFFICIENCY EXPERT, THE
Lawrence, C'Esca
RAPID FIRE
Lawrence, Cary
CANVAS
Lawrence, David
SLUMBER PARTY MASSACRE 3
Lawrence, Harry
FLIRTING
Lawrence, Joey
CHAINS OF GOLD
Lawrence, Josie
ENCHANTED APRIL
Lawrence, Marc
NEWSIES
RUBY
Lawrence, Martin
BOOMERANG
Lawrence, Patricia
HOWARDS END
Lawrence, Ron
HONEY, I BLEW UP THE KID
Lawrence, Scott
RUBY
Lawrence, Steven
LONDON KILLS ME

Lennix, Harry J.
BOB ROBERTS
MO' MONEY
Lennon, Jarrett
HIGHWAY TO HELL
Lennon, Julian
LINGUINI INCIDENT, THE
Lennox, Annie
EDWARD II
Leno, Jay
COLLISION COURSE
Lentini, Susan
RUNESTONE, THE
Lenz, Cliff
HAND THAT ROCKS THE CRADLE, THE
Lenz, Kay
FALLING FROM GRACE
Leo, Melissa
VENICE/VENICE
Leol, Robert
SUNSET STRIP
Leon, Reggie
WHITE MEN CAN'T JUMP
Leonard, Jacqueline
CHAPLIN
Leonard, Lu
KUFFS
Leonard, Sean
WIND
Leonard, Sheldon
COLOR ADJUSTMENT
Leong, Al
RAPID FIRE
Leong, Darren
SOUTH CENTRAL
Leong, Willie
KUFFS
Leoni, Tea
LEAGUE OF THEIR OWN, A
Leppell, Jonathan J.
TWIN PEAKS: FIRE WALK WITH ME
Lerer, Joe
ARTICLE 99
Lerer, Shifra
STRANGER AMONG US, A
Lerner, Allen Michael
SOUTH CENTRAL
STOP! OR MY MOM WILL SHOOT
Lerner, Ken
UNLAWFUL ENTRY
Lerner, Michael
NEWSIES
Lerner, Neal
BATMAN RETURNS
LeRoy, Gloria
BODY WAVES
IN THE HEAT OF PASSION
Lesko, Ruth
BOB ROBERTS
PASSED AWAY
Lesley, Bradley Jay "Animal"
MR. BASEBALL
Leslie, Tina
HOWARDS END
Lessard, Bob
MANIAC WARRIORS
Lesseos, Louie
PUSHED TO THE LIMIT
Lesseos, Mimi
FINAL IMPACT
PUSHED TO THE LIMIT
Lesseos-Lypher, Eva
PUSHED TO THE LIMIT
Lester, Eleese
CONFESSIONS OF A SERIAL KILLER
Lester, Ken
MANIAC WARRIORS
Lester, Loren
PRAYER OF THE ROLLERBOYS
Letts, Dennis
PASSENGER 57
Letts, Tracy
STRAIGHT TALK
Leung, Tony
HARD-BOILED
LOVER, THE
Levasseur, Aline
UNFORGIVEN
Levels, Calvin
JOHNNY SUEDE
Levenstein, Janna
I DON'T BUY KISSES ANYMORE
Levi, Ro'ee
STRANGER AMONG US, A
Levien, Philip
PATRIOT GAMES
Levin, Stu
DISTINGUISHED GENTLEMAN, THE
Levine, Emily
WISECRACKS
Levingston, Henry
ARTICLE 99
Levinson, G.J.
HELLROLLER
Levinson, Sam
TOYS
Levisetti, Emile
SEXUAL RESPONSE
Levy, Anne
FAVOUR, THE WATCH, AND THE VERY BIG FISH, THE
Levy, Benjamin
DAY IN OCTOBER, A
Levy, Eugene
STAY TUNED
Levy, Geula
HUMAN SHIELD, THE
Levy, Gussie
MY NEW GUN
Levy, Lawrence
POISON IVY
Levy, Marc
LEAVING NORMAL
Levy, Matthew
UNLAWFUL ENTRY
Levy, Philip
HUSBANDS AND WIVES
WHISPERS IN THE DARK
Levy, Shuki
ROUND TRIP TO HEAVEN
Lew, James
DO OR DIE
Lewis, Al
MY GRANDPA IS A VAMPIRE
Lewis, Brittnew
RUBIN & ED
Lewis, Charlotte
STORYVILLE
Lewis, Clea
HERO
Lewis, Craig C.
BASIC INSTINCT
Lewis, Don
BRAM STOKER'S DRACULA
Lewis, Emma
CHAPLIN
Lewis, Fred
STORYVILLE
Lewis, Geoffrey
LAWNMOWER MAN, THE
Lewis, Gilbert
CANDYMAN
Lewis, Glean
DEATH BECOMES HER
Lewis, Howard "Lew"
CHAPLIN
Lewis, Jay
GIVING, THE
Lewis, Jeff
MY COUSIN VINNY
Lewis, Jenifer
FROZEN ASSETS
SISTER ACT
Lewis, Jenny
BIG GIRLS DON'T CRY . . . THEY GET EVEN
Lewis, Jerry
MR. SATURDAY NIGHT
Lewis, Joe
BLOODFIST III: FORCED TO FIGHT
Lewis, Joseph H.
LEATHER JACKETS
Lewis, Juliette
HUSBANDS AND WIVES
Lewis, Karen
CHAPLIN
Lewis, Keith
MALCOLM X
Lewis, Naomi
FERNGULLY: THE LAST RAINFOREST
Lewis, Phill
ACES: IRON EAGLE III
Lewis, Richard
ONCE UPON A CRIME
Lewis, Sheryl Mary
FROZEN ASSETS
Lewis, Thomas
SOCIETY
Lewy, Eric
GIVING, THE
Lexsee, Richar
GLADIATOR
Leybourne, Audrey
CHAPLIN
Leyton, Yvonne
CABEZA DE VACA

Leyva, Norma
DANZON
Li, Donald
MEMOIRS OF AN INVISIBLE MAN
RAPID FIRE
Licciardello, Elmer
MALCOLM X
Liddy, G. Gordon
ADVENTURES IN SPYING
Liebenson, Ken
BASIC INSTINCT
Lieberman, Rick
WATERDANCE, THE
Liebowitz, Barry
SWOON
Lierras, Anibal
LAWS OF GRAVITY
Lifford, Tina
BEBE'S KIDS
Lill, Dennis
BERNARD AND THE GENIE
Lilley, Clay
FAR AND AWAY
HARD PROMISES
Lilley, Clint
BUFFY THE VAMPIRE SLAYER
Lilley, Jack
HARD PROMISES
Lillie, Beatrice
WISECRACKS
Lilly, Brenda
RAMPAGE
Lilly, Sarah
GHOULIES III:
GHOULIES GO TO COLLEGE
Lin, Ben
MO' MONEY
NIGHT AND THE CITY
Lind, Roy
TERMINAL BLISS
Lind, Traci
VOYAGER
Lindeman, Susan
HOWARDS END
Linder, Emile
CTHULHU MANSION
Linder, Steve
COMPLEX WORLD
Lindfors, Viveca
EXILED IN AMERICA
LINGUINI INCIDENT, THE
Lindholm, Terry
NEWSIES
Lindo, Delroy
MALCOLM X
Lindo, Robert
PRELUDE TO A KISS
Lindsay, Josh
BEBE'S KIDS
Lindsey, Kent
PASSENGER 57
Lingenberg, Kira
BECOMING COLETTE
Lingley, Erika
BOB ROBERTS
Linh Dan-pham
INDOCHINE
Linn, Rex
THUNDERHEART
Linn, Susan Gale
RADIO FLYER
Linn-Baker, Mark
NOISES OFF
Linney, Laura
LORENZO'S OIL
Linthicum, Brooke
BABE, THE
Linville, Larry
BODY WAVES
Lionel, Evan
FOLKS!
Liotta, Ray
ARTICLE 99
UNLAWFUL ENTRY
Lip, Tony
INNOCENT BLOOD
Lipari, Joanna
HONEYMOON IN VEGAS
Lipovsek, Edita
CAPTAIN AMERICA
Lippin, Renee
THIS IS MY LIFE
Lipscomb, Dennis
UNDER SIEGE
Lipson, Brian
CHAPLIN
HOWARDS END
Lipton, Peggy
TWIN PEAKS: FIRE WALK WITH ME
Lipton, Robert
WOMAN, HER MEN AND HER
FUTON, A
Lira, Johnny
GLADIATOR
Lisenco, Michael
SCENT OF A WOMAN
Lish, Becca
COMPLEX WORLD
Lishner, Dan
MONTANA RUN, THE
Lisi, Joe
TRACES OF RED
Liss, Joe
HOME ALONE 2:
LOST IN NEW YORK
Lister, Jr., Tom "Tiny"
UNIVERSAL SOLDIER
Lister, Tiny
TRESPASS
Lithgow, John
RAISING CAIN
Litman, Ron
HELLROLLER
MAXIMUM BREAKOUT
Little, Chris
BEETHOVEN
Little, Ira
MALCOLM X
Little, Michelle
ARTICLE 99
Little, Rich
BEBE'S KIDS
Liu, Carolyn
DO OR DIE
Liu Zhongyuan
LIFE ON A STRING
Livane, Lisa
INSPECTOR LAVARDIN
Livans, Eric Ray
PROJECT: SHADOWCHASER
Lively, Ernie
PASSENGER 57
STEPHEN KING'S SLEEPWALKERS
STOP! OR MY MOM WILL SHOOT
Lively, Jason
MAXIMUM FORCE
Lively, Steve
MR. SATURDAY NIGHT
Livingston, Jo
LOVE HURTS
Livingston, Ron
STRAIGHT TALK
Lizarraga, Anna
AMERICAN ME
Ljoka, Linda
NETHERWORLD
Llewellyn, Roger
DAMAGE
Lloyd, Caleb
CHRISTOPHER COLUMBUS:
THE DISCOVERY
Lloyd, Emily
RIVER RUNS THROUGH IT, A
SCORCHERS
Lloyd, Lauren
BACKTRACK
Lloyd, May
CROSSING, THE
Lloyd, Norman
JOURNEY OF HONOR
Lloyd, Peter
PRELUDE TO A KISS
Lloyd-Breed, Helen
PASSED AWAY
Lo Lieh
SUPERCOP: POLICE STORY III
Lobell, Anna
HONEYMOON IN VEGAS
Locane, Amy
SCHOOL TIES
Locascio, James T.
NETHERWORLD
Lochran, Derek Mark
VAGRANT, THE
Locker, Phil
PUBLIC EYE, THE
Lockhart, Calvin
TWIN PEAKS: FIRE WALK WITH ME
Locklear, Heather
ILLUSIONS
Lockwood, Vera
ALADDIN
Lodge, Suzanne
MAN TROUBLE
Loeb, Caroline
FAVOUR, THE WATCH, AND THE
VERY BIG FISH, THE
Loeffler, Annie
LORENZO'S OIL
Loewen, Dale
MANIAC WARRIORS

Loffler, Gianin
LITTLE NOISES
Lofton, Cirroc
BEETHOVEN
Logan, Angela
BOOMERANG
Logan, Jason
CHAPLIN
Logan, Pat
BOB ROBERTS
Logan, Phyllis
FREDDIE AS F.R.O.7
Logan, Rick
MR. SATURDAY NIGHT
Logan, Ricky Dean
BUFFY THE VAMPIRE SLAYER
Logan, Tracye
BODYGUARD, THE
Loggia, Robert
CODE NAME: CHAOS
GLADIATOR
INNOCENT BLOOD
Logrono, Emannuel
CAPTAIN RON
Logue, Donal
SNEAKERS
Lohr, Aaron
NEWSIES
Lohr, Heidi
BRIDE OF KILLER NERD
Lom, Herbert
DEVIL'S DAUGHTER, THE
POPE MUST DIET!, THE
Lomas, Caroline
SOCIETY
Lombardo, Coleby
RADIO FLYER
Lombart, Daniel
FAVOUR, THE WATCH, AND THE VERY BIG FISH, THE
Londez, Guilaine
NIGHT AND DAY
Londner, Eitan
HUMAN SHIELD, THE
London, Alexandra
VAN GOGH
London, Roy
RAMPAGE
Long, Andrew
MANIAC WARRIORS
Long, Joseph
CHRISTOPHER COLUMBUS: THE DISCOVERY
Long, Mark
CHAPLIN
CHRISTOPHER COLUMBUS: THE DISCOVERY
Long, Shelley
FROZEN ASSETS
Longhi, Anna
ENCHANTED APRIL
Longinidus, Stan
BLOODFIST III: FORCED TO FIGHT
Longo, Tony
RAPID FIRE
UNLAWFUL ENTRY

Longwell, Anya
DEATH BECOMES HER
Longwell, Karen
WHISPERS IN THE DARK
Longworth, Adam
MANIAC WARRIORS
Lonow, Mark
MR. SATURDAY NIGHT
Lonsdale, Kim
HIRED TO KILL
Lonza, Tonko
CAPTAIN AMERICA
Loomis, Tim
SHADOWS AND FOG
Lopez, Eliseo
CAPTAIN RON
Lopez, Fredrick
WHITE SANDS
Lopez, Irene Olga
BASIC INSTINCT
Lopez, Kamala
DEEP COVER
EXILED IN AMERICA
Lopez, Lauro
MO' MONEY
Lopez, Sal
AMERICAN ME
COLD HEAVEN
Lopez, Santiago
CABEZA DE VACA
Lord, Lisa
CLASS ACT
Lords, Traci
LASER MOON
Lorenzo, Blas
WE'RE TALKIN' SERIOUS MONEY
Lorian, Owen
OVER HER DEAD BODY
Loriaux, Fabienne
TOTO LE HEROS
Los Pegamoides
PEPI, LUCI, BOM AND OTHER GIRLS ON THE HEAP
Loska, Bill
HONEY, I BLEW UP THE KID
Lotito, Mark
JUST LIKE IN THE MOVIES
Lottimer, Eb
FIELD OF FIRE
FINEST HOUR, THE
Louise, Tina
JOHNNY SUEDE
Louiso, Todd
SCENT OF A WOMAN
Louret, Guy
INSPECTOR LAVARDIN
Love, Darlene
LETHAL WEAPON 3
Love, Faizon
BEBE'S KIDS
Love, Nicholas
JENNIFER EIGHT
OVER HER DEAD BODY
Love, Pee Wee
MALCOLM X
Love, Victor
HEAVEN IS A PLAYGROUND

Lovelett, James
STRANGER AMONG US, A
Lover, Ed
JUICE
Lovett, Alan
FATHER
Lovett, Dale
DAY IN OCTOBER, A
Lovett, Lyle
PLAYER, THE
Lovitz, Jon
LEAGUE OF THEIR OWN, A
MOM AND DAD SAVE THE WORLD
Low, Chuck
NIGHT AND THE CITY
Low, Mitchell Tex
NIGHT AND THE CITY
Lowe, Alex
PETER'S FRIENDS
Lowe, Chad
HIGHWAY TO HELL
Lowe, Chuck
MISTRESS
Lowe, Jr., Arvie
BEBE'S KIDS
NEWSIES
Lowe, Lawrence
FEW GOOD MEN, A
Lowe, Rob
FINEST HOUR, THE
WAYNE'S WORLD
Lowell, Carey
ROAD TO RUIN
Lowens, Curt
MIDNIGHT CLEAR, A
Lowensohn, Elina
SIMPLE MEN
Lowenstein, Cary
WILD ORCHID 2: TWO SHADES OF BLUE
Lowenthal, Mark
ARTICLE 99
NEWSIES
Lowery, Andrew
BUFFY THE VAMPIRE SLAYER
SCHOOL TIES
Lowery, Carolyn
CANDYMAN
Lowery, H. Wayne
KILL LINE
Lowrey, Marcella
JUST LIKE IN THE MOVIES
Lowry, Michael
NETHERWORLD
Loya, Marcos
KISS ME A KILLER
Loya, Willie
KISS ME A KILLER
Lozano, Jose Luis
ENCINO MAN
Lubega, Bonnie M.
MISSISSIPPI MASALA
Lubotsky, Dana
BABE, THE
STRAIGHT TALK
Luca, Bracuitti
VENICE/VENICE

Lucas, Deborah
CONSENTING ADULTS
Lucas, Delaney
FATE
Lucas, George
MAGICAL WORLD OF CHUCK JONES, THE
Lucas, Jan
MR. SATURDAY NIGHT
Lucero, Dominic
NEWSIES
Lucey, Scott
FATHER
Luchini, Fabrice
DISCRETE, LA
Lucia, Charles
SOCIETY
Lucia, Chip
HAND THAT ROCKS THE CRADLE, THE
Luciano, Michael
JOHNNY SUEDE
Luciano, Silvio
JUST LIKE IN THE MOVIES
Lucy, Tom
FAR AND AWAY
Ludwig, Pamela
PALE BLOOD
Lugg, George
PUBLIC EYE, THE
Lujan, Daniel
AMERICAN ME
Luke, Ned
ROVER DANGERFIELD
Lumbers, Emily
CROSSING, THE
Lumbly, Carl
SOUTH CENTRAL
Lumpkin, Furley
ENCINO MAN
Luna, Ernesto
COMPLEX WORLD
Lund, Deanna
ROOTS OF EVIL
Lund, Graci
GAS FOOD LODGING
Lund, Zoe Tamarlaine
BAD LIEUTENANT
Lundgren, Dolph
UNIVERSAL SOLDIER
Lundquist, Steve
KILLER TOMATOES EAT FRANCE!
Lundy, Jessica
SINGLE WHITE FEMALE
Lundy, Mike
RUBY
Lunn, Harry
DAMNED IN THE USA
Lupo, Miriam
COMPLEX WORLD
Lupo, Rich
COMPLEX WORLD
Luport, Steve
LETHAL WEAPON 3
Lurie, Evan
MARTIAL LAW 2: UNDERCOVER
Lustig, Aaron
BAD CHANNELS
MEMOIRS OF AN INVISIBLE MAN
ROADSIDE PROPHETS
Luu, An
DOES THIS MEAN WE'RE MARRIED?
Luzietti, Alan
NEWSIES
Lyden, Jerry
INNOCENT BLOOD
Lydon, Colin F.
SCHOOL TIES
Lyell, Paul
FATAL INSTINCT
Lykes, Theorn "Touche"
GLADIATOR
Lykins, Ray
LAWNMOWER MAN, THE
Lyman, Will
SCHOOL TIES
Lymboura, Anthony
MUPPET CHRISTMAS CAROL, THE
Lynch, Barry
DEMONIC TOYS
DESERT KICKBOXER
Lynch, Charles
COMPLEX WORLD
Lynch, David
TWIN PEAKS: FIRE WALK WITH ME
Lynch, Dinah
HOFFA
Lynch, Jack
BEBE'S KIDS
Lynch, Jane
STRAIGHT TALK
Lynch, Jimmy
HIGHWAY 61
Lynch, John
EDWARD II
MONKEY BOY
Lynch, Peter
HIGHWAY 61
Lynch, Raymond
CHAPLIN
Lynch, Richard
INSIDE EDGE
MAXIMUM FORCE
Lynley, Carol
SPIRITS
Lynn
35 UP
Lynn, Cheryl M.
FATE
Lynn, Jerry
CROSSING THE BRIDGE
Lynn, Sherry
ALADDIN
LITTLE NEMO: ADVENTURES IN SLUMBERLAND
Lyon-Buchanan, Jennifer
BODYGUARD, THE
Lyons, Emilio
TEXAS TENOR: THE ILLINOIS JACQUET STORY
Lyons, Jim
SWOON
Lyttleton, Danielle
FLIRTING
Ma Jingwu
RAISE THE RED LANTERN
Ma Ling
LIFE ON A STRING
Maat, Jaloe
LILY WAS HERE
Mabli, Christopher
LIVING END, THE
Mabray, Stuart
DEATH BECOMES HER
Mac, Bernie
MO' MONEY
Macabe, Christopher
SCANNERS III: THE TAKEOVER
Macarelli, Cameron
INVASION OF THE SPACE PREACHERS
Macarthur, Scott K.
SWOON
Macat, Sandra
HOME ALONE 2: LOST IN NEW YORK
Macauley, Marc
PASSENGER 57
MacCarron, Lauretta
MANIAC WARRIORS
Macchio, Ralph
MY COUSIN VINNY
MacDonald, James
MALCOLM X
MacDonald, Ryan
NEWSIES
MacDonald, Scott
CUTTING EDGE, THE
MacDonald, Wendy
NAKED OBSESSION
MacDowell, Andie
PLAYER, THE
MacFadyen, Christie
SWOON
MacGregor, Andrew
MANIAC WARRIORS
Machado, Victor
NIGHT AND THE CITY
Macht, Stephen
AMITYVILLE 1992: IT'S ABOUT TIME
TRANCERS III: DETH LIVES
Machuca, Eli "Chupadera"
CABEZA DE VACA
MacHugh, Doug
CANDYMAN
MacInnes, Angus
CODE NAME: CHAOS
Mack, Jerome
THUNDERHEART
Mack, Rana
SOUTH CENTRAL
Mack, Terry
PUSHED TO THE LIMIT
MacKay, John Alexander
SIMPLE MEN
MacKay, Lizabeth
MALCOLM X

Mackay, Michael Reid
STEPHEN KING'S SLEEPWALKERS
MacKechnie, Keith
BIG GIRLS DON'T CRY . . . THEY GET EVEN
STRAIGHT TALK
MacKenzie, Evan
CHILDREN OF THE NIGHT
GHOULIES III: GHOULIES GO TO COLLEGE
MacKenzie, Peter
LORENZO'S OIL
Mackiewicz, Lech
TILL THERE WAS YOU
Mackintosh, Steven
LONDON KILLS ME
MUPPET CHRISTMAS CAROL, THE
Macklin, Peter
LIGHT SLEEPER
MacLachlan, Kyle
TWIN PEAKS: FIRE WALK WITH ME
WHERE THE DAY TAKES YOU
MacLaine, Shirley
USED PEOPLE
MacLeod, Tracey
LONDON KILLS ME
MacMenamin, Tim
BEAUTIFUL DREAMERS
MacMillan, Lorna
TWIN PEAKS: FIRE WALK WITH ME
MacNamara, Pete
MAMBO KINGS, THE
Macnee, Patrick
WAXWORK II: LOST IN TIME
MacNeil, Patricia
CUTTING EDGE, THE
MacNeille, Tress
LITTLE NEMO: ADVENTURES IN SLUMBERLAND
MacNicol, Peter
HARD PROMISES
HOUSESITTER
MacPherson, Harold
INSIDE EDGE
MacPherson, Rand
PASSENGER 57
MacRae, Rachel C.
CONSENTING ADULTS
MacTaggart, Kyla
VENICE/VENICE
Macy, W.H.
SHADOWS AND FOG
Madden, Patricia
HOUSESITTER
Maddox, Chalmer
WHITE MEN CAN'T JUMP
Madio, James
HERO
Madison, Spider
UNLAWFUL ENTRY
Madison-Ciu, Chelsea
WATERDANCE, THE
Madjerac, Lena
ROADSIDE PROPHETS
Madonna
LEAGUE OF THEIR OWN, A
SHADOWS AND FOG
Madrigal, Humberto
AMERICAN ME
Madsen, Michael
FATAL INSTINCT
INSIDE EDGE
RESERVOIR DOGS
STRAIGHT TALK
Madsen, Virginia
BECOMING COLETTE
CANDYMAN
Maenpaa, Outi
MATCH FACTORY GIRL, THE
Maffei, Joe
MANIAC WARRIORS
Maffia, Robert
HOFFA
MaGee, Ken
CHAPLIN
Maggard, Jon
LOVE FIELD
Magill, Mark
GUN IN BETTY LOU'S HANDBAG, THE
Magnano, Matt
SINGLES
Magner, Frank
CHINA O'BRIEN II
Magnin, Claire
FAVOUR, THE WATCH, AND THE VERY BIG FISH, THE
Magnuson, Britt
DR. GIGGLES
Maguire, Josh
CHAPLIN
Maguire, Michael
WHERE THE DAY TAKES YOU
Magwili, Dom
KUFFS
Mahal, Camillia
MANIAC WARRIORS
Mahan, Kerrigan
BEBE'S KIDS
PROFESSIONAL, THE
VAMPIRE HUNTER D
Mahard, Thomas D.
HOFFA
Maher, Joseph
SISTER ACT
Mahon, Michael C.
MALCOLM X
Mahoney, John
ARTICLE 99
LOVE HURTS
Mahoney, Victoria
WILD ORCHID 2: TWO SHADES OF BLUE
Mahoney, William
PASSION FISH
Mai Chau
INDOCHINE
Mai, Larissa
MANIAC WARRIORS
Maiello, Michael
RADIO FLYER
Mailer, Stephen
LEAGUE OF THEIR OWN, A
Makasutji, Gino
LADY DRAGON
Makeba, Miriam
SARAFINA!
Makkena, Wendy
SISTER ACT
Makuwachuma, Dominic
POWER OF ONE, THE
Malaczech, Ruth
IN THE SOUP
Malamud, Allan
WHITE MEN CAN'T JUMP
Malave, Chu Chu
DO OR DIE
Malavoy, Christophe
CRY OF THE OWL, THE
Maldonado, Dominic
NEWSIES
Maldonatti, Frankie
PATRIOT GAMES
Malele, Dixon
SARAFINA!
Malesci, Artie
TRACES OF RED
Malet, Arthur
BEASTMASTER 2: THROUGH THE PORTAL OF TIME
RUNESTONE, THE
TOYS
Malhotra, Pavan
CITY OF JOY
Malik
WHISPERS IN THE DARK
Malik, Art
CITY OF JOY
YEAR OF THE COMET
Malik, Keira Jane
CITY OF JOY
Malik, Serge
CHRISTOPHER COLUMBUS: THE DISCOVERY
Malina, Josh
FEW GOOD MEN, A
Malkovich, John
JENNIFER EIGHT
OF MICE AND MEN
SHADOWS AND FOG
Mall, Korey
MIRROR IMAGES
Malloff, Rosalind
NIGHT AND THE CITY
Mallow, Dave
FERNGULLY: THE LAST RAINFOREST
Malloy, John
HOFFA
SHAKING THE TREE
Malloy, Matt
MY NEW GUN
SIMPLE MEN
WIND
Malm, Mona
BEST INTENTIONS, THE
Malone, Dorothy
BASIC INSTINCT
Malone, Joseph
UNIVERSAL SOLDIER

Malone, Mike
TWIN PEAKS: FIRE WALK WITH ME
Malone, Oswaldo
PROOF
Malone, Patrick
ORIGINAL INTENT
Maloney, Peter
PUBLIC EYE, THE
Maltin, Leonard
MAGICAL WORLD OF CHUCK JONES, THE
Mamanzi, Cecil Zilla
POWER OF ONE, THE
Mammone, Robert
CROSSING, THE
Manard, Biff
DESERT KICKBOXER
Manas, Achero
1492: THE CONQUEST OF PARADISE
Mancini, Al
PUBLIC EYE, THE
Mancini, Ray
ACES: IRON EAGLE III
DEADLY BET
Mancuso, Nick
RAPID FIRE
UNDER SIEGE
Mandel, Babaloo
MR. SATURDAY NIGHT
Manderson, Bill
FATHER
Mandirosian, Tom
JUST LIKE IN THE MOVIES
Mandley, Lawrence
BEASTMASTER 2: THROUGH THE PORTAL OF TIME
Mandon, Jeff
PATRIOT GAMES
Manfredi, Nino
ALBERTO EXPRESS
Mangiu, Carlo Amedeo
JOHNNY STECCHINO
Mango, Daniela
JOHNNY STECCHINO
Mangwarara, Winston
POWER OF ONE, THE
Mankuma, Blu
K2
Mann, Cheryl
BOB ROBERTS
Mann, Danny
FERNGULLY: THE LAST RAINFOREST
LITTLE NEMO: ADVENTURES IN SLUMBERLAND
Mann, Douglas
MONKEY BOY
Mann, Howard
MR. SATURDAY NIGHT
Mann, Peter
BECOMING COLETTE
Mann, Sonny
BABE, THE
Mann, Terrence
CRITTERS 4
Mannix, Ed
PROFESSIONAL, THE

Manqele, David
SARAFINA!
Mansion, Gracie
ALL THE VERMEERS IN NEW YORK
Mantell, Michael
PASSION FISH
Mantle, Clive
ALIEN3
Mantz, Delphine T.
MALCOLM X
Manuli, Davide
ENCHANTED APRIL
Manver, Kiti
PEPI, LUCI, BOM AND OTHER GIRLS ON THE HEAP
Manzo, Diane
MAMBO KINGS, THE
SOUTH CENTRAL
Maphumulo, Khanyo
SARAFINA!
Mapp, Andrew
NOISES OFF
Mappin, Jefferson
BEAUTIFUL DREAMERS
Mara, Mary
LOVE POTION NO. 9
MR. SATURDAY NIGHT
Maracle, Mark J.
LAST OF THE MOHICANS, THE
Marc, Peter
WE'RE TALKIN' SERIOUS MONEY
Marceau, Sophie
POUR SACHA
Marcenko, Dennis
LEAVING NORMAL
March, Jane
LOVER, THE
Marchado, Maria
FINE ROMANCE, A
Marchand, Mitchell
FATHERS AND SONS
JUICE
Marchand, Nancy
BRAIN DONORS
Marcum, Staci
BOB ROBERTS
HOFFA
Marcus, Boni Sue
HUMAN SHIELD, THE
Marcus, Dominic
WHISPERS IN THE DARK
Marcus, Steven
JUST LIKE IN THE MOVIES
Mardirosian, Tom
BOOMERANG
Marescotti, Ivano
JOHNNY STECCHINO
Marga, Lorraine
BEETHOVEN
Margetts, Noah
CHAPLIN
Margo, Guy
CLASS ACT
Margolis, Mark
1492: THE CONQUEST OF PARADISE
JUST LIKE IN THE MOVIES

Margot, Sandra
SPIRITS
Margulies, David
OUT ON A LIMB
STRANGER AMONG US, A
Maria, Anna
PUSHED TO THE LIMIT
Mariano, John
FINISHING TOUCH, THE
Marich, Marietta
LEAP OF FAITH
SIMPLE MEN
Marie, Louisa
FAR AND AWAY
Marielle, Jean-Pierre
TOUS LES MATINS DU MONDE
Marin, Jason
ROCK-A-DOODLE
Marin, Richard "Cheech"
FERNGULLY: THE LAST RAINFOREST
Marini, Giulio
CAPTAIN AMERICA
Marino, Rick
HONEYMOON IN VEGAS
Marino, Ron
BABE, THE
Markel, Richard
RAMPAGE
Markham, Monte
NEON CITY
Markota, Ivan
WAXWORK II: LOST IN TIME
Marks, Harlow
CHINA O'BRIEN II
Marley, Bob
BOB MARLEY: TIME WILL TELL
Marley, Dana
NOISES OFF
Marlowe, Nancy
DOUBLE TROUBLE
Marlyn, Jan
FATAL INSTINCT
Maronna, Michael C.
HOME ALONE 2: LOST IN NEW YORK
Marquez, Roberto Martin
AMERICAN ME
Marquez, William
FOREVER YOUNG
Marr, Jo Jo
SNEAKERS
Marr, Periel
WHITE TRASH
Marrero, Ralph
BABE, THE
JOHNNY SUEDE
JUST LIKE IN THE MOVIES
Marruzzo, Eugenia
ALBERTO EXPRESS
Mars, Kenneth
SHADOWS AND FOG
Marsden, Jason
MR. SATURDAY NIGHT
Marsh, Bernard
MALCOLM X

Marshall, David Anthony
CRISSCROSS
ROADSIDE PROPHETS
Marshall, E.G.
CONSENTING ADULTS
Marshall, Garry
LEAGUE OF THEIR OWN, A
Marshall, James
FEW GOOD MEN, A
GLADIATOR
TWIN PEAKS: FIRE WALK WITH ME
Marshall, John
INVASION OF THE SPACE PREACHERS
Marshall, Joshua
FLIRTING
Marshall, Kathleen
LEAGUE OF THEIR OWN, A
Marshall, Meredith
WHITE SANDS
Marshall, Paula
HELLRAISER III: HELL ON EARTH
Marshall, Rosalyn
RAMPAGE
Marsland, Helen
WHITE TRASH
Marta, Darcy
LIVING END, THE
Marteau, Henri
INDOCHINE
Marthouret, Francois
HOT CHOCOLATE
Martial, Jacques
VOYAGER
Martin, Christopher
CLASS ACT
Martin, Christy
CRISSCROSS
Martin, Damon
AMITYVILLE 1992: IT'S ABOUT TIME
Martin, Dan
BLOODFIST IV: DIE TRYING
STEPHEN KING'S SLEEPWALKERS
Martin, David
HOT CHOCOLATE
Martin, Duane
WHITE MEN CAN'T JUMP
Martin, Greg Allan
FOREVER YOUNG
Martin, Gregory Paul
MEMOIRS OF AN INVISIBLE MAN
Martin, Greta
MALCOLM X
Martin, Janis
SHINING THROUGH
Martin, John
LOVE HURTS
Martin, Latesha
CANDYMAN
Martin, Laurie
MANIAC WARRIORS
Martin, Melissa
DEATH BECOMES HER
Martin, Russell
MUPPET CHRISTMAS CAROL, THE
Martin, Steve
HOUSESITTER
LEAP OF FAITH
Martin, Timothy
LOVE POTION NO. 9
Martin, William E.
LITTLE NEMO: ADVENTURES IN SLUMBERLAND
Martindale, Margo
LORENZO'S OIL
Martinelli, Elsa
ONCE UPON A CRIME
Martinez, Adrian
MAMBO KINGS, THE
Martinez, Alma
DOLLY DEAREST
PANAMA DECEPTION, THE
Martinez, Geraldo
CABEZA DE VACA
Martinez, Juan Carlos
CABEZA DE VACA
Martinez, Leo
EYE OF THE EAGLE 3
Martinez, Ruben
WHITE MEN CAN'T JUMP
Martinez, Sharmeek
MALCOLM X
Martinozzi, Marco
ONCE UPON A CRIME
Martir, Carlos A.
BRENDA STARR
Martorana, Marc
ADVENTURES IN DINOSAUR CITY
Marvalous, Simply
CLASS ACT
Marx, Salomon
BIG GIRLS DON'T CRY . . . THEY GET EVEN
Marynczak, Julian
SWOON
Marzan, Rick
RUNESTONE, THE
Mascis, J.
GAS FOOD LODGING
Masenda, Tonderai
POWER OF ONE, THE
Masenko, Valentina
RASPAD
Mashigo, Billy
SARAFINA!
Mask, Ace
MUNCHIE
Mason, Colleen
FROZEN ASSETS
Mason, Edward
HOUSESITTER
Mason, Hilary
AFRAID OF THE DARK
Mason, Holaday
KICK OR DIE
Mason, Margery
HOWARDS END
Masses, Michael
MY FATHER IS COMING
Massett, Patrick
THUNDERHEART
Massimi, Massimilio
CAPTAIN AMERICA
Massman, Stephanie
BEETHOVEN
Masten, Gordon
BEAUTIFUL DREAMERS
Masterson, Christopher Kennedy
SINGLES
Masterson, Fay
POWER OF ONE, THE
Masterson, Rod
DELTA HEAT
Mastrandea, Nicholas
DR. GIGGLES
Mastrantonio, Mary Elizabeth
CONSENTING ADULTS
WHITE SANDS
Mastrodominico, Joseph
THIS IS MY LIFE
Mastroianni, Marcello
FINE ROMANCE, A
USED PEOPLE
Masumoto, Hiroshi
MR. BASEBALL
Masur, Richard
ENCINO MAN
Matacena, Orestes
DIGGSTOWN
Matalon, Shmuel
HUMAN SHIELD, THE
Mataras, Krystle
SINGLE WHITE FEMALE
Mataras, Tiffany
SINGLE WHITE FEMALE
Matheson, Michelle
LITTLE SISTER
Matheson, Pamela
SOCIETY
Mathews, James
VOYAGER
Mathews, John M.
FEW GOOD MEN, A
Mathis, Samantha
FERNGULLY: THE LAST RAINFOREST
THIS IS MY LIFE
Mathou, Jacques
DELICATESSEN
HAIRDRESSER'S HUSBAND, THE
YEAR OF THE COMET
Matiezen, Kathleen
VOYAGER
Matis, Stanley
COMPLEX WORLD
Matlin, Marlee
LINGUINI INCIDENT, THE
PLAYER, THE
Matson, Ericka
HAND THAT ROCKS THE CRADLE, THE
Matson, Kathleen
VENICE/VENICE
Matsubara, Kazuma
GODZILLA VS. BIOLLANTE
Matsunami, Nobuhiko
MR. BASEBALL

Matsushita, Jeff
GIVING, THE
Matsuzaki, Masanao
MR. BASEBALL
Matthews, Dennis
FINAL ANALYSIS
Matthews, Lawrence
LEAP OF FAITH
Matthews, Lionel
DEEP COVER
Matthews, Reverend Fred
MISSISSIPPI MASALA
Maugans, Wayne
JOHNNY SUEDE
Maura, Carmen
PEPI, LUCI, BOM AND OTHER GIRLS ON THE HEAP
Maurice, Cedric
BASKET CASE 3: THE PROGENY
Maurin, Mado
FAVOUR, THE WATCH, AND THE VERY BIG FISH, THE
Mavers, Gary
MONKEY BOY
Mavros, Claudine
FAVOUR, THE WATCH, AND THE VERY BIG FISH, THE
Maxwell, Ara
FOREVER YOUNG
Maxwell, David
WHITE MEN CAN'T JUMP
Maxwell, Don
FROZEN ASSETS
Maxwell, Tony
BUFFY THE VAMPIRE SLAYER
May, Charmain
DEMON IN MY VIEW, A
May, Deborah
CAGED FEAR
May, Jodhi
LAST OF THE MOHICANS, THE
May, Mathilda
BECOMING COLETTE
CRY OF THE OWL, THE
Mayall, Rik
LITTLE NOISES
Mayberry, James
LOVE CRIMES
Mayberry, Michelle
WILDFIRE
Mayer, Jerry
SINGLE WHITE FEMALE
Mayer, Roger
MAGICAL WORLD OF CHUCK JONES, THE
Mayes, Darrell
LEAVING NORMAL
Mayes, Winston
HAPPY HELL NIGHT
Mayeux, Rosalee
LAWNMOWER MAN, THE
Mayfield, Tracy
RIVER RUNS THROUGH IT, A
Mayhook, Rebecca
PATRIOT GAMES
Maynard, Bill
ODDBALL HALL
Maynard, Mimi
ADVENTURES IN DINOSAUR CITY
FROZEN ASSETS
PLAY NICE
Mayo, Jonjo
LOVE CRIMES
Mayron, Gale
GUN IN BETTY LOU'S HANDBAG, THE
Maywood, Patricia
MANIAC WARRIORS
Mazar, Debi
IN THE SOUP
MALCOLM X
TOYS
Mazet, Robert
INSPECTOR LAVARDIN
Mazibuko, Brian "Jazz"
SARAFINA!
Mazie, Sherri
HOFFA
Mazursky, Paul
MAN TROUBLE
Mazzello, John
RADIO FLYER
Mazzello, Joseph
RADIO FLYER
Mbandu, Konga
MISSISSIPPI MASALA
Mbatha, Sindane
SARAFINA!
Mbili, Sduduzo
SARAFINA!
McArthur, Alex
RAMPAGE
McArthur, Benny
PURE COUNTRY
McAteer, Joanne
FAR AND AWAY
McBee, Deron
OUT FOR BLOOD
McBride, Jeff
BOOMERANG
McCafferty, Dee
CLEARCUT
McCafferty, Frankie
FAR AND AWAY
McCall, Andrida
PASSED AWAY
McCall, Jack
NOISES OFF
McCall, Ross
WATERLAND
McCallany, Holt
ALIEN3
McCallie, Douglas
ENCINO MAN
McCamus, Tom
BEAUTIFUL DREAMERS
McCann, Chuck
STORYVILLE
McCarthy, Andrew
ONLY YOU
McCarthy, Elizabeth Ann
TWIN PEAKS: FIRE WALK WITH ME
McCarthy, Jeanne
ROADSIDE PROPHETS
WHITE MEN CAN'T JUMP
McCarthy, Jeff
RAPID FIRE
McCarthy, Julia
YEAR OF THE COMET
McCarthy, Julianna
DISTINGUISHED GENTLEMAN, THE
McCarthy, Kevin
DISTINGUISHED GENTLEMAN, THE
GHOULIES III: GHOULIES GO TO COLLEGE
McCarthy, Moira J.
HOUSESITTER
McCarthy, Sheila
BEAUTIFUL DREAMERS
BEETHOVEN LIVES UPSTAIRS
McCarthy, Thomas
CROSSING THE BRIDGE
McCarty, Bruce
LOVE POTION NO. 9
McCarty, Sean
SAVAGE INSTINCT
McCarver, Tim
LOVE HURTS
MR. BASEBALL
McCasland, Kevin
NEWSIES
McCaslim, Keith
HARD PROMISES
McCauley, James
LAWS OF GRAVITY
McCauley, John
GUN IN BETTY LOU'S HANDBAG, THE
McCay, Rodney
ARTICLE 99
McClendon, Michael
BRIDE OF KILLER NERD
McClure, Gordon
MO' MONEY
McClure, Mark
VAGRANT, THE
McClure, Molly
PURE COUNTRY
McClurg, Edie
RIVER RUNS THROUGH IT, A
McCluskey, Kenneth
FAR AND AWAY
McColl, Catriona
AFRAID OF THE DARK
McComb, Heather
STAY TUNED
McConnachie, Brian
HUSBANDS AND WIVES
McConnell, David
TROLL 2
McConnell, John "Spud"
DELTA HEAT
McConnell, Michael
LAST OF THE MOHICANS, THE
McConnico, Hilton
FAVOUR, THE WATCH, AND THE VERY BIG FISH, THE
McConnochie, Rhys
HUNTING

McConnohie, Michael
LITTLE NEMO: ADVENTURES IN SLUMBERLAND
PROFESSIONAL, THE
VAMPIRE HUNTER D
McCormack, John
FOLKS!
McCourt, Emer
LONDON KILLS ME
McCown, Cort
AUNTIE LEE'S MEAT PIES
McCoy, Larry
MALCOLM X
McCoy, Matt
HAND THAT ROCKS THE CRADLE, THE
McCoy, Timothy
SWOON
McCree, Brian
LUNATICS: A LOVE STORY
McCullough, Julie
ROUND TRIP TO HEAVEN
McCullough, Kimberly
CONSENTING ADULTS
McCurdy, Gregory
HONEY, I BLEW UP THE KID
McCusker, Stella
PLAYBOYS, THE
McDade, Sandy
LONDON KILLS ME
McDaniel, Hattie
WISECRACKS
McDaniel, James
MALCOLM X
McDaniel, Keith
DEATH BECOMES HER
McDaniel, Keith A.
BASIC INSTINCT
McDaniel, Xavier
SINGLES
McDermott, Carolyn
PUERTO RICAN MAMBO (NOT A MUSICAL), THE
McDonald, Belle
HOUSESITTER
McDonald, Bill
HOUSESITTER
McDonald, Brenda
LEAVING NORMAL
McDonald, Christopher
WILD ORCHID 2: TWO SHADES OF BLUE
McDonald, Jeffrey
GAS FOOD LODGING
McDonald, Jim
PASSENGER 57
McDonald, Keiko
LORENZO'S OIL
McDonald, Michael James
BODY WAVES
DANCE WITH DEATH
McDonald, Pat
MANIAC WARRIORS
McDonald, Robin
HOURS AND TIMES, THE
McDonald, Scott
MANIAC WARRIORS

McDonnell, Mary
PASSION FISH
SNEAKERS
McDonnell, Tim
FAR AND AWAY
McDonough, Ann
LORENZO'S OIL
McDonough, Sean
MR. BASEBALL
McDormand, Frances
PASSED AWAY
McDowall, Roddy
DOUBLE TROUBLE
MAGICAL WORLD OF CHUCK JONES, THE
McDowell, Lisa
WHITE MEN CAN'T JUMP
McDowell, Malcolm
LIGHT IN THE JUNGLE, THE
PLAYER, THE
McDuffie, Kay
GUN IN BETTY LOU'S HANDBAG, THE
McElduff, Ellen
GUN IN BETTY LOU'S HANDBAG, THE
PUBLIC EYE, THE
McElheron, Maureen
TUNE, THE
McElhinney, Ian
PLAYBOYS, THE
McElroy, Brian
BAD LIEUTENANT
McElroy, Nan
CONSENTING ADULTS
McEnnan, Jaime
MUNCHIE
McEnroe, Annie
CRISSCROSS
McEvoy, Teri
FOLKS!
HOME ALONE 2: LOST IN NEW YORK
McFadden, Beth
FAVOUR, THE WATCH, AND THE VERY BIG FISH, THE
McFadden, Davenia
ARTICLE 99
McFadden, David
LORENZO'S OIL
McFadden, Sandy
PUERTO RICAN MAMBO (NOT A MUSICAL), THE
McFadden, Stephanie
LOVE FIELD
McFarland, C.K.
HARD PROMISES
McFarland, Connie
TROLL 2
McFarlane, David
HIGHWAY 61
McFliker, Dean
NEWSIES
McGann, Paul
AFRAID OF THE DARK
ALIEN3
McGarrigle, Pat
MANIAC WARRIORS

McGarry, Jonathan
TOYS
McGauley, Henry J.
PASSENGER 57
McGavin, Darren
CAPTAIN AMERICA
HAPPY HELL NIGHT
McGee, Carl A.
WHITE MEN CAN'T JUMP
McGee, Fran
HOME ALONE 2: LOST IN NEW YORK
McGee, Jack
BASIC INSTINCT
McGee, John
SWOON
McGee, Michael
GIVING, THE
McGee, Michi
IN GOLD WE TRUST
McGee, Robin
STEELE'S LAW
McGhee, Johnny Ray
LOVE FIELD
UNLAWFUL ENTRY
McGhee, Tony
MISSISSIPPI MASALA
McGill, Bruce
LITTLE VEGAS
MY COUSIN VINNY
PLAY NICE
McGill, Michael
CANVAS
McGillis, Kelly
BABE, THE
McGinley, John
LITTLE NOISES
McGinley, John C
MIDNIGHT CLEAR, A
McGinley, John C.
ARTICLE 99
McGlone, Mike
GIVING, THE
McGoohan, Catherine
BLIND VISION
McGovern, Barry
FAR AND AWAY
McGovern, Mick
PUBLIC EYE, THE
McGowan, Charles
DEATH BECOMES HER
McGowan, Mickie
ALADDIN
McGowan, Rose
ENCINO MAN
McGowan, Thomas John
LAST OF THE MOHICANS, THE
McGowan, Tom
CAPTAIN RON
McGrady, Michael
BABE, THE
DIGGSTOWN
MR. BASEBALL
McGrath, Matt
BOB ROBERTS
McGraw, Sean
RUBY

McGraw, Tom
OUT ON A LIMB
McGregor, Angela Punch
EFFICIENCY EXPERT, THE
McGregor, Ken
PROM NIGHT IV - DELIVER US FROM EVIL
McGregor-Stewart, Kate
THIS IS MY LIFE
McGruder, Jasper
MALCOLM X
McGuire, Bruce
NEAR MISSES
McGuire, Jason
LEAP OF FAITH
PET SEMATARY II
McGuire, Sean
WATERLAND
McHallem, Chris
EDWARD II
McHoney, Tiffany
LOVE FIELD
Mchunu, Velile
SARAFINA!
McIlvain, James Terry
PURE COUNTRY
McIntosh, Michelle
VENICE/VENICE
McIntosh, Valerie
MAMBO KINGS, THE
McInturff, T.J.
UNLAWFUL ENTRY
McIntyre, Judith
FAR AND AWAY
McKamy, Kim
FATAL INSTINCT
McKanna, Robert
SWOON
McKay, Cole
FAR AND AWAY
McKay, Johanna
BABE, THE
McKean, Michael
MAN TROUBLE
MEMOIRS OF AN INVISIBLE MAN
McKee, Lonette
MALCOLM X
McKee, Monty
WE'RE TALKIN' SERIOUS MONEY
McKellar, Don
ADJUSTER, THE
HIGHWAY 61
McKenna, Breffini
CRYING GAME, THE
McKenna, Kilian
PLAYBOYS, THE
McKenna, Travis
BATMAN RETURNS
McKennon, Dallas
FROZEN ASSETS
McKenzie, Andres
BEETHOVEN
McKenzie, Mary
SIMPLE MEN
McKenzie, Nicolette
UNDER SUSPICION

McKeon, Nancy
WHERE THE DAY TAKES YOU
McKernan, Jr., Peter
RAMPAGE
McKerras, Ross
I DON'T BUY KISSES ANYMORE
McKewan, Marny
MANIAC WARRIORS
McKibbin, Tod
BASIC INSTINCT
McKinney, Gregory
BLOODFIST III: FORCED TO FIGHT
DOUBLE TROUBLE
McKinney, Kirk
ARMED FOR ACTION
McKinnie, Gerald
TOYS
McKinnon, Ray
GUN IN BETTY LOU'S HANDBAG, THE
McKinster, Dawn
MAMBO KINGS, THE
McKnight, David
UNDER SIEGE
McKuen, Kellie A.
GIVING, THE
McLane, Harley
LOVE HURTS
McLaughlin, Jack
MALCOLM X
McLaughlin, John Patrick
JUICE
McLaughlin, Maya
CHILDREN OF THE NIGHT
Mclaughlin, Suzi
LEAP OF FAITH
McLauglin, Kevin
CROSSING THE BRIDGE
McLean, Shawn
BAD LIEUTENANT
McLemore, Zachary
PASSENGER 57
McLeod, Janell
LOVE FIELD
McLeod, Ken
OUT FOR BLOOD
TRAINED TO FIGHT
McLin, Eugenia
LEAGUE OF THEIR OWN, A
McLish, Rachel
ACES: IRON EAGLE III
McLure, Tane
DEATH HOUSE
McLuskie, Carolyn
VENICE/VENICE
McLynn, Pauline
FAR AND AWAY
McMahon, John
HONEYMOON IN VEGAS
McMillan, Mary
ALAN & NAOMI
McMillen, Michael
MIND, BODY & SOUL
McMurdo-Wallis, Cristine
HAND THAT ROCKS THE CRADLE, THE

McMurray, Sam
CLASS ACT
McNab, Michael
SOUTH CENTRAL
McNair, Chris
MY GRANDPA IS A VAMPIRE
McNair, Heather
CHAPLIN
McNarland, Laura
MANIAC WARRIORS
McNarland, Robert
MANIAC WARRIORS
McNeal, Heidi
HERO
McNeice, Ian
SECRET FRIENDS
YEAR OF THE COMET
McNeil, Kevin
MISSISSIPPI MASALA
McPherson, Jane
PASSENGER 57
McQuarry, Chuck
TWIN PEAKS: FIRE WALK WITH ME
McQuary, Chuck
SINGLES
McRae, Alan
3 NINJAS
McRae, Basil
MIGHTY DUCKS, THE
McRae, Rick
PURE COUNTRY
McReynolds, Tracy
MAXIMUM BREAKOUT
McRobbie, Peter
JOHNNY SUEDE
SCHOOL TIES
SHADOWS AND FOG
McShane, Timothy
BABE, THE
McTeigue, Mark
WIND
McWilliams, Mary
HOWARDS END
Mead, Phil
OVER HER DEAD BODY
Meadows, Jayne
PLAYER, THE
Meadows, Stephen
ULTRAVIOLET
Meaney, Colm
FAR AND AWAY
LAST OF THE MOHICANS, THE
UNDER SIEGE
Means, Randy
MALCOLM X
Means, Russell
LAST OF THE MOHICANS, THE
Means, Scott
LAST OF THE MOHICANS, THE
Meara, Anne
HIGHWAY TO HELL
Meat Loaf
GUN IN BETTY LOU'S HANDBAG, THE
LEAP OF FAITH
WAYNE'S WORLD

Mechoso, Julio Oscar
DEEP COVER
TOYS
Medalis, Joseph G.
SISTER ACT
Medina, Arcoiris
LIGHT SLEEPER
Medina, Hazel
MALCOLM X
Medina, James
ARTICLE 99
Medina, Jr., Albert Joe
AMERICAN ME
Medlock, Ken
AMERICAN ME
MR. BASEBALL
Medvesek, Rene
CAPTAIN AMERICA
Medvesek, Sven
CAPTAIN AMERICA
Meghangi, Evelina
WHERE ANGELS FEAR TO TREAD
Megia, Dalila
KISS ME A KILLER
Megowan, Alva
BEASTMASTER 2: THROUGH THE PORTAL OF TIME
Mehana, Richard
MR. SATURDAY NIGHT
Mehdizadeh, Soleiman
GODZILLA VS. BIOLLANTE
Meier, Shane
UNFORGIVEN
Meininger, Frederique
LOVER, THE
Meintjes, Tertius
SARAFINA!
Meisle, William
SCHOOL TIES
Meistrich, Larry
LAWS OF GRAVITY
Mejdi, Hadji
K2
Mejia, Carla Lizzette
BODYGUARD, THE
Mekka, Eddie
LEAGUE OF THEIR OWN, A
Melamed, Fred
SHADOWS AND FOG
Melander, Ashley
HAND THAT ROCKS THE CRADLE, THE
Melander, Eric
HAND THAT ROCKS THE CRADLE, THE
Melander, Jennifer
HAND THAT ROCKS THE CRADLE, THE
Meldrum, Wendel
BEAUTIFUL DREAMERS
Melendez, Maria
LIFE ON THE EDGE
Melhuse, Peder
WAYNE'S WORLD
Melissen, Beppie
LILY WAS HERE
Mellencamp, Joe
FALLING FROM GRACE
Mellencamp, John
FALLING FROM GRACE
Mellencamp, Teddi Jo
FALLING FROM GRACE
Melocchi, Vince
ARTICLE 99
Meloy, Tammara
CROSSING THE BRIDGE
Melson, Sara
DR. GIGGLES
Melton, Kim
INNOCENT BLOOD
Melvoin, Wendy
TOYS
Mende, Lisa
HONEY, I BLEW UP THE KID
Mendelsohn, Ben
EFFICIENCY EXPERT, THE
Mendelsohn, Eric R.
THIS IS MY LIFE
Mendes, Luis Carlos
EMMANUELLE 6
Mendez, Agustin
SEX CRIMES
Mendicino, Gerry
GATE II
Mendoza, Arturo
PUSHED TO THE LIMIT
Mendoza, Frank
MR. BASEBALL
Mendoza, Indio
DANZON
Mendoza, John
MEATBALLS 4
Mendoza, Lucia
PUERTO RICAN MAMBO (NOT A MUSICAL), THE
Mendozo, Arthur
DEEP COVER
Mengel, Eran
HUMAN SHIELD, THE
Menick, Jon
FOREVER YOUNG
Menning, Sam
RUNESTONE, THE
Menzies, Michelle
CUTTING EDGE, THE
Mercado, Hector
PLAY NICE
Mercant, Marsha
OUT ON A LIMB
Mercer, Marian
OUT ON A LIMB
Mercier, Mary
MISTRESS
Merck, Ken
MIND, BODY & SOUL
Mercury, Bruce
HELLROLLER
Merdis, Thomas
MY COUSIN VINNY
Meredith, Burgess
ODDBALL HALL
Merediz, Olga
BOOMERANG
Merhi, Jalal
TALONS OF THE EAGLE
TIGER CLAWS
Meril, Macha
DOUBLE VISION
Merino, Jackie
PUSHED TO THE LIMIT
Merrem, Anne
RIVER RUNS THROUGH IT, A
Merrill, C. John
SOCIETY
Merrill, Dina
PLAYER, THE
Merrill, James
LORENZO'S OIL
Merrill, John
HERO
Merriman, Christine
LORENZO'S OIL
Merscher, April
LORENZO'S OIL
Merten, Michael Tony
SOCIETY
Meshover-Iorg, Jason
LETHAL WEAPON 3
Mesko, Sabrina
SECRET GAMES
Messaline, Peter
CUTTING EDGE, THE
Messeri, Marco
ALBERTO EXPRESS
Messina, Frank
IN THE SOUP
Messina, Richard
LILY WAS HERE
Messing, Susan
STRAIGHT TALK
Messmer, Wayne
BABE, THE
Messner, Kristin
SHAKING THE TREE
Mestre, Adelaide
HUSBANDS AND WIVES
Metallica
FOR THOSE ABOUT TO ROCK
Metcalf, Joe
WHITE MEN CAN'T JUMP
Metcalf, Laurie
MISTRESS
Metcalf, Toby
PURE COUNTRY
Metcalfe, Michael
MANIAC WARRIORS
Metrano, Art
TOYS
Metropolis, Nick
HUSBANDS AND WIVES
Mette, Nancy
PASSION FISH
Metzler, Jim
ONE FALSE MOVE
WAXWORK II: LOST IN TIME
Metzman, Irving
USED PEOPLE

Meyer, Con
LILY WAS HERE
Meyer, Jennifer
WATERLAND
Meyers, Ari
DARK HORSE
Meyers, David
COLD HEAVEN
Meyers, Jimmy
LOVE CRIMES
Meyers, Larry John
BOB ROBERTS
HOFFA
PASSED AWAY
WATERLAND
Meyers, Pauline
MY COUSIN VINNY
Meyerson, Ben
SOCIETY
Meyrand, Pierre
HAIRDRESSER'S HUSBAND, THE
Mhlongo, Batho
SARAFINA!
Mhlongo, Futhi
SARAFINA!
Mhlongo, Somizi "Whacko"
SARAFINA!
Miano, Robert
BIKINI SUMMER 2
OUT FOR BLOOD
Michaels, Julie
DOCTOR MORDRID
Michaels, Keo
HOMEBOYS
Michaels, Kevin
NEWSIES
Michaels, Kristen
PURE COUNTRY
Michaels, Lou
LOVE HURTS
Michaels, Rhino
UNIVERSAL SOLDIER
Michaud, Francoise
FINE ROMANCE, A
Michaux, Leroy
WHITE MEN CAN'T JUMP
Michel, Delaune
WOMAN, HER MEN AND HER FUTON, A
Michelle, Diane
PROFESSIONAL, THE
Michelle, Julianne
I DON'T BUY KISSES ANYMORE
Michelle, Shelley
SUNSET STRIP
Michelson, Roger
NOISES OFF
Michie, Edward
CHILDREN, THE
Micklesen, Elaine
HAND THAT ROCKS THE CRADLE, THE
Midden, Robert
PASSENGER 57
Midkiff, Dale
LOVE POTION NO. 9

Mifune, Toshiro
JOURNEY OF HONOR
Migita, Kazuhiko
MR. BASEBALL
Migre, Eduardo
UNLAWFUL ENTRY
Miguel, Nigel
HEAVEN IS A PLAYGROUND
WHITE MEN CAN'T JUMP
Miguelito
DANZON
Mihailoff, R.A.
TRANCERS III: DETH LIVES
Mikesell, Mark
STOP! OR MY MOM WILL SHOOT
Mikita, Stan
WAYNE'S WORLD
Mikitenko, Taracik
RASPAD
Milano, Alyssa
LITTLE SISTER
WHERE THE DAY TAKES YOU
Milanovich, Tom
FOLKS!
HERO
Milburn, Jane
LEAP OF FAITH
Miler, John
WHITE TRASH
Miles, George Lee
MALCOLM X
Milford, David
BASKET CASE 3: THE PROGENY
Milford, Penelope
COLD JUSTICE
Milgrom, Michael
LOVE FIELD
UNLAWFUL ENTRY
Milhoan, Michael
HONEY, I BLEW UP THE KID
ROUND TRIP TO HEAVEN
Military, Frank
CRISSCROSS
Millan, Jim
USED PEOPLE
Millar, Gregory
LETHAL WEAPON 3
Millar, Michael
CLEARCUT
Millardet, Patricia
HOT CHOCOLATE
Miller, Andrea
EDWARD II
Miller, Andrew
OH, WHAT A NIGHT
Miller, Betty
LEAGUE OF THEIR OWN, A
Miller, Bob
MIGHTY DUCKS, THE
Miller, Dick
BODY WAVES
UNLAWFUL ENTRY
Miller, Eric
PRELUDE TO A KISS
Miller, Eric W.
TOYS

Miller, George
LONDON KILLS ME
Miller, Greg Marc
WHO SHOT PATAKANGO?
Miller, Harvey
THIS IS MY LIFE
Miller, James Earl
NEWSIES
Miller, Jeanette
COLD HEAVEN
Miller, Jeff
SUNSET STRIP
Miller, Jeffrey R.
TOYS
Miller, Joel McKinnon
FOREVER YOUNG
Miller, Joseph
FOLKS!
Miller, Kelly
RUNESTONE, THE
Miller, Kristy E.
TOYS
Miller, Larry
FROZEN ASSETS
Miller, Lisa Sheldon
HELL MASTER
Miller, Marisa
GUN IN BETTY LOU'S HANDBAG, THE
Miller, Mark
LOVE FIELD
Miller, Melanie
CUTTING EDGE, THE
Miller, Michael
CHAPLIN
Miller, Michael George
LETHAL WEAPON 3
Miller, Norma
MALCOLM X
Miller, Penelope Ann
CHAPLIN
GUN IN BETTY LOU'S HANDBAG, THE
YEAR OF THE COMET
Miller, Pola
BRENDA STARR
Miller, Rebecca
CONSENTING ADULTS
WIND
Miller, Sidney
LITTLE NEMO: ADVENTURES IN SLUMBERLAND
Miller, Taira
DAUGHTERS OF THE DUST
Millian, Andra
LOVE POTION NO. 9
Milligan, Henry
NIGHT AND THE CITY
Milligan, Tuck
OF MICE AND MEN
Milliken, Martha
COLD HEAVEN
Mills, Albert G. "Zeke"
HARD PROMISES
Mills, Michael
DEATH BECOMES HER

Mills, Ronald
FINE ROMANCE, A
Milnes, Kristopher
MUPPET CHRISTMAS CAROL, THE
Milo, Candy
COOL WORLD
I DON'T BUY KISSES ANYMORE
Miltes, John T.
BABE, THE
Milton, Clifford
RAMPAGE
Miltsakakis, Stefanos
DOUBLE TROUBLE
Milutin, Savic
JOURNEY OF HONOR
Minegishi, Toru
GODZILLA VS. BIOLLANTE
Minja, Stevan
JOURNEY OF HONOR
Minns, Byron
TRESPASS
Minns, Byron Keith
SOUTH CENTRAL
Minor, Bob
ACES: IRON EAGLE III
INNOCENT BLOOD
LOVE FIELD
UNLAWFUL ENTRY
Minor, Royce
UNLAWFUL ENTRY
Minsker, Andy
BROKEN NOSES
Minter, Kristin
PASSED AWAY
Minutoli, Domenico
JOHNNY STECCHINO
Miralles, Pedro
PEPI, LUCI, BOM AND OTHER GIRLS ON THE HEAP
Miranda, Althea
KICKBOXER 3: THE ART OF WAR
Miranda, Carlos
CAPTAIN RON
Miranda, Dianna
GUN IN BETTY LOU'S HANDBAG, THE
Miranda, Robert
SISTER ACT
Miranda, Salvador
MAMBO KINGS, THE
Mirandola, Vasco
MEDITERRANEO
Mirman, Edie
PROFESSIONAL, THE
VAMPIRE HUNTER D
Mirren, Helen
WHERE ANGELS FEAR TO TREAD
Mischwitzki, Gertrud
AFFENGEIL
Mishkin, Phil
KUFFS
Mishra, Loveleen
CITY OF JOY
Miskolczy, Victoria
SNEAKERS
Mita, Yoshiko
SILK ROAD, THE
Mitamura, Kunihiko
GODZILLA VS. BIOLLANTE
Mitani, Manami
JOURNEY OF HONOR
Mitchell, Aleta
MALCOLM X
Mitchell, Ben
FATHER
Mitchell, Billy
MALCOLM X
Mitchell, Brian
EDWARD II
Mitchell, Daryl "Chill"
BOOMERANG
Mitchell, Derek
SEX CRIMES
Mitchell, Heather
PROOF
Mitchell, Sasha
KICKBOXER 3: THE ART OF WAR
Mitchell, Scott
FATAL INSTINCT
Mitchell, Truce
ESCAPE FROM . . . SURVIVAL ZONE
Mitchum, Bentley
DEMONIC TOYS
MEATBALLS 4
Mitra, Rana
CITY OF JOY
Mittleman, Jonathan
PUSHED TO THE LIMIT
Miura, Kenji
JOURNEY OF HONOR
Miura, Shinichiro
MR. BASEBALL
Mixon, Mary Ann
CAN IT BE LOVE
Miyazaki, Gerrielani
MAN TROUBLE
Mize, Nicolas
BEETHOVEN
Mizer, Bob
DADDY AND THE MUSCLE ACADEMY
Mizushima, Shintaro
MR. BASEBALL
Mizutari, Craig
UNLAWFUL ENTRY
Mkhize, Gugu
SARAFINA!
Mkhize, Khanya
BOOMERANG
Mnisi, Jeremiah
POWER OF ONE, THE
Mo Chow
TIGER CLAWS
Mo, Teresa
HARD-BOILED
Mochnik, Paul
PASSED AWAY
Mock, Wild Bill
SOLDIER'S FORTUNE
Mockus, Jr., Tony
FOLKS!
Modano, Michael
MIGHTY DUCKS, THE
Model, Ben
PUERTO RICAN MAMBO (NOT A MUSICAL), THE
Modine, Matthew
WIND
Moeller, Gary
WHITE MEN CAN'T JUMP
Moeller, Ralph
UNIVERSAL SOLDIER
Moen, Marianna
DANCE MACABRE
Moericke, Costanze
BECOMING COLETTE
Moffat, Donald
HOUSESITTER
Moffett, Michelle
DEATHSTALKER IV: MATCH OF TITANS
HIRED TO KILL
Mofokeng, Thulani
SARAFINA!
Mogeridge, Ross
FATHER
Mogilevskaya, Marina
RASPAD
Moherlein, John
COLD JUSTICE
Mohrlein, John
HERO
Moio, John
SNEAKERS
Moir, Alison
JOHNNY SUEDE
Mok, Harry
TALONS OF THE EAGLE
Molero, Darlene
NETHERWORLD
Molina, Alfred
ENCHANTED APRIL
Molina, Angela
1492: THE CONQUEST OF PARADISE
Molina, Javier
DANZON
Molina, Rolando
AMERICAN ME
Molinare, Richard
RUNESTONE, THE
Molinari, Stefano
EVIL CLUTCH
Molinaro, Ursule
MY FATHER IS COMING
Moll, Randy
BABE, THE
Moloney, Aedin
FAR AND AWAY
Moloney, Terry
SHAKING THE TREE
Momo, Joseph
DOES THIS MEAN WE'RE MARRIED?
Monaco, Ralph
I DON'T BUY KISSES ANYMORE
RUNESTONE, THE
SNEAKERS
Monda, Youichi
MR. BASEBALL

Mondae, Brooks
TOYS

Moneta, Tullio
ODDBALL HALL

Monfort, Jean Claude
SWOON

Monich, Tim
FAR AND AWAY

Monjauze, Liza
STEAL AMERICA

Monk, Debra
PRELUDE TO A KISS

Monk, Isabell
CROSSING THE BRIDGE

Monks, Michael
OUT ON A LIMB

Monson, Lex
MALCOLM X

Montague, Helen
FAR AND AWAY

Montalvo, Miguel
WATERLAND

Monteaqudo, Rene
MAMBO KINGS, THE

Montes, Vira
AMERICAN ME

Montgomery, Elizabeth
PANAMA DECEPTION, THE

Montgomery, Julia
STOP! OR MY MOM WILL SHOOT

Montgomery, Lisa
LORENZO'S OIL

Montgomery, Peter
WIND

Montgomery, Reggie
MALCOLM X

Montini, Luigi
MEDITERRANEO

Montoya, Noe
RAISING CAIN

Montoya, Richard
ENCINO MAN
HERO

Moody, William A.
GIVING, THE

Moon, Lonnie
DAUGHTERS OF THE DUST

Moon, Philip
LETHAL WEAPON 3

Mooney, David
CHAPLIN

Mooney, John
SEEDPEOPLE

Mooney, Laura
LITTLE NEMO: ADVENTURES IN SLUMBERLAND

Moore, Argentina
MISSISSIPPI MASALA

Moore, Bennie
AMERICAN ME

Moore, Christopher Michael
ALMOST PREGNANT

Moore, Corwin
JUICE

Moore, Deborah Maria
CHAPLIN
INTO THE SUN

Moore, Demi
FEW GOOD MEN, A

Moore, Denis
FATHER

Moore, Dudley
BLAME IT ON THE BELLBOY

Moore, E.J.
POISON IVY

Moore, Jack
UNIVERSAL SOLDIER

Moore, Jeanie
WE'RE TALKIN' SERIOUS MONEY

Moore, Julianne
GUN IN BETTY LOU'S HANDBAG, THE
HAND THAT ROCKS THE CRADLE, THE

Moore, Kaycee
DAUGHTERS OF THE DUST

Moore, Kevin
UNDER SUSPICION

Moore, Kyle
PUBLIC EYE, THE

Moore, Lori June
BIG GIRLS DON'T CRY . . . THEY GET EVEN

Moore, Mahcoe
WHITE MEN CAN'T JUMP

Moore, Mary Ellen
FOREVER YOUNG
HONEY, I BLEW UP THE KID

Moore, Melissa
INTO THE SUN
OTHER WOMAN, THE
SORORITY HOUSE MASSACRE 2

Moore, Michelle
CONSENTING ADULTS

Moore, Muriel
MY COUSIN VINNY

Moore, Roger
BED & BREAKFAST

Moore, Sandy
BOOMERANG

Moore, Sheila
COMMON BONDS

Moore, Stephen
UNDER SUSPICION

Moosekian, Duke
PATRIOT GAMES

Mor, Juliano
DEADLY CURRENTS

Morales, Armando
KISS ME A KILLER

Morales, Esai
FREEJACK
ULTRAVIOLET

Morales, Gerald
FAVOUR, THE WATCH, AND THE VERY BIG FISH, THE

Moran, David Taylor
UNLAWFUL ENTRY

Moran, Joan
SEX CRIMES

Moran, Lauren
FROZEN ASSETS

Moran, Tim
INTO THE SUN

Moranis, Rick
HONEY, I BLEW UP THE KID

Morano, David M.
BODYGUARD, THE

Moreau, Jeanne
ALBERTO EXPRESS
LOVER, THE

Moreau, Marguerite
MIGHTY DUCKS, THE

Moreau, Marsha
BEAUTIFUL DREAMERS

Moreira, Angelo Barra
MEDICINE MAN

Morell, Jason
DAMAGE

Morelli, Robert
TWIN SISTERS

Moreno, Sergio
HOURS AND TIMES, THE

Moreno-Orrison, Laura
RAMPAGE

Morettini, Mark
HOME ALONE 2: LOST IN NEW YORK

Morgan, Frances
MALCOLM X

Morgan, Jaye P.
HOME ALONE 2: LOST IN NEW YORK

Morgan, Leah
LOVE CRIMES

Morgan, Mark
GIVING, THE

Morgan, Robert
FATHER

Morgan, Stafford
WILD ORCHID 2: TWO SHADES OF BLUE

Morgan, Steven
SOCIETY

Morgenroth, Robert
PUSHED TO THE LIMIT

Morgenstern, Dan
TEXAS TENOR: THE ILLINOIS JACQUET STORY

Moriarity, Daniel
OTHER WOMAN, THE

Moriarty, Cathy
GUN IN BETTY LOU'S HANDBAG, THE
MAMBO KINGS, THE

Moriarty, P.H.
CHAPLIN
PATRIOT GAMES

Morin, D. David
HERO

Morinaga, Kenji
MR. BASEBALL

Morita, Pat
AUNTIE LEE'S MEAT PIES
COLLISION COURSE
DO OR DIE
HONEYMOON IN VEGAS
MIRACLE BEACH

Morita, Yoshiya
MR. BASEBALL
Mork, Erik
ZENTROPA
Morkeborg, Peer
BECOMING COLETTE
Morley, Grace
AMERICAN ME
SEX CRIMES
Morley, J.R.
KILLER TOMATOES EAT FRANCE!
Morrell, Carla
BASKET CASE 3: THE PROGENY
Morrell, Carmen
BASKET CASE 3: THE PROGENY
Morrell, Carolyn
RAISING CAIN
Morris, Ann
MY GRANDPA IS A VAMPIRE
Morris, Colleen
DEATH BECOMES HER
Morris, Dean
BRENDA STARR
Morris, Garrett
CHILDREN OF THE NIGHT
SEVERED TIES
Morris, James
PLAYBOYS, THE
Morris, James T.
DEEP COVER
STREET CRIMES
Morris, Leslie
MEGAVILLE
Morris, Michael
PROJECT: SHADOWCHASER
Morris, Peter
PLAYBOYS, THE
Morris, Wolfe
SHINING THROUGH
Morrisette, Billy
SEVERED TIES
Morrison, Carlin Orville
THUNDERHEART
Morrison, Robert
ULTIMATE DESIRES
Morrison, Rudy E.
HOFFA
Morrissey, David
WATERLAND
Morse, Natalie
POWER OF ONE, THE
Morshower, Glenn
UNDER SIEGE
Mortato, Lucia
HELLROLLER
Mortil, Janne
COMMON BONDS
Morton, Amy
STRAIGHT TALK
Morton, Chad
BEETHOVEN
Morton, Joe
FOREVER YOUNG
OF MICE AND MEN
Morton, Rob
LEAVING NORMAL

Mortorff, Lawrence
HELLRAISER III: HELL ON EARTH
Moscaritola, Vincent
MALCOLM X
Moscow, David
NEWSIES
Moseley, Bill
HONEY, I BLEW UP THE KID
Moseley, Stacy
ALAN & NAOMI
Moses, Senta
HOME ALONE 2:
LOST IN NEW YORK
Mosiman, Marnie
HERO
Mosley, Roger E.
UNLAWFUL ENTRY
Moss, Jim
FIELD OF FIRE
Moss, Lambert
BAD LIEUTENANT
Moss, Michael
PASSENGER 57
Motiv, Lieutenant Kobi
DEADLY CURRENTS
Motloung, Phakiso
SARAFINA!
Mount Scott Boxing Club Members
BROKEN NOSES
Moussati, Karim
TOTO LE HEROS
Mousseau, Steve
CLEARCUT
Moussilides, Poll
FAR AND AWAY
Mouton, Benjamin
BASIC INSTINCT
Mowod, John
LORENZO'S OIL
Moy, Wood
FINAL ANALYSIS
Moya, Bercelio
1492: THE CONQUEST OF PARADISE
Moya, Pat
IN THE SOUP
Moynahan, Bill
DOUBLE TROUBLE
Moyo, Alois
POWER OF ONE, THE
Moyo, Banele Dala
POWER OF ONE, THE
Moyo, Peggy
POWER OF ONE, THE
Mqadi, Bheki
SARAFINA!
Mr. Shaban
K2
Msala, Princess
SARAFINA!
Mseleku, Wendy
SARAFINA!
Msini, Velaphi
SARAFINA!
Mtethwa, Sduduzo
SARAFINA!

Mthoba, James
SARAFINA!
Mucci, David
UNFORGIVEN
Mudara, Emanuel
MISSISSIPPI MASALA
Mudd, John A.
SWOON
Mueller, Julia
REFRIGERATOR, THE
Mueller, Marcus "Wally the Wall"
CAN IT BE LOVE
Mueller, Maureen
OVER HER DEAD BODY
Mueller, Rafael
VENICE/VENICE
Mueller, Tracy
BECOMING COLETTE
Mueller-Stahl, Armin
NIGHT ON EARTH
POWER OF ONE, THE
Muellerleile, Marianne
PASSION FISH
Muglia, Nick
MALCOLM X
Muhammad, Zaahir
MALCOLM X
Muir, Mike
ENCINO MAN
Muir, Tiina
CUTTING EDGE, THE
Mujumdar, Anashua
CITY OF JOY
Mukherjee, Manu
CITY OF JOY
Mukherjee, Sujan
CITY OF JOY
Mukherjee, Sunil
CITY OF JOY
Mulheren, Michael
JOHNNY SUEDE
Mulherin, Joe
CONSENTING ADULTS
Mulholland, George
SOUTH CENTRAL
Mulholland, Mark
FAR AND AWAY
Mulkey, Chris
DEADBOLT
GAS FOOD LODGING
Mull, Martin
DANCE WITH DEATH
MIRACLE BEACH
PLAYER, THE
Mullane, Larry
BAD LIEUTENANT
Mullen, Bill
GUN IN BETTY LOU'S
HANDBAG, THE
Mullen, Michael
HERO
Mullen, Monique
SAVAGE INSTINCT
Muller, Terry "Turk"
HERO
SHAKING THE TREE

Muller, Wolfgang W.
SHINING THROUGH
Mullerleile, Mary Ann
LITTLE SISTER
Mullin, Peter L.
MIGHTY DUCKS, THE
Mulrean, Peter
CAPTAIN AMERICA
Mulroney, Dermot
WHERE THE DAY TAKES YOU
Mumy, Bill
CAPTAIN AMERICA
DOUBLE TROUBLE
Munch, Gary
KUFFS
Munford, Tricia
BABE, THE
Munic, Robert
RADIO FLYER
Munn, Brian
FAR AND AWAY
Munn, Colin James
LEAVING NORMAL
Munns, Robert
FOREVER YOUNG
HERO
Munro, Neil
BEETHOVEN LIVES UPSTAIRS
GATE II
Munro, Sharon
EDWARD II
Munroe, Jan
FEW GOOD MEN, A
Munster, Klaus
SHINING THROUGH
Munuz, Erol
WITCHCRAFT IV: VIRGIN HEART
Murdoch, Lachlan
LEAVING NORMAL
Murdock, George
FINAL ANALYSIS
Murillo-Carr, Gerardo
HERO
Murphy, Barri
ARMED FOR ACTION
Murphy, Eddie
BOOMERANG
DISTINGUISHED GENTLEMAN, THE
Murphy, Gerry
NIGHT AND THE CITY
Murphy, Harmony
BIG GIRLS DON'T CRY . . . THEY GET EVEN
Murphy, Margaret
FOLKS!
Murphy, Michael
BATMAN RETURNS
BIG GIRLS DON'T CRY . . . THEY GET EVEN
FOLKS!
Murphy, Reilly
BIG GIRLS DON'T CRY . . . THEY GET EVEN
Murphy, Sally
PRELUDE TO A KISS
SCENT OF A WOMAN
Murphy, Shaggy
BIG GIRLS DON'T CRY . . . THEY GET EVEN
Murphy, Thomas
DEATH BECOMES HER
Murphy, Wesley
FAR AND AWAY
Murrah, Joyce
MISSISSIPPI MASALA
Murray, Bill
MANIAC WARRIORS
Murray, Brian
BOB ROBERTS
Murray, Carrie
MAXIMUM BREAKOUT
Murray, James
BRAM STOKER'S DRACULA
Murray, Joel
SHAKES THE CLOWN
Murray, Mary Gordon
POISON IVY
Murray, Rosemary
LUNATIC, THE
Murray, Steve
UNDER SUSPICION
Murtagh, Kate
ROOTS OF EVIL
Murtaugh, James
MALCOLM X
Musafar, Fakir
MY FATHER IS COMING
Musaka, Naomasa
TETSUO: THE IRON MAN
Mussetter, Jude
HIRED TO KILL
Mustain, Minor
SNAKEEATER III . . . HIS LAW
Mustillo, Louis
PASSED AWAY
Muta, Masashi
JOURNEY OF HONOR
Muti, Ornella
ONCE UPON A CRIME
Mutnick, Andrew
COMPLEX WORLD
Mutoh, Kazukuni
MR. BASEBALL
Muzadi, Pascal
CTHULHU MANSION
Muzila, Tom
UNDER SIEGE
Mvicane, Olga
SARAFINA!
Mwale, Akim
POWER OF ONE, THE
Myers, Mike
WAYNE'S WORLD
Myers, Toby
FALLING FROM GRACE
Myles, Ken
BODYGUARD, THE
Myles, Rayhana
SARAFINA!
Myra
24 HOURS TO MIDNIGHT
Myra J.
BEBE'S KIDS
Mzolo, Nkosana
SARAFINA!
N'Gom, Abdoulaye
HOME ALONE 2: LOST IN NEW YORK
Nacho, Father
ACES: IRON EAGLE III
Nadal, Vincent
BECOMING COLETTE
Nadarevic, Mustafa
CAPTAIN AMERICA
Nader, Michael
FINISHING TOUCH, THE
Nagae, Hiro
MR. BASEBALL
Nagan, Rebecca
MUPPET CHRISTMAS CAROL, THE
Nagano, Hirokazu
MR. BASEBALL
Nagashima, Toshiyuki
GODZILLA VS. BIOLLANTE
Nagy, Michelle
BOB ROBERTS
Nahyr, Maite
DOES THIS MEAN WE'RE MARRIED?
Nair, John
CITY OF JOY
Nair, Mira
MISSISSIPPI MASALA
Nair, Sahira
MISSISSIPPI MASALA
Najeeullah, Mansoor
MALCOLM X
SCENT OF A WOMAN
Najera, Miguel
RAMPAGE
Najimy, Kathy
SISTER ACT
THIS IS MY LIFE
Nakagawa, Anna
SILK ROAD, THE
Nakajima, Shogo
MR. BASEBALL
Nakane, Masahiro
MR. BASEBALL
Nalis, Autun
CAPTAIN AMERICA
Nance, Jack
MEATBALLS 4
Nann, Erika
ANIMAL INSTINCTS
FINAL IMPACT
NIGHT RHYTHMS
Napaul, Neriah
BIKINI CARWASH COMPANY, THE
Napier, Charles
CENTER OF THE WEB
HOMICIDAL IMPULSE
INDIO 2 - THE REVOLT
LONELY HEARTS
SOLDIER'S FORTUNE
Napier, Markus
SHINING THROUGH

Napier, Marshall
FLIRTING
Napio, David
MANIAC WARRIORS
Naples, Toni
MUNCHIE
Nardi, Tony
ADJUSTER, THE
Narita, Richard
UNLAWFUL ENTRY
Nasaka, Yuki
JOURNEY OF HONOR
Nash, Jennifer
PLAYER, THE
Nash, Mary
HOWARDS END
Nasrallah, Dana
SWOON
Naufts, Geoffrey
FEW GOOD MEN, A
Navarre, Louis
FAVOUR, THE WATCH, AND THE VERY BIG FISH, THE
Navarro, Martha
DANZON
Navon, Shim
DEADLY CURRENTS
Navratil, Borivoj
EAR, THE
Naya, Ernique
PEPI, LUCI, BOM AND OTHER GIRLS ON THE HEAP
Naylor, Brian
BABE, THE
Naylor, Marcus
MALCOLM X
Nayyar, Harsh
NIGHT AND THE CITY
Ndlovu, Alfred
SARAFINA!
Ndlovu, Patrick
SARAFINA!
Neal, Billie
CONSENTING ADULTS
GUN IN BETTY LOU'S HANDBAG, THE
Neal, Rome
MALCOLM X
Neal, Siri
CHILDREN, THE
WATERLAND
Neale, Leslie
HONEY, I BLEW UP THE KID
Neer, Joanne
HOFFA
Neeson, Liam
HUSBANDS AND WIVES
LEAP OF FAITH
SHINING THROUGH
UNDER SUSPICION
Negoda, Natalya
BACK IN THE U.S.S.R.
Negret, Francois
NIGHT AND DAY
Neil
35 UP
Neil, Ed
BREATHING FIRE
Neill, Sam
MEMOIRS OF AN INVISIBLE MAN
Nelligan, Kate
SHADOWS AND FOG
Nelson, Bob
BRAIN DONORS
THIS IS MY LIFE
Nelson, Ed
BRENDA STARR
Nelson, Guy
INVASION OF THE SPACE PREACHERS
Nelson, Jerry
MUPPET CHRISTMAS CAROL, THE
Nelson, Josh
HONEYMOON IN VEGAS
Nelson, Judd
PRIMARY MOTIVE
Nelson, Linda
LIFE ON THE EDGE
Nelson, Marty
TUNE, THE
Nelson, Peter
EYE OF THE EAGLE 3
Nelson, Race
3 NINJAS
Nelson, Tim Blake
THIS IS MY LIFE
Nementz, Rudy Francis
SNEAKERS
Neri, Francesca
CAPTAIN AMERICA
Nero, Franco
TOUCH AND DIE
Nesbitt, Michael L.
CONSENTING ADULTS
Nesci, John
CRISSCROSS
Nesline, Michael
SWOON
Nettles, Irene
WHITE MEN CAN'T JUMP
Nettles-Bey, Marctwaine
GLADIATOR
Neukirch, Rob
OUT ON A LIMB
Neuman, Leonard
RAMPAGE
Neville, Kimberly
NOISES OFF
New, Barbara
EDWARD II
Newbern, George
LITTLE SISTER
Newcomb, Deana
LOVE HURTS
Newhouse, Sarah
HOUSE ON TOMBSTONE HILL, THE
Newman, Andrew Hill
LETHAL WEAPON 3
Newman, Daniel
BRAM STOKER'S DRACULA
Newman, David
RUNESTONE, THE
Newman, William
HERO
Newsome, Paula
STRAIGHT TALK
Newson, Lloyd
EDWARD II
Newton, John Haymes
DESERT KICKBOXER
Newton, Thandie
FLIRTING
Ng, Craig
LEATHER JACKETS
Ngakane, Sam
SARAFINA!
Ngcamu, Siphamandla
SARAFINA!
Ngcobe, Siya
SARAFINA!
Ngema, Mbongeni
SARAFINA!
Ngema, Nhlanhla
SARAFINA!
Ngema, Sibusiso
SARAFINA!
Ngobese, Vincent
SARAFINA!
Nguyen, Dustin
RAPID FIRE
Nguyen, Eric
INDOCHINE
Ngwenya, Liz
POWER OF ONE, THE
Nhlangothi, Ayanda
SARAFINA!
Nicholas
35 UP
Nicholas, Anna
FINAL ANALYSIS
Nicholas, Thomas Ian
RADIO FLYER
Nicholls, Allan
BOB ROBERTS
Nichols, Jane
SCHOOL TIES
Nichols, Jeff
SCHOOL TIES
Nichols, Robert
UNDER SIEGE
Nichols, Susan
TERMINAL BLISS
Nicholson, Jack
FEW GOOD MEN, A
HOFFA
MAN TROUBLE
Nicholson, Jennifer
HOFFA
Nickles, Michael A.
DEATH BECOMES HER
Nickman, Bob
CROSSING THE BRIDGE
SHAKES THE CLOWN
Nicksay, Alexander
WHITE SANDS
Nickson-Soul, Julia
K2

Nicola, Larry
GIVING, THE
Nicoli, Vincenzo
ALIEN3
Nicolosi, Michael
BABE, THE
Nicotero, Sam
HOFFA
Nieden, Daniel
TUNE, THE
Nielsen, Barbara
LIGHT IN THE JUNGLE, THE
Nielsen, Brigitte
MISSION OF JUSTICE
976-EVIL II
Nielsen, Joshua
DR. GIGGLES
Niemeyer, Shelly
LEAGUE OF THEIR OWN, A
Nieves, Mario
FOLKS!
Nikkari, Esko
MATCH FACTORY GIRL, THE
Nimerfro, Scott Lloyd
RADIO FLYER
NiMhuiri, Aine
PLAYBOYS, THE
Nino, Miguel
UNDER SIEGE
Nipar, Yvette
DOCTOR MORDRID
Nipote, Joe
WATERDANCE, THE
Nirvana
1991: THE YEAR PUNK BROKE
Nisbett, Joanne
CUTTING EDGE, THE
Nishida, Toshiyuki
SILK ROAD, THE
Nishimura, Joh
MR. BASEBALL
Nitschke, Ronald
SHINING THROUGH
Nixon, DeVaughn
BEBE'S KIDS
BODYGUARD, THE
Nobbs, Eric
POWER OF ONE, THE
Nobis, Felix
FLIRTING
Noble, Bob
BRENDA STARR
Noble, Maurice
MAGICAL WORLD OF CHUCK JONES, THE
Nocerino, Anthony
HUSBANDS AND WIVES
MALCOLM X
Nogulich, Natalija
HOFFA
Nolan, Robert
TIGER CLAWS
Nolan, Roger
RAMPAGE
STEPHEN KING'S SLEEPWALKERS
Noland, Charles
WAYNE'S WORLD
Nolen, Dean
ARMED FOR ACTION
BLOOD ON THE BADGE
Nolte, Nick
LORENZO'S OIL
PLAYER, THE
Noonan, Kate
FALLING FROM GRACE
Noonan, Tom
COLLISION COURSE
Norby, Ghita
BEST INTENTIONS, THE
Nordling, Jeffrey
RUBY
Norman, Zack
VENICE/VENICE
Normandeau, Raymond
LIGHT SLEEPER
Norris, Dean
LAWNMOWER MAN, THE
Norris, Eric
UNIVERSAL SOLDIER
Norris, William J.
BABE, THE
Norstrom, Bertil
BEST INTENTIONS, THE
Norte, Victor
WINTER IN LISBON, THE
Northrup, Christopher Todd
LIGHT SLEEPER
Northup, Harry
HERO
UNLAWFUL ENTRY
Norton, Alex
BLAME IT ON THE BELLBOY
PATRIOT GAMES
UNDER SUSPICION
Norton, Dee Dee
CONFESSIONS OF A SERIAL KILLER
Norton, Dennis
LOVE CRIMES
Norton, James
EDWARD II
Norton, Jim
MEMOIRS OF AN INVISIBLE MAN
Norton, Richard
CHINA O'BRIEN II
LADY DRAGON
Norton, Terry
KICK OR DIE
Nosek, Dionne Lynn
STRAIGHT TALK
Noseworthy, Jack
ENCINO MAN
Noto, Vic
INNOCENT BLOOD
Nouri, Michael
BLACK ICE
CAPTAIN AMERICA
LITTLE VEGAS
PSYCHIC
Novak, Frank
NEWSIES
STEPHEN KING'S SLEEPWALKERS
Novak, Kim
CHILDREN, THE
Novinski, Billy Joe
LIGHT SLEEPER
Now, Michael
LIVING END, THE
Nowe, Keri
BOB ROBERTS
Nowicki, Tom
PASSENGER 57
NRBQ
COMPLEX WORLD
Ntshona, Winston
POWER OF ONE, THE
Nugent, Patrick
BABE, THE
Nugent-Head, Marie
LORENZO'S OIL
Nunes, Delroy
LONDON KILLS ME
Nunez, Jr., Miguel
ROUND TRIP TO HEAVEN
Nunez, Miguel
LETHAL WEAPON 3
Nungray, Johnny
PUSHED TO THE LIMIT
Nunn, Bill
SISTER ACT
Nurse, Michael
HOUSESITTER
Nussbaum, Mike
GLADIATOR
Nutini, Jean Pierre
PASSED AWAY
Nuttall, Jeff
DAMAGE
Nyroos, Gunilla
BEST INTENTIONS, THE
Nzonzi, Pascal
NIGHT ON EARTH
O, Barbara
DAUGHTERS OF THE DUST
O, George
FOLKS!
O'Brey, Larry
GATE II
O'Brien, Austin
LAWNMOWER MAN, THE
O'Brien, Barret
NETHERWORLD
O'Brien, Donald
DEVIL'S DAUGHTER, THE
O'Brien, Giorgia
JOHNNY STECCHINO
O'Brien, Joycelyn
MAMBO KINGS, THE
O'Brien, Kevin
HOUSESITTER
O'Brien, Laurie
GAS FOOD LODGING
O'Brien, Marlane
LEAVING NORMAL
O'Brien, Niall
PLAYBOYS, THE
O'Brien, Quentin
RAPID FIRE
O'Bryan, Patrick
976-EVIL II

O'Bryan, Sean
CHAPLIN
O'Byrne, Kehli
K2
O'Connell, Bridget
COLD JUSTICE
O'Connell, Deirdre
COOL WORLD
CRISSCROSS
FALLING FROM GRACE
LEAVING NORMAL
STRAIGHT TALK
O'Connell, Patricia
PASSED AWAY
O'Connor, Donald
TOYS
O'Connor, Helen
TILL THERE WAS YOU
O'Connor, Kevin J.
HERO
O'Connor, Raymond
MEGAVILLE
O'Connor, Rosie
BATMAN RETURNS
O'Doherty, James
BASKET CASE 3: THE PROGENY
O'Donell, Steven
DEMON IN MY VIEW, A
O'Donnell, Chris
SCENT OF A WOMAN
SCHOOL TIES
O'Donnell, Rosie
LEAGUE OF THEIR OWN, A
O'Donnell, Steven
FAR AND AWAY
POPE MUST DIET!, THE
O'Donovan, Noel
FAR AND AWAY
O'Dwyer, Michael
HERO
O'Fatharta, MacDara
FAR AND AWAY
O'Grady, Rynagh
FAR AND AWAY
O'Gulihur, Jason
WITCHCRAFT IV: VIRGIN HEART
O'Haco, Daniel
BEASTMASTER 2:
THROUGH THE PORTAL OF TIME
O'Haco, Jeff
GUN IN BETTY LOU'S
HANDBAG, THE
O'Hara, Catherine
HOME ALONE 2:
LOST IN NEW YORK
LITTLE VEGAS
O'Hara, Colleen
BEETHOVEN
O'Hara, Joan
FAR AND AWAY
O'Hurley, John
MIRROR IMAGES
NIGHT EYES 2
O'Leary, Brian
PLAYBOYS, THE
O'Leary, Hal
BOB ROBERTS
O'Leary, Harold
PASSED AWAY
O'Leary, Pat
TEXAS TENOR:
THE ILLINOIS JACQUET STORY
O'Leary, Tara
RAMPAGE
O'Malley, Bingo
BOB ROBERTS
O'Meara, Brian A.
THUNDERHEART
O'Neal, Cleveland
NOISES OFF
O'Neal, Granvile
ARTICLE 99
O'Neal, Griffin
GHOULIES III:
GHOULIES GO TO COLLEGE
O'Neal, Patrick
UNDER SIEGE
O'Neal, Ron
DEATH HOUSE
O'Neal, Tatum
LITTLE NOISES
O'Neil, Dink
HELLROLLER
O'Neil, Shaun
MALCOLM X
O'Neil, William Dean
OUT ON A LIMB
O'Neill, Amy
HONEY, I BLEW UP THE KID
O'Neill, Ed
WAYNE'S WORLD
O'Neill, Maggie
UNDER SUSPICION
O'Neill, Michael
GUN IN BETTY LOU'S
HANDBAG, THE
JENNIFER EIGHT
LORENZO'S OIL
O'Neill, Robert James
PROOF
O'Quinn, Terry
CUTTING EDGE, THE
O'Reilly, Robert
DESERT KICKBOXER
O'Ross, Ed
PLAY NICE
UNIVERSAL SOLDIER
O'Shaughnessy, Brian
POWER OF ONE, THE
O'Shea, Brian
GLADIATOR
O'Shea, Milo
PLAYBOYS, THE
Oakland, Fred
RIVER RUNS THROUGH IT, A
Oakland, Leonard A.
WHITE MEN CAN'T JUMP
Oberheu, Ken
I DON'T BUY KISSES ANYMORE
Oberman, Charles
K2
Oberman, Claire
PATRIOT GAMES
Obodiac, Hadley
HIGHWAY 61
Obrand, Amy
SOCIETY
Obregon, Rodrigo
EXILED IN AMERICA
Obst, Oly
THIS IS MY LIFE
Ocampo, Isaac
RADIO FLYER
Ocean, Ivory
BIG GIRLS DON'T CRY . . . THEY
GET EVEN
CLASS ACT
PLAY MURDER FOR ME
SOUTH CENTRAL
Ochlan, P.J.
LITTLE VEGAS
Ochs, Jim
HOFFA
Odajima, Takashi
JOURNEY OF HONOR
Odaka, Megumi
GODZILLA VS. BIOLLANTE
Oddo, Lynn
HERO
Odom, George T.
MALCOLM X
Odriozola, Ron
HOMEBOYS
Offner, Deborah
LOVE FIELD
UNLAWFUL ENTRY
Ogasawara, Tadashi
JOURNEY OF HONOR
Ogilvy, Ian
DEATH BECOMES HER
Ogiwara, Toshimi
JOURNEY OF HONOR
Ohoki, Shoji
MR. BASEBALL
Ohrman, Ward
PRELUDE TO A KISS
Ohsumi, Masato
MR. BASEBALL
Ojeda, Juan
BREATHING FIRE
Okada, Janine
CAPTAIN RON
Olajuwon, Hakeen
HEAVEN IS A PLAYGROUND
Oldfield, Brian
SAVAGE INSTINCT
Oldman, Gary
BRAM STOKER'S DRACULA
Olekceenko, Vladimir
RASPAD
Olin, Tom
TEXAS TENOR:
THE ILLINOIS JACQUET STORY
Olita, Joseph
MISSISSIPPI MASALA
Oliver, Allen
COMPLEX WORLD
Oliver, David
EDWARD II
PROJECT: SHADOWCHASER

Oliver, James
LETHAL WEAPON 3
RADIO FLYER
Oliver, John
MIGHTY DUCKS, THE
Oliver, Leslie
VENICE/VENICE
Oliver, Natalie
MISSISSIPPI MASALA
Oliver, Rochelle
SCENT OF A WOMAN
Oliveri, Robert
HONEY, I BLEW UP THE KID
Olivier, Dhan
FAVOUR, THE WATCH, AND THE VERY BIG FISH, THE
Olivis, Lamar
LORENZO'S OIL
Olivo, Maria A. Ferrari
MR. SATURDAY NIGHT
Olkewicz, Walter
TWIN PEAKS: FIRE WALK WITH ME
Olmedo, Juan
FOLKS!
Olmos, Edward James
AMERICAN ME
Olsen, "Crazy Steve"
SINGLES
Olsen, Patrick Lars
NEWSIES
Olsen, Richard K.
ALAN & NAOMI
Olsen, Ryan
LEAGUE OF THEIR OWN, A
Olson, Heather Lauren
BLOODFIST IV: DIE TRYING
Oman, Bernarda
CAPTAIN AMERICA
Ommaya, Ayub
LORENZO'S OIL
Onate, Erik
BATMAN RETURNS
Ong, Jack
I DON'T BUY KISSES ANYMORE
Ontiveros, Lupe
DOLLY DEAREST
UNIVERSAL SOLDIER
Ooms, Michael
MIGHTY DUCKS, THE
Oparei, Dhobi
ALIEN3
Opocensky, Gustav
EAR, THE
Oppenheimer, Alan
LITTLE NEMO: ADVENTURES IN SLUMBERLAND
LOVE FIELD
Oppenheimer, Michael
STRAIGHT TALK
Opper, Don Keith
CRITTERS 4
GUN IN BETTY LOU'S HANDBAG, THE
Orbach, Jerry
MR. SATURDAY NIGHT
STRAIGHT TALK
UNIVERSAL SOLDIER

Orbach, Ron
LOVE CRIMES
Orcier, Fabien
POUR SACHA
Orgolini, Lisa
SHINING THROUGH
Ormsby, Robert
TROLL 2
Orniga, Miguel
KICKBOXER 3: THE ART OF WAR
Orsatti, Frank
RUBY
Orsini, Tino
PUSHED TO THE LIMIT
Ortega, Chick
DELICATESSEN
Ortelli, Dyana
AMERICAN ME
Ortiz, Cecelia Neal
MAMBO KINGS, THE
Ortiz, Jessica Neal
MAMBO KINGS, THE
Ortiz, Jose Angel
CAPTAIN RON
Ortiz, Roberto
DANZON
Ortlieb, Jim
BABE, THE
Orton, Tanya
MANIAC WARRIORS
Osborn, Bill
MIDNIGHT CLEAR, A
Osborne, John
POWER OF ONE, THE
Osborne, Kent
SCHOOL TIES
Oss, Eniko
BRAM STOKER'S DRACULA
Osteen, Aubrey J.
MY COUSIN VINNY
Osterhage, Jeffrey
SEX CRIMES
Osterweil, Richard
PAINTING THE TOWN
Ostos, Auturo
BARBARIAN QUEEN II: THE EMPRESS STRIKES BACK
Ostrin, Greg
PUSHED TO THE LIMIT
Ostrow, Ron
FEW GOOD MEN, A
Otoin, Bazil
TOUCH AND DIE
Otrin, John
CHAPLIN
Ott, Margaret Rose
RAMPAGE
Ottavino, John
BOB ROBERTS
MALCOLM X
Ottley, Rachelle
CUTTING EDGE, THE
Otto, Christopher
HOFFA
Otto, Kevin
WHO SHOT PATAKANGO?

Ouimette, Stephen
ADJUSTER, THE
Outinen, Kati
MATCH FACTORY GIRL, THE
Outlaw, Patrick
GLADIATOR
Overton, Kristina
EDWARD II
Oviedo, Adrian A.
ACES: IRON EAGLE III
Owczarek, Bob
COMPLEX WORLD
Owen, Mary Anne
HAND THAT ROCKS THE CRADLE, THE
Owen, Timothy
TERMINAL BLISS
Owens, Gerald
FOLKS!
Owens, Jack
DEEP BLUES
Owens, Mel
DISTINGUISHED GENTLEMAN, THE
Owens, Michael George
TRACES OF RED
Owens, Richard
MALCOLM X
Oxenberg, Catherine
SEXUAL RESPONSE
Oxenberg, Jan
THANK YOU AND GOOD NIGHT!
Oxford, Diane
BASKET CASE 3: THE PROGENY
Oxley, Stephen
UNDER SUSPICION
Oz, Frank
INNOCENT BLOOD
MUPPET CHRISTMAS CAROL, THE
Ozermuller, Thomass
EMMANUELLE 6
Ozier, William
ZEBRAHEAD
P., Miller
MAMBO KINGS, THE
Pabst, Robert
HERO
Pace-Rhodes, Shun
LEAP OF FAITH
Pacino, Al
GLENGARRY GLEN ROSS
SCENT OF A WOMAN
Pack, Stephanie
HOURS AND TIMES, THE
Packalen, Marja
MATCH FACTORY GIRL, THE
Packer-Phillips, Mary K.E.
CONSENTING ADULTS
Pacula, Joanna
BLACK ICE
HUSBANDS AND LOVERS
Padick, Lauren
MALCOLM X
Padilla, George
AMERICAN ME
Padunov, Vladimir
LORENZO'S OIL

Page, Don
BRIEF HISTORY OF TIME, A
Page, LaWanda
SHAKES THE CLOWN
Pageon, Daniel Andre
AFRAID OF THE DARK
Pagett, Gary
COLD HEAVEN
Pahor, Galliano
CAPTAIN AMERICA
Pai, Liana
ZEBRAHEAD
Paige, Ken
LOVE HURTS
Paige, Raymond
DAUGHTERS OF THE DUST
Paik, Greg
GUYVER, THE
MR. SATURDAY NIGHT
Palillo, Ron
WIND
Palis, Jonathan
CANVAS
Pall, Robert
MIGHTY DUCKS, THE
Palm, Michael
PALE BLOOD
Palmas, Joseph
SCENT OF A WOMAN
Palmer, Adam James
MANIAC WARRIORS
Palmer, Greg
FLIRTING
Palmer, Kalvin
WATERLAND
Palmer, Marion
HONEY, I BLEW UP THE KID
Palmer, Robert
DEEP BLUES
Palminteri, Chazz
INNOCENT BLOOD
Palminteri, Lorenzo
NIGHT AND THE CITY
Palmisano, Conrad E.
UNDER SIEGE
Palombi, Luciana
JOHNNY STECCHINO
Palomino, Carlos
RAMPAGE
Pan Qing-fu
TALONS OF THE EAGLE
Panda, Gouri Sankar
CITY OF JOY
Panesar, Amrit
MISSISSIPPI MASALA
Pankin, Stuart
VAGRANT, THE
Pankiw, Alex
MANIAC WARRIORS
Pankow, John
STRANGER AMONG US, A
Panos, Greg
WHITE TRASH
Pansullo, Ed
ROADSIDE PROPHETS
Pantaleo, Peter
HOME ALONE 2:
LOST IN NEW YORK
Pantera
FOR THOSE ABOUT TO ROCK
Pantoliano, Joe
USED PEOPLE
Paoli, Cecile
NEAR MISSES
Paolone, Catherine
UNLAWFUL ENTRY
WE'RE TALKIN' SERIOUS MONEY
Papaioannou, Penny
CUTTING EDGE, THE
Papajohn, Michael
BABE, THE
MR. BASEBALL
Papalia, Fedele
DOES THIS MEAN WE'RE
MARRIED?
FAVOUR, THE WATCH, AND THE
VERY BIG FISH, THE
Papia, Frank
CAPTAIN AMERICA
Papick, Barry
LITTLE NOISES
Papineau, Alice
LAST OF THE MOHICANS, THE
Pappalardo, Ignazio
JOHNNY STECCHINO
Paquet, Lucina
PRELUDE TO A KISS
Paradise, James
BUFFY THE VAMPIRE SLAYER
Paragon, John
DOUBLE TROUBLE
HONEY, I BLEW UP THE KID
Paramore, Kiri
FLIRTING
Parbario, Phavin
MISSISSIPPI MASALA
Pare, Michael
BLINK OF AN EYE
INTO THE SUN
Parenti, Rose
SISTER ACT
Parfitt, Bill
PETER'S FRIENDS
Parham, Wendy
BASKET CASE 3: THE PROGENY
Parian, Levon
LIFE ON THE EDGE
Parigot, Guy
INSPECTOR LAVARDIN
Parillaud, Anne
INNOCENT BLOOD
Paris, Freddie
FLIRTING
Paris, Gerald
HOWARDS END
Parish, T.J.
FOLKS!
Park, Steve
KUFFS
TOYS
Parke, Greg
ROCK & ROLL COWBOYS
Parke, Sean
STEAL AMERICA
Parker, Brad
CHAPLIN
Parker, Carl
RUNESTONE, THE
Parker, David M.
SISTER ACT
Parker, David Shaw
MUPPET CHRISTMAS CAROL, THE
Parker, Dewitt
DAUGHTERS OF THE DUST
Parker, Ginny
CONSENTING ADULTS
Parker, Jackie
DAUGHTERS OF THE DUST
Parker, Joel "Wolf"
GIVING, THE
Parker, Leonard
MALCOLM X
Parker, Michael
KILL LINE
SINGLES
Parker, Nathaniel
BODYGUARD, THE
Parker, Ray
COMPLEX WORLD
Parker, Sarah Jessica
HONEYMOON IN VEGAS
Parker, Shanna
DAUGHTERS OF THE DUST
Parker, Trey
NEWSIES
Parkes, Gerard
ADJUSTER, THE
Parks, James
TWIN PEAKS: FIRE WALK WITH ME
Parks, John
MALCOLM X
Parks, Michael
STORYVILLE
Parks, Muhammad
MALCOLM X
Parks, Tom
LADYBUGS
Parlato, Dennis
JOHNNY SUEDE
Paroux, Patrick
DELICATESSEN
Parrish, Steve
SCANNERS III: THE TAKEOVER
Parry, Chinere
MALCOLM X
Parry, Luke
HOWARDS END
Parsons, Karyn
CLASS ACT
Parsons, Nancy
LADYBUGS
Parton, Dolly
STRAIGHT TALK
Partridge, Ross
KUFFS
Parvanova, Radestina
BECOMING COLETTE

Pascual, Christina S.
PEPI, LUCI, BOM AND OTHER GIRLS ON THE HEAP

Pask, John
ARMED FOR ACTION

Pasmur, Jr., Alexander
STRANGER AMONG US, A

Pass, Cyndi
DEADBOLT
MISSION OF JUSTICE
ROUND TRIP TO HEAVEN

Passantino, Joann
BIG GIRLS DON'T CRY . . . THEY GET EVEN

Passard, Colleen
AFRAID OF THE DARK

Passero, Lisa
POISON IVY

Passmore, Angie
MUPPET CHRISTMAS CAROL, THE

Passmore, Peter
MUPPET CHRISTMAS CAROL, THE

Pasternak, John
PROJECT: SHADOWCHASER

Pastko, Earl
HIGHWAY 61

Pastor, Kathy
HONEY, I BLEW UP THE KID

Pastorelli, Robert
FERNGULLY: THE LAST RAINFOREST
FOLKS!

Pataki, Michael
DEATH HOUSE

Pataki, Nancy
MANIAC WARRIORS

Patarot, Helene
LOVER, THE

Paterson, Bill
CHAPLIN

Paterson, Florence
GETTING MARRIED IN BUFFALO JUMP

Pathak, Sanjay
CITY OF JOY

Patno, Regan
DEATH BECOMES HER

Paton, Morris
SPLIT SECOND

Patrick, Brian
WHITE TRASH

Patrick, James
PRAYER OF THE ROLLERBOYS

Patrick, John
HONEYMOON IN VEGAS

Patrick, Robert
WAYNE'S WORLD

Patterson, Gordon
THUNDERHEART

Patterson, J. Michael
CHAPLIN

Patterson, Jay
HIGHWAY 61

Patterson, Oliver
GIVING, THE

Patterson, Rocky
ARMED FOR ACTION
BLOOD ON THE BADGE

Patton, Will
COLD HEAVEN
IN THE SOUP
WILDFIRE

Patullo, Carole
PROOF

Paul
35 UP

Paul, Adrian
LOVE POTION NO. 9

Paul, Bonnie
FATE

Paul, Chen Baoer
RAPID FIRE

Paul, David
DOUBLE TROUBLE

Paul, Eric
PATRIOT GAMES

Paul, Peter
DOUBLE TROUBLE

Paul, Richard
BLOODFIST III: FORCED TO FIGHT

Paul, Stuart
FATE

Paul-Thompson, Mayme
MONTANA RUN, THE

Paulin, Scott
CAPTAIN AMERICA

Paull, Craig
SWOON
SWOON

Paulsen, Pat
AUNTIE LEE'S MEAT PIES

Pauly, Rebecca
NEAR MISSES
ROAD TO RUIN

Pauzer, Irene
GATE II

Pavia, Ria
CANDYMAN

Pavitt, Bruce
SINGLES

Paxton, Bill
ONE FALSE MOVE
TRESPASS
VAGRANT, THE

Paymer, David
MR. SATURDAY NIGHT

Payne, Bruce
PASSENGER 57

Payne, Cecil
TEXAS TENOR: THE ILLINOIS JACQUET STORY

Payne, Eric
JUICE
MALCOLM X

Payne, Travis
NEWSIES

Paysinger, Sherri
BEETHOVEN

Payton, Mark
HOWARDS END

Pearce, Guy
HUNTING

Pearlman, Stephen
MY NEW GUN

Pearson, Clive
WITCHCRAFT IV: VIRGIN HEART

Pearson, Sarah Luck
WILDFIRE

Peck, Craig
THERE'S NOTHING OUT THERE

Peck, Jim
PET SEMATARY II

Peck, Jonathan
MALCOLM X

Peck, Tony
BRENDA STARR
INSIDE EDGE

Pecoraro, Joseph
RUBY

Pedegana, Timothy J.
SISTER ACT

Pedersen, Chris
TWIN PEAKS: FIRE WALK WITH ME

Peeks, Kevin
CUTTING EDGE, THE

Peel, Ben
LONDON KILLS ME

Peeples, Nia
I DON'T BUY KISSES ANYMORE

Peery, Sarah
NIGHT EYES 2

Pegram, Nigel
POWER OF ONE, THE

Peldon, Courtney
OUT ON A LIMB

Pellegrino, Mark
LETHAL WEAPON 3
PRAYER OF THE ROLLERBOYS

Pellett, Adrian
CUTTING EDGE, THE

Pellonpaa, Matti
NIGHT ON EARTH

Peloquin, Pierre
CUTTING EDGE, THE

Peltier, Leonard
INCIDENT AT OGLALA

Pelton, Patti
LEAGUE OF THEIR OWN, A

Peluso, Mike
CHAPLIN

Pemberton, Lenore
MALCOLM X

Pena, Anthony
BACKTRACK

Pena, Elizabeth
WATERDANCE, THE

Pena, Hector
GLADIATOR

Pencheva, Anya
DEATHSTALKER IV: MATCH OF TITANS

Pendleton, Austin
MY COUSIN VINNY

Penhale, David A.
DISTINGUISHED GENTLEMAN, THE

Penhall, Bruce
DO OR DIE

Penn, Christopher
LEATHER JACKETS
RESERVOIR DOGS

Pennell, Larry
MR. BASEBALL

Pennelo, Anthony T.
LETHAL WEAPON 3

Penner, Jonathan
AMITYVILLE 1992: IT'S ABOUT TIME

Penny, Bob
MY COUSIN VINNY

Penot, Jacques
CRY OF THE OWL, THE

Penrose, Roger
BRIEF HISTORY OF TIME, A

Pentangelo, Joe
MALCOLM X

Pepeli, Rocky
DIGGSTOWN

Peploe, Lola
AFRAID OF THE DARK

Pera, Len
WE'RE TALKIN' SERIOUS MONEY

Pere, Wayne
BEASTMASTER 2: THROUGH THE PORTAL OF TIME

Perea, Pierre
BASKET CASE 3: THE PROGENY

Pereira, Sergio
BRENDA STARR

Perez, Gil
RUNESTONE, THE

Perez, Guillermo
AMERICAN ME

Perez, Inez
ACES: IRON EAGLE III

Perez, Lazaro
MAMBO KINGS, THE

Perez, Mary
PUERTO RICAN MAMBO (NOT A MUSICAL), THE

Perez, Rosie
NIGHT ON EARTH
WHITE MEN CAN'T JUMP

Perez, Vincent
INDOCHINE

Perez-Lee, Fernando
BASKET CASE 3: THE PROGENY

Perier, Francois
ELEGANT CRIMINEL, L'

Perkin, Danny
DR. GIGGLES

Perkins, Anthony
DEMON IN MY VIEW, A

Perkins, David Spence
GLADIATOR

Perkins, Elizabeth
OVER HER DEAD BODY

Perkins, Jo
SIMPLE MEN

Perkins, Stephen
ENCINO MAN

Perkovich, Roger
SEVERED TIES

Perlard, Roger
CUTTING EDGE, THE

Perlman, Philip
CLASS ACT
HOFFA

Perlman, Rhea
CLASS ACT
OVER HER DEAD BODY

Perlman, Ron
STEPHEN KING'S SLEEPWALKERS

Perlov, Marty
HOFFA

Perot, Ross
FEED

Perri, Paul
MEMOIRS OF AN INVISIBLE MAN

Perriam, Claire
CHAPLIN

Perrier, Don
MANIAC WARRIORS

Perrier, Jean-Francois
DELICATESSEN

Perrier, Mireille
TOTO LE HEROS

Perrigo, Howe F.
HOUSESITTER

Perrin, Jacques
TOUCH AND DIE

Perron, Michel
SCANNERS III: THE TAKEOVER

Perrotti, Riccardo Parisio
ONCE UPON A CRIME

Perruccio, Giuseppe
ONCE UPON A CRIME

Perry, Brian
MIRACLE BEACH

Perry, David
AUNTIE LEE'S MEAT PIES

Perry, Dwain A.
GLADIATOR

Perry, Jeff
HARD PROMISES
LIFE ON THE EDGE
STORYVILLE

Perry, Jr., Ernest
COLD JUSTICE

Perry, Louise
MY GRANDPA IS A VAMPIRE

Perry, Luke
BUFFY THE VAMPIRE SLAYER
SCORCHERS
TERMINAL BLISS

Perry, Manny
AMERICAN ME

Perry, Manuel
STOP! OR MY MOM WILL SHOOT

Persaud, Jenna
OTHER WOMAN, THE

Person, Tycie
ZEBRAHEAD

Persons, Fern
PRELUDE TO A KISS

Pertwee, Sean
LONDON KILLS ME

Pesce, Frank
PAMELA PRINCIPLE, THE

Pesci, Joe
BACKTRACK
HOME ALONE 2: LOST IN NEW YORK
LETHAL WEAPON 3
MY COUSIN VINNY
PUBLIC EYE, THE

Pesqueira, Eric
NEWSIES

Peter
35 UP

Peterkoch, Lydia
DEATH BECOMES HER

Peters, Brock
IMPORTANCE OF BEING EARNEST, THE

Peters, Christine
MANIAC WARRIORS

Peters, Helmut
MANIAC WARRIORS

Petersen, Donald
STEPHEN KING'S SLEEPWALKERS

Petersen, William
HARD PROMISES
PASSED AWAY

Peterson, Brad
MIGHTY DUCKS, THE

Peterson, Diane
CANDYMAN

Peterson, Kurt
JUST LIKE IN THE MOVIES

Peterson, Tashequa J.
TOYS

Peterson, Tord
BEST INTENTIONS, THE

Petievich, John
RAMPAGE

Petit, Yvette
FINE ROMANCE, A

Petraglia, Ricardo
KICKBOXER 3: THE ART OF WAR

Petri, Hella
HOT CHOCOLATE

Petrie, George O.
FOLKS!

Petrie, Jr., Daniel
DISTINGUISHED GENTLEMAN, THE

Petrov, Nicolas
LORENZO'S OIL

Petruzzi, Joe
MAMBO KINGS, THE

Pettis, Tom
BRIDE OF KILLER NERD

Petts, Theresa
CHAPLIN

Petty, Lori
LEAGUE OF THEIR OWN, A

Pettyman, Jeff
PURE COUNTRY

Pfeifer, Ben
KILL LINE

Pfeifer, Chuck
BOOMERANG

Pfeiffer, Dedee
DRIVE

Pfeiffer, Michelle
BATMAN RETURNS
LOVE FIELD
Pfleiger, Jeanne
BEASTMASTER 2: THROUGH THE PORTAL OF TIME
Pflieger, Jean
DEATH BECOMES HER
Pfulger, Vanessa
WATERLAND
Phelan, Shawn
BREAKING THE RULES
Phelps, Peter
ROCK & ROLL COWBOYS
Phelps, Verland Theodore
THUNDERHEART
Philbin, Joy
NIGHT AND THE CITY
Philbin, Regis
NIGHT AND THE CITY
Philip Moore, Charles
IN THE HEAT OF PASSION
Philips, Brian
MANIAC WARRIORS
Philipson, Adam
CANDYMAN
Phillips, Brian
MANIAC WARRIORS
Phillips, Doc
WHITE SANDS
Phillips, G. Elvis
BAD LIEUTENANT
Phillips, Grace
ALL THE VERMEERS IN NEW YORK
Phillips, Jacqy
CROSSING, THE
Phillips, James
IN GOLD WE TRUST
Phillips, Jeffrey Daniel
SNEAKERS
Phillips, John
FINEST HOUR, THE
Phillips, Lacy Darryl
DEATH BECOMES HER
Phillips, Lou Diamond
PANAMA DECEPTION, THE
Phillips, Marc
MALCOLM X
Phillips, Maurice
OVER HER DEAD BODY
Phillips, Mike
LAST OF THE MOHICANS, THE
Phillips, Neville
ENCHANTED APRIL
Phillips, Russell
BABE, THE
Phillips, Sydney Coale
MAXIMUM BREAKOUT
Philpot, Susan
STRAIGHT TALK
Phipps, Bunny
BASKET CASE 3: THE PROGENY
Phiri, Joel
POWER OF ONE, THE
Phoenix, River
SNEAKERS
Phun, Dennis
WHERE THE DAY TAKES YOU
Pia, Marti C.
MAN TROUBLE
Picard, Connie
HUSBANDS AND WIVES
Picart, Delilah
MALCOLM X
Piccini, Carmen
LORENZO'S OIL
Pichon, Christophe
BEATING HEART, A
HAIRDRESSER'S HUSBAND, THE
Pickells, Bill
TIGER CLAWS
Pickens, Jr., James
TRESPASS
Picker, Josh
FLIRTING
Pickering, Steve
RAPID FIRE
Pickering, Vincent
CHRISTOPHER COLUMBUS: THE DISCOVERY
Pickett, Blake
CAN IT BE LOVE
Pickett, Cindy
ORIGINAL INTENT
STEPHEN KING'S SLEEPWALKERS
Pickett, Manual
BREAKING THE RULES
Pickles, Chris
PETER'S FRIENDS
Pickup, Ronald
JOURNEY OF HONOR
Picot, Genevieve
PROOF
Picoy, Kane
MY NEW GUN
Piculjan, Gordon
CAPTAIN AMERICA
Piddock, Jim
TRACES OF RED
Piemonte, II, Stephen
JENNIFER EIGHT
Piemonte, Richard
UNDER SIEGE
Pierce, Ann
TERMINAL BLISS
Pierce, Bradley
CHAPLIN
Pierce, Brock
MIGHTY DUCKS, THE
Pierce, Denney
LAWNMOWER MAN, THE
Pierce, Katheryn Culliver
TRACES OF RED
Pierce, Shirley
HERO
Pierce, Stack
24 HOURS TO MIDNIGHT
Pierce, Tony
BODYGUARD, THE
TRANCERS III: DETH LIVES
Pierce, Wendell
MALCOLM X
Pierpont, Eric
FOREVER YOUNG
Pierre, Olivier
YEAR OF THE COMET
Pierre, Rickey
UNDER SIEGE
Pierson, Rex
BEASTMASTER 2: THROUGH THE PORTAL OF TIME
BRENDA STARR
Pietropinto, Angela
HONEYMOON IN VEGAS
Pilavin, Barbara
I DON'T BUY KISSES ANYMORE
LEAGUE OF THEIR OWN, A
Pileggi, Mitch
BASIC INSTINCT
Pilon, Daniel
SCANNERS III: THE TAKEOVER
Pilorge, Michel
DOES THIS MEAN WE'RE MARRIED?
Pinchot, Bronson
BLAME IT ON THE BELLBOY
Pine, Larry
JUST LIKE IN THE MOVIES
Pineau, Patrick
ELEGANT CRIMINEL, L'
Pink, Steve
BOB ROBERTS
Pinkard, Craig
BEETHOVEN
UNDER SIEGE
Pinkston, Karen
MISSISSIPPI MASALA
Pinney, Patrick
ALADDIN
COOL WORLD
Pinon, Dominique
ALBERTO EXPRESS
DELICATESSEN
Pinsent, Charlie
WHERE ANGELS FEAR TO TREAD
Pinsky, Shelly
CONSENTING ADULTS
Pinson, Julie
MAMBO KINGS, THE
Pipkin, Turk
HARD PROMISES
Pippin, Hollis
MISSISSIPPI MASALA
Piro, Gaetano
WHERE ANGELS FEAR TO TREAD
Pisani, Anne-Marie
DELICATESSEN
DOES THIS MEAN WE'RE MARRIED?
HAIRDRESSER'S HUSBAND, THE
Pisarenkov, Albert
WHISPERS IN THE DARK
Pitchford, Lonnie
DEEP BLUES
Pitillo, Maria
CHAPLIN

Pitt, Brad
COOL WORLD
JOHNNY SUEDE
RIVER RUNS THROUGH IT, A

Pittman, Reggie
MALCOLM X

Pitts-Wiley, Ricardo
HOUSESITTER

Piven, Jeremy
BOB ROBERTS
PLAYER, THE
SINGLES

Piven, Joyce Hiller
STRAIGHT TALK

Piven, Shira
BOB ROBERTS

Place, Heather
BASKET CASE 3: THE PROGENY

Place, Mary Kay
CAPTAIN RON

Place, Robin
INNOCENT BLOOD

Plachta, Nance
CONSENTING ADULTS

Plana, Tony
PANAMA DECEPTION, THE

Plank, Jane
MIGHTY DUCKS, THE

Plank, Scott
MR. BASEBALL

Plankers, Claus
SHINING THROUGH

Planting, Jeroen
LILY WAS HERE

Plaskitt, Nigel
MUPPET CHRISTMAS CAROL, THE

Plastina, Rick
HERO

Platt, Oliver
BEETHOVEN
DIGGSTOWN

Pleasants, Dean
ENCINO MAN

Pleasence, Angela
FAVOUR, THE WATCH, AND THE
VERY BIG FISH, THE

Pleasence, Donald
HOUSE OF USHER, THE
SHADOWS AND FOG

Plohotniuk, Natalia
RASPAD

Plowright, Joan
ENCHANTED APRIL

Plummer, Amanda
FREEJACK

Plummer, Christopher
MALCOLM X
ROCK-A-DOODLE

Plummer, Glenn
SOUTH CENTRAL
TRESPASS

Pochran, Jon
LEATHER JACKETS

Pock, Bernie
24 HOURS TO MIDNIGHT

Podwal, Murray
COOL WORLD

Poe, IV, Edgar Allen
TRACES OF RED

Poggi, Lisa
HONEYMOON IN VEGAS

Poggi, Lisa Ann
CANDYMAN

Pogue, Ken
COMMON BONDS

Poirer, Jean-Marie
TOUS LES MATINS DU MONDE

Poiret, Jean
ELEGANT CRIMINEL, L'
INSPECTOR LAVARDIN

Poisson, Michael
COMPLEX WORLD

Poitier, Barbara
LORENZO'S OIL

Poitier, Sidney
SNEAKERS

Polak, Marty
BASKET CASE 3: THE PROGENY

Polanco, Iraida
BAD LIEUTENANT

Poland, Greg
MALCOLM X

Polanski, Roman
BACK IN THE U.S.S.R.

Polce, John
NIGHT AND THE CITY

Polic, II, Henry
DOUBLE TROUBLE

Polit, Katie
BRIDE OF KILLER NERD

Polito, Jon
LEATHER JACKETS

Poliy, Stevo
RESERVOIR DOGS

Polk, E. Keith
KUFFS

Pollack, Paige Nan
FERNGULLY:
THE LAST RAINFOREST

Pollack, Sydney
DEATH BECOMES HER
HUSBANDS AND WIVES
PLAYER, THE

Pollak, Cheryl
CROSSING THE BRIDGE

Pollak, Kevin
FEW GOOD MEN, A

Pollak, Roberto
HUMAN SHIELD, THE

Pollan, Tracy
STRANGER AMONG US, A

Pollard, Michael J.
OVER HER DEAD BODY
SPLIT SECOND

Pollock, Daniel
PROOF

Pollock, Eileen
FAR AND AWAY

Pollupec, Zoran
CAPTAIN AMERICA

Polo, Lou
NIGHT AND THE CITY

Polo, Teri
PASSED AWAY

Pombo, Amanda
RAISING CAIN

Pon, Patrick
RESURRECTED, THE

Poncelis, Jose Manuel
CABEZA DE VACA

Ponomarenko, Oleg
FAVOUR, THE WATCH, AND THE
VERY BIG FISH, THE

Pook, Jocelyn
EDWARD II

Pool, Gene
WILD WHEELS

Poole, Regina
INNOCENT BLOOD

Pope, Tony
FROZEN ASSETS

Poppick, Eric
BASIC INSTINCT
HERO
SINGLE WHITE FEMALE

Porco, Elena
BOB ROBERTS

Port, Nina
SWOON

Portel, Manny
TOYS

Porter, Adina
SWOON

Porter, Bob
TEXAS TENOR:
THE ILLINOIS JACQUET STORY

Porter, Fia
MALCOLM X

Porter, Liz
CHAPLIN

Portillo, Anthony
NIGHT ON EARTH

Portillo, Rose
PANAMA DECEPTION, THE

Portney, Charles
BASKET CASE 3: THE PROGENY

Portnow, Richard
SISTER ACT

Porto, Daniel
WHITE MEN CAN'T JUMP

Portser, Mary
PASSION FISH

Posen, Steven
LIGHT SLEEPER

Posey, John
OUT ON A LIMB

Post, Saskia
PROOF

Postlethwaite, Pete
ALIEN3
LAST OF THE MOHICANS, THE
SPLIT SECOND
WATERLAND

Poston, Tiffanie
ADVENTURES IN DINOSAUR CITY

Potin, Jacques
FAVOUR, THE WATCH, AND THE
VERY BIG FISH, THE

Potter, Trek
CAPTAIN AMERICA

Potts, Annie
BREAKING THE RULES
Poulten, Benari
SCHOOL TIES
Pounder, C.C.H.
IMPORTANCE OF BEING EARNEST, THE
Pounds-Taylor, Connie
LEAGUE OF THEIR OWN, A
Poundstone, Paula
WISECRACKS
Poupaud, Melvil
LOVER, THE
Poussaint, Alvin
COLOR ADJUSTMENT
Povall, David
PROFESSIONAL, THE
Powell, Brian
BOB ROBERTS
Powell, Clifton
3 NINJAS
Powell, Ella
DAUGHTERS OF THE DUST
Powell, Sandy
EDWARD II
Powell, Susan
LIFE ON THE EDGE
Power, Chad
3 NINJAS
Power, Derry
FAR AND AWAY
Power, Henry
DAMAGE
Power, Udana
FROZEN ASSETS
Powers, Alexandra
PLAYER, THE
Powers, Anthony
WE'RE TALKIN' SERIOUS MONEY
Powers, Matthew
STOP! OR MY MOM WILL SHOOT
Powladge, David
LITTLE SISTER
Powney, Derek
BRIEF HISTORY OF TIME, A
Prager, Elizabeth J.
RAMPAGE
Pratt, Sean
OVER HER DEAD BODY
Pravda, Hana Maria
SHINING THROUGH
Prawer, Siegbert
HOWARDS END
Preece, Judy
MUPPET CHRISTMAS CAROL, THE
Preisig, Sally
MUPPET CHRISTMAS CAROL, THE
Prell, Karen
MUPPET CHRISTMAS CAROL, THE
Presles, Nathalie
ROAD TO RUIN
Press, Fiona
FLIRTING
Prestia, Shirley
FINAL ANALYSIS
HOFFA
Preston, Edward
TEXAS TENOR: THE ILLINOIS JACQUET STORY
Preston, J.A.
CAPTAIN RON
FEW GOOD MEN, A
Preston, Kelly
ONLY YOU
Preston, Tom
CHAPLIN
Preston, Wayde
CAPTAIN AMERICA
Preston, William
FAR AND AWAY
Prey, Margo
TROLL 2
Price, Chestley
LOVE FIELD
Price, Douglas
BODYGUARD, THE
Price, Gary
DISTINGUISHED GENTLEMAN, THE
Price, Louis
WHITE MEN CAN'T JUMP
Price, Marc
KILLER TOMATOES EAT FRANCE!
Price, Richard
NIGHT AND THE CITY
Price, Vincent
BACKTRACK
Priest, Martin
ZEBRAHEAD
Primus, Barry
NIGHT AND THE CITY
Primus, Raphaela Rose
MISTRESS
Prince
SARAFINA!
Prince, James
HARD PROMISES
Prince, James Hansen
SIMPLE MEN
Prince, Taylor
MANIAC WARRIORS
Prine, Andrew
LIFE ON THE EDGE
Prine, John
FALLING FROM GRACE
Prinz, Isabel
1492: THE CONQUEST OF PARADISE
Prior, Ted
CENTER OF THE WEB
Pritchard, Elizabeth
HIGHWAY 61
Probst, Eva
BECOMING COLETTE
Prochnow, Jurgen
HURRICANE SMITH
KILL CRUISE
TWIN PEAKS: FIRE WALK WITH ME
Proctor, Andrew
CLEARCUT
Proctor, Phil
ALADDIN
Profy, Hugues
DOES THIS MEAN WE'RE MARRIED?
Prosky, Robert
FAR AND AWAY
HOFFA
Prosper, Gloria Grace
MAN TROUBLE
Prouder, Cynthia
PUSHED TO THE LIMIT
Proval, David
INNOCENT BLOOD
Provence, Todd A.
MR. BASEBALL
Prud'homme, Michel
DOES THIS MEAN WE'RE MARRIED?
Pruzelius, Gosta
BEST INTENTIONS, THE
Pryce, Jonathan
FREDDIE AS F.R.O.7
GLENGARRY GLEN ROSS
Pryor, Nicholas
HOFFA
Prytz, Agneta
OX, THE
Psaros, Steve
LETHAL WEAPON 3
Pucci, Robert
AMERICAN ME
Puente, Tito
MAMBO KINGS, THE
Pugh, Sharrieff
NIGHT AND THE CITY
Pugh, Willard
GUYVER, THE
Pugsley, Don
AMERICAN ME
HERO
Pulliam, Jaqueline
BREATHING FIRE
Pullman, Bill
LEAGUE OF THEIR OWN, A
NEWSIES
SINGLES
Pumpkin Seed, Sylvan
THUNDERHEART
Purdie, Bernard
TEXAS TENOR: THE ILLINOIS JACQUET STORY
Puri, Om
CITY OF JOY
Puri, Rajika
MISSISSIPPI MASALA
Purtak, Evelyn
PURE COUNTRY
Purviance, Douglas
MALCOLM X
Purvis-Smith, Esther
PRIMO BABY
Puzzo, Michael
WHO SHOT PATAKANGO?
Pyeritz, Matthew
LORENZO'S OIL
Pyper-Ferguson, John
KILLER IMAGE
Quach Van-an
LOVER, THE
Quadros, Steven
AUNTIE LEE'S MEAT PIES

Quai, Tricia
CHINA O'BRIEN II
Quaid, Brady
LOVE HURTS
Qualls, ShanaLedet
PASSION FISH
Quan, Jonathan
ENCINO MAN
Quarry, Robert
SPIRITS
Quasarano, Joe
HOFFA
Quastel, Jonas
JENNIFER EIGHT
Quayle, Dan
INNOCENT BLOOD
Queen Latifah
JUICE
Quentin, John
EDWARD II
Quesenberry, Lincoln
RIVER RUNS THROUGH IT, A
Quester, Hugues
CONTE DE PRINTEMPS
Quigley, Gerry
BEAUTIFUL DREAMERS
Quigley, Linnea
GUYVER, THE
INNOCENT BLOOD
Quigley, William
HELLROLLER
Quijano, Diana
WELCOME TO OBLIVION
Quiles, Ian
MALCOLM X
Quine, Robbie
WHITE TRASH
Quinn, Aidan
PLAYBOYS, THE
Quinn, Francesco
DEAD CERTAIN
Quinn, Glenn
DR. GIGGLES
Quinn, J.C.
ALL-AMERICAN MURDER
BABE, THE
CRISSCROSS
MEGAVILLE
PRAYER OF THE ROLLERBOYS
Quinn, James
SCHOOL TIES
Quinn, John
NIGHT AND THE CITY
Quinn, Kathy
ARTICLE 99
Quinn, Martha
BAD CHANNELS
Quinn, Paul
BOB ROBERTS
Quintanilla, Marcos
MAMBO KINGS, THE
Quintard, Mika
CANDYMAN
Quiring, Frederic
POUR SACHA
Quiroz, Eva
SHAKING THE TREE
Quon, J.B.
POISON IVY
Quynh, Nhu
INDOCHINE
Raab, Ellie
ROADSIDE PROPHETS
Raasch, Amy
HELL MASTER
Raballo, Robert Louis
RAMPAGE
Rabineer, Ellen
MAN TROUBLE
Raci, Paul
SMOOTH TALKER
Raclawski, Craig
NEWSIES
Raczkowski, Paul
UNIVERSAL SOLDIER
Radebe, Congo
SARAFINA!
Radebe, Zanele
SARAFINA!
Radevic, Miomir
JOURNEY OF HONOR
Radford, Mathew
ENCHANTED APRIL
Radloff, Toby
BRIDE OF KILLER NERD
Rae, Melody
BABE, THE
Rae Prior, Teddi
MAXIMUM BREAKOUT
Rael, Tony
KISS ME A KILLER
Raeuker, Ralf
BECOMING COLETTE
Raff, Mark Phillip
GLADIATOR
Raffe
INTO THE SUN
Rafferty, George
MALCOLM X
Raft, Francesca
FLIRTING
Ragno, Joe
BABE, THE
Ragon, Laurence
HAIRDRESSER'S HUSBAND, THE
Ragsdale, Roddy
HONEYMOON IN VEGAS
Ragusa, Antonino
NIGHT ON EARTH
Raguz, Matko
CAPTAIN AMERICA
Raichowdhury, Tamal
CITY OF JOY
Raimi, Sam
INNOCENT BLOOD
Raimi, Ted
CANDYMAN
FINISHING TOUCH, THE
LUNATICS: A LOVE STORY
PATRIOT GAMES
Rainer, Josef
RUNESTONE, THE
Raines, Howard
TO RENDER A LIFE
Rainey, Ford
BED & BREAKFAST
Rainone, Tom
SOCIETY
Raja, Rania
EMMANUELLE 6
Rally, Steve
MAXIMUM BREAKOUT
Ralph, Ken
MANIAC WARRIORS
Ralph, Michael
MALCOLM X
Ralph, Sheryl Lee
DISTINGUISHED GENTLEMAN, THE
MISTRESS
Ralston, Mark
NICKEL & DIME
Rambo, Dack
WELCOME TO OBLIVION
Rambo, T. Mychael
CROSSING THE BRIDGE
Ramirez, Alicia
UNLAWFUL ENTRY
Ramirez, Juan
FOLKS!
Ramos, Jorge Luis
CAPTAIN RON
Ramos, Marco
WATERDANCE, THE
Ramos, Norma
DAMNED IN THE USA
Ramos, Ruben
FIELD OF FIRE
Ramos, Rudy
TO PROTECT AND SERVE
Ramoupi, Mmabatho
SARAFINA!
Ramsay, Anne Elizabeth
CRITTERS 4
LEAGUE OF THEIR OWN, A
Ramsey, Jeff
FAR AND AWAY
Ramsey, Remak
SHADOWS AND FOG
Randall, Addison
OUT FOR BLOOD
Randall, Brad
WHO SHOT PATAKANGO?
Randall, Chad
KUFFS
Randall, Eric
PURE COUNTRY
Randazzo, Steven
HUSBANDS AND WIVES
IN THE SOUP
MALCOLM X
Randelman, Mike
CHAPLIN
Randle, Theresa
MALCOLM X
Randolph, David
BEBE'S KIDS

Randolph, Larry
CHAPLIN
Rands, Sylvia
MY GRANDPA IS A VAMPIRE
Ranft, Owen H.
SWOON
Rangel, John
AMERICAN ME
Ranger, Ulf
PUSHED TO THE LIMIT
Ranken, Liz
EDWARD II
Rankin, Steve
JUST LIKE IN THE MOVIES
Ranni, Rodolfo
PLAY MURDER FOR ME
Ransom, Kenny
FOREVER YOUNG
Raoul, Dale
LAWNMOWER MAN, THE
Rapaport, Michael
ZEBRAHEAD
Rapley, Brooks
HIGHWAY 61
Raposa, Jim
NEWSIES
Rapp, Anthony
SCHOOL TIES
Rapport, Louise
DEATH BECOMES HER
Rasberry, Robin
MANIAC WARRIORS
Rasmussen-Novros, Paula
MAN TROUBLE
Rasmusson, Lindy
BASIC INSTINCT
Rastel, Anne-Marie
BECOMING COLETTE
Rasulala, Thalmus
LIFE ON THE EDGE
MOM AND DAD SAVE THE WORLD
Ratajczak, David
PET SEMATARY II
Ratliff, Elden
MIGHTY DUCKS, THE
RADIO FLYER
Ratliff, Garette
CAPTAIN AMERICA
RADIO FLYER
Ratner, Ben
LEAVING NORMAL
Ratner, Nic
ROADSIDE PROPHETS
Ratray, Devin
HOME ALONE 2:
LOST IN NEW YORK
Rauh, Richard
PASSED AWAY
Rauseo, Mike
UNIVERSAL SOLDIER
Ravarra, Gina
STEAL AMERICA
Rawcliffe, Mary Heller
MAN TROUBLE
Rawling, Anthony
PROOF

Ray, Fred Olen
MUNCHIE
NAKED OBSESSION
Ray, Lynette
BRIDE OF KILLER NERD
Ray, William Earl
DR. GIGGLES
Raye, Martha
WISECRACKS
Raymond, Bill
MY NEW GUN
Raymond, Devon
SINGLES
Raymond, Sid
FOLKS!
Razowsky, David
MO' MONEY
Rea, Brad
UNDER SIEGE
Rea, Peggy
LOVE FIELD
Rea, Stephen
CRYING GAME, THE
Read, James
LOVE CRIMES
Read, Robert
SWOON
Reagan, Resa
LOVE FIELD
Reagan, Ronald
WISECRACKS
Reardon, Noreen
BEBE'S KIDS
Reardon, Rick
BABE, THE
Reatha, Bean
BRENDA STARR
Reaux, Romel
BAD CHANNELS
Rebel
CRISSCROSS
Rebelo, Nicky
SARAFINA!
Reber, Fred
MANIAC WARRIORS
Rebhorn, James
BASIC INSTINCT
LORENZO'S OIL
MY COUSIN VINNY
SCENT OF A WOMAN
SHADOWS AND FOG
WHITE SANDS
WIND
Reckord, Lloyd
LUNATIC, THE
Record, Jeff
MAN TROUBLE
MIND, BODY & SOUL
Recter, Jerry
FATAL INSTINCT
Rector, Jeff
HELL MASTER
Red Bow, Buddy
THUNDERHEART
Red Elk, Ernest
THUNDERHEART

Red Elk, Sr., Calvin Timothy
THUNDERHEART
Redd, Mary Robin
MAN TROUBLE
Reddin, Keith
LORENZO'S OIL
Redfern, Damon
BEAUTIFUL DREAMERS
Redford, Robert
INCIDENT AT OGLALA
RIVER RUNS THROUGH IT, A
SNEAKERS
Redglare, Rockets
IN THE SOUP
Redgrave, Jemma
HOWARDS END
Redgrave, Vanessa
HOWARDS END
Redmann, Marysue
BABE, THE
Redmond, Tim
BRIDE OF KILLER NERD
Redow, Ann
ARTICLE 99
Redrow, Phil
BODYGUARD, THE
Reed, Bobby
SWOON
Reed, Deborah
TROLL 2
Reed, Gary Lee
FATAL INSTINCT
Reed, Jr., Verrel Lester
PUSHED TO THE LIMIT
Reed, Lance
WILD ORCHID 2:
TWO SHADES OF BLUE
Reed, Lou
DAMNED IN THE USA
Reed, Oliver
HIRED TO KILL
HOUSE OF USHER, THE
SEVERED TIES
Reed, Pamela
BOB ROBERTS
PASSED AWAY
Reed, Penelope
HIRED TO KILL
Reed, Peter
DAMNED IN THE USA
Reed, Reye
RADIO FLYER
Reed, Rick
ARTICLE 99
Reed, Robert Thomas
POWER OF ONE, THE
Reed, Rondi
MO' MONEY
Reed, Steve
MALCOLM X
Reehling, Joyce
JUST LIKE IN THE MOVIES
LORENZO'S OIL
Reenberg, Jorgen
ZENTROPA
Rees, Roger
STOP! OR MY MOM WILL SHOOT

Reeve, Christopher
NOISES OFF
Reeves, Frank
FINAL IMPACT
Reeves, Keanu
BRAM STOKER'S DRACULA
Regal, David
HOFFA
Regehr, Duncan
PRIMO BABY
Regnaut, Maurice
INSPECTOR LAVARDIN
Reichman, Karl
LIFE ON THE EDGE
Reid, Christopher
CLASS ACT
Reid, Daphne
COLOR ADJUSTMENT
Reid, Fiona
BEETHOVEN LIVES UPSTAIRS
Reid, R.D.
BEAUTIFUL DREAMERS
CUTTING EDGE, THE
Reid, Roger
DISTINGUISHED GENTLEMAN, THE
Reid, Ron
MONTANA RUN, THE
Reid, Tim
COLOR ADJUSTMENT
Reidy, John
MALCOLM X
Reiland, Jeff
ARTICLE 99
Reilly, Charles Nelson
ROCK-A-DOODLE
Reilly, Dave
NIGHT AND THE CITY
Reilly, David
MALCOLM X
Reilly, Joe
DAMNED IN THE USA
Reilly, John C.
HOFFA
OUT ON A LIMB
SHADOWS AND FOG
Reilly, Luke
ZEBRAHEAD
Reilly, Tom
ANIMAL INSTINCTS
Reily, Brian
TERMINAL BLISS
Reinemann, Peter J.
HOFFA
Reiner, Nicholas
WHO SHOT PATAKANGO?
Reiner, Tracy
LEAGUE OF THEIR OWN, A
Reinhart, Gordon
MAN TROUBLE
Reinhold, Judge
NEAR MISSES
OVER HER DEAD BODY
SOLDIER'S TALE, A
Reissa, Eleanor
STRANGER AMONG US, A

Reitinger, Richard
MATCH FACTORY GIRL, THE
Reitmeier, Robert
CAPTAIN AMERICA
Reitz, Ric
LOVE POTION NO. 9
Reivers, David
MALCOLM X
Remele, Julie Marie
LORENZO'S OIL
Remsen, Bert
BODYGUARD, THE
PLAYER, THE
Remsen, Guy
PLAYER, THE
Renaday, Peter
BEBE'S KIDS
Renaldo, Enrique
DOLLY DEAREST
Renee, Carol
OVER HER DEAD BODY
Renee, Julene
DANCE MACABRE
Renfrey, Debra
MANIAC WARRIORS
Renfrey, Derek
MANIAC WARRIORS
Renfrey, Gary
MANIAC WARRIORS
Renneisen, Charles
STOP! OR MY MOM WILL SHOOT
Rensenhouse, John
CANDYMAN
Renzi, Maggie
PASSION FISH
Repo-Martell, Liisa
UNFORGIVEN
Rereme, Francisco Tsirene Tsere
MEDICINE MAN
Rergis, Daniel
DANZON
Resnick, Patricia
PLAYER, THE
Resto, Eddie
KISS ME A KILLER
Retigan, Shannon
NIGHT EYES 2
Reubens, Madonna
RIVER RUNS THROUGH IT, A
Reubens, Paul
BATMAN RETURNS
BUFFY THE VAMPIRE SLAYER
Rey, Fernando
1492: THE CONQUEST OF PARADISE
Rey, Reynaldo
BEBE'S KIDS
WHITE MEN CAN'T JUMP
Reyes, Chato
DANZON
Reyes, Estrella
ACES: IRON EAGLE III
Reyes, Jose
HERO
Reyes, Pia
AUNTIE LEE'S MEAT PIES

Reyes, Richard
SIMPLE MEN
Reynolds, Burt
PLAYER, THE
Reynolds, Debbie
BODYGUARD, THE
Reynolds, John S.
CAPTAIN AMERICA
Reynolds, Judy
MANIAC WARRIORS
Reynolds, Michael J.
CLEARCUT
Reynolds, Mike
PROFESSIONAL, THE
Reynolds, Ned
TUNE, THE
Reynolds, Simon
GATE II
Reynolds, Tom
UNDER SIEGE
Reynolds, Vickilyn
SOUTH CENTRAL
Rhames, Ving
STOP! OR MY MOM WILL SHOOT
Rhee, Simon
UNIVERSAL SOLDIER
Rhys, Paul
BECOMING COLETTE
CHAPLIN
Rhys-Davies, John
CANVAS
JOURNEY OF HONOR
Ribes, Jean-Michel
FAVOUR, THE WATCH, AND THE VERY BIG FISH, THE
Ribon, Diego
EVIL CLUTCH
Ricard, Adrian
LOVE HURTS
Riccardo, Steev
HARD PROMISES
Ricci, Shane
SHAKES THE CLOWN
Rice, James Brett
PASSENGER 57
Rice, Justin M.
LAST OF THE MOHICANS, THE
Rice, Sean
CUTTING EDGE, THE
Rice, W.C.
WILD WHEELS
Rice, Warren
HOME ALONE 2: LOST IN NEW YORK
Rich, Allan
NICKEL & DIME
Rich, Delphine
BECOMING COLETTE
Rich, Kate
NOISES OFF
Richard, Beth
OTHER WOMAN, THE
Richard, Judine Hawkins
MALCOLM X
Richards, Bethany
OUT ON A LIMB

Richards, Charles David
UNLAWFUL ENTRY
Richards, Evan
MIDNIGHT FEAR
SOCIETY
Richards, Jami
LITTLE SISTER
Richards, Jerome F.
SWOON
Richards, Kenneth J.
THUNDERHEART
Richards, Lisa
VENICE/VENICE
Richards, Mark
WIND
Richards, Michele Lamar
BODYGUARD, THE
Richardson, Arnold
RIVER RUNS THROUGH IT, A
Richardson, Ian
YEAR OF THE COMET
Richardson, Jack
HUSBANDS AND WIVES
Richardson, Jane
USED PEOPLE
Richardson, Janet
USED PEOPLE
Richardson, Jay
HONEYMOON IN VEGAS
MIND, BODY & SOUL
MUNCHIE
ORIGINAL INTENT
Richardson, Joely
SHINING THROUGH
Richardson, Latanya
JUICE
LORENZO'S OIL
MALCOLM X
Richardson, Lee
STRANGER AMONG US, A
Richardson, Mark
MIND, BODY & SOUL
Richardson, Miranda
CRYING GAME, THE
DAMAGE
ENCHANTED APRIL
Richardson, Natasha
FAVOUR, THE WATCH, AND THE VERY BIG FISH, THE
Richardson, Peter
POPE MUST DIET!, THE
Richardson, Salli
MO' MONEY
PRELUDE TO A KISS
Richardson, Stevie Lee
BABE, THE
Richardson, Sy
BACKTRACK
Richelmy, Nino
ONCE UPON A CRIME
Richert, Carole
TOUS LES MATINS DU MONDE
Richman, Orien
WITCHCRAFT IV: VIRGIN HEART
Richman, Stewart
WATERLAND
Richman, Stuart
CHAPLIN
Richmond, Angie Hill
PROJECT: SHADOWCHASER
Richmond, Branscombe
ACES: IRON EAGLE III
BATMAN RETURNS
CHRISTOPHER COLUMBUS: THE DISCOVERY
INSIDE EDGE
Richter, Gregory L.
TRACES OF RED
Richter, Thomas
FOLKS!
Richwine, Maria
SEX CRIMES
Richwood, Patrick
LITTLE SISTER
Rickardson, Marie
BEST INTENTIONS, THE
Rickles, Don
INNOCENT BLOOD
Rickman, Alan
BOB ROBERTS
Rickman, Patrick
MALCOLM X
Ricks, John
INVASION OF THE SPACE PREACHERS
Ricupero, Michael
USED PEOPLE
Riegert, Peter
PASSED AWAY
RUNESTONE, THE
Riehle, Richard
HERO
OF MICE AND MEN
PRELUDE TO A KISS
PUBLIC EYE, THE
SHADOWS AND FOG
Rifkin, Ron
HUSBANDS AND WIVES
Rigby, Terence
CHILDREN, THE
Rigg, Rebecca
EFFICIENCY EXPERT, THE
HUNTING
Riggins, Terrence
CANDYMAN
Rigsby, Gordon
HUSBANDS AND WIVES
Riley, Jack
PLAYER, THE
Riley, Rob
PRELUDE TO A KISS
Rimada, Fernando Garcia
1492: THE CONQUEST OF PARADISE
Rimkus, Stevan
LONDON KILLS ME
Rimmer, Shane
YEAR OF THE COMET
Rincon, Rodney
AMERICAN ME
Ring, Theresa
NIGHT RHYTHMS
Ringkvist, Elias
BEST INTENTIONS, THE
Ringuette, Lor-Michael
SAVAGE INSTINCT
Rioseco, Carmela
COLD HEAVEN
Rippy, Leon
EYE OF THE STORM
KUFFS
UNIVERSAL SOLDIER
Ristie, Yvonne
LILY WAS HERE
Ritchie, Michael
INNOCENT BLOOD
Ritschel, Jack
CHAPLIN
Ritter, John
NOISES OFF
STAY TUNED
Riva, Emmanuelle
POUR SACHA
Rivera, Rene
LIGHT SLEEPER
Rivers, Frank
BOOMERANG
Rivers, Victor
DISTINGUISHED GENTLEMAN, THE
TWIN PEAKS: FIRE WALK WITH ME
Rizacos, Angelo
BEAUTIFUL DREAMERS
Rizzo, Willy
HOFFA
Roach, Daryl
IMPORTANCE OF BEING EARNEST, THE
Roach, James
WATERDANCE, THE
Robards, Jason
STORYVILLE
Robbins, Adele
BOB ROBERTS
Robbins, Gabrielle
BOB ROBERTS
Robbins, Gil
BOB ROBERTS
Robbins, Lee
BOB ROBERTS
Robbins, Peter
MUPPET CHRISTMAS CAROL, THE
Robbins, Tim
BOB ROBERTS
PLAYER, THE
Roberson, David
WHITE MEN CAN'T JUMP
Roberts, Adrian
LOVE CRIMES
Roberts, C. Alex
LORENZO'S OIL
Roberts, Cameron
PASSENGER 57
Roberts, Chapman
YEAR OF THE COMET
Roberts, Chick
CUTTING EDGE, THE
Roberts, Cindy
FATE
Roberts, Doris
USED PEOPLE

Roberts, Eric
FINAL ANALYSIS
LONELY HEARTS
Roberts, Francesca P.
GLADIATOR
Roberts, Ian
POWER OF ONE, THE
Roberts, Jackye
FOLKS!
Roberts, Jake
WHITE MEN CAN'T JUMP
Roberts, Jeremy
DIGGSTOWN
SISTER ACT
Roberts, Jimmy N.
BUFFY THE VAMPIRE SLAYER
Roberts, Julia
PLAYER, THE
Roberts, K.J.
PASSED AWAY
Roberts, Mark
BEASTMASTER 2: THROUGH THE PORTAL OF TIME
Roberts, Rikki
WHITE TRASH
Roberts, Sally Ann
STORYVILLE
Roberts, Tanya
ALMOST PREGNANT
Roberts, Yvonne
TWIN PEAKS: FIRE WALK WITH ME
Robertson, Andrew
YEAR OF THE COMET
Robertson, Barbara
SHAKING THE TREE
Robertson, Cliff
WIND
Robertson, Malcolm
FLIRTING
Robertson, R.J.
MUNCHIE
Robertson, Simone
FATHER
Robertson, Tim
FATHER
Robey
PLAY NICE
Robic, Gillie
MUPPET CHRISTMAS CAROL, THE
Robillard, Kim
DIGGSTOWN
KUFFS
Robin, Michel
TOTO LE HEROS
Robin, Sophie
CONTE DE PRINTEMPS
Robinson, Allison
HOFFA
Robinson, Andrew
TRANCERS III: DETH LIVES
Robinson, Dalisia
DAUGHTERS OF THE DUST
Robinson, Dan
MANIAC WARRIORS
Robinson, Dean
BOB ROBERTS
Robinson, Eartha
DAUGHTERS OF THE DUST
MALCOLM X
Robinson, Emma
DAUGHTERS OF THE DUST
Robinson, Hank
BABE, THE
Robinson, Jay
BRAM STOKER'S DRACULA
Robinson, John
CUTTING EDGE, THE
Robinson, Kasey
FALLING FROM GRACE
Robinson, Max
SHADOWS AND FOG
Robinson, Michelle
MALCOLM X
Robinson, Nate
UNDER SIEGE
Robinson, Niko
WHITE TRASH
Robinson, Patrick
MANIAC WARRIORS
Robinson, Robby
AMERICAN ME
Robinson, Scot Anthony
MALCOLM X
Robinson, Tad
UNDER SIEGE
Robinson, Traci
MALCOLM X
Robinson, William
PUSHED TO THE LIMIT
Robison, Karin
TWIN PEAKS: FIRE WALK WITH ME
Robledo, Rafael H.
AMERICAN ME
Robles, Mike
PUERTO RICAN MAMBO (NOT A MUSICAL), THE
Robles, Walter R.
UNIVERSAL SOLDIER
Rocco, Alex
POPE MUST DIET!, THE
Roche, Sebastian
LAST OF THE MOHICANS, THE
Roche, Suzzy
MY NEW GUN
Rochefort, Jean
HAIRDRESSER'S HUSBAND, THE
Rochefort, Thomas
HAIRDRESSER'S HUSBAND, THE
Rochon, Lela
BOOMERANG
Rock, Chris
BOOMERANG
Rock, Kevin
MALCOLM X
Rockell, Sam
LIGHT SLEEPER
Rockwell, Rick
KILLER TOMATOES EAT FRANCE!
Roder, Paul
SAVAGE INSTINCT
Rodger, Struan
AFRAID OF THE DARK
Rodgers, Katheleen
LOVE CRIMES
Rodgers, Mary Ann
BASIC INSTINCT
Rodgers, Rick
SCHOOL TIES
Rodriguez, Agustin
FINAL ANALYSIS
Rodriguez, Carlos
SWOON
Rodriguez, Claudia
DANZON
Rodriguez, David
COLD HEAVEN
Rodriguez, Edgar
WATERDANCE, THE
Rodriguez, Eva
WATERDANCE, THE
Rodriguez, Gustavo
CAPTAIN RON
EMMANUELLE 6
Rodriguez, Lucy
PANAMA DECEPTION, THE
Rodriguez, Rocio
DANZON
Rodriguez Terracina, Nydia
FOLKS!
Rodriguez, Victor Emilio
CAPTAIN RON
Rodriquez, Rolando
MR. BASEBALL
Roeder, Peggy
HERO
Roeves, Maurice
LAST OF THE MOHICANS, THE
Rogers, Alva
DAUGHTERS OF THE DUST
Rogers, Alysia
CLASS ACT
Rogers, Bill
UNLAWFUL ENTRY
Rogers, Erica
ROADSIDE PROPHETS
Rogers, Harriet
BED & BREAKFAST
Rogers, Heather
TOYS
Rogers, III, Ed
STRANGER AMONG US, A
Rogers, Ivan
ESCAPE FROM . . . SURVIVAL ZONE
Rogers, Ken Leigh
MALCOLM X
Rogers, Mimi
DARK HORSE
PLAYER, THE
SHOOTING ELIZABETH
WHITE SANDS
Rogers, Ray
AMERICAN DREAM
Rogers, Sally
DEMON IN MY VIEW, A
Rogers, Victor
BAD CHANNELS
Rogge, David
MIKEY

Rohr, Tony
PLAYBOYS, THE
Rohrbacher, Michael
NEWSIES
Rohrer, Paul
KILL LINE
Rojo, Jaime
REFRIGERATOR, THE
Rojo, Maria
DANZON
Rolen, Tracy
INNOCENT BLOOD
Rolle, Esther
COLOR ADJUSTMENT
Rollins, Sonny
TEXAS TENOR: THE ILLINOIS JACQUET STORY
Roman, Todd
HELLROLLER
Romano, Andy
GUN IN BETTY LOU'S HANDBAG, THE
RAMPAGE
UNDER SIEGE
UNLAWFUL ENTRY
Romano, Carlos
BARBARIAN QUEEN II: THE EMPRESS STRIKES BACK
Romano, Gerardo
PLAY MURDER FOR ME
Romanus, Richard
RESURRECTED, THE
TO PROTECT AND SERVE
Romer, Kim
DAY IN OCTOBER, A
Romero, Cesar
MORTUARY ACADEMY
Romero, David
KISS ME A KILLER
Romero, Kaylan
RADIO FLYER
Romero, Ned
HOUSE IV
Romito, Loredana
JOHNNY STECCHINO
Ronan, Martin
SPLIT SECOND
Rondell, Craig
CAPTAIN RON
Rondell, Erik
KUFFS
Rook, Roger
KUFFS
LAWNMOWER MAN, THE
Roomful of Blues
COMPLEX WORLD
Rooney, Mickey
LITTLE NEMO: ADVENTURES IN SLUMBERLAND
MAXIMUM FORCE
Root, Stephen
BED & BREAKFAST
BUFFY THE VAMPIRE SLAYER
Roper, Alicia
SINGLES
Roper, Gil
BASKET CASE 3: THE PROGENY

Roquette, Suzanne
SHINING THROUGH
Rorman, Gary
PASSENGER 57
Rosal, Angela
1492: THE CONQUEST OF PARADISE
Rosales, Thomas
UNIVERSAL SOLDIER
Rosario, Bert
COLD JUSTICE
Rosario, Efrain "Chico"
CAPTAIN RON
Rosas, Paul H.
GIVING, THE
Rosato, Mary Lou
BRENDA STARR
Rose, Bartholomew
FLIRTING
Rose, Bernard
CANDYMAN
Rose, Gabrielle
ADJUSTER, THE
Rose, Kristine
NIGHT RHYTHMS
ROUND TRIP TO HEAVEN
Rose, Kristine Anne
AUNTIE LEE'S MEAT PIES
Rose, Myim
UNLAWFUL ENTRY
Rose, Patrick
THIS IS MY LIFE
Rose, Sherrie
DEADLY BET
IN GOLD WE TRUST
MARTIAL LAW 2: UNDERCOVER
MAXIMUM FORCE
UNLAWFUL ENTRY
Rose, Tim
MUPPET CHRISTMAS CAROL, THE
Roselius, John
FINAL ANALYSIS
RUBY
Roseman, Joshua
TEXAS TENOR: THE ILLINOIS JACQUET STORY
Rosen, Edward
LETHAL WEAPON 3
Rosen, Michael
PALE BLOOD
Rosenbaum, Anina Ritterband
DAY IN OCTOBER, A
Rosenbaum, David
STRANGER AMONG US, A
Rosenblatt, Mark
BREAKING THE RULES
Rosenfeld, Robyn
VENICE/VENICE
Rosenthal, Phil
WHO SHOT PATAKANGO?
Roshell, Antoine
GLADIATOR
Ross, Annie
BASKET CASE 3: THE PROGENY
PLAYER, THE
Ross, Chelcie
BASIC INSTINCT

Ross, David Colin
VENICE/VENICE
Ross, Gene
BABE, THE
Ross, Hugh
PATRIOT GAMES
Ross, Jaclyn
CROSSING THE BRIDGE
Ross, Liza
PROJECT: SHADOWCHASER
Ross, Margery Jane
HERO
Ross, Monty
MALCOLM X
Ross, Neil
FERNGULLY: THE LAST RAINFOREST
LITTLE NEMO: ADVENTURES IN SLUMBERLAND
Ross, Ramsay
WELCOME TO OBLIVION
Ross, Ricco
PROJECT: SHADOWCHASER
Ross-Magenty, Adrian
HOWARDS END
Ross-Norris, Vickie
LOVE FIELD
Rosselini, Isabella
DEATH BECOMES HER
Rossi, Frank
WHITE MEN CAN'T JUMP
Rossi, Leo
WE'RE TALKIN' SERIOUS MONEY
WHERE THE DAY TAKES YOU
Rossi, Roberto
VENICE/VENICE
Rossi, Vittorio
CANVAS
Rossitch, Jocko
DEATHSTALKER IV: MATCH OF TITANS
Rossitto, Susan
BATMAN RETURNS
Rossomando, Sicily
ENCINO MAN
Rotaeta, Felix
PEPI, LUCI, BOM AND OTHER GIRLS ON THE HEAP
Roth, Andrea
PSYCHIC
SEEDPEOPLE
Roth, Cecilia
PEPI, LUCI, BOM AND OTHER GIRLS ON THE HEAP
Roth, Ron
INNOCENT BLOOD
Roth, Tim
JUMPIN' AT THE BONEYARD
RESERVOIR DOGS
Rothrock, Cynthia
CHINA O'BRIEN II
LADY DRAGON
MARTIAL LAW 2: UNDERCOVER
TIGER CLAWS
24 HOURS TO MIDNIGHT
Rothwell, Robert
BACKTRACK

Rotko, Bill
MISTRESS
Rottger, John
UNDER SIEGE
Roudette, Lisa
SPLIT SECOND
Roulette-Mosely, Sherry
ARTICLE 99
Roundtree, Richard
BLOODFIST III: FORCED TO FIGHT
Rourke, Mickey
WHITE SANDS
Rovere, Liliane
DOES THIS MEAN WE'RE MARRIED?
Rowan, John
SWOON
Rowan, Tom
LOVE CRIMES
Rowden, David
BUFFY THE VAMPIRE SLAYER
Rowe, Stephen
BASIC INSTINCT
Rowell, Victoria
DISTINGUISHED GENTLEMAN, THE
Rowland, Chris
BOOMERANG
Rowlands, Gena
NIGHT ON EARTH
Rowsell, Arthur
CUTTING EDGE, THE
Roxiane
DOES THIS MEAN WE'RE MARRIED?
Roy, Debraj
CITY OF JOY
Roy, Deep
RESURRECTED, THE
Roy, Siddharth
CITY OF JOY
Royal, Cornell "Kofi"
DAUGHTERS OF THE DUST
Royale, Maxine
DAUGHTERS OF THE DUST
Roychoudhury, Aloke
CITY OF JOY
Ruben, Sandy Roth
POISON IVY
Ruben, Tom
POISON IVY
Rubenstein, Zelda
GUILTY AS CHARGED
Rubin, Christopher
JUICE
MALCOLM X
Rubin, Ira
STRANGER AMONG US, A
Rubin, Jennifer
WOMAN, HER MEN AND HER FUTON, A
Rubin, Paul
SWOON
Rubinek, Saul
MAN TROUBLE
QUARREL, THE
UNFORGIVEN
Rubini, Sergio
STATION, THE
Rubinstein, Ora
VENICE/VENICE
Ruck, Alan
JUST LIKE IN THE MOVIES
Rucker, Tina
RUBY
Rudall, Nicholas
BABE, THE
Rude, Dick
ROADSIDE PROPHETS
Rudge, Dennis
LILY WAS HERE
Rudman, David
MUPPET CHRISTMAS CAROL, THE
Rudner, Rita
PETER'S FRIENDS
Rudolph, Alan
PLAYER, THE
Rue, Sara
PASSED AWAY
Rueben, Gloria
WILD ORCHID 2: TWO SHADES OF BLUE
Ruffelle, Alison
UNDER SUSPICION
Ruffin, Roger
ALL THE VERMEERS IN NEW YORK
Rufo, John
COMPLEX WORLD
Rufus
DELICATESSEN
Ruge, George Marshall
BRENDA STARR
MALCOLM X
Ruggiero, Anthony
BAD LIEUTENANT
Ruglio, Tony
ROADSIDE PROPHETS
Ruiz, Luis
LORENZO'S OIL
Rumph, Sky
CHAPLIN
Ruoti, Helena
LORENZO'S OIL
PASSED AWAY
Rupnik, Amy
BRIDE OF KILLER NERD
Ruschell, Niva
WHITE TRASH
Ruscio, Al
I DON'T BUY KISSES ANYMORE
ROUND TRIP TO HEAVEN
Rush, Debra
PASSED AWAY
Rush, Maggie
JUICE
Rushing, Larry
MALCOLM X
Rushton, Jared
PET SEMATARY II
Russ
COMPLEX WORLD
Russ, Tim
MR. SATURDAY NIGHT
NIGHT EYES 2
Russ, William
TRACES OF RED
Russell, Barbara
LEAVING NORMAL
Russell, Betsy
DELTA HEAT
Russell, Carlton L.
TWIN PEAKS: FIRE WALK WITH ME
Russell, Catherine
NIGHT AND THE CITY
Russell, Clive
POWER OF ONE, THE
Russell, Gail
LASER MOON
Russell, Gregg
NEWSIES
Russell, Karen
DEAD CERTAIN
Russell, Keri
HONEY, I BLEW UP THE KID
Russell, Kurt
CAPTAIN RON
UNLAWFUL ENTRY
Russell, Peter
RAPID FIRE
Russell, T.E.
GLADIATOR
TRESPASS
Russell, Theresa
COLD HEAVEN
Russell, Thomas
PATRIOT GAMES
Russell-Pavier, Nicholas
SECRET FRIENDS
Russo, Chris "Mad Dog"
BAD LIEUTENANT
Russo, James
COLD HEAVEN
Russo, John D.
MAN TROUBLE
Russo, Michael
DEMONIC TOYS
Russo, Rene
FREEJACK
LETHAL WEAPON 3
Russo, Rosario
USED PEOPLE
Ruth, Rebeca
WATERDANCE, THE
Ruth, Robert
RESERVOIR DOGS
Rutherford, Rudy
TEXAS TENOR: THE ILLINOIS JACQUET STORY
Rutherford, Sally
LEAGUE OF THEIR OWN, A
Rutledge, Stephen
SINGLES
Ruud, Michael
FAR AND AWAY
Ruud, Sif
BEST INTENTIONS, THE
Ruzan, Robin
WAYNE'S WORLD
Ryabova, Svetlana
ADAM'S RIB

Ryals, Patrick
HAND THAT ROCKS THE CRADLE, THE
Ryan, Anna Livia
PLAYBOYS, THE
Ryan, Bridgit
WILD ORCHID 2: TWO SHADES OF BLUE
Ryan, Chanel
SOCIETY
Ryan, Colin
SECRET FRIENDS
Ryan, Holly
FERNGULLY: THE LAST RAINFOREST
Ryan, Jennifer
WATERDANCE, THE
Ryan, Jim
RUBY
Ryan, John P.
HOFFA
Ryan, Jonathan
PATRIOT GAMES
Ryan, Joseph R.
FOLKS!
Ryan, Leslie
976-EVIL II
Ryan, Meg
PRELUDE TO A KISS
Ryan, Mitchell
ACES: IRON EAGLE III
Ryan, Tim
RUNESTONE, THE
Ryan, Will
ROCK-A-DOODLE
Ryder, Richard
FOREVER YOUNG
Ryder, Winona
BRAM STOKER'S DRACULA
NIGHT ON EARTH
Rydstrom, Gary
MAGICAL WORLD OF CHUCK JONES, THE
Rymell, Rodney
HOWARDS END
Saadi, Isaac
HUMAN SHIELD, THE
Saavedra, Eddie
BREATHING FIRE
Sabir, Nazir
K2
Sabordo, Roe
LOVE CRIMES
Sacchari, Micki
MANIAC WARRIORS
Saccio, Thomas
CONSENTING ADULTS
Sacco, Dennis Ryan
AMERICAN ME
Sach, Terence
HOWARDS END
Sacha, Kenny
BUFFY THE VAMPIRE SLAYER
Sacha, Orlando
WELCOME TO OBLIVION
Sachs, Leslie
HARD PROMISES
Sacker, Elion
SWOON
Saddington, Tina
LIFE ON THE EDGE
Saderup, Robin J.
THUNDERHEART
Sadgrove, Mark
MY GRANDPA IS A VAMPIRE
Sadler, Nicholas
SCENT OF A WOMAN
STOP! OR MY MOM WILL SHOOT
Sadler, William
TRESPASS
Safra, Jaqui
OX, THE
Sagal, Joey
OUT FOR BLOOD
Sagal, Liz
LIFE ON THE EDGE
Sage, Nandan
NIGHT AND THE CITY
Sage, William
LAWS OF GRAVITY
SIMPLE MEN
Sahagan, Elena
DANCE WITH DEATH
NAKED OBSESSION
Saiko, Johnnie
GUYVER, THE
Saint-Macary, Hubert
INDOCHINE
Saitoh, Ikuko
MR. BASEBALL
Saiz, Rita
PALE BLOOD
Sakata, Jeanne
POISON IVY
Saks, Matthew
FEW GOOD MEN, A
Sakura, Kinzoh
MR. BASEBALL
Salazar, Ruby
UNLAWFUL ENTRY
Salazar, Sigrid
HOMEBOYS
Salcedo, Victor Hugo
CABEZA DE VACA
Saldana, Ramon
BRENDA STARR
Salem, Kario
1492: THE CONQUEST OF PARADISE
Salinas, Carmen
DANZON
Salinas, Jose
CABEZA DE VACA
Salinas, Raul
GLADIATOR
Salinas, Ric
ENCINO MAN
Salinas, Ricardo
HERO
Salinger, Diane
BATMAN RETURNS
VENICE/VENICE
Salinger, Matt
CAPTAIN AMERICA
Salisbury, Benjamin
CAPTAIN RON
Salkilld, Gordon
UNDER SUSPICION
Salmela, Tomi
NIGHT ON EARTH
Salo, Elina
MATCH FACTORY GIRL, THE
Salonga, Lea
ALADDIN
Salt, James Asher
GIVING, THE
Salt, Karen
CHAPLIN
Salt-N-Pepa
STAY TUNED
Samir, Sami
CUP FINAL
Samms, Emma
ILLUSIONS
Sammy
HONEY, I BLEW UP THE KID
Sampsel, Charla
POISON IVY
Sampson, DonRe
FAR AND AWAY
Sampson, Robert
NETHERWORLD
Sampson, Roy
UNDER SUSPICION
Samrai, Rocky
DEMON IN MY VIEW, A
Samuda, Jacqueline
ADJUSTER, THE
San Giacomo, Laura
UNDER SUSPICION
WHERE THE DAY TAKES YOU
San Martino, Rose-Ann
HOUSESITTER
Sanabria, Eddie
MALCOLM X
Sanchez, Alicia
CABEZA DE VACA
Sanchez, Blanca
PEPI, LUCI, BOM AND OTHER GIRLS ON THE HEAP
Sanchez, Gerardo
CABEZA DE VACA
Sanchez, Jamie
BAD LIEUTENANT
Sanchez, Mario Ernesto
TRACES OF RED
Sanchez, Modesto M.
AMERICAN ME
Sanchez, Monica
KISS ME A KILLER
Sanchez, Pancho
KISS ME A KILLER
Sanchez, Pedro
NIGHT AND THE CITY
Sanchez, Roselyn
CAPTAIN RON
Sanchez, Sara Iliana
CABEZA DE VACA
Sand, Paul
FROZEN ASSETS

Sandel, Jr., Wantland L.
LEAGUE OF THEIR OWN, A
Sanders, Alix Henry
MISSISSIPPI MASALA
Sanders, Alix W.
MISSISSIPPI MASALA
Sanders, Brad
BEBE'S KIDS
Sanders, Edward
MUPPET CHRISTMAS CAROL, THE
Sanders, Elizabeth
BATMAN RETURNS
Sanders, Fred
JUST LIKE IN THE MOVIES
Sanders, Gisela I.
CABEZA DE VACA
Sanders, Henry G.
KUFFS
Sanders, Jay O.
JUST LIKE IN THE MOVIES
Sanders, Kurtis Epper
BUFFY THE VAMPIRE SLAYER
Sanders, Richard
NEON CITY
Sanders, Theo
MUPPET CHRISTMAS CAROL, THE
Sandgren, Eric D.
LAST OF THE MOHICANS, THE
Sandler, Adam
SHAKES THE CLOWN
Sandlund, Debra
GLADIATOR
Sandoval, Miguel
WHITE SANDS
Sandow, Wendy
MINDWARP
Sands, Julian
HUSBANDS AND LOVERS
Sanford, Naydia
BOOMERANG
Sanghyuk Shin
WATERDANCE, THE
Sangmeister, John
WIND
Sangweni, Zanele
SARAFINA!
Sank, Leslie A.
SINGLE WHITE FEMALE
Santa Cruz, A.C.
NETHERWORLD
Santangelo, Melody
NEWSIES
Santesson, Kare
BEST INTENTIONS, THE
Santoro, Michael
SCENT OF A WOMAN
Santos, A.C.
KISS ME A KILLER
Santos, Cynthia
MAMBO KINGS, THE
Santos, Joe
MO' MONEY
Santoyo, Jorge
CABEZA DE VACA
Santucci, John
HOUSE IV

Sanz, Jorge
AMANTES
Sanz, Phyllis
REFRIGERATOR, THE
Sapp, Lindsey Jayde
TRACES OF RED
Sara, Mia
STRANGER AMONG US, A
Sarafian, Richard
RUBY
Sarandon, Chris
COLLISION COURSE
RESURRECTED, THE
Sarandon, Susan
BOB ROBERTS
LIGHT SLEEPER
LORENZO'S OIL
PLAYER, THE
Sarda, Anthony
CHRISTOPHER COLUMBUS: THE DISCOVERY
Sarelle, Leilani
BASIC INSTINCT
LITTLE SISTER
Sargeant, Kate
3 NINJAS
Sargent, Gary
TEXAS TENOR: THE ILLINOIS JACQUET STORY
Sarkisyan, Rose
ADJUSTER, THE
Sarkka, Jari
CLEARCUT
Sarna, Martin
COMPLEX WORLD
Sartain, Gailard
STOP! OR MY MOM WILL SHOOT
Sarviss, John
STOP! OR MY MOM WILL SHOOT
Sassi, Khedija
POPE MUST DIET!, THE
Sasso, Dick
SHAKING THE TREE
Sassoon, Catya
BLOODFIST IV: DIE TRYING
DANCE WITH DEATH
SECRET GAMES
Sato, Koichi
SILK ROAD, THE
Satoni, Reni
WATERDANCE, THE
Satoris, Susan
TERMINAL BLISS
Satriano, Nicholas
BABE, THE
Satterlee, C. Craig
ARTICLE 99
Saucedo, Denise J.
TOYS
Saucedo, Lisette Yvonne
TOYS
Saunders, Greg
LONDON KILLS ME
Saunders, Mark
GATE II
Saurez, Maiquel
MAMBO KINGS, THE

Sautner, Eugene
HOUSE ON TOMBSTONE HILL, THE
Savage, Ben
BIG GIRLS DON'T CRY . . . THEY GET EVEN
Savage, John
HUNTING
PRIMARY MOTIVE
Savage, Lisa
FOREVER YOUNG
Savant, Doug
SHAKING THE TREE
Savarin, Charisse
VENICE/VENICE
Savident, John
BRAIN DONORS
Savin, Jody
CLASS ACT
Savini, Tom
INNOCENT BLOOD
Savino, Joe
CRYING GAME, THE
Saviola, Camille
SHADOWS AND FOG
Savoia, John
BED & BREAKFAST
COMPLEX WORLD
Savoy, Suzanne
HARD PROMISES
Sawaguchi, Yasuko
GODZILLA VS. BIOLLANTE
Sawayama, Yuji
JOURNEY OF HONOR
Sawyer, David
CHILDREN OF THE NIGHT
HIRED TO KILL
Sawyer-Young, Kat
LIFE ON THE EDGE
Saxenmeyer, James
LIGHT SLEEPER
Saxon, John
ANIMAL INSTINCTS
DEATH HOUSE
HELL MASTER
MAXIMUM FORCE
Saxon, Pamela
PATRIOT GAMES
Sayles, John
LITTLE VEGAS
MALCOLM X
STRAIGHT TALK
Sayles, Michael
FINAL ANALYSIS
Sbaratto, Roberto
ONCE UPON A CRIME
Sbardellati, James
LOVE POTION NO. 9
Scacchi, Greta
PLAYER, THE
Scaggs, Pat "Soul"
MO' MONEY
Scales, Prunella
FREDDIE AS F.R.O.7
HOWARDS END
Scallia, Salvatore
JOHNNY STECCHINO

Scanduzzi, Gian-Carlo
PUBLIC EYE, THE
Scannell, Kevin
PLAYER, THE
Scarabelli, Michele
DEADBOLT
I DON'T BUY KISSES ANYMORE
Scarbro, Robert
WHITE TRASH
Scarfe, Alan
LETHAL WEAPON 3
Scarlett, Lori
BRIDE OF KILLER NERD
Scarwid, Diana
BRENDA STARR
Scates, David
HONEY, I BLEW UP THE KID
Schafer, Frank
AFFENGEIL
Schaffer, Sharon
BUFFY THE VAMPIRE SLAYER
Scharler, Kathy
RIVER RUNS THROUGH IT, A
Schaufuss, Ann
LOVER, THE
Schechner, Richard
SWOON
Scheibner, Ed
HERO
Scheine, Raynor
MY COUSIN VINNY
Schell, Maurice
STRANGER AMONG US, A
Schell, Ronnie
ROVER DANGERFIELD
Scheller, Justin
LEAGUE OF THEIR OWN, A
Schelling, Susan
KUFFS
Schepps, Shawn
OUT ON A LIMB
Schettino, Gianni
NIGHT ON EARTH
Schiavelli, Vincent
BATMAN RETURNS
FREEJACK
MIRACLE BEACH
Schick, Stephanie
DO OR DIE
Schickel, Erika
RUNESTONE, THE
Schienle, Martin
HERO
Schiff, Richard
BODYGUARD, THE
HOFFA
MALCOLM X
PUBLIC EYE, THE
RAPID FIRE
STOP! OR MY MOM WILL SHOOT
Schill, Steve
RAISING CAIN
Schiller, Danny
UNDER SUSPICION
Schindler, Klaus
TOTO LE HEROS

Schipper, Michael
SOCIETY
Schlachet, Daniel
SWOON
Schlatter, Charlie
ALL-AMERICAN MURDER
Schlesinger, Renate
TRACES OF RED
Schlossman, Don
KUFFS
Schmidt, Benno
HUSBANDS AND WIVES
Schmidt, Karl Dick
BECOMING COLETTE
Schmidt, Paul
SWOON
Schmidt, Scot
ONE LAST RUN
Schmidtke, Ned
BABE, THE
SHAKING THE TREE
Schmoeller, David
NETHERWORLD
Schnarre, Monika
WAXWORK II: LOST IN TIME
Schneider, Carol Jeanne
JENNIFER EIGHT
Schneider, Michael
DOUBLE EDGE
Schneider, Rob
HOME ALONE 2:
LOST IN NEW YORK
Schock, Bridgit P.
THUNDERHEART
Schoelen, Jill
ADVENTURES IN SPYING
Schoeller, Anna
WAYNE'S WORLD
Schofield, David
LAST OF THE MOHICANS, THE
Schons, Caleen
LIFE ON THE EDGE
Schoppert, Bill
CROSSING THE BRIDGE
MIGHTY DUCKS, THE
Schott, Bob
OUT FOR BLOOD
Schram, Bitty
LEAGUE OF THEIR OWN, A
Schrum, Pete
DEMONIC TOYS
Schryver, Dave
LEAVING NORMAL
Schub, Steven
LITTLE NOISES
Schultz, Albert
BEAUTIFUL DREAMERS
BEETHOVEN LIVES UPSTAIRS
PSYCHIC
Schultz, Armand
MALCOLM X
Schulz, Richard C.W.
PRELUDE TO A KISS
Schulzie, Paul
LAWS OF GRAVITY
Schumacher Garth
MIGHTY DUCKS, THE

Schuyler, Lonnie
HONEYMOON IN VEGAS
Schwade, Hans Peter
AFFENGEIL
Schwartz, Aaron
MIGHTY DUCKS, THE
Schwartz, Gary
BEBE'S KIDS
FERNGULLY:
THE LAST RAINFOREST
Schwartz, Marty Eli
CAPTAIN RON
Schwartz-Hartley, Steven
OVER HER DEAD BODY
Schwartzberg, Hattie
RADIO FLYER
Schwarzenegger, Arnold
FEED
Schweig, Eric
LAST OF THE MOHICANS, THE
Schweiger, Carola
BECOMING COLETTE
Schwenk, Joan
GLADIATOR
Schwidde, Jess
RIVER RUNS THROUGH IT, A
Schwimmer, David
CROSSING THE BRIDGE
Schwimmer, Rusty
CANDYMAN
STEPHEN KING'S SLEEPWALKERS
Sciacca, Joey
BIG GIRLS DON'T CRY . . . THEY
GET EVEN
Scialla, Fred
HOFFA
Sciama, Dennis
BRIEF HISTORY OF TIME, A
Sciorra, Annabella
HAND THAT ROCKS THE
CRADLE, THE
WHISPERS IN THE DARK
Scmitt, Lita
LEAGUE OF THEIR OWN, A
Scoggins, Tracy
DEMONIC TOYS
ONE LAST RUN
PLAY MURDER FOR ME
ULTIMATE DESIRES
Sconduto, David
HOFFA
Scorby, Don
FROZEN ASSETS
Scorrar, Jim
MY GRANDPA IS A VAMPIRE
Scott, Alex
PETER'S FRIENDS
Scott, Ben R.
BUFFY THE VAMPIRE SLAYER
Scott, Campbell
SINGLES
Scott, Dawan
RADIO FLYER
RUNESTONE, THE
Scott, Debra
MAMBO KINGS, THE

Scott, Esther
ENCINO MAN
Scott I, Alan Randolph
NIGHT ON EARTH
Scott, Ian
HUNTING
Scott, James
BASKET CASE 3: THE PROGENY
Scott, Jessie
LIFE ON THE EDGE
Scott, John-Clay
FAR AND AWAY
Scott, Kennan
NIGHT AND THE CITY
Scott, Kimberly
WATERDANCE, THE
Scott, Renata
CHAPLIN
Scott, TaiNesha
MALCOLM X
Scott, Virginia
BRIDE OF KILLER NERD
Scotty
GIVING, THE
Scriba, Mik
GLADIATOR
MO' MONEY
SHAKING THE TREE
Scrimm, Angus
MINDWARP
MUNCHIE
Scrivano, Rae
CAFE ROMEO
Scully, Bill
BASKET CASE 3: THE PROGENY
Scully, David
HAND THAT ROCKS THE CRADLE, THE
Scurlock, Connie
FOLKS!
Seacat, Sandra
WILDFIRE
Seagal, Steven
UNDER SIEGE
Seale, Bobby
MALCOLM X
Seale, Douglas
ALADDIN
Seals, Jr., Frank
PASSED AWAY
Seamon, Edward
CONSENTING ADULTS
SCHOOL TIES
Searcy, Nick
LOVE FIELD
Sears, Steve
CUTTING EDGE, THE
Sebastian, Kim
NOISES OFF
Sebban, Michel
FAVOUR, THE WATCH, AND THE VERY BIG FISH, THE
Seboko, Louis
SARAFINA!
Sebrasky, Dolores E.
TOYS

Secundo, Frank
COMPLEX WORLD
Seda, Jon
GLADIATOR
ZEBRAHEAD
Sederholm, David
BEASTMASTER 2: THROUGH THE PORTAL OF TIME
Sedgwick, Kyra
SINGLES
Sedwick, Shannon
HARD PROMISES
Seely, Jessica
BIG GIRLS DON'T CRY . . . THEY GET EVEN
Seema, Eric
SARAFINA!
Segal, Barton
GUN IN BETTY LOU'S HANDBAG, THE
Segal, Nena
REFRIGERATOR, THE
Segall, Pamela
FERNGULLY: THE LAST RAINFOREST
GATE II
Segerstrom, Mikael
BEST INTENTIONS, THE
Segure, Kristan Rai
MALCOLM X
Sehula, Doris
SARAFINA!
Seibel, Mary
FOLKS!
Seibert, Jaime
BUFFY THE VAMPIRE SLAYER
Seide, Maximilien
FAVOUR, THE WATCH, AND THE VERY BIG FISH, THE
Seide, Stuart
NEAR MISSES
Sekae, Sith
SCANNERS III: THE TAKEOVER
Sekiguchi, Ken
JOURNEY OF HONOR
Selby, Nicholas
CHRISTOPHER COLUMBUS: THE DISCOVERY
Selby, William
DEATH HOUSE
Seldes, Marian
GUN IN BETTY LOU'S HANDBAG, THE
Seliger, Gwen
BODYGUARD, THE
Selkirk, Willie
HIGHWAY 61
Sell, Rod
HOME ALONE 2: LOST IN NEW YORK
Selleck, Tom
CHRISTOPHER COLUMBUS: THE DISCOVERY
FOLKS!
MR. BASEBALL
Sellers, Trevor
CHRISTOPHER COLUMBUS: THE DISCOVERY

Sells, Susan
COLD HEAVEN
Selman, Suzi
CONSENTING ADULTS
Selzer, Jim
UNLAWFUL ENTRY
Semenoff, Sasha
HONEYMOON IN VEGAS
Sen, Chitra
CITY OF JOY
Sen Sharma, Subrata
CITY OF JOY
Seneca, Joe
MALCOLM X
MISSISSIPPI MASALA
Sengupta, Rudraprasad
CITY OF JOY
Sengupta, Shyamal
CITY OF JOY
Sengupta, Suneeta
CITY OF JOY
Sengupta, Swatilekha
CITY OF JOY
Senko, Jennifer
TUNE, THE
Senkumba, Sammy E.D.
MISSISSIPPI MASALA
Senn, Rick
MISSISSIPPI MASALA
Senzy, Arthur
FEW GOOD MEN, A
Seppala, Silu
MATCH FACTORY GIRL, THE
Septien, Al
3 NINJAS
Serbulo, Mayra
CABEZA DE VACA
Sercelj, Karyn
STEPHEN KING'S SLEEPWALKERS
Serdar, Igor
CAPTAIN AMERICA
Sergeyev, Alexander
DANCE MACABRE
Sergott, Matt
DEATH BECOMES HER
Seri, Mati
HUMAN SHIELD, THE
Sermon, Erik
JUICE
Serna, Assumpta
PEPI, LUCI, BOM AND OTHER GIRLS ON THE HEAP
Serna, Pepe
AMERICAN ME
Serrano, Andres
DAMNED IN THE USA
Serrano, Frank
LOVE HURTS
Serrano, Julieta
PEPI, LUCI, BOM AND OTHER GIRLS ON THE HEAP
Serrano, Nestor
BRENDA STARR
Serret, Jean
AFRAID OF THE DARK

Serrio Dos Santos, Edinei Maria
MEDICINE MAN

Servadio, Donatella
NIGHT ON EARTH

Sessions, John
FREDDIE AS F.R.O.7
POPE MUST DIET!, THE

Sestak, Slvko
CAPTAIN AMERICA

Setala, Minna
MANIAC WARRIORS

Seth, Roshan
LONDON KILLS ME
MISSISSIPPI MASALA

Settimi, Tim
CRISSCROSS

Sety, Gerard
VAN GOGH

Severance, Joan
ALMOST PREGNANT
RUNESTONE, THE

Seward, Bill
RUBY

Seweryn, Andrzej
INDOCHINE

Seymour, Phillip
MY NEW GUN

Seyrig, Coralie
BEATING HEART, A

Sgan-Cohen, Natan
FINEST HOUR, THE

Sguerri, Clementina
WHERE ANGELS FEAR TO TREAD

Shabalala, Mazwe
SARAFINA!

Shaban, Nabil
CITY OF JOY

Shabazz, Ilyasah
MALCOLM X

Shadix, Glenn
STEPHEN KING'S SLEEPWALKERS

Shafer, Rick
HOME ALONE 2:
LOST IN NEW YORK

Shaff, Edmund L.
MEMOIRS OF AN INVISIBLE MAN

Shaga, Lad
HIGHWAY 61

Shah, Jamal
K2

Shah, Rajeb
K2

Shai, Patrick
LIGHT IN THE JUNGLE, THE

Shaiman, Marc
MR. SATURDAY NIGHT

Shakur, Tupac
JUICE

Shakurov, Sergei
RASPAD

Shalet, Victoria
SHINING THROUGH

Shalhoub, Tony
HONEYMOON IN VEGAS

Shalikar, Daniel
HONEY, I BLEW UP THE KID

Shalikar, Joshua
HONEY, I BLEW UP THE KID

Shallo, Karen
SCHOOL TIES

Shamas, Sandra
WISECRACKS

Shandu, Cyprian
SARAFINA!

Shaner, Michael A.
AMERICAN ME

Shangraw, Howard
FINISHING TOUCH, THE

Shankman, Adam
GUN IN BETTY LOU'S
HANDBAG, THE

Sharif, Abdul Hassan
ZEBRAHEAD

Sharif, Omar
BEYOND JUSTICE

Shark, David
INSIDE EDGE

Sharkey, Ray
CAGED FEAR
ROUND TRIP TO HEAVEN
ZEBRAHEAD

Sharp, Sara Jennifer
HAND THAT ROCKS THE
CRADLE, THE

Sharpton, Al
MALCOLM X

Sharron, Nitzan
CHRISTOPHER COLUMBUS:
THE DISCOVERY

Shatner, Melanie
CTHULHU MANSION

Shattuck, Shari
LOWER LEVEL
OUT FOR BLOOD

Shaud, Grant
DISTINGUISHED GENTLEMAN, THE

Shaver, Helen
ZEBRAHEAD

Shavers, Ernie
HONEYMOON IN VEGAS

Shaw, Crystal
LASER MOON

Shaw, Fiona
LONDON KILLS ME

Shaw, Kaefan
MUPPET CHRISTMAS CAROL, THE

Shaw, Rick
PUSHED TO THE LIMIT

Shaw, Sebastian
MONKEY BOY

Shaw, Susan
BOB ROBERTS

Shaw, Tina
SPLIT SECOND

Shaw, Vinessa
LADYBUGS

Shawn, Wallace
MOM AND DAD SAVE THE WORLD
NICKEL & DIME
SHADOWS AND FOG

Shay, Maureen Elisabeth
HOME ALONE 2:
LOST IN NEW YORK

Shaye, Lin
ROADSIDE PROPHETS

Shayne, Linda
MUNCHIE

Shayne, Michael
DO OR DIE

Shea, Ann
PASSED AWAY

Shea, Joe
MR. SATURDAY NIGHT

Shea, John
FREEJACK
HONEY, I BLEW UP THE KID

Shea, Lisa
HELLROLLER

Shearer, Harry
LEAGUE OF THEIR OWN, A

Shearer, Jack
FINAL ANALYSIS

Sheedy, Ally
HOME ALONE 2:
LOST IN NEW YORK

Sheehan, John Charles
WHITE MEN CAN'T JUMP

Sheehan, Michael
LITTLE NEMO: ADVENTURES IN
SLUMBERLAND

Sheen, Charlie
BACKTRACK

Sheen, Martin
ORIGINAL INTENT
TOUCH AND DIE

Sheffer, Craig
EYE OF THE STORM
RIVER RUNS THROUGH IT, A

Sheinkopf, David
NEWSIES

Shelby, LaRita
SOUTH CENTRAL

Sheldon, Jana
WATERLAND

Shellen, Stephen
BODYGUARD, THE
RIVER RUNS THROUGH IT, A

Shelley, Carole
LITTLE NOISES

Shellito, Chilton
GLADIATOR

Shellman, Eddie
MALCOLM X

Shelly, Adrienne
BIG GIRLS DON'T CRY . . . THEY
GET EVEN

Shelly, Ron
LOVE FIELD

Shelton, Deborah
BLIND VISION

Shelton, Glenn
AMERICAN ME

Shemo, Dave
HOFFA

Shen, Freda Foh
BASIC INSTINCT

Shepard, Hilary
I DON'T BUY KISSES ANYMORE

Shepard, John
PATRIOT GAMES

Shepard, Karen
MISSION OF JUSTICE
Shepard, Sam
THUNDERHEART
VOYAGER
Shepherd, Cybill
ONCE UPON A CRIME
Shepherd, Gerda
CAPTAIN AMERICA
Shepherd, Gwendolyn
ARTICLE 99
Shepherd, John
SNEAKERS
Sheppard, Delia
ANIMAL INSTINCTS
MIRROR IMAGES
NIGHT RHYTHMS
ROOTS OF EVIL
SECRET GAMES
Sheppard, Jewell
ROOTS OF EVIL
Sheptekita, Valerii
RASPAD
Sheridan, Jamey
STRANGER AMONG US, A
WHISPERS IN THE DARK
Sheridan, Kim
WIND
Sheridan, Nicollette
NOISES OFF
Sherinian, Derek
WAYNE'S WORLD
Sherman, Daniel
CHAPLIN
Sherman, Emily
SWOON
Sherrer, Renee
WILD WHEELS
Sherrill, David
BUFFY THE VAMPIRE SLAYER
Sherrill, Sam
MISSISSIPPI MASALA
Shidell, Gerald
SEVERED TIES
Shields, Brooke
BRENDA STARR
Shields, Majorie
ACES: IRON EAGLE III
Shiff, Caleb
RIVER RUNS THROUGH IT, A
Shigemizu, Naoto
JOURNEY OF HONOR
Shikartsi, Ofer
HUMAN SHIELD, THE
Shillo, Michael
HUMAN SHIELD, THE
Shiloh, Shmuel
DOUBLE EDGE
Shiner, David
LORENZO'S OIL
Shiono, Ryonosuke
LORENZO'S OIL
Shioya, Toshi
MR. BASEBALL
Shipman, Ann
HIGHWAY 61

Shirakura, Shinsuke
JOURNEY OF HONOR
Shire, Talia
BED & BREAKFAST
COLD HEAVEN
Shoemaker, Tim
MIDNIGHT CLEAR, A
Shoenberg, Aimee
VENICE/VENICE
Shoji, Tomohisa
MR. BASEBALL
Sholto, Pamela
UNDER SUSPICION
Shonka, Ted
ARTICLE 99
Shore, Harris
WAYNE'S WORLD
Shore, Jeff
COMPLEX WORLD
Shore, Pauly
CLASS ACT
ENCINO MAN
Short, James
PASSENGER 57
Short, John
BRENDA STARR
DIGGSTOWN
Short, Joy
BOB ROBERTS
Short, Martin
CAPTAIN RON
Short, Paul
BIG GIRLS DON'T CRY . . . THEY GET EVEN
Short, Sylvia
NEWSIES
Shorter, Wayne
LOVE CRIMES
Show, Grant
WOMAN, HER MEN AND HER FUTON, A
Showler, Dave
MUPPET CHRISTMAS CAROL, THE
Shrog, Maurice
NIGHT AND THE CITY
Shroyer, Sonny
LOVE CRIMES
Shuler, Larry
MY COUSIN VINNY
Shuler-Donner, Lauren
LETHAL WEAPON 3
Shull, Richard B.
HOUSESITTER
Shuman, Danielle
LOVE CRIMES
Shuman, David
LOVE CRIMES
Shumba, Simon
POWER OF ONE, THE
Shung Moo Joo
MISSISSIPPI MASALA
Sibanda, Lungani
POWER OF ONE, THE
Sibanda, Rosemary Chikobwe
POWER OF ONE, THE
Sibbald, Tony
SPLIT SECOND

Sibbett, Jane
RESURRECTED, THE
Sibray, Carolyn
BOB ROBERTS
Sicotte, Nancy L.
RAMPAGE
Sidel, Jon
JUST LIKE IN THE MOVIES
Sidell, Tom
PALE BLOOD
Sidney, Sylvia
USED PEOPLE
Sidoni, David
NEWSIES
Siegel, Adam
ENCINO MAN
Siegler, Marc
WILDFIRE
Siemaszko, Casey
NEAR MISSES
OF MICE AND MEN
Siemaszko, Nina
BED & BREAKFAST
LITTLE NOISES
WILD ORCHID 2: TWO SHADES OF BLUE
Sierra, Gregory
DEEP COVER
HONEY, I BLEW UP THE KID
Sierra, Miguel
BRONX WAR, THE
LAWS OF GRAVITY
Siguenza, Herbert
ENCINO MAN
HERO
Sihol, Caroline
TOUS LES MATINS DU MONDE
Siilas, Kurt
MATCH FACTORY GIRL, THE
Silberg, Tusse
SHINING THROUGH
Silla, Felix
BATMAN RETURNS
Sillas, Karen
SIMPLE MEN
Silo, Susan
BEBE'S KIDS
Silva, Frank
TWIN PEAKS: FIRE WALK WITH ME
Silva, Geno
NIGHT EYES 2
Silva, Luis J.
UNDER SIEGE
Silver, Daniel
LAWNMOWER MAN, THE
Silver, Johnny
SHAKES THE CLOWN
Silver, Robert
SHADOWS AND FOG
Silver, Ron
MR. SATURDAY NIGHT
Silverman, Jonathan
BREAKING THE RULES
DEATH BECOMES HER
LITTLE SISTER
Silvestri, Stewart
WIND

Sim, Gerald
CHAPLIN
PATRIOT GAMES
Simaan, Summer
TOYS
Simek, Vasek
HOUSESITTER
MISTRESS
Simmonds, Buck
RIVER RUNS THROUGH IT, A
Simmons, Ernest
BLACKBELT
Simmons, Jr., Leroy
DAUGHTERS OF THE DUST
Simmons, Thom C.
BABE, THE
Simmons, Thomas Charles
GLADIATOR
Simmrin, Mike
MUNCHIE
RADIO FLYER
Simms, George C.
LIFE ON THE EDGE
Simms, Leslie
AUNTIE LEE'S MEAT PIES
Simms, Phil
AUNTIE LEE'S MEAT PIES
Simon, Adam
BOB ROBERTS
PLAYER, THE
Simon, Fawzy
CROSSING THE BRIDGE
Simon, John
TEXAS TENOR: THE ILLINOIS JACQUET STORY
Simon, Michel
SCENT OF A WOMAN
Simon, Rogers
MALCOLM X
Simonds, David
REFRIGERATOR, THE
Simonds, Lincoln
BUFFY THE VAMPIRE SLAYER
Simonneau, Odette
INSPECTOR LAVARDIN
Simons, Robyn
LEAVING NORMAL
Simons, Talbot Perry
MR. SATURDAY NIGHT
Simotes, Tony
CLASS ACT
WATERDANCE, THE
Simpkins, Kelli
LEAGUE OF THEIR OWN, A
Simpkins, Michael
DEMON IN MY VIEW, A
Simpson, Brock
PROM NIGHT IV - DELIVER US FROM EVIL
Simpson, Byron
MISTRESS
Simpson, Doug
GUYVER, THE
Simpson, Freddie
LEAGUE OF THEIR OWN, A
Simpson, Mark
SWOON
Simpson, Michael
MY COUSIN VINNY
Simrin, Joey
LAWNMOWER MAN, THE
Sinaiko, David
BOB ROBERTS
Sinatra, Jr., Frank
COOL WORLD
Sinclair, Graham
CHAPLIN
Sinclair, Ken
HIGHWAY 61
Sinclair, Paul
CHAPLIN
Sinden, Donald
CHILDREN, THE
Singer, Marc
BEASTMASTER 2: THROUGH THE PORTAL OF TIME
ULTIMATE DESIRES
Singer, Ritchie
TILL THERE WAS YOU
Singh, Desi
GLADIATOR
Sinise, Gary
MIDNIGHT CLEAR, A
OF MICE AND MEN
Sinisi, Erica
DEVIL'S DAUGHTER, THE
Sinovoi, Maxwell
MALCOLM X
Siragusa, Peter
BABE, THE
Siraj, Nadia
WATERLAND
Sirico, G. Anthony
BACKTRACK
Sirico, Tony
INNOCENT BLOOD
Sirtis, Mirina
WAXWORK II: LOST IN TIME
Sisson, Chuck
BABE, THE
Sisto, Meadow
CAPTAIN RON
Sisto, Rocco
FAR AND AWAY
INNOCENT BLOOD
LORENZO'S OIL
Sithole, Khululiwe
SARAFINA!
Sithole, Nonhlanhla
SARAFINA!
Siva, Eva
PEPI, LUCI, BOM AND OTHER GIRLS ON THE HEAP
Siverio, Manny
MALCOLM X
Sizemore, Tom
PASSENGER 57
Skarsgard, Stellan
OX, THE
WIND
Skeaping, Colin
SPLIT SECOND
Skefile, Tiny
ODDBALL HALL
Skelly, Deborah
VENICE/VENICE
Skerritt, Tom
POISON IVY
RIVER RUNS THROUGH IT, A
SINGLES
WILD ORCHID 2: TWO SHADES OF BLUE
Skiljevic, Ljubomir
JOURNEY OF HONOR
Skingle, Trevor
EDWARD II
Skipper, Pat
MEMOIRS OF AN INVISIBLE MAN
Skorohod, Anatolii
RASPAD
Skosana, Dominic
SARAFINA!
Skousen, Kevin
HAND THAT ROCKS THE CRADLE, THE
Skutch, Christopher
MALCOLM X
Skye, Ione
GAS FOOD LODGING
WAYNE'S WORLD
Slack, Ben
SOCIETY
Slade, Max Elliott
3 NINJAS
Slany, Sonia
EDWARD II
Slate, Jeremy
LAWNMOWER MAN, THE
Slater, Christian
FERNGULLY: THE LAST RAINFOREST
KUFFS
WHERE THE DAY TAKES YOU
Slater, Rick
SAVAGE INSTINCT
Slattery, Tony
CRYING GAME, THE
PETER'S FRIENDS
Slaughter, Lance
GLADIATOR
Slavin, Millie
FOREVER YOUNG
Slezak, Victor
BED & BREAKFAST
Slim, Magic
FOLKS!
Sloat, Tracy
ARTICLE 99
Sloman, Larry "Ratso"
PRIMARY MOTIVE
Sloop, Helga
AFFENGEIL
Slotky, Anna
HOME ALONE 2: LOST IN NEW YORK
Slotnick, Joseph
LEAGUE OF THEIR OWN, A
Smack, Jr., Dion
MALCOLM X
Smailes, Rick
BASKET CASE 3: THE PROGENY

Small, Nina
MISTRESS
Smalls, Marie
DAUGHTERS OF THE DUST
Smart, Jean
MISTRESS
Smart, Jonathan
LAWNMOWER MAN, THE
Smart, Sam
DEMON IN MY VIEW, A
Smart, Veronica
LONDON KILLS ME
Smeeton, Phil
SPLIT SECOND
Smertcov, Adrian
MR. SATURDAY NIGHT
Smeysters, Christine
TOTO LE HEROS
Smiar, Brian
SHADOWS AND FOG
Smiley, Desmond
LEAVING NORMAL
Smillie, Bill
SINGLES
Smith, A.C. Tony
MO' MONEY
Smith, Albert
BABE, THE
Smith, Barbara
MALCOLM X
Smith, Brandon
HARD PROMISES
Smith, Brenda
VENICE/VENICE
Smith, Bryan Travis
PUBLIC EYE, THE
Smith, C.E.
MALCOLM X
Smith, Cary
SHAKES THE CLOWN
Smith, Chad
DARK HORSE
Smith, Charles Martin
DEEP COVER
Smith, Cheryl Tyre
BEBE'S KIDS
Smith, Darnell
MALCOLM X
Smith, David Anthony
FIELD OF FIRE
Smith, Ebbe Roe
ROADSIDE PROPHETS
Smith, Ebonie
LETHAL WEAPON 3
Smith, Eddie "Bo"
MO' MONEY
Smith, Erica Catherine
BOOMERANG
Smith, Evan Lionel
MO' MONEY
Smith, Eve
LOVE HURTS
Smith, Frazer
PALE BLOOD
Smith, Fred
ACES: IRON EAGLE III
Smith, Greg
WAYNE'S WORLD
Smith, Hillary Bailey
LOVE POTION NO. 9
Smith, Howard
GIVING, THE
Smith, Jaffar
SINGLES
Smith, Jasmine
MALCOLM X
Smith, Josie
UNFORGIVEN
Smith, Jr., Eddie Bo
UNDER SIEGE
Smith, Jr., Lonnie R.
LOVE CRIMES
Smith, K.
MALCOLM X
Smith, Keith
MALCOLM X
Smith, Kurtwood
SHADOWS AND FOG
Smith, Lane
DISTINGUISHED GENTLEMAN, THE
MIGHTY DUCKS, THE
MY COUSIN VINNY
Smith, Lewis
DIARY OF A HITMAN
Smith, Liz
BUFFY THE VAMPIRE SLAYER
Smith, Lois
HARD PROMISES
Smith, Lonnie
CONSENTING ADULTS
Smith, Maggie
SISTER ACT
Smith, Mary Alice
MALCOLM X
Smith, Mary Ann
LOVE HURTS
Smith, Matt
SCENT OF A WOMAN
Smith, Maurice
BLOODFIST III: FORCED TO FIGHT
Smith, Mel
BRAIN DONORS
Smith, Melanie
TRANCERS III: DETH LIVES
Smith, Michelle
CONSENTING ADULTS
Smith, Parrish
JUICE
Smith, Paul L.
DESERT KICKBOXER
Smith, Paul Stockman
LIGHT SLEEPER
Smith, Rhett
CHAPLIN
Smith, Roger Guenveur
DEEP COVER
MALCOLM X
Smith, Russell
GIVING, THE
Smith, Sly
HONEYMOON IN VEGAS
Smith, Stephen Wolfe
UNIVERSAL SOLDIER
Smith, Ted
GUYVER, THE
Smith, Tia
CLEARCUT
Smith, Tina
SPLIT SECOND
Smith, Troy A.
DIGGSTOWN
Smith, Valentino
MALCOLM X
Smith, Will
WHERE THE DAY TAKES YOU
Smith, William
AMERICAN ME
MANIAC WARRIORS
Smith, Yeardley
TOYS
Smith-Brown, Erika
MALCOLM X
Smithwick, Jane
GUN IN BETTY LOU'S HANDBAG, THE
Smolek, Jeff
FINAL ANALYSIS
Smollett, Jussie
MIGHTY DUCKS, THE
Sneddon, Kahli
FATHER
Sneed, Maurice
MALCOLM X
Snegoff, Gregory
COOL WORLD
PROFESSIONAL, THE
Snell, Terrie
HOME ALONE 2: LOST IN NEW YORK
Sniffen, Elsie
BASIC INSTINCT
Snipes, Wesley
PASSENGER 57
WATERDANCE, THE
WHITE MEN CAN'T JUMP
Snow, Carrie
WISECRACKS
Snow, Ron
WILD WHEELS
Snow, Victoria
GETTING MARRIED IN BUFFALO JUMP
Snowden, Van
BRAM STOKER'S DRACULA
Snyder, Bonnie
WILD ORCHID 2: TWO SHADES OF BLUE
Snyder, Drew
DANCE WITH DEATH
UNIVERSAL SOLDIER
Snyder, Jacob
RIVER RUNS THROUGH IT, A
Snyder, Jennifer
LEAP OF FAITH
Snyder, John
ROADSIDE PROPHETS
Snyder, Noah
RIVER RUNS THROUGH IT, A

Soban, Gisele
FAVOUR, THE WATCH, AND THE VERY BIG FISH, THE
Sobieski, Greg
STRAIGHT TALK
Soble, Lisa-Marie
VENICE/VENICE
Sobrevals, Cesar
DANZON
Sofer, Rena
STRANGER AMONG US, A
Sokhela, Sindisiwe
SARAFINA!
Sokolow, Diane
THIS IS MY LIFE
Solann, Evelyn
JOHNNY SUEDE
Solari, John
RUBY
Soler, Tanya
CAPTAIN RON
Soles, P.J.
SOLDIER'S FORTUNE
Soles, Paul
BEETHOVEN LIVES UPSTAIRS
Solis, Alex
AMERICAN ME
Solomon, Charles
WITCHCRAFT IV: VIRGIN HEART
Solomon, Ed
LEAVING NORMAL
Somerville, Phyllis
LEAP OF FAITH
Sommer, Elke
SEVERED TIES
Sommer, Josef
MIGHTY DUCKS, THE
SHADOWS AND FOG
Song, Magie
LIVING END, THE
VENICE/VENICE
Sonic Youth
1991: THE YEAR PUNK BROKE
Soo Hoo, Hayward
SNEAKERS
Soo Lam, Papillion
SPLIT SECOND
Soon-Teck Ho
COLLISION COURSE
Sorkin, Aaron
FEW GOOD MEN, A
Sorkin, Arleen
I DON'T BUY KISSES ANYMORE
Sorko-Ram, Ari
FINEST HOUR, THE
Sosa, Roberto
CABEZA DE VACA
Sosic, Toni
JOURNEY OF HONOR
Soter, Tiffany
CHINA O'BRIEN II
Sothoane, Seipati
SARAFINA!
Sothoane, Sibonakaliso
SARAFINA!
Soto, Talisa
MAMBO KINGS, THE
Sottile, Michael
RESERVOIR DOGS
Southern Comfort
GIVING, THE
Southwic, Shawn
ROVER DANGERFIELD
Souza, Blaine
OUT ON A LIMB
Souza, Tammara
HELLROLLER
Sova, Peter
STRAIGHT TALK
Spaan, Art
BODYGUARD, THE
Spacek, Sissy
HARD PROMISES
Spacey, Kevin
CONSENTING ADULTS
GLENGARRY GLEN ROSS
Spade, David
LIGHT SLEEPER
Spader, James
BOB ROBERTS
STORYVILLE
Spahr, Wendy
HELLROLLER
Spano, Nealla
JUST LIKE IN THE MOVIES
Spat, Andrew
K2
Spatt, Edward
K2
Spaulding, Tracy
ARMED FOR ACTION
Spearman, Tre'demont
MISSISSIPPI MASALA
Spector, Deborah
GUN IN BETTY LOU'S HANDBAG, THE
JENNIFER EIGHT
Speer, Connie
LOVE HURTS
Speir, Dona
DO OR DIE
MORTUARY ACADEMY
Speller, Mike
PASSENGER 57
Spellos, Peter
GUYVER, THE
HOFFA
Speltz, David
SNEAKERS
Spencer, Dan
SHAKES THE CLOWN
Spencer, Danielle
CROSSING, THE
Spencer, Fred
BRAM STOKER'S DRACULA
Spencer, John
WE'RE TALKIN' SERIOUS MONEY
Spengler-Jacobs, Shirley
CHILDREN OF THE NIGHT
Sperandeo, Gaetano
JOHNNY STECCHINO
Sperberg, Fritz
PATRIOT GAMES
Spiegler-Jacobs, Shirley
BABE, THE
Spielberg, Steven
MAGICAL WORLD OF CHUCK JONES, THE
Spinadel, Lisa
FLIRTING
Spinak, Larry
DESIRE AND HELL AT SUNSET MOTEL
Spinks, James
MO' MONEY
STRAIGHT TALK
Spires, Bud
DEEP BLUES
Spooner, Jimmy
TOYS
Sporledder, Greg "Spoonie"
ROADSIDE PROPHETS
Sporleder, Gregory
LEAGUE OF THEIR OWN, A
Spradling, Charlie
BAD CHANNELS
Spratt, Jack
WILDFIRE
Sprerdakos, John
SCHOOL TIES
Sprinkle, Annie
MY FATHER IS COMING
Squibb, June
SCENT OF A WOMAN
Squitieri, Barry
NIGHT AND THE CITY
Srivastava, Anjan
MISSISSIPPI MASALA
Srubar, Jeanette
WHITE MEN CAN'T JUMP
Ssekasi, Mayambala
MISSISSIPPI MASALA
St. Amant, Buddy
MISSISSIPPI MASALA
St. Gerard, Michael
INTO THE SUN
St. Clair, Andrew
HOWARDS END
St. James, David
MAN TROUBLE
St. James, Mark
WAYNE'S WORLD
St. John, Jill
PLAYER, THE
St. John, Sandi
FROZEN ASSETS
Staab, Rebecca
LOVE POTION NO. 9
Stables, Jonathan
EDWARD II
Stack, Tim
DOUBLE TROUBLE
Stafford, Jamie
NIGHT RHYTHMS
Staller, Eric
WILD WHEELS

Stallone, Sylvester
STOP! OR MY MOM WILL SHOOT
Stamm, Deena
BRIDE OF KILLER NERD
Standen, Donald
CAPTAIN AMERICA
Standing, John
CHAPLIN
Stanec, Dagmar
BRAM STOKER'S DRACULA
Stanford, Natalie
SWOON
Stanilias, Peter
LOVE CRIMES
Stankevich, Stanislas
RASPAD
Stanley, Don
LETHAL WEAPON 3
Stanley, Paul
LEAVING NORMAL
Stanojevic-Kameni, Dragomir
JOURNEY OF HONOR
Stanton, Harry Dean
MAN TROUBLE
TWIN PEAKS: FIRE WALK WITH ME
Stanton, Philip
SWOON
Stanton, Randall
PUBLIC EYE, THE
Stanton, Robert
BOB ROBERTS
LEAGUE OF THEIR OWN, A
Stapenhorst, Steve
MALCOLM X
Stapleton, Maureen
PASSED AWAY
Starbuck, Cheryl
MORTUARY ACADEMY
Starbuck, Jojo
CUTTING EDGE, THE
Stark, Douglas
WILD ORCHID 2:
TWO SHADES OF BLUE
Stark, Mary
CHAPLIN
Starr, Mike
BODYGUARD, THE
Staunton, Imelda
PETER'S FRIENDS
Stavrou, Sarah
WHITE MEN CAN'T JUMP
Stea, Kevin
NEWSIES
Steadman, Alison
BLAME IT ON THE BELLBOY
Steadman, Jason
TROLL 2
Steady, Maduka
LORENZO'S OIL
Stearn, Barry
DAMAGE
Stebner, Greg
SHADOWS AND FOG
Stedelin, Claudia
VENICE/VENICE

Steedman, Tony
SPLIT SECOND
Steel, Amy
PLAY NICE
Steelman, Ron
OUT FOR BLOOD
Steen, David
OF MICE AND MEN
RESERVOIR DOGS
RUBY
Steers, Burr
RESERVOIR DOGS
Steger, Shannon M.
HONEY, I BLEW UP THE KID
Steig, Maggie
HOUSESITTER
Steiger, Rod
GUILTY AS CHARGED
PLAYER, THE
Stein, Ben
HONEYMOON IN VEGAS
Stein, Julian
SCENT OF A WOMAN
Stein, June
BOB ROBERTS
Stein, Max
SCENT OF A WOMAN
Stein, Ron
DEATH BECOMES HER
Stein, Saul
LAWS OF GRAVITY
Steinberg, Robert Martin
SINGLE WHITE FEMALE
UNLAWFUL ENTRY
Steindal, Vivian
OUT ON A LIMB
Steinmeyer, Randy
BABE, THE
Stenberg, Brigitta
RAPID FIRE
STOP! OR MY MOM WILL SHOOT
Stenberg, Gaby
BEST INTENTIONS, THE
Stengel, Casey
INTO THE SUN
WATERDANCE, THE
Stephen, Valerie
DOES THIS MEAN WE'RE
MARRIED?
Stephens, Jean
LOVE HURTS
Stephens, Robert
AFRAID OF THE DARK
CHAPLIN
CHILDREN, THE
POPE MUST DIET!, THE
Stephens, Stephanie
LEAP OF FAITH
Stephenson, Edwin
CUTTING EDGE, THE
Stephenson, John
LITTLE NEMO: ADVENTURES IN
SLUMBERLAND
Stephenson, Jolyon
WATERLAND

Stephenson, Michael
BEYOND DARKNESS
TROLL 2
Stepp, Craig
OTHER WOMAN, THE
Sterling, Lynn
MALCOLM X
Sterlini, John
BARBARIAN QUEEN II:
THE EMPRESS STRIKES BACK
Stern, Daniel
HOME ALONE 2:
LOST IN NEW YORK
Stern, Gilya
FINEST HOUR, THE
HUMAN SHIELD, THE
Sternhagen, Frances
RAISING CAIN
Sterry, David
HELLROLLER
LOWER LEVEL
Stetor, Jennifer
BOB ROBERTS
Steuer, Monica
BARBARIAN QUEEN II:
THE EMPRESS STRIKES BACK
Stevens, Andrew
MUNCHIE
NIGHT EYES 2
Stevens, Brinke
MUNCHIE
ROOTS OF EVIL
SPIRITS
Stevens, Chris
LEAVING NORMAL
Stevens, Dalton
WILD WHEELS
Stevens, Dana
LEAVING NORMAL
Stevens, David P.B.
COMPLEX WORLD
Stevens, Edward
HELL MASTER
Stevens, Fisher
BOB ROBERTS
Stevens, Joe
SIMPLE MEN
Stevens, John
TOYS
Stevens, Leon B.
SCHOOL TIES
Stevens, Ronnie
BLAME IT ON THE BELLBOY
Stevens, Sally
MAN TROUBLE
Stevens, Shadoe
MR. SATURDAY NIGHT
Stevens, Stella
EXILED IN AMERICA
Stevens, Susan Danielle
MAN TROUBLE
Stevenson, Cynthia
PLAYER, THE
Stevenson, David
TIGER CLAWS
Stewardson, Joe
KICK OR DIE

Stewart, Barbara
THIS IS MY LIFE
Stewart, Brad
MANIAC WARRIORS
Stewart, Catherine Mary
CAFE ROMEO
PSYCHIC
Stewart, David A.
DEEP BLUES
Stewart, Harriet
HOWARDS END
Stewart, Jan Bick
BEYOND JUSTICE
Stewart, John
JOURNEY OF HONOR
ROUND TRIP TO HEAVEN
Stewart, Lynne Marie
DOUBLE TROUBLE
Stewart, Maggie
PASSED AWAY
Stewart, Paul Anthony
SHADOWS AND FOG
Stewart, Suzanne
CONSENTING ADULTS
Stewart, Wendell Wayne
UNDER SIEGE
Stickney, Mollie
OUT ON A LIMB
Stickney, Phyllis Yvonne
MALCOLM X
Stickney, Timothy
LIGHT SLEEPER
Stier, Hans Martin
SHINING THROUGH
Stiers, David Ogden
SHADOWS AND FOG
Still, Jeff
BABE, THE
Stiller, Amy
HIGHWAY TO HELL
Stiller, Ben
HIGHWAY TO HELL
Stiller, Jerry
HIGHWAY TO HELL
LITTLE VEGAS
Stillwell, Susie
MAMBO KINGS, THE
Stimpson, Phillip
COMRADES IN ARMS
Stiteler, Elena
K2
Stites, Todd
TOGETHER ALONE
Stobart, Ed
AFRAID OF THE DARK
Stock, Alan
POISON IVY
Stock, Francine
DAMAGE
Stock, Mario
KILL CRUISE
Stockbridge, Paula
HOWARDS END
Stockbridge, Sarah
SPLIT SECOND

Stocker, Paul
LIGHT SLEEPER
SCENT OF A WOMAN
Stockman, Laura
BLOODFIST III: FORCED TO FIGHT
Stocks, Alan
SPLIT SECOND
UNDER SUSPICION
Stockwell, Dean
BACKTRACK
PLAYER, THE
Stoddard, Ken
LIFE ON THE EDGE
Stojanovic, Bora
JOURNEY OF HONOR
Stokes, Irwin
TEXAS TENOR:
THE ILLINOIS JACQUET STORY
Stokes, Nelle
PASSION FISH
Stoler, Shirley
MALCOLM X
Stolti, Christian
PUBLIC EYE, THE
Stoltz, Eric
SINGLES
WATERDANCE, THE
Stona, Winston
LUNATIC, THE
Stone, James
PASSENGER 57
Stone, Julian
NIGHT EYES 2
Stone, Madison
NAKED OBSESSION
Stone, Oliver
PATRIOT GAMES
Stone, Pam
WISECRACKS
Stone, Sharon
BASIC INSTINCT
DIARY OF A HITMAN
Stone, Stuart
USED PEOPLE
Stone, Terrence
CHAPLIN
Stoneburner, Sam
LOVE HURTS
Stoneham, Lionel
GIVING, THE
Stoneham, Marilyn
GIVING, THE
Stoppelwerth, Josh
HARD PROMISES
Storch, Larry
I DON'T BUY KISSES ANYMORE
Storey, Don
SOCIETY
Storey, John
UNIVERSAL SOLDIER
Storke, Adam
DEATH BECOMES HER
HIGHWAY TO HELL
Storm, Emy
BEST INTENTIONS, THE
Stormare, Peter
DAMAGE

Storry, Malcolm
LAST OF THE MOHICANS, THE
UNDER SUSPICION
Stout, Craig
ALL-AMERICAN MURDER
Stowe, Madeleine
LAST OF THE MOHICANS, THE
UNLAWFUL ENTRY
Stoyanov, Michael
MOM AND DAD SAVE THE WORLD
Stradi, Anne
HOUSE OF USHER, THE
Stradling, Charlie
CAGED FEAR
Strain, Julie
KUFFS
MIRROR IMAGES
NIGHT RHYTHMS
WITCHCRAFT IV: VIRGIN HEART
Strain, Luke
CHAPLIN
Strait, George
PURE COUNTRY
Strasberg, Susan
LIGHT IN THE JUNGLE, THE
Strassman, Marcia
HONEY, I BLEW UP THE KID
Straten, L.B.
NOISES OFF
Strathairn, David
BIG GIRLS DON'T CRY . . . THEY
GET EVEN
BOB ROBERTS
LEAGUE OF THEIR OWN, A
PASSION FISH
SNEAKERS
Strauss, Daryl
BAD CHANNELS
Strauss, Virgil
GLADIATOR
Streep, Meryl
DEATH BECOMES HER
Stremikis, Hasmin
WATERLAND
Strgacic, Ljubomir
CAPTAIN AMERICA
Stribling, Angela
DISTINGUISHED GENTLEMAN, THE
Strobel, Al
TWIN PEAKS: FIRE WALK WITH ME
Strode, Woody
STORYVILLE
Strong, Gwynneth
AFRAID OF THE DARK
Strong, John
BATMAN RETURNS
Strong, Ken
LOVE POTION NO. 9
Strong, Natalie
BOB ROBERTS
PLAYER, THE
Strouth, Jeffrey
AMERICAN FABULOUS
Strova, Maria
RESERVOIR DOGS
Strzalkowski, Henry
FIELD OF FIRE

Stuart, Cassie
AFRAID OF THE DARK
Stubbert, Gabrielle
LIGHT SLEEPER
Stubbs, Dave
MANIAC WARRIORS
Studi, Wes
LAST OF THE MOHICANS, THE
Stumm, Michael
SWOON
Stump, Gregory G.
UNDER SIEGE
Sturges, Shannon
DESIRE AND HELL AT SUNSET MOTEL
Sturtevant, Hobson
SWOON
Sturzbecher, Ulricke
BECOMING COLETTE
Su, Michael
SINGLES
Suddaby, Don
LORENZO'S OIL
Sugar, Bert Randolph
NIGHT AND THE CITY
Sugden, James
FATHER
Suggett, Richard
STOP! OR MY MOM WILL SHOOT
Sugimura, Yuki
JOURNEY OF HONOR
Sukoff, David
LIGHT SLEEPER
Sukowa, Barbara
VOYAGER
ZENTROPA
Sullivan, Billy
1492: THE CONQUEST OF PARADISE
Sullivan, Frankie
CHAPLIN
Sullivan, J. Christopher
NOISES OFF
Sullivan, Patricia
LAWS OF GRAVITY
Sullivan, Rob
BODYGUARD, THE
Sullivan, Robert
SWOON
Sullivan, Sean Gregory
WAYNE'S WORLD
Summers, Lee
MALCOLM X
Sumter, Terry
MALCOLM X
Surentu, Henry
LADY DRAGON
Surovy, Nicholas
FOREVER YOUNG
Susan
35 UP
Susi, Carol Ann
DEATH BECOMES HER
Sussman, Joshua
BRENDA STARR
PHANTOM OF THE RITZ

Suthar, Dipti
MISSISSIPPI MASALA
Sutherland, Donald
BUFFY THE VAMPIRE SLAYER
Sutherland, Kiefer
ARTICLE 99
FEW GOOD MEN, A
TWIN PEAKS: FIRE WALK WITH ME
Sutton, David A.
CLEARCUT
Sutton, Dudley
EDWARD II
Suurballe, Morten
DAY IN OCTOBER, A
Suzuki, Rinzoh
MR. BASEBALL
Suzy
35 UP
Svenson, Bo
STEELE'S LAW
Swago, Jennifer
CONSENTING ADULTS
Swain, Bob
DEATH BECOMES HER
Swain, Chuck
DESIRE AND HELL AT SUNSET MOTEL
Swain, James L.
MALCOLM X
Swallow, Randy
HONEY, I BLEW UP THE KID
Swan, Bob
BABE, THE
Swan, Dale
WE'RE TALKIN' SERIOUS MONEY
Swan, Robert
MO' MONEY
Swank, Hilary
BUFFY THE VAMPIRE SLAYER
Swann, Bill
INSIDE EDGE
Swanson, Bob "Swanie"
BUFFY THE VAMPIRE SLAYER
Swanson, Kristy
BUFFY THE VAMPIRE SLAYER
HIGHWAY TO HELL
Swart, Rufus
HOUSE OF USHER, THE
Swayze, Patrick
CITY OF JOY
Sweaney, Debra
SAVAGE INSTINCT
Sweeney, Birdie
CRYING GAME, THE
Sweeney, D.B.
CUTTING EDGE, THE
DAY IN OCTOBER, A
HEAVEN IS A PLAYGROUND
LEATHER JACKETS
Sweeney, Julia
HONEY, I BLEW UP THE KID
Sweeney, Sean
HELL MASTER
Sweet, Vonte
GLADIATOR
Sweety Dog
HIGHWAY 61

Swetow, Joel
3 NINJAS
Swift, David
SECRET FRIENDS
Swift, Francie
SCENT OF A WOMAN
Swinford, Stacy
MISSISSIPPI MASALA
Swinson, David
ROADSIDE PROPHETS
Swinton, Tilda
EDWARD II
Swinton, William
MALCOLM X
Swirsly, Eric
MALCOLM X
Swope, Tracy Brooks
POWER OF ONE, THE
Sykes, Baldwin C.
CLASS ACT
SOUTH CENTRAL
Sykes, Cynthia
LOVE HURTS
Sykes, Kim
SINGLE WHITE FEMALE
Sylvers, Ronald
LIGHT SLEEPER
Sylvester, Jules
BRAM STOKER'S DRACULA
Symon
35 UP
Syms, Sylvia
SHINING THROUGH
Syner, Tom
VAMPIRE HUNTER D
Syrett, Peter
TERMINAL BLISS
Syvertsen, Peter
MIGHTY DUCKS, THE
Szapolowska, Grazyna
KILL CRUISE
Szeibert, Joseph "Simon"
TWIN PEAKS: FIRE WALK WITH ME
Szigeti, Cynthia
WHERE THE DAY TAKES YOU
Szmidt, Sharon
LEAGUE OF THEIR OWN, A
Tabaka, Victoria
LOVE POTION NO. 9
Tabakin, Ralph
TOYS
Tabassi, Leah
PATRIOT GAMES
Tabsch, Imad
BECOMING COLETTE
Tagawa, Cary-Hiroyuki
AMERICAN ME
Taggart, Julie
LEAVING NORMAL
Taggart, Rita
CROSSING THE BRIDGE
Taggart, Tim Owen
THUNDERHEART
Taglang, Tom
UNIVERSAL SOLDIER

Tagore, Sharmila
MISSISSIPPI MASALA
Taguchi, Tomoroh
TETSUO: THE IRON MAN
Tai Thai
UNIVERSAL SOLDIER
Taikeff, Elliot
WHITE TRASH
Taipale, Reijo
MATCH FACTORY GIRL, THE
Tait, Tristan
PASSED AWAY
Takada, Miwa
JOURNEY OF HONOR
Takahashi, Koji
GODZILLA VS. BIOLLANTE
Takakura, Ken
MR. BASEBALL
Takanashi, Aya
MR. BASEBALL
Takano, Hikari
MR. BASEBALL
Takano, Mak
MR. BASEBALL
Takashima, Masanobu
GODZILLA VS. BIOLLANTE
Taketoshi, Kazuhiro
JOURNEY OF HONOR
Tal, Gregory
FINEST HOUR, THE
Talaskivi, Jaakko
NIGHT ON EARTH
Talbot, Alan
UNDER SUSPICION
Talbot, Michael
LITTLE VEGAS
Talbot, Nita
AMITYVILLE 1992:
IT'S ABOUT TIME
Talbott, Michael
HERO
Talkington, Clement
CAPTAIN RON
Tallman, Bob
PURE COUNTRY
Talman, Ann
BOB ROBERTS
Tamayo, Alejandro
CABEZA DE VACA
Tamberelli, Daniel
MIGHTY DUCKS, THE
Tambor, Jeffrey
ARTICLE 99
BRENDA STARR
CROSSING THE BRIDGE
Tamburrelli, Karla
FOREVER YOUNG
Tamburro, Charles A.
MAN TROUBLE
Tamburro, Michael
MAN TROUBLE
RAMPAGE
Tamira
EMMANUELLE 6
Tamma, Nanni
ALBERTO EXPRESS
Tammi, Emma
USED PEOPLE
Tamura, Takahiro
SILK ROAD, THE
Tanaka
LADY DRAGON
Tanaka, Toru
3 NINJAS
Tanaka, Yoshiko
GODZILLA VS. BIOLLANTE
Tandy, Jessica
USED PEOPLE
Tandy, Mark
HOWARDS END
Tang Tak Wing
TRAINED TO FIGHT
Tangkilisan, Diaz
LADY DRAGON
Tannenbaum, Neri Kyle
LORENZO'S OIL
Tannenbaum, Shirley
LORENZO'S OIL
PASSED AWAY
Tanner, Jeff
FINAL ANALYSIS
Tanner, Joy
PROM NIGHT IV - DELIVER US
FROM EVIL
Tarabshi, Nagy
HUMAN SHIELD, THE
Tarantino, Quentin
RESERVOIR DOGS
Tarkanian, Jerry
HONEYMOON IN VEGAS
Tarleton, Neezer
LEAGUE OF THEIR OWN, A
Tarsia, Frank
BOOMERANG
Tarver, Catherine
DAUGHTERS OF THE DUST
Tarver, Pamela
RAMPAGE
Tassoni, Coralina C.
EVIL CLUTCH
Tate, Buddy
TEXAS TENOR:
THE ILLINOIS JACQUET STORY
Tate, Laura Mae
DIGGSTOWN
Tate, Nick
PUBLIC EYE, THE
Tate, Sean A.
MO' MONEY
Taub, Stanley
SWOON
Taylor, Bruce
TERMINAL BLISS
Taylor, Chad
PRAYER OF THE ROLLERBOYS
Taylor, Curtis
LIFE ON THE EDGE
Taylor, Dean
CONSENTING ADULTS
Taylor, Dub
FALLING FROM GRACE
Taylor, Femi
FLIRTING
Taylor, Gary
MANIAC WARRIORS
Taylor, J.T.
MAMBO KINGS, THE
Taylor, Jack
1492: THE CONQUEST OF PARADISE
Taylor, Joe
DAUGHTERS OF THE DUST
Taylor, John
BRIEF HISTORY OF TIME, A
Taylor, Kory
BEAUTIFUL DREAMERS
Taylor, L. Charles
MARTIAL LAW 2: UNDERCOVER
Taylor, Meshach
CLASS ACT
WELCOME TO OBLIVION
Taylor, Noah
FLIRTING
Taylor, Rip
HOME ALONE 2:
LOST IN NEW YORK
Taylor, Sergeant Johnson
LOVE CRIMES
Taylor, Tanya
SWOON
Taylor, Tessa
NIGHT EYES 2
Taylor, W. Allen
RAISING CAIN
Taylor, Wendy E.
MALCOLM X
Taylor, Willis
MANIAC WARRIORS
Teigen, Trenton
BIG GIRLS DON'T CRY . . . THEY
GET EVEN
Telford, Robert S.
RUBY
Tellez, Hector
CABEZA DE VACA
Telvi, Jeff
LIGHT SLEEPER
Temple, Kate
EDWARD II
Tennant, Deborah
BEAUTIFUL DREAMERS
Tennon, Julius
HARD PROMISES
Tephany, Arlette
HAIRDRESSER'S HUSBAND, THE
Tepper, Leonard
HOME ALONE 2:
LOST IN NEW YORK
Tepper, Paul
STEELE'S LAW
Terese, Emma
JUST LIKE IN THE MOVIES
Tergesen, Lee
WAYNE'S WORLD
Termo, Leonard
RUBY
Teron, Nadege
TOUS LES MATINS DU MONDE

Terranova, Michael
SAVAGE INSTINCT
Terrell, John Canada
BOOMERANG
Terris, Malcolm
CHAPLIN
Terry, Clark
TEXAS TENOR: THE ILLINOIS JACQUET STORY
Terry, John
OF MICE AND MEN
RESURRECTED, THE
Terry, Nigel
CHRISTOPHER COLUMBUS: THE DISCOVERY
EDWARD II
Tetrault, Ernie
SNEAKERS
Teufenkjian, Tamar
HERO
TeWiata, Beryl
MY GRANDPA IS A VAMPIRE
Tewkesbury, Joan
PLAYER, THE
Teyssedre, Anne
CONTE DE PRINTEMPS
Teytaud, Jorgen
DAY IN OCTOBER, A
Thai, Tai
WATERDANCE, THE
Thaker, Jaimini
MISSISSIPPI MASALA
Thaker, Varsha
MISSISSIPPI MASALA
Thal, Eric
GUN IN BETTY LOU'S HANDBAG, THE
STRANGER AMONG US, A
Thalken, Meg
BABE, THE
Thatcher, Kirk
SHAKING THE TREE
Thaw, John
CHAPLIN
The Alexander Sisters
WISECRACKS
The Association of Former Fish Drill Team Members of Cadets at Texas A & M University
FEW GOOD MEN, A
The Black Crowes
FOR THOSE ABOUT TO ROCK
The Capoeira Dancers
BRENDA STARR
The Clichettes
WISECRACKS
The Coasters
PHANTOM OF THE RITZ
The Glass Family
TO RENDER A LIFE
The Ramones
1991: THE YEAR PUNK BROKE
The Shend
SPLIT SECOND
The Smithereens
COMPLEX WORLD
The Upbeaters
PRELUDE TO A KISS
Theaker, Deborah
WISECRACKS
Thebeault, Maya
BECOMING COLETTE
Thebus, Mary Ann
STRAIGHT TALK
Theodore, Robert
HIGHWAY 61
Thevenet, Virginie
CRY OF THE OWL, THE
Thewlis, David
AFRAID OF THE DARK
DAMAGE
Thexton, Winnie
WHITE TRASH
Thi Hoe Tranh Huu Trieu
INDOCHINE
Thigpen, Lynne
ARTICLE 99
BOB ROBERTS
Thin Elk, Chief Ted
THUNDERHEART
Thirtle, John
MUPPET CHRISTMAS CAROL, THE
Thom, Christy
MEATBALLS 4
Thom, Ian
MUPPET CHRISTMAS CAROL, THE
Thomas, Archie
DAUGHTERS OF THE DUST
Thomas, Cynthia
MALCOLM X
Thomas, D. Paul
INSIDE EDGE
Thomas, Diane O.
MAN TROUBLE
Thomas, Ernest
MALCOLM X
Thomas, Frank
MR. BASEBALL
Thomas, Gareth
WATERLAND
Thomas, Giles
WATERLAND
Thomas, Jade Marisa
ZEBRAHEAD
Thomas, Jay
LITTLE VEGAS
STRAIGHT TALK
Thomas, Jeffrey
HUNTING
WHITE TRASH
Thomas, Jr., David
MALCOLM X
Thomas, Jr., William
MAMBO KINGS, THE
Thomas, Keith
MALCOLM X
Thomas, Kevin
HOME ALONE 2: LOST IN NEW YORK
Thomas, Leonard
BAD LIEUTENANT
MALCOLM X
Thomas, Matt
UNIVERSAL SOLDIER
Thomas, Raymond Anthony
MALCOLM X
Thomas, Robert
VENICE/VENICE
Thomas, Rohn
INNOCENT BLOOD
WATERLAND
Thomas, Ryan
LORENZO'S OIL
Thomas, Sharon
PURE COUNTRY
Thomas, Susan
RAMPAGE
Thomason, Donna
ARTICLE 99
Thomerson, Tim
TRANCERS III: DETH LIVES
Thompson, Brian
DOCTOR MORDRID
HIRED TO KILL
Thompson, Cherrie
LEAP OF FAITH
Thompson, Emma
HOWARDS END
PETER'S FRIENDS
Thompson, Fred Dalton
ACES: IRON EAGLE III
THUNDERHEART
Thompson, Jack
WIND
Thompson, Lauren
JUST LIKE IN THE MOVIES
Thompson, Lea
ARTICLE 99
Thompson, Linda
BODYGUARD, THE
LOVE CRIMES
ORIGINAL INTENT
Thompson, Randall
BRENDA STARR
Thompson, Randy
MONTANA RUN, THE
SINGLES
Thompson, Rick
MANIAC WARRIORS
Thompson, Ron
AMERICAN ME
MAMBO KINGS, THE
Thompson, Stephan
BRENDA STARR
Thompson, Taylor
DAUGHTERS OF THE DUST
Thomson, Anna
UNFORGIVEN
Thomson, Anna Levine
CRISSCROSS
Thomson, R.H.
QUARREL, THE
Thor, Cameron
FEW GOOD MEN, A
Thorley, Ken
MAN TROUBLE
WHITE SANDS
Thorn, Frankie
BAD LIEUTENANT

Thornburgh, Maurita L.
MAN TROUBLE
Thorne, Kip
BRIEF HISTORY OF TIME, A
Thornhill, Ann Harris
OVER HER DEAD BODY
Thornton, Billy Bob
ONE FALSE MOVE
Thornton, Howard
WHITE TRASH
Thornton, Kirk
VAMPIRE HUNTER D
Thorpe, Paul
DEATH BECOMES HER
Thorsen, Sven-Ole
LETHAL WEAPON 3
Threlfall, David
PATRIOT GAMES
Throne, Malachi
PRIMARY MOTIVE
Thrower, Emmitt
SWOON
Thunder
KUFFS
Thunhurst, Jr., William
LORENZO'S OIL
PASSED AWAY
Thurman, Judith
ROADSIDE PROPHETS
Thurman, Lesa
PASSENGER 57
Thurman, Uma
FINAL ANALYSIS
JENNIFER EIGHT
Thysell, Jeff
NEWSIES
Thysell, Scott
NEWSIES
Tia, Donamari
SOCIETY
Ticotin, Rachel
WHERE THE DAY TAKES YOU
Tidgewell, Todd
CROSSING THE BRIDGE
Tien Tho
INDOCHINE
Tiernan, Andrew
EDWARD II
Tiernan, Michael
CAFE ROMEO
Tierney, Lawrence
RESERVOIR DOGS
RUNESTONE, THE
Tierney, Maura
LINGUINI INCIDENT, THE
WHITE SANDS
Tiffe, Jerry
DEADLY BET
Tigar, Kenneth
LETHAL WEAPON 3
Tiger, Steve
BRENDA STARR
Tighe, Kevin
NEWSIES
SCHOOL TIES

Tijerina, Cecilia
BARBARIAN QUEEN II:
THE EMPRESS STRIKES BACK
Tillery, Lester T.
PATRIOT GAMES
Tilley, Don
LAST OF THE MOHICANS, THE
Tillman, Ashley
BATMAN RETURNS
Tillman, Lynne
MY FATHER IS COMING
Tilly, Jennifer
SCORCHERS
Tilly, Meg
LEAVING NORMAL
Tilton, Charlene
CENTER OF THE WEB
DEADLY BET
Timbes, Graham
STORYVILLE
Timko, Johnny
WE'RE TALKIN' SERIOUS MONEY
Timoney, William
WHISPERS IN THE DARK
Tingay, Paul
POWER OF ONE, THE
Tingle, Jimmy
DAMNED IN THE USA
Tinling, Therese Xavier
HAND THAT ROCKS THE
CRADLE, THE
Tipple, Gordon
LEAVING NORMAL
Tippo, Patti
ROADSIDE PROPHETS
Tipton, Jade Rodell
BABE, THE
Tisdall, Bill
FATHER
Tisman, Daniel
MR. SATURDAY NIGHT
Tobeck, Joel
MY GRANDPA IS A VAMPIRE
Tobey, Ken
HONEY, I BLEW UP THE KID
SINGLE WHITE FEMALE
Tobey, Kenneth
DESIRE AND HELL AT SUNSET
MOTEL
Tobolowsky, Stephen
BASIC INSTINCT
HERO
MEMOIRS OF AN INVISIBLE MAN
ROADSIDE PROPHETS
SINGLE WHITE FEMALE
SNEAKERS
WHERE THE DAY TAKES YOU
Tocha, Paula
DEATH BECOMES HER
Tochi, Brian
PLAYER, THE
Todd, Jeffrey
WHITE MEN CAN'T JUMP
Todd, Mark Alexander
MUPPET CHRISTMAS CAROL, THE
Todd, Russell
ONE LAST RUN

Todd, Tony
CANDYMAN
Todde, Mickael
DELICATESSEN
Todisco, Mario
HOME ALONE 2:
LOST IN NEW YORK
Toibin, Niall
FAR AND AWAY
Toita, Kensuke
MR. BASEBALL
Tokos, Lubor
EAR, THE
Tolbert, Berlinda
PATRIOT GAMES
Tolces, Todd
DR. GIGGLES
Toledano, Alberto
MR. SATURDAY NIGHT
Toler, Ray
STRAIGHT TALK
Toles-Bey, John
LEAP OF FAITH
TRESPASS
Tolkach, Dennis
HOFFA
Tolkan, James
BLOODFIST IV: DIE TRYING
Tolkin, Michael
PLAYER, THE
Tolkin, Stephen
PLAYER, THE
Toloubeyev, Andrei
ADAM'S RIB
Tom, David
STAY TUNED
Tom, Lauren
MAN TROUBLE
Tom, Nicholle
BEETHOVEN
Tom of Finland/Touko Laaksonen
DADDY AND THE MUSCLE
ACADEMY
Toma, Fred
PATRIOT GAMES
Tomac, Petar
CAPTAIN AMERICA
Toman, Maya
CUTTING EDGE, THE
Tomasello, Duchess
PASSENGER 57
Tomaska, Joey
SHAKING THE TREE
Tomei, Marisa
CHAPLIN
MY COUSIN VINNY
Tomlin, Lily
PLAYER, THE
SHADOWS AND FOG
Tomlin, Melanie
TRACES OF RED
Tommie
LOVE HURTS
Tone-Loc
BEBE'S KIDS
FERNGULLY:
THE LAST RAINFOREST

Toney, Demp
CONFESSIONS OF A SERIAL KILLER
Toney, Mike
DEADLY BET
FINAL IMPACT
Tony
35 UP
Tony V.
SHAKES THE CLOWN
Tootoosis, Gordon
LEAVING NORMAL
Topazio, Sonia
HUSBANDS AND LOVERS
Topolski, Ted
MO' MONEY
Torisaka, Tsukumo
MR. BASEBALL
Torn, Rip
BEAUTIFUL DREAMERS
DOLLY DEAREST
Tornando, Hengky
LADY DRAGON
Torrens, Pip
MONKEY BOY
PATRIOT GAMES
Torrens, Tania
LOVER, THE
Torres, Liz
BLOODFIST IV: DIE TRYING
Tostado, Francisco
BARBARIAN QUEEN II: THE EMPRESS STRIKES BACK
Totenberg, Nina
DISTINGUISHED GENTLEMAN, THE
Toth, Les
FATHER
Totheroh, David
CHAPLIN
Totheroh, Jack
CHAPLIN
Toumarkine, Francois
DISCRETE, LA
TOTO LE HEROS
Tousey, Sheila
THUNDERHEART
Tova, Theresa
THIS IS MY LIFE
Townley, Scott
RAISING CAIN
Townsend, Tommy
TOYS
Townson, Jacklin
GIVING, THE
Towson, Elizabeth
SWOON
Toy, Patty
DEADLY BET
Toyohara, Kohsuke
MR. BASEBALL
Trader, Dal
PRAYER OF THE ROLLERBOYS
Traeger, Michael
HOMICIDAL IMPULSE
Trainor, Mary Ellen
DEATH BECOMES HER
KUFFS
LETHAL WEAPON 3

Tranchina, Frank
PHANTOM OF THE RITZ
Trancz, Jeremy
USED PEOPLE
Trash
SWOON
Trasharama
SWOON
Travanti, Daniel J.
MEGAVILLE
Travis, Bobby Joe
ZEBRAHEAD
Travis, Chandler
COMPLEX WORLD
Travis, Dianne Turley
DISTINGUISHED GENTLEMAN, THE
Travis, Greg
SHAKES THE CLOWN
Travis, Nancy
CHAPLIN
PASSED AWAY
Travolta, Joey
ROUND TRIP TO HEAVEN
Travolta, John
CHAINS OF GOLD
Traylor, Susan
BODYGUARD, THE
RIVER RUNS THROUGH IT, A
Treanor, Michael
3 NINJAS
Treas, Charles
GUN IN BETTY LOU'S HANDBAG, THE
Treas, Terri
HOUSE IV
Trebek, Alex
WHITE MEN CAN'T JUMP
Trebor, Robert
UNIVERSAL SOLDIER
Tregonning, Ian
MUPPET CHRISTMAS CAROL, THE
Trejo, Danny
SEX CRIMES
Trejo, Frank
PUSHED TO THE LIMIT
Trenas, Tote
PEPI, LUCI, BOM AND OTHER GIRLS ON THE HEAP
Trese, Adam
LAWS OF GRAVITY
Trestini, Giorgio
JOHNNY STECCHINO
Treuil, Bertrand
BECOMING COLETTE
Treveiler, Robert C.
CONSENTING ADULTS
Trevino, Vic
AMERICAN ME
BEASTMASTER 2: THROUGH THE PORTAL OF TIME
Trevor, Dudi
LEATHER JACKETS
Trew, Grafton
MALCOLM X
Trilling, Zoe
DR. GIGGLES
TO PROTECT AND SERVE

Trimble, Jerry
BREATHING FIRE
Trini Tran
UNIVERSAL SOLDIER
Trinidad, Arsenio "Sonny"
NEON CITY
Trintignant, Marie
ALBERTO EXPRESS
Tripp, Louis
GATE II
Tripplehorn, Jeanne
BASIC INSTINCT
Tristancho, Carlos
PEPI, LUCI, BOM AND OTHER GIRLS ON THE HEAP
Trivino, Johny
KISS ME A KILLER
Troup, David
LAWS OF GRAVITY
Troy, Michael P.
SHADOWS AND FOG
Troy-Keitt, Juanita
JUICE
Truchon, Isabelle
DEADBOLT
Trudell, John
INCIDENT AT OGLALA
THUNDERHEART
True, Jim
SINGLES
Trujillo, Raoul
ADJUSTER, THE
CLEARCUT
Trujillo, Robert
ENCINO MAN
Trujillo, Sergio
DEATH BECOMES HER
Truman, Jeff
EFFICIENCY EXPERT, THE
FLIRTING
TILL THERE WAS YOU
Trump, Donald
HOME ALONE 2: LOST IN NEW YORK
Trung, Nguyen Lan
INDOCHINE
Truong, Jean-Marc
DOES THIS MEAN WE'RE MARRIED?
Truro, Victor
HUSBANDS AND WIVES
Tryphon, Georg
BECOMING COLETTE
Tsai, Laura
BRIDE OF KILLER NERD
Tsang Kong
SUPERCOP: POLICE STORY III
Tschiersch, Jockel
BECOMING COLETTE
Tsongas, Paul
FEED
Tsukamoto, Shinya
TETSUO: THE IRON MAN

Tucci, Stanley
BEETHOVEN
IN THE SOUP
PRELUDE TO A KISS
PUBLIC EYE, THE
Tucker, Aubrey
TEXAS TENOR: THE ILLINOIS JACQUET STORY
Tucker, Ben
LOVE CRIMES
Tucker, Brian
GIVING, THE
Tucker, Deborah
DR. GIGGLES
MEATBALLS 4
Tucker, Kendra
TRAINED TO FIGHT
Tucker, Sophie
WISECRACKS
Tuerpe, Paul
LETHAL WEAPON 3
RADIO FLYER
Tulaska, Laura
SOCIETY
Tulin, Michael
LIFE ON THE EDGE
Tully, Thomas Lee
FROZEN ASSETS
Tully, Tom
BOB ROBERTS
PASSED AWAY
Tung Biao
SUPERCOP: POLICE STORY III
Tunney, Robin
ENCINO MAN
Turco, Tony
HUSBANDS AND WIVES
Turek, Ron
SHADOWS AND FOG
Turley, Michelle
HUSBANDS AND WIVES
Turman, Glynn
DEEP COVER
Turner, John
POWER OF ONE, THE
Turner, Leon P.
LEAP OF FAITH
Turner, Raymond D.
DIGGSTOWN
SEX CRIMES
Turner, Rich
RESERVOIR DOGS
Turpin, Bahni
DAUGHTERS OF THE DUST
MALCOLM X
Turrin, Enzo
BLAME IT ON THE BELLBOY
Turturro, John
BACKTRACK
BRAIN DONORS
Turturro, Nick
MALCOLM X
Tuscan, Darko
PROOF
Tuttle, Dave
LAWS OF GRAVITY
Twala, Mary
SARAFINA!
Tweed, Chuck
RIVER RUNS THROUGH IT, A
Tweed, Shannon
NIGHT EYES 2
SEXUAL RESPONSE
Tweed, Tracy
NIGHT RHYTHMS
Tygner, Rob
MUPPET CHRISTMAS CAROL, THE
Tyler, Robin
WISECRACKS
Tyler, Scott
HAPPY HELL NIGHT
Tyler, Steven
WHITE SANDS
Tyner, Charles
OVER HER DEAD BODY
Tyson, Richard
BABE, THE
Tzelniker, Anna
SHINING THROUGH
Tzi Ma
RAPID FIRE
Ubdurrahman, Umar
DAUGHTERS OF THE DUST
Uher, Natalie
EMMANUELLE 6
Uhl, Brian
GODZILLA VS. BIOLLANTE
Uhland, Mary
RAISING CAIN
Uhlen, Gisela
TOTO LE HEROS
Uhley, Janis
KUFFS
Ullmann, Liv
OX, THE
Ulm, Tammy
INNOCENT BLOOD
Uneke, Showman
MALCOLM X
Unger, Deborah
TILL THERE WAS YOU
WHISPERS IN THE DARK
Unger, Joe
BODYGUARD, THE
LOVE FIELD
Ungerman, William
TWIN PEAKS: FIRE WALK WITH ME
Upadhyay, Mansi
CITY OF JOY
Upton, Richard R.
SWOON
Uren, Tania
PROOF
Urena, Fabio
BRONX WAR, THE
Urla, Joe
BODYGUARD, THE
Urney, William Shaw
LOVE FIELD
Urquidez, Benny
DIGGSTOWN
Ustinov, Peter
LORENZO'S OIL
Utay, William
RUNESTONE, THE
Utley, Byron
MALCOLM X
NIGHT AND THE CITY
Utley, Scott
FIELD OF FIRE
Utsumi, Hidekazu
JOURNEY OF HONOR
Uzzaman, Badi
K2
V., Tony
HOUSESITTER
Vaananen, Kari
NIGHT ON EARTH
Vacchiann, Carmen
MANIAC WARRIORS
Vachtiline, Nikolai
CLOSE TO EDEN
Vadim, Christian
WINTER IN LISBON, THE
Vail, Bretton
LIVING END, THE
Valdez, C.R.
KILL LINE
Valentine, Scott
HOMICIDAL IMPULSE
Valentino, Venessia
HOME ALONE 2: LOST IN NEW YORK
Valerie, Jean
HUSBANDS AND LOVERS
Valero, Carolina
BARBARIAN QUEEN II: THE EMPRESS STRIKES BACK
Valkenburg, Stacey
HUNTING
Vallee, Ed
COMPLEX WORLD
Vallin, Bekki
SEVERED TIES
Valois, Valerie
SCANNERS III: THE TAKEOVER
Valtierra, Marina
RAMPAGE
Valverde, Mike
LAWNMOWER MAN, THE
Van Alyn, Abigail
FINAL ANALYSIS
Van, Billy
THIS IS MY LIFE
Van Buren, Shula
ZEBRAHEAD
Van Damme, Jean-Claude
UNIVERSAL SOLDIER
Van De Ven, Monique
LILY WAS HERE
Van Dohlen, Lenny
TWIN PEAKS: FIRE WALK WITH ME
Van Dreelen, John
BECOMING COLETTE
Van Harper, James
RAISING CAIN

Van Helsdingen, Mouchette
PUSHED TO THE LIMIT
Van Hentenryck, Kevin
BASKET CASE 3: THE PROGENY
Van Hool, Jan
SPLIT SECOND
Van Horn, Patrick
ENCINO MAN
Van Niekerk, Gart
POWER OF ONE, THE
Van Norden, Peter
LOVE HURTS
Van Patten, Nels
MIRROR IMAGES
ONE LAST RUN
Van Patten, Pat
BODYGUARD, THE
Van Peebles, Melvin
BOOMERANG
Van Rellim, Tim
K2
Van Thijn, Marion
LILY WAS HERE
Van Tiem, Sr., Thomas A.
HOFFA
Van Valkenburg, Deborah
PHANTOM OF THE RITZ
Van Valkenburgh, Deborah
RAMPAGE
Van Vrijburghe DeConingh, Coen
LILY WAS HERE
Van Vuuren, Reverend Peter
POWER OF ONE, THE
Van Zuiden, Berta
LORENZO'S OIL
Van Zyl, Dee Dee
HAND THAT ROCKS THE CRADLE, THE
Van-thinh, Trinh
INDOCHINE
Vancao, Colin
FATHER
Vance, Danitra
JUMPIN' AT THE BONEYARD
Vance, Kenny
HUSBANDS AND WIVES
Vander, Musetta
ROUND TRIP TO HEAVEN
Vanity
NEON CITY
Vannucci, Elena
LIGHT SLEEPER
Vantriglia, Damian
CRISSCROSS
Varda, Brenda
ARTICLE 99
Vargas, Jacob
AMERICAN ME
GAS FOOD LODGING
Vargas, John
EYE OF THE EAGLE 3
Vargo, Don
HOFFA
Vasconcelos, Tito
DANZON
Vasconcelos, Victor
DANZON
Vasques, Tony
WELCOME TO OBLIVION
Vasquez, Joseph B.
BRONX WAR, THE
Vasquez, Roberta
DO OR DIE
OUT FOR BLOOD
Vaughan, Paris
BUFFY THE VAMPIRE SLAYER
Vaughn, Judson
CONSENTING ADULTS
Vaughn, Ned
WIND
Vaughn, Robert
BLIND VISION
Vawter, Ron
JOHNNY SUEDE
SWOON
Vazquez, Jesus
CABEZA DE VACA
Vazquez, Robert
SWOON
Vazquez, Yul
MAMBO KINGS, THE
Vean, Alex
SWOON
Vecchia, Kiki Della
MALCOLM X
Vedder, Eddie
SINGLES
Vega, Johnny
OUT ON A LIMB
Vegh, Mark
CHAPLIN
Vela, Rosie
INSIDE EDGE
Velasco, Marta
BODYGUARD, THE
Veldink, Wes
NEWSIES
Velez, Derrick
CRISSCROSS
Velez, Fernando
BAD LIEUTENANT
Velez, Martha
PANAMA DECEPTION, THE
Venantini, Luca
TOUCH AND DIE
Vendruscolo, Michael
HIGHWAY 61
Venegas, Arturo
YEAR OF THE COMET
Ventimiglia, John
SWOON
Ventimiglia, Tom S.
AMERICAN ME
Ventulett, Suzanne
MOM AND DAD SAVE THE WORLD
Venture, Richard
SCENT OF A WOMAN
Verdu, Maribel
AMANTES
Verduzco, Abraham
AMERICAN ME
RADIO FLYER
Verduzco, Noah
KICKBOXER 3: THE ART OF WAR
RADIO FLYER
Verell, Jack
BLACKBELT
Verhaeghe, Victor
HOUSE ON TOMBSTONE HILL, THE
Verkaik, Petra
AUNTIE LEE'S MEAT PIES
Vernes, Edith
ROAD TO RUIN
Vernon, Howard
DELICATESSEN
Vernon, Kate
MALCOLM X
Vero, Dennis
CHAPLIN
Verran, Michelle
SORORITY HOUSE MASSACRE 2
Vestunis, Dennis
SHADOWS AND FOG
Viard, Karin
DELICATESSEN
Vicino, Cyndi
BRENDA STARR
Vick, Linda
PASSENGER 57
Vickers, Taylor
LOVE CRIMES
Vickery, John
DR. GIGGLES
RAPID FIRE
Victor, Hayden
STEPHEN KING'S SLEEPWALKERS
Victor, Ray
KISS ME A KILLER
Victor, Vanessa
SPLIT SECOND
Vidal, Albert
1492: THE CONQUEST OF PARADISE
Vidal, Gore
BOB ROBERTS
Vidal, Jacques
VAN GOGH
Vidal, Lisa
NIGHT AND THE CITY
WHISPERS IN THE DARK
Vieira, Asia
USED PEOPLE
Viera, Abidah
VENICE/VENICE
Vierikko, Vesa
MATCH FACTORY GIRL, THE
Vigil, Erick
WATERDANCE, THE
Vikouloff, Sacha
FAVOUR, THE WATCH, AND THE VERY BIG FISH, THE
Vilas
MAN TROUBLE
Viljanen, Helga
MATCH FACTORY GIRL, THE
Villa, Isreal
CABEZA DE VACA

Villalobos, Sabino
AMERICAN ME
Villani, Mike
CHAPLIN
Villard, Tom
SHAKES THE CLOWN
Villarreal, Daniel
AMERICAN ME
Villarreal, Dulce Maria
CABEZA DE VACA
Villarreal, Gerardo
CABEZA DE VACA
Villarreal, Javier Escobar
CABEZA DE VACA
Villella, Michael
WILD ORCHID 2: TWO SHADES OF BLUE
Villemaire, James
GATE II
Villeret, Jacques
FAVOUR, THE WATCH, AND THE VERY BIG FISH, THE
Vilpas, Eija
NIGHT ON EARTH
Vincent, Alex
JUST LIKE IN THE MOVIES
Vincent, Jan-Michael
ANIMAL INSTINCTS
IN GOLD WE TRUST
Vincent, Mark C.
DR. GIGGLES
Vincino, Cindy
PHANTOM OF THE RITZ
Vine, Abbey
BODYGUARD, THE
Vines, Dion B.
WHITE MEN CAN'T JUMP
Vinson, Jackey
BREAKING THE RULES
Vinson, Viva
ROADSIDE PROPHETS
Viola, Giuseppe
JOHNNY STECCHINO
Viper
LEATHER JACKETS
Vishnevskii, Anatolii
RASPAD
Vismale, Preston
MALCOLM X
Visser, Angela
KILLER TOMATOES EAT FRANCE!
Vitale, Angelo M.
RAMPAGE
Viterelli, Joe
RUBY
Vivenzio, Giuseppe
WHERE ANGELS FEAR TO TREAD
Vives, Pepe
SWOON
Vlahos, Sam
COLD HEAVEN
KISS ME A KILLER
Vlerick, Jean-Francois
FAVOUR, THE WATCH, AND THE VERY BIG FISH, THE
Vogel, Tony
WATERLAND
Voges, Mark
HARD PROMISES
Voils, Andy
BABE, THE
Volpi, Franco
JOHNNY STECCHINO
Volz, Nedra
MORTUARY ACADEMY
Von Bargen, Daniel
BASIC INSTINCT
COMPLEX WORLD
SHADOWS AND FOG
Von Bibra, Eve
FATHER
Von Dohlen, Lenny
BLIND VISION
JENNIFER EIGHT
LEAVING NORMAL
Von Franckenstein, Clement
DEATH BECOMES HER
SHINING THROUGH
Von Furstenberg, Tatiana
BRAM STOKER'S DRACULA
LIGHT SLEEPER
Von Holstein, Mark
BRENDA STARR
Von Homburg, Wilhelm
DIGGSTOWN
Von Leer, Hunter
INTO THE SUN
TRANCERS III: DETH LIVES
Von Praunheim, Rosa
AFFENGEIL
Von Sydow, Max
BEST INTENTIONS, THE
FATHER
OX, THE
ZENTROPA
Von Trier, Lars
ZENTROPA
Vool, Ruth
STRANGER AMONG US, A
Vosbein, Gary
TEXAS TENOR: THE ILLINOIS JACQUET STORY
Vose, Vicky
FROZEN ASSETS
Vosloo, Arnold
FINISHING TOUCH, THE
1492: THE CONQUEST OF PARADISE
Voth, Tomas R.
MISTRESS
Votrian, Ralph
CHAPLIN
Voves, Stephanie
USED PEOPLE
Vozoff, Lorinne
SHINING THROUGH
Vrana, Vlasta
TWIN SISTERS
Vujnovic, Dusko
JOURNEY OF HONOR
Vyent, Louise
BOOMERANG
Wack, Joe
BRIDE OF KILLER NERD
Wackler, Rebecca
LOVE CRIMES
Waddington, Steven
EDWARD II
1492: THE CONQUEST OF PARADISE
LAST OF THE MOHICANS, THE
Wade, Lonn
HELLROLLER
Wade, Sean
HELLROLLER
Wagner, Frank
BREAKING THE RULES
Wagner, Jack
PLAY MURDER FOR ME
Wagner, Natasha Gregson
BUFFY THE VAMPIRE SLAYER
DARK HORSE
FATHERS AND SONS
Wagner, Rachel
UNIVERSAL SOLDIER
Wagner, Robert
PLAYER, THE
Wahbah, Ali Abdul
MALCOLM X
Wahlstrom, Becky
STRAIGHT TALK
Waite, Ralph
BODYGUARD, THE
Waite, Todd
GATE II
Waits, Tom
BRAM STOKER'S DRACULA
Wakefield, Julia
WILD ORCHID 2: TWO SHADES OF BLUE
Wakins, Jason
SPLIT SECOND
Wakio, Mary
LORENZO'S OIL
Walcott, III, Noel L.
ENCINO MAN
Walczak, Diana
LIFE ON THE EDGE
Walczak, Eric
LIFE ON THE EDGE
Waldegrave, Lyn
MY GRANDPA IS A VAMPIRE
Waleffe, Patrick
TOTO LE HEROS
Walken, Christopher
ALL-AMERICAN MURDER
BATMAN RETURNS
MISTRESS
Walken, Jesse
HAPPY HELL NIGHT
Walker, Albertina
LEAP OF FAITH
Walker, Ally
SINGLES
UNIVERSAL SOLDIER
Walker, Amanda
LEAGUE OF THEIR OWN, A
Walker, Amelia "Mimi"
MALCOLM X
Walker, Arnetia
LOVE CRIMES

Walker, Carolyn L.A.
LIGHT SLEEPER
Walker, Cathy
SPLIT SECOND
Walker, Dominic
POWER OF ONE, THE
Walker, Gerald L.
AMERICAN ME
Walker, Jeffrey
PROOF
Walker, Jimmie
GUYVER, THE
HOME ALONE 2: LOST IN NEW YORK
Walker, Jimmy
INVASION OF THE SPACE PREACHERS
Walker, Lou
MY COUSIN VINNY
Walker, Polly
ENCHANTED APRIL
JOURNEY OF HONOR
PATRIOT GAMES
Walker, Robert
INNOCENT BLOOD
Walker, Sydney
PRELUDE TO A KISS
Walker, Theresa F.
BEYOND DARKNESS
Walker, Wyatt T.
MALCOLM X
Wall, Mary Chris
RUBY
Wall, Stuart
HELLROLLER
Wallace, Barbara Faye
BABE, THE
Wallace, Basil
RAPID FIRE
Wallace, Billie
FATE
Wallace, Denise
SEVERED TIES
Wallace, George
BEBE'S KIDS
DIGGSTOWN
Wallace, Julie T.
LUNATIC, THE
Wallace, Lee
USED PEOPLE
Wallace, Marcia
GHOULIES III: GHOULIES GO TO COLLEGE
Wallace, Tim
KICK OR DIE
Wallach, Eli
ARTICLE 99
MISTRESS
NIGHT AND THE CITY
Wallach, Roberta
MISTRESS
Wallenstein, Carlos
WINTER IN LISBON, THE
Walsh, Gerry
FAR AND AWAY
Walsh, J.T.
FEW GOOD MEN, A
HOFFA
Walsh, Jack
STRAIGHT TALK
Walsh, Kerry E.
MAN TROUBLE
Walsh, M. Emmet
KILLER IMAGE
WHITE SANDS
Walsh, Mark
WIND
Walston, Ray
OF MICE AND MEN
PLAYER, THE
Walter, Perla
VOYAGER
Walter, Tracey
MORTUARY ACADEMY
Walters, Anthony
SHINING THROUGH
Walters, Jamie
BED & BREAKFAST
Walters, Mark
LEAP OF FAITH
PURE COUNTRY
Walters, Melora
BEETHOVEN
Walters, William
SWOON
Waltman, Sean
CROSSING THE BRIDGE
Walton, John
EFFICIENCY EXPERT, THE
Walton, Wade
DEEP BLUES
Waltz, Lisa
PET SEMATARY II
Wanberg, Annie
DR. GIGGLES
Wang Zhiyong
CLOSE TO EDEN
Ward, Burt
SMOOTH TALKER
Ward, Colin
LORENZO'S OIL
Ward, Delbert
BROTHER'S KEEPER
Ward, Fred
BACKTRACK
BOB ROBERTS
PLAYER, THE
THUNDERHEART
Ward, Jonathan
FERNGULLY: THE LAST RAINFOREST
Ward, Lyman
BROTHER'S KEEPER
MIKEY
STEPHEN KING'S SLEEPWALKERS
Ward, Lymon
GUILTY AS CHARGED
Ward, Mac
NAKED OBSESSION
Ward, Megan
AMITYVILLE 1992: IT'S ABOUT TIME
ENCINO MAN
TRANCERS III: DETH LIVES
Ward, Patrick
CROSSING, THE
Ward, Rachel
CHRISTOPHER COLUMBUS: THE DISCOVERY
Ward, Roscoe
BROTHER'S KEEPER
Ward, Sandy
UNDER SIEGE
Ward, Skip
DO OR DIE
Ward, Sophie
DEMON IN MY VIEW, A
WAXWORK II: LOST IN TIME
Ward, Theara
MALCOLM X
Warda, Yussef Abu
CUP FINAL
Wardell, Greg
GIVING, THE
Warden, Jack
NIGHT AND THE CITY
PASSED AWAY
TOYS
Ware, Herta
LONELY HEARTS
Ware, Tim
BASKET CASE 3: THE PROGENY
Warfield, Emily
LOVE HURTS
Warlock, Billy
SOCIETY
Warlock, Dick
BEASTMASTER 2: THROUGH THE PORTAL OF TIME
Warnecke, Gordon
LONDON KILLS ME
Warner, David
CODE NAME: CHAOS
DRIVE
Warner, Julie
MR. SATURDAY NIGHT
Warner, Martin Charles
MAMBO KINGS, THE
SHAKES THE CLOWN
Warnock, Grant
WATERLAND
Warren, Andre
BUFFY THE VAMPIRE SLAYER
Warren, Jared
DAUGHTERS OF THE DUST
Warren, Judette
STEPHEN KING'S SLEEPWALKERS
Warren, Kai Lynn
DAUGHTERS OF THE DUST
Warren, Lesley Ann
PURE COUNTRY
Warren, Michael
HEAVEN IS A PLAYGROUND
STORYVILLE
Wartman, Dan
SINGLES
Warwick, Michael
NEWSIES
Washburn, Rick
COMRADES IN ARMS

Washington, Denzel
MALCOLM X
MISSISSIPPI MASALA
Washington, Grover
LEAP OF FAITH
Washington, III, Lulanger
LEAP OF FAITH
Washington, John David
MALCOLM X
Washington, Lennis
MALCOLM X
Washington, Sharon
MALCOLM X
Washizukan, Michiyo
MR. BASEBALL
Wasik, Ray
SWOON
Wasserman, Irving
MR. SATURDAY NIGHT
Wasson, Craig
MALCOLM X
MIDNIGHT FEAR
Wasson, Sarah
CAPTAIN AMERICA
Watas, Chief Telkon
TILL THERE WAS YOU
Watase, Tsunehiko
SILK ROAD, THE
Waterhouse, Eric
BEASTMASTER 2: THROUGH THE PORTAL OF TIME
Waterman, Annie
CHAPLIN
Waterman, Dennis
COLD JUSTICE
Waterman, Felicity
MIRACLE BEACH
Waters, Merl
MAXIMUM BREAKOUT
Watkin, Ian
MY GRANDPA IS A VAMPIRE
Watkins, Art
MANIAC WARRIORS
Watkins, Deborah
NIGHT AND THE CITY
Watkins, Gary
LOVE POTION NO. 9
Watkins, Michael
EDWARD II
Watson, Alberta
ZEBRAHEAD
Watson, Brenda
LEAGUE OF THEIR OWN, A
Watson, Cory
CUTTING EDGE, THE
Watson, Jimmy
HIGHWAY 61
Watson, Sr., John M.
GLADIATOR
HERO
PUBLIC EYE, THE
Watson, Woody
ALL-AMERICAN MURDER
HARD PROMISES
Watt, Tom
PATRIOT GAMES

Watters, Alithea
HIGHWAY 61
Watts, Naomi
FLIRTING
Waugh, Ric
KUFFS
Wawuyo, Michael
MISSISSIPPI MASALA
Waxman, Al
COLLISION COURSE
Way, Ann
ONCE UPON A CRIME
Way, Michael Ryan
PATRIOT GAMES
Wayans, Damon
MO' MONEY
Wayans, Kem
WISECRACKS
Wayans, Marlon
MO' MONEY
Wayne, "Big Daddy"
SOUTH CENTRAL
Weatherley, David
MY GRANDPA IS A VAMPIRE
Weatherly, Shawn
AMITYVILLE 1992: IT'S ABOUT TIME
Weathers, Carl
HURRICANE SMITH
Weaver, Beau
LITTLE NEMO: ADVENTURES IN SLUMBERLAND
Weaver, Robin
MUPPET CHRISTMAS CAROL, THE
Weaver, Sigourney
ALIEN3
1492: THE CONQUEST OF PARADISE
Weaving, Hugo
PROOF
Webb, Alyce
BOOMERANG
Webb, Audrey
THIS IS MY LIFE
Webb, Danny
ALIEN3
Webb, John
BABE, THE
Webb, Marni
RAMPAGE
Webb, Tom
STRAIGHT TALK
Webb, Veronica
MALCOLM X
Webber, Jake
BED & BREAKFAST
Webber, Timothy
LEAVING NORMAL
Weber, Franz
ONE LAST RUN
Weber, Jacques
ELEGANT CRIMINEL, L'
Weber, Jake
STRANGER AMONG US, A
Weber, Paul
ACES: IRON EAGLE III

Weber, Steven
SINGLE WHITE FEMALE
Webster, Bonnie
PATRIOT GAMES
Webster, David
UNDER SIEGE
Webster, Harry
FAR AND AWAY
Webster, John
TIGER CLAWS
Weddington, Stacy
INVASION OF THE SPACE PREACHERS
Wedgeworth, Ann
HARD PROMISES
Weenick, Annabelle
LOVE HURTS
Weickgenant, Blair
SMOOTH TALKER
Weiding, Lily
DAY IN OCTOBER, A
Weigel, Teri
AUNTIE LEE'S MEAT PIES
INNOCENT BLOOD
Weil, Robert
BRENDA STARR
Weillich, Lutz
SHINING THROUGH
Wein, Dean
WATERDANCE, THE
Weiner, John
COMRADES IN ARMS
Weiner, Michael
MR. SATURDAY NIGHT
Weingardt, Ellie
LEAGUE OF THEIR OWN, A
Weinger, Scott
ALADDIN
Weinstock, Lotus
WISECRACKS
Weisman, Michael
FROZEN ASSETS
Weiss, Gordon Joseph
ALL THE VERMEERS IN NEW YORK
Weiss, Pete
ROADSIDE PROPHETS
Weiss, Shaun
MIGHTY DUCKS, THE
Weisser, Morgan
PRAYER OF THE ROLLERBOYS
Weisser, Norbert
CAPTAIN AMERICA
CHAPLIN
Welch, Dan
COMPLEX WORLD
Welch, Eric
DESIRE AND HELL AT SUNSET MOTEL
Welch, Patrick
BARBARIAN QUEEN II: THE EMPRESS STRIKES BACK
Weldon, Ann
IMPORTANCE OF BEING EARNEST, THE
Weldon, Charles
MALCOLM X

Whitman, Parker
DESIRE AND HELL AT SUNSET MOTEL
Whitman, Sally
LONDON KILLS ME
Whitman, Stuart
SMOOTH TALKER
Whitmey, Nigel
SHINING THROUGH
Whitmire, Steve
MUPPET CHRISTMAS CAROL, THE
Whitney, Christopher
CAPTAIN AMERICA
Whitrow, Ben
CHAPLIN
Whitrow, Benjamin
DAMAGE
Whitt, Brian
BRIEF HISTORY OF TIME, A
Whittaker, Stephen
HUNTING
Whitted, Earl
MALCOLM X
Whittemore, Libby
LOVE POTION NO. 9
Whittingham, Christopher
UNDER SUSPICION
Whittington, Gene
FEW GOOD MEN, A
Whitton, Margaret
BIG GIRLS DON'T CRY . . . THEY GET EVEN
Whitworth, Cathy-Anne
LEAVING NORMAL
Whyle, James
SARAFINA!
Whyte, Laura
BABE, THE
GLADIATOR
Wickes, Mary
SISTER ACT
Wickliffe, Vivian
PUSHED TO THE LIMIT
Widerker, Jack
FINEST HOUR, THE
Widman, Rick
SOCIETY
Wiebe, Lesley
MANIAC WARRIORS
Wieberker, Jack
BLINK OF AN EYE
Wieland, David
FLIRTING
Wiener, Joshua
NEWSIES
Wiese, Nicholas
LORENZO'S OIL
Wigan, Jonathan
LOVE FIELD
MEMOIRS OF AN INVISIBLE MAN
Wiggins, Georgia
DAUGHTERS OF THE DUST
Wiggins, III, Eric J.
SWOON
Wiggins, Jerone
MISSISSIPPI MASALA
UNDER SIEGE
Wiggins, Kevin
RUBY
Wilberforce, Muteta
MISSISSIPPI MASALA
Wilby, James
HOWARDS END
Wilcox, Steve
AMERICAN ME
Wilde, Steven
SHAKING THE TREE
Wildeman, Lerato
SARAFINA!
Wildeman, Pheto
SARAFINA!
Wilder, Alan
LEAGUE OF THEIR OWN, A
STRAIGHT TALK
Wilder, Cara
FAR AND AWAY
Wilder, James
SCORCHERS
Wildman, Valerie
NEON CITY
Wildmon, Reverend Donald
DAMNED IN THE USA
Wiley, David
SOCIETY
Wiley, Margaret
HARD PROMISES
Wilheim, Michael
CANDYMAN
Wilhoite, Kathleen
BRENDA STARR
LORENZO'S OIL
Wiliams, Gwyneth
MANIAC WARRIORS
Wilkens, Claudia
MIGHTY DUCKS, THE
Wilker, Jose
MEDICINE MAN
Wilkins, Ozzie
PRELUDE TO A KISS
Wilkins, Tessa
WATERLAND
Wilkinson, Eileen
MISTRESS
Wilkof, Lee
HERO
Willett, Janine
BOB ROBERTS
Williams, Barbara
OH, WHAT A NIGHT
Williams, Billy Sly
MISSION OF JUSTICE
Williams, Candice
NETHERWORLD
Williams, Chino "Fats"
BEBE'S KIDS
STORYVILLE
Williams, Curt
MALCOLM X
Williams, Cynda
ONE FALSE MOVE
Williams, Debbie
MALCOLM X
Williams, Denalda
CAFE ROMEO
Williams, Eugene
SOUTH CENTRAL
Williams, Freeman
WHITE MEN CAN'T JUMP
Williams, Gareth
MALCOLM X
Williams, Gene
LETHAL WEAPON 3
Williams, Germain
LETHAL WEAPON 3
Williams, Haley
CUTTING EDGE, THE
Williams, Harold
PRELUDE TO A KISS
Williams, Hywel
POWER OF ONE, THE
Williams, Ian Patrick
BAD CHANNELS
Williams, III, Clarence
DEEP COVER
Williams, J.D.
DISTINGUISHED GENTLEMAN, THE
Williams, Jason
SOCIETY
Williams, JoBeth
STOP! OR MY MOM WILL SHOOT
Williams, John Louis
GLADIATOR
Williams, Johnny
HONEYMOON IN VEGAS
Williams, Kimberly
SECRET GAMES
Williams, L.B.
JUICE
Williams, Leroy
LEAP OF FAITH
Williams, Mark
KILL LINE
TRAINED TO FIGHT
Williams, Michael
FLIRTING
Williams, Nelson C.
CROSSING THE BRIDGE
Williams, Phaeder
MANIAC WARRIORS
Williams, Philip
USED PEOPLE
Williams, Randy
ALAN & NAOMI
Williams, Robin
ALADDIN
FERNGULLY: THE LAST RAINFOREST
SHAKES THE CLOWN
TOYS
Williams, Roldan Nill
TOYS
Williams, Satch
SAVAGE INSTINCT
Williams, Sharon
MISSISSIPPI MASALA
Williams, Spice
GUYVER, THE
Williams, Steven Lloyd
DANCE WITH DEATH

Wolper, David
COLOR ADJUSTMENT
Wong, Anderson
FERNGULLY:
THE LAST RAINFOREST
Wong, Anthony
HARD-BOILED
Wong, Gary
TIGER CLAWS
Wong, Quincy
MO' MONEY
Wong, Victor
3 NINJAS
Wood, Elijah
FOREVER YOUNG
RADIO FLYER
Wood, Hannah
RADIO FLYER
Wood, Mark
CONSENTING ADULTS
Wood, Rebecca
BARBARIAN QUEEN II:
THE EMPRESS STRIKES BACK
Wood, Tom
MISSION OF JUSTICE
THIS IS MY LIFE
UNDER SIEGE
Woodard, Alfre
GUN IN BETTY LOU'S
HANDBAG, THE
PASSION FISH
Woodard, Alma
LOVE FIELD
Woodard, Jimmy
MO' MONEY
Woodcock, John
MANIAC WARRIORS
Wooden, Nashom
SWOON
Woodfine, Phil
MUPPET CHRISTMAS CAROL, THE
Woodhouse, Donna
FATHER
Woodruff, Dennis
WE'RE TALKIN' SERIOUS MONEY
Woods, Barbara Alyn
DANCE WITH DEATH
WATERDANCE, THE
WE'RE TALKIN' SERIOUS MONEY
Woods, Carol
NIGHT AND THE CITY
Woods, James
CHAPLIN
DIGGSTOWN
STRAIGHT TALK
Woods, Johnathon
FATE
Woods, Michael Jeffrey
STRAIGHT TALK
Woodward, Lorraine Pascal
SPLIT SECOND
Woodworth, Cristin
LORENZO'S OIL
Woolrich, Abel
CABEZA DE VACA
Woolridge, Susan
AFRAID OF THE DARK

Woolvett, Jaimz
UNFORGIVEN
Worcester, David
WHITE TRASH
Wordsworth, Roy
BEAUTIFUL DREAMERS
Woren, Dan
BEASTMASTER 2:
THROUGH THE PORTAL OF TIME
Woronov, Mary
HELLROLLER
LIVING END, THE
MORTUARY ACADEMY
Wortell, Holly
BEETHOVEN
Worth, Mike
FINAL IMPACT
STREET CRIMES
Worth, Sarah
LONDON KILLS ME
Worth, Stephen
COOL WORLD
Worthington, Rick
MANIAC WARRIORS
Wrangler, Greg
BARBARIAN QUEEN II:
THE EMPRESS STRIKES BACK
RUNESTONE, THE
Wright, Amy
HARD PROMISES
LOVE HURTS
Wright, Bethany
SIMPLE MEN
Wright, Burt
SWOON
Wright, Jason
TROLL 2
Wright, Jeff
HELLROLLER
Wright, Jeffrey
JUMPIN' AT THE BONEYARD
Wright, Jenny
LAWNMOWER MAN, THE
Wright, Karon
ARTICLE 99
Wright, Ken
EYE OF THE EAGLE 3
Wright, Michael
BIKINI CARWASH COMPANY, THE
Wright, N'Bushe
ZEBRAHEAD
Wright, Nicki
PETER'S FRIENDS
Wright, Patrick
FATE
Wright, Peter
SCANNERS III: THE TAKEOVER
Wright, Robert
RAMPAGE
Wright, Robin
PLAYBOYS, THE
TOYS
Wright, Steven
RESERVOIR DOGS
Wright, Tom
PASSION FISH

Wright, Tommy
CHAPLIN
UNDER SUSPICION
Wright, Tracy
HIGHWAY 61
Wright, Victor R.
MAXIMUM BREAKOUT
Wu, Vivian
GUYVER, THE
Wuhl, Robert
BODYGUARD, THE
MISTRESS
Wuhrer, Kari
BEASTMASTER 2:
THROUGH THE PORTAL OF TIME
Wurinile
CLOSE TO EDEN
Wyanabi, Paul
PUSHED TO THE LIMIT
Wyands, Richard
TEXAS TENOR:
THE ILLINOIS JACQUET STORY
Wyatt, Jr., Allan
UNIVERSAL SOLDIER
Wyerch, Harold
MANIAC WARRIORS
Wyett, Paul
SOLDIER'S TALE, A
Wyle, Noah
FEW GOOD MEN, A
Wylie, Adam
OUT ON A LIMB
Wyllie, Dan
EFFICIENCY EXPERT, THE
Wynands, Danny
LETHAL WEAPON 3
Wynn, Bobby
LETHAL WEAPON 3
Wynn, Irwin
VOYAGER
Wynn, Jena
GLADIATOR
Wyss, Amanda
BLOODFIST IV: DIE TRYING
Xavier-Zimmerman, Nicole
BECOMING COLETTE
Xiem Mang
LOVER, THE
Xu Qing
LIFE ON A STRING
Yacoub, Hayan
DEADLY CURRENTS
Yagher, Jeff
LOWER LEVEL
Yago, Art T.
STOP! OR MY MOM WILL SHOOT
Yale, Stanley
PRAYER OF THE ROLLERBOYS
Yama, Michael
BACKTRACK
Yamadera, William
MR. SATURDAY NIGHT
Yamaguchi, Katsushi
MR. BASEBALL
Yamaguchi, Toshimi
JOURNEY OF HONOR

Yamamoto, Kay
DEATH BECOMES HER
Yamanlar, Aijdin
GODZILLA VS. BIOLLANTE
Yang, Jennifer
MAN TROUBLE
Yanne, Jean
INDOCHINE
Yansick, Eddie
INTO THE SUN
Yao Jingou
LIFE ON A STRING
Yarbrough, Joani
LOVE CRIMES
Yardley, Jonathan
TO RENDER A LIFE
Yarnell, Chris
OVER HER DEAD BODY
Yaroshefsky, Lois D.
GIVING, THE
Yasunaga, Kenji
JOURNEY OF HONOR
Yasutake, Patti
STOP! OR MY MOM WILL SHOOT
Yates, Art
MANIAC WARRIORS
Yates, Cassie
I DON'T BUY KISSES ANYMORE
Yayama, Osamu
JOURNEY OF HONOR
Yazel, Carrie
DEATH BECOMES HER
MR. BASEBALL
Yeager, Biff
BATMAN RETURNS
ROADSIDE PROPHETS
Yeaoh, Michelle
SUPERCOP: POLICE STORY III
Yeck, Janice
CUTTING EDGE, THE
Yee, Sarah
TOYS
Yenawine, Philip
DAMNED IN THE USA
Yerkes, Bob
MR. SATURDAY NIGHT
Yesko, Jeffrey Scott
WATERDANCE, THE
Yesso, Don
HERO
Yeung, Bolo
BREATHING FIRE
TIGER CLAWS
Yevdokimov, Alexei
BACK IN THE U.S.S.R.
Yip, Violet
RAMPAGE
Ynovskii, Leonid
RASPAD
Yoldi, Oscar
CABEZA DE VACA
York, Susannah
FATE
ILLUSIONS
Yorozuyo, Mineko
MR. BASEBALL

Young, Andrea
WATERDANCE, THE
Young Bear, Melvin David
THUNDERHEART
Young Bear, Sr., Severt
THUNDERHEART
Young, Blumen
BODYGUARD, THE
Young, Bruce A.
BASIC INSTINCT
TRESPASS
Young, Cedric
HOME ALONE 2:
LOST IN NEW YORK
RAPID FIRE
Young, Charles
BEASTMASTER 2:
THROUGH THE PORTAL OF TIME
Young, Charles F.
MALCOLM X
Young, Chris
RUNESTONE, THE
Young, Dale
HOFFA
Young, Damian
SIMPLE MEN
Young, De'Von
BOOMERANG
Young, Dey
BACK IN THE U.S.S.R.
Young, IV, Eugene
LEAP OF FAITH
Young, Jeff Alan
WILD ORCHID 2:
TWO SHADES OF BLUE
Young, Karen
HOFFA
Young, Keone
HONEYMOON IN VEGAS
Young, L. Warren
CONSENTING ADULTS
LOVE CRIMES
TRESPASS
Young, Lois
NEWSIES
Young, Marvin
PLAYER, THE
Young, Sean
LOVE CRIMES
ONCE UPON A CRIME
Young, William Allen
CODE NAME: CHAOS
WATERDANCE, THE
Youngs, Jennifer
PRIMARY MOTIVE
Yribar, Jason
NEWSIES
Yuen Biao
ONCE UPON A TIME IN CHINA
Yuen Wah
SUPERCOP: POLICE STORY III
Yuzna, Conan
SOCIETY
Z'Dar, Robert
BEASTMASTER 2:
THROUGH THE PORTAL OF TIME

Zabalelta, Jairo
KISS ME A KILLER
Zabriskie, Grace
FERNGULLY:
THE LAST RAINFOREST
MEGAVILLE
RAMPAGE
TWIN PEAKS: FIRE WALK WITH ME
Zabrosky, Joseph
BODYGUARD, THE
Zagarino, Frank
PROJECT: SHADOWCHASER
Zagrodnick, Terri
RUBY
Zahid, Ibrahim
K2
Zahradnick, Pete
MO' MONEY
Zahrn, Will
MO' MONEY
Zaks, Jerry
HUSBANDS AND WIVES
Zalaznick, Lauren
SWOON
Zalcberg, Gerard
FAVOUR, THE WATCH, AND THE
VERY BIG FISH, THE
Zanck, Bernard
RAMPAGE
Zand, Michael
PLAY NICE
Zane, Billy
MEGAVILLE
Zaoui, Vanessa
ALAN & NAOMI
Zapata, Carmen
PANAMA DECEPTION, THE
SISTER ACT
Zappa, Moon
LITTLE SISTER
Zappala, Vito
JOHNNY STECCHINO
Zaragoza, Gregory
LAST OF THE MOHICANS, THE
Zardi, Dominique
DELICATESSEN
Zaremby, Justin
HAND THAT ROCKS THE
CRADLE, THE
Zarish, Janet
MALCOLM X
Zarzour, Jean
PUBLIC EYE, THE
Zediker, Kara
BABE, THE
Zeek
COMPLEX WORLD
Zehentmayr, Patricia
STREET CRIMES
Zeitlin, Michelle
DANCE MACABRE
Zeller, Ben
WHITE SANDS
Zeller, Rick
FATAL INSTINCT
Zeman, Richard
TWIN SISTERS

Zenda, John
BACKTRACK
Zenil, Amanda
GUN IN BETTY LOU'S HANDBAG, THE
Zepeda, Nayelli
CABEZA DE VACA
Zeta-Jones, Catherine
CHRISTOPHER COLUMBUS: THE DISCOVERY
Zetlina, Ahbaru
INTO THE SUN
Zette, Bernard
STORYVILLE
Zhang Zhenguan
LIFE ON A STRING
Zhao Qi
RAISE THE RED LANTERN
Zhivago, Stacia
SORORITY HOUSE MASSACRE 2
Zidel, Bob
THIS IS MY LIFE
Ziegler, Ronald Edward
BOOMERANG
Ziesmer, Jerry
SINGLES
Zigic, Dragana
CAPTAIN AMERICA
Zim, Paul
STRANGER AMONG US, A
Zima, Madeline
HAND THAT ROCKS THE CRADLE, THE
Zimmerman, J.R.
BEAUTIFUL DREAMERS
Zimmerman, Joe
LIFE ON THE EDGE
Zimmerman, Leigh
HOME ALONE 2: LOST IN NEW YORK
Zimmerman, Marlene
KILL LINE
Zimmerman, Natalie
MAMBO KINGS, THE
Zion, Rabbi, Dr. Joel Y.
THIS IS MY LIFE
Zipp, William
CENTER OF THE WEB
Zirner, August
VOYAGER
Ziskie, Dan
ZEBRAHEAD
Zmed, Adrian
OTHER WOMAN, THE
Zobian, Mark
HOUSE ON TOMBSTONE HILL, THE
Zocopoulos, George
FATHER
Zohar, Rita
FINAL ANALYSIS
Zolli, Maribe
INNOCENT BLOOD
Zorer, Ayelet
POUR SACHA
Zorn, Danny
THIS IS MY LIFE
Zuamut, Bassam
CUP FINAL
Zubia, Edward Paul
PUSHED TO THE LIMIT
Zubiaga, Antonio
BARBARIAN QUEEN II: THE EMPRESS STRIKES BACK
Zucchero, Joe
EYE OF THE EAGLE 3
Zully, Stewart J.
MALCOLM X
Zumwalt, Rick
BATMAN RETURNS
Zuniga, Jennifer
WOMAN, HER MEN AND HER FUTON, A
Zylberstein, Elsa
VAN GOGH

ANIMATORS

Altieri, Kathy
ALADDIN
Anderson, Tamara
ROCK-A-DOODLE
Azadani, Rasoul
ALADDIN
Buck, Chris
BEBE'S KIDS
Fawdry, Richard
FREDDIE AS F.R.O.7
Fucile, Tony
FERNGULLY: THE LAST RAINFOREST
Goldberg, Steve
ALADDIN
Gombert, Ed
ALADDIN
Graves, Lennie
BEBE'S KIDS
Guy, Tony
FREDDIE AS F.R.O.7
Haylor, Jan
ROCK-A-DOODLE
Higgins, Tom
ROCK-A-DOODLE
Jones, Chuck
STAY TUNED
Kelly, Paul
ROCK-A-DOODLE
Lanpher, Vera
ALADDIN
Paul, Don
ALADDIN
Richardson, Charles Leland
FERNGULLY: THE LAST RAINFOREST
Stewart, Mike
FREDDIE AS F.R.O.7
Tokyo Movie Shinsha Company Ltd.
LITTLE NEMO: ADVENTURES IN SLUMBERLAND
Tomizawa, Nobuo
LITTLE NEMO: ADVENTURES IN SLUMBERLAND
Vischer, Frans
BEBE'S KIDS
Woodside, Bruce
COOL WORLD
Young, Sue
BOB MARLEY: TIME WILL TELL

ART DIRECTORS

Aguilar, Jose Luis
CABEZA DE VACA
Ako, Yehuda
HUMAN SHIELD, THE
Ako, Yudo
SEXUAL RESPONSE
Albertini, Gianni
EVIL CLUTCH
Alberto, Mario
WINTER IN LISBON, THE
Albournac, Michel
FINE ROMANCE, A
Allen, Ian
TILL THERE WAS YOU
Ames, Paul
GETTING MARRIED IN BUFFALO JUMP
Ancona, Amy
DANCE WITH DEATH
KISS ME A KILLER
Andrev, Ivan
DEATHSTALKER IV: MATCH OF TITANS
Ashida, Toyoo
VAMPIRE HUNTER D
Asman, Jayne
BLIND VISION
Baille, Ian
SPLIT SECOND
Baker, Cherie
VOYAGER
Ballance, Jack D.L.
CROSSING THE BRIDGE
Ballou, Bill
THUNDERHEART
Bangham, Humphrey
SPLIT SECOND
Barbosa, Carlos
LONELY HEARTS
Barclay, Bill
GLENGARRY GLEN ROSS
Barclay, William
BOOMERANG
Barrows, James
BUFFY THE VAMPIRE SLAYER
Bateup, Hugh
EFFICIENCY EXPERT, THE
Beal, Charley
NIGHT AND THE CITY
Becher, Sophie
CODE NAME: CHAOS
Benjamin, Susan
WE'RE TALKIN' SERIOUS MONEY
Benoit-Fresco
INSPECTOR LAVARDIN
Biagetti, Paolo
JOHNNY STECCHINO
Bickel, Daniel W.
DEEP COVER

Billerman, Mark
RAISING CAIN
Blackman, Jack
HOUSESITTER
Blaymires, Colin
LONDON KILLS ME
Boll, Bradford
INVASION OF THE SPACE PREACHERS
Bomba, David James
COOL WORLD
GUN IN BETTY LOU'S HANDBAG, THE
Bonnie, Louisa
LITTLE SISTER
Bose, Asoke
CITY OF JOY
Bosher, Dennis
MUPPET CHRISTMAS CAROL, THE
Bradford, Dennis
LEAP OF FAITH
LORENZO'S OIL
Breen, Charles
BEETHOVEN
TRESPASS
Brewer, Daniel
LITTLE VEGAS
Brock, Ian
HIGHWAY 61
Brock, Laura
JOHNNY SUEDE
Brody, Alan
HELLROLLER
Brothers, Andrew D.
SOUTH CENTRAL
Brown, Tom
DOUBLE VISION
Brunton, Richard
ILLUSIONS
ULTRAVIOLET
Buenrostro, Jesus
MEDICINE MAN
Bufnoir, Jacques
ELEGANT CRIMINEL, L'
Butcher, Charles
RAPID FIRE
Byggdin, Doug
RESURRECTED, THE
Cao Jiuping
RAISE THE RED LANTERN
Cassie, Alan
MUPPET CHRISTMAS CAROL, THE
Chichester, John
WAXWORK II: LOST IN TIME
Chong, Joel
HARD-BOILED
Clements, Carol
RAMPAGE
Close, Michael
TIGER CLAWS
Coates, Nelson
UNIVERSAL SOLDIER
Cochrane, Sandy
LEAVING NORMAL
Conklin, Kate
JUST LIKE IN THE MOVIES
Conti, Juan Carlos
FAVOUR, THE WATCH, AND THE VERY BIG FISH, THE
Cornyn, Alison
LITTLE NOISES
Costanza, Mike
CAGED FEAR
Crew, Rosalind
SCORCHERS
Crone, Bruce
MEMOIRS OF AN INVISIBLE MAN
UNLAWFUL ENTRY
Crowe, Desmond
SHINING THROUGH
YEAR OF THE COMET
Cruz, Ronnie
FIELD OF FIRE
Dancklefsen, Diane
LONDON KILLS ME
Darby, Kim
CROSSING, THE
Davick, Tom
LOVE CRIMES
Davis, Dan
CUTTING EDGE, THE
OF MICE AND MEN
De M. Yates, Hayden
NAKED OBSESSION
DeForrest, Kelle
SOCIETY
Delauria, Java
WITCHCRAFT IV: VIRGIN HEART
Delira, Ben
EYE OF THE EAGLE 3
Denker, Lisa
GAS FOOD LODGING
DePrez, Therese
SIMPLE MEN
REFRIGERATOR, THE
DeVilla, Debbie
KILLER TOMATOES EAT FRANCE!
Diers, Don
MEDICINE MAN
Dong Huamiao
RAISE THE RED LANTERN
Douret, Dominique
NIGHT AND DAY
Driskill, Lionel
WHO SHOT PATAKANGO?
Drummond-Hay, Cecil
MANIAC WARRIORS
Durrell, Bill
COLLISION COURSE
Durrell, Jr., William
JENNIFER EIGHT
Earl, Richard
DAMAGE
Eckel, Tim
HELLRAISER III: HELL ON EARTH
Eggleston, Ralph
FERNGULLY: THE LAST RAINFOREST
Eriksen, Randy
WILD ORCHID 2: TWO SHADES OF BLUE
Eyres, Rick
EDWARD II
Fanning, Tony
MIGHTY DUCKS, THE
Feng, Jim
LIGHT SLEEPER
Fernandez, Benjamin
1492: THE CONQUEST OF PARADISE
Ferrari, Giorgio
LUNATIC, THE
Fleming, Jerry
PLAYER, THE
Ford, Marianne
WHERE ANGELS FEAR TO TREAD
Ford, Robin
MY FATHER IS COMING
Fortune, Roger
WHITE MEN CAN'T JUMP
Francois, Thierry
VOYAGER
Fraser, Eric
VAGRANT, THE
Fraser, James
NETHERWORLD
French, Jim
ALL-AMERICAN MURDER
Galbraith, Rick
MIDNIGHT FEAR
Galvin, Tim
LEAGUE OF THEIR OWN, A
Gantly, Arden
PLAYBOYS, THE
Ginsburg, Gershon
OVER HER DEAD BODY
Goldstein, Dan
BLOODFIST IV: DIE TRYING
Gorton, Adrian
UNFORGIVEN
Gracie, Ian
ROCK & ROLL COWBOYS
Graham, Angelo
FINAL ANALYSIS
Graham, W. Steven
PRELUDE TO A KISS
SCENT OF A WOMAN
STRANGER AMONG US, A
Grande, Greg
3 NINJAS
Grickson, Randy
MISTRESS
Griffiths, Reston
SOLDIER'S TALE, A
Guerra, Robert
LAST OF THE MOHICANS, THE
Haack, Mark
SINGLES
Hardy, Ian
GUILTY AS CHARGED
Hardy, Kenneth A.
RUBY
Hatfield, Todd
FALLING FROM GRACE
Heinrichs, Rick
BATMAN RETURNS
Hemmings, Prudence
DARK HORSE
Hidalgo, Eduardo
CTHULHU MANSION

Hiney, Bill
UNDER SIEGE
Hitchcock, Martin
POWER OF ONE, THE
Hoimark, Peter
OX, THE
Hole, Fred
ALIEN3
Holland, Richard
LAST OF THE MOHICANS, THE
Hopkins, Speed
HUSBANDS AND WIVES
SHADOWS AND FOG
Hudolin, Richard
K2
STAY TUNED
Hugon, Jean Michel
FINE ROMANCE, A
Hyde, Bernard
DARK HORSE
Iankova, Tsvetana
DEATHSTALKER IV: MATCH OF TITANS
Irwin, Janice
HOUSE ON TOMBSTONE HILL, THE
Jett, Billy
DEMONIC TOYS
NETHERWORLD
Johnson, Bo
LINGUINI INCIDENT, THE
PUBLIC EYE, THE
Johnston, P. Michael
SINGLE WHITE FEMALE
Jost, Jon
ALL THE VERMEERS IN NEW YORK
Joy, Michael
QUARREL, THE
Keen, Gregory Paul
USED PEOPLE
Keywan, Alicia
CONSENTING ADULTS
King, John
CHAPLIN
King, Lance
LOVE FIELD
Kirchener, Ken
3 NINJAS
Kirkland, Geoffrey
WILDFIRE
Klassen, David
FEW GOOD MEN, A
Klassen, David Frederick
RADIO FLYER
Klein, Jay
PRAYER OF THE ROLLERBOYS
Klotz, Clyde
COMMON BONDS
Koldo, Luis
CHRISTOPHER COLUMBUS: THE DISCOVERY
Kosko, Gary
BOB ROBERTS
Kou Honglie
SILK ROAD, THE
Kretschmer, Barbara Kahn
ALAN & NAOMI
Kroyer, Susan
FERNGULLY: THE LAST RAINFOREST
Lamont, Simon
PROJECT: SHADOWCHASER
Lazan, David
CANDYMAN
Lee, David
BRIEF HISTORY OF TIME, A
Lee, Dayna
CRISSCROSS
Lee, Gary
HOME ALONE 2: LOST IN NEW YORK
Lees, Patrick
IN THE HEAT OF PASSION
Leguillon, Jacques
CRY OF THE OWL, THE
Lennox, Thomas S.
BEYOND DARKNESS
Lewis, Linda
CENTER OF THE WEB
Lipton, Dina
PUBLIC EYE, THE
Locke, Alan
DR. GIGGLES
Lubin, David
MIDNIGHT CLEAR, A
Lucky, Joseph P.
PATRIOT GAMES
Magallon, Francisco
BARBARIAN QUEEN II: THE EMPRESS STRIKES BACK
Maltese, Daniel E.
NOISES OFF
Mansbridge, Mark
CHAPLIN
Manson, Michael
EYE OF THE STORM
Marchione, Luigi
WHERE ANGELS FEAR TO TREAD
Marcotte, Paul
BACKTRACK
Martin, Greg
DEADLY BET
Martishius, Walter
RIVER RUNS THROUGH IT, A
Marty, John E. "Jack"
LOVE CRIMES
Mason, Lee
SAVAGE INSTINCT
Matis, Barbra
THIS IS MY LIFE
Maussion, Ivan
HAIRDRESSER'S HUSBAND, THE
Maxey, Caty
BASKET CASE 3: THE PROGENY
McDonald, Leslie
HERO
McKernin, Kathleen M.
STORYVILLE
McKinnon, Gary
LIFE ON THE EDGE
Mercier, Gilbert
PASSED AWAY
Meyer, Carey
MUNCHIE
Miller, Bruce
FOREVER YOUNG
GLADIATOR
WAYNE'S WORLD
Miller, Paul
MIRACLE BEACH
Miller, Scott
DRIVE
Minton, Thomas
LOVE POTION NO. 9
Moe, David
OH, WHAT A NIGHT
Moore, Don
ROCK-A-DOODLE
Moore, Randy
BUFFY THE VAMPIRE SLAYER
MOM AND DAD SAVE THE WORLD
Morahan, James
ALIEN3
Muraoka, Alan
PASSENGER 57
Muzio, Craig
BLACKBELT
Myers, Troy
MEGAVILLE
Nelson, Steven
WHITE TRASH
New, Gary
MORTUARY ACADEMY
Oehler, Greg P.
LIFE ON THE EDGE
Okac, Oldrich
EAR, THE
Okowita
DIGGSTOWN
Oxley, Ray
MONSTER IN A BOX
Papalia, Greg
LETHAL WEAPON 3
Patton, Nancy
NEWSIES
Pecanins, Marisa
DANZON
Pereira, Jackie
CAN IT BE LOVE
Perkins, Bill
ALADDIN
Perrin, Richard
ARMED FOR ACTION
Perry, Michael T.
STRAIGHT TALK
Peterson, Barbara
CHAINS OF GOLD
Phipps, Kevin
POWER OF ONE, THE
SHINING THROUGH
Poses, David
TERMINAL BLISS
Pouille, Hubert
TOTO LE HEROS
Precht, Andrew
BRAM STOKER'S DRACULA
Prier, Nicolas
NEAR MISSES
Pritchard, Terry
CHRISTOPHER COLUMBUS: THE DISCOVERY

Ralph, John
HOWARDS END
Randall, Gary
MISSION OF JUSTICE
Raney, Pat
COLD JUSTICE
Rayner, Helen
WATERLAND
Reading, Tony
UNDER SUSPICION
Richardson, Edward
TOYS
Richardson, Mark
MIND, BODY & SOUL
Richardson, Scott
ULTIMATE DESIRES
Richwood, Frank
BRAIN DONORS
Ricker, Brad
BIG GIRLS DON'T CRY . . . THEY GET EVEN
Ridney, Leith
HOUSE OF USHER, THE
Rizzo, Michael
MY COUSIN VINNY
WHITE SANDS
Roberts, Florina
WOMAN, HER MEN AND HER FUTON, A
Roberts, Rick
UNFORGIVEN
Robinson, Dave
PALE BLOOD
Rosell, Josep
AMANTES
Ross, Heather
ROUND TRIP TO HEAVEN
Rothschild, Andrew
DEMON IN MY VIEW, A
Roussell, Peter
BLAME IT ON THE BELLBOY
Rudot, Olivier
LOVER, THE
Ruscio, Nina
COLD HEAVEN
Sage, Jeff
HOUSESITTER
Sage, Jefferson
MISSISSIPPI MASALA
Sanchez, Ferran
SHOOTING ELIZABETH
Sanchez, Norberto
DANZON
Sarlad, Steve
MAMBO KINGS, THE
Schmook, Randall
MY COUSIN VINNY
Schulze, Douglas
HELL MASTER
Schwartz, Steven
BRENDA STARR
Scott, Stephen
AFRAID OF THE DARK
Seagers, Chris
CRYING GAME, THE
YEAR OF THE COMET
Senter, Jack
FAR AND AWAY
Shahid, Sam
BROKEN NOSES
Shao Ruigang
LIFE ON A STRING
Shardlow, Paul
FREDDIE AS F.R.O.7
Shaw, Mike
MIRROR IMAGES
Shaw, Jr., Robert K.
GLENGARRY GLEN ROSS
Shouler, Kirsten
MY GRANDPA IS A VAMPIRE
Silvertone, Jill
MAXIMUM BREAKOUT
Simmonds, Stephen
K2
Sinski, Bruce
KILLER IMAGE
Skinner, William Ladd
BODYGUARD, THE
Smith, Rusty
DIARY OF A HITMAN
Stefanovic, Jasna
PSYCHIC
TALONS OF THE EAGLE
Steward, Karen
PET SEMATARY II
Tatopoulos, Patrick
BEASTMASTER 2: THROUGH THE PORTAL OF TIME
Taylor, Jim
FREEJACK
Teegarden, Jim
DEATH BECOMES HER
Tinglof, Sig
STEPHEN KING'S SLEEPWALKERS
Tokuda, Hiroshi
SILK ROAD, THE
Told, John
CHINA O'BRIEN II
Tomkins, Leslie
1492: THE CONQUEST OF PARADISE
Torrey, Dana
INTO THE SUN
ONE FALSE MOVE
Tougas, Ginger
IN THE SOUP
Trabbie, Lou
ALMOST PREGNANT
Trout, Lynn
SCANNERS III: THE TAKEOVER
Truesdale, James
CAPTAIN RON
Tsukamoto, Shinya
TETSUO: THE IRON MAN
Tuers, Pepie
DOLLY DEAREST
Tunney, Edward T.E.
SOLDIER'S FORTUNE
Tunny, Ted
SPIRITS
Van Der Linden, Dorus
LILY WAS HERE
Verreaux, Ed
DISTINGUISHED GENTLEMAN, THE
HONEY, I BLEW UP THE KID
Vetter, Arlan Jay
ONLY YOU
Wager, Diane
SNEAKERS
Wallace, Jeff
CRITTERS 4
Walters, Mark
NAKED OBSESSION
Wang, Stella
RUNESTONE, THE
Warnke, John
HONEYMOON IN VEGAS
Warren, Tom
MALCOLM X
Watkins, Kenneth
CLEARCUT
Weber, Carla
GAS FOOD LODGING
Weimer, Pauly
FATHERS AND SONS
Werner, Axel
PRIMARY MOTIVE
Whifler, Dan
ZEBRAHEAD
White, Nick
DEAD CERTAIN
Willett, John
JENNIFER EIGHT
Williams, Michael Kelly
DAUGHTERS OF THE DUST
Willson, David
LOVE FIELD
Wilson, Everett D.
SEEDPEOPLE
Wilson, Ron
BED & BREAKFAST
Wissner, Gary
HOFFA
Wolff, Steven
SCHOOL TIES
Wong, Oliver
SUPERCOP: POLICE STORY III
Wood, Carol Winstead
MR. SATURDAY NIGHT
Wynack, Bernadette
FATHER
HUNTING
Yates, Diane
STOP! OR MY MOM WILL SHOOT
Yates, Hayden
POISON IVY
Yee Chung-man
ONCE UPON A TIME IN CHINA
Young, Brian
INVASION OF THE SPACE PREACHERS
Zuelzke, Mark
HAND THAT ROCKS THE CRADLE, THE

CHOREOGRAPHERS

Armitage, Karole
KUFFS

Charnock, Nigel
EDWARD II
Cousins, Robin
CUTTING EDGE, THE
Garrett, Pat
MUPPET CHRISTMAS CAROL, THE
Holmes, Peggy
NEWSIES
Mitchell, Jerry
SCENT OF A WOMAN
Newson, Lloyd
EDWARD II
Ortega, Kenny
NEWSIES
Pellicoro, Paul
SCENT OF A WOMAN
Peters, Michael
MAMBO KINGS, THE
SARAFINA!
Thomas, Anthony
TOYS

CINEMATOGRAPHERS

Achs, Robert
DAMNED IN THE USA
Ahern, Lloyd
TRESPASS
Ahlberg, Mac
INNOCENT BLOOD
Alazraki, Robert
POUR SACHA
Albert, Arthur
PASSED AWAY
Alberti, Maryse
INCIDENT AT OGLALA
ZEBRAHEAD
Alcaine, Jose Luis
AMANTES
Aliphat, Jean-Pierre
HOT CHOCOLATE
Alonzo, John A.
COOL WORLD
HOUSESITTER
Anao, Vic
EYE OF THE EAGLE 3
FIELD OF FIRE
Anderson, Eric D.
DOLLY DEAREST
Anderson, Jamie
UNLAWFUL ENTRY
Anderson, Michael
COLOR ADJUSTMENT
Angell, Mark
IMPORTANCE OF BEING EARNEST, THE
Angelo, Yves
BEATING HEART, A
TOUS LES MATINS DU MONDE
Araki, Gregg
LIVING END, THE
Armenaki, Arledge
AUNTIE LEE'S MEAT PIES
Arvantis, Yorgos
VOYAGER
Baer, Hanania
VENICE/VENICE
Baggot, King
LITTLE VEGAS
WHERE THE DAY TAKES YOU
Bailey, John
BRIEF HISTORY OF TIME, A
Baker, Fred
WHITE TRASH
Baker, Ian
MR. BASEBALL
Ballhaus, Michael
BRAM STOKER'S DRACULA
MAMBO KINGS, THE
Banks, Larry
JUICE
Barrett, Jim
STEAL AMERICA
Barrio, Cusi
WELCOME TO OBLIVION
Bartkowiak, Andrzej
HARD PROMISES
STRANGER AMONG US, A
Bartoli, Adolfo
BAD CHANNELS
DEMONIC TOYS
DOCTOR MORDRID
NETHERWORLD
SEEDPEOPLE
TRANCERS III: DETH LIVES
Baszak, Miroslaw
HIGHWAY 61
Batac, Joe
EYE OF THE EAGLE 3
FIELD OF FIRE
Baum, Jurgen
SLUMBER PARTY MASSACRE 3
Baum, William Brooks
MONTANA RUN, THE
Bazelli, Bojan
DEEP COVER
Beato, Affonso
OVER HER DEAD BODY
Becker, Manuel
PANAMA DECEPTION, THE
Bellis, Andreas
HIRED TO KILL
Bendtsen, Henning
ZENTROPA
Benjamin, Mark
DAMNED IN THE USA
Bennett, Dean
KILLER IMAGE
Benvenuti, Roberto
INDIO 2 - THE REVOLT
Beristain, Gabriel
DISTINGUISHED GENTLEMAN, THE
K2
Berrie, John
QUARREL, THE
Biddle, Adrian
1492: THE CONQUEST OF PARADISE
Biziou, Peter
CITY OF JOY
DAMAGE
Blakey, Ken
MAXIMUM FORCE
SUNSET STRIP
Blank, Harrod
WILD WHEELS
Blank, Les
WILD WHEELS
Blaylock, Layton
CONFESSIONS OF A SERIAL KILLER
Blood, D.H.
ARMED FOR ACTION
Blood, David
STEELE'S LAW
Bode, Ralf
LEAVING NORMAL
LOVE FIELD
Bogner, Ludek
PSYCHIC
Bojorques, Francisco
BARBARIAN QUEEN II: THE EMPRESS STRIKES BACK
Bollinger, Alun
SOLDIER'S TALE, A
Bonilla, Peter
MAGICAL WORLD OF CHUCK JONES, THE
Bota, Rick
BLOODFIST III: FORCED TO FIGHT
Bowen, Richard
ARTICLE 99
PURE COUNTRY
Boyd, Russell
FOREVER YOUNG
WHITE MEN CAN'T JUMP
Brabbee, Kurt
HOMEBOYS
Bragado, Julio
CTHULHU MANSION
Brinkmann, Robert
ENCINO MAN
Brooks, Robert
WHO SHOT PATAKANGO?
Bruhne, Frank
DEMON IN MY VIEW, A
Buckley, Dick
NAKED OBSESSION
Bukowski, Bobby
SHAKES THE CLOWN
Burberry, Vance
MEATBALLS 4
Burgess, Don
MO' MONEY
Burstall, Dan
FATHER
HUNTING
LADYBUGS
Burton, Geoff
FLIRTING
Burum, Stephen H.
HOFFA
MAN TROUBLE
RAISING CAIN
Butler, Bill
WILDFIRE
Butler, Rick
COLOR ADJUSTMENT
Byers, Frank
BLIND VISION
Byrne, Bobby
THIS IS MY LIFE

Callaway, Thomasy
ONE LAST RUN
Callaway, Tom
CRITTERS 4
Carlson, Van
HUGH HEFNER: ONCE UPON A TIME
Carmack, Kenneth
LASER MOON
Carpenter, Russell
LAWNMOWER MAN, THE
PET SEMATARY II
Carter, James L.
ONE FALSE MOVE
Caso, Alan
CAGED FEAR
Catonne, Francois
INDOCHINE
Chan Pui-kai
ONCE UPON A TIME IN CHINA
Chan Tung-chuen
ONCE UPON A TIME IN CHINA
Chapman, Michael
WHISPERS IN THE DARK
Charters, Rodney
STEPHEN KING'S SLEEPWALKERS
Chinon, Henry
BREATHING FIRE
Chressanthis, James
LEATHER JACKETS
Chung, David
ONCE UPON A TIME IN CHINA
Collin, Francoise
BEATING HEART, A
Connell, David
HUNTING
Connor, John
JOURNEY OF HONOR
Connor, John J.
VAGRANT, THE
Conroy, Jack
PLAYBOYS, THE
Cooper, Douglas
BROTHER'S KEEPER
Cope, Paul
WILD WHEELS
Coulter, Michael
MONSTER IN A BOX
WHERE ANGELS FEAR TO TREAD
Crain, Michael
MIDNIGHT FEAR
Cronenweth, Jordan
FINAL ANALYSIS
Cundey, Dean
DEATH BECOMES HER
Czapsky, Stefan
BATMAN RETURNS
BRIEF HISTORY OF TIME, A
PRELUDE TO A KISS
Dahan, Yves
DOES THIS MEAN WE'RE MARRIED?
NEAR MISSES
Dakota, Reno
AMERICAN FABULOUS
Darling, Jeff
CROSSING, THE

Darrow, Jenny
FEED
David, Zoltan
MEGAVILLE
Davis, Elliot
CUTTING EDGE, THE
SHAKES THE CLOWN
Davis, Michael
WOMAN, HER MEN AND HER FUTON, A
De Bont, Jan
BASIC INSTINCT
LETHAL WEAPON 3
SHINING THROUGH
De Keyzer, Bruno
DOUBLE VISION
De Segonzac, Jean
LAWS OF GRAVITY
Deakins, Roger
PASSION FISH
THUNDERHEART
DeBorman, John
DEAD CERTAIN
Dechant, David
TOGETHER ALONE
DeHaeck, Hughes
SCANNERS III: THE TAKEOVER
DeKeyzer, Bruno
AFRAID OF THE DARK
ELEGANT CRIMINEL, L'
Del Ruth, Thomas
KUFFS
LITTLE SISTER
MIGHTY DUCKS, THE
Delville, Bernard
NIGHT AND DAY
Deming, Peter
MY COUSIN VINNY
SCORCHERS
DeNove, Thomas F.
SECRET GAMES
DeSalvo, Joe
JOHNNY SUEDE
Desatoff, Paul
MIRROR IMAGES
Dessalles, Olivier
NIGHT AND DAY
Di Battista, Giorgio
BEYOND JUSTICE
Diamond, Ron
PHANTOM OF THE RITZ
Dickerson, Ernest
COUSIN BOBBY
MALCOLM X
DiGiacomo, Franco
FINE ROMANCE, A
DiPalma, Carlo
HUSBANDS AND WIVES
SHADOWS AND FOG
Dirlam, John
FATAL INSTINCT
Dirse, Zoe
WISECRACKS
Dobo, Michael
PANAMA DECEPTION, THE
Donnelly, John
TUNE, THE

Dougherty, Jeff
LUNATICS: A LOVE STORY
Drake, John
PRIMARY MOTIVE
Draper, Robert
DR. GIGGLES
Duggan, Bryan
RUBIN & ED
Dunn, Andrew
BLAME IT ON THE BELLBOY
BODYGUARD, THE
Durham, Sarah
FEED
Elmes, Frederick
NIGHT ON EARTH
Elswit, Robert
HAND THAT ROCKS THE CRADLE, THE
WATERLAND
Emir, Florence
BEATING HEART, A
England, Brian
ONLY YOU
England, Bryan
GATE II
Evdemon, Nikos
GETTING MARRIED IN BUFFALO JUMP
Fante, John
DEATH HOUSE
Fante, John V.
ORIGINAL INTENT
Fauntleroy, Don E.
MUNCHIE
Fenner, John
MUPPET CHRISTMAS CAROL, THE
Fermenia, Paco
PEPI, LUCI, BOM AND OTHER GIRLS ON THE HEAP
Fernberger, Peter
JUST LIKE IN THE MOVIES
MARTIAL LAW 2: UNDERCOVER
MINDWARP
MISSION OF JUSTICE
Ferris, Michael
I DON'T BUY KISSES ANYMORE
Fichter, Rick
ADVENTURES IN DINOSAUR CITY
SOCIETY
Fisher, Gerry
DIGGSTOWN
Fortier, Jacques
SNAKEEATER III . . . HIS LAW
Fortunato, Ron
FATHERS AND SONS
Fraisse, Robert
LOVER, THE
Fraker, William A.
HONEYMOON IN VEGAS
MEMOIRS OF AN INVISIBLE MAN
Francis, Freddie
BRENDA STARR
SCHOOL TIES
Fraser, Larry J.
BEYOND DARKNESS
Fraser, Tom
LIFE ON THE EDGE

Fresco, Bob
WISECRACKS
Fujimoto, Tak
GLADIATOR
NIGHT AND THE CITY
Fujiwara, Kei
TETSUO: THE IRON MAN
Galfas, Timothy
NEON CITY
Garcia, Rodrigo
DANZON
Garcia, Ron
STORYVILLE
TWIN PEAKS: FIRE WALK WITH ME
Geddes, David
BLACK ICE
Gell, Frank
POPE MUST DIET!, THE
Gelsini, Alessio
STATION, THE
Gibbons, Rodney
DEADBOLT
TWIN SISTERS
Gibson, Paul
REFRIGERATOR, THE
Gibson, Sue
SECRET FRIENDS
Gilbert, Peter
AMERICAN DREAM
Godet, Serge
EMMANUELLE 6
Goi, Michael
HELL MASTER
Goldblatt, Stephen
CONSENTING ADULTS
Goldfine, Lloyd
JUMPIN' AT THE BONEYARD
Gondre, Jean Francis
WINTER IN LISBON, THE
Goodnoff, Irv
TO PROTECT AND SERVE
Goodnoff, Irvin
RESURRECTED, THE
Gordower, Pierre
NIGHT AND DAY
Grass, Steve
INTO THE SUN
Graver, Gary
ROOTS OF EVIL
SPIRITS
Greatrex, Richard
LUNATIC, THE
Green, Jack N.
LOVE CRIMES
UNFORGIVEN
Greenberg, Adam
LOVE HURTS
SISTER ACT
TOYS
Grumman, Francis
EXILED IN AMERICA
Gu Changwei
LIFE ON A STRING
Gurfinkel, David
BLINK OF AN EYE
Haagensen, Craig
COUSIN BOBBY
Haitkin, Jacques
MOM AND DAD SAVE THE WORLD
WE'RE TALKIN' SERIOUS MONEY
Hall, Conrad L.
JENNIFER EIGHT
Hammer, Victor
FALLING FROM GRACE
Hayes, Robert
MIND, BODY & SOUL
Hayes, William
SOLDIER'S FORTUNE
Hayman, James
BREAKING THE RULES
BUFFY THE VAMPIRE SLAYER
Hayward, Kevin
MY GRANDPA IS A VAMPIRE
Hazard, John
THANK YOU AND GOOD NIGHT!
Hebb, Brian
OH, WHAT A NIGHT
Henri, Gilles
VAN GOGH
Herrington, David
PRIMO BABY
Hershberger, Ed
THERE'S NOTHING OUT THERE
Heschong, Gregg
ULTRAVIOLET
Hochstatter, Zoran
976-EVIL II
Hogan, Bill
INVASION OF THE SPACE PREACHERS
Holland, Keith
SEX CRIMES
Holst, Bodo
PUSHED TO THE LIMIT
Hora, John
HONEY, I BLEW UP THE KID
Hosek, George
ILLUSIONS
Hyams, Peter
STAY TUNED
Illik, Josef
EAR, THE
Irwin, Mark
PASSENGER 57
Isaacks, Levie
GUYVER, THE
Isoli, Marco
EVIL CLUTCH
Jafa, Arthur
DAUGHTERS OF THE DUST
Jannelli, Tony
COUSIN BOBBY
Janschewski, Klaus
AFFENGEIL
Jewett, Tom
MIKEY
Jost, Jon
ALL THE VERMEERS IN NEW YORK
Kaluta, Villenn
CLOSE TO EDEN
Kaman, Steven
COMRADES IN ARMS
Karpick, Avi
DELTA HEAT
ODDBALL HALL
Karpik, Avi
FINEST HOUR, THE
Kato, Yudai
GODZILLA VS. BIOLLANTE
Keating, Kevin
AMERICAN DREAM
Kelsch, Ken
BAD LIEUTENANT
Kemper, Victor J.
BEETHOVEN
Kenny, Francis
CLASS ACT
COLD HEAVEN
Kershaw, Glen
ALMOST PREGNANT
Khondji, Darius
DELICATESSEN
Kirsten, Sven
MISTRESS
Klosinski, Edward
KILL CRUISE
ZENTROPA
Knovak, Danny
ULTIMATE DESIRES
Knowland, Nic
CHILDREN, THE
Koestner, Paul A.
PUERTO RICAN MAMBO (NOT A MUSICAL), THE
Kovacs, Laszlo
RADIO FLYER
Kristiansen, Henning
DAY IN OCTOBER, A
Kuchar, Mike
AFFENGEIL
Kuras, Ellen
SWOON
Lachman, Edward
BACKTRACK
LIGHT SLEEPER
LONDON KILLS ME
MISSISSIPPI MASALA
MY NEW GUN
Lagerroos, Kjell
DADDY AND THE MUSCLE ACADEMY
Lam Kwok-wah
ONCE UPON A TIME IN CHINA
SUPERCOP: POLICE STORY III
Lambert, John
FATE
Lanci, Giuseppe
HUSBANDS AND LOVERS
JOHNNY STECCHINO
Lanser, Roger
PETER'S FRIENDS
Laskus, Jacek
COUSIN BOBBY
Laszlo, Andrew
NEWSIES
Latoure, Ron
FROZEN ASSETS
Layton, Vernon
UNDER SUSPICION

Lazan, Stan
SMOOTH TALKER
Lebedev, Pavel
ADAM'S RIB
Lebo, Henry M.
NICKEL & DIME
LeMener, Jean-Yves
ROAD TO RUIN
Lent, Dean
GAS FOOD LODGING
Leonetti, Matthew F.
LEAP OF FAITH
Lepine, Jean
BOB ROBERTS
PLAYER, THE
Levinson, G.J.
HELLROLLER
Lhomme, Pierre
VOYAGER
Lieberman, Charlie
SOUTH CENTRAL
Lindenlaub, Karl Walter
EYE OF THE STORM
UNIVERSAL SOLDIER
Lindley, John
SNEAKERS
Linzey, Philip
CAFE ROMEO
Lively, Gerry
HELLRAISER III: HELL ON EARTH
PALE BLOOD
WAXWORK II: LOST IN TIME
Loiseleux, Jacques
VAN GOGH
Macat, Julio
HOME ALONE 2:
LOST IN NEW YORK
Machuel, Emmanuel
VAN GOGH
MacKay, Mark
DEADLY CURRENTS
MacMillan, Kenneth
OF MICE AND MEN
Maidment, Rex
ENCHANTED APRIL
Maloney, Denis
COMPLEX WORLD
Manes, Vincent
PUERTO RICAN MAMBO
(NOT A MUSICAL), THE
Markey, Dave
1991: THE YEAR PUNK BROKE
Mathers, Jim
HOUSE IV
ROUND TRIP TO HEAVEN
Maynard, Gordon
BRONX WAR, THE
McAlpine, Donald
MEDICINE MAN
PATRIOT GAMES
McGrath, Martin
PROOF
Meheux, Phil
RUBY
Menzies, Jr., Peter
WHITE SANDS
Mertes, Raffaele
DEVIL'S DAUGHTER, THE
Meurisse, Jean-Paul
ZENTROPA
Michaels, James
OTHER WOMAN, THE
Michalak, Richard
CHILDREN OF THE NIGHT
DOUBLE TROUBLE
GUILTY AS CHARGED
3 NINJAS
Mikesch, Elfi
MY FATHER IS COMING
Miller, Dusty
COLD JUSTICE
Mills, Alec
ACES: IRON EAGLE III
CHRISTOPHER COLUMBUS:
THE DISCOVERY
Minsky, Charles
GUN IN BETTY LOU'S
HANDBAG, THE
Mokri, Amir
FREEJACK
Molina, Bill
DANCE WITH DEATH
Montheillet, Max
EMMANUELLE 6
Morris, Mark
DO OR DIE
Morrisey, Kevin
KILLER TOMATOES EAT FRANCE!
WITCHCRAFT IV: VIRGIN HEART
Moura, Edgar
KICKBOXER 3: THE ART OF WAR
Munch, Christopher
HOURS AND TIMES, THE
Munzi, Maximo
KILL LINE
Myhrman, Dan
OX, THE
Namir, David "Dudy"
DESERT KICKBOXER
Navarro, Guillermo
CABEZA DE VACA
Neckelbrouck, Jean-Claude
NIGHT AND DAY
Negrin, Sol
HAPPY HELL NIGHT
Neville, Rex
FREDDIE AS F.R.O.7
Neyman, Yuri
BACK IN THE U.S.S.R.
Nowak, Danny
MANIAC WARRIORS
Nunn, Adam
BLOOD ON THE BADGE
Nykvist, Sven
CHAPLIN
Okada, Daryn
CAPTAIN RON
Omens, Woody
BOOMERANG
Ondricek, Miroslav
LEAGUE OF THEIR OWN, A
Orona, Gary
BIKINI CARWASH COMPANY, THE
Pages, Luc
CONTE DE PRINTEMPS
Paone, Bob
BASKET CASE 3: THE PROGENY
BODY WAVES
Papamichael, Phedon
POISON IVY
PRAYER OF THE ROLLERBOYS
Parke, Andrew
CENTER OF THE WEB
Parmet, Phil
IN THE SOUP
Parry, Mark
FINISHING TOUCH, THE
Pepin, Richard
DEADLY BET
FINAL IMPACT
OUT FOR BLOOD
STREET CRIMES
Perrault, David
BEETHOVEN LIVES UPSTAIRS
Perry, Hart
AMERICAN DREAM
Persson, Jorgen
BEST INTENTIONS, THE
Peterman, Donald
MR. SATURDAY NIGHT
Petersen, Curtis
TALONS OF THE EAGLE
TIGER CLAWS
Petersson, Mark
AMERICAN DREAM
Petriccione, Italo
MEDITERRANEO
Pfister, Wally
ANIMAL INSTINCTS
IN THE HEAT OF PASSION
LOWER LEVEL
NIGHT RHYTHMS
SECRET GAMES
Pickering, Joseph
ROCK & ROLL COWBOYS
Pierce, Mike
SAVAGE INSTINCT
Pierce-Roberts, Tony
HOWARDS END
Pinter, Tom
LANDSLIDE
Pizer, Larry
FOLKS!
Plenert, Thomas
LOCKED-UP TIME
Plummer, Mark
WATERDANCE, THE
Pratt, Roger
BERNARD AND THE GENIE
YEAR OF THE COMET
Priess, Jeff
BROKEN NOSES
Protat, Francois
BEAUTIFUL DREAMERS
CLEARCUT
Quinn, Declan
COUSIN BOBBY

Rabier, Jean
CRY OF THE OWL, THE
INSPECTOR LAVARDIN
Rafferty, Kevin
FEED
Reizes, Stephen
CANVAS
Renaut, Philippe
CONTE DE PRINTEMPS
Reshovsky, Mark
WILD ORCHID 2:
TWO SHADES OF BLUE
Reynolds, Buster
LIGHT IN THE JUNGLE, THE
Richardson, Robert
FEW GOOD MEN, A
Richmond, Anthony B.
CANDYMAN
Richmond, Tom
HEAVEN IS A PLAYGROUND
MIDNIGHT CLEAR, A
ROADSIDE PROPHETS
Roberts, Mathieu
AMERICAN DREAM
Rogers, Richard P.
PICTURES FROM A REVOLUTION
Roland, Erich
DEEP BLUES
Rosenberg, Ilan
SEXUAL RESPONSE
Rotunno, Giuseppe
ONCE UPON A CRIME
Rousselot, Philippe
RIVER RUNS THROUGH IT, A
Ruiz-Anchia, Juan
GLENGARRY GLEN ROSS
Ruse, Travis
AMERICAN FABULOUS
Ryan, Ellery
EFFICIENCY EXPERT, THE
Ryan, Paul
ALAN & NAOMI
LONELY HEARTS
Sacher, Luke
DAMNED IN THE USA
Salminen, Timo
MATCH FACTORY GIRL, THE
Salmones, Javier G.
SHOOTING ELIZABETH
Salomon, Amnon
CUP FINAL
DOUBLE EDGE
Salomon, Mikael
FAR AND AWAY
Salzmann, Bernard
MIRACLE BEACH
Sandtroen, Morten
TEXAS TENOR:
THE ILLINOIS JACQUET STORY
Santhavee, Visidh
IN GOLD WE TRUST
Sarossy, Paul
ADJUSTER, THE
Scantlebury, Glen
STEAL AMERICA
Schaaf, Geoff
ALL-AMERICAN MURDER
Schlair, Doron
ROCK SOUP
Schliessler, Tobias
COMMON BONDS
Schmidt, Ronn
BEASTMASTER 2:
THROUGH THE PORTAL OF TIME
GHOULIES III:
GHOULIES GO TO COLLEGE
SHAKING THE TREE
Schreiber, Nancy
KISS ME A KILLER
Seale, John
LORENZO'S OIL
Sebaldt, Christian
BLOODFIST IV: DIE TRYING
Sekula, Andrzej
RESERVOIR DOGS
Semler, Dean
POWER OF ONE, THE
Serra, Eduardo
HAIRDRESSER'S HUSBAND, THE
Shagayev, Alexander
RASPAD
Shams, Hamid
PAINTING THE TOWN
Shizuka, Akira
SILK ROAD, THE
Sigel, Tomy
CROSSING THE BRIDGE
Simpson, Geoffrey
TILL THERE WAS YOU
Sinkovics, Geza
FROZEN ASSETS
SEVERED TIES
Sissel, Sandi
THANK YOU AND GOOD NIGHT!
Slonisko, Federiko
TROLL 2
Smith, Dan
PAMELA PRINCIPLE, THE
Smith, Gregory
TERMINAL BLISS
Sokol, Yuri
DIARY OF A HITMAN
Soriano, Antonio
GIVING, THE
Southon, Mike
CODE NAME: CHAOS
Sova, Peter
BED & BREAKFAST
STRAIGHT TALK
Spears, Ross
TO RENDER A LIFE
Spiller, Michael
SIMPLE MEN
Spinotti, Dante
LAST OF THE MOHICANS, THE
Stapleton, Oliver
HERO
Steiger, Ueli
SINGLES
Stevens, Alan
BRIDE OF KILLER NERD
Stokes, John
HURRICANE SMITH
Strasburg, Ivan
CRISSCROSS
Stringer, Michael
HIRED TO KILL
Suhrstedt, Timothy
NOISES OFF
TRACES OF RED
Surtees, Bruce
CHAINS OF GOLD
Suschitzky, Peter
PUBLIC EYE, THE
Suslov, Misha
RUNESTONE, THE
Takahashi, Hirokata
PROFESSIONAL, THE
Taylor, Christopher
AMITYVILLE 1992:
IT'S ABOUT TIME
Teel, Dustin
HUGH HEFNER: ONCE UPON A TIME
Thompson, Jamie
DESIRE AND HELL AT SUNSET
MOTEL
Thomson, Alex
ALIEN3
Thorin, Donald E.
COLLISION COURSE
OUT ON A LIMB
SCENT OF A WOMAN
Tickner, Clive
SPLIT SECOND
Tidy, Frank
STOP! OR MY MOM WILL SHOOT
UNDER SIEGE
Toll, John
WIND
Tomosky-Franco, Rosemary
PUERTO RICAN MAMBO
(NOT A MUSICAL), THE
Tovoli, Luciano
SINGLE WHITE FEMALE
Treu, Wolfgang
BECOMING COLETTE
Trow, Alan M.
PROJECT: SHADOWCHASER
Truschkovski, Vassili
RASPAD
Tsukamoto, Shinya
TETSUO: THE IRON MAN
Turner, George Jesse
35 UP
Ulyanov, John
BLACKBELT
Van De Sande, Theo
BIG GIRLS DON'T CRY . . . THEY
GET EVEN
WAYNE'S WORLD
Van Haren Noman, Eric
INSIDE EDGE
Vanden Ende, Walther
TOTO LE HEROS
Vicente, Mark
SARAFINA!
Vidgeon, Robin
HIGHWAY TO HELL
Villalobos, Reynaldo
AMERICAN ME

Von Sternberg, Nick
LIFE ON THE EDGE
Wacks, Steven
DRIVE
Wagenstein, Emil
DEATHSTALKER IV: MATCH OF TITANS
Wages, William
LOVE POTION NO. 9
Wagner, Roy H.
MORTUARY ACADEMY
Waite, Ric
RAPID FIRE
Wakeford, Kent
CHINA O'BRIEN II
NIGHT EYES 2
Walker, Jon
ESCAPE FROM . . . SURVIVAL ZONE
Wallner, Jack
VAGRANT, THE
Walsh, David M.
BRAIN DONORS
Walther, Jurg
TRAINED TO FIGHT
Wang Wing-heng
HARD-BOILED
Warrilow, Peter
ADVENTURES IN SPYING
Watanabe, Makoto
LITTLE NOISES
Waters, Philip Alan
CAPTAIN AMERICA
Watkin, David
USED PEOPLE
Weber, Alicia
THANK YOU AND GOOD NIGHT!
Wein, Yossi
HOUSE OF USHER, THE
HUMAN SHIELD, THE
Welt, Philippe
ALBERTO EXPRESS
Wertwijn, Lex
LILY WAS HERE
Westbury, Ken
MONKEY BOY
Wexler, Haskell
BABE, THE
Willis, Mark
TIGER CLAWS
Wilson, Barry
MAXIMUM BREAKOUT
Wilson, Ian
CRYING GAME, THE
EDWARD II
Wincenty, Rick
PROM NIGHT IV - DELIVER US FROM EVIL
Winding, Romain
DISCRETE, LA
Wolfe, Jerry
CAN IT BE LOVE
Wolski, Dariusz
CHAINS OF GOLD
Wong, Arthur
ONCE UPON A TIME IN CHINA
Wong, Bill
ONCE UPON A TIME IN CHINA
Worth, David
LADY DRAGON
Yaconelli, Steve
DARK HORSE
Yeoman, Robert
LINGUINI INCIDENT, THE
RAMPAGE
Zapata, Tony
HUGH HEFNER: ONCE UPON A TIME
Zhao Fei
RAISE THE RED LANTERN
Zitzermann, Bernard
FAVOUR, THE WATCH, AND THE VERY BIG FISH, THE

COSTUMES

Adey-Jones, Del
COLD HEAVEN
Aguilar, Ignacia
BARBARIAN QUEEN II: THE EMPRESS STRIKES BACK
Allen, Marit
SHINING THROUGH
WIND
Anttila, Ann Mari
BEST INTENTIONS, THE
Armani, Giorgio
HUSBANDS AND LOVERS
Aroff-Lane, Libbie
LONELY HEARTS
Artinano, Javier
WINTER IN LISBON, THE
Atwood, Colleen
LORENZO'S OIL
LOVE FIELD
Bafaloukos, Eugenie
MY NEW GUN
Barbara, Gordon
NIGHT ON EARTH
Barnett, Ccerri
PROOF
Baron, Lenny
CENTER OF THE WEB
Baum, Barbara
BECOMING COLETTE
VOYAGER
Bava, Magda
NIGHT ON EARTH
Beavan, Jenny
HOWARDS END
Bergstrom, Cynthia
BACK IN THE U.S.S.R.
Bertram, Susan
GAS FOOD LODGING
SEVERED TIES
Berwick, Donna
JUICE
Blondeel, Michele
NIGHT AND DAY
Bloomfield, John
CHRISTOPHER COLUMBUS: THE DISCOVERY
Bonmati, Nereida
AMANTES
Boudreaux, Christine
DEADLY BET
SUNSET STRIP
Boyle, Consolata
PLAYBOYS, THE
Bracco, Elizabeth
IN THE SOUP
Braga, Isabela
KICKBOXER 3: THE ART OF WAR
Brewer, Miv
TILL THERE WAS YOU
Bridges, Mark
WAXWORK II: LOST IN TIME
Bright, John
HOWARDS END
Bronson, Tom
HONEY, I BLEW UP THE KID
Bronson-Howard, Aude
FINAL ANALYSIS
SCENT OF A WOMAN
Bruno, Richard
NIGHT AND THE CITY
UNDER SIEGE
Burks, Arline
DAUGHTERS OF THE DUST
Burrows, Jami
LOWER LEVEL
Cacavas, Lisa
MUNCHIE
Caceres, Maria
CTHULHU MANSION
Cain, Candice
BLIND VISION
Calin, Angela
MEATBALLS 4
Camacho, Manuela
PEPI, LUCI, BOM AND OTHER GIRLS ON THE HEAP
Cameron, Jeannie
FATHER
Camusi, Susan F.
ORIGINAL INTENT
Canonero, Milena
DAMAGE
SINGLE WHITE FEMALE
Carter, Ruth E.
MALCOLM X
Chance, Stacey
DELTA HEAT
Cheek, Taylor
LITTLE NOISES
Chudej, Stephen M.
SHAKES THE CLOWN
Cilliers, Dianna
HOUSE OF USHER, THE
Coates, Susan
PETER'S FRIENDS
Cole, Lawane
RUBIN & ED
Cole, Michelle
MO' MONEY
Collie, Stephanie
PETER'S FRIENDS
Cone, Nancy
BACKTRACK
Corbett, Elizabeth
BIKINI SUMMER 2
Corbett, Hilary
GETTING MARRIED IN BUFFALO JUMP

Cox, Betsy
HOUSESITTER
Cozzolino, Vera
DEVIL'S DAUGHTER, THE
Crichton, Philip
PROJECT: SHADOWCHASER
Culotta, Ann
FROZEN ASSETS
Cunliffe, Shay
OF MICE AND MEN
D'Arcy, Timothy
LOVE POTION NO. 9
Dandanell, Lotte
DAY IN OCTOBER, A
Daniel, Malissa
COOL WORLD
Dee, Patte
I DON'T BUY KISSES ANYMORE
Delgado, Lothar
MIRROR IMAGES
NIGHT RHYTHMS
OTHER WOMAN, THE
PAMELA PRINCIPLE, THE
WOMAN, HER MEN AND HER FUTON, A
Delgado, Ricardo
MIRROR IMAGES
NIGHT RHYTHMS
OTHER WOMAN, THE
PAMELA PRINCIPLE, THE
SECRET GAMES
DeNesle, Yvonne Sassinot
ELEGANT CRIMINEL, L'
LOVER, THE
Denny, Keith
K2
DeSanto, Susie
RUBY
DiBorgo, Valerie Pozzo
DELICATESSEN
Dickson, Ngila
MY GRANDPA IS A VAMPIRE
DiGagni, Tess
AUNTIE LEE'S MEAT PIES
Dillon, Rudy
ARTICLE 99
Donfeld
GLADIATOR
Dover, Katherine D.
VAGRANT, THE
Dresbach, Terry
LITTLE SISTER
RUNESTONE, THE
Drew, Laurie
SCANNERS III: THE TAKEOVER
Ducoulombier, Annie
NEAR MISSES
Dunn, John A.
WHISPERS IN THE DARK
Emir, Florence
BEATING HEART, A
Englesman, Julie
PRIMARY MOTIVE
Evans, Leesa
ULTRAVIOLET
Everton, Deborah
WHITE SANDS
Farrell, Peggy
BRENDA STARR
Fedoruk, Sharon
BLACK ICE
Ferry, April
BABE, THE
RADIO FLYER
UNLAWFUL ENTRY
Figueroa, Totita
CABEZA DE VACA
Filipe, Ruy
LIGHT IN THE JUNGLE, THE
Finkelman, Wayne A.
DIGGSTOWN
Finlayson, Bruce
MR. BASEBALL
Fisher, Linda
JUST LIKE IN THE MOVIES
Flynt, Cynthia
LEAGUE OF THEIR OWN, A
LITTLE VEGAS
PASSION FISH
Fort, Mary Jane
LAWNMOWER MAN, THE
Fraisse, Claire
NIGHT ON EARTH
France, Marie
BUFFY THE VAMPIRE SLAYER
ENCINO MAN
STOP! OR MY MOM WILL SHOOT
Frogley, Louise
STORYVILLE
Fujiwara, Kei
TETSUO: THE IRON MAN
Fustier, Magali
INSPECTOR LAVARDIN
Gammie, Susan
HARD PROMISES
Gant, Arlene
DEEP COVER
Gayraud, Pierre-Yves
INDOCHINE
Gemser, Laura M.
BEYOND DARKNESS
Giammona, Ted
INSIDE EDGE
Gilmore, Aline
DEADBOLT
PSYCHIC
Gissi, Gianna
JOHNNY STECCHINO
Gorlan, Valentia
RASPAD
Granata, Dona
DARK HORSE
Greenwood, Jane
GLENGARRY GLEN ROSS
Gregory, Antoinette
SPLIT SECOND
Gresham, Gloria
FEW GOOD MEN, A
Griffiths, Pat
LUNATIC, THE
Gross, Ellen
POISON IVY
Guinno, Irina
CLOSE TO EDEN
Hanafin, Hope
MISSISSIPPI MASALA
PHANTOM OF THE RITZ
Harwood, Shuna
DEMON IN MY VIEW, A
DOUBLE VISION
Haston, Jessica
JOHNNY SUEDE
SWOON
Healey, Kate
TIGER CLAWS
Heimann, Betsy
RESERVOIR DOGS
Hemming, Lindy
BLAME IT ON THE BELLBOY
WATERLAND
Hendrickson, Calista
DIARY OF A HITMAN
Henriksen, Laurie
EYE OF THE STORM
Hetland, Carla
CAFE ROMEO
Hibbs, John
CHILDREN, THE
Hicklin, Walker
PRELUDE TO A KISS
Hilkamo, Tuula
MATCH FACTORY GIRL, THE
Hooper, Helen
ROCK & ROLL COWBOYS
Hornung, Richard
HERO
Howe, Monica
WHERE ANGELS FEAR TO TREAD
Huang Lihua
RAISE THE RED LANTERN
Hung Wei-Chuk
SUPERCOP: POLICE STORY III
Hurley, Jay
COLD JUSTICE
FOLKS!
HOME ALONE 2: LOST IN NEW YORK
Ishioka, Eiko
BRAM STOKER'S DRACULA
Jamison-Tanchuck, Francine
BOOMERANG
DISTINGUISHED GENTLEMAN, THE
Jardine, Meta
IN THE HEAT OF PASSION
KISS ME A KILLER
Jensen, Lisa
CRISSCROSS
FREEJACK
GUN IN BETTY LOU'S HANDBAG, THE
OVER HER DEAD BODY
Jensen, Sandra Araya
SLUMBER PARTY MASSACRE 3
Johnston, Joanna
DEATH BECOMES HER
FAR AND AWAY
Jones, Gary
CONSENTING ADULTS
MAMBO KINGS, THE
STRANGER AMONG US, A

Jorry, Corrine
TOUS LES MATINS DU MONDE
Julian, Alexander
PLAYER, THE
Kaczenski, Heidi
CAPTAIN AMERICA
SCORCHERS
Kaplan, Sashanna
DESERT KICKBOXER
Kaufman, Susan Michel
SHAKING THE TREE
Kaufmann, Susan
HEAVEN IS A PLAYGROUND
Kawasaki, Kanji
GODZILLA VS. BIOLLANTE
Kelly, Bridget
BOB ROBERTS
MAMBO KINGS, THE
Kemper, Florence
HIGHWAY TO HELL
King, Terri
ALMOST PREGNANT
Knode, Charles
1492: THE CONQUEST OF PARADISE
Kondos, Aphrodite
HUNTING
Krumbachova, Ester
EAR, THE
Kurland, Jeffrey
HUSBANDS AND WIVES
SHADOWS AND FOG
THIS IS MY LIFE
L'Annee, Valerie
ROAD TO RUIN
Lambert, Ann
NICKEL & DIME
Landau, Natasha
JUMPIN' AT THE BONEYARD
Larner-Corbett, Erika
TALONS OF THE EAGLE
LaVoi, Greg
DOUBLE TROUBLE
NIGHT EYES 2
976-EVIL II
Leamon, Ron
ONE FALSE MOVE
Leavell, Shawna
LEATHER JACKETS
MEGAVILLE
Lecours, Francoise
TWIN SISTERS
Lempicka, Mimi
POUR SACHA
Leone, Caroline
WITCHCRAFT IV: VIRGIN HEART
Levy, Rakefet
DOUBLE EDGE
Lewis, Robin
DEMONIC TOYS
Libby, Paris
NAKED OBSESSION
Lichmanova, Tatiana
BACK IN THE U.S.S.R.
Lisle, David
COMMON BONDS
Little, Debrae
SMOOTH TALKER
Long, William Ivey
CUTTING EDGE, THE
Lutter, Ellen
THANK YOU AND GOOD NIGHT!
Lyall, Susan
THUNDERHEART
Madden, Betty
BEASTMASTER 2: THROUGH THE PORTAL OF TIME
DESIRE AND HELL AT SUNSET MOTEL
Maginnis, Molly
ONCE UPON A CRIME
SISTER ACT
Malterre, Marie
DISCRETE, LA
Mangus, Imogen
CODE NAME: CHAOS
Mani, Maya
ADJUSTER, THE
Massone, Nicoletta
CANVAS
May, Mona
HOUSE IV
3 NINJAS
McBride, Elizabeth
LOVE HURTS
McKinley, Tom
WE'RE TALKIN' SERIOUS MONEY
Meltzer, Linda "Lulu"
GUYVER, THE
Mirojnick, Ellen
BASIC INSTINCT
CHAPLIN
Mitchell, Peter
LOVE FIELD
Mollo, John
CHAPLIN
Moorcroft, Judy
CITY OF JOY
Moore, Dan
TRESPASS
Morgan, Bernardine
DOUBLE EDGE
Moriaty, Prudence
ROADSIDE PROPHETS
Moriceau, Norma
PATRIOT GAMES
Murray-Walsh, Merrily
PRAYER OF THE ROLLERBOYS
Mussenden, Isis
LADYBUGS
WATERDANCE, THE
Myers, Ruth
MR. SATURDAY NIGHT
Nadoolman, Deborah
INNOCENT BLOOD
Napier, Sheena
ENCHANTED APRIL
Nicholson, Lesley
ACES: IRON EAGLE III
Nierhaus, Brigitte
NIGHT AND DAY
Nininger, Susan
BODYGUARD, THE
MISTRESS
Norris, Patricia
LEAVING NORMAL
TWIN PEAKS: FIRE WALK WITH ME
Oditz, Carol
ZEBRAHEAD
Ottobe-Melton, Giovanna
BREAKING THE RULES
Panni, Francesco
MEDITERRANEO
Pasternak, Beth
GATE II
Pasztor, Beatrix Aruna
GHOULIES III: GHOULIES GO TO COLLEGE
Patch, Karen
MIDNIGHT FEAR
Pehrsson, Inger
OX, THE
Perry, David
ALIEN3
Pescucci, Gabriella
INDOCHINE
Petrovich, Victoria
KILLER TOMATOES EAT FRANCE!
Phillips, Erica Edell
RAPID FIRE
Phipps, Diana
STREET CRIMES
Pickering, Loretta
DANCE WITH DEATH
Pickwell, Lynn
FATHERS AND SONS
Polcsa, Juliet
TERMINAL BLISS
Pollack, Bernie
RIVER RUNS THROUGH IT, A
SNEAKERS
Pollack, Leonard
CANDYMAN
HELLRAISER III: HELL ON EARTH
Powell, Sandy
CRYING GAME, THE
POPE MUST DIET!, THE
Pye, Katie
CROSSING, THE
Quesnel-Boursaus, Annie
HOT CHOCOLATE
Ramsey, Carol
CROSSING THE BRIDGE
Rand, Tom
POWER OF ONE, THE
Rasmussen, Manon
ZENTROPA
Read, Bobbie
RAISING CAIN
Reichek, Robyn
MOM AND DAD SAVE THE WORLD
Ringwood, Bob
ALIEN3
BATMAN RETURNS
Roberts, Amy
LONDON KILLS ME
Roberts, Rikki
WHITE TRASH
Robertson, Marcella
RESURRECTED, THE

Robinson, Jane
PUBLIC EYE, THE
Rosado, Carleen
BASKET CASE 3: THE PROGENY
PET SEMATARY II
Rose, Penny
UNDER SUSPICION
Rosenfeld, Hilary
TRACES OF RED
Roth, Ann
CONSENTING ADULTS
MAMBO KINGS, THE
SCHOOL TIES
STRANGER AMONG US, A
Routh, May
NEWSIES
Ruhm, Jane
BIG GIRLS DON'T CRY . . . THEY GET EVEN
Ruskin, Judy
MAN TROUBLE
Rutter, Barbara
1492: THE CONQUEST OF PARADISE
Samples, Nile
CHAINS OF GOLD
Sawaryn, David
BAD LIEUTENANT
Schklair, Julia
MIRACLE BEACH
Schnitzer, Peggy
LONELY HEARTS
Schofield, Tess
EFFICIENCY EXPERT, THE
Schutte, Ulrike
KILL CRUISE
Scott, Alexis
SEXUAL RESPONSE
Scott, Deborah L.
HOFFA
Secord, Ruth
BEAUTIFUL DREAMERS
OH, WHAT A NIGHT
Shine, Debbie
NEON CITY
Simbach, Lois
NETHERWORLD
SEEDPEOPLE
Slate, Deborah
ILLUSIONS
Slaughter, Jane
ARMED FOR ACTION
Smith, Polly
MUPPET CHRISTMAS CAROL, THE
Spiazzi, Alberto
HUSBANDS AND LOVERS
Stjernsward, Louise
AFRAID OF THE DARK
Syrkin, Yana
MARTIAL LAW 2: UNDERCOVER
MISSION OF JUSTICE
Talsky, Ron
COLLISION COURSE
Tavernier, Elisabeth
FAVOUR, THE WATCH, AND THE VERY BIG FISH, THE
Tax, Yan
LILY WAS HERE
Tfank, Barbara
MIDNIGHT CLEAR, A
Tillen, Jodie
STRAIGHT TALK
Tomlinson, Scott
DOLLY DEAREST
Tompkins, Joe
STAY TUNED
Turturice, Robert
BRAIN DONORS
Van Runkle, Theadora
LEAP OF FAITH
WILDFIRE
Van Well, Suzanne
TOTO LE HEROS
Vance-Straker, Marilyn
MEDICINE MAN
USED PEOPLE
YEAR OF THE COMET
Vega-Vasquez, Sylvia
AMERICAN ME
Versace, Gianni
FINE ROMANCE, A
Vieira, Kathy
CLEARCUT
Vogt, Mary
BATMAN RETURNS
KUFFS
Von Ernst, Richard
LINGUINI INCIDENT, THE
Von Mayrhauser, Jennifer
BED & BREAKFAST
CAPTAIN RON
HAND THAT ROCKS THE CRADLE, THE
PASSED AWAY
Von Puttkamer, Sheera
DEATH HOUSE
Waknin, Deborah
ONLY YOU
Weir, Mary Law
SOUTH CENTRAL
Weiss, Julie
HONEYMOON IN VEGAS
Welker, Alexandra
NIGHT ON EARTH
SIMPLE MEN
Wilson, Alonzo V.
ALAN & NAOMI
Wolsky, Albert
TOYS
Wood, Carol
MY COUSIN VINNY
Yu Ka-on
ONCE UPON A TIME IN CHINA
Zaltzman, Rochelle
FINEST HOUR, THE
Zbroniec, Ewa
EXILED IN AMERICA
Ziv, Rina
BLINK OF AN EYE

DIRECTORS

Abernathy, Lewis
HOUSE IV
Acevski, Jon
FREDDIE AS F.R.O.7
Adams, Daniel
PRIMARY MOTIVE
Akerman, Chantal
NIGHT AND DAY
Alan, Jordan
TERMINAL BLISS
Allen, Woody
HUSBANDS AND WIVES
SHADOWS AND FOG
Almodovar, Pedro
PEPI, LUCI, BOM AND OTHER GIRLS ON THE HEAP
Altman, Robert
PLAYER, THE
Anders, Allison
GAS FOOD LODGING
Anderson, Kurt
MARTIAL LAW 2: UNDERCOVER
Anderson, Steve
SOUTH CENTRAL
Annaud, Jean-Jacques
LOVER, THE
Apted, Michael
INCIDENT AT OGLALA
35 UP
THUNDERHEART
Araki, Gregg
LIVING END, THE
Aranda, Vicente
AMANTES
Arcady, Alexandre
POUR SACHA
Ardolino, Emile
SISTER ACT
Ashida, Toyoo
VAMPIRE HUNTER D
Attenborough, Richard
CHAPLIN
August, Bille
BEST INTENTIONS, THE
Avildsen, John G.
POWER OF ONE, THE
Baker, Kurt
IMPORTANCE OF BEING EARNEST, THE
Baker, Fred
WHITE TRASH
Bakshi, Ralph
COOL WORLD
Ballard, Carroll
WIND
Band, Charles
DOCTOR MORDRID
Band, Albert
DOCTOR MORDRID
Barnett, Steve
MINDWARP
MISSION OF JUSTICE
Beaird, David
SCORCHERS
Becker, Josh
LUNATICS: A LOVE STORY
Beeman, Greg
MOM AND DAD SAVE THE WORLD

Behar, Andrew
PAINTING THE TOWN
Belikov, Mikhail
RASPAD
Benigni, Roberto
JOHNNY STECCHINO
Bergman, Andrew
HONEYMOON IN VEGAS
Berlinger, Joe
BROTHER'S KEEPER
Berry, Tom
TWIN SISTERS
Binder, Mike
CROSSING THE BRIDGE
Birkinshaw, Alan
HOUSE OF USHER, THE
Blair, Mark
CONFESSIONS OF A SERIAL KILLER
Blank, Harrod
WILD WHEELS
Bluth, Don
ROCK-A-DOODLE
Blyth, David
MY GRANDPA IS A VAMPIRE
Bogdanovich, Peter
NOISES OFF
Bolognini, Mauro
HUSBANDS AND LOVERS
Borden, Lizzie
LOVE CRIMES
Borris, Clay
PROM NIGHT IV - DELIVER US FROM EVIL
Bosko, Mark Steven
BRIDE OF KILLER NERD
Boyd, Daniel
INVASION OF THE SPACE PREACHERS
Branagh, Kenneth
PETER'S FRIENDS
Brandstrom, Charlotte
ROAD TO RUIN
Brest, Martin
SCENT OF A WOMAN
Britton, Tracy Lynch
MAXIMUM BREAKOUT
Bromfield, Rex
CAFE ROMEO
Brooks, Robert
WHO SHOT PATAKANGO?
Broomfield, Nick
MONSTER IN A BOX
Budds, Colin
HURRICANE SMITH
Buechler, John Carl
GHOULIES III: GHOULIES GO TO COLLEGE
Bugajski, Richard
CLEARCUT
Burton, Tim
BATMAN RETURNS
Cain, Christopher
PURE COUNTRY
Caro, Marc
DELICATESSEN
Carpenter, John
MEMOIRS OF AN INVISIBLE MAN
Carroll, Willard
RUNESTONE, THE
Castellaneta, P.J.
TOGETHER ALONE
Castle, Alan
DESIRE AND HELL AT SUNSET MOTEL
Chabrol, Claude
CRY OF THE OWL, THE
INSPECTOR LAVARDIN
Chalong Pakdivijit
IN GOLD WE TRUST
Chen Kaige
LIFE ON A STRING
Clark, Greydon
DANCE MACABRE
Clark, Warren
INSIDE EDGE
Clark, Duane
SHAKING THE TREE
Clements, Ron
ALADDIN
Clouse, Robert
CHINA O'BRIEN II
Cochran, Stacy
MY NEW GUN
Cohen, Howard R.
DEATHSTALKER IV: MATCH OF TITANS
Cohen, Eli
QUARREL, THE
Columbus, Chris
HOME ALONE 2: LOST IN NEW YORK
Conaway, Jeff
BIKINI SUMMER 2
Coppola, Francis Ford
BRAM STOKER'S DRACULA
Corneau, Alain
TOUS LES MATINS DU MONDE
Coto, Manny
DR. GIGGLES
Covington, Hil
ADVENTURES IN SPYING
Crain, Bill
MIDNIGHT FEAR
Creme, Lol
LUNATIC, THE
Crowe, Cameron
SINGLES
Crowe, Christopher
WHISPERS IN THE DARK
Crystal, Billy
MR. SATURDAY NIGHT
Dakota, Reno
AMERICAN FABULOUS
Dash, Julie
DAUGHTERS OF THE DUST
Daugherty, George
MAGICAL WORLD OF CHUCK JONES, THE
Davidson, Martin
HARD PROMISES
Davis, Andrew
UNDER SIEGE
Dawson, Anthony M.
INDIO 2 - THE REVOLT
Dayan, Josee
HOT CHOCOLATE
De Jong, Ate
HIGHWAY TO HELL
De Palma, Brian
RAISING CAIN
De Vito, Danny
HOFFA
DeBello, John
KILLER TOMATOES EAT FRANCE!
DeLeon, Marcus
KISS ME A KILLER
DeLuise, Michael
ALMOST PREGNANT
Demetrios, Eames
GIVING, THE
Demme, Jonathan
COUSIN BOBBY
Deutch, Howard
ARTICLE 99
Devine, David
BEETHOVEN LIVES UPSTAIRS
DeWilde, Brandon
BREATHING FIRE
Dezaki, Osamu
PROFESSIONAL, THE
DiCillo, Tom
JOHNNY SUEDE
Dickerson, Ernest
JUICE
Dimster-Denk, Dennis
MIKEY
Dirlam, John
FATAL INSTINCT
Donahue, Patrick G.
SAVAGE INSTINCT
Donaldson, Roger
WHITE SANDS
Donner, Richard
LETHAL WEAPON 3
RADIO FLYER
Dotan, Shimon
FINEST HOUR, THE
Drazan, Anthony
ZEBRAHEAD
Drysdale, Lee
LEATHER JACKETS
Dugan, Dennis
BRAIN DONORS
Duguay, Christian
SCANNERS III: THE TAKEOVER
Duigan, John
FLIRTING
Duke, Bill
DEEP COVER
Dupeyron, Francois
BEATING HEART, A
Eastwood, Clint
UNFORGIVEN
Eberhardt, Thom
CAPTAIN RON
Echevarria, Nicolas
CABEZA DE VACA
Egoyan, Atom
ADJUSTER, THE

Elgear, Sandra
VOICES FROM THE FRONT
Elgort, Arthur
TEXAS TENOR: THE ILLINOIS JACQUET STORY
Emmerich, Roland
UNIVERSAL SOLDIER
Ephron, Nora
THIS IS MY LIFE
Erschbamer, George
SNAKEEATER III . . . HIS LAW
Evans, Bruce A.
KUFFS
Eyres, John E.
PROJECT: SHADOWCHASER
Fearnley, Neill
BLACK ICE
Ferrara, Abel
BAD LIEUTENANT
Fincher, David
ALIEN3
Finley, Joe
BARBARIAN QUEEN II: THE EMPRESS STRIKES BACK
Fischa, Michael
DELTA HEAT
Flender, Rodman
IN THE HEAT OF PASSION
Florentine, Isaac
DESERT KICKBOXER
Floyd, Drago
TROLL 2
Foley, James
GLENGARRY GLEN ROSS
Fong, Leo T.
24 HOURS TO MIDNIGHT
Fragasso, Claudio
BEYOND DARKNESS
Franklin, Carl
ONE FALSE MOVE
Franklin, Howard
PUBLIC EYE, THE
Frears, Stephen
HERO
Fried, Randall
HEAVEN IS A PLAYGROUND
Friedkin, William
RAMPAGE
Frost, Mark
STORYVILLE
Furie, Sidney J.
LADYBUGS
Gallo, Fred
FINISHING TOUCH, THE
Garcia, David
SEX CRIMES
Garris, Mick
STEPHEN KING'S SLEEPWALKERS
Gebhard, Glenn
ONE LAST RUN
George, James
ROVER DANGERFIELD
Girod, Francis
ELEGANT CRIMINEL, L'
Glaser, Paul M.
CUTTING EDGE, THE
Glen, John
ACES: IRON EAGLE III
CHRISTOPHER COLUMBUS: THE DISCOVERY
Glimcher, Arne
MAMBO KINGS, THE
Golden, Dan
NAKED OBSESSION
Goldstein, Allan A.
COMMON BONDS
Goldthwait, Bobcat
SHAKES THE CLOWN
Gomez, Nick
LAWS OF GRAVITY
Gordon, Keith
MIDNIGHT CLEAR, A
Gordon-Clark, Lawrence
MONKEY BOY
Graver, Gary
ROOTS OF EVIL
Green, Terry
COLD JUSTICE
Griffiths, Mark
ULTRAVIOLET
Grimm, Douglas K.
LASER MOON
Guzzetti, Alfred
PICTURES FROM A REVOLUTION
Gyllenhaal, Stephen
WATERLAND
Haffter, Petra
DEMON IN MY VIEW, A
Halliday, Mark
JUST LIKE IN THE MOVIES
Hansen, Ed
BIKINI CARWASH COMPANY, THE
Hanson, Curtis
HAND THAT ROCKS THE CRADLE, THE
Harold, Wayne A.
BRIDE OF KILLER NERD
Harris, Trent
RUBIN & ED
Harrison, John Kent
BEAUTIFUL DREAMERS
Hartley, Hal
SIMPLE MEN
Harvey, Rupert
CRITTERS 4
Hata, Masami
LITTLE NEMO: ADVENTURES IN SLUMBERLAND
Heath, Robert
HUGH HEFNER: ONCE UPON A TIME
Hemmings, David
DARK HORSE
Henenlotter, Frank
BASKET CASE 3: THE PROGENY
Henson, Brian
MUPPET CHRISTMAS CAROL, THE
Herek, Stephen
MIGHTY DUCKS, THE
Herman, Mark
BLAME IT ON THE BELLBOY
Herrington, Rowdy
GLADIATOR
Hessler, Gordon
JOURNEY OF HONOR
Hickox, Anthony
HELLRAISER III: HELL ON EARTH
WAXWORK II: LOST IN TIME
Hill, Walter
TRESPASS
Hiller, Arthur
BABE, THE
Hippolyte, A. Gregory
ANIMAL INSTINCTS
MIRROR IMAGES
NIGHT RHYTHMS
SECRET GAMES
Hofmyer, Gray
LIGHT IN THE JUNGLE, THE
Holcomb, Rod
CHAINS OF GOLD
Hooks, Kevin
PASSENGER 57
Hopper, Dennis
BACKTRACK
Houston, Bobby
CAGED FEAR
Howard, Ron
FAR AND AWAY
Howson, Frank
HUNTING
Hsu, V. Dachin
PALE BLOOD
Hudlin, Reginald
BOOMERANG
Hunsicker, Jackson
ODDBALL HALL
Hurtz, William T.
LITTLE NEMO: ADVENTURES IN SLUMBERLAND
Huston, Danny
BECOMING COLETTE
Hutt, Robyn
VOICES FROM THE FRONT
Hyams, Peter
STAY TUNED
Ingvordsen, J. Christian
COMRADES IN ARMS
Irvin, Sam
GUILTY AS CHARGED
Isham, Wayne
FOR THOSE ABOUT TO ROCK
Israel, Neal
BREAKING THE RULES
Ivory, James
HOWARDS END
Jackson, Mick
BODYGUARD, THE
Jackson, Doug
DEADBOLT
Jacobovici, Simcha
DEADLY CURRENTS
Jacobs, Nicholas A.E.
REFRIGERATOR, THE
Jaglom, Henry
VENICE/VENICE
Jarman, Derek
EDWARD II
Jarmusch, Jim
NIGHT ON EARTH

Jeunet, Jean-Pierre
DELICATESSEN
Jimenez, Neal
WATERDANCE, THE
Joanou, Phil
FINAL ANALYSIS
Joffe, Arthur
ALBERTO EXPRESS
Joffe, Roland
CITY OF JOY
Joffe, Mark
EFFICIENCY EXPERT, THE
Jones, Chris
ESCAPE FROM . . . SURVIVAL ZONE
Jordan, Neil
CRYING GAME, THE
Jost, Jon
ALL THE VERMEERS IN NEW YORK
Joyner, C. Courtney
TRANCERS III: DETH LIVES
Kachyna, Karel
EAR, THE
Kalin, Tom
SWOON
Kanefsky, Rolfe
THERE'S NOTHING OUT THERE
Kaplan, Jonathan
LOVE FIELD
UNLAWFUL ENTRY
Kaurismaki, Aki
MATCH FACTORY GIRL, THE
Keglevic, Peter
KILL CRUISE
Kellman, Barnet
STRAIGHT TALK
Kennedy, Lou
BREATHING FIRE
Kennedy, Michael
TALONS OF THE EAGLE
Kidron, Beeban
USED PEOPLE
Kiersch, Fritz
INTO THE SUN
Kim, Richard H.
KILL LINE
King, Rick
KICKBOXER 3: THE ART OF WAR
PRAYER OF THE ROLLERBOYS
King, Zalman
WILD ORCHID 2:
TWO SHADES OF BLUE
WILDFIRE
Kleiser, Randal
HONEY, I BLEW UP THE KID
Knights, Robert
DOUBLE VISION
Kollek, Amos
DOUBLE EDGE
Kopple, Barbara
AMERICAN DREAM
Kotcheff, Ted
FOLKS!
Kowalski, Lech
ROCK SOUP
Krishtofovich, Vyacheslav
ADAM'S RIB

Kroyer, Bill
FERNGULLY:
THE LAST RAINFOREST
Kulle, Victor
ILLUSIONS
Kureishi, Hanif
LONDON KILLS ME
Kuzui, Fran Rubel
BUFFY THE VAMPIRE SLAYER
Lambert, Mary
PET SEMATARY II
Landis, John
INNOCENT BLOOD
Lane, Andrew
LONELY HEARTS
Lang, Perry
LITTLE VEGAS
Launer, Dale
LOVE POTION NO. 9
Lease, Maria A.
DOLLY DEAREST
Leconte, Patrice
HAIRDRESSER'S HUSBAND, THE
Leder, Paul
EXILED IN AMERICA
Lee, Spike
MALCOLM X
Lehner, Peter
MEGAVILLE
Leighton, Michael W.
PALE BLOOD
Lemmo, James
WE'RE TALKIN' SERIOUS MONEY
Leonard, Brett
LAWNMOWER MAN, THE
Levant, Brian
BEETHOVEN
Levinson, G.J.
HELLROLLER
Levinson, Barry
TOYS
Levy, Shuki
BLIND VISION
Levy, Jefery
DRIVE
Levy, Eugene
ONCE UPON A CRIME
Lewin, Ben
FAVOUR, THE WATCH, AND THE
VERY BIG FISH, THE
Lishman, Eda Lever
PRIMO BABY
Little, Dwight H.
RAPID FIRE
Logan, Bob
MEATBALLS 4
London, Roy
DIARY OF A HITMAN
Lord, Jean-Claude
LANDSLIDE
Lowney, Declan
BOB MARLEY: TIME WILL TELL
Lumet, Sidney
STRANGER AMONG US, A
Lynch, David
TWIN PEAKS: FIRE WALK WITH ME

Lynn, Jonathan
DISTINGUISHED GENTLEMAN, THE
MY COUSIN VINNY
Macdonald, Peter
MO' MONEY
Macek, Carl
PROFESSIONAL, THE
VAMPIRE HUNTER D
MacKenzie, John
RUBY
MacKinnon, Gillies
PLAYBOYS, THE
Madsen, Kenneth
DAY IN OCTOBER, A
Makin, Kelly
TIGER CLAWS
Malle, Louis
DAMAGE
Mandel, Robert
SCHOOL TIES
Mann, Michael
LAST OF THE MOHICANS, THE
Manoogian, Peter
DEMONIC TOYS
SEEDPEOPLE
Marcarelli, Robert
I DON'T BUY KISSES ANYMORE
Marcarelli, Rob
ORIGINAL INTENT
Marfori, Andreas
EVIL CLUTCH
Maris, Peter
CAN IT BE LOVE
Markey, Dave
1991: THE YEAR PUNK BROKE
Markham, Monte
NEON CITY
Marshall, Penny
LEAGUE OF THEIR OWN, A
Mastorakis, Nico
HIRED TO KILL
Mattison, Sally
SLUMBER PARTY MASSACRE 3
Mayfield, Les
ENCINO MAN
Maylam, Tony
SPLIT SECOND
Mazo, Michael
MANIAC WARRIORS
McCormick, Bret
ARMED FOR ACTION
BLOOD ON THE BADGE
McDonald, Bruce
HIGHWAY 61
McDonald, Rodney
NIGHT EYES 2
McTiernan, John
MEDICINE MAN
Meiesan, David
VOICES FROM THE FRONT
Meiselas, Susan
PICTURES FROM A REVOLUTION
Mele, Arthur N.
SOLDIER'S FORTUNE
Mellencamp, John
FALLING FROM GRACE

Menges, Chris
CRISSCROSS
Merendino, James
WITCHCRAFT IV: VIRGIN HEART
Merhi, Joseph
FINAL IMPACT
MAXIMUM FORCE
Mihalka, George
PSYCHIC
Mikhalkov, Nikita
CLOSE TO EDEN
Mileham, Michael
PUSHED TO THE LIMIT
Miller, Robert Ellis
BED & BREAKFAST
BRENDA STARR
Miller, Randall
CLASS ACT
Miller, George
FROZEN ASSETS
LORENZO'S OIL
Milo, Tom E.
SMOOTH TALKER
Miner, Steve
FOREVER YOUNG
Misiorowski, Bob
BLINK OF AN EYE
Model, Ben
PUERTO RICAN MAMBO (NOT A MUSICAL), THE
Mohr, Henro
KICK OR DIE
Mones, Paul
FATHERS AND SONS
Moore, Charles Philip
BLACKBELT
DANCE WITH DEATH
Moore, Simon
UNDER SUSPICION
Moorhouse, Jocelyn
PROOF
Morris, Errol
BRIEF HISTORY OF TIME, A
Moses, Ben
NICKEL & DIME
Moyle, Allan
GUN IN BETTY LOU'S HANDBAG, THE
Mugge, Robert
DEEP BLUES
Munch, Christopher
HOURS AND TIMES, THE
Munchkin, Richard W.
DEADLY BET
OUT FOR BLOOD
Mundhra, Jag
OTHER WOMAN, THE
Murphy, Geoff
FREEJACK
Musker, John
ALADDIN
Nair, Mira
MISSISSIPPI MASALA
Newell, Mike
ENCHANTED APRIL
Nicolaou, Ted
BAD CHANNELS

Norgard, Lindsay
HOMEBOYS
Novaro, Maria
DANZON
Noyce, Phillip
PATRIOT GAMES
Nykvist, Sven
OX, THE
O'Bannon, Dan
RESURRECTED, THE
Ogilvie, George
CROSSING, THE
Olivera, Hector
PLAY MURDER FOR ME
Olmos, Edward James
AMERICAN ME
Omori, Kazuki
GODZILLA VS. BIOLLANTE
Ortega, Kenny
NEWSIES
Owens, Brian
HAPPY HELL NIGHT
Oxenberg, Jan
THANK YOU AND GOOD NIGHT!
Oz, Frank
HOUSESITTER
Pakula, Alan J.
CONSENTING ADULTS
Palm, Anders
DEAD CERTAIN
Palmer, Tony
CHILDREN, THE
Paragon, John
DOUBLE TROUBLE
Parr, Larry
SOLDIER'S TALE, A
Paul, Stuart
FATE
Pearce, Richard
LEAP OF FAITH
Peploe, Mark
AFRAID OF THE DARK
Pesce, P.J.
BODY WAVES
Peters, Charlie
PASSED AWAY
Peterson, Kristine
LOWER LEVEL
Phillips, Maurice
OVER HER DEAD BODY
Phillips, Toby
PAMELA PRINCIPLE, THE
Phillips, Lucy
STEAL AMERICA
Pialat, Maurice
VAN GOGH
Plone, Allen
PHANTOM OF THE RITZ
Plympton, Bill
TUNE, THE
Pohjola, Ilppo
DADDY AND THE MUSCLE ACADEMY
Post, Ted
HUMAN SHIELD, THE

Potter, Dennis
SECRET FRIENDS
Power, John
FATHER
Primus, Barry
MISTRESS
Prior, David A.
CENTER OF THE WEB
Pyun, Albert
CAPTAIN AMERICA
Rader, Peter
HIRED TO KILL
Rafelson, Bob
MAN TROUBLE
Rafferty, Kevin
FEED
Randel, Tony
AMITYVILLE 1992: IT'S ABOUT TIME
CHILDREN OF THE NIGHT
Ray, Fred Olen
SPIRITS
Redford, Robert
RIVER RUNS THROUGH IT, A
Reiner, Rob
FEW GOOD MEN, A
Rene, Norman
PRELUDE TO A KISS
Richardson, Peter
POPE MUST DIET!, THE
Ridgeway, James
FEED
Riffel, J.
HOUSE ON TOMBSTONE HILL, THE
Riggs, Marlon T.
COLOR ADJUSTMENT
Riklis, Eran
CUP FINAL
Ritchie, Michael
DIGGSTOWN
Robbins, Tim
BOB ROBERTS
Roberts, Alan
ROUND TRIP TO HEAVEN
Roberts, Richard
SEVERED TIES
Robertson, Joseph F.
AUNTIE LEE'S MEAT PIES
Robinson, Bruce
JENNIFER EIGHT
Robinson, Phil Alden
SNEAKERS
Rocco, Marc
WHERE THE DAY TAKES YOU
Rockwell, Alexandre
IN THE SOUP
Roddam, Franc
K2
Roeg, Nicolas
COLD HEAVEN
Rogers, Richard P.
PICTURES FROM A REVOLUTION
Rohmer, Eric
CONTE DE PRINTEMPS
Roodt, Darrell James
SARAFINA!

Rose, Bernard
CANDYMAN
Rubini, Sergio
STATION, THE
Saks, Gene
FINE ROMANCE, A
Salvatores, Gabriele
MEDITERRANEO
Santiago, Cirio
EYE OF THE EAGLE 3
FIELD OF FIRE
Santostefano, Damon
SEVERED TIES
Sarafian, Deran
BACK IN THE U.S.S.R.
Sassone, Oley
BLOODFIST III: FORCED TO FIGHT
Sato, Junya
SILK ROAD, THE
Saxon, John
DEATH HOUSE
Sayles, John
PASSION FISH
Schepisi, Fred
MR. BASEBALL
Schlondorff, Volker
VOYAGER
Schmoeller, David
NETHERWORLD
Schonemann, Sibylle
LOCKED-UP TIME
Schrader, Paul
LIGHT SLEEPER
Schroeder, Michael
MORTUARY ACADEMY
Schroeder, Barbet
SINGLE WHITE FEMALE
Schulze, Douglas
HELL MASTER
Scott, Ridley
1492: THE CONQUEST OF PARADISE
Screaming Mad George
GUYVER, THE
Seale, John
TILL THERE WAS YOU
Seeley, Robert
ROVER DANGERFIELD
Seltzer, David
SHINING THROUGH
Shea Ruben, Katt
POISON IVY
Shelton, Ron
WHITE MEN CAN'T JUMP
Shepard, Richard
LINGUINI INCIDENT, THE
Sherman, Eric
TRAINED TO FIGHT
Sibay, Mussef
WOMAN, HER MEN AND HER FUTON, A
Sidaris, Andy
DO OR DIE
Silver, Joan Micklin
BIG GIRLS DON'T CRY . . . THEY GET EVEN
Simandl, Lloyd
MANIAC WARRIORS
ULTIMATE DESIRES
Simon, J.P.
CTHULHU MANSION
Singer, Gail
WISECRACKS
Sinise, Gary
OF MICE AND MEN
Sinofski, Bruce
BROTHER'S KEEPER
Sloane, Rick
MIND, BODY & SOUL
Smith, Bruce
BEBE'S KIDS
Smoke, Stephen
FINAL IMPACT
STREET CRIMES
Snider, Skott
MIRACLE BEACH
Soavi, Michele
DEVIL'S DAUGHTER, THE
Solinas, Piernico
TOUCH AND DIE
Spears, Ross
TO RENDER A LIFE
Spencer, Jane
LITTLE NOISES
Spheeris, Penelope
WAYNE'S WORLD
Spottiswoode, Roger
STOP! OR MY MOM WILL SHOOT
Stanzler, Jeff
JUMPIN' AT THE BONEYARD
Steinberg, Michael
WATERDANCE, THE
Stewart, Rob
ROCK & ROLL COWBOYS
Sturridge, Charles
WHERE ANGELS FEAR TO TREAD
Tabet, Sylvio
BEASTMASTER 2: THROUGH THE PORTAL OF TIME
Takacs, Tibor
GATE II
Tamayo, Augusto
WELCOME TO OBLIVION
Tarantino, Quentin
RESERVOIR DOGS
Tausik, David
HOMICIDAL IMPULSE
Taylor, Baz
NEAR MISSES
SHOOTING ELIZABETH
Teague, Lewis
COLLISION COURSE
Tent, Kevin
WELCOME TO OBLIVION
Tessari, Duccio
BEYOND JUSTICE
Thomas, Anthony
CODE NAME: CHAOS
Thomas, Betty
ONLY YOU
Thompson, Brett
ADVENTURES IN DINOSAUR CITY
Thompson, Randy
MONTANA RUN, THE
Till, Eric
GETTING MARRIED IN BUFFALO JUMP
OH, WHAT A NIGHT
Tong, Stanley
SUPERCOP: POLICE STORY III
Towbin, Bram
JUST LIKE IN THE MOVIES
Treas, Teri
PLAY NICE
Trent, Barbara
PANAMA DECEPTION, THE
Treut, Monika
MY FATHER IS COMING
Tsui Hark
ONCE UPON A TIME IN CHINA
Tsukamoto, Shinya
TETSUO: THE IRON MAN
Turteltaub, Jon
3 NINJAS
Van Dormael, Jaco
TOTO LE HEROS
VanWagenen, Sterling
ALAN & NAOMI
Vasquez, Joseph B.
BRONX WAR, THE
Veber, Francis
OUT ON A LIMB
Verbong, Ben
LILY WAS HERE
Verhoeven, Paul
BASIC INSTINCT
Vincent, Christian
DISCRETE, LA
Volk, Paul G.
SUNSET STRIP
Von Praunheim, Rosa
AFFENGEIL
Von Trier, Lars
ZENTROPA
Walas, Chris
VAGRANT, THE
Wang, Steve
GUYVER, THE
Wargnier, Regis
INDOCHINE
Weber, Bruce
BROKEN NOSES
Weiland, Paul
BERNARD AND THE GENIE
Weisser, Otto
EMMANUELLE 6
Weston, Eric
TO PROTECT AND SERVE
Williams, Anson
ALL-AMERICAN MURDER
Williamson, Fred
STEELE'S LAW
Winkler, Irwin
NIGHT AND THE CITY
Winning, David
KILLER IMAGE
Winograd, Peter
ONE LAST RUN

Wiseman, Carol
DOES THIS MEAN WE'RE MARRIED?
Wolk, Andy
TRACES OF RED
Wolpaw, James
COMPLEX WORLD
Woo, John
HARD-BOILED
Wool, Abbe
ROADSIDE PROPHETS
Worth, David
LADY DRAGON
Wynorski, Jim
MUNCHIE
976-EVIL II
SORORITY HOUSE MASSACRE 2
Yates, Andrew
LIFE ON THE EDGE
Yates, Peter
YEAR OF THE COMET
Yorkin, Bud
LOVE HURTS
Yosha, Yaky
SEXUAL RESPONSE
Yule, Paul
DAMNED IN THE USA
Yuzna, Brian
SOCIETY
Zaloum, Alain
CANVAS
Zellinger, Jimmy
LITTLE SISTER
Zeltser, Yuri
EYE OF THE STORM
Zemeckis, Robert
DEATH BECOMES HER
Zhang Yimou
RAISE THE RED LANTERN
Ziller, Paul
BLOODFIST IV: DIE TRYING
Zincone, Bruno
EMMANUELLE 6
Zorrilla, Jose Antonio
WINTER IN LISBON, THE
Zwick, Edward
LEAVING NORMAL

EDITORS

Accomando, Beth
KILLER TOMATOES EAT FRANCE!
Adair, Sandra
SMOOTH TALKER
Akers, George
EDWARD II
Alan, David
MAXIMUM BREAKOUT
Aleso, Ivan
WINTER IN LISBON, THE
Alexander, Tracy
IMPORTANCE OF BEING EARNEST, THE
Allen, Dick
ENCHANTED APRIL
Amyx, Tim
SLUMBER PARTY MASSACRE 3
Anbar, Netaya
FINEST HOUR, THE
Anderson, Pippa
HURRICANE SMITH
Anderson, William
1492: THE CONQUEST OF PARADISE
Angelo, Lou
HEAVEN IS A PLAYGROUND
Anwar, Tariq
UNDER SUSPICION
Ara, Maruli
LADY DRAGON
Araki, Gregg
LIVING END, THE
Audsley, Mick
HERO
Avildsen, John G.
POWER OF ONE, THE
Aviles, Paul
CTHULHU MANSION
Baird, Stuart
RADIO FLYER
Baragali, Nino
MEDITERRANEO
Baragli, Nino
JOHNNY STECCHINO
Barius, Moune
DEMON IN MY VIEW, A
Barraque, Martine
POUR SACHA
Barrett, Tom
SEEDPEOPLE
Barrow, Bruce
GIVING, THE
Barton, Sean
K2
Baumgarten, Alan
LAWNMOWER MAN, THE
Beason, Eric L.
BLOODFIST III: FORCED TO FIGHT
Beatty, David
BLOODFIST IV: DIE TRYING
Beauman, Nicholas
EFFICIENCY EXPERT, THE
WHITE SANDS
Bedford, James Gavin
DESIRE AND HELL AT SUNSET MOTEL
Behar, Andrew
PAINTING THE TOWN
Beldin, Dale
INNOCENT BLOOD
Bell, Geraint
DEADLY BET
FINAL IMPACT
STREET CRIMES
Bensimon, Peter
BOB MARLEY: TIME WILL TELL
Benwick, Richard
CAFE ROMEO
Benwick, Rick
PRIMO BABY
Berger, Peter E.
MAGICAL WORLD OF CHUCK JONES, THE
STAY TUNED
Berlinger, Joe
BROTHER'S KEEPER
Bernardi, Adam
BEASTMASTER 2: THROUGH THE PORTAL OF TIME
Bernhardi, Adam
GHOULIES III: GHOULIES GO TO COLLEGE
Bernstein, Martin L.
SHAKING THE TREE
Berroyer, Marie-Josephe
TOUS LES MATINS DU MONDE
Beyda, Kent
MR. SATURDAY NIGHT
Bilcock, Jill
TILL THERE WAS YOU
Billeskov-Jansen, Janus
BEST INTENTIONS, THE
Blair, Gary
DEATH HOUSE
Blank, Harrod
WILD WHEELS
Bloom, John
DAMAGE
Board, Timothy N.
LADYBUGS
Bock, Larry
FROZEN ASSETS
MIGHTY DUCKS, THE
Boden, Kristina
LIGHT SLEEPER
Boisson, Noelle
LOVER, THE
Bonnot, Francoise
1492: THE CONQUEST OF PARADISE
Booth, Matthew
HUMAN SHIELD, THE
Bowers, George
LEAGUE OF THEIR OWN, A
Boyd, Daniel
INVASION OF THE SPACE PREACHERS
Braga-Mermet, Angela
INSPECTOR LAVARDIN
Braun, Jonathon
BLIND VISION
Brenner, David
NIGHT AND THE CITY
Brochu, Don
UNDER SIEGE
Brochu, Donald
MIDNIGHT CLEAR, A
Brooks, Halle
WHO SHOT PATAKANGO?
Brooks, Robert
WHO SHOT PATAKANGO?
Brown, Barry Alexander
MALCOLM X
Brown, O. Nicholas
STEPHEN KING'S SLEEPWALKERS
Brown, Robert
LETHAL WEAPON 3
Brown, Steve
MY FATHER IS COMING
Brozhovskaya, Inna
ADAM'S RIB

Bryan, Doug
STEELE'S LAW
Bryant, John
BLIND VISION
Buff, Conrad
JENNIFER EIGHT
Burge, Roy
DEAD CERTAIN
Burnett, John F.
BED & BREAKFAST
CLASS ACT
LEAP OF FAITH
Burton, Joseph
DAUGHTERS OF THE DUST
Bush, Bert
MANIAC WARRIORS
Butler, Bill
JOURNEY OF HONOR
Butler, Mark Talbot
ESCAPE FROM . . . SURVIVAL ZONE
Cabreros, Ron
OUT FOR BLOOD
STREET CRIMES
Cahn, Daniel
HUMAN SHIELD, THE
Cambas, Jacqueline
SCHOOL TIES
Cambern, Donn
BODYGUARD, THE
Campbell, Malcolm
BRAIN DONORS
OVER HER DEAD BODY
WAYNE'S WORLD
Candib, Richard
AMERICAN ME
Canney, Elizabeth
ADVENTURES IN DINOSAUR CITY
Caplan, Cathy
AMERICAN DREAM
Caputo, Bernie
ROCK-A-DOODLE
Carey, Amy
DAUGHTERS OF THE DUST
Carmody, Jacqeline
PRIMARY MOTIVE
Carter, John
DEEP COVER
Castanedo, Rafael
CABEZA DE VACA
Castellaneta, P.J.
TOGETHER ALONE
Castro-Brechignac
ALBERTO EXPRESS
Ceppi, Francois
DISCRETE, LA
Chandler, Michael
WIND
Chapman, Joan E.
FOLKS!
NICKEL & DIME
Charles, Peter
IN GOLD WE TRUST
Cheung Kai-fei
SUPERCOP: POLICE STORY III
Cheunng Yaeo-chung
SUPERCOP: POLICE STORY III

Chew, Richard
SINGLES
Chiu, Francisco
BARBARIAN QUEEN II:
THE EMPRESS STRIKES BACK
Churgin, Lisa
BOB ROBERTS
Cibelli, Christopher
HELLRAISER III: HELL ON EARTH
WAXWORK II: LOST IN TIME
Cipriani, Angela
INDIO 2 - THE REVOLT
Clark, Jim
CODE NAME: CHAOS
Clayton, Curtiss
UNLAWFUL ENTRY
Coates, Anne V.
CHAPLIN
Coburn, Arthur R.
AMERICAN ME
Cohen, Peter
PUSHED TO THE LIMIT
SEX CRIMES
Cole, Stan
PROM NIGHT IV - DELIVER US
FROM EVIL
Collin, Francoise
BEATING HEART, A
Collins, Alan
KILLER IMAGE
Congdon, Dana
IN THE SOUP
Connell, Michael
LUNATIC, THE
Conte, Mark
STOP! OR MY MOM WILL SHOOT
Coughlin, Cari
ALAN & NAOMI
Coulson, Peter
WHERE ANGELS FEAR TO TREAD
Cox, Joel
UNFORGIVEN
Crafford, Ian
BACK IN THE U.S.S.R.
THUNDERHEART
Crain, Brian
MIDNIGHT FEAR
Crivallero, Michel
EMMANUELLE 6
Crutcher, Susan R.
ORIGINAL INTENT
D'Antonio, Joanne
I DON'T BUY KISSES ANYMORE
D'Arcy, Marcus
LORENZO'S OIL
Dakota, Reno
AMERICAN FABULOUS
Dalva, Robert
RAISING CAIN
Dangar, Henry
CROSSING, THE
Davies, Carmel
BLINK OF AN EYE
Davies, Freeman
TRESPASS
Davis, Battle
LETHAL WEAPON 3

Davis, Kaye
LUNATICS: A LOVE STORY
Day, Lisa
NOISES OFF
De La Bouillerie, Hubert C.
MO' MONEY
Dedet, Yann
VAN GOGH
DeGraaff, Ton
LILY WAS HERE
Del Amo, Pablo G.
WINTER IN LISBON, THE
Dennison, Reid
TALONS OF THE EAGLE
TIGER CLAWS
Dixon, Humphrey
PLAYBOYS, THE
Dorney, Lisa
ROCK-A-DOODLE
Douglas, Clare
SECRET FRIENDS
Du Yuan
RAISE THE RED LANTERN
DuBois, Victor
LEAVING NORMAL
Ducsay, Bob
FINEST HOUR, THE
Durham, Sarah
FEED
Duthie, Michael J.
EYE OF THE STORM
HOUSE OF USHER, THE
UNIVERSAL SOLDIER
Edwards, Rob
DELTA HEAT
Elgear, Sandra
VOICES FROM THE FRONT
Ellis, Michael
BLAME IT ON THE BELLBOY
Estrin, Robert
RIVER RUNS THROUGH IT, A
Famiglietti, Phyllis
BROKEN NOSES
Fardoulis, Monique
CRY OF THE OWL, THE
INSPECTOR LAVARDIN
Farr, Glenn
OUT ON A LIMB
Ferretti, Robert A.
UNDER SIEGE
Finan, Tom
PET SEMATARY II
Finney, Rick
AMITYVILLE 1992:
IT'S ABOUT TIME
Fitzpatrick
MANIAC WARRIORS
Flaum, Erica
CAGED FEAR
Font, Teresa
AMANTES
Francis-Bruce, Richard
LORENZO'S OIL
Freeman, Jeff
WATERDANCE, THE
Freeman-Fox, Lois
STOP! OR MY MOM WILL SHOOT

Fritz, Ernie
LITTLE NOISES
Fuller, Brad
BRIEF HISTORY OF TIME, A
Galloway, Sheri
CONFESSIONS OF A SERIAL KILLER
Garcia, Maria-Luisa
CONTE DE PRINTEMPS
Garfield, David
SCORCHERS
Garland, Glenn
FINISHING TOUCH, THE
KISS ME A KILLER
Garrett, Okuwah
MOM AND DAD SAVE THE WORLD
Gaster, Nicolas
DAY IN OCTOBER, A
Gavin, James
WILD ORCHID 2:
TWO SHADES OF BLUE
Gavin, Seth
HOUSE IV
Gentile, Steven
COMPLEX WORLD
Gentner, Rich
MUNCHIE
Gibson, J. Kathleen
SHAKES THE CLOWN
Gibson, Robert
FLIRTING
Gilbert, John
SUNSET STRIP
Gilbert-Reeves, Gabrielle
NAKED OBSESSION
Gilberti, Nina
LOWER LEVEL
976-EVIL II
Glatstein, Bert
SEEDPEOPLE
Glen, Matthew
CHRISTOPHER COLUMBUS:
THE DISCOVERY
Gomez, Nick
LAWS OF GRAVITY
Gordean, William
WILDFIRE
Gordean, William D.
BEETHOVEN
Gordon, Robert
DELTA HEAT
Gosnell, Raja
HOME ALONE 2:
LOST IN NEW YORK
Goursaud, Anne
BRAM STOKER'S DRACULA
Gradidge, Havelock
QUARREL, THE
Granger, Tracy S.
GAS FOOD LODGING
Green, Crispin
COLD JUSTICE
Greenberg, Jerry
COLLISION COURSE
SCHOOL TIES
Greene, Danford B.
WILDFIRE
Greenwald, David
COUSIN BOBBY
Gregory, Jon
LONDON KILLS ME
Gribble, Bernard
ACES: IRON EAGLE III
Grimley, Simon
KICK OR DIE
Grosett, Peter
LIGHT IN THE JUNGLE, THE
Gross, Michael
HUGH HEFNER: ONCE UPON A TIME
Grossman, Marc
WILD ORCHID 2:
TWO SHADES OF BLUE
Grover, John
FAVOUR, THE WATCH, AND THE
VERY BIG FISH, THE
Hache, Joelle
CLOSE TO EDEN
HAIRDRESSER'S HUSBAND, THE
Hagar, David
NEON CITY
Haglund, Terje
LANDSLIDE
Haight, Michael
DO OR DIE
Halsey, Richard
ARTICLE 99
SISTER ACT
Hambling, Gerry
CITY OF JOY
Hamilton, Steve
SIMPLE MEN
Hampton, Janice
BIG GIRLS DON'T CRY . . . THEY
GET EVEN
GUN IN BETTY LOU'S
HANDBAG, THE
Hanek, Miroslav
EAR, THE
Haneke, Tom
AMERICAN DREAM
Hanley, Daniel
FAR AND AWAY
Harrah, Mark
CHINA O'BRIEN II
Harris, Richard A.
BODYGUARD, THE
Hartley, Hal
SIMPLE MEN
Heard, Howard
WOMAN, HER MEN AND HER
FUTON, A
Heldmyer, W.F.
HELLROLLER
Heredia, Paula
TEXAS TENOR:
THE ILLINOIS JACQUET STORY
Hiatt, Vicki
DOUBLE EDGE
Hickox, Emma
MIRACLE BEACH
Hietner, David
SARAFINA!
Hill, Michael
FAR AND AWAY
Hirsch, Paul
RAISING CAIN
Hirsch, Tina
CAPTAIN RON
Hirtz, Dagmar
VOYAGER
Hitner, Harry
HONEY, I BLEW UP THE KID
Hoenig, Dov
LAST OF THE MOHICANS, THE
UNDER SIEGE
Hoffman, Deborah
COLOR ADJUSTMENT
Hofstra, Jack
PURE COUNTRY
Hollywood, Peter
SARAFINA!
Honess, Peter
MR. BASEBALL
Horger, John C.
LOVE HURTS
Hori, Jorma
DADDY AND THE MUSCLE
ACADEMY
Horn, Karen
DESERT KICKBOXER
Horton, Kim
35 UP
Horton, Michael
SOLDIER'S TALE, A
Horvitch, Andy
DEMONIC TOYS
GUYVER, THE
Hoy, Maysie
PLAYER, THE
Hoy, William
PATRIOT GAMES
Hubert, Nathalie
VAN GOGH
Huggett, David
MY GRANDPA IS A VAMPIRE
Huggins, Erica
GUN IN BETTY LOU'S
HANDBAG, THE
Huggins, Jere
RAMPAGE
Humphreys, Ned
LEATHER JACKETS
Huntley, Tim
ONE LAST RUN
Hutchings, Graham
MONSTER IN A BOX
Hutshing, Gillian
FERNGULLY:
THE LAST RAINFOREST
Hutt, Robyn
VOICES FROM THE FRONT
Igel, Rachel
FATAL INSTINCT
Ignaszewski, Jay
VAGRANT, THE
Ikeda, Michiko
GODZILLA VS. BIOLLANTE
Jablow, Michael
MUPPET CHRISTMAS CAROL, THE
Jackson, Mike
LOVE CRIMES

Jacobs, Nicholas
REFRIGERATOR, THE
Jaffe, Gib
RAPID FIRE
Jean, Jacques
SNAKEEATER III . . . HIS LAW
Jones, Robert C.
BABE, THE
Jost, Jon
ALL THE VERMEERS IN NEW YORK
Jympson, John
HOUSESITTER
Kahn, Sheldon
BEETHOVEN
Kai Kit-wai
HARD-BOILED
Kalin, Tom
SWOON
Kaman, Steven
COMRADES IN ARMS
Kanefsky, Victor
THERE'S NOTHING OUT THERE
Kasper, David
PANAMA DECEPTION, THE
Kaurismaki, Aki
MATCH FACTORY GIRL, THE
Kelly, Michael
ENCINO MAN
Keneshea, Ellen
MORTUARY ACADEMY
Kennedy, Patrick
ONCE UPON A CRIME
Keramidas, Harry
PASSED AWAY
Kertarahardja, Amin
LADY DRAGON
Keunelian, Janice
FATHERS AND SONS
Keuper, Jay
JUST LIKE IN THE MOVIES
Keusch, Michael
INSIDE EDGE
Kling, Elizabeth
ZEBRAHEAD
Klingman, Lynzee
HOFFA
RIVER RUNS THROUGH IT, A
Koehler, Bonnie
HARD PROMISES
RAISING CAIN
Koenig, Ken
LASER MOON
Kowalski, Lech
ROCK SOUP
Kravitz, Carole
ONE FALSE MOVE
Kurson, Jane
LOVE FIELD
Lang-Willar, Suzanne
DOES THIS MEAN WE'RE MARRIED?
Lange, Bruce
GETTING MARRIED IN BUFFALO JUMP
Langlois, Yves
DEADBOLT
SCANNERS III: THE TAKEOVER
TWIN SISTERS
Lark, Tony
BLIND VISION
Lawson, Tony
COLD HEAVEN
CRISSCROSS
Lebenzon, Chris
BATMAN RETURNS
Leder, Paul
EXILED IN AMERICA
Lee, Alan
BLACK ICE
Lee, Allan
COMMON BONDS
Lee, Maria
TOGETHER ALONE
Leighton, Michael W.
PALE BLOOD
Leighton, Robert
FEW GOOD MEN, A
Leirer, Barry B.
DISTINGUISHED GENTLEMAN, THE
Levy, Shuki
BLIND VISION
Lewis, Claire
35 UP
Linder, Stu
TOYS
Link, John F.
HAND THAT ROCKS THE CRADLE, THE
MIGHTY DUCKS, THE
Livingstone, Russell
RESURRECTED, THE
WHERE THE DAY TAKES YOU
Lloyd, David H.
NIGHT EYES 2
SEXUAL RESPONSE
Loewenthal, Daniel
KICKBOXER 3: THE ART OF WAR
Lombardo, Tony
DISTINGUISHED GENTLEMAN, THE
MY COUSIN VINNY
Lottman, Evan
PUBLIC EYE, THE
Lovejoy, Ray
YEAR OF THE COMET
Lowenthal, Daniel
PRAYER OF THE ROLLERBOYS
Lubarsky, Anat
CUP FINAL
Magalis, Tatiana
RASPAD
Mak Chi-sin
ONCE UPON A TIME IN CHINA
Malanowski, Tony
CENTER OF THE WEB
Malkin, Barry
HONEYMOON IN VEGAS
Marcus, Andrew
HOWARDS END
PETER'S FRIENDS
Markey, Dave
1991: THE YEAR PUNK BROKE
McArdle, Tom
LAWS OF GRAVITY
McBride, Randall C.
KILL LINE
McClellan, Gordon
WISECRACKS
McKay, Craig
SHINING THROUGH
Meiesan, David
VOICES FROM THE FRONT
Melnick, Mark
BRENDA STARR
Menke, Sally
RESERVOIR DOGS
Miller, Michael R.
MEDICINE MAN
Miller, Tony
WITCHCRAFT IV: VIRGIN HEART
Miller, W. Peter
ADVENTURES IN DINOSAUR CITY
Miller, III, Harry B.
GLADIATOR
Minasian, Armen
LIFE ON THE EDGE
Mirkovich, Steve
COOL WORLD
Mitchell, David
HAPPY HELL NIGHT
Mitchell, Rick
MIND, BODY & SOUL
Mittleman, Gina
POISON IVY
Mizgalski, Tony
ROVER DANGERFIELD
Model, Ben
PUERTO RICAN MAMBO (NOT A MUSICAL), THE
Mondshein, Andrew
STRANGER AMONG US, A
Montanari, Sergio
HUSBANDS AND LOVERS
Moore, Patrick
CANVAS
Morden, Rick
BEETHOVEN LIVES UPSTAIRS
Morra, Mario
BEYOND JUSTICE
Morrish, Tom
COLD JUSTICE
Morse, Susan E.
HUSBANDS AND WIVES
SHADOWS AND FOG
Mugge, Robert
DEEP BLUES
Munch, Christopher
HOURS AND TIMES, THE
Myers, Dick
BRIDE OF KILLER NERD
Neil, Debra
DR. GIGGLES
Nelson, Chris
CHAINS OF GOLD
Nevius, Steve
SOUTH CENTRAL
WE'RE TALKIN' SERIOUS MONEY

Nicoloni, Angelo
STATION, THE
Nirobk, Trebor
CAN IT BE LOVE
Noble, Thom
FINAL ANALYSIS
Nord, Richard
FINE ROMANCE, A
PASSENGER 57
Novaro, Maria
DANZON
O'Connel, Marjorie
DARK HORSE
O'Connor, Dennis
ADVENTURES IN SPYING
O'Steen, Sam
CONSENTING ADULTS
Oblath, Carol
BAD CHANNELS
NETHERWORLD
Oldcorn, Christopher
REFRIGERATOR, THE
Pacek, Michael
HIGHWAY 61
Palmer, Tony
CHILDREN, THE
Pan, Kant
CRYING GAME, THE
Pankow, Bill
WHISPERS IN THE DARK
Parker, Nancy
GIVING, THE
Pattillo, Alan
MONKEY BOY
Pei Xiaonan
LIFE ON A STRING
Percy, Lee
SINGLE WHITE FEMALE
Peroni, Geraldine
JOHNNY SUEDE
PLAYER, THE
Pesce, P.J.
REFRIGERATOR, THE
Peterson, H. Lee
ALADDIN
Pettit, Suzanne
LOVE POTION NO. 9
Pillsbury, Suzanne
REFRIGERATOR, THE
Polakow, Michael E.
CUTTING EDGE, THE
Poll, Jon
CAPTAIN AMERICA
FOREVER YOUNG
Pollard, Sam
JUICE
Polonsky, Sonya
LINGUINI INCIDENT, THE
Polverari, Fabrizio
EVIL CLUTCH
Ponce, Jose
BIKINI CARWASH COMPANY, THE
Poscetti, Anna
FINE ROMANCE, A
Puett, Dallas
RADIO FLYER

Rabinowitz, Jay
NIGHT ON EARTH
Rae, Dan
CANDYMAN
SPLIT SECOND
Rafferty, Kevin
FEED
Ramsey, Todd
HIGHWAY TO HELL
Rand, Patrick
IN THE HEAT OF PASSION
Rasch, Steve
HOMEBOYS
Rawlings, Terry
ALIEN3
Rawlins, David
BACKTRACK
Ray, Kimberly
WHITE MEN CAN'T JUMP
Rayment, Alex
FREDDIE AS F.R.O.7
Raz, Irit
ALMOST PREGNANT
Rea, Michael
CLEARCUT
Redman, Anthony
BAD LIEUTENANT
Reeves, Gabrielle Gilbert
BLACKBELT
Regan, Kerry
FATHER
Reid, Philip
HUNTING
Reitano, Robert
THIS IS MY LIFE
Rennie, David
3 NINJAS
Resnais, Camille Bordes
NIGHT AND DAY
Resnick, Ron
OTHER WOMAN, THE
Reynolds, William
NEWSIES
Richardson, Nancy
ROADSIDE PROPHETS
Ripps, Michael
LITTLE SISTER
Robert-Lauliac, Michele
HOT CHOCOLATE
NEAR MISSES
ROAD TO RUIN
Roberts, Richard
SEVERED TIES
Roberts, Rick
CHILDREN OF THE NIGHT
Robson, Amanda
ROCK & ROLL COWBOYS
Rogriguez, Nelson
DANZON
Rolf, Tom
SNEAKERS
Roose, Ronald
HOFFA
Rosenstock, Harvey
SCENT OF A WOMAN

Ross, Chris
SPIRITS
Rossberg, Susana
TOTO LE HEROS
Rostock, Susanne
INCIDENT AT OGLALA
Roth, Chris
DANCE WITH DEATH
SOLDIER'S FORTUNE
Rothman, Marion
MEMOIRS OF AN INVISIBLE MAN
Rotter, Stephen A.
PRELUDE TO A KISS
Rowland, Geoffrey
DOLLY DEAREST
Sackner, Sara
PAINTING THE TOWN
Salcedo, Pepe
PEPI, LUCI, BOM AND OTHER GIRLS ON THE HEAP
Sallows, Ken
PROOF
Sanchez, Melisa
BIKINI SUMMER 2
Sandberg, Francine
NIGHT AND DAY
Sanders, Greg
ROUND TRIP TO HEAVEN
Sanders, Ronald
GATE II
Savitt, Jill
BUFFY THE VAMPIRE SLAYER
Sayles, John
PASSION FISH
Scalia, Pietro
MEGAVILLE
Scantlebury, Glen
BRAM STOKER'S DRACULA
STEAL AMERICA
Schaeffer, William
ROOTS OF EVIL
Schaffer, Lauren
DOCTOR MORDRID
TRANCERS III: DETH LIVES
Schalk, Dan
WELCOME TO OBLIVION
Schett, Susanne
KILL CRUISE
Schill, Stewart
PALE BLOOD
Schmidt, Arthur
DEATH BECOMES HER
LAST OF THE MOHICANS, THE
Schneid, Herve
DELICATESSEN
ZENTROPA
Schoenfeld, Brent
MISSION OF JUSTICE
RUBIN & ED
Schroeder, Roger
LASER MOON
Schulze, Douglas
HELL MASTER
Schwartz, Valerie
HOUSE ON TOMBSTONE HILL, THE
Schweitzer, Michael
BRONX WAR, THE

Sears, B.J.
STORYVILLE
Sears, Eric
ENCINO MAN
Semel, Stephen
KUFFS
Semilian, Julian
LONELY HEARTS
Seydor, Paul
WHITE MEN CAN'T JUMP
Shaine, Rick
HARD PROMISES
Sheldon, Greg
BASKET CASE 3: THE PROGENY
Shephard, Mike
AFFENGEIL
Shepphird, John
BODY WAVES
Ship, Trudy
TRACES OF RED
Shipton, Susan
ADJUSTER, THE
OH, WHAT A NIGHT
Silk, Larry
AMERICAN DREAM
Silvi, Roberto
BECOMING COLETTE
MISSISSIPPI MASALA
Simpson, Claire
MAMBO KINGS, THE
Simpson, Robert
WHITE TRASH
Sinise, Robert L.
OF MICE AND MEN
Sinofsky, Bruce
BROTHER'S KEEPER
TERMINAL BLISS
Smedley-Aston, Brian
DIARY OF A HITMAN
Smith, Howard
GLENGARRY GLEN ROSS
Smith, Kent
ANIMAL INSTINCTS
MIRROR IMAGES
NIGHT RHYTHMS
PAMELA PRINCIPLE, THE
SECRET GAMES
Smith, Lee
LORENZO'S OIL
Smith, Margaret-Anne
LIGHT IN THE JUNGLE, THE
TRANCERS III: DETH LIVES
Smith, Nicholas C.
BRAM STOKER'S DRACULA
LOVE CRIMES
Southerland, Lynne
BEBE'S KIDS
RUNESTONE, THE
Steinbruck, Gudrun
LOCKED-UP TIME
Steiner, Gerald M.
AUNTIE LEE'S MEAT PIES
Steinkamp, William
MAN TROUBLE
SCENT OF A WOMAN
Stern, Merril
TUNE, THE
Stevenson, Michael A.
HONEY, I BLEW UP THE KID
Stokes, Terry
CRITTERS 4
Stratton, Kathleen
BEYOND DARKNESS
Street, John
DAMNED IN THE USA
Strigenoff, Vania
TROLL 2
Summanen, Lasse
OX, THE
Suzuki, Akira
SILK ROAD, THE
Sweeney, Mary
TWIN PEAKS: FIRE WALK WITH ME
Szanto, Annamaria
COOL WORLD
Tal, Omer
MIKEY
Tamayo, Augusto
WELCOME TO OBLIVION
Taylor, Peter
BECOMING COLETTE
Tellefsen, Chris
JUMPIN' AT THE BONEYARD
Tent, Kevin
GUILTY AS CHARGED
ULTRAVIOLET
Teschner, Peter
ONLY YOU
SOCIETY
Thaler, Jonas
ALL-AMERICAN MURDER
DOUBLE TROUBLE
Thibault, Michael
MARTIAL LAW 2: UNDERCOVER
Thomas, Sarah
SARAFINA!
Thomas, Scott
AFRAID OF THE DARK
Thompson, Blue
ARMED FOR ACTION
BLOOD ON THE BADGE
Thornton, Randy
HIGHWAY TO HELL
Thornton-Allen, Tim
BOB MARLEY: TIME WILL TELL
Tintori, John
LITTLE VEGAS
USED PEOPLE
Toniolo, Camilla
BUFFY THE VAMPIRE SLAYER
MY NEW GUN
Torres, Brunilda
JUICE
Tour, David
DOUBLE EDGE
Trader, Rick
MAGICAL WORLD OF CHUCK JONES, THE
Travis, Neil
PATRIOT GAMES
Trayler, Fiona
ROCK-A-DOODLE
Trevor, Richard
RUBY
Tronick, Michael
SCENT OF A WOMAN
STRAIGHT TALK
Tsenova, Nadia
DEATHSTALKER IV: MATCH OF TITANS
Tsukamoto, Shinya
TETSUO: THE IRON MAN
Tsurubuchi, Mitsuo
PROFESSIONAL, THE
Tucker, Jack
FATE
ILLUSIONS
Urioste, Frank J.
BASIC INSTINCT
Varaday, Brian
TRAINED TO FIGHT
Varity, Peter H.
MEATBALLS 4
Vinarao, Edgardo
EYE OF THE EAGLE 3
FIELD OF FIRE
Virkler, Dennis
FALLING FROM GRACE
FREEJACK
UNDER SIEGE
Volk, Paul G.
OUT FOR BLOOD
SUNSET STRIP
Walker, Lesley
WATERLAND
Walls, Tom
BREAKING THE RULES
Warner, Mark
LEAP OF FAITH
Watson, Earl
BOOMERANG
DANCE MACABRE
Weidner, John
DEADLY BET
FINAL IMPACT
MAXIMUM FORCE
OUT FOR BLOOD
Weil, Ian
BERNARD AND THE GENIE
Weisberg, Steven
MISTRESS
Weisbrot, Howie
BROKEN NOSES
Weiss, Adam
CROSSING THE BRIDGE
Wenning, Katherine
POPE MUST DIET!, THE
Weslak, Steve
DEADLY CURRENTS
Wheeler, John W.
LADYBUGS
Whelan, Derek
ULTIMATE DESIRES
Wimble, Chris
DOUBLE VISION
Winding, Genevieve
ELEGANT CRIMINEL, L'
INDOCHINE
Winer, Lucy
THANK YOU AND GOOD NIGHT!

Wisman, Ron
BEAUTIFUL DREAMERS
Wolfe, Adam
MINDWARP
Wreen, Delhak
PROJECT: SHADOWCHASER
Wu, David
HARD-BOILED
Young, William
BREATHING FIRE
Zahavi, Natan
MIKEY
Zetlin, Barry
INTO THE SUN
Ziller, Paul
PSYCHIC
Zimmerman, Don
DIGGSTOWN
LEAP OF FAITH
Zinner, Peter
GLADIATOR
Zuckerman, Lauren
DRIVE

MAKEUP

McCarthy, Tom C.
BRAM STOKER'S DRACULA
Bienkowsky, James
COMPLEX WORLD
Blake, John
HOFFA
Cannom, Greg
HOFFA
Constantinides, Michele
DISCRETE, LA
Johnson, Steve
INNOCENT BLOOD
Kindlon, Dave
BASKET CASE 3: THE PROGENY
Neill, Ve
BATMAN RETURNS
HOFFA
Reusch, Christa
ARTICLE 99
Specter, Ronnie
BATMAN RETURNS
Stone, David E.
BRAM STOKER'S DRACULA
Winston, Stan
BATMAN RETURNS

MUSIC COMPOSERS

Alabardo, Wayne
TOGETHER ALONE
Allaman, Eric
MIRACLE BEACH
Allen, Stephen
FATAL INSTINCT
Anderson, Laurie
MONSTER IN A BOX
Angelique
ALBERTO EXPRESS
Antonelli, Paul F.
CHINA O'BRIEN II
Armiger, Martin
CROSSING, THE
Artzi, Shlomo
LEATHER JACKETS
Asher, Jay
EXILED IN AMERICA
Aulepp, Glenn
INSIDE EDGE
SEX CRIMES
Avgerinos, Paul
COMRADES IN ARMS
Bach, Nenad
HAPPY HELL NIGHT
Badalamenti, Angelo
TWIN PEAKS: FIRE WALK WITH ME
Badarou, Wally
LUNATIC, THE
Bahtia, Amin
BLACK ICE
Baker, Fred
WHITE TRASH
Band, Richard
DOCTOR MORDRID
RESURRECTED, THE
TRANCERS III: DETH LIVES
Barber, Stephen
HUMAN SHIELD, THE
Barnes, John
BEBE'S KIDS
DAUGHTERS OF THE DUST
Barnes, Ricky
PANAMA DECEPTION, THE
Barry, John
CHAPLIN
Bartek, Steve
GUILTY AS CHARGED
Beck, Jeff
POPE MUST DIET!, THE
Becker, Frank W.
TERMINAL BLISS
Been, Michael
LIGHT SLEEPER
Beethoven, Ludwig van
BEETHOVEN LIVES UPSTAIRS
Bellon, Roger
DARK HORSE
Benford, Vassal
CLASS ACT
Bennet, Richard Rodney
ENCHANTED APRIL
Bennett, James
SWOON
Bergeaud, David
TRAINED TO FIGHT
Berger, Richard
SEXUAL RESPONSE
Bernstein, Elmer
BABE, THE
Best, Peter
FATHER
Bhalia, Amin
CAFE ROMEO
Bhatia, Amin
PRIMO BABY
Bigazzi, Giancarlo
MEDITERRANEO
Bisharat, Charles H.
DRIVE
Blanchard, Terence
MALCOLM X
Blue Oyster Cult
BAD CHANNELS
Bob Marley and the Wailers
BOB MARLEY: TIME WILL TELL
Bock, Jerry
STRANGER AMONG US, A
Broughton, Bruce
HONEY, I BLEW UP THE KID
STAY TUNED
Browne, Jackson
PANAMA DECEPTION, THE
Bryan, David
NETHERWORLD
Bryarly, Kelly
KILL LINE
Burke, Chris
REFRIGERATOR, THE
Burning Flames
LUNATIC, THE
Burwell, Carter
BUFFY THE VAMPIRE SLAYER
STORYVILLE
WATERLAND
Bussinger, Cobb
I DON'T BUY KISSES ANYMORE
Carlin, Sean
BRIDE OF KILLER NERD
Castle, Doug Walter
DESIRE AND HELL AT SUNSET MOTEL
Chabrol, Mathieu
CRY OF THE OWL, THE
INSPECTOR LAVARDIN
Chang, Gary
HOUSE OF USHER, THE
UNDER SIEGE
Charles, John
SOLDIER'S TALE, A
Chase, Thomas
LITTLE NEMO: ADVENTURES IN SLUMBERLAND
Cirino, Chuck
MUNCHIE
SOLDIER'S FORTUNE
Clapton, Eric
LETHAL WEAPON 3
Clarke, Stanley
PASSENGER 57
Clinton, George
WILD ORCHID 2: TWO SHADES OF BLUE
Clinton, George A.
HOUSE OF USHER, THE
Clinton, George S.
HARD PROMISES
Cocciante, Riccardo
MEDITERRANEO
Cohn, Stephen
NICKEL & DIME
Coleman, Graeme
COMMON BONDS

Halfpenny, Jim
BIKINI SUMMER 2
Harry, James
BODY WAVES
Hartley, Hal
SIMPLE MEN
Harvey, Shane
CLEARCUT
Havelka, Svatopluk
EAR, THE
Haycock, Peter
ONE FALSE MOVE
Heim, George Blond
GATE II
Herouet, Marc
NIGHT AND DAY
Hertzog, Paul
BREATHING FIRE
Herzog, David
HUNTING
Hess, Nigel
MONKEY BOY
Hewer, Mike
CANVAS
Hidden Faces
HIGHWAY TO HELL
Hill, John
JUST LIKE IN THE MOVIES
Himmelman, Peter
CROSSING THE BRIDGE
Hoffman, Kurt
LITTLE NOISES
Holbek, Joakim
ZENTROPA
Holt, Derek
ONE FALSE MOVE
Holton, Nigel
BLOODFIST III: FORCED TO FIGHT
KISS ME A KILLER
Hooper, Les
BACK IN THE U.S.S.R.
Horn, Trevor
TOYS
Horner, James
PATRIOT GAMES
SNEAKERS
THUNDERHEART
UNLAWFUL ENTRY
Horunzhy, Vladimir
BLINK OF AN EYE
Howard, James Newton
DIGGSTOWN
GLENGARRY GLEN ROSS
NIGHT AND THE CITY
Hunter, Steve
MEATBALLS 4
Hyman, Dick
ALAN & NAOMI
Irwin, Ashley
NIGHT RHYTHMS
Irwin, Pat
MY NEW GUN
Isham, Mark
COOL WORLD
MIDNIGHT CLEAR, A
OF MICE AND MEN
PUBLIC EYE, THE
RIVER RUNS THROUGH IT, A
Ishikawa, Chu
TETSUO: THE IRON MAN
Jankel, Chaz
K2
Jarre, Maurice
SCHOOL TIES
WILDFIRE
Jones, Brynmor
KILL CRUISE
Jones, Gregory
STEAL AMERICA
Jones, Trevor
BLAME IT ON THE BELLBOY
CHAINS OF GOLD
CRISSCROSS
FREEJACK
LAST OF THE MOHICANS, THE
Kaczenski, Heidi
SCORCHERS
Kaczmarek, Jan A.P.
PALE BLOOD
Kahane, Thomas
LOCKED-UP TIME
Kamen, Michael
LETHAL WEAPON 3
SHINING THROUGH
Kaniel, Noam
ROUND TRIP TO HEAVEN
Khrapatchev, Vadim
ADAM'S RIB
Kilar, Wojciech
BRAM STOKER'S DRACULA
Kitay, David
BREAKING THE RULES
Klingler, Kevin
WELCOME TO OBLIVION
Kraft, Robert
MAMBO KINGS, THE
Kymlicka, Milan
DEADBOLT
Lambert, Dennis
AMERICAN ME
Landers, Tim
SPIRITS
Lang, K.D.
GETTING MARRIED IN BUFFALO JUMP
Lansberg, Charlotte
HUGH HEFNER: ONCE UPON A TIME
Lavista, Mario
CABEZA DE VACA
Lazarov, Simo
DEATHSTALKER IV: MATCH OF TITANS
Lee Chun Shing
SUPERCOP: POLICE STORY III
Legrand, Michel
FATE
Leiber, Jed
LOVE POTION NO. 9
Levy, Shuki
BLIND VISION
ROUND TRIP TO HEAVEN
Licht, Daniel
AMITYVILLE 1992: IT'S ABOUT TIME
CHILDREN OF THE NIGHT
SEVERED TIES
Lipton, Michael
INVASION OF THE SPACE PREACHERS
Lloyd, Michael
GHOULIES III: GHOULIES GO TO COLLEGE
Logan, Mike
STEELE'S LAW
Lord, Justin
EYE OF THE EAGLE 3
FIELD OF FIRE
Lurie, Evan
JOHNNY STECCHINO
Lyons, Richard
DO OR DIE
Lysdal, Jens
DAY IN OCTOBER, A
MacDermot, Galt
MISTRESS
MacLachlan, Scott Douglas
INSIDE EDGE
SEX CRIMES
Madara, John
PHANTOM OF THE RITZ
Mader
IN THE SOUP
Mandel, Johnny
BRENDA STARR
Manfredini, Harry
ACES: IRON EAGLE III
HOUSE IV
KICKBOXER 3: THE ART OF WAR
Mann, Hummie
IN GOLD WE TRUST
YEAR OF THE COMET
Manska, Clay
INSIDE EDGE
SEX CRIMES
Manzie, Jim
MY GRANDPA IS A VAMPIRE
Marquard, Thomas
AFFENGEIL
Marsalis, Branford
SNEAKERS
Marshall, Phil
NOISES OFF
Marvin, Rick
3 NINJAS
Mascis, J.
GAS FOOD LODGING
Mason, Molly
BROTHER'S KEEPER
Massari, John
SNAKEEATER III . . . HIS LAW
May, Brian
DR. GIGGLES
McElheron, Maureen
TUNE, THE

McHugh, David
LONELY HEARTS
Menken, Alan
ALADDIN
NEWSIES
Miller, Marcus
BOOMERANG
Miller, Randy
HELLRAISER III: HELL ON EARTH
INTO THE SUN
Mithoff, Bob
LANDSLIDE
Mithoff, Boby
SEEDPEOPLE
Mixon, Donald
BIKINI CARWASH COMPANY, THE
Mole, Charlie
DEAD CERTAIN
Morgan, Mark
WHERE THE DAY TAKES YOU
Morricone, Ennio
BEYOND JUSTICE
CITY OF JOY
HUSBANDS AND LOVERS
RAMPAGE
Morse, Matthew
GUYVER, THE
Myers, Stanley
COLD HEAVEN
SARAFINA!
VOYAGER
Myrow, Fredric
RUBIN & ED
Nachon, Jean-Claude
ALBERTO EXPRESS
Nash the Slash
HIGHWAY 61
Natola, Cos
CAFE ROMEO
Newborn, Ira
BRAIN DONORS
COLLISION COURSE
INNOCENT BLOOD
Newman, David
HOFFA
HONEYMOON IN VEGAS
MIGHTY DUCKS, THE
ROVER DANGERFIELD
RUNESTONE, THE
Newman, Thomas
LINGUINI INCIDENT, THE
PLAYER, THE
SCENT OF A WOMAN
WHISPERS IN THE DARK
Niehaus, Lennie
UNFORGIVEN
Nieto, Jose
AMANTES
Nilsson, Stefan
BEST INTENTIONS, THE
Not Drowning Waving
PROOF
Nyman, Michael
HAIRDRESSER'S HUSBAND, THE
O'Hearn, Patrick
HEAVEN IS A PLAYGROUND
WHITE SANDS

Offenbach, Jacques
PETER'S FRIENDS
Omori, Toshiyuki
PROFESSIONAL, THE
Osborn, Jason
AFRAID OF THE DARK
Palmieri, Eddie
PUERTO RICAN MAMBO (NOT A MUSICAL), THE
Parks, Van Dyke
OUT ON A LIMB
Parsons, Stephen
SPLIT SECOND
Patrick, Cameron
MAGICAL WORLD OF CHUCK JONES, THE
Patterson, Rick
KILLER TOMATOES EAT FRANCE!
Penn, William
CONFESSIONS OF A SERIAL KILLER
Peterkofsky, Don
REFRIGERATOR, THE
Petit, Jean-Claude
PLAYBOYS, THE
Petitgirard, Laurent
ELEGANT CRIMINEL, L'
Pike, Nicholas
CAPTAIN RON
STEPHEN KING'S SLEEPWALKERS
Pinder, Gary
PROJECT: SHADOWCHASER
Plumeri, Terry
LOWER LEVEL
Poledouris, Basil
WIND
Poore, Dennis
MAXIMUM BREAKOUT
Portman, Rachel
USED PEOPLE
WHERE ANGELS FEAR TO TREAD
Postel, Steve
JUMPIN' AT THE BONEYARD
Powell, Reg
GHOULIES III: GHOULIES GO TO COLLEGE
Pray For Rain
ROADSIDE PROPHETS
Preisner, Zbigniew
DAMAGE
Price, Stephen
DEADLY CURRENTS
Qu Xiaosong
LIFE ON A STRING
Rachtman, Karyn
RESERVOIR DOGS
Rarick, Ken
IN THE HEAT OF PASSION
Ravio, Roy J.
DESERT KICKBOXER
Redford, J.A.C.
NEWSIES
Remote Control Music
HOUSE ON TOMBSTONE HILL, THE
Renzetti, Joe
BASKET CASE 3: THE PROGENY
Rettino, Debby Kerner
ORIGINAL INTENT

Rettino, Ernie
ORIGINAL INTENT
Revell, Graeme
HAND THAT ROCKS THE CRADLE, THE
LOVE CRIMES
TILL THERE WAS YOU
TRACES OF RED
Rivera, Ismael
PANAMA DECEPTION, THE
Robbins, David
BOB ROBERTS
Robbins, Richard
HOWARDS END
Robertson, C. Barny
ORIGINAL INTENT
Robertson, Eric N.
GETTING MARRIED IN BUFFALO JUMP
Robinson, J. Peter
ENCINO MAN
WAYNE'S WORLD
Robinson, Peter Manning
CRITTERS 4
Roman, Tony
SMOOTH TALKER
Roth, Adam
REFRIGERATOR, THE
Rothe, Walter Christian
FINEST HOUR, THE
Rucker, Steve
LITTLE NEMO: ADVENTURES IN SLUMBERLAND
Russell-Pavier, Nicholas
SECRET FRIENDS
Russo, David E.
SHAKING THE TREE
Ryder, Mark
SOCIETY
TRANCERS III: DETH LIVES
Sacher, Graham
DOUBLE VISION
Safan, Craig
OVER HER DEAD BODY
Sanborn, David
LETHAL WEAPON 3
Sanko, Anton
COUSIN BOBBY
Sarde, Philippe
POUR SACHA
Sarhandi, Sarah
LONDON KILLS ME
Sato, Masaru
SILK ROAD, THE
Savall, Jordi
TOUS LES MATINS DU MONDE
Schiff, Steve
WAXWORK II: LOST IN TIME
Schumann, Robert
CONTE DE PRINTEMPS
Sciacqua, Duane
ROOTS OF EVIL
Scott, John
BECOMING COLETTE
HOMEBOYS
JOURNEY OF HONOR
RUBY

Scott, Tom
SHAKES THE CLOWN
Senchuk, Igor
RASPAD
Sereda, John
MANIAC WARRIORS
Shaiman, Marc
FEW GOOD MEN, A
MR. SATURDAY NIGHT
SISTER ACT
Sharp, Elliot
DADDY AND THE MUSCLE ACADEMY
Sheriff, Jamie
SLUMBER PARTY MASSACRE 3
Shire, David
BED & BREAKFAST
Shore, Howard
PRELUDE TO A KISS
SINGLE WHITE FEMALE
Silvestri, Alan
BODYGUARD, THE
DEATH BECOMES HER
FERNGULLY: THE LAST RAINFOREST
STOP! OR MY MOM WILL SHOOT
Simon, Carly
THIS IS MY LIFE
Simon, Marty
SCANNERS III: THE TAKEOVER
Singer, Scott
NAKED OBSESSION
Skinner, David
ROCK & ROLL COWBOYS
Slane, Rod
ALL-AMERICAN MURDER
Slider, Dan
DANCE MACABRE
Small, Michael
AMERICAN DREAM
CONSENTING ADULTS
Smart, Robert
ULTIMATE DESIRES
Smith, Bruce
LONDON KILLS ME
Smith, Joseph
ANIMAL INSTINCTS
MIRROR IMAGES
OTHER WOMAN, THE
PAMELA PRINCIPLE, THE
Snow, Mark
DOLLY DEAREST
Snyder, Steven
COMPLEX WORLD
Sobel, Curt
BACKTRACK
Solomon, Elliot
MARTIAL LAW 2: UNDERCOVER
Solomon, Maribeth
WISECRACKS
Souster, Tim
CTHULHU MANSION
Spear, David
MORTUARY ACADEMY
Spektor, Mira J.
DOUBLE EDGE
Spotts, Roger Hamilton
IMPORTANCE OF BEING EARNEST, THE
Springer, Mark
LONDON KILLS ME
Standish, John
LASER MOON
Static Effect
HELLROLLER
Stemple, James
ADVENTURES IN SPYING
Stewart, David A.
LILY WAS HERE
Sting
PANAMA DECEPTION, THE
Stromberg, William T.
ODDBALL HALL
Strunz, Jorge
PANAMA DECEPTION, THE
Subramaniam, L.
MISSISSIPPI MASALA
Sugiyama, Koichi
GODZILLA VS. BIOLLANTE
Suozzo, Mark
THANK YOU AND GOOD NIGHT!
Taj Mahal
ZEBRAHEAD
Tavera, Michael
FROZEN ASSETS
Teetsel, Fredric
ADVENTURES IN DINOSAUR CITY
The Bomb Squad
JUICE
Thomas, Christopher
THERE'S NOTHING OUT THERE
Thomas, Ian
OH, WHAT A NIGHT
Thompson, Randy
MONTANA RUN, THE
Tomney, Ed
ULTRAVIOLET
Traynor, John
HELL MASTER
Trench, Fiachra
CODE NAME: CHAOS
Troob, Danny
NEWSIES
Truman, Tim
MIKEY
SOUTH CENTRAL
Turner, Greg
CENTER OF THE WEB
Turner, Simon Fisher
EDWARD II
Tyng, Christopher
DELTA HEAT
Ungar, Jay
BROTHER'S KEEPER
Valero, Jean-Louis
CONTE DE PRINTEMPS
Van Beethoven, Ludwig
CONTE DE PRINTEMPS
Van Dormael, Pierre
TOTO LE HEROS
Van Orden, Fritz
LITTLE NOISES
Van Tieghem, David
MY FATHER IS COMING
Vangelis
1492: THE CONQUEST OF PARADISE
VaRouje
TALONS OF THE EAGLE
TIGER CLAWS
Vasseur, Didier
NEAR MISSES
Vesperini, Edith
VAN GOGH
Vitali, Adriano M.
EVIL CLUTCH
Waits, Tom
NIGHT ON EARTH
Walden, W.G. Snuffy
LEAVING NORMAL
Walker, Shirley
MEMOIRS OF AN INVISIBLE MAN
Wallace, Bennie
WHITE MEN CAN'T JUMP
Watkins, Mary
COLOR ADJUSTMENT
Way, Darryl
FINISHING TOUCH, THE
Weill, Kurt
SHADOWS AND FOG
Weiss, Steve
CAN IT BE LOVE
Wentworth, Rick
FREDDIE AS F.R.O.7
West, Jim
LADY DRAGON
Westerberg, Paul
SINGLES
Wheatley, David
CHINA O'BRIEN II
White, Dave
PHANTOM OF THE RITZ
Widelitz, Stacy
MEGAVILLE
PRAYER OF THE ROLLERBOYS
Wild, Chuck
PANAMA DECEPTION, THE
Williams, John
FAR AND AWAY
HOME ALONE 2: LOST IN NEW YORK
Williams, Patrick
BIG GIRLS DON'T CRY . . . THEY GET EVEN
CUTTING EDGE, THE
Wong, James
ONCE UPON A TIME IN CHINA
Wood, Art
IN THE HEAT OF PASSION
Wurst, David
BLACKBELT
BLOODFIST IV: DIE TRYING
Wurst, Eric
BLACKBELT
BLOODFIST IV: DIE TRYING
Wyman, Dan
LAWNMOWER MAN, THE
Yared, Gabriel
LOVER, THE

Young, Chris
BARBARIAN QUEEN II: THE EMPRESS STRIKES BACK
Young, Christopher
JENNIFER EIGHT
RAPID FIRE
VAGRANT, THE
Zapanti, Tasso
BRONX WAR, THE
Zaza, Paul
PROM NIGHT IV - DELIVER US FROM EVIL
Zhao Jiping
RAISE THE RED LANTERN
Zimmer, Hans
CODE NAME: CHAOS
LEAGUE OF THEIR OWN, A
POWER OF ONE, THE
RADIO FLYER
TOYS

MUSIC DIRECTORS

Massara, Natale
FINE ROMANCE, A
Matsuura, Noriyoshi
VAMPIRE HUNTER D
Palmer, Robert
DEEP BLUES

PRODUCERS

Abbott, Elliot
LEAGUE OF THEIR OWN, A
Abbott, Steve
BLAME IT ON THE BELLBOY
Abrams, Peter
MIKEY
Acevski, Jon
FREDDIE AS F.R.O.7
Adams, Geoff
COMPLEX WORLD
Albert, Richard L.
DELTA HEAT
Amigo, Angel
WINTER IN LISBON, THE
Amritraj, Ashok
LIGHT IN THE JUNGLE, THE
NIGHT EYES 2
SEXUAL RESPONSE
Anderson, David
ALAN & NAOMI
Anderson, Kurt
MISSION OF JUSTICE
Annaud, Monique
DOES THIS MEAN WE'RE MARRIED?
HOT CHOCOLATE
NEAR MISSES
ROAD TO RUIN
SHOOTING ELIZABETH
Apted, Michael
35 UP
Aras, Ruta K.
CENTER OF THE WEB
MAXIMUM BREAKOUT
Arcady, Alexandre
POUR SACHA
Argento, Dario
DEVIL'S DAUGHTER, THE
Attenborough, Richard
CHAPLIN
Avneri, Ronit
TEXAS TENOR: THE ILLINOIS JACQUET STORY
Avnet, Jon
MIGHTY DUCKS, THE
Baden-Powell, Sue
PUBLIC EYE, THE
Baker, Fred
WHITE TRASH
Baker, Martin G.
MUPPET CHRISTMAS CAROL, THE
Balian, Haig
LILY WAS HERE
Balsam, Mark
ALAN & NAOMI
Band, Albert
TRANCERS III: DETH LIVES
Band, Charles
DOCTOR MORDRID
Bandini, Filiberto
INDIO 2 - THE REVOLT
Bank, Keith
HEAVEN IS A PLAYGROUND
Barichello, Rudy
KILLER IMAGE
Bateman, Kent
BREAKING THE RULES
Battista, Franco
DEADBOLT
TWIN SISTERS
Baum, Carol
SHINING THROUGH
Baumgarten, Craig
UNIVERSAL SOLDIER
Bean, Henry
DEEP COVER
Beaton, Jesse
ONE FALSE MOVE
Begun, Jeff
NEON CITY
Belzberg, Leslie
INNOCENT BLOOD
Bender, Lawrence
RESERVOIR DOGS
Berlinger, Joe
BROTHER'S KEEPER
Bernart, Maurice
ALBERTO EXPRESS
Berner, Fred
STRAIGHT TALK
Berri, Claude
LOVER, THE
Berry, Tom
DEADBOLT
PSYCHIC
TWIN SISTERS
Besser, Stuart M.
DR. GIGGLES
Betzer, Just
DAY IN OCTOBER, A
Bevan, Tim
LONDON KILLS ME
Biber, Michael J.
SOLDIER'S FORTUNE
Bibo, Heinz
BECOMING COLETTE
Bienstock, Ric Esther
DEADLY CURRENTS
Bjalkeskog, Lars
BEST INTENTIONS, THE
Black, Todd
CLASS ACT
Blair, Jon
MONSTER IN A BOX
Blank, Harrod
WILD WHEELS
Blumenthal, Hank
IN THE SOUP
Bluth, Don
ROCK-A-DOODLE
Bodner, Bruce
MEMOIRS OF AN INVISIBLE MAN
Borchers, Donald P.
DESIRE AND HELL AT SUNSET MOTEL
MEATBALLS 4
Borde, Mark
RESURRECTED, THE
Borden, Bill
MIDNIGHT CLEAR, A
Borden, Lizzie
LOVE CRIMES
Border, W.K.
LOWER LEVEL
Borgnine, Nancee
SUNSET STRIP
Bosanquet, Simon
AFRAID OF THE DARK
Bosko, Mark Steven
BRIDE OF KILLER NERD
Bouygues, Francis
TWIN PEAKS: FIRE WALK WITH ME
Boyd, Daniel
INVASION OF THE SPACE PREACHERS
Bradford, Thomas
NETHERWORLD
Branagh, Kenneth
PETER'S FRIENDS
Brandes, David
QUARREL, THE
Braun, Jonathon
BLIND VISION
Bregman, Martin
WHISPERS IN THE DARK
Bregman, Michael S.
WHISPERS IN THE DARK
Brennan, Richard
EFFICIENCY EXPERT, THE
Brest, Martin
SCENT OF A WOMAN
Brezner, Larry
PASSED AWAY
Brooks, Halle
WHO SHOT PATAKANGO?
Brouwer, Chris
LILY WAS HERE

Brown, David
FEW GOOD MEN, A
PLAYER, THE

Brubaker, James D.
BRAIN DONORS

Bruce-Clayton, Martin
DEMON IN MY VIEW, A

Brunton, Colin
HIGHWAY 61

Burkhardt, Bernd
LOCKED-UP TIME

Burton, Tim
BATMAN RETURNS

Byers, John
HIGHWAY TO HELL

Cady, Daniel
DOLLY DEAREST

Cameron, Ross
COLD JUSTICE

Campbell, Bruce
LUNATICS: A LOVE STORY

Canal Plus
TOUS LES MATINS DU MONDE

Canale, Michael
ILLUSIONS

Cantero, Mate
SHOOTING ELIZABETH

Cantin, Marie
WATERDANCE, THE

Canton, Neil
TRESPASS

Carroll, Gordon
ALIEN3

Carroll, Willard
BEBE'S KIDS
ROVER DANGERFIELD

Cartlidge, William P.
PLAYBOYS, THE

Cassavetti, Patrick
WATERLAND

Castellaneta, P.J.
TOGETHER ALONE

Cathell, Cevin
GIVING, THE

Cecchi Gori, Mario
DEVIL'S DAUGHTER, THE
JOHNNY STECCHINO
MEDITERRANEO

Cecchi Gori, Vittorio
DEVIL'S DAUGHTER, THE
JOHNNY STECCHINO
MEDITERRANEO

Chalong Pakdivijit
IN GOLD WE TRUST

Chan, Willie
SUPERCOP: POLICE STORY III

Chang, Martha
3 NINJAS

Chang, Terence
HARD-BOILED

Chartoff, Robert
STRAIGHT TALK

Chaudhri, Amin Q.
DIARY OF A HITMAN

Chiu Fu-sheng
RAISE THE RED LANTERN

Chobanian, Arthur
INCIDENT AT OGLALA

Chow, Raymond
ONCE UPON A TIME IN CHINA

Chubb, Caldecott
HOFFA

Chvatal, Cindy
HARD PROMISES

Cingolani, Luigi
ADVENTURES IN DINOSAUR CITY
PLAY NICE

Clark, Dick
BACKTRACK

Clark-Hall, Steve
EDWARD II

Claybourne, Doug
MR. BASEBALL

Cleitman, Rene
BEATING HEART, A

Clements, Ron
ALADDIN

Codikow, Stacy
FATAL INSTINCT

Cohen, Howard R.
DEATHSTALKER IV: MATCH OF TITANS

Cohen, Rudy
DELTA HEAT

Cohen, Steve
MARTIAL LAW 2: UNDERCOVER

Cohn, Arthur
AMERICAN DREAM

Cohn, Elie
HUMAN SHIELD, THE

Colichman, Paul
SHAKES THE CLOWN

Coppola, Francis Ford
BRAM STOKER'S DRACULA

Corman, Roger
BLOODFIST III: FORCED TO FIGHT
FIELD OF FIRE
PLAY MURDER FOR ME

Corominas, Pepon
PEPI, LUCI, BOM AND OTHER GIRLS ON THE HEAP

Cort, Robert W.
COLLISION COURSE
CUTTING EDGE, THE

Costa, Pedro
AMANTES

Costner, Kevin
BODYGUARD, THE

Cox, Brian
TERMINAL BLISS

Crow, Nancy Carter
IMPORTANCE OF BEING EARNEST, THE

Crowe, Cameron
SINGLES

Cruz, Rafael
CABEZA DE VACA

Crystal, Billy
MR. SATURDAY NIGHT

Cunningham, Sean S.
HOUSE IV

Curtis, John A.
MANIAC WARRIORS
ULTIMATE DESIRES

Cutforth, Mark
DEAD CERTAIN

Cyran, Catherine
KISS ME A KILLER
SLUMBER PARTY MASSACRE 3
ULTRAVIOLET

Dakota, Reno
AMERICAN FABULOUS

Daniel, Don
PLAY NICE

Daniel, Sean
AMERICAN ME

Danielson, Lynn
NICKEL & DIME

Danton, Sylvie
VAN GOGH

Dash, Julie
DAUGHTERS OF THE DUST

Daugherty, George
MAGICAL WORLD OF CHUCK JONES, THE

Davey, Bruce
FOREVER YOUNG

David, Pierre
DEEP COVER
MISSION OF JUSTICE

Davies, Chris
KICK OR DIE

Davis, John
CODE NAME: CHAOS

Davis, John A.
OVER HER DEAD BODY

Davis, Richard
CAFE ROMEO
COMMON BONDS

De Niro, Robert
MISTRESS
THUNDERHEART

DeBello, John
KILLER TOMATOES EAT FRANCE!

DeBroca, Michelle
FAVOUR, THE WATCH, AND THE VERY BIG FISH, THE

DeFaria, Christopher
AMITYVILLE 1992: IT'S ABOUT TIME

DeGanay, Thierry
HAIRDRESSER'S HUSBAND, THE

DeLaurentiis, Dino
ONCE UPON A CRIME

Demetrios, Eames
GIVING, THE

Devine, David
BEETHOVEN LIVES UPSTAIRS

DeVito, Danny
HOFFA

DiNovi, Denise
BATMAN RETURNS

Disney, Tim
GIVING, THE

Donahue, Patrick G.
SAVAGE INSTINCT

Donner, Richard
LETHAL WEAPON 3

Doran, Lindsay
LEAVING NORMAL
Doroshow, Joanne
PANAMA DECEPTION, THE
Doumanian, Jean
OX, THE
Dowd, Jeff
ZEBRAHEAD
Drai, Victor
FOLKS!
Driver, Charla
STREET CRIMES
Drouot, Pierre
TOTO LE HEROS
Dubrow, Donna
MEDICINE MAN
Dunn, Jr., William G.
DESERT KICKBOXER
Dunning, John
SNAKEEATER III . . . HIS LAW
DuPlantier, Daniel Toscan
VAN GOGH
Eastman, Brian
UNDER SUSPICION
Eastman, Carole
MAN TROUBLE
Eastwood, Clint
UNFORGIVEN
Eberle, Oliver
EYE OF THE STORM
Eberts, Jake
CITY OF JOY
Egoyan, Atom
ADJUSTER, THE
Eisenman, Morrie
ONLY YOU
SCORCHERS
Eisenman, Rafael
WILD ORCHID 2: TWO SHADES OF BLUE
Elbert, Ed
CAGED FEAR
Elgear, Sandra
VOICES FROM THE FRONT
Elliott, Mike
BLACKBELT
BLOODFIST IV: DIE TRYING
BODY WAVES
DANCE WITH DEATH
HOMICIDAL IMPULSE
MUNCHIE
Elwes, Cassian
LEATHER JACKETS
Ephraim, Lionel A.
KICK OR DIE
Everett, Gimel
LAWNMOWER MAN, THE
Ewart, William
GAS FOOD LODGING
Eyres, John E.
PROJECT: SHADOWCHASER
Faiman, Peter
FERNGULLY: THE LAST RAINFOREST
Feldman, Edward S.
HONEY, I BLEW UP THE KID

Field, Ted
COLLISION COURSE
CUTTING EDGE, THE
Fienberg, Gregg
TWIN PEAKS: FIRE WALK WITH ME
Finnell, Michael
NEWSIES
Flender, Rodman
IN THE HEAT OF PASSION
Flick, Steve
MIND, BODY & SOUL
Flower, Buck
BIKINI CARWASH COMPANY, THE
Flynn, Michael
MY NEW GUN
Fontana, Agnese
EVIL CLUTCH
Foppa, Julio Solorzano
CABEZA DE VACA
Frankel, Elizabeth
BRONX WAR, THE
Frankfurt, Peter
JUICE
French Ministry of Culture
TOUS LES MATINS DU MONDE
Fuchs, Fred
BRAM STOKER'S DRACULA
Fujioka, Yutaka
LITTLE NEMO: ADVENTURES IN SLUMBERLAND
PROFESSIONAL, THE
Fusco, John
BABE, THE
THUNDERHEART
Gale, Randolph
GUILTY AS CHARGED
Gallager, Bob
CAN IT BE LOVE
Gallagher, A.V.
INVASION OF THE SPACE PREACHERS
Garcia, David
SEX CRIMES
Garroni, Andrew
ANIMAL INSTINCTS
MIRROR IMAGES
NIGHT RHYTHMS
OTHER WOMAN, THE
PAMELA PRINCIPLE, THE
SECRET GAMES
Gazzano, Liz
STEAL AMERICA
Gebhard, Glenn
ONE LAST RUN
Gerrans, Jon
LIVING END, THE
Geys, Dany
TOTO LE HEROS
Gideon, Raynold
KUFFS
Gilbert, Brad
LITTLE NOISES
Gilbert, Bruce
MAN TROUBLE
Giler, David
ALIEN3

Gillott, Nick
MONKEY BOY
Glaser, Allan
DARK HORSE
Glimcher, Arne
MAMBO KINGS, THE
Golan, Menahem
CAPTAIN AMERICA
DANCE MACABRE
FINEST HOUR, THE
Goldberg, Leonard
DISTINGUISHED GENTLEMAN, THE
Goldfine, Lloyd
JUMPIN' AT THE BONEYARD
Goldman, Alain
1492: THE CONQUEST OF PARADISE
Goldman, Gary
ROCK-A-DOODLE
Golin, Steve
CANDYMAN
RUBY
STRANGER AMONG US, A
Gordon, Charles
UNLAWFUL ENTRY
Gordon, Mark
TRACES OF RED
Gosse, Bob
LAWS OF GRAVITY
Gould, Jr., Harry E.
RUNESTONE, THE
Grais, Michael
STEPHEN KING'S SLEEPWALKERS
Granger, Derek
WHERE ANGELS FEAR TO TREAD
Grazer, Brian
BOOMERANG
FAR AND AWAY
HOUSESITTER
Green, Sarah
PASSION FISH
Greenhut, Robert
HUSBANDS AND WIVES
LEAGUE OF THEIR OWN, A
SHADOWS AND FOG
Gregory, Eileen
DEEP BLUES
Gregory, Laura
SPLIT SECOND
Griffiths, Geoff
PROJECT: SHADOWCHASER
Gross, Michael C.
BEETHOVEN
STOP! OR MY MOM WILL SHOOT
Grossman, Gary H.
HUGH HEFNER: ONCE UPON A TIME
Gruenberg, Tom
PRIMARY MOTIVE
Gruskoff, Michael
ARTICLE 99
PRELUDE TO A KISS
Guzzetti, Alfred
PICTURES FROM A REVOLUTION
Haboush, Ray
ALMOST PREGNANT
Hadar, Ronnie
ROUND TRIP TO HEAVEN

Halpern, Elliott
DEADLY CURRENTS
Hamori, Andras
GATE II
Harding, Malcolm R.
FOLKS!
Harold, Wayne A.
BRIDE OF KILLER NERD
Haruna, Kazuo
SILK ROAD, THE
Harvey, Bruce
KILLER IMAGE
Harvey, Rupert
CRITTERS 4
Hashimoto, Richard
SINGLES
Hassid, Daniel
GAS FOOD LODGING
Hayes, Terry
FLIRTING
Heath, Robert
HUGH HEFNER: ONCE UPON A TIME
Heller, Paul
LUNATIC, THE
Hellman, Richard
SCORCHERS
Henson, Brian
MUPPET CHRISTMAS CAROL, THE
Hertzberg, Michael
OUT ON A LIMB
Hertzberg, Paul
976-EVIL II
WE'RE TALKIN' SERIOUS MONEY
WHERE THE DAY TAKES YOU
Hess, Oliver G.
INTO THE SUN
Heumann, Eric
INDOCHINE
Heyman, David
JUICE
Hickman, David
BRIEF HISTORY OF TIME, A
Higgins, Bill
HEAVEN IS A PLAYGROUND
Hill, Walter
ALIEN3
Hippolyte, Alexander Gregory
OTHER WOMAN, THE
PAMELA PRINCIPLE, THE
Hogue, Jeffrey C.
SOLDIER'S FORTUNE
Holt, James A.
HOMEBOYS
House, Lynda
PROOF
Howard, Ron
FAR AND AWAY
Howarth, Jennie
BLAME IT ON THE BELLBOY
Howson, Frank
HUNTING
Hu, Marcus
LIVING END, THE
Hudecek, Robert
COLD JUSTICE
Hudlin, Warrington
BOOMERANG
Hughes, John
HOME ALONE 2:
LOST IN NEW YORK
Hurd, Gale Anne
RAISING CAIN
WATERDANCE, THE
Hurmer, Alfred
LOCKED-UP TIME
Hutt, Robyn
VOICES FROM THE FRONT
Hyman, Myron A.
BRENDA STARR
Ievins, Edgar
BASKET CASE 3: THE PROGENY
Inada, Nobuo
PROFESSIONAL, THE
Ingvordsen, J. Christian
COMRADES IN ARMS
Jacobovici, Simcha
DEADLY CURRENTS
Jafa, Arthur
DAUGHTERS OF THE DUST
Jaffe, Stanley R.
SCHOOL TIES
Jarmusch, Jim
NIGHT ON EARTH
Jensen, Peter Aalbaek
ZENTROPA
Joffe, Roland
CITY OF JOY
Johannson, Signe
WISECRACKS
Johnson, Mark
TOYS
Jolliffe, Genevieve
ESCAPE FROM . . . SURVIVAL ZONE
Jones, Chris
ESCAPE FROM . . . SURVIVAL ZONE
Junkersdorf, Eberhard
VOYAGER
Juso, Galliano
HUSBANDS AND LOVERS
Kaczmarczyk, Omar
PALE BLOOD
Kahn, Terry
CAGED FEAR
Kallberg, Kevin M.
INTO THE SUN
Kaman, Steven
COMRADES IN ARMS
Kane, Mary
BAD LIEUTENANT
Kanefsky, Victor
THERE'S NOTHING OUT THERE
Karmitz, Marin
INSPECTOR LAVARDIN
Kasdan, Lawrence
BODYGUARD, THE
Kasha, Alon
JUST LIKE IN THE MOVIES
Kasper, David
PANAMA DECEPTION, THE
Kassar, Mario
CHAPLIN
Kastenbaum, Michael
ALMOST PREGNANT
Kato, Hiroshi
VAMPIRE HUNTER D
Kaurismaki, Aki
MATCH FACTORY GIRL, THE
Kelly, Anne
DEMONIC TOYS
SEEDPEOPLE
Kelly, David
DEMON IN MY VIEW, A
Kenner, Robert
LONELY HEARTS
Kerner, Jordan
MIGHTY DUCKS, THE
Kilik, Jon
FATHERS AND SONS
Kim, Robert W.
KILL LINE
Kleiman, Vivian
COLOR ADJUSTMENT
Klein, Don
FROZEN ASSETS
Koch, Jr., Howard W.
COLLISION COURSE
Koeda, Mitsuhisa
VAMPIRE HUNTER D
Kollek, Amos
DOUBLE EDGE
Kolsrud, Dan
MEMOIRS OF AN INVISIBLE MAN
Kopple, Barbara
AMERICAN DREAM
Koster-Paul, Dorothy
FATE
Kosugi, Sho
JOURNEY OF HONOR
Kotzky, Jacob
BLINK OF AN EYE
Kowalski, Lech
ROCK SOUP
Krane, Jonathan D.
BREAKING THE RULES
CHAINS OF GOLD
COLD HEAVEN
Krevoy, Brad
DOUBLE TROUBLE
MIRACLE BEACH
Krone, Alan
BARBARIAN QUEEN II:
THE EMPRESS STRIKES BACK
Kroopf, Scott
GUN IN BETTY LOU'S
HANDBAG, THE
Kuk, Linda
HARD-BOILED
Kurys, Diane
POUR SACHA
Kuzui, Kaz
BUFFY THE VAMPIRE SLAYER
Labadie, Jean
INDOCHINE
Lane, Andrew
LONELY HEARTS
Langlais, Randy
LOVE CRIMES

Lankford, T.L.
SPIRITS
Lansing, Sherry
SCHOOL TIES
LaPegna, Arturo
FINE ROMANCE, A
LaPegna, Massimiliano
FINE ROMANCE, A
Lasker, Lawrence
SNEAKERS
Launer, Dale
LOVE POTION NO. 9
MY COUSIN VINNY
Lawrence, Robert
RAPID FIRE
Leahy, Michael
LOWER LEVEL
Leder, Paul
EXILED IN AMERICA
Lee, Spike
MALCOLM X
Leighton, Michael W.
PALE BLOOD
Lesseos, Mimi
PUSHED TO THE LIMIT
Lester, David
WHITE MEN CAN'T JUMP
Levine, Jean
BIKINI SUMMER 2
Levinson, Barry
TOYS
Levinson, G.J.
HELLROLLER
Levy, Jefery
DRIVE
Levy, John
CODE NAME: CHAOS
Levy, Michael I.
ARTICLE 99
PRELUDE TO A KISS
Levy, Robert
MIKEY
Lewald, Eric
LIFE ON THE EDGE
Lewis, Melisse
HOUSE ON TOMBSTONE HILL, THE
Lieb, Stephen
WITCHCRAFT IV: VIRGIN HEART
Lishman, Eda Lever
PRIMO BABY
Litinsky, Irene
SNAKEEATER III . . . HIS LAW
Livi, Jean-Louis
TOUS LES MATINS DU MONDE
Llosa, Luis
WELCOME TO OBLIVION
Lobell, Mike
HONEYMOON IN VEGAS
Lorenz, Carsten H.W.
EYE OF THE STORM
Lowry, Hunt
LAST OF THE MOHICANS, THE
Lucchesi, Gary
JENNIFER EIGHT
Luddy, Tom
WIND
Luly-Goldthwait, Ann
SHAKES THE CLOWN
Lupo, Rich
COMPLEX WORLD
Ma, Nicole
MY FATHER IS COMING
MacConkey, Holly
WITCHCRAFT IV: VIRGIN HEART
Macdonald, Flora
GETTING MARRIED IN BUFFALO JUMP
Macek, Carl
PROFESSIONAL, THE
VAMPIRE HUNTER D
MacGregor-Scott, Peter
LITTLE VEGAS
MacLear, Michael
BEAUTIFUL DREAMERS
Madden, David
HAND THAT ROCKS THE CRADLE, THE
Madec, Evelyne
TOUCH AND DIE
Maesso, Jose G.
CTHULHU MANSION
Mahoney, Raymond
BREATHING FIRE
Malin, Howard
OVER HER DEAD BODY
Malle, Louis
DAMAGE
Malo, Rene
SCANNERS III: THE TAKEOVER
Maloney, Denis
COMPLEX WORLD
Mancuso, Jr., Frank
COOL WORLD
Mandel, Yoram
JOHNNY SUEDE
Manheim, Michael
LEAP OF FAITH
Mann, Michael
LAST OF THE MOHICANS, THE
Marcarelli, Rob
ORIGINAL INTENT
Marcus-Plone, Carol
PHANTOM OF THE RITZ
Marignac, Martine
NIGHT AND DAY
Marino, Nick
DEATH HOUSE
Markey, Patrick
RIVER RUNS THROUGH IT, A
Marshall, Alan
BASIC INSTINCT
Marshall, Frank
NOISES OFF
Marvis, Curt
FOR THOSE ABOUT TO ROCK
Marx, Timothy
PASSED AWAY
Mastorakis, Isabelle
HIRED TO KILL
Mastorakis, Nico
HIRED TO KILL
Matovich, Mitchel
I DON'T BUY KISSES ANYMORE
Mayfield, Les
ENCINO MAN
Mazzola, Eugene
ADVENTURES IN SPYING
McCarthy, Peter
ROADSIDE PROPHETS
McCormick, Bret
BLOOD ON THE BADGE
McDonald, Bruce
HIGHWAY 61
McDougall, Ian
CLEARCUT
McElroy, Hal
TILL THERE WAS YOU
McElroy, Jim
TILL THERE WAS YOU
McGuinness, Katy
WATERLAND
Medjuck, Joe
BEETHOVEN
STOP! OR MY MOM WILL SHOOT
Mehri, Jalal
TALONS OF THE EAGLE
TIGER CLAWS
Mehri, Joseph
OUT FOR BLOOD
STREET CRIMES
Meiesan, David
VOICES FROM THE FRONT
Meiselas, Susan
PICTURES FROM A REVOLUTION
Meistrich, Larry
LAWS OF GRAVITY
Menegoz, Margaret
CONTE DE PRINTEMPS
Merchant, Ismail
HOWARDS END
Merhi, Joseph
DEADLY BET
FINAL IMPACT
MAXIMUM FORCE
Michaels, Joel B.
UNIVERSAL SOLDIER
Michaels, Lorne
WAYNE'S WORLD
Mickelson, Robert
PRAYER OF THE ROLLERBOYS
Milchan, Arnon
MAMBO KINGS, THE
POWER OF ONE, THE
UNDER SIEGE
Miller, Chip
MORTUARY ACADEMY
Miller, Don
WHITE MEN CAN'T JUMP
Miller, George
FLIRTING
LORENZO'S OIL
Minervini, Gianni
MEDITERRANEO
Mitchell, Charles
ZEBRAHEAD
Mitchell, Doug
FLIRTING
LORENZO'S OIL

Model, Ben
PUERTO RICAN MAMBO (NOT A MUSICAL), THE

Mogulesco, Miles
ADVENTURES IN SPYING

Monn-Iversen, Stein
LANDSLIDE

Montes, Eduardo
SMOOTH TALKER

Morgan, Andre E.
LADYBUGS

Moritz, Neal H.
JUICE

Mortorff, Lawrence
HELLRAISER III: HELL ON EARTH

Moses, Ben
NICKEL & DIME

Mozer, Richard
BEETHOVEN LIVES UPSTAIRS

Mulvehill, Charles
BRAM STOKER'S DRACULA

Munch, Christopher
HOURS AND TIMES, THE

Munro, Alan
ODDBALL HALL

Murphy, Karen
CUTTING EDGE, THE

Murray, Forrest
BOB ROBERTS

Musker, John
ALADDIN

Myron, Ben
ONE FALSE MOVE

Nagasaki, Yukio
VAMPIRE HUNTER D

Nair, Mira
MISSISSIPPI MASALA

Navarro, Bertha
CABEZA DE VACA

Netter, Gil
BRAIN DONORS

Neufeld, Mace
PATRIOT GAMES

Neuman, Jeffrey
LITTLE SISTER

Newey, Murray
MY GRANDPA IS A VAMPIRE

Newmyer, Robert
CROSSING THE BRIDGE
MR. BASEBALL

Nicolaou, Ted
BAD CHANNELS

Niekerk, Sidney
ROOTS OF EVIL

Norgard, Lindsay
HOMEBOYS

Norway, Tony
BARBARIAN QUEEN II: THE EMPRESS STRIKES BACK

Novodor, Bill
ALL-AMERICAN MURDER

Nozik, Michael
MISSISSIPPI MASALA

O'Toole, Daniel
HURRICANE SMITH

O'Toole, Stanley
HURRICANE SMITH

Obst, Lynda
THIS IS MY LIFE

Oken, Stuart
FREEJACK

Oldcorn, Christopher
REFRIGERATOR, THE

Oldham, Rocky
BOB MARLEY: TIME WILL TELL

Olmos, Edward James
AMERICAN ME

Olson, Gerald T.
BIG GIRLS DON'T CRY . . . THEY GET EVEN

Oppenheimer, Peer
BECOMING COLETTE

Opper, Barry
CRITTERS 4

Orgolini, Arnold
LINGUINI INCIDENT, THE

Ossard, Claude
DELICATESSEN

Oxenberg, Jan
THANK YOU AND GOOD NIGHT!

Page, Mary Anne
HIGHWAY TO HELL

Paglia, Mark
LASER MOON

Pakula, Alan J.
CONSENTING ADULTS

Paland, Jean Mark
TWIN SISTERS

Paljakka, Kari
DADDY AND THE MUSCLE ACADEMY

Palm, Anders
DEAD CERTAIN

Palmer, Tony
CHILDREN, THE

Paloian, Nancy
WAXWORK II: LOST IN TIME

Panigutti, Nico
PANAMA DECEPTION, THE

Pardo, Alvaro
DADDY AND THE MUSCLE ACADEMY

Parer, Damien
FATHER

Pariser, Michael D.
KICKBOXER 3: THE ART OF WAR

Parkes, Walter F.
SNEAKERS

Parr, Larry
SOLDIER'S TALE, A

Passalia, Antonio
CRY OF THE OWL, THE

Paterson, Iain
GHOULIES III: GHOULIES GO TO COLLEGE

Paul, Hank
FATE

Paul, Steven
ILLUSIONS

Paulson, Dan
BACKTRACK
PASSENGER 57

Payson, Keith
BAD CHANNELS

Peace, J. Stephen
KILLER TOMATOES EAT FRANCE!

Pearce, Christopher
HUMAN SHIELD, THE

Peel, Jacinta
BERNARD AND THE GENIE

Pepin, Richard
DEADLY BET
FINAL IMPACT
MAXIMUM FORCE
OUT FOR BLOOD
STREET CRIMES

Perlman, Laurie
BIG GIRLS DON'T CRY . . . THEY GET EVEN

Permut, David
CAPTAIN RON
CONSENTING ADULTS

Perry, Simon
PLAYBOYS, THE

Petersen, William
HARD PROMISES

Peyser, Michael
DISTINGUISHED GENTLEMAN, THE

Pfaeffli, Andres
MEGAVILLE

Phillips, Lucy
STEAL AMERICA

Phillips, Michael S.
MOM AND DAD SAVE THE WORLD

Picker, David V.
LEAP OF FAITH
TRACES OF RED

Pillsbury, Sarah
LOVE FIELD

Plympton, Bill
TUNE, THE

Pollock, Dale
MIDNIGHT CLEAR, A

Pomeroy, John
ROCK-A-DOODLE

Poul, Alan
CANDYMAN

Preisler, Gary
ILLUSIONS

Pressman, Edward R.
BAD LIEUTENANT
HOFFA
STORYVILLE

Price, Frank
GLADIATOR

Priggen, Norman
FREDDIE AS F.R.O.7

Pringle, John
LUNATIC, THE

Procacci, Domenico
STATION, THE

Proevska, Pavlina
HAPPY HELL NIGHT

Rabiner, Steve
DEATHSTALKER IV: MATCH OF TITANS
FINISHING TOUCH, THE

Rachmil, Michael
MO' MONEY

Rafferty, Kevin
FEED
Raich, Kenneth M.
RESURRECTED, THE
Rajski, Peggy
USED PEOPLE
Ranvaud, Don
LIFE ON A STRING
Rassam, Paul
LOVER, THE
Raven, Max
ARMED FOR ACTION
Redford, Robert
RIVER RUNS THROUGH IT, A
Rehme, Robert
PATRIOT GAMES
Reibenbach, Rafi
DOUBLE EDGE
Reiner, Rob
FEW GOOD MEN, A
Reisman, Linda
LIGHT SLEEPER
Reitman, Ivan
STOP! OR MY MOM WILL SHOOT
Renzi, Maggie
PASSION FISH
Reuther, Steven
UNDER SIEGE
Rexrode, Cecyle Osgood
CONFESSIONS OF A SERIAL KILLER
Rice, Wayne Allan
ONLY YOU
Rich, Lee
INNOCENT BLOOD
PASSENGER 57
Richardson, Gillian
VAGRANT, THE
Ridgeway, James
FEED
Riffel, James
HOUSE ON TOMBSTONE HILL, THE
Riggs, Marlon T.
COLOR ADJUSTMENT
Rivier, Philippe
DAY IN OCTOBER, A
Rocca, Alain
DISCRETE, LA
Roe, David
STORYVILLE
Rogers, Richard P.
PICTURES FROM A REVOLUTION
Root, Antony
EDWARD II
Rosenbloom, Dale
WOMAN, HER MEN AND HER FUTON, A
Rosenman, Howard
BUFFY THE VAMPIRE SLAYER
SHINING THROUGH
STRANGER AMONG US, A
Rosenthal, Henry S.
ALL THE VERMEERS IN NEW YORK
Rosenthal, Jane
NIGHT AND THE CITY
THUNDERHEART
Roth, Stephen J.
CLEARCUT
Roth, Steve
GLADIATOR
Roven, Charles
FINAL ANALYSIS
Ruben, Andy
POISON IVY
Ruddy, Albert S.
LADYBUGS
Rudin, Scott
WHITE SANDS
Sackheim, William
WHITE SANDS
Sackner, Sara
PAINTING THE TOWN
Sadowsky, Nina R.
JUMPIN' AT THE BONEYARD
Sager, Ray
PROM NIGHT IV - DELIVER US FROM EVIL
Salkind, Ilya
CHRISTOPHER COLUMBUS: THE DISCOVERY
Salven, David
RAMPAGE
Samtani, Gope T.
LADY DRAGON
Samuels, Ron
ACES: IRON EAGLE III
Sanchez, Jorge
CABEZA DE VACA
DANZON
Sandler, Harry
FALLING FROM GRACE
Sanford, Midge
LOVE FIELD
Saunders, David
WILD ORCHID 2: TWO SHADES OF BLUE
Saxon, Edward
COUSIN BOBBY
Schaffel, Robert
DIGGSTOWN
Schapiro, Angela
TO PROTECT AND SERVE
Scharfenberg, E.
MY FATHER IS COMING
Scheinman, Andrew
FEW GOOD MEN, A
Schepisi, Fred
MR. BASEBALL
Schiff, Paul
MY COUSIN VINNY
Schmidlin, Christina
MEGAVILLE
Schouweiler, John
NEON CITY
Schroeder, Barbet
SINGLE WHITE FEMALE
Schulze, Douglas
HELL MASTER
Schwartz, Teri
SISTER ACT
Schwartzman, Jack
BED & BREAKFAST
Scott, Allan
COLD HEAVEN
Scott, Ann
ENCHANTED APRIL
Scott, Ridley
1492: THE CONQUEST OF PARADISE
Seagal, Steven
UNDER SIEGE
Seeary, Sue
CROSSING, THE
Sellers, Dylan
PASSENGER 57
Shapiro, Allen
UNIVERSAL SOLDIER
Shapiro, Craig
SMOOTH TALKER
Shapiro, Leonard
BASKET CASE 3: THE PROGENY
Sharfshtein, Michael
CUP FINAL
Shea Ruben, Katt
POISON IVY
Shuler-Donner, Lauren
RADIO FLYER
Shusett, Ronald
FREEJACK
Shuster, Brian
CAN IT BE LOVE
Sibay, Mussef
WOMAN, HER MEN AND HER FUTON, A
Sidaris, Arlene
DO OR DIE
Sighvatsson, Sigurjon
CANDYMAN
RUBY
STRANGER AMONG US, A
Silver, Jeffrey
CROSSING THE BRIDGE
Silver, Joel
LETHAL WEAPON 3
Simandl, Lloyd
MANIAC WARRIORS
ULTIMATE DESIRES
Simon, J.P.
CTHULHU MANSION
Simpson, Paige
CAPTAIN RON
Simpson, Peter R.
OH, WHAT A NIGHT
Singer, Gail
WISECRACKS
Singh, Anant
SARAFINA!
Singleton, Ralph S.
PET SEMATARY II
Sinise, Gary
OF MICE AND MEN
Sinofski, Bruce
BROTHER'S KEEPER
Siritzky, Alain
EMMANUELLE 6
Sloane, Rick
MIND, BODY & SOUL
Smith, Lindsay
BACK IN THE U.S.S.R.
Smith, Russ
OF MICE AND MEN

Spielberg, Michael
LITTLE NOISES
Stabler, Steve
MIRACLE BEACH
Stabler, Steven
DOUBLE TROUBLE
Stark, Jim
IN THE SOUP
Starkey, Steve
DEATH BECOMES HER
Steakley, William B.
SOUTH CENTRAL
Steel, Dawn
HONEY, I BLEW UP THE KID
Steiner, Gerald M.
AUNTIE LEE'S MEAT PIES
Stewart, John
DEEP BLUES
Stoker, Shelly
SORORITY HOUSE MASSACRE 2
Sunshine, Leslie
HAPPY HELL NIGHT
Swinson, David
ROADSIDE PROPHETS
Sylbert, Anthea
CRISSCROSS
Tabet, Sylvio
BEASTMASTER 2: THROUGH THE PORTAL OF TIME
Tagliaferro, Pat
MIDNIGHT FEAR
Takeda, Atsushi
SILK ROAD, THE
Tang King-sung
SUPERCOP: POLICE STORY III
Tannen, William
INSIDE EDGE
Taplin, Jonathan
K2
Taska, Ilmar
BACK IN THE U.S.S.R.
Teper, Meir
MISTRESS
Thomas, Maynell
CLASS ACT
Thomas, Tony
FINAL ANALYSIS
Thompson, David M.
SARAFINA!
Thompson, Randy
MONTANA RUN, THE
Tinchant, Maurice
NIGHT AND DAY
Todd, Kim
QUARREL, THE
Tokofsky, Jerry
GLENGARRY GLEN ROSS
WILDFIRE
Tolkin, Michael
PLAYER, THE
Tomiyama, Shogo
GODZILLA VS. BIOLLANTE
Tornberg, Ralph
EXILED IN AMERICA
Towers, Alan Harry
HOUSE OF USHER, THE
Trent, Barbara
PANAMA DECEPTION, THE
Treut, Monika
MY FATHER IS COMING
Tsukamoto, Shinya
TETSUO: THE IRON MAN
Tyrell, Jan
ROCK & ROLL COWBOYS
Vachon, Christine
SWOON
Vajna, Andrew G.
MEDICINE MAN
Van Rellim, Tim
K2
Vanger, Gregory
CAGED FEAR
Vejrik, Karel
EAR, THE
Vernon, James Michael
ROCK & ROLL COWBOYS
Victor, Mark
STEPHEN KING'S SLEEPWALKERS
Vince, Robert
BLACK ICE
CAFE ROMEO
Von Helmolt, Vonnie
BLACK ICE
Von Praunheim, Rosa
AFFENGEIL
Waldburger, Ruth
JOHNNY SUEDE
Wall, Stuart
HELLROLLER
Walley, Keith
SOCIETY
Walsh, Steve
DOUBLE VISION
Walters, Martin
BEAUTIFUL DREAMERS
Waterman, Dennis
COLD JUSTICE
Webb, William
PSYCHIC
Webster, Christopher
CHILDREN OF THE NIGHT
MINDWARP
SEVERED TIES
Webster, Paul
RUBIN & ED
Wechsler, Nick
PLAYER, THE
Weiner, John
COMRADES IN ARMS
Weiner, Marilyn
K2
Weintraub, Fred
CHINA O'BRIEN II
Weintraub, Jerry
PURE COUNTRY
Weintraub, Sandra
CHINA O'BRIEN II
Wendlandt, Matthias
KILL CRUISE
White, Timothy
EFFICIENCY EXPERT, THE
Whitman, Rosemarie
SECRET FRIENDS
Wilhite, Thomas L.
BEBE'S KIDS
ROVER DANGERFIELD
RUNESTONE, THE
Willenson, Seth M.
GAS FOOD LODGING
Willett, William F.
ZEBRAHEAD
Williams, Anson
ALL-AMERICAN MURDER
Williamson, Fred
STEELE'S LAW
Wilson, Jim
BODYGUARD, THE
Wilson, Robert J.
SHAKING THE TREE
Wimbury, David
JENNIFER EIGHT
Winfrey, Dennis
MORTUARY ACADEMY
Winkler, Irwin
NIGHT AND THE CITY
Winning, David
KILLER IMAGE
Winograd, Peter
ONE LAST RUN
Witt, Paul Junger
FINAL ANALYSIS
Wohl, David
INVASION OF THE SPACE PREACHERS
Wolf, Schmidt
NEON CITY
Wolinsky, Judith
VENICE/VENICE
Wong, David Ka Lik
MAGICAL WORLD OF CHUCK JONES, THE
Woo, Theresa
TRAINED TO FIGHT
Wooll, Nigel
YEAR OF THE COMET
Woolley, Stephen
CRYING GAME, THE
POPE MUST DIET!, THE
Worth, Marvin
MALCOLM X
Yamamoto, Mata
WIND
Yamamoto, Mataichiro
PROFESSIONAL, THE
Yang, Janet
SOUTH CENTRAL
Yates, Andrew
LIFE ON THE EDGE
Yates, Peter
YEAR OF THE COMET
Yorkin, Bud
LOVE HURTS
Young, Robert M.
AMERICAN ME
Young, Wayne
FERNGULLY: THE LAST RAINFOREST

Yuen, William
TRAINED TO FIGHT
Yule, Paul
DAMNED IN THE USA
Yuzna, Brian
GUYVER, THE
Zahavi, Natan
MIKEY
Zahid, Nabeel
STEPHEN KING'S SLEEPWALKERS
Zaloom, George
ENCINO MAN
Zaloum, Jean
CANVAS
Zeitoun, Ariel
ELEGANT CRIMINEL, L'
Zemeckis, Robert
DEATH BECOMES HER
Ziskin, Laura
HERO
Zupnik, Stanley R.
GLENGARRY GLEN ROSS
Zwang, Ron
NAKED OBSESSION
Zwicker-Ritz, Ulla
MY FATHER IS COMING

PRODUCTION DESIGNERS

Albalak, Itzik
HUMAN SHIELD, THE
Allen, James
ENCINO MAN
Alonso, Pablo
CTHULHU MANSION
Altman, Stephen
PLAYER, THE
Alves, Joe
FREEJACK
Amend, Richard
WILD ORCHID 2: TWO SHADES OF BLUE
Amies, Caroline
AFRAID OF THE DARK
DOUBLE VISION
Angelo, Yves
TOUS LES MATINS DU MONDE
Argentina, Regina
DEATH HOUSE
Arnold, Bill
COLD JUSTICE
Arnold, William
MO' MONEY
Arrighi, Luciana
HOWARDS END
Asp, Anna
BEST INTENTIONS, THE
Aubel, Joe
AMERICAN ME
Avellana, Joe Mari
FIELD OF FIRE
Avivi, Avi
FINEST HOUR, THE
Bafaloukos, Ted
BRIEF HISTORY OF TIME, A
Bahs, Henning
ZENTROPA
Barbosa, Carlos
ILLUSIONS
ULTRAVIOLET
Barclay, William
BASKET CASE 3: THE PROGENY
Barkham, David
SARAFINA!
Basile, Pier Luigi
ONCE UPON A CRIME
Beard, John
BERNARD AND THE GENIE
Beecroft, Jeffrey
BODYGUARD, THE
Beeton, William
GATE II
Bell, Mary Jane
WHITE TRASH
Benedict, Robert
ROUND TRIP TO HEAVEN
Bishop, Dan
PASSION FISH
THUNDERHEART
TRACES OF RED
Blatt, Stuart
MUNCHIE
Bolton, Gregory William
HEAVEN IS A PLAYGROUND
Bolton, Michael
VAGRANT, THE
Bourne, Mel
MAN TROUBLE
Bradley, Chris
CHILDREN, THE
Brenner, Albert
MR. SATURDAY NIGHT
Bretherton, Monica
LAWS OF GRAVITY
Brill, Robert
KILLER TOMATOES EAT FRANCE!
Brisbin, David
RUBY
Brock, Ian
PROM NIGHT IV - DELIVER US FROM EVIL
Brown, Dennis
LOWER LEVEL
Bueno, Clovis
KICKBOXER 3: THE ART OF WAR
Bumstead, Henry
UNFORGIVEN
Burns, Robert A.
CONFESSIONS OF A SERIAL KILLER
Cagli, Leonardo Coen
HOUSE OF USHER, THE
Cahours De Virgile, Richard
HOT CHOCOLATE
Calosio, Marcia
MIKEY
Cameron, Allan
FAR AND AWAY
Canonero, Milena
SINGLE WHITE FEMALE
Carp, Jean-Philippe
DELICATESSEN
Carter, Rick
DEATH BECOMES HER
Casey, Steven Michael
ORIGINAL INTENT
Cassidy, William J.
BRAIN DONORS
Cauley, Eve
FATHERS AND SONS
Cavedon, Suzanne
BED & BREAKFAST
Chapman, David
THIS IS MY LIFE
Cheng, Fu Ding
NEON CITY
Cinini, Claudio
HUSBANDS AND LOVERS
Clark, Diane Romine
GIVING, THE
Clausen, Michael
DESIRE AND HELL AT SUNSET MOTEL
Clay, Jim
CRYING GAME, THE
Cline, Fred
BEBE'S KIDS
ROVER DANGERFIELD
Clinker, Nigel
MIKEY
Coates, Kathleen
BODY WAVES
Cohen, Lester
JUICE
Collis, Jack T.
FAR AND AWAY
Cone, Buddyy
RAMPAGE
Corbett, Toby
MY NEW GUN
Corenblith, Michael
COOL WORLD
GUN IN BETTY LOU'S HANDBAG, THE
Corsillo, George
FALLING FROM GRACE
Costello, George
NICKEL & DIME
Craig, Stuart
CHAPLIN
Creber, William J.
FOLKS!
Crew, A. Rosalind
ONLY YOU
Danielson, Dins
WE'RE TALKIN' SERIOUS MONEY
Day, Don
DELTA HEAT
SEVERED TIES
De Rouin, Colin
BLACKBELT
Dearborn, Richard
SUNSET STRIP
DeCuir, Jr., John
STEPHEN KING'S SLEEPWALKERS
DeGovia, Jackson
SISTER ACT
Del Rosario, Linda
ADJUSTER, THE
DeLeeuw, Willem
LILY WAS HERE

Densmore, Brian
SMOOTH TALKER
Deprez, Therese
SWOON
Dilley, Leslie
DISTINGUISHED GENTLEMAN, THE
HONEY, I BLEW UP THE KID
DiSanto, Byrnadette
GUILTY AS CHARGED
I DON'T BUY KISSES ANYMORE
Dobrowolski, Marek
JUST LIKE IN THE MOVIES
Douy, Berge
BECOMING COLETTE
Dowding, John
HUNTING
Eastwood, Laurence
WIND
Ebden, John
POPE MUST DIET!, THE
Edwards, Chris
MONKEY BOY
SPLIT SECOND
Egry, Tony
POUR SACHA
Eigenbrodt, Bill
SCORCHERS
Elliott, William A.
HONEYMOON IN VEGAS
Epstein, Mitch
MISSISSIPPI MASALA
Farthing, Robert
FATE
Ferrara, Carolina
STATION, THE
Flannery, Seamus
BEAUTIFUL DREAMERS
Fonseca, Gregg
FOREVER YOUNG
GLADIATOR
WAYNE'S WORLD
Ford, Roger
FLIRTING
Foreman, Philip Dean
CRITTERS 4
HIGHWAY TO HELL
Foreman, Ron
BACKTRACK
RAPID FIRE
Fox, J. Rae
ROADSIDE PROPHETS
Freas, Dianna
PASSION FISH
TRACES OF RED
Freeborn, Mark
LOVE FIELD
Friedberg, Mark
IN THE SOUP
Ganz, Armin
KUFFS
LOVE CRIMES
LOVE HURTS
Gassner, Dennis
HERO
Gilliland, Steve
INVASION OF THE SPACE
PREACHERS
Gobbi, Luca
STATION, THE
Goetz, Dave
ROCK-A-DOODLE
Goodridge, George
ALAN & NAOMI
CHAINS OF GOLD
Gorrara, Perri
DEADBOLT
PSYCHIC
Gorrara, Perry
CLEARCUT
Gorton, Adrian
JOURNEY OF HONOR
Graham, Angelo
SCENT OF A WOMAN
Graysmark, John
WHITE SANDS
Greenberg, Stephen
GHOULIES III:
GHOULIES GO TO COLLEGE
Groom, Bill
LEAGUE OF THEIR OWN, A
Gropman, David
CUTTING EDGE, THE
OF MICE AND MEN
Gross, Holger
UNIVERSAL SOLDIER
Gurski, Peter
LUNATICS: A LOVE STORY
Hall, Roger
POWER OF ONE, THE
Hardie, Steve
HELLRAISER III: HELL ON EARTH
WAXWORK II: LOST IN TIME
Hardwicke, Catherine
PASSED AWAY
Harris, Andy
PLAYBOYS, THE
Harris, Mark
PROJECT: SHADOWCHASER
Harrison, Philip
STAY TUNED
Hartog, Michael
LITTLE VEGAS
Harvey, Tim
PETER'S FRIENDS
Haworth, Ted
MR. BASEBALL
Hendrickson, Stephen
DIARY OF A HITMAN
DIGGSTOWN
Hinds, Marcia
LINGUINI INCIDENT, THE
Hinds-Johnson, Marcia
PUBLIC EYE, THE
Hinkle, Jaymes
PASSENGER 57
Hitchcock, Martin
HURRICANE SMITH
Hix, Kim
AMITYVILLE 1992:
IT'S ABOUT TIME
CHILDREN OF THE NIGHT
MINDWARP
Hoang, Thanh At
LOVER, THE
Hobbs, Christopher
EDWARD II
Hoffman, Jane
BODY WAVES
Holland, Simon
WHERE ANGELS FEAR TO TREAD
Hoover, Richard
BOB ROBERTS
STORYVILLE
Hornung, Richard
LIGHT SLEEPER
Howard, Jeffrey
PURE COUNTRY
Hunter, Clark
RUBIN & ED
Hutchinson, Tim
UNDER SUSPICION
Hutman, Jon
RIVER RUNS THROUGH IT, A
TRESPASS
Ikuno, Shigekazu
GODZILLA VS. BIOLLANTE
Jackness, Andrew
PRELUDE TO A KISS
Jackson, Gemma
BLAME IT ON THE BELLBOY
CODE NAME: CHAOS
Jacobs, Matthew C.
GUYVER, THE
SOCIETY
Jones, Allen
BEASTMASTER 2:
THROUGH THE PORTAL OF TIME
Joy, Michael
CANVAS
QUARREL, THE
SCANNERS III: THE TAKEOVER
Kennedy, Chris
EFFICIENCY EXPERT, THE
Kenney, Bill
UNDER SIEGE
Kieser, Marina
SOUTH CENTRAL
King, Robb Wilson
ACES: IRON EAGLE III
LADYBUGS
Kirkland, Geoffrey
WILDFIRE
Kjnakovic, Kreka
DELICATESSEN
Kljakovic, Miljen
HAPPY HELL NIGHT
Kraner, Doug
RAISING CAIN
Kroeger, Wolf
LAST OF THE MOHICANS, THE
Krumbachova, Ester
EAR, THE
Lagola, Charles
BAD LIEUTENANT
LITTLE NOISES
Larkin, Peter
NIGHT AND THE CITY
Lau Man-hung
ONCE UPON A TIME IN CHINA
Ledwith, Cherie Day
DO OR DIE

Lee, Virginia
ONE LAST RUN
POISON IVY
Legler, Steve
COLD HEAVEN
Leigh, Dan
HARD PROMISES
Leonard, Douglas
CAPTAIN AMERICA
LeTenoux, Johan
DOUBLE TROUBLE
NAKED OBSESSION
Leung, James
HARD-BOILED
Levtchenko, Aleksei
CLOSE TO EDEN
Levy, Eytan
BLINK OF AN EYE
Levy, J.
DRIVE
Liddle, George
TILL THERE WAS YOU
Light-Harris, Donald
BREAKING THE RULES
Lineweaver, Stephen J.
SINGLES
Lloyd, John
BRENDA STARR
Logevall, Robert
CAFE ROMEO
Loquasto, Santo
HUSBANDS AND WIVES
SHADOWS AND FOG
Luczyc-Wyhowski, Hugo
WATERLAND
Lytar, Stephanie
SLUMBER PARTY MASSACRE 3
MacDonald, Richard
JENNIFER EIGHT
Maginnis, Scott
STREET CRIMES
Malley, Bill
DR. GIGGLES
Mannion, Sean
SHAKING THE TREE
Marsh, Stephen
OUT ON A LIMB
Marsh, Terence
BASIC INSTINCT
Marshall, Kerry
DAUGHTERS OF THE DUST
Martin, Blair
ANIMAL INSTINCTS
MIRROR IMAGES
NIGHT RHYTHMS
OTHER WOMAN, THE
SECRET GAMES
Martin, Greg
DEADLY BET
MAXIMUM FORCE
Martin, William
OUT FOR BLOOD
Matthews, William F.
CAPTAIN RON
Maussion, Ivan
HAIRDRESSER'S HUSBAND, THE
SOLDIER'S TALE, A

McDowell, Alex
LAWNMOWER MAN, THE
McLean, Rod
BERNARD AND THE GENIE
Medlon, Damon
ALMOST PREGNANT
Miller, David Brian
SOUTH CENTRAL
Miller, Lawrence
BUFFY THE VAMPIRE SLAYER
Milo
DOCTOR MORDRID
TRANCERS III: DETH LIVES
Minch, Michelle
PET SEMATARY II
Moore, John Jay
WHISPERS IN THE DARK
Moore, Russell
INSIDE EDGE
Morris, Brian
DAMAGE
Munchin, Joseph
DEATHSTALKER IV: MATCH OF TITANS
Musky, Jane
BOOMERANG
GLENGARRY GLEN ROSS
Nay, Igor
CROSSING, THE
Needles, Milo
HOUSE IV
MEGAVILLE
NIGHT EYES 2
Nelsen, Shane
PALE BLOOD
Nemec, III, Joseph
PATRIOT GAMES
New, Gary T.
INTO THE SUN
ONE FALSE MOVE
Newberry, Norman
NOISES OFF
Nichols, David
MIDNIGHT CLEAR, A
Nixson, Robin
BLOODFIST IV: DIE TRYING
Norris, Patricia
LEAVING NORMAL
TWIN PEAKS: FIRE WALK WITH ME
O'Reilly, Ed
PAMELA PRINCIPLE, THE
Ouellette, Daniel
SIMPLE MEN
Pallut, Philippe
VAN GOGH
Paris, Richard
ADJUSTER, THE
Parrondo, Gil
CHRISTOPHER COLUMBUS: THE DISCOVERY
Paul, Victoria
BIG GIRLS DON'T CRY . . . THEY GET EVEN
KUFFS
MY COUSIN VINNY

Paull, Lawrence G.
MEMOIRS OF AN INVISIBLE MAN
UNLAWFUL ENTRY
Pearl, Linda
LOVE POTION NO. 9
Perakis, Nicos
VOYAGER
Peters, Paul
OVER HER DEAD BODY
Peters, Phil
FATHER
MISTRESS
Petruccelli, Kirk
3 NINJAS
WHERE THE DAY TAKES YOU
Philippov, Vladimir
BACK IN THE U.S.S.R.
Philips, Michael
LIGHT IN THE JUNGLE, THE
Pisoni, Edward
HAND THAT ROCKS THE CRADLE, THE
Porteous, Cameron
BEETHOVEN LIVES UPSTAIRS
Pottle, Harry
COLLISION COURSE
Pratt, Anthony
SHINING THROUGH
YEAR OF THE COMET
Ralph, Michael
ROCK & ROLL COWBOYS
Randall, Gary
976-EVIL II
MIRACLE BEACH
SLUMBER PARTY MASSACRE 3
Randolph, Virginia L.
ARTICLE 99
Random, Ida
HOFFA
HOUSESITTER
Raubertas, Peter Paul
WOMAN, HER MEN AND HER FUTON, A
Raymond, Deborah
FROZEN ASSETS
MEATBALLS 4
Reardon, Patrick
PROOF
Reed, Gary Lee
FATAL INSTINCT
Reinhart, Jr., John Krenz
MEDICINE MAN
Reynolds, Norman
ALIEN3
Rhode, Deanna
BLACK ICE
Richardson, Mark
HOMEBOYS
Riva, J. Michael
FEW GOOD MEN, A
RADIO FLYER
Roberts, Rick
PRIMO BABY
Rosen, Charles
STOP! OR MY MOM WILL SHOOT
Rosenberg, Philip
STRANGER AMONG US, A

Ross, Heather Lynn
DESERT KICKBOXER
Rothschild, Jon
MORTUARY ACADEMY
Sackner, Sara
PAINTING THE TOWN
Sagoni, Luciano
BEYOND JUSTICE
Sallis, Crispian
CRISSCROSS
Sanders, Andrew
K2
Sanders, Thomas
BRAM STOKER'S DRACULA
Sanktjohanser, Josef
DEMON IN MY VIEW, A
Sawyer, Richard
INNOCENT BLOOD
Scarfiotti, Ferdinando
TOYS
Scarpulla, Clare
CAGED FEAR
Schlubach, Jan
BECOMING COLETTE
Schmidt, Phil
COMMON BONDS
Searcy, R. Clifford
SEEDPEOPLE
Seitz, Bertrand
ROAD TO RUIN
Ser, Randy
MIGHTY DUCKS, THE
Shane, Lee
GIVING, THE
Shohan, Naomi
ZEBRAHEAD
Shumaker, James R.
AUNTIE LEE'S MEAT PIES
BLOODFIST III: FORCED TO FIGHT
DANCE WITH DEATH
KISS ME A KILLER
MARTIAL LAW 2: UNDERCOVER
Sichenkova, Inna
RASPAD
Sinclair, Kim
MY GRANDPA IS A VAMPIRE
Snyder, David L.
CLASS ACT
Spencer, James
LETHAL WEAPON 3
Spencer, Norris
1492: THE CONQUEST OF PARADISE
Spier, Carol
CONSENTING ADULTS
Stearns, Craig
CROSSING THE BRIDGE
MOM AND DAD SAVE THE WORLD
Steele, Jon Gary
LITTLE SISTER
RUNESTONE, THE
Stewart, Jane Ann
CANDYMAN
GAS FOOD LODGING
Stock, Mario
KILL CRUISE
Strazovec, Val
MUPPET CHRISTMAS CAROL, THE
Stringer, Michael
HIRED TO KILL
Stuart, Michael
ADVENTURES IN DINOSAUR CITY
Tangkilisan, Hendro
LADY DRAGON
Tasse, Richard
SNAKEEATER III . . . HIS LAW
TWIN SISTERS
Tavoularis, Alex
BEETHOVEN
Tavoularis, Dean
FINAL ANALYSIS
Templeman, Paul
CHILDREN, THE
Thomas, Brent
RESURRECTED, THE
Thomas, Phillip G.
LEATHER JACKETS
Thomas, Wynn
MALCOLM X
Thornton, Malcolm
ENCHANTED APRIL
Tirr, Catherine
TERMINAL BLISS
Townsend, Jeffrey
STRAIGHT TALK
Tunney, Ted
SOLDIER'S FORTUNE
Van Tries, Amy
LIFE ON THE EDGE
Vance, James D.
BABE, THE
Velez, Hector
FINISHING TOUCH, THE
IN THE HEAT OF PASSION
Veneziano, Sandy
HOME ALONE 2:
LOST IN NEW YORK
Vernacchio, Dorian
FROZEN ASSETS
MEATBALLS 4
Vetter, Arlan Jay
SEXUAL RESPONSE
Vischkof, Katia
VAN GOGH
Von Brandenstein, Patrizia
LEAP OF FAITH
SNEAKERS
Walker, Roy
CITY OF JOY
Walker, Stuart
LONDON KILLS ME
Wallner, Caroline
JUMPIN' AT THE BONEYARD
Walsh, Thomas A.
PRAYER OF THE ROLLERBOYS
Warfield, Todd
WITCHCRAFT IV: VIRGIN HEART
Warner, Pam
DEEP COVER
Wasco, David
RESERVOIR DOGS
Washington, Dennis
WHITE MEN CAN'T JUMP
Welch, Bo
BATMAN RETURNS
Wheeler, Brooke
DOLLY DEAREST
Wichmann, Sven
DAY IN OCTOBER, A
Williamson, Gary
SECRET FRIENDS
Wilson, Everett
BAD CHANNELS
Winkelhofer, Ladislav
EAR, THE
Woodbridge, Pamela
LONELY HEARTS
SHAKES THE CLOWN
THANK YOU AND GOOD NIGHT!
Woodbridge, Patricia
JOHNNY SUEDE
Wurtzel, Stuart
MAMBO KINGS, THE
USED PEOPLE
Yarhi, Daniel
PRIMARY MOTIVE
Zaruva, Vasilli
RASPAD
Zea, Kristi
LORENZO'S OIL
Ziembicki, Bob
WATERDANCE, THE

SCREENWRITERS

Abrams, Jeffrey
FOREVER YOUNG
Acevski, Jon
FREDDIE AS F.R.O.7
Adams, Daniel
PRIMARY MOTIVE
Akerman, Chantal
NIGHT AND DAY
Alan, Jordan
TERMINAL BLISS
Allan, Ranald
CROSSING, THE
Allen, Woody
HUSBANDS AND WIVES
SHADOWS AND FOG
Almodovar, Pedro
PEPI, LUCI, BOM AND OTHER
GIRLS ON THE HEAP
Als, Hilton
SWOON
Anders, Allison
GAS FOOD LODGING
Anderson, Clyde
TROLL 2
Anderson, Steve
SOUTH CENTRAL
Andrews, Peter
IMPORTANCE OF BEING
EARNEST, THE
Anjou, Erik
976-EVIL II
ROAD TO RUIN
Annaud, Jean-Jacques
LOVER, THE
Apted, Michael
35 UP

Araki, Gregg
LIVING END, THE
Aranda, Vicente
AMANTES
Arcady, Alexandre
POUR SACHA
Argento, Dario
DEVIL'S DAUGHTER, THE
Arlorio, Giorgio
ONCE UPON A CRIME
Ascione, Gianfilippo
STATION, THE
Ashton, David
FREDDIE AS F.R.O.7
Asproon, Sarah
BEYOND DARKNESS
Atkins, Peter
HELLRAISER III: HELL ON EARTH
Attanasio, Paul
RAPID FIRE
Avrech, Robert J.
STRANGER AMONG US, A
Aylward, Alan
COMMON BONDS
Baker, Kurt
IMPORTANCE OF BEING EARNEST, THE
Baldwin, James
MALCOLM X
Baloff, Peter I.
NEAR MISSES
Bandini, Filiberto
INDIO 2 - THE REVOLT
Barnes, Peter
ENCHANTED APRIL
Baronet, Willie
ADVENTURES IN DINOSAUR CITY
Barr, Jackson
BAD CHANNELS
SEEDPEOPLE
Barski, Odile
CRY OF THE OWL, THE
Bates, Cary
CHRISTOPHER COLUMBUS: THE DISCOVERY
Bazzini, Sergio
HUSBANDS AND LOVERS
Beaird, David
SCORCHERS
Bean, Henry
DEEP COVER
Beattie, Richard
PROM NIGHT IV - DELIVER US FROM EVIL
Becker, Josh
LUNATICS: A LOVE STORY
Begun, Jeff
NEON CITY
Belikov, Mikhail
RASPAD
Benderson, Bruce
MY FATHER IS COMING
Benigni, Roberto
JOHNNY STECCHINO
Benoit, Jean-Louis
ALBERTO EXPRESS
Berg, Adam
ROOTS OF EVIL
Bergman, Andrew
HONEYMOON IN VEGAS
Bergman, Ingmar
BEST INTENTIONS, THE
Bergman, Martin
PETER'S FRIENDS
Bergstein, Eleanor
SISTER ACT
Berlinger, Joe
BROTHER'S KEEPER
Berry, Tom
TWIN SISTERS
Bickley, Grace Cary
GUN IN BETTY LOU'S HANDBAG, THE
Billette, Christian
ALBERTO EXPRESS
Binder, Mike
CROSSING THE BRIDGE
Bindley, Scott
MIRACLE BEACH
Blair, Mark
CONFESSIONS OF A SERIAL KILLER
Blaustein, Barry W.
BOOMERANG
Boam, Jeffrey
LETHAL WEAPON 3
Bolotin, Craig
STRAIGHT TALK
Bolzoni, Adriano
BEYOND JUSTICE
Bonitzer, Pascal
NIGHT AND DAY
Bosch, Roselyne
1492: THE CONQUEST OF PARADISE
Bosko, Mark Steven
BRIDE OF KILLER NERD
Boyd, Daniel
INVASION OF THE SPACE PREACHERS
Boyd, William
CHAPLIN
Brach, Gerard
LOVER, THE
Brancato, John
INTO THE SUN
Brandes, David
QUARREL, THE
Brandes, Richard
MARTIAL LAW 2: UNDERCOVER
Bright, Matthew
WILDFIRE
Briley, John
CHRISTOPHER COLUMBUS: THE DISCOVERY
Brill, Steven
MIGHTY DUCKS, THE
Brooks, Halle
WHO SHOT PATAKANGO?
Brooks, Robert
WHO SHOT PATAKANGO?
Brott, Tamara
LINGUINI INCIDENT, THE
Brown, Gerard
JUICE
Bucceri, Gianfranco
INDIO 2 - THE REVOLT
Buchanan, James David
BRENDA STARR
Burch, Curtis
LADYBUGS
Burnett, Allison
BLOODFIST III: FORCED TO FIGHT
Burrell, Maryedith
HOT CHOCOLATE
Butler, Ken
EDWARD II
Butler, Mark Talbot
ESCAPE FROM . . . SURVIVAL ZONE
Cacliasso, Dan
EYE OF THE EAGLE 3
Carl, Michelle J.
MAXIMUM BREAKOUT
Carroll, Willard
RUNESTONE, THE
Cash, Jim
SISTER ACT
Cassidy, Gordon
ULTRAVIOLET
Castellaneta, P.J.
TOGETHER ALONE
Castle, Alan
DESIRE AND HELL AT SUNSET MOTEL
Cavanaugh, Tony
FATHER
Cerami, Vincenzo
JOHNNY STECCHINO
Cercone, Janus
LEAP OF FAITH
Cerrella, Ginny
HOT CHOCOLATE
Chabrol, Claude
CRY OF THE OWL, THE
INSPECTOR LAVARDIN
Chapman, Matthew
CONSENTING ADULTS
Chavis, Gordon
MEGAVILLE
Chen Kaige
LIFE ON A STRING
Chicago, Billy
NETHERWORLD
Cianetti, John
BLOOD ON THE BADGE
Cidre, Cynthia
MAMBO KINGS, THE
Cirile, Cindy
RAPID FIRE
Clark, Duane
SHAKING THE TREE
Clark, Greydon
DANCE MACABRE
Clay, Mel
WHITE TRASH
Clements, Ron
ALADDIN
Clyde, Craig
CHINA O'BRIEN II
Cochran, Stacy
MY NEW GUN

Cohen, Catherine
INDOCHINE

Cohen, Howard R.
DEATHSTALKER IV: MATCH OF TITANS

Colick, Lewis
UNLAWFUL ENTRY

Collector, Robert
MEMOIRS OF AN INVISIBLE MAN

Colley, Peter
ILLUSIONS

Columbus, Chris
LITTLE NEMO: ADVENTURES IN SLUMBERLAND

Conchon, Georges
ELEGANT CRIMINEL, L'

Conkie, Heather
BEETHOVEN LIVES UPSTAIRS

Connaughton, Shane
PLAYBOYS, THE

Corneau, Alain
TOUS LES MATINS DU MONDE

Cotler, Lanny
BACKTRACK

Cotler, Stephen L.
BACKTRACK

Coto, Manny
DR. GIGGLES

Covington, Hil
ADVENTURES IN SPYING

Cox, Jim
FERNGULLY: THE LAST RAINFOREST

Crabbe, Kerry
PLAYBOYS, THE

Crain, Bill
MIDNIGHT FEAR

Crawford, Mark McQuade
PSYCHIC

Crawford, William
PSYCHIC

Crowe, Cameron
SINGLES

Crowe, Christopher
LAST OF THE MOHICANS, THE
WHISPERS IN THE DARK

Crystal, Billy
MR. SATURDAY NIGHT

Curtin, Valerie
TOYS

Curtis, Richard
BERNARD AND THE GENIE

Cutler, Ron
ARTICLE 99

Cyran, Catherine
SLUMBER PARTY MASSACRE 3

Dalton, Darren
TO PROTECT AND SERVE

Dangerfield, Rodney
ROVER DANGERFIELD

Daniels, R.E.
LONELY HEARTS

Dann, Max
EFFICIENCY EXPERT, THE

Dash, Julie
DAUGHTERS OF THE DUST

Daugherty, George
MAGICAL WORLD OF CHUCK JONES, THE

Davies, William
STOP! OR MY MOM WILL SHOOT

Davis, Stephen
RUBY

De Palma, Brian
RAISING CAIN

DeBello, John
KILLER TOMATOES EAT FRANCE!

DeFaria, Christopher
AMITYVILLE 1992: IT'S ABOUT TIME

Del Amo, Alvaro
AMANTES

DeLeon, Marcus
KISS ME A KILLER

Demetrios, Eames
GIVING, THE

Dempsey, Tom
PHANTOM OF THE RITZ

Des Esseintes, Georges
ANIMAL INSTINCTS
OTHER WOMAN, THE
SECRET GAMES

Devlin, Dean
UNIVERSAL SOLDIER

Dhawee, Buncherd
IN GOLD WE TRUST

Diamond, Eric
SEXUAL RESPONSE

DiCillo, Tom
JOHNNY SUEDE

Dickerson, Ernest
JUICE

Dillon, Constantine
KILLER TOMATOES EAT FRANCE!

Dodson, Robert
NAKED OBSESSION

Dolman, Bob
FAR AND AWAY

Dominic, Henry
MINDWARP
SEVERED TIES

Donahue, Patrick G.
SAVAGE INSTINCT

Donati, Sergio
BEYOND JUSTICE

Donovan, Martin
DEATH BECOMES HER

Dotan, Shimon
FINEST HOUR, THE

Downes, Anson
CHAINS OF GOLD

Drazan, Anthony
ZEBRAHEAD

Drysdale, Lee
LEATHER JACKETS

Duigan, John
FLIRTING

Dunne, Philip
LAST OF THE MOHICANS, THE

Dunning, John
SNAKEEATER III . . . HIS LAW

Dupeyron, Francois
BEATING HEART, A

Dwyer, John
CAPTAIN RON

Eastman, Carole
MAN TROUBLE

Eberhardt, Thom
CAPTAIN RON
HONEY, I BLEW UP THE KID

Echevarria, Nicolas
CABEZA DE VACA

Edens, Mark
LIFE ON THE EDGE

Edmonds, Stan
KILLER IMAGE

Egoyan, Atom
ADJUSTER, THE

Eisinger, Jo
NIGHT AND THE CITY

Elbling, Peter
HONEY, I BLEW UP THE KID

Elders, Kevin
ACES: IRON EAGLE III

Elliot, Ted
ALADDIN

Ellis, Kirk
HIRED TO KILL

Emanuel, Edward
3 NINJAS

Engels, Robert
TWIN PEAKS: FIRE WALK WITH ME

Enright, Nick
LORENZO'S OIL

Ephron, Delia
BRENDA STARR
THIS IS MY LIFE

Ephron, Nora
THIS IS MY LIFE

Epperson, Tom
ONE FALSE MOVE

Epps, Jr., Jack
SISTER ACT

Eszterhas, Joe
BASIC INSTINCT

Evans, Bruce A.
KUFFS

Evans, David Mickey
RADIO FLYER

Everett, Gimel
LAWNMOWER MAN, THE

Falacci, Nicolas
CHILDREN OF THE NIGHT

Falls, Jeff
SPIRITS

Favila, Linda
CHAINS OF GOLD

Feinman, J.P.
PLAY MURDER FOR ME

Ferguson, Larry
ALIEN3

Ferrara, Abel
BAD LIEUTENANT

Ferris, Michael
INTO THE SUN

Finch, Buck
NEON CITY

Fisher, Carrie
SISTER ACT

Fitzgerald, Jiles
MARTIAL LAW 2: UNDERCOVER
Fitzpatrick, Michael
HAPPY HELL NIGHT
Flender, Rodman
IN THE HEAT OF PASSION
Florentine, Isaac
DESERT KICKBOXER
Flower, Buck
BIKINI CARWASH COMPANY, THE
Foldy, Peter
HOMEBOYS
Fong, Leo T.
24 HOURS TO MIDNIGHT
Foote, Horton
OF MICE AND MEN
Forbes, Bryan
CHAPLIN
Forsyth, Rob
CLEARCUT
Fox, Robbie
SHOOTING ELIZABETH
Fragasso, Claudio
BEYOND DARKNESS
Frank, Laurie
LOVE CRIMES
Franklin, Carl
EYE OF THE EAGLE 3
Franklin, Howard
PUBLIC EYE, THE
Frazer, Devin
DEATH HOUSE
Freidlob, Cynthia
CLASS ACT
Fried, Randall
HEAVEN IS A PLAYGROUND
Friedenberg, Richard
RIVER RUNS THROUGH IT, A
Friedkin, William
RAMPAGE
Friedman, Brent V.
RESURRECTED, THE
Frizzell, John
GETTING MARRIED IN BUFFALO JUMP
Front, Seth
NICKEL & DIME
Frost, Mark
STORYVILLE
Fry, Rick
SOCIETY
Funk, Mason
WINTER IN LISBON, THE
Fusco, John
BABE, THE
THUNDERHEART
Gale, Bob
TRESPASS
Gale, Charles
GUILTY AS CHARGED
Gallagher, Stephen
MONKEY BOY
Ganz, Lowell
LEAGUE OF THEIR OWN, A
MR. SATURDAY NIGHT
Garcia, David
SEX CRIMES
Gardel, Louis
INDOCHINE
Gebhard, Glenn
ONE LAST RUN
Gerard, Michael Paul
WITCHCRAFT IV: VIRGIN HEART
Gidding, Nelson
JOURNEY OF HONOR
Gideon, Raynold
KUFFS
Giler, David
ALIEN3
Gilles, Adrien
DELICATESSEN
Gilroy, Dan
FREEJACK
Gilroy, Tony
CUTTING EDGE, THE
Girod, Francis
ELEGANT CRIMINEL, L'
Glassner, Jonathan
MIKEY
Goldin, Daniel
OUT ON A LIMB
Goldin, Joshua
OUT ON A LIMB
Goldman, Bo
SCENT OF A WOMAN
Goldman, William
CHAPLIN
MEMOIRS OF AN INVISIBLE MAN
YEAR OF THE COMET
Goldthwait, Bobcat
SHAKES THE CLOWN
Gomez, Nick
LAWS OF GRAVITY
Goodrow, Garry
HONEY, I BLEW UP THE KID
Gordon, Dan
PASSENGER 57
Gordon, Keith
MIDNIGHT CLEAR, A
Goyer, David S.
DEMONIC TOYS
Graff, Todd
USED PEOPLE
Graham, Ruth
BECOMING COLETTE
Grais, Michael
COOL WORLD
Granger, Derek
WHERE ANGELS FEAR TO TREAD
Gray, Spalding
MONSTER IN A BOX
Green, David S.
OUT FOR BLOOD
Green, Terry
COLD JUSTICE
Greene, Anthony L.
FINISHING TOUCH, THE
Gries, Alan
NIGHT RHYTHMS
PAMELA PRINCIPLE, THE
Grimm, Douglas K.
LASER MOON
Grisoni, Tony
DOUBLE VISION
Gross, Larry
COOL WORLD
WIND
Gross, Michael
HUGH HEFNER: ONCE UPON A TIME
Grossman, Gary H.
HUGH HEFNER: ONCE UPON A TIME
Gudgeon, Mac
WIND
Gutierrez, Vincent
INSIDE EDGE
Haffter, Petra
DEMON IN MY VIEW, A
Halfon, Eyal
CUP FINAL
Hamm, Sam
BATMAN RETURNS
Haney, Daryl
DANCE WITH DEATH
Hansen, Ed
BIKINI CARWASH COMPANY, THE
Hare, David
DAMAGE
Harling, Robert
SISTER ACT
Harold, Wayne A.
BRIDE OF KILLER NERD
Harris, Trent
RUBIN & ED
Harrison, John Kent
BEAUTIFUL DREAMERS
Hart, James V.
BRAM STOKER'S DRACULA
Hartley, Grahame
FATHER
Hartley, Hal
SIMPLE MEN
Harwood, Ronald
FINE ROMANCE, A
Hauser, Ken
BEASTMASTER 2: THROUGH THE PORTAL OF TIME
Hawking, Stephen
BRIEF HISTORY OF TIME, A
Heath, Michael
MY GRANDPA IS A VAMPIRE
Heath, Robert
HUGH HEFNER: ONCE UPON A TIME
Hedberg, John Bryant
MISSION OF JUSTICE
Heikin-Pepin, Nancy
DOES THIS MEAN WE'RE MARRIED?
Helgeland, Brian
HIGHWAY TO HELL
Henenlotter, Frank
BASKET CASE 3: THE PROGENY
Hennessy, James
CHINA O'BRIEN II
Herman, Mark
BLAME IT ON THE BELLBOY

Hickox, Anthony
WAXWORK II: LOST IN TIME
Higgins, Deirdre
HOUSE IV
Hill, Walter
ALIEN3
Hirano, Yasuhi
VAMPIRE HUNTER D
Hitchcock, Michael
WHERE THE DAY TAKES YOU
Hogue, Jeffrey C.
SOLDIER'S FORTUNE
Hohlfield, Brian
MIGHTY DUCKS, THE
Holden-Jones, Amy
BEETHOVEN
Holliday, Tom
CHILDREN OF THE NIGHT
Hopkins, William
CHILDREN OF THE NIGHT
Horowitz, Jordan
ALAN & NAOMI
Houston, Bobby
CAGED FEAR
Howlett, John
TOUCH AND DIE
Howson, Frank
HUNTING
Hsu, V. Dachin
PALE BLOOD
Hubert, Ted
ULTIMATE DESIRES
Hudlin, Reginald
BEBE'S KIDS
Hughes, Craig
MIDNIGHT FEAR
Hughes, John
BEETHOVEN
HOME ALONE 2:
LOST IN NEW YORK
Hunsicker, Jackson
ODDBALL HALL
Ibraguimbekov, Roustam
CLOSE TO EDEN
Iliff, W. Peter
PATRIOT GAMES
PRAYER OF THE ROLLERBOYS
Ingvordsen, J. Christian
COMRADES IN ARMS
Ironside, Michael
COMMON BONDS
Jacobs, Nicholas A.E.
REFRIGERATOR, THE
Jaglom, Henry
VENICE/VENICE
Jarman, Derek
EDWARD II
Jarmusch, Jim
NIGHT ON EARTH
Jeffries, Richard
VAGRANT, THE
Jenkin, Len
WELCOME TO OBLIVION
Jennewein, Jim
STAY TUNED
Jhabvala, Ruth Prawer
HOWARDS END
Jimenez, Neal
WATERDANCE, THE
Joffe, Arthur
ALBERTO EXPRESS
John, Wayne
BREATHING FIRE
Johnson, Charles
STEELE'S LAW
Jones, Chris
ESCAPE FROM . . . SURVIVAL ZONE
Jordan, Neil
CRYING GAME, THE
Jost, Jon
ALL THE VERMEERS IN NEW YORK
Joyner, C. Courtney
DOCTOR MORDRID
TRANCERS III: DETH LIVES
Juhl, Jerry
MUPPET CHRISTMAS CAROL, THE
Kachyna, Karel
EAR, THE
Kalin, Tom
SWOON
Kaman, Steven
COMRADES IN ARMS
Kamen, Robert Mark
GLADIATOR
LETHAL WEAPON 3
POWER OF ONE, THE
Kanefsky, Rolfe
THERE'S NOTHING OUT THERE
Kanganis, Charles A.
BIKINI SUMMER 2
Kaplan, Marty
DISTINGUISHED GENTLEMAN, THE
NOISES OFF
Kartozian, Thomas
FROZEN ASSETS
Kasdan, Lawrence
BODYGUARD, THE
Kasper, David
PANAMA DECEPTION, THE
Kaurismaki, Aki
MATCH FACTORY GIRL, THE
Keglevic, Peter
KILL CRUISE
Keith, Woody
SOCIETY
Kelman, William
MORTUARY ACADEMY
Kerns, Jeffrey
DOUBLE TROUBLE
Kersusan, Silvia
TO RENDER A LIFE
Kessler, Lyle
GLADIATOR
Kim, Richard H.
KILL LINE
King, Freeman
TO PROTECT AND SERVE
King, R.U.
SPIRITS
King, Stephen
STEPHEN KING'S SLEEPWALKERS
King, Zalman
WILD ORCHID 2:
TWO SHADES OF BLUE
WILDFIRE
Kinloch, Peter A.
HURRICANE SMITH
Kissell, Tim
IN THE SOUP
Klane, Robert
FOLKS!
Klein, Don
FROZEN ASSETS
Kleinman, Dan
WELCOME TO OBLIVION
Klotz, Claude
HAIRDRESSER'S HUSBAND, THE
Kluger, Steve
ONCE UPON A CRIME
Knight, Andrew
EFFICIENCY EXPERT, THE
Knop, Patricia Louisiana
WILD ORCHID 2:
TWO SHADES OF BLUE
Koepp, David
DEATH BECOMES HER
Kollek, Amos
DOUBLE EDGE
Koster-Paul, Dorothy
FATE
Kounine, Vladimir
ADAM'S RIB
Kourtchatkin, Anatol
ADAM'S RIB
Kovach, Edward
BLINK OF AN EYE
Koval, Paul
PSYCHIC
Kronstadt-Mann, Rachel
BACKTRACK
Kureishi, Hanif
LONDON KILLS ME
Lacomblez, Antoine
POUR SACHA
Lamplugh, Ken
MAXIMUM FORCE
Lane, Andrew
LONELY HEARTS
Lang, Perry
LITTLE VEGAS
Lasker, Lawrence
SNEAKERS
Launer, Dale
LOVE POTION NO. 9
MY COUSIN VINNY
Lawton, J.F.
MISTRESS
UNDER SIEGE
Lease, Maria A.
DOLLY DEAREST
Leconte, Patrice
HAIRDRESSER'S HUSBAND, THE
Leder, Paul
EXILED IN AMERICA
Lee, Patrick
LIGHT IN THE JUNGLE, THE
Lee, Spike
MALCOLM X

Lee Wei-yee
SUPERCOP: POLICE STORY III
Lehner, Peter
MEGAVILLE
Leitch, Christopher
UNIVERSAL SOLDIER
Lemay, Charles Douglas
SOLDIER'S FORTUNE
Lemmo, James
WE'RE TALKIN' SERIOUS MONEY
Leonard, Brett
LAWNMOWER MAN, THE
Lesseos, Mimi
PUSHED TO THE LIMIT
Leung Yiu-ming
ONCE UPON A TIME IN CHINA
Lever, A.A.
PRIMO BABY
Levinson, Barry
TOYS
Levinson, G.J.
HELLROLLER
Levy, Jefery
DRIVE
Levy, Shuki
BLIND VISION
ROUND TRIP TO HEAVEN
Lewin, Ben
FAVOUR, THE WATCH, AND THE VERY BIG FISH, THE
Lindsell, Jonnie
I DON'T BUY KISSES ANYMORE
Lishner, Dan
MONTANA RUN, THE
Lister, Steven
PROJECT: SHADOWCHASER
Logan, Bob
MEATBALLS 4
Lotfi, Jim
DESERT KICKBOXER
Loughery, David
PASSENGER 57
Lucas, Craig
PRELUDE TO A KISS
Lund, Zoe Tamarlaine
BAD LIEUTENANT
Lyle, Joseph
CRITTERS 4
Lynch, David
TWIN PEAKS: FIRE WALK WITH ME
Ma Mei-ping
SUPERCOP: POLICE STORY III
MacLean, J.E.
DARK HORSE
MacLeod, Colin
DRIVE
Malo, Rene
SCANNERS III: THE TAKEOVER
Mamet, David
GLENGARRY GLEN ROSS
HOFFA
Mandel, Babaloo
LEAGUE OF THEIR OWN, A
MR. SATURDAY NIGHT
Mann, Michael
LAST OF THE MOHICANS, THE
Marcarelli, Joyce
ORIGINAL INTENT
Marcarelli, Rob
ORIGINAL INTENT
Marfori, Andreas
EVIL CLUTCH
Marino, Umberto
STATION, THE
Markham, Monte
NEON CITY
Martin, Robert
BASKET CASE 3: THE PROGENY
Marx, Rick
MIRROR IMAGES
Mason, John
UNDER SIEGE
Mastorakis, Nico
HIRED TO KILL
Matheson, Chris
MOM AND DAD SAVE THE WORLD
Matsuokoa, Takashi
PALE BLOOD
Mattera, Charles
BLOODFIST III: FORCED TO FIGHT
Maunder, J. Stephen
TALONS OF THE EAGLE
TIGER CLAWS
McBride, Stephen
EDWARD II
McCollum, Chuck
PLAY NICE
McCormick, Bret
BLOOD ON THE BADGE
McElheron, Maureen
TUNE, THE
McElroy, Alan B.
RAPID FIRE
McGee, Rex
PURE COUNTRY
McKay, Steven
DIGGSTOWN
McKellar, Don
HIGHWAY 61
McMurtry, Larry
FALLING FROM GRACE
Medoff, Mark
CITY OF JOY
Merendino, James
WITCHCRAFT IV: VIRGIN HEART
Merhi, Joseph
BIKINI SUMMER 2
DEADLY BET
Merinero, Carlos Perez
AMANTES
Merrick, Monte
MR. BASEBALL
Meyers, Nancy
ONCE UPON A CRIME
SISTER ACT
Meyers, Patrick
K2
Mikhalkov, Nikita
CLOSE TO EDEN
Miles, Doug
BEASTMASTER 2: THROUGH THE PORTAL OF TIME
Miller, Geof
HOUSE IV
Miller, George
LORENZO'S OIL
Miller, Grant Hinden
SOLDIER'S TALE, A
Milling, William R.
CAN IT BE LOVE
Model, Ben
PUERTO RICAN MAMBO (NOT A MUSICAL), THE
Mohoney, Raymond
BREATHING FIRE
Mohr, Clifford
LADY DRAGON
Mohr, Henro
KICK OR DIE
Mones, Paul
FATHERS AND SONS
Montefiori, Luigi
BEYOND JUSTICE
Monteleone, Vincenzo
MEDITERRANEO
Moore, Charles Philip
BLACKBELT
Moore, Simon
UNDER SUSPICION
Moorhouse, Jocelyn
PROOF
Moran, Joan
SEX CRIMES
Morris, Brent
SEXUAL RESPONSE
Morris, Grant
DOES THIS MEAN WE'RE MARRIED?
Morton, Lisa
ADVENTURES IN DINOSAUR CITY
Moyle, Allan
LOVE CRIMES
Mugavero, Frank
BIG GIRLS DON'T CRY . . . THEY GET EVEN
Munch, Christopher
HOURS AND TIMES, THE
Murray, Michael J.
DANCE MACABRE
HOUSE OF USHER, THE
Musker, John
ALADDIN
Mutrux, Floyd
AMERICAN ME
Myers, Cindy
BED & BREAKFAST
Myers, Mike
WAYNE'S WORLD
Nakano, Desmond
AMERICAN ME
Namei, Frank Darius
COLLISION COURSE
Nankin, Michael
GATE II
Nelson, B.J.
SCANNERS III: THE TAKEOVER
Newman, Brenda
CANVAS

Ngema, Mbongeni
SARAFINA!
Ni Zhen
RAISE THE RED LANTERN
Nicholson, William
SARAFINA!
Nielsen, Richard
OH, WHAT A NIGHT
Novaro, Beatriz
DANZON
Novaro, Maria
DANZON
Nykvist, Sven
OX, THE
Nystrom, John
SEVERED TIES
Nyswaner, Ron
LOVE HURTS
Olsen, Arne
BLACK ICE
Olsen, Dana
MEMOIRS OF AN INVISIBLE MAN
Olson, Brent
GHOULIES III: GHOULIES GO TO COLLEGE
Omori, Kazuki
GODZILLA VS. BIOLLANTE
Orsenna, Erik
INDOCHINE
Osborne, Chuck
DOUBLE TROUBLE
Osborne, William
STOP! OR MY MOM WILL SHOOT
Osterweil, Richard
PAINTING THE TOWN
Outten, Richard
LITTLE NEMO: ADVENTURES IN SLUMBERLAND
PET SEMATARY II
Owens, Brian
HAPPY HELL NIGHT
Oxenberg, Jan
THANK YOU AND GOOD NIGHT!
Palliser, Peter
LANDSLIDE
Palm, Anders
DEAD CERTAIN
Parker, Tom S.
STAY TUNED
Parkes, Walter F.
SNEAKERS
Parr, Larry
SOLDIER'S TALE, A
Paul, Stuart
FATE
Peace, J. Stephen
KILLER TOMATOES EAT FRANCE!
Peoples, David Webb
HERO
UNFORGIVEN
Peploe, Mark
AFRAID OF THE DARK
Perkins, Kent
TO PROTECT AND SERVE
Perl, Arnold
MALCOLM X
Perry, Fred C.
HIRED TO KILL
Pesce, P.J.
BODY WAVES
Peters, Charlie
PASSED AWAY
Petersen, Ron
HAPPY HELL NIGHT
Petz, John
CHAINS OF GOLD
Phillips, Lucy
STEAL AMERICA
Phillips, Maurice
OVER HER DEAD BODY
Phillips, Toby
PAMELA PRINCIPLE, THE
Pialat, Maurice
VAN GOGH
Piddock, Jim
TRACES OF RED
Plone, Allen
PHANTOM OF THE RITZ
Plympton, Bill
TUNE, THE
Pohjola, Ilppo
DADDY AND THE MUSCLE ACADEMY
Pollon, Eddy
NICKEL & DIME
Ponicsan, Darryl
SCHOOL TIES
Potter, Dennis
SECRET FRIENDS
Potts, Michel
LIGHT IN THE JUNGLE, THE
Pratt, Dennis A.
KICKBOXER 3: THE ART OF WAR
Pressfield, Steven
FREEJACK
Pressman, Kenneth
DIARY OF A HITMAN
Preston, David
SCANNERS III: THE TAKEOVER
TWIN SISTERS
Preston, Trevor
COLD JUSTICE
Price, Richard
NIGHT AND THE CITY
Pridhodko, Oleg
RASPAD
Primus, Barry
MISTRESS
Prince, Peter
WATERLAND
Prior, David A.
CENTER OF THE WEB
Prior, Ted
ARMED FOR ACTION
Prochazka, Jan
EAR, THE
Procopio, Frank
CAFE ROMEO
Proft, Pat
BRAIN DONORS
Purdy, Jon
GUYVER, THE
Putnam, George D.
FATAL INSTINCT
Puzo, Mario
CHRISTOPHER COLUMBUS: THE DISCOVERY
Pyne, Daniel
WHITE SANDS
Quignard, Pascal
TOUS LES MATINS DU MONDE
Rae, Michael
UNDER SIEGE
Reaver, Roxanne
TRAINED TO FIGHT
Rehwaldt, Frank
DEADBOLT
Reid, Ron
MONTANA RUN, THE
Rephun, Hesh
CAN IT BE LOVE
Resnick, Patricia
STRAIGHT TALK
Resnikoff, Robert
COLLISION COURSE
Reynolds, Lee
STORYVILLE
Rice, Wayne Allan
ONLY YOU
Richard, Julie
SCANNERS III: THE TAKEOVER
Richards, Winston
ROUND TRIP TO HEAVEN
Richardson, Peter
POPE MUST DIET!, THE
Richens, Pete
POPE MUST DIET!, THE
Rickard, Winston
BLIND VISION
Riffel, J.
HOUSE ON TOMBSTONE HILL, THE
Riggs, Marlon T.
COLOR ADJUSTMENT
Robbins, Tim
BOB ROBERTS
Roberts, Scott
K2
Robertson, Joseph F.
AUNTIE LEE'S MEAT PIES
Robertson, R.J.
BEASTMASTER 2: THROUGH THE PORTAL OF TIME
MUNCHIE
Robinson, Bruce
JENNIFER EIGHT
Robinson, Phil Alden
SNEAKERS
Robinson, Sally
MEDICINE MAN
Rocco, Marc
WHERE THE DAY TAKES YOU
Rockwell, Alexandre
IN THE SOUP
Rogers, James B.
SORORITY HOUSE MASSACRE 2
Rohmer, Eric
CONTE DE PRINTEMPS

Rollin, Jean
EMMANUELLE 6
Romoli, Giovanni
DEVIL'S DAUGHTER, THE
Ronssin, Jean-Pierre
DISCRETE, LA
Roos, Don
LOVE FIELD
SINGLE WHITE FEMALE
Rose, Bernard
CANDYMAN
Ross, Gary
MR. BASEBALL
Rossi, Leo
WE'RE TALKIN' SERIOUS MONEY
Rossio, Terry
ALADDIN
Rothstein, Richard
UNIVERSAL SOLDIER
Roulet, Dominique
INSPECTOR LAVARDIN
Ruben, Andy
POISON IVY
Rubin, Mann
HUMAN SHIELD, THE
Rubini, Sergio
STATION, THE
Rudner, Rita
PETER'S FRIENDS
Rudnick, Paul
SISTER ACT
Saint-Hamont, Daniel
POUR SACHA
Sandler, Barry
ALL-AMERICAN MURDER
Sato, Junya
SILK ROAD, THE
Saunders, George
MISSION OF JUSTICE
Sayles, John
PASSION FISH
Scantlebury, Glen
STEAL AMERICA
Schepps, Shawn
ENCINO MAN
Schlondorff, Volker
VOYAGER
Schoffman, Stuart
FINEST HOUR, THE
Schow, David J.
CRITTERS 4
Schrader, Paul
LIGHT SLEEPER
Schulman, Tom
MEDICINE MAN
Schulze, Douglas
HELL MASTER
Schwartz, John Alan
BLACK ICE
Scott, Allan
COLD HEAVEN
Scribner, Sam A.
DELTA HEAT
Seidel, Frederick
AFRAID OF THE DARK
Selbo, Jule
HARD PROMISES
Selby, William
DEATH HOUSE
Seltzer, David
SHINING THROUGH
Semper, John
CLASS ACT
Shapiro, Paul
BREAKING THE RULES
Shea Ruben, Katt
POISON IVY
Sheffield, David
BOOMERANG
Shelton, Ron
WHITE MEN CAN'T JUMP
Shepard, Richard
LINGUINI INCIDENT, THE
Sheridan, Bob
SORORITY HOUSE MASSACRE 2
Sheridan, Guillermo
CABEZA DE VACA
Shusett, Ronald
FREEJACK
Shyer, Charles
ONCE UPON A CRIME
Sibay, Mussef
WOMAN, HER MEN AND HER FUTON, A
Sidaris, Andy
DO OR DIE
Silver, Amanda
HAND THAT ROCKS THE CRADLE, THE
Simon, J.P.
CTHULHU MANSION
Sinofski, Bruce
BROTHER'S KEEPER
Slattery, Damian F.
DAY IN OCTOBER, A
Sloane, Rick
MIND, BODY & SOUL
Smith, Lindsay
BACK IN THE U.S.S.R.
Smoke, Stephen
FINAL IMPACT
STREET CRIMES
Snowden, William
PRIMARY MOTIVE
Snyder, Blake
STOP! OR MY MOM WILL SHOOT
Soavi, Michele
DEVIL'S DAUGHTER, THE
Soisson, Joel
LOWER LEVEL
Solinas, Piernico
TOUCH AND DIE
Solomon, Ed
LEAVING NORMAL
MOM AND DAD SAVE THE WORLD
Solomon, M.A.
EYE OF THE EAGLE 3
Sommer, Scott
CRISSCROSS
Sonego, Rodolfo
ONCE UPON A CRIME
Sorkin, Aaron
FEW GOOD MEN, A
Spencer, Jane
LITTLE NOISES
Stanzler, Jeff
JUMPIN' AT THE BONEYARD
Stein, Mark
HOUSESITTER
Steiner, Gerald M.
AUNTIE LEE'S MEAT PIES
Stewart, Donald
PATRIOT GAMES
Stewart, Michael
EYE OF THE STORM
Stone, Nick
SUNSET STRIP
Stone, Noreen
BRENDA STARR
Strick, Wesley
FINAL ANALYSIS
Stroppel, Fred
ALMOST PREGNANT
Strouth, Jeffrey
AMERICAN FABULOUS
Strucchi, Stefano
ONCE UPON A CRIME
Sturridge, Charles
WHERE ANGELS FEAR TO TREAD
Sullivan, Tim
WHERE ANGELS FEAR TO TREAD
Sullivent, Robyn
NIGHT RHYTHMS
PAMELA PRINCIPLE, THE
Summanen, Lasse
OX, THE
Summers, Jaron
KILLER IMAGE
Sutton, Lisa
CAGED FEAR
Suvat, Tony S.
IN GOLD WE TRUST
Tabet, Sylvio
BEASTMASTER 2: THROUGH THE PORTAL OF TIME
Tang King-sung
SUPERCOP: POLICE STORY III
Tang Pik-yin
ONCE UPON A TIME IN CHINA
Tannen, William
INSIDE EDGE
Tarantino, Quentin
RESERVOIR DOGS
Taraporevala, Sooni
MISSISSIPPI MASALA
Tausik, David
HOMICIDAL IMPULSE
Tejada-Flores, Miguel
PSYCHIC
Thomas, Anthony
CODE NAME: CHAOS
Thomas, David A.
FIELD OF FIRE
Thomas, Michael
TILL THERE WAS YOU
Thompson, Gary Scott
SPLIT SECOND

Thompson, Randy
MONTANA RUN, THE
Thornton, Billy Bob
ONE FALSE MOVE
Tiffe, Robert
DEADLY BET
Tipping, A. J.
OVER HER DEAD BODY
Tolkin, Michael
DEEP COVER
PLAYER, THE
Tolkin, Stephen
CAPTAIN AMERICA
Toro, Antonio
AMITYVILLE 1992:
IT'S ABOUT TIME
Towbin, Bram
JUST LIKE IN THE MOVIES
Trafficante, Mara
DEADBOLT
Travolta, John
CHAINS OF GOLD
Treut, Monika
MY FATHER IS COMING
Tsui Hark
ONCE UPON A TIME IN CHINA
Tsukamoto, Shinya
TETSUO: THE IRON MAN
Turner, Bonnie
WAYNE'S WORLD
Turner, Terry
WAYNE'S WORLD
Tzudiker, Bob
NEWSIES
Van Der Laan, Sytze
LILY WAS HERE
Van Dormael, Jaco
TOTO LE HEROS
Vasquez, Joseph B.
BRONX WAR, THE
Verbong, Ben
LILY WAS HERE
Vey, P.C.
TUNE, THE
Victor, Mark
COOL WORLD
Vincent, Christian
DISCRETE, LA
Vincenzoni, Luciano
ONCE UPON A CRIME
Von Arnim, Elizabeth
ENCHANTED APRIL
Von Praunheim, Rosa
AFFENGEIL
Von Trier, Lars
ZENTROPA
Vorsel, Niels
ZENTROPA
Voss, Kurt
WHERE THE DAY TAKES YOU
Wade, Kevin
MR. BASEBALL
Wall, Stuart
HELLROLLER
Ward, Simon Louis
NIGHT EYES 2
Wargnier, Regis
INDOCHINE
Wasson, Craig
MIDNIGHT FEAR
Waterman, Dennis
COLD JUSTICE
Waters, Daniel
BATMAN RETURNS
Wayans, Damon
MO' MONEY
Weidner, John
MAXIMUM FORCE
Weiner, John
COMRADES IN ARMS
Weinshanker, Burt
BECOMING COLETTE
Weiss, David N.
ROCK-A-DOODLE
Wertenbaker, Timberlake
CHILDREN, THE
Weston, Eric
TO PROTECT AND SERVE
Whaley, James
OVER HER DEAD BODY
Whedon, Joss
BUFFY THE VAMPIRE SLAYER
Whifler, Graeme
DR. GIGGLES
Whitaker, Darrah
SMOOTH TALKER
White, Noni
NEWSIES
Wilde, Steven
SHAKING THE TREE
Wimmer, Kurt
DOUBLE TROUBLE
Winkler, Anthony C.
LUNATIC, THE
Winning, David
KILLER IMAGE
Winograd, Peter
ONE LAST RUN
Wittcomb, Kate
DEATH HOUSE
Wolf, Dick
SCHOOL TIES
Wolk, Michael
INNOCENT BLOOD
Wollert, David W.
NEAR MISSES
Wolpaw, James
COMPLEX WORLD
Wong, Barry
HARD-BOILED
Woo, Teresa
TRAINED TO FIGHT
Wooden, Christopher
KISS ME A KILLER
Wool, Abbe
ROADSIDE PROPHETS
Wurlitzer, Rudy
VOYAGER
WIND
Wynorski, Jim
BEASTMASTER 2:
THROUGH THE PORTAL OF TIME
MUNCHIE
Yoshida, Tsuyoshi
SILK ROAD, THE
Young, David R.
ROCK & ROLL COWBOYS
Yuen Kai-chi
ONCE UPON A TIME IN CHINA
Zaloum, Alain
CANVAS
Zand, Michael
PLAY NICE
Zeiderman, Jon
LITTLE NOISES
Zellinger, Jimmy
LITTLE SISTER
Zeltser, Yuri
EYE OF THE STORM
Zemeckis, Robert
TRESPASS
Zenga, Bo
BODY WAVES
Ziller, Paul
BLOODFIST IV: DIE TRYING
Zorrilla, Jose Antonio
WINTER IN LISBON, THE

SET DECORATORS

Ahrens, Anne H.
SINGLE WHITE FEMALE
Alan, Jean
FOLKS!
Ancona, Amy
MIRACLE BEACH
976-EVIL II
Armour, Rik
IN THE SOUP
Arnold, Nancy
LITTLE SISTER
RUNESTONE, THE
Arvaniti, Pepeta
VOYAGER
Barrett, Penny
ZEBRAHEAD
Beattie, Julie Brooke
GUYVER, THE
Benjamin, Susan
NICKEL & DIME
PET SEMATARY II
Benton, Robert R.
WHITE MEN CAN'T JUMP
Bernard, Andy
BREAKING THE RULES
VAGRANT, THE
Berstrom, Jan K.
PUBLIC EYE, THE
Blackie-Goodine, Janice
UNFORGIVEN
Bode, Susan
HUSBANDS AND WIVES
Bonetto, Aline
DELICATESSEN
Boswell, Merideth
COOL WORLD

Bowin, Claire
BUFFY THE VAMPIRE SLAYER
Boxer, Daniel
ACES: IRON EAGLE III
Bradette, Jacques
PRIMARY MOTIVE
Brandenburg, Rosemary
SCHOOL TIES
Braunstein, Sharon
BASKET CASE 3: THE PROGENY
Brink, Gary
STRANGER AMONG US, A
Brookes, Karen
POWER OF ONE, THE
Bruck, Karen
HEAVEN IS A PLAYGROUND
Burbank, Lynda
HIGHWAY TO HELL
Buri, Mary
WE'RE TALKIN' SERIOUS MONEY
Burt, Amy
DEADBOLT
Butler, Chris A.
CHAPLIN
Carasick, Cheryl
BATMAN RETURNS
Carle, Alexander
UNIVERSAL SOLDIER
Carr, Cindy
PRELUDE TO A KISS
Carr, Jackie
DEATH BECOMES HER
Carroll, Stephanie
BAD LIEUTENANT
Chamberland, Andre
SCANNERS III: THE TAKEOVER
Charbonnet, Merideth Boswell
GUN IN BETTY LOU'S HANDBAG, THE
Childs, Martin
CRYING GAME, THE
Claypool, Michael
MO' MONEY
Cook, Sandi
FALLING FROM GRACE
Cooper, Dorree
DISTINGUISHED GENTLEMAN, THE
HONEY, I BLEW UP THE KID
MOM AND DAD SAVE THE WORLD
Crew, A. Rosaline
INTO THE SUN
Crew, Rosalind
SCORCHERS
Cummings, Peg
INNOCENT BLOOD
OUT ON A LIMB
Cunningham, Cliff
COLD HEAVEN
D'Amico, Archie
PALE BLOOD
Davis, Catherine
MY NEW GUN
Davis, Deb
COMPLEX WORLD
Dean, Lisa
BODYGUARD, THE
Dehaan, Catie
LITTLE NOISES
Del Rosario, Linda
ADJUSTER, THE
Dersjant, Helen
LEATHER JACKETS
DeScenna, Linda
HONEYMOON IN VEGAS
TOYS
DeTitta, Jr., George
LEAGUE OF THEIR OWN, A
SCENT OF A WOMAN
SHADOWS AND FOG
Dick, Jaro
THIS IS MY LIFE
Doyle, Tracey A.
HOUSESITTER
Drake, Barbara
DIGGSTOWN
Duffy, Jim
NOISES OFF
Duffy, Jr., Irvin E. Jim
CAPTAIN RON
Dwyer, John M.
PATRIOT GAMES
Edwards, Belinda
ALIEN3
Elmblad, Donald
DEEP COVER
Emshwiller, Susan
PLAYER, THE
Erickson, Jim
LAST OF THE MOHICANS, THE
LOVE FIELD
Etevez, Enrique
MEDICINE MAN
Fanton, Julie Kaye
MIGHTY DUCKS, THE
Fettis, Gary
BEETHOVEN
Ford, Michael
MUPPET CHRISTMAS CAROL, THE
Fox, K.O.
MISTRESS
Franco, Robert J.
GLENGARRY GLEN ROSS
NIGHT AND THE CITY
Frankenheimer, Leslie
RAPID FIRE
Freas, Dianna
THUNDERHEART
Fumagalli, Gianfranco
ONCE UPON A CRIME
Gaffin, Lauri
RUBY
Gee, Carolyn
PSYCHIC
Gentz, Rick
UNDER SIEGE
Gibeson, Bruce
FREEJACK
Gibeson, Bruce A.
STEPHEN KING'S SLEEPWALKERS
Gilstrap, Joyce Anne
BIG GIRLS DON'T CRY . . . THEY GET EVEN
OF MICE AND MEN
Glass, Ted
MALCOLM X
Goddard, Richard
FAR AND AWAY
LETHAL WEAPON 3
Gould, Robert
NEWSIES
Greco, Anthony
BEAUTIFUL DREAMERS
Griffith, Clay
SINGLES
Gunn, Jeannie
BRAIN DONORS
Haigh, Nancy
HERO
Haley, Jeff
CAPTAIN RON
Hallenbeck, Casey C.
JENNIFER EIGHT
Hart, Jay R.
FOREVER YOUNG
GLADIATOR
WAYNE'S WORLD
Hartmann, Jeff
SIMPLE MEN
Hepburn, Rob
TALONS OF THE EAGLE
Hicks, Alan
BOOMERANG
Hill, Derek R.
PURE COUNTRY
Hislop, Mary
DARK HORSE
Holinko, Roberta
FATHERS AND SONS
Hotte, Paul
CANVAS
Howitt, Peter
SHINING THROUGH
Huyette, Marty
LONELY HEARTS
Ivey, Don K.
PASSENGER 57
Jacobson, Scott
FOLKS!
Jimenez, Marisol
DOUBLE TROUBLE
Jones, Stacey
SWOON
Kasch, Brian
BOB ROBERTS
STORYVILLE
Kearney, Cheryal
ENCINO MAN
Kelter, Jerie
LINGUINI INCIDENT, THE
Kemp, Barry
COMMON BONDS
Kent, James V.
LAST OF THE MOHICANS, THE
Kittel, Lance
BRIDE OF KILLER NERD
Klopp, Kathe
MR. SATURDAY NIGHT
Koneff, David
HELLRAISER III: HELL ON EARTH

Koneff, David A.
WAXWORK II: LOST IN TIME

Kremer, Richard
BEASTMASTER 2: THROUGH THE PORTAL OF TIME

Kuchera, Ted
K2

Laughlin, Jeannie
BACKTRACK

Lauzier, Frederque
VOYAGER

Lee, Steven
NEON CITY

Lemmon, Jacqueline
DESIRE AND HELL AT SUNSET MOTEL

LeTenoux, Johan
NIGHT ON EARTH

Lewis, Garrett
BRAM STOKER'S DRACULA
COLLISION COURSE

Lichter, Amiram
BLINK OF AN EYE

Lindstrom, Kara
MAMBO KINGS, THE

Litsch, Joseph
LOVE CRIMES

Lubin, Janis
MIDNIGHT CLEAR, A

MacLean, Christine
RESURRECTED, THE

Magnusson, Magnus
OX, THE

March, Marvin
HOME ALONE 2: LOST IN NEW YORK

Marrett, John
JUST LIKE IN THE MOVIES

Marshall, Amy
SHADOWS AND FOG

Martel, Sophie
LOVER, THE

Martin, Maggie
GHOULIES III: GHOULIES GO TO COLLEGE

Martinez, Angeles
CABEZA DE VACA

Marz, Volker
AFFENGEIL

Mayer, Augusto
WINTER IN LISBON, THE

McMillan, Stephen
YEAR OF THE COMET

McMillan, Stephenie
CHAPLIN
UNDER SUSPICION

McSherry, Rose Marie
STAY TUNED

Medlen, Damon
NICKEL & DIME

Meeks, Mary
GAS FOOD LODGING

Mollo, Ann
1492: THE CONQUEST OF PARADISE

Morales, Leslie
CRISSCROSS
TWIN PEAKS: FIRE WALK WITH ME

Morrison, Todd
DEATH HOUSE

Munch, Barbara
RAISING CAIN

Munoz, Muchele
POISON IVY

Murphy, Jennifer
ORIGINAL INTENT

Murphy, Tamara
ULTRAVIOLET

Myers, Troy
ONE FALSE MOVE

Nelson, Bob
FINAL ANALYSIS

Nicolaou, Sally
LOVE POTION NO. 9

Nikolaidou, Doxi
VOYAGER

Nye, Nancy
RAMPAGE

O'Hara, Karen A.
LORENZO'S OIL

Olive, Sylvie
DISCRETE, LA

Osborne, Aaron
IN THE HEAT OF PASSION
KISS ME A KILLER

Osipenko, Yuri
BACK IN THE U.S.S.R.

Paris, Richard
ADJUSTER, THE

Pedersen, Torben Baekmark
DAY IN OCTOBER, A

Perreau, Brigitte
DOES THIS MEAN WE'RE MARRIED?

Perzan, Caroline
FROZEN ASSETS

Pesquer, Frederic
FAVOUR, THE WATCH, AND THE VERY BIG FISH, THE

Peters, Kathryn
CANDYMAN

Peyton, Robin
CLASS ACT

Pope, Natalie K.
PRAYER OF THE ROLLERBOYS

Pressman, Carol
3 NINJAS

Prihoda, Joel
COLD JUSTICE

Quertier, Jill
DAMAGE

Rau, Gretchen
CONSENTING ADULTS
LEAP OF FAITH
RIVER RUNS THROUGH IT, A

Rearden, Chance
WILD ORCHID 2: TWO SHADES OF BLUE

Reed, Sharo
MARTIAL LAW 2: UNDERCOVER

Reed, Sharon
MISSION OF JUSTICE

Remacle, Don
STOP! OR MY MOM WILL SHOOT

Reynolds-Wasco, Sandy
HAND THAT ROCKS THE CRADLE, THE

Ricardi, Anthony
PHANTOM OF THE RITZ

Roberts, Nicki
NIGHT EYES 2

Robitaille, Ginette
CANVAS

Rodarte, C.C.
DR. GIGGLES

Rollins, Leslie
HARD PROMISES
LOVE HURTS

Rosemarin, Hilton
THIS IS MY LIFE
USED PEOPLE

Ross, Heather
ROUND TRIP TO HEAVEN

Rowell, Victoria
HUNTING

Rubino, Beth
TRESPASS

Sampson, Laura
ALMOST PREGNANT

Sanna, Frank
TWIN SISTERS

Scandariato, Itala
VOYAGER

Schaefer, Kendal
DANCE WITH DEATH

Schaffer, Samara
MAN TROUBLE
SNEAKERS

Schneider, Robin
VOYAGER

Schulz, Karen
OF MICE AND MEN

Schulze, Douglas
HELL MASTER

Scoppa, Jr., Justin
WHISPERS IN THE DARK

Scott, Jeanette
MISSISSIPPI MASALA

Seirton, Michael
MY COUSIN VINNY
WHITE SANDS

Sensidoni, Giancarlo
JOHNNY STECCHINO

Serdena, Gene
PASSED AWAY

Shannon, Elizabeth
NETHERWORLD

Shaw, William J.
LIFE ON THE EDGE

Shewchuk, Steve
CUTTING EDGE, THE

Shingleton, Rosalind
CITY OF JOY

Simpson, Rick
MEMOIRS OF AN INVISIBLE MAN
UNLAWFUL ENTRY

Spaddro, Michelle
RUBIN & ED

Stabley, Anthony
BLACKBELT

SOURCE AUTHORS

Fujioka, Yutaka
LITTLE NEMO: ADVENTURES IN SLUMBERLAND
Funk, Mason
WINTER IN LISBON, THE
Furie, Sidney J.
ACES: IRON EAGLE III
Galbally, Frank
STORYVILLE
Gallagher, Stephen
MONKEY BOY
Gidding, Nelson
JOURNEY OF HONOR
Giraud, Jean Moebius
LITTLE NEMO: ADVENTURES IN SLUMBERLAND
Gitelson, Richard
ROAD TO RUIN
Goddard, Mark
BIG GIRLS DON'T CRY . . . THEY GET EVEN
Goddard, Melissa
BIG GIRLS DON'T CRY . . . THEY GET EVEN
POISON IVY
Golden, Dan
NAKED OBSESSION
Goldman, Gary
ROCK-A-DOODLE
Goodrow, Garry
HONEY, I BLEW UP THE KID
Gordon, Dan
PASSENGER 57
Gordon, Stuart
HONEY, I BLEW UP THE KID
Grade, Chaim
QUARREL, THE
Graff, Todd
USED PEOPLE
Gray, Spalding
MONSTER IN A BOX
Grazer, Brian
HOUSESITTER
Greene, Anthony L.
FINISHING TOUCH, THE
Grossman, Rodger S.
FINISHING TOUCH, THE
Gutierrez, Vincent
INSIDE EDGE
Haley, Alex
MALCOLM X
Haley, Susan
GETTING MARRIED IN BUFFALO JUMP
Harris, Robin
BEBE'S KIDS
Hart, Josephine
DAMAGE
Hawkins, Diana
CHAPLIN
Higgins, Deirdre
HOUSE IV
Highsmith, Patricia
CRY OF THE OWL, THE
Hijuelos, Oscar
MAMBO KINGS, THE
Hopkins, William
CHILDREN OF THE NIGHT
Houston, Bobby
CAGED FEAR
Howard, Ron
FAR AND AWAY
Hughes, John
HOME ALONE 2: LOST IN NEW YORK
Hunter, Tab
DARK HORSE
Ibraguimbekov, Roustam
CLOSE TO EDEN
Inoue, Yasushi
SILK ROAD, THE
Isaacs, Susan
SHINING THROUGH
Jan Otten, Willem
LILY WAS HERE
Jennewein, Jim
STAY TUNED
Jensen, Karen
PRIMO BABY
Jones, John G.
AMITYVILLE 1992: IT'S ABOUT TIME
Joseph, M.K.
SOLDIER'S TALE, A
Jost, Jon
ALL THE VERMEERS IN NEW YORK
Junkerman, John
MR. BASEBALL
Kahn, Terry
CAGED FEAR
Kamen, Robert Mark
GLADIATOR
Kane, Bob
BATMAN RETURNS
Kaplan, Marty
DISTINGUISHED GENTLEMAN, THE
Kasdan, Lawrence
BODYGUARD, THE
Katchmer, John
UNLAWFUL ENTRY
Kelly, M.T.
CLEARCUT
Kerchner, Robert
BLOODFIST IV: DIE TRYING
Kersh, Gerald
NIGHT AND THE CITY
Kim, Kenny
3 NINJAS
King, Stephen
LAWNMOWER MAN, THE
Kirby, Jack
CAPTAIN AMERICA
Kobayashi, Shinichiro
GODZILLA VS. BIOLLANTE
Koob, Andre
TWIN SISTERS
Kosugi, Sho
JOURNEY OF HONOR
Kourtchatkin, Anatol
ADAM'S RIB
Kronstadt-Mann, Rachel
BACKTRACK
Kuenster, T.J.
ROCK-A-DOODLE
Lapierre, Dominique
CITY OF JOY
Leahy, Michael
LOWER LEVEL
Lease, Maria A.
DOLLY DEAREST
Leconte, Patrice
HAIRDRESSER'S HUSBAND, THE
Leroux, Gaston
PHANTOM OF THE RITZ
Levoy, Myron
ALAN & NAOMI
Levy, Jeffery
GHOULIES III: GHOULIES GO TO COLLEGE
Livingston, Kimball
WIND
Lovecraft, H.P.
CTHULHU MANSION
RESURRECTED, THE
Lucas, Craig
PRELUDE TO A KISS
Lutz, Jon
SINGLE WHITE FEMALE
Maccari, Ruggero
SCENT OF A WOMAN
Macklin, Robert
STORYVILLE
MacLean, Norman
RIVER RUNS THROUGH IT, A
Magee, Allan
HIGHWAY 61
Mamet, David
GLENGARRY GLEN ROSS
Mancuso, Jr., Frank
COOL WORLD
Marino, Umberto
STATION, THE
Marlowe, Christopher
EDWARD II
Marti, Jose
MAMBO KINGS, THE
Mastorakis, Nico
HIRED TO KILL
McCollum, Chuck
PLAY NICE
McDonald, Bruce
HIGHWAY 61
McElroy, Alan B.
RAPID FIRE
McKay, Winsor
LITTLE NEMO: ADVENTURES IN SLUMBERLAND
McKellar, Don
HIGHWAY 61
Messick, Dale
BRENDA STARR
Meyers, Patrick
K2
Mikhalkov, Nikita
CLOSE TO EDEN
Milicevic, Djordje
GLADIATOR

Webster, Christopher
CHILDREN OF THE NIGHT

Weintraub, Sandra
CHINA O'BRIEN II

Weiss, David N.
ROCK-A-DOODLE

Werb, Michael
HUMAN SHIELD, THE

Wharton, Edith
CHILDREN, THE

Wharton, William
MIDNIGHT CLEAR, A

Wilde, Oscar
IMPORTANCE OF BEING EARNEST, THE

Wilson, Kim
LEAGUE OF THEIR OWN, A

Wimmer, Kurt
DOUBLE TROUBLE

Winkler, Anthony C.
LUNATIC, THE

Wise, Leonard
DIGGSTOWN

Wolf, Dick
SCHOOL TIES

Wolitzer, Meg
THIS IS MY LIFE

Woo, John
HARD-BOILED

Wood, William P.
RAMPAGE

Worth, David
LADY DRAGON

Wynorski, Jim
BEASTMASTER 2: THROUGH THE PORTAL OF TIME
HOUSE IV

Young, Diana
FERNGULLY: THE LAST RAINFOREST

Yuzna, Brian
HONEY, I BLEW UP THE KID

Zaloom, George
ENCINO MAN

Zand, Michael
PLAY NICE

Ziskin, Laura
HERO

SPECIAL EFFECTS

Angel Studios
LAWNMOWER MAN, THE

Barr, Craig
BATMAN RETURNS

Bartalos, Gabe
BASKET CASE 3: THE PROGENY

Bruno, John
BATMAN RETURNS

Buechler, John
DEMONIC TOYS

Carere, Frank
GATE II

Ceglia, Frank
CRITTERS 4
LAWNMOWER MAN, THE

Ceglia, Tom
LAWNMOWER MAN, THE

Chiang, Doug
DEATH BECOMES HER

Cook, Randall William
GATE II

David Stipes Productions
LAWNMOWER MAN, THE

Edlund, Richard
ALIEN3

Fink, Michael
BATMAN RETURNS

Gibbs, George
ALIEN3

Gillis, Alec
ALIEN3

Haines, Paul
LAWNMOWER MAN, THE

Homer & Associates Inc.
LAWNMOWER MAN, THE

Keen, Bob
CANDYMAN

Magical Media Industries
LAWNMOWER MAN, THE

Moore, Randy
BLOOD ON THE BADGE

Ralston, Ken
DEATH BECOMES HER

Reel EFX Inc.
LAWNMOWER MAN, THE

Reel Time
LAWNMOWER MAN, THE

Skotak, Dennis
BATMAN RETURNS

Smythe, Doug
DEATH BECOMES HER

The Goosney Company
LAWNMOWER MAN, THE

Tsukamoto, Shinya
TETSUO: THE IRON MAN

Woodruff, Tom
DEATH BECOMES HER

Woodruff, Jr., Tom
ALIEN3

Xaos Inc.
LAWNMOWER MAN, THE

STUNTS

Cheung Jue-luh
HARD-BOILED

Razatos, Spiro
976-EVIL II

Tong, Stanley
SUPERCOP: POLICE STORY III

REVIEW ATTRIBUTION

Bartholomew, David
AUNTIE LEE'S MEAT PIES
BLIND VISION
COMRADES IN ARMS
DEADLY BET
DESERT KICKBOXER
EMMANUELLE 6
GETTING MARRIED IN BUFFALO JUMP
I DON'T BUY KISSES ANYMORE
IMPORTANCE OF BEING EARNEST, THE
INSIDE EDGE
JUST LIKE IN THE MOVIES
LADY DRAGON
LEATHER JACKETS
MARTIAL LAW 2: UNDERCOVER
NICKEL & DIME
NIGHT RHYTHMS
OUT FOR BLOOD
PAMELA PRINCIPLE, THE
POUR SACHA
RASPAD
ROAD TO RUIN
SEX CRIMES
SNAKEEATER III . . . HIS LAW
STREET CRIMES
TALONS OF THE EAGLE
WELCOME TO OBLIVION
WILD WHEELS

Brenner, Paul
BABE, THE
BIG GIRLS DON'T CRY . . . THEY GET EVEN
BIKINI CARWASH COMPANY, THE
BOB MARLEY: TIME WILL TELL
BODYGUARD, THE
CLASS ACT
DESIRE AND HELL AT SUNSET MOTEL
ESCAPE FROM . . . SURVIVAL ZONE
FATAL INSTINCT
HAPPY HELL NIGHT
HOFFA
INCIDENT AT OGLALA
KICK OR DIE
LAST OF THE MOHICANS, THE
MIGHTY DUCKS, THE
MISTRESS
MOM AND DAD SAVE THE WORLD
ONCE UPON A CRIME
OTHER WOMAN, THE
PASSENGER 57
POPE MUST DIET!, THE
PUSHED TO THE LIMIT
RADIO FLYER
ROVER DANGERFIELD
SAVAGE INSTINCT
SILK ROAD, THE
STAY TUNED
TERMINAL BLISS
35 UP
TOYS
24 HOURS TO MIDNIGHT
WIND

Cassady, Jr., Charles
ALMOST PREGNANT
BEASTMASTER 2: THROUGH THE PORTAL OF TIME
BEETHOVEN
BEETHOVEN LIVES UPSTAIRS
BERNARD AND THE GENIE
BLOOD ON THE BADGE
BLOODFIST IV: DIE TRYING
BLOODFIST III: FORCED TO FIGHT
BREATHING FIRE
CAPTAIN AMERICA
CHAINS OF GOLD
CHINA O'BRIEN II
COLLISION COURSE
COLOR ADJUSTMENT
COMMON BONDS
COMPLEX WORLD
DEAD CERTAIN
DEATH HOUSE
DELTA HEAT
DIARY OF A HITMAN
DO OR DIE
DOUBLE TROUBLE
EXILED IN AMERICA
FATE
FINAL IMPACT
GHOULIES III: GHOULIES GO TO COLLEGE
HEAVEN IS A PLAYGROUND
HELL MASTER
HIGHWAY 61
HIRED TO KILL
HOURS AND TIMES, THE
HOUSE OF USHER, THE
HOUSE ON TOMBSTONE HILL, THE
IN THE HEAT OF PASSION
INDIO 2 – THE REVOLT
INTO THE SUN
INVASION OF THE SPACE PREACHERS
KILL LINE
KILLER TOMATOES EAT FRANCE!
KISS ME A KILLER
LIFE ON A STRING
LIGHT IN THE JUNGLE, THE
LILY WAS HERE
LITTLE VEGAS
LONELY HEARTS
LOWER LEVEL
MEGAVILLE
MIDNIGHT FEAR
MIRACLE BEACH
MIRROR IMAGES
MORTUARY ACADEMY
MUNCHIE
MY FATHER IS COMING
NAKED OBSESSION
NEAR MISSES
NEON CITY
NIGHT EYES 2
NIGHT ON EARTH
ONE LAST RUN
ORIGINAL INTENT
OVER HER DEAD BODY
PALE BLOOD
PRAYER OF THE ROLLERBOYS
PRIMO BABY
PROJECT: SHADOWCHASER
PSYCHIC
RAISE THE RED LANTERN
ROCK & ROLL COWBOYS
SHAKES THE CLOWN
SLUMBER PARTY MASSACRE 3
SMOOTH TALKER
SPIRITS
STATION, THE
STEELE'S LAW
STOP! OR MY MOM WILL SHOOT
TIGER CLAWS
TOTO LE HEROS
TRAINED TO FIGHT
TWIN SISTERS
ULTIMATE DESIRES

Cramer, Barbara Browne
CHAPLIN
HOWARDS END
K2
OX, THE
PETER'S FRIENDS
TOUS LES MATINS DU MONDE
WHERE ANGELS FEAR TO TREAD

Gingold, Michael
ALIEN3
AMITYVILLE 1992: IT'S ABOUT TIME
BAD CHANNELS
BASKET CASE 3: THE PROGENY
BEYOND DARKNESS
BRENDA STARR
BRIDE OF KILLER NERD
CANDYMAN
CHILDREN OF THE NIGHT
CONFESSIONS OF A SERIAL KILLER
CRITTERS 4
CTHULHU MANSION
DANCE MACABRE
DEMONIC TOYS
DR. GIGGLES
DOCTOR MORDRID
DOLLY DEAREST
EVIL CLUTCH
FERNGULLY: THE LAST RAINFOREST
GODZILLA VS. BIOLLANTE
GUYVER, THE
HARD – BOILED
HELLRAISER III: HELL ON EARTH
HELLROLLER
HIGHWAY TO HELL
HOUSE IV
INNOCENT BLOOD
JUICE

LADYBUGS
LASER MOON
MALCOLM X
MINDWARP
MISSISSIPPI MASALA
MONKEY BOY
976 – EVIL II
PET SEMATARY II
PHANTOM OF THE RITZ
POISON IVY
PROM NIGHT IV – DELIVER US FROM EVIL
RAISING CAIN
RESURRECTED, THE
RUNESTONE, THE
SCANNERS III: THE TAKEOVER
SEEDPEOPLE
SOCIETY
SORORITY HOUSE MASSACRE 2
SUPERCOP: POLICE STORY III
THIS IS MY LIFE
TRANCERS III: DETH LIVES
TROLL 2
TUNE, THE
VAGRANT, THE
WAXWORK II: LOST IN TIME
WAYNE'S WORLD
WITCHCRAFT IV: VIRGIN HEART

Glines, Carole
BEBE'S KIDS
CONSENTING ADULTS
DAMAGE
DIGGSTOWN
FEW GOOD MEN, A
1492: THE CONQUEST OF PARADISE
LEAGUE OF THEIR OWN, A
LEAP OF FAITH
PUBLIC EYE, THE
RIVER RUNS THROUGH IT, A

Goldman, David
ALADDIN
ALBERTO EXPRESS
COOL WORLD
DEEP BLUES
FALLING FROM GRACE
MR. SATURDAY NIGHT
1991: THE YEAR PUNK BROKE
PASSION FISH
ROADSIDE PROPHETS
SCENT OF A WOMAN
SINGLES
USED PEOPLE

Gonzalez, Francisco
ADVENTURES IN SPYING
AMANTES
BREAKING THE RULES
CABEZA DE VACA
DANZON
ROOTS OF EVIL

Green, Douglas
DISTINGUISHED GENTLEMAN, THE
FOREVER YOUNG
HOME ALONE 2: LOST IN NEW YORK
HUSBANDS AND WIVES
LETHAL WEAPON 3
LORENZO'S OIL
SARAFINA!
SHADOWS AND FOG

Greene, Kent
AFFENGEIL
BACK IN THE U.S.S.R.
BIKINI SUMMER 2
DOUBLE VISION
MAXIMUM FORCE
SCORCHERS

Hinckley, Tom
ACES: IRON EAGLE III
ARTICLE 99
BASIC INSTINCT
BATMAN RETURNS
BEATING HEART, A
BED & BREAKFAST
BLAME IT ON THE BELLBOY
BOOMERANG
BRAM STOKER'S DRACULA
BUFFY THE VAMPIRE SLAYER
CAPTAIN RON
CHRISTOPHER COLUMBUS: THE DISCOVERY
CLEARCUT
COLD HEAVEN
CONTE DE PRINTEMPS
COUSIN BOBBY
CRISSCROSS
CROSSING THE BRIDGE
CROSSING, THE
CRY OF THE OWL, THE
DEADBOLT
DEATH BECOMES HER
DEEP COVER
DELICATESSEN
DISCRETE, LA
DRIVE
ELEGANT CRIMINEL, L'
ENCHANTED APRIL
ENCINO MAN
FAR AND AWAY
FAVOUR, THE WATCH, AND THE VERY BIG FISH, THE
FINEST HOUR, THE
FOLKS!
FREEJACK
FROZEN ASSETS
GIVING, THE
GLENGARRY GLEN ROSS
GUILTY AS CHARGED
GUN IN BETTY LOU'S HANDBAG, THE
HAIRDRESSER'S HUSBAND, THE
HAND THAT ROCKS THE CRADLE, THE
HARD PROMISES
HERO
HONEY, I BLEW UP THE KID
HONEYMOON IN VEGAS
HOUSESITTER
HUGH HEFNER: ONCE UPON A TIME
HUMAN SHIELD, THE
INSPECTOR LAVARDIN
JENNIFER EIGHT
JOURNEY OF HONOR
KILL CRUISE
LEAVING NORMAL
LOVE CRIMES
LOVE FIELD
LUNATICS: A LOVE STORY
MAGICAL WORLD OF CHUCK JONES, THE
MAN TROUBLE
MEMOIRS OF AN INVISIBLE MAN
MIDNIGHT CLEAR, A
MONSTER IN A BOX
MONTANA RUN, THE
MR. BASEBALL
MUPPET CHRISTMAS CAROL, THE
MY COUSIN VINNY
NIGHT AND THE CITY
NOISES OFF
OH, WHAT A NIGHT
ONE FALSE MOVE
PASSED AWAY
PLAYBOYS, THE
PLAYER, THE
POWER OF ONE, THE
PRELUDE TO A KISS
PRIMARY MOTIVE
PROOF
PURE COUNTRY
RAPID FIRE
RESERVOIR DOGS
RUBIN & ED
RUBY
SCHOOL TIES
SECRET GAMES
SISTER ACT
SNEAKERS
STORYVILLE
STRAIGHT TALK
STRANGER AMONG US, A
THUNDERHEART
TRACES OF RED
TRESPASS
TWIN PEAKS: FIRE WALK WITH ME
UNDER SIEGE
UNFORGIVEN
UNIVERSAL SOLDIER
UNLAWFUL ENTRY
VAN GOGH
VENICE/VENICE
WATERDANCE, THE
WHISPERS IN THE DARK
WHITE MEN CAN'T JUMP
WHITE SANDS
WILD ORCHID 2: TWO SHADES OF BLUE
YEAR OF THE COMET

Hubbard, James
STEAL AMERICA
VOICES FROM THE FRONT

McDonagh, Maitland
ADJUSTER, THE
AMERICAN ME
BACKTRACK
BAD LIEUTENANT
BRAIN DONORS
CENTER OF THE WEB
CRYING GAME, THE
CUTTING EDGE, THE
DEVIL'S DAUGHTER, THE

EDWARD II
GAS FOOD LODGING
GATE II
GLADIATOR
LAWNMOWER MAN, THE
LIGHT SLEEPER
LINGUINI INCIDENT, THE
MAXIMUM BREAKOUT
MEDICINE MAN
NETHERWORLD
ONCE UPON A TIME IN CHINA
PATRIOT GAMES
STEPHEN KING'S SLEEPWALKERS
SWOON
THERE'S NOTHING OUT THERE
UNDER SUSPICION
WHITE TRASH

McKennon, Mark D.
CITY OF JOY
FINAL ANALYSIS

Miller-Monzon, John
AMERICAN FABULOUS
CLOSE TO EDEN
DADDY AND THE MUSCLE ACADEMY
DAMNED IN THE USA
DEADLY CURRENTS
LIVING END, THE
NIGHT AND DAY
PAINTING THE TOWN
PANAMA DECEPTION, THE
SIMPLE MEN
TOGETHER ALONE
WATERLAND

Mills, Thomas
BECOMING COLETTE
BRIEF HISTORY OF TIME, A
BRONX WAR, THE
FINE ROMANCE, A
FLIRTING
IN THE SOUP
JOHNNY STECCHINO
JOHNNY SUEDE
JUMPIN' AT THE BONEYARD
LAWS OF GRAVITY
LONDON KILLS ME
LOVE POTION NO. 9
MY NEW GUN
PROFESSIONAL, THE
REFRIGERATOR, THE
SINGLE WHITE FEMALE
SOUTH CENTRAL
TEXAS TENOR: THE ILLINOIS JACQUET STORY
WHERE THE DAY TAKES YOU
WINTER IN LISBON, THE
ZEBRAHEAD

Munroe, Dale
ADVENTURES IN DINOSAUR CITY
ALAN & NAOMI
FREDDIE AS F.R.O.7
KUFFS
LITTLE NEMO: ADVENTURES IN SLUMBERLAND
MY GRANDPA IS A VAMPIRE
NEWSIES
ROCK-A-DOODLE
SHAKING THE TREE
SHINING THROUGH
3 NINJAS

Noh, David
BOB ROBERTS
INDOCHINE
LOVER, THE
MAMBO KINGS, THE
OF MICE AND MEN

Pardi, Robert
ALL – AMERICAN MURDER
ANIMAL INSTINCTS
BARBARIAN QUEEN II: THE EMPRESS STRIKES BACK
BEYOND JUSTICE
BLACK ICE
BLACKBELT
BLINK OF AN EYE
CAFE ROMEO
CAGED FEAR
CAN IT BE LOVE
CANVAS
CODE NAME: CHAOS
COLD JUSTICE
DANCE WITH DEATH
DEATHSTALKER IV: MATCH OF TITANS
DEMON IN MY VIEW, A
EYE OF THE EAGLE 3
FIELD OF FIRE
FINISHING TOUCH, THE
HOMICIDAL IMPULSE
HOT CHOCOLATE
HUNTING
HURRICANE SMITH
HUSBANDS AND LOVERS
ILLUSIONS
IN GOLD WE TRUST
KICKBOXER 3: THE ART OF WAR
KILLER IMAGE
LITTLE NOISES
LUNATIC, THE
MANIAC WARRIORS
MEATBALLS 4
ONLY YOU
OUT ON A LIMB
PLAY MURDER FOR ME
PLAY NICE
ROUND TRIP TO HEAVEN
SECRET FRIENDS
SEVERED TIES
SEXUAL RESPONSE
SHOOTING ELIZABETH
SOLDIER'S FORTUNE
TILL THERE WAS YOU
TO PROTECT AND SERVE
TOUCH AND DIE
ULTRAVIOLET
VOYAGER
WE'RE TALKIN' SERIOUS MONEY
WHO SHOT PATAKANGO?

Rubenstein, Leonard
ADAM'S RIB
ALL THE VERMEERS IN NEW YORK
AMERICAN DREAM
BROTHER'S KEEPER
CUP FINAL
DAY IN OCTOBER, A
DOUBLE EDGE
EAR, THE
EFFICIENCY EXPERT, THE
FATHER
FATHERS AND SONS
FEED
LIFE ON THE EDGE
LOCKED-UP TIME
MATCH FACTORY GIRL, THE
PICTURES FROM A REVOLUTION
PUERTO RICAN MAMBO (NOT A MUSICAL), THE
QUARREL, THE
RAMPAGE
ROCK SOUP
SOLDIER'S TALE, A
SPLIT SECOND
TETSUO: THE IRON MAN
THANK YOU AND GOOD NIGHT!
TO RENDER A LIFE
WISECRACKS
ZENTROPA

Stewart, Linda J.
ARMED FOR ACTION
BEAUTIFUL DREAMERS
BODY WAVES
CHILDREN, THE
DARK HORSE
DOES THIS MEAN WE'RE MARRIED?
EYE OF THE STORM
LITTLE SISTER
MIKEY
MIND, BODY & SOUL
SUNSET STRIP
WILDFIRE
WOMAN, HER MEN AND HER FUTON, A

Streible, Dan
BROKEN NOSES
FOR THOSE ABOUT TO ROCK
HOMEBOYS
LANDSLIDE
MISSION OF JUSTICE
ODDBALL HALL
VAMPIRE HUNTER D

Weir, Sarah B.
AFRAID OF THE DARK
BEST INTENTIONS, THE
DAUGHTERS OF THE DUST
LOVE HURTS
MEDITERRANEO
MO' MONEY
PEPI, LUCI, BOM AND OTHER GIRLS ON THE HEAP